PRESENTED TO:

_____

BY:

_____

OCCASION:

_____

DATE:

_____

FRESH START BIBLE

FRESH START BIBLE

DIRECTION FOR EVERY DAY

FRESH START BIBLE

DIRECTION FOR EVERY DAY

Fresh Start Bible
Copyright © 2019 by Gateway Press

ISBN: 978-1-949399-58-5 Softcover
ISBN: 978-1-949399-59-2 Hardcover
ISBN: 978-1-949399-60-8 Imitation Leather
ISBN: 978-1-949399-61-5 Genuine Leather

Library of Congress Control Number: 2019942909

Gateway Press, an imprint of Gateway Publishing
700 Blessed Way
Southlake, Texas 76092
gatewaypublishing.com

Printed in the United States of America

19 20 21 22 23 — 5 4 3 2 1

Design and typesetting by 2K/DENMARK A/S

TABLE OF CONTENTS

BOOKS OF THE BIBLE

OLD TESTAMENT

NEW TESTAMENT

NEW TESTAMENT

CONTRIBUTORS

PUBLISHER

Craig Dunnagan

EDITOR-IN-CHIEF

John Andersen, PhD

EXECUTIVE EDITOR

Jenny Morgan

GATEWAY EDITORIAL TEAM

John Andersen, PhD   Caleb Jobe   Kathy Krenzien
Stacy Burnett   Dennis Krenzien   Jenny Morgan
Craig Dunnagan   Peyton Sepeda

FEATURE ARTICLES

Marcus Brecheen   Phillip Hunter   Robert Morris
Aaron Crider, DMin   Jon Huntzinger, PhD   Preston Morrison
Steve Dulin   Mark Jobe   Zach Neese
Jimmy Evans   Todd Lane   Mary Jo Pierce
Benjamin Gilmore   Tom Lane   James Robison
Olen Griffing   Thomas Miller   Tim Ross
Mark Harris   Debbie Morris   Elizabeth Settle
Jack W. Hayford   Joel Stockstill

CONTRIBUTING WRITERS

John Andersen, PhD
Steve Bontrager, DMin
Aaron Crider, DMin
Ron Kramer
Jenny Morgan
Erin Vilchez

CONTENT REVIEWERS

Sion Alford, PharmD
Stacy Burnett
Aaron Crider, DMin
Mark Jobe
Cassie Reid, PhD
Chelsea Seaton
S. George Thomas

CREATIVE DESIGN

Peyton Sepeda
2K/Denmark

AN INVITATION TO YOU

Welcome to your fresh start!

I am so glad you have chosen to read the *Fresh Start Bible*. This is a wonderful tool for you to use in your walk with the Lord.

If you're a new believer or have recently recommitted your life to Christ, I want to be among the first to congratulate you on your decision to follow Christ. You have made the greatest decision of your life! I am so proud of you and am honored to welcome you into God's family.

Now that you've received Jesus Christ as your Lord and Savior, you have a fresh start. In 2 Corinthians 5:17, the apostle Paul writes, "Anyone who belongs to Christ has become a new person. The old life is gone; a new life has begun!" As a new believer, your next step is to turn from your old lifestyle and start living for the Lord.

The best way to start living a godly lifestyle is by adopting habits that encourage growth in your relationship with Christ. This is why I'm so excited for you to start reading the *Fresh Start Bible*. The Bible is your standard for living a godly life. Each word is the very heart and breath of God and is a valuable gift to you in your Christian walk.

Even if you have been a believer for a long time, reading God's Word gives you the spiritual sustenance and direction you need to grow in your relationship with the Lord. You may have even heard someone refer to the Bible as the Bread of Life. It's because the Bible is nourishment to us.

Not too long ago, I had a full and emotionally exhausting week, followed by a very busy Saturday. My day started early with a haircut at eight o'clock in the morning, followed by a doctor's appointment and a visit to the chiropractor. Then I went to my office to spend some time in prayer and to finish studying for the message I was delivering that evening at church. By that afternoon, I was exhausted, so I took a nap. When I arrived at church, I was feeling weak and depleted, even though I had taken a nap. Then I realized I hadn't eaten all day, so I ate a sandwich before the service, and immediately I felt better.

When we don't eat food, our physical bodies become tired and weak. In the same way, when we don't "eat" the Word by reading it every day, we feel spiritually tired and weak. When Jesus taught His disciples to pray, He said, "Give us today the food we need" (Matthew 6:11). He understood that we need food, both physical and spiritual, to live. It isn't an option; it's necessary to stay alive. In order to stay spiritually strong and to keep growing in your relationship with God, you need to "eat" His Word every day.

One of the first habits I encourage you to adopt is reading your Bible daily. The first thing I do every morning—before I shower, have breakfast, or get on my computer—is read my Bible. I hope you will make a commitment to read your Bible every day. If you do, you'll gain a greater understanding of God's Word, and things will start to come into order as you begin to experience the power of God in your life.

The *Fresh Start Bible* is filled with hundreds of study resources created specifically to help equip and disciple you in your walk with the Lord. It took many people to put this together, specifically John Andersen and Jenny Morgan, who worked diligently to compile the in-depth teachings, Bible studies, and message notes. I also want to extend a special thank you to the numerous contributors, including Jimmy Evans, Jack W. Hayford, Jon Huntzinger, Marcus Brecheen, Tom Lane, Todd Lane, Olen Griffing, Thomas Miller, Preston Morrison, Tim Ross, Elizabeth Settle, Benjamin Gilmore, Mark Jobe, James Robison, Steve Dulin, Debbie Morris, Joel Stockstill, Mark Harris, Zach Neese, Aaron Crider, Mary Jo Pierce, and Phillip Hunter. These men and women have enabled us to give you dynamic and expository teachings that reflect the heart of Gateway Church. These teachings will strengthen your faith. I hope you will read through this entire Bible and experience all it has to offer.

Putting this Bible together has been a gift of love, and it is my greatest desire that as you encounter God's Word, you will grow in your love for the Lord and be healed, set free, discipled, equipped, and empowered. It's also my desire for you to find a good church home where you can begin serving. Attending a church that teaches the Bible will have a tremendous impact on your spiritual growth and fulfillment as a Christian.

I am so grateful to have the opportunity to share this wonderful resource with you. I know it will help you learn how to live victoriously each and every day, and I can't wait for you to get started.

I invite you to open your heart and ask the Holy Spirit to start speaking to you and revealing things to you as you read.

Father, I pray You will draw each person reading this Bible to You. I ask You to speak clearly and directly to them. I pray You will make the words in this Book come alive and bring revelation and understanding through Your Holy Spirit. In Jesus' name, Amen.

May God bless you abundantly as you begin your new life in Christ!

Pastor Robert Morris
Founding Lead Senior Pastor
Gateway Church

INTRODUCING YOUR BIBLE

The Gospel of John begins and ends with a life-changing invitation: "Follow me" (John 1:43; 21:19). Today, Jesus calls you to do the same—*follow Him*.

To be a follower of Jesus, you have to know Him and learn to hear His voice. You are holding the best source for understanding what Jesus says and does and what He wants you to say and do. The Bible is the inspired Word of God (2 Timothy 3:16), which means its words are *from* God. In its pages, God reveals the perfect plan for every person, including you.

The *Fresh Start Bible* comes from the heart of Gateway Church, where our motto is "We're all about people." Why? Because God is all about people! The *Fresh Start Bible* was designed with people in mind. In this Bible, you will learn many important spiritual truths, but even more importantly, you will begin to hear God's voice and understand His heart. His greatest desire is to have a real, intimate relationship with you.

No matter who you are or what you have done, Jesus wants to give you a fresh start. If you have accepted Him as your Lord and Savior, this Bible will give you many tools to live a successful Christian life. If you are not yet a follower of Jesus but want to know more about being a "Christian," this Bible will introduce you to important truths about God's plan for you. Even if you have been a believer for a very long time, this Bible will remind you of important principles for living as a victorious follower of Jesus.

—The Editors

WHAT WILL YOU FIND IN THIS BIBLE?

The *Fresh Start Bible* includes two in-depth programs that can each be explored at your own pace or used weekly over the course of a year. This Bible also includes several shorter studies and hundreds of helpful notes and articles. Each program or study can be used by individuals or small groups and features open-ended questions designed to make the lessons applicable to everyday life. For those interested in facilitating group meetings, we have provided a Leader Guide for Small Groups. We recommend every individual or group begin with the program called Fresh Start Journey, which answers many questions about the foundations of Christian faith and will enable readers to understand and engage with the other content on a deeper level.

The following is a description of the primary features of this Bible:

Fresh Start Journey

Written by Jimmy Evans, this program consists of 52 lessons adapted from *Ten Steps Toward Christ, I Changed My Mind*, and various sermons. It focuses on the basics of Christian living and addresses fundamental issues of faith, such as sin, salvation, baptism, and the Holy Spirit. Jimmy also offers practical advice on living victoriously in the Kingdom of God and shares the importance of godly relationships, financial stewardship, and daily meditation on God's Word.

Intersections

This program explores major characters of the Bible in an overarching narrative that begins with God in Genesis and concludes with Jesus in Revelation. These 59 lessons weave a thread through Scripture of God's faithfulness and His relationship with men and women throughout history.

Road Signs

Located throughout the *Fresh Start Bible*, Road Signs are brief and practical teachings from key communicators connected to Gateway Church. These articles illuminate Scripture and inspire spiritual growth.

Worship Way

This four-part study answers essential questions about worship:
— *What* Is Worship?
— *Whom* Do We Worship?
— *Why* Do We Worship?
— *How* Do We Worship?

Freedom Path

This four-part study explores the spiritual freedom available to every believer:
— Barking Up the Wrong Tree
— Unbound
— Promised Land or Prison
— Bound for Freedom

Bible Reading Breakthrough

This four-part study explains the importance of reading God's Word every day:
— Daily Journey
— 15-Minute Breakthrough
— Traveling the Scriptures
— The Promise Principle™

ADDITIONAL FEATURES

The *Fresh Start Bible* provides several helpful resources throughout the text, including:
— Introductions to each book of the Bible
— Historical and cultural background articles
— Visual aids

The following resources are located at the back of this Bible:
— One-Year Bible Reading Plan
— Select Famous Bible Passages
— Tables of Weights and Measures
— Maps

For more information, visit
www.freshstartbible.com.

LEADER GUIDE FOR SMALL GROUPS

The *Fresh Start Bible* includes two in-depth programs (Fresh Start Journey and Intersections) and several shorter studies (Bible Reading Breakthrough, Worship Way, and Freedom Path). All of these programs and studies can be explored individually or in a small group setting. Each lesson is self-paced and includes questions for reflection and/or group discussion. We recommend beginning with Fresh Start Journey as this program answers many questions about the foundations of the Christian faith and will enable readers to engage with other content on a deeper level.

The following is a suggested method for using a *Fresh Start Bible* program or study in a small group:

BEFORE YOU MEET

— Ask God to prepare the hearts and minds of the people in your group. Ask Him to show you how to encourage each person to integrate the principles all of you discover into your daily lives.
— Read the key Scripture passage and any other Scripture references in the lesson.
— Read the lesson and make notes that will help you as you lead the group.
— Plan how much time you'll give to each portion of your meeting (see the suggested schedule below).

SUGGESTED SMALL GROUP SCHEDULE

1. Engage and Recap (10 Minutes)
2. Read (15 Minutes)
3. Talk (25 Minutes)
4. Pray (10 minutes)

HOW TO USE THE LESSONS

Engage the group with an icebreaker question.
Prepare one or more icebreaker questions to help get people talking and feeling comfortable with one another.

Recap the previous lesson.
Recap the previous meeting and invite members to talk about any opportunities they have encountered to apply what they have learned. (This instruction doesn't apply to the first meeting.) At the first meeting, provide an overview of the program or study and encourage everyone to read and prepare before each meeting.

Read or summarize the key Scripture and the lesson.
Many lessons begin with a key Scripture reference. Before your group meets, decide if you will read the entire Scripture passage aloud or only selections. You may want to read selections and summarize the rest of the passage if your time is limited. In any case, make sure you encourage the participants to read all the Scriptures for each lesson. Lessons usually include multiple Scripture references, which you may read or summarize for the group. Additionally, read or summarize the lesson aloud. If time is limited or for late arrivals, prepare a brief summary of the lesson.

Talk.
The questions in these lessons are intentionally open-ended. Use them to help the group members reflect on Scripture and the lesson. As you allow open discussion, the Holy Spirit will work within the group. Look for opportunities to encourage the members with God's Word. Be careful not to allow any discussions to turn into debates or arguments. You may prepare additional questions for the discussion time, but avoid questions with simple "yes" or "no" answers.

Pray.
Ask members to share their concerns and then pray together. Be sensitive to the Holy Spirit and the needs of the group.

KEYS TO A DYNAMIC SMALL GROUP

Relationships
Meaningful, encouraging relationships are the foundation of a dynamic small group. Teaching, discussion, worship, and prayer are important elements of a group meeting, but the depth of each element is often dependent upon the depth of the relationships among members.

Availability
Building a sense of community within your group requires members to prioritize their relationships with one another. This means being available to listen, care for one another, and meet each other's needs.

Mutual Respect
Mutual respect is shown when members value each other's opinions (even when they disagree) and are careful never to put down or embarrass others in the group (including their spouses, who may or may not be present).

Openness
A healthy small group environment encourages sincerity and transparency. Members treat each other with grace in areas of weakness, allowing each other room to grow.

Confidentiality
To develop authenticity and a sense of safety within the group, each member must be able to trust that things discussed within the group will not be shared outside the group.

Shared Responsibility

Group members will share the responsibility of group meetings by using their God-given abilities to serve at each gathering. Some may greet, some may host, some may teach, etc. Ideally, each person should be available to care for others as needed.

Sensitivity

Dynamic small groups are born when the leader consistently seeks and is responsive to the guidance of the Holy Spirit, following His leading throughout the meeting as opposed to sticking to the "agenda." This guidance is especially important during the discussion and ministry times.

Fun!

Dynamic small groups take the time to have fun. Create an atmosphere for fun and be willing to laugh at yourself every now and then!

NLT INTRODUCTION CONTENT

A NOTE TO READERS

The *Holy Bible,* New Living Translation, was first published in 1996. It quickly became one of the most popular Bible translations in the English-speaking world. While the NLT's influence was rapidly growing, the Bible Translation Committee determined that an additional investment in scholarly review and text refinement could make it even better. So shortly after its initial publication, the committee began an eight-year process with the purpose of increasing the level of the NLT's precision without sacrificing its easy-to-understand quality. This second-generation text was completed in 2004 and is reflected in this edition of the New Living Translation. An additional update with minor changes was subsequently introduced in 2007, 2013, and 2015.

The goal of any Bible translation is to convey the meaning and content of the ancient Hebrew, Aramaic, and Greek texts as accurately as possible to contemporary readers. The challenge for our translators was to create a text that would communicate as clearly and powerfully to today's readers as the original texts did to readers and listeners in the ancient biblical world. The resulting translation is easy to read and understand, while also accurately communicating the meaning and content of the original biblical texts. The NLT is a general-purpose text especially good for study, devotional reading, and reading aloud in worship services.

We believe that the New Living Translation—which combines the latest biblical scholarship with a clear, dynamic writing style—will communicate God's word powerfully to all who read it. We publish it with the prayer that God will use it to speak his timeless truth to the church and the world in a fresh, new way.

The Publishers

INTRODUCTION TO THE NEW LIVING TRANSLATION

TRANSLATION PHILOSOPHY AND METHODOLOGY

English Bible translations tend to be governed by one of two general translation theories. The first theory has been called "formal-equivalence," "literal," or "word-for-word" translation. According to this theory, the translator attempts to render each word of the original language into English and seeks to preserve the original syntax and sentence structure as much as possible in translation. The second theory has been called "dynamic-equivalence," "functional-equivalence," or "thought-for-thought" translation. The goal of this translation theory is to produce in English the closest natural equivalent of the message expressed by the original-language text, both in meaning and in style.

Both of these translation theories have their strengths. A formal-equivalence translation preserves aspects of the original text—including ancient idioms, term consistency, and original-language syntax—that are valuable for scholars and professional study. It allows a reader to trace formal elements of the original-language text through the English translation. A dynamic-equivalence translation, on the other hand, focuses on translating the message of the original-language text. It ensures that the meaning of the text is readily apparent to the contemporary reader. This allows the message to come through with immediacy, without requiring the reader to struggle with foreign idioms and awkward syntax. It also facilitates serious study of the text's message and clarity in both devotional and public reading.

The pure application of either of these translation philosophies would create translations at opposite ends of the translation spectrum. But in reality, all translations contain a mixture of these two philosophies. A purely formal-equivalence translation would be unintelligible in English, and a purely dynamic-equivalence translation would risk being unfaithful to the original. That is why translations shaped by dynamic-equivalence theory are usually quite literal when the original text is relatively clear, and the translations shaped by formal-equivalence theory are sometimes quite dynamic when the original text is obscure.

The translators of the New Living Translation set out to render the message of the original texts of Scripture into clear, contemporary English. As they did so, they kept the concerns of both formal-equivalence and dynamic-equivalence in mind. On the one hand, they translated as simply and literally as possible when that approach yielded an accurate, clear, and natural English text. Many words and phrases were rendered literally and consistently into English, preserving essential literary and rhetorical devices, ancient metaphors, and word choices that give structure to the text and provide echoes of meaning from one passage to the next.

On the other hand, the translators rendered the message more dynamically when the literal rendering was hard to understand, was misleading, or yielded archaic or foreign wording. They clarified difficult metaphors and terms to aid in the reader's understanding. The translators first struggled with the meaning of the words and phrases in the ancient context; then they rendered the message into clear, natural English. Their goal was to be both faithful to the ancient texts and eminently readable. The result is a translation that is both exegetically accurate and idiomatically powerful.

TRANSLATION PROCESS AND TEAM

To produce an accurate translation of the Bible into contemporary English, the translation team needed the skills necessary to enter into the thought patterns of the ancient authors and then to render their ideas, connotations, and effects into clear, contemporary English. To begin this process, qualified biblical scholars were needed to interpret the meaning of the original text and to check it against our base English translation. In order to guard against personal and theological biases, the scholars needed to represent a diverse group of evangelicals who would employ the best exegetical tools. Then to work alongside the scholars, skilled English stylists were needed to shape the text into clear, contemporary English.

With these concerns in mind, the Bible Translation Committee recruited teams of scholars that represented a broad spectrum of denominations, theological perspectives, and backgrounds within the worldwide evangelical community. (These scholars are listed at the end of this introduction.) Each book of the Bible was assigned to three different scholars with proven expertise in the book or group of books to be reviewed. Each of these scholars made a thorough review of a base translation and submitted suggested revisions to the appropriate Senior Translator. The Senior Translator then reviewed and summarized these suggestions and proposed a first-draft revision of the base text. This draft served as the basis for several additional phases of exegetical and stylistic committee review. Then the Bible Translation Committee jointly reviewed and approved every verse of the final translation.

Throughout the translation and editing process, the Senior Translators and their scholar teams were given a chance to review the editing done by the team of stylists. This ensured that exegetical errors would not be introduced late in the process and that the entire Bible Translation Committee was happy with the final result. By choosing a team of qualified scholars and skilled stylists and by setting up a process that allowed their interaction throughout the process, the New Living Translation has been refined to preserve the essential formal elements of the original biblical texts, while also creating a clear, understandable English text.

The New Living Translation was first published in 1996. Shortly after its initial publication, the Bible Translation Committee began a process of further committee review and translation refinement. The purpose of this continued revision was to increase the level of precision without sacrificing the text's easy-to-understand quality. This second-edition text was completed in 2004, with minor changes subsequently introduced in 2007, 2013, and 2015.

WRITTEN TO BE READ ALOUD

It is evident in Scripture that the biblical documents were written to be read aloud, often in public worship (see Nehemiah 8; Luke 4:16-20; 1 Timothy 4:13; Revelation 1:3). It is still the case today that more people will hear the Bible read aloud in church than are likely to read it for themselves. Therefore, a new translation must communicate with clarity and power when it is read publicly. Clarity was a primary goal for the NLT translators, not only to facilitate private reading and understanding, but also to ensure that it would be excellent for public reading and make an immediate and powerful impact on any listener.

THE TEXTS BEHIND THE NEW LIVING TRANSLATION

The Old Testament translators used the Masoretic Text of the Hebrew Bible as represented in *Biblia Hebraica Stuttgartensia* (1977), with its extensive system of textual notes; this is an update of Rudolf Kittel's *Biblia Hebraica* (Stuttgart, 1937). The translators also further compared the Dead Sea Scrolls, the Septuagint and other Greek manuscripts, the Samaritan Pentateuch, the Syriac Peshitta, the Latin Vulgate, and any other versions or manuscripts that shed light on the meaning of difficult passages.

The New Testament translators used the two standard editions of the Greek New Testament: the *Greek New Testament*, published by the United Bible Societies (UBS, fourth revised edition, 1993), and *Novum Testamentum Graece*, edited by Nestle and Aland (NA, twenty-seventh edition, 1993). These two editions, which have the same text but differ in punctuation and textual notes, represent, for the most part, the best in modern textual scholarship. However, in cases where strong textual or other scholarly evidence supported the decision, the translators sometimes chose to differ from the UBS and NA Greek texts and followed variant readings found in other ancient witnesses. Significant textual variants of this sort are always noted in the textual notes of the New Living Translation.

TRANSLATION ISSUES

The translators have made a conscious effort to provide a text that can be easily understood by the typical reader of modern English. To this end, we sought to use only vocabulary and language structures in common use today. We avoided using language likely to become quickly dated or that reflects only a narrow subdialect of English, with the goal of making the New Living Translation as broadly useful and timeless as possible.

But our concern for readability goes beyond the concerns of vocabulary and sentence structure. We are also concerned about historical and cultural barriers to understanding the Bible, and we have sought to translate terms shrouded in history and culture in ways that can be immediately understood. To this end:

— We have converted ancient weights and measures (for example, "ephah" [a unit of dry volume] or "cubit" [a unit of length]) to modern English

(American) equivalents, since the ancient measures are not generally meaningful to today's readers. Then in the textual footnotes we offer the literal Hebrew, Aramaic, or Greek measures, along with modern metric equivalents.

— Instead of translating ancient currency values literally, we have expressed them in common terms that communicate the message. For example, in the Old Testament, "ten shekels of silver" becomes "ten pieces of silver" to convey the intended message. In the New Testament, we have often translated the "denarius" as "the normal daily wage" to facilitate understanding. Then a footnote offers: "Greek *a denarius,* the payment for a full day's labor." In general, we give a clear English rendering and then state the literal Hebrew, Aramaic, or Greek in a textual footnote.

— Since the names of Hebrew months are unknown to most contemporary readers, and since the Hebrew lunar calendar fluctuates from year to year in relation to the solar calendar used today, we have looked for clear ways to communicate the time of year the Hebrew months (such as Abib) refer to. When an expanded or interpretive rendering is given in the text, a textual note gives the literal rendering. Where it is possible to define a specific ancient date in terms of our modern calendar, we use modern dates in the text. A textual footnote then gives the literal Hebrew date and states the rationale for our rendering. For example, Ezra 6:15 pinpoints the date when the postexilic Temple was completed in Jerusalem: "the third day of the month Adar." This was during the sixth year of King Darius's reign (that is, 515 B.C.). We have translated that date as March 12, with a footnote giving the Hebrew and identifying the year as 515 B.C.

— Since ancient references to the time of day differ from our modern methods of denoting time, we have used renderings that are instantly understandable to the modern reader. Accordingly, we have rendered specific times of day by using approximate equivalents in terms of our common "o'clock" system. On occasion, translations such as "at dawn the next morning" or "as the sun was setting" have been used when the biblical reference is more general.

— When the meaning of a proper name (or a wordplay inherent in a proper name) is relevant to the message of the text, its meaning is often illuminated with a textual footnote. For example, in Exodus 2:10 the text reads: "The princess named him Moses, for she explained, 'I lifted him out of the water.'" The accompanying footnote reads: "*Moses* sounds like a Hebrew term that means 'to lift out.'"

Sometimes, when the actual meaning of a name is clear, that meaning is included in parentheses within the text itself. For example, the text at Genesis 16:11 reads: "You are to name him Ishmael *(which means 'God hears'),* for the LORD has heard your cry of distress." Since the original hearers and readers would have instantly understood the meaning of the name "Ishmael," we have provided modern readers with the same information so they can experience the text in a similar way.

— Many words and phrases carry a great deal of cultural meaning that was obvious to the original readers but needs explanation in our own culture. For example, the phrase "they beat their breasts" (Luke 23:48) in ancient times meant that people were very upset, often in mourning. In our translation we chose to translate this phrase dynamically for clarity: "They went home *in deep sorrow.*" Then we included a footnote with the literal Greek, which reads: "Greek *went home beating their breasts.*" In other similar cases, however, we have sometimes chosen to illuminate the existing literal expression to make it immediately understandable. For example, here we might have expanded the literal Greek phrase to read: "They went home beating their breasts *in sorrow.*" If we had done this, we would not have included a textual footnote, since the literal Greek clearly appears in translation.

— Metaphorical language is sometimes difficult for contemporary readers to understand, so at times we have chosen to translate or illuminate the meaning of a metaphor. For example, the ancient poet writes, "Your neck is *like* the tower of David" (Song of Songs 4:4). We have rendered it "Your neck is *as beautiful as* the tower of David" to clarify the intended positive meaning of the simile. Another example comes in Ecclesiastes 12:3, which can be literally rendered: "Remember him . . . when the grinding women cease because they are few, and the women who look through the windows see dimly." We have rendered it: "Remember him before your teeth—your few remaining servants—stop grinding; and before your eyes—the women looking through the windows—see dimly." We clarified such metaphors only when we believed a typical reader might be confused by the literal text.

— When the content of the original language text is poetic in character, we have rendered it in English poetic form. We sought to break lines in ways that clarify and highlight the relationships between phrases of the text. Hebrew poetry often uses parallelism, a literary form where a second phrase (or in some instances a third or fourth) echoes the initial phrase in some way. In Hebrew parallelism, the subsequent parallel phrases continue, while also furthering and sharpening, the thought expressed in the initial line or phrase. Whenever possible, we sought to represent these parallel phrases in natural poetic English.

— The Greek term *hoi Ioudaioi* is literally translated "the Jews" in many English translations. In the Gospel of John, however, this term doesn't always refer to the Jewish people generally. In some contexts, it refers more particularly to the Jewish religious leaders. We have attempted to capture the meaning in these different contexts by using terms such as "the people" (with a footnote: Greek *the Jewish people*) or "the Jewish leaders," where appropriate.

— One challenge we faced was how to translate accurately the ancient biblical text that was originally written in a context where male-oriented terms were used to refer to humanity generally. We needed to respect the nature of the ancient context while also trying to make the translation clear to a modern audience that tends to read male-oriented language as applying only to males. Often the original text, though using masculine nouns and pronouns, clearly intends that the message be applied to both men and women. A typical example is found in the New Testament letters, where the believers are called "brothers" (*adelphoi*). Yet it is clear from the content of these letters that they were addressed to all the believers—male and female. Thus, we have usually translated this Greek word as "brothers and sisters" in order to represent the historical situation more accurately.

We have also been sensitive to passages where the text applies generally to human beings or to the human condition. In some instances we have used plural pronouns (they, them) in place of the masculine singular (he, him). For example, a traditional rendering of Proverbs 22:6 is: "Train up a child in the way he should go, and when he is old he will not turn from it." We have rendered it: "Direct your children onto the right path, and when they are older, they will not leave it." At times, we have also replaced third person pronouns with the second person to ensure clarity. A traditional rendering of Proverbs 26:27 is: "He who digs a pit will fall into it, and he who rolls a stone, it will come back on him." We have rendered it: "If you set a trap for others, you will get caught in it yourself. If you roll a boulder down on others, it will crush you instead."

We should emphasize, however, that all masculine nouns and pronouns used to represent God (for example, "Father") have been maintained without exception. All decisions of this kind have been driven by the concern to reflect accurately the intended meaning of the original texts of Scripture.

LEXICAL CONSISTENCY IN TERMINOLOGY

For the sake of clarity, we have translated certain original-language terms consistently, especially within synoptic passages and for commonly repeated rhetorical phrases, and within certain word categories such as divine names and non-theological technical terminology (e.g., liturgical, legal, cultural, zoological, and botanical terms). For theological terms, we have allowed a greater semantic range of acceptable English words or phrases for a single Hebrew or Greek word. We have avoided some theological terms that are not readily understood by many modern readers. For example, we avoided using words such as "justification" and "sanctification," which are carryovers from Latin translations. In place of these words, we have provided renderings such as "made right with God" and "made holy."

THE SPELLING OF PROPER NAMES

Many individuals in the Bible, especially the Old Testament, are known by more than one name (e.g., Uzziah/Azariah). For the sake of clarity, we have tried to use a single spelling for any one individual, footnoting the literal spelling whenever we differ from it. This is especially helpful in delineating the kings of Israel and Judah. King Joash/Jehoash of Israel has been consistently called Jehoash, while King Joash/Jehoash of Judah is called Joash. A similar distinction has been used to distinguish between Joram/Jehoram of Israel and Joram/Jehoram of Judah. All such decisions were made with the goal of clarifying the text for the reader. When the ancient biblical writers clearly had a theological purpose in their choice of a variant name (e.g., Esh-baal/Ishbosheth), the different names have been maintained with an explanatory footnote.

For the names Jacob and Israel, which are used interchangeably for both the individual patriarch and the nation, we generally render it "Israel" when it refers to the nation and "Jacob" when it refers to the individual. When our rendering of the name differs from the underlying Hebrew text, we provide a textual footnote, which includes this explanation: "The names 'Jacob' and 'Israel' are often interchanged throughout the Old Testament, referring sometimes to the individual patriarch and sometimes to the nation."

THE RENDERING OF DIVINE NAMES

In the Old Testament, all appearances of *'el, 'elohim,* or *'eloah* have been translated "God," except where the context demands the translation "god(s)." We have generally rendered the tetragrammaton (*YHWH*) consistently as "the LORD," utilizing a form with small capitals that is common among English translations. This will distinguish it from the name *'adonai,* which we render "Lord." When *'adonai* and *YHWH* appear together, we have rendered it "Sovereign LORD." When *'elohim* and *YHWH* appear together, we have rendered it "LORD God." When *YH* (the short form of *YHWH*) and *YHWH* appear together, we have rendered it

"Lord God." When *YHWH* appears with the term *tseba'oth,* we have rendered it "Lord of Heaven's Armies" to translate the meaning of the name. In a few cases, we have utilized the transliteration, *Yahweh,* when the personal character of the name is being invoked in contrast to another divine name or the name of some other god (for example, see Exodus 3:15; 6:2-3).

In the Gospels and Acts, the Greek word *christos* has normally been translated as "Messiah" when the context assumes a Jewish audience. When a Gentile audience can be assumed (which is consistently the case for the Epistles and Revelation), *christos* has been translated as "Christ." The Greek word *kurios* is consistently translated "Lord," except that it is translated "Lord" wherever the New Testament text explicitly quotes from the Old Testament, and the text there has it in small capitals.

TEXTUAL FOOTNOTES

The New Living Translation provides several kinds of textual footnotes, all designated in the text with an asterisk:

— When for the sake of clarity the NLT renders a difficult or potentially confusing phrase dynamically, we generally give the literal rendering in a textual footnote. This allows the reader to see the literal source of our dynamic rendering and how our translation relates to other more literal translations. These notes are prefaced with "Hebrew," "Aramaic," or "Greek," identifying the language of the underlying source text. For example, in Acts 2:42 we translated the literal "breaking of bread" (from the Greek) as "the Lord's Supper" to clarify that this verse refers to the ceremonial practice of the church rather than just an ordinary meal. Then we attached a footnote to "the Lord's Supper," which reads: "Greek *the breaking of bread.*"

— Textual footnotes are also used to show alternative renderings, prefaced with the word "Or." These normally occur for passages where an aspect of the meaning is debated. On occasion, we also provide notes on words or phrases that represent a departure from long-standing tradition. These notes are prefaced with "Traditionally rendered." For example, the footnote to the translation "serious skin disease" at Leviticus 13:2 says: "Traditionally rendered *leprosy.* The Hebrew word used throughout this passage is used to describe various skin diseases."

— When our translators follow a textual variant that differs significantly from our standard Hebrew or Greek texts (listed earlier), we document that difference with a footnote. We also footnote cases when the NLT excludes a passage that is included in the Greek text known as the *Textus Receptus* (and familiar to readers through its translation in the King James Version). In such cases, we offer a translation of the excluded text in a footnote, even though it is generally recognized as a later addition to the Greek text and not part of the original Greek New Testament.

— All Old Testament passages that are quoted in the New Testament are identified by a textual footnote at the New Testament location. When the New Testament clearly quotes from the Greek translation of the Old Testament, and when it differs significantly in wording from the Hebrew text, we also place a textual footnote at the Old Testament location. This note includes a rendering of the Greek version, along with a cross-reference to the New Testament passage(s) where it is cited (for example, see notes on Psalms 8:2; 53:3; Proverbs 3:12).

— Some textual footnotes provide cultural and historical information on places, things, and people in the Bible that are probably obscure to modern readers. Such notes should aid the reader in understanding the message of the text. For example, in Acts 12:1, "King Herod" is named in this translation as "King Herod Agrippa" and is identified in a footnote as being "the nephew of Herod Antipas and a grandson of Herod the Great."

— When the meaning of a proper name (or a word-play inherent in a proper name) is relevant to the meaning of the text, it is either illuminated with a textual footnote or included within parentheses in the text itself. For example, the footnote concerning the name "Eve" at Genesis 3:20 reads: "*Eve* sounds like a Hebrew term that means 'to give life.'" This wordplay in the Hebrew illuminates the meaning of the text, which goes on to say that Eve "would be the mother of all who live."

As we submit this translation for publication, we recognize that any translation of the Scriptures is subject to limitations and imperfections. Anyone who has attempted to communicate the richness of God's word into another language will realize it is impossible to make a perfect translation. Recognizing these limitations, we sought God's guidance and wisdom throughout this project. Now we pray that he will accept our efforts and use this translation for the benefit of the church and of all people.

We pray that the New Living Translation will overcome some of the barriers of history, culture, and language that have kept people from reading and understanding God's word. We hope that readers unfamiliar with the Bible will find the words clear and easy to understand and that readers well versed in the Scriptures will gain a fresh perspective. We pray that readers will gain insight and wisdom for living, but most of all that they will meet the God of the Bible and be forever changed by knowing him.

The Bible Translation Committee

BIBLE TRANSLATION TEAM

HOLY BIBLE, NEW LIVING TRANSLATION

PENTATEUCH

Daniel I. Block, Senior Translator
Wheaton College

GENESIS

Allen Ross, *Beeson Divinity School, Samford University*
Gordon Wenham, *Trinity Theological College, Bristol*

EXODUS

Robert Bergen, *Hannibal-LaGrange College*
Daniel I. Block, *Wheaton College*
Eugene Carpenter, *Bethel College, Mishawaka, Indiana*

LEVITICUS

David Baker, *Ashland Theological Seminary*
Victor Hamilton, *Asbury University*
Kenneth Mathews, *Beeson Divinity School, Samford University*

NUMBERS

Dale A. Brueggemann, *Assemblies of God Division of Foreign Missions*
R. K. Harrison, *Wycliffe College*
Paul R. House, *Beeson Divinity School, Samford University*
Gerald L. Mattingly, *Johnson Bible College*

DEUTERONOMY

J. Gordon McConville, *University of Gloucester*
Eugene H. Merrill, *Dallas Theological Seminary*
John A. Thompson, *University of Melbourne*

HISTORICAL BOOKS

Barry J. Beitzel, Senior Translator
Trinity Evangelical Divinity School

JOSHUA, JUDGES

Carl E. Armerding, *Schloss Mittersill Study Centre*
Barry J. Beitzel, *Trinity Evangelical Divinity School*
Lawson Stone, *Asbury Theological Seminary*

1 & 2 SAMUEL

Robert Gordon, *Cambridge University*
V. Philips Long, *Regent College*
J. Robert Vannoy, *Biblical Theological Seminary*

1 & 2 KINGS

Bill T. Arnold, *Asbury Theological Seminary*
William H. Barnes, *North Central University*
Frederic W. Bush, *Fuller Theological Seminary*

1 & 2 CHRONICLES

Raymond B. Dillard, *Westminster Theological Seminary*
David A. Dorsey, *Evangelical School of Theology*
Terry Eves, *Erskine College*

RUTH, EZRA—ESTHER

William C. Williams, *Vanguard University*
H. G. M. Williamson, *Oxford University*

WISDOM BOOKS

Tremper Longman III, Senior Translator
Westmont College

JOB

August Konkel, *Providence Theological Seminary*
Tremper Longman III, *Westmont College*
Al Wolters, *Redeemer College*

PSALMS 1–75

Mark D. Futato, *Reformed Theological Seminary*
Douglas Green, *Westminster Theological Seminary*
Richard Pratt, *Reformed Theological Seminary*

PSALMS 76–150

David M. Howard Jr., *Bethel Theological Seminary*
Raymond C. Ortlund Jr., *Immanuel Church, Nashville, Tennessee*
Willem VanGemeren, *Trinity Evangelical Divinity School*

PROVERBS

Ted Hildebrandt, *Gordon College*
Richard Schultz, *Wheaton College*
Raymond C. Van Leeuwen, *Eastern College*

ECCLESIASTES, SONG OF SONGS

Daniel C. Fredericks, *Belhaven College*
David Hubbard, *Fuller Theological Seminary*
Tremper Longman III, *Westmont College*

PROPHETS

John N. Oswalt, Senior Translator
Asbury Theological Seminary

ISAIAH

John N. Oswalt, *Asbury Theological Seminary*
Gary Smith, *Union University*
John Walton, *Wheaton College*

JEREMIAH, LAMENTATIONS

G. Herbert Livingston, *Asbury Theological Seminary*
Elmer A. Martens, *Mennonite Brethren Biblical Seminary*

EZEKIEL

Daniel I. Block, *Wheaton College*
David H. Engelhard, *Calvin Theological Seminary*
David Thompson, *Asbury Theological Seminary*

DANIEL, HAGGAI—MALACHI

Joyce Baldwin Caine, *Trinity Theological College, Bristol*
Douglas Gropp, *Catholic University of America*

Roy Hayden, *Oral Roberts School of Theology*
Andrew Hill, *Wheaton College*
Tremper Longman III, *Westmont College*

HOSEA—ZEPHANIAH

Joseph Coleson, *Nazarene Theological Seminary*
Roy Hayden, *Oral Roberts School of Theology*
Andrew Hill, *Wheaton College*
Richard Patterson, *Liberty University*

GOSPELS AND ACTS

Grant R. Osborne, Senior Translator
Trinity Evangelical Divinity School

MATTHEW

Craig Blomberg, *Denver Seminary*
Donald A. Hagner, *Fuller Theological Seminary*
David Turner, *Grand Rapids Baptist Seminary*

MARK

Robert Guelich, *Fuller Theological Seminary*
George Guthrie, *Union University*
Grant R. Osborne, *Trinity Evangelical Divinity School*

LUKE

Darrell Bock, *Dallas Theological Seminary*
Scot McKnight, *North Park University*
Robert Stein, *The Southern Baptist Theological Seminary*

JOHN

Gary M. Burge, *Wheaton College*
Philip W. Comfort, *Coastal Carolina University*
Marianne Meye Thompson, *Fuller Theological Seminary*

ACTS

D. A. Carson, *Trinity Evangelical Divinity School*
William J. Larkin, *Columbia International University*
Roger Mohrlang, *Whitworth University*

LETTERS AND REVELATION

Norman R. Ericson, Senior Translator
Wheaton College

ROMANS, GALATIANS

Gerald Borchert, *Northern Baptist Theological Seminary*
Douglas J. Moo, *Wheaton College*
Thomas R. Schreiner, *The Southern Baptist Theological Seminary*

1 & 2 CORINTHIANS

Joseph Alexanian, *Trinity International University*
Linda Belleville, *Bethel College, Mishawaka, Indiana*
Douglas A. Oss, *Central Bible College*
Robert Sloan, *Houston Baptist University*

EPHESIANS—PHILEMON

Harold W. Hoehner, *Dallas Theological Seminary*
Moises Silva, *Gordon-Conwell Theological Seminary*
Klyne Snodgrass, *North Park Theological Seminary*

HEBREWS, JAMES, 1 & 2 PETER, JUDE

Peter Davids, *St. Stephen's University*
Norman R. Ericson, *Wheaton College*
William Lane, *Seattle Pacific University*
J. Ramsey Michaels, *S. W. Missouri State University*

1–3 JOHN, REVELATION

Greg Beale, *Westminster Theological Seminary*
Robert Mounce, *Whitworth University*
M. Robert Mulholland Jr., *Asbury Theological Seminary*

SPECIAL REVIEWERS

F. F. Bruce, *University of Manchester*
Kenneth N. Taylor, *Translator,* The Living Bible

COORDINATING TEAM

Mark D. Taylor, *Director and Chief Stylist*
Ronald A. Beers, *Executive Director and Stylist*
Mark R. Norton, *Managing Editor and O.T. Coordinating Editor*
Philip W. Comfort, *N.T. Coordinating Editor*
Daniel W. Taylor, *Bethel University, Senior Stylist*
Sean A. Harrison, *Editor and Stylist*
James A. Swanson, *Lexical Reviewer*

FRESH START
JOURNEY

JIMMY EVANS

1 WHO MADE ME?

GENESIS 2:7

The book of Genesis says God created everything. *Everything!* It also says everything God made was "good." After God made humans, He said all His creation was "very good" (Genesis 1:31). Believe this truth: God made you and everything in the natural world around you. He also made everything good. When you see things in this world that are not good, remember that this is not how God created them to be.

When God created Adam and Eve, He breathed life into their nostrils, and they became living persons. Some translations of the Bible say they became "living soul(s)" (Genesis 2:7, KJV). God didn't simply breathe air into their lungs; His Spirit breathed life into their spirits. Thus, humans became alive as three-part beings—each with a body, soul, and spirit.

You are alive because God is the source your life. Without Him, you would not exist. In fact, without God, nothing would exist. You are not an accident. You were in God's plan from the very beginning, and you are in His plan now.

1. If God created you, what do you think His plan is for your life?
2. How do you think God feels when He sees the current state of the world?
3. How do you think God feels about the way humans live?
4. What does God think about the way you live?

2 WHAT SHOULD I BELIEVE ABOUT GOD?

JOHN 6:29

What should you believe about God? This is a very small question with a very big answer. The apostle Paul writes,

> Oh, how great are God's riches and wisdom and knowledge! How impossible it is for us to understand his decisions and his ways!
>
> For who can know the LORD's thoughts?
>   Who knows enough to give him advice?
> And who has given him so much
>   that he needs to pay it back?
>
> For everything comes from him and exists by his power and is intended for his glory. All glory to him forever! Amen (Romans 11:33-36).

Indeed, it is a difficult task to describe God. An entire library full of books couldn't tell the whole story about Him. Even so, every person should know these important truths about God:

God is good (Psalm 119:68).

— The very first sin came with the idea that God is not good. Satan told Adam and Eve that God was withholding good things from them, and therefore, He could not be trusted. When we don't believe in God's goodness, we will not believe He can (or wants to) meet our needs. When we don't trust Him to have our best interests in mind, we won't want to have a close relationship with Him. God's goodness is an essential truth for people to grasp. He sent His Son, Jesus, so we could see His goodness face-to-face. Then Jesus died on the cross as the ultimate demonstration of God's goodness.

God is God, and we are not (Romans 1:21-23).

— Satan did not trust God; instead, he wanted *to be God*. Then he convinced Adam and Eve that they could "be like God" too (Genesis 3:5). No person and no thing can ever be God, except for God Himself. When we disobey God, we are telling Him we don't need Him. Whenever we try to control our own lives, we are putting ourselves on His throne. Rebellion always says, *I want to be God*. However, God is the only One who has the right to sit on His throne and on the throne of your life. Everything and everyone else will always come second to Him.

God is always near (Psalm 16:8).

— If we believe God is far away, we may pray, read our Bibles, or go to church, but we will still believe He does not care about us. You can be as close to God as you choose. He is a *gentleman*, meaning He will not force His way into your life or make your choices for you. Instead, He waits patiently for you to allow Him to move into the deepest places of your heart. This may seem scary at first because we all have hurts and wounds. You have to trust God enough to let Him shine His light in those dark places. He is good, gentle, and patient, and His healing is available if you will receive it. God cares about everything you have experienced, and He will meet all your needs (Philippians 4:19; 1 Peter 5:7).

God is powerful (Hebrews 1:3).

— If we truly believe God is powerful, then we will know He can do the impossible. God is not limited by our small imaginations or by anything in the physical or spiritual universe. King Nebuchadnezzar threatened to throw Shadrach, Meshach, and Abednego (three Hebrew slaves in Babylon) into the fiery furnace if they would not bow down and worship a statue of him. Still, these men chose to believe God was powerful enough to rescue them, and they refused to bow (Daniel 3:16-18). Nebuchadnezzar had them tossed into the furnace, but a miracle happened: God was with them in the fire, and He didn't allow the fire to singe a single hair on their heads. Their clothing didn't even smell like smoke! God is powerful. He can save, heal, and deliver all who call on Him.

God speaks the truth in His Word (Ephesians 6:17).

— The Bible is God's Word, and through it, He speaks personally to each of us. If you want to

live a successful life in Christ and resist Satan's tricks, you must know God's Word.

"And you will know the truth, and the truth will set you free" (John 8:32).

God is love (1 John 4:7-8).

— God is love, and Jesus is the proof of how much He loves us (John 3:16). Jesus took your sins on Himself when He died in your place on the cross. Nothing and no one will ever again be able to separate you from God or His love (Romans 8:31-39). He loves you unconditionally and more deeply than you can imagine.

1. Read Daniel 3. What was the result of Shadrach, Meshach, and Abednego's belief in God's goodness, nearness, and power?
2. What do we have when we believe in Jesus, according to John 20:31?
3. Read John 14:12-14. What is Jesus' promise to those who believe in Him?

3 WHY DO PEOPLE DIE?

GENESIS 2:17

Why do people die? The answer is simple: *sin*. At the beginning of the world, no sin existed. Adam and Eve, the very first humans, walked continually in God's presence, which means they constantly experienced perfect love, joy, and peace. God gave them everything they needed. Adam and Eve had no reason to feel shame even though they weren't wearing clothes (Genesis 2:25). Without sin, they would have lived forever.

God told Adam and Eve they could eat the fruit of all the trees in the Garden of Eden except one. He warned them not to eat the fruit from the tree of the knowledge of good and evil. He said they would die if they ate it (Genesis 2:17).

One day, Satan approached Adam and Eve in the form of a serpent and tempted them to eat the fruit from the forbidden tree. He said the fruit would make them "like God, knowing both good and evil" (Genesis 3:5). Adam and Eve ate the fruit, and sin immediately entered the world. Bible scholars often call this event "the fall of man." Because of their sin, the Spirit of God departed from them. Their bodies and souls did not die immediately, but their spirits did. They could no longer walk and talk with God in the intimate way they had before.

Sin darkened Adam and Eve's minds, corrupted their emotions, and caused their bodies to age and decay. It also spoiled their relationships with each other. They passed on their fallen, sinful nature to their children, and eventually, the entire human race became completely evil (Genesis 6:5-6). To this day, humans still rebel against God and experience spiritual death because of their disobedience (Romans 7:14-21).

Today, all living things decay and die. Adam and Eve became old and died, but their physical deaths began when they sinned against God, the source of all life. We are descendants of Adam and Eve and have inherited their sinful nature (Deuteronomy 5:9). We may think we are "good" people, but *everyone* has sinned (Romans 3:23). Even on our best days, we cannot be good enough or do enough good works to make ourselves right with God again.

1. According to Ephesians 2:8-9, can you do anything in your own power to make things right with God? Why or why not?
2. Read Genesis 3:5-6. How do you think God felt when Adam and Eve disobeyed Him?
3. What has God done about the problem of sin and death?

4 WHAT CAN BE DONE ABOUT SIN?

JOHN 3:16-17

God has only one solution for sin: *Jesus*. God loves us so much that He gave His own Son, Jesus, as the payment for our sin (John 3:16-17). Both fully God and fully human, Jesus gave His life on a Roman cross to pay for our sins and save us.

In the first five books of the Bible, God gave Moses the Law so the people could know God's will and direction. Sadly, the people could not keep the Law perfectly, so they remained separated from God (Isaiah 59:2). Sin is "missing the mark," like an archer shooting an arrow and completely missing the target. Consequently, there is no such thing as a "small" sin. Either we obey God perfectly, or we miss His will entirely. In the Old Testament, God gave the people a way to deal with sin. They were to offer blood sacrifices of spotless, perfect animals (Leviticus 5:10; 17:11). Blood was the only way they could purify themselves because there could be no forgiveness of sins without shedding blood (Hebrews 9:22). In those days, the high priest of the Tabernacle sacrificed animals on the altar as a temporary covering for sin (also known as *atonement*). However, this solution was not permanent.

That is why God sent His Son, Jesus. He wanted to make us right with Him, once and for all (Hebrews 7:27; 9:26-28). When Jesus died on the cross, His sacrifice was permanent because He was also God in the flesh and He never sinned (1 Peter 1:19). Jesus became the offering for our sin so we could become right with God and experience the personal, intimate relationship with Him that Adam and Eve lost in the Garden of Eden (2 Corinthians 5:21).

Jesus gave His life for you. Even if you were the only person who would ever accept His gift of salvation, He still would have gone through with it. That's how much He loves you! When Jesus gave Himself to be nailed to the cross and die, your salvation was in His plans. His deepest desire was and is to have a close, personal relationship with you.

1. According to John 3:16, how does God feel about people? How does He feel about you?
2. What do you think God expects you to do, now that you know what Jesus did for you?
3. Read Luke 15:20-24. How do you think Jesus feels when someone accepts Him as Lord and Savior? How do you feel when someone you know decides to follow Jesus?

5 WHY IS JESUS IMPORTANT?

1 TIMOTHY 2:5

You may have heard one or more of the following statements:

— "I'm spiritual, but I'm not religious."
— "I believe God exists, but I don't follow any particular view or teaching."
— "All religions basically teach the same thing."
— "As long as I do more good things than bad, I'll go to heaven."

What is the problem with these statements? They aren't true, and they don't line up with Scripture. God's Word clearly says Jesus is the *only* way for us to be right with God, experience freedom in this world, and then go to heaven (John 14:6). There is simply no alternative option.

God gave the Law of Moses to the people of Israel so they could have successful relationships with Him and each other. However, the people failed miserably at keeping God's commandments, and so do we. Since the days of Adam and Eve, every person has been born with a sinful nature (Psalm 51:5). Sin separates us from God, and nothing in our human power can bridge this gap.

This is why God's Good News is so amazing: God gave His own Son, Jesus, to be the bridge to reconnect us with Him. Jesus was and is both fully God and fully man (Colossians 2:9; 2 John 7). He is the only perfect human ever to exist. Hebrews 4:15 says, "He faced all of the same testings we do, yet he did not sin." Because He was sinless, Jesus was able to do for us what we could never do—He gave Himself as the perfect sacrifice to pay for our sins. In a divine exchange, Jesus traded our sins for His righteousness and made a way for us to be right with God (2 Corinthians 5:21).

Old Testament prophets wrote about a Messiah who would come from God and rescue humanity. The people of Israel eagerly waited for this Savior, but many failed to recognize that Jesus fulfilled every Messianic prophecy when He was on this earth.

— He was a Jew, from King David's family line (Isaiah 11:1-5; Matthew 1:1-6).
— He was born in Bethlehem in Judea (Micah 5:2; Matthew 2:1).
— John the Baptist prepared for His coming, and Isaiah and Malachi prophesied about it (Matthew 3:1-3; Isaiah 40:3-5; Malachi 3:1).

— He was rejected by God's people (Isaiah 53:3; John 1:11).
— He fulfilled every Messianic prophecy through His birth, life, death, and resurrection (Psalm 16:10; Luke 24:44-48; Acts 2:30-32).

The story of Jesus is not simply a story. There are verifiable records of the events of His life in ancient historical documents. Jesus actually lived, walked on earth, died, and rose again three days later. No one will ever find a tomb with His body. He is alive in heaven and "seated in the place of power at God's right hand" (Mark 14:62).

Jesus fully embodied God's character and love. He can relate to all our human struggles because He experienced them. He showed us how to live and love by His example. He took upon Himself our sin, shame, and death and gave us His righteousness, freedom, and life.

Jesus paid for our sins, which means we have hope for this life and beyond. He gives us new tender hearts in exchange for our old hardened ones (Ezekiel 36:26). When we accept Him as our Lord, He changes us in ways we never thought possible. In fact, these changes truly are impossible without Him. Jesus raises our spirits from death so we can live in relationship with Him, both now and for eternity (John 11:25-26).

1. According to 1 Timothy 2:5, who is the only person who could bring God and humanity back together?
2. Read John 14:6-7. How can we know God?
3. Why is the resurrection of Jesus important, according to 1 Corinthians 15:12-20?
4. Read Acts 4:11-12. What would you say to someone who believes there are many paths to heaven?

6 HOW CAN I BE SAVED?

ROMANS 10:9-10

God loves us so much that He sent Jesus, His only Son, into the world to pay the price for our sins. Through His sacrifice on the cross, Jesus broke the power of sin and death over our lives. God wants to save us from eternal punishment and separation from Him, and He offers us the incredible gift of salvation. In order to be saved or "born again" (John 3:1-21), we must put our faith in Jesus as the Lord of our lives and the only Savior of the world.

We must confess with our mouths.
— The apostle Paul writes, "If you openly declare that Jesus is Lord and believe in your heart that God raised him from the dead, you will be saved" (Romans 10:9). If we do not acknowledge Jesus as Lord, then we are simply trying to buy "fire insurance" to save us from hell and make us feel better. A confession of faith that doesn't acknowledge Jesus as Lord fails to change the root of the problem between God and humans—rebellion (Matthew 7:22-23).

We must believe in our hearts.
— Believing God raised Jesus from the dead is essential to our salvation because we are acknowledging that Jesus alone satisfied God's requirements to save us from our sins. We can't give ourselves or any other religious leader credit for saving us. If we trust God's Word, then we must choose to believe in our hearts that Jesus paid for our sins on the cross. His resurrection from death proves He was right (Isaiah 53:3-5; Romans 1:3-4; Galatians 3:13-14). By faith, we also believe and confess that Jesus is Lord of our lives (Romans 10:9). The title Lord means He is completely in

charge. When we say, "Jesus is Lord," and mean it, we step down from the throne of our own lives and ask Him to rule over us in the way God planned from the beginning of creation.

We must repent.
— Repentance means we change our hearts and minds, turn from our sins and rebellion against God, confess Jesus as our Lord, and invite Him to take charge of our lives. Then He comes in, forgives us of all our sins, and gives us the gift of eternal life (John 17:3). Jesus makes us capable of having a spiritual relationship and communion with God. Faith in Jesus and the salvation He offers isn't a dead religion; it's a dynamic, personal relationship with God (James 2:17).

We must choose to follow Jesus.
— Following Jesus is a choice. To be saved doesn't simply mean we now believe something we didn't believe before. True believing requires following. You are born again when you make the radical decision to change your life's purpose and follow Him. You no longer live for self and sin; instead, you surrender your life to Christ and choose to follow Him as your Lord.

1. Read Ephesians 2:8-9. Can you be saved by doing "good things" like attending church, reading the Bible, or serving other people? Why or why not?
2. According to Romans 10:9-10, what two steps must a person take in order to be saved? Have you taken those steps?
3. How would you respond to someone who says, "I believe in Jesus, but I don't want to give up control over my life"?

7 HOW DO I ACCEPT JESUS?

JOHN 3:16

Have you decided to make Jesus your Lord? If yes, then pray this prayer:

Lord Jesus, I have sinned and rebelled against You, a holy God. I have no excuse. I confess my sins to You now and turn away from rebelling against You. I ask You to forgive me. I believe You died for my sins on the cross. I receive Your forgiveness and believe Your blood is more powerful than my worst sins. I accept that I am now totally forgiven by You, and I also forgive myself. The past is behind me. I confess You as my Lord and Savior. I step down from the throne of my heart and ask You to sit on that throne as my Lord and King. Come into my heart and give me the gift of eternal life. I know I don't deserve it, but I receive it by faith as a free gift of grace. I believe I am forgiven, saved, and on my way to heaven. I will live the rest of my life for You. Please fill me with Your Holy Spirit. Lead me, speak to me, and give me the power to change, make right decisions, and live for You. In Jesus' name, Amen.

A prayer such as this one is not magical, but its words are important. If you just prayed and asked Jesus to be the Lord of your life, God has saved you.

He has eternally changed you and made your salvation secure in Christ. Your name is written in God's Book of Life in heaven (Philippians 4:3; Revelation 21:27). You may feel very emotional, or you may have very few feelings. Either way, your salvation does not depend upon your feelings. You are saved by faith in Jesus and His death on the cross. He is faithful to do what He has promised in the Bible. He simply wants you to believe and receive His gift of salvation.

Perhaps you think that being saved means you will never sin again. Many new believers have this thought and are quickly disappointed. Hold on to this truth: Jesus was perfect, so you don't have to be. God lives in your heart now (Ephesians 3:17). He's never going to leave you (Psalm 16:8), and no one can take you out of His hand (John 10:29). You invited Him in, and He will change the way you think and behave. Be patient with yourself and keep your eyes on Him.

1. According to John 13:34–35, how will others know you have given your life to Jesus?
2. Read Mark 16:15 and Matthew 10:32-33. Why is it important to share your faith with other people?
3. Read Ephesians 4:2. How should you interact with other believers, especially when they make mistakes?

MY STORY

ROBERT MORRIS

Every person has a story worth telling, and mine began even before I was born. When my mother was 16 years old, her father—a preacher named Robert—was shot and killed. Years later, when my parents were choosing a name for me, they named me after him and dedicated me to God to be a preacher. Their prayer was that I would carry on the ministry my grandfather never had a chance to complete. It would take a move of the Holy Spirit for this to become a reality.

Growing up, I was very accident-prone. When I was just three years old, I was riding my tricycle and attempted to negotiate a turn, but I went into a ravine instead. My two front teeth dug into my bottom lip and had to be removed surgically. About a year later, doctors removed some scar tissue, but I never felt like they removed enough. (To this day, I can still feel some scar tissue in my lip.) I remember looking in the mirror as a little boy and thinking, *You have the biggest bottom lip of any person I've ever seen!* This thought was reinforced when people would comment about my lips, saying, "Your bottom lip is kind of big, isn't it?" When I joined the school band, the director looked at me and said, "You need to play the trombone because you've got big lips." I think he was trying to be complimentary, but to me, he was just another person saying, "Boy, you are one freaky-looking kid!" There was a man in our church who played the trombone, and he had huge lips too. I thought, *If I play the trombone, my lips are just going to get bigger, and one day I'm going to stick my head out the window of the car, and my lips are going to beat me to death.* I decided I didn't want to play the trombone. I chose to play the saxophone instead because I could pull my lips in. I thought this would make them a little smaller, but it never worked.

I was also a *really* skinny kid. I never thought I looked normal. Whenever I looked at other people, I thought, *There's a normal looking person. I'm just goofy-looking and skinny.*

It's why I hated Physical Education. My legs were so skinny, and the gym shorts we wore only brought more attention to them. The label inside read, "One size fits all," but it was a lie. I remember coming out of the locker room one day, and one of the bigger and stronger students shouted out in front of everyone, "Hey Robert, let me help you. You got a string hanging off your shorts . . . Oh, I'm sorry. That's your leg."

As I grew up, I thought, *I look different from everyone. I'm awkward.* And to top it off, I had a speech impediment. I hadn't learned to pronounce my Rs, and when your name is "Wobewt Mowwis," you're doomed! On the first day of school, the kids asked, "What's your name?" When I told them, they all laughed. I went straight home and told my parents I was *never* going to school again. They explained to me why I had to go and said they would send me to speech therapy. But even this was problematic. The speech therapist would come get me from class every day, which was embarrassing and made me feel singled out. Every day, I sat in class and prayed she wouldn't come.

I continued to feel out of place as I was growing up. I ran for class president. I didn't win. Then I ran for vice president, and I didn't get it. I even ran for secretary, and guess what? I didn't get it. I didn't get *any* of the positions I wanted. I didn't get picked for sports either. One time, a girl and I were the last two left. I thought, *Dear God, please don't let me be the last person picked.* Finally, the guy chose me and said, "Alright, we'll take Robert, and you can have the girl." I thought, *Thank God I wasn't the last person!*

My life at church wasn't much different. My first memory of church was when I was eight years old and they served "refreshments." Of course, I now know it's called *communion.* I thought, *Man, they've come up with a great idea! They finally figured out that if they don't give us something to eat, we're not going to make it through the whole service.* The plate came by, and there were little pieces of bread on it. I thought, *They're small, but 10 or 12 pieces will probably tide me over until the end of the service.* I went to grab a handful, but my dad said, "You can't take that until you're a Christian." I bucked up and said, "It looks like someone stepped on it, anyway. I don't want it!" Then another tray, this one with grape juice, came along. I *love* grape juice, but when I reached to get some, my dad said again, "You can't have that." I asked, "Why not?" "Because you're not a Christian yet," he replied. If Christians get refreshments in church and nonChristians don't, then *I* wanted to be a Christian. I looked over at my dad and said, "I would like to become a Christian." My dad said, "We'll have the pastor come over and talk to you." The pastor came over and said, "If you ask Jesus into your heart, then when you die, you'll go to heaven. If you don't ask Jesus into your heart, when you die you'll go to hell. Would you like to ask Jesus into your heart?" I thought, *If I ask Jesus into my heart, I'll go to heaven; if I don't, I'll fry like a French fry.* Well, I wasn't stupid, so I said, "Yes, I want to ask Jesus into my heart." The pastor asked me to repeat a prayer, and I did. *But I didn't get saved that day.* You have to be drawn by the Holy Spirit, and I wasn't drawn by the Holy Spirit—I was drawn by the grape juice.

The older I got, the more I wanted to be accepted, and I found I received a lot of attention and acceptance by doing bad things. In junior high, I found a group of friends who accepted me. They were rebellious—they smoked, drank, and did drugs. I smoked my first joint when I was 13 years old. A couple of years later, I tried cocaine and speed. I also became a very immoral person. I thought I was saved, but in reality, I was in terrible bondage.

Still, I continued going to church and even had a great youth pastor who came up with lots of great ways for students to "get right with God" at youth camp. The problem was none of these ways seemed to work for me. One year at camp, the youth pastor told each of us to go into the woods and get a stick. Then we were supposed to throw our sticks in a big bonfire and say, "This is my life for God. I'm going to burn up for God." But when I threw my stick, it hit another stick, rolled out of the fire, and fell into the lake! The youth pastor looked at me and said, "Go get your stick." I got my stick, put it back in the fire, and thought, *Please, stay in the fire.* Thirty minutes later, my stick was still in the fire, but it wasn't burning. Three hours later, it *still* wasn't burning. What I didn't know was that I had picked up a piece of petrified wood. No other kid got petrified wood! Just me! The whole fire burned out, but my stick was still there.

The next year the youth pastor went to Dairy Queen and got little plastic boats, the ones made to hold banana splits. He put candles in them, and then he asked us to walk down to the lake, light our candle, and say, "This is my life for God." The problem this time was my candle kept going out. So I pulled out the switchblade I bought while on a mission trip to Mexico and trimmed the wick so my candle would stay lit. I relit the candle, and everything was going well. Not wanting to mess up again, I watched the way the kids put their boats in the water. On the other side of the lake was a cross that was lit up, and all the boats were floating toward it. I suddenly realized I was the last one to go, so I went to the edge of the water and thought, *Dear God, please help me.* I pushed my boat toward the cross, but I pushed it a little too hard. Everybody's boats were going toward the cross, but my boat went out a few feet and stopped. The youth pastor started to share something, but no one was paying attention. Everybody was watching my boat. And then it happened. The candle fell over, and my boat caught on fire, burned, and sank. All I could think was, *My life for God just burned and sank.* It was actually a perfect metaphor because I never really knew Jesus. I knew *about* Him, but I didn't *know* Him.

Then an evangelist came to our church when I was 16 years old. Until then, church had always been a very solemn place, almost like a funeral home. But this guy was funny and energetic, and I thought, *Man, this is cool! I need to live for God.* So I rededicated my life to God. After the service, the evangelist came up to me and said, "Hey, why don't you come with me next week, and we'll do a skit for a youth fellowship?" I started traveling with him, and one night he asked me to share my testimony. I said I was saved when I was eight years old, but I didn't read my Bible or grow spiritually, so I fell away from the Lord. But I rededicated my life, and everything was fine. The problem was everything wasn't "fine." I was still getting high and being immoral, even while I was preaching at youth revivals. Why? Because I was still the one in control of my life.

During this time, I met Debbie and was very attracted to her. I was totally intrigued by her love for God. She had something I didn't have, and I fell in love with her. We got married, and I slowly came out of the drug lifestyle. I still wasn't saved yet, even though I was still preaching.

Here's a funny thing about preaching when you're not saved: in order to preach, you have to read the Bible and use Scripture in your messages. One day while I was preaching, I got convicted by one of my own sermons. I was sharing about the wheat and the tares, and I said, "The only difference between wheat and a tare is a tare looks exactly like wheat, but it's empty on the inside." Later, when I got in the car with Debbie, I said to her, "If I believe everything I preached today, then I'm not saved."

Soon after that day, I got on a plane to Kentucky and checked into Jake's Motel. It was in room 12 that I began to think about my life. The first time I ever smoked a cigarette was behind the church sanctuary. The first time I ever smoked marijuana was between the Sunday school buildings. The first time I was ever immoral with a girl was in a Sunday school classroom. If anyone deserved to go to hell, I did. And that's exactly what I said to God in that motel room. I said, "God, I can't change. I've tried. I've prayed the prayers and rededicated my life, but I cannot escape this bondage. I can't do it. I give up. God, please change me." And that was all He was waiting for. It was as though God reached down, picked me up like a small child, and said, "You're My child now." I was saved that day.

You may need to be truly saved too. You've prayed prayers, but you've never given control of your life to Jesus. If you're still in charge of your life, you're going to hell. The way you go to heaven is by giving Jesus control of your life. Nothing changed in my life until I let Jesus be in charge. God saved me, and He can save you too!

---

8 WHY SHOULD I BE BAPTIZED?

MARK 16:16

Before He ascended into heaven, Jesus instructed His followers to make disciples of people and baptize them (Matthew 28:19). Baptism, like salvation, is an act of faith and obedience. The Greek word translated *baptism* means 'to immerse.' Therefore, New Testament baptism means to be immersed in water. Baptism is important because Jesus commands it, and He personally submitted to baptism as an act of obedience to God His Father (Matthew 3:13–16). Many times, as Christians, we will need to obey faithfully what God asks us to do, even when it makes us uncomfortable or we don't understand it.

Baptism shows your life has changed.
— Baptism is an outward, public demonstration to the world of what has happened inside a believer. Going into the water symbolizes the death and burial of the old, sinful nature (Romans 6:3). Coming out of the water symbolizes being raised with Christ into new life and

freedom from sin (Romans 6:4, 7). By faith, we believe our old selves died and Christ now lives in us.

Baptism tells God you will obey Him.

— Baptism is the first test of obedience for followers of Jesus. When you follow Him in baptism, you tell everyone through your actions that you are dead to sin. It no longer has any control over

you because you have begun the new life Jesus has for you (Romans 6:8- 14).

1. According to Galatians 2:20, what happened to your old self when Jesus saved you?
2. Read Romans 8:9. Does sin have the power to control you? Whose Spirit now lives in you?
3. Read Matthew 3:13-16. Why did Jesus submit to baptism even though He never sinned?

---

9 CAN I BE SAVED WITHOUT BAPTISM?

EPHESIANS 2:8-9

Can you be saved without being baptized? The short answer is *yes*.

But here's the long answer. Before Jesus' time on earth, baptism was a sign of repentance for the Jewish people. They were not baptized for salvation. The Temple priests practiced ceremonial washing with water before and after performing their duties (Leviticus 16:4, 23-24). Christian baptism may be linked to this practice.

The thief on the cross next to Jesus recognized Him as Lord and King (Luke 23:39-43). He believed Jesus was who He said He was. The thief said, "Jesus, remember me when you come into your Kingdom" (v. 42). Jesus replied, "Today you will be with me in paradise" (v. 43). Of course, the thief could not have been baptized because it was physically impossible to do so on the cross. Even so, Jesus took him into heaven.

Some people today, like the thief on the cross, receive Christ shortly before death or in other circumstances in which water baptism isn't practical or possible. Some choose to follow Christ but never learn about water baptism. However, repentance and faith in Jesus are what save us (Romans 10:9-10). The thief showed he had a

repentant heart. He recognized he was on that cross for his own bad choices (Luke 23:40-41). When we get saved, our hearts develop a desire to follow Jesus and obey His commands. One of these commands is to follow Him in baptism. Baptism is a visible sign that Jesus has changed our hearts as we have surrendered to His Lordship.

Some people are baptized as children, a practice often referred to as being "sprinkled." They are taught that their baptism as an infant is all that is necessary for salvation; however, this doctrine does not align with God's Word. No one can make the decision for you to be saved or baptized except you. Each person must make the decision to receive Christ, and the act of water baptism is meaningful only after making a personal commitment to Him.

1. According to 1 Peter 3:21, what makes baptism effective?
2. Read Colossians 2:12. How does baptism symbolize Jesus' death and resurrection?
3. What would you say to someone who wants to be a follower of Jesus but doesn't want to be baptized?

---

10 WHAT DOES WATER BAPTISM MEAN?

ROMANS 6:4

Through baptism, we publicly identify ourselves as followers of Jesus and declare our love and loyalty to Him. This public act signifies two personal decisions:

Baptism declares we have chosen to die to sin and live for Christ.

— The original Greek word used in the Bible for baptism is *baptizo*. A similar word is *bapto*, but the two words have important distinctions. *Bapto* means 'to dip,' such as dipping a vegetable into water to cleanse it. However, *baptizo* means 'to soak,' such as soaking a vegetable in a vinegar

brine to pickle it. *Bapto* is temporary while *baptizo* is permanent. When a new believer is baptized (*baptizo*) in water, it symbolizes that person's death to sin and self, along with their resurrection as a new person who now lives for Christ. It signifies they have truly been born again as a new creation in Christ (2 Corinthians 5:17).

Baptism demonstrates we receive Christ's death as the payment for our sin and failure.

— The apostle Peter says baptism is "a response to God from a clean conscience. It is effective because of the resurrection of Jesus Christ"

(1 Peter 3:21-22). When we accept salvation and put our faith in Jesus' finished work on the cross, God purifies our consciences. We are free from the past and can now enjoy an intimate relationship with Him (Hebrews 9:14).

Water baptism is an important act that symbolizes powerful spiritual truths. However, something supernatural also happens to us in the baptismal waters. God meets us there and changes our hearts, something only He can do.

1. Read 2 Corinthians 5:14. What controls us after Jesus saves us?
2. According to 1 John 5:6, how was Jesus revealed as God's Son?
3. Read Romans 6:1-4. What happens to sin's power when we are saved and baptized?

11 WHAT IS THE LORD'S SUPPER?

1 CORINTHIANS 11:23-32

The Lord's Supper (also called *communion*) is an important sign of our covenant relationship with God. When Jesus gave His disciples the first Lord's Supper, He gave new meaning to the ancient Jewish ritual feast called the Seder, a celebration of the Israelites' release from Egyptian slavery. In a Seder ceremony, the participants recall the night of Passover, when God rescued His people from the death of the firstborn sons and from bondage in Egypt (Exodus 12:11-13).

Jesus is our Passover Lamb. The bread represents His body, and the wine (or juice) represents His blood. Every time we take the bread and the wine during the Lord's Supper, we celebrate the fullness and freedom Jesus gained for us by dying as our substitute on the cross. Because of His blood poured out for us, we receive spiritual life and freedom from death and sin. We are "announcing the Lord's death," declaring by His death that we are healed and He has removed the curse of sin from us (1 Corinthians 11:26).

The Lord's Supper is a time to recommit to our covenant relationship with Jesus and to remind ourselves of God's grace and love for us. This meal keeps us from forgetting about Jesus' loving act when He took our place on the cross. At this time, each of us should consider whether something else has taken God's place in our lives and if we have compromised our relationship with Him in any way. If so, we must be willing to either do away with that thing or put it in its right place. This covenant process with the Lord keeps our relationship intimate and genuine.

In our human nature, we may never feel worthy to receive this meal—*because we're not*. We needed Jesus to take our place on the cross. After we focus on God's love and grace, we can celebrate the benefits that come because Jesus gave His body and blood to supply us with abundant life. Take the Lord's Supper regularly because all of us need to remember what Jesus has done for us. We should frequently examine our lives and recommit ourselves to Him.

1. Read Exodus 12:1-13. What was the purpose of the Passover lamb for the Israelites?
2. How is Jesus our "Passover Lamb" today (1 Corinthians 5:7)?
3. According to 1 Corinthians 10:16, what do the cup and the bread represent?

12 WHY SHOULD I GO TO CHURCH?

HEBREWS 10:24-25

As followers of Jesus, we need to meet regularly with other believers to encourage one another. Together, we motivate each other to serve God faithfully and love Him and others (Hebrews 10:24-25). Jesus promises to be with us as we come together and worship God (Matthew 18:20). As we enter His presence, Jesus reminds us that we are His beloved people, and He humbles our hearts and comforts us when we surrender to Him as our Savior and King (Psalm 95:6; 2 Corinthians 1:3-4).

Our faith grows and strengthens as we hear God's Word read, taught, and proclaimed (Romans 10:17). In our personal lives, we should read and listen to the Bible every day; however, when a Holy Spirit-inspired pastor teaches from it in our churches, we can receive additional clarity and insight, which builds our faith even more. God gives us faith as our shield against the lies and temptations of Satan (Ephesians 6:16). Our enemy, the devil, wants to stop our encouragement and stunt our faith. He definitely doesn't want us to go to church. Ask God to remove anything keeping you from gathering with other believers every week.

We live in a world with much evil. We need the constant love and encouragement of other practicing Christians. Without it, we will not be able to withstand the forces of temptation, deception, and persecution. With a strong foundation of fellowship, not only can you prosper, but you can also make a difference in the lives of others and lead them to Christ, which is our highest calling as believers.

1. Read Psalm 27:4. What is the one thing David says he wants to do?
2. According to Matthew 18:19, why is it important to pray with other believers?
3. Read Psalm 133. What does David say happens to those who live together in harmony? How can you experience this kind of unity with others?

13 HOW DO I FIND THE RIGHT CHURCH?

ACTS 2:42–47

When you make Jesus the Lord of your life, God adopts you as His child, and you instantly gain acceptance into a global family of brothers and sisters—the body of Christ (Romans 8:15; 1 Corinthians 12:27). The apostle Paul tells us that Jesus is "the head of the church, which is his body" (Colossians 1:18). Even though you are part of the global Church, it is also important to belong to a local church where you can serve and grow in Christ.

Perhaps you already belong to a wonderful, healthy church. Or maybe you are still looking. Finding the right local church can seem daunting, especially when churches vary so much in size, teaching style, and special interests. How do you know which church is right for you? A simple way to start is by asking your Christian friends where they go to church. You can also find out what kinds of ministries the churches near you offer (such as children's ministry, youth services, community outreaches, etc.).

As you begin visiting churches, ask yourself these questions:

Does this church believe in the authority of the Bible?
— While this question may seem simple, it is actually a fundamental issue facing churches today. Some people, even sincere Christians, have stopped believing the Bible is the ultimate truth without any mistake or error at all. Instead, they believe each person should interpret the Bible according to what seems right to them. However, this is simply not scriptural. Proverbs 14:12 says,

There is a path before each person that seems right,
but it ends in death.

If you are unsure of what a certain church believes, ask to see its statement of faith. The right church is one that uses Scripture to interpret and give meaning to life, not the other way around.

Does the leadership of this church surrender to the power of the Holy Spirit?
— The Holy Spirit is not chaotic, weird, or disorganized, and neither are church leaders who

have surrendered to His power (Titus 1:5–9). When the Holy Spirit is welcome in a church, you will be able to feel His presence, see things mostly in order, and witness the fruit of the Spirit in the lives of church leaders and members alike.

Does this church have a balance of grace and truth?
— Some churches believe in the authority of God's Word but have a very legalistic atmosphere in which they treat sinful people like the enemy. These churches see right living as a means to achieve perfection, rather than a sign of love and obedience to the Lord. Other churches take the opposite approach. In an attempt to be inviting, they water down the truth and refuse to take a stand against sin. Neither method is healthy. Both grace and truth are essential to the gospel. A healthy, Spirit-empowered church will always have a godly balance of these two elements.

Does this church evangelize and equip?
— To evangelize means to share the Good News of Jesus Christ with people who are not saved. To equip means to train people who are saved to do the work of ministry. The right church actively grows in two ways: salvation and maturation. Jesus told His followers, "Go and make disciples of all the nations" (Matthew 28:19). A church that ministers only to already-saved people does not fulfill the Great Commission. On the other hand, a church that focuses solely on unbelievers misses the opportunity to help current Christians grow and mature in their faith (1 Thessalonians 5:11). The right church will reach people who are lost while also training and strengthening believers.

Does this church have both corporate and small group gatherings?
— Acts 2:46 says the early church "worshiped together at the Temple each day, met in homes for the Lord's Supper, and shared their meals with great joy and generosity." We experience God's presence in a powerful way when we meet corporately as a church congregation, and we experience rewarding and fulfilling

relationships with other believers when we meet in small groups. The right church should provide both opportunities.

Does this church serve people and influence the world around it with God's love?
— The right church cares not only for those who are educated, successful, and wealthy but also for those who are vulnerable, wounded, and broken (Matthew 25:34–40).

When looking for the right church, don't look for perfection; instead, watch for integrity, sincerity,

and faithfulness to God's Word. Remember, the best church on its best day is made up of imperfect people who need God's grace just as much as you do. Ask God to direct your search. He will guide you to the right church.

1. Describe the early church in Acts 2:42–47.
2. How does the apostle Paul describe orderly worship in 1 Corinthians 14:26?
3. Read Titus 1:5–9. What are the qualifications of an elder?
4. According to Matthew 18:15–18, how should believers deal with offenses?

14 WHAT IS THE BIBLE?

JOHN 17:17

The Bible is God's Word. It is the Christian's standard for all truth without any error (John 17:17). God's Word guides us and gives us wisdom so we can live in a way that honors Him (Psalm 119:105). When we take delight in His Word, God says we will prosper (Psalm 1:1–3).

The Holy Spirit inspired the writers of the books of the Bible. *Inspired* means 'God-breathed.' The entire Bible is God-breathed and life-giving (2 Timothy 3:16). When we read it, we don't simply learn facts; we experience the living God.

The Bible consists of 66 books. The first 39, from Genesis to Malachi, make up the Old Testament. The New Testament begins with Matthew and ends with Revelation. The earliest Bible manuscripts were probably written around 1400 BC, and the latest was written around AD 95. That's a span of over 1,000 years. Most of the Bible's writers did not know one another, but their messages correlate

and prove the same Holy Spirit inspired them all. God never changes (Hebrews 13:8). He's the same God today as He was thousands of years ago.

One message repeats throughout the entire Bible: "They will be my people, and I will be their God" (Ezekiel 14:11; see 2 Corinthians 6:16; Hebrews 8:10). The Bible constantly portrays a God who is trying to save His people so they can have a relationship with Him. He wants us to know Him and His goodness. When we know God's character, we can trust Him in both good and difficult times. And to know Him, we must know His Word.

1. Read John 14:6 and Ephesians 4:21. Who is Truth? What does this say about His character?
2. According to Ephesians 4:15, what should we do in order to grow and become more like Jesus?
3. Read Revelation 21:6–7. What does God want to give His children?

15 WHY SHOULD I READ THE BIBLE?

PSALM 119:105

The Bible is God's Word to you. In the same way that He breathed Scripture (2 Timothy 3:16), God breathes life into you as you read it. Here are four great reasons to read the Bible every day:

The Word of God creates intimacy with Jesus.
— Reading and meditating on the Word of God creates intimacy with the Lord Jesus. John says Jesus Christ *is* the Word (John 1:1–4). He is God and the Creator of all things. Jesus is the perfect living portrayal of God's truth. His life embodies everything the Bible has to say. Thus, John calls Jesus "the Word." As you read God's Word, you will personally encounter and come to know Jesus.

The Word of God renews our minds.
— The Word of God renews our minds to know the truth (Romans 12:2). As you read the Bible, it will bring the light of God into you. Jesus told us His words are "spirit and life" (John 6:63). As God's Word enters your mind and spirit, it wages war against every work of Satan in your life. Hebrews 4:12 calls it "sharper than the sharpest two-edged sword." God's Word examines every thought and intention of your heart, and it will remove anything that is harmful. You may have grown up with faulty teachings about God and the Bible, but with the Holy Spirit's help, you can learn the truth as you study His Word.

The Word of God gives us power over the enemy.

— The Word of God will empower you for victory over the devil (Luke 10:19). The apostle Paul says to put on the whole armor of God to defend yourself against the enemy, and God's Word is the sword of the Spirit (Ephesians 6:11, 17). Authority comes from speaking and believing what the Bible says. The devil tempted Jesus in the wilderness, but Jesus defeated him by using God's Word to overcome temptation (Matthew 4:3–11). Victory over the enemy isn't automatic simply because we believe in Jesus. If Jesus was tempted, then we can expect testing in similar ways. We must use the authority God gives us in His Word to succeed and live victoriously.

The Word of God heals us.

— The Word of God heals us and makes us whole. You can choose life or death with the words you speak (Proverbs 18:21). When our words agree with God's Word, we enable Jesus to fulfill His ministry to us. When we put our faith in God's Word and confess it over our lives, we allow Jesus to change both our circumstances and us.

1. Read Psalm 107:20. What healed God's children and saved them from death?
2. What is Scripture useful for, according to 2 Timothy 3:16–17?
3. Read Matthew 7:24, Luke 11:28, and James 1:22. What should people do after they hear God's Word?

16   CAN I TRUST THE BIBLE?

PSALM 119

No book has gone through greater scrutiny than the Bible. Theologians, historians, and scientists have debated its accuracy and reliability for centuries. Some people think the Bible is simply an old book full of interesting stories and good advice. However, it is so much more. It is God's Word, "alive and powerful" (Hebrews 4:12). Why does Satan work so hard to make people, even believers, doubt the Bible's trustworthiness? Because if he can convince people not to trust the Bible, then he is one step closer to convincing them not to trust God.

However, there is a big problem with the enemy's plan: the Bible is completely accurate, totally reliable, and archaeologically verifiable. In his book *How Do I Know?* Pastor Robert Morris thoroughly explains the different tests used to prove just how valid the Bible really is. For example, the New Testament has more supporting evidence than any other ancient writing—over 25,000 existing manuscripts! In comparison, *The Iliad* by Homer has just 643 manuscripts, and Caesar's writings have only 10. Even more remarkable, the New Testament's oldest existing manuscripts say exactly what is in the Bible today! Pastor Robert says,

> If any one of the writers of the Gospels or the book of Acts had embellished, then we would have contradictions in persons, places, dates, and events. And if any of the transcribers throughout history had chosen to construct stories and/or fabricate events, then massive contradictions would exist in the ancient manuscripts. But they don't.

The Bible contains 66 books that were written over the span of 1,500 years by 40 different people. God inspired these writers. There is simply no other way to explain how their writings could be so consistent, especially considering that most of them never met.

Old Testament writers wrote about things that would happen hundreds of years later. Isaiah wrote, "The virgin will conceive a child" (Isaiah 7:14) centuries before Jesus was born. Micah said the "ruler of Israel" (Jesus) would come from Bethlehem (Micah 5:2), which is especially incredible because Mary and Joseph did not live in Bethlehem. They only traveled there because Rome had ordered a census, and Joseph's family was from Bethlehem. "While they were there, the time came for her baby to be born" (Luke 2:6). Jesus fulfilled this prophecy about His birthplace, and He fulfilled every other prophecy about Him in Scripture too. Only the Son of God could have done this!

Several New Testament writers had the incredible experience of seeing Scripture fulfilled right in front of them. These "eyewitness reports" (Luke 1:2–4), shared by those who were with Jesus from the beginning of His earthly ministry, maintained the consistent message of Jesus' birth, death, and resurrection. Many of the first Christians were persecuted for teaching about Jesus, and every apostle except one died as a martyr. These early believers, as well as Christians throughout history, were willing to risk everything, even their lives, because they were convinced that Jesus was exactly who He claimed to be—*the Son of God.*

> For we were not making up clever stories when we told you about the powerful coming of our Lord Jesus Christ. We saw his majestic splendor with our own eyes . . . Because of that experience, we have even greater confidence in the message proclaimed by the prophets. . . . You must realize that no prophecy in

Scripture ever came from the prophet's own understanding, or from human initiative. No, those prophets were moved by the Holy Spirit, and they spoke from God (2 Peter 1:16, 19–21).

What does God have to say about the Bible? In John 17:17, Jesus prays for His followers and asks God to "make them holy by your truth; teach them your word, which is truth." Inspired by the Holy Spirit, the psalmist repeatedly declares in Psalm 119:

All your commands are trustworthy (v. 86).

Your eternal word, O LORD,
    stands firm in heaven (v. 89).

Your laws are perfect
    and completely trustworthy (v. 138).

Your promises have been thoroughly tested
    (v. 140).

All your commands are true (v. 151).

I have known from my earliest days
    that your laws will last forever (v. 152).

The very essence of your words is truth;
    all your just regulations will stand forever
    (v. 160).

Perhaps you want to believe the Bible is true, but you feel as if you don't have enough faith. The apostle Paul says, "Faith comes from hearing, that is, hearing the Good News about Christ" (Romans 10:17). Ask God to reveal the truth to you about His Word. It's reliable. It's accurate. It's trustworthy.

1. What does 2 Samuel 7:28 say about God's Word?
2. Read John 1:17. What is the difference between God's word given through Moses and God's Word given through Jesus?
3. How would you encourage someone who has questions about trusting the Bible?

17 WHY SHOULD I READ THE OLD TESTAMENT?

LUKE 24:44–48

The writing of the Old Testament dates from approximately 1450 to 430 BC. It consists of 39 books written in Hebrew and Aramaic. Jewish scholars have traditionally divided these books into three primary categories. The first five books are known as the *Pentateuch*, meaning 'five books,' or *Torah*, meaning 'law.' They contain the Ten Commandments and instructions for living a godly life. The second category includes books written by prophets—people who were inspired by God to deliver His messages. The rest of the Old Testament is comprised of poetry, songs, wise sayings, and narratives.

When Jesus and the apostles read the Scriptures, they read the Old Testament. It was the only Bible they knew at that time, and they referred to it frequently. By the time of Jesus' ministry, most Jewish people had memorized or at least heard of the Old Testament Scriptures. They knew the prophecies regarding a Messiah who would restore the world (2 Timothy 3:15–17). In John 4:26, Jesus revealed His true identity to the woman at the well: "I AM the Messiah!"

Since we now have the New Testament, why should Christians continue to read the Old Testament as well?

The Old Testament validates the New Testament.
— The Old Testament speaks to the truth of the New Testament. It encourages believers to persevere because God will always fulfill His promises. Many things God said He would do in the Old Testament find fulfillment in the New Testament, the most important example being the coming of the Messiah (Jesus). The New Testament echoes many things not yet fulfilled, such as prophecies about the end times. If we do not read the Old Testament, then we cannot adequately understand our place in the story of God's people or the reasons Jesus came to die for us.

The Old Testament gives deeper meaning to the New Testament.
— For example, the New Testament refers to Jesus as the "sinless, spotless Lamb of God" (1 Peter 1:19). This phrase holds great significance because Jesus forever changed the way God addressed sin in the lives of His people. Before Jesus' death and resurrection, the people of Israel had to offer sacrifices regularly to atone for their sins. (The instructions for sacrifices are located in the Old Testament book of Leviticus.) These sacrifices had to be perfect, spotless animals, but even so, they were only a temporary solution. Nothing the people of Israel could bring to God could eradicate sin from their lives. When Jesus died on the cross, His blood served as the final, permanent sacrifice that destroyed sin's power and restored humanity's relationship with God.

The Old Testament introduces us to the people of God.
— Through Abraham, a loving God called a particular group of people (the Israelites) to be His

special, chosen nation. Generations of Israelites wavered between loving the one true God and worshipping false gods, between serving Him and serving as slaves to other nations. Even the best leaders failed to follow God's instructions perfectly. God wanted to protect and bless His people, but they chose their own way instead of His. Today, you are part of this story. Even though you were born into the human race as a sinner, God the Father adopted you into Abraham's (and Jesus') family the moment you received salvation. You are now God's child and an heir of His promises to Abraham. The Old Testament is the story of your heritage (Galatians 3:29; 4:7).

1. Why was the Old Testament written, according to Romans 15:4?
2. Read John 5:39–40 and Luke 24:25–27, 44. To whom do the Old Testament Scriptures point us?
3. Read Hosea 11:1 and Psalm 103:13. What kind of relationship did God want to have with Israel?

18 WHY SHOULD I READ THE NEW TESTAMENT?

MATTHEW 5:17

The New Testament tells us the Good News: God sent His Son, Jesus, to save people from sin, death, and hell. The word *testament* can also be translated *covenant*. New *Testament* means God has made a new *covenant* with us. The old covenant required God's people to abide by His Law perfectly, or they would be separated from Him until a proper sacrifice was made. Only then could His people enter His presence. The new covenant did away with the problem of our sinful nature once and for all (Hebrews 10:10). Because of Jesus' sacrifice for our sins, we can now freely enter into God's presence. Nothing can separate us from His love (Romans 8:38).

Originally written in Greek, the New Testament is the second part of the Bible and begins with the four Gospels—four separate accounts of Jesus' life, ministry, death, and resurrection. These books demonstrate the way Jesus fulfilled the long-awaited Messianic prophecies of the Old Testament (Matthew 5:17).

The book of Acts follows the Gospels and tells about the founding of the Church through the power of the Holy Spirit. Acts 2 gives the account of Jesus' followers being filled with the Holy Spirit and thousands of people coming to believe in Jesus on the Day of Pentecost. The Church grew as more people believed and spread the Good News. Jesus' followers performed many miracles in the power He had given them through the Holy Spirit. The same Holy Spirit who raised Jesus from the dead now lived inside them, and they were unstoppable (Romans 8:31).

Other books in the New Testament are letters, mostly written by the apostle Paul but also by a few others. These letters remind believers of what the apostles had seen and heard. They give instructions about how to live and work together, and they encourage followers of Christ not to waver from the truth (2 Timothy 1:13–14). Paul and the other writers communicated some things in these letters to give comfort and encouragement to those who were suffering persecution or going through trials. They also wrote for the believers' correction. Even today, these letters give us guidance, comfort, and encouragement. The words are as relevant for the modern Church as they were for those who originally read them (John 17:20–23).

Revelation is the last book of the Bible, but instead of concluding humanity's history, this ending points to a new beginning. It gives crucial insight into God's ongoing message to the Church as well as depicting specific events leading up to and following Christ's return. It describes a future day when God will abolish all sin and evil, and those who have trusted in Christ for their salvation will live and reign with Him for all eternity. Revelation does not tell us exactly when this day will occur, but we should live in expectation of it. Jesus says, "Look, I am coming soon!" (Revelation 22:7).

1. In Matthew 5:17, what does Jesus say He came to fulfill?
2. According to John 17:20–23, how will the world believe in Jesus?
3. Read 2 Timothy 3:15–17. What is the purpose of Scripture?

19 HOW DO I READ THE BIBLE?

DEUTERONOMY 6:6–9

You will want to hear good teaching about the Bible. However, if you want to know Jesus and His Word, then you must discipline yourself to read the Bible every day. There are many reading plans available to help you read through the Bible in a year or less. You can also find daily Bible-based devotionals on the internet or from a bookstore.

There are varieties of methods for reading the Bible. If you are a new believer, you may benefit from starting with Romans, Galatians, or John. Some devotionals provide daily selections from both the Old and New Testaments as well as Psalms and Proverbs. Conveniently, Proverbs has thirty-one chapters, one for each day of the month. Regardless of your approach, you will want to do the most important thing—*read God's Word*. Jesus tells us it takes more than bread to keep us alive; we must also consume a steady diet of God's Word (Matthew 4:4).

Jesus says He is the "living bread," and "anyone who eats this bread will live forever" (John 6:51). What does He mean? When we eat food, we chew it and then swallow it. Spiritually speaking, we take Jesus' life and teachings into our spirits. As we read God's Word and reflect on it, we are "eating" the food that gives us the most life.

The most important thing for you to do as you read God's Word is to pray and ask Him to help you understand it. After all, God is the Author who told the writers of the Bible what to write (2 Timothy 3:16). How wonderful it is for you to be able to speak to the Author as you read and try to understand His Book! The more you read the Bible, the more you will see the life it brings. You will also recognize how spiritually weak and tired you feel when you have not been in God's Word for several days. You will feel like you have gone through an entire day without eating or even breathing. Consider how you will make reading the Bible a priority in your schedule. Start reading now, and you will see how the Holy Spirit revives you as He breathes His life into your soul (Psalm 119:50).

1. Read Matthew 4:4 and Deuteronomy 8:3. What do you think will happen if you try to live without God's Word?
2. According to Deuteronomy 6:6–9, how should we study the Bible?
3. Read Psalm 119:25–40. What is the psalmist asking God to do for him?

20 WHY SHOULD I MEDITATE ON GOD'S WORD?

PSALM 1:1–3

Meditating is the process of reading God's Word and bringing it back into your mind to think upon it. As you ponder Scripture, you are memorizing truth. When you know the truth, it will set you free (John 8:32). The benefits of meditating on God's Word are eternal and include spiritual freedom, growth, healing, and truly knowing the God who uniquely created and loves you.

In Psalm 1, God promises we will succeed in everything we do if we meditate on His Word day and night. Jesus is our Mediator who reconciles us to God (1 Timothy 2:5), and He is also our messenger and High Priest in heaven (Hebrews 3:1). This means when the words of your mouth are in agreement with God's Word, you enable Jesus to fulfill the promises God has made. Part of the healing God's Word brings will take place within you as you meditate on it.

When you meditate on Scripture, you are more likely to remember it. Then the Holy Spirit can bring it back to your mind when you need it most. That's how God helps you use His Word to defeat the devil. God Himself is your defender (Psalm 119:114). When you are tempted, grieving, or prideful, the Holy Spirit can bring verses into your mind to encourage, comfort, or correct you. The more you meditate on God's Word, the more ammunition you give the Holy Spirit to defend you with against the enemy.

Meditating on God's Word is also one of the best ways for you to learn to hear God's voice clearly. When you know God's Word, you know His character, and when you know His character, you know *Him*. In John 10:27, Jesus says, "My sheep listen to my voice; I know them, and they follow me." We are His sheep (Psalm 100:3). When you learn to know His voice, you also learn how to follow Him.

1. According to Philippians 4:8, on what things should you meditate?
2. Read Joshua 1:8. What are the results of meditating on God's Word day and night?
3. What is David's desire in Psalm 19:14?

21 WHY DO I NEED TO SPEND TIME WITH GOD EVERY DAY?

JOHN 15

Life can get really busy. Perhaps you have a demanding job that requires a reply to every message and a checkmark next to every task. Maybe you have a growing family in which everyone has different needs, schedules, and hobbies. Technology is supposed to make life easier, but somehow our to-do lists are always growing while our time to complete them is always shrinking.

Do you ever find yourself crawling into bed at night and realizing, "I haven't talked to God at all today!" Most believers know they should spend time with God. They may even have an idea of what this time should look like. However, since it is not presently as demanding as the piles of dirty laundry or the promotion-earning presentation, they move time with God to the end of the list day after day.

So why is it important to spend *daily* time with God? Why is attending church on the weekend not enough? Simply put, God made you to be in a relationship with Him. His greatest desire, above everything else in the universe, is you! 1 John 3:1 says, "See how very much our Father loves us, for he calls us his children, and that is what we are!"

When Adam and Even ate the forbidden fruit in the Garden of Eden, sin entered the world and created a devastating rift between God and humanity. The relationship was broken, and there was only one way to repair it—a perfect sacrifice. In Romans 5:8, the apostle Paul writes, "God showed his great love for us by sending Christ to die for us while we were still sinners." God gave His perfect, sinless Son, Jesus, to fix what humanity had broken and restore the relationship for which He created us.

God is all-powerful, so He could force us to love Him in return. However, that would violate who He is. God will never make you love Him, and He will never make you spend time with Him. He wants you to choose to make Him a priority—to move Him to the top of your list. If you want to have an intimate relationship with the King of all kings and Lord of all lords (Revelation 19:16), you absolutely can! Just like any other intimate relationship, though, it will only happen when you spend time in His presence.

First John 2:6 says, "Those who say they live in God should live their lives as Jesus did." Our world is full of distractions and temptations, so how can we *really* live like Jesus did? By spending time with Him. When you spend time with God, you will begin to think as He thinks and understand His will for your life (Romans 12:2).

Having a relationship with God does not mean your life will be free from frustrations or difficulties. We live in a fallen world, and the devil is constantly looking for ways to discourage believers and make them doubt God's goodness. Jesus said, "Here on earth you will have many trials and sorrows. But take heart, because I have overcome the world" (John 16:33).

Some people think a "quiet time" is a boring formality that requires rising before dawn, dutifully reading Scripture, and then praying for hours (all while hoping you don't fall asleep). While it is certainly beneficial to begin your day with God, He cares more about your heart than how many verses you read or how "holy" your prayers are. You should not base your quiet time on a set formula; rather, set time aside for you to connect with the One who knows and loves you better than anyone else.

Are you facing challenges? Tell God. Do you need the answer to an important question? Ask Him. Praying is not just talking to God; it's also listening to Him talk to you. One of the ways God often speaks is through His Word. Reading God's Word will build your faith and put your focus on His eternal promises instead of your present circumstances.

Some people struggle with finding the right words to share their faith with others. However, when you spend time with God, talking about Him will come naturally (Psalm 73:28). Most people who have had something great happen, such as an engagement, promotion, or the birth of a child, want to share their news with the world. As a believer, you have the best news of all—the Good News of eternal salvation and hope in Christ!

1. Read Matthew 14:23 and Mark 1:35. What did Jesus do in these verses? Why was this important?

2. How does Matthew 6:6-13 teach us to pray?

3. According to 2 Corinthians 3:18, how does God change us as we spend time with Him?

---

22   HOW DOES GOD SPEAK TO ME?

JOHN 10:27-28

As you read the Bible, you will discover God is not limited in the ways He can speak. In Numbers 22:28-39, He even uses the mouth of a donkey! Most often, though, God speaks in one of the following ways:

A gentle whisper (1 Kings 19:11-12)
— When you hear from God, it will always be loving, consistent, and in accordance with the Bible. Practice obeying when you hear Him speak. Train yourself to recognize God's

voice. Everyone makes mistakes when they are beginning to hear His voice, but don't give up! Eventually, you will be confident in recognizing God's voice.

His written Word (Romans 10:17)
— When you read your Bible daily, you give God the opportunity to speak to you. All Scripture is the divinely-inspired Word of God, and the Holy Spirit will often speak to specific situations in your life through the verses you read. Ask God to speak to you as you read His Word.

A sense of peace (Colossians 3:15)

— God will guide you with His peace through every situation. There will be times when everything in the physical, natural world looks right, but you just don't feel peace about it. That feeling can be God telling you *no*. There are also times when everything around you is falling apart and seems impossible, but for some reason you feel peace about it. That could be God telling you *yes* or that things will be okay and to continue on your path.

Other people (Proverbs 15:22)

— As you pray for guidance, be sure to listen to the wise people around you and ask them to confirm what you believe God is saying to you. Listen for times when a wise believer says something to you that could be a word from God.

Open and closed doors of opportunity (Revelation 3:7-8)

— At times, you will pray for God's guidance, and He will use circumstances to answer you. For example, when a door of opportunity closes, He could be protecting you. He loves you and may have a better plan. Other times, He could be saying, "Not now." Ask God to bring you opportunities that align with His purpose for you. When God opens a door, no one can shut it.

1. What is the Holy Spirit's purpose, according to John 14:26-27?
2. Read Acts 2:17. What are some ways God speaks to His people?
3. What is God saying to you right now?

23 WHAT CAN KEEP ME FROM HEARING GOD?

ISAIAH 59:1-3

Even though God speaks on a regular basis, many believers do not hear Him because of one or more of the following issues in their lives:

Unconfessed Sin

— You don't have to be perfect for God to speak to you. He is a very gracious God. However, He is also a holy God, and when we willfully sin, we separate ourselves from Him (Isaiah 59:2). Things such as unforgiveness, immorality, and vulgar or hateful speech all offend God and create obstacles to our prayers. As you pray daily, it is important for you to confess your sins and be sensitive to the Holy Spirit's conviction (John 16:8). As you confess your sins, God forgives you and completely restores your relationship with Him.

Rebellion

— God loves us passionately, and when He tells us something, He expects us to obey. As a good Father, God will give you guidance to protect you and lead you into a better life. He doesn't give you rules to keep you from having fun but to give you the full and abundant life He has promised (John 10:10). If you don't obey, you are choosing not to listen to God or His Word. It pleases God when His children obey Him and

saddens Him when they don't (Psalm 119:136). If you are rebelling, God will seem far away, and it will be very difficult to hear His voice. But He is only one choice away from you. If you have made Jesus your Lord, show your love for Him by obeying Him (Luke 6:46; John 14:15). He cares for you and has good plans for you (1 Peter 5:7).

Busyness and Distraction

— We must discipline ourselves to find a quiet, private place every day to pray and hear God. God is always ready to speak to you, but you must make time to be still and listen. When you get quiet and pray to Him, it slows you down and establishes your priorities. One word from God can change your life. His voice will make you wiser than your adversaries and give you the tools you need for victory in every area of your life.

Ask God if any of these issues affect your life. When we repent, He forgives us and enables us to hear Him when He speaks.

1. According to James 4:3, what can keep us from receiving what we ask of God?
2. Read John 14:15. How can we show our love to God?
3. What does God promise in 2 Chronicles 7:14?

24 HOW SHOULD I PRAY?

1 THESSALONIANS 5:17

When you are learning to pray, it is important to understand who God really is. Most of us have

developed our concepts of God based on our parents, especially our earthly fathers. The way we think about our fathers, whether good or bad, is often the same way we think about God. We must come to an important place in our spiritual lives that will set us free to grow in God and develop true faith and intimacy with Him. We must learn to disassociate our parents' failures and flaws from who God is. Regardless of what your earthly parents are or were like, you can rejoice that your perfect Father has adopted you (1 John 3:1). He rejoices over you, sings songs over you, and blesses you (Zephaniah 3:17). He wants to care for you every day as His child (Matthew 6:26; 1 Peter 5:7). He loves you!

Many of the Jewish leaders of Jesus' day were prideful, so they prayed long, religious prayers to make themselves look very holy in the eyes of the people. However, Jesus says we should pray privately and without a lot of fancy words. Find a quiet spot where you won't be disturbed. It could be your room with the door closed, a solitary place in the woods, your car, or even a closet. It may take some trial and error to find a place where you feel comfortable. The point is to get alone with God and put your focus on Him.

Once you are in your quiet spot, thank, praise, and worship Him. Ask the Holy Spirit to be with you while you spend time with Him. God dwells in our praises (Psalm 22:3), and when we worship Him, He is faithful to be present. Praise and worship will also get your mind off yourself and your problems and onto the One who can help you do something about them.

Prayer is talking with God as if He is sitting right next to you. He wants to be your best friend and trusted confidant because He cares so much about you. If you have trouble expressing your feelings or knowing what to say to God, read the book of Psalms. Psalms is an entire book of prayers, and it will give you some ideas. Some people find it helpful to write their prayers in a notebook or journal. Talk to God about what is happening in your life—things that make you sad or angry, concerning questions, and any doubts you have. He is listening, and He has great love for you.

1. According to 1 Thessalonians 5:17, how often should we pray?
2. Read Psalm 27:10. Will God ever abandon you? How does it make you feel to know this truth?
3. How does David express his problems in Psalm 142:1-2?

25 WHAT SHOULD I PRAY?

MATTHEW 6:9-13

Jesus teaches His followers how to pray in Matthew 6:9-13, a passage often referred to as "The Lord's Prayer." First, worship God as a holy God who is worthy of all your worship: "May your name be kept holy" (v. 9). Thank Him for all He has done for you and ask Him to show you who He really is.

Next, surrender yourself to God's will and direction: "May your will be done" (v. 10). Submit every aspect of your life to God and ask Him for His guidance, wisdom, protection, and blessings. Bring every decision, anxiety, and relationship issue to Him. Tell God about what you are going through, what you desire, what you struggle with, and what worries you.

Then pray for provision: "Give us today the food we need" (v. 11). After you surrender to God and begin walking in His will, He provides for you as your Father. He is gracious, generous, and faithful. Tell God your needs and desires regarding finances, friends, favor, jobs, houses, your children, or any other concerns you have. When you have a need, bring it to God every day until He provides. Then praise Him when He does it.

Ask God to forgive you for things you have done wrong and admit any area where you have fallen short of His holy standards: "Forgive us our sins . . ." (v. 12). Confess to Him what you did wrong and ask for forgiveness for it. We also must forgive others who have sinned against us (v. 12). Forgiveness doesn't make the offender or the offense right, but it will set you free from any power it has over you.

Then ask for guidance and protection: "Rescue us from the evil one" (v. 13). When you are walking in God's will, you are under His protective covering; however, if you disobey Him, you step out from under that covering. Walk with God, and things will be more peaceful, successful, and safe.

Some versions of the Bible include a final phrase that is not in every manuscript. However, it is still a true statement about God: "For yours is the kingdom and the power and the glory forever. Amen" (v. 13). Acknowledge God's divine right over all creation, which means you refuse any kingdom, power, or glory you may want to take for yourself. Declare that God is the only true King of the only true kingdom, the only real power, and the only One with a right to glory. Orient your heart to serve God, rely on His power, and bring Him glory in the way you live.

Jesus says whatever we ask the Father in His name will be granted to us (John 15:16; 16:23). *Amen* means 'let it be so.' Praying in Jesus' name means we have aligned our lives and prayers with His authority and purposes for us.

1. How does Paul say we should pray in Philippians 4:6-7?

2. Read James 5:16. Why should we confess our sins to each other?

3. Read James 5:17–18. How does Elijah's life demonstrate the power of prayer?

26 WHY DO I NEED THE BAPTISM IN THE HOLY SPIRIT?

ACTS 1:5

Once you have been saved and baptized in water, there is another important step for you to take to live a successful Christian life: the baptism in the Holy Spirit. This experience comes after salvation, but it doesn't automatically happen just because you are saved.

The Holy Spirit is God and is equal with God the Son (Jesus) and God the Father. We often say He is the third person of the Trinity—Father, Son, and *Holy Spirit*. He always speaks and acts in harmony with God's Word and character. Just as water baptism is immersion in water, the baptism in the Holy Spirit is being immersed into a relationship with Him. We become saturated with the Holy Spirit's presence from the inside out.

After rising from death and before ascending into heaven, Jesus told His disciples to stay in Jerusalem until they were filled with the Holy Spirit. Once they received the Holy Spirit, they would be empowered to be His witnesses throughout the world (Acts 1:8). The baptism in the Holy Spirit helps us live for God, grow in our knowledge of Him, accomplish His will, and overcome sin. We need an ongoing partnership with the Holy Spirit,

which is why Jesus spoke of the Holy Spirit so often and commanded His disciples to wait for the Spirit to come.

The Holy Spirit draws us to Jesus and comes to dwell in every believer when we receive salvation. He is our Helper and is always with us (John 14:16). He shows us the truth (John 14:17), teaches us (John 14:26), and provides correction (John 16:8). However, it is not until we receive the baptism in the Holy Spirit that we receive all His benefits. We begin to see His fruit in our lives—love, joy, peace, patience, kindness, goodness, faithfulness, gentleness, and self-control (Galatians 5:22–23). The Holy Spirit empowers us to become the persons He created us to be (Acts 1:8), and He gives us spiritual gifts (1 Corinthians 12:4–7) to help us fulfill His calling on our lives.

1. Read Acts 1:4–5 and Acts 2:38. What is the *gift* believers should receive after they have been saved and water-baptized?
2. According to Acts 19:2, is it possible to be saved and not be baptized in the Holy Spirit?
3. Read John 14:16–17; 15:26; and Isaiah 11:2. What are some other names for the Holy Spirit? What do you think these names mean?

27 HOW DO I RECEIVE THE BAPTISM IN THE HOLY SPIRIT?

MATTHEW 3:11

Once we receive salvation, Jesus will baptize us in the Holy Spirit if we ask Him to do so (Matthew 3:11). To be a disciple of Jesus Christ, the Bible says we must repent (which means to change our hearts and minds), submit to (water) baptism, and receive the Holy Spirit (Acts 2:38). Jesus commanded His disciples, "Do not leave Jerusalem until the Father sends you the gift he promised" (Acts 1:4). The Holy Spirit is that promised gift, and He is still available to us today (Acts 2:39).

The baptism in the Holy Spirit makes us more like Jesus, and it makes living for Him possible and exciting. Have you received the baptism in the Holy Spirit since you were saved? The Bible places importance on the laying on of hands, especially as it relates to imparting the Holy Spirit (Acts 8:17; 19:6). You may want to ask a pastor or another Spirit-filled believer to pray for you. If you'd like to

receive the baptism in the Holy Spirit now, then pray this prayer:

Father, thank You for the promise of the Holy Spirit and for sending Him into my life. I repent of my sins. I also choose to forgive others who have hurt me, sinned against me, or brought harm to my loved ones. By faith, I ask You to baptize me in Your Holy Spirit. I surrender my life to You. Holy Spirit, fill me. I ask You to lead me closer to Jesus and empower me to live in victory for Him. Impart spiritual gifts into my life and use me to glorify God and help others. I surrender my tongue to You and pray that You will give me a personal prayer language to enable me to pray more effectively. In Jesus' name, Amen.

1. According to Luke 11:13, who gives us the Holy Spirit?

2. Read Galatians 3:1-14. How did Abraham receive God's promise? Can we receive God's promises the same way?

3. Read Acts 8:9-23. What prevented Simon from receiving the baptism in the Holy Spirit?

28 WHY SHOULD I PRAY IN TONGUES?

1 CORINTHIANS 14:15

When believers talk about the practice of *speaking in tongues*, they can be referring to one or both of two definitions. Speaking in tongues can be a message from God that is interpreted for the strengthening and encouragement of others (Acts 2:4-8; 1 Corinthians 14:5-13). Speaking in tongues can also be a private prayer language that strengthens an individual as he or she prays in the Spirit (Romans 8:26; 1 Corinthians 14:2-5, 14-15). God will not force you to speak in tongues, but you can choose to speak in this prayer language by faith as the Holy Spirit leads.

Occasionally, you may hear someone compare praying in tongues to the way a baby learns to speak. It may sound like repeating the same syllables over and over. Ask the Holy Spirit to put a syllable in your mind, and once He gives it to you, simply speak it. It will require faith for you to do this. However, just like any other language, it will get easier with practice.

Some people fear speaking in tongues or yielding completely to the Holy Spirit because they are concerned about losing control. However, it is just the opposite. In Galatians 5:22-23, the apostle Paul lists "self-control" as one characteristic of the fruit of the Holy Spirit. The Holy Spirit is gentle, gracious, and orderly in how He operates. Everything about Him is a blessing, and we never need to be afraid of Him.

The Holy Spirit helps us in our weaknesses, and when we pray in tongues, He can intercede on our behalf in ways we don't even know we need (Romans 8:26). Through a prayer language, the Holy Spirit also leads us into greater intimacy with God. Even though our minds may not understand as we pray or praise in tongues, our spirits are still edified and blessed.

1. Read Acts 2:4, 14. What did the believers do once they were filled with the Holy Spirit? What was Peter's response?
2. According to 1 Corinthians 14:4, what is a benefit of speaking in tongues?
3. Read Romans 8:26-27. When you pray in tongues, will the Holy Spirit ever lead you to pray for anything that goes against God's will? Why or why not?

29 HOW CAN I LIVE IN THE SPIRIT?

GALATIANS 5:16-26

The apostle Paul instructs believers to "let the Holy Spirit guide your lives" (Galatians 5:16). But how does this work? Do we make to-do lists full of good things and try to check enough items off each day to make God happy?

Think about your human relationships. Did you become close with your dearest friends by following a formula? Of course not. You have good relationships with them because you spend time with them. You've learned their likes and dislikes. You know how they talk and respond to things, and you can almost guess what they will say before they say it. You know you can trust them because you have seen them in action. All these aspects have helped build your relationships with your friends.

Now, think about the Holy Spirit. You have a relationship with Him too. It can be either weak and distant or strong and intimate—the choice is yours. The more you listen to the Holy Spirit's voice, the more you will recognize it. You will know how He responds to situations because you will have seen Him in action. You will be able to trust His goodness during difficult times because you will know He is faithful. The more time you spend with the Holy Spirit, the more you will know Him. And the more you know Him, the more you will be able to avoid "what your sinful nature craves" (Galatians 5:16).

Here are some ways you can live in the Spirit every day:

Give God control over your thoughts.
— When your mind goes unchecked, it can lead you toward pride, bitterness, fear, and many other negative thought patterns. These can inhibit your relationship with God. Ask the Holy Spirit to reveal and uproot any thoughts or beliefs that don't produce good fruit (Galatians 5:22-23). When you become saved, your spirit comes alive, but your soul (your mind, will, and emotions) is still accustomed to being in charge. God wants to purify every part of you. In His Word, He promises to give you the desire and power to obey Him (Philippians 2:13; Romans 8:9).

Resist temptation.

— Everyone faces temptation, even Christians. However, we have this promise: "God is faithful. He will not allow the temptation to be more than you can stand. When you are tempted, he will show you a way out so that you can endure" (1 Corinthians 10:13). The Holy Spirit has better plans for you than you could ever make for yourself. When you humbly submit to God's authority, temptation loses its power, and the devil "will flee from you" (James 4:7).

Listen for God's voice.

— When a close friend or relative calls you on the telephone, you don't have to ask, "Who is this?" Why? Because you recognize the voice. And how do you recognize someone's voice? By spending time with that person. The only way to learn to recognize God's voice is to spend time with Him. We do this through worship, praying, reading His Word, and even fasting. These actions help us learn to quiet our flesh and open our spiritual ears. God wants to talk to us, but He will not force us to listen.

Trust God's plan.

— Sometimes you may think the way God is leading you doesn't make sense. When God freed the Israelites from slavery in Egypt, the people struggled to trust Him. There was always something to complain about—food, water, sickness, etc. They questioned God's instructions, and they doubted His goodness, even after He did many miracles that proved His love and saving power (Exodus 13:17–17:13). Because of their disobedience, God did not allow that generation of Israelites to enter the Promised Land. Don't miss out on the promises God has in store for you because you let doubt and unbelief control your mind. You have already experienced one great miracle: when Jesus became your Lord and Savior. Trust Him to continue working for your good.

1. According to Romans 8:6-14, how can you have life and peace?
2. Read John 5:19-20. How did Jesus live in the Spirit? How can you follow His example?
3. Read Ephesians 4:21-24. How can you throw off your sinful nature?

30 WHAT IS THE BATTLE FOR MY MIND?

ISAIAH 26:3

Satan's weapon of choice is mental deception. He subtly introduces thoughts into our minds that covertly oppose God's Word and then tries to get us to accept them as truth. As followers of Christ, we can't experience freedom until we unmask those false beliefs and change the way we think.

To solve a problem, you have to deal with the root issue before you can find a real solution. Many people experience chronic problems such as sickness, fear, depression, sexual bondage, and eating disorders. False answers only provide temporary relief, and after many failed attempts, people often give up trying to find a solution.

The battle is not between you and Satan; it is between Satan and God's Word. You just have to decide whom you will believe. During Jesus' temptation in the wilderness, Satan attacked Him with half-truths and seductive offers (Matthew 4:1-11). Jesus responded to each thought with God's Word. He used the "sword of the Spirit" (Ephesians 6:17) to win the battle for His mind, and so can you.

The battle begins with taking every thought captive (2 Corinthians 10:3-5). Whenever a thought enters, it must submit to the authority of Jesus Christ—the Word (John 1:1). For example, when we are lonely, we may think no one cares about us. However, this thought does not agree with God's Word, so we must reject it. Find Scriptures

to counteract this lie, such as Psalm 16:8 ("The LORD is always with me") and 1 Peter 5:7 ("He cares about you"). Ask God to comfort you as you focus on the truth of His Word.

In Deuteronomy 6:7, God directs us to meditate on His Word during four specific times of day: when we are at home, when we are going somewhere, when we wake up, and when we go to bed. Identify the negative thoughts and false beliefs you struggle with and find Scriptures that declare God's truth on these issues. Write the Scriptures on notecards and tape them to places you'll see at the four times mentioned above. You can also save them to your phone or computer to help you meditate on God's truth. Then fight the battle for your freedom.

Jesus says if we abide in His Word, we will know the truth, and the truth will set us free (John 8:31-32). You must read His Word, meditate on it, and decide that it has the final say in your life. Only then will you be set free.

1. Read Matthew 4:1-11. How did Satan attack Jesus? Has he ever attacked you in a similar way?
2. According to Matthew 4:4, how did Jesus overcome Satan's attacks? How can you use the same method?
3. How can we have the "perfect peace" mentioned in Isaiah 26:3?

31 HOW DO I CHANGE MY ATTITUDE?

1 PETER 4:1-2

What determines a person's happiness? Is it an impressive career and an ever-growing bank account? Or perhaps a stable family unit and many supportive friends? While each of these factors can have a significant influence on your life, there is one thing, next to salvation, that will have the single greatest effect on your behavior and success: *your attitude.*

1 Peter 4:1-2 says believers should have the same attitude as Christ. So why do we still struggle with bitterness, anger, envy, and pride? To have the "mind of Christ" the apostle Paul writes about in 1 Corinthians 2:16, we must begin *by changing our attitude.*

Attitudes precede and predict our future. In Luke 6:45, Jesus says,

> "A good person produces good things from the treasury of a good heart, and an evil person produces evil things from the treasury of an evil heart. What you say flows from what is in your heart."

As you think about the past events of your life, are you grateful or ungrateful? Forgiving or bitter? A bad attitude about the past will keep you from having the future God wants to give you.

Bad attitudes begin as negative thought patterns, such as false expectations, comparison with others, entitlement, and self-pity. These negative patterns cause us to focus inwardly, leaving no room for the Holy Spirit to work in us. When we allow a bad attitude to plant itself in our minds, it is never for our benefit. It will only lead to failure, displeasure, and demotion.

The Bible is your attitude indicator. When you go through difficulties, turn your eyes and heart toward God's Word. The Holy Spirit is your Helper, and He will help you change your attitude. Thought patterns that build a good attitude include gratitude, faith, humility, and respect. Good attitudes lead to success, favor, and promotion.

Attitudes are always a choice. Some people have miserable circumstances and decide everyone else should be miserable as well. Others choose to find happiness, even though they too have experienced misery. Happiness is not a byproduct of your circumstances—it is a chosen attitude.

Attitudes also have consequences. This truth is essential for parents to understand if they want to raise godly children. Discipline cannot wait until bad behaviors and habits surface; instead, parents must address problems while they are still in the attitude stage. Our heavenly Father understands the importance of our attitudes. Because He loves us, God rewards good attitudes and disciplines bad ones (Hebrews 12:7-8).

Paul writes, "Don't copy the behavior and customs of this world, but let God transform you into a new person by changing the way you think" (Romans 12:2). Allow God to transform your attitude today. When it seems impossible to have a good attitude, remember Jesus' promise: "With God everything is possible" (Matthew 19:26).

1. According to Romans 14:17-18, what kind of attitude pleases God?
2. Read Matthew 5:5 and Proverbs 11:2. What are some benefits of having a humble attitude?
3. What was God's warning to Cain regarding his attitude in Genesis 4:5-7?
4. Read Acts 16:22-34. What happened when Paul and Silas chose to have the right attitude, even in a very difficult situation?

32 HOW SHOULD I DEFINE SUCCESS?

JOHN 6:29

What makes a person successful? According to the world's standard, success comes through wealth, education, popularity, and power. A "successful" person may be a hard worker or simply blessed, but either way, that person enjoys security and happiness in every area of life. There is one problem with this definition of success, though. It does not examine the most important detail: the spiritual condition of humanity.

During His earthly ministry, Jesus certainly did not meet the world's standard for success. Crowds enjoyed His miracles and followed Him for a short time, but then they turned against Him. Onlookers taunted Jesus as He hung on the cross, saying, "He saved others . . . but he can't save himself!" (Mark 15:31). Jesus never had financial wealth, and after the crucifixion, His followers buried His body in a borrowed tomb. In a prophetic message about the Messiah, Isaiah writes,

> There was nothing beautiful or majestic about his appearance,
> nothing to attract us to him.

He was despised and rejected—
a man of sorrows, acquainted with deepest grief.
We turned our back on him and looked the other way.
He was despised, and we did not care (Isaiah 53:2-3).

Jesus may have been a "failure" according to society, but through His blood, He paid the penalty for every sin we ever have and ever will commit. Sin created an impossible gap between God and us, and Jesus Himself became the bridge.

Earthly success only brings temporary happiness. If you want to be eternally successful, the Bible's standards are clear:

Have a personal relationship with Jesus.

— Salvation is not just a religious exercise, and becoming a Christian is much more than joining a social club. Through His sacrifice, Jesus offers us a personal relationship with God. Every person has a free will to choose to accept this offer or not. If we surrender the authority of our lives to Christ, we become children of God. In Hebrews 13:5, God promises He will never fail or abandon His people. However, if we reject Jesus' gift of eternal life, we will be permanently separated from Him.

Live for God, not only yourself.

— Salvation is by grace through faith, not works. However, God has given every believer gifts to further His Kingdom. We will all be held accountable for how we use our gifts. God values people more than anything else, and He wants us to share His love with the lost and hurting people in our lives. When we get to heaven, we will receive an eternal reward for what we have allowed God to do through us in this life.

Treat others with compassion and respect.

— Many "successful" people in the world are hard-hearted and self-centered. As believers, we should be different. We know that Jesus guarantees eternal life for us. If we truly love and want to obey Him, we should treat others with love and compassion, regardless of what they have done or can do for us.

God is just and fair. Acts 10:34-35 says, "God shows no favoritism. In every nation he accepts those who fear him and do what is right." It doesn't matter what possessions you own, how much money you make, or how educated you are. If you know Jesus, live for Him, and treat others with love, you will have everything you need to be successful— both now and for eternity.

1. Read Luke 16:19-31. What benefit are your earthly possessions and riches when you die?
2. Read Matthew 25:14-30. What does God want you to do with the talents He has given you?
3. Why should we treat others with compassion and respect, according to Matthew 25:34-36?

33 HOW DO I DEAL WITH ANXIETY AND WORRY?

PHILIPPIANS 4:6-7

Anxiety and worry are common problems in today's society, and even mature believers can struggle with these issues. *Anxiety* is a feeling of unease about an event, person, or problem you cannot control. *Worry* is usually the milder of the two emotions and relates to thinking about a specific difficulty. Anxiety and worry are both related to fear and are rooted in not understanding just how much God loves us.

We often experience worry and anxiety because we accept them as normal feelings. However, they are neither normal nor inevitable. Worry distracts us from God's promises, and anxiety robs us of our joy. In Matthew 6, Jesus says,

"I tell you not to worry about everyday life— whether you have enough food and drink, or enough clothes to wear. Isn't life more than food and your body more than clothing?. . . So don't worry about these things, saying, 'What will we eat? What will we drink? What will we wear?' These things dominate the thoughts of unbelievers, but your heavenly Father already knows all your needs. Seek the Kingdom of God above all else, and live righteously, and he will give you everything you need" (Matthew 6:25-33).

There are three ways to overcome worry and anxiety:

Consider them as enemies.

— The devil has no ability or authority to harm you, but he will do his best to intimidate you. You may experience difficulties in your finances, your relationships, or your health; however, don't allow anxiety and worry to rob you of God's promises. The apostle Paul writes, "This same God who takes care of me will supply all your needs from his glorious riches, which have been given to us in Christ Jesus" (Philippians 4:19).

Turn thoughts into prayers.

— When we try to pray, our minds often wander to the things bothering us. Write these worries down and add them to your prayer list. Continue to turn every anxious or worrisome thought into a prayer until you have victory (Philippians 4:6-7). The devil wants you to think you have to solve your own problems, but he is a liar. God is a loving Father who wants to help you with every circumstance. Thank Him today that He loves you, hears you, and will answer your prayers.

Believe in faith and confess God's love.

— Sometimes we feel discouraged when our prayers do not receive an immediate answer. The devil tries to plant doubts in our minds

about God's faithfulness, so it is important to stay firmly rooted in God's Word. Romans 10:17 says, "Faith comes from hearing, that is, hearing the Good News about Christ." Whenever you feel worry and anxiety lurking nearby, hold tightly to God's promises.

1. As believers, what should we seek above all else, according to Matthew 6:31-33?
2. Read Psalm 138:8. Will God ever stop caring about us? Why or why not?
3. Read John 16:33. How should Christians react when they face difficulties?

---

34 HOW CAN I OVERCOME INSECURITY AND FEAR?

2 TIMOTHY 1:7

Every person deals with insecurity and fear at some point in life. The devil wants believers to live in bondage, ashamed of their weaknesses and too afraid to ask for help. However, God wants to set us free, and He shows us the path to freedom in His Word.

Insecurity is a lack of confidence on a personal level. Some people may be insecure about one or two areas while others feel insecure about almost everything. How can we deal with insecurity? The world's cures include money, physical appearance, and comparing oneself with others. However, the only true remedy is a personal relationship with Jesus Christ. Without knowing Him, any security we feel is fleeting and false.

King Saul was a very insecure man. As the first king of Israel, he had an opportunity to be an incredible leader; however, he allowed his insecurities to dictate his actions. King Saul became angry and jealous (1 Samuel 18:8-9), unable to accept responsibility (1 Samuel 15:15), and emotionally unstable (1 Samuel 18:10-11). Due to his unteachable spirit, God rejected Saul in favor of David, "a man after my own heart" (Acts 13:22).

The apostle Paul also faced insecurity. He had a "thorn in the flesh" (a physical affliction), and even though he asked God to remove it three times, the thorn remained. Unlike King Saul, though, Paul chose to trust God's promise: "My grace is all you need. My power works best in weakness" (2 Corinthians 12:9).

If we want to defeat insecurity, we must first turn to God. He is our refuge in every time of trouble (Psalm 91:1-3). Placing our confidence in anyone or anything else will only lead to disappointment. Second, we should embrace our weaknesses. We may not be able to change our situation, but our hope is in God our heavenly Father, who loves us and will never disappoint us (Romans 5:3-5). Finally, we need to put our faith in God's grace. We don't have to do anything to deserve it; in fact, it's impossible to earn it. God's

grace is a *free* gift that comes with unconditional love, unending joy, and eternal security.

God did not design us to live with insecurity, and He does not want us to live with fear either. Next to the command to love, "Do not fear" is one of the most often repeated instructions in the Bible. But if Jesus is our Prince of Peace (Isaiah 9:6), then why do believers still experience fear?

Satan uses fear to try to stop us from doing God's will. He even tried to stop Jesus from sacrificing Himself for humanity's sins. In the Garden of Gethsemane, just before His arrest, Jesus experienced tremendous, agonizing fear. He prayed, "Father, if you are willing, please take this cup of suffering away from me. Yet I want your will to be done, not mine" (Luke 22:42).

Yes, Jesus experienced fear, but He also defeated it, and we can too. Remember—fear is always from the enemy. God will never use fear to control you (2 Timothy 1:7). First Peter 5:8 calls the devil "a roaring lion, looking for someone to devour." He cannot control your thoughts, but he will try to influence them. To defeat fear, you must:

Admit your fear.

— The enemy wants to keep you trapped in shame and darkness, but the Holy Spirit is ready and willing to help you if you will bring your fear into the light.

Submit your fear to God.

— God sent an angel to strengthen Jesus in the garden of Gethsemane, and He will come to your rescue as well. He will give you the ability to act above your fear and discern the truth (John 8:32).

Focus on God's presence and love.

— Remind yourself that God is bigger, stronger, and more powerful than the enemy. Even while fleeing for his life from King Saul, David refused to give into fear. He wrote,

I will not be afraid,
> for you are close beside me
> (Psalm 23:4).

Faith is not the absence of reality; it is reality *plus* God. Hebrews 13:5 promises God will never fail or abandon us. No matter what insecurities or fears the devil may try to distract you with, remain confident and boldly declare,

I know the LORD is always with me.
> I will not be shaken, for he is right beside me
> (Psalm 16:8).

1. Read 1 Samuel 18:6-12. Why did King Saul want to kill David?
2. What gives Paul the confidence to overcome insecurity in 2 Corinthians 12:7-10?
3. Read 1 John 4:8, 18. Does God ever use fear to instruct or punish us?

---

35 WHAT SHOULD I DO WHEN I DON'T FEEL JOYFUL?

PSALM 42

Jesus' disciples expected Him to be a conquering hero, freeing the people of Israel from centuries of oppression and leading them to a life of ease and success. Like many believers today, they were surprised to hear Jesus say, "Here on earth you will have many trials and sorrows" (John 16:33). What's the point of following God, then? What difference does it make? Jesus answers in the second part of the verse: "But take heart, because I have overcome the world" (John 16:33).

No matter the situation or circumstance, Jesus is our hope. Before He went to the cross, Jesus promised His disciples a gift: "peace of mind and heart" (John 14:27). As believers, we have the Holy Spirit, who is our constant Advocate, Comforter, and Encourager (John 14:16).

Salvation does not insulate us from the fallen world in which we live, but it does give us a choice. When we face disappointment, discontentment, or even disaster, how will we respond? James 1:2-4 offers an answer:

> Dear brothers and sisters, when troubles of any kind come your way, consider it an opportunity for great *joy*. For you know that when your faith is tested, your endurance has a chance to grow. So let it grow, for when your endurance is fully developed, you will be perfect and complete, needing nothing (emphasis added).

You may not have had a choice about some of the difficulties in your life. Factors may be entirely out of your control, leaving you with a feeling of hopelessness. For some, this hopelessness can be so consuming that any escape, even death, seems preferable to continuing this life. In these moments, our only hope is to cry out to God. He is not distant nor ambivalent. God called David "a man after my own heart" (Acts 13:22), but David was no stranger to adversity. He faced death on a daily basis for years, both from foreign enemies and from King Saul. In one of his most famous psalms, David writes,

The LORD is my shepherd;
> I have all that I need. . . .

Even when I walk
> through the darkest valley,
> I will not be afraid,
> for you are close beside me (Psalm 23:1, 4).

The apostle Paul also knew hardship. If anyone had the right to feel less than joyful, it was him; after all, he had "worked harder, been put in prison more often, been whipped times without number, and faced death again and again" (2 Corinthians 11:23). What was Paul's secret to keeping his joy through all these troubles?

> I have learned the secret of living in every situation, whether it is with a full stomach or empty, with plenty or little. For I can do everything through Christ, who gives me strength (Philippians 4:12-13).

If we allow our thoughts and feelings to control us, we will always find a reason to be discontented or dissatisfied. It is easy to think, "I deserve better, and if God *really* cared about me, He would . . ." Satan wants you to doubt God's goodness, and he will lie to you as long as you will let him.

So how can you trust God and be joyful regardless of your circumstances?

Ask the Holy Spirit to examine your heart.
— The Holy Spirit can help you identify the reason for your discontent (Psalm 42:11; 139:23-24). He will use your emotions to tell you when you need to make something right. Perhaps you need to grieve a loss, reconcile with someone, or get your expectations in line with God's plan for you. You won't know if you don't seek Him.

Let the Holy Spirit comfort you.
— God is the source of all comfort, and He will give you rest in exchange for your burdens (2 Corinthians 1:3-5; Matthew 11:28). Ask the Holy Spirit what He says about your situation

and what He wants you to do about it. Listen to His reply and obey. God will turn your mourning into dancing and clothe you with joy (Psalm 30:11–12).

Give God thanks in all things.
— When you go through difficult times, thank and praise God for His presence. All God's promises in the Bible are for you, so take the time to read and live in His Word. He has power over every storm (Matthew 8:23–27), and He is bringing about good for you (Romans 8:28).

Resist the enemy.
— The devil wants to steal from you and then kill and destroy you (John 10:10). He wants you to believe God is not good, powerful, or interested in your life. Don't fall for his lies. Call on God— He will deliver you (Joel 2:32). Put on the armor of God, pray in the Spirit, and worship God every day (Ephesians 6:10–18). Fix your thoughts on

the Lord, and He will guard your heart and mind and give you peace (Isaiah 26:3; Philippians 4:8).

Reach out to other believers.
— It is easy to become fixated on your own problems. Other believers can help redirect your focus to God and offer life-giving instruction (Proverbs 13:14). Find several mature, trustworthy believers who can build you up when you need encouragement, hold you up when you need strength, and straighten you up when you need correction.

1. What does God give us when we are going through troubles, according to 2 Corinthians 1:3–5?
2. Read Psalms 42 and 103. What does David say and do when he is discouraged?
3. Read Job 1. After losing everything, what is Job's response in verses 20–21?
4. What does God do when the righteous cry out for help in Psalm 34:17–20?

---

36 HOW CAN I GET FREEDOM FROM GENERATIONAL SIN?

1 JOHN 1:9

In biblical terms, an *iniquity* is a tendency toward sin or error because of a parent's influence or a family's history. Another term for iniquity is *generational sin*. These tendencies negatively influence our lives, and God wants us to have freedom from them. What steps should you take to gain freedom from generational sin?

Learn to recognize the iniquities of your parents.
— An iniquity is any form of behavior you recognize in your family history as being unbiblical, unrepresentative of God's character, and having a generational influence. Some common iniquities include (but are not limited to) anger, bitterness, judgmentalism, abuse, fear, manipulation, irresponsibility, rebellion, moral impurity, and addiction. Freedom begins with recognizing the presence of iniquities in your family.

Forgive your parents and family for the influence their iniquities had on you.
— Once you forgive them, realize you are also responsible for your own behavior and then repent. If your family influenced you negatively, you likely do many of the same things your parents did to you. Ask God and those you have harmed through your behavior for forgiveness. Get help so you will not continue on the same path. Sin destroys families because we fail to recognize and deal with it properly. However, if we call sin what it is, forgive those who have sinned, and repent for our own sins, then Jesus' blood erases the power of that sin from our lives.

Submit yourself to Jesus.
— Iniquities begin when parents rebel against God's authority and the truth of His Word. The resulting sin twists and distorts their children's lives and perceptions. You can only break the cycle by recognizing the original sin and making things right. Ask Jesus to heal and change this area in your life. Admit your problem and submit to the Word of God. Ask the Holy Spirit to show you the truth and correct you.

Pray.

Father, I recognize this iniquity and repent of my involvement in it. I forgive the members of my family for anything they have done wrong, and I bless them in Jesus' name. I ask for Your forgiveness and receive it. I also break the power of this iniquity off my life in Jesus' name. I break [name the iniquity] off my life and all future generations. I renounce it and pray that You will heal me and teach me how to change in this area and walk in obedience to You. I thank You for forgiving me and setting me free. In Jesus' name, Amen.

1. According to Deuteronomy 5:9–10, how many generations experience the effects of generational sin? How many generations will God show His love to when people obey His commands?
2. What does 1 John 1:9 say God is faithful to do if we confess our sins?
3. Read Matthew 6:14–15. Why is forgiving others an essential part of having victory of generational sins?

37 WHAT ARE INNER VOWS?

MATTHEW 5:33-37

An *inner vow* is a self-oriented commitment made in response to a person, experience, or desire in life. Whenever we focus a commitment inward, it becomes an inner vow. We often make inner vows in response to pain or frustration in an attempt to comfort ourselves regarding the future. Rather than freeing us from the problem, though, inner vows act as tethers that tie us to the past in an unhealthy way. Some common examples of inner vows include:
— "No one will ever hurt me again!"
— "I'll never be vulnerable again to anyone."
— "I'm never going to be like my parents."

Regardless of how noble our motives are, there are three major problems with inner vows.

Inner vows go against God's Word.
— If we make significant commitments in our lives, we should focus them toward God and fulfill them as acts of worship and obedience to Him. Inner vows perform the exact opposite function. Instead of submitting everything to the lordship of Christ, inner vows take control of an individual's life away from God and set a course without His approval or blessing.

Inner vows have unforeseen effects on our lives.
— They have a powerful influence on us, whether we realize it or not. Inner vows have the power to pull the strongest of us in directions we don't even realize. After we have made inner vows, they can become a part of our subconscious mind until something provokes them. The most dangerous aspect of inner vows is that they influence our daily decisions instead of God.

Inner vows are our highest level of commitment.
— If we swear to ourselves that we will or will not do something, then this commitment subconsciously overrides any commitment we have to God. Consequently, many sincere Christians say they love God but have areas of their lives operating in opposition to His purposes. Without realizing it, their commitment has become a competitor with Christ.

If we realize there are commitments we have made to ourselves and withheld from God, we must quickly submit them to God, or they will keep us from fully living for Him.

1. Read Matthew 5:33-37. Why does Jesus say we should not make vows?
2. According to Psalm 37:4-5, what should we do instead of making inner vows?
3. What inner vows do you need to submit to God today?

38 HOW CAN I GET FREEDOM FROM INNER VOWS?

MATTHEW 5:33-37

If you want God to set you free from the inner vows you have made, you must first recognize what those vows are. Think about how you responded to difficult or negative circumstances in the past. Did you make promises to yourself about relationships, money, pain, or anything else? Can you easily fill in one of the following blanks?
— "I will never allow _____ to happen."
— "My children will always have _____."
— "I will never trust _____ again."

When you recognize a specific judgment and the resulting vow you made to yourself while growing up or even as an adult, renounce it and repent for trying to take control of your own life. Then submit that area to God. Give the Lord control over every area of your life and ask Him to break the power of your inner vow. Find out what the Bible says to do in that situation and obey God's Word (James 1:22).

Submit your judgments and release unforgiveness to God. Almost all inner vows go back to some level of judgmentalism or unforgiveness. If you have made inner vows, you almost always have someone to forgive and judgments to break.

God wants to help and bless us in every area. Whenever we reject His wise counsel and grace, we make a terrible mistake. Inner vows threaten to distract us from God because they pull our loyalties away from Him and toward our own self-governing agendas. Even if your inner vow has a positive and healthy commitment attached to it, it should be made to the Lord, not to yourself. God will give you the freedom and power to fulfill His will for your life.

1. Read Matthew 23:16-22. Why does Jesus dislike the way the Pharisees make vows?
2. Read Colossians 3:23-24. To whom should we commit our efforts?
3. According to John 15:5, can we do anything by our own efforts? Why or why not?

39   HOW DO I BUILD GODLY RELATIONSHIPS?

ACTS 2:46

The easiest way to find godly relationships is in a Bible-believing, Holy Spirit-empowered church. Once you find this kind of church, get involved in a small group that will help you develop closer relationships with other believers.

The earliest Christians met together in the Temple, the synagogues, and individual houses, which established intimate fellowship (Acts 2:46). These first believers had large group meetings and small group gatherings on a regular basis. Their model is still significant for believers today. You will experience God in a powerful way as you meet corporately in larger groups, and you will experience rich Christian fellowship when you become part of a small group. Both the large and small settings are essential for making godly friends and living a successful Christian life.

When you're searching for friends, don't look for perfection. Instead, seek people who are sincere, humble, and have a desire to love and obey God. No one is perfect, but you will soon recognize the difference between people who are sincere and those who are not. Don't judge them based on rumors but on things you know to be true from your personal experience (Exodus 23:1). Learn healthy ways of relating to others and put those behaviors into practice. God intends for your relationships to be a blessing to you. A godly relationship includes these important elements: boundaries, accountability, trustworthiness, integrity, mutual respect, honesty, fairness, and equality. Look for people who will care about you and share sound biblical advice with you.

You will become like the people you spend time with, so commit your search for friends to God. Seek out believers who love the Lord and are not simply "religious." Trust God, and He will help you find godly friends with whom you can develop Christ-centered relationships (Psalm 37:5).

1. Read Exodus 20 and Deuteronomy 5. What boundaries has God given us for relating to one another?
2. According to Ecclesiastes 4:12, why are godly relationships important?
3. Read Proverbs 27:17. What is a benefit of Christ-centered friendships?

40   WHY SHOULD I AVOID UNGODLY RELATIONSHIPS?

2 CORINTHIANS 6:14-18

When we choose to follow Jesus and obey the Bible, God blesses our lives (Psalm 1:2-3). Scripture is God's guidance for us, and He means for it to be a blessing if we will obey it (Psalm 119:105). God commands us to separate ourselves and live a different lifestyle from that of unbelievers. He doesn't mean we can't be friendly and kind to everyone. However, unbelievers cannot be our source of fellowship and friendship. Our closest relational circle needs to consist of godly believers. God warns us not to be deceived: immoral company will corrupt good character and endanger our souls (1 Corinthians 15:33; Proverbs 22:24-25).

Immoral people should not have an influential position in your life (Psalm 1:5). If you want to prosper, do not take spiritual or moral advice from immoral people, go into business with them, or spend a lot of time with them (Psalm 1:1). You can walk closely with seasoned believers and become wise as you spend time with them, or you can associate with immoral people and get yourself into trouble (Proverbs 13:20).

Jesus' friends were His disciples. He did spend a lot of time with unbelievers but not in situations in which they had influence on Him. Jesus always had influence on others, and He invited unbelievers to follow Him and learn His ways (Matthew 9:9-13). He met their needs by casting out evil spirits and healing them (Matthew 8:16-17). Jesus was always connected to God the Father (John 10:30, 38). He listened for the Father's voice and only did what He was led to do (John 5:19).

As believers in an unbelieving world, Jesus compares us to "sheep among wolves." He commands us to be "as shrewd as snakes and harmless as doves" (Matthew 10:16). Be wise about your choices and glorify God as you allow Him to guide you. When you trust Him and seek what He wants, He will show you what to do (Proverbs 3:5-6).

1. According to Exodus 34:12, what happens when believers make covenant relationships with unbelievers?
2. Read Deuteronomy 28:1-14 and 30:19. What does God guarantee for us if we listen to His Word and obey what He says?
3. Read Proverbs 4:18-19. How is the way of the righteous different from the way of the wicked?

41 WHAT IF SOMEONE OFFENDS ME?

MATTHEW 18:15-17

Bumps and bruises in our relationships are inevitable. There is no genuine relationship in which conflict doesn't happen. When we are in committed, long-term relationships, we can expect problems, and we should deal with them maturely and according to God's Word. Prayer is often the solution that brings healing to our hurts and disappointments (1 John 5:16-17).

When someone offends or sins against us, Jesus says we should first go to the offender privately and attempt to talk about what happened. This approach is essential for building healthy relationships. When offenders confess and change their behavior, we should forgive them and celebrate. If they don't repent, Jesus says to go back again with one or two people as witnesses. If the offender still doesn't repent or confess wrongdoing, we should then bring the matter to our church leaders. After all these attempts, if the offender still hasn't repented, we should break off close relations with them until they do, even though we still love and pray for them (Matthew 18:15-17).

The worst situations occur when a serious offense, such as a moral, legal, or spiritual sin, is involved, and the guilty party will not repent or acknowledge any wrongdoing. This can be especially difficult if the person we must confront is a church leader or friend. If the sin is with a pastor or prominent leader of the church, and if the other leaders of the church won't address it, we may have to consider leaving the church. This step must be taken with extreme caution, though. We should never consider separation too quickly. The devil is an accuser (Revelation 12:10), and his full-time job is to make us offended at God, our family members, our church, and our Christian friends. He hates godly, wholesome, and healthy relationships, and he is always trying to produce confusion and division.

We should only separate after much prayer and doing everything we can to reconcile with others. Most of the time, when we speak the truth in love to others and are willing to take responsibility for our own problems and mistakes, situations will be resolved.

1. Read Colossians 3:13. What should we do when others offend us?
2. According to 1 Peter 3:9, how should we treat those who have sinned against us?
3. What sign in Ephesians 4:15 shows we are growing to be more like Christ?
4. Read James 5:19-20. What do you think James means by "the forgiveness of many sins"?

42 HOW DO I FORGIVE?

MATTHEW 6:14-15

Relationships can be very messy. In a world full of imperfect people, it's impossible to avoid being hurt by others. When someone commits an offense against us, God wants us to forgive that person. Forgiveness is for our benefit. When we don't forgive someone, we are tied to that person in bondage. However, Jesus sets us free when we forgive. Forgiveness doesn't make the offense right, but it frees us as we continue to love and live in freedom.

If you have never actively practiced forgiveness, you may have many people you need to forgive. How do you do it?

— Ask the Holy Spirit to help you write a list of everyone who has ever hurt you and what those people did. Tell Jesus you choose to forgive the people on your list. Ask Him to cover their sins with His blood as you release them of the debt you've been holding against them. This does not mean you condone their actions; instead, you simply remove yourself from being their judge. God alone will be their judge now. Ask Him to heal the wounds and traumas in your

heart and set you free from their effects (Psalm 147:3). As you do this, it may help to speak out loud or write in a journal.

— Acknowledge the high value God places on those people who have offended you. The people you despise or hold bitterness toward are God's children, and He loves them. Declare yourself incompetent to judge them. Only God knows their hearts and the reasons they behaved as they did (1 Samuel 16:7). You can trust God to judge righteously.

— Recognize forgiveness is a choice. God wants you to do what is right, regardless of your feelings (Galatians 6:9). Your feelings are valid and real and may not change for a while; however, if you continue to choose to forgive, God will heal you. When you bless those who curse you and pray for those who mistreat you (Luke 6:27-28), you open the door for God to heal you from feelings of anger, bitterness, hate, hurt, and offense.

— Finally, forgive yourself. Give shame, anger, and any other negative emotions about yourself to Jesus. Ask the Holy Spirit to show you anything you hold against yourself. Choose to love yourself the way Jesus loves you (1 John 3:1) and speak His truth over your life. Declare, "Through the power of what Jesus did for me on the cross, I am worthy, pure, and righteous. Jesus calls me loved, precious, and valuable, and because He says it, I choose to believe

it!" Ask the Holy Spirit to fill you and set you free. Wherever He is, there is freedom (2 Corinthians 3:17).

1. Read Matthew 6:14-15. What must we do for God to forgive us?
2. How does Paul say we should relate to one another in Ephesians 4:2-3?
3. According to Matthew 7:1-2, why is it dangerous to judge others?

43 WHY SHOULD I CARE ABOUT THE WORLD?

JOHN 13:34-35

Sometimes Christians are confused about how they should relate to the world. The apostle John says,

Do not love this world nor the things it offers you, for when you love the world, you do not have the love of the Father in you. For the world offers only a craving for physical pleasure, a craving for everything we see, and pride in our achievements and possessions. These are not from the Father, but are from this world. And this world is fading away, along with everything that people crave. But anyone who does what pleases God will live forever (1 John 2:15-17).

Are these verses saying Christians should only interact with other Christians and shut themselves off from anyone or anything outside the church? Of course not. God cares about the world—about people. He loves them so much He gave His own Son to save them (John 3:16). Jesus says God's greatest commandments are to love Him and love others (Matthew 22:36-40). Some Christians have wrongly taken this as an excuse to continue doing wrong things or to seek out sinful relationships. Instead, as believers, our lives should be significantly different, to the point that others notice and wonder how they too can experience such healing and freedom.

God has given you the responsibility to share His Good News with others (Matthew 28:19). Remember, someone cared enough about you to tell you about Jesus. You know firsthand the incredible truth about God's love and His promise

of eternal life. You will want to share this news with others. How could you keep it a secret?

The apostle Paul says it is God's kindness that turns us away from sin (Romans 2:4). As we are kind to others, showing them love and grace, we demonstrate to them the character of our Father. God is patient, and He waits for us to turn away from our mistakes and bad choices. He cares for us (1 Peter 5:7), and when the Holy Spirit lives inside us, we begin to care about others. Our love for others is the proof that we are truly followers of Christ (John 13:35). Jesus says when we care for others, we are also caring for Him (Matthew 25:40).

Can you remember what your life was like before you met Jesus? Perhaps your past was very troubled. Maybe you regret some of your words or actions. Do you ever wish someone had told you about Jesus sooner? People who still live in the world urgently need to know and experience the love you have found.

Jesus says His followers are "the light of the world" (Matthew 5:14). If we hide our light by keeping the Good News confined to the comfort of our homes or circles of Christian friends, the darkness in the world will grow stronger and stronger. The only way people will know how much Jesus loves and values them is if we tell them!

1. Read Luke 16:19-31. Why was it too late for the rich man to warn his brothers?
2. What will we do if we really are Jesus' "friends," according to John 15:13-17?
3. According to Galatians 6:9, what will happen if we obey God's commands?

44 HOW CAN I WITNESS TO OTHERS?

1 JOHN 1:1-4

God loves you and has done a wonderful thing in your life: He has adopted you as His child through the work of His Son, Jesus. Naturally,

you will want to tell others what has happened to you. Telling others about Jesus is often called *witnessing*. What is the right way to be a witness for Jesus?

Adopt an attitude of humility.

— God did a great and powerful thing for you when you surrendered your life to Him. Remember, He loved you and chose you before you ever chose Him. It is only by God's grace you have been saved. He now calls you to obey Him by telling others about His amazing work. As you do what God tells you to do, you will begin to see His goodness and favor on your life like never before. We call that being blessed!

Tell your story.

— Your testimony is the most authentic and effective tool you have for witnessing. It is the best story you have *because it is yours*. Always be prepared to share it. The Bible says believers overcome Satan as they share their testimonies (Revelation 12:11). Have you seen the goodness of God? Then tell others about what He has done (Acts 4:20). God has saved you *from* eternal death and separation from Him. But *for what* has He saved you? You know what your life was like before you heard about Jesus and asked Him to be your Lord. How has your life changed since then? Perhaps you were sick in your body or spirit. How has He healed you? Everything good comes from God (James 1:17). Now you have the opportunity to tell others about His love, mercy, and goodness (Isaiah 63:7).

Be ready to serve.

— Jesus drew many people to Himself because He met their needs for compassion, truth, freedom, healing, hope, and even food. God has given you skills, gifts, and talents so you can serve others. As you listen and obey, He will give you fresh opportunities to share His Good News. Ask the Holy Spirit to teach you what to say and do (Exodus 4:12).

Trust the Holy Spirit.

— Jesus promised the Holy Spirit would help us be His witnesses all over the world (Acts 1:8). You can certainly share your testimony at church with other believers, but most people who have never heard about Jesus are outside the church. Ask God to tell you where to go and when to talk about Him with other people. Pray for opportunities to witness and tell others about God's goodness.

Turn away from fear.

— Don't let the fear of rejection keep you from witnessing (1 John 4:18). You may have some unpleasant interactions with others, but remember that many people have a deep desire to experience God in a real way. Paul writes in Romans 10:14, "How can they hear about him unless someone tells them?" God promises to help you as you obey Him (Hebrews 13:6). Know who you are in Christ—a child of God, forgiven of your sins, and a new creation in Him (2 Corinthians 5:17). Don't be swayed by what anyone else says. Jesus is your friend, so join in a close and intimate relationship with Him first. When you know what God thinks and says about you, you will have security in His love. Other people will notice your confidence and ask for the reason behind your joy and hope. Then you will be prepared to answer them. Pray today for boldness to speak God's truth (Acts 4:29-31).

1. According to 1 Peter 3:15, what should believers always be ready to do?
2. Read Matthew 28:18-20. How do we fulfill this "Great Commission"?
3. What does Jesus tell His disciples to do in Mark 16:15-18? Can we do the same things today?
4. How did you first hear about Jesus?

45 WHY IS MY TESTIMONY IMPORTANT?

REVELATION 12:11

Why is your testimony so important? Just as a witness is called to testify in a court of law, so you are called to tell the truth about Jesus to others. Your testimony is your story of what Jesus has done for you, and it has great power to help others believe in Him too.

You will overcome the lies of Satan.

— The words you speak "can bring death or life" (Proverbs 18:21). If you speak lies, curses, negativity, and gossip, then you speak death. If you speak God's Word, love, and truth, then you speak life. In addition, when you honor God by telling others what He has done for you,

you speak life, and your testimony defeats the enemy (Revelation 12:11).

God will build faith in the hearts of those who hear.

— As you share your testimony, you plant seeds of faith in others (Romans 10:17). God loves people and wants everyone to be saved (2 Peter 3:9), but if we are unwilling to tell others about the free gift of salvation, we rob them of the opportunity to know Him (Romans 10:14-15). You honor and thank God for His salvation and freedom by sharing your story. As others come to know Christ and accept Him as their Savior, they will then gain the faith to share their own testimonies.

People will come to believe.

— In the Bible, many people heard about Jesus and then believed in Him because they heard testimonies. After Jesus raised Lazarus from death, many people believed (John 12:9-11). Jesus talked with the Samaritan woman at a water well. Then she gave her testimony to the people in her town, and they came to meet Jesus. As a result, many believed (John 4:4-42). Some of the details of the Samaritan woman's story were personally embarrassing, but she told them anyway. What would have happened if she had kept her story to herself?

Some people welcome an argument. However, your testimony is not likely to start one because it is your unique, personal experience. God has called you to be a light to others, but if you hide your light, the world will only grow dimmer (Matthew 5:14-16). Jesus says He is the light of the world (John 8:12), and now His light is in us (Ephesians 5:8). Today, He wants you to use your testimony to tell everyone about His light (John 1:7).

1. In Philippians 3:4-17, whose story does Paul use to share God's Good News?
2. What needs to happen for people to be saved, according to Romans 10:14-15?
3. Write down your testimony and practice sharing it in two minutes or less. Use these questions as a guide:
— What was your life like before you believed in Jesus?
— How did you hear about Him?
— How did you realize you needed His salvation and love?
— What is your life like now?

46 WHAT DO I DO WHEN THOSE I LOVE DON'T BELIEVE?

MATTHEW 5:14-16

Becoming a follower of Jesus changes the way you relate to others, especially your family and friends. The Holy Spirit begins to work in your life, changing your words, thoughts, actions, and beliefs. Over time, as you listen to His voice, you will become more and more like Christ (Philippians 2:13). In Romans 12:18, the apostle Paul instructs believers to "do all that you can to live in peace with everyone." God wants you to live in such a way that unbelievers will see the good things you do and glorify Him as a result (Matthew 5:16).

One of the biggest challenges for a believer is relating to loved ones who don't yet believe. In some situations, your faith will awaken a spiritual hunger in them; other times, they may be completely disinterested or even hostile. Whatever the case, God has resources available to help you as you relate to them.

Rely on God's power, and He will give you strength.
— Spend time with the Holy Spirit and let your loved ones see the fruit of your new life in Christ (John 15:8). Ask God to help you become more and more like Jesus. Even though becoming like Christ is a lifelong journey, God has already given you a new heart (Ezekiel 36:26). He is showing you a new way to live. When people see the fruit of the Spirit in you (Galatians 5:22-23), they will be more willing to acknowledge and accept your decision to follow Jesus. They may even decide to accept Jesus for themselves.

The Holy Spirit will give you wisdom for your circumstances.
— You may be a believer who lives with someone who is not. Be ready to talk about what God has done for you and invite your family member to join you in following Jesus. Learn how to have healthier relationships with your loved ones by reading God's Word and asking for help from other believers who have successful relationships. Practice what you learn (James 1:22-25) and humbly ask for forgiveness when you make mistakes. The Holy Spirit will gently lead you and provide correction when you need it. Trust Him, and He will help you (Psalm 37:23). If you are married, God's Word provides specific instructions about your continuing relationship with a spouse who does not yet believe (1 Corinthians 7:12-16).

Jesus is your Advocate.
— You can live without fear because Jesus is working on your behalf (1 John 2:1-2). Take comfort in knowing that Jesus can relate to your experiences in every way (Hebrews 2:17). Even Jesus had earthly siblings who did not always believe in Him (John 7:5). At one time, they did not even think He was in His right mind (Mark 3:21). They did not trust Jesus as Lord until after He went back to heaven (Acts 1:14). However, they finally believed and were saved. Pray for your loved ones and trust God to work in their lives just as He has in yours.

1. What happens when others see our "good deeds," according to Matthew 5:15-16?
2. Read Acts 16:16-34. What effect did Paul and Silas have on the jailor and his family?
3. What is God's promise to us in James 1:22-25?

47 HOW SHOULD I RESPOND TO FALSE BELIEFS?

2 TIMOTHY 2:23-26

It is only a matter of time before you will encounter someone with false beliefs. The apostle Paul says the time will come when people will not accept "sound and wholesome teaching" (2 Timothy 4:3). In many ways, today is such a time. As followers of Jesus, we do not have the option to pick and choose our own truth. God's Word is the one and only truth (Psalm 119:160; John 17:17). How, then, can you respond to false beliefs?

Resist the urge to correct someone immediately.
— When we encounter someone with false beliefs, we sometimes feel compelled to offer correction right away. However, people do not often change their minds simply because they lose an argument. They believe what they do for particular reasons, so telling them they are wrong is not an effective way to change their thinking. If you frequently speak with someone who believes something in error, it is probably better to get to know this person over time and try to understand the reasons for their false beliefs. For example, someone who had an abusive parent may have difficulty believing in God as a loving heavenly Father. A person who grew up in a very different culture or with parents who were not believers may have difficulty even imagining a personal God. Listen to other people's stories, try to understand their unique experiences, and ask God to help you see them through His eyes before you attempt to correct their false beliefs.

Live your testimony.
— One of the best ways to lead others to the truth is to live it for yourself. Always be ready to share your faith and the good things God has done for you (1 Peter 3:15). When someone

tries to get you to violate what you know to be the truth, stand firm in gentle kindness and respect.

Seek common ground and interests.
— The apostle Paul worked very hard to find common ground with everyone he met so he could spread the Good News about Jesus. When he was with Jews, Paul behaved like a Jew, taking part in their customs. When he was with the Greeks, he had a different set of social practices. In other words, Paul did whatever it took, short of sinning, to relate to all people (1 Corinthians 9:19-23). You should look for opportunities to relate to others while maintaining godly character.

Show love in your actions and speech.
— Paul writes, "Whatever you do or say, do it as a representative of the Lord Jesus" (Colossians 3:17). If you say the right things but don't do them, you are not living consistently. If you want to show God's love to others, be ready to lay down your own preferences, comforts, and biases. You may think you are making a huge sacrifice, but remember that Jesus laid down His life for us.

1. In Galatians 2:1-5, what was the goal of the "so-called believers"? How was Paul's goal different?
2. What will happen in the "last times" according to 1 Timothy 4:1-5? How should we as believers respond?
3. What warning does Colossians 2:8 give us?
4. Read Ephesians 4:1-3, 14-16. What does Paul beg believers to do so they won't be tricked into false beliefs?

48 HOW SHOULD I FACE TRIALS AND TEMPTATIONS?

1 PETER 4:12-13

Becoming a Christian does not make you immune to difficulty. The apostle Peter writes, "Don't be surprised at the fiery trials you are going through, as if something strange were happening to you" (1 Peter 4:12). Everyone, even the most faithful and steadfast Christians, will go through hard times. Trials and temptations are difficult to endure, but God uses these experiences to grow believers into mature and complete followers of Christ (James 1:2-4).

God uses some trials to bring us closer to Him. Other times, He uses trials to discipline us. Don't

confuse discipline with punishment, though. God does not punish His children—Jesus already took *all* our punishment on the cross (Romans 3:21-31). Just as a loving parent trains and disciplines his children, our heavenly Father trains and disciplines us because He loves us (Proverbs 13:24; Hebrews 12:5-7). Trials may arise as consequences for negative choices we have made, or they can simply be hardships unrelated to our actions. In either case, God wants to use our uncomfortable or painful circumstances to bring us closer to Him and shape our character to better reflect His (Romans 5:3-5).

We can rejoice when we experience trials because God has promised that He is always working for our good (Romans 8:28). We can even accept them with thanksgiving. Thankfulness is a sacrifice to God (Psalm 107:22), and it softens our hearts. When you go through trials, put your trust in God and witness the comfort and strength He will give you (Psalm 18:32; Isaiah 40:31).

Temptation has many forms but always one goal: to draw us away from our relationship with God (James 1:13). Satan has used the same tactics ever since He tempted Adam and Eve in the Garden of Eden (Genesis 3:1-4). He is constantly trying to get us to mistrust God's character and misunderstand our identity in Christ.

What can you do when temptation comes?

Identify your weaknesses and make a battle plan.
— If you know you have a weakness in any area, begin asking the Holy Spirit to give you a battle plan to defeat your enemy. The Holy Spirit can give you grace and truth to face any circumstance. Also, talk to a mature, trustworthy believer, such as a friend, pastor, or counselor. That person will be able to help you understand why you are often tempted in a particular area and how to get freedom from that stronghold.

To the best of your ability, avoid those things that most often lead you into temptation and decide even now what you will do when the devil tries to entice you (Mark 9:47; Proverbs 4:14-15).

Use your Sword—God's Word.
— When the devil tried to tempt Jesus, he could not overcome the power of God's Word that came from Jesus' mouth (Matthew 4:1-11). The same is true for you. As you feed your spirit by reading the Bible, God will give you the right spiritual weapons. Find Scriptures that speak about God's character and who you are through your relationship with Him. Write these verses down and post them in places where you will see them often. The truth of God's Word will always defeat the enemy (Ephesians 6:17).

1. Read Genesis 37 and 39. What trials and temptations did Joseph face? According to Genesis 50:20, for what purpose was God preparing him?
2. Read James 1:12. What will we receive when we "patiently endure testing and temptation"?
3. According to Romans 5:3-5, how can difficulties lead to hope?

49 WHY DOES GOD WANT ME TO REMAIN SEXUALLY PURE?

1 CORINTHIANS 6:13-20

God commands His people to abstain from sexual acts until marriage (Exodus 20:14) and to run away from sexual sin (1 Corinthians 6:18). As a believer, your body is not your own. Paul says it is the Holy Spirit's house, and God bought it for a very high price with His own Son's blood (1 Corinthians 6:19-20). We should honor our bodies as His holy dwelling place because together, we make up the body of Christ (1 Corinthians 12:27). God created you, and He knows what is best for you.

God wants to bless you (Matthew 5:8). Many times in His Word, God gives the choice between blessings and curses. If we obey and depend on Him for wisdom and strength, we will be blessed (Psalm 24:4-5). However, if we disobey, we are cursed. The Bible warns us that adultery is sinning against our own bodies (1 Corinthians 6:18). When we have sex with someone, our souls join and meld together (1 Corinthians 6:16). Because sex gives part of your soul to another person, you should save this experience for a committed marriage relationship. Otherwise, we risk destroying ourselves by giving away our hearts piece by precious piece. God created sex to reflect His goodness, not to be defiled by worldly views and actions.

God cares about the condition of your soul (your mind, will, and emotions). Proverbs 4:23 says,

Guard your heart above all else,
    for it determines the course of your life.

God loves people and knows sex outside of marriage will only hurt them. If you will humbly let God lead you and teach you His ways, you will prosper (Psalm 32:8; Deuteronomy 28:8).

Sin always keeps God at an arm's length. When we consider sex outside the boundaries of marriage, we take our minds off Christ and open ourselves up to the enemy's attack. God grieves when you sin (Psalm 78:40) because He wants you to be close to Him (Isaiah 40:11). He promises to give you peace if you will fix your thoughts on Him and meditate on His Word and things that are pure (Isaiah 26:3; Philippians 4:8).

1. Read Proverbs 5:15-21. Who is the only person with whom we should have sexual relations?
2. According to Proverbs 6:32, what happens to a person who commits adultery?
3. Read Genesis 2:24 and 1 Corinthians 6:16. What happens when one person joins to another sexually?
4. According to Romans 6:12-14, what should we do with our bodies now that Christ has given us new life?

50 WHAT KIND OF EMPLOYEE SHOULD I BE?

COLOSSIANS 3:23–24

The story of Joseph provides a model for believers to follow as they honor God with their employment. God was with Joseph and blessed everything he did because he served humbly and without complaining (Genesis 39:3; 1 Peter 5:5). Although Joseph's brothers abused him and sold him into slavery, he forgave them. His circumstances humbled him, yet he always chose to trust God.

We can learn these principles from Joseph's example:

Work hard and work willingly.

— As a slave, Joseph did not receive payment for his work. Still, he worked hard, and God honored his efforts. Work in such a way that you honor God with your accomplishments (2 Timothy 2:15). If you work as though you are working for God, He will reward you (Colossians 3:23–24).

Have integrity and be trustworthy.

— Joseph honored God with his work even when no one was looking. The only time he disobeyed those in authority over him was when they tempted him to disobey God (Genesis 39:8–12; Acts 5:29). Joseph had administrative responsibility in Potiphar's house, respect in the prison, and great authority under Pharaoh. He received honor and responsibility because he was trustworthy.

Remain humble and be ready to use your gifts at all times.

— Potiphar's wife wrongly accused Joseph, and Potiphar put him in jail where he was forgotten (Genesis 40:23). Even so, Joseph remained humble and used his gifts regardless of his circumstances (Genesis 41:16). Eventually, Pharaoh made him a ruler over "the entire land

of Egypt" (Genesis 41:41). Only Pharaoh had a higher rank than Joseph. When we are faithful with little, we will be rewarded and given more (Luke 19:17).

Be quick to listen and slow to speak (James 1:19).

— Joseph was not a natural-born Egyptian. He had to learn the cultural expectations and customs of the land. He spoke humbly and kindly to those in authority over him (Genesis 41:16). If you practice listening to what others have to say, then you will learn and grow in wisdom (Proverbs 19:20).

Know your responsibilities and do them well.

— Working in a lazy way leads to hardship and fruitlessness (Proverbs 14:23; 18:9). When we do our work eagerly and joyfully, we honor God and make Jesus attractive to others (Titus 2:9–10). Your coworkers may come to know the Lord by watching your life. Completing your work in a timely and excellent manner shows you care about your responsibilities.

Acknowledge the Owner.

— Everything belongs to God (Psalm 24:1). We are simply stewards of what He owns. God has given us the responsibility to treat people as He does and manage resources as He would (Matthew 25:14–30). Jesus will return one day, and He will call us to give an account for all we have done. Let us be found faithful.

1. Read Genesis 39–41. How did Joseph honor God, and how did God bless him in return?
2. How can we gain wisdom, according to Proverbs 19:20?
3. Read Philippians 2:3–4, 14–15. How should we treat our coworkers?

51 WHY IS MY RELATIONSHIP WITH MONEY IMPORTANT?

2 CORINTHIANS 9:7–8

When God entrusts money to us, it is our responsibility to be good stewards of it. How we manage money is a matter of the heart, and we cannot separate it from our relationship with Christ. Jesus instructs His followers not to center their lives on worldly, short-term things. If we focus on material things and try to be our own providers, it will lead to anxiety, stress, and depression. We can become blind to God's intent to bless us. On the other hand, if we focus on God and allow

Him to change our perspective on money, we will become grateful and can rest in the knowledge that He is our provider. When we give our time, money, assets, and talents to serve God and the local church, we store up treasures in heaven (Matthew 6:19–21).

Financial stewardship shows if we have focused our hearts on God or the world. The way you relate to money directly affects how you will relate to God and vice versa. You will choose to put your trust in God or in money. Jesus says we can trust our Father in heaven with all our needs, and He will provide for us faithfully (Matthew 6:33).

God wants to establish a relationship with you characterized by intimate trust and dependence. He wants to bless and provide for you in ways you cannot imagine. But He cannot do those things when your trust is in money and not in Him. The apostle Paul reminds Timothy, "The *love* of money is the root of all kinds of evil" (1 Timothy 6:10, emphasis added). God commands us to love Him and have no idols before Him (Deuteronomy 5:7).

When God is your source and focus, your relationship with money will align with His principles for a blessed life.

1. According to Matthew 6:24-26, can a person serve two masters? Why or why not?
2. Read 2 Corinthians 9:6-10. Who provides everything you need? How do you know this is true?
3. Read 2 Corinthians 9:11-15. What two good things happen when believers give?

52 HOW DO I BECOME A GOOD STEWARD?

PROVERBS 3:9-10

The first step toward godly stewardship is realizing you do not own anything (Psalm 24:1). Everything in your possession actually belongs to God. You came into the world with nothing, and you will leave the same way. All of us will stand in judgment before God and give an account for how we have stewarded (or managed) what belongs to Him (Matthew 25:14-30).

If we live as though we are the owners of our possessions, several problems arise:
— We believe a lie.
— We attempt to control our possessions and put our trust in them rather than God, which is a form of idolatry.
— We keep our possessions away from God and do not allow Him to be Lord over them.

God cannot bless and provide for us if we do not trust Him with this area of our lives.

The second step toward godly stewardship is surrendering everything to God's ownership. We can enjoy a life of incredible blessing, but it begins by recognizing that the "best" (or first) belongs to God (Proverbs 3:9-10). Giving God the first of your time means taking a Sabbath—setting aside one day per week to rest (Exodus 20:9-11). You should also give God the first part of every day to pray and seek Him. If you're not a morning person, then give Him the best time of your day.

Giving God the first of your talents means giving to the Lord by using your gifts and abilities to serve the local church and those in need. Giving God the first of your money means paying tithes and giving offerings to your local church. The word *tithe* means 'ten percent.' Give the first ten percent of your income to the Lord. Everything after that is called "offerings." When you tithe, God promises to "pour out a blessing so great you won't have enough room to take it in!" (Malachi 3:10).

The third step toward godly stewardship is submitting your life to God (2 Corinthians 8:5). Successful stewardship cannot happen until you have submitted to Him. God wants to partner with you so you can live a successful life. He has a purpose for you. Not only can you live with financial and personal blessings, but you can also know you're fulfilling God's higher purpose. Begin by surrendering to God and committing everything you have to serving Him and furthering His kingdom.

1. What will we receive if we put God first, according to Matthew 6:33?
2. Read Matthew 25:14-30. Why does the master call the first two servants "faithful"? Why did he call the third servant "wicked and lazy"?
3. Read Malachi 3:8-11. Why were the people of Israel cursed? Is it possible to be cursed in the same way today?

OLD TESTAMENT

GENESIS

JON HUNTZINGER, PHD

The book of Genesis takes its name from a word that means 'origin' or 'beginning.' This is a book of beginnings. Not only is Genesis the first book of the Bible, but it also describes the beginnings of Creation, human existence, human sin against God, and God's redemptive work to save His special relationship with all people through Abraham. Jewish tradition, as represented by Josephus, Philo of Alexandria, the Mishnah, and even Jesus, identifies Moses as the writer of Genesis, along with the books of Exodus, Numbers, Leviticus, and Deuteronomy. These five books comprise the *Torah*, also known as the Pentateuch. The Bible itself claims God appeared and gave His Law to Moses on Mount Sinai (Exodus 19-20; Deuteronomy 5). God spoke to Moses face-to-face (Numbers 12:6-8) and at times directed him to record events that happened (Exodus 17:14; Numbers 33:2). God also gave the laws to Moses and the Israelites (Exodus 24:3-14). According to Deuteronomy, Moses even wrote a song at God's direction (Deuteronomy 31:16-32:47). Later biblical texts indicate these writings are the Book of Moses (Ezra 6:16-18; Nehemiah 13:1).

Two major sections constitute the book of Genesis:
— Chapters 1-11 describe *primeval history*, which means they tell about events that happened before people used written language. These first chapters outline the Creation of the earth, the formation of Adam and Eve, the growth of the human race, the great Flood, and the movement of people throughout the earth.
— Chapters 12-50 recount the story of Abraham and his family.

Genesis contains the stories of many important people that help us make sense of the rest of the Bible. It tells about how God
— created Adam and Eve and placed them in the Garden of Eden,
— rescued Noah and his family from the great Flood,

— chose Abraham because of his faith and promised to bless all people through him,
— remained faithful to Abraham's descendants Isaac and Jacob, and
— saved His people and the Egyptians through Joseph.

In each of these stories, God speaks and makes Himself known through His words and actions:
— He speaks creation into existence through ten words or declarations.
— He speaks to Adam and Eve in the Garden of Eden when the breeze blows in the evening.
— He speaks to Noah, telling him to build a boat that will save his family and the animals of the creation God loves so much.
— He promises many descendants to Abraham when he and his wife, Sarah, are old and do not yet have any children.
— He speaks to Abraham's grandson Jacob and Jacob's son Joseph in dreams that reveal what He plans to do in their lives for the sake of other people.

Yes, the God of Genesis is a God who speaks. He is neither mute nor silent. He talks and tells people who He is and what He wants to do in their lives.

The God of Genesis is a God who is good:
— The first chapter uses the word *good* seven times to describe the creation God speaks into existence.
— When Adam discovers he is naked, God clothes him.
— When the people do evil in His sight, God gives Noah instructions to build a boat that will save his family and the animals of God's creation.
— When Abraham despairs of not having any descendants, God enables him and Sarah to have a baby in their old age.

The picture of God in Genesis is one of a good God who speaks to His people.

THE ACCOUNT OF CREATION

1 In the beginning God created the heavens and the earth.* ²The earth was formless and empty, and darkness covered the deep waters. And the Spirit of God was hovering over the surface of the waters.

³Then God said, "Let there be light," and there was light. ⁴And God saw that the light was good. Then he separated the light from the darkness. ⁵God called the light "day" and the darkness "night."

And evening passed and morning came, marking the first day.

⁶Then God said, "Let there be a space between the waters, to separate the waters of the heavens from the waters of the earth." ⁷And that is what happened. God made this space to separate the waters of the earth from the waters of the heavens. ⁸God called the space "sky."

And evening passed and morning came, marking the second day.

⁹Then God said, "Let the waters beneath the sky flow together into one place, so dry ground may appear." And that is what happened. ¹⁰God called the dry ground "land" and the waters "seas." And God saw that it was good. ¹¹Then God said, "Let the land sprout with vegetation—every sort of seed-bearing plant, and trees that grow seed-bearing fruit. These seeds will then produce the kinds of plants and trees from which they came." And that is what happened. ¹²The land produced vegetation—all sorts of seed-bearing plants, and trees with seed-bearing fruit. Their seeds produced plants and trees of the same kind. And God saw that it was good.

¹³And evening passed and morning came, marking the third day.

¹⁴Then God said, "Let lights appear in the sky to separate the day from the night. Let them be signs to mark the seasons, days, and years. ¹⁵Let these lights in the sky shine down on the earth." And that is what happened. ¹⁶God made two great lights—the larger one to govern the day, and the smaller one to govern the night. He also made the stars. ¹⁷God set these lights in the sky to light the earth, ¹⁸to govern the day and night, and to separate the light from the darkness. And God saw that it was good.

¹⁹And evening passed and morning came, marking the fourth day.

²⁰Then God said, "Let the waters swarm with fish and other life. Let the skies be filled with birds of every kind." ²¹So God created

GOD'S GREATEST DESIRE
Genesis 1:11, 24 ROBERT MORRIS

All people come from God, are sustained by God, and will go back to God. God made us like Him, and just like God, we desire communion. The truth is God's greatest desire is to commune with us and to be with us *forever*. He created us to love and be loved by Him.

God's plan is to present His Son, Jesus, with a bride—a companion. And we are His desired bride and companion. Throughout the Bible, the cry of God's heart is His desire for us to be His people and for Him to be our God. He created us for Himself, but He also created us with a free will. We can choose to love or not love Him. I hope you will choose to love God as much as He loves you.

great sea creatures and every living thing that scurries and swarms in the water, and every sort of bird—each producing offspring of the same kind. And God saw that it was good. ²²Then God blessed them, saying, "Be fruitful and multiply. Let the fish fill the seas, and let the birds multiply on the earth."

²³And evening passed and morning came, marking the fifth day.

²⁴Then God said, "Let the earth produce every sort of animal, each producing offspring of the same kind—livestock, small animals that scurry along the ground, and wild animals." And that is what happened. ²⁵God made all sorts of wild animals, livestock, and small animals, each able to produce offspring of the same kind. And God saw that it was good.

²⁶Then God said, "Let us make human beings* in our image, to be like us. They will reign over the fish in the sea, the birds in the sky, the livestock, all the wild animals on the earth,* and the small animals that scurry along the ground."

²⁷ So God created human beings* in his own image.
　　In the image of God he created them;
　　male and female he created them.

²⁸Then God blessed them and said, "Be fruitful and multiply. Fill the earth and govern it. Reign over the fish in the sea, the birds in the sky, and all the animals that scurry along the ground."

1:1 Or *In the beginning when God created the heavens and the earth, . . .* Or *When God began to create the heavens and the earth, . . .* 1:26a Or *man;* Hebrew reads *adam.* 1:26b As in Syriac version; Hebrew reads *all the earth.* 1:27 Or *the man;* Hebrew reads *ha-adam.*

HOW CAN I KNOW GOD WANTS ME?
Genesis 1:26–27   ROBERT MORRIS

God created you in His image. Before we ever existed, God the Father, God the Son, and God the Holy Spirit lived in perfect relationship. God does not need us for relationship, but He *wants* to have a relationship with us. *God created you because He wants you!*

He redeemed you with His blood. God sent Jesus, His one and only Son, to pay the penalty for our sins by dying on the cross. Could He have redeemed you any other way? According to Hebrews 9:22, "Without the shedding of blood, there is no forgiveness." Without forgiveness, our sins would doom us to eternal punishment and separation from God.

He perfected you by His grace. How can a *perfect God* have a relationship with an *imperfect you* unless He does something to perfect you? First John 1:7 says, "The blood of Jesus, his Son, cleanses us from all sin." Jesus' blood covers all our failures and shortcomings and makes us perfect in God's sight. Isn't that amazing?

LIFE, NOT LAW
Genesis 2:15–17   ROBERT MORRIS

Tithing is a principle that runs throughout the Word of God, predating the Law of Moses by thousands of years. When God gave Adam and Eve stewardship over the Garden of Eden, He allowed them to eat from every tree except one. Being faithful stewards meant *life* to Adam and Eve. However, when they chose to eat fruit from the forbidden tree, they acted like owners rather than stewards.

The same principle applies to us today. God gives us stewardship over our lives. Though everything belongs to Him, He "richly gives us all we need for our enjoyment" (1 Timothy 6:17). All God asks is that we not touch the firstfruits because they belong to Him. When we give Him our firstfruits (our tithes), we demonstrate faithful stewardship and show God that we realize we are not owners. When you begin to see tithing as life instead of law, your heart will change, and tithing will become a blessing instead of a burden.

---

²⁹Then God said, "Look! I have given you every seed-bearing plant throughout the earth and all the fruit trees for your food. ³⁰And I have given every green plant as food for all the wild animals, the birds in the sky, and the small animals that scurry along the ground—everything that has life." And that is what happened.

³¹Then God looked over all he had made, and he saw that it was very good!

And evening passed and morning came, marking the sixth day.

2 So the creation of the heavens and the earth and everything in them was completed. ²On the seventh day God had finished his work of creation, so he rested* from all his work. ³And God blessed the seventh day and declared it holy, because it was the day when he rested from all his work of creation.

⁴This is the account of the creation of the heavens and the earth.

THE MAN AND WOMAN IN EDEN

When the LORD God made the earth and the heavens, ⁵neither wild plants nor grains were growing on the earth. For the LORD God had not yet sent rain to water the earth, and there were no people to cultivate the soil. ⁶Instead, springs* came up from the ground and watered all the land. ⁷Then the LORD God formed the man from the dust of the ground. He breathed the breath of life into the man's nostrils, and the man became a living person.

⁸Then the LORD God planted a garden in Eden in the east, and there he placed the man he had made. ⁹The LORD God made all sorts of trees grow up from the ground—trees that were beautiful and that produced delicious fruit. In the middle of the garden he placed the tree of life and the tree of the knowledge of good and evil.

¹⁰A river flowed from the land of Eden, watering the garden and then dividing into four branches. ¹¹The first branch, called the Pishon, flowed around the entire land of Havilah, where gold is found. ¹²The gold of that land is exceptionally pure; aromatic resin and onyx stone are also found there. ¹³The second branch, called the Gihon, flowed around the entire land of Cush. ¹⁴The third branch, called the Tigris, flowed east of the land of Asshur. The fourth branch is called the Euphrates.

¹⁵The LORD God placed the man in the Garden of Eden to tend and watch over it. ¹⁶But the LORD God warned him, "You may freely eat the fruit of every tree in the garden—¹⁷except the tree of the knowledge of good and evil. If you eat its fruit, you are sure to die."

¹⁸Then the LORD God said, "It is not good for the man to be alone. I will make a helper who is just right for him." ¹⁹So the LORD God formed from the ground all the wild animals and all the birds of the sky. He brought them to the man* to see what he would call them, and the man chose a name for each one. ²⁰He gave names to all the livestock, all the birds of the sky, and all the wild animals. But still there was no helper just right for him.

2:2 Or *ceased;* also in 2:3. 2:6 Or *mist.* 2:19 Or *Adam,* and so throughout the chapter.

I AM PROTECTED
Genesis 2:16-17

MARCUS BRECHEEN

People often think of Scripture as being hard and rigid, but our Father in heaven wants to protect us, not limit or restrict us. When God placed Adam in the Garden of Eden, He said, "You may freely eat the fruit of every tree in the garden—except the tree of the knowledge of good and evil. If you eat its fruit, you are sure to die" (Genesis 2:16-17). This was the very first time God sowed His word in a person's heart.

Since Satan can't attack God, he comes against us and hurts us so he can hurt *God*.

Disguised as a serpent, Satan told Eve that God's word about the tree wasn't true. He convinced her that God was withholding something good from her and made her think God's command was a punishment instead of protection.

God loves us and wants to bless us. Once we understand that His Word is meant to protect us, we'll stop seeing Him as an enforcer and start seeing Him as our Father and protector.

WHAT DOES GOD NEED?
Genesis 2:19-20

ROBERT MORRIS

God is completely self-existent, self-sufficient, and self-sustaining. He does not need anything to exist. However, He has decided to need you—not to exist but to coexist!

God decided to need us to partner with Him to accomplish things on the earth. Why did He give Adam the responsibility of naming the animals? Because Adam was going to have authority over the animals. Authority and responsibility go hand in hand. God's power is limitless, but He has chosen to share His

authority—and therefore responsibility—over the earth with us.

Have you decided to need God in *every* area of your life—relationships, finances, work, etc.? Have you chosen to cooperate with Him every day? If people are going to get saved, it's going to be because we shared our faith. If people are going to get healed, it's going to be because we prayed. This world is not going to be saved independently by God. God has decided to partner with us and use us to see His purposes fulfilled.

EXPOSING THE DEVIL
Genesis 3:1-5

JIMMY EVANS

The devil is an accuser who tries to divide us from every healthy, godly relationship. He wants to separate you from God, your spouse, your family, and the body of Christ. His desire is for you to live in rebellion against authority. However, God has equipped you to overcome the enemy's accusations by the blood of Jesus and the Word of God.

How can you know the difference between the devil's voice and the Holy Spirit's voice?

The devil's voice shouts condemnation that is general, hateful, and gives no way out. The Holy Spirit, however, brings conviction that is specific, loving, and helpful.

The devil wants to keep you away from those who will encourage you in your walk with the Lord. There is a special anointing of God's power and protection when you meet with other believers. When you are under the covering of authority, the devil cannot touch you.

²¹ So the Lord God caused the man to fall into a deep sleep. While the man slept, the Lord God took out one of the man's ribs* and closed up the opening. ²² Then the Lord God made a woman from the rib, and he brought her to the man.

²³ "At last!" the man exclaimed.

> "This one is bone from my bone,
>   and flesh from my flesh!
> She will be called 'woman,'
>   because she was taken from 'man.'"

²⁴ This explains why a man leaves his father and mother and is joined to his wife, and the two are united into one.

²⁵ Now the man and his wife were both naked, but they felt no shame.

THE MAN AND WOMAN SIN

3 The serpent was the shrewdest of all the wild animals the Lord God had made. One day he asked the woman, "Did God really say you must not eat the fruit from any of the trees in the garden?"

² "Of course we may eat fruit from the trees in the garden," the woman replied. ³ "It's only the fruit from the tree in the middle of the garden that we are not allowed to eat. God said, 'You

2:21 Or *took a part of the man's side.*

THE FALL OF THE FIRST FAMILY
Genesis 3:1-19

ROBERT MORRIS

As descendants of Adam and Eve, we all have biological characteristics inherited from them. However, we also have spiritual characteristics or spiritual genetic tendencies because of the first family. Adam and Eve once enjoyed perfect relationships with God and each other, but the moment they ate the forbidden fruit, their relationships splintered and broke. Sin entered the world and brought painful side effects that still influence us today.

1. Shame
The very first result of sin was shame. After they sinned, Adam and Eve hid from God and each other. We too try to hide from God and cover our sins; however, only the righteousness of Jesus can cover us. On the cross, Jesus bore your sin *and* your shame. His blood cleanses you of everything you have ever done wrong, both before and after you got saved. He wants us to live shame free!

2. Blame
Sin brings separation, first from God and then from each other. In the same way that Adam blamed Eve and God for his sin, we look for someone on whom we can place the blame

for our own sins. We say, "It's not *my* fault!" Another word for blame is *accusation*, and accusations only come from one source—the devil (Revelation 12:10).

3. Fame
Everyone has the desire to be recognized. When God first created woman, Adam called her "bone from my bone, and flesh from my flesh" (Genesis 2:23). Man and woman were one. After sinning, though, Adam separated from the woman and named her *Eve*, "because she would be the mother of all who live" (Genesis 3:20). By giving her a different name, Adam declared that Eve's primary purpose in life was to bear and raise children. While family certainly is important, motherhood is not a woman's highest calling. The highest calling of every person, whether male or female, is to be a child of God.

Jesus came to redeem us from the fall of the first family so we too can be children of God. When we are born again, we join God's family, and He sets us free from the curse of shame, blame, and fame.

GOD'S MANIFEST PRESENCE
Genesis 3:8

ROBERT MORRIS

Sin makes us try to hide from God's presence, even when we're in church. If you messed up last week, Satan will do everything he can to tell you, "You shouldn't worship today because it will mean you're a hypocrite." But the truth is the times you mess up are the times when you really need to enter the presence of God. Even when you make mistakes, Scripture says you can boldly enter His presence.

You may wonder, *How can I "enter" God's presence? Isn't He everywhere?* Yes, God is omnipresent (everywhere at all times), but we have the choice to enter or leave His manifest presence. Genesis 3:8 says Adam and Eve "hid from the LORD God among the trees" after they sinned. God manifests—or makes known—His presence in times when we sincerely seek Him, such as when we worship, pray, or study His Word. He wants to make His presence known to us so He can do something in our lives that we can't do ourselves.

In Genesis 4, Adam and Eve's son Cain murders his brother Abel out of jealous anger.

However, instead of repenting, "Cain left the LORD's presence and settled in the land of Nod, east of Eden" (Genesis 4:16). When God tells you to do something and you don't do it, you begin leaving His manifest presence. Yes, we're all humans, and we all make mistakes; however, when you're willfully disobedient (i.e., you remember His instructions and then ignore them), you leave God's manifest presence.

So how do we enter the Lord's manifest presence? There are many ways, but I want to focus on worshipping and praising the One who is worthy of praise (Psalm 95:1-2; 100:1-2). When you start singing, whether you sing well or not, you are going to sense God's presence. Sadly, some people only enter His presence once a week when they go to church. Then they try to make it the whole week without ever entering His presence again. Lamentations 3:23 declares, "His mercies begin afresh each morning." We all need God's mercy, and the most important thing we can do is begin each and every day in His presence.

must not eat it or even touch it; if you do, you will die.'"

⁴"You won't die!" the serpent replied to the woman. ⁵"God knows that your eyes will be

opened as soon as you eat it, and you will be like God, knowing both good and evil."

⁶The woman was convinced. She saw that the tree was beautiful and its fruit looked delicious,

GOD STILL SPEAKS
Genesis 3:8–9
ROBERT MORRIS

God talks to people throughout the Bible, beginning with Adam in the Garden of Eden and ending with John on the island of Patmos. To believe He has suddenly stopped talking to us makes no sense. How can we tell people they can have a personal relationship with Jesus and then say, "Oh, by the way, He doesn't talk to us anymore. He left the Bible as an instruction manual, so do your best to figure it out!"? Now, I believe the Bible is God's divinely inspired Word. However, I also believe Jesus' word that He would not "abandon [us] as orphans" (John 14:18). He promised to send the Holy Spirit to talk to us. Since the Holy Spirit *is* God, I can confidently say God still speaks!

Before sin came into the world, Adam and Eve were never afraid of the voice of God. In fact, He walked and talked with them on a regular basis. We should not be afraid of hearing God's voice either. Our highest priority should be spending time in His presence and walking and talking with Him every day.

and she wanted the wisdom it would give her. So she took some of the fruit and ate it. Then she gave some to her husband, who was with her, and he ate it, too. 7 At that moment their eyes were opened, and they suddenly felt shame at their nakedness. So they sewed fig leaves together to cover themselves.

8 When the cool evening breezes were blowing, the man* and his wife heard the Lᴏʀᴅ God walking about in the garden. So they hid from the Lᴏʀᴅ God among the trees. 9 Then the Lᴏʀᴅ God called to the man, "Where are you?"

10 He replied, "I heard you walking in the garden, so I hid. I was afraid because I was naked."

11 "Who told you that you were naked?" the Lᴏʀᴅ God asked. "Have you eaten from the tree whose fruit I commanded you not to eat?"

12 The man replied, "It was the woman you gave me who gave me the fruit, and I ate it."

13 Then the Lᴏʀᴅ God asked the woman, "What have you done?"

"The serpent deceived me," she replied. "That's why I ate it."

14 Then the Lᴏʀᴅ God said to the serpent,

"Because you have done this, you are cursed
    more than all animals, domestic and wild.
You will crawl on your belly,
    groveling in the dust as long as you live.
15 And I will cause hostility between you and
    the woman,
    and between your offspring and
    her offspring.
He will strike* your head,
    and you will strike his heel."

16 Then he said to the woman,

"I will sharpen the pain of your pregnancy,
    and in pain you will give birth.
And you will desire to control your husband,
    but he will rule over you.*"

17 And to the man he said,

"Since you listened to your wife and ate
    from the tree
    whose fruit I commanded you not to eat,
the ground is cursed because of you.
    All your life you will struggle to scratch
    a living from it.
18 It will grow thorns and thistles for you,
    though you will eat of its grains.
19 By the sweat of your brow
    will you have food to eat
until you return to the ground
    from which you were made.
For you were made from dust,
    and to dust you will return."

PARADISE LOST: GOD'S JUDGMENT

20 Then the man—Adam—named his wife Eve, because she would be the mother of all who live.* 21 And the Lᴏʀᴅ God made clothing from animal skins for Adam and his wife.

22 Then the Lᴏʀᴅ God said, "Look, the human beings* have become like us, knowing both good and evil. What if they reach out, take fruit from the tree of life, and eat it? Then they will live forever!" 23 So the Lᴏʀᴅ God banished them from the Garden of Eden, and he sent Adam out to cultivate the ground from which he had been made. 24 After sending them out, the Lᴏʀᴅ God stationed mighty cherubim to the east of the Garden of Eden. And he placed a flaming sword that flashed back and forth to guard the way to the tree of life.

CAIN AND ABEL

4 Now Adam* had sexual relations with his wife, Eve, and she became pregnant. When she gave birth to Cain, she said, "With the Lᴏʀᴅ's help, I have produced* a man!" 2 Later she gave birth to his brother and named him Abel.

When they grew up, Abel became a shepherd, while Cain cultivated the ground. 3 When it was time for the harvest, Cain presented some of his crops as a gift to the Lᴏʀᴅ. 4 Abel also brought a gift—the best portions of the firstborn lambs from his flock. The Lᴏʀᴅ accepted Abel and his gift, 5 but he did not accept Cain and his gift. This made Cain very angry, and he looked dejected.

3:8 Or *Adam,* and so throughout the chapter.   3:15 Or *bruise;* also in 3:15b.   3:16 Or *And though you will have desire for your husband, / he will rule over you.*   3:20 *Eve* sounds like a Hebrew term that means "to give life."   3:22 Or *the man;* Hebrew reads *ha-adam.*   4:1a Or *the man;* also in 4:25.   4:1b Or *I have acquired. Cain* sounds like a Hebrew term that can mean "produce" or "acquire."

THE PRINCIPLE OF FIRST
Genesis 4:2-5   ROBERT MORRIS

The principle of first is about putting God first in our lives. Throughout Scripture, the first of everything always belonged to the Lord. In Genesis 4, God honors Abel's gift, "the best portions of the firstborn lambs from his flock" (Genesis 4:4). However, the Lord rejects Cain's offering of crops because it was not from his firstfruits.

Our obedience to God's principles reveals the conditions of our hearts. When we honor the Lord with the best parts of everything we have, we invite His provision and protection into our lives. Many blessings go along with tithing, but it is the principle of putting God first that initiates those blessings. God does not want a legalistic, begrudging response to His commands. Instead, He desires for us to submit our hearts to Him joyfully, in faith that His principles are true.

⁶ "Why are you so angry?" the LORD asked Cain. "Why do you look so dejected? ⁷ You will be accepted if you do what is right. But if you refuse to do what is right, then watch out! Sin is crouching at the door, eager to control you. But you must subdue it and be its master."

⁸ One day Cain suggested to his brother, "Let's go out into the fields."* And while they were in the field, Cain attacked his brother, Abel, and killed him.

⁹ Afterward the LORD asked Cain, "Where is your brother? Where is Abel?"

"I don't know," Cain responded. "Am I my brother's guardian?"

¹⁰ But the LORD said, "What have you done? Listen! Your brother's blood cries out to me from the ground! ¹¹ Now you are cursed and banished from the ground, which has swallowed your brother's blood. ¹² No longer will the ground yield good crops for you, no matter how hard you work! From now on you will be a homeless wanderer on the earth."

¹³ Cain replied to the LORD, "My punishment* is too great for me to bear! ¹⁴ You have banished me from the land and from your presence; you have made me a homeless wanderer. Anyone who finds me will kill me!"

¹⁵ The LORD replied, "No, for I will give a seven-fold punishment to anyone who kills you." Then the LORD put a mark on Cain to warn anyone who might try to kill him. ¹⁶ So Cain left the LORD's presence and settled in the land of Nod,* east of Eden.

THE DESCENDANTS OF CAIN

¹⁷ Cain had sexual relations with his wife, and she became pregnant and gave birth to Enoch. Then Cain founded a city, which he named Enoch, after his son. ¹⁸ Enoch had a son named Irad. Irad became the father of* Mehujael. Mehujael became the father of Methushael. Methushael became the father of Lamech.

¹⁹ Lamech married two women. The first was named Adah, and the second was Zillah. ²⁰ Adah gave birth to Jabal, who was the first of those who raise livestock and live in tents. ²¹ His brother's name was Jubal, the first of all who play the harp and flute. ²² Lamech's other wife, Zillah, gave birth to a son named Tubal-cain. He became an expert in forging tools of bronze and iron. Tubal-cain had a sister named Naamah. ²³ One day Lamech said to his wives,

"Adah and Zillah, hear my voice;
    listen to me, you wives of Lamech.
I have killed a man who attacked me,
    a young man who wounded me.
²⁴ If someone who kills Cain is punished seven times,
    then the one who kills me will be
        punished seventy-seven times!"

THE BIRTH OF SETH

²⁵ Adam had sexual relations with his wife again, and she gave birth to another son. She named him Seth,* for she said, "God has granted me another son in place of Abel, whom Cain killed." ²⁶ When Seth grew up, he had a son and named him Enosh. At that time people first began to worship the LORD by name.

THE DESCENDANTS OF ADAM

5 This is the written account of the descendants of Adam. When God created human beings,* he made them to be like himself. ² He created them male and female, and he blessed them and called them "human."

³ When Adam was 130 years old, he became the father of a son who was just like him—in his very image. He named his son Seth. ⁴ After the birth of Seth, Adam lived another 800 years, and he had other sons and daughters. ⁵ Adam lived 930 years, and then he died.

⁶ When Seth was 105 years old, he became the father of* Enosh. ⁷ After the birth of* Enosh, Seth lived another 807 years, and he had other sons and daughters. ⁸ Seth lived 912 years, and then he died.

⁹ When Enosh was 90 years old, he became the father of Kenan. ¹⁰ After the birth of Kenan, Enosh lived another 815 years, and he had

---

4:8 As in Samaritan Pentateuch, Greek and Syriac versions, and Latin Vulgate; Masoretic Text lacks "Let's go out into the fields." 4:13 Or *My sin.* 4:16 *Nod* means "wandering." 4:18 Or *the ancestor of,* and so throughout the verse. 4:25 *Seth* probably means "granted"; the name may also mean "appointed." 5:1 Or *man;* Hebrew reads *adam;* similarly in 5:2. 5:6 Or *the ancestor of;* also in 5:9, 12, 15, 18, 21, 25. 5:7 Or *the birth of this ancestor of;* also in 5:10, 13, 16, 19, 22, 26.

other sons and daughters. [11]Enosh lived 905 years, and then he died.

[12]When Kenan was 70 years old, he became the father of Mahalalel. [13]After the birth of Mahalalel, Kenan lived another 840 years, and he had other sons and daughters. [14]Kenan lived 910 years, and then he died.

[15]When Mahalalel was 65 years old, he became the father of Jared. [16]After the birth of Jared, Mahalalel lived another 830 years, and he had other sons and daughters. [17]Mahalalel lived 895 years, and then he died.

[18]When Jared was 162 years old, he became the father of Enoch. [19]After the birth of Enoch, Jared lived another 800 years, and he had other sons and daughters. [20]Jared lived 962 years, and then he died.

[21]When Enoch was 65 years old, he became the father of Methuselah. [22]After the birth of Methuselah, Enoch lived in close fellowship with God for another 300 years, and he had other sons and daughters. [23]Enoch lived 365 years, [24]walking in close fellowship with God. Then one day he disappeared, because God took him.

[25]When Methuselah was 187 years old, he became the father of Lamech. [26]After the birth of Lamech, Methuselah lived another 782 years, and he had other sons and daughters. [27]Methuselah lived 969 years, and then he died.

[28]When Lamech was 182 years old, he became the father of a son. [29]Lamech named his son Noah, for he said, "May he bring us relief* from our work and the painful labor of farming this ground that the LORD has cursed." [30]After the birth of Noah, Lamech lived another 595 years, and he had other sons and daughters. [31]Lamech lived 777 years, and then he died.

[32]After Noah was 500 years old, he became the father of Shem, Ham, and Japheth.

A WORLD GONE WRONG

6 Then the people began to multiply on the earth, and daughters were born to them. [2]The sons of God saw the beautiful women* and took any they wanted as their wives. [3]Then the LORD said, "My Spirit will not put up with* humans for such a long time, for they are only mortal flesh. In the future, their normal lifespan will be no more than 120 years."

[4]In those days, and for some time after, giant Nephilites lived on the earth, for whenever the sons of God had intercourse with women, they gave birth to children who became the heroes and famous warriors of ancient times.

[5]The LORD observed the extent of human wickedness on the earth, and he saw that everything they thought or imagined was consistently and totally evil. [6]So the LORD was sorry he had ever made them and put them on the earth. It

---

NOAH WAS CRAZY
Genesis 6:9   PRESTON MORRISON

It's easy to think what God called Noah to do was crazy. You might even find yourself saying, "I'm glad God didn't call *me* to build a huge boat." But God has called all of us to build something, whether it's a ministry, business, family, or life legacy. Walking in God's call may feel crazy at times, but you can put your trust in God because He is faithful. In Isaiah 43:1-2, God promises to be with us no matter what difficulties we face.

When God calls us to do something, He is also gracious to give us confirmation. God told Noah, "I will confirm my covenant with you. So enter the boat—you and your wife and your sons and their wives" (Genesis 6:18). Just as God called Noah to what might seem like *crazy* faith, we too are called to have radical obedience to God.

---

broke his heart. [7]And the LORD said, "I will wipe this human race I have created from the face of the earth. Yes, and I will destroy every living thing—all the people, the large animals, the small animals that scurry along the ground, and even the birds of the sky. I am sorry I ever made them." [8]But Noah found favor with the LORD.

THE STORY OF NOAH

[9]This is the account of Noah and his family. Noah was a righteous man, the only blameless person living on earth at the time, and he walked in close fellowship with God. [10]Noah was the father of three sons: Shem, Ham, and Japheth.

[11]Now God saw that the earth had become corrupt and was filled with violence. [12]God observed all this corruption in the world, for everyone on earth was corrupt. [13]So God said to Noah, "I have decided to destroy all living creatures, for they have filled the earth with violence. Yes, I will wipe them all out along with the earth!

[14]"Build a large boat* from cypress wood* and waterproof it with tar, inside and out. Then construct decks and stalls throughout its interior. [15]Make the boat 450 feet long, 75 feet wide, and 45 feet high.* [16]Leave an 18-inch opening* below the roof all the way around the boat. Put the door on the side, and build three decks inside the boat—lower, middle, and upper.

[17]"Look! I am about to cover the earth with a flood that will destroy every living thing that breathes. Everything on earth will die. [18]But I will confirm my covenant with you. So enter the boat—you and your wife and your sons and

---

5:29 *Noah* sounds like a Hebrew term that can mean "relief" or "comfort." 6:2 Hebrew *daughters of men;* also in 6:4. 6:3 Greek version reads *will not remain in.* 6:14a Traditionally rendered *an ark.* 6:14b Or *gopher wood.* 6:15 Hebrew *300 cubits* [138 meters] *long, 50 cubits* [23 meters] *wide, and 30 cubits* [13.8 meters] *high.* 6:16 Hebrew *an opening of 1 cubit* [46 centimeters].

their wives. 19 Bring a pair of every kind of animal—a male and a female—into the boat with you to keep them alive during the flood. 20 Pairs of every kind of bird, and every kind of animal, and every kind of small animal that scurries along the ground, will come to you to be kept alive. 21 And be sure to take on board enough food for your family and for all the animals."

22 So Noah did everything exactly as God had commanded him.

THE FLOOD COVERS THE EARTH

7 When everything was ready, the LORD said to Noah, "Go into the boat with all your family, for among all the people of the earth, I can see that you alone are righteous. 2 Take with you seven pairs—male and female—of each animal I have approved for eating and for sacrifice,* and take one pair of each of the others. 3 Also take seven pairs of every kind of bird. There must be a male and a female in each pair to ensure that all life will survive on the earth after the flood. 4 Seven days from now I will make the rains pour down on the earth. And it will rain for forty days and forty nights, until I have wiped from the earth all the living things I have created."

5 So Noah did everything as the LORD commanded him.

6 Noah was 600 years old when the flood covered the earth. 7 He went on board the boat to escape the flood—he and his wife and his sons and their wives. 8 With them were all the various kinds of animals—those approved for eating and for sacrifice and those that were not—along with all the birds and the small animals that scurry along the ground. 9 They entered the boat in pairs, male and female, just as God had commanded Noah. 10 After seven days, the waters of the flood came and covered the earth.

11 When Noah was 600 years old, on the seventeenth day of the second month, all the underground waters erupted from the earth, and the rain fell in mighty torrents from the sky. 12 The rain continued to fall for forty days and forty nights.

13 That very day Noah had gone into the boat with his wife and his sons—Shem, Ham, and Japheth—and their wives. 14 With them in the boat were pairs of every kind of animal—domestic and wild, large and small—along with birds of every kind. 15 Two by two they came into the boat, representing every living thing that breathes. 16 A male and female of each kind entered, just as God had commanded Noah. Then the LORD closed the door behind them.

17 For forty days the floodwaters grew deeper, covering the ground and lifting the boat high above the earth. 18 As the waters rose higher and higher above the ground, the boat floated safely on the surface. 19 Finally, the water covered even the highest mountains on the earth, 20 rising more than twenty-two feet* above the highest

peaks. 21 All the living things on earth died—birds, domestic animals, wild animals, small animals that scurry along the ground, and all the people. 22 Everything that breathed and lived on dry land died. 23 God wiped out every living thing on the earth—people, livestock, small animals that scurry along the ground, and the birds of the sky. All were destroyed. The only people who survived were Noah and those with him in the boat. 24 And the floodwaters covered the earth for 150 days.

THE FLOOD RECEDES

8 But God remembered Noah and all the wild animals and livestock with him in the boat. He sent a wind to blow across the earth, and the floodwaters began to recede. 2 The underground waters stopped flowing, and the torrential rains from the sky were stopped. 3 So the floodwaters gradually receded from the earth. After 150 days, 4 exactly five months from the time the flood began,* the boat came to rest on the mountains of Ararat. 5 Two and a half months later,* as the waters continued to go down, other mountain peaks became visible.

6 After another forty days, Noah opened the window he had made in the boat 7 and released a raven. The bird flew back and forth until the floodwaters on the earth had dried up. 8 He also released a dove to see if the water had receded and it could find dry ground. 9 But the dove could find no place to land because the water still covered the ground. So it returned to the boat, and Noah held out his hand and drew the dove back inside. 10 After waiting another seven days, Noah released the dove again. 11 This time the dove returned to him in the evening with a fresh olive leaf in its beak. Then Noah knew that the floodwaters were almost gone. 12 He waited another seven days and then released the dove again. This time it did not come back.

13 Noah was now 601 years old. On the first day of the new year, ten and a half months after the flood began,* the floodwaters had almost dried up from the earth. Noah lifted back the covering of the boat and saw that the surface of the ground was drying. 14 Two more months went by,* and at last the earth was dry!

15 Then God said to Noah, 16 "Leave the boat, all of you—you and your wife, and your sons and their wives. 17 Release all the animals—the birds, the livestock, and the small animals that scurry along the ground—so they can be fruitful and multiply throughout the earth."

18 So Noah, his wife, and his sons and their wives left the boat. 19 And all of the large and small animals and birds came out of the boat, pair by pair.

7:2 Hebrew *of each clean animal;* similarly in 7:8.   7:20 Hebrew *15 cubits* [6.9 meters].   8:4 Hebrew *on the seventeenth day of the seventh month;* see 7:11.   8:5 Hebrew *On the first day of the tenth month;* see 7:11 and note on 8:4.   8:13 Hebrew *On the first day of the first month;* see 7:11.   8:14 Hebrew *The twenty-seventh day of the second month arrived;* see note on 8:13.

[20]Then Noah built an altar to the LORD, and there he sacrificed as burnt offerings the animals and birds that had been approved for that purpose.* [21]And the LORD was pleased with the aroma of the sacrifice and said to himself, "I will never again curse the ground because of the human race, even though everything they think or imagine is bent toward evil from childhood. I will never again destroy all living things. [22]As long as the earth remains, there will be planting and harvest, cold and heat, summer and winter, day and night."

GOD CONFIRMS HIS COVENANT

9 Then God blessed Noah and his sons and told them, "Be fruitful and multiply. Fill the earth. [2]All the animals of the earth, all the birds of the sky, all the small animals that scurry along the ground, and all the fish in the sea will look on you with fear and terror. I have placed them in your power. [3]I have given them to you for food, just as I have given you grain and vegetables. [4]But you must never eat any meat that still has the lifeblood in it.

[5]"And I will require the blood of anyone who takes another person's life. If a wild animal kills a person, it must die. And anyone who murders a fellow human must die. [6]If anyone takes a human life, that person's life will also be taken by human hands. For God made human beings* in his own image. [7]Now be fruitful and multiply, and repopulate the earth."

[8]Then God told Noah and his sons, [9]"I hereby confirm my covenant with you and your descendants, [10]and with all the animals that were on the boat with you—the birds, the livestock, and all the wild animals—every living creature on earth. [11]Yes, I am confirming my covenant with you. Never again will floodwaters kill all living creatures; never again will a flood destroy the earth."

[12]Then God said, "I am giving you a sign of my covenant with you and with all living creatures, for all generations to come. [13]I have placed my rainbow in the clouds. It is the sign of my covenant with you and with all the earth. [14]When I send clouds over the earth, the rainbow will appear in the clouds, [15]and I will remember my covenant with you and with all living creatures. Never again will the floodwaters destroy all life. [16]When I see the rainbow in the clouds, I will remember the eternal covenant between God and every living creature on earth." [17]Then God said to Noah, "Yes, this rainbow is the sign of the covenant I am confirming with all the creatures on earth."

NOAH'S SONS

[18]The sons of Noah who came out of the boat with their father were Shem, Ham, and Japheth. (Ham is the father of Canaan.) [19]From these three sons of Noah came all the people who now populate the earth.

[20]After the flood, Noah began to cultivate the ground, and he planted a vineyard. [21]One day he drank some wine he had made, and he became drunk and lay naked inside his tent. [22]Ham, the father of Canaan, saw that his father was naked and went outside and told his brothers. [23]Then Shem and Japheth took a robe, held it over their shoulders, and backed into the tent to cover their father. As they did this, they looked the other way so they would not see him naked.

[24]When Noah woke up from his stupor, he learned what Ham, his youngest son, had done. [25]Then he cursed Canaan, the son of Ham:

"May Canaan be cursed!
  May he be the lowest of servants to his
    relatives."

[26]Then Noah said,

"May the LORD, the God of Shem,
  be blessed,
  and may Canaan be his servant!
[27] May God expand the territory of Japheth!
May Japheth share the prosperity
    of Shem,*
  and may Canaan be his servant."

[28]Noah lived another 350 years after the great flood. [29]He lived 950 years, and then he died.

10 This is the account of the families of Shem, Ham, and Japheth, the three sons of Noah. Many children were born to them after the great flood.

DESCENDANTS OF JAPHETH

[2]The descendants of Japheth were Gomer, Magog, Madai, Javan, Tubal, Meshech, and Tiras.
[3]The descendants of Gomer were Ashkenaz, Riphath, and Togarmah.
[4]The descendants of Javan were Elishah, Tarshish, Kittim, and Rodanim.* [5]Their descendants became the seafaring peoples that spread out to various lands, each identified by its own language, clan, and national identity.

DESCENDANTS OF HAM

[6]The descendants of Ham were Cush, Mizraim, Put, and Canaan.
[7]The descendants of Cush were Seba, Havilah, Sabtah, Raamah, and Sabteca. The descendants of Raamah were Sheba and Dedan.
[8]Cush was also the ancestor of Nimrod, who was the first heroic warrior on earth.

8:20 Hebrew every clean animal and every clean bird.   9:6 Or man; Hebrew reads ha-adam.   9:27 Hebrew May he live in the tents of Shem.   10:4 As in some Hebrew manuscripts and Greek version (see also 1 Chr 1:7); most Hebrew manuscripts read Dodanim.

⁹Since he was the greatest hunter in the world,* his name became proverbial. People would say, "This man is like Nimrod, the greatest hunter in the world." ¹⁰He built his kingdom in the land of Babylonia,* with the cities of Babylon, Erech, Akkad, and Calneh. ¹¹From there he expanded his territory to Assyria,* building the cities of Nineveh, Rehoboth-ir, Calah, ¹²and Resen (the great city located between Nineveh and Calah). ¹³Mizraim was the ancestor of the Ludites, Anamites, Lehabites, Naphtuhites, ¹⁴Pathrusites, Casluhites, and the Caphtorites, from whom the Philistines came.* ¹⁵Canaan's oldest son was Sidon, the ancestor of the Sidonians. Canaan was also the ancestor of the Hittites,* ¹⁶Jebusites, Amorites, Girgashites, ¹⁷Hivites, Arkites, Sinites, ¹⁸Arvadites, Zemarites, and Hamathites. The Canaanite clans eventually spread out, ¹⁹and the territory of Canaan extended from Sidon in the north to Gerar and Gaza in the south, and east as far as Sodom, Gomorrah, Admah, and Zeboiim, near Lasha. ²⁰These were the descendants of Ham, identified by clan, language, territory, and national identity.

DESCENDANTS OF SHEM

²¹Sons were also born to Shem, the older brother of Japheth.* Shem was the ancestor of all the descendants of Eber. ²²The descendants of Shem were Elam, Asshur, Arphaxad, Lud, and Aram. ²³The descendants of Aram were Uz, Hul, Gether, and Mash. ²⁴Arphaxad was the father of Shelah,* and Shelah was the father of Eber. ²⁵Eber had two sons. The first was named Peleg (which means "division"), for during his lifetime the people of the world were divided into different language groups. His brother's name was Joktan. ²⁶Joktan was the ancestor of Almodad, Sheleph, Hazarmaveth, Jerah, ²⁷Hadoram, Uzal, Diklah, ²⁸Obal, Abimael, Sheba, ²⁹Ophir, Havilah, and Jobab. All these were descendants of Joktan. ³⁰The territory they occupied extended from Mesha all the way to Sephar in the eastern mountains. ³¹These were the descendants of Shem, identified by clan, language, territory, and national identity.

CONCLUSION

³²These are the clans that descended from Noah's sons, arranged by nation according to their lines of descent. All the nations of the earth descended from these clans after the great flood.

THE TOWER OF BABEL

11 At one time all the people of the world spoke the same language and used the same words. ²As the people migrated to the east, they found a plain in the land of Babylonia* and settled there.

³They began saying to each other, "Let's make bricks and harden them with fire." (In this region bricks were used instead of stone, and tar was used for mortar.) ⁴Then they said, "Come, let's build a great city for ourselves with a tower that reaches into the sky. This will make us famous and keep us from being scattered all over the world."

⁵But the LORD came down to look at the city and the tower the people were building. ⁶"Look!" he said. "The people are united, and they all speak the same language. After this, nothing they set out to do will be impossible for them! ⁷Come, let's go down and confuse the people with different languages. Then they won't be able to understand each other."

⁸In that way, the LORD scattered them all over the world, and they stopped building the city. ⁹That is why the city was called Babel,* because that is where the LORD confused the people with different languages. In this way he scattered them all over the world.

THE LINE OF DESCENT FROM SHEM TO ABRAM

¹⁰This is the account of Shem's family.

Two years after the great flood, when Shem was 100 years old, he became the father of* Arphaxad. ¹¹After the birth of* Arphaxad, Shem lived another 500 years and had other sons and daughters.

¹²When Arphaxad was 35 years old, he became the father of Shelah. ¹³After the birth of Shelah, Arphaxad lived another 403 years and had other sons and daughters.* ¹⁴When Shelah was 30 years old, he became the father of Eber. ¹⁵After the birth of Eber, Shelah lived another 403 years and had other sons and daughters. ¹⁶When Eber was 34 years old, he became the father of Peleg. ¹⁷After the birth of Peleg, Eber lived another 430 years and had other sons and daughters.

10:9 Hebrew *a great hunter before the LORD;* also in 10:9b. 10:10 Hebrew *Shinar.* 10:11 Or *From that land Assyria went out.* 10:14 Hebrew *Casluhites, from whom the Philistines came, and Caphtorites.* Compare Jer 47:4; Amos 9:7. 10:15 Hebrew *ancestor of Heth.* 10:21 Or *Shem, whose older brother was Japheth.* 10:24 Greek version reads *Arphaxad was the father of Cainan, Cainan was the father of Shelah.* Compare Luke 3:36. 11:2 Hebrew *Shinar.* 11:9 Or *Babylon.* Babel sounds like a Hebrew term that means "confusion." 11:10 Or *the ancestor of;* also in 11:12, 14, 16, 18, 20, 22, 24. 11:11 Or *the birth of this ancestor of;* also in 11:13, 15, 17, 19, 21, 23, 25. 11:12-13 Greek version reads *¹²When Arphaxad was 135 years old, he became the father of Cainan. ¹³After the birth of Cainan, Arphaxad lived another 430 years and had other sons and daughters, and then he died. When Cainan was 130 years old, he became the father of Shelah. After the birth of Shelah, Cainan lived another 330 years and had other sons and daughters, and then he died.* Compare Luke 3:35-36.

THANKS GIVEN
Genesis 12–13   MARCUS BRECHEEN

The primary way we mature in our love for God is by being thankful. Abraham displayed his thankfulness to God by building altars, described in Genesis 12-13. An *altar* is a statement of your values, which extends into your future and bends your life around God. When we build altars from our earthly difficulties, we will see the greatness of God at work in our lives.

When Abraham received a promise from God, he made room in his life to receive it and built an altar to represent God doing a work that changed his life. He built an *altar of provision*, calling on the name (the character) of the Lord, prophetically thanking God for His provision. When Abraham stepped away from God's promise, God brought him back, and Abraham built an *altar of redemption*. Abraham's *altar of trust* demonstrated his belief that God would make a way for him when all seemed lost.

18 When Peleg was 30 years old, he became the father of Reu. 19 After the birth of Reu, Peleg lived another 209 years and had other sons and daughters.
20 When Reu was 32 years old, he became the father of Serug. 21 After the birth of Serug, Reu lived another 207 years and had other sons and daughters.
22 When Serug was 30 years old, he became the father of Nahor. 23 After the birth of Nahor, Serug lived another 200 years and had other sons and daughters.
24 When Nahor was 29 years old, he became the father of Terah. 25 After the birth of Terah, Nahor lived another 119 years and had other sons and daughters.
26 After Terah was 70 years old, he became the father of Abram, Nahor, and Haran.

THE FAMILY OF TERAH

27 This is the account of Terah's family. Terah was the father of Abram, Nahor, and Haran; and Haran was the father of Lot. 28 But Haran died in Ur of the Chaldeans, the land of his birth, while his father, Terah, was still living. 29 Meanwhile, Abram and Nahor both married. The name of Abram's wife was Sarai, and the name of Nahor's wife was Milcah. (Milcah and her sister Iscah were daughters of Nahor's brother Haran.) 30 But Sarai was unable to become pregnant and had no children.
31 One day Terah took his son Abram, his daughter-in-law Sarai (his son Abram's wife), and his grandson Lot (his son Haran's child) and moved away from Ur of the Chaldeans. He was headed for the land of Canaan, but they stopped at Haran and settled there. 32 Terah lived for 205 years* and died while still in Haran.

THE CALL OF ABRAM

12 The Lord had said to Abram, "Leave your native country, your relatives, and your father's family, and go to the land that I will show you. 2 I will make you into a great nation. I will bless you and make you famous, and you will be a blessing to others. 3 I will bless those who bless you and curse those who treat you with contempt. All the families on earth will be blessed through you."

4 So Abram departed as the Lord had instructed, and Lot went with him. Abram was seventy-five years old when he left Haran. 5 He took his wife, Sarai, his nephew Lot, and all his wealth—his livestock and all the people he had taken into his household at Haran—and headed for the land of Canaan. When they arrived in Canaan, 6 Abram traveled through the land as far as Shechem. There he set up camp beside the oak of Moreh. At that time, the area was inhabited by Canaanites.

7 Then the Lord appeared to Abram and said, "I will give this land to your descendants.*" And Abram built an altar there and dedicated it to the Lord, who had appeared to him. 8 After that, Abram traveled south and set up camp in the hill country, with Bethel to the west and Ai to the east. There he built another altar and dedicated it to the Lord, and he worshiped the Lord. 9 Then Abram continued traveling south by stages toward the Negev.

ABRAM AND SARAI IN EGYPT

10 At that time a severe famine struck the land of Canaan, forcing Abram to go down to Egypt, where he lived as a foreigner. 11 As he was approaching the border of Egypt, Abram said to his wife, Sarai, "Look, you are a very beautiful woman. 12 When the Egyptians see you, they will say, 'This is his wife. Let's kill him; then we can have her!' 13 So please tell them you are my sister. Then they will spare my life and treat me well because of their interest in you."

14 And sure enough, when Abram arrived in Egypt, everyone noticed Sarai's beauty. 15 When the palace officials saw her, they sang her praises to Pharaoh, their king, and Sarai was taken into his palace. 16 Then Pharaoh gave Abram many gifts because of her—sheep, goats, cattle, male and female donkeys, male and female servants, and camels.

17 But the Lord sent terrible plagues upon Pharaoh and his household because of Sarai, Abram's wife. 18 So Pharaoh summoned Abram and accused him sharply. "What have you done to me?" he demanded. "Why didn't you tell me she was your wife? 19 Why did you say, 'She is my sister,' and allow me to take her as my wife? Now then, here is your wife. Take her and get out of

11:32 Some ancient versions read *145 years;* compare 11:26 and 12:4.   12:7 Hebrew *seed.*

here!" ²⁰Pharaoh ordered some of his men to escort them, and he sent Abram out of the country, along with his wife and all his possessions.

ABRAM AND LOT SEPARATE

13 So Abram left Egypt and traveled north into the Negev, along with his wife and Lot and all that they owned. ²(Abram was very rich in livestock, silver, and gold.) ³From the Negev, they continued traveling by stages toward Bethel, and they pitched their tents between Bethel and Ai, where they had camped before. ⁴This was the same place where Abram had built the altar, and there he worshiped the LORD again.

⁵Lot, who was traveling with Abram, had also become very wealthy with flocks of sheep and goats, herds of cattle, and many tents. ⁶But the land could not support both Abram and Lot with all their flocks and herds living so close together. ⁷So disputes broke out between the herdsmen of Abram and Lot. (At that time Canaanites and Perizzites were also living in the land.)

⁸Finally Abram said to Lot, "Let's not allow this conflict to come between us or our herdsmen. After all, we are close relatives! ⁹The whole countryside is open to you. Take your choice of any section of the land you want, and we will separate. If you want the land to the left, then I'll take the land on the right. If you prefer the land on the right, then I'll go to the left."

¹⁰Lot took a long look at the fertile plains of the Jordan Valley in the direction of Zoar. The whole area was well watered everywhere, like the garden of the LORD or the beautiful land of Egypt. (This was before the LORD destroyed Sodom and Gomorrah.) ¹¹Lot chose for himself the whole Jordan Valley to the east of them. He went there with his flocks and servants and parted company with his uncle Abram. ¹²So Abram settled in the land of Canaan, and Lot moved his tents to a place near Sodom and settled among the cities of the plain. ¹³But the people of this area were extremely wicked and constantly sinned against the LORD.

¹⁴After Lot had gone, the LORD said to Abram, "Look as far as you can see in every direction— north and south, east and west. ¹⁵I am giving all this land, as far as you can see, to you and your descendants* as a permanent possession. ¹⁶And I will give you so many descendants that, like the dust of the earth, they cannot be counted! ¹⁷Go and walk through the land in every direction, for I am giving it to you."

¹⁸So Abram moved his camp to Hebron and settled near the oak grove belonging to Mamre. There he built another altar to the LORD.

ABRAM RESCUES LOT

14 About this time war broke out in the region. King Amraphel of Babylonia,* King Arioch of Ellasar, King Kedorlaomer of Elam, and King Tidal of Goiim ²fought against King Bera of Sodom, King Birsha of Gomorrah, King Shinab of Admah, King Shemeber of Zeboiim, and the king of Bela (also called Zoar).

³This second group of kings joined forces in Siddim Valley (that is, the valley of the Dead Sea*). ⁴For twelve years they had been subject to King Kedorlaomer, but in the thirteenth year they rebelled against him.

⁵One year later Kedorlaomer and his allies arrived and defeated the Rephaites at Ashteroth-karnaim, the Zuzites at Ham, the Emites at Shaveh-kiriathaim, ⁶and the Horites at Mount Seir, as far as El-paran at the edge of the wilderness. ⁷Then they turned back and came to En-mishpat (now called Kadesh) and conquered all the territory of the Amalekites, and also the Amorites living in Hazazon-tamar.

⁸Then the rebel kings of Sodom, Gomorrah, Admah, Zeboiim, and Bela (also called Zoar) prepared for battle in the valley of the Dead Sea.* ⁹They fought against King Kedorlaomer of Elam, King Tidal of Goiim, King Amraphel of Babylonia, and King Arioch of Ellasar—four kings against five. ¹⁰As it happened, the valley of the Dead Sea was filled with tar pits. And as the army of the kings of Sodom and Gomorrah fled, some fell into the tar pits, while the rest escaped into the mountains. ¹¹The victorious invaders then plundered Sodom and Gomorrah and headed for home, taking with them all the spoils of war and the food supplies. ¹²They also captured Lot—Abram's nephew who lived in Sodom—and carried off everything he owned.

¹³But one of Lot's men escaped and reported everything to Abram the Hebrew, who was living near the oak grove belonging to Mamre the Amorite. Mamre and his relatives, Eshcol and Aner, were Abram's allies.

¹⁴When Abram heard that his nephew Lot had been captured, he mobilized the 318 trained men who had been born into his household. Then he pursued Kedorlaomer's army until he caught up with them at Dan. ¹⁵There he divided his men and attacked during the night. Kedorlaomer's army fled, but Abram chased them as far as Hobah, north of Damascus. ¹⁶Abram recovered all the goods that had been taken, and he brought back his nephew Lot with his possessions and all the women and other captives.

MELCHIZEDEK BLESSES ABRAM

¹⁷After Abram returned from his victory over Kedorlaomer and all his allies, the king of Sodom went out to meet him in the valley of Shaveh (that is, the King's Valley).

¹⁸And Melchizedek, the king of Salem and a priest of God Most High,* brought Abram some bread and wine. ¹⁹Melchizedek blessed Abram with this blessing:

13:15 Hebrew *seed;* also in 13:16.   **14:1** Hebrew *Shinar;* also in 14:9.
14:3 Hebrew *Salt Sea.*   **14:8** Hebrew *Siddim Valley* (see 14:3); also
in 14:10.   **14:18** Hebrew *El-Elyon;* also in 14:19, 20, 22.

"Blessed be Abram by God Most High,
Creator of heaven and earth.
20 And blessed be God Most High,
who has defeated your enemies for you."

Then Abram gave Melchizedek a tenth of all the goods he had recovered.

21 The king of Sodom said to Abram, "Give back my people who were captured. But you may keep for yourself all the goods you have recovered."

22 Abram replied to the king of Sodom, "I solemnly swear to the LORD, God Most High, Creator of heaven and earth, 23 that I will not take so much as a single thread or sandal thong from what belongs to you. Otherwise you might say, 'I am the one who made Abram rich.' 24 I will accept only what my young warriors have already eaten, and I request that you give a fair share of the goods to my allies—Aner, Eshcol, and Mamre."

THE LORD'S COVENANT PROMISE TO ABRAM

15 Some time later, the LORD spoke to Abram in a vision and said to him, "Do not be afraid, Abram, for I will protect you, and your reward will be great."

2 But Abram replied, "O Sovereign LORD, what good are all your blessings when I don't even have a son? Since you've given me no children, Eliezer of Damascus, a servant in my household, will inherit all my wealth. 3 You have given me no descendants of my own, so one of my servants will be my heir."

4 Then the LORD said to him, "No, your servant will not be your heir, for you will have a son of your own who will be your heir." 5 Then the LORD took Abram outside and said to him, "Look up into the sky and count the stars if you can. That's how many descendants you will have!"

6 And Abram believed the LORD, and the LORD counted him as righteous because of his faith.

7 Then the LORD told him, "I am the LORD who brought you out of Ur of the Chaldeans to give you this land as your possession."

8 But Abram replied, "O Sovereign LORD, how can I be sure that I will actually possess it?"

9 The LORD told him, "Bring me a three-year-old heifer, a three-year-old female goat, a three-year-old ram, a turtledove, and a young pigeon." 10 So Abram presented all these to him and killed them. Then he cut each animal down the middle and laid the halves side by side; he did not, however, cut the birds in half. 11 Some vultures swooped down to eat the carcasses, but Abram chased them away.

12 As the sun was going down, Abram fell into a deep sleep, and a terrifying darkness came down over him. 13 Then the LORD said to Abram, "You can be sure that your descendants will be strangers in a foreign land, where they will be oppressed as slaves for 400 years. 14 But I will punish the nation that enslaves them, and in the end they will come away with great wealth. 15 (As for you, you will die in peace and be buried at a ripe old age.) 16 After four generations your descendants will return here to this land, for the sins of the Amorites do not yet warrant their destruction."

17 After the sun went down and darkness fell, Abram saw a smoking firepot and a flaming torch pass between the halves of the carcasses. 18 So the LORD made a covenant with Abram that day and said, "I have given this land to your descendants, all the way from the border of Egypt* to the great Euphrates River—19 the land now occupied by the Kenites, Kenizzites, Kadmonites, 20 Hittites, Perizzites, Rephaites, 21 Amorites, Canaanites, Girgashites, and Jebusites."

THE BIRTH OF ISHMAEL

16 Now Sarai, Abram's wife, had not been able to bear children for him. But she had an Egyptian servant named Hagar. 2 So Sarai said to Abram, "The LORD has prevented me from having children. Go and sleep with my servant. Perhaps I can have children through her." And Abram agreed with Sarai's proposal. 3 So Sarai, Abram's wife, took Hagar the Egyptian servant and gave her to Abram as a wife. (This happened ten years after Abram had settled in the land of Canaan.)

4 So Abram had sexual relations with Hagar, and she became pregnant. But when Hagar knew she was pregnant, she began to treat her mistress, Sarai, with contempt. 5 Then Sarai said to Abram, "This is all your fault! I put my servant into your arms, but now that she's pregnant she treats me with contempt. The LORD will show who's wrong—you or me!"

6 Abram replied, "Look, she is your servant, so deal with her as you see fit." Then Sarai treated Hagar so harshly that she finally ran away.

7 The angel of the LORD found Hagar beside a spring of water in the wilderness, along the road to Shur. 8 The angel said to her, "Hagar, Sarai's servant, where have you come from, and where are you going?"

"I'm running away from my mistress, Sarai," she replied.

9 The angel of the LORD said to her, "Return to your mistress, and submit to her authority." 10 Then he added, "I will give you more descendants than you can count."

11 And the angel also said, "You are now pregnant and will give birth to a son. You are to name him Ishmael (which means 'God hears'), for the LORD has heard your cry of distress. 12 This son of yours will be a wild man, as untamed as a wild donkey! He will raise his fist against everyone, and everyone will be against him. Yes, he will live in open hostility against all his relatives."

15:18 Hebrew *the river of Egypt*, referring either to an eastern branch of the Nile River or to the Brook of Egypt in the Sinai (see Num 34:5).

¹³ Thereafter, Hagar used another name to refer to the Lord, who had spoken to her. She said, "You are the God who sees me."* She also said, "Have I truly seen the One who sees me?" ¹⁴ So that well was named Beer-lahai-roi (which means "well of the Living One who sees me"). It can still be found between Kadesh and Bered.

¹⁵ So Hagar gave Abram a son, and Abram named him Ishmael. ¹⁶ Abram was eighty-six years old when Ishmael was born.

ABRAM IS NAMED ABRAHAM

17 When Abram was ninety-nine years old, the Lord appeared to him and said, "I am El-Shaddai—'God Almighty.' Serve me faithfully and live a blameless life. ² I will make a covenant with you, by which I will guarantee to give you countless descendants."

³ At this, Abram fell face down on the ground. Then God said to him, ⁴ "This is my covenant with you: I will make you the father of a multitude of nations! ⁵ What's more, I am changing your name. It will no longer be Abram. Instead, you will be called Abraham,* for you will be the father of many nations. ⁶ I will make you extremely fruitful. Your descendants will become many nations, and kings will be among them!

⁷ "I will confirm my covenant with you and your descendants* after you, from generation to generation. This is the everlasting covenant: I will always be your God and the God of your descendants after you. ⁸ And I will give the entire land of Canaan, where you now live as a foreigner, to you and your descendants. It will be their possession forever, and I will be their God."

THE MARK OF THE COVENANT

⁹ Then God said to Abraham, "Your responsibility is to obey the terms of the covenant. You and all your descendants have this continual responsibility. ¹⁰ This is the covenant that you and your descendants must keep: Each male among you must be circumcised. ¹¹ You must cut off the flesh of your foreskin as a sign of the covenant between me and you. ¹² From generation to generation, every male child must be circumcised on the eighth day after his birth. This applies not only to members of your family but also to the servants born in your household and the foreign-born servants whom you have purchased. ¹³ All must be circumcised. Your bodies will bear the mark of my everlasting covenant. ¹⁴ Any male who fails to be circumcised will be cut off from the covenant family for breaking the covenant."

SARAI IS NAMED SARAH

¹⁵ Then God said to Abraham, "Regarding Sarai, your wife—her name will no longer be Sarai. From now on her name will be Sarah.* ¹⁶ And I will bless her and give you a son from her! Yes, I will bless her richly, and she will become the mother of many nations. Kings of nations will be among her descendants."

¹⁷ Then Abraham bowed down to the ground, but he laughed to himself in disbelief. "How could I become a father at the age of 100?" he thought. "And how can Sarah have a baby when she is ninety years old?" ¹⁸ So Abraham said to God, "May Ishmael live under your special blessing!"

¹⁹ But God replied, "No—Sarah, your wife, will give birth to a son for you. You will name him Isaac,* and I will confirm my covenant with him and his descendants as an everlasting covenant. ²⁰ As for Ishmael, I will bless him also, just as you have asked. I will make him extremely fruitful and multiply his descendants. He will become the father of twelve princes, and I will make him a great nation. ²¹ But my covenant will be confirmed with Isaac, who will be born to you and Sarah about this time next year." ²² When God had finished speaking, he left Abraham.

²³ On that very day Abraham took his son, Ishmael, and every male in his household, including those born there and those he had bought. Then he circumcised them, cutting off their foreskins, just as God had told him. ²⁴ Abraham was ninety-nine years old when he was circumcised, ²⁵ and Ishmael, his son, was thirteen. ²⁶ Both Abraham and his son, Ishmael, were circumcised on that same day, ²⁷ along with all the other men and boys of the household, whether they were born there or bought as servants. All were circumcised with him.

A SON IS PROMISED TO SARAH

18 The Lord appeared again to Abraham near the oak grove belonging to Mamre. One day Abraham was sitting at the entrance to his tent during the hottest part of the day. ² He looked up and noticed three men standing nearby. When he saw them, he ran to meet them and welcomed them, bowing low to the ground.

³ "My lord," he said, "if it pleases you, stop here for a while. ⁴ Rest in the shade of this tree while water is brought to wash your feet. ⁵ And since you've honored your servant with this visit, let me prepare some food to refresh you before you continue on your journey."

"All right," they said. "Do as you have said."

⁶ So Abraham ran back to the tent and said to Sarah, "Hurry! Get three large measures* of your best flour, knead it into dough, and bake some bread." ⁷ Then Abraham ran out to the herd and chose a tender calf and gave it to his servant, who quickly prepared it. ⁸ When the food was ready, Abraham took some yogurt and milk and the roasted meat, and he served it to the men.

16:13 Hebrew *El-roi.* 17:5 *Abram* means "exalted father"; *Abraham* sounds like a Hebrew term that means "father of many." 17:7 Hebrew *seed;* also in 17:7b, 8, 9, 10, 19. 17:15 *Sarai* and *Sarah* both mean "princess"; the change in spelling may reflect the difference in dialect between Ur and Canaan. 17:19 *Isaac* means "he laughs." 18:6 Hebrew *3 seahs,* about half a bushel or 22 liters.

As they ate, Abraham waited on them in the shade of the trees.

⁹"Where is Sarah, your wife?" the visitors asked.

"She's inside the tent," Abraham replied.

¹⁰Then one of them said, "I will return to you about this time next year, and your wife, Sarah, will have a son!"

Sarah was listening to this conversation from the tent. ¹¹Abraham and Sarah were both very old by this time, and Sarah was long past the age of having children. ¹²So she laughed silently to herself and said, "How could a worn-out woman like me enjoy such pleasure, especially when my master—my husband—is also so old?"

¹³Then the LORD said to Abraham, "Why did Sarah laugh? Why did she say, 'Can an old woman like me have a baby?' ¹⁴Is anything too hard for the LORD? I will return about this time next year, and Sarah will have a son."

¹⁵Sarah was afraid, so she denied it, saying, "I didn't laugh."

But the LORD said, "No, you did laugh."

ABRAHAM INTERCEDES FOR SODOM

¹⁶Then the men got up from their meal and looked out toward Sodom. As they left, Abraham went with them to send them on their way. ¹⁷"Should I hide my plan from Abraham?" the LORD asked. ¹⁸"For Abraham will certainly become a great and mighty nation, and all the nations of the earth will be blessed through him. ¹⁹I have singled him out so that he will direct his sons and their families to keep the way of the LORD by doing what is right and just. Then I will do for Abraham all that I have promised."

²⁰So the LORD told Abraham, "I have heard a great outcry from Sodom and Gomorrah, because their sin is so flagrant. ²¹I am going down to see if their actions are as wicked as I have heard. If not, I want to know."

²²The other men turned and headed toward Sodom, but the LORD remained with Abraham. ²³Abraham approached him and said, "Will you sweep away both the righteous and the wicked? ²⁴Suppose you find fifty righteous people living there in the city—will you still sweep it away and not spare it for their sakes? ²⁵Surely you wouldn't do such a thing, destroying the righteous along with the wicked. Why, you would be treating the righteous and the wicked exactly the same! Surely you wouldn't do that! Should not the Judge of all the earth do what is right?"

²⁶And the LORD replied, "If I find fifty righteous people in Sodom, I will spare the entire city for their sake."

²⁷Then Abraham spoke again. "Since I have begun, let me speak further to my Lord, even though I am but dust and ashes. ²⁸Suppose there are only forty-five righteous people rather than fifty? Will you destroy the whole city for lack of five?"

And the LORD said, "I will not destroy it if I find forty-five righteous people there."

²⁹Then Abraham pressed his request further. "Suppose there are only forty?"

And the LORD replied, "I will not destroy it for the sake of the forty."

³⁰"Please don't be angry, my Lord," Abraham pleaded. "Let me speak—suppose only thirty righteous people are found?"

And the LORD replied, "I will not destroy it if I find thirty."

³¹Then Abraham said, "Since I have dared to speak to the Lord, let me continue—suppose there are only twenty?"

And the LORD replied, "Then I will not destroy it for the sake of the twenty."

³²Finally, Abraham said, "Lord, please don't be angry with me if I speak one more time. Suppose only ten are found there?"

And the LORD replied, "Then I will not destroy it for the sake of the ten."

³³When the LORD had finished his conversation with Abraham, he went on his way, and Abraham returned to his tent.

SODOM AND GOMORRAH DESTROYED

19 That evening the two angels came to the entrance of the city of Sodom. Lot was sitting there, and when he saw them, he stood up to meet them. Then he welcomed them and bowed with his face to the ground. ²"My lords," he said, "come to my home to wash your feet, and be my guests for the night. You may then get up early in the morning and be on your way again."

"Oh no," they replied. "We'll just spend the night out here in the city square."

³But Lot insisted, so at last they went home with him. Lot prepared a feast for them, complete with fresh bread made without yeast, and they ate. ⁴But before they retired for the night, all the men of Sodom, young and old, came from all over the city and surrounded the house. ⁵They shouted to Lot, "Where are the men who came to spend the night with you? Bring them out to us so we can have sex with them!"

⁶So Lot stepped outside to talk to them, shutting the door behind him. ⁷"Please, my brothers," he begged, "don't do such a wicked thing. ⁸Look, I have two virgin daughters. Let me bring them out to you, and you can do with them as you wish. But please, leave these men alone, for they are my guests and are under my protection."

⁹"Stand back!" they shouted. "This fellow came to town as an outsider, and now he's acting like our judge! We'll treat you far worse than those other men!" And they lunged toward Lot to break down the door.

¹⁰But the two angels* reached out, pulled Lot into the house, and bolted the door. ¹¹Then they blinded all the men, young and old, who were

_____
19:10 Hebrew *men*; also in 19:12, 16.

at the door of the house, so they gave up trying to get inside.

¹² Meanwhile, the angels questioned Lot. "Do you have any other relatives here in the city?" they asked. "Get them out of this place—your sons-in-law, sons, daughters, or anyone else. ¹³ For we are about to destroy this city completely. The outcry against this place is so great it has reached the LORD, and he has sent us to destroy it."

¹⁴ So Lot rushed out to tell his daughters' fiancés, "Quick, get out of the city! The LORD is about to destroy it." But the young men thought he was only joking.

¹⁵ At dawn the next morning the angels became insistent. "Hurry," they said to Lot. "Take your wife and your two daughters who are here. Get out right now, or you will be swept away in the destruction of the city!"

¹⁶ When Lot still hesitated, the angels seized his hand and the hands of his wife and two daughters and rushed them to safety outside the city, for the LORD was merciful. ¹⁷ When they were safely out of the city, one of the angels ordered, "Run for your lives! And don't look back or stop anywhere in the valley! Escape to the mountains, or you will be swept away!"

¹⁸ "Oh no, my lord!" Lot begged. ¹⁹ "You have been so gracious to me and saved my life, and you have shown such great kindness. But I cannot go to the mountains. Disaster would catch up to me there, and I would soon die. ²⁰ See, there is a small village nearby. Please let me go there instead; don't you see how small it is? Then my life will be saved."

²¹ "All right," the angel said, "I will grant your request. I will not destroy the little village. ²² But hurry! Escape to it, for I can do nothing until you arrive there." (This explains why that village was known as Zoar, which means "little place.")

²³ Lot reached the village just as the sun was rising over the horizon. ²⁴ Then the LORD rained down fire and burning sulfur from the sky on Sodom and Gomorrah. ²⁵ He utterly destroyed them, along with the other cities and villages of the plain, wiping out all the people and every bit of vegetation. ²⁶ But Lot's wife looked back as she was following behind him, and she turned into a pillar of salt.

²⁷ Abraham got up early that morning and hurried out to the place where he had stood in the LORD's presence. ²⁸ He looked out across the plain toward Sodom and Gomorrah and watched as columns of smoke rose from the cities like smoke from a furnace.

²⁹ But God had listened to Abraham's request and kept Lot safe, removing him from the disaster that engulfed the cities on the plain.

LOT AND HIS DAUGHTERS

³⁰ Afterward Lot left Zoar because he was afraid of the people there, and he went to live in a cave in the mountains with his two daughters. ³¹ One day the older daughter said to her sister, "There are no men left anywhere in this entire area, so we can't get married like everyone else. And our father will soon be too old to have children. ³² Come, let's get him drunk with wine, and then we will have sex with him. That way we will preserve our family line through our father."

³³ So that night they got him drunk with wine, and the older daughter went in and had intercourse with her father. He was unaware of her lying down or getting up again.

³⁴ The next morning the older daughter said to her younger sister, "I had sex with our father last night. Let's get him drunk with wine again tonight, and you go in and have sex with him. That way we will preserve our family line through our father." ³⁵ So that night they got him drunk with wine again, and the younger daughter went in and had intercourse with him. As before, he was unaware of her lying down or getting up again.

³⁶ As a result, both of Lot's daughters became pregnant by their own father. ³⁷ When the older daughter gave birth to a son, she named him Moab.* He became the ancestor of the nation now known as the Moabites. ³⁸ When the younger daughter gave birth to a son, she named him Ben-ammi.* He became the ancestor of the nation now known as the Ammonites.

ABRAHAM DECEIVES ABIMELECH

20 Abraham moved south to the Negev and lived for a while between Kadesh and Shur, and then he moved on to Gerar. While living there as a foreigner, ² Abraham introduced his wife, Sarah, by saying, "She is my sister." So King Abimelech of Gerar sent for Sarah and had her brought to him at his palace.

³ But that night God came to Abimelech in a dream and told him, "You are a dead man, for that woman you have taken is already married!"

⁴ But Abimelech had not slept with her yet, so he said, "Lord, will you destroy an innocent nation? ⁵ Didn't Abraham tell me, 'She is my sister'? And she herself said, 'Yes, he is my brother.' I acted in complete innocence! My hands are clean."

⁶ In the dream God responded, "Yes, I know you are innocent. That's why I kept you from sinning against me, and why I did not let you touch her. ⁷ Now return the woman to her husband, and he will pray for you, for he is a prophet. Then you will live. But if you don't return her to him, you can be sure that you and all your people will die."

⁸ Abimelech got up early the next morning and quickly called all his servants together. When he told them what had happened, his men were terrified. ⁹ Then Abimelech called for Abraham.

19:37 *Moab* sounds like a Hebrew term that means "from father."
19:38 *Ben-ammi* means "son of my kinsman."

"What have you done to us?" he demanded. "What crime have I committed that deserves treatment like this, making me and my kingdom guilty of this great sin? No one should ever do what you have done! ¹⁰Whatever possessed you to do such a thing?"

¹¹Abraham replied, "I thought, 'This is a godless place. They will want my wife and will kill me to get her.' ¹²And she really is my sister, for we both have the same father, but different mothers. And I married her. ¹³When God called me to leave my father's home and to travel from place to place, I told her, 'Do me a favor. Wherever we go, tell the people that I am your brother.'"

¹⁴Then Abimelech took some of his sheep and goats, cattle, and male and female servants, and he presented them to Abraham. He also returned his wife, Sarah, to him. ¹⁵Then Abimelech said, "Look over my land and choose any place where you would like to live." ¹⁶And he said to Sarah, "Look, I am giving your 'brother' 1,000 pieces of silver* in the presence of all these witnesses. This is to compensate you for any wrong I may have done to you. This will settle any claim against me, and your reputation is cleared."

¹⁷Then Abraham prayed to God, and God healed Abimelech, his wife, and his female servants, so they could have children. ¹⁸For the LORD had caused all the women to be infertile because of what happened with Abraham's wife, Sarah.

THE BIRTH OF ISAAC

21 The LORD kept his word and did for Sarah exactly what he had promised. ²She became pregnant, and she gave birth to a son for Abraham in his old age. This happened at just the time God had said it would. ³And Abraham named their son Isaac. ⁴Eight days after Isaac was born, Abraham circumcised him as God had commanded. ⁵Abraham was 100 years old when Isaac was born.

⁶And Sarah declared, "God has brought me laughter.* All who hear about this will laugh with me. ⁷Who would have said to Abraham that Sarah would nurse a baby? Yet I have given Abraham a son in his old age!"

HAGAR AND ISHMAEL ARE SENT AWAY

⁸When Isaac grew up and was about to be weaned, Abraham prepared a huge feast to celebrate the occasion. ⁹But Sarah saw Ishmael—the son of Abraham and her Egyptian servant Hagar—making fun of her son, Isaac.* ¹⁰So she turned to Abraham and demanded, "Get rid of that slave woman and her son. He is not going to share the inheritance with my son, Isaac. I won't have it!"

¹¹This upset Abraham very much because Ishmael was his son. ¹²But God told Abraham, "Do not be upset over the boy and your servant. Do whatever Sarah tells you, for Isaac is the son through whom your descendants will be

counted. ¹³But I will also make a nation of the descendants of Hagar's son because he is your son, too."

¹⁴So Abraham got up early the next morning, prepared food and a container of water, and strapped them on Hagar's shoulders. Then he sent her away with their son, and she wandered aimlessly in the wilderness of Beersheba.

¹⁵When the water was gone, she put the boy in the shade of a bush. ¹⁶Then she went and sat down by herself about a hundred yards* away. "I don't want to watch the boy die," she said, as she burst into tears.

¹⁷But God heard the boy crying, and the angel of God called to Hagar from heaven, "Hagar, what's wrong? Do not be afraid! God has heard the boy crying as he lies there. ¹⁸Go to him and comfort him, for I will make a great nation from his descendants."

¹⁹Then God opened Hagar's eyes, and she saw a well full of water. She quickly filled her water container and gave the boy a drink.

²⁰And God was with the boy as he grew up in the wilderness. He became a skillful archer, ²¹and he settled in the wilderness of Paran. His mother arranged for him to marry a woman from the land of Egypt.

ABRAHAM'S COVENANT WITH ABIMELECH

²²About this time, Abimelech came with Phicol, his army commander, to visit Abraham. "God is obviously with you, helping you in everything you do," Abimelech said. ²³"Swear to me in God's name that you will never deceive me, my children, or any of my descendants. I have been loyal to you, so now swear that you will be loyal to me and to this country where you are living as a foreigner."

²⁴Abraham replied, "Yes, I swear to it!" ²⁵Then Abraham complained to Abimelech about a well that Abimelech's servants had taken by force from Abraham's servants.

²⁶"This is the first I've heard of it," Abimelech answered. "I have no idea who is responsible. You have never complained about this before."

²⁷Abraham then gave some of his sheep, goats, and cattle to Abimelech, and they made a treaty. ²⁸But Abraham also took seven additional female lambs and set them off by themselves. ²⁹Abimelech asked, "Why have you set these seven apart from the others?"

³⁰Abraham replied, "Please accept these seven lambs to show your agreement that I dug this well." ³¹Then he named the place Beersheba (which means "well of the oath"), because that was where they had sworn the oath.

³²After making their covenant at Beersheba, Abimelech left with Phicol, the commander of

---

20:16 Hebrew *1,000 [shekels] of silver*, about 25 pounds or 11.4 kilograms in weight. 21:6 The name *Isaac* means "he laughs." 21:9 As in Greek version and Latin Vulgate; Hebrew lacks *of her son, Isaac.* 21:16 Hebrew *a bowshot.*

THE POWER OF SURRENDER
Genesis 22:1–19   JIMMY EVANS

God will never tempt us, but He does test us. In Genesis 22, God tests Abraham's faithfulness through his beloved son, Isaac. God had made promises to Abraham, and Isaac represented those promises coming to life. But then God asks Abraham to sacrifice Isaac. What does Abraham do? He immediately obeys. God sees that Abraham's heart is faithful, and He provides a ram for the sacrifice instead of Isaac.

Just as Abraham is blessed for being willing to lay down Isaac, we too will be blessed when we lay down anything that competes with God for first place in our lives. There will be moments when God will challenge you to surrender specific things to Him. These things may include your finances, business, ministry, relationships, personal habits, and time. Whenever you surrender the things of this life completely to God, He will always take you to another level of provision and blessing.

his army, and they returned home to the land of the Philistines. ³³Then Abraham planted a tamarisk tree at Beersheba, and there he worshiped the LORD, the Eternal God.* ³⁴And Abraham lived as a foreigner in Philistine country for a long time.

ABRAHAM'S FAITH TESTED

22 Some time later, God tested Abraham's faith. "Abraham!" God called.

"Yes," he replied. "Here I am."

²"Take your son, your only son—yes, Isaac, whom you love so much—and go to the land of Moriah. Go and sacrifice him as a burnt offering on one of the mountains, which I will show you."

³The next morning Abraham got up early. He saddled his donkey and took two of his servants with him, along with his son, Isaac. Then he chopped wood for a fire for a burnt offering and set out for the place God had told him about. ⁴On the third day of their journey, Abraham looked up and saw the place in the distance. ⁵"Stay here with the donkey," Abraham told the servants. "The boy and I will travel a little farther. We will worship there, and then we will come right back."

⁶So Abraham placed the wood for the burnt offering on Isaac's shoulders, while he himself carried the fire and the knife. As the two of them walked on together, ⁷Isaac turned to Abraham and said, "Father?"

"Yes, my son?" Abraham replied.

"We have the fire and the wood," the boy said, "but where is the sheep for the burnt offering?"

⁸"God will provide a sheep for the burnt offering, my son," Abraham answered. And they both walked on together.

⁹When they arrived at the place where God had told him to go, Abraham built an altar and arranged the wood on it. Then he tied his son, Isaac, and laid him on the altar on top of the wood. ¹⁰And Abraham picked up the knife to kill his son as a sacrifice. ¹¹At that moment the angel of the LORD called to him from heaven, "Abraham! Abraham!"

"Yes," Abraham replied. "Here I am!"

¹²"Don't lay a hand on the boy!" the angel said. "Do not hurt him in any way, for now I know that you truly fear God. You have not withheld from me even your son, your only son."

¹³Then Abraham looked up and saw a ram caught by its horns in a thicket. So he took the ram and sacrificed it as a burnt offering in place of his son. ¹⁴Abraham named the place Yahweh-Yireh (which means "the LORD will provide"). To this day, people still use that name as a proverb: "On the mountain of the LORD it will be provided."

¹⁵Then the angel of the LORD called again to Abraham from heaven. ¹⁶"This is what the LORD says: Because you have obeyed me and have not withheld even your son, your only son, I swear by my own name that ¹⁷I will certainly bless you. I will multiply your descendants* beyond number, like the stars in the sky and the sand on the seashore. Your descendants will conquer the cities of their enemies. ¹⁸And through your descendants all the nations of the earth will be blessed—all because you have obeyed me."

¹⁹Then they returned to the servants and traveled back to Beersheba, where Abraham continued to live.

²⁰Soon after this, Abraham heard that Milcah, his brother Nahor's wife, had borne Nahor eight sons. ²¹The oldest was named Uz, the next oldest was Buz, followed by Kemuel (the ancestor of the Arameans), ²²Kesed, Hazo, Pildash, Jidlaph, and Bethuel. ²³(Bethuel became the father of Rebekah.) In addition to these eight sons from Milcah, ²⁴Nahor had four other children from his concubine Reumah. Their names were Tebah, Gaham, Tahash, and Maacah.

THE BURIAL OF SARAH

23 When Sarah was 127 years old, ²she died at Kiriath-arba (now called Hebron) in the land of Canaan. There Abraham mourned and wept for her.

³Then, leaving her body, he said to the Hittite elders, ⁴"Here I am, a stranger and a foreigner among you. Please sell me a piece of land so I can give my wife a proper burial."

⁵The Hittites replied to Abraham, ⁶"Listen, my lord, you are an honored prince among us. Choose the finest of our tombs and bury her there. No one here will refuse to help you in this way."

21:33 Hebrew *El-Olam.*   22:17 Hebrew *seed;* also in 22:17b, 18.

7 Then Abraham bowed low before the Hittites 8 and said, "Since you are willing to help me in this way, be so kind as to ask Ephron son of Zohar 9 to let me buy his cave at Machpelah, down at the end of his field. I will pay the full price in the presence of witnesses, so I will have a permanent burial place for my family."

10 Ephron was sitting there among the others, and he answered Abraham as the others listened, speaking publicly before all the Hittite elders of the town. 11 "No, my lord," he said to Abraham, "please listen to me. I will give you the field and the cave. Here in the presence of my people, I give it to you. Go and bury your dead."

12 Abraham again bowed low before the citizens of the land, 13 and he replied to Ephron as everyone listened. "No, listen to me. I will buy it from you. Let me pay the full price for the field so I can bury my dead there."

14 Ephron answered Abraham, 15 "My lord, please listen to me. The land is worth 400 pieces* of silver, but what is that between friends? Go ahead and bury your dead."

16 So Abraham agreed to Ephron's price and paid the amount he had suggested—400 pieces of silver, weighed according to the market standard. The Hittite elders witnessed the transaction.

17 So Abraham bought the plot of land belonging to Ephron at Machpelah, near Mamre. This included the field itself, the cave that was in it, and all the surrounding trees. 18 It was transferred to Abraham as his permanent possession in the presence of the Hittite elders at the city gate. 19 Then Abraham buried his wife, Sarah, there in Canaan, in the cave of Machpelah, near Mamre (also called Hebron). 20 So the field and the cave were transferred from the Hittites to Abraham for use as a permanent burial place.

A WIFE FOR ISAAC

24 Abraham was now a very old man, and the LORD had blessed him in every way. 2 One day Abraham said to his oldest servant, the man in charge of his household, "Take an oath by putting your hand under my thigh. 3 Swear by the LORD, the God of heaven and earth, that you will not allow my son to marry one of these local Canaanite women. 4 Go instead to my homeland, to my relatives, and find a wife there for my son Isaac."

5 The servant asked, "But what if I can't find a young woman who is willing to travel so far from home? Should I then take Isaac there to live among your relatives in the land you came from?"

6 "No!" Abraham responded. "Be careful never to take my son there. 7 For the LORD, the God of heaven, who took me from my father's house and my native land, solemnly promised to give this land to my descendants.* He will send his angel ahead of you, and he will see to it that you find a wife there for my son. 8 If she is unwilling to come back with you, then you are free from this oath of mine. But under no circumstances are you to take my son there."

9 So the servant took an oath by putting his hand under the thigh of his master, Abraham. He swore to follow Abraham's instructions. 10 Then he loaded ten of Abraham's camels with all kinds of expensive gifts from his master, and he traveled to distant Aram-naharaim. There he went to the town where Abraham's brother Nahor had settled. 11 He made the camels kneel beside a well just outside the town. It was evening, and the women were coming out to draw water.

12 "O LORD, God of my master, Abraham," he prayed. "Please give me success today, and show unfailing love to my master, Abraham. 13 See, I am standing here beside this spring, and the young women of the town are coming out to draw water. 14 This is my request. I will ask one of them, 'Please give me a drink from your jug.' If she says, 'Yes, have a drink, and I will water your camels, too!'—let her be the one you have selected as Isaac's wife. This is how I will know that you have shown unfailing love to my master."

15 Before he had finished praying, he saw a young woman named Rebekah coming out with her water jug on her shoulder. She was the daughter of Bethuel, who was the son of Abraham's brother Nahor and his wife, Milcah. 16 Rebekah was very beautiful and old enough to be married, but she was still a virgin. She went down to the spring, filled her jug, and came up again. 17 Running over to her, the servant said, "Please give me a little drink of water from your jug."

18 "Yes, my lord," she answered, "have a drink." And she quickly lowered her jug from her shoulder and gave him a drink. 19 When she had given him a drink, she said, "I'll draw water for your camels, too, until they have had enough to drink." 20 So she quickly emptied her jug into the watering trough and ran back to the well to draw water for all his camels.

21 The servant watched her in silence, wondering whether or not the LORD had given him success in his mission. 22 Then at last, when the camels had finished drinking, he took out a gold ring for her nose and two large gold bracelets* for her wrists.

23 "Whose daughter are you?" he asked. "And please tell me, would your father have any room to put us up for the night?"

24 "I am the daughter of Bethuel," she replied. "My grandparents are Nahor and Milcah. 25 Yes, we have plenty of straw and feed for the camels, and we have room for guests."

26 The man bowed low and worshiped the LORD. 27 "Praise the LORD, the God of my master,

23:15 Hebrew 400 shekels, about 10 pounds or 4.6 kilograms in weight; also in 23:16. 24:7 Hebrew seed; also in 24:60. 24:22 Hebrew a gold nose-ring weighing a beka [0.2 ounces or 6 grams] and two gold bracelets weighing 10 [shekels] [4 ounces or 114 grams].

Abraham," he said. "The LORD has shown unfailing love and faithfulness to my master, for he has led me straight to my master's relatives."

²⁸The young woman ran home to tell her family everything that had happened. ²⁹Now Rebekah had a brother named Laban, who ran out to meet the man at the spring. ³⁰He had seen the nose-ring and the bracelets on his sister's wrists, and had heard Rebekah tell what the man had said. So he rushed out to the spring, where the man was still standing beside his camels. ³¹Laban said to him, "Come and stay with us, you who are blessed by the LORD! Why are you standing here outside the town when I have a room all ready for you and a place prepared for the camels?"

³²So the man went home with Laban, and Laban unloaded the camels, gave him straw for their bedding, fed them, and provided water for the man and the camel drivers to wash their feet. ³³Then food was served. But Abraham's servant said, "I don't want to eat until I have told you why I have come."

"All right," Laban said, "tell us."

³⁴"I am Abraham's servant," he explained. ³⁵"And the LORD has greatly blessed my master; he has become a wealthy man. The LORD has given him flocks of sheep and goats, herds of cattle, a fortune in silver and gold, and many male and female servants and camels and donkeys. ³⁶When Sarah, my master's wife, was very old, she gave birth to my master's son, and my master has given him everything he owns. ³⁷And my master made me take an oath. He said, 'Do not allow my son to marry one of these local Canaanite women. ³⁸Go instead to my father's house, to my relatives, and find a wife there for my son.'

³⁹"But I said to my master, 'What if I can't find a young woman who is willing to go back with me?' ⁴⁰He responded, 'The LORD, in whose presence I have lived, will send his angel with you and will make your mission successful. Yes, you must find a wife for my son from among my relatives, from my father's family. ⁴¹Then you will have fulfilled your obligation. But if you go to my relatives and they refuse to let her go with you, you will be free from your oath.'

⁴²"So today when I came to the spring, I prayed this prayer: 'O LORD, God of my master, Abraham, please give me success on this mission. ⁴³See, I am standing here beside this spring. This is my request. When a young woman comes to draw water, I will say to her, "Please give me a little drink of water from your jug." ⁴⁴If she says, "Yes, have a drink, and I will draw water for your camels, too," let her be the one you have selected to be the wife of my master's son.'

⁴⁵"Before I had finished praying in my heart, I saw Rebekah coming out with her water jug on her shoulder. She went down to the spring and drew water. So I said to her, 'Please give me a drink.' ⁴⁶She quickly lowered her jug from her shoulder and said, 'Yes, have a drink, and I will water your camels, too!' So I drank, and then she watered the camels.

⁴⁷"Then I asked, 'Whose daughter are you?' She replied, 'I am the daughter of Bethuel, and my grandparents are Nahor and Milcah.' So I put the ring on her nose, and the bracelets on her wrists. ⁴⁸"Then I bowed low and worshiped the LORD. I praised the LORD, the God of my master, Abraham, because he had led me straight to my master's niece to be his son's wife. ⁴⁹So tell me—will you or won't you show unfailing love and faithfulness to my master? Please tell me yes or no, and then I'll know what to do next."

⁵⁰Then Laban and Bethuel replied, "The LORD has obviously brought you here, so there is nothing we can say. ⁵¹Here is Rebekah; take her and go. Yes, let her be the wife of your master's son, as the LORD has directed."

⁵²When Abraham's servant heard their answer, he bowed down to the ground and worshiped the LORD. ⁵³Then he brought out silver and gold jewelry and clothing and presented them to Rebekah. He also gave expensive presents to her brother and mother. ⁵⁴Then they ate their meal, and the servant and the men with him stayed there overnight.

But early the next morning, Abraham's servant said, "Send me back to my master."

⁵⁵"But we want Rebekah to stay with us at least ten days," her brother and mother said. "Then she can go."

⁵⁶But he said, "Don't delay me. The LORD has made my mission successful; now send me back so I can return to my master."

⁵⁷"Well," they said, "we'll call Rebekah and ask her what she thinks." ⁵⁸So they called Rebekah. "Are you willing to go with this man?" they asked her.

And she replied, "Yes, I will go."

⁵⁹So they said good-bye to Rebekah and sent her away with Abraham's servant and his men. The woman who had been Rebekah's childhood nurse went along with her. ⁶⁰They gave her this blessing as she parted:

"Our sister, may you become
    the mother of many millions!
May your descendants be strong
    and conquer the cities of their enemies."

⁶¹Then Rebekah and her servant girls mounted the camels and followed the man. So Abraham's servant took Rebekah and went on his way.

⁶²Meanwhile, Isaac, whose home was in the Negev, had returned from Beer-lahai-roi. ⁶³One evening as he was walking and meditating in the fields, he looked up and saw the camels coming. ⁶⁴When Rebekah looked up and saw Isaac, she quickly dismounted from her camel. ⁶⁵"Who is that man walking through the fields to meet us?" she asked the servant.

And he replied, "It is my master." So Rebekah covered her face with her veil. ⁶⁶ Then the servant told Isaac everything he had done.

⁶⁷ And Isaac brought Rebekah into his mother Sarah's tent, and she became his wife. He loved her deeply, and she was a special comfort to him after the death of his mother.

THE DEATH OF ABRAHAM

25 Abraham married another wife, whose name was Keturah. ² She gave birth to Zimran, Jokshan, Medan, Midian, Ishbak, and Shuah. ³ Jokshan was the father of Sheba and Dedan. Dedan's descendants were the Asshurites, Letushites, and Leummites. ⁴ Midian's sons were Ephah, Epher, Hanoch, Abida, and Eldaah. These were all descendants of Abraham through Keturah.

⁵ Abraham gave everything he owned to his son Isaac. ⁶ But before he died, he gave gifts to the sons of his concubines and sent them off to a land in the east, away from Isaac.

⁷ Abraham lived for 175 years, ⁸ and he died at a ripe old age, having lived a long and satisfying life. He breathed his last and joined his ancestors in death. ⁹ His sons Isaac and Ishmael buried him in the cave of Machpelah, near Mamre, in the field of Ephron son of Zohar the Hittite. ¹⁰ This was the field Abraham had purchased from the Hittites and where he had buried his wife Sarah. ¹¹ After Abraham's death, God blessed his son Isaac, who settled near Beer-lahai-roi in the Negev.

ISHMAEL'S DESCENDANTS

¹² This is the account of the family of Ishmael, the son of Abraham through Hagar, Sarah's Egyptian servant. ¹³ Here is a list, by their names and clans, of Ishmael's descendants: The oldest was Nebaioth, followed by Kedar, Adbeel, Mibsam, ¹⁴ Mishma, Dumah, Massa, ¹⁵ Hadad, Tema, Jetur, Naphish, and Kedemah. ¹⁶ These twelve sons of Ishmael became the founders of twelve tribes named after them, listed according to the places they settled and camped. ¹⁷ Ishmael lived for 137 years. Then he breathed his last and joined his ancestors in death. ¹⁸ Ishmael's descendants occupied the region from Havilah to Shur, which is east of Egypt in the direction of Asshur. There they lived in open hostility toward all their relatives.*

THE BIRTHS OF ESAU AND JACOB

¹⁹ This is the account of the family of Isaac, the son of Abraham. ²⁰ When Isaac was forty years old, he married Rebekah, the daughter of Bethuel the Aramean from Paddan-aram and the sister of Laban the Aramean.

²¹ Isaac pleaded with the LORD on behalf of his wife, because she was unable to have children. The LORD answered Isaac's prayer, and Rebekah became pregnant with twins. ²² But

the two children struggled with each other in her womb. So she went to ask the LORD about it. "Why is this happening to me?" she asked.

²³ And the LORD told her, "The sons in your womb will become two nations. From the very beginning, the two nations will be rivals. One nation will be stronger than the other; and your older son will serve your younger son."

²⁴ And when the time came to give birth, Rebekah discovered that she did indeed have twins! ²⁵ The first one was very red at birth and covered with thick hair like a fur coat. So they named him Esau.* ²⁶ Then the other twin was born with his hand grasping Esau's heel. So they named him Jacob.* Isaac was sixty years old when the twins were born.

ESAU SELLS HIS BIRTHRIGHT

²⁷ As the boys grew up, Esau became a skillful hunter. He was an outdoorsman, but Jacob had a quiet temperament, preferring to stay at home. ²⁸ Isaac loved Esau because he enjoyed eating the wild game Esau brought home, but Rebekah loved Jacob.

²⁹ One day when Jacob was cooking some stew, Esau arrived home from the wilderness exhausted and hungry. ³⁰ Esau said to Jacob, "I'm starved! Give me some of that red stew!" (This is how Esau got his other name, Edom, which means "red.")

³¹ "All right," Jacob replied, "but trade me your rights as the firstborn son."

³² "Look, I'm dying of starvation!" said Esau. "What good is my birthright to me now?"

³³ But Jacob said, "First you must swear that your birthright is mine." So Esau swore an oath, thereby selling all his rights as the firstborn to his brother, Jacob.

³⁴ Then Jacob gave Esau some bread and lentil stew. Esau ate the meal, then got up and left. He showed contempt for his rights as the firstborn.

ISAAC DECEIVES ABIMELECH

26 A severe famine now struck the land, as had happened before in Abraham's time. So Isaac moved to Gerar, where Abimelech, king of the Philistines, lived.

² The LORD appeared to Isaac and said, "Do not go down to Egypt, but do as I tell you. ³ Live here as a foreigner in this land, and I will be with you and bless you. I hereby confirm that I will give all these lands to you and your descendants,* just as I solemnly promised Abraham, your father. ⁴ I will cause your descendants to become as numerous as the stars of the sky, and I will give them all these lands. And through your descendants all the nations of the earth will be blessed. ⁵ I will do this because Abraham listened to me and obeyed

25:18 The meaning of the Hebrew is uncertain. 25:25 *Esau* sounds like a Hebrew term that means "hair." 25:26 *Jacob* sounds like the Hebrew words for "heel" and "deceiver." 26:3 Hebrew *seed*; also in 26:4, 24.

all my requirements, commands, decrees, and instructions." ⁶ So Isaac stayed in Gerar.

⁷ When the men who lived there asked Isaac about his wife, Rebekah, he said, "She is my sister." He was afraid to say, "She is my wife." He thought, "They will kill me to get her, because she is so beautiful." ⁸ But some time later, Abimelech, king of the Philistines, looked out his window and saw Isaac caressing Rebekah.

⁹ Immediately, Abimelech called for Isaac and exclaimed, "She is obviously your wife! Why did you say, 'She is my sister'?"

"Because I was afraid someone would kill me to get her from me," Isaac replied.

¹⁰ "How could you do this to us?" Abimelech exclaimed. "One of my people might easily have taken your wife and slept with her, and you would have made us guilty of great sin."

¹¹ Then Abimelech issued a public proclamation: "Anyone who touches this man or his wife will be put to death!"

CONFLICT OVER WATER RIGHTS

¹² When Isaac planted his crops that year, he harvested a hundred times more grain than he planted, for the LORD blessed him. ¹³ He became a very rich man, and his wealth continued to grow. ¹⁴ He acquired so many flocks of sheep and goats, herds of cattle, and servants that the Philistines became jealous of him. ¹⁵ So the Philistines filled up all of Isaac's wells with dirt. These were the wells that had been dug by the servants of his father, Abraham.

¹⁶ Finally, Abimelech ordered Isaac to leave the country. "Go somewhere else," he said, "for you have become too powerful for us."

¹⁷ So Isaac moved away to the Gerar Valley, where he set up their tents and settled down. ¹⁸ He reopened the wells his father had dug, which the Philistines had filled in after Abraham's death. Isaac also restored the names Abraham had given them.

¹⁹ Isaac's servants also dug in the Gerar Valley and discovered a well of fresh water. ²⁰ But then the shepherds from Gerar came and claimed the spring. "This is our water," they said, and they argued over it with Isaac's herdsmen. So Isaac named the well Esek (which means "argument"). ²¹ Isaac's men then dug another well, but again there was a dispute over it. So Isaac named it Sitnah (which means "hostility"). ²² Abandoning that one, Isaac moved on and dug another well. This time there was no dispute over it, so Isaac named the place Rehoboth (which means "open space"), for he said, "At last the LORD has created enough space for us to prosper in this land."

²³ From there Isaac moved to Beersheba, ²⁴ where the LORD appeared to him on the night of his arrival. "I am the God of your father, Abraham," he said. "Do not be afraid, for I am with you and will bless you. I will multiply your descendants, and they will become a great nation. I will do this because of my promise to Abraham, my servant." ²⁵ Then Isaac built an altar there and worshiped the LORD. He set up his camp at that place, and his servants dug another well.

ISAAC'S COVENANT WITH ABIMELECH

²⁶ One day King Abimelech came from Gerar with his adviser, Ahuzzath, and also Phicol, his army commander. ²⁷ "Why have you come here?" Isaac asked. "You obviously hate me, since you kicked me off your land."

²⁸ They replied, "We can plainly see that the LORD is with you. So we want to enter into a sworn treaty with you. Let's make a covenant. ²⁹ Swear that you will not harm us, just as we have never troubled you. We have always treated you well, and we sent you away from us in peace. And now look how the LORD has blessed you!"

³⁰ So Isaac prepared a covenant feast to celebrate the treaty, and they ate and drank together. ³¹ Early the next morning, they each took a solemn oath not to interfere with each other. Then Isaac sent them home again, and they left him in peace.

³² That very day Isaac's servants came and told him about a new well they had dug. "We've found water!" they exclaimed. ³³ So Isaac named the well Shibah (which means "oath"). And to this day the town that grew up there is called Beersheba (which means "well of the oath").

³⁴ At the age of forty, Esau married two Hittite wives: Judith, the daughter of Beeri, and Basemath, the daughter of Elon. ³⁵ But Esau's wives made life miserable for Isaac and Rebekah.

JACOB STEALS ESAU'S BLESSING

27 One day when Isaac was old and turning blind, he called for Esau, his older son, and said, "My son."

"Yes, Father?" Esau replied.

² "I am an old man now," Isaac said, "and I don't know when I may die. ³ Take your bow and a quiver full of arrows, and go out into the open country to hunt some wild game for me. ⁴ Prepare my favorite dish, and bring it here for me to eat. Then I will pronounce the blessing that belongs to you, my firstborn son, before I die."

⁵ But Rebekah overheard what Isaac had said to his son Esau. So when Esau left to hunt for the wild game, ⁶ she said to her son Jacob, "Listen. I overheard your father say to Esau, ⁷ 'Bring me some wild game and prepare me a delicious meal. Then I will bless you in the LORD's presence before I die.' ⁸ Now, my son, listen to me. Do exactly as I tell you. ⁹ Go out to the flocks, and bring me two fine young goats. I'll use them to prepare your father's favorite dish. ¹⁰ Then take the food to your father so he can eat it and bless you before he dies."

¹¹ "But look," Jacob replied to Rebekah, "my brother, Esau, is a hairy man, and my skin is smooth. ¹² What if my father touches me? He'll

see that I'm trying to trick him, and then he'll curse me instead of blessing me."

[13] But his mother replied, "Then let the curse fall on me, my son! Just do what I tell you. Go out and get the goats for me!"

[14] So Jacob went out and got the young goats for his mother. Rebekah took them and prepared a delicious meal, just the way Isaac liked it. [15] Then she took Esau's favorite clothes, which were there in the house, and gave them to her younger son, Jacob. [16] She covered his arms and the smooth part of his neck with the skin of the young goats. [17] Then she gave Jacob the delicious meal, including freshly baked bread.

[18] So Jacob took the food to his father. "My father?" he said.

"Yes, my son," Isaac answered. "Who are you—Esau or Jacob?"

[19] Jacob replied, "It's Esau, your firstborn son. I've done as you told me. Here is the wild game. Now sit up and eat it so you can give me your blessing."

[20] Isaac asked, "How did you find it so quickly, my son?"

"The LORD your God put it in my path!" Jacob replied.

[21] Then Isaac said to Jacob, "Come closer so I can touch you and make sure that you really are Esau." [22] So Jacob went closer to his father, and Isaac touched him. "The voice is Jacob's, but the hands are Esau's," Isaac said. [23] But he did not recognize Jacob, because Jacob's hands felt hairy just like Esau's. So Isaac prepared to bless Jacob. [24] "But are you really my son Esau?" he asked.

"Yes, I am," Jacob replied.

[25] Then Isaac said, "Now, my son, bring me the wild game. Let me eat it, and then I will give you my blessing." So Jacob took the food to his father, and Isaac ate it. He also drank the wine that Jacob served him. [26] Then Isaac said to Jacob, "Please come a little closer and kiss me, my son."

[27] So Jacob went over and kissed him. And when Isaac caught the smell of his clothes, he was finally convinced, and he blessed his son. He said, "Ah! The smell of my son is like the smell of the outdoors, which the LORD has blessed!

[28] "From the dew of heaven
    and the richness of the earth,
    may God always give you abundant harvests
        of grain
    and bountiful new wine.
[29] May many nations become your servants,
    and may they bow down to you.
May you be the master over your brothers,
    and may your mother's sons bow down
        to you.
All who curse you will be cursed,
    and all who bless you will be blessed."

[30] As soon as Isaac had finished blessing Jacob, and almost before Jacob had left his father, Esau returned from his hunt. [31] Esau prepared a delicious meal and brought it to his father. Then he said, "Sit up, my father, and eat my wild game so you can give me your blessing."

[32] But Isaac asked him, "Who are you?"

Esau replied, "It's your son, your firstborn son, Esau."

[33] Isaac began to tremble uncontrollably and said, "Then who just served me wild game? I have already eaten it, and I blessed him just before you came. And yes, that blessing must stand!"

[34] When Esau heard his father's words, he let out a loud and bitter cry. "Oh my father, what about me? Bless me, too!" he begged.

[35] But Isaac said, "Your brother was here, and he tricked me. He has taken away your blessing."

[36] Esau exclaimed, "No wonder his name is Jacob, for now he has cheated me twice.* First he took my rights as the firstborn, and now he has stolen my blessing. Oh, haven't you saved even one blessing for me?"

[37] Isaac said to Esau, "I have made Jacob your master and have declared that all his brothers will be his servants. I have guaranteed him an abundance of grain and wine—what is left for me to give you, my son?"

[38] Esau pleaded, "But do you have only one blessing? Oh my father, bless me, too!" Then Esau broke down and wept.

[39] Finally, his father, Isaac, said to him,

"You will live away from the richness of
        the earth,
    and away from the dew of the heaven
        above.
[40] You will live by your sword,
    and you will serve your brother.
But when you decide to break free,
    you will shake his yoke from your neck."

JACOB FLEES TO PADDAN-ARAM

[41] From that time on, Esau hated Jacob because their father had given Jacob the blessing. And Esau began to scheme: "I will soon be mourning my father's death. Then I will kill my brother, Jacob."

[42] But Rebekah heard about Esau's plans. So she sent for Jacob and told him, "Listen, Esau is consoling himself by plotting to kill you. [43] So listen carefully, my son. Get ready and flee to my brother, Laban, in Haran. [44] Stay there with him until your brother cools off. [45] When he calms down and forgets what you have done to him, I will send for you to come back. Why should I lose both of you in one day?"

[46] Then Rebekah said to Isaac, "I'm sick and tired of these local Hittite women! I would rather die than see Jacob marry one of them."

27:36 *Jacob* sounds like the Hebrew words for "heel" and "deceiver."

GATEWAY TO HEAVEN
Genesis 28:16-17

ROBERT MORRIS

The Lord gave me the name for Gateway Church in my quiet time one morning. A few days later, I came across the passage in Genesis in which Jacob dreams of heaven opening up and angels ascending and descending between heaven and earth. In this dream, Jacob has an encounter with God Himself in which God makes a remarkable promise to him. When he wakes up, Jacob exclaims, "What an awesome place this is! It is none other than the house of God, the very gateway to heaven!" (Genesis 28:17). That one phrase leaped out at me—*the very gateway to heaven.*

It was exactly what I wanted Gateway Church to be—a place where people encountered the presence of God. I wanted it to be a place where people who had never experienced the love, power, and peace of God would feel His presence the moment they walked in the door, and they would declare, "Surely the LORD is in this place!" (Genesis 28:16).

I had been feeling like Southlake, Texas, was the place we were to begin the church. Then one night, my wife, Debbie, and I drove out there to have dinner with some friends. As we were taking the exit onto Southlake Boulevard, I said to Debbie,

"I feel like the Lord gave me the name of the church."
"Oh! What is it?" she asked.
"Gateway!"

At that exact moment, we saw a huge sign that said, "Coming soon! Gateway Shopping Plaza."

We picked up our friends, and I began telling them about the name and seeing the sign. We drove back to show them the sign, but when we looked, there was *no sign*. We thought maybe we couldn't see it from that angle because we were driving in a different direction. So after we ate, we drove back and took the exact same exit. As we turned left to drive over the bridge, I said, "Look, you'll be able to see it really well." But there was *no sign*. We never saw the "coming soon" sign again.

---

28 So Isaac called for Jacob, blessed him, and said, "You must not marry any of these Canaanite women. ² Instead, go at once to Paddan-aram, to the house of your grandfather Bethuel, and marry one of your uncle Laban's daughters. ³ May God Almighty* bless you and give you many children. And may your descendants multiply and become many nations! ⁴ May God pass on to you and your descendants* the blessings he promised to Abraham. May you own this land where you are now living as a foreigner, for God gave this land to Abraham."

⁵ So Isaac sent Jacob away, and he went to Paddan-aram to stay with his uncle Laban, his mother's brother, the son of Bethuel the Aramean.

⁶ Esau knew that his father, Isaac, had blessed Jacob and sent him to Paddan-aram to find a wife, and that he had warned Jacob, "You must not marry a Canaanite woman." ⁷ He also knew that Jacob had obeyed his parents and gone to Paddan-aram. ⁸ It was now very clear to Esau that his father did not like the local Canaanite women. ⁹ So Esau visited his uncle Ishmael's family and married one of Ishmael's daughters, in addition to the wives he already had. His new wife's name was Mahalath. She was the sister of Nebaioth and the daughter of Ishmael, Abraham's son.

JACOB'S DREAM AT BETHEL

¹⁰ Meanwhile, Jacob left Beersheba and traveled toward Haran. ¹¹ At sundown he arrived at a good place to set up camp and stopped there for the night. Jacob found a stone to rest his head against and lay down to sleep. ¹² As he slept, he dreamed of a stairway that reached from the earth up to heaven. And he saw the angels of God going up and down the stairway.

¹³ At the top of the stairway stood the LORD, and he said, "I am the LORD, the God of your grandfather Abraham, and the God of your father, Isaac. The ground you are lying on belongs to you. I am giving it to you and your descendants. ¹⁴ Your descendants will be as numerous as the dust of the earth! They will spread out in all directions—to the west and the east, to the north and the south. And all the families of the earth will be blessed through you and your descendants. ¹⁵ What's more, I am with you, and I will protect you wherever you go. One day I will bring you back to this land. I will not leave you until I have finished giving you everything I have promised you."

¹⁶ Then Jacob awoke from his sleep and said, "Surely the LORD is in this place, and I wasn't even aware of it!" ¹⁷ But he was also afraid and said, "What an awesome place this is! It is none other than the house of God, the very gateway to heaven!"

¹⁸ The next morning Jacob got up very early. He took the stone he had rested his head against, and he set it upright as a memorial pillar. Then he poured olive oil over it. ¹⁹ He named that place Bethel (which means "house of God"), although it was previously called Luz.

28:3 Hebrew *El-Shaddai*. 28:4 Hebrew *seed*; also in 28:13, 14.

20Then Jacob made this vow: "If God will indeed be with me and protect me on this journey, and if he will provide me with food and clothing, 21and if I return safely to my father's home, then the LORD will certainly be my God. 22And this memorial pillar I have set up will become a place for worshiping God, and I will present to God a tenth of everything he gives me."

JACOB ARRIVES AT PADDAN-ARAM

29 Then Jacob hurried on, finally arriving in the land of the east. 2He saw a well in the distance. Three flocks of sheep and goats lay in an open field beside it, waiting to be watered. But a heavy stone covered the mouth of the well. 3It was the custom there to wait for all the flocks to arrive before removing the stone and watering the animals. Afterward the stone would be placed back over the mouth of the well. 4Jacob went over to the shepherds and asked, "Where are you from, my friends?"

"We are from Haran," they answered.

5"Do you know a man there named Laban, the grandson of Nahor?" he asked.

"Yes, we do," they replied.

6"Is he doing well?" Jacob asked.

"Yes, he's well," they answered. "Look, here comes his daughter Rachel with the flock now."

7Jacob said, "Look, it's still broad daylight—too early to round up the animals. Why don't you water the sheep and goats so they can get back out to pasture?"

8"We can't water the animals until all the flocks have arrived," they replied. "Then the shepherds move the stone from the mouth of the well, and we water all the sheep and goats."

9Jacob was still talking with them when Rachel arrived with her father's flock, for she was a shepherd. 10And because Rachel was his cousin—the daughter of Laban, his mother's brother—and because the sheep and goats belonged to his uncle Laban, Jacob went over to the well and moved the stone from its mouth and watered his uncle's flock. 11Then Jacob kissed Rachel, and he wept aloud. 12He explained to Rachel that he was her cousin on her father's side—the son of her aunt Rebekah. So Rachel quickly ran and told her father, Laban.

13As soon as Laban heard that his nephew Jacob had arrived, he ran out to meet him. He embraced and kissed him and brought him home. When Jacob had told him his story, 14Laban exclaimed, "You really are my own flesh and blood!"

JACOB MARRIES LEAH AND RACHEL

After Jacob had stayed with Laban for about a month, 15Laban said to him, "You shouldn't work for me without pay just because we are relatives. Tell me how much your wages should be."

16Now Laban had two daughters. The older daughter was named Leah, and the younger one was Rachel. 17There was no sparkle in Leah's eyes,* but Rachel had a beautiful figure and a lovely face. 18Since Jacob was in love with Rachel, he told her father, "I'll work for you for seven years if you'll give me Rachel, your younger daughter, as my wife."

19"Agreed!" Laban replied. "I'd rather give her to you than to anyone else. Stay and work with me." 20So Jacob worked seven years to pay for Rachel. But his love for her was so strong that it seemed to him but a few days.

21Finally, the time came for him to marry her. "I have fulfilled my agreement," Jacob said to Laban. "Now give me my wife so I can sleep with her."

22So Laban invited everyone in the neighborhood and prepared a wedding feast. 23But that night, when it was dark, Laban took Leah to Jacob, and he slept with her. 24(Laban had given Leah a servant, Zilpah, to be her maid.)

25But when Jacob woke up in the morning—it was Leah! "What have you done to me?" Jacob raged at Laban. "I worked seven years for Rachel! Why have you tricked me?"

26"It's not our custom here to marry off a younger daughter ahead of the firstborn," Laban replied. 27"But wait until the bridal week is over; then we'll give you Rachel, too—provided you promise to work another seven years for me."

28So Jacob agreed to work seven more years. A week after Jacob had married Leah, Laban gave him Rachel, too. 29(Laban gave Rachel a servant, Bilhah, to be her maid.) 30So Jacob slept with Rachel, too, and he loved her much more than Leah. He then stayed and worked for Laban the additional seven years.

JACOB'S MANY CHILDREN

31When the LORD saw that Leah was unloved, he enabled her to have children, but Rachel could not conceive. 32So Leah became pregnant and gave birth to a son. She named him Reuben,* for she said, "The LORD has noticed my misery, and now my husband will love me."

33She soon became pregnant again and gave birth to another son. She named him Simeon,* for she said, "The LORD heard that I was unloved and has given me another son."

34Then she became pregnant a third time and gave birth to another son. He was named Levi,* for she said, "Surely this time my husband will feel affection for me, since I have given him three sons!"

35Once again Leah became pregnant and gave birth to another son. She named him Judah,* for she said, "Now I will praise the LORD!" And then she stopped having children.

29:17 Or *Leah had dull eyes,* or *Leah had soft eyes.* The meaning of the Hebrew is uncertain. 29:32 *Reuben* means "Look, a son!" It also sounds like the Hebrew for "He has seen my misery." 29:33 *Simeon* probably means "one who hears." 29:34 *Levi* sounds like a Hebrew term that means "being attached" or "feeling affection for." 29:35 *Judah* is related to the Hebrew term for "praise."

30 When Rachel saw that she wasn't having any children for Jacob, she became jealous of her sister. She pleaded with Jacob, "Give me children, or I'll die!"

²Then Jacob became furious with Rachel. "Am I God?" he asked. "He's the one who has kept you from having children!"

³Then Rachel told him, "Take my maid, Bilhah, and sleep with her. She will bear children for me,* and through her I can have a family, too." ⁴So Rachel gave her servant, Bilhah, to Jacob as a wife, and he slept with her. ⁵Bilhah became pregnant and presented him with a son. ⁶Rachel named him Dan,* for she said, "God has vindicated me! He has heard my request and given me a son." ⁷Then Bilhah became pregnant again and gave Jacob a second son. ⁸Rachel named him Naphtali,* for she said, "I have struggled hard with my sister, and I'm winning!"

⁹Meanwhile, Leah realized that she wasn't getting pregnant anymore, so she took her servant, Zilpah, and gave her to Jacob as a wife. ¹⁰Soon Zilpah presented him with a son. ¹¹Leah named him Gad,* for she said, "How fortunate I am!" ¹²Then Zilpah gave Jacob a second son. ¹³And Leah named him Asher,* for she said, "What joy is mine! Now the other women will celebrate with me."

¹⁴One day during the wheat harvest, Reuben found some mandrakes growing in a field and brought them to his mother, Leah. Rachel begged Leah, "Please give me some of your son's mandrakes."

¹⁵But Leah angrily replied, "Wasn't it enough that you stole my husband? Now will you steal my son's mandrakes, too?"

Rachel answered, "I will let Jacob sleep with you tonight if you give me some of the mandrakes."

¹⁶So that evening, as Jacob was coming home from the fields, Leah went out to meet him. "You must come and sleep with me tonight!" she said. "I have paid for you with some mandrakes that my son found." So that night he slept with Leah. ¹⁷And God answered Leah's prayers. She became pregnant again and gave birth to a fifth son for Jacob. ¹⁸She named him Issachar,* for she said, "God has rewarded me for giving my servant to my husband as a wife." ¹⁹Then Leah became pregnant again and gave birth to a sixth son for Jacob. ²⁰She named him Zebulun,* for she said, "God has given me a good reward. Now my husband will treat me with respect, for I have given him six sons." ²¹Later she gave birth to a daughter and named her Dinah.

²²Then God remembered Rachel's plight and answered her prayers by enabling her to have children. ²³She became pregnant and gave birth to a son. "God has removed my disgrace," she said. ²⁴And she named him Joseph,* for she said, "May the LORD add yet another son to my family."

JACOB'S WEALTH INCREASES

²⁵Soon after Rachel had given birth to Joseph, Jacob said to Laban, "Please release me so I can go home to my own country. ²⁶Let me take my wives and children, for I have earned them by serving you, and let me be on my way. You certainly know how hard I have worked for you."

²⁷"Please listen to me," Laban replied. "I have become wealthy, for* the LORD has blessed me because of you. ²⁸Tell me how much I owe you. Whatever it is, I'll pay it."

²⁹Jacob replied, "You know how hard I've worked for you, and how your flocks and herds have grown under my care. ³⁰You had little indeed before I came, but your wealth has increased enormously. The LORD has blessed you through everything I've done. But now, what about me? When can I start providing for my own family?"

³¹"What wages do you want?" Laban asked again.

Jacob replied, "Don't give me anything. Just do this one thing, and I'll continue to tend and watch over your flocks. ³²Let me inspect your flocks today and remove all the sheep and goats that are speckled or spotted, along with all the black sheep. Give these to me as my wages. ³³In the future, when you check on the animals you have given me as my wages, you'll see that I have been honest. If you find in my flock any goats without speckles or spots, or any sheep that are not black, you will know that I have stolen them from you."

³⁴"All right," Laban replied. "It will be as you say." ³⁵But that very day Laban went out and removed the male goats that were streaked and spotted, all the female goats that were speckled and spotted or had white patches, and all the black sheep. He placed them in the care of his own sons, ³⁶who took them a three-days' journey from where Jacob was. Meanwhile, Jacob stayed and cared for the rest of Laban's flock.

³⁷Then Jacob took some fresh branches from poplar, almond, and plane trees and peeled off strips of bark, making white streaks on them. ³⁸Then he placed these peeled branches in the watering troughs where the flocks came to drink, for that was where they mated. ³⁹And when they mated in front of the white-streaked branches, they gave birth to young that were streaked, speckled, and spotted. ⁴⁰Jacob separated those lambs from Laban's flock. And at mating time he turned the flock to face Laban's animals that were streaked or black. This is how he built his own flock instead of increasing Laban's.

⁴¹Whenever the stronger females were ready to mate, Jacob would place the peeled branches in the watering troughs in front of them. Then

---

30:3 Hebrew *bear children on my knees.* 30:6 *Dan* means "he judged" or "he vindicated." 30:8 *Naphtali* means "my struggle." 30:11 *Gad* means "good fortune." 30:13 *Asher* means "happy." 30:18 *Issachar* sounds like a Hebrew term that means "reward." 30:20 *Zebulun* probably means "honor." 30:24 *Joseph* means "may he add." 30:27 Or *I have learned by divination that.*

they would mate in front of the branches. ⁴² But he didn't do this with the weaker ones, so the weaker lambs belonged to Laban, and the stronger ones were Jacob's. ⁴³ As a result, Jacob became very wealthy, with large flocks of sheep and goats, female and male servants, and many camels and donkeys.

JACOB FLEES FROM LABAN

31 But Jacob soon learned that Laban's sons were grumbling about him. "Jacob has robbed our father of everything!" they said. "He has gained all his wealth at our father's expense." ² And Jacob began to notice a change in Laban's attitude toward him.

³ Then the Lord said to Jacob, "Return to the land of your father and grandfather and to your relatives there, and I will be with you."

⁴ So Jacob called Rachel and Leah out to the field where he was watching his flock. ⁵ He said to them, "I have noticed that your father's attitude toward me has changed. But the God of my father has been with me. ⁶ You know how hard I have worked for your father, ⁷ but he has cheated me, changing my wages ten times. But God has not allowed him to do me any harm. ⁸ For if he said, 'The speckled animals will be your wages,' the whole flock began to produce speckled young. And when he changed his mind and said, 'The striped animals will be your wages,' then the whole flock produced striped young. ⁹ In this way, God has taken your father's animals and given them to me.

¹⁰ "One time during the mating season, I had a dream and saw that the male goats mating with the females were streaked, speckled, and spotted. ¹¹ Then in my dream, the angel of God said to me, 'Jacob!' And I replied, 'Yes, here I am.'

¹² "The angel said, 'Look up, and you will see that only the streaked, speckled, and spotted males are mating with the females of your flock. For I have seen how Laban has treated you. ¹³ I am the God who appeared to you at Bethel,* the place where you anointed the pillar of stone and made your vow to me. Now get ready and leave this country and return to the land of your birth.'"

¹⁴ Rachel and Leah responded, "That's fine with us! We won't inherit any of our father's wealth anyway. ¹⁵ He has reduced our rights to those of foreign women. And after he sold us, he wasted the money you paid him for us. ¹⁶ All the wealth God has given you from our father legally belongs to us and our children. So go ahead and do whatever God has told you."

¹⁷ So Jacob put his wives and children on camels, ¹⁸ and he drove all his livestock in front of him. He packed all the belongings he had acquired in Paddan-aram and set out for the land of Canaan, where his father, Isaac, lived. ¹⁹ At the time they left, Laban was some distance away, shearing his sheep. Rachel stole her father's household idols and took them with her. ²⁰ Jacob outwitted Laban the Aramean, for they set out secretly and never told Laban they were leaving. ²¹ So Jacob took all his possessions with him and crossed the Euphrates River,* heading for the hill country of Gilead.

LABAN PURSUES JACOB

²² Three days later, Laban was told that Jacob had fled. ²³ So he gathered a group of his relatives and set out in hot pursuit. He caught up with Jacob seven days later in the hill country of Gilead. ²⁴ But the previous night God had appeared to Laban the Aramean in a dream and told him, "I'm warning you—leave Jacob alone!"

²⁵ Laban caught up with Jacob as he was camped in the hill country of Gilead, and he set up his camp not far from Jacob's. ²⁶ "What do you mean by deceiving me like this?" Laban demanded. "How dare you drag my daughters away like prisoners of war? ²⁷ Why did you slip away secretly? Why did you deceive me? And why didn't you say you wanted to leave? I would have given you a farewell feast, with singing and music, accompanied by tambourines and harps. ²⁸ Why didn't you let me kiss my daughters and grandchildren and tell them good-bye? You have acted very foolishly! ²⁹ I could destroy you, but the God of your father appeared to me last night and warned me, 'Leave Jacob alone!' ³⁰ I can understand your feeling that you must go, and your intense longing for your father's home. But why have you stolen my gods?"

³¹ "I rushed away because I was afraid," Jacob answered. "I thought you would take your daughters from me by force. ³² But as for your gods, see if you can find them, and let the person who has taken them die! And if you find anything else that belongs to you, identify it before all these relatives of ours, and I will give it back!" But Jacob did not know that Rachel had stolen the household idols.

³³ Laban went first into Jacob's tent to search there, then into Leah's, and then the tents of the two servant wives—but he found nothing. Finally, he went into Rachel's tent. ³⁴ But Rachel had taken the household idols and hidden them in her camel saddle, and now she was sitting on them. When Laban had thoroughly searched her tent without finding them, ³⁵ she said to her father, "Please, sir, forgive me if I don't get up for you. I'm having my monthly period." So Laban continued his search, but he could not find the household idols.

³⁶ Then Jacob became very angry, and he challenged Laban. "What's my crime?" he demanded. "What have I done wrong to make you chase after me as though I were a criminal? ³⁷ You have rummaged through everything I own. Now show me what you found that belongs to you! Set it out

---

31:13 As in Greek version and an Aramaic Targum; Hebrew reads the God of Bethel.   31:21 Hebrew the river.

here in front of us, before our relatives, for all to see. Let them judge between us! ³⁸"For twenty years I have been with you, caring for your flocks. In all that time your sheep and goats never miscarried. In all those years I never used a single ram of yours for food. ³⁹If any were attacked and killed by wild animals, I never showed you the carcass and asked you to reduce the count of your flock. No, I took the loss myself! You made me pay for every stolen animal, whether it was taken in broad daylight or in the dark of night.

⁴⁰"I worked for you through the scorching heat of the day and through cold and sleepless nights. ⁴¹Yes, for twenty years I slaved in your house! I worked for fourteen years earning your two daughters, and then six more years for your flock. And you changed my wages ten times! ⁴²In fact, if the God of my father had not been on my side—the God of Abraham and the fearsome God of Isaac*—you would have sent me away empty-handed. But God has seen your abuse and my hard work. That is why he appeared to you last night and rebuked you!"

JACOB'S TREATY WITH LABAN

⁴³Then Laban replied to Jacob, "These women are my daughters, these children are my grandchildren, and these flocks are my flocks—in fact, everything you see is mine. But what can I do now about my daughters and their children? ⁴⁴So come, let's make a covenant, you and I, and it will be a witness to our commitment."

⁴⁵So Jacob took a stone and set it up as a monument. ⁴⁶Then he told his family members, "Gather some stones." So they gathered stones and piled them in a heap. Then Jacob and Laban sat down beside the pile of stones to eat a covenant meal. ⁴⁷To commemorate the event, Laban called the place Jegar-sahadutha (which means "witness pile" in Aramaic), and Jacob called it Galeed (which means "witness pile" in Hebrew).

⁴⁸Then Laban declared, "This pile of stones will stand as a witness to remind us of the covenant we have made today." This explains why it was called Galeed—"Witness Pile." ⁴⁹But it was also called Mizpah (which means "watchtower"), for Laban said, "May the LORD keep watch between us to make sure that we keep this covenant when we are out of each other's sight. ⁵⁰If you mistreat my daughters or if you marry other wives, God will see it even if no one else does. He is a witness to this covenant between us.

⁵¹"See this pile of stones," Laban continued, "and see this monument I have set between us. ⁵²They stand between us as witnesses of our vows. I will never pass this pile of stones to harm you, and you must never pass these stones or this monument to harm me. ⁵³I call on the God of our ancestors—the God of your grandfather Abraham and the God of my grandfather Nahor—to serve as a judge between us."

So Jacob took an oath before the fearsome God of his father, Isaac,* to respect the boundary line. ⁵⁴Then Jacob offered a sacrifice to God there on the mountain and invited everyone to a covenant feast. After they had eaten, they spent the night on the mountain.

⁵⁵*Laban got up early the next morning, and he kissed his grandchildren and his daughters and blessed them. Then he left and returned home.

32 ¹*As Jacob started on his way again, angels of God came to meet him. ²When Jacob saw them, he exclaimed, "This is God's camp!" So he named the place Mahanaim.*

JACOB SENDS GIFTS TO ESAU

³Then Jacob sent messengers ahead to his brother, Esau, who was living in the region of Seir in the land of Edom. ⁴He told them, "Give this message to my master Esau: 'Humble greetings from your servant Jacob. Until now I have been living with Uncle Laban, ⁵and now I own cattle, donkeys, flocks of sheep and goats, and many servants, both men and women. I have sent these messengers to inform my lord of my coming, hoping that you will be friendly to me.'"

⁶After delivering the message, the messengers returned to Jacob and reported, "We met your brother, Esau, and he is already on his way to meet you—with an army of 400 men!" ⁷Jacob was terrified at the news. He divided his household, along with the flocks and herds and camels, into two groups. ⁸He thought, "If Esau meets one group and attacks it, perhaps the other group can escape."

⁹Then Jacob prayed, "O God of my grandfather Abraham, and God of my father, Isaac—O LORD, you told me, 'Return to your own land and to your relatives.' And you promised me, 'I will treat you kindly.' ¹⁰I am not worthy of all the unfailing love and faithfulness you have shown to me, your servant. When I left home and crossed the Jordan River, I owned nothing except a walking stick. Now my household fills two large camps! ¹¹O LORD, please rescue me from the hand of my brother, Esau. I am afraid that he is coming to attack me, along with my wives and children. ¹²But you promised me, 'I will surely treat you kindly, and I will multiply your descendants until they become as numerous as the sands along the seashore—too many to count.'"

¹³Jacob stayed where he was for the night. Then he selected these gifts from his possessions to present to his brother, Esau: ¹⁴200 female goats, 20 male goats, 200 ewes, 20 rams, ¹⁵30 female camels with their young, 40 cows, 10 bulls,

20 female donkeys, and 10 male donkeys. [16] He divided these animals into herds and assigned each to different servants. Then he told his servants, "Go ahead of me with the animals, but keep some distance between the herds."

[17] He gave these instructions to the men leading the first group: "When my brother, Esau, meets you, he will ask, 'Whose servants are you? Where are you going? Who owns these animals?' [18] You must reply, 'They belong to your servant Jacob, but they are a gift for his master Esau. Look, he is coming right behind us.'"

[19] Jacob gave the same instructions to the second and third herdsmen and to all who followed behind the herds: "You must say the same thing to Esau when you meet him. [20] And be sure to say, 'Look, your servant Jacob is right behind us.'"

Jacob thought, "I will try to appease him by sending gifts ahead of me. When I see him in person, perhaps he will be friendly to me." [21] So the gifts were sent on ahead, while Jacob himself spent that night in the camp.

JACOB WRESTLES WITH GOD

[22] During the night Jacob got up and took his two wives, his two servant wives, and his eleven sons and crossed the Jabbok River with them. [23] After taking them to the other side, he sent over all his possessions.

[24] This left Jacob all alone in the camp, and a man came and wrestled with him until the dawn began to break. [25] When the man saw that he would not win the match, he touched Jacob's hip and wrenched it out of its socket. [26] Then the man said, "Let me go, for the dawn is breaking!"

But Jacob said, "I will not let you go unless you bless me."

[27] "What is your name?" the man asked.

He replied, "Jacob."

[28] "Your name will no longer be Jacob," the man told him. "From now on you will be called Israel,* because you have fought with God and with men and have won."

[29] "Please tell me your name," Jacob said.

"Why do you want to know my name?" the man replied. Then he blessed Jacob there.

[30] Jacob named the place Peniel (which means "face of God"), for he said, "I have seen God face to face, yet my life has been spared." [31] The sun was rising as Jacob left Peniel,* and he was limping because of the injury to his hip. [32] (Even today the people of Israel don't eat the tendon near the hip socket because of what happened that night when the man strained the tendon of Jacob's hip.)

JACOB AND ESAU MAKE PEACE

33 Then Jacob looked up and saw Esau coming with his 400 men. So he divided the children among Leah, Rachel, and his two servant wives. [2] He put the servant wives and their children at the front, Leah and her children next, and Rachel and Joseph last. [3] Then Jacob went on ahead. As he approached his brother, he bowed to the ground seven times before him. [4] Then Esau ran to meet him and embraced him, threw his arms around his neck, and kissed him. And they both wept.

[5] Then Esau looked at the women and children and asked, "Who are these people with you?"

"These are the children God has graciously given to me, your servant," Jacob replied. [6] Then the servant wives came forward with their children and bowed before him. [7] Next came Leah with her children, and they bowed before him. Finally, Joseph and Rachel came forward and bowed before him.

[8] "And what were all the flocks and herds I met as I came?" Esau asked.

Jacob replied, "They are a gift, my lord, to ensure your friendship."

[9] "My brother, I have plenty," Esau answered. "Keep what you have for yourself."

[10] But Jacob insisted, "No, if I have found favor with you, please accept this gift from me. And what a relief to see your friendly smile. It is like seeing the face of God! [11] Please take this gift I have brought you, for God has been very gracious to me. I have more than enough." And because Jacob insisted, Esau finally accepted the gift.

[12] "Well," Esau said, "let's be going. I will lead the way."

[13] But Jacob replied, "You can see, my lord, that some of the children are very young, and the flocks and herds have their young, too. If they are driven too hard, even for one day, all the animals could die. [14] Please, my lord, go ahead of your servant. We will follow slowly, at a pace that is comfortable for the livestock and the children. I will meet you at Seir."

[15] "All right," Esau said, "but at least let me assign some of my men to guide and protect you."

Jacob responded, "That's not necessary. It's enough that you've received me warmly, my lord!"

[16] So Esau turned around and started back to Seir that same day. [17] Jacob, on the other hand, traveled on to Succoth. There he built himself a house and made shelters for his livestock. That is why the place was named Succoth (which means "shelters").

[18] Later, having traveled all the way from Paddan-aram, Jacob arrived safely at the town of Shechem, in the land of Canaan. There he set up camp outside the town. [19] Jacob bought the plot of land where he camped from the family of Hamor, the father of Shechem, for 100 pieces of silver.* [20] And there he built an altar and named it El-Elohe-Israel.*

32:28 *Jacob* sounds like the Hebrew words for "heel" and "deceiver." *Israel* means "God fights." 32:31 Hebrew *Penuel*, a variant spelling of Peniel. 33:19 Hebrew *100 kesitahs;* the value or weight of the kesitah is no longer known. 33:20 *El-Elohe-Israel* means "God, the God of Israel."

REVENGE AGAINST SHECHEM

34 One day Dinah, the daughter of Jacob and Leah, went to visit some of the young women who lived in the area. [2] But when the local prince, Shechem son of Hamor the Hivite, saw Dinah, he seized her and raped her. [3] But then he fell in love with her, and he tried to win her affection with tender words. [4] He said to his father, Hamor, "Get me this young girl. I want to marry her."

[5] Soon Jacob heard that Shechem had defiled his daughter, Dinah. But since his sons were out in the fields herding his livestock, he said nothing until they returned. [6] Hamor, Shechem's father, came to discuss the matter with Jacob. [7] Meanwhile, Jacob's sons had come in from the field as soon as they heard what had happened. They were shocked and furious that their sister had been raped. Shechem had done a disgraceful thing against Jacob's family,* something that should never be done.

[8] Hamor tried to speak with Jacob and his sons. "My son Shechem is truly in love with your daughter," he said. "Please let him marry her. [9] In fact, let's arrange other marriages, too. You give us your daughters for our sons, and we will give you our daughters for your sons. [10] And you may live among us; the land is open to you! Settle here and trade with us. And feel free to buy property in the area."

[11] Then Shechem himself spoke to Dinah's father and brothers. "Please be kind to me, and let me marry her," he begged. "I will give you whatever you ask. [12] No matter what dowry or gift you demand, I will gladly pay it—just give me the girl as my wife."

[13] But since Shechem had defiled their sister, Dinah, Jacob's sons responded deceitfully to Shechem and his father, Hamor. [14] They said to them, "We couldn't possibly allow this, because you're not circumcised. It would be a disgrace for our sister to marry a man like you! [15] But here is a solution. If every man among you will be circumcised like we are, [16] then we will give you our daughters, and we'll take your daughters for ourselves. We will live among you and become one people. [17] But if you don't agree to be circumcised, we will take her and be on our way."

[18] Hamor and his son Shechem agreed to their proposal. [19] Shechem wasted no time in acting on this request, for he wanted Jacob's daughter desperately. Shechem was a highly respected member of his family, [20] and he went with his father, Hamor, to present this proposal to the leaders at the town gate.

[21] "These men are our friends," they said. "Let's invite them to live here among us and trade freely. Look, the land is large enough to hold them. We can take their daughters as wives and let them marry ours. [22] But they will consider staying here and becoming one people with us only if all of our men are circumcised, just as they are. [23] But if we do this, all their livestock and possessions will eventually be ours. Come, let's agree to their terms and let them settle here among us."

[24] So all the men in the town council agreed with Hamor and Shechem, and every male in the town was circumcised. [25] But three days later, when their wounds were still sore, two of Jacob's sons, Simeon and Levi, who were Dinah's full brothers, took their swords and entered the town without opposition. Then they slaughtered every male there, [26] including Hamor and his son Shechem. They killed them with their swords, then took Dinah from Shechem's house and returned to their camp.

[27] Meanwhile, the rest of Jacob's sons arrived. Finding the men slaughtered, they plundered the town because their sister had been defiled there. [28] They seized all the flocks and herds and donkeys—everything they could lay their hands on, both inside the town and outside in the fields. [29] They looted all their wealth and plundered their houses. They also took all their little children and wives and led them away as captives.

[30] Afterward Jacob said to Simeon and Levi, "You have ruined me! You've made me stink among all the people of this land—among all the Canaanites and Perizzites. We are so few that they will join forces and crush us. I will be ruined, and my entire household will be wiped out!"

[31] "But why should we let him treat our sister like a prostitute?" they retorted angrily.

JACOB'S RETURN TO BETHEL

35 Then God said to Jacob, "Get ready and move to Bethel and settle there. Build an altar there to the God who appeared to you when you fled from your brother, Esau."

[2] So Jacob told everyone in his household, "Get rid of all your pagan idols, purify yourselves, and put on clean clothing. [3] We are now going to Bethel, where I will build an altar to the God who answered my prayers when I was in distress. He has been with me wherever I have gone."

[4] So they gave Jacob all their pagan idols and earrings, and he buried them under the great tree near Shechem. [5] As they set out, a terror from God spread over the people in all the towns of that area, so no one attacked Jacob's family.

[6] Eventually, Jacob and his household arrived at Luz (also called Bethel) in Canaan. [7] Jacob built an altar there and named the place El-bethel (which means "God of Bethel"), because God had appeared to him there when he was fleeing from his brother, Esau.

[8] Soon after this, Rebekah's old nurse, Deborah, died. She was buried beneath the oak tree in the valley below Bethel. Ever since, the tree has been called Allon-bacuth (which means "oak of weeping").

34:7 Hebrew *a disgraceful thing in Israel.*

⁹Now that Jacob had returned from Paddan-aram, God appeared to him again at Bethel. God blessed him, ¹⁰saying, "Your name is Jacob, but you will not be called Jacob any longer. From now on your name will be Israel."* So God renamed him Israel.

¹¹Then God said, "I am El-Shaddai—'God Almighty.' Be fruitful and multiply. You will become a great nation, even many nations. Kings will be among your descendants! ¹²And I will give you the land I once gave to Abraham and Isaac. Yes, I will give it to you and your descendants after you." ¹³Then God went up from the place where he had spoken to Jacob.

¹⁴Jacob set up a stone pillar to mark the place where God had spoken to him. Then he poured wine on it as an offering to God and anointed the pillar with olive oil. ¹⁵And Jacob named the place Bethel (which means "house of God"), because God had spoken to him there.

THE DEATHS OF RACHEL AND ISAAC

¹⁶Leaving Bethel, Jacob and his clan moved on toward Ephrath. But Rachel went into labor while they were still some distance away. Her labor pains were intense. ¹⁷After a very hard delivery, the midwife finally exclaimed, "Don't be afraid—you have another son!" ¹⁸Rachel was about to die, but with her last breath she named the baby Ben-oni (which means "son of my sorrow"). The baby's father, however, called him Benjamin (which means "son of my right hand"). ¹⁹So Rachel died and was buried on the way to Ephrath (that is, Bethlehem). ²⁰Jacob set up a stone monument over Rachel's grave, and it can be seen there to this day.

²¹Then Jacob* traveled on and camped beyond Migdal-eder. ²²While he was living there, Reuben had intercourse with Bilhah, his father's concubine, and Jacob soon heard about it.

These are the names of the twelve sons of Jacob:

²³The sons of Leah were Reuben (Jacob's oldest son), Simeon, Levi, Judah, Issachar, and Zebulun.
²⁴The sons of Rachel were Joseph and Benjamin.
²⁵The sons of Bilhah, Rachel's servant, were Dan and Naphtali.
²⁶The sons of Zilpah, Leah's servant, were Gad and Asher.
These are the names of the sons who were born to Jacob at Paddan-aram.

²⁷So Jacob returned to his father, Isaac, in Mamre, which is near Kiriath-arba (now called Hebron), where Abraham and Isaac had both lived as foreigners. ²⁸Isaac lived for 180 years. ²⁹Then he breathed his last and died at a ripe old age, joining his ancestors in death. And his sons, Esau and Jacob, buried him.

DESCENDANTS OF ESAU

36 This is the account of the descendants of Esau (also known as Edom). ²Esau married two young women from Canaan: Adah, the daughter of Elon the Hittite; and Oholibamah, the daughter of Anah and granddaughter of Zibeon the Hivite. ³He also married his cousin Basemath, who was the daughter of Ishmael and the sister of Nebaioth. ⁴Adah gave birth to a son named Eliphaz for Esau. Basemath gave birth to a son named Reuel. ⁵Oholibamah gave birth to sons named Jeush, Jalam, and Korah. All these sons were born to Esau in the land of Canaan.

⁶Esau took his wives, his children, and his entire household, along with his livestock and cattle—all the wealth he had acquired in the land of Canaan—and moved away from his brother, Jacob. ⁷There was not enough land to support them both because of all the livestock and possessions they had acquired. ⁸So Esau (also known as Edom) settled in the hill country of Seir.

⁹This is the account of Esau's descendants, the Edomites, who lived in the hill country of Seir.

¹⁰These are the names of Esau's sons: Eliphaz, the son of Esau's wife Adah; and Reuel, the son of Esau's wife Basemath. ¹¹The descendants of Eliphaz were Teman, Omar, Zepho, Gatam, and Kenaz. ¹²Timna, the concubine of Esau's son Eliphaz, gave birth to a son named Amalek. These are the descendants of Esau's wife Adah. ¹³The descendants of Reuel were Nahath, Zerah, Shammah, and Mizzah. These are the descendants of Esau's wife Basemath. ¹⁴Esau also had sons through Oholibamah, the daughter of Anah and granddaughter of Zibeon. Their names were Jeush, Jalam, and Korah.

¹⁵These are the descendants of Esau who became the leaders of various clans:

The descendants of Esau's oldest son, Eliphaz, became the leaders of the clans of Teman, Omar, Zepho, Kenaz, ¹⁶Korah, Gatam, and Amalek. These are the clan leaders in the land of Edom who descended from Eliphaz. All these were descendants of Esau's wife Adah.

¹⁷The descendants of Esau's son Reuel became the leaders of the clans of Nahath, Zerah, Shammah, and Mizzah. These are the clan leaders in the land of Edom who descended from Reuel. All these were descendants of Esau's wife Basemath.

35:10 *Jacob* sounds like the Hebrew words for "heel" and "deceiver." *Israel* means "God fights." 35:21 Hebrew *Israel;* also in 35:22a. The names "Jacob" and "Israel" are often interchanged throughout the Old Testament, referring sometimes to the individual patriarch and sometimes to the nation.

¹⁸ The descendants of Esau and his wife Oholibamah became the leaders of the clans of Jeush, Jalam, and Korah. These are the clan leaders who descended from Esau's wife Oholibamah, the daughter of Anah.
¹⁹ These are the clans descended from Esau (also known as Edom), identified by their clan leaders.

ORIGINAL PEOPLES OF EDOM

²⁰ These are the names of the tribes that descended from Seir the Horite. They lived in the land of Edom: Lotan, Shobal, Zibeon, Anah, ²¹ Dishon, Ezer, and Dishan. These were the Horite clan leaders, the descendants of Seir, who lived in the land of Edom.

²² The descendants of Lotan were Hori and Hemam. Lotan's sister was named Timna.
²³ The descendants of Shobal were Alvan, Manahath, Ebal, Shepho, and Onam.
²⁴ The descendants of Zibeon were Aiah and Anah. (This is the Anah who discovered the hot springs in the wilderness while he was grazing his father's donkeys.)
²⁵ The descendants of Anah were his son, Dishon, and his daughter, Oholibamah.
²⁶ The descendants of Dishon* were Hemdan, Eshban, Ithran, and Keran.
²⁷ The descendants of Ezer were Bilhan, Zaavan, and Akan.
²⁸ The descendants of Dishan were Uz and Aran.
²⁹ So these were the leaders of the Horite clans: Lotan, Shobal, Zibeon, Anah, ³⁰ Dishon, Ezer, and Dishan. The Horite clans are named after their clan leaders, who lived in the land of Seir.

RULERS OF EDOM

³¹ These are the kings who ruled in the land of Edom before any king ruled over the Israelites*:

³² Bela son of Beor, who ruled in Edom from his city of Dinhabah.
³³ When Bela died, Jobab son of Zerah from Bozrah became king in his place.
³⁴ When Jobab died, Husham from the land of the Temanites became king in his place.
³⁵ When Husham died, Hadad son of Bedad became king in his place and ruled from the city of Avith. He was the one who defeated the Midianites in the land of Moab.
³⁶ When Hadad died, Samlah from the city of Masrekah became king in his place.
³⁷ When Samlah died, Shaul from the city of Rehoboth-on-the-River became king in his place.
³⁸ When Shaul died, Baal-hanan son of Acbor became king in his place.
³⁹ When Baal-hanan son of Acbor died, Hadad* became king in his place and ruled from the city of Pau. His wife was Mehetabel, the daughter of Matred and granddaughter of Me-zahab.

⁴⁰ These are the names of the leaders of the clans descended from Esau, who lived in the places named for them: Timna, Alvah, Jetheth, ⁴¹ Oholibamah, Elah, Pinon, ⁴² Kenaz, Teman, Mibzar, ⁴³ Magdiel, and Iram. These are the leaders of the clans of Edom, listed according to their settlements in the land they occupied. They all descended from Esau, the ancestor of the Edomites.

JOSEPH'S DREAMS

37 So Jacob settled again in the land of Canaan, where his father had lived as a foreigner.
² This is the account of Jacob and his family. When Joseph was seventeen years old, he often tended his father's flocks. He worked for his half brothers, the sons of his father's wives Bilhah and Zilpah. But Joseph reported to his father some of the bad things his brothers were doing.
³ Jacob* loved Joseph more than any of his other children because Joseph had been born to him in his old age. So one day Jacob had a special gift made for Joseph—a beautiful robe.* ⁴ But his brothers hated Joseph because their father loved him more than the rest of them. They couldn't say a kind word to him.
⁵ One night Joseph had a dream, and when he told his brothers about it, they hated him more than ever. ⁶ "Listen to this dream," he said. ⁷ "We were out in the field, tying up bundles of grain. Suddenly my bundle stood up, and your bundles all gathered around and bowed low before mine!"

36:26 Hebrew *Dishan*, a variant spelling of Dishon; compare 36:21, 28.   36:31 Or *before an Israelite king ruled over them.* 36:39 As in some Hebrew manuscripts, Samaritan Pentateuch, and Syriac version (see also 1 Chr 1:50); most Hebrew manuscripts read *Hadar.*   37:3a Hebrew *Israel;* also in 37:13. See note on 35:21.   37:3b Traditionally rendered *a coat of many colors.* The exact meaning of the Hebrew is uncertain.

⁸His brothers responded, "So you think you will be our king, do you? Do you actually think you will reign over us?" And they hated him all the more because of his dreams and the way he talked about them.

⁹Soon Joseph had another dream, and again he told his brothers about it. "Listen, I have had another dream," he said. "The sun, moon, and eleven stars bowed low before me!"

¹⁰This time he told the dream to his father as well as to his brothers, but his father scolded him. "What kind of dream is that?" he asked. "Will your mother and I and your brothers actually come and bow to the ground before you?" ¹¹But while his brothers were jealous of Joseph, his father wondered what the dreams meant.

¹²Soon after this, Joseph's brothers went to pasture their father's flocks at Shechem. ¹³When they had been gone for some time, Jacob said to Joseph, "Your brothers are pasturing the sheep at Shechem. Get ready, and I will send you to them."

"I'm ready to go," Joseph replied.

¹⁴"Go and see how your brothers and the flocks are getting along," Jacob said. "Then come back and bring me a report." So Jacob sent him on his way, and Joseph traveled to Shechem from their home in the valley of Hebron.

¹⁵When he arrived there, a man from the area noticed him wandering around the countryside. "What are you looking for?" he asked.

¹⁶"I'm looking for my brothers," Joseph replied. "Do you know where they are pasturing their sheep?"

¹⁷"Yes," the man told him. "They have moved on from here, but I heard them say, 'Let's go on to Dothan.'" So Joseph followed his brothers to Dothan and found them there.

JOSEPH SOLD INTO SLAVERY

¹⁸When Joseph's brothers saw him coming, they recognized him in the distance. As he approached, they made plans to kill him. ¹⁹"Here comes the dreamer!" they said. ²⁰"Come on, let's kill him and throw him into one of these cisterns. We can tell our father, 'A wild animal has eaten him.' Then we'll see what becomes of his dreams!"

²¹But when Reuben heard of their scheme, he came to Joseph's rescue. "Let's not kill him," he said. ²²"Why should we shed any blood? Let's just throw him into this empty cistern here in the wilderness. Then he'll die without our laying a hand on him." Reuben was secretly planning to rescue Joseph and return him to his father.

²³So when Joseph arrived, his brothers ripped off the beautiful robe he was wearing. ²⁴Then they grabbed him and threw him into the cistern. Now the cistern was empty; there was no water in it. ²⁵Then, just as they were sitting down to eat, they looked up and saw a caravan of camels in the distance coming toward them. It was a group of Ishmaelite traders taking a load of gum, balm, and aromatic resin from Gilead down to Egypt.

²⁶Judah said to his brothers, "What will we gain by killing our brother? We'd have to cover up the crime.* ²⁷Instead of hurting him, let's sell him to those Ishmaelite traders. After all, he is our brother—our own flesh and blood!" And his brothers agreed. ²⁸So when the Ishmaelites, who were Midianite traders, came by, Joseph's brothers pulled him out of the cistern and sold him to them for twenty pieces* of silver. And the traders took him to Egypt.

²⁹Some time later, Reuben returned to get Joseph out of the cistern. When he discovered that Joseph was missing, he tore his clothes in grief. ³⁰Then he went back to his brothers and lamented, "The boy is gone! What will I do now?"

³¹Then the brothers killed a young goat and dipped Joseph's robe in its blood. ³²They sent the beautiful robe to their father with this message: "Look at what we found. Doesn't this robe belong to your son?"

³³Their father recognized it immediately. "Yes," he said, "it is my son's robe. A wild animal must have eaten him. Joseph has clearly been torn to pieces!" ³⁴Then Jacob tore his clothes and dressed himself in burlap. He mourned deeply for his son for a long time. ³⁵His family all tried to comfort him, but he refused to be comforted. "I will go to my grave* mourning for my son," he would say, and then he would weep.

³⁶Meanwhile, the Midianite traders* arrived in Egypt, where they sold Joseph to Potiphar, an officer of Pharaoh, the king of Egypt. Potiphar was captain of the palace guard.

JUDAH AND TAMAR

38 About this time, Judah left home and moved to Adullam, where he stayed with a man named Hirah. ²There he saw a Canaanite woman, the daughter of Shua, and he married her. When he slept with her, ³she became pregnant and gave birth to a son, and he named the boy Er. ⁴Then she became pregnant again and gave birth to another son, and she named him Onan. ⁵And when she gave birth to a third son, she named him Shelah. At the time of Shelah's birth, they were living at Kezib.

⁶In the course of time, Judah arranged for his firstborn son, Er, to marry a young woman named Tamar. ⁷But Er was a wicked man in the LORD's sight, so the LORD took his life. ⁸Then Judah said to Er's brother Onan, "Go and marry Tamar, as our law requires of the brother of a man who has died. You must produce an heir for your brother."

⁹But Onan was not willing to have a child who would not be his own heir. So whenever he had intercourse with his brother's wife, he spilled

---

37:26 Hebrew *cover his blood.* 37:28 Hebrew *20 [shekels],* about 8 ounces or 228 grams in weight. 37:35 Hebrew *go down to Sheol.* 37:36 Hebrew *the Medanites.* The relationship between the Midianites and Medanites is unclear; compare 37:28. See also 25:2.

the semen on the ground. This prevented her from having a child who would belong to his brother. [10] But the LORD considered it evil for Onan to deny a child to his dead brother. So the LORD took Onan's life, too.

[11] Then Judah said to Tamar, his daughter-in-law, "Go back to your parents' home and remain a widow until my son Shelah is old enough to marry you." (But Judah didn't really intend to do this because he was afraid Shelah would also die, like his two brothers.) So Tamar went back to live in her father's home.

[12] Some years later Judah's wife died. After the time of mourning was over, Judah and his friend Hirah the Adullamite went up to Timnah to supervise the shearing of his sheep. [13] Someone told Tamar, "Look, your father-in-law is going up to Timnah to shear his sheep."

[14] Tamar was aware that Shelah had grown up, but no arrangements had been made for her to come and marry him. So she changed out of her widow's clothing and covered herself with a veil to disguise herself. Then she sat beside the road at the entrance to the village of Enaim, which is on the road to Timnah. [15] Judah noticed her and thought she was a prostitute, since she had covered her face. [16] So he stopped and propositioned her. "Let me have sex with you," he said, not realizing that she was his own daughter-in-law.

"How much will you pay to have sex with me?" Tamar asked.

[17] "I'll send you a young goat from my flock," Judah promised.

"But what will you give me to guarantee that you will send the goat?" she asked.

[18] "What kind of guarantee do you want?" he replied.

She answered, "Leave me your identification seal and its cord and the walking stick you are carrying." So Judah gave them to her. Then he had intercourse with her, and she became pregnant. [19] Afterward she went back home, took off her veil, and put on her widow's clothing as usual.

[20] Later Judah asked his friend Hirah the Adullamite to take the young goat to the woman and to pick up the things he had given her as his guarantee. But Hirah couldn't find her. [21] So he asked the men who lived there, "Where can I find the shrine prostitute who was sitting beside the road at the entrance to Enaim?"

"We've never had a shrine prostitute here," they replied.

[22] So Hirah returned to Judah and told him, "I couldn't find her anywhere, and the men of the village claim they've never had a shrine prostitute there."

[23] "Then let her keep the things I gave her," Judah said. "I sent the young goat as we agreed, but you couldn't find her. We'd be the laughingstock of the village if we went back again to look for her."

[24] About three months later, Judah was told, "Tamar, your daughter-in-law, has acted like a prostitute. And now, because of this, she's pregnant."

"Bring her out, and let her be burned!" Judah demanded.

[25] But as they were taking her out to kill her, she sent this message to her father-in-law: "The man who owns these things made me pregnant. Look closely. Whose seal and cord and walking stick are these?"

[26] Judah recognized them immediately and said, "She is more righteous than I am, because I didn't arrange for her to marry my son Shelah." And Judah never slept with Tamar again.

[27] When the time came for Tamar to give birth, it was discovered that she was carrying twins. [28] While she was in labor, one of the babies reached out his hand. The midwife grabbed it and tied a scarlet string around the child's wrist, announcing, "This one came out first." [29] But then he pulled back his hand, and out came his brother! "What!" the midwife exclaimed. "How did you break out first?" So he was named Perez.* [30] Then the baby with the scarlet string on his wrist was born, and he was named Zerah.*

JOSEPH IN POTIPHAR'S HOUSE

39 When Joseph was taken to Egypt by the Ishmaelite traders, he was purchased by Potiphar, an Egyptian officer. Potiphar was captain of the guard for Pharaoh, the king of Egypt. [2] The LORD was with Joseph, so he succeeded in everything he did as he served in the home of his Egyptian master. [3] Potiphar noticed this and realized that the LORD was with Joseph, giving him success in everything he did. [4] This pleased Potiphar, so he soon made Joseph his personal attendant. He put him in charge of his entire household and everything he owned. [5] From the day Joseph was put in charge of his master's household and property, the LORD began to bless Potiphar's household for Joseph's sake. All his household affairs ran smoothly, and his crops and livestock flourished. [6] So Potiphar gave Joseph complete administrative responsibility over everything he owned. With Joseph there, he didn't worry about a thing—except what kind of food to eat!

Joseph was a very handsome and well-built young man, [7] and Potiphar's wife soon began to look at him lustfully. "Come and sleep with me," she demanded.

[8] But Joseph refused. "Look," he told her, "my master trusts me with everything in his entire household. [9] No one here has more authority than I do. He has held back nothing from me except you, because you are his wife. How could

---

38:29 *Perez* means "breaking out." **38:30** *Zerah* means "scarlet" or "brightness."

I do such a wicked thing? It would be a great sin against God."

¹⁰ She kept putting pressure on Joseph day after day, but he refused to sleep with her, and he kept out of her way as much as possible. ¹¹ One day, however, no one else was around when he went in to do his work. ¹² She came and grabbed him by his cloak, demanding, "Come on, sleep with me!" Joseph tore himself away, but he left his cloak in her hand as he ran from the house.

¹³ When she saw that she was holding his cloak and he had fled, ¹⁴ she called out to her servants. Soon all the men came running. "Look!" she said. "My husband has brought this Hebrew slave here to make fools of us! He came into my room to rape me, but I screamed. ¹⁵ When he heard me scream, he ran outside and got away, but he left his cloak behind with me."

¹⁶ She kept the cloak with her until her husband came home. ¹⁷ Then she told him her story. "That Hebrew slave you've brought into our house tried to come in and fool around with me," she said. ¹⁸ "But when I screamed, he ran outside, leaving his cloak with me!"

JOSEPH PUT IN PRISON

¹⁹ Potiphar was furious when he heard his wife's story about how Joseph had treated her. ²⁰ So he took Joseph and threw him into the prison where the king's prisoners were held, and there he remained. ²¹ But the LORD was with Joseph in the prison and showed him his faithful love. And the LORD made Joseph a favorite with the prison warden. ²² Before long, the warden put Joseph in charge of all the other prisoners and over everything that happened in the prison. ²³ The warden had no more worries, because Joseph took care of everything. The LORD was with him and caused everything he did to succeed.

JOSEPH INTERPRETS TWO DREAMS

40 Some time later, Pharaoh's chief cup-bearer and chief baker offended their royal master. ² Pharaoh became angry with these two officials, ³ and he put them in the prison where Joseph was, in the palace of the captain of the guard. ⁴ They remained in prison for quite some time, and the captain of the guard assigned them to Joseph, who looked after them.

⁵ While they were in prison, Pharaoh's cup-bearer and baker each had a dream one night, and each dream had its own meaning. ⁶ When Joseph saw them the next morning, he noticed that they both looked upset. ⁷ "Why do you look so worried today?" he asked them.

⁸ And they replied, "We both had dreams last night, but no one can tell us what they mean."

"Interpreting dreams is God's business," Joseph replied. "Go ahead and tell me your dreams."

⁹ So the chief cup-bearer told Joseph his dream first. "In my dream," he said, "I saw a grapevine in front of me. ¹⁰ The vine had three branches that began to bud and blossom, and soon it produced clusters of ripe grapes. ¹¹ I was holding Pharaoh's wine cup in my hand, so I took a cluster of grapes and squeezed the juice into the cup. Then I placed the cup in Pharaoh's hand."

¹² "This is what the dream means," Joseph said. "The three branches represent three days. ¹³ Within three days Pharaoh will lift you up and restore you to your position as his chief cup-bearer. ¹⁴ And please remember me and do me a favor when things go well for you. Mention me to Pharaoh, so he might let me out of this place. ¹⁵ For I was kidnapped from my homeland, the land of the Hebrews, and now I'm here in prison, but I did nothing to deserve it."

¹⁶ When the chief baker saw that Joseph had given the first dream such a positive interpretation, he said to Joseph, "I had a dream, too. In my dream there were three baskets of white pastries stacked on my head. ¹⁷ The top basket contained all kinds of pastries for Pharaoh, but the birds came and ate them from the basket on my head."

¹⁸ "This is what the dream means," Joseph told him. "The three baskets also represent three days. ¹⁹ Three days from now Pharaoh will lift you up and impale your body on a pole. Then birds will come and peck away at your flesh."

²⁰ Pharaoh's birthday came three days later, and he prepared a banquet for all his officials and staff. He summoned* his chief cup-bearer and chief baker to join the other officials. ²¹ He then restored the chief cup-bearer to his former position, so he could again hand Pharaoh his cup. ²² But Pharaoh impaled the chief baker, just as Joseph had predicted when he interpreted his dream. ²³ Pharaoh's chief cup-bearer, however, forgot all about Joseph, never giving him another thought.

PHARAOH'S DREAMS

41 Two full years later, Pharaoh dreamed that he was standing on the bank of the Nile River. ² In his dream he saw seven fat, healthy cows come up out of the river and begin grazing in the marsh grass. ³ Then he saw seven more cows come up behind them from the Nile, but these were scrawny and thin. These cows stood beside the fat cows on the riverbank. ⁴ Then the scrawny, thin cows ate the seven healthy, fat cows! At this point in the dream, Pharaoh woke up.

⁵ But he fell asleep again and had a second dream. This time he saw seven heads of grain, plump and beautiful, growing on a single stalk. ⁶ Then seven more heads of grain appeared, but these were shriveled and withered by the east wind. ⁷ And these thin heads swallowed up the seven plump, well-formed heads! Then Pharaoh woke up again and realized it was a dream.

40:20 Hebrew *He lifted up the head of.*

⁸ The next morning Pharaoh was very disturbed by the dreams. So he called for all the magicians and wise men of Egypt. When Pharaoh told them his dreams, not one of them could tell him what they meant.

⁹ Finally, the king's chief cup-bearer spoke up. "Today I have been reminded of my failure," he told Pharaoh. ¹⁰ "Some time ago, you were angry with the chief baker and me, and you imprisoned us in the palace of the captain of the guard. ¹¹ One night the chief baker and I each had a dream, and each dream had its own meaning. ¹² There was a young Hebrew man with us in the prison who was a slave of the captain of the guard. We told him our dreams, and he told us what each of our dreams meant. ¹³ And everything happened just as he had predicted. I was restored to my position as cup-bearer, and the chief baker was executed and impaled on a pole."

¹⁴ Pharaoh sent for Joseph at once, and he was quickly brought from the prison. After he shaved and changed his clothes, he went in and stood before Pharaoh. ¹⁵ Then Pharaoh said to Joseph, "I had a dream last night, and no one here can tell me what it means. But I have heard that when you hear about a dream you can interpret it."

¹⁶ "It is beyond my power to do this," Joseph replied. "But God can tell you what it means and set you at ease."

¹⁷ So Pharaoh told Joseph his dream. "In my dream," he said, "I was standing on the bank of the Nile River, ¹⁸ and I saw seven fat, healthy cows come up out of the river and begin grazing in the marsh grass. ¹⁹ But then I saw seven sick-looking cows, scrawny and thin, come up after them. I've never seen such sorry-looking animals in all the land of Egypt. ²⁰ These thin, scrawny cows ate the seven fat cows. ²¹ But afterward you wouldn't have known it, for they were still as thin and scrawny as before! Then I woke up.

²² "In my dream I also saw seven heads of grain, full and beautiful, growing on a single stalk. ²³ Then seven more heads of grain appeared, but these were blighted, shriveled, and withered by the east wind. ²⁴ And the shriveled heads swallowed the seven healthy heads. I told these dreams to the magicians, but no one could tell me what they mean."

²⁵ Joseph responded, "Both of Pharaoh's dreams mean the same thing. God is telling Pharaoh in advance what he is about to do. ²⁶ The seven healthy cows and the seven healthy heads of grain both represent seven years of prosperity. ²⁷ The seven thin, scrawny cows that came up later and the seven thin heads of grain, withered by the east wind, represent seven years of famine.

²⁸ "This will happen just as I have described it, for God has revealed to Pharaoh in advance what he is about to do. ²⁹ The next seven years will be a period of great prosperity throughout the land of Egypt. ³⁰ But afterward there will be seven years of famine so great that all the prosperity will be forgotten in Egypt. Famine will destroy the land. ³¹ This famine will be so severe that even the memory of the good years will be erased. ³² As for having two similar dreams, it means that these events have been decreed by God, and he will soon make them happen.

³³ "Therefore, Pharaoh should find an intelligent and wise man and put him in charge of the entire land of Egypt. ³⁴ Then Pharaoh should appoint supervisors over the land and let them collect one-fifth of all the crops during the seven good years. ³⁵ Have them gather all the food produced in the good years that are just ahead and bring it to Pharaoh's storehouses. Store it away, and guard it so there will be food in the cities. ³⁶ That way there will be enough to eat when the seven years of famine come to the land of Egypt. Otherwise this famine will destroy the land."

JOSEPH MADE RULER OF EGYPT

³⁷ Joseph's suggestions were well received by Pharaoh and his officials. ³⁸ So Pharaoh asked his officials, "Can we find anyone else like this man so obviously filled with the spirit of God?" ³⁹ Then Pharaoh said to Joseph, "Since God has revealed the meaning of the dreams to you, clearly no one else is as intelligent or wise as you are. ⁴⁰ You will be in charge of my court, and all my people will take orders from you. Only I, sitting on my throne, will have a rank higher than yours."

⁴¹ Pharaoh said to Joseph, "I hereby put you in charge of the entire land of Egypt." ⁴² Then Pharaoh removed his signet ring from his hand and placed it on Joseph's finger. He dressed him in fine linen clothing and hung a gold chain around his neck. ⁴³ Then he had Joseph ride in the chariot reserved for his second-in-command. And wherever Joseph went, the command was shouted, "Kneel down!" So Pharaoh put Joseph in charge of all Egypt. ⁴⁴ And Pharaoh said to him, "I am Pharaoh, but no one will lift a hand or foot in the entire land of Egypt without your approval."

⁴⁵ Then Pharaoh gave Joseph a new Egyptian name, Zaphenath-paneah.* He also gave him a wife, whose name was Asenath. She was the daughter of Potiphera, the priest of On.* So Joseph took charge of the entire land of Egypt. ⁴⁶ He was thirty years old when he began serving in the court of Pharaoh, the king of Egypt. And when Joseph left Pharaoh's presence, he inspected the entire land of Egypt.

⁴⁷ As predicted, for seven years the land produced bumper crops. ⁴⁸ During those years, Joseph gathered all the crops grown in Egypt and stored the grain from the surrounding fields in the cities. ⁴⁹ He piled up huge amounts of grain like sand on the seashore. Finally, he stopped keeping records because there was too much to measure.

41:45a *Zaphenath-paneah* probably means "God speaks and lives."
41:45b Greek version reads *of Heliopolis;* also in 41:50.

⁵⁰During this time, before the first of the famine years, two sons were born to Joseph and his wife, Asenath, the daughter of Potiphera, the priest of On. ⁵¹Joseph named his older son Manasseh,* for he said, "God has made me forget all my troubles and everyone in my father's family." ⁵²Joseph named his second son Ephraim,* for he said, "God has made me fruitful in this land of my grief."

⁵³At last the seven years of bumper crops throughout the land of Egypt came to an end. ⁵⁴Then the seven years of famine began, just as Joseph had predicted. The famine also struck all the surrounding countries, but throughout Egypt there was plenty of food. ⁵⁵Eventually, however, the famine spread throughout the land of Egypt as well. And when the people cried out to Pharaoh for food, he told them, "Go to Joseph, and do whatever he tells you." ⁵⁶So with severe famine everywhere, Joseph opened up the storehouses and distributed grain to the Egyptians, for the famine was severe throughout the land of Egypt. ⁵⁷And people from all around came to Egypt to buy grain from Joseph because the famine was severe throughout the world.

JOSEPH'S BROTHERS GO TO EGYPT

42 When Jacob heard that grain was available in Egypt, he said to his sons, "Why are you standing around looking at one another? ²I have heard there is grain in Egypt. Go down there, and buy enough grain to keep us alive. Otherwise we'll die."

³So Joseph's ten older brothers went down to Egypt to buy grain. ⁴But Jacob wouldn't let Joseph's younger brother, Benjamin, go with them, for fear some harm might come to him. ⁵So Jacob's* sons arrived in Egypt along with others to buy food, for the famine was in Canaan as well.

⁶Since Joseph was governor of all Egypt and in charge of selling grain to all the people, it was to him that his brothers came. When they arrived, they bowed before him with their faces to the ground. ⁷Joseph recognized his brothers instantly, but he pretended to be a stranger and spoke harshly to them. "Where are you from?" he demanded.

"From the land of Canaan," they replied. "We have come to buy food."

⁸Although Joseph recognized his brothers, they didn't recognize him. ⁹And he remembered the dreams he'd had about them many years before. He said to them, "You are spies! You have come to see how vulnerable our land has become."

¹⁰"No, my lord!" they exclaimed. "Your servants have simply come to buy food. ¹¹We are all brothers—members of the same family. We are honest men, sir! We are not spies!"

¹²"Yes, you are!" Joseph insisted. "You have come to see how vulnerable our land has become."

¹³"Sir," they said, "there are actually twelve of us. We, your servants, are all brothers, sons of a man living in the land of Canaan. Our youngest brother is back there with our father right now, and one of our brothers is no longer with us."

¹⁴But Joseph insisted, "As I said, you are spies! ¹⁵This is how I will test your story. I swear by the life of Pharaoh that you will never leave Egypt unless your youngest brother comes here! ¹⁶One of you must go and get your brother. I'll keep the rest of you here in prison. Then we'll find out whether or not your story is true. By the life of Pharaoh, if it turns out that you don't have a younger brother, then I'll know you are spies."

¹⁷So Joseph put them all in prison for three days. ¹⁸On the third day Joseph said to them, "I am a God-fearing man. If you do as I say, you will live. ¹⁹If you really are honest men, choose one of your brothers to remain in prison. The rest of you may go home with grain for your starving families. ²⁰But you must bring your youngest brother back to me. This will prove that you are telling the truth, and you will not die." To this they agreed.

²¹Speaking among themselves, they said, "Clearly we are being punished because of what we did to Joseph long ago. We saw his anguish when he pleaded for his life, but we wouldn't listen. That's why we're in this trouble." ²²"Didn't I tell you not to sin against the boy?" Reuben asked. "But you wouldn't listen. And now we have to answer for his blood!"

²³Of course, they didn't know that Joseph understood them, for he had been speaking to them through an interpreter. ²⁴Now he turned away from them and began to weep. When he regained his composure, he spoke to them again. Then he chose Simeon from among them and had him tied up right before their eyes.

²⁵Joseph then ordered his servants to fill the men's sacks with grain, but he also gave secret instructions to return each brother's payment at the top of his sack. He also gave them supplies for their journey home. ²⁶So the brothers loaded their donkeys with the grain and headed for home.

²⁷But when they stopped for the night and one of them opened his sack to get grain for his donkey, he found his money in the top of his sack. ²⁸"Look!" he exclaimed to his brothers. "My money has been returned; it's here in my sack!" Then their hearts sank. Trembling, they said to each other, "What has God done to us?"

²⁹When the brothers came to their father, Jacob, in the land of Canaan, they told him everything that had happened to them. ³⁰"The man who is governor of the land spoke very harshly to us," they told him. "He accused us of being spies scouting the land. ³¹But we said, 'We are honest

---

41:51 *Manasseh* sounds like a Hebrew term that means "causing to forget." 41:52 *Ephraim* sounds like a Hebrew term that means "fruitful." 42:5 Hebrew *Israel's*. See note on 35:21.

men, not spies. ³²We are twelve brothers, sons of one father. One brother is no longer with us, and the youngest is at home with our father in the land of Canaan.'

³³"Then the man who is governor of the land told us, 'This is how I will find out if you are honest men. Leave one of your brothers here with me, and take grain for your starving families and go on home. ³⁴But you must bring your youngest brother back to me. Then I will know you are honest men and not spies. Then I will give you back your brother, and you may trade freely in the land.'"

³⁵As they emptied out their sacks, there in each man's sack was the bag of money he had paid for the grain! The brothers and their father were terrified when they saw the bags of money. ³⁶Jacob exclaimed, "You are robbing me of my children! Joseph is gone! Simeon is gone! And now you want to take Benjamin, too. Everything is going against me!"

³⁷Then Reuben said to his father, "You may kill my two sons if I don't bring Benjamin back to you. I'll be responsible for him, and I promise to bring him back."

³⁸But Jacob replied, "My son will not go down with you. His brother Joseph is dead, and he is all I have left. If anything should happen to him on your journey, you would send this grieving, white-haired man to his grave.*"

THE BROTHERS RETURN TO EGYPT

43 But the famine continued to ravage the land of Canaan. ²When the grain they had brought from Egypt was almost gone, Jacob said to his sons, "Go back and buy us a little more food."

³But Judah said, "The man was serious when he warned us, 'You won't see my face again unless your brother is with you.' ⁴If you send Benjamin with us, we will go down and buy more food. ⁵But if you don't let Benjamin go, we won't go either. Remember, the man said, 'You won't see my face again unless your brother is with you.'"

⁶"Why were you so cruel to me?" Jacob* moaned. "Why did you tell him you had another brother?"

⁷"The man kept asking us questions about our family," they replied. "He asked, 'Is your father still alive? Do you have another brother?' So we answered his questions. How could we know he would say, 'Bring your brother down here'?"

⁸Judah said to his father, "Send the boy with me, and we will be on our way. Otherwise we will all die of starvation—and not only we, but you and our little ones. ⁹I personally guarantee his safety. You may hold me responsible if I don't bring him back to you. Then let me bear the blame forever. ¹⁰If we hadn't wasted all this time, we could have gone and returned twice by now."

¹¹So their father, Jacob, finally said to them, "If it can't be avoided, then at least do this. Pack your bags with the best products of this land. Take them down to the man as gifts—balm, honey, gum, aromatic resin, pistachio nuts, and almonds. ¹²Also take double the money that was put back in your sacks, as it was probably someone's mistake. ¹³Then take your brother, and go back to the man. ¹⁴May God Almighty* give you mercy as you go before the man, so that he will release Simeon and let Benjamin return. But if I must lose my children, so be it."

¹⁵So the men packed Jacob's gifts and double the money and headed off with Benjamin. They finally arrived in Egypt and presented themselves to Joseph. ¹⁶When Joseph saw Benjamin with them, he said to the manager of his household, "These men will eat with me this noon. Take them inside the palace. Then go slaughter an animal, and prepare a big feast." ¹⁷So the man did as Joseph told him and took them into Joseph's palace.

¹⁸The brothers were terrified when they saw that they were being taken into Joseph's house. "It's because of the money someone put in our sacks last time we were here," they said. "He plans to pretend that we stole it. Then he will seize us, make us slaves, and take our donkeys."

A FEAST AT JOSEPH'S PALACE

¹⁹The brothers approached the manager of Joseph's household and spoke to him at the entrance to the palace. ²⁰"Sir," they said, "we came to Egypt once before to buy food. ²¹But as we were returning home, we stopped for the night and opened our sacks. Then we discovered that each man's money—the exact amount paid—was in the top of his sack! Here it is; we have brought it back with us. ²²We also have additional money to buy more food. We have no idea who put our money in our sacks."

²³"Relax. Don't be afraid," the household manager told them. "Your God, the God of your father, must have put this treasure into your sacks. I know I received your payment." Then he released Simeon and brought him out to them.

²⁴The manager then led the men into Joseph's palace. He gave them water to wash their feet and provided food for their donkeys. ²⁵They were told they would be eating there, so they prepared their gifts for Joseph's arrival at noon.

²⁶When Joseph came home, they gave him the gifts they had brought him, then bowed low to the ground before him. ²⁷After greeting them, he asked, "How is your father, the old man you spoke about? Is he still alive?"

²⁸"Yes," they replied. "Our father, your servant, is alive and well." And they bowed low again.

²⁹Then Joseph looked at his brother Benjamin, the son of his own mother. "Is this your youngest brother, the one you told me about?" Joseph

---

42:38 Hebrew *to Sheol.* **43:6** Hebrew *Israel;* also in 43:11. See note on 35:21. **43:14** Hebrew *El-Shaddai.*

asked. "May God be gracious to you, my son." [30]Then Joseph hurried from the room because he was overcome with emotion for his brother. He went into his private room, where he broke down and wept. [31]After washing his face, he came back out, keeping himself under control. Then he ordered, "Bring out the food!"

[32]The waiters served Joseph at his own table, and his brothers were served at a separate table. The Egyptians who ate with Joseph sat at their own table, because Egyptians despise Hebrews and refuse to eat with them. [33]Joseph told each of his brothers where to sit, and to their amazement, he seated them according to age, from oldest to youngest. [34]And Joseph filled their plates with food from his own table, giving Benjamin five times as much as he gave the others. So they feasted and drank freely with him.

JOSEPH'S SILVER CUP

44 When his brothers were ready to leave, Joseph gave these instructions to his palace manager: "Fill each of their sacks with as much grain as they can carry, and put each man's money back into his sack. [2]Then put my personal silver cup at the top of the youngest brother's sack, along with the money for his grain." So the manager did as Joseph instructed him.

[3]The brothers were up at dawn and were sent on their journey with their loaded donkeys. [4]But when they had gone only a short distance and were barely out of the city, Joseph said to his palace manager, "Chase after them and stop them. When you catch up with them, ask them, 'Why have you repaid my kindness with such evil? [5]Why have you stolen my master's silver cup,* which he uses to predict the future? What a wicked thing you have done!'"

[6]When the palace manager caught up with the men, he spoke to them as he had been instructed. [7]"What are you talking about?" the brothers responded. "We are your servants and would never do such a thing! [8]Didn't we return the money we found in our sacks? We brought it back all the way from the land of Canaan. Why would we steal silver or gold from your master's house? [9]If you find his cup with any one of us, let that man die. And all the rest of us, my lord, will be your slaves."

[10]"That's fair," the man replied. "But only the one who stole the cup will be my slave. The rest of you may go free."

[11]They all quickly took their sacks from the backs of their donkeys and opened them. [12]The palace manager searched the brothers' sacks, from the oldest to the youngest. And the cup was found in Benjamin's sack! [13]When the brothers saw this, they tore their clothing in despair. Then they loaded their donkeys again and returned to the city.

[14]Joseph was still in his palace when Judah and his brothers arrived, and they fell to the ground before him. [15]"What have you done?" Joseph demanded. "Don't you know that a man like me can predict the future?"

[16]Judah answered, "Oh, my lord, what can we say to you? How can we explain this? How can we prove our innocence? God is punishing us for our sins. My lord, we have all returned to be your slaves—all of us, not just our brother who had your cup in his sack."

[17]"No," Joseph said. "I would never do such a thing! Only the man who stole the cup will be my slave. The rest of you may go back to your father in peace."

JUDAH SPEAKS FOR HIS BROTHERS

[18]Then Judah stepped forward and said, "Please, my lord, let your servant say just one word to you. Please, do not be angry with me, even though you are as powerful as Pharaoh himself.

[19]"My lord, previously you asked us, your servants, 'Do you have a father or a brother?' [20]And we responded, 'Yes, my lord, we have a father who is an old man, and his youngest son is a child of his old age. His full brother is dead, and he alone is left of his mother's children, and his father loves him very much.'

[21]"And you said to us, 'Bring him here so I can see him with my own eyes.' [22]But we said to you, 'My lord, the boy cannot leave his father, for his father would die.' [23]But you told us, 'Unless your youngest brother comes with you, you will never see my face again.'

[24]"So we returned to your servant, our father, and told him what you had said. [25]Later, when he said, 'Go back again and buy us more food,' [26]we replied, 'We can't go unless you let our youngest brother go with us. We'll never get to see the man's face unless our youngest brother is with us.'

[27]"Then my father said to us, 'As you know, my wife had two sons, [28]and one of them went away and never returned. Doubtless he was torn to pieces by some wild animal. I have never seen him since. [29]Now if you take his brother away from me, and any harm comes to him, you will send this grieving, white-haired man to his grave.*'

[30]"And now, my lord, I cannot go back to my father without the boy. Our father's life is bound up in the boy's life. [31]If he sees that the boy is not with us, our father will die. We, your servants, will indeed be responsible for sending that grieving, white-haired man to his grave. [32]My lord, I guaranteed to my father that I would take care of the boy. I told him, 'If I don't bring him back to you, I will bear the blame forever.' [33]So please, my lord, let me stay here as a slave instead of the boy, and let the boy return with his brothers. [34]For how can I return to my father if the boy is not with me? I couldn't bear to see the anguish this would cause my father!"

44:5 As in Greek version; Hebrew lacks this phrase.
44:29 Hebrew to Sheol; also in 44:31.

JOSEPH REVEALS HIS IDENTITY

45 Joseph could stand it no longer. There were many people in the room, and he said to his attendants, "Out, all of you!" So he was alone with his brothers when he told them who he was. ²Then he broke down and wept. He wept so loudly the Egyptians could hear him, and word of it quickly carried to Pharaoh's palace.

³"I am Joseph!" he said to his brothers. "Is my father still alive?" But his brothers were speechless! They were stunned to realize that Joseph was standing there in front of them. ⁴"Please, come closer," he said to them. So they came closer. And he said again, "I am Joseph, your brother, whom you sold into slavery in Egypt. ⁵But don't be upset, and don't be angry with yourselves for selling me to this place. It was God who sent me here ahead of you to preserve your lives. ⁶This famine that has ravaged the land for two years will last five more years, and there will be neither plowing nor harvesting. ⁷God has sent me ahead of you to keep you and your families alive and to preserve many survivors.* ⁸So it was God who sent me here, not you! And he is the one who made me an adviser* to Pharaoh—the manager of his entire palace and the governor of all Egypt.

⁹"Now hurry back to my father and tell him, 'This is what your son Joseph says: God has made me master over all the land of Egypt. So come down to me immediately! ¹⁰You can live in the region of Goshen, where you can be near me with all your children and grandchildren, your flocks and herds, and everything you own. ¹¹I will take care of you there, for there are still five years of famine ahead of us. Otherwise you, your household, and all your animals will starve.'"

¹²Then Joseph added, "Look! You can see for yourselves, and so can my brother Benjamin, that I really am Joseph! ¹³Go tell my father of my honored position here in Egypt. Describe for him everything you have seen, and then bring my father here quickly." ¹⁴Weeping with joy, he embraced Benjamin, and Benjamin did the same. ¹⁵Then Joseph kissed each of his brothers and wept over them, and after that they began talking freely with him.

PHARAOH INVITES JACOB TO EGYPT

¹⁶The news soon reached Pharaoh's palace: "Joseph's brothers have arrived!" Pharaoh and his officials were all delighted to hear this.

¹⁷Pharaoh said to Joseph, "Tell your brothers, 'This is what you must do: Load your pack animals, and hurry back to the land of Canaan. ¹⁸Then get your father and all of your families, and return here to me. I will give you the very best land in Egypt, and you will eat from the best that the land produces.'"

¹⁹Then Pharaoh said to Joseph, "Tell your brothers, 'Take wagons from the land of Egypt to carry your little children and your wives, and bring your father here. ²⁰Don't worry about your personal belongings, for the best of all the land of Egypt is yours.'"

²¹So the sons of Jacob* did as they were told. Joseph provided them with wagons, as Pharaoh had commanded, and he gave them supplies for the journey. ²²And he gave each of them new clothes—but to Benjamin he gave five changes of clothes and 300 pieces* of silver. ²³He also sent his father ten male donkeys loaded with the finest products of Egypt, and ten female donkeys loaded with grain and bread and other supplies he would need on his journey.

²⁴So Joseph sent his brothers off, and as they left, he called after them, "Don't quarrel about all this along the way!" ²⁵And they left Egypt and returned to their father, Jacob, in the land of Canaan.

²⁶"Joseph is still alive!" they told him. "And he is governor of all the land of Egypt!" Jacob was stunned at the news—he couldn't believe it. ²⁷But when they repeated to Jacob everything Joseph had told them, and when he saw the wagons Joseph had sent to carry him, their father's spirits revived.

²⁸Then Jacob exclaimed, "It must be true! My son Joseph is alive! I must go and see him before I die."

JACOB'S JOURNEY TO EGYPT

46 So Jacob* set out for Egypt with all his possessions. And when he came to Beersheba, he offered sacrifices to the God of his father, Isaac. ²During the night God spoke to him in a vision. "Jacob! Jacob!" he called.

"Here I am," Jacob replied.

³"I am God,* the God of your father," the voice said. "Do not be afraid to go down to Egypt, for there I will make your family into a great nation. ⁴I will go with you down to Egypt, and I will bring you back again. You will die in Egypt, but Joseph will be with you to close your eyes."

⁵So Jacob left Beersheba, and his sons took him to Egypt. They carried him and their little ones and their wives in the wagons Pharaoh had provided for them. ⁶They also took all their livestock and all the personal belongings they had acquired in the land of Canaan. So Jacob and his entire family went to Egypt—⁷sons and grandsons, daughters and granddaughters—all his descendants.

⁸These are the names of the descendants of Israel—the sons of Jacob—who went to Egypt:

Reuben was Jacob's oldest son. ⁹The sons of Reuben were Hanoch, Pallu, Hezron, and Carmi.

45:7 Or *and to save you with an extraordinary rescue.* The meaning of the Hebrew is uncertain. **45:8** Hebrew *a father.*
45:21 Hebrew *Israel;* also in 45:28. See note on 35:21.
45:22 Hebrew *300 [shekels],* about 7.5 pounds or 3.4 kilograms in weight. **46:1** Hebrew *Israel;* also in 46:29, 30. See note on 35:21.
46:3 Hebrew *I am El.*

¹⁰ The sons of Simeon were Jemuel, Jamin, Ohad, Jakin, Zohar, and Shaul. (Shaul's mother was a Canaanite woman.)

¹¹ The sons of Levi were Gershon, Kohath, and Merari.

¹² The sons of Judah were Er, Onan, Shelah, Perez, and Zerah (though Er and Onan had died in the land of Canaan). The sons of Perez were Hezron and Hamul.

¹³ The sons of Issachar were Tola, Puah,* Jashub,* and Shimron.

¹⁴ The sons of Zebulun were Sered, Elon, and Jahleel.

¹⁵ These were the sons of Leah and Jacob who were born in Paddan-aram, in addition to their daughter, Dinah. The number of Jacob's descendants (male and female) through Leah was thirty-three.

¹⁶ The sons of Gad were Zephon,* Haggi, Shuni, Ezbon, Eri, Arodi, and Areli.

¹⁷ The sons of Asher were Imnah, Ishvah, Ishvi, and Beriah. Their sister was Serah. Beriah's sons were Heber and Malkiel.

¹⁸ These were the sons of Zilpah, the servant given to Leah by her father, Laban. The number of Jacob's descendants through Zilpah was sixteen.

¹⁹ The sons of Jacob's wife Rachel were Joseph and Benjamin.

²⁰ Joseph's sons, born in the land of Egypt, were Manasseh and Ephraim. Their mother was Asenath, daughter of Potiphera, the priest of On.*

²¹ Benjamin's sons were Bela, Beker, Ashbel, Gera, Naaman, Ehi, Rosh, Muppim, Huppim, and Ard.

²² These were the sons of Rachel and Jacob. The number of Jacob's descendants through Rachel was fourteen.

²³ The son of Dan was Hushim.

²⁴ The sons of Naphtali were Jahzeel, Guni, Jezer, and Shillem.

²⁵ These were the sons of Bilhah, the servant given to Rachel by her father, Laban. The number of Jacob's descendants through Bilhah was seven.

²⁶ The total number of Jacob's direct descendants who went with him to Egypt, not counting his sons' wives, was sixty-six. ²⁷ In addition, Joseph had two sons* who were born in Egypt. So altogether, there were seventy* members of Jacob's family in the land of Egypt.

JACOB'S FAMILY ARRIVES IN GOSHEN

²⁸ As they neared their destination, Jacob sent Judah ahead to meet Joseph and get directions to the region of Goshen. And when they finally arrived there, ²⁹ Joseph prepared his chariot and traveled to Goshen to meet his father, Jacob. When Joseph arrived, he embraced his father and wept, holding him for a long time. ³⁰ Finally, Jacob said to Joseph, "Now I am ready to die, since I have seen your face again and know you are still alive."

³¹ And Joseph said to his brothers and to his father's entire family, "I will go to Pharaoh and tell him, 'My brothers and my father's entire family have come to me from the land of Canaan. ³² These men are shepherds, and they raise livestock. They have brought with them their flocks and herds and everything they own.'"

³³ Then he said, "When Pharaoh calls for you and asks you about your occupation, ³⁴ you must tell him, 'We, your servants, have raised livestock all our lives, as our ancestors have always done.' When you tell him this, he will let you live here in the region of Goshen, for the Egyptians despise shepherds."

JACOB BLESSES PHARAOH

47 Then Joseph went to see Pharaoh and told him, "My father and my brothers have arrived from the land of Canaan. They have come with all their flocks and herds and possessions, and they are now in the region of Goshen." ² Joseph took five of his brothers with him and presented them to Pharaoh. ³ And Pharaoh asked the brothers, "What is your occupation?"

They replied, "We, your servants, are shepherds, just like our ancestors. ⁴ We have come to live here in Egypt for a while, for there is no pasture for our flocks in Canaan. The famine is very severe there. So please, we request permission to live in the region of Goshen."

⁵ Then Pharaoh said to Joseph, "Now that your father and brothers have joined you here, ⁶ choose any place in the entire land of Egypt for them to live. Give them the best land of Egypt. Let them live in the region of Goshen. And if any of them have special skills, put them in charge of my livestock, too."

⁷ Then Joseph brought in his father, Jacob, and presented him to Pharaoh. And Jacob blessed Pharaoh.

⁸ "How old are you?" Pharaoh asked him.

⁹ Jacob replied, "I have traveled this earth for 130 hard years. But my life has been short compared to the lives of my ancestors." ¹⁰ Then Jacob blessed Pharaoh again before leaving his court.

¹¹ So Joseph assigned the best land of Egypt— the region of Rameses—to his father and his brothers, and he settled them there, just as Pharaoh had commanded. ¹² And Joseph provided food for his father and his brothers in amounts

---

46:13a As in Syriac version and Samaritan Pentateuch (see also 1 Chr 7:1); Hebrew reads *Puvah*. 46:13b As in some Greek manuscripts and Samaritan Pentateuch (see also Num 26:24; 1 Chr 7:1); Hebrew reads *Iob*. 46:16 As in Greek version and Samaritan Pentateuch (see also Num 26:15); Hebrew reads *Ziphion*. 46:20 Greek version reads *of Heliopolis*. 46:27a Greek version reads *nine sons*, probably including Joseph's grandsons through Ephraim and Manasseh (see 1 Chr 7:14-20). 46:27b Greek version reads *seventy-five*; see note on Exod 1:5.

appropriate to the number of their dependents, including the smallest children.

JOSEPH'S LEADERSHIP IN THE FAMINE

[13] Meanwhile, the famine became so severe that all the food was used up, and people were starving throughout the lands of Egypt and Canaan. [14] By selling grain to the people, Joseph eventually collected all the money in Egypt and Canaan, and he put the money in Pharaoh's treasury. [15] When the people of Egypt and Canaan ran out of money, all the Egyptians came to Joseph. "Our money is gone!" they cried. "But please give us food, or we will die before your very eyes!"

[16] Joseph replied, "Since your money is gone, bring me your livestock. I will give you food in exchange for your livestock." [17] So they brought their livestock to Joseph in exchange for food. In exchange for their horses, flocks of sheep and goats, herds of cattle, and donkeys, Joseph provided them with food for another year.

[18] But that year ended, and the next year they came again and said, "We cannot hide the truth from you, my lord. Our money is gone, and all our livestock and cattle are yours. We have nothing left to give but our bodies and our land. [19] Why should we die before your very eyes? Buy us and our land in exchange for food; we offer our land and ourselves as slaves for Pharaoh. Just give us grain so we may live and not die, and so the land does not become empty and desolate."

[20] So Joseph bought all the land of Egypt for Pharaoh. All the Egyptians sold him their fields because the famine was so severe, and soon all the land belonged to Pharaoh. [21] As for the people, he made them all slaves,* from one end of Egypt to the other. [22] The only land he did not buy was the land belonging to the priests. They received an allotment of food directly from Pharaoh, so they didn't need to sell their land.

[23] Then Joseph said to the people, "Look, today I have bought you and your land for Pharaoh. I will provide you with seed so you can plant the fields. [24] Then when you harvest it, one-fifth of your crop will belong to Pharaoh. You may keep the remaining four-fifths as seed for your fields and as food for you, your households, and your little ones."

[25] "You have saved our lives!" they exclaimed. "May it please you, my lord, to let us be Pharaoh's servants." [26] Joseph then issued a decree still in effect in the land of Egypt, that Pharaoh should receive one-fifth of all the crops grown on his land. Only the land belonging to the priests was not given to Pharaoh.

[27] Meanwhile, the people of Israel settled in the region of Goshen in Egypt. There they acquired property, and they were fruitful, and their population grew rapidly. [28] Jacob lived for seventeen years after his arrival in Egypt, so he lived 147 years in all.

[29] As the time of his death drew near, Jacob* called for his son Joseph and said to him, "Please do me this favor. Put your hand under my thigh and swear that you will treat me with unfailing love by honoring this last request: Do not bury me in Egypt. [30] When I die, please take my body out of Egypt and bury me with my ancestors."

So Joseph promised, "I will do as you ask."

[31] "Swear that you will do it," Jacob insisted. So Joseph gave his oath, and Jacob bowed humbly at the head of his bed.*

JACOB BLESSES MANASSEH AND EPHRAIM

48 One day not long after this, word came to Joseph, "Your father is failing rapidly." So Joseph went to visit his father, and he took with him his two sons, Manasseh and Ephraim.

[2] When Joseph arrived, Jacob was told, "Your son Joseph has come to see you." So Jacob* gathered his strength and sat up in his bed.

[3] Jacob said to Joseph, "God Almighty* appeared to me at Luz in the land of Canaan and blessed me. [4] He said to me, 'I will make you fruitful, and I will multiply your descendants. I will make you a multitude of nations. And I will give this land of Canaan to your descendants* after you as an everlasting possession.'

[5] "Now I am claiming as my own sons these two boys of yours, Ephraim and Manasseh, who were born here in the land of Egypt before I arrived. They will be my sons, just as Reuben and Simeon are. [6] But any children born to you in the future will be your own, and they will inherit land within the territories of their brothers Ephraim and Manasseh.

[7] "Long ago, as I was returning from Paddan-aram,* Rachel died in the land of Canaan. We were still on the way, some distance from Ephrath (that is, Bethlehem). So with great sorrow I buried her there beside the road to Ephrath."

[8] Then Jacob looked over at the two boys. "Are these your sons?" he asked.

[9] "Yes," Joseph told him, "these are the sons God has given me here in Egypt."

And Jacob said, "Bring them closer to me, so I can bless them."

[10] Jacob was half blind because of his age and could hardly see. So Joseph brought the boys close to him, and Jacob kissed and embraced them. [11] Then Jacob said to Joseph, "I never thought I would see your face again, but now God has let me see your children, too!"

[12] Joseph moved the boys, who were at their grandfather's knees, and he bowed with his face to the ground. [13] Then he positioned the boys in

---

47:21 As in Greek version and Samaritan Pentateuch; Hebrew reads *he moved them all into the towns.* 47:29 Hebrew *Israel;* also in 47:31b. See note on 35:21. 47:31 Greek version reads *and Israel bowed in worship as he leaned on his staff.* Compare Heb 11:21. 48:2 Hebrew *Israel;* also in 48:8, 10, 11, 13, 14, 21. See note on 35:21. 48:3 Hebrew *El-Shaddai.* 48:4 Hebrew *seed;* also in 48:19. 48:7 Hebrew *Paddan,* referring to Paddan-aram; compare Gen 35:9.

front of Jacob. With his right hand he directed Ephraim toward Jacob's left hand, and with his left hand he put Manasseh at Jacob's right hand. ¹⁴But Jacob crossed his arms as he reached out to lay his hands on the boys' heads. He put his right hand on the head of Ephraim, though he was the younger boy, and his left hand on the head of Manasseh, though he was the firstborn. ¹⁵Then he blessed Joseph and said,

"May the God before whom my grandfather
    Abraham
  and my father, Isaac, walked—
the God who has been my shepherd
  all my life, to this very day,
¹⁶ the Angel who has redeemed me from
    all harm—
  may he bless these boys.
May they preserve my name
  and the names of Abraham and Isaac.
And may their descendants multiply
    greatly
  throughout the earth."

¹⁷But Joseph was upset when he saw that his father placed his right hand on Ephraim's head. So Joseph lifted it to move it from Ephraim's head to Manasseh's head. ¹⁸"No, my father," he said. "This one is the firstborn. Put your right hand on his head."

¹⁹But his father refused. "I know, my son; I know," he replied. "Manasseh will also become a great people, but his younger brother will become even greater. And his descendants will become a multitude of nations."

²⁰So Jacob blessed the boys that day with this blessing: "The people of Israel will use your names when they give a blessing. They will say, 'May God make you as prosperous as Ephraim and Manasseh.'" In this way, Jacob put Ephraim ahead of Manasseh.

²¹Then Jacob said to Joseph, "Look, I am about to die, but God will be with you and will take you back to Canaan, the land of your ancestors. ²²And beyond what I have given your brothers, I am giving you an extra portion of the land* that I took from the Amorites with my sword and bow."

JACOB'S LAST WORDS TO HIS SONS

49 Then Jacob called together all his sons and said, "Gather around me, and I will tell you what will happen to each of you in the days to come.

² "Come and listen, you sons of Jacob;
  listen to Israel, your father.

³ "Reuben, you are my firstborn, my strength,
  the child of my vigorous youth.
  You are first in rank and first in power.
⁴ But you are as unruly as a flood,
  and you will be first no longer.

For you went to bed with my wife;
  you defiled my marriage couch.

⁵ "Simeon and Levi are two of a kind;
  their weapons are instruments of
    violence.
⁶ May I never join in their meetings;
  may I never be a party to their plans.
For in their anger they murdered men,
  and they crippled oxen just for sport.
⁷ A curse on their anger, for it is fierce;
  a curse on their wrath, for it is cruel.
I will scatter them among the descendants
    of Jacob;
  I will disperse them throughout Israel.

⁸ "Judah, your brothers will praise you.
  You will grasp your enemies by the neck.
  All your relatives will bow before you.
⁹ Judah, my son, is a young lion
  that has finished eating its prey.
Like a lion he crouches and lies down;
  like a lioness—who dares to rouse him?
¹⁰ The scepter will not depart from Judah,
  nor the ruler's staff from his
    descendants,*
until the coming of the one to whom it
    belongs,*
  the one whom all nations will honor.
¹¹ He ties his foal to a grapevine,
  the colt of his donkey to a choice vine.
He washes his clothes in wine,
  his robes in the blood of grapes.
¹² His eyes are darker than wine,
  and his teeth are whiter than milk.

¹³ "Zebulun will settle by the seashore
  and will be a harbor for ships;
  his borders will extend to Sidon.

¹⁴ "Issachar is a sturdy donkey,
  resting between two saddlepacks.*
¹⁵ When he sees how good the countryside is
  and how pleasant the land,
he will bend his shoulder to the load
  and submit himself to hard labor.

¹⁶ "Dan will govern his people,
  like any other tribe in Israel.
¹⁷ Dan will be a snake beside the road,
  a poisonous viper along the path
that bites the horse's hooves
  so its rider is thrown off.
¹⁸ I trust in you for salvation, O LORD!

¹⁹ "Gad will be attacked by marauding bands,
  but he will attack them when they
    retreat.

48:22 Or *an extra ridge of land.* The meaning of the Hebrew is uncertain. 49:10a Hebrew *from between his feet.* 49:10b Or *until tribute is brought to him and the peoples obey;* traditionally rendered *until Shiloh comes.* 49:14 Or *sheepfolds,* or *hearths.*

20 "Asher will dine on rich foods
  and produce food fit for kings.

21 "Naphtali is a doe set free
  that bears beautiful fawns.

22 "Joseph is the foal of a wild donkey,
  the foal of a wild donkey at a spring—
  one of the wild donkeys on the ridge.*

23 Archers attacked him savagely;
  they shot at him and harassed him.

24 But his bow remained taut,
  and his arms were strengthened
by the hands of the Mighty One of Jacob,
  by the Shepherd, the Rock of Israel.

25 May the God of your father help you;
  may the Almighty bless you
with the blessings of the heavens above,
  and blessings of the watery depths below,
  and blessings of the breasts and womb.

26 May my fatherly blessings on you
  surpass the blessings of my ancestors,*
  reaching to the heights of the eternal hills.
May these blessings rest on the head of
  Joseph,
  who is a prince among his brothers.

27 "Benjamin is a ravenous wolf,
  devouring his enemies in the morning
  and dividing his plunder in the evening."

28 These are the twelve tribes of Israel, and this is what their father said as he told his sons good-bye. He blessed each one with an appropriate message.

JACOB'S DEATH AND BURIAL

29 Then Jacob instructed them, "Soon I will die and join my ancestors. Bury me with my father and grandfather in the cave in the field of Ephron the Hittite. 30 This is the cave in the field of Machpelah, near Mamre in Canaan, that Abraham bought from Ephron the Hittite as a permanent burial site. 31 There Abraham and his wife Sarah are buried. There Isaac and his wife, Rebekah, are buried. And there I buried Leah. 32 It is the plot of land and the cave that my grandfather Abraham bought from the Hittites."

33 When Jacob had finished this charge to his sons, he drew his feet into the bed, breathed his last, and joined his ancestors in death.

50 Joseph threw himself on his father and wept over him and kissed him. 2 Then Joseph told the physicians who served him to embalm his father's body; so Jacob* was embalmed. 3 The embalming process took the usual forty days. And the Egyptians mourned his death for seventy days.

4 When the period of mourning was over, Joseph approached Pharaoh's advisers and said, "Please do me this favor and speak to Pharaoh on my behalf. 5 Tell him that my father made me swear an oath. He said to me, 'Listen, I am about to die. Take my body back to the land of Canaan, and bury me in the tomb I prepared for myself.' So please allow me to go and bury my father. After his burial, I will return without delay."

6 Pharaoh agreed to Joseph's request. "Go and bury your father, as he made you promise," he said. 7 So Joseph went up to bury his father. He was accompanied by all of Pharaoh's officials, all the senior members of Pharaoh's household, and all the senior officers of Egypt. 8 Joseph also took his entire household and his brothers and their households. But they left their little children and flocks and herds in the land of Goshen. 9 A great number of chariots and charioteers accompanied Joseph.

10 When they arrived at the threshing floor of Atad, near the Jordan River, they held a very great and solemn memorial service, with a seven-day period of mourning for Joseph's father. 11 The local residents, the Canaanites, watched them mourning at the threshing floor of Atad. Then they renamed that place (which is near the Jordan) Abel-mizraim,* for they said, "This is a place of deep mourning for these Egyptians."

12 So Jacob's sons did as he had commanded them. 13 They carried his body to the land of Canaan and buried him in the cave in the field of Machpelah, near Mamre. This is the cave that Abraham had bought as a permanent burial site from Ephron the Hittite.

JOSEPH REASSURES HIS BROTHERS

14 After burying Jacob, Joseph returned to Egypt with his brothers and all who had accompanied him to his father's burial. 15 But now that their father was dead, Joseph's brothers became fearful. "Now Joseph will show his anger and pay us back for all the wrong we did to him," they said.

16 So they sent this message to Joseph: "Before your father died, he instructed us17 to say to you: 'Please forgive your brothers for the great wrong they did to you—for their sin in treating you so cruelly.' So we, the servants of the God of your father, beg you to forgive our sin." When Joseph received the message, he broke down and wept. 18 Then his brothers came and threw themselves down before Joseph. "Look, we are your slaves!" they said.

19 But Joseph replied, "Don't be afraid of me. Am I God, that I can punish you? 20 You intended to harm me, but God intended it all for good. He brought me to this position so I could save the lives of many people. 21 No, don't be afraid. I will continue to take care of you and your children." So he reassured them by speaking kindly to them.

49:22 Or *Joseph is a fruitful tree, / a fruitful tree beside a spring. / His branches reach over the wall.* The meaning of the Hebrew is uncertain.   49:26 Or *of the ancient mountains.*   50:2 Hebrew *Israel.* See note on 35:21.   50:11 *Abel-mizraim* means "mourning of the Egyptians."

THE DEATH OF JOSEPH

[22] So Joseph and his brothers and their families continued to live in Egypt. Joseph lived to the age of 110. [23] He lived to see three generations of descendants of his son Ephraim, and he lived to see the birth of the children of Manasseh's son Makir, whom he claimed as his own. *

[24] "Soon I will die," Joseph told his brothers, "but God will surely come to help you and lead you out of this land of Egypt. He will bring you back to the land he solemnly promised to give to Abraham, to Isaac, and to Jacob."

[25] Then Joseph made the sons of Israel swear an oath, and he said, "When God comes to help you and lead you back, you must take my bones with you." [26] So Joseph died at the age of 110. The Egyptians embalmed him, and his body was placed in a coffin in Egypt.

50:23 Hebrew *who were born on Joseph's knees.*

ARTICLES

THE PRIDE TEST

Genesis 37:1-11   ROBERT MORRIS

In the process of moving from our dreams to our destinies, we all go through tests. Joseph was 17 years old when he received his dream from God, but he did not enter his destiny until he was 30, and he did not see its complete fulfillment until he was in his 40s. Joseph was destined for great power and influence, but he had to endure a series of tests, the first of which was the *pride test.*

Joseph saw himself as better than others, especially his brothers. He was critical of them and gave their father a bad report about them (Genesis 37:2). Then Joseph had two dreams about being bowed down to, and he immediately bragged about the dreams to his brothers. Without a doubt, Joseph failed the pride test.

Any time we turn the conversation away from God and onto ourselves, it's bragging. Bragging is a sign of immaturity. The problem isn't your mouth, though—it's your heart (Matthew 12:34; 15:18). If pride is in your heart, it will come out of your mouth. Pride is rooted in insecurity and makes us feel like we have to tell everyone who we are, what we've done, and all the things we're going to do. Insecurity is always desperate for acceptance. Yet even Jesus was not always accepted. In fact, He was often rejected, even by His family and friends! No matter what, Jesus remained perfectly secure because He knew Who and Whose He was. If we want to overcome pride, we must learn to be content with who we are in God, not in what others think about us.

God gave Joseph a big dream at a young age for a reason—He knew the young man would not pass the pride test the first time. Thankfully, when God gives us a test, it's not "pass or fail." Instead, it's "pass or take again." You may have to take a test over and over again, but through God's grace, you will eventually pass it. God began rooting pride out of Joseph's heart when he was 17 so he would be ready to enter his destiny when he was 30.

If God has given you a big dream too, I encourage you to allow Him to begin working in your heart today so you can step into your destiny at the right time. ▲

THE PIT TEST

Genesis 37:12-24   ROBERT MORRIS

Many people never fulfill the destiny God has for them because their character is not ready to support it. Sometimes after receiving our dreams, we find ourselves in the same position as Joseph—in a pit.

Although they discussed killing him, Joseph's brothers decided to "throw him into this empty cistern here in the wilderness. Then he'll die without our laying a hand on him" (Genesis 37:22). The cistern was a deep, dry pit. Joseph had no food, no water, and no way to escape. I'm sure this pit was the last place he expected to be after having such incredible dreams, and Joseph probably asked himself the same questions we ask ourselves when we are undergoing the *pit test.*

1. How did I get in this position?
   Joseph's brothers hated him, but did he ever consider their reasons? Did he ever wonder,

Does the way I talk about my dreams bother my brothers? We live in a blame-filled society where personal responsibility is frequently avoided. For example, I know people who go from one financial pit to another, yet they never consider that they're robbing God of the tithe. They are under giving and overspending, but they think they are in the pit for reasons other than poor financial stewardship. We must learn to ask, *Have I done anything to contribute to this problem?* and then honestly answer the question.

2. What is God doing in my life through the pit?
Every time you're in a pit, Satan, the accuser, will show up to condemn you by saying,

"You're just a bad person, worse than everyone else, and you'll never do anything for God or accomplish anything." We must not listen to the enemy's perspective. Instead, we must remind ourselves that God sent Jesus to save us from condemnation (John 3:17). God never condemns us, but He does convict us of what we have done wrong.

3. What is the purpose of the pit?
The purpose of every pit is to get us to cry out to God. You can't do anything on your own; you need God for every breath. If you're in a pit, I encourage you to say, "God, I need You!" He will deliver you and restore you when you trust in Him. ▲

THE PALACE TEST
Genesis 39:1-6   ROBERT MORRIS

Instead of dying in the pit, Joseph was sold to slave traders, taken to Egypt, and bought by Potiphar, Pharaoh's captain of the guard. Genesis 39:2 says, "The LORD was with Joseph, so he succeeded in everything he did ... in the home of his Egyptian master." The *palace test* is a test of stewardship, and Joseph passed it because he was faithful even in the midst of difficult circumstances.

God wants to bless you. His favor is available to everyone, and there are four simple keys to living in it.

1. The presence of the Lord
God wants you to prosper and succeed (see Genesis 26:12-13; Deuteronomy 29:9; 2 Kings 18:7). The Hebrew word for prospering means 'to push forward,' and the Greek equivalent means 'to help along the road.' In other words, if you help someone along the road or push them forward, then you prosper them. Do you want God to push you forward? The key is for Him to be present with you. God prospers and succeeds in everything He does, so if He is with you, then you're going to be successful too.

Potiphar didn't know the Lord, but he promoted Joseph because he recognized that God was with him. The palace test examines if you can serve others—even

unbelievers—well. If you cannot have the right attitude, you'll never move forward to your destiny.

2. Obedience
Most of us don't like the word *obedience* unless it refers to others obeying us. However, God walks with obedient servants (see Deuteronomy 11:26-28; Job 36:11-12; Isaiah 1:19-20). This is not a matter of our salvation; we are saved by grace through faith. However, if we want to be blessed in this life, we must obey God. Obedience is the key to His presence (Psalm 51:11-12).

3. Faith
Faith produces obedience in our lives. If you believe God is going to reward you for doing the right thing, then you do it (see Exodus 19:5; Ephesians 6:1-3). Joseph was promoted everywhere he went because no matter whom he worked for, he worked first for God.

4. Hearing the Word
If faith produces obedience, then what produces faith? The answer is hearing the Word of God (Romans 10:17). The more you hear it, the more faith you have, and the more you will follow in obedience. The more you obey, the more you will experience God's manifest presence and succeed in life. Every believer has the ability to live in God's favor and blessing, and it begins with hearing His Word. ▲

THE PURITY TEST

Genesis 39:7-12

ROBERT MORRIS

Joseph had an opportunity to have an impure relationship with Potiphar's wife, but he chose to run away from temptation. The apostle Paul may have been thinking of Joseph when he wrote, "Run from sexual sin! No other sin so clearly affects the body as this one does. For sexual immorality is a sin against your own body" (1 Corinthians 6:18).

1. **Impurity begins in the eyes.**
Genesis 39:7 says, "Potiphar's wife soon began to look at him lustfully." She lusted after Joseph because she *looked* at him. If you don't want to commit sexual sin, train yourself not to look. Jesus said, "Anyone who even looks at a woman with lust has already committed adultery with her in his heart" (Matthew 5:28). By the way, lust is never love. If Potiphar's wife loved Joseph, she wouldn't have let him sit in prison for 13 years because of her lie.

2. **Impurity affects your family.**
Satan lies to us about lust. He tells us that as long as we don't cross the line physically, it won't affect our families. However, sin is an inward motivation that leads to an outward movement. If lust is in your heart, it *will* affect

your family. King David fell morally, and this weakness prevented him from helping his children when they fell (see 2 Samuel 11, 13).

3. **Impurity affects your faith.**
When God tells us not to do something, it's not because He doesn't want us to have fun. It's because He doesn't want our lives to be destroyed. Sexual immorality opens the doors to other sins, such as manipulation and deception. When you allow impurity to remain in your life, you learn to be so deceptive with God that you no longer feel convicted of your sin. You cannot walk in immorality *and* have intimacy with God.

4. **Impurity affects your future.**
Joseph was separated from his family and living as a slave in a foreign land. What did he have to lose by giving in to sexual temptation? Actually, he had everything to lose! There is only one person in the world who can hinder God's plan for your life—*you*. If Joseph had failed the *purity test*, his family, future, and destiny would have been jeopardized. Thankfully, God is gracious and offers forgiveness when we fail in this area, but we must confess our weakness and seek the Holy Spirit's help (1 John 1:9). ▲

THE PRISON TEST

Genesis 39:13-40:23

ROBERT MORRIS

Furious at Joseph's rejection of her advances, Potiphar's wife claimed he tried to assault her. Joseph passed the purity test, but instead of receiving a reward, he found himself in an even more difficult situation: prison. The *prison test* builds perseverance as God develops our character through our experiences. In Romans 5, the apostle Paul presents the formula for this character development:

1. **Problems and trials develop endurance (v. 3).**
Every person experiences trouble; it's part of living on this earth (John 16:33; James 1:2-3). We can either be discouraged or learn to endure. *Endure* means to wait with contentment. We may see only the battle, but we can choose to keep our hearts focused on God's promises.

2. **Endurance develops character (v. 4).**
The worst thing you can do for someone is to deliver him out of a trial through which God is working character into his life.

Joseph was a man of great ability, but his character needed time to grow. God's grace did not allow Joseph to enter his destiny before his character was strong enough to support it.

3. **Character strengthens hope (v. 4).**
Character is not only how we act; it's also how we *react*. Joseph did the right thing and suffered the wrong consequences. Rather than giving into self-pity, though, he kept his heart right before God. Hope says, *Even if my circumstances don't change, God loves me and is working in my life right now.*

4. **Hope produces appointments (v. 5).**
Paul says our hope "will not lead to disappointment." Instead, hope prepares us for divine appointments. Joseph's hope allowed him to be sensitive to the needs of others. He ministered to his fellow prisoners, one of whom eventually produced Joseph's appointment to get out of prison and step into his destiny. ▲

THE PROPHETIC TEST

Genesis 41:1-7

ROBERT MORRIS

Genesis 41 begins with Pharaoh's dreams, which set in motion the fulfillment of the prophetic word God spoke over Joseph's life. God has also spoken a specific word over your life. Like Joseph, it's our responsibility to obey and honor the Word of God as we pass the tests on the way to our destinies. God tests our faith with prophetic words, and He tests our character with His written Word.

In order to see your destiny fulfilled, you must do the following:

1. **Submit your word to His Word.**

   Paul writes, "Our knowledge is partial and incomplete, and even the gift of prophecy reveals only part of the whole picture!" (1 Corinthians 13:9). We don't know everything. Since we know only partially, we also prophesy only partially. Prophecy contains encouraging words from God that lead us to seek Him, but they're not the whole picture. We must submit prophecy to the perfect Word of God.

2. **Test your word.**

   There is always a human element in prophecy. God's Word must be the standard to which we hold up and test our words (Deuteronomy 13:1-3; 1 Corinthians 14:29). Never allow yourself to follow a prophecy that doesn't line up with the Bible.

3. **Hold on to your word.**

   God has a destiny for every person. He builds our character and faith by speaking to us and then allowing time to pass before He fulfills His word. If God has spoken something to you, then hold on to it and don't let go. Joseph held on to his word through slavery, accusations, and imprisonment. He passed the *prophetic test*, and 13 years later, he finally glimpsed the beginning of his destiny. ◢

THE PROSPERITY TEST

Genesis 41:25-36

ROBERT MORRIS

Every time we get paid or receive extra money, we take the *prosperity test*. Are we faithful with our finances, or do we waste them and then beg God for more? According to Matthew 6:21, our heart follows our money. As believers, we must ask ourselves, *Does money control me? Or do I control money?*

1. **Let God be first.**

   When God blesses you with extra money, do you tithe on it? Do you honor Him first? Joseph honored God with his firstfruits in everything he did, including naming his sons and setting apart the land of the priests for God (Genesis 41:50-52; 47:26). It takes faith to give the *first* 10 percent of what we have to God, but if we want to be blessed, we must put Him first.

2. **Learn to wait.**

   Joseph led the Egyptians to store up grain for *seven years* so they would have enough food to survive the coming years of famine. In today's world, many people are tempted by "get rich quick" schemes, but the Bible teaches us to wait and be faithful stewards of our resources. Setting a budget and sticking to it builds character and discipline, which are essential to fulfilling your destiny.

3. **Live below your means.**

   God wants you to be content. He doesn't want you to live stressed out and in debt. When you live above your means, you tell God *I'm not content with Your provision, and I'm not content with You. I'm going to figure out a way to get more.* Many people blame God for not blessing them when their actual problem lies in poor financial management. ◢

THE POWER TEST

Genesis 41:37-46

ROBERT MORRIS

Joseph was 30 years old when he interpreted Pharaoh's dreams and stepped into his destiny (although it would be years before he completely fulfilled it). He went to sleep as a slave and prisoner, but the next day he became a ruler over Egypt. How would Joseph handle such authority and responsibility? He would have to pass the *power test*.

Many people expect to be tested by adversity, and they easily pass the prison test. However, they often don't realize they'll also be tested by success. The power test is the first test we take as we step into God's destiny for our life, and it includes three important questions:

1. From where does power come?
   All power comes from God (Psalm 62:11; John 19:10-11). Satan tries to twist it into a selfish desire, but the original, pure desire for power comes from God. Power is for our own good, and its purpose is to help people. The power test recognizes that God's blessing and power are in our lives as we respond and do the right thing. God gave Joseph power so he could feed multitudes and bless people. Joseph understood this and used his power correctly.

2. To whom does power come?
   God gives power to the humble (James 4:10; 1 Peter 5:5-6). People are often humble when they begin something new, but after a while, they tend to lose some of their humility. Pride is ugly, and we need to remember the lower we put ourselves, the higher God puts us.

3. Why does God give power?
   God gives power to help people because He loves them (Acts 10:38). God has all the resources in the world and all the supply to meet all the demands. He is simply looking for humble stewards—you and me—to channel His resources and power. ▲

THE PURPOSE TEST

Genesis 45:3-8

ROBERT MORRIS

The seven abundant years had passed, and Egypt and all the surrounding lands were now two years into the seven years of famine. Joseph's brothers came to Egypt in desperate need of food, and they unknowingly knelt before the brother they had sold into slavery 20 years earlier. At the age of 39, Joseph finally realized God's purpose for his life—"to keep you and your families alive and to preserve many survivors" (Genesis 45:7).

Every person has a purpose. The *purpose test* examines if you will discover and step into God's purpose for your life, thereby fulfilling your destiny. Here are four keys to passing the purpose test:

1. Believe you have a purpose.
   Deep in our hearts, every person wonders, *What purpose does God have for me?* Ecclesiastes 3:1 assures us there is a season and a reason for everything God does. He had a specific purpose in mind when He designed you. God has a destiny for you, and you are the only person who can fulfill it.

2. Understand God is in control.
   You will experience setbacks and complications on the way to your destiny. Everyone does. Joseph went through many difficulties, but no matter what, he always believed God was in control. No one can derail your destiny except you. When God speaks His word, He will accomplish His purpose (Isaiah 55:10-11; Romans 8:28).

3. Discover your gift and your direction.
   God has given you a gift (Romans 12:4-8). You need to find out what this gift is so you can fulfill your destiny. Joseph had a dream, but he didn't know his purpose. However, he knew he had the gift of leadership. He led in Potiphar's house, in prison, and in the palace as Pharaoh's second-in-command. Many people say they will use their gifts when they get in the right position, but the way you get in the right position is to use your gifts. Remember, Joseph started in the pit. No matter where you are, you can start right now.

4. Determine your direction and be faithful.
   Joseph didn't know the specific details of his purpose for many years. He simply used his gift and followed God's leading. Begin moving in the direction God leads you today. His Word will direct your path (Psalm 119:105-112). Take one step at a time, be faithful, change to you'll find yourself operating in your calling. ▲

THE PARDON TEST

Genesis 50:15–21   ROBERT MORRIS

The *pardon test* is the test of forgiveness. Joseph's brothers were going to murder him, but they changed their minds and decided to sell him into slavery (Genesis 37:26–28). Joseph followed God throughout his difficulties, and God blessed and prospered him. In order to step into his destiny fully, though, Joseph had to forgive those who had wronged him. The same is true for us today.

The word *forgive* means to absolve or to release fully. Unforgiveness, on the other hand, is like drinking poison and hoping it hurts someone else. In reality, you are the one who is going to be hurt.

Here are three words to help you understand how to pardon or forgive:

1. **Release**

   After their father's death, Jacob's sons feared Joseph would finally seek revenge, so they tried to manipulate their brother. However, instead of holding on to unforgiveness, Joseph chose to let God vindicate him. Can you forgive someone who refuses to admit they're wrong or, even worse, continues with their hurtful behavior? Though it may be difficult, this model of release is throughout Scripture

(Leviticus 19:18; Romans 12:17–21). Remember, God is the *only* One who has the right to judge. Whenever you hold unforgiveness against someone, you make yourself the judge and jury and leave God out of the picture. Only by releasing unforgiveness can you free yourself from bondage and allow God to bring His perfect justice to the situation.

2. **Receive**

   The Bible ties forgiving others to God forgiving us. Many people don't believe God has completely forgiven them for their wrongdoings, so they cannot extend the same forgiveness to others. If you believe you must somehow earn God's forgiveness, then you'll make other people earn your forgiveness as well.

3. **Believe**

   Once you receive Jesus as your Savior, God removes your sin as far from you "as the east is from the west" (Psalm 103:12). You are forgiven—completely pardoned by the sacrifice of Jesus Christ. Because you have been pardoned, you can now pardon others. You *can* forgive. It doesn't matter what anyone has done to you. What you have done to God is worse, and He forgave you. ◢

EXODUS

JON HUNTZINGER, PHD

The book of Exodus follows Genesis in the Bible. It continues the story of God's promise to bless Abraham and the patriarchs (the founding fathers): Isaac, Jacob, and Joseph and their descendants. The word *exodus* means 'a mass departure of people.' In Exodus Abraham's descendants (the Israelites or the Hebrew people) escape from Egypt, where they lived for several hundred years after their ancestor Joseph. As with Genesis, Jewish tradition identifies Moses as the writer of Exodus. Several passages refer to Moses' writing activity, such as Exodus 17:14.

The book of Exodus comprises three major divisions:
— Chapters 1-18 record the circumstances of the Hebrew people in Egypt from the birth of Moses to their deliverance through the Red Sea and to their encampment at Mount Sinai.
— Chapters 19-24 recount the gift of God's words to the Israelites instructing them how to live in relationship with Him and with one another.
— Chapters 25-40 describe the building of the Tabernacle in which God makes Himself personally present among them. Then this section moves from Egypt, where the people live in ignorance and fear, to Mount Sinai, where God speaks to Moses and the people to give them knowledge about how to live with and worship Him once they are free from slavery.

Exodus tells many important stories:
— How Pharaoh's daughter found Moses in the Nile River
— About the ten signs (or plagues)
— How God parted the Red Sea, drowning the Egyptian army and saving the Hebrews
— Of the first Passover and the protection of the Hebrew people
— How God provided manna (bread-like food) to His people in the wilderness and took care of their needs
— How God gave His words at Mount Sinai
— About the building of the Tabernacle

— How the people disobeyed God and forged a golden calf to worship
— About the fear of all the changes the people experienced in their deliverance

Throughout Exodus, God is revealed as a God who saves His people:
— He does not permit the death angel to enter the Hebrews' houses.
— He provides manna for them in the wilderness.
— He delivers them from their ignorance by giving knowledge and wisdom at Mount Sinai.
— He gives them instructions for a building for worship, freeing them from the false worship they learned in Egypt.
— He gives His name to them, revealing Himself as "I Am Who I Am" (Exodus 3:14).

God does not want His people to know Him only by a title, such as "Creator" or "King" but *by His name*. And His name means that He exists and is a Person they can know and trust.

Exodus also shows that God is merciful. He is patient with His people even when they act with fear toward Him. God knows they need help to trust Him since they have been in slavery for a very long time, so He gives signs to help them trust what He is doing:
— He gives the sign of a leprous hand and turns a rod into a snake and back again to show the Hebrews His power and His desire to cleanse them of their past.
— He sends the plagues as signs of His power.
— He institutes Passover as a sign of communion with His people.
— He parts the Red Sea as a sign of new life.
— He sends the manna as a sign of His provision.
— He places the cloud and the fire to hover over the camp as signs of His presence with them.

From beginning to end, the book of Exodus is a book of signs describing who God is and what He is doing in the midst of His people.

THE ISRAELITES IN EGYPT

1 These are the names of the sons of Israel (that is, Jacob) who moved to Egypt with their father, each with his family: ² Reuben, Simeon, Levi, Judah, ³ Issachar, Zebulun, Benjamin, ⁴ Dan, Naphtali, Gad, and Asher. ⁵ In all, Jacob had seventy* descendants in Egypt, including Joseph, who was already there.

⁶ In time, Joseph and all of his brothers died, ending that entire generation. ⁷ But their descendants, the Israelites, had many children and grandchildren. In fact, they multiplied so greatly that they became extremely powerful and filled the land.

⁸ Eventually, a new king came to power in Egypt who knew nothing about Joseph or what he had done. ⁹ He said to his people, "Look, the people of Israel now outnumber us and are stronger than we are. ¹⁰ We must make a plan to keep them from growing even more. If we don't, and if war breaks out, they will join our enemies and fight against us. Then they will escape from the country.*"

¹¹ So the Egyptians made the Israelites their slaves. They appointed brutal slave drivers over them, hoping to wear them down with crushing labor. They forced them to build the cities of Pithom and Rameses as supply centers for the king. ¹² But the more the Egyptians oppressed them, the more the Israelites multiplied and spread, and the more alarmed the Egyptians became. ¹³ So the Egyptians worked the people of Israel without mercy. ¹⁴ They made their lives bitter, forcing them to mix mortar and make bricks and do all the work in the fields. They were ruthless in all their demands.

¹⁵ Then Pharaoh, the king of Egypt, gave this order to the Hebrew midwives, Shiphrah and Puah: ¹⁶ "When you help the Hebrew women as they give birth, watch as they deliver.* If the baby is a boy, kill him; if it is a girl, let her live." ¹⁷ But because the midwives feared God, they refused to obey the king's orders. They allowed the boys to live, too.

¹⁸ So the king of Egypt called for the midwives. "Why have you done this?" he demanded. "Why have you allowed the boys to live?"

¹⁹ "The Hebrew women are not like the Egyptian women," the midwives replied. "They are more vigorous and have their babies so quickly that we cannot get there in time."

²⁰ So God was good to the midwives, and the Israelites continued to multiply, growing more and more powerful. ²¹ And because the midwives feared God, he gave them families of their own.

²² Then Pharaoh gave this order to all his people: "Throw every newborn Hebrew boy into the Nile River. But you may let the girls live."

THE BIRTH OF MOSES

2 About this time, a man and woman from the tribe of Levi got married. ² The woman became pregnant and gave birth to a son. She saw that he was a special baby and kept him hidden for three months. ³ But when she could no longer hide him, she got a basket made of papyrus reeds and waterproofed it with tar and pitch. She put the baby in the basket and laid it among the reeds along the bank of the Nile River. ⁴ The baby's sister then stood at a distance, watching to see what would happen to him.

⁵ Soon Pharaoh's daughter came down to bathe in the river, and her attendants walked along the riverbank. When the princess saw the basket among the reeds, she sent her maid to get it for her. ⁶ When the princess opened it, she saw the baby. The little boy was crying, and she felt sorry for him. "This must be one of the Hebrew children," she said.

⁷ Then the baby's sister approached the princess. "Should I go and find one of the Hebrew women to nurse the baby for you?" she asked.

⁸ "Yes, do!" the princess replied. So the girl went and called the baby's mother.

⁹ "Take this baby and nurse him for me," the princess told the baby's mother. "I will pay you for your help." So the woman took her baby home and nursed him.

¹⁰ Later, when the boy was older, his mother brought him back to Pharaoh's daughter, who adopted him as her own son. The princess named him Moses,* for she explained, "I lifted him out of the water."

MOSES ESCAPES TO MIDIAN

¹¹ Many years later, when Moses had grown up, he went out to visit his own people, the Hebrews, and he saw how hard they were forced to work. During his visit, he saw an Egyptian beating one of his fellow Hebrews. ¹² After looking in all directions to make sure no one was watching, Moses killed the Egyptian and hid the body in the sand.

¹³ The next day, when Moses went out to visit his people again, he saw two Hebrew men fighting. "Why are you beating up your friend?" Moses said to the one who had started the fight.

¹⁴ The man replied, "Who appointed you to be our prince and judge? Are you going to kill me as you killed that Egyptian yesterday?"

Then Moses was afraid, thinking, "Everyone knows what I did." ¹⁵ And sure enough, Pharaoh heard what had happened, and he tried to kill Moses. But Moses fled from Pharaoh and went to live in the land of Midian.

When Moses arrived in Midian, he sat down beside a well. ¹⁶ Now the priest of Midian had seven daughters who came as usual to draw water and fill the water troughs for their father's flocks. ¹⁷ But some other shepherds came and

---

1:5 Dead Sea Scrolls and Greek version read *seventy-five*; see notes on Gen 46:27. 1:10 Or *will take the country.* 1:16 Hebrew *look upon the two stones*; perhaps the reference is to a birthstool. 2:10 *Moses* sounds like a Hebrew term that means "to lift out."

chased them away. So Moses jumped up and rescued the girls from the shepherds. Then he drew water for their flocks.

[18]When the girls returned to Reuel, their father, he asked, "Why are you back so soon today?"

[19]"An Egyptian rescued us from the shepherds," they answered. "And then he drew water for us and watered our flocks."

[20]"Then where is he?" their father asked. "Why did you leave him there? Invite him to come and eat with us."

[21]Moses accepted the invitation, and he settled there with him. In time, Reuel gave Moses his daughter Zipporah to be his wife. [22]Later she gave birth to a son, and Moses named him Gershom,* for he explained, "I have been a foreigner in a foreign land."

[23]Years passed, and the king of Egypt died. But the Israelites continued to groan under their burden of slavery. They cried out for help, and their cry rose up to God. [24]God heard their groaning, and he remembered his covenant promise to Abraham, Isaac, and Jacob. [25]He looked down on the people of Israel and knew it was time to act.*

MOSES AND THE BURNING BUSH

3 One day Moses was tending the flock of his father-in-law, Jethro,* the priest of Midian. He led the flock far into the wilderness and came to Sinai,* the mountain of God. [2]There the angel of the LORD appeared to him in a blazing fire from the middle of a bush. Moses stared in amazement. Though the bush was engulfed in flames, it didn't burn up. [3]"This is amazing," Moses said to himself. "Why isn't that bush burning up? I must go see it."

[4]When the LORD saw Moses coming to take a closer look, God called to him from the middle of the bush, "Moses! Moses!"

"Here I am!" Moses replied.

[5]"Do not come any closer," the LORD warned. "Take off your sandals, for you are standing on holy ground. [6]I am the God of your father*—the God of Abraham, the God of Isaac, and the God of Jacob." When Moses heard this, he covered his face because he was afraid to look at God.

[7]Then the LORD told him, "I have certainly seen the oppression of my people in Egypt. I have heard their cries of distress because of their harsh slave drivers. Yes, I am aware of their suffering. [8]So I have come down to rescue them from the power of the Egyptians and lead them out of Egypt into their own fertile and spacious land. It is a land flowing with milk and honey— the land where the Canaanites, Hittites, Amorites, Perizzites, Hivites, and Jebusites now live. [9]Look! The cry of the people of Israel has reached me, and I have seen how harshly the Egyptians abuse them. [10]Now go, for I am sending you to Pharaoh. You must lead my people Israel out of Egypt."

WHAT'S SO IMPORTANT ABOUT WORSHIP?
Exodus 3:1-5   ROBERT MORRIS

Every time I enter into God's presence through worship, He speaks. In fact, I've never entered His presence without hearing Him speak to my heart. I want you to experience this too. Here are three simple words to help you as you enter into God's presence through worship:

1. Look
   When you begin worshipping, turn away from every distraction and look at God. At Gateway Church, we sing songs about God's greatness, goodness, and glory. We focus on His attributes because worship is a time for us to look at God—not just glance in His direction but also *focus on Him*. When you become a believer, the veil over your spiritual eyes is removed, and you can see Jesus clearly (2 Corinthians 3:18).

2. Listen
   When my children were young, I used to say, "Look at me!" before giving them instructions. I knew if they weren't looking at me, they weren't *listening* to me. God waited to speak until He knew Moses was listening. All of us want to hear God, but many of us aren't willing to give Him our undivided attention. God wants to speak to you, so spend time in His presence and practice listening for His voice.

3. Learn
   When God told Moses to remove his sandals (Exodus 3:5), Moses learned that *anything* God touches is holy. Psalm 103:7 says God "revealed his character to Moses," and as a result, this man who was "more humble than any other person on earth" (Numbers 12:3) wrote the first five books of the Bible. Today, many people expect their pastor to meet with God as their representative, but God says, "I want to meet directly with *you*."

[11]But Moses protested to God, "Who am I to appear before Pharaoh? Who am I to lead the people of Israel out of Egypt?"

[12]God answered, "I will be with you. And this is your sign that I am the one who has sent you: When you have brought the people out of Egypt, you will worship God at this very mountain."

[13]But Moses protested, "If I go to the people of Israel and tell them, 'The God of your ancestors has sent me to you,' they will ask me, 'What is his name?' Then what should I tell them?"

2:22 Gershom sounds like a Hebrew term that means "a foreigner there." 2:25 Or and acknowledged his obligation to help them. 3:1a Moses' father-in-law went by two names, Jethro and Reuel. 3:1b Hebrew Horeb, another name for Sinai. 3:6 Greek version reads your fathers.

THE FOUNDATIONS OF WORSHIP
Exodus 3:1-12   JACK HAYFORD

Worship is the starting place for God's movement. When Moses approaches the burning bush, he is an 80-year-old shepherd who has spent the last 40 years hiding in the wilderness. Once a prince of Egypt, he had to flee for his life after killing an Egyptian who was beating a Hebrew slave. Moses tried using his own strength to help his people, but it ended in disaster. From the burning bush, God now says He will rescue the Hebrews and use Moses to "lead my people Israel out of Egypt" (Exodus 3:10). God chooses people as the channels to accomplish His purposes, but He is their power source.

Worship is a fire that won't wear you out or burn you up. When Moses meets God, he encounters a fire that doesn't consume the bush. The fire doesn't destroy or eat away life. God calls Moses to draw near and stand on His lasting work rather than on Moses' own efforts. Our efforts will wear us out and burn us up. God's fire accomplishes His objectives without destroying either the bush or the man.

Worship gets you to the place God wants to take you. Moses becomes the world's greatest emancipator, a prolific author and songwriter, and the architect of the Tabernacle—God's dwelling place on earth. Worship is the key that unlocks your creative potential and intended destiny.

---

[14] God replied to Moses, "I AM WHO I AM.* Say this to the people of Israel: I AM has sent me to you." [15] God also said to Moses, "Say this to the people of Israel: Yahweh,* the God of your ancestors—the God of Abraham, the God of Isaac, and the God of Jacob—has sent me to you.

This is my eternal name,
    my name to remember for all generations.

[16] "Now go and call together all the elders of Israel. Tell them, 'Yahweh, the God of your ancestors—the God of Abraham, Isaac, and Jacob—has appeared to me. He told me, "I have been watching closely, and I see how the Egyptians are treating you. [17] I have promised to rescue you from your oppression in Egypt. I will lead you to a land flowing with milk and honey—the land where the Canaanites, Hittites, Amorites, Perizzites, Hivites, and Jebusites now live."'

[18] "The elders of Israel will accept your message. Then you and the elders must go to the king of Egypt and tell him, 'The LORD, the God of the Hebrews, has met with us. So please let us take a three-day journey into the wilderness to offer sacrifices to the LORD, our God.'

[19] "But I know that the king of Egypt will not let you go unless a mighty hand forces him.* [20] So I will raise my hand and strike the Egyptians, performing all kinds of miracles among them. Then at last he will let you go. [21] And I will cause the Egyptians to look favorably on you. They will give you gifts when you go so you will not leave empty-handed. [22] Every Israelite woman will ask for articles of silver and gold and fine clothing from her Egyptian neighbors and from the foreign women in their houses. You will dress your sons and daughters with these, stripping the Egyptians of their wealth."

SIGNS OF THE LORD'S POWER

4 But Moses protested again, "What if they won't believe me or listen to me? What if they say, 'The LORD never appeared to you'?"

[2] Then the LORD asked him, "What is that in your hand?"

"A shepherd's staff," Moses replied.

[3] "Throw it down on the ground," the LORD told him. So Moses threw down the staff, and it turned into a snake! Moses jumped back.

[4] Then the LORD told him, "Reach out and grab its tail." So Moses reached out and grabbed it, and it turned back into a shepherd's staff in his hand.

[5] "Perform this sign," the LORD told him. "Then they will believe that the LORD, the God of their ancestors—the God of Abraham, the God of Isaac, and the God of Jacob—really has appeared to you."

[6] Then the LORD said to Moses, "Now put your hand inside your cloak." So Moses put his hand inside his cloak, and when he took it out again, his hand was white as snow with a severe skin disease.* [7] "Now put your hand back into your cloak," the LORD said. So Moses put his hand back in, and when he took it out again, it was as healthy as the rest of his body.

[8] The LORD said to Moses, "If they do not believe you and are not convinced by the first miraculous sign, they will be convinced by the second sign. [9] And if they don't believe you or listen to you even after these two signs, then take some water from the Nile River and pour it out on the dry ground. When you do, the water from the Nile will turn to blood on the ground."

[10] But Moses pleaded with the LORD, "O Lord, I'm not very good with words. I never have been, and I'm not now, even though you have spoken to me. I get tongue-tied, and my words get tangled."

[11] Then the LORD asked Moses, "Who makes a person's mouth? Who decides whether people speak or do not speak, hear or do not hear, see or do not see? Is it not I, the LORD? [12] Now go! I

3:14 Or I WILL BE WHAT I WILL BE. · 3:15 *Yahweh* (also in 3:16) is a transliteration of the proper name *YHWH* that is sometimes rendered "Jehovah"; in this translation it is usually rendered "the LORD" (note the use of small capitals). 3:19 As in Greek and Latin versions; Hebrew reads *will not let you go, not by a mighty hand.* 4:6 Or *with leprosy.* The Hebrew word used here can describe various skin diseases.

will be with you as you speak, and I will instruct you in what to say."

[13] But Moses again pleaded, "Lord, please! Send anyone else."

[14] Then the LORD became angry with Moses. "All right," he said. "What about your brother, Aaron the Levite? I know he speaks well. And look! He is on his way to meet you now. He will be delighted to see you. [15] Talk to him, and put the words in his mouth. I will be with both of you as you speak, and I will instruct you both in what to do. [16] Aaron will be your spokesman to the people. He will be your mouthpiece, and you will stand in the place of God for him, telling him what to say. [17] And take your shepherd's staff with you, and use it to perform the miraculous signs I have shown you."

MOSES RETURNS TO EGYPT

[18] So Moses went back home to Jethro, his father-in-law. "Please let me return to my relatives in Egypt," Moses said. "I don't even know if they are still alive."

"Go in peace," Jethro replied.

[19] Before Moses left Midian, the LORD said to him, "Return to Egypt, for all those who wanted to kill you have died."

[20] So Moses took his wife and sons, put them on a donkey, and headed back to the land of Egypt. In his hand he carried the staff of God.

[21] And the LORD told Moses, "When you arrive back in Egypt, go to Pharaoh and perform all the miracles I have empowered you to do. But I will harden his heart so he will refuse to let the people go. [22] Then you will tell him, 'This is what the LORD says: Israel is my firstborn son. [23] I commanded you, "Let my son go, so he can worship me." But since you have refused, I will now kill your firstborn son!'"

[24] On the way to Egypt, at a place where Moses and his family had stopped for the night, the LORD confronted him and was about to kill him. [25] But Moses' wife, Zipporah, took a flint knife and circumcised her son. She touched his feet* with the foreskin and said, "Now you are a bridegroom of blood to me." [26] (When she said "a bridegroom of blood," she was referring to the circumcision.) After that, the LORD left him alone.

[27] Now the LORD had said to Aaron, "Go out into the wilderness to meet Moses." So Aaron went and met Moses at the mountain of God, and he embraced him. [28] Moses then told Aaron everything the LORD had commanded him to say. And he told him about the miraculous signs the LORD had commanded him to perform.

[29] Then Moses and Aaron returned to Egypt and called all the elders of Israel together. [30] Aaron told them everything the LORD had told Moses, and Moses performed the miraculous signs as they watched. [31] Then the people of Israel were convinced that the LORD had sent Moses and Aaron. When they heard that the LORD was concerned about them and had seen their misery, they bowed down and worshiped.

MOSES AND AARON SPEAK TO PHARAOH

5 After this presentation to Israel's leaders, Moses and Aaron went and spoke to Pharaoh. They told him, "This is what the LORD, the God of Israel, says: Let my people go so they may hold a festival in my honor in the wilderness."

[2] "Is that so?" retorted Pharaoh. "And who is the LORD? Why should I listen to him and let Israel go? I don't know the LORD, and I will not let Israel go."

[3] But Aaron and Moses persisted. "The God of the Hebrews has met with us," they declared. "So let us take a three-day journey into the wilderness so we can offer sacrifices to the LORD our God. If we don't, he will kill us with a plague or with the sword."

[4] Pharaoh replied, "Moses and Aaron, why are you distracting the people from their tasks? Get back to work! [5] Look, there are many of your people in the land, and you are stopping them from their work."

MAKING BRICKS WITHOUT STRAW

[6] That same day Pharaoh sent this order to the Egyptian slave drivers and the Israelite foremen: [7] "Do not supply any more straw for making bricks. Make the people get it themselves! [8] But still require them to make the same number of bricks as before. Don't reduce the quota. They are lazy. That's why they are crying out, 'Let us go and offer sacrifices to our God.' [9] Load them down with more work. Make them sweat! That will teach them to listen to lies!"

[10] So the slave drivers and foremen went out and told the people: "This is what Pharaoh says: I will not provide any more straw for you. [11] Go and get it yourselves. Find it wherever you can. But you must produce just as many bricks as before!" [12] So the people scattered throughout the land of Egypt in search of stubble to use as straw.

[13] Meanwhile, the Egyptian slave drivers continued to push hard. "Meet your daily quota of bricks, just as you did when we provided you with straw!" they demanded. [14] Then they whipped the Israelite foremen they had put in charge of the work crews. "Why haven't you met your quotas either yesterday or today?" they demanded.

[15] So the Israelite foremen went to Pharaoh and pleaded with him. "Please don't treat your servants like this," they begged. [16] "We are given no straw, but the slave drivers still demand, 'Make bricks!' We are being beaten, but it isn't our fault! Your own people are to blame!"

[17] But Pharaoh shouted, "You're just lazy! Lazy! That's why you're saying, 'Let us go and offer sacrifices to the LORD.' [18] Now get back to work!

4:25 The Hebrew word for "feet" may refer here to the male sex organ.

No straw will be given to you, but you must still produce the full quota of bricks."

[19]The Israelite foremen could see that they were in serious trouble when they were told, "You must not reduce the number of bricks you make each day." [20]As they left Pharaoh's court, they confronted Moses and Aaron, who were waiting outside for them. [21]The foremen said to them, "May the LORD judge and punish you for making us stink before Pharaoh and his officials. You have put a sword into their hands, an excuse to kill us!"

[22]Then Moses went back to the LORD and protested, "Why have you brought all this trouble on your own people, Lord? Why did you send me? [23]Ever since I came to Pharaoh as your spokesman, he has been even more brutal to your people. And you have done nothing to rescue them!"

PROMISES OF DELIVERANCE

6 Then the LORD told Moses, "Now you will see what I will do to Pharaoh. When he feels the force of my strong hand, he will let the people go. In fact, he will force them to leave his land!"

[2]And God said to Moses, "I am Yahweh—'the LORD.'* [3]I appeared to Abraham, to Isaac, and to Jacob as El-Shaddai—'God Almighty'*—but I did not reveal my name, Yahweh, to them. [4]And I reaffirmed my covenant with them. Under its terms, I promised to give them the land of Canaan, where they were living as foreigners. [5]You can be sure that I have heard the groans of the people of Israel, who are now slaves to the Egyptians. And I am well aware of my covenant with them.

[6]"Therefore, say to the people of Israel: 'I am the LORD. I will free you from your oppression and will rescue you from your slavery in Egypt. I will redeem you with a powerful arm and great acts of judgment. [7]I will claim you as my own people, and I will be your God. Then you will know that I am the LORD your God who has freed you from your oppression in Egypt. [8]I will bring you into the land I swore to give to Abraham, Isaac, and Jacob. I will give it to you as your very own possession. I am the LORD!'"

[9]So Moses told the people of Israel what the LORD had said, but they refused to listen anymore. They had become too discouraged by the brutality of their slavery.

[10]Then the LORD said to Moses, [11]"Go back to Pharaoh, the king of Egypt, and tell him to let the people of Israel leave his country."

[12]"But LORD!" Moses objected. "My own people won't listen to me anymore. How can I expect Pharaoh to listen? I'm such a clumsy speaker!*"

[13]But the LORD spoke to Moses and Aaron and gave them orders for the Israelites and for Pharaoh, the king of Egypt. The LORD commanded Moses and Aaron to lead the people of Israel out of Egypt.

THE ANCESTORS OF MOSES AND AARON

[14]These are the ancestors of some of the clans of Israel:

The sons of Reuben, Israel's oldest son, were Hanoch, Pallu, Hezron, and Carmi. Their descendants became the clans of Reuben. [15]The sons of Simeon were Jemuel, Jamin, Ohad, Jakin, Zohar, and Shaul. (Shaul's mother was a Canaanite woman.) Their descendants became the clans of Simeon.

[16]These are the descendants of Levi, as listed in their family records: The sons of Levi were Gershon, Kohath, and Merari. (Levi lived to be 137 years old.)

[17]The descendants of Gershon included Libni and Shimei, each of whom became the ancestor of a clan.

[18]The descendants of Kohath included Amram, Izhar, Hebron, and Uzziel. (Kohath lived to be 133 years old.)

[19]The descendants of Merari included Mahli and Mushi.

These are the clans of the Levites, as listed in their family records.

[20]Amram married his father's sister Jochebed, and she gave birth to his sons, Aaron and Moses. (Amram lived to be 137 years old.) [21]The sons of Izhar were Korah, Nepheg, and Zicri. [22]The sons of Uzziel were Mishael, Elzaphan, and Sithri.

[23]Aaron married Elisheba, the daughter of Amminadab and sister of Nahshon, and she gave birth to his sons, Nadab, Abihu, Eleazar, and Ithamar. [24]The sons of Korah were Assir, Elkanah, and Abiasaph. Their descendants became the clans of Korah.

[25]Eleazar son of Aaron married one of the daughters of Putiel, and she gave birth to his son, Phinehas.

These are the ancestors of the Levite families, listed according to their clans.

[26]The Aaron and Moses named in this list are the same ones to whom the LORD said, "Lead the people of Israel out of the land of Egypt like an army." [27]It was Moses and Aaron who spoke to Pharaoh, the king of Egypt, about leading the people of Israel out of Egypt.

[28]When the LORD spoke to Moses in the land of Egypt, [29]he said to him, "I am the LORD! Tell Pharaoh, the king of Egypt, everything I am telling you." [30]But Moses argued with the LORD, saying,

---

6:2 Yahweh is a transliteration of the proper name YHWH that is sometimes rendered "Jehovah"; in this translation it is usually rendered "the LORD" (note the use of small capitals). 6:3 El-Shaddai, which means "God Almighty," is the name for God used in Gen 17:1; 28:3; 35:11; 43:14; 48:3. 6:12 Hebrew I have uncircumcised lips; also in 6:30.

"I can't do it! I'm such a clumsy speaker! Why should Pharaoh listen to me?"

AARON'S STAFF BECOMES A SERPENT

7 Then the LORD said to Moses, "Pay close attention to this. I will make you seem like God to Pharaoh, and your brother, Aaron, will be your prophet. [2] Tell Aaron everything I command you, and Aaron must command Pharaoh to let the people of Israel leave his country. [3] But I will make Pharaoh's heart stubborn so I can multiply my miraculous signs and wonders in the land of Egypt. [4] Even then Pharaoh will refuse to listen to you. So I will bring down my fist on Egypt. Then I will rescue my forces—my people, the Israelites—from the land of Egypt with great acts of judgment. [5] When I raise my powerful hand and bring out the Israelites, the Egyptians will know that I am the LORD."

[6] So Moses and Aaron did just as the LORD had commanded them. [7] Moses was eighty years old, and Aaron was eighty-three when they made their demands to Pharaoh.

[8] Then the LORD said to Moses and Aaron, [9] "Pharaoh will demand, 'Show me a miracle.' When he does this, say to Aaron, 'Take your staff and throw it down in front of Pharaoh, and it will become a serpent.*'"

[10] So Moses and Aaron went to Pharaoh and did what the LORD had commanded them. Aaron threw down his staff before Pharaoh and his officials, and it became a serpent! [11] Then Pharaoh called in his own wise men and sorcerers, and these Egyptian magicians did the same thing with their magic. [12] They threw down their staffs, which also became serpents! But then Aaron's staff swallowed up their staffs. [13] Pharaoh's heart, however, remained hard. He still refused to listen, just as the LORD had predicted.

A PLAGUE OF BLOOD

[14] Then the LORD said to Moses, "Pharaoh's heart is stubborn,* and he still refuses to let the people go. [15] So go to Pharaoh in the morning as he goes down to the river. Stand on the bank of the Nile and meet him there. Be sure to take along the staff that turned into a snake. [16] Then announce to him, 'The LORD, the God of the Hebrews, has sent me to tell you, "Let my people go, so they can worship me in the wilderness." Until now, you have refused to listen to him. [17] So this is what the LORD says: "I will show you that I am the LORD." Look! I will strike the water of the Nile with this staff in my hand, and the river will turn to blood. [18] The fish in it will die, and the river will stink. The Egyptians will not be able to drink any water from the Nile.'"

[19] Then the LORD said to Moses: "Tell Aaron, 'Take your staff and raise your hand over the waters of Egypt—all its rivers, canals, ponds, and all the reservoirs. Turn all the water to blood. Everywhere in Egypt the water will turn to blood, even the water stored in wooden bowls and stone pots.'"

[20] So Moses and Aaron did just as the LORD commanded them. As Pharaoh and all of his officials watched, Aaron raised his staff and struck the water of the Nile. Suddenly, the whole river turned to blood! [21] The fish in the river died, and the water became so foul that the Egyptians couldn't drink it. There was blood everywhere throughout the land of Egypt. [22] But again the magicians of Egypt used their magic, and they, too, turned water into blood. So Pharaoh's heart remained hard. He refused to listen to Moses and Aaron, just as the LORD had predicted. [23] Pharaoh returned to his palace and put the whole thing out of his mind. [24] Then all the Egyptians dug along the riverbank to find drinking water, for they couldn't drink the water from the Nile.

[25] Seven days passed from the time the LORD struck the Nile.

A PLAGUE OF FROGS

8 [1*] Then the LORD said to Moses, "Go back to Pharaoh and announce to him, 'This is what the LORD says: Let my people go, so they can worship me. [2] If you refuse to let them go, I will send a plague of frogs across your entire land. [3] The Nile River will swarm with frogs. They will come up out of the river and into your palace, even into your bedroom and onto your bed! They will enter the houses of your officials and your people. They will even jump into your ovens and your kneading bowls. [4] Frogs will jump on you, your people, and all your officials.'"

[5*] Then the LORD said to Moses, "Tell Aaron, 'Raise the staff in your hand over all the rivers, canals, and ponds of Egypt, and bring up frogs over all the land.'" [6] So Aaron raised his hand over the waters of Egypt, and frogs came up and covered the whole land! [7] But the magicians were able to do the same thing with their magic. They, too, caused frogs to come up on the land of Egypt.

[8] Then Pharaoh summoned Moses and Aaron and begged, "Plead with the LORD to take the frogs away from me and my people. I will let your people go, so they can offer sacrifices to the LORD."

[9] "You set the time!" Moses replied. "Tell me when you want me to pray for you, your officials, and your people. Then you and your houses will be rid of the frogs. They will remain only in the Nile River."

[10] "Do it tomorrow," Pharaoh said.

"All right," Moses replied, "it will be as you have said. Then you will know that there is no one like the LORD our God. [11] The frogs will leave

---

7:9 Hebrew tannin, which elsewhere refers to a sea monster. Greek version translates it "dragon." 7:14 Hebrew heavy. 8:1 Verses 8:1-4 are numbered 7:26-29 in Hebrew text. 8:5 Verses 8:5-32 are numbered 8:1-28 in Hebrew text.

you and your houses, your officials, and your people. They will remain only in the Nile River."

¹² So Moses and Aaron left Pharaoh's palace, and Moses cried out to the LORD about the frogs he had inflicted on Pharaoh. ¹³ And the LORD did just what Moses had predicted. The frogs in the houses, the courtyards, and the fields all died. ¹⁴ The Egyptians piled them into great heaps, and a terrible stench filled the land. ¹⁵ But when Pharaoh saw that relief had come, he became stubborn.* He refused to listen to Moses and Aaron, just as the LORD had predicted.

A PLAGUE OF GNATS

¹⁶ So the LORD said to Moses, "Tell Aaron, 'Raise your staff and strike the ground. The dust will turn into swarms of gnats throughout the land of Egypt.'" ¹⁷ So Moses and Aaron did just as the LORD had commanded them. When Aaron raised his hand and struck the ground with his staff, gnats infested the entire land, covering the Egyptians and their animals. All the dust in the land of Egypt turned into gnats. ¹⁸ Pharaoh's magicians tried to do the same thing with their secret arts, but this time they failed. And the gnats covered everyone, people and animals alike.

¹⁹ "This is the finger of God!" the magicians exclaimed to Pharaoh. But Pharaoh's heart remained hard. He wouldn't listen to them, just as the LORD had predicted.

A PLAGUE OF FLIES

²⁰ Then the LORD told Moses, "Get up early in the morning and stand in Pharaoh's way as he goes down to the river. Say to him, 'This is what the LORD says: Let my people go, so they can worship me. ²¹ If you refuse, then I will send swarms of flies on you, your officials, your people, and all the houses. The Egyptian homes will be filled with flies, and the ground will be covered with them. ²² But this time I will spare the region of Goshen, where my people live. No flies will be found there. Then you will know that I am the LORD and that I am present even in the heart of your land. ²³ I will make a clear distinction between* my people and your people. This miraculous sign will happen tomorrow.'"

²⁴ And the LORD did just as he had said. A thick swarm of flies filled Pharaoh's palace and the houses of his officials. The whole land of Egypt was thrown into chaos by the flies.

²⁵ Pharaoh called for Moses and Aaron. "All right! Go ahead and offer sacrifices to your God," he said. "But do it here in this land."

²⁶ But Moses replied, "That wouldn't be right. The Egyptians detest the sacrifices that we offer to the LORD our God. Look, if we offer our sacrifices here where the Egyptians can see us, they will stone us. ²⁷ We must take a three-day trip into the wilderness to offer sacrifices to the LORD our God, just as he has commanded us."

²⁸ "All right, go ahead," Pharaoh replied. "I will let you go into the wilderness to offer sacrifices to the LORD your God. But don't go too far away. Now hurry and pray for me."

²⁹ Moses answered, "As soon as I leave you, I will pray to the LORD, and tomorrow the swarms of flies will disappear from you and your officials and all your people. But I am warning you, Pharaoh, don't lie to us again and refuse to let the people go to sacrifice to the LORD."

³⁰ So Moses left Pharaoh's palace and pleaded with the LORD to remove all the flies. ³¹ And the LORD did as Moses asked and caused the swarms of flies to disappear from Pharaoh, his officials, and his people. Not a single fly remained. ³² But Pharaoh again became stubborn and refused to let the people go.

A PLAGUE AGAINST LIVESTOCK

9 "Go back to Pharaoh," the LORD commanded Moses. "Tell him, 'This is what the LORD, the God of the Hebrews, says: Let my people go, so they can worship me. ² If you continue to hold them and refuse to let them go, ³ the hand of the LORD will strike all your livestock—your horses, donkeys, camels, cattle, sheep, and goats—with a deadly plague. ⁴ But the LORD will again make a distinction between the livestock of the Israelites and that of the Egyptians. Not a single one of Israel's animals will die! ⁵ The LORD has already set the time for the plague to begin. He has declared that he will strike the land tomorrow.'"

⁶ And the LORD did just as he had said. The next morning all the livestock of the Egyptians died, but the Israelites didn't lose a single animal. ⁷ Pharaoh sent his officials to investigate, and they discovered that the Israelites had not lost a single animal! But even so, Pharaoh's heart remained stubborn,* and he still refused to let the people go.

A PLAGUE OF FESTERING BOILS

⁸ Then the LORD said to Moses and Aaron, "Take handfuls of soot from a brick kiln, and have Moses toss it into the air while Pharaoh watches. ⁹ The ashes will spread like fine dust over the whole land of Egypt, causing festering boils to break out on people and animals throughout the land."

¹⁰ So they took soot from a brick kiln and went and stood before Pharaoh. As Pharaoh watched, Moses threw the soot into the air, and boils broke out on people and animals alike. ¹¹ Even the magicians were unable to stand before Moses, because the boils had broken out on them and all the Egyptians. ¹² But the LORD hardened Pharaoh's heart, and just as the LORD had predicted to Moses, Pharaoh refused to listen.

8:15 Hebrew *made his heart heavy;* also in 8:32.   8:23 As in Greek and Latin versions; Hebrew reads *I will set redemption between.*
9:7 Hebrew *heavy.*

A PLAGUE OF HAIL

¹³Then the LORD said to Moses, "Get up early in the morning and stand before Pharaoh. Tell him, 'This is what the LORD, the God of the Hebrews, says: Let my people go, so they can worship me. ¹⁴If you don't, I will send more plagues on you* and your officials and your people. Then you will know that there is no one like me in all the earth. ¹⁵By now I could have lifted my hand and struck you and your people with a plague to wipe you off the face of the earth. ¹⁶But I have spared you for a purpose—to show you my power* and to spread my fame throughout the earth. ¹⁷But you still lord it over my people and refuse to let them go. ¹⁸So tomorrow at this time I will send a hailstorm more devastating than any in all the history of Egypt. ¹⁹Quick! Order your livestock and servants to come in from the fields to find shelter. Any person or animal left outside will die when the hail falls.'"

²⁰Some of Pharaoh's officials were afraid because of what the LORD had said. They quickly brought their servants and livestock in from the fields. ²¹But those who paid no attention to the word of the LORD left theirs out in the open.

²²Then the LORD said to Moses, "Lift your hand toward the sky so hail may fall on the people, the livestock, and all the plants throughout the land of Egypt." ²³So Moses lifted his staff toward the sky, and the LORD sent thunder and hail, and lightning flashed toward the earth. The LORD sent a tremendous hailstorm against all the land of Egypt. ²⁴Never in all the history of Egypt had there been a storm like that, with such devastating hail and continuous lightning. ²⁵It left all of Egypt in ruins. The hail struck down everything in the open field—people, animals, and plants alike. Even the trees were destroyed. ²⁶The only place without hail was the region of Goshen, where the people of Israel lived.

²⁷Then Pharaoh quickly summoned Moses and Aaron. "This time I have sinned," he confessed. "The LORD is the righteous one, and my people and I are wrong. ²⁸Please beg the LORD to end this terrifying thunder and hail. We've had enough. I will let you go; you don't need to stay any longer."

²⁹"All right," Moses replied. "As soon as I leave the city, I will lift my hands and pray to the LORD. Then the thunder and hail will stop, and you will know that the earth belongs to the LORD. ³⁰But I know that you and your officials still do not fear the LORD God."

³¹(All the flax and barley were ruined by the hail, because the barley had formed heads and the flax was budding. ³²But the wheat and the emmer wheat were spared, because they had not yet sprouted from the ground.)

³³So Moses left Pharaoh's court and went out of the city. When he lifted his hands to the LORD, the thunder and hail stopped, and the downpour ceased. ³⁴But when Pharaoh saw that the rain, hail, and thunder had stopped, he and his officials sinned again, and Pharaoh again became stubborn. * ³⁵Because his heart was hard, Pharaoh refused to let the people leave, just as the LORD had predicted through Moses.

A PLAGUE OF LOCUSTS

10 Then the LORD said to Moses, "Return to Pharaoh and make your demands again. I have made him and his officials stubborn* so I can display my miraculous signs among them. ²I've also done it so you can tell your children and grandchildren about how I made a mockery of the Egyptians and about the signs I displayed among them—and so you will know that I am the LORD."

³So Moses and Aaron went to Pharaoh and said, "This is what the LORD, the God of the Hebrews, says: How long will you refuse to submit to me? Let my people go, so they can worship me. ⁴If you refuse, watch out! For tomorrow I will bring a swarm of locusts on your country. ⁵They will cover the land so that you won't be able to see the ground. They will devour what little is left of your crops after the hailstorm, including all the trees growing in the fields. ⁶They will overrun your palaces and the homes of your officials and all the houses in Egypt. Never in the history of Egypt have your ancestors seen a plague like this one!" And with that, Moses turned and left Pharaoh.

⁷Pharaoh's officials now came to Pharaoh and appealed to him. "How long will you let this man hold us hostage? Let the men go to worship the LORD their God! Don't you realize that Egypt lies in ruins?"

⁸So Moses and Aaron were brought back to Pharaoh. "All right," he told them, "go and worship the LORD your God. But who exactly will be going with you?"

⁹Moses replied, "We will all go—young and old, our sons and daughters, and our flocks and herds. We must all join together in celebrating a festival to the LORD."

¹⁰Pharaoh retorted, "The LORD will certainly need to be with you if I let you take your little ones! I can see through your evil plan. ¹¹Never! Only the men may go and worship the LORD, since that is what you requested." And Pharaoh threw them out of the palace.

¹²Then the LORD said to Moses, "Raise your hand over the land of Egypt to bring on the locusts. Let them cover the land and devour every plant that survived the hailstorm."

¹³So Moses raised his staff over Egypt, and the LORD caused an east wind to blow over the land all that day and through the night. When morning arrived, the east wind had brought the locusts. ¹⁴And the locusts swarmed over the whole land of Egypt, settling in dense swarms

---

9:14 Hebrew *on your heart.* 9:16 Greek version reads *to display my power in you;* compare Rom 9:17. 9:34 Hebrew *made his heart heavy.* 10:1 Hebrew *have made his heart and his officials' hearts heavy.*

from one end of the country to the other. It was the worst locust plague in Egyptian history, and there has never been another one like it. ¹⁵ For the locusts covered the whole country and darkened the land. They devoured every plant in the fields and all the fruit on the trees that had survived the hailstorm. Not a single leaf was left on the trees and plants throughout the land of Egypt.

¹⁶ Pharaoh quickly summoned Moses and Aaron. "I have sinned against the LORD your God and against you," he confessed. ¹⁷ "Forgive my sin, just this once, and plead with the LORD your God to take away this death from me."

¹⁸ So Moses left Pharaoh's court and pleaded with the LORD. ¹⁹ The LORD responded by shifting the wind, and the strong west wind blew the locusts into the Red Sea.* Not a single locust remained in all the land of Egypt. ²⁰ But the LORD hardened Pharaoh's heart again, so he refused to let the people go.

A PLAGUE OF DARKNESS

²¹ Then the LORD said to Moses, "Lift your hand toward heaven, and the land of Egypt will be covered with a darkness so thick you can feel it." ²² So Moses lifted his hand to the sky, and a deep darkness covered the entire land of Egypt for three days. ²³ During all that time the people could not see each other, and no one moved. But there was light as usual where the people of Israel lived.

²⁴ Finally, Pharaoh called for Moses. "Go and worship the LORD," he said. "But leave your flocks and herds here. You may even take your little ones with you."

²⁵ "No," Moses said, "you must provide us with animals for sacrifices and burnt offerings to the LORD our God. ²⁶ All our livestock must go with us, too; not a hoof can be left behind. We must choose our sacrifices for the LORD our God from among these animals. And we won't know how we are to worship the LORD until we get there."

²⁷ But the LORD hardened Pharaoh's heart once more, and he would not let them go. ²⁸ "Get out of here!" Pharaoh shouted at Moses. "I'm warning you. Never come back to see me again! The day you see my face, you will die!"

²⁹ "Very well," Moses replied. "I will never see your face again."

DEATH FOR EGYPT'S FIRSTBORN

11 Then the LORD said to Moses, "I will strike Pharaoh and the land of Egypt with one more blow. After that, Pharaoh will let you leave this country. In fact, he will be so eager to get rid of you that he will force you all to leave. ² Tell all the Israelite men and women to ask their Egyptian neighbors for articles of silver and gold." ³ (Now the LORD had caused the Egyptians to look favorably on the people of Israel. And Moses was considered a very great man in the land of Egypt, respected by Pharaoh's officials and the Egyptian people alike.)

⁴ Moses had announced to Pharaoh, "This is what the LORD says: At midnight tonight I will pass through the heart of Egypt. ⁵ All the firstborn sons will die in every family in Egypt, from the oldest son of Pharaoh, who sits on his throne, to the oldest son of his lowliest servant girl who grinds the flour. Even the firstborn of all the livestock will die. ⁶ Then a loud wail will rise throughout the land of Egypt, a wail like no one has heard before or will ever hear again. ⁷ But among the Israelites it will be so peaceful that not even a dog will bark. Then you will know that the LORD makes a distinction between the Egyptians and the Israelites. ⁸ All the officials of Egypt will run to me and fall to the ground before me. 'Please leave!' they will beg. 'Hurry! And take all your followers with you.' Only then will I go!" Then, burning with anger, Moses left Pharaoh.

⁹ Now the LORD had told Moses earlier, "Pharaoh will not listen to you, but then I will do even more mighty miracles in the land of Egypt." ¹⁰ Moses and Aaron performed these miracles in Pharaoh's presence, but the LORD hardened Pharaoh's heart, and he wouldn't let the Israelites leave the country.

THE FIRST PASSOVER

12 While the Israelites were still in the land of Egypt, the LORD gave the following instructions to Moses and Aaron: ² "From now on, this month will be the first month of the year for you. ³ Announce to the whole community of Israel that on the tenth day of this month each family must choose a lamb or a young goat for a sacrifice, one animal for each household. ⁴ If a family is too small to eat a whole animal, let them share with another family in the neighborhood. Divide the animal according to the size of each family and how much they can eat. ⁵ The animal you select must be a one-year-old male, either a sheep or a goat, with no defects.

⁶ "Take special care of this chosen animal until the evening of the fourteenth day of this first month. Then the whole assembly of the community of Israel must slaughter their lamb or young goat at twilight. ⁷ They are to take some of the blood and smear it on the sides and top of the doorframes of the houses where they eat the animal. ⁸ That same night they must roast the meat over a fire and eat it along with bitter salad greens and bread made without yeast. ⁹ Do not eat any of the meat raw or boiled in water. The whole animal—including the head, legs, and internal organs—must be roasted over a fire. ¹⁰ Do not leave any of it until the next morning. Burn whatever is not eaten before morning.

¹¹ "These are your instructions for eating this meal: Be fully dressed,* wear your sandals, and carry your walking stick in your hand. Eat the meal with urgency, for this is the LORD's

10:19 Hebrew *sea of reeds.* 12:11 Hebrew *Bind up your loins.*

Passover. ¹²On that night I will pass through the land of Egypt and strike down every firstborn son and firstborn male animal in the land of Egypt. I will execute judgment against all the gods of Egypt, for I am the LORD! ¹³But the blood on your doorposts will serve as a sign, marking the houses where you are staying. When I see the blood, I will pass over you. This plague of death will not touch you when I strike the land of Egypt.

¹⁴"This is a day to remember. Each year, from generation to generation, you must celebrate it as a special festival to the LORD. This is a law for all time. ¹⁵For seven days the bread you eat must be made without yeast. On the first day of the festival, remove every trace of yeast from your homes. Anyone who eats bread made with yeast during the seven days of the festival will be cut off from the community of Israel. ¹⁶On the first day of the festival and again on the seventh day, all the people must observe an official day for holy assembly. No work of any kind may be done on these days except in the preparation of food.

¹⁷"Celebrate this Festival of Unleavened Bread, for it will remind you that I brought your forces out of the land of Egypt on this very day. This festival will be a permanent law for you; celebrate this day from generation to generation. ¹⁸The bread you eat must be made without yeast from the evening of the fourteenth day of the first month until the evening of the twenty-first day of that month. ¹⁹During those seven days, there must be no trace of yeast in your homes. Anyone who eats anything made with yeast during this week will be cut off from the community of Israel. These regulations apply both to the foreigners living among you and to the native-born Israelites. ²⁰During those days you must not eat anything made with yeast. Wherever you live, eat only bread made without yeast."

²¹Then Moses called all the elders of Israel together and said to them, "Go, pick out a lamb or young goat for each of your families, and slaughter the Passover animal. ²²Drain the blood into a basin. Then take a bundle of hyssop branches and dip it into the blood. Brush the hyssop across the top and sides of the doorframes of your houses. And no one may go out through the door until morning. ²³For the LORD will pass through the land to strike down the Egyptians. But when he sees the blood on the top and sides of the doorframe, the LORD will pass over your home. He will not permit his death angel to enter your house and strike you down.

²⁴"Remember, these instructions are a permanent law that you and your descendants must observe forever. ²⁵When you enter the land the LORD has promised to give you, you will continue to observe this ceremony. ²⁶Then your children will ask, 'What does this ceremony mean?' ²⁷And you will reply, 'It is the Passover sacrifice to the LORD, for he passed over the houses of the Israelites in Egypt. And though he struck the Egyptians, he spared our families.'" When Moses had finished speaking, all the people bowed down to the ground and worshiped.

²⁸So the people of Israel did just as the LORD had commanded through Moses and Aaron. ²⁹And that night at midnight, the LORD struck down all the firstborn sons in the land of Egypt, from the firstborn son of Pharaoh, who sat on his throne, to the firstborn son of the prisoner in the dungeon. Even the firstborn of their livestock were killed. ³⁰Pharaoh and all his officials and all the people of Egypt woke up during the night, and loud wailing was heard throughout the land of Egypt. There was not a single house where someone had not died.

ISRAEL'S EXODUS FROM EGYPT

³¹Pharaoh sent for Moses and Aaron during the night. "Get out!" he ordered. "Leave my people—and take the rest of the Israelites with you! Go and worship the LORD as you have requested. ³²Take your flocks and herds, as you said, and be gone. Go, but bless me as you leave." ³³All the Egyptians urged the people of Israel to get out of the land as quickly as possible, for they thought, "We will all die!"

³⁴The Israelites took their bread dough before yeast was added. They wrapped their kneading boards in their cloaks and carried them on their shoulders. ³⁵And the people of Israel did as Moses had instructed; they asked the Egyptians for clothing and articles of silver and gold. ³⁶The LORD caused the Egyptians to look favorably on the Israelites, and they gave the Israelites whatever they asked for. So they stripped the Egyptians of their wealth!

³⁷That night the people of Israel left Rameses and started for Succoth. There were about 600,000 men,* plus all the women and children. ³⁸A rabble of non-Israelites went with them, along with great flocks and herds of livestock. ³⁹For bread they baked flat cakes from the dough

12:37 Or *fighting men*; Hebrew reads *men on foot.*

without yeast they had brought from Egypt. It was made without yeast because the people were driven out of Egypt in such a hurry that they had no time to prepare the bread or other food. ⁴⁰The people of Israel had lived in Egypt* for 430 years. ⁴¹In fact, it was on the last day of the 430th year that all the LORD's forces left the land. ⁴²On this night the LORD kept his promise to bring his people out of the land of Egypt. So this night belongs to him, and it must be commemorated every year by all the Israelites, from generation to generation.

INSTRUCTIONS FOR THE PASSOVER

⁴³Then the LORD said to Moses and Aaron, "These are the instructions for the festival of Passover. No outsiders are allowed to eat the Passover meal. ⁴⁴But any slave who has been purchased may eat it if he has been circumcised. ⁴⁵Temporary residents and hired servants may not eat it. ⁴⁶Each Passover lamb must be eaten in one house. Do not carry any of its meat outside, and do not break any of its bones. ⁴⁷The whole community of Israel must celebrate this Passover festival.

⁴⁸"If there are foreigners living among you who want to celebrate the LORD's Passover, let all their males be circumcised. Only then may they celebrate the Passover with you like any native-born Israelite. But no uncircumcised male may ever eat the Passover meal. ⁴⁹This instruction applies to everyone, whether a native-born Israelite or a foreigner living among you."

⁵⁰So all the people of Israel followed all the LORD's commands to Moses and Aaron. ⁵¹On that very day the LORD brought the people of Israel out of the land of Egypt like an army.

DEDICATION OF THE FIRSTBORN

13 Then the LORD said to Moses, ²"Dedicate to me every firstborn among the Israelites. The first offspring to be born, of both humans and animals, belongs to me."

³So Moses said to the people, "This is a day to remember forever—the day you left Egypt, the place of your slavery. Today the LORD has brought you out by the power of his mighty hand. (Remember, eat no food containing yeast.) ⁴On this day in early spring, in the month of Abib,* you have been set free. ⁵You must celebrate this event in this month each year after the LORD brings you into the land of the Canaanites, Hittites, Amorites, Hivites, and Jebusites. (He swore to your ancestors that he would give you this land—a land flowing with milk and honey.) ⁶For seven days the bread you eat must be made without yeast. Then on the seventh day, celebrate a feast to the LORD. ⁷Eat bread without yeast during those seven days. In fact, there must be no yeast bread or any yeast at all found within the borders of your land during this time.

⁸"On the seventh day you must explain to your children, 'I am celebrating what the LORD did

for me when I left Egypt.' ⁹This annual festival will be a visible sign to you, like a mark branded on your hand or your forehead. Let it remind you always to recite this teaching of the LORD: 'With a strong hand, the LORD rescued you from Egypt.'* ¹⁰So observe the decree of this festival at the appointed time each year.

¹¹"This is what you must do when the LORD fulfills the promise he swore to you and to your ancestors. When he gives you the land where the Canaanites now live, ¹²you must present all firstborn sons and firstborn male animals to the LORD, for they belong to him. ¹³A firstborn donkey may be bought back from the LORD by presenting a lamb or young goat in its place. But if you do not buy it back, you must break its neck. However, you must buy back every firstborn son.

¹⁴"And in the future, your children will ask you, 'What does all this mean?' Then you will tell them, 'With the power of his mighty hand, the LORD brought us out of Egypt, the place of our slavery. ¹⁵Pharaoh stubbornly refused to let us go, so the LORD killed all the firstborn males throughout the land of Egypt, both people and animals. That is why I now sacrifice all the firstborn males to the LORD—except that the firstborn sons are always bought back.' ¹⁶This ceremony will be like a mark branded on your hand or your forehead. It is a reminder that the power of the LORD's mighty hand brought us out of Egypt."

12:40 Samaritan Pentateuch reads *in Canaan and Egypt;* Greek version reads *in Egypt and Canaan.* 13:4 Hebrew *On this day in the month of Abib.* This first month of the ancient Hebrew lunar calendar usually occurs within the months of March and April. 13:9 Or *Let it remind you always to keep the instructions of the LORD on the tip of your tongue,* because *with a strong hand, the LORD rescued you from Egypt.*

PASS DOWN THE PRINCIPLE
Exodus 13:14-15   ROBERT MORRIS

When my children were young, they would look at the amount on our tithe check and ask, "Why do we give so much to the church?" I would reply, "Daddy wasn't always a Christian. Before I met Jesus, my life was a total wreck. I was a slave to sin, but God delivered me with His mighty hand. That's why I gladly give God the first of everything with which He blesses us. I want Him to know that He is first in my life."

The truth is God has rescued each one of us from bondage. We must pass down these truths to our children so they can live lives of blessing as well. It begins by giving them a clear understanding of biblical principles regarding money. Without that understanding, it's impossible to move on to the greater adventures God has in store for those who put Him first.

ISRAEL'S WILDERNESS DETOUR

[17] When Pharaoh finally let the people go, God did not lead them along the main road that runs through Philistine territory, even though that was the shortest route to the Promised Land. God said, "If the people are faced with a battle, they might change their minds and return to Egypt." [18] So God led them in a roundabout way through the wilderness toward the Red Sea.* Thus the Israelites left Egypt like an army ready for battle.*

[19] Moses took the bones of Joseph with him, for Joseph had made the sons of Israel swear to do this. He said, "God will certainly come to help you. When he does, you must take my bones with you from this place."

[20] The Israelites left Succoth and camped at Etham on the edge of the wilderness. [21] The LORD went ahead of them. He guided them during the day with a pillar of cloud, and he provided light at night with a pillar of fire. This allowed them to travel by day or by night. [22] And the LORD did not remove the pillar of cloud or pillar of fire from its place in front of the people.

14 Then the LORD gave these instructions to Moses: [2] "Order the Israelites to turn back and camp by Pi-hahiroth between Migdol and the sea. Camp there along the shore, across from Baal-zephon. [3] Then Pharaoh will think, 'The Israelites are confused. They are trapped in the wilderness!' [4] And once again I will harden Pharaoh's heart, and he will chase after you.* I have planned this in order to display my glory through Pharaoh and his whole army. After this the Egyptians will know that I am the LORD!" So the Israelites camped there as they were told.

THE EGYPTIANS PURSUE ISRAEL

[5] When word reached the king of Egypt that the Israelites had fled, Pharaoh and his officials changed their minds. "What have we done, letting all those Israelite slaves get away?" they asked. [6] So Pharaoh harnessed his chariot and called up his troops. [7] He took with him 600 of Egypt's best chariots, along with the rest of the chariots of Egypt, each with its commander. [8] The LORD hardened the heart of Pharaoh, the king of Egypt, so he chased after the people of Israel, who had left with fists raised in defiance. [9] The Egyptians chased after them with all the forces in Pharaoh's army—all his horses and chariots, his charioteers, and his troops. The Egyptians caught up with the people of Israel as they were camped beside the shore near Pi-hahiroth, across from Baal-zephon.

[10] As Pharaoh approached, the people of Israel looked up and panicked when they saw the Egyptians overtaking them. They cried out to the LORD, [11] and they said to Moses, "Why did you bring us out here to die in the wilderness? Weren't there enough graves for us in Egypt? What have you done to us? Why did you make us leave Egypt? [12] Didn't we tell you this would happen while we were still in Egypt? We said, 'Leave us alone! Let us be slaves to the Egyptians. It's better to be a slave in Egypt than a corpse in the wilderness!'"

[13] But Moses told the people, "Don't be afraid. Just stand still and watch the LORD rescue you today. The Egyptians you see today will never be seen again. [14] The LORD himself will fight for you. Just stay calm."

ESCAPE THROUGH THE RED SEA

[15] Then the LORD said to Moses, "Why are you crying out to me? Tell the people to get moving! [16] Pick up your staff and raise your hand over the sea. Divide the water so the Israelites can walk through the middle of the sea on dry ground. [17] And I will harden the hearts of the Egyptians, and they will charge in after the Israelites. My great glory will be displayed through Pharaoh and his troops, his chariots, and his charioteers. [18] When my glory is displayed through them, all Egypt will see my glory and know that I am the LORD!"

[19] Then the angel of God, who had been leading the people of Israel, moved to the rear of the camp. The pillar of cloud also moved from the front and stood behind them. [20] The cloud settled between the Egyptian and Israelite camps. As darkness fell, the cloud turned to fire, lighting up the night. But the Egyptians and Israelites did not approach each other all night.

[21] Then Moses raised his hand over the sea, and the LORD opened up a path through the water with a strong east wind. The wind blew all that night, turning the seabed into dry land. [22] So the

---

13:18a Hebrew *sea of reeds.*   13:18b Greek version reads *left Egypt in the fifth generation.*   14:4 Hebrew *after them.*

people of Israel walked through the middle of the sea on dry ground, with walls of water on each side!

²³Then the Egyptians—all of Pharaoh's horses, chariots, and charioteers—chased them into the middle of the sea. ²⁴But just before dawn the LORD looked down on the Egyptian army from the pillar of fire and cloud, and he threw their forces into total confusion. ²⁵He twisted* their chariot wheels, making their chariots difficult to drive. "Let's get out of here—away from these Israelites!" the Egyptians shouted. "The LORD is fighting for them against Egypt!"

²⁶When all the Israelites had reached the other side, the LORD said to Moses, "Raise your hand over the sea again. Then the waters will rush back and cover the Egyptians and their chariots and charioteers." ²⁷So as the sun began to rise, Moses raised his hand over the sea, and the water rushed back into its usual place. The Egyptians tried to escape, but the LORD swept them into the sea. ²⁸Then the waters returned and covered all the chariots and charioteers—the entire army of Pharaoh. Of all the Egyptians who had chased the Israelites into the sea, not a single one survived.

²⁹But the people of Israel had walked through the middle of the sea on dry ground, as the water stood up like a wall on both sides. ³⁰That is how the LORD rescued Israel from the hand of the Egyptians that day. And the Israelites saw the bodies of the Egyptians washed up on the seashore. ³¹When the people of Israel saw the mighty power that the LORD had unleashed against the Egyptians, they were filled with awe before him. They put their faith in the LORD and in his servant Moses.

A SONG OF DELIVERANCE

15 Then Moses and the people of Israel sang this song to the LORD:

"I will sing to the LORD,
 for he has triumphed gloriously;
he has hurled both horse and rider
 into the sea.
² The LORD is my strength and my song;
 he has given me victory.
This is my God, and I will praise him—
 my father's God, and I will exalt him!
³ The LORD is a warrior;
 Yahweh* is his name!
⁴ Pharaoh's chariots and army
 he has hurled into the sea.
The finest of Pharaoh's officers
 are drowned in the Red Sea.*
⁵ The deep waters gushed over them;
 they sank to the bottom like a stone.

⁶ "Your right hand, O LORD,
 is glorious in power.
Your right hand, O LORD,
 smashes the enemy.

⁷ In the greatness of your majesty,
 you overthrow those who rise against you.
You unleash your blazing fury;
 it consumes them like straw.
⁸ At the blast of your breath,
 the waters piled up!
The surging waters stood straight like a wall;
 in the heart of the sea the deep waters
  became hard.

⁹ "The enemy boasted, 'I will chase them
 and catch up with them.
I will plunder them
 and consume them.
I will flash my sword;
 my powerful hand will destroy them.'
¹⁰ But you blew with your breath,
 and the sea covered them.
They sank like lead
 in the mighty waters.

¹¹ "Who is like you among the gods, O LORD—
 glorious in holiness,
awesome in splendor,
 performing great wonders?
¹² You raised your right hand,
 and the earth swallowed our enemies.

¹³ "With your unfailing love you lead
 the people you have redeemed.
In your might, you guide them
 to your sacred home.
¹⁴ The peoples hear and tremble;
 anguish grips those who live in Philistia.
¹⁵ The leaders of Edom are terrified;
 the nobles of Moab tremble.
All who live in Canaan melt away;
¹⁶ terror and dread fall upon them.
The power of your arm
 makes them lifeless as stone
until your people pass by, O LORD,
 until the people you purchased pass by.
¹⁷ You will bring them in and plant them on
  your own mountain—
 the place, O LORD, reserved for your own
  dwelling,
 the sanctuary, O Lord, that your hands
  have established.
¹⁸ The LORD will reign forever and ever!"

¹⁹When Pharaoh's horses, chariots, and charioteers rushed into the sea, the LORD brought the water crashing down on them. But the people of Israel had walked through the middle of the sea on dry ground!

²⁰Then Miriam the prophet, Aaron's sister, took a tambourine and led all the women as they

---

14:25 As in Greek version, Samaritan Pentateuch, and Syriac version; Hebrew reads *He removed.* 15:3 *Yahweh* is a transliteration of the proper name YHWH that is sometimes rendered "Jehovah"; in this translation it is usually rendered "the LORD" (note the use of small capitals). 15:4 Hebrew *sea of reeds;* also in 15:22.

played their tambourines and danced. ²¹ And Miriam sang this song:

> "Sing to the LORD,
>   for he has triumphed gloriously;
> he has hurled both horse and rider
>   into the sea."

BITTER WATER AT MARAH

²² Then Moses led the people of Israel away from the Red Sea, and they moved out into the desert of Shur. They traveled in this desert for three days without finding any water. ²³ When they came to the oasis of Marah, the water was too bitter to drink. So they called the place Marah (which means "bitter").

²⁴ Then the people complained and turned against Moses. "What are we going to drink?" they demanded. ²⁵ So Moses cried out to the LORD for help, and the LORD showed him a piece of wood. Moses threw it into the water, and this made the water good to drink.

It was there at Marah that the LORD set before them the following decree as a standard to test their faithfulness to him. ²⁶ He said, "If you will listen carefully to the voice of the LORD your God and do what is right in his sight, obeying his commands and keeping all his decrees, then I will not make you suffer any of the diseases I sent on the Egyptians; for I am the LORD who heals you."

²⁷ After leaving Marah, the Israelites traveled on to the oasis of Elim, where they found twelve springs and seventy palm trees. They camped there beside the water.

MANNA AND QUAIL FROM HEAVEN

16 Then the whole community of Israel set out from Elim and journeyed into the wilderness of Sin,* between Elim and Mount Sinai. They arrived there on the fifteenth day of the second month, one month after leaving the land of Egypt.* ² There, too, the whole community of Israel complained about Moses and Aaron.

³ "If only the LORD had killed us back in Egypt," they moaned. "There we sat around pots filled with meat and ate all the bread we wanted. But now you have brought us into this wilderness to starve us all to death."

⁴ Then the LORD said to Moses, "Look, I'm going to rain down food from heaven for you. Each day the people can go out and pick up as much food as they need for that day. I will test them in this to see whether or not they will follow my instructions. ⁵ On the sixth day they will gather food, and when they prepare it, there will be twice as much as usual."

⁶ So Moses and Aaron said to all the people of Israel, "By evening you will realize it was the LORD who brought you out of the land of Egypt. ⁷ In the morning you will see the glory of the LORD, because he has heard your complaints, which are against him, not against us. What have we done

that you should complain about us?" ⁸ Then Moses added, "The LORD will give you meat to eat in the evening and bread to satisfy you in the morning, for he has heard all your complaints against him. What have we done? Yes, your complaints are against the LORD, not against us."

⁹ Then Moses said to Aaron, "Announce this to the entire community of Israel: 'Present yourselves before the LORD, for he has heard your complaining.'" ¹⁰ And as Aaron spoke to the whole community of Israel, they looked out toward the wilderness. There they could see the awesome glory of the LORD in the cloud.

¹¹ Then the LORD said to Moses, ¹² "I have heard the Israelites' complaints. Now tell them, 'In the evening you will have meat to eat, and in the morning you will have all the bread you want. Then you will know that I am the LORD your God.'"

¹³ That evening vast numbers of quail flew in and covered the camp. And the next morning the area around the camp was wet with dew. ¹⁴ When the dew evaporated, a flaky substance as fine as frost blanketed the ground. ¹⁵ The Israelites were puzzled when they saw it. "What is it?" they asked each other. They had no idea what it was.

And Moses told them, "It is the food the LORD has given you to eat. ¹⁶ These are the LORD's instructions: Each household should gather as much as it needs. Pick up two quarts* for each person in your tent."

¹⁷ So the people of Israel did as they were told. Some gathered a lot, some only a little. ¹⁸ But when they measured it out,* everyone had just enough. Those who gathered a lot had nothing left over, and those who gathered only a little had enough. Each family had just what it needed.

¹⁹ Then Moses told them, "Do not keep any of it until morning." ²⁰ But some of them didn't listen and kept some of it until morning. But by then it was full of maggots and had a terrible smell. Moses was very angry with them.

²¹ After this the people gathered the food morning by morning, each family according to its need. And as the sun became hot, the flakes they had not picked up melted and disappeared. ²² On the sixth day, they gathered twice as much as usual—four quarts* for each person instead of two. Then all the leaders of the community came and asked Moses for an explanation. ²³ He told them, "This is what the LORD commanded: Tomorrow will be a day of complete rest, a holy Sabbath day set apart for the LORD. So bake or boil as much as you want today, and set aside what is left for tomorrow."

²⁴ So they put some aside until morning, just as Moses had commanded. And in the morning the leftover food was wholesome and good, without

---

16:1a The geographical name *Sin* is related to *Sinai* and should not be confused with the English word *sin*.   16:1b The Exodus had occurred on the fifteenth day of the first month (see Num 33:3).   16:16 Hebrew *1 omer* [2.2 liters]; also in 16:32, 33.   16:18 Hebrew *measured it with an omer*.   16:22 Hebrew *2 omers* [4.4 liters].

maggots or odor. [25] Moses said, "Eat this food today, for today is a Sabbath day dedicated to the LORD. There will be no food on the ground today. [26] You may gather the food for six days, but the seventh day is the Sabbath. There will be no food on the ground that day."

[27] Some of the people went out anyway on the seventh day, but they found no food. [28] The LORD asked Moses, "How long will these people refuse to obey my commands and instructions? [29] They must realize that the Sabbath is the LORD's gift to you. That is why he gives you a two-day supply on the sixth day, so there will be enough for two days. On the Sabbath day you must stay in your place. Do not go out to pick up food on the seventh day." [30] So the people did not gather any food on the seventh day.

[31] The Israelites called the food manna.* It was white like coriander seed, and it tasted like honey wafers.

[32] Then Moses said, "This is what the LORD has commanded: Fill a two-quart container with manna to preserve it for your descendants. Then later generations will be able to see the food I gave you in the wilderness when I set you free from Egypt."

[33] Moses said to Aaron, "Get a jar and fill it with two quarts of manna. Then put it in a sacred place before the LORD to preserve it for all future generations." [34] Aaron did just as the LORD had commanded Moses. He eventually placed it in the Ark of the Covenant—in front of the stone tablets inscribed with the terms of the covenant.* [35] So the people of Israel ate manna for forty years until they arrived at the land where they would settle. They ate manna until they came to the border of the land of Canaan.

[36] The container used to measure the manna was an omer, which was one-tenth of an ephah; it held about two quarts.*

WATER FROM THE ROCK

17 At the LORD's command, the whole community of Israel left the wilderness of Sin* and moved from place to place. Eventually they camped at Rephidim, but there was no water there for the people to drink. [2] So once more the people complained against Moses. "Give us water to drink!" they demanded.

"Quiet!" Moses replied. "Why are you complaining against me? And why are you testing the LORD?"

[3] But tormented by thirst, they continued to argue with Moses. "Why did you bring us out of Egypt? Are you trying to kill us, our children, and our livestock with thirst?"

[4] Then Moses cried out to the LORD, "What should I do with these people? They are ready to stone me!"

[5] The LORD said to Moses, "Walk out in front of the people. Take your staff, the one you used when you struck the water of the Nile, and call some of the elders of Israel to join you. [6] I will stand before you on the rock at Mount Sinai.* Strike the rock, and water will come gushing out. Then the people will be able to drink." So Moses struck the rock as he was told, and water gushed out as the elders looked on.

[7] Moses named the place Massah (which means "test") and Meribah (which means "arguing") because the people of Israel argued with Moses and tested the LORD by saying, "Is the LORD here with us or not?"

ISRAEL DEFEATS THE AMALEKITES

[8] While the people of Israel were still at Rephidim, the warriors of Amalek attacked them. [9] Moses commanded Joshua, "Choose some men to go out and fight the army of Amalek for us. Tomorrow, I will stand at the top of the hill, holding the staff of God in my hand."

[10] So Joshua did what Moses had commanded and fought the army of Amalek. Meanwhile, Moses, Aaron, and Hur climbed to the top of a nearby hill. [11] As long as Moses held up the staff in his hand, the Israelites had the advantage. But whenever he dropped his hand, the Amalekites gained the advantage. [12] Moses' arms soon became so tired he could no longer hold them up. So Aaron and Hur found a stone for him to sit on. Then they stood on each side of Moses, holding up his hands. So his hands held steady until sunset. [13] As a result, Joshua overwhelmed the army of Amalek in battle.

[14] After the victory, the LORD instructed Moses, "Write this down on a scroll as a permanent reminder, and read it aloud to Joshua: I will erase the memory of Amalek from under heaven." [15] Moses built an altar there and named it Yahweh-Nissi (which means "the LORD is my banner"). [16] He said, "They have raised their fist against the LORD's throne, so now* the LORD will be at war with Amalek generation after generation."

JETHRO'S VISIT TO MOSES

18 Moses' father-in-law, Jethro, the priest of Midian, heard about everything God had done for Moses and his people, the Israelites. He heard especially about how the LORD had rescued them from Egypt.

[2] Earlier, Moses had sent his wife, Zipporah, and his two sons back to Jethro, who had taken them in. [3] (Moses' first son was named Gershom,* for Moses had said when the boy was born, "I have been a foreigner in a foreign land." [4] His second son was named Eliezer,* for Moses had said, "The God of my ancestors was my helper; he

16:31 *Manna* means "What is it?" See 16:15. 16:34 Hebrew *He placed it in front of the Testimony;* see note on 25:16. 16:36 Hebrew *An omer is one-tenth of an ephah.* 17:1 The geographical name *Sin* is related to *Sinai* and should not be confused with the English word *sin.* 17:6 Hebrew *Horeb,* another name for Sinai. 17:16 Or *Hands have been lifted up to the LORD's throne, and now.* 18:3 *Gershom* sounds like a Hebrew term that means "a foreigner there." 18:4 *Eliezer* means "God is my helper."

rescued me from the sword of Pharaoh.") ⁵Jethro, Moses' father-in-law, now came to visit Moses in the wilderness. He brought Moses' wife and two sons with him, and they arrived while Moses and the people were camped near the mountain of God. ⁶Jethro had sent a message to Moses, saying, "I, Jethro, your father-in-law, am coming to see you with your wife and your two sons."

⁷So Moses went out to meet his father-in-law. He bowed low and kissed him. They asked about each other's welfare and then went into Moses' tent. ⁸Moses told his father-in-law everything the LORD had done to Pharaoh and Egypt on behalf of Israel. He also told about all the hardships they had experienced along the way and how the LORD had rescued his people from all their troubles. ⁹Jethro was delighted when he heard about all the good things the LORD had done for Israel as he rescued them from the hand of the Egyptians.

¹⁰"Praise the LORD," Jethro said, "for he has rescued you from the Egyptians and from Pharaoh. Yes, he has rescued Israel from the powerful hand of Egypt! ¹¹I know now that the LORD is greater than all other gods, because he rescued his people from the oppression of the proud Egyptians."

¹²Then Jethro, Moses' father-in-law, brought a burnt offering and sacrifices to God. Aaron and all the elders of Israel came out and joined him in a sacrificial meal in God's presence.

JETHRO'S WISE ADVICE

¹³The next day, Moses took his seat to hear the people's disputes against each other. They waited before him from morning till evening.

¹⁴When Moses' father-in-law saw all that Moses was doing for the people, he asked, "What are you really accomplishing here? Why are you trying to do all this alone while everyone stands around you from morning till evening?"

¹⁵Moses replied, "Because the people come to me to get a ruling from God. ¹⁶When a dispute arises, they come to me, and I am the one who settles the case between the quarreling parties. I inform the people of God's decrees and give them his instructions."

¹⁷"This is not good!" Moses' father-in-law exclaimed. ¹⁸"You're going to wear yourself out—and the people, too. This job is too heavy a burden for you to handle all by yourself. ¹⁹Now listen to me, and let me give you a word of advice, and may God be with you. You should continue to be the people's representative before God, bringing their disputes to him. ²⁰Teach them God's decrees, and give them his instructions. Show them how to conduct their lives. ²¹But select from all the people some capable, honest men who fear God and hate bribes. Appoint them as leaders over groups of one thousand, one hundred, fifty, and ten. ²²They should always be available to solve the people's common disputes,

but have them bring the major cases to you. Let the leaders decide the smaller matters themselves. They will help you carry the load, making the task easier for you. ²³If you follow this advice, and if God commands you to do so, then you will be able to endure the pressures, and all these people will go home in peace."

²⁴Moses listened to his father-in-law's advice and followed his suggestions. ²⁵He chose capable men from all over Israel and appointed them as leaders over the people. He put them in charge of groups of one thousand, one hundred, fifty, and ten. ²⁶These men were always available to solve the people's common disputes. They brought the major cases to Moses, but they took care of the smaller matters themselves.

²⁷Soon after this, Moses said good-bye to his father-in-law, who returned to his own land.

THE LORD REVEALS HIMSELF AT SINAI

19 Exactly two months after the Israelites left Egypt,* they arrived in the wilderness of Sinai. ²After breaking camp at Rephidim, they came to the wilderness of Sinai and set up camp there at the base of Mount Sinai.

³Then Moses climbed the mountain to appear before God. The LORD called to him from the mountain and said, "Give these instructions to the family of Jacob; announce it to the descendants of Israel: ⁴'You have seen what I did to the Egyptians. You know how I carried you on eagles' wings and brought you to myself. ⁵Now if you will obey me and keep my covenant, you will be my own special treasure from among all the peoples on earth; for all the earth belongs to me. ⁶And you will be my kingdom of priests, my holy nation.' This is the message you must give to the people of Israel."

⁷So Moses returned from the mountain and called together the elders of the people and told them everything the LORD had commanded him. ⁸And all the people responded together, "We will do everything the LORD has commanded." So Moses brought the people's answer back to the LORD.

⁹Then the LORD said to Moses, "I will come to you in a thick cloud, Moses, so the people themselves can hear me when I speak with you. Then they will always trust you."

Moses told the LORD what the people had said. ¹⁰Then the LORD told Moses, "Go down and prepare the people for my arrival. Consecrate them today and tomorrow, and have them wash their clothing. ¹¹Be sure they are ready on the third day, for on that day the LORD will come down on Mount Sinai as all the people watch. ¹²Mark off a boundary all around the mountain. Warn the people, 'Be careful! Do not go up on the

------

19:1 Hebrew *In the third month after the Israelites left Egypt, on the very day,* i.e., two lunar months to the day after leaving Egypt. Compare Num 33:3.

VALUE HIS VOICE
Exodus 19:10-11   ROBERT MORRIS

Do you value hearing God's voice? I think we would all say, "Of course!" But are you willing to devote the time and effort necessary to hear Him? Here are some simple ways you can hear God's voice:

1. Set an appointment.
   In Exodus 10:10-11, God set an appointment to meet with His people. He spoke to Moses, and Moses relayed His message to the Israelites. We need to set a time and place to meet with God. If you don't make an appointment, you'll miss Him, and a missed appointment becomes a disappointment.

2. Be still and worship.
   Moses stood on the edge of the Red Sea with the Egyptian army in pursuit. Then he turned to the people and said, "Don't be afraid. Just stand still and watch the Lord rescue you today" (Exodus 14:13). Many people go straight to praying and reading the Bible, and they forget to enter God's presence first. We must learn to wait on the Lord and take time to worship Him.

3. Pray and read the Bible.
   Pray about whatever is on your heart. It's much easier to hear God when you give Him the burdens you've been carrying. Then read His Word.

4. Listen and write.
   This is the best way to start hearing God. Write what's on your heart. Write your prayers and what you believe God is saying to you through the Scriptures you read. Try it for a month and see what happens!

mountain or even touch its boundaries. Anyone who touches the mountain will certainly be put to death. ¹³No hand may touch the person or animal that crosses the boundary; instead, stone them or shoot them with arrows. They must be put to death.' However, when the ram's horn sounds a long blast, then the people may go up on the mountain.*"

¹⁴So Moses went down to the people. He consecrated them for worship, and they washed their clothes. ¹⁵He told them, "Get ready for the third day, and until then abstain from having sexual intercourse."

¹⁶On the morning of the third day, thunder roared and lightning flashed, and a dense cloud came down on the mountain. There was a long, loud blast from a ram's horn, and all the people trembled. ¹⁷Moses led them out from the camp to meet with God, and they stood at the foot of the mountain. ¹⁸All of Mount Sinai was covered with smoke because the Lord had descended on it in the form of fire. The smoke billowed into the

sky like smoke from a brick kiln, and the whole mountain shook violently. ¹⁹As the blast of the ram's horn grew louder and louder, Moses spoke, and God thundered his reply. ²⁰The Lord came down on the top of Mount Sinai and called Moses to the top of the mountain. So Moses climbed the mountain.

²¹Then the Lord told Moses, "Go back down and warn the people not to break through the boundaries to see the Lord, or they will die. ²²Even the priests who regularly come near to the Lord must purify themselves so that the Lord does not break out and destroy them."

²³"But Lord," Moses protested, "the people cannot come up to Mount Sinai. You already warned us. You told me, 'Mark off a boundary all around the mountain to set it apart as holy.'"

²⁴But the Lord said, "Go down and bring Aaron back up with you. In the meantime, do not let the priests or the people break through to approach the Lord, or he will break out and destroy them."

²⁵So Moses went down to the people and told them what the Lord had said.

TEN COMMANDMENTS FOR THE COVENANT COMMUNITY

20 Then God gave the people all these instructions*:

²"I am the Lord your God, who rescued you from the land of Egypt, the place of your slavery.

³"You must not have any other god but me.

⁴"You must not make for yourself an idol of any kind or an image of anything in the heavens or on the earth or in the sea. ⁵You must not bow down to them or worship them, for I, the Lord your God, am a jealous God who will not tolerate your affection for any other gods. I lay the sins of the parents upon their children; the entire family is affected—even children in the third and fourth generations of those who reject me. ⁶But I lavish unfailing love for a thousand generations* on those who love me and obey my commands.

⁷"You must not misuse the name of the Lord your God. The Lord will not let you go unpunished if you misuse his name.

⁸"Remember to observe the Sabbath day by keeping it holy. ⁹You have six days each week for your ordinary work, ¹⁰but the seventh day is a Sabbath day of rest dedicated to the Lord your God. On that day no one in your household may do any work. This includes you, your sons and daughters, your male and female servants, your livestock, and any foreigners living among you. ¹¹For in six days the Lord made the heavens, the earth, the sea,

19:13 Or *up to the mountain.* 20:1 Hebrew *all these words.* 20:6 Hebrew *for thousands of those.*

RELAT**10**NSHIP
FINDING RELATIONSHIP THROUGH GOD'S TOP 10
Exodus 20:1-17

ROBERT MORRIS

When God gave the Ten Commandments to Moses, He intended them to be much more than a set of rules. Each commandment contains a principle designed to enhance our relationship with God and others.

1. "You must not have any other god but me" (v. 3).

The Israelites had spent the past four centuries immersed in Egypt's worship of many gods (polytheism). Egyptians at that time worshipped 29 main gods and over 2,000 lesser gods. As His people transitioned from slavery to freedom, God wanted the Israelites to understand that He is the *one and only* God.

God began the Ten Commandments with this principle of priority because He wanted to have a relationship with His people. It's the very reason why He created and redeemed us. But this relationship only works when we put God first in our lives.

2. "You must not make for yourself an idol of any kind or an image of anything in the heavens or on the earth or in the sea" (v. 4).

The word *image* comes from *imagination*. When we begin to imagine having something other than what God has provided, we set up an idol in our minds. Idols steal our love, gratitude, and worship of God. However, God is a jealous God, and He refuses to share His glory with any other person or thing. After all, He made us in *His* image.

Idolatry was very common in Canaan, the land God had promised as Israel's inheritance. Israel was the only nation that worshipped a deity they could not see. God wanted to protect His people, and He warned them that the consequences of idol worship would affect their grandchildren and great-grandchildren. For those who kept this principle of purity, though, He promised to "lavish unfailing love for a thousand generations" (Exodus 20:6).

3. "You must not misuse the name of the LORD your God" (v. 7).

We misuse God's name when we pray for selfish purposes or when we claim to have heard from Him but are really sharing our own opinions. A person shows extreme arrogance when they use God's name to curse, and Scripture warns that He "will not let you go unpunished if you misuse his name" (Exodus 20:7). Centuries before Christ was born, Israel went into exile because they profaned God's name by worshipping idols.

Since God's name and His character are interchangeable, this principle of humility should influence how we live. The best way to proclaim the Lord's name is to praise Him with gratitude. We also correctly use His name when we pray for His will to be done. If we are going to claim to be children of God, we must honor Him by living in a holy and righteous manner.

4. "Remember to observe the Sabbath day by keeping it holy. . . . On that day no one in your household may do any work" (vv. 8, 10).

The Sabbath is God's gift of rest to us. It is meant to revive us emotionally, mentally, physically, and spiritually. God Himself modeled this principle of rest by creating the world in six days and then resting on the seventh day (Genesis 2:2-3; Exodus 31:17).

The Sabbath gave God an opportunity to provide supernaturally for the Israelites. For five days a week, they gathered enough manna to eat for each day. On the sixth day, though, they gathered enough for two days. God wanted the people of Israel to trust Him by accepting His rest on the seventh day. If we want His blessings in our lives as well, we too must obey God and keep the Sabbath holy.

5. "Honor your father and mother. Then you will live a long, full life in the land the LORD your God is giving you" (v. 12).

When God told Moses to lead the people of Israel out of slavery, He knew they would need faith to enter the Promised Land. Honor produces faith, and only the Israelites who honored God's word were able to enter the land of their inheritance.

As children, our first command is to obey our parents. As we mature, we are told to honor them, and in doing so, we learn to honor God and those in authority. Today, many people fail to enter their destinies because they refuse to honor authority. By honoring those in authority over you, you choose to live out this principle of honor and receive the blessings God has in store for you.

6. "You must not murder" (v. 13).

When someone fails to do something we expected them to do, we may become offended and angry. Anger is a natural emotion, but when we allow it to remain unresolved inside us, it grows into hate. First John 3:15 says, "Anyone who hates another brother or sister is really a murderer at heart." Hate is the seed of murder.

If we allow it to go unchecked, it will destroy our lives.

The opposite of hate is love. How can we love our enemies even when they have offended us? We must remind ourselves that we do not have to earn our forgiveness from God. This principle of love recognizes that because God freely forgives us, we too can freely forgive others. Our battle is not with people but with the devil who wants to separate us from God and each other.

7. "You must not commit adultery" (v. 14).

Adultery causes a spouse to leave and join to someone else spiritually. You can have a wrong relationship with someone in your body, mind, or emotions. According to Matthew 5:27-28, looking at someone other than your spouse with lustful thoughts or unrestrained imagination is adultery. Premarital sex also causes spiritual separation from the Lord and creates inappropriate appetites and habits.

One of Satan's common lies is that sex is dirty or wrong. However, God gave us this principle of intimacy because He designed you to have an appetite for sex and to experience pleasure with your spouse. Sexual intimacy involves a supernatural joining together, and God blesses this union under the covenant of marriage.

8. "You must not steal" (v. 15).

People may have various excuses for stealing, but there is only one *real* reason—they do not trust God to provide for them. Stealing involves taking anything that does not belong to you. This includes taking more of something than you are supposed to take. God owns everything, so when we steal, we are ultimately stealing from Him. A person who steals learns to function in deceit and darkness, which is where Satan operates.

God wants us to trust Him for all provision, including finances, health, relationships, and children. When we live out this principle of trust, we no longer feel the need to take what doesn't belong to us. Instead, we find satisfaction and peace in working hard and seeing the

Lord as our Provider. To have everything we need, we simply need to trust and obey Him.

9. "You must not testify falsely against your neighbor" (v. 16).

Even as believers, we often allow dishonesty into our lives in seemingly small ways. For example, instead of "lying," we *exaggerate*. However, honesty is the foundation of our relationship with God and other people. No one can have a real relationship with a dishonest person. Dishonesty and deceit keep us in bondage, and the only way to be free is to repent and tell the truth.

We must learn to be completely honest with ourselves, others, and God. James 5:16 says, "Confess your sins to each other and pray for each other so that you may be healed." Confession brings humility and accountability into our lives. We can freely admit our mistakes and ask for forgiveness. This principle of honesty allows us to have a better relationship with God and everyone else with whom we interact.

10. "You must not covet your neighbor's house. . . . or anything else that belongs to your neighbor" (v. 17).

The word *covet* means to desire in a strong way. When we covet what others have, we stop being grateful for what God has given to us and begin seeing only the things that we don't have.

God gave us this principle of contentment to strengthen our relationship with Him. Psalm 37:4 says,

> Take delight in the LORD,
>   and he will give you your heart's desires.

Contentment is a state of satisfaction that comes from trusting God for your provision. When we don't trust God, we compare ourselves with others and see ourselves as inferior or superior to them. This leads to *contention*, a state of constant competition and dissatisfaction. Trust God for your provision. He will put the right desires in your heart and fill you with contentment.

and everything in them; but on the seventh day he rested. That is why the LORD blessed the Sabbath day and set it apart as holy.
12 "Honor your father and mother. Then you will live a long, full life in the land the LORD your God is giving you.
13 "You must not murder.
14 "You must not commit adultery.
15 "You must not steal.
16 "You must not testify falsely against your neighbor.

17 "You must not covet your neighbor's house. You must not covet your neighbor's wife, male or female servant, ox or donkey, or anything else that belongs to your neighbor."

18 When the people heard the thunder and the loud blast of the ram's horn, and when they saw the flashes of lightning and the smoke billowing from the mountain, they stood at a distance, trembling with fear.

19And they said to Moses, "You speak to us, and we will listen. But don't let God speak directly to us, or we will die!"

20"Don't be afraid," Moses answered them, "for God has come in this way to test you, and so that your fear of him will keep you from sinning!"

21As the people stood in the distance, Moses approached the dark cloud where God was.

PROPER USE OF ALTARS

22And the LORD said to Moses, "Say this to the people of Israel: You saw for yourselves that I spoke to you from heaven. 23Remember, you must not make any idols of silver or gold to rival me. 24"Build for me an altar made of earth, and offer your sacrifices to me—your burnt offerings and peace offerings, your sheep and goats, and your cattle. Build my altar wherever I cause my name to be remembered, and I will come to you and bless you. 25If you use stones to build my altar, use only natural, uncut stones. Do not shape the stones with a tool, for that would make the altar unfit for holy use. 26And do not approach my altar by going up steps. If you do, someone might look up under your clothing and see your nakedness.

FAIR TREATMENT OF SLAVES

21 "These are the regulations you must present to Israel.

2"If you buy a Hebrew slave, he may serve for no more than six years. Set him free in the seventh year, and he will owe you nothing for his freedom. 3If he was single when he became your slave, he shall leave single. But if he was married before he became a slave, then his wife must be freed with him.

4"If his master gave him a wife while he was a slave and they had sons or daughters, then only the man will be free in the seventh year, but his wife and children will still belong to his master. 5But the slave may declare, 'I love my master, my wife, and my children. I don't want to go free.' 6If he does this, his master must present him before God.* Then his master must take him to the door or doorpost and publicly pierce his ear with an awl. After that, the slave will serve his master for life.

7"When a man sells his daughter as a slave, she will not be freed at the end of six years as the men are. 8If she does not satisfy her owner, he must allow her to be bought back again. But he is not allowed to sell her to foreigners, since he is the one who broke the contract with her. 9But if the slave's owner arranges for her to marry his son, he may no longer treat her as a slave but as a daughter. 10"If a man who has married a slave wife takes another wife for himself, he must not neglect the rights of the first wife to food, clothing, and sexual intimacy. 11If he fails in any of these three obligations, she may leave as a free woman without making any payment.

CASES OF PERSONAL INJURY

12"Anyone who assaults and kills another person must be put to death. 13But if it was simply an accident permitted by God, I will appoint a place of refuge where the slayer can run for safety. 14However, if someone deliberately kills another person, then the slayer must be dragged even from my altar and be put to death.

15"Anyone who strikes father or mother must be put to death.

16"Kidnappers must be put to death, whether they are caught in possession of their victims or have already sold them as slaves.

17"Anyone who dishonors* father or mother must be put to death.

18"Now suppose two men quarrel, and one hits the other with a stone or fist, and the injured person does not die but is confined to bed. 19If he is later able to walk outside again, even with a crutch, the assailant will not be punished but must compensate his victim for lost wages and provide for his full recovery.

20"If a man beats his male or female slave with a club and the slave dies as a result, the owner must be punished. 21But if the slave recovers within a day or two, then the owner shall not be punished, since the slave is his property.

22"Now suppose two men are fighting, and in the process they accidentally strike a pregnant woman so she gives birth prematurely.* If no further injury results, the man who struck the woman must pay the amount of compensation the woman's husband demands and the judges approve. 23But if there is further injury, the punishment must match the injury: a life for a life, 24an eye for an eye, a tooth for a tooth, a hand for a hand, a foot for a foot, 25a burn for a burn, a wound for a wound, a bruise for a bruise.

26"If a man hits his male or female slave in the eye and the eye is blinded, he must let the slave go free to compensate for the eye. 27And if a man knocks out the tooth of his male or female slave, he must let the slave go free to compensate for the tooth.

28"If an ox* gores a man or woman to death, the ox must be stoned, and its flesh may not be eaten. In such a case, however, the owner will not be held liable. 29But suppose the ox had a reputation for goring, and the owner had been informed but failed to keep it under control. If the ox then kills someone, it must be stoned, and the owner must also be put to death. 30However, the dead person's relatives may accept payment to compensate for the loss of life. The owner of the ox may redeem his life by paying whatever is demanded.

31"The same regulation applies if the ox gores a boy or a girl. 32But if the ox gores a slave, either male or female, the animal's owner must pay

---

21:6 Or before the judges.   21:17 Greek version reads Anyone who speaks disrespectfully of. Compare Matt 15:4; Mark 7:10.   21:22 Or so she has a miscarriage; Hebrew reads so her children come out. 21:28 Or bull, or cow; also in 21:29-36.

the slave's owner thirty silver coins,* and the ox must be stoned.

³³ "Suppose someone digs or uncovers a pit and fails to cover it, and then an ox or a donkey falls into it. ³⁴ The owner of the pit must pay full compensation to the owner of the animal, but then he gets to keep the dead animal.

³⁵ "If someone's ox injures a neighbor's ox and the injured ox dies, then the two owners must sell the live ox and divide the price equally between them. They must also divide the dead animal. ³⁶ But if the ox had a reputation for goring, yet its owner failed to keep it under control, he must pay full compensation—a live ox for the dead one—but he may keep the dead ox.

PROTECTION OF PROPERTY

22 ¹* "If someone steals an ox* or sheep and then kills or sells it, the thief must pay back five oxen for each ox stolen, and four sheep for each sheep stolen.

²* "If a thief is caught in the act of breaking into a house and is struck and killed in the process, the person who killed the thief is not guilty of murder. ³ But if it happens in daylight, the one who killed the thief is guilty of murder.

"A thief who is caught must pay in full for everything he stole. If he cannot pay, he must be sold as a slave to pay for his theft. ⁴ If someone steals an ox or a donkey or a sheep and it is found in the thief's possession, then the thief must pay double the value of the stolen animal.

⁵ "If an animal is grazing in a field or vineyard and the owner lets it stray into someone else's field to graze, then the animal's owner must pay compensation from the best of his own grain or grapes.

⁶ "If you are burning thornbushes and the fire gets out of control and spreads into another person's field, destroying the sheaves or the uncut grain or the whole crop, the one who started the fire must pay for the lost crop.

⁷ "Suppose someone leaves money or goods with a neighbor for safekeeping, and they are stolen from the neighbor's house. If the thief is caught, the compensation is double the value of what was stolen. ⁸ But if the thief is not caught, the neighbor must appear before God,* who will determine if he stole the property.

⁹ "Suppose there is a dispute between two people who both claim to own a particular ox, donkey, sheep, article of clothing, or any lost property. Both parties must come before God, and the person whom God declares* guilty must pay double compensation to the other.

¹⁰ "Now suppose someone leaves a donkey, ox, sheep, or any other animal with a neighbor for safekeeping, but it dies or is injured or is taken away, and no one sees what happened. ¹¹ The neighbor must then take an oath in the presence of the LORD. If the LORD confirms that the neighbor did not steal the property, the owner must accept the verdict, and no payment will be required. ¹² But if the animal was indeed stolen, the guilty person must pay compensation to the owner. ¹³ If it was torn to pieces by a wild animal, the remains of the carcass must be shown as evidence, and no compensation will be required.

¹⁴ "If someone borrows an animal from a neighbor and it is injured or dies when the owner is absent, the person who borrowed it must pay full compensation. ¹⁵ But if the owner was present, no compensation is required. And no compensation is required if the animal was rented, for this loss is covered by the rental fee.

SOCIAL RESPONSIBILITY

¹⁶ "If a man seduces a virgin who is not engaged to anyone and has sex with her, he must pay the customary bride price and marry her. ¹⁷ But if her father refuses to let him marry her, the man must still pay him an amount equal to the bride price of a virgin.

¹⁸ "You must not allow a sorceress to live.

¹⁹ "Anyone who has sexual relations with an animal must certainly be put to death.

²⁰ "Anyone who sacrifices to any god other than the LORD must be destroyed.*

²¹ "You must not mistreat or oppress foreigners in any way. Remember, you yourselves were once foreigners in the land of Egypt.

²² "You must not exploit a widow or an orphan. ²³ If you exploit them in any way and they cry out to me, then I will certainly hear their cry. ²⁴ My anger will blaze against you, and I will kill you with the sword. Then your wives will be widows and your children fatherless.

²⁵ "If you lend money to any of my people who are in need, do not charge interest as a money lender would. ²⁶ If you take your neighbor's cloak as security for a loan, you must return it before sunset. ²⁷ This coat may be the only blanket your neighbor has. How can a person sleep without it? If you do not return it and your neighbor cries out to me for help, then I will hear, for I am merciful.

²⁸ "You must not dishonor God or curse any of your rulers.

²⁹ "You must not hold anything back when you give me offerings from your crops and your wine.

"You must give me your firstborn sons.

³⁰ "You must also give me the firstborn of your cattle, sheep, and goats. But leave the newborn animal with its mother for seven days; then give it to me on the eighth day.

³¹ "You must be my holy people. Therefore, do not eat any animal that has been torn up and killed by wild animals. Throw it to the dogs.

21:32 Hebrew *30 shekels of silver*, about 12 ounces or 342 grams in weight. **22:1a** Verse 22:1 is numbered 21:37 in Hebrew text. **22:1b** Or *bull,* or *cow;* also in 22:4, 9, 10. **22:2** Verses 22:2-31 are numbered 22:1-30 in Hebrew text. **22:8** Or *before the judges.* **22:9** Or *before the judges, and the person whom the judges declare.* **22:20** The Hebrew term used here refers to the complete consecration of things or people to the LORD, either by destroying them or by giving them as an offering.

A CALL FOR JUSTICE

23 "You must not pass along false rumors. You must not cooperate with evil people by lying on the witness stand.

[2] "You must not follow the crowd in doing wrong. When you are called to testify in a dispute, do not be swayed by the crowd to twist justice. [3] And do not slant your testimony in favor of a person just because that person is poor.

[4] "If you come upon your enemy's ox or donkey that has strayed away, take it back to its owner. [5] If you see that the donkey of someone who hates you has collapsed under its load, do not walk by. Instead, stop and help.

[6] "In a lawsuit, you must not deny justice to the poor.

[7] "Be sure never to charge anyone falsely with evil. Never sentence an innocent or blameless person to death, for I never declare a guilty person to be innocent.

[8] "Take no bribes, for a bribe makes you ignore something that you clearly see. A bribe makes even a righteous person twist the truth.

[9] "You must not oppress foreigners. You know what it's like to be a foreigner, for you yourselves were once foreigners in the land of Egypt.

[10] "Plant and harvest your crops for six years, [11] but let the land be renewed and lie uncultivated during the seventh year. Then let the poor among you harvest whatever grows on its own. Leave the rest for wild animals to eat. The same applies to your vineyards and olive groves.

[12] "You have six days each week for your ordinary work, but on the seventh day you must stop working. This gives your ox and your donkey a chance to rest. It also allows your slaves and the foreigners living among you to be refreshed.

[13] "Pay close attention to all my instructions. You must not call on the name of any other gods. Do not even speak their names.

THREE ANNUAL FESTIVALS

[14] "Each year you must celebrate three festivals in my honor. [15] First, celebrate the Festival of Unleavened Bread. For seven days the bread you eat must be made without yeast, just as I commanded you. Celebrate this festival annually at the appointed time in early spring, in the month of Abib,* for that is the anniversary of your departure from Egypt. No one may appear before me without an offering.

[16] "Second, celebrate the Festival of Harvest,* when you bring me the first crops of your harvest.

"Finally, celebrate the Festival of the Final Harvest* at the end of the harvest season, when you have harvested all the crops from your fields. [17] At these three times each year, every man in Israel must appear before the Sovereign, the LORD.

[18] "You must not offer the blood of my sacrificial offerings together with any baked goods containing yeast. And do not leave the fat from the festival offerings until the next morning.

FIRST OF THE FIRST
Exodus 23:19   ROBERT MORRIS

The Bible makes it clear that we need to honor the Lord with the first of our increase. Exodus 23:19 says, "As you harvest your crops, bring the very best of the first harvest to the house of the LORD your God." Is it really an act of faith to give 10 percent *after* all your other bills are paid? What does it say about our priorities when we willingly pay everyone else first and then see if there's enough left to give God His portion? The first portion we spend should always be the tithe—the first of the first. According to Exodus 13, the first portion is the redemptive portion. However, if we take the first portion for ourselves, it becomes a curse because we've stolen from God. I promise you a redeemed 90 percent can go a lot further than a cursed 100 percent.

[19] "As you harvest your crops, bring the very best of the first harvest to the house of the LORD your God.

"You must not cook a young goat in its mother's milk.

A PROMISE OF THE LORD'S PRESENCE

[20] "See, I am sending an angel before you to protect you on your journey and lead you safely to the place I have prepared for you. [21] Pay close attention to him, and obey his instructions. Do not rebel against him, for he is my representative, and he will not forgive your rebellion. [22] But if you are careful to obey him, following all my instructions, then I will be an enemy to your enemies, and I will oppose those who oppose you. [23] For my angel will go before you and bring you into the land of the Amorites, Hittites, Perizzites, Canaanites, Hivites, and Jebusites, so you may live there. And I will destroy them completely. [24] You must not worship the gods of these nations or serve them in any way or imitate their evil practices. Instead, you must utterly destroy them and smash their sacred pillars.

[25] "You must serve only the LORD your God. If you do, I* will bless you with food and water, and I will protect you from illness. [26] There will be no miscarriages or infertility in your land, and I will give you long, full lives.

[27] "I will send my terror ahead of you and create panic among all the people whose lands you invade. I will make all your enemies turn and run.

23:15 Hebrew *appointed time in the month of Abib.* This first month of the ancient Hebrew lunar calendar usually occurs within the months of March and April.   23:16a Or *Festival of Weeks.* This was later called the Festival of Pentecost (see Acts 2:1). It is celebrated today as Shavuot (or Shabuoth).   23:16b Or *Festival of Ingathering.* This was later called the Festival of Shelters or Festival of Tabernacles (see Lev 23:33-36). It is celebrated today as Sukkot (or Succoth).   23:25 As in Greek and Latin versions; Hebrew reads *he.*

[28] I will send terror* ahead of you to drive out the Hivites, Canaanites, and Hittites. [29] But I will not drive them out in a single year, because the land would become desolate and the wild animals would multiply and threaten you. [30] I will drive them out a little at a time until your population has increased enough to take possession of the land. [31] And I will fix your boundaries from the Red Sea to the Mediterranean Sea,* and from the eastern wilderness to the Euphrates River.* I will hand over to you the people now living in the land, and you will drive them out ahead of you. [32] "Make no treaties with them or their gods. [33] They must not live in your land, or they will cause you to sin against me. If you serve their gods, you will be caught in the trap of idolatry."

ISRAEL ACCEPTS THE LORD'S COVENANT

24 Then the LORD instructed Moses: "Come up here to me, and bring along Aaron, Nadab, Abihu, and seventy of Israel's elders. All of you must worship from a distance. [2] Only Moses is allowed to come near to the LORD. The others must not come near, and none of the other people are allowed to climb up the mountain with him."

[3] Then Moses went down to the people and repeated all the instructions and regulations the LORD had given him. All the people answered with one voice, "We will do everything the LORD has commanded."

[4] Then Moses carefully wrote down all the LORD's instructions. Early the next morning Moses got up and built an altar at the foot of the mountain. He also set up twelve pillars, one for each of the twelve tribes of Israel. [5] Then he sent some of the young Israelite men to present burnt offerings and to sacrifice bulls as peace offerings to the LORD. [6] Moses drained half the blood from these animals into basins. The other half he splattered against the altar.

[7] Then he took the Book of the Covenant and read it aloud to the people. Again they all responded, "We will do everything the LORD has commanded. We will obey."

[8] Then Moses took the blood from the basins and splattered it over the people, declaring, "Look, this blood confirms the covenant the LORD has made with you in giving you these instructions."

[9] Then Moses, Aaron, Nadab, Abihu, and the seventy elders of Israel climbed up the mountain. [10] There they saw the God of Israel. Under his feet there seemed to be a surface of brilliant blue lapis lazuli, as clear as the sky itself. [11] And though these nobles of Israel gazed upon God, he did not destroy them. In fact, they ate a covenant meal, eating and drinking in his presence!

[12] Then the LORD said to Moses, "Come up to me on the mountain. Stay there, and I will give you the tablets of stone on which I have inscribed the instructions and commands so you can teach the people." [13] So Moses and his assistant Joshua set out, and Moses climbed up the mountain of God.

[14] Moses told the elders, "Stay here and wait for us until we come back. Aaron and Hur are here with you. If anyone has a dispute while I am gone, consult with them."

[15] Then Moses climbed up the mountain, and the cloud covered it. [16] And the glory of the LORD settled down on Mount Sinai, and the cloud covered it for six days. On the seventh day the LORD called to Moses from inside the cloud. [17] To the Israelites at the foot of the mountain, the glory of the LORD appeared at the summit like a consuming fire. [18] Then Moses disappeared into the cloud as he climbed higher up the mountain. He remained on the mountain forty days and forty nights.

OFFERINGS FOR THE TABERNACLE

25 The LORD said to Moses, [2] "Tell the people of Israel to bring me their sacred offerings. Accept the contributions from all whose hearts are moved to offer them. [3] Here is a list of sacred offerings you may accept from them:

gold, silver, and bronze;
[4] blue, purple, and scarlet thread;
fine linen and goat hair for cloth;
[5] tanned ram skins and fine goatskin leather;
acacia wood;
[6] olive oil for the lamps;
spices for the anointing oil and the fragrant incense;
[7] onyx stones, and other gemstones to be set in the ephod and the priest's chestpiece.

[8] "Have the people of Israel build me a holy sanctuary so I can live among them. [9] You must build this Tabernacle and its furnishings exactly according to the pattern I will show you.

PLANS FOR THE ARK OF THE COVENANT

[10] "Have the people make an Ark of acacia wood—a sacred chest 45 inches long, 27 inches wide, and 27 inches high.* [11] Overlay it inside and outside with pure gold, and run a molding of gold all around it. [12] Cast four gold rings and attach them to its four feet, two rings on each side. [13] Make poles from acacia wood, and overlay them with gold. [14] Insert the poles into the rings at the sides of the Ark to carry it. [15] These carrying poles must stay inside the rings; never remove them. [16] When the Ark is finished, place inside it the stone tablets inscribed with the terms of the covenant,* which I will give to you.

23:28 Often rendered the hornet. The meaning of the Hebrew is uncertain. 23:31a Hebrew from the sea of reeds to the sea of the Philistines. 23:31b Hebrew from the wilderness to the river. 25:10 Hebrew 2.5 cubits [115 centimeters] long, 1.5 cubits [69 centimeters] wide, and 1.5 cubits high. 25:16 Hebrew Place inside the Ark the Testimony; similarly in 25:21. The Hebrew word for "testimony" refers to the terms of the LORD's covenant with Israel as written on stone tablets, and also to the covenant itself.

ENCOUNTERING GOD
Exodus 25:22   ROBERT MORRIS

One of the most frequent things I hear people say about Gateway Church is, "When I walked in, it felt like home!" But what makes a place feel like home? *Love.* When we sense love in a place, we are really sensing the presence of God. In Exodus 25:22, the Lord gives Moses instructions for the Ark of the Covenant and says, "I will meet with you there and talk to you." God wants to meet and talk with *you* too!

Scripture tells us several ways we can encounter God. First, you can encounter Him when you are alone (Genesis 28:16-17). God loves to encourage the lonely, and He will happily meet with you anytime, anywhere. You can also encounter God with a few others (Matthew 18:20), a small group (Acts 2:46), or a "vast crowd" (Revelation 7:9). No matter the size of the gathering, there is something powerful about coming together with other believers and worshipping our King!

¹⁷ "Then make the Ark's cover—the place of atonement—from pure gold. It must be 45 inches long and 27 inches wide.* ¹⁸ Then make two cherubim from hammered gold, and place them on the two ends of the atonement cover. ¹⁹ Mold the cherubim on each end of the atonement cover, making it all of one piece of gold. ²⁰ The cherubim will face each other and look down on the atonement cover. With their wings spread above it, they will protect it. ²¹ Place inside the Ark the stone tablets inscribed with the terms of the covenant, which I will give to you. Then put the atonement cover on top of the Ark. ²² I will meet with you there and talk to you from above the atonement cover between the gold cherubim that hover over the Ark of the Covenant.* From there I will give you my commands for the people of Israel.

PLANS FOR THE TABLE

²³ "Then make a table of acacia wood, 36 inches long, 18 inches wide, and 27 inches high.* ²⁴ Overlay it with pure gold and run a gold molding around the edge. ²⁵ Decorate it with a 3-inch border* all around, and run a gold molding along the border. ²⁶ Make four gold rings for the table and attach them at the four corners next to the four legs. ²⁷ Attach the rings near the border to hold the poles that are used to carry the table. ²⁸ Make these poles from acacia wood, and overlay them with gold. ²⁹ Make special containers of pure gold for the table—bowls, ladles, pitchers, and jars—to be used in pouring out liquid offerings. ³⁰ Place the Bread of the Presence on the table to remain before me at all times.

PLANS FOR THE LAMPSTAND

³¹ "Make a lampstand of pure, hammered gold. Make the entire lampstand and its decorations of one piece—the base, center stem, lamp cups, buds, and petals. ³² Make it with six branches going out from the center stem, three on each side. ³³ Each of the six branches will have three lamp cups shaped like almond blossoms, complete with buds and petals. ³⁴ Craft the center stem of the lampstand with four lamp cups shaped like almond blossoms, complete with buds and petals. ³⁵ There will also be an almond bud beneath each pair of branches where the six branches extend from the center stem. ³⁶ The almond buds and branches must all be of one piece with the center stem, and they must be hammered from pure gold. ³⁷ Then make the seven lamps for the lampstand, and set them so they reflect their light forward. ³⁸ The lamp snuffers and trays must also be made of pure gold. ³⁹ You will need 75 pounds* of pure gold for the lampstand and its accessories.

⁴⁰ "Be sure that you make everything according to the pattern I have shown you here on the mountain.

PLANS FOR THE TABERNACLE

26 "Make the Tabernacle from ten curtains of finely woven linen. Decorate the curtains with blue, purple, and scarlet thread and with skillfully embroidered cherubim. ² These ten curtains must all be exactly the same size—42 feet long and 6 feet wide.* ³ Join five of these curtains together to make one long curtain, then join the other five into a second long curtain. ⁴ Put loops of blue yarn along the edge of the last curtain in each set. ⁵ The fifty loops along the edge of one curtain are to match the fifty loops along the edge of the other curtain. ⁶ Then make fifty gold clasps and fasten the long curtains together with the clasps. In this way, the Tabernacle will be made of one continuous piece.

⁷ "Make eleven curtains of goat-hair cloth to serve as a tent covering for the Tabernacle. ⁸ These eleven curtains must all be exactly the same size—45 feet long and 6 feet wide.* ⁹ Join five of these curtains together to make one long curtain, and join the other six into a second long curtain. Allow 3 feet of material from the second set of curtains to hang over the front* of the sacred tent. ¹⁰ Make fifty loops for one edge of each large curtain. ¹¹ Then make fifty bronze clasps, and fasten the loops of the long curtains with the clasps. In this way, the tent covering will be made of one continuous piece.

25:17 Hebrew *2.5 cubits* [115 centimeters] *long and 1.5 cubits* [69 centimeters] *wide.*   25:22 Or *Ark of the Testimony.*
25:23 Hebrew *2 cubits* [92 centimeters] *long, 1 cubit* [46 centimeters] *wide, and 1.5 cubits* [69 centimeters] *high.*
25:25 Hebrew *a border of a handbreadth* [8 centimeters].
25:39 Hebrew *1 talent* [34 kilograms].   26:2 Hebrew *28 cubits* [12.9 meters] *long and 4 cubits* [1.8 meters] *wide.*   26:8 Hebrew *30 cubits* [13.8 meters] *long and 4 cubits* [1.8 meters] *wide.*
26:9 Hebrew *Double over the sixth sheet at the front.*

¹²The remaining 3 feet* of this tent covering will be left to hang over the back of the Tabernacle. ¹³Allow 18 inches* of remaining material to hang down over each side, so the Tabernacle is completely covered. ¹⁴Complete the tent covering with a protective layer of tanned ram skins and a layer of fine goatskin leather.

¹⁵"For the framework of the Tabernacle, construct frames of acacia wood. ¹⁶Each frame must be 15 feet high and 27 inches wide,* ¹⁷with two pegs under each frame. Make all the frames identical. ¹⁸Make twenty of these frames to support the curtains on the south side of the Tabernacle. ¹⁹Also make forty silver bases—two bases under each frame, with the pegs fitting securely into the bases. ²⁰For the north side of the Tabernacle, make another twenty frames, ²¹with their forty silver bases, two bases under each frame. ²²Make six frames for the rear—the west side of the Tabernacle—²³along with two additional frames to reinforce the rear corners of the Tabernacle. ²⁴These corner frames will be matched at the bottom and firmly attached at the top with a single ring, forming a single corner unit. Make both of these corner units the same way. ²⁵So there will be eight frames at the rear of the Tabernacle, set in sixteen silver bases—two bases under each frame.

²⁶"Make crossbars of acacia wood to link the frames, five crossbars for the north side of the Tabernacle ²⁷and five for the south side. Also make five crossbars for the rear of the Tabernacle, which will face west. ²⁸The middle crossbar, attached halfway up the frames, will run all the way from one end of the Tabernacle to the other. ²⁹Overlay the frames with gold, and make gold rings to hold the crossbars. Overlay the crossbars with gold as well.

³⁰"Set up this Tabernacle according to the pattern you were shown on the mountain.

³¹"For the inside of the Tabernacle, make a special curtain of finely woven linen. Decorate it with blue, purple, and scarlet thread and with skillfully embroidered cherubim. ³²Hang this curtain on gold hooks attached to four posts of acacia wood. Overlay the posts with gold, and set them in four silver bases. ³³Hang the inner curtain from clasps, and put the Ark of the Covenant* in the room behind it. This curtain will separate the Holy Place from the Most Holy Place. ³⁴Then put the Ark's cover—the place of atonement—on top of the Ark of the Covenant inside the Most Holy Place. ³⁵Place the table outside the inner curtain on the north side of the Tabernacle, and place the lampstand across the room on the south side.

³⁶"Make another curtain for the entrance to the sacred tent. Make it of finely woven linen and embroider it with exquisite designs, using blue, purple, and scarlet thread. ³⁷Craft five posts from acacia wood. Overlay them with gold, and hang the curtain from them with gold hooks. Cast five bronze bases for the posts.

PLANS FOR THE ALTAR OF BURNT OFFERING

27 "Using acacia wood, construct a square altar 7½ feet wide, 7½ feet long, and 4½ feet high.* ²Make horns for each of its four corners so that the horns and altar are all one piece. Overlay the altar with bronze. ³Make ash buckets, shovels, basins, meat forks, and firepans, all of bronze. ⁴Make a bronze grating for it, and attach four bronze rings at its four corners. ⁵Install the grating halfway down the side of the altar, under the ledge. ⁶For carrying the altar, make poles from acacia wood, and overlay them with bronze. ⁷Insert the poles through the rings on the two sides of the altar. ⁸The altar must be hollow, made from planks. Build it just as you were shown on the mountain.

PLANS FOR THE COURTYARD

⁹"Then make the courtyard for the Tabernacle, enclosed with curtains made of finely woven linen. On the south side, make the curtains 150 feet long.* ¹⁰They will be held up by twenty posts set securely in twenty bronze bases. Hang the curtains with silver hooks and rings. ¹¹Make the curtains the same on the north side—150 feet of curtains held up by twenty posts set securely in bronze bases. Hang the curtains with silver hooks and rings. ¹²The curtains on the west end of the courtyard will be 75 feet long,* supported by ten posts set into ten bases. ¹³The east end of the courtyard, the front, will also be 75 feet long. ¹⁴The courtyard entrance will be on the east end, flanked by two curtains. The curtain on the right side will be 22½ feet long,* supported by three posts set into three bases. ¹⁵The curtain on the left side will also be 22½ feet long, supported by three posts set into three bases.

¹⁶"For the entrance to the courtyard, make a curtain that is 30 feet long.* Make it from finely woven linen, and decorate it with beautiful embroidery in blue, purple, and scarlet thread. Support it with four posts, each securely set in its own base. ¹⁷All the posts around the courtyard must have silver rings and hooks and bronze bases. ¹⁸So the entire courtyard will be 150 feet long and 75 feet wide, with curtain walls 7½ feet high,* made from finely woven linen. The bases for the posts will be made of bronze.

¹⁹"All the articles used in the rituals of the Tabernacle, including all the tent pegs used to support the Tabernacle and the courtyard curtains, must be made of bronze.

26:12 Hebrew *The half sheet that is left over.* 26:13 Hebrew *1 cubit* [46 centimeters]. 26:16 Hebrew *10 cubits* [4.6 meters] *high and 1.5 cubits* [69 centimeters] *wide.* 26:33 Or *Ark of the Testimony;* also in 26:34. 27:1 Hebrew *5 cubits* [2.3 meters] *wide, 5 cubits long, a square, and 3 cubits* [1.4 meters] *high.* 27:9 Hebrew *100 cubits* [46 meters]; also in 27:11. 27:12 Hebrew *50 cubits* [23 meters]; also in 27:13. 27:14 Hebrew *15 cubits* [6.9 meters]; also in 27:15. 27:16 Hebrew *20 cubits* [9.2 meters]. 27:18 Hebrew *100 cubits* [46 meters] *long and 50 by 50* [23 meters] *wide and 5 cubits* [2.3 meters] *high.*

LIGHT FOR THE TABERNACLE

20 "Command the people of Israel to bring you pure oil of pressed olives for the light, to keep the lamps burning continually. 21 The lampstand will stand in the Tabernacle, in front of the inner curtain that shields the Ark of the Covenant.* Aaron and his sons must keep the lamps burning in the LORD's presence all night. This is a permanent law for the people of Israel, and it must be observed from generation to generation.

CLOTHING FOR THE PRIESTS

28 "Call for your brother, Aaron, and his sons, Nadab, Abihu, Eleazar, and Ithamar. Set them apart from the rest of the people of Israel so they may minister to me and be my priests. 2 Make sacred garments for Aaron that are glorious and beautiful. 3 Instruct all the skilled craftsmen whom I have filled with the spirit of wisdom. Have them make garments for Aaron that will distinguish him as a priest set apart for my service. 4 These are the garments they are to make: a chestpiece, an ephod, a robe, a patterned tunic, a turban, and a sash. They are to make these sacred garments for your brother, Aaron, and his sons to wear when they serve me as priests. 5 So give them fine linen cloth, gold thread, and blue, purple, and scarlet thread.

DESIGN OF THE EPHOD

6 "The craftsmen must make the ephod of finely woven linen and skillfully embroider it with gold and with blue, purple, and scarlet thread. 7 It will consist of two pieces, front and back, joined at the shoulders with two shoulder-pieces. 8 The decorative sash will be made of the same materials: finely woven linen embroidered with gold and with blue, purple, and scarlet thread.

9 "Take two onyx stones, and engrave on them the names of the tribes of Israel. 10 Six names will be on each stone, arranged in the order of the births of the original sons of Israel. 11 Engrave these names on the two stones in the same way a jeweler engraves a seal. Then mount the stones in settings of gold filigree. 12 Fasten the two stones on the shoulder-pieces of the ephod as a reminder that Aaron represents the people of Israel. Aaron will carry these names on his shoulders as a constant reminder whenever he goes before the LORD. 13 Make the settings of gold filigree, 14 then braid two cords of pure gold and attach them to the filigree settings on the shoulders of the ephod.

DESIGN OF THE CHESTPIECE

15 "Then, with great skill and care, make a chestpiece to be worn for seeking a decision from God.* Make it to match the ephod, using finely woven linen embroidered with gold and with blue, purple, and scarlet thread. 16 Make the chestpiece of a single piece of cloth folded to form a pouch nine inches* square. 17 Mount four rows of gemstones* on it. The first row will contain a red carnelian, a pale-green peridot, and an emerald. 18 The second row will contain a turquoise, a blue lapis lazuli, and a white moonstone. 19 The third row will contain an orange jacinth, an agate, and a purple amethyst. 20 The fourth row will contain a blue-green beryl, an onyx, and a green jasper. All these stones will be set in gold filigree. 21 Each stone will represent one of the twelve sons of Israel, and the name of that tribe will be engraved on it like a seal.

22 "To attach the chestpiece to the ephod, make braided cords of pure gold thread. 23 Then make two gold rings and attach them to the top corners of the chestpiece. 24 Tie the two gold cords to the two rings on the chestpiece. 25 Tie the other ends of the cords to the gold settings on the shoulder-pieces of the ephod. 26 Then make two more gold rings and attach them to the inside edges of the chestpiece next to the ephod. 27 And make two more gold rings and attach them to the front of the ephod, below the shoulder-pieces, just above the knot where the decorative sash is fastened to the ephod. 28 Then attach the bottom rings of the chestpiece to the rings on the ephod with blue cords. This will hold the chestpiece securely to the ephod above the decorative sash.

29 "In this way, Aaron will carry the names of the tribes of Israel on the sacred chestpiece* over his heart when he goes into the Holy Place. This will be a continual reminder that he represents the people when he comes before the LORD. 30 Insert the Urim and Thummim into the sacred chestpiece so they will be carried over Aaron's heart when he goes into the LORD's presence. In this way, Aaron will always carry over his heart the objects used to determine the LORD's will for his people whenever he goes in before the LORD.

ADDITIONAL CLOTHING FOR THE PRIESTS

31 "Make the robe that is worn with the ephod from a single piece of blue cloth, 32 with an opening for Aaron's head in the middle of it. Reinforce the opening with a woven collar* so it will not tear. 33 Make pomegranates out of blue, purple, and scarlet yarn, and attach them to the hem of the robe, with gold bells between them. 34 The gold bells and pomegranates are to alternate all around the hem. 35 Aaron will wear this robe whenever he ministers before the LORD, and the bells will tinkle as he goes in and out of the LORD's presence in the Holy Place. If he wears it, he will not die.

36 "Next make a medallion of pure gold, and engrave it like a seal with these words: HOLY TO THE LORD. 37 Attach the medallion with a blue cord to the front of Aaron's turban, where it must remain. 38 Aaron must wear it on his forehead so

---

27:21 Hebrew in the Tent of Meeting, outside the inner curtain that is in front of the Testimony. See note on 25:16. 28:15 Hebrew a chestpiece for decision. 28:16 Hebrew 1 span [23 centimeters]. 28:17 The identification of some of these gemstones is uncertain. 28:29 Hebrew the chestpiece for decision; also in 28:30. See 28:15. 28:32 The meaning of the Hebrew is uncertain.

THE LAMB
Exodus 29:38–41

ROBERT MORRIS

For centuries, God's people offered two lambs every day for their sins—one for sins committed during the day and one for those committed during the night. I grew up in a church that taught me to confess all my sins every morning and every night, but I was always afraid that I would forget one. I'm so grateful to know salvation isn't based on remembering and confessing. Salvation comes from trusting in Jesus, "the Lamb of God who takes away the sin of the world" (John 1:29). He is my Lord and Savior, and His blood covers all my sins.

Here are three things to remember about the Lamb:

1. The Lamb was provided.

God told Abraham to sacrifice his son Isaac as a burnt offering. On the way up the mountain, Isaac asked Abraham where the lamb was. Abraham replied, "God will provide" (Genesis 22:8). No matter what you're going through right now, those three words are the answer—*God will provide*. God provided a ram for Abraham, and two thousand years later, He provided a Lamb—His Son, Jesus—for everyone.

2. The Lamb was pure.

In the Old Testament, sacrificial lambs had to be pure, with no defects (Exodus 12:5). The apostle Peter said Jesus was a "sinless, spotless Lamb of God" (1 Peter 1:19.) Jesus is absolutely pure; there is no fault, blemish, or defect in Him. Many preachers say we had better straighten up our acts because Jesus is coming back for a Bride "without a spot or wrinkle" (Ephesians 5:27). But we'll never be holy enough through our works. The reason Jesus is coming back for a pure Bride is that He paid the price for all our sins. His blood makes us pure.

3. The Lamb is perfect.

No one is perfect, but the good news is there *is* a perfect Lamb, and you can put your faith in Him. It's how you get to heaven—by grace through faith in Jesus Christ.

---

he may take on himself any guilt of the people of Israel when they consecrate their sacred offerings. He must always wear it on his forehead so the LORD will accept the people.

[39] "Weave Aaron's patterned tunic from fine linen cloth. Fashion the turban from this linen as well. Also make a sash, and decorate it with colorful embroidery.

[40] "For Aaron's sons, make tunics, sashes, and special head coverings that are glorious and beautiful. [41] Clothe your brother, Aaron, and his sons with these garments, and then anoint and ordain them. Consecrate them so they can serve as my priests. [42] Also make linen undergarments for them, to be worn next to their bodies, reaching from their hips to their thighs. [43] These must be worn whenever Aaron and his sons enter the Tabernacle* or approach the altar in the Holy Place to perform their priestly duties. Then they will not incur guilt and die. This is a permanent law for Aaron and all his descendants after him.

DEDICATION OF THE PRIESTS

29 "This is the ceremony you must follow when you consecrate Aaron and his sons to serve me as priests: Take a young bull and two rams with no defects. [2] Then, using choice wheat flour and no yeast, make loaves of bread, thin cakes mixed with olive oil, and wafers spread with oil. [3] Place them all in a single basket, and present them at the entrance of the Tabernacle, along with the young bull and the two rams.

[4] "Present Aaron and his sons at the entrance of the Tabernacle,* and wash them with water. [5] Dress Aaron in his priestly garments—the tunic, the robe worn with the ephod, the ephod itself, and the chestpiece. Then wrap the decorative sash of the ephod around him. [6] Place the turban on his head, and fasten the sacred medallion to the turban. [7] Then anoint him by pouring the anointing oil over his head. [8] Next present his sons, and dress them in their tunics. [9] Wrap the sashes around the waists of Aaron and his sons, and put their special head coverings on them. Then the right to the priesthood will be theirs by law forever. In this way, you will ordain Aaron and his sons.

[10] "Bring the young bull to the entrance of the Tabernacle, where Aaron and his sons will lay their hands on its head. [11] Then slaughter the bull in the LORD's presence at the entrance of the Tabernacle. [12] Put some of its blood on the horns of the altar with your finger, and pour out the rest at the base of the altar. [13] Take all the fat around the internal organs, the long lobe of the liver, and the two kidneys and the fat around them, and burn it all on the altar. [14] Then take the rest of the bull, including its hide, meat, and dung, and burn it outside the camp as a sin offering.

[15] "Next Aaron and his sons must lay their hands on the head of one of the rams. [16] Then slaughter the ram, and splatter its blood against all sides of the altar. [17] Cut the ram into pieces, and wash off the internal organs and the legs. Set them alongside the head and the other pieces of the body, [18] then burn the entire animal on the altar. This is a burnt offering to the LORD; it is a pleasing aroma, a special gift presented to the LORD.

28:43 Hebrew *Tent of Meeting.* 29:4 Hebrew *Tent of Meeting;* also in 29:10, 11, 30, 32, 42, 44.

¹⁹"Now take the other ram, and have Aaron and his sons lay their hands on its head. ²⁰Then slaughter it, and apply some of its blood to the right earlobes of Aaron and his sons. Also put it on the thumbs of their right hands and the big toes of their right feet. Splatter the rest of the blood against all sides of the altar. ²¹Then take some of the blood from the altar and some of the anointing oil, and sprinkle it on Aaron and his sons and on their garments. In this way, they and their garments will be set apart as holy.

²²"Since this is the ram for the ordination of Aaron and his sons, take the fat of the ram, including the fat of the broad tail, the fat around the internal organs, the long lobe of the liver, and the two kidneys and the fat around them, along with the right thigh. ²³Then take one round loaf of bread, one thin cake mixed with olive oil, and one wafer from the basket of bread without yeast that was placed in the LORD's presence. ²⁴Put all these in the hands of Aaron and his sons to be lifted up as a special offering to the LORD. ²⁵Afterward take the various breads from their hands, and burn them on the altar along with the burnt offering. It is a pleasing aroma to the LORD, a special gift for him. ²⁶Then take the breast of Aaron's ordination ram, and lift it up in the LORD's presence as a special offering to him. Then keep it as your own portion.

²⁷"Set aside the portions of the ordination ram that belong to Aaron and his sons. This includes the breast and the thigh that were lifted up before the LORD as a special offering. ²⁸In the future, whenever the people of Israel lift up a peace offering, a portion of it must be set aside for Aaron and his descendants. This is their permanent right, and it is a sacred offering from the Israelites to the LORD.

²⁹"Aaron's sacred garments must be preserved for his descendants who succeed him, and they will wear them when they are anointed and ordained. ³⁰The descendant who succeeds him as high priest will wear these clothes for seven days as he ministers in the Tabernacle and the Holy Place.

³¹"Take the ram used in the ordination ceremony, and boil its meat in a sacred place. ³²Then Aaron and his sons will eat this meat, along with the bread in the basket, at the Tabernacle entrance. ³³They alone may eat the meat and bread used for their purification* in the ordination ceremony. No one else may eat them, for these things are set apart and holy. ³⁴If any of the ordination meat or bread remains until the morning, it must be burned. It may not be eaten, for it is holy.

³⁵"This is how you will ordain Aaron and his sons to their offices, just as I have commanded you. The ordination ceremony will go on for seven days. ³⁶Each day you must sacrifice a young bull as a sin offering to purify them, making them right with the LORD.* Afterward, cleanse the altar by purifying it*; make it holy by anointing it with oil. ³⁷Purify the altar, and consecrate it every day for seven days. After that, the altar will be absolutely holy, and whatever touches it will become holy.

³⁸"These are the sacrifices you are to offer regularly on the altar. Each day, offer two lambs that are a year old, ³⁹one in the morning and the other in the evening. ⁴⁰With one of them, offer two quarts of choice flour mixed with one quart of pure oil of pressed olives; also, offer one quart of wine* as a liquid offering. ⁴¹Offer the other lamb in the evening, along with the same offerings of flour and wine as in the morning. It will be a pleasing aroma, a special gift presented to the LORD.

⁴²"These burnt offerings are to be made each day from generation to generation. Offer them in the LORD's presence at the Tabernacle entrance; there I will meet with you and speak with you. ⁴³I will meet the people of Israel there, in the place made holy by my glorious presence. ⁴⁴Yes, I will consecrate the Tabernacle and the altar, and I will consecrate Aaron and his sons to serve me as priests. ⁴⁵Then I will live among the people of Israel and be their God, ⁴⁶and they will know that I am the LORD their God. I am the one who brought them out of the land of Egypt so that I could live among them. I am the LORD their God.

PLANS FOR THE INCENSE ALTAR

30 "Then make another altar of acacia wood for burning incense. ²Make it 18 inches square and 36 inches high,* with horns at the corners carved from the same piece of wood as the altar itself. ³Overlay the top, sides, and horns of the altar with pure gold, and run a gold molding around the entire altar. ⁴Make two gold rings, and attach them on opposite sides of the altar below the gold molding to hold the carrying poles. ⁵Make the poles of acacia wood and overlay them with gold. ⁶Place the incense altar just outside the inner curtain that shields the Ark of the Covenant,* in front of the Ark's cover—the place of atonement—that covers the tablets inscribed with the terms of the covenant.* I will meet with you there.

⁷"Every morning when Aaron maintains the lamps, he must burn fragrant incense on the altar. ⁸And each evening when he lights the lamps, he must again burn incense in the LORD's presence. This must be done from generation to generation. ⁹Do not offer any unholy incense on this altar, or any burnt offerings, grain offerings, or liquid offerings.

29:33 Or their atonement.   29:36a Or to make atonement.
29:36b Or by making atonement for it; similarly in 29:37.
29:40 Hebrew ¹⁄₁₀ [of an ephah] [2.2 liters] of choice flour . . . ¼ of a hin [1 liter] of pure oil . . . ¼ of a hin of wine.   30:2 Hebrew 1 cubit [46 centimeters] long and 1 cubit wide, a square, and 2 cubits [92 centimeters] high.   30:6a Or Ark of the Testimony; also in 30:26.   30:6b Hebrew that covers the Testimony; see note on 25:16.

¹⁰ "Once a year Aaron must purify* the altar by smearing its horns with blood from the offering made to purify the people from their sin. This will be a regular, annual event from generation to generation, for this is the LORD's most holy altar."

MONEY FOR THE TABERNACLE

¹¹ Then the LORD said to Moses, ¹² "Whenever you take a census of the people of Israel, each man who is counted must pay a ransom for himself to the LORD. Then no plague will strike the people as you count them. ¹³ Each person who is counted must give a small piece of silver as a sacred offering to the LORD. (This payment is half a shekel,* based on the sanctuary shekel, which equals twenty gerahs.) ¹⁴ All who have reached their twentieth birthday must give this sacred offering to the LORD. ¹⁵ When this offering is given to the LORD to purify your lives, making you right with him,* the rich must not give more than the specified amount, and the poor must not give less. ¹⁶ Receive this ransom money from the Israelites, and use it for the care of the Tabernacle.* It will bring the Israelites to the LORD's attention, and it will purify your lives."

PLANS FOR THE WASHBASIN

¹⁷ Then the LORD said to Moses, ¹⁸ "Make a bronze washbasin with a bronze stand. Place it between the Tabernacle and the altar, and fill it with water. ¹⁹ Aaron and his sons will wash their hands and feet there. ²⁰ They must wash with water whenever they go into the Tabernacle to appear before the LORD and when they approach the altar to burn up their special gifts to the LORD—or they will die! ²¹ They must always wash their hands and feet, or they will die. This is a permanent law for Aaron and his descendants, to be observed from generation to generation."

THE ANOINTING OIL

²² Then the LORD said to Moses, ²³ "Collect choice spices—12½ pounds of pure myrrh, 6¼ pounds of fragrant cinnamon, 6¼ pounds of fragrant calamus,* ²⁴ and 12½ pounds of cassia*—as measured by the weight of the sanctuary shekel. Also get one gallon of olive oil.* ²⁵ Like a skilled incense maker, blend these ingredients to make a holy anointing oil. ²⁶ Use this sacred oil to anoint the Tabernacle, the Ark of the Covenant, ²⁷ the table and all its utensils, the lampstand and all its accessories, the incense altar, ²⁸ the altar of burnt offering and all its utensils, and the washbasin with its stand. ²⁹ Consecrate them to make them absolutely holy. After this, whatever touches them will also become holy.

³⁰ "Anoint Aaron and his sons also, consecrating them to serve me as priests. ³¹ And say to the people of Israel, 'This holy anointing oil is reserved for me from generation to generation. ³² It must never be used to anoint anyone else, and you must never make any blend like it for yourselves. It is holy, and you must treat it as holy. ³³ Anyone who makes a blend like it or anoints someone other than a priest will be cut off from the community.'"

THE INCENSE

³⁴ Then the LORD said to Moses, "Gather fragrant spices—resin droplets, mollusk shell, and galbanum—and mix these fragrant spices with pure frankincense, weighed out in equal amounts. ³⁵ Using the usual techniques of the incense maker, blend the spices together and sprinkle them with salt to produce a pure and holy incense. ³⁶ Grind some of the mixture into a very fine powder and put it in front of the Ark of the Covenant,* where I will meet with you in the Tabernacle. You must treat this incense as most holy. ³⁷ Never use this formula to make this incense for yourselves. It is reserved for the LORD, and you must treat it as holy. ³⁸ Anyone who makes incense like this for personal use will be cut off from the community."

CRAFTSMEN: BEZALEL AND OHOLIAB

31 Then the LORD said to Moses, ² "Look, I have specifically chosen Bezalel son of Uri, grandson of Hur, of the tribe of Judah. ³ I have filled him with the Spirit of God, giving him great wisdom, ability, and expertise in all kinds of crafts. ⁴ He is a master craftsman, expert in working with gold, silver, and bronze. ⁵ He is skilled in engraving and mounting gemstones and in carving wood. He is a master at every craft!

⁶ "And I have personally appointed Oholiab son of Ahisamach, of the tribe of Dan, to be his assistant. Moreover, I have given special skill to all the gifted craftsmen so they can make all the things I have commanded you to make:

⁷ the Tabernacle;*
the Ark of the Covenant;*
the Ark's cover—the place of atonement;
all the furnishings of the Tabernacle;
⁸ the table and its utensils;
the pure gold lampstand with all its accessories;
the incense altar;
⁹ the altar of burnt offering with all its utensils;
the washbasin with its stand;

30:10 Or *make atonement for;* also in 30:10b. 30:13 Or *0.2 ounces* [6 grams]. 30:15 Or *to make atonement for your lives;* similarly in 30:16. 30:16 Hebrew *Tent of Meeting;* also in 30:18, 20, 26, 36. 30:23 Hebrew *500* [shekels] [5.7 kilograms] *of pure myrrh, 250* [shekels] [2.9 kilograms] *of fragrant cinnamon, 250* [shekels] *of fragrant calamus.* 30:24a Hebrew *500* [shekels] [5.7 kilograms] *of cassia.* 30:24b Hebrew *1 hin* [3.8 liters] *of olive oil.* 30:36 Hebrew *in front of the Testimony;* see note on 25:16. 31:7a Hebrew *the Tent of Meeting.* 31:7b Hebrew *the Ark of the Testimony.*

10 the beautifully stitched garments—the sacred garments for Aaron the priest, and the garments for his sons to wear as they minister as priests;

11 the anointing oil;

the fragrant incense for the Holy Place.

The craftsmen must make everything as I have commanded you."

INSTRUCTIONS FOR THE SABBATH

12 The LORD then gave these instructions to Moses: 13 "Tell the people of Israel: 'Be careful to keep my Sabbath day, for the Sabbath is a sign of the covenant between me and you from generation to generation. It is given so you may know that I am the LORD, who makes you holy. 14 You must keep the Sabbath day, for it is a holy day for you. Anyone who desecrates it must be put to death; anyone who works on that day will be cut off from the community. 15 You have six days each week for your ordinary work, but the seventh day must be a Sabbath day of complete rest, a holy day dedicated to the LORD. Anyone who works on the Sabbath must be put to death. 16 The people of Israel must keep the Sabbath day by observing it from generation to generation. This is a covenant obligation for all time. 17 It is a permanent sign of my covenant with the people of Israel. For in six days the LORD made heaven and earth, but on the seventh day he stopped working and was refreshed.'"

18 When the LORD finished speaking with Moses on Mount Sinai, he gave him the two stone tablets inscribed with the terms of the covenant,* written by the finger of God.

THE GOLD CALF

32 When the people saw how long it was taking Moses to come back down the mountain, they gathered around Aaron. "Come on," they said, "make us some gods who can lead us. We don't know what happened to this fellow Moses, who brought us here from the land of Egypt."

2 So Aaron said, "Take the gold rings from the ears of your wives and sons and daughters, and bring them to me."

3 All the people took the gold rings from their ears and brought them to Aaron. 4 Then Aaron took the gold, melted it down, and molded it into the shape of a calf. When the people saw it, they exclaimed, "O Israel, these are the gods who brought you out of the land of Egypt!"

5 Aaron saw how excited the people were, so he built an altar in front of the calf. Then he announced, "Tomorrow will be a festival to the LORD!"

6 The people got up early the next morning to sacrifice burnt offerings and peace offerings. After this, they celebrated with feasting and drinking, and they indulged in pagan revelry.

7 The LORD told Moses, "Quick! Go down the mountain! Your people whom you brought from the land of Egypt have corrupted themselves. 8 How quickly they have turned away from the way I commanded them to live! They have melted down gold and made a calf, and they have bowed down and sacrificed to it. They are saying, 'These are your gods, O Israel, who brought you out of the land of Egypt.'"

9 Then the LORD said, "I have seen how stubborn and rebellious these people are. 10 Now leave me alone so my fierce anger can blaze against them, and I will destroy them. Then I will make you, Moses, into a great nation."

11 But Moses tried to pacify the LORD his God. "O LORD!" he said. "Why are you so angry with your own people whom you brought from the land of Egypt with such great power and such a strong hand? 12 Why let the Egyptians say, 'Their God rescued them with the evil intention of slaughtering them in the mountains and wiping them from the face of the earth'? Turn away from your fierce anger. Change your mind about this terrible disaster you have threatened against your people! 13 Remember your servants Abraham, Isaac, and Jacob.* You bound yourself with an oath to them, saying, 'I will make your descendants as numerous as the stars of heaven. And I will give them all of this land that I have promised to your descendants, and they will possess it forever.'"

14 So the LORD changed his mind about the terrible disaster he had threatened to bring on his people.

15 Then Moses turned and went down the mountain. He held in his hands the two stone tablets inscribed with the terms of the covenant.* They were inscribed on both sides, front and back. 16 These tablets were God's work; the words on them were written by God himself.

17 When Joshua heard the boisterous noise of the people shouting below them, he exclaimed to Moses, "It sounds like war in the camp!"

18 But Moses replied, "No, it's not a shout of victory nor the wailing of defeat. I hear the sound of a celebration."

19 When they came near the camp, Moses saw the calf and the dancing, and he burned with anger. He threw the stone tablets to the ground, smashing them at the foot of the mountain. 20 He took the calf they had made and burned it. Then he ground it into powder, threw it into the water, and forced the people to drink it.

21 Finally, he turned to Aaron and demanded, "What did these people do to you to make you bring such terrible sin upon them?"

31:18 Hebrew the two tablets of the Testimony; see note on 25:16. 32:13 Hebrew Israel. The names "Jacob" and "Israel" are often interchanged throughout the Old Testament, referring sometimes to the individual patriarch and sometimes to the nation. 32:15 Hebrew the two tablets of the Testimony; see note on 25:16.

[22] "Don't get so upset, my lord," Aaron replied. "You yourself know how evil these people are. [23] They said to me, 'Make us gods who will lead us. We don't know what happened to this fellow Moses, who brought us here from the land of Egypt.' [24] So I told them, 'Whoever has gold jewelry, take it off.' When they brought it to me, I simply threw it into the fire—and out came this calf!"

[25] Moses saw that Aaron had let the people get completely out of control, much to the amusement of their enemies.* [26] So he stood at the entrance to the camp and shouted, "All of you who are on the LORD's side, come here and join me." And all the Levites gathered around him.

[27] Moses told them, "This is what the LORD, the God of Israel, says: Each of you, take your swords and go back and forth from one end of the camp to the other. Kill everyone—even your brothers, friends, and neighbors." [28] The Levites obeyed Moses' command, and about 3,000 people died that day.

[29] Then Moses told the Levites, "Today you have ordained yourselves* for the service of the LORD, for you obeyed him even though it meant killing your own sons and brothers. Today you have earned a blessing."

MOSES INTERCEDES FOR ISRAEL

[30] The next day Moses said to the people, "You have committed a terrible sin, but I will go back up to the LORD on the mountain. Perhaps I will be able to obtain forgiveness* for your sin."

[31] So Moses returned to the LORD and said, "Oh, what a terrible sin these people have committed. They have made gods of gold for themselves. [32] But now, if you will only forgive their sin—but if not, erase my name from the record you have written!"

[33] But the LORD replied to Moses, "No, I will erase the name of everyone who has sinned against me. [34] Now go, lead the people to the place I told you about. Look! My angel will lead the way before you. And when I come to call the people to account, I will certainly hold them responsible for their sins."

[35] Then the LORD sent a great plague upon the people because they had worshiped the calf Aaron had made.

33 The LORD said to Moses, "Get going, you and the people you brought up from the land of Egypt. Go up to the land I swore to give to Abraham, Isaac, and Jacob. I told them, 'I will give this land to your descendants.' [2] And I will send an angel before you to drive out the Canaanites, Amorites, Hittites, Perizzites, Hivites, and Jebusites. [3] Go up to this land that flows with milk and honey. But I will not travel among you, for you are a stubborn and rebellious people. If I did, I would surely destroy you along the way."

[4] When the people heard these stern words, they went into mourning and stopped wearing their jewelry and fine clothes. [5] For the LORD had told Moses to tell them, "You are a stubborn and rebellious people. If I were to travel with you for even a moment, I would destroy you. Remove your jewelry and fine clothes while I decide what to do with you." [6] So from the time they left Mount Sinai,* the Israelites wore no more jewelry or fine clothes.

[7] It was Moses' practice to take the Tent of Meeting* and set it up some distance from the camp. Everyone who wanted to make a request of the LORD would go to the Tent of Meeting outside the camp.

[8] Whenever Moses went out to the Tent of Meeting, all the people would get up and stand in the entrances of their own tents. They would all watch Moses until he disappeared inside. [9] As he went into the tent, the pillar of cloud would come down and hover at its entrance while the LORD spoke with Moses. [10] When the people saw the cloud standing at the entrance of the tent, they would stand and bow down in front of their own tents. [11] Inside the Tent of Meeting, the LORD would speak to Moses face to face, as one speaks to a friend. Afterward Moses would return to the camp, but the young man who assisted him, Joshua son of Nun, would remain behind in the Tent of Meeting.

MOSES' STORY
Exodus 33
TIM ROSS

Moses had a taste of God's presence, but he wanted *more*. He said, "Let me know your ways so I may understand you more fully and continue to enjoy your favor" (Exodus 33:13). Like Moses, we need three things to say we have met God.

First, we need a miracle. The children of Israel had a miracle when God delivered them from slavery in Egypt. Our miracle occurs when God delivers us from sin and reconciles us through Jesus' sacrifice on the cross. Second, we need an experience. Moses wanted to see God's glory, so he asked God to reveal Himself. We can experience God's presence when we continually pursue Him. Every difficult situation we encounter is an opportunity for God to reveal His glory. Finally, we need a testimony. Our testimonies are the stories of what God has done in our lives. Moses knew he could not lead the Israelites by himself. He told the Lord, "Your presence among us sets your people and me apart from all other people on the earth" (Exodus 33:16).

33:25 Or *out of control, and they mocked anyone who opposed them.* The meaning of the Hebrew is uncertain. 32:29 As in Greek and Latin versions; Hebrew reads *Today ordain yourselves.* 32:30 Or *to make atonement.* 33:6 Hebrew *Horeb,* another name for Sinai. 33:7 This "Tent of Meeting" is different from the Tabernacle described in chapters 26 and 36.

MOSES SEES THE LORD'S GLORY

12 One day Moses said to the LORD, "You have been telling me, 'Take these people up to the Promised Land.' But you haven't told me whom you will send with me. You have told me, 'I know you by name, and I look favorably on you.' 13 If it is true that you look favorably on me, let me know your ways so I may understand you more fully and continue to enjoy your favor. And remember that this nation is your very own people."

14 The LORD replied, "I will personally go with you, Moses, and I will give you rest—everything will be fine for you."

15 Then Moses said, "If you don't personally go with us, don't make us leave this place. 16 How will anyone know that you look favorably on me—on me and on your people—if you don't go with us? For your presence among us sets your people and me apart from all other people on the earth."

17 The LORD replied to Moses, "I will indeed do what you have asked, for I look favorably on you, and I know you by name."

18 Moses responded, "Then show me your glorious presence."

19 The LORD replied, "I will make all my goodness pass before you, and I will call out my name, Yahweh,* before you. For I will show mercy to anyone I choose, and I will show compassion to anyone I choose. 20 But you may not look directly at my face, for no one may see me and live." 21 The LORD continued, "Look, stand near me on this rock. 22 As my glorious presence passes by, I will hide you in the crevice of the rock and cover you with my hand until I have passed by. 23 Then I will remove my hand and let you see me from behind. But my face will not be seen."

A NEW COPY OF THE COVENANT

34 Then the LORD told Moses, "Chisel out two stone tablets like the first ones. I will write on them the same words that were on the tablets you smashed. 2 Be ready in the morning to climb up Mount Sinai and present yourself to me on the top of the mountain. 3 No one else may come with you. In fact, no one is to appear anywhere on the mountain. Do not even let the flocks or herds graze near the mountain."

4 So Moses chiseled out two tablets of stone like the first ones. Early in the morning he climbed Mount Sinai as the LORD had commanded him, and he carried the two stone tablets in his hands.

5 Then the LORD came down in a cloud and stood there with him; and he called out his own name, Yahweh.* 6 The LORD passed in front of Moses, calling out,

"Yahweh!* The LORD!
    The God of compassion and mercy!
I am slow to anger
    and filled with unfailing love and
        faithfulness.

7 I lavish unfailing love to a thousand
        generations.*
    I forgive iniquity, rebellion, and sin.
But I do not excuse the guilty.
    I lay the sins of the parents upon their
        children and grandchildren;
the entire family is affected—
    even children in the third and fourth
        generations."

8 Moses immediately threw himself to the ground and worshiped. 9 And he said, "O Lord, if it is true that I have found favor with you, then please travel with us. Yes, this is a stubborn and rebellious people, but please forgive our iniquity and our sins. Claim us as your own special possession."

10 The LORD replied, "Listen, I am making a covenant with you in the presence of all your people. I will perform miracles that have never been performed anywhere in all the earth or in any nation. And all the people around you will see the power of the LORD—the awesome power I will display for you. 11 But listen carefully to everything I command you today. Then I will go ahead of you and drive out the Amorites, Canaanites, Hittites, Perizzites, Hivites, and Jebusites.

12 "Be very careful never to make a treaty with the people who live in the land where you are going. If you do, you will follow their evil ways and be trapped. 13 Instead, you must break down their pagan altars, smash their sacred pillars, and cut down their Asherah poles. 14 You must worship no other gods, for the LORD, whose very name is Jealous, is a God who is jealous about his relationship with you.

15 "You must not make a treaty of any kind with the people living in the land. They lust after their gods, offering sacrifices to them. They will invite you to join them in their sacrificial meals, and you will go with them. 16 Then you will accept their daughters, who sacrifice to other gods, as wives for your sons. And they will seduce your sons to commit adultery against me by worshiping other gods. 17 You must not make any gods of molten metal for yourselves.

18 "You must celebrate the Festival of Unleavened Bread. For seven days the bread you eat must be made without yeast, just as I commanded you. Celebrate this festival annually at the appointed time in early spring, in the month of Abib,* for that is the anniversary of your departure from Egypt.

33:19 Yahweh is a transliteration of the proper name YHWH that is sometimes rendered "Jehovah"; in this translation it is usually rendered "the LORD" (note the use of small capitals). 34:5 Yahweh is a transliteration of the proper name YHWH that is sometimes rendered "Jehovah"; in this translation it is usually rendered "the LORD" (note the use of small capitals). 34:6 See note on 34:5. 34:7 Hebrew for thousands. 34:18 Hebrew appointed time in the month of Abib. This first month of the ancient Hebrew lunar calendar usually occurs within the months of March and April.

[19] "The firstborn of every animal belongs to me, including the firstborn males* from your herds of cattle and your flocks of sheep and goats. [20] A firstborn donkey may be bought back from the LORD by presenting a lamb or young goat in its place. But if you do not buy it back, you must break its neck. However, you must buy back every firstborn son.

"No one may appear before me without an offering.

[21] "You have six days each week for your ordinary work, but on the seventh day you must stop working, even during the seasons of plowing and harvest.

[22] "You must celebrate the Festival of Harvest* with the first crop of the wheat harvest, and celebrate the Festival of the Final Harvest* at the end of the harvest season. [23] Three times each year every man in Israel must appear before the Sovereign, the LORD, the God of Israel. [24] I will drive out the other nations ahead of you and expand your territory, so no one will covet and conquer your land while you appear before the LORD your God three times each year.

[25] "You must not offer the blood of my sacrificial offerings together with any baked goods containing yeast. And none of the meat of the Passover sacrifice may be kept over until the next morning.

[26] "As you harvest your crops, bring the very best of the first harvest to the house of the LORD your God.

"You must not cook a young goat in its mother's milk."

[27] Then the LORD said to Moses, "Write down all these instructions, for they represent the terms of the covenant I am making with you and with Israel."

[28] Moses remained there on the mountain with the LORD forty days and forty nights. In all that time he ate no bread and drank no water. And the LORD* wrote the terms of the covenant—the Ten Commandments*—on the stone tablets.

[29] When Moses came down Mount Sinai carrying the two stone tablets inscribed with the terms of the covenant,* he wasn't aware that his face had become radiant because he had spoken to the LORD. [30] So when Aaron and the people of Israel saw the radiance of Moses' face, they were afraid to come near him.

[31] But Moses called out to them and asked Aaron and all the leaders of the community to come over, and he talked with them. [32] Then all the people of Israel approached him, and Moses gave them all the instructions the LORD had given him on Mount Sinai. [33] When Moses finished speaking with them, he covered his face with a veil. [34] But whenever he went into the Tent of Meeting to speak with the LORD, he would remove the veil until he came out again. Then he would give the people whatever instructions the LORD had given him, [35] and the people of Israel

would see the radiant glow of his face. So he would put the veil over his face until he returned to speak with the LORD.

INSTRUCTIONS FOR THE SABBATH

35 Then Moses called together the whole community of Israel and told them, "These are the instructions the LORD has commanded you to follow. [2] You have six days each week for your ordinary work, but the seventh day must be a Sabbath day of complete rest, a holy day dedicated to the LORD. Anyone who works on that day must be put to death. [3] You must not even light a fire in any of your homes on the Sabbath."

OFFERINGS FOR THE TABERNACLE

[4] Then Moses said to the whole community of Israel, "This is what the LORD has commanded: [5] Take a sacred offering for the LORD. Let those with generous hearts present the following gifts to the LORD:

gold, silver, and bronze;
[6] blue, purple, and scarlet thread;
fine linen and goat hair for cloth;
[7] tanned ram skins and fine goatskin leather;
acacia wood;
[8] olive oil for the lamps;
spices for the anointing oil and the fragrant incense;
[9] onyx stones, and other gemstones to be set in the ephod and the priest's chestpiece.

[10] "Come, all of you who are gifted craftsmen. Construct everything that the LORD has commanded:

[11] the Tabernacle and its sacred tent, its covering, clasps, frames, crossbars, posts, and bases;
[12] the Ark and its carrying poles;
the Ark's cover—the place of atonement;
the inner curtain to shield the Ark;
[13] the table, its carrying poles,
and all its utensils;
the Bread of the Presence;
[14] for light, the lampstand, its accessories, the lamp cups, and the olive oil for lighting;
[15] the incense altar and its carrying poles;
the anointing oil and fragrant incense;
the curtain for the entrance of the Tabernacle;

34:19 As in Greek version; the meaning of the Hebrew word is uncertain. 34:22a Hebrew *Festival of Weeks;* compare 23:16. This was later called the Festival of Pentecost. It is celebrated today as Shavuot (or Shabuoth). 34:22b Or *Festival of Ingathering.* This was later called the Festival of Shelters or Festival of Tabernacles (see Lev 23:33-36). It is celebrated today as Sukkot (or Succoth). 34:28a Hebrew *he.* 34:28b Hebrew *the ten words.* 34:29 Hebrew *the two tablets of the Testimony;* see note on 25:16.

16 the altar of burnt offering;
the bronze grating of the altar and its
carrying poles and utensils;
the washbasin with its stand;
17 the curtains for the walls of the courtyard;
the posts and their bases;
the curtain for the entrance to the
courtyard;
18 the tent pegs of the Tabernacle and
courtyard and their ropes;
19 the beautifully stitched garments for the
priests to wear while ministering in the
Holy Place—the sacred garments for
Aaron the priest, and the garments for his
sons to wear as they minister as priests."

20 So the whole community of Israel left Moses and returned to their tents. 21 All whose hearts were stirred and whose spirits were moved came and brought their sacred offerings to the LORD. They brought all the materials needed for the Tabernacle,* for the performance of its rituals, and for the sacred garments. 22 Both men and women came, all whose hearts were willing. They brought to the LORD their offerings of gold—brooches, earrings, rings from their fingers, and necklaces. They presented gold objects of every kind as a special offering to the LORD. 23 All those who owned the following items willingly brought them: blue, purple, and scarlet thread; fine linen and goat hair for cloth; and tanned ram skins and fine goatskin leather. 24 And all who had silver and bronze objects gave them as a sacred offering to the LORD. And those who had acacia wood brought it for use in the project. 25 All the women who were skilled in sewing and spinning prepared blue, purple, and scarlet thread, and fine linen cloth. 26 All the women who were willing used their skills to spin the goat hair into yarn. 27 The leaders brought onyx stones and the special gemstones to be set in the ephod and the priest's chestpiece. 28 They also brought spices and olive oil for the light, the anointing oil, and the fragrant incense. 29 So the people of Israel—every man and woman who was eager to help in the work the LORD had given them through Moses—brought their gifts and gave them freely to the LORD.

30 Then Moses told the people of Israel, "The LORD has specifically chosen Bezalel son of Uri, grandson of Hur, of the tribe of Judah. 31 The LORD has filled Bezalel with the Spirit of God, giving him great wisdom, ability, and expertise in all kinds of crafts. 32 He is a master craftsman, expert in working with gold, silver, and bronze. 33 He is skilled in engraving and mounting gemstones and in carving wood. He is a master at every craft. 34 And the LORD has given both him and Oholiab son of Ahisamach, of the tribe of Dan, the ability to teach their skills to others. 35 The LORD has given them special skills as engravers, designers, embroiderers in blue, purple, and scarlet thread on fine linen cloth, and weavers. They excel as craftsmen and as designers.

36 "The LORD has gifted Bezalel, Oholiab, and the other skilled craftsmen with wisdom and ability to perform any task involved in building the sanctuary. Let them construct and furnish the Tabernacle, just as the LORD has commanded."

2 So Moses summoned Bezalel and Oholiab and all the others who were specially gifted by the LORD and were eager to get to work. 3 Moses gave them the materials donated by the people of Israel as sacred offerings for the completion of the sanctuary. But the people continued to bring additional gifts each morning. 4 Finally the craftsmen who were working on the sanctuary left their work. 5 They went to Moses and reported, "The people have given more than enough materials to complete the job the LORD has commanded us to do!"

6 So Moses gave the command, and this message was sent throughout the camp: "Men and women, don't prepare any more gifts for the sanctuary. We have enough!" So the people stopped bringing their sacred offerings. 7 Their contributions were more than enough to complete the whole project.

BUILDING THE TABERNACLE

8 The skilled craftsmen made ten curtains of finely woven linen for the Tabernacle. Then Bezalel* decorated the curtains with blue, purple, and scarlet thread and with skillfully embroidered cherubim. 9 All ten curtains were exactly the same size—42 feet long and 6 feet wide.* 10 Five of these curtains were joined together to make one long curtain, and the other five were joined to make a second long curtain. 11 He made fifty loops of blue yarn and put them along the edge of the last curtain in each set. 12 The fifty loops along the edge of one curtain matched the fifty loops along the edge of the other curtain. 13 Then he made fifty gold clasps and fastened the long curtains together with the clasps. In this way, the Tabernacle was made of one continuous piece.

14 He made eleven curtains of goat-hair cloth to serve as a tent covering for the Tabernacle. 15 These eleven curtains were all exactly the same size—45 feet long and 6 feet wide.* 16 Bezalel joined five of these curtains together to make one long curtain, and the other six were joined to make a second long curtain. 17 He made fifty loops for the edge of each large curtain. 18 He also made fifty bronze clasps to fasten the long curtains together. In this way, the tent covering was made of one continuous piece. 19 He completed the tent

---

35:21 Hebrew *Tent of Meeting.* 36:8 Hebrew *he;* also in 36:16, 20, 35. See 37:1. 36:9 Hebrew *28 cubits* [12.9 meters] *long and 4 cubits* [1.8 meters] *wide.* 36:15 Hebrew *30 cubits* [13.8 meters] *long and 4 cubits* [1.8 meters] *wide.*

covering with a layer of tanned ram skins and a layer of fine goatskin leather.

²⁰ For the framework of the Tabernacle, Bezalel constructed frames of acacia wood. ²¹ Each frame was 15 feet high and 27 inches wide,* ²² with two pegs under each frame. All the frames were identical. ²³ He made twenty of these frames to support the curtains on the south side of the Tabernacle. ²⁴ He also made forty silver bases—two bases under each frame, with the pegs fitting securely into the bases. ²⁵ For the north side of the Tabernacle, he made another twenty frames, ²⁶ with their forty silver bases, two bases under each frame. ²⁷ He made six frames for the rear—the west side of the Tabernacle—²⁸ along with two additional frames to reinforce the rear corners of the Tabernacle. ²⁹ These corner frames were matched at the bottom and firmly attached at the top with a single ring, forming a single corner unit. Both of these corner units were made the same way. ³⁰ So there were eight frames at the rear of the Tabernacle, set in sixteen silver bases—two bases under each frame.

³¹ Then he made crossbars of acacia wood to link the frames, five crossbars for the north side of the Tabernacle ³² and five for the south side. He also made five crossbars for the rear of the Tabernacle, which faced west. ³³ He made the middle crossbar to attach halfway up the frames; it ran all the way from one end of the Tabernacle to the other. ³⁴ He overlaid the frames with gold and made gold rings to hold the crossbars. Then he overlaid the crossbars with gold as well.

³⁵ For the inside of the Tabernacle, Bezalel made a special curtain of finely woven linen. He decorated it with blue, purple, and scarlet thread and with skillfully embroidered cherubim. ³⁶ For the curtain, he made four posts of acacia wood and four gold hooks. He overlaid the posts with gold and set them in four silver bases.

³⁷ Then he made another curtain for the entrance to the sacred tent. He made it of finely woven linen and embroidered it with exquisite designs using blue, purple, and scarlet thread. ³⁸ This curtain was hung on gold hooks attached to five posts. The posts with their decorated tops and hooks were overlaid with gold, and the five bases were cast from bronze.

BUILDING THE ARK OF THE COVENANT

37 Next Bezalel made the Ark of acacia wood—a sacred chest 45 inches long, 27 inches wide, and 27 inches high.* ² He overlaid it inside and outside with pure gold, and he ran a molding of gold all around it. ³ He cast four gold rings and attached them to its four feet, two rings on each side. ⁴ Then he made poles from acacia wood and overlaid them with gold. ⁵ He inserted the poles into the rings at the sides of the Ark to carry it.

⁶ Then he made the Ark's cover—the place of atonement—from pure gold. It was 45 inches long and 27 inches wide.* ⁷ He made two cherubim from hammered gold and placed them on the two ends of the atonement cover. ⁸ He molded the cherubim on each end of the atonement cover, making it all of one piece of gold. ⁹ The cherubim faced each other and looked down on the atonement cover. With their wings spread above it, they protected it.

BUILDING THE TABLE

¹⁰ Then Bezalel* made the table of acacia wood, 36 inches long, 18 inches wide, and 27 inches high.* ¹¹ He overlaid it with pure gold and ran a gold molding around the edge. ¹² He decorated it with a 3-inch border* all around, and he ran a gold molding along the border. ¹³ Then he cast four gold rings for the table and attached them at the four corners next to the four legs. ¹⁴ The rings were attached near the border to hold the poles that were used to carry the table. ¹⁵ He made these poles from acacia wood and overlaid them with gold. ¹⁶ Then he made special containers of pure gold for the table—bowls, ladles, jars, and pitchers—to be used in pouring out liquid offerings.

BUILDING THE LAMPSTAND

¹⁷ Then Bezalel made the lampstand of pure, hammered gold. He made the entire lampstand and its decorations of one piece—the base, center stem, lamp cups, buds, and petals. ¹⁸ The lampstand had six branches going out from the center stem, three on each side. ¹⁹ Each of the six branches had three lamp cups shaped like almond blossoms, complete with buds and petals. ²⁰ The center stem of the lampstand was crafted with four lamp cups shaped like almond blossoms, complete with buds and petals. ²¹ There was an almond bud beneath each pair of branches where the six branches extended from the center stem, all made of one piece. ²² The almond buds and branches were all of one piece with the center stem, and they were hammered from pure gold.

²³ He also made seven lamps for the lampstand, lamp snuffers, and trays, all of pure gold. ²⁴ The entire lampstand, along with its accessories, was made from 75 pounds* of pure gold.

BUILDING THE INCENSE ALTAR

²⁵ Then Bezalel made the incense altar of acacia wood. It was 18 inches square and 36 inches high,* with horns at the corners carved from the same piece of wood as the altar itself. ²⁶ He

---

36:21 Hebrew *10 cubits* [4.6 meters] *high and 1.5 cubits* [69 centimeters] *wide.*   37:1 Hebrew *2.5 cubits* [115 centimeters] *long, 1.5 cubits* [69 centimeters] *wide, and 1.5 cubits high.*
37:6 Hebrew *2.5 cubits* [115 centimeters] *long and 1.5 cubits* [69 centimeters] *wide.*   37:10a Hebrew *he;* also in 37:17, 25.   37:10b Hebrew *2 cubits* [92 centimeters] *long, 1 cubit* [46 centimeters] *wide, and 1.5 cubits* [69 centimeters] *high.*
37:12 Hebrew *a border of a handbreadth* [8 centimeters].
37:24 Hebrew *1 talent* [34 kilograms].   37:25 Hebrew *1 cubit* [46 centimeters] *long and 1 cubit wide, a square, and 2 cubits* [92 centimeters] *high.*

overlaid the top, sides, and horns of the altar with pure gold, and he ran a gold molding around the entire altar. ²⁷He made two gold rings and attached them on opposite sides of the altar below the gold molding to hold the carrying poles. ²⁸He made the poles of acacia wood and overlaid them with gold.

²⁹Then he made the sacred anointing oil and the fragrant incense, using the techniques of a skilled incense maker.

BUILDING THE ALTAR OF BURNT OFFERING

38 Next Bezalel* used acacia wood to construct the square altar of burnt offering. It was 7½ feet wide, 7½ feet long, and 4½ feet high.* ²He made horns for each of its four corners so that the horns and altar were all one piece. He overlaid the altar with bronze. ³Then he made all the altar utensils of bronze—the ash buckets, shovels, basins, meat forks, and firepans. ⁴Next he made a bronze grating and installed it halfway down the side of the altar, under the ledge. ⁵He cast four rings and attached them to the corners of the bronze grating to hold the carrying poles. ⁶He made the poles from acacia wood and overlaid them with bronze. ⁷He inserted the poles through the rings on the sides of the altar. The altar was hollow and was made from planks.

BUILDING THE WASHBASIN

⁸Bezalel made the bronze washbasin and its bronze stand from bronze mirrors donated by the women who served at the entrance of the Tabernacle.*

BUILDING THE COURTYARD

⁹Then Bezalel made the courtyard, which was enclosed with curtains made of finely woven linen. On the south side the curtains were 150 feet long.* ¹⁰They were held up by twenty posts set securely in twenty bronze bases. He hung the curtains with silver hooks and rings. ¹¹He made a similar set of curtains for the north side—150 feet of curtains held up by twenty posts set securely in bronze bases. He hung the curtains with silver hooks and rings. ¹²The curtains on the west end of the courtyard were 75 feet long,* hung with silver hooks and rings and supported by ten posts set into ten bases. ¹³The east end, the front, was also 75 feet long.

¹⁴The courtyard entrance was on the east end, flanked by two curtains. The curtain on the right side was 22½ feet long* and was supported by three posts set into three bases. ¹⁵The curtain on the left side was also 22½ feet long and was supported by three posts set into three bases. ¹⁶All the curtains used in the courtyard were made of finely woven linen. ¹⁷Each post had a bronze base, and all the hooks and rings were silver. The tops of the posts of the courtyard were overlaid with silver, and the rings to hold up the curtains were made of silver.

¹⁸He made the curtain for the entrance to the courtyard of finely woven linen, and he decorated it with beautiful embroidery in blue, purple, and scarlet thread. It was 30 feet long, and its height was 7½ feet,* just like the curtains of the courtyard walls. ¹⁹It was supported by four posts, each set securely in its own bronze base. The tops of the posts were overlaid with silver, and the hooks and rings were also made of silver.

²⁰All the tent pegs used in the Tabernacle and courtyard were made of bronze.

INVENTORY OF MATERIALS

²¹This is an inventory of the materials used in building the Tabernacle of the Covenant.* The Levites compiled the figures, as Moses directed, and Ithamar son of Aaron the priest served as recorder. ²²Bezalel son of Uri, grandson of Hur, of the tribe of Judah, made everything just as the LORD had commanded Moses. ²³He was assisted by Oholiab son of Ahisamach, of the tribe of Dan, a craftsman expert at engraving, designing, and embroidering with blue, purple, and scarlet thread on fine linen cloth.

²⁴The people brought special offerings of gold totaling 2,193 pounds,* as measured by the weight of the sanctuary shekel. This gold was used throughout the Tabernacle.

²⁵The whole community of Israel gave 7,545 pounds* of silver, as measured by the weight of the sanctuary shekel. ²⁶This silver came from the tax collected from each man registered in the census. (The tax is one beka, which is half a shekel,* based on the sanctuary shekel.) The tax was collected from 603,550 men who had reached their twentieth birthday. ²⁷The hundred bases for the frames of the sanctuary walls and for the posts supporting the inner curtain required 7,500 pounds of silver, about 75 pounds for each base.* ²⁸The remaining 45 pounds* of silver was used to make the hooks and rings and to overlay the tops of the posts.

²⁹The people also brought as special offerings 5,310 pounds* of bronze, ³⁰which was used for casting the bases for the posts at the entrance to the Tabernacle, and for the bronze altar with its bronze grating and all the altar utensils. ³¹Bronze was also used to make the bases for the posts that supported the curtains around the courtyard,

38:1a Hebrew he; also in 38:8, 9. 38:1b Hebrew 5 cubits [2.3 meters] wide, 5 cubits long, a square, and 3 cubits [1.4 meters] high. 38:8 Hebrew Tent of Meeting; also in 38:30. 38:9 Hebrew 100 cubits [46 meters]; also in 38:11. 38:12 Hebrew 50 cubits [23 meters]; also in 38:13. 38:14 Hebrew 15 cubits [6.9 meters]; also in 38:15. 38:18 Hebrew 20 cubits [9.2 meters] long and 5 cubits [2.3 meters] high. 38:21 Hebrew the Tabernacle, the Tabernacle of the Testimony. 38:24 Hebrew 29 talents and 730 shekels [994 kilograms]. Each shekel weighed about 0.4 ounces or 11 grams. 38:25 Hebrew 100 talents and 1,775 shekels [3,420 kilograms]. 38:26 Or 0.2 ounces [6 grams]. 38:27 Hebrew 100 talents [3,400 kilograms] of silver, 1 talent [34 kilograms] for each base. 38:28 Hebrew 1,775 [shekels] [20.2 kilograms]. 38:29 Hebrew 70 talents and 2,400 shekels [2,407 kilograms].

the bases for the curtain at the entrance of the courtyard, and all the tent pegs for the Tabernacle and the courtyard.

CLOTHING FOR THE PRIESTS

39 The craftsmen made beautiful sacred garments of blue, purple, and scarlet cloth—clothing for Aaron to wear while ministering in the Holy Place, just as the LORD had commanded Moses.

MAKING THE EPHOD

[2] Bezalel* made the ephod of finely woven linen and embroidered it with gold and with blue, purple, and scarlet thread. [3] He made gold thread by hammering out thin sheets of gold and cutting it into fine strands. With great skill and care, he worked it into the fine linen with the blue, purple, and scarlet thread.

[4] The ephod consisted of two pieces, front and back, joined at the shoulders with two shoulder-pieces. [5] The decorative sash was made of the same materials: finely woven linen embroidered with gold and with blue, purple, and scarlet thread, just as the LORD had commanded Moses. [6] They mounted the two onyx stones in settings of gold filigree. The stones were engraved with the names of the tribes of Israel, just as a seal is engraved. [7] He fastened these stones on the shoulder-pieces of the ephod as a reminder that the priest represents the people of Israel. All this was done just as the LORD had commanded Moses.

MAKING THE CHESTPIECE

[8] Bezalel made the chestpiece with great skill and care. He made it to match the ephod, using finely woven linen embroidered with gold and with blue, purple, and scarlet thread. [9] He made the chestpiece of a single piece of cloth folded to form a pouch nine inches* square. [10] They mounted four rows of gemstones* on it. The first row contained a red carnelian, a pale-green peridot, and an emerald. [11] The second row contained a turquoise, a blue lapis lazuli, and a white moonstone. [12] The third row contained an orange jacinth, an agate, and a purple amethyst. [13] The fourth row contained a blue-green beryl, an onyx, and a green jasper. All these stones were set in gold filigree. [14] Each stone represented one of the twelve sons of Israel, and the name of that tribe was engraved on it like a seal.

[15] To attach the chestpiece to the ephod, they made braided cords of pure gold thread. [16] They also made two settings of gold filigree and two gold rings and attached them to the top corners of the chestpiece. [17] They tied the two gold cords to the rings on the chestpiece. [18] They tied the other ends of the cords to the gold settings on the shoulder-pieces of the ephod. [19] Then they made two more gold rings and attached them to the inside edges of the chestpiece next to the ephod. [20] Then they made two more gold rings and attached them to the front of the ephod, below the shoulder-pieces, just above the knot where the decorative sash was fastened to the ephod. [21] They attached the bottom rings of the chestpiece to the rings on the ephod with blue cords. In this way, the chestpiece was held securely to the ephod above the decorative sash. All this was done just as the LORD had commanded Moses.

ADDITIONAL CLOTHING FOR THE PRIESTS

[22] Bezalel made the robe that is worn with the ephod from a single piece of blue woven cloth, [23] with an opening for Aaron's head in the middle of it. The opening was reinforced with a woven collar* so it would not tear. [24] They made pomegranates of blue, purple, and scarlet yarn, and attached them to the hem of the robe. [25] They also made bells of pure gold and placed them between the pomegranates along the hem of the robe, [26] with bells and pomegranates alternating all around the hem. This robe was to be worn whenever the priest ministered before the LORD, just as the LORD had commanded Moses.

[27] They made tunics for Aaron and his sons from fine linen cloth. [28] The turban and the special head coverings were made of fine linen, and the undergarments were also made of finely woven linen. [29] The sashes were made of finely woven linen and embroidered with blue, purple, and scarlet thread, just as the LORD had commanded Moses.

[30] Finally, they made the sacred medallion—the badge of holiness—of pure gold. They engraved it like a seal with these words: HOLY TO THE LORD. [31] They attached the medallion with a blue cord to Aaron's turban, just as the LORD had commanded Moses.

MOSES INSPECTS THE WORK

[32] And so at last the Tabernacle* was finished. The Israelites had done everything just as the LORD had commanded Moses. [33] And they brought the entire Tabernacle to Moses:

the sacred tent with all its furnishings, clasps, frames, crossbars, posts, and bases;
[34] the tent coverings of tanned ram skins and fine goatskin leather;
the inner curtain to shield the Ark;
[35] the Ark of the Covenant* and its carrying poles;
the Ark's cover—the place of atonement;
[36] the table and all its utensils;
the Bread of the Presence;

39:2 Hebrew He; also in 39:8, 22.   39:9 Hebrew 1 span [23 centimeters].   39:10 The identification of some of these gemstones is uncertain.   39:23 The meaning of the Hebrew is uncertain.   39:32 Hebrew the Tabernacle, the Tent of Meeting; also in 39:40.   39:35 Or Ark of the Testimony.

37 the pure gold lampstand with its symmetrical lamp cups, all its accessories, and the olive oil for lighting; 38 the gold altar;

the anointing oil and fragrant incense;

the curtain for the entrance of the sacred tent; 39 the bronze altar;

the bronze grating and its carrying poles and utensils;

the washbasin with its stand; 40 the curtains for the walls of the courtyard;

the posts and their bases;

the curtain for the entrance to the courtyard;

the ropes and tent pegs;

all the furnishings to be used in worship at the Tabernacle; 41 the beautifully stitched garments for the priests to wear while ministering in the Holy Place—the sacred garments for Aaron the priest, and the garments for his sons to wear as they minister as priests.

42 So the people of Israel followed all of the LORD's instructions to Moses. 43 Then Moses inspected all their work. When he found it had been done just as the LORD had commanded him, he blessed them.

THE TABERNACLE COMPLETED

40 Then the LORD said to Moses, 2 "Set up the Tabernacle* on the first day of the new year.* 3 Place the Ark of the Covenant* inside, and install the inner curtain to enclose the Ark within the Most Holy Place. 4 Then bring in the table, and arrange the utensils on it. And bring in the lampstand, and set up the lamps.

5 "Place the gold incense altar in front of the Ark of the Covenant. Then hang the curtain at the entrance of the Tabernacle. 6 Place the altar of burnt offering in front of the Tabernacle entrance. 7 Set the washbasin between the Tabernacle* and the altar, and fill it with water. 8 Then set up the courtyard around the outside of the tent, and hang the curtain for the courtyard entrance.

9 "Take the anointing oil and anoint the Tabernacle and all its furnishings to consecrate them and make them holy. 10 Anoint the altar of burnt offering and its utensils to consecrate them. Then the altar will become absolutely holy. 11 Next anoint the washbasin and its stand to consecrate them.

12 "Present Aaron and his sons at the entrance of the Tabernacle, and wash them with water. 13 Dress Aaron with the sacred garments and anoint him, consecrating him to serve me as a priest. 14 Then present his sons and dress them in their tunics. 15 Anoint them as you did their father, so they may also serve me as priests.

With their anointing, Aaron's descendants are set apart for the priesthood forever, from generation to generation."

16 Moses proceeded to do everything just as the LORD had commanded him. 17 So the Tabernacle was set up on the first day of the first month of the second year. 18 Moses erected the Tabernacle by setting down its bases, inserting the frames, attaching the crossbars, and setting up the posts. 19 Then he spread the coverings over the Tabernacle framework and put on the protective layers, just as the LORD had commanded him.

20 He took the stone tablets inscribed with the terms of the covenant and placed them* inside the Ark. Then he attached the carrying poles to the Ark, and he set the Ark's cover—the place of atonement—on top of it. 21 Then he brought the Ark of the Covenant into the Tabernacle and hung the inner curtain to shield it from view, just as the LORD had commanded him.

22 Next Moses placed the table in the Tabernacle, along the north side of the Holy Place, just outside the inner curtain. 23 And he arranged the Bread of the Presence on the table before the LORD, just as the LORD had commanded him.

24 He set the lampstand in the Tabernacle across from the table on the south side of Holy Place. 25 Then he lit the lamps in the LORD's presence, just as the LORD had commanded him. 26 He also placed the gold incense altar in the Tabernacle, in the Holy Place in front of the inner curtain. 27 On it he burned the fragrant incense, just as the LORD had commanded him.

28 He hung the curtain at the entrance of the Tabernacle, 29 and he placed the altar of burnt offering near the Tabernacle entrance. On it he offered a burnt offering and a grain offering, just as the LORD had commanded him.

30 Next Moses placed the washbasin between the Tabernacle and the altar. He filled it with water so the priests could wash themselves. 31 Moses and Aaron and Aaron's sons used water from it to wash their hands and feet. 32 Whenever they approached the altar and entered the Tabernacle, they washed themselves, just as the LORD had commanded Moses.

33 Then he hung the curtains forming the courtyard around the Tabernacle and the altar. And he set up the curtain at the entrance of the courtyard. So at last Moses finished the work.

THE LORD'S GLORY FILLS
THE TABERNACLE

34 Then the cloud covered the Tabernacle, and the glory of the LORD filled the Tabernacle. 35 Moses

---

40:2a Hebrew *the Tabernacle, the Tent of Meeting;* also in 40:6, 29.
40:2b Hebrew *the first day of the first month.* This day of the ancient Hebrew lunar calendar occurred in March or April. 40:3 Or *Ark of the Testimony;* also in 40:5, 21.   40:7 Hebrew *Tent of Meeting;* also in 40:12, 22, 24, 26, 30, 32, 34, 35.
40:20 Hebrew *He placed the Testimony;* see note on 25:16.

could no longer enter the Tabernacle because the cloud had settled down over it, and the glory of the LORD filled the Tabernacle.

[36] Now whenever the cloud lifted from the Tabernacle, the people of Israel would set out on their journey, following it. [37] But if the cloud did not rise, they remained where they were until it lifted. [38] The cloud of the LORD hovered over the Tabernacle during the day, and at night fire glowed inside the cloud so the whole family of Israel could see it. This continued throughout all their journeys.

LEVITICUS

JON HUNTZINGER, PHD

The book of Leviticus contains instructions given to Moses on Mount Sinai for the worship of God by the Israelites. It follows Exodus, which itself concludes with instructions for the building of the Tabernacle (the place of worship) and its furnishings to facilitate that worship. Leviticus begins where Exodus ends and shifts the focus from the construction of the Tabernacle to
— the *sacrifices* offered there,
— the *priests* who will oversee the worship, and
— the behavior of the *people* who will participate.

Jewish tradition recognizes Moses as the writer of Leviticus in the same way it names him as the writer of Genesis and Exodus: by virtue of the fact that Leviticus reports numerous instances when God spoke to him. The book takes its name from the Levites from the tribe of Levi to whom God gave the privilege of leading Israel in worshipping Him.

Leviticus has four primary divisions:
— Chapters 1–7 describe five sacrifices the people were to offer God at the Tabernacle. These sacrifices included the burnt offering, the grain offering, the peace or fellowship offering, the sin offering, and the trespass or guilt offering.
— Chapters 8–10 provide information about the priests who officiated these offerings. These chapters describe the garments they were to wear as well as the anointing they were to receive to carry out their ministry.
— Chapters 11–16 outline laws distinguishing conditions and behaviors that are clean and acceptable from those that are unclean and unacceptable. This section concludes with a discussion of the Day of Atonement, when all the people and priests offered sacrifices for purification from sin so that they might remain in relationship with God and worship Him.

— Chapters 17–27 are often described by Bible scholars as the Holiness Code. This section provides a framework for how the people were to show God's holiness in the way they lived with one another. It also includes a list of the various days and festivals the people were to celebrate together throughout the year: the Sabbath, Passover and the Festival of Unleavened Bread, Celebration of First Harvest, the Festival of Harvest, the Festival of Trumpets, the Day of Atonement, and the Festival of Shelters, along with the Year of Jubilee.

Leviticus reveals that God is holy. God is not only worthy of worship because He delivered the Hebrew people from slavery in Egypt but also because He is holy. Because God is holy, the people are exhorted—*commanded* even—to be holy too. In fact, the exhortation "Be holy, because I am holy" occurs several times in the book (11:44–45; 19:2; 20:26). How were the people to be holy? They were to be holy in relationship to a holy God by
— giving the necessary offerings to God,
— celebrating the special times given for their benefit, and
— living in God-honoring ways as outlined in the laws of Leviticus that involved everything from the foods they ate to the intimate relationships they had with one another.

When the Hebrew people live according to the laws given by God and participate in the life of the community with one another as outlined in the book of Leviticus, they will fulfill the calling God gave them at Mount Sinai to be "my kingdom of priests, my holy nation" (Exodus 19:6). To live as a holy nation before God is, at the same time, to exercise their privilege and responsibility to the nations of the earth to be their priesthood and to lead them in the worship of God, who is Himself holy.

PROCEDURES FOR THE BURNT OFFERING

1 The LORD called to Moses from the Tabernacle* and said to him, ²"Give the following instructions to the people of Israel. When you present an animal as an offering to the LORD, you may take it from your herd of cattle or your flock of sheep and goats.

³"If the animal you present as a burnt offering is from the herd, it must be a male with no defects. Bring it to the entrance of the Tabernacle so you* may be accepted by the LORD. ⁴Lay your hand on the animal's head, and the LORD will accept its death in your place to purify you, making you right with him.* ⁵Then slaughter the young bull in the LORD's presence, and Aaron's sons, the priests, will present the animal's blood by splattering it against all sides of the altar that stands at the entrance to the Tabernacle. ⁶Then skin the animal and cut it into pieces. ⁷The sons of Aaron the priest will build a wood fire on the altar. ⁸They will arrange the pieces of the offering, including the head and fat, on the wood burning on the altar. ⁹But the internal organs and the legs must first be washed with water. Then the priest will burn the entire sacrifice on the altar as a burnt offering. It is a special gift, a pleasing aroma to the LORD.

¹⁰"If the animal you present as a burnt offering is from the flock, it may be either a sheep or a goat, but it must be a male with no defects. ¹¹Slaughter the animal on the north side of the altar in the LORD's presence, and Aaron's sons, the priests, will splatter its blood against all sides of the altar. ¹²Then cut the animal in pieces, and the priests will arrange the pieces of the offering, including the head and fat, on the wood burning on the altar. ¹³But the internal organs and the legs must first be washed with water. Then the priest will burn the entire sacrifice on the altar as a burnt offering. It is a special gift, a pleasing aroma to the LORD.

¹⁴"If you present a bird as a burnt offering to the LORD, choose either a turtledove or a young pigeon. ¹⁵The priest will take the bird to the altar, wring off its head, and burn it on the altar. But first he must drain its blood against the side of the altar. ¹⁶The priest must also remove the crop and the feathers* and throw them in the ashes on the east side of the altar. ¹⁷Then, grasping the bird by its wings, the priest will tear the bird open, but without tearing it apart. Then he will burn it as a burnt offering on the wood burning on the altar. It is a special gift, a pleasing aroma to the LORD.

PROCEDURES FOR THE GRAIN OFFERING

2 "When you present grain as an offering to the LORD, the offering must consist of choice flour. You are to pour olive oil on it, sprinkle it with frankincense, ²and bring it to Aaron's sons, the priests. The priest will scoop out a handful of the flour moistened with oil, together with all the frankincense, and burn this representative portion on the altar. It is a special gift, a pleasing aroma to the LORD. ³The rest of the grain offering will then be given to Aaron and his sons. This offering will be considered a most holy part of the special gifts presented to the LORD.

⁴"If your offering is a grain offering baked in an oven, it must be made of choice flour, but without any yeast. It may be presented in the form of thin cakes mixed with olive oil or wafers spread with olive oil. ⁵If your grain offering is cooked on a griddle, it must be made of choice flour mixed with olive oil but without any yeast. ⁶Break it in pieces and pour olive oil on it; it is a grain offering. ⁷If your grain offering is prepared in a pan, it must be made of choice flour and olive oil.

⁸"No matter how a grain offering for the LORD has been prepared, bring it to the priest, who will present it at the altar. ⁹The priest will take a representative portion of the grain offering and burn it on the altar. It is a special gift, a pleasing aroma to the LORD. ¹⁰The rest of the grain offering will then be given to Aaron and his sons as their food. This offering will be considered a most holy part of the special gifts presented to the LORD.

¹¹"Do not use yeast in preparing any of the grain offerings you present to the LORD, because no yeast or honey may be burned as a special gift presented to the LORD. ¹²You may add yeast and honey to an offering of the first crops of your harvest, but these must never be offered on the altar as a pleasing aroma to the LORD. ¹³Season all your grain offerings with salt to remind you of God's eternal covenant. Never forget to add salt to your grain offerings.

¹⁴"If you present a grain offering to the LORD from the first portion of your harvest, bring fresh grain that is coarsely ground and roasted on a fire. ¹⁵Put olive oil on this grain offering, and sprinkle it with frankincense. ¹⁶The priest will take a representative portion of the grain moistened with oil, together with all the frankincense, and burn it as a special gift presented to the LORD.

PROCEDURES FOR THE PEACE OFFERING

3 "If you present an animal from the herd as a peace offering to the LORD, it may be a male or a female, but it must have no defects. ²Lay your hand on the animal's head, and slaughter it at the entrance of the Tabernacle.* Then Aaron's sons, the priests, will splatter its blood against all sides of the altar. ³The priest must present part of this peace offering as a special gift to the LORD. This includes all the fat around the internal organs, ⁴the two kidneys and the fat around them near the loins, and the long lobe of the liver. These must be removed with the kidneys, ⁵and Aaron's

---

1:1 Hebrew *Tent of Meeting;* also in 1:3, 5.   1:3 Or *it.*   1:4 Or *to make atonement for you.*   1:16 Or *the crop and its contents.* The meaning of the Hebrew is uncertain.   3:2 Hebrew *Tent of Meeting;* also in 3:8, 13.

sons will burn them on top of the burnt offering on the wood burning on the altar. It is a special gift, a pleasing aroma to the LORD.

6 "If you present an animal from the flock as a peace offering to the LORD, it may be a male or a female, but it must have no defects. 7 If you present a sheep as your offering, bring it to the LORD, 8 lay your hand on its head, and slaughter it in front of the Tabernacle. Aaron's sons will then splatter the sheep's blood against all sides of the altar. 9 The priest must present the fat of this peace offering as a special gift to the LORD. This includes the fat of the broad tail cut off near the backbone, all the fat around the internal organs, 10 the two kidneys and the fat around them near the loins, and the long lobe of the liver. These must be removed with the kidneys, 11 and the priest will burn them on the altar. It is a special gift of food presented to the LORD.

12 "If you present a goat as your offering, bring it to the LORD, 13 lay your hand on its head, and slaughter it in front of the Tabernacle. Aaron's sons will then splatter the goat's blood against all sides of the altar. 14 The priest must present part of this offering as a special gift to the LORD. This includes all the fat around the internal organs, 15 the two kidneys and the fat around them near the loins, and the long lobe of the liver. These must be removed with the kidneys, 16 and the priest will burn them on the altar. It is a special gift of food, a pleasing aroma to the LORD. All the fat belongs to the LORD.

17 "You must never eat any fat or blood. This is a permanent law for you, and it must be observed from generation to generation, wherever you live."

PROCEDURES FOR THE SIN OFFERING

4 Then the LORD said to Moses, 2 "Give the following instructions to the people of Israel. This is how you are to deal with those who sin unintentionally by doing anything that violates one of the LORD's commands.

3 "If the high priest* sins, bringing guilt upon the entire community, he must give a sin offering for the sin he has committed. He must present to the LORD a young bull with no defects. 4 He must bring the bull to the LORD at the entrance of the Tabernacle,* lay his hand on the bull's head, and slaughter it before the LORD. 5 The high priest will then take some of the bull's blood into the Tabernacle, 6 dip his finger in the blood, and sprinkle it seven times before the LORD in front of the inner curtain of the sanctuary. 7 The priest will then put some of the blood on the horns of the altar for fragrant incense that stands in the LORD's presence inside the Tabernacle. He will pour out the rest of the bull's blood at the base of the altar for burnt offerings at the entrance of the Tabernacle. 8 Then the priest must remove all the fat of the bull to be offered as a sin offering. This includes all the fat around the internal organs,

9 the two kidneys and the fat around them near the loins, and the long lobe of the liver. He must remove these along with the kidneys, 10 just as he does with cattle offered as a peace offering, and burn them on the altar of burnt offerings. 11 But he must take whatever is left of the bull— its hide, meat, head, legs, internal organs, and dung—12 and carry it away to a place outside the camp that is ceremonially clean, the place where the ashes are dumped. There, on the ash heap, he will burn it on a wood fire.

13 "If the entire Israelite community sins by violating one of the LORD's commands, but the people don't realize it, they are still guilty. 14 When they become aware of their sin, the people must bring a young bull as an offering for their sin and present it before the Tabernacle. 15 The elders of the community must then lay their hands on the bull's head and slaughter it before the LORD. 16 The high priest will then take some of the bull's blood into the Tabernacle, 17 dip his finger in the blood, and sprinkle it seven times before the LORD in front of the inner curtain. 18 He will then put some of the blood on the horns of the altar for fragrant incense that stands in the LORD's presence inside the Tabernacle. He will pour out the rest of the blood at the base of the altar for burnt offerings at the entrance of the Tabernacle. 19 Then the priest must remove all the animal's fat and burn it on the altar, 20 just as he does with the bull offered as a sin offering for the high priest. Through this process, the priest will purify the people, making them right with the LORD,* and they will be forgiven. 21 Then the priest must take what is left of the bull and carry it outside the camp and burn it there, just as is done with the sin offering for the high priest. This offering is for the sin of the entire congregation of Israel.

22 "If one of Israel's leaders sins by violating one of the commands of the LORD his God but doesn't realize it, he is still guilty. 23 When he becomes aware of his sin, he must bring as his offering a male goat with no defects. 24 He must lay his hand on the goat's head and slaughter it at the place where burnt offerings are slaughtered before the LORD. This is an offering for his sin. 25 Then the priest will dip his finger in the blood of the sin offering and put it on the horns of the altar for burnt offerings. He will pour out the rest of the blood at the base of the altar. 26 Then he must burn all the goat's fat on the altar, just as he does with the peace offering. Through this process, the priest will purify the leader from his sin, making him right with the LORD, and he will be forgiven.

27 "If any of the common people sin by violating one of the LORD's commands, but they don't realize it, they are still guilty. 28 When they become

---

4:3 Hebrew *the anointed priest;* also in 4:5, 16.   4:4 Hebrew *Tent of Meeting;* also in 4:5, 7, 14, 16, 18.   4:20 Or *will make atonement for the people;* similarly in 4:26, 31, 35.

aware of their sin, they must bring as an offering for their sin a female goat with no defects. ²⁹ They must lay a hand on the head of the sin offering and slaughter it at the place where burnt offerings are slaughtered. ³⁰ Then the priest will dip his finger in the blood and put it on the horns of the altar for burnt offerings. He will pour out the rest of the blood at the base of the altar. ³¹ Then he must remove all the goat's fat, just as he does with the fat of the peace offering. He will burn the fat on the altar, and it will be a pleasing aroma to the Lord. Through this process, the priest will purify the people, making them right with the Lord, and they will be forgiven.

³² "If the people bring a sheep as their sin offering, it must be a female with no defects. ³³ They must lay a hand on the head of the sin offering and slaughter it at the place where burnt offerings are slaughtered. ³⁴ Then the priest will dip his finger in the blood of the sin offering and put it on the horns of the altar for burnt offerings. He will pour out the rest of the blood at the base of the altar. ³⁵ Then he must remove all the sheep's fat, just as he does with the fat of a sheep presented as a peace offering. He will burn the fat on the altar on top of the special gifts presented to the Lord. Through this process, the priest will purify the people from their sin, making them right with the Lord, and they will be forgiven.

SINS REQUIRING A SIN OFFERING

5 "If you are called to testify about something you have seen or that you know about, it is sinful to refuse to testify, and you will be punished for your sin.

² "Or suppose you unknowingly touch something that is ceremonially unclean, such as the carcass of an unclean animal. When you realize what you have done, you must admit your defilement and your guilt. This is true whether it is a wild animal, a domestic animal, or an animal that scurries along the ground.

³ "Or suppose you unknowingly touch something that makes a person unclean. When you realize what you have done, you must admit your guilt.

⁴ "Or suppose you make a foolish vow of any kind, whether its purpose is for good or for bad. When you realize its foolishness, you must admit your guilt.

⁵ "When you become aware of your guilt in any of these ways, you must confess your sin. ⁶ Then you must bring to the Lord as the penalty for your sin a female from the flock, either a sheep or a goat. This is a sin offering with which the priest will purify you from your sin, making you right with the Lord.*

⁷ "But if you cannot afford to bring a sheep, you may bring to the Lord two turtledoves or two young pigeons as the penalty for your sin. One of the birds will be for a sin offering, and the other for a burnt offering. ⁸ You must bring

them to the priest, who will present the first bird as the sin offering. He will wring its neck but without severing its head from the body. ⁹ Then he will sprinkle some of the blood of the sin offering against the sides of the altar, and the rest of the blood will be drained out at the base of the altar. This is an offering for sin. ¹⁰ The priest will then prepare the second bird as a burnt offering, following all the procedures that have been prescribed. Through this process the priest will purify you from your sin, making you right with the Lord, and you will be forgiven.

¹¹ "If you cannot afford to bring two turtledoves or two young pigeons, you may bring two quarts* of choice flour for your sin offering. Since it is an offering for sin, you must not moisten it with olive oil or put any frankincense on it. ¹² Take the flour to the priest, who will scoop out a handful as a representative portion. He will burn it on the altar on top of the special gifts presented to the Lord. It is an offering for sin. ¹³ Through this process, the priest will purify those who are guilty of any of these sins, making them right with the Lord, and they will be forgiven. The rest of the flour will belong to the priest, just as with the grain offering."

PROCEDURES FOR THE GUILT OFFERING

¹⁴ Then the Lord said to Moses, ¹⁵ "If one of you commits a sin by unintentionally defiling the Lord's sacred property, you must bring a guilt offering to the Lord. The offering must be your own ram with no defects, or you may buy one of equal value with silver, as measured by the weight of the sanctuary shekel.* ¹⁶ You must make restitution for the sacred property you have harmed by paying for the loss, plus an additional 20 percent. When you give the payment to the priest, he will purify you with the ram sacrificed as a guilt offering, making you right with the Lord, and you will be forgiven.

¹⁷ "Suppose you sin by violating one of the Lord's commands. Even if you are unaware of what you have done, you are guilty and will be punished for your sin. ¹⁸ For a guilt offering, you must bring to the priest your own ram with no defects, or you may buy one of equal value. Through this process the priest will purify you from your unintentional sin, making you right with the Lord, and you will be forgiven. ¹⁹ This is a guilt offering, for you have been guilty of an offense against the Lord."

SINS REQUIRING A GUILT OFFERING

6 ^{1*} Then the Lord said to Moses, ² "Suppose one of you sins against your associate and is unfaithful to the Lord. Suppose you cheat in a deal involving a security deposit, or you steal

---

5:6 Or *will make atonement for you for your sin;* similarly in 5:10, 13, 16, 18.   5:11 Hebrew ⅒ *of an ephah* [2.2 liters].   5:15 Each shekel was about 0.4 ounces or 11 grams in weight.   6:1 Verses 6:1-7 are numbered 5:20-26 in Hebrew text.

or commit fraud, ³or you find lost property and lie about it, or you lie while swearing to tell the truth, or you commit any other such sin. ⁴If you have sinned in any of these ways, you are guilty. You must give back whatever you stole, or the money you took by extortion, or the security deposit, or the lost property you found, ⁵or anything obtained by swearing falsely. You must make restitution by paying the full price plus an additional 20 percent to the person you have harmed. On the same day you must present a guilt offering. ⁶As a guilt offering to the LORD, you must bring to the priest your own ram with no defects, or you may buy one of equal value. ⁷Through this process, the priest will purify you before the LORD, making you right with him,* and you will be forgiven for any of these sins you have committed."

FURTHER INSTRUCTIONS FOR THE BURNT OFFERING

⁸*Then the LORD said to Moses, ⁹"Give Aaron and his sons the following instructions regarding the burnt offering. The burnt offering must be left on top of the altar until the next morning, and the fire on the altar must be kept burning all night. ¹⁰In the morning, after the priest on duty has put on his official linen clothing and linen undergarments, he must clean out the ashes of the burnt offering and put them beside the altar. ¹¹Then he must take off these garments, change back into his regular clothes, and carry the ashes outside the camp to a place that is ceremonially clean. ¹²Meanwhile, the fire on the altar must be kept burning; it must never go out. Each morning the priest will add fresh wood to the fire and arrange the burnt offering on it. He will then burn the fat of the peace offerings on it. ¹³Remember, the fire must be kept burning on the altar at all times. It must never go out.

FURTHER INSTRUCTIONS FOR THE GRAIN OFFERING

¹⁴"These are the instructions regarding the grain offering. Aaron's sons must present this offering to the LORD in front of the altar. ¹⁵The priest on duty will take from the grain offering a handful of the choice flour moistened with olive oil, together with all the frankincense. He will burn this representative portion on the altar as a pleasing aroma to the LORD. ¹⁶Aaron and his sons may eat the rest of the flour, but it must be baked without yeast and eaten in a sacred place within the courtyard of the Tabernacle.* ¹⁷Remember, it must never be prepared with yeast. I have given it to the priests as their share of the special gifts presented to me. Like the sin offering and the guilt offering, it is most holy. ¹⁸Any of Aaron's male descendants may eat from the special gifts presented to the LORD. This is their permanent right from generation to generation. Anyone or anything that touches these offerings will become holy."

PROCEDURES FOR THE ORDINATION OFFERING

¹⁹Then the LORD said to Moses, ²⁰"On the day Aaron and his sons are anointed, they must present to the LORD the standard grain offering of two quarts* of choice flour, half to be offered in the morning and half to be offered in the evening. ²¹It must be carefully mixed with olive oil and cooked on a griddle. Then slice* this grain offering and present it as a pleasing aroma to the LORD. ²²In each generation, the high priest* who succeeds Aaron must prepare this same offering. It belongs to the LORD and must be burned up completely. This is a permanent law. ²³All such grain offerings of a priest must be burned up entirely. None of it may be eaten."

FURTHER INSTRUCTIONS FOR THE SIN OFFERING

²⁴Then the LORD said to Moses, ²⁵"Give Aaron and his sons the following instructions regarding the sin offering. The animal given as an offering for sin is a most holy offering, and it must be slaughtered in the LORD's presence at the place where the burnt offerings are slaughtered. ²⁶The priest who offers the sacrifice as a sin offering must eat his portion in a sacred place within the courtyard of the Tabernacle. ²⁷Anyone or anything that touches the sacrificial meat will become holy. If any of the sacrificial blood spatters on a person's clothing, the soiled garment must be washed in a sacred place. ²⁸If a clay pot is used to boil the sacrificial meat, it must then be broken. If a bronze pot is used, it must be scoured and thoroughly rinsed with water. ²⁹Any male from a priest's family may eat from this offering; it is most holy. ³⁰But the offering for sin may not be eaten if its blood was brought into the Tabernacle as an offering for purification* in the Holy Place. It must be completely burned with fire.

FURTHER INSTRUCTIONS FOR THE GUILT OFFERING

7 "These are the instructions for the guilt offering. It is most holy. ²The animal sacrificed as a guilt offering must be slaughtered at the place where the burnt offerings are slaughtered, and its blood must be splattered against all sides of the altar. ³The priest will then offer all its fat on the altar, including the fat of the broad tail, the fat around the internal organs, ⁴the two kidneys and the fat around them near the loins, and the long lobe of the liver. These are to be removed with the kidneys, ⁵and the priests will burn them on the altar as a special gift presented to the LORD. This is the guilt offering. ⁶Any male from

---

6:7 Or *will make atonement for you before the LORD.* 6:8 Verses 6:8-30 are numbered 6:1-23 in Hebrew text. 6:16 Hebrew *Tent of Meeting;* also in 6:26, 30. 6:20 Hebrew ¹⁄₁₀ *of an ephah* [2.2 liters]. 6:21 The meaning of this Hebrew term is uncertain. 6:22 Hebrew *the anointed priest.* 6:30 Or *an offering to make atonement.*

a priest's family may eat the meat. It must be eaten in a sacred place, for it is most holy.

⁷ "The same instructions apply to both the guilt offering and the sin offering. Both belong to the priest who uses them to purify someone, making that person right with the LORD.* ⁸ In the case of the burnt offering, the priest may keep the hide of the sacrificed animal. ⁹ Any grain offering that has been baked in an oven, prepared in a pan, or cooked on a griddle belongs to the priest who presents it. ¹⁰ All other grain offerings, whether made of dry flour or flour moistened with olive oil, are to be shared equally among all the priests, the descendants of Aaron.

FURTHER INSTRUCTIONS FOR THE PEACE OFFERING

¹¹ "These are the instructions regarding the different kinds of peace offerings that may be presented to the LORD. ¹² If you present your peace offering as an expression of thanksgiving, the usual animal sacrifice must be accompanied by various kinds of bread made without yeast—thin cakes mixed with olive oil, wafers spread with oil, and cakes made of choice flour mixed with olive oil. ¹³ This peace offering of thanksgiving must also be accompanied by loaves of bread made with yeast. ¹⁴ One of each kind of bread must be presented as a gift to the LORD. It will then belong to the priest who splatters the blood of the peace offering against the altar. ¹⁵ The meat of the peace offering of thanksgiving must be eaten on the same day it is offered. None of it may be saved for the next morning.

¹⁶ "If you bring an offering to fulfill a vow or as a voluntary offering, the meat must be eaten on the same day the sacrifice is offered, but whatever is left over may be eaten on the second day. ¹⁷ Any meat left over until the third day must be completely burned up. ¹⁸ If any of the meat from the peace offering is eaten on the third day, the person who presented it will not be accepted by the LORD. You will receive no credit for offering it. By then the meat will be contaminated; if you eat it, you will be punished for your sin.

¹⁹ "Meat that touches anything ceremonially unclean may not be eaten; it must be completely burned up. The rest of the meat may be eaten, but only by people who are ceremonially clean. ²⁰ If you are ceremonially unclean and you eat meat from a peace offering that was presented to the LORD, you will be cut off from the community. ²¹ If you touch anything that is unclean (whether it is human defilement or an unclean animal or any other unclean, detestable thing) and then eat meat from a peace offering presented to the LORD, you will be cut off from the community."

THE FORBIDDEN BLOOD AND FAT

²² Then the LORD said to Moses, ²³ "Give the following instructions to the people of Israel. You must never eat fat, whether from cattle, sheep, or goats. ²⁴ The fat of an animal found dead or torn to pieces by wild animals must never be eaten, though it may be used for any other purpose. ²⁵ Anyone who eats fat from an animal presented as a special gift to the LORD will be cut off from the community. ²⁶ No matter where you live, you must never consume the blood of any bird or animal. ²⁷ Anyone who consumes blood will be cut off from the community."

A PORTION FOR THE PRIESTS

²⁸ Then the LORD said to Moses, ²⁹ "Give the following instructions to the people of Israel. When you present a peace offering to the LORD, bring part of it as a gift to the LORD. ³⁰ Present it to the LORD with your own hands as a special gift to the LORD. Bring the fat of the animal, together with the breast, and lift up the breast as a special offering to the LORD. ³¹ Then the priest will burn the fat on the altar, but the breast will belong to Aaron and his descendants. ³² Give the right thigh of your peace offering to the priest as a gift. ³³ The right thigh must always be given to the priest who offers the blood and the fat of the peace offering. ³⁴ For I have reserved the breast of the special offering and the right thigh of the sacred offering for the priests. It is the permanent right of Aaron and his descendants to share in the peace offerings brought by the people of Israel. ³⁵ This is their rightful share. The special gifts presented to the LORD have been reserved for Aaron and his descendants from the time they were set apart to serve the LORD as priests. ³⁶ On the day they were anointed, the LORD commanded the Israelites to give these portions to the priests as their permanent share from generation to generation."

³⁷ These are the instructions for the burnt offering, the grain offering, the sin offering, and the guilt offering, as well as the ordination offering and the peace offering. ³⁸ The LORD gave these instructions to Moses on Mount Sinai when he commanded the Israelites to present their offerings to the LORD in the wilderness of Sinai.

ORDINATION OF THE PRIESTS

8 Then the LORD said to Moses, ² "Bring Aaron and his sons, along with their sacred garments, the anointing oil, the bull for the sin offering, the two rams, and the basket of bread made without yeast, ³ and call the entire community of Israel together at the entrance of the Tabernacle.*"

⁴ So Moses followed the LORD's instructions, and the whole community assembled at the Tabernacle entrance. ⁵ Moses announced to them, "This is what the LORD has commanded us to do!" ⁶ Then he presented Aaron and his sons and

---

7:7 Or to make atonement.   8:3 Hebrew Tent of Meeting; also in 8:4, 31, 33, 35.

washed them with water. ⁷He put the official tunic on Aaron and tied the sash around his waist. He dressed him in the robe, placed the ephod on him, and attached the ephod securely with its decorative sash. ⁸Then Moses placed the chestpiece on Aaron and put the Urim and the Thummim inside it. ⁹He placed the turban on Aaron's head and attached the gold medallion—the badge of holiness—to the front of the turban, just as the LORD had commanded him.

¹⁰Then Moses took the anointing oil and anointed the Tabernacle and everything in it, making them holy. ¹¹He sprinkled the oil on the altar seven times, anointing it and all its utensils, as well as the washbasin and its stand, making them holy. ¹²Then he poured some of the anointing oil on Aaron's head, anointing him and making him holy for his work. ¹³Next Moses presented Aaron's sons. He clothed them in their tunics, tied their sashes around them, and put their special head coverings on them, just as the LORD had commanded him.

¹⁴Then Moses presented the bull for the sin offering. Aaron and his sons laid their hands on the bull's head, ¹⁵and Moses slaughtered it. Moses took some of the blood, and with his finger he put it on the four horns of the altar to purify it. He poured out the rest of the blood at the base of the altar. Through this process, he made the altar holy by purifying it.* ¹⁶Then Moses took all the fat around the internal organs, the long lobe of the liver, and the two kidneys and the fat around them, and he burned it all on the altar. ¹⁷He took the rest of the bull, including its hide, meat, and dung, and burned it on a fire outside the camp, just as the LORD had commanded him.

¹⁸Then Moses presented the ram for the burnt offering. Aaron and his sons laid their hands on the ram's head, ¹⁹and Moses slaughtered it. Then Moses took the ram's blood and splattered it against all sides of the altar. ²⁰Then he cut the ram into pieces, and he burned the head, some of its pieces, and the fat on the altar. ²¹After washing the internal organs and the legs with water, Moses burned the entire ram on the altar as a burnt offering. It was a pleasing aroma, a special gift presented to the LORD, just as the LORD had commanded him.

²²Then Moses presented the other ram, which was the ram of ordination. Aaron and his sons laid their hands on the ram's head, ²³and Moses slaughtered it. Then Moses took some of its blood and applied it to the lobe of Aaron's right ear, the thumb of his right hand, and the big toe of his right foot. ²⁴Next Moses presented Aaron's sons and applied some of the blood to the lobes of their right ears, the thumbs of their right hands, and the big toes of their right feet. He then splattered the rest of the blood against all sides of the altar.

²⁵Next Moses took the fat, including the fat of the broad tail, the fat around the internal organs, the long lobe of the liver, and the two kidneys and the fat around them, along with the right thigh. ²⁶On top of these he placed a thin cake of bread made without yeast, a cake of bread mixed with olive oil, and a wafer spread with olive oil. All these were taken from the basket of bread made without yeast that was placed in the LORD's presence. ²⁷He put all these in the hands of Aaron and his sons, and he lifted these gifts as a special offering to the LORD. ²⁸Moses then took all the offerings back from them and burned them on the altar on top of the burnt offering. This was the ordination offering. It was a pleasing aroma, a special gift presented to the LORD. ²⁹Then Moses took the breast and lifted it up as a special offering to the LORD. This was Moses' portion of the ram of ordination, just as the LORD had commanded him.

³⁰Next Moses took some of the anointing oil and some of the blood that was on the altar, and he sprinkled them on Aaron and his garments and on his sons and their garments. In this way, he made Aaron and his sons and their garments holy.

³¹Then Moses said to Aaron and his sons, "Boil the remaining meat of the offerings at the Tabernacle entrance, and eat it there, along with the bread that is in the basket of offerings for the ordination, just as I commanded when I said, 'Aaron and his sons will eat it.' ³²Any meat or bread that is left over must then be burned up. ³³You must not leave the Tabernacle entrance for seven days, for that is when the ordination ceremony will be completed. ³⁴Everything we have done today was commanded by the LORD in order to purify you, making you right with him.* ³⁵Now stay at the entrance of the Tabernacle day and night for seven days, and do everything the LORD requires. If you fail to do this, you will die, for this is what the LORD has commanded." ³⁶So Aaron and his sons did everything the LORD had commanded through Moses.

THE PRIESTS BEGIN THEIR WORK

9 After the ordination ceremony, on the eighth day, Moses called together Aaron and his sons and the elders of Israel. ²He said to Aaron, "Take a young bull for a sin offering and a ram for a burnt offering, both without defects, and present them to the LORD. ³Then tell the Israelites, 'Take a male goat for a sin offering, and take a calf and a lamb, both a year old and without defects, for a burnt offering. ⁴Also take a bull* and a ram for a peace offering and flour moistened with olive oil for a grain offering. Present all these offerings to the LORD because the LORD will appear to you today.'"

⁵So the people presented all these things at the entrance of the Tabernacle,* just as Moses

8:15 Or by making atonement for it; or that offerings for purification might be made on it. 8:34 Or to make atonement for you. 9:4 Or cow; also in 9:18, 19. 9:5 Hebrew Tent of Meeting; also in 9:23.

had commanded. Then the whole community came forward and stood before the Lord. ⁶And Moses said, "This is what the Lord has commanded you to do so that the glory of the Lord may appear to you."

⁷Then Moses said to Aaron, "Come to the altar and sacrifice your sin offering and your burnt offering to purify yourself and the people. Then present the offerings of the people to purify them, making them right with the Lord,* just as he has commanded."

⁸So Aaron went to the altar and slaughtered the calf as a sin offering for himself. ⁹His sons brought him the blood, and he dipped his finger in it and put it on the horns of the altar. He poured out the rest of the blood at the base of the altar. ¹⁰Then he burned on the altar the fat, the kidneys, and the long lobe of the liver from the sin offering, just as the Lord had commanded Moses. ¹¹The meat and the hide, however, he burned outside the camp.

¹²Next Aaron slaughtered the animal for the burnt offering. His sons brought him the blood, and he splattered it against all sides of the altar. ¹³Then they handed him each piece of the burnt offering, including the head, and he burned them on the altar. ¹⁴Then he washed the internal organs and the legs and burned them on the altar along with the rest of the burnt offering.

¹⁵Next Aaron presented the offerings of the people. He slaughtered the people's goat and presented it as an offering for their sin, just as he had first done with the offering for his own sin. ¹⁶Then he presented the burnt offering and sacrificed it in the prescribed way. ¹⁷He also presented the grain offering, burning a handful of the flour mixture on the altar, in addition to the regular burnt offering for the morning.

¹⁸Then Aaron slaughtered the bull and the ram for the people's peace offering. His sons brought him the blood, and he splattered it against all sides of the altar. ¹⁹Then he took the fat of the bull and the ram—the fat of the broad tail and from around the internal organs—along with the kidneys and the long lobes of the livers. ²⁰He placed these fat portions on top of the breasts of these animals and burned them on the altar. ²¹Aaron then lifted up the breasts and right thighs as a special offering to the Lord, just as Moses had commanded.

²²After that, Aaron raised his hands toward the people and blessed them. Then, after presenting the sin offering, the burnt offering, and the peace offering, he stepped down from the altar. ²³Then Moses and Aaron went into the Tabernacle, and when they came back out, they blessed the people again, and the glory of the Lord appeared to the whole community. ²⁴Fire blazed forth from the Lord's presence and consumed the burnt offering and the fat on the altar. When the people saw this, they shouted with joy and fell face down on the ground.

THE SIN OF NADAB AND ABIHU

10 Aaron's sons Nadab and Abihu put coals of fire in their incense burners and sprinkled incense over them. In this way, they disobeyed the Lord by burning before him the wrong kind of fire, different than he had commanded. ²So fire blazed forth from the Lord's presence and burned them up, and they died there before the Lord.

³Then Moses said to Aaron, "This is what the Lord meant when he said,

'I will display my holiness
    through those who come near me.
I will display my glory
    before all the people.'"

And Aaron was silent.

⁴Then Moses called for Mishael and Elzaphan, Aaron's cousins, the sons of Aaron's uncle Uzziel. He said to them, "Come forward and carry away the bodies of your relatives from in front of the sanctuary to a place outside the camp." ⁵So they came forward and picked them up by their garments and carried them out of the camp, just as Moses had commanded.

⁶Then Moses said to Aaron and his sons Eleazar and Ithamar, "Do not show grief by leaving your hair uncombed* or by tearing your clothes. If you do, you will die, and the Lord's anger will strike the whole community of Israel. However, the rest of the Israelites, your relatives, may mourn because of the Lord's fiery destruction of Nadab and Abihu. ⁷But you must not leave the entrance of the Tabernacle* or you will die, for you have been anointed with the Lord's anointing oil." So they did as Moses commanded.

INSTRUCTIONS FOR PRIESTLY CONDUCT

⁸Then the Lord said to Aaron, ⁹"You and your descendants must never drink wine or any other alcoholic drink before going into the Tabernacle. If you do, you will die. This is a permanent law for you, and it must be observed from generation to generation. ¹⁰You must distinguish between what is sacred and what is common, between what is ceremonially unclean and what is clean. ¹¹And you must teach the Israelites all the decrees that the Lord has given them through Moses."

¹²Then Moses said to Aaron and his remaining sons, Eleazar and Ithamar, "Take what is left of the grain offering after a portion has been presented as a special gift to the Lord, and eat it beside the altar. Make sure it contains no yeast, for it is most holy. ¹³You must eat it in a sacred place, for it has been given to you and your descendants as your portion of the special gifts presented to the Lord. These are the commands I have been given. ¹⁴But the breast and thigh that were lifted up as a special offering

9:7 Or to make atonement for them. 10:6 Or by uncovering your heads. 10:7 Hebrew Tent of Meeting; also in 10:9.

may be eaten in any place that is ceremonially clean. These parts have been given to you and your descendants as your portion of the peace offerings presented by the people of Israel. ¹⁵ You must lift up the thigh and breast as a special offering to the LORD, along with the fat of the special gifts. These parts will belong to you and your descendants as your permanent right, just as the LORD has commanded."

¹⁶ Moses then asked them what had happened to the goat of the sin offering. When he discovered it had been burned up, he became very angry with Eleazar and Ithamar, Aaron's remaining sons. ¹⁷ "Why didn't you eat the sin offering in the sacred area?" he demanded. "It is a holy offering! The LORD has given it to you to remove the guilt of the community and to purify the people, making them right with the LORD.* ¹⁸ Since the animal's blood was not brought into the Holy Place, you should have eaten the meat in the sacred area as I ordered you."

¹⁹ Then Aaron answered Moses, "Today my sons presented both their sin offering and their burnt offering to the LORD. And yet this tragedy has happened to me. If I had eaten the people's sin offering on such a tragic day as this, would the LORD have been pleased?" ²⁰ And when Moses heard this, he was satisfied.

CEREMONIALLY CLEAN AND UNCLEAN ANIMALS

11 Then the LORD said to Moses and Aaron, ² "Give the following instructions to the people of Israel.

"Of all the land animals, these are the ones you may use for food. ³ You may eat any animal that has completely split hooves and chews the cud. ⁴ You may not, however, eat the following animals* that have split hooves or that chew the cud, but not both. The camel chews the cud but does not have split hooves, so it is ceremonially unclean for you. ⁵ The hyrax* chews the cud but does not have split hooves, so it is unclean. ⁶ The hare chews the cud but does not have split hooves, so it is unclean. ⁷ The pig has evenly split hooves but does not chew the cud, so it is unclean. ⁸ You may not eat the meat of these animals or even touch their carcasses. They are ceremonially unclean for you.

⁹ "Of all the marine animals, these are ones you may use for food. You may eat anything from the water if it has both fins and scales, whether taken from salt water or from streams. ¹⁰ But you must never eat animals from the sea or from rivers that do not have both fins and scales. They are detestable to you. This applies both to little creatures that live in shallow water and to all creatures that live in deep water. ¹¹ They will always be detestable to you. You must never eat their meat or even touch their dead bodies. ¹² Any marine animal that does not have both fins and scales is detestable to you.

¹³ "These are the birds that are detestable to you. You must never eat them: the griffon vulture, the bearded vulture, the black vulture, ¹⁴ the kite, falcons of all kinds, ¹⁵ ravens of all kinds, ¹⁶ the eagle owl, the short-eared owl, the seagull, hawks of all kinds, ¹⁷ the little owl, the cormorant, the great owl, ¹⁸ the barn owl, the desert owl, the Egyptian vulture, ¹⁹ the stork, herons of all kinds, the hoopoe, and the bat.

²⁰ "You must not eat winged insects that walk along the ground; they are detestable to you. ²¹ You may, however, eat winged insects that walk along the ground and have jointed legs so they can jump. ²² The insects you are permitted to eat include all kinds of locusts, bald locusts, crickets, and grasshoppers. ²³ All other winged insects that walk along the ground are detestable to you.

²⁴ "The following creatures will make you ceremonially unclean. If any of you touch their carcasses, you will be defiled until evening. ²⁵ If you pick up their carcasses, you must wash your clothes, and you will remain defiled until evening.

²⁶ "Any animal that has split hooves that are not evenly divided or that does not chew the cud is unclean for you. If you touch the carcass of such an animal, you will be defiled. ²⁷ Of the animals that walk on all fours, those that have paws are unclean. If you touch the carcass of such an animal, you will be defiled until evening. ²⁸ If you pick up its carcass, you must wash your clothes, and you will remain defiled until evening. These animals are unclean for you.

²⁹ "Of the small animals that scurry along the ground, these are unclean for you: the mole rat, the rat, large lizards of all kinds, ³⁰ the gecko, the monitor lizard, the common lizard, the sand lizard, and the chameleon. ³¹ All these small animals are unclean for you. If any of you touch the dead body of such an animal, you will be defiled until evening. ³² If such an animal dies and falls on something, that object will be unclean. This is true whether the object is made of wood, cloth, leather, or burlap. Whatever its use, you must dip it in water, and it will remain defiled until evening. After that, it will be ceremonially clean and may be used again.

³³ "If such an animal falls into a clay pot, everything in the pot will be defiled, and the pot must be smashed. ³⁴ If the water from such a container spills on any food, the food will be defiled. And any beverage in such a container will be defiled. ³⁵ Any object on which the carcass of such an animal falls will be defiled. If it is an oven or hearth, it must be destroyed, for it is defiled, and you must treat it accordingly.

³⁶ "However, if the carcass of such an animal falls into a spring or a cistern, the water will still be clean. But anyone who touches the carcass

---

10:17 Or *to make atonement for the people before the LORD.*
11:4 The identification of some of the animals, birds, and insects in this chapter is uncertain. 11:5 Or *coney,* or *rock badger.*

will be defiled. ³⁷ If the carcass falls on seed grain to be planted in the field, the seed will still be considered clean. ³⁸ But if the seed is wet when the carcass falls on it, the seed will be defiled.

³⁹ "If an animal you are permitted to eat dies and you touch its carcass, you will be defiled until evening. ⁴⁰ If you eat any of its meat or carry away its carcass, you must wash your clothes, and you will remain defiled until evening.

⁴¹ "All small animals that scurry along the ground are detestable, and you must never eat them. ⁴² This includes all animals that slither along on their bellies, as well as those with four legs and those with many feet. All such animals that scurry along the ground are detestable, and you must never eat them. ⁴³ Do not defile yourselves by touching them. You must not make yourselves ceremonially unclean because of them. ⁴⁴ For I am the LORD your God. You must consecrate yourselves and be holy, because I am holy. So do not defile yourselves with any of these small animals that scurry along the ground. ⁴⁵ For I, the LORD, am the one who brought you up from the land of Egypt, that I might be your God. Therefore, you must be holy because I am holy.

⁴⁶ "These are the instructions regarding land animals, birds, marine creatures, and animals that scurry along the ground. ⁴⁷ By these instructions you will know what is unclean and clean, and which animals may be eaten and which may not be eaten."

PURIFICATION AFTER CHILDBIRTH

12 The LORD said to Moses, ² "Give the following instructions to the people of Israel. If a woman becomes pregnant and gives birth to a son, she will be ceremonially unclean for seven days, just as she is unclean during her menstrual period. ³ On the eighth day the boy's foreskin must be circumcised. ⁴ After waiting thirty-three days, she will be purified from the bleeding of childbirth. During this time of purification, she must not touch anything that is set apart as holy. And she must not enter the sanctuary until her time of purification is over. ⁵ If a woman gives birth to a daughter, she will be ceremonially unclean for two weeks, just as she is unclean during her menstrual period. After waiting sixty-six days, she will be purified from the bleeding of childbirth.

⁶ "When the time of purification is completed for either a son or a daughter, the woman must bring a one-year-old lamb for a burnt offering and a young pigeon or turtledove for a purification offering. She must bring her offerings to the priest at the entrance of the Tabernacle.* ⁷ The priest will then present them to the LORD to purify her.* Then she will be ceremonially clean again after her bleeding at childbirth. These are the instructions for a woman after the birth of a son or a daughter.

⁸ "If a woman cannot afford to bring a lamb, she must bring two turtledoves or two young pigeons. One will be for the burnt offering and the other for the purification offering. The priest will sacrifice them to purify her, and she will be ceremonially clean."

SERIOUS SKIN DISEASES

13 The LORD said to Moses and Aaron, ² "If anyone has a swelling or a rash or discolored skin that might develop into a serious skin disease,* that person must be brought to Aaron the priest or to one of his sons.* ³ The priest will examine the affected area of the skin. If the hair in the affected area has turned white and the problem appears to be more than skin-deep, it is a serious skin disease, and the priest who examines it must pronounce the person ceremonially unclean.

⁴ "But if the affected area of the skin is only a white discoloration and does not appear to be more than skin-deep, and if the hair on the spot has not turned white, the priest will quarantine the person for seven days. ⁵ On the seventh day the priest will make another examination. If he finds the affected area has not changed and the problem has not spread on the skin, the priest will quarantine the person for seven more days. ⁶ On the seventh day the priest will make another examination. If he finds the affected area has faded and has not spread, the priest will pronounce the person ceremonially clean. It was only a rash. The person's clothing must be washed, and the person will be ceremonially clean. ⁷ But if the rash continues to spread after the person has been examined by the priest and has been pronounced clean, the infected person must return to be examined again. ⁸ If the priest finds that the rash has spread, he must pronounce the person ceremonially unclean, for it is indeed a skin disease.

⁹ "Anyone who develops a serious skin disease must go to the priest for an examination. ¹⁰ If the priest finds a white swelling on the skin, and some hair on the spot has turned white, and there is an open sore in the affected area, ¹¹ it is a chronic skin disease, and the priest must pronounce the person ceremonially unclean. In such cases the person need not be quarantined, for it is obvious that the skin is defiled by the disease.

¹² "Now suppose the disease has spread all over the person's skin, covering the body from head to foot. ¹³ When the priest examines the infected person and finds that the disease covers the entire body, he will pronounce the person ceremonially clean. Since the skin has turned completely white, the person is clean. ¹⁴ But if any

12:6 Hebrew *Tent of Meeting.* 12:7 Or *to make atonement for her;* also in 12:8. 13:2a Traditionally rendered *leprosy.* The Hebrew word used throughout this passage is used to describe various skin diseases. 13:2b Or *one of his descendants.*

open sores appear, the infected person will be pronounced ceremonially unclean. ¹⁵ The priest must make this pronouncement as soon as he sees an open sore, since open sores indicate the presence of a skin disease. ¹⁶ However, if the open sores heal and turn white like the rest of the skin, the person must return to the priest ¹⁷ for another examination. If the affected areas have indeed turned white, the priest will then pronounce the person ceremonially clean by declaring, 'You are clean!'

¹⁸ "If anyone has a boil on the skin that has started to heal, ¹⁹ but a white swelling or a reddish white spot develops in its place, that person must go to the priest to be examined. ²⁰ If the priest examines it and finds it to be more than skin-deep, and if the hair in the affected area has turned white, the priest must pronounce the person ceremonially unclean. The boil has become a serious skin disease. ²¹ But if the priest finds no white hair on the affected area and the problem appears to be no more than skin-deep and has faded, the priest must quarantine the person for seven days. ²² If during that time the affected area spreads on the skin, the priest must pronounce the person ceremonially unclean, because it is a serious disease. ²³ But if the area grows no larger and does not spread, it is merely the scar from the boil, and the priest will pronounce the person ceremonially clean.

²⁴ "If anyone has suffered a burn on the skin and the burned area changes color, becoming either reddish white or shiny white, ²⁵ the priest must examine it. If he finds that the hair in the affected area has turned white and the problem appears to be more than skin-deep, a skin disease has broken out in the burn. The priest must then pronounce the person ceremonially unclean, for it is clearly a serious skin disease. ²⁶ But if the priest finds no white hair on the affected area and the problem appears to be no more than skin-deep and has faded, the priest must quarantine the infected person for seven days. ²⁷ On the seventh day the priest must examine the person again. If the affected area has spread on the skin, the priest must pronounce that person ceremonially unclean, for it is clearly a serious skin disease. ²⁸ But if the affected area has not changed or spread on the skin and has faded, it is simply a swelling from the burn. The priest will then pronounce the person ceremonially clean, for it is only the scar from the burn.

²⁹ "If anyone, either a man or woman, has a sore on the head or chin, ³⁰ the priest must examine it. If he finds it is more than skin-deep and has fine yellow hair on it, the priest must pronounce the person ceremonially unclean. It is a scabby sore of the head or chin. ³¹ If the priest examines the scabby sore and finds that it is only skin-deep but there is no black hair on it, he must quarantine the person for seven days. ³² On the seventh day the priest must examine the sore

again. If he finds that the scabby sore has not spread, and there is no yellow hair on it, and it appears to be only skin-deep, ³³ the person must shave off all hair except the hair on the affected area. Then the priest must quarantine the person for another seven days. ³⁴ On the seventh day he will examine the sore again. If it has not spread and appears to be no more than skin-deep, the priest will pronounce the person ceremonially clean. The person's clothing must be washed, and the person will be ceremonially clean. ³⁵ But if the scabby sore begins to spread after the person is pronounced clean, ³⁶ the priest must do another examination. If he finds that the sore has spread, the priest does not need to look for yellow hair. The infected person is ceremonially unclean. ³⁷ But if the color of the scabby sore does not change and black hair has grown on it, it has healed. The priest will then pronounce the person ceremonially clean.

³⁸ "If anyone, either a man or woman, has shiny white patches on the skin, ³⁹ the priest must examine the affected area. If he finds that the shiny patches are only pale white, this is a harmless skin rash, and the person is ceremonially clean.

⁴⁰ "If a man loses his hair and his head becomes bald, he is still ceremonially clean. ⁴¹ And if he loses hair on his forehead, he simply has a bald forehead; he is still clean. ⁴² However, if a reddish white sore appears on the bald area on top of his head or on his forehead, this is a skin disease. ⁴³ The priest must examine him, and if he finds swelling around the reddish white sore anywhere on the man's head and it looks like a skin disease, ⁴⁴ the man is indeed infected with a skin disease and is unclean. The priest must pronounce him ceremonially unclean because of the sore on his head.

⁴⁵ "Those who suffer from a serious skin disease must tear their clothing and leave their hair uncombed.* They must cover their mouth and call out, 'Unclean! Unclean!' ⁴⁶ As long as the serious disease lasts, they will be ceremonially unclean. They must live in isolation in their place outside the camp.

TREATMENT OF CONTAMINATED CLOTHING

⁴⁷ "Now suppose mildew* contaminates some woolen or linen clothing, ⁴⁸ woolen or linen fabric, the hide of an animal, or anything made of leather. ⁴⁹ If the contaminated area in the clothing, the animal hide, the fabric, or the leather article has turned greenish or reddish, it is contaminated with mildew and must be shown to the priest. ⁵⁰ After examining the affected spot, the priest will put the article in quarantine for seven days. ⁵¹ On the seventh day the priest must

13:45 Or *and uncover their heads.* 13:47 Traditionally rendered *leprosy.* The Hebrew term used throughout this passage is the same term used for the various skin diseases described in 13:1-46.

inspect it again. If the contaminated area has spread, the clothing or fabric or leather is clearly contaminated by a serious mildew and is ceremonially unclean. [52] The priest must burn the item—the clothing, the woolen or linen fabric, or piece of leather—for it has been contaminated by a serious mildew. It must be completely destroyed by fire.

[53] "But if the priest examines it and finds that the contaminated area has not spread in the clothing, the fabric, or the leather, [54] the priest will order the object to be washed and then quarantined for seven more days. [55] Then the priest must examine the object again. If he finds that the contaminated area has not changed color after being washed, even if it did not spread, the object is defiled. It must be completely burned up, whether the contaminated spot* is on the inside or outside. [56] But if the priest examines it and finds that the contaminated area has faded after being washed, he must cut the spot from the clothing, the fabric, or the leather. [57] If the spot later reappears on the clothing, the fabric, or the leather article, the mildew is clearly spreading, and the contaminated object must be burned up. [58] But if the spot disappears from the clothing, the fabric, or the leather article after it has been washed, it must be washed again; then it will be ceremonially clean.

[59] "These are the instructions for dealing with mildew that contaminates woolen or linen clothing or fabric or anything made of leather. This is how the priest will determine whether these items are ceremonially clean or unclean."

CLEANSING FROM SKIN DISEASES

14 And the LORD said to Moses, [2] "The following instructions are for those seeking ceremonial purification from a skin disease.* Those who have been healed must be brought to the priest, [3] who will examine them at a place outside the camp. If the priest finds that someone has been healed of a serious skin disease, [4] he will perform a purification ceremony, using two live birds that are ceremonially clean, a stick of cedar,* some scarlet yarn, and a hyssop branch. [5] The priest will order that one bird be slaughtered over a clay pot filled with fresh water. [6] He will take the live bird, the cedar stick, the scarlet yarn, and the hyssop branch, and dip them into the blood of the bird that was slaughtered over the fresh water. [7] The priest will then sprinkle the blood of the dead bird seven times on the person being purified of the skin disease. When the priest has purified the person, he will release the live bird in the open field to fly away.

[8] "The persons being purified must then wash their clothes, shave off all their hair, and bathe themselves in water. Then they will be ceremonially clean and may return to the camp. However, they must remain outside their tents for seven days. [9] On the seventh day they must again shave all the hair from their heads, including the hair of the beard and eyebrows. They must also wash their clothes and bathe themselves in water. Then they will be ceremonially clean.

[10] "On the eighth day each person being purified must bring two male lambs and a one-year-old female lamb, all with no defects, along with a grain offering of six quarts* of choice flour moistened with olive oil, and a cup* of olive oil. [11] Then the officiating priest will present that person for purification, along with the offerings, before the LORD at the entrance of the Tabernacle.* [12] The priest will take one of the male lambs and the olive oil and present them as a guilt offering, lifting them up as a special offering before the LORD. [13] He will then slaughter the male lamb in the sacred area where sin offerings and burnt offerings are slaughtered. As with the sin offering, the guilt offering belongs to the priest. It is a most holy offering. [14] The priest will then take some of the blood of the guilt offering and apply it to the lobe of the right ear, the thumb of the right hand, and the big toe of the right foot of the person being purified.

[15] "Then the priest will pour some of the olive oil into the palm of his own left hand. [16] He will dip his right finger into the oil in his palm and sprinkle some of it with his finger seven times before the LORD. [17] The priest will then apply some of the oil in his palm over the blood from the guilt offering that is on the lobe of the right ear, the thumb of the right hand, and the big toe of the right foot of the person being purified. [18] The priest will apply the oil remaining in his hand to the head of the person being purified. Through this process, the priest will purify* the person before the LORD.

[19] "Then the priest must present the sin offering to purify the person who was cured of the skin disease. After that, the priest will slaughter the burnt offering [20] and offer it on the altar along with the grain offering. Through this process, the priest will purify the person who was healed, and the person will be ceremonially clean.

[21] "But anyone who is too poor and cannot afford these offerings may bring one male lamb for a guilt offering, to be lifted up as a special offering for purification. The person must also bring two quarts* of choice flour moistened with olive oil for the grain offering and a cup of olive oil. [22] The offering must also include two turtledoves or two young pigeons, whichever the person can afford. One of the pair must be used for the sin offering and the other for a burnt offering. [23] On the eighth day of the purification ceremony, the person being purified must bring the offerings to the priest in the LORD's presence at the

---

13:55 The meaning of the Hebrew is uncertain. 14:2 Traditionally rendered *leprosy;* see note on 13:2a. 14:4 Or *juniper;* also in 14:6, 49, 51. 14:10a Hebrew *⅒ of an ephah* [6.6 liters]. 14:10b Hebrew *1 log* [0.3 liters]; also in 14:21. 14:11 Hebrew *Tent of Meeting;* also in 14:23. 14:18 Or *will make atonement for;* similarly in 14:19, 20, 21, 29, 31, 53. 14:21 Hebrew *⅒ of an ephah* [2.2 liters].

entrance of the Tabernacle. 24 The priest will take the lamb for the guilt offering, along with the olive oil, and lift them up as a special offering to the LORD. 25 Then the priest will slaughter the lamb for the guilt offering. He will take some of its blood and apply it to the lobe of the right ear, the thumb of the right hand, and the big toe of the right foot of the person being purified.

26 "The priest will also pour some of the olive oil into the palm of his own left hand. 27 He will dip his right finger into the oil in his palm and sprinkle some of it seven times before the LORD. 28 The priest will then apply some of the oil in his palm over the blood from the guilt offering that is on the lobe of the right ear, the thumb of the right hand, and the big toe of the right foot of the person being purified. 29 The priest will apply the oil remaining in his hand to the head of the person being purified. Through this process, the priest will purify the person before the LORD.

30 "Then the priest will offer the two turtledoves or the two young pigeons, whichever the person can afford. 31 One of them is for a sin offering and the other for a burnt offering, to be presented along with the grain offering. Through this process, the priest will purify the person before the LORD. 32 These are the instructions for purification for those who have recovered from a serious skin disease but who cannot afford to bring the offerings normally required for the ceremony of purification."

TREATMENT OF CONTAMINATED HOUSES

33 Then the LORD said to Moses and Aaron, 34 "When you arrive in Canaan, the land I am giving you as your own possession, I may contaminate some of the houses in your land with mildew.* 35 The owner of such a house must then go to the priest and say, 'It appears that my house has some kind of mildew.' 36 Before the priest goes in to inspect the house, he must have the house emptied so nothing inside will be pronounced ceremonially unclean. 37 Then the priest will go in and examine the mildew on the walls. If he finds greenish or reddish streaks and the contamination appears to go deeper than the wall's surface, 38 the priest will step outside the door and put the house in quarantine for seven days. 39 On the seventh day the priest must return for another inspection. If he finds that the mildew on the walls of the house has spread, 40 the priest must order that the stones from those areas be removed. The contaminated material will then be taken outside the town to an area designated as ceremonially unclean. 41 Next the inside walls of the entire house must be scraped thoroughly and the scrapings dumped in the unclean place outside the town. 42 Other stones will be brought in to replace the ones that were removed, and the walls will be replastered.

43 "But if the mildew reappears after all the stones have been replaced and the house has been scraped and replastered, 44 the priest must return and inspect the house again. If he finds that the mildew has spread, the walls are clearly contaminated with a serious mildew, and the house is defiled. 45 It must be torn down, and all its stones, timbers, and plaster must be carried out of town to the place designated as ceremonially unclean. 46 Those who enter the house during the period of quarantine will be ceremonially unclean until evening, 47 and all who sleep or eat in the house must wash their clothing.

48 "But if the priest returns for his inspection and finds that the mildew has not reappeared in the house after the fresh plastering, he will pronounce it clean because the mildew is clearly gone. 49 To purify the house the priest must take two birds, a stick of cedar, some scarlet yarn, and a hyssop branch. 50 He will slaughter one of the birds over a clay pot filled with fresh water. 51 He will take the cedar stick, the hyssop branch, the scarlet yarn, and the live bird, and dip them into the blood of the slaughtered bird and into the fresh water. Then he will sprinkle the house seven times. 52 When the priest has purified the house in exactly this way, 53 he will release the live bird in the open fields outside the town. Through this process, the priest will purify the house, and it will be ceremonially clean.

54 "These are the instructions for dealing with serious skin diseases,* including scabby sores; 55 and mildew,* whether on clothing or in a house; 56 and a swelling on the skin, a rash, or discolored skin. 57 This procedure will determine whether a person or object is ceremonially clean or unclean.

"These are the instructions regarding skin diseases and mildew."

BODILY DISCHARGES

15 The LORD said to Moses and Aaron, 2 "Give the following instructions to the people of Israel.

"Any man who has a bodily discharge is ceremonially unclean. 3 This defilement is caused by his discharge, whether the discharge continues or stops. In either case the man is unclean. 4 Any bed on which the man with the discharge lies and anything on which he sits will be ceremonially unclean. 5 So if you touch the man's bed, you must wash your clothes and bathe yourself in water, and you will remain unclean until evening. 6 If you sit where the man with the discharge has sat, you must wash your clothes and bathe yourself in water, and you will remain unclean until evening. 7 If you touch the man with the discharge, you must wash your clothes and bathe yourself in water, and you will remain unclean until evening. 8 If the man spits on you, you must wash your clothes and bathe yourself in water, and

14:34 Traditionally rendered *leprosy;* see note on 13:47.
14:54 Traditionally rendered *leprosy;* see note on 13:2a.
14:55 Traditionally rendered *leprosy;* see note on 13:47.

you will remain unclean until evening. ⁹Any saddle blanket on which the man rides will be ceremonially unclean. ¹⁰If you touch anything that was under the man, you will be unclean until evening. You must wash your clothes and bathe yourself in water, and you will remain unclean until evening. ¹¹If the man touches you without first rinsing his hands, you must wash your clothes and bathe yourself in water, and you will remain unclean until evening. ¹²Any clay pot the man touches must be broken, and any wooden utensil he touches must be rinsed with water.

¹³"When the man with the discharge is healed, he must count off seven days for the period of purification. Then he must wash his clothes and bathe himself in fresh water, and he will be ceremonially clean. ¹⁴On the eighth day he must get two turtledoves or two young pigeons and come before the LORD at the entrance of the Tabernacle* and give his offerings to the priest. ¹⁵The priest will offer one bird for a sin offering and the other for a burnt offering. Through this process, the priest will purify* the man before the LORD for his discharge.

¹⁶"Whenever a man has an emission of semen, he must bathe his entire body in water, and he will remain ceremonially unclean until the next evening.* ¹⁷Any clothing or leather with semen on it must be washed in water, and it will remain unclean until evening. ¹⁸After a man and a woman have sexual intercourse, they must each bathe in water, and they will remain unclean until the next evening.

¹⁹"Whenever a woman has her menstrual period, she will be ceremonially unclean for seven days. Anyone who touches her during that time will be unclean until evening. ²⁰Anything on which the woman lies or sits during the time of her period will be unclean. ²¹If any of you touch her bed, you must wash your clothes and bathe yourself in water, and you will remain unclean until evening. ²²If you touch any object she has sat on, you must wash your clothes and bathe yourself in water, and you will remain unclean until evening. ²³This includes her bed or any other object she has sat on; you will be unclean until evening if you touch it. ²⁴If a man has sexual intercourse with her and her blood touches him, her menstrual impurity will be transmitted to him. He will remain unclean for seven days, and any bed on which he lies will be unclean.

²⁵"If a woman has a flow of blood for many days that is unrelated to her menstrual period, or if the blood continues beyond the normal period, she is ceremonially unclean. As during her menstrual period, the woman will be unclean as long as the discharge continues. ²⁶Any bed she lies on and any object she sits on during that time will be unclean, just as during her normal menstrual period. ²⁷If any of you touch these things, you will be ceremonially unclean. You must wash your clothes and bathe yourself in water, and you will remain unclean until evening.

²⁸"When the woman's bleeding stops, she must count off seven days. Then she will be ceremonially clean. ²⁹On the eighth day she must bring two turtledoves or two young pigeons and present them to the priest at the entrance of the Tabernacle. ³⁰The priest will offer one for a sin offering and the other for a burnt offering. Through this process, the priest will purify her before the LORD for the ceremonial impurity caused by her bleeding.

³¹"This is how you will guard the people of Israel from ceremonial uncleanness. Otherwise they would die, for their impurity would defile my Tabernacle that stands among them. ³²These are the instructions for dealing with anyone who has a bodily discharge—a man who is unclean because of an emission of semen ³³or a woman during her menstrual period. It applies to any man or woman who has a bodily discharge, and to a man who has sexual intercourse with a woman who is ceremonially unclean."

THE DAY OF ATONEMENT

16 The LORD spoke to Moses after the death of Aaron's two sons, who died after they entered the LORD's presence and burned the wrong kind of fire before him. ²The LORD said to Moses, "Warn your brother, Aaron, not to enter the Most Holy Place behind the inner curtain whenever he chooses; if he does, he will die. For the Ark's cover—the place of atonement—is there, and I myself am present in the cloud above the atonement cover.

³"When Aaron enters the sanctuary area, he must follow these instructions fully. He must bring a young bull for a sin offering and a ram for a burnt offering. ⁴He must put on his linen tunic and the linen undergarments worn next to his body. He must tie the linen sash around his waist and put the linen turban on his head. These are sacred garments, so he must bathe himself in water before he puts them on. ⁵Aaron must take from the community of Israel two male goats for a sin offering and a ram for a burnt offering.

⁶"Aaron will present his own bull as a sin offering to purify himself and his family, making them right with the LORD.* ⁷Then he must take the two male goats and present them to the LORD at the entrance of the Tabernacle.* ⁸He is to cast sacred lots to determine which goat will be reserved as an offering to the LORD and which will carry the sins of the people to the wilderness of Azazel. ⁹Aaron will then present as a sin offering the goat chosen by lot for the LORD. ¹⁰The other goat, the scapegoat chosen by lot to be sent away, will be

---

15:14 Hebrew *Tent of Meeting;* also in 15:29. **15:15** Or *will make atonement for;* also in 15:30. **15:16** Hebrew *until evening;* also in 15:18. **16:6** Or *to make atonement for himself and his family;* similarly in 16:11, 17b, 24, 34. **16:7** Hebrew *Tent of Meeting;* also in 16:16, 17, 20, 23, 33.

kept alive, standing before the LORD. When it is sent away to Azazel in the wilderness, the people will be purified and made right with the LORD.*

11 "Aaron will present his own bull as a sin offering to purify himself and his family, making them right with the LORD. After he has slaughtered the bull as a sin offering, 12 he will fill an incense burner with burning coals from the altar that stands before the LORD. Then he will take two handfuls of fragrant powdered incense and will carry the burner and the incense behind the inner curtain. 13 There in the LORD's presence he will put the incense on the burning coals so that a cloud of incense will rise over the Ark's cover—the place of atonement—that rests on the Ark of the Covenant.* If he follows these instructions, he will not die. 14 Then he must take some of the blood of the bull, dip his finger in it, and sprinkle it on the east side of the atonement cover. He must sprinkle blood seven times with his finger in front of the atonement cover.

15 "Then Aaron must slaughter the first goat as a sin offering for the people and carry its blood behind the inner curtain. There he will sprinkle the goat's blood over the atonement cover and in front of it, just as he did with the bull's blood. 16 Through this process, he will purify* the Most Holy Place, and he will do the same for the entire Tabernacle, because of the defiling sin and rebellion of the Israelites. 17 No one else is allowed inside the Tabernacle when Aaron enters it for the purification ceremony in the Most Holy Place. No one may enter until he comes out again after purifying himself, his family, and all the congregation of Israel, making them right with the LORD.

18 "Then Aaron will come out to purify the altar that stands before the LORD. He will do this by taking some of the blood from the bull and the goat and putting it on each of the horns of the altar. 19 Then he must sprinkle the blood with his finger seven times over the altar. In this way, he will cleanse it from Israel's defilement and make it holy.

20 "When Aaron has finished purifying the Most Holy Place and the Tabernacle and the altar, he must present the live goat. 21 He will lay both of his hands on the goat's head and confess over it all the wickedness, rebellion, and sins of the people of Israel. In this way, he will transfer the people's sins to the head of the goat. Then a man specially chosen for the task will drive the goat into the wilderness. 22 As the goat goes into the wilderness, it will carry all the people's sins upon itself into a desolate land.

23 "When Aaron goes back into the Tabernacle, he must take off the linen garments he was wearing when he entered the Most Holy Place, and he must leave the garments there. 24 Then he must bathe himself with water in a sacred place, put on his regular garments, and go out to sacrifice a burnt offering for himself and a burnt offering for the people. Through this process, he will purify himself and the people, making them right with the LORD. 25 He must then burn all the fat of the sin offering on the altar.

26 "The man chosen to drive the scapegoat into the wilderness of Azazel must wash his clothes and bathe himself in water. Then he may return to the camp.

27 "The bull and the goat presented as sin offerings, whose blood Aaron takes into the Most Holy Place for the purification ceremony, will be carried outside the camp. The animals' hides, internal organs, and dung are all to be burned. 28 The man who burns them must wash his clothes and bathe himself in water before returning to the camp.

29 "On the tenth day of the appointed month in early autumn,* you must deny yourselves.* Neither native-born Israelites nor foreigners living among you may do any kind of work. This is a permanent law for you. 30 On that day offerings of purification will be made for you,* and you will be purified in the LORD's presence from all your sins. 31 It will be a Sabbath day of complete rest for you, and you must deny yourselves. This is a permanent law for you. 32 In future generations, the purification* ceremony will be performed by the priest who has been anointed and ordained to serve as high priest in place of his ancestor Aaron. He will put on the holy linen garments 33 and purify the Most Holy Place, the Tabernacle, the altar, the priests, and the entire congregation. 34 This is a permanent law for you, to purify the people of Israel from their sins, making them right with the LORD once each year."

Moses followed all these instructions exactly as the LORD had commanded him.

PROHIBITIONS AGAINST EATING BLOOD

17 Then the LORD said to Moses, 2 "Give the following instructions to Aaron and his sons and all the people of Israel. This is what the LORD has commanded.

3 "If any native Israelite sacrifices a bull* or a lamb or a goat anywhere inside or outside the camp 4 instead of bringing it to the entrance of the Tabernacle* to present it as an offering to the LORD, that person will be as guilty as a murderer.* Such a person has shed blood and will be cut off from the community. 5 The purpose of this rule is to stop the Israelites from sacrificing animals in the open fields. It will ensure that they bring their sacrifices to the priest at the entrance of the Tabernacle, so he can present them to the LORD as peace offerings. 6 Then the priest will

---

16:10 Or *wilderness, it will make atonement for the people.*
16:13 Hebrew *that is above the Testimony.* The Hebrew word for "testimony" refers to the terms of the LORD's covenant with Israel as written on stone tablets, which were kept in the Ark, and also to the covenant itself. 16:16 Or *make atonement for;* similarly in 16:17a, 18, 20, 27, 33. 16:29a Hebrew *On the tenth day of the seventh month.* This day in the ancient Hebrew lunar calendar occurred in September or October. 16:29b Or *must fast;* also in 16:31. 16:30 Or *atonement will be made for you, to purify you.* 16:32 Or *atonement.* 17:3 Or *cow.* 17:4a Hebrew *Tent of Meeting;* also in 17:5, 6, 9. 17:4b Hebrew *will be guilty of blood.*

be able to splatter the blood against the LORD's altar at the entrance of the Tabernacle, and he will burn the fat as a pleasing aroma to the LORD. [7]The people must no longer be unfaithful to the LORD by offering sacrifices to the goat idols.* This is a permanent law for them, to be observed from generation to generation.

[8]"Give them this command as well. If any native Israelite or foreigner living among you offers a burnt offering or a sacrifice [9]but does not bring it to the entrance of the Tabernacle to offer it to the LORD, that person will be cut off from the community.

[10]"And if any native Israelite or foreigner living among you eats or drinks blood in any form, I will turn against that person and cut him off from the community of your people, [11]for the life of the body is in its blood. I have given you the blood on the altar to purify you, making you right with the LORD.* It is the blood, given in exchange for a life, that makes purification possible. [12]That is why I have said to the people of Israel, 'You must never eat or drink blood—neither you nor the foreigners living among you.'

[13]"And if any native Israelite or foreigner living among you goes hunting and kills an animal or bird that is approved for eating, he must drain its blood and cover it with earth. [14]The life of every creature is in its blood. That is why I have said to the people of Israel, 'You must never eat or drink blood, for the life of any creature is in its blood.' So whoever consumes blood will be cut off from the community.

[15]"And if any native-born Israelites or foreigners eat the meat of an animal that died naturally or was torn up by wild animals, they must wash their clothes and bathe themselves in water. They will remain ceremonially unclean until evening, but then they will be clean. [16]But if they do not wash their clothes and bathe themselves, they will be punished for their sin."

FORBIDDEN SEXUAL PRACTICES

18 Then the LORD said to Moses, [2]"Give the following instructions to the people of Israel. I am the LORD your God. [3]So do not act like the people in Egypt, where you used to live, or like the people of Canaan, where I am taking you. You must not imitate their way of life. [4]You must obey all my regulations and be careful to obey my decrees, for I am the LORD your God. [5]If you obey my decrees and my regulations, you will find life through them. I am the LORD.

[6]"You must never have sexual relations with a close relative, for I am the LORD.

[7]"Do not violate your father by having sexual relations with your mother. She is your mother; you must not have sexual relations with her.

[8]"Do not have sexual relations with any of your father's wives, for this would violate your father.

[9]"Do not have sexual relations with your sister or half sister, whether she is your father's daughter or your mother's daughter, whether she was born into your household or someone else's.

[10]"Do not have sexual relations with your granddaughter, whether she is your son's daughter or your daughter's daughter, for this would violate yourself.

[11]"Do not have sexual relations with your stepsister, the daughter of any of your father's wives, for she is your sister.

[12]"Do not have sexual relations with your father's sister, for she is your father's close relative.

[13]"Do not have sexual relations with your mother's sister, for she is your mother's close relative.

[14]"Do not violate your uncle, your father's brother, by having sexual relations with his wife, for she is your aunt.

[15]"Do not have sexual relations with your daughter-in-law; she is your son's wife, so you must not have sexual relations with her.

[16]"Do not have sexual relations with your brother's wife, for this would violate your brother.

[17]"Do not have sexual relations with both a woman and her daughter. And do not take* her granddaughter, whether her son's daughter or her daughter's daughter, and have sexual relations with her. They are close relatives, and this would be a wicked act.

[18]"While your wife is living, do not marry her sister and have sexual relations with her, for they would be rivals.

[19]"Do not have sexual relations with a woman during her period of menstrual impurity.

[20]"Do not defile yourself by having sexual intercourse with your neighbor's wife.

[21]"Do not permit any of your children to be offered as a sacrifice to Molech, for you must not bring shame on the name of your God. I am the LORD.

[22]"Do not practice homosexuality, having sex with another man as with a woman. It is a detestable sin.

[23]"A man must not defile himself by having sex with an animal. And a woman must not offer herself to a male animal to have intercourse with it. This is a perverse act.

[24]"Do not defile yourselves in any of these ways, for the people I am driving out before you have defiled themselves in all these ways. [25]Because the entire land has become defiled, I am punishing the people who live there. I will cause the land to vomit them out. [26]You must obey all my decrees and regulations. You must not commit any of these detestable sins. This applies both to native-born Israelites and to the foreigners living among you.

[27]"All these detestable activities are practiced by the people of the land where I am taking you,

---

17:7 Or goat demons. 17:11 Or to make atonement for you.
18:17 Or do not marry.

and this is how the land has become defiled. [28] So do not defile the land and give it a reason to vomit you out, as it will vomit out the people who live there now. [29] Whoever commits any of these detestable sins will be cut off from the community of Israel. [30] So obey my instructions, and do not defile yourselves by committing any of these detestable practices that were committed by the people who lived in the land before you. I am the LORD your God."

HOLINESS IN PERSONAL CONDUCT

19 The LORD also said to Moses, [2] "Give the following instructions to the entire community of Israel. You must be holy because I, the LORD your God, am holy.

[3] "Each of you must show great respect for your mother and father, and you must always observe my Sabbath days of rest. I am the LORD your God.

[4] "Do not put your trust in idols or make metal images of gods for yourselves. I am the LORD your God.

[5] "When you sacrifice a peace offering to the LORD, offer it properly so you* will be accepted by God. [6] The sacrifice must be eaten on the same day you offer it or on the next day. Whatever is left over until the third day must be completely burned up. [7] If any of the sacrifice is eaten on the third day, it will be contaminated, and I will not accept it. [8] Anyone who eats it on the third day will be punished for defiling what is holy to the LORD and will be cut off from the community.

[9] "When you harvest the crops of your land, do not harvest the grain along the edges of your fields, and do not pick up what the harvesters drop. [10] It is the same with your grape crop—do not strip every last bunch of grapes from the vines, and do not pick up the grapes that fall to the ground. Leave them for the poor and the foreigners living among you. I am the LORD your God.

[11] "Do not steal.

"Do not deceive or cheat one another.

[12] "Do not bring shame on the name of your God by using it to swear falsely. I am the LORD.

[13] "Do not defraud or rob your neighbor.

"Do not make your hired workers wait until the next day to receive their pay.

[14] "Do not insult the deaf or cause the blind to stumble. You must fear your God; I am the LORD.

[15] "Do not twist justice in legal matters by favoring the poor or being partial to the rich and powerful. Always judge people fairly.

[16] "Do not spread slanderous gossip among your people.*

"Do not stand idly by when your neighbor's life is threatened. I am the LORD.

[17] "Do not nurse hatred in your heart for any of your relatives.* Confront people directly so you will not be held guilty for their sin.

[18] "Do not seek revenge or bear a grudge against a fellow Israelite, but love your neighbor as yourself. I am the LORD.

[19] "You must obey all my decrees.

"Do not mate two different kinds of animals. Do not plant your field with two different kinds of seed. Do not wear clothing woven from two different kinds of thread.

[20] "If a man has sex with a slave girl whose freedom has never been purchased but who is committed to become another man's wife, he must pay full compensation to her master. But since she is not a free woman, neither the man nor the woman will be put to death. [21] The man, however, must bring a ram as a guilt offering and present it to the LORD at the entrance of the Tabernacle.* [22] The priest will then purify him* before the LORD with the ram of the guilt offering, and the man's sin will be forgiven.

[23] "When you enter the land and plant fruit trees, leave the fruit unharvested for the first three years and consider it forbidden.* Do not eat it. [24] In the fourth year the entire crop must be consecrated to the LORD as a celebration of praise. [25] Finally, in the fifth year you may eat the fruit. If you follow this pattern, your harvest will increase. I am the LORD your God.

[26] "Do not eat meat that has not been drained of its blood.

"Do not practice fortune-telling or witchcraft.

[27] "Do not trim off the hair on your temples or trim your beards.

[28] "Do not cut your bodies for the dead, and do not mark your skin with tattoos. I am the LORD.

[29] "Do not defile your daughter by making her a prostitute, or the land will be filled with prostitution and wickedness.

[30] "Keep my Sabbath days of rest, and show reverence toward my sanctuary. I am the LORD.

[31] "Do not defile yourselves by turning to mediums or to those who consult the spirits of the dead. I am the LORD your God.

[32] "Stand up in the presence of the elderly, and show respect for the aged. Fear your God. I am the LORD.

[33] "Do not take advantage of foreigners who live among you in your land. [34] Treat them like native-born Israelites, and love them as you love yourself. Remember that you were once foreigners living in the land of Egypt. I am the LORD your God.

[35] "Do not use dishonest standards when measuring length, weight, or volume. [36] Your scales and weights must be accurate. Your containers for measuring dry materials or liquids must be accurate.* I am the LORD your God who brought you out of the land of Egypt.

[37] "You must be careful to keep all of my decrees and regulations by putting them into practice. I am the LORD."

19:5 Or it. 19:16 Hebrew Do not act as a merchant toward your own people. 19:17 Hebrew for your brother. 19:21 Hebrew Tent of Meeting. 19:22 Or make atonement for him. 19:23 Hebrew consider it uncircumcised. 19:36 Hebrew Use an honest ephah [a dry measure] and an honest hin [a liquid measure].

PUNISHMENTS FOR DISOBEDIENCE

20 The LORD said to Moses, ²"Give the people of Israel these instructions, which apply both to native Israelites and to the foreigners living in Israel.

"If any of them offer their children as a sacrifice to Molech, they must be put to death. The people of the community must stone them to death. ³ I myself will turn against them and cut them off from the community, because they have defiled my sanctuary and brought shame on my holy name by offering their children to Molech. ⁴And if the people of the community ignore those who offer their children to Molech and refuse to execute them, ⁵ I myself will turn against them and their families and will cut them off from the community. This will happen to all who commit spiritual prostitution by worshiping Molech.

⁶"I will also turn against those who commit spiritual prostitution by putting their trust in mediums or in those who consult the spirits of the dead. I will cut them off from the community. ⁷ So set yourselves apart to be holy, for I am the LORD your God. ⁸ Keep all my decrees by putting them into practice, for I am the LORD who makes you holy.

⁹"Anyone who dishonors* father or mother must be put to death. Such a person is guilty of a capital offense.

¹⁰"If a man commits adultery with his neighbor's wife, both the man and the woman who have committed adultery must be put to death. ¹¹"If a man violates his father by having sex with one of his father's wives, both the man and the woman must be put to death, for they are guilty of a capital offense.

¹²"If a man has sex with his daughter-in-law, both must be put to death. They have committed a perverse act and are guilty of a capital offense.

¹³"If a man practices homosexuality, having sex with another man as with a woman, both men have committed a detestable act. They must both be put to death, for they are guilty of a capital offense.

¹⁴"If a man marries both a woman and her mother, he has committed a wicked act. The man and both women must be burned to death to wipe out such wickedness from among you.

¹⁵"If a man has sex with an animal, he must be put to death, and the animal must be killed.

¹⁶"If a woman presents herself to a male animal to have intercourse with it, she and the animal must both be put to death. You must kill both, for they are guilty of a capital offense.

¹⁷"If a man marries his sister, the daughter of either his father or his mother, and they have sexual relations, it is a shameful disgrace. They must be publicly cut off from the community. Since the man has violated his sister, he will be punished for his sin.

¹⁸"If a man has sexual relations with a woman during her menstrual period, both of them must be cut off from the community, for together they have exposed the source of her blood flow.

¹⁹"Do not have sexual relations with your aunt, whether your mother's sister or your father's sister. This would dishonor a close relative. Both parties are guilty and will be punished for their sin.

²⁰"If a man has sex with his uncle's wife, he has violated his uncle. Both the man and woman will be punished for their sin, and they will die childless.

²¹"If a man marries his brother's wife, it is an act of impurity. He has violated his brother, and the guilty couple will remain childless.

²²"You must keep all my decrees and regulations by putting them into practice; otherwise the land to which I am bringing you as your new home will vomit you out. ²³ Do not live according to the customs of the people I am driving out before you. It is because they do these shameful things that I detest them. ²⁴ But I have promised you, 'You will possess their land because I will give it to you as your possession—a land flowing with milk and honey.' I am the LORD your God, who has set you apart from all other people.

²⁵"You must therefore make a distinction between ceremonially clean and unclean animals, and between clean and unclean birds. You must not defile yourselves by eating any unclean animal or bird or creature that scurries along the ground. I have identified them as being unclean for you. ²⁶ You must be holy because I, the LORD, am holy. I have set you apart from all other people to be my very own.

²⁷"Men and women among you who act as mediums or who consult the spirits of the dead must be put to death by stoning. They are guilty of a capital offense."

INSTRUCTIONS FOR THE PRIESTS

21 The LORD said to Moses, "Give the following instructions to the priests, the descendants of Aaron.

"A priest must not make himself ceremonially unclean by touching the dead body of a relative. ² The only exceptions are his closest relatives— his mother or father, son or daughter, brother, ³ or his virgin sister who depends on him because she has no husband. ⁴ But a priest must not defile himself and make himself unclean for someone who is related to him only by marriage.

⁵"The priests must not shave their heads or trim their beards or cut their bodies. ⁶ They must be set apart as holy to their God and must never bring shame on the name of God. They must be holy, for they are the ones who present the special gifts to the LORD, gifts of food for their God.

⁷"Priests may not marry a woman defiled by prostitution, and they may not marry a woman

---

20:9 Greek version reads *Anyone who speaks disrespectfully of.* Compare Matt 15:4; Mark 7:10.

who is divorced from her husband, for the priests are set apart as holy to their God. ⁸ You must treat them as holy because they offer up food to your God. You must consider them holy because I, the LORD, am holy, and I make you holy.

⁹ "If a priest's daughter defiles herself by becoming a prostitute, she also defiles her father's holiness, and she must be burned to death.

¹⁰ "The high priest has the highest rank of all the priests. The anointing oil has been poured on his head, and he has been ordained to wear the priestly garments. He must never leave his hair uncombed* or tear his clothing. ¹¹ He must not defile himself by going near a dead body. He may not make himself ceremonially unclean even for his father or mother. ¹² He must not defile the sanctuary of his God by leaving it to attend to a dead person, for he has been made holy by the anointing oil of his God. I am the LORD.

¹³ "The high priest may marry only a virgin. ¹⁴ He may not marry a widow, a woman who is divorced, or a woman who has defiled herself by prostitution. She must be a virgin from his own clan, ¹⁵ so that he will not dishonor his descendants among his clan, for I am the LORD who makes him holy."

¹⁶ Then the LORD said to Moses, ¹⁷ "Give the following instructions to Aaron: In all future generations, none of your descendants who has any defect will qualify to offer food to his God. ¹⁸ No one who has a defect qualifies, whether he is blind, lame, disfigured, deformed, ¹⁹ or has a broken foot or arm, ²⁰ or is hunchbacked or dwarfed, or has a defective eye, or skin sores or scabs, or damaged testicles. ²¹ No descendant of Aaron who has a defect may approach the altar to present special gifts to the LORD. Since he has a defect, he may not approach the altar to offer food to his God. ²² However, he may eat from the food offered to God, including the holy offerings and the most holy offerings. ²³ Yet because of his physical defect, he may not enter the room behind the inner curtain or approach the altar, for this would defile my holy places. I am the LORD who makes them holy."

²⁴ So Moses gave these instructions to Aaron and his sons and to all the Israelites.

22 The LORD said to Moses, ² "Tell Aaron and his sons to be very careful with the sacred gifts that the Israelites set apart for me, so they do not bring shame on my holy name. I am the LORD. ³ Give them the following instructions.

"In all future generations, if any of your descendants is ceremonially unclean when he approaches the sacred offerings that the people of Israel consecrate to the LORD, he must be cut off from my presence. I am the LORD.

⁴ "If any of Aaron's descendants has a skin disease* or any kind of discharge that makes him ceremonially unclean, he may not eat from the sacred offerings until he has been pronounced clean. He also becomes unclean by touching a corpse, or by having an emission of semen, ⁵ or by touching a small animal that is unclean, or by touching someone who is ceremonially unclean for any reason. ⁶ The man who is defiled in any of these ways will remain unclean until evening. He may not eat from the sacred offerings until he has bathed himself in water. ⁷ When the sun goes down, he will be ceremonially clean again and may eat from the sacred offerings, for this is his food. ⁸ He may not eat an animal that has died a natural death or has been torn apart by wild animals, for this would defile him. I am the LORD.

⁹ "The priests must follow my instructions carefully. Otherwise they will be punished for their sin and will die for violating my instructions. I am the LORD who makes them holy.

¹⁰ "No one outside a priest's family may eat the sacred offerings. Even guests and hired workers in a priest's home are not allowed to eat them. ¹¹ However, if the priest buys a slave for himself, the slave may eat from the sacred offerings. And if his slaves have children, they also may share his food. ¹² If a priest's daughter marries someone outside the priestly family, she may no longer eat the sacred offerings. ¹³ But if she becomes a widow or is divorced and has no children to support her, and she returns to live in her father's home as in her youth, she may eat her father's food again. Otherwise, no one outside a priest's family may eat the sacred offerings.

¹⁴ "Any such person who eats the sacred offerings without realizing it must pay the priest for the amount eaten, plus an additional 20 percent. ¹⁵ The priests must not let the Israelites defile the sacred offerings brought to the LORD ¹⁶ by allowing unauthorized people to eat them. This would bring guilt upon them and require them to pay compensation. I am the LORD who makes them holy."

WORTHY AND UNWORTHY OFFERINGS

¹⁷ And the LORD said to Moses, ¹⁸ "Give Aaron and his sons and all the Israelites these instructions, which apply both to native Israelites and to the foreigners living among you.

"If you present a gift as a burnt offering to the LORD, whether it is to fulfill a vow or is a voluntary offering, ¹⁹ you* will be accepted only if your offering is a male animal with no defects. It may be a bull, a ram, or a male goat. ²⁰ Do not present an animal with defects, because the LORD will not accept it on your behalf.

²¹ "If you present a peace offering to the LORD from the herd or the flock, whether it is to fulfill a vow or is a voluntary offering, you must offer a perfect animal. It may have no defect of any kind. ²² You must not offer an animal that is blind, crippled, or injured, or that has a wart, a skin

---

21:10 Or *never uncover his head.*   22:4 Traditionally rendered *leprosy;* see note on 13:2a.   22:19 Or *it.*

sore, or scabs. Such animals must never be offered on the altar as special gifts to the LORD. 23 If a bull* or lamb has a leg that is too long or too short, it may be offered as a voluntary offering, but it may not be offered to fulfill a vow. 24 If an animal has damaged testicles or is castrated, you may not offer it to the LORD. You must never do this in your own land, 25 and you must not accept such an animal from foreigners and then offer it as a sacrifice to your God. Such animals will not be accepted on your behalf, for they are mutilated or defective."

26 And the LORD said to Moses, 27 "When a calf or lamb or goat is born, it must be left with its mother for seven days. From the eighth day on, it will be acceptable as a special gift to the LORD. 28 But you must not slaughter a mother animal and her offspring on the same day, whether from the herd or the flock. 29 When you bring a thanksgiving offering to the LORD, sacrifice it properly so you will be accepted. 30 Eat the entire sacrificial animal on the day it is presented. Do not leave any of it until the next morning. I am the LORD.

31 "You must faithfully keep all my commands by putting them into practice, for I am the LORD. 32 Do not bring shame on my holy name, for I will display my holiness among the people of Israel. I am the LORD who makes you holy. 33 It was I who rescued you from the land of Egypt, that I might be your God. I am the LORD."

THE APPOINTED FESTIVALS

23 The LORD said to Moses, 2 "Give the following instructions to the people of Israel. These are the LORD's appointed festivals, which you are to proclaim as official days for holy assembly.

3 "You have six days each week for your ordinary work, but the seventh day is a Sabbath day of complete rest, an official day for holy assembly. It is the LORD's Sabbath day, and it must be observed wherever you live.

4 "In addition to the Sabbath, these are the LORD's appointed festivals, the official days for holy assembly that are to be celebrated at their proper times each year.

PASSOVER AND THE FESTIVAL OF UNLEAVENED BREAD

5 "The LORD's Passover begins at sundown on the fourteenth day of the first month.* 6 On the next day, the fifteenth day of the month, you must begin celebrating the Festival of Unleavened Bread. This festival to the LORD continues for seven days, and during that time the bread you eat must be made without yeast. 7 On the first day of the festival, all the people must stop their ordinary work and observe an official day for holy assembly. 8 For seven days you must present special gifts to the LORD. On the seventh day the people must again stop all their ordinary work to observe an official day for holy assembly."

CELEBRATION OF FIRST HARVEST

9 Then the LORD said to Moses, 10 "Give the following instructions to the people of Israel. When you enter the land I am giving you and you harvest its first crops, bring the priest a bundle of grain from the first cutting of your grain harvest. 11 On the day after the Sabbath, the priest will lift it up before the LORD so it may be accepted on your behalf. 12 On that same day you must sacrifice a one-year-old male lamb with no defects as a burnt offering to the LORD. 13 With it you must present a grain offering consisting of four quarts* of choice flour moistened with olive oil. It will be a special gift, a pleasing aroma to the LORD. You must also offer one quart* of wine as a liquid offering. 14 Do not eat any bread or roasted grain or fresh kernels on that day until you bring this offering to your God. This is a permanent law for you, and it must be observed from generation to generation wherever you live.

THE FESTIVAL OF HARVEST

15 "From the day after the Sabbath—the day you bring the bundle of grain to be lifted up as a special offering—count off seven full weeks. 16 Keep counting until the day after the seventh Sabbath, fifty days later. Then present an offering of new grain to the LORD. 17 From wherever you live, bring two loaves of bread to be lifted up before the LORD as a special offering. Make these loaves from four quarts of choice flour, and bake them with yeast. They will be an offering to the LORD from the first of your crops. 18 Along with the bread, present seven one-year-old male lambs with no defects, one young bull, and two rams as burnt offerings to the LORD. These burnt offerings, together with the grain offerings and liquid offerings, will be a special gift, a pleasing aroma to the LORD. 19 Then you must offer one male goat as a sin offering and two one-year-old male lambs as a peace offering.

20 "The priest will lift up the two lambs as a special offering to the LORD, together with the loaves representing the first of your crops. These offerings, which are holy to the LORD, belong to the priests. 21 That same day will be proclaimed an official day for holy assembly, a day on which you do no ordinary work. This is a permanent law for you, and it must be observed from generation to generation wherever you live.*

22 "When you harvest the crops of your land, do not harvest the grain along the edges of your fields, and do not pick up what the harvesters drop. Leave it for the poor and the foreigners living among you. I am the LORD your God."

23:23 Or cow. 23:5 This day in the ancient Hebrew lunar calendar occurred in late March, April, or early May. 23:13a Hebrew ⅒ of an ephah [4.4 liters]; also in 23:17. 23:13b Hebrew ¼ of a hin [1 liter]. 23:21 This celebration, called the Festival of Harvest or the Festival of Weeks, was later called the Festival of Pentecost (see Acts 2:1). It is celebrated today as Shavuot (or Shabuoth).

THE FESTIVAL OF TRUMPETS

23 The LORD said to Moses, 24 "Give the following instructions to the people of Israel. On the first day of the appointed month in early autumn,* you are to observe a day of complete rest. It will be an official day for holy assembly, a day commemorated with loud blasts of a trumpet. 25 You must do no ordinary work on that day. Instead, you are to present special gifts to the LORD."

THE DAY OF ATONEMENT

26 Then the LORD said to Moses, 27 "Be careful to celebrate the Day of Atonement on the tenth day of that same month—nine days after the Festival of Trumpets.* You must observe it as an official day for holy assembly, a day to deny yourselves* and present special gifts to the LORD. 28 Do no work during that entire day because it is the Day of Atonement, when offerings of purification are made for you, making you right with* the LORD your God. 29 All who do not deny themselves that day will be cut off from God's people. 30 And I will destroy anyone among you who does any work on that day. 31 You must not do any work at all! This is a permanent law for you, and it must be observed from generation to generation wherever you live. 32 This will be a Sabbath day of complete rest for you, and on that day you must deny yourselves. This day of rest will begin at sundown on the ninth day of the month and extend until sundown on the tenth day."

THE FESTIVAL OF SHELTERS

33 And the LORD said to Moses, 34 "Give the following instructions to the people of Israel. Begin celebrating the Festival of Shelters* on the fifteenth day of the appointed month—five days after the Day of Atonement.* This festival to the LORD will last for seven days. 35 On the first day of the festival you must proclaim an official day for holy assembly, when you do no ordinary work. 36 For seven days you must present special gifts to the LORD. The eighth day is another holy day on which you present your special gifts to the LORD. This will be a solemn occasion, and no ordinary work may be done that day.

37 ("These are the LORD's appointed festivals. Celebrate them each year as official days for holy assembly by presenting special gifts to the LORD—burnt offerings, grain offerings, sacrifices, and liquid offerings—each on its proper day. 38 These festivals must be observed in addition to the LORD's regular Sabbath days, and the offerings are in addition to your personal gifts, the offerings you give to fulfill your vows, and the voluntary offerings you present to the LORD.)

39 "Remember that this seven-day festival to the LORD—the Festival of Shelters—begins on the fifteenth day of the appointed month,* after you have harvested all the produce of the land. The first day and the eighth day of the festival will be days of complete rest. 40 On the first day gather branches from magnificent trees*—palm fronds, boughs from leafy trees, and willows that grow by the streams. Then celebrate with joy before the LORD your God for seven days. 41 You must observe this festival to the LORD for seven days every year. This is a permanent law for you, and it must be observed in the appointed month* from generation to generation. 42 For seven days you must live outside in little shelters. All native-born Israelites must live in shelters. 43 This will remind each new generation of Israelites that I made their ancestors live in shelters when I rescued them from the land of Egypt. I am the LORD your God."

44 So Moses gave the Israelites these instructions regarding the annual festivals of the LORD.

PURE OIL AND HOLY BREAD

24 The LORD said to Moses, 2 "Command the people of Israel to bring you pure oil of pressed olives for the light, to keep the lamps burning continually. 3 This is the lampstand that stands in the Tabernacle, in front of the inner curtain that shields the Ark of the Covenant.* Aaron must keep the lamps burning in the LORD's presence all night. This is a permanent law for you, and it must be observed from generation to generation. 4 Aaron and the priests must tend the lamps on the pure gold lampstand continually in the LORD's presence.

5 "You must bake twelve flat loaves of bread from choice flour, using four quarts* of flour for each loaf. 6 Place the bread before the LORD on the pure gold table, and arrange the loaves in two stacks, with six loaves in each stack. 7 Put some pure frankincense near each stack to serve as a representative offering, a special gift presented to the LORD. 8 Every Sabbath day this bread must be laid out before the LORD as a gift from the Israelites; it is an ongoing expression of the eternal covenant. 9 The loaves of bread will belong to Aaron and his descendants, who must eat them in a sacred place, for they are most holy. It is the permanent right of the priests to claim this portion of the special gifts presented to the LORD."

AN EXAMPLE OF JUST PUNISHMENT

10 One day a man who had an Israelite mother and an Egyptian father came out of his tent and

---

23:24 Hebrew *On the first day of the seventh month.* This day in the ancient Hebrew lunar calendar occurred in September or October. This festival is celebrated today as Rosh Hashanah, the Jewish new year.   23:27a Hebrew *on the tenth day of the seventh month;* see 23:24 and the note there. This day in the ancient Hebrew lunar calendar occurred in September or October. It is celebrated today as Yom Kippur.   23:27b Or *to fast;* similarly in 23:29, 32.   23:28 Or *when atonement is made for you before.*   23:34a Or *Festival of Booths,* or *Festival of Tabernacles.* This was earlier called the Festival of the Final Harvest or Festival of Ingathering (see Exod 23:16b). It is celebrated today as Sukkot (or Succoth).   23:34b Hebrew *on the fifteenth day of the seventh month;* see 23:27a and the note there.   23:39 Hebrew *on the fifteenth day of the seventh month.*   23:40 Or *gather fruit from majestic trees.*   23:41 Hebrew *the seventh month.*   24:3 Hebrew *in the Tent of Meeting, outside the inner curtain of the Testimony;* see note on 16:13.   24:5 Hebrew ⁴⁄₁₀ *of an ephah* [4.4 liters].

got into a fight with one of the Israelite men. [11] During the fight, this son of an Israelite woman blasphemed the Name of the LORD* with a curse. So the man was brought to Moses for judgment. His mother was Shelomith, the daughter of Dibri of the tribe of Dan. [12] They kept the man in custody until the LORD's will in the matter should become clear to them.

[13] Then the LORD said to Moses, [14] "Take the blasphemer outside the camp, and tell all those who heard the curse to lay their hands on his head. Then let the entire community stone him to death. [15] Say to the people of Israel: Those who curse their God will be punished for their sin. [16] Anyone who blasphemes the Name of the LORD must be stoned to death by the whole community of Israel. Any native-born Israelite or foreigner among you who blasphemes the Name of the LORD must be put to death.

[17] "Anyone who takes another person's life must be put to death.

[18] "Anyone who kills another person's animal must pay for it in full—a live animal for the animal that was killed.

[19] "Anyone who injures another person must be dealt with according to the injury inflicted— [20] a fracture for a fracture, an eye for an eye, a tooth for a tooth. Whatever anyone does to injure another person must be paid back in kind.

[21] "Whoever kills an animal must pay for it in full, but whoever kills another person must be put to death.

[22] "This same standard applies both to native-born Israelites and to the foreigners living among you. I am the LORD your God."

[23] After Moses gave all these instructions to the Israelites, they took the blasphemer outside the camp and stoned him to death. The Israelites did just as the LORD had commanded Moses.

THE SABBATH YEAR

25 While Moses was on Mount Sinai, the LORD said to him, [2] "Give the following instructions to the people of Israel. When you have entered the land I am giving you, the land itself must observe a Sabbath rest before the LORD every seventh year. [3] For six years you may plant your fields and prune your vineyards and harvest your crops, [4] but during the seventh year the land must have a Sabbath year of complete rest. It is the LORD's Sabbath. Do not plant your fields or prune your vineyards during that year. [5] And don't store away the crops that grow on their own or gather the grapes from your unpruned vines. The land must have a year of complete rest. [6] But you may eat whatever the land produces on its own during its Sabbath. This applies to you, your male and female servants, your hired workers, and the temporary residents who live with you. [7] Your livestock and the wild animals in your land will also be allowed to eat what the land produces.

THE YEAR OF JUBILEE

[8] "In addition, you must count off seven Sabbath years, seven sets of seven years, adding up to forty-nine years in all. [9] Then on the Day of Atonement in the fiftieth year,* blow the ram's horn loud and long throughout the land. [10] Set this year apart as holy, a time to proclaim freedom throughout the land for all who live there. It will be a jubilee year for you, when each of you may return to the land that belonged to your ancestors and return to your own clan. [11] This fiftieth year will be a jubilee for you. During that year you must not plant your fields or store away any of the crops that grow on their own, and don't gather the grapes from your unpruned vines. [12] It will be a jubilee year for you, and you must keep it holy. But you may eat whatever the land produces on its own. [13] In the Year of Jubilee each of you may return to the land that belonged to your ancestors.

[14] "When you make an agreement with your neighbor to buy or sell property, you must not take advantage of each other. [15] When you buy land from your neighbor, the price you pay must be based on the number of years since the last jubilee. The seller must set the price by taking into account the number of years remaining until the next Year of Jubilee. [16] The more years until the next jubilee, the higher the price; the fewer years, the lower the price. After all, the person selling the land is actually selling you a certain number of harvests. [17] Show your fear of God by not taking advantage of each other. I am the LORD your God.

[18] "If you want to live securely in the land, follow my decrees and obey my regulations. [19] Then the land will yield large crops, and you will eat your fill and live securely in it. [20] But you might ask, 'What will we eat during the seventh year, since we are not allowed to plant or harvest crops that year?' [21] Be assured that I will send my blessing for you in the sixth year, so the land will produce a crop large enough for three years. [22] When you plant your fields in the eighth year, you will still be eating from the large crop of the sixth year. In fact, you will still be eating from that large crop when the new crop is harvested in the ninth year.

REDEMPTION OF PROPERTY

[23] "The land must never be sold on a permanent basis, for the land belongs to me. You are only foreigners and tenant farmers working for me.

[24] "With every purchase of land you must grant the seller the right to buy it back. [25] If one of your fellow Israelites falls into poverty and is forced to sell some family land, then a close relative should buy it back for him. [26] If there is no close relative to buy the land, but the person who sold it gets enough money to buy it back, [27] he then

---

24:11 Hebrew *the Name;* also in 24:16b.   25:9 Hebrew *on the tenth day of the seventh month, on the Day of Atonement;* see 23:27a and the note there.

has the right to redeem it from the one who bought it. The price of the land will be discounted according to the number of years until the next Year of Jubilee. In this way the original owner can then return to the land. ²⁸But if the original owner cannot afford to buy back the land, it will remain with the new owner until the next Year of Jubilee. In the jubilee year, the land must be returned to the original owners so they can return to their family land.

²⁹"Anyone who sells a house inside a walled town has the right to buy it back for a full year after its sale. During that year, the seller retains the right to buy it back. ³⁰But if it is not bought back within a year, the sale of the house within the walled town cannot be reversed. It will become the permanent property of the buyer. It will not be returned to the original owner in the Year of Jubilee. ³¹But a house in a village—a settlement without fortified walls—will be treated like property in the countryside. Such a house may be bought back at any time, and it must be returned to the original owner in the Year of Jubilee.

³²"The Levites always have the right to buy back a house they have sold within the towns allotted to them. ³³And any property that is sold by the Levites—all houses within the Levitical towns—must be returned in the Year of Jubilee. After all, the houses in the towns reserved for the Levites are the only property they own in all Israel. ³⁴The open pastureland around the Levitical towns may never be sold. It is their permanent possession.

REDEMPTION OF THE POOR AND ENSLAVED

³⁵"If one of your fellow Israelites falls into poverty and cannot support himself, support him as you would a foreigner or a temporary resident and allow him to live with you. ³⁶Do not charge interest or make a profit at his expense. Instead, show your fear of God by letting him live with you as your relative. ³⁷Remember, do not charge interest on money you lend him or make a profit on food you sell him. ³⁸I am the LORD your God, who brought you out of the land of Egypt to give you the land of Canaan and to be your God.

³⁹"If one of your fellow Israelites falls into poverty and is forced to sell himself to you, do not treat him as a slave. ⁴⁰Treat him instead as a hired worker or as a temporary resident who lives with you, and he will serve you only until the Year of Jubilee. ⁴¹At that time he and his children will no longer be obligated to you, and they will return to their clans and go back to the land originally allotted to their ancestors. ⁴²The people of Israel are my servants, whom I brought out of the land of Egypt, so they must never be sold as slaves. ⁴³Show your fear of God by not treating them harshly.

⁴⁴"However, you may purchase male and female slaves from among the nations around you. ⁴⁵You may also purchase the children of temporary residents who live among you, including those who have been born in your land. You may treat them as your property, ⁴⁶passing them on to your children as a permanent inheritance. You may treat them as slaves, but you must never treat your fellow Israelites this way.

⁴⁷"Suppose a foreigner or temporary resident becomes rich while living among you. If any of your fellow Israelites fall into poverty and are forced to sell themselves to such a foreigner or to a member of his family, ⁴⁸they still retain the right to be bought back, even after they have been purchased. They may be bought back by a brother, ⁴⁹an uncle, or a cousin. In fact, anyone from the extended family may buy them back. They may also redeem themselves if they have prospered. ⁵⁰They will negotiate the price of their freedom with the person who bought them. The price will be based on the number of years from the time they were sold until the next Year of Jubilee—whatever it would cost to hire a worker for that period of time. ⁵¹If many years still remain until the jubilee, they will repay the proper proportion of what they received when they sold themselves. ⁵²If only a few years remain until the Year of Jubilee, they will repay a small amount for their redemption. ⁵³The foreigner must treat them as workers hired on a yearly basis. You must not allow a foreigner to treat any of your fellow Israelites harshly. ⁵⁴If any Israelites have not been bought back by the time the Year of Jubilee arrives, they and their children must be set free at that time. ⁵⁵For the people of Israel belong to me. They are my servants, whom I brought out of the land of Egypt. I am the LORD your God.

BLESSINGS FOR OBEDIENCE

26 "Do not make idols or set up carved images, or sacred pillars, or sculptured stones in your land so you may worship them. I am the LORD your God. ²You must keep my Sabbath days of rest and show reverence for my sanctuary. I am the LORD.

³"If you follow my decrees and are careful to obey my commands, ⁴I will send you the seasonal rains. The land will then yield its crops, and the trees of the field will produce their fruit. ⁵Your threshing season will overlap with the grape harvest, and your grape harvest will overlap with the season of planting grain. You will eat your fill and live securely in your own land.

⁶"I will give you peace in the land, and you will be able to sleep with no cause for fear. I will rid the land of wild animals and keep your enemies out of your land. ⁷In fact, you will chase down your enemies and slaughter them with your swords. ⁸Five of you will chase a hundred, and a hundred of you will chase ten thousand! All your enemies will fall beneath your sword.

⁹"I will look favorably upon you, making you fertile and multiplying your people. And I will fulfill my covenant with you. ¹⁰You will have such a surplus of crops that you will need to clear out the old grain to make room for the new harvest! ¹¹I will live among you, and I will not despise you. ¹²I will walk among you; I will be your God, and you will be my people. ¹³I am the LORD your God, who brought you out of the land of Egypt so you would no longer be their slaves. I broke the yoke of slavery from your neck so you can walk with your heads held high.

PUNISHMENTS FOR DISOBEDIENCE

¹⁴"However, if you do not listen to me or obey all these commands, ¹⁵and if you break my covenant by rejecting my decrees, treating my regulations with contempt, and refusing to obey my commands, ¹⁶I will punish you. I will bring sudden terrors upon you—wasting diseases and burning fevers that will cause your eyes to fail and your life to ebb away. You will plant your crops in vain because your enemies will eat them. ¹⁷I will turn against you, and you will be defeated by your enemies. Those who hate you will rule over you, and you will run even when no one is chasing you!

¹⁸"And if, in spite of all this, you still disobey me, I will punish you seven times over for your sins. ¹⁹I will break your proud spirit by making the skies as unyielding as iron and the earth as hard as bronze. ²⁰All your work will be for nothing, for your land will yield no crops, and your trees will bear no fruit.

²¹"If even then you remain hostile toward me and refuse to obey me, I will inflict disaster on you seven times over for your sins. ²²I will send wild animals that will rob you of your children and destroy your livestock. Your numbers will dwindle, and your roads will be deserted.

²³"And if you fail to learn the lesson and continue your hostility toward me, ²⁴then I myself will be hostile toward you. I will personally strike you with calamity seven times over for your sins. ²⁵I will send armies against you to carry out the curse of the covenant you have broken. When you run to your towns for safety, I will send a plague to destroy you there, and you will be handed over to your enemies. ²⁶I will destroy your food supply, so that ten women will need only one oven to bake bread for their families. They will ration your food by weight, and though you have food to eat, you will not be satisfied.

²⁷"If in spite of all this you still refuse to listen and still remain hostile toward me, ²⁸then I will give full vent to my hostility. I myself will punish you seven times over for your sins. ²⁹Then you will eat the flesh of your own sons and daughters. ³⁰I will destroy your pagan shrines and knock down your places of worship. I will leave your lifeless corpses piled on top of your lifeless idols,* and I will despise you. ³¹I will make your cities desolate and destroy your places of pagan worship. I will take no pleasure in your offerings that should be a pleasing aroma to me. ³²Yes, I myself will devastate your land, and your enemies who come to occupy it will be appalled at what they see. ³³I will scatter you among the nations and bring out my sword against you. Your land will become desolate, and your cities will lie in ruins. ³⁴Then at last the land will enjoy its neglected Sabbath years as it lies desolate while you are in exile in the land of your enemies. Then the land will finally rest and enjoy the Sabbaths it missed. ³⁵As long as the land lies in ruins, it will enjoy the rest you never allowed it to take every seventh year while you lived in it.

³⁶"And for those of you who survive, I will demoralize you in the land of your enemies. You will live in such fear that the sound of a leaf driven by the wind will send you fleeing. You will run as though fleeing from a sword, and you will fall even when no one pursues you. ³⁷Though no one is chasing you, you will stumble over each other as though fleeing from a sword. You will have no power to stand up against your enemies. ³⁸You will die among the foreign nations and be devoured in the land of your enemies. ³⁹Those of you who survive will waste away in your enemies' lands because of their sins and the sins of their ancestors.

⁴⁰"But at last my people will confess their sins and the sins of their ancestors for betraying me and being hostile toward me. ⁴¹When I have turned their hostility back on them and brought them to the land of their enemies, then at last their stubborn hearts will be humbled, and they will pay for their sins. ⁴²Then I will remember my covenant with Jacob and my covenant with Isaac and my covenant with Abraham, and I will remember the land. ⁴³For the land must be abandoned to enjoy its years of Sabbath rest as it lies deserted. At last the people will pay for their sins, for they have continually rejected my regulations and despised my decrees.

⁴⁴"But despite all this, I will not utterly reject or despise them while they are in exile in the land of their enemies. I will not cancel my covenant with them by wiping them out, for I am the LORD their God. ⁴⁵For their sakes I will remember my ancient covenant with their ancestors, whom I brought out of the land of Egypt in the sight of all the nations, that I might be their God. I am the LORD."

⁴⁶These are the decrees, regulations, and instructions that the LORD gave through Moses on Mount Sinai as evidence of the relationship between himself and the Israelites.

26:30 The Hebrew term (literally *round things*) probably alludes to dung.

REDEMPTION OF GIFTS OFFERED TO THE LORD

27 The LORD said to Moses, [2] "Give the following instructions to the people of Israel. If anyone makes a special vow to dedicate someone to the LORD by paying the value of that person, [3] here is the scale of values to be used. A man between the ages of twenty and sixty is valued at fifty shekels* of silver, as measured by the sanctuary shekel. [4] A woman of that age is valued at thirty shekels* of silver. [5] A boy between the ages of five and twenty is valued at twenty shekels of silver; a girl of that age is valued at ten shekels* of silver. [6] A boy between the ages of one month and five years is valued at five shekels of silver; a girl of that age is valued at three shekels* of silver. [7] A man older than sixty is valued at fifteen shekels of silver; a woman of that age is valued at ten shekels* of silver. [8] If you desire to make such a vow but cannot afford to pay the required amount, take the person to the priest. He will determine the amount for you to pay based on what you can afford.

[9] "If your vow involves giving an animal that is acceptable as an offering to the LORD, any gift to the LORD will be considered holy. [10] You may not exchange or substitute it for another animal—neither a good animal for a bad one nor a bad animal for a good one. But if you do exchange one animal for another, then both the original animal and its substitute will be considered holy. [11] If your vow involves an unclean animal—one that is not acceptable as an offering to the LORD—then you must bring the animal to the priest. [12] He will assess its value, and his assessment will be final, whether high or low. [13] If you want to buy back the animal, you must pay the value set by the priest, plus 20 percent.

[14] "If someone dedicates a house to the LORD, the priest will come to assess its value. The priest's assessment will be final, whether high or low. [15] If the person who dedicated the house wants to buy it back, he must pay the value set by the priest, plus 20 percent. Then the house will again be his.

[16] "If someone dedicates to the LORD a piece of his family property, its value will be assessed according to the amount of seed required to plant it—fifty shekels of silver for a field planted with five bushels of barley seed.* [17] If the field is dedicated to the LORD in the Year of Jubilee, then the entire assessment will apply. [18] But if the field is dedicated after the Year of Jubilee, the priest will assess the land's value in proportion to the number of years left until the next Year of Jubilee. Its assessed value is reduced each year. [19] If the person who dedicated the field wants to buy it back, he must pay the value set by the priest, plus 20 percent. Then the field will again be legally his. [20] But if he does not want to buy it back, and it is sold to someone else, the field can no longer be bought back. [21] When the field is released in the Year of Jubilee, it will be holy, a field specially set apart* for the LORD. It will become the property of the priests.

[22] "If someone dedicates to the LORD a field he has purchased but which is not part of his family property, [23] the priest will assess its value based on the number of years left until the next Year of Jubilee. On that day he must give the assessed value of the land as a sacred donation to the LORD. [24] In the Year of Jubilee the field must be returned to the person from whom he purchased it, the one who inherited it as family property. [25] (All the payments must be measured by the weight of the sanctuary shekel,* which equals twenty gerahs.)

[26] "You may not dedicate a firstborn animal to the LORD, for the firstborn of your cattle, sheep, and goats already belong to him. [27] However, you may buy back the firstborn of a ceremonially unclean animal by paying the priest's assessment of its worth, plus 20 percent. If you do not buy it back, the priest will sell it at its assessed value.

[28] "However, anything specially set apart for the LORD—whether a person, an animal, or family property—must never be sold or bought back. Anything devoted in this way has been set apart as holy, and it belongs to the LORD. [29] No person specially set apart for destruction may be bought back. Such a person must be put to death.

[30] "One-tenth of the produce of the land, whether grain from the fields or fruit from the trees, belongs to the LORD and must be set apart to him as holy. [31] If you want to buy back the LORD's tenth of the grain or fruit, you must pay its value, plus 20 percent. [32] Count off every tenth animal from your herds and flocks and set them apart for the LORD as holy. [33] You may not pick and choose between good and bad animals, and you may not substitute one for another. But if you do exchange one animal for another, then both the original animal and its substitute will be considered holy and cannot be bought back."

[34] These are the commands that the LORD gave through Moses on Mount Sinai for the Israelites.

27:3 Or *20 ounces* [570 grams].   27:4 Or *12 ounces* [342 grams].
27:5 Or *A boy . . . 8 ounces* [228 grams] *of silver; a girl . . .
4 ounces* [114 grams].   27:6 Or *A boy . . . 2 ounces* [57 grams]
of silver; a girl . . . 1.2 ounces [34 grams].   27:7 Or *A man . . .
6 ounces* [171 grams] *of silver; a woman . . . 4 ounces* [114 grams].
27:16 Hebrew *50 shekels* [20 ounces or 570 grams] *of silver for a
homer* [220 liters] *of barley seed.*   27:21 The Hebrew term used
here refers to the complete consecration of things or people
to the LORD, either by destroying them or by giving them as
an offering; also in 27:28, 29.   27:25 Each shekel was about
0.4 ounces [11 grams] in weight.

NUMBERS

JON HUNTZINGER, PHD

The book of Numbers gets its name from the listing and numbering of the families and tribes of Israel whom God delivered from Egypt (1:1-46; 3:14-43; 26:1-51). Just as Leviticus continues the account from Exodus (which ends with a description of the Tabernacle) by describing how the people should worship at the Tabernacle, so also Numbers continues the story after the people leave Mount Sinai. Numbers continues to describe what happened after Moses received God's commandments and the instructions for the worship at the Tabernacle. Once again, Jewish tradition recognizes Moses as the writer because of the internal testimony of God's direct speech to him.

Numbers describes the wilderness experience of the Hebrew people after they left Mount Sinai. They arrive at the border of the Promised Land (Canaan) and send out spies for reconnaissance. The spies return with vines of grapes, proving God's description of a land "flowing with milk and honey" (Exodus 3:8). However, the people turn away from the land God promised and give in to the fear of the giants who live there. They are afraid to go into the land and complain to Moses. In their fear, they turn away from Canaan and wander in the wilderness for the next 38 years. Numbers reveals how difficult the wilderness years were for Moses and the people.

The generation that came out of Egypt spends the wilderness years rebelling against Moses and complaining against God. Almost everyone criticizes Moses, including his family, the chosen leaders, and even the people. Indirectly, they complain against God, who had chosen Moses to lead them. Specifically, they complain about God's provision of food for them, and they long to go back to Egypt (11:4-6). Furthermore, the people intermarry with the Moabites despite God's command not to do so (25:1-18). Throughout the Israelites' rebellion, two men stand out from the rest for their faithfulness toward God:

— Joshua son of Nun, who is chosen to lead the new generation of Hebrew people into the land of promise (27:12-23)

— Caleb son of Jephunneh, who is ready to act in response to what God has promised

Thus, the book of Numbers describes a time of transition from the first generation of Israelites whom God delivered out of Egypt to the second generation He is preparing to enter into Canaan. Numbers can be divided into two major sections:

— Chapters 1-25 describe the struggles of the first generation who will eventually die in the wilderness short of the Promised Land.

— Chapters 26-36 tell of the emergence of the sons and daughters of the second generation who are reminded of the offerings and worship they are to give God and the vows they must keep once they enter the land (chapters 28-30). They are also told about battles that lie ahead and the boundaries they are to establish after they become victorious (33:50-34:15).

Numbers depicts Moses as a humble leader (12:3) who carries heavy responsibilities (11:10-15) and sometimes gives in to the pressure he feels, such as when he strikes a rock with his staff in anger in response to the people's complaints.

At the same time, Numbers presents God as faithful to the people by keeping His word to them:

— He causes Aaron's staff to blossom as a sign of His provision (17:1-11).

— He heals the people after a plague of poisonous snakes (21:4-9).

— He speaks through a foreign prophet of His good plans for them (chapters 22-24).

— He selects Joshua to lead the people after Moses dies so that they will not be without a leader (27:12-23).

— He draws the boundaries of the land that He is giving them to inherit (34:1-29).

God describes the land as an inheritance for the people: He gives it to them due to the special relationship they have with Him through the covenant He made with them, and they must keep it, in part, by offering sacrifices and keeping vows (chapters 28-30).

REGISTRATION OF ISRAEL'S TROOPS

1 A year after Israel's departure from Egypt, the LORD spoke to Moses in the Tabernacle* in the wilderness of Sinai. On the first day of the second month* of that year he said, 2 "From the whole community of Israel, record the names of all the warriors by their clans and families. List all the men 3 twenty years old or older who are able to go to war. You and Aaron must register the troops, 4 and you will be assisted by one family leader from each tribe.

5 "These are the tribes and the names of the leaders who will assist you:

Tribe	Leader
Reuben	Elizur son of Shedeur
6 Simeon	Shelumiel son of Zurishaddai
7 Judah	Nahshon son of Amminadab
8 Issachar	Nethanel son of Zuar
9 Zebulun	Eliab son of Helon
10 Ephraim son of Joseph	Elishama son of Ammihud
Manasseh son of Joseph	Gamaliel son of Pedahzur
11 Benjamin	Abidan son of Gideoni
12 Dan	Ahiezer son of Ammishaddai
13 Asher	Pagiel son of Ocran
14 Gad	Eliasaph son of Deuel
15 Naphtali	Ahira son of Enan

16 These are the chosen leaders of the community, the leaders of their ancestral tribes, the heads of the clans of Israel."

17 So Moses and Aaron called together these chosen leaders, 18 and they assembled the whole community of Israel on that very day.* All the people were registered according to their ancestry by their clans and families. The men of Israel who were twenty years old or older were listed one by one, 19 just as the LORD had commanded Moses. So Moses recorded their names in the wilderness of Sinai.

20-21 This is the number of men twenty years old or older who were able to go to war, as their names were listed in the records of their clans and families*:

Tribe	Number
Reuben (Jacob's* oldest son)	46,500
22-23 Simeon	59,300
24-25 Gad	45,650
26-27 Judah	74,600
28-29 Issachar	54,400
30-31 Zebulun	57,400
32-33 Ephraim son of Joseph	40,500
34-35 Manasseh son of Joseph	32,200
36-37 Benjamin	35,400
38-39 Dan	62,700
40-41 Asher	41,500
42-43 Naphtali	53,400

44 These were the men registered by Moses and Aaron and the twelve leaders of Israel, all listed according to their ancestral descent. 45 They were registered by families—all the men of Israel who were twenty years old or older and able to go to war. 46 The total number was 603,550.

47 But this total did not include the Levites. 48 For the LORD had said to Moses, 49 "Do not include the tribe of Levi in the registration; do not count them with the rest of the Israelites. 50 Put the Levites in charge of the Tabernacle of the Covenant,* along with all its furnishings and equipment. They must carry the Tabernacle and all its furnishings as you travel, and they must take care of it and camp around it. 51 Whenever it is time for the Tabernacle to move, the Levites will take it down. And when it is time to stop, they will set it up again. But any unauthorized person who goes too near the Tabernacle must be put to death. 52 Each tribe of Israel will camp in a designated area with its own family banner. 53 But the Levites will camp around the Tabernacle of the Covenant to protect the community of Israel from the LORD's anger. The Levites are responsible to stand guard around the Tabernacle."

54 So the Israelites did everything just as the LORD had commanded Moses.

ORGANIZATION FOR ISRAEL'S CAMP

2 Then the LORD gave these instructions to Moses and Aaron: 2 "When the Israelites set up camp, each tribe will be assigned its own area. The tribal divisions will camp beneath their family banners on all four sides of the Tabernacle,* but at some distance from it.

3-4 "The divisions of Judah, Issachar, and Zebulun are to camp toward the sunrise on the east side of the Tabernacle, beneath their family banners. These are the names of the tribes, their leaders, and the numbers of their registered troops:

Tribe	Leader	Number
Judah	Nahshon son of Amminadab	74,600
5-6 Issachar	Nethanel son of Zuar	54,400
7-8 Zebulun	Eliab son of Helon	57,400

9 So the total of all the troops on Judah's side of the camp is 186,400. These three tribes are to lead the way whenever the Israelites travel to a new campsite.

1:1a Hebrew the Tent of Meeting. 1:1b This day in the ancient Hebrew lunar calendar occurred in April or May. 1:18 Hebrew on the first day of the second month; see 1:1. 1:20-21a In the Hebrew text, this sentence (This is the number of men twenty years old or older who were able to go to war, as their names were listed in the records of their clans and families) is repeated in 1:22, 24, 26, 28, 30, 32, 34, 36, 38, 40, 42. 1:20-21b Hebrew Israel's. The names "Jacob" and "Israel" are often interchanged throughout the Old Testament, referring sometimes to the individual patriarch and sometimes to the nation. 1:50 Or Tabernacle of the Testimony; also in 1:53. 2:2 Hebrew the Tent of Meeting; also in 2:17.

[10-11]"The divisions of Reuben, Simeon, and Gad are to camp on the south side of the Tabernacle, beneath their family banners. These are the names of the tribes, their leaders, and the numbers of their registered troops:

Tribe	Leader	Number
Reuben	Elizur son of Shedeur	46,500
[12-13] Simeon	Shelumiel son of Zurishaddai	59,300
[14-15] Gad	Eliasaph son of Deuel*	45,650

[16]So the total of all the troops on Reuben's side of the camp is 151,450. These three tribes will be second in line whenever the Israelites travel.

[17]"Then the Tabernacle, carried by the Levites, will set out from the middle of the camp. All the tribes are to travel in the same order that they camp, each in position under the appropriate family banner.

[18-19]"The divisions of Ephraim, Manasseh, and Benjamin are to camp on the west side of the Tabernacle, beneath their family banners. These are the names of the tribes, their leaders, and the numbers of their registered troops:

Tribe	Leader	Number
Ephraim	Elishama son of Ammihud	40,500
[20-21] Manasseh	Gamaliel son of Pedahzur	32,200
[22-23] Benjamin	Abidan son of Gideoni	35,400

[24]So the total of all the troops on Ephraim's side of the camp is 108,100. These three tribes will be third in line whenever the Israelites travel.

[25-26]"The divisions of Dan, Asher, and Naphtali are to camp on the north side of the Tabernacle, beneath their family banners. These are the names of the tribes, their leaders, and the numbers of their registered troops:

Tribe	Leader	Number
Dan	Ahiezer son of Ammishaddai	62,700
[27-28] Asher	Pagiel son of Ocran	41,500
[29-30] Naphtali	Ahira son of Enan	53,400

[31]So the total of all the troops on Dan's side of the camp is 157,600. These three tribes will be last, marching under their banners whenever the Israelites travel."

[32]In summary, the troops of Israel listed by their families totaled 603,550. [33]But as the LORD had commanded, the Levites were not included in this registration. [34]So the people of Israel did everything as the LORD had commanded Moses. Each clan and family set up camp and marched under their banners exactly as the LORD had instructed them.

LEVITES APPOINTED FOR SERVICE

3 This is the family line of Aaron and Moses as it was recorded when the LORD spoke to Moses on Mount Sinai: [2]The names of Aaron's sons were Nadab (the oldest), Abihu, Eleazar, and Ithamar. [3]These sons of Aaron were anointed and ordained to minister as priests. [4]But Nadab and Abihu died in the LORD's presence in the wilderness of Sinai when they burned before the LORD the wrong kind of fire, different than he had commanded. Since they had no sons, this left only Eleazar and Ithamar to serve as priests with their father, Aaron.

[5]Then the LORD said to Moses, [6]"Call forward the tribe of Levi, and present them to Aaron the priest to serve as his assistants. [7]They will serve Aaron and the whole community, performing their sacred duties in and around the Tabernacle.* [8]They will also maintain all the furnishings of the sacred tent,* serving in the Tabernacle on behalf of all the Israelites. [9]Assign the Levites to Aaron and his sons. They have been given from among all the people of Israel to serve as their assistants. [10]Appoint Aaron and his sons to carry out the duties of the priesthood. But any unauthorized person who goes too near the sanctuary must be put to death."

[11]And the LORD said to Moses, [12]"Look, I have chosen the Levites from among the Israelites to serve as substitutes for all the firstborn sons of the people of Israel. The Levites belong to me, [13]for all the firstborn males are mine. On the day I struck down all the firstborn sons of the Egyptians, I set apart for myself all the firstborn in Israel, both of people and of animals. They are mine; I am the LORD."

REGISTRATION OF THE LEVITES

[14]The LORD spoke again to Moses in the wilderness of Sinai. He said, [15]"Record the names of the members of the tribe of Levi by their families and clans. List every male who is one month old or older." [16]So Moses listed them, just as the LORD had commanded.

[17]Levi had three sons, whose names were Gershon, Kohath, and Merari.
[18]The clans descended from Gershon were named after two of his descendants, Libni and Shimei.
[19]The clans descended from Kohath were named after four of his descendants, Amram, Izhar, Hebron, and Uzziel.
[20]The clans descended from Merari were named after two of his descendants, Mahli and Mushi.
These were the Levite clans, listed according to their family groups.

2:14-15 As in many Hebrew manuscripts, Samaritan Pentateuch, and Latin Vulgate (see also 1:14); most Hebrew manuscripts read *son of Reuel*. 3:7 Hebrew *around the Tent of Meeting, doing service at the Tabernacle*. 3:8 Hebrew *the Tent of Meeting*; also in 3:25.

21 The descendants of Gershon were composed of the clans descended from Libni and Shimei. 22 There were 7,500 males one month old or older among these Gershonite clans. 23 They were assigned the area to the west of the Tabernacle for their camp. 24 The leader of the Gershonite clans was Eliasaph son of Lael. 25 These two clans were responsible to care for the Tabernacle, including the sacred tent with its layers of coverings, the curtain at its entrance, 26 the curtains of the courtyard that surrounded the Tabernacle and altar, the curtain at the courtyard entrance, the ropes, and all the equipment related to their use.

27 The descendants of Kohath were composed of the clans descended from Amram, Izhar, Hebron, and Uzziel. 28 There were 8,600* males one month old or older among these Kohathite clans. They were responsible for the care of the sanctuary, 29 and they were assigned the area south of the Tabernacle for their camp. 30 The leader of the Kohathite clans was Elizaphan son of Uzziel. 31 These four clans were responsible for the care of the Ark, the table, the lampstand, the altars, the various articles used in the sanctuary, the inner curtain, and all the equipment related to their use. 32 Eleazar, son of Aaron the priest, was the chief administrator over all the Levites, with special responsibility for the oversight of the sanctuary.

33 The descendants of Merari were composed of the clans descended from Mahli and Mushi. 34 There were 6,200 males one month old or older among these Merarite clans. 35 They were assigned the area north of the Tabernacle for their camp. The leader of the Merarite clans was Zuriel son of Abihail. 36 These two clans were responsible for the care of the frames supporting the Tabernacle, the crossbars, the pillars, the bases, and all the equipment related to their use. 37 They were also responsible for the posts of the courtyard and all their bases, pegs, and ropes.

38 The area in front of the Tabernacle, in the east toward the sunrise,* was reserved for the tents of Moses and of Aaron and his sons, who had the final responsibility for the sanctuary on behalf of the people of Israel. Anyone other than a priest or Levite who went too near the sanctuary was to be put to death.

39 When Moses and Aaron counted the Levite clans at the LORD's command, the total number was 22,000 males one month old or older.

REDEEMING THE FIRSTBORN SONS

40 Then the LORD said to Moses, "Now count all the firstborn sons in Israel who are one month old or older, and make a list of their names. 41 The Levites must be reserved for me as substitutes for the firstborn sons of Israel; I am the LORD. And the Levites' livestock must be reserved for me as substitutes for the firstborn livestock of the whole nation of Israel."

42 So Moses counted the firstborn sons of the people of Israel, just as the LORD had commanded. 43 The number of firstborn sons who were one month old or older was 22,273.

44 Then the LORD said to Moses, 45 "Take the Levites as substitutes for the firstborn sons of the people of Israel. And take the livestock of the Levites as substitutes for the firstborn livestock of the people of Israel. The Levites belong to me; I am the LORD. 46 There are 273 more firstborn sons of Israel than there are Levites. To redeem these extra firstborn sons, 47 collect five pieces of silver* for each of them (each piece weighing the same as the sanctuary shekel, which equals twenty gerahs). 48 Give the silver to Aaron and his sons as the redemption price for the extra firstborn sons."

49 So Moses collected the silver for redeeming the firstborn sons of Israel who exceeded the number of Levites. 50 He collected 1,365 pieces of silver* on behalf of these firstborn sons of Israel (each piece weighing the same as the sanctuary shekel). 51 And Moses gave the silver for the redemption to Aaron and his sons, just as the LORD had commanded.

DUTIES OF THE KOHATHITE CLAN

4 Then the LORD said to Moses and Aaron, 2 "Record the names of the members of the clans and families of the Kohathite division of the tribe of Levi. 3 List all the men between the ages of thirty and fifty who are eligible to serve in the Tabernacle.*

4 "The duties of the Kohathites at the Tabernacle will relate to the most sacred objects. 5 When the camp moves, Aaron and his sons must enter the Tabernacle first to take down the inner curtain and cover the Ark of the Covenant* with it. 6 Then they must cover the inner curtain with fine goatskin leather and spread over that a single piece of blue cloth. Finally, they must put the carrying poles of the Ark in place.

7 "Next they must spread a blue cloth over the table where the Bread of the Presence is displayed, and on the cloth they will place the bowls, ladles, jars, pitchers, and the special bread. 8 They must spread a scarlet cloth over all of this, and finally a covering of fine goatskin leather on top of the scarlet cloth. Then they must insert the carrying poles into the table.

9 "Next they must cover the lampstand with a blue cloth, along with its lamps, lamp snuffers, trays, and special jars of olive oil. 10 Then they must cover the lampstand and its accessories with fine goatskin leather and place the bundle on a carrying frame.

3:28 Some Greek manuscripts read 8,300; see total in 3:39.
3:38 Hebrew toward the sunrise, in front of the Tent of Meeting.
3:47 Hebrew 5 shekels [2 ounces or 57 grams]. 3:50 Hebrew 1,365 [shekels] of silver [34 pounds or 15.5 kilograms]. 4:3 Hebrew the Tent of Meeting; also in 4:4, 15, 23, 25, 28, 30, 31, 33, 35, 37, 39, 41, 43, 47. 4:5 Or Ark of the Testimony.

¹¹"Next they must spread a blue cloth over the gold incense altar and cover this cloth with fine goatskin leather. Then they must attach the carrying poles to the altar. ¹²They must take all the remaining furnishings of the sanctuary and wrap them in a blue cloth, cover them with fine goatskin leather, and place them on the carrying frame.

¹³"They must remove the ashes from the altar for sacrifices and cover the altar with a purple cloth. ¹⁴All the altar utensils—the firepans, meat forks, shovels, basins, and all the containers—must be placed on the cloth, and a covering of fine goatskin leather must be spread over them. Finally, they must put the carrying poles in place. ¹⁵The camp will be ready to move when Aaron and his sons have finished covering the sanctuary and all the sacred articles. The Ko-hath-ites will come and carry these things to the next destination. But they must not touch the sacred objects, or they will die. So these are the things from the Tabernacle that the Kohathites must carry.

¹⁶"Eleazar son of Aaron the priest will be responsible for the oil of the lampstand, the fragrant incense, the daily grain offering, and the anointing oil. In fact, Eleazar will be responsible for the entire Tabernacle and everything in it, including the sanctuary and its furnishings."

¹⁷Then the LORD said to Moses and Aaron, ¹⁸"Do not let the Kohathite clans be destroyed from among the Levites! ¹⁹This is what you must do so they will live and not die when they approach the most sacred objects. Aaron and his sons must always go in with them and assign a specific duty or load to each person. ²⁰The Kohathites must never enter the sanctuary to look at the sacred objects for even a moment, or they will die."

DUTIES OF THE GERSHONITE CLAN

²¹And the LORD said to Moses, ²²"Record the names of the members of the clans and families of the Gershonite division of the tribe of Levi. ²³List all the men between the ages of thirty and fifty who are eligible to serve in the Tabernacle.

²⁴"These Gershonite clans will be responsible for general service and carrying loads. ²⁵They must carry the curtains of the Tabernacle, the Tabernacle itself with its coverings, the outer covering of fine goatskin leather, and the curtain for the Tabernacle entrance. ²⁶They are also to carry the curtains for the courtyard walls that surround the Tabernacle and altar, the curtain across the courtyard entrance, the ropes, and all the equipment related to their use. The Gershonites are responsible for all these items. ²⁷Aaron and his sons will direct the Gershonites regarding all their duties, whether it involves moving the equipment or doing other work. They must assign the Gershonites responsibility

for the loads they are to carry. ²⁸So these are the duties assigned to the Gershonite clans at the Tabernacle. They will be directly responsible to Ithamar son of Aaron the priest.

DUTIES OF THE MERARITE CLAN

²⁹"Now record the names of the members of the clans and families of the Merarite division of the tribe of Levi. ³⁰List all the men between the ages of thirty and fifty who are eligible to serve in the Tabernacle.

³¹"Their only duty at the Tabernacle will be to carry loads. They will carry the frames of the Tabernacle, the crossbars, the posts, and the bases; ³²also the posts for the courtyard walls with their bases, pegs, and ropes; and all the accessories and everything else related to their use. Assign the various loads to each man by name. ³³So these are the duties of the Merarite clans at the Tabernacle. They are directly responsible to Ithamar son of Aaron the priest."

SUMMARY OF THE REGISTRATION

³⁴So Moses, Aaron, and the other leaders of the community listed the members of the Kohathite division by their clans and families. ³⁵The list included all the men between thirty and fifty years of age who were eligible for service in the Tabernacle, ³⁶and the total number came to 2,750. ³⁷So this was the total of all those from the Kohathite clans who were eligible to serve at the Tabernacle. Moses and Aaron listed them, just as the LORD had commanded through Moses.

³⁸The Gershonite division was also listed by its clans and families. ³⁹The list included all the men between thirty and fifty years of age who were eligible for service in the Tabernacle, ⁴⁰and the total number came to 2,630. ⁴¹So this was the total of all those from the Gershonite clans who were eligible to serve at the Tabernacle. Moses and Aaron listed them, just as the LORD had commanded.

⁴²The Merarite division was also listed by its clans and families. ⁴³The list included all the men between thirty and fifty years of age who were eligible for service in the Tabernacle, ⁴⁴and the total number came to 3,200. ⁴⁵So this was the total of all those from the Merarite clans who were eligible for service. Moses and Aaron listed them, just as the LORD had commanded through Moses.

⁴⁶So Moses, Aaron, and the leaders of Israel listed all the Levites by their clans and families. ⁴⁷All the men between thirty and fifty years of age who were eligible for service in the Tabernacle and for its transportation ⁴⁸numbered 8,580. ⁴⁹When their names were recorded, as the LORD had commanded through Moses, each man was assigned his task and told what to carry.

And so the registration was completed, just as the LORD had commanded Moses.

PURITY IN ISRAEL'S CAMP

5 The LORD gave these instructions to Moses: ²"Command the people of Israel to remove from the camp anyone who has a skin disease* or a discharge, or who has become ceremonially unclean by touching a dead person. ³This command applies to men and women alike. Remove them so they will not defile the camp in which I live among them." ⁴So the Israelites did as the LORD had commanded Moses and removed such people from the camp.

⁵Then the LORD said to Moses, ⁶"Give the following instructions to the people of Israel: If any of the people—men or women—betray the LORD by doing wrong to another person, they are guilty. ⁷They must confess their sin and make full restitution for what they have done, adding an additional 20 percent and returning it to the person who was wronged. ⁸But if the person who was wronged is dead, and there are no near relatives to whom restitution can be made, the payment belongs to the LORD and must be given to the priest. Those who are guilty must also bring a ram as a sacrifice, and they will be purified and made right with the LORD.* ⁹All the sacred offerings that the Israelites bring to a priest will belong to him. ¹⁰Each priest may keep all the sacred donations that he receives."

PROTECTING MARITAL FAITHFULNESS

¹¹And the LORD said to Moses, ¹²"Give the following instructions to the people of Israel.

"Suppose a man's wife goes astray, and she is unfaithful to her husband ¹³and has sex with another man, but neither her husband nor anyone else knows about it. She has defiled herself, even though there was no witness and she was not caught in the act. ¹⁴If her husband becomes jealous and is suspicious of his wife and needs to know whether or not she has defiled herself, ¹⁵the husband must bring his wife to the priest. He must also bring an offering of two quarts* of barley flour to be presented on her behalf. Do not mix it with olive oil or frankincense, for it is a jealousy offering—an offering to prove whether or not she is guilty.

¹⁶"The priest will then present her to stand trial before the LORD. ¹⁷He must take some holy water in a clay jar and pour into it dust he has taken from the Tabernacle floor. ¹⁸When the priest has presented the woman before the LORD, he must unbind her hair and place in her hands the offering of proof—the jealousy offering to determine whether her husband's suspicions are justified. The priest will stand before her, holding the jar of bitter water that brings a curse to those who are guilty. ¹⁹The priest will then put the woman under oath and say to her, 'If no other man has had sex with you, and you have not gone astray and defiled yourself while under your husband's authority, may you be immune from the effects of this bitter water that brings on the curse. ²⁰But if you have gone astray by being unfaithful to your husband, and have defiled yourself by having sex with another man—'

²¹"At this point the priest must put the woman under oath by saying, 'May the people know that the LORD's curse is upon you when he makes you infertile, causing your womb to shrivel* and your abdomen to swell. ²²Now may this water that brings the curse enter your body and cause your abdomen to swell and your womb to shrivel.*' And the woman will be required to say, 'Yes, let it be so.' ²³And the priest will write these curses on a piece of leather and wash them off into the bitter water. ²⁴He will make the woman drink the bitter water that brings on the curse. When the water enters her body, it will cause bitter suffering if she is guilty.

²⁵"The priest will take the jealousy offering from the woman's hand, lift it up before the LORD, and carry it to the altar. ²⁶He will take a handful of the flour as a token portion and burn it on the altar, and he will require the woman to drink the water. ²⁷If she has defiled herself by being unfaithful to her husband, the water that brings on the curse will cause bitter suffering. Her abdomen will swell and her womb will shrink,* and her name will become a curse among her people. ²⁸But if she has not defiled herself and is pure, then she will be unharmed and will still be able to have children.

²⁹"This is the ritual law for dealing with suspicion. If a woman goes astray and defiles herself while under her husband's authority, ³⁰or if a man becomes jealous and is suspicious that his wife has been unfaithful, the husband must present his wife before the LORD, and the priest will apply this entire ritual law to her. ³¹The husband will be innocent of any guilt in this matter, but his wife will be held accountable for her sin."

NAZIRITE LAWS

6 Then the LORD said to Moses, ²"Give the following instructions to the people of Israel.

"If any of the people, either men or women, take the special vow of a Nazirite, setting themselves apart to the LORD in a special way, ³they must give up wine and other alcoholic drinks. They must not use vinegar made from wine or from other alcoholic drinks, they must not drink fresh grape juice, and they must not eat grapes or raisins. ⁴As long as they are bound by their Nazirite vow, they are not allowed to eat or drink anything that comes from a grapevine—not even the grape seeds or skins.

⁵"They must never cut their hair throughout the time of their vow, for they are holy and set apart to the LORD. Until the time of their vow has

---

5:2 Traditionally rendered *leprosy*. The Hebrew word used here describes various skin diseases. 5:8 Or *bring a ram for atonement, which will make atonement for them.* 5:15 Hebrew *¹⁄₁₀ of an ephah* [2.2 liters]. 5:21 Hebrew *when he causes your thigh to waste away.* 5:22 Hebrew *and your thigh to waste away.* 5:27 Hebrew *and her thigh will waste away.*

been fulfilled, they must let their hair grow long. ⁶And they must not go near a dead body during the entire period of their vow to the LORD. ⁷Even if the dead person is their own father, mother, brother, or sister, they must not defile themselves, for the hair on their head is the symbol of their separation to God. ⁸This requirement applies as long as they are set apart to the LORD.

⁹"If someone falls dead beside them, the hair they have dedicated will be defiled. They must wait for seven days and then shave their heads. Then they will be cleansed from their defilement. ¹⁰On the eighth day they must bring two turtledoves or two young pigeons to the priest at the entrance of the Tabernacle.* ¹¹The priest will offer one of the birds for a sin offering and the other for a burnt offering. In this way, he will purify them* from the guilt they incurred through contact with the dead body. Then they must reaffirm their commitment and let their hair begin to grow again. ¹²The days of their vow that were completed before their defilement no longer count. They must rededicate themselves to the LORD as a Nazirite for the full term of their vow, and each must bring a one-year-old male lamb for a guilt offering.

¹³"This is the ritual law for Nazirites. At the conclusion of their time of separation as Nazirites, they must each go to the entrance of the Tabernacle ¹⁴and offer their sacrifices to the LORD: a one-year-old male lamb without defect for a burnt offering, a one-year-old female lamb without defect for a sin offering, a ram without defect for a peace offering, ¹⁵a basket of bread made without yeast—cakes of choice flour mixed with olive oil and wafers spread with olive oil—along with their prescribed grain offerings and liquid offerings. ¹⁶The priest will present these offerings before the LORD: first the sin offering and the burnt offering; ¹⁷then the ram for a peace offering, along with the basket of bread made without yeast. The priest must also present the prescribed grain offering and liquid offering to the LORD.

¹⁸"Then the Nazirites will shave their heads at the entrance of the Tabernacle. They will take the hair that had been dedicated and place it on the fire beneath the peace-offering sacrifice. ¹⁹After the Nazirite's head has been shaved, the priest will take for each of them the boiled shoulder of the ram, and he will take from the basket a cake and a wafer made without yeast. He will put them all into the Nazirite's hands. ²⁰Then the priest will lift them up as a special offering before the LORD. These are holy portions for the priest, along with the breast of the special offering and the thigh of the sacred offering that are lifted up before the LORD. After this ceremony the Nazirites may again drink wine.

²¹"This is the ritual law of the Nazirites, who vow to bring these offerings to the LORD. They may also bring additional offerings if they can afford it. And they must be careful to do whatever they vowed when they set themselves apart as Nazirites."

THE PRIESTLY BLESSING

²²Then the LORD said to Moses, ²³"Tell Aaron and his sons to bless the people of Israel with this special blessing:

²⁴ 'May the LORD bless you
and protect you.
²⁵ May the LORD smile on you
and be gracious to you.
²⁶ May the LORD show you his favor
and give you his peace.'

²⁷Whenever Aaron and his sons bless the people of Israel in my name, I myself will bless them."

OFFERINGS OF DEDICATION

7 On the day Moses set up the Tabernacle, he anointed it and set it apart as holy. He also anointed and set apart all its furnishings and the altar with its utensils. ²Then the leaders of Israel—the tribal leaders who had registered the troops—came and brought their offerings. ³Together they brought six large wagons and twelve oxen. There was a wagon for every two leaders and an ox for each leader. They presented these to the LORD in front of the Tabernacle.

⁴Then the LORD said to Moses, ⁵"Receive their gifts, and use these oxen and wagons for transporting the Tabernacle.* Distribute them among the Levites according to the work they have to do." ⁶So Moses took the wagons and oxen and presented them to the Levites. ⁷He gave two wagons and four oxen to the Gershonite division for their work, ⁸and he gave four wagons and eight oxen to the Merarite division for their work. All their work was done under the leadership of Ithamar son of Aaron the priest. ⁹But he gave none of the wagons or oxen to the Kohathite division, since they were required to carry the sacred objects of the Tabernacle on their shoulders.

¹⁰The leaders also presented dedication gifts for the altar at the time it was anointed. They each placed their gifts before the altar. ¹¹The LORD said to Moses, "Let one leader bring his gift each day for the dedication of the altar."

¹²On the first day Nahshon son of Amminadab, leader of the tribe of Judah, presented his offering.

¹³His offering consisted of a silver platter weighing 3¼ pounds and a silver basin weighing 1¾ pounds* (as measured by the weight of the sanctuary shekel). These were

---

6:10 Hebrew *the Tent of Meeting;* also in 6:13, 18.   6:11 Or *make atonement for them.*   7:5 Hebrew *the Tent of Meeting;* also in 7:89. 7:13 Hebrew *silver platter weighing 130 [shekels]* [1.5 kilograms] *and a silver basin weighing 70 shekels* [800 grams]; also in 7:19, 25, 31, 37, 43, 49, 55, 61, 67, 73, 79, 85.

both filled with grain offerings of choice flour moistened with olive oil. ¹⁴ He also brought a gold container weighing four ounces,* which was filled with incense. ¹⁵ He brought a young bull, a ram, and a one-year-old male lamb for a burnt offering, ¹⁶ and a male goat for a sin offering. ¹⁷ For a peace offering he brought two bulls, five rams, five male goats, and five one-year-old male lambs. This was the offering brought by Nahshon son of Amminadab.

¹⁸ On the second day Nethanel son of Zuar, leader of the tribe of Issachar, presented his offering. ¹⁹ His offering consisted of a silver platter weighing 3¼ pounds and a silver basin weighing 1¾ pounds (as measured by the weight of the sanctuary shekel). These were both filled with grain offerings of choice flour moistened with olive oil. ²⁰ He also brought a gold container weighing four ounces, which was filled with incense. ²¹ He brought a young bull, a ram, and a one-year-old male lamb for a burnt offering, ²² and a male goat for a sin offering. ²³ For a peace offering he brought two bulls, five rams, five male goats, and five one-year-old male lambs. This was the offering brought by Nethanel son of Zuar.

²⁴ On the third day Eliab son of Helon, leader of the tribe of Zebulun, presented his offering. ²⁵ His offering consisted of a silver platter weighing 3¼ pounds and a silver basin weighing 1¾ pounds (as measured by the weight of the sanctuary shekel). These were both filled with grain offerings of choice flour moistened with olive oil. ²⁶ He also brought a gold container weighing four ounces, which was filled with incense. ²⁷ He brought a young bull, a ram, and a one-year-old male lamb for a burnt offering, ²⁸ and a male goat for a sin offering. ²⁹ For a peace offering he brought two bulls, five rams, five male goats, and five one-year-old male lambs. This was the offering brought by Eliab son of Helon.

³⁰ On the fourth day Elizur son of Shedeur, leader of the tribe of Reuben, presented his offering. ³¹ His offering consisted of a silver platter weighing 3¼ pounds and a silver basin weighing 1¾ pounds (as measured by the weight of the sanctuary shekel). These were both filled with grain offerings of choice flour moistened with olive oil. ³² He also brought a gold container weighing four ounces, which was filled with incense. ³³ He brought a young bull, a ram, and a one-year-old male lamb for a burnt offering, ³⁴ and a male goat for a sin offering. ³⁵ For a peace offering he brought two bulls, five

rams, five male goats, and five one-year-old male lambs. This was the offering brought by Elizur son of Shedeur.

³⁶ On the fifth day Shelumiel son of Zurishaddai, leader of the tribe of Simeon, presented his offering. ³⁷ His offering consisted of a silver platter weighing 3¼ pounds and a silver basin weighing 1¾ pounds (as measured by the weight of the sanctuary shekel). These were both filled with grain offerings of choice flour moistened with olive oil. ³⁸ He also brought a gold container weighing four ounces, which was filled with incense. ³⁹ He brought a young bull, a ram, and a one-year-old male lamb for a burnt offering, ⁴⁰ and a male goat for a sin offering. ⁴¹ For a peace offering he brought two bulls, five rams, five male goats, and five one-year-old male lambs. This was the offering brought by Shelumiel son of Zurishaddai.

⁴² On the sixth day Eliasaph son of Deuel, leader of the tribe of Gad, presented his offering. ⁴³ His offering consisted of a silver platter weighing 3¼ pounds and a silver basin weighing 1¾ pounds (as measured by the weight of the sanctuary shekel). These were both filled with grain offerings of choice flour moistened with olive oil. ⁴⁴ He also brought a gold container weighing four ounces, which was filled with incense. ⁴⁵ He brought a young bull, a ram, and a one-year-old male lamb for a burnt offering, ⁴⁶ and a male goat for a sin offering. ⁴⁷ For a peace offering he brought two bulls, five rams, five male goats, and five one-year-old male lambs. This was the offering brought by Eliasaph son of Deuel.

⁴⁸ On the seventh day Elishama son of Ammihud, leader of the tribe of Ephraim, presented his offering. ⁴⁹ His offering consisted of a silver platter weighing 3¼ pounds and a silver basin weighing 1¾ pounds (as measured by the weight of the sanctuary shekel). These were both filled with grain offerings of choice flour moistened with olive oil. ⁵⁰ He also brought a gold container weighing four ounces, which was filled with incense. ⁵¹ He brought a young bull, a ram, and a one-year-old male lamb for a burnt offering, ⁵² and a male goat for a sin offering. ⁵³ For a peace offering he brought two bulls, five rams, five male goats, and five one-year-old male lambs. This was the offering brought by Elishama son of Ammihud.

7:14 Hebrew *10 [shekels]* [114 grams]; also in 7:20, 26, 32, 38, 44, 50, 56, 62, 68, 74, 80, 86.

⁵⁴On the eighth day Gamaliel son of Pedahzur, leader of the tribe of Manasseh, presented his offering.

⁵⁵His offering consisted of a silver platter weighing 3¼ pounds and a silver basin weighing 1¾ pounds (as measured by the weight of the sanctuary shekel). These were both filled with grain offerings of choice flour moistened with olive oil. ⁵⁶He also brought a gold container weighing four ounces, which was filled with incense. ⁵⁷He brought a young bull, a ram, and a one-year-old male lamb for a burnt offering, ⁵⁸and a male goat for a sin offering. ⁵⁹For a peace offering he brought two bulls, five rams, five male goats, and five one-year-old male lambs. This was the offering brought by Gamaliel son of Pedahzur.

⁶⁰On the ninth day Abidan son of Gideoni, leader of the tribe of Benjamin, presented his offering. ⁶¹His offering consisted of a silver platter weighing 3¼ pounds and a silver basin weighing 1¾ pounds (as measured by the weight of the sanctuary shekel). These were both filled with grain offerings of choice flour moistened with olive oil. ⁶²He also brought a gold container weighing four ounces, which was filled with incense. ⁶³He brought a young bull, a ram, and a one-year-old male lamb for a burnt offering, ⁶⁴and a male goat for a sin offering. ⁶⁵For a peace offering he brought two bulls, five rams, five male goats, and five one-year-old male lambs. This was the offering brought by Abidan son of Gideoni.

⁶⁶On the tenth day Ahiezer son of Ammishaddai, leader of the tribe of Dan, presented his offering. ⁶⁷His offering consisted of a silver platter weighing 3¼ pounds and a silver basin weighing 1¾ pounds (as measured by the weight of the sanctuary shekel). These were both filled with grain offerings of choice flour moistened with olive oil. ⁶⁸He also brought a gold container weighing four ounces, which was filled with incense. ⁶⁹He brought a young bull, a ram, and a one-year-old male lamb for a burnt offering, ⁷⁰and a male goat for a sin offering. ⁷¹For a peace offering he brought two bulls, five rams, five male goats, and five one-year-old male lambs. This was the offering brought by Ahiezer son of Ammishaddai.

⁷²On the eleventh day Pagiel son of Ocran, leader of the tribe of Asher, presented his offering. ⁷³His offering consisted of a silver platter weighing 3¼ pounds and a silver basin weighing 1¾ pounds (as measured by the weight of the sanctuary shekel). These were both filled with grain offerings of choice flour moistened with olive oil. ⁷⁴He also brought a gold container weighing four ounces, which was filled with incense. ⁷⁵He brought a young bull, a ram, and a one-year-old male lamb for a burnt offering, ⁷⁶and a male goat for a sin offering. ⁷⁷For a peace offering he brought two bulls, five rams, five male goats, and five one-year-old male lambs. This was the offering brought by Pagiel son of Ocran.

⁷⁸On the twelfth day Ahira son of Enan, leader of the tribe of Naphtali, presented his offering. ⁷⁹His offering consisted of a silver platter weighing 3¼ pounds and a silver basin weighing 1¾ pounds (as measured by the weight of the sanctuary shekel). These were both filled with grain offerings of choice flour moistened with olive oil. ⁸⁰He also brought a gold container weighing four ounces, which was filled with incense. ⁸¹He brought a young bull, a ram, and a one-year-old male lamb for a burnt offering, ⁸²and a male goat for a sin offering. ⁸³For a peace offering he brought two bulls, five rams, five male goats, and five one-year-old male lambs. This was the offering brought by Ahira son of Enan.

⁸⁴So this was the dedication offering brought by the leaders of Israel at the time the altar was anointed: twelve silver platters, twelve silver basins, and twelve gold incense containers. ⁸⁵Each silver platter weighed 3¼ pounds, and each silver basin weighed 1¾ pounds. The total weight of the silver was 60 pounds* (as measured by the weight of the sanctuary shekel). ⁸⁶Each of the twelve gold containers that was filled with incense weighed four ounces (as measured by the weight of the sanctuary shekel). The total weight of the gold was three pounds.* ⁸⁷Twelve young bulls, twelve rams, and twelve one-year-old male lambs were donated for the burnt offerings, along with their prescribed grain offerings. Twelve male goats were brought for the sin offerings. ⁸⁸Twenty-four bulls, sixty rams, sixty male goats, and sixty one-year-old male lambs were donated for the peace offerings. This was the dedication offering for the altar after it was anointed.

⁸⁹Whenever Moses went into the Tabernacle to speak with the Lord, he heard the voice speaking to him from between the two cherubim above the Ark's cover—the place of atonement—that rests on the Ark of the Covenant.* The Lord spoke to him from there.

PREPARING THE LAMPS

8 The Lord said to Moses, ²"Give Aaron the following instructions: When you set up the seven lamps in the lampstand, place them so

---

7:85 Hebrew 2,400 [shekels] [27.6 kilograms].   7:86 Hebrew 120 [shekels] [1.4 kilograms].   7:89 Or Ark of the Testimony.

their light shines forward in front of the lampstand." ³ So Aaron did this. He set up the seven lamps so they reflected their light forward, just as the LORD had commanded Moses. ⁴ The entire lampstand, from its base to its decorative blossoms, was made of beaten gold. It was built according to the exact design the LORD had shown Moses.

THE LEVITES DEDICATED

⁵ Then the LORD said to Moses, ⁶ "Now set the Levites apart from the rest of the people of Israel and make them ceremonially clean. ⁷ Do this by sprinkling them with the water of purification, and have them shave their entire body and wash their clothing. Then they will be ceremonially clean. ⁸ Have them bring a young bull and a grain offering of choice flour moistened with olive oil, along with a second young bull for a sin offering. ⁹ Then assemble the whole community of Israel, and present the Levites at the entrance of the Tabernacle.* ¹⁰ When you present the Levites before the LORD, the people of Israel must lay their hands on them. ¹¹ Raising his hands, Aaron must then present the Levites to the LORD as a special offering from the people of Israel, thus dedicating them to the LORD's service.

¹² "Next the Levites will lay their hands on the heads of the young bulls. Present one as a sin offering and the other as a burnt offering to the LORD, to purify the Levites and make them right with the LORD.* ¹³ Then have the Levites stand in front of Aaron and his sons, and raise your hands and present them as a special offering to the LORD. ¹⁴ In this way, you will set the Levites apart from the rest of the people of Israel, and the Levites will belong to me. ¹⁵ After this, they may go into the Tabernacle to do their work, because you have purified them and presented them as a special offering.

¹⁶ "Of all the people of Israel, the Levites are reserved for me. I have claimed them for myself in place of all the firstborn sons of the Israelites; I have taken the Levites as their substitutes. ¹⁷ For all the firstborn males among the people of Israel are mine, both of people and of animals. I set them apart for myself on the day I struck down all the firstborn sons of the Egyptians. ¹⁸ Yes, I have claimed the Levites in place of all the firstborn sons of Israel. ¹⁹ And of all the Israelites, I have assigned the Levites to Aaron and his sons. They will serve in the Tabernacle on behalf of the Israelites and make sacrifices to purify* the people so no plague will strike them when they approach the sanctuary."

²⁰ So Moses, Aaron, and the whole community of Israel dedicated the Levites, carefully following all the LORD's instructions to Moses. ²¹ The Levites purified themselves from sin and washed their clothes, and Aaron lifted them up and presented them to the LORD as a special offering. He then offered a sacrifice to purify them and make them right with the LORD.* ²² After that the Levites went into the Tabernacle to perform their duties, assisting Aaron and his sons. So they carried out all the commands that the LORD gave Moses concerning the Levites.

²³ The LORD also instructed Moses, ²⁴ "This is the rule the Levites must follow: They must begin serving in the Tabernacle at the age of twenty-five, ²⁵ and they must retire at the age of fifty. ²⁶ After retirement they may assist their fellow Levites by serving as guards at the Tabernacle, but they may not officiate in the service. This is how you must assign duties to the Levites."

THE SECOND PASSOVER

9 A year after Israel's departure from Egypt, the LORD spoke to Moses in the wilderness of Sinai. In the first month* of that year he said, ² "Tell the Israelites to celebrate the Passover at the prescribed time, ³ at twilight on the fourteenth day of the first month.* Be sure to follow all my decrees and regulations concerning this celebration."

⁴ So Moses told the people to celebrate the Passover ⁵ in the wilderness of Sinai as twilight fell on the fourteenth day of the month. And they celebrated the festival there, just as the LORD had commanded Moses. ⁶ But some of the men had been ceremonially defiled by touching a dead body, so they could not celebrate the Passover that day. They came to Moses and Aaron that day ⁷ and said, "We have become ceremonially unclean by touching a dead body. But why should we be prevented from presenting the LORD's offering at the proper time with the rest of the Israelites?"

⁸ Moses answered, "Wait here until I have received instructions for you from the LORD."

⁹ This was the LORD's reply to Moses. ¹⁰ "Give the following instructions to the people of Israel: If any of the people now or in future generations are ceremonially unclean at Passover time because of touching a dead body, or if they are on a journey and cannot be present at the ceremony, they may still celebrate the LORD's Passover. ¹¹ They must offer the Passover sacrifice one month later, at twilight on the fourteenth day of the second month.* They must eat the Passover lamb at that time with bitter salad greens and bread made without yeast. ¹² They must not leave any of the lamb until the next morning, and they must not break any of its bones. They must follow all the normal regulations concerning the Passover.

8:9 Hebrew *the Tent of Meeting;* also in 8:15, 19, 22, 24, 26.　8:12 Or *to make atonement for the Levites.*　8:19 Or *make atonement for.*　8:21 Or *then made atonement for them to purify them.*　9:1 The first month of the ancient Hebrew lunar calendar usually occurs within the months of March and April.　9:3 This day in the ancient Hebrew lunar calendar occurred in late March, April, or early May.　9:11 This day in the ancient Hebrew lunar calendar occurred in late April, May, or early June.

[13] "But those who neglect to celebrate the Passover at the regular time, even though they are ceremonially clean and not away on a trip, will be cut off from the community of Israel. If they fail to present the LORD's offering at the proper time, they will suffer the consequences of their guilt. [14] And if foreigners living among you want to celebrate the Passover to the LORD, they must follow these same decrees and regulations. The same laws apply both to native-born Israelites and to the foreigners living among you."

THE FIERY CLOUD

[15] On the day the Tabernacle was set up, the cloud covered it.* But from evening until morning the cloud over the Tabernacle looked like a pillar of fire. [16] This was the regular pattern—at night the cloud that covered the Tabernacle had the appearance of fire. [17] Whenever the cloud lifted from over the sacred tent, the people of Israel would break camp and follow it. And wherever the cloud settled, the people of Israel would set up camp. [18] In this way, they traveled and camped at the LORD's command wherever he told them to go. Then they remained in their camp as long as the cloud stayed over the Tabernacle. [19] If the cloud remained over the Tabernacle for a long time, the Israelites stayed and performed their duty to the LORD. [20] Sometimes the cloud would stay over the Tabernacle for only a few days, so the people would stay for only a few days, as the LORD commanded. Then at the LORD's command they would break camp and move on. [21] Sometimes the cloud stayed only overnight and lifted the next morning. But day or night, when the cloud lifted, the people broke camp and moved on. [22] Whether the cloud stayed above the Tabernacle for two days, a month, or a year, the people of Israel stayed in camp and did not move on. But as soon as it lifted, they broke camp and moved on. [23] So they camped or traveled at the LORD's command, and they did whatever the LORD told them through Moses.

THE SILVER TRUMPETS

10 Now the LORD said to Moses, [2] "Make two trumpets of hammered silver for calling the community to assemble and for signaling the breaking of camp. [3] When both trumpets are blown, everyone must gather before you at the entrance of the Tabernacle.* [4] But if only one trumpet is blown, then only the leaders—the heads of the clans of Israel—must present themselves to you.

[5] "When you sound the signal to move on, the tribes camped on the east side of the Tabernacle must break camp and move forward. [6] When you sound the signal a second time, the tribes camped on the south will follow. You must sound short blasts as the signal for moving on. [7] But when you call the people to an assembly, blow the trumpets with a different signal. [8] Only the priests, Aaron's descendants, are allowed to blow the trumpets. This is a permanent law for you, to be observed from generation to generation.

[9] "When you arrive in your own land and go to war against your enemies who attack you, sound the alarm with the trumpets. Then the LORD your God will remember you and rescue you from your enemies. [10] Blow the trumpets in times of gladness, too, sounding them at your annual festivals and at the beginning of each month. And blow the trumpets over your burnt offerings and peace offerings. The trumpets will remind your God of his covenant with you. I am the LORD your God."

THE ISRAELITES LEAVE SINAI

[11] In the second year after Israel's departure from Egypt—on the twentieth day of the second month*—the cloud lifted from the Tabernacle of the Covenant.* [12] So the Israelites set out from the wilderness of Sinai and traveled on from place to place until the cloud stopped in the wilderness of Paran.

[13] When the people set out for the first time, following the instructions the LORD had given through Moses, [14] Judah's troops led the way. They marched behind their banner, and their leader was Nahshon son of Amminadab. [15] They were joined by the troops of the tribe of Issachar, led by Nethanel son of Zuar, [16] and the troops of the tribe of Zebulun, led by Eliab son of Helon.

[17] Then the Tabernacle was taken down, and the Gershonite and Merarite divisions of the Levites were next in the line of march, carrying the Tabernacle with them. [18] Reuben's troops went next, marching behind their banner. Their leader was Elizur son of Shedeur. [19] They were joined by the troops of the tribe of Simeon, led by Shelumiel son of Zurishaddai, [20] and the troops of the tribe of Gad, led by Eliasaph son of Deuel.

[21] Next came the Kohathite division of the Levites, carrying the sacred objects from the Tabernacle. Before they arrived at the next camp, the Tabernacle would already be set up at its new location. [22] Ephraim's troops went next, marching behind their banner. Their leader was Elishama son of Ammihud. [23] They were joined by the troops of the tribe of Manasseh, led by Gamaliel son of Pedahzur, [24] and the troops of the tribe of Benjamin, led by Abidan son of Gideoni.

[25] Dan's troops went last, marching behind their banner and serving as the rear guard for all the tribal camps. Their leader was Ahiezer son of Ammishaddai. [26] They were joined by the troops of the tribe of Asher, led by Pagiel son of Ocran, [27] and the troops of the tribe of Naphtali, led by Ahira son of Enan.

[28] This was the order in which the Israelites marched, division by division.

9:15 Hebrew *covered the Tabernacle, the Tent of the Testimony.*
10:3 Hebrew *Tent of Meeting.* **10:11a** This day in the ancient Hebrew lunar calendar occurred in late April, May, or early June.
10:11b Or *Tabernacle of the Testimony.*

29 One day Moses said to his brother-in-law, Hobab son of Reuel the Midianite, "We are on our way to the place the LORD promised us, for he said, 'I will give it to you.' Come with us and we will treat you well, for the LORD has promised wonderful blessings for Israel!"

30 But Hobab replied, "No, I will not go. I must return to my own land and family."

31 "Please don't leave us," Moses pleaded. "You know the places in the wilderness where we should camp. Come, be our guide. 32 If you do, we'll share with you all the blessings the LORD gives us."

33 They marched for three days after leaving the mountain of the LORD, with the Ark of the LORD's Covenant moving ahead of them to show them where to stop and rest. 34 As they moved on each day, the cloud of the LORD hovered over them. 35 And whenever the Ark set out, Moses would shout, "Arise, O LORD, and let your enemies be scattered! Let them flee before you!" 36 And when the Ark was set down, he would say, "Return, O LORD, to the countless thousands of Israel!"

THE PEOPLE COMPLAIN TO MOSES

11 Soon the people began to complain about their hardship, and the LORD heard everything they said. Then the LORD's anger blazed against them, and he sent a fire to rage among them, and he destroyed some of the people in the outskirts of the camp. 2 Then the people screamed to Moses for help, and when he prayed to the LORD, the fire stopped. 3 After that, the area was known as Taberah (which means "the place of burning"), because fire from the LORD had burned among them there.

4 Then the foreign rabble who were traveling with the Israelites began to crave the good things of Egypt. And the people of Israel also began to complain. "Oh, for some meat!" they exclaimed. 5 "We remember the fish we used to eat for free in Egypt. And we had all the cucumbers, melons, leeks, onions, and garlic we wanted. 6 But now our appetites are gone. All we ever see is this manna!"

7 The manna looked like small coriander seeds, and it was pale yellow like gum resin. 8 The people would go out and gather it from the ground. They made flour by grinding it with hand mills or pounding it in mortars. Then they boiled it in a pot and made it into flat cakes. These cakes tasted like pastries baked with olive oil. 9 The manna came down on the camp with the dew during the night.

10 Moses heard all the families standing in the doorways of their tents whining, and the LORD became extremely angry. Moses was also very aggravated. 11 And Moses said to the LORD, "Why are you treating me, your servant, so harshly? Have mercy on me! What did I do to deserve the burden of all these people? 12 Did I give birth to them? Did I bring them into the world? Why did you tell me to carry them in my arms like a mother carries a nursing baby? How can I carry them to the land you swore to give their ancestors? 13 Where am I supposed to get meat for all these people? They keep whining to me, saying, 'Give us meat to eat!' 14 I can't carry all these people by myself! The load is far too heavy! 15 If this is how you intend to treat me, just go ahead and kill me. Do me a favor and spare me this misery!"

MOSES CHOOSES SEVENTY LEADERS

16 Then the LORD said to Moses, "Gather before me seventy men who are recognized as elders and leaders of Israel. Bring them to the Tabernacle* to stand there with you. 17 I will come down and talk to you there. I will take some of the Spirit that is upon you, and I will put the Spirit upon them also. They will bear the burden of the people along with you, so you will not have to carry it alone.

18 "And say to the people, 'Purify yourselves, for tomorrow you will have meat to eat. You were whining, and the LORD heard you when you cried, "Oh, for some meat! We were better off in Egypt!" Now the LORD will give you meat, and you will have to eat it. 19 And it won't be for just a day or two, or for five or ten or even twenty. 20 You will eat it for a whole month until you gag and are sick of it. For you have rejected the LORD, who is here among you, and you have whined to him, saying, "Why did we ever leave Egypt?"'"

21 But Moses responded to the LORD, "There are 600,000 foot soldiers here with me, and yet you say, 'I will give them meat for a whole month!' 22 Even if we butchered all our flocks and herds, would that satisfy them? Even if we caught all the fish in the sea, would that be enough?"

23 Then the LORD said to Moses, "Has my arm lost its power? Now you will see whether or not my word comes true!"

24 So Moses went out and reported the LORD's words to the people. He gathered the seventy elders and stationed them around the Tabernacle.* 25 And the LORD came down in the cloud and spoke to Moses. Then he gave the seventy elders the same Spirit that was upon Moses. And when the Spirit rested upon them, they prophesied. But this never happened again.

26 Two men, Eldad and Medad, had stayed behind in the camp. They were listed among the elders, but they had not gone out to the Tabernacle. Yet the Spirit rested upon them as well, so they prophesied there in the camp. 27 A young man ran and reported to Moses, "Eldad and Medad are prophesying in the camp!"

28 Joshua son of Nun, who had been Moses' assistant since his youth, protested, "Moses, my master, make them stop!"

11:16 Hebrew *the Tent of Meeting.* 11:24 Hebrew *the tent;* also in 11:26.

I'M A PROPHET
Numbers 11:24-30   ROBERT MORRIS

God wants us to desire His spiritual gifts, "especially the ability to prophesy" (1 Corinthians 14:1). The idea of *prophesying* can be intimidating to some people, but it simply means hearing what God is saying and using His words to encourage others. Here are three important truths about the spiritual gift of prophecy:

1. All can prophesy.
   Wouldn't it be great if God put His Spirit on all of His people? In Acts 2, it happened. Peter reminded those present that God had promised to pour out His Spirit: "Your sons and daughters will prophesy" (Acts 2:16-17). What happened at Pentecost was a fulfillment of Moses' prayer: "I wish that *all* the Lord's people were prophets and that the Lord would put his Spirit upon them *all*!" (Numbers 11:29, emphasis added). When you receive the baptism in the Holy Spirit, He comes on you and remains with you. The Holy Spirit wants to walk and talk with you every day.

   Prophecy is not manipulative.
   Prophecy does not try to get people to do what you want them to do. Selfish motives cloud our ability to hear God, and we need to be very careful about saying, "The Lord told me . . ." It's better to say, "I was praying for you, and I felt like the Lord impressed me to say this."

2. Prophecy is encouraging.
   The apostle Paul says, "One who prophesies strengthens others, encourages them, and comforts them" (1 Corinthians 14:3). *Encourage* means to put courage in. We can all learn to hear God so He can use us to encourage people.

²⁹But Moses replied, "Are you jealous for my sake? I wish that all the Lord's people were prophets and that the Lord would put his Spirit upon them all!" ³⁰Then Moses returned to the camp with the elders of Israel.

THE LORD SENDS QUAIL
³¹Now the Lord sent a wind that brought quail from the sea and let them fall all around the camp. For miles in every direction there were quail flying about three feet above the ground.* ³²So the people went out and caught quail all that day and throughout the night and all the next day, too. No one gathered less than fifty bushels*! They spread the quail all around the camp to dry. ³³But while they were gorging themselves on the meat—while it was still in their mouths—the anger of the Lord blazed against the people, and he struck them with a severe plague. ³⁴So that place was called Kibroth-hattaavah (which means "graves of gluttony") because there they buried the people who had craved meat from Egypt. ³⁵From Kibroth-hattaavah the Israelites traveled to Hazeroth, where they stayed for some time.

THE COMPLAINTS OF MIRIAM AND AARON
12 While they were at Hazeroth, Miriam and Aaron criticized Moses because he had married a Cushite woman. ²They said, "Has the Lord spoken only through Moses? Hasn't he spoken through us, too?" But the Lord heard them. ³(Now Moses was very humble—more humble than any other person on earth.)

⁴So immediately the Lord called to Moses, Aaron, and Miriam and said, "Go out to the Tabernacle,* all three of you!" So the three of them went to the Tabernacle. ⁵Then the Lord descended in the pillar of cloud and stood at the entrance of the Tabernacle.* "Aaron and Miriam!" he called, and they stepped forward. ⁶And the Lord said to them, "Now listen to what I say:

"If there were prophets among you,
   I, the Lord, would reveal myself in
      visions.
   I would speak to them in dreams.
⁷ But not with my servant Moses.
   Of all my house, he is the one I trust.
⁸ I speak to him face to face,
   clearly, and not in riddles!
   He sees the Lord as he is.
So why were you not afraid
   to criticize my servant Moses?"

⁹The Lord was very angry with them, and he departed. ¹⁰As the cloud moved from above the Tabernacle, there stood Miriam, her skin as white as snow from leprosy.* When Aaron saw what had happened to her, ¹¹he cried out to Moses, "Oh, my master! Please don't punish us for this sin we have so foolishly committed. ¹²Don't let her be like a stillborn baby, already decayed at birth."

¹³So Moses cried out to the Lord, "O God, I beg you, please heal her!"

¹⁴But the Lord said to Moses, "If her father had done nothing more than spit in her face, wouldn't she be defiled for seven days? So keep her outside the camp for seven days, and after that she may be accepted back."

¹⁵So Miriam was kept outside the camp for seven days, and the people waited until she was brought back before they traveled again. ¹⁶Then they left Hazeroth and camped in the wilderness of Paran.

11:31 Or *there were quail about 3 feet* [2 cubits or 92 centimeters] *deep on the ground.*   11:32 Hebrew *10 homers* [2.2 kiloliters].   12:4 Hebrew *the Tent of Meeting.*   12:5 Hebrew *the tent;* also in 12:10.   12:10 Or *with a skin disease.* The Hebrew word used here can describe various skin diseases.

TWELVE SCOUTS EXPLORE CANAAN

13 The Lord now said to Moses, ²"Send out men to explore the land of Canaan, the land I am giving to the Israelites. Send one leader from each of the twelve ancestral tribes." ³So Moses did as the Lord commanded him. He sent out twelve men, all tribal leaders of Israel, from their camp in the wilderness of Paran. ⁴These were the tribes and the names of their leaders:

Tribe	Leader
Reuben	Shammua son of Zaccur
⁵ Simeon	Shaphat son of Hori
⁶ Judah	Caleb son of Jephunneh
⁷ Issachar	Igal son of Joseph
⁸ Ephraim	Hoshea son of Nun
⁹ Benjamin	Palti son of Raphu
¹⁰ Zebulun	Gaddiel son of Sodi
¹¹ Manasseh son of Joseph	Gaddi son of Susi
¹² Dan	Ammiel son of Gemalli
¹³ Asher	Sethur son of Michael
¹⁴ Naphtali	Nahbi son of Vophsi
¹⁵ Gad	Geuel son of Maki

¹⁶These are the names of the men Moses sent out to explore the land. (Moses called Hoshea son of Nun by the name Joshua.)

¹⁷Moses gave the men these instructions as he sent them out to explore the land: "Go north through the Negev into the hill country. ¹⁸See what the land is like, and find out whether the people living there are strong or weak, few or many. ¹⁹See what kind of land they live in. Is it good or bad? Do their towns have walls, or are they unprotected like open camps? ²⁰Is the soil fertile or poor? Are there many trees? Do your best to bring back samples of the crops you see." (It happened to be the season for harvesting the first ripe grapes.)

²¹So they went up and explored the land from the wilderness of Zin as far as Rehob, near Lebo-hamath. ²²Going north, they passed through the Negev and arrived at Hebron, where Ahiman, Sheshai, and Talmai—all descendants of Anak—lived. (The ancient town of Hebron was founded seven years before the Egyptian city of Zoan.) ²³When they came to the valley of Eshcol, they cut down a branch with a single cluster of grapes so large that it took two of them to carry it on a pole between them! They also brought back samples of the pomegranates and figs. ²⁴That place was called the valley of Eshcol (which means "cluster"), because of the cluster of grapes the Israelite men cut there.

THE SCOUTING REPORT

²⁵After exploring the land for forty days, the men returned ²⁶to Moses, Aaron, and the whole community of Israel at Kadesh in the wilderness of Paran. They reported to the whole community what they had seen and showed them the fruit they had taken from the land. ²⁷This was their report to Moses: "We entered the land you sent us to explore, and it is indeed a bountiful country—a land flowing with milk and honey. Here is the kind of fruit it produces. ²⁸But the people living there are powerful, and their towns are large and fortified. We even saw giants there, the descendants of Anak! ²⁹The Amalekites live in the Negev, and the Hittites, Jebusites, and Amorites live in the hill country. The Canaanites live along the coast of the Mediterranean Sea* and along the Jordan Valley."

³⁰But Caleb tried to quiet the people as they stood before Moses. "Let's go at once to take the land," he said. "We can certainly conquer it!"

³¹But the other men who had explored the land with him disagreed. "We can't go up against them! They are stronger than we are!" ³²So they spread this bad report about the land among the Israelites: "The land we traveled through and explored will devour anyone who goes to live there. All the people we saw were huge. ³³We even saw giants* there, the descendants of Anak. Next to them we felt like grasshoppers, and that's what they thought, too!"

THE PEOPLE REBEL

14 Then the whole community began weeping aloud, and they cried all night. ²Their voices rose in a great chorus of protest against Moses and Aaron. "If only we had died in Egypt, or even here in the wilderness!" they complained. ³"Why is the Lord taking us to this country only to have us die in battle? Our wives and our little ones will be carried off as plunder! Wouldn't it be better for us to return to Egypt?" ⁴Then they plotted among themselves, "Let's choose a new leader and go back to Egypt!"

⁵Then Moses and Aaron fell face down on the ground before the whole community of Israel. ⁶Two of the men who had explored the land, Joshua son of Nun and Caleb son of Jephunneh, tore their clothing. ⁷They said to all the people of Israel, "The land we traveled through and explored is a wonderful land! ⁸And if the Lord is pleased with us, he will bring us safely into that land and give it to us. It is a rich land flowing with milk and honey. ⁹Do not rebel against the Lord, and don't be afraid of the people of the land. They are only helpless prey to us! They have no protection, but the Lord is with us! Don't be afraid of them!"

¹⁰But the whole community began to talk about stoning Joshua and Caleb. Then the glorious presence of the Lord appeared to all the Israelites at the Tabernacle.* ¹¹And the Lord said to Moses, "How long will these people treat me with contempt? Will they never believe me, even after all the miraculous signs I have done among them? ¹²I will disown them and destroy them with a plague. Then I will make you into a nation greater and mightier than they are!"

MOSES INTERCEDES FOR THE PEOPLE

¹³ But Moses objected. "What will the Egyptians think when they hear about it?" he asked the LORD. "They know full well the power you displayed in rescuing your people from Egypt. ¹⁴ Now if you destroy them, the Egyptians will send a report to the inhabitants of this land, who have already heard that you live among your people. They know, LORD, that you have appeared to your people face to face and that your pillar of cloud hovers over them. They know that you go before them in the pillar of cloud by day and the pillar of fire by night. ¹⁵ Now if you slaughter all these people with a single blow, the nations that have heard of your fame will say, ¹⁶ 'The LORD was not able to bring them into the land he swore to give them, so he killed them in the wilderness.'

¹⁷ "Please, Lord, prove that your power is as great as you have claimed. For you said, ¹⁸ 'The LORD is slow to anger and filled with unfailing love, forgiving every kind of sin and rebellion. But he does not excuse the guilty. He lays the sins of the parents upon their children; the entire family is affected—even children in the third and fourth generations.' ¹⁹ In keeping with your magnificent, unfailing love, please pardon the sins of this people, just as you have forgiven them ever since they left Egypt."

²⁰ Then the LORD said, "I will pardon them as you have requested. ²¹ But as surely as I live, and as surely as the earth is filled with the LORD's glory, ²² not one of these people will ever enter that land. They have all seen my glorious presence and the miraculous signs I performed both in Egypt and in the wilderness, but again and again they have tested me by refusing to listen to my voice. ²³ They will never even see the land I swore to give their ancestors. None of those who have treated me with contempt will ever see it. ²⁴ But my servant Caleb has a different attitude than the others have. He has remained loyal to me, so I will bring him into the land he explored. His descendants will possess their full share of that land. ²⁵ Now turn around, and don't go on toward the land where the Amalekites and Canaanites live. Tomorrow you must set out for the wilderness in the direction of the Red Sea.*"

THE LORD PUNISHES THE ISRAELITES

²⁶ Then the LORD said to Moses and Aaron, ²⁷ "How long must I put up with this wicked community and its complaints about me? Yes, I have heard the complaints the Israelites are making against me. ²⁸ Now tell them this: 'As surely as I live, declares the LORD, I will do to you the very things I heard you say. ²⁹ You will all drop dead in this wilderness! Because you complained against me, every one of you who is twenty years old or older and was included in the registration will die. ³⁰ You will not enter and occupy the land I swore to give you. The only exceptions will be Caleb son of Jephunneh and Joshua son of Nun.

³¹ "'You said your children would be carried off as plunder. Well, I will bring them safely into the land, and they will enjoy what you have despised. ³² But as for you, you will drop dead in this wilderness. ³³ And your children will be like shepherds, wandering in the wilderness for forty years. In this way, they will pay for your faithlessness, until the last of you lies dead in the wilderness.

³⁴ "'Because your men explored the land for forty days, you must wander in the wilderness for forty years—a year for each day, suffering the consequences of your sins. Then you will discover what it is like to have me for an enemy.' ³⁵ I, the LORD, have spoken! I will certainly do these things to every member of the community who has conspired against me. They will be destroyed here in this wilderness, and here they will die!"

³⁶ The ten men Moses had sent to explore the land—the ones who incited rebellion against the LORD with their bad report—³⁷ were struck dead with a plague before the LORD. ³⁸ Of the twelve who had explored the land, only Joshua and Caleb remained alive.

³⁹ When Moses reported the LORD's words to all the Israelites, the people were filled with grief. ⁴⁰ Then they got up early the next morning and went to the top of the range of hills. "Let's go," they said. "We realize that we have sinned, but now we are ready to enter the land the LORD has promised us."

⁴¹ But Moses said, "Why are you now disobeying the LORD's orders to return to the wilderness? It won't work. ⁴² Do not go up into the land now. You will only be crushed by your enemies because the LORD is not with you. ⁴³ When you face the Amalekites and Canaanites in battle, you will be slaughtered. The LORD will abandon you because you have abandoned the LORD."

⁴⁴ But the people defiantly pushed ahead toward the hill country, even though neither Moses nor the Ark of the LORD's Covenant left the camp. ⁴⁵ Then the Amalekites and the Canaanites who lived in those hills came down and attacked them and chased them back as far as Hormah.

LAWS CONCERNING OFFERINGS

15 Then the LORD told Moses, ² "Give the following instructions to the people of Israel. "When you finally settle in the land I am giving you, ³ you will offer special gifts as a pleasing aroma to the LORD. These gifts may take the form of a burnt offering, a sacrifice to fulfill a vow, a voluntary offering, or an offering at any of your annual festivals, and they may be taken from your herds of cattle or your flocks of sheep and goats. ⁴ When you present these offerings, you must also give the LORD a grain offering of two quarts* of choice flour mixed with one quart* of olive oil. ⁵ For each lamb offered as a

14:25 Hebrew *sea of reeds.* 15:4a Hebrew ¹⁄₁₀ *of an ephah* [2.2 liters]. 15:4b Hebrew ¼ *of a hin* [1 liter]; also in 15:5.

burnt offering or a special sacrifice, you must also present one quart of wine as a liquid offering.

⁶"If the sacrifice is a ram, give a grain offering of four quarts* of choice flour mixed with a third of a gallon* of olive oil, ⁷and give a third of a gallon of wine as a liquid offering. This will be a pleasing aroma to the LORD.

⁸"When you present a young bull as a burnt offering or as a sacrifice to fulfill a vow or as a peace offering to the LORD, ⁹you must also give a grain offering of six quarts* of choice flour mixed with two quarts* of olive oil, ¹⁰and give two quarts of wine as a liquid offering. This will be a special gift, a pleasing aroma to the LORD.

¹¹"Each sacrifice of a bull, ram, lamb, or young goat should be prepared in this way. ¹²Follow these instructions with each offering you present. ¹³All of you native-born Israelites must follow these instructions when you offer a special gift as a pleasing aroma to the LORD. ¹⁴And if any foreigners visit you or live among you and want to present a special gift as a pleasing aroma to the LORD, they must follow these same procedures. ¹⁵Native-born Israelites and foreigners are equal before the LORD and are subject to the same decrees. This is a permanent law for you, to be observed from generation to generation. ¹⁶The same instructions and regulations will apply both to you and to the foreigners living among you."

¹⁷Then the LORD said to Moses, ¹⁸"Give the following instructions to the people of Israel.

"When you arrive in the land where I am taking you, ¹⁹and you eat the crops that grow there, you must set some aside as a sacred offering to the LORD. ²⁰Present a cake from the first of the flour you grind, and set it aside as a sacred offering, as you do with the first grain from the threshing floor. ²¹Throughout the generations to come, you are to present a sacred offering to the LORD each year from the first of your ground flour.

²²"But suppose you unintentionally fail to carry out all these commands that the LORD has given you through Moses. ²³And suppose your descendants in the future fail to do everything the LORD has commanded through Moses. ²⁴If the mistake was made unintentionally, and the community was unaware of it, the whole community must present a young bull for a burnt offering as a pleasing aroma to the LORD. It must be offered along with its prescribed grain offering and liquid offering and with one male goat for a sin offering. ²⁵With it the priest will purify the whole community of Israel, making them right with the LORD,* and they will be forgiven. For it was an unintentional sin, and they have corrected it with their offerings to the LORD— the special gift and the sin offering. ²⁶The whole community of Israel will be forgiven, including the foreigners living among you, for all the people were involved in the sin.

²⁷"If one individual commits an unintentional sin, the guilty person must bring a one-year-old female goat for a sin offering. ²⁸The priest will sacrifice it to purify* the guilty person before the LORD, and that person will be forgiven. ²⁹These same instructions apply both to native-born Israelites and to the foreigners living among you.

³⁰"But those who brazenly violate the LORD's will, whether native-born Israelites or foreigners, have blasphemed the LORD, and they must be cut off from the community. ³¹Since they have treated the LORD's word with contempt and deliberately disobeyed his command, they must be completely cut off and suffer the punishment for their guilt."

PENALTY FOR BREAKING THE SABBATH

³²One day while the people of Israel were in the wilderness, they discovered a man gathering wood on the Sabbath day. ³³The people who found him doing this took him before Moses, Aaron, and the rest of the community. ³⁴They held him in custody because they did not know what to do with him. ³⁵Then the LORD said to Moses, "The man must be put to death! The whole community must stone him outside the camp." ³⁶So the whole community took the man outside the camp and stoned him to death, just as the LORD had commanded Moses.

TASSELS ON CLOTHING

³⁷Then the LORD said to Moses, ³⁸"Give the following instructions to the people of Israel: Throughout the generations to come you must make tassels for the hems of your clothing and attach them with a blue cord. ³⁹When you see the tassels, you will remember and obey all the commands of the LORD instead of following your own desires and defiling yourselves, as you are prone to do. ⁴⁰The tassels will help you remember that you must obey all my commands and be holy to your God. ⁴¹I am the LORD your God who brought you out of the land of Egypt that I might be your God. I am the LORD your God!"

KORAH'S REBELLION

16 One day Korah son of Izhar, a descendant of Kohath son of Levi, conspired with Dathan and Abiram, the sons of Eliab, and On son of Peleth, from the tribe of Reuben. ²They incited a rebellion against Moses, along with 250 other leaders of the community, all prominent members of the assembly. ³They united against Moses and Aaron and said, "You have gone too far! The whole community of Israel has been set apart by the LORD, and he is with all of us. What right do you have to act as though you are greater than the rest of the LORD's people?"

15:6a Hebrew ²⁄₁₀ of an ephah [4.4 liters].　15:6b Hebrew ⅓ of a hin [1.3 liters]; also in 15:7.　15:9a Hebrew ³⁄₁₀ of an ephah [6.6 liters]. 15:9b Hebrew ½ of a hin [2 liters]; also in 15:10.　15:25 Or will make atonement for the whole community of Israel.　15:28 Or to make atonement for.

⁴When Moses heard what they were saying, he fell face down on the ground. ⁵Then he said to Korah and his followers, "Tomorrow morning the LORD will show us who belongs to him* and who is holy. The LORD will allow only those whom he selects to enter his own presence. ⁶Korah, you and all your followers must prepare your incense burners. ⁷Light fires in them tomorrow, and burn incense before the LORD. Then we will see whom the LORD chooses as his holy one. You Levites are the ones who have gone too far!"

⁸Then Moses spoke again to Korah: "Now listen, you Levites! ⁹Does it seem insignificant to you that the God of Israel has chosen you from among all the community of Israel to be near him so you can serve in the LORD's Tabernacle and stand before the people to minister to them? ¹⁰Korah, he has already given this special ministry to you and your fellow Levites. Are you now demanding the priesthood as well? ¹¹The LORD is the one you and your followers are really revolting against! For who is Aaron that you are complaining about him?"

¹²Then Moses summoned Dathan and Abiram, the sons of Eliab, but they replied, "We refuse to come before you! ¹³Isn't it enough that you brought us out of Egypt, a land flowing with milk and honey, to kill us here in this wilderness, and that you now treat us like your subjects? ¹⁴What's more, you haven't brought us into another land flowing with milk and honey. You haven't given us a new homeland with fields and vineyards. Are you trying to fool these men?* We will not come."

¹⁵Then Moses became very angry and said to the LORD, "Do not accept their grain offerings! I have not taken so much as a donkey from them, and I have never hurt a single one of them." ¹⁶And Moses said to Korah, "You and all your followers must come here tomorrow and present yourselves before the LORD. Aaron will also be here. ¹⁷You and each of your 250 followers must prepare an incense burner and put incense on it, so you can all present them before the LORD. Aaron will also bring his incense burner."

¹⁸So each of these men prepared an incense burner, lit the fire, and placed incense on it. Then they all stood at the entrance of the Tabernacle* with Moses and Aaron. ¹⁹Meanwhile, Korah had stirred up the entire community against Moses and Aaron, and they all gathered at the Tabernacle entrance. Then the glorious presence of the LORD appeared to the whole community, ²⁰and the LORD said to Moses and Aaron, ²¹"Get away from all these people so that I may instantly destroy them!"

²²But Moses and Aaron fell face down on the ground. "O God," they pleaded, "you are the God who gives breath to all creatures. Must you be angry with all the people when only one man sins?"

²³And the LORD said to Moses, ²⁴"Then tell all the people to get away from the tents of Korah, Dathan, and Abiram."

²⁵So Moses got up and rushed over to the tents of Dathan and Abiram, followed by the elders of Israel. ²⁶"Quick!" he told the people. "Get away from the tents of these wicked men, and don't touch anything that belongs to them. If you do, you will be destroyed for their sins." ²⁷So all the people stood back from the tents of Korah, Dathan, and Abiram. Then Dathan and Abiram came out and stood at the entrances of their tents, together with their wives and children and little ones.

²⁸And Moses said, "This is how you will know that the LORD has sent me to do all these things that I have done—for I have not done them on my own. ²⁹If these men die a natural death, or if nothing unusual happens, then the LORD has not sent me. ³⁰But if the LORD does something entirely new and the ground opens its mouth and swallows them and all their belongings, and they go down alive into the grave,* then you will know that these men have shown contempt for the LORD."

³¹He had hardly finished speaking the words when the ground suddenly split open beneath them. ³²The earth opened its mouth and swallowed the men, along with their households and all their followers who were standing with them, and everything they owned. ³³So they went down alive into the grave, along with all their belongings. The earth closed over them, and they all vanished from among the people of Israel. ³⁴All the people around them fled when they heard their screams. "The earth will swallow us, too!" they cried. ³⁵Then fire blazed forth from the LORD and burned up the 250 men who were offering incense.

³⁶*And the LORD said to Moses, ³⁷"Tell Eleazar son of Aaron the priest to pull all the incense burners from the fire, for they are holy. Also tell him to scatter the burning coals. ³⁸Take the incense burners of these men who have sinned at the cost of their lives, and hammer the metal into a thin sheet to overlay the altar. Since these burners were used in the LORD's presence, they have become holy. Let them serve as a warning to the people of Israel."

³⁹So Eleazar the priest collected the 250 bronze incense burners that had been used by the men who died in the fire, and the bronze was hammered into a thin sheet to overlay the altar. ⁴⁰This would warn the Israelites that no unauthorized person—no one who was not a descendant of Aaron—should ever enter the LORD's presence to burn incense. If anyone did, the same thing would happen to him as happened to Korah and his followers. So the LORD's instructions to Moses were carried out.

16:5 Greek version reads *God has visited and knows those who are his*. Compare 2 Tim 2:19. 16:14 Hebrew *Are you trying to put out the eyes of these men?* 16:18 Hebrew *the Tent of Meeting*; also in 16:19, 42, 43, 50. 16:30 Hebrew *into Sheol*; also in 16:33. 16:36 Verses 16:36-50 are numbered 17:1-15 in Hebrew text.

⁴¹But the very next morning the whole community of Israel began muttering again against Moses and Aaron, saying, "You have killed the LORD's people!" ⁴²As the community gathered to protest against Moses and Aaron, they turned toward the Tabernacle and saw that the cloud had covered it, and the glorious presence of the LORD appeared.

⁴³Moses and Aaron came and stood in front of the Tabernacle, ⁴⁴and the LORD said to Moses, ⁴⁵"Get away from all these people so that I can instantly destroy them!" But Moses and Aaron fell face down on the ground.

⁴⁶And Moses said to Aaron, "Quick, take an incense burner and place burning coals on it from the altar. Lay incense on it, and carry it out among the people to purify them and make them right with the LORD.* The LORD's anger is blazing against them—the plague has already begun."

⁴⁷Aaron did as Moses told him and ran out among the people. The plague had already begun to strike down the people, but Aaron burned the incense and purified* the people. ⁴⁸He stood between the dead and the living, and the plague stopped. ⁴⁹But 14,700 people died in that plague, in addition to those who had died in the affair involving Korah. ⁵⁰Then because the plague had stopped, Aaron returned to Moses at the entrance of the Tabernacle.

THE BUDDING OF AARON'S STAFF

17 ¹*Then the LORD said to Moses, ²"Tell the people of Israel to bring you twelve wooden staffs, one from each leader of Israel's ancestral tribes, and inscribe each leader's name on his staff. ³Inscribe Aaron's name on the staff of the tribe of Levi, for there must be one staff for the leader of each ancestral tribe. ⁴Place these staffs in the Tabernacle in front of the Ark containing the tablets of the Covenant,* where I meet with you. ⁵Buds will sprout on the staff belonging to the man I choose. Then I will finally put an end to the people's murmuring and complaining against you."

⁶So Moses gave the instructions to the people of Israel, and each of the twelve tribal leaders, including Aaron, brought Moses a staff. ⁷Moses placed the staffs in the LORD's presence in the Tabernacle of the Covenant.* ⁸When he went into the Tabernacle of the Covenant the next day, he found that Aaron's staff, representing the tribe of Levi, had sprouted, budded, blossomed, and produced ripe almonds!

⁹When Moses brought all the staffs out from the LORD's presence, he showed them to the people. Each man claimed his own staff. ¹⁰And the LORD said to Moses: "Place Aaron's staff permanently before the Ark of the Covenant* to serve as a warning to rebels. This should put an end to their complaints against me and prevent any further deaths." ¹¹So Moses did as the LORD commanded him.

¹²Then the people of Israel said to Moses, "Look, we are doomed! We are dead! We are ruined! ¹³Everyone who even comes close to the Tabernacle of the LORD dies. Are we all doomed to die?"

DUTIES OF PRIESTS AND LEVITES

18 Then the LORD said to Aaron: "You, your sons, and your relatives from the tribe of Levi will be held responsible for any offenses related to the sanctuary. But you and your sons alone will be held responsible for violations connected with the priesthood.

²"Bring your relatives of the tribe of Levi—your ancestral tribe—to assist you and your sons as you perform the sacred duties in front of the Tabernacle of the Covenant.* ³But as the Levites go about all their assigned duties at the Tabernacle, they must be careful not to go near any of the sacred objects or the altar. If they do, both you and they will die. ⁴The Levites must join you in fulfilling their responsibilities for the care and maintenance of the Tabernacle,* but no unauthorized person may assist you.

⁵"You yourselves must perform the sacred duties inside the sanctuary and at the altar. If you follow these instructions, the LORD's anger will never again blaze against the people of Israel. ⁶I myself have chosen your fellow Levites from among the Israelites to be your special assistants. They are a gift to you, dedicated to the LORD for service in the Tabernacle. ⁷But you and your sons, the priests, must personally handle all the priestly rituals associated with the altar and with everything behind the inner curtain. I am giving you the priesthood as your special privilege of service. Any unauthorized person who comes too near the sanctuary will be put to death."

SUPPORT FOR THE PRIESTS AND LEVITES

⁸The LORD gave these further instructions to Aaron: "I myself have put you in charge of all the holy offerings that are brought to me by the people of Israel. I have given all these consecrated offerings to you and your sons as your permanent share. ⁹You are allotted the portion of the most holy offerings that is not burned on the fire. This portion of all the most holy offerings—including the grain offerings, sin offerings, and guilt offerings—will be most holy, and it belongs to you and your sons. ¹⁰You must eat it as a most holy offering. All the males may eat of it, and you must treat it as most holy.

16:46 Or *to make atonement for them.* 16:47 Or *and made atonement for.* 17:1 Verses 17:1-13 are numbered 17:16-28 in Hebrew text. 17:4 Hebrew *in the Tent of Meeting before the Testimony.* The Hebrew word for "testimony" refers to the terms of the LORD's covenant with Israel as written on stone tablets, which were kept in the Ark, and also to the covenant itself. 17:7 Or *Tabernacle of the Testimony;* also in 17:8. 17:10 Hebrew *before the Testimony;* see note on 17:4. 18:2 Or *Tabernacle of the Testimony.* 18:4 Hebrew *the Tent of Meeting;* also in 18:6, 21, 22, 23, 31.

[11] "All the sacred offerings and special offerings presented to me when the Israelites lift them up before the altar also belong to you. I have given them to you and to your sons and daughters as your permanent share. Any member of your family who is ceremonially clean may eat of these offerings.

[12] "I also give you the harvest gifts brought by the people as offerings to the LORD—the best of the olive oil, new wine, and grain. [13] All the first crops of their land that the people present to the LORD belong to you. Any member of your family who is ceremonially clean may eat this food.

[14] "Everything in Israel that is specially set apart for the LORD* also belongs to you.

[15] "The firstborn of every mother, whether human or animal, that is offered to the LORD will be yours. But you must always redeem your firstborn sons and the firstborn of ceremonially unclean animals. [16] Redeem them when they are one month old. The redemption price is five pieces of silver* (as measured by the weight of the sanctuary shekel, which equals twenty gerahs).

[17] "However, you may not redeem the firstborn of cattle, sheep, or goats. They are holy and have been set apart for the LORD. Sprinkle their blood on the altar, and burn their fat as a special gift, a pleasing aroma to the LORD. [18] The meat of these animals will be yours, just like the breast and right thigh that are presented by lifting them up as a special offering before the altar. [19] Yes, I am giving you all these holy offerings that the people of Israel bring to the LORD. They are for you and your sons and daughters, to be eaten as your permanent share. This is an eternal and unbreakable covenant* between the LORD and you, and it also applies to your descendants."

[20] And the LORD said to Aaron, "You priests will receive no allotment of land or share of property among the people of Israel. I am your share and your allotment. [21] As for the tribe of Levi, your relatives, I will compensate them for their service in the Tabernacle. Instead of an allotment of land, I will give them the tithes from the entire land of Israel.

[22] "From now on, no Israelites except priests or Levites may approach the Tabernacle. If they come too near, they will be judged guilty and will die. [23] Only the Levites may serve at the Tabernacle, and they will be held responsible for any offenses against it. This is a permanent law for you, to be observed from generation to generation. The Levites will receive no allotment of land among the Israelites, [24] because I have given them the Israelites' tithes, which have been presented as sacred offerings to the LORD. This will be the Levites' share. That is why I said they would receive no allotment of land among the Israelites."

[25] The LORD also told Moses, [26] "Give these instructions to the Levites: When you receive from the people of Israel the tithes I have assigned as your allotment, give a tenth of the tithes you receive—a tithe of the tithe—to the LORD as a sacred offering. [27] The LORD will consider this offering to be your harvest offering, as though it were the first grain from your own threshing floor or wine from your own winepress. [28] You must present one-tenth of the tithe received from the Israelites as a sacred offering to the LORD. This is the LORD's sacred portion, and you must present it to Aaron the priest. [29] Be sure to give to the LORD the best portions of the gifts given to you.

[30] "Also, give these instructions to the Levites: When you present the best part as your offering, it will be considered as though it came from your own threshing floor or winepress. [31] You Levites and your families may eat this food anywhere you wish, for it is your compensation for serving in the Tabernacle. [32] You will not be considered guilty for accepting the LORD's tithes if you give the best portion to the priests. But be careful not to treat the holy gifts of the people of Israel as though they were common. If you do, you will die."

THE WATER OF PURIFICATION

19 The LORD said to Moses and Aaron, [2] "Here is another legal requirement commanded by the LORD: Tell the people of Israel to bring you a red heifer, a perfect animal that has no defects and has never been yoked to a plow. [3] Give it to Eleazar the priest, and it will be taken outside the camp and slaughtered in his presence. [4] Eleazar will take some of its blood on his finger and sprinkle it seven times toward the front of the Tabernacle.* [5] As Eleazar watches, the heifer must be burned—its hide, meat, blood, and dung. [6] Eleazar the priest must then take a stick of cedar,* a hyssop branch, and some scarlet yarn and throw them into the fire where the heifer is burning.

[7] "Then the priest must wash his clothes and bathe himself in water. Afterward he may return to the camp, though he will remain ceremonially unclean until evening. [8] The man who burns the animal must also wash his clothes and bathe himself in water, and he, too, will remain unclean until evening. [9] Then someone who is ceremonially clean will gather up the ashes of the heifer and deposit them in a purified place outside the camp. They will be kept there for the community of Israel to use in the water for the purification ceremony. This ceremony is performed for the removal of sin. [10] The man who gathers up the ashes of the heifer must also wash his clothes, and he will remain ceremonially unclean until evening. This is a permanent law

---

18:14 The Hebrew term used here refers to the complete consecration of things or people to the LORD, either by destroying them or by giving them as an offering. 18:16 Hebrew 5 shekels [2 ounces or 57 grams] of silver. 18:19 Hebrew a covenant of salt. 19:4 Hebrew the Tent of Meeting. 19:6 Or juniper.

for the people of Israel and any foreigners who live among them.

[11] "All those who touch a dead human body will be ceremonially unclean for seven days. [12] They must purify themselves on the third and seventh days with the water of purification; then they will be purified. But if they do not do this on the third and seventh days, they will continue to be unclean even after the seventh day. [13] All those who touch a dead body and do not purify themselves in the proper way defile the LORD's Tabernacle, and they will be cut off from the community of Israel. Since the water of purification was not sprinkled on them, their defilement continues.

[14] "This is the ritual law that applies when someone dies inside a tent: All those who enter that tent and those who were inside when the death occurred will be ceremonially unclean for seven days. [15] Any open container in the tent that was not covered with a lid is also defiled. [16] And if someone in an open field touches the corpse of someone who was killed with a sword or who died a natural death, or if someone touches a human bone or a grave, that person will be defiled for seven days.

[17] "To remove the defilement, put some of the ashes from the burnt purification offering in a jar, and pour fresh water over them. [18] Then someone who is ceremonially clean must take a hyssop branch and dip it into the water. That person must sprinkle the water on the tent, on all the furnishings in the tent, and on the people who were in the tent; also on the person who touched a human bone, or touched someone who was killed or who died naturally, or touched a grave. [19] On the third and seventh days the person who is ceremonially clean must sprinkle the water on those who are defiled. Then on the seventh day the people being cleansed must wash their clothes and bathe themselves, and that evening they will be cleansed of their defilement.

[20] "But those who become defiled and do not purify themselves will be cut off from the community, for they have defiled the sanctuary of the LORD. Since the water of purification has not been sprinkled on them, they remain defiled. [21] This is a permanent law for the people. Those who sprinkle the water of purification must afterward wash their clothes, and anyone who then touches the water used for purification will remain defiled until evening. [22] Anything and anyone that a defiled person touches will be ceremonially unclean until evening."

MOSES STRIKES THE ROCK

20 In the first month of the year,* the whole community of Israel arrived in the wilderness of Zin and camped at Kadesh. While they were there, Miriam died and was buried.

[2] There was no water for the people to drink at that place, so they rebelled against Moses and Aaron. [3] The people blamed Moses and said, "If only we had died in the LORD's presence with our brothers! [4] Why have you brought the congregation of the LORD's people into this wilderness to die, along with all our livestock? [5] Why did you make us leave Egypt and bring us here to this terrible place? This land has no grain, no figs, no grapes, no pomegranates, and no water to drink!"

[6] Moses and Aaron turned away from the people and went to the entrance of the Tabernacle,* where they fell face down on the ground. Then the glorious presence of the LORD appeared to them, [7] and the LORD said to Moses, [8] "You and Aaron must take the staff and assemble the entire community. As the people watch, speak to the rock over there, and it will pour out its water. You will provide enough water from the rock to satisfy the whole community and their livestock."

[9] So Moses did as he was told. He took the staff from the place where it was kept before the LORD. [10] Then he and Aaron summoned the people to come and gather at the rock. "Listen, you rebels!" he shouted. "Must we bring you water from this rock?" [11] Then Moses raised his hand and struck the rock twice with the staff, and water gushed out. So the entire community and their livestock drank their fill.

[12] But the LORD said to Moses and Aaron, "Because you did not trust me enough to demonstrate my holiness to the people of Israel, you will not lead them into the land I am giving them!" [13] This place was known as the waters of Meribah (which means "arguing") because there the people of Israel argued with the LORD, and there he demonstrated his holiness among them.

EDOM REFUSES ISRAEL PASSAGE

[14] While Moses was at Kadesh, he sent ambassadors to the king of Edom with this message:

"This is what your relatives, the people of Israel, say: You know all the hardships we have been through. [15] Our ancestors went down to Egypt, and we lived there a long time, and we and our ancestors were brutally mistreated by the Egyptians. [16] But when we cried out to the LORD, he heard us and sent an angel who brought us out of Egypt. Now we are camped at Kadesh, a town on the border of your land. [17] Please let us travel through your land. We will be careful not to go through your fields and vineyards. We won't even drink water from your wells. We will stay on the king's road and never leave it until we have passed through your territory."

20:1 The first month of the ancient Hebrew lunar calendar usually occurs within the months of March and April. The number of years since leaving Egypt is not specified.
20:6 Hebrew the Tent of Meeting.

18 But the king of Edom said, "Stay out of my land, or I will meet you with an army!" 19 The Israelites answered, "We will stay on the main road. If our livestock drink your water, we will pay for it. Just let us pass through your country. That's all we ask." 20 But the king of Edom replied, "Stay out! You may not pass through our land." With that he mobilized his army and marched out against them with an imposing force. 21 Because Edom refused to allow Israel to pass through their country, Israel was forced to turn around.

THE DEATH OF AARON

22 The whole community of Israel left Kadesh and arrived at Mount Hor. 23 There, on the border of the land of Edom, the Lord said to Moses and Aaron, 24 "The time has come for Aaron to join his ancestors in death. He will not enter the land I am giving the people of Israel, because the two of you rebelled against my instructions concerning the water at Meribah. 25 Now take Aaron and his son Eleazar up Mount Hor. 26 There you will remove Aaron's priestly garments and put them on Eleazar, his son. Aaron will die there and join his ancestors."

27 So Moses did as the Lord commanded. The three of them went up Mount Hor together as the whole community watched. 28 At the summit, Moses removed the priestly garments from Aaron and put them on Eleazar, Aaron's son. Then Aaron died there on top of the mountain, and Moses and Eleazar went back down. 29 When the people realized that Aaron had died, all Israel mourned for him thirty days.

VICTORY OVER THE CANAANITES

21 The Canaanite king of Arad, who lived in the Negev, heard that the Israelites were approaching on the road through Atharim. So he attacked the Israelites and took some of them as prisoners. 2 Then the people of Israel made this vow to the Lord: "If you will hand these people over to us, we will completely destroy* all their towns." 3 The Lord heard the Israelites' request and gave them victory over the Canaanites. The Israelites completely destroyed them and their towns, and the place has been called Hormah* ever since.

THE BRONZE SNAKE

4 Then the people of Israel set out from Mount Hor, taking the road to the Red Sea* to go around the land of Edom. But the people grew impatient with the long journey, 5 and they began to speak against God and Moses. "Why have you brought us out of Egypt to die here in the wilderness?" they complained. "There is nothing to eat here and nothing to drink. And we hate this horrible manna!"

6 So the Lord sent poisonous snakes among the people, and many were bitten and died.

7 Then the people came to Moses and cried out, "We have sinned by speaking against the Lord and against you. Pray that the Lord will take away the snakes." So Moses prayed for the people. 8 Then the Lord told him, "Make a replica of a poisonous snake and attach it to a pole. All who are bitten will live if they simply look at it!" 9 So Moses made a snake out of bronze and attached it to a pole. Then anyone who was bitten by a snake could look at the bronze snake and be healed!

ISRAEL'S JOURNEY TO MOAB

10 The Israelites traveled next to Oboth and camped there. 11 Then they went on to Iye-abarim, in the wilderness on the eastern border of Moab. 12 From there they traveled to the valley of Zered Brook and set up camp. 13 Then they moved out and camped on the far side of the Arnon River, in the wilderness adjacent to the territory of the Amorites. The Arnon is the boundary line between the Moabites and the Amorites. 14 For this reason The Book of the Wars of the Lord speaks of "the town of Waheb in the area of Suphah, and the ravines of the Arnon River, 15 and the ravines that extend as far as the settlement of Ar on the border of Moab."

16 From there the Israelites traveled to Beer,* which is the well where the Lord said to Moses, "Assemble the people, and I will give them water." 17 There the Israelites sang this song:

"Spring up, O well!
    Yes, sing its praises!
18 Sing of this well,
    which princes dug,
    which great leaders hollowed out
    with their scepters and staffs."

Then the Israelites left the wilderness and proceeded on through Mattanah, 19 Nahaliel, and Bamoth. 20 After that they went to the valley in Moab where Pisgah Peak overlooks the wasteland.*

VICTORY OVER SIHON AND OG

21 The Israelites sent ambassadors to King Sihon of the Amorites with this message:

22 "Let us travel through your land. We will be careful not to go through your fields and vineyards. We won't even drink water from your wells. We will stay on the king's road until we have passed through your territory."

23 But King Sihon refused to let them cross his territory. Instead, he mobilized his entire army and attacked Israel in the wilderness, engaging

---

21:2 The Hebrew term used here refers to the complete consecration of things or people to the Lord, either by destroying them or by giving them as an offering; also in 21:3. 21:3 Hormah means "destruction." 21:4 Hebrew sea of reeds. 21:16 Beer means "well." 21:20 Or overlooks Jeshimon.

them in battle at Jahaz. ²⁴ But the Israelites slaughtered them with their swords and occupied their land from the Arnon River to the Jabbok River. They went only as far as the Ammonite border because the boundary of the Ammonites was fortified.*

²⁵ So Israel captured all the towns of the Amorites and settled in them, including the city of Heshbon and its surrounding villages. ²⁶ Heshbon had been the capital of King Sihon of the Amorites. He had defeated a former Moabite king and seized all his land as far as the Arnon River. ²⁷ Therefore, the ancient poets wrote this about him:

"Come to Heshbon and let it be rebuilt!
    Let the city of Sihon be restored.
²⁸ A fire flamed forth from Heshbon,
    a blaze from the city of Sihon.
It burned the city of Ar in Moab;
    it destroyed the rulers of the Arnon
        heights.
²⁹ What sorrow awaits you, O people of Moab!
    You are finished, O worshipers of
        Chemosh!
Chemosh has left his sons as refugees,
    his daughters as captives of Sihon, the
        Amorite king.
³⁰ We have utterly destroyed them,
    from Heshbon to Dibon.
We have completely wiped them out
    as far away as Nophah and Medeba.*"

³¹ So the people of Israel occupied the territory of the Amorites. ³² After Moses sent men to explore the Jazer area, they captured all the towns in the region and drove out the Amorites who lived there. ³³ Then they turned and marched up the road to Bashan, but King Og of Bashan and all his people attacked them at Edrei. ³⁴ The LORD said to Moses, "Do not be afraid of him, for I have handed him over to you, along with all his people and his land. Do the same to him as you did to King Sihon of the Amorites, who ruled in Heshbon." ³⁵ And Israel killed King Og, his sons, and all his subjects; not a single survivor remained. Then Israel occupied their land.

BALAK SENDS FOR BALAAM

22 Then the people of Israel traveled to the plains of Moab and camped east of the Jordan River, across from Jericho. ² Balak son of Zippor, the Moabite king, had seen everything the Israelites did to the Amorites. ³ And when the people of Moab saw how many Israelites there were, they were terrified. ⁴ The king of Moab said to the elders of Midian, "This mob will devour everything in sight, like an ox devours grass in the field!"

So Balak, king of Moab, ⁵ sent messengers to call Balaam son of Beor, who was living in his native land of Pethor* near the Euphrates River.* His message said:

"Look, a vast horde of people has arrived from Egypt. They cover the face of the earth and are threatening me. ⁶ Please come and curse these people for me because they are too powerful for me. Then perhaps I will be able to conquer them and drive them from the land. I know that blessings fall on any people you bless, and curses fall on people you curse."

⁷ Balak's messengers, who were elders of Moab and Midian, set out with money to pay Balaam to place a curse upon Israel.* They went to Balaam and delivered Balak's message to him. ⁸ "Stay here overnight," Balaam said. "In the morning I will tell you whatever the LORD directs me to say." So the officials from Moab stayed there with Balaam.

⁹ That night God came to Balaam and asked him, "Who are these men visiting you?"

¹⁰ Balaam said to God, "Balak son of Zippor, king of Moab, has sent me this message: ¹¹ 'Look, a vast horde of people has arrived from Egypt, and they cover the face of the earth. Come and curse these people for me. Then perhaps I will be able to stand up to them and drive them from the land.'"

¹² But God told Balaam, "Do not go with them. You are not to curse these people, for they have been blessed!"

¹³ The next morning Balaam got up and told Balak's officials, "Go on home! The LORD will not let me go with you."

¹⁴ So the Moabite officials returned to King Balak and reported, "Balaam refused to come with us." ¹⁵ Then Balak tried again. This time he sent a larger number of even more distinguished officials than those he had sent the first time. ¹⁶ They went to Balaam and delivered this message to him:

"This is what Balak son of Zippor says:
Please don't let anything stop you from coming to help me. ¹⁷ I will pay you very well and do whatever you tell me. Just come and curse these people for me!"

¹⁸ But Balaam responded to Balak's messengers, "Even if Balak were to give me his palace filled with silver and gold, I would be powerless to do anything against the will of the LORD my God. ¹⁹ But stay here one more night, and I will see if the LORD has anything else to say to me."

²⁰ That night God came to Balaam and told him, "Since these men have come for you, get up and go with them. But do only what I tell you to do."

21:24 Or because the terrain of the Ammonite frontier was rugged; Hebrew reads because the boundary of the Ammonites was strong. 21:30 Or until fire spread to Medeba. The meaning of the Hebrew is uncertain. 22:5a Or who was at Pethor in the land of the Amavites. 22:5b Hebrew the river. 22:7 Hebrew set out with the money of divination in their hand.

BALAAM AND HIS DONKEY

²¹ So the next morning Balaam got up, saddled his donkey, and started off with the Moabite officials. ²² But God was angry that Balaam was going, so he sent the angel of the Lord to stand in the road to block his way. As Balaam and two servants were riding along, ²³ Balaam's donkey saw the angel of the Lord standing in the road with a drawn sword in his hand. The donkey bolted off the road into a field, but Balaam beat it and turned it back onto the road. ²⁴ Then the angel of the Lord stood at a place where the road narrowed between two vineyard walls. ²⁵ When the donkey saw the angel of the Lord, it tried to squeeze by and crushed Balaam's foot against the wall. So Balaam beat the donkey again. ²⁶ Then the angel of the Lord moved farther down the road and stood in a place too narrow for the donkey to get by at all. ²⁷ This time when the donkey saw the angel, it lay down under Balaam. In a fit of rage Balaam beat the animal again with his staff.

²⁸ Then the Lord gave the donkey the ability to speak. "What have I done to you that deserves your beating me three times?" it asked Balaam.

²⁹ "You have made me look like a fool!" Balaam shouted. "If I had a sword with me, I would kill you!"

³⁰ "But I am the same donkey you have ridden all your life," the donkey answered. "Have I ever done anything like this before?"

"No," Balaam admitted.

³¹ Then the Lord opened Balaam's eyes, and he saw the angel of the Lord standing in the roadway with a drawn sword in his hand. Balaam bowed his head and fell face down on the ground before him.

³² "Why did you beat your donkey those three times?" the angel of the Lord demanded. "Look, I have come to block your way because you are stubbornly resisting me. ³³ Three times the donkey saw me and shied away; otherwise, I would certainly have killed you by now and spared the donkey."

³⁴ Then Balaam confessed to the angel of the Lord, "I have sinned. I didn't realize you were standing in the road to block my way. I will return home if you are against my going."

³⁵ But the angel of the Lord told Balaam, "Go with these men, but say only what I tell you to say." So Balaam went on with Balak's officials. ³⁶ When King Balak heard that Balaam was on the way, he went out to meet him at a Moabite town on the Arnon River at the farthest border of his land.

³⁷ "Didn't I send you an urgent invitation? Why didn't you come right away?" Balak asked Balaam. "Didn't you believe me when I said I would reward you richly?"

³⁸ Balaam replied, "Look, now I have come, but I have no power to say whatever I want. I will speak only the message that God puts in my mouth." ³⁹ Then Balaam accompanied Balak to Kiriath-huzoth, ⁴⁰ where the king sacrificed cattle and sheep. He sent portions of the meat to Balaam and the officials who were with him. ⁴¹ The next morning Balak took Balaam up to Bamoth-baal. From there he could see some of the people of Israel spread out below him.

BALAAM BLESSES ISRAEL

23 Then Balaam said to King Balak, "Build me seven altars here, and prepare seven young bulls and seven rams for me to sacrifice." ² Balak followed his instructions, and the two of them sacrificed a young bull and a ram on each altar.

³ Then Balaam said to Balak, "Stand here by your burnt offerings, and I will go to see if the Lord will respond to me. Then I will tell you whatever he reveals to me." So Balaam went alone to the top of a bare hill, ⁴ and God met him there. Balaam said to him, "I have prepared seven altars and have sacrificed a young bull and a ram on each altar."

⁵ The Lord gave Balaam a message for King Balak. Then he said, "Go back to Balak and give him my message."

⁶ So Balaam returned and found the king standing beside his burnt offerings with all the officials of Moab. ⁷ This was the message Balaam delivered:

"Balak summoned me to come from Aram;
  the king of Moab brought me from the
    eastern hills.
'Come,' he said, 'curse Jacob for me!
  Come and announce Israel's doom.'
⁸ But how can I curse those
  whom God has not cursed?
How can I condemn those
  whom the Lord has not condemned?
⁹ I see them from the cliff tops;
  I watch them from the hills.
I see a people who live by themselves,
  set apart from other nations.
¹⁰ Who can count Jacob's descendants, as
    numerous as dust?
  Who can count even a fourth of Israel's
    people?
Let me die like the righteous;
  let my life end like theirs."

¹¹ Then King Balak demanded of Balaam, "What have you done to me? I brought you to curse my enemies. Instead, you have blessed them!"

¹² But Balaam replied, "I will speak only the message that the Lord puts in my mouth."

BALAAM'S SECOND MESSAGE

¹³ Then King Balak told him, "Come with me to another place. There you will see another part of the nation of Israel, but not all of them. Curse at least that many!" ¹⁴ So Balak took Balaam to the plateau of Zophim on Pisgah Peak. He built seven altars there and offered a young bull and a ram on each altar.

[15] Then Balaam said to the king, "Stand here by your burnt offerings while I go over there to meet the LORD."

[16] And the LORD met Balaam and gave him a message. Then he said, "Go back to Balak and give him my message."

[17] So Balaam returned and found the king standing beside his burnt offerings with all the officials of Moab. "What did the LORD say?" Balak asked eagerly.

[18] This was the message Balaam delivered:

"Rise up, Balak, and listen!
  Hear me, son of Zippor.
[19] God is not a man, so he does not lie.
  He is not human, so he does not change
    his mind.
Has he ever spoken and failed to act?
  Has he ever promised and not carried it
    through?
[20] Listen, I received a command to bless;
  God has blessed, and I cannot reverse it!
[21] No misfortune is in his plan for Jacob;
  no trouble is in store for Israel.
For the LORD their God is with them;
  he has been proclaimed their king.
[22] God brought them out of Egypt;
  for them he is as strong as a wild ox.
[23] No curse can touch Jacob;
  no magic has any power against Israel.
For now it will be said of Jacob,
  'What wonders God has done
    for Israel!'
[24] These people rise up like a lioness,
  like a majestic lion rousing itself.
They refuse to rest
  until they have feasted on prey,
  drinking the blood of the slaughtered!"

[25] Then Balak said to Balaam, "Fine, but if you won't curse them, at least don't bless them!"

[26] But Balaam replied to Balak, "Didn't I tell you that I can do only what the LORD tells me?"

BALAAM'S THIRD MESSAGE

[27] Then King Balak said to Balaam, "Come, I will take you to one more place. Perhaps it will please God to let you curse them from there." [28] So Balak took Balaam to the top of Mount Peor, overlooking the wasteland.* [29] Balaam again told Balak, "Build me seven altars, and prepare seven young bulls and seven rams for me to sacrifice." [30] So Balak did as Balaam ordered and offered a young bull and a ram on each altar.

24 By now Balaam realized that the LORD was determined to bless Israel, so he did not resort to divination as before. Instead, he turned and looked out toward the wilderness, [2] where he saw the people of Israel camped, tribe by tribe. Then the Spirit of God came upon him, [3] and this is the message he delivered:

"This is the message of Balaam son of Beor,
  the message of the man whose eyes see
    clearly,
[4] the message of one who hears the words
    of God,
  who sees a vision from the Almighty,
  who bows down with eyes wide open:
[5] How beautiful are your tents, O Jacob;
  how lovely are your homes, O Israel!
[6] They spread before me like palm groves,*
  like gardens by the riverside.
They are like tall trees planted by the LORD,
  like cedars beside the waters.
[7] Water will flow from their buckets;
  their offspring have all they need.
Their king will be greater than Agag;
  their kingdom will be exalted.
[8] God brought them out of Egypt;
  for them he is as strong as a wild ox.
He devours all the nations that oppose him,
  breaking their bones in pieces,
  shooting them with arrows.
[9] Like a lion, Israel crouches and lies down;
  like a lioness, who dares to arouse her?
Blessed is everyone who blesses you,
    O Israel,
  and cursed is everyone who curses you."

[10] King Balak flew into a rage against Balaam. He angrily clapped his hands and shouted, "I called you to curse my enemies! Instead, you have blessed them three times. [11] Now get out of here! Go back home! I promised to reward you richly, but the LORD has kept you from your reward."

[12] Balaam told Balak, "Don't you remember what I told your messengers? I said, [13] 'Even if Balak were to give me his palace filled with silver and gold, I would be powerless to do anything against the will of the LORD.' I told you that I could say only what the LORD says! [14] Now I am returning to my own people. But first let me tell you what the Israelites will do to your people in the future."

BALAAM'S FINAL MESSAGES

[15] This is the message Balaam delivered:

"This is the message of Balaam son of Beor,
  the message of the man whose eyes see
    clearly,
[16] the message of one who hears the words
    of God,
  who has knowledge from the Most High,
  who sees a vision from the Almighty,
  who bows down with eyes wide open:
[17] I see him, but not here and now.
  I perceive him, but far in the distant
    future.
A star will rise from Jacob;
  a scepter will emerge from Israel.

23:28 Or *overlooking Jeshimon.*   24:6 Or *like a majestic valley.*

It will crush the heads of Moab's people,
cracking the skulls* of the people of
Sheth.
[18] Edom will be taken over,
and Seir, its enemy, will be conquered,
while Israel marches on in triumph.
[19] A ruler will rise in Jacob
who will destroy the survivors of Ir."

[20] Then Balaam looked over toward the people of Amalek and delivered this message:

"Amalek was the greatest of nations,
but its destiny is destruction!"

[21] Then he looked over toward the Kenites and delivered this message:

"Your home is secure;
your nest is set in the rocks.
[22] But the Kenites will be destroyed
when Assyria* takes you captive."

[23] Balaam concluded his messages by saying:

"Alas, who can survive
unless God has willed it?
[24] Ships will come from the coasts of Cyprus*;
they will oppress Assyria and afflict Eber,
but they, too, will be utterly destroyed."

[25] Then Balaam left and returned home, and Balak also went on his way.

MOAB SEDUCES ISRAEL

25 While the Israelites were camped at Acacia Grove,* some of the men defiled themselves by having* sexual relations with local Moabite women. [2] These women invited them to attend sacrifices to their gods, so the Israelites feasted with them and worshiped the gods of Moab. [3] In this way, Israel joined in the worship of Baal of Peor, causing the LORD's anger to blaze against his people.

[4] The LORD issued the following command to Moses: "Seize all the ringleaders and execute them before the LORD in broad daylight, so his fierce anger will turn away from the people of Israel."

[5] So Moses ordered Israel's judges, "Each of you must put to death the men under your authority who have joined in worshiping Baal of Peor."

[6] Just then one of the Israelite men brought a Midianite woman into his tent, right before the eyes of Moses and all the people, as everyone was weeping at the entrance of the Tabernacle.* [7] When Phinehas son of Eleazar and grandson of Aaron the priest saw this, he jumped up and left the assembly. He took a spear [8] and rushed after the man into his tent. Phinehas thrust the spear all the way through the man's body and into the woman's stomach. So the plague against the Israelites was stopped, [9] but not before 24,000 people had died.

[10] Then the LORD said to Moses, [11] "Phinehas son of Eleazar and grandson of Aaron the priest has turned my anger away from the Israelites by being as zealous among them as I was. So I stopped destroying all Israel as I had intended to do in my zealous anger. [12] Now tell him that I am making my special covenant of peace with him. [13] In this covenant, I give him and his descendants a permanent right to the priesthood, for in his zeal for me, his God, he purified the people of Israel, making them right with me.*"

[14] The Israelite man killed with the Midianite woman was named Zimri son of Salu, the leader of a family from the tribe of Simeon. [15] The woman's name was Cozbi; she was the daughter of Zur, the leader of a Midianite clan.

[16] Then the LORD said to Moses, [17] "Attack the Midianites and destroy them, [18] because they assaulted you with deceit and tricked you into worshiping Baal of Peor, and because of Cozbi, the daughter of a Midianite leader, who was killed at the time of the plague because of what happened at Peor."

THE SECOND REGISTRATION OF ISRAEL'S TROOPS

26 After the plague had ended,* the LORD said to Moses and to Eleazar son of Aaron the priest, [2] "From the whole community of Israel, record the names of all the warriors by their families. List all the men twenty years old or older who are able to go to war."

[3] So there on the plains of Moab beside the Jordan River, across from Jericho, Moses and Eleazar the priest issued these instructions to the leaders of Israel: [4] "List all the men of Israel twenty years old and older, just as the LORD commanded Moses."

This is the record of all the descendants of Israel who came out of Egypt.

THE TRIBE OF REUBEN

[5] These were the clans descended from the sons of Reuben, Jacob's* oldest son:
The Hanochite clan, named after their ancestor Hanoch.
The Palluite clan, named after their ancestor Pallu.
[6] The Hezronite clan, named after their ancestor Hezron.
The Carmite clan, named after their ancestor Carmi.

[7] These were the clans of Reuben. Their registered troops numbered 43,730.

24:17 As in Samaritan Pentateuch; the meaning of the Hebrew word is uncertain. 24:22 Hebrew *Asshur;* also in 24:24. 24:24 Hebrew *Kittim.* 25:1a Hebrew *Shittim.* 25:1b As in Greek version; Hebrew reads *some of the men began having.* 25:6 Hebrew *the Tent of Meeting.* 25:13 Or *he made atonement for the people of Israel.* 26:1 The initial phrase in verse 26:1 is numbered 25:19 in Hebrew text. 26:5 Hebrew *Israel's;* see note on 1:20-21b.

[8] Pallu was the ancestor of Eliab, [9] and Eliab was the father of Nemuel, Dathan, and Abiram. This Dathan and Abiram are the same community leaders who conspired with Korah against Moses and Aaron, rebelling against the LORD. [10] But the earth opened up its mouth and swallowed them with Korah, and fire devoured 250 of their followers. This served as a warning to the entire nation of Israel. [11] However, the sons of Korah did not die that day.

THE TRIBE OF SIMEON

[12] These were the clans descended from the sons of Simeon:

The Jemuelite clan, named after their ancestor Jemuel.*

The Jaminite clan, named after their ancestor Jamin.

The Jakinite clan, named after their ancestor Jakin.

[13] The Zoharite clan, named after their ancestor Zohar.*

The Shaulite clan, named after their ancestor Shaul.

[14] These were the clans of Simeon. Their registered troops numbered 22,200.

THE TRIBE OF GAD

[15] These were the clans descended from the sons of Gad:

The Zephonite clan, named after their ancestor Zephon.

The Haggite clan, named after their ancestor Haggi.

The Shunite clan, named after their ancestor Shuni.

[16] The Oznite clan, named after their ancestor Ozni.

The Erite clan, named after their ancestor Eri.

[17] The Arodite clan, named after their ancestor Arodi.*

The Arelite clan, named after their ancestor Areli.

[18] These were the clans of Gad. Their registered troops numbered 40,500.

THE TRIBE OF JUDAH

[19] Judah had two sons, Er and Onan, who had died in the land of Canaan. [20] These were the clans descended from Judah's surviving sons:

The Shelanite clan, named after their ancestor Shelah.

The Perezite clan, named after their ancestor Perez.

The Zerahite clan, named after their ancestor Zerah.

[21] These were the subclans descended from the Perezites:

The Hezronites, named after their ancestor Hezron.

The Hamulites, named after their ancestor Hamul.

[22] These were the clans of Judah. Their registered troops numbered 76,500.

THE TRIBE OF ISSACHAR

[23] These were the clans descended from the sons of Issachar:

The Tolaite clan, named after their ancestor Tola.

The Puite clan, named after their ancestor Puah.*

[24] The Jashubite clan, named after their ancestor Jashub.

The Shimronite clan, named after their ancestor Shimron.

[25] These were the clans of Issachar. Their registered troops numbered 64,300.

THE TRIBE OF ZEBULUN

[26] These were the clans descended from the sons of Zebulun:

The Seredite clan, named after their ancestor Sered.

The Elonite clan, named after their ancestor Elon.

The Jahleelite clan, named after their ancestor Jahleel.

[27] These were the clans of Zebulun. Their registered troops numbered 60,500.

THE TRIBE OF MANASSEH

[28] Two clans were descended from Joseph through Manasseh and Ephraim.

[29] These were the clans descended from Manasseh:

The Makirite clan, named after their ancestor Makir.

The Gileadite clan, named after their ancestor Gilead, Makir's son.

[30] These were the subclans descended from the Gileadites:

The Iezerites, named after their ancestor Iezer.

The Helekites, named after their ancestor Helek.

[31] The Asrielites, named after their ancestor Asriel.

26:12 As in Syriac version (see also Gen 46:10; Exod 6:15); Hebrew reads *Nemuelite . . . Nemuel*.   26:13 As in parallel texts at Gen 46:10 and Exod 6:15; Hebrew reads *Zerahite . . . Zerah*.   26:17 As in Samaritan Pentateuch and Greek and Syriac versions (see also Gen 46:16); Hebrew reads *Arod*.   26:23 As in Samaritan Pentateuch, Greek and Syriac versions, and Latin Vulgate (see also 1 Chr 7:1); Hebrew reads *The Punite clan, named after its ancestor Puvah*.

The Shechemites, named after their ancestor Shechem.

[32] The Shemidaites, named after their ancestor Shemida.

The Hepherites, named after their ancestor Hepher.

[33] (One of Hepher's descendants, Zelophehad, had no sons, but his daughters' names were Mahlah, Noah, Hoglah, Milcah, and Tirzah.)

[34] These were the clans of Manasseh. Their registered troops numbered 52,700.

THE TRIBE OF EPHRAIM

[35] These were the clans descended from the sons of Ephraim:

The Shuthelahite clan, named after their ancestor Shuthelah.

The Bekerite clan, named after their ancestor Beker.

The Tahanite clan, named after their ancestor Tahan.

[36] This was the subclan descended from the Shuthelahites:

The Eranites, named after their ancestor Eran.

[37] These were the clans of Ephraim. Their registered troops numbered 32,500.

These clans of Manasseh and Ephraim were all descendants of Joseph.

THE TRIBE OF BENJAMIN

[38] These were the clans descended from the sons of Benjamin:

The Belaite clan, named after their ancestor Bela.

The Ashbelite clan, named after their ancestor Ashbel.

The Ahiramite clan, named after their ancestor Ahiram.

[39] The Shuphamite clan, named after their ancestor Shupham.*

The Huphamite clan, named after their ancestor Hupham.

[40] These were the subclans descended from the Belaites:

The Ardites, named after their ancestor Ard.*

The Naamites, named after their ancestor Naaman.

[41] These were the clans of Benjamin. Their registered troops numbered 45,600.

THE TRIBE OF DAN

[42] These were the clans descended from the sons of Dan:

The Shuhamite clan, named after their ancestor Shuham.

[43] These were the Shuhamite clans of Dan. Their registered troops numbered 64,400.

THE TRIBE OF ASHER

[44] These were the clans descended from the sons of Asher:

The Imnite clan, named after their ancestor Imnah.

The Ishvite clan, named after their ancestor Ishvi.

The Beriite clan, named after their ancestor Beriah.

[45] These were the subclans descended from the Beriites:

The Heberites, named after their ancestor Heber.

The Malkielites, named after their ancestor Malkiel.

[46] Asher also had a daughter named Serah.

[47] These were the clans of Asher. Their registered troops numbered 53,400.

THE TRIBE OF NAPHTALI

[48] These were the clans descended from the sons of Naphtali:

The Jahzeelite clan, named after their ancestor Jahzeel.

The Gunite clan, named after their ancestor Guni.

[49] The Jezerite clan, named after their ancestor Jezer.

The Shillemite clan, named after their ancestor Shillem.

[50] These were the clans of Naphtali. Their registered troops numbered 45,400.

RESULTS OF THE REGISTRATION

[51] In summary, the registered troops of all Israel numbered 601,730.

[52] Then the LORD said to Moses, [53] "Divide the land among the tribes, and distribute the grants of land in proportion to the tribes' populations, as indicated by the number of names on the list. [54] Give the larger tribes more land and the smaller tribes less land, each group receiving a grant in proportion to the size of its population. [55] But you must assign the land by lot, and give land to each ancestral tribe according to the number of names on the list. [56] Each grant of land must be assigned by lot among the larger and smaller tribal groups."

26:39 As in some Hebrew manuscripts, Samaritan Pentateuch, Greek and Syriac versions, and Latin Vulgate; most Hebrew manuscripts read *Shephupham*. 26:40 As in Samaritan Pentateuch, some Greek manuscripts, and Latin Vulgate; Hebrew lacks *named after their ancestor Ard*.

THE TRIBE OF LEVI

⁵⁷ This is the record of the Levites who were counted according to their clans:

The Gershonite clan, named after their ancestor Gershon.

The Kohathite clan, named after their ancestor Kohath.

The Merarite clan, named after their ancestor Merari.

⁵⁸ The Libnites, the Hebronites, the Mahlites, the Mushites, and the Korahites were all subclans of the Levites.

Now Kohath was the ancestor of Amram, ⁵⁹ and Amram's wife was named Jochebed. She also was a descendant of Levi, born among the Levites in the land of Egypt. Amram and Jochebed became the parents of Aaron, Moses, and their sister, Miriam. ⁶⁰ To Aaron were born Nadab, Abihu, Eleazar, and Ithamar. ⁶¹ But Nadab and Abihu died when they burned before the LORD the wrong kind of fire, different than he had commanded.

⁶² The men from the Levite clans who were one month old or older numbered 23,000. But the Levites were not included in the registration of the rest of the people of Israel because they were not given an allotment of land when it was divided among the Israelites.

⁶³ So these are the results of the registration of the people of Israel as conducted by Moses and Eleazar the priest on the plains of Moab beside the Jordan River, across from Jericho. ⁶⁴ Not one person on this list had been among those listed in the previous registration taken by Moses and Aaron in the wilderness of Sinai. ⁶⁵ For the LORD had said of them, "They will all die in the wilderness." Not one of them survived except Caleb son of Jephunneh and Joshua son of Nun.

THE DAUGHTERS OF ZELOPHEHAD

27 One day a petition was presented by the daughters of Zelophehad—Mahlah, Noah, Hoglah, Milcah, and Tirzah. Their father, Zelophehad, was a descendant of Hepher son of Gilead, son of Makir, son of Manasseh, son of Joseph. ² These women stood before Moses, Eleazar the priest, the tribal leaders, and the entire community at the entrance of the Tabernacle.* ³ "Our father died in the wilderness," they said. "He was not among Korah's followers, who rebelled against the LORD; he died because of his own sin. But he had no sons. ⁴ Why should the name of our father disappear from his clan just because he had no sons? Give us property along with the rest of our relatives."

⁵ So Moses brought their case before the LORD. ⁶ And the LORD replied to Moses, ⁷ "The claim of the daughters of Zelophehad is legitimate. You must give them a grant of land along with their father's relatives. Assign them the property that would have been given to their father.

⁸ "And give the following instructions to the people of Israel: If a man dies and has no son, then give his inheritance to his daughters. ⁹ And if he has no daughter either, transfer his inheritance to his brothers. ¹⁰ If he has no brothers, give his inheritance to his father's brothers. ¹¹ But if his father has no brothers, give his inheritance to the nearest relative in his clan. This is a legal requirement for the people of Israel, just as the LORD commanded Moses."

JOSHUA CHOSEN TO LEAD ISRAEL

¹² One day the LORD said to Moses, "Climb one of the mountains east of the river,* and look out over the land I have given the people of Israel. ¹³ After you have seen it, you will die like your brother, Aaron, ¹⁴ for you both rebelled against my instructions in the wilderness of Zin. When the people of Israel rebelled, you failed to demonstrate my holiness to them at the waters." (These are the waters of Meribah at Kadesh* in the wilderness of Zin.)

¹⁵ Then Moses said to the LORD, ¹⁶ "O LORD, you are the God who gives breath to all creatures. Please appoint a new man as leader for the community. ¹⁷ Give them someone who will guide them wherever they go and will lead them into battle, so the community of the LORD will not be like sheep without a shepherd."

¹⁸ The LORD replied, "Take Joshua son of Nun, who has the Spirit in him, and lay your hands on him. ¹⁹ Present him to Eleazar the priest before the whole community, and publicly commission him to lead the people. ²⁰ Transfer some of your authority to him so the whole community of Israel will obey him. ²¹ When direction from the LORD is needed, Joshua will stand before Eleazar the priest, who will use the Urim—one of the sacred lots cast before the LORD—to determine his will. This is how Joshua and the rest of the community of Israel will determine everything they should do."

²² So Moses did as the LORD commanded. He presented Joshua to Eleazar the priest and the whole community. ²³ Moses laid his hands on him and commissioned him to lead the people, just as the LORD had commanded through Moses.

THE DAILY OFFERINGS

28 The LORD said to Moses, ² "Give these instructions to the people of Israel: The offerings you present as special gifts are a pleasing aroma to me; they are my food. See to it that they are brought at the appointed times and offered according to my instructions.

27:2 Hebrew the Tent of Meeting.   27:12 Or the mountains of Abarim.   27:14 Hebrew waters of Meribath-kadesh.

³ "Say to the people: This is the special gift you must present to the LORD as your daily burnt offering. You must offer two one-year-old male lambs with no defects. ⁴ Sacrifice one lamb in the morning and the other in the evening. ⁵ With each lamb you must offer a grain offering of two quarts* of choice flour mixed with one quart* of pure oil of pressed olives. ⁶ This is the regular burnt offering instituted at Mount Sinai as a special gift, a pleasing aroma to the LORD. ⁷ Along with it you must present the proper liquid offering of one quart of alcoholic drink with each lamb, poured out in the Holy Place as an offering to the LORD. ⁸ Offer the second lamb in the evening with the same grain offering and liquid offering. It, too, is a special gift, a pleasing aroma to the LORD.

THE SABBATH OFFERINGS

⁹ "On the Sabbath day, sacrifice two one-year-old male lambs with no defects. They must be accompanied by a grain offering of four quarts* of choice flour moistened with olive oil, and a liquid offering. ¹⁰ This is the burnt offering to be presented each Sabbath day, in addition to the regular burnt offering and its accompanying liquid offering.

THE MONTHLY OFFERINGS

¹¹ "On the first day of each month, present an extra burnt offering to the LORD of two young bulls, one ram, and seven one-year-old male lambs, all with no defects. ¹² These must be accompanied by grain offerings of choice flour moistened with olive oil—six quarts* with each bull, four quarts with the ram, ¹³ and two quarts with each lamb. This burnt offering will be a special gift, a pleasing aroma to the LORD. ¹⁴ You must also present a liquid offering with each sacrifice: two quarts* of wine for each bull, a third of a gallon* for the ram, and one quart* for each lamb. Present this monthly burnt offering on the first day of each month throughout the year. ¹⁵ "On the first day of each month, you must also offer one male goat for a sin offering to the LORD. This is in addition to the regular burnt offering and its accompanying liquid offering.

OFFERINGS FOR THE PASSOVER

¹⁶ "On the fourteenth day of the first month,* you must celebrate the LORD's Passover. ¹⁷ On the following day—the fifteenth day of the month—a joyous, seven-day festival will begin, but no bread made with yeast may be eaten. ¹⁸ The first day of the festival will be an official day for holy assembly, and no ordinary work may be done on that day. ¹⁹ As a special gift you must present a burnt offering to the LORD—two young bulls, one ram, and seven one-year-old male lambs, all with no defects. ²⁰ These will be accompanied by grain offerings of choice flour moistened with olive oil—six quarts with

each bull, four quarts with the ram, ²¹ and two quarts with each of the seven lambs. ²² You must also offer a male goat as a sin offering to purify yourselves and make yourselves right with the LORD.* ²³ Present these offerings in addition to your regular morning burnt offering. ²⁴ On each of the seven days of the festival, this is how you must prepare the food offering that is presented as a special gift, a pleasing aroma to the LORD. These will be offered in addition to the regular burnt offerings and liquid offerings. ²⁵ The seventh day of the festival will be another official day for holy assembly, and no ordinary work may be done on that day.

OFFERINGS FOR THE FESTIVAL OF HARVEST

²⁶ "At the Festival of Harvest,* when you present the first of your new grain to the LORD, you must call an official day for holy assembly, and you may do no ordinary work on that day. ²⁷ Present a special burnt offering on that day as a pleasing aroma to the LORD. It will consist of two young bulls, one ram, and seven one-year-old male lambs. ²⁸ These will be accompanied by grain offerings of choice flour moistened with olive oil—six quarts with each bull, four quarts with the ram, ²⁹ and two quarts with each of the seven lambs. ³⁰ Also, offer one male goat to purify yourselves and make yourselves right with the LORD. ³¹ Prepare these special burnt offerings, along with their liquid offerings, in addition to the regular burnt offering and its accompanying grain offering. Be sure that all the animals you sacrifice have no defects.

OFFERINGS FOR THE FESTIVAL OF TRUMPETS

29 "Celebrate the Festival of Trumpets each year on the first day of the appointed month in early autumn.* You must call an official day for holy assembly, and you may do no ordinary work. ² On that day you must present a burnt offering as a pleasing aroma to the LORD. It will consist of one young bull, one ram, and seven one-year-old male lambs, all with no defects. ³ These must be accompanied by grain offerings of choice flour moistened with olive oil—six quarts* with the bull, four quarts* with the ram, ⁴ and two quarts* with each of the seven lambs.

28:5a Hebrew ¹⁄₁₀ of an ephah [2.2 liters]; also in 28:13, 21, 29. 28:5b Hebrew ¼ of a hin [1 liter]; also in 28:7. 28:9 Hebrew ²⁄₁₀ of an ephah [4.4 liters]; also in 28:12, 20, 28. 28:12 Hebrew ³⁄₁₀ of an ephah [6.6 liters]; also in 28:20, 28. 28:14a Hebrew ½ of a hin [2 liters]. 28:14b Hebrew ⅓ of a hin [1.3 liters]. 28:14c Hebrew ¼ of a hin [1 liter]. 28:16 This day in the ancient Hebrew lunar calendar occurred in late March, April, or early May. 28:22 Or to make atonement for yourselves; also in 28:30. 28:26 Hebrew Festival of Weeks. This was later called the Festival of Pentecost (see Acts 2:1). It is celebrated today as Shavuot (or Shabuoth). 29:1 Hebrew the first day of the seventh month. This day in the ancient Hebrew lunar calendar occurred in September or October. This festival is celebrated today as Rosh Hashanah, the Jewish new year. 29:3a Hebrew ³⁄₁₀ of an ephah [6.6 liters]; also in 29:9, 14. 29:3b Hebrew ²⁄₁₀ of an ephah [4.4 liters]; also in 29:9, 14. 29:4 Hebrew ¹⁄₁₀ of an ephah [2.2 liters]; also in 29:10, 15.

⁵ In addition, you must sacrifice a male goat as a sin offering to purify yourselves and make yourselves right with the LORD.* ⁶ These special sacrifices are in addition to your regular monthly and daily burnt offerings, and they must be given with their prescribed grain offerings and liquid offerings. These offerings are given as a special gift to the LORD, a pleasing aroma to him.

OFFERINGS FOR THE DAY OF ATONEMENT

⁷ "Ten days later, on the tenth day of the same month,* you must call another holy assembly. On that day, the Day of Atonement, the people must go without food and must do no ordinary work. ⁸ You must present a burnt offering as a pleasing aroma to the LORD. It will consist of one young bull, one ram, and seven one-year-old male lambs, all with no defects. ⁹ These offerings must be accompanied by the prescribed grain offerings of choice flour moistened with olive oil—six quarts of choice flour with the bull, four quarts of choice flour with the ram, ¹⁰ and two quarts of choice flour with each of the seven lambs. ¹¹ You must also sacrifice one male goat for a sin offering. This is in addition to the sin offering of atonement and the regular daily burnt offering with its grain offering, and their accompanying liquid offerings.

OFFERINGS FOR THE FESTIVAL OF SHELTERS

¹² "Five days later, on the fifteenth day of the same month,* you must call another holy assembly of all the people, and you may do no ordinary work on that day. It is the beginning of the Festival of Shelters,* a seven-day festival to the LORD. ¹³ On the first day of the festival, you must present a burnt offering as a special gift, a pleasing aroma to the LORD. It will consist of thirteen young bulls, two rams, and fourteen one-year-old male lambs, all with no defects. ¹⁴ Each of these offerings must be accompanied by a grain offering of choice flour moistened with olive oil—six quarts for each of the thirteen bulls, four quarts for each of the two rams, ¹⁵ and two quarts for each of the fourteen lambs. ¹⁶ You must also sacrifice a male goat as a sin offering, in addition to the regular burnt offering with its accompanying grain offering and liquid offering.

¹⁷ "On the second day of this seven-day festival, sacrifice twelve young bulls, two rams, and fourteen one-year-old male lambs, all with no defects. ¹⁸ Each of these offerings of bulls, rams, and lambs must be accompanied by its prescribed grain offering and liquid offering. ¹⁹ You must also sacrifice a male goat as a sin offering, in addition to the regular burnt offering with its accompanying grain offering and liquid offering.

²⁰ "On the third day of the festival, sacrifice eleven young bulls, two rams, and fourteen one-year-old male lambs, all with no defects. ²¹ Each of these offerings of bulls, rams, and lambs must be accompanied by its prescribed grain offering and liquid offering. ²² You must also sacrifice a male goat as a sin offering, in addition to the regular burnt offering with its accompanying grain offering and liquid offering.

²³ "On the fourth day of the festival, sacrifice ten young bulls, two rams, and fourteen one-year-old male lambs, all with no defects. ²⁴ Each of these offerings of bulls, rams, and lambs must be accompanied by its prescribed grain offering and liquid offering. ²⁵ You must also sacrifice a male goat as a sin offering, in addition to the regular burnt offering with its accompanying grain offering and liquid offering.

²⁶ "On the fifth day of the festival, sacrifice nine young bulls, two rams, and fourteen one-year-old male lambs, all with no defects. ²⁷ Each of these offerings of bulls, rams, and lambs must be accompanied by its prescribed grain offering and liquid offering. ²⁸ You must also sacrifice a male goat as a sin offering, in addition to the regular burnt offering with its accompanying grain offering and liquid offering.

²⁹ "On the sixth day of the festival, sacrifice eight young bulls, two rams, and fourteen one-year-old male lambs, all with no defects. ³⁰ Each of these offerings of bulls, rams, and lambs must be accompanied by its prescribed grain offering and liquid offering. ³¹ You must also sacrifice a male goat as a sin offering, in addition to the regular burnt offering with its accompanying grain offering and liquid offering.

³² "On the seventh day of the festival, sacrifice seven young bulls, two rams, and fourteen one-year-old male lambs, all with no defects. ³³ Each of these offerings of bulls, rams, and lambs must be accompanied by its prescribed grain offering and liquid offering. ³⁴ You must also sacrifice one male goat as a sin offering, in addition to the regular burnt offering with its accompanying grain offering and liquid offering.

³⁵ "On the eighth day of the festival, proclaim another holy day. You must do no ordinary work on that day. ³⁶ You must present a burnt offering as a special gift, a pleasing aroma to the LORD. It will consist of one young bull, one ram, and seven one-year-old male lambs, all with no defects. ³⁷ Each of these offerings must be accompanied by its prescribed grain offering and liquid offering. ³⁸ You must also sacrifice one male goat as a sin offering, in addition to the regular burnt offering with its accompanying grain offering and liquid offering.

29:5 Or *to make atonement for yourselves.* 29:7 Hebrew *On the tenth day of the seventh month;* see 29:1 and the note there. This day in the ancient Hebrew lunar calendar occurred in September or October. It is celebrated today as Yom Kippur. 29:12a Hebrew *On the fifteenth day of the seventh month;* see 29:1, 7 and the notes there. This day in the ancient Hebrew lunar calendar occurred in late September, October, or early November. 29:12b Or *Festival of Booths,* or *Festival of Tabernacles.* This was earlier called the Festival of the Final Harvest or Festival of Ingathering (see Exod 23:16b). It is celebrated today as Sukkot (or Succoth).

³⁹"You must present these offerings to the LORD at your annual festivals. These are in addition to the sacrifices and offerings you present in connection with vows, or as voluntary offerings, burnt offerings, grain offerings, liquid offerings, or peace offerings."

⁴⁰*So Moses gave all of these instructions to the people of Israel as the LORD had commanded him.

LAWS CONCERNING VOWS

30 ¹*Then Moses summoned the leaders of the tribes of Israel and told them, "This is what the LORD has commanded: ²A man who makes a vow to the LORD or makes a pledge under oath must never break it. He must do exactly what he said he would do.

³"If a young woman makes a vow to the LORD or a pledge under oath while she is still living at her father's home, ⁴and her father hears of the vow or pledge and does not object to it, then all her vows and pledges will stand. ⁵But if her father refuses to let her fulfill the vow or pledge on the day he hears of it, then all her vows and pledges will become invalid. The LORD will forgive her because her father would not let her fulfill them. ⁶"Now suppose a young woman makes a vow or binds herself with an impulsive pledge and later marries. ⁷If her husband learns of her vow or pledge and does not object on the day he hears of it, her vows and pledges will stand. ⁸But if her husband refuses to accept her vow or impulsive pledge on the day he hears of it, he nullifies her commitments, and the LORD will forgive her. ⁹If, however, a woman is a widow or is divorced, she must fulfill all her vows and pledges.

¹⁰"But suppose a woman is married and living in her husband's home when she makes a vow or binds herself with a pledge. ¹¹If her husband hears of it and does not object to it, her vow or pledge will stand. ¹²But if her husband refuses to accept it on the day he hears of it, her vow or pledge will be nullified, and the LORD will forgive her. ¹³So her husband may either confirm or nullify any vows or pledges she makes to deny herself. ¹⁴But if he does not object on the day he hears of it, then he is agreeing to all her vows and pledges. ¹⁵If he waits more than a day and then tries to nullify a vow or pledge, he will be punished for her guilt."

¹⁶These are the regulations the LORD gave Moses concerning relationships between a man and his wife, and between a father and a young daughter who still lives at home.

CONQUEST OF THE MIDIANITES

31 Then the LORD said to Moses, ²"On behalf of the people of Israel, take revenge on the Midianites for leading them into idolatry. After that, you will die and join your ancestors."

³So Moses said to the people, "Choose some men, and arm them to fight the LORD's war of revenge against Midian. ⁴From each tribe of Israel, send 1,000 men into battle." ⁵So they chose 1,000 men from each tribe of Israel, a total of 12,000 men armed for battle. ⁶Then Moses sent them out, 1,000 men from each tribe, and Phinehas son of Eleazar the priest led them into battle. They carried along the holy objects of the sanctuary and the trumpets for sounding the charge. ⁷They attacked Midian as the LORD had commanded Moses, and they killed all the men. ⁸All five of the Midianite kings—Evi, Rekem, Zur, Hur, and Reba—died in the battle. They also killed Balaam son of Beor with the sword.

⁹Then the Israelite army captured the Midianite women and children and seized their cattle and flocks and all their wealth as plunder. ¹⁰They burned all the towns and villages where the Midianites had lived. ¹¹After they had gathered the plunder and captives, both people and animals, ¹²they brought them all to Moses and Eleazar the priest, and to the whole community of Israel, which was camped on the plains of Moab beside the Jordan River, across from Jericho. ¹³Moses, Eleazar the priest, and all the leaders of the community went to meet them outside the camp. ¹⁴But Moses was furious with all the generals and captains* who had returned from the battle.

¹⁵"Why have you let all the women live?" he demanded. ¹⁶"These are the very ones who followed Balaam's advice and caused the people of Israel to rebel against the LORD at Mount Peor. They are the ones who caused the plague to strike the LORD's people. ¹⁷So kill all the boys and all the women who have had intercourse with a man. ¹⁸Only the young girls who are virgins may live; you may keep them for yourselves. ¹⁹And all of you who have killed anyone or touched a dead body must stay outside the camp for seven days. You must purify yourselves and your captives on the third and seventh days. ²⁰Purify all your clothing, too, and everything made of leather, goat hair, or wood."

²¹Then Eleazar the priest said to the men who were in the battle, "The LORD has given Moses this legal requirement: ²²Anything made of gold, silver, bronze, iron, tin, or lead—²³that is, all metals that do not burn—must be passed through fire in order to be made ceremonially pure. These metal objects must then be further purified with the water of purification. But everything that burns must be purified by the water alone. ²⁴On the seventh day you must wash your clothes and be purified. Then you may return to the camp."

DIVISION OF THE PLUNDER

²⁵And the LORD said to Moses, ²⁶"You and Eleazar the priest and the family leaders of each tribe are to make a list of all the plunder taken in the battle, including the people and animals. ²⁷Then

29:40 Verse 29:40 is numbered 30:1 in Hebrew text.
30:1 Verses 30:1-16 are numbered 30:2-17 in Hebrew text.
31:14 Hebrew *the commanders of thousands, and the commanders of hundreds;* also in 31:48, 52, 54.

divide the plunder into two parts, and give half to the men who fought the battle and half to the rest of the people. [28] From the army's portion, first give the Lord his share of the plunder—one of every 500 of the prisoners and of the cattle, donkeys, sheep, and goats. [29] Give this share of the army's half to Eleazar the priest as an offering to the Lord. [30] From the half that belongs to the people of Israel, take one of every fifty of the prisoners and of the cattle, donkeys, sheep, goats, and other animals. Give this share to the Levites, who are in charge of maintaining the Lord's Tabernacle." [31] So Moses and Eleazar the priest did as the Lord commanded Moses.

[32] The plunder remaining from everything the fighting men had taken totaled 675,000 sheep and goats, [33] 72,000 cattle, [34] 61,000 donkeys, [35] and 32,000 virgin girls.

[36] Half of the plunder was given to the fighting men. It totaled 337,500 sheep and goats, [37] of which 675 were the Lord's share; [38] 36,000 cattle, of which 72 were the Lord's share; [39] 30,500 donkeys, of which 61 were the Lord's share; [40] and 16,000 virgin girls, of whom 32 were the Lord's share. [41] Moses gave all the Lord's share to Eleazar the priest, just as the Lord had directed him.

[42] Half of the plunder belonged to the people of Israel, and Moses separated it from the half belonging to the fighting men. [43] It totaled 337,500 sheep and goats, [44] 36,000 cattle, [45] 30,500 donkeys, [46] and 16,000 virgin girls. [47] From the half-share given to the people, Moses took one of every fifty prisoners and animals and gave them to the Levites, who maintained the Lord's Tabernacle. All this was done as the Lord had commanded Moses.

[48] Then all the generals and captains came to Moses [49] and said, "We, your servants, have accounted for all the men who went out to battle under our command; not one of us is missing! [50] So we are presenting the items of gold we captured as an offering to the Lord from our share of the plunder—armbands, bracelets, rings, earrings, and necklaces. This will purify our lives before the Lord and make us right with him.*"

[51] So Moses and Eleazar the priest received the gold from all the military commanders—all kinds of jewelry and crafted objects. [52] In all, the gold that the generals and captains presented as a gift to the Lord weighed about 420 pounds.* [53] All the fighting men had taken some of the plunder for themselves. [54] So Moses and Eleazar the priest accepted the gifts from the generals and captains and brought the gold to the Tabernacle* as a reminder to the Lord that the people of Israel belong to him.

THE TRIBES EAST OF THE JORDAN

32 The tribes of Reuben and Gad owned vast numbers of livestock. So when they saw that the lands of Jazer and Gilead were ideally suited for their flocks and herds, [2] they came to Moses, Eleazar the priest, and the other leaders of the community. They said, [3] "Notice the towns of Ataroth, Dibon, Jazer, Nimrah, Heshbon, Elealeh, Sibmah,* Nebo, and Beon. [4] The Lord has conquered this whole area for the community of Israel, and it is ideally suited for all our livestock. [5] If we have found favor with you, please let us have this land as our property instead of giving us land across the Jordan River."

[6] "Do you intend to stay here while your brothers go across and do all the fighting?" Moses asked the men of Gad and Reuben. [7] "Why do you want to discourage the rest of the people of Israel from going across to the land the Lord has given them? [8] Your ancestors did the same thing when I sent them from Kadesh-barnea to explore the land. [9] After they went up to the valley of Eshcol and explored the land, they discouraged the people of Israel from entering the land the Lord was giving them. [10] Then the Lord was very angry with them, and he vowed, [11] 'Of all those I rescued from Egypt, no one who is twenty years old or older will ever see the land I swore to give to Abraham, Isaac, and Jacob, for they have not obeyed me wholeheartedly. [12] The only exceptions are Caleb son of Jephunneh the Kenizzite and Joshua son of Nun, for they have wholeheartedly followed the Lord.'

[13] "The Lord was angry with Israel and made them wander in the wilderness for forty years until the entire generation that sinned in the Lord's sight had died. [14] But here you are, a brood of sinners, doing exactly the same thing! You are making the Lord even angrier with Israel. [15] If you turn away from him like this and he abandons them again in the wilderness, you will be responsible for destroying this entire nation!"

[16] But they approached Moses and said, "We simply want to build pens for our livestock and fortified towns for our wives and children. [17] Then we will arm ourselves and lead our fellow Israelites into battle until we have brought them safely to their land. Meanwhile, our families will stay in the fortified towns we build here, so they will be safe from any attacks by the local people. [18] We will not return to our homes until all the people of Israel have received their portions of land. [19] But we do not claim any of the land on the other side of the Jordan. We would rather live here on the east side and accept this as our grant of land."

[20] Then Moses said, "If you keep your word and arm yourselves for the Lord's battles, [21] and if your troops cross the Jordan and keep fighting until the Lord has driven out his enemies, [22] then you may return when the Lord has conquered the land. You will have fulfilled your duty to the

31:50 Or will make atonement for our lives before the Lord. 31:52 Hebrew 16,750 shekels [191 kilograms]. 31:54 Hebrew the Tent of Meeting. 32:3 As in Samaritan Pentateuch and Greek version (see also 32:38); Hebrew reads Sebam.

LORD and to the rest of the people of Israel. And the land on the east side of the Jordan will be your property from the LORD. [23] But if you fail to keep your word, then you will have sinned against the LORD, and you may be sure that your sin will find you out. [24] Go ahead and build towns for your families and pens for your flocks, but do everything you have promised."

[25] Then the men of Gad and Reuben replied, "We, your servants, will follow your instructions exactly. [26] Our children, wives, flocks, and cattle will stay here in the towns of Gilead. [27] But all who are able to bear arms will cross over to fight for the LORD, just as you have said."

[28] So Moses gave orders to Eleazar the priest, Joshua son of Nun, and the leaders of the clans of Israel. [29] He said, "The men of Gad and Reuben who are armed for battle must cross the Jordan with you to fight for the LORD. If they do, give them the land of Gilead as their property when the land is conquered. [30] But if they refuse to arm themselves and cross over with you, then they must accept land with the rest of you in the land of Canaan."

[31] The tribes of Gad and Reuben said again, "We are your servants, and we will do as the LORD has commanded! [32] We will cross the Jordan into Canaan fully armed to fight for the LORD, but our property will be here on this side of the Jordan."

[33] So Moses assigned land to the tribes of Gad, Reuben, and half the tribe of Manasseh son of Joseph. He gave them the territory of King Sihon of the Amorites and the land of King Og of Bashan—the whole land with its cities and surrounding lands.

[34] The descendants of Gad built the towns of Dibon, Ataroth, Aroer, [35] Atroth-shophan, Jazer, Jogbehah, [36] Beth-nimrah, and Beth-haran. These were all fortified towns with pens for their flocks.

[37] The descendants of Reuben built the towns of Heshbon, Elealeh, Kiriathaim, [38] Nebo, Baal-meon, and Sibmah. They changed the names of some of the towns they conquered and rebuilt.

[39] Then the descendants of Makir of the tribe of Manasseh went to Gilead and conquered it, and they drove out the Amorites living there. [40] So Moses gave Gilead to the Makirites, descendants of Manasseh, and they settled there. [41] The people of Jair, another clan of the tribe of Manasseh, captured many of the towns in Gilead and changed the name of that region to the Towns of Jair.* [42] Meanwhile, a man named Nobah captured the town of Kenath and its surrounding villages, and he renamed that area Nobah after himself.

REMEMBERING ISRAEL'S JOURNEY

33 This is the route the Israelites followed as they marched out of Egypt under the leadership of Moses and Aaron. [2] At the LORD's direction, Moses kept a written record of their progress. These are the stages of their march, identified by the different places where they stopped along the way.

[3] They set out from the city of Rameses in early spring—on the fifteenth day of the first month*—on the morning after the first Passover celebration. The people of Israel left defiantly, in full view of all the Egyptians. [4] Meanwhile, the Egyptians were burying all their firstborn sons, whom the LORD had killed the night before. The LORD had defeated the gods of Egypt that night with great acts of judgment!

[5] After leaving Rameses, the Israelites set up camp at Succoth.

[6] Then they left Succoth and camped at Etham on the edge of the wilderness.

[7] They left Etham and turned back toward Pi-hahiroth, opposite Baal-zephon, and camped near Migdol.

[8] They left Pi-hahiroth* and crossed the Red Sea* into the wilderness beyond. Then they traveled for three days into the Etham wilderness and camped at Marah.

[9] They left Marah and camped at Elim, where there were twelve springs of water and seventy palm trees.

[10] They left Elim and camped beside the Red Sea.*

[11] They left the Red Sea and camped in the wilderness of Sin.*

[12] They left the wilderness of Sin and camped at Dophkah.

[13] They left Dophkah and camped at Alush.

[14] They left Alush and camped at Rephidim, where there was no water for the people to drink.

[15] They left Rephidim and camped in the wilderness of Sinai.

[16] They left the wilderness of Sinai and camped at Kibroth-hattaavah.

[17] They left Kibroth-hattaavah and camped at Hazeroth.

[18] They left Hazeroth and camped at Rithmah.

[19] They left Rithmah and camped at Rimmon-perez.

[20] They left Rimmon-perez and camped at Libnah.

[21] They left Libnah and camped at Rissah.

[22] They left Rissah and camped at Kehelathah.

[23] They left Kehelathah and camped at Mount Shepher.

[24] They left Mount Shepher and camped at Haradah.

[25] They left Haradah and camped at Makheloth.

32:41 Hebrew *Havvoth-jair.* **33:3** This day in the ancient Hebrew lunar calendar occurred in late March, April, or early May. **33:8a** As in many Hebrew manuscripts, Samaritan Pentateuch, and Latin Vulgate (see also 33:7); most Hebrew manuscripts read *left from in front of Hahiroth.* **33:8b** Hebrew *the sea.* **33:10** Hebrew *sea of reeds;* also in 33:11. **33:11** The geographical name *Sin* is related to *Sinai* and should not be confused with the English word *sin.*

²⁶ They left Makheloth and camped at Tahath.

²⁷ They left Tahath and camped at Terah.

²⁸ They left Terah and camped at Mithcah.

²⁹ They left Mithcah and camped at Hashmonah.

³⁰ They left Hashmonah and camped at Moseroth.

³¹ They left Moseroth and camped at Bene-jaakan.

³² They left Bene-jaakan and camped at Hor-haggidgad.

³³ They left Hor-haggidgad and camped at Jotbathah.

³⁴ They left Jotbathah and camped at Abronah.

³⁵ They left Abronah and camped at Ezion-geber.

³⁶ They left Ezion-geber and camped at Kadesh in the wilderness of Zin.

³⁷ They left Kadesh and camped at Mount Hor, at the border of Edom. ³⁸ While they were at the foot of Mount Hor, Aaron the priest was directed by the LORD to go up the mountain, and there he died. This happened in midsummer, on the first day of the fifth month* of the fortieth year after Israel's departure from Egypt. ³⁹ Aaron was 123 years old when he died there on Mount Hor.

⁴⁰ At that time the Canaanite king of Arad, who lived in the Negev in the land of Canaan, heard that the people of Israel were approaching his land.

⁴¹ Meanwhile, the Israelites left Mount Hor and camped at Zalmonah.

⁴² Then they left Zalmonah and camped at Punon.

⁴³ They left Punon and camped at Oboth.

⁴⁴ They left Oboth and camped at Iye-abarim on the border of Moab.

⁴⁵ They left Iye-abarim* and camped at Dibon-gad.

⁴⁶ They left Dibon-gad and camped at Almon-diblathaim.

⁴⁷ They left Almon-diblathaim and camped in the mountains east of the river,* near Mount Nebo.

⁴⁸ They left the mountains east of the river and camped on the plains of Moab beside the Jordan River, across from Jericho. ⁴⁹ Along the Jordan River they camped from Beth-jeshimoth as far as the meadows of Acacia* on the plains of Moab.

⁵⁰ While they were camped near the Jordan River on the plains of Moab opposite Jericho, the LORD said to Moses, ⁵¹ "Give the following instructions to the people of Israel: When you cross the Jordan River into the land of Canaan, ⁵² you must drive out all the people living there. You must destroy all their carved and molten images and demolish all their pagan shrines. ⁵³ Take possession of the land and settle in it, because I have given it to you to occupy. ⁵⁴ You must distribute the land among the clans by sacred lot and in proportion to their size. A larger portion of land will be allotted to each of the larger clans, and a smaller portion will be allotted to each of the smaller clans. The decision of the sacred lot is final. In this way, the portions of land will be divided among your ancestral tribes. ⁵⁵ But if you fail to drive out the people who live in the land, those who remain will be like splinters in your eyes and thorns in your sides. They will harass you in the land where you live. ⁵⁶ And I will do to you what I had planned to do to them."

BOUNDARIES OF THE LAND

34 Then the LORD said to Moses, ² "Give these instructions to the Israelites: When you come into the land of Canaan, which I am giving you as your special possession, these will be the boundaries. ³ The southern portion of your country will extend from the wilderness of Zin, along the edge of Edom. The southern boundary will begin on the east at the Dead Sea.* ⁴ It will then run south past Scorpion Pass* in the direction of Zin. Its southernmost point will be Kadesh-barnea, from which it will go to Hazar-addar, and on to Azmon. ⁵ From Azmon the boundary will turn toward the Brook of Egypt and end at the Mediterranean Sea.*

⁶ "Your western boundary will be the coastline of the Mediterranean Sea.

⁷ "Your northern boundary will begin at the Mediterranean Sea and run east to Mount Hor, ⁸ then to Lebo-hamath, and on through Zedad ⁹ and Ziphron to Hazar-enan. This will be your northern boundary.

¹⁰ "The eastern boundary will start at Hazar-enan and run south to Shepham, ¹¹ then down to Riblah on the east side of Ain. From there the boundary will run down along the eastern edge of the Sea of Galilee,* ¹² and then along the Jordan River to the Dead Sea. These are the boundaries of your land."

¹³ Then Moses told the Israelites, "This territory is the homeland you are to divide among yourselves by sacred lot. The LORD has commanded that the land be divided among the nine and a half remaining tribes. ¹⁴ The families of the tribes of Reuben, Gad, and half the tribe of Manasseh have already received their grants of land ¹⁵ on the east side of the Jordan River, across from Jericho toward the sunrise."

LEADERS TO DIVIDE THE LAND

¹⁶ And the LORD said to Moses, ¹⁷ "Eleazar the priest and Joshua son of Nun are the men designated to divide the grants of land among the

---

33:38 This day in the ancient Hebrew lunar calendar occurred in July or August.   33:45 As in 33:44; Hebrew reads *Iyim*, another name for Iye-abarim.   33:47 Or *the mountains of Abarim;* also in 33:48.   33:49 Hebrew *as far as Abel-shittim.*   34:3 Hebrew *Salt Sea;* also in 34:12.   34:4 Or *the ascent of Akrabbim.*   34:5 Hebrew *the sea;* also in 34:6, 7.   34:11 Hebrew *Sea of Kinnereth.*

RULES OF REFUGE
Numbers 35:9-21

ROBERT MORRIS

When the people of Israel settled in the Promised Land, God instructed them to "designate six cities of refuge" (Numbers 35:13). If anyone unintentionally killed another person, he could flee to one of these cities and be safe. However, if he left the city of refuge, he forfeited his right of protection.

Every person needs a refuge. Many people turn to food, sex, alcohol, or drugs, but these will never truly protect us. God offers Himself as our refuge, but to remain under His protection, we must understand two things:

1. **Refuge is for the righteous.**
   God told the people of Israel that if they wanted to have their prayers answered and live in peace and safety, they had to be righteous. No one can live up to God's standard of righteousness through their own merit, but through Jesus, God graciously offers us right standing with Him. Believers who want to live under God's refuge must acknowledge their

sin and turn away from it. Refuge is for the person who says, "I want to live my life God's way." When you have this attitude, you're living under His protection.

2. **Refuge is not for the rebellious.**

"But there is no peace for the wicked,"
   says the LORD (Isaiah 48:22).

Even if you're a believer, you will not have peace, joy, or protection if you choose to walk continually in sin. The Lord says if you leave His refuge, the avenger is going to chase you. Do you know who the avenger is? It's God (Deuteronomy 32:35; Romans 12:17-19). When you run away from God, both He *and* the devil will pursue you. The devil wants to bring destruction, but God wants to bring righteousness into your life. Our sins make us guilty of death, but Jesus released us from judgment by dying in our place. He is our Redeemer, and He invites us to take refuge in Him today.

---

people. [18] Enlist one leader from each tribe to help them with the task. [19] These are the tribes and the names of the leaders:

Tribe	Leader
Judah	Caleb son of Jephunneh
[20] Simeon	Shemuel son of Ammihud
[21] Benjamin	Elidad son of Kislon
[22] Dan	Bukki son of Jogli
[23] Manasseh son of Joseph	Hanniel son of Ephod
[24] Ephraim son of Joseph	Kemuel son of Shiphtan
[25] Zebulun	Elizaphan son of Parnach
[26] Issachar	Paltiel son of Azzan
[27] Asher	Ahihud son of Shelomi
[28] Naphtali	Pedahel son of Ammihud

[29] These are the men the LORD has appointed to divide the grants of land in Canaan among the Israelites."

TOWNS FOR THE LEVITES

35 While Israel was camped beside the Jordan on the plains of Moab across from Jericho, the LORD said to Moses, [2] "Command the people of Israel to give to the Levites from their property certain towns to live in, along with the surrounding pasturelands. [3] These towns will be for the Levites to live in, and the surrounding lands will provide pasture for their cattle, flocks, and other livestock. [4] The pastureland assigned to the Levites around these towns will extend 1,500 feet* from the town walls in every direction. [5] Measure off 3,000 feet* outside the town walls in

every direction—east, south, west, north—with the town at the center. This area will serve as the larger pastureland for the towns.

[6] "Six of the towns you give the Levites will be cities of refuge, where a person who has accidentally killed someone can flee for safety. In addition, give them forty-two other towns. [7] In all, forty-eight towns with the surrounding pastureland will be given to the Levites. [8] These towns will come from the property of the people of Israel. The larger tribes will give more towns to the Levites, while the smaller tribes will give fewer. Each tribe will give property in proportion to the size of its land."

CITIES OF REFUGE

[9] The LORD said to Moses, [10] "Give the following instructions to the people of Israel.

"When you cross the Jordan into the land of Canaan, [11] designate cities of refuge to which people can flee if they have killed someone accidentally. [12] These cities will be places of protection from a dead person's relatives who want to avenge the death. The slayer must not be put to death before being tried by the community. [13] Designate six cities of refuge for yourselves, [14] three on the east side of the Jordan River and three on the west in the land of Canaan. [15] These cities are for the protection of Israelites, foreigners living among you, and traveling merchants. Anyone who accidentally kills someone may flee there for safety.

35:4 Hebrew *1,000 cubits* [460 meters].   **35:5** Hebrew *2,000 cubits* [920 meters].

THE RELATIONSHIPS OF REFUGE
Numbers 35:22-33 ROBERT MORRIS

Israel's cities of refuge didn't have walls around them. Instead, they were protected by the people, "the community" (v. 24). The way God protects us and gives us refuge is through *relationships*—with God and with God's people. Sadly, we often seek refuge in possessions, isolation, busyness, and unrighteous relationships. Many people look to religion for comfort, but God did not create us for religion. He created us for relationship.

Have you ever thought, *I wish God would have made the Bible simple?* Actually, He did. In Matthew 22, Jesus gives us the most important commandment: "Love the LORD your God with all your heart, all your soul, and all your mind" (v. 37). He immediately follows this with a second commandment "equally important": "Love your neighbor as yourself" (v. 39). Jesus summarizes the entire Bible in our relationships with God and God's people. Only in these relationships will we find our refuge.

16 "But if someone strikes and kills another person with a piece of iron, it is murder, and the murderer must be executed. 17 Or if someone with a stone in his hand strikes and kills another person, it is murder, and the murderer must be put to death. 18 Or if someone strikes and kills another person with a wooden object, it is murder, and the murderer must be put to death. 19 The victim's nearest relative is responsible for putting the murderer to death. When they meet, the avenger must put the murderer to death. 20 So if someone hates another person and waits in ambush, then pushes him or throws something at him and he dies, it is murder. 21 Or if someone hates another person and hits him with a fist and he dies, it is murder. In such cases, the avenger must put the murderer to death when they meet.

22 "But suppose someone pushes another person without having shown previous hostility, or throws something that unintentionally hits another person, 23 or accidentally drops a huge stone on someone, though they were not enemies, and the person dies. 24 If this should happen, the community must follow these regulations in making a judgment between the slayer and the avenger, the victim's nearest relative: 25 The community must protect the slayer from the avenger and must escort the slayer back to live in the city of refuge to which he fled. There he must remain until the death of the high priest, who was anointed with the sacred oil.

26 "But if the slayer ever leaves the limits of the city of refuge, 27 and the avenger finds him outside the city and kills him, it will not be considered murder. 28 The slayer should have stayed inside the city of refuge until the death of the high priest. But after the death of the high priest, the slayer may return to his own property. 29 These are legal requirements for you to observe from generation to generation, wherever you may live.

30 "All murderers must be put to death, but only if evidence is presented by more than one witness. No one may be put to death on the testimony of only one witness. 31 Also, you must never accept a ransom payment for the life of someone judged guilty of murder and subject to execution; murderers must always be put to death. 32 And never accept a ransom payment from someone who has fled to a city of refuge, allowing a slayer to return to his property before the death of the high priest. 33 This will ensure that the land where you live will not be polluted, for murder pollutes the land. And no sacrifice except the execution of the murderer can purify the land from murder.* 34 You must not defile the land where you live, for I live there myself. I am the LORD, who lives among the people of Israel."

WOMEN WHO INHERIT PROPERTY

36 Then the heads of the clans of Gilead—descendants of Makir, son of Manasseh, son of Joseph—came to Moses and the family leaders of Israel with a petition. 2 They said, "Sir, the LORD instructed you to divide the land by sacred lot among the people of Israel. You were told by the LORD to give the grant of land owned by our brother Zelophehad to his daughters. 3 But if they marry men from another tribe, their grants of land will go with them to the tribe into which they marry. In this way, the total area of our tribal land will be reduced. 4 Then when the Year of Jubilee comes, their portion of land will be added to that of the new tribe, causing it to be lost forever to our ancestral tribe."

5 So Moses gave the Israelites this command from the LORD: "The claim of the men of the tribe of Joseph is legitimate. 6 This is what the LORD commands concerning the daughters of Zelophehad: Let them marry anyone they like, as long as it is within their own ancestral tribe. 7 None of the territorial land may pass from tribe to tribe, for all the land given to each tribe must remain within the tribe to which it was first allotted. 8 The daughters throughout the tribes of Israel who are in line to inherit property must marry within their tribe, so that all the Israelites will keep their ancestral property. 9 No grant of land may pass from one tribe to another; each tribe of Israel must keep its allotted portion of land."

10 The daughters of Zelophehad did as the LORD commanded Moses. 11 Mahlah, Tirzah,

Hoglah, Milcah, and Noah all married cousins on their father's side. ¹²They married into the clans of Manasseh son of Joseph. Thus, their inheritance of land remained within their ancestral tribe.

¹³These are the commands and regulations that the LORD gave to the people of Israel through Moses while they were camped on the plains of Moab beside the Jordan River, across from Jericho.

DEUTERONOMY

JON HUNTZINGER, PHD

The book of Deuteronomy records the teaching of Moses to the second generation of Israelites. He delivers this message while they camp on the plains of Moab, preparing to enter Canaan—the Promised Land—after the long journey through the wilderness with their parents. Moses reviews the previous 40 years while, at the same time, he directs their attention forward to Canaan and the new leadership of Joshua. Deuteronomy concludes with a description of how Moses wrote the law and gave it to the priests for the people to follow (31:9). The book takes its name from a term meaning 'second law.' It includes a second version of the Ten Commandments and the laws given at Mount Sinai that were already preserved in parts of Exodus, Leviticus, and Numbers.

Deuteronomy depicts Moses as Israel's teacher and prophet. He speaks God's words to the people and, like any good teacher, reviews the lessons that God's people should know and must now be prepared to put into practice as they go into Canaan. The book can be divided into three messages by Moses and a conclusion:

— Chapters 1–4 contain Moses' first message as he recalls Israel's experience in the wilderness.
— Chapters 5–28 comprise the second and longest message. Moses looks forward to Israel's life in Canaan as the people live in obedience to the covenant God made with them in the law given at Mount Sinai.
— Chapters 29–32 encompass Moses' final message. He leads the people in a renewal of the covenant as they ready themselves to go into Canaan.
— Chapters 33–34 conclude with a description of Moses' death.

So important is the instruction that Moses gives to the Israelites that he promises another prophet will come after him to continue to speak God's words to them (18:15–22). The Gospel writers identify Jesus as this prophet about whom Moses speaks (John 5:43–47; 6:14).

Central to Deuteronomy is the giving of the commandments at Mount Sinai and the prayer that the people are to pray to God as part of their relationship with Him, known as the Shema. The word shema means 'hear and obey' and comes from the first word of the prayer, which is "Listen, O Israel! The LORD is our God, the LORD alone." (6:4). The law God gives to the people is designed for their blessing and intended to enhance their lives with each other in the presence of God. This kind of life is distinctive from that of other people and is expected by God to give an example to surrounding peoples of a way of life that is not only attractive but rich and meaningful as well (28:1–14). This way is contrasted with a diminished life that is barren and unfruitful (28:15–68). The people must walk in the way of God by living according to the words He has given them from the mountain (5:33; 8:6; 10:12–13). These words come from His fiery presence, which is a symbol of His Spirit (5:22–27). God establishes His way for the Israelites by the word He speaks to them through His Spirit. Throughout the Bible, God gives both His Word and His Spirit to His people to help them live in relation to Him and with each other.

Throughout Deuteronomy, Moses underscores the warnings against idolatry (4:15–31; 12:29–31; 29:16–28). He reminds the people in the Shema that God is One. God is unified in His being, and because He is unified in His being, His people should be one as well. They are to worship Him in the unity of their collective life. They are not to fashion any other gods of their own creation to worship. God has created His people in His image (Genesis 1:26–27), and He forbids them from trying to make Him into their own images.

INTRODUCTION TO MOSES' FIRST ADDRESS

1 These are the words that Moses spoke to all the people of Israel while they were in the wilderness east of the Jordan River. They were camped in the Jordan Valley* near Suph, between Paran on one side and Tophel, Laban, Hazeroth, and Di-zahab on the other.

2 Normally it takes only eleven days to travel from Mount Sinai* to Kadesh-barnea, going by way of Mount Seir. 3 But forty years after the Israelites left Egypt, on the first day of the eleventh month,* Moses addressed the people of Israel, telling them everything the LORD had commanded him to say. 4 This took place after he had defeated King Sihon of the Amorites, who ruled in Heshbon, and at Edrei had defeated King Og of Bashan, who ruled in Ashtaroth.

5 While the Israelites were in the land of Moab east of the Jordan River, Moses carefully explained the LORD's instructions as follows.

THE COMMAND TO LEAVE SINAI

6 "When we were at Mount Sinai, the LORD our God said to us, 'You have stayed at this mountain long enough. 7 It is time to break camp and move on. Go to the hill country of the Amorites and to all the neighboring regions—the Jordan Valley, the hill country, the western foothills,* the Negev, and the coastal plain. Go to the land of the Canaanites and to Lebanon, and all the way to the great Euphrates River. 8 Look, I am giving all this land to you! Go in and occupy it, for it is the land the LORD swore to give to your ancestors Abraham, Isaac, and Jacob, and to all their descendants.'"

MOSES APPOINTS LEADERS FROM EACH TRIBE

9 Moses continued, "At that time I told you, 'You are too great a burden for me to carry all by myself. 10 The LORD your God has increased your population, making you as numerous as the stars! 11 And may the LORD, the God of your ancestors, multiply you a thousand times more and bless you as he promised! 12 But you are such a heavy load to carry! How can I deal with all your problems and bickering? 13 Choose some well-respected men from each tribe who are known for their wisdom and understanding, and I will appoint them as your leaders.'

14 "Then you responded, 'Your plan is a good one.' 15 So I took the wise and respected men you had selected from your tribes and appointed them to serve as judges and officials over you. Some were responsible for a thousand people, some for a hundred, some for fifty, and some for ten.

16 "At that time I instructed the judges, 'You must hear the cases of your fellow Israelites and the foreigners living among you. Be perfectly fair in your decisions 17 and impartial in your judgments. Hear the cases of those who are poor as well as those who are rich. Don't be afraid of anyone's anger, for the decision you make is God's decision. Bring me any cases that are too difficult for you, and I will handle them.'

18 "At that time I gave you instructions about everything you were to do.

SCOUTS EXPLORE THE LAND

19 "Then, just as the LORD our God commanded us, we left Mount Sinai and traveled through the great and terrifying wilderness, as you yourselves remember, and headed toward the hill country of the Amorites. When we arrived at Kadesh-barnea, 20 I said to you, 'You have now reached the hill country of the Amorites that the LORD our God is giving us. 21 Look! He has placed the land in front of you. Go and occupy it as the LORD, the God of your ancestors, has promised you. Don't be afraid! Don't be discouraged!'

22 "But you all came to me and said, 'First, let's send out scouts to explore the land for us. They will advise us on the best route to take and which towns we should enter.'

23 "This seemed like a good idea to me, so I chose twelve scouts, one from each of your tribes. 24 They headed for the hill country and came to the valley of Eshcol and explored it. 25 They picked some of its fruit and brought it back to us. And they reported, 'The land the LORD our God has given us is indeed a good land.'

ISRAEL'S REBELLION AGAINST THE LORD

26 "But you rebelled against the command of the LORD your God and refused to go in. 27 You complained in your tents and said, 'The LORD must hate us. That's why he has brought us here from Egypt—to hand us over to the Amorites to be slaughtered. 28 Where can we go? Our brothers have demoralized us with their report. They tell us, "The people of the land are taller and more powerful than we are, and their towns are large, with walls rising high into the sky! We even saw giants there—the descendants of Anak!"'

29 "But I said to you, 'Don't be shocked or afraid of them! 30 The LORD your God is going ahead of you. He will fight for you, just as you saw him do in Egypt. 31 And you saw how the LORD your God cared for you all along the way as you traveled through the wilderness, just as a father cares for his child. Now he has brought you to this place.'

32 "But even after all he did, you refused to trust the LORD your God, 33 who goes before you looking for the best places to camp, guiding you with a pillar of fire by night and a pillar of cloud by day.

34 "When the LORD heard your complaining, he became very angry. So he solemnly swore, 35 'Not one of you from this wicked generation will live to see the good land I swore to give your

1:1 Hebrew the Arabah; also in 1:7. 1:2 Hebrew Horeb, another name for Sinai; also in 1:6, 19. 1:3 Hebrew In the fortieth year, on the first day of the eleventh month. This day in the ancient Hebrew lunar calendar occurred in January or February. 1:7 Hebrew the Shephelah.

ancestors, [36] except Caleb son of Jephunneh. He will see this land because he has followed the LORD completely. I will give to him and his descendants some of the very land he explored during his scouting mission.'

[37] "And the LORD was also angry with me because of you. He said to me, 'Moses, not even you will enter the Promised Land! [38] Instead, your assistant, Joshua son of Nun, will lead the people into the land. Encourage him, for he will lead Israel as they take possession of it. [39] I will give the land to your little ones—your innocent children. You were afraid they would be captured, but they will be the ones who occupy it. [40] As for you, turn around now and go on back through the wilderness toward the Red Sea.*'

[41] "Then you confessed, 'We have sinned against the LORD! We will go into the land and fight for it, as the LORD our God has commanded us.' So your men strapped on their weapons, thinking it would be easy to attack the hill country.

[42] "But the LORD told me to tell you, 'Do not attack, for I am not with you. If you go ahead on your own, you will be crushed by your enemies.'

[43] "This is what I told you, but you would not listen. Instead, you again rebelled against the LORD's command and arrogantly went into the hill country to fight. [44] But the Amorites who lived there came out against you like a swarm of bees. They chased and battered you all the way from Seir to Hormah. [45] Then you returned and wept before the LORD, but he refused to listen. [46] So you stayed there at Kadesh for a long time.

REMEMBERING ISRAEL'S WANDERINGS

2 "Then we turned around and headed back across the wilderness toward the Red Sea,* just as the LORD had instructed me, and we wandered around in the region of Mount Seir for a long time.

[2] "Then at last the LORD said to me, [3] 'You have been wandering around in this hill country long enough; turn to the north. [4] Give these orders to the people: "You will pass through the country belonging to your relatives the Edomites, the descendants of Esau, who live in Seir. The Edomites will feel threatened, so be careful. [5] Do not bother them, for I have given them all the hill country around Mount Seir as their property, and I will not give you even one square foot of their land. [6] If you need food to eat or water to drink, pay them for it. [7] For the LORD your God has blessed you in everything you have done. He has watched your every step through this great wilderness. During these forty years, the LORD your God has been with you, and you have lacked nothing."'

[8] "So we bypassed the territory of our relatives, the descendants of Esau, who live in Seir. We avoided the road through the Arabah Valley that comes up from Elath and Ezion-geber.

"Then as we turned north along the desert route through Moab, [9] the LORD warned us, 'Do not bother the Moabites, the descendants of Lot, or start a war with them. I have given them Ar as their property, and I will not give you any of their land.'"

[10] (A race of giants called the Emites had once lived in the area of Ar. They were as strong and numerous and tall as the Anakites, another race of giants. [11] Both the Emites and the Anakites are also known as the Rephaites, though the Moabites call them Emites. [12] In earlier times the Horites had lived in Seir, but they were driven out and displaced by the descendants of Esau, just as Israel drove out the people of Canaan when the LORD gave Israel their land.)

[13] Moses continued, "Then the LORD said to us, 'Get moving. Cross the Zered Brook.' So we crossed the brook.

[14] "Thirty-eight years passed from the time we first left Kadesh-barnea until we finally crossed the Zered Brook! By then, all the men old enough to fight in battle had died in the wilderness, as the LORD had vowed would happen. [15] The LORD struck them down until they had all been eliminated from the community.

[16] "When all the men of fighting age had died, [17] the LORD said to me, [18] 'Today you will cross the border of Moab at Ar [19] and enter the land of the Ammonites, the descendants of Lot. But do not bother them or start a war with them. I have given the land of Ammon to them as their property, and I will not give you any of their land.'"

[20] (That area was once considered the land of the Rephaites, who had lived there, though the Ammonites call them Zamzummites. [21] They were also as strong and numerous and tall as the Anakites. But the LORD destroyed them so the Ammonites could occupy their land. [22] He had done the same for the descendants of Esau who lived in Seir, for he destroyed the Horites so they could settle there in their place. The descendants of Esau live there to this day. [23] A similar thing happened when the Caphtorites from Crete* invaded and destroyed the Avvites, who had lived in villages in the area of Gaza.)

[24] Moses continued, "Then the LORD said, 'Now get moving! Cross the Arnon Gorge. Look, I will hand over to you Sihon the Amorite, king of Heshbon, and I will give you his land. Attack him and begin to occupy the land. [25] Beginning today I will make people throughout the earth terrified because of you. When they hear reports about you, they will tremble with dread and fear.'"

VICTORY OVER SIHON OF HESHBON

[26] Moses continued, "From the wilderness of Kedemoth I sent ambassadors to King Sihon of Heshbon with this proposal of peace:

1:40 Hebrew *sea of reeds.*   2:1 Hebrew *sea of reeds.*   2:23 Hebrew *from Caphtor.*

²⁷ 'Let us travel through your land. We will stay on the main road and won't turn off into the fields on either side. ²⁸ Sell us food to eat and water to drink, and we will pay for it. All we want is permission to pass through your land. ²⁹ The descendants of Esau who live in Seir allowed us to go through their country, and so did the Moabites, who live in Ar. Let us pass through until we cross the Jordan into the land the LORD our God is giving us.'

³⁰ "But King Sihon of Heshbon refused to allow us to pass through, because the LORD your God made Sihon stubborn and defiant so he could help you defeat him, as he has now done. ³¹ "Then the LORD said to me, 'Look, I have begun to hand King Sihon and his land over to you. Begin now to conquer and occupy his land.' ³² "Then King Sihon declared war on us and mobilized his forces at Jahaz. ³³ But the LORD our God handed him over to us, and we crushed him, his sons, and all his people. ³⁴ We conquered all his towns and completely destroyed* everyone—men, women, and children. Not a single person was spared. ³⁵ We took all the livestock as plunder for ourselves, along with anything of value from the towns we ransacked.

³⁶ "The LORD our God also helped us conquer Aroer on the edge of the Arnon Gorge, and the town in the gorge, and the whole area as far as Gilead. No town had walls too strong for us. ³⁷ However, we avoided the land of the Ammonites all along the Jabbok River and the towns in the hill country—all the places the LORD our God had commanded us to leave alone.

VICTORY OVER OG OF BASHAN

3 "Next we turned and headed for the land of Bashan, where King Og and his entire army attacked us at Edrei. ² But the LORD told me, 'Do not be afraid of him, for I have given you victory over Og and his entire army, and I will give you all his land. Treat him just as you treated King Sihon of the Amorites, who ruled in Heshbon.'

³ "So the LORD our God handed King Og and all his people over to us, and we killed them all. Not a single person survived. ⁴ We conquered all sixty of his towns—the entire Argob region in his kingdom of Bashan. Not a single town escaped our conquest. ⁵ These towns were all fortified with high walls and barred gates. We also took many unwalled villages at the same time. ⁶ We completely destroyed* the kingdom of Bashan, just as we had destroyed King Sihon of Heshbon. We destroyed all the people in every town we conquered—men, women, and children alike. ⁷ But we kept all the livestock for ourselves and took plunder from all the towns.

⁸ "So we took the land of the two Amorite kings east of the Jordan River—all the way from the Arnon Gorge to Mount Hermon. ⁹ (Mount Hermon is called Sirion by the Sidonians, and the Amorites call it Senir.) ¹⁰ We had now conquered all the cities on the plateau and all Gilead and Bashan, as far as the towns of Salecah and Edrei, which were part of Og's kingdom in Bashan. ¹¹ (King Og of Bashan was the last survivor of the giant Rephaites. His bed was made of iron and was more than thirteen feet long and six feet wide.* It can still be seen in the Ammonite city of Rabbah.)

LAND DIVISION EAST OF THE JORDAN

¹² "When we took possession of this land, I gave to the tribes of Reuben and Gad the territory beyond Aroer along the Arnon Gorge, plus half of the hill country of Gilead with its towns. ¹³ Then I gave the rest of Gilead and all of Bashan—Og's former kingdom—to the half-tribe of Manasseh. (This entire Argob region of Bashan used to be known as the land of the Rephaites. ¹⁴ Jair, a leader from the tribe of Manasseh, conquered the whole Argob region in Bashan, all the way to the border of the Geshurites and Maacathites. Jair renamed this region after himself, calling it the Towns of Jair,* as it is still known today.) ¹⁵ I gave Gilead to the clan of Makir. ¹⁶ But I also gave part of Gilead to the tribes of Reuben and Gad. The area I gave them extended from the middle of the Arnon Gorge in the south to the Jabbok River on the Ammonite frontier. ¹⁷ They also received the Jordan Valley, all the way from the Sea of Galilee down to the Dead Sea,* with the Jordan River serving as the western boundary. To the east were the slopes of Pisgah.

¹⁸ "At that time I gave this command to the tribes that would live east of the Jordan: 'Although the LORD your God has given you this land as your property, all your fighting men must cross the Jordan ahead of your Israelite relatives, armed and ready to assist them. ¹⁹ Your wives, children, and numerous livestock, however, may stay behind in the towns I have given you. ²⁰ When the LORD has given security to the rest of the Israelites, as he has to you, and when they occupy the land the LORD your God is giving them across the Jordan River, then you may all return here to the land I have given you.'

MOSES FORBIDDEN TO ENTER THE LAND

²¹ "At that time I gave Joshua this charge: 'You have seen for yourself everything the LORD your God has done to these two kings. He will do the same to all the kingdoms on the west side of the Jordan. ²² Do not be afraid of the nations there, for the LORD your God will fight for you.'

2:34 The Hebrew term used here refers to the complete consecration of things or people to the LORD, either by destroying them or by giving them as an offering. 3:6 The Hebrew term used here refers to the complete consecration of things or people to the LORD, either by destroying them or by giving them as an offering; also in 3:6b. 3:11 Hebrew *9 cubits* [4.1 meters] *long and 4 cubits* [1.8 meters] *wide.* 3:14 Hebrew *Havvoth-jair.* 3:17 Hebrew *from Kinnereth to the Sea of the Arabah, the Salt Sea.*

²³"At that time I pleaded with the Lord and said, ²⁴'O Sovereign Lord, you have only begun to show your greatness and the strength of your hand to me, your servant. Is there any god in heaven or on earth who can perform such great and mighty deeds as you do? ²⁵Please let me cross the Jordan to see the wonderful land on the other side, the beautiful hill country and the Lebanon mountains.'

²⁶"But the Lord was angry with me because of you, and he would not listen to me. 'That's enough!' he declared. 'Speak of it no more. ²⁷But go up to Pisgah Peak, and look over the land in every direction. Take a good look, but you may not cross the Jordan River. ²⁸Instead, commission Joshua and encourage and strengthen him, for he will lead the people across the Jordan. He will give them all the land you now see before you as their possession.' ²⁹So we stayed in the valley near Beth-peor.

MOSES URGES ISRAEL TO OBEY

4 "And now, Israel, listen carefully to these decrees and regulations that I am about to teach you. Obey them so that you may live, so you may enter and occupy the land that the Lord, the God of your ancestors, is giving you. ²Do not add to or subtract from these commands I am giving you. Just obey the commands of the Lord your God that I am giving you.

³"You saw for yourself what the Lord did to you at Baal-peor. There the Lord your God destroyed everyone who had worshiped Baal, the god of Peor. ⁴But all of you who were faithful to the Lord your God are still alive today—every one of you.

⁵"Look, I now teach you these decrees and regulations just as the Lord my God commanded me, so that you may obey them in the land you are about to enter and occupy. ⁶Obey them completely, and you will display your wisdom and intelligence among the surrounding nations. When they hear all these decrees, they will exclaim, 'How wise and prudent are the people of this great nation!' ⁷For what great nation has a god as near to them as the Lord our God is near to us whenever we call on him? ⁸And what great nation has decrees and regulations as righteous and fair as this body of instructions that I am giving you today?

⁹"But watch out! Be careful never to forget what you yourself have seen. Do not let these memories escape from your mind as long as you live! And be sure to pass them on to your children and grandchildren. ¹⁰Never forget the day when you stood before the Lord your God at Mount Sinai,* where he told me, 'Summon the people before me, and I will personally instruct them. Then they will learn to fear me as long as they live, and they will teach their children to fear me also.'

¹¹"You came near and stood at the foot of the mountain, while flames from the mountain shot into the sky. The mountain was shrouded in black clouds and deep darkness. ¹²And the Lord spoke to you from the heart of the fire. You heard the sound of his words but didn't see his form; there was only a voice. ¹³He proclaimed his covenant—the Ten Commandments*—which he commanded you to keep, and which he wrote on two stone tablets. ¹⁴It was at that time that the Lord commanded me to teach you his decrees and regulations so you would obey them in the land you are about to enter and occupy.

A WARNING AGAINST IDOLATRY

¹⁵"But be very careful! You did not see the Lord's form on the day he spoke to you from the heart of the fire at Mount Sinai. ¹⁶So do not corrupt yourselves by making an idol in any form—whether of a man or a woman, ¹⁷an animal on the ground, a bird in the sky, ¹⁸a small animal that scurries along the ground, or a fish in the deepest sea. ¹⁹And when you look up into the sky and see the sun, moon, and stars—all the forces of heaven—don't be seduced into worshiping them. The Lord your God gave them to all the peoples of the earth. ²⁰Remember that the Lord rescued you from the iron-smelting furnace of Egypt in order to make you his very own people and his special possession, which is what you are today.

²¹"But the Lord was angry with me because of you. He vowed that I would not cross the Jordan River into the good land the Lord your God is giving you as your special possession. ²²You will cross the Jordan to occupy the land, but I will not. Instead, I will die here on the east side of the river. ²³So be careful not to break the covenant the Lord your God has made with you. Do not make idols of any shape or form, for the Lord your God has forbidden this. ²⁴The Lord your God is a devouring fire; he is a jealous God.

²⁵"In the future, when you have children and grandchildren and have lived in the land a long time, do not corrupt yourselves by making idols of any kind. This is evil in the sight of the Lord your God and will arouse his anger.

²⁶"Today I call on heaven and earth as witnesses against you. If you break my covenant, you will quickly disappear from the land you are crossing the Jordan to occupy. You will live there only a short time; then you will be utterly destroyed. ²⁷For the Lord will scatter you among the nations, where only a few of you will survive. ²⁸There, in a foreign land, you will worship idols made from wood and stone—gods that neither see nor hear nor eat nor smell. ²⁹But from there you will search again for the Lord your God. And if you search for him with all your heart and soul, you will find him.

³⁰"In the distant future, when you are suffering all these things, you will finally return to the

4:10 Hebrew *Horeb*, another name for Sinai; also in 4:15.
4:13 Hebrew *the ten words.*

THE FATHER IS SOVEREIGN
Deuteronomy 4:34-40 — TOM LANE

God is sovereign. He does not answer to anyone or anything, yet He always does what is right, best, and of the highest good.

Through His sovereign authority, God is guiding all of history to the glorious return of His Son, Jesus. God also has a personal, sovereign plan for each of us. Through His gift of free will, He offers us a choice: will we actively participate in His plan, or will we watch from the sidelines?

Jesus had the opportunity to opt out of God's plan in the Garden of Gethsemane. He knew He was about to suffer and die an excruciating death on the cross for all of humanity's sins. However, Jesus told the Father, "I want your will to be done, not mine" (Luke 22:42).

God loves you, and He is directing the world's affairs for His glory and your good. Choose to opt into His plan today.

LORD your God and listen to what he tells you. ³¹For the LORD your God is a merciful God; he will not abandon you or destroy you or forget the solemn covenant he made with your ancestors.

THERE IS ONLY ONE GOD

³²"Now search all of history, from the time God created people on the earth until now, and search from one end of the heavens to the other. Has anything as great as this ever been seen or heard before? ³³Has any nation ever heard the voice of God* speaking from fire—as you did—and survived? ³⁴Has any other god dared to take a nation for himself out of another nation by means of trials, miraculous signs, wonders, war, a strong hand, a powerful arm, and terrifying acts? Yet that is what the LORD your God did for you in Egypt, right before your eyes.

³⁵"He showed you these things so you would know that the LORD is God and there is no other. ³⁶He let you hear his voice from heaven so he could instruct you. He let you see his great fire here on earth so he could speak to you from it. ³⁷Because he loved your ancestors, he chose to bless their descendants, and he personally brought you out of Egypt with a great display of power. ³⁸He drove out nations far greater than you, so he could bring you in and give you their land as your special possession, as it is today.

³⁹"So remember this and keep it firmly in mind: The LORD is God both in heaven and on earth, and there is no other. ⁴⁰If you obey all the decrees and commands I am giving you today, all will be well with you and your children. I am giving you these instructions so you will enjoy a long life in the land the LORD your God is giving you for all time."

EASTERN CITIES OF REFUGE

⁴¹Then Moses set apart three cities of refuge east of the Jordan River. ⁴²Anyone who killed another person unintentionally, without previous hostility, could flee there to live in safety. ⁴³These were the cities: Bezer on the wilderness plateau for the tribe of Reuben; Ramoth in Gilead for the tribe of Gad; Golan in Bashan for the tribe of Manasseh.

INTRODUCTION TO MOSES' SECOND ADDRESS

⁴⁴This is the body of instruction that Moses presented to the Israelites. ⁴⁵These are the laws, decrees, and regulations that Moses gave to the people of Israel when they left Egypt, ⁴⁶and as they camped in the valley near Beth-peor east of the Jordan River. (This land was formerly occupied by the Amorites under King Sihon, who ruled from Heshbon. But Moses and the Israelites destroyed him and his people when they came up from Egypt. ⁴⁷Israel took possession of his land and that of King Og of Bashan—the two Amorite kings east of the Jordan. ⁴⁸So Israel conquered the entire area from Aroer at the edge of the Arnon Gorge all the way to Mount Sirion,* also called Mount Hermon. ⁴⁹And they conquered the eastern bank of the Jordan River as far south as the Dead Sea,* below the slopes of Pisgah.)

TEN COMMANDMENTS FOR THE COVENANT COMMUNITY

5 Moses called all the people of Israel together and said, "Listen carefully, Israel. Hear the decrees and regulations I am giving you today, so you may learn them and obey them!

²"The LORD our God made a covenant with us at Mount Sinai.* ³The LORD did not make this covenant with our ancestors, but with all of us who are alive today. ⁴At the mountain the LORD spoke to you face to face from the heart of the fire. ⁵I stood as an intermediary between you and the LORD, for you were afraid of the fire and did not want to approach the mountain. He spoke to me, and I passed his words on to you. This is what he said:

⁶"I am the LORD your God, who rescued you from the land of Egypt, the place of your slavery.

⁷"You must not have any other god but me.

⁸"You must not make for yourself an idol of any kind, or an image of anything in the heavens or on the earth or in the sea. ⁹You must not bow down to them or worship them, for I, the LORD your God, am a jealous God who will not tolerate your affection for any other gods. I lay the sins of the parents upon their children; the entire family is affected—even children in the third and fourth generations of those who reject me.

4:33 Or *voice of a god.*   4:48 As in Syriac version (see also 3:9); Hebrew reads *Mount Sion.*   4:49 Hebrew *took the Arabah on the east side of the Jordan as far as the sea of the Arabah.*   5:2 Hebrew *Horeb,* another name for Sinai.

¹⁰But I lavish unfailing love for a thousand generations on those* who love me and obey my commands.

¹¹"You must not misuse the name of the LORD your God. The LORD will not let you go unpunished if you misuse his name.

¹²"Observe the Sabbath day by keeping it holy, as the LORD your God has commanded you. ¹³You have six days each week for your ordinary work, ¹⁴but the seventh day is a Sabbath day of rest dedicated to the LORD your God. On that day no one in your household may do any work. This includes you, your sons and daughters, your male and female servants, your oxen and donkeys and other livestock, and any foreigners living among you. All your male and female servants must rest as you do. ¹⁵Remember that you were once slaves in Egypt, but the LORD your God brought you out with his strong hand and powerful arm. That is why the LORD your God has commanded you to rest on the Sabbath day.

¹⁶"Honor your father and mother, as the LORD your God commanded you. Then you will live a long, full life in the land the LORD your God is giving you.

¹⁷"You must not murder.

¹⁸"You must not commit adultery.

¹⁹"You must not steal.

²⁰"You must not testify falsely against your neighbor.

²¹"You must not covet your neighbor's wife. You must not covet your neighbor's house or land, male or female servant, ox or donkey, or anything else that belongs to your neighbor.

²²"The LORD spoke these words to all of you assembled there at the foot of the mountain. He spoke with a loud voice from the heart of the fire, surrounded by clouds and deep darkness. This was all he said at that time, and he wrote his words on two stone tablets and gave them to me.

²³"But when you heard the voice from the heart of the darkness, while the mountain was blazing with fire, all your tribal leaders and elders came to me. ²⁴They said, 'Look, the LORD our God has shown us his glory and greatness, and we have heard his voice from the heart of the fire. Today we have seen that God can speak to us humans, and yet we live! ²⁵But now, why should we risk death again? If the LORD our God speaks to us again, we will certainly die and be consumed by this awesome fire. ²⁶Can any living thing hear the voice of the living God from the heart of the fire as we did and yet survive? ²⁷Go yourself and listen to what the LORD our God says. Then come and tell us everything he tells you, and we will listen and obey.'

²⁸"The LORD heard the request you made to me. And he said, 'I have heard what the people said to you, and they are right. ²⁹Oh, that they would always have hearts like this, that they might fear me and obey all my commands! If they did, they and their descendants would prosper forever. ³⁰Go and tell them, "Return to your tents." ³¹But you stand here with me so I can give you all my commands, decrees, and regulations. You must teach them to the people so they can obey them in the land I am giving them as their possession.'"

³²So Moses told the people, "You must be careful to obey all the commands of the LORD your God, following his instructions in every detail. ³³Stay on the path that the LORD your God has commanded you to follow. Then you will live long and prosperous lives in the land you are about to enter and occupy.

A CALL FOR WHOLEHEARTED COMMITMENT

6 "These are the commands, decrees, and regulations that the LORD your God commanded me to teach you. You must obey them in the land you are about to enter and occupy, ²and you and your children and grandchildren must fear the LORD your God as long as you live. If you obey all his decrees and commands, you will enjoy a long life. ³Listen closely, Israel, and be careful to obey. Then all will go well with you, and you will have many children in the land flowing with milk and honey, just as the LORD, the God of your ancestors, promised you.

⁴"Listen, O Israel! The LORD is our God, the LORD alone.* ⁵And you must love the LORD your God with all your heart, all your soul, and all your strength. ⁶And you must commit yourselves wholeheartedly to these commands that I am giving you today. ⁷Repeat them again and again to your children. Talk about them when you are at home and when you are on the road, when you are going to bed and when you are getting up. ⁸Tie them to your hands and wear them on your forehead as reminders. ⁹Write them on the doorposts of your house and on your gates.

¹⁰"The LORD your God will soon bring you into the land he swore to give you when he made a vow to your ancestors Abraham, Isaac, and Jacob. It is a land with large, prosperous cities that you did not build. ¹¹The houses will be richly stocked with goods you did not produce. You will draw water from cisterns you did not dig, and you will eat from vineyards and olive trees you did not plant. When you have eaten your fill in this land, ¹²be careful not to forget the LORD, who rescued you from slavery in the land of Egypt. ¹³You must fear the LORD your God and serve him. When you take an oath, you must use only his name.

¹⁴"You must not worship any of the gods of neighboring nations, ¹⁵for the LORD your God,

5:10 Hebrew *for thousands of those.* 6:4 Or *The LORD our God is one LORD;* or *The LORD our God, the LORD is one;* or *The LORD is our God, the LORD is one.*

HOW CAN I EXPRESS WORSHIP?
Deuteronomy 6:5 — ROBERT MORRIS

Deuteronomy 6:5 tells us to "love the LORD your God with all your heart, all your soul, and all your strength." If worship is love expressed (and it is!), then is it possible that God wants us to *express* our love to Him with all our heart, soul, and strength?

Here are six biblical expressions of worship:

1. Clapping (Psalm 98:8; Isaiah 55:12; Nahum 3:19)
   When we clap our hands, we express our joy to the Lord and declare our victory over the enemy.
2. Shouting (Psalm 47:1; Galatians 4:27)
   Worship is an act of faith. Shouting is declaring victory, sometimes even before it happens. No matter what we are going through, God is worthy of our worship.
3. Singing (Numbers 21:16-17; Psalm 95:1; 96:1)
   When we sing to God, we express our joy and exercise our faith. Do you have any barren or dry places in your life right now? Sing over your business, your family, and your marriage. If you will sing, then they will flourish.
4. Bowing and Kneeling (Psalm 95:6; Philippians 2:10)
   Bowing represents submission. When the wise men bowed before the Child (Matthew 2:11), they were submitting to the authority of the Lord Jesus Christ. Kneeling represents honor and adoration. Satan offered Jesus power over the world, with one condition: "Kneel down and worship me" (Matthew 4:9). Even Satan knows true worship is always expressed.
5. Lifting Hands (Psalm 63:4; 134:2; Luke 24:50)
   In Scripture, lifting hands represents blessing. The one to whom you lift your hands is *blessed*, which means happy. God is happy when we express our love to Him!
6. Dancing (Psalm 149:3; 150:4)
   In Luke 7:31-34, Jesus says the Jewish leaders are missing their opportunity because the Messiah is right in front of them, and they don't even realize it. Today is our day of opportunity. Are you going to worship the Messiah? Are you going to express your love to Him?

A FATHER'S LASTING LEGACY
Deuteronomy 6:6-7 — TOM LANE

God wants to empower fathers to leave a lasting legacy to their children. According to the principle of transference, we can only pass on to our children the values and character demonstrated in our own lives. In other words, our values must be modeled by our behavior if we want them to transfer to our children. This system of influence is the method God intends parents to use as they build and prepare the next generation.

A father also trains for success. Training is a process that incorporates discipleship for constructive purposes. God's discipleship is redemptive and life-giving. Thus, our discipleship of our children (or those we are leading) also needs to be redemptive and life-giving. Training requires a consistent response to disobedience and recognizes that attitudes are a precursor to behavior.

A father guides toward purpose and success. God desires earthly fathers who will help their children discover His will for them. God is our ultimate Father, and if we are lacking in any area, He will gladly supply all our needs when we come to Him.

who lives among you, is a jealous God. His anger will flare up against you, and he will wipe you from the face of the earth. ¹⁶ You must not test the LORD your God as you did when you complained at Massah. ¹⁷ You must diligently obey the commands of the LORD your God—all the laws and decrees he has given you. ¹⁸ Do what is right and good in the LORD's sight, so all will go well with you. Then you will enter and occupy the good land that the LORD swore to give your ancestors. ¹⁹ You will drive out all the enemies living in the land, just as the LORD said you would.

²⁰ "In the future your children will ask you, 'What is the meaning of these laws, decrees, and regulations that the LORD our God has commanded us to obey?'

²¹ "Then you must tell them, 'We were Pharaoh's slaves in Egypt, but the LORD brought us out of Egypt with his strong hand. ²² The LORD did miraculous signs and wonders before our eyes, dealing terrifying blows against Egypt and Pharaoh and all his people. ²³ He brought us out of Egypt so he could give us this land he had sworn to give our ancestors. ²⁴ And the LORD our God commanded us to obey all these decrees and to fear him so he can continue to bless us and preserve our lives, as he has done to this day. ²⁵ For we will be counted as righteous when we obey all the commands the LORD our God has given us.'

THE PRIVILEGE OF HOLINESS

7 "When the LORD your God brings you into the land you are about to enter and occupy, he will clear away many nations ahead of you: the Hittites, Girgashites, Amorites, Canaanites, Perizzites, Hivites, and Jebusites. These seven nations are greater and more numerous than

you. ² When the LORD your God hands these nations over to you and you conquer them, you must completely destroy* them. Make no treaties with them and show them no mercy. ³ You must not intermarry with them. Do not let your daughters and sons marry their sons and daughters, ⁴ for they will lead your children away from me to worship other gods. Then the anger of the LORD will burn against you, and he will quickly destroy you. ⁵ This is what you must do. You must break down their pagan altars and shatter their sacred pillars. Cut down their Asherah poles and burn their idols. ⁶ For you are a holy people, who belong to the LORD your God. Of all the people on earth, the LORD your God has chosen you to be his own special treasure.

⁷ "The LORD did not set his heart on you and choose you because you were more numerous than other nations, for you were the smallest of all nations! ⁸ Rather, it was simply that the LORD loves you, and he was keeping the oath he had sworn to your ancestors. That is why the LORD rescued you with such a strong hand from your slavery and from the oppressive hand of Pharaoh, king of Egypt. ⁹ Understand, therefore, that the LORD your God is indeed God. He is the faithful God who keeps his covenant for a thousand generations and lavishes his unfailing love on those who love him and obey his commands. ¹⁰ But he does not hesitate to punish and destroy those who reject him. ¹¹ Therefore, you must obey all these commands, decrees, and regulations I am giving you today.

¹² "If you listen to these regulations and faithfully obey them, the LORD your God will keep his covenant of unfailing love with you, as he promised with an oath to your ancestors. ¹³ He will love you and bless you, and he will give you many children. He will give fertility to your land and your animals. When you arrive in the land he swore to give your ancestors, you will have large harvests of grain, new wine, and olive oil, and great herds of cattle, sheep, and goats. ¹⁴ You will be blessed above all the nations of the earth. None of your men or women will be childless, and all your livestock will bear young. ¹⁵ And the LORD will protect you from all sickness. He will not let you suffer from the terrible diseases you knew in Egypt, but he will inflict them on all your enemies!

¹⁶ "You must destroy all the nations the LORD your God hands over to you. Show them no mercy, and do not worship their gods, or they will trap you. ¹⁷ Perhaps you will think to yourselves, 'How can we ever conquer these nations that are so much more powerful than we are?' ¹⁸ But don't be afraid of them! Just remember what the LORD your God did to Pharaoh and to all the land of Egypt. ¹⁹ Remember the great terrors the LORD your God sent against them. You saw it all with your own eyes! And remember the miraculous signs and wonders, and the strong hand and powerful arm with which he brought you out of Egypt. The LORD your God will use this same power against all the people you fear. ²⁰ And then the LORD your God will send terror* to drive out the few survivors still hiding from you!

²¹ "No, do not be afraid of those nations, for the LORD your God is among you, and he is a great and awesome God. ²² The LORD your God will drive those nations out ahead of you little by little. You will not clear them away all at once, otherwise the wild animals would multiply too quickly for you. ²³ But the LORD your God will hand them over to you. He will throw them into complete confusion until they are destroyed. ²⁴ He will put their kings in your power, and you will erase their names from the face of the earth. No one will be able to stand against you, and you will destroy them all.

²⁵ "You must burn their idols in fire, and you must not covet the silver or gold that covers them. You must not take it or it will become a trap to you, for it is detestable to the LORD your God. ²⁶ Do not bring any detestable objects into your home, for then you will be destroyed, just like them. You must utterly detest such things, for they are set apart for destruction.

A CALL TO REMEMBER AND OBEY

8 "Be careful to obey all the commands I am giving you today. Then you will live and multiply, and you will enter and occupy the land the LORD swore to give your ancestors. ² Remember how the LORD your God led you through the wilderness for these forty years, humbling you and testing you to prove your character, and to find out whether or not you would obey his commands. ³ Yes, he humbled you by letting you go hungry and then feeding you with manna, a food previously unknown to you and your ancestors. He did it to teach you that people do not live by bread alone; rather, we live by every word that comes from the mouth of the LORD. ⁴ For all these forty years your clothes didn't wear out, and your feet didn't blister or swell. ⁵ Think about it: Just as a parent disciplines a child, the LORD your God disciplines you for your own good.

⁶ "So obey the commands of the LORD your God by walking in his ways and fearing him. ⁷ For the LORD your God is bringing you into a good land of flowing streams and pools of water, with fountains and springs that gush out in the valleys and hills. ⁸ It is a land of wheat and barley; of grapevines, fig trees, and pomegranates; of olive oil and honey. ⁹ It is a land where food is plentiful and nothing is lacking. It is a land where iron is as common as stone, and copper is abundant in the hills. ¹⁰ When you have eaten

---

7:2 The Hebrew term used here refers to the complete consecration of things or people to the LORD, either by destroying them or by giving them as an offering; also in 7:26. 7:20 Often rendered *the hornet.* The meaning of the Hebrew is uncertain.

your fill, be sure to praise the LORD your God for the good land he has given you.

11 "But that is the time to be careful! Beware that in your plenty you do not forget the LORD your God and disobey his commands, regulations, and decrees that I am giving you today. 12 For when you have become full and prosperous and have built fine homes to live in, 13 and when your flocks and herds have become very large and your silver and gold have multiplied along with everything else, be careful! 14 Do not become proud at that time and forget the LORD your God, who rescued you from slavery in the land of Egypt. 15 Do not forget that he led you through the great and terrifying wilderness with its poisonous snakes and scorpions, where it was so hot and dry. He gave you water from the rock! 16 He fed you with manna in the wilderness, a food unknown to your ancestors. He did this to humble you and test you for your own good. 17 He did all this so you would never say to yourself, 'I have achieved this wealth with my own strength and energy.' 18 Remember the LORD your God. He is the one who gives you power to be successful, in order to fulfill the covenant he confirmed to your ancestors with an oath.

19 "But I assure you of this: If you ever forget the LORD your God and follow other gods, worshiping and bowing down to them, you will certainly be destroyed. 20 Just as the LORD has destroyed other nations in your path, you also will be destroyed if you refuse to obey the LORD your God.

VICTORY BY GOD'S GRACE

9 "Listen, O Israel! Today you are about to cross the Jordan River to take over the land belonging to nations much greater and more powerful than you. They live in cities with walls that reach to the sky! 2 The people are strong and tall—descendants of the famous Anakite giants. You've heard the saying, 'Who can stand up to the Anakites?' 3 But recognize today that the LORD your God is the one who will cross over ahead of you like a devouring fire to destroy them. He will subdue them so that you will quickly conquer them and drive them out, just as the LORD has promised.

4 "After the LORD your God has done this for you, don't say in your hearts, 'The LORD has given us this land because we are such good people!' No, it is because of the wickedness of the other nations that he is pushing them out of your way. 5 It is not because you are so good or have such integrity that you are about to occupy their land. The LORD your God will drive these nations out ahead of you only because of their wickedness, and to fulfill the oath he swore to your ancestors Abraham, Isaac, and Jacob. 6 You must recognize that the LORD your God is not giving you this good land because you are good, for you are not—you are a stubborn people.

REMEMBERING THE GOLD CALF

7 "Remember and never forget how angry you made the LORD your God out in the wilderness. From the day you left Egypt until now, you have been constantly rebelling against him. 8 Even at Mount Sinai* you made the LORD so angry he was ready to destroy you. 9 This happened when I was on the mountain receiving the tablets of stone inscribed with the words of the covenant that the LORD had made with you. I was there for forty days and forty nights, and all that time I ate no food and drank no water. 10 The LORD gave me the two tablets on which God had written with his own finger all the words he had spoken to you from the heart of the fire when you were assembled at the mountain.

11 "At the end of the forty days and nights, the LORD handed me the two stone tablets inscribed with the words of the covenant. 12 Then the LORD said to me, 'Get up! Go down immediately, for the people you brought out of Egypt have corrupted themselves. How quickly they have turned away from the way I commanded them to live! They have melted gold and made an idol for themselves!'

13 "The LORD also said to me, 'I have seen how stubborn and rebellious these people are. 14 Leave me alone so I may destroy them and erase their name from under heaven. Then I will make a mighty nation of your descendants, a nation larger and more powerful than they are.'

15 "So while the mountain was blazing with fire I turned and came down, holding in my hands the two stone tablets inscribed with the terms of the covenant. 16 There below me I could see that you had sinned against the LORD your God. You had melted gold and made a calf idol for yourselves. How quickly you had turned away from the path the LORD had commanded you to follow! 17 So I took the stone tablets and threw them to the ground, smashing them before your eyes.

18 "Then, as before, I threw myself down before the LORD for forty days and nights. I ate no bread and drank no water because of the great sin you had committed by doing what the LORD hated, provoking him to anger. 19 I feared that the furious anger of the LORD, which turned him against you, would drive him to destroy you. But again he listened to me. 20 The LORD was so angry with Aaron that he wanted to destroy him, too. But I prayed for Aaron, and the LORD spared him. 21 I took your sin—the calf you had made—and I melted it down in the fire and ground it into fine dust. Then I threw the dust into the stream that flows down the mountain.

22 "You also made the LORD angry at Taberah,* Massah,* and Kibroth-hattaavah.* 23 And at Kadesh-barnea the LORD sent you out with this

9:8 Hebrew Horeb, another name for Sinai. 9:22a Taberah means "place of burning." See Num 11:1-3. 9:22b Massah means "place of testing." See Exod 17:1-7. 9:22c Kibroth-hattaavah means "graves of gluttony." See Num 11:31-34.

command: 'Go up and take over the land I have given you.' But you rebelled against the command of the LORD your God and refused to put your trust in him or obey him. [24] Yes, you have been rebelling against the LORD as long as I have known you.

[25] "That is why I threw myself down before the LORD for forty days and nights—for the LORD said he would destroy you. [26] I prayed to the LORD and said, 'O Sovereign LORD, do not destroy them. They are your own people. They are your special possession, whom you redeemed from Egypt by your mighty power and your strong hand. [27] Please overlook the stubbornness and the awful sin of these people, and remember instead your servants Abraham, Isaac, and Jacob. [28] If you destroy these people, the Egyptians will say, "The Israelites died because the LORD wasn't able to bring them to the land he had promised to give them." Or they might say, "He destroyed them because he hated them; he deliberately took them into the wilderness to slaughter them." [29] But they are your people and your special possession, whom you brought out of Egypt by your great strength and powerful arm.'

A NEW COPY OF THE COVENANT

10 "At that time the LORD said to me, 'Chisel out two stone tablets like the first ones. Also make a wooden Ark—a sacred chest to store them in. Come up to me on the mountain, [2] and I will write on the tablets the same words that were on the ones you smashed. Then place the tablets in the Ark.'

[3] "So I made an Ark of acacia wood and cut two stone tablets like the first two. Then I went up the mountain with the tablets in my hand. [4] Once again the LORD wrote the Ten Commandments* on the tablets and gave them to me. They were the same words the LORD had spoken to you from the heart of the fire on the day you were assembled at the foot of the mountain. [5] Then I turned and came down the mountain and placed the tablets in the Ark of the Covenant, which I had made, just as the LORD commanded me. And the tablets are still there in the Ark."

[6] (The people of Israel set out from the wells of the people of Jaakan* and traveled to Moserah, where Aaron died and was buried. His son Eleazar ministered as high priest in his place. [7] Then they journeyed to Gudgodah, and from there to Jotbathah, a land with many brooks and streams. [8] At that time the LORD set apart the tribe of Levi to carry the Ark of the LORD's Covenant, and to stand before the LORD as his ministers, and to pronounce blessings in his name. These are their duties to this day. [9] That is why the Levites have no share of property or possession of land among the other Israelite tribes. The LORD himself is their special possession, as the LORD your God told them.)

[10] "As for me, I stayed on the mountain in the LORD's presence for forty days and nights, as I had done the first time. And once again the LORD listened to my pleas and agreed not to destroy you. [11] Then the LORD said to me, 'Get up and resume the journey, and lead the people to the land I swore to give to their ancestors, so they may take possession of it.'

A CALL TO LOVE AND OBEDIENCE

[12] "And now, Israel, what does the LORD your God require of you? He requires only that you fear the LORD your God, and live in a way that pleases him, and love him and serve him with all your heart and soul. [13] And you must always obey the LORD's commands and decrees that I am giving you today for your own good.

[14] "Look, the highest heavens and the earth and everything in it all belong to the LORD your God. [15] Yet the LORD chose your ancestors as the objects of his love. And he chose you, their descendants, above all other nations, as is evident today. [16] Therefore, change your hearts* and stop being stubborn.

[17] "For the LORD your God is the God of gods and Lord of lords. He is the great God, the mighty and awesome God, who shows no partiality and cannot be bribed. [18] He ensures that orphans and widows receive justice. He shows love to the foreigners living among you and gives them food and clothing. [19] So you, too, must show love to foreigners, for you yourselves were once foreigners in the land of Egypt. [20] You must fear the LORD your God and worship him and cling to him. Your oaths must be in his name alone. [21] He alone is your God, the only one who is worthy of your praise, the one who has done these mighty miracles that you have seen with your own eyes. [22] When your ancestors went down into Egypt, there were only seventy of them. But now the LORD your God has made you as numerous as the stars in the sky!

11 "You must love the LORD your God and always obey his requirements, decrees, regulations, and commands. [2] Keep in mind that I am not talking now to your children, who have never experienced the discipline of the LORD your God or seen his greatness and his strong hand and powerful arm. [3] They didn't see the miraculous signs and wonders he performed in Egypt against Pharaoh and all his land. [4] They didn't see what the LORD did to the armies of Egypt and to their horses and chariots—how he drowned them in the Red Sea* as they were chasing you. He destroyed them, and they have not recovered to this very day!

[5] "Your children didn't see how the LORD cared for you in the wilderness until you arrived here. [6] They didn't see what he did to Dathan and Abiram (the sons of Eliab, a descendant of Reuben) when the earth opened its mouth in the Israelite

---

10:4 Hebrew *the ten words.*   10:6 Or *set out from Beeroth of Bene-jaakan.*   10:16 Hebrew *circumcise the foreskin of your hearts.*
11:4 Hebrew *sea of reeds.*

LOVE EXPRESSED
Deuteronomy 11:1, 13   ROBERT MORRIS

Do you ever wonder, *Is this all there is to life?* Do you have an intense longing for more? There's a reason for that—God created you for *more*. He created you for a greater purpose: to be a worshipper. The question is "Whom or what are you worshipping?"

The simplest and most accurate definition of worship is *love expressed.* In order to worship God, you must first have love in your heart, and then you must express that love. If it's not expressed, it's not worship. Deuteronomy 11:1 tells us what God wants. So many times, we think we're supposed to serve God by doing a bunch of stuff for Him. However, the truth is the greatest thing you can do is love God. Worship is communicating your love to God and God communicating His love to you. You *were* created for more—to love and be loved. So express your love to God in worship!

camp and swallowed them, along with their households and tents and every living thing that belonged to them. ⁷But you have seen the LORD perform all these mighty deeds with your own eyes!

THE BLESSINGS OF OBEDIENCE

⁸"Therefore, be careful to obey every command I am giving you today, so you may have strength to go in and take over the land you are about to enter. ⁹If you obey, you will enjoy a long life in the land the LORD swore to give to your ancestors and to you, their descendants—a land flowing with milk and honey! ¹⁰For the land you are about to enter and take over is not like the land of Egypt from which you came, where you planted your seed and made irrigation ditches with your foot as in a vegetable garden. ¹¹Rather, the land you will soon take over is a land of hills and valleys with plenty of rain—¹²a land that the LORD your God cares for. He watches over it through each season of the year!

¹³"If you carefully obey the commands I am giving you today, and if you love the LORD your God and serve him with all your heart and soul, ¹⁴then he will send the rains in their proper seasons—the early and late rains—so you can bring in your harvests of grain, new wine, and olive oil. ¹⁵He will give you lush pastureland for your livestock, and you yourselves will have all you want to eat. ¹⁶"But be careful. Don't let your heart be deceived so that you turn away from the LORD and serve and worship other gods. ¹⁷If you do, the LORD's anger will burn against you. He will shut up the sky and hold back the rain, and the ground will fail to produce its harvests. Then you will quickly die in that good land the LORD is giving you.

¹⁸"So commit yourselves wholeheartedly to these words of mine. Tie them to your hands and wear them on your forehead as reminders. ¹⁹Teach them to your children. Talk about them when you are at home and when you are on the road, when you are going to bed and when you are getting up. ²⁰Write them on the doorposts of your house and on your gates, ²¹so that as long as the sky remains above the earth, you and your children may flourish in the land the LORD swore to give your ancestors.

²²"Be careful to obey all these commands I am giving you. Show love to the LORD your God by walking in his ways and holding tightly to him. ²³Then the LORD will drive out all the nations ahead of you, though they are much greater and stronger than you, and you will take over their land. ²⁴Wherever you set foot, that land will be yours. Your frontiers will stretch from the wilderness in the south to Lebanon in the north, and from the Euphrates River in the east to the Mediterranean Sea in the west.* ²⁵No one will be able to stand against you, for the LORD your God will cause the people to fear and dread you, as he promised, wherever you go in the whole land.

²⁶"Look, today I am giving you the choice between a blessing and a curse! ²⁷You will be blessed if you obey the commands of the LORD your God that I am giving you today. ²⁸But you will be cursed if you reject the commands of the LORD your God and turn away from him and worship gods you have not known before.

²⁹"When the LORD your God brings you into the land and helps you take possession of it, you must pronounce the blessing at Mount Gerizim and the curse at Mount Ebal. ³⁰(These two mountains are west of the Jordan River in the land of the Canaanites who live in the Jordan Valley,* near the town of Gilgal, not far from the oaks of Moreh.) ³¹For you are about to cross the Jordan River to take over the land the LORD your God is giving you. When you take that land and are living in it, ³²you must be careful to obey all the decrees and regulations I am giving you today.

THE LORD'S CHOSEN PLACE FOR WORSHIP

12 "These are the decrees and regulations you must be careful to obey when you live in the land that the LORD, the God of your ancestors, is giving you. You must obey them as long as you live.

²"When you drive out the nations that live there, you must destroy all the places where they worship their gods—high on the mountains, up on the hills, and under every green tree. ³Break down their altars and smash their sacred pillars. Burn their Asherah poles and cut down their carved idols. Completely erase the names of their gods!

11:24 Hebrew *to the western sea.*   **11:30** Hebrew *the Arabah.*

[4] "Do not worship the LORD your God in the way these pagan peoples worship their gods. [5] Rather, you must seek the LORD your God at the place of worship he himself will choose from among all the tribes—the place where his name will be honored. [6] There you will bring your burnt offerings, your sacrifices, your tithes, your sacred offerings, your offerings to fulfill a vow, your voluntary offerings, and your offerings of the firstborn animals of your herds and flocks. [7] There you and your families will feast in the presence of the LORD your God, and you will rejoice in all you have accomplished because the LORD your God has blessed you.

[8] "Your pattern of worship will change. Today all of you are doing as you please, [9] because you have not yet arrived at the place of rest, the land the LORD your God is giving you as your special possession. [10] But you will soon cross the Jordan River and live in the land the LORD your God is giving you. When he gives you rest from all your enemies and you're living safely in the land, [11] you must bring everything I command you—your burnt offerings, your sacrifices, your tithes, your sacred offerings, and your offerings to fulfill a vow—to the designated place of worship, the place the LORD your God chooses for his name to be honored.

[12] "You must celebrate there in the presence of the LORD your God with your sons and daughters and all your servants. And remember to include the Levites who live in your towns, for they will receive no allotment of land among you. [13] Be careful not to sacrifice your burnt offerings just anywhere you like. [14] You may do so only at the place the LORD will choose within one of your tribal territories. There you must offer your burnt offerings and do everything I command you.

[15] "But you may butcher your animals and eat their meat in any town whenever you want. You may freely eat the animals with which the LORD your God blesses you. All of you, whether ceremonially clean or unclean, may eat that meat, just as you now eat gazelle and deer. [16] But you must not consume the blood. You must pour it out on the ground like water.

[17] "But you may not eat your offerings in your hometown—neither the tithe of your grain and new wine and olive oil, nor the firstborn of your flocks and herds, nor any offering to fulfill a vow, nor your voluntary offerings, nor your sacred offerings. [18] You must eat these in the presence of the LORD your God at the place he will choose. Eat them there with your children, your servants, and the Levites who live in your towns, celebrating in the presence of the LORD your God in all you do. [19] And be very careful never to neglect the Levites as long as you live in your land.

[20] "When the LORD your God expands your territory as he has promised, and you have the urge to eat meat, you may freely eat meat whenever you want. [21] It might happen that the designated place of worship—the place the LORD your God chooses for his name to be honored—is a long way from your home. If so, you may butcher any of the cattle, sheep, or goats the LORD has given you, and you may freely eat the meat in your hometown, as I have commanded you. [22] Anyone, whether ceremonially clean or unclean, may eat that meat, just as you do now with gazelle and deer. [23] But never consume the blood, for the blood is the life, and you must not consume the lifeblood with the meat. [24] Instead, pour out the blood on the ground like water. [25] Do not consume the blood, so that all may go well with you and your children after you, because you will be doing what pleases the LORD.

[26] "Take your sacred gifts and your offerings given to fulfill a vow to the place the LORD chooses. [27] You must offer the meat and blood of your burnt offerings on the altar of the LORD your God. The blood of your other sacrifices must be poured out on the altar of the LORD your God, but you may eat the meat. [28] Be careful to obey all my commands, so that all will go well with you and your children after you, because you will be doing what is good and pleasing to the LORD your God.

[29] "When the LORD your God goes ahead of you and destroys the nations and you drive them out and live in their land, [30] do not fall into the trap of following their customs and worshiping their gods. Do not inquire about their gods, saying, 'How do these nations worship their gods? I want to follow their example.' [31] You must not worship the LORD your God the way the other nations worship their gods, for they perform for their gods every detestable act that the LORD hates. They even burn their sons and daughters as sacrifices to their gods.

[32]* "So be careful to obey all the commands I give you. You must not add anything to them or subtract anything from them.

A WARNING AGAINST IDOLATRY

13 [1]* "Suppose there are prophets among you or those who dream dreams about the future, and they promise you signs or miracles, [2] and the predicted signs or miracles occur. If they then say, 'Come, let us worship other gods'— gods you have not known before—[3] do not listen to them. The LORD your God is testing you to see if you truly love him with all your heart and soul. [4] Serve only the LORD your God and fear him alone. Obey his commands, listen to his voice, and cling to him. [5] The false prophets or visionaries who try to lead you astray must be put to death, for they encourage rebellion against the LORD your God, who redeemed you from slavery and brought you out of the land of Egypt. Since they try to lead you astray from the way the LORD

12:32 Verse 12:32 is numbered 13:1 in Hebrew text. 13:1 Verses 13:1-18 are numbered 13:2-19 in Hebrew text.

your God commanded you to live, you must put them to death. In this way you will purge the evil from among you.

⁶ "Suppose someone secretly entices you—even your brother, your son or daughter, your beloved wife, or your closest friend—and says, 'Let us go worship other gods'—gods that neither you nor your ancestors have known. ⁷ They might suggest that you worship the gods of peoples who live nearby or who come from the ends of the earth. ⁸ But do not give in or listen. Have no pity, and do not spare or protect them. ⁹ You must put them to death! Strike the first blow yourself, and then all the people must join in. ¹⁰ Stone the guilty ones to death because they have tried to draw you away from the LORD your God, who rescued you from the land of Egypt, the place of slavery. ¹¹ Then all Israel will hear about it and be afraid, and no one will act so wickedly again.

¹² "When you begin living in the towns the LORD your God is giving you, you may hear ¹³ that scoundrels among you are leading their fellow citizens astray by saying, 'Let us go worship other gods'—gods you have not known before. ¹⁴ In such cases, you must examine the facts carefully. If you find that the report is true and such a detestable act has been committed among you, ¹⁵ you must attack that town and completely destroy* all its inhabitants, as well as all the livestock. ¹⁶ Then you must pile all the plunder in the middle of the open square and burn it. Burn the entire town as a burnt offering to the LORD your God. That town must remain a ruin forever; it may never be rebuilt. ¹⁷ Keep none of the plunder that has been set apart for destruction. Then the LORD will turn from his fierce anger and be merciful to you. He will have compassion on you and make you a large nation, just as he swore to your ancestors.

¹⁸ "The LORD your God will be merciful only if you listen to his voice and keep all his commands that I am giving you today, doing what pleases him.

CEREMONIALLY CLEAN AND UNCLEAN ANIMALS

14 "Since you are the people of the LORD your God, never cut yourselves or shave the hair above your foreheads in mourning for the dead. ² You have been set apart as holy to the LORD your God, and he has chosen you from all the nations of the earth to be his own special treasure.

³ "You must not eat any detestable animals that are ceremonially unclean. ⁴ These are the animals* you may eat: the ox, the sheep, the goat, ⁵ the deer, the gazelle, the roe deer, the wild goat, the addax, the antelope, and the mountain sheep.

⁶ "You may eat any animal that has completely split hooves and chews the cud, ⁷ but if the animal doesn't have both, it may not be eaten. So you may not eat the camel, the hare, or the hyrax.*

They chew the cud but do not have split hooves, so they are ceremonially unclean for you. ⁸ And you may not eat the pig. It has split hooves but does not chew the cud, so it is ceremonially unclean for you. You may not eat the meat of these animals or even touch their carcasses.

⁹ "Of all the marine animals, you may eat whatever has both fins and scales. ¹⁰ You may not, however, eat marine animals that do not have both fins and scales. They are ceremonially unclean for you.

¹¹ "You may eat any bird that is ceremonially clean. ¹² These are the birds you may not eat: the griffon vulture, the bearded vulture, the black vulture, ¹³ the kite, the falcon, buzzards of all kinds, ¹⁴ ravens of all kinds, ¹⁵ the eagle owl, the short-eared owl, the seagull, hawks of all kinds, ¹⁶ the little owl, the great owl, the barn owl, ¹⁷ the desert owl, the Egyptian vulture, the cormorant, ¹⁸ the stork, herons of all kinds, the hoopoe, and the bat.

¹⁹ "All winged insects that walk along the ground are ceremonially unclean for you and may not be eaten. ²⁰ But you may eat any winged bird or insect that is ceremonially clean.

²¹ "You must not eat anything that has died a natural death. You may give it to a foreigner living in your town, or you may sell it to a stranger. But do not eat it yourselves, for you are set apart as holy to the LORD your God.

"You must not cook a young goat in its mother's milk.

THE GIVING OF TITHES

²² "You must set aside a tithe of your crops—one-tenth of all the crops you harvest each year. ²³ Bring this tithe to the designated place of worship—the place the LORD your God chooses for his name to be honored—and eat it there in his presence. This applies to your tithes of grain, new wine, olive oil, and the firstborn males of your flocks and herds. Doing this will teach you always to fear the LORD your God.

²⁴ "Now when the LORD your God blesses you with a good harvest, the place of worship he chooses for his name to be honored might be too far for you to bring the tithe. ²⁵ If so, you may sell the tithe portion of your crops and herds, put the money in a pouch, and go to the place the LORD your God has chosen. ²⁶ When you arrive, you may use the money to buy any kind of food you want—cattle, sheep, goats, wine, or other alcoholic drink. Then feast there in the presence of the LORD your God and celebrate with your household. ²⁷ And do not neglect the Levites in your town, for they will receive no allotment of land among you.

13:15 The Hebrew term used here refers to the complete consecration of things or people to the LORD, either by destroying them or by giving them as an offering; similarly in 13:17. 14:4 The identification of some of the animals and birds listed in this chapter is uncertain. 14:7 Or *coney, or rock badger.*

THE RIGHT ATTITUDE
Deuteronomy 15:9-10   ROBERT MORRIS

Have you ever had buyer's remorse? Maybe you made a big purchase, such as a car or a house, and after the excitement wore off, you experienced that panicky "What have I done?" feeling. A similar emotion can occur after you're obedient to give as the Holy Spirit leads. Deuteronomy 15:10 says, "Give generously to the poor, not grudgingly, for the LORD your God will bless you in everything you do." Sometimes overcoming a selfish heart is the first step. The next step is to protect your heart from forming a grudge over what you have given.

The best way to avoid such a grudge is to maintain a proper perspective regarding "your" money. The truth is, everything we have, including our finances, belongs to God. When we truly believe this, we won't have a giving grudge. Instead, we'll feel joy and gratitude knowing that God has blessed us so much that we can bless others.

A HEART OF GRATITUDE
Deuteronomy 15:15   ROBERT MORRIS

One of my favorite sayings is, "I was born selfish, but I was born again generous." I can't begin to tell you how much joy giving has brought to our lives as a family. Being givers in God's Kingdom has resulted in a more exciting life than we could have ever imagined.

Deuteronomy 15:15 says, "Remember that you were once slaves in the land of Egypt and the LORD your God redeemed you!" Why did God instruct the Israelites to remember they had been slaves? Because it would fill their hearts with gratitude for what He had done for them.

From time to time, God reminds me of my past. He doesn't do it to produce guilt or condemnation. It's because He knows it produces deep gratitude. I was on a road of heartache and self-destruction, and then He saved me and put me on the road of life and blessing.

²⁸"At the end of every third year, bring the entire tithe of that year's harvest and store it in the nearest town. ²⁹Give it to the Levites, who will receive no allotment of land among you, as well as to the foreigners living among you, the orphans, and the widows in your towns, so they can eat and be satisfied. Then the LORD your God will bless you in all your work.

RELEASE FOR DEBTORS

15 "At the end of every seventh year you must cancel the debts of everyone who owes you money. ²This is how it must be done. Everyone must cancel the loans they have made to their fellow Israelites. They must not demand payment from their neighbors or relatives, for the LORD's time of release has arrived. ³This release from debt, however, applies only to your fellow Israelites—not to the foreigners living among you.

⁴"There should be no poor among you, for the LORD your God will greatly bless you in the land he is giving you as a special possession. ⁵You will receive this blessing if you are careful to obey all the commands of the LORD your God that I am giving you today. ⁶The LORD your God will bless you as he has promised. You will lend money to many nations but will never need to borrow. You will rule many nations, but they will not rule over you.

⁷"But if there are any poor Israelites in your towns when you arrive in the land the LORD your God is giving you, do not be hard-hearted or tightfisted toward them. ⁸Instead, be generous and lend them whatever they need. ⁹Do not be mean-spirited and refuse someone a loan because the year for canceling debts is close at hand. If you refuse to make the loan and the needy person cries out to the LORD, you will be considered guilty of sin. ¹⁰Give generously to the poor, not grudgingly, for the LORD your God will bless you in everything you do. ¹¹There will always be some in the land who are poor. That is why I am commanding you to share freely with the poor and with other Israelites in need.

RELEASE FOR HEBREW SLAVES

¹²"If a fellow Hebrew sells himself or herself to be your servant* and serves you for six years, in the seventh year you must set that servant free. ¹³"When you release a male servant, do not send him away empty-handed. ¹⁴Give him a generous farewell gift from your flock, your threshing floor, and your winepress. Share with him some of the bounty with which the LORD your God has blessed you. ¹⁵Remember that you were once slaves in the land of Egypt and the LORD your God redeemed you! That is why I am giving you this command.

¹⁶"But suppose your servant says, 'I will not leave you,' because he loves you and your family, and he has done well with you. ¹⁷In that case, take an awl and push it through his earlobe into the door. After that, he will be your servant for life. And do the same for your female servants.

¹⁸"You must not consider it a hardship when you release your servants. Remember that for six years they have given you services worth double the wages of hired workers, and the LORD your God will bless you in all you do.

SACRIFICING FIRSTBORN MALE ANIMALS

¹⁹"You must set aside for the LORD your God all the firstborn males from your flocks and herds. Do not use the firstborn of your herds to work

15:12 Or *If a Hebrew man or woman is sold to you.*

your fields, and do not shear the firstborn of your flocks. 20 Instead, you and your family must eat these animals in the presence of the LORD your God each year at the place he chooses. 21 But if this firstborn animal has any defect, such as lameness or blindness, or if anything else is wrong with it, you must not sacrifice it to the LORD your God. 22 Instead, use it for food for your family in your hometown. Anyone, whether ceremonially clean or unclean, may eat it, just as anyone may eat a gazelle or deer. 23 But you must not consume the blood. You must pour it out on the ground like water.

PASSOVER AND THE FESTIVAL OF UNLEAVENED BREAD

16 "In honor of the LORD your God, celebrate the Passover each year in the early spring, in the month of Abib,* for that was the month in which the LORD your God brought you out of Egypt by night. 2 Your Passover sacrifice may be from either the flock or the herd, and it must be sacrificed to the LORD your God at the designated place of worship—the place he chooses for his name to be honored. 3 Eat it with bread made without yeast. For seven days the bread you eat must be made without yeast, as when you escaped from Egypt in such a hurry. Eat this bread—the bread of suffering—so that as long as you live you will remember the day you departed from Egypt. 4 Let no yeast be found in any house throughout your land for those seven days. And when you sacrifice the Passover lamb on the evening of the first day, do not let any of the meat remain until the next morning.

5 "You may not sacrifice the Passover in just any of the towns that the LORD your God is giving you. 6 You must offer it only at the designated place of worship—the place the LORD your God chooses for his name to be honored. Sacrifice it there in the evening as the sun goes down on the anniversary of your exodus from Egypt. 7 Roast the lamb and eat it in the place the LORD your God chooses. Then you may go back to your tents the next morning. 8 For the next six days you may not eat any bread made with yeast. On the seventh day proclaim another holy day in honor of the LORD your God, and no work may be done on that day.

THE FESTIVAL OF HARVEST

9 "Count off seven weeks from when you first begin to cut the grain at the time of harvest. 10 Then celebrate the Festival of Harvest* to honor the LORD your God. Bring him a voluntary offering in proportion to the blessings you have received from him. 11 This is a time to celebrate before the LORD your God at the designated place of worship he will choose for his name to be honored. Celebrate with your sons and daughters, your male and female servants, the Levites from your towns, and the foreigners, orphans, and

widows who live among you. 12 Remember that you were once slaves in Egypt, so be careful to obey all these decrees.

THE FESTIVAL OF SHELTERS

13 "You must observe the Festival of Shelters* for seven days at the end of the harvest season, after the grain has been threshed and the grapes have been pressed. 14 This festival will be a happy time of celebrating with your sons and daughters, your male and female servants, and the Levites, foreigners, orphans, and widows from your towns. 15 For seven days you must celebrate this festival to honor the LORD your God at the place he chooses, for it is he who blesses you with bountiful harvests and gives you success in all your work. This festival will be a time of great joy for all.

16 "Each year every man in Israel must celebrate these three festivals: the Festival of Unleavened Bread, the Festival of Harvest, and the Festival of Shelters. On each of these occasions, all men must appear before the LORD your God at the place he chooses, but they must not appear before the LORD without a gift for him. 17 All must give as they are able, according to the blessings given to them by the LORD your God.

JUSTICE FOR THE PEOPLE

18 "Appoint judges and officials for yourselves from each of your tribes in all the towns the LORD your God is giving you. They must judge the people fairly. 19 You must never twist justice or show partiality. Never accept a bribe, for bribes blind the eyes of the wise and corrupt the decisions of the godly. 20 Let true justice prevail, so you may live and occupy the land that the LORD your God is giving you.

21 "You must never set up a wooden Asherah pole beside the altar you build for the LORD your God. 22 And never set up sacred pillars for worship, for the LORD your God hates them.

17 "Never sacrifice sick or defective cattle, sheep, or goats to the LORD your God, for he detests such gifts.

2 "When you begin living in the towns the LORD your God is giving you, a man or woman among you might do evil in the sight of the LORD your God and violate the covenant. 3 For instance, they might serve other gods or worship the sun, the moon, or any of the stars—the forces of heaven—which I have strictly forbidden. 4 When you hear about it, investigate the

16:1 Hebrew *Observe the month of Abib, and keep the Passover unto the LORD your God.* Abib, the first month of the ancient Hebrew lunar calendar, usually occurs within the months of March and April. 16:10 Hebrew *Festival of Weeks;* also in 16:16. This was later called the Festival of Pentecost (see Acts 2:1). It is celebrated today as Shavuot (or Shabuoth). 16:13 Or *Festival of Booths,* or *Festival of Tabernacles;* also in 16:16. This was earlier called the Festival of the Final Harvest or Festival of Ingathering (see Exod 23:16b). It is celebrated today as Sukkot (or Succoth).

matter thoroughly. If it is true that this detestable thing has been done in Israel, ⁵ then the man or woman who has committed such an evil act must be taken to the gates of the town and stoned to death. ⁶ But never put a person to death on the testimony of only one witness. There must always be two or three witnesses. ⁷ The witnesses must throw the first stones, and then all the people may join in. In this way, you will purge the evil from among you.

⁸ "Suppose a case arises in a local court that is too hard for you to decide—for instance, whether someone is guilty of murder or only of manslaughter, or a difficult lawsuit, or a case involving different kinds of assault. Take such legal cases to the place the LORD your God will choose, ⁹ and present them to the Levitical priests or the judge on duty at that time. They will hear the case and declare the verdict. ¹⁰ You must carry out the verdict they announce and the sentence they prescribe at the place the LORD chooses. You must do exactly what they say. ¹¹ After they have interpreted the law and declared their verdict, the sentence they impose must be fully executed; do not modify it in any way. ¹² Anyone arrogant enough to reject the verdict of the judge or of the priest who represents the LORD your God must die. In this way you will purge the evil from Israel. ¹³ Then everyone else will hear about it and be afraid to act so arrogantly.

GUIDELINES FOR A KING

¹⁴ "You are about to enter the land the LORD your God is giving you. When you take it over and settle there, you may think, 'We should select a king to rule over us like the other nations around us.' ¹⁵ If this happens, be sure to select as king the man the LORD your God chooses. You must appoint a fellow Israelite; he may not be a foreigner.

¹⁶ "The king must not build up a large stable of horses for himself or send his people to Egypt to buy horses, for the LORD has told you, 'You must never return to Egypt.' ¹⁷ The king must not take many wives for himself, because they will turn his heart away from the LORD. And he must not accumulate large amounts of wealth in silver and gold for himself.

¹⁸ "When he sits on the throne as king, he must copy for himself this body of instruction on a scroll in the presence of the Levitical priests. ¹⁹ He must always keep that copy with him and read it daily as long as he lives. That way he will learn to fear the LORD his God by obeying all the terms of these instructions and decrees. ²⁰ This regular reading will prevent him from becoming proud and acting as if he is above his fellow citizens. It will also prevent him from turning away from these commands in the smallest way. And it will ensure that he and his descendants will reign for many generations in Israel.

GIFTS FOR THE PRIESTS AND LEVITES

18 "Remember that the Levitical priests— that is, the whole of the tribe of Levi—will receive no allotment of land among the other tribes in Israel. Instead, the priests and Levites will eat from the special gifts given to the LORD, for that is their share. ² They will have no land of their own among the Israelites. The LORD himself is their special possession, just as he promised them.

³ "These are the parts the priests may claim as their share from the cattle, sheep, and goats that the people bring as offerings: the shoulder, the cheeks, and the stomach. ⁴ You must also give to the priests the first share of the grain, the new wine, the olive oil, and the wool at shearing time. ⁵ For the LORD your God chose the tribe of Levi out of all your tribes to minister in the LORD's name forever.

⁶ "Suppose a Levite chooses to move from his town in Israel, wherever he is living, to the place the LORD chooses for worship. ⁷ He may minister there in the name of the LORD his God, just like all his fellow Levites who are serving the LORD there. ⁸ He may eat his share of the sacrifices and offerings, even if he also receives support from his family.

A CALL TO HOLY LIVING

⁹ "When you enter the land the LORD your God is giving you, be very careful not to imitate the detestable customs of the nations living there. ¹⁰ For example, never sacrifice your son or daughter as a burnt offering.* And do not let your people practice fortune-telling, or use sorcery, or interpret omens, or engage in witchcraft, ¹¹ or cast spells, or function as mediums or psychics, or call forth the spirits of the dead. ¹² Anyone who does these things is detestable to the LORD. It is because the other nations have done these detestable things that the LORD your God will drive them out ahead of you. ¹³ But you must be blameless before the LORD your God. ¹⁴ The nations you are about to displace consult sorcerers and fortune-tellers, but the LORD your God forbids you to do such things.

TRUE AND FALSE PROPHETS

¹⁵ Moses continued, "The LORD your God will raise up for you a prophet like me from among your fellow Israelites. You must listen to him. ¹⁶ For this is what you yourselves requested of the LORD your God when you were assembled at Mount Sinai.* You said, 'Don't let us hear the voice of the LORD our God anymore or see this blazing fire, for we will die.'

¹⁷ "Then the LORD said to me, 'What they have said is right. ¹⁸ I will raise up a prophet like you from among their fellow Israelites. I will put my

18:10 Or never make your son or daughter pass through the fire.
18:16 Hebrew Horeb, another name for Sinai.

words in his mouth, and he will tell the people everything I command him. ¹⁹I will personally deal with anyone who will not listen to the messages the prophet proclaims on my behalf. ²⁰But any prophet who falsely claims to speak in my name or who speaks in the name of another god must die.'

²¹"But you may wonder, 'How will we know whether or not a prophecy is from the LORD?' ²²If the prophet speaks in the LORD's name but his prediction does not happen or come true, you will know that the LORD did not give that message. That prophet has spoken without my authority and need not be feared.

CITIES OF REFUGE

19 "When the LORD your God destroys the nations whose land he is giving you, you will take over their land and settle in their towns and homes. ²Then you must set apart three cities of refuge in the land the LORD your God is giving you. ³Survey the territory,* and divide the land the LORD your God is giving you into three districts, with one of these cities in each district. Then anyone who has killed someone can flee to one of the cities of refuge for safety.

⁴"If someone kills another person unintentionally, without previous hostility, the slayer may flee to any of these cities to live in safety. ⁵For example, suppose someone goes into the forest with a neighbor to cut wood. And suppose one of them swings an ax to chop down a tree, and the ax head flies off the handle, killing the other person. In such cases, the slayer may flee to one of the cities of refuge to live in safety.

⁶"If the distance to the nearest city of refuge is too far, an enraged avenger might be able to chase down and kill the person who caused the death. Then the slayer would die unfairly, since he had never shown hostility toward the person who died. ⁷That is why I am commanding you to set aside three cities of refuge.

⁸"And if the LORD your God enlarges your territory, as he swore to your ancestors, and gives you all the land he promised them, ⁹you must designate three additional cities of refuge. (He will give you this land if you are careful to obey all the commands I have given you—if you always love the LORD your God and walk in his ways.) ¹⁰That way you will prevent the death of innocent people in the land the LORD your God is giving you as your special possession. You will not be held responsible for the death of innocent people.

¹¹"But suppose someone is hostile toward a neighbor and deliberately ambushes and murders him and then flees to one of the cities of refuge. ¹²In that case, the elders of the murderer's hometown must send agents to the city of refuge to bring him back and hand him over to the dead person's avenger to be put to death. ¹³Do not feel sorry for that murderer! Purge from Israel the guilt of murdering innocent people; then all will go well with you.

CONCERN FOR JUSTICE

¹⁴"When you arrive in the land the LORD your God is giving you as your special possession, you must never steal anyone's land by moving the boundary markers your ancestors set up to mark their property.

¹⁵"You must not convict anyone of a crime on the testimony of only one witness. The facts of the case must be established by the testimony of two or three witnesses.

¹⁶"If a malicious witness comes forward and accuses someone of a crime, ¹⁷then both the accuser and accused must appear before the LORD by coming to the priests and judges in office at that time. ¹⁸The judges must investigate the case thoroughly. If the accuser has brought false charges against his fellow Israelite, ¹⁹you must impose on the accuser the sentence he intended for the other person. In this way, you will purge such evil from among you. ²⁰Then the rest of the people will hear about it and be afraid to do such an evil thing. ²¹You must show no pity for the guilty! Your rule should be life for life, eye for eye, tooth for tooth, hand for hand, foot for foot.

REGULATIONS CONCERNING WAR

20 "When you go out to fight your enemies and you face horses and chariots and an army greater than your own, do not be afraid. The LORD your God, who brought you out of the land of Egypt, is with you! ²When you prepare for battle, the priest must come forward to speak to the troops. ³He will say to them, 'Listen to me, all you men of Israel! Do not be afraid as you go out to fight your enemies today! Do not lose heart or panic or tremble before them. ⁴For the LORD your God is going with you! He will fight for you against your enemies, and he will give you victory!'

⁵"Then the officers of the army must address the troops and say, 'Has anyone here just built a new house but not yet dedicated it? If so, you may go home! You might be killed in the battle, and someone else would dedicate your house. ⁶Has anyone here just planted a vineyard but not yet eaten any of its fruit? If so, you may go home! You might die in battle, and someone else would eat the first fruit. ⁷Has anyone here just become engaged to a woman but not yet married her? Well, you may go home and get married! You might die in the battle, and someone else would marry her.'

⁸"Then the officers will also say, 'Is anyone here afraid or worried? If you are, you may go home before you frighten anyone else.' ⁹When the officers have finished speaking to their troops, they will appoint the unit commanders.

19:3 Or *Keep the roads in good repair.*

[10] "As you approach a town to attack it, you must first offer its people terms for peace. [11] If they accept your terms and open the gates to you, then all the people inside will serve you in forced labor. [12] But if they refuse to make peace and prepare to fight, you must attack the town. [13] When the LORD your God hands the town over to you, use your swords to kill every man in the town. [14] But you may keep for yourselves all the women, children, livestock, and other plunder. You may enjoy the plunder from your enemies that the LORD your God has given you.

[15] "But these instructions apply only to distant towns, not to the towns of the nations in the land you will enter. [16] In those towns that the LORD your God is giving you as a special possession, destroy every living thing. [17] You must completely destroy* the Hittites, Amorites, Canaanites, Perizzites, Hivites, and Jebusites, just as the LORD your God has commanded you. [18] This will prevent the people of the land from teaching you to imitate their detestable customs in the worship of their gods, which would cause you to sin deeply against the LORD your God.

[19] "When you are attacking a town and the war drags on, you must not cut down the trees with your axes. You may eat the fruit, but do not cut down the trees. Are the trees your enemies, that you should attack them? [20] You may only cut down trees that you know are not valuable for food. Use them to make the equipment you need to attack the enemy town until it falls.

CLEANSING FOR UNSOLVED MURDER

21 "When you are in the land the LORD your God is giving you, someone may be found murdered in a field, and you don't know who committed the murder. [2] In such a case, your elders and judges must measure the distance from the site of the crime to the nearby towns. [3] When the nearest town has been determined, that town's elders must select from the herd a heifer that has never been trained or yoked to a plow. [4] They must lead it down to a valley that has not been plowed or planted and that has a stream running through it. There in the valley they must break the heifer's neck. [5] Then the Levitical priests must step forward, for the LORD your God has chosen them to minister before him and to pronounce blessings in the LORD's name. They are to decide all legal and criminal cases.

[6] "The elders of the town must wash their hands over the heifer whose neck was broken. [7] Then they must say, 'Our hands did not shed this person's blood, nor did we see it happen. [8] O LORD, forgive your people Israel whom you have redeemed. Do not charge your people with the guilt of murdering an innocent person.' Then they will be absolved of the guilt of this person's blood. [9] By following these instructions, you will do what is right in the LORD's sight and will cleanse the guilt of murder from your community.

MARRIAGE TO A CAPTIVE WOMAN

[10] "Suppose you go out to war against your enemies and the LORD your God hands them over to you, and you take some of them as captives. [11] And suppose you see among the captives a beautiful woman, and you are attracted to her and want to marry her. [12] If this happens, you may take her to your home, where she must shave her head, cut her nails, [13] and change the clothes she was wearing when she was captured. She will stay in your home, but let her mourn for her father and mother for a full month. Then you may marry her, and you will be her husband and she will be your wife. [14] But if you marry her and she does not please you, you must let her go free. You may not sell her or treat her as a slave, for you have humiliated her.

RIGHTS OF THE FIRSTBORN

[15] "Suppose a man has two wives, but he loves one and not the other, and both have given him sons. And suppose the firstborn son is the son of the wife he does not love. [16] When the man divides his inheritance, he may not give the larger inheritance to his younger son, the son of the wife he loves, as if he were the firstborn son. [17] He must recognize the rights of his oldest son, the son of the wife he does not love, by giving him a double portion. He is the first son of his father's virility, and the rights of the firstborn belong to him.

DEALING WITH A REBELLIOUS SON

[18] "Suppose a man has a stubborn and rebellious son who will not obey his father or mother, even though they discipline him. [19] In such a case, the father and mother must take the son to the elders as they hold court at the town gate. [20] The parents must say to the elders, 'This son of ours is stubborn and rebellious and refuses to obey. He is a glutton and a drunkard.' [21] Then all the men of his town must stone him to death. In this way, you will purge this evil from among you, and all Israel will hear about it and be afraid.

VARIOUS REGULATIONS

[22] "If someone has committed a crime worthy of death and is executed and hung on a tree,* [23] the body must not remain hanging from the tree overnight. You must bury the body that same day, for anyone who is hung* is cursed in the sight of God. In this way, you will prevent the defilement of the land the LORD your God is giving you as your special possession.

20:17 The Hebrew term used here refers to the complete consecration of things or people to the LORD, either by destroying them or by giving them as an offering.   21:22 Or impaled on a pole; similarly in 21:23.   21:23 Greek version reads for everyone who is hung on a tree. Compare Gal 3:13.

22
"If you see your neighbor's ox or sheep or goat wandering away, don't ignore your responsibility.* Take it back to its owner. ²If its owner does not live nearby or you don't know who the owner is, take it to your place and keep it until the owner comes looking for it. Then you must return it. ³Do the same if you find your neighbor's donkey, clothing, or anything else your neighbor loses. Don't ignore your responsibility.

⁴"If you see that your neighbor's donkey or ox has collapsed on the road, do not look the other way. Go and help your neighbor get it back on its feet!

⁵"A woman must not put on men's clothing, and a man must not wear women's clothing. Anyone who does this is detestable in the sight of the LORD your God.

⁶"If you happen to find a bird's nest in a tree or on the ground, and there are young ones or eggs in it with the mother sitting in the nest, do not take the mother with the young. ⁷You may take the young, but let the mother go, so that you may prosper and enjoy a long life.

⁸"When you build a new house, you must build a railing around the edge of its flat roof. That way you will not be considered guilty of murder if someone falls from the roof.

⁹"You must not plant any other crop between the rows of your vineyard. If you do, you are forbidden to use either the grapes from the vineyard or the other crop.

¹⁰"You must not plow with an ox and a donkey harnessed together.

¹¹"You must not wear clothing made of wool and linen woven together.

¹²"You must put four tassels on the hem of the cloak with which you cover yourself—on the front, back, and sides.

REGULATIONS FOR SEXUAL PURITY

¹³"Suppose a man marries a woman, but after sleeping with her, he turns against her ¹⁴and publicly accuses her of shameful conduct, saying, 'When I married this woman, I discovered she was not a virgin.' ¹⁵Then the woman's father and mother must bring the proof of her virginity to the elders as they hold court at the town gate. ¹⁶Her father must say to them, 'I gave my daughter to this man to be his wife, and now he has turned against her. ¹⁷He has accused her of shameful conduct, saying, "I discovered that your daughter was not a virgin." But here is the proof of my daughter's virginity.' Then they must spread her bed sheet before the elders. ¹⁸The elders must then take the man and punish him. ¹⁹They must also fine him 100 pieces of silver,* which he must pay to the woman's father because he publicly accused a virgin of Israel of shameful conduct. The woman will then remain the man's wife, and he may never divorce her.

²⁰"But suppose the man's accusations are true, and he can show that she was not a virgin. ²¹The

woman must be taken to the door of her father's home, and there the men of the town must stone her to death, for she has committed a disgraceful crime in Israel by being promiscuous while living in her parents' home. In this way, you will purge this evil from among you.

²²"If a man is discovered committing adultery, both he and the woman must die. In this way, you will purge Israel of such evil.

²³"Suppose a man meets a young woman, a virgin who is engaged to be married, and he has sexual intercourse with her. If this happens within a town, ²⁴you must take both of them to the gates of that town and stone them to death. The woman is guilty because she did not scream for help. The man must die because he violated another man's wife. In this way, you will purge this evil from among you.

²⁵"But if the man meets the engaged woman out in the country, and he rapes her, then only the man must die. ²⁶Do nothing to the young woman; she has committed no crime worthy of death. She is as innocent as a murder victim. ²⁷Since the man raped her out in the country, it must be assumed that she screamed, but there was no one to rescue her.

²⁸"Suppose a man has intercourse with a young woman who is a virgin but is not engaged to be married. If they are discovered, ²⁹he must pay her father fifty pieces of silver.* Then he must marry the young woman because he violated her, and he may never divorce her as long as he lives.

³⁰*"A man must not marry his father's former wife, for this would violate his father.

REGULATIONS CONCERNING WORSHIP

23
¹*"If a man's testicles are crushed or his penis is cut off, he may not be admitted to the assembly of the LORD.

²"If a person is illegitimate by birth, neither he nor his descendants for ten generations may be admitted to the assembly of the LORD.

³"No Ammonite or Moabite or any of their descendants for ten generations may be admitted to the assembly of the LORD. ⁴These nations did not welcome you with food and water when you came out of Egypt. Instead, they hired Balaam son of Beor from Pethor in distant Aram-naharaim to curse you. ⁵But the LORD your God refused to listen to Balaam. He turned the intended curse into a blessing because the LORD your God loves you. ⁶As long as you live, you must never promote the welfare and prosperity of the Ammonites or Moabites.

⁷"Do not detest the Edomites or the Egyptians, because the Edomites are your relatives and you lived as foreigners among the Egyptians. ⁸The

---

22:1 Hebrew *don't hide yourself;* similarly in 22:3.   22:19 Hebrew *100 [shekels] of silver,* about 2.5 pounds or 1.1 kilograms in weight.   22:29 Hebrew *50 [shekels] of silver,* about 1.25 pounds or 570 grams in weight.   22:30 Verse 22:30 is numbered 23:1 in Hebrew text.   23:1 Verses 23:1-25 are numbered 23:2-26 in Hebrew text.

third generation of Edomites and Egyptians may enter the assembly of the LORD.

MISCELLANEOUS REGULATIONS

⁹ "When you go to war against your enemies, be sure to stay away from anything that is impure. ¹⁰ "Any man who becomes ceremonially defiled because of a nocturnal emission must leave the camp and stay away all day. ¹¹ Toward evening he must bathe himself, and at sunset he may return to the camp.

¹² "You must have a designated area outside the camp where you can go to relieve yourself. ¹³ Each of you must have a spade as part of your equipment. Whenever you relieve yourself, dig a hole with the spade and cover the excrement. ¹⁴ The camp must be holy, for the LORD your God moves around in your camp to protect you and to defeat your enemies. He must not see any shameful thing among you, or he will turn away from you.

¹⁵ "If slaves should escape from their masters and take refuge with you, you must not hand them over to their masters. ¹⁶ Let them live among you in any town they choose, and do not oppress them.

¹⁷ "No Israelite, whether man or woman, may become a temple prostitute. ¹⁸ When you are bringing an offering to fulfill a vow, you must not bring to the house of the LORD your God any offering from the earnings of a prostitute, whether a man* or a woman, for both are detestable to the LORD your God.

¹⁹ "Do not charge interest on the loans you make to a fellow Israelite, whether you loan money, or food, or anything else. ²⁰ You may charge interest to foreigners, but you may not charge interest to Israelites, so that the LORD your God may bless you in everything you do in the land you are about to enter and occupy.

²¹ "When you make a vow to the LORD your God, be prompt in fulfilling whatever you promised him. For the LORD your God demands that you promptly fulfill all your vows, or you will be guilty of sin. ²² However, it is not a sin to refrain from making a vow. ²³ But once you have voluntarily made a vow, be careful to fulfill your promise to the LORD your God.

²⁴ "When you enter your neighbor's vineyard, you may eat your fill of grapes, but you must not carry any away in a basket. ²⁵ And when you enter your neighbor's field of grain, you may pluck the heads of grain with your hand, but you must not harvest it with a sickle.

24 "Suppose a man marries a woman but she does not please him. Having discovered something wrong with her, he writes a document of divorce, hands it to her, and sends her away from his house. ² When she leaves his house, she is free to marry another man. ³ But if the second husband also turns against her,

writes a document of divorce, hands it to her, and sends her away, or if he dies, ⁴ the first husband may not marry her again, for she has been defiled. That would be detestable to the LORD. You must not bring guilt upon the land the LORD your God is giving you as a special possession.

⁵ "A newly married man must not be drafted into the army or be given any other official responsibilities. He must be free to spend one year at home, bringing happiness to the wife he has married.

⁶ "It is wrong to take a set of millstones, or even just the upper millstone, as security for a loan, for the owner uses it to make a living.

⁷ "If anyone kidnaps a fellow Israelite and treats him as a slave or sells him, the kidnapper must die. In this way, you will purge the evil from among you.

⁸ "In all cases involving serious skin diseases,* be careful to follow the instructions of the Levitical priests; obey all the commands I have given them. ⁹ Remember what the LORD your God did to Miriam as you were coming from Egypt.

¹⁰ "If you lend anything to your neighbor, do not enter his house to pick up the item he is giving as security. ¹¹ You must wait outside while he goes in and brings it out to you. ¹² If your neighbor is poor and gives you his cloak as security for a loan, do not keep the cloak overnight. ¹³ Return the cloak to its owner by sunset so he can stay warm through the night and bless you, and the LORD your God will count you as righteous.

¹⁴ "Never take advantage of poor and destitute laborers, whether they are fellow Israelites or foreigners living in your towns. ¹⁵ You must pay them their wages each day before sunset because they are poor and are counting on it. If you don't, they might cry out to the LORD against you, and it would be counted against you as sin.

¹⁶ "Parents must not be put to death for the sins of their children, nor children for the sins of their parents. Those deserving to die must be put to death for their own crimes.

¹⁷ "True justice must be given to foreigners living among you and to orphans, and you must never accept a widow's garment as security for her debt. ¹⁸ Always remember that you were slaves in Egypt and that the LORD your God redeemed you from your slavery. That is why I have given you this command.

¹⁹ "When you are harvesting your crops and forget to bring in a bundle of grain from your field, don't go back to get it. Leave it for the foreigners, orphans, and widows. Then the LORD your God will bless you in all you do. ²⁰ When you beat the olives from your olive trees, don't go over the boughs twice. Leave the remaining olives for the foreigners, orphans, and widows.

23:18 Hebrew *a dog*.   24:8 Traditionally rendered *leprosy*. The Hebrew word used here can describe various skin diseases.

²¹When you gather the grapes in your vineyard, don't glean the vines after they are picked. Leave the remaining grapes for the foreigners, orphans, and widows. ²²Remember that you were slaves in the land of Egypt. That is why I am giving you this command.

25 "Suppose two people take a dispute to court, and the judges declare that one is right and the other is wrong. ²If the person in the wrong is sentenced to be flogged, the judge must command him to lie down and be beaten in his presence with the number of lashes appropriate to the crime. ³But never give more than forty lashes; more than forty lashes would publicly humiliate your neighbor.

⁴"You must not muzzle an ox to keep it from eating as it treads out the grain.

⁵"If two brothers are living together on the same property and one of them dies without a son, his widow may not be married to anyone from outside the family. Instead, her husband's brother should marry her and have intercourse with her to fulfill the duties of a brother-in-law. ⁶The first son she bears to him will be considered the son of the dead brother, so that his name will not be forgotten in Israel.

⁷"But if the man refuses to marry his brother's widow, she must go to the town gate and say to the elders assembled there, 'My husband's brother refuses to preserve his brother's name in Israel—he refuses to fulfill the duties of a brother-in-law by marrying me.' ⁸The elders of the town will then summon him and talk with him. If he still refuses and says, 'I don't want to marry her,' ⁹the widow must walk over to him in the presence of the elders, pull his sandal from his foot, and spit in his face. Then she must declare, 'This is what happens to a man who refuses to provide his brother with children.' ¹⁰Ever afterward in Israel his family will be referred to as 'the family of the man whose sandal was pulled off'!

¹¹"If two Israelite men get into a fight and the wife of one tries to rescue her husband by grabbing the testicles of the other man, ¹²you must cut off her hand. Show her no pity.

¹³"You must use accurate scales when you weigh out merchandise, ¹⁴and you must use full and honest measures. ¹⁵Yes, always use honest weights and measures, so that you may enjoy a long life in the land the LORD your God is giving you. ¹⁶All who cheat with dishonest weights and measures are detestable to the LORD your God.

¹⁷"Never forget what the Amalekites did to you as you came from Egypt. ¹⁸They attacked you when you were exhausted and weary, and they struck down those who were straggling behind. They had no fear of God. ¹⁹Therefore, when the LORD your God has given you rest from all your enemies in the land he is giving you as a special possession, you must destroy the Amalekites and erase their memory from under heaven. Never forget this!

HARVEST OFFERINGS AND TITHES

26 "When you enter the land the LORD your God is giving you as a special possession and you have conquered it and settled there, ²put some of the first produce from each crop you harvest into a basket and bring it to the designated place of worship—the place the LORD your God chooses for his name to be honored. ³Go to the priest in charge at that time and say to him, 'With this gift I acknowledge to the LORD your God that I have entered the land he swore to our ancestors he would give us.' ⁴The priest will then take the basket from your hand and set it before the altar of the LORD your God.

⁵"You must then say in the presence of the LORD your God, 'My ancestor Jacob was a wandering Aramean who went to live as a foreigner in Egypt. His family arrived few in number, but in Egypt they became a large and mighty nation. ⁶When the Egyptians oppressed and humiliated us by making us their slaves, ⁷we cried out to the LORD, the God of our ancestors. He heard our cries and saw our hardship, toil, and oppression. ⁸So the LORD brought us out of Egypt with a strong hand and powerful arm, with overwhelming terror, and with miraculous signs and wonders. ⁹He brought us to this place and gave us this land flowing with milk and honey! ¹⁰And now, O LORD, I have brought you the first portion of the harvest you have given me from the ground.' Then place the produce before the LORD your God, and bow to the ground in worship before him. ¹¹Afterward you may go and celebrate because of all the good things the LORD your God has given to you and your household. Remember to include the Levites and the foreigners living among you in the celebration.

¹²"Every third year you must offer a special tithe of your crops. In this year of the special tithe you must give your tithes to the Levites, foreigners, orphans, and widows, so that they will have enough to eat in your towns. ¹³Then you must declare in the presence of the LORD your God, 'I have taken the sacred gift from my house and have given it to the Levites, foreigners, orphans, and widows, just as you commanded me. I have not violated or forgotten any of your commands. ¹⁴I have not eaten any of it while in mourning; I have not handled it while I was ceremonially unclean; and I have not offered any of it to the dead. I have obeyed the LORD my God and have done everything you commanded me. ¹⁵Now look down from your holy dwelling place in heaven and bless your people Israel and the land you swore to our ancestors to give us—a land flowing with milk and honey.'

A CALL TO OBEY THE LORD'S COMMANDS

16 "Today the LORD your God has commanded you to obey all these decrees and regulations. So be careful to obey them wholeheartedly. 17 You have declared today that the LORD is your God. And you have promised to walk in his ways, and to obey his decrees, commands, and regulations, and to do everything he tells you. 18 The LORD has declared today that you are his people, his own special treasure, just as he promised, and that you must obey all his commands. 19 And if you do, he will set you high above all the other nations he has made. Then you will receive praise, honor, and renown. You will be a nation that is holy to the LORD your God, just as he promised."

THE ALTAR ON MOUNT EBAL

27 Then Moses and the leaders of Israel gave this charge to the people: "Obey all these commands that I am giving you today. 2 When you cross the Jordan River and enter the land the LORD your God is giving you, set up some large stones and coat them with plaster. 3 Write this whole body of instruction on them when you cross the river to enter the land the LORD your God is giving you—a land flowing with milk and honey, just as the LORD, the God of your ancestors, promised you. 4 When you cross the Jordan, set up these stones at Mount Ebal and coat them with plaster, as I am commanding you today.

5 "Then build an altar there to the LORD your God, using natural, uncut stones. You must not shape the stones with an iron tool. 6 Build the altar of uncut stones, and use it to offer burnt offerings to the LORD your God. 7 Also sacrifice peace offerings on it, and celebrate by feasting there before the LORD your God. 8 You must clearly write all these instructions on the stones coated with plaster."

9 Then Moses and the Levitical priests addressed all Israel as follows: "O Israel, be quiet and listen! Today you have become the people of the LORD your God. 10 So you must obey the LORD your God by keeping all these commands and decrees that I am giving you today."

CURSES FROM MOUNT EBAL

11 That same day Moses also gave this charge to the people: 12 "When you cross the Jordan River, the tribes of Simeon, Levi, Judah, Issachar, Joseph, and Benjamin must stand on Mount Gerizim to proclaim a blessing over the people. 13 And the tribes of Reuben, Gad, Asher, Zebulun, Dan, and Naphtali must stand on Mount Ebal to proclaim a curse. 14 "Then the Levites will shout to all the people of Israel:

15 'Cursed is anyone who carves or casts an idol and secretly sets it up. These idols, the work of craftsmen, are detestable to the LORD.'
And all the people will reply, 'Amen.'

16 'Cursed is anyone who dishonors father or mother.'
And all the people will reply, 'Amen.'

17 'Cursed is anyone who steals property from a neighbor by moving a boundary marker.'
And all the people will reply, 'Amen.'

18 'Cursed is anyone who leads a blind person astray on the road.'
And all the people will reply, 'Amen.'

19 'Cursed is anyone who denies justice to foreigners, orphans, or widows.'
And all the people will reply, 'Amen.'

20 'Cursed is anyone who has sexual intercourse with one of his father's wives, for he has violated his father.'
And all the people will reply, 'Amen.'

21 'Cursed is anyone who has sexual intercourse with an animal.'
And all the people will reply, 'Amen.'

22 'Cursed is anyone who has sexual intercourse with his sister, whether she is the daughter of his father or his mother.'
And all the people will reply, 'Amen.'

23 'Cursed is anyone who has sexual intercourse with his mother-in-law.'
And all the people will reply, 'Amen.'

24 'Cursed is anyone who attacks a neighbor in secret.'
And all the people will reply, 'Amen.'

25 'Cursed is anyone who accepts payment to kill an innocent person.'
And all the people will reply, 'Amen.'

26 'Cursed is anyone who does not affirm and obey the terms of these instructions.'
And all the people will reply, 'Amen.'

BLESSINGS FOR OBEDIENCE

28 "If you fully obey the LORD your God and carefully keep all his commands that I am giving you today, the LORD your God will set you high above all the nations of the world. 2 You will experience all these blessings if you obey the LORD your God:

3 Your towns and your fields
will be blessed.

4 Your children and your crops
will be blessed.
The offspring of your herds and flocks
will be blessed.

5 Your fruit baskets and breadboards
will be blessed.

⁶ Wherever you go and whatever you do,
  you will be blessed.

⁷ "The LORD will conquer your enemies when they attack you. They will attack you from one direction, but they will scatter from you in seven!
⁸ "The LORD will guarantee a blessing on everything you do and will fill your storehouses with grain. The LORD your God will bless you in the land he is giving you.
⁹ "If you obey the commands of the LORD your God and walk in his ways, the LORD will establish you as his holy people as he swore he would do.
¹⁰ Then all the nations of the world will see that you are a people claimed by the LORD, and they will stand in awe of you.
¹¹ "The LORD will give you prosperity in the land he swore to your ancestors to give you, blessing you with many children, numerous livestock, and abundant crops. ¹² The LORD will send rain at the proper time from his rich treasury in the heavens and will bless all the work you do. You will lend to many nations, but you will never need to borrow from them. ¹³ If you listen to these commands of the LORD your God that I am giving you today, and if you carefully obey them, the LORD will make you the head and not the tail, and you will always be on top and never at the bottom. ¹⁴ You must not turn away from any of the commands I am giving you today, nor follow after other gods and worship them.

CURSES FOR DISOBEDIENCE

¹⁵ "But if you refuse to listen to the LORD your God and do not obey all the commands and decrees I am giving you today, all these curses will come and overwhelm you:

¹⁶ Your towns and your fields
  will be cursed.
¹⁷ Your fruit baskets and breadboards
  will be cursed.
¹⁸ Your children and your crops
  will be cursed.
The offspring of your herds and flocks
  will be cursed.
¹⁹ Wherever you go and whatever you do,
  you will be cursed.

²⁰ "The LORD himself will send on you curses, confusion, and frustration in everything you do, until at last you are completely destroyed for doing evil and abandoning me. ²¹ The LORD will afflict you with diseases until none of you are left in the land you are about to enter and occupy. ²² The LORD will strike you with wasting diseases, fever, and inflammation, with scorching heat and drought, and with blight and mildew. These disasters will pursue you until you die. ²³ The skies above will be as unyielding as bronze, and the earth beneath will be as hard as iron. ²⁴ The LORD will change the rain that falls on your land into powder, and dust will pour down from the sky until you are destroyed.
²⁵ "The LORD will cause you to be defeated by your enemies. You will attack your enemies from one direction, but you will scatter from them in seven! You will be an object of horror to all the kingdoms of the earth. ²⁶ Your corpses will be food for all the scavenging birds and wild animals, and no one will be there to chase them away.
²⁷ "The LORD will afflict you with the boils of Egypt and with tumors, scurvy, and the itch, from which you cannot be cured. ²⁸ The LORD will strike you with madness, blindness, and panic. ²⁹ You will grope around in broad daylight like a blind person groping in the darkness, but you will not find your way. You will be oppressed and robbed continually, and no one will come to save you.
³⁰ "You will be engaged to a woman, but another man will sleep with her. You will build a house, but someone else will live in it. You will plant a vineyard, but you will never enjoy its fruit. ³¹ Your ox will be butchered before your eyes, but you will not eat a single bite of the meat. Your donkey will be taken from you, never to be returned. Your sheep and goats will be given to your enemies, and no one will be there to help you. ³² You will watch as your sons and daughters are taken away as slaves. Your heart will break for them, but you won't be able to help them. ³³ A foreign nation you have never heard about will eat the crops you worked so hard to grow. You will suffer under constant oppression and harsh treatment. ³⁴ You will go mad because of all the tragedy you see around you. ³⁵ The LORD will cover your knees and legs with incurable boils. In fact, you will be covered from head to foot.
³⁶ "The LORD will exile you and your king to a nation unknown to you and your ancestors. There in exile you will worship gods of wood and stone! ³⁷ You will become an object of horror, ridicule, and mockery among all the nations to which the LORD sends you.
³⁸ "You will plant much but harvest little, for locusts will eat your crops. ³⁹ You will plant vineyards and care for them, but you will not drink the wine or eat the grapes, for worms will destroy the vines. ⁴⁰ You will grow olive trees throughout your land, but you will never use the olive oil, for the fruit will drop before it ripens. ⁴¹ You will have sons and daughters, but you will lose them, for they will be led away into captivity. ⁴² Swarms of insects will destroy your trees and crops.
⁴³ "The foreigners living among you will become stronger and stronger, while you become weaker and weaker. ⁴⁴ They will lend money to you, but you will not lend to them. They will be the head, and you will be the tail!
⁴⁵ "If you refuse to listen to the LORD your God and to obey the commands and decrees he has given you, all these curses will pursue and overtake you until you are destroyed. ⁴⁶ These horrors

will serve as a sign and warning among you and your descendants forever. [47]If you do not serve the LORD your God with joy and enthusiasm for the abundant benefits you have received, [48]you will serve your enemies whom the LORD will send against you. You will be left hungry, thirsty, naked, and lacking in everything. The LORD will put an iron yoke on your neck, oppressing you harshly until he has destroyed you.

[49]"The LORD will bring a distant nation against you from the end of the earth, and it will swoop down on you like a vulture. It is a nation whose language you do not understand, [50]a fierce and heartless nation that shows no respect for the old and no pity for the young. [51]Its armies will devour your livestock and crops, and you will be destroyed. They will leave you no grain, new wine, olive oil, calves, or lambs, and you will starve to death. [52]They will attack your cities until all the fortified walls in your land—the walls you trusted to protect you—are knocked down. They will attack all the towns in the land the LORD your God has given you.

[53]"The siege and terrible distress of the enemy's attack will be so severe that you will eat the flesh of your own sons and daughters, whom the LORD your God has given you. [54]The most tenderhearted man among you will have no compassion for his own brother, his beloved wife, and his surviving children. [55]He will refuse to share with them the flesh he is devouring—the flesh of one of his own children—because he has nothing else to eat during the siege and terrible distress that your enemy will inflict on all your towns. [56]The most tender and delicate woman among you—so delicate she would not so much as touch the ground with her foot—will be selfish toward the husband she loves and toward her own son or daughter. [57]She will hide from them the afterbirth and the new baby she has borne, so that she herself can secretly eat them. She will have nothing else to eat during the siege and terrible distress that your enemy will inflict on all your towns.

[58]"If you refuse to obey all the words of instruction that are written in this book, and if you do not fear the glorious and awesome name of the LORD your God, [59]then the LORD will overwhelm you and your children with indescribable plagues. These plagues will be intense and without relief, making you miserable and unbearably sick. [60]He will afflict you with all the diseases of Egypt that you feared so much, and you will have no relief. [61]The LORD will afflict you with every sickness and plague there is, even those not mentioned in this Book of Instruction, until you are destroyed. [62]Though you become as numerous as the stars in the sky, few of you will be left because you would not listen to the LORD your God.

[63]"Just as the LORD has found great pleasure in causing you to prosper and multiply, the LORD will find pleasure in destroying you. You will be torn from the land you are about to enter and occupy. [64]For the LORD will scatter you among all the nations from one end of the earth to the other. There you will worship foreign gods that neither you nor your ancestors have known, gods made of wood and stone! [65]There among those nations you will find no peace or place to rest. And the LORD will cause your heart to tremble, your eyesight to fail, and your soul to despair. [66]Your life will constantly hang in the balance. You will live night and day in fear, unsure if you will survive. [67]In the morning you will say, 'If only it were night!' And in the evening you will say, 'If only it were morning!' For you will be terrified by the awful horrors you see around you. [68]Then the LORD will send you back to Egypt in ships, to a destination I promised you would never see again. There you will offer to sell yourselves to your enemies as slaves, but no one will buy you."

29

[1]*These are the terms of the covenant the LORD commanded Moses to make with the Israelites while they were in the land of Moab, in addition to the covenant he had made with them at Mount Sinai.*

MOSES REVIEWS THE COVENANT

[2]*Moses summoned all the Israelites and said to them, "You have seen with your own eyes everything the LORD did in the land of Egypt to Pharaoh and to all his servants and to his whole country— [3]all the great tests of strength, the miraculous signs, and the amazing wonders. [4]But to this day the LORD has not given you minds that understand, nor eyes that see, nor ears that hear! [5]For forty years I led you through the wilderness, yet your clothes and sandals did not wear out. [6]You ate no bread and drank no wine or other alcoholic drink, but he provided for you so you would know that he is the LORD your God.

[7]"When we came here, King Sihon of Heshbon and King Og of Bashan came out to fight against us, but we defeated them. [8]We took their land and gave it to the tribes of Reuben and Gad and to the half-tribe of Manasseh as their grant of land.

[9]"Therefore, obey the terms of this covenant so that you will prosper in everything you do. [10]All of you—tribal leaders, elders, officers, all the men of Israel—are standing today in the presence of the LORD your God. [11]Your little ones and your wives are with you, as well as the foreigners living among you who chop your wood and carry your water. [12]You are standing here today to enter into the covenant of the LORD your God. The LORD is making this covenant, including the curses. [13]By entering into the covenant today, he will establish you as his people and

---

29:1a Verse 29:1 is numbered 28:69 in Hebrew text.
29:1b Hebrew *Horeb*, another name for Sinai. 29:2 Verses 29:2-29 are numbered 29:1-28 in Hebrew text.

confirm that he is your God, just as he promised you and as he swore to your ancestors Abraham, Isaac, and Jacob.

¹⁴"But you are not the only ones with whom I am making this covenant with its curses. ¹⁵I am making this covenant both with you who stand here today in the presence of the LORD our God, and also with the future generations who are not standing here today.

¹⁶"You remember how we lived in the land of Egypt and how we traveled through the lands of enemy nations as we left. ¹⁷You have seen their detestable practices and their idols* made of wood, stone, silver, and gold. ¹⁸I am making this covenant with you so that no one among you—no man, woman, clan, or tribe—will turn away from the LORD our God to worship these gods of other nations, and so that no root among you bears bitter and poisonous fruit.

¹⁹"Those who hear the warnings of this curse should not congratulate themselves, thinking, 'I am safe, even though I am following the desires of my own stubborn heart.' This would lead to utter ruin! ²⁰The LORD will never pardon such people. Instead his anger and jealousy will burn against them. All the curses written in this book will come down on them, and the LORD will erase their names from under heaven. ²¹The LORD will separate them from all the tribes of Israel, to pour out on them all the curses of the covenant recorded in this Book of Instruction.

²²"Then the generations to come, both your own descendants and the foreigners who come from distant lands, will see the devastation of the land and the diseases the LORD inflicts on it. ²³They will exclaim, 'The whole land is devastated by sulfur and salt. It is a wasteland with nothing planted and nothing growing, not even a blade of grass. It is like the cities of Sodom and Gomorrah, Admah and Zeboiim, which the LORD destroyed in his intense anger.'

²⁴"And all the surrounding nations will ask, 'Why has the LORD done this to this land? Why was he so angry?'

²⁵"And the answer will be, 'This happened because the people of the land abandoned the covenant that the LORD, the God of their ancestors, made with them when he brought them out of the land of Egypt. ²⁶Instead, they turned away to serve and worship gods they had not known before, gods that were not from the LORD. ²⁷That is why the LORD's anger has burned against this land, bringing down on it every curse recorded in this book. ²⁸In great anger and fury the LORD uprooted his people from their land and banished them to another land, where they still live today!'

²⁹"The LORD our God has secrets known to no one. We are not accountable for them, but we and our children are accountable forever for all that he has revealed to us, so that we may obey all the terms of these instructions.

A CALL TO RETURN TO THE LORD

30 "In the future, when you experience all these blessings and curses I have listed for you, and when you are living among the nations to which the LORD your God has exiled you, take to heart all these instructions. ²If at that time you and your children return to the LORD your God, and if you obey with all your heart and all your soul all the commands I have given you today, ³then the LORD your God will restore your fortunes. He will have mercy on you and gather you back from all the nations where he has scattered you. ⁴Even though you are banished to the ends of the earth,* the LORD your God will gather you from there and bring you back again. ⁵The LORD your God will return you to the land that belonged to your ancestors, and you will possess that land again. Then he will make you even more prosperous and numerous than your ancestors!

⁶"The LORD your God will change your heart* and the hearts of all your descendants, so that you will love him with all your heart and soul and so you may live! ⁷The LORD your God will inflict all these curses on your enemies and on those who hate and persecute you. ⁸Then you will again obey the LORD and keep all his commands that I am giving you today.

⁹"The LORD your God will then make you successful in everything you do. He will give you many children and numerous livestock, and he will cause your fields to produce abundant harvests, for the LORD will again delight in being good to you as he was to your ancestors. ¹⁰The LORD your God will delight in you if you obey his voice and keep the commands and decrees written in this Book of Instruction, and if you turn to the LORD your God with all your heart and soul.

THE CHOICE OF LIFE OR DEATH

¹¹"This command I am giving you today is not too difficult for you, and it is not beyond your reach. ¹²It is not kept in heaven, so distant that you must ask, 'Who will go up to heaven and bring it down so we can hear it and obey?' ¹³It is not kept beyond the sea, so far away that you must ask, 'Who will cross the sea to bring it to us so we can hear it and obey?' ¹⁴No, the message is very close at hand; it is on your lips and in your heart so that you can obey it.

¹⁵"Now listen! Today I am giving you a choice between life and death, between prosperity and disaster. ¹⁶For I command you this day to love the LORD your God and to keep his commands, decrees, and regulations by walking in his ways. If you do this, you will live and multiply, and the LORD your God will bless you and the land you are about to enter and occupy.

¹⁷"But if your heart turns away and you refuse to listen, and if you are drawn away to serve and

---

29:17 The Hebrew term (literally *round things*) probably alludes to dung. 30:4 Hebrew *of the heavens.* 30:6 Hebrew *circumcise your heart.*

worship other gods, [18] then I warn you now that you will certainly be destroyed. You will not live a long, good life in the land you are crossing the Jordan to occupy.

[19] "Today I have given you the choice between life and death, between blessings and curses. Now I call on heaven and earth to witness the choice you make. Oh, that you would choose life, so that you and your descendants might live! [20] You can make this choice by loving the LORD your God, obeying him, and committing yourself firmly to him. This[*] is the key to your life. And if you love and obey the LORD, you will live long in the land the LORD swore to give your ancestors Abraham, Isaac, and Jacob."

JOSHUA BECOMES ISRAEL'S LEADER

31 When Moses had finished giving these instructions[*] to all the people of Israel, [2] he said, "I am now 120 years old, and I am no longer able to lead you. The LORD has told me, 'You will not cross the Jordan River.' [3] But the LORD your God himself will cross over ahead of you. He will destroy the nations living there, and you will take possession of their land. Joshua will lead you across the river, just as the LORD promised.

[4] "The LORD will destroy the nations living in the land, just as he destroyed Sihon and Og, the kings of the Amorites. [5] The LORD will hand over to you the people who live there, and you must deal with them as I have commanded you. [6] So be strong and courageous! Do not be afraid and do not panic before them. For the LORD your God will personally go ahead of you. He will neither fail you nor abandon you."

[7] Then Moses called for Joshua, and as all Israel watched, he said to him, "Be strong and courageous! For you will lead these people into the land that the LORD swore to their ancestors he would give them. You are the one who will divide it among them as their grants of land. [8] Do not be afraid or discouraged, for the LORD will personally go ahead of you. He will be with you; he will neither fail you nor abandon you."

PUBLIC READING OF THE BOOK OF INSTRUCTION

[9] So Moses wrote this entire body of instruction in a book and gave it to the priests, who carried the Ark of the LORD's Covenant, and to the elders of Israel. [10] Then Moses gave them this command: "At the end of every seventh year, the Year of Release, during the Festival of Shelters, [11] you must read this Book of Instruction to all the people of Israel when they assemble before the LORD your God at the place he chooses. [12] Call them all together—men, women, children, and the foreigners living in your towns—so they may hear this Book of Instruction and learn to fear the LORD your God and carefully obey all the terms of these instructions. [13] Do this so that your children who have not known these instructions will hear them and will learn to fear the LORD your God. Do this as long as you live in the land you are crossing the Jordan to occupy."

ISRAEL'S DISOBEDIENCE PREDICTED

[14] Then the LORD said to Moses, "The time has come for you to die. Call Joshua and present yourselves at the Tabernacle,[*] so that I may commission him there." So Moses and Joshua went and presented themselves at the Tabernacle. [15] And the LORD appeared to them in a pillar of cloud that stood at the entrance to the sacred tent.

[16] The LORD said to Moses, "You are about to die and join your ancestors. After you are gone, these people will begin to worship foreign gods, the gods of the land where they are going. They will abandon me and break my covenant that I have made with them. [17] Then my anger will blaze forth against them. I will abandon them, hiding my face from them, and they will be devoured. Terrible trouble will come down on them, and on that day they will say, 'These disasters have come down on us because God is no longer among us!' [18] At that time I will hide my face from them on account of all the evil they commit by worshiping other gods.

[19] "So write down the words of this song, and teach it to the people of Israel. Help them learn it, so it may serve as a witness for me against them. [20] For I will bring them into the land I swore to give their ancestors—a land flowing with milk and honey. There they will become prosperous, eat all the food they want, and become fat. But they will begin to worship other gods; they will despise me and break my covenant. [21] And when great disasters come down on them, this song will stand as evidence against them, for it will never be forgotten by their descendants. I know the intentions of these people, even now before they have entered the land I swore to give them."

[22] So that very day Moses wrote down the words of the song and taught it to the Israelites.

[23] Then the LORD commissioned Joshua son of Nun with these words: "Be strong and courageous, for you must bring the people of Israel into the land I swore to give them. I will be with you."

[24] When Moses had finished writing this entire body of instruction in a book, [25] he gave this command to the Levites who carried the Ark of the LORD's Covenant: [26] "Take this Book of Instruction and place it beside the Ark of the Covenant of the LORD your God, so it may remain there as a witness against the people of Israel. [27] For I know how rebellious and stubborn you are. Even now, while I am still alive and am here with you, you have rebelled against the LORD. How much more rebellious will you be after my death!

[28] "Now summon all the elders and officials of your tribes, so that I can speak to them directly

---

30:20 Or He. 31:1 As in Dead Sea Scrolls and Greek version; Masoretic Text reads Moses went and spoke. 31:14 Hebrew Tent of Meeting; also in 31:14b.

and call heaven and earth to witness against them. ²⁹ I know that after my death you will become utterly corrupt and will turn from the way I have commanded you to follow. In the days to come, disaster will come down on you, for you will do what is evil in the Lord's sight, making him very angry with your actions."

THE SONG OF MOSES

³⁰ So Moses recited this entire song publicly to the assembly of Israel:

32 ¹ "Listen, O heavens, and I will speak!
   Hear, O earth, the words that I say!
² Let my teaching fall on you like rain;
   let my speech settle like dew.
Let my words fall like rain on tender grass,
   like gentle showers on young plants.
³ I will proclaim the name of the Lord;
   how glorious is our God!
⁴ He is the Rock; his deeds are perfect.
   Everything he does is just and fair.
He is a faithful God who does no wrong;
   how just and upright he is!

⁵ "But they have acted corruptly toward him;
   when they act so perversely,
are they really his children?*
   They are a deceitful and twisted
      generation.
⁶ Is this the way you repay the Lord,
   you foolish and senseless people?
Isn't he your Father who created you?
   Has he not made you and established you?
⁷ Remember the days of long ago;
   think about the generations past.
Ask your father, and he will inform you.
   Inquire of your elders, and they will
      tell you.
⁸ When the Most High assigned lands to the
      nations,
   when he divided up the human race,
he established the boundaries of the peoples
   according to the number in his heavenly
      court.*

⁹ "For the people of Israel belong to the Lord;
   Jacob is his special possession.
¹⁰ He found them in a desert land,
   in an empty, howling wasteland.
He surrounded them and watched
      over them;
   he guarded them as he would guard his
      own eyes.*
¹¹ Like an eagle that rouses her chicks
   and hovers over her young,
so he spread his wings to take them up
   and carried them safely on his pinions.
¹² The Lord alone guided them;
   they followed no foreign gods.
¹³ He let them ride over the highlands
   and feast on the crops of the fields.

He nourished them with honey from
      the rock
   and olive oil from the stony ground.
¹⁴ He fed them yogurt from the herd
   and milk from the flock,
   together with the fat of lambs.
He gave them choice rams from Bashan,
      and goats,
   together with the choicest wheat.
You drank the finest wine,
   made from the juice of grapes.

¹⁵ "But Israel* soon became fat and unruly;
   the people grew heavy, plump, and
      stuffed!
Then they abandoned the God who had
      made them;
   they made light of the Rock of their
      salvation.
¹⁶ They stirred up his jealousy by worshiping
      foreign gods;
   they provoked his fury with detestable
      deeds.
¹⁷ They offered sacrifices to demons,
      which are not God,
   to gods they had not known before,
to new gods only recently arrived,
   to gods their ancestors had never feared.
¹⁸ You neglected the Rock who had
      fathered you;
   you forgot the God who had given you
      birth.

¹⁹ "The Lord saw this and drew back,
   provoked to anger by his own sons and
      daughters.
²⁰ He said, 'I will abandon them;
   then see what becomes of them.
For they are a twisted generation,
   children without integrity.
²¹ They have roused my jealousy by worshiping
      things that are not God;
   they have provoked my anger with their
      useless idols.
Now I will rouse their jealousy through
      people who are not even a people;
   I will provoke their anger through the
      foolish Gentiles.
²² For my anger blazes forth like fire
   and burns to the depths of the grave.*
It devours the earth and all its crops
   and ignites the foundations of the
      mountains.
²³ I will heap disasters upon them
   and shoot them down with my arrows.
²⁴ I will weaken them with famine,
   burning fever, and deadly disease.

32:5 The meaning of the Hebrew is uncertain. 32:8 As in Dead Sea Scrolls, which read *the number of the sons of God*, and Greek version, which reads *the number of the angels of God*; Masoretic Text reads *the number of the sons of Israel*. 32:10 Hebrew *as the pupil of his eye*. 32:15 Hebrew *Jeshurun*, a term of endearment for Israel. 32:22 Hebrew *of Sheol*.

I will send the fangs of wild beasts
and poisonous snakes that glide in the dust.
25 Outside, the sword will bring death,
and inside, terror will strike
both young men and young women,
both infants and the aged.
26 I would have annihilated them,
wiping out even the memory of them.
27 But I feared the taunt of Israel's enemy,
who might misunderstand and say,
"Our own power has triumphed!
The LORD had nothing to do with this!'"

28 "But Israel is a senseless nation;
the people are foolish, without
understanding.
29 Oh, that they were wise and could
understand this!
Oh, that they might know their fate!
30 How could one person chase a thousand
of them,
and two people put ten thousand
to flight,
unless their Rock had sold them,
unless the LORD had given them up?
31 But the rock of our enemies is not like
our Rock,
as even they recognize.*
32 Their vine grows from the vine of Sodom,
from the vineyards of Gomorrah.
Their grapes are poison,
and their clusters are bitter.
33 Their wine is the venom of serpents,
the deadly poison of cobras.

34 "The LORD says, 'Am I not storing up
these things,
sealing them away in my treasury?
35 I will take revenge; I will pay them back.
In due time their feet will slip.
Their day of disaster will arrive,
and their destiny will overtake them.'

36 "Indeed, the LORD will give justice to
his people,
and he will change his mind about*
his servants,
when he sees their strength is gone
and no one is left, slave or free.
37 Then he will ask, 'Where are their gods,
the rocks they fled to for refuge?
38 Where now are those gods,
who ate the fat of their sacrifices
and drank the wine of their offerings?
Let those gods arise and help you!
Let them provide you with shelter!
39 Look now; I myself am he!
There is no other god but me!
I am the one who kills and gives life;
I am the one who wounds and heals;
no one can be rescued from my
powerful hand!

40 Now I raise my hand to heaven
and declare, "As surely as I live,
41 when I sharpen my flashing sword
and begin to carry out justice,
I will take revenge on my enemies
and repay those who reject me.
42 I will make my arrows drunk with blood,
and my sword will devour flesh—
the blood of the slaughtered and the
captives,
and the heads of the enemy leaders."'

43 "Rejoice with him, you heavens,
and let all of God's angels worship him.*
Rejoice with his people, you Gentiles,
and let all the angels be strengthened
in him.*
For he will avenge the blood of
his children*;
he will take revenge against
his enemies.
He will repay those who hate him*
and cleanse his people's land."

44 So Moses came with Joshua* son of Nun
and recited all the words of this song to the
people.

45 When Moses had finished reciting all these
words to the people of Israel, 46 he added: "Take
to heart all the words of warning I have given
you today. Pass them on as a command to your
children so they will obey every word of these
instructions. 47 These instructions are not empty
words—they are your life! By obeying them you
will enjoy a long life in the land you will occupy
when you cross the Jordan River."

MOSES' DEATH FORETOLD

48 That same day the LORD said to Moses, 49 "Go
to Moab, to the mountains east of the river,* and
climb Mount Nebo, which is across from Jericho.
Look out across the land of Canaan, the land I
am giving to the people of Israel as their own
special possession. 50 Then you will die there on
the mountain. You will join your ancestors, just
as Aaron, your brother, died on Mount Hor and
joined his ancestors. 51 For both of you betrayed
me with the Israelites at the waters of Meribah
at Kadesh* in the wilderness of Zin. You failed to
demonstrate my holiness to the people of Israel
there. 52 So you will see the land from a distance,
but you may not enter the land I am giving to
the people of Israel."

32:31 The meaning of the Hebrew is uncertain; Greek version reads *our enemies are fools.* 32:36 Or *will take revenge for.* 32:43a As in Dead Sea Scrolls and Greek version; Masoretic Text lacks the first two lines. Compare Heb 1:6. 32:43b As in Greek version; Hebrew text lacks this sentence. Compare Rom 15:10. 32:43c As in Dead Sea Scrolls and Greek version; Masoretic Text reads *his servants.* 32:43d As in Dead Sea Scrolls and Greek version; Masoretic Text lacks this line. 32:44 Hebrew *Hoshea,* a variant name for Joshua. 32:49 Hebrew *the mountains of Abarim.* 32:51 Hebrew *waters of Meribath-kadesh.*

MOSES BLESSES THE PEOPLE

33 This is the blessing that Moses, the man of God, gave to the people of Israel before his death:

2 "The LORD came from Mount Sinai
    and dawned upon us* from Mount Seir;
he shone forth from Mount Paran
    and came from Meribah-kadesh
    with flaming fire at his right hand.*
3 Indeed, he loves his people;*
    all his holy ones are in his hands.
They follow in his steps
    and accept his teaching.
4 Moses gave us the LORD's instruction,
    the special possession of the people of
        Israel.*
5 The LORD became king in Israel*—
    when the leaders of the people
        assembled,
    when the tribes of Israel gathered as one."

6 Moses said this about the tribe of Reuben:*

"Let the tribe of Reuben live and not
    die out,
    though they are few in number."

7 Moses said this about the tribe of Judah:

"O LORD, hear the cry of Judah
    and bring them together as a people.
Give them strength to defend their cause;
    help them against their enemies!"

8 Moses said this about the tribe of Levi:

"O LORD, you have given your Thummim
    and Urim—the sacred lots—
    to your faithful servants the Levites.*
You put them to the test at Massah
    and struggled with them at the waters
        of Meribah.
9 The Levites obeyed your word
    and guarded your covenant.
They were more loyal to you
    than to their own parents.
They ignored their relatives
    and did not acknowledge their own
        children.
10 They teach your regulations to Jacob;
    they give your instructions to Israel.
They present incense before you
    and offer whole burnt offerings on the
        altar.
11 Bless the ministry of the Levites, O LORD,
    and accept all the work of their hands.
Hit their enemies where it hurts the most;
    strike down their foes so they never
        rise again."

12 Moses said this about the tribe of Benjamin:

"The people of Benjamin are loved by
    the LORD
    and live in safety beside him.
He surrounds them continuously
    and preserves them from every harm."

13 Moses said this about the tribes of Joseph:

"May their land be blessed by the LORD
    with the precious gift of dew from the
        heavens
    and water from beneath the earth;
14 with the rich fruit that grows in the sun,
    and the rich harvest produced each
        month;
15 with the finest crops of the ancient
        mountains,
    and the abundance from the
        everlasting hills;
16 with the best gifts of the earth and its
        bounty,
    and the favor of the one who appeared in
        the burning bush.
May these blessings rest on Joseph's head,
    crowning the brow of the prince among
        his brothers.
17 Joseph has the majesty of a young bull;
    he has the horns of a wild ox.
He will gore distant nations,
    even to the ends of the earth.
This is my blessing for the multitudes
        of Ephraim
    and the thousands of Manasseh."

18 Moses said this about the tribes of Zebulun
and Issachar*:

"May the people of Zebulun prosper in their
        travels.
    May the people of Issachar prosper at
        home in their tents.
19 They summon the people to the mountain
    to offer proper sacrifices there.
They benefit from the riches of the sea
    and the hidden treasures in the sand."

20 Moses said this about the tribe of Gad:

"Blessed is the one who enlarges
        Gad's territory!
Gad is poised there like a lion
    to tear off an arm or a head.

33:2a As in Greek and Syriac versions; Hebrew reads *upon them.* 33:2b Or *came from myriads of holy ones, from the south, from his mountain slopes.* The meaning of the Hebrew is uncertain. 33:3 As in Greek version; Hebrew reads *Indeed, lover of the peoples.* 33:4 Hebrew *of Jacob.* The names "Jacob" and "Israel" are often interchanged throughout the Old Testament, referring sometimes to the individual patriarch and sometimes to the nation. 33:5 Hebrew *in Jeshurun,* a term of endearment for Israel. 33:6 Hebrew lacks *Moses said this about the tribe of Reuben.* 33:8 As in Greek version; Hebrew lacks *the Levites.* 33:18 Hebrew lacks *and Issachar.*

²¹ The people of Gad took the best land for
themselves;
a leader's share was assigned to them.
When the leaders of the people were
assembled,
they carried out the Lord's justice
and obeyed his regulations for Israel."

²² Moses said this about the tribe of Dan:

"Dan is a lion's cub,
leaping out from Bashan."

²³ Moses said this about the tribe of Naphtali:

"O Naphtali, you are rich in favor
and full of the Lord's blessings;
may you possess the west and the south."

²⁴ Moses said this about the tribe of Asher:

"May Asher be blessed above other sons;
may he be esteemed by his brothers;
may he bathe his feet in olive oil.
²⁵ May the bolts of your gates be of iron
and bronze;
may you be secure all your days."

²⁶ "There is no one like the God of Israel.*
He rides across the heavens to help you,
across the skies in majestic splendor.
²⁷ The eternal God is your refuge,
and his everlasting arms are under you.
He drives out the enemy before you;
he cries out, 'Destroy them!'
²⁸ So Israel will live in safety,
prosperous Jacob in security,
in a land of grain and new wine,
while the heavens drop down dew.
²⁹ How blessed you are, O Israel!
Who else is like you, a people saved
by the Lord?
He is your protecting shield
and your triumphant sword!

Your enemies will cringe before you,
and you will stomp on their backs!"

THE DEATH OF MOSES

34 Then Moses went up to Mount Nebo from
the plains of Moab and climbed Pisgah
Peak, which is across from Jericho. And the
Lord showed him the whole land, from Gilead as far as Dan; ²all the land of Naphtali; the
land of Ephraim and Manasseh; all the land of
Judah, extending to the Mediterranean Sea*;
³the Negev; the Jordan Valley with Jericho—the
city of palms—as far as Zoar. ⁴Then the Lord said
to Moses, "This is the land I promised on oath
to Abraham, Isaac, and Jacob when I said, 'I will
give it to your descendants.' I have now allowed
you to see it with your own eyes, but you will
not enter the land."

⁵So Moses, the servant of the Lord, died there
in the land of Moab, just as the Lord had said.
⁶The Lord buried him* in a valley near Bethpeor in Moab, but to this day no one knows the
exact place. ⁷Moses was 120 years old when he
died, yet his eyesight was clear, and he was as
strong as ever. ⁸The people of Israel mourned
for Moses on the plains of Moab for thirty days,
until the customary period of mourning was
over.

⁹Now Joshua son of Nun was full of the spirit
of wisdom, for Moses had laid his hands on him.
So the people of Israel obeyed him, doing just as
the Lord had commanded Moses.

¹⁰There has never been another prophet in
Israel like Moses, whom the Lord knew face
to face. ¹¹The Lord sent him to perform all the
miraculous signs and wonders in the land of
Egypt against Pharaoh, and all his servants, and
his entire land. ¹²With mighty power, Moses performed terrifying acts in the sight of all Israel.

33:26 Hebrew *of Jeshurun*, a term of endearment for Israel.
34:2 Hebrew *the western sea.* 34:6 Hebrew *He buried him;*
Samaritan Pentateuch and some Greek manuscripts read
They buried him.

JOSHUA

JON HUNTZINGER, PHD

The book of Joshua describes Israel's entry into Canaan after 40 years in the wilderness. It is named after Moses' assistant Joshua son of Nun, who leads the people into the land God promised to give them (Exodus 3:7-8, 17; Deuteronomy 6:10-12; 11:8-12). As with the books of Genesis, Exodus, Leviticus, Numbers, and Deuteronomy, the book of Joshua recounts God's active work among the Israelites and reports His directions to them through His chosen leader. That leader is now Joshua, and this phrase is repeated throughout the book: "The Lord said to Joshua . . ."

The book of Joshua picks up where the book of Deuteronomy leaves off. Just as Deuteronomy includes Moses' exhortation near the end for the people to live by the commandments God has given to them (Deuteronomy 28:1-14), so also Joshua begins with an exhortation to the people to be courageous and live by the words God has given them (Joshua 1:1-9). Their fathers and mothers, who came out of Egypt and went through the wilderness, were filled with fear, and because of it, they did not enter Canaan. They were afraid they would not have enough food or water. They feared the people of the land, who appeared as giants to them, and so they turned back to the wilderness (Numbers 13:25-33). The man who leads them now is one who "has the Spirit in him" (Numbers 27:18). The Spirit of God in Joshua will give him the courage he needs to lead the people and overcome any of his own fears. God wants Joshua to keep the Book of Instruction (Law) and "meditate on it day and night" (Joshua 1:8). This means that the words God spoke to Moses had been collected and written in a book and that Joshua and the Israelites are to remember the things God said to Moses as they make their way into Canaan.

The book of Joshua records a series of battles the Israelites waged against the Canaanites, including the battle at Jericho, where the city walls fell when the priests of Israel blew their rams' horns (Joshua 6:1-27). Following the record of the battles is a report of the allotment of the land they had conquered. The lists of the names of the tribes and families and the parcels of land given to them may make for tedious reading (chapters 13-21), but these events are important to the theme of the book. They confirm that God keeps His promises. Not only does He keep His promise to give the people a rich and abundant land, but He also preserves His promise for every family in particular. Every family was allotted a specific place in the land, and the parcel each received was a tangible sign to them of God's faithfulness to the words He had spoken to them.

Two important questions arise when reading the book of Joshua:

— *When did the events of the conquest of Canaan occur?*

Bible scholars point to two primary dates for the conquest based on their interpretation of the archaeological evidence of cities that existed in ancient Canaan: the fifteenth century BC (1400s) and the thirteenth century BC (1200s). The earlier date fits well with 1 Kings 6:1, which says King Solomon built the Temple in Jerusalem 480 years after the Exodus of the Israelites from Egypt. Since Solomon began to build the Temple in the fourth year of his reign (967 BC), this would date the Exodus to 1447 BC and the entry into Canaan shortly afterward in the late 1400s.

— *What are the implications of the wars that God led the Israelites to fight?*

This second question is a more difficult one. The writer of Joshua placed great importance on God's passionate commitment to one particular people—the Israelites—which reveals His potential and ultimate commitment to all people. By showing His willingness to give salvation and victory to the Israelites, who are smaller and weaker than their foes, God gives us reason to believe He will do the same for anyone else. The writer of the book of Joshua gives an uncompromising record of the battles fought and won by the Israelites to show the dramatic action God takes in response to the agony of His people in slavery (Exodus 2:23-25) so they might have a home where they can know Him and live in freedom. By returning them to the land that He had promised to Abraham hundreds of years earlier and to Moses a generation before, God proves He hears the cries of His people and He keeps His promises. What God does for the small, poor, and fearful Israelites by overthrowing those larger and stronger nations is a sign of the victory and salvation He will give to all peoples if they will receive His Word, just as the second generation of Israelites did under Moses and Joshua.

The entry into Canaan described in Joshua parallels the departure of the people from Egypt. Just as the Israelites passed through the Red Sea, so also their sons and daughters pass through the Jordan River. Prior to the Red Sea, the Israelites observed a Passover meal, just as their children eat a Passover prior to crossing into Canaan. And just as God is described as a warrior who delivered the Israelites from Egypt (Exodus 15:3), so also "the commander of the LORD's army" leads the people in victory over the tribes of Canaan (Joshua 5:13-15). Those two events of deliverance from Egypt and entry into Canaan are parts of one great, saving work God does for the Israelites. He not only saves the people by bringing them out of an old way of slavery and suffering in Egypt, but He also continues to save them by leading them into Canaan and a new way of life.

THE LORD'S CHARGE TO JOSHUA

1 After the death of Moses the LORD's servant, the LORD spoke to Joshua son of Nun, Moses' assistant. He said, ² "Moses my servant is dead. Therefore, the time has come for you to lead these people, the Israelites, across the Jordan River into the land I am giving them. ³ I promise you what I promised Moses: 'Wherever you set foot, you will be on land I have given you—⁴ from the Negev wilderness in the south to the Lebanon mountains in the north, from the Euphrates River in the east to the Mediterranean Sea* in the west, including all the land of the Hittites.' ⁵ No one will be able to stand against you as long as you live. For I will be with you as I was with Moses. I will not fail you or abandon you.

⁶ "Be strong and courageous, for you are the one who will lead these people to possess all the land I swore to their ancestors I would give them. ⁷ Be strong and very courageous. Be careful to obey all the instructions Moses gave you. Do not deviate from them, turning either to the right or to the left. Then you will be successful in everything you do. ⁸ Study this Book of Instruction continually. Meditate on it day and night so you will be sure to obey everything written in it. Only then will you prosper and succeed in all you do. ⁹ This is my command—be strong and courageous! Do not be afraid or discouraged. For the LORD your God is with you wherever you go."

JOSHUA'S CHARGE TO THE ISRAELITES

¹⁰ Joshua then commanded the officers of Israel, ¹¹ "Go through the camp and tell the people to get their provisions ready. In three days you will cross the Jordan River and take possession of the land the LORD your God is giving you."

¹² Then Joshua called together the tribes of Reuben, Gad, and the half-tribe of Manasseh. He told them, ¹³ "Remember what Moses, the servant of the LORD, commanded you: 'The LORD your God is giving you a place of rest. He has given you this land.' ¹⁴ Your wives, children, and livestock may remain here in the land Moses assigned to you on the east side of the Jordan River. But your strong warriors, fully armed, must lead the other tribes across the Jordan to help them conquer their territory. Stay with them ¹⁵ until the LORD gives them rest, as he has given you rest, and until they, too, possess the land the LORD your God is giving them. Only then may you return and settle here on the east side of the Jordan River in the land that Moses, the servant of the LORD, assigned to you."

¹⁶ They answered Joshua, "We will do whatever you command us, and we will go wherever you send us. ¹⁷ We will obey you just as we obeyed Moses. And may the LORD your God be with you as he was with Moses. ¹⁸ Anyone who rebels against your orders and does not obey your words and everything you command will be put to death. So be strong and courageous!"

RAHAB PROTECTS THE SPIES

2 Then Joshua secretly sent out two spies from the Israelite camp at Acacia Grove.* He instructed them, "Scout out the land on the other side of the Jordan River, especially around Jericho." So the two men set out and came to the house of a prostitute named Rahab and stayed there that night.

² But someone told the king of Jericho, "Some Israelites have come here tonight to spy out the land." ³ So the king of Jericho sent orders to Rahab: "Bring out the men who have come into your house, for they have come here to spy out the whole land."

⁴ Rahab had hidden the two men, but she replied, "Yes, the men were here earlier, but I didn't know where they were from. ⁵ They left the

---

THE MIRACLE OF MEDITATION
Joshua 1:8   ROBERT MORRIS

Joshua told the people of Israel to meditate on God's Word. He said, "Study this Book of Instruction continually. Meditate on it day and night so you will be sure to obey everything written in it. Only then will you prosper and succeed in all you do" (Joshua 1:8). *In all you do* refers to every area of your life—family, health, finances, relationships, career, etc. Reading the Word sets supernatural things in motion.

How do you meditate on God's Word? The word *meditate* means to focus on something deliberately. Write a Scripture on a notecard in the morning and think about it throughout the day. Spend time in the Word while you eat during your lunch hour. As you put these practices into your schedule, you'll gain a greater understanding of God's Word, and things will start to come into order as you begin to experience the power of God in your life.

1:4 Hebrew *the Great Sea.*   2:1 Hebrew *Shittim.*

WHEN YOU HAVE A BAD PAST
Joshua 2   ROBERT MORRIS

Rahab didn't know anything about the God of Israel. She was a prostitute who lived in a heathen culture. You may compare her background to yours and think, *Well, at least I'm not as bad as her.* But according to Scripture, we all have a bad past. Romans 3:23 says, "Everyone has sinned; we all fall short of God's glorious standard" (emphasis added). All of us have done things we wish we hadn't done and said things we wish we wouldn't have said. And all of us have had things happen to us in the past we wish wouldn't have happened.

Rahab had a bad past, and yet God looked at her and saw a woman He could use. How is this possible? He saw her heart. Rahab had heard of the great and powerful deeds of the God of Israel, and even though her past was filled with sin, she decided to trust God with her future. She declared to the Hebrew spies, "The LORD your God is the supreme God of the heavens above and the earth below" (Joshua 2:11).

Every person God used in the Bible (except for His Son, Jesus) had a bad past, but He used them anyway. God wants to use you too. No matter how bad your past is, God can and will use you for His glory if you will put your trust in Him.

---

town at dusk, as the gates were about to close. I don't know where they went. If you hurry, you can probably catch up with them." ⁶(Actually, she had taken them up to the roof and hidden them beneath bundles of flax she had laid out.) ⁷So the king's men went looking for the spies along the road leading to the shallow crossings of the Jordan River. And as soon as the king's men had left, the gate of Jericho was shut.

⁸Before the spies went to sleep that night, Rahab went up on the roof to talk with them. ⁹"I know the LORD has given you this land," she told them. "We are all afraid of you. Everyone in the land is living in terror. ¹⁰For we have heard how the LORD made a dry path for you through the Red Sea* when you left Egypt. And we know what you did to Sihon and Og, the two Amorite kings east of the Jordan River, whose people you completely destroyed.* ¹¹No wonder our hearts have melted in fear! No one has the courage to fight after hearing such things. For the LORD your God is the supreme God of the heavens above and the earth below.

¹²"Now swear to me by the LORD that you will be kind to me and my family since I have helped you. Give me some guarantee that ¹³when Jericho is conquered, you will let me live, along with my father and mother, my brothers and sisters, and all their families."

¹⁴"We offer our own lives as a guarantee for your safety," the men agreed. "If you don't betray us, we will keep our promise and be kind to you when the LORD gives us the land."

¹⁵Then, since Rahab's house was built into the town wall, she let them down by a rope through the window. ¹⁶"Escape to the hill country," she told them. "Hide there for three days from the men searching for you. Then, when they have returned, you can go on your way."

¹⁷Before they left, the men told her, "We will be bound by the oath we have taken only if you follow these instructions. ¹⁸When we come into the land, you must leave this scarlet rope hanging from the window through which you let us down. And all your family members—your father, mother, brothers, and all your relatives—must be here inside the house. ¹⁹If they go out into the street and are killed, it will not be our fault. But if anyone lays a hand on people inside this house, we will accept the responsibility for their death. ²⁰If you betray us, however, we are not bound by this oath in any way."

²¹"I accept your terms," she replied. And she sent them on their way, leaving the scarlet rope hanging from the window.

²²The spies went up into the hill country and stayed there three days. The men who were chasing them searched everywhere along the road, but they finally returned without success. ²³Then the two spies came down from the hill country, crossed the Jordan River, and reported to Joshua all that had happened to them. ²⁴"The LORD has given us the whole land," they said, "for all the people in the land are terrified of us."

THE ISRAELITES CROSS THE JORDAN

3 Early the next morning Joshua and all the Israelites left Acacia Grove* and arrived at the banks of the Jordan River, where they camped before crossing. ²Three days later the Israelite officers went through the camp, ³giving these instructions to the people: "When you see the Levitical priests carrying the Ark of the Covenant of the LORD your God, move out from your positions and follow them. ⁴Since you have never traveled this way before, they will guide you. Stay about half a mile* behind them, keeping a clear distance between you and the Ark. Make sure you don't come any closer."

⁵Then Joshua told the people, "Purify yourselves, for tomorrow the LORD will do great wonders among you."

⁶In the morning Joshua said to the priests, "Lift up the Ark of the Covenant and lead the people across the river." And so they started out and went ahead of the people.

2:10a Hebrew *sea of reeds.* 2:10b The Hebrew term used here refers to the complete consecration of things or people to the LORD, either by destroying them or by giving them as an offering. 3:1 Hebrew *Shittim.* 3:4 Hebrew *about 2,000 cubits* [920 meters].

[7] The LORD told Joshua, "Today I will begin to make you a great leader in the eyes of all the Israelites. They will know that I am with you, just as I was with Moses. [8] Give this command to the priests who carry the Ark of the Covenant: 'When you reach the banks of the Jordan River, take a few steps into the river and stop there.'"

[9] So Joshua told the Israelites, "Come and listen to what the LORD your God says. [10] Today you will know that the living God is among you. He will surely drive out the Canaanites, Hittites, Hivites, Perizzites, Girgashites, Amorites, and Jebusites ahead of you. [11] Look, the Ark of the Covenant, which belongs to the Lord of the whole earth, will lead you across the Jordan River! [12] Now choose twelve men from the tribes of Israel, one from each tribe. [13] The priests will carry the Ark of the LORD, the Lord of all the earth. As soon as their feet touch the water, the flow of water will be cut off upstream, and the river will stand up like a wall."

[14] So the people left their camp to cross the Jordan, and the priests who were carrying the Ark of the Covenant went ahead of them. [15] It was the harvest season, and the Jordan was overflowing its banks. But as soon as the feet of the priests who were carrying the Ark touched the water at the river's edge, [16] the water above that point began backing up a great distance away at a town called Adam, which is near Zarethan. And the water below that point flowed on to the Dead Sea* until the riverbed was dry. Then all the people crossed over near the town of Jericho.

[17] Meanwhile, the priests who were carrying the Ark of the LORD's Covenant stood on dry ground in the middle of the riverbed as the people passed by. They waited there until the whole nation of Israel had crossed the Jordan on dry ground.

MEMORIALS TO THE JORDAN CROSSING

4 When all the people had crossed the Jordan, the LORD said to Joshua, [2] "Now choose twelve men, one from each tribe. [3] Tell them, 'Take twelve stones from the very place where the priests are standing in the middle of the Jordan. Carry them out and pile them up at the place where you will camp tonight.'"

[4] So Joshua called together the twelve men he had chosen—one from each of the tribes of Israel. [5] He told them, "Go into the middle of the Jordan, in front of the Ark of the LORD your God. Each of you must pick up one stone and carry it out on your shoulder—twelve stones in all, one for each of the twelve tribes of Israel. [6] We will use these stones to build a memorial. In the future your children will ask you, 'What do these stones mean?' [7] Then you can tell them, 'They remind us that the Jordan River stopped flowing when the Ark of the LORD's Covenant went across.' These stones will stand as a memorial among the people of Israel forever."

[8] So the men did as Joshua had commanded them. They took twelve stones from the middle of the Jordan River, one for each tribe, just as the LORD had told Joshua. They carried them to the place where they camped for the night and constructed the memorial there.

[9] Joshua also set up another pile of twelve stones in the middle of the Jordan, at the place where the priests who carried the Ark of the Covenant were standing. And they are there to this day.

[10] The priests who were carrying the Ark stood in the middle of the river until all of the LORD's commands that Moses had given to Joshua were carried out. Meanwhile, the people hurried across the riverbed. [11] And when everyone was safely on the other side, the priests crossed over with the Ark of the LORD as the people watched.

[12] The armed warriors from the tribes of Reuben, Gad, and the half-tribe of Manasseh led the Israelites across the Jordan, just as Moses had directed. [13] These armed men—about 40,000 strong—were ready for battle, and the LORD was with them as they crossed over to the plains of Jericho.

[14] That day the LORD made Joshua a great leader in the eyes of all the Israelites, and for the rest of his life they revered him as much as they had revered Moses.

[15] The LORD had said to Joshua, [16] "Command the priests carrying the Ark of the Covenant* to come up out of the riverbed." [17] So Joshua gave the command. [18] As soon as the priests carrying the Ark of the LORD's Covenant came up out of the riverbed and their feet were on high ground, the water of the Jordan returned and overflowed its banks as before.

[19] The people crossed the Jordan on the tenth day of the first month.* Then they camped at Gilgal, just east of Jericho. [20] It was there at Gilgal that Joshua piled up the twelve stones taken from the Jordan River.

[21] Then Joshua said to the Israelites, "In the future your children will ask, 'What do these stones mean?' [22] Then you can tell them, 'This is where the Israelites crossed the Jordan on dry ground.' [23] For the LORD your God dried up the river right before your eyes, and he kept it dry until you were all across, just as he did at the Red Sea* when he dried it up until we had all crossed over. [24] He did this so all the nations of the earth might know that the LORD's hand is powerful, and so you might fear the LORD your God forever."

5 When all the Amorite kings west of the Jordan and all the Canaanite kings who lived along the Mediterranean coast* heard how the LORD had dried up the Jordan River so the people

---

3:16 Hebrew *the sea of the Arabah, the Salt Sea.*   4:16 Hebrew *Ark of the Testimony.*   4:19 This day in the ancient Hebrew lunar calendar occurred in late March, April, or early May.   4:23 Hebrew *sea of reeds.*   5:1 Hebrew *along the sea.*

of Israel could cross, they lost heart and were paralyzed with fear because of them.

ISRAEL REESTABLISHES COVENANT CEREMONIES

²At that time the LORD told Joshua, "Make flint knives and circumcise this second generation of Israelites.*" ³So Joshua made flint knives and circumcised the entire male population of Israel at Gibeath-haaraloth.*

⁴Joshua had to circumcise them because all the men who were old enough to fight in battle when they left Egypt had died in the wilderness. ⁵Those who left Egypt had all been circumcised, but none of those born after the Exodus, during the years in the wilderness, had been circumcised. ⁶The Israelites had traveled in the wilderness for forty years until all the men who were old enough to fight in battle when they left Egypt had died. For they had disobeyed the LORD, and the LORD vowed he would not let them enter the land he had sworn to give us—a land flowing with milk and honey. ⁷So Joshua circumcised their sons—those who had grown up to take their fathers' places—for they had not been circumcised on the way to the Promised Land. ⁸After all the males had been circumcised, they rested in the camp until they were healed.

⁹Then the LORD said to Joshua, "Today I have rolled away the shame of your slavery in Egypt." So that place has been called Gilgal* to this day.

¹⁰While the Israelites were camped at Gilgal on the plains of Jericho, they celebrated Passover on the evening of the fourteenth day of the first month.* ¹¹The very next day they began to eat unleavened bread and roasted grain harvested from the land. ¹²No manna appeared on the day they first ate from the crops of the land, and it was never seen again. So from that time on the Israelites ate from the crops of Canaan.

THE LORD'S COMMANDER CONFRONTS JOSHUA

¹³When Joshua was near the town of Jericho, he looked up and saw a man standing in front of him with sword in hand. Joshua went up to him and demanded, "Are you friend or foe?"

¹⁴"Neither one," he replied. "I am the commander of the LORD's army."

At this, Joshua fell with his face to the ground in reverence. "I am at your command," Joshua said. "What do you want your servant to do?"

¹⁵The commander of the LORD's army replied, "Take off your sandals, for the place where you are standing is holy." And Joshua did as he was told.

THE FALL OF JERICHO

6 Now the gates of Jericho were tightly shut because the people were afraid of the Israelites. No one was allowed to go out or in. ²But the LORD said to Joshua, "I have given you Jericho, its king, and all its strong warriors. ³You and your fighting men should march around the town once a day for six days. ⁴Seven priests will walk ahead of the Ark, each carrying a ram's horn. On the seventh day you are to march around the town seven times, with the priests blowing the horns. ⁵When you hear the priests give one long blast on the rams' horns, have all the people shout as loud as they can. Then the walls of the town will collapse, and the people can charge straight into the town."

⁶So Joshua called together the priests and said, "Take up the Ark of the LORD's Covenant, and assign seven priests to walk in front of it, each carrying a ram's horn." ⁷Then he gave orders to the people: "March around the town, and the armed men will lead the way in front of the Ark of the LORD."

⁸After Joshua spoke to the people, the seven priests with the rams' horns started marching in the presence of the LORD, blowing the horns as they marched. And the Ark of the LORD's Covenant followed behind them. ⁹Some of the armed men marched in front of the priests with the horns and some behind the Ark, with the priests continually blowing the horns. ¹⁰"Do not shout; do not even talk," Joshua commanded. "Not a single word from any of you until I tell you to shout. Then shout!" ¹¹So the Ark of the LORD was carried around the town once that day, and then everyone returned to spend the night in the camp.

¹²Joshua got up early the next morning, and the priests again carried the Ark of the LORD. ¹³The seven priests with the rams' horns marched in front of the Ark of the LORD, blowing their horns. Again the armed men marched both in front of the priests with the horns and behind the Ark of the LORD. All this time the priests were blowing their horns. ¹⁴On the second day they again marched around the town once and returned to the camp. They followed this pattern for six days.

¹⁵On the seventh day the Israelites got up at dawn and marched around the town as they had done before. But this time they went around the town seven times. ¹⁶The seventh time around, as the priests sounded the long blast on their horns, Joshua commanded the people, "Shout! For the LORD has given you the town! ¹⁷Jericho and everything in it must be completely destroyed* as an offering to the LORD. Only Rahab the prostitute and the others in her house will be spared, for she protected our spies.

¹⁸"Do not take any of the things set apart for destruction, or you yourselves will be completely

5:2 Or circumcise the Israelites a second time. 5:3 Gibeath-haaraloth means "hill of foreskins." 5:9 Gilgal sounds like the Hebrew word galal, meaning "to roll." 5:10 This day in the ancient Hebrew lunar calendar occurred in late March, April, or early May. 6:17 The Hebrew term used here refers to the complete consecration of things or people to the LORD, either by destroying them or by giving them as an offering; similarly in 6:18, 21.

destroyed, and you will bring trouble on the camp of Israel. [19] Everything made from silver, gold, bronze, or iron is sacred to the LORD and must be brought into his treasury."

[20] When the people heard the sound of the rams' horns, they shouted as loud as they could. Suddenly, the walls of Jericho collapsed, and the Israelites charged straight into the town and captured it. [21] They completely destroyed everything in it with their swords—men and women, young and old, cattle, sheep, goats, and donkeys.

[22] Meanwhile, Joshua said to the two spies, "Keep your promise. Go to the prostitute's house and bring her out, along with all her family."

[23] The men who had been spies went in and brought out Rahab, her father, mother, brothers, and all the other relatives who were with her. They moved her whole family to a safe place near the camp of Israel.

[24] Then the Israelites burned the town and everything in it. Only the things made from silver, gold, bronze, or iron were kept for the treasury of the LORD's house. [25] So Joshua spared Rahab the prostitute and her relatives who were with her in the house, because she had hidden the spies Joshua sent to Jericho. And she lives among the Israelites to this day.

[26] At that time Joshua invoked this curse:

"May the curse of the LORD fall on anyone
who tries to rebuild the town of Jericho.
At the cost of his firstborn son,
he will lay its foundation.
At the cost of his youngest son,
he will set up its gates."

[27] So the LORD was with Joshua, and his reputation spread throughout the land.

AI DEFEATS THE ISRAELITES

7 But Israel violated the instructions about the things set apart for the LORD.* A man named Achan had stolen some of these dedicated things, so the LORD was very angry with the Israelites. Achan was the son of Carmi, a descendant of Zimri* son of Zerah, of the tribe of Judah.

[2] Joshua sent some of his men from Jericho to spy out the town of Ai, east of Bethel, near Beth-aven. [3] When they returned, they told Joshua, "There's no need for all of us to go up there; it won't take more than two or three thousand men to attack Ai. Since there are so few of them, don't make all our people struggle to go up there."

[4] So approximately 3,000 warriors were sent, but they were soundly defeated. The men of Ai [5] chased the Israelites from the town gate as far as the quarries,* and they killed about thirty-six who were retreating down the slope. The Israelites were paralyzed with fear at this turn of events, and their courage melted away.

[6] Joshua and the elders of Israel tore their clothing in dismay, threw dust on their heads, and bowed face down to the ground before the Ark of the LORD until evening. [7] Then Joshua cried out, "Oh, Sovereign LORD, why did you bring us across the Jordan River if you are going to let the Amorites kill us? If only we had been content to stay on the other side! [8] Lord, what can I say now that Israel has fled from its enemies? [9] For when the Canaanites and all the other people living in the land hear about it, they will surround us and wipe our name off the face of the earth. And then what will happen to the honor of your great name?"

[10] But the LORD said to Joshua, "Get up! Why are you lying on your face like this? [11] Israel has sinned and broken my covenant! They have stolen some of the things that I commanded must be set apart for me. And they have not only stolen them but have lied about it and hidden the things among their own belongings. [12] That is why the Israelites are running from their enemies in defeat. For now Israel itself has been set apart for destruction. I will not remain with you any longer unless you destroy the things among you that were set apart for destruction.

[13] "Get up! Command the people to purify themselves in preparation for tomorrow. For this is what the LORD, the God of Israel, says: Hidden among you, O Israel, are things set apart for the LORD. You will never defeat your enemies until you remove these things from among you.

[14] "In the morning you must present yourselves by tribes, and the LORD will point out the tribe to which the guilty man belongs. That tribe must come forward with its clans, and the LORD will point out the guilty clan. That clan will then come forward, and the LORD will point out the guilty family. Finally, each member of the guilty family must come forward one by one. [15] The one who has stolen what was set apart for destruction will himself be burned with fire, along with everything he has, for he has broken the covenant of the LORD and has done a horrible thing in Israel."

ACHAN'S SIN

[16] Early the next morning Joshua brought the tribes of Israel before the LORD, and the tribe of Judah was singled out. [17] Then the clans of Judah came forward, and the clan of Zerah was singled out. Then the families of Zerah came forward, and the family of Zimri was singled out. [18] Every member of Zimri's family was brought forward person by person, and Achan was singled out.

[19] Then Joshua said to Achan, "My son, give glory to the LORD, the God of Israel, by telling the truth. Make your confession and tell me what you have done. Don't hide it from me."

7:1a The Hebrew term used here refers to the complete consecration of things or people to the LORD, either by destroying them or by giving them as an offering; similarly in 7:11, 12, 13, 15.   7:1b As in parallel text at 1 Chr 2:6; Hebrew reads *Zabdi*. Also in 7:17, 18.   7:5 Or *as far as Shebarim*.

²⁰Achan replied, "It is true! I have sinned against the LORD, the God of Israel. ²¹Among the plunder I saw a beautiful robe from Babylon,* 200 silver coins,* and a bar of gold weighing more than a pound.* I wanted them so much that I took them. They are hidden in the ground beneath my tent, with the silver buried deeper than the rest."

²²So Joshua sent some men to make a search. They ran to the tent and found the stolen goods hidden there, just as Achan had said, with the silver buried beneath the rest. ²³They took the things from the tent and brought them to Joshua and all the Israelites. Then they laid them on the ground in the presence of the LORD.

²⁴Then Joshua and all the Israelites took Achan, the silver, the robe, the bar of gold, his sons, daughters, cattle, donkeys, sheep, goats, tent, and everything he had, and they brought them to the valley of Achor. ²⁵Then Joshua said to Achan, "Why have you brought trouble on us? The LORD will now bring trouble on you." And all the Israelites stoned Achan and his family and burned their bodies. ²⁶They piled a great heap of stones over Achan, which remains to this day. That is why the place has been called the Valley of Trouble* ever since. So the LORD was no longer angry.

THE ISRAELITES DEFEAT AI

8 Then the LORD said to Joshua, "Do not be afraid or discouraged. Take all your fighting men and attack Ai, for I have given you the king of Ai, his people, his town, and his land. ²You will destroy them as you destroyed Jericho and its king. But this time you may keep the plunder and the livestock for yourselves. Set an ambush behind the town."

³So Joshua and all the fighting men set out to attack Ai. Joshua chose 30,000 of his best warriors and sent them out at night ⁴with these orders: "Hide in ambush close behind the town and be ready for action. ⁵When our main army attacks, the men of Ai will come out to fight as they did before, and we will run away from them. ⁶We will let them chase us until we have drawn them away from the town. For they will say, 'The Israelites are running away from us as they did before.' Then, while we are running from them, ⁷you will jump up from your ambush and take possession of the town, for the LORD your God will give it to you. ⁸Set the town on fire, as the LORD has commanded. You have your orders."

⁹So they left and went to the place of ambush between Bethel and the west side of Ai. But Joshua remained among the people in the camp that night. ¹⁰Early the next morning Joshua roused his men and started toward Ai, accompanied by the elders of Israel. ¹¹All the fighting men who were with Joshua marched in front of the town and camped on the north side of Ai, with a valley between them and the town. ¹²That night

Joshua sent about 5,000 men to lie in ambush between Bethel and Ai, on the west side of the town. ¹³So they stationed the main army north of the town and the ambush west of the town. Joshua himself spent that night in the valley.

¹⁴When the king of Ai saw the Israelites across the valley, he and all his army hurried out early in the morning and attacked the Israelites at a place overlooking the Jordan Valley.* But he didn't realize there was an ambush behind the town. ¹⁵Joshua and the Israelite army fled toward the wilderness as though they were badly beaten. ¹⁶Then all the men in the town were called out to chase after them. In this way, they were lured away from the town. ¹⁷There was not a man left in Ai or Bethel* who did not chase after the Israelites, and the town was left wide open.

¹⁸Then the LORD said to Joshua, "Point the spear in your hand toward Ai, for I will hand the town over to you." Joshua did as he was commanded. ¹⁹As soon as Joshua gave this signal, all the men in ambush jumped up from their position and poured into the town. They quickly captured it and set it on fire.

²⁰When the men of Ai looked behind them, smoke from the town was filling the sky, and they had nowhere to go. For the Israelites who had fled in the direction of the wilderness now turned on their pursuers. ²¹When Joshua and all the other Israelites saw that the ambush had succeeded and that smoke was rising from the town, they turned and attacked the men of Ai. ²²Meanwhile, the Israelites who were inside the town came out and attacked the enemy from the rear. So the men of Ai were caught in the middle, with Israelite fighters on both sides. Israel attacked them, and not a single person survived or escaped. ²³Only the king of Ai was taken alive and brought to Joshua.

²⁴When the Israelite army finished chasing and killing all the men of Ai in the open fields, they went back and finished off everyone inside. ²⁵So the entire population of Ai, including men and women, was wiped out that day—12,000 in all. ²⁶For Joshua kept holding out his spear until everyone who had lived in Ai was completely destroyed.* ²⁷Only the livestock and the treasures of the town were not destroyed, for the Israelites kept these as plunder for themselves, as the LORD had commanded Joshua. ²⁸So Joshua burned the town of Ai,* and it became a permanent mound of ruins, desolate to this very day. ²⁹Joshua impaled the king of Ai on a sharpened pole and left him there until evening. At sunset the Israelites took down the body, as Joshua

7:21a Hebrew *Shinar.*   7:21b Hebrew *200 shekels of silver,* about 5 pounds or 2.3 kilograms in weight.   7:21c Hebrew *50 shekels,* about 20 ounces or 570 grams in weight.   7:26 Hebrew *valley of Achor.*   8:14 Hebrew *the Arabah.*   8:17 Some manuscripts lack *or Bethel.*   8:26 The Hebrew term used here refers to the complete consecration of things or people to the LORD, either by destroying them or by giving them as an offering.   8:28 *Ai* means "ruin."

commanded, and threw it in front of the town gate. They piled a great heap of stones over him that can still be seen today.

THE LORD'S COVENANT RENEWED

30 Then Joshua built an altar to the LORD, the God of Israel, on Mount Ebal. 31 He followed the commands that Moses the LORD's servant had written in the Book of Instruction: "Make me an altar from stones that are uncut and have not been shaped with iron tools."* Then on the altar they presented burnt offerings and peace offerings to the LORD. 32 And as the Israelites watched, Joshua copied onto the stones of the altar* the instructions Moses had given them.

33 Then all the Israelites—foreigners and native-born alike—along with the elders, officers, and judges, were divided into two groups. One group stood in front of Mount Gerizim, the other in front of Mount Ebal. Each group faced the other, and between them stood the Levitical priests carrying the Ark of the LORD's Covenant. This was all done according to the commands that Moses, the servant of the LORD, had previously given for blessing the people of Israel.

34 Joshua then read to them all the blessings and curses Moses had written in the Book of Instruction. 35 Every word of every command that Moses had ever given was read to the entire assembly of Israel, including the women and children and the foreigners who lived among them.

THE GIBEONITES DECEIVE ISRAEL

9 Now all the kings west of the Jordan River heard about what had happened. These were the kings of the Hittites, Amorites, Canaanites, Perizzites, Hivites, and Jebusites, who lived in the hill country, in the western foothills,* and along the coast of the Mediterranean Sea* as far north as the Lebanon mountains. 2 These kings combined their armies to fight as one against Joshua and the Israelites.

3 But when the people of Gibeon heard what Joshua had done to Jericho and Ai, 4 they resorted to deception to save themselves. They sent ambassadors to Joshua, loading their donkeys with weathered saddlebags and old, patched wineskins. 5 They put on worn-out, patched sandals and ragged clothes. And the bread they took with them was dry and moldy. 6 When they arrived at the camp of Israel at Gilgal, they told Joshua and the men of Israel, "We have come from a distant land to ask you to make a peace treaty with us."

7 The Israelites replied to these Hivites, "How do we know you don't live nearby? For if you do, we cannot make a treaty with you."

8 They replied, "We are your servants."

"But who are you?" Joshua demanded. "Where do you come from?"

9 They answered, "Your servants have come from a very distant country. We have heard of the might of the LORD your God and of all he did in Egypt. 10 We have also heard what he did to the two Amorite kings east of the Jordan River—King Sihon of Heshbon and King Og of Bashan (who lived in Ashtaroth). 11 So our elders and all our people instructed us, 'Take supplies for a long journey. Go meet with the people of Israel and tell them, "We are your servants; please make a treaty with us."'

12 "This bread was hot from the ovens when we left our homes. But now, as you can see, it is dry and moldy. 13 These wineskins were new when we filled them, but now they are old and split open. And our clothing and sandals are worn out from our very long journey."

14 So the Israelites examined their food, but they did not consult the LORD. 15 Then Joshua made a peace treaty with them and guaranteed their safety, and the leaders of the community ratified their agreement with a binding oath.

16 Three days after making the treaty, they learned that these people actually lived nearby! 17 The Israelites set out at once to investigate and reached their towns in three days. The names of these towns were Gibeon, Kephirah, Beeroth, and Kiriath-jearim. 18 But the Israelites did not attack the towns, for the Israelite leaders had made a vow to them in the name of the LORD, the God of Israel.

The people of Israel grumbled against their leaders because of the treaty. 19 But the leaders replied, "Since we have sworn an oath in the presence of the LORD, the God of Israel, we cannot touch them. 20 This is what we must do. We must let them live, for divine anger would come upon us if we broke our oath. 21 Let them live." So they made them woodcutters and water carriers for the entire community, as the Israelite leaders directed.

22 Joshua called together the Gibeonites and said, "Why did you lie to us? Why did you say that you live in a distant land when you live right here among us? 23 May you be cursed! From now on you will always be servants who cut wood and carry water for the house of my God."

24 They replied, "We did it because we—your servants—were clearly told that the LORD your God commanded his servant Moses to give you this entire land and to destroy all the people living in it. So we feared greatly for our lives because of you. That is why we have done this. 25 Now we are at your mercy—do to us whatever you think is right."

26 So Joshua did not allow the people of Israel to kill them. 27 But that day he made the Gibeonites the woodcutters and water carriers for the community of Israel and for the altar of the LORD—wherever the LORD would choose to build it. And that is what they do to this day.

8:31 Exod 20:25; Deut 27:5-6.   8:32 Hebrew *onto the stones*.
9:1a Hebrew *the Shephelah*.   9:1b Hebrew *the Great Sea*.

ISRAEL DEFEATS THE SOUTHERN ARMIES

10 Adoni-zedek, king of Jerusalem, heard that Joshua had captured and completely destroyed* Ai and killed its king, just as he had destroyed the town of Jericho and killed its king. He also learned that the Gibeonites had made peace with Israel and were now their allies. ²He and his people became very afraid when they heard all this because Gibeon was a large town— as large as the royal cities and larger than Ai. And the Gibeonite men were strong warriors.

³So King Adoni-zedek of Jerusalem sent messengers to several other kings: Hoham of Hebron, Piram of Jarmuth, Japhia of Lachish, and Debir of Eglon. ⁴"Come and help me destroy Gibeon," he urged them, "for they have made peace with Joshua and the people of Israel." ⁵So these five Amorite kings combined their armies for a united attack. They moved all their troops into place and attacked Gibeon.

⁶The men of Gibeon quickly sent messengers to Joshua at his camp in Gilgal. "Don't abandon your servants now!" they pleaded. "Come at once! Save us! Help us! For all the Amorite kings who live in the hill country have joined forces to attack us."

⁷So Joshua and his entire army, including his best warriors, left Gilgal and set out for Gibeon. ⁸"Do not be afraid of them," the LORD said to Joshua, "for I have given you victory over them. Not a single one of them will be able to stand up to you."

⁹Joshua traveled all night from Gilgal and took the Amorite armies by surprise. ¹⁰The LORD threw them into a panic, and the Israelites slaughtered great numbers of them at Gibeon. Then the Israelites chased the enemy along the road to Beth-horon, killing them all along the way to Azekah and Makkedah. ¹¹As the Amorites retreated down the road from Beth-horon, the LORD destroyed them with a terrible hailstorm from heaven that continued until they reached Azekah. The hail killed more of the enemy than the Israelites killed with the sword.

¹²On the day the LORD gave the Israelites victory over the Amorites, Joshua prayed to the LORD in front of all the people of Israel. He said,

"Let the sun stand still over Gibeon,
and the moon over the valley of Aijalon."

¹³So the sun stood still and the moon stayed in place until the nation of Israel had defeated its enemies.

Is this event not recorded in *The Book of Jashar*? The sun stayed in the middle of the sky, and it did not set as on a normal day.* ¹⁴There has never been a day like this one before or since, when the LORD answered such a prayer. Surely the LORD fought for Israel that day!

¹⁵Then Joshua and the Israelite army returned to their camp at Gilgal.

JOSHUA KILLS THE FIVE SOUTHERN KINGS

¹⁶During the battle the five kings escaped and hid in a cave at Makkedah. ¹⁷When Joshua heard that they had been found, ¹⁸he issued this command: "Cover the opening of the cave with large rocks, and place guards at the entrance to keep the kings inside. ¹⁹The rest of you continue chasing the enemy and cut them down from the rear. Don't give them a chance to get back to their towns, for the LORD your God has given you victory over them."

²⁰So Joshua and the Israelite army continued the slaughter and completely crushed the enemy. They totally wiped out the five armies except for a tiny remnant that managed to reach their fortified towns. ²¹Then the Israelites returned safely to Joshua in the camp at Makkedah. After that, no one dared to speak even a word against Israel.

²²Then Joshua said, "Remove the rocks covering the opening of the cave, and bring the five kings to me." ²³So they brought the five kings out of the cave—the kings of Jerusalem, Hebron, Jarmuth, Lachish, and Eglon. ²⁴When they brought them out, Joshua told the commanders of his army, "Come and put your feet on the kings' necks." And they did as they were told.

²⁵"Don't ever be afraid or discouraged," Joshua told his men. "Be strong and courageous, for the LORD is going to do this to all of your enemies." ²⁶Then Joshua killed each of the five kings and impaled them on five sharpened poles, where they hung until evening.

²⁷As the sun was going down, Joshua gave instructions for the bodies of the kings to be taken down from the poles and thrown into the cave where they had been hiding. Then they covered the opening of the cave with a pile of large rocks, which remains to this very day.

ISRAEL DESTROYS THE SOUTHERN TOWNS

²⁸That same day Joshua captured and destroyed the town of Makkedah. He killed everyone in it, including the king, leaving no survivors. He destroyed them all, and he killed the king of Makkedah as he had killed the king of Jericho. ²⁹Then Joshua and the Israelites went to Libnah and attacked it. ³⁰There, too, the LORD gave them the town and its king. He killed everyone in it, leaving no survivors. Then Joshua killed the king of Libnah as he had killed the king of Jericho.

³¹From Libnah, Joshua and the Israelites went to Lachish and attacked it. ³²Here again, the LORD gave them Lachish. Joshua took it on the second day and killed everyone in it, just as he had done at Libnah. ³³During the attack on Lachish, King Horam of Gezer arrived with his army to help defend the town. But Joshua's men killed him and his army, leaving no survivors.

10:1 The Hebrew term used here refers to the complete consecration of things or people to the LORD, either by destroying them or by giving them as an offering; also in 10:28, 35, 37, 39, 40.   10:13a Or *The Book of the Upright.*   10:13b Or *did not set for about a whole day.*

³⁴Then Joshua and the Israelite army went on to Eglon and attacked it. ³⁵They captured it that day and killed everyone in it. He completely destroyed everyone, just as he had done at Lachish. ³⁶From Eglon, Joshua and the Israelite army went up to Hebron and attacked it. ³⁷They captured the town and killed everyone in it, including its king, leaving no survivors. They did the same thing to all of its surrounding villages. And just as he had done at Eglon, he completely destroyed the entire population.

³⁸Then Joshua and the Israelites turned back and attacked Debir. ³⁹He captured the town, its king, and all of its surrounding villages. He completely destroyed everyone in it, leaving no survivors. He did to Debir and its king just what he had done to Hebron and to Libnah and its king.

⁴⁰So Joshua conquered the whole region—the kings and people of the hill country, the Negev, the western foothills,* and the mountain slopes. He completely destroyed everyone in the land, leaving no survivors, just as the LORD, the God of Israel, had commanded. ⁴¹Joshua slaughtered them from Kadesh-barnea to Gaza and from the region around the town of Goshen up to Gibeon. ⁴²Joshua conquered all these kings and their land in a single campaign, for the LORD, the God of Israel, was fighting for his people. ⁴³Then Joshua and the Israelite army returned to their camp at Gilgal.

ISRAEL DEFEATS THE NORTHERN ARMIES

11 When King Jabin of Hazor heard what had happened, he sent messages to the following kings: King Jobab of Madon; the king of Shimron; the king of Acshaph; ²all the kings of the northern hill country; the kings in the Jordan Valley south of Galilee*; the kings in the Galilean foothills*; the kings of Naphoth-dor on the west; ³the kings of Canaan, both east and west; the kings of the Amorites, the Hittites, the Perizzites, the Jebusites in the hill country, and the Hivites in the towns on the slopes of Mount Hermon in the land of Mizpah.

⁴All these kings came out to fight. Their combined armies formed a vast horde. And with all their horses and chariots, they covered the landscape like the sand on the seashore. ⁵The kings joined forces and established their camp around the water near Merom to fight against Israel.

⁶Then the LORD said to Joshua, "Do not be afraid of them. By this time tomorrow I will hand all of them over to Israel as dead men. Then you must cripple their horses and burn their chariots."

⁷So Joshua and all his fighting men traveled to the water near Merom and attacked suddenly. ⁸And the LORD gave them victory over their enemies. The Israelites chased them as far as Greater Sidon and Misrephoth-maim, and eastward into the valley of Mizpah, until not one enemy warrior was left alive. ⁹Then Joshua crippled the horses and burned all the chariots, as the LORD had instructed.

¹⁰Joshua then turned back and captured Hazor and killed its king. (Hazor had at one time been the capital of all these kingdoms.) ¹¹The Israelites completely destroyed* every living thing in the city, leaving no survivors. Not a single person was spared. And then Joshua burned the city.

¹²Joshua slaughtered all the other kings and their people, completely destroying them, just as Moses, the servant of the LORD, had commanded. ¹³But the Israelites did not burn any of the towns built on mounds except Hazor, which Joshua burned. ¹⁴And the Israelites took all the plunder and livestock of the ravaged towns for themselves. But they killed all the people, leaving no survivors. ¹⁵As the LORD had commanded his servant Moses, so Moses commanded Joshua. And Joshua did as he was told, carefully obeying all the commands that the LORD had given to Moses.

¹⁶So Joshua conquered the entire region—the hill country, the entire Negev, the whole area around the town of Goshen, the western foothills, the Jordan Valley,* the mountains of Israel, and the Galilean foothills. ¹⁷The Israelite territory now extended all the way from Mount Halak, which leads up to Seir in the south, as far north as Baal-gad at the foot of Mount Hermon in the valley of Lebanon. Joshua killed all the kings of those territories, ¹⁸waging war for a long time to accomplish this. ¹⁹No one in this region made peace with the Israelites except the Hivites of Gibeon. All the others were defeated. ²⁰For the LORD hardened their hearts and caused them to fight the Israelites. So they were completely destroyed without mercy, as the LORD had commanded Moses.

²¹During this period Joshua destroyed all the descendants of Anak, who lived in the hill country of Hebron, Debir, Anab, and the entire hill country of Judah and Israel. He killed them all and completely destroyed their towns. ²²None of the descendants of Anak were left in all the land of Israel, though some still remained in Gaza, Gath, and Ashdod.

²³So Joshua took control of the entire land, just as the LORD had instructed Moses. He gave it to the people of Israel as their special possession, dividing the land among the tribes. So the land finally had rest from war.

KINGS DEFEATED EAST OF THE JORDAN

12 These are the kings east of the Jordan River who had been killed by the Israelites and whose land was taken. Their territory extended from the Arnon Gorge to Mount Hermon and included all the land east of the Jordan Valley.*

10:40 Hebrew *the Shephelah.* 11:2a Hebrew *in the Arabah south of Kinnereth.* 11:2b Hebrew *the Shephelah;* also in 11:16. 11:11 The Hebrew term used here refers to the complete consecration of things or people to the LORD, either by destroying them or by giving them as an offering; also in 11:12, 20, 21. 11:16 Hebrew *the Shephelah, the Arabah.* 12:1 Hebrew *the Arabah;* also in 12:3, 8.

² King Sihon of the Amorites, who lived in Heshbon, was defeated. His kingdom included Aroer, on the edge of the Arnon Gorge, and extended from the middle of the Arnon Gorge to the Jabbok River, which serves as a border for the Ammonites. This territory included the southern half of the territory of Gilead. ³ Sihon also controlled the Jordan Valley and regions to the east—from as far north as the Sea of Galilee to as far south as the Dead Sea,* including the road to Beth-jeshimoth and southward to the slopes of Pisgah.

⁴ King Og of Bashan, the last of the Rephaites, lived at Ashtaroth and Edrei. ⁵ He ruled a territory stretching from Mount Hermon to Salecah in the north and to all of Bashan in the east, and westward to the borders of the kingdoms of Geshur and Maacah. This territory included the northern half of Gilead, as far as the boundary of King Sihon of Heshbon.

⁶ Moses, the servant of the LORD, and the Israelites had destroyed the people of King Sihon and King Og. And Moses gave their land as a possession to the tribes of Reuben, Gad, and the half-tribe of Manasseh.

KINGS DEFEATED WEST OF THE JORDAN

⁷ The following is a list of the kings that Joshua and the Israelite armies defeated on the west side of the Jordan, from Baal-gad in the valley of Lebanon to Mount Halak, which leads up to Seir. (Joshua gave this land to the tribes of Israel as their possession, ⁸ including the hill country, the western foothills,* the Jordan Valley, the mountain slopes, the Judean wilderness, and the Negev. The people who lived in this region were the Hittites, the Amorites, the Canaanites, the Perizzites, the Hivites, and the Jebusites.) These are the kings Israel defeated:

⁹ The king of Jericho
   The king of Ai, near Bethel
¹⁰ The king of Jerusalem
   The king of Hebron
¹¹ The king of Jarmuth
   The king of Lachish
¹² The king of Eglon
   The king of Gezer
¹³ The king of Debir
   The king of Geder
¹⁴ The king of Hormah
   The king of Arad
¹⁵ The king of Libnah
   The king of Adullam
¹⁶ The king of Makkedah
   The king of Bethel
¹⁷ The king of Tappuah
   The king of Hepher
¹⁸ The king of Aphek
   The king of Lasharon
¹⁹ The king of Madon
   The king of Hazor

²⁰ The king of Shimron-meron
   The king of Acshaph
²¹ The king of Taanach
   The king of Megiddo
²² The king of Kedesh
   The king of Jokneam in Carmel
²³ The king of Dor in the town of Naphoth-dor*
   The king of Goyim in Gilgal*
²⁴ The king of Tirzah.

In all, thirty-one kings were defeated.

THE LAND YET TO BE CONQUERED

13 When Joshua was an old man, the LORD said to him, "You are growing old, and much land remains to be conquered. ² This is the territory that remains: all the regions of the Philistines and the Geshurites, ³ and the larger territory of the Canaanites, extending from the stream of Shihor on the border of Egypt, northward to the boundary of Ekron. It includes the territory of the five Philistine rulers of Gaza, Ashdod, Ashkelon, Gath, and Ekron. The land of the Avvites ⁴ in the south also remains to be conquered. In the north, the following area has not yet been conquered: all the land of the Canaanites, including Mearah (which belongs to the Sidonians), stretching northward to Aphek on the border of the Amorites; ⁵ the land of the Gebalites and all of the Lebanon mountain area to the east, from Baal-gad below Mount Hermon to Lebo-hamath; ⁶ and all the hill country from Lebanon to Misrephoth-maim, including all the land of the Sidonians.

"I myself will drive these people out of the land ahead of the Israelites. So be sure to give this land to Israel as a special possession, just as I have commanded you. ⁷ Include all this territory as Israel's possession when you divide this land among the nine tribes and the half-tribe of Manasseh."

THE LAND DIVIDED EAST OF THE JORDAN

⁸ Half the tribe of Manasseh and the tribes of Reuben and Gad had already received their grants of land on the east side of the Jordan, for Moses, the servant of the LORD, had previously assigned this land to them.

⁹ Their territory extended from Aroer on the edge of the Arnon Gorge (including the town in the middle of the gorge) to the plain beyond Medeba, as far as Dibon. ¹⁰ It also included all the towns of King Sihon of the Amorites, who had reigned in Heshbon, and extended as far as the borders of Ammon. ¹¹ It included Gilead, the territory of the kingdoms of Geshur and Maacah, all

12:3 Hebrew from the Sea of Kinnereth to the Sea of the Arabah, which is the Salt Sea.   12:8 Hebrew the Shephelah.   12:23a Hebrew Naphath-dor, a variant spelling of Naphoth-dor.   12:23b Greek version reads Goyim in Galilee.

of Mount Hermon, all of Bashan as far as Salecah, [12] and all the territory of King Og of Bashan, who had reigned in Ashtaroth and Edrei. King Og was the last of the Rephaites, for Moses had attacked them and driven them out. [13] But the Israelites failed to drive out the people of Geshur and Maacah, so they continue to live among the Israelites to this day.

AN ALLOTMENT FOR THE TRIBE OF LEVI

[14] Moses did not assign any allotment of land to the tribe of Levi. Instead, as the LORD had promised them, their allotment came from the offerings burned on the altar to the LORD, the God of Israel.

THE LAND GIVEN TO THE TRIBE OF REUBEN

[15] Moses had assigned the following area to the clans of the tribe of Reuben.

[16] Their territory extended from Aroer on the edge of the Arnon Gorge (including the town in the middle of the gorge) to the plain beyond Medeba. [17] It included Heshbon and the other towns on the plain—Dibon, Bamoth-baal, Beth-baal-meon, [18] Jahaz, Kedemoth, Mephaath, [19] Kiriathaim, Sibmah, Zereth-shahar on the hill above the valley, [20] Beth-peor, the slopes of Pisgah, and Beth-jeshimoth.

[21] The land of Reuben also included all the towns of the plain and the entire kingdom of Sihon. Sihon was the Amorite king who had reigned in Heshbon and was killed by Moses along with the leaders of Midian—Evi, Rekem, Zur, Hur, and Reba—princes living in the region who were allied with Sihon. [22] The Israelites had also killed Balaam son of Beor, who used magic to tell the future. [23] The Jordan River marked the western boundary for the tribe of Reuben. The towns and their surrounding villages in this area were given as a homeland to the clans of the tribe of Reuben.

THE LAND GIVEN TO THE TRIBE OF GAD

[24] Moses had assigned the following area to the clans of the tribe of Gad.

[25] Their territory included Jazer, all the towns of Gilead, and half of the land of Ammon, as far as the town of Aroer just west of* Rabbah. [26] It extended from Heshbon to Ramath-mizpeh and Betonim, and from Mahanaim to the territory of Lo-debar.* [27] In the valley were Beth-haram, Beth-nimrah, Succoth, Zaphon, and the rest of the kingdom of King Sihon of Heshbon. The western boundary ran along the Jordan River, extended as far north as the tip of the Sea of Galilee,* and then turned eastward. [28] The towns and their surrounding villages in this area were given as a homeland to the clans of the tribe of Gad.

THE LAND GIVEN TO THE HALF-TRIBE OF MANASSEH

[29] Moses had assigned the following area to the clans of the half-tribe of Manasseh.

[30] Their territory extended from Mahanaim, including all of Bashan, all the former kingdom of King Og, and the sixty towns of Jair in Bashan. [31] It also included half of Gilead and King Og's royal cities of Ashtaroth and Edrei. All this was given to the clans of the descendants of Makir, who was Manasseh's son.

[32] These are the allotments Moses had made while he was on the plains of Moab, across the Jordan River, east of Jericho. [33] But Moses gave no allotment of land to the tribe of Levi, for the LORD, the God of Israel, had promised that he himself would be their allotment.

THE LAND DIVIDED WEST OF THE JORDAN

14 The remaining tribes of Israel received land in Canaan as allotted by Eleazar the priest, Joshua son of Nun, and the tribal leaders. [2] These nine and a half tribes received their grants of land by means of sacred lots, in accordance with the LORD's command through Moses. [3] Moses had already given a grant of land to the two and a half tribes on the east side of the Jordan River, but he had given the Levites no such allotment. [4] The descendants of Joseph had become two separate tribes—Manasseh and Ephraim. And the Levites were given no land at all, only towns to live in with surrounding pasturelands for their livestock and all their possessions. [5] So the land was distributed in strict accordance with the LORD's commands to Moses.

CALEB REQUESTS HIS LAND

[6] A delegation from the tribe of Judah, led by Caleb son of Jephunneh the Kenizzite, came to Joshua at Gilgal. Caleb said to Joshua, "Remember what the LORD said to Moses, the man of God, about you and me when we were at Kadesh-barnea. [7] I was forty years old when Moses, the servant of the LORD, sent me from Kadesh-barnea to explore the land of Canaan. I returned and gave an honest report, [8] but my brothers who went with me frightened the people from entering the Promised Land. For my part, I wholeheartedly followed the LORD my God. [9] So that

---

13:25 Hebrew *in front of.*   13:26 Hebrew *Li-debir,* apparently a variant spelling of Lo-debar (compare 2 Sam 9:4; 17:27; Amos 6:13).   13:27 Hebrew *Sea of Kinnereth.*

day Moses solemnly promised me, 'The land of Canaan on which you were just walking will be your grant of land and that of your descendants forever, because you wholeheartedly followed the LORD my God.'

10 "Now, as you can see, the LORD has kept me alive and well as he promised for all these forty-five years since Moses made this promise—even while Israel wandered in the wilderness. Today I am eighty-five years old. 11 I am as strong now as I was when Moses sent me on that journey, and I can still travel and fight as well as I could then. 12 So give me the hill country that the LORD promised me. You will remember that as scouts we found the descendants of Anak living there in great, walled towns. But if the LORD is with me, I will drive them out of the land, just as the LORD said."

13 So Joshua blessed Caleb son of Jephunneh and gave Hebron to him as his portion of land. 14 Hebron still belongs to the descendants of Caleb son of Jephunneh the Kenizzite because he wholeheartedly followed the LORD, the God of Israel. 15 (Previously Hebron had been called Kiriath-arba. It had been named after Arba, a great hero of the descendants of Anak.)

And the land had rest from war.

THE LAND GIVEN TO THE TRIBE OF JUDAH

15 The allotment for the clans of the tribe of Judah reached southward to the border of Edom, as far south as the wilderness of Zin.

2 The southern boundary began at the south bay of the Dead Sea,* 3 ran south of Scorpion Pass* into the wilderness of Zin, and then went south of Kadesh-barnea to Hezron. Then it went up to Addar, where it turned toward Karka. 4 From there it passed to Azmon until it finally reached the Brook of Egypt, which it followed to the Mediterranean Sea.* This was their* southern boundary.

5 The eastern boundary extended along the Dead Sea to the mouth of the Jordan River.

The northern boundary began at the bay where the Jordan River empties into the Dead Sea, 6 went up from there to Beth-hoglah, then proceeded north of Beth-arabah to the Stone of Bohan. (Bohan was Reuben's son.) 7 From that point it went through the valley of Achor to Debir, turning north toward Gilgal, which is across from the slopes of Adummim on the south side of the valley. From there the boundary extended to the springs at En-shemesh and on to En-rogel. 8 The boundary then passed through the valley of Ben-Hinnom, along the southern slopes of the Jebusites, where the city of Jerusalem is located. Then it went west to the top of the mountain above the valley of Hinnom, and on up to the northern end of the valley of Rephaim. 9 From there the boundary extended from the top of the mountain to the spring at the waters of Nephtoah,* and from there to the towns on Mount Ephron. Then it turned toward Baalah (that is, Kiriath-jearim). 10 The boundary circled west of Baalah to Mount Seir, passed along to the town of Kesalon on the northern slope of Mount Jearim, and went down to Beth-shemesh and on to Timnah. 11 The boundary then proceeded to the slope of the hill north of Ekron, where it turned toward Shikkeron and Mount Baalah. It passed Jabneel and ended at the Mediterranean Sea.

12 The western boundary was the shoreline of the Mediterranean Sea.*

These are the boundaries for the clans of the tribe of Judah.

THE LAND GIVEN TO CALEB

13 The LORD commanded Joshua to assign some of Judah's territory to Caleb son of Jephunneh. So Caleb was given the town of Kiriath-arba (that is, Hebron), which had been named after Anak's ancestor. 14 Caleb drove out the three groups of Anakites—the descendants of Sheshai, Ahiman, and Talmai, the sons of Anak.

15 From there he went to fight against the people living in the town of Debir (formerly called Kiriath-sepher). 16 Caleb said, "I will give my daughter Acsah in marriage to the one who attacks and captures Kiriath-sepher." 17 Othniel, the son of Caleb's brother Kenaz, was the one who conquered it, so Acsah became Othniel's wife.

18 When Acsah married Othniel, she urged him* to ask her father for a field. As she got down off her donkey, Caleb asked her, "What's the matter?"

19 She said, "Give me another gift. You have already given me land in the Negev; now please give me springs of water, too." So Caleb gave her the upper and lower springs.

THE TOWNS ALLOTTED TO JUDAH

20 This was the homeland allocated to the clans of the tribe of Judah.

21 The towns of Judah situated along the borders of Edom in the extreme south were Kabzeel, Eder, Jagur, 22 Kinah, Dimonah, Adadah, 23 Kedesh, Hazor, Ithnan, 24 Ziph, Telem, Bealoth, 25 Hazor-hadattah, Kerioth-hezron (that is, Hazor), 26 Amam, Shema, Moladah, 27 Hazar-gaddah,

15:2 Hebrew the Salt Sea; also in 15:5.   15:3 Hebrew Akrabbim.   15:4a Hebrew the sea; also in 15:11.   15:4b Hebrew your.   15:9 Or the spring at Me-nephtoah.   15:12 Hebrew the Great Sea; also in 15:47.   15:18 Some Greek manuscripts read he urged her.

Heshmon, Beth-pelet, 28 Hazar-shual, Beersheba, Biziothiah, 29 Baalah, Iim, Ezem, 30 Eltolad, Kesil, Hormah, 31 Ziklag, Madmannah, Sansannah, 32 Lebaoth, Shilhim, Ain, and Rimmon—twenty-nine towns with their surrounding villages.

33 The following towns situated in the western foothills* were also given to Judah: Eshtaol, Zorah, Ashnah, 34 Zanoah, En-gannim, Tappuah, Enam, 35 Jarmuth, Adullam, Socoh, Azekah, 36 Shaaraim, Adithaim, Gederah, and Gederothaim—fourteen towns with their surrounding villages.

37 Also included were Zenan, Hadashah, Migdal-gad, 38 Dilean, Mizpeh, Joktheel, 39 Lachish, Bozkath, Eglon, 40 Cabbon, Lahmam, Kitlish, 41 Gederoth, Beth-dagon, Naamah, and Makkedah—sixteen towns with their surrounding villages.

42 Besides these, there were Libnah, Ether, Ashan, 43 Iphtah, Ashnah, Nezib, 44 Keilah, Aczib, and Mareshah—nine towns with their surrounding villages.

45 The territory of the tribe of Judah also included Ekron and its surrounding settlements and villages. 46 From Ekron the boundary extended west and included the towns near Ashdod with their surrounding villages. 47 It also included Ashdod with its surrounding settlements and villages and Gaza with its settlements and villages, as far as the Brook of Egypt and along the coast of the Mediterranean Sea.

48 Judah also received the following towns in the hill country: Shamir, Jattir, Socoh, 49 Dannah, Kiriath-sannah (that is, Debir), 50 Anab, Eshtemoh, Anim, 51 Goshen, Holon, and Giloh—eleven towns with their surrounding villages.

52 Also included were the towns of Arab, Dumah, Eshan, 53 Janim, Beth-tappuah, Aphekah, 54 Humtah, Kiriath-arba (that is, Hebron), and Zior—nine towns with their surrounding villages.

55 Besides these, there were Maon, Carmel, Ziph, Juttah, 56 Jezreel, Jokdeam, Zanoah, 57 Kain, Gibeah, and Timnah—ten towns with their surrounding villages.

58 In addition, there were Halhul, Beth-zur, Gedor, 59 Maarath, Beth-anoth, and Eltekon—six towns with their surrounding villages.

60 There were also Kiriath-baal (that is, Kiriath-jearim) and Rabbah—two towns with their surrounding villages.

61 In the wilderness there were the towns of Beth-arabah, Middin, Secacah, 62 Nibshan, the City of Salt, and En-gedi—six towns with their surrounding villages.

63 But the tribe of Judah could not drive out the Jebusites, who lived in the city of Jerusalem, so the Jebusites live there among the people of Judah to this day.

THE LAND GIVEN TO EPHRAIM AND WEST MANASSEH

16 The allotment for the descendants of Joseph extended from the Jordan River near Jericho, east of the springs of Jericho, through the wilderness and into the hill country of Bethel. 2 From Bethel (that is, Luz)* it ran over to Ataroth in the territory of the Arkites. 3 Then it descended westward to the territory of the Japhletites as far as Lower Beth-horon, then to Gezer and over to the Mediterranean Sea.*

4 This was the homeland allocated to the families of Joseph's sons, Manasseh and Ephraim.

THE LAND GIVEN TO EPHRAIM

5 The following territory was given to the clans of the tribe of Ephraim.

The boundary of their homeland began at Ataroth-addar in the east. From there it ran to Upper Beth-horon, 6 then on to the Mediterranean Sea. From Micmethath on the north, the boundary curved eastward past Taanath-shiloh to the east of Janoah. 7 From Janoah it turned southward to Ataroth and Naarah, touched Jericho, and ended at the Jordan River. 8 From Tappuah the boundary extended westward, following the Kanah Ravine to the Mediterranean Sea. This is the homeland allocated to the clans of the tribe of Ephraim.

9 In addition, some towns with their surrounding villages in the territory allocated to the half-tribe of Manasseh were set aside for the tribe of Ephraim. 10 They did not drive the Canaanites out of Gezer, however, so the people of Gezer live as slaves among the people of Ephraim to this day.

THE LAND GIVEN TO WEST MANASSEH

17 The next allotment of land was given to the half-tribe of Manasseh, the descendants of Joseph's older son. Makir, the firstborn son of Manasseh, was the father of Gilead. Because his descendants were experienced soldiers, the regions of Gilead and Bashan on the east side of the Jordan had already been given to them. 2 So the allotment on the west side of the Jordan was for the remaining families within the clans of the tribe of Manasseh: Abiezer, Helek, Asriel, Shechem, Hepher, and Shemida. These clans represent the male descendants of Manasseh son of Joseph.

15:33 Hebrew the Shephelah. 16:2 As in Greek version (also see 18:13); Hebrew reads From Bethel to Luz. 16:3 Hebrew the sea; also in 16:6, 8.

³ However, Zelophehad, a descendant of Hepher son of Gilead, son of Makir, son of Manasseh, had no sons. He had only daughters, whose names were Mahlah, Noah, Hoglah, Milcah, and Tirzah. ⁴ These women came to Eleazar the priest, Joshua son of Nun, and the Israelite leaders and said, "The LORD commanded Moses to give us a grant of land along with the men of our tribe."

So Joshua gave them a grant of land along with their uncles, as the LORD had commanded. ⁵ As a result, Manasseh's total allocation came to ten parcels of land, in addition to the land of Gilead and Bashan across the Jordan River, ⁶ because the female descendants of Manasseh received a grant of land along with the male descendants. (The land of Gilead was given to the rest of the male descendants of Manasseh.)

⁷ The boundary of the tribe of Manasseh extended from the border of Asher to Micmethath, near Shechem. Then the boundary went south from Micmethath to the settlement near the spring of Tappuah. ⁸ The land surrounding Tappuah belonged to Manasseh, but the town of Tappuah itself, on the border of Manasseh's territory, belonged to the tribe of Ephraim. ⁹ From the spring of Tappuah, the boundary of Manasseh followed the Kanah Ravine to the Mediterranean Sea.* Several towns south of the ravine were inside Manasseh's territory, but they actually belonged to the tribe of Ephraim. ¹⁰ In general, however, the land south of the ravine belonged to Ephraim, and the land north of the ravine belonged to Manasseh. Manasseh's boundary ran along the northern side of the ravine and ended at the Mediterranean Sea. North of Manasseh was the territory of Asher, and to the east was the territory of Issachar. ¹¹ The following towns within the territory of Issachar and Asher, however, were given to Manasseh: Beth-shan,* Ibleam, Dor (that is, Naphoth-dor),* Endor, Taanach, and Megiddo, each with their surrounding settlements.

¹² But the descendants of Manasseh were unable to occupy these towns because the Canaanites were determined to stay in that region. ¹³ Later, however, when the Israelites became strong enough, they forced the Canaanites to work as slaves. But they did not drive them out of the land.

¹⁴ The descendants of Joseph came to Joshua and asked, "Why have you given us only one portion of land as our homeland when the LORD has blessed us with so many people?"

¹⁵ Joshua replied, "If there are so many of you, and if the hill country of Ephraim is not large enough for you, clear out land for yourselves in the forest where the Perizzites and Rephaites live."

¹⁶ The descendants of Joseph responded, "It's true that the hill country is not large enough for us. But all the Canaanites in the lowlands have iron chariots, both those in Beth-shan and its surrounding settlements and those in the valley of Jezreel. They are too strong for us."

¹⁷ Then Joshua said to the tribes of Ephraim and Manasseh, the descendants of Joseph, "Since you are so large and strong, you will be given more than one portion. ¹⁸ The forests of the hill country will be yours as well. Clear as much of the land as you wish, and take possession of its farthest corners. And you will drive out the Canaanites from the valleys, too, even though they are strong and have iron chariots."

THE ALLOTMENTS OF THE REMAINING LAND

18 Now that the land was under Israelite control, the entire community of Israel gathered at Shiloh and set up the Tabernacle.* ² But there remained seven tribes who had not yet been allotted their grants of land.

³ Then Joshua asked them, "How long are you going to wait before taking possession of the remaining land the LORD, the God of your ancestors, has given to you? ⁴ Select three men from each tribe, and I will send them out to explore the land and map it out. They will then return to me with a written report of their proposed divisions of their new homeland. ⁵ Let them divide the land into seven sections, excluding Judah's territory in the south and Joseph's territory in the north. ⁶ And when you record the seven divisions of the land and bring them to me, I will cast sacred lots in the presence of the LORD our God to assign land to each tribe.

⁷ "The Levites, however, will not receive any allotment of land. Their role as priests of the LORD is their allotment. And the tribes of Gad, Reuben, and the half-tribe of Manasseh won't receive any more land, for they have already received their grant of land, which Moses, the servant of the LORD, gave them on the east side of the Jordan River."

⁸ As the men started on their way to map out the land, Joshua commanded them, "Go and explore the land and write a description of it. Then return to me, and I will assign the land to the tribes by casting sacred lots here in the presence of the LORD at Shiloh." ⁹ The men did as they were told and mapped the entire territory into seven sections, listing the towns in each section. They made a written record and then returned to Joshua in the camp at Shiloh. ¹⁰ And there at Shiloh, Joshua cast sacred lots in the presence of the LORD to determine which tribe should have each section.

17:9 Hebrew *the sea;* also in 17:10.   17:11a Hebrew *Beth-shean,* a variant spelling of Beth-shan; also in 17:16.   17:11b The meaning of the Hebrew here is uncertain.   18:1 Hebrew *Tent of Meeting.*

THE LAND GIVEN TO BENJAMIN

11 The first allotment of land went to the clans of the tribe of Benjamin. It lay between the territory assigned to the tribes of Judah and Joseph.

12 The northern boundary of Benjamin's land began at the Jordan River, went north of the slope of Jericho, then west through the hill country and the wilderness of Beth-aven. 13 From there the boundary went south to Luz (that is, Bethel) and proceeded down to Ataroth-addar on the hill that lies south of Lower Beth-horon.

14 The boundary then made a turn and swung south along the western edge of the hill facing Beth-horon, ending at the village of Kiriath-baal (that is, Kiriath-jearim), a town belonging to the tribe of Judah. This was the western boundary.

15 The southern boundary began at the outskirts of Kiriath-jearim. From that western point it ran* to the spring at the waters of Nephtoah,* 16 and down to the base of the mountain beside the valley of Ben-Hinnom, at the northern end of the valley of Rephaim. From there it went down the valley of Hinnom, crossing south of the slope where the Jebusites lived, and continued down to En-rogel. 17 From En-rogel the boundary proceeded in a northerly direction and came to En-shemesh and on to Geliloth (which is across from the slopes of Adummim). Then it went down to the Stone of Bohan. (Bohan was Reuben's son.) 18 From there it passed along the north side of the slope overlooking the Jordan Valley.* The border then went down into the valley, 19 ran past the north slope of Beth-hoglah, and ended at the north bay of the Dead Sea,* which is the southern end of the Jordan River. This was the southern boundary. 20 The eastern boundary was the Jordan River.

These were the boundaries of the homeland allocated to the clans of the tribe of Benjamin.

THE TOWNS GIVEN TO BENJAMIN

21 These were the towns given to the clans of the tribe of Benjamin.

Jericho, Beth-hoglah, Emek-keziz, 22 Beth-arabah, Zemaraim, Bethel, 23 Avvim, Parah, Ophrah, 24 Kephar-ammoni, Ophni, and Geba—twelve towns with their surrounding villages. 25 Also Gibeon, Ramah, Beeroth, 26 Mizpah, Kephirah, Mozah, 27 Rekem, Irpeel, Taralah, 28 Zela, Haeleph, the Jebusite town (that is, Jerusalem), Gibeah, and Kiriath-jearim*—fourteen towns with their surrounding villages.

This was the homeland allocated to the clans of the tribe of Benjamin.

THE LAND GIVEN TO SIMEON

19 The second allotment of land went to the clans of the tribe of Simeon. Their homeland was surrounded by Judah's territory.

2 Simeon's homeland included Beersheba, Sheba, Moladah, 3 Hazar-shual, Balah, Ezem, 4 Eltolad, Bethul, Hormah, 5 Ziklag, Beth-marcaboth, Hazar-susah, 6 Beth-lebaoth, and Sharuhen—thirteen towns with their surrounding villages. 7 It also included Ain, Rimmon, Ether, and Ashan—four towns with their villages, 8 including all the surrounding villages as far south as Baalath-beer (also known as Ramah of the Negev).

This was the homeland allocated to the clans of the tribe of Simeon. 9 Their allocation of land came from part of what had been given to Judah because Judah's territory was too large for them. So the tribe of Simeon received an allocation within the territory of Judah.

THE LAND GIVEN TO ZEBULUN

10 The third allotment of land went to the clans of the tribe of Zebulun.

The boundary of Zebulun's homeland started at Sarid. 11 From there it went west, going past Maralah, touching Dabbesheth, and proceeding to the brook east of Jokneam. 12 In the other direction, the boundary went east from Sarid to the border of Kisloth-tabor, and from there to Daberath and up to Japhia. 13 Then it continued east to Gath-hepher, Eth-kazin, and Rimmon and turned toward Neah. 14 The northern boundary of Zebulun passed Hannathon and ended at the valley of Iphtah-el. 15 The towns in these areas included Kattath, Nahalal, Shimron, Idalah, and Bethlehem—twelve towns with their surrounding villages.

16 The homeland allocated to the clans of the tribe of Zebulun included these towns and their surrounding villages.

THE LAND GIVEN TO ISSACHAR

17 The fourth allotment of land went to the clans of the tribe of Issachar.

18 Its boundaries included the following towns: Jezreel, Kesulloth, Shunem, 19 Hapharaim, Shion, Anaharath, 20 Rabbith,

---

18:15a Or *From there it went to Mozah*. The meaning of the Hebrew is uncertain. 18:15b Or *the spring at Me-nephtoah*. 18:18 Hebrew *overlooking the Arabah*, or *overlooking Beth-arabah*. 18:19 Hebrew *Salt Sea*. 18:28 As in Greek version; Hebrew reads *Kiriath*.

Kishion, Ebez, ²¹Remeth, En-gannim, En-haddah, and Beth-pazzez. ²²The boundary also touched Tabor, Shahazumah, and Beth-shemesh, ending at the Jordan River—sixteen towns with their surrounding villages.

²³The homeland allocated to the clans of the tribe of Issachar included these towns and their surrounding villages.

THE LAND GIVEN TO ASHER

²⁴The fifth allotment of land went to the clans of the tribe of Asher.

²⁵Its boundaries included these towns: Helkath, Hali, Beten, Acshaph, ²⁶Allammelech, Amad, and Mishal. The boundary on the west touched Carmel and Shihor-libnath, ²⁷then it turned east toward Beth-dagon, and ran as far as Zebulun in the valley of Iphtah-el, going north to Beth-emek and Neiel. It then continued north to Cabul, ²⁸Abdon,* Rehob, Hammon, Kanah, and as far as Greater Sidon. ²⁹Then the boundary turned toward Ramah and the fortress of Tyre, where it turned toward Hosah and came to the Mediterranean Sea.* The territory also included Mehebel, Aczib, ³⁰Ummah, Aphek, and Rehob—twenty-two towns with their surrounding villages.

³¹The homeland allocated to the clans of the tribe of Asher included these towns and their surrounding villages.

THE LAND GIVEN TO NAPHTALI

³²The sixth allotment of land went to the clans of the tribe of Naphtali.

³³Its boundary ran from Heleph, from the oak at Zaanannim, and extended across to Adami-nekeb, Jabneel, and as far as Lakkum, ending at the Jordan River. ³⁴The western boundary ran past Aznoth-tabor, then to Hukkok, and touched the border of Zebulun in the south, the border of Asher on the west, and the Jordan River* on the east. ³⁵The fortified towns included in this territory were Ziddim, Zer, Hammath, Rakkath, Kinnereth, ³⁶Adamah, Ramah, Hazor, ³⁷Kedesh, Edrei, En-hazor, ³⁸Yiron, Migdal-el, Horem, Beth-anath, and Beth-shemesh—nineteen towns with their surrounding villages.

³⁹The homeland allocated to the clans of the tribe of Naphtali included these towns and their surrounding villages.

THE LAND GIVEN TO DAN

⁴⁰The seventh allotment of land went to the clans of the tribe of Dan.

⁴¹The land allocated as their homeland included the following towns: Zorah, Eshtaol, Ir-shemesh, ⁴²Shaalabbin, Aijalon, Ithlah, ⁴³Elon, Timnah, Ekron, ⁴⁴Eltekeh, Gibbethon, Baalath, ⁴⁵Jehud, Bene-berak, Gath-rimmon, ⁴⁶Me-jarkon, Rakkon, and the territory across from Joppa.

⁴⁷But the tribe of Dan had trouble taking possession of their land,* so they attacked the town of Laish.* They captured it, slaughtered its people, and settled there. They renamed the town Dan after their ancestor.

⁴⁸The homeland allocated to the clans of the tribe of Dan included these towns and their surrounding villages.

THE LAND GIVEN TO JOSHUA

⁴⁹After all the land was divided among the tribes, the Israelites gave a piece of land to Joshua as his allocation. ⁵⁰For the LORD had said he could have any town he wanted. He chose Timnath-serah in the hill country of Ephraim. He rebuilt the town and lived there.

⁵¹These are the territories that Eleazar the priest, Joshua son of Nun, and the tribal leaders allocated as grants of land to the tribes of Israel by casting sacred lots in the presence of the LORD at the entrance of the Tabernacle* at Shiloh. So the division of the land was completed.

THE CITIES OF REFUGE

20 The LORD said to Joshua, ²"Now tell the Israelites to designate the cities of refuge, as I instructed Moses. ³Anyone who kills another person accidentally and unintentionally can run to one of these cities; they will be places of refuge from relatives seeking revenge for the person who was killed.

⁴"Upon reaching one of these cities, the one who caused the death will appear before the elders at the city gate and present his case. They must allow him to enter the city and give him a place to live among them. ⁵If the relatives of the victim come to avenge the killing, the leaders must not release the slayer to them, for he killed the other person unintentionally and without previous hostility. ⁶But the slayer must stay in that city and be tried by the local assembly, which will render a judgment. And he must continue to live in that city until the death of the high priest who was in office at the time of the accident. After that, he is free to return to his own home in the town from which he fled."

⁷The following cities were designated as cities of refuge: Kedesh of Galilee, in the hill

---

19:28 As in some Hebrew manuscripts (see also 21:30); most Hebrew manuscripts read *Ebron.* 19:29 Hebrew *the sea.* 19:34 Hebrew *and Judah at the Jordan River.* 19:47a Or *had trouble holding on to their land.* 19:47b Hebrew *Leshem,* a variant spelling of Laish. 19:51 Hebrew *Tent of Meeting.*

country of Naphtali; Shechem, in the hill country of Ephraim; and Kiriath-arba (that is, Hebron), in the hill country of Judah. ⁸On the east side of the Jordan River, across from Jericho, the following cities were designated: Bezer, in the wilderness plain of the tribe of Reuben; Ramoth in Gilead, in the territory of the tribe of Gad; and Golan in Bashan, in the land of the tribe of Manasseh. ⁹These cities were set apart for all the Israelites as well as the foreigners living among them. Anyone who accidentally killed another person could take refuge in one of these cities. In this way, they could escape being killed in revenge prior to standing trial before the local assembly.

THE TOWNS GIVEN TO THE LEVITES

21 Then the leaders of the tribe of Levi came to consult with Eleazar the priest, Joshua son of Nun, and the leaders of the other tribes of Israel. ²They came to them at Shiloh in the land of Canaan and said, "The LORD commanded Moses to give us towns to live in and pasturelands for our livestock." ³So by the command of the LORD the people of Israel gave the Levites the following towns and pasturelands out of their own grants of land.

⁴The descendants of Aaron, who were members of the Kohathite clan within the tribe of Levi, were allotted thirteen towns that were originally assigned to the tribes of Judah, Simeon, and Benjamin. ⁵The other families of the Kohathite clan were allotted ten towns from the tribes of Ephraim, Dan, and the half-tribe of Manasseh.

⁶The clan of Gershon was allotted thirteen towns from the tribes of Issachar, Asher, Naphtali, and the half-tribe of Manasseh in Bashan.

⁷The clan of Merari was allotted twelve towns from the tribes of Reuben, Gad, and Zebulun.

⁸So the Israelites obeyed the LORD's command to Moses and assigned these towns and pasturelands to the Levites by casting sacred lots.

⁹The Israelites gave the following towns from the tribes of Judah and Simeon ¹⁰to the descendants of Aaron, who were members of the Kohathite clan within the tribe of Levi, since the sacred lot fell to them first: ¹¹Kiriath-arba (that is, Hebron), in the hill country of Judah, along with its surrounding pasturelands. (Arba was an ancestor of Anak.) ¹²But the open fields beyond the town and the surrounding villages were given to Caleb son of Jephunneh as his possession.

¹³The following towns with their pasturelands were given to the descendants of Aaron the priest: Hebron (a city of refuge for those who accidentally killed someone), Libnah, ¹⁴Jattir, Eshtemoa, ¹⁵Holon, Debir, ¹⁶Ain, Juttah, and Beth-shemesh—nine towns from these two tribes.

¹⁷From the tribe of Benjamin the priests were given the following towns with their pasturelands: Gibeon, Geba, ¹⁸Anathoth, and Almon—four towns. ¹⁹So in all, thirteen towns with their pasturelands were given to the priests, the descendants of Aaron.

²⁰The rest of the Kohathite clan from the tribe of Levi was allotted the following towns and pasturelands from the tribe of Ephraim: ²¹Shechem in the hill country of Ephraim (a city of refuge for those who accidentally killed someone), Gezer, ²²Kibzaim, and Beth-horon—four towns.

²³The following towns and pasturelands were allotted to the priests from the tribe of Dan: Eltekeh, Gibbethon, ²⁴Aijalon, and Gath-rimmon—four towns.

²⁵The half-tribe of Manasseh allotted the following towns with their pasturelands to the priests: Taanach and Gath-rimmon—two towns. ²⁶So in all, ten towns with their pasturelands were given to the rest of the Kohathite clan.

²⁷The descendants of Gershon, another clan within the tribe of Levi, received the following towns with their pasturelands from the half-tribe of Manasseh: Golan in Bashan (a city of refuge for those who accidentally killed someone) and Be-eshterah—two towns.

²⁸From the tribe of Issachar they received the following towns with their pasturelands: Kishion, Daberath, ²⁹Jarmuth, and En-gannim—four towns.

³⁰From the tribe of Asher they received the following towns with their pasturelands: Mishal, Abdon, ³¹Helkath, and Rehob—four towns.

³²From the tribe of Naphtali they received the following towns with their pasturelands: Kedesh in Galilee (a city of refuge for those who accidentally killed someone), Hammoth-dor, and Kartan—three towns. ³³So in all, thirteen towns with their pasturelands were allotted to the clan of Gershon.

³⁴The rest of the Levites—the Merari clan—were given the following towns with their pasturelands from the tribe of Zebulun: Jokneam, Kartah, ³⁵Dimnah, and Nahalal—four towns.

³⁶From the tribe of Reuben they received the following towns with their pasturelands: Bezer, Jahaz,* ³⁷Kedemoth, and Mephaath—four towns.

³⁸From the tribe of Gad they received the following towns with their pasturelands: Ramoth in Gilead (a city of refuge for those who accidentally killed someone), Mahanaim, ³⁹Heshbon, and Jazer—four towns. ⁴⁰So in all, twelve towns were allotted to the clan of Merari.

⁴¹The total number of towns and pasturelands within Israelite territory given to the Levites came to forty-eight. ⁴²Every one of these towns had pasturelands surrounding it.

21:36 Hebrew *Jahzah,* a variant spelling of Jahaz.

⁴³ So the LORD gave to Israel all the land he had sworn to give their ancestors, and they took possession of it and settled there. ⁴⁴ And the LORD gave them rest on every side, just as he had solemnly promised their ancestors. None of their enemies could stand against them, for the LORD helped them conquer all their enemies. ⁴⁵ Not a single one of all the good promises the LORD had given to the family of Israel was left unfulfilled; everything he had spoken came true.

THE EASTERN TRIBES RETURN HOME

22 Then Joshua called together the tribes of Reuben, Gad, and the half-tribe of Manasseh. ² He told them, "You have done as Moses, the servant of the LORD, commanded you, and you have obeyed every order I have given you. ³ During all this time you have not deserted the other tribes. You have been careful to obey the commands of the LORD your God right up to the present day. ⁴ And now the LORD your God has given the other tribes rest, as he promised them. So go back home to the land that Moses, the servant of the LORD, gave you as your possession on the east side of the Jordan River. ⁵ But be very careful to obey all the commands and the instructions that Moses gave to you. Love the LORD your God, walk in all his ways, obey his commands, hold firmly to him, and serve him with all your heart and all your soul." ⁶ So Joshua blessed them and sent them away, and they went home.

⁷ Moses had given the land of Bashan, east of the Jordan River, to the half-tribe of Manasseh. (The other half of the tribe was given land west of the Jordan.) As Joshua sent them away and blessed them, ⁸ he said to them, "Go back to your homes with the great wealth you have taken from your enemies—the vast herds of livestock, the silver, gold, bronze, and iron, and the large supply of clothing. Share the plunder with your relatives."

⁹ So the men of Reuben, Gad, and the half-tribe of Manasseh left the rest of Israel at Shiloh in the land of Canaan. They started the journey back to their own land of Gilead, the territory that belonged to them according to the LORD's command through Moses.

THE EASTERN TRIBES BUILD AN ALTAR

¹⁰ But while they were still in Canaan, and when they came to a place called Geliloth* near the Jordan River, the men of Reuben, Gad, and the half-tribe of Manasseh stopped to build a large and imposing altar.

¹¹ The rest of Israel heard that the people of Reuben, Gad, and the half-tribe of Manasseh had built an altar at Geliloth at the edge of the land of Canaan, on the west side of the Jordan River. ¹² So the whole community of Israel gathered at Shiloh and prepared to go to war against them. ¹³ First, however, they sent a delegation led by Phinehas son of Eleazar, the priest, to talk with the tribes of Reuben, Gad, and the half-tribe of Manasseh. ¹⁴ In this delegation were ten leaders of Israel, one from each of the ten tribes, and each the head of his family within the clans of Israel.

¹⁵ When they arrived in the land of Gilead, they said to the tribes of Reuben, Gad, and the half-tribe of Manasseh, ¹⁶ "The whole community of the LORD demands to know why you are betraying the God of Israel. How could you turn away from the LORD and build an altar for yourselves in rebellion against him? ¹⁷ Was our sin at Peor not enough? To this day we are not fully cleansed of it, even after the plague that struck the entire community of the LORD. ¹⁸ And yet today you are turning away from following the LORD. If you rebel against the LORD today, he will be angry with all of us tomorrow.

¹⁹ "If you need the altar because the land you possess is defiled, then join us in the LORD's land, where the Tabernacle of the LORD is situated, and share our land with us. But do not rebel against the LORD or against us by building an altar other than the one true altar of the LORD our God. ²⁰ Didn't divine anger fall on the entire community of Israel when Achan, a member of the clan of Zerah, sinned by stealing the things set apart for the LORD*? He was not the only one who died because of his sin."

²¹ Then the people of Reuben, Gad, and the half-tribe of Manasseh answered the heads of the clans of Israel: ²² "The LORD, the Mighty One, is God! The LORD, the Mighty One, is God! He knows the truth, and may Israel know it, too! We have not built the altar in treacherous rebellion against the LORD. If we have done so, do not spare our lives this day. ²³ If we have built an altar for ourselves to turn away from the LORD or to offer burnt offerings or grain offerings or peace offerings, may the LORD himself punish us.

²⁴ "The truth is, we have built this altar because we fear that in the future your descendants will say to ours, 'What right do you have to worship the LORD, the God of Israel? ²⁵ The LORD has placed the Jordan River as a barrier between our people and you people of Reuben and Gad. You have no claim to the LORD.' So your descendants may prevent our descendants from worshiping the LORD.

²⁶ "So we decided to build the altar, not for burnt offerings or sacrifices, ²⁷ but as a memorial. It will remind our descendants and your descendants that we, too, have the right to worship the LORD at his sanctuary with our burnt offerings, sacrifices, and peace offerings. Then your descendants will not be able to say to ours, 'You have no claim to the LORD.'

22:10 Or *to the circle of stones;* similarly in 22:11.   22:20 The Hebrew term used here refers to the complete consecration of things or people to the LORD, either by destroying them or by giving them as an offering.

[28] "If they say this, our descendants can reply, 'Look at this copy of the LORD's altar that our ancestors made. It is not for burnt offerings or sacrifices; it is a reminder of the relationship both of us have with the LORD.' [29] Far be it from us to rebel against the LORD or turn away from him by building our own altar for burnt offerings, grain offerings, or sacrifices. Only the altar of the LORD our God that stands in front of the Tabernacle may be used for that purpose."

[30] When Phinehas the priest and the leaders of the community—the heads of the clans of Israel—heard this from the tribes of Reuben, Gad, and the half-tribe of Manasseh, they were satisfied. [31] Phinehas son of Eleazar, the priest, replied to them, "Today we know the LORD is among us because you have not committed this treachery against the LORD as we thought. Instead, you have rescued Israel from being destroyed by the hand of the LORD."

[32] Then Phinehas son of Eleazar, the priest, and the other leaders left the tribes of Reuben and Gad in Gilead and returned to the land of Canaan to tell the Israelites what had happened. [33] And all the Israelites were satisfied and praised God and spoke no more of war against Reuben and Gad.

[34] The people of Reuben and Gad named the altar "Witness,"* for they said, "It is a witness between us and them that the LORD is our God, too."

JOSHUA'S FINAL WORDS TO ISRAEL

23 The years passed, and the LORD had given the people of Israel rest from all their enemies. Joshua, who was now very old, [2] called together all the elders, leaders, judges, and officers of Israel. He said to them, "I am now a very old man. [3] You have seen everything the LORD your God has done for you during my lifetime. The LORD your God has fought for you against your enemies. [4] I have allotted to you as your homeland all the land of the nations yet unconquered, as well as the land of those we have already conquered—from the Jordan River to the Mediterranean Sea* in the west. [5] This land will be yours, for the LORD your God will himself drive out all the people living there now. You will take possession of their land, just as the LORD your God promised you.

[6] "So be very careful to follow everything Moses wrote in the Book of Instruction. Do not deviate from it, turning either to the right or to the left. [7] Make sure you do not associate with the other people still remaining in the land. Do not even mention the names of their gods, much less swear by them or serve them or worship them. [8] Rather, cling tightly to the LORD your God as you have done until now.

[9] "For the LORD has driven out great and powerful nations for you, and no one has yet been able to defeat you. [10] Each one of you will put to flight a thousand of the enemy, for the LORD your God fights for you, just as he has promised. [11] So be very careful to love the LORD your God.

[12] "But if you turn away from him and cling to the customs of the survivors of these nations remaining among you, and if you intermarry with them, [13] then know for certain that the LORD your God will no longer drive them out of your land. Instead, they will be a snare and a trap to you, a whip for your backs and thorny brambles in your eyes, and you will vanish from this good land the LORD your God has given you.

[14] "Soon I will die, going the way of everything on earth. Deep in your hearts you know that every promise of the LORD your God has come true. Not a single one has failed! [15] But as surely as the LORD your God has given you the good things he promised, he will also bring disaster on you if you disobey him. He will completely destroy you from this good land he has given you. [16] If you break the covenant of the LORD your God by worshiping and serving other gods, his anger will burn against you, and you will quickly vanish from the good land he has given you."

THE LORD'S COVENANT RENEWED

24 Then Joshua summoned all the tribes of Israel to Shechem, including their elders, leaders, judges, and officers. So they came and presented themselves to God.

[2] Joshua said to the people, "This is what the LORD, the God of Israel, says: Long ago your ancestors, including Terah, the father of Abraham and Nahor, lived beyond the Euphrates River,* and they worshiped other gods. [3] But I took your ancestor Abraham from the land beyond the Euphrates and led him into the land of Canaan. I gave him many descendants through his son Isaac. [4] To Isaac I gave Jacob and Esau. To Esau I gave the mountains of Seir, while Jacob and his children went down into Egypt.

[5] "Then I sent Moses and Aaron, and I brought terrible plagues on Egypt; and afterward I brought you out as a free people. [6] But when your ancestors arrived at the Red Sea,* the Egyptians chased after you with chariots and charioteers. [7] When your ancestors cried out to the LORD, I put darkness between you and the Egyptians. I brought the sea crashing down on the Egyptians, drowning them. With your very own eyes you saw what I did. Then you lived in the wilderness for many years.

[8] "Finally, I brought you into the land of the Amorites on the east side of the Jordan. They fought against you, but I destroyed them before you. I gave you victory over them, and you took possession of their land. [9] Then Balak son of Zippor, king of Moab, started a war against Israel.

22:34 Some manuscripts lack this word.   23:4 Hebrew *the Great Sea.*   24:2 Hebrew *the river;* also in 24:3, 14, 15.   24:6 Hebrew *sea of reeds.*

He summoned Balaam son of Beor to curse you, [10] but I would not listen to him. Instead, I made Balaam bless you, and so I rescued you from Balak.

[11] "When you crossed the Jordan River and came to Jericho, the men of Jericho fought against you, as did the Amorites, the Perizzites, the Canaanites, the Hittites, the Girgashites, the Hivites, and the Jebusites. But I gave you victory over them. [12] And I sent terror* ahead of you to drive out the two kings of the Amorites. It was not your swords or bows that brought you victory. [13] I gave you land you had not worked on, and I gave you towns you did not build—the towns where you are now living. I gave you vineyards and olive groves for food, though you did not plant them.

[14] "So fear the LORD and serve him wholeheartedly. Put away forever the idols your ancestors worshiped when they lived beyond the Euphrates River and in Egypt. Serve the LORD alone. [15] But if you refuse to serve the LORD, then choose today whom you will serve. Would you prefer the gods your ancestors served beyond the Euphrates? Or will it be the gods of the Amorites in whose land you now live? But as for me and my family, we will serve the LORD."

[16] The people replied, "We would never abandon the LORD and serve other gods. [17] For the LORD our God is the one who rescued us and our ancestors from slavery in the land of Egypt. He performed mighty miracles before our very eyes. As we traveled through the wilderness among our enemies, he preserved us. [18] It was the LORD who drove out the Amorites and the other nations living here in the land. So we, too, will serve the LORD, for he alone is our God."

[19] Then Joshua warned the people, "You are not able to serve the LORD, for he is a holy and jealous God. He will not forgive your rebellion and your sins. [20] If you abandon the LORD and serve other gods, he will turn against you and destroy you, even though he has been so good to you."

[21] But the people answered Joshua, "No, we will serve the LORD!"

[22] "You are a witness to your own decision," Joshua said. "You have chosen to serve the LORD."

"Yes," they replied, "we are witnesses to what we have said."

[23] "All right then," Joshua said, "destroy the idols among you, and turn your hearts to the LORD, the God of Israel."

[24] The people said to Joshua, "We will serve the LORD our God. We will obey him alone."

[25] So Joshua made a covenant with the people that day at Shechem, committing them to follow the decrees and regulations of the LORD. [26] Joshua recorded these things in the Book of God's Instructions. As a reminder of their agreement, he took a huge stone and rolled it beneath the terebinth tree beside the Tabernacle of the LORD.

[27] Joshua said to all the people, "This stone has heard everything the LORD said to us. It will be a witness to testify against you if you go back on your word to God."

[28] Then Joshua sent all the people away to their own homelands.

LEADERS BURIED IN THE PROMISED LAND

[29] After this, Joshua son of Nun, the servant of the LORD, died at the age of 110. [30] They buried him in the land he had been allocated, at Timnath-serah in the hill country of Ephraim, north of Mount Gaash.

[31] The people of Israel served the LORD throughout the lifetime of Joshua and of the elders who outlived him—those who had personally experienced all that the LORD had done for Israel.

[32] The bones of Joseph, which the Israelites had brought along with them when they left Egypt, were buried at Shechem, in the plot of land Jacob had bought from the sons of Hamor for 100 pieces of silver.* This land was located in the territory allotted to the descendants of Joseph.

[33] Eleazar son of Aaron also died. He was buried in the hill country of Ephraim, in the town of Gibeah, which had been given to his son Phinehas.

24:12 Often rendered the hornet. The meaning of the Hebrew is uncertain. 24:32 Hebrew 100 kesitahs; the value or weight of the kesitah is no longer known.

JUDGES

JON HUNTZINGER, PHD

The book of Judges narrates the events that followed the settlement of the land by the Israelites recounted in the book of Joshua. These events are also prior to the establishment of the monarchy (fourteenth-eleventh centuries BC). This book describes the difficulties the Israelites encountered in settling the land of Canaan. Before the book of Joshua, the Israelites wandered as nomads in the wilderness for 40 years. Consequently, the adjustment to a more settled, agrarian way of life in Canaan was hard. The name of the book comes from the "judges"—minor rulers God appointed to lead the people after Joshua's death. The writer of the book is unknown, which is the case for all of the historical books of the Old Testament. The book of Judges was written sometime after the monarchy was first founded in Israel in the eleventh century BC (17:6; 18:1; 19:1; 21:25).

The major section of the book (chapters 2–16) follows a recurring cycle of idolatry, judgment, and deliverance:
— In story after story, the people "did evil in the LORD's sight" (2:11; 3:7; 3:12; 4:1; 6:1; 10:6; 13:1) by worshipping the idols of Canaan.
— God judges the people by allowing foreign powers to rule over them (2:14; 3:8; 4:2; 10:9).
— The people then cry out for help (3:9; 3:15; 6:6-7; 10:10).
— God hears their cries and raises up a judge to overthrow the people who are oppressing them (2:16; 3:9; 3:15; 10:1; 10:12).
— Then the people worship God in peace until the judge dies.

This pattern repeats itself throughout the book, with each successive period resulting in judgment more severe than the previous one and with each judge more questionable than the one who went before.

The book of Judges names 12 leaders who judged Israel. Of those 12, the book of Judges only gives a brief mention to half: Shamgar, Tola, Jair, Ibzan, Elon, and Abdon. The book contains extended stories of the other six:
— Othniel defeats the king of Mesopotamia (3:7-11).
— Ehud defeats the king of Moab (3:12-30).
— Deborah defeats the king of Canaan (chapters 4–5).
— Gideon defeats the Midianites (chapters 6–8).

— Jephthah overthrows the Ammonites (chapters 11–12).
— Samson overthrows the Philistines (chapters 13–16).

After Samson, the land descends into civil war, and there is no further judge to save the people (chapters 17–21).

Throughout the stories of the judges, God gives His Spirit to them, by which they save the people (3:10; 6:34; 11:29; 13:25; 14:6; 14:19). All of these judges have features that would normally disqualify them from leadership:
— Othniel is not a descendant of Joshua's family as might be expected.
— Ehud is a left-handed man rather than right-handed.
— Deborah is a woman living in a male-dominated culture.
— Gideon is a member of Israel's smallest tribe, the tribe of Benjamin, rather than the largest.
— Jephthah is the son of a prostitute and does not have a recognized father.
— Samson is a foolish man rather than a man of wisdom, and he carelessly tells God's plans to Delilah.

Nonetheless, God chooses each of these people to show that their success is not due to their own ability, greatness, or wisdom but due to His presence with them by His Spirit.

Why did the Israelites keep returning to idol worship during this time? Why did they need one judge after another to deliver them from other nations? The simple explanation is the ancient people of the Near East believed farming had a religious component. Since they saw agriculture as dependent on the favor of the gods for rain, sunshine, and protection from storms and drought, the farmers often made offerings to those gods they thought could give them the weather they needed to plant, grow, and harvest their crops. The Israelites, who had recently been nomads, learned how to farm from these people and so adopted their practices. They had a hard time separating proven agricultural techniques from superstitious ones, especially when those practices seemed effective for growing crops.

JUDAH AND SIMEON CONQUER THE LAND

1 After the death of Joshua, the Israelites asked the LORD, "Which tribe should go first to attack the Canaanites?"

[2] The LORD answered, "Judah, for I have given them victory over the land."

[3] The men of Judah said to their relatives from the tribe of Simeon, "Join with us to fight against the Canaanites living in the territory allotted to us. Then we will help you conquer your territory." So the men of Simeon went with Judah.

[4] When the men of Judah attacked, the LORD gave them victory over the Canaanites and Perizzites, and they killed 10,000 enemy warriors at the town of Bezek. [5] While at Bezek they encountered King Adoni-bezek and fought against him, and the Canaanites and Perizzites were defeated. [6] Adoni-bezek escaped, but the Israelites soon captured him and cut off his thumbs and big toes.

[7] Adoni-bezek said, "I once had seventy kings with their thumbs and big toes cut off, eating scraps from under my table. Now God has paid me back for what I did to them." They took him to Jerusalem, and he died there.

[8] The men of Judah attacked Jerusalem and captured it, killing all its people and setting the city on fire. [9] Then they went down to fight the Canaanites living in the hill country, the Negev, and the western foothills.* [10] Judah marched against the Canaanites in Hebron (formerly called Kiriath-arba), defeating the forces of Sheshai, Ahiman, and Talmai.

[11] From there they went to fight against the people living in the town of Debir (formerly called Kiriath-sepher). [12] Caleb said, "I will give my daughter Acsah in marriage to the one who attacks and captures Kiriath-sepher." [13] Othniel, the son of Caleb's younger brother, Kenaz, was the one who conquered it, so Acsah became Othniel's wife.

[14] When Acsah married Othniel, she urged him* to ask her father for a field. As she got down off her donkey, Caleb asked her, "What's the matter?"

[15] She said, "Let me have another gift. You have already given me land in the Negev; now please give me springs of water, too." So Caleb gave her the upper and lower springs.

[16] When the tribe of Judah left Jericho—the city of palms—the Kenites, who were descendants of Moses' father-in-law, traveled with them into the wilderness of Judah. They settled among the people there, near the town of Arad in the Negev.

[17] Then Judah joined with Simeon to fight against the Canaanites living in Zephath, and they completely destroyed* the town. So the town was named Hormah.* [18] In addition, Judah captured the towns of Gaza, Ashkelon, and Ekron, along with their surrounding territories.

ISRAEL FAILS TO CONQUER THE LAND

[19] The LORD was with the people of Judah, and they took possession of the hill country. But they failed to drive out the people living in the plains, who had iron chariots. [20] The town of Hebron was given to Caleb as Moses had promised. And Caleb drove out the people living there, who were descendants of the three sons of Anak.

[21] The tribe of Benjamin, however, failed to drive out the Jebusites, who were living in Jerusalem. So to this day the Jebusites live in Jerusalem among the people of Benjamin.

[22] The descendants of Joseph attacked the town of Bethel, and the LORD was with them. [23] They sent men to scout out Bethel (formerly known as Luz). [24] They confronted a man coming out of the town and said to him, "Show us a way into the town, and we will have mercy on you." [25] So he showed them a way in, and they killed everyone in the town except that man and his family. [26] Later the man moved to the land of the Hittites, where he built a town. He named it Luz, which is its name to this day.

[27] The tribe of Manasseh failed to drive out the people living in Beth-shan,* Taanach, Dor, Ibleam, Megiddo, and all their surrounding settlements, because the Canaanites were determined to stay in that region. [28] When the Israelites grew stronger, they forced the Canaanites to work as slaves, but they never did drive them completely out of the land.

[29] The tribe of Ephraim failed to drive out the Canaanites living in Gezer, so the Canaanites continued to live there among them.

[30] The tribe of Zebulun failed to drive out the residents of Kitron and Nahalol, so the Canaanites continued to live among them. But the Canaanites were forced to work as slaves for the people of Zebulun.

[31] The tribe of Asher failed to drive out the residents of Acco, Sidon, Ahlab, Aczib, Helbah, Aphik, and Rehob. [32] Instead, the people of Asher moved in among the Canaanites, who controlled the land, for they failed to drive them out.

[33] Likewise, the tribe of Naphtali failed to drive out the residents of Beth-shemesh and Beth-anath. Instead, they moved in among the Canaanites, who controlled the land. Nevertheless, the people of Beth-shemesh and Beth-anath were forced to work as slaves for the people of Naphtali.

[34] As for the tribe of Dan, the Amorites forced them back into the hill country and would not let them come down into the plains. [35] The Amorites were determined to stay in Mount Heres, Aijalon, and Shaalbim, but when the descendants of Joseph became stronger, they forced the Amorites to work as slaves. [36] The boundary of the Amorites ran from Scorpion Pass* to Sela and continued upward from there.

1:9 Hebrew *the Shephelah.* 1:14 Greek version and Latin Vulgate read *he urged her.* 1:17a The Hebrew term used here refers to the complete consecration of things or people to the LORD, either by destroying them or by giving them as an offering. 1:17b *Hormah* means "destruction." 1:27 Hebrew *Beth-shean,* a variant spelling of Beth-shan. 1:36 Hebrew *Akrabbim.*

THE LORD'S MESSENGER COMES TO BOKIM

2 The angel of the LORD went up from Gilgal to Bokim and said to the Israelites, "I brought you out of Egypt into this land that I swore to give your ancestors, and I said I would never break my covenant with you. ²For your part, you were not to make any covenants with the people living in this land; instead, you were to destroy their altars. But you disobeyed my command. Why did you do this? ³So now I declare that I will no longer drive out the people living in your land. They will be thorns in your sides,* and their gods will be a constant temptation to you."

⁴When the angel of the LORD finished speaking to all the Israelites, the people wept loudly. ⁵So they called the place Bokim (which means "weeping"), and they offered sacrifices there to the LORD.

THE DEATH OF JOSHUA

⁶After Joshua sent the people away, each of the tribes left to take possession of the land allotted to them. ⁷And the Israelites served the LORD throughout the lifetime of Joshua and the leaders who outlived him—those who had seen all the great things the LORD had done for Israel.

⁸Joshua son of Nun, the servant of the LORD, died at the age of 110. ⁹They buried him in the land he had been allocated, at Timnath-serah* in the hill country of Ephraim, north of Mount Gaash.

ISRAEL DISOBEYS THE LORD

¹⁰After that generation died, another generation grew up who did not acknowledge the LORD or remember the mighty things he had done for Israel.

¹¹The Israelites did evil in the LORD's sight and served the images of Baal. ¹²They abandoned the LORD, the God of their ancestors, who had brought them out of Egypt. They went after other gods, worshiping the gods of the people around them. And they angered the LORD. ¹³They abandoned the LORD to serve Baal and the images of Ashtoreth. ¹⁴This made the LORD burn with anger against Israel, so he handed them over to raiders who stole their possessions. He turned them over to their enemies all around, and they were no longer able to resist them. ¹⁵Every time Israel went out to battle, the LORD fought against them, causing them to be defeated, just as he had warned. And the people were in great distress.

THE LORD RESCUES HIS PEOPLE

¹⁶Then the LORD raised up judges to rescue the Israelites from their attackers. ¹⁷Yet Israel did not listen to the judges but prostituted themselves by worshiping other gods. How quickly they turned away from the path of their ancestors, who had walked in obedience to the LORD's commands.

¹⁸Whenever the LORD raised up a judge over Israel, he was with that judge and rescued the people from their enemies throughout the judge's lifetime. For the LORD took pity on his people, who were burdened by oppression and suffering. ¹⁹But when the judge died, the people returned to their corrupt ways, behaving worse than those who had lived before them. They went after other gods, serving and worshiping them. And they refused to give up their evil practices and stubborn ways.

²⁰So the LORD burned with anger against Israel. He said, "Because these people have violated my covenant, which I made with their ancestors, and have ignored my commands, ²¹I will no longer drive out the nations that Joshua left unconquered when he died. ²²I did this to test Israel—to see whether or not they would follow the ways of the LORD as their ancestors did." ²³That is why the LORD left those nations in place. He did not quickly drive them out or allow Joshua to conquer them all.

THE NATIONS LEFT IN CANAAN

3 These are the nations that the LORD left in the land to test those Israelites who had not experienced the wars of Canaan. ²He did this to teach warfare to generations of Israelites who had no experience in battle. ³These are the nations: the Philistines (those living under the five Philistine rulers), all the Canaanites, the Sidonians, and the Hivites living in the mountains of Lebanon from Mount Baal-hermon to Lebo-hamath. ⁴These people were left to test the Israelites—to see whether they would obey the commands the LORD had given to their ancestors through Moses.

⁵So the people of Israel lived among the Canaanites, Hittites, Amorites, Perizzites, Hivites, and Jebusites, ⁶and they intermarried with them. Israelite sons married their daughters, and Israelite daughters were given in marriage to their sons. And the Israelites served their gods.

OTHNIEL BECOMES ISRAEL'S JUDGE

⁷The Israelites did evil in the LORD's sight. They forgot about the LORD their God, and they served the images of Baal and the Asherah poles. ⁸Then the LORD burned with anger against Israel, and he turned them over to King Cushan-rishathaim of Aram-naharaim.* And the Israelites served Cushan-rishathaim for eight years.

⁹But when the people of Israel cried out to the LORD for help, the LORD raised up a rescuer to save them. His name was Othniel, the son of Caleb's younger brother, Kenaz. ¹⁰The Spirit of the LORD came upon him, and he became Israel's

---

2:3 Hebrew *They will be in your sides;* compare Num 33:55.   2:9 As in parallel text at Josh 24:30; Hebrew reads *Timnath-heres,* a variant spelling of Timnath-serah.   3:8 *Aram-naharaim* means "Aram of the two rivers," thought to have been located between the Euphrates and Balih Rivers in northwestern Mesopotamia.

judge. He went to war against King Cushan-rishathaim of Aram, and the LORD gave Othniel victory over him. [11]So there was peace in the land for forty years. Then Othniel son of Kenaz died.

EHUD BECOMES ISRAEL'S JUDGE

[12]Once again the Israelites did evil in the LORD's sight, and the LORD gave King Eglon of Moab control over Israel because of their evil. [13]Eglon enlisted the Ammonites and Amalekites as allies, and then he went out and defeated Israel, taking possession of Jericho, the city of palms. [14]And the Israelites served Eglon of Moab for eighteen years.

[15]But when the people of Israel cried out to the LORD for help, the LORD again raised up a rescuer to save them. His name was Ehud son of Gera, a left-handed man of the tribe of Benjamin. The Israelites sent Ehud to deliver their tribute money to King Eglon of Moab. [16]So Ehud made a double-edged dagger that was about a foot* long, and he strapped it to his right thigh, keeping it hidden under his clothing. [17]He brought the tribute money to Eglon, who was very fat.

[18]After delivering the payment, Ehud started home with those who had helped carry the tribute. [19]But when Ehud reached the stone idols near Gilgal, he turned back. He came to Eglon and said, "I have a secret message for you."

So the king commanded his servants, "Be quiet!" and he sent them all out of the room.

[20]Ehud walked over to Eglon, who was sitting alone in a cool upstairs room. And Ehud said, "I have a message from God for you!" As King Eglon rose from his seat, [21]Ehud reached with his left hand, pulled out the dagger strapped to his right thigh, and plunged it into the king's belly. [22]The dagger went so deep that the handle disappeared beneath the king's fat. So Ehud did not pull out the dagger, and the king's bowels emptied.* [23]Then Ehud closed and locked the doors of the room and escaped down the latrine.*

[24]After Ehud was gone, the king's servants returned and found the doors to the upstairs room locked. They thought he might be using the latrine in the room, [25]so they waited. But when the king didn't come out after a long delay, they became concerned and got a key. And when they opened the doors, they found their master dead on the floor.

[26]While the servants were waiting, Ehud escaped, passing the stone idols on his way to Seirah. [27]When he arrived in the hill country of Ephraim, Ehud sounded a call to arms. Then he led a band of Israelites down from the hills.

[28]"Follow me," he said, "for the LORD has given you victory over Moab your enemy." So they followed him. And the Israelites took control of the shallow crossings of the Jordan River across from Moab, preventing anyone from crossing.

[29]They attacked the Moabites and killed about 10,000 of their strongest and most able-bodied warriors. Not one of them escaped. [30]So Moab was conquered by Israel that day, and there was peace in the land for eighty years.

SHAMGAR BECOMES ISRAEL'S JUDGE

[31]After Ehud, Shamgar son of Anath rescued Israel. He once killed 600 Philistines with an ox goad.

DEBORAH BECOMES ISRAEL'S JUDGE

4 After Ehud's death, the Israelites again did evil in the LORD's sight. [2]So the LORD turned them over to King Jabin of Hazor, a Canaanite king. The commander of his army was Sisera, who lived in Harosheth-haggoyim. [3]Sisera, who had 900 iron chariots, ruthlessly oppressed the Israelites for twenty years. Then the people of Israel cried out to the LORD for help.

[4]Deborah, the wife of Lappidoth, was a prophet who was judging Israel at that time. [5]She would sit under the Palm of Deborah, between Ramah and Bethel in the hill country of Ephraim, and the Israelites would go to her for judgment. [6]One day she sent for Barak son of Abinoam, who lived in Kedesh in the land of Naphtali. She said to him, "This is what the LORD, the God of Israel, commands you: Call out 10,000 warriors from the tribes of Naphtali and Zebulun at Mount Tabor. [7]And I will call out Sisera, commander of Jabin's army, along with his chariots and warriors, to the Kishon River. There I will give you victory over him."

[8]Barak told her, "I will go, but only if you go with me."

[9]"Very well," she replied, "I will go with you. But you will receive no honor in this venture, for the LORD's victory over Sisera will be at the hands of a woman." So Deborah went with Barak to Kedesh. [10]At Kedesh, Barak called together the tribes of Zebulun and Naphtali, and 10,000 warriors went up with him. Deborah also went with him.

[11]Now Heber the Kenite, a descendant of Moses' brother-in-law* Hobab, had moved away from the other members of his tribe and pitched his tent by the oak of Zaanannim near Kedesh.

[12]When Sisera was told that Barak son of Abinoam had gone up to Mount Tabor, [13]he called for all 900 of his iron chariots and all of his warriors, and they marched from Harosheth-haggoyim to the Kishon River.

[14]Then Deborah said to Barak, "Get ready! This is the day the LORD will give you victory over Sisera, for the LORD is marching ahead of you." So Barak led his 10,000 warriors down the slopes of Mount Tabor into battle. [15]When Barak attacked, the LORD threw Sisera and all his chariots and warriors into a panic. Sisera leaped down from his chariot and escaped on foot. [16]Then Barak chased the chariots and the enemy army all the

---

3:16 Hebrew *gomed*, the length of which is uncertain.   3:22 Or *and it came out behind.*   3:23 Or *and went out through the porch;* the meaning of the Hebrew is uncertain.   4:11 Or *father-in-law.*

way to Harosheth-haggoyim, killing all of Sisera's warriors. Not a single one was left alive.

17 Meanwhile, Sisera ran to the tent of Jael, the wife of Heber the Kenite, because Heber's family was on friendly terms with King Jabin of Hazor. 18 Jael went out to meet Sisera and said to him, "Come into my tent, sir. Come in. Don't be afraid." So he went into her tent, and she covered him with a blanket.

19 "Please give me some water," he said. "I'm thirsty." So she gave him some milk from a leather bag and covered him again.

20 "Stand at the door of the tent," he told her. "If anybody comes and asks you if there is anyone here, say no."

21 But when Sisera fell asleep from exhaustion, Jael quietly crept up to him with a hammer and tent peg in her hand. Then she drove the tent peg through his temple and into the ground, and so he died.

22 When Barak came looking for Sisera, Jael went out to meet him. She said, "Come, and I will show you the man you are looking for." So he followed her into the tent and found Sisera lying there dead, with the tent peg through his temple.

23 So on that day Israel saw God defeat Jabin, the Canaanite king. 24 And from that time on Israel became stronger and stronger against King Jabin until they finally destroyed him.

THE SONG OF DEBORAH

5 On that day Deborah and Barak son of Abinoam sang this song:

2 "Israel's leaders took charge,
   and the people gladly followed.
 Praise the LORD!

3 "Listen, you kings!
   Pay attention, you mighty rulers!
 For I will sing to the LORD.
 I will make music to the LORD, the God
   of Israel.

4 "LORD, when you set out from Seir
   and marched across the fields of Edom,
 the earth trembled,
   and the cloudy skies poured down rain.
5 The mountains quaked in the presence of
   the LORD,
   the God of Mount Sinai—
 in the presence of the LORD,
   the God of Israel.

6 "In the days of Shamgar son of Anath,
   and in the days of Jael,
 people avoided the main roads,
   and travelers stayed on winding pathways.
7 There were few people left in the villages
   of Israel*—
   until Deborah arose as a mother for Israel.
8 When Israel chose new gods,

war erupted at the city gates.
 Yet not a shield or spear could be seen
   among forty thousand warriors in Israel!
9 My heart is with the commanders of Israel,
   with those who volunteered for war.
 Praise the LORD!

10 "Consider this, you who ride on fine donkeys,
   you who sit on fancy saddle blankets,
   and you who walk along the road.
11 Listen to the village musicians*
   gathered at the watering holes.
 They recount the righteous victories of
   the LORD
   and the victories of his villagers in Israel.
 Then the people of the LORD
   marched down to the city gates.

12 "Wake up, Deborah, wake up!
   Wake up, wake up, and sing a song!
 Arise, Barak!
   Lead your captives away, son of Abinoam!

13 "Down from Tabor marched the few against
   the nobles.
 The people of the LORD marched down
   against mighty warriors.
14 They came down from Ephraim—
   a land that once belonged to the
     Amalekites;
   they followed you, Benjamin, with your
     troops.
 From Makir the commanders marched down;
   from Zebulun came those who carry a
     commander's staff.
15 The princes of Issachar were with Deborah
   and Barak.
 They followed Barak, rushing into the
   valley.
 But in the tribe of Reuben
   there was great indecision.*
16 Why did you sit at home among the
   sheepfolds—
   to hear the shepherds whistle for their
     flocks?
 Yes, in the tribe of Reuben
   there was great indecision.
17 Gilead remained east of the Jordan.
   And why did Dan stay home?
 Asher sat unmoved at the seashore,
   remaining in his harbors.
18 But Zebulun risked his life,
   as did Naphtali, on the heights of the
     battlefield.

19 "The kings of Canaan came and fought,
   at Taanach near Megiddo's springs,
   but they carried off no silver treasures.

5:7 The meaning of the Hebrew is uncertain. 5:11 The meaning of the Hebrew is uncertain. 5:15 As in some Hebrew manuscripts and Syriac version, which read *searchings of heart;* Masoretic Text reads *resolve of heart.*

²⁰ The stars fought from heaven.
  The stars in their orbits fought
    against Sisera.
²¹ The Kishon River swept them away—
    that ancient torrent, the Kishon.
  March on with courage, my soul!
²² Then the horses' hooves hammered the
    ground,
    the galloping, galloping of Sisera's
      mighty steeds.
²³ 'Let the people of Meroz be cursed,' said the
    angel of the LORD.
  'Let them be utterly cursed,
  because they did not come to help
    the LORD—
  to help the LORD against the mighty
    warriors.'

²⁴ "Most blessed among women is Jael,
    the wife of Heber the Kenite.
  May she be blessed above all women who
    live in tents.
²⁵ Sisera asked for water,
    and she gave him milk.
  In a bowl fit for nobles,
    she brought him yogurt.
²⁶ Then with her left hand she reached for
      a tent peg,
    and with her right hand for the
      workman's hammer.
  She struck Sisera with the hammer,
    crushing his head.
  With a shattering blow, she pierced
    his temples.
²⁷ He sank, he fell,
    he lay still at her feet.
  And where he sank,
    there he died.

²⁸ "From the window Sisera's mother
    looked out.
    Through the window she watched for his
      return, saying,
  'Why is his chariot so long in coming?
  Why don't we hear the sound of chariot
    wheels?'

²⁹ "Her wise women answer,
    and she repeats these words to herself:
³⁰ 'They must be dividing the captured
      plunder—
    with a woman or two for every man.
  There will be colorful robes for Sisera,
    and colorful, embroidered robes for me.
  Yes, the plunder will include
    colorful robes embroidered on both sides.'

³¹ "LORD, may all your enemies die like Sisera!
    But may those who love you rise like the
      sun in all its power!"

Then there was peace in the land for forty years.

GIDEON BECOMES ISRAEL'S JUDGE

6 The Israelites did evil in the LORD's sight. So the LORD handed them over to the Midianites for seven years. ² The Midianites were so cruel that the Israelites made hiding places for themselves in the mountains, caves, and strongholds. ³ Whenever the Israelites planted their crops, marauders from Midian, Amalek, and the people of the east would attack Israel, ⁴ camping in the land and destroying crops as far away as Gaza. They left the Israelites with nothing to eat, taking all the sheep, goats, cattle, and donkeys. ⁵ These enemy hordes, coming with their livestock and tents, were as thick as locusts; they arrived on droves of camels too numerous to count. And they stayed until the land was stripped bare. ⁶ So Israel was reduced to starvation by the Midianites. Then the Israelites cried out to the LORD for help.

⁷ When they cried out to the LORD because of Midian, ⁸ the LORD sent a prophet to the Israelites. He said, "This is what the LORD, the God of Israel, says: I brought you up out of slavery in Egypt. ⁹ I rescued you from the Egyptians and from all who oppressed you. I drove out your enemies and gave you their land. ¹⁰ I told you, 'I am the LORD your God. You must not worship the gods of the Amorites, in whose land you now live.' But you have not listened to me."

¹¹ Then the angel of the LORD came and sat beneath the great tree at Ophrah, which belonged to Joash of the clan of Abiezer. Gideon son of Joash was threshing wheat at the bottom of a winepress to hide the grain from the Midianites. ¹² The angel of the LORD appeared to him and said, "Mighty hero, the LORD is with you!"

¹³ "Sir," Gideon replied, "if the LORD is with us, why has all this happened to us? And where are all the miracles our ancestors told us about? Didn't they say, 'The LORD brought us up out of Egypt'? But now the LORD has abandoned us and handed us over to the Midianites."

¹⁴ Then the LORD turned to him and said, "Go with the strength you have, and rescue Israel from the Midianites. I am sending you!"

¹⁵ "But Lord," Gideon replied, "how can I rescue Israel? My clan is the weakest in the whole tribe of Manasseh, and I am the least in my entire family!"

¹⁶ The LORD said to him, "I will be with you. And you will destroy the Midianites as if you were fighting against one man."

¹⁷ Gideon replied, "If you are truly going to help me, show me a sign to prove that it is really the LORD speaking to me. ¹⁸ Don't go away until I come back and bring my offering to you."

He answered, "I will stay here until you return."

¹⁹ Gideon hurried home. He cooked a young goat, and with a basket* of flour he baked some

---

6:19 Hebrew *an ephah* [20 quarts or 22 liters].

ROBERT MORRIS

CALL FOR CONFIRMATION
Judges 6:16–39

The number one question people have asked me over 35 years of ministry is, "How can I hear God?" And the second question is, "How can I know it's *really* Him?"

Asking for confirmation isn't wrong. In fact, it's biblical. God will always confirm His Word, and we need confirmation to make sure we're hearing Him correctly.

Most people know the story of Gideon's fleece, but before he asked for the fleece, Gideon asked God to confirm His word with a sign (Judges 6:17). God was not offended by Gideon, and He is not offended when we ask for signs either.

Scripture provides three ways we can know with certainty if what we're hearing is really God or just our own thoughts and desires:

1. **Does it line up with the Bible?**
   A word from God will never disagree with His written Word. People often take one Scripture out of context in an attempt to prove just about anything with it. The Bible will never contradict itself, but your interpretation of a Scripture might contradict the Bible as a whole. So ask yourself, "Does the *whole* Word agree with what I'm hearing?"

2. **Does godly counsel agree?**
   People will often ask one person after another about a word until they finally find someone who says, "Yes, I think that's God!" However, godly counsel is not simply finding someone who agrees with you. Godly counsel is finding people who really know God, His Word, and you. Share your word with godly, mature believers and be willing to hear them say, "No, I don't think that's God."

3. **Do I have peace?**
   God created you with an internal gauge to measure peace. The apostle Paul says, "Let the peace that comes from Christ rule in your hearts" (Colossians 3:15). The word translated *peace* in this verse actually means 'umpire'— let the peace of God *umpire* in your heart. How many times have you not had peace about a word or situation? God never leads through fear; He always leads through faith. If you don't have peace, then it's not from God.

bread without yeast. Then, carrying the meat in a basket and the broth in a pot, he brought them out and presented them to the angel, who was under the great tree.

²⁰The angel of God said to him, "Place the meat and the unleavened bread on this rock, and pour the broth over it." And Gideon did as he was told. ²¹Then the angel of the LORD touched the meat and bread with the tip of the staff in his hand, and fire flamed up from the rock and consumed all he had brought. And the angel of the LORD disappeared.

²²When Gideon realized that it was the angel of the LORD, he cried out, "Oh, Sovereign LORD, I'm doomed! I have seen the angel of the LORD face to face!"

²³"It is all right," the LORD replied. "Do not be afraid. You will not die." ²⁴And Gideon built an altar to the LORD there and named it Yahweh-Shalom (which means "the LORD is peace"). The altar remains in Ophrah in the land of the clan of Abiezer to this day.

²⁵That night the LORD said to Gideon, "Take the second bull from your father's herd, the one that is seven years old. Pull down your father's altar to Baal, and cut down the Asherah pole standing beside it. ²⁶Then build an altar to the LORD your God here on this hilltop sanctuary, laying the stones carefully. Sacrifice the bull as a burnt offering on the altar, using as fuel the wood of the Asherah pole you cut down."

²⁷So Gideon took ten of his servants and did as the LORD had commanded. But he did it at night because he was afraid of the other members of his father's household and the people of the town.

²⁸Early the next morning, as the people of the town began to stir, someone discovered that the altar of Baal had been broken down and that the Asherah pole beside it had been cut down. In their place a new altar had been built, and on it were the remains of the bull that had been sacrificed. ²⁹The people said to each other, "Who did this?" And after asking around and making a careful search, they learned that it was Gideon, the son of Joash.

³⁰"Bring out your son," the men of the town demanded of Joash. "He must die for destroying the altar of Baal and for cutting down the Asherah pole."

³¹But Joash shouted to the mob that confronted him, "Why are you defending Baal? Will you argue his case? Whoever pleads his case will be put to death by morning! If Baal truly is a god, let him defend himself and destroy the one who broke down his altar!" ³²From then on Gideon was called Jerub-baal, which means "Let Baal defend himself," because he broke down Baal's altar.

GIDEON ASKS FOR A SIGN

³³Soon afterward the armies of Midian, Amalek, and the people of the east formed an alliance against Israel and crossed the Jordan, camping in the valley of Jezreel. ³⁴Then the Spirit of the LORD clothed Gideon with power. He blew a ram's horn as a call to arms, and the men of

the clan of Abiezer came to him. ³⁵ He also sent messengers throughout Manasseh, Asher, Zebulun, and Naphtali, summoning their warriors, and all of them responded.

³⁶ Then Gideon said to God, "If you are truly going to use me to rescue Israel as you promised, ³⁷ prove it to me in this way. I will put a wool fleece on the threshing floor tonight. If the fleece is wet with dew in the morning but the ground is dry, then I will know that you are going to help me rescue Israel as you promised." ³⁸ And that is just what happened. When Gideon got up early the next morning, he squeezed the fleece and wrung out a whole bowlful of water.

³⁹ Then Gideon said to God, "Please don't be angry with me, but let me make one more request. Let me use the fleece for one more test. This time let the fleece remain dry while the ground around it is wet with dew." ⁴⁰ So that night God did as Gideon asked. The fleece was dry in the morning, but the ground was covered with dew.

GIDEON DEFEATS THE MIDIANITES

7 So Jerub-baal (that is, Gideon) and his army got up early and went as far as the spring of Harod. The armies of Midian were camped north of them in the valley near the hill of Moreh. ² The LORD said to Gideon, "You have too many warriors with you. If I let all of you fight the Midianites, the Israelites will boast to me that they saved themselves by their own strength. ³ Therefore, tell the people, 'Whoever is timid or afraid may leave this mountain* and go home.'" So 22,000 of them went home, leaving only 10,000 who were willing to fight.

⁴ But the LORD told Gideon, "There are still too many! Bring them down to the spring, and I will test them to determine who will go with you and who will not." ⁵ When Gideon took his warriors down to the water, the LORD told him, "Divide the men into two groups. In one group put all those who cup water in their hands and lap it up with their tongues like dogs. In the other group put all those who kneel down and drink with their mouths in the stream." ⁶ Only 300 of the men drank from their hands. All the others got down on their knees and drank with their mouths in the stream.

⁷ The LORD told Gideon, "With these 300 men I will rescue you and give you victory over the Midianites. Send all the others home." ⁸ So Gideon collected the provisions and rams' horns of the other warriors and sent them home. But he kept the 300 men with him.

The Midianite camp was in the valley just below Gideon. ⁹ That night the LORD said, "Get up! Go down into the Midianite camp, for I have given you victory over them! ¹⁰ But if you are afraid to attack, go down to the camp with your servant Purah. ¹¹ Listen to what the Midianites are saying, and you will be greatly encouraged. Then you will be eager to attack."

So Gideon took Purah and went down to the edge of the enemy camp. ¹² The armies of Midian, Amalek, and the people of the east had settled in the valley like a swarm of locusts. Their camels were like grains of sand on the seashore—too many to count! ¹³ Gideon crept up just as a man was telling his companion about a dream. The man said, "I had this dream, and in my dream a loaf of barley bread came tumbling down into the Midianite camp. It hit a tent, turned it over, and knocked it flat!"

¹⁴ His companion answered, "Your dream can mean only one thing—God has given Gideon son of Joash, the Israelite, victory over Midian and all its allies!"

¹⁵ When Gideon heard the dream and its interpretation, he bowed in worship before the LORD.* Then he returned to the Israelite camp and shouted, "Get up! For the LORD has given you victory over the Midianite hordes!" ¹⁶ He divided the 300 men into three groups and gave each man a ram's horn and a clay jar with a torch in it.

¹⁷ Then he said to them, "Keep your eyes on me. When I come to the edge of the camp, do just as I do. ¹⁸ As soon as I and those with me blow the rams' horns, blow your horns, too, all around the entire camp, and shout, 'For the LORD and for Gideon!'"

¹⁹ It was just after midnight,* after the changing of the guard, when Gideon and the 100 men with him reached the edge of the Midianite camp. Suddenly, they blew the rams' horns and broke their clay jars. ²⁰ Then all three groups blew their horns and broke their jars. They held the blazing torches in their left hands and the horns in their right hands, and they all shouted, "A sword for the LORD and for Gideon!"

²¹ Each man stood at his position around the camp and watched as all the Midianites rushed around in a panic, shouting as they ran to escape. ²² When the 300 Israelites blew their rams' horns, the LORD caused the warriors in the camp to fight against each other with their swords. Those who were not killed fled to places as far away as Beth-shittah near Zererah and to the border of Abel-meholah near Tabbath.

²³ Then Gideon sent for the warriors of Naphtali, Asher, and Manasseh, who joined in chasing the army of Midian. ²⁴ Gideon also sent messengers throughout the hill country of Ephraim, saying, "Come down to attack the Midianites. Cut them off at the shallow crossings of the Jordan River at Beth-barah."

So all the men of Ephraim did as they were told. ²⁵ They captured Oreb and Zeeb, the two Midianite commanders, killing Oreb at the rock of Oreb, and Zeeb at the winepress of Zeeb. And they continued to chase the Midianites. Afterward the

---

7:3 Hebrew *may leave Mount Gilead.* The identity of Mount Gilead is uncertain in this context. It is perhaps used here as another name for Mount Gilboa.   7:15 As in Greek version; Hebrew reads *he bowed.*   7:19 Hebrew *at the beginning of the second watch.*

Israelites brought the heads of Oreb and Zeeb to Gideon, who was by the Jordan River.

GIDEON KILLS ZEBAH AND ZALMUNNA

8 Then the people of Ephraim asked Gideon, "Why have you treated us this way? Why didn't you send for us when you first went out to fight the Midianites?" And they argued heatedly with Gideon.

²But Gideon replied, "What have I accomplished compared to you? Aren't even the leftover grapes of Ephraim's harvest better than the entire crop of my little clan of Abiezer? ³God gave you victory over Oreb and Zeeb, the commanders of the Midianite army. What have I accomplished compared to that?" When the men of Ephraim heard Gideon's answer, their anger subsided.

⁴Gideon then crossed the Jordan River with his 300 men, and though exhausted, they continued to chase the enemy. ⁵When they reached Succoth, Gideon asked the leaders of the town, "Please give my warriors some food. They are very tired. I am chasing Zebah and Zalmunna, the kings of Midian."

⁶But the officials of Succoth replied, "Catch Zebah and Zalmunna first, and then we will feed your army."

⁷So Gideon said, "After the LORD gives me victory over Zebah and Zalmunna, I will return and tear your flesh with the thorns and briers from the wilderness."

⁸From there Gideon went up to Peniel* and again asked for food, but he got the same answer. ⁹So he said to the people of Peniel, "After I return in victory, I will tear down this tower."

¹⁰By this time Zebah and Zalmunna were in Karkor with about 15,000 warriors—all that remained of the allied armies of the east, for 120,000 had already been killed. ¹¹Gideon circled around by the caravan route east of Nobah and Jogbehah, taking the Midianite army by surprise. ¹²Zebah and Zalmunna, the two Midianite kings, fled, but Gideon chased them down and captured all their warriors.

¹³After this, Gideon returned from the battle by way of Heres Pass. ¹⁴There he captured a young man from Succoth and demanded that he write down the names of all the seventy-seven officials and elders in the town. ¹⁵Gideon then returned to Succoth and said to the leaders, "Here are Zebah and Zalmunna. When we were here before, you taunted me, saying, 'Catch Zebah and Zalmunna first, and then we will feed your exhausted army.'" ¹⁶Then Gideon took the elders of the town and taught them a lesson, punishing them with thorns and briers from the wilderness. ¹⁷He also tore down the tower of Peniel and killed all the men in the town.

¹⁸Then Gideon asked Zebah and Zalmunna, "The men you killed at Tabor—what were they like?"

"Like you," they replied. "They all had the look of a king's son."

¹⁹"They were my brothers, the sons of my own mother!" Gideon exclaimed. "As surely as the LORD lives, I wouldn't kill you if you hadn't killed them."

²⁰Turning to Jether, his oldest son, he said, "Kill them!" But Jether did not draw his sword, for he was only a boy and was afraid.

²¹Then Zebah and Zalmunna said to Gideon, "Be a man! Kill us yourself!" So Gideon killed them both and took the royal ornaments from the necks of their camels.

GIDEON'S SACRED EPHOD

²²Then the Israelites said to Gideon, "Be our ruler! You and your son and your grandson will be our rulers, for you have rescued us from Midian."

²³But Gideon replied, "I will not rule over you, nor will my son. The LORD will rule over you! ²⁴However, I do have one request—that each of you give me an earring from the plunder you collected from your fallen enemies." (The enemies, being Ishmaelites, all wore gold earrings.)

²⁵"Gladly!" they replied. They spread out a cloak, and each one threw in a gold earring he had gathered from the plunder. ²⁶The weight of the gold earrings was forty-three pounds,* not including the royal ornaments and pendants, the purple clothing worn by the kings of Midian, or the chains around the necks of their camels.

²⁷Gideon made a sacred ephod from the gold and put it in Ophrah, his hometown. But soon all the Israelites prostituted themselves by worshiping it, and it became a trap for Gideon and his family.

²⁸That is the story of how the people of Israel defeated Midian, which never recovered. Throughout the rest of Gideon's lifetime—about forty years—there was peace in the land. ²⁹Then Gideon* son of Joash returned home. ³⁰He had seventy sons born to him, for he had many wives. ³¹He also had a concubine in Shechem, who gave birth to a son, whom he named Abimelech. ³²Gideon died when he was very old, and he was buried in the grave of his father, Joash, at Ophrah in the land of the clan of Abiezer.

³³As soon as Gideon died, the Israelites prostituted themselves by worshiping the images of Baal, making Baal-berith their god. ³⁴They forgot the LORD their God, who had rescued them from all their enemies surrounding them. ³⁵Nor did they show any loyalty to the family of Jerub-baal (that is, Gideon), despite all the good he had done for Israel.

8:8 Hebrew *Penuel,* a variant spelling of Peniel; also in 8:9, 17. 8:26 Hebrew *1,700* [*shekels*] [19.4 kilograms]. 8:29 Hebrew *Jerub-baal;* see 6:32.

ABIMELECH RULES OVER SHECHEM

9 One day Gideon's* son Abimelech went to Shechem to visit his uncles—his mother's brothers. He said to them and to the rest of his mother's family, ²"Ask the leading citizens of Shechem whether they want to be ruled by all seventy of Gideon's sons or by one man. And remember that I am your own flesh and blood!"

³So Abimelech's uncles gave his message to all the citizens of Shechem on his behalf. And after listening to this proposal, the people of Shechem decided in favor of Abimelech because he was their relative. ⁴They gave him seventy silver coins from the temple of Baal-berith, which he used to hire some reckless troublemakers who agreed to follow him. ⁵He went to his father's home at Ophrah, and there, on one stone, they killed all seventy of his half brothers, the sons of Gideon.* But the youngest brother, Jotham, escaped and hid.

⁶Then all the leading citizens of Shechem and Beth-millo called a meeting under the oak beside the pillar* at Shechem and made Abimelech their king.

JOTHAM'S PARABLE

⁷When Jotham heard about this, he climbed to the top of Mount Gerizim and shouted,

"Listen to me, citizens of Shechem!
    Listen to me if you want God to listen
        to you!
⁸ Once upon a time the trees decided to
        choose a king.
    First they said to the olive tree,
        'Be our king!'
⁹ But the olive tree refused, saying,
    'Should I quit producing the olive oil
        that blesses both God and people,
    just to wave back and forth over the trees?'
¹⁰ "Then they said to the fig tree,
        'You be our king!'
¹¹ But the fig tree also refused, saying,
    'Should I quit producing my sweet fruit
        just to wave back and forth over the trees?'
¹² "Then they said to the grapevine,
        'You be our king!'
¹³ But the grapevine also refused, saying,
    'Should I quit producing the wine
        that cheers both God and people,
    just to wave back and forth over the trees?'
¹⁴ "Then all the trees finally turned to the
        thornbush and said,
        'Come, you be our king!'
¹⁵ And the thornbush replied to the trees,
    'If you truly want to make me your king,
        come and take shelter in my shade.
    If not, let fire come out from me
        and devour the cedars of Lebanon.'"

¹⁶Jotham continued, "Now make sure you have acted honorably and in good faith by making Abimelech your king, and that you have done right by Gideon and all of his descendants. Have you treated him with the honor he deserves for all he accomplished? ¹⁷For he fought for you and risked his life when he rescued you from the Midianites. ¹⁸But today you have revolted against my father and his descendants, killing his seventy sons on one stone. And you have chosen his slave woman's son, Abimelech, to be your king just because he is your relative.

¹⁹"If you have acted honorably and in good faith toward Gideon and his descendants today, then may you find joy in Abimelech, and may he find joy in you. ²⁰But if you have not acted in good faith, then may fire come out from Abimelech and devour the leading citizens of Shechem and Beth-millo; and may fire come out from the citizens of Shechem and Beth-millo and devour Abimelech!"

²¹Then Jotham escaped and lived in Beer because he was afraid of his brother Abimelech.

SHECHEM REBELS AGAINST ABIMELECH

²²After Abimelech had ruled over Israel for three years, ²³God sent a spirit that stirred up trouble between Abimelech and the leading citizens of Shechem, and they revolted. ²⁴God was punishing Abimelech for murdering Gideon's seventy sons, and the citizens of Shechem for supporting him in this treachery of murdering his brothers. ²⁵The citizens of Shechem set an ambush for Abimelech on the hilltops and robbed everyone who passed that way. But someone warned Abimelech about their plot.

²⁶One day Gaal son of Ebed moved to Shechem with his brothers and gained the confidence of the leading citizens of Shechem. ²⁷During the annual harvest festival at Shechem, held in the temple of the local god, the wine flowed freely, and everyone began cursing Abimelech. ²⁸"Who is Abimelech?" Gaal shouted. "He's not a true son of Shechem,* so why should we be his servants? He's merely the son of Gideon, and this Zebul is merely his deputy. Serve the true sons of Hamor, the founder of Shechem. Why should we serve Abimelech? ²⁹If I were in charge here, I would get rid of Abimelech. I would say* to him, 'Get some soldiers, and come out and fight!'"

³⁰But when Zebul, the leader of the city, heard what Gaal was saying, he was furious. ³¹He sent messengers to Abimelech in Arumah,* telling him, "Gaal son of Ebed and his brothers have come to live in Shechem, and now they are inciting the city to rebel against you. ³²Come by night with an army and hide out in the fields. ³³In the

9:1 Hebrew *Jerub-baal's* (see 6:32); also in 9:2, 24.   9:5 Hebrew *Jerub-baal* (see 6:32); also in 9:16, 19, 28, 57.   9:6 The meaning of the Hebrew is uncertain.   9:28 Hebrew *Who is Shechem?* 9:29 As in Greek version; Hebrew reads *And he said.*   9:31 Or *in secret;* Hebrew reads *in Tormah;* compare 9:41.

morning, as soon as it is daylight, attack the city. When Gaal and those who are with him come out against you, you can do with them as you wish."

³⁴So Abimelech and all his men went by night and split into four groups, stationing themselves around Shechem. ³⁵Gaal was standing at the city gates when Abimelech and his army came out of hiding. ³⁶When Gaal saw them, he said to Zebul, "Look, there are people coming down from the hilltops!"

Zebul replied, "It's just the shadows on the hills that look like men."

³⁷But again Gaal said, "No, people are coming down from the hills.* And another group is coming down the road past the Diviners' Oak.*"

³⁸Then Zebul turned on him and asked, "Now where is that big mouth of yours? Wasn't it you that said, 'Who is Abimelech, and why should we be his servants?' The men you mocked are right outside the city! Go out and fight them!"

³⁹So Gaal led the leading citizens of Shechem into battle against Abimelech. ⁴⁰But Abimelech chased him, and many of Shechem's men were wounded and fell along the road as they retreated to the city gate. ⁴¹Abimelech returned to Arumah, and Zebul drove Gaal and his brothers out of Shechem.

⁴²The next day the people of Shechem went out into the fields to battle. When Abimelech heard about it, ⁴³he divided his men into three groups and set an ambush in the fields. When Abimelech saw the people coming out of the city, he and his men jumped up from their hiding places and attacked them. ⁴⁴Abimelech and his group stormed the city gate to keep the men of Shechem from getting back in, while Abimelech's other two groups cut them down in the fields. ⁴⁵The battle went on all day before Abimelech finally captured the city. He killed the people, leveled the city, and scattered salt all over the ground.

⁴⁶When the leading citizens who lived in the tower of Shechem heard what had happened, they ran and hid in the temple of Baal-berith.* ⁴⁷Someone reported to Abimelech that the citizens had gathered in the temple, ⁴⁸so he led his forces to Mount Zalmon. He took an ax and chopped some branches from a tree, then put them on his shoulder. "Quick, do as I have done!" he told his men. ⁴⁹So each of them cut down some branches, following Abimelech's example. They piled the branches against the walls of the temple and set them on fire. So all the people who had lived in the tower of Shechem died—about 1,000 men and women.

⁵⁰Then Abimelech attacked the town of Thebez and captured it. ⁵¹But there was a strong tower inside the town, and all the men and women—the entire population—fled to it. They barricaded themselves in and climbed up to the roof of the tower. ⁵²Abimelech followed them to attack the tower. But as he prepared to set fire to the entrance, ⁵³a woman on the roof dropped a millstone that landed on Abimelech's head and crushed his skull.

⁵⁴He quickly said to his young armor bearer, "Draw your sword and kill me! Don't let it be said that a woman killed Abimelech!" So the young man ran him through with his sword, and he died. ⁵⁵When Abimelech's men saw that he was dead, they disbanded and returned to their homes.

⁵⁶In this way, God punished Abimelech for the evil he had done against his father by murdering his seventy brothers. ⁵⁷God also punished the men of Shechem for all their evil. So the curse of Jotham son of Gideon was fulfilled.

TOLA BECOMES ISRAEL'S JUDGE

10 After Abimelech died, Tola son of Puah, son of Dodo, was the next person to rescue Israel. He was from the tribe of Issachar but lived in the town of Shamir in the hill country of Ephraim. ²He judged Israel for twenty-three years. When he died, he was buried in Shamir.

JAIR BECOMES ISRAEL'S JUDGE

³After Tola died, Jair from Gilead judged Israel for twenty-two years. ⁴His thirty sons rode around on thirty donkeys, and they owned thirty towns in the land of Gilead, which are still called the Towns of Jair.* ⁵When Jair died, he was buried in Kamon.

THE AMMONITES OPPRESS ISRAEL

⁶Again the Israelites did evil in the LORD's sight. They served the images of Baal and Ashtoreth, and the gods of Aram, Sidon, Moab, Ammon, and Philistia. They abandoned the LORD and no longer served him at all. ⁷So the LORD burned with anger against Israel, and he turned them over to the Philistines and the Ammonites, ⁸who began to oppress them that year. For eighteen years they oppressed all the Israelites east of the Jordan River in the land of the Amorites (that is, in Gilead). ⁹The Ammonites also crossed to the west side of the Jordan and attacked Judah, Benjamin, and Ephraim.

The Israelites were in great distress. ¹⁰Finally, they cried out to the LORD for help, saying, "We have sinned against you because we have abandoned you as our God and have served the images of Baal."

¹¹The LORD replied, "Did I not rescue you from the Egyptians, the Amorites, the Ammonites, the Philistines, ¹²the Sidonians, the Amalekites, and the Maonites? When they oppressed you, you cried out to me for help, and I rescued you. ¹³Yet you have abandoned me and served other gods. So I will not rescue you anymore. ¹⁴Go and cry out to the gods you have chosen! Let them rescue you in your hour of distress!"

9:37a Or *the center of the land.* 9:37b Hebrew *Elon-meonenim.* 9:46 Hebrew *El-berith,* another name for Baal-berith; compare 9:4. 10:4 Hebrew *Havvoth-jair.*

¹⁵But the Israelites pleaded with the LORD and said, "We have sinned. Punish us as you see fit, only rescue us today from our enemies." ¹⁶Then the Israelites put aside their foreign gods and served the LORD. And he was grieved by their misery.

¹⁷At that time the armies of Ammon had gathered for war and were camped in Gilead, and the people of Israel assembled and camped at Mizpah. ¹⁸The leaders of Gilead said to each other, "Whoever attacks the Ammonites first will become ruler over all the people of Gilead."

JEPHTHAH BECOMES ISRAEL'S JUDGE

11 Now Jephthah of Gilead was a great warrior. He was the son of Gilead, but his mother was a prostitute. ²Gilead's wife also had several sons, and when these half brothers grew up, they chased Jephthah off the land. "You will not get any of our father's inheritance," they said, "for you are the son of a prostitute." ³So Jephthah fled from his brothers and lived in the land of Tob. Soon he had a band of worthless rebels following him.

⁴At about this time, the Ammonites began their war against Israel. ⁵When the Ammonites attacked, the elders of Gilead sent for Jephthah in the land of Tob. ⁶The elders said, "Come and be our commander! Help us fight the Ammonites!"

⁷But Jephthah said to them, "Aren't you the ones who hated me and drove me from my father's house? Why do you come to me now when you're in trouble?"

⁸"Because we need you," the elders replied. "If you lead us in battle against the Ammonites, we will make you ruler over all the people of Gilead."

⁹Jephthah said to the elders, "Let me get this straight. If I come with you and if the LORD gives me victory over the Ammonites, will you really make me ruler over all the people?"

¹⁰"The LORD is our witness," the elders replied. "We promise to do whatever you say."

¹¹So Jephthah went with the elders of Gilead, and the people made him their ruler and commander of the army. At Mizpah, in the presence of the LORD, Jephthah repeated what he had said to the elders.

¹²Then Jephthah sent messengers to the king of Ammon, asking, "Why have you come out to fight against my land?"

¹³The king of Ammon answered Jephthah's messengers, "When the Israelites came out of Egypt, they stole my land from the Arnon River to the Jabbok River and all the way to the Jordan. Now then, give back the land peaceably."

¹⁴Jephthah sent this message back to the Ammonite king:

¹⁵"This is what Jephthah says: Israel did not steal any land from Moab or Ammon. ¹⁶When the people of Israel arrived at Kadesh on their journey from Egypt after crossing the Red Sea,* ¹⁷they sent messengers to the king of Edom asking for permission to pass through his land. But their request was denied. Then they asked the king of Moab for similar permission, but he wouldn't let them pass through either. So the people of Israel stayed in Kadesh.

¹⁸"Finally, they went around Edom and Moab through the wilderness. They traveled along Moab's eastern border and camped on the other side of the Arnon River. But they never once crossed the Arnon River into Moab, for the Arnon was the border of Moab.

¹⁹"Then Israel sent messengers to King Sihon of the Amorites, who ruled from Heshbon, asking for permission to cross through his land to get to their destination. ²⁰But King Sihon didn't trust Israel to pass through his land. Instead, he mobilized his army at Jahaz and attacked them. ²¹But the LORD, the God of Israel, gave his people victory over King Sihon. So Israel took control of all the land of the Amorites, who lived in that region, ²²from the Arnon River to the Jabbok River, and from the eastern wilderness to the Jordan.

²³"So you see, it was the LORD, the God of Israel, who took away the land from the Amorites and gave it to Israel. Why, then, should we give it back to you? ²⁴You keep whatever your god Chemosh gives you, and we will keep whatever the LORD our God gives us. ²⁵Are you any better than Balak son of Zippor, king of Moab? Did he try to make a case against Israel for disputed land? Did he go to war against them?

²⁶"Israel has been living here for 300 years, inhabiting Heshbon and its surrounding settlements, all the way to Aroer and its settlements, and in all the towns along the Arnon River. Why have you made no effort to recover it before now? ²⁷Therefore, I have not sinned against you. Rather, you have wronged me by attacking me. Let the LORD, who is judge, decide today which of us is right—Israel or Ammon."

²⁸But the king of Ammon paid no attention to Jephthah's message.

JEPHTHAH'S VOW

²⁹At that time the Spirit of the LORD came upon Jephthah, and he went throughout the land of Gilead and Manasseh, including Mizpah in Gilead, and from there he led an army against the Ammonites. ³⁰And Jephthah made a vow to the LORD. He said, "If you give me victory over the Ammonites, ³¹I will give to the LORD whatever comes out of my house to meet me when I return in triumph. I will sacrifice it as a burnt offering."

11:16 Hebrew *sea of reeds.*

³²So Jephthah led his army against the Ammonites, and the LORD gave him victory. ³³He crushed the Ammonites, devastating about twenty towns from Aroer to an area near Minnith and as far away as Abel-keramim. In this way Israel defeated the Ammonites.

³⁴When Jephthah returned home to Mizpah, his daughter came out to meet him, playing on a tambourine and dancing for joy. She was his one and only child; he had no other sons or daughters. ³⁵When he saw her, he tore his clothes in anguish. "Oh, my daughter!" he cried out. "You have completely destroyed me! You've brought disaster on me! For I have made a vow to the LORD, and I cannot take it back."

³⁶And she said, "Father, if you have made a vow to the LORD, you must do to me what you have vowed, for the LORD has given you a great victory over your enemies, the Ammonites. ³⁷But first let me do this one thing: Let me go up and roam in the hills and weep with my friends for two months, because I will die a virgin."

³⁸"You may go," Jephthah said. And he sent her away for two months. She and her friends went into the hills and wept because she would never have children. ³⁹When she returned home, her father kept the vow he had made, and she died a virgin.

So it has become a custom in Israel ⁴⁰for young Israelite women to go away for four days each year to lament the fate of Jephthah's daughter.

EPHRAIM FIGHTS WITH JEPHTHAH

12 Then the people of Ephraim mobilized an army and crossed over the Jordan River to Zaphon. They sent this message to Jephthah: "Why didn't you call for us to help you fight against the Ammonites? We are going to burn down your house with you in it!"

²Jephthah replied, "I summoned you at the beginning of the dispute, but you refused to come! You failed to help us in our struggle against Ammon. ³So when I realized you weren't coming, I risked my life and went to battle without you, and the LORD gave me victory over the Ammonites. So why have you now come to fight me?"

⁴The people of Ephraim responded, "You men of Gilead are nothing more than fugitives from Ephraim and Manasseh." So Jephthah gathered all the men of Gilead and attacked the men of Ephraim and defeated them.

⁵Jephthah captured the shallow crossings of the Jordan River, and whenever a fugitive from Ephraim tried to go back across, the men of Gilead would challenge him. "Are you a member of the tribe of Ephraim?" they would ask. If the man said, "No, I'm not," ⁶they would tell him to say "Shibboleth." If he was from Ephraim, he would say "Sibboleth," because people from Ephraim cannot pronounce the word correctly. Then they would take him and kill him at the shallow crossings of the Jordan. In all, 42,000 Ephraimites were killed at that time.

⁷Jephthah judged Israel for six years. When he died, he was buried in one of the towns of Gilead.

IBZAN BECOMES ISRAEL'S JUDGE

⁸After Jephthah died, Ibzan from Bethlehem judged Israel. ⁹He had thirty sons and thirty daughters. He sent his daughters to marry men outside his clan, and he brought in thirty young women from outside his clan to marry his sons. Ibzan judged Israel for seven years. ¹⁰When he died, he was buried at Bethlehem.

ELON BECOMES ISRAEL'S JUDGE

¹¹After Ibzan died, Elon from the tribe of Zebulun judged Israel for ten years. ¹²When he died, he was buried at Aijalon in Zebulun.

ABDON BECOMES ISRAEL'S JUDGE

¹³After Elon died, Abdon son of Hillel, from Pirathon, judged Israel. ¹⁴He had forty sons and thirty grandsons, who rode on seventy donkeys. He judged Israel for eight years. ¹⁵When he died, he was buried at Pirathon in Ephraim, in the hill country of the Amalekites.

THE BIRTH OF SAMSON

13 Again the Israelites did evil in the LORD's sight, so the LORD handed them over to the Philistines, who oppressed them for forty years.

²In those days a man named Manoah from the tribe of Dan lived in the town of Zorah. His wife was unable to become pregnant, and they had no children. ³The angel of the LORD appeared to Manoah's wife and said, "Even though you have been unable to have children, you will soon become pregnant and give birth to a son. ⁴So be careful; you must not drink wine or any other alcoholic drink nor eat any forbidden food.* ⁵You will become pregnant and give birth to a son, and his hair must never be cut. For he will be dedicated to God as a Nazirite from birth. He will begin to rescue Israel from the Philistines."

⁶The woman ran and told her husband, "A man of God appeared to me! He looked like one of God's angels, terrifying to see. I didn't ask where he was from, and he didn't tell me his name. ⁷But he told me, 'You will become pregnant and give birth to a son. You must not drink wine or any other alcoholic drink nor eat any forbidden food. For your son will be dedicated to God as a Nazirite from the moment of his birth until the day of his death.'"

⁸Then Manoah prayed to the LORD, saying, "Lord, please let the man of God come back to us again and give us more instructions about this son who is to be born."

⁹God answered Manoah's prayer, and the angel of God appeared once again to his wife as she was

13:4 Hebrew *any unclean thing;* also in 13:7, 14.

sitting in the field. But her husband, Manoah, was not with her. ¹⁰So she quickly ran and told her husband, "The man who appeared to me the other day is here again!"

¹¹Manoah ran back with his wife and asked, "Are you the man who spoke to my wife the other day?"

"Yes," he replied, "I am."

¹²So Manoah asked him, "When your words come true, what kind of rules should govern the boy's life and work?"

¹³The angel of the LORD replied, "Be sure your wife follows the instructions I gave her. ¹⁴She must not eat grapes or raisins, drink wine or any other alcoholic drink, or eat any forbidden food."

¹⁵Then Manoah said to the angel of the LORD, "Please stay here until we can prepare a young goat for you to eat."

¹⁶"I will stay," the angel of the LORD replied, "but I will not eat anything. However, you may prepare a burnt offering as a sacrifice to the LORD." (Manoah didn't realize it was the angel of the LORD.)

¹⁷Then Manoah asked the angel of the LORD, "What is your name? For when all this comes true, we want to honor you."

¹⁸"Why do you ask my name?" the angel of the LORD replied. "It is too wonderful for you to understand."

¹⁹Then Manoah took a young goat and a grain offering and offered it on a rock as a sacrifice to the LORD. And as Manoah and his wife watched, the LORD did an amazing thing. ²⁰As the flames from the altar shot up toward the sky, the angel of the LORD ascended in the fire. When Manoah and his wife saw this, they fell with their faces to the ground.

²¹The angel did not appear again to Manoah and his wife. Manoah finally realized it was the angel of the LORD, ²²and he said to his wife, "We will certainly die, for we have seen God!"

²³But his wife said, "If the LORD were going to kill us, he wouldn't have accepted our burnt offering and grain offering. He wouldn't have appeared to us and told us this wonderful thing and done these miracles."

²⁴When her son was born, she named him Samson. And the LORD blessed him as he grew up. ²⁵And the Spirit of the LORD began to stir him while he lived in Mahaneh-dan, which is located between the towns of Zorah and Eshtaol.

SAMSON'S RIDDLE

14 One day when Samson was in Timnah, one of the Philistine women caught his eye. ²When he returned home, he told his father and mother, "A young Philistine woman in Timnah caught my eye. I want to marry her. Get her for me."

³His father and mother objected. "Isn't there even one woman in our tribe or among all the Israelites you could marry?" they asked. "Why must you go to the pagan Philistines to find a wife?"

But Samson told his father, "Get her for me! She looks good to me." ⁴His father and mother didn't realize the LORD was at work in this, creating an opportunity to work against the Philistines, who ruled over Israel at that time.

⁵As Samson and his parents were going down to Timnah, a young lion suddenly attacked Samson near the vineyards of Timnah. ⁶At that moment the Spirit of the LORD came powerfully upon him, and he ripped the lion's jaws apart with his bare hands. He did it as easily as if it were a young goat. But he didn't tell his father or mother about it. ⁷When Samson arrived in Timnah, he talked with the woman and was very pleased with her.

⁸Later, when he returned to Timnah for the wedding, he turned off the path to look at the carcass of the lion. And he found that a swarm of bees had made some honey in the carcass. ⁹He scooped some of the honey into his hands and ate it along the way. He also gave some to his father and mother, and they ate it. But he didn't tell them he had taken the honey from the carcass of the lion.

¹⁰As his father was making final arrangements for the marriage, Samson threw a party at Timnah, as was the custom for elite young men. ¹¹When the bride's parents* saw him, they selected thirty young men from the town to be his companions.

¹²Samson said to them, "Let me tell you a riddle. If you solve my riddle during these seven days of the celebration, I will give you thirty fine linen robes and thirty sets of festive clothing. ¹³But if you can't solve it, then you must give me thirty fine linen robes and thirty sets of festive clothing."

"All right," they agreed, "let's hear your riddle."

¹⁴So he said:

"Out of the one who eats came something
      to eat;
   out of the strong came something sweet."

Three days later they were still trying to figure it out. ¹⁵On the fourth* day they said to Samson's wife, "Entice your husband to explain the riddle for us, or we will burn down your father's house with you in it. Did you invite us to this party just to make us poor?"

¹⁶So Samson's wife came to him in tears and said, "You don't love me; you hate me! You have given my people a riddle, but you haven't told me the answer."

"I haven't even given the answer to my father or mother," he replied. "Why should I tell you?"

14:11 Hebrew *they.* 14:15 As in Greek version; Hebrew reads *seventh.*

17 So she cried whenever she was with him and kept it up for the rest of the celebration. At last, on the seventh day he told her the answer because she was tormenting him with her nagging. Then she explained the riddle to the young men.

18 So before sunset of the seventh day, the men of the town came to Samson with their answer:

"What is sweeter than honey?
What is stronger than a lion?"

Samson replied, "If you hadn't plowed with my heifer, you wouldn't have solved my riddle!"

19 Then the Spirit of the LORD came powerfully upon him. He went down to the town of Ashkelon, killed thirty men, took their belongings, and gave their clothing to the men who had solved his riddle. But Samson was furious about what had happened, and he went back home to live with his father and mother. 20 So his wife was given in marriage to the man who had been Samson's best man at the wedding.

SAMSON'S VENGEANCE ON THE PHILISTINES

15 Later on, during the wheat harvest, Samson took a young goat as a present to his wife. He said, "I'm going into my wife's room to sleep with her," but her father wouldn't let him in.

2 "I truly thought you must hate her," her father explained, "so I gave her in marriage to your best man. But look, her younger sister is even more beautiful than she is. Marry her instead."

3 Samson said, "This time I cannot be blamed for everything I am going to do to you Philistines." 4 Then he went out and caught 300 foxes. He tied their tails together in pairs, and he fastened a torch to each pair of tails. 5 Then he lit the torches and let the foxes run through the grain fields of the Philistines. He burned all their grain to the ground, including the sheaves and the uncut grain. He also destroyed their vineyards and olive groves.

6 "Who did this?" the Philistines demanded.

"Samson," was the reply, "because his father-in-law from Timnah gave Samson's wife to be married to his best man." So the Philistines went and got the woman and her father and burned them to death.

7 "Because you did this," Samson vowed, "I won't rest until I take my revenge on you!" 8 So he attacked the Philistines with great fury and killed many of them. Then he went to live in a cave in the rock of Etam.

9 The Philistines retaliated by setting up camp in Judah and spreading out near the town of Lehi. 10 The men of Judah asked the Philistines, "Why are you attacking us?"

The Philistines replied, "We've come to capture Samson. We've come to pay him back for what he did to us."

11 So 3,000 men of Judah went down to get Samson at the cave in the rock of Etam. They said to Samson, "Don't you realize the Philistines rule over us? What are you doing to us?"

But Samson replied, "I only did to them what they did to me."

12 But the men of Judah told him, "We have come to tie you up and hand you over to the Philistines."

"All right," Samson said. "But promise that you won't kill me yourselves."

13 "We will only tie you up and hand you over to the Philistines," they replied. "We won't kill you." So they tied him up with two new ropes and brought him up from the rock.

14 As Samson arrived at Lehi, the Philistines came shouting in triumph. But the Spirit of the LORD came powerfully upon Samson, and he snapped the ropes on his arms as if they were burnt strands of flax, and they fell from his wrists. 15 Then he found the jawbone of a recently killed donkey. He picked it up and killed 1,000 Philistines with it. 16 Then Samson said,

"With the jawbone of a donkey,
I've piled them in heaps!
With the jawbone of a donkey,
I've killed a thousand men!"

17 When he finished his boasting, he threw away the jawbone; and the place was named Jawbone Hill.*

18 Samson was now very thirsty, and he cried out to the LORD, "You have accomplished this great victory by the strength of your servant. Must I now die of thirst and fall into the hands of these pagans?" 19 So God caused water to gush out of a hollow in the ground at Lehi, and Samson was revived as he drank. Then he named that place "The Spring of the One Who Cried Out,"* and it is still in Lehi to this day.

20 Samson judged Israel for twenty years during the period when the Philistines dominated the land.

SAMSON CARRIES AWAY GAZA'S GATES

16 One day Samson went to the Philistine town of Gaza and spent the night with a prostitute. 2 Word soon spread* that Samson was there, so the men of Gaza gathered together and waited all night at the town gates. They kept quiet during the night, saying to themselves, "When the light of morning comes, we will kill him."

3 But Samson stayed in bed only until midnight. Then he got up, took hold of the doors of the town gate, including the two posts, and lifted them up, bar and all. He put them on his shoulders and carried them all the way to the top of the hill across from Hebron.

15:17 Hebrew *Ramath-lehi.*   15:19 Hebrew *En-hakkore.*   16:2 As in Greek and Syriac versions and Latin Vulgate; Hebrew lacks *Word soon spread.*

SAMSON AND DELILAH

⁴ Some time later Samson fell in love with a woman named Delilah, who lived in the valley of Sorek. ⁵ The rulers of the Philistines went to her and said, "Entice Samson to tell you what makes him so strong and how he can be overpowered and tied up securely. Then each of us will give you 1,100 pieces* of silver."

⁶ So Delilah said to Samson, "Please tell me what makes you so strong and what it would take to tie you up securely."

⁷ Samson replied, "If I were tied up with seven new bowstrings that have not yet been dried, I would become as weak as anyone else."

⁸ So the Philistine rulers brought Delilah seven new bowstrings, and she tied Samson up with them. ⁹ She had hidden some men in one of the inner rooms of her house, and she cried out, "Samson! The Philistines have come to capture you!" But Samson snapped the bowstrings as a piece of string snaps when it is burned by a fire. So the secret of his strength was not discovered.

¹⁰ Afterward Delilah said to him, "You've been making fun of me and telling me lies! Now please tell me how you can be tied up securely."

¹¹ Samson replied, "If I were tied up with brand-new ropes that had never been used, I would become as weak as anyone else."

¹² So Delilah took new ropes and tied him up with them. The men were hiding in the inner room as before, and again Delilah cried out, "Samson! The Philistines have come to capture you!" But again Samson snapped the ropes from his arms as if they were thread.

¹³ Then Delilah said, "You've been making fun of me and telling me lies! Now tell me how you can be tied up securely."

Samson replied, "If you were to weave the seven braids of my hair into the fabric on your loom and tighten it with the loom shuttle, I would become as weak as anyone else."

So while he slept, Delilah wove the seven braids of his hair into the fabric. ¹⁴ Then she tightened it with the loom shuttle.* Again she cried out, "Samson! The Philistines have come to capture you!" But Samson woke up, pulled back the loom shuttle, and yanked his hair away from the loom and the fabric.

¹⁵ Then Delilah pouted, "How can you tell me, 'I love you,' when you don't share your secrets with me? You've made fun of me three times now, and you still haven't told me what makes you so strong!" ¹⁶ She tormented him with her nagging day after day until he was sick to death of it.

¹⁷ Finally, Samson shared his secret with her. "My hair has never been cut," he confessed, "for I was dedicated to God as a Nazirite from birth. If my head were shaved, my strength would leave me, and I would become as weak as anyone else."

¹⁸ Delilah realized he had finally told her the truth, so she sent for the Philistine rulers.

"Come back one more time," she said, "for he has finally told me his secret." So the Philistine rulers returned with the money in their hands. ¹⁹ Delilah lulled Samson to sleep with his head in her lap, and then she called in a man to shave off the seven locks of his hair. In this way she began to bring him down,* and his strength left him.

²⁰ Then she cried out, "Samson! The Philistines have come to capture you!"

When he woke up, he thought, "I will do as before and shake myself free." But he didn't realize the LORD had left him.

²¹ So the Philistines captured him and gouged out his eyes. They took him to Gaza, where he was bound with bronze chains and forced to grind grain in the prison.

²² But before long, his hair began to grow back.

SAMSON'S FINAL VICTORY

²³ The Philistine rulers held a great festival, offering sacrifices and praising their god, Dagon. They said, "Our god has given us victory over our enemy Samson!"

²⁴ When the people saw him, they praised their god, saying, "Our god has delivered our enemy to us! The one who killed so many of us is now in our power!"

²⁵ Half drunk by now, the people demanded, "Bring out Samson so he can amuse us!" So he was brought from the prison to amuse them, and they had him stand between the pillars supporting the roof.

²⁶ Samson said to the young servant who was leading him by the hand, "Place my hands against the pillars that hold up the temple. I want to rest against them." ²⁷ Now the temple was completely filled with people. All the Philistine rulers were there, and there were about 3,000 men and women on the roof who were watching as Samson amused them.

²⁸ Then Samson prayed to the LORD, "Sovereign LORD, remember me again. O God, please strengthen me just one more time. With one blow let me pay back the Philistines for the loss of my two eyes." ²⁹ Then Samson put his hands on the two center pillars that held up the temple. Pushing against them with both hands, ³⁰ he prayed, "Let me die with the Philistines." And the temple crashed down on the Philistine rulers and all the people. So he killed more people when he died than he had during his entire lifetime.

³¹ Later his brothers and other relatives went down to get his body. They took him back home and buried him between Zorah and Eshtaol, where his father, Manoah, was buried. Samson had judged Israel for twenty years.

16:5 Hebrew *1,100 [shekels]*, about 28 pounds or 12.5 kilograms in weight. 16:13-14 As in Greek version and Latin Vulgate; Hebrew lacks *I would become as weak as anyone else. / So while he slept, Delilah wove the seven braids of his hair into the fabric.* 14Then she *tightened it with the loom shuttle.* 16:19 Or *she began to torment him.* Greek version reads *He began to grow weak.*

MICAH'S IDOLS

17 There was a man named Micah, who lived in the hill country of Ephraim. ²One day he said to his mother, "I heard you place a curse on the person who stole 1,100 pieces* of silver from you. Well, I have the money. I was the one who took it."

"The LORD bless you for admitting it," his mother replied. ³He returned the money to her, and she said, "I now dedicate these silver coins to the LORD. In honor of my son, I will have an image carved and an idol cast."

⁴So when he returned the money to his mother, she took 200 silver coins and gave them to a silversmith, who made them into an image and an idol. And these were placed in Micah's house. ⁵Micah set up a shrine for the idol, and he made a sacred ephod and some household idols. Then he installed one of his sons as his personal priest.

⁶In those days Israel had no king; all the people did whatever seemed right in their own eyes.

⁷One day a young Levite, who had been living in Bethlehem in Judah, arrived in that area. ⁸He had left Bethlehem in search of another place to live, and as he traveled, he came to the hill country of Ephraim. He happened to stop at Micah's house as he was traveling through. ⁹"Where are you from?" Micah asked him.

He replied, "I am a Levite from Bethlehem in Judah, and I am looking for a place to live."

¹⁰"Stay here with me," Micah said, "and you can be a father and priest to me. I will give you ten pieces of silver* a year, plus a change of clothes and your food." ¹¹The Levite agreed to this, and the young man became like one of Micah's sons.

¹²So Micah installed the Levite as his personal priest, and he lived in Micah's house. ¹³"I know the LORD will bless me now," Micah said, "because I have a Levite serving as my priest."

IDOLATRY IN THE TRIBE OF DAN

18 Now in those days Israel had no king. And the tribe of Dan was trying to find a place where they could settle, for they had not yet moved into the land assigned to them when the land was divided among the tribes of Israel. ²So the men of Dan chose from their clans five capable warriors from the towns of Zorah and Eshtaol to scout out a land for them to settle in.

When these warriors arrived in the hill country of Ephraim, they came to Micah's house and spent the night there. ³While at Micah's house, they recognized the young Levite's accent, so they went over and asked him, "Who brought you here, and what are you doing in this place? Why are you here?" ⁴He told them about his agreement with Micah and that he had been hired as Micah's personal priest.

⁵Then they said, "Ask God whether or not our journey will be successful."

⁶"Go in peace," the priest replied. "For the LORD is watching over your journey."

⁷So the five men went on to the town of Laish, where they noticed the people living carefree lives, like the Sidonians; they were peaceful and secure.* The people were also wealthy because their land was very fertile. And they lived a great distance from Sidon and had no allies nearby.

⁸When the men returned to Zorah and Eshtaol, their relatives asked them, "What did you find?"

⁹The men replied, "Come on, let's attack them! We have seen the land, and it is very good. What are you waiting for? Don't hesitate to go and take possession of it. ¹⁰When you get there, you will find the people living carefree lives. God has given us a spacious and fertile land, lacking in nothing!"

¹¹So 600 men from the tribe of Dan, armed with weapons of war, set out from Zorah and Eshtaol. ¹²They camped at a place west of Kiriath-jearim in Judah, which is called Mahaneh-dan* to this day. ¹³Then they went on from there into the hill country of Ephraim and came to the house of Micah.

¹⁴The five men who had scouted out the land around Laish explained to the others, "These buildings contain a sacred ephod, as well as some household idols, a carved image, and a cast idol. What do you think you should do?" ¹⁵Then the five men turned off the road and went over to Micah's house, where the young Levite lived, and greeted him kindly. ¹⁶As the 600 armed warriors from the tribe of Dan stood at the entrance of the gate, ¹⁷the five scouts entered the shrine and removed the carved image, the sacred ephod, the household idols, and the cast idol. Meanwhile, the priest was standing at the gate with the 600 armed warriors.

¹⁸When the priest saw the men carrying all the sacred objects out of Micah's shrine, he said, "What are you doing?"

¹⁹"Be quiet and come with us," they said. "Be a father and priest to all of us. Isn't it better to be a priest for an entire tribe and clan of Israel than for the household of just one man?"

²⁰The young priest was quite happy to go with them, so he took along the sacred ephod, the household idols, and the carved image. ²¹They turned and started on their way again, placing their children, livestock, and possessions in front of them.

²²When the people from the tribe of Dan were quite a distance from Micah's house, the people who lived near Micah came chasing after them. ²³They were shouting as they caught up with them. The men of Dan turned around and said to Micah, "What's the matter? Why have you called these men together and chased after us like this?"

17:2 Hebrew *1,100 [shekels]*, about 28 pounds or 12.5 kilograms in weight.   17:10 Hebrew *10 [shekels] of silver*, about 4 ounces or 114 grams in weight.   18:7 The meaning of the Hebrew is uncertain.   18:12 *Mahaneh-dan* means "the camp of Dan."

24 "What do you mean, 'What's the matter?'" Micah replied. "You've taken away all the gods I have made, and my priest, and I have nothing left!"

25 The men of Dan said, "Watch what you say! There are some short-tempered men around here who might get angry and kill you and your family." 26 So the men of Dan continued on their way. When Micah saw that there were too many of them for him to attack, he turned around and went home.

27 Then, with Micah's idols and his priest, the men of Dan came to the town of Laish, whose people were peaceful and secure. They attacked with swords and burned the town to the ground. 28 There was no one to rescue the people, for they lived a great distance from Sidon and had no allies nearby. This happened in the valley near Beth-rehob.

Then the people of the tribe of Dan rebuilt the town and lived there. 29 They renamed the town Dan after their ancestor, Israel's son, but it had originally been called Laish.

30 Then they set up the carved image, and they appointed Jonathan son of Gershom, son of Moses,* as their priest. This family continued as priests for the tribe of Dan until the Exile. 31 So Micah's carved image was worshiped by the tribe of Dan as long as the Tabernacle of God remained at Shiloh.

THE LEVITE AND HIS CONCUBINE

19 Now in those days Israel had no king. There was a man from the tribe of Levi living in a remote area of the hill country of Ephraim. One day he brought home a woman from Bethlehem in Judah to be his concubine. 2 But she became angry with him* and returned to her father's home in Bethlehem.

After about four months, 3 her husband set out for Bethlehem to speak personally to her and persuade her to come back. He took with him a servant and a pair of donkeys. When he arrived at* her father's house, her father saw him and welcomed him. 4 Her father urged him to stay awhile, so he stayed three days, eating, drinking, and sleeping there.

5 On the fourth day the man was up early, ready to leave, but the woman's father said to his son-in-law, "Have something to eat before you go." 6 So the two men sat down together and had something to eat and drink. Then the woman's father said, "Please stay another night and enjoy yourself." 7 The man got up to leave, but his father-in-law kept urging him to stay, so he finally gave in and stayed the night.

8 On the morning of the fifth day he was up early again, ready to leave, and again the woman's father said, "Have something to eat; then you can leave later this afternoon." So they had another day of feasting. 9 Later, as the man and his concubine and servant were preparing to

leave, his father-in-law said, "Look, it's almost evening. Stay the night and enjoy yourself. Tomorrow you can get up early and be on your way."

10 But this time the man was determined to leave. So he took his two saddled donkeys and his concubine and headed in the direction of Jebus (that is, Jerusalem). 11 It was late in the day when they neared Jebus, and the man's servant said to him, "Let's stop at this Jebusite town and spend the night there."

12 "No," his master said, "we can't stay in this foreign town where there are no Israelites. Instead, we will go on to Gibeah. 13 Come on, let's try to get as far as Gibeah or Ramah, and we'll spend the night in one of those towns." 14 So they went on. The sun was setting as they came to Gibeah, a town in the land of Benjamin, 15 so they stopped there to spend the night. They rested in the town square, but no one took them in for the night.

16 That evening an old man came home from his work in the fields. He was from the hill country of Ephraim, but he was living in Gibeah, where the people were from the tribe of Benjamin. 17 When he saw the travelers sitting in the town square, he asked them where they were from and where they were going.

18 "We have been in Bethlehem in Judah," the man replied. "We are on our way to a remote area in the hill country of Ephraim, which is my home. I traveled to Bethlehem, and now I'm returning home.* But no one has taken us in for the night, 19 even though we have everything we need. We have straw and feed for our donkeys and plenty of bread and wine for ourselves."

20 "You are welcome to stay with me," the old man said. "I will give you anything you might need. But whatever you do, don't spend the night in the square." 21 So he took them home with him and fed the donkeys. After they washed their feet, they ate and drank together.

22 While they were enjoying themselves, a crowd of troublemakers from the town surrounded the house. They began beating at the door and shouting to the old man, "Bring out the man who is staying with you so we can have sex with him."

23 The old man stepped outside to talk to them. "No, my brothers, don't do such an evil thing. For this man is a guest in my house, and such a thing would be shameful. 24 Here, take my virgin daughter and this man's concubine. I will bring them out to you, and you can abuse them and do whatever you like. But don't do such a shameful thing to this man."

[25] But they wouldn't listen to him. So the Levite took hold of his concubine and pushed her out the door. The men of the town abused her all night, taking turns raping her until morning. Finally, at dawn they let her go. [26] At daybreak the woman returned to the house where her husband was staying. She collapsed at the door of the house and lay there until it was light.

[27] When her husband opened the door to leave, there lay his concubine with her hands on the threshold. [28] He said, "Get up! Let's go!" But there was no answer.* So he put her body on his donkey and took her home.

[29] When he got home, he took a knife and cut his concubine's body into twelve pieces. Then he sent one piece to each tribe throughout all the territory of Israel.

[30] Everyone who saw it said, "Such a horrible crime has not been committed in all the time since Israel left Egypt. Think about it! What are we going to do? Who's going to speak up?"

ISRAEL'S WAR WITH BENJAMIN

20 Then all the Israelites were united as one man, from Dan in the north to Beersheba in the south, including those from across the Jordan in the land of Gilead. The entire community assembled in the presence of the LORD at Mizpah. [2] The leaders of all the people and all the tribes of Israel—400,000 warriors armed with swords—took their positions in the assembly of the people of God. [3] (Word soon reached the land of Benjamin that the other tribes had gone up to Mizpah.) The Israelites then asked how this terrible crime had happened.

[4] The Levite, the husband of the woman who had been murdered, said, "My concubine and I came to spend the night in Gibeah, a town that belongs to the people of Benjamin. [5] That night some of the leading citizens of Gibeah surrounded the house, planning to kill me, and they raped my concubine until she was dead. [6] So I cut her body into twelve pieces and sent the pieces throughout the territory assigned to Israel, for these men have committed a terrible and shameful crime. [7] Now then, all of you—the entire community of Israel—must decide here and now what should be done about this!"

[8] And all the people rose to their feet in unison and declared, "None of us will return home! No, not even one of us! [9] Instead, this is what we will do to Gibeah; we will draw lots to decide who will attack it. [10] One-tenth of the men* from each tribe will be chosen to supply the warriors with food, and the rest of us will take revenge on Gibeah* of Benjamin for this shameful thing they have done in Israel." [11] So all the Israelites were completely united, and they gathered together to attack the town.

[12] The Israelites sent messengers to the tribe of Benjamin, saying, "What a terrible thing has been done among you! [13] Give up those evil men, those troublemakers from Gibeah, so we can execute them and purge Israel of this evil."

But the people of Benjamin would not listen. [14] Instead, they came from their towns and gathered at Gibeah to fight the Israelites. [15] In all, 26,000 of their warriors armed with swords arrived in Gibeah to join the 700 elite troops who lived there. [16] Among Benjamin's elite troops, 700 were left-handed, and each of them could sling a rock and hit a target within a hairsbreadth without missing. [17] Israel had 400,000 experienced soldiers armed with swords, not counting Benjamin's warriors.

[18] Before the battle the Israelites went to Bethel and asked God, "Which tribe should go first to attack the people of Benjamin?"

The LORD answered, "Judah is to go first."

[19] So the Israelites left early the next morning and camped near Gibeah. [20] Then they advanced toward Gibeah to attack the men of Benjamin. [21] But Benjamin's warriors, who were defending the town, came out and killed 22,000 Israelites on the battlefield that day.

[22] But the Israelites encouraged each other and took their positions again at the same place they had fought the previous day. [23] For they had gone up to Bethel and wept in the presence of the LORD until evening. They had asked the LORD, "Should we fight against our relatives from Benjamin again?"

And the LORD had said, "Go out and fight against them."

[24] So the next day they went out again to fight against the men of Benjamin, [25] but the men of Benjamin killed another 18,000 Israelites, all of whom were experienced with the sword.

[26] Then all the Israelites went up to Bethel and wept in the presence of the LORD and fasted until evening. They also brought burnt offerings and peace offerings to the LORD. [27] The Israelites went up seeking direction from the LORD. (In those days the Ark of the Covenant of God was in Bethel, [28] and Phinehas son of Eleazar and grandson of Aaron was the priest.) The Israelites asked the LORD, "Should we fight against our relatives from Benjamin again, or should we stop?"

The LORD said, "Go! Tomorrow I will hand them over to you."

[29] So the Israelites set an ambush all around Gibeah. [30] They went out on the third day and took their positions at the same place as before. [31] When the men of Benjamin came out to attack, they were drawn away from the town. And as they had done before, they began to kill the Israelites. About thirty Israelites died in the open fields and along the roads, one leading to Bethel and the other leading back to Gibeah.

19:28 Greek version adds *for she was dead.* 20:10a Hebrew *10 men from every hundred, 100 men from every thousand, and 1,000 men from every 10,000.* 20:10b Hebrew *Geba*, in this case a variant spelling of Gibeah; also in 20:33.

³²Then the warriors of Benjamin shouted, "We're defeating them as we did before!" But the Israelites had planned in advance to run away so that the men of Benjamin would chase them along the roads and be drawn away from the town.

³³When the main group of Israelite warriors reached Baal-tamar, they turned and took up their positions. Meanwhile, the Israelites hiding in ambush to the west* of Gibeah jumped up to fight. ³⁴There were 10,000 elite Israelite troops who advanced against Gibeah. The fighting was so heavy that Benjamin didn't realize the impending disaster. ³⁵So the LORD helped Israel defeat Benjamin, and that day the Israelites killed 25,100 of Benjamin's warriors, all of whom were experienced swordsmen. ³⁶Then the men of Benjamin saw that they were beaten.

The Israelites had retreated from Benjamin's warriors in order to give those hiding in ambush more room to maneuver against Gibeah. ³⁷Then those who were hiding rushed in from all sides and killed everyone in the town. ³⁸They had arranged to send up a large cloud of smoke from the town as a signal. ³⁹When the Israelites saw the smoke, they turned and attacked Benjamin's warriors.

By that time Benjamin's warriors had killed about thirty Israelites, and they shouted, "We're defeating them as we did in the first battle!" ⁴⁰But when the warriors of Benjamin looked behind them and saw the smoke rising into the sky from every part of the town, ⁴¹the men of Israel turned and attacked. At this point the men of Benjamin became terrified, because they realized disaster was close at hand. ⁴²So they turned around and fled before the Israelites toward the wilderness. But they couldn't escape the battle, and the people who came out of the nearby towns were also killed.* ⁴³The Israelites surrounded the men of Benjamin and chased them relentlessly, finally overtaking them east of Gibeah.* ⁴⁴That day 18,000 of Benjamin's strongest warriors died in battle. ⁴⁵The survivors fled into the wilderness toward the rock of Rimmon, but Israel killed 5,000 of them along the road. They continued the chase until they had killed another 2,000 near Gidom.

⁴⁶So that day the tribe of Benjamin lost 25,000 strong warriors armed with swords, ⁴⁷leaving only 600 men who escaped to the rock of Rimmon, where they lived for four months. ⁴⁸And the Israelites returned and slaughtered every living thing in all the towns—the people, the livestock, and everything they found. They also burned down all the towns they came to.

ISRAEL PROVIDES WIVES FOR BENJAMIN

21 The Israelites had vowed at Mizpah, "We will never give our daughters in marriage to a man from the tribe of Benjamin." ²Now the people went to Bethel and sat in the presence of God until evening, weeping loudly and bitterly. ³"O LORD, God of Israel," they cried out, "why has this happened in Israel? Now one of our tribes is missing from Israel!"

⁴Early the next morning the people built an altar and presented their burnt offerings and peace offerings on it. ⁵Then they said, "Who among the tribes of Israel did not join us at Mizpah when we held our assembly in the presence of the LORD?" At that time they had taken a solemn oath in the LORD's presence, vowing that anyone who refused to come would be put to death.

⁶The Israelites felt sorry for their brother Benjamin and said, "Today one of the tribes of Israel has been cut off. ⁷How can we find wives for the few who remain, since we have sworn by the LORD not to give them our daughters in marriage?"

⁸So they asked, "Who among the tribes of Israel did not join us at Mizpah when we assembled in the presence of the LORD?" And they discovered that no one from Jabesh-gilead had attended the assembly. ⁹For after they counted all the people, no one from Jabesh-gilead was present.

¹⁰So the assembly sent 12,000 of their best warriors to Jabesh-gilead with orders to kill everyone there, including women and children. ¹¹"This is what you are to do," they said. "Completely destroy* all the males and every woman who is not a virgin." ¹²Among the residents of Jabesh-gilead they found 400 young virgins who had never slept with a man, and they brought them to the camp at Shiloh in the land of Canaan.

¹³The Israelite assembly sent a peace delegation to the remaining people of Benjamin who were living at the rock of Rimmon. ¹⁴Then the men of Benjamin returned to their homes, and the 400 women of Jabesh-gilead who had been spared were given to them as wives. But there were not enough women for all of them.

¹⁵The people felt sorry for Benjamin because the LORD had made this gap among the tribes of Israel. ¹⁶So the elders of the assembly asked, "How can we find wives for the few who remain, since the women of the tribe of Benjamin are dead? ¹⁷There must be heirs for the survivors so that an entire tribe of Israel is not wiped out. ¹⁸But we cannot give them our own daughters in marriage because we have sworn with a solemn oath that anyone who does this will fall under God's curse."

¹⁹Then they thought of the annual festival of the LORD held in Shiloh, south of Lebonah and north of Bethel, along the east side of the road

---

20:33 As in Greek and Syriac versions and Latin Vulgate; Hebrew reads *hiding in the open space.* 20:42 Or *battle, for the people from the nearby towns also came out and killed them.* 20:43 The meaning of the Hebrew is uncertain. 21:11 The Hebrew term used here refers to the complete consecration of things or people to the LORD, either by destroying them or by giving them as an offering.

that goes from Bethel to Shechem. ²⁰They told the men of Benjamin who still needed wives, "Go and hide in the vineyards. ²¹When you see the young women of Shiloh come out for their dances, rush out from the vineyards, and each of you can take one of them home to the land of Benjamin to be your wife! ²²And when their fathers and brothers come to us in protest, we will tell them, 'Please be sympathetic. Let them have your daughters, for we didn't find wives for all of them when we destroyed Jabesh-gilead. And you are not guilty of breaking the vow since you did not actually give your daughters to them in marriage.'"

²³So the men of Benjamin did as they were told. Each man caught one of the women as she danced in the celebration and carried her off to be his wife. They returned to their own land, and they rebuilt their towns and lived in them.

²⁴Then the people of Israel departed by tribes and families, and they returned to their own homes.

²⁵In those days Israel had no king; all the people did whatever seemed right in their own eyes.

RUTH

JON HUNTZINGER, PHD

The book of Ruth tells the story of a Moabite woman named Ruth. She remains faithful to her widowed Israelite mother-in-law, Naomi, long after Naomi's son, who was also Ruth's husband, dies. Naomi would have been left all alone, except Ruth stays by her side. Ruth then cares for her by gathering leftover grain from surrounding fields as allowed by law so they would have food to eat. The owner of the field, a man named Boaz, observes Ruth's devotion and is so moved by what he sees that he eventually marries her.

The story is set during the time of the judges, as described in the book of Judges, which is why it is placed after Judges in the Bible. In the Jewish collection of Old Testament books written in Hebrew and known as the Hebrew Bible, however, the book comes after Proverbs because Ruth is seen as the perfect example of the strong, compassionate, and industrious woman described in the last chapter of that book. The writer of the story is unknown but possessed an understanding of the historical period prior to the beginning of the monarchy in the eleventh century BC.

The country of Moab sat east of the Dead Sea. Moses and the Israelites passed through it on their journey to Canaan (Numbers 22–24). It is also one of the nations God used to judge the Israelites for their idolatry after they settled in the land (Judges 3:12–30).

Naomi's condition as described in the story resembles the historical situation of Israel during the time of the judges. Her husband has died, as have her sons, leaving her a widow without children to support her. Ruth becomes a symbol of the nations who support Israel by choosing to remain with Naomi and live among the Israelites even though she is a Moabite. The story shows that even though Israel and the surrounding nations often lived in tension, their relationships were not exclusively negative and confrontational.

When Ruth declares to Naomi, "Your people will be my people, and your God will be my God" (1:16), she fulfills the goal that God laid out for Israel since the time He delivered them from Egypt. He had said that they would be a kingdom of priests (Exodus 19:6) who would lead the nations in recognition and worship of Him. Ruth's declaration recognizes that the Lord is her God, just as He is the God of all people. An interesting feature of the book of Ruth is that the divine name of God (Yahweh) is given more than 20 times in the story. The Lord (Yahweh) is the God of Israel, and He is the God of the Moabites, such as Ruth, who commits to a relationship with His people and worships Him in doing so.

Boaz is Naomi's relative. He recognizes Ruth's faithfulness, marries her, and redeems the name and legacy of Ruth's deceased husband according to the law of the family redeemer. This law prescribed a way for people who had suffered loss to redeem what they had lost through the help of family members (Leviticus 25:25–57). Even though the law specifically concerned the redemption of property, its application in a situation such as that described in the book of Ruth would have been acceptable to people at that time.

Though once a poor, Gentile widow, the Bible remembers Ruth as the remarkable great-grandmother of King David. Consequently, the story of Ruth is both the story of one woman's loyalty to her mother-in-law and of the lineage God gives to her for her loyalty. It is also a story of mutuality between Israel and the other nations. Ruth serves as a representative of those nations. Boaz blesses her for the love she shows to Naomi, who is herself a representative of Israel. Because of Ruth's love, she is given the privilege of sharing in God's plans for all people.

ELIMELECH MOVES HIS FAMILY TO MOAB

1 In the days when the judges ruled in Israel, a severe famine came upon the land. So a man from Bethlehem in Judah left his home and went to live in the country of Moab, taking his wife and two sons with him. ² The man's name was Elimelech, and his wife was Naomi. Their two sons were Mahlon and Kilion. They were Ephrathites from Bethlehem in the land of Judah. And when they reached Moab, they settled there.

³ Then Elimelech died, and Naomi was left with her two sons. ⁴ The two sons married Moabite women. One married a woman named Orpah, and the other a woman named Ruth. But about ten years later, ⁵ both Mahlon and Kilion died. This left Naomi alone, without her two sons or her husband.

NAOMI AND RUTH RETURN

⁶ Then Naomi heard in Moab that the LORD had blessed his people in Judah by giving them good crops again. So Naomi and her daughters-in-law got ready to leave Moab to return to her homeland. ⁷ With her two daughters-in-law she set out from the place where she had been living, and they took the road that would lead them back to Judah.

⁸ But on the way, Naomi said to her two daughters-in-law, "Go back to your mothers' homes. And may the LORD reward you for your kindness to your husbands and to me. ⁹ May the LORD bless you with the security of another marriage." Then she kissed them good-bye, and they all broke down and wept.

¹⁰ "No," they said. "We want to go with you to your people."

¹¹ But Naomi replied, "Why should you go on with me? Can I still give birth to other sons who could grow up to be your husbands? ¹² No, my daughters, return to your parents' homes, for I am too old to marry again. And even if it were possible, and I were to get married tonight and bear sons, then what? ¹³ Would you wait for them to grow up and refuse to marry someone else? No, of course not, my daughters! Things are far more bitter for me than for you, because the LORD himself has raised his fist against me."

¹⁴ And again they wept together, and Orpah kissed her mother-in-law good-bye. But Ruth clung tightly to Naomi. ¹⁵ "Look," Naomi said to her, "your sister-in-law has gone back to her people and to her gods. You should do the same."

¹⁶ But Ruth replied, "Don't ask me to leave you and turn back. Wherever you go, I will go; wherever you live, I will live. Your people will be my people, and your God will be my God. ¹⁷ Wherever you die, I will die, and there I will be buried. May the LORD punish me severely if I allow anything but death to separate us!" ¹⁸ When Naomi saw that Ruth was determined to go with her, she said nothing more.

¹⁹ So the two of them continued on their journey. When they came to Bethlehem, the entire town was excited by their arrival. "Is it really Naomi?" the women asked.

²⁰ "Don't call me Naomi," she responded. "Instead, call me Mara,* for the Almighty has made life very bitter for me. ²¹ I went away full, but the LORD has brought me home empty. Why call me Naomi when the LORD has caused me to suffer* and the Almighty has sent such tragedy upon me?"

²² So Naomi returned from Moab, accompanied by her daughter-in-law Ruth, the young Moabite woman. They arrived in Bethlehem in late spring, at the beginning of the barley harvest.

RUTH WORKS IN BOAZ'S FIELD

2 Now there was a wealthy and influential man in Bethlehem named Boaz, who was a relative of Naomi's husband, Elimelech.

² One day Ruth the Moabite said to Naomi, "Let me go out into the harvest fields to pick up the stalks of grain left behind by anyone who is kind enough to let me do it."

Naomi replied, "All right, my daughter, go ahead." ³ So Ruth went out to gather grain behind the harvesters. And as it happened, she found herself working in a field that belonged to Boaz, the relative of her father-in-law, Elimelech.

⁴ While she was there, Boaz arrived from Bethlehem and greeted the harvesters. "The LORD be with you!" he said.

"The LORD bless you!" the harvesters replied.

⁵ Then Boaz asked his foreman, "Who is that young woman over there? Who does she belong to?"

⁶ And the foreman replied, "She is the young woman from Moab who came back with Naomi. ⁷ She asked me this morning if she could gather grain behind the harvesters. She has been hard at work ever since, except for a few minutes' rest in the shelter."

⁸ Boaz went over and said to Ruth, "Listen, my daughter. Stay right here with us when you gather grain; don't go to any other fields. Stay right behind the young women working in my field. ⁹ See which part of the field they are harvesting, and then follow them. I have warned the young men not to treat you roughly. And when you are thirsty, help yourself to the water they have drawn from the well."

¹⁰ Ruth fell at his feet and thanked him warmly. "What have I done to deserve such kindness?" she asked. "I am only a foreigner."

¹¹ "Yes, I know," Boaz replied. "But I also know about everything you have done for your mother-in-law since the death of your husband. I have heard how you left your father and mother and your own land to live here among complete

---

1:20 *Naomi* means "pleasant"; *Mara* means "bitter." 1:21 Or *has testified against me.*

strangers. ¹²May the Lᴏʀᴅ, the God of Israel, under whose wings you have come to take refuge, reward you fully for what you have done."

¹³"I hope I continue to please you, sir," she replied. "You have comforted me by speaking so kindly to me, even though I am not one of your workers."

¹⁴At mealtime Boaz called to her, "Come over here, and help yourself to some food. You can dip your bread in the sour wine." So she sat with his harvesters, and Boaz gave her some roasted grain to eat. She ate all she wanted and still had some left over.

¹⁵When Ruth went back to work again, Boaz ordered his young men, "Let her gather grain right among the sheaves without stopping her. ¹⁶And pull out some heads of barley from the bundles and drop them on purpose for her. Let her pick them up, and don't give her a hard time!"

¹⁷So Ruth gathered barley there all day, and when she beat out the grain that evening, it filled an entire basket.* ¹⁸She carried it back into town and showed it to her mother-in-law. Ruth also gave her the roasted grain that was left over from her meal.

¹⁹"Where did you gather all this grain today?" Naomi asked. "Where did you work? May the Lᴏʀᴅ bless the one who helped you!"

So Ruth told her mother-in-law about the man in whose field she had worked. She said, "The man I worked with today is named Boaz."

²⁰"May the Lᴏʀᴅ bless him!" Naomi told her daughter-in-law. "He is showing his kindness to us as well as to your dead husband.* That man is one of our closest relatives, one of our family redeemers."

²¹Then Ruth* said, "What's more, Boaz even told me to come back and stay with his harvesters until the entire harvest is completed."

²²"Good!" Naomi exclaimed. "Do as he said, my daughter. Stay with his young women right through the whole harvest. You might be harassed in other fields, but you'll be safe with him."

²³So Ruth worked alongside the women in Boaz's fields and gathered grain with them until the end of the barley harvest. Then she continued working with them through the wheat harvest in early summer. And all the while she lived with her mother-in-law.

RUTH AT THE THRESHING FLOOR

3 One day Naomi said to Ruth, "My daughter, it's time that I found a permanent home for you, so that you will be provided for. ²Boaz is a close relative of ours, and he's been very kind by letting you gather grain with his young women. Tonight he will be winnowing barley at the threshing floor. ³Now do as I tell you—take a bath and put on perfume and dress in your nicest clothes. Then go to the threshing floor, but don't let Boaz see you until he has finished eating and

drinking. ⁴Be sure to notice where he lies down; then go and uncover his feet and lie down there. He will tell you what to do."

⁵"I will do everything you say," Ruth replied. ⁶So she went down to the threshing floor that night and followed the instructions of her mother-in-law.

⁷After Boaz had finished eating and drinking and was in good spirits, he lay down at the far end of the pile of grain and went to sleep. Then Ruth came quietly, uncovered his feet, and lay down. ⁸Around midnight Boaz suddenly woke up and turned over. He was surprised to find a woman lying at his feet! ⁹"Who are you?" he asked.

"I am your servant Ruth," she replied. "Spread the corner of your covering over me, for you are my family redeemer."

¹⁰"The Lᴏʀᴅ bless you, my daughter!" Boaz exclaimed. "You are showing even more family loyalty now than you did before, for you have not gone after a younger man, whether rich or poor. ¹¹Now don't worry about a thing, my daughter. I will do what is necessary, for everyone in town knows you are a virtuous woman. ¹²But while it's true that I am one of your family redeemers, there is another man who is more closely related to you than I am. ¹³Stay here tonight, and in the morning I will talk to him. If he is willing to redeem you, very well. Let him marry you. But if he is not willing, then as surely as the Lᴏʀᴅ lives, I will redeem you myself! Now lie down here until morning."

¹⁴So Ruth lay at Boaz's feet until the morning, but she got up before it was light enough for people to recognize each other. For Boaz had said, "No one must know that a woman was here at the threshing floor." ¹⁵Then Boaz said to her, "Bring your cloak and spread it out." He measured six scoops* of barley into the cloak and placed it on her back. Then he* returned to the town.

¹⁶When Ruth went back to her mother-in-law, Naomi asked, "What happened, my daughter?"

Ruth told Naomi everything Boaz had done for her, ¹⁷and she added, "He gave me these six scoops of barley and said, 'Don't go back to your mother-in-law empty-handed.'"

¹⁸Then Naomi said to her, "Just be patient, my daughter, until we hear what happens. The man won't rest until he has settled things today."

BOAZ MARRIES RUTH

4 Boaz went to the town gate and took a seat there. Just then the family redeemer he had mentioned came by, so Boaz called out to him, "Come over here and sit down, friend. I want to talk to you." So they sat down together. ²Then Boaz called ten leaders from the town and asked

---

2:17 Hebrew *it was about an ephah* [20 quarts or 22 liters].
2:20 Hebrew *to the living and to the dead.*   2:21 Hebrew *Ruth the Moabite.*   3:15a Hebrew *six measures,* an unknown quantity.
3:15b Most Hebrew manuscripts read *he;* many Hebrew manuscripts, Syriac version, and Latin Vulgate read *she.*

IT'S MORE ABOUT THE JOURNEY THAN YOU THINK
Ruth 4:17   TODD LANE

Determination, devotion, and the desire for redemption are all qualities of a hero. Ruth was an ordinary Moabite woman who left her family, country, and gods because she had a glimpse of the one, true God through her mother-in-law Naomi. Ruth worked hard to provide for herself and Naomi, and her devotion caused her to find favor with Boaz, one of their family redeemers. Ruth married Boaz and eventually became the great-grand-mother of King David as well as an ancestor of Jesus.

We can learn much from Ruth's example of determination as we follow God and keep His Word as our priority. When we faithfully serve others, even without recognition, we are truly serving Him. Like Ruth, we too have a family redeemer—Jesus Christ. When we accept Him as our Lord and Savior, the Holy Spirit begins to work in us and develop a godly heritage for future generations.

---

them to sit as witnesses. ³And Boaz said to the family redeemer, "You know Naomi, who came back from Moab. She is selling the land that belonged to our relative Elimelech. ⁴I thought I should speak to you about it so that you can redeem it if you wish. If you want the land, then buy it here in the presence of these witnesses. But if you don't want it, let me know right away, because I am next in line to redeem it after you."

The man replied, "All right, I'll redeem it."

⁵Then Boaz told him, "Of course, your purchase of the land from Naomi also requires that you marry Ruth, the Moabite widow. That way she can have children who will carry on her husband's name and keep the land in the family."

⁶"Then I can't redeem it," the family redeemer replied, "because this might endanger my own estate. You redeem the land; I cannot do it."

⁷Now in those days it was the custom in Israel for anyone transferring a right of purchase to remove his sandal and hand it to the other party. This publicly validated the transaction. ⁸So the other family redeemer drew off his sandal as he said to Boaz, "You buy the land."

⁹Then Boaz said to the elders and to the crowd standing around, "You are witnesses that today I have bought from Naomi all the property of Elimelech, Kilion, and Mahlon. ¹⁰And with the land I have acquired Ruth, the Moabite widow of Mahlon, to be my wife. This way she can have a son to carry on the family name of her dead husband and to inherit the family property here in his hometown. You are all witnesses today."

¹¹Then the elders and all the people standing in the gate replied, "We are witnesses! May the LORD make this woman who is coming into your home like Rachel and Leah, from whom all the nation of Israel descended! May you prosper in Ephrathah and be famous in Bethlehem. ¹²And may the LORD give you descendants by this young woman who will be like those of our ancestor Perez, the son of Tamar and Judah."

THE DESCENDANTS OF BOAZ

¹³So Boaz took Ruth into his home, and she became his wife. When he slept with her, the LORD enabled her to become pregnant, and she gave birth to a son. ¹⁴Then the women of the town said to Naomi, "Praise the LORD, who has now provided a redeemer for your family! May this child be famous in Israel. ¹⁵May he restore your youth and care for you in your old age. For he is the son of your daughter-in-law who loves you and has been better to you than seven sons!"

¹⁶Naomi took the baby and cuddled him to her breast. And she cared for him as if he were her own. ¹⁷The neighbor women said, "Now at last Naomi has a son again!" And they named him Obed. He became the father of Jesse and the grandfather of David.

¹⁸This is the genealogical record of their ancestor Perez:

Perez was the father of Hezron.
¹⁹ Hezron was the father of Ram.
Ram was the father of Amminadab.
²⁰ Amminadab was the father of Nahshon.
Nahshon was the father of Salmon.*
²¹ Salmon was the father of Boaz.
Boaz was the father of Obed.
²² Obed was the father of Jesse.
Jesse was the father of David.

4:20 As in some Greek manuscripts (see also 4:21); Hebrew reads *Salma.*

1-2 SAMUEL

JON HUNTZINGER, PHD

The two books of Samuel describe the making of Israel's first king, his fall, and the installation of a second king who leads Israel to become a small but powerful nation. As a result, the books of Samuel feature three men: Samuel, Saul, and David. These two books were *originally one book*, which was divided at some point into two smaller ones to make it easier to read and study. The book of 1 Samuel begins with the birth of Samuel and ends with the death of Saul. The book of 2 Samuel features the rise and rule of King David. The anonymous writer compiled and wrote the content of these books long after David's rule ended in the early tenth century BC. The books bear the name of the prophet Samuel, the last of the judges appointed by God to lead the people.

The name Samuel means 'God hears.' When the people clamor for a king after the Philistines capture the Ark of the Covenant (1 Samuel 8:19–22), God hears them and, though it is not His desire, He gives to them what they ask through Samuel. The exceptional nature of Samuel's prophetic ministry is evident in the statement the writer of the book makes about him, that "everything Samuel said proved to be reliable" (1 Samuel 3:19). Everything he said happened because he only spoke what God wanted him to speak and not his own words. Samuel is a true prophet, and through him, God appoints the first kings of Israel. For this reason, these books depict God as a kingmaker who Himself is sovereign over the affairs of His people. *He raises up rulers, and He can bring them down.*

The original single book of Samuel is a long narrative that begins with a poetic passage containing Hannah's prayer for a son (1 Samuel 2:1–10) and concludes with David's song of deliverance (2 Samuel 22:1–23:7). Just as Hannah's prayer anticipates the future king (verse 10), so also David's song gives praise for God's faithfulness to him as king. Between these poetic passages, the writer recounts the story of Israel's transition from being a people under God to a people under a king.

The book of 1 Samuel contains four major sections:
— Chapters 1–3 include the stories of Samuel's birth in response to his mother's prayers and God's call to Samuel to speak His words.
— Chapters 4–8 recount the events that led to the loss of the Ark of the Covenant to the Philistines and its return, and the demand by the people for a king as a result.
— Chapters 9–15 tell about the selection of Saul to be king, his battles with the Philistines, and his ultimate failure for not honoring God's word.
— Chapters 16–31 record the choice of David as king after Saul and Saul's struggle against him, during which time David defeats the giant Goliath, befriends Saul's son Jonathan, and spares Saul's life.

The book of 2 Samuel can be divided into five major sections:
— Chapters 1–7 include the installation of David as king, the placement of the Ark of the Covenant in Jerusalem, and the covenant God makes with David.
— Chapters 8–10 outline David's battles with his enemies.
— Chapters 11–18 consist of David's adultery with Bathsheba and the birth of Solomon, followed by the struggles David has with his son Absalom.
— Chapters 19–21 relate the continued conflict with other tribes.
— Chapters 22–24 conclude with David's song of deliverance and a census of all the people.

These two books depict David primarily as a man who wants the things God wants and who receives correction when he places his own desires before those of God. His life corresponds to God's words to Samuel when He directs him to anoint the young David as king: "The LORD doesn't see things the way you see them. People judge by outward appearance, but the LORD looks at the heart" (1 Samuel 16:7). The story confirms God's choice of David as king after Saul because David's heart was similar to God's own. When the prophet Nathan later rebukes David for his adultery with Bathsheba, David immediately acknowledges his sin and repents of it (2 Samuel 12:7–14). Unlike Saul, who acts on his own without waiting for God's word only to explain away his failure to follow that word (1 Samuel 13:8–14), David listens to the words God speaks to him through prophets like Nathan and acts upon them. The humility David exemplifies in his life separates him from his predecessor, Saul, who fell from grace with God due to his pride.

Nonetheless, the books of Samuel depict David as a complex character. David is both *a man of warfare and a man of worship*. He battles the Philistines and other tribes as he expands the territory of his kingdom and kills thousands of men in the process. At the same time, David brings the Ark of the Covenant to Jerusalem while dancing in uninhibited celebration before the Lord. He is *a man of both passion and compassion*. Though David has many wives and concubines, he still commits adultery with Bathsheba and has her husband sent into battle to be killed. Yet he spares Saul's life on more than one occasion and shows mercy to Saul's family, even though the king actively pursued David to kill him.

God makes a covenant with David (2 Samuel 7:1–17), recalling those He made earlier with Abraham (Genesis 15:1–20) and Moses (Deuteronomy 5–6). In the earlier covenants, God promised to give Abraham innumerable descendants and a land in which to live, and to Moses, He promised blessing upon the people and a land flowing with milk and honey. To David, God promises an eternal kingdom and future descendants who will follow and live in relationship with Him. To all three, God promises to give them a name by which they will be known to Him and to the nations (Genesis 12:2; Exodus 19:5–6). God makes these covenants despite the fact that Abraham and Moses are imperfect men, as is David.

Abraham gives his wife, Sarah, to a foreign ruler as a type of peace offering out of fear (Genesis 20:1–13). Moses strikes a rock in anger over the people's complaints (Numbers 20:10–13). Like them, David is flawed due to his adultery with Bathsheba, the census he takes of the people, and his inability to lead his own family while leading the nation. Nonetheless, God makes a covenant with each of these men because each one is committed to the words God speaks to them. Abraham leaves his family, people, and country in response to God's promise of a greater land (Genesis 12:1–9). Moses returns to Egypt and speaks God's promise to the Israelites and to Pharaoh of a land of milk and honey (Exodus 3:7–4:20). And David responds to the words God speaks through His prophets like Nathan throughout David's reign as king.

1 SAMUEL

ELKANAH AND HIS FAMILY

1 There was a man named Elkanah who lived in Ramah in the region of Zuph* in the hill country of Ephraim. He was the son of Jeroham, son of Elihu, son of Tohu, son of Zuph, of Ephraim. ²Elkanah had two wives, Hannah and Peninnah. Peninnah had children, but Hannah did not.

³Each year Elkanah would travel to Shiloh to worship and sacrifice to the LORD of Heaven's Armies at the Tabernacle. The priests of the LORD at that time were the two sons of Eli—Hophni and Phinehas. ⁴On the days Elkanah presented his sacrifice, he would give portions of the meat to Peninnah and each of her children. ⁵And though he loved Hannah, he would give her only one choice portion* because the LORD had given her no children. ⁶So Peninnah would taunt Hannah and make fun of her because the LORD had kept her from having children. ⁷Year after year it was the same—Peninnah would taunt Hannah as they went to the Tabernacle.* Each time, Hannah would be reduced to tears and would not even eat.

⁸"Why are you crying, Hannah?" Elkanah would ask. "Why aren't you eating? Why be downhearted just because you have no children? You have me—isn't that better than having ten sons?"

HANNAH'S PRAYER FOR A SON

⁹Once after a sacrificial meal at Shiloh, Hannah got up and went to pray. Eli the priest was sitting at his customary place beside the entrance of the Tabernacle.* ¹⁰Hannah was in deep anguish, crying bitterly as she prayed to the LORD. ¹¹And

she made this vow: "O LORD of Heaven's Armies, if you will look upon my sorrow and answer my prayer and give me a son, then I will give him back to you. He will be yours for his entire lifetime, and as a sign that he has been dedicated to the LORD, his hair will never be cut.*"

¹²As she was praying to the LORD, Eli watched her. ¹³Seeing her lips moving but hearing no sound, he thought she had been drinking. ¹⁴"Must you come here drunk?" he demanded. "Throw away your wine!"

¹⁵"Oh no, sir!" she replied. "I haven't been drinking wine or anything stronger. But I am very discouraged, and I was pouring out my heart to the LORD. ¹⁶Don't think I am a wicked woman! For I have been praying out of great anguish and sorrow."

¹⁷"In that case," Eli said, "go in peace! May the God of Israel grant the request you have asked of him."

¹⁸"Oh, thank you, sir!" she exclaimed. Then she went back and began to eat again, and she was no longer sad.

SAMUEL'S BIRTH AND DEDICATION

¹⁹The entire family got up early the next morning and went to worship the LORD once more. Then they returned home to Ramah. When Elkanah slept with Hannah, the LORD remembered her

---

1:1 As in Greek version; Hebrew reads in Ramathaim-zophim; compare 1:19. 1:5 Or And because he loved Hannah, he would give her a choice portion. The meaning of the Hebrew is uncertain. 1:7 Hebrew the house of the LORD; also in 1:24. 1:9 Hebrew the Temple of the LORD. 1:11 Some manuscripts add He will drink neither wine nor intoxicants.

plea, [20] and in due time she gave birth to a son. She named him Samuel,* for she said, "I asked the LORD for him."

[21] The next year Elkanah and his family went on their annual trip to offer a sacrifice to the LORD and to keep his vow. [22] But Hannah did not go. She told her husband, "Wait until the boy is weaned. Then I will take him to the Tabernacle and leave him there with the LORD permanently.*"

[23] "Whatever you think is best," Elkanah agreed. "Stay here for now, and may the LORD help you keep your promise.*" So she stayed home and nursed the boy until he was weaned.

[24] When the child was weaned, Hannah took him to the Tabernacle in Shiloh. They brought along a three-year-old bull* for the sacrifice and a basket* of flour and some wine. [25] After sacrificing the bull, they brought the boy to Eli. [26] "Sir, do you remember me?" Hannah asked. "I am the very woman who stood here several years ago praying to the LORD. [27] I asked the LORD to give me this boy, and he has granted my request. [28] Now I am giving him to the LORD, and he will belong to the LORD his whole life." And they* worshiped the LORD there.

HANNAH'S PRAYER OF PRAISE

2 Then Hannah prayed:

"My heart rejoices in the LORD!
 The LORD has made me strong.*
Now I have an answer for my enemies;
 I rejoice because you rescued me.

[2] No one is holy like the LORD!
 There is no one besides you;
 there is no Rock like our God.

[3] "Stop acting so proud and haughty!
 Don't speak with such arrogance!
For the LORD is a God who knows what you
 have done;
 he will judge your actions.

[4] The bow of the mighty is now broken,
 and those who stumbled are now strong.

[5] Those who were well fed are now starving,
 and those who were starving are now full.
The childless woman now has seven
 children,
 and the woman with many children
 wastes away.

[6] The LORD gives both death and life;
 he brings some down to the grave* but
 raises others up.

[7] The LORD makes some poor and others rich;
 he brings some down and lifts others up.

[8] He lifts the poor from the dust
 and the needy from the garbage dump.
He sets them among princes,
 placing them in seats of honor.
For all the earth is the LORD's,
 and he has set the world in order.

[9] "He will protect his faithful ones,
 but the wicked will disappear in darkness.
No one will succeed by strength alone.

[10] Those who fight against the LORD will
 be shattered.
He thunders against them from heaven;
 the LORD judges throughout the earth.
He gives power to his king;
 he increases the strength* of his
 anointed one."

[11] Then Elkanah returned home to Ramah without Samuel. And the boy served the LORD by assisting Eli the priest.

ELI'S WICKED SONS

[12] Now the sons of Eli were scoundrels who had no respect for the LORD [13] or for their duties as priests. Whenever anyone offered a sacrifice, Eli's sons would send over a servant with a three-pronged fork. While the meat of the sacrificed animal was still boiling, [14] the servant would stick the fork into the pot and demand that whatever it brought up be given to Eli's sons. All the Israelites who came to worship at Shiloh were treated this way. [15] Sometimes the servant would come even before the animal's fat had been burned on the altar. He would demand raw meat before it had been boiled so that it could be used for roasting. [16] The man offering the sacrifice might reply, "Take as much as you want, but the fat must be burned first." Then the servant would demand, "No, give it to me now, or I'll take it by force." [17] So the sin of these young men was very serious in the LORD's sight, for they treated the LORD's offerings with contempt.

[18] But Samuel, though he was only a boy, served the LORD. He wore a linen garment like that of a priest.* [19] Each year his mother made a small coat for him and brought it to him when she came with her husband for the sacrifice. [20] Before they returned home, Eli would bless Elkanah and his wife and say, "May the LORD give you other children to take the place of this one she gave to the LORD.*" [21] And the LORD blessed Hannah, and she conceived and gave birth to three sons and two daughters. Meanwhile, Samuel grew up in the presence of the LORD.

[22] Now Eli was very old, but he was aware of what his sons were doing to the people of Israel. He knew, for instance, that his sons were seducing the young women who assisted at the entrance of the Tabernacle.* [23] Eli said to them, "I have been

---

2:20 *Samuel* sounds like the Hebrew term for "asked of God" or "heard by God." 2:22 Some manuscripts add *I will offer him as a Nazirite for all time.* 2:23 As in Dead Sea Scrolls and Greek version; Masoretic Text reads *may the LORD keep his promise.* 2:24a As in Dead Sea Scrolls, Greek and Syriac versions; Masoretic Text reads *three bulls.* 2:24b Hebrew *and an ephah* [20 quarts or 22 liters]. 2:28 Hebrew *he.* 2:1 Hebrew *has exalted my horn.* 2:6 Hebrew *to Sheol.* 2:10 Hebrew *he exalts the horn.* 2:18 Hebrew *He wore a linen ephod.* 2:20 As in Dead Sea Scrolls and Greek version; Masoretic Text reads *this one he requested of the LORD.* 2:22 Hebrew *Tent of Meeting.* Some manuscripts lack this entire sentence.

hearing reports from all the people about the wicked things you are doing. Why do you keep sinning? ²⁴ You must stop, my sons! The reports I hear among the LORD's people are not good. ²⁵ If someone sins against another person, God* can mediate for the guilty party. But if someone sins against the LORD, who can intercede?" But Eli's sons wouldn't listen to their father, for the LORD was already planning to put them to death.

²⁶ Meanwhile, the boy Samuel grew taller and grew in favor with the LORD and with the people.

A WARNING FOR ELI'S FAMILY

²⁷ One day a man of God came to Eli and gave him this message from the LORD: "I revealed myself* to your ancestors when they were Pharaoh's slaves in Egypt. ²⁸ I chose your ancestor Aaron* from among all the tribes of Israel to be my priest, to offer sacrifices on my altar, to burn incense, and to wear the priestly vest* as he served me. And I assigned the sacrificial offerings to you priests. ²⁹ So why do you scorn my sacrifices and offerings? Why do you give your sons more honor than you give me—for you and they have become fat from the best offerings of my people Israel!

³⁰ "Therefore, the LORD, the God of Israel, says: I promised that your branch of the tribe of Levi* would always be my priests. But I will honor those who honor me, and I will despise those who think lightly of me. ³¹ The time is coming when I will put an end to your family, so it will no longer serve as my priests. All the members of your family will die before their time. None will reach old age. ³² You will watch with envy as I pour out prosperity on the people of Israel. But no members of your family will ever live out their days. ³³ The few not cut off from serving at my altar will survive, but only so their eyes can go blind and their hearts break, and their children will die a violent death.* ³⁴ And to prove that what I have said will come true, I will cause your two sons, Hophni and Phinehas, to die on the same day!

³⁵ "Then I will raise up a faithful priest who will serve me and do what I desire. I will establish his family, and they will be priests to my anointed kings forever. ³⁶ Then all of your surviving family will bow before him, begging for money and food. 'Please,' they will say, 'give us jobs among the priests so we will have enough to eat.'"

THE LORD SPEAKS TO SAMUEL

3 Meanwhile, the boy Samuel served the LORD by assisting Eli. Now in those days messages from the LORD were very rare, and visions were quite uncommon.

² One night Eli, who was almost blind by now, had gone to bed. ³ The lamp of God had not yet gone out, and Samuel was sleeping in the Tabernacle* near the Ark of God. ⁴ Suddenly the LORD called out, "Samuel!"

VALUE HIS WORD
1 Samuel 3:1   ROBERT MORRIS

First Samuel 3:1 says, "The boy Samuel served the LORD by assisting Eli. Now in those days messages from the LORD were very rare." This verse is frequently misunderstood. We mistakenly think that if the word of the Lord was "rare," God wasn't speaking much during this time. However, the actual problem was in the *hearing* of the word of God. God was—and is—still speaking. In Hebrew, the word *rare* means 'something that is precious and valuable.' Samuel valued the word of the Lord, so he heard it. Other people at this time did not value it, so they didn't hear it. God's word was available to them just as it was to Samuel, but they weren't listening.

Is the Word of the Lord precious to you? Is it valuable? Is it a treasure? God is speaking to you. The more you value His Word, the more you'll hear and understand it.

"Yes?" Samuel replied. "What is it?" ⁵ He got up and ran to Eli. "Here I am. Did you call me?"

"I didn't call you," Eli replied. "Go back to bed." So he did.

⁶ Then the LORD called out again, "Samuel!"

Again Samuel got up and went to Eli. "Here I am. Did you call me?"

"I didn't call you, my son," Eli said. "Go back to bed."

⁷ Samuel did not yet know the LORD because he had never had a message from the LORD before. ⁸ So the LORD called a third time, and once more Samuel got up and went to Eli. "Here I am. Did you call me?"

Then Eli realized it was the LORD who was calling the boy. ⁹ So he said to Samuel, "Go and lie down again, and if someone calls again, say, 'Speak, LORD, your servant is listening.'" So Samuel went back to bed.

¹⁰ And the LORD came and called as before, "Samuel! Samuel!"

And Samuel replied, "Speak, your servant is listening."

¹¹ Then the LORD said to Samuel, "I am about to do a shocking thing in Israel. ¹² I am going to carry out all my threats against Eli and his family, from beginning to end. ¹³ I have warned him that judgment is coming upon his family forever, because his sons are blaspheming God* and he hasn't disciplined them. ¹⁴ So I have vowed that the sins of Eli and his sons will never be forgiven by sacrifices or offerings."

2:25 Or *the judges.*   2:27 As in Greek and Syriac versions; Hebrew reads *Did I reveal myself.*   2:28a Hebrew *your father.* 2:28b Hebrew *an ephod.*   2:30 Hebrew *that your house and your father's house.*   2:33 As in Dead Sea Scrolls and Greek version, which read *die by the sword;* Masoretic Text reads *die like mortals.* 3:3 Hebrew *the Temple of the LORD.*   3:13 As in Greek version; Hebrew reads *his sons have made themselves contemptible.*

SAMUEL SPEAKS FOR THE LORD

15Samuel stayed in bed until morning, then got up and opened the doors of the Tabernacle* as usual. He was afraid to tell Eli what the LORD had said to him. 16But Eli called out to him, "Samuel, my son."

"Here I am," Samuel replied.

17"What did the LORD say to you? Tell me everything. And may God strike you and even kill you if you hide anything from me!" 18So Samuel told Eli everything; he didn't hold anything back. "It is the LORD's will," Eli replied. "Let him do what he thinks best."

19As Samuel grew up, the LORD was with him, and everything Samuel said proved to be reliable. 20And all Israel, from Dan in the north to Beersheba in the south, knew that Samuel was confirmed as a prophet of the LORD. 21The LORD continued to appear at Shiloh and gave messages to Samuel there at the Tabernacle. 4:1And Samuel's words went out to all the people of Israel.

THE PHILISTINES CAPTURE THE ARK

4 At that time Israel was at war with the Philistines. The Israelite army was camped near Ebenezer, and the Philistines were at Aphek. 2The Philistines attacked and defeated the army of Israel, killing 4,000 men. 3After the battle was over, the troops retreated to their camp, and the elders of Israel asked, "Why did the LORD allow us to be defeated by the Philistines?" Then they said, "Let's bring the Ark of the Covenant of the LORD from Shiloh. If we carry it into battle with us, it* will save us from our enemies."

4So they sent men to Shiloh to bring the Ark of the Covenant of the LORD of Heaven's Armies, who is enthroned between the cherubim. Hophni and Phinehas, the sons of Eli, were also there with the Ark of the Covenant of God. 5When all the Israelites saw the Ark of the Covenant of the LORD coming into the camp, their shout of joy was so loud it made the ground shake!

6"What's going on?" the Philistines asked. "What's all the shouting about in the Hebrew camp?" When they were told it was because the Ark of the LORD had arrived, 7they panicked. "The gods have* come into their camp!" they cried. "This is a disaster! We have never had to face anything like this before! 8Help! Who can save us from these mighty gods of Israel? They are the same gods who destroyed the Egyptians with plagues when Israel was in the wilderness. 9Fight as never before, Philistines! If you don't, we will become the Hebrews' slaves just as they have been ours! Stand up like men and fight!"

10So the Philistines fought desperately, and Israel was defeated again. The slaughter was great; 30,000 Israelite soldiers died that day. The survivors turned and fled to their tents. 11The Ark of God was captured, and Hophni and Phinehas, the two sons of Eli, were killed.

THE DEATH OF ELI

12A man from the tribe of Benjamin ran from the battlefield and arrived at Shiloh later that same day. He had torn his clothes and put dust on his head to show his grief. 13Eli was waiting beside the road to hear the news of the battle, for his heart trembled for the safety of the Ark of God. When the messenger arrived and told what had happened, an outcry resounded throughout the town.

14"What is all the noise about?" Eli asked.

The messenger rushed over to Eli, 15who was ninety-eight years old and blind. 16He said to Eli, "I have just come from the battlefield—I was there this very day."

"What happened, my son?" Eli demanded.

17"Israel has been defeated by the Philistines," the messenger replied. "The people have been slaughtered, and your two sons, Hophni and Phinehas, were also killed. And the Ark of God has been captured."

18When the messenger mentioned what had happened to the Ark of God, Eli fell backward from his seat beside the gate. He broke his neck and died, for he was old and overweight. He had been Israel's judge for forty years.

19Eli's daughter-in-law, the wife of Phinehas, was pregnant and near her time of delivery. When she heard that the Ark of God had been captured and that her father-in-law and husband were dead, she went into labor and gave birth. 20She died in childbirth, but before she passed away the midwives tried to encourage her. "Don't be afraid," they said. "You have a baby boy!" But she did not answer or pay attention to them.

21She named the child Ichabod (which means "Where is the glory?"), for she said, "Israel's glory is gone." She named him this because the Ark of God had been captured and because her father-in-law and husband were dead. 22Then she said, "The glory has departed from Israel, for the Ark of God has been captured."

THE ARK IN PHILISTIA

5 After the Philistines captured the Ark of God, they took it from the battleground at Ebenezer to the town of Ashdod. 2They carried the Ark of God into the temple of Dagon and placed it beside an idol of Dagon. 3But when the citizens of Ashdod went to see it the next morning, Dagon had fallen with his face to the ground in front of the Ark of the LORD! So they took Dagon and put him in his place again. 4But the next morning the same thing happened—Dagon had fallen face down before the Ark of the LORD again. This time his head and hands had broken off and were lying in the doorway. Only the trunk of his body was left intact. 5That is why to this day neither the priests of Dagon nor anyone who

enters the temple of Dagon in Ashdod will step on its threshold.

⁶ Then the LORD's heavy hand struck the people of Ashdod and the nearby villages with a plague of tumors.* ⁷ When the people realized what was happening, they cried out, "We can't keep the Ark of the God of Israel here any longer! He is against us! We will all be destroyed along with Dagon, our god." ⁸ So they called together the rulers of the Philistine towns and asked, "What should we do with the Ark of the God of Israel?"

The rulers discussed it and replied, "Move it to the town of Gath." So they moved the Ark of the God of Israel to Gath. ⁹ But when the Ark arrived at Gath, the LORD's heavy hand fell on its men, young and old; he struck them with a plague of tumors, and there was a great panic.

¹⁰ So they sent the Ark of God to the town of Ekron, but when the people of Ekron saw it coming they cried out, "They are bringing the Ark of the God of Israel here to kill us, too!" ¹¹ The people summoned the Philistine rulers again and begged them, "Please send the Ark of the God of Israel back to its own country, or it* will kill us all." For the deadly plague from God had already begun, and great fear was sweeping across the town. ¹² Those who didn't die were afflicted with tumors; and the cry from the town rose to heaven.

THE PHILISTINES RETURN THE ARK

6 The Ark of the LORD remained in Philistine territory seven months in all. ² Then the Philistines called in their priests and diviners and asked them, "What should we do about the Ark of the LORD? Tell us how to return it to its own country."

³ "Send the Ark of the God of Israel back with a gift," they were told. "Send a guilt offering so the plague will stop. Then, if you are healed, you will know it was his hand that caused the plague."

⁴ "What sort of guilt offering should we send?" they asked.

And they were told, "Since the plague has struck you and your five rulers, make five gold tumors and five gold rats, just like those that have ravaged your land. ⁵ Make these things to show honor to the God of Israel. Perhaps then he will stop afflicting you, your gods, and your land. ⁶ Don't be stubborn and rebellious as Pharaoh and the Egyptians were. By the time God was finished with them, they were eager to let Israel go.

⁷ "Now build a new cart, and find two cows that have just given birth to calves. Make sure the cows have never been yoked to a cart. Hitch the cows to the cart, but shut their calves away from them in a pen. ⁸ Put the Ark of the LORD on the cart, and beside it place a chest containing the gold rats and gold tumors you are sending as a guilt offering. Then let the cows go wherever they want. ⁹ If they cross the border of our land and go to Beth-shemesh, we will know it was the LORD who brought this great disaster upon us. If they don't, we will know it was not his hand that caused the plague. It came simply by chance."

¹⁰ So these instructions were carried out. Two cows were hitched to the cart, and their newborn calves were shut up in a pen. ¹¹ Then the Ark of the LORD and the chest containing the gold rats and gold tumors were placed on the cart. ¹² And sure enough, without veering off in other directions, the cows went straight along the road toward Beth-shemesh, lowing as they went. The Philistine rulers followed them as far as the border of Beth-shemesh.

¹³ The people of Beth-shemesh were harvesting wheat in the valley, and when they saw the Ark, they were overjoyed! ¹⁴ The cart came into the field of a man named Joshua and stopped beside a large rock. So the people broke up the wood of the cart for a fire and killed the cows and sacrificed them to the LORD as a burnt offering. ¹⁵ Several men of the tribe of Levi lifted the Ark of the LORD and the chest containing the gold rats and gold tumors from the cart and placed them on the large rock. Many sacrifices and burnt offerings were offered to the LORD that day by the people of Beth-shemesh. ¹⁶ The five Philistine rulers watched all this and then returned to Ekron that same day.

¹⁷ The five gold tumors sent by the Philistines as a guilt offering to the LORD were gifts from the rulers of Ashdod, Gaza, Ashkelon, Gath, and Ekron. ¹⁸ The five gold rats represented the five Philistine towns and their surrounding villages, which were controlled by the five rulers. The large rock* at Beth-shemesh, where they set the Ark of the LORD, still stands in the field of Joshua as a witness to what happened there.

THE ARK MOVED TO KIRIATH-JEARIM

¹⁹ But the LORD killed seventy men* from Beth-shemesh because they looked into the Ark of the LORD. And the people mourned greatly because of what the LORD had done. ²⁰ "Who is able to stand in the presence of the LORD, this holy God?" they cried out. "Where can we send the Ark from here?"

²¹ So they sent messengers to the people at Kiriath-jearim and told them, "The Philistines have returned the Ark of the LORD. Come here and get it!"

7 So the men of Kiriath-jearim came to get the Ark of the LORD. They took it to the hillside home of Abinadab and ordained Eleazar, his son,

---

5:6 Greek version and Latin Vulgate read *tumors; and rats appeared in their land, and death and destruction were throughout the city.* 5:11 Or *he.* 6:18 As in some Hebrew manuscripts and Greek version; most Hebrew manuscripts read *great meadow* or *Abel-haggedolah.* 6:19 As in a few Hebrew manuscripts; most Hebrew manuscripts read *70 men, 50,000 men.* Perhaps the text should be understood to read *the LORD killed 70 men and 50 oxen.*

to be in charge of it. ²The Ark remained in Kiriath-jearim for a long time—twenty years in all. During that time all Israel mourned because it seemed the LORD had abandoned them.

SAMUEL LEADS ISRAEL TO VICTORY

³Then Samuel said to all the people of Israel, "If you want to return to the LORD with all your hearts, get rid of your foreign gods and your images of Ashtoreth. Turn your hearts to the LORD and obey him alone; then he will rescue you from the Philistines." ⁴So the Israelites got rid of their images of Baal and Ashtoreth and worshiped only the LORD.

⁵Then Samuel told them, "Gather all of Israel to Mizpah, and I will pray to the LORD for you." ⁶So they gathered at Mizpah and, in a great ceremony, drew water from a well and poured it out before the LORD. They also went without food all day and confessed that they had sinned against the LORD. (It was at Mizpah that Samuel became Israel's judge.)

⁷When the Philistine rulers heard that Israel had gathered at Mizpah, they mobilized their army and advanced. The Israelites were badly frightened when they learned that the Philistines were approaching. ⁸"Don't stop pleading with the LORD our God to save us from the Philistines!" they begged Samuel. ⁹So Samuel took a young lamb and offered it to the LORD as a whole burnt offering. He pleaded with the LORD to help Israel, and the LORD answered him.

¹⁰Just as Samuel was sacrificing the burnt offering, the Philistines arrived to attack Israel. But the LORD spoke with a mighty voice of thunder from heaven that day, and the Philistines were thrown into such confusion that the Israelites defeated them. ¹¹The men of Israel chased them from Mizpah to a place below Beth-car, slaughtering them all along the way.

¹²Samuel then took a large stone and placed it between the towns of Mizpah and Jeshanah.* He named it Ebenezer (which means "the stone of help"), for he said, "Up to this point the LORD has helped us!"

¹³So the Philistines were subdued and didn't invade Israel again for some time. And throughout Samuel's lifetime, the LORD's powerful hand was raised against the Philistines. ¹⁴The Israelite villages near Ekron and Gath that the Philistines had captured were restored to Israel, along with the rest of the territory that the Philistines had taken. And there was peace between Israel and the Amorites in those days.

¹⁵Samuel continued as Israel's judge for the rest of his life. ¹⁶Each year he traveled around, setting up his court first at Bethel, then at Gilgal, and then at Mizpah. He judged the people of Israel at each of these places. ¹⁷Then he would return to his home at Ramah, and he would hear cases there, too. And Samuel built an altar to the LORD at Ramah.

ISRAEL REQUESTS A KING

8 As Samuel grew old, he appointed his sons to be judges over Israel. ²Joel and Abijah, his oldest sons, held court in Beersheba. ³But they were not like their father, for they were greedy for money. They accepted bribes and perverted justice.

⁴Finally, all the elders of Israel met at Ramah to discuss the matter with Samuel. ⁵"Look," they told him, "you are now old, and your sons are not like you. Give us a king to judge us like all the other nations have."

⁶Samuel was displeased with their request and went to the LORD for guidance. ⁷"Do everything they say to you," the LORD replied, "for they are rejecting me, not you. They don't want me to be their king any longer. ⁸Ever since I brought them from Egypt they have continually abandoned me and followed other gods. And now they are giving you the same treatment. ⁹Do as they ask, but solemnly warn them about the way a king will reign over them."

SAMUEL WARNS AGAINST A KINGDOM

¹⁰So Samuel passed on the LORD's warning to the people who were asking him for a king. ¹¹"This is how a king will reign over you," Samuel said. "The king will draft your sons and assign them to his chariots and his charioteers, making them run before his chariots. ¹²Some will be generals and captains in his army,* some will be forced to plow in his fields and harvest his crops, and some will make his weapons and chariot equipment. ¹³The king will take your daughters from you and force them to cook and bake and make perfumes for him. ¹⁴He will take away the best of your fields and vineyards and olive groves and give them to his own officials. ¹⁵He will take a tenth of your grain and your grape harvest and distribute it among his officers and attendants. ¹⁶He will take your male and female slaves and demand the finest of your cattle* and donkeys for his own use. ¹⁷He will demand a tenth of your flocks, and you will be his slaves. ¹⁸When that day comes, you will beg for relief from this king you are demanding, but then the LORD will not help you."

¹⁹But the people refused to listen to Samuel's warning. "Even so, we still want a king," they said. ²⁰"We want to be like the nations around us. Our king will judge us and lead us into battle."

²¹So Samuel repeated to the LORD what the people had said, ²²and the LORD replied, "Do as they say, and give them a king." Then Samuel agreed and sent the people home.

SAUL MEETS SAMUEL

9 There was a wealthy, influential man named Kish from the tribe of Benjamin. He was the son of Abiel, son of Zeror, son of Becorath, son of

---

7:12 As in Greek and Syriac versions; Hebrew reads *Shen.*
8:12 Hebrew *commanders of thousands and commanders of fifties.*
8:16 As in Greek version; Hebrew reads *young men.*

Aphiah, of the tribe of Benjamin. ²His son Saul was the most handsome man in Israel—head and shoulders taller than anyone else in the land.

³One day Kish's donkeys strayed away, and he told Saul, "Take a servant with you, and go look for the donkeys." ⁴So Saul took one of the servants and traveled through the hill country of Ephraim, the land of Shalishah, the Shaalim area, and the entire land of Benjamin, but they couldn't find the donkeys anywhere.

⁵Finally, they entered the region of Zuph, and Saul said to his servant, "Let's go home. By now my father will be more worried about us than about the donkeys!"

⁶But the servant said, "I've just thought of something! There is a man of God who lives here in this town. He is held in high honor by all the people because everything he says comes true. Let's go find him. Perhaps he can tell us which way to go."

⁷"But we don't have anything to offer him," Saul replied. "Even our food is gone, and we don't have a thing to give him."

⁸"Well," the servant said, "I have one small silver piece.* We can at least offer it to the man of God and see what happens!" ⁹(In those days if people wanted a message from God, they would say, "Let's go and ask the seer," for prophets used to be called seers.)

¹⁰"All right," Saul agreed, "let's try it!" So they started into the town where the man of God lived.

¹¹As they were climbing the hill to the town, they met some young women coming out to draw water. So Saul and his servant asked, "Is the seer here today?"

¹²"Yes," they replied. "Stay right on this road. He is at the town gates. He has just arrived to take part in a public sacrifice up at the place of worship. ¹³Hurry and catch him before he goes up there to eat. The guests won't begin eating until he arrives to bless the food."

¹⁴So they entered the town, and as they passed through the gates, Samuel was coming out toward them to go up to the place of worship.

¹⁵Now the LORD had told Samuel the previous day, ¹⁶"About this time tomorrow I will send you a man from the land of Benjamin. Anoint him to be the leader of my people, Israel. He will rescue them from the Philistines, for I have looked down on my people in mercy and have heard their cry."

¹⁷When Samuel saw Saul, the LORD said, "That's the man I told you about! He will rule my people."

¹⁸Just then Saul approached Samuel at the gateway and asked, "Can you please tell me where the seer's house is?"

¹⁹"I am the seer!" Samuel replied. "Go up to the place of worship ahead of me. We will eat there together, and in the morning I'll tell you what you want to know and send you on your way. ²⁰And don't worry about those donkeys that were lost three days ago, for they have been found. And I am here to tell you that you and your family are the focus of all Israel's hopes."

²¹Saul replied, "But I'm only from the tribe of Benjamin, the smallest tribe in Israel, and my family is the least important of all the families of that tribe! Why are you talking like this to me?"

²²Then Samuel brought Saul and his servant into the hall and placed them at the head of the table, honoring them above the thirty special guests. ²³Samuel then instructed the cook to bring Saul the finest cut of meat, the piece that had been set aside for the guest of honor. ²⁴So the cook brought in the meat and placed it before Saul. "Go ahead and eat it," Samuel said. "I was saving it for you even before I invited these others!" So Saul ate with Samuel that day.

²⁵When they came down from the place of worship and returned to town, Samuel took Saul up to the roof of the house and prepared a bed for him there.* ²⁶At daybreak the next morning, Samuel called to Saul, "Get up! It's time you were on your way." So Saul got ready, and he and Samuel left the house together. ²⁷When they reached the edge of town, Samuel told Saul to send his servant on ahead. After the servant was gone, Samuel said, "Stay here, for I have received a special message for you from God."

SAMUEL ANOINTS SAUL AS KING

10 Then Samuel took a flask of olive oil and poured it over Saul's head. He kissed Saul and said, "I am doing this because the LORD has appointed you to be the ruler over Israel, his special possession.* ²When you leave me today, you will see two men beside Rachel's tomb at Zelzah, on the border of Benjamin. They will tell you that the donkeys have been found and that your father has stopped worrying about them and is now worried about you. He is asking, 'Have you seen my son?'

³"When you get to the oak of Tabor, you will see three men coming toward you who are on their way to worship God at Bethel. One will be bringing three young goats, another will have three loaves of bread, and the third will be carrying a wineskin full of wine. ⁴They will greet you and offer you two of the loaves, which you are to accept.

⁵"When you arrive at Gibeah of God,* where the garrison of the Philistines is located, you will meet a band of prophets coming down from the place of worship. They will be playing a harp, a tambourine, a flute, and a lyre, and they will be prophesying. ⁶At that time the Spirit of the LORD will come powerfully upon you, and you will prophesy with them. You will be changed

---

9:8 Hebrew ¼ *shekel of silver*, about 0.1 ounces or 3 grams in weight. 9:25 As in Greek version; Hebrew reads *and talked with him there.* 10:1 Greek version reads *over Israel. And you will rule over the LORD's people and save them from their enemies around them. This will be the sign to you that the LORD has appointed you to be leader over his special possession.* 10:5 Hebrew *Gibeath-haelohim.*

into a different person. ⁷After these signs take place, do what must be done, for God is with you. ⁸Then go down to Gilgal ahead of me. I will join you there to sacrifice burnt offerings and peace offerings. You must wait for seven days until I arrive and give you further instructions."

SAMUEL'S SIGNS ARE FULFILLED

⁹As Saul turned and started to leave, God gave him a new heart, and all Samuel's signs were fulfilled that day. ¹⁰When Saul and his servant arrived at Gibeah, they saw a group of prophets coming toward them. Then the Spirit of God came powerfully upon Saul, and he, too, began to prophesy. ¹¹When those who knew Saul heard about it, they exclaimed, "What? Is even Saul a prophet? How did the son of Kish become a prophet?"

¹²And one of those standing there said, "Can anyone become a prophet, no matter who his father is?"* So that is the origin of the saying "Is even Saul a prophet?"

¹³When Saul had finished prophesying, he went up to the place of worship. ¹⁴"Where have you been?" Saul's uncle asked him and his servant.

"We were looking for the donkeys," Saul replied, "but we couldn't find them. So we went to Samuel to ask him where they were."

¹⁵"Oh? And what did he say?" his uncle asked.

¹⁶"He told us that the donkeys had already been found," Saul replied. But Saul didn't tell his uncle what Samuel said about the kingdom.

SAUL IS ACCLAIMED KING

¹⁷Later Samuel called all the people of Israel to meet before the LORD at Mizpah. ¹⁸And he said, "This is what the LORD, the God of Israel, has declared: I brought you from Egypt and rescued you from the Egyptians and from all of the nations that were oppressing you. ¹⁹But though I have rescued you from your misery and distress, you have rejected your God today and have said, 'No, we want a king instead!' Now, therefore, present yourselves before the LORD by tribes and clans."

²⁰So Samuel brought all the tribes of Israel before the LORD, and the tribe of Benjamin was chosen by lot. ²¹Then he brought each family of the tribe of Benjamin before the LORD, and the family of the Matrites was chosen. And finally Saul son of Kish was chosen from among them. But when they looked for him, he had disappeared! ²²So they asked the LORD, "Where is he?"

And the LORD replied, "He is hiding among the baggage." ²³So they found him and brought him out, and he stood head and shoulders above anyone else.

²⁴Then Samuel said to all the people, "This is the man the LORD has chosen as your king. No one in all Israel is like him!"

And all the people shouted, "Long live the king!"

²⁵Then Samuel told the people what the rights and duties of a king were. He wrote them down on a scroll and placed it before the LORD. Then Samuel sent the people home again.

²⁶When Saul returned to his home at Gibeah, a group of men whose hearts God had touched went with him. ²⁷But there were some scoundrels who complained, "How can this man save us?" And they scorned him and refused to bring him gifts. But Saul ignored them.

[Nahash, king of the Ammonites, had been grievously oppressing the people of Gad and Reuben who lived east of the Jordan River. He gouged out the right eye of each of the Israelites living there, and he didn't allow anyone to come and rescue them. In fact, of all the Israelites east of the Jordan, there wasn't a single one whose right eye Nahash had not gouged out. But there were 7,000 men who had escaped from the Ammonites, and they had settled in Jabesh-gilead.]*

SAUL DEFEATS THE AMMONITES

11 About a month later,* King Nahash of Ammon led his army against the Israelite town of Jabesh-gilead. But all the citizens of Jabesh asked for peace. "Make a treaty with us, and we will be your servants," they pleaded.

²"All right," Nahash said, "but only on one condition. I will gouge out the right eye of every one of you as a disgrace to all Israel!"

³"Give us seven days to send messengers throughout Israel!" replied the elders of Jabesh. "If no one comes to save us, we will agree to your terms."

⁴When the messengers came to Gibeah of Saul and told the people about their plight, everyone broke into tears. ⁵Saul had been plowing a field with his oxen, and when he returned to town, he asked, "What's the matter? Why is everyone crying?" So they told him about the message from Jabesh.

⁶Then the Spirit of God came powerfully upon Saul, and he became very angry. ⁷He took two oxen and cut them into pieces and sent the messengers to carry them throughout Israel with this message: "This is what will happen to the oxen of anyone who refuses to follow Saul and Samuel into battle!" And the LORD made the people afraid of Saul's anger, and all of them came out together as one. ⁸When Saul mobilized them at Bezek, he found that there were 300,000 men from Israel and 30,000* men from Judah.

⁹So Saul sent the messengers back to Jabesh-gilead to say, "We will rescue you by noontime tomorrow!" There was great joy throughout the town when that message arrived!

10:12 Hebrew said, "Who is their father?" 10:27 This paragraph, which is not included in the Masoretic Text, is found in Dead Sea Scroll 4QSamᵃ. 11:1 As in Dead Sea Scroll 4QSamᵃ and Greek version; Masoretic Text lacks About a month later. 11:8 Dead Sea Scrolls and Greek version read 70,000.

CONFIRMATION
1 Samuel 11:8   ROBERT MORRIS

I want you to build a church of 30,000 people, which reaches 300,000 in the Dallas/Fort Worth Metroplex. I also want this church to reach 3 million people in Texas, 30 million people in America, and 300 million people around the world.

God gave me this vision for ministry in a dream one night in 1993. I had been reading through the Bible during my quiet time, and the very next morning I read 1 Samuel 11:8. Immediately, the Lord confirmed in my heart that the dream I had the night before was from Him!

At the time, I was on staff at Shady Grove Church (which is now Gateway Church Grand Prairie Campus), and Pastor Olen Griffing, the founding senior pastor, had been talking to me about being a senior pastor one day. Almost seven years later, I went to the Prayer Center to spend the day with the Lord, and He started speaking to me about planting a church in the Dallas/Fort Worth Metroplex. I shared what the Lord had spoken to me with Pastor Olen. He was disappointed to see me leave but knew it was the Lord. Pastor Olen and the elders gave me their blessing and said I should travel and rest for a season before planting a church. They graciously gave me a two-month sabbatical.

Later that day, I called my friend Pastor Jimmy Evans to let him know I was taking a break and traveling some. I told him I wasn't jumping into a new church plant right away, so I was available if he needed me for any speaking engagements. Pastor Jimmy immediately said, "I want you to travel and speak to our Trinity Fellowship Association of Churches—about 70 churches. Whatever Shady Grove has been paying you, I'll pay you." I had resigned not knowing where my next paycheck was going to come from, and within a few hours, Trinity Fellowship Church hired me at the *exact same salary.*

I obeyed the Lord's leading and stepped out in faith, and God immediately provided. It's as if I had taken a step, but my back foot left before my front foot landed. To me, it was another confirmation the Lord was in the planting of Gateway Church.

[10] The men of Jabesh then told their enemies, "Tomorrow we will come out to you, and you can do to us whatever you wish." [11] But before dawn the next morning, Saul arrived, having divided his army into three detachments. He launched a surprise attack against the Ammonites and slaughtered them the whole morning. The remnant of their army was so badly scattered that no two of them were left together.

[12] Then the people exclaimed to Samuel, "Now where are those men who said, 'Why should Saul rule over us?' Bring them here, and we will kill them!"

[13] But Saul replied, "No one will be executed today, for today the LORD has rescued Israel!"

[14] Then Samuel said to the people, "Come, let us all go to Gilgal to renew the kingdom." [15] So they all went to Gilgal, and in a solemn ceremony before the LORD they made Saul king. Then they offered peace offerings to the LORD, and Saul and all the Israelites were filled with joy.

SAMUEL'S FAREWELL ADDRESS

12 Then Samuel addressed all Israel: "I have done as you asked and given you a king. [2] Your king is now your leader. I stand here before you—an old, gray-haired man—and my sons serve you. I have served as your leader from the time I was a boy to this very day. [3] Now testify against me in the presence of the LORD and before his anointed one. Whose ox or donkey have I stolen? Have I ever cheated any of you? Have I ever oppressed you? Have I ever taken a bribe and perverted justice? Tell me and I will make right whatever I have done wrong."

[4] "No," they replied, "you have never cheated or oppressed us, and you have never taken even a single bribe."

[5] "The LORD and his anointed one are my witnesses today," Samuel declared, "that my hands are clean."

"Yes, he is a witness," they replied.

[6] "It was the LORD who appointed Moses and Aaron," Samuel continued. "He brought your ancestors out of the land of Egypt. [7] Now stand here quietly before the LORD as I remind you of all the great things the LORD has done for you and your ancestors.

[8] "When the Israelites were* in Egypt and cried out to the LORD, he sent Moses and Aaron to rescue them from Egypt and to bring them into this land. [9] But the people soon forgot about the LORD their God, so he handed them over to Sisera, the commander of Hazor's army, and also to the Philistines and to the king of Moab, who fought against them.

[10] "Then they cried to the LORD again and confessed, 'We have sinned by turning away from the LORD and worshiping the images of Baal and Ashtoreth. But we will worship you and you alone if you will rescue us from our enemies.' [11] Then the LORD sent Gideon,* Bedan,* Jephthah, and Samuel* to save you, and you lived in safety.

12:8 Hebrew *When Jacob was.* The names "Jacob" and "Israel" are often interchanged throughout the Old Testament, referring sometimes to the individual patriarch and sometimes to the nation. 12:11a Hebrew *Jerub-baal,* another name for Gideon; see Judg 6:32. 12:11b Greek and Syriac versions read *Barak.* 12:11c Greek and Syriac versions read *Samson.*

¹² "But when you were afraid of Nahash, the king of Ammon, you came to me and said that you wanted a king to reign over you, even though the LORD your God was already your king. ¹³ All right, here is the king you have chosen. You asked for him, and the LORD has granted your request.

¹⁴ "Now if you fear and worship the LORD and listen to his voice, and if you do not rebel against the LORD's commands, then both you and your king will show that you recognize the LORD as your God. ¹⁵ But if you rebel against the LORD's commands and refuse to listen to him, then his hand will be as heavy upon you as it was upon your ancestors.

¹⁶ "Now stand here and see the great thing the LORD is about to do. ¹⁷ You know that it does not rain at this time of the year during the wheat harvest. I will ask the LORD to send thunder and rain today. Then you will realize how wicked you have been in asking the LORD for a king!"

¹⁸ So Samuel called to the LORD, and the LORD sent thunder and rain that day. And all the people were terrified of the LORD and of Samuel. ¹⁹ "Pray to the LORD your God for us, or we will die!" they all said to Samuel. "For now we have added to our sins by asking for a king."

²⁰ "Don't be afraid," Samuel reassured them. "You have certainly done wrong, but make sure now that you worship the LORD with all your heart, and don't turn your back on him. ²¹ Don't go back to worshiping worthless idols that cannot help or rescue you—they are totally useless! ²² The LORD will not abandon his people, because that would dishonor his great name. For it has pleased the LORD to make you his very own people.

²³ "As for me, I will certainly not sin against the LORD by ending my prayers for you. And I will continue to teach you what is good and right. ²⁴ But be sure to fear the LORD and faithfully serve him. Think of all the wonderful things he has done for you. ²⁵ But if you continue to sin, you and your king will be swept away."

CONTINUED WAR WITH PHILISTIA

13 Saul was thirty* years old when he became king, and he reigned for forty-two years.* ² Saul selected 3,000 special troops from the army of Israel and sent the rest of the men home. He took 2,000 of the chosen men with him to Micmash and the hill country of Bethel. The other 1,000 went with Saul's son Jonathan to Gibeah in the land of Benjamin.

³ Soon after this, Jonathan attacked and defeated the garrison of Philistines at Geba. The news spread quickly among the Philistines. So Saul blew the ram's horn throughout the land, saying, "Hebrews, hear this! Rise up in revolt!" ⁴ All Israel heard the news that Saul had destroyed the Philistine garrison at Geba and that the Philistines now hated the Israelites more than ever. So the entire Israelite army was summoned to join Saul at Gilgal.

⁵ The Philistines mustered a mighty army of 3,000* chariots, 6,000 charioteers, and as many warriors as the grains of sand on the seashore! They camped at Micmash east of Beth-aven. ⁶ The men of Israel saw what a tight spot they were in; and because they were hard pressed by the enemy, they tried to hide in caves, thickets, rocks, holes, and cisterns. ⁷ Some of them crossed the Jordan River and escaped into the land of Gad and Gilead.

SAUL'S DISOBEDIENCE AND SAMUEL'S REBUKE

Meanwhile, Saul stayed at Gilgal, and his men were trembling with fear. ⁸ Saul waited there seven days for Samuel, as Samuel had instructed him earlier, but Samuel still didn't come. Saul realized that his troops were rapidly slipping away. ⁹ So he demanded, "Bring me the burnt offering and the peace offerings!" And Saul sacrificed the burnt offering himself.

¹⁰ Just as Saul was finishing with the burnt offering, Samuel arrived. Saul went out to meet and welcome him, ¹¹ but Samuel said, "What is this you have done?"

Saul replied, "I saw my men scattering from me, and you didn't arrive when you said you would, and the Philistines are at Micmash ready for battle. ¹² So I said, 'The Philistines are ready to march against us at Gilgal, and I haven't even

13:1a As in a few Greek manuscripts; the number is missing in the Hebrew. 13:1b Hebrew *reigned . . . and two;* the number is incomplete in the Hebrew. Compare Acts 13:21. 13:5 As in Greek and Syriac versions; Hebrew reads *30,000.*

asked for the Lord's help!' So I felt compelled to offer the burnt offering myself before you came."

¹³"How foolish!" Samuel exclaimed. "You have not kept the command the Lord your God gave you. Had you kept it, the Lord would have established your kingdom over Israel forever. ¹⁴But now your kingdom must end, for the Lord has sought out a man after his own heart. The Lord has already appointed him to be the leader of his people, because you have not kept the Lord's command."

ISRAEL'S MILITARY DISADVANTAGE

¹⁵Samuel then left Gilgal and went on his way, but the rest of the troops went with Saul to meet the army. They went up from Gilgal to Gibeah in the land of Benjamin.* When Saul counted the men who were still with him, he found only 600 were left! ¹⁶Saul and Jonathan and the troops with them were staying at Geba in the land of Benjamin. The Philistines set up their camp at Micmash. ¹⁷Three raiding parties soon left the camp of the Philistines. One went north toward Ophrah in the land of Shual, ¹⁸another went west to Beth-horon, and the third moved toward the border above the valley of Zeboim near the wilderness.

¹⁹There were no blacksmiths in the land of Israel in those days. The Philistines wouldn't allow them for fear they would make swords and spears for the Hebrews. ²⁰So whenever the Israelites needed to sharpen their plowshares, picks, axes, or sickles,* they had to take them to a Philistine blacksmith. ²¹The charges were as follows: a quarter of an ounce* of silver for sharpening a plowshare or a pick, and an eighth of an ounce* for sharpening an ax or making the point of an ox goad. ²²So on the day of the battle none of the people of Israel had a sword or spear, except for Saul and Jonathan.

²³The pass at Micmash had meanwhile been secured by a contingent of the Philistine army.

JONATHAN'S DARING PLAN

14 One day Jonathan said to his armor bearer, "Come on, let's go over to where the Philistines have their outpost." But Jonathan did not tell his father what he was doing.

²Meanwhile, Saul and his 600 men were camped on the outskirts of Gibeah, around the pomegranate tree* at Migron. ³Among Saul's men was Ahijah the priest, who was wearing the ephod, the priestly vest. Ahijah was the son of Ichabod's brother Ahitub, son of Phinehas, son of Eli, the priest of the Lord who had served at Shiloh.

No one realized that Jonathan had left the Israelite camp. ⁴To reach the Philistine outpost, Jonathan had to go down between two rocky cliffs that were called Bozez and Seneh. ⁵The cliff on the north was in front of Micmash, and the one on the south was in front of Geba. ⁶"Let's go across to the outpost of those pagans," Jonathan said to his armor bearer. "Perhaps the Lord will help us, for nothing can hinder the Lord. He can win a battle whether he has many warriors or only a few!"

⁷"Do what you think is best," the armor bearer replied. "I'm with you completely, whatever you decide."

⁸"All right, then," Jonathan told him. "We will cross over and let them see us. ⁹If they say to us, 'Stay where you are or we'll kill you,' then we will stop and not go up to them. ¹⁰But if they say, 'Come on up and fight,' then we will go up. That will be the Lord's sign that he will help us defeat them."

¹¹When the Philistines saw them coming, they shouted, "Look! The Hebrews are crawling out of their holes!" ¹²Then the men from the outpost shouted to Jonathan, "Come on up here, and we'll teach you a lesson!"

"Come on, climb right behind me," Jonathan said to his armor bearer, "for the Lord will help us defeat them!"

¹³So they climbed up using both hands and feet, and the Philistines fell before Jonathan, and his armor bearer killed those who came behind them. ¹⁴They killed some twenty men in all, and their bodies were scattered over about half an acre.*

¹⁵Suddenly, panic broke out in the Philistine army, both in the camp and in the field, including even the outposts and raiding parties. And just then an earthquake struck, and everyone was terrified.

ISRAEL DEFEATS THE PHILISTINES

¹⁶Saul's lookouts in Gibeah of Benjamin saw a strange sight—the vast army of Philistines began to melt away in every direction.* ¹⁷"Call the roll and find out who's missing," Saul ordered. And when they checked, they found that Jonathan and his armor bearer were gone.

¹⁸Then Saul shouted to Ahijah, "Bring the ephod here!" For at that time Ahijah was wearing the ephod in front of the Israelites.* ¹⁹But while Saul was talking to the priest, the confusion in the Philistine camp grew louder and louder. So Saul said to the priest, "Never mind; let's get going!"*

²⁰Then Saul and all his men rushed out to the battle and found the Philistines killing each other. There was terrible confusion everywhere. ²¹Even the Hebrews who had previously gone over to the Philistine army revolted and joined in with Saul, Jonathan, and the rest of the Israelites. ²²Likewise, the men of Israel who were hiding in the hill country of Ephraim joined the

13:15 As in Greek version; Hebrew reads *Samuel then left Gilgal and went to Gibeah in the land of Benjamin.* 13:20 As in Greek version; Hebrew reads or *plowshares.* 13:21a Hebrew *1 pim* [8 grams]. 13:21b Hebrew *⅓ [of a shekel]* [4 grams]. 14:2 Or *around the rock of Rimmon;* compare Judg 20:45, 47; 21:13. 14:14 Hebrew *half a yoke;* a "yoke" was the amount of land plowed by a pair of yoked oxen in one day. 14:16 As in Greek version; Hebrew reads *they went and there.* 14:18 As in some Greek manuscripts; Hebrew reads *"Bring the Ark of God." For at that time the Ark of God was with the Israelites.* 14:19 Hebrew *Withdraw your hand.*

chase when they saw the Philistines running away. ²³So the LORD saved Israel that day, and the battle continued to rage even beyond Beth-aven.

SAUL'S FOOLISH OATH

²⁴Now the men of Israel were pressed to exhaustion that day, because Saul had placed them under an oath, saying, "Let a curse fall on anyone who eats before evening—before I have full revenge on my enemies." So no one ate anything all day, ²⁵even though they had all found honeycomb on the ground in the forest. ²⁶They didn't dare touch the honey because they all feared the oath they had taken.

²⁷But Jonathan had not heard his father's command, and he dipped the end of his stick into a piece of honeycomb and ate the honey. After he had eaten it, he felt refreshed.* ²⁸But one of the men saw him and said, "Your father made the army take a strict oath that anyone who eats food today will be cursed. That is why everyone is weary and faint."

²⁹"My father has made trouble for us all!" Jonathan exclaimed. "A command like that only hurts us. See how refreshed I am now that I have eaten this little bit of honey. ³⁰If the men had been allowed to eat freely from the food they found among our enemies, think how many more Philistines we could have killed!"

³¹They chased and killed the Philistines all day from Micmash to Aijalon, growing more and more faint. ³²That evening they rushed for the battle plunder and butchered the sheep, goats, cattle, and calves, but they ate them without draining the blood. ³³Someone reported to Saul, "Look, the men are sinning against the LORD by eating meat that still has blood in it."

"That is very wrong," Saul said. "Find a large stone and roll it over here. ³⁴Then go out among the troops and tell them, 'Bring the cattle, sheep, and goats here to me. Kill them here, and drain the blood before you eat them. Do not sin against the LORD by eating meat with the blood still in it.'"

So that night all the troops brought their animals and slaughtered them there. ³⁵Then Saul built an altar to the LORD; it was the first of the altars he built to the LORD.

³⁶Then Saul said, "Let's chase the Philistines all night and plunder them until sunrise. Let's destroy every last one of them."

His men replied, "We'll do whatever you think is best."

But the priest said, "Let's ask God first."

³⁷So Saul asked God, "Should we go after the Philistines? Will you help us defeat them?" But God made no reply that day.

³⁸Then Saul said to the leaders, "Something's wrong! I want all my army commanders to come here. We must find out what sin was committed today. ³⁹I vow by the name of the LORD who rescued Israel that the sinner will surely die, even

if it is my own son Jonathan!" But no one would tell him what the trouble was.

⁴⁰Then Saul said, "Jonathan and I will stand over here, and all of you stand over there."

And the people responded to Saul, "Whatever you think is best."

⁴¹Then Saul prayed, "O LORD, God of Israel, please show us who is guilty and who is innocent.*" Then they cast sacred lots, and Jonathan and Saul were chosen as the guilty ones, and the people were declared innocent.

⁴²Then Saul said, "Now cast lots again and choose between me and Jonathan." And Jonathan was shown to be the guilty one.

⁴³"Tell me what you have done," Saul demanded of Jonathan.

"I tasted a little honey," Jonathan admitted. "It was only a little bit on the end of my stick. Does that deserve death?"

⁴⁴"Yes, Jonathan," Saul said, "you must die! May God strike me and even kill me if you do not die for this."

⁴⁵But the people broke in and said to Saul, "Jonathan has won this great victory for Israel. Should he die? Far from it! As surely as the LORD lives, not one hair on his head will be touched, for God helped him do a great deed today." So the people rescued Jonathan, and he was not put to death.

⁴⁶Then Saul called back the army from chasing the Philistines, and the Philistines returned home.

SAUL'S MILITARY SUCCESSES

⁴⁷Now when Saul had secured his grasp on Israel's throne, he fought against his enemies in every direction—against Moab, Ammon, Edom, the kings of Zobah, and the Philistines. And wherever he turned, he was victorious.* ⁴⁸He performed great deeds and conquered the Amalekites, saving Israel from all those who had plundered them.

⁴⁹Saul's sons included Jonathan, Ishbosheth,* and Malkishua. He also had two daughters: Merab, who was older, and Michal. ⁵⁰Saul's wife was Ahinoam, the daughter of Ahimaaz. The commander of Saul's army was Abner, the son of Saul's uncle Ner. ⁵¹Saul's father, Kish, and Abner's father, Ner, were both sons of Abiel.

⁵²The Israelites fought constantly with the Philistines throughout Saul's lifetime. So whenever Saul observed a young man who was brave and strong, he drafted him into his army.

SAUL DEFEATS THE AMALEKITES

15 One day Samuel said to Saul, "It was the LORD who told me to anoint you as king of his people, Israel. Now listen to this message

---

14:27 Or *his eyes brightened;* similarly in 14:29.   14:41 Greek version adds *If the fault is with me or my son Jonathan, respond with Urim; but if the men of Israel are at fault, respond with Thummim.*   14:47 As in Greek version; Hebrew reads *he acted wickedly.*   14:49 Hebrew *Ishvi,* a variant name for Ishbosheth; also known as Esh-baal.

from the LORD! [2] This is what the LORD of Heaven's Armies has declared: I have decided to settle accounts with the nation of Amalek for opposing Israel when they came from Egypt. [3] Now go and completely destroy* the entire Amalekite nation—men, women, children, babies, cattle, sheep, goats, camels, and donkeys."

[4] So Saul mobilized his army at Telaim. There were 200,000 soldiers from Israel and 10,000 men from Judah. [5] Then Saul and his army went to a town of the Amalekites and lay in wait in the valley. [6] Saul sent this warning to the Kenites: "Move away from where the Amalekites live, or you will die with them. For you showed kindness to all the people of Israel when they came up from Egypt." So the Kenites packed up and left.

[7] Then Saul slaughtered the Amalekites from Havilah all the way to Shur, east of Egypt. [8] He captured Agag, the Amalekite king, but completely destroyed everyone else. [9] Saul and his men spared Agag's life and kept the best of the sheep and goats, the cattle, the fat calves, and the lambs—everything, in fact, that appealed to them. They destroyed only what was worthless or of poor quality.

THE LORD REJECTS SAUL

[10] Then the LORD said to Samuel, [11] "I am sorry that I ever made Saul king, for he has not been loyal to me and has refused to obey my command." Samuel was so deeply moved when he heard this that he cried out to the LORD all night.

[12] Early the next morning Samuel went to find Saul. Someone told him, "Saul went to the town of Carmel to set up a monument to himself; then he went on to Gilgal."

[13] When Samuel finally found him, Saul greeted him cheerfully. "May the LORD bless you," he said. "I have carried out the LORD's command!"

[14] "Then what is all the bleating of sheep and goats and the lowing of cattle I hear?" Samuel demanded.

[15] "It's true that the army spared the best of the sheep, goats, and cattle," Saul admitted. "But they are going to sacrifice them to the LORD your God. We have destroyed everything else."

[16] Then Samuel said to Saul, "Stop! Listen to what the LORD told me last night!"

"What did he tell you?" Saul asked.

[17] And Samuel told him, "Although you may think little of yourself, are you not the leader of the tribes of Israel? The LORD has anointed you king of Israel. [18] And the LORD sent you on a mission and told you, 'Go and completely destroy the sinners, the Amalekites, until they are all dead.' [19] Why haven't you obeyed the LORD? Why did you rush for the plunder and do what was evil in the LORD's sight?"

[20] "But I did obey the LORD," Saul insisted. "I carried out the mission he gave me. I brought back King Agag, but I destroyed everyone else.

[21] Then my troops brought in the best of the sheep, goats, cattle, and plunder to sacrifice to the LORD your God in Gilgal."

[22] But Samuel replied,

"What is more pleasing to the LORD:
    your burnt offerings and sacrifices
    or your obedience to his voice?
Listen! Obedience is better than sacrifice,
    and submission is better than offering
        the fat of rams.
[23] Rebellion is as sinful as witchcraft,
    and stubbornness as bad as
        worshiping idols.
So because you have rejected the command
        of the LORD,
    he has rejected you as king."

SAUL PLEADS FOR FORGIVENESS

[24] Then Saul admitted to Samuel, "Yes, I have sinned. I have disobeyed your instructions and the LORD's command, for I was afraid of the people and did what they demanded. [25] But now, please forgive my sin and come back with me so that I may worship the LORD."

[26] But Samuel replied, "I will not go back with you! Since you have rejected the LORD's command, he has rejected you as king of Israel."

[27] As Samuel turned to go, Saul tried to hold him back and tore the hem of his robe. [28] And Samuel said to him, "The LORD has torn the kingdom of Israel from you today and has given it to someone else—one who is better than you. [29] And he who is the Glory of Israel will not lie, nor will he change his mind, for he is not human that he should change his mind!"

[30] Then Saul pleaded again, "I know I have sinned. But please, at least honor me before the elders of my people and before Israel by coming back with me so that I may worship the LORD your God." [31] So Samuel finally agreed and went back with him, and Saul worshiped the LORD.

SAMUEL EXECUTES KING AGAG

[32] Then Samuel said, "Bring King Agag to me." Agag arrived full of hope, for he thought, "Surely the worst is over, and I have been spared!"* [33] But Samuel said, "As your sword has killed the sons of many mothers, now your mother will be childless." And Samuel cut Agag to pieces before the LORD at Gilgal.

[34] Then Samuel went home to Ramah, and Saul returned to his house at Gibeah of Saul. [35] Samuel never went to meet with Saul again, but he mourned constantly for him. And the LORD was sorry he had ever made Saul king of Israel.

15:3 The Hebrew term used here refers to the complete consecration of things or people to the LORD, either by destroying them or by giving them as an offering; also in 15:8, 9, 15, 18, 20, 21. 15:32 Dead Sea Scrolls and Greek version read *Agag arrived hesitantly, for he thought, "Surely this is the bitterness of death."*

SAMUEL ANOINTS DAVID AS KING

16 Now the LORD said to Samuel, "You have mourned long enough for Saul. I have rejected him as king of Israel, so fill your flask with olive oil and go to Bethlehem. Find a man named Jesse who lives there, for I have selected one of his sons to be my king."

2 But Samuel asked, "How can I do that? If Saul hears about it, he will kill me."

"Take a heifer with you," the LORD replied, "and say that you have come to make a sacrifice to the LORD. 3 Invite Jesse to the sacrifice, and I will show you which of his sons to anoint for me."

4 So Samuel did as the LORD instructed. When he arrived at Bethlehem, the elders of the town came trembling to meet him. "What's wrong?" they asked. "Do you come in peace?"

5 "Yes," Samuel replied. "I have come to sacrifice to the LORD. Purify yourselves and come with me to the sacrifice." Then Samuel performed the purification rite for Jesse and his sons and invited them to the sacrifice, too.

6 When they arrived, Samuel took one look at Eliab and thought, "Surely this is the LORD's anointed!"

7 But the LORD said to Samuel, "Don't judge by his appearance or height, for I have rejected him. The LORD doesn't see things the way you see them. People judge by outward appearance, but the LORD looks at the heart."

8 Then Jesse told his son Abinadab to step forward and walk in front of Samuel. But Samuel said, "This is not the one the LORD has chosen." 9 Next Jesse summoned Shimea,* but Samuel said, "Neither is this the one the LORD has chosen." 10 In the same way all seven of Jesse's sons were presented to Samuel. But Samuel said to Jesse, "The LORD has not chosen any of these." 11 Then Samuel asked, "Are these all the sons you have?"

"There is still the youngest," Jesse replied. "But he's out in the fields watching the sheep and goats."

"Send for him at once," Samuel said. "We will not sit down to eat until he arrives."

12 So Jesse sent for him. He was dark and handsome, with beautiful eyes.

And the LORD said, "This is the one; anoint him."

13 So as David stood there among his brothers, Samuel took the flask of olive oil he had brought and anointed David with the oil. And the Spirit of the LORD came powerfully upon David from that day on. Then Samuel returned to Ramah.

DAVID SERVES IN SAUL'S COURT

14 Now the Spirit of the LORD had left Saul, and the LORD sent a tormenting spirit* that filled him with depression and fear.

15 Some of Saul's servants said to him, "A tormenting spirit from God is troubling you. 16 Let us find a good musician to play the harp whenever the tormenting spirit troubles you. He will play soothing music, and you will soon be well again."

17 "All right," Saul said. "Find me someone who plays well, and bring him here."

18 One of the servants said to Saul, "One of Jesse's sons from Bethlehem is a talented harp player. Not only that—he is a brave warrior, a man of war, and has good judgment. He is also a fine-looking young man, and the LORD is with him."

19 So Saul sent messengers to Jesse to say, "Send me your son David, the shepherd." 20 Jesse responded by sending David to Saul, along with a young goat, a donkey loaded with bread, and a wineskin full of wine.

21 So David went to Saul and began serving him. Saul loved David very much, and David became his armor bearer.

22 Then Saul sent word to Jesse asking, "Please let David remain in my service, for I am very pleased with him."

23 And whenever the tormenting spirit from God troubled Saul, David would play the harp. Then Saul would feel better, and the tormenting spirit would go away.

GOLIATH CHALLENGES THE ISRAELITES

17 The Philistines now mustered their army for battle and camped between Socoh in Judah and Azekah at Ephes-dammim. 2 Saul countered by gathering his Israelite troops near the valley of Elah. 3 So the Philistines and Israelites faced each other on opposite hills, with the valley between them.

4 Then Goliath, a Philistine champion from Gath, came out of the Philistine ranks to face the forces of Israel. He was over nine feet* tall! 5 He wore a bronze helmet, and his bronze coat of mail weighed 125 pounds.* 6 He also wore bronze leg armor, and he carried a bronze javelin on his shoulder. 7 The shaft of his spear was as heavy and thick as a weaver's beam, tipped with an iron spearhead that weighed 15 pounds.* His armor bearer walked ahead of him carrying a shield.

8 Goliath stood and shouted a taunt across to the Israelites. "Why are you all coming out to fight?" he called. "I am the Philistine champion, but you are only the servants of Saul. Choose one man to come down here and fight me! 9 If he kills me, then we will be your slaves. But if I kill him, you will be our slaves! 10 I defy the armies of Israel today! Send me a man who will fight me!" 11 When Saul and the Israelites heard this, they were terrified and deeply shaken.

16:9 Hebrew *Shammah*, a variant spelling of Shimea; compare 1 Chr 2:13; 20:7.   16:14 Or *an evil spirit;* also in 16:15, 16, 23.   17:4 Hebrew *6 cubits and 1 span* [which totals about 9.75 feet or 3 meters]; Dead Sea Scrolls and Greek version read *4 cubits and 1 span* [which totals about 6.75 feet or 2 meters].   17:5 Hebrew *5,000 shekels* [57 kilograms].   17:7 Hebrew *600 shekels* [6.8 kilograms].

JESSE SENDS DAVID TO SAUL'S CAMP

¹²Now David was the son of a man named Jesse, an Ephrathite from Bethlehem in the land of Judah. Jesse was an old man at that time, and he had eight sons. ¹³Jesse's three oldest sons—Eliab, Abinadab, and Shimea*—had already joined Saul's army to fight the Philistines. ¹⁴David was the youngest son. David's three oldest brothers stayed with Saul's army, ¹⁵but David went back and forth so he could help his father with the sheep in Bethlehem.

¹⁶For forty days, every morning and evening, the Philistine champion strutted in front of the Israelite army.

¹⁷One day Jesse said to David, "Take this basket* of roasted grain and these ten loaves of bread, and carry them quickly to your brothers. ¹⁸And give these ten cuts of cheese to their captain. See how your brothers are getting along, and bring back a report on how they are doing.*" ¹⁹David's brothers were with Saul and the Israelite army at the valley of Elah, fighting against the Philistines.

²⁰So David left the sheep with another shepherd and set out early the next morning with the gifts, as Jesse had directed him. He arrived at the camp just as the Israelite army was leaving for the battlefield with shouts and battle cries. ²¹Soon the Israelite and Philistine forces stood facing each other, army against army. ²²David left his things with the keeper of supplies and hurried out to the ranks to greet his brothers. ²³As he was talking with them, Goliath, the Philistine champion from Gath, came out from the Philistine ranks. Then David heard him shout his usual taunt to the army of Israel.

²⁴As soon as the Israelite army saw him, they began to run away in fright. ²⁵"Have you seen the giant?" the men asked. "He comes out each day to defy Israel. The king has offered a huge reward to anyone who kills him. He will give that man one of his daughters for a wife, and the man's entire family will be exempted from paying taxes!"

²⁶David asked the soldiers standing nearby, "What will a man get for killing this Philistine and ending his defiance of Israel? Who is this pagan Philistine anyway, that he is allowed to defy the armies of the living God?"

²⁷And these men gave David the same reply. They said, "Yes, that is the reward for killing him."

²⁸But when David's oldest brother, Eliab, heard David talking to the men, he was angry. "What are you doing around here anyway?" he demanded. "What about those few sheep you're supposed to be taking care of? I know about your pride and deceit. You just want to see the battle!"

²⁹"What have I done now?" David replied. "I was only asking a question!" ³⁰He walked over to some others and asked them the same thing and received the same answer. ³¹Then David's

question was reported to King Saul, and the king sent for him.

DAVID KILLS GOLIATH

³²"Don't worry about this Philistine," David told Saul. "I'll go fight him!"

³³"Don't be ridiculous!" Saul replied. "There's no way you can fight this Philistine and possibly win! You're only a boy, and he's been a man of war since his youth."

³⁴But David persisted. "I have been taking care of my father's sheep and goats," he said. "When a lion or a bear comes to steal a lamb from the flock, ³⁵I go after it with a club and rescue the lamb from its mouth. If the animal turns on me, I catch it by the jaw and club it to death. ³⁶I have done this to both lions and bears, and I'll do it to this pagan Philistine, too, for he has defied the armies of the living God! ³⁷The LORD who rescued me from the claws of the lion and the bear will rescue me from this Philistine!"

Saul finally consented. "All right, go ahead," he said. "And may the LORD be with you!"

³⁸Then Saul gave David his own armor—a bronze helmet and a coat of mail. ³⁹David put it on, strapped the sword over it, and took a step or two to see what it was like, for he had never worn such things before.

"I can't go in these," he protested to Saul. "I'm not used to them." So David took them off again. ⁴⁰He picked up five smooth stones from a stream and put them into his shepherd's bag. Then, armed only with his shepherd's staff and sling, he started across the valley to fight the Philistine.

⁴¹Goliath walked out toward David with his shield bearer ahead of him, ⁴²sneering in contempt at this ruddy-faced boy. ⁴³"Am I a dog," he roared at David, "that you come at me with a stick?" And he cursed David by the names of his gods. ⁴⁴"Come over here, and I'll give your flesh to the birds and wild animals!" Goliath yelled.

⁴⁵David replied to the Philistine, "You come to me with sword, spear, and javelin, but I come to you in the name of the LORD of Heaven's Armies—the God of the armies of Israel, whom you have defied. ⁴⁶Today the LORD will conquer you, and I will kill you and cut off your head. And then I will give the dead bodies of your men to the birds and wild animals, and the whole world will know that there is a God in Israel! ⁴⁷And everyone assembled here will know that the LORD rescues his people, but not with sword and spear. This is the LORD's battle, and he will give you to us!"

⁴⁸As Goliath moved closer to attack, David quickly ran out to meet him. ⁴⁹Reaching into his shepherd's bag and taking out a stone, he hurled it with his sling and hit the Philistine in the forehead. The stone sank in, and Goliath stumbled and fell face down on the ground.

17:13 Hebrew *Shammah*, a variant spelling of Shimea; compare 1 Chr 2:13; 20:7. 17:17 Hebrew *ephah* [20 quarts or 22 liters]. 17:18 Hebrew *and take their pledge*.

⁵⁰So David triumphed over the Philistine with only a sling and a stone, for he had no sword. ⁵¹Then David ran over and pulled Goliath's sword from its sheath. David used it to kill him and cut off his head.

ISRAEL ROUTS THE PHILISTINES

When the Philistines saw that their champion was dead, they turned and ran. ⁵²Then the men of Israel and Judah gave a great shout of triumph and rushed after the Philistines, chasing them as far as Gath* and the gates of Ekron. The bodies of the dead and wounded Philistines were strewn all along the road from Shaaraim, as far as Gath and Ekron. ⁵³Then the Israelite army returned and plundered the deserted Philistine camp. ⁵⁴(David took the Philistine's head to Jerusalem, but he stored the man's armor in his own tent.)

⁵⁵As Saul watched David go out to fight the Philistine, he asked Abner, the commander of his army, "Abner, whose son is this young man?"

"I really don't know," Abner declared.

⁵⁶"Well, find out who he is!" the king told him.

⁵⁷As soon as David returned from killing Goliath, Abner brought him to Saul with the Philistine's head still in his hand. ⁵⁸"Tell me about your father, young man," Saul said.

And David replied, "His name is Jesse, and we live in Bethlehem."

SAUL BECOMES JEALOUS OF DAVID

18 After David had finished talking with Saul, he met Jonathan, the king's son. There was an immediate bond between them, for Jonathan loved David. ²From that day on Saul kept David with him and wouldn't let him return home. ³And Jonathan made a solemn pact with David, because he loved him as he loved himself. ⁴Jonathan sealed the pact by taking off his robe and giving it to David, together with his tunic, sword, bow, and belt.

⁵Whatever Saul asked David to do, David did it successfully. So Saul made him a commander over the men of war, an appointment that was welcomed by the people and Saul's officers alike.

⁶When the victorious Israelite army was returning home after David had killed the Philistine, women from all the towns of Israel came out to meet King Saul. They sang and danced for joy with tambourines and cymbals.* ⁷This was their song:

"Saul has killed his thousands,
    and David his ten thousands!"

⁸This made Saul very angry. "What's this?" he said. "They credit David with ten thousands and me with only thousands. Next they'll be making him their king!" ⁹So from that time on Saul kept a jealous eye on David.

¹⁰The very next day a tormenting spirit* from God overwhelmed Saul, and he began to rave in his house like a madman. David was playing the harp, as he did each day. But Saul had a spear in his hand, ¹¹and he suddenly hurled it at David, intending to pin him to the wall. But David escaped him twice.

¹²Saul was then afraid of David, for the LORD was with David and had turned away from Saul. ¹³Finally, Saul sent him away and appointed him commander over 1,000 men, and David faithfully led his troops into battle.

¹⁴David continued to succeed in everything he did, for the LORD was with him. ¹⁵When Saul recognized this, he became even more afraid of him. ¹⁶But all Israel and Judah loved David because he was so successful at leading his troops into battle.

DAVID MARRIES SAUL'S DAUGHTER

¹⁷One day Saul said to David, "I am ready to give you my older daughter, Merab, as your wife. But first you must prove yourself to be a real warrior by fighting the LORD's battles." For Saul thought, "I'll send him out against the Philistines and let them kill him rather than doing it myself."

¹⁸"Who am I, and what is my family in Israel that I should be the king's son-in-law?" David exclaimed. "My father's family is nothing!" ¹⁹So* when the time came for Saul to give his daughter Merab in marriage to David, he gave her instead to Adriel, a man from Meholah.

²⁰In the meantime, Saul's daughter Michal had fallen in love with David, and Saul was delighted when he heard about it. ²¹"Here's another chance to see him killed by the Philistines!" Saul said to himself. But to David he said, "Today you have a second chance to become my son-in-law!"

²²Then Saul told his men to say to David, "The king really likes you, and so do we. Why don't you accept the king's offer and become his son-in-law?"

²³When Saul's men said these things to David, he replied, "How can a poor man from a humble family afford the bride price for the daughter of a king?"

²⁴When Saul's men reported this back to the king, ²⁵he told them, "Tell David that all I want for the bride price is 100 Philistine foreskins! Vengeance on my enemies is all I really want." But what Saul had in mind was that David would be killed in the fight.

²⁶David was delighted to accept the offer. Before the time limit expired, ²⁷he and his men went out and killed 200 Philistines. Then David fulfilled the king's requirement by presenting all their foreskins to him. So Saul gave his daughter Michal to David to be his wife.

²⁸When Saul realized that the LORD was with David and how much his daughter Michal loved him, ²⁹Saul became even more afraid of him, and he remained David's enemy for the rest of his life.

17:52 As in some Greek manuscripts; Hebrew reads *a valley*.
18:6 The type of instrument represented by the word *cymbals* is uncertain.   18:10 Or *an evil spirit*.   18:19 Or *But*.

³⁰Every time the commanders of the Philistines attacked, David was more successful against them than all the rest of Saul's officers. So David's name became very famous.

SAUL TRIES TO KILL DAVID

19 Saul now urged his servants and his son Jonathan to assassinate David. But Jonathan, because of his strong affection for David, ²told him what his father was planning. "Tomorrow morning," he warned him, "you must find a hiding place out in the fields. ³I'll ask my father to go out there with me, and I'll talk to him about you. Then I'll tell you everything I can find out."

⁴The next morning Jonathan spoke with his father about David, saying many good things about him. "The king must not sin against his servant David," Jonathan said. "He's never done anything to harm you. He has always helped you in any way he could. ⁵Have you forgotten about the time he risked his life to kill the Philistine giant and how the LORD brought a great victory to all Israel as a result? You were certainly happy about it then. Why should you murder an innocent man like David? There is no reason for it at all!"

⁶So Saul listened to Jonathan and vowed, "As surely as the LORD lives, David will not be killed."

⁷Afterward Jonathan called David and told him what had happened. Then he brought David to Saul, and David served in the court as before.

⁸War broke out again after that, and David led his troops against the Philistines. He attacked them with such fury that they all ran away.

⁹But one day when Saul was sitting at home, with spear in hand, the tormenting spirit* from the LORD suddenly came upon him again. As David played his harp, ¹⁰Saul hurled his spear at David. But David dodged out of the way, and leaving the spear stuck in the wall, he fled and escaped into the night.

MICHAL SAVES DAVID'S LIFE

¹¹Then Saul sent troops to watch David's house. They were told to kill David when he came out the next morning. But Michal, David's wife, warned him, "If you don't escape tonight, you will be dead by morning." ¹²So she helped him climb out through a window, and he fled and escaped. ¹³Then she took an idol* and put it in his bed, covered it with blankets, and put a cushion of goat's hair at its head.

¹⁴When the troops came to arrest David, she told them he was sick and couldn't get out of bed. ¹⁵But Saul sent the troops back to get David. He ordered, "Bring him to me in his bed so I can kill him!" ¹⁶But when they came to carry David out, they discovered that it was only an idol in the bed with a cushion of goat's hair at its head.

¹⁷"Why have you betrayed me like this and let my enemy escape?" Saul demanded of Michal.

"I had to," Michal replied. "He threatened to kill me if I didn't help him."

¹⁸So David escaped and went to Ramah to see Samuel, and he told him all that Saul had done to him. Then Samuel took David with him to live at Naioth. ¹⁹When the report reached Saul that David was at Naioth in Ramah, ²⁰he sent troops to capture him. But when they arrived and saw Samuel leading a group of prophets who were prophesying, the Spirit of God came upon Saul's men, and they also began to prophesy. ²¹When Saul heard what had happened, he sent other troops, but they, too, prophesied! The same thing happened a third time. ²²Finally, Saul himself went to Ramah and arrived at the great well in Secu. "Where are Samuel and David?" he demanded.

"They are at Naioth in Ramah," someone told him.

²³But on the way to Naioth in Ramah the Spirit of God came even upon Saul, and he, too, began to prophesy all the way to Naioth! ²⁴He tore off his clothes and lay naked on the ground all day and all night, prophesying in the presence of Samuel. The people who were watching exclaimed, "What? Is even Saul a prophet?"

JONATHAN HELPS DAVID

20 David now fled from Naioth in Ramah and found Jonathan. "What have I done?" he exclaimed. "What is my crime? How have I offended your father that he is so determined to kill me?"

²"That's not true!" Jonathan protested. "You're not going to die. He always tells me everything he's going to do, even the little things. I know my father wouldn't hide something like this from me. It just isn't so!"

³Then David took an oath before Jonathan and said, "Your father knows perfectly well about our friendship, so he has said to himself, 'I won't tell Jonathan—why should I hurt him?' But I swear to you that I am only a step away from death! I swear it by the LORD and by your own soul!"

⁴"Tell me what I can do to help you," Jonathan exclaimed.

⁵David replied, "Tomorrow we celebrate the new moon festival. I've always eaten with the king on this occasion, but tomorrow I'll hide in the field and stay there until the evening of the third day. ⁶If your father asks where I am, tell him I asked permission to go home to Bethlehem for an annual family sacrifice. ⁷If he says, 'Fine!' you will know all is well. But if he is angry and loses his temper, you will know he is determined to kill me. ⁸Show me this loyalty as my sworn friend—for we made a solemn pact before the LORD—or kill me yourself if I have sinned against your father. But please don't betray me to him!"

19:9 Or *evil spirit.* 19:13 Hebrew *teraphim;* also in 19:16.

⁹"Never!" Jonathan exclaimed. "You know that if I had the slightest notion my father was planning to kill you, I would tell you at once."

¹⁰Then David asked, "How will I know whether or not your father is angry?"

¹¹"Come out to the field with me," Jonathan replied. And they went out there together. ¹²Then Jonathan told David, "I promise by the LORD, the God of Israel, that by this time tomorrow, or the next day at the latest, I will talk to my father and let you know at once how he feels about you. If he speaks favorably about you, I will let you know. ¹³But if he is angry and wants you killed, may the LORD strike me and even kill me if I don't warn you so you can escape and live. May the LORD be with you as he used to be with my father. ¹⁴And may you treat me with the faithful love of the LORD as long as I live. But if I die, ¹⁵treat my family with this faithful love, even when the LORD destroys all your enemies from the face of the earth."

¹⁶So Jonathan made a solemn pact with David,* saying, "May the LORD destroy all your enemies!" ¹⁷And Jonathan made David reaffirm his vow of friendship again, for Jonathan loved David as he loved himself.

¹⁸Then Jonathan said, "Tomorrow we celebrate the new moon festival. You will be missed when your place at the table is empty. ¹⁹The day after tomorrow, toward evening, go to the place where you hid before, and wait there by the stone pile.* ²⁰I will come out and shoot three arrows to the side of the stone pile as though I were shooting at a target. ²¹Then I will send a boy to bring the arrows back. If you hear me tell him, 'They're on this side,' then you will know, as surely as the LORD lives, that all is well, and there is no trouble. ²²But if I tell him, 'Go farther—the arrows are still ahead of you,' then it will mean that you must leave immediately, for the LORD is sending you away. ²³And may the LORD make us keep our promises to each other, for he has witnessed them."

²⁴So David hid himself in the field, and when the new moon festival began, the king sat down to eat. ²⁵He sat at his usual place against the wall, with Jonathan sitting opposite him* and Abner beside him. But David's place was empty. ²⁶Saul didn't say anything about it that day, for he said to himself, "Something must have made David ceremonially unclean." ²⁷But when David's place was empty again the next day, Saul asked Jonathan, "Why hasn't the son of Jesse been here for the meal either yesterday or today?"

²⁸Jonathan replied, "David earnestly asked me if he could go to Bethlehem. ²⁹He said, 'Please let me go, for we are having a family sacrifice. My brother demanded that I be there. So please let me get away to see my brothers.' That's why he isn't here at the king's table."

³⁰Saul boiled with rage at Jonathan. "You stupid son of a whore!"* he swore at him. "Do you think I don't know that you want him to be king in your place, shaming yourself and your mother? ³¹As long as that son of Jesse is alive, you'll never be king. Now go and get him so I can kill him!"

³²"But why should he be put to death?" Jonathan asked his father. "What has he done?" ³³Then Saul hurled his spear at Jonathan, intending to kill him. So at last Jonathan realized that his father was really determined to kill David.

³⁴Jonathan left the table in fierce anger and refused to eat on that second day of the festival, for he was crushed by his father's shameful behavior toward David.

³⁵The next morning, as agreed, Jonathan went out into the field and took a young boy with him to gather his arrows. ³⁶"Start running," he told the boy, "so you can find the arrows as I shoot them." So the boy ran, and Jonathan shot an arrow beyond him. ³⁷When the boy had almost reached the arrow, Jonathan shouted, "The arrow is still ahead of you. ³⁸Hurry, hurry, don't wait." So the boy quickly gathered up the arrows and ran back to his master. ³⁹He, of course, suspected nothing; only Jonathan and David understood the signal. ⁴⁰Then Jonathan gave his bow and arrows to the boy and told him to take them back to town.

⁴¹As soon as the boy was gone, David came out from where he had been hiding near the stone pile.* Then David bowed three times to Jonathan with his face to the ground. Both of them were in tears as they embraced each other and said good-bye, especially David.

⁴²At last Jonathan said to David, "Go in peace, for we have sworn loyalty to each other in the LORD's name. The LORD is the witness of a bond between us and our children forever." Then David left, and Jonathan returned to the town.*

DAVID RUNS FROM SAUL

21 ¹*David went to the town of Nob to see Ahimelech the priest. Ahimelech trembled when he saw him. "Why are you alone?" he asked. "Why is no one with you?"

²"The king has sent me on a private matter," David said. "He told me not to tell anyone why I am here. I have told my men where to meet me later. ³Now, what is there to eat? Give me five loaves of bread or anything else you have."

⁴"We don't have any regular bread," the priest replied. "But there is the holy bread, which you can have if your young men have not slept with any women recently."

⁵"Don't worry," David replied. "I never allow my men to be with women when we are on a campaign. And since they stay clean even on ordinary trips, how much more on this one!"

20:16 Hebrew *with the house of David.* 20:19 Hebrew *the stone Ezel.* The meaning of the Hebrew is uncertain. 20:25 As in Greek version; Hebrew reads *with Jonathan standing.* 20:30 Hebrew *You son of a perverse and rebellious woman.* 20:41 As in Greek version; Hebrew reads *near the south edge.* 20:42 This sentence is numbered 21:1 in Hebrew text. 21:1 Verses 21:1-15 are numbered 21:2-16 in Hebrew text.

⁶Since there was no other food available, the priest gave him the holy bread—the Bread of the Presence that was placed before the LORD in the Tabernacle. It had just been replaced that day with fresh bread.

⁷Now Doeg the Edomite, Saul's chief herdsman, was there that day, having been detained before the LORD.*

⁸David asked Ahimelech, "Do you have a spear or sword? The king's business was so urgent that I didn't even have time to grab a weapon!"

⁹"I only have the sword of Goliath the Philistine, whom you killed in the valley of Elah," the priest replied. "It is wrapped in a cloth behind the ephod. Take that if you want it, for there is nothing else here."

"There is nothing like it!" David replied. "Give it to me!"

¹⁰So David escaped from Saul and went to King Achish of Gath. ¹¹But the officers of Achish were unhappy about his being there. "Isn't this David, the king of the land?" they asked. "Isn't he the one the people honor with dances, singing,

'Saul has killed his thousands,
  and David his ten thousands'?"

¹²David heard these comments and was very afraid of what King Achish of Gath might do to him. ¹³So he pretended to be insane, scratching on doors and drooling down his beard.

¹⁴Finally, King Achish said to his men, "Must you bring me a madman? ¹⁵We already have enough of them around here! Why should I let someone like this be my guest?"

DAVID AT THE CAVE OF ADULLAM

22 So David left Gath and escaped to the cave of Adullam. Soon his brothers and all his other relatives joined him there. ²Then others began coming—men who were in trouble or in debt or who were just discontented—until David was the captain of about 400 men.

³Later David went to Mizpeh in Moab, where he asked the king, "Please allow my father and mother to live here with you until I know what God is going to do for me." ⁴So David's parents stayed in Moab with the king during the entire time David was living in his stronghold.

⁵One day the prophet Gad told David, "Leave the stronghold and return to the land of Judah." So David went to the forest of Hereth.

⁶The news of his arrival in Judah soon reached Saul. At the time, the king was sitting beneath the tamarisk tree on the hill at Gibeah, holding his spear and surrounded by his officers.

⁷"Listen here, you men of Benjamin!" Saul shouted to his officers when he heard the news. "Has that son of Jesse promised every one of you fields and vineyards? Has he promised to make you all generals and captains in his army?* ⁸Is that why you have conspired against me? For not one

of you told me when my own son made a solemn pact with the son of Jesse. You're not even sorry for me. Think of it! My own son—encouraging him to kill me, as he is trying to do this very day!"

⁹Then Doeg the Edomite, who was standing there with Saul's men, spoke up. "When I was at Nob," he said, "I saw the son of Jesse talking to the priest, Ahimelech son of Ahitub. ¹⁰Ahimelech consulted the LORD for him. Then he gave him food and the sword of Goliath the Philistine."

THE SLAUGHTER OF THE PRIESTS

¹¹King Saul immediately sent for Ahimelech and all his family, who served as priests at Nob. ¹²When they arrived, Saul shouted at him, "Listen to me, you son of Ahitub!"

"What is it, my king?" Ahimelech asked.

¹³"Why have you and the son of Jesse conspired against me?" Saul demanded. "Why did you give him food and a sword? Why have you consulted God for him? Why have you encouraged him to kill me, as he is trying to do this very day?"

¹⁴"But sir," Ahimelech replied, "is anyone among all your servants as faithful as David, your son-in-law? Why, he is the captain of your bodyguard and a highly honored member of your household! ¹⁵This was certainly not the first time I had consulted God for him! May the king not accuse me and my family in this matter, for I knew nothing at all of any plot against you."

¹⁶"You will surely die, Ahimelech, along with your entire family!" the king shouted. ¹⁷And he ordered his bodyguards, "Kill these priests of the LORD, for they are allies and conspirators with David! They knew he was running away from me, but they didn't tell me!" But Saul's men refused to kill the LORD's priests.

¹⁸Then the king said to Doeg, "You do it." So Doeg the Edomite turned on them and killed them that day, eighty-five priests in all, still wearing their priestly garments. ¹⁹Then he went to Nob, the town of the priests, and killed the priests' families—men and women, children and babies—and all the cattle, donkeys, sheep, and goats.

²⁰Only Abiathar, one of the sons of Ahimelech, escaped and fled to David. ²¹When he told David that Saul had killed the priests of the LORD, ²²David exclaimed, "I knew it! When I saw Doeg the Edomite there that day, I knew he was sure to tell Saul. Now I have caused the death of all your father's family. ²³Stay here with me, and don't be afraid. I will protect you with my own life, for the same person wants to kill us both."

DAVID PROTECTS THE TOWN OF KEILAH

23 One day news came to David that the Philistines were at Keilah stealing grain from the threshing floors. ²David asked the LORD, "Should I go and attack them?"

21:7 The meaning of the Hebrew is uncertain. 22:7 Hebrew *commanders of thousands and commanders of hundreds?*

"Yes, go and save Keilah," the LORD told him. ³But David's men said, "We're afraid even here in Judah. We certainly don't want to go to Keilah to fight the whole Philistine army!"

⁴So David asked the LORD again, and again the LORD replied, "Go down to Keilah, for I will help you conquer the Philistines."

⁵So David and his men went to Keilah. They slaughtered the Philistines and took all their livestock and rescued the people of Keilah. ⁶Now when Abiathar son of Ahimelech fled to David at Keilah, he brought the ephod with him.

⁷Saul soon learned that David was at Keilah. "Good!" he exclaimed. "We've got him now! God has handed him over to me, for he has trapped himself in a walled town!" ⁸So Saul mobilized his entire army to march to Keilah and besiege David and his men.

⁹But David learned of Saul's plan and told Abiathar the priest to bring the ephod and ask the LORD what he should do. ¹⁰Then David prayed, "O LORD, God of Israel, I have heard that Saul is planning to come and destroy Keilah because I am here. ¹¹Will the leaders of Keilah betray me to him?* And will Saul actually come as I have heard? O LORD, God of Israel, please tell me."

And the LORD said, "He will come."

¹²Again David asked, "Will the leaders of Keilah betray me and my men to Saul?"

And the LORD replied, "Yes, they will betray you."

DAVID HIDES IN THE WILDERNESS

¹³So David and his men—about 600 of them now—left Keilah and began roaming the countryside. Word soon reached Saul that David had escaped, so he didn't go to Keilah after all. ¹⁴David now stayed in the strongholds of the wilderness and in the hill country of Ziph. Saul hunted him day after day, but God didn't let Saul find him.

¹⁵One day near Horesh, David received the news that Saul was on the way to Ziph to search for him and kill him. ¹⁶Jonathan went to find David and encouraged him to stay strong in his faith in God. ¹⁷"Don't be afraid," Jonathan reassured him. "My father will never find you! You are going to be the king of Israel, and I will be next to you, as my father, Saul, is well aware." ¹⁸So the two of them renewed their solemn pact before the LORD. Then Jonathan returned home, while David stayed at Horesh.

¹⁹But now the men of Ziph went to Saul in Gibeah and betrayed David to him. "We know where David is hiding," they said. "He is in the strongholds of Horesh on the hill of Hakilah, which is in the southern part of Jeshimon. ²⁰Come down whenever you're ready, O king, and we will catch him and hand him over to you!"

²¹"The LORD bless you," Saul said. "At last someone is concerned about me! ²²Go and check again to be sure of where he is staying and who has seen him there, for I know that he is very crafty. ²³Discover his hiding places, and come back when you are sure. Then I'll go with you. And if he is in the area at all, I'll track him down, even if I have to search every hiding place in Judah!" ²⁴So the men of Ziph returned home ahead of Saul.

Meanwhile, David and his men had moved into the wilderness of Maon in the Arabah Valley south of Jeshimon. ²⁵When David heard that Saul and his men were searching for him, he went even farther into the wilderness to the great rock, and he remained there in the wilderness of Maon. But Saul kept after him in the wilderness.

²⁶Saul and David were now on opposite sides of a mountain. Just as Saul and his men began to close in on David and his men, ²⁷an urgent message reached Saul that the Philistines were raiding Israel again. ²⁸So Saul quit chasing David and returned to fight the Philistines. Ever since that time, the place where David was camped has been called the Rock of Escape.* ²⁹*David then went to live in the strongholds of En-gedi.

DAVID SPARES SAUL'S LIFE

24 ¹*After Saul returned from fighting the Philistines, he was told that David had gone into the wilderness of En-gedi. ²So Saul chose 3,000 elite troops from all Israel and went to search for David and his men near the rocks of the wild goats.

³At the place where the road passes some sheepfolds, Saul went into a cave to relieve himself. But as it happened, David and his men were hiding farther back in that very cave!

⁴"Now's your opportunity!" David's men whispered to him. "Today the LORD is telling you, 'I will certainly put your enemy into your power, to do with as you wish.'" So David crept forward and cut off a piece of the hem of Saul's robe.

⁵But then David's conscience began bothering him because he had cut Saul's robe. ⁶He said to his men, "The LORD forbid that I should do this to my lord the king. I shouldn't attack the LORD's anointed one, for the LORD himself has chosen him." ⁷So David restrained his men and did not let them kill Saul.

After Saul had left the cave and gone on his way, ⁸David came out and shouted after him, "My lord the king!" And when Saul looked around, David bowed low before him.

⁹Then he shouted to Saul, "Why do you listen to the people who say I am trying to harm you? ¹⁰This very day you can see with your own eyes it isn't true. For the LORD placed you at my mercy back there in the cave. Some of my men told me to kill you, but I spared you. For I said, 'I will never harm the king—he is the LORD's anointed one.' ¹¹Look, my father, at what I have

---

23:11 Some manuscripts lack the first sentence of 23:11.
23:28 Hebrew *Sela-hammahlekoth*.   23:29 Verse 23:29 is numbered 24:1 in Hebrew text.   24:1 Verses 24:1-22 are numbered 24:2-23 in Hebrew text.

DAVID: THE KING IN WAITING
1 Samuel 24

JIMMY EVANS

All authority comes from God. As believers, we must reject the rebellious attitude so pervasive in modern culture. Rebellion only has one source—the devil. We need to accept and honor the biblical principle of submission to authority. Only then can we grow spiritually, increase our understanding of God, and experience His favor, blessing, and protection.

From the life of King David, we learn there are four tests of our submission to authority:

1. The Arrogance Test

    David had been anointed king by Samuel (1 Samuel 16:13), and he was not afraid of the Philistine giant Goliath. However, David also recognized that King Saul was still the *appointed* king, so he humbled himself and waited for the king's permission and blessing to fight the giant (1 Samuel 17:32-37).

2. The Abuse Test

    God is the only perfect authority. He gives us the opportunity to honor imperfect leaders, but He also allows us to remove ourselves from abusive or damaging situations. King Saul tried to kill David out of jealousy (1 Samuel 19:9-11), but instead of retaliating, David secretly escaped.

3. The Advantage Test

    David had every advantage over King Saul—he was younger, smarter, stronger, and much more popular with the people of Israel. He even had multiple opportunities to overpower and kill King Saul (1 Samuel 24:16-30; 26:7-11). However, David always chose to use his strengths to honor and serve the king instead of usurping his authority.

4. The Association Test

    David ordered one of his men to execute the man who claimed to kill King Saul (2 Samuel 1:13-16). He knew if he let the man live, he would be guilty of Saul's blood by association. Associations with rebellious people will always influence us toward having our own rebellious attitudes.

---

in my hand. It is a piece of the hem of your robe! I cut it off, but I didn't kill you. This proves that I am not trying to harm you and that I have not sinned against you, even though you have been hunting for me to kill me.

[12] "May the LORD judge between us. Perhaps the LORD will punish you for what you are trying to do to me, but I will never harm you. [13] As that old proverb says, 'From evil people come evil deeds.' So you can be sure I will never harm you. [14] Who is the king of Israel trying to catch anyway? Should he spend his time chasing one who is as worthless as a dead dog or a single flea? [15] May the LORD therefore judge which of us is right and punish the guilty one. He is my advocate, and he will rescue me from your power!"

[16] When David had finished speaking, Saul called back, "Is that really you, my son David?" Then he began to cry. [17] And he said to David, "You are a better man than I am, for you have repaid me good for evil. [18] Yes, you have been amazingly kind to me today, for when the LORD put me in a place where you could have killed me, you didn't do it. [19] Who else would let his enemy get away when he had him in his power? May the LORD reward you well for the kindness you have shown me today. [20] And now I realize that you are surely going to be king, and that the kingdom of Israel will flourish under your rule. [21] Now swear to me by the LORD that when that happens you will not kill my family and destroy my line of descendants!"

[22] So David promised this to Saul with an oath. Then Saul went home, but David and his men went back to their stronghold.

THE DEATH OF SAMUEL

25 Now Samuel died, and all Israel gathered for his funeral. They buried him at his house in Ramah.

NABAL ANGERS DAVID

Then David moved down to the wilderness of Maon.* [2] There was a wealthy man from Maon who owned property near the town of Carmel. He had 3,000 sheep and 1,000 goats, and it was sheep-shearing time. [3] This man's name was Nabal, and his wife, Abigail, was a sensible and beautiful woman. But Nabal, a descendant of Caleb, was crude and mean in all his dealings.

[4] When David heard that Nabal was shearing his sheep, [5] he sent ten of his young men to Carmel with this message for Nabal: [6] "Peace and prosperity to you, your family, and everything you own! [7] I am told that it is sheep-shearing time. While your shepherds stayed among us near Carmel, we never harmed them, and nothing was ever stolen from them. [8] Ask your own men, and they will tell you this is true. So would you be kind to us, since we have come at a time of celebration? Please share any provisions you might have on hand with us and with your friend David." [9] David's young men gave this message to Nabal in David's name, and they waited for a reply.

[10] "Who is this fellow David?" Nabal sneered to the young men. "Who does this son of Jesse think he is? There are lots of servants these days who run away from their masters. [11] Should I take

---

25:1 As in Greek version (see also 25:2); Hebrew reads *Paran*.

my bread and my water and my meat that I've slaughtered for my shearers and give it to a band of outlaws who come from who knows where?" ¹²So David's young men returned and told him what Nabal had said. ¹³"Get your swords!" was David's reply as he strapped on his own. Then 400 men started off with David, and 200 remained behind to guard their equipment.

¹⁴Meanwhile, one of Nabal's servants went to Abigail and told her, "David sent messengers from the wilderness to greet our master, but he screamed insults at them. ¹⁵These men have been very good to us, and we never suffered any harm from them. Nothing was stolen from us the whole time they were with us. ¹⁶In fact, day and night they were like a wall of protection to us and the sheep. ¹⁷You need to know this and figure out what to do, for there is going to be trouble for our master and his whole family. He's so ill-tempered that no one can even talk to him!"

¹⁸Abigail wasted no time. She quickly gathered 200 loaves of bread, two wineskins full of wine, five sheep that had been slaughtered, nearly a bushel* of roasted grain, 100 clusters of raisins, and 200 fig cakes. She packed them on donkeys ¹⁹and said to her servants, "Go on ahead. I will follow you shortly." But she didn't tell her husband Nabal what she was doing.

²⁰As she was riding her donkey into a mountain ravine, she saw David and his men coming toward her. ²¹David had just been saying, "A lot of good it did to help this fellow. We protected his flocks in the wilderness, and nothing he owned was lost or stolen. But he has repaid me evil for good. ²²May God strike me and kill me* if even one man of his household is still alive tomorrow morning!"

ABIGAIL INTERCEDES FOR NABAL

²³When Abigail saw David, she quickly got off her donkey and bowed low before him. ²⁴She fell at his feet and said, "I accept all blame in this matter, my lord. Please listen to what I have to say. ²⁵I know Nabal is a wicked and ill-tempered man; please don't pay any attention to him. He is a fool, just as his name suggests.* But I never even saw the young men you sent.

²⁶"Now, my lord, as surely as the LORD lives and you yourself live, since the LORD has kept you from murdering and taking vengeance into your own hands, let all your enemies and those who try to harm you be as cursed as Nabal is. ²⁷And here is a present that I, your servant, have brought to you and your young men. ²⁸Please forgive me if I have offended you in any way. The LORD will surely reward you with a lasting dynasty, for you are fighting the LORD's battles. And you have not done wrong throughout your entire life.

²⁹"Even when you are chased by those who seek to kill you, your life is safe in the care of the LORD your God, secure in his treasure pouch!

But the lives of your enemies will disappear like stones shot from a sling! ³⁰When the LORD has done all he promised and has made you leader of Israel, ³¹don't let this be a blemish on your record. Then your conscience won't have to bear the staggering burden of needless bloodshed and vengeance. And when the LORD has done these great things for you, please remember me, your servant!"

³²David replied to Abigail, "Praise the LORD, the God of Israel, who has sent you to meet me today! ³³Thank God for your good sense! Bless you for keeping me from murder and from carrying out vengeance with my own hands. ³⁴For I swear by the LORD, the God of Israel, who has kept me from hurting you, that if you had not hurried out to meet me, not one of Nabal's men would still be alive tomorrow morning." ³⁵Then David accepted her present and told her, "Return home in peace. I have heard what you said. We will not kill your husband."

³⁶When Abigail arrived home, she found that Nabal was throwing a big party and was celebrating like a king. He was very drunk, so she didn't tell him anything about her meeting with David until dawn the next day. ³⁷In the morning when Nabal was sober, his wife told him what had happened. As a result he had a stroke,* and he lay paralyzed on his bed like a stone. ³⁸About ten days later, the LORD struck him, and he died.

DAVID MARRIES ABIGAIL

³⁹When David heard that Nabal was dead, he said, "Praise the LORD, who has avenged the insult I received from Nabal and has kept me from doing it myself. Nabal has received the punishment for his sin." Then David sent messengers to Abigail to ask her to become his wife.

⁴⁰When the messengers arrived at Carmel, they told Abigail, "David has sent us to take you back to marry him."

⁴¹She bowed low to the ground and responded, "I, your servant, would be happy to marry David. I would even be willing to become a slave, washing the feet of his servants!" ⁴²Quickly getting ready, she took along five of her servant girls as attendants, mounted her donkey, and went with David's messengers. And so she became his wife. ⁴³David also married Ahinoam from Jezreel, making both of them his wives. ⁴⁴Saul, meanwhile, had given his daughter Michal, David's wife, to a man from Gallim named Palti son of Laish.

DAVID SPARES SAUL AGAIN

26 Now some men from Ziph came to Saul at Gibeah to tell him, "David is hiding on the hill of Hakilah, which overlooks Jeshimon."

25:18 Hebrew 5 seahs [36.5 liters].   25:22 As in Greek version; Hebrew reads May God strike and kill the enemies of David.
25:25 The name Nabal means "fool."   25:37 Hebrew his heart failed him.

[2] So Saul took 3,000 of Israel's elite troops and went to hunt him down in the wilderness of Ziph. [3] Saul camped along the road beside the hill of Hakilah, near Jeshimon, where David was hiding. When David learned that Saul had come after him into the wilderness, [4] he sent out spies to verify the report of Saul's arrival.

[5] David slipped over to Saul's camp one night to look around. Saul and Abner son of Ner, the commander of his army, were sleeping inside a ring formed by the slumbering warriors. [6] "Who will volunteer to go in there with me?" David asked Ahimelech the Hittite and Abishai son of Zeruiah, Joab's brother.

"I'll go with you," Abishai replied. [7] So David and Abishai went right into Saul's camp and found him asleep, with his spear stuck in the ground beside his head. Abner and the soldiers were lying asleep around him.

[8] "God has surely handed your enemy over to you this time!" Abishai whispered to David. "Let me pin him to the ground with one thrust of the spear; I won't need to strike twice!"

[9] "No!" David said. "Don't kill him. For who can remain innocent after attacking the LORD's anointed one? [10] Surely the LORD will strike Saul down someday, or he will die of old age or in battle. [11] The LORD forbid that I should kill the one he has anointed! But take his spear and that jug of water beside his head, and then let's get out of here!"

[12] So David took the spear and jug of water that were near Saul's head. Then he and Abishai got away without anyone seeing them or even waking up, because the LORD had put Saul's men into a deep sleep.

[13] David climbed the hill opposite the camp until he was at a safe distance. [14] Then he shouted down to the soldiers and to Abner son of Ner, "Wake up, Abner!"

"Who is it?" Abner demanded.

[15] "Well, Abner, you're a great man, aren't you?" David taunted. "Where in all Israel is there anyone as mighty? So why haven't you guarded your master the king when someone came to kill him? [16] This isn't good at all! I swear by the LORD that you and your men deserve to die, because you failed to protect your master, the LORD's anointed! Look around! Where are the king's spear and the jug of water that were beside his head?"

[17] Saul recognized David's voice and called out, "Is that you, my son David?"

And David replied, "Yes, my lord the king. [18] Why are you chasing me? What have I done? What is my crime? [19] But now let my lord the king listen to his servant. If the LORD has stirred you up against me, then let him accept my offering. But if this is simply a human scheme, then may those involved be cursed by the LORD. For they have driven me from my home, so I can no longer live among the LORD's people, and they have said, 'Go, worship pagan gods.' [20] Must I die on foreign soil, far from the presence of the LORD? Why has the king of Israel come out to search for a single flea? Why does he hunt me down like a partridge on the mountains?"

[21] Then Saul confessed, "I have sinned. Come back home, my son, and I will no longer try to harm you, for you valued my life today. I have been a fool and very, very wrong."

[22] "Here is your spear, O king," David replied. "Let one of your young men come over and get it. [23] The LORD gives his own reward for doing good and for being loyal, and I refused to kill you even when the LORD placed you in my power, for you are the LORD's anointed one. [24] Now may the LORD value my life, even as I have valued yours today. May he rescue me from all my troubles."

[25] And Saul said to David, "Blessings on you, my son David. You will do many heroic deeds, and you will surely succeed." Then David went away, and Saul returned home.

DAVID AMONG THE PHILISTINES

27 But David kept thinking to himself, "Someday Saul is going to get me. The best thing I can do is escape to the Philistines. Then Saul will stop hunting for me in Israelite territory, and I will finally be safe."

[2] So David took his 600 men and went over and joined Achish son of Maoch, the king of Gath. [3] David and his men and their families settled there with Achish at Gath. David brought his two wives along with him—Ahinoam from Jezreel and Abigail, Nabal's widow from Carmel. [4] Word soon reached Saul that David had fled to Gath, so he stopped hunting for him.

[5] One day David said to Achish, "If it is all right with you, we would rather live in one of the country towns instead of here in the royal city."

[6] So Achish gave him the town of Ziklag (which still belongs to the kings of Judah to this day), [7] and they lived there among the Philistines for a year and four months.

[8] David and his men spent their time raiding the Geshurites, the Girzites, and the Amalekites—people who had lived near Shur, toward the land of Egypt, since ancient times. [9] David did not leave one person alive in the villages he attacked. He took the sheep, goats, cattle, donkeys, camels, and clothing before returning home to see King Achish.

[10] "Where did you make your raid today?" Achish would ask.

And David would reply, "Against the south of Judah, the Jerahmeelites, and the Kenites."

[11] No one was left alive to come to Gath and tell where he had really been. This happened again and again while he was living among the Philistines. [12] Achish believed David and thought to himself, "By now the people of Israel must hate him bitterly. Now he will have to stay here and serve me forever!"

SAUL CONSULTS A MEDIUM

28 About that time the Philistines mustered their armies for another war with Israel. King Achish told David, "You and your men will be expected to join me in battle."

[2] "Very well!" David agreed. "Now you will see for yourself what we can do."

Then Achish told David, "I will make you my personal bodyguard for life."

[3] Meanwhile, Samuel had died, and all Israel had mourned for him. He was buried in Ramah, his hometown. And Saul had banned from the land of Israel all mediums and those who consult the spirits of the dead.

[4] The Philistines set up their camp at Shunem, and Saul gathered all the army of Israel and camped at Gilboa. [5] When Saul saw the vast Philistine army, he became frantic with fear. [6] He asked the LORD what he should do, but the LORD refused to answer him, either by dreams or by sacred lots* or by the prophets. [7] Saul then said to his advisers, "Find a woman who is a medium, so I can go and ask her what to do."

His advisers replied, "There is a medium at Endor."

[8] So Saul disguised himself by wearing ordinary clothing instead of his royal robes. Then he went to the woman's home at night, accompanied by two of his men.

"I have to talk to a man who has died," he said. "Will you call up his spirit for me?"

[9] "Are you trying to get me killed?" the woman demanded. "You know that Saul has outlawed all the mediums and all who consult the spirits of the dead. Why are you setting a trap for me?"

[10] But Saul took an oath in the name of the LORD and promised, "As surely as the LORD lives, nothing bad will happen to you for doing this."

[11] Finally, the woman said, "Well, whose spirit do you want me to call up?"

"Call up Samuel," Saul replied.

[12] When the woman saw Samuel, she screamed, "You've deceived me! You are Saul!"

[13] "Don't be afraid!" the king told her. "What do you see?"

"I see a god* coming up out of the earth," she said.

[14] "What does he look like?" Saul asked.

"He is an old man wrapped in a robe," she replied. Saul realized it was Samuel, and he fell to the ground before him.

[15] "Why have you disturbed me by calling me back?" Samuel asked Saul.

"Because I am in deep trouble," Saul replied. "The Philistines are at war with me, and God has left me and won't reply by prophets or dreams. So I have called for you to tell me what to do."

[16] But Samuel replied, "Why ask me, since the LORD has left you and has become your enemy? [17] The LORD has done just as he said he would. He has torn the kingdom from you and given it to your rival, David. [18] The LORD has done this to you today because you refused to carry out his fierce anger against the Amalekites. [19] What's more, the LORD will hand you and the army of Israel over to the Philistines tomorrow, and you and your sons will be here with me. The LORD will bring down the entire army of Israel in defeat."

[20] Saul fell full length on the ground, paralyzed with fright because of Samuel's words. He was also faint with hunger, for he had eaten nothing all day and all night.

[21] When the woman saw how distraught he was, she said, "Sir, I obeyed your command at the risk of my life. [22] Now do what I say, and let me give you a little something to eat so you can regain your strength for the trip back."

[23] But Saul refused to eat anything. Then his advisers joined the woman in urging him to eat, so he finally yielded and got up from the ground and sat on the couch.

[24] The woman had been fattening a calf, so she hurried out and killed it. She took some flour, kneaded it into dough and baked unleavened bread. [25] She brought the meal to Saul and his advisers, and they ate it. Then they went out into the night.

THE PHILISTINES REJECT DAVID

29 The entire Philistine army now mobilized at Aphek, and the Israelites camped at the spring in Jezreel. [2] As the Philistine rulers were leading out their troops in groups of hundreds and thousands, David and his men marched at the rear with King Achish. [3] But the Philistine commanders demanded, "What are these Hebrews doing here?"

And Achish told them, "This is David, the servant of King Saul of Israel. He's been with me for years, and I've never found a single fault in him from the day he arrived until today."

[4] But the Philistine commanders were angry. "Send him back to the town you've given him!" they demanded. "He can't go into the battle with us. What if he turns against us in battle and becomes our adversary? Is there any better way for him to reconcile himself with his master than by handing our heads over to him? [5] Isn't this the same David about whom the women of Israel sing in their dances,

'Saul has killed his thousands,
    and David his ten thousands'?"

[6] So Achish finally summoned David and said to him, "I swear by the LORD that you have been a trustworthy ally. I think you should go with me into battle, for I've never found a single flaw in you from the day you arrived until today. But the other Philistine rulers won't hear of it. [7] Please don't upset them, but go back quietly."

28:6 Hebrew *by Urim.* 28:13 Or *gods.*

[8] "What have I done to deserve this treatment?" David demanded. "What have you ever found in your servant, that I can't go and fight the enemies of my lord the king?"

[9] But Achish insisted, "As far as I'm concerned, you're as perfect as an angel of God. But the Philistine commanders are afraid to have you with them in the battle. [10] Now get up early in the morning, and leave with your men as soon as it gets light."

[11] So David and his men headed back into the land of the Philistines, while the Philistine army went on to Jezreel.

DAVID DESTROYS THE AMALEKITES

30 Three days later, when David and his men arrived home at their town of Ziklag, they found that the Amalekites had made a raid into the Negev and Ziklag; they had crushed Ziklag and burned it to the ground. [2] They had carried off the women and children and everyone else but without killing anyone.

[3] When David and his men saw the ruins and realized what had happened to their families, [4] they wept until they could weep no more. [5] David's two wives, Ahinoam from Jezreel and Abigail, the widow of Nabal from Carmel, were among those captured. [6] David was now in great danger because all his men were very bitter about losing their sons and daughters, and they began to talk of stoning him. But David found strength in the LORD his God.

[7] Then he said to Abiathar the priest, "Bring me the ephod!" So Abiathar brought it. [8] Then David asked the LORD, "Should I chase after this band of raiders? Will I catch them?"

And the LORD told him, "Yes, go after them. You will surely recover everything that was taken from you!"

[9] So David and his 600 men set out, and they came to the brook Besor. [10] But 200 of the men were too exhausted to cross the brook, so David continued the pursuit with 400 men.

[11] Along the way they found an Egyptian man in a field and brought him to David. They gave him some bread to eat and water to drink. [12] They also gave him part of a fig cake and two clusters of raisins, for he hadn't had anything to eat or drink for three days and nights. Before long his strength returned.

[13] "To whom do you belong, and where do you come from?" David asked him.

"I am an Egyptian—the slave of an Amalekite," he replied. "My master abandoned me three days ago because I was sick. [14] We were on our way back from raiding the Kerethites in the Negev, the territory of Judah, and the land of Caleb, and we had just burned Ziklag."

[15] "Will you lead me to this band of raiders?" David asked.

The young man replied, "If you take an oath in God's name that you will not kill me or give me back to my master, then I will guide you to them."

[16] So he led David to them, and they found the Amalekites spread out across the fields, eating and drinking and dancing with joy because of the vast amount of plunder they had taken from the Philistines and the land of Judah. [17] David and his men rushed in among them and slaughtered them throughout that night and the entire next day until evening. None of the Amalekites escaped except 400 young men who fled on camels. [18] David got back everything the Amalekites had taken, and he rescued his two wives. [19] Nothing was missing: small or great, son or daughter, nor anything else that had been taken. David brought everything back. [20] He also recovered all the flocks and herds, and his men drove them ahead of the other livestock. "This plunder belongs to David!" they said.

[21] Then David returned to the brook Besor and met up with the 200 men who had been left behind because they were too exhausted to go with him. They went out to meet David and his men, and David greeted them joyfully. [22] But some evil troublemakers among David's men said, "They didn't go with us, so they can't have any of the plunder we recovered. Give them their wives and children, and tell them to be gone."

[23] But David said, "No, my brothers! Don't be selfish with what the LORD has given us. He has kept us safe and helped us defeat the band of raiders that attacked us. [24] Who will listen when you talk like this? We share and share alike—those who go to battle and those who guard the equipment." [25] From then on David made this a decree and regulation for Israel, and it is still followed today.

[26] When he arrived at Ziklag, David sent part of the plunder to the elders of Judah, who were his friends. "Here is a present for you, taken from the LORD's enemies," he said.

[27] The gifts were sent to the people of the following towns David had visited: Bethel, Ramoth-negev, Jattir, [28] Aroer, Siphmoth, Eshtemoa, [29] Racal,* the towns of the Jerahmeelites, the towns of the Kenites, [30] Hormah, Bor-ashan, Athach, [31] Hebron, and all the other places David and his men had visited.

THE DEATH OF SAUL

31 Now the Philistines attacked Israel, and the men of Israel fled before them. Many were slaughtered on the slopes of Mount Gilboa. [2] The Philistines closed in on Saul and his sons, and they killed three of his sons—Jonathan, Abinadab, and Malkishua. [3] The fighting grew very fierce around Saul, and the Philistine archers caught up with him and wounded him severely.

[4] Saul groaned to his armor bearer, "Take your sword and kill me before these pagan Philistines come to run me through and taunt and torture me."

30:29 Greek version reads *Carmel*.

But his armor bearer was afraid and would not do it. So Saul took his own sword and fell on it. [5] When his armor bearer realized that Saul was dead, he fell on his own sword and died beside the king. [6] So Saul, his three sons, his armor bearer, and his troops all died together that same day.

[7] When the Israelites on the other side of the Jezreel Valley and beyond the Jordan saw that the Israelite army had fled and that Saul and his sons were dead, they abandoned their towns and fled. So the Philistines moved in and occupied their towns.

[8] The next day, when the Philistines went out to strip the dead, they found the bodies of Saul and his three sons on Mount Gilboa. [9] So they cut off Saul's head and stripped off his armor. Then they proclaimed the good news of Saul's death in their pagan temple and to the people throughout the land of Philistia. [10] They placed his armor in the temple of the Ashtoreths, and they fastened his body to the wall of the city of Beth-shan.

[11] But when the people of Jabesh-gilead heard what the Philistines had done to Saul, [12] all their mighty warriors traveled through the night to Beth-shan and took the bodies of Saul and his sons down from the wall. They brought them to Jabesh, where they burned the bodies. [13] Then they took their bones and buried them beneath the tamarisk tree at Jabesh, and they fasted for seven days.

2 SAMUEL

DAVID LEARNS OF SAUL'S DEATH

1 After the death of Saul, David returned from his victory over the Amalekites and spent two days in Ziklag. ²On the third day a man arrived from Saul's army camp. He had torn his clothes and put dirt on his head to show that he was in mourning. He fell to the ground before David in deep respect.

³"Where have you come from?" David asked.

"I escaped from the Israelite camp," the man replied.

⁴"What happened?" David demanded. "Tell me how the battle went."

The man replied, "Our entire army fled from the battle. Many of the men are dead, and Saul and his son Jonathan are also dead."

⁵"How do you know Saul and Jonathan are dead?" David demanded of the young man.

⁶The man answered, "I happened to be on Mount Gilboa, and there was Saul leaning on his spear with the enemy chariots and charioteers closing in on him. ⁷When he turned and saw me, he cried out for me to come to him. 'How can I help?' I asked him.

⁸"He responded, 'Who are you?'

"'I am an Amalekite,' I told him.

⁹"Then he begged me, 'Come over here and put me out of my misery, for I am in terrible pain and want to die.'

¹⁰"So I killed him," the Amalekite told David, "for I knew he couldn't live. Then I took his crown and his armband, and I have brought them here to you, my lord."

¹¹David and his men tore their clothes in sorrow when they heard the news. ¹²They mourned and wept and fasted all day for Saul and his son Jonathan, and for the LORD's army and the nation of Israel, because they had died by the sword that day.

¹³Then David said to the young man who had brought the news, "Where are you from?"

And he replied, "I am a foreigner, an Amalekite, who lives in your land."

¹⁴"Why were you not afraid to kill the LORD's anointed one?" David asked.

¹⁵Then David said to one of his men, "Kill him!" So the man thrust his sword into the Amalekite and killed him. ¹⁶"You have condemned yourself," David said, "for you yourself confessed that you killed the LORD's anointed one."

DAVID'S SONG FOR SAUL AND JONATHAN

¹⁷Then David composed a funeral song for Saul and Jonathan, ¹⁸and he commanded that it be taught to the people of Judah. It is known as the Song of the Bow, and it is recorded in *The Book of Jashar*.*

¹⁹ Your pride and joy, O Israel, lies dead on
    the hills!
  Oh, how the mighty heroes have fallen!
²⁰ Don't announce the news in Gath,
    don't proclaim it in the streets of
    Ashkelon,
  or the daughters of the Philistines will
    rejoice
    and the pagans will laugh in triumph.

²¹ O mountains of Gilboa,
    let there be no dew or rain upon you,
    nor fruitful fields producing offerings
    of grain.*
  For there the shield of the mighty heroes
    was defiled;
    the shield of Saul will no longer be
    anointed with oil.
²² The bow of Jonathan was powerful,
    and the sword of Saul did its mighty work.
  They shed the blood of their enemies
    and pierced the bodies of mighty heroes.

²³ How beloved and gracious were Saul and
    Jonathan!
  They were together in life and in death.
  They were swifter than eagles,
    stronger than lions.
²⁴ O women of Israel, weep for Saul,
  for he dressed you in luxurious scarlet
    clothing,
    in garments decorated with gold.

²⁵ Oh, how the mighty heroes have fallen in
    battle!
  Jonathan lies dead on the hills.
²⁶ How I weep for you, my brother Jonathan!
  Oh, how much I loved you!
  And your love for me was deep,
    deeper than the love of women!

²⁷ Oh, how the mighty heroes have fallen!
  Stripped of their weapons, they lie dead.

DAVID ANOINTED KING OF JUDAH

2 After this, David asked the LORD, "Should I move back to one of the towns of Judah?"

"Yes," the LORD replied.

Then David asked, "Which town should I go to?"

"To Hebron," the LORD answered.

²David's two wives were Ahinoam from Jezreel and Abigail, the widow of Nabal from Carmel. So David and his wives ³and his men and their

---

1:18 Or *The Book of the Upright.* 1:21 The meaning of the Hebrew is uncertain.

families all moved to Judah, and they settled in the villages near Hebron. ⁴Then the men of Judah came to David and anointed him king over the people of Judah.

When David heard that the men of Jabesh-gilead had buried Saul, ⁵he sent them this message: "May the LORD bless you for being so loyal to your master Saul and giving him a decent burial. ⁶May the LORD be loyal to you in return and reward you with his unfailing love! And I, too, will reward you for what you have done. ⁷Now that Saul is dead, I ask you to be my strong and loyal subjects like the people of Judah, who have anointed me as their new king."

ISHBOSHETH PROCLAIMED KING OF ISRAEL

⁸But Abner son of Ner, the commander of Saul's army, had already gone to Mahanaim with Saul's son Ishbosheth.* ⁹There he proclaimed Ishbosheth king over Gilead, Jezreel, Ephraim, Benjamin, the land of the Ashurites, and all the rest of Israel.

¹⁰Ishbosheth, Saul's son, was forty years old when he became king, and he ruled from Mahanaim for two years. Meanwhile, the people of Judah remained loyal to David. ¹¹David made Hebron his capital, and he ruled as king of Judah for seven and a half years.

WAR BETWEEN ISRAEL AND JUDAH

¹²One day Abner led Ishbosheth's troops from Mahanaim to Gibeon. ¹³About the same time, Joab son of Zeruiah led David's troops out and met them at the pool of Gibeon. The two groups sat down there, facing each other from opposite sides of the pool.

¹⁴Then Abner suggested to Joab, "Let's have a few of our warriors fight hand to hand here in front of us."

"All right," Joab agreed. ¹⁵So twelve men were chosen to fight from each side—twelve men of Benjamin representing Ishbosheth son of Saul, and twelve representing David. ¹⁶Each one grabbed his opponent by the hair and thrust his sword into the other's side so that all of them died. So this place at Gibeon has been known ever since as the Field of Swords.*

¹⁷A fierce battle followed that day, and Abner and the men of Israel were defeated by the forces of David.

THE DEATH OF ASAHEL

¹⁸Joab, Abishai, and Asahel—the three sons of Zeruiah—were among David's forces that day. Asahel could run like a gazelle, ¹⁹and he began chasing Abner. He pursued him relentlessly, not stopping for anything. ²⁰When Abner looked back and saw him coming, he called out, "Is that you, Asahel?"

"Yes, it is," he replied.

²¹"Go fight someone else!" Abner warned. "Take on one of the younger men, and strip him of his weapons." But Asahel kept right on chasing Abner.

²²Again Abner shouted to him, "Get away from here! I don't want to kill you. How could I ever face your brother Joab again?"

²³But Asahel refused to turn back, so Abner thrust the butt end of his spear through Asahel's stomach, and the spear came out through his back. He stumbled to the ground and died there. And everyone who came by that spot stopped and stood still when they saw Asahel lying there.

²⁴When Joab and Abishai found out what had happened, they set out after Abner. The sun was just going down as they arrived at the hill of Ammah near Giah, along the road to the wilderness of Gibeon. ²⁵Abner's troops from the tribe of Benjamin regrouped there at the top of the hill to take a stand.

²⁶Abner shouted down to Joab, "Must we always be killing each other? Don't you realize that bitterness is the only result? When will you call off your men from chasing their Israelite brothers?"

²⁷Then Joab said, "God only knows what would have happened if you hadn't spoken, for we would have chased you all night if necessary." ²⁸So Joab blew the ram's horn, and his men stopped chasing the troops of Israel.

²⁹All that night Abner and his men retreated through the Jordan Valley.* They crossed the Jordan River, traveling all through the morning,* and didn't stop until they arrived at Mahanaim.

³⁰Meanwhile, Joab and his men also returned home. When Joab counted his casualties, he discovered that only 19 men were missing in addition to Asahel. ³¹But 360 of Abner's men had been killed, all from the tribe of Benjamin. ³²Joab and his men took Asahel's body to Bethlehem and buried him there in his father's tomb. Then they traveled all night and reached Hebron at daybreak.

3 That was the beginning of a long war between those who were loyal to Saul and those loyal to David. As time passed David became stronger and stronger, while Saul's dynasty became weaker and weaker.

DAVID'S SONS BORN IN HEBRON

²These are the sons who were born to David in Hebron:

The oldest was Amnon, whose mother was
    Ahinoam from Jezreel.
³ The second was Daniel,* whose mother was
    Abigail, the widow of Nabal from Carmel.

2:8 *Ishbosheth* is another name for Esh-baal. **2:16** Hebrew *Helkath-hazzurim.* **2:29a** Hebrew *the Arabah.* **2:29b** Or *continued on through the Bithron.* The meaning of the Hebrew is uncertain. **3:3** As in parallel text at 1 Chr 3:1 (see also Greek version, which reads *Daluia,* and possible support by Dead Sea Scrolls); Hebrew reads *Kileab.*

The third was Absalom, whose mother was Maacah, the daughter of Talmai, king of Geshur.

⁴ The fourth was Adonijah, whose mother was Haggith.

The fifth was Shephatiah, whose mother was Abital.

⁵ The sixth was Ithream, whose mother was Eglah, David's wife.

These sons were all born to David in Hebron.

ABNER JOINS FORCES WITH DAVID

⁶ As the war between the house of Saul and the house of David went on, Abner became a powerful leader among those loyal to Saul. ⁷ One day Ishbosheth,* Saul's son, accused Abner of sleeping with one of his father's concubines, a woman named Rizpah, daughter of Aiah.

⁸ Abner was furious. "Am I some Judean dog to be kicked around like this?" he shouted. "After all I have done for your father, Saul, and his family and friends by not handing you over to David, is this my reward—that you find fault with me about this woman? ⁹ May God strike me and even kill me if I don't do everything I can to help David get what the LORD has promised him! ¹⁰ I'm going to take Saul's kingdom and give it to David. I will establish the throne of David over Israel as well as Judah, all the way from Dan in the north to Beersheba in the south." ¹¹ Ishbosheth didn't dare say another word because he was afraid of what Abner might do.

¹² Then Abner sent messengers to David, saying, "Doesn't the entire land belong to you? Make a solemn pact with me, and I will help turn over all of Israel to you."

¹³ "All right," David replied, "but I will not negotiate with you unless you bring back my wife Michal, Saul's daughter, when you come."

¹⁴ David then sent this message to Ishbosheth, Saul's son: "Give me back my wife Michal, for I bought her with the lives* of 100 Philistines."

¹⁵ So Ishbosheth took Michal away from her husband, Palti* son of Laish. ¹⁶ Palti followed along behind her as far as Bahurim, weeping as he went. Then Abner told him, "Go back home!" So Palti returned.

¹⁷ Meanwhile, Abner had consulted with the elders of Israel. "For some time now," he told them, "you have wanted to make David your king. ¹⁸ Now is the time! For the LORD has said, 'I have chosen David to save my people Israel from the hands of the Philistines and from all their other enemies.'" ¹⁹ Abner also spoke with the men of Benjamin. Then he went to Hebron to tell David that all the people of Israel and Benjamin had agreed to support him.

²⁰ When Abner and twenty of his men came to Hebron, David entertained them with a great feast. ²¹ Then Abner said to David, "Let me go and call an assembly of all Israel to support my lord the king. They will make a covenant with you to make you their king, and you will rule over everything your heart desires." So David sent Abner safely on his way.

JOAB MURDERS ABNER

²² But just after David had sent Abner away in safety, Joab and some of David's troops returned from a raid, bringing much plunder with them. ²³ When Joab arrived, he was told that Abner had just been there visiting the king and had been sent away in safety.

²⁴ Joab rushed to the king and demanded, "What have you done? What do you mean by letting Abner get away? ²⁵ You know perfectly well that he came to spy on you and find out everything you're doing!"

²⁶ Joab then left David and sent messengers to catch up with Abner, asking him to return. They found him at the well of Sirah and brought him back, though David knew nothing about it. ²⁷ When Abner arrived back at Hebron, Joab took him aside at the gateway as if to speak with him privately. But then he stabbed Abner in the stomach and killed him in revenge for killing his brother Asahel.

²⁸ When David heard about it, he declared, "I vow by the LORD that I and my kingdom are forever innocent of this crime against Abner son of Ner. ²⁹ Joab and his family are the guilty ones. May the family of Joab be cursed in every generation with a man who has open sores or leprosy* or who walks on crutches* or dies by the sword or begs for food!"

³⁰ So Joab and his brother Abishai killed Abner because Abner had killed their brother Asahel at the battle of Gibeon.

DAVID MOURNS ABNER'S DEATH

³¹ Then David said to Joab and all those who were with him, "Tear your clothes and put on burlap. Mourn for Abner." And King David himself walked behind the procession to the grave. ³² They buried Abner in Hebron, and the king and all the people wept at his graveside. ³³ Then the king sang this funeral song for Abner:

"Should Abner have died as fools die?
³⁴ Your hands were not bound;
    your feet were not chained.
No, you were murdered—
    the victim of a wicked plot."

All the people wept again for Abner. ³⁵ David had refused to eat anything on the day of the funeral, and now everyone begged him to eat. But David had made a vow, saying, "May God

---

3:7 *Ishbosheth* is another name for Esh-baal. 3:14 Hebrew *the foreskins.* 3:15 As in 1 Sam 25:44; Hebrew reads *Paltiel,* a variant spelling of Palti. 3:29a Or *or a contagious skin disease.* The Hebrew word used here can describe various skin diseases. 3:29b Or *who is effeminate;* Hebrew reads *who handles a spindle.*

strike me and even kill me if I eat anything before sundown."

36 This pleased the people very much. In fact, everything the king did pleased them! 37 So everyone in Judah and all Israel understood that David was not responsible for Abner's murder.

38 Then King David said to his officials, "Don't you realize that a great commander has fallen today in Israel? 39 And even though I am the anointed king, these two sons of Zeruiah—Joab and Abishai—are too strong for me to control. So may the LORD repay these evil men for their evil deeds."

THE MURDER OF ISHBOSHETH

4 When Ishbosheth,* Saul's son, heard about Abner's death at Hebron, he lost all courage, and all Israel became paralyzed with fear. 2 Now there were two brothers, Baanah and Recab, who were captains of Ishbosheth's raiding parties. They were sons of Rimmon, a member of the tribe of Benjamin who lived in Beeroth. The town of Beeroth is now part of Benjamin's territory 3 because the original people of Beeroth fled to Gittaim, where they still live as foreigners.

4 (Saul's son Jonathan had a son named Mephibosheth,* who was crippled as a child. He was five years old when the report came from Jezreel that Saul and Jonathan had been killed in battle. When the child's nurse heard the news, she picked him up and fled. But as she hurried away, she dropped him, and he became crippled.)

5 One day Recab and Baanah, the sons of Rimmon from Beeroth, went to Ishbosheth's house around noon as he was taking his midday rest. 6 The doorkeeper, who had been sifting wheat, became drowsy and fell asleep. So Recab and Baanah slipped past her.* 7 They went into the house and found Ishbosheth sleeping on his bed. They struck and killed him and cut off his head. Then, taking his head with them, they fled across the Jordan Valley* through the night. 8 When they arrived at Hebron, they presented Ishbosheth's head to David. "Look!" they exclaimed to the king. "Here is the head of Ishbosheth, the son of your enemy Saul who tried to kill you. Today the LORD has given my lord the king revenge on Saul and his entire family!"

9 But David said to Recab and Baanah, "The LORD, who saves me from all my enemies, is my witness. 10 Someone once told me, 'Saul is dead,' thinking he was bringing me good news. But I seized him and killed him at Ziklag. That's the reward I gave him for his news! 11 How much more should I reward evil men who have killed an innocent man in his own house and on his own bed? Shouldn't I hold you responsible for his blood and rid the earth of you?"

12 So David ordered his young men to kill them, and they did. They cut off their hands and feet and hung their bodies beside the pool in Hebron.

Then they took Ishbosheth's head and buried it in Abner's tomb in Hebron.

DAVID BECOMES KING OF ALL ISRAEL

5 Then all the tribes of Israel went to David at Hebron and told him, "We are your own flesh and blood. 2 In the past,* when Saul was our king, you were the one who really led the forces of Israel. And the LORD told you, 'You will be the shepherd of my people Israel. You will be Israel's leader.'"

3 So there at Hebron, King David made a covenant before the LORD with all the elders of Israel. And they anointed him king of Israel. 4 David was thirty years old when he began to reign, and he reigned forty years in all. 5 He had reigned over Judah from Hebron for seven years and six months, and from Jerusalem he reigned over all Israel and Judah for thirty-three years.

DAVID CAPTURES JERUSALEM

6 David then led his men to Jerusalem to fight against the Jebusites, the original inhabitants of the land who were living there. The Jebusites taunted David, saying, "You'll never get in here! Even the blind and lame could keep you out!" For the Jebusites thought they were safe. 7 But David captured the fortress of Zion, which is now called the City of David.

8 On the day of the attack, David said to his troops, "I hate those 'lame' and 'blind' Jebusites.* Whoever attacks them should strike by going into the city through the water tunnel.*" That is the origin of the saying, "The blind and the lame may not enter the house."*

9 So David made the fortress his home, and he called it the City of David. He extended the city, starting at the supporting terraces* and working inward. 10 And David became more and more powerful, because the LORD God of Heaven's Armies was with him.

11 Then King Hiram of Tyre sent messengers to David, along with cedar timber and carpenters and stonemasons, and they built David a palace. 12 And David realized that the LORD had confirmed him as king over Israel and had blessed his kingdom for the sake of his people Israel.

13 After moving from Hebron to Jerusalem, David married more concubines and wives, and they had more sons and daughters. 14 These are the names of David's sons who were born in Jerusalem: Shammua, Shobab, Nathan, Solomon, 15 Ibhar, Elishua, Nepheg, Japhia, 16 Elishama, Eliada, and Eliphelet.

4:1 *Ishbosheth* is another name for Esh-baal. 4:4 *Mephibosheth* is another name for Merib-baal. 4:6 As in Greek version; Hebrew reads *So they went into the house pretending to fetch wheat, but they stabbed him in the stomach. Then Recab and Baanah escaped.* 4:7 Hebrew *the Arabah.* 5:2 Or *For some time.* 5:8a Or *Those 'lame' and 'blind' Jebusites hate me.* 5:8b Or *with scaling hooks.* The meaning of the Hebrew is uncertain. 5:8c The meaning of this saying is uncertain. 5:9 Hebrew *the millo.* The meaning of the Hebrew is uncertain.

DAVID CONQUERS THE PHILISTINES

[17] When the Philistines heard that David had been anointed king of Israel, they mobilized all their forces to capture him. But David was told they were coming, so he went into the stronghold. [18] The Philistines arrived and spread out across the valley of Rephaim. [19] So David asked the LORD, "Should I go out to fight the Philistines? Will you hand them over to me?"

The LORD replied to David, "Yes, go ahead. I will certainly hand them over to you."

[20] So David went to Baal-perazim and defeated the Philistines there. "The LORD did it!" David exclaimed. "He burst through my enemies like a raging flood!" So he named that place Baal-perazim (which means "the Lord who bursts through"). [21] The Philistines had abandoned their idols there, so David and his men confiscated them.

[22] But after a while the Philistines returned and again spread out across the valley of Rephaim. [23] And again David asked the LORD what to do. "Do not attack them straight on," the LORD replied. "Instead, circle around behind and attack them near the poplar* trees. [24] When you hear a sound like marching feet in the tops of the poplar trees, be on the alert! That will be the signal that the LORD is moving ahead of you to strike down the Philistine army." [25] So David did what the LORD commanded, and he struck down the Philistines all the way from Gibeon* to Gezer.

MOVING THE ARK TO JERUSALEM

6 Then David again gathered all the elite troops in Israel, 30,000 in all. [2] He led them to Baalah of Judah* to bring back the Ark of God, which bears the name of the LORD of Heaven's Armies,* who is enthroned between the cherubim. [3] They placed the Ark of God on a new cart and brought it from Abinadab's house, which was on a hill. Uzzah and Ahio, Abinadab's sons, were guiding the cart [4] that carried the Ark of God.* Ahio walked in front of the Ark. [5] David and all the people of Israel were celebrating before the LORD, singing songs* and playing all kinds of musical instruments—lyres, harps, tambourines, castanets, and cymbals.

[6] But when they arrived at the threshing floor of Nacon, the oxen stumbled, and Uzzah reached out his hand and steadied the Ark of God. [7] Then the LORD's anger was aroused against Uzzah, and God struck him dead because of this.* So Uzzah died right there beside the Ark of God.

[8] David was angry because the LORD's anger had burst out against Uzzah. He named that place Perez-uzzah (which means "to burst out against Uzzah"), as it is still called today.

[9] David was now afraid of the LORD, and he asked, "How can I ever bring the Ark of the LORD back into my care?" [10] So David decided not to move the Ark of the LORD into the City of David. Instead, he took it to the house of Obed-edom

of Gath. [11] The Ark of the LORD remained there in Obed-edom's house for three months, and the LORD blessed Obed-edom and his entire household.

[12] Then King David was told, "The LORD has blessed Obed-edom's household and everything he has because of the Ark of God." So David went there and brought the Ark of God from the house of Obed-edom to the City of David with a great celebration. [13] After the men who were carrying the Ark of the LORD had gone six steps, David sacrificed a bull and a fattened calf. [14] And David danced before the LORD with all his might, wearing a priestly garment.* [15] So David and all the people of Israel brought up the Ark of the LORD with shouts of joy and the blowing of rams' horns.

MICHAL'S CONTEMPT FOR DAVID

[16] But as the Ark of the LORD entered the City of David, Michal, the daughter of Saul, looked down from her window. When she saw King David leaping and dancing before the LORD, she was filled with contempt for him.

[17] They brought the Ark of the LORD and set it in its place inside the special tent David had prepared for it. And David sacrificed burnt offerings and peace offerings to the LORD. [18] When he had finished his sacrifices, David blessed the people in the name of the LORD of Heaven's Armies. [19] Then he gave to every Israelite man and woman in the crowd a loaf of bread, a cake of dates,* and a cake of raisins. Then all the people returned to their homes.

[20] When David returned home to bless his own family, Michal, the daughter of Saul, came out to meet him. She said in disgust, "How distinguished the king of Israel looked today, shamelessly exposing himself to the servant girls like any vulgar person might do!"

[21] David retorted to Michal, "I was dancing before the LORD, who chose me above your father and all his family! He appointed me as the leader of Israel, the people of the LORD, so I celebrate before the LORD. [22] Yes, and I am willing to look even more foolish than this, even to be humiliated in my own eyes! But those servant girls you mentioned will indeed think I am distinguished!" [23] So Michal, the daughter of Saul, remained childless throughout her entire life.

5:23 Or *aspen,* or *balsam;* also in 5:24. The exact identification of this tree is uncertain.   5:25 As in Greek version (see also 1 Chr 14:16); Hebrew reads *Geba.*   6:2a Hebrew *Baale of Judah,* another name for Kiriath-jearim; compare 1 Chr 13:6.   6:2b Or *the Ark of God where the Name is proclaimed—the name of the LORD of Heaven's Armies.*   6:4 As in Dead Sea Scrolls and some Greek manuscripts; Masoretic Text reads *'and they brought it from Abinadab's house, which was on a hill, with the Ark of God.*   6:5 As in Dead Sea Scrolls and Greek version (see also 1 Chr 13:8); Masoretic Text reads *before the LORD with all manner of cypress wood.*   6:7 As in Dead Sea Scrolls; Masoretic Text reads *because of his irreverence.*   6:14 Hebrew *a linen ephod.*   6:19 Or *a portion of meat.* The meaning of the Hebrew is uncertain.

THE LORD'S COVENANT PROMISE TO DAVID

7 When King David was settled in his palace and the LORD had given him rest from all the surrounding enemies, ² the king summoned Nathan the prophet. "Look," David said, "I am living in a beautiful cedar palace,* but the Ark of God is out there in a tent!"

³ Nathan replied to the king, "Go ahead and do whatever you have in mind, for the LORD is with you."

⁴ But that same night the LORD said to Nathan,

⁵ "Go and tell my servant David, 'This is what the LORD has declared: Are you the one to build a house for me to live in? ⁶ I have never lived in a house, from the day I brought the Israelites out of Egypt until this very day. I have always moved from one place to another with a tent and a Tabernacle as my dwelling. ⁷ Yet no matter where I have gone with the Israelites, I have never once complained to Israel's tribal leaders, the shepherds of my people Israel. I have never asked them, "Why haven't you built me a beautiful cedar house?"'

⁸ "Now go and say to my servant David, 'This is what the LORD of Heaven's Armies has declared: I took you from tending sheep in the pasture and selected you to be the leader of my people Israel. ⁹ I have been with you wherever you have gone, and I have destroyed all your enemies before your eyes. Now I will make your name as famous as anyone who has ever lived on the earth! ¹⁰ And I will provide a homeland for my people Israel, planting them in a secure place where they will never be disturbed. Evil nations won't oppress them as they've done in the past, ¹¹ starting from the time I appointed judges to rule my people Israel. And I will give you rest from all your enemies.

"'Furthermore, the LORD declares that he will make a house for you—a dynasty of kings! ¹² For when you die and are buried with your ancestors, I will raise up one of your descendants, your own offspring, and I will make his kingdom strong. ¹³ He is the one who will build a house—a temple—for my name. And I will secure his royal throne forever. ¹⁴ I will be his father, and he will be my son. If he sins, I will correct and discipline him with the rod, like any father would do. ¹⁵ But my favor will not be taken from him as I took it from Saul, whom I removed from your sight. ¹⁶ Your house and your kingdom will continue before me* for all time, and your throne will be secure forever.'"

¹⁷ So Nathan went back to David and told him everything the LORD had said in this vision.

DAVID'S PRAYER OF THANKS

¹⁸ Then King David went in and sat before the LORD and prayed,

"Who am I, O Sovereign LORD, and what is my family, that you have brought me this far? ¹⁹ And now, Sovereign LORD, in addition to everything else, you speak of giving your servant a lasting dynasty! Do you deal with everyone this way, O Sovereign LORD?* ²⁰ "What more can I say to you? You know what your servant is really like, Sovereign LORD. ²¹ Because of your promise and according to your will, you have done all these great things and have made them known to your servant.

²² "How great you are, O Sovereign LORD! There is no one like you. We have never even heard of another God like you! ²³ What other nation on earth is like your people Israel? What other nation, O God, have you redeemed from slavery to be your own people? You made a great name for yourself when you redeemed your people from Egypt. You performed awesome miracles and drove out the nations and gods that stood in their way.* ²⁴ You made Israel your very own people forever, and you, O LORD, became their God. ²⁵ "And now, O LORD God, I am your servant; do as you have promised concerning me and my family. Confirm it as a promise that will last forever. ²⁶ And may your name be honored forever so that everyone will say, 'The LORD of Heaven's Armies is God over Israel!' And may the house of your servant David continue before you forever.

²⁷ "O LORD of Heaven's Armies, God of Israel, I have been bold enough to pray this prayer to you because you have revealed all this to your servant, saying, 'I will build a house for you—a dynasty of kings!' ²⁸ For you are God, O Sovereign LORD. Your words are truth, and you have promised these good things to your servant. ²⁹ And now, may it please you to bless the house of your servant, so that it may continue forever before you. For you have spoken, and when you grant a blessing to your servant, O Sovereign LORD, it is an eternal blessing!"

DAVID'S MILITARY VICTORIES

8 After this, David defeated and subdued the Philistines by conquering Gath, their largest town.* ² David also conquered the land of Moab. He made the people lie down on the ground in a row, and he measured them off in groups with a length of rope. He measured off two groups to be executed for every one group to be spared. The Moabites who were spared became David's subjects and paid him tribute money.

³David also destroyed the forces of Hadadezer son of Rehob, king of Zobah, when Hadadezer marched out to strengthen his control along the Euphrates River. ⁴David captured 1,000 chariots, 7,000 charioteers,* and 20,000 foot soldiers. He crippled all the chariot horses except enough for 100 chariots.

⁵When Arameans from Damascus arrived to help King Hadadezer, David killed 22,000 of them. ⁶Then he placed several army garrisons in Damascus, the Aramean capital, and the Arameans became David's subjects and paid him tribute money. So the LORD made David victorious wherever he went.

⁷David brought the gold shields of Hadadezer's officers to Jerusalem, ⁸along with a large amount of bronze from Hadadezer's towns of Tebah* and Berothai.

⁹When King Toi of Hamath heard that David had destroyed the entire army of Hadadezer, ¹⁰he sent his son Joram to congratulate King David for his successful campaign. Hadadezer and Toi had been enemies and were often at war. Joram presented David with many gifts of silver, gold, and bronze.

¹¹King David dedicated all these gifts to the LORD, as he did with the silver and gold from the other nations he had defeated—¹²from Edom,* Moab, Ammon, Philistia, and Amalek—and from Hadadezer son of Rehob, king of Zobah.

¹³So David became even more famous when he returned from destroying 18,000 Edomites* in the Valley of Salt. ¹⁴He placed army garrisons throughout Edom, and all the Edomites became David's subjects. In fact, the LORD made David victorious wherever he went.

¹⁵So David reigned over all Israel and did what was just and right for all his people. ¹⁶Joab son of Zeruiah was commander of the army. Jehoshaphat son of Ahilud was the royal historian. ¹⁷Zadok son of Ahitub and Ahimelech son of Abiathar were the priests. Seraiah was the court secretary. ¹⁸Benaiah son of Jehoiada was captain of the king's bodyguard.* And David's sons served as priestly leaders.*

DAVID'S KINDNESS TO MEPHIBOSHETH

9 One day David asked, "Is anyone in Saul's family still alive—anyone to whom I can show kindness for Jonathan's sake?" ²He summoned a man named Ziba, who had been one of Saul's servants. "Are you Ziba?" the king asked.

"Yes sir, I am," Ziba replied.

³The king then asked him, "Is anyone still alive from Saul's family? If so, I want to show God's kindness to them."

Ziba replied, "Yes, one of Jonathan's sons is still alive. He is crippled in both feet."

⁴"Where is he?" the king asked.

"In Lo-debar," Ziba told him, "at the home of Makir son of Ammiel."

⁵So David sent for him and brought him from Makir's home. ⁶His name was Mephibosheth*; he was Jonathan's son and Saul's grandson. When he came to David, he bowed low to the ground in deep respect. David said, "Greetings, Mephibosheth."

Mephibosheth replied, "I am your servant."

⁷"Don't be afraid!" David said. "I intend to show kindness to you because of my promise to your father, Jonathan. I will give you all the property that once belonged to your grandfather Saul, and you will eat here with me at the king's table!"

⁸Mephibosheth bowed respectfully and exclaimed, "Who is your servant, that you should show such kindness to a dead dog like me?"

⁹Then the king summoned Saul's servant Ziba and said, "I have given your master's grandson everything that belonged to Saul and his family. ¹⁰You and your sons and servants are to farm the land for him to produce food for your master's household.* But Mephibosheth, your master's

---

FUELED BY INHERITANCE
2 Samuel 9   MARCUS BRECHEEN

God has given us "vehicles" to carry us back to a renewed sense of our position as His children. He has given each of us an inheritance through Jesus that is "pure and undefiled, beyond the reach of change and decay" (1 Peter 1:4).

King David sought out Jonathan's descendants so he could bless them as he promised he would. Jonathan's son Mephibosheth, who was crippled, was the only one remaining. According to the law, he was not allowed to enter the royal palace. Nevertheless, because of David's covenant with Jonathan, Mephibosheth lived the rest of his life inside the palace with the blessing of the king.

By God's covenant made through Jesus, we too receive an inheritance. Our identity in Christ is greater than our brokenness, weaknesses, iniquities, or limitations. God is not ashamed of us, nor does He merely tolerate us. He loves us and desires friendship with each one of us.

8:4 As in Dead Sea Scrolls and Greek version (see also 1 Chr 18:4); Masoretic Text reads *captured 1,700 charioteers.* 8:8 As in some Greek manuscripts (see also 1 Chr 18:8); Hebrew reads *Betah.* 8:12 As in a few Hebrew manuscripts and Greek and Syriac versions (see also 8:14; 1 Chr 18:11); most Hebrew manuscripts read *Aram.* 8:13 As in a few Hebrew manuscripts and Greek and Syriac versions (see also 8:14; 1 Chr 18:12); most Hebrew manuscripts read *Arameans.* 8:18a Hebrew *of the Kerethites and Pelethites.* 8:18b Hebrew *David's sons were priests;* compare parallel text at 1 Chr 18:17. 9:6 *Mephibosheth* is another name for *Merib-baal.* 9:10 As in Greek version; Hebrew reads *your master's grandson.*

grandson, will eat here at my table." (Ziba had fifteen sons and twenty servants.)

¹¹Ziba replied, "Yes, my lord the king; I am your servant, and I will do all that you have commanded." And from that time on, Mephibosheth ate regularly at David's table,* like one of the king's own sons.

¹²Mephibosheth had a young son named Mica. From then on, all the members of Ziba's household were Mephibosheth's servants. ¹³And Mephibosheth, who was crippled in both feet, lived in Jerusalem and ate regularly at the king's table.

DAVID DEFEATS THE AMMONITES

10 Some time after this, King Nahash* of the Ammonites died, and his son Hanun became king. ²David said, "I am going to show loyalty to Hanun just as his father, Nahash, was always loyal to me." So David sent ambassadors to express sympathy to Hanun about his father's death.

But when David's ambassadors arrived in the land of Ammon, ³the Ammonite commanders said to Hanun, their master, "Do you really think these men are coming here to honor your father? No! David has sent them to spy out the city so they can come in and conquer it!" ⁴So Hanun seized David's ambassadors and shaved off half of each man's beard, cut off their robes at the buttocks, and sent them back to David in shame.

⁵When David heard what had happened, he sent messengers to tell the men, "Stay at Jericho until your beards grow out, and then come back." For they felt deep shame because of their appearance.

⁶When the people of Ammon realized how seriously they had angered David, they sent and hired 20,000 Aramean foot soldiers from the lands of Beth-rehob and Zobah, 1,000 from the king of Maacah, and 12,000 from the land of Tob. ⁷When David heard about this, he sent Joab and all his warriors to fight them. ⁸The Ammonite troops came out and drew up their battle lines at the entrance of the city gate, while the Arameans from Zobah and Rehob and the men from Tob and Maacah positioned themselves to fight in the open fields.

⁹When Joab saw that he would have to fight on both the front and the rear, he chose some of Israel's elite troops and placed them under his personal command to fight the Arameans in the fields. ¹⁰He left the rest of the army under the command of his brother Abishai, who was to attack the Ammonites. ¹¹"If the Arameans are too strong for me, then come over and help me," Joab told his brother. "And if the Ammonites are too strong for you, I will come and help you. ¹²Be courageous! Let us fight bravely for our people and the cities of our God. May the LORD's will be done."

¹³When Joab and his troops attacked, the Arameans began to run away. ¹⁴And when the Ammonites saw the Arameans running, they ran from Abishai and retreated into the city. After the battle was over, Joab returned to Jerusalem.

¹⁵The Arameans now realized that they were no match for Israel. So when they regrouped, ¹⁶they were joined by additional Aramean troops summoned by Hadadezer from the other side of the Euphrates River.* These troops arrived at Helam under the command of Shobach, the commander of Hadadezer's forces.

¹⁷When David heard what was happening, he mobilized all Israel, crossed the Jordan River, and led the army to Helam. The Arameans positioned themselves in battle formation and fought against David. ¹⁸But again the Arameans fled from the Israelites. This time David's forces killed 700 charioteers and 40,000 foot soldiers,* including Shobach, the commander of their army. ¹⁹When all the kings allied with Hadadezer saw that they had been defeated by Israel, they surrendered to Israel and became their subjects. After that, the Arameans were afraid to help the Ammonites.

DAVID AND BATHSHEBA

11 In the spring of the year,* when kings normally go out to war, David sent Joab and the Israelite army to fight the Ammonites. They destroyed the Ammonite army and laid siege to the city of Rabbah. However, David stayed behind in Jerusalem.

²Late one afternoon, after his midday rest, David got out of bed and was walking on the roof of the palace. As he looked out over the city, he noticed a woman of unusual beauty taking a bath. ³He sent someone to find out who she was, and he was told, "She is Bathsheba, the daughter of Eliam and the wife of Uriah the Hittite." ⁴Then David sent messengers to get her; and when she came to the palace, he slept with her. She had just completed the purification rites after having her menstrual period. Then she returned home. ⁵Later, when Bathsheba discovered that she was pregnant, she sent David a message, saying, "I'm pregnant."

⁶Then David sent word to Joab: "Send me Uriah the Hittite." So Joab sent him to David. ⁷When Uriah arrived, David asked him how Joab and the army were getting along and how the war was progressing. ⁸Then he told Uriah, "Go on home and relax.*" David even sent a gift to Uriah after he had left the palace. ⁹But Uriah didn't go home. He slept that night at the palace entrance with the king's palace guard.

¹⁰When David heard that Uriah had not gone home, he summoned him and asked, "What's

9:11 As in Greek version; Hebrew reads *my table.* **10:1** As in parallel text at 1 Chr 19:1; Hebrew reads *the king.* **10:16** Hebrew *the river.* **10:18** As in some Greek manuscripts (see also 1 Chr 19:18); Hebrew reads *charioteers.* **11:1** Hebrew *At the turn of the year.* The first day of the year in the ancient Hebrew lunar calendar occurred in March or April. **11:8** Hebrew *and wash your feet,* an expression that may also have a connotation of ritualistic washing.

the matter? Why didn't you go home last night after being away for so long?"

¹¹Uriah replied, "The Ark and the armies of Israel and Judah are living in tents,* and Joab and my master's men are camping in the open fields. How could I go home to wine and dine and sleep with my wife? I swear that I would never do such a thing."

¹²"Well, stay here today," David told him, "and tomorrow you may return to the army." So Uriah stayed in Jerusalem that day and the next. ¹³Then David invited him to dinner and got him drunk. But even then he couldn't get Uriah to go home to his wife. Again he slept at the palace entrance with the king's palace guard.

DAVID ARRANGES FOR URIAH'S DEATH

¹⁴So the next morning David wrote a letter to Joab and gave it to Uriah to deliver. ¹⁵The letter instructed Joab, "Station Uriah on the front lines where the battle is fiercest. Then pull back so that he will be killed." ¹⁶So Joab assigned Uriah to a spot close to the city wall where he knew the enemy's strongest men were fighting. ¹⁷And when the enemy soldiers came out of the city to fight, Uriah the Hittite was killed along with several other Israelite soldiers.

¹⁸Then Joab sent a battle report to David. ¹⁹He told his messenger, "Report all the news of the battle to the king. ²⁰But he might get angry and ask, 'Why did the troops go so close to the city? Didn't they know there would be shooting from the walls? ²¹Wasn't Abimelech son of Gideon* killed at Thebez by a woman who threw a millstone down on him from the wall? Why would you get so close to the wall?' Then tell him, 'Uriah the Hittite was killed, too.'"

²²So the messenger went to Jerusalem and gave a complete report to David. ²³"The enemy came out against us in the open fields," he said. "And as we chased them back to the city gate, ²⁴the archers on the wall shot arrows at us. Some of the king's men were killed, including Uriah the Hittite."

²⁵"Well, tell Joab not to be discouraged," David said. "The sword devours this one today and that one tomorrow! Fight harder next time, and conquer the city!"

²⁶When Uriah's wife heard that her husband was dead, she mourned for him. ²⁷When the period of mourning was over, David sent for her and brought her to the palace, and she became one of his wives. Then she gave birth to a son. But the LORD was displeased with what David had done.

NATHAN REBUKES DAVID

12 So the LORD sent Nathan the prophet to tell David this story: "There were two men in a certain town. One was rich, and one was poor. ²The rich man owned a great many sheep and cattle. ³The poor man owned nothing but one little lamb he had bought. He raised that little lamb, and it grew up with his children. It ate from the man's own plate and drank from his cup. He cuddled it in his arms like a baby daughter. ⁴One day a guest arrived at the home of the rich man. But instead of killing an animal from his own flock or herd, he took the poor man's lamb and killed it and prepared it for his guest."

⁵David was furious. "As surely as the LORD lives," he vowed, "any man who would do such a thing deserves to die! ⁶He must repay four lambs to the poor man for the one he stole and for having no pity."

⁷Then Nathan said to David, "You are that man! The LORD, the God of Israel, says: I anointed you king of Israel and saved you from the power of Saul. ⁸I gave you your master's house and his wives and the kingdoms of Israel and Judah. And if that had not been enough, I would have given you much, much more. ⁹Why, then, have you despised the word of the LORD and done this horrible deed? For you have murdered Uriah the Hittite with the sword of the Ammonites and stolen his wife. ¹⁰From this time on, your family will live by the sword because you have despised me by taking Uriah's wife to be your own.

¹¹"This is what the LORD says: Because of what you have done, I will cause your own household to rebel against you. I will give your wives to another man before your very eyes, and he will go to bed with them in public view. ¹²You did it secretly, but I will make this happen to you openly in the sight of all Israel."

DAVID CONFESSES HIS GUILT

¹³Then David confessed to Nathan, "I have sinned against the LORD."

Nathan replied, "Yes, but the LORD has forgiven you, and you won't die for this sin. ¹⁴Nevertheless, because you have shown utter contempt for the word of the LORD* by doing this, your child will die."

¹⁵After Nathan returned to his home, the LORD sent a deadly illness to the child of David and Uriah's wife. ¹⁶David begged God to spare the child. He went without food and lay all night on the bare ground. ¹⁷The elders of his household pleaded with him to get up and eat with them, but he refused.

¹⁸Then on the seventh day the child died. David's advisers were afraid to tell him. "He wouldn't listen to reason while the child was ill," they said. "What drastic thing will he do when we tell him the child is dead?"

¹⁹When David saw them whispering, he realized what had happened. "Is the child dead?" he asked.

11:11 Or at Succoth.   11:21 Hebrew son of Jerub-besheth. Jerub-besheth is a variation on the name Jerub-baal, which is another name for Gideon; see Judg 6:32.   12:14 As in Dead Sea Scrolls; Masoretic Text reads the enemies of the LORD.

"Yes," they replied, "he is dead."

[20] Then David got up from the ground, washed himself, put on lotions,* and changed his clothes. He went to the Tabernacle and worshiped the LORD. After that, he returned to the palace and was served food and ate.

[21] His advisers were amazed. "We don't understand you," they told him. "While the child was still living, you wept and refused to eat. But now that the child is dead, you have stopped your mourning and are eating again."

[22] David replied, "I fasted and wept while the child was alive, for I said, 'Perhaps the LORD will be gracious to me and let the child live.' [23] But why should I fast when he is dead? Can I bring him back again? I will go to him one day, but he cannot return to me."

[24] Then David comforted Bathsheba, his wife, and slept with her. She became pregnant and gave birth to a son, and David* named him Solomon. The LORD loved the child [25] and sent word through Nathan the prophet that they should name him Jedidiah (which means "beloved of the LORD"), as the LORD had commanded.*

DAVID CAPTURES RABBAH

[26] Meanwhile, Joab was fighting against Rabbah, the capital of Ammon, and he captured the royal fortifications.* [27] Joab sent messengers to tell David, "I have fought against Rabbah and captured its water supply.* [28] Now bring the rest of the army and capture the city. Otherwise, I will capture it and get credit for the victory."

[29] So David gathered the rest of the army and went to Rabbah, and he fought against it and captured it. [30] David removed the crown from the king's head,* and it was placed on his own head. The crown was made of gold and set with gems, and it weighed seventy-five pounds.* David took a vast amount of plunder from the city. [31] He also made slaves of the people of Rabbah and forced them to labor with* saws, iron picks, and iron axes, and to work in the brick kilns.* That is how he dealt with the people of all the Ammonite towns. Then David and all the army returned to Jerusalem.

THE RAPE OF TAMAR

13 Now David's son Absalom had a beautiful sister named Tamar. And Amnon, her half brother, fell desperately in love with her. [2] Amnon became so obsessed with Tamar that he became ill. She was a virgin, and Amnon thought he could never have her.

[3] But Amnon had a very crafty friend—his cousin Jonadab. He was the son of David's brother Shimea.* [4] One day Jonadab said to Amnon, "What's the trouble? Why should the son of a king look so dejected morning after morning?"

So Amnon told him, "I am in love with Tamar, my brother Absalom's sister."

[5] "Well," Jonadab said, "I'll tell you what to do. Go back to bed and pretend you are ill. When your father comes to see you, ask him to let Tamar come and prepare some food for you. Tell him you'll feel better if she prepares it as you watch and feeds you with her own hands."

[6] So Amnon lay down and pretended to be sick. And when the king came to see him, Amnon asked him, "Please let my sister Tamar come and cook my favorite dish* as I watch. Then I can eat it from her own hands." [7] So David agreed and sent Tamar to Amnon's house to prepare some food for him.

[8] When Tamar arrived at Amnon's house, she went to the place where he was lying down so he could watch her mix some dough. Then she baked his favorite dish for him. [9] But when she set the serving tray before him, he refused to eat. "Everyone get out of here," Amnon told his servants. So they all left.

[10] Then he said to Tamar, "Now bring the food into my bedroom and feed it to me here." So Tamar took his favorite dish to him. [11] But as she was feeding him, he grabbed her and demanded, "Come to bed with me, my darling sister."

[12] "No, my brother!" she cried. "Don't be foolish! Don't do this to me! Such wicked things aren't done in Israel. [13] Where could I go in my shame? And you would be called one of the greatest fools in Israel. Please, just speak to the king about it, and he will let you marry me."

[14] But Amnon wouldn't listen to her, and since he was stronger than she was, he raped her. [15] Then suddenly Amnon's love turned to hate, and he hated her even more than he had loved her. "Get out of here!" he snarled at her.

[16] "No, no!" Tamar cried. "Sending me away now is worse than what you've already done to me."

But Amnon wouldn't listen to her. [17] He shouted for his servant and demanded, "Throw this woman out, and lock the door behind her!"

[18] So the servant put her out and locked the door behind her. She was wearing a long, beautiful robe,* as was the custom in those days for the king's virgin daughters. [19] But now Tamar tore her robe and put ashes on her head. And then, with her face in her hands, she went away crying.

[20] Her brother Absalom saw her and asked, "Is it true that Amnon has been with you? Well, my sister, keep quiet for now, since he's your brother.

12:20 Hebrew *anointed himself.* 12:24 Hebrew *he;* an alternate Hebrew reading and some Hebrew manuscripts read *she.* 12:25 As in Greek version; Hebrew reads *because of the* LORD. 12:26 Or *the royal city.* 12:27 Or *captured the city of water.* 12:30a Or *from the head of Milcom* (as in Greek version). Milcom, also called Molech, was the god of the Ammonites. 12:30b Hebrew *1 talent* [34 kilograms]. 12:31a Hebrew *He also brought out the people [of Rabbah] and put them under.* 12:31b Hebrew *and he made them pass through the brick kilns.* 13:3 Hebrew *Shimeah* (also in 13:32), a variant spelling of Shimea; compare 1 Chr 2:13. 13:6 Or *a couple of cakes;* also in 13:8, 10. 13:18 Or *a robe with sleeves,* or *an ornamented robe.* The meaning of the Hebrew is uncertain.

Don't you worry about it." So Tamar lived as a desolate woman in her brother Absalom's house.

²¹ When King David heard what had happened, he was very angry.* ²² And though Absalom never spoke to Amnon about this, he hated Amnon deeply because of what he had done to his sister.

ABSALOM'S REVENGE ON AMNON

²³ Two years later, when Absalom's sheep were being sheared at Baal-hazor near Ephraim, Absalom invited all the king's sons to come to a feast. ²⁴ He went to the king and said, "My sheep-shearers are now at work. Would the king and his servants please come to celebrate the occasion with me?"

²⁵ The king replied, "No, my son. If we all came, we would be too much of a burden on you." Absalom pressed him, but the king would not come, though he gave Absalom his blessing.

²⁶ "Well, then," Absalom said, "if you can't come, how about sending my brother Amnon with us?"

"Why Amnon?" the king asked. ²⁷ But Absalom kept on pressing the king until he finally agreed to let all his sons attend, including Amnon. So Absalom prepared a feast fit for a king.*

²⁸ Absalom told his men, "Wait until Amnon gets drunk; then at my signal, kill him! Don't be afraid. I'm the one who has given the command. Take courage and do it!" ²⁹ So at Absalom's signal they murdered Amnon. Then the other sons of the king jumped on their mules and fled.

³⁰ As they were on the way back to Jerusalem, this report reached David: "Absalom has killed all the king's sons; not one is left alive!" ³¹ The king got up, tore his robe, and threw himself on the ground. His advisers also tore their clothes in horror and sorrow.

³² But just then Jonadab, the son of David's brother Shimea, arrived and said, "No, don't believe that all the king's sons have been killed! It was only Amnon! Absalom has been plotting this ever since Amnon raped his sister Tamar. ³³ No, my lord the king, your sons aren't all dead! It was only Amnon." ³⁴ Meanwhile Absalom escaped.

Then the watchman on the Jerusalem wall saw a great crowd coming down the hill on the road from the west. He ran to tell the king, "I see a crowd of people coming from the Horonaim road along the side of the hill."*

³⁵ "Look!" Jonadab told the king. "There they are now! The king's sons are coming, just as I said."

³⁶ They soon arrived, weeping and sobbing, and the king and all his servants wept bitterly with them. ³⁷ And David mourned many days for his son Amnon.

Absalom fled to his grandfather, Talmai son of Ammihud, the king of Geshur. ³⁸ He stayed there in Geshur for three years. ³⁹ And King David,* now reconciled to Amnon's death, longed to be reunited with his son Absalom.*

JOAB ARRANGES FOR ABSALOM'S RETURN

14 Joab realized how much the king longed to see Absalom. ² So he sent for a woman from Tekoa who had a reputation for great wisdom. He said to her, "Pretend you are in mourning; wear mourning clothes and don't put on lotions.* Act like a woman who has been mourning for the dead for a long time. ³ Then go to the king and tell him the story I am about to tell you." Then Joab told her what to say.

⁴ When the woman from Tekoa approached* the king, she bowed with her face to the ground in deep respect and cried out, "O king! Help me!"

⁵ "What's the trouble?" the king asked.

"Alas, I am a widow!" she replied. "My husband is dead. ⁶ My two sons had a fight out in the field. And since no one was there to stop it, one of them was killed. ⁷ Now the rest of the family is demanding, 'Let us have your son. We will execute him for murdering his brother. He doesn't deserve to inherit his family's property.' They want to extinguish the only coal I have left, and my husband's name and family will disappear from the face of the earth."

⁸ "Leave it to me," the king told her. "Go home, and I'll see to it that no one touches him."

⁹ "Oh, thank you, my lord the king," the woman from Tekoa replied. "If you are criticized for helping me, let the blame fall on me and on my father's house, and let the king and his throne be innocent."

¹⁰ "If anyone objects," the king said, "bring him to me. I can assure you he will never harm you again!"

¹¹ Then she said, "Please swear to me by the LORD your God that you won't let anyone take vengeance against my son. I want no more bloodshed."

"As surely as the LORD lives," he replied, "not a hair on your son's head will be disturbed!"

¹² "Please allow me to ask one more thing of my lord the king," she said.

"Go ahead and speak," he responded.

¹³ She replied, "Why don't you do as much for the people of God as you have promised to do for me? You have convicted yourself in making this decision, because you have refused to bring home your own banished son. ¹⁴ All of us must die eventually. Our lives are like water spilled out on the ground, which cannot be gathered up again. But God does not just sweep life away; instead, he devises ways to bring us back when we have been separated from him.

¹⁵ "I have come to plead with my lord the king because people have threatened me. I said to

13:21 Dead Sea Scrolls and Greek version add *But he did not punish his son Amnon, because he loved him, for he was his firstborn.* 13:27 As in Greek and Latin versions (compare also Dead Sea Scrolls); the Hebrew text lacks this sentence. 13:34 As in Greek version; Hebrew lacks this sentence. 13:39a Dead Sea Scrolls and Greek version read *And the spirit of the king.* 13:39b Or *no longer felt a need to go out after Absalom.* 14:2 Hebrew *don't anoint yourself with oil.* 14:4 As in many Hebrew manuscripts and Greek and Syriac versions; Masoretic Text reads *spoke to.*

myself, 'Perhaps the king will listen to me [16] and rescue us from those who would cut us off from the inheritance* God has given us. [17] Yes, my lord the king will give us peace of mind again.' I know that you are like an angel of God in discerning good from evil. May the LORD your God be with you."

[18] "I must know one thing," the king replied, "and tell me the truth."

"Yes, my lord the king," she responded.

[19] "Did Joab put you up to this?"

And the woman replied, "My lord the king, how can I deny it? Nobody can hide anything from you. Yes, Joab sent me and told me what to say. [20] He did it to place the matter before you in a different light. But you are as wise as an angel of God, and you understand everything that happens among us!"

[21] So the king sent for Joab and told him, "All right, go and bring back the young man Absalom."

[22] Joab bowed with his face to the ground in deep respect and said, "At last I know that I have gained your approval, my lord the king, for you have granted me this request!"

[23] Then Joab went to Geshur and brought Absalom back to Jerusalem. [24] But the king gave this order: "Absalom may go to his own house, but he must never come into my presence." So Absalom did not see the king.

ABSALOM RECONCILED TO DAVID

[25] Now Absalom was praised as the most handsome man in all Israel. He was flawless from head to foot. [26] He cut his hair only once a year, and then only because it was so heavy. When he weighed it out, it came to five pounds!* [27] He had three sons and one daughter. His daughter's name was Tamar, and she was very beautiful.

[28] Absalom lived in Jerusalem for two years, but he never got to see the king. [29] Then Absalom sent for Joab to ask him to intercede for him, but Joab refused to come. Absalom sent for him a second time, but again Joab refused to come. [30] So Absalom said to his servants, "Go and set fire to Joab's barley field, the field next to mine." So they set his field on fire, as Absalom had commanded.

[31] Then Joab came to Absalom at his house and demanded, "Why did your servants set my field on fire?"

[32] And Absalom replied, "Because I wanted you to ask the king why he brought me back from Geshur if he didn't intend to see me. I might as well have stayed there. Let me see the king; if he finds me guilty of anything, then let him kill me."

[33] So Joab told the king what Absalom had said. Then at last David summoned Absalom, who came and bowed low before the king, and the king kissed him.

ABSALOM'S REBELLION

15 After this, Absalom bought a chariot and horses, and he hired fifty bodyguards to run ahead of him. [2] He got up early every morning and went out to the gate of the city. When people brought a case to the king for judgment, Absalom would ask where in Israel they were from, and they would tell him their tribe. [3] Then Absalom would say, "You've really got a strong case here! It's too bad the king doesn't have anyone to hear it. [4] I wish I were the judge. Then everyone could bring their cases to me for judgment, and I would give them justice!"

[5] When people tried to bow before him, Absalom wouldn't let them. Instead, he took them by the hand and kissed them. [6] Absalom did this with everyone who came to the king for judgment, and so he stole the hearts of all the people of Israel.

[7] After four years,* Absalom said to the king, "Let me go to Hebron to offer a sacrifice to the LORD and fulfill a vow I made to him. [8] For while your servant was at Geshur in Aram, I promised to sacrifice to the LORD in Hebron* if he would bring me back to Jerusalem."

[9] "All right," the king told him. "Go and fulfill your vow."

So Absalom went to Hebron. [10] But while he was there, he sent secret messengers to all the tribes of Israel to stir up a rebellion against the king. "As soon as you hear the ram's horn," his message read, "you are to say, 'Absalom has been crowned king in Hebron.'" [11] He took 200 men from Jerusalem with him as guests, but they knew nothing of his intentions. [12] While Absalom was offering the sacrifices, he sent for Ahithophel, one of David's counselors who lived in Giloh. Soon many others also joined Absalom, and the conspiracy gained momentum.

DAVID ESCAPES FROM JERUSALEM

[13] A messenger soon arrived in Jerusalem to tell David, "All Israel has joined Absalom in a conspiracy against you!"

[14] "Then we must flee at once, or it will be too late!" David urged his men. "Hurry! If we get out of the city before Absalom arrives, both we and the city of Jerusalem will be spared from disaster."

[15] "We are with you," his advisers replied. "Do what you think is best."

[16] So the king and all his household set out at once. He left no one behind except ten of his concubines to look after the palace. [17] The king and all his people set out on foot, pausing at the last house [18] to let all the king's men move past to lead the way. There were 600 men from Gath who had come with David, along with the king's bodyguard.*

14:16 Or *the property;* or *the people.* 14:26 Hebrew *200 shekels* [2.3 kilograms] *by the royal standard.* 15:7 As in Greek and Syriac versions; Hebrew reads *forty years.* 15:8 As in some Greek manuscripts; Hebrew lacks *in Hebron.* 15:18 Hebrew *the Kerethites and Pelethites.*

¹⁹Then the king turned and said to Ittai, a leader of the men from Gath, "Why are you coming with us? Go on back to King Absalom, for you are a guest in Israel, a foreigner in exile. ²⁰You arrived only recently, and should I force you today to wander with us? I don't even know where we will go. Go on back and take your kinsmen with you, and may the LORD show you his unfailing love and faithfulness.*"

²¹But Ittai said to the king, "I vow by the LORD and by your own life that I will go wherever my lord the king goes, no matter what happens—whether it means life or death."

²²David replied, "All right, come with us." So Ittai and all his men and their families went along.

²³Everyone cried loudly as the king and his followers passed by. They crossed the Kidron Valley and then went out toward the wilderness. ²⁴Zadok and all the Levites also came along, carrying the Ark of the Covenant of God. They set down the Ark of God, and Abiathar offered sacrifices* until everyone had passed out of the city.

²⁵Then the king instructed Zadok to take the Ark of God back into the city. "If the LORD sees fit," David said, "he will bring me back to see the Ark and the Tabernacle* again. ²⁶But if he is through with me, then let him do what seems best to him."

²⁷The king also told Zadok the priest, "Look,* here is my plan. You and Abiathar* should return quietly to the city with your son Ahimaaz and Abiathar's son Jonathan. ²⁸I will stop at the shallows of the Jordan River* and wait there for a report from you." ²⁹So Zadok and Abiathar took the Ark of God back to the city and stayed there.

³⁰David walked up the road to the Mount of Olives, weeping as he went. His head was covered and his feet were bare as a sign of mourning. And the people who were with him covered their heads and wept as they climbed the hill. ³¹When someone told David that his adviser Ahithophel was now backing Absalom, David prayed, "O LORD, let Ahithophel give Absalom foolish advice!"

³²When David reached the summit of the Mount of Olives where people worshiped God, Hushai the Arkite was waiting there for him. Hushai had torn his clothing and put dirt on his head as a sign of mourning. ³³But David told him, "If you go with me, you will only be a burden. ³⁴Return to Jerusalem and tell Absalom, 'I will now be your adviser, O king, just as I was your father's adviser in the past.' Then you can frustrate and counter Ahithophel's advice. ³⁵Zadok and Abiathar, the priests, will be there. Tell them about the plans being made in the king's palace, ³⁶and they will send their sons Ahimaaz and Jonathan to tell me what is going on."

³⁷So David's friend Hushai returned to Jerusalem, getting there just as Absalom arrived.

DAVID AND ZIBA

16 When David had gone a little beyond the summit of the Mount of Olives, Ziba, the servant of Mephibosheth,* was waiting there for him. He had two donkeys loaded with 200 loaves of bread, 100 clusters of raisins, 100 bunches of summer fruit, and a wineskin full of wine.

²"What are these for?" the king asked Ziba.

Ziba replied, "The donkeys are for the king's people to ride on, and the bread and summer fruit are for the young men to eat. The wine is for those who become exhausted in the wilderness."

³"And where is Mephibosheth, Saul's grandson?" the king asked him.

"He stayed in Jerusalem," Ziba replied. "He said, 'Today I will get back the kingdom of my grandfather Saul.'"

⁴"In that case," the king told Ziba, "I give you everything Mephibosheth owns."

"I bow before you," Ziba replied. "May I always be pleasing to you, my lord the king."

SHIMEI CURSES DAVID

⁵As King David came to Bahurim, a man came out of the village cursing them. It was Shimei son of Gera, from the same clan as Saul's family. ⁶He threw stones at the king and the king's officers and all the mighty warriors who surrounded him. ⁷"Get out of here, you murderer, you scoundrel!" he shouted at David. ⁸"The LORD is paying you back for all the bloodshed in Saul's clan. You stole his throne, and now the LORD has given it to your son Absalom. At last you will taste some of your own medicine, for you are a murderer!"

⁹"Why should this dead dog curse my lord the king?" Abishai son of Zeruiah demanded. "Let me go over and cut off his head!"

¹⁰"No!" the king said. "Who asked your opinion, you sons of Zeruiah! If the LORD has told him to curse me, who are you to stop him?"

¹¹Then David said to Abishai and to all his servants, "My own son is trying to kill me. Doesn't this relative of Saul* have even more reason to do so? Leave him alone and let him curse, for the LORD has told him to do it. ¹²And perhaps the LORD will see that I am being wronged* and will bless me because of these curses today." ¹³So David and his men continued down the road, and Shimei kept pace with them on a nearby hillside, cursing and throwing stones and dirt at David.

¹⁴The king and all who were with him grew weary along the way, so they rested when they reached the Jordan River.*

15:20 As in Greek version; Hebrew reads *and may unfailing love and faithfulness go with you.* 15:24 Or *Abiathar went up.* 15:25 Hebrew *and his dwelling place.* 15:27a As in Greek version; Hebrew reads *Are you a seer?* or *Do you see?* 15:27b Hebrew lacks *and Abiathar;* compare 15:29. 15:28 Hebrew *at the crossing points of the wilderness.* 16:1 *Mephibosheth* is another name for Merib-baal. 16:11 Hebrew *this Benjaminite.* 16:12 As in Greek and Syriac versions; Hebrew reads *see my iniquity.* 16:14 As in Greek version (see also 17:16); Hebrew reads *when they reached their destination.*

AHITHOPHEL ADVISES ABSALOM

¹⁵ Meanwhile, Absalom and all the army of Israel arrived at Jerusalem, accompanied by Ahithophel. ¹⁶ When David's friend Hushai the Arkite arrived, he went immediately to see Absalom. "Long live the king!" he exclaimed. "Long live the king!"

¹⁷ "Is this the way you treat your friend David?" Absalom asked him. "Why aren't you with him?"

¹⁸ "I'm here because I belong to the man who is chosen by the LORD and by all the men of Israel," Hushai replied. ¹⁹ "And anyway, why shouldn't I serve you? Just as I was your father's adviser, now I will be your adviser!"

²⁰ Then Absalom turned to Ahithophel and asked him, "What should I do next?"

²¹ Ahithophel told him, "Go and sleep with your father's concubines, for he has left them here to look after the palace. Then all Israel will know that you have insulted your father beyond hope of reconciliation, and they will throw their support to you." ²² So they set up a tent on the palace roof where everyone could see it, and Absalom went in and had sex with his father's concubines.

²³ Absalom followed Ahithophel's advice, just as David had done. For every word Ahithophel spoke seemed as wise as though it had come directly from the mouth of God.

17 Now Ahithophel urged Absalom, "Let me choose 12,000 men to start out after David tonight. ² I will catch up with him while he is weary and discouraged. He and his troops will panic, and everyone will run away. Then I will kill only the king, ³ and I will bring all the people back to you as a bride returns to her husband. After all, it is only one man's life that you seek.* Then you will be at peace with all the people." ⁴ This plan seemed good to Absalom and to all the elders of Israel.

HUSHAI COUNTERS AHITHOPHEL'S ADVICE

⁵ But then Absalom said, "Bring in Hushai the Arkite. Let's see what he thinks about this." ⁶ When Hushai arrived, Absalom told him what Ahithophel had said. Then he asked, "What is your opinion? Should we follow Ahithophel's advice? If not, what do you suggest?"

⁷ "Well," Hushai replied to Absalom, "this time Ahithophel has made a mistake. ⁸ You know your father and his men; they are mighty warriors. Right now they are as enraged as a mother bear who has been robbed of her cubs. And remember that your father is an experienced man of war. He won't be spending the night among the troops. ⁹ He has probably already hidden in some pit or cave. And when he comes out and attacks and a few of your men fall, there will be panic among your troops, and the word will spread that Absalom's men are being slaughtered. ¹⁰ Then even the bravest soldiers, though

they have the heart of a lion, will be paralyzed with fear. For all Israel knows what a mighty warrior your father is and how courageous his men are.

¹¹ "I recommend that you mobilize the entire army of Israel, bringing them from as far away as Dan in the north and Beersheba in the south. That way you will have an army as numerous as the sand on the seashore. And I advise that you personally lead the troops. ¹² When we find David, we'll fall on him like dew that falls on the ground. Then neither he nor any of his men will be left alive. ¹³ And if David were to escape into some town, you will have all Israel there at your command. Then we can take ropes and drag the walls of the town into the nearest valley until every stone is torn down."

¹⁴ Then Absalom and all the men of Israel said, "Hushai's advice is better than Ahithophel's." For the LORD had determined to defeat the counsel of Ahithophel, which really was the better plan, so that he could bring disaster on Absalom!

HUSHAI WARNS DAVID TO ESCAPE

¹⁵ Hushai told Zadok and Abiathar, the priests, what Ahithophel had said to Absalom and the elders of Israel and what he himself had advised instead. ¹⁶ "Quick!" he told them. "Find David and urge him not to stay at the shallows of the Jordan River* tonight. He must go across at once into the wilderness beyond. Otherwise he will die and his entire army with him."

¹⁷ Jonathan and Ahimaaz had been staying at En-rogel so as not to be seen entering and leaving the city. Arrangements had been made for a servant girl to bring them the message they were to take to King David. ¹⁸ But a boy spotted them at En-rogel, and he told Absalom about it. So they quickly escaped to Bahurim, where a man hid them down inside a well in his courtyard. ¹⁹ The man's wife put a cloth over the top of the well and scattered grain on it to dry in the sun; so no one suspected they were there.

²⁰ When Absalom's men arrived, they asked her, "Have you seen Ahimaaz and Jonathan?"

The woman replied, "They were here, but they crossed over the brook." Absalom's men looked for them without success and returned to Jerusalem.

²¹ Then the two men crawled out of the well and hurried on to King David. "Quick!" they told him, "cross the Jordan tonight!" And they told him how Ahithophel had advised that he be captured and killed. ²² So David and all the people with him went across the Jordan River during the night, and they were all on the other bank before dawn.

²³ When Ahithophel realized that his advice had not been followed, he saddled his donkey,

---

17:3 As in Greek version; Hebrew reads *like the return of all is the man whom you seek.* 17:16 Hebrew *at the crossing points of the wilderness.*

went to his hometown, set his affairs in order, and hanged himself. He died there and was buried in the family tomb.

²⁴David soon arrived at Mahanaim. By now, Absalom had mobilized the entire army of Israel and was leading his troops across the Jordan River. ²⁵Absalom had appointed Amasa as commander of his army, replacing Joab, who had been commander under David. (Amasa was Joab's cousin. His father was Jether,* an Ishmaelite.* His mother, Abigail daughter of Nahash, was the sister of Joab's mother, Zeruiah.) ²⁶Absalom and the Israelite army set up camp in the land of Gilead.

²⁷When David arrived at Mahanaim, he was warmly greeted by Shobi son of Nahash, who came from Rabbah of the Ammonites, and by Makir son of Ammiel from Lo-debar, and by Barzillai of Gilead from Rogelim. ²⁸They brought sleeping mats, cooking pots, serving bowls, wheat and barley, flour and roasted grain, beans, lentils, ²⁹honey, butter, sheep, goats, and cheese for David and those who were with him. For they said, "You must all be very hungry and tired and thirsty after your long march through the wilderness."

ABSALOM'S DEFEAT AND DEATH

18 David now mustered the men who were with him and appointed generals and captains* to lead them. ²He sent the troops out in three groups, placing one group under Joab, one under Joab's brother Abishai son of Zeruiah, and one under Ittai, the man from Gath. The king told his troops, "I am going out with you."

³But his men objected strongly. "You must not go," they urged. "If we have to turn and run—and even if half of us die—it will make no difference to Absalom's troops; they will be looking only for you. You are worth 10,000 of us,* and it is better that you stay here in the town and send help if we need it."

⁴"If you think that's the best plan, I'll do it," the king answered. So he stood alongside the gate of the town as all the troops marched out in groups of hundreds and of thousands.

⁵And the king gave this command to Joab, Abishai, and Ittai: "For my sake, deal gently with young Absalom." And all the troops heard the king give this order to his commanders.

⁶So the battle began in the forest of Ephraim, ⁷and the Israelite troops were beaten back by David's men. There was a great slaughter that day, and 20,000 men laid down their lives. ⁸The battle raged all across the countryside, and more men died because of the forest than were killed by the sword.

⁹During the battle, Absalom happened to come upon some of David's men. He tried to escape on his mule, but as he rode beneath the thick branches of a great tree, his hair* got caught in the tree. His mule kept going and left him dangling in the air. ¹⁰One of David's men saw what

had happened and told Joab, "I saw Absalom dangling from a great tree."

¹¹"What?" Joab demanded. "You saw him there and didn't kill him? I would have rewarded you with ten pieces of silver* and a hero's belt!"

¹²"I would not kill the king's son for even a thousand pieces of silver,*" the man replied to Joab. "We all heard the king say to you and Abishai and Ittai, 'For my sake, please spare young Absalom.' ¹³And if I had betrayed the king by killing his son—and the king would certainly find out who did it—you yourself would be the first to abandon me."

¹⁴"Enough of this nonsense," Joab said. Then he took three daggers and plunged them into Absalom's heart as he dangled, still alive, in the great tree. ¹⁵Ten of Joab's young armor bearers then surrounded Absalom and killed him.

¹⁶Then Joab blew the ram's horn, and his men returned from chasing the army of Israel. ¹⁷They threw Absalom's body into a deep pit in the forest and piled a great heap of stones over it. And all Israel fled to their homes.

¹⁸During his lifetime, Absalom had built a monument to himself in the King's Valley, for he said, "I have no son to carry on my name." He named the monument after himself, and it is known as Absalom's Monument to this day.

DAVID MOURNS ABSALOM'S DEATH

¹⁹Then Zadok's son Ahimaaz said, "Let me run to the king with the good news that the LORD has rescued him from his enemies."

²⁰"No," Joab told him, "it wouldn't be good news to the king that his son is dead. You can be my messenger another time, but not today."

²¹Then Joab said to a man from Ethiopia,* "Go tell the king what you have seen." The man bowed and ran off.

²²But Ahimaaz continued to plead with Joab, "Whatever happens, please let me go, too."

"Why should you go, my son?" Joab replied. "There will be no reward for your news."

²³"Yes, but let me go anyway," he begged.

Joab finally said, "All right, go ahead." So Ahimaaz took the less demanding route by way of the plain and ran to Mahanaim ahead of the Ethiopian.

²⁴While David was sitting between the inner and outer gates of the town, the watchman climbed to the roof of the gateway by the wall. As he looked, he saw a lone man running toward them. ²⁵He shouted the news down to David, and the king replied, "If he is alone, he has news."

17:25a Hebrew *Ithra*, a variant spelling of Jether.   17:25b As in some Greek manuscripts (see also 1 Chr 2:17); Hebrew reads *an Israelite*.   18:1 Hebrew *appointed commanders of thousands and commanders of hundreds*.   18:3 As in two Hebrew manuscripts and some Greek and Latin manuscripts; most Hebrew manuscripts read *Now there are 10,000 like us*.   18:9 Hebrew *his head*.   18:11 Hebrew *10 [shekels] of silver*, about 4 ounces or 114 grams in weight.   18:12 Hebrew *1,000 [shekels] of silver*, about 25 pounds or 11.4 kilograms in weight.   18:21 Hebrew *from Cush*; similarly in 18:23, 31, 32.

As the messenger came closer, [26] the watchman saw another man running toward them. He shouted down, "Here comes another one!"

The king replied, "He also will have news."

[27] "The first man runs like Ahimaaz son of Zadok," the watchman said.

"He is a good man and comes with good news," the king replied.

[28] Then Ahimaaz cried out to the king, "Everything is all right!" He bowed before the king with his face to the ground and said, "Praise to the LORD your God, who has handed over the rebels who dared to stand against my lord the king."

[29] "What about young Absalom?" the king demanded. "Is he all right?"

Ahimaaz replied, "When Joab told me to come, there was a lot of commotion. But I didn't know what was happening."

[30] "Wait here," the king told him. So Ahimaaz stepped aside.

[31] Then the man from Ethiopia arrived and said, "I have good news for my lord the king. Today the LORD has rescued you from all those who rebelled against you."

[32] "What about young Absalom?" the king demanded. "Is he all right?"

And the Ethiopian replied, "May all of your enemies, my lord the king, both now and in the future, share the fate of that young man!"

[33] *The king was overcome with emotion. He went up to the room over the gateway and burst into tears. And as he went, he cried, "O my son Absalom! My son, my son Absalom! If only I had died instead of you! O Absalom, my son, my son."

JOAB REBUKES THE KING

19 [1] *Word soon reached Joab that the king was weeping and mourning for Absalom. [2] As all the people heard of the king's deep grief for his son, the joy of that day's victory was turned into deep sadness. [3] They crept back into the town that day as though they were ashamed and had deserted in battle. [4] The king covered his face with his hands and kept on crying, "O my son Absalom! O my son, my son, my son!"

[5] Then Joab went to the king's room and said to him, "We saved your life today and the lives of your sons, your daughters, and your wives and concubines. Yet you act like this, making us feel ashamed of ourselves. [6] You seem to love those who hate you and hate those who love you. You have made it clear today that your commanders and troops mean nothing to you. It seems that if Absalom had lived and all of us had died, you would be pleased. [7] Now go out there and congratulate your troops, for I swear by the LORD that if you don't go out, not a single one of them will remain here tonight. Then you will be worse off than ever before."

[8] So the king went out and took his seat at the town gate, and as the news spread throughout the town that he was there, everyone went to him.

Meanwhile, the Israelites who had supported Absalom fled to their homes. [9] And throughout all the tribes of Israel there was much discussion and argument going on. The people were saying, "The king rescued us from our enemies and saved us from the Philistines, but Absalom chased him out of the country. [10] Now Absalom, whom we anointed to rule over us, is dead. Why not ask David to come back and be our king again?"

[11] Then King David sent Zadok and Abiathar, the priests, to say to the elders of Judah, "Why are you the last ones to welcome back the king into his palace? For I have heard that all Israel is ready. [12] You are my relatives, my own tribe, my own flesh and blood! So why are you the last ones to welcome back the king?" [13] And David told them to tell Amasa, "Since you are my own flesh and blood, like Joab, may God strike me and even kill me if I do not appoint you as commander of my army in his place."

[14] Then Amasa* convinced all the men of Judah, and they responded unanimously. They sent word to the king, "Return to us, and bring back all who are with you."

DAVID'S RETURN TO JERUSALEM

[15] So the king started back to Jerusalem. And when he arrived at the Jordan River, the people of Judah came to Gilgal to meet him and escort him across the river. [16] Shimei son of Gera, the man from Bahurim in Benjamin, hurried across with the men of Judah to welcome King David. [17] A thousand other men from the tribe of Benjamin were with him, including Ziba, the chief servant of the house of Saul, and Ziba's fifteen sons and twenty servants. They rushed down to the Jordan to meet the king. [18] They crossed the shallows of the Jordan to bring the king's household across the river, helping him in every way they could.

DAVID'S MERCY TO SHIMEI

As the king was about to cross the river, Shimei fell down before him. [19] "My lord the king, please forgive me," he pleaded. "Forget the terrible thing your servant did when you left Jerusalem. May the king put it out of his mind. [20] I know how much I sinned. That is why I have come here today, the very first person in all Israel* to greet my lord the king."

[21] Then Abishai son of Zeruiah said, "Shimei should die, for he cursed the LORD's anointed king!"

[22] "Who asked your opinion, you sons of Zeruiah!" David exclaimed. "Why have you become my adversary* today? This is not a day for execution, for today I am once again the king of Israel!" [23] Then, turning to Shimei, David vowed, "Your life will be spared."

18:33 Verse 18:33 is numbered 19:1 in Hebrew text. **19:1** Verses 19:1-43 are numbered 19:2-44 in Hebrew text. **19:14** Or *David;* Hebrew reads *he.* **19:20** Hebrew *in the house of Joseph.* **19:22** Or *my prosecutor.*

DAVID'S KINDNESS TO MEPHIBOSHETH

24 Now Mephibosheth,* Saul's grandson, came down from Jerusalem to meet the king. He had not cared for his feet, trimmed his beard, or washed his clothes since the day the king left Jerusalem. 25 "Why didn't you come with me, Mephibosheth?" the king asked him.

26 Mephibosheth replied, "My lord the king, my servant Ziba deceived me. I told him, 'Saddle my donkey* so I can go with the king.' For as you know I am crippled. 27 Ziba has slandered me by saying that I refused to come. But I know that my lord the king is like an angel of God, so do what you think is best. 28 All my relatives and I could expect only death from you, my lord, but instead you have honored me by allowing me to eat at your own table! What more can I ask?"

29 "You've said enough," David replied. "I've decided that you and Ziba will divide your land equally between you."

30 "Give him all of it," Mephibosheth said. "I am content just to have you safely back again, my lord the king!"

DAVID'S KINDNESS TO BARZILLAI

31 Barzillai of Gilead had come down from Rogelim to escort the king across the Jordan. 32 He was very old—eighty years of age—and very wealthy. He was the one who had provided food for the king during his stay in Mahanaim. 33 "Come across with me and live in Jerusalem," the king said to Barzillai. "I will take care of you there."

34 "No," he replied, "I am far too old to go with the king to Jerusalem. 35 I am eighty years old today, and I can no longer enjoy anything. Food and wine are no longer tasty, and I cannot hear the singers as they sing. I would only be a burden to my lord the king. 36 Just to go across the Jordan River with the king is all the honor I need! 37 Then let me return again to die in my own town, where my father and mother are buried. But here is your servant, my son Kimham. Let him go with my lord the king and receive whatever you want to give him."

38 "Good," the king agreed. "Kimham will go with me, and I will help him in any way you would like. And I will do for you anything you want." 39 So all the people crossed the Jordan with the king. After David had blessed Barzillai and kissed him, Barzillai returned to his own home.

40 The king then crossed over to Gilgal, taking Kimham with him. All the troops of Judah and half the troops of Israel escorted the king on his way.

AN ARGUMENT OVER THE KING

41 But all the men of Israel complained to the king, "The men of Judah stole the king and didn't give us the honor of helping take you, your household, and all your men across the Jordan."

42 The men of Judah replied, "The king is one of our own kinsmen. Why should this make you angry? We haven't eaten any of the king's food or received any special favors!"

43 "But there are ten tribes in Israel," the others replied. "So we have ten times as much right to the king as you do. What right do you have to treat us with such contempt? Weren't we the first to speak of bringing him back to be our king again?" The argument continued back and forth, and the men of Judah spoke even more harshly than the men of Israel.

THE REVOLT OF SHEBA

20 There happened to be a troublemaker there named Sheba son of Bicri, a man from the tribe of Benjamin. Sheba blew a ram's horn and began to chant:

"Down with the dynasty of David!
We have no interest in the son of Jesse.
Come on, you men of Israel,
back to your homes!"

2 So all the men of Israel deserted David and followed Sheba son of Bicri. But the men of Judah stayed with their king and escorted him from the Jordan River to Jerusalem.

3 When David came to his palace in Jerusalem, he took the ten concubines he had left to look after the palace and placed them in seclusion. Their needs were provided for, but he no longer slept with them. So each of them lived like a widow until she died.

4 Then the king told Amasa, "Mobilize the army of Judah within three days, and report back at that time." 5 So Amasa went out to notify Judah, but it took him longer than the time he had been given.

6 Then David said to Abishai, "Sheba son of Bicri is going to hurt us more than Absalom did. Quick, take my troops and chase after him before he gets into a fortified town where we can't reach him."

7 So Abishai and Joab,* together with the king's bodyguard* and all the mighty warriors, set out from Jerusalem to go after Sheba. 8 As they arrived at the great stone in Gibeon, Amasa met them. Joab was wearing his military tunic with a dagger strapped to his belt. As he stepped forward to greet Amasa, he slipped the dagger from its sheath.*

9 "How are you, my cousin?" Joab said and took him by the beard with his right hand as though to kiss him. 10 Amasa didn't notice the dagger in his left hand, and Joab stabbed him in the stomach with it so that his insides gushed out onto the ground. Joab did not need to strike again, and Amasa soon died. Joab and his brother Abishai left him lying there and continued after Sheba.

19:24 Mephibosheth is another name for Merib-baal.   19:26 As in Greek, Syriac, and Latin versions; Hebrew reads I will saddle a donkey for myself.   20:7a Hebrew So Joab's men.   20:7b Hebrew the Kerethites and Pelethites; also in 20:23.   20:8 Hebrew As he stepped forward, it fell out.

[11] One of Joab's young men shouted to Amasa's troops, "If you are for Joab and David, come and follow Joab." [12] But Amasa lay in his blood in the middle of the road, and Joab's man saw that everyone was stopping to stare at him. So he pulled him off the road into a field and threw a cloak over him. [13] With Amasa's body out of the way, everyone went on with Joab to capture Sheba son of Bicri.

[14] Meanwhile, Sheba traveled through all the tribes of Israel and eventually came to the town of Abel-beth-maacah. All the members of his own clan, the Bicrites,* assembled for battle and followed him into the town. [15] When Joab's forces arrived, they attacked Abel-beth-maacah. They built a siege ramp against the town's fortifications and began battering down the wall. [16] But a wise woman in the town called out to Joab, "Listen to me, Joab. Come over here so I can talk to you." [17] As he approached, the woman asked, "Are you Joab?"

"I am," he replied.

So she said, "Listen carefully to your servant."

"I'm listening," he said.

[18] Then she continued, "There used to be a saying, 'If you want to settle an argument, ask advice at the town of Abel.' [19] I am one who is peace loving and faithful in Israel. But you are destroying an important town in Israel.* Why do you want to devour what belongs to the LORD?"

[20] And Joab replied, "Believe me, I don't want to devour or destroy your town! [21] That's not my purpose. All I want is a man named Sheba son of Bicri from the hill country of Ephraim, who has revolted against King David. If you hand over this one man to me, I will leave the town in peace."

"All right," the woman replied, "we will throw his head over the wall to you." [22] Then the woman went to all the people with her wise advice, and they cut off Sheba's head and threw it out to Joab. So he blew the ram's horn and called his troops back from the attack. They all returned to their homes, and Joab returned to the king at Jerusalem.

[23] Now Joab was the commander of the army of Israel. Benaiah son of Jehoiada was captain of the king's bodyguard. [24] Adoniram* was in charge of forced labor. Jehoshaphat son of Ahilud was the royal historian. [25] Sheva was the court secretary. Zadok and Abiathar were the priests. [26] And Ira, a descendant of Jair, was David's personal priest.

DAVID AVENGES THE GIBEONITES

21 There was a famine during David's reign that lasted for three years, so David asked the LORD about it. And the LORD said, "The famine has come because Saul and his family are guilty of murdering the Gibeonites."

[2] So the king summoned the Gibeonites. They were not part of Israel but were all that was left of the nation of the Amorites. The people of Israel had sworn not to kill them, but Saul, in his zeal for Israel and Judah, had tried to wipe them out.

[3] David asked them, "What can I do for you? How can I make amends so that you will bless the LORD's people again?"

[4] "Well, money can't settle this matter between us and the family of Saul," the Gibeonites replied. "Neither can we demand the life of anyone in Israel."

"What can I do then?" David asked. "Just tell me and I will do it for you."

[5] Then they replied, "It was Saul who planned to destroy us, to keep us from having any place at all in the territory of Israel. [6] So let seven of Saul's sons be handed over to us, and we will execute them before the LORD at Gibeon, on the mountain of the LORD.*"

"All right," the king said, "I will do it." [7] The king spared Jonathan's son Mephibosheth,* who was Saul's grandson, because of the oath David and Jonathan had sworn before the LORD. [8] But he gave them Saul's two sons Armoni and Mephibosheth, whose mother was Rizpah daughter of Aiah. He also gave them the five sons of Saul's daughter Merab,* the wife of Adriel son of Barzillai from Meholah. [9] The men of Gibeon executed them on the mountain before the LORD. So all seven of them died together at the beginning of the barley harvest.

[10] Then Rizpah daughter of Aiah, the mother of two of the men, spread burlap on a rock and stayed there the entire harvest season. She prevented the scavenger birds from tearing at their bodies during the day and stopped wild animals from eating them at night. [11] When David learned what Rizpah, Saul's concubine, had done, [12] he went to the people of Jabesh-gilead and retrieved the bones of Saul and his son Jonathan. (When the Philistines had killed Saul and Jonathan on Mount Gilboa, the people of Jabesh-gilead stole their bodies from the public square of Beth-shan, where the Philistines had hung them.) [13] So David obtained the bones of Saul and Jonathan, as well as the bones of the men the Gibeonites had executed.

[14] Then the king ordered that they bury the bones in the tomb of Kish, Saul's father, at the town of Zela in the land of Benjamin. After that, God ended the famine in the land.

BATTLES AGAINST PHILISTINE GIANTS

[15] Once again the Philistines were at war with Israel. And when David and his men were in the thick of battle, David became weak and exhausted. [16] Ishbi-benob was a descendant of the giants*; his bronze spearhead weighed more than seven pounds,* and he was armed with a

---

20:14 As in Greek and Latin versions; Hebrew reads *All the Berites*. 20:19 Hebrew *a town that is a mother in Israel*. 20:24 As in Greek version (see also 1 Kgs 4:6; 5:14); Hebrew reads *Adoram*. 21:6 As in Greek version (see also 21:9); Hebrew reads *at Gibeah of Saul, the chosen of the LORD*. 21:7 *Mephibosheth* is another name for Merib-baal. 21:8 As in a few Hebrew and Greek manuscripts and Syriac version (see also 1 Sam 18:19); most Hebrew manuscripts read *Michal*. 21:16a Or *a descendant of the Rapha; also in 21:18, 20, 22.* 21:16b Hebrew *300 [shekels]* [3.4 kilograms].

new sword. He had cornered David and was about to kill him. ¹⁷But Abishai son of Zeruiah came to David's rescue and killed the Philistine. Then David's men declared, "You are not going out to battle with us again! Why risk snuffing out the light of Israel?"

¹⁸After this, there was another battle against the Philistines at Gob. As they fought, Sibbecai from Hushah killed Saph, another descendant of the giants.

¹⁹During another battle at Gob, Elhanan son of Jair* from Bethlehem killed the brother of Goliath of Gath.* The handle of his spear was as thick as a weaver's beam!

²⁰In another battle with the Philistines at Gath, they encountered a huge man* with six fingers on each hand and six toes on each foot, twenty-four in all, who was also a descendant of the giants. ²¹But when he defied and taunted Israel, he was killed by Jonathan, the son of David's brother Shimea.*

²²These four Philistines were descendants of the giants of Gath, but David and his warriors killed them.

DAVID'S SONG OF PRAISE

22 David sang this song to the LORD on the day the LORD rescued him from all his enemies and from Saul. ²He sang:

"The LORD is my rock, my fortress,
    and my savior;
³   my God is my rock, in whom I find
        protection.
He is my shield, the power that saves me,
    and my place of safety.
He is my refuge, my savior,
    the one who saves me from violence.
⁴ I called on the LORD, who is worthy
        of praise,
    and he saved me from my enemies.

⁵ "The waves of death overwhelmed me;
    floods of destruction swept over me.
⁶ The grave* wrapped its ropes around me;
    death laid a trap in my path.
⁷ But in my distress I cried out to the LORD;
    yes, I cried to my God for help.
He heard me from his sanctuary;
    my cry reached his ears.

⁸ "Then the earth quaked and trembled.
    The foundations of the heavens shook;
    they quaked because of his anger.
⁹ Smoke poured from his nostrils;
    fierce flames leaped from his mouth.
    Glowing coals blazed forth from him.
¹⁰ He opened the heavens and came down;
    dark storm clouds were beneath his feet.
¹¹ Mounted on a mighty angelic being,*
        he flew,
    soaring* on the wings of the wind.

¹² He shrouded himself in darkness,
    veiling his approach with dense rain
        clouds.
¹³ A great brightness shone around him,
    and burning coals* blazed forth.
¹⁴ The LORD thundered from heaven;
    the voice of the Most High resounded.
¹⁵ He shot arrows and scattered his enemies;
    his lightning flashed, and they were
        confused.
¹⁶ Then at the command of the LORD,
    at the blast of his breath,
the bottom of the sea could be seen,
    and the foundations of the earth were
        laid bare.

¹⁷ "He reached down from heaven and
        rescued me;
    he drew me out of deep waters.
¹⁸ He rescued me from my powerful enemies,
    from those who hated me and were too
        strong for me.
¹⁹ They attacked me at a moment when I was
        in distress,
    but the LORD supported me.
²⁰ He led me to a place of safety;
    he rescued me because he delights in me.
²¹ The LORD rewarded me for doing right;
    he restored me because of my innocence.
²² For I have kept the ways of the LORD;
    I have not turned from my God to follow
        evil.
²³ I have followed all his regulations;
    I have never abandoned his decrees.
²⁴ I am blameless before God;
    I have kept myself from sin.
²⁵ The LORD rewarded me for doing right.
    He has seen my innocence.

²⁶ "To the faithful you show yourself faithful;
    to those with integrity you
        show integrity.
²⁷ To the pure you show yourself pure,
    but to the crooked you show yourself
        shrewd.
²⁸ You rescue the humble,
    but your eyes watch the proud and
        humiliate them.
²⁹ O LORD, you are my lamp.
    The LORD lights up my darkness.
³⁰ In your strength I can crush an army;
    with my God I can scale any wall.

³¹ "God's way is perfect.
    All the LORD's promises prove true.

21:19a As in parallel text at 1 Chr 20:5; Hebrew reads *son of Jaare-oregim.* 21:19b As in parallel text at 1 Chr 20:5; Hebrew reads *killed Goliath of Gath.* 21:20 As in parallel text at 1 Chr 20:6; Hebrew reads *a Midianite.* 21:21 As in parallel text at 1 Chr 20:7; Hebrew reads *Shimei,* a variant spelling of Shimea. 22:6 Hebrew *Sheol.* 22:11a Hebrew *a cherub.* 22:11b As in some Hebrew manuscripts (see also Ps 18:10); other Hebrew manuscripts read *appearing.* 22:13 Or *and lightning bolts.*

He is a shield for all who look to him
    for protection.
³² For who is God except the LORD?
    Who but our God is a solid rock?
³³ God is my strong fortress,
    and he makes my way perfect.
³⁴ He makes me as surefooted as a deer,
    enabling me to stand on mountain
    heights.
³⁵ He trains my hands for battle;
    he strengthens my arm to draw
    a bronze bow.
³⁶ You have given me your shield of victory;
    your help* has made me great.
³⁷ You have made a wide path for my feet
    to keep them from slipping.

³⁸ "I chased my enemies and destroyed them;
    I did not stop until they were conquered.
³⁹ I consumed them;
    I struck them down so they did not get up;
    they fell beneath my feet.
⁴⁰ You have armed me with strength for the
    battle;
    you have subdued my enemies under my
    feet.
⁴¹ You placed my foot on their necks.
    I have destroyed all who hated me.
⁴² They looked for help, but no one came to
    their rescue.
    They even cried to the LORD, but he
    refused to answer.
⁴³ I ground them as fine as the dust of
    the earth;
    I trampled them* in the gutter like dirt.

⁴⁴ "You gave me victory over my accusers.
    You preserved me as the ruler over
    nations;
    people I don't even know now serve me.
⁴⁵ Foreign nations cringe before me;
    as soon as they hear of me, they submit.
⁴⁶ They all lose their courage
    and come trembling* from their
    strongholds.

⁴⁷ "The LORD lives! Praise to my Rock!
    May God, the Rock of my salvation, be
    exalted!
⁴⁸ He is the God who pays back those who
    harm me;
    he brings down the nations under me
⁴⁹   and delivers me from my enemies.
    You hold me safe beyond the reach of my
    enemies;
    you save me from violent opponents.
⁵⁰ For this, O LORD, I will praise you among the
    nations;
    I will sing praises to your name.
⁵¹ You give great victories to your king;
    you show unfailing love to your anointed,
    to David and all his descendants forever."

DAVID'S LAST WORDS

23 These are the last words of David:

"David, the son of Jesse, speaks—
    David, the man who was raised up so high,
David, the man anointed by the God of Jacob,
    David, the sweet psalmist of Israel.*

² "The Spirit of the LORD speaks through me;
    his words are upon my tongue.
³ The God of Israel spoke.
    The Rock of Israel said to me:
'The one who rules righteously,
    who rules in the fear of God,
⁴ is like the light of morning at sunrise,
    like a morning without clouds,
like the gleaming of the sun
    on new grass after rain.'

⁵ "Is it not my family God has chosen?
    Yes, he has made an everlasting covenant
    with me.
His agreement is arranged and guaranteed
    in every detail.
He will ensure my safety and success.
⁶ But the godless are like thorns to be
    thrown away,
    for they tear the hand that touches them.
⁷ One must use iron tools to chop them down;
    they will be totally consumed by fire."

DAVID'S MIGHTIEST WARRIORS

⁸These are the names of David's mightiest warriors. The first was Jashobeam the Hacmonite,* who was leader of the Three*—the three mightiest warriors among David's men. He once used his spear to kill 800 enemy warriors in a single battle.* ⁹Next in rank among the Three was Eleazar son of Dodai, a descendant of Ahoah. Once Eleazar and David stood together against the Philistines when the entire Israelite army had fled. ¹⁰He killed Philistines until his hand was too tired to lift his sword, and the LORD gave him a great victory that day. The rest of the army did not return until it was time to collect the plunder!

¹¹Next in rank was Shammah son of Agee from Harar. One time the Philistines gathered at Lehi and attacked the Israelites in a field full of lentils. The Israelite army fled, ¹²but Shammah* held his ground in the middle of the field and beat back the Philistines. So the LORD brought about a great victory.

22:36 As in Dead Sea Scrolls; Masoretic Text reads *your answering.*
22:43 As in Dead Sea Scrolls (see also Ps 18:42); Masoretic Text reads *I crushed and trampled them.*   22:46 As in parallel text at Ps 18:45; Hebrew reads *come girding themselves.*   23:1 Or *the favorite subject of the songs of Israel;* or *the favorite of the Strong One of Israel.*   23:8a As in parallel text at 1 Chr 11:11; Hebrew reads *Josheb-basshebeth the Tahkemonite.*   23:8b As in Greek and Latin versions (see also 1 Chr 11:11); the meaning of the Hebrew is uncertain.   23:8c As in some Greek manuscripts (see also 1 Chr 11:11); the meaning of the Hebrew is uncertain, though it might be rendered *the Three. It was Adino the Eznite who killed 800 men at one time.*   23:12 Hebrew *he.*

¹³Once during the harvest, when David was at the cave of Adullam, the Philistine army was camped in the valley of Rephaim. The Three (who were among the Thirty—an elite group among David's fighting men) went down to meet him there. ¹⁴David was staying in the stronghold at the time, and a Philistine detachment had occupied the town of Bethlehem.

¹⁵David remarked longingly to his men, "Oh, how I would love some of that good water from the well by the gate in Bethlehem." ¹⁶So the Three broke through the Philistine lines, drew some water from the well by the gate in Bethlehem, and brought it back to David. But he refused to drink it. Instead, he poured it out as an offering to the LORD. ¹⁷"The LORD forbid that I should drink this!" he exclaimed. "This water is as precious as the blood of these men* who risked their lives to bring it to me." So David did not drink it. These are examples of the exploits of the Three.

DAVID'S THIRTY MIGHTY MEN

¹⁸Abishai son of Zeruiah, the brother of Joab, was the leader of the Thirty.* He once used his spear to kill 300 enemy warriors in a single battle. It was by such feats that he became as famous as the Three. ¹⁹Abishai was the most famous of the Thirty* and was their commander, though he was not one of the Three.

²⁰There was also Benaiah son of Jehoiada, a valiant warrior* from Kabzeel. He did many heroic deeds, which included killing two champions* of Moab. Another time, on a snowy day, he chased a lion down into a pit and killed it. ²¹Once, armed only with a club, he killed an imposing Egyptian warrior who was armed with a spear. Benaiah wrenched the spear from the Egyptian's hand and killed him with it. ²²Deeds like these made Benaiah as famous as the Three mightiest warriors. ²³He was more honored than the other members of the Thirty, though he was not one of the Three. And David made him captain of his bodyguard.

²⁴Other members of the Thirty included:

Asahel, Joab's brother;
Elhanan son of Dodo from Bethlehem;
²⁵ Shammah from Harod;
Elika from Harod;
²⁶ Helez from Pelon*;
Ira son of Ikkesh from Tekoa;
²⁷ Abiezer from Anathoth;
Sibbecai* from Hushah;
²⁸ Zalmon from Ahoah;
Maharai from Netophah;
²⁹ Heled* son of Baanah from Netophah;
Ithai* son of Ribai from Gibeah
(in the land of Benjamin);
³⁰ Benaiah from Pirathon;
Hurai* from Nahale-gaash*;
³¹ Abi-albon from Arabah;
Azmaveth from Bahurim;
³² Eliahba from Shaalbon;
the sons of Jashen;
Jonathan ³³son of Shagee* from Harar;
Ahiam son of Sharar from Harar;
³⁴ Eliphelet son of Ahasbai from Maacah;
Eliam son of Ahithophel from Giloh;
³⁵ Hezro from Carmel;
Paarai from Arba;
³⁶ Igal son of Nathan from Zobah;
Bani from Gad;
³⁷ Zelek from Ammon;
Naharai from Beeroth, the armor bearer
of Joab son of Zeruiah;
³⁸ Ira from Jattir;
Gareb from Jattir;
³⁹ Uriah the Hittite.

There were thirty-seven in all.

DAVID TAKES A CENSUS

24 Once again the anger of the LORD burned against Israel, and he caused David to harm them by taking a census. "Go and count the people of Israel and Judah," the LORD told him.

²So the king said to Joab and the commanders* of the army, "Take a census of all the tribes of Israel—from Dan in the north to Beersheba in the south—so I may know how many people there are."

³But Joab replied to the king, "May the LORD your God let you live to see a hundred times as many people as there are now! But why, my lord the king, do you want to do this?"

⁴But the king insisted that they take the census, so Joab and the commanders of the army went out to count the people of Israel. ⁵First they crossed the Jordan and camped at Aroer, south of the town in the valley, in the direction of Gad. Then they went on to Jazer, ⁶then to Gilead in the land of Tahtim-hodshi* and to Dan-jaan and around to Sidon. ⁷Then they came to the fortress of Tyre, and all the towns of the Hivites and Canaanites. Finally, they went south to Judah* as far as Beersheba.

⁸Having gone through the entire land for nine months and twenty days, they returned to Jerusalem. ⁹Joab reported the number of people to the king. There were 800,000 capable warriors in Israel who could handle a sword, and 500,000 in Judah.

23:17 Hebrew Shall I drink the blood of these men? 23:18 As in a few Hebrew manuscripts and Syriac version; most Hebrew manuscripts read the Three. 23:19 As in Syriac version; Hebrew reads the Three. 23:20a Or son of Jehoiada, son of Ish-hai. 23:20b Hebrew two of Ariel. 23:26 As in parallel text at 1 Chr 11:27 (see also 1 Chr 27:10); Hebrew reads from Palti. 23:27 As in some Greek manuscripts (see also 1 Chr 11:29); Hebrew reads Mebunnai. 23:29a As in some Hebrew manuscripts (see also 1 Chr 11:30); most Hebrew manuscripts read Heleb. 23:29b As in parallel text at 1 Chr 11:31; Hebrew reads Ittai. 23:30a As in some Greek manuscripts (see also 1 Chr 11:32); Hebrew reads Hiddai. 23:30b Or from the ravines of Gaash. 23:33 As in parallel text at 1 Chr 11:34; Hebrew reads Jonathan, Shammah; some Greek manuscripts read Jonathan son of Shammah. 24:2 As in Greek version (see also 24:4 and 1 Chr 21:2); Hebrew reads Joab the commander. 24:6 Greek version reads to Gilead and to Kadesh in the land of the Hittites. 24:7 Or they went to the Negev of Judah.

JUDGMENT FOR DAVID'S SIN

[10] But after he had taken the census, David's conscience began to bother him. And he said to the LORD, "I have sinned greatly by taking this census. Please forgive my guilt, LORD, for doing this foolish thing."

[11] The next morning the word of the LORD came to the prophet Gad, who was David's seer. This was the message: [12] "Go and say to David, 'This is what the LORD says: I will give you three choices. Choose one of these punishments, and I will inflict it on you.'"

[13] So Gad came to David and asked him, "Will you choose three* years of famine throughout your land, three months of fleeing from your enemies, or three days of severe plague throughout your land? Think this over and decide what answer I should give the LORD who sent me."

[14] "I'm in a desperate situation!" David replied to Gad. "But let us fall into the hands of the LORD, for his mercy is great. Do not let me fall into human hands."

[15] So the LORD sent a plague upon Israel that morning, and it lasted for three days.* A total of 70,000 people died throughout the nation, from Dan in the north to Beersheba in the south. [16] But as the angel was preparing to destroy Jerusalem, the LORD relented and said to the death angel, "Stop! That is enough!" At that moment the angel of the LORD was by the threshing floor of Araunah the Jebusite.

[17] When David saw the angel, he said to the LORD, "I am the one who has sinned and done wrong! But these people are as innocent as sheep—what have they done? Let your anger fall against me and my family."

DAVID BUILDS AN ALTAR

[18] That day Gad came to David and said to him, "Go up and build an altar to the LORD on the threshing floor of Araunah the Jebusite."

[19] So David went up to do what the LORD had commanded him. [20] When Araunah saw the king and his men coming toward him, he came and bowed before the king with his face to the ground. [21] "Why have you come, my lord the king?" Araunah asked.

David replied, "I have come to buy your threshing floor and to build an altar to the LORD there, so that he will stop the plague."

[22] "Take it, my lord the king, and use it as you wish," Araunah said to David. "Here are oxen for the burnt offering, and you can use the threshing boards and ox yokes for wood to build a fire on the altar. [23] I will give it all to you, Your Majesty, and may the LORD your God accept your sacrifice."

[24] But the king replied to Araunah, "No, I insist on buying it, for I will not present burnt offerings to the LORD my God that have cost me nothing." So David paid him fifty pieces of silver* for the threshing floor and the oxen.

[25] David built an altar there to the LORD and sacrificed burnt offerings and peace offerings. And the LORD answered his prayer for the land, and the plague on Israel was stopped.

24:13 As in Greek version (see also 1 Chr 21:12); Hebrew reads *seven.* **24:15** Hebrew *for the designated time.* **24:24** Hebrew *50 shekels of silver,* about 20 ounces or 570 grams in weight.

THE LANDS OF THE ANCIENT NEAR EAST

JON HUNTZINGER, PHD

Three regions constitute the lands of the Bible in the ancient Near East: Egypt, Syria-Israel, and Mesopotamia.

EGYPT

The Nile River flows from the south to the north through Egypt for more than 600 miles (966 km). It divides the land into east and west. The ancient Egyptians called the land surrounding the Nile the "black" land because of its rich, fertile soil. More than 90 percent of all Egyptians in the ancient world lived in the 10-mile-wide (16 km) valley along the Nile. Many Egyptians thought of Pharaoh as a god who released the annual floods that deposited soil throughout the valley. Because the kingdom of Egypt was relatively isolated, with deserts to the east, west, and south, its political institutions were secure from outside invasion and more stable than other kingdoms of the ancient world.

SYRIA-ISRAEL

The lands of Syria and Israel are a land bridge for the continents of Europe, Asia, and Africa. Four subareas divide Syria-Israel: Coastal Plain, central mountains, Jordan Rift, and Transjordan highlands. The highest point is Mount Hermon at 9,232 feet (2,814 m), and the lowest point is the Dead Sea at 1,300 feet (400 m) below sea level. The Assyrian people lived in the north of Syria, with their capital in Nineveh. They sent many Israelites into exile in the eighth century BC.

MESOPOTAMIA

Mesopotamia means 'between the rivers' and describes the land between and surrounding the Tigris and Euphrates Rivers. Because of its rich agricultural land, it is one of the earliest inhabited areas on earth. It was the land where the people of Babylon lived and where many Israelites were taken into exile in 587 BC.

TWO HIGHWAYS

Two main highways connected these three regions:
— The Via Maris (the Way of the Sea) was an international road that ran north and south near the coast of the Mediterranean and passed through the city of Megiddo in Israel. Because of its strategic location, Megiddo was the site of 25 major battles over the course of its long history.
— The King's Highway ran north and south as well, inland along the Transjordan highlands to the east of the Sea of Galilee and the Dead Sea. ▲

THE KINGS OF JUDAH AND ISRAEL

JON HUNTZINGER, PHD

The kingdom established by David and preserved by his son Solomon was divided into two kingdoms in 930 BC: a northern realm and a southern realm. The Bible describes most of the kings of Israel (northern kingdom) and Judah (southern kingdom) as evil or wicked. They were seen this way because they failed to maintain the covenant God made with them. They did not keep the laws of Moses or give complete devotion to God in worship. Thus, a king could oversee a successful economic or foreign policy and still be regarded as having done evil. The line of kings in both kingdoms ended in exile. The northern kingdom of Israel fell to Assyria in 722 BC, and the southern kingdom of Judah fell to Babylon in 586 BC. *Select* kings from the northern and southern kingdoms are listed in the following table:

SOUTHERN KINGS	DATES (BC)	DESCRIPTION	NORTHERN KINGS	DATES (BC)	DESCRIPTION
Rehoboam	930–913	Continued Solomon's policies and lost the support of the people.	Jeroboam I	930–909	Built shrines to keep the north separate from the south. Appointed priests outside the tribe of Levi. Changed date of Passover.
Asa	910–869	Enjoyed a long rule and was regarded as a good king.	Omri	885–873	Established Samaria as the capital of the northern kingdom. Oversaw building projects. Made treaty with Phoenician Tyre and sealed treaty with the marriage of Ahab to Jezebel.
			Ahab	873–853	Embraced the worship of Baal. Opposed Israel's ancient faith and the ministry of Elijah.
			Joram	852–841	Lost control of Moab. Ruled during the ministry of Elisha.
			Jehu	841–813	Led a bloody purge of the royal house.
			Jeroboam II	793–753	Expanded borders of the northern kingdom of Syria and the Dead Sea. Oversaw period of economic prosperity. Amos critical of social inequity during his rule.
Hezekiah	715–686	Learned from the northern kingdom's experience and attempted to break with Assyria. Renewed covenant by destroying foreign shrines. Ruled during the time of Isaiah.	Hoshea	731–722	Asked Egypt for help when besieged by Assyria but was eventually defeated in 722 BC.
Manasseh	686–641	Longest reign of any king of Judah. Compromised with Assyria and adopted idolatrous practices. Openly opposed the prophets.			
Josiah	639–609	Found the Book of the Law in 621 BC. Instituted reforms as Assyria was in decline. Purged temple of idols and destroyed foreign shrines. Died in battle at Megiddo.			
Jehoiakim	609–598	Resisted the Babylonians.			
Zedekiah	597–586	Blinded by the Babylonians after seeing his sons killed.			

1-2 KINGS

JON HUNTZINGER, PHD

The two books of Kings survey the history of Israel after the reign of David, beginning with his son Solomon. As with 1 and 2 Samuel, 1 and 2 Kings originally constituted one book. They were divided sometime later because the single book was too large to use with ease. After Solomon's rule (970-930 BC), the single kingdom established by David was divided into the northern kingdom of Israel and the southern kingdom of Judah (930 BC). The northern kingdom fell to the Assyrians in 722 BC, and the southern kingdom eventually collapsed before the Babylonian Empire in 586 BC. According to 1 and 2 Kings, the fortunes of the people and that of the nation during this period rose or fell with the righteousness of their kings, who are described as either good or evil. Good kings worshipped God and lived by the covenant He made with Moses, resulting in blessing for the people. Evil kings did not live by the covenant, leading to hardship for the nation.

The book of 1 Kings contains three major sections:

— Chapters 1-11 open with the conclusion of David's reign, recount Solomon's rise to power, and tell about Solomon's story with a description of his remarkable wisdom and great wealth.

— Chapters 12-14 give an account of the division of the northern and southern tribes into two kingdoms.

— Chapters 15-22 outline the histories of the two kingdoms by highlighting the rules of their kings, giving particular attention to the rule of King Ahab in the northern kingdom.

The book of 1 Kings identifies two major problems with Solomon's kingship, one having to do with his foreign policy and the other with his domestic policy.

Solomon's foreign policy problem: Solomon attempted to strengthen Israel's standing with other nations through many marriages. Leaders and nations consolidated power in the ancient world through intermarriage. Solomon's many wives and concubines represented the various foreign alliances he entered into with other nations. Predictably, those alliances usually involved religious commitments. Solomon participated in the sacred rites of his wives' religions as part of his marital obligations to them, which weakened his own commitment to the worship of the God of Israel. His example influenced later kings and the people themselves to mix the worship of the God of Israel with the gods of other nations. This practice is also known as religious syncretism, which is a form of idolatry. Often, the people did not reject the God of Israel outright. Instead, they tried to worship God *and* the gods of the other nations. Consequently, the kings and the people worshipped the Lord their God who had delivered their ancestors out of Egypt, but they also participated in the religious rituals of the tribes and peoples with whom they had entered into foreign treaties, as well as the tribes who had remained in the land after the conquest during the time of Joshua.

Solomon's domestic policy problem: Shortly after Solomon's rule, the unified kingdom established by David split into two kingdoms. This division occurred because some parts of the country believed they were not being fairly taxed. Fiscal inequity developed during Solomon's reign between the tribes of Judah and Benjamin in the south and the other tribes in the north. Taxes collected in the north were primarily distributed in Jerusalem and Judah in the south where the king lived. While the tribes of Judah and Benjamin prospered, the other tribes struggled. This inequity led to the separation of the northern tribes from Judah and the eventual rule of King Ahab over the north.

After the reign of Solomon, the next most significant story in 1 Kings centers on King Ahab's rule in the north (16:29-22:40). He married Jezebel, the daughter of the king of Tyre, and on her account instituted the worship of Baal in his kingdom. Baal was a major deity for Jezebel and her people. Ahab built a temple in Samaria, the new capital of Israel, to compete with the Temple in Jerusalem, and he placed an idol of Baal in the new temple (16:31-33). The prophet Elijah, whose name means 'My God is Yah,' opposed Ahab and prophesied a drought on the land: "There will be no dew or rain during the next few years until I give the word!" (17:1). Since Baal was the god of fresh water, Elijah essentially declared war on Ahab's god with these words.

Chapter 18 records the contest between the God of Israel and the Phoenician god Baal. Two bulls are placed on separate altars, one for Baal and one for the God of Israel. The deity who consumed the sacrifice with fire from the sky would prove himself as the true God. Though the priests of Baal pray, dance, and cut themselves throughout the day, fire does not fall on their sacrifice. For his part, Elijah pours 12 pots of water over his sacrifice. He intentionally puts Baal and the element associated with his power (water) side-by-side against the God of Israel and the element associated with His glory (fire). When fire falls upon Elijah's sacrifice and vaporizes all the water around the altar, the people shout, "The LORD—he is God! Yes, the LORD is God!" (18:38-39), showing their conversion from idolatry (religious syncretism) to the worship of the one true God of Elijah (monotheism). After this event, 1 Kings describes Ahab's continued struggle with the Lord's prophets and concludes with a description of his death in battle (22:29-40). Despite the resistance of kings like Ahab, 1 and 2 Kings depicts Israel's God as worthy of the exclusive worship of His people.

The book of 2 Kings comprises five major sections:
— Chapters 1:1-8:15 begin with the departure of Elijah into heaven, riding in a chariot of fire. Elisha's prophetic ministry follows with accounts of several miracles.
— Chapters 8:16-17:40 chronicle the good and evil actions of both the northern and southern kings.
— Chapters 18-21 tell about the reigns of the good king Hezekiah and his evil son, Manasseh, who follows.

— Chapters 22:1-23:30 give an account of King Josiah's commitment to renew the covenant.
— Chapters 23:31-25:30 record the reigns of the kings who followed Josiah. They "do evil in the LORD's sight," and for that reason, God brings judgment upon the nation in the form of the destruction of Jerusalem and its Temple by the Babylonians.

In several passages of 1 and 2 Kings, the writer identifies the kings as either good or evil, depending on whether they do good or evil "in the LORD's sight," revealing that God is all-knowing. Nothing escapes His vision. Since God knows all and sees both good and evil, He is able to distinguish between them. Consequently, the God of Israel is a moral being qualified to act on behalf of His people. Remarkably, God's moral action on their behalf will involve the judgment of the Exile, described in historical detail at the end of the book (chapters 24-25). This point is one that many people would struggle to understand at that time.

1 KINGS

DAVID IN HIS OLD AGE

1 King David was now very old, and no matter how many blankets covered him, he could not keep warm. ²So his advisers told him, "Let us find a young virgin to wait on you and look after you, my lord. She will lie in your arms and keep you warm."

³So they searched throughout the land of Israel for a beautiful girl, and they found Abishag from Shunem and brought her to the king. ⁴The girl was very beautiful, and she looked after the king and took care of him. But the king had no sexual relations with her.

ADONIJAH CLAIMS THE THRONE

⁵About that time David's son Adonijah, whose mother was Haggith, began boasting, "I will make myself king." So he provided himself with chariots and charioteers and recruited fifty men to run in front of him. ⁶Now his father, King David, had never disciplined him at any time, even by asking, "Why are you doing that?" Adonijah had been born next after Absalom, and he was very handsome.

⁷Adonijah took Joab son of Zeruiah and Abiathar the priest into his confidence, and they agreed to help him become king. ⁸But Zadok the priest, Benaiah son of Jehoiada, Nathan the prophet, Shimei, Rei, and David's personal bodyguard refused to support Adonijah.

⁹Adonijah went to the Stone of Zoheleth* near the spring of En-rogel, where he sacrificed sheep, cattle, and fattened calves. He invited all his brothers—the other sons of King David—and all the royal officials of Judah. ¹⁰But he did not invite Nathan the prophet or Benaiah or the king's bodyguard or his brother Solomon.

¹¹Then Nathan went to Bathsheba, Solomon's mother, and asked her, "Haven't you heard that Haggith's son, Adonijah, has made himself king, and our lord David doesn't even know about it? ¹²If you want to save your own life and the life of your son Solomon, follow my advice. ¹³Go at once to King David and say to him, 'My lord the king, didn't you make a vow and say to me, "Your son Solomon will surely be the next king and will sit on my throne"? Why then has Adonijah become king?' ¹⁴And while you are still talking with him, I will come and confirm everything you have said."

¹⁵So Bathsheba went into the king's bedroom. (He was very old now, and Abishag was taking care of him.) ¹⁶Bathsheba bowed down before the king.

"What can I do for you?" he asked her.

¹⁷She replied, "My lord, you made a vow before the LORD your God when you said to me, 'Your son Solomon will surely be the next king and

1:9 Or to the Serpent's Stone; Greek version supports reading Zoheleth as a proper name.

will sit on my throne.' ¹⁸ But instead, Adonijah has made himself king, and my lord the king does not even know about it. ¹⁹ He has sacrificed many cattle, fattened calves, and sheep, and he has invited all the king's sons to attend the celebration. He also invited Abiathar the priest and Joab, the commander of the army. But he did not invite your servant Solomon. ²⁰ And now, my lord the king, all Israel is waiting for you to announce who will become king after you. ²¹ If you do not act, my son Solomon and I will be treated as criminals as soon as my lord the king has died."

²² While she was still speaking with the king, Nathan the prophet arrived. ²³ The king's officials told him, "Nathan the prophet is here to see you."

Nathan went in and bowed before the king with his face to the ground. ²⁴ Nathan asked, "My lord the king, have you decided that Adonijah will be the next king and that he will sit on your throne? ²⁵ Today he has sacrificed many cattle, fattened calves, and sheep, and he has invited all the king's sons to attend the celebration. He also invited the commanders of the army and Abiathar the priest. They are feasting and drinking with him and shouting, 'Long live King Adonijah!' ²⁶ But he did not invite me or Zadok the priest or Benaiah or your servant Solomon. ²⁷ Has my lord the king really done this without letting any of his officials know who should be the next king?"

DAVID MAKES SOLOMON KING

²⁸ King David responded, "Call Bathsheba!" So she came back in and stood before the king. ²⁹ And the king repeated his vow: "As surely as the LORD lives, who has rescued me from every danger, ³⁰ your son Solomon will be the next king and will sit on my throne this very day, just as I vowed to you before the LORD, the God of Israel."

³¹ Then Bathsheba bowed down with her face to the ground before the king and exclaimed, "May my lord King David live forever!"

³² Then King David ordered, "Call Zadok the priest, Nathan the prophet, and Benaiah son of Jehoiada." When they came into the king's presence, ³³ the king said to them, "Take Solomon and my officials down to Gihon Spring. Solomon is to ride on my own mule. ³⁴ There Zadok the priest and Nathan the prophet are to anoint him king over Israel. Blow the ram's horn and shout, 'Long live King Solomon!' ³⁵ Then escort him back here, and he will sit on my throne. He will succeed me as king, for I have appointed him to be ruler over Israel and Judah."

³⁶ "Amen!" Benaiah son of Jehoiada replied. "May the LORD, the God of my lord the king, decree that it happen. ³⁷ And may the LORD be with Solomon as he has been with you, my lord the king, and may he make Solomon's reign even greater than yours!"

³⁸ So Zadok the priest, Nathan the prophet, Benaiah son of Jehoiada, and the king's bodyguard* took Solomon down to Gihon Spring,

with Solomon riding on King David's own mule. ³⁹ There Zadok the priest took the flask of olive oil from the sacred tent and anointed Solomon with the oil. Then they sounded the ram's horn and all the people shouted, "Long live King Solomon!" ⁴⁰ And all the people followed Solomon into Jerusalem, playing flutes and shouting for joy. The celebration was so joyous and noisy that the earth shook with the sound.

⁴¹ Adonijah and his guests heard the celebrating and shouting just as they were finishing their banquet. When Joab heard the sound of the ram's horn, he asked, "What's going on? Why is the city in such an uproar?"

⁴² And while he was still speaking, Jonathan son of Abiathar the priest arrived. "Come in," Adonijah said to him, "for you are a good man. You must have good news."

⁴³ "Not at all!" Jonathan replied. "Our lord King David has just declared Solomon king! ⁴⁴ The king sent him down to Gihon Spring with Zadok the priest, Nathan the prophet, and Benaiah son of Jehoiada, protected by the king's bodyguard. They had him ride on the king's own mule, ⁴⁵ and Zadok and Nathan have anointed him at Gihon Spring as the new king. They have just returned, and the whole city is celebrating and rejoicing. That's what all the noise is about. ⁴⁶ What's more, Solomon is now sitting on the royal throne as king. ⁴⁷ And all the royal officials have gone to King David and congratulated him, saying, 'May your God make Solomon's fame even greater than your own, and may Solomon's reign be even greater than yours!' Then the king bowed his head in worship as he lay in his bed, ⁴⁸ and he said, 'Praise the LORD, the God of Israel, who today has chosen a successor to sit on my throne while I am still alive to see it.'"

⁴⁹ Then all of Adonijah's guests jumped up in panic from the banquet table and quickly scattered. ⁵⁰ Adonijah was afraid of Solomon, so he rushed to the sacred tent and grabbed on to the horns of the altar. ⁵¹ Word soon reached Solomon that Adonijah had seized the horns of the altar in fear, and that he was pleading, "Let King Solomon swear today that he will not kill me!"

⁵² Solomon replied, "If he proves himself to be loyal, not a hair on his head will be touched. But if he makes trouble, he will die." ⁵³ So King Solomon summoned Adonijah, and they brought him down from the altar. He came and bowed respectfully before King Solomon, who dismissed him, saying, "Go on home."

DAVID'S FINAL INSTRUCTIONS TO SOLOMON

2 As the time of King David's death approached, he gave this charge to his son Solomon:
² "I am going where everyone on earth must someday go. Take courage and be a man. ³ Observe

---

1:38 Hebrew *the Kerethites and Pelethites;* also in 1:44.

the requirements of the LORD your God, and follow all his ways. Keep the decrees, commands, regulations, and laws written in the Law of Moses so that you will be successful in all you do and wherever you go. ⁴If you do this, then the LORD will keep the promise he made to me. He told me, 'If your descendants live as they should and follow me faithfully with all their heart and soul, one of them will always sit on the throne of Israel.'

⁵"And there is something else. You know what Joab son of Zeruiah did to me when he murdered my two army commanders, Abner son of Ner and Amasa son of Jether. He pretended that it was an act of war, but it was done in a time of peace,* staining his belt and sandals with innocent blood.* ⁶Do with him what you think best, but don't let him grow old and go to his grave in peace.*

⁷"Be kind to the sons of Barzillai of Gilead. Make them permanent guests at your table, for they took care of me when I fled from your brother Absalom.

⁸"And remember Shimei son of Gera, the man from Bahurim in Benjamin. He cursed me with a terrible curse as I was fleeing to Mahanaim. When he came down to meet me at the Jordan River, I swore by the LORD that I would not kill him. ⁹But that oath does not make him innocent. You are a wise man, and you will know how to arrange a bloody death for him.*"

¹⁰Then David died and was buried with his ancestors in the City of David. ¹¹David had reigned over Israel for forty years, seven of them in Hebron and thirty-three in Jerusalem. ¹²Solomon became king and sat on the throne of David his father, and his kingdom was firmly established.

SOLOMON ESTABLISHES HIS RULE

¹³One day Adonijah, whose mother was Haggith, came to see Bathsheba, Solomon's mother. "Have you come with peaceful intentions?" she asked him.

"Yes," he said, "I come in peace. ¹⁴In fact, I have a favor to ask of you."

"What is it?" she asked.

¹⁵He replied, "As you know, the kingdom was rightfully mine; all Israel wanted me to be the next king. But the tables were turned, and the kingdom went to my brother instead; for that is the way the LORD wanted it. ¹⁶So now I have just one favor to ask of you. Please don't turn me down."

"What is it?" she asked.

¹⁷He replied, "Speak to King Solomon on my behalf, for I know he will do anything you request. Ask him to let me marry Abishag, the girl from Shunem."

¹⁸"All right," Bathsheba replied. "I will speak to the king for you."

¹⁹So Bathsheba went to King Solomon to speak on Adonijah's behalf. The king rose from his throne to meet her, and he bowed down before her. When he sat down on his throne again, the king ordered that a throne be brought for his mother, and she sat at his right hand.

²⁰"I have one small request to make of you," she said. "I hope you won't turn me down."

"What is it, my mother?" he asked. "You know I won't refuse you."

²¹"Then let your brother Adonijah marry Abishag, the girl from Shunem," she replied.

²²"How can you possibly ask me to give Abishag to Adonijah?" King Solomon demanded. "You might as well ask me to give him the kingdom! You know that he is my older brother, and that he has Abiathar the priest and Joab son of Zeruiah on his side."

²³Then King Solomon made a vow before the LORD: "May God strike me and even kill me if Adonijah has not sealed his fate with this request. ²⁴The LORD has confirmed me and placed me on the throne of my father, David; he has established my dynasty as he promised. So as surely as the LORD lives, Adonijah will die this very day!" ²⁵So King Solomon ordered Benaiah son of Jehoiada to execute him, and Adonijah was put to death.

²⁶Then the king said to Abiathar the priest, "Go back to your home in Anathoth. You deserve to die, but I will not kill you now, because you carried the Ark of the Sovereign LORD for David my father and you shared all his hardships." ²⁷So Solomon deposed Abiathar from his position as priest of the LORD, thereby fulfilling the prophecy the LORD had given at Shiloh concerning the descendants of Eli.

²⁸Joab had not joined Absalom's earlier rebellion, but he had joined Adonijah's rebellion. So when Joab heard about Adonijah's death, he ran to the sacred tent of the LORD and grabbed on to the horns of the altar. ²⁹When this was reported to King Solomon, he sent Benaiah son of Jehoiada to execute him.

³⁰Benaiah went to the sacred tent of the LORD and said to Joab, "The king orders you to come out!"

But Joab answered, "No, I will die here."

So Benaiah returned to the king and told him what Joab had said.

³¹"Do as he said," the king replied. "Kill him there beside the altar and bury him. This will remove the guilt of Joab's senseless murders from me and from my father's family. ³²The LORD will repay him* for the murders of two men who were more righteous and better than he. For my father knew nothing about the deaths of Abner son of Ner, commander of the army of Israel, and of Amasa son of Jether, commander of

2:5a Or *He murdered them during a time of peace as revenge for deaths they had caused in time of war.*   2:5b As in some Greek and Old Latin manuscripts; Hebrew reads *with the blood of war.*
2:6 Hebrew *don't let his white head go down to Sheol in peace.*
2:9 Hebrew *how to bring his white head down to Sheol in blood.*
2:32 Hebrew *will return his blood on his own head.*

the army of Judah. ³³ May their blood be on Joab and his descendants forever, and may the LORD grant peace forever to David, his descendants, his dynasty, and his throne."

³⁴ So Benaiah son of Jehoiada returned to the sacred tent and killed Joab, and he was buried at his home in the wilderness. ³⁵ Then the king appointed Benaiah to command the army in place of Joab, and he installed Zadok the priest to take the place of Abiathar.

³⁶ The king then sent for Shimei and told him, "Build a house here in Jerusalem and live there. But don't step outside the city to go anywhere else. ³⁷ On the day you so much as cross the Kidron Valley, you will surely die; and your blood will be on your own head."

³⁸ Shimei replied, "Your sentence is fair; I will do whatever my lord the king commands." So Shimei lived in Jerusalem for a long time.

³⁹ But three years later two of Shimei's slaves ran away to King Achish son of Maacah of Gath. When Shimei learned where they were, ⁴⁰ he saddled his donkey and went to Gath to search for them. When he found them, he brought them back to Jerusalem.

⁴¹ Solomon heard that Shimei had left Jerusalem and had gone to Gath and returned. ⁴² So the king sent for Shimei and demanded, "Didn't I make you swear by the LORD and warn you not to go anywhere else or you would surely die? And you replied, 'The sentence is fair; I will do as you say.' ⁴³ Then why haven't you kept your oath to the LORD and obeyed my command?"

⁴⁴ The king also said to Shimei, "You certainly remember all the wicked things you did to my father, David. May the LORD now bring that evil on your own head. ⁴⁵ But may I, King Solomon, receive the LORD's blessings, and may one of David's descendants always sit on this throne in the presence of the LORD." ⁴⁶ Then, at the king's command, Benaiah son of Jehoiada took Shimei outside and killed him.

So the kingdom was now firmly in Solomon's grip.

SOLOMON ASKS FOR WISDOM

3 Solomon made an alliance with Pharaoh, the king of Egypt, and married one of his daughters. He brought her to live in the City of David until he could finish building his palace and the Temple of the LORD and the wall around the city. ² At that time the people of Israel sacrificed their offerings at local places of worship, for a temple honoring the name of the LORD had not yet been built.

³ Solomon loved the LORD and followed all the decrees of his father, David, except that Solomon, too, offered sacrifices and burned incense at the local places of worship. ⁴ The most important of these places of worship was at Gibeon, so the king went there and sacrificed 1,000 burnt offerings. ⁵ That night the LORD appeared to Solomon in a dream, and God said, "What do you want? Ask, and I will give it to you!"

⁶ Solomon replied, "You showed great and faithful love to your servant my father, David, because he was honest and true and faithful to you. And you have continued to show this great and faithful love to him today by giving him a son to sit on his throne.

⁷ "Now, O LORD my God, you have made me king instead of my father, David, but I am like a little child who doesn't know his way around. ⁸ And here I am in the midst of your own chosen people, a nation so great and numerous they cannot be counted! ⁹ Give me an understanding heart so that I can govern your people well and know the difference between right and wrong. For who by himself is able to govern this great people of yours?"

¹⁰ The Lord was pleased that Solomon had asked for wisdom. ¹¹ So God replied, "Because you have asked for wisdom in governing my people with justice and have not asked for a long life or wealth or the death of your enemies—¹² I will give you what you asked for! I will give you a wise and understanding heart such as no one else has had or ever will have! ¹³ And I will also give you what you did not ask for—riches and fame! No other king in all the world will be compared to you for the rest of your life! ¹⁴ And if you follow me and obey my decrees and my commands as your father, David, did, I will give you a long life."

¹⁵ Then Solomon woke up and realized it had been a dream. He returned to Jerusalem and stood before the Ark of the Lord's Covenant, where he sacrificed burnt offerings and peace offerings. Then he invited all his officials to a great banquet.

SOLOMON JUDGES WISELY

¹⁶ Some time later two prostitutes came to the king to have an argument settled. ¹⁷ "Please, my lord," one of them began, "this woman and I live in the same house. I gave birth to a baby while she was with me in the house. ¹⁸ Three days later this woman also had a baby. We were alone; there were only two of us in the house.

¹⁹ "But her baby died during the night when she rolled over on it. ²⁰ Then she got up in the night and took my son from beside me while I was asleep. She laid her dead child in my arms and took mine to sleep beside her. ²¹ And in the morning when I tried to nurse my son, he was dead! But when I looked more closely in the morning light, I saw that it wasn't my son at all."

²² Then the other woman interrupted, "It certainly was your son, and the living child is mine."

"No," the first woman said, "the living child is mine, and the dead one is yours." And so they argued back and forth before the king.

²³ Then the king said, "Let's get the facts straight. Both of you claim the living child is

yours, and each says that the dead one belongs to the other. ²⁴All right, bring me a sword." So a sword was brought to the king.

²⁵Then he said, "Cut the living child in two, and give half to one woman and half to the other!"

²⁶Then the woman who was the real mother of the living child, and who loved him very much, cried out, "Oh no, my lord! Give her the child—please do not kill him!"

But the other woman said, "All right, he will be neither yours nor mine; divide him between us!"

²⁷Then the king said, "Do not kill the child, but give him to the woman who wants him to live, for she is his mother!"

²⁸When all Israel heard the king's decision, the people were in awe of the king, for they saw the wisdom God had given him for rendering justice.

SOLOMON'S OFFICIALS AND GOVERNORS

4 King Solomon now ruled over all Israel, ²and these were his high officials:

Azariah son of Zadok was the priest.
³ Elihoreph and Ahijah, the sons of Shisha, were court secretaries.
Jehoshaphat son of Ahilud was the royal historian.
⁴ Benaiah son of Jehoiada was commander of the army.
Zadok and Abiathar were priests.
⁵ Azariah son of Nathan was in charge of the district governors.
Zabud son of Nathan, a priest, was a trusted adviser to the king.
⁶ Ahishar was manager of the palace property.
Adoniram son of Abda was in charge of forced labor.

⁷Solomon also had twelve district governors who were over all Israel. They were responsible for providing food for the king's household. Each of them arranged provisions for one month of the year. ⁸These are the names of the twelve governors:

Ben-hur, in the hill country of Ephraim.
⁹ Ben-deker, in Makaz, Shaalbim, Beth-shemesh, and Elon-bethhanan.
¹⁰ Ben-hesed, in Arubboth, including Socoh and all the land of Hepher.
¹¹ Ben-abinadab, in all of Naphoth-dor.* (He was married to Taphath, one of Solomon's daughters.)
¹² Baana son of Ahilud, in Taanach and Megiddo, all of Beth-shan* near Zarethan below Jezreel, and all the territory from Beth-shan to Abel-meholah and over to Jokmeam.
¹³ Ben-geber, in Ramoth-gilead, including the Towns of Jair (named for Jair of the tribe of Manasseh*) in Gilead, and in the Argob

region of Bashan, including sixty large fortified towns with bronze bars on their gates.
¹⁴ Ahinadab son of Iddo, in Mahanaim.
¹⁵ Ahimaaz, in Naphtali. (He was married to Basemath, another of Solomon's daughters.)
¹⁶ Baana son of Hushai, in Asher and in Aloth.
¹⁷ Jehoshaphat son of Paruah, in Issachar.
¹⁸ Shimei son of Ela, in Benjamin.
¹⁹ Geber son of Uri, in the land of Gilead,* including the territories of King Sihon of the Amorites and King Og of Bashan. There was also one governor over the land of Judah.*

SOLOMON'S PROSPERITY AND WISDOM

²⁰The people of Judah and Israel were as numerous as the sand on the seashore. They were very contented, with plenty to eat and drink. ²¹*Solomon ruled over all the kingdoms from the Euphrates River* in the north to the land of the Philistines and the border of Egypt in the south. The conquered peoples of those lands sent tribute money to Solomon and continued to serve him throughout his lifetime.

²²The daily food requirements for Solomon's palace were 150 bushels of choice flour and 300 bushels of meal*; ²³also 10 oxen from the fattening pens, 20 pasture-fed cattle, 100 sheep or goats, as well as deer, gazelles, roe deer, and choice poultry.*

²⁴Solomon's dominion extended over all the kingdoms west of the Euphrates River, from Tiphsah to Gaza. And there was peace on all his borders. ²⁵During the lifetime of Solomon, all of Judah and Israel lived in peace and safety. And from Dan in the north to Beersheba in the south, each family had its own home and garden.*

²⁶Solomon had 4,000* stalls for his chariot horses, and he had 12,000 horses.*

²⁷The district governors faithfully provided food for King Solomon and his court; each made sure nothing was lacking during the month assigned to him. ²⁸They also brought the necessary barley and straw for the royal horses in the stables.

²⁹God gave Solomon very great wisdom and understanding, and knowledge as vast as the sands of the seashore. ³⁰In fact, his wisdom exceeded that of all the wise men of the East and the wise men of Egypt. ³¹He was wiser than anyone else, including Ethan the Ezrahite and

4:11 Hebrew *Naphath-dor*, a variant spelling of Naphoth-dor. 4:12 Hebrew *Beth-shean*, a variant spelling of Beth-shan; also in 4:12b. 4:13 Hebrew *Jair son of Manasseh*; compare 1 Chr 2:22. 4:19a Greek version reads *of Gad*; compare 4:13. 4:19b As in some Greek manuscripts; Hebrew lacks *of Judah*. The meaning of the Hebrew is uncertain. 4:21a Verses 4:21-34 are numbered 5:1-14 in Hebrew text. 4:21b Hebrew *the river*; also in 4:24. 4:22 Hebrew *30 cors* [6.6 kiloliters] *of choice flour and 60 cors* [13.2 kiloliters] *of meal.* 4:23 Or *and fattened geese.* 4:25 Hebrew *each family lived under its own grapevine and under its own fig tree.* 4:26a As in some Greek manuscripts (see also 2 Chr 9:25); Hebrew reads *40,000.* 4:26b Or *12,000 charioteers.*

the sons of Mahol—Heman, Calcol, and Darda. His fame spread throughout all the surrounding nations. ³²He composed some 3,000 proverbs and wrote 1,005 songs. ³³He could speak with authority about all kinds of plants, from the great cedar of Lebanon to the tiny hyssop that grows from cracks in a wall. He could also speak about animals, birds, small creatures, and fish. ³⁴And kings from every nation sent their ambassadors to listen to the wisdom of Solomon.

PREPARATIONS FOR BUILDING THE TEMPLE

5 ¹*King Hiram of Tyre had always been a loyal friend of David. When Hiram learned that David's son Solomon was the new king of Israel, he sent ambassadors to congratulate him.

²Then Solomon sent this message back to Hiram:

³"You know that my father, David, was not able to build a Temple to honor the name of the LORD his God because of the many wars waged against him by surrounding nations. He could not build until the LORD gave him victory over all his enemies. ⁴But now the LORD my God has given me peace on every side; I have no enemies, and all is well. ⁵So I am planning to build a Temple to honor the name of the LORD my God, just as he had instructed my father, David. For the LORD told him, 'Your son, whom I will place on your throne, will build the Temple to honor my name.'

⁶"Therefore, please command that cedars from Lebanon be cut for me. Let my men work alongside yours, and I will pay your men whatever wages you ask. As you know, there is no one among us who can cut timber like you Sidonians!"

⁷When Hiram received Solomon's message, he was very pleased and said, "Praise the LORD today for giving David a wise son to be king of the great nation of Israel." ⁸Then he sent this reply to Solomon:

"I have received your message, and I will supply all the cedar and cypress timber you need. ⁹My servants will bring the logs from the Lebanon mountains to the Mediterranean Sea* and make them into rafts and float them along the coast to whatever place you choose. Then we will break the rafts apart so you can carry the logs away. You can pay me by supplying me with food for my household."

¹⁰So Hiram supplied as much cedar and cypress timber as Solomon desired. ¹¹In return, Solomon sent him an annual payment of 100,000 bushels* of wheat for his household and 110,000 gallons* of pure olive oil. ¹²So the LORD gave wisdom to Solomon, just as he had promised. And Hiram and Solomon made a formal alliance of peace.

¹³Then King Solomon conscripted a labor force of 30,000 men from all Israel. ¹⁴He sent them to Lebanon in shifts, 10,000 every month, so that each man would be one month in Lebanon and two months at home. Adoniram was in charge of this labor force. ¹⁵Solomon also had 70,000 common laborers, 80,000 quarry workers in the hill country, ¹⁶and 3,600* foremen to supervise the work. ¹⁷At the king's command, they quarried large blocks of high-quality stone and shaped them to make the foundation of the Temple. ¹⁸Men from the city of Gebal helped Solomon's and Hiram's builders prepare the timber and stone for the Temple.

SOLOMON BUILDS THE TEMPLE

6 It was in midspring, in the month of Ziv,* during the fourth year of Solomon's reign, that he began to construct the Temple of the LORD. This was 480 years after the people of Israel were rescued from their slavery in the land of Egypt.

²The Temple that King Solomon built for the LORD was 90 feet long, 30 feet wide, and 45 feet high.* ³The entry room at the front of the Temple was 30 feet* wide, running across the entire width of the Temple. It projected outward 15 feet* from the front of the Temple. ⁴Solomon also made narrow recessed windows throughout the Temple.

⁵He built a complex of rooms against the outer walls of the Temple, all the way around the sides and rear of the building. ⁶The complex was three stories high, the bottom floor being 7½ feet wide, the second floor 9 feet wide, and the top floor 10½ feet wide.* The rooms were connected to the walls of the Temple by beams resting on ledges built out from the wall. So the beams were not inserted into the walls themselves.

⁷The stones used in the construction of the Temple were finished at the quarry, so there was no sound of hammer, ax, or any other iron tool at the building site.

⁸The entrance to the bottom floor* was on the south side of the Temple. There were winding stairs going up to the second floor, and another flight of stairs between the second and third floors. ⁹After completing the Temple structure, Solomon put in a ceiling made of cedar beams

5:1 Verses 5:1-18 are numbered 5:15-32 in Hebrew text. 5:9 Hebrew *the sea.* 5:11a Hebrew *20,000 cors* [4,400 kiloliters]. 5:11b As in Greek version, which reads *20,000 baths* [420 kiloliters] (see also 2 Chr 2:10); Hebrew reads *20 cors,* about 1,000 gallons or 4.4 kiloliters in volume. 5:16 As in some Greek manuscripts (see also 2 Chr 2:2, 18); Hebrew reads *3,300.* 6:1 Hebrew *It was in the month of Ziv, which is the second month.* This month of the ancient Hebrew lunar calendar usually occurs within the months of April and May. 6:2 Hebrew *60 cubits* [27.6 meters] *long, 20 cubits* [9.2 meters] *wide, and 30 cubits* [13.8 meters] *high.* 6:3a Hebrew *20 cubits* [9.2 meters]; also in 6:16, 20. 6:3b Hebrew *10 cubits* [4.6 meters]. 6:6 Hebrew *the bottom floor being 5 cubits* [2.3 meters] *wide, the second floor 6 cubits* [2.8 meters] *wide, and the top floor 7 cubits* [3.2 meters] *wide.* 6:8 As in Greek version; Hebrew reads *middle floor.*

and planks. ¹⁰As already stated, he built a complex of rooms along the sides of the building, attached to the Temple walls by cedar timbers. Each story of the complex was 7½ feet* high.

¹¹Then the LORD gave this message to Solomon: ¹²"Concerning this Temple you are building, if you keep all my decrees and regulations and obey all my commands, I will fulfill through you the promise I made to your father, David. ¹³I will live among the Israelites and will never abandon my people Israel."

THE TEMPLE'S INTERIOR

¹⁴So Solomon finished building the Temple. ¹⁵The entire inside, from floor to ceiling, was paneled with wood. He paneled the walls and ceilings with cedar, and he used planks of cypress for the floors. ¹⁶He partitioned off an inner sanctuary—the Most Holy Place—at the far end of the Temple. It was 30 feet deep and was paneled with cedar from floor to ceiling. ¹⁷The main room of the Temple, outside the Most Holy Place, was 60 feet* long. ¹⁸Cedar paneling completely covered the stone walls throughout the Temple, and the paneling was decorated with carvings of gourds and open flowers.

¹⁹He prepared the inner sanctuary at the far end of the Temple, where the Ark of the LORD's Covenant would be placed. ²⁰This inner sanctuary was 30 feet long, 30 feet wide, and 30 feet high. He overlaid the inside with solid gold. He also overlaid the altar made of cedar.* ²¹Then Solomon overlaid the rest of the Temple's interior with solid gold, and he made gold chains to protect the entrance* to the Most Holy Place. ²²So he finished overlaying the entire Temple with gold, including the altar that belonged to the Most Holy Place.

²³He made two cherubim of wild olive* wood, each 15 feet* tall, and placed them in the inner sanctuary. ²⁴The wingspan of each of the cherubim was 15 feet, each wing being 7½ feet* long. ²⁵The two cherubim were identical in shape and size; ²⁶each was 15 feet tall. ²⁷He placed them side by side in the inner sanctuary of the Temple. Their outspread wings reached from wall to wall, while their inner wings touched at the center of the room. ²⁸He overlaid the two cherubim with gold.

²⁹He decorated all the walls of the inner sanctuary and the main room with carvings of cherubim, palm trees, and open flowers. ³⁰He overlaid the floor in both rooms with gold.

³¹For the entrance to the inner sanctuary, he made double doors of wild olive wood with five-sided doorposts.* ³²These double doors were decorated with carvings of cherubim, palm trees, and open flowers. The doors, including the decorations of cherubim and palm trees, were overlaid with gold.

³³Then he made four-sided doorposts of wild olive wood for the entrance to the Temple.

³⁴There were two folding doors of cypress wood, and each door was hinged to fold back upon itself. ³⁵These doors were decorated with carvings of cherubim, palm trees, and open flowers—all overlaid evenly with gold.

³⁶The walls of the inner courtyard were built so that there was one layer of cedar beams between every three layers of finished stone.

³⁷The foundation of the LORD's Temple was laid in midspring, in the month of Ziv,* during the fourth year of Solomon's reign. ³⁸The entire building was completed in every detail by midautumn, in the month of Bul,* during the eleventh year of his reign. So it took seven years to build the Temple.

SOLOMON BUILDS HIS PALACE

7 Solomon also built a palace for himself, and it took him thirteen years to complete the construction.

²One of Solomon's buildings was called the Palace of the Forest of Lebanon. It was 150 feet long, 75 feet wide, and 45 feet high.* There were four rows of cedar pillars, and great cedar beams rested on the pillars. ³The hall had a cedar roof. Above the beams on the pillars were forty-five side rooms,* arranged in three tiers of fifteen each. ⁴On each end of the long hall were three rows of windows facing each other. ⁵All the doorways and doorposts* had rectangular frames and were arranged in sets of three, facing each other.

⁶Solomon also built the Hall of Pillars, which was 75 feet long and 45 feet wide.* There was a porch in front, along with a canopy supported by pillars.

⁷Solomon also built the throne room, known as the Hall of Justice, where he sat to hear legal matters. It was paneled with cedar from floor to ceiling.* ⁸Solomon's living quarters surrounded a courtyard behind this hall, and they were constructed the same way. He also built similar living quarters for Pharaoh's daughter, whom he had married.

⁹From foundation to eaves, all these buildings were built from huge blocks of high-quality stone, cut with saws and trimmed to exact measure on all sides. ¹⁰Some of the huge foundation stones were 15 feet long, and some were 12 feet* long.

6:10 Hebrew 5 cubits [2.3 meters].   6:17 Hebrew 40 cubits [18.4 meters].   6:20 Or overlaid the altar with cedar. The meaning of the Hebrew is uncertain.   6:21 Or to draw curtains across. The meaning of the Hebrew is uncertain.   6:23a Or pine; Hebrew reads oil tree; also in 6:31, 33.   6:23b Hebrew 10 cubits [4.6 meters]; also in 6:24, 26.   6:24 Hebrew 5 cubits [2.3 meters]. 6:31 The meaning of the Hebrew is uncertain.   6:37 Hebrew was laid in the month of Ziv. This month of the ancient Hebrew lunar calendar usually occurs within the months of April and May.   6:38 Hebrew by the month of Bul, which is the eighth month. This month of the ancient Hebrew lunar calendar usually occurs within the months of October and November.   7:2 Hebrew 100 cubits [46 meters] long, 50 cubits [23 meters] wide, and 30 cubits [13.8 meters] high.   7:3 Or 45 rafters, or 45 beams, or 45 pillars. The architectural details in 7:2-6 can be interpreted in many different ways.   7:5 Greek version reads windows.   7:6 Hebrew 50 cubits [23 meters] long and 30 cubits [13.8 meters] wide.   7:7 As in Syriac version and Latin Vulgate; Hebrew reads from floor to floor. 7:10 Hebrew 10 cubits [4.6 meters] . . . 8 cubits [3.7 meters].

¹¹The blocks of high-quality stone used in the walls were also cut to measure, and cedar beams were also used. ¹²The walls of the great courtyard were built so that there was one layer of cedar beams between every three layers of finished stone, just like the walls of the inner courtyard of the LORD's Temple with its entry room.

FURNISHINGS FOR THE TEMPLE

¹³King Solomon then asked for a man named Huram* to come from Tyre. ¹⁴He was half Israelite, since his mother was a widow from the tribe of Naphtali, and his father had been a craftsman in bronze from Tyre. Huram was extremely skillful and talented in any work in bronze, and he came to do all the metal work for King Solomon.

¹⁵Huram cast two bronze pillars, each 27 feet tall and 18 feet in circumference.* ¹⁶For the tops of the pillars he cast bronze capitals, each 7½ feet* tall. ¹⁷Each capital was decorated with seven sets of latticework and interwoven chains. ¹⁸He also encircled the latticework with two rows of pomegranates to decorate the capitals over the pillars. ¹⁹The capitals on the columns inside the entry room were shaped like water lilies, and they were six feet* tall. ²⁰The capitals on the two pillars had 200 pomegranates in two rows around them, beside the rounded surface next to the latticework. ²¹Huram set the pillars at the entrance of the Temple, one toward the south and one toward the north. He named the one on the south Jakin, and the one on the north Boaz.* ²²The capitals on the pillars were shaped like water lilies. And so the work on the pillars was finished.

²³Then Huram cast a great round basin, 15 feet across from rim to rim, called the Sea. It was 7½ feet deep and about 45 feet in circumference.* ²⁴It was encircled just below its rim by two rows of decorative gourds. There were about six gourds per foot* all the way around, and they were cast as part of the basin.

²⁵The Sea was placed on a base of twelve bronze oxen,* all facing outward. Three faced north, three faced west, three faced south, and three faced east, and the Sea rested on them. ²⁶The walls of the Sea were about three inches* thick, and its rim flared out like a cup and resembled a water lily blossom. It could hold about 11,000 gallons* of water.

²⁷Huram also made ten bronze water carts, each 6 feet long, 6 feet wide, and 4½ feet tall.* ²⁸They were constructed with side panels braced with crossbars. ²⁹Both the panels and the crossbars were decorated with carved lions, oxen, and cherubim. Above and below the lions and oxen were wreath decorations. ³⁰Each of these carts had four bronze wheels and bronze axles. There were supporting posts for the bronze basins at the corners of the carts; these supports were decorated on each side with carvings of wreaths.

³¹The top of each cart had a rounded frame for the basin. It projected 1½ feet* above the cart's top like a round pedestal, and its opening was 2¼ feet* across; it was decorated on the outside with carvings of wreaths. The panels of the carts were square, not round. ³²Under the panels were four wheels that were connected to axles that had been cast as one unit with the cart. The wheels were 2¼ feet in diameter ³³and were similar to chariot wheels. The axles, spokes, rims, and hubs were all cast from molten bronze.

³⁴There were handles at each of the four corners of the carts, and these, too, were cast as one unit with the cart. ³⁵Around the top of each cart was a rim nine inches wide.* The corner supports and side panels were cast as one unit with the cart. ³⁶Carvings of cherubim, lions, and palm trees decorated the panels and corner supports wherever there was room, and there were wreaths all around. ³⁷All ten water carts were the same size and were made alike, for each was cast from the same mold.

³⁸Huram also made ten smaller bronze basins, one for each cart. Each basin was six feet across and could hold 220 gallons* of water. ³⁹He set five water carts on the south side of the Temple and five on the north side. The great bronze basin called the Sea was placed near the southeast corner of the Temple. ⁴⁰He also made the necessary washbasins, shovels, and bowls.

So at last Huram completed everything King Solomon had assigned him to make for the Temple of the LORD:

⁴¹ the two pillars;
the two bowl-shaped capitals on top of the pillars;
the two networks of interwoven chains that decorated the capitals;
⁴² the 400 pomegranates that hung from the chains on the capitals (two rows of pomegranates for each of the chain networks that decorated the capitals on top of the pillars);
⁴³ the ten water carts holding the ten basins;
⁴⁴ the Sea and the twelve oxen under it;
⁴⁵ the ash buckets, the shovels, and the bowls.

Huram made all these things of burnished bronze for the Temple of the LORD, just as King

7:13 Hebrew *Hiram* (also in 7:40, 45); compare 2 Chr 2:13. This is not the same person mentioned in 5:1.   7:15 Hebrew *18 cubits* [8.3 meters] *tall and 12 cubits* [5.5 meters] *in circumference.*   7:16 Hebrew *5 cubits* [2.3 meters].   7:19 Hebrew *4 cubits* [1.8 meters]; also in 7:38.   7:21 *Jakin* probably means "he establishes"; *Boaz* probably means "in him is strength."   7:23 Hebrew *10 cubits* [4.6 meters] *across. . . . 5 cubits* [2.3 meters] *deep and 30 cubits* [13.8 meters] *in circumference.*   7:24 Or *20 gourds per meter;* Hebrew reads *10 per cubit.*   7:25 Hebrew *12 oxen;* compare 2 Kgs 16:17, which specifies *bronze oxen.*   7:26a Hebrew *a handbreadth* [8 centimeters].   7:26b Hebrew *2,000 baths* [42 kiloliters].   7:27 Hebrew *4 cubits* [1.8 meters] *long, 4 cubits wide, and 3 cubits* [1.4 meters] *high.*   7:31a Hebrew *a cubit* [46 centimeters].   7:31b Hebrew *1½ cubits* [69 centimeters]; also in 7:32.   7:35 Hebrew *half a cubit wide* [23 centimeters].   7:38 Hebrew *40 baths* [840 liters].

Solomon had directed. ⁴⁶The king had them cast in clay molds in the Jordan Valley between Succoth and Zarethan. ⁴⁷Solomon did not weigh all these things because there were so many; the weight of the bronze could not be measured.

⁴⁸Solomon also made all the furnishings of the Temple of the LORD:

the gold altar;
the gold table for the Bread of the Presence;
⁴⁹ the lampstands of solid gold, five on the
    south and five on the north, in front of
    the Most Holy Place;
the flower decorations, lamps, and tongs—
    all of gold;
⁵⁰ the small bowls, lamp snuffers, bowls, ladles,
    and incense burners—all of solid gold;
the doors for the entrances to the Most Holy
    Place and the main room of the Temple,
    with their fronts overlaid with gold.

⁵¹So King Solomon finished all his work on the Temple of the LORD. Then he brought all the gifts his father, David, had dedicated—the silver, the gold, and the various articles—and he stored them in the treasuries of the LORD's Temple.

THE ARK BROUGHT TO THE TEMPLE

8 Solomon then summoned to Jerusalem the elders of Israel and all the heads of the tribes—the leaders of the ancestral families of the Israelites. They were to bring the Ark of the LORD's Covenant to the Temple from its location in the City of David, also known as Zion. ²So all the men of Israel assembled before King Solomon at the annual Festival of Shelters, which is held in early autumn in the month of Ethanim.*

³When all the elders of Israel arrived, the priests picked up the Ark. ⁴The priests and Levites brought up the Ark of the LORD along with the special tent* and all the sacred items that had been in it. ⁵There, before the Ark, King Solomon and the entire community of Israel sacrificed so many sheep, goats, and cattle that no one could keep count!

⁶Then the priests carried the Ark of the LORD's Covenant into the inner sanctuary of the Temple—the Most Holy Place—and placed it beneath the wings of the cherubim. ⁷The cherubim spread their wings over the Ark, forming a canopy over the Ark and its carrying poles. ⁸These poles were so long that their ends could be seen from the Holy Place, which is in front of the Most Holy Place, but not from the outside. They are still there to this day. ⁹Nothing was in the Ark except the two stone tablets that Moses had placed in it at Mount Sinai,* where the LORD made a covenant with the people of Israel when they left the land of Egypt.

¹⁰When the priests came out of the Holy Place, a thick cloud filled the Temple of the LORD. ¹¹The priests could not continue their service because

of the cloud, for the glorious presence of the LORD filled the Temple of the LORD.

SOLOMON PRAISES THE LORD

¹²Then Solomon prayed, "O LORD, you have said that you would live in a thick cloud of darkness. ¹³Now I have built a glorious Temple for you, a place where you can live forever!*"

¹⁴Then the king turned around to the entire community of Israel standing before him and gave this blessing: ¹⁵"Praise the LORD, the God of Israel, who has kept the promise he made to my father, David. For he told my father, ¹⁶'From the day I brought my people Israel out of Egypt, I have never chosen a city among any of the tribes of Israel as the place where a Temple should be built to honor my name. But I have chosen David to be king over my people Israel.'

¹⁷Then Solomon said, "My father, David, wanted to build this Temple to honor the name of the LORD, the God of Israel. ¹⁸But the LORD told him, 'You wanted to build the Temple to honor my name. Your intention is good, ¹⁹but you are not the one to do it. One of your own sons will build the Temple to honor me.'

²⁰"And now the LORD has fulfilled the promise he made, for I have become king in my father's place, and now I sit on the throne of Israel, just as the LORD promised. I have built this Temple to honor the name of the LORD, the God of Israel. ²¹And I have prepared a place there for the Ark, which contains the covenant that the LORD made with our ancestors when he brought them out of Egypt."

SOLOMON'S PRAYER OF DEDICATION

²²Then Solomon stood before the altar of the LORD in front of the entire community of Israel. He lifted his hands toward heaven, ²³and he prayed,

"O LORD, God of Israel, there is no God like you in all of heaven above or on the earth below. You keep your covenant and show unfailing love to all who walk before you in wholehearted devotion. ²⁴You have kept your promise to your servant David, my father. You made that promise with your own mouth, and with your own hands you have fulfilled it today.

²⁵"And now, O LORD, God of Israel, carry out the additional promise you made to your servant David, my father. For you said to him, 'If your descendants guard their behavior and faithfully follow me as you

8:2 Hebrew *at the festival in the month Ethanim, which is the seventh month.* The Festival of Shelters began on the fifteenth day of the seventh month of the ancient Hebrew lunar calendar. This day occurred in late September, October, or early November. 8:4 Hebrew *the Tent of Meeting;* i.e., the tent mentioned in 2 Sam 6:17 and 1 Chr 16:1. 8:9 Hebrew *at Horeb,* another name for Sinai. 8:13 Some Greek texts add the line *Is this not written in the Book of Jashar?*

have done, one of them will always sit on the throne of Israel.' ²⁶ Now, O God of Israel, fulfill this promise to your servant David, my father.

²⁷ "But will God really live on earth? Why, even the highest heavens cannot contain you. How much less this Temple I have built! ²⁸ Nevertheless, listen to my prayer and my plea, O Lord my God. Hear the cry and the prayer that your servant is making to you today. ²⁹ May you watch over this Temple night and day, this place where you have said, 'My name will be there.' May you always hear the prayers I make toward this place. ³⁰ May you hear the humble and earnest requests from me and your people Israel when we pray toward this place. Yes, hear us from heaven where you live, and when you hear, forgive.

³¹ "If someone wrongs another person and is required to take an oath of innocence in front of your altar in this Temple, ³² then hear from heaven and judge between your servants—the accuser and the accused. Punish the guilty as they deserve. Acquit the innocent because of their innocence.

³³ "If your people Israel are defeated by their enemies because they have sinned against you, and if they turn to you and acknowledge your name and pray to you here in this Temple, ³⁴ then hear from heaven and forgive the sin of your people Israel and return them to this land you gave their ancestors.

³⁵ "If the skies are shut up and there is no rain because your people have sinned against you, and if they pray toward this Temple and acknowledge your name and turn from their sins because you have punished them, ³⁶ then hear from heaven and forgive the sins of your servants, your people Israel. Teach them to follow the right path, and send rain on your land that you have given to your people as their special possession.

³⁷ "If there is a famine in the land or a plague or crop disease or attacks of locusts or caterpillars, or if your people's enemies are in the land besieging their towns—whatever disaster or disease there is—³⁸ and if your people Israel pray about their troubles, raising their hands toward this Temple, ³⁹ then hear from heaven where you live, and forgive. Give your people what their actions deserve, for you alone know each human heart. ⁴⁰ Then they will fear you as long as they live in the land you gave to our ancestors.

⁴¹ "In the future, foreigners who do not belong to your people Israel will hear of you. They will come from distant lands because of your name, ⁴² for they will hear of your great name and your strong hand and your powerful arm. And when they pray toward this Temple, ⁴³ then hear from heaven where you live, and grant what they ask of you. In this way, all the people of the earth will come to know and fear you, just as your own people Israel do. They, too, will know that this Temple I have built honors your name.

⁴⁴ "If your people go out where you send them to fight their enemies, and if they pray to the Lord by turning toward this city you have chosen and toward this Temple I have built to honor your name, ⁴⁵ then hear their prayers from heaven and uphold their cause.

⁴⁶ "If they sin against you—and who has never sinned?—you might become angry with them and let their enemies conquer them and take them captive to their land far away or near. ⁴⁷ But in that land of exile, they might turn to you in repentance and pray, 'We have sinned, done evil, and acted wickedly.' ⁴⁸ If they turn to you with their whole heart and soul in the land of their enemies and pray toward the land you gave to their ancestors—toward this city you have chosen, and toward this Temple I have built to honor your name—⁴⁹ then hear their prayers and their petition from heaven where you live, and uphold their cause. ⁵⁰ Forgive your people who have sinned against you. Forgive all the offenses they have committed against you. Make their captors merciful to them, ⁵¹ for they are your people—your special possession—whom you brought out of the iron-smelting furnace of Egypt.

⁵² "May your eyes be open to my requests and to the requests of your people Israel. May you hear and answer them whenever they cry out to you. ⁵³ For when you brought our ancestors out of Egypt, O Sovereign Lord, you told your servant Moses that you had set Israel apart from all the nations of the earth to be your own special possession."

THE DEDICATION OF THE TEMPLE

⁵⁴ When Solomon finished making these prayers and petitions to the Lord, he stood up in front of the altar of the Lord, where he had been kneeling with his hands raised toward heaven. ⁵⁵ He stood and in a loud voice blessed the entire congregation of Israel:

⁵⁶ "Praise the Lord who has given rest to his people Israel, just as he promised. Not one word has failed of all the wonderful promises he gave through his servant Moses. ⁵⁷ May the Lord our God be with us as he was with our ancestors; may he never leave us or abandon us. ⁵⁸ May he give us the desire to do his will in everything and to obey all the commands, decrees, and regulations that he gave our ancestors. ⁵⁹ And may these words that I have prayed in the presence of the Lord be before him constantly, day and night, so that

the LORD our God may give justice to me and to his people Israel, according to each day's needs. ⁶⁰Then people all over the earth will know that the LORD alone is God and there is no other. ⁶¹And may you be completely faithful to the LORD our God. May you always obey his decrees and commands, just as you are doing today."

⁶²Then the king and all Israel with him offered sacrifices to the LORD. ⁶³Solomon offered to the LORD a peace offering of 22,000 cattle and 120,000 sheep and goats. And so the king and all the people of Israel dedicated the Temple of the LORD.

⁶⁴That same day the king consecrated the central area of the courtyard in front of the LORD's Temple. He offered burnt offerings, grain offerings, and the fat of peace offerings there, because the bronze altar in the LORD's presence was too small to hold all the burnt offerings, grain offerings, and the fat of the peace offerings.

⁶⁵Then Solomon and all Israel celebrated the Festival of Shelters* in the presence of the LORD our God. A large congregation had gathered from as far away as Lebo-hamath in the north and the Brook of Egypt in the south. The celebration went on for fourteen days in all—seven days for the dedication of the altar and seven days for the Festival of Shelters.* ⁶⁶After the festival was over,* Solomon sent the people home. They blessed the king and went to their homes joyful and glad because the LORD had been good to his servant David and to his people Israel.

THE LORD'S RESPONSE TO SOLOMON

9 So Solomon finished building the Temple of the LORD, as well as the royal palace. He completed everything he had planned to do. ²Then the LORD appeared to Solomon a second time, as he had done before at Gibeon. ³The LORD said to him,

"I have heard your prayer and your petition. I have set this Temple apart to be holy—this place you have built where my name will be honored forever. I will always watch over it, for it is dear to my heart.

⁴"As for you, if you will follow me with integrity and godliness, as David your father did, obeying all my commands, decrees, and regulations, ⁵then I will establish the throne of your dynasty over Israel forever. For I made this promise to your father, David: 'One of your descendants will always sit on the throne of Israel.'

⁶"But if you or your descendants abandon me and disobey the commands and decrees I have given you, and if you serve and worship other gods, ⁷then I will uproot Israel from this land that I have given them. I will reject this Temple that I have made holy to honor my name. I will make Israel an object of mockery and ridicule among the nations. ⁸And though this Temple is impressive now,

all who pass by will be appalled and will gasp in horror. They will ask, 'Why did the LORD do such terrible things to this land and to this Temple?' ⁹"And the answer will be, 'Because his people abandoned the LORD their God, who brought their ancestors out of Egypt, and they worshiped other gods instead and bowed down to them. That is why the LORD has brought all these disasters on them.'"

SOLOMON'S AGREEMENT WITH HIRAM

¹⁰It took Solomon twenty years to build the LORD's Temple and his own royal palace. At the end of that time, ¹¹he gave twenty towns in the land of Galilee to King Hiram of Tyre. (Hiram had previously provided all the cedar and cypress timber and gold that Solomon had requested.) ¹²But when Hiram came from Tyre to see the towns Solomon had given him, he was not at all pleased with them. ¹³"What kind of towns are these, my brother?" he asked. So Hiram called that area Cabul (which means "worthless"), as it is still known today. ¹⁴Nevertheless, Hiram paid* Solomon 9,000 pounds* of gold.

SOLOMON'S MANY ACHIEVEMENTS

¹⁵This is the account of the forced labor that King Solomon conscripted to build the LORD's Temple, the royal palace, the supporting terraces,* the wall of Jerusalem, and the cities of Hazor, Megiddo, and Gezer. ¹⁶(Pharaoh, the king of Egypt, had attacked and captured Gezer, killing the Canaanite population and burning it down. He gave the city to his daughter as a wedding gift when she married Solomon. ¹⁷So Solomon rebuilt the city of Gezer.) He also built up the towns of Lower Beth-horon, ¹⁸Baalath, and Tamar* in the wilderness within his land. ¹⁹He built towns as supply centers and constructed towns where his chariots and horses* could be stationed. He built everything he desired in Jerusalem and Lebanon and throughout his entire realm.

²⁰There were still some people living in the land who were not Israelites, including Amorites, Hittites, Perizzites, Hivites, and Jebusites. ²¹These were descendants of the nations whom the people of Israel had not completely destroyed.* So Solomon conscripted them as slaves, and they serve as forced laborers to this day. ²²But Solomon did not conscript any of the Israelites for forced labor. Instead, he assigned them to serve as fighting men, government

---

8:65a Hebrew *the festival;* see note on 8:2. 8:65b Hebrew *seven days and seven days, fourteen days;* compare parallel text at 2 Chr 7:8-10. 8:66 Hebrew *On the eighth day,* probably referring to the day following the seven-day Festival of Shelters; compare parallel text at 2 Chr 7:9-10. 9:14a Or *For Hiram had paid.* 9:14b Hebrew *120 talents* [4,000 kilograms]. 9:15 Hebrew *the millo;* also in 9:24. The meaning of the Hebrew is uncertain. 9:18 An alternate reading in the Masoretic Text reads *Tadmor.* 9:19 Or *and charioteers.* 9:21 The Hebrew term used here refers to the complete consecration of things or people to the LORD, either by destroying them or by giving them as an offering.

officials, officers and captains in his army, commanders of his chariots, and charioteers. [23] Solomon appointed 550 of them to supervise the people working on his various projects.

[24] Solomon moved his wife, Pharaoh's daughter, from the City of David to the new palace he had built for her. Then he constructed the supporting terraces.

[25] Three times each year Solomon presented burnt offerings and peace offerings on the altar he had built for the LORD. He also burned incense to the LORD. And so he finished the work of building the Temple.

[26] King Solomon also built a fleet of ships at Ezion-geber, a port near Elath* in the land of Edom, along the shore of the Red Sea.* [27] Hiram sent experienced crews of sailors to sail the ships with Solomon's men. [28] They sailed to Ophir and brought back to Solomon some sixteen tons* of gold.

VISIT OF THE QUEEN OF SHEBA

10 When the queen of Sheba heard of Solomon's fame, which brought honor to the name of the LORD,* she came to test him with hard questions. [2] She arrived in Jerusalem with a large group of attendants and a great caravan of camels loaded with spices, large quantities of gold, and precious jewels. When she met with Solomon, she talked with him about everything she had on her mind. [3] Solomon had answers for all her questions; nothing was too hard for the king to explain to her. [4] When the queen of Sheba realized how very wise Solomon was, and when she saw the palace he had built, [5] she was overwhelmed. She was also amazed at the food on his tables, the organization of his officials and their splendid clothing, the cup-bearers, and the burnt offerings Solomon made at the Temple of the LORD.

[6] She exclaimed to the king, "Everything I heard in my country about your achievements* and wisdom is true! [7] I didn't believe what was said until I arrived here and saw it with my own eyes. In fact, I had not heard the half of it! Your wisdom and prosperity are far beyond what I was told. [8] How happy your people* must be! What a privilege for your officials to stand here day after day, listening to your wisdom! [9] Praise the LORD your God, who delights in you and has placed you on the throne of Israel. Because of the LORD's eternal love for Israel, he has made you king so you can rule with justice and righteousness."

[10] Then she gave the king a gift of 9,000 pounds* of gold, great quantities of spices, and precious jewels. Never again were so many spices brought in as those the queen of Sheba gave to King Solomon.

[11] (In addition, Hiram's ships brought gold from Ophir, and they also brought rich cargoes of red sandalwood* and precious jewels. [12] The king used the sandalwood to make railings for the Temple of the LORD and the royal palace, and to construct lyres and harps for the musicians. Never before or since has there been such a supply of sandalwood.)

[13] King Solomon gave the queen of Sheba whatever she asked for, besides all the customary gifts he had so generously given. Then she and all her attendants returned to their own land.

SOLOMON'S WEALTH AND SPLENDOR

[14] Each year Solomon received about 25 tons* of gold. [15] This did not include the additional revenue he received from merchants and traders, all the kings of Arabia, and the governors of the land.

[16] King Solomon made 200 large shields of hammered gold, each weighing more than fifteen pounds.* [17] He also made 300 smaller shields of hammered gold, each weighing nearly four pounds.* The king placed these shields in the Palace of the Forest of Lebanon.

[18] Then the king made a huge throne, decorated with ivory and overlaid with fine gold. [19] The throne had six steps and a rounded back. There were armrests on both sides of the seat, and the figure of a lion stood on each side of the throne. [20] There were also twelve other lions, one standing on each end of the six steps. No other throne in all the world could be compared with it!

[21] All of King Solomon's drinking cups were solid gold, as were all the utensils in the Palace of the Forest of Lebanon. They were not made of silver, for silver was considered worthless in Solomon's day!

[22] The king had a fleet of trading ships of Tarshish that sailed with Hiram's fleet. Once every three years the ships returned, loaded with gold, silver, ivory, apes, and peacocks.*

[23] So King Solomon became richer and wiser than any other king on earth. [24] People from every nation came to consult him and to hear the wisdom God had given him. [25] Year after year everyone who visited brought him gifts of silver and gold, clothing, weapons, spices, horses, and mules.

[26] Solomon built up a huge force of chariots and horses.* He had 1,400 chariots and 12,000 horses. He stationed some of them in the chariot cities and some near him in Jerusalem. [27] The king made silver as plentiful in Jerusalem as stone. And valuable cedar timber was as common as the sycamore-fig trees that grow in the foothills of Judah.* [28] Solomon's horses were imported from Egypt* and from Cilicia*; the king's traders

---

9:26a As in Greek version (see also 2 Kgs 14:22; 16:6); Hebrew reads *Eloth*, a variant spelling of Elath.   9:26b Hebrew *sea of reeds.*   9:28 Hebrew *420 talents* [14 metric tons].   10:1 Or *which was due to the name of the LORD.* The meaning of the Hebrew is uncertain.   10:6 Hebrew *your words.*   10:8 Greek and Syriac versions and Latin Vulgate read *your wives.*   10:10 Hebrew *120 talents* [4,000 kilograms].   10:11 Hebrew *almug wood;* also in 10:12.   10:14 Hebrew *666 talents* [23 metric tons].   10:16 Hebrew *600* [shekels] *of gold* [6.8 kilograms].   10:17 Hebrew *3 minas* [1.8 kilograms].   10:22 Or *and baboons.*   10:26 Or *charioteers;* also in 10:26b.   10:27 Hebrew *the Shephelah.*   10:28a Possibly *Muzur,* a district near Cilicia; also in 10:29.   10:28b Hebrew *Kue,* probably another name for Cilicia.

acquired them from Cilicia at the standard price. [29]At that time chariots from Egypt could be purchased for 600 pieces of silver,* and horses for 150 pieces of silver.* They were then exported to the kings of the Hittites and the kings of Aram.

SOLOMON'S MANY WIVES

11 Now King Solomon loved many foreign women. Besides Pharaoh's daughter, he married women from Moab, Ammon, Edom, Sidon, and from among the Hittites. [2]The LORD had clearly instructed the people of Israel, "You must not marry them, because they will turn your hearts to their gods." Yet Solomon insisted on loving them anyway. [3]He had 700 wives of royal birth and 300 concubines. And in fact, they did turn his heart away from the LORD.

[4]In Solomon's old age, they turned his heart to worship other gods instead of being completely faithful to the LORD his God, as his father, David, had been. [5]Solomon worshiped Ashtoreth, the goddess of the Sidonians, and Molech,* the detestable god of the Ammonites. [6]In this way, Solomon did what was evil in the LORD's sight; he refused to follow the LORD completely, as his father, David, had done.

[7]On the Mount of Olives, east of Jerusalem,* he even built a pagan shrine for Chemosh, the detestable god of Moab, and another for Molech, the detestable god of the Ammonites. [8]Solomon built such shrines for all his foreign wives to use for burning incense and sacrificing to their gods.

[9]The LORD was very angry with Solomon, for his heart had turned away from the LORD, the God of Israel, who had appeared to him twice. [10]He had warned Solomon specifically about worshiping other gods, but Solomon did not listen to the LORD's command. [11]So now the LORD said to him, "Since you have not kept my covenant and have disobeyed my decrees, I will surely tear the kingdom away from you and give it to one of your servants. [12]But for the sake of your father, David, I will not do this while you are still alive. I will take the kingdom away from your son. [13]And even so, I will not take away the entire kingdom; I will let him be king of one tribe for the sake of my servant David and for the sake of Jerusalem, my chosen city."

SOLOMON'S ADVERSARIES

[14]Then the LORD raised up Hadad the Edomite, a member of Edom's royal family, to be Solomon's adversary. [15]Years before, David had defeated Edom. Joab, his army commander, had stayed to bury some of the Israelite soldiers who had died in battle. While there, they killed every male in Edom. [16]Joab and the army of Israel had stayed there for six months, killing them.

[17]But Hadad and a few of his father's royal officials escaped and headed for Egypt. (Hadad was just a boy at the time.) [18]They set out from Midian and went to Paran, where others joined them. Then they traveled to Egypt and went to Pharaoh, who gave them a home, food, and some land. [19]Pharaoh grew very fond of Hadad, and he gave him his wife's sister in marriage—the sister of Queen Tahpenes. [20]She bore him a son named Genubath. Tahpenes raised him* in Pharaoh's palace among Pharaoh's own sons.

[21]When the news reached Hadad in Egypt that David and his commander Joab were both dead, he said to Pharaoh, "Let me return to my own country."

[22]"Why?" Pharaoh asked him. "What do you lack here that makes you want to go home?"

"Nothing," he replied. "But even so, please let me return home."

[23]God also raised up Rezon son of Eliada as Solomon's adversary. Rezon had fled from his master, King Hadadezer of Zobah, [24]and had become the leader of a gang of rebels. After David conquered Hadadezer, Rezon and his men fled to Damascus, where he became king. [25]Rezon was Israel's bitter adversary for the rest of Solomon's reign, and he made trouble, just as Hadad did. Rezon hated Israel intensely and continued to reign in Aram.

JEROBOAM REBELS AGAINST SOLOMON

[26]Another rebel leader was Jeroboam son of Nebat, one of Solomon's own officials. He came from the town of Zeredah in Ephraim, and his mother was Zeruah, a widow.

[27]This is the story behind his rebellion. Solomon was rebuilding the supporting terraces* and repairing the walls of the city of his father, David. [28]Jeroboam was a very capable young man, and when Solomon saw how industrious he was, he put him in charge of the labor force from the tribes of Ephraim and Manasseh, the descendants of Joseph.

[29]One day as Jeroboam was leaving Jerusalem, the prophet Ahijah from Shiloh met him along the way. Ahijah was wearing a new cloak. The two of them were alone in a field, [30]and Ahijah took hold of the new cloak he was wearing and tore it into twelve pieces. [31]Then he said to Jeroboam, "Take ten of these pieces, for this is what the LORD, the God of Israel, says: 'I am about to tear the kingdom from the hand of Solomon, and I will give ten of the tribes to you! [32]But I will leave him one tribe for the sake of my servant David and for the sake of Jerusalem, which I have chosen out of all the tribes of Israel. [33]For Solomon has* abandoned me and worshiped Ashtoreth, the goddess of the Sidonians; Chemosh,

---

10:29a Hebrew 600 [shekels] of silver, about 15 pounds or 6.8 kilograms in weight.   10:29b Hebrew 150 [shekels], about 3.8 pounds or 1.7 kilograms in weight.   11:5 Hebrew Milcom, a variant spelling of Molech; also in 11:33.   11:7 Hebrew On the mountain east of Jerusalem.   11:20 As in Greek version; Hebrew reads weaned him.   11:27 Hebrew the millo. The meaning of the Hebrew is uncertain.   11:33 As in Greek, Syriac, and Latin Vulgate; Hebrew reads For they have.

the god of Moab; and Molech, the god of the Ammonites. He has not followed my ways and done what is pleasing in my sight. He has not obeyed my decrees and regulations as David his father did. [34]"But I will not take the entire kingdom from Solomon at this time. For the sake of my servant David, the one whom I chose and who obeyed my commands and decrees, I will keep Solomon as leader for the rest of his life. [35]But I will take the kingdom away from his son and give ten of the tribes to you. [36]His son will have one tribe so that the descendants of David my servant will continue to reign, shining like a lamp in Jerusalem, the city I have chosen to be the place for my name. [37]And I will place you on the throne of Israel, and you will rule over all that your heart desires. [38]If you listen to what I tell you and follow my ways and do whatever I consider to be right, and if you obey my decrees and commands, as my servant David did, then I will always be with you. I will establish an enduring dynasty for you as I did for David, and I will give Israel to you. [39]Because of Solomon's sin I will punish the descendants of David—though not forever.'"

[40]Solomon tried to kill Jeroboam, but he fled to King Shishak of Egypt and stayed there until Solomon died.

SUMMARY OF SOLOMON'S REIGN

[41]The rest of the events in Solomon's reign, including all his deeds and his wisdom, are recorded in *The Book of the Acts of Solomon*. [42]Solomon ruled in Jerusalem over all Israel for forty years. [43]When he died, he was buried in the City of David, named for his father. Then his son Rehoboam became the next king.

THE NORTHERN TRIBES REVOLT

12 Rehoboam went to Shechem, where all Israel had gathered to make him king. [2]When Jeroboam son of Nebat heard of this, he returned from Egypt,* for he had fled to Egypt to escape from King Solomon. [3]The leaders of Israel summoned him, and Jeroboam and the whole assembly of Israel went to speak with Rehoboam. [4]"Your father was a hard master," they said. "Lighten the harsh labor demands and heavy taxes that your father imposed on us. Then we will be your loyal subjects."

[5]Rehoboam replied, "Give me three days to think this over. Then come back for my answer." So the people went away.

[6]Then King Rehoboam discussed the matter with the older men who had counseled his father, Solomon. "What is your advice?" he asked. "How should I answer these people?"

[7]The older counselors replied, "If you are willing to be a servant to these people today and give them a favorable answer, they will always be your loyal subjects."

[8]But Rehoboam rejected the advice of the older men and instead asked the opinion of the young men who had grown up with him and were now his advisers. [9]"What is your advice?" he asked them. "How should I answer these people who want me to lighten the burdens imposed by my father?"

[10]The young men replied, "This is what you should tell those complainers who want a lighter burden: 'My little finger is thicker than my father's waist! [11]Yes, my father laid heavy burdens on you, but I'm going to make them even heavier! My father beat you with whips, but I will beat you with scorpions!'"

[12]Three days later Jeroboam and all the people returned to hear Rehoboam's decision, just as the king had ordered. [13]But Rehoboam spoke harshly to the people, for he rejected the advice of the older counselors [14]and followed the counsel of his younger advisers. He told the people, "My father laid heavy burdens on you, but I'm going to make them even heavier! My father beat you with whips, but I will beat you with scorpions!"

[15]So the king paid no attention to the people. This turn of events was the will of the LORD, for it fulfilled the LORD's message to Jeroboam son of Nebat through the prophet Ahijah from Shiloh.

[16]When all Israel realized that the king had refused to listen to them, they responded,

"Down with the dynasty of David!
    We have no interest in the son of Jesse.
Back to your homes, O Israel!
    Look out for your own house, O David!"

So the people of Israel returned home. [17]But Rehoboam continued to rule over the Israelites who lived in the towns of Judah.

[18]King Rehoboam sent Adoniram,* who was in charge of forced labor, to restore order, but the people of Israel stoned him to death. When this news reached King Rehoboam, he quickly jumped into his chariot and fled to Jerusalem. [19]And to this day the northern tribes of Israel have refused to be ruled by a descendant of David.

[20]When the people of Israel learned of Jeroboam's return from Egypt, they called an assembly and made him king over all Israel. So only the tribe of Judah remained loyal to the family of David.

SHEMAIAH'S PROPHECY

[21]When Rehoboam arrived at Jerusalem, he mobilized the men of Judah and the tribe of Benjamin—180,000 select troops—to fight against

---

12:2 As in Greek version and Latin Vulgate (see also 2 Chr 10:2); Hebrew reads *he lived in Egypt*. 12:18 As in some Greek manuscripts and Syriac version (see also 4:6; 5:14); Hebrew reads *Adoram*.

the men of Israel and to restore the kingdom to himself. ²²But God said to Shemaiah, the man of God, ²³"Say to Rehoboam son of Solomon, king of Judah, and to all the people of Judah and Benjamin, and to the rest of the people, ²⁴'This is what the LORD says: Do not fight against your relatives, the Israelites. Go back home, for what has happened is my doing!'" So they obeyed the message of the LORD and went home, as the LORD had commanded.

JEROBOAM MAKES GOLD CALVES

²⁵Jeroboam then built up the city of Shechem in the hill country of Ephraim, and it became his capital. Later he went and built up the town of Peniel.*

²⁶Jeroboam thought to himself, "Unless I am careful, the kingdom will return to the dynasty of David. ²⁷When these people go to Jerusalem to offer sacrifices at the Temple of the LORD, they will again give their allegiance to King Rehoboam of Judah. They will kill me and make him their king instead."

²⁸So on the advice of his counselors, the king made two gold calves. He said to the people,* "It is too much trouble for you to worship in Jerusalem. Look, Israel, these are the gods who brought you out of Egypt!"

²⁹He placed these calf idols in Bethel and in Dan—at either end of his kingdom. ³⁰But this became a great sin, for the people worshiped the idols, traveling as far north as Dan to worship the one there.

³¹Jeroboam also erected buildings at the pagan shrines and ordained priests from the common people—those who were not from the priestly tribe of Levi. ³²And Jeroboam instituted a religious festival in Bethel, held on the fifteenth day of the eighth month,* in imitation of the annual Festival of Shelters in Judah. There at Bethel he himself offered sacrifices to the calves he had made, and he appointed priests for the pagan shrines he had made. ³³So on the fifteenth day of the eighth month, a day that he himself had designated, Jeroboam offered sacrifices on the altar at Bethel. He instituted a religious festival for Israel, and he went up to the altar to burn incense.

A PROPHET DENOUNCES JEROBOAM

13 At the LORD's command, a man of God from Judah went to Bethel, arriving there just as Jeroboam was approaching the altar to burn incense. ²Then at the LORD's command, he shouted, "O altar, altar! This is what the LORD says: A child named Josiah will be born into the dynasty of David. On you he will sacrifice the priests from the pagan shrines who come here to burn incense, and human bones will be burned on you." ³That same day the man of God gave a sign to prove his message. He said, "The LORD

has promised to give this sign: This altar will split apart, and its ashes will be poured out on the ground."

⁴When King Jeroboam heard the man of God speaking against the altar at Bethel, he pointed at him and shouted, "Seize that man!" But instantly the king's hand became paralyzed in that position, and he couldn't pull it back. ⁵At the same time a wide crack appeared in the altar, and the ashes poured out, just as the man of God had predicted in his message from the LORD.

⁶The king cried out to the man of God, "Please ask the LORD your God to restore my hand again!" So the man of God prayed to the LORD, and the king's hand was restored and he could move it again.

⁷Then the king said to the man of God, "Come to the palace with me and have something to eat, and I will give you a gift."

⁸But the man of God said to the king, "Even if you gave me half of everything you own, I would not go with you. I would not eat or drink anything in this place. ⁹For the LORD gave me this command: 'You must not eat or drink anything while you are there, and do not return to Judah by the same way you came.'" ¹⁰So he left Bethel and went home another way.

¹¹As it happened, there was an old prophet living in Bethel, and his sons* came home and told him what the man of God had done in Bethel that day. They also told their father what the man had said to the king. ¹²The old prophet asked them, "Which way did he go?" So they showed their father* which road the man of God had taken. ¹³"Quick, saddle the donkey," the old man said. So they saddled the donkey for him, and he mounted it.

¹⁴Then he rode after the man of God and found him sitting under a great tree. The old prophet asked him, "Are you the man of God who came from Judah?"

"Yes, I am," he replied.

¹⁵Then he said to the man of God, "Come home with me and eat some food."

¹⁶"No, I cannot," he replied. "I am not allowed to eat or drink anything here in this place. ¹⁷For the LORD gave me this command: 'You must not eat or drink anything while you are there, and do not return to Judah by the same way you came.'"

¹⁸But the old prophet answered, "I am a prophet, too, just as you are. And an angel gave me this command from the LORD: 'Bring him home with you so he can have something to eat and drink.'" But the old man was lying to him. ¹⁹So they went back together, and the man of God ate and drank at the prophet's home.

12:25 Hebrew *Penuel*, a variant spelling of Peniel.   12:28 Hebrew *to them*.   12:32 This day of the ancient Hebrew lunar calendar occurred in late October or early November, exactly one month after the annual Festival of Shelters in Judah (see Lev 23:34).   13:11 As in Greek version; Hebrew reads *son*.   13:12 As in Greek version; Hebrew reads *They had seen*.

²⁰ Then while they were sitting at the table, a command from the LORD came to the old prophet. ²¹ He cried out to the man of God from Judah, "This is what the LORD says: You have defied the word of the LORD and have disobeyed the command the LORD your God gave you. ²² You came back to this place and ate and drank where he told you not to eat or drink. Because of this, your body will not be buried in the grave of your ancestors."

²³ After the man of God had finished eating and drinking, the old prophet saddled his own donkey for him, ²⁴ and the man of God started off again. But as he was traveling along, a lion came out and killed him. His body lay there on the road, with the donkey and the lion standing beside it. ²⁵ People who passed by saw the body lying in the road and the lion standing beside it, and they went and reported it in Bethel, where the old prophet lived.

²⁶ When the prophet heard the report, he said, "It is the man of God who disobeyed the LORD's command. The LORD has fulfilled his word by causing the lion to attack and kill him."

²⁷ Then the prophet said to his sons, "Saddle a donkey for me." So they saddled a donkey, ²⁸ and he went out and found the body lying in the road. The donkey and lion were still standing there beside it, for the lion had not eaten the body nor attacked the donkey. ²⁹ So the prophet laid the body of the man of God on the donkey and took it back to the town to mourn over him and bury him. ³⁰ He laid the body in his own grave, crying out in grief, "Oh, my brother!"

³¹ Afterward the prophet said to his sons, "When I die, bury me in the grave where the man of God is buried. Lay my bones beside his bones. ³² For the message the LORD told him to proclaim against the altar in Bethel and against the pagan shrines in the towns of Samaria will certainly come true."

³³ But even after this, Jeroboam did not turn from his evil ways. He continued to choose priests from the common people. He appointed anyone who wanted to become a priest for the pagan shrines. ³⁴ This became a great sin and resulted in the utter destruction of Jeroboam's dynasty from the face of the earth.

AHIJAH'S PROPHECY AGAINST JEROBOAM

14 At that time Jeroboam's son Abijah became very sick. ² So Jeroboam told his wife, "Disguise yourself so that no one will recognize you as my wife. Then go to the prophet Ahijah at Shiloh—the man who told me I would become king. ³ Take him a gift of ten loaves of bread, some cakes, and a jar of honey, and ask him what will happen to the boy."

⁴ So Jeroboam's wife went to Ahijah's home at Shiloh. He was an old man now and could no longer see. ⁵ But the LORD had told Ahijah, "Jeroboam's wife will come here, pretending to be someone else. She will ask you about her son, for he is very sick. Give her the answer I give you."

⁶ So when Ahijah heard her footsteps at the door, he called out, "Come in, wife of Jeroboam! Why are you pretending to be someone else?" Then he told her, "I have bad news for you. ⁷ Give your husband, Jeroboam, this message from the LORD, the God of Israel: 'I promoted you from the ranks of the common people and made you ruler over my people Israel. ⁸ I ripped the kingdom away from the family of David and gave it to you. But you have not been like my servant David, who obeyed my commands and followed me with all his heart and always did whatever I wanted. ⁹ You have done more evil than all who lived before you. You have made other gods for yourself and have made me furious with your gold calves. And since you have turned your back on me, ¹⁰ I will bring disaster on your dynasty and will destroy every one of your male descendants, slave and free alike, anywhere in Israel. I will burn up your royal dynasty as one burns up trash until it is all gone. ¹¹ The members of Jeroboam's family who die in the city will be eaten by dogs, and those who die in the field will be eaten by vultures. I, the LORD, have spoken.'"

¹² Then Ahijah said to Jeroboam's wife, "Go on home, and when you enter the city, the child will die. ¹³ All Israel will mourn for him and bury him. He is the only member of your family who will have a proper burial, for this child is the only good thing that the LORD, the God of Israel, sees in the entire family of Jeroboam.

¹⁴ "In addition, the LORD will raise up a king over Israel who will destroy the family of Jeroboam. This will happen today, even now! ¹⁵ Then the LORD will shake Israel like a reed whipped about in a stream. He will uproot the people of Israel from this good land that he gave their ancestors and will scatter them beyond the Euphrates River,* for they have angered the LORD with the Asherah poles they have set up for worship. ¹⁶ He will abandon Israel because Jeroboam sinned and made Israel sin along with him."

¹⁷ So Jeroboam's wife returned to Tirzah, and the child died just as she walked through the door of her home. ¹⁸ And all Israel buried him and mourned for him, as the LORD had promised through the prophet Ahijah.

¹⁹ The rest of the events in Jeroboam's reign, including all his wars and how he ruled, are recorded in *The Book of the History of the Kings of Israel.* ²⁰ Jeroboam reigned in Israel twenty-two years. When Jeroboam died, his son Nadab became the next king.

REHOBOAM RULES IN JUDAH

²¹ Meanwhile, Rehoboam son of Solomon was king in Judah. He was forty-one years old when he became king, and he reigned seventeen years

---

14:15 Hebrew *the river.*

in Jerusalem, the city the LORD had chosen from among all the tribes of Israel as the place to honor his name. Rehoboam's mother was Naamah, an Ammonite woman.

²²During Rehoboam's reign, the people of Judah did what was evil in the LORD's sight, provoking his anger with their sin, for it was even worse than that of their ancestors. ²³For they also built for themselves pagan shrines and set up sacred pillars and Asherah poles on every high hill and under every green tree. ²⁴There were even male and female shrine prostitutes throughout the land. The people imitated the detestable practices of the pagan nations the LORD had driven from the land ahead of the Israelites.

²⁵In the fifth year of King Rehoboam's reign, King Shishak of Egypt came up and attacked Jerusalem. ²⁶He ransacked the treasuries of the LORD's Temple and the royal palace; he stole everything, including all the gold shields Solomon had made. ²⁷King Rehoboam later replaced them with bronze shields as substitutes, and he entrusted them to the care of the commanders of the guard who protected the entrance to the royal palace. ²⁸Whenever the king went to the Temple of the LORD, the guards would also take the shields and then return them to the guardroom.

²⁹The rest of the events in Rehoboam's reign and everything he did are recorded in *The Book of the History of the Kings of Judah*. ³⁰There was constant war between Rehoboam and Jeroboam. ³¹When Rehoboam died, he was buried among his ancestors in the City of David. His mother was Naamah, an Ammonite woman. Then his son Abijam* became the next king.

ABIJAM RULES IN JUDAH

15 Abijam* began to rule over Judah in the eighteenth year of Jeroboam's reign in Israel. ²He reigned in Jerusalem three years. His mother was Maacah, the granddaughter of Absalom.*

³He committed the same sins as his father before him, and he was not faithful to the LORD his God, as his ancestor David had been. ⁴But for David's sake, the LORD his God allowed his descendants to continue ruling, shining like a lamp, and he gave Abijam a son to rule after him in Jerusalem. ⁵For David had done what was pleasing in the LORD's sight and had obeyed the LORD's commands throughout his life, except in the affair concerning Uriah the Hittite.

⁶There was war between Abijam and Jeroboam* throughout Abijam's reign. ⁷The rest of the events in Abijam's reign and everything he did are recorded in *The Book of the History of the Kings of Judah*. There was constant war between Abijam and Jeroboam. ⁸When Abijam died, he was buried in the City of David. Then his son Asa became the next king.

ASA RULES IN JUDAH

⁹Asa began to rule over Judah in the twentieth year of Jeroboam's reign in Israel. ¹⁰He reigned in Jerusalem forty-one years. His grandmother* was Maacah, the granddaughter of Absalom.

¹¹Asa did what was pleasing in the LORD's sight, as his ancestor David had done. ¹²He banished the male and female shrine prostitutes from the land and got rid of all the idols* his ancestors had made. ¹³He even deposed his grandmother Maacah from her position as queen mother because she had made an obscene Asherah pole. He cut down her obscene pole and burned it in the Kidron Valley. ¹⁴Although the pagan shrines were not removed, Asa's heart remained completely faithful to the LORD throughout his life. ¹⁵He brought into the Temple of the LORD the silver and gold and the various items that he and his father had dedicated.

¹⁶There was constant war between King Asa of Judah and King Baasha of Israel. ¹⁷King Baasha of Israel invaded Judah and fortified Ramah in order to prevent anyone from entering or leaving King Asa's territory in Judah.

¹⁸Asa responded by removing all the silver and gold that was left in the treasuries of the Temple of the LORD and the royal palace. He sent it with some of his officials to Ben-hadad son of Tabrimmon, son of Hezion, the king of Aram, who was ruling in Damascus, along with this message:

¹⁹"Let there be a treaty* between you and me like the one between your father and my father. See, I am sending you a gift of silver and gold. Break your treaty with King Baasha of Israel so that he will leave me alone."

²⁰Ben-hadad agreed to King Asa's request and sent the commanders of his army to attack the towns of Israel. They conquered the towns of Ijon, Dan, Abel-beth-maacah, and all Kinnereth, and all the land of Naphtali. ²¹As soon as Baasha of Israel heard what was happening, he abandoned his project of fortifying Ramah and withdrew to Tirzah. ²²Then King Asa sent an order throughout Judah, requiring that everyone, without exception, help to carry away the building stones and timbers that Baasha had been using to fortify Ramah. Asa used these materials to fortify the town of Geba in Benjamin and the town of Mizpah.

²³The rest of the events in Asa's reign—the extent of his power, everything he did, and the

---

14:31 Also known as *Abijah*. 15:1 Also known as *Abijah*.
15:2 Hebrew *Abishalom* (also in 15:10), a variant spelling of Absalom; compare 2 Chr 11:20. 15:6 As in a few Hebrew and Greek manuscripts; most Hebrew manuscripts read *between Rehoboam and Jeroboam*. 15:10 Or *The queen mother;* Hebrew reads *His mother* (also in 15:13); compare 15:2. 15:12 The Hebrew term (literally *round things*) probably alludes to dung. 15:19 As in Greek version; Hebrew reads *There is a treaty*.

names of the cities he built—are recorded in *The Book of the History of the Kings of Judah.* In his old age his feet became diseased. ²⁴ When Asa died, he was buried with his ancestors in the City of David.

Then Jehoshaphat, Asa's son, became the next king.

NADAB RULES IN ISRAEL

²⁵ Nadab son of Jeroboam began to rule over Israel in the second year of King Asa's reign in Judah. He reigned in Israel two years. ²⁶ But he did what was evil in the LORD's sight and followed the example of his father, continuing the sins that Jeroboam had led Israel to commit.

²⁷ Then Baasha son of Ahijah, from the tribe of Issachar, plotted against Nadab and assassinated him while he and the Israelite army were laying siege to the Philistine town of Gibbethon. ²⁸ Baasha killed Nadab in the third year of King Asa's reign in Judah, and he became the next king of Israel.

²⁹ He immediately slaughtered all the descendants of King Jeroboam, so that not one of the royal family was left, just as the LORD had promised concerning Jeroboam by the prophet Ahijah from Shiloh. ³⁰ This was done because Jeroboam had provoked the anger of the LORD, the God of Israel, by the sins he had committed and the sins he had led Israel to commit.

³¹ The rest of the events in Nadab's reign and everything he did are recorded in *The Book of the History of the Kings of Israel.*

BAASHA RULES IN ISRAEL

³² There was constant war between King Asa of Judah and King Baasha of Israel. ³³ Baasha son of Ahijah began to rule over all Israel in the third year of King Asa's reign in Judah. Baasha reigned in Tirzah twenty-four years. ³⁴ But he did what was evil in the LORD's sight and followed the example of Jeroboam, continuing the sins that Jeroboam had led Israel to commit.

16 This message from the LORD was delivered to King Baasha by the prophet Jehu son of Hanani: ² "I lifted you out of the dust to make you ruler of my people Israel, but you have followed the evil example of Jeroboam. You have provoked my anger by causing my people Israel to sin. ³ So now I will destroy you and your family, just as I destroyed the descendants of Jeroboam son of Nebat. ⁴ The members of Baasha's family who die in the city will be eaten by dogs, and those who die in the field will be eaten by vultures."

⁵ The rest of the events in Baasha's reign and the extent of his power are recorded in *The Book of the History of the Kings of Israel.* ⁶ When Baasha died, he was buried in Tirzah. Then his son Elah became the next king.

⁷ The message from the LORD against Baasha and his family came through the prophet Jehu son of Hanani. It was delivered because Baasha had done what was evil in the LORD's sight (just as the family of Jeroboam had done), and also because Baasha had destroyed the family of Jeroboam. The LORD's anger was provoked by Baasha's sins.

ELAH RULES IN ISRAEL

⁸ Elah son of Baasha began to rule over Israel in the twenty-sixth year of King Asa's reign in Judah. He reigned in the city of Tirzah for two years.

⁹ Then Zimri, who commanded half of the royal chariots, made plans to kill him. One day in Tirzah, Elah was getting drunk at the home of Arza, the supervisor of the palace. ¹⁰ Zimri walked in and struck him down and killed him. This happened in the twenty-seventh year of King Asa's reign in Judah. Then Zimri became the next king.

¹¹ Zimri immediately killed the entire royal family of Baasha, leaving him not even a single male child. He even destroyed distant relatives and friends. ¹² So Zimri destroyed the dynasty of Baasha as the LORD had promised through the prophet Jehu. ¹³ This happened because of all the sins Baasha and his son Elah had committed, and because of the sins they led Israel to commit. They provoked the anger of the LORD, the God of Israel, with their worthless idols.

¹⁴ The rest of the events in Elah's reign and everything he did are recorded in *The Book of the History of the Kings of Israel.*

ZIMRI RULES IN ISRAEL

¹⁵ Zimri began to rule over Israel in the twenty-seventh year of King Asa's reign in Judah, but his reign in Tirzah lasted only seven days. The army of Israel was then attacking the Philistine town of Gibbethon. ¹⁶ When they heard that Zimri had committed treason and had assassinated the king, that very day they chose Omri, commander of the army, as the new king of Israel. ¹⁷ So Omri led the entire army of Israel up from Gibbethon to attack Tirzah, Israel's capital. ¹⁸ When Zimri saw that the city had been taken, he went into the citadel of the palace and burned it down over himself and died in the flames. ¹⁹ For he, too, had done what was evil in the LORD's sight. He followed the example of Jeroboam in all the sins he had committed and led Israel to commit.

²⁰ The rest of the events in Zimri's reign and his conspiracy are recorded in *The Book of the History of the Kings of Israel.*

OMRI RULES IN ISRAEL

²¹ But now the people of Israel were split into two factions. Half the people tried to make Tibni son of Ginath their king, while the other half supported Omri. ²² But Omri's supporters defeated the supporters of Tibni. So Tibni was killed, and Omri became the next king.

²³ Omri began to rule over Israel in the thirty-first year of King Asa's reign in Judah. He reigned twelve years in all, six of them in Tirzah. ²⁴ Then Omri bought the hill now known as Samaria from its owner, Shemer, for 150 pounds of silver.* He built a city on it and called the city Samaria in honor of Shemer.

²⁵ But Omri did what was evil in the LORD's sight, even more than any of the kings before him. ²⁶ He followed the example of Jeroboam son of Nebat in all the sins he had committed and led Israel to commit. The people provoked the anger of the LORD, the God of Israel, with their worthless idols.

²⁷ The rest of the events in Omri's reign, the extent of his power, and everything he did are recorded in *The Book of the History of the Kings of Israel.* ²⁸ When Omri died, he was buried in Samaria. Then his son Ahab became the next king.

AHAB RULES IN ISRAEL

²⁹ Ahab son of Omri began to rule over Israel in the thirty-eighth year of King Asa's reign in Judah. He reigned in Samaria twenty-two years. ³⁰ But Ahab son of Omri did what was evil in the LORD's sight, even more than any of the kings before him. ³¹ And as though it were not enough to follow the sinful example of Jeroboam, he married Jezebel, the daughter of King Ethbaal of the Sidonians, and he began to bow down in worship of Baal. ³² First Ahab built a temple and an altar for Baal in Samaria. ³³ Then he set up an Asherah pole. He did more to provoke the anger of the LORD, the God of Israel, than any of the other kings of Israel before him.

³⁴ It was during his reign that Hiel, a man from Bethel, rebuilt Jericho. When he laid its foundations, it cost him the life of his oldest son, Abiram. And when he completed it and set up its gates, it cost him the life of his youngest son, Segub.* This all happened according to the message from the LORD concerning Jericho spoken by Joshua son of Nun.

ELIJAH FED BY RAVENS

17 Now Elijah, who was from Tishbe in Gilead, told King Ahab, "As surely as the LORD, the God of Israel, lives—the God I serve—there will be no dew or rain during the next few years until I give the word!"

² Then the LORD said to Elijah, ³ "Go to the east and hide by Kerith Brook, near where it enters the Jordan River. ⁴ Drink from the brook and eat what the ravens bring you, for I have commanded them to bring you food."

⁵ So Elijah did as the LORD told him and camped beside Kerith Brook, east of the Jordan. ⁶ The ravens brought him bread and meat each morning and evening, and he drank from the brook. ⁷ But after a while the brook dried up, for there was no rainfall anywhere in the land.

ALWAYS ENOUGH
1 Kings 17:13–16   ROBERT MORRIS

During a time of severe drought, God sent the prophet Elijah to a widow who had only enough flour and oil to make one last meal for herself and her son. The prophet told her not to fear but to make some food for him first. Elijah prophesied, "There will always be flour and olive oil left in your containers until the time when the LORD sends rain and the crops grow again!" (1 Kings 17:14). So the widow did what Elijah told her to do, and God gave her enough food to last through the drought.

There are many times when we feel just like that widow. We think we have only a small amount of serving, giving, prayer, etc. But when we give that small amount to God, He always provides more for us. As we determine to be a blessing to other people, God blesses us as well.

THE WIDOW AT ZAREPHATH

⁸ Then the LORD said to Elijah, ⁹ "Go and live in the village of Zarephath, near the city of Sidon. I have instructed a widow there to feed you."

¹⁰ So he went to Zarephath. As he arrived at the gates of the village, he saw a widow gathering sticks, and he asked her, "Would you please bring me a little water in a cup?" ¹¹ As she was going to get it, he called to her, "Bring me a bite of bread, too."

¹² But she said, "I swear by the LORD your God that I don't have a single piece of bread in the house. And I have only a handful of flour left in the jar and a little cooking oil in the bottom of the jug. I was just gathering a few sticks to cook this last meal, and then my son and I will die."

¹³ But Elijah said to her, "Don't be afraid! Go ahead and do just what you've said, but make a little bread for me first. Then use what's left to prepare a meal for yourself and your son. ¹⁴ For this is what the LORD, the God of Israel, says: There will always be flour and olive oil left in your containers until the time when the LORD sends rain and the crops grow again!"

¹⁵ So she did as Elijah said, and she and Elijah and her family continued to eat for many days. ¹⁶ There was always enough flour and olive oil left in the containers, just as the LORD had promised through Elijah.

¹⁷ Some time later the woman's son became sick. He grew worse and worse, and finally he died. ¹⁸ Then she said to Elijah, "O man of God, what have you done to me? Have you come here to point out my sins and kill my son?"

16:24 Hebrew *for 2 talents* [68 kilograms] *of silver.*   16:34 An ancient Hebrew scribal tradition reads *He killed his oldest son when he laid its foundations, and he killed his youngest son when he set up its gates.*

¹⁹But Elijah replied, "Give me your son." And he took the child's body from her arms, carried him up the stairs to the room where he was staying, and laid the body on his bed. ²⁰Then Elijah cried out to the LORD, "O LORD my God, why have you brought tragedy to this widow who has opened her home to me, causing her son to die?"

²¹And he stretched himself out over the child three times and cried out to the LORD, "O LORD my God, please let this child's life return to him." ²²The LORD heard Elijah's prayer, and the life of the child returned, and he revived! ²³Then Elijah brought him down from the upper room and gave him to his mother. "Look!" he said. "Your son is alive!"

²⁴Then the woman told Elijah, "Now I know for sure that you are a man of God, and that the LORD truly speaks through you."

THE CONTEST ON MOUNT CARMEL

18 Later on, in the third year of the drought, the LORD said to Elijah, "Go and present yourself to King Ahab. Tell him that I will soon send rain!" ²So Elijah went to appear before Ahab.

Meanwhile, the famine had become very severe in Samaria. ³So Ahab summoned Obadiah, who was in charge of the palace. (Obadiah was a devoted follower of the LORD. ⁴Once when Jezebel had tried to kill all the LORD's prophets, Obadiah had hidden 100 of them in two caves. He put fifty prophets in each cave and supplied them with food and water.) ⁵Ahab said to Obadiah, "We must check every spring and valley in the land to see if we can find enough grass to save at least some of my horses and mules." ⁶So they divided the land between them. Ahab went one way by himself, and Obadiah went another way by himself.

⁷As Obadiah was walking along, he suddenly saw Elijah coming toward him. Obadiah recognized him at once and bowed low to the ground before him. "Is it really you, my lord Elijah?" he asked.

⁸"Yes, it is," Elijah replied. "Now go and tell your master, 'Elijah is here.'"

⁹"Oh, sir," Obadiah protested, "what harm have I done to you that you are sending me to my death at the hands of Ahab? ¹⁰For I swear by the LORD your God that the king has searched every nation and kingdom on earth from end to end to find you. And each time he was told, 'Elijah isn't here,' King Ahab forced the king of that nation to swear to the truth of his claim. ¹¹And now you say, 'Go and tell your master, "Elijah is here."' ¹²But as soon as I leave you, the Spirit of the LORD will carry you away to who knows where. When Ahab comes and cannot find you, he will kill me. Yet I have been a true servant of the LORD all my life. ¹³Has no one told you, my lord, about the time when Jezebel was trying to kill the LORD's prophets? I hid 100 of them in two caves and supplied them with food and

water. ¹⁴And now you say, 'Go and tell your master, "Elijah is here."' Sir, if I do that, Ahab will certainly kill me."

¹⁵But Elijah said, "I swear by the LORD Almighty, in whose presence I stand, that I will present myself to Ahab this very day."

¹⁶So Obadiah went to tell Ahab that Elijah had come, and Ahab went out to meet Elijah. ¹⁷When Ahab saw him, he exclaimed, "So, is it really you, you troublemaker of Israel?"

¹⁸"I have made no trouble for Israel," Elijah replied. "You and your family are the troublemakers, for you have refused to obey the commands of the LORD and have worshiped the images of Baal instead. ¹⁹Now summon all Israel to join me at Mount Carmel, along with the 450 prophets of Baal and the 400 prophets of Asherah who are supported by Jezebel.*"

²⁰So Ahab summoned all the people of Israel and the prophets to Mount Carmel. ²¹Then Elijah stood in front of them and said, "How much longer will you waver, hobbling between two opinions? If the LORD is God, follow him! But if Baal is God, then follow him!" But the people were completely silent.

²²Then Elijah said to them, "I am the only prophet of the LORD who is left, but Baal has 450 prophets. ²³Now bring two bulls. The prophets of Baal may choose whichever one they wish and cut it into pieces and lay it on the wood of their altar, but without setting fire to it. I will prepare the other bull and lay it on the wood on the altar, but not set fire to it. ²⁴Then call on the name of your god, and I will call on the name of the LORD. The god who answers by setting fire to the wood is the true God!" And all the people agreed.

²⁵Then Elijah said to the prophets of Baal, "You go first, for there are many of you. Choose one of

---

18:19 Hebrew *who eat at Jezebel's table.*

the bulls, and prepare it and call on the name of your god. But do not set fire to the wood."

²⁶So they prepared one of the bulls and placed it on the altar. Then they called on the name of Baal from morning until noontime, shouting, "O Baal, answer us!" But there was no reply of any kind. Then they danced, hobbling around the altar they had made.

²⁷About noontime Elijah began mocking them. "You'll have to shout louder," he scoffed, "for surely he is a god! Perhaps he is daydreaming, or is relieving himself.* Or maybe he is away on a trip, or is asleep and needs to be wakened!"

²⁸So they shouted louder, and following their normal custom, they cut themselves with knives and swords until the blood gushed out. ²⁹They raved all afternoon until the time of the evening sacrifice, but still there was no sound, no reply, no response.

³⁰Then Elijah called to the people, "Come over here!" They all crowded around him as he repaired the altar of the LORD that had been torn down. ³¹He took twelve stones, one to represent each of the tribes of Israel,* ³²and he used the stones to rebuild the altar in the name of the LORD. Then he dug a trench around the altar large enough to hold about three gallons.* ³³He piled wood on the altar, cut the bull into pieces, and laid the pieces on the wood.*

Then he said, "Fill four large jars with water, and pour the water over the offering and the wood."

³⁴After they had done this, he said, "Do the same thing again!" And when they were finished, he said, "Now do it a third time!" So they did as he said, ³⁵and the water ran around the altar and even filled the trench.

³⁶At the usual time for offering the evening sacrifice, Elijah the prophet walked up to the altar and prayed, "O LORD, God of Abraham, Isaac, and Jacob,* prove today that you are God in Israel and that I am your servant. Prove that I have done all this at your command. ³⁷O LORD, answer me! Answer me so these people will know that you, O LORD, are God and that you have brought them back to yourself."

³⁸Immediately the fire of the LORD flashed down from heaven and burned up the young bull, the wood, the stones, and the dust. It even licked up all the water in the trench! ³⁹And when all the people saw it, they fell face down on the ground and cried out, "The LORD—he is God! Yes, the LORD is God!"

⁴⁰Then Elijah commanded, "Seize all the prophets of Baal. Don't let a single one escape!" So the people seized them all, and Elijah took them down to the Kishon Valley and killed them there.

ELIJAH PRAYS FOR RAIN

⁴¹Then Elijah said to Ahab, "Go get something to eat and drink, for I hear a mighty rainstorm coming!"

⁴²So Ahab went to eat and drink. But Elijah climbed to the top of Mount Carmel and bowed low to the ground and prayed with his face between his knees.

⁴³Then he said to his servant, "Go and look out toward the sea."

The servant went and looked, then returned to Elijah and said, "I didn't see anything."

Seven times Elijah told him to go and look. ⁴⁴Finally the seventh time, his servant told him, "I saw a little cloud about the size of a man's hand rising from the sea."

Then Elijah shouted, "Hurry to Ahab and tell him, 'Climb into your chariot and go back home. If you don't hurry, the rain will stop you!'"

⁴⁵And soon the sky was black with clouds. A heavy wind brought a terrific rainstorm, and Ahab left quickly for Jezreel. ⁴⁶Then the LORD gave special strength to Elijah. He tucked his cloak into his belt* and ran ahead of Ahab's chariot all the way to the entrance of Jezreel.

ELIJAH FLEES TO SINAI

19 When Ahab got home, he told Jezebel everything Elijah had done, including the way he had killed all the prophets of Baal. ²So Jezebel sent this message to Elijah: "May the gods strike me and even kill me if by this time tomorrow I have not killed you just as you killed them."

³Elijah was afraid and fled for his life. He went to Beersheba, a town in Judah, and he left his servant there. ⁴Then he went on alone into the wilderness, traveling all day. He sat down under a solitary broom tree and prayed that he might die. "I have had enough, LORD," he said. "Take my life, for I am no better than my ancestors who have already died."

⁵Then he lay down and slept under the broom tree. But as he was sleeping, an angel touched him and told him, "Get up and eat!" ⁶He looked around and there beside his head was some bread baked on hot stones and a jar of water! So he ate and drank and lay down again.

⁷Then the angel of the LORD came again and touched him and said, "Get up and eat some more, or the journey ahead will be too much for you."

⁸So he got up and ate and drank, and the food gave him enough strength to travel forty days and forty nights to Mount Sinai,* the mountain of God. ⁹There he came to a cave, where he spent the night.

THE LORD SPEAKS TO ELIJAH

But the LORD said to him, "What are you doing here, Elijah?"

18:27 Or *is busy somewhere else, or is engaged in business.* 18:31 Hebrew *each of the tribes of the sons of Jacob to whom the LORD had said, "Your name will be Israel."* 18:32 Hebrew *2 seahs* [14.6 liters] *of seed.* 18:33 Verse 18:34 in the Hebrew text begins here. 18:36 Hebrew *and Israel.* The names "Jacob" and "Israel" are often interchanged throughout the Old Testament, referring sometimes to the individual patriarch and sometimes to the nation. 18:46 Hebrew *He bound up his loins.* 19:8 Hebrew *to Horeb,* another name for Sinai.

THE WAYS GOD SPEAKS?   ROBERT MORRIS

Did you know God speaks to us all the time? You may think, *Then why don't I hear Him?* Here's a tough question: are you sure you're really listening? God can speak to us in many different ways, but if we're not listening, we'll never hear Him.

Here are 10 ways God often speaks to us:

1. **Circumstances (Jonah 1:4)**
God spoke to the prophet Jonah with His voice. However, Jonah didn't obey God's instructions, so the Lord then spoke to him through circumstances.

2. **Counsel (Proverbs 19:20)**
The book of Proverbs contains many verses about godly counsel.

3. **Peace (Philippians 4:7)**
God speaks by giving you peace in your heart and mind.

4. **People (Acts 21:10-12)**
Agabus, a prophet, gave a word from God to Paul.

5. **Dreams and Visions (Genesis 28:12; 37:5-7; 1 Kings 3:5-15; Acts 10:9-16; Revelation 1-21)**
God used dreams and visions to speak to many people in the Bible, including Jacob, Joseph, Solomon, Peter, and John.

6. **Thoughts (John 14:26)**
Jesus promised the Holy Spirit will "teach you everything and will remind you of everything I have told you."

7. **Natural Manifestations (Romans 1:18-20)**
Paul writes, "Through everything God made, they can clearly see his invisible qualities." And in the book of Revelation, God speaks through many forms of nature, including the sun, mountains, trees, and water.

8. **Supernatural Manifestations (Exodus 3:1-17)**
The Bible includes numerous examples of supernatural activity, including the burning bush, Gideon's fleece, and Balaam's donkey.

9. **The Bible (Romans 10:17)**
Paul writes, "Faith comes from hearing, that is, hearing the Good News about Christ." Every time we read God's Word, our faith grows.

10. **A Gentle Whisper (1 Kings 19:12)**
Some Bible versions refer to this as "a still, small voice." Sometimes God speaks very quietly and deliberately.

---

[10] Elijah replied, "I have zealously served the LORD God Almighty. But the people of Israel have broken their covenant with you, torn down your altars, and killed every one of your prophets. I am the only one left, and now they are trying to kill me, too."

[11] "Go out and stand before me on the mountain," the LORD told him. And as Elijah stood there, the LORD passed by, and a mighty windstorm hit the mountain. It was such a terrible blast that the rocks were torn loose, but the LORD was not in the wind. After the wind there was an earthquake, but the LORD was not in the earthquake. [12] And after the earthquake there was a fire, but the LORD was not in the fire. And after the fire there was the sound of a gentle whisper. [13] When Elijah heard it, he wrapped his face in his cloak and went out and stood at the entrance of the cave.

And a voice said, "What are you doing here, Elijah?"

[14] He replied again, "I have zealously served the LORD God Almighty. But the people of Israel have broken their covenant with you, torn down your altars, and killed every one of your prophets.

I am the only one left, and now they are trying to kill me, too."

¹⁵Then the LORD told him, "Go back the same way you came, and travel to the wilderness of Damascus. When you arrive there, anoint Hazael to be king of Aram. ¹⁶Then anoint Jehu grandson of Nimshi* to be king of Israel, and anoint Elisha son of Shaphat from the town of Abel-meholah to replace you as my prophet. ¹⁷Anyone who escapes from Hazael will be killed by Jehu, and those who escape Jehu will be killed by Elisha! ¹⁸Yet I will preserve 7,000 others in Israel who have never bowed down to Baal or kissed him!"

THE CALL OF ELISHA

¹⁹So Elijah went and found Elisha son of Shaphat plowing a field. There were twelve teams of oxen in the field, and Elisha was plowing with the twelfth team. Elijah went over to him and threw his cloak across his shoulders and then walked away. ²⁰Elisha left the oxen standing there, ran after Elijah, and said to him, "First let me go and kiss my father and mother good-bye, and then I will go with you!"

Elijah replied, "Go on back, but think about what I have done to you."

²¹So Elisha returned to his oxen and slaughtered them. He used the wood from the plow to build a fire to roast their flesh. He passed around the meat to the townspeople, and they all ate. Then he went with Elijah as his assistant.

BEN-HADAD ATTACKS SAMARIA

20 About that time King Ben-hadad of Aram mobilized his army, supported by the chariots and horses of thirty-two allied kings. They went to besiege Samaria, the capital of Israel, and launched attacks against it. ²Ben-hadad sent messengers into the city to relay this message to King Ahab of Israel: "This is what Ben-hadad says: ³'Your silver and gold are mine, and so are your wives and the best of your children!'"

⁴"All right, my lord the king," Israel's king replied. "All that I have is yours!"

⁵Soon Ben-hadad's messengers returned again and said, "This is what Ben-hadad says: 'I have already demanded that you give me your silver, gold, wives, and children. ⁶But about this time tomorrow I will send my officials to search your palace and the homes of your officials. They will take away everything you consider valuable!'"

⁷Then Ahab summoned all the elders of the land and said to them, "Look how this man is stirring up trouble! I already agreed with his demand that I give him my wives and children and silver and gold."

⁸"Don't give in to any more demands," all the elders and the people advised.

⁹So Ahab told the messengers from Ben-hadad, "Say this to my lord the king: 'I will give you everything you asked for the first time, but I cannot accept this last demand of yours.'" So the messengers returned to Ben-hadad with that response.

¹⁰Then Ben-hadad sent this message to Ahab: "May the gods strike me and even kill me if there remains enough dust from Samaria to provide even a handful for each of my soldiers."

¹¹The king of Israel sent back this answer: "A warrior putting on his sword for battle should not boast like a warrior who has already won."

¹²Ahab's reply reached Ben-hadad and the other kings as they were drinking in their tents.* "Prepare to attack!" Ben-hadad commanded his officers. So they prepared to attack the city.

AHAB'S VICTORY OVER BEN-HADAD

¹³Then a certain prophet came to see King Ahab of Israel and told him, "This is what the LORD says: Do you see all these enemy forces? Today I will hand them all over to you. Then you will know that I am the LORD."

¹⁴Ahab asked, "How will he do it?"

And the prophet replied, "This is what the LORD says: The troops of the provincial commanders will do it."

"Should we attack first?" Ahab asked.

"Yes," the prophet answered.

¹⁵So Ahab mustered the troops of the 232 provincial commanders. Then he called out the rest of the army of Israel, some 7,000 men. ¹⁶About noontime, as Ben-hadad and the thirty-two allied kings were still in their tents drinking themselves into a stupor, ¹⁷the troops of the provincial commanders marched out of the city as the first contingent.

As they approached, Ben-hadad's scouts reported to him, "Some troops are coming from Samaria."

¹⁸"Take them alive," Ben-hadad commanded, "whether they have come for peace or for war."

¹⁹But Ahab's provincial commanders and the entire army had now come out to fight. ²⁰Each Israelite soldier killed his Aramean opponent, and suddenly the entire Aramean army panicked and fled. The Israelites chased them, but King Ben-hadad and a few of his charioteers escaped on horses. ²¹However, the king of Israel destroyed the other horses and chariots and slaughtered the Arameans.

²²Afterward the prophet said to King Ahab, "Get ready for another attack. Begin making plans now, for the king of Aram will come back next spring.*"

BEN-HADAD'S SECOND ATTACK

²³After their defeat, Ben-hadad's officers said to him, "The Israelite gods are gods of the hills; that is why they won. But we can beat them easily on the plains. ²⁴Only this time replace the kings with field commanders! ²⁵Recruit another army

---

19:16 Hebrew *descendant of Nimshi*; compare 2 Kgs 9:2, 14. 20:12 Or *in Succoth*; also in 20:16. 20:22 Hebrew *at the turn of the year*; similarly in 20:26. The first day of the year in the ancient Hebrew lunar calendar occurred in March or April.

like the one you lost. Give us the same number of horses, chariots, and men, and we will fight against them on the plains. There's no doubt that we will beat them." So King Ben-hadad did as they suggested.

²⁶The following spring he called up the Aramean army and marched out against Israel, this time at Aphek. ²⁷Israel then mustered its army, set up supply lines, and marched out for battle. But the Israelite army looked like two little flocks of goats in comparison to the vast Aramean forces that filled the countryside!

²⁸Then the man of God went to the king of Israel and said, "This is what the LORD says: The Arameans have said, 'The LORD is a god of the hills and not of the plains.' So I will defeat this vast army for you. Then you will know that I am the LORD."

²⁹The two armies camped opposite each other for seven days, and on the seventh day the battle began. The Israelites killed 100,000 Aramean foot soldiers in one day. ³⁰The rest fled into the town of Aphek, but the wall fell on them and killed another 27,000. Ben-hadad fled into the town and hid in a secret room.

³¹Ben-hadad's officers said to him, "Sir, we have heard that the kings of Israel are merciful. So let's humble ourselves by wearing burlap around our waists and putting ropes on our heads, and surrender to the king of Israel. Then perhaps he will let you live."

³²So they put on burlap and ropes, and they went to the king of Israel and begged, "Your servant Ben-hadad says, 'Please let me live!'"

The king of Israel responded, "Is he still alive? He is my brother!"

³³The men took this as a good sign and quickly picked up on his words. "Yes," they said, "your brother Ben-hadad!"

"Go and get him," the king of Israel told them. And when Ben-hadad arrived, Ahab invited him up into his chariot.

³⁴Ben-hadad told him, "I will give back the towns my father took from your father, and you may establish places of trade in Damascus, as my father did in Samaria."

Then Ahab said, "I will release you under these conditions." So they made a new treaty, and Ben-hadad was set free.

A PROPHET CONDEMNS AHAB

³⁵Meanwhile, the LORD instructed one of the group of prophets to say to another man, "Hit me!" But the man refused to hit the prophet. ³⁶Then the prophet told him, "Because you have not obeyed the voice of the LORD, a lion will kill you as soon as you leave me." And when he had gone, a lion did attack and kill him.

³⁷Then the prophet turned to another man and said, "Hit me!" So he struck the prophet and wounded him.

³⁸The prophet placed a bandage over his eyes to disguise himself and then waited beside the road for the king. ³⁹As the king passed by, the prophet called out to him, "Sir, I was in the thick of battle, and suddenly a man brought me a prisoner. He said, 'Guard this man; if for any reason he gets away, you will either die or pay a fine of seventy-five pounds* of silver!' ⁴⁰But while I was busy doing something else, the prisoner disappeared!"

"Well, it's your own fault," the king replied. "You have brought the judgment on yourself."

⁴¹Then the prophet quickly pulled the bandage from his eyes, and the king of Israel recognized him as one of the prophets. ⁴²The prophet said to him, "This is what the LORD says: Because you have spared the man I said must be destroyed,* now you must die in his place, and your people will die instead of his people." ⁴³So the king of Israel went home to Samaria angry and sullen.

NABOTH'S VINEYARD

21 Now there was a man named Naboth, from Jezreel, who owned a vineyard in Jezreel beside the palace of King Ahab of Samaria. ²One day Ahab said to Naboth, "Since your vineyard is so convenient to my palace, I would like to buy it to use as a vegetable garden. I will give you a better vineyard in exchange, or if you prefer, I will pay you for it."

³But Naboth replied, "The LORD forbid that I should give you the inheritance that was passed down by my ancestors."

⁴So Ahab went home angry and sullen because of Naboth's answer. The king went to bed with his face to the wall and refused to eat!

⁵"What's the matter?" his wife Jezebel asked him. "What's made you so upset that you're not eating?"

⁶"I asked Naboth to sell me his vineyard or trade it, but he refused!" Ahab told her.

⁷"Are you the king of Israel or not?" Jezebel demanded. "Get up and eat something, and don't worry about it. I'll get you Naboth's vineyard!"

⁸So she wrote letters in Ahab's name, sealed them with his seal, and sent them to the elders and other leaders of the town where Naboth lived. ⁹In her letters she commanded: "Call the citizens together for a time of fasting, and give Naboth a place of honor. ¹⁰And then seat two scoundrels across from him who will accuse him of cursing God and the king. Then take him out and stone him to death."

¹¹So the elders and other town leaders followed the instructions Jezebel had written in the letters. ¹²They called for a fast and put Naboth at a prominent place before the people. ¹³Then the two scoundrels came and sat down across from him. And they accused Naboth before all the people, saying, "He cursed God and the king." So he was dragged outside the town and stoned

---

20:39 Hebrew *1 talent* [34 kilograms]. 20:42 The Hebrew term used here refers to the complete consecration of things or people to the LORD, either by destroying them or by giving them as an offering.

to death. [14] The town leaders then sent word to Jezebel, "Naboth has been stoned to death."

[15] When Jezebel heard the news, she said to Ahab, "You know the vineyard Naboth wouldn't sell you? Well, you can have it now! He's dead!" [16] So Ahab immediately went down to the vineyard of Naboth to claim it.

[17] But the LORD said to Elijah,[*] [18] "Go down to meet King Ahab of Israel, who rules in Samaria. He will be at Naboth's vineyard in Jezreel, claiming it for himself. [19] Give him this message: 'This is what the LORD says: Wasn't it enough that you killed Naboth? Must you rob him, too? Because you have done this, dogs will lick your blood at the very place where they licked the blood of Naboth!'"

[20] "So, my enemy, you have found me!" Ahab exclaimed to Elijah.

"Yes," Elijah answered, "I have come because you have sold yourself to what is evil in the LORD's sight. [21] So now the LORD says,[*] 'I will bring disaster on you and consume you. I will destroy every one of your male descendants, slave and free alike, anywhere in Israel! [22] I am going to destroy your family as I did the family of Jeroboam son of Nebat and the family of Baasha son of Ahijah, for you have made me very angry and have led Israel into sin.'

[23] "And regarding Jezebel, the LORD says, 'Dogs will eat Jezebel's body at the plot of land in Jezreel.'[*]

[24] "The members of Ahab's family who die in the city will be eaten by dogs, and those who die in the field will be eaten by vultures."

[25] (No one else so completely sold himself to what was evil in the LORD's sight as Ahab did under the influence of his wife Jezebel. [26] His worst outrage was worshiping idols[*] just as the Amorites had done—the people whom the LORD had driven out from the land ahead of the Israelites.)

[27] But when Ahab heard this message, he tore his clothing, dressed in burlap, and fasted. He even slept in burlap and went about in deep mourning.

[28] Then another message from the LORD came to Elijah: [29] "Do you see how Ahab has humbled himself before me? Because he has done this, I will not do what I promised during his lifetime. It will happen to his sons; I will destroy his dynasty."

JEHOSHAPHAT AND AHAB

22 For three years there was no war between Aram and Israel. [2] Then during the third year, King Jehoshaphat of Judah went to visit King Ahab of Israel. [3] During the visit, the king of Israel said to his officials, "Do you realize that the town of Ramoth-gilead belongs to us? And yet we've done nothing to recapture it from the king of Aram!"

[4] Then he turned to Jehoshaphat and asked, "Will you join me in battle to recover Ramoth-gilead?"

Jehoshaphat replied to the king of Israel, "Why, of course! You and I are as one. My troops are your troops, and my horses are your horses." [5] Then Jehoshaphat added, "But first let's find out what the LORD says."

[6] So the king of Israel summoned the prophets, about 400 of them, and asked them, "Should I go to war against Ramoth-gilead, or should I hold back?"

They all replied, "Yes, go right ahead! The Lord will give the king victory."

[7] But Jehoshaphat asked, "Is there not also a prophet of the LORD here? We should ask him the same question."

[8] The king of Israel replied to Jehoshaphat, "There is one more man who could consult the LORD for us, but I hate him. He never prophesies anything but trouble for me! His name is Micaiah son of Imlah."

Jehoshaphat replied, "That's not the way a king should talk! Let's hear what he has to say."

[9] So the king of Israel called one of his officials and said, "Quick! Bring Micaiah son of Imlah."

MICAIAH PROPHESIES AGAINST AHAB

[10] King Ahab of Israel and King Jehoshaphat of Judah, dressed in their royal robes, were sitting on thrones at the threshing floor near the gate of Samaria. All of Ahab's prophets were prophesying there in front of them. [11] One of them, Zedekiah son of Kenaanah, made some iron horns and proclaimed, "This is what the LORD says: With these horns you will gore the Arameans to death!"

[12] All the other prophets agreed. "Yes," they said, "go up to Ramoth-gilead and be victorious, for the LORD will give the king victory!"

[13] Meanwhile, the messenger who went to get Micaiah said to him, "Look, all the prophets are promising victory for the king. Be sure that you agree with them and promise success."

[14] But Micaiah replied, "As surely as the LORD lives, I will say only what the LORD tells me to say."

[15] When Micaiah arrived before the king, Ahab asked him, "Micaiah, should we go to war against Ramoth-gilead, or should we hold back?"

Micaiah replied sarcastically, "Yes, go up and be victorious, for the LORD will give the king victory!"

[16] But the king replied sharply, "How many times must I demand that you speak only the truth to me when you speak for the LORD?"

[17] Then Micaiah told him, "In a vision I saw all Israel scattered on the mountains, like sheep without a shepherd. And the LORD said, 'Their master has been killed.[*] Send them home in peace.'"

[18] "Didn't I tell you?" the king of Israel exclaimed to Jehoshaphat. "He never prophesies anything but trouble for me."

21:17 Hebrew *Elijah the Tishbite;* also in 21:28. 21:21 As in Greek version; Hebrew lacks *So now the LORD says.* 21:23 As in several Hebrew manuscripts, Syriac, and Latin Vulgate (see also 2 Kgs 9:26, 36); most Hebrew manuscripts read *at the city wall.* 21:26 The Hebrew term (literally *round things*) probably alludes to dung. 22:17 Hebrew *These people have no master.*

¹⁹ Then Micaiah continued, "Listen to what the LORD says! I saw the LORD sitting on his throne with all the armies of heaven around him, on his right and on his left. ²⁰ And the LORD said, 'Who can entice Ahab to go into battle against Ramoth-gilead so he can be killed?'

"There were many suggestions, ²¹ and finally a spirit approached the LORD and said, 'I can do it!'

²² "'How will you do this?' the LORD asked.

"And the spirit replied, 'I will go out and inspire all of Ahab's prophets to speak lies.'

"'You will succeed,' said the LORD. 'Go ahead and do it.'

²³ "So you see, the LORD has put a lying spirit in the mouths of all your prophets. For the LORD has pronounced your doom."

²⁴ Then Zedekiah son of Kenaanah walked up to Micaiah and slapped him across the face. "Since when did the Spirit of the LORD leave me to speak to you?" he demanded.

²⁵ And Micaiah replied, "You will find out soon enough when you are trying to hide in some secret room!"

²⁶ "Arrest him!" the king of Israel ordered. "Take him back to Amon, the governor of the city, and to my son Joash. ²⁷ Give them this order from the king: 'Put this man in prison, and feed him nothing but bread and water until I return safely from the battle!'"

²⁸ But Micaiah replied, "If you return safely, it will mean that the LORD has not spoken through me!" Then he added to those standing around, "Everyone mark my words!"

THE DEATH OF AHAB

²⁹ So King Ahab of Israel and King Jehoshaphat of Judah led their armies against Ramoth-gilead. ³⁰ The king of Israel said to Jehoshaphat, "As we go into battle, I will disguise myself so no one will recognize me, but you wear your royal robes." So the king of Israel disguised himself, and they went into battle.

³¹ Meanwhile, the king of Aram had issued these orders to his thirty-two chariot commanders: "Attack only the king of Israel. Don't bother with anyone else!" ³² So when the Aramean chariot commanders saw Jehoshaphat in his royal robes, they went after him. "There is the king of Israel!" they shouted. But when Jehoshaphat called out, ³³ the chariot commanders realized he was not the king of Israel, and they stopped chasing him.

³⁴ An Aramean soldier, however, randomly shot an arrow at the Israelite troops and hit the king of Israel between the joints of his armor. "Turn the horses* and get me out of here!" Ahab groaned to the driver of his chariot. "I'm badly wounded!"

³⁵ The battle raged all that day, and the king remained propped up in his chariot facing the Arameans. The blood from his wound ran down to the floor of his chariot, and as evening arrived he died. ³⁶ Just as the sun was setting, the cry ran through his troops: "We're done for! Run for your lives!"

³⁷ So the king died, and his body was taken to Samaria and buried there. ³⁸ Then his chariot was washed beside the pool of Samaria, and dogs came and licked his blood at the place where the prostitutes bathed,* just as the LORD had promised.

³⁹ The rest of the events in Ahab's reign and everything he did, including the story of the ivory palace and the towns he built, are recorded in *The Book of the History of the Kings of Israel.* ⁴⁰ So Ahab died, and his son Ahaziah became the next king.

JEHOSHAPHAT RULES IN JUDAH

⁴¹ Jehoshaphat son of Asa began to rule over Judah in the fourth year of King Ahab's reign in Israel. ⁴² Jehoshaphat was thirty-five years old when he became king, and he reigned in Jerusalem twenty-five years. His mother was Azubah, the daughter of Shilhi.

⁴³ Jehoshaphat was a good king, following the example of his father, Asa. He did what was pleasing in the LORD's sight. *During his reign, however, he failed to remove all the pagan shrines, and the people still offered sacrifices and burned incense there. ⁴⁴ Jehoshaphat also made peace with the king of Israel.

⁴⁵ The rest of the events in Jehoshaphat's reign, the extent of his power, and the wars he waged are recorded in *The Book of the History of the Kings of Judah.* ⁴⁶ He banished from the land the rest of the male and female shrine prostitutes, who still continued their practices from the days of his father, Asa.

⁴⁷ (There was no king in Edom at that time, only a deputy.)

⁴⁸ Jehoshaphat also built a fleet of trading ships* to sail to Ophir for gold. But the ships never set sail, for they met with disaster in their home port of Ezion-geber. ⁴⁹ At one time Ahaziah son of Ahab had proposed to Jehoshaphat, "Let my men sail with your men in the ships." But Jehoshaphat refused the request.

⁵⁰ When Jehoshaphat died, he was buried with his ancestors in the City of David. Then his son Jehoram became the next king.

AHAZIAH RULES IN ISRAEL

⁵¹ Ahaziah son of Ahab began to rule over Israel in the seventeenth year of King Jehoshaphat's reign in Judah. He reigned in Samaria two years. ⁵² But he did what was evil in the LORD's sight, following the example of his father and mother and the example of Jeroboam son of Nebat, who had led Israel to sin. ⁵³ He served Baal and worshiped him, provoking the anger of the LORD, the God of Israel, just as his father had done.

22:34 Hebrew *Turn your hand.* 22:38 Or *his blood, and the prostitutes bathed [in it]; or his blood, and they washed his armor.* 22:43 Verses 22:43b-53 are numbered 22:44-54 in Hebrew text. 22:48 Hebrew *fleet of ships of Tarshish.*

2 KINGS

ELIJAH CONFRONTS KING AHAZIAH

1 After King Ahab's death, the land of Moab rebelled against Israel.

2 One day Israel's new king, Ahaziah, fell through the latticework of an upper room at his palace in Samaria and was seriously injured. So he sent messengers to the temple of Baal-zebub, the god of Ekron, to ask whether he would recover. 3 But the angel of the LORD told Elijah, who was from Tishbe, "Go and confront the messengers of the king of Samaria and ask them, 'Is there no God in Israel? Why are you going to Baal-zebub, the god of Ekron, to ask whether the king will recover? 4 Now, therefore, this is what the LORD says: You will never leave the bed you are lying on; you will surely die.'" So Elijah went to deliver the message.

5 When the messengers returned to the king, he asked them, "Why have you returned so soon?"

6 They replied, "A man came up to us and told us to go back to the king and give him this message. 'This is what the LORD says: Is there no God in Israel? Why are you sending men to Baal-zebub, the god of Ekron, to ask whether you will recover? Therefore, because you have done this, you will never leave the bed you are lying on; you will surely die.'"

7 "What sort of man was he?" the king demanded. "What did he look like?"

8 They replied, "He was a hairy man,* and he wore a leather belt around his waist."

"Elijah from Tishbe!" the king exclaimed.

9 Then he sent an army captain with fifty soldiers to arrest him. They found him sitting on top of a hill. The captain said to him, "Man of God, the king has commanded you to come down with us."

10 But Elijah replied to the captain, "If I am a man of God, let fire come down from heaven and destroy you and your fifty men!" Then fire fell from heaven and killed them all.

11 So the king sent another captain with fifty men. The captain said to him, "Man of God, the king demands that you come down at once."

12 Elijah replied, "If I am a man of God, let fire come down from heaven and destroy you and your fifty men!" And again the fire of God fell from heaven and killed them all.

13 Once more the king sent a third captain with fifty men. But this time the captain went up the hill and fell to his knees before Elijah. He pleaded with him, "O man of God, please spare my life and the lives of these, your fifty servants. 14 See how the fire from heaven came down and destroyed the first two groups. But now please spare my life!"

15 Then the angel of the LORD said to Elijah, "Go down with him, and don't be afraid of him." So Elijah got up and went with him to the king.

16 And Elijah said to the king, "This is what the LORD says: Why did you send messengers to Baal-zebub, the god of Ekron, to ask whether you will recover? Is there no God in Israel to answer your question? Therefore, because you have done this, you will never leave the bed you are lying on; you will surely die."

17 So Ahaziah died, just as the LORD had promised through Elijah. Since Ahaziah did not have a son to succeed him, his brother Joram* became the next king. This took place in the second year of the reign of Jehoram son of Jehoshaphat, king of Judah.

18 The rest of the events in Ahaziah's reign and everything he did are recorded in *The Book of the History of the Kings of Israel.*

ELIJAH TAKEN INTO HEAVEN

2 When the LORD was about to take Elijah up to heaven in a whirlwind, Elijah and Elisha were traveling from Gilgal. 2 And Elijah said to Elisha, "Stay here, for the LORD has told me to go to Bethel."

But Elisha replied, "As surely as the LORD lives and you yourself live, I will never leave you!" So they went down together to Bethel.

3 The group of prophets from Bethel came to Elisha and asked him, "Did you know that the LORD is going to take your master away from you today?"

"Of course I know," Elisha answered. "But be quiet about it."

4 Then Elijah said to Elisha, "Stay here, for the LORD has told me to go to Jericho."

But Elisha replied again, "As surely as the LORD lives and you yourself live, I will never leave you." So they went on together to Jericho.

5 Then the group of prophets from Jericho came to Elisha and asked him, "Did you know that the LORD is going to take your master away from you today?"

"Of course I know," Elisha answered. "But be quiet about it."

6 Then Elijah said to Elisha, "Stay here, for the LORD has told me to go to the Jordan River."

But again Elisha replied, "As surely as the LORD lives and you yourself live, I will never leave you." So they went on together.

7 Fifty men from the group of prophets also went and watched from a distance as Elijah and Elisha stopped beside the Jordan River. 8 Then

1:8 Or *He was wearing clothing made of hair.*   1:17 Hebrew *Jehoram,* a variant spelling of Joram.

Elijah folded his cloak together and struck the water with it. The river divided, and the two of them went across on dry ground!

⁹ When they came to the other side, Elijah said to Elisha, "Tell me what I can do for you before I am taken away."

And Elisha replied, "Please let me inherit a double share of your spirit and become your successor."

¹⁰ "You have asked a difficult thing," Elijah replied. "If you see me when I am taken from you, then you will get your request. But if not, then you won't."

¹¹ As they were walking along and talking, suddenly a chariot of fire appeared, drawn by horses of fire. It drove between the two men, separating them, and Elijah was carried by a whirlwind into heaven. ¹² Elisha saw it and cried out, "My father! My father! I see the chariots and charioteers of Israel!" And as they disappeared from sight, Elisha tore his clothes in distress.

¹³ Elisha picked up Elijah's cloak, which had fallen when he was taken up. Then Elisha returned to the bank of the Jordan River. ¹⁴ He struck the water with Elijah's cloak and cried out, "Where is the LORD, the God of Elijah?" Then the river divided, and Elisha went across.

¹⁵ When the group of prophets from Jericho saw from a distance what happened, they exclaimed, "Elijah's spirit rests upon Elisha!" And they went to meet him and bowed to the ground before him. ¹⁶ "Sir," they said, "just say the word and fifty of our strongest men will search the wilderness for your master. Perhaps the Spirit of the LORD has left him on some mountain or in some valley."

"No," Elisha said, "don't send them." ¹⁷ But they kept urging him until they shamed him into agreeing, and he finally said, "All right, send them." So fifty men searched for three days but did not find Elijah. ¹⁸ Elisha was still at Jericho when they returned. "Didn't I tell you not to go?" he asked.

ELISHA'S FIRST MIRACLES

¹⁹ One day the leaders of the town of Jericho visited Elisha. "We have a problem, my lord," they told him. "This town is located in pleasant surroundings, as you can see. But the water is bad, and the land is unproductive."

²⁰ Elisha said, "Bring me a new bowl with salt in it." So they brought it to him. ²¹ Then he went out to the spring that supplied the town with water and threw the salt into it. And he said, "This is what the LORD says: I have purified this water. It will no longer cause death or infertility.*" ²² And the water has remained pure ever since, just as Elisha said.

²³ Elisha left Jericho and went up to Bethel. As he was walking along the road, a group of boys from the town began mocking and making fun of him. "Go away, baldy!" they chanted. "Go away,

baldy!" ²⁴ Elisha turned around and looked at them, and he cursed them in the name of the LORD. Then two bears came out of the woods and mauled forty-two of them. ²⁵ From there Elisha went to Mount Carmel and finally returned to Samaria.

WAR BETWEEN ISRAEL AND MOAB

3 Ahab's son Joram* began to rule over Israel in the eighteenth year of King Jehoshaphat's reign in Judah. He reigned in Samaria twelve years. ² He did what was evil in the LORD's sight, but not to the same extent as his father and mother. He at least tore down the sacred pillar of Baal that his father had set up. ³ Nevertheless, he continued in the sins that Jeroboam son of Nebat had committed and led the people of Israel to commit.

⁴ King Mesha of Moab was a sheep breeder. He used to pay the king of Israel an annual tribute of 100,000 lambs and the wool of 100,000 rams. ⁵ But after Ahab's death, the king of Moab rebelled against the king of Israel. ⁶ So King Joram promptly mustered the army of Israel and marched from Samaria. ⁷ On the way, he sent this message to King Jehoshaphat of Judah: "The king of Moab has rebelled against me. Will you join me in battle against him?"

And Jehoshaphat replied, "Why, of course! You and I are as one. My troops are your troops, and my horses are your horses." ⁸ Then Jehoshaphat asked, "What route will we take?"

"We will attack from the wilderness of Edom," Joram replied.

⁹ The king of Edom and his troops joined them, and all three armies traveled along a roundabout route through the wilderness for seven days. But there was no water for the men or their animals.

¹⁰ "What should we do?" the king of Israel cried out. "The LORD has brought the three of us here to let the king of Moab defeat us."

¹¹ But King Jehoshaphat of Judah asked, "Is there no prophet of the LORD with us? If there is, we can ask the LORD what to do through him."

One of King Joram's officers replied, "Elisha son of Shaphat is here. He used to be Elijah's personal assistant.*"

¹² Jehoshaphat said, "Yes, the LORD speaks through him." So the king of Israel, King Jehoshaphat of Judah, and the king of Edom went to consult with Elisha.

¹³ "Why are you coming to me?"* Elisha asked the king of Israel. "Go to the pagan prophets of your father and mother!"

But King Joram of Israel said, "No! For it was the LORD who called us three kings here—only to be defeated by the king of Moab!"

¹⁴ Elisha replied, "As surely as the LORD Almighty lives, whom I serve, I wouldn't even

2:21 Or or make the land unproductive; Hebrew reads or barrenness.
3:1 Hebrew Jehoram, a variant spelling of Joram; also in
3:6.   3:11 Hebrew He used to pour water on the hands of Elijah.
3:13 Hebrew What is there in common between you and me?

bother with you except for my respect for King Jehoshaphat of Judah. ¹⁵ Now bring me someone who can play the harp."

While the harp was being played, the power* of the LORD came upon Elisha, ¹⁶ and he said, "This is what the LORD says: This dry valley will be filled with pools of water! ¹⁷ You will see neither wind nor rain, says the LORD, but this valley will be filled with water. You will have plenty for yourselves and your cattle and other animals. ¹⁸ But this is only a simple thing for the LORD, for he will make you victorious over the army of Moab! ¹⁹ You will conquer the best of their towns, even the fortified ones. You will cut down all their good trees, stop up all their springs, and ruin all their good land with stones."

²⁰ The next day at about the time when the morning sacrifice was offered, water suddenly appeared! It was flowing from the direction of Edom, and soon there was water everywhere.

²¹ Meanwhile, when the people of Moab heard about the three armies marching against them, they mobilized every man who was old enough to strap on a sword, and they stationed themselves along their border. ²² But when they got up the next morning, the sun was shining across the water, making it appear red to the Moabites—like blood. ²³ "It's blood!" the Moabites exclaimed. "The three armies must have attacked and killed each other! Let's go, men of Moab, and collect the plunder!"

²⁴ But when the Moabites arrived at the Israelite camp, the army of Israel rushed out and attacked them until they turned and ran. The army of Israel chased them into the land of Moab, destroying everything as they went.* ²⁵ They destroyed the towns, covered their good land with stones, stopped up all the springs, and cut down all the good trees. Finally, only Kirhareseth and its stone walls were left, but men with slings surrounded and attacked it.

²⁶ When the king of Moab saw that he was losing the battle, he led 700 of his swordsmen in a desperate attempt to break through the enemy lines near the king of Edom, but they failed. ²⁷ Then the king of Moab took his oldest son, who would have been the next king, and sacrificed him as a burnt offering on the wall. So there was great anger against Israel,* and the Israelites withdrew and returned to their own land.

ELISHA HELPS A POOR WIDOW

4 One day the widow of a member of the group of prophets came to Elisha and cried out, "My husband who served you is dead, and you know how he feared the LORD. But now a creditor has come, threatening to take my two sons as slaves."

² "What can I do to help you?" Elisha asked. "Tell me, what do you have in the house?"

"Nothing at all, except a flask of olive oil," she replied.

³ And Elisha said, "Borrow as many empty jars as you can from your friends and neighbors. ⁴ Then go into your house with your sons and shut the door behind you. Pour olive oil from your flask into the jars, setting each one aside when it is filled."

⁵ So she did as she was told. Her sons kept bringing jars to her, and she filled one after another. ⁶ Soon every container was full to the brim!

"Bring me another jar," she said to one of her sons.

"There aren't any more!" he told her. And then the olive oil stopped flowing.

⁷ When she told the man of God what had happened, he said to her, "Now sell the olive oil and pay your debts, and you and your sons can live on what is left over."

ELISHA AND THE WOMAN FROM SHUNEM

⁸ One day Elisha went to the town of Shunem. A wealthy woman lived there, and she urged him to come to her home for a meal. After that, whenever he passed that way, he would stop there for something to eat.

⁹ She said to her husband, "I am sure this man who stops in from time to time is a holy man of God. ¹⁰ Let's build a small room for him on the roof and furnish it with a bed, a table, a chair, and a lamp. Then he will have a place to stay whenever he comes by."

¹¹ One day Elisha returned to Shunem, and he went up to this upper room to rest. ¹² He said to his servant Gehazi, "Tell the woman from Shunem I want to speak to her." When she appeared, ¹³ Elisha said to Gehazi, "Tell her, 'We appreciate the kind concern you have shown us. What can we do for you? Can we put in a good word for you to the king or to the commander of the army?'"

"No," she replied, "my family takes good care of me."

¹⁴ Later Elisha asked Gehazi, "What can we do for her?"

Gehazi replied, "She doesn't have a son, and her husband is an old man."

¹⁵ "Call her back again," Elisha told him. When the woman returned, Elisha said to her as she stood in the doorway, ¹⁶ "Next year at this time you will be holding a son in your arms!"

"No, my lord!" she cried. "O man of God, don't deceive me and get my hopes up like that."

¹⁷ But sure enough, the woman soon became pregnant. And at that time the following year she had a son, just as Elisha had said.

¹⁸ One day when her child was older, he went out to help his father, who was working with the harvesters. ¹⁹ Suddenly he cried out, "My head hurts! My head hurts!"

3:15 Hebrew *the hand.* 3:24 The meaning of the Hebrew is uncertain. 3:27 Or *So Israel's anger was great.* The meaning of the Hebrew is uncertain.

His father said to one of the servants, "Carry him home to his mother."

20 So the servant took him home, and his mother held him on her lap. But around noontime he died. 21 She carried him up and laid him on the bed of the man of God, then shut the door and left him there. 22 She sent a message to her husband: "Send one of the servants and a donkey so that I can hurry to the man of God and come right back."

23 "Why go today?" he asked. "It is neither a new moon festival nor a Sabbath."

But she said, "It will be all right."

24 So she saddled the donkey and said to the servant, "Hurry! Don't slow down unless I tell you to."

25 As she approached the man of God at Mount Carmel, Elisha saw her in the distance. He said to Gehazi, "Look, the woman from Shunem is coming. 26 Run out to meet her and ask her, 'Is everything all right with you, your husband, and your child?'"

"Yes," the woman told Gehazi, "everything is fine."

27 But when she came to the man of God at the mountain, she fell to the ground before him and caught hold of his feet. Gehazi began to push her away, but the man of God said, "Leave her alone. She is deeply troubled, but the LORD has not told me what it is."

28 Then she said, "Did I ask you for a son, my lord? And didn't I say, 'Don't deceive me and get my hopes up'?"

29 Then Elisha said to Gehazi, "Get ready to travel*; take my staff and go! Don't talk to anyone along the way. Go quickly and lay the staff on the child's face."

30 But the boy's mother said, "As surely as the LORD lives and you yourself live, I won't go home unless you go with me." So Elisha returned with her.

31 Gehazi hurried on ahead and laid the staff on the child's face, but nothing happened. There was no sign of life. He returned to meet Elisha and told him, "The child is still dead."

32 When Elisha arrived, the child was indeed dead, lying there on the prophet's bed. 33 He went in alone and shut the door behind him and prayed to the LORD. 34 Then he lay down on the child's body, placing his mouth on the child's mouth, his eyes on the child's eyes, and his hands on the child's hands. And as he stretched out on him, the child's body began to grow warm again! 35 Elisha got up, walked back and forth across the room once, and then stretched himself out again on the child. This time the boy sneezed seven times and opened his eyes!

36 Then Elisha summoned Gehazi. "Call the child's mother!" he said. And when she came in, Elisha said, "Here, take your son!" 37 She fell at his feet and bowed before him, overwhelmed with gratitude. Then she took her son in her arms and carried him downstairs.

MIRACLES DURING A FAMINE

38 Elisha now returned to Gilgal, and there was a famine in the land. One day as the group of prophets was seated before him, he said to his servant, "Put a large pot on the fire, and make some stew for the rest of the group."

39 One of the young men went out into the field to gather herbs and came back with a pocketful of wild gourds. He shredded them and put them into the pot without realizing they were poisonous. 40 Some of the stew was served to the men. But after they had eaten a bite or two they cried out, "Man of God, there's poison in this stew!" So they would not eat it.

41 Elisha said, "Bring me some flour." Then he threw it into the pot and said, "Now it's all right; go ahead and eat." And then it did not harm them.

42 One day a man from Baal-shalishah brought the man of God a sack of fresh grain and twenty loaves of barley bread made from the first grain of his harvest. Elisha said, "Give it to the people so they can eat."

43 "What?" his servant exclaimed. "Feed a hundred people with only this?"

But Elisha repeated, "Give it to the people so they can eat, for this is what the LORD says: Everyone will eat, and there will even be some left over!" 44 And when they gave it to the people, there was plenty for all and some left over, just as the LORD had promised.

THE HEALING OF NAAMAN

5 The king of Aram had great admiration for Naaman, the commander of his army, because through him the LORD had given Aram great victories. But though Naaman was a mighty warrior, he suffered from leprosy.*

2 At this time Aramean raiders had invaded the land of Israel, and among their captives was a young girl who had been given to Naaman's wife as a maid. 3 One day the girl said to her mistress, "I wish my master would go to see the prophet in Samaria. He would heal him of his leprosy."

4 So Naaman told the king what the young girl from Israel had said. 5 "Go and visit the prophet," the king of Aram told him. "I will send a letter of introduction for you to take to the king of Israel." So Naaman started out, carrying as gifts 750 pounds of silver, 150 pounds of gold,* and ten sets of clothing. 6 The letter to the king of Israel said: "With this letter I present my servant Naaman. I want you to heal him of his leprosy."

7 When the king of Israel read the letter, he tore his clothes in dismay and said, "Am I God, that I can give life and take it away? Why is this man

---

4:29 Hebrew *Bind up your loins.* 5:1 Or *from a contagious skin disease.* The Hebrew word used here and throughout this passage can describe various skin diseases. 5:5 Hebrew *10 talents* [340 kilograms] *of silver, 6,000 [shekels]* [68 kilograms] *of gold.*

asking me to heal someone with leprosy? I can see that he's just trying to pick a fight with me."

⁸ But when Elisha, the man of God, heard that the king of Israel had torn his clothes in dismay, he sent this message to him: "Why are you so upset? Send Naaman to me, and he will learn that there is a true prophet here in Israel."

⁹ So Naaman went with his horses and chariots and waited at the door of Elisha's house. ¹⁰ But Elisha sent a messenger out to him with this message: "Go and wash yourself seven times in the Jordan River. Then your skin will be restored, and you will be healed of your leprosy."

¹¹ But Naaman became angry and stalked away. "I thought he would certainly come out to meet me!" he said. "I expected him to wave his hand over the leprosy and call on the name of the LORD his God and heal me! ¹² Aren't the rivers of Damascus, the Abana and the Pharpar, better than any of the rivers of Israel? Why shouldn't I wash in them and be healed?" So Naaman turned and went away in a rage.

¹³ But his officers tried to reason with him and said, "Sir,* if the prophet had told you to do something very difficult, wouldn't you have done it? So you should certainly obey him when he says simply, 'Go and wash and be cured!'" ¹⁴ So Naaman went down to the Jordan River and dipped himself seven times, as the man of God had instructed him. And his skin became as healthy as the skin of a young child, and he was healed!

¹⁵ Then Naaman and his entire party went back to find the man of God. They stood before him, and Naaman said, "Now I know that there is no God in all the world except in Israel. So please accept a gift from your servant."

¹⁶ But Elisha replied, "As surely as the LORD lives, whom I serve, I will not accept any gifts." And though Naaman urged him to take the gift, Elisha refused.

¹⁷ Then Naaman said, "All right, but please allow me to load two of my mules with earth from this place, and I will take it back home with me. From now on I will never again offer burnt offerings or sacrifices to any other god except the LORD. ¹⁸ However, may the LORD pardon me in this one thing: When my master the king goes into the temple of the god Rimmon to worship there and leans on my arm, may the LORD pardon me when I bow, too."

¹⁹ "Go in peace," Elisha said. So Naaman started home again.

THE GREED OF GEHAZI

²⁰ But Gehazi, the servant of Elisha, the man of God, said to himself, "My master should not have let this Aramean get away without accepting any of his gifts. As surely as the LORD lives, I will chase after him and get something from him." ²¹ So Gehazi set off after Naaman.

When Naaman saw Gehazi running after him, he climbed down from his chariot and went to meet him. "Is everything all right?" Naaman asked.

²² "Yes," Gehazi said, "but my master has sent me to tell you that two young prophets from the hill country of Ephraim have just arrived. He would like 75 pounds* of silver and two sets of clothing to give to them."

²³ "By all means, take twice as much* silver," Naaman insisted. He gave him two sets of clothing, tied up the money in two bags, and sent two of his servants to carry the gifts for Gehazi. ²⁴ But when they arrived at the citadel,* Gehazi took the gifts from the servants and sent the men back. Then he went and hid the gifts inside the house.

²⁵ When he went in to his master, Elisha asked him, "Where have you been, Gehazi?"

"I haven't been anywhere," he replied.

²⁶ But Elisha asked him, "Don't you realize that I was there in spirit when Naaman stepped down from his chariot to meet you? Is this the time to receive money and clothing, olive groves and vineyards, sheep and cattle, and male and female servants? ²⁷ Because you have done this, you and your descendants will suffer from Naaman's leprosy forever." When Gehazi left the room, he was covered with leprosy; his skin was white as snow.

THE FLOATING AX HEAD

6 One day the group of prophets came to Elisha and told him, "As you can see, this place where we meet with you is too small. ² Let's go down to the Jordan River, where there are plenty of logs. There we can build a new place for us to meet."

"All right," he told them, "go ahead." ³ "Please come with us," someone suggested.

"I will," he said. ⁴ So he went with them.

When they arrived at the Jordan, they began cutting down trees. ⁵ But as one of them was cutting a tree, his ax head fell into the river. "Oh, sir!" he cried. "It was a borrowed ax!"

⁶ "Where did it fall?" the man of God asked. When he showed him the place, Elisha cut a stick and threw it into the water at that spot. Then the ax head floated to the surface. ⁷ "Grab it," Elisha said. And the man reached out and grabbed it.

ELISHA TRAPS THE ARAMEANS

⁸ When the king of Aram was at war with Israel, he would confer with his officers and say, "We will mobilize our forces at such and such a place."

⁹ But immediately Elisha, the man of God, would warn the king of Israel, "Do not go near that place, for the Arameans are planning to mobilize their troops there." ¹⁰ So the king of Israel would send word to the place indicated by the man of God. Time and again Elisha warned the king, so that he would be on the alert there.

5:13 Hebrew *My father.*   5:22 Hebrew *1 talent* [34 kilograms].
5:23 Hebrew *take 2 talents* [150 pounds or 68 kilograms].
5:24 Hebrew *the Ophel.*

¹¹The king of Aram became very upset over this. He called his officers together and demanded, "Which of you is the traitor? Who has been informing the king of Israel of my plans?"

¹²"It's not us, my lord the king," one of the officers replied. "Elisha, the prophet in Israel, tells the king of Israel even the words you speak in the privacy of your bedroom!"

¹³"Go and find out where he is," the king commanded, "so I can send troops to seize him."

And the report came back: "Elisha is at Dothan." ¹⁴So one night the king of Aram sent a great army with many chariots and horses to surround the city.

¹⁵When the servant of the man of God got up early the next morning and went outside, there were troops, horses, and chariots everywhere. "Oh, sir, what will we do now?" the young man cried to Elisha.

¹⁶"Don't be afraid!" Elisha told him. "For there are more on our side than on theirs!" ¹⁷Then Elisha prayed, "O LORD, open his eyes and let him see!" The LORD opened the young man's eyes, and when he looked up, he saw that the hillside around Elisha was filled with horses and chariots of fire.

¹⁸As the Aramean army advanced toward him, Elisha prayed, "O LORD, please make them blind." So the LORD struck them with blindness as Elisha had asked.

¹⁹Then Elisha went out and told them, "You have come the wrong way! This isn't the right city! Follow me, and I will take you to the man you are looking for." And he led them to the city of Samaria.

²⁰As soon as they had entered Samaria, Elisha prayed, "O LORD, now open their eyes and let them see." So the LORD opened their eyes, and they discovered that they were in the middle of Samaria.

²¹When the king of Israel saw them, he shouted to Elisha, "My father, should I kill them? Should I kill them?"

²²"Of course not!" Elisha replied. "Do we kill prisoners of war? Give them food and drink and send them home again to their master."

²³So the king made a great feast for them and then sent them home to their master. After that, the Aramean raiders stayed away from the land of Israel.

BEN-HADAD BESIEGES SAMARIA

²⁴Some time later, however, King Ben-hadad of Aram mustered his entire army and besieged Samaria. ²⁵As a result, there was a great famine in the city. The siege lasted so long that a donkey's head sold for eighty pieces of silver, and a cup of dove's dung sold for five pieces* of silver.

²⁶One day as the king of Israel was walking along the wall of the city, a woman called to him, "Please help me, my lord the king!"

²⁷He answered, "If the LORD doesn't help you, what can I do? I have neither food from the threshing floor nor wine from the press to give you." ²⁸But then the king asked, "What is the matter?"

She replied, "This woman said to me: 'Come on, let's eat your son today, then we will eat my son tomorrow.' ²⁹So we cooked my son and ate him. Then the next day I said to her, 'Kill your son so we can eat him,' but she has hidden her son."

³⁰When the king heard this, he tore his clothes in despair. And as the king walked along the wall, the people could see that he was wearing burlap under his robe next to his skin. ³¹"May God strike me and even kill me if I don't separate Elisha's head from his shoulders this very day," the king vowed.

³²Elisha was sitting in his house with the elders of Israel when the king sent a messenger to summon him. But before the messenger arrived, Elisha said to the elders, "A murderer has sent a man to cut off my head. When he arrives, shut the door and keep him out. We will soon hear his master's steps following him."

³³While Elisha was still saying this, the messenger arrived. And the king* said, "All this misery is from the LORD! Why should I wait for the LORD any longer?"

7 Elisha replied, "Listen to this message from the LORD! This is what the LORD says: By this time tomorrow in the markets of Samaria, six quarts of choice flour will cost only one piece of silver,* and twelve quarts of barley grain will cost only one piece of silver.*"

²The officer assisting the king said to the man of God, "That couldn't happen even if the LORD opened the windows of heaven!"

But Elisha replied, "You will see it happen with your own eyes, but you won't be able to eat any of it!"

OUTCASTS VISIT THE ENEMY CAMP

³Now there were four men with leprosy* sitting at the entrance of the city gates. "Why should we sit here waiting to die?" they asked each other. ⁴"We will starve if we stay here, but with the famine in the city, we will starve if we go back there. So we might as well go out and surrender to the Aramean army. If they let us live, so much the better. But if they kill us, we would have died anyway."

⁵So at twilight they set out for the camp of the Arameans. But when they came to the edge of the camp, no one was there! ⁶For the Lord had caused the Aramean army to hear the clatter of speeding

6:25 Hebrew sold for 80 [shekels] [2 pounds or 0.9 kilograms] of silver, and ¼ of a cab [0.3 liters] of dove's dung sold for 5 [shekels] [2 ounces or 57 grams]. Dove's dung may be a variety of wild vegetable. 6:33 Hebrew he. 7:1a Hebrew 1 seah [7.3 liters] of choice flour will cost 1 shekel [0.4 ounces or 11 grams]; also in 7:16, 18. 7:1b Hebrew 2 seahs [14.6 liters] of barley grain will cost 1 shekel [0.4 ounces or 11 grams]; also in 7:16, 18. 7:3 Or with a contagious skin disease. The Hebrew word used here and throughout this passage can describe various skin diseases.

chariots and the galloping of horses and the sounds of a great army approaching. "The king of Israel has hired the Hittites and Egyptians* to attack us!" they cried to one another. ⁷ So they panicked and ran into the night, abandoning their tents, horses, donkeys, and everything else, as they fled for their lives.

⁸ When the men with leprosy arrived at the edge of the camp, they went into one tent after another, eating and drinking wine; and they carried off silver and gold and clothing and hid it. ⁹ Finally, they said to each other, "This is not right. This is a day of good news, and we aren't sharing it with anyone! If we wait until morning, some calamity will certainly fall upon us. Come on, let's go back and tell the people at the palace."

¹⁰ So they went back to the city and told the gatekeepers what had happened. "We went out to the Aramean camp," they said, "and no one was there! The horses and donkeys were tethered and the tents were all in order, but there wasn't a single person around!" ¹¹ Then the gatekeepers shouted the news to the people in the palace.

ISRAEL PLUNDERS THE CAMP

¹² The king got out of bed in the middle of the night and told his officers, "I know what has happened. The Arameans know we are starving, so they have left their camp and have hidden in the fields. They are expecting us to leave the city, and then they will take us alive and capture the city."

¹³ One of his officers replied, "We had better send out scouts to check into this. Let them take five of the remaining horses. If something happens to them, it will be no worse than if they stay here and die with the rest of us."

¹⁴ So two chariots with horses were prepared, and the king sent scouts to see what had happened to the Aramean army. ¹⁵ They went all the way to the Jordan River, following a trail of clothing and equipment that the Arameans had thrown away in their mad rush to escape. The scouts returned and told the king about it. ¹⁶ Then the people of Samaria rushed out and plundered the Aramean camp. So it was true that six quarts of choice flour were sold that day for one piece of silver, and twelve quarts of barley grain were sold for one piece of silver, just as the LORD had promised. ¹⁷ The king appointed his officer to control the traffic at the gate, but he was knocked down and trampled to death as the people rushed out.

So everything happened exactly as the man of God had predicted when the king came to his house. ¹⁸ The man of God had said to the king, "By this time tomorrow in the markets of Samaria, six quarts of choice flour will cost one piece of silver, and twelve quarts of barley grain will cost one piece of silver."

¹⁹ The king's officer had replied, "That couldn't happen even if the LORD opened the windows of heaven!" And the man of God had said, "You will see it happen with your own eyes, but you won't be able to eat any of it!" ²⁰ And so it was, for the people trampled him to death at the gate!

THE WOMAN FROM SHUNEM RETURNS HOME

8 Elisha had told the woman whose son he had brought back to life, "Take your family and move to some other place, for the LORD has called for a famine on Israel that will last for seven years." ² So the woman did as the man of God instructed. She took her family and settled in the land of the Philistines for seven years.

³ After the famine ended she returned from the land of the Philistines, and she went to see the king about getting back her house and land. ⁴ As she came in, the king was talking with Gehazi, the servant of the man of God. The king had just said, "Tell me some stories about the great things Elisha has done." ⁵ And Gehazi was telling the king about the time Elisha had brought a boy back to life. At that very moment, the mother of the boy walked in to make her appeal to the king about her house and land.

"Look, my lord the king!" Gehazi exclaimed. "Here is the woman now, and this is her son—the very one Elisha brought back to life!"

⁶ "Is this true?" the king asked her. And she told him the story. So he directed one of his officials to see that everything she had lost was restored to her, including the value of any crops that had been harvested during her absence.

HAZAEL MURDERS BEN-HADAD

⁷ Elisha went to Damascus, the capital of Aram, where King Ben-hadad lay sick. When someone told the king that the man of God had come, ⁸ the king said to Hazael, "Take a gift to the man of God. Then tell him to ask the LORD, 'Will I recover from this illness?'"

⁹ So Hazael loaded down forty camels with the finest products of Damascus as a gift for Elisha. He went to him and said, "Your servant Ben-hadad, the king of Aram, has sent me to ask, 'Will I recover from this illness?'"

¹⁰ And Elisha replied, "Go and tell him, 'You will surely recover.' But actually the LORD has shown me that he will surely die!" ¹¹ Elisha stared at Hazael* with a fixed gaze until Hazael became uneasy.* Then the man of God started weeping.

¹² "What's the matter, my lord?" Hazael asked him.

Elisha replied, "I know the terrible things you will do to the people of Israel. You will burn their fortified cities, kill their young men with the sword, dash their little children to the ground, and rip open their pregnant women!"

¹³ Hazael responded, "How could a nobody like me* ever accomplish such great things?"

7:6 Possibly *and the people of Muzur,* a district near Cilicia. 8:11a Hebrew *He stared at him.* 8:11b The meaning of the Hebrew is uncertain. 8:13 Hebrew *a dog.*

Elisha answered, "The LORD has shown me that you are going to be the king of Aram."

¹⁴ When Hazael left Elisha and went back, the king asked him, "What did Elisha tell you?"

And Hazael replied, "He told me that you will surely recover."

¹⁵ But the next day Hazael took a blanket, soaked it in water, and held it over the king's face until he died. Then Hazael became the next king of Aram.

JEHORAM RULES IN JUDAH

¹⁶ Jehoram son of King Jehoshaphat of Judah began to rule over Judah in the fifth year of the reign of Joram son of Ahab, king of Israel. ¹⁷ Jehoram was thirty-two years old when he became king, and he reigned in Jerusalem eight years. ¹⁸ But Jehoram followed the example of the kings of Israel and was as wicked as King Ahab, for he had married one of Ahab's daughters. So Jehoram did what was evil in the LORD's sight. ¹⁹ But the LORD did not want to destroy Judah, for he had promised his servant David that his descendants would continue to rule, shining like a lamp forever.

²⁰ During Jehoram's reign, the Edomites revolted against Judah and crowned their own king. ²¹ So Jehoram* went with all his chariots to attack the town of Zair.* The Edomites surrounded him and his chariot commanders, but he went out at night and attacked them* under cover of darkness. But Jehoram's army deserted him and fled to their homes. ²² So Edom has been independent from Judah to this day. The town of Libnah also revolted about that same time.

²³ The rest of the events in Jehoram's reign and everything he did are recorded in *The Book of the History of the Kings of Judah.* ²⁴ When Jehoram died, he was buried with his ancestors in the City of David. Then his son Ahaziah became the next king.

AHAZIAH RULES IN JUDAH

²⁵ Ahaziah son of Jehoram began to rule over Judah in the twelfth year of the reign of Joram son of Ahab, king of Israel. ²⁶ Ahaziah was twenty-two years old when he became king, and he reigned in Jerusalem one year. His mother was Athaliah, a granddaughter of King Omri of Israel. ²⁷ Ahaziah followed the evil example of King Ahab's family. He did what was evil in the LORD's sight, just as Ahab's family had done, for he was related by marriage to the family of Ahab.

²⁸ Ahaziah joined Joram son of Ahab in his war against King Hazael of Aram at Ramoth-gilead. When the Arameans wounded King Joram in the battle, ²⁹ he returned to Jezreel to recover from the wounds he had received at Ramoth.* Because Joram was wounded, King Ahaziah of Judah went to Jezreel to visit him.

JEHU ANOINTED KING OF ISRAEL

9 Meanwhile, Elisha the prophet had summoned a member of the group of prophets. "Get ready to travel,"* he told him, "and take this flask of olive oil with you. Go to Ramoth-gilead, ² and find Jehu son of Jehoshaphat, son of Nimshi. Call him into a private room away from his friends, ³ and pour the oil over his head. Say to him, 'This is what the LORD says: I anoint you to be the king over Israel.' Then open the door and run for your life!"

⁴ So the young prophet did as he was told and went to Ramoth-gilead. ⁵ When he arrived there, he found Jehu sitting around with the other army officers. "I have a message for you, Commander," he said.

"For which one of us?" Jehu asked.

"For you, Commander," he replied.

⁶ So Jehu left the others and went into the house. Then the young prophet poured the oil over Jehu's head and said, "This is what the LORD, the God of Israel, says: I anoint you king over the LORD's people, Israel. ⁷ You are to destroy the family of Ahab, your master. In this way, I will avenge the murder of my prophets and all the LORD's servants who were killed by Jezebel. ⁸ The entire family of Ahab must be wiped out. I will destroy every one of his male descendants, slave and free alike, anywhere in Israel. ⁹ I will destroy the family of Ahab as I destroyed the families of Jeroboam son of Nebat and of Baasha son of Ahijah. ¹⁰ Dogs will eat Ahab's wife Jezebel at the plot of land in Jezreel, and no one will bury her." Then the young prophet opened the door and ran.

¹¹ Jehu went back to his fellow officers, and one of them asked him, "What did that madman want? Is everything all right?"

"You know how a man like that babbles on," Jehu replied.

¹² "You're hiding something," they said. "Tell us."

So Jehu told them, "He said to me, 'This is what the LORD says: I have anointed you to be king over Israel.'"

¹³ Then they quickly spread out their cloaks on the bare steps and blew the ram's horn, shouting, "Jehu is king!"

JEHU KILLS JORAM AND AHAZIAH

¹⁴ So Jehu son of Jehoshaphat, son of Nimshi, led a conspiracy against King Joram. (Now Joram had been with the army at Ramoth-gilead, defending Israel against the forces of King Hazael of Aram. ¹⁵ But King Joram* was wounded in the fighting and returned to Jezreel to recover from his wounds.) So Jehu told the men with him, "If you want me to be king,

---

8:21a Hebrew *Joram,* a variant spelling of Jehoram; also in 8:23, 24.   8:21b Greek version reads *Seir.*   8:21c Or *he went out and escaped.* The meaning of the Hebrew is uncertain.   8:29 Hebrew *Ramah,* a variant spelling of Ramoth.   9:1 Hebrew *Bind up your loins.*   9:15 Hebrew *Jehoram,* a variant spelling of Joram; also in 9:17, 21, 22, 23, 24.

don't let anyone leave town and go to Jezreel to report what we have done."

¹⁶Then Jehu got into a chariot and rode to Jezreel to find King Joram, who was lying there wounded. King Ahaziah of Judah was there, too, for he had gone to visit him. ¹⁷The watchman on the tower of Jezreel saw Jehu and his company approaching, so he shouted to Joram, "I see a company of troops coming!"

"Send out a rider to ask if they are coming in peace," King Joram ordered.

¹⁸So a horseman went out to meet Jehu and said, "The king wants to know if you are coming in peace."

Jehu replied, "What do you know about peace? Fall in behind me!"

The watchman called out to the king, "The messenger has met them, but he's not returning."

¹⁹So the king sent out a second horseman. He rode up to them and said, "The king wants to know if you come in peace."

Again Jehu answered, "What do you know about peace? Fall in behind me!"

²⁰The watchman exclaimed, "The messenger has met them, but he isn't returning either! It must be Jehu son of Nimshi, for he's driving like a madman."

²¹"Quick! Get my chariot ready!" King Joram commanded.

Then King Joram of Israel and King Ahaziah of Judah rode out in their chariots to meet Jehu. They met him at the plot of land that had belonged to Naboth of Jezreel. ²²King Joram demanded, "Do you come in peace, Jehu?"

Jehu replied, "How can there be peace as long as the idolatry and witchcraft of your mother, Jezebel, are all around us?"

²³Then King Joram turned the horses around* and fled, shouting to King Ahaziah, "Treason, Ahaziah!" ²⁴But Jehu drew his bow and shot Joram between the shoulders. The arrow pierced his heart, and he sank down dead in his chariot.

²⁵Jehu said to Bidkar, his officer, "Throw him into the plot of land that belonged to Naboth of Jezreel. Do you remember when you and I were riding along behind his father, Ahab? The LORD pronounced this message against him: ²⁶'I solemnly swear that I will repay him here on this plot of land, says the LORD, for the murder of Naboth and his sons that I saw yesterday.' So throw him out on Naboth's property, just as the LORD said."

²⁷When King Ahaziah of Judah saw what was happening, he fled along the road to Beth-haggan. Jehu rode after him, shouting, "Shoot him, too!" So they shot Ahaziah* in his chariot at the Ascent of Gur, near Ibleam. He was able to go on as far as Megiddo, but he died there. ²⁸His servants took him by chariot to Jerusalem, where they buried him with his ancestors in the City of David. ²⁹Ahaziah had become king over Judah in the eleventh year of the reign of Joram son of Ahab.

THE DEATH OF JEZEBEL

³⁰When Jezebel, the queen mother, heard that Jehu had come to Jezreel, she painted her eyelids and fixed her hair and sat at a window. ³¹When Jehu entered the gate of the palace, she shouted at him, "Have you come in peace, you murderer? You're just like Zimri, who murdered his master!"*

³²Jehu looked up and saw her at the window and shouted, "Who is on my side?" And two or three eunuchs looked out at him. ³³"Throw her down!" Jehu yelled. So they threw her out the window, and her blood spattered against the wall and on the horses. And Jehu trampled her body under his horses' hooves.

³⁴Then Jehu went into the palace and ate and drank. Afterward he said, "Someone go and bury this cursed woman, for she is the daughter of a king." ³⁵But when they went out to bury her, they found only her skull, her feet, and her hands.

³⁶When they returned and told Jehu, he stated, "This fulfills the message from the LORD, which he spoke through his servant Elijah from Tishbe: 'At the plot of land in Jezreel, dogs will eat Jezebel's body. ³⁷Her remains will be scattered like dung on the plot of land in Jezreel, so that no one will be able to recognize her.'"

JEHU KILLS AHAB'S FAMILY

10 Ahab had seventy sons living in the city of Samaria. So Jehu wrote letters and sent them to Samaria, to the elders and officials of the city,* and to the guardians of King Ahab's sons. He said, ²"The king's sons are with you, and you have at your disposal chariots, horses, a fortified city, and weapons. As soon as you receive this letter, ³select the best qualified of your master's sons to be your king, and prepare to fight for Ahab's dynasty."

⁴But they were paralyzed with fear and said, "We've seen that two kings couldn't stand against this man! What can we do?"

⁵So the palace and city administrators, together with the elders and the guardians of the king's sons, sent this message to Jehu: "We are your servants and will do anything you tell us. We will not make anyone king; do whatever you think is best."

⁶Jehu responded with a second letter: "If you are on my side and are going to obey me, bring the heads of your master's sons to me at Jezreel by this time tomorrow." Now the seventy sons of the king were being cared for by the leaders of Samaria, where they had been raised since childhood. ⁷When the letter arrived, the leaders killed all seventy of the king's sons. They placed their heads in baskets and presented them to Jehu at Jezreel.

9:23 Hebrew *turned his hands.*   9:27 As in Greek and Syriac versions; Hebrew lacks *So they shot Ahaziah.*   9:31 See 1 Kgs 16:9-10, where Zimri killed his master, King Elah.   10:1 As in some Greek manuscripts and Latin Vulgate (see also 10:6); Hebrew reads *of Jezreel.*

[8] A messenger went to Jehu and said, "They have brought the heads of the king's sons."

So Jehu ordered, "Pile them in two heaps at the entrance of the city gate, and leave them there until morning."

[9] In the morning he went out and spoke to the crowd that had gathered around them. "You are not to blame," he told them. "I am the one who conspired against my master and killed him. But who killed all these? [10] You can be sure that the message of the LORD that was spoken concerning Ahab's family will not fail. The LORD declared through his servant Elijah that this would happen." [11] Then Jehu killed all who were left of Ahab's relatives living in Jezreel and all his important officials, his personal friends, and his priests. So Ahab was left without a single survivor.

[12] Then Jehu set out for Samaria. Along the way, while he was at Beth-eked of the Shepherds, [13] he met some relatives of King Ahaziah of Judah. "Who are you?" he asked them.

And they replied, "We are relatives of King Ahaziah. We are going to visit the sons of King Ahab and the sons of the queen mother."

[14] "Take them alive!" Jehu shouted to his men. And they captured all forty-two of them and killed them at the well of Beth-eked. None of them escaped.

[15] When Jehu left there, he met Jehonadab son of Recab, who was coming to meet him. After they had greeted each other, Jehu said to him, "Are you as loyal to me as I am to you?"

"Yes, I am," Jehonadab replied.

"If you are," Jehu said, "then give me your hand." So Jehonadab put out his hand, and Jehu helped him into the chariot. [16] Then Jehu said, "Now come with me, and see how devoted I am to the LORD." So Jehonadab rode along with him.

[17] When Jehu arrived in Samaria, he killed everyone who was left there from Ahab's family, just as the LORD had promised through Elijah.

JEHU KILLS THE PRIESTS OF BAAL

[18] Then Jehu called a meeting of all the people of the city and said to them, "Ahab's worship of Baal was nothing compared to the way I will worship him! [19] Therefore, summon all the prophets and worshipers of Baal, and call together all his priests. See to it that every one of them comes, for I am going to offer a great sacrifice to Baal. Anyone who fails to come will be put to death." But Jehu's cunning plan was to destroy all the worshipers of Baal.

[20] Then Jehu ordered, "Prepare a solemn assembly to worship Baal!" So they did. [21] He sent messengers throughout all Israel summoning those who worshiped Baal. They all came—not a single one remained behind—and they filled the temple of Baal from one end to the other. [22] And Jehu instructed the keeper of the wardrobe, "Be sure that every worshiper of Baal wears one of these robes." So robes were given to them.

[23] Then Jehu went into the temple of Baal with Jehonadab son of Recab. Jehu said to the worshipers of Baal, "Make sure no one who worships the LORD is here—only those who worship Baal." [24] So they were all inside the temple to offer sacrifices and burnt offerings. Now Jehu had stationed eighty of his men outside the building and had warned them, "If you let anyone escape, you will pay for it with your own life."

[25] As soon as Jehu had finished sacrificing the burnt offering, he commanded his guards and officers, "Go in and kill all of them. Don't let a single one escape!" So they killed them all with their swords, and the guards and officers dragged their bodies outside.* Then Jehu's men went into the innermost fortress* of the temple of Baal. [26] They dragged out the sacred pillar* used in the worship of Baal and burned it. [27] They smashed the sacred pillar and wrecked the temple of Baal, converting it into a public toilet, as it remains to this day.

[28] In this way, Jehu destroyed every trace of Baal worship from Israel. [29] He did not, however, destroy the gold calves at Bethel and Dan, with which Jeroboam son of Nebat had caused Israel to sin.

[30] Nonetheless the LORD said to Jehu, "You have done well in following my instructions to destroy the family of Ahab. Therefore, your descendants will be kings of Israel down to the fourth generation." [31] But Jehu did not obey the Law of the LORD, the God of Israel, with all his heart. He refused to turn from the sins that Jeroboam had led Israel to commit.

THE DEATH OF JEHU

[32] At about that time the LORD began to cut down the size of Israel's territory. King Hazael conquered several sections of the country [33] east of the Jordan River, including all of Gilead, Gad, Reuben, and Manasseh. He conquered the area from the town of Aroer by the Arnon Gorge to as far north as Gilead and Bashan.

[34] The rest of the events in Jehu's reign—everything he did and all his achievements—are recorded in *The Book of the History of the Kings of Israel*.

[35] When Jehu died, he was buried in Samaria. Then his son Jehoahaz became the next king. [36] In all, Jehu reigned over Israel from Samaria for twenty-eight years.

QUEEN ATHALIAH RULES IN JUDAH

11 When Athaliah, the mother of King Ahaziah of Judah, learned that her son was dead, she began to destroy the rest of the royal family. [2] But Ahaziah's sister Jehosheba, the daughter

10:25a Or *and they left their bodies lying there;* or *and they threw them out into the outermost court.* 10:25b Hebrew *city.* 10:26 As in Greek and Syriac versions and Latin Vulgate; Hebrew reads *sacred pillars.*

of King Jehoram,* took Ahaziah's infant son, Joash, and stole him away from among the rest of the king's children, who were about to be killed. She put Joash and his nurse in a bedroom, and they hid him from Athaliah, so the child was not murdered. ³Joash remained hidden in the Temple of the LORD for six years while Athaliah ruled over the land.

REVOLT AGAINST ATHALIAH

⁴In the seventh year of Athaliah's reign, Jehoiada the priest summoned the commanders, the Carite mercenaries, and the palace guards to come to the Temple of the LORD. He made a solemn pact with them and made them swear an oath of loyalty there in the LORD's Temple; then he showed them the king's son.

⁵Jehoiada told them, "This is what you must do. A third of you who are on duty on the Sabbath are to guard the royal palace itself. ⁶Another third of you are to stand guard at the Sur Gate. And the final third must stand guard behind the palace guard. These three groups will all guard the palace. ⁷The other two units who are off duty on the Sabbath must stand guard for the king at the LORD's Temple. ⁸Form a bodyguard around the king and keep your weapons in hand. Kill anyone who tries to break through. Stay with the king wherever he goes."

⁹So the commanders did everything as Jehoiada the priest ordered. The commanders took charge of the men reporting for duty that Sabbath, as well as those who were going off duty. They brought them all to Jehoiada the priest, ¹⁰and he supplied them with the spears and small shields that had once belonged to King David and were stored in the Temple of the LORD. ¹¹The palace guards stationed themselves around the king, with their weapons ready. They formed a line from the south side of the Temple around to the north side and all around the altar.

¹²Then Jehoiada brought out Joash, the king's son, placed the crown on his head, and presented him with a copy of God's laws.* They anointed him and proclaimed him king, and everyone clapped their hands and shouted, "Long live the king!"

THE DEATH OF ATHALIAH

¹³When Athaliah heard the noise made by the palace guards and the people, she hurried to the LORD's Temple to see what was happening. ¹⁴When she arrived, she saw the newly crowned king standing in his place of authority by the pillar, as was the custom at times of coronation. The commanders and trumpeters were surrounding him, and people from all over the land were rejoicing and blowing trumpets. When Athaliah saw all this, she tore her clothes in despair and shouted, "Treason! Treason!"

¹⁵Then Jehoiada the priest ordered the commanders who were in charge of the troops, "Take her to the soldiers in front of the Temple,* and

kill anyone who tries to rescue her." For the priest had said, "She must not be killed in the Temple of the LORD." ¹⁶So they seized her and led her out to the gate where horses enter the palace grounds, and she was killed there.

JEHOIADA'S RELIGIOUS REFORMS

¹⁷Then Jehoiada made a covenant between the LORD and the king and the people that they would be the LORD's people. He also made a covenant between the king and the people. ¹⁸And all the people of the land went over to the temple of Baal and tore it down. They demolished the altars and smashed the idols to pieces, and they killed Mattan the priest of Baal in front of the altars.

Jehoiada the priest stationed guards at the Temple of the LORD. ¹⁹Then the commanders, the Carite mercenaries, the palace guards, and all the people of the land escorted the king from the Temple of the LORD. They went through the gate of the guards and into the palace, and the king took his seat on the royal throne. ²⁰So all the people of the land rejoiced, and the city was peaceful because Athaliah had been killed at the king's palace.

²¹*Joash* was seven years old when he became king.

JOASH REPAIRS THE TEMPLE

12 ¹*Joash* began to rule over Judah in the seventh year of King Jehu's reign in Israel. He reigned in Jerusalem forty years. His mother was Zibiah from Beersheba. ²All his life Joash did what was pleasing in the LORD's sight because Jehoiada the priest instructed him. ³Yet even so, he did not destroy the pagan shrines, and the people still offered sacrifices and burned incense there.

⁴One day King Joash said to the priests, "Collect all the money brought as a sacred offering to the LORD's Temple, whether it is a regular assessment, a payment of vows, or a voluntary gift. ⁵Let the priests take some of that money to pay for whatever repairs are needed at the Temple."

⁶But by the twenty-third year of Joash's reign, the priests still had not repaired the Temple. ⁷So King Joash called for Jehoiada and the other priests and asked them, "Why haven't you repaired the Temple? Don't use any more money for your own needs. From now on, it must all be spent on Temple repairs." ⁸So the priests agreed not to accept any more money from the people, and they also agreed to let others take responsibility for repairing the Temple.

11:2 Hebrew *Joram*, a variant spelling of Jehoram. 11:12 Or *a copy of the covenant*. 11:15 Or *Bring her out from between the ranks;* or *Take her out of the Temple precincts*. The meaning of the Hebrew is uncertain. 11:21a Verse 11:21 is numbered 12:1 in Hebrew text. 11:21b Hebrew *Jehoash*, a variant spelling of Joash. 12:1a Verses 12:1-21 are numbered 12:2-22 in Hebrew text. 12:1b Hebrew *Jehoash*, a variant spelling of Joash; also in 12:2, 4, 6, 7, 18.

⁹Then Jehoiada the priest bored a hole in the lid of a large chest and set it on the right-hand side of the altar at the entrance of the Temple of the LORD. The priests guarding the entrance put all of the people's contributions into the chest. ¹⁰Whenever the chest became full, the court secretary and the high priest counted the money that had been brought to the LORD's Temple and put it into bags. ¹¹Then they gave the money to the construction supervisors, who used it to pay the people working on the LORD's Temple—the carpenters, the builders, ¹²the masons, and the stonecutters. They also used the money to buy the timber and the finished stone needed for repairing the LORD's Temple, and they paid any other expenses related to the Temple's restoration.

¹³The money brought to the Temple was not used for making silver bowls, lamp snuffers, basins, trumpets, or other articles of gold or silver for the Temple of the LORD. ¹⁴It was paid to the workmen, who used it for the Temple repairs. ¹⁵No accounting of this money was required from the construction supervisors, because they were honest and trustworthy men. ¹⁶However, the money that was contributed for guilt offerings and sin offerings was not brought into the LORD's Temple. It was given to the priests for their own use.

THE END OF JOASH'S REIGN

¹⁷About this time King Hazael of Aram went to war against Gath and captured it. Then he turned to attack Jerusalem. ¹⁸King Joash collected all the sacred objects that Jehoshaphat, Jehoram, and Ahaziah, the previous kings of Judah, had dedicated, along with what he himself had dedicated. He sent them all to Hazael, along with all the gold in the treasuries of the LORD's Temple and the royal palace. So Hazael called off his attack on Jerusalem.

¹⁹The rest of the events in Joash's reign and everything he did are recorded in *The Book of the History of the Kings of Judah*.

²⁰Joash's officers plotted against him and assassinated him at Beth-millo on the road to Silla. ²¹The assassins were Jozacar* son of Shimeath and Jehozabad son of Shomer—both trusted advisers. Joash was buried with his ancestors in the City of David. Then his son Amaziah became the next king.

JEHOAHAZ RULES IN ISRAEL

13 Jehoahaz son of Jehu began to rule over Israel in the twenty-third year of King Joash's reign in Judah. He reigned in Samaria seventeen years. ²But he did what was evil in the LORD's sight. He followed the example of Jeroboam son of Nebat, continuing the sins that Jeroboam had led Israel to commit. ³So the LORD was very angry with Israel, and he allowed King Hazael of Aram and his son Ben-hadad to defeat them repeatedly.

⁴Then Jehoahaz prayed for the LORD's help, and the LORD heard his prayer, for he could see how severely the king of Aram was oppressing Israel. ⁵So the LORD provided someone to rescue the Israelites from the tyranny of the Arameans. Then Israel lived in safety again as they had in former days.

⁶But they continued to sin, following the evil example of Jeroboam. They also allowed the Asherah pole in Samaria to remain standing. ⁷Finally, Jehoahaz's army was reduced to 50 charioteers, 10 chariots, and 10,000 foot soldiers. The king of Aram had killed the others, trampling them like dust under his feet.

⁸The rest of the events in Jehoahaz's reign—everything he did and the extent of his power—are recorded in *The Book of the History of the Kings of Israel*. ⁹When Jehoahaz died, he was buried in Samaria. Then his son Jehoash* became the next king.

JEHOASH RULES IN ISRAEL

¹⁰Jehoash son of Jehoahaz began to rule over Israel in the thirty-seventh year of King Joash's reign in Judah. He reigned in Samaria sixteen years. ¹¹But he did what was evil in the LORD's sight. He refused to turn from the sins that Jeroboam son of Nebat had led Israel to commit.

¹²The rest of the events in Jehoash's reign and everything he did, including the extent of his power and his war with King Amaziah of Judah, are recorded in *The Book of the History of the Kings of Israel*. ¹³When Jehoash died, he was buried in Samaria with the kings of Israel. Then his son Jeroboam II became the next king.

ELISHA'S FINAL PROPHECY

¹⁴When Elisha was in his last illness, King Jehoash of Israel visited him and wept over him. "My father! My father! I see the chariots and charioteers of Israel!" he cried.

¹⁵Elisha told him, "Get a bow and some arrows." And the king did as he was told. ¹⁶Elisha told him, "Put your hand on the bow," and Elisha laid his own hands on the king's hands.

¹⁷Then he commanded, "Open that eastern window," and he opened it. Then he said, "Shoot!" So he shot an arrow. Elisha proclaimed, "This is the LORD's arrow, an arrow of victory over Aram, for you will completely conquer the Arameans at Aphek."

¹⁸Then he said, "Now pick up the other arrows and strike them against the ground." So the king picked them up and struck the ground three times. ¹⁹But the man of God was angry with him. "You should have struck the ground five or six times!" he exclaimed. "Then you would have beaten Aram until it was entirely destroyed. Now you will be victorious only three times."

12:21 As in Greek and Syriac versions; Hebrew reads *Jozabad*.
13:9 Hebrew *Joash*, a variant spelling of Jehoash; also in 13:10, 12, 13, 14, 25.

2 KINGS 14:27 | 321

[20] Then Elisha died and was buried.

Groups of Moabite raiders used to invade the land each spring. [21] Once when some Israelites were burying a man, they spied a band of these raiders. So they hastily threw the corpse into the tomb of Elisha and fled. But as soon as the body touched Elisha's bones, the dead man revived and jumped to his feet!

[22] King Hazael of Aram had oppressed Israel during the entire reign of King Jehoahaz. [23] But the LORD was gracious and merciful to the people of Israel, and they were not totally destroyed. He pitied them because of his covenant with Abraham, Isaac, and Jacob. And to this day he still has not completely destroyed them or banished them from his presence.

[24] King Hazael of Aram died, and his son Ben-hadad became the next king. [25] Then Jehoash son of Jehoahaz recaptured from Ben-hadad son of Hazael the towns that had been taken from Jehoash's father, Jehoahaz. Jehoash defeated Ben-hadad on three occasions, and he recovered the Israelite towns.

AMAZIAH RULES IN JUDAH

14 Amaziah son of Joash began to rule over Judah in the second year of the reign of King Jehoash* of Israel. [2] Amaziah was twenty-five years old when he became king, and he reigned in Jerusalem twenty-nine years. His mother was Jehoaddin from Jerusalem. [3] Amaziah did what was pleasing in the LORD's sight, but not like his ancestor David. Instead, he followed the example of his father, Joash. [4] Amaziah did not destroy the pagan shrines, and the people still offered sacrifices and burned incense there.

[5] When Amaziah was well established as king, he executed the officials who had assassinated his father. [6] However, he did not kill the children of the assassins, for he obeyed the command of the LORD as written by Moses in the Book of the Law: "Parents must not be put to death for the sins of their children, nor children for the sins of their parents. Those deserving to die must be put to death for their own crimes."*

[7] Amaziah also killed 10,000 Edomites in the Valley of Salt. He also conquered Sela and changed its name to Joktheel, as it is called to this day.

[8] One day Amaziah sent messengers with this challenge to Israel's king Jehoash, the son of Jehoahaz and grandson of Jehu: "Come and meet me in battle!"*

[9] But King Jehoash of Israel replied to King Amaziah of Judah with this story: "Out in the Lebanon mountains, a thistle sent a message to a mighty cedar tree: 'Give your daughter in marriage to my son.' But just then a wild animal of Lebanon came by and stepped on the thistle, crushing it!

[10] "You have indeed defeated Edom, and you are proud of it. But be content with your victory and stay at home! Why stir up trouble that will only bring disaster on you and the people of Judah?"

[11] But Amaziah refused to listen, so King Jehoash of Israel mobilized his army against King Amaziah of Judah. The two armies drew up their battle lines at Beth-shemesh in Judah. [12] Judah was routed by the army of Israel, and its army scattered and fled for home. [13] King Jehoash of Israel captured Judah's king, Amaziah son of Joash and grandson of Ahaziah, at Beth-shemesh. Then he marched to Jerusalem, where he demolished 600 feet* of Jerusalem's wall, from the Ephraim Gate to the Corner Gate. [14] He carried off all the gold and silver and all the articles from the Temple of the LORD. He also seized the treasures from the royal palace, along with hostages, and then returned to Samaria.

[15] The rest of the events in Jehoash's reign and everything he did, including the extent of his power and his war with King Amaziah of Judah, are recorded in *The Book of the History of the Kings of Israel.* [16] When Jehoash died, he was buried in Samaria with the kings of Israel. And his son Jeroboam II became the next king.

[17] King Amaziah of Judah lived for fifteen years after the death of King Jehoash of Israel. [18] The rest of the events in Amaziah's reign are recorded in *The Book of the History of the Kings of Judah.*

[19] There was a conspiracy against Amaziah's life in Jerusalem, and he fled to Lachish. But his enemies sent assassins after him, and they killed him there. [20] They brought his body back to Jerusalem on a horse, and he was buried with his ancestors in the City of David.

[21] All the people of Judah had crowned Amaziah's sixteen-year-old son, Uzziah,* as king in place of his father, Amaziah. [22] After his father's death, Uzziah rebuilt the town of Elath and restored it to Judah.

JEROBOAM II RULES IN ISRAEL

[23] Jeroboam II, the son of Jehoash, began to rule over Israel in the fifteenth year of King Amaziah's reign in Judah. He reigned in Samaria forty-one years. [24] He did what was evil in the LORD's sight. He refused to turn from the sins that Jeroboam son of Nebat had led Israel to commit. [25] Jeroboam II recovered the territories of Israel between Lebo-hamath and the Dead Sea,* just as the LORD, the God of Israel, had promised through Jonah son of Amittai, the prophet from Gath-hepher.

[26] For the LORD saw the bitter suffering of everyone in Israel, and that there was no one in Israel, slave or free, to help them. [27] And because the LORD had not said he would blot out the name of Israel completely, he used Jeroboam II, the son of Jehoash, to save them.

14:1 Hebrew *Joash,* a variant spelling of Jehoash; also in 14:13, 23, 27. 14:6 Deut 24:16. 14:8 Hebrew *Come, let us look one another in the face.* 14:13 Hebrew *400 cubits* [180 meters]. 14:21 Hebrew *Azariah,* a variant spelling of Uzziah. 14:25 Hebrew *the sea of the Arabah.*

28 The rest of the events in the reign of Jeroboam II and everything he did—including the extent of his power, his wars, and how he recovered for Israel both Damascus and Hamath, which had belonged to Judah*—are recorded in *The Book of the History of the Kings of Israel.* 29 When Jeroboam II died, he was buried in Samaria* with the kings of Israel. Then his son Zechariah became the next king.

UZZIAH RULES IN JUDAH

15 Uzziah* son of Amaziah began to rule over Judah in the twenty-seventh year of the reign of King Jeroboam II of Israel. 2 He was sixteen years old when he became king, and he reigned in Jerusalem fifty-two years. His mother was Jecoliah from Jerusalem.

3 He did what was pleasing in the LORD's sight, just as his father, Amaziah, had done. 4 But he did not destroy the pagan shrines, and the people still offered sacrifices and burned incense there. 5 The LORD struck the king with leprosy,* which lasted until the day he died. He lived in isolation in a separate house. The king's son Jotham was put in charge of the royal palace, and he governed the people of the land.

6 The rest of the events in Uzziah's reign and everything he did are recorded in *The Book of the History of the Kings of Judah.* 7 When Uzziah died, he was buried with his ancestors in the City of David. And his son Jotham became the next king.

ZECHARIAH RULES IN ISRAEL

8 Zechariah son of Jeroboam II began to rule over Israel in the thirty-eighth year of King Uzziah's reign in Judah. He reigned in Samaria six months. 9 Zechariah did what was evil in the LORD's sight, as his ancestors had done. He refused to turn from the sins that Jeroboam son of Nebat had led Israel to commit. 10 Then Shallum son of Jabesh conspired against Zechariah, assassinated him in public,* and became the next king.

11 The rest of the events in Zechariah's reign are recorded in *The Book of the History of the Kings of Israel.* 12 So the LORD's message to Jehu came true: "Your descendants will be kings of Israel down to the fourth generation."

SHALLUM RULES IN ISRAEL

13 Shallum son of Jabesh began to rule over Israel in the thirty-ninth year of King Uzziah's reign in Judah. Shallum reigned in Samaria only one month. 14 Then Menahem son of Gadi went to Samaria from Tirzah and assassinated him, and he became the next king.

15 The rest of the events in Shallum's reign, including his conspiracy, are recorded in *The Book of the History of the Kings of Israel.*

MENAHEM RULES IN ISRAEL

16 At that time Menahem destroyed the town of Tappuah* and all the surrounding countryside as far as Tirzah, because its citizens refused to surrender the town. He killed the entire population and ripped open the pregnant women.

17 Menahem son of Gadi began to rule over Israel in the thirty-ninth year of King Uzziah's reign in Judah. He reigned in Samaria ten years. 18 But Menahem did what was evil in the LORD's sight. During his entire reign, he refused to turn from the sins that Jeroboam son of Nebat had led Israel to commit.

19 Then King Tiglath-pileser* of Assyria invaded the land. But Menahem paid him thirty-seven tons* of silver to gain his support in tightening his grip on royal power. 20 Menahem extorted the money from the rich of Israel, demanding that each of them pay fifty pieces* of silver to the king of Assyria. So the king of Assyria turned from attacking Israel and did not stay in the land.

21 The rest of the events in Menahem's reign and everything he did are recorded in *The Book of the History of the Kings of Israel.* 22 When Menahem died, his son Pekahiah became the next king.

PEKAHIAH RULES IN ISRAEL

23 Pekahiah son of Menahem began to rule over Israel in the fiftieth year of King Uzziah's reign in Judah. He reigned in Samaria two years. 24 But Pekahiah did what was evil in the LORD's sight. He refused to turn from the sins that Jeroboam son of Nebat had led Israel to commit.

25 Then Pekah son of Remaliah, the commander of Pekahiah's army, conspired against him. With fifty men from Gilead, Pekah assassinated the king, along with Argob and Arieh, in the citadel of the palace at Samaria. And Pekah reigned in his place.

26 The rest of the events in Pekahiah's reign and everything he did are recorded in *The Book of the History of the Kings of Israel.*

PEKAH RULES IN ISRAEL

27 Pekah son of Remaliah began to rule over Israel in the fifty-second year of King Uzziah's reign in Judah. He reigned in Samaria twenty years. 28 But Pekah did what was evil in the LORD's sight. He refused to turn from the sins that Jeroboam son of Nebat had led Israel to commit.

29 During Pekah's reign, King Tiglath-pileser of Assyria attacked Israel again, and he captured the towns of Ijon, Abel-beth-maacah, Janoah, Kedesh, and Hazor. He also conquered the regions of Gilead, Galilee, and all of Naphtali, and he took the people to Assyria as captives. 30 Then Hoshea son of Elah conspired against Pekah and

14:28 Or *to Yaudi.* The meaning of the Hebrew is uncertain. 14:29 As in some Greek manuscripts; Hebrew lacks *he was buried in Samaria.* 15:1 Hebrew *Azariah,* a variant spelling of Uzziah; also in 15:6, 7, 8, 17, 23, 27. 15:5 Or *with a contagious skin disease.* The Hebrew word used here and throughout this passage can describe various skin diseases. 15:10 Or *at Ibleam.* 15:16 As in some Greek manuscripts; Hebrew reads *Tiphsah.* 15:19a Hebrew *Pul,* another name for Tiglath-pileser. 15:19b Hebrew *1,000 talents* [34 metric tons]. 15:20 Hebrew *50 shekels* [20 ounces or 570 grams].

assassinated him. He began to rule over Israel in the twentieth year of Jotham son of Uzziah. ³¹The rest of the events in Pekah's reign and everything he did are recorded in *The Book of the History of the Kings of Israel.*

JOTHAM RULES IN JUDAH

³²Jotham son of Uzziah began to rule over Judah in the second year of King Pekah's reign in Israel. ³³He was twenty-five years old when he became king, and he reigned in Jerusalem sixteen years. His mother was Jerusha, the daughter of Zadok.

³⁴Jotham did what was pleasing in the LORD's sight. He did everything his father, Uzziah, had done. ³⁵But he did not destroy the pagan shrines, and the people still offered sacrifices and burned incense there. He rebuilt the upper gate of the Temple of the LORD.

³⁶The rest of the events in Jotham's reign and everything he did are recorded in *The Book of the History of the Kings of Judah.* ³⁷In those days the LORD began to send King Rezin of Aram and King Pekah of Israel to attack Judah. ³⁸When Jotham died, he was buried with his ancestors in the City of David. And his son Ahaz became the next king.

AHAZ RULES IN JUDAH

16 Ahaz son of Jotham began to rule over Judah in the seventeenth year of King Pekah's reign in Israel. ²Ahaz was twenty years old when he became king, and he reigned in Jerusalem sixteen years. He did not do what was pleasing in the sight of the LORD his God, as his ancestor David had done. ³Instead, he followed the example of the kings of Israel, even sacrificing his own son in the fire.* In this way, he followed the detestable practices of the pagan nations the LORD had driven from the land ahead of the Israelites. ⁴He offered sacrifices and burned incense at the pagan shrines and on the hills and under every green tree.

⁵Then King Rezin of Aram and King Pekah of Israel came up to attack Jerusalem. They besieged Ahaz but could not conquer him. ⁶At that time the king of Edom* recovered the town of Elath for Edom.* He drove out the people of Judah and sent Edomites* to live there, as they do to this day.

⁷King Ahaz sent messengers to King Tiglath-pileser of Assyria with this message: "I am your servant and your vassal.* Come up and rescue me from the attacking armies of Aram and Israel." ⁸Then Ahaz took the silver and gold from the Temple of the LORD and the palace treasury and sent it as a payment to the Assyrian king. ⁹So the king of Assyria attacked the Aramean capital of Damascus and led its population away as captives, resettling them in Kir. He also killed King Rezin.

¹⁰King Ahaz then went to Damascus to meet with King Tiglath-pileser of Assyria. While he was there, he took special note of the altar. Then he sent a model of the altar to Uriah the priest, along with its design in full detail. ¹¹Uriah followed the king's instructions and built an altar just like it, and it was ready before the king returned from Damascus. ¹²When the king returned, he inspected the altar and made offerings on it. ¹³He presented a burnt offering and a grain offering, he poured out a liquid offering, and he sprinkled the blood of peace offerings on the altar.

¹⁴Then King Ahaz removed the old bronze altar from its place in front of the LORD's Temple, between the entrance and the new altar, and placed it on the north side of the new altar. ¹⁵He told Uriah the priest, "Use the new altar* for the morning sacrifices of burnt offering, the evening grain offering, the king's burnt offering and grain offering, and the burnt offerings of all the people, as well as their grain offerings and liquid offerings. Sprinkle the blood from all the burnt offerings and sacrifices on the new altar. The bronze altar will be for my personal use only." ¹⁶Uriah the priest did just as King Ahaz commanded him.

¹⁷Then the king removed the side panels and basins from the portable water carts. He also removed the great bronze basin called the Sea from the backs of the bronze oxen and placed it on the stone pavement. ¹⁸In deference to the king of Assyria, he also removed the canopy that had been constructed inside the palace for use on the Sabbath day,* as well as the king's outer entrance to the Temple of the LORD.

¹⁹The rest of the events in Ahaz's reign and everything he did are recorded in *The Book of the History of the Kings of Judah.* ²⁰When Ahaz died, he was buried with his ancestors in the City of David. Then his son Hezekiah became the next king.

HOSHEA RULES IN ISRAEL

17 Hoshea son of Elah began to rule over Israel in the twelfth year of King Ahaz's reign in Judah. He reigned in Samaria nine years. ²He did what was evil in the LORD's sight, but not to the same extent as the kings of Israel who ruled before him.

³King Shalmaneser of Assyria attacked King Hoshea, so Hoshea was forced to pay heavy tribute to Assyria. ⁴But Hoshea stopped paying the annual tribute and conspired against the king of Assyria by asking King So of Egypt* to help him shake free of Assyria's power. When the king of Assyria discovered this treachery, he seized Hoshea and put him in prison.

16:3 Or *even making his son pass through the fire.* 16:6a As in Latin Vulgate; Hebrew reads *Rezin king of Aram.* 16:6b As in Latin Vulgate; Hebrew reads *Aram.* 16:6c As in Greek version, Latin Vulgate, and an alternate reading of the Masoretic Text; the other alternate reads *Arameans.* 16:7 Hebrew *your son.* 16:15 Hebrew *the great altar.* 16:18 The meaning of the Hebrew is uncertain. 17:4 Or *by asking the king of Egypt at Sais.*

SAMARIA FALLS TO ASSYRIA

⁵Then the king of Assyria invaded the entire land, and for three years he besieged the city of Samaria. ⁶Finally, in the ninth year of King Hoshea's reign, Samaria fell, and the people of Israel were exiled to Assyria. They were settled in colonies in Halah, along the banks of the Habor River in Gozan, and in the cities of the Medes.

⁷This disaster came upon the people of Israel because they worshiped other gods. They sinned against the LORD their God, who had brought them safely out of Egypt and had rescued them from the power of Pharaoh, the king of Egypt. ⁸They had followed the practices of the pagan nations the LORD had driven from the land ahead of them, as well as the practices the kings of Israel had introduced. ⁹The people of Israel had also secretly done many things that were not pleasing to the LORD their God. They built pagan shrines for themselves in all their towns, from the smallest outpost to the largest walled city. ¹⁰They set up sacred pillars and Asherah poles at the top of every hill and under every green tree. ¹¹They offered sacrifices on all the hilltops, just like the nations the LORD had driven from the land ahead of them. So the people of Israel had done many evil things, arousing the LORD's anger. ¹²Yes, they worshiped idols,* despite the LORD's specific and repeated warnings.

¹³Again and again the LORD had sent his prophets and seers to warn both Israel and Judah: "Turn from all your evil ways. Obey my commands and decrees—the entire law that I commanded your ancestors to obey, and that I gave you through my servants the prophets." ¹⁴But the Israelites would not listen. They were as stubborn as their ancestors who had refused to believe in the LORD their God. ¹⁵They rejected his decrees and the covenant he had made with their ancestors, and they despised all his warnings. They worshiped worthless idols, so they became worthless themselves. They followed the example of the nations around them, disobeying the LORD's command not to imitate them.

¹⁶They rejected all the commands of the LORD their God and made two calves from metal. They set up an Asherah pole and worshiped Baal and all the forces of heaven. ¹⁷They even sacrificed their own sons and daughters in the fire.* They consulted fortune-tellers and practiced sorcery and sold themselves to evil, arousing the LORD's anger.

¹⁸Because the LORD was very angry with Israel, he swept them away from his presence. Only the tribe of Judah remained in the land. ¹⁹But even the people of Judah refused to obey the commands of the LORD their God, for they followed the evil practices that Israel had introduced. ²⁰The LORD rejected all the descendants of Israel. He punished them by handing them over to their attackers until he had banished Israel from his presence.

²¹For when the LORD* tore Israel away from the kingdom of David, they chose Jeroboam son of Nebat as their king. But Jeroboam drew Israel away from following the LORD and made them commit a great sin. ²²And the people of Israel persisted in all the evil ways of Jeroboam. They did not turn from these sins ²³until the LORD finally swept them away from his presence, just as all his prophets had warned. So Israel was exiled from their land to Assyria, where they remain to this day.

FOREIGNERS SETTLE IN ISRAEL

²⁴The king of Assyria transported groups of people from Babylon, Cuthah, Avva, Hamath, and Sepharvaim and resettled them in the towns of Samaria, replacing the people of Israel. They took possession of Samaria and lived in its towns. ²⁵But since these foreign settlers did not worship the LORD when they first arrived, the LORD sent lions among them, which killed some of them. ²⁶So a message was sent to the king of Assyria: "The people you have sent to live in the towns of Samaria do not know the religious customs of the God of the land. He has sent lions among them to destroy them because they have not worshiped him correctly."

²⁷The king of Assyria then commanded, "Send one of the exiled priests back to Samaria. Let him live there and teach the new residents the religious customs of the God of the land." ²⁸So one of the priests who had been exiled from Samaria returned to Bethel and taught the new residents how to worship the LORD.

²⁹But these various groups of foreigners also continued to worship their own gods. In town after town where they lived, they placed their idols at the pagan shrines that the people of Samaria had built. ³⁰Those from Babylon worshiped idols of their god Succoth-benoth. Those from Cuthah worshiped their god Nergal. And those from Hamath worshiped Ashima. ³¹The Avvites worshiped their gods Nibhaz and Tartak. And the people from Sepharvaim even burned their own children as sacrifices to their gods Adrammelech and Anammelech.

³²These new residents worshiped the LORD, but they also appointed from among themselves all sorts of people as priests to offer sacrifices at their places of worship. ³³And though they worshiped the LORD, they continued to follow their own gods according to the religious customs of the nations from which they came. ³⁴And this is still going on today. They continue to follow their former practices instead of truly worshiping the LORD and obeying the decrees, regulations, instructions, and commands he gave the descendants of Jacob, whose name he changed to Israel.

17:12 The Hebrew term (literally *round things*) probably alludes to dung.   17:17 Or *They even made their sons and daughters pass through the fire.*   17:21 Hebrew *he;* compare 1 Kgs 11:31-32.

[35] For the LORD had made a covenant with the descendants of Jacob and commanded them: "Do not worship any other gods or bow before them or serve them or offer sacrifices to them. [36] But worship only the LORD, who brought you out of Egypt with great strength and a powerful arm. Bow down to him alone, and offer sacrifices only to him. [37] Be careful at all times to obey the decrees, regulations, instructions, and commands that he wrote for you. You must not worship other gods. [38] Do not forget the covenant I made with you, and do not worship other gods. [39] You must worship only the LORD your God. He is the one who will rescue you from all your enemies."

[40] But the people would not listen and continued to follow their former practices. [41] So while these new residents worshiped the LORD, they also worshiped their idols. And to this day their descendants do the same.

HEZEKIAH RULES IN JUDAH

18 Hezekiah son of Ahaz began to rule over Judah in the third year of King Hoshea's reign in Israel. [2] He was twenty-five years old when he became king, and he reigned in Jerusalem twenty-nine years. His mother was Abijah,* the daughter of Zechariah. [3] He did what was pleasing in the LORD's sight, just as his ancestor David had done. [4] He removed the pagan shrines, smashed the sacred pillars, and cut down the Asherah poles. He broke up the bronze serpent that Moses had made, because the people of Israel had been offering sacrifices to it. The bronze serpent was called Nehushtan.*

[5] Hezekiah trusted in the LORD, the God of Israel. There was no one like him among all the kings of Judah, either before or after his time. [6] He remained faithful to the LORD in everything, and he carefully obeyed all the commands the LORD had given Moses. [7] So the LORD was with him, and Hezekiah was successful in everything he did. He revolted against the king of Assyria and refused to pay him tribute. [8] He also conquered the Philistines as far distant as Gaza and its territory, from their smallest outpost to their largest walled city.

[9] During the fourth year of Hezekiah's reign, which was the seventh year of King Hoshea's reign in Israel, King Shalmaneser of Assyria attacked the city of Samaria and began a siege against it. [10] Three years later, during the sixth year of King Hezekiah's reign and the ninth year of King Hoshea's reign in Israel, Samaria fell. [11] At that time the king of Assyria exiled the Israelites to Assyria and placed them in colonies in Halah, along the banks of the Habor River in Gozan, and in the cities of the Medes. [12] For they refused to listen to the LORD their God and obey him. Instead, they violated his covenant—all the laws that Moses the LORD's servant had commanded them to obey.

ASSYRIA INVADES JUDAH

[13] In the fourteenth year of King Hezekiah's reign,* King Sennacherib of Assyria came to attack the fortified towns of Judah and conquered them. [14] King Hezekiah sent this message to the king of Assyria at Lachish: "I have done wrong. I will pay whatever tribute money you demand if you will only withdraw." The king of Assyria then demanded a settlement of more than eleven tons of silver and one ton of gold.* [15] To gather this amount, King Hezekiah used all the silver stored in the Temple of the LORD and in the palace treasury. [16] Hezekiah even stripped the gold from the doors of the LORD's Temple and from the doorposts he had overlaid with gold, and he gave it all to the Assyrian king.

[17] Nevertheless, the king of Assyria sent his commander in chief, his field commander, and his chief of staff* from Lachish with a huge army to confront King Hezekiah in Jerusalem. The Assyrians took up a position beside the aqueduct that feeds water into the upper pool, near the road leading to the field where cloth is washed.* [18] They summoned King Hezekiah, but the king sent these officials to meet with them: Eliakim son of Hilkiah, the palace administrator; Shebna the court secretary; and Joah son of Asaph, the royal historian.

SENNACHERIB THREATENS JERUSALEM

[19] Then the Assyrian king's chief of staff told them to give this message to Hezekiah:

"This is what the great king of Assyria says: What are you trusting in that makes you so confident? [20] Do you think that mere words can substitute for military skill and strength? Who are you counting on, that you have rebelled against me? [21] On Egypt? If you lean on Egypt, it will be like a reed that splinters beneath your weight and pierces your hand. Pharaoh, the king of Egypt, is completely unreliable!

[22] "But perhaps you will say to me, 'We are trusting in the LORD our God!' But isn't he the one who was insulted by Hezekiah? Didn't Hezekiah tear down his shrines and altars and make everyone in Judah and Jerusalem worship only at the altar here in Jerusalem?

[23] "I'll tell you what! Strike a bargain with my master, the king of Assyria. I will give you 2,000 horses if you can find that many men to ride on them! [24] With your tiny army, how can you think of challenging even the weakest contingent of my master's troops,

18:2 As in parallel text at 2 Chr 29:1; Hebrew reads *Abi*, a variant spelling of Abijah. 18:4 *Nehushtan* sounds like the Hebrew terms that mean "snake," "bronze," and "unclean thing." 18:13 The fourteenth year of Hezekiah's reign was 701 B.C. 18:14 Hebrew *300 talents* [10 metric tons] *of silver and 30 talents* [1 metric ton] *of gold.* 18:17a Or *the rabshakeh;* also in 18:19, 26, 27, 28, 37. 18:17b Or *bleached.*

even with the help of Egypt's chariots and charioteers? [25] What's more, do you think we have invaded your land without the LORD's direction? The LORD himself told us, 'Attack this land and destroy it!'"

[26] Then Eliakim son of Hilkiah, Shebna, and Joah said to the Assyrian chief of staff, "Please speak to us in Aramaic, for we understand it well. Don't speak in Hebrew,* for the people on the wall will hear."

[27] But Sennacherib's chief of staff replied, "Do you think my master sent this message only to you and your master? He wants all the people to hear it, for when we put this city under siege, they will suffer along with you. They will be so hungry and thirsty that they will eat their own dung and drink their own urine."

[28] Then the chief of staff stood and shouted in Hebrew to the people on the wall, "Listen to this message from the great king of Assyria! [29] This is what the king says: Don't let Hezekiah deceive you. He will never be able to rescue you from my power. [30] Don't let him fool you into trusting in the LORD by saying, 'The LORD will surely rescue us. This city will never fall into the hands of the Assyrian king!'

[31] "Don't listen to Hezekiah! These are the terms the king of Assyria is offering: Make peace with me—open the gates and come out. Then each of you can continue eating from your own grapevine and fig tree and drinking from your own well. [32] Then I will arrange to take you to another land like this one—a land of grain and new wine, bread and vineyards, olive groves and honey. Choose life instead of death!

"Don't listen to Hezekiah when he tries to mislead you by saying, 'The LORD will rescue us!' [33] Have the gods of any other nations ever saved their people from the king of Assyria? [34] What happened to the gods of Hamath and Arpad? And what about the gods of Sepharvaim, Hena, and Ivvah? Did any god rescue Samaria from my power? [35] What god of any nation has ever been able to save its people from my power? So what makes you think that the LORD can rescue Jerusalem from me?"

[36] But the people were silent and did not utter a word because Hezekiah had commanded them, "Do not answer him."

[37] Then Eliakim son of Hilkiah, the palace administrator; Shebna the court secretary; and Joah son of Asaph, the royal historian, went back to Hezekiah. They tore their clothes in despair, and they went in to see the king and told him what the Assyrian chief of staff had said.

HEZEKIAH SEEKS THE LORD'S HELP

19 When King Hezekiah heard their report, he tore his clothes and put on burlap and went into the Temple of the LORD. [2] And he sent Eliakim the palace administrator, Shebna the court secretary, and the leading priests, all dressed in burlap, to the prophet Isaiah son of Amoz. [3] They told him, "This is what King Hezekiah says: Today is a day of trouble, insults, and disgrace. It is like when a child is ready to be born, but the mother has no strength to deliver the baby. [4] But perhaps the LORD your God has heard the Assyrian chief of staff,* sent by the king to defy the living God, and will punish him for his words. Oh, pray for those of us who are left!"

[5] After King Hezekiah's officials delivered the king's message to Isaiah, [6] the prophet replied, "Say to your master, 'This is what the LORD says: Do not be disturbed by this blasphemous speech against me from the Assyrian king's messengers. [7] Listen! I myself will move against him,* and the king will receive a message that he is needed at home. So he will return to his land, where I will have him killed with a sword.'"

[8] Meanwhile, the Assyrian chief of staff left Jerusalem and went to consult the king of Assyria, who had left Lachish and was attacking Libnah.

[9] Soon afterward King Sennacherib received word that King Tirhakah of Ethiopia* was leading an army to fight against him. Before leaving to meet the attack, he sent messengers back to Hezekiah in Jerusalem with this message:

[10] "This message is for King Hezekiah of Judah. Don't let your God, in whom you trust, deceive you with promises that Jerusalem will not be captured by the king of Assyria. [11] You know perfectly well what the kings of Assyria have done wherever they have gone. They have completely destroyed everyone who stood in their way! Why should you be any different? [12] Have the gods of other nations rescued them—such nations as Gozan, Haran, Rezeph, and the people of Eden who were in Tel-assar? My predecessors destroyed them all! [13] What happened to the king of Hamath and the king of Arpad? What happened to the kings of Sepharvaim, Hena, and Ivvah?"

[14] After Hezekiah received the letter from the messengers and read it, he went up to the LORD's Temple and spread it out before the LORD. [15] And Hezekiah prayed this prayer before the LORD: "O LORD, God of Israel, you are enthroned between the mighty cherubim! You alone are God of all the kingdoms of the earth. You alone created the heavens and the earth. [16] Bend down, O LORD, and listen! Open your eyes, O LORD, and see! Listen to Sennacherib's words of defiance against the living God.

18:26 Hebrew *in the dialect of Judah;* also in 18:28.   19:4 Or *the rabshakeh;* also in 19:8.   19:7 Hebrew *I will put a spirit in him.* 19:9 Hebrew *of Cush.*

[17] "It is true, LORD, that the kings of Assyria have destroyed all these nations. [18] And they have thrown the gods of these nations into the fire and burned them. But of course the Assyrians could destroy them! They were not gods at all—only idols of wood and stone shaped by human hands. [19] Now, O LORD our God, rescue us from his power; then all the kingdoms of the earth will know that you alone, O LORD, are God."

ISAIAH PREDICTS JUDAH'S DELIVERANCE

[20] Then Isaiah son of Amoz sent this message to Hezekiah: "This is what the LORD, the God of Israel, says: I have heard your prayer about King Sennacherib of Assyria. [21] And the LORD has spoken this word against him:

"The virgin daughter of Zion
  despises you and laughs at you.
The daughter of Jerusalem
  shakes her head in derision as you flee.

[22] "Whom have you been defying and
    ridiculing?
  Against whom did you raise your voice?
At whom did you look with such
    haughty eyes?
  It was the Holy One of Israel!
[23] By your messengers you have defied
    the Lord.
  You have said, 'With my many chariots
I have conquered the highest mountains—
  yes, the remotest peaks of Lebanon.
I have cut down its tallest cedars
  and its finest cypress trees.
I have reached its farthest corners
  and explored its deepest forests.
[24] I have dug wells in many foreign lands
  and refreshed myself with their water.
With the sole of my foot
  I stopped up all the rivers of Egypt!'

[25] "But have you not heard?
  I decided this long ago.
Long ago I planned it,
  and now I am making it happen.
I planned for you to crush fortified cities
  into heaps of rubble.
[26] That is why their people have so little power
  and are so frightened and confused.
They are as weak as grass,
  as easily trampled as tender green shoots.
They are like grass sprouting on a housetop,
  scorched before it can grow lush and tall.

[27] "But I know you well—
  where you stay
and when you come and go.
  I know the way you have raged against me.
[28] And because of your raging against me
  and your arrogance, which I have heard
    for myself,

I will put my hook in your nose
  and my bit in your mouth.
I will make you return
  by the same road on which you came."

[29] Then Isaiah said to Hezekiah, "Here is the proof that what I say is true:

"This year you will eat only what grows up
    by itself,
  and next year you will eat what springs
    up from that.
But in the third year you will plant crops
    and harvest them;
  you will tend vineyards and eat their fruit.
[30] And you who are left in Judah,
  who have escaped the ravages of
    the siege,
will put roots down in your own soil
  and will grow up and flourish.
[31] For a remnant of my people will spread out
    from Jerusalem,
  a group of survivors from Mount Zion.
The passionate commitment of the LORD of
    Heaven's Armies*
  will make this happen!

[32] "And this is what the LORD says about the king of Assyria:

"His armies will not enter Jerusalem.
  They will not even shoot an arrow at it.
They will not march outside its gates with
    their shields
  nor build banks of earth against its walls.
[33] The king will return to his own country
  by the same road on which he came.
He will not enter this city,
  says the LORD.
[34] For my own honor and for the sake of my
    servant David,
  I will defend this city and protect it."

[35] That night the angel of the LORD went out to the Assyrian camp and killed 185,000 Assyrian soldiers. When the surviving Assyrians* woke up the next morning, they found corpses everywhere. [36] Then King Sennacherib of Assyria broke camp and returned to his own land. He went home to his capital of Nineveh and stayed there.

[37] One day while he was worshiping in the temple of his god Nisroch, his sons* Adrammelech and Sharezer killed him with their swords. They then escaped to the land of Ararat, and another son, Esarhaddon, became the next king of Assyria.

19:31 As in Greek and Syriac versions, Latin Vulgate, and an alternate reading of the Masoretic Text (see also Isa 37:32); the other alternate reads the LORD. 19:35 Hebrew When they. 19:37 As in Greek version and an alternate reading of the Masoretic Text (see also Isa 37:38); the other alternate reading lacks his sons.

HEZEKIAH'S SICKNESS AND RECOVERY

20 About that time Hezekiah became deathly ill, and the prophet Isaiah son of Amoz went to visit him. He gave the king this message: "This is what the LORD says: Set your affairs in order, for you are going to die. You will not recover from this illness."

2 When Hezekiah heard this, he turned his face to the wall and prayed to the LORD, 3 "Remember, O LORD, how I have always been faithful to you and have served you single-mindedly, always doing what pleases you." Then he broke down and wept bitterly.

4 But before Isaiah had left the middle courtyard,* this message came to him from the LORD: 5 "Go back to Hezekiah, the leader of my people. Tell him, 'This is what the LORD, the God of your ancestor David, says: I have heard your prayer and seen your tears. I will heal you, and three days from now you will get out of bed and go to the Temple of the LORD. 6 I will add fifteen years to your life, and I will rescue you and this city from the king of Assyria. I will defend this city for my own honor and for the sake of my servant David.'"

7 Then Isaiah said, "Make an ointment from figs." So Hezekiah's servants spread the ointment over the boil, and Hezekiah recovered!

8 Meanwhile, Hezekiah had said to Isaiah, "What sign will the LORD give to prove that he will heal me and that I will go to the Temple of the LORD three days from now?"

9 Isaiah replied, "This is the sign from the LORD to prove that he will do as he promised. Would you like the shadow on the sundial to go forward ten steps or backward ten steps?*"

10 "The shadow always moves forward," Hezekiah replied, "so that would be easy. Make it go ten steps backward instead." 11 So Isaiah the prophet asked the LORD to do this, and he caused the shadow to move ten steps backward on the sundial* of Ahaz!

ENVOYS FROM BABYLON

12 Soon after this, Merodach-baladan* son of Baladan, king of Babylon, sent Hezekiah his best wishes and a gift, for he had heard that Hezekiah had been very sick. 13 Hezekiah received the Babylonian envoys and showed them everything in his treasure-houses—the silver, the gold, the spices, and the aromatic oils. He also took them to see his armory and showed them everything in his royal treasuries! There was nothing in his palace or kingdom that Hezekiah did not show them.

14 Then Isaiah the prophet went to King Hezekiah and asked him, "What did those men want? Where were they from?"

Hezekiah replied, "They came from the distant land of Babylon."

15 "What did they see in your palace?" Isaiah asked.

"They saw everything," Hezekiah replied. "I showed them everything I own—all my royal treasuries."

16 Then Isaiah said to Hezekiah, "Listen to this message from the LORD: 17 The time is coming when everything in your palace—all the treasures stored up by your ancestors until now—will be carried off to Babylon. Nothing will be left, says the LORD. 18 Some of your very own sons will be taken away into exile. They will become eunuchs who will serve in the palace of Babylon's king."

19 Then Hezekiah said to Isaiah, "This message you have given me from the LORD is good." For the king was thinking, "At least there will be peace and security during my lifetime."

20 The rest of the events in Hezekiah's reign, including the extent of his power and how he built a pool and dug a tunnel* to bring water into the city, are recorded in *The Book of the History of the Kings of Judah.* 21 Hezekiah died, and his son Manasseh became the next king.

MANASSEH RULES IN JUDAH

21 Manasseh was twelve years old when he became king, and he reigned in Jerusalem fifty-five years. His mother was Hephzibah. 2 He did what was evil in the LORD's sight, following the detestable practices of the pagan nations that the LORD had driven from the land ahead of the Israelites. 3 He rebuilt the pagan shrines his father, Hezekiah, had destroyed. He constructed altars for Baal and set up an Asherah pole, just as King Ahab of Israel had done. He also bowed before all the powers of the heavens and worshiped them.

4 He built pagan altars in the Temple of the LORD, the place where the LORD had said, "My name will remain in Jerusalem forever." 5 He built these altars for all the powers of the heavens in both courtyards of the LORD's Temple. 6 Manasseh also sacrificed his own son in the fire.* He practiced sorcery and divination, and he consulted with mediums and psychics. He did much that was evil in the LORD's sight, arousing his anger.

7 Manasseh even made a carved image of Asherah and set it up in the Temple, the very place where the LORD had told David and his son Solomon: "My name will be honored forever in this Temple and in Jerusalem—the city I have chosen from among all the tribes of Israel. 8 If the Israelites will be careful to obey my commands—all the laws my servant Moses gave them—I will not send them into exile from this land that I gave

20:4 As in Greek version and an alternate reading in the Masoretic Text; the other alternate reads *the middle of the city.* 20:9 Or *The shadow on the sundial has gone forward ten steps; do you want it to go backward ten steps?* 20:11 Hebrew *the steps.* 20:12 As in some Hebrew manuscripts and Greek and Syriac versions (see also Isa 39:1); Masoretic Text reads *Berodach-baladan.* 20:20 Hebrew *watercourse.* 21:6 Or *also made his son pass through the fire.*

their ancestors." [9] But the people refused to listen, and Manasseh led them to do even more evil than the pagan nations that the LORD had destroyed when the people of Israel entered the land.

[10] Then the LORD said through his servants the prophets: [11] "King Manasseh of Judah has done many detestable things. He is even more wicked than the Amorites, who lived in this land before Israel. He has caused the people of Judah to sin with his idols.* [12] So this is what the LORD, the God of Israel, says: I will bring such disaster on Jerusalem and Judah that the ears of those who hear about it will tingle with horror. [13] I will judge Jerusalem by the same standard I used for Samaria and the same measure* I used for the family of Ahab. I will wipe away the people of Jerusalem as one wipes a dish and turns it upside down. [14] Then I will reject even the remnant of my own people who are left, and I will hand them over as plunder for their enemies. [15] For they have done great evil in my sight and have angered me ever since their ancestors came out of Egypt."

[16] Manasseh also murdered many innocent people until Jerusalem was filled from one end to the other with innocent blood. This was in addition to the sin that he caused the people of Judah to commit, leading them to do evil in the LORD's sight.

[17] The rest of the events in Manasseh's reign and everything he did, including the sins he committed, are recorded in *The Book of the History of the Kings of Judah*. [18] When Manasseh died, he was buried in the palace garden, the garden of Uzza. Then his son Amon became the next king.

AMON RULES IN JUDAH

[19] Amon was twenty-two years old when he became king, and he reigned in Jerusalem two years. His mother was Meshullemeth, the daughter of Haruz from Jotbah. [20] He did what was evil in the LORD's sight, just as his father, Manasseh, had done. [21] He followed the example of his father, worshiping the same idols his father had worshiped. [22] He abandoned the LORD, the God of his ancestors, and he refused to follow the LORD's ways.

[23] Then Amon's own officials conspired against him and assassinated him in his palace. [24] But the people of the land killed all those who had conspired against King Amon, and they made his son Josiah the next king.

[25] The rest of the events in Amon's reign and what he did are recorded in *The Book of the History of the Kings of Judah*. [26] He was buried in his tomb in the garden of Uzza. Then his son Josiah became the next king.

JOSIAH RULES IN JUDAH

22 Josiah was eight years old when he became king, and he reigned in Jerusalem thirty-one years. His mother was Jedidah, the daughter of Adaiah from Bozkath. [2] He did what was pleasing in the LORD's sight and followed the example of his ancestor David. He did not turn away from doing what was right.

[3] In the eighteenth year of his reign, King Josiah sent Shaphan son of Azaliah and grandson of Meshullam, the court secretary, to the Temple of the LORD. He told him, [4] "Go to Hilkiah the high priest and have him count the money the gatekeepers have collected from the people at the LORD's Temple. [5] Entrust this money to the men assigned to supervise the restoration of the LORD's Temple. Then they can use it to pay workers to repair the Temple. [6] They will need to hire carpenters, builders, and masons. Also have them buy the timber and the finished stone needed to repair the Temple. [7] But don't require the construction supervisors to keep account of the money they receive, for they are honest and trustworthy men."

HILKIAH DISCOVERS GOD'S LAW

[8] Hilkiah the high priest said to Shaphan the court secretary, "I have found the Book of the Law in the LORD's Temple!" Then Hilkiah gave the scroll to Shaphan, and he read it.

[9] Shaphan went to the king and reported, "Your officials have turned over the money collected at the Temple of the LORD to the workers and supervisors at the Temple." [10] Shaphan also told the king, "Hilkiah the priest has given me a scroll." So Shaphan read it to the king.

[11] When the king heard what was written in the Book of the Law, he tore his clothes in despair. [12] Then he gave these orders to Hilkiah the priest, Ahikam son of Shaphan, Acbor son of Micaiah, Shaphan the court secretary, and Asaiah the king's personal adviser: [13] "Go to the Temple and speak to the LORD for me and for the people and for all Judah. Inquire about the words written in this scroll that has been found. For the LORD's great anger is burning against us because our ancestors have not obeyed the words in this scroll. We have not been doing everything it says we must do."

[14] So Hilkiah the priest, Ahikam, Acbor, Shaphan, and Asaiah went to the New Quarter* of Jerusalem to consult with the prophet Huldah. She was the wife of Shallum son of Tikvah, son of Harhas, the keeper of the Temple wardrobe.

[15] She said to them, "The LORD, the God of Israel, has spoken! Go back and tell the man who sent you, [16] 'This is what the LORD says: I am going to bring disaster on this city* and its people. All the words written in the scroll that the king of Judah has read will come true. [17] For my people have abandoned me and offered sacrifices to pagan gods, and I am very angry with them for

---

21:11 The Hebrew term (literally *round things*) probably alludes to dung; also in 21:21. 21:13 Hebrew *the same plumb line I used for Samaria and the same plumb bob*. 22:14 Or *the Second Quarter*, a newer section of Jerusalem. Hebrew reads *the Mishneh*. 22:16 Hebrew *this place*; also in 22:19, 20.

everything they have done. My anger will burn against this place, and it will not be quenched.'

¹⁸ "But go to the king of Judah who sent you to seek the Lord and tell him: 'This is what the Lord, the God of Israel, says concerning the message you have just heard: ¹⁹ You were sorry and humbled yourself before the Lord when you heard what I said against this city and its people—that this land would be cursed and become desolate. You tore your clothing in despair and wept before me in repentance. And I have indeed heard you, says the Lord. ²⁰ So I will not send the promised disaster until after you have died and been buried in peace. You will not see the disaster I am going to bring on this city.'"

So they took her message back to the king.

JOSIAH'S RELIGIOUS REFORMS

23 Then the king summoned all the elders of Judah and Jerusalem. ² And the king went up to the Temple of the Lord with all the people of Judah and Jerusalem, along with the priests and the prophets—all the people from the least to the greatest. There the king read to them the entire Book of the Covenant that had been found in the Lord's Temple. ³ The king took his place of authority beside the pillar and renewed the covenant in the Lord's presence. He pledged to obey the Lord by keeping all his commands, laws, and decrees with all his heart and soul. In this way, he confirmed all the terms of the covenant that were written in the scroll, and all the people pledged themselves to the covenant.

⁴ Then the king instructed Hilkiah the high priest and the priests of the second rank and the Temple gatekeepers to remove from the Lord's Temple all the articles that were used to worship Baal, Asherah, and all the powers of the heavens. The king had all these things burned outside Jerusalem on the terraces of the Kidron Valley, and he carried the ashes away to Bethel. ⁵ He did away with the idolatrous priests, who had been appointed by the previous kings of Judah, for they had offered sacrifices at the pagan shrines throughout Judah and even in the vicinity of Jerusalem. They had also offered sacrifices to Baal, and to the sun, the moon, the constellations, and to all the powers of the heavens. ⁶ The king removed the Asherah pole from the Lord's Temple and took it outside Jerusalem to the Kidron Valley, where he burned it. Then he ground the ashes of the pole to dust and threw the dust over the graves of the people. ⁷ He also tore down the living quarters of the male and female shrine prostitutes that were inside the Temple of the Lord, where the women wove coverings for the Asherah pole.

⁸ Josiah brought to Jerusalem all the priests who were living in other towns of Judah. He also defiled the pagan shrines, where they had offered sacrifices—all the way from Geba to Beersheba. He destroyed the shrines at the entrance to the gate of Joshua, the governor of Jerusalem. This gate was located to the left of the city gate as one enters the city. ⁹ The priests who had served at the pagan shrines were not allowed to serve at* the Lord's altar in Jerusalem, but they were allowed to eat unleavened bread with the other priests.

¹⁰ Then the king defiled the altar of Topheth in the valley of Ben-Hinnom, so no one could ever again use it to sacrifice a son or daughter in the fire* as an offering to Molech. ¹¹ He removed from the entrance of the Lord's Temple the horse statues that the former kings of Judah had dedicated to the sun. They were near the quarters of Nathan-melech the eunuch, an officer of the court.* The king also burned the chariots dedicated to the sun.

¹² Josiah tore down the altars that the kings of Judah had built on the palace roof above the upper room of Ahaz. The king destroyed the altars that Manasseh had built in the two courtyards of the Lord's Temple. He smashed them to bits* and scattered the pieces in the Kidron Valley. ¹³ The king also desecrated the pagan shrines east of Jerusalem, to the south of the Mount of Corruption, where King Solomon of Israel had built shrines for Ashtoreth, the detestable goddess of the Sidonians; and for Chemosh, the detestable god of the Moabites; and for Molech,* the vile god of the Ammonites. ¹⁴ He smashed the sacred pillars and cut down the Asherah poles. Then he desecrated these places by scattering human bones over them.

¹⁵ The king also tore down the altar at Bethel—the pagan shrine that Jeroboam son of Nebat had made when he caused Israel to sin. He burned down the shrine and ground it to dust, and he burned the Asherah pole. ¹⁶ Then Josiah turned around and noticed several tombs in the side of the hill. He ordered that the bones be brought out, and he burned them on the altar at Bethel to desecrate it. (This happened just as the Lord had promised through the man of God when Jeroboam stood beside the altar at the festival.)

Then Josiah turned and looked up at the tomb of the man of God* who had predicted these things. ¹⁷ "What is that monument over there?" Josiah asked.

And the people of the town told him, "It is the tomb of the man of God who came from Judah and predicted the very things that you have just done to the altar at Bethel!"

¹⁸ Josiah replied, "Leave it alone. Don't disturb his bones." So they did not burn his bones or those of the old prophet from Samaria.

23:9 Hebrew did not come up to. 23:10 Or to make a son or daughter pass through the fire. 23:11 The meaning of the Hebrew is uncertain. 23:12 Or He quickly removed them. 23:13 Hebrew Milcom, a variant spelling of Molech. 23:16 As in Greek version; Hebrew lacks when Jeroboam stood beside the altar at the festival. Then Josiah turned and looked up at the tomb of the man of God.

[19] Then Josiah demolished all the buildings at the pagan shrines in the towns of Samaria, just as he had done at Bethel. They had been built by the various kings of Israel and had made the LORD* very angry. [20] He executed the priests of the pagan shrines on their own altars, and he burned human bones on the altars to desecrate them. Finally, he returned to Jerusalem.

JOSIAH CELEBRATES PASSOVER

[21] King Josiah then issued this order to all the people: "You must celebrate the Passover to the LORD your God, as required in this Book of the Covenant." [22] There had not been a Passover celebration like that since the time when the judges ruled in Israel, nor throughout all the years of the kings of Israel and Judah. [23] But in the eighteenth year of King Josiah's reign, this Passover was celebrated to the LORD in Jerusalem.

[24] Josiah also got rid of the mediums and psychics, the household gods, the idols,* and every other kind of detestable practice, both in Jerusalem and throughout the land of Judah. He did this in obedience to the laws written in the scroll that Hilkiah the priest had found in the LORD's Temple. [25] Never before had there been a king like Josiah, who turned to the LORD with all his heart and soul and strength, obeying all the laws of Moses. And there has never been a king like him since.

[26] Even so, the LORD was very angry with Judah because of all the wicked things Manasseh had done to provoke him. [27] For the LORD said, "I will also banish Judah from my presence just as I have banished Israel. And I will reject my chosen city of Jerusalem and the Temple where my name was to be honored."

[28] The rest of the events in Josiah's reign and all his deeds are recorded in *The Book of the History of the Kings of Judah.*

[29] While Josiah was king, Pharaoh Neco, king of Egypt, went to the Euphrates River to help the king of Assyria. King Josiah and his army marched out to fight him,* but King Neco* killed him when they met at Megiddo. [30] Josiah's officers took his body back in a chariot from Megiddo to Jerusalem and buried him in his own tomb. Then the people of the land anointed Josiah's son Jehoahaz and made him the next king.

JEHOAHAZ RULES IN JUDAH

[31] Jehoahaz was twenty-three years old when he became king, and he reigned in Jerusalem three months. His mother was Hamutal, the daughter of Jeremiah from Libnah. [32] He did what was evil in the LORD's sight, just as his ancestors had done.

[33] Pharaoh Neco put Jehoahaz in prison at Riblah in the land of Hamath to prevent him from ruling* in Jerusalem. He also demanded that Judah pay 7,500 pounds of silver and 75 pounds of gold* as tribute.

JEHOIAKIM RULES IN JUDAH

[34] Pharaoh Neco then installed Eliakim, another of Josiah's sons, to reign in place of his father, and he changed Eliakim's name to Jehoiakim. Jehoahaz was taken to Egypt as a prisoner, where he died.

[35] In order to get the silver and gold demanded as tribute by Pharaoh Neco, Jehoiakim collected a tax from the people of Judah, requiring them to pay in proportion to their wealth.

[36] Jehoiakim was twenty-five years old when he became king, and he reigned in Jerusalem eleven years. His mother was Zebidah, the daughter of Pedaiah from Rumah. [37] He did what was evil in the LORD's sight, just as his ancestors had done.

24 During Jehoiakim's reign, King Nebuchadnezzar of Babylon invaded the land of Judah. Jehoiakim surrendered and paid him tribute for three years but then rebelled. [2] Then the LORD sent bands of Babylonian,* Aramean, Moabite, and Ammonite raiders against Judah to destroy it, just as the LORD had promised through his prophets. [3] These disasters happened to Judah because of the LORD's command. He had decided to banish Judah from his presence because of the many sins of Manasseh, [4] who had filled Jerusalem with innocent blood. The LORD would not forgive this.

[5] The rest of the events in Jehoiakim's reign and all his deeds are recorded in *The Book of the History of the Kings of Judah.* [6] When Jehoiakim died, his son Jehoiachin became the next king.

[7] The king of Egypt did not venture out of his country after that, for the king of Babylon captured the entire area formerly claimed by Egypt—from the Brook of Egypt to the Euphrates River.

JEHOIACHIN RULES IN JUDAH

[8] Jehoiachin was eighteen years old when he became king, and he reigned in Jerusalem three months. His mother was Nehushta, the daughter of Elnathan from Jerusalem. [9] Jehoiachin did what was evil in the LORD's sight, just as his father had done.

[10] During Jehoiachin's reign, the officers of King Nebuchadnezzar of Babylon came up against Jerusalem and besieged it. [11] Nebuchadnezzar himself arrived at the city during the siege. [12] Then King Jehoiachin, along with the queen mother, his advisers, his commanders, and his officials, surrendered to the Babylonians.

In the eighth year of Nebuchadnezzar's reign, he took Jehoiachin prisoner. [13] As the LORD had

---

23:19 As in Greek and Syriac versions and Latin Vulgate; Hebrew lacks *the LORD.* 23:24 The Hebrew term (literally *round things*) probably alludes to dung. 23:29a Or *Josiah went out to meet him.* 23:29b Hebrew *he.* 23:33a The meaning of the Hebrew is uncertain. 23:33b Hebrew *100 talents* [3,400 kilograms] *of silver and 1 talent* [34 kilograms] *of gold.* 24:2 Or *Chaldean.*

said beforehand, Nebuchadnezzar carried away all the treasures from the LORD's Temple and the royal palace. He stripped away* all the gold objects that King Solomon of Israel had placed in the Temple. ¹⁴King Nebuchadnezzar took all of Jerusalem captive, including all the commanders and the best of the soldiers, craftsmen, and artisans—10,000 in all. Only the poorest people were left in the land.

¹⁵Nebuchadnezzar led King Jehoiachin away as a captive to Babylon, along with the queen mother, his wives and officials, and all Jerusalem's elite. ¹⁶He also exiled 7,000 of the best troops and 1,000 craftsmen and artisans, all of whom were strong and fit for war. ¹⁷Then the king of Babylon installed Mattaniah, Jehoiachin's* uncle, as the next king, and he changed Mattaniah's name to Zedekiah.

ZEDEKIAH RULES IN JUDAH

¹⁸Zedekiah was twenty-one years old when he became king, and he reigned in Jerusalem eleven years. His mother was Hamutal, the daughter of Jeremiah from Libnah. ¹⁹But Zedekiah did what was evil in the LORD's sight, just as Jehoiakim had done. ²⁰These things happened because of the LORD's anger against the people of Jerusalem and Judah, until he finally banished them from his presence and sent them into exile.

THE FALL OF JERUSALEM

Zedekiah rebelled against the king of Babylon.

25 So on January 15,* during the ninth year of Zedekiah's reign, King Nebuchadnezzar of Babylon led his entire army against Jerusalem. They surrounded the city and built siege ramps against its walls. ²Jerusalem was kept under siege until the eleventh year of King Zedekiah's reign.

³By July 18 in the eleventh year of Zedekiah's reign,* the famine in the city had become very severe, and the last of the food was entirely gone. ⁴Then a section of the city wall was broken down. Since the city was surrounded by the Babylonians,* the soldiers waited for nightfall and escaped* through the gate between the two walls behind the king's garden. Then they headed toward the Jordan Valley.*

⁵But the Babylonian* troops chased the king and overtook him on the plains of Jericho, for his men had all deserted him and scattered. ⁶They captured the king and took him to the king of Babylon at Riblah, where they pronounced judgment upon Zedekiah. ⁷They made Zedekiah watch as they slaughtered his sons. Then they gouged out Zedekiah's eyes, bound him in bronze chains, and led him away to Babylon.

THE TEMPLE DESTROYED

⁸On August 14 of that year,* which was the nineteenth year of King Nebuchadnezzar's reign, Nebuzaradan, the captain of the guard and an official of the Babylonian king, arrived in Jerusalem. ⁹He burned down the Temple of the LORD, the royal palace, and all the houses of Jerusalem. He destroyed all the important buildings* in the city. ¹⁰Then he supervised the entire Babylonian army as they tore down the walls of Jerusalem on every side. ¹¹Then Nebuzaradan, the captain of the guard, took as exiles the rest of the people who remained in the city, the defectors who had declared their allegiance to the king of Babylon, and the rest of the population. ¹²But the captain of the guard allowed some of the poorest people to stay behind to care for the vineyards and fields.

¹³The Babylonians broke up the bronze pillars in front of the LORD's Temple, the bronze water carts, and the great bronze basin called the Sea, and they carried all the bronze away to Babylon. ¹⁴They also took all the ash buckets, shovels, lamp snuffers, ladles, and all the other bronze articles used for making sacrifices at the Temple. ¹⁵The captain of the guard also took the incense burners and basins, and all the other articles made of pure gold or silver.

¹⁶The weight of the bronze from the two pillars, the Sea, and the water carts was too great to be measured. These things had been made for the LORD's Temple in the days of Solomon. ¹⁷Each of the pillars was 27 feet* tall. The bronze capital on top of each pillar was 7½ feet* high and was decorated with a network of bronze pomegranates all the way around.

¹⁸Nebuzaradan, the captain of the guard, took with him as prisoners Seraiah the high priest, Zephaniah the priest of the second rank, and the three chief gatekeepers. ¹⁹And from among the people still hiding in the city, he took an officer who had been in charge of the Judean army; five of the king's personal advisers; the army commander's chief secretary, who was in charge of recruitment; and sixty other citizens. ²⁰Nebuzaradan, the captain of the guard, took them all to the king of Babylon at Riblah. ²¹And there at Riblah, in the land of Hamath, the king of Babylon had them all put to death. So the people of Judah were sent into exile from their land.

24:13 Or *He cut apart.* 24:17 Hebrew *his.* 25:1 Hebrew *on the tenth day of the tenth month,* of the ancient Hebrew lunar calendar. A number of events in 2 Kings can be cross-checked with dates in surviving Babylonian records and related accurately to our modern calendar. This day was January 15, 588 B.C. 25:3 Hebrew *By the ninth day of the [fourth] month* [in the eleventh year of Zedekiah's reign] (compare Jer 39:2; 52:6 and the notes there). This day was July 18, 586 B.C.; also see note on 25:1. 25:4a Or *the Chaldeans;* also in 25:13, 25, 26. 25:4b As in Greek version (see also Jer 39:4; 52:7); Hebrew lacks *escaped.* 25:4c Hebrew *the Arabah.* 25:5 Or *Chaldean;* also in 25:10, 24. 25:8 Hebrew *On the seventh day of the fifth month,* of the ancient Hebrew lunar calendar. This day was August 14, 586 B.C.; also see note on 25:1. 25:9 Or *destroyed the houses of all the important people.* 25:17a Hebrew *18 cubits* [8.3 meters]. 25:17b As in parallel texts at 1 Kgs 7:16, 2 Chr 3:15, and Jer 52:22, all of which read *5 cubits* [2.3 meters]; Hebrew reads *3 cubits,* which is 4.5 feet or 1.4 meters.

GEDALIAH GOVERNS IN JUDAH

²² Then King Nebuchadnezzar appointed Gedaliah son of Ahikam and grandson of Shaphan as governor over the people he had left in Judah. ²³ When all the army commanders and their men learned that the king of Babylon had appointed Gedaliah as governor, they went to see him at Mizpah. These included Ishmael son of Nethaniah, Johanan son of Kareah, Seraiah son of Tanhumeth the Netophathite, Jezaniah* son of the Maacathite, and all their men.

²⁴ Gedaliah vowed to them that the Babylonian officials meant them no harm. "Don't be afraid of them. Live in the land and serve the king of Babylon, and all will go well for you," he promised.

²⁵ But in midautumn of that year,* Ishmael son of Nethaniah and grandson of Elishama, who was a member of the royal family, went to Mizpah with ten men and killed Gedaliah. He also killed all the Judeans and Babylonians who were with him at Mizpah.

²⁶ Then all the people of Judah, from the least to the greatest, as well as the army commanders, fled in panic to Egypt, for they were afraid of what the Babylonians would do to them.

HOPE FOR ISRAEL'S ROYAL LINE

²⁷ In the thirty-seventh year of the exile of King Jehoiachin of Judah, Evil-merodach ascended to the Babylonian throne. He was kind to* Jehoiachin and released him* from prison on April 2 of that year.* ²⁸ He spoke kindly to Jehoiachin and gave him a higher place than all the other exiled kings in Babylon. ²⁹ He supplied Jehoiachin with new clothes to replace his prison garb and allowed him to dine in the king's presence for the rest of his life. ³⁰ So the king gave him a regular food allowance as long as he lived.

25:23 As in parallel text at Jer 40:8; Hebrew reads *Jaazaniah,* a variant spelling of Jezaniah.   25:25 Hebrew *in the seventh month,* of the ancient Hebrew lunar calendar. This month occurred within the months of October and November 586 B.C.; also see note on 25:1.   25:27a Hebrew *He raised the head of.*   25:27b As in some Hebrew manuscripts and Greek and Syriac versions (see also Jer 52:31); Masoretic Text lacks *released him.*   25:27c Hebrew *on the twenty-seventh day of the twelfth month,* of the ancient Hebrew lunar calendar. This day was April 2, 561 B.C.; also see note on 25:1.

1-2 CHRONICLES

JON HUNTZINGER, PHD

The books of 1 and 2 Chronicles were originally one book, just as 1 and 2 Samuel and 1 and 2 Kings were when written. Through genealogies, the Chronicles trace the history of the people of Israel from the time of Adam through Abraham, Moses, David, and Solomon down to the present time of the writer. The title "Chronicles" means that these books take a comprehensive view of Jewish history from the beginning of the human race to the time of the writing. The Persian king Cyrus permitted the return of the Babylonian exiles to Judah in 538 BC. Based on the reference to him in 2 Chronicles 36:22-23, the books were written sometime in the fifth century (400s) BC. The writer (or the Chronicler), who remains anonymous, drew upon various sources to write his history. Those sources included the biblical books (Samuel, Kings, Jeremiah) and prophetic records (1 Chronicles 29:29; 2 Chronicles 12:15; 13:22; 20:34; 32:32). Because the writer presents a very positive view of David and Solomon, he likely wanted to inspire his Jewish readers with hope for the future by reminding them of their glorious past.

The book of 1 Chronicles contains four major sections:

— Chapters 1-9 open with the genealogies of Adam, Abraham, and David, continue with those of the 12 sons of Jacob, and conclude with a genealogy of the people who returned from exile to resettle the land.

— Chapters 10-17 recount the deeds of David, with special attention given to the Ark of God and the new covenant God makes with him.

— Chapters 18-27 tell about David's role in preparing for the construction of the Temple and the worship of God therein. Lists of Israelite leaders follow.

— Chapters 28-29 conclude the book with a record of the instructions David gave to Solomon for the Temple and for the provisions for the offerings to be made, the anointing of Solomon to be king, and David's death.

The Ark of God (the Ark of the Covenant), which is central to 1 Chronicles, was a sacred, wooden box covered with gold and containing pieces of the manna God provided for Israel in the wilderness, Aaron's rod that blossomed, and the two stone tablets with the Ten Commandments God had given to Moses on Mount Sinai (Exodus 25:10-22). The Ark was a powerful symbol of the life-giving nature of God's Word and the provision for His people in the covenant He made with them.

The several genealogies at the beginning of 1 Chronicles make for difficult reading. Many contemporary readers simply glance at this material before turning to the narrative in the remainder of the book. What, then, is the significance of these genealogies? As noted previously, the writer composed the Chronicles sometime after the Exile when the people returned. They would have naturally wondered about their relationship to the past. Did the Exile mean they were no longer God's chosen people? These genealogies reminded them of their importance in relation to David, Moses, and Abraham and told them once again of their responsibility to keep the covenant God made with their ancestors, especially with David, the greatest of Israel's kings. This setting explains the extensive attention the Chronicler gave to David in 1 Chronicles. He intended to show David as a man of worship, whom the people in postexilic Judah were to imitate in their own worship. The Chronicler records David's devotion to the Ark of God (1 Chronicles 13-16), his plans for the Temple and instructions to Solomon to build it (1 Chronicles 22:2-19), and the provision he makes for the offerings to be given at the Temple (1 Chronicles 29:1-9). These events hold David up as a man committed to the praise and honor of God. The first readers would have understood this message. They would have understood that God's covenant with His people remained in effect and He called them to continue in their worship of Him.

Although the books of 1 and 2 Chronicles cover the same period as that of 2 Samuel with respect to David and 1 and 2 Kings with respect to Solomon and the later kings, the Chronicler looks at that period in a different way. He wrote at a different time for a different group of people. Since the books of Samuel and Kings were written during the Exile or soon afterward, their writer attempted to make sense of all that had happened in Judah's history up to that time. The writer of Samuel and Kings concluded that the Exile was God's judgment for the many years of sin and idolatry by the kings and the people. Thus, his writing recounted the failures and sins of the people to show the Exile as the consequence. He reports David's adultery with Bathsheba, for example, because it shows that even Israel's greatest king had sinned. However, at the time of the Chronicles, the people asked a different question. They did not ask, "Why has this happened?" Instead, they asked, "Does God still have a purpose for us?" The Chronicler's response is that God has a purpose, and it is for His people to keep the covenant He has made with them and to give worship to Him as David did. For this reason, the Chronicler did not report David's adultery with Bathsheba. That story would take away from the urgent and important message he had for them. In this way, the books of Chronicles complement the books of Kings, much like the four Gospels of Matthew, Mark, Luke, and John present different but complementary portraits of Jesus because they were written to different groups for different reasons.

One important feature of the genealogical lists in 1 Chronicles is the inclusion of the northern tribes along with the southern tribes of Judah and Benjamin. This inclusion means that the writer saw all Israel as a unified people of north and south, even after years of exile and division between them. For this reason, he repeatedly refers to "all Israel" throughout his writing in both 1 and 2 Chronicles. The Chronicler's conviction is that just as God's covenant remained in effect with His people, so too the people of north and south made up one nation that belonged to Him.

The book of 2 Chronicles includes two major sections:
— Chapters 1-7 highlight the building of the Temple and the institution of worship during the rule of Solomon.
— Chapters 8-36 depict Solomon as a king who worshipped God, and the kings of Judah who follow him are generally presented in a positive way for their support of the Temple. For example, the acts of idolatry by certain kings are noted but without detail. The evil King Manasseh commits idolatry, but he is also depicted as remorseful for his faithlessness to the covenant.

Throughout 2 Chronicles, the writer shows interest in the Temple and support for the worship given there:

— Asa brings gifts to the Temple (chapter 15).
— Jehoshaphat initiates reforms at the Temple (chapter 19).
— Jotham repairs the gates of the Temple (chapter 27).
— Hezekiah repairs the doors of the Temple, restores worship there, and celebrates Passover (chapters 29-31).
— Josiah discovers the Book of the Law in the Temple and, like Hezekiah, celebrates Passover (34:8-35:19).

The best-known passage in 1 and 2 Chronicles describes Israel's God as ready, even anxious, to intervene on His people's behalf: "If my people who are called by my name will humble themselves and pray and seek my face and turn from their wicked ways, I will hear from heaven and will forgive their sins and restore their land" (2 Chronicles 7:14). The Chronicler describes God as immediately available and present. He is not distant nor far off, even though the people may feel that way. He is closer than they think. If they pray to Him and worship like David, then He will make them a whole people once again.

1 CHRONICLES

FROM ADAM TO NOAH'S SONS

1 The descendants of Adam were Seth, Enosh, [2] Kenan, Mahalalel, Jared, [3] Enoch, Methuselah, Lamech, [4] and Noah.
The sons of Noah were* Shem, Ham, and Japheth.

DESCENDANTS OF JAPHETH

[5] The descendants of Japheth were Gomer, Magog, Madai, Javan, Tubal, Meshech, and Tiras.
[6] The descendants of Gomer were Ashkenaz, Riphath,* and Togarmah.
[7] The descendants of Javan were Elishah, Tarshish, Kittim, and Rodanim.

DESCENDANTS OF HAM

[8] The descendants of Ham were Cush, Mizraim,* Put, and Canaan.
[9] The descendants of Cush were Seba, Havilah, Sabtah, Raamah, and Sabteca. The descendants of Raamah were Sheba and Dedan. [10] Cush was also the ancestor of

Nimrod, who was the first heroic warrior on earth.
[11] Mizraim was the ancestor of the Ludites, Anamites, Lehabites, Naphtuhites, [12] Pathrusites, Casluhites, and the Caphtorites, from whom the Philistines came.*
[13] Canaan's oldest son was Sidon, the ancestor of the Sidonians. Canaan was also the ancestor of the Hittites,* [14] Jebusites, Amorites, Girgashites, [15] Hivites, Arkites, Sinites, [16] Arvadites, Zemarites, and Hamathites.

DESCENDANTS OF SHEM

[17] The descendants of Shem were Elam, Asshur, Arphaxad, Lud, and Aram.

1:4 As in Greek version (see also Gen 5:3-32); Hebrew lacks The sons of Noah were.   1:6 As in some Hebrew manuscripts and Greek version (see also Gen 10:3); most Hebrew manuscripts read Diphath.   1:8 Or Egypt; also in 1:11.   1:12 Hebrew Casluhites, from whom the Philistines came, Caphtorites. See Jer 47:4; Amos 9:7.   1:13 Hebrew ancestor of Heth.

The descendants of Aram were* Uz, Hul, Gether, and Mash.*

¹⁸Arphaxad was the father of Shelah. Shelah was the father of Eber.

¹⁹Eber had two sons. The first was named Peleg (which means "division"), for during his lifetime the people of the world were divided into different language groups. His brother's name was Joktan.

²⁰Joktan was the ancestor of Almodad, Sheleph, Hazarmaveth, Jerah, ²¹Hadoram, Uzal, Diklah, ²²Obal,* Abimael, Sheba, ²³Ophir, Havilah, and Jobab. All these were descendants of Joktan.

²⁴So this is the family line descended from Shem: Arphaxad, Shelah,* ²⁵Eber, Peleg, Reu, ²⁶Serug, Nahor, Terah, ²⁷and Abram, later known as Abraham.

DESCENDANTS OF ABRAHAM

²⁸The sons of Abraham were Isaac and Ishmael. ²⁹These are their genealogical records:

The sons of Ishmael were Nebaioth (the oldest), Kedar, Adbeel, Mibsam, ³⁰Mishma, Dumah, Massa, Hadad, Tema, ³¹Jetur, Naphish, and Kedemah. These were the sons of Ishmael.

³²The sons of Keturah, Abraham's concubine, were Zimran, Jokshan, Medan, Midian, Ishbak, and Shuah.

The sons of Jokshan were Sheba and Dedan.

³³The sons of Midian were Ephah, Epher, Hanoch, Abida, and Eldaah.

All these were descendants of Abraham through his concubine Keturah.

DESCENDANTS OF ISAAC

³⁴Abraham was the father of Isaac. The sons of Isaac were Esau and Israel.*

DESCENDANTS OF ESAU

³⁵The sons of Esau were Eliphaz, Reuel, Jeush, Jalam, and Korah.

³⁶The descendants of Eliphaz were Teman, Omar, Zepho,* Gatam, Kenaz, and Amalek, who was born to Timna.*

³⁷The descendants of Reuel were Nahath, Zerah, Shammah, and Mizzah.

ORIGINAL PEOPLES OF EDOM

³⁸The descendants of Seir were Lotan, Shobal, Zibeon, Anah, Dishon, Ezer, and Dishan.

³⁹The descendants of Lotan were Hori and Hemam.* Lotan's sister was named Timna.

⁴⁰The descendants of Shobal were Alvan,* Manahath, Ebal, Shepho,* and Onam.

The descendants of Zibeon were Aiah and Anah.

⁴¹The son of Anah was Dishon.

The descendants of Dishon were Hemdan,* Eshban, Ithran, and Keran.

⁴²The descendants of Ezer were Bilhan, Zaavan, and Akan.*

The descendants of Dishan* were Uz and Aran.

RULERS OF EDOM

⁴³These are the kings who ruled in the land of Edom before any king ruled over the Israelites*:

Bela son of Beor, who ruled from his city of Dinhabah.

⁴⁴When Bela died, Jobab son of Zerah from Bozrah became king in his place.

⁴⁵When Jobab died, Husham from the land of the Temanites became king in his place.

⁴⁶When Husham died, Hadad son of Bedad became king in his place and ruled from the city of Avith. He was the one who destroyed the Midianite army in the land of Moab.

⁴⁷When Hadad died, Samlah from the city of Masrekah became king in his place.

⁴⁸When Samlah died, Shaul from the city of Rehoboth-on-the-River became king in his place.

⁴⁹When Shaul died, Baal-hanan son of Acbor became king in his place.

⁵⁰When Baal-hanan died, Hadad became king in his place and ruled from the city of Pau.* His wife was Mehetabel, the daughter of Matred and granddaughter of Me-zahab.

⁵¹Then Hadad died.

The clan leaders of Edom were Timna, Alvah,* Jetheth, ⁵²Oholibamah, Elah, Pinon, ⁵³Kenaz, Teman, Mibzar, ⁵⁴Magdiel, and Iram. These are the clan leaders of Edom.

DESCENDANTS OF ISRAEL

2 The sons of Israel* were Reuben, Simeon, Levi, Judah, Issachar, Zebulun, ²Dan, Joseph, Benjamin, Naphtali, Gad, and Asher.

1:17a As in one Hebrew manuscript and some Greek manuscripts (see also Gen 10:23); most Hebrew manuscripts lack *The descendants of Aram were.*   1:17b As in parallel text at Gen 10:23; Hebrew reads *and Meshech.*   1:22 As in some Hebrew manuscripts and Syriac version (see also Gen 10:28); most Hebrew manuscripts read *Ebal.*   1:24 Some Greek manuscripts read *Arphaxad, Cainan, Shelah.* See notes on Gen 10:24; 11:12-13.   1:34 *Israel* is the name that God gave to Jacob.   1:36a As in many Hebrew manuscripts and a few Greek manuscripts (see also Gen 36:11); most Hebrew manuscripts read *Zephi.*   1:36b As in some Greek manuscripts (see also Gen 36:12); Hebrew reads *Kenaz, Timna, and Amalek.*   1:39 As in parallel text at Gen 36:22; Hebrew reads *and Homam.*   1:40a As in many Hebrew manuscripts and a few Greek manuscripts (see also Gen 36:23); most Hebrew manuscripts read *Alian.*   1:40b As in some Hebrew manuscripts (see also Gen 36:23); most Hebrew manuscripts read *Shephi.*   1:41 As in many Hebrew manuscripts and some Greek manuscripts (see also Gen 36:26); most Hebrew manuscripts read *Hamran.*   1:42a As in many Hebrew and Greek manuscripts (see also Gen 36:27); most Hebrew manuscripts read *Jaakan.*   1:42b Hebrew *Dishon;* compare 1:38 and parallel text at Gen 36:28.   1:43 Or *before an Israelite king ruled over them.*   1:50 As in many Hebrew manuscripts, some Greek manuscripts, Syriac version, and Latin Vulgate (see also Gen 36:39); most Hebrew manuscripts read *Pai.*   1:51 As in an alternate reading of the Masoretic Text (see also Gen 36:40); the other alternate reads *Aliah.*   2:1 *Israel* is the name that God gave to Jacob.

DESCENDANTS OF JUDAH

³Judah had three sons from Bathshua, a Canaanite woman. Their names were Er, Onan, and Shelah. But the LORD saw that the oldest son, Er, was a wicked man, so he killed him. ⁴Later Judah had twin sons from Tamar, his widowed daughter-in-law. Their names were Perez and Zerah. So Judah had five sons in all.

⁵The sons of Perez were Hezron and Hamul.

⁶The sons of Zerah were Zimri, Ethan, Heman, Calcol, and Darda*—five in all.

⁷The son of Carmi (a descendant of Zimri) was Achan,* who brought disaster on Israel by taking plunder that had been set apart for the LORD.*

⁸The son of Ethan was Azariah.

FROM JUDAH'S GRANDSON HEZRON TO DAVID

⁹The sons of Hezron were Jerahmeel, Ram, and Caleb.*

¹⁰ Ram was the father of Amminadab. Amminadab was the father of Nahshon, a leader of Judah.

¹¹ Nahshon was the father of Salmon.* Salmon was the father of Boaz.

¹² Boaz was the father of Obed. Obed was the father of Jesse.

¹³Jesse's first son was Eliab, his second was Abinadab, his third was Shimea, ¹⁴his fourth was Nethanel, his fifth was Raddai, ¹⁵his sixth was Ozem, and his seventh was David.

¹⁶Their sisters were named Zeruiah and Abigail. Zeruiah had three sons named Abishai, Joab, and Asahel. ¹⁷Abigail married a man named Jether, an Ishmaelite, and they had a son named Amasa.

OTHER DESCENDANTS OF HEZRON

¹⁸Hezron's son Caleb had sons from his wife Azubah and from Jerioth.* Her sons were named Jesher, Shobab, and Ardon. ¹⁹After Azubah died, Caleb married Ephrathah,* and they had a son named Hur. ²⁰Hur was the father of Uri. Uri was the father of Bezalel.

²¹When Hezron was sixty years old, he married Gilead's sister, the daughter of Makir. They had a son named Segub. ²²Segub was the father of Jair, who ruled twenty-three towns in the land of Gilead. ²³(But Geshur and Aram captured the Towns of Jair* and also took Kenath and its sixty surrounding villages.) All these were descendants of Makir, the father of Gilead.

²⁴Soon after Hezron died in the town of Caleb-ephrathah, his wife Abijah gave birth to a son named Ashhur (the father of* Tekoa).

DESCENDANTS OF HEZRON'S SON JERAHMEEL

²⁵The sons of Jerahmeel, the oldest son of Hezron, were Ram (the firstborn), Bunah, Oren, Ozem, and Ahijah. ²⁶Jerahmeel had a second wife named Atarah. She was the mother of Onam.

²⁷The sons of Ram, the oldest son of Jerahmeel, were Maaz, Jamin, and Eker.

²⁸The sons of Onam were Shammai and Jada. The sons of Shammai were Nadab and Abishur.

²⁹The sons of Abishur and his wife Abihail were Ahban and Molid.

³⁰The sons of Nadab were Seled and Appaim. Seled died without children, ³¹but Appaim had a son named Ishi. The son of Ishi was Sheshan. Sheshan had a descendant named Ahlai.

³²The sons of Jada, Shammai's brother, were Jether and Jonathan. Jether died without children, ³³but Jonathan had two sons named Peleth and Zaza.

These were all descendants of Jerahmeel.

³⁴Sheshan had no sons, though he did have daughters. He also had an Egyptian servant named Jarha. ³⁵Sheshan gave one of his daughters to be the wife of Jarha, and they had a son named Attai.

³⁶Attai was the father of Nathan. Nathan was the father of Zabad.

³⁷Zabad was the father of Ephlal. Ephlal was the father of Obed.

³⁸Obed was the father of Jehu. Jehu was the father of Azariah.

³⁹Azariah was the father of Helez. Helez was the father of Eleasah.

⁴⁰Eleasah was the father of Sismai. Sismai was the father of Shallum.

⁴¹Shallum was the father of Jekamiah. Jekamiah was the father of Elishama.

DESCENDANTS OF HEZRON'S SON CALEB

⁴²The descendants of Caleb, the brother of Jerahmeel, included Mesha (the firstborn), who became the father of Ziph. Caleb's descendants also included the sons of Mareshah, the father of Hebron.*

⁴³The sons of Hebron were Korah, Tappuah, Rekem, and Shema. ⁴⁴Shema was the father of Raham. Raham was the father of Jorkeam. Rekem was the father of Shammai.

2:6 As in many Hebrew manuscripts, some Greek manuscripts, and Syriac version (see also 1 Kgs 4:31); Hebrew reads *Dara.*   2:7a Hebrew *Achar;* compare Josh 7:1. *Achar* means "disaster."   2:7b The Hebrew term used here refers to the complete consecration of things or people to the LORD, either by destroying them or by giving them as an offering.   2:9 Hebrew *Kelubai,* a variant spelling of Caleb; compare 2:18.   2:11 As in Greek version (see also Ruth 4:20); Hebrew reads *Salma.*   2:18 Or *Caleb had a daughter named Jerioth from his wife, Azubah.* The meaning of the Hebrew is uncertain.   2:19 Hebrew *Ephrath,* a variant spelling of Ephrathah; compare 2:50 and 4:4.   2:23 Or *captured Havvoth-jair;* also in 2:42, 45, 49.   2:42 Or *who founded Hebron.* The meaning of the Hebrew is uncertain.

⁴⁵The son of Shammai was Maon. Maon was the father of Beth-zur.

⁴⁶Caleb's concubine Ephah gave birth to Haran, Moza, and Gazez. Haran was the father of Gazez.

⁴⁷The sons of Jahdai were Regem, Jotham, Geshan, Pelet, Ephah, and Shaaph.

⁴⁸Another of Caleb's concubines, Maacah, gave birth to Sheber and Tirhanah. ⁴⁹She also gave birth to Shaaph (the father of Madmannah) and Sheva (the father of Macbenah and Gibea). Caleb also had a daughter named Acsah.

⁵⁰These were all descendants of Caleb.

DESCENDANTS OF CALEB'S SON HUR

The sons of Hur, the oldest son of Caleb's wife Ephrathah, were Shobal (the founder of Kiriath-jearim), ⁵¹Salma (the founder of Bethlehem), and Hareph (the founder of Beth-gader).

⁵²The descendants of Shobal (the founder of Kiriath-jearim) were Haroeh, half the Manahathites, ⁵³and the families of Kiriath-jearim—the Ithrites, Puthites, Shumathites, and Mishraites, from whom came the people of Zorah and Eshtaol.

⁵⁴The descendants of Salma were the people of Bethlehem, the Netophathites, Atroth-beth-joab, the other half of the Manahathites, the Zorites, ⁵⁵and the families of scribes living at Jabez—the Tirathites, Shimeathites, and Sucathites. All these were Kenites who descended from Hammath, the father of the family of Recab.*

DESCENDANTS OF DAVID

3 These are the sons of David who were born in Hebron:

The oldest was Amnon, whose mother was Ahinoam from Jezreel.

The second was Daniel, whose mother was Abigail from Carmel.

²The third was Absalom, whose mother was Maacah, the daughter of Talmai, king of Geshur.

The fourth was Adonijah, whose mother was Haggith.

³The fifth was Shephatiah, whose mother was Abital.

The sixth was Ithream, whose mother was Eglah, David's wife.

⁴These six sons were born to David in Hebron, where he reigned seven and a half years.

Then David reigned another thirty-three years in Jerusalem. ⁵The sons born to David in Jerusalem included Shammua,* Shobab, Nathan, and Solomon. Their mother was Bathsheba,* the daughter of Ammiel. ⁶David also had nine other sons: Ibhar, Elishua,* Elpelet,* ⁷Nogah, Nepheg, Japhia, ⁸Elishama, Eliada, and Eliphelet.

⁹These were the sons of David, not including his sons born to his concubines. Their sister was named Tamar.

DESCENDANTS OF SOLOMON

¹⁰The descendants of Solomon were Rehoboam, Abijah, Asa, Jehoshaphat, ¹¹Jehoram,* Ahaziah, Joash, ¹²Amaziah, Uzziah,* Jotham, ¹³Ahaz, Hezekiah, Manasseh, ¹⁴Amon, and Josiah.

¹⁵The sons of Josiah were Johanan (the oldest), Jehoiakim (the second), Zedekiah (the third), and Jehoahaz* (the fourth).

¹⁶The successors of Jehoiakim were his son Jehoiachin and his brother Zedekiah.*

DESCENDANTS OF JEHOIACHIN

¹⁷The sons of Jehoiachin,* who was taken prisoner by the Babylonians, were Shealtiel, ¹⁸Malkiram, Pedaiah, Shenazzar, Jekamiah, Hoshama, and Nedabiah.

¹⁹The sons of Pedaiah were Zerubbabel and Shimei.

The sons of Zerubbabel were Meshullam and Hananiah. (Their sister was Shelomith.) ²⁰His five other sons were Hashubah, Ohel, Berekiah, Hasadiah, and Jushab-hesed.

²¹The sons of Hananiah were Pelatiah and Jeshaiah. Jeshaiah's son was Rephaiah. Rephaiah's son was Arnan. Arnan's son was Obadiah. Obadiah's son was Shecaniah.

²²The descendants of Shecaniah were Shemaiah and his sons, Hattush, Igal, Bariah, Neariah, and Shaphat—six in all.

²³The sons of Neariah were Elioenai, Hizkiah, and Azrikam—three in all.

²⁴The sons of Elioenai were Hodaviah, Eliashib, Pelaiah, Akkub, Johanan, Delaiah, and Anani—seven in all.

OTHER DESCENDANTS OF JUDAH

4 The descendants of Judah were Perez, Hezron, Carmi, Hur, and Shobal.

²Shobal's son Reaiah was the father of Jahath. Jahath was the father of Ahumai and Lahad. These were the families of the Zorathites.

³The descendants of* Etam were Jezreel, Ishma, Idbash, their sister Hazzelelponi, ⁴Penuel (the father of* Gedor), and Ezer (the father of Hushah). These were the descendants of Hur (the firstborn of Ephrathah), the ancestor of Bethlehem.

2:55 Or *the founder of Beth-recab.* 3:5a As in Syriac version (see also 14:4; 2 Sam 5:14); Hebrew reads *Shimea.* 3:5b Hebrew *Bathshua,* a variant spelling of Bathsheba. 3:6a As in some Hebrew and Greek manuscripts (see also 14:5-7 and 2 Sam 5:15); most Hebrew manuscripts read *Elishama.* 3:6b Hebrew *Eliphelet;* compare parallel text at 14:5-7. 3:11 Hebrew *Joram,* a variant spelling of Jehoram. 3:12 Hebrew *Azariah,* a variant spelling of Uzziah. 3:15 Hebrew *Shallum,* another name for Jehoahaz. 3:16 Hebrew *The sons of Jehoiakim were his son Jeconiah* [a variant spelling of Jehoiachin] *and his son Zedekiah.* 3:17 Hebrew *Jeconiah,* a variant spelling of Jehoiachin. 4:3 As in Greek version; Hebrew reads *father of.* The meaning of the Hebrew is uncertain. 4:4 Or *the founder of;* also in 4:5, 12, 14, 17, 18, and perhaps other instances where the text reads *the father of.*

⁵Ashhur (the father of Tekoa) had two wives, named Helah and Naarah. ⁶Naarah gave birth to Ahuzzam, Hepher, Temeni, and Haahashtari. ⁷Helah gave birth to Zereth, Izhar,* Ethnan, ⁸and Koz, who became the ancestor of Anub, Zobebah, and all the families of Aharhel son of Harum.

⁹There was a man named Jabez who was more honorable than any of his brothers. His mother named him Jabez* because his birth had been so painful. ¹⁰He was the one who prayed to the God of Israel, "Oh, that you would bless me and expand my territory! Please be with me in all that I do, and keep me from all trouble and pain!" And God granted him his request.

¹¹Kelub (the brother of Shuhah) was the father of Mehir. Mehir was the father of Eshton. ¹²Eshton was the father of Beth-rapha, Paseah, and Tehinnah. Tehinnah was the father of Ir-nahash. These were the descendants of Recah.

¹³The sons of Kenaz were Othniel and Seraiah. Othniel's sons were Hathath and Meonothai.* ¹⁴Meonothai was the father of Ophrah. Seraiah was the father of Joab, the founder of the Valley of Craftsmen,* so called because they were craftsmen.

¹⁵The sons of Caleb son of Jephunneh were Iru, Elah, and Naam. The son of Elah was Kenaz.

¹⁶The sons of Jehallelel were Ziph, Ziphah, Tiria, and Asarel.

¹⁷The sons of Ezrah were Jether, Mered, Epher, and Jalon. One of Mered's wives became* the mother of Miriam, Shammai, and Ishbah (the father of Eshtemoa). ¹⁸He married a woman from Judah, who became the mother of Jered (the father of Gedor), Heber (the father of Soco), and Jekuthiel (the father of Zanoah). Mered also married Bithia, a daughter of Pharaoh, and she bore him children.

¹⁹Hodiah's wife was the sister of Naham. One of her sons was the father of Keilah the Garmite, and another was the father of Eshtemoa the Maacathite.

²⁰The sons of Shimon were Amnon, Rinnah, Ben-hanan, and Tilon. The descendants of Ishi were Zoheth and Ben-zoheth.

DESCENDANTS OF JUDAH'S SON SHELAH

²¹Shelah was one of Judah's sons. The descendants of Shelah were Er (the father of Lecah); Laadah (the father of Mareshah); the families of linen workers at Beth-ashbea; ²²Jokim; the men of Cozeba; and Joash and Saraph, who ruled over Moab and Jashubi-lehem. These names all come from ancient records. ²³They were the pottery makers who lived in Netaim and Gederah. They lived there and worked for the king.

DESCENDANTS OF SIMEON

²⁴The sons of Simeon were Jemuel,* Jamin, Jarib, Zohar,* and Shaul.
²⁵The descendants of Shaul were Shallum, Mibsam, and Mishma.
²⁶The descendants of Mishma were Hammuel, Zaccur, and Shimei.
²⁷Shimei had sixteen sons and six daughters, but none of his brothers had large families. So Simeon's tribe never grew as large as the tribe of Judah.
²⁸They lived in Beersheba, Moladah, Hazar-shual, ²⁹Bilhah, Ezem, Tolad, ³⁰Bethuel, Hormah, Ziklag, ³¹Beth-marcaboth, Hazar-susim, Beth-biri, and Shaaraim. These towns were under their control until the time of King David. ³²Their descendants also lived in Etam, Ain, Rimmon, Token, and Ashan—five towns ³³and their surrounding villages as far away as Baalath.* This was their territory, and these names are listed in their genealogical records.
³⁴Other descendants of Simeon included Meshobab, Jamlech, Joshah son of Amaziah, ³⁵Joel, Jehu son of Joshibiah, son of Seraiah, son of Asiel, ³⁶Elioenai, Jaakobah, Jeshohaiah, Asaiah, Adiel, Jesimiel, Benaiah, ³⁷and Ziza son of Shiphi, son of Allon, son of Jedaiah, son of Shimri, son of Shemaiah.

³⁸These were the names of some of the leaders of Simeon's wealthy clans. Their families grew, ³⁹and they traveled to the region of Gerar,* in the east part of the valley, seeking pasture-land for their flocks. ⁴⁰They found lush pastures there, and the land was spacious, quiet, and peaceful.

Some of Ham's descendants had been living in that region. ⁴¹But during the reign of King Hezekiah of Judah, these leaders of Simeon invaded the region and completely destroyed* the homes of the descendants of Ham and of the Meunites. No trace of them remains today. They killed everyone who lived there and took the land for themselves, because they wanted its good pastureland for their flocks. ⁴²Five hundred of these invaders from the tribe of Simeon went to Mount Seir, led by Pelatiah, Neariah, Rephaiah, and Uzziel—all sons of Ishi. ⁴³They destroyed the few Amalekites who had survived, and they have lived there ever since.

4:7 As in an alternate reading in the Masoretic Text (see also Latin Vulgate); the other alternate and the Greek version read *Zohar.*   4:9 *Jabez* sounds like a Hebrew word meaning "distress" or "pain."   4:13 As in some Greek manuscripts and Latin Vulgate; Hebrew lacks *and Meonothai.*   4:14 Or *Joab, the father of Ge-harashim.*   4:17 Or *Jether's wife became;* Hebrew reads *She became.*   4:24a As in Syriac version (see also Gen 46:10; Exod 6:15); Hebrew reads *Nemuel.*   4:24b As in parallel texts at Gen 46:10 and Exod 6:15; Hebrew reads *Zerah.*   4:33 As in some Greek manuscripts (see also Josh 19:8); Hebrew reads *Baal.*   4:39 As in Greek version; Hebrew reads *Gedor.*   4:41 The Hebrew term used here refers to the complete consecration of things or people to the LORD, either by destroying them or by giving them as an offering.

DESCENDANTS OF REUBEN

5 The oldest son of Israel* was Reuben. But since he dishonored his father by sleeping with one of his father's concubines, his birthright was given to the sons of his brother Joseph. For this reason, Reuben is not listed in the genealogical records as the firstborn son. ²The descendants of Judah became the most powerful tribe and provided a ruler for the nation,* but the birthright belonged to Joseph.

³ The sons of Reuben, the oldest son of Israel, were Hanoch, Pallu, Hezron, and Carmi.
⁴ The descendants of Joel were Shemaiah, Gog, Shimei, ⁵ Micah, Reaiah, Baal, ⁶ and Beerah. Beerah was the leader of the Reubenites when they were taken into captivity by King Tiglath-pileser* of Assyria.
⁷ Beerah's* relatives are listed in their genealogical records by their clans: Jeiel (the leader), Zechariah, ⁸ and Bela son of Azaz, son of Shema, son of Joel.
The Reubenites lived in the area that stretches from Aroer to Nebo and Baal-meon. ⁹And since they had so many livestock in the land of Gilead, they spread east toward the edge of the desert that stretches to the Euphrates River.
¹⁰ During the reign of Saul, the Reubenites defeated the Hagrites in battle. Then they moved into the Hagrite settlements all along the eastern edge of Gilead.

DESCENDANTS OF GAD

¹¹ Next to the Reubenites, the descendants of Gad lived in the land of Bashan as far east as Salecah. ¹² Joel was the leader in the land of Bashan, and Shapham was second-in-command, followed by Janai and Shaphat.
¹³ Their relatives, the leaders of seven other clans, were Michael, Meshullam, Sheba, Jorai, Jacan, Zia, and Eber. ¹⁴ These were all descendants of Abihail son of Huri, son of Jaroah, son of Gilead, son of Michael, son of Jeshishai, son of Jahdo, son of Buz. ¹⁵Ahi son of Abdiel, son of Guni, was the leader of their clans.

¹⁶ The Gadites lived in the land of Gilead, in Bashan and its villages, and throughout all the pasturelands of Sharon. ¹⁷All of these were listed in the genealogical records during the days of King Jotham of Judah and King Jeroboam of Israel.

THE TRIBES EAST OF THE JORDAN

¹⁸ There were 44,760 capable warriors in the armies of Reuben, Gad, and the half-tribe of Manasseh. They were all skilled in combat and armed with shields, swords, and bows. ¹⁹ They waged war against the Hagrites, the Jeturites, the Naphishites, and the Nodabites. ²⁰ They cried out to God during the battle, and he answered their prayer because they trusted in him. So the Hagrites and all their allies were defeated. ²¹The plunder taken from the Hagrites included 50,000 camels, 250,000 sheep and goats, 2,000 donkeys, and 100,000 captives. ²² Many of the Hagrites were killed in the battle because God was fighting against them. The people of Reuben, Gad, and Manasseh lived in their land until they were taken into exile.

²³ The half-tribe of Manasseh was very large and spread through the land from Bashan to Baal-hermon, Senir, and Mount Hermon. ²⁴ These were the leaders of their clans: Epher,* Ishi, Eliel, Azriel, Jeremiah, Hodaviah, and Jahdiel. These men had a great reputation as mighty warriors and leaders of their clans.

²⁵ But these tribes were unfaithful to the God of their ancestors. They worshiped the gods of the nations that God had destroyed. ²⁶ So the God of Israel caused King Pul of Assyria (also known as Tiglath-pileser) to invade the land and take away the people of Reuben, Gad, and the half-tribe of Manasseh as captives. The Assyrians exiled them to Halah, Habor, Hara, and the Gozan River, where they remain to this day.

THE PRIESTLY LINE

6 ¹* The sons of Levi were Gershon, Kohath, and Merari.
² The descendants of Kohath included Amram, Izhar, Hebron, and Uzziel.
³ The children of Amram were Aaron, Moses, and Miriam.
The sons of Aaron were Nadab, Abihu, Eleazar, and Ithamar.
⁴ Eleazar was the father of Phinehas. Phinehas was the father of Abishua.
⁵ Abishua was the father of Bukki. Bukki was the father of Uzzi.
⁶ Uzzi was the father of Zerahiah. Zerahiah was the father of Meraioth.
⁷ Meraioth was the father of Amariah. Amariah was the father of Ahitub.
⁸ Ahitub was the father of Zadok. Zadok was the father of Ahimaaz.
⁹ Ahimaaz was the father of Azariah. Azariah was the father of Johanan.
¹⁰ Johanan was the father of Azariah, the high priest at the Temple* built by Solomon in Jerusalem.
¹¹ Azariah was the father of Amariah. Amariah was the father of Ahitub.
¹² Ahitub was the father of Zadok. Zadok was the father of Shallum.
¹³ Shallum was the father of Hilkiah. Hilkiah was the father of Azariah.

5:1 Israel is the name that God gave to Jacob.   5:2 Or and from Judah came a prince.   5:6 Hebrew Tilgath-pilneser, a variant spelling of Tiglath-pileser; also in 5:26.   5:7 Hebrew His.
5:24 As in Greek version and Latin Vulgate; Hebrew reads and Epher.   6:1 Verses 6:1-15 are numbered 5:27-41 in Hebrew text.
6:10 Hebrew the house.

¹⁴ Azariah was the father of Seraiah. Seraiah was the father of Jehozadak, ¹⁵who went into exile when the LORD sent the people of Judah and Jerusalem into captivity under Nebuchadnezzar.

THE LEVITE CLANS

¹⁶* The sons of Levi were Gershon,* Kohath, and Merari.
¹⁷The descendants of Gershon included Libni and Shimei.
¹⁸The descendants of Kohath included Amram, Izhar, Hebron, and Uzziel.
¹⁹The descendants of Merari included Mahli and Mushi.

The following were the Levite clans, listed according to their ancestral descent:

²⁰The descendants of Gershon included Libni, Jahath, Zimmah, ²¹Joah, Iddo, Zerah, and Jeatherai.
²²The descendants of Kohath included Amminadab, Korah, Assir, ²³Elkanah, Abiasaph,* Assir, ²⁴Tahath, Uriel, Uzziah, and Shaul.
²⁵The descendants of Elkanah included Amasai, Ahimoth, ²⁶Elkanah, Zophai, Nahath, ²⁷Eliab, Jeroham, Elkanah, and Samuel.*
²⁸The sons of Samuel were Joel* (the older) and Abijah (the second).
²⁹The descendants of Merari included Mahli, Libni, Shimei, Uzzah, ³⁰Shimea, Haggiah, and Asaiah.

THE TEMPLE MUSICIANS

³¹David assigned the following men to lead the music at the house of the LORD after the Ark was placed there. ³²They ministered with music at the Tabernacle* until Solomon built the Temple of the LORD in Jerusalem. They carried out their work, following all the regulations handed down to them. ³³These are the men who served, along with their sons:

Heman the musician was from the clan of Kohath. His genealogy was traced back through Joel, Samuel, ³⁴Elkanah, Jeroham, Eliel, Toah, ³⁵Zuph, Elkanah, Mahath, Amasai, ³⁶Elkanah, Joel, Azariah, Zephaniah, ³⁷Tahath, Assir, Abiasaph, Korah, ³⁸Izhar, Kohath, Levi, and Israel.*
³⁹Heman's first assistant was Asaph from the clan of Gershon.* Asaph's genealogy was traced back through Berekiah, Shimea, ⁴⁰Michael, Baaseiah, Malkijah, ⁴¹Ethni, Zerah, Adaiah, ⁴²Ethan, Zimmah, Shimei, ⁴³Jahath, Gershon, and Levi.
⁴⁴Heman's second assistant was Ethan from the clan of Merari. Ethan's genealogy was traced back through Kishi, Abdi, Malluch,

⁴⁵Hashabiah, Amaziah, Hilkiah, ⁴⁶Amzi, Bani, Shemer, ⁴⁷Mahli, Mushi, Merari, and Levi.

⁴⁸Their fellow Levites were appointed to various other tasks in the Tabernacle, the house of God.

AARON'S DESCENDANTS

⁴⁹Only Aaron and his descendants served as priests. They presented the offerings on the altar of burnt offering and the altar of incense, and they performed all the other duties related to the Most Holy Place. They made atonement for Israel by doing everything that Moses, the servant of God, had commanded them.

⁵⁰The descendants of Aaron were Eleazar, Phinehas, Abishua, ⁵¹Bukki, Uzzi, Zerahiah, ⁵²Meraioth, Amariah, Ahitub, ⁵³Zadok, and Ahimaaz.

TERRITORY FOR THE LEVITES

⁵⁴This is a record of the towns and territory assigned by means of sacred lots to the descendants of Aaron, who were from the clan of Kohath. ⁵⁵This territory included Hebron and its surrounding pasturelands in Judah, ⁵⁶but the fields and outlying areas belonging to the city were given to Caleb son of Jephunneh. ⁵⁷So the descendants of Aaron were given the following towns, each with its pasturelands: Hebron (a city of refuge),* Libnah, Jattir, Eshtemoa, ⁵⁸Holon,* Debir, ⁵⁹Ain,* Juttah,* and Beth-shemesh. ⁶⁰And from the territory of Benjamin they were given Gibeon,* Geba, Alemeth, and Anathoth, each with its pasturelands. So thirteen towns were given to the descendants of Aaron. ⁶¹The remaining descendants of Kohath received ten towns from the territory of the half-tribe of Manasseh by means of sacred lots.

⁶²The descendants of Gershon received by sacred lots thirteen towns from the territories of Issachar, Asher, Naphtali, and from the Bashan area of Manasseh, east of the Jordan.

⁶³The descendants of Merari received by sacred lots twelve towns from the territories of Reuben, Gad, and Zebulun.

⁶⁴So the people of Israel assigned all these towns and pasturelands to the Levites. ⁶⁵The towns in the territories of Judah, Simeon, and

6:16a Verses 6:16-81 are numbered 6:1-66 in Hebrew text. 6:16b Hebrew *Gershom*, a variant spelling of Gershon (see 6:1); also in 6:17, 20, 43, 62, 71. 6:23 Hebrew *Ebiasaph*, a variant spelling of Abiasaph (also in 6:37); compare parallel text at Exod 6:24. 6:27 As in some Greek manuscripts (see also 6:33-34); Hebrew lacks *and Samuel*. 6:28 As in some Greek manuscripts and the Syriac version (see also 6:33 and 1 Sam 8:2); Hebrew lacks *Joel*. 6:32 Hebrew *the Tabernacle, the Tent of Meeting*. 6:38 *Israel* is the name that God gave to Jacob. 6:39 Hebrew lacks *from the clan of Gershon;* see 6:57. 6:57 As in parallel text at Josh 21:13; Hebrew reads *were given the cities of refuge: Hebron, and the following towns, each with its pasturelands.* 6:58 As in parallel text at Josh 21:15; Masoretic Text reads *Hilez;* other manuscripts read *Hilen.* 6:59a As in parallel text at Josh 21:16; Hebrew reads *Ashan.* 6:59b As in Syriac version (see also Josh 21:16); Hebrew lacks *Juttah.* 6:60 As in parallel text at Josh 21:17; Hebrew lacks *Gibeon.*

Benjamin, mentioned above, were assigned to them by means of sacred lots.

⁶⁶ The descendants of Kohath were given the following towns from the territory of Ephraim, each with its pasturelands: ⁶⁷ Shechem (a city of refuge in the hill country of Ephraim),* Gezer, ⁶⁸ Jokmeam, Beth-horon, ⁶⁹ Aijalon, and Gath-rimmon. ⁷⁰ The remaining descendants of Kohath were assigned the towns of Aner and Bileam from the territory of the half-tribe of Manasseh, each with its pasturelands.

⁷¹ The descendants of Gershon received the towns of Golan (in Bashan) and Ashtaroth from the territory of the half-tribe of Manasseh, each with its pasturelands. ⁷² From the territory of Issachar, they were given Kedesh, Daberath, ⁷³ Ramoth, and Anem, each with its pasture-lands. ⁷⁴ From the territory of Asher, they received Mashal, Abdon, ⁷⁵ Hukok, and Rehob, each with its pasturelands. ⁷⁶ From the territory of Naphtali, they were given Kedesh in Galilee, Hammon, and Kiriathaim, each with its pasturelands.

⁷⁷ The remaining descendants of Merari received the towns of Jokneam, Kartah,* Rimmon,* and Tabor from the territory of Zebulun, each with its pasturelands. ⁷⁸ From the territory of Reuben, east of the Jordan River opposite Jericho, they received Bezer (a desert town), Jahaz,* ⁷⁹ Kedemoth, and Mephaath, each with its pasturelands. ⁸⁰ And from the territory of Gad, they received Ramoth in Gilead, Mahanaim, ⁸¹ Heshbon, and Jazer, each with its pasturelands.

DESCENDANTS OF ISSACHAR

7 The four sons of Issachar were Tola, Puah, Jashub, and Shimron. ²The sons of Tola were Uzzi, Rephaiah, Jeriel, Jahmai, Ibsam, and Shemuel. Each of them was the leader of an ancestral clan. At the time of King David, the total number of mighty warriors listed in the records of these clans was 22,600. ³The son of Uzzi was Izrahiah. The sons of Izrahiah were Michael, Obadiah, Joel, and Isshiah. These five became the leaders of clans. ⁴All of them had many wives and many sons, so the total number of men available for military service among their descendants was 36,000. ⁵The total number of mighty warriors from all the clans of the tribe of Issachar was 87,000. All of them were listed in their genealogical records.

DESCENDANTS OF BENJAMIN

⁶Three of Benjamin's sons were Bela, Beker, and Jediael. ⁷The five sons of Bela were Ezbon, Uzzi, Uzziel, Jerimoth, and Iri. Each of them was the leader of an ancestral clan. The total number of mighty warriors from these clans was 22,034, as listed in their genealogical records.

⁸The sons of Beker were Zemirah, Joash, Eliezer, Elioenai, Omri, Jeremoth, Abijah, Anathoth, and Alemeth. ⁹Each of them was the leader of an ancestral clan. The total number of mighty warriors and leaders from these clans was 20,200, as listed in their genealogical records.

¹⁰The son of Jediael was Bilhan. The sons of Bilhan were Jeush, Benjamin, Ehud, Kenaanah, Zethan, Tarshish, and Ahishahar. ¹¹Each of them was the leader of an ancestral clan. From these clans the total number of mighty warriors ready for war was 17,200. ¹²The sons of Ir were Shuppim and Huppim. Hushim was the son of Aher.

DESCENDANTS OF NAPHTALI

¹³The sons of Naphtali were Jahzeel,* Guni, Jezer, and Shillem.* They were all descendants of Jacob's concubine Bilhah.

DESCENDANTS OF MANASSEH

¹⁴The descendants of Manasseh through his Aramean concubine included Asriel. She also bore Makir, the father of Gilead. ¹⁵Makir found wives for* Huppim and Shuppim. Makir had a sister named Maacah. One of his descendants was Zelophehad, who had only daughters.

¹⁶Makir's wife, Maacah, gave birth to a son whom she named Peresh. His brother's name was Sheresh. The sons of Peresh were Ulam and Rakem. ¹⁷The son of Ulam was Bedan. All these were considered Gileadites, descendants of Makir son of Manasseh. ¹⁸Makir's sister Hammoleketh gave birth to Ishhod, Abiezer, and Mahlah. ¹⁹The sons of Shemida were Ahian, Shechem, Likhi, and Aniam.

DESCENDANTS OF EPHRAIM

²⁰The descendants of Ephraim were Shuthelah, Bered, Tahath, Eleadah, Tahath, ²¹Zabad, Shuthelah, Ezer, and Elead. These two were killed trying to steal livestock from the local farmers near Gath. ²²Their father, Ephraim, mourned for them a long time, and his relatives came to comfort him. ²³Afterward Ephraim slept with his wife, and she became pregnant and gave birth to a son. Ephraim named him Beriah* because of the tragedy his family had suffered. ²⁴He had a daughter named Sheerah. She built the

---

6:66-67 As in parallel text at Josh 21:21; Hebrew text reads *were given the cities of refuge: Shechem in the hill country of Ephraim, and the following towns, each with its pasturelands.* 6:77a As in Greek version (see also Josh 21:34); Hebrew lacks *Jokneam, Kartah.* 6:77b As in Greek version (see also Josh 19:13); Hebrew reads *Rimmono.* 6:78 Hebrew *Jahzah,* a variant spelling of Jahaz. 7:13a As in parallel text at Gen 46:24; Hebrew reads *Jahziel,* a variant spelling of Jahzeel. 7:13b As in some Hebrew and Greek manuscripts (see also Gen 46:24; Num 26:49); most Hebrew manuscripts read *Shallum.* 7:15 Or *Makir took a wife from.* The meaning of the Hebrew is uncertain. 7:23 *Beriah* sounds like a Hebrew term meaning "tragedy" or "misfortune."

towns of Lower and Upper Beth-horon and Uzzen-sheerah.

²⁵The descendants of Ephraim included Rephah, Resheph, Telah, Tahan, ²⁶Ladan, Ammihud, Elishama, ²⁷Nun, and Joshua.

²⁸The descendants of Ephraim lived in the territory that included Bethel and its surrounding towns to the south, Naaran to the east, Gezer and its villages to the west, and Shechem and its surrounding villages to the north as far as Ayyah and its towns. ²⁹Along the border of Manasseh were the towns of Beth-shan,* Taanach, Megiddo, Dor, and their surrounding villages. The descendants of Joseph son of Israel* lived in these towns.

DESCENDANTS OF ASHER

³⁰The sons of Asher were Imnah, Ishvah, Ishvi, and Beriah. They had a sister named Serah.
³¹The sons of Beriah were Heber and Malkiel (the father of Birzaith).
³²The sons of Heber were Japhlet, Shomer, and Hotham. They had a sister named Shua.
³³The sons of Japhlet were Pasach, Bimhal, and Ashvath.
³⁴The sons of Shomer were Ahi,* Rohgah, Hubbah, and Aram.
³⁵The sons of his brother Helem* were Zophah, Imna, Shelesh, and Amal.
³⁶The sons of Zophah were Suah, Harnepher, Shual, Beri, Imrah, ³⁷Bezer, Hod, Shamma, Shilshah, Ithran,* and Beera.
³⁸The sons of Jether were Jephunneh, Pispah, and Ara.
³⁹The sons of Ulla were Arah, Hanniel, and Rizia.
⁴⁰Each of these descendants of Asher was the head of an ancestral clan. They were all select men—mighty warriors and outstanding leaders. The total number of men available for military service was 26,000, as listed in their genealogical records.

DESCENDANTS OF BENJAMIN

8 Benjamin's first son was Bela, the second was Ashbel, the third was Aharah, ²the fourth was Nohah, and the fifth was Rapha.
³The sons of Bela were Addar, Gera, Abihud,* ⁴Abishua, Naaman, Ahoah, ⁵Gera, Shephuphan, and Huram.
⁶The sons of Ehud, leaders of the clans living at Geba, were exiled to Manahath. ⁷Ehud's sons were Naaman, Ahijah, and Gera. Gera, who led them into exile, was the father of Uzza and Ahihud.*
⁸After Shaharaim divorced his wives Hushim and Baara, he had children in the land of Moab. ⁹His wife Hodesh gave birth to Jobab, Zibia, Mesha, Malcam, ¹⁰Jeuz, Sakia, and Mirmah. These sons all became the leaders of clans.
¹¹Shaharaim's wife Hushim had already given birth to Abitub and Elpaal. ¹²The sons of Elpaal were Eber, Misham, Shemed (who built the towns of Ono and Lod and their nearby villages), ¹³Beriah, and Shema. They were the leaders of the clans living in Aijalon, and they drove out the inhabitants of Gath.

¹⁴Ahio, Shashak, Jeremoth, ¹⁵Zebadiah, Arad, Eder, ¹⁶Michael, Ishpah, and Joha were the sons of Beriah.
¹⁷Zebadiah, Meshullam, Hizki, Heber, ¹⁸Ishmerai, Izliah, and Jobab were the sons of Elpaal.
¹⁹Jakim, Zicri, Zabdi, ²⁰Elienai, Zillethai, Eliel, ²¹Adaiah, Beraiah, and Shimrath were the sons of Shimei.
²²Ishpan, Eber, Eliel, ²³Abdon, Zicri, Hanan, ²⁴Hananiah, Elam, Anthothijah, ²⁵Iphdeiah, and Penuel were the sons of Shashak.
²⁶Shamsherai, Shehariah, Athaliah, ²⁷Jaareshiah, Elijah, and Zicri were the sons of Jeroham.
²⁸These were the leaders of the ancestral clans; they were listed in their genealogical records, and they all lived in Jerusalem.

THE FAMILY OF SAUL

²⁹Jeiel* (the father of* Gibeon) lived in the town of Gibeon. His wife's name was Maacah, ³⁰and his oldest son was named Abdon. Jeiel's other sons were Zur, Kish, Baal, Ner,* Nadab, ³¹Gedor, Ahio, Zechariah,* ³²and Mikloth, who was the father of Shimeam.* All these families lived near each other in Jerusalem.

³³ Ner was the father of Kish.
Kish was the father of Saul.
Saul was the father of Jonathan, Malkishua, Abinadab, and Esh-baal.
³⁴ Jonathan was the father of Merib-baal.
Merib-baal was the father of Micah.
³⁵ Micah was the father of Pithon, Melech, Tahrea,* and Ahaz.
³⁶ Ahaz was the father of Jadah.*
Jadah was the father of Alemeth, Azmaveth, and Zimri.
Zimri was the father of Moza.
³⁷ Moza was the father of Binea.
Binea was the father of Rephaiah.*
Rephaiah was the father of Eleasah.
Eleasah was the father of Azel.

7:29a Hebrew *Beth-shean*, a variant spelling of Beth-shan.
7:29b *Israel* is the name that God gave to Jacob. 7:34 Or *The sons of Shomer, his brother, were.* 7:35 Possibly another name for *Hotham;* compare 7:32. 7:37 Possibly another name for *Jether;* compare 7:38. 8:3 Possibly *Gera the father of Ehud;* compare 8:6. 8:7 Or *Gera, that is Heglam, was the father of Uzza and Ahihud.* 8:29a As in some Greek manuscripts (see also 9:35); Hebrew lacks *Jeiel.* 8:29b Or *the founder of.* 8:30 As in some Greek manuscripts (see also 9:36); Hebrew lacks *Ner.* 8:31 As in parallel text at 9:37; Hebrew reads *Zeker,* a variant spelling of Zechariah. 8:32 As in parallel text at 9:38; Hebrew reads *Shimeah,* a variant spelling of Shimeam. 8:35 As in parallel text at 9:41; Hebrew reads *Tarea,* a variant spelling of Tahrea. 8:36 As in parallel text at 9:42; Hebrew reads *Jehoaddah,* a variant spelling of Jadah. 8:37 As in parallel text at 9:43; Hebrew reads *Raphah,* a variant spelling of Rephaiah.

³⁸Azel had six sons: Azrikam, Bokeru, Ishmael, Sheariah, Obadiah, and Hanan. These were the sons of Azel. ³⁹Azel's brother Eshek had three sons: the first was Ulam, the second was Jeush, and the third was Eliphelet. ⁴⁰Ulam's sons were all mighty warriors and expert archers. They had many sons and grandsons—150 in all.

All these were descendants of Benjamin.

9 So all Israel was listed in the genealogical records in *The Book of the Kings of Israel*.

THE RETURNING EXILES

The people of Judah were exiled to Babylon because they were unfaithful to the LORD. ²The first of the exiles to return to their property in their former towns were priests, Levites, Temple servants, and other Israelites. ³Some of the people from the tribes of Judah, Benjamin, Ephraim, and Manasseh came and settled in Jerusalem.

⁴One family that returned was that of Uthai son of Ammihud, son of Omri, son of Imri, son of Bani, a descendant of Perez son of Judah. ⁵Others returned from the Shilonite clan, including Asaiah (the oldest) and his sons. ⁶From the Zerahite clan, Jeuel returned with his relatives.
In all, 690 families from the tribe of Judah returned.

⁷From the tribe of Benjamin came Sallu son of Meshullam, son of Hodaviah, son of Hassenuah; ⁸Ibneiah son of Jeroham; Elah son of Uzzi, son of Micri; and Meshullam son of Shephatiah, son of Reuel, son of Ibnijah. ⁹These men were all leaders of clans, and they were listed in their genealogical records. In all, 956 families from the tribe of Benjamin returned.

THE RETURNING PRIESTS

¹⁰Among the priests who returned were Jedaiah, Jehoiarib, Jakin, ¹¹Azariah son of Hilkiah, son of Meshullam, son of Zadok, son of Meraioth, son of Ahitub. Azariah was the chief officer of the house of God. ¹²Other returning priests were Adaiah son of Jeroham, son of Pashhur, son of Malkijah, and Maasai son of Adiel, son of Jahzerah, son of Meshullam, son of Meshillemith, son of Immer. ¹³In all, 1,760 priests returned. They were heads of clans and very able men. They were responsible for ministering at the house of God.

THE RETURNING LEVITES

¹⁴The Levites who returned were Shemaiah son of Hasshub, son of Azrikam, son of Hashabiah, a descendant of Merari; ¹⁵Bakbakkar; Heresh; Galal; Mattaniah son of Mica, son of Zicri, son of Asaph; ¹⁶Obadiah son of Shemaiah, son of Galal, son of Jeduthun; and Berekiah son of Asa, son of Elkanah, who lived in the area of Netophah.

¹⁷The gatekeepers who returned were Shallum, Akkub, Talmon, Ahiman, and their relatives. Shallum was the chief gatekeeper. ¹⁸Prior to this time, they were responsible for the King's Gate on the east side. These men served as gatekeepers for the camps of the Levites. ¹⁹Shallum was the son of Kore, a descendant of Abiasaph,* from the clan of Korah. He and his relatives, the Korahites, were responsible for guarding the entrance to the sanctuary, just as their ancestors had guarded the Tabernacle in the camp of the LORD.

²⁰Phinehas son of Eleazar had been in charge of the gatekeepers in earlier times, and the LORD had been with him. ²¹And later Zechariah son of Meshelemiah was responsible for guarding the entrance to the Tabernacle.*

²²In all, there were 212 gatekeepers in those days, and they were listed according to the genealogies in their villages. David and Samuel the seer had appointed their ancestors because they were reliable men. ²³These gatekeepers and their descendants, by their divisions, were responsible for guarding the entrance to the house of the LORD when that house was a tent. ²⁴The gatekeepers were stationed on all four sides—east, west, north, and south. ²⁵Their relatives in the villages came regularly to share their duties for seven-day periods.

²⁶The four chief gatekeepers, all Levites, were trusted officials, for they were responsible for the rooms and treasuries at the house of God. ²⁷They would spend the night around the house of God, since it was their duty to guard it and to open the gates every morning.

²⁸Some of the gatekeepers were assigned to care for the various articles used in worship. They checked them in and out to avoid any loss. ²⁹Others were responsible for the furnishings, the items in the sanctuary, and the supplies, such as choice flour, wine, olive oil, frankincense, and spices. ³⁰But it was the priests who blended the spices. ³¹Mattithiah, a Levite and the oldest son of Shallum the Korahite, was entrusted with baking the bread used in the offerings. ³²And some members of the clan of Kohath were in charge of preparing the bread to be set on the table each Sabbath day.

³³The musicians, all prominent Levites, lived at the Temple. They were exempt from other responsibilities since they were on duty at all hours. ³⁴All these men lived in Jerusalem. They were the heads of Levite families and were listed as prominent leaders in their genealogical records.

9:19 Hebrew *Ebiasaph*, a variant spelling of Abiasaph; compare Exod 6:24.   9:21 Hebrew *Tent of Meeting*.

KING SAUL'S FAMILY TREE

35 Jeiel (the father of* Gibeon) lived in the town of Gibeon. His wife's name was Maacah, 36 and his oldest son was named Abdon. Jeiel's other sons were Zur, Kish, Baal, Ner, Nadab, 37 Gedor, Ahio, Zechariah, and Mikloth. 38 Mikloth was the father of Shimeam. All these families lived near each other in Jerusalem.

39 Ner was the father of Kish.
Kish was the father of Saul.
Saul was the father of Jonathan, Malkishua, Abinadab, and Esh-baal.

40 Jonathan was the father of Merib-baal.
Merib-baal was the father of Micah.

41 The sons of Micah were Pithon, Melech, Tahrea, and Ahaz.*

42 Ahaz was the father of Jadah.*
Jadah was the father of Alemeth, Azmaveth, and Zimri.
Zimri was the father of Moza.

43 Moza was the father of Binea.
Binea's son was Rephaiah.
Rephaiah's son was Eleasah.
Eleasah's son was Azel.

44 Azel had six sons, whose names were Azrikam, Bokeru, Ishmael, Sheariah, Obadiah, and Hanan. These were the sons of Azel.

THE DEATH OF KING SAUL

10 Now the Philistines attacked Israel, and the men of Israel fled before them. Many were slaughtered on the slopes of Mount Gilboa. 2 The Philistines closed in on Saul and his sons, and they killed three of his sons—Jonathan, Abinadab, and Malkishua. 3 The fighting grew very fierce around Saul, and the Philistine archers caught up with him and wounded him.

4 Saul groaned to his armor bearer, "Take your sword and kill me before these pagan Philistines come to taunt and torture me."

But his armor bearer was afraid and would not do it. So Saul took his own sword and fell on it. 5 When his armor bearer realized that Saul was dead, he fell on his own sword and died. 6 So Saul and his three sons died there together, bringing his dynasty to an end.

7 When all the Israelites in the Jezreel Valley saw that their army had fled and that Saul and his sons were dead, they abandoned their towns and fled. So the Philistines moved in and occupied their towns.

8 The next day, when the Philistines went out to strip the dead, they found the bodies of Saul and his sons on Mount Gilboa. 9 So they stripped off Saul's armor and cut off his head. Then they proclaimed the good news of Saul's death before their idols and to the people throughout the land of Philistia. 10 They placed his armor in the temple of their gods, and they fastened his head to the temple of Dagon.

11 But when everyone in Jabesh-gilead heard about everything the Philistines had done to Saul, 12 all their mighty warriors brought the bodies of Saul and his sons back to Jabesh. Then they buried their bones beneath the great tree at Jabesh, and they fasted for seven days.

13 So Saul died because he was unfaithful to the LORD. He failed to obey the LORD's command, and he even consulted a medium 14 instead of asking the LORD for guidance. So the LORD killed him and turned the kingdom over to David son of Jesse.

DAVID BECOMES KING OF ALL ISRAEL

11 Then all Israel gathered before David at Hebron and told him, "We are your own flesh and blood. 2 In the past,* even when Saul was king, you were the one who really led the forces of Israel. And the LORD your God told you, 'You will be the shepherd of my people Israel. You will be the leader of my people Israel.'"

3 So there at Hebron, David made a covenant before the LORD with all the elders of Israel. And they anointed him king of Israel, just as the LORD had promised through Samuel.

DAVID CAPTURES JERUSALEM

4 Then David and all Israel went to Jerusalem (or Jebus, as it used to be called), where the Jebusites, the original inhabitants of the land, were living. 5 The people of Jebus taunted David, saying, "You'll never get in here!" But David captured the fortress of Zion, which is now called the City of David.

6 David had said to his troops, "Whoever is first to attack the Jebusites will become the commander of my armies!" And Joab, the son of David's sister Zeruiah, was first to attack, so he became the commander of David's armies.

7 David made the fortress his home, and that is why it is called the City of David. 8 He extended the city from the supporting terraces* to the surrounding area, while Joab rebuilt the rest of Jerusalem. 9 And David became more and more powerful, because the LORD of Heaven's Armies was with him.

DAVID'S MIGHTIEST WARRIORS

10 These are the leaders of David's mighty warriors. Together with all Israel, they decided to make David their king, just as the LORD had promised concerning Israel.

11 Here is the record of David's mightiest warriors: The first was Jashobeam the Hacmonite, who was leader of the Three—the mightiest warriors among David's men.* He once used his spear to kill 300 enemy warriors in a single battle.

9:35 Or the founder of. 9:41 As in Syriac version and Latin Vulgate (see also 8:35); Hebrew lacks and Ahaz. 9:42 As in some Hebrew manuscripts and Greek version (see also 8:36); Hebrew reads Jarah. 11:2 Or For some time. 11:8 Hebrew the millo. The meaning of the Hebrew is uncertain. 11:11 As in some Greek manuscripts (see also 2 Sam 23:8); Hebrew reads leader of the Thirty, or leader of the captains.

¹²Next in rank among the Three was Eleazar son of Dodai,* a descendant of Ahoah. ¹³He was with David when the Philistines gathered for battle at Pas-dammim and attacked the Israelites in a field full of barley. The Israelite army fled, ¹⁴but Eleazar and David* held their ground in the middle of the field and beat back the Philistines. So the LORD saved them by giving them a great victory.

¹⁵Once when David was at the rock near the cave of Adullam, the Philistine army was camped in the valley of Rephaim. The Three (who were among the Thirty—an elite group among David's fighting men) went down to meet him there. ¹⁶David was staying in the stronghold at the time, and a Philistine detachment had occupied the town of Bethlehem.

¹⁷David remarked longingly to his men, "Oh, how I would love some of that good water from the well by the gate in Bethlehem." ¹⁸So the Three broke through the Philistine lines, drew some water from the well by the gate in Bethlehem, and brought it back to David. But David refused to drink it. Instead, he poured it out as an offering to the LORD. ¹⁹"God forbid that I should drink this!" he exclaimed. "This water is as precious as the blood of these men* who risked their lives to bring it to me." So David did not drink it. These are examples of the exploits of the Three.

DAVID'S THIRTY MIGHTY MEN

²⁰Abishai, the brother of Joab, was the leader of the Thirty.* He once used his spear to kill 300 enemy warriors in a single battle. It was by such feats that he became as famous as the Three. ²¹Abishai was the most famous of the Thirty and was their commander, though he was not one of the Three.

²²There was also Benaiah son of Jehoiada, a valiant warrior from Kabzeel. He did many heroic deeds, which included killing two champions* of Moab. Another time, on a snowy day, he chased a lion down into a pit and killed it. ²³Once, armed only with a club, he killed an Egyptian warrior who was 7½ feet* tall and who was armed with a spear as thick as a weaver's beam. Benaiah wrenched the spear from the Egyptian's hand and killed him with it. ²⁴Deeds like these made Benaiah as famous as the three mightiest warriors. ²⁵He was more honored than the other members of the Thirty, though he was not one of the Three. And David made him captain of his bodyguard.

²⁶David's mighty warriors also included:

Asahel, Joab's brother;
Elhanan son of Dodo from Bethlehem;
²⁷Shammah from Harod;*
Helez from Pelon;
²⁸Ira son of Ikkesh from Tekoa;
Abiezer from Anathoth;
²⁹Sibbecai from Hushah;
Zalmon* from Ahoah;
³⁰Maharai from Netophah;
Heled son of Baanah from Netophah;
³¹Ithai son of Ribai from Gibeah
(in the land of Benjamin);
Benaiah from Pirathon;
³²Hurai from near Nahale-gaash*;
Abi-albon* from Arabah;
³³Azmaveth from Bahurim*;
Eliahba from Shaalbon;
³⁴the sons of Jashen* from Gizon;
Jonathan son of Shagee from Harar;
³⁵Ahiam son of Sharar* from Harar;
Eliphal son of Ur;
³⁶Hepher from Mekerah;
Ahijah from Pelon;
³⁷Hezro from Carmel;
Paarai* son of Ezbai;
³⁸Joel, the brother of Nathan;
Mibhar son of Hagri;
³⁹Zelek from Ammon;
Naharai from Beeroth, the armor bearer of Joab son of Zeruiah;
⁴⁰Ira from Jattir;
Gareb from Jattir;
⁴¹Uriah the Hittite;
Zabad son of Ahlai;
⁴²Adina son of Shiza, the Reubenite leader who had thirty men with him;
⁴³Hanan son of Maacah;
Joshaphat from Mithna;
⁴⁴Uzzia from Ashtaroth;
Shama and Jeiel, the sons of Hotham, from Aroer;
⁴⁵Jediael son of Shimri;
Joha, his brother, from Tiz;
⁴⁶Eliel from Mahavah;
Jeribai and Joshaviah, the sons of Elnaam;
Ithmah from Moab;
⁴⁷Eliel and Obed;
Jaasiel from Zobah.*

WARRIORS JOIN DAVID'S ARMY

12 The following men joined David at Ziklag while he was hiding from Saul son of Kish. They were among the warriors who fought beside David in battle. ²All of them were expert archers, and they could shoot arrows or sling stones with their left hand as well as their right. They were all relatives of Saul from the tribe of Benjamin. ³Their leader was Ahiezer son of Shemaah from Gibeah; his brother Joash was

11:12 As in parallel text at 2 Sam 23:9 (see also 1 Chr 27:4); Hebrew reads *Dodo,* a variant spelling of Dodai. 11:14 Hebrew *they.* 11:19 Hebrew *Shall I drink the lifeblood of these men?* 11:20 As in Syriac version; Hebrew reads *the Three;* also in 11:21. 11:22 Or *two champions of Ariel.* 11:23 Hebrew *5 cubits* [2.3 meters]. 11:27 As in parallel text at 2 Sam 23:25; Hebrew reads *Shammoth from Haror.* 11:29 As in parallel text at 2 Sam 23:28; Hebrew reads *Ilai.* 11:32a Or *from the ravines of Gaash.* 11:32b As in parallel text at 2 Sam 23:31; Hebrew reads *Abiel.* 11:33 As in parallel text at 2 Sam 23:31; Hebrew reads *Baharum.* 11:34 As in parallel text at 2 Sam 23:32; Hebrew reads *sons of Hashem.* 11:35 As in parallel text at 2 Sam 23:33; Hebrew reads *son of Sacar.* 11:37 As in parallel text at 2 Sam 23:35; Hebrew reads *Naarai.* 11:47 Or *the Mezobaite.*

second-in-command. These were the other warriors:

Jeziel and Pelet, sons of Azmaveth;
Beracah;
Jehu from Anathoth;
⁴ Ishmaiah from Gibeon, a famous warrior and leader among the Thirty;
*Jeremiah, Jahaziel, Johanan, and Jozabad from Gederah;
⁵ Eluzai, Jerimoth, Bealiah, Shemariah, and Shephatiah from Haruph;
⁶ Elkanah, Isshiah, Azarel, Joezer, and Jashobeam, who were Korahites;
⁷ Joelah and Zebadiah, sons of Jeroham from Gedor.

⁸ Some brave and experienced warriors from the tribe of Gad also defected to David while he was at the stronghold in the wilderness. They were expert with both shield and spear, as fierce as lions and as swift as deer on the mountains.

⁹ Ezer was their leader.
Obadiah was second.
Eliab was third.
¹⁰ Mishmannah was fourth.
Jeremiah was fifth.
¹¹ Attai was sixth.
Eliel was seventh.
¹² Johanan was eighth.
Elzabad was ninth.
¹³ Jeremiah was tenth.
Macbannai was eleventh.

¹⁴ These warriors from Gad were army commanders. The weakest among them could take on a hundred regular troops, and the strongest could take on a thousand! ¹⁵ These were the men who crossed the Jordan River during its seasonal flooding at the beginning of the year and drove out all the people living in the lowlands on both the east and west banks.

¹⁶ Others from Benjamin and Judah came to David at the stronghold. ¹⁷ David went out to meet them and said, "If you have come in peace to help me, we are friends. But if you have come to betray me to my enemies when I am innocent, then may the God of our ancestors see it and punish you." ¹⁸ Then the Spirit came upon Amasai, the leader of the Thirty, and he said,

"We are yours, David!
We are on your side, son of Jesse.
Peace and prosperity be with you,
and success to all who help you,
for your God is the one who helps you."

So David let them join him, and he made them officers over his troops.

¹⁹ Some men from Manasseh defected from the Israelite army and joined David when he set out with the Philistines to fight against Saul. But as it turned out, the Philistine rulers refused to let David and his men go with them. After much discussion, they sent them back, for they said, "It will cost us our heads if David switches loyalties to Saul and turns against us."

²⁰ Here is a list of the men from Manasseh who defected to David as he was returning to Ziklag: Adnah, Jozabad, Jediael, Michael, Jozabad, Elihu, and Zillethai. Each commanded 1,000 troops from the tribe of Manasseh. ²¹ They helped David chase down bands of raiders, for they were all brave and able warriors who became commanders in his army. ²² Day after day more men joined David until he had a great army, like the army of God.

²³ These are the numbers of armed warriors who joined David at Hebron. They were all eager to see David become king instead of Saul, just as the LORD had promised.

²⁴ From the tribe of Judah, there were 6,800 warriors armed with shields and spears.
²⁵ From the tribe of Simeon, there were 7,100 brave warriors.
²⁶ From the tribe of Levi, there were 4,600 warriors. ²⁷ This included Jehoiada, leader of the family of Aaron, who had 3,700 under his command. ²⁸ This also included Zadok, a brave young warrior, with 22 members of his family who were all officers.
²⁹ From the tribe of Benjamin, Saul's relatives, there were 3,000 warriors. Most of the men from Benjamin had remained loyal to Saul until this time.
³⁰ From the tribe of Ephraim, there were 20,800 brave warriors, each highly respected in his own clan.
³¹ From the half-tribe of Manasseh west of the Jordan, 18,000 men were designated by name to help David become king.
³² From the tribe of Issachar, there were 200 leaders of the tribe with their relatives. All these men understood the signs of the times and knew the best course for Israel to take.
³³ From the tribe of Zebulun, there were 50,000 skilled warriors. They were fully armed and prepared for battle and completely loyal to David.
³⁴ From the tribe of Naphtali, there were 1,000 officers and 37,000 warriors armed with shields and spears.
³⁵ From the tribe of Dan, there were 28,600 warriors, all prepared for battle.
³⁶ From the tribe of Asher, there were 40,000 trained warriors, all prepared for battle.
³⁷ From the east side of the Jordan River— where the tribes of Reuben and Gad and the half-tribe of Manasseh lived—there were 120,000 troops armed with every kind of weapon.

12:4 Verses 12:4b-40 are numbered 12:5-41 in Hebrew text.

³⁸All these men came in battle array to Hebron with the single purpose of making David the king over all Israel. In fact, everyone in Israel agreed that David should be their king. ³⁹They feasted and drank with David for three days, for preparations had been made by their relatives for their arrival. ⁴⁰And people from as far away as Issachar, Zebulun, and Naphtali brought food on donkeys, camels, mules, and oxen. Vast supplies of flour, fig cakes, clusters of raisins, wine, olive oil, cattle, sheep, and goats were brought to the celebration. There was great joy throughout the land of Israel.

DAVID ATTEMPTS TO MOVE THE ARK

13 David consulted with all his officials, including the generals and captains of his army.* ²Then he addressed the entire assembly of Israel as follows: "If you approve and if it is the will of the LORD our God, let us send messages to all the Israelites throughout the land, including the priests and Levites in their towns and pasturelands. Let us invite them to come and join us. ³It is time to bring back the Ark of our God, for we neglected it during the reign of Saul."

⁴The whole assembly agreed to this, for the people could see it was the right thing to do. ⁵So David summoned all Israel, from the Shihor Brook of Egypt in the south all the way to the town of Lebo-hamath in the north, to join in bringing the Ark of God from Kiriath-jearim. ⁶Then David and all Israel went to Baalah of Judah (also called Kiriath-jearim) to bring back the Ark of God, which bears the name* of the LORD who is enthroned between the cherubim. ⁷They placed the Ark of God on a new cart and brought it from Abinadab's house. Uzzah and Ahio were guiding the cart. ⁸David and all Israel were celebrating before God with all their might, singing songs and playing all kinds of musical instruments—lyres, harps, tambourines, cymbals, and trumpets.

⁹But when they arrived at the threshing floor of Nacon,* the oxen stumbled, and Uzzah reached out his hand to steady the Ark. ¹⁰Then the LORD's anger was aroused against Uzzah, and he struck him dead because he had laid his hand on the Ark. So Uzzah died there in the presence of God.

¹¹David was angry because the LORD's anger had burst out against Uzzah. He named that place Perez-uzzah (which means "to burst out against Uzzah"), as it is still called today. ¹²David was now afraid of God, and he asked, "How can I ever bring the Ark of God back into my care?" ¹³So David did not move the Ark into the City of David. Instead, he took it to the house of Obed-edom of Gath. ¹⁴The Ark of God remained there in Obed-edom's house for three months, and the LORD blessed the household of Obed-edom and everything he owned.

DAVID'S PALACE AND FAMILY

14 Then King Hiram of Tyre sent messengers to David, along with cedar timber, and stonemasons and carpenters to build him a palace. ²And David realized that the LORD had confirmed him as king over Israel and had greatly blessed his kingdom for the sake of his people Israel.

³Then David married more wives in Jerusalem, and they had more sons and daughters. ⁴These are the names of David's sons who were born in Jerusalem: Shammua, Shobab, Nathan, Solomon, ⁵Ibhar, Elishua, Elpelet, ⁶Nogah, Nepheg, Japhia, ⁷Elishama, Eliada,* and Eliphelet.

DAVID CONQUERS THE PHILISTINES

⁸When the Philistines heard that David had been anointed king over all Israel, they mobilized all their forces to capture him. But David was told they were coming, so he marched out to meet them. ⁹The Philistines arrived and made a raid in the valley of Rephaim. ¹⁰So David asked God, "Should I go out to fight the Philistines? Will you hand them over to me?"

The LORD replied, "Yes, go ahead. I will hand them over to you."

¹¹So David and his troops went up to Baal-perazim and defeated the Philistines there. "God did it!" David exclaimed. "He used me to burst through my enemies like a raging flood!" So they named that place Baal-perazim (which means "the Lord who bursts through"). ¹²The Philistines

---

13:1 Hebrew *the commanders of thousands and of hundreds.*　13:6 Or *the Ark of God, where the Name is proclaimed—the name.*　13:9 As in parallel text at 2 Sam 6:6; Hebrew reads *Kidon.*　14:7 Hebrew *Beeliada,* a variant spelling of Eliada; compare 3:8 and parallel text at 2 Sam 5:16.

had abandoned their gods there, so David gave orders to burn them.

[13] But after a while the Philistines returned and raided the valley again. [14] And once again David asked God what to do. "Do not attack them straight on," God replied. "Instead, circle around behind and attack them near the poplar* trees. [15] When you hear a sound like marching feet in the tops of the poplar trees, go out and attack! That will be the signal that God is moving ahead of you to strike down the Philistine army." [16] So David did what God commanded, and they struck down the Philistine army all the way from Gibeon to Gezer.

[17] So David's fame spread everywhere, and the LORD caused all the nations to fear David.

PREPARING TO MOVE THE ARK

15 David now built several buildings for himself in the City of David. He also prepared a place for the Ark of God and set up a special tent for it. [2] Then he commanded, "No one except the Levites may carry the Ark of God. The LORD has chosen them to carry the Ark of the LORD and to serve him forever."

[3] Then David summoned all Israel to Jerusalem to bring the Ark of the LORD to the place he had prepared for it. [4] This is the number of the descendants of Aaron (the priests) and the Levites who were called together:

[5] From the clan of Kohath, 120, with Uriel as their leader.
[6] From the clan of Merari, 220, with Asaiah as their leader.
[7] From the clan of Gershon,* 130, with Joel as their leader.
[8] From the descendants of Elizaphan, 200, with Shemaiah as their leader.
[9] From the descendants of Hebron, 80, with Eliel as their leader.
[10] From the descendants of Uzziel, 112, with Amminadab as their leader.

[11] Then David summoned the priests, Zadok and Abiathar, and these Levite leaders: Uriel, Asaiah, Joel, Shemaiah, Eliel, and Amminadab. [12] He said to them, "You are the leaders of the Levite families. You must purify yourselves and all your fellow Levites, so you can bring the Ark of the LORD, the God of Israel, to the place I have prepared for it. [13] Because you Levites did not carry the Ark the first time, the anger of the LORD our God burst out against us. We failed to ask God how to move it properly." [14] So the priests and the Levites purified themselves in order to bring the Ark of the LORD, the God of Israel, to Jerusalem. [15] Then the Levites carried the Ark of God on their shoulders with its carrying poles, just as the LORD had instructed Moses.

[16] David also ordered the Levite leaders to appoint a choir of Levites who were singers and musicians to sing joyful songs to the accompaniment of harps, lyres, and cymbals. [17] So the Levites appointed Heman son of Joel along with his fellow Levites: Asaph son of Berekiah, and Ethan son of Kushaiah from the clan of Merari. [18] The following men were chosen as their assistants: Zechariah, Jaaziel,* Shemiramoth, Jehiel, Unni, Eliab, Benaiah, Maaseiah, Mattithiah, Eliphelehu, Mikneiah, and the gatekeepers—Obed-edom and Jeiel.

[19] The musicians Heman, Asaph, and Ethan were chosen to sound the bronze cymbals. [20] Zechariah, Aziel, Shemiramoth, Jehiel, Unni, Eliab, Maaseiah, and Benaiah were chosen to play the harps.* [21] Mattithiah, Eliphelehu, Mikneiah, Obed-edom, Jeiel, and Azaziah were chosen to play the lyres.* [22] Kenaniah, the head Levite, was chosen as the choir leader because of his skill.

[23] Berekiah and Elkanah were chosen to guard* the Ark. [24] Shebaniah, Joshaphat, Nethanel, Amasai, Zechariah, Benaiah, and Eliezer—all of whom were priests—were chosen to blow the trumpets as they marched in front of the Ark of God. Obed-edom and Jehiah were chosen to guard the Ark.

MOVING THE ARK TO JERUSALEM

[25] Then David and the elders of Israel and the generals of the army* went to the house of Obed-edom to bring the Ark of the LORD's Covenant up to Jerusalem with a great celebration. [26] And because God was clearly helping the Levites as they carried the Ark of the LORD's Covenant, they sacrificed seven bulls and seven rams.

[27] David was dressed in a robe of fine linen, as were all the Levites who carried the Ark, and also the singers, and Kenaniah the choir leader. David was also wearing a priestly garment.* [28] So all Israel brought up the Ark of the LORD's Covenant with shouts of joy, the blowing of rams' horns and trumpets, the crashing of cymbals, and loud playing on harps and lyres.

[29] But as the Ark of the LORD's Covenant entered the City of David, Michal, the daughter of Saul, looked down from her window. When she saw King David skipping about and laughing with joy, she was filled with contempt for him.

16 They brought the Ark of God and placed it inside the special tent David had prepared for it. And they presented burnt offerings and peace offerings to God. [2] When he had finished his sacrifices, David blessed the people in the

---

14:14 Or *aspen,* or *balsam;* also in 14:15. The exact identification of this tree is uncertain. 15:7 Hebrew *Gershom,* a variant spelling of Gershon. 15:18 As in several Hebrew manuscripts and Greek version (see also parallel lists in 15:20; 16:5); Masoretic Text reads *Zechariah ben Jaaziel.* 15:20 Hebrew adds *according to Alamoth,* which is probably a musical term. The meaning of the Hebrew is uncertain. 15:21 Hebrew adds *according to the Sheminith,* which is probably a musical term. The meaning of the Hebrew is uncertain. 15:23 Hebrew *chosen as gatekeepers for;* also in 15:24. 15:25 Hebrew *the commanders of thousands.* 15:27 Hebrew *a linen ephod.*

name of the LORD. ³Then he gave to every man and woman in all Israel a loaf of bread, a cake of dates,* and a cake of raisins.

⁴David appointed the following Levites to lead the people in worship before the Ark of the LORD—to invoke his blessings, to give thanks, and to praise the LORD, the God of Israel. ⁵Asaph, the leader of this group, sounded the cymbals. Second to him was Zechariah, followed by Jeiel, Shemiramoth, Jehiel, Mattithiah, Eliab, Benaiah, Obed-edom, and Jeiel. They played the harps and lyres. ⁶The priests, Benaiah and Jahaziel, played the trumpets regularly before the Ark of God's Covenant.

DAVID'S SONG OF PRAISE

⁷On that day David gave to Asaph and his fellow Levites this song of thanksgiving to the LORD:

⁸ Give thanks to the LORD and proclaim his
    greatness.
  Let the whole world know what he
    has done.
⁹ Sing to him; yes, sing his praises.
  Tell everyone about his wonderful deeds.
¹⁰ Exult in his holy name;
  rejoice, you who worship the LORD.
¹¹ Search for the LORD and for his strength;
  continually seek him.
¹² Remember the wonders he has performed,
  his miracles, and the rulings he has given,
¹³ you children of his servant Israel,
  you descendants of Jacob, his chosen ones.

¹⁴ He is the LORD our God.
  His justice is seen throughout the land.
¹⁵ Remember his covenant forever—
  the commitment he made to a thousand
    generations.
¹⁶ This is the covenant he made with Abraham
  and the oath he swore to Isaac.
¹⁷ He confirmed it to Jacob as a decree,
  and to the people of Israel as a
    never-ending covenant:
¹⁸ "I will give you the land of Canaan
  as your special possession."

¹⁹ He said this when you were few in number,
  a tiny group of strangers in Canaan.
²⁰ They wandered from nation to nation,
  from one kingdom to another.
²¹ Yet he did not let anyone oppress them.
  He warned kings on their behalf:
²² "Do not touch my chosen people,
  and do not hurt my prophets."

²³ Let the whole earth sing to the LORD!
  Each day proclaim the good news that
    he saves.
²⁴ Publish his glorious deeds among the nations.
  Tell everyone about the amazing things
    he does.

²⁵ Great is the LORD! He is most worthy of
    praise!
  He is to be feared above all gods.
²⁶ The gods of other nations are mere idols,
  but the LORD made the heavens!
²⁷ Honor and majesty surround him;
  strength and joy fill his dwelling.

²⁸ O nations of the world, recognize the LORD,
  recognize that the LORD is glorious and
    strong.
²⁹ Give to the LORD the glory he deserves!
  Bring your offering and come into his
    presence.
  Worship the LORD in all his holy splendor.
³⁰ Let all the earth tremble before him.
  The world stands firm and cannot be
    shaken.

³¹ Let the heavens be glad, and the earth
    rejoice!
  Tell all the nations, "The LORD reigns!"
³² Let the sea and everything in it shout
    his praise!
  Let the fields and their crops burst out
    with joy!
³³ Let the trees of the forest sing for joy before
    the LORD,
  for he is coming to judge the earth.

³⁴ Give thanks to the LORD, for he is good!
  His faithful love endures forever.
³⁵ Cry out, "Save us, O God of our salvation!
  Gather and rescue us from among the
    nations,
  so we can thank your holy name
    and rejoice and praise you."

³⁶ Praise the LORD, the God of Israel,
  who lives from everlasting to everlasting!

And all the people shouted "Amen!" and praised the LORD.

WORSHIP AT JERUSALEM AND GIBEON

³⁷David arranged for Asaph and his fellow Levites to serve regularly before the Ark of the LORD's Covenant, doing whatever needed to be done each day. ³⁸This group included Obed-edom (son of Jeduthun), Hosah, and sixty-eight other Levites as gatekeepers.

³⁹Meanwhile, David stationed Zadok the priest and his fellow priests at the Tabernacle of the LORD at the place of worship in Gibeon, where they continued to minister before the LORD. ⁴⁰They sacrificed the regular burnt offerings to the LORD each morning and evening on the altar set aside for that purpose, obeying everything written in the Law of the LORD, as he

---

16:3 Or *a portion of meat*. The meaning of the Hebrew is uncertain.

had commanded Israel. [41]David also appointed Heman, Jeduthun, and the others chosen by name to give thanks to the LORD, for "his faithful love endures forever." [42]They used their trumpets, cymbals, and other instruments to accompany their songs of praise to God.* And the sons of Jeduthun were appointed as gatekeepers.

[43]Then all the people returned to their homes, and David turned and went home to bless his own family.

THE LORD'S COVENANT PROMISE TO DAVID

17 When David was settled in his palace, he summoned Nathan the prophet. "Look," David said, "I am living in a beautiful cedar palace,* but the Ark of the LORD's Covenant is out there under a tent!"

[2]Nathan replied to David, "Do whatever you have in mind, for God is with you."

[3]But that same night God said to Nathan,

[4]"Go and tell my servant David, 'This is what the LORD has declared: You are not the one to build a house for me to live in. [5]I have never lived in a house, from the day I brought the Israelites out of Egypt until this very day. My home has always been a tent, moving from one place to another in a Tabernacle. [6]Yet no matter where I have gone with the Israelites, I have never once complained to Israel's leaders, the shepherds of my people. I have never asked them, "Why haven't you built me a beautiful cedar house?"'

[7]"Now go and say to my servant David, 'This is what the LORD of Heaven's Armies has declared: I took you from tending sheep in the pasture and selected you to be the leader of my people Israel. [8]I have been with you wherever you have gone, and I have destroyed all your enemies before your eyes. Now I will make your name as famous as anyone who has ever lived on the earth! [9]And I will provide a homeland for my people Israel, planting them in a secure place where they will never be disturbed. Evil nations won't oppress them as they've done in the past, [10]starting from the time I appointed judges to rule my people Israel. And I will defeat all your enemies.

"'Furthermore, I declare that the LORD will build a house for you—a dynasty of kings! [11]For when you die and join your ancestors, I will raise up one of your descendants, one of your sons, and I will make his kingdom strong. [12]He is the one who will build a house—a temple—for me. And I will secure his throne forever. [13]I will be his father, and he will be my son. I will never take my favor from him as I took it from the one who ruled before you. [14]I will confirm him as king over my house and my kingdom for all time, and his throne will be secure forever.'"

[15]So Nathan went back to David and told him everything the LORD had said in this vision.

DAVID'S PRAYER OF THANKS

[16]Then King David went in and sat before the LORD and prayed,

"Who am I, O LORD God, and what is my family, that you have brought me this far? [17]And now, O God, in addition to everything else, you speak of giving your servant a lasting dynasty! You speak as though I were someone very great,* O LORD God!

[18]"What more can I say to you about the way you have honored me? You know what your servant is really like. [19]For the sake of your servant, O LORD, and according to your will, you have done all these great things and have made them known.

[20]"O LORD, there is no one like you. We have never even heard of another God like you! [21]What other nation on earth is like your people Israel? What other nation, O God, have you redeemed from slavery to be your own people? You made a great name for yourself when you redeemed your people from Egypt. You performed awesome miracles and drove out the nations that stood in their way. [22]You chose Israel to be your very own people forever, and you, O LORD, became their God.

[23]"And now, O LORD, I am your servant; do as you have promised concerning me and my family. May it be a promise that will last forever. [24]And may your name be established and honored forever so that everyone will say, 'The LORD of Heaven's Armies, the God of Israel, is Israel's God!' And may the house of your servant David continue before you forever.

[25]"O my God, I have been bold enough to pray to you because you have revealed to your servant that you will build a house for him—a dynasty of kings! [26]For you are God, O LORD. And you have promised these good things to your servant. [27]And now, it has pleased you to bless the house of your servant, so that it will continue forever before you. For when you grant a blessing, O LORD, it is an eternal blessing!"

DAVID'S MILITARY VICTORIES

18 After this, David defeated and subdued the Philistines by conquering Gath and its surrounding towns. [2]David also conquered

---

16:42 Or *to accompany the sacred music;* or *to accompany singing to God.* 17:1 Hebrew *a house of cedar.* 17:17 The meaning of the Hebrew is uncertain.

the land of Moab, and the Moabites who were spared became David's subjects and paid him tribute money.

³David also destroyed the forces of Hadadezer, king of Zobah, as far as Hamath,* when Hadadezer marched out to strengthen his control along the Euphrates River. ⁴David captured 1,000 chariots, 7,000 charioteers, and 20,000 foot soldiers. He crippled all the chariot horses except enough for 100 chariots.

⁵When Arameans from Damascus arrived to help King Hadadezer, David killed 22,000 of them. ⁶Then he placed several army garrisons* in Damascus, the Aramean capital, and the Arameans became David's subjects and paid him tribute money. So the Lord made David victorious wherever he went.

⁷David brought the gold shields of Hadadezer's officers to Jerusalem, ⁸along with a large amount of bronze from Hadadezer's towns of Tebah* and Cun. Later Solomon melted the bronze and molded it into the great bronze basin called the Sea, the pillars, and the various bronze articles used at the Temple.

⁹When King Toi* of Hamath heard that David had destroyed the entire army of King Hadadezer of Zobah, ¹⁰he sent his son Joram* to congratulate King David for his successful campaign. Hadadezer and Toi had been enemies and were often at war. Joram presented David with many gifts of gold, silver, and bronze.

¹¹King David dedicated all these gifts to the Lord, along with the silver and gold he had taken from the other nations—from Edom, Moab, Ammon, Philistia, and Amalek.

¹²Abishai son of Zeruiah destroyed 18,000 Edomites in the Valley of Salt. ¹³He placed army garrisons in Edom, and all the Edomites became David's subjects. In fact, the Lord made David victorious wherever he went.

¹⁴So David reigned over all Israel and did what was just and right for all his people. ¹⁵Joab son of Zeruiah was commander of the army. Jehoshaphat son of Ahilud was the royal historian. ¹⁶Zadok son of Ahitub and Ahimelech* son of Abiathar were the priests. Seraiah* was the court secretary. ¹⁷Benaiah son of Jehoiada was captain of the king's bodyguard.* And David's sons served as the king's chief assistants.

DAVID DEFEATS THE AMMONITES

19 Some time after this, King Nahash of the Ammonites died, and his son Hanun* became king. ²David said, "I am going to show loyalty to Hanun because his father, Nahash, was always loyal to me." So David sent messengers to express sympathy to Hanun about his father's death.

But when David's ambassadors arrived in the land of Ammon, ³the Ammonite commanders said to Hanun, "Do you really think these men are coming here to honor your father? No!

David has sent them to spy out the land so they can come in and conquer it!" ⁴So Hanun seized David's ambassadors and shaved them, cut off their robes at the buttocks, and sent them back to David in shame.

⁵When David heard what had happened to the men, he sent messengers to tell them, "Stay at Jericho until your beards grow out, and then come back." For they felt deep shame because of their appearance.

⁶When the people of Ammon realized how seriously they had angered David, Hanun and the Ammonites sent 75,000 pounds* of silver to hire chariots and charioteers from Aram-naharaim, Aram-maacah, and Zobah. ⁷They also hired 32,000 chariots and secured the support of the king of Maacah and his army. These forces camped at Medeba, where they were joined by the Ammonite troops that Hanun had recruited from his own towns. ⁸When David heard about this, he sent Joab and all his warriors to fight them. ⁹The Ammonite troops came out and drew up their battle lines at the entrance of the city, while the other kings positioned themselves to fight in the open fields.

¹⁰When Joab saw that he would have to fight on both the front and the rear, he chose some of Israel's elite troops and placed them under his personal command to fight the Arameans in the fields. ¹¹He left the rest of the army under the command of his brother Abishai, who was to attack the Ammonites. ¹²"If the Arameans are too strong for me, then come over and help me," Joab told his brother. "And if the Ammonites are too strong for you, I will help you. ¹³Be courageous! Let us fight bravely for our people and the cities of our God. May the Lord's will be done."

¹⁴When Joab and his troops attacked, the Arameans began to run away. ¹⁵And when the Ammonites saw the Arameans running, they also ran from Abishai and retreated into the city. Then Joab returned to Jerusalem.

¹⁶The Arameans now realized that they were no match for Israel, so they sent messengers and summoned additional Aramean troops from the other side of the Euphrates River.* These troops were under the command of Shobach,* the commander of Hadadezer's forces.

¹⁷When David heard what was happening, he mobilized all Israel, crossed the Jordan River,

18:3 The meaning of the Hebrew is uncertain. 18:6 As in Greek version and Latin Vulgate (see also 2 Sam 8:6); Hebrew lacks several army garrisons. 18:8 Hebrew reads Tibhah, a variant spelling of Tebah; compare parallel text at 2 Sam 8:8. 18:9 As in parallel text at 2 Sam 8:9; Hebrew reads Tou; also in 18:10. 18:10 As in parallel text at 2 Sam 8:10; Hebrew reads Hadoram, a variant spelling of Joram. 18:16a As in some Hebrew manuscripts, Syriac version, and Latin Vulgate (see also 2 Sam 8:17); most Hebrew manuscripts read Abimelech. 18:16b As in parallel text at 2 Sam 8:17; Hebrew Shavsha. 18:17 Hebrew of the Kerethites and Pelethites. 19:1 As in parallel text at 2 Sam 10:1; Hebrew lacks Hanun. 19:6 Hebrew 1,000 talents [34,000 kilograms]. 19:16a Hebrew the river. 19:16b As in parallel text at 2 Sam 10:16; Hebrew reads Shophach; also in 19:18.

and positioned his troops in battle formation. Then David engaged the Arameans in battle, and they fought against him. ¹⁸ But again the Arameans fled from the Israelites. This time David's forces killed 7,000 charioteers and 40,000 foot soldiers, including Shobach, the commander of their army. ¹⁹ When Hadadezer's allies saw that they had been defeated by Israel, they surrendered to David and became his subjects. After that, the Arameans were no longer willing to help the Ammonites.

DAVID CAPTURES RABBAH

20 In the spring of the year,* when kings normally go out to war, Joab led the Israelite army in successful attacks against the land of the Ammonites. In the process he laid siege to the city of Rabbah, attacking and destroying it. However, David stayed behind in Jerusalem.

² Then David went to Rabbah and removed the crown from the king's head,* and it was placed on his own head. The crown was made of gold and set with gems, and he found that it weighed seventy-five pounds.* David took a vast amount of plunder from the city. ³ He also made slaves of the people of Rabbah and forced them to labor with saws, iron picks, and iron axes.* That is how David dealt with the people of all the Ammonite towns. Then David and all the army returned to Jerusalem.

BATTLES AGAINST PHILISTINE GIANTS

⁴ After this, war broke out with the Philistines at Gezer. As they fought, Sibbecai from Hushah killed Saph,* a descendant of the giants,* and so the Philistines were subdued.

⁵ During another battle with the Philistines, Elhanan son of Jair killed Lahmi, the brother of Goliath of Gath. The handle of Lahmi's spear was as thick as a weaver's beam!

⁶ In another battle with the Philistines at Gath, they encountered a huge man with six fingers on each hand and six toes on each foot, twenty-four in all, who was also a descendant of the giants. ⁷ But when he defied and taunted Israel, he was killed by Jonathan, the son of David's brother Shimea.

⁸ These Philistines were descendants of the giants of Gath, but David and his warriors killed them.

DAVID TAKES A CENSUS

21 Satan rose up against Israel and caused David to take a census of the people of Israel. ² So David said to Joab and the commanders of the army, "Take a census of all the people of Israel—from Beersheba in the south to Dan in the north—and bring me a report so I may know how many there are."

³ But Joab replied, "May the LORD increase the number of his people a hundred times over! But why, my lord the king, do you want to do this? Are they not all your servants? Why must you cause Israel to sin?"

⁴ But the king insisted that they take the census, so Joab traveled throughout all Israel to count the people. Then he returned to Jerusalem ⁵ and reported the number of people to David. There were 1,100,000 warriors in all Israel who could handle a sword, and 470,000 in Judah. ⁶ But Joab did not include the tribes of Levi and Benjamin in the census because he was so distressed at what the king had made him do.

JUDGMENT FOR DAVID'S SIN

⁷ God was very displeased with the census, and he punished Israel for it. ⁸ Then David said to God, "I have sinned greatly by taking this census. Please forgive my guilt for doing this foolish thing."

⁹ Then the LORD spoke to Gad, David's seer. This was the message: ¹⁰ "Go and say to David, 'This is what the LORD says: I will give you three choices. Choose one of these punishments, and I will inflict it on you.'"

¹¹ So Gad came to David and said, "These are the choices the LORD has given you. ¹² You may choose three years of famine, three months of destruction by the sword of your enemies, or three days of severe plague as the angel of the LORD brings devastation throughout the land of Israel. Decide what answer I should give the LORD who sent me."

¹³ "I'm in a desperate situation!" David replied to Gad. "But let me fall into the hands of the LORD, for his mercy is very great. Do not let me fall into human hands."

¹⁴ So the LORD sent a plague upon Israel, and 70,000 people died as a result. ¹⁵ And God sent an angel to destroy Jerusalem. But just as the angel was preparing to destroy it, the LORD relented and said to the death angel, "Stop! That is enough!" At that moment the angel of the LORD was standing by the threshing floor of Araunah* the Jebusite.

¹⁶ David looked up and saw the angel of the LORD standing between heaven and earth with his sword drawn, reaching out over Jerusalem. So David and the leaders of Israel put on burlap to show their deep distress and fell face down on the ground. ¹⁷ And David said to God, "I am the one who called for the census! I am the one who has sinned and done wrong! But these people are as innocent as sheep—what have they done? O LORD my God, let your anger fall against me and my family, but do not destroy your people."

20:1 Hebrew *At the turn of the year*. The first day of the year in the ancient Hebrew lunar calendar occurred in March or April.   20:2a Or *from the head of Milcom* (as in Greek version and Latin Vulgate). Milcom, also called Molech, was the god of the Ammonites.   20:2b Hebrew *1 talent* [34 kilograms].   20:3 As in parallel text at 2 Sam 12:31; Hebrew reads *and cut them with saws, iron picks, and saws*.   20:4a As in parallel text at 2 Sam 21:18; Hebrew reads *Sippai*.   20:4b Hebrew *descendant of the Rephaites;* also in 20:6, 8.   21:15 As in parallel text at 2 Sam 24:16; Hebrew reads *Ornan*, another name for Araunah; also in 21:18-28.

DAVID BUILDS AN ALTAR

¹⁸Then the angel of the LORD told Gad to instruct David to go up and build an altar to the LORD on the threshing floor of Araunah the Jebusite. ¹⁹So David went up to do what the LORD had commanded him through Gad. ²⁰Araunah, who was busy threshing wheat at the time, turned and saw the angel there. His four sons, who were with him, ran away and hid. ²¹When Araunah saw David approaching, he left his threshing floor and bowed before David with his face to the ground.

²²David said to Araunah, "Let me buy this threshing floor from you at its full price. Then I will build an altar to the LORD there, so that he will stop the plague."

²³"Take it, my lord the king, and use it as you wish," Araunah said to David. "I will give the oxen for the burnt offerings, and the threshing boards for wood to build a fire on the altar, and the wheat for the grain offering. I will give it all to you."

²⁴But King David replied to Araunah, "No, I insist on buying it for the full price. I will not take what is yours and give it to the LORD. I will not present burnt offerings that have cost me nothing!" ²⁵So David gave Araunah 600 pieces of gold* in payment for the threshing floor.

²⁶David built an altar there to the LORD and sacrificed burnt offerings and peace offerings. And when David prayed, the LORD answered him by sending fire from heaven to burn up the offering on the altar. ²⁷Then the LORD spoke to the angel, who put the sword back into its sheath.

²⁸When David saw that the LORD had answered his prayer, he offered sacrifices there at Araunah's threshing floor. ²⁹At that time the Tabernacle of the LORD and the altar of burnt offering that Moses had made in the wilderness were located at the place of worship in Gibeon. ³⁰But David was not able to go there to inquire of God, because he was terrified by the drawn sword of the angel of the LORD.

22 Then David said, "This will be the location for the Temple of the LORD God and the place of the altar for Israel's burnt offerings!"

PREPARATIONS FOR THE TEMPLE

²So David gave orders to call together the foreigners living in Israel, and he assigned them the task of preparing finished stone for building the Temple of God. ³David provided large amounts of iron for the nails that would be needed for the doors in the gates and for the clamps, and he gave more bronze than could be weighed. ⁴He also provided innumerable cedar logs, for the men of Tyre and Sidon had brought vast amounts of cedar to David.

⁵David said, "My son Solomon is still young and inexperienced. And since the Temple to be built for the LORD must be a magnificent structure, famous and glorious throughout the world, I will begin making preparations for it now." So David collected vast amounts of building materials before his death.

⁶Then David sent for his son Solomon and instructed him to build a Temple for the LORD, the God of Israel. ⁷"My son, I wanted to build a Temple to honor the name of the LORD my God," David told him. ⁸"But the LORD said to me, 'You have killed many men in the battles you have fought. And since you have shed so much blood in my sight, you will not be the one to build a Temple to honor my name. ⁹But you will have a son who will be a man of peace. I will give him peace with his enemies in all the surrounding lands. His name will be Solomon,* and I will give peace and quiet to Israel during his reign. ¹⁰He is the one who will build a Temple to honor my name. He will be my son, and I will be his father. And I will secure the throne of his kingdom over Israel forever.'

¹¹"Now, my son, may the LORD be with you and give you success as you follow his directions in building the Temple of the LORD your God. ¹²And may the LORD give you wisdom and understanding, that you may obey the Law of the LORD your God as you rule over Israel. ¹³For you will be successful if you carefully obey the decrees and regulations that the LORD gave to Israel through Moses. Be strong and courageous; do not be afraid or lose heart!

¹⁴"I have worked hard to provide materials for building the Temple of the LORD—nearly 4,000 tons of gold, 40,000 tons of silver,* and so much iron and bronze that it cannot be weighed. I have also gathered timber and stone for the walls, though you may need to add more. ¹⁵You have a large number of skilled stonemasons and carpenters and craftsmen of every kind. ¹⁶You have expert goldsmiths and silversmiths and workers of bronze and iron. Now begin the work, and may the LORD be with you!"

¹⁷Then David ordered all the leaders of Israel to assist Solomon in this project. ¹⁸"The LORD your God is with you," he declared. "He has given you peace with the surrounding nations. He has handed them over to me, and they are now subject to the LORD and his people. ¹⁹Now seek the LORD your God with all your heart and soul. Build the sanctuary of the LORD God so that you can bring the Ark of the LORD's Covenant and the holy vessels of God into the Temple built to honor the LORD's name."

DUTIES OF THE LEVITES

23 When David was an old man, he appointed his son Solomon to be king over Israel. ²David summoned all the leaders of Israel, together with the priests and Levites. ³All the Levites who were thirty years old or older were

---

21:25 Hebrew *600 shekels of gold*, about 15 pounds or 6.8 kilograms in weight.   22:9 *Solomon* sounds like and is probably derived from the Hebrew word for "peace."   22:14 Hebrew *100,000 talents* [3,400 metric tons] *of gold*, *1,000,000 talents* [34,000 metric tons] *of silver*.

counted, and the total came to 38,000. ⁴Then David said, "From all the Levites, 24,000 will supervise the work at the Temple of the LORD. Another 6,000 will serve as officials and judges. ⁵Another 4,000 will work as gatekeepers, and 4,000 will praise the LORD with the musical instruments I have made." ⁶Then David divided the Levites into divisions named after the clans descended from the three sons of Levi—Gershon, Kohath, and Merari.

THE GERSHONITES

⁷The Gershonite family units were defined by their lines of descent from Libni* and Shimei, the sons of Gershon. ⁸Three of the descendants of Libni were Jehiel (the family leader), Zetham, and Joel. ⁹These were the leaders of the family of Libni.

Three of the descendants of Shimei were Shelomoth, Haziel, and Haran. ¹⁰Four other descendants of Shimei were Jahath, Ziza,* Jeush, and Beriah. ¹¹Jahath was the family leader, and Ziza was next. Jeush and Beriah were counted as a single family because neither had many sons.

THE KOHATHITES

¹²Four of the descendants of Kohath were Amram, Izhar, Hebron, and Uzziel. ¹³The sons of Amram were Aaron and Moses. Aaron and his descendants were set apart to dedicate the most holy things, to offer sacrifices in the LORD's presence, to serve the LORD, and to pronounce blessings in his name forever.

¹⁴As for Moses, the man of God, his sons were included with the tribe of Levi. ¹⁵The sons of Moses were Gershom and Eliezer. ¹⁶The descendants of Gershom included Shebuel, the family leader. ¹⁷Eliezer had only one son, Rehabiah, the family leader. Rehabiah had numerous descendants. ¹⁸The descendants of Izhar included Shelomith, the family leader. ¹⁹The descendants of Hebron included Jeriah (the family leader), Amariah (the second), Jahaziel (the third), and Jekameam (the fourth). ²⁰The descendants of Uzziel included Micah (the family leader) and Isshiah (the second).

THE MERARITES

²¹The descendants of Merari included Mahli and Mushi.

The sons of Mahli were Eleazar and Kish. ²²Eleazar died with no sons, only daughters. His daughters married their cousins, the sons of Kish. ²³Three of the descendants of Mushi were Mahli, Eder, and Jerimoth.

²⁴These were the descendants of Levi by clans, the leaders of their family groups, registered carefully by name. Each had to be twenty years old or older to qualify for service in the house of the LORD. ²⁵For David said, "The LORD, the God of Israel, has given us peace, and he will always live in Jerusalem. ²⁶Now the Levites will no longer need to carry the Tabernacle and its furnishings from place to place." ²⁷In accordance with David's final instructions, all the Levites twenty years old or older were registered for service.

²⁸The work of the Levites was to assist the priests, the descendants of Aaron, as they served at the house of the LORD. They also took care of the courtyards and side rooms, helped perform the ceremonies of purification, and served in many other ways in the house of God. ²⁹They were in charge of the sacred bread that was set out on the table, the choice flour for the grain offerings, the wafers made without yeast, the cakes cooked in olive oil, and the other mixed breads. They were also responsible to check all the weights and measures. ³⁰And each morning and evening they stood before the LORD to sing songs of thanks and praise to him. ³¹They assisted with the burnt offerings that were presented to the LORD on Sabbath days, at new moon celebrations, and at all the appointed festivals. The required number of Levites served in the LORD's presence at all times, following all the procedures they had been given.

³²And so, under the supervision of the priests, the Levites watched over the Tabernacle and the Temple* and faithfully carried out their duties of service at the house of the LORD.

DUTIES OF THE PRIESTS

24 This is how Aaron's descendants, the priests, were divided into groups for service. The sons of Aaron were Nadab, Abihu, Eleazar, and Ithamar. ²But Nadab and Abihu died before their father, and they had no sons. So only Eleazar and Ithamar were left to carry on as priests. ³With the help of Zadok, who was a descendant of Eleazar, and of Ahimelech, who was a descendant of Ithamar, David divided Aaron's descendants into groups according to their various duties. ⁴Eleazar's descendants were divided into sixteen groups and Ithamar's into eight, for there were more family leaders among the descendants of Eleazar.

⁵All tasks were assigned to the various groups by means of sacred lots so that no preference would be shown, for there were many qualified officials serving God in the sanctuary from among the descendants of both Eleazar and Ithamar. ⁶Shemaiah son of Nethanel, a Levite, acted as secretary and wrote down the names and assignments in the presence of the king, the

officials, Zadok the priest, Ahimelech son of Abiathar, and the family leaders of the priests and Levites. The descendants of Eleazar and Ithamar took turns casting lots.

7 The first lot fell to Jehoiarib.
The second lot fell to Jedaiah.
8 The third lot fell to Harim.
The fourth lot fell to Seorim.
9 The fifth lot fell to Malkijah.
The sixth lot fell to Mijamin.
10 The seventh lot fell to Hakkoz.
The eighth lot fell to Abijah.
11 The ninth lot fell to Jeshua.
The tenth lot fell to Shecaniah.
12 The eleventh lot fell to Eliashib.
The twelfth lot fell to Jakim.
13 The thirteenth lot fell to Huppah.
The fourteenth lot fell to Jeshebeab.
14 The fifteenth lot fell to Bilgah.
The sixteenth lot fell to Immer.
15 The seventeenth lot fell to Hezir.
The eighteenth lot fell to Happizzez.
16 The nineteenth lot fell to Pethahiah.
The twentieth lot fell to Jehezkel.
17 The twenty-first lot fell to Jakin.
The twenty-second lot fell to Gamul.
18 The twenty-third lot fell to Delaiah.
The twenty-fourth lot fell to Maaziah.

19 Each group carried out its appointed duties in the house of the LORD according to the procedures established by their ancestor Aaron in obedience to the commands of the LORD, the God of Israel.

FAMILY LEADERS AMONG THE LEVITES
20 These were the other family leaders descended from Levi:

From the descendants of Amram, the leader was Shebuel.*
From the descendants of Shebuel, the leader was Jehdeiah.
21 From the descendants of Rehabiah, the leader was Isshiah.
22 From the descendants of Izhar, the leader was Shelomith.*
From the descendants of Shelomith, the leader was Jahath.
23 From the descendants of Hebron, Jeriah was the leader,* Amariah was second, Jahaziel was third, and Jekameam was fourth.
24 From the descendants of Uzziel, the leader was Micah.
From the descendants of Micah, the leader was Shamir, 25 along with Isshiah, the brother of Micah.
From the descendants of Isshiah, the leader was Zechariah.
26 From the descendants of Merari, the leaders were Mahli and Mushi.

From the descendants of Jaaziah, the leader was Beno.
27 From the descendants of Merari through Jaaziah, the leaders were Beno, Shoham, Zaccur, and Ibri.
28 From the descendants of Mahli, the leader was Eleazar, though he had no sons.
29 From the descendants of Kish, the leader was Jerahmeel.
30 From the descendants of Mushi, the leaders were Mahli, Eder, and Jerimoth.

These were the descendants of Levi in their various families. 31 Like the descendants of Aaron, they were assigned to their duties by means of sacred lots, without regard to age or rank. Lots were drawn in the presence of King David, Zadok, Ahimelech, and the family leaders of the priests and the Levites.

DUTIES OF THE MUSICIANS
25 David and the army commanders then appointed men from the families of Asaph, Heman, and Jeduthun to proclaim God's messages to the accompaniment of lyres, harps, and cymbals. Here is a list of their names and their work:

2 From the sons of Asaph, there were Zaccur, Joseph, Nethaniah, and Asarelah. They worked under the direction of their father, Asaph, who proclaimed God's messages by the king's orders.
3 From the sons of Jeduthun, there were Gedaliah, Zeri, Jeshaiah, Shimei,* Hashabiah, and Mattithiah, six in all. They worked under the direction of their father, Jeduthun, who proclaimed God's messages to the accompaniment of the lyre, offering thanks and praise to the LORD.
4 From the sons of Heman, there were Bukkiah, Mattaniah, Uzziel, Shubael,* Jerimoth, Hananiah, Hanani, Eliathah, Giddalti, Romamti-ezer, Joshbekashah, Mallothi, Hothir, and Mahazioth. 5 All these were the sons of Heman, the king's seer, for God had honored him with fourteen sons and three daughters.

6 All these men were under the direction of their fathers as they made music at the house of the LORD. Their responsibilities included the playing of cymbals, harps, and lyres at the house of God. Asaph, Jeduthun, and Heman reported directly to the king. 7 They and their families

24:20 Hebrew *Shubael* (also in 24:20b), a variant spelling of Shebuel; compare 23:16 and 26:24.   24:22 Hebrew *Shelomoth* (also in 24:22b), a variant spelling of Shelomith; compare 23:18.   24:23 Hebrew *From the descendants of Jeriah;* compare 23:19.   25:3 As in one Hebrew manuscript and some Greek manuscripts (see also 25:17); most Hebrew manuscripts lack *Shimei.*   25:4 Hebrew *Shebuel,* a variant spelling of Shubael; compare 25:20.

were all trained in making music before the LORD, and each of them—288 in all—was an accomplished musician. ⁸The musicians were appointed to their term of service by means of sacred lots, without regard to whether they were young or old, teacher or student.

⁹ The first lot fell to Joseph of the Asaph clan and twelve of his sons and relatives.*
The second lot fell to Gedaliah and twelve of his sons and relatives.

¹⁰ The third lot fell to Zaccur and twelve of his sons and relatives.

¹¹ The fourth lot fell to Zeri* and twelve of his sons and relatives.

¹² The fifth lot fell to Nethaniah and twelve of his sons and relatives.

¹³ The sixth lot fell to Bukkiah and twelve of his sons and relatives.

¹⁴ The seventh lot fell to Asarelah* and twelve of his sons and relatives.

¹⁵ The eighth lot fell to Jeshaiah and twelve of his sons and relatives.

¹⁶ The ninth lot fell to Mattaniah and twelve of his sons and relatives.

¹⁷ The tenth lot fell to Shimei and twelve of his sons and relatives.

¹⁸ The eleventh lot fell to Uzziel* and twelve of his sons and relatives.

¹⁹ The twelfth lot fell to Hashabiah and twelve of his sons and relatives.

²⁰ The thirteenth lot fell to Shubael and twelve of his sons and relatives.

²¹ The fourteenth lot fell to Mattithiah and twelve of his sons and relatives.

²² The fifteenth lot fell to Jerimoth* and twelve of his sons and relatives.

²³ The sixteenth lot fell to Hananiah and twelve of his sons and relatives.

²⁴ The seventeenth lot fell to Joshbekashah* and twelve of his sons and relatives.

²⁵ The eighteenth lot fell to Hanani and twelve of his sons and relatives.

²⁶ The nineteenth lot fell to Mallothi and twelve of his sons and relatives.

²⁷ The twentieth lot fell to Eliathah and twelve of his sons and relatives.

²⁸ The twenty-first lot fell to Hothir and twelve of his sons and relatives.

²⁹ The twenty-second lot fell to Giddalti and twelve of his sons and relatives.

³⁰ The twenty-third lot fell to Mahazioth and twelve of his sons and relatives.

³¹ The twenty-fourth lot fell to Romamti-ezer and twelve of his sons and relatives.

DUTIES OF THE GATEKEEPERS

26 These are the divisions of the gatekeepers:

From the Korahites, there was Meshelemiah son of Kore, of the family of Abiasaph.* ²The sons of Meshelemiah were Zechariah

(the oldest), Jediael (the second), Zebadiah (the third), Jathniel (the fourth), ³Elam (the fifth), Jehohanan (the sixth), and Eliehoenai (the seventh).

⁴The sons of Obed-edom, also gatekeepers, were Shemaiah (the oldest), Jehozabad (the second), Joah (the third), Sacar (the fourth), Nethanel (the fifth), ⁵Ammiel (the sixth), Issachar (the seventh), and Peullethai (the eighth). God had richly blessed Obed-edom.

⁶Obed-edom's son Shemaiah had sons with great ability who earned positions of great authority in the clan. ⁷Their names were Othni, Rephael, Obed, and Elzabad. Their relatives, Elihu and Semakiah, were also very capable men.

⁸All of these descendants of Obed-edom, including their sons and grandsons—sixty-two of them in all—were very capable men, well qualified for their work. ⁹Meshelemiah's eighteen sons and relatives were also very capable men.

¹⁰Hosah, of the Merari clan, appointed Shimri as the leader among his sons, though he was not the oldest. ¹¹His other sons included Hilkiah (the second), Tebaliah (the third), and Zechariah (the fourth). Hosah's sons and relatives, who served as gatekeepers, numbered thirteen in all.

¹²These divisions of the gatekeepers were named for their family leaders, and like the other Levites, they served at the house of the LORD. ¹³They were assigned by families for guard duty at the various gates, without regard to age or training, for it was all decided by means of sacred lots.

¹⁴The responsibility for the east gate went to Meshelemiah* and his group. The north gate was assigned to his son Zechariah, a man of unusual wisdom. ¹⁵The south gate went to Obed-edom, and his sons were put in charge of the storehouse. ¹⁶Shuppim and Hosah were assigned the west gate and the gateway leading up to the Temple.* Guard duties were divided evenly. ¹⁷Six Levites were assigned each day to the east gate, four to the north gate, four to the south gate, and two pairs at the storehouse. ¹⁸Six were assigned each day to the west gate, four to the gateway leading up to the Temple, and two to the courtyard.* ¹⁹These were the divisions of the gatekeepers from the clans of Korah and Merari.

25:9 As in Greek version; Hebrew lacks *and twelve of his sons and relatives.* 25:11 Hebrew *Izri,* a variant spelling of Zeri; compare 25:3. 25:14 Hebrew *Jesarelah,* a variant spelling of Asarelah; compare 25:2. 25:18 Hebrew *Azarel,* a variant spelling of Uzziel; compare 25:4. 25:22 Hebrew *Jeremoth,* a variant spelling of Jerimoth; compare 25:4. 25:24 Hebrew *Joshbekasha,* a variant spelling of Joshbekashah; compare 25:4. 26:1 As in Greek version (see also Exod 6:24); Hebrew reads *Asaph.* 26:14 Hebrew *Shelemiah,* a variant spelling of Meshelemiah; compare 26:2. 26:16 Or *the gate of Shalleketh on the upper road* (also in 26:18). The meaning of the Hebrew is uncertain. 26:18 Or *the colonnade.* The meaning of the Hebrew is uncertain.

TREASURERS AND OTHER OFFICIALS

20 Other Levites, led by Ahijah, were in charge of the treasuries of the house of God and the treasuries of the gifts dedicated to the LORD. 21 From the family of Libni* in the clan of Gershon, Jehiel* was the leader. 22 The sons of Jehiel, Zetham and his brother Joel, were in charge of the treasuries of the house of the LORD.

23 These are the leaders that descended from Amram, Izhar, Hebron, and Uzziel:

24 From the clan of Amram, Shebuel was a descendant of Gershom son of Moses. He was the chief officer of the treasuries. 25 His relatives through Eliezer were Rehabiah, Jeshaiah, Joram, Zicri, and Shelomoth.

26 Shelomoth and his relatives were in charge of the treasuries containing the gifts that King David, the family leaders, and the generals and captains* and other officers of the army had dedicated to the LORD. 27 These men dedicated some of the plunder they had gained in battle to maintain the house of the LORD. 28 Shelomoth* and his relatives also cared for the gifts dedicated to the LORD by Samuel the seer, Saul son of Kish, Abner son of Ner, and Joab son of Zeruiah. All the other dedicated gifts were in their care, too.

29 From the clan of Izhar came Kenaniah. He and his sons were given administrative responsibilities* over Israel as officials and judges.

30 From the clan of Hebron came Hashabiah. He and his relatives—1,700 capable men—were put in charge of the Israelite lands west of the Jordan River. They were responsible for all matters related to the things of the LORD and the service of the king in that area.

31 Also from the clan of Hebron came Jeriah,* who was the leader of the Hebronites according to the genealogical records. (In the fortieth year of David's reign, a search was made in the records, and capable men from the clan of Hebron were found at Jazer in the land of Gilead.) 32 There were 2,700 capable men among the relatives of Jeriah. King David sent them to the east side of the Jordan River and put them in charge of the tribes of Reuben and Gad and the half-tribe of Manasseh. They were responsible for all matters related to God and to the king.

MILITARY COMMANDERS AND DIVISIONS

27 This is the list of Israelite generals and captains,* and their officers, who served the king by supervising the army divisions that were on duty each month of the year. Each division served for one month and had 24,000 troops.

2 Jashobeam son of Zabdiel was commander of the first division of 24,000 troops, which was on duty during the first month. 3 He was a descendant of Perez and was in charge of all the army officers for the first month.

4 Dodai, a descendant of Ahoah, was commander of the second division of 24,000 troops, which was on duty during the second month. Mikloth was his chief officer.

5 Benaiah son of Jehoiada the priest was commander of the third division of 24,000 troops, which was on duty during the third month. 6 This was the Benaiah who commanded David's elite military group known as the Thirty. His son Ammizabad was his chief officer.

7 Asahel, the brother of Joab, was commander of the fourth division of 24,000 troops, which was on duty during the fourth month. Asahel was succeeded by his son Zebadiah.

8 Shammah* the Izrahite was commander of the fifth division of 24,000 troops, which was on duty during the fifth month.

9 Ira son of Ikkesh from Tekoa was commander of the sixth division of 24,000 troops, which was on duty during the sixth month.

10 Helez, a descendant of Ephraim from Pelon, was commander of the seventh division of 24,000 troops, which was on duty during the seventh month.

11 Sibbecai, a descendant of Zerah from Hushah, was commander of the eighth division of 24,000 troops, which was on duty during the eighth month.

12 Abiezer from Anathoth in the territory of Benjamin was commander of the ninth division of 24,000 troops, which was on duty during the ninth month.

13 Maharai, a descendant of Zerah from Netophah, was commander of the tenth division of 24,000 troops, which was on duty during the tenth month.

14 Benaiah from Pirathon in Ephraim was commander of the eleventh division of 24,000 troops, which was on duty during the eleventh month.

15 Heled,* a descendant of Othniel from Netophah, was commander of the twelfth division of 24,000 troops, which was on duty during the twelfth month.

LEADERS OF THE TRIBES

16 The following were the tribes of Israel and their leaders:

26:21a Hebrew Ladan, a variant spelling of Libni; compare 6:17. 26:21b Hebrew Jehieli (also in 26:22), a variant spelling of Jehiel; compare 23:8. 26:26 Hebrew the commanders of thousands and of hundreds. 26:28 Hebrew Shelomith, a variant spelling of Shelomoth. 26:29 Or were given outside work; or were given work away from the Temple area. 26:31 Hebrew Jerijah, a variant spelling of Jeriah; compare 23:19. 27:1 Hebrew commanders of thousands and of hundreds. 27:8 Hebrew Shamhuth, a variant spelling of Shammah; compare 11:27 and 2 Sam 23:25. 27:15 Hebrew Heldai, a variant spelling of Heled; compare 11:30 and 2 Sam 23:29.

Tribe	Leader
Reuben	Eliezer son of Zicri
Simeon	Shephatiah son of Maacah
17 Levi	Hashabiah son of Kemuel
Aaron (the priests)	Zadok
18 Judah	Elihu (a brother of David)
Issachar	Omri son of Michael
19 Zebulun	Ishmaiah son of Obadiah
Naphtali	Jeremoth son of Azriel
20 Ephraim	Hoshea son of Azaziah
Manasseh (west)	Joel son of Pedaiah
21 Manasseh in Gilead (east)	Iddo son of Zechariah
Benjamin	Jaasiel son of Abner
22 Dan	Azarel son of Jeroham

These were the leaders of the tribes of Israel.

23 When David took his census, he did not count those who were younger than twenty years of age, because the LORD had promised to make the Israelites as numerous as the stars in heaven. 24 Joab son of Zeruiah began the census but never finished it because* the anger of God fell on Israel. The total number was never recorded in King David's official records.

OFFICIALS OF DAVID'S KINGDOM

25 Azmaveth son of Adiel was in charge of the palace treasuries.

Jonathan son of Uzziah was in charge of the regional treasuries throughout the towns, villages, and fortresses of Israel.

26 Ezri son of Kelub was in charge of the field workers who farmed the king's lands.

27 Shimei from Ramah was in charge of the king's vineyards.

Zabdi from Shepham was responsible for the grapes and the supplies of wine.

28 Baal-hanan from Geder was in charge of the king's olive groves and sycamore-fig trees in the foothills of Judah.*

Joash was responsible for the supplies of olive oil.

29 Shitrai from Sharon was in charge of the cattle on the Sharon Plain.

Shaphat son of Adlai was responsible for the cattle in the valleys.

30 Obil the Ishmaelite was in charge of the camels.

Jehdeiah from Meronoth was in charge of the donkeys.

31 Jaziz the Hagrite was in charge of the king's flocks of sheep and goats.

All these officials were overseers of King David's property.

32 Jonathan, David's uncle, was a wise counselor to the king, a man of great insight, and a scribe. Jehiel the Hacmonite was responsible for teaching the king's sons. 33 Ahithophel was the royal adviser. Hushai the Arkite was the king's friend. 34 Ahithophel was succeeded by Jehoiada son of Benaiah and by Abiathar. Joab was commander of the king's army.

DAVID'S INSTRUCTIONS TO SOLOMON

28 David summoned all the officials of Israel to Jerusalem—the leaders of the tribes, the commanders of the army divisions, the other generals and captains,* the overseers of the royal property and livestock, the palace officials, the mighty men, and all the other brave warriors in the kingdom. 2 David rose to his feet and said: "My brothers and my people! It was my desire to build a Temple where the Ark of the LORD's Covenant, God's footstool, could rest permanently. I made the necessary preparations for building it, 3 but God said to me, 'You must not build a Temple to honor my name, for you are a warrior and have shed much blood.'

4 "Yet the LORD, the God of Israel, has chosen me from among all my father's family to be king over Israel forever. For he has chosen the tribe of Judah to rule, and from among the families of Judah he chose my father's family. And from among my father's sons the LORD was pleased to make me king over all Israel. 5 And from among my sons—for the LORD has given me many—he chose Solomon to succeed me on the throne of Israel and to rule over the LORD's kingdom. 6 He said to me, 'Your son Solomon will build my Temple and its courtyards, for I have chosen him as my son, and I will be his father. 7 And if he continues to obey my commands and regulations as he does now, I will make his kingdom last forever.'

8 "So now, with God as our witness, and in the sight of all Israel—the LORD's assembly—I give you this charge. Be careful to obey all the commands of the LORD your God, so that you may continue to possess this good land and leave it to your children as a permanent inheritance.

9 "And Solomon, my son, learn to know the God of your ancestors intimately. Worship and serve him with your whole heart and a willing mind. For the LORD sees every heart and knows every plan and thought. If you seek him, you will find him. But if you forsake him, he will reject you forever. 10 So take this seriously. The LORD has chosen you to build a Temple as his sanctuary. Be strong, and do the work."

11 Then David gave Solomon the plans for the Temple and its surroundings, including the entry room, the storerooms, the upstairs rooms, the inner rooms, and the inner sanctuary—which was the place of atonement. 12 David also gave Solomon all the plans he had in mind* for the courtyards of the LORD's Temple, the outside rooms, the treasuries, and the rooms for the gifts dedicated to the LORD. 13 The king also gave

---

27:24 Or never finished it, and yet. 27:28 Hebrew the Shephelah.
28:1 Hebrew the commanders of thousands and commanders of hundreds. 28:12 Or the plans of the spirit that was with him.

Solomon the instructions concerning the work of the various divisions of priests and Levites in the Temple of the LORD. And he gave specifications for the items in the Temple that were to be used for worship.

¹⁴David gave instructions regarding how much gold and silver should be used to make the items needed for service. ¹⁵He told Solomon the amount of gold needed for the gold lampstands and lamps, and the amount of silver for the silver lampstands and lamps, depending on how each would be used. ¹⁶He designated the amount of gold for the table on which the Bread of the Presence would be placed and the amount of silver for other tables.

¹⁷David also designated the amount of gold for the solid gold meat hooks used to handle the sacrificial meat and for the basins, pitchers, and dishes, as well as the amount of silver for every dish. ¹⁸He designated the amount of refined gold for the altar of incense. Finally, he gave him a plan for the LORD's "chariot"—the gold cherubim* whose wings were stretched out over the Ark of the LORD's Covenant. ¹⁹"Every part of this plan," David told Solomon, "was given to me in writing from the hand of the LORD.*"

²⁰Then David continued, "Be strong and courageous, and do the work. Don't be afraid or discouraged, for the LORD God, my God, is with you. He will not fail you or forsake you. He will see to it that all the work related to the Temple of the LORD is finished correctly. ²¹The various divisions of priests and Levites will serve in the Temple of God. Others with skills of every kind will volunteer, and the officials and the entire nation are at your command."

GIFTS FOR BUILDING THE TEMPLE

29 Then King David turned to the entire assembly and said, "My son Solomon, whom God has clearly chosen as the next king of Israel, is still young and inexperienced. The work ahead of him is enormous, for the Temple he will build is not for mere mortals—it is for the LORD God himself! ²Using every resource at my command, I have gathered as much as I could for building the Temple of my God. Now there is enough gold, silver, bronze, iron, and wood, as well as great quantities of onyx, other precious stones, costly jewels, and all kinds of fine stone and marble.

³"And now, because of my devotion to the Temple of my God, I am giving all of my own private treasures of gold and silver to help in the construction. This is in addition to the building materials I have already collected for his holy Temple. ⁴I am donating more than 112 tons of gold* from Ophir and 262 tons of refined silver* to be used for overlaying the walls of the buildings ⁵and for the other gold and silver work to be done by the craftsmen. Now then, who will follow my example and give offerings to the LORD today?"

⁶Then the family leaders, the leaders of the tribes of Israel, the generals and captains of the army,* and the king's administrative officers all gave willingly. ⁷For the construction of the Temple of God, they gave about 188 tons of gold,* 10,000 gold coins,* 375 tons of silver,* 675 tons of bronze,* and 3,750 tons of iron.* ⁸They also contributed numerous precious stones, which were deposited in the treasury of the house of the LORD under the care of Jehiel, a descendant of Gershon. ⁹The people rejoiced over the offerings, for they had given freely and wholeheartedly to the LORD, and King David was filled with joy.

DAVID'S PRAYER OF PRAISE

¹⁰Then David praised the LORD in the presence of the whole assembly:

"O LORD, the God of our ancestor Israel,*
may you be praised forever and ever!
¹¹Yours, O LORD, is the greatness, the power,
the glory, the victory, and the majesty.
Everything in the heavens and on earth is
yours, O LORD, and this is your kingdom.
We adore you as the one who is over all
things. ¹²Wealth and honor come from you
alone, for you rule over everything. Power
and might are in your hand, and at your
discretion people are made great and given
strength.

¹³"O our God, we thank you and praise
your glorious name! ¹⁴But who am I, and
who are my people, that we could give
anything to you? Everything we have has
come from you, and we give you only what
you first gave us! ¹⁵We are here for only a
moment, visitors and strangers in the land
as our ancestors were before us. Our days
on earth are like a passing shadow, gone so
soon without a trace.

¹⁶"O LORD our God, even this material
we have gathered to build a Temple to
honor your holy name comes from you! It
all belongs to you! ¹⁷I know, my God, that
you examine our hearts and rejoice when
you find integrity there. You know I have
done all this with good motives, and I
have watched your people offer their gifts
willingly and joyously.

¹⁸"O LORD, the God of our ancestors
Abraham, Isaac, and Israel, make your
people always want to obey you. See to it

28:18 Hebrew *for the gold cherub chariot.*   28:19 Or *was written under the direction of the LORD.*   29:4a Hebrew *3,000 talents* [102 metric tons] *of gold.*   29:4b Hebrew *7,000 talents* [238 metric tons] *of silver.*   29:6 Hebrew *the commanders of thousands and commanders of hundreds.*   29:7a Hebrew *5,000 talents* [170 metric tons] *of gold.*   29:7b Hebrew *10,000 darics* [a Persian coin] *of gold,* about 185 pounds or 84 kilograms in weight.   29:7c Hebrew *10,000 talents* [340 metric tons] *of silver.*   29:7d Hebrew *18,000 talents* [612 metric tons] *of bronze.*   29:7e Hebrew *100,000 talents* [3,400 metric tons] *of iron.*   29:10 *Israel* is the name that God gave to Jacob.

that their love for you never changes. [19]Give my son Solomon the wholehearted desire to obey all your commands, laws, and decrees, and to do everything necessary to build this Temple, for which I have made these preparations."

[20]Then David said to the whole assembly, "Give praise to the LORD your God!" And the entire assembly praised the LORD, the God of their ancestors, and they bowed low and knelt before the LORD and the king.

SOLOMON NAMED AS KING

[21]The next day they brought 1,000 bulls, 1,000 rams, and 1,000 male lambs as burnt offerings to the LORD. They also brought liquid offerings and many other sacrifices on behalf of all Israel. [22]They feasted and drank in the LORD's presence with great joy that day.

And again they crowned David's son Solomon as their new king. They anointed him before the LORD as their leader, and they anointed Zadok as priest. [23]So Solomon took the throne of the LORD in place of his father, David, and he succeeded in everything, and all Israel obeyed him. [24]All the officials, the warriors, and the sons of King David pledged their loyalty to King Solomon. [25]And the LORD exalted Solomon in the sight of all Israel, and he gave Solomon greater royal splendor than any king in Israel before him.

SUMMARY OF DAVID'S REIGN

[26]So David son of Jesse reigned over all Israel. [27]He reigned over Israel for forty years, seven of them in Hebron and thirty-three in Jerusalem. [28]He died at a ripe old age, having enjoyed long life, wealth, and honor. Then his son Solomon ruled in his place.

[29]All the events of King David's reign, from beginning to end, are written in *The Record of Samuel the Seer, The Record of Nathan the Prophet,* and *The Record of Gad the Seer.* [30]These accounts include the mighty deeds of his reign and everything that happened to him and to Israel and to all the surrounding kingdoms.

2 CHRONICLES

SOLOMON ASKS FOR WISDOM

1 Solomon son of David took firm control of his kingdom, for the LORD his God was with him and made him very powerful.

²Solomon called together all the leaders of Israel—the generals and captains of the army,* the judges, and all the political and clan leaders. ³Then he led the entire assembly to the place of worship in Gibeon, for God's Tabernacle* was located there. (This was the Tabernacle that Moses, the LORD's servant, had made in the wilderness.)

⁴David had already moved the Ark of God from Kiriath-jearim to the tent he had prepared for it in Jerusalem. ⁵But the bronze altar made by Bezalel son of Uri and grandson of Hur was there* at Gibeon in front of the Tabernacle of the LORD. So Solomon and the people gathered in front of it to consult the LORD.* ⁶There in front of the Tabernacle, Solomon went up to the bronze altar in the LORD's presence and sacrificed 1,000 burnt offerings on it.

⁷That night God appeared to Solomon and said, "What do you want? Ask, and I will give it to you!"

⁸Solomon replied to God, "You showed great and faithful love to David, my father, and now you have made me king in his place. ⁹O LORD God, please continue to keep your promise to David my father, for you have made me king over a people as numerous as the dust of the earth! ¹⁰Give me the wisdom and knowledge to lead them properly,* for who could possibly govern this great people of yours?"

¹¹God said to Solomon, "Because your greatest desire is to help your people, and you did not ask for wealth, riches, fame, or even the death of your enemies or a long life, but rather you asked for wisdom and knowledge to properly govern my people—¹²I will certainly give you the wisdom and knowledge you requested. But I will also give you wealth, riches, and fame such as no other king has before you or will ever have in the future!"

¹³Then Solomon returned to Jerusalem from the Tabernacle at the place of worship in Gibeon, and he reigned over Israel.

¹⁴Solomon built up a huge force of chariots and horses.* He had 1,400 chariots and 12,000 horses. He stationed some of them in the chariot cities and some near him in Jerusalem. ¹⁵The king made silver and gold as plentiful in Jerusalem as stone. And valuable cedar timber was as common as the sycamore-fig trees that grow in the foothills of Judah.* ¹⁶Solomon's horses were imported from Egypt* and from Cilicia*; the king's traders acquired them from Cilicia at the standard price. ¹⁷At that time chariots from Egypt could be purchased for 600 pieces of silver,* and horses for 150 pieces of silver.* They were then exported to the kings of the Hittites and the kings of Aram.

PREPARATIONS FOR BUILDING THE TEMPLE

2 ¹*Solomon decided to build a Temple to honor the name of the LORD, and also a royal palace for himself. ²*He enlisted a force of 70,000 laborers, 80,000 men to quarry stone in the hill country, and 3,600 foremen.

³Solomon also sent this message to King Hiram* at Tyre:

"Send me cedar logs as you did for my father, David, when he was building his palace. ⁴I am about to build a Temple to honor the name of the LORD my God. It will be a place set apart to burn fragrant incense before him, to display the special sacrificial bread, and to sacrifice burnt offerings each morning and evening, on the Sabbaths, at new moon celebrations, and at the other appointed festivals of the LORD our God. He has commanded Israel to do these things forever.

⁵"This must be a magnificent Temple because our God is greater than all other gods. ⁶But who can really build him a worthy home? Not even the highest heavens can contain him! So who am I to consider building a Temple for him, except as a place to burn sacrifices to him?

⁷"So send me a master craftsman who can work with gold, silver, bronze, and iron, as well as with purple, scarlet, and blue cloth. He must be a skilled engraver who can work with the craftsmen of Judah and Jerusalem who were selected by my father, David.

⁸"Also send me cedar, cypress, and red sandalwood* logs from Lebanon, for I know that your men are without equal at cutting timber in Lebanon. I will send my men to help them. ⁹An immense amount of timber will be needed, for the Temple I am going to build will be very large and magnificent. ¹⁰In payment for your woodcutters, I will send

---

1:2 Hebrew *the commanders of thousands and of hundreds.*
1:3 Hebrew *Tent of Meeting;* also in 1:6, 13.   1:5a As in Greek version and Latin Vulgate, and some Hebrew manuscripts; Masoretic Text reads *he placed.*   1:5b Hebrew *to consult him.*   1:10 Hebrew *to go out and come in before this people.*   1:14 Or *charioteers;* also in 1:14b.   1:15 Hebrew *the Shephelah.*   1:16a Possibly *Muzur,* a district near Cilicia; also in 1:17.   1:16b Hebrew *Kue,* probably another name for Cilicia.   1:17a Hebrew *600 [shekels] of silver,* about 15 pounds or 6.8 kilograms in weight.   1:17b Hebrew *150 [shekels],* about 3.8 pounds or 1.7 kilograms in weight.   2:1 Verse 2:1 is numbered 1:18 in Hebrew text.   2:2 Verses 2:2-18 are numbered 2:1-17 in Hebrew text.   2:3 Hebrew *Huram,* a variant spelling of Hiram; also in 2:11.   2:8 Or *juniper;* Hebrew reads *algum,* perhaps a variant spelling of *almug;* compare 9:10-11 and parallel text at 1 Kgs 10:11-12.

100,000 bushels of crushed wheat, 100,000 bushels of barley,* 110,000 gallons of wine, and 110,000 gallons of olive oil.*"

¹¹King Hiram sent this letter of reply to Solomon:

"It is because the LORD loves his people that he has made you their king! ¹²Praise the LORD, the God of Israel, who made the heavens and the earth! He has given King David a wise son, gifted with skill and understanding, who will build a Temple for the LORD and a royal palace for himself.

¹³"I am sending you a master craftsman named Huram-abi, who is extremely talented. ¹⁴His mother is from the tribe of Dan in Israel, and his father is from Tyre. He is skillful at making things from gold, silver, bronze, and iron, and he also works with stone and wood. He can work with purple, blue, and scarlet cloth and fine linen. He is also an engraver and can follow any design given to him. He will work with your craftsmen and those appointed by my lord David, your father.

¹⁵"Send along the wheat, barley, olive oil, and wine that my lord has mentioned. ¹⁶We will cut whatever timber you need from the Lebanon mountains and will float the logs in rafts down the coast of the Mediterranean Sea* to Joppa. From there you can transport the logs up to Jerusalem."

¹⁷Solomon took a census of all foreigners in the land of Israel, like the census his father had taken, and he counted 153,600. ¹⁸He assigned 70,000 of them as common laborers, 80,000 as quarry workers in the hill country, and 3,600 as foremen.

SOLOMON BUILDS THE TEMPLE

3 So Solomon began to build the Temple of the LORD in Jerusalem on Mount Moriah, where the LORD had appeared to David, his father. The Temple was built on the threshing floor of Araunah* the Jebusite, the site that David had selected. ²The construction began in midspring,* during the fourth year of Solomon's reign.

³These are the dimensions Solomon used for the foundation of the Temple of God (using the old standard of measurement).* It was 90 feet long and 30 feet wide.* ⁴The entry room at the front of the Temple was 30 feet* wide, running across the entire width of the Temple, and 30 feet* high. He overlaid the inside with pure gold.

⁵He paneled the main room of the Temple with cypress wood, overlaid it with fine gold, and decorated it with carvings of palm trees and chains. ⁶He decorated the walls of the Temple with beautiful jewels and with gold from the land of Parvaim. ⁷He overlaid the beams, thresholds, walls, and doors throughout the Temple with gold, and he carved figures of cherubim on the walls.

⁸He made the Most Holy Place 30 feet wide, corresponding to the width of the Temple, and 30 feet deep. He overlaid its interior with 23 tons* of fine gold. ⁹The gold nails that were used weighed 20 ounces* each. He also overlaid the walls of the upper rooms with gold.

¹⁰He made two figures shaped like cherubim, overlaid them with gold, and placed them in the Most Holy Place. ¹¹The total wingspan of the two cherubim standing side by side was 30 feet. One wing of the first figure was 7½ feet* long, and it touched the Temple wall. The other wing, also 7½ feet long, touched one of the wings of the second figure. ¹²In the same way, the second figure had one wing 7½ feet long that touched the opposite wall. The other wing, also 7½ feet long, touched the wing of the first figure. ¹³So the wingspan of the two cherubim side by side was 30 feet. They stood on their feet and faced out toward the main room of the Temple.

¹⁴Across the entrance of the Most Holy Place he hung a curtain made of fine linen, decorated with blue, purple, and scarlet thread and embroidered with figures of cherubim.

¹⁵For the front of the Temple, he made two pillars that were 27 feet* tall, each topped by a capital extending upward another 7½ feet. ¹⁶He made a network of interwoven chains* and used them to decorate the tops of the pillars. He also made 100 decorative pomegranates and attached them to the chains. ¹⁷Then he set up the two pillars at the entrance of the Temple, one to the south of the entrance and the other to the north. He named the one on the south Jakin, and the one on the north Boaz.*

FURNISHINGS FOR THE TEMPLE

4 Solomon* also made a bronze altar 30 feet long, 30 feet wide, and 15 feet high.* ²Then he cast a great round basin, 15 feet across from rim to rim, called the Sea. It was 7½ feet deep and about 45 feet in circumference.* ³It was encircled just below its rim by two rows of figures that

2:10a Hebrew 20,000 cors [4,400 kiloliters] of crushed wheat, 20,000 cors of barley. 2:10b Hebrew 20,000 baths [420 kiloliters] of wine, and 20,000 baths of olive oil. 2:16 Hebrew the sea. 3:1 Hebrew reads Ornan, a variant spelling of Araunah; compare 2 Sam 24:16. 3:2 Hebrew on the second [day] of the second month. This day of the ancient Hebrew lunar calendar occurred in April or May. 3:3a The "old standard of measurement" was a cubit equal to 18 inches [46 centimeters]. The new standard was a cubit of approximately 21 inches [53 centimeters]. 3:3b Hebrew 60 cubits [27.6 meters] long and 20 cubits [9.2 meters] wide. 3:4a Hebrew 20 cubits [9.2 meters]; also in 3:8, 11, 13. 3:4b As in some Greek and Syriac manuscripts, which read 20 cubits [9.2 meters]; Hebrew reads 120 [cubits], which is 180 feet or 55 meters. 3:8 Hebrew 600 talents [20.4 metric tons]. 3:9 Hebrew 50 shekels [570 grams]. 3:11 Hebrew 5 cubits [2.3 meters]; also in 3:11b, 12, 15. 3:15 As in Syriac version (see also 1 Kgs 7:15; 2 Kgs 25:17; Jer 52:21), which reads 18 cubits [8.3 meters]; Hebrew reads 35 cubits, which is 52.5 feet or 16.5 meters. 3:16 Hebrew He made chains in the inner sanctuary. The meaning of the Hebrew is uncertain. 3:17 Jakin probably means "he establishes"; Boaz probably means "in him is strength." 4:1a Or Huram-abi; Hebrew reads He. 4:1b Hebrew 20 cubits [9.2 meters] long, 20 cubits wide, and 10 cubits [4.6 meters] high. 4:2 Hebrew 10 cubits [4.6 meters] across . . . 5 cubits [2.3 meters] deep and 30 cubits [13.8 meters] in circumference.

resembled oxen. There were about six oxen per foot* all the way around, and they were cast as part of the basin.

⁴The Sea was placed on a base of twelve bronze oxen, all facing outward. Three faced north, three faced west, three faced south, and three faced east, and the Sea rested on them. ⁵The walls of the Sea were about three inches* thick, and its rim flared out like a cup and resembled a water lily blossom. It could hold about 16,500 gallons* of water.

⁶He also made ten smaller basins for washing the utensils for the burnt offerings. He set five on the south side and five on the north. But the priests washed themselves in the Sea.

⁷He then cast ten gold lampstands according to the specifications that had been given, and he put them in the Temple. Five were placed against the south wall, and five were placed against the north wall.

⁸He also built ten tables and placed them in the Temple, five along the south wall and five along the north wall. Then he molded 100 gold basins.

⁹He then built a courtyard for the priests, and also the large outer courtyard. He made doors for the courtyard entrances and overlaid them with bronze. ¹⁰The great bronze basin called the Sea was placed near the southeast corner of the Temple.

¹¹Huram-abi also made the necessary washbasins, shovels, and bowls.

So at last Huram-abi completed everything King Solomon had assigned him to make for the Temple of God:

¹² the two pillars;
the two bowl-shaped capitals on top of the pillars;
the two networks of interwoven chains that decorated the capitals;
¹³ the 400 pomegranates that hung from the chains on the capitals (two rows of pomegranates for each of the chain networks that decorated the capitals on top of the pillars);
¹⁴ the water carts holding the basins;
¹⁵ the Sea and the twelve oxen under it;
¹⁶ the ash buckets, the shovels, the meat hooks, and all the related articles.

Huram-abi made all these things of burnished bronze for the Temple of the LORD, just as King Solomon had directed. ¹⁷The king had them cast in clay molds in the Jordan Valley between Succoth and Zarethan.* ¹⁸Solomon used such great quantities of bronze that its weight could not be determined.

¹⁹Solomon also made all the furnishings for the Temple of God:

the gold altar;
the tables for the Bread of the Presence;

BUILDING A HOUSE OF WORSHIP: THE FOUNDATION
2 Chronicles 5:1–14　　　　　JACK HAYFORD

Solomon built the Temple with the resources his father, David, had saved for that very purpose. David, a warrior, recognized that the fountainhead of life in the Kingdom was worship. He knew victory comes not through human strength but through the worship of the living God.

No matter how efficient or proficient you become, your "house" will only succeed to the degree that worship becomes a priority in your life. I am speaking of the kind of worship that walks with God, recognizing every good and perfect gift comes from Him (James 1:17). The foundation of worship is based on the realization that it penetrates everything central to our lives, everything over which we have some sort of responsibility. David understood that his skills and success were always secondary to the power of God at work through His presence.

²⁰ the lampstands and their lamps of solid gold, to burn in front of the Most Holy Place as prescribed;
²¹ the flower decorations, lamps, and tongs—all of the purest gold;
²² the lamp snuffers, bowls, ladles, and incense burners—all of solid gold;
the doors for the entrances to the Most Holy Place and the main room of the Temple, overlaid with gold.

5 So Solomon finished all his work on the Temple of the LORD. Then he brought all the gifts his father, David, had dedicated—the silver, the gold, and the various articles—and he stored them in the treasuries of the Temple of God.

THE ARK BROUGHT TO THE TEMPLE

²Solomon then summoned to Jerusalem the elders of Israel and all the heads of tribes—the leaders of the ancestral families of Israel. They were to bring the Ark of the LORD's Covenant to the Temple from its location in the City of David, also known as Zion. ³So all the men of Israel assembled before the king at the annual Festival of Shelters, which is held in early autumn.* ⁴When all the elders of Israel arrived, the Levites picked up the Ark. ⁵The priests and Levites

4:3 Or *20 oxen per meter;* Hebrew reads *10 per cubit.*
4:5a Hebrew *a handbreadth* [8 centimeters].　**4:5b** Hebrew *3,000 baths* [63 kiloliters].　**4:17** As in parallel text at 1 Kgs 7:46; Hebrew reads *Zeredah.*　**5:3** Hebrew *at the festival that is in the seventh month.* The Festival of Shelters began on the fifteenth day of the seventh month of the ancient Hebrew lunar calendar. This day occurred in late September, October, or early November.

brought up the Ark along with the special tent* and all the sacred items that had been in it. ⁶There, before the Ark, King Solomon and the entire community of Israel sacrificed so many sheep, goats, and cattle that no one could keep count!

⁷Then the priests carried the Ark of the LORD's Covenant into the inner sanctuary of the Temple—the Most Holy Place—and placed it beneath the wings of the cherubim. ⁸The cherubim spread their wings over the Ark, forming a canopy over the Ark and its carrying poles. ⁹These poles were so long that their ends could be seen from the Holy Place,* which is in front of the Most Holy Place, but not from the outside. They are still there to this day. ¹⁰Nothing was in the Ark except the two stone tablets that Moses had placed in it at Mount Sinai,* where the LORD made a covenant with the people of Israel when they left Egypt.

¹¹Then the priests left the Holy Place. All the priests who were present had purified themselves, whether or not they were on duty that day. ¹²And the Levites who were musicians—Asaph, Heman, Jeduthun, and all their sons and brothers—were dressed in fine linen robes and stood at the east side of the altar playing cymbals, lyres, and harps. They were joined by 120 priests who were playing trumpets. ¹³The trumpeters and singers performed together in unison to praise and give thanks to the LORD. Accompanied by trumpets, cymbals, and other instruments, they raised their voices and praised the LORD with these words:

"He is good!
His faithful love endures forever!"

At that moment a thick cloud filled the Temple of the LORD. ¹⁴The priests could not continue their service because of the cloud, for the glorious presence of the LORD filled the Temple of God.

SOLOMON PRAISES THE LORD

6 Then Solomon prayed, "O LORD, you have said that you would live in a thick cloud of darkness. ²Now I have built a glorious Temple for you, a place where you can live forever!"

³Then the king turned around to the entire community of Israel standing before him and gave this blessing: ⁴"Praise the LORD, the God of Israel, who has kept the promise he made to my father, David. For he told my father, ⁵'From the day I brought my people out of the land of Egypt, I have never chosen a city among any of the tribes of Israel as the place where a Temple should be built to honor my name. Nor have I chosen a king to lead my people Israel. ⁶But now I have chosen Jerusalem as the place for my name to be honored, and I have chosen David to be king over my people Israel.'"

⁷Then Solomon said, "My father, David, wanted to build this Temple to honor the name of the LORD, the God of Israel. ⁸But the LORD told him, 'You wanted to build the Temple to honor my name. Your intention is good, ⁹but you are not the one to do it. One of your own sons will build the Temple to honor me.'

¹⁰"And now the LORD has fulfilled the promise he made, for I have become king in my father's place, and now I sit on the throne of Israel, just as the LORD promised. I have built this Temple to honor the name of the LORD, the God of Israel. ¹¹There I have placed the Ark, which contains the covenant that the LORD made with the people of Israel."

SOLOMON'S PRAYER OF DEDICATION

¹²Then Solomon stood before the altar of the LORD in front of the entire community of Israel, and he lifted his hands in prayer. ¹³Now Solomon had made a bronze platform 7½ feet long, 7½ feet wide, and 4½ feet high* and had placed it at the center of the Temple's outer courtyard. He stood on the platform, and then he knelt in front of the entire community of Israel and lifted his hands toward heaven. ¹⁴He prayed,

"O LORD, God of Israel, there is no God like you in all of heaven and earth. You keep your covenant and show unfailing love to all who walk before you in wholehearted devotion. ¹⁵You have kept your promise to your servant David, my father. You made that promise with your own mouth, and with your own hands you have fulfilled it today.

¹⁶"And now, O LORD, God of Israel, carry out the additional promise you made to your servant David, my father. For you said to him, 'If your descendants guard their behavior and faithfully follow my Law as you have done, one of them will always sit on the throne of Israel.' ¹⁷Now, O LORD, God of Israel, fulfill this promise to your servant David.

¹⁸"But will God really live on earth among people? Why, even the highest heavens cannot contain you. How much less this Temple I have built! ¹⁹Nevertheless, listen to my prayer and my plea, O LORD my God. Hear the cry and the prayer that your servant is making to you. ²⁰May you watch over this Temple day and night, this place where you have said you would put your name. May you always hear the prayers I make toward this place. ²¹May you hear the humble and earnest requests from me and your people Israel when we pray toward this

---

5:5 Hebrew *the Tent of Meeting;* i.e., the tent mentioned in 2 Sam 6:17 and 1 Chr 16:1. 5:9 As in some Hebrew manuscripts and Greek version (see also 1 Kgs 8:8); Masoretic Text reads *from the Ark.* 5:10 Hebrew *Horeb,* another name for Sinai. 6:13 Hebrew *5 cubits [2.3 meters] long, 5 cubits wide, and 3 cubits [1.4 meters] high.*

place. Yes, hear us from heaven where you live, and when you hear, forgive.

[22] "If someone wrongs another person and is required to take an oath of innocence in front of your altar at this Temple, [23] then hear from heaven and judge between your servants—the accuser and the accused. Pay back the guilty as they deserve. Acquit the innocent because of their innocence.

[24] "If your people Israel are defeated by their enemies because they have sinned against you, and if they turn back and acknowledge your name and pray to you here in this Temple, [25] then hear from heaven and forgive the sin of your people Israel and return them to this land you gave to them and to their ancestors.

[26] "If the skies are shut up and there is no rain because your people have sinned against you, and if they pray toward this Temple and acknowledge your name and turn from their sins because you have punished them, [27] then hear from heaven and forgive the sins of your servants, your people Israel. Teach them to follow the right path, and send rain on your land that you have given to your people as their special possession.

[28] "If there is a famine in the land or a plague or crop disease or attacks of locusts or caterpillars, or if your people's enemies are in the land besieging their towns—whatever disaster or disease there is—[29] and if your people Israel pray about their troubles or sorrow, raising their hands toward this Temple, [30] then hear from heaven where you live, and forgive. Give your people what their actions deserve, for you alone know each human heart. [31] Then they will fear you and walk in your ways as long as they live in the land you gave to our ancestors.

[32] "In the future, foreigners who do not belong to your people Israel will hear of you. They will come from distant lands when they hear of your great name and your strong hand and your powerful arm. And when they pray toward this Temple, [33] then hear from heaven where you live, and grant what they ask of you. In this way, all the people of the earth will come to know and fear you, just as your own people Israel do. They, too, will know that this Temple I have built honors your name.

[34] "If your people go out where you send them to fight their enemies, and if they pray to you by turning toward this city you have chosen and toward this Temple I have built to honor your name, [35] then hear their prayers from heaven and uphold their cause.

[36] "If they sin against you—and who has never sinned?—you might become angry with them and let their enemies conquer them and take them captive to a foreign land far away or near. [37] But in that land of exile, they might turn to you in repentance and pray, 'We have sinned, done evil, and acted wickedly.' [38] If they turn to you with their whole heart and soul in the land of their captivity and pray toward the land you gave to their ancestors—toward this city you have chosen, and toward this Temple I have built to honor your name—[39] then hear their prayers and their petitions from heaven where you live, and uphold their cause. Forgive your people who have sinned against you.

[40] "O my God, may your eyes be open and your ears attentive to all the prayers made to you in this place.

[41] "And now arise, O LORD God, and enter
   your resting place,
   along with the Ark, the symbol of your
      power.
May your priests, O LORD God, be clothed
      with salvation;
   may your loyal servants rejoice in your
      goodness.
[42] O LORD God, do not reject the king you
      have anointed.
   Remember your unfailing love for your
      servant David."

THE DEDICATION OF THE TEMPLE

7 When Solomon finished praying, fire flashed down from heaven and burned up the burnt offerings and sacrifices, and the glorious presence of the LORD filled the Temple. [2] The priests could not enter the Temple of the LORD because the glorious presence of the LORD filled it. [3] When all the people of Israel saw the fire coming down and the glorious presence of the LORD filling the Temple, they fell face down on the ground and worshiped and praised the LORD, saying,

"He is good!
   His faithful love endures forever!"

[4] Then the king and all the people offered sacrifices to the LORD. [5] King Solomon offered a sacrifice of 22,000 cattle and 120,000 sheep and goats. And so the king and all the people dedicated the Temple of God. [6] The priests took their assigned positions, and so did the Levites who were singing, "His faithful love endures forever!" They accompanied the singing with music from the instruments King David had made for praising the LORD. Across from the Levites, the priests blew the trumpets, while all Israel stood.

[7] Solomon then consecrated the central area of the courtyard in front of the LORD's Temple. He offered burnt offerings and the fat of peace offerings there, because the bronze altar he had

built could not hold all the burnt offerings, grain offerings, and sacrificial fat.

⁸ For the next seven days Solomon and all Israel celebrated the Festival of Shelters.* A large congregation had gathered from as far away as Lebo-hamath in the north and the Brook of Egypt in the south. ⁹ On the eighth day they had a closing ceremony, for they had celebrated the dedication of the altar for seven days and the Festival of Shelters for seven days. ¹⁰ Then at the end of the celebration,* Solomon sent the people home. They were all joyful and glad because the LORD had been so good to David and to Solomon and to his people Israel.

THE LORD'S RESPONSE TO SOLOMON

¹¹ So Solomon finished the Temple of the LORD, as well as the royal palace. He completed everything he had planned to do in the construction of the Temple and the palace. ¹² Then one night the LORD appeared to Solomon and said,

"I have heard your prayer and have chosen this Temple as the place for making sacrifices. ¹³ At times I might shut up the heavens so that no rain falls, or command grasshoppers to devour your crops, or send plagues among you. ¹⁴ Then if my people who are called by my name will humble themselves and pray and seek my face and turn from their wicked ways, I will hear from heaven and will forgive their sins and restore their land. ¹⁵ My eyes will be open and my ears attentive to every prayer made in this place. ¹⁶ For I have chosen this Temple and set it apart to be holy—a place where my name will be honored forever. I will always watch over it, for it is dear to my heart.

¹⁷ "As for you, if you faithfully follow me as David your father did, obeying all my commands, decrees, and regulations, ¹⁸ then I will establish the throne of your dynasty. For I made this covenant with your father, David, when I said, 'One of your descendants will always rule over Israel.'

¹⁹ "But if you or your descendants abandon me and disobey the decrees and commands I have given you, and if you serve and worship other gods, ²⁰ then I will uproot the people from this land that I have given them. I will reject this Temple that I have made holy to honor my name. I will make it an object of mockery and ridicule among the nations. ²¹ And though this Temple is impressive now, all who pass by will be appalled. They will ask, 'Why did the LORD do such terrible things to this land and to this Temple?'

²² "And the answer will be, 'Because his people abandoned the LORD, the God of their ancestors, who brought them out of Egypt, and they worshiped other gods instead and

bowed down to them. That is why he has brought all these disasters on them.'"

SOLOMON'S MANY ACHIEVEMENTS

8 It took Solomon twenty years to build the LORD's Temple and his own royal palace. At the end of that time, ² Solomon turned his attention to rebuilding the towns that King Hiram* had given him, and he settled Israelites in them.

³ Solomon also fought against the town of Hamath-zobah and conquered it. ⁴ He rebuilt Tadmor in the wilderness and built towns in the region of Hamath as supply centers. ⁵ He fortified the towns of Upper Beth-horon and Lower Beth-horon, rebuilding their walls and installing barred gates. ⁶ He also rebuilt Baalath and other supply centers and constructed towns where his chariots and horses* could be stationed. He built everything he desired in Jerusalem and Lebanon and throughout his entire realm.

⁷ There were still some people living in the land who were not Israelites, including the Hittites, Amorites, Perizzites, Hivites, and Jebusites. ⁸ These were descendants of the nations whom the people of Israel had not destroyed. So Solomon conscripted them for his labor force, and they serve as forced laborers to this day. ⁹ But Solomon did not conscript any of the Israelites for his labor force. Instead, he assigned them to serve as fighting men, officers in his army, commanders of his chariots, and charioteers. ¹⁰ King Solomon appointed 250 of them to supervise the people.

¹¹ Solomon moved his wife, Pharaoh's daughter, from the City of David to the new palace he had built for her. He said, "My wife must not live in King David's palace, for the Ark of the LORD has been there, and it is holy ground."

¹² Then Solomon presented burnt offerings to the LORD on the altar he had built for him in front of the entry room of the Temple. ¹³ He offered the sacrifices for the Sabbaths, the new moon festivals, and the three annual festivals—the Passover celebration, the Festival of Harvest,* and the Festival of Shelters—as Moses had commanded.

¹⁴ In assigning the priests to their duties, Solomon followed the regulations of his father, David. He also assigned the Levites to lead the people in praise and to assist the priests in their daily duties. And he assigned the gatekeepers to their gates by their divisions, following the commands of David, the man of God. ¹⁵ Solomon did not deviate in any way from David's commands concerning the priests and Levites and the treasuries.

7:8 Hebrew *the festival* (also in 7:9); see note on 5:3.
7:10 Hebrew *Then on the twenty-third day of the seventh month.* This day of the ancient Hebrew lunar calendar occurred in October or early November. 8:2 Hebrew *Huram,* a variant spelling of Hiram; also in 8:18. 8:6 Or *and chariots.* 8:13 Or *Festival of Weeks.*

[16] So Solomon made sure that all the work related to building the Temple of the LORD was carried out, from the day its foundation was laid to the day of its completion. [17] Later Solomon went to Ezion-geber and Elath,* ports along the shore of the Red Sea* in the land of Edom. [18] Hiram sent him ships commanded by his own officers and manned by experienced crews of sailors. These ships sailed to Ophir with Solomon's men and brought back to Solomon almost seventeen tons* of gold.

VISIT OF THE QUEEN OF SHEBA

9 When the queen of Sheba heard of Solomon's fame, she came to Jerusalem to test him with hard questions. She arrived with a large group of attendants and a great caravan of camels loaded with spices, large quantities of gold, and precious jewels. When she met with Solomon, she talked with him about everything she had on her mind. [2] Solomon had answers for all her questions; nothing was too hard for him to explain to her. [3] When the queen of Sheba realized how wise Solomon was, and when she saw the palace he had built, [4] she was overwhelmed. She was also amazed at the food on his tables, the organization of his officials and their splendid clothing, the cup-bearers and their robes, and the burnt offerings* Solomon made at the Temple of the LORD.

[5] She exclaimed to the king, "Everything I heard in my country about your achievements* and wisdom is true! [6] I didn't believe what was said until I arrived here and saw it with my own eyes. In fact, I had not heard the half of your great wisdom! It is far beyond what I was told. [7] How happy your people must be! What a privilege for your officials to stand here day after day, listening to your wisdom! [8] Praise the LORD your God, who delights in you and has placed you on the throne as king to rule for him. Because God loves Israel and desires this kingdom to last forever, he has made you king over them so you can rule with justice and righteousness."

[9] Then she gave the king a gift of 9,000 pounds* of gold, great quantities of spices, and precious jewels. Never before had there been spices as fine as those the queen of Sheba gave to King Solomon.

[10] (In addition, the crews of Hiram and Solomon brought gold from Ophir, and they also brought red sandalwood* and precious jewels. [11] The king used the sandalwood to make steps* for the Temple of the LORD and the royal palace, and to construct lyres and harps for the musicians. Never before had such beautiful things been seen in Judah.)

[12] King Solomon gave the queen of Sheba whatever she asked for—gifts of greater value than the gifts she had given him. Then she and all her attendants returned to their own land.

SOLOMON'S WEALTH AND SPLENDOR

[13] Each year Solomon received about 25 tons* of gold. [14] This did not include the additional revenue he received from merchants and traders. All the kings of Arabia and the governors of the provinces also brought gold and silver to Solomon.

[15] King Solomon made 200 large shields of hammered gold, each weighing more than 15 pounds.* [16] He also made 300 smaller shields of hammered gold, each weighing more than 7½ pounds.* The king placed these shields in the Palace of the Forest of Lebanon.

[17] Then the king made a huge throne, decorated with ivory and overlaid with pure gold. [18] The throne had six steps, with a footstool of gold. There were armrests on both sides of the seat, and the figure of a lion stood on each side of the throne. [19] There were also twelve other lions, one standing on each end of the six steps. No other throne in all the world could be compared with it!

[20] All of King Solomon's drinking cups were solid gold, as were all the utensils in the Palace of the Forest of Lebanon. They were not made of silver, for silver was considered worthless in Solomon's day!

[21] The king had a fleet of trading ships of Tarshish manned by the sailors sent by Hiram.* Once every three years the ships returned, loaded with gold, silver, ivory, apes, and peacocks.*

[22] So King Solomon became richer and wiser than any other king on earth. [23] Kings from every nation came to consult him and to hear the wisdom God had given him. [24] Year after year everyone who visited brought him gifts of silver and gold, clothing, weapons, spices, horses, and mules.

[25] Solomon had 4,000 stalls for his horses and chariots, and he had 12,000 horses.* He stationed some of them in the chariot cities, and some near him in Jerusalem. [26] He ruled over all the kings from the Euphrates River* in the north to the land of the Philistines and the border of Egypt in the south. [27] The king made silver as plentiful in Jerusalem as stone. And valuable cedar timber was as common as the sycamore-fig trees that grow in the foothills of Judah.* [28] Solomon's horses were imported from Egypt* and many other countries.

8:17a As in Greek version (see also 2 Kgs 14:22; 16:6); Hebrew reads *Eloth*, a variant spelling of Elath. 8:17b As in parallel text at 1 Kgs 9:26; Hebrew reads *the sea*. 8:18 Hebrew *450 talents* [15.3 metric tons]. 9:4 As in Greek and Syriac versions (see also 1 Kgs 10:5); Hebrew reads *and the ascent*. 9:5 Hebrew *your words*. 9:9 Hebrew *120 talents* [4,000 kilograms]. 9:10 Hebrew *algum wood* (also in 9:11); perhaps a variant spelling of *almug*. Compare parallel text at 1 Kgs 10:11-12. 9:11 Or *gateways*. The meaning of the Hebrew is uncertain. 9:13 Hebrew *666 talents* [23 metric tons]. 9:15 Hebrew *600 [shekels] of hammered gold* [6.8 kilograms]. 9:16 Hebrew *300 [shekels] of gold* [3.4 kilograms]. 9:21a Hebrew *Huram*, a variant spelling of Hiram. 9:21b Or *and baboons*. 9:25 Or *12,000 charioteers*. 9:26 Hebrew *the river*. 9:27 Hebrew *the Shephelah*. 9:28 Possibly *Muzur*, a district near Cilicia.

SUMMARY OF SOLOMON'S REIGN

²⁹The rest of the events of Solomon's reign, from beginning to end, are recorded in *The Record of Nathan the Prophet,* and *The Prophecy of Ahijah from Shiloh,* and also in *The Visions of Iddo the Seer,* concerning Jeroboam son of Nebat. ³⁰Solomon ruled in Jerusalem over all Israel for forty years. ³¹When he died, he was buried in the City of David, named for his father. Then his son Rehoboam became the next king.

THE NORTHERN TRIBES REVOLT

10 Rehoboam went to Shechem, where all Israel had gathered to make him king. ²When Jeroboam son of Nebat heard of this, he returned from Egypt, for he had fled to Egypt to escape from King Solomon. ³The leaders of Israel summoned him, and Jeroboam and all Israel went to speak with Rehoboam. ⁴"Your father was a hard master," they said. "Lighten the harsh labor demands and heavy taxes that your father imposed on us. Then we will be your loyal subjects."

⁵Rehoboam replied, "Come back in three days for my answer." So the people went away.

⁶Then King Rehoboam discussed the matter with the older men who had counseled his father, Solomon. "What is your advice?" he asked. "How should I answer these people?"

⁷The older counselors replied, "If you are good to these people and do your best to please them and give them a favorable answer, they will always be your loyal subjects."

⁸But Rehoboam rejected the advice of the older men and instead asked the opinion of the young men who had grown up with him and were now his advisers. ⁹"What is your advice?" he asked them. "How should I answer these people who want me to lighten the burdens imposed by my father?"

¹⁰The young men replied, "This is what you should tell those complainers who want a lighter burden: 'My little finger is thicker than my father's waist! ¹¹Yes, my father laid heavy burdens on you, but I'm going to make them even heavier! My father beat you with whips, but I will beat you with scorpions!'"

¹²Three days later Jeroboam and all the people returned to hear Rehoboam's decision, just as the king had ordered. ¹³But Rehoboam spoke harshly to them, for he rejected the advice of the older counselors ¹⁴and followed the counsel of his younger advisers. He told the people, "My father laid* heavy burdens on you, but I'm going to make them even heavier! My father beat you with whips, but I will beat you with scorpions!"

¹⁵So the king paid no attention to the people. This turn of events was the will of God, for it fulfilled the LORD's message to Jeroboam son of Nebat through the prophet Ahijah from Shiloh.

¹⁶When all Israel realized* that the king had refused to listen to them, they responded,

"Down with the dynasty of David!
We have no interest in the son of Jesse.
Back to your homes, O Israel!
Look out for your own house, O David!"

So all the people of Israel returned home. ¹⁷But Rehoboam continued to rule over the Israelites who lived in the towns of Judah.

¹⁸King Rehoboam sent Adoniram,* who was in charge of forced labor, to restore order, but the people of Israel stoned him to death. When this news reached King Rehoboam, he quickly jumped into his chariot and fled to Jerusalem. ¹⁹And to this day the northern tribes of Israel have refused to be ruled by a descendant of David.

SHEMAIAH'S PROPHECY

11 When Rehoboam arrived at Jerusalem, he mobilized the men of Judah and Benjamin—180,000 select troops—to fight against Israel and to restore the kingdom to himself.

²But the LORD said to Shemaiah, the man of God, ³"Say to Rehoboam son of Solomon, king of Judah, and to all the Israelites in Judah and Benjamin: ⁴'This is what the LORD says: Do not fight against your relatives. Go back home, for what has happened is my doing!'" So they obeyed the message of the LORD and did not fight against Jeroboam.

REHOBOAM FORTIFIES JUDAH

⁵Rehoboam remained in Jerusalem and fortified various towns for the defense of Judah. ⁶He built up Bethlehem, Etam, Tekoa, ⁷Beth-zur, Soco, Adullam, ⁸Gath, Mareshah, Ziph, ⁹Adoraim, Lachish, Azekah, ¹⁰Zorah, Aijalon, and Hebron. These became the fortified towns of Judah and Benjamin. ¹¹Rehoboam strengthened their defenses and stationed commanders in them, and he stored supplies of food, olive oil, and wine. ¹²He also put shields and spears in these towns as a further safety measure. So only Judah and Benjamin remained under his control.

¹³But all the priests and Levites living among the northern tribes of Israel sided with Rehoboam. ¹⁴The Levites even abandoned their pasturelands and property and moved to Judah and Jerusalem, because Jeroboam and his sons would not allow them to serve the LORD as priests. ¹⁵Jeroboam appointed his own priests to serve at the pagan shrines, where they worshiped the goat and calf idols he had made. ¹⁶From all the tribes of Israel, those who sincerely wanted to worship the LORD, the God of Israel, followed the Levites to Jerusalem, where they could offer sacrifices to the LORD, the God of their ancestors. ¹⁷This strengthened the kingdom of Judah, and

---

10:14 As in Greek version and many Hebrew manuscripts (see also 1 Kgs 12:14); Masoretic Text reads *I will lay.* **10:16** As in Syriac version, Latin Vulgate, and many Hebrew manuscripts (see also 1 Kgs 12:16); Masoretic Text lacks *realized.* **10:18** Hebrew *Hadoram,* a variant spelling of Adoniram; compare 1 Kgs 4:6; 5:14; 12:18.

for three years they supported Rehoboam son of Solomon, for during those years they faithfully followed in the footsteps of David and Solomon.

REHOBOAM'S FAMILY

¹⁸Rehoboam married his cousin Mahalath, the daughter of David's son Jerimoth and of Abihail, the daughter of Eliab son of Jesse. ¹⁹Mahalath had three sons—Jeush, Shemariah, and Zaham. ²⁰Later Rehoboam married another cousin, Maacah, the granddaughter of Absalom. Maacah gave birth to Abijah, Attai, Ziza, and Shelomith. ²¹Rehoboam loved Maacah more than any of his other wives and concubines. In all, he had eighteen wives and sixty concubines, and they gave birth to twenty-eight sons and sixty daughters. ²²Rehoboam appointed Maacah's son Abijah as leader among the princes, making it clear that he would be the next king. ²³Rehoboam also wisely gave responsibilities to his other sons and stationed some of them in the fortified towns throughout the land of Judah and Benjamin. He provided them with generous provisions, and he found many wives for them.

EGYPT INVADES JUDAH

12 But when Rehoboam was firmly established and strong, he abandoned the Law of the LORD, and all Israel followed him in this sin. ²Because they were unfaithful to the LORD, King Shishak of Egypt came up and attacked Jerusalem in the fifth year of King Rehoboam's reign. ³He came with 1,200 chariots, 60,000 horses,* and a countless army of foot soldiers, including Libyans, Sukkites, and Ethiopians.* ⁴Shishak conquered Judah's fortified towns and then advanced to attack Jerusalem.

⁵The prophet Shemaiah then met with Rehoboam and Judah's leaders, who had all fled to Jerusalem because of Shishak. Shemaiah told them, "This is what the LORD says: You have abandoned me, so I am abandoning you to Shishak."

⁶Then the leaders of Israel and the king humbled themselves and said, "The LORD is right in doing this to us!"

⁷When the LORD saw their change of heart, he gave this message to Shemaiah: "Since the people have humbled themselves, I will not completely destroy them and will soon give them some relief. I will not use Shishak to pour out my anger on Jerusalem. ⁸But they will become his subjects, so they will know the difference between serving me and serving earthly rulers."

⁹So King Shishak of Egypt came up and attacked Jerusalem. He ransacked the treasuries of the LORD's Temple and the royal palace; he stole everything, including all the gold shields Solomon had made. ¹⁰King Rehoboam later replaced them with bronze shields as substitutes, and he entrusted them to the care of the commanders of the guard who protected the entrance to the royal palace. ¹¹Whenever the king went to the Temple of the LORD, the guards would also take the shields and then return them to the guardroom. ¹²Because Rehoboam humbled himself, the LORD's anger was turned away, and he did not destroy him completely. There were still some good things in the land of Judah.

SUMMARY OF REHOBOAM'S REIGN

¹³King Rehoboam firmly established himself in Jerusalem and continued to rule. He was forty-one years old when he became king, and he reigned seventeen years in Jerusalem, the city the LORD had chosen from among all the tribes of Israel as the place to honor his name. Rehoboam's mother was Naamah, a woman from Ammon. ¹⁴But he was an evil king, for he did not seek the LORD with all his heart.

¹⁵The rest of the events of Rehoboam's reign, from beginning to end, are recorded in *The Record of Shemaiah the Prophet* and *The Record of Iddo the Seer,* which are part of the genealogical record. Rehoboam and Jeroboam were continually at war with each other. ¹⁶When Rehoboam died, he was buried in the City of David. Then his son Abijah became the next king.

ABIJAH'S WAR WITH JEROBOAM

13 Abijah began to rule over Judah in the eighteenth year of Jeroboam's reign in Israel. ²He reigned in Jerusalem three years. His mother was Maacah,* the daughter of Uriel from Gibeah.

Then war broke out between Abijah and Jeroboam. ³Judah, led by King Abijah, fielded 400,000 select warriors, while Jeroboam mustered 800,000 select troops from Israel.

⁴When the army of Judah arrived in the hill country of Ephraim, Abijah stood on Mount Zemaraim and shouted to Jeroboam and all Israel: "Listen to me! ⁵Don't you realize that the LORD, the God of Israel, made a lasting covenant* with David, giving him and his descendants the throne of Israel forever? ⁶Yet Jeroboam son of Nebat, a mere servant of David's son Solomon, rebelled against his master. ⁷Then a whole gang of scoundrels joined him, defying Solomon's son Rehoboam when he was young and inexperienced and could not stand up to them.

⁸"Do you really think you can stand against the kingdom of the LORD that is led by the descendants of David? You may have a vast army, and you have those gold calves that Jeroboam made as your gods. ⁹But you have chased away the priests of the LORD (the descendants of Aaron) and the Levites, and you have appointed your own priests, just like the pagan nations. You let anyone become a priest these days! Whoever comes to be

---

12:3a Or *charioteers,* or *horsemen.*   12:3b Hebrew *and Cushites.*   13:2 As in most Greek manuscripts and Syriac version (see also 2 Chr 11:20-21; 1 Kgs 15:2); Hebrew reads *Micaiah,* a variant spelling of Maacah.   13:5 Hebrew *a covenant of salt.*

dedicated with a young bull and seven rams can become a priest of these so-called gods of yours! ¹⁰"But as for us, the LORD is our God, and we have not abandoned him. Only the descendants of Aaron serve the LORD as priests, and the Levites alone may help them in their work. ¹¹They present burnt offerings and fragrant incense to the LORD every morning and evening. They place the Bread of the Presence on the holy table, and they light the gold lampstand every evening. We are following the instructions of the LORD our God, but you have abandoned him. ¹²So you see, God is with us. He is our leader. His priests blow their trumpets and lead us into battle against you. O people of Israel, do not fight against the LORD, the God of your ancestors, for you will not succeed!"

¹³Meanwhile, Jeroboam had secretly sent part of his army around behind the men of Judah to ambush them. ¹⁴When Judah realized that they were being attacked from the front and the rear, they cried out to the LORD for help. Then the priests blew the trumpets, ¹⁵and the men of Judah began to shout. At the sound of their battle cry, God defeated Jeroboam and all Israel and routed them before Abijah and the army of Judah. ¹⁶The Israelite army fled from Judah, and God handed them over to Judah in defeat. ¹⁷Abijah and his army inflicted heavy losses on them; 500,000 of Israel's select troops were killed that day. ¹⁸So Judah defeated Israel on that occasion because they trusted in the LORD, the God of their ancestors. ¹⁹Abijah and his army pursued Jeroboam's troops and captured some of his towns, including Bethel, Jeshanah, and Ephron, along with their surrounding villages.

²⁰So Jeroboam of Israel never regained his power during Abijah's lifetime, and finally the LORD struck him down and he died. ²¹Meanwhile, Abijah of Judah grew more and more powerful. He married fourteen wives and had twenty-two sons and sixteen daughters. ²²The rest of the events of Abijah's reign, including his words and deeds, are recorded in *The Commentary of Iddo the Prophet.*

EARLY YEARS OF ASA'S REIGN

14 ¹*When Abijah died, he was buried in the City of David. Then his son Asa became the next king. There was peace in the land for ten years. ²*Asa did what was pleasing and good in the sight of the LORD his God. ³He removed the foreign altars and the pagan shrines. He smashed the sacred pillars and cut down the Asherah poles. ⁴He commanded the people of Judah to seek the LORD, the God of their ancestors, and to obey his law and his commands. ⁵Asa also removed the pagan shrines, as well as the incense altars from every one of Judah's towns. So Asa's kingdom enjoyed a period of peace. ⁶During those peaceful years, he was able to build up the fortified towns throughout Judah. No one

tried to make war against him at this time, for the LORD was giving him rest from his enemies. ⁷Asa told the people of Judah, "Let us build towns and fortify them with walls, towers, gates, and bars. The land is still ours because we sought the LORD our God, and he has given us peace on every side." So they went ahead with these projects and brought them to completion.

⁸King Asa had an army of 300,000 warriors from the tribe of Judah, armed with large shields and spears. He also had an army of 280,000 warriors from the tribe of Benjamin, armed with small shields and bows. Both armies were composed of well-trained fighting men.

⁹Once an Ethiopian* named Zerah attacked Judah with an army of 1,000,000 men* and 300 chariots. They advanced to the town of Mareshah, ¹⁰so Asa deployed his armies for battle in the valley north of Mareshah.* ¹¹Then Asa cried out to the LORD his God, "O LORD, no one but you can help the powerless against the mighty! Help us, O LORD our God, for we trust in you alone. It is in your name that we have come against this vast horde. O LORD, you are our God; do not let mere men prevail against you!"

¹²So the LORD defeated the Ethiopians* in the presence of Asa and the army of Judah, and the enemy fled. ¹³Asa and his army pursued them as far as Gerar, and so many Ethiopians fell that they were unable to rally. They were destroyed by the LORD and his army, and the army of Judah carried off a vast amount of plunder. ¹⁴While they were at Gerar, they attacked all the towns in that area, and terror from the LORD came upon the people there. As a result, a vast amount of plunder was taken from these towns, too. ¹⁵They also attacked the camps of herdsmen and captured many sheep, goats, and camels before finally returning to Jerusalem.

ASA'S RELIGIOUS REFORMS

15 Then the Spirit of God came upon Azariah son of Oded, ²and he went out to meet King Asa as he was returning from the battle. "Listen to me, Asa!" he shouted. "Listen, all you people of Judah and Benjamin! The LORD will stay with you as long as you stay with him! Whenever you seek him, you will find him. But if you abandon him, he will abandon you. ³For a long time Israel was without the true God, without a priest to teach them, and without the Law to instruct them. ⁴But whenever they were in trouble and turned to the LORD, the God of Israel, and sought him out, they found him.

⁵"During those dark times, it was not safe to travel. Problems troubled the people of every land. ⁶Nation fought against nation, and city

14:1 Verse 14:1 is numbered 13:23 in Hebrew text. 14:2 Verses 14:2-15 are numbered 14:1-14 in Hebrew text. 14:9a Hebrew *a Cushite.* 14:9b Or *an army of thousands and thousands;* Hebrew reads *an army of a thousand thousands.* 14:10 As in Greek version; Hebrew reads *valley of Zephathah near Mareshah.* 14:12 Hebrew *Cushites;* also in 14:13.

against city, for God was troubling them with every kind of problem. [7] But as for you, be strong and courageous, for your work will be rewarded."

[8] When Asa heard this message from Azariah the prophet,* he took courage and removed all the detestable idols from the land of Judah and Benjamin and in the towns he had captured in the hill country of Ephraim. And he repaired the altar of the LORD, which stood in front of the entry room of the LORD's Temple.

[9] Then Asa called together all the people of Judah and Benjamin, along with the people of Ephraim, Manasseh, and Simeon who had settled among them. For many from Israel had moved to Judah during Asa's reign when they saw that the LORD his God was with him. [10] The people gathered at Jerusalem in late spring,* during the fifteenth year of Asa's reign.

[11] On that day they sacrificed to the LORD 700 cattle and 7,000 sheep and goats from the plunder they had taken in the battle. [12] Then they entered into a covenant to seek the LORD, the God of their ancestors, with all their heart and soul. [13] They agreed that anyone who refused to seek the LORD, the God of Israel, would be put to death—whether young or old, man or woman. [14] They shouted out their oath of loyalty to the LORD with trumpets blaring and rams' horns sounding. [15] All in Judah were happy about this covenant, for they had entered into it with all their heart. They earnestly sought after God, and they found him. And the LORD gave them rest from their enemies on every side.

[16] King Asa even deposed his grandmother* Maacah from her position as queen mother because she had made an obscene Asherah pole. He cut down her obscene pole, broke it up, and burned it in the Kidron Valley. [17] Although the pagan shrines were not removed from Israel, Asa's heart remained completely faithful throughout his life. [18] He brought into the Temple of God the silver and gold and the various items that he and his father had dedicated.

[19] So there was no more war until the thirty-fifth year of Asa's reign.

FINAL YEARS OF ASA'S REIGN

16 In the thirty-sixth year of Asa's reign, King Baasha of Israel invaded Judah and fortified Ramah in order to prevent anyone from entering or leaving King Asa's territory in Judah.

[2] Asa responded by removing the silver and gold from the treasuries of the Temple of the LORD and the royal palace. He sent it to King Ben-hadad of Aram, who was ruling in Damascus, along with this message:

[3] "Let there be a treaty* between you and me like the one between your father and my father. See, I am sending you silver and gold. Break your treaty with King Baasha of Israel so that he will leave me alone."

[4] Ben-hadad agreed to King Asa's request and sent the commanders of his army to attack the towns of Israel. They conquered the towns of Ijon, Dan, Abel-beth-maacah,* and all the store cities in Naphtali. [5] As soon as Baasha of Israel heard what was happening, he abandoned his project of fortifying Ramah and stopped all work on it. [6] Then King Asa called out all the men of Judah to carry away the building stones and timbers that Baasha had been using to fortify Ramah. Asa used these materials to fortify the towns of Geba and Mizpah.

[7] At that time Hanani the seer came to King Asa and told him, "Because you have put your trust in the king of Aram instead of in the LORD your God, you missed your chance to destroy the army of the king of Aram. [8] Don't you remember what happened to the Ethiopians* and Libyans and their vast army, with all of their chariots and charioteers?* At that time you relied on the LORD, and he handed them over to you. [9] The eyes of the LORD search the whole earth in order to strengthen those whose hearts are fully committed to him. What a fool you have been! From now on you will be at war."

[10] Asa became so angry with Hanani for saying this that he threw him into prison and put him in stocks. At that time Asa also began to oppress some of his people.

SUMMARY OF ASA'S REIGN

[11] The rest of the events of Asa's reign, from beginning to end, are recorded in *The Book of the Kings of Judah and Israel.* [12] In the thirty-ninth year of his reign, Asa developed a serious foot disease. Yet even with the severity of his disease, he did not seek the LORD's help but turned only to his physicians. [13] So he died in the forty-first year of his reign. [14] He was buried in the tomb he had carved out for himself in the City of David. He was laid on a bed perfumed with sweet spices and fragrant ointments, and the people built a huge funeral fire in his honor.

JEHOSHAPHAT RULES IN JUDAH

17 Then Jehoshaphat, Asa's son, became the next king. He strengthened Judah to stand against any attack from Israel. [2] He stationed troops in all the fortified towns of Judah, and he assigned additional garrisons to the land of Judah and to the towns of Ephraim that his father, Asa, had captured.

[3] The LORD was with Jehoshaphat because he followed the example of his father's early years* and did not worship the images of Baal.

15:8 As in Syriac version and Latin Vulgate (see also 15:1); Hebrew reads *from Oded the prophet.* 15:10 Hebrew *in the third month.* This month of the ancient Hebrew lunar calendar usually occurs within the months of May and June. 15:16 Hebrew *his mother.* 16:3 As in Greek version; Hebrew reads *There is a treaty.* 16:4 As in parallel text at 1 Kgs 15:20; Hebrew reads *Abel-maim,* another name for Abel-beth-maacah. 16:8a Hebrew *Cushites.* 16:8b Or *and horsemen?* 17:3 Some Hebrew manuscripts read *the example of his father, David.*

[4] He sought his father's God and obeyed his commands instead of following the evil practices of the kingdom of Israel. [5] So the LORD established Jehoshaphat's control over the kingdom of Judah. All the people of Judah brought gifts to Jehoshaphat, so he became very wealthy and highly esteemed. [6] He was deeply committed to* the ways of the LORD. He removed the pagan shrines and Asherah poles from Judah.

[7] In the third year of his reign Jehoshaphat sent his officials to teach in all the towns of Judah. These officials included Ben-hail, Obadiah, Zechariah, Nethanel, and Micaiah. [8] He sent Levites along with them, including Shemaiah, Nethaniah, Zebadiah, Asahel, Shemiramoth, Jehonathan, Adonijah, Tobijah, and Tobadonijah. He also sent out the priests Elishama and Jehoram. [9] They took copies of the Book of the Law of the LORD and traveled around through all the towns of Judah, teaching the people.

[10] Then the fear of the LORD fell over all the surrounding kingdoms so that none of them wanted to declare war on Jehoshaphat. [11] Some of the Philistines brought him gifts and silver as tribute, and the Arabs brought 7,700 rams and 7,700 male goats.

[12] So Jehoshaphat became more and more powerful and built fortresses and storage cities throughout Judah. [13] He stored numerous supplies in Judah's towns and stationed an army of seasoned troops at Jerusalem. [14] His army was enrolled according to ancestral clans.

From Judah there were 300,000 troops organized in units of 1,000, under the command of Adnah. [15] Next in command was Jehohanan, who commanded 280,000 troops. [16] Next was Amasiah son of Zicri, who volunteered for the LORD's service, with 200,000 troops under his command.

[17] From Benjamin there were 200,000 troops equipped with bows and shields. They were under the command of Eliada, a veteran soldier. [18] Next in command was Jehozabad, who commanded 180,000 armed men.

[19] These were the troops stationed in Jerusalem to serve the king, besides those Jehoshaphat stationed in the fortified towns throughout Judah.

JEHOSHAPHAT AND AHAB

18 Jehoshaphat enjoyed great riches and high esteem, and he made an alliance with Ahab of Israel by having his son marry Ahab's daughter. [2] A few years later he went to Samaria to visit Ahab, who prepared a great banquet for him and his officials. They butchered great numbers of sheep, goats, and cattle for the feast. Then Ahab enticed Jehoshaphat to join forces with him to recover Ramoth-gilead.

[3] "Will you go with me to Ramoth-gilead?" King Ahab of Israel asked King Jehoshaphat of Judah.

Jehoshaphat replied, "Why, of course! You and I are as one, and my troops are your troops. We will certainly join you in battle." [4] Then Jehoshaphat added, "But first let's find out what the LORD says."

[5] So the king of Israel summoned the prophets, 400 of them, and asked them, "Should we go to war against Ramoth-gilead, or should I hold back?"

They all replied, "Yes, go right ahead! God will give the king victory."

[6] But Jehoshaphat asked, "Is there not also a prophet of the LORD here? We should ask him the same question."

[7] The king of Israel replied to Jehoshaphat, "There is one more man who could consult the LORD for us, but I hate him. He never prophesies anything but trouble for me! His name is Micaiah son of Imlah."

Jehoshaphat replied, "That's not the way a king should talk! Let's hear what he has to say."

[8] So the king of Israel called one of his officials and said, "Quick! Bring Micaiah son of Imlah."

MICAIAH PROPHESIES AGAINST AHAB

[9] King Ahab of Israel and King Jehoshaphat of Judah, dressed in their royal robes, were sitting on thrones at the threshing floor near the gate of Samaria. All of Ahab's prophets were prophesying there in front of them. [10] One of them, Zedekiah son of Kenaanah, made some iron horns and proclaimed, "This is what the LORD says: With these horns you will gore the Arameans to death!"

[11] All the other prophets agreed. "Yes," they said, "go up to Ramoth-gilead and be victorious, for the LORD will give the king victory!"

[12] Meanwhile, the messenger who went to get Micaiah said to him, "Look, all the prophets are promising victory for the king. Be sure that you agree with them and promise success."

[13] But Micaiah replied, "As surely as the LORD lives, I will say only what my God says."

[14] When Micaiah arrived before the king, Ahab asked him, "Micaiah, should we go to war against Ramoth-gilead, or should I hold back?"

Micaiah replied sarcastically, "Yes, go up and be victorious, for you will have victory over them!"

[15] But the king replied sharply, "How many times must I demand that you speak only the truth to me when you speak for the LORD?"

[16] Then Micaiah told him, "In a vision I saw all Israel scattered on the mountains, like sheep without a shepherd. And the LORD said, 'Their master has been killed.* Send them home in peace.'"

[17] "Didn't I tell you?" the king of Israel exclaimed to Jehoshaphat. "He never prophesies anything but trouble for me."

17:6 Hebrew *His heart was courageous in.* 18:16 Hebrew *These people have no master.*

[18] Then Micaiah continued, "Listen to what the LORD says! I saw the LORD sitting on his throne with all the armies of heaven around him, on his right and on his left. [19] And the LORD said, 'Who can entice King Ahab of Israel to go into battle against Ramoth-gilead so he can be killed?'

"There were many suggestions, [20] and finally a spirit approached the LORD and said, 'I can do it!'

"'How will you do this?' the LORD asked.

[21] "And the spirit replied, 'I will go out and inspire all of Ahab's prophets to speak lies.'

"'You will succeed,' said the LORD. 'Go ahead and do it.'

[22] "So you see, the LORD has put a lying spirit in the mouths of your prophets. For the LORD has pronounced your doom."

[23] Then Zedekiah son of Kenaanah walked up to Micaiah and slapped him across the face. "Since when did the Spirit of the LORD leave me to speak to you?" he demanded.

[24] And Micaiah replied, "You will find out soon enough when you are trying to hide in some secret room!"

[25] "Arrest him!" the king of Israel ordered. "Take him back to Amon, the governor of the city, and to my son Joash. [26] Give them this order from the king: 'Put this man in prison, and feed him nothing but bread and water until I return safely from the battle!'"

[27] But Micaiah replied, "If you return safely, it will mean that the LORD has not spoken through me!" Then he added to those standing around, "Everyone mark my words!"

THE DEATH OF AHAB

[28] So King Ahab of Israel and King Jehoshaphat of Judah led their armies against Ramoth-gilead. [29] The king of Israel said to Jehoshaphat, "As we go into battle, I will disguise myself so no one will recognize me, but you wear your royal robes." So the king of Israel disguised himself, and they went into battle.

[30] Meanwhile, the king of Aram had issued these orders to his chariot commanders: "Attack only the king of Israel! Don't bother with anyone else." [31] So when the Aramean chariot commanders saw Jehoshaphat in his royal robes, they went after him. "There is the king of Israel!" they shouted. But Jehoshaphat called out, and the LORD saved him. God helped him by turning the attackers away from him. [32] As soon as the chariot commanders realized he was not the king of Israel, they stopped chasing him.

[33] An Aramean soldier, however, randomly shot an arrow at the Israelite troops and hit the king of Israel between the joints of his armor. "Turn the horses* and get me out of here!" Ahab groaned to the driver of the chariot. "I'm badly wounded!"

[34] The battle raged all that day, and the king of Israel propped himself up in his chariot facing the Arameans. In the evening, just as the sun was setting, he died.

JEHOSHAPHAT APPOINTS JUDGES

19 When King Jehoshaphat of Judah arrived safely home in Jerusalem, [2] Jehu son of Hanani the seer went out to meet him. "Why should you help the wicked and love those who hate the LORD?" he asked the king. "Because of what you have done, the LORD is very angry with you. [3] Even so, there is some good in you, for you have removed the Asherah poles throughout the land, and you have committed yourself to seeking God."

[4] Jehoshaphat lived in Jerusalem, but he went out among the people, traveling from Beersheba to the hill country of Ephraim, encouraging the people to return to the LORD, the God of their ancestors. [5] He appointed judges throughout the nation in all the fortified towns, [6] and he said to them, "Always think carefully before pronouncing judgment. Remember that you do not judge to please people but to please the LORD. He will be with you when you render the verdict in each case. [7] Fear the LORD and judge with integrity, for the LORD our God does not tolerate perverted justice, partiality, or the taking of bribes."

[8] In Jerusalem, Jehoshaphat appointed some of the Levites and priests and clan leaders in Israel to serve as judges* for cases involving the LORD's regulations and for civil disputes. [9] These were his instructions to them: "You must always act in the fear of the LORD, with faithfulness and an undivided heart. [10] Whenever a case comes to you from fellow citizens in an outlying town, whether a murder case or some other violation of God's laws, commands, decrees, or regulations, you must warn them not to sin against the LORD, so that he will not be angry with you and them. Do this and you will not be guilty.

[11] "Amariah the high priest will have final say in all cases involving the LORD. Zebadiah son of Ishmael, a leader from the tribe of Judah, will have final say in all civil cases. The Levites will assist you in making sure that justice is served. Take courage as you fulfill your duties, and may the LORD be with those who do what is right."

WAR WITH SURROUNDING NATIONS

20 After this, the armies of the Moabites, Ammonites, and some of the Meunites* declared war on Jehoshaphat. [2] Messengers came and told Jehoshaphat, "A vast army from Edom* is marching against you from beyond the Dead Sea.* They are already at Hazazon-tamar." (This was another name for En-gedi.)

[3] Jehoshaphat was terrified by this news and begged the LORD for guidance. He also ordered everyone in Judah to begin fasting. [4] So people

---

18:33 Hebrew *Turn your hand.*   19:8 As in Greek version; the meaning of the Hebrew is uncertain.   20:1 As in some Greek manuscripts (see also 26:7); Hebrew repeats *Ammonites.*   20:2a As in one Hebrew manuscript; most Hebrew manuscripts and ancient versions read *Aram.*   20:2b Hebrew *the sea.*

from all the towns of Judah came to Jerusalem to seek the LORD's help.

⁵Jehoshaphat stood before the community of Judah and Jerusalem in front of the new courtyard at the Temple of the LORD. ⁶He prayed, "O LORD, God of our ancestors, you alone are the God who is in heaven. You are ruler of all the kingdoms of the earth. You are powerful and mighty; no one can stand against you! ⁷O our God, did you not drive out those who lived in this land when your people Israel arrived? And did you not give this land forever to the descendants of your friend Abraham? ⁸Your people settled here and built this Temple to honor your name. ⁹They said, 'Whenever we are faced with any calamity such as war,* plague, or famine, we can come to stand in your presence before this Temple where your name is honored. We can cry out to you to save us, and you will hear us and rescue us.'

¹⁰"And now see what the armies of Ammon, Moab, and Mount Seir are doing. You would not let our ancestors invade those nations when Israel left Egypt, so they went around them and did not destroy them. ¹¹Now see how they reward us! For they have come to throw us out of your land, which you gave us as an inheritance. ¹²O our God, won't you stop them? We are powerless against this mighty army that is about to attack us. We do not know what to do, but we are looking to you for help."

¹³As all the men of Judah stood before the LORD with their little ones, wives, and children, ¹⁴the Spirit of the LORD came upon one of the men standing there. His name was Jahaziel son of Zechariah, son of Benaiah, son of Jeiel, son of Mattaniah, a Levite who was a descendant of Asaph.

¹⁵He said, "Listen, all you people of Judah and Jerusalem! Listen, King Jehoshaphat! This is what the LORD says: Do not be afraid! Don't be discouraged by this mighty army, for the battle is not yours, but God's. ¹⁶Tomorrow, march out against them. You will find them coming up through the ascent of Ziz at the end of the valley that opens into the wilderness of Jeruel. ¹⁷But you will not even need to fight. Take your positions; then stand still and watch the LORD's victory. He is with you, O people of Judah and Jerusalem. Do not be afraid or discouraged. Go out against them tomorrow, for the LORD is with you!"

¹⁸Then King Jehoshaphat bowed low with his face to the ground. And all the people of Judah and Jerusalem did the same, worshiping the LORD. ¹⁹Then the Levites from the clans of Kohath and Korah stood to praise the LORD, the God of Israel, with a very loud shout.

²⁰Early the next morning the army of Judah went out into the wilderness of Tekoa. On the way Jehoshaphat stopped and said, "Listen to me, all you people of Judah and Jerusalem! Believe in the LORD your God, and you will be able to stand firm. Believe in his prophets, and you will succeed."

²¹After consulting the people, the king appointed singers to walk ahead of the army, singing to the LORD and praising him for his holy splendor. This is what they sang:

"Give thanks to the LORD;
 his faithful love endures forever!"

²²At the very moment they began to sing and give praise, the LORD caused the armies of Ammon, Moab, and Mount Seir to start fighting among themselves. ²³The armies of Moab and Ammon turned against their allies from Mount Seir and killed every one of them. After they had destroyed the army of Seir, they began attacking each other. ²⁴So when the army of Judah arrived at the lookout point in the wilderness, all they saw were dead bodies lying on the ground as far as they could see. Not a single one of the enemy had escaped.

²⁵King Jehoshaphat and his men went out to gather the plunder. They found vast amounts of equipment, clothing,* and other valuables—more than they could carry. There was so much plunder that it took them three days just to collect it all! ²⁶On the fourth day they gathered in the Valley of Blessing,* which got its name that day because the people praised and thanked the LORD there. It is still called the Valley of Blessing today.

²⁷Then all the men returned to Jerusalem, with Jehoshaphat leading them, overjoyed that the LORD had given them victory over their enemies. ²⁸They marched into Jerusalem to the music of harps, lyres, and trumpets, and they proceeded to the Temple of the LORD.

²⁹When all the surrounding kingdoms heard that the LORD himself had fought against the enemies of Israel, the fear of God came over them. ³⁰So Jehoshaphat's kingdom was at peace, for his God had given him rest on every side.

SUMMARY OF JEHOSHAPHAT'S REIGN

³¹So Jehoshaphat ruled over the land of Judah. He was thirty-five years old when he became king, and he reigned in Jerusalem twenty-five years. His mother was Azubah, the daughter of Shilhi. ³²Jehoshaphat was a good king, following the ways of his father, Asa. He did what was pleasing in the LORD's sight. ³³During his reign, however, he failed to remove all the pagan shrines, and the people never fully committed themselves to follow the God of their ancestors.

³⁴The rest of the events of Jehoshaphat's reign, from beginning to end, are recorded in *The Record of Jehu Son of Hanani*, which is included in *The Book of the Kings of Israel*.

³⁵Some time later King Jehoshaphat of Judah made an alliance with King Ahaziah of Israel, who

20:9 Or *sword of judgment;* or *sword, judgment.* 20:25 As in some Hebrew manuscripts and Latin Vulgate; most Hebrew manuscripts read *corpses.* 20:26 Hebrew *valley of Beracah.*

was very wicked.* ³⁶Together they built a fleet of trading ships* at the port of Ezion-geber. ³⁷Then Eliezer son of Dodavahu from Mareshah prophesied against Jehoshaphat. He said, "Because you have allied yourself with King Ahaziah, the LORD will destroy your work." So the ships met with disaster and never put out to sea.*

JEHORAM RULES IN JUDAH

21 When Jehoshaphat died, he was buried with his ancestors in the City of David. Then his son Jehoram became the next king. ²Jehoram's brothers—the other sons of Jehoshaphat—were Azariah, Jehiel, Zechariah, Azariahu, Michael, and Shephatiah; all these were the sons of Jehoshaphat king of Judah.* ³Their father had given each of them valuable gifts of silver, gold, and costly items, and also some of Judah's fortified towns. However, he designated Jehoram as the next king because he was the oldest. ⁴But when Jehoram had become solidly established as king, he killed all his brothers and some of the other leaders of Judah.

⁵Jehoram was thirty-two years old when he became king, and he reigned in Jerusalem eight years. ⁶But Jehoram followed the example of the kings of Israel and was as wicked as King Ahab, for he had married one of Ahab's daughters. So Jehoram did what was evil in the LORD's sight. ⁷But the LORD did not want to destroy David's dynasty, for he had made a covenant with David and promised that his descendants would continue to rule, shining like a lamp forever.

⁸During Jehoram's reign, the Edomites revolted against Judah and crowned their own king. ⁹So Jehoram went out with his full army and all his chariots. The Edomites surrounded him and his chariot commanders, but he went out at night and attacked them* under cover of darkness. ¹⁰Even so, Edom has been independent from Judah to this day. The town of Libnah also revolted about that same time. All this happened because Jehoram had abandoned the LORD, the God of his ancestors. ¹¹He had built pagan shrines in the hill country of Judah and had led the people of Jerusalem and Judah to give themselves to pagan gods and to go astray.

¹²Then Elijah the prophet wrote Jehoram this letter:

"This is what the LORD, the God of your ancestor David, says: You have not followed the good example of your father, Jehoshaphat, or your grandfather King Asa of Judah. ¹³Instead, you have been as evil as the kings of Israel. You have led the people of Jerusalem and Judah to worship idols, just as King Ahab did in Israel. And you have even killed your own brothers, men who were better than you. ¹⁴So now the LORD is about to strike you, your people, your children, your wives, and all that is yours

with a heavy blow. ¹⁵You yourself will suffer with a severe intestinal disease that will get worse each day until your bowels come out."

¹⁶Then the LORD stirred up the Philistines and the Arabs, who lived near the Ethiopians,* to attack Jehoram. ¹⁷They marched against Judah, broke down its defenses, and carried away everything of value in the royal palace, including the king's sons and his wives. Only his youngest son, Ahaziah,* was spared.

¹⁸After all this, the LORD struck Jehoram with an incurable intestinal disease. ¹⁹The disease grew worse and worse, and at the end of two years it caused his bowels to come out, and he died in agony. His people did not build a great funeral fire to honor him as they had done for his ancestors.

²⁰Jehoram was thirty-two years old when he became king, and he reigned in Jerusalem eight years. No one was sorry when he died. They buried him in the City of David, but not in the royal cemetery.

AHAZIAH RULES IN JUDAH

22 Then the people of Jerusalem made Ahaziah, Jehoram's youngest son, their next king, since the marauding bands who came with the Arabs* had killed all the older sons. So Ahaziah son of Jehoram reigned as king of Judah.

²Ahaziah was twenty-two* years old when he became king, and he reigned in Jerusalem one year. His mother was Athaliah, a granddaughter of King Omri. ³Ahaziah also followed the evil example of King Ahab's family, for his mother encouraged him in doing wrong. ⁴He did what was evil in the LORD's sight, just as Ahab's family had done. They even became his advisers after the death of his father, and they led him to ruin.

⁵Following their evil advice, Ahaziah joined Joram,* the son of King Ahab of Israel, in his war against King Hazael of Aram at Ramoth-gilead. When the Arameans* wounded Joram in the battle, ⁶he returned to Jezreel to recover from the wounds he had received at Ramoth.* Because Joram was wounded, King Ahaziah* of Judah went to Jezreel to visit him.

⁷But God had decided that this visit would be Ahaziah's downfall. While he was there, Ahaziah went out with Joram to meet Jehu grandson

20:35 Or who made him do what was wicked. 20:36 Hebrew fleet of ships that could go to Tarshish. 20:37 Hebrew never set sail for Tarshish. 21:2 Masoretic Text reads of Israel; also in 21:4. The author of Chronicles sees Judah as representative of the true Israel. (Some Hebrew manuscripts, Greek and Syriac versions, and Latin Vulgate read of Judah.) 21:9 Or he went out and escaped. The meaning of the Hebrew is uncertain. 21:16 Hebrew the Cushites. 21:17 Hebrew Jehoahaz, a variant spelling of Ahaziah; compare 22:1. 22:1 Or marauding bands of Arabs. 22:2 As in some Greek manuscripts and Syriac version (see also 2 Kgs 8:26); Hebrew reads forty-two. 22:5a Hebrew Jehoram, a variant spelling of Joram; also in 22:6, 7. 22:5b As in two Hebrew manuscripts and Latin Vulgate (see also 2 Kgs 8:28); Masoretic Text reads the archers. 22:6a Hebrew Ramah, a variant spelling of Ramoth. 22:6b As in some Hebrew manuscripts, Greek and Syriac versions, and Latin Vulgate (see also 2 Kgs 8:29); most Hebrew manuscripts read Azariah.

2 CHRONICLES 23:19 | 377

of Nimshi,* whom the LORD had appointed to destroy the dynasty of Ahab.

⁸While Jehu was executing judgment against the family of Ahab, he happened to meet some of Judah's officials and Ahaziah's relatives* who were traveling with Ahaziah. So Jehu killed them all. ⁹Then Jehu's men searched for Ahaziah, and they found him hiding in the city of Samaria. They brought him to Jehu, who killed him. Ahaziah was given a decent burial because the people said, "He was the grandson of Jehoshaphat—a man who sought the LORD with all his heart." But none of the surviving members of Ahaziah's family was capable of ruling the kingdom.

QUEEN ATHALIAH RULES IN JUDAH

¹⁰When Athaliah, the mother of King Ahaziah of Judah, learned that her son was dead, she began to destroy the rest of Judah's royal family. ¹¹But Ahaziah's sister Jehosheba,* the daughter of King Jehoram, took Ahaziah's infant son, Joash, and stole him away from among the rest of the king's children, who were about to be killed. She put Joash and his nurse in a bedroom. In this way, Jehosheba, wife of Jehoiada the priest and sister of Ahaziah, hid the child so that Athaliah could not murder him. ¹²Joash remained hidden in the Temple of God for six years while Athaliah ruled over the land.

REVOLT AGAINST ATHALIAH

23 In the seventh year of Athaliah's reign, Jehoiada the priest decided to act. He summoned his courage and made a pact with five army commanders: Azariah son of Jeroham, Ishmael son of Jehohanan, Azariah son of Obed, Maaseiah son of Adaiah, and Elishaphat son of Zicri. ²These men traveled secretly throughout Judah and summoned the Levites and clan leaders in all the towns to come to Jerusalem. ³They all gathered at the Temple of God, where they made a solemn pact with Joash, the young king.

Jehoiada said to them, "Here is the king's son! The time has come for him to reign! The LORD has promised that a descendant of David will be our king. ⁴This is what you must do. When you priests and Levites come on duty on the Sabbath, a third of you will serve as gatekeepers. ⁵Another third will go over to the royal palace, and the final third will be at the Foundation Gate. Everyone else should stay in the courtyards of the LORD's Temple. ⁶Remember, only the priests and Levites on duty may enter the Temple of the LORD, for they are set apart as holy. The rest of the people must obey the LORD's instructions and stay outside. ⁷You Levites, form a bodyguard around the king and keep your weapons in hand. Kill anyone who tries to enter the Temple. Stay with the king wherever he goes."

⁸So the Levites and all the people of Judah did everything as Jehoiada the priest ordered. The commanders took charge of the men reporting for duty that Sabbath, as well as those who were going off duty. Jehoiada the priest did not let anyone go home after their shift ended. ⁹Then Jehoiada supplied the commanders with the spears and the large and small shields that had once belonged to King David and were stored in the Temple of God. ¹⁰He stationed all the people around the king, with their weapons ready. They formed a line from the south side of the Temple around to the north side and all around the altar. ¹¹Then Jehoiada and his sons brought out Joash, the king's son, placed the crown on his head, and presented him with a copy of God's laws.* They anointed him and proclaimed him king, and everyone shouted, "Long live the king!"

THE DEATH OF ATHALIAH

¹²When Athaliah heard the noise of the people running and the shouts of praise to the king, she hurried to the LORD's Temple to see what was happening. ¹³When she arrived, she saw the newly crowned king standing in his place of authority by the pillar at the Temple entrance. The commanders and trumpeters were surrounding him, and people from all over the land were rejoicing and blowing trumpets. Singers with musical instruments were leading the people in a great celebration. When Athaliah saw all this, she tore her clothes in despair and shouted, "Treason! Treason!"

¹⁴Then Jehoiada the priest ordered the commanders who were in charge of the troops, "Take her to the soldiers in front of the Temple,* and kill anyone who tries to rescue her." For the priest had said, "She must not be killed in the Temple of the LORD." ¹⁵So they seized her and led her out to the entrance of the Horse Gate on the palace grounds, and they killed her there.

JEHOIADA'S RELIGIOUS REFORMS

¹⁶Then Jehoiada made a covenant between himself and the king and the people that they would be the LORD's people. ¹⁷And all the people went over to the temple of Baal and tore it down. They demolished the altars and smashed the idols, and they killed Mattan the priest of Baal in front of the altars.

¹⁸Jehoiada now put the priests and Levites in charge of the Temple of the LORD, following all the directions given by David. He also commanded them to present burnt offerings to the LORD, as prescribed by the Law of Moses, and to sing and rejoice as David had instructed. ¹⁹He also stationed gatekeepers at the gates of the LORD's Temple to keep out those who for any reason were ceremonially unclean.

22:7 Hebrew *descendant of Nimshi;* compare 2 Kgs 9:2, 14.
22:8 As in Greek version (see also 2 Kgs 10:13); Hebrew reads *and sons of the brothers of Ahaziah.* 22:11 As in parallel text at 2 Kgs 11:2; Hebrew lacks *Ahaziah's sister* and reads *Jehoshabeath* [a variant spelling of Jehosheba]. 23:11 Or *a copy of the covenant.* 23:14 Or *Bring her out from between the ranks;* or *Take her out of the Temple precincts.* The meaning of the Hebrew is uncertain.

²⁰ Then the commanders, nobles, rulers, and all the people of the land escorted the king from the Temple of the Lᴏʀᴅ. They went through the upper gate and into the palace, and they seated the king on the royal throne. ²¹ So all the people of the land rejoiced, and the city was peaceful because Athaliah had been killed.

JOASH REPAIRS THE TEMPLE

24 Joash was seven years old when he became king, and he reigned in Jerusalem forty years. His mother was Zibiah from Beersheba. ² Joash did what was pleasing in the Lᴏʀᴅ's sight throughout the lifetime of Jehoiada the priest. ³ Jehoiada chose two wives for Joash, and he had sons and daughters.

⁴ At one point Joash decided to repair and restore the Temple of the Lᴏʀᴅ. ⁵ He summoned the priests and Levites and gave them these instructions: "Go to all the towns of Judah and collect the required annual offerings, so that we can repair the Temple of your God. Do not delay!" But the Levites did not act immediately.

⁶ So the king called for Jehoiada the high priest and asked him, "Why haven't you demanded that the Levites go out and collect the Temple taxes from the towns of Judah and from Jerusalem? Moses, the servant of the Lᴏʀᴅ, levied this tax on the community of Israel in order to maintain the Tabernacle of the Covenant.*"

⁷ Over the years the followers of wicked Athaliah had broken into the Temple of God, and they had used all the dedicated things from the Temple of the Lᴏʀᴅ to worship the images of Baal.

⁸ So now the king ordered a chest to be made and set outside the gate leading to the Temple of the Lᴏʀᴅ. ⁹ Then a proclamation was sent throughout Judah and Jerusalem, telling the people to bring to the Lᴏʀᴅ the tax that Moses, the servant of God, had required of the Israelites in the wilderness. ¹⁰ This pleased all the leaders and the people, and they gladly brought their money and filled the chest with it.

¹¹ Whenever the chest became full, the Levites would carry it to the king's officials. Then the court secretary and an officer of the high priest would come and empty the chest and take it back to the Temple again. This went on day after day, and a large amount of money was collected. ¹² The king and Jehoiada gave the money to the construction supervisors, who hired masons and carpenters to restore the Temple of the Lᴏʀᴅ. They also hired metalworkers, who made articles of iron and bronze for the Lᴏʀᴅ's Temple.

¹³ The men in charge of the renovation worked hard and made steady progress. They restored the Temple of God according to its original design and strengthened it. ¹⁴ When all the repairs were finished, they brought the remaining money to the king and Jehoiada. It was used to make various articles for the Temple of the Lᴏʀᴅ—articles for worship services and for burnt offerings, including ladles and other articles made of gold and silver. And the burnt offerings were sacrificed continually in the Temple of the Lᴏʀᴅ during the lifetime of Jehoiada the priest.

¹⁵ Jehoiada lived to a very old age, finally dying at 130. ¹⁶ He was buried among the kings in the City of David, because he had done so much good in Israel for God and his Temple.

JEHOIADA'S REFORMS REVERSED

¹⁷ But after Jehoiada's death, the leaders of Judah came and bowed before King Joash and persuaded him to listen to their advice. ¹⁸ They decided to abandon the Temple of the Lᴏʀᴅ, the God of their ancestors, and they worshiped Asherah poles and idols instead! Because of this sin, divine anger fell on Judah and Jerusalem. ¹⁹ Yet the Lᴏʀᴅ sent prophets to bring them back to him. The prophets warned them, but still the people would not listen.

²⁰ Then the Spirit of God came upon Zechariah son of Jehoiada the priest. He stood before the people and said, "This is what God says: Why do you disobey the Lᴏʀᴅ's commands and keep yourselves from prospering? You have abandoned the Lᴏʀᴅ, and now he has abandoned you!"

²¹ Then the leaders plotted to kill Zechariah, and King Joash ordered that they stone him to death in the courtyard of the Lᴏʀᴅ's Temple. ²² That was how King Joash repaid Jehoiada for his loyalty—by killing his son. Zechariah's last words as he died were, "May the Lᴏʀᴅ see what they are doing and avenge my death!"

THE END OF JOASH'S REIGN

²³ In the spring of the year* the Aramean army marched against Joash. They invaded Judah and Jerusalem and killed all the leaders of the nation. Then they sent all the plunder back to their king in Damascus. ²⁴ Although the Arameans attacked with only a small army, the Lᴏʀᴅ helped them conquer the much larger army of Judah. The people of Judah had abandoned the Lᴏʀᴅ, the God of their ancestors, so judgment was carried out against Joash.

²⁵ The Arameans withdrew, leaving Joash severely wounded. But his own officials plotted to kill him for murdering the son* of Jehoiada the priest. They assassinated him as he lay in bed. Then he was buried in the City of David, but not in the royal cemetery. ²⁶ The assassins were Jozacar,* the son of an Ammonite woman named Shimeath, and Jehozabad, the son of a Moabite woman named Shomer.*

²⁷ The account of the sons of Joash, the prophecies about him, and the record of his restoration of the Temple of God are written in *The*

24:6 Hebrew *Tent of the Testimony.* 24:23 Hebrew *At the turn of the year.* The first day of the year in the ancient Hebrew lunar calendar occurred in March or April. 24:25 As in Greek version and Latin Vulgate; Hebrew reads *sons.* 24:26a As in parallel text at 2 Kgs 12:21; Hebrew reads *Zabad.* 24:26b As in parallel text at 2 Kgs 12:21; Hebrew reads *Shimrith,* a variant spelling of Shomer.

Commentary on the Book of the Kings. His son Amaziah became the next king.

AMAZIAH RULES IN JUDAH

25 Amaziah was twenty-five years old when he became king, and he reigned in Jerusalem twenty-nine years. His mother was Jehoaddin* from Jerusalem. ²Amaziah did what was pleasing in the LORD's sight, but not wholeheartedly.

³When Amaziah was well established as king, he executed the officials who had assassinated his father. ⁴However, he did not kill the children of the assassins, for he obeyed the command of the LORD as written by Moses in the Book of the Law: "Parents must not be put to death for the sins of their children, nor children for the sins of their parents. Those deserving to die must be put to death for their own crimes."*

⁵Then Amaziah organized the army, assigning generals and captains* for all Judah and Benjamin. He took a census and found that he had an army of 300,000 select troops, twenty years old and older, all trained in the use of spear and shield. ⁶He also paid about 7,500 pounds* of silver to hire 100,000 experienced fighting men from Israel.

⁷But a man of God came to him and said, "Your Majesty, do not hire troops from Israel, for the LORD is not with Israel. He will not help those people of Ephraim! ⁸If you let them go with your troops into battle, you will be defeated by the enemy no matter how well you fight. God will overthrow you, for he has the power to help you or to trip you up."

⁹Amaziah asked the man of God, "But what about all that silver I paid to hire the army of Israel?"

The man of God replied, "The LORD is able to give you much more than this!" ¹⁰So Amaziah discharged the hired troops and sent them back to Ephraim. This made them very angry with Judah, and they returned home in a great rage.

¹¹Then Amaziah summoned his courage and led his army to the Valley of Salt, where they killed 10,000 Edomite troops from Seir. ¹²They captured another 10,000 and took them to the top of a cliff and threw them off, dashing them to pieces on the rocks below.

¹³Meanwhile, the hired troops that Amaziah had sent home raided several of the towns of Judah between Samaria and Beth-horon. They killed 3,000 people and carried off great quantities of plunder.

¹⁴When King Amaziah returned from slaughtering the Edomites, he brought with him idols taken from the people of Seir. He set them up as his own gods, bowed down in front of them, and offered sacrifices to them! ¹⁵This made the LORD very angry, and he sent a prophet to ask, "Why do you turn to gods who could not even save their own people from you?"

¹⁶But the king interrupted him and said, "Since when have I made you the king's counselor? Be quiet now before I have you killed!"

So the prophet stopped with this warning: "I know that God has determined to destroy you because you have done this and have refused to accept my counsel."

¹⁷After consulting with his advisers, King Amaziah of Judah sent this challenge to Israel's king Jehoash,* the son of Jehoahaz and grandson of Jehu: "Come and meet me in battle!"*

¹⁸But King Jehoash of Israel replied to King Amaziah of Judah with this story: "Out in the Lebanon mountains, a thistle sent a message to a mighty cedar tree: 'Give your daughter in marriage to my son.' But just then a wild animal of Lebanon came by and stepped on the thistle, crushing it!

¹⁹"You are saying, 'I have defeated Edom,' and you are very proud of it. But my advice is to stay at home. Why stir up trouble that will only bring disaster on you and the people of Judah?"

²⁰But Amaziah refused to listen, for God was determined to destroy him for turning to the gods of Edom. ²¹So King Jehoash of Israel mobilized his army against King Amaziah of Judah. The two armies drew up their battle lines at Beth-shemesh in Judah. ²²Judah was routed by the army of Israel, and its army scattered and fled for home. ²³King Jehoash of Israel captured Judah's king, Amaziah son of Joash and grandson of Ahaziah, at Beth-shemesh. Then he brought him to Jerusalem, where he demolished 600 feet* of Jerusalem's wall, from the Ephraim Gate to the Corner Gate. ²⁴He carried off all the gold and silver and all the articles from the Temple of God that had been in the care of Obed-edom. He also seized the treasures of the royal palace, along with hostages, and then returned to Samaria.

²⁵King Amaziah of Judah lived for fifteen years after the death of King Jehoash of Israel. ²⁶The rest of the events in Amaziah's reign, from beginning to end, are recorded in *The Book of the Kings of Judah and Israel.*

²⁷After Amaziah turned away from the LORD, there was a conspiracy against his life in Jerusalem, and he fled to Lachish. But his enemies sent assassins after him, and they killed him there. ²⁸They brought his body back on a horse, and he was buried with his ancestors in the City of David.*

UZZIAH RULES IN JUDAH

26 All the people of Judah had crowned Amaziah's sixteen-year-old son, Uzziah,

---

25:1 As in parallel text at 2 Kgs 14:2; Hebrew reads *Jehoaddan,* a variant spelling of Jehoaddin.　25:4 Deut 24:16.　25:5 Hebrew *commanders of thousands and commanders of hundreds.*
25:6 Hebrew *100 talents* [3,400 kilograms].　25:17a Hebrew *Joash,* a variant spelling of Jehoash; also in 25:18, 21, 23, 25.　25:17b Hebrew *Come, let us look one another in the face.*
25:23 Hebrew *400 cubits* [180 meters].　25:28 As in some Hebrew manuscripts and other ancient versions (see also 2 Kgs 14:20); most Hebrew manuscripts read *the city of Judah.*

as king in place of his father. ²After his father's death, Uzziah rebuilt the town of Elath* and restored it to Judah.

³Uzziah was sixteen years old when he became king, and he reigned in Jerusalem fifty-two years. His mother was Jecoliah from Jerusalem. ⁴He did what was pleasing in the LORD's sight, just as his father, Amaziah, had done. ⁵Uzziah sought God during the days of Zechariah, who taught him to fear God.* And as long as the king sought guidance from the LORD, God gave him success.

⁶Uzziah declared war on the Philistines and broke down the walls of Gath, Jabneh, and Ashdod. Then he built new towns in the Ashdod area and in other parts of Philistia. ⁷God helped him in his wars against the Philistines, his battles with the Arabs of Gur,* and his wars with the Meunites. ⁸The Meunites* paid annual tribute to him, and his fame spread even to Egypt, for he had become very powerful.

⁹Uzziah built fortified towers in Jerusalem at the Corner Gate, at the Valley Gate, and at the angle in the wall. ¹⁰He also constructed forts in the wilderness and dug many water cisterns, because he kept great herds of livestock in the foothills of Judah* and on the plains. He was also a man who loved the soil. He had many workers who cared for his farms and vineyards, both on the hillsides and in the fertile valleys.

¹¹Uzziah had an army of well-trained warriors, ready to march into battle, unit by unit. This army had been mustered and organized by Jeiel, the secretary of the army, and his assistant, Maaseiah. They were under the direction of Hananiah, one of the king's officials. ¹²These regiments of mighty warriors were commanded by 2,600 clan leaders. ¹³The army consisted of 307,500 men, all elite troops. They were prepared to assist the king against any enemy.

¹⁴Uzziah provided the entire army with shields, spears, helmets, coats of mail, bows, and sling stones. ¹⁵And he built structures on the walls of Jerusalem, designed by experts to protect those who shot arrows and hurled large stones* from the towers and the corners of the wall. His fame spread far and wide, for the LORD gave him marvelous help, and he became very powerful.

UZZIAH'S SIN AND PUNISHMENT

¹⁶But when he had become powerful, he also became proud, which led to his downfall. He sinned against the LORD his God by entering the sanctuary of the LORD's Temple and personally burning incense on the incense altar. ¹⁷Azariah the high priest went in after him with eighty other priests of the LORD, all brave men. ¹⁸They confronted King Uzziah and said, "It is not for you, Uzziah, to burn incense to the LORD. That is the work of the priests alone, the descendants of Aaron who are set apart for this work. Get out

of the sanctuary, for you have sinned. The LORD God will not honor you for this!"

¹⁹Uzziah, who was holding an incense burner, became furious. But as he was standing there raging at the priests before the incense altar in the LORD's Temple, leprosy* suddenly broke out on his forehead. ²⁰When Azariah the high priest and all the other priests saw the leprosy, they rushed him out. And the king himself was eager to get out because the LORD had struck him. ²¹So King Uzziah had leprosy until the day he died. He lived in isolation in a separate house, for he was excluded from the Temple of the LORD. His son Jotham was put in charge of the royal palace, and he governed the people of the land.

²²The rest of the events of Uzziah's reign, from beginning to end, are recorded by the prophet Isaiah son of Amoz. ²³When Uzziah died, he was buried with his ancestors; his grave was in a nearby burial field belonging to the kings, for the people said, "He had leprosy." And his son Jotham became the next king.

JOTHAM RULES IN JUDAH

27 Jotham was twenty-five years old when he became king, and he reigned in Jerusalem sixteen years. His mother was Jerusha, the daughter of Zadok.

²Jotham did what was pleasing in the LORD's sight. He did everything his father, Uzziah, had done, except that Jotham did not sin by entering the Temple of the LORD. But the people continued in their corrupt ways.

³Jotham rebuilt the upper gate of the Temple of the LORD. He also did extensive rebuilding on the wall at the hill of Ophel. ⁴He built towns in the hill country of Judah and constructed fortresses and towers in the wooded areas. ⁵Jotham went to war against the Ammonites and conquered them. Over the next three years he received from them an annual tribute of 7,500 pounds* of silver, 50,000 bushels of wheat, and 50,000 bushels of barley.*

⁶King Jotham became powerful because he was careful to live in obedience to the LORD his God.

⁷The rest of the events of Jotham's reign, including all his wars and other activities, are recorded in *The Book of the Kings of Israel and Judah.* ⁸He was twenty-five years old when he became king, and he reigned in Jerusalem sixteen years. ⁹When Jotham died, he was buried in the City of David. And his son Ahaz became the next king.

26:2 As in Greek version (see also 2 Kgs 14:22; 16:6); Hebrew reads *Eloth*, a variant spelling of Elath.   26:5 As in Syriac and Greek versions; Hebrew reads *who instructed him in divine visions.* 26:7 As in Greek version; Hebrew reads *Gur-baal.*   26:8 As in Greek version; Hebrew reads *Ammonites.* Compare 26:7. 26:10 Hebrew *the Shephelah.*   26:15 Or *to shoot arrows and hurl large stones.*   26:19 Or *a contagious skin disease.* The Hebrew word used here and throughout this passage can describe various skin diseases.   27:5a Hebrew *100 talents* [3,400 kilograms]. 27:5b Hebrew *10,000 cors* [2,200 kiloliters] *of wheat, and 10,000 cors of barley.*

AHAZ RULES IN JUDAH

28 Ahaz was twenty years old when he became king, and he reigned in Jerusalem sixteen years. He did not do what was pleasing in the sight of the LORD, as his ancestor David had done. ²Instead, he followed the example of the kings of Israel. He cast metal images for the worship of Baal. ³He offered sacrifices in the valley of Ben-Hinnom, even sacrificing his own sons in the fire.* In this way, he followed the detestable practices of the pagan nations the LORD had driven from the land ahead of the Israelites. ⁴He offered sacrifices and burned incense at the pagan shrines and on the hills and under every green tree.

⁵Because of all this, the LORD his God allowed the king of Aram to defeat Ahaz and to exile large numbers of his people to Damascus. The armies of the king of Israel also defeated Ahaz and inflicted many casualties on his army. ⁶In a single day Pekah son of Remaliah, Israel's king, killed 120,000 of Judah's troops, all of them experienced warriors, because they had abandoned the LORD, the God of their ancestors. ⁷Then Zicri, a warrior from Ephraim, killed Maaseiah, the king's son; Azrikam, the king's palace commander; and Elkanah, the king's second-in-command. ⁸The armies of Israel captured 200,000 women and children from Judah and seized tremendous amounts of plunder, which they took back to Samaria.

⁹But a prophet of the LORD named Oded was there in Samaria when the army of Israel returned home. He went out to meet them and said, "The LORD, the God of your ancestors, was angry with Judah and let you defeat them. But you have gone too far, killing them without mercy, and all heaven is disturbed. ¹⁰And now you are planning to make slaves of these people from Judah and Jerusalem. What about your own sins against the LORD your God? ¹¹Listen to me and return these prisoners you have taken, for they are your own relatives. Watch out, because now the LORD's fierce anger has been turned against you!"

¹²Then some of the leaders of Israel*—Azariah son of Jehohanan, Berekiah son of Meshillemoth, Jehizkiah son of Shallum, and Amasa son of Hadlai—agreed with this and confronted the men returning from battle. ¹³"You must not bring the prisoners here!" they declared. "We cannot afford to add to our sins and guilt. Our guilt is already great, and the LORD's fierce anger is already turned against Israel."

¹⁴So the warriors released the prisoners and handed over the plunder in the sight of the leaders and all the people. ¹⁵Then the four men just mentioned by name came forward and distributed clothes from the plunder to the prisoners who were naked. They provided clothing and sandals to wear, gave them enough food and drink, and dressed their wounds with olive oil.

They put those who were weak on donkeys and took all the prisoners back to their own people in Jericho, the city of palms. Then they returned to Samaria.

AHAZ CLOSES THE TEMPLE

¹⁶At that time King Ahaz of Judah asked the king of Assyria for help. ¹⁷The armies of Edom had again invaded Judah and taken captives. ¹⁸And the Philistines had raided towns located in the foothills of Judah* and in the Negev of Judah. They had already captured and occupied Beth-shemesh, Aijalon, Gederoth, Soco with its villages, Timnah with its villages, and Gimzo with its villages. ¹⁹The LORD was humbling Judah because of King Ahaz of Judah,* for he had encouraged his people to sin and had been utterly unfaithful to the LORD. ²⁰So when King Tiglath-pileser* of Assyria arrived, he attacked Ahaz instead of helping him. ²¹Ahaz took valuable items from the LORD's Temple, the royal palace, and from the homes of his officials and gave them to the king of Assyria as tribute. But this did not help him.

²²Even during this time of trouble, King Ahaz continued to reject the LORD. ²³He offered sacrifices to the gods of Damascus who had defeated him, for he said, "Since these gods helped the kings of Aram, they will help me, too, if I sacrifice to them." But instead, they led to his ruin and the ruin of all Judah.

²⁴The king took the various articles from the Temple of God and broke them into pieces. He shut the doors of the LORD's Temple so that no one could worship there, and he set up altars to pagan gods in every corner of Jerusalem. ²⁵He made pagan shrines in all the towns of Judah for offering sacrifices to other gods. In this way, he aroused the anger of the LORD, the God of his ancestors.

²⁶The rest of the events of Ahaz's reign and everything he did, from beginning to end, are recorded in *The Book of the Kings of Judah and Israel.* ²⁷When Ahaz died, he was buried in Jerusalem but not in the royal cemetery of the kings of Judah. Then his son Hezekiah became the next king.

HEZEKIAH RULES IN JUDAH

29 Hezekiah was twenty-five years old when he became the king of Judah, and he reigned in Jerusalem twenty-nine years. His mother was Abijah, the daughter of Zechariah. ²He did what was pleasing in the LORD's sight, just as his ancestor David had done.

28:3 Or *even making his sons pass through the fire.* 28:12 Hebrew *Ephraim,* referring to the northern kingdom of Israel. 28:18 Hebrew *the Shephelah.* 28:19 Masoretic Text reads *of Israel;* also in 28:23, 27. The author of Chronicles sees Judah as representative of the true Israel. (Some Hebrew manuscripts and Greek version read *of Judah.*) 28:20 Hebrew *Tilgath-pilneser,* a variant spelling of Tiglath-pileser.

HEZEKIAH REOPENS THE TEMPLE

³ In the very first month of the first year of his reign, Hezekiah reopened the doors of the Temple of the LORD and repaired them. ⁴ He summoned the priests and Levites to meet him at the courtyard east of the Temple. ⁵ He said to them, "Listen to me, you Levites! Purify yourselves, and purify the Temple of the LORD, the God of your ancestors. Remove all the defiled things from the sanctuary. ⁶ Our ancestors were unfaithful and did what was evil in the sight of the LORD our God. They abandoned the LORD and his dwelling place; they turned their backs on him. ⁷ They also shut the doors to the Temple's entry room, and they snuffed out the lamps. They stopped burning incense and presenting burnt offerings at the sanctuary of the God of Israel.

⁸ "That is why the LORD's anger has fallen upon Judah and Jerusalem. He has made them an object of dread, horror, and ridicule, as you can see with your own eyes. ⁹ Because of this, our fathers have been killed in battle, and our sons and daughters and wives have been captured. ¹⁰ But now I will make a covenant with the LORD, the God of Israel, so that his fierce anger will turn away from us. ¹¹ My sons, do not neglect your duties any longer! The LORD has chosen you to stand in his presence, to minister to him, and to lead the people in worship and present offerings to him."

¹² Then these Levites got right to work:

From the clan of Kohath: Mahath son of Amasai and Joel son of Azariah.
From the clan of Merari: Kish son of Abdi and Azariah son of Jehallelel.
From the clan of Gershon: Joah son of Zimmah and Eden son of Joah.
¹³ From the family of Elizaphan: Shimri and Jeiel.
From the family of Asaph: Zechariah and Mattaniah.
¹⁴ From the family of Heman: Jehiel and Shimei.
From the family of Jeduthun: Shemaiah and Uzziel.

¹⁵ These men called together their fellow Levites, and they all purified themselves. Then they began to cleanse the Temple of the LORD, just as the king had commanded. They were careful to follow all the LORD's instructions in their work. ¹⁶ The priests went into the sanctuary of the Temple of the LORD to cleanse it, and they took out to the Temple courtyard all the defiled things they found. From there the Levites carted it all out to the Kidron Valley.

¹⁷ They began the work in early spring, on the first day of the new year,* and in eight days they had reached the entry room of the LORD's Temple. Then they purified the Temple of the LORD itself, which took another eight days. So the entire task was completed in sixteen days.

THE TEMPLE REDEDICATION

¹⁸ Then the Levites went to King Hezekiah and gave him this report: "We have cleansed the entire Temple of the LORD, the altar of burnt offering with all its utensils, and the table of the Bread of the Presence with all its utensils. ¹⁹ We have also recovered all the items discarded by King Ahaz when he was unfaithful and closed the Temple. They are now in front of the altar of the LORD, purified and ready for use."

²⁰ Early the next morning King Hezekiah gathered the city officials and went to the Temple of the LORD. ²¹ They brought seven bulls, seven rams, and seven male lambs as a burnt offering, together with seven male goats as a sin offering for the kingdom, for the Temple, and for Judah. The king commanded the priests, who were descendants of Aaron, to sacrifice the animals on the altar of the LORD.

²² So they killed the bulls, and the priests took the blood and sprinkled it on the altar. Next they killed the rams and sprinkled their blood on the altar. And finally, they did the same with the male lambs. ²³ The male goats for the sin offering were then brought before the king and the assembly of people, who laid their hands on them. ²⁴ The priests then killed the goats as a sin offering and sprinkled their blood on the altar to make atonement for the sins of all Israel. The king had specifically commanded that this burnt offering and sin offering should be made for all Israel.

²⁵ King Hezekiah then stationed the Levites at the Temple of the LORD with cymbals, lyres, and harps. He obeyed all the commands that the LORD had given to King David through Gad, the king's seer, and the prophet Nathan. ²⁶ The Levites then took their positions around the Temple with the instruments of David, and the priests took their positions with the trumpets. ²⁷ Then Hezekiah ordered that the burnt offering be placed on the altar. As the burnt offering was presented, songs of praise to the LORD were begun, accompanied by the trumpets and other instruments of David, the former king of Israel. ²⁸ The entire assembly worshiped the LORD as the singers sang and the trumpets blew, until all the burnt offerings were finished. ²⁹ Then the king and everyone with him bowed down in worship. ³⁰ King Hezekiah and the officials ordered the Levites to praise the LORD with the psalms written by David and by Asaph the seer. So they offered joyous praise and bowed down in worship.

³¹ Then Hezekiah declared, "Now that you have consecrated yourselves to the LORD, bring your sacrifices and thanksgiving offerings to the Temple of the LORD." So the people brought their sacrifices and thanksgiving offerings, and all whose hearts were willing brought burnt offerings, too. ³² The people brought to the LORD

29:17 Hebrew *on the first day of the first month.* This day in the ancient Hebrew lunar calendar occurred in March or early April, 715 B.C.

70 bulls, 100 rams, and 200 male lambs for burnt offerings. ³³They also brought 600 cattle and 3,000 sheep and goats as sacred offerings.

³⁴But there were too few priests to prepare all the burnt offerings. So their relatives the Levites helped them until the work was finished and more priests had been purified, for the Levites had been more conscientious about purifying themselves than the priests had been. ³⁵There was an abundance of burnt offerings, along with the usual liquid offerings, and a great deal of fat from the many peace offerings.

So the Temple of the LORD was restored to service. ³⁶And Hezekiah and all the people rejoiced because of what God had done for the people, for everything had been accomplished so quickly.

PREPARATIONS FOR PASSOVER

30 King Hezekiah now sent word to all Israel and Judah, and he wrote letters of invitation to the people of Ephraim and Manasseh. He asked everyone to come to the Temple of the LORD at Jerusalem to celebrate the Passover of the LORD, the God of Israel. ²The king, his officials, and all the community of Jerusalem decided to celebrate Passover a month later than usual.* ³They were unable to celebrate it at the prescribed time because not enough priests could be purified by then, and the people had not yet assembled at Jerusalem.

⁴This plan for keeping the Passover seemed right to the king and all the people. ⁵So they sent a proclamation throughout all Israel, from Beersheba in the south to Dan in the north, inviting everyone to come to Jerusalem to celebrate the Passover of the LORD, the God of Israel. The people had not been celebrating it in great numbers as required in the Law.

⁶At the king's command, runners were sent throughout Israel and Judah. They carried letters that said:

"O people of Israel, return to the LORD, the God of Abraham, Isaac, and Israel,* so that he will return to the few of us who have survived the conquest of the Assyrian kings. ⁷Do not be like your ancestors and relatives who abandoned the LORD, the God of their ancestors, and became an object of derision, as you yourselves can see. ⁸Do not be stubborn, as they were, but submit yourselves to the LORD. Come to his Temple, which he has set apart as holy forever. Worship the LORD your God so that his fierce anger will turn away from you. ⁹For if you return to the LORD, your relatives and your children will be treated mercifully by their captors, and they will be able to return to this land. For the LORD your God is gracious and merciful. If you return to him, he will not continue to turn his face from you."

CELEBRATION OF PASSOVER

¹⁰The runners went from town to town throughout Ephraim and Manasseh and as far as the territory of Zebulun. But most of the people just laughed at the runners and made fun of them. ¹¹However, some people from Asher, Manasseh, and Zebulun humbled themselves and went to Jerusalem.

¹²At the same time, God's hand was on the people in the land of Judah, giving them all one heart to obey the orders of the king and his officials, who were following the word of the LORD. ¹³So a huge crowd assembled at Jerusalem in midspring* to celebrate the Festival of Unleavened Bread. ¹⁴They set to work and removed the pagan altars from Jerusalem. They took away all the incense altars and threw them into the Kidron Valley.

¹⁵On the fourteenth day of the second month, one month later than usual,* the people slaughtered the Passover lamb. This shamed the priests and Levites, so they purified themselves and brought burnt offerings to the Temple of the LORD. ¹⁶Then they took their places at the Temple as prescribed in the Law of Moses, the man of God. The Levites brought the sacrificial blood to the priests, who then sprinkled it on the altar.

¹⁷Since many of the people had not purified themselves, the Levites had to slaughter their Passover lamb for them, to set them apart for the LORD. ¹⁸Most of those who came from Ephraim, Manasseh, Issachar, and Zebulun had not purified themselves. But King Hezekiah prayed for them, and they were allowed to eat the Passover meal anyway, even though this was contrary to the requirements of the Law. For Hezekiah said, "May the LORD, who is good, pardon those ¹⁹who decide to follow the LORD, the God of their ancestors, even though they are not properly cleansed for the ceremony." ²⁰And the LORD listened to Hezekiah's prayer and healed the people.

²¹So the people of Israel who were present in Jerusalem joyously celebrated the Festival of Unleavened Bread for seven days. Each day the Levites and priests sang to the LORD, accompanied by loud instruments.* ²²Hezekiah encouraged all the Levites regarding the skill they displayed as they served the LORD. The celebration continued for seven days. Peace offerings were sacrificed, and the people gave thanks to the LORD, the God of their ancestors.

²³The entire assembly then decided to continue the festival another seven days, so they celebrated joyfully for another week. ²⁴King Hezekiah gave the people 1,000 bulls and 7,000

30:2 Hebrew *in the second month.* Passover was normally observed in the first month (of the ancient Hebrew lunar calendar). 30:6 *Israel* is the name that God gave to Jacob. 30:13 Hebrew *in the second month.* The second month of the ancient Hebrew lunar calendar usually occurs within the months of April and May. 30:15 Hebrew *On the fourteenth day of the second month.* Passover normally began on the fourteenth day of the first month (see Lev 23:5). 30:21 Or *sang to the LORD with all their strength.*

sheep and goats for offerings, and the officials donated 1,000 bulls and 10,000 sheep and goats. Meanwhile, many more priests purified themselves.

²⁵ The entire assembly of Judah rejoiced, including the priests, the Levites, all who came from the land of Israel, the foreigners who came to the festival, and all those who lived in Judah. ²⁶ There was great joy in the city, for Jerusalem had not seen a celebration like this one since the days of Solomon, King David's son. ²⁷ Then the priests and Levites stood and blessed the people, and God heard their prayer from his holy dwelling in heaven.

HEZEKIAH'S RELIGIOUS REFORMS

31 When the festival ended, the Israelites who attended went to all the towns of Judah, Benjamin, Ephraim, and Manasseh, and they smashed all the sacred pillars, cut down the Asherah poles, and removed the pagan shrines and altars. After this, the Israelites returned to their own towns and homes.

² Hezekiah then organized the priests and Levites into divisions to offer the burnt offerings and peace offerings, and to worship and give thanks and praise to the LORD at the gates of the Temple. ³ The king also made a personal contribution of animals for the daily morning and evening burnt offerings, the weekly Sabbath festivals, the monthly new moon festivals, and the annual festivals as prescribed in the Law of the LORD. ⁴ In addition, he required the people in Jerusalem to bring a portion of their goods to the priests and Levites, so they could devote themselves fully to the Law of the LORD.

⁵ When the people of Israel heard these requirements, they responded generously by bringing the first share of their grain, new wine, olive oil, honey, and all the produce of their fields. They brought a large quantity—a tithe of all they produced. ⁶ The people who had moved to Judah from Israel, and the people of Judah themselves, brought in the tithes of their cattle, sheep, and goats and a tithe of the things that had been dedicated to the LORD their God, and they piled them up in great heaps. ⁷ They began piling them up in late spring, and the heaps continued to grow until early autumn.* ⁸ When Hezekiah and his officials came and saw these huge piles, they thanked the LORD and his people Israel!

⁹ "Where did all this come from?" Hezekiah asked the priests and Levites.

¹⁰ And Azariah the high priest, from the family of Zadok, replied, "Since the people began bringing their gifts to the LORD's Temple, we have had enough to eat and plenty to spare. The LORD has blessed his people, and all this is left over."

¹¹ Hezekiah ordered that storerooms be prepared in the Temple of the LORD. When this was done, ¹² the people faithfully brought all the gifts, tithes, and other items dedicated for use in the

---

BLESSINGS AND BENEFITS
2 Chronicles 31:10   ROBERT MORRIS

Can you imagine what the body of Christ could accomplish if every believer tithed?

Think about what God's people could do on the earth if they faithfully gave Him the first 10 percent so the remaining 90 percent could be redeemed and blessed!

When Hezekiah became king, he "did what was pleasing in the LORD's sight" (2 Chronicles 29:2). He reinstituted tithing in Jerusalem, and the people responded with great enthusiasm. The king and his officials were amazed to see everything the people brought, and the priest Azariah explained, "Since the people began bringing their gifts to the LORD's Temple, we have had enough to eat and plenty to spare. The LORD has blessed his people, and all this is left over" (2 Chronicles 31:10).

Tithing isn't a grim duty or a dry religious exercise. It's an opportunity that blesses the church and greatly benefits the giver as well.

Temple. Conaniah the Levite was put in charge, assisted by his brother Shimei. ¹³ The supervisors under them were Jehiel, Azaziah, Nahath, Asahel, Jerimoth, Jozabad, Eliel, Ismakiah, Mahath, and Benaiah. These appointments were made by King Hezekiah and Azariah, the chief official in the Temple of God.

¹⁴ Kore son of Imnah the Levite, who was the gatekeeper at the East Gate, was put in charge of distributing the voluntary offerings given to God, the gifts, and the things that had been dedicated to the LORD. ¹⁵ His faithful assistants were Eden, Miniamin, Jeshua, Shemaiah, Amariah, and Shecaniah. They distributed the gifts among the families of priests in their towns by their divisions, dividing the gifts fairly among old and young alike. ¹⁶ They distributed the gifts to all males three years old or older, regardless of their place in the genealogical records. The distribution went to all who would come to the LORD's Temple to perform their daily duties according to their divisions. ¹⁷ They distributed gifts to the priests who were listed by their families in the genealogical records, and to the Levites twenty years old or older who were listed according to their jobs and their divisions. ¹⁸ Food allotments were also given to the families of all those listed in the genealogical records, including their little babies, wives, sons, and daughters. For they had all been faithful in purifying themselves.

¹⁹ As for the priests, the descendants of Aaron, who were living in the open villages around the

---

31:7 Hebrew *in the third month . . . until the seventh month.* The third month of the ancient Hebrew lunar calendar usually occurs within the months of May and June; the seventh month usually occurs within September and October.

towns, men were appointed by name to distribute portions to every male among the priests and to all the Levites listed in the genealogical records. ²⁰ In this way, King Hezekiah handled the distribution throughout all Judah, doing what was pleasing and good in the sight of the LORD his God. ²¹ In all that he did in the service of the Temple of God and in his efforts to follow God's laws and commands, Hezekiah sought his God wholeheartedly. As a result, he was very successful.

ASSYRIA INVADES JUDAH

32 After Hezekiah had faithfully carried out this work, King Sennacherib of Assyria invaded Judah. He laid siege to the fortified towns, giving orders for his army to break through their walls. ² When Hezekiah realized that Sennacherib also intended to attack Jerusalem, ³ he consulted with his officials and military advisers, and they decided to stop the flow of the springs outside the city. ⁴ They organized a huge work crew to stop the flow of the springs, cutting off the brook that ran through the fields. For they said, "Why should the kings of Assyria come here and find plenty of water?"

⁵ Then Hezekiah worked hard at repairing all the broken sections of the wall, erecting towers, and constructing a second wall outside the first. He also reinforced the supporting terraces* in the City of David and manufactured large numbers of weapons and shields. ⁶ He appointed military officers over the people and assembled them before him in the square at the city gate. Then Hezekiah encouraged them by saying: ⁷ "Be strong and courageous! Don't be afraid or discouraged because of the king of Assyria or his mighty army, for there is a power far greater on our side! ⁸ He may have a great army, but they are merely men. We have the LORD our God to help us and to fight our battles for us!" Hezekiah's words greatly encouraged the people.

SENNACHERIB THREATENS JERUSALEM

⁹ While King Sennacherib of Assyria was still besieging the town of Lachish, he sent his officers to Jerusalem with this message for Hezekiah and all the people in the city:

¹⁰ "This is what King Sennacherib of Assyria says: What are you trusting in that makes you think you can survive my siege of Jerusalem? ¹¹ Hezekiah has said, 'The LORD our God will rescue us from the king of Assyria.' Surely Hezekiah is misleading you, sentencing you to death by famine and thirst! ¹² Don't you realize that Hezekiah is the very person who destroyed all the LORD's shrines and altars? He commanded Judah and Jerusalem to worship only at the altar at the Temple and to offer sacrifices on it alone.

¹³ "Surely you must realize what I and the other kings of Assyria before me have done to all the people of the earth! Were any of the gods of those nations able to rescue their people from my power? ¹⁴ Which of their gods was able to rescue its people from the destructive power of my predecessors? What makes you think your God can rescue you from me? ¹⁵ Don't let Hezekiah deceive you! Don't let him fool you like this! I say it again—no god of any nation or kingdom has ever yet been able to rescue his people from me or my ancestors. How much less will your God rescue you from my power!"

¹⁶ And Sennacherib's officers further mocked the LORD God and his servant Hezekiah, heaping insult upon insult. ¹⁷ The king also sent letters scorning the LORD, the God of Israel. He wrote, "Just as the gods of all the other nations failed to rescue their people from my power, so the God of Hezekiah will also fail." ¹⁸ The Assyrian officials who brought the letters shouted this in Hebrew* to the people gathered on the walls of the city, trying to terrify them so it would be easier to capture the city. ¹⁹ These officers talked about the God of Jerusalem as though he were one of the pagan gods, made by human hands.

²⁰ Then King Hezekiah and the prophet Isaiah son of Amoz cried out in prayer to God in heaven. ²¹ And the LORD sent an angel who destroyed the Assyrian army with all its commanders and officers. So Sennacherib was forced to return home in disgrace to his own land. And when he entered the temple of his god, some of his own sons killed him there with a sword.

²² That is how the LORD rescued Hezekiah and the people of Jerusalem from King Sennacherib of Assyria and from all the others who threatened them. So there was peace throughout the land. ²³ From then on King Hezekiah became highly respected among all the surrounding nations, and many gifts for the LORD arrived at Jerusalem, with valuable presents for King Hezekiah, too.

HEZEKIAH'S SICKNESS AND RECOVERY

²⁴ About that time Hezekiah became deathly ill. He prayed to the LORD, who healed him and gave him a miraculous sign. ²⁵ But Hezekiah did not respond appropriately to the kindness shown him, and he became proud. So the LORD's anger came against him and against Judah and Jerusalem. ²⁶ Then Hezekiah humbled himself and repented of his pride, as did the people of Jerusalem. So the LORD's anger did not fall on them during Hezekiah's lifetime.

²⁷ Hezekiah was very wealthy and highly honored. He built special treasury buildings for his

32:5 Hebrew *the millo*. The meaning of the Hebrew is uncertain.
32:18 Hebrew *in the dialect of Judah*.

silver, gold, precious stones, and spices, and for his shields and other valuable items. 28 He also constructed many storehouses for his grain, new wine, and olive oil; and he made many stalls for his cattle and pens for his flocks of sheep and goats. 29 He built many towns and acquired vast flocks and herds, for God had given him great wealth. 30 He blocked up the upper spring of Gihon and brought the water down through a tunnel to the west side of the City of David. And so he succeeded in everything he did.

31 However, when ambassadors arrived from Babylon to ask about the remarkable events that had taken place in the land, God withdrew from Hezekiah in order to test him and to see what was really in his heart.

SUMMARY OF HEZEKIAH'S REIGN

32 The rest of the events in Hezekiah's reign and his acts of devotion are recorded in *The Vision of the Prophet Isaiah Son of Amoz,* which is included in *The Book of the Kings of Judah and Israel.* 33 When Hezekiah died, he was buried in the upper area of the royal cemetery, and all Judah and Jerusalem honored him at his death. And his son Manasseh became the next king.

MANASSEH RULES IN JUDAH

33 Manasseh was twelve years old when he became king, and he reigned in Jerusalem fifty-five years. 2 He did what was evil in the LORD's sight, following the detestable practices of the pagan nations that the LORD had driven from the land ahead of the Israelites. 3 He rebuilt the pagan shrines his father, Hezekiah, had broken down. He constructed altars for the images of Baal and set up Asherah poles. He also bowed before all the powers of the heavens and worshiped them.

4 He built pagan altars in the Temple of the LORD, the place where the LORD had said, "My name will remain in Jerusalem forever." 5 He built these altars for all the powers of the heavens in both courtyards of the LORD's Temple. 6 Manasseh also sacrificed his own sons in the fire* in the valley of Ben-Hinnom. He practiced sorcery, divination, and witchcraft, and he consulted with mediums and psychics. He did much that was evil in the LORD's sight, arousing his anger.

7 Manasseh even took a carved idol he had made and set it up in God's Temple, the very place where God had told David and his son Solomon: "My name will be honored forever in this Temple and in Jerusalem—the city I have chosen from among all the tribes of Israel. 8 If the Israelites will be careful to obey my commands—all the laws, decrees, and regulations given through Moses—I will not send them into exile from this land that I set aside for your ancestors." 9 But Manasseh led the people of Judah and Jerusalem to do even more evil than the pagan nations

that the LORD had destroyed when the people of Israel entered the land.

10 The LORD spoke to Manasseh and his people, but they ignored all his warnings. 11 So the LORD sent the commanders of the Assyrian armies, and they took Manasseh prisoner. They put a ring through his nose, bound him in bronze chains, and led him away to Babylon. 12 But while in deep distress, Manasseh sought the LORD his God and sincerely humbled himself before the God of his ancestors. 13 And when he prayed, the LORD listened to him and was moved by his request. So the LORD brought Manasseh back to Jerusalem and to his kingdom. Then Manasseh finally realized that the LORD alone is God!

14 After this Manasseh rebuilt the outer wall of the City of David, from west of the Gihon Spring in the Kidron Valley to the Fish Gate, and continuing around the hill of Ophel. He built the wall very high. And he stationed his military officers in all of the fortified towns of Judah. 15 Manasseh also removed the foreign gods and the idol from the LORD's Temple. He tore down all the altars he had built on the hill where the Temple stood and all the altars that were in Jerusalem, and he dumped them outside the city. 16 Then he restored the altar of the LORD and sacrificed peace offerings and thanksgiving offerings on it. He also encouraged the people of Judah to worship the LORD, the God of Israel. 17 However, the people still sacrificed at the pagan shrines, though only to the LORD their God.

18 The rest of the events of Manasseh's reign, his prayer to God, and the words the seers spoke to him in the name of the LORD, the God of Israel, are recorded in *The Book of the Kings of Israel.* 19 Manasseh's prayer, the account of the way God answered him, and an account of all his sins and unfaithfulness are recorded in *The Record of the Seers.* It includes a list of the locations where he built pagan shrines and set up Asherah poles and idols before he humbled himself and repented. 20 When Manasseh died, he was buried in his palace. Then his son Amon became the next king.

AMON RULES IN JUDAH

21 Amon was twenty-two years old when he became king, and he reigned in Jerusalem two years. 22 He did what was evil in the LORD's sight, just as his father, Manasseh, had done. He worshiped and sacrificed to all the idols his father had made. 23 But unlike his father, he did not humble himself before the LORD. Instead, Amon sinned even more.

24 Then Amon's own officials conspired against him and assassinated him in his palace. 25 But the people of the land killed all those who had conspired against King Amon, and they made his son Josiah the next king.

33:6 Or *also made his sons pass through the fire.* 33:19 Or *The Record of Hozai.*

JOSIAH RULES IN JUDAH

34 Josiah was eight years old when he became king, and he reigned in Jerusalem thirty-one years. [2] He did what was pleasing in the LORD's sight and followed the example of his ancestor David. He did not turn away from doing what was right.

[3] During the eighth year of his reign, while he was still young, Josiah began to seek the God of his ancestor David. Then in the twelfth year he began to purify Judah and Jerusalem, destroying all the pagan shrines, the Asherah poles, and the carved idols and cast images. [4] He ordered that the altars of Baal be demolished and that the incense altars which stood above them be broken down. He also made sure that the Asherah poles, the carved idols, and the cast images were smashed and scattered over the graves of those who had sacrificed to them. [5] He burned the bones of the pagan priests on their own altars, and so he purified Judah and Jerusalem.

[6] He did the same thing in the towns of Manasseh, Ephraim, and Simeon, even as far as Naphtali, and in the regions* all around them. [7] He destroyed the pagan altars and the Asherah poles, and he crushed the idols into dust. He cut down all the incense altars throughout the land of Israel. Finally, he returned to Jerusalem. [8] In the eighteenth year of his reign, after he had purified the land and the Temple, Josiah appointed Shaphan son of Azaliah, Maaseiah the governor of Jerusalem, and Joah son of Joahaz, the royal historian, to repair the Temple of the LORD his God. [9] They gave Hilkiah the high priest the money that had been collected by the Levites who served as gatekeepers at the Temple of God. The gifts were brought by people from Manasseh, Ephraim, and from all the remnant of Israel, as well as from all Judah, Benjamin, and the people of Jerusalem.

[10] He entrusted the money to the men assigned to supervise the restoration of the LORD's Temple. Then they paid the workers who did the repairs and renovation of the Temple. [11] They hired carpenters and builders, who purchased finished stone for the walls and timber for the rafters and beams. They restored what earlier kings of Judah had allowed to fall into ruin. [12] The workers served faithfully under the leadership of Jahath and Obadiah, Levites of the Merarite clan, and Zechariah and Meshullam, Levites of the Kohathite clan. Other Levites, all of whom were skilled musicians, [13] were put in charge of the laborers of the various trades. Still others assisted as secretaries, officials, and gatekeepers.

HILKIAH DISCOVERS GOD'S LAW

[14] While they were bringing out the money collected at the LORD's Temple, Hilkiah the priest found the Book of the Law of the LORD that was written by Moses. [15] Hilkiah said to Shaphan the court secretary, "I have found the Book of the Law in the LORD's Temple!" Then Hilkiah gave the scroll to Shaphan.

[16] Shaphan took the scroll to the king and reported, "Your officials are doing everything they were assigned to do. [17] The money that was collected at the Temple of the LORD has been turned over to the supervisors and workmen." [18] Shaphan also told the king, "Hilkiah the priest has given me a scroll." So Shaphan read it to the king.

[19] When the king heard what was written in the Law, he tore his clothes in despair. [20] Then he gave these orders to Hilkiah, Ahikam son of Shaphan, Acbor son of Micaiah,* Shaphan the court secretary, and Asaiah the king's personal adviser: [21] "Go to the Temple and speak to the LORD for me and for all the remnant of Israel and Judah. Inquire about the words written in the scroll that has been found. For the LORD's great anger has been poured out on us because our ancestors have not obeyed the word of the LORD. We have not been doing everything this scroll says we must do."

[22] So Hilkiah and the other men went to the New Quarter* of Jerusalem to consult with the prophet Huldah. She was the wife of Shallum son of Tikvah, son of Harhas,* the keeper of the Temple wardrobe.

[23] She said to them, "The LORD, the God of Israel, has spoken! Go back and tell the man who sent you, [24] 'This is what the LORD says: I am going to bring disaster on this city* and its people. All the curses written in the scroll that was read to the king of Judah will come true. [25] For my people have abandoned me and offered sacrifices to pagan gods, and I am very angry with them for everything they have done. My anger will be poured out on this place, and it will not be quenched.'

[26] "But go to the king of Judah who sent you to seek the LORD and tell him: 'This is what the LORD, the God of Israel, says concerning the message you have just heard: [27] You were sorry and humbled yourself before God when you heard his words against this city and its people. You humbled yourself and tore your clothing in despair and wept before me in repentance. And I have indeed heard you, says the LORD. [28] So I will not send the promised disaster until after you have died and been buried in peace. You yourself will not see the disaster I am going to bring on this city and its people.'"

So they took her message back to the king.

34:6 As in Syriac version; Hebrew reads *in their temples*, or *in their ruins*. The meaning of the Hebrew is uncertain. 34:20 As in parallel text at 2 Kgs 22:12; Hebrew reads *Abdon son of Micah.* 34:22a Or *the Second Quarter*, a newer section of Jerusalem. Hebrew reads *the Mishneh.* 34:22b As in parallel text at 2 Kgs 22:14; Hebrew reads *son of Tokhath, son of Hasrah.* 34:24 Hebrew *this place;* also in 34:27, 28.

JOSIAH'S RELIGIOUS REFORMS

29 Then the king summoned all the elders of Judah and Jerusalem. 30 And the king went up to the Temple of the LORD with all the people of Judah and Jerusalem, along with the priests and the Levites—all the people from the greatest to the least. There the king read to them the entire Book of the Covenant that had been found in the LORD's Temple. 31 The king took his place of authority beside the pillar and renewed the covenant in the LORD's presence. He pledged to obey the LORD by keeping all his commands, laws, and decrees with all his heart and soul. He promised to obey all the terms of the covenant that were written in the scroll. 32 And he required everyone in Jerusalem and the people of Benjamin to make a similar pledge. The people of Jerusalem did so, renewing their covenant with God, the God of their ancestors.

33 So Josiah removed all detestable idols from the entire land of Israel and required everyone to worship the LORD their God. And throughout the rest of his lifetime, they did not turn away from the LORD, the God of their ancestors.

JOSIAH CELEBRATES PASSOVER

35 Then Josiah announced that the Passover of the LORD would be celebrated in Jerusalem, and so the Passover lamb was slaughtered on the fourteenth day of the first month.* 2 Josiah also assigned the priests to their duties and encouraged them in their work at the Temple of the LORD. 3 He issued this order to the Levites, who were to teach all Israel and who had been set apart to serve the LORD: "Put the holy Ark in the Temple that was built by Solomon son of David, the king of Israel. You no longer need to carry it back and forth on your shoulders. Now spend your time serving the LORD your God and his people Israel. 4 Report for duty according to the family divisions of your ancestors, following the directions of King David of Israel and the directions of his son Solomon.

5 "Then stand in the sanctuary at the place appointed for your family division and help the families assigned to you as they bring their offerings to the Temple. 6 Slaughter the Passover lambs, purify yourselves, and prepare to help those who come. Follow all the directions that the LORD gave through Moses."

7 Then Josiah provided 30,000 lambs and young goats for the people's Passover offerings, along with 3,000 cattle, all from the king's own flocks and herds. 8 The king's officials also made willing contributions to the people, priests, and Levites. Hilkiah, Zechariah, and Jehiel, the administrators of God's Temple, gave the priests 2,600 lambs and young goats and 300 cattle as Passover offerings. 9 The Levite leaders—Conaniah and his brothers Shemaiah and Nethanel, as well as Hashabiah, Jeiel, and Jozabad—gave 5,000 lambs and young goats and 500 cattle to the Levites for their Passover offerings.

10 When everything was ready for the Passover celebration, the priests and the Levites took their places, organized by their divisions, as the king had commanded. 11 The Levites then slaughtered the Passover lambs and presented the blood to the priests, who sprinkled the blood on the altar while the Levites prepared the animals. 12 They divided the burnt offerings among the people by their family groups, so they could offer them to the LORD as prescribed in the Book of Moses. They did the same with the cattle. 13 Then they roasted the Passover lambs as prescribed; and they boiled the holy offerings in pots, kettles, and pans, and brought them out quickly so the people could eat them.

14 Afterward the Levites prepared Passover offerings for themselves and for the priests—the descendants of Aaron—because the priests had been busy from morning till night offering the burnt offerings and the fat portions. The Levites took responsibility for all these preparations.

15 The musicians, descendants of Asaph, were in their assigned places, following the commands that had been given by David, Asaph, Heman, and Jeduthun, the king's seer. The gatekeepers guarded the gates and did not need to leave their posts of duty, for their Passover offerings were prepared for them by their fellow Levites.

16 The entire ceremony for the LORD's Passover was completed that day. All the burnt offerings were sacrificed on the altar of the LORD, as King Josiah had commanded. 17 All the Israelites present in Jerusalem celebrated Passover and the Festival of Unleavened Bread for seven days. 18 Never since the time of the prophet Samuel had there been such a Passover. None of the kings of Israel had ever kept a Passover as Josiah did, involving all the priests and Levites, all the people of Jerusalem, and people from all over Judah and Israel. 19 This Passover was celebrated in the eighteenth year of Josiah's reign.

JOSIAH DIES IN BATTLE

20 After Josiah had finished restoring the Temple, King Neco of Egypt led his army up from Egypt to do battle at Carchemish on the Euphrates River, and Josiah and his army marched out to fight him.* 21 But King Neco sent messengers to Josiah with this message:

"What do you want with me, king of Judah? I have no quarrel with you today! I am on my way to fight another nation, and God has told me to hurry! Do not interfere with God, who is with me, or he will destroy you."

35:1 This day in the ancient Hebrew lunar calendar was April 5, 622 B.C.   35:20 Or *Josiah went out to meet him.*

²²But Josiah refused to listen to Neco, to whom God had indeed spoken, and he would not turn back. Instead, he disguised himself and led his army into battle on the plain of Megiddo. ²³But the enemy archers hit King Josiah with their arrows and wounded him. He cried out to his men, "Take me from the battle, for I am badly wounded!"

²⁴So they lifted Josiah out of his chariot and placed him in another chariot. Then they brought him back to Jerusalem, where he died. He was buried there in the royal cemetery. And all Judah and Jerusalem mourned for him. ²⁵The prophet Jeremiah composed funeral songs for Josiah, and to this day choirs still sing these sad songs about his death. These songs of sorrow have become a tradition and are recorded in *The Book of Laments.*

²⁶The rest of the events of Josiah's reign and his acts of devotion (carried out according to what was written in the Law of the LORD), ²⁷from beginning to end—all are recorded in *The Book of the Kings of Israel and Judah.*

JEHOAHAZ RULES IN JUDAH

36 Then the people of the land took Josiah's son Jehoahaz and made him the next king in Jerusalem.

²Jehoahaz* was twenty-three years old when he became king, and he reigned in Jerusalem three months.

³Then he was deposed by the king of Egypt, who demanded that Judah pay 7,500 pounds of silver and 75 pounds of gold* as tribute.

JEHOIAKIM RULES IN JUDAH

⁴The king of Egypt then installed Eliakim, the brother of Jehoahaz, as the next king of Judah and Jerusalem, and he changed Eliakim's name to Jehoiakim. Then Neco took Jehoahaz to Egypt as a prisoner.

⁵Jehoiakim was twenty-five years old when he became king, and he reigned in Jerusalem eleven years. He did what was evil in the sight of the LORD his God.

⁶Then King Nebuchadnezzar of Babylon came to Jerusalem and captured it, and he bound Jehoiakim in bronze chains and led him away to Babylon. ⁷Nebuchadnezzar also took some of the treasures from the Temple of the LORD, and he placed them in his palace* in Babylon.

⁸The rest of the events in Jehoiakim's reign, including all the evil things he did and everything found against him, are recorded in *The Book of the Kings of Israel and Judah.* Then his son Jehoiachin became the next king.

JEHOIACHIN RULES IN JUDAH

⁹Jehoiachin was eighteen* years old when he became king, and he reigned in Jerusalem three months and ten days. Jehoiachin did what was evil in the LORD's sight.

¹⁰In the spring of the year* King Nebuchadnezzar took Jehoiachin to Babylon. Many treasures from the Temple of the LORD were also taken to Babylon at that time. And Nebuchadnezzar installed Jehoiachin's uncle,* Zedekiah, as the next king in Judah and Jerusalem.

ZEDEKIAH RULES IN JUDAH

¹¹Zedekiah was twenty-one years old when he became king, and he reigned in Jerusalem eleven years. ¹²But Zedekiah did what was evil in the sight of the LORD his God, and he refused to humble himself when the prophet Jeremiah spoke to him directly from the LORD. ¹³He also rebelled against King Nebuchadnezzar, even though he had taken an oath of loyalty in God's name. Zedekiah was a hard and stubborn man, refusing to turn to the LORD, the God of Israel.

¹⁴Likewise, all the leaders of the priests and the people became more and more unfaithful. They followed all the pagan practices of the surrounding nations, desecrating the Temple of the LORD that had been consecrated in Jerusalem.

¹⁵The LORD, the God of their ancestors, repeatedly sent his prophets to warn them, for he had compassion on his people and his Temple. ¹⁶But the people mocked these messengers of God and despised their words. They scoffed at the prophets until the LORD's anger could no longer be restrained and nothing could be done.

THE FALL OF JERUSALEM

¹⁷So the LORD brought the king of Babylon against them. The Babylonians* killed Judah's young men, even chasing after them into the Temple. They had no pity on the people, killing both young men and young women, the old and the infirm. God handed all of them over to Nebuchadnezzar. ¹⁸The king took home to Babylon all the articles, large and small, used in the Temple of God, and the treasures from both the LORD's Temple and from the palace of the king and his officials. ¹⁹Then his army burned the Temple of God, tore down the walls of Jerusalem, burned all the palaces, and completely destroyed everything of value.* ²⁰The few who survived were taken as exiles to Babylon, and they became servants to the king and his sons until the kingdom of Persia came to power.

²¹So the message of the LORD spoken through Jeremiah was fulfilled. The land finally enjoyed its Sabbath rest, lying desolate until the seventy years were fulfilled, just as the prophet had said.

36:2 Hebrew *Joahaz,* a variant spelling of Jehoahaz; also in 36:4. **36:3** Hebrew *100 talents* [3,400 kilograms] *of silver and 1 talent* [34 kilograms] *of gold.* **36:7** Or *temple.* **36:9** As in one Hebrew manuscript, some Greek manuscripts, and Syriac version (see also 2 Kgs 24:8); most Hebrew manuscripts read *eight.* **36:10a** Hebrew *At the turn of the year.* The first day of this year in the ancient Hebrew lunar calendar was April 13, 597 B.C. **36:10b** As in parallel text at 2 Kgs 24:17; Hebrew reads *brother,* or *relative.* **36:17** Or *Chaldeans.* **36:19** Or *destroyed all the valuable articles from the Temple.*

CYRUS ALLOWS THE EXILES TO RETURN

²² In the first year of King Cyrus of Persia,* the LORD fulfilled the prophecy he had given through Jeremiah.* He stirred the heart of Cyrus to put this proclamation in writing and to send it throughout his kingdom:

²³ "This is what King Cyrus of Persia says:

"The LORD, the God of heaven, has given me all the kingdoms of the earth. He has appointed me to build him a Temple at Jerusalem, which is in Judah. Any of you who are his people may go there for this task. And may the LORD your God be with you!"

36:22a The first year of Cyrus's reign over Babylon was 538 B.C.
36:22b See Jer 25:11-12; 29:10.

EZRA AND NEHEMIAH

JON HUNTZINGER, PHD

Ancient Jewish tradition viewed the two books of Ezra and Nehemiah as one volume telling one story. These books recorded the return of the exiles from Judea to their homeland to rebuild their Temple (538–515 BC) as well as the return of Ezra and Nehemiah to rebuild the walls of the city of Jerusalem and lead the people in religious renewal (458–433 BC). Just as the name *Nehemiah* means 'Yahweh comforts,' the book describes God's comfort to His people at that time in the restoration of Jerusalem's security with rebuilt walls. Not all the exiles chose to return, but this one combined book tells the story of those who did. This story was written sometime in the late fifth century (400s) BC by an anonymous writer.

The outline of these two books contains five major sections:

— Ezra 1:1-3 begins with the decree by Cyrus the king of Persia to allow the exiles to return home.
— Ezra 1:4-6:22 reports the events related to the rebuilding of the Temple.
— Ezra 7-10 describes the return of Ezra the priest.
— Nehemiah 1-6 tells about the return of Nehemiah, an administrator authorized by King Artaxerxes to oversee the reconstruction of the walls of Jerusalem.
— Nehemiah 7-13 shows how, together, Ezra and Nehemiah lead the people in a renewed commitment to the Book of the Law of Moses and God's covenant with the people.

According to Ezra-Nehemiah, the people returned to their ancestral home to start their lives over and to rebuild the Jerusalem Temple, which the Babylonians had destroyed. The Temple rebuilding occurs prior to the building of the city walls. This order of construction indicates that a primary theme of the book, in addition to the comfort God gives the people, is the restoration of the worship of God among His people. As noted, the book begins with a record of Cyrus's decree and lists the people who returned to the land (Ezra 1). Then it describes the rebuilding of the Temple altar and its foundations in the midst of local opposition, which eventually brings the project to a halt (Ezra 3-4). The project is completed later under orders from King Darius. Next, the people dedicate the rebuilt Temple and celebrate Passover (Ezra 5-6). Then Ezra returns to Jerusalem to teach the people God's laws so they can live in fidelity with Him and one another, which involves the divorce of their foreign spouses (Ezra 7-10). The Book of Moses is read to the people, and they celebrate the festival of shelters (Nehemiah 8-9). After that, the priests and Levites are instructed about their service at the Temple (Nehemiah 12:44-47).

Ezra-Nehemiah recounts the rebuilding of the Temple, the celebration of the festivals, and the worship by the people at the Temple. The people are restored to their primary calling, which is the worship of God.

The ministries of Ezra and Nehemiah, then, are about more than the restoration of the Temple and the city walls—they are about the rebuilding of the people. After the writer reports on the restoration of the Temple (Ezra 6:13-18), he turns his attention to the people who needed to be restored in their collective identity as worshippers of God. He does this by reporting the return of the Levites, who lead the people in giving offerings to God (Ezra 8:24-36), and by describing Ezra's decree for the people to divorce their foreign spouses (Ezra 9-10). Given that ancient intermarriage involved commitment to the gods of both spouses, Ezra's command was not so much a racial action as it was a spiritual one designed to strengthen the people's exclusive commitment to God and His worship. Ezra reads from the Book of the Law of Moses to the people (Nehemiah 8:1-8), and the priests lead the people in a confession of their sins and renewal of their commitment to the covenant (Nehemiah 9:1-10:39). Nehemiah then institutes some final reforms for the benefit of the people (Nehemiah 13).

Related to the theme of rebuilding is that of community, given the people themselves rebuild the Temple (Ezra 3:1-13) and the walls and gates of the city (Nehemiah 3). Moreover, the people celebrate Passover (Ezra 6:19-22) and the festival of shelters (Nehemiah 8:13-18). The people also confess their sins (Ezra 10:1-17; Nehemiah 9:1-38) and renew their commitment to the covenant (Nehemiah 10:1-39). Ezra and Nehemiah prepare them for their work and give direction, but the focus of the book is not on these two men as much as it is on the restoration of the people to the worship of God and to life with one another.

Since Ezra-Nehemiah includes letters and lists in the account of the rebuilding of the Temple and the city walls, and because it records several first-person accounts of Ezra and Nehemiah themselves, most scholars classify it as a book of history. This history is closely connected with the book of Chronicles and contains several passages that are the same in both books. Not only does Ezra-Nehemiah identify numerous written documents to tell its story, but it also emphasizes the importance of the written Torah for the life of the people, in that Ezra reads and teaches the people from the Torah (Ezra 7:1-6). All of this means that Ezra-Nehemiah attests to the growing importance and authority of the *written* word within the oral culture of Judah at that time.

EZRA

CYRUS ALLOWS THE EXILES TO RETURN

1 In the first year of King Cyrus of Persia,* the LORD fulfilled the prophecy he had given through Jeremiah.* He stirred the heart of Cyrus to put this proclamation in writing and to send it throughout his kingdom:

2 "This is what King Cyrus of Persia says:

"The LORD, the God of heaven, has given me all the kingdoms of the earth. He has appointed me to build him a Temple at Jerusalem, which is in Judah. 3 Any of you who are his people may go to Jerusalem in Judah to rebuild this Temple of the LORD, the God of Israel, who lives in Jerusalem. And may your God be with you! 4 Wherever this Jewish remnant is found, let their neighbors contribute toward their expenses by giving them silver and gold, supplies for the journey, and livestock, as well as a voluntary offering for the Temple of God in Jerusalem."

5 Then God stirred the hearts of the priests and Levites and the leaders of the tribes of Judah and Benjamin to go to Jerusalem to rebuild the Temple of the LORD. 6 And all their neighbors assisted by giving them articles of silver and gold, supplies for the journey, and livestock. They gave them many valuable gifts in addition to all the voluntary offerings.

7 King Cyrus himself brought out the articles that King Nebuchadnezzar had taken from the LORD's Temple in Jerusalem and had placed in the temple of his own gods. 8 Cyrus directed Mithredath, the treasurer of Persia, to count these items and present them to Sheshbazzar, the leader of the exiles returning to Judah.* 9 This is a list of the items that were returned:

gold basins	30
silver basins	1,000
silver incense burners*	29
10 gold bowls	30
silver bowls	410
other items	1,000

11 In all, there were 5,400 articles of gold and silver. Sheshbazzar brought all of these along when the exiles went from Babylon to Jerusalem.

EXILES WHO RETURNED WITH ZERUBBABEL

2 Here is the list of the Jewish exiles of the provinces who returned from their captivity. King Nebuchadnezzar had deported them to Babylon, but now they returned to Jerusalem and the other towns in Judah where they originally lived. 2 Their leaders were Zerubbabel, Jeshua, Nehemiah, Seraiah, Reelaiah, Mordecai, Bilshan, Mispar, Bigvai, Rehum, and Baanah.

This is the number of the men of Israel who returned from exile:

3 The family of Parosh	2,172
4 The family of Shephatiah	372
5 The family of Arah	775
6 The family of Pahath-moab (descendants of Jeshua and Joab)	2,812
7 The family of Elam	1,254
8 The family of Zattu	945
9 The family of Zaccai	760
10 The family of Bani	642
11 The family of Bebai	623
12 The family of Azgad	1,222
13 The family of Adonikam	666
14 The family of Bigvai	2,056
15 The family of Adin	454
16 The family of Ater (descendants of Hezekiah)	98
17 The family of Bezai	323
18 The family of Jorah	112
19 The family of Hashum	223
20 The family of Gibbar	95
21 The people of Bethlehem	123
22 The people of Netophah	56
23 The people of Anathoth	128
24 The people of Beth-azmaveth*	42
25 The people of Kiriath-jearim,* Kephirah, and Beeroth	743
26 The people of Ramah and Geba	621
27 The people of Micmash	122
28 The people of Bethel and Ai	223
29 The citizens of Nebo	52
30 The citizens of Magbish	156
31 The citizens of West Elam*	1,254
32 The citizens of Harim	320
33 The citizens of Lod, Hadid, and Ono	725
34 The citizens of Jericho	345
35 The citizens of Senaah	3,630

36 These are the priests who returned from exile:

The family of Jedaiah (through the line of Jeshua)	973
37 The family of Immer	1,052
38 The family of Pashhur	1,247
39 The family of Harim	1,017

40 These are the Levites who returned from exile:

1:1a The first year of Cyrus's reign over Babylon was 538 B.C.
1:1b See Jer 25:11-12; 29:10.   1:8 Hebrew *Sheshbazzar, the prince of Judah.*   1:9 The meaning of this Hebrew word is uncertain.
2:24 As in parallel text at Neh 7:28; Hebrew reads *Azmaveth.*
2:25 As in some Hebrew manuscripts and Greek version (see also Neh 7:29); Hebrew reads *Kiriath-arim.*   2:31 Or *of the other Elam.*

43 The descendants of the following Temple servants returned from exile:
Ziha, Hasupha, Tabbaoth,
44 Keros, Siaha, Padon,
45 Lebanah, Hagabah, Akkub,
46 Hagab, Shalmai,* Hanan,
47 Giddel, Gahar, Reaiah,
48 Rezin, Nekoda, Gazzam,
49 Uzza, Paseah, Besai,
50 Asnah, Meunim, Nephusim,
51 Bakbuk, Hakupha, Harhur,
52 Bazluth, Mehida, Harsha,
53 Barkos, Sisera, Temah,
54 Neziah, and Hatipha.

55 The descendants of these servants of King Solomon returned from exile:
Sotai, Hassophereth, Peruda,
56 Jaalah, Darkon, Giddel,
57 Shephatiah, Hattil, Pokereth-hazzebaim,
and Ami.

58 In all, the Temple servants and the descendants of Solomon's servants numbered 392.

59 Another group returned at this time from the towns of Tel-melah, Tel-harsha, Kerub, Addan, and Immer. However, they could not prove that they or their families were descendants of Israel. 60 This group included the families of Delaiah, Tobiah, and Nekoda—a total of 652 people.
61 Three families of priests—Hobaiah, Hakkoz, and Barzillai—also returned. (This Barzillai had married a woman who was a descendant of Barzillai of Gilead, and he had taken her family name.) 62 They searched for their names in the genealogical records, but they were not found, so they were disqualified from serving as priests. 63 The governor told them not to eat the priests' share of food from the sacrifices until a priest could consult the LORD about the matter by using the Urim and Thummim—the sacred lots.
64 So a total of 42,360 people returned to Judah, 65 in addition to 7,337 servants and 200 singers, both men and women. 66 They took with them 736 horses, 245 mules, 67 435 camels, and 6,720 donkeys.
68 When they arrived at the Temple of the LORD in Jerusalem, some of the family leaders made voluntary offerings toward the rebuilding of God's Temple on its original site, 69 and each leader gave as much as he could. The total of their gifts came to 61,000 gold coins,* 6,250 pounds* of silver, and 100 robes for the priests.

70 So the priests, the Levites, the singers, the gatekeepers, the Temple servants, and some of the common people settled in villages near Jerusalem. The rest of the people returned to their own towns throughout Israel.

THE ALTAR IS REBUILT

3 In early autumn,* when the Israelites had settled in their towns, all the people assembled in Jerusalem with a unified purpose. 2 Then Jeshua son of Jehozadak* joined his fellow priests and Zerubbabel son of Shealtiel with his family in rebuilding the altar of the God of Israel. They wanted to sacrifice burnt offerings on it, as instructed in the Law of Moses, the man of God. 3 Even though the people were afraid of the local residents, they rebuilt the altar at its old site. Then they began to sacrifice burnt offerings on the altar to the LORD each morning and evening.
4 They celebrated the Festival of Shelters as prescribed in the Law, sacrificing the number of burnt offerings specified for each day of the festival. 5 They also offered the regular burnt offerings and the offerings required for the new moon celebrations and the annual festivals as prescribed by the LORD. The people also gave voluntary offerings to the LORD. 6 Fifteen days before the Festival of Shelters began,* the priests had begun to sacrifice burnt offerings to the LORD. This was even before they had started to lay the foundation of the LORD's Temple.

THE PEOPLE BEGIN TO REBUILD THE TEMPLE

7 Then the people hired masons and carpenters and bought cedar logs from the people of Tyre and Sidon, paying them with food, wine, and olive oil. The logs were brought down from the Lebanon mountains and floated along the coast of the Mediterranean Sea* to Joppa, for King Cyrus had given permission for this.
8 The construction of the Temple of God began in midspring,* during the second year after they arrived in Jerusalem. The work force was made up of everyone who had returned from exile, including Zerubbabel son of Shealtiel, Jeshua son of Jehozadak and his fellow priests, and all the Levites. The Levites who were twenty years old or older were put in charge of rebuilding the LORD's

2:46 As in an alternate reading of the Masoretic Text (see also Neh 7:48); the other alternate reads *Shamlai.* 2:69a Hebrew *61,000 darics of gold,* about 1,100 pounds or 500 kilograms in weight. 2:69b Hebrew *5,000 minas* [3,000 kilograms]. 3:1 Hebrew *In the seventh month.* The year is not specified, so it may have been during Cyrus's first year (538 B.C.) or second year (537 B.C.). The seventh month of the ancient Hebrew lunar calendar occurred within the months of September/October 538 B.C. and October/November 537 B.C. 3:2 Hebrew *Jozadak,* a variant spelling of Jehozadak; also in 3:8. 3:6 Hebrew *On the first day of the seventh month.* This day in the ancient Hebrew lunar calendar occurred in September or October. The Festival of Shelters began on the fifteenth day of the seventh month. 3:7 Hebrew *the sea.* 3:8 Hebrew *in the second month.* This month in the ancient Hebrew lunar calendar occurred within the months of April and May 536 B.C.

Temple. ⁹ The workers at the Temple of God were supervised by Jeshua with his sons and relatives, and Kadmiel and his sons, all descendants of Hodaviah.* They were helped in this task by the Levites of the family of Henadad.

¹⁰ When the builders completed the foundation of the LORD's Temple, the priests put on their robes and took their places to blow their trumpets. And the Levites, descendants of Asaph, clashed their cymbals to praise the LORD, just as King David had prescribed. ¹¹ With praise and thanks, they sang this song to the LORD:

"He is so good!
His faithful love for Israel endures
forever!"

Then all the people gave a great shout, praising the LORD because the foundation of the LORD's Temple had been laid.

¹² But many of the older priests, Levites, and other leaders who had seen the first Temple wept aloud when they saw the new Temple's foundation. The others, however, were shouting for joy. ¹³ The joyful shouting and weeping mingled together in a loud noise that could be heard far in the distance.

ENEMIES OPPOSE THE REBUILDING

4 The enemies of Judah and Benjamin heard that the exiles were rebuilding a Temple to the LORD, the God of Israel. ² So they approached Zerubbabel and the other leaders and said, "Let us build with you, for we worship your God just as you do. We have sacrificed to him ever since King Esarhaddon of Assyria brought us here."

³ But Zerubbabel, Jeshua, and the other leaders of Israel replied, "You may have no part in this work. We alone will build the Temple for the LORD, the God of Israel, just as King Cyrus of Persia commanded us."

⁴ Then the local residents tried to discourage and frighten the people of Judah to keep them from their work. ⁵ They bribed agents to work against them and to frustrate their plans. This went on during the entire reign of King Cyrus of Persia and lasted until King Darius of Persia took the throne.*

LATER OPPOSITION UNDER XERXES AND ARTAXERXES

⁶ Years later when Xerxes* began his reign, the enemies of Judah wrote a letter of accusation against the people of Judah and Jerusalem.

⁷ Even later, during the reign of King Artaxerxes of Persia,* the enemies of Judah, led by Bishlam, Mithredath, and Tabeel, sent a letter to Artaxerxes in the Aramaic language, and it was translated for the king.

⁸* Rehum the governor and Shimshai the court secretary wrote the letter, telling King Artaxerxes about the situation in Jerusalem. ⁹ They greeted the king for all their colleagues—the judges and local leaders, the people of Tarpel, the Persians, the Babylonians, and the people of Erech and Susa (that is, Elam). ¹⁰ They also sent greetings from the rest of the people whom the great and noble Ashurbanipal* had deported and relocated in Samaria and throughout the neighboring lands of the province west of the Euphrates River.* ¹¹ This is a copy of their letter:

"To King Artaxerxes, from your loyal subjects in the province west of the Euphrates River.

¹² "The king should know that the Jews who came here to Jerusalem from Babylon are rebuilding this rebellious and evil city. They have already laid the foundation and will soon finish its walls. ¹³ And the king should know that if this city is rebuilt and its walls are completed, it will be much to your disadvantage, for the Jews will then refuse to pay their tribute, customs, and tolls to you.

¹⁴ "Since we are your loyal subjects* and do not want to see the king dishonored in this way, we have sent the king this information. ¹⁵ We suggest that a search be made in your ancestors' records, where you will discover what a rebellious city this has been in the past. In fact, it was destroyed because of its long and troublesome history of revolt against the kings and countries who controlled it. ¹⁶ We declare to the king that if this city is rebuilt and its walls are completed, the province west of the Euphrates River will be lost to you."

¹⁷ Then King Artaxerxes sent this reply:

"To Rehum the governor, Shimshai the court secretary, and their colleagues living in Samaria and throughout the province west of the Euphrates River. Greetings.

¹⁸ "The letter you sent has been translated and read to me. ¹⁹ I ordered a search of the records and have found that Jerusalem has indeed been a hotbed of insurrection against many kings. In fact, rebellion and revolt are normal there! ²⁰ Powerful kings have ruled over Jerusalem and the entire province west of the Euphrates River, receiving tribute, customs, and tolls. ²¹ Therefore, issue orders to have these men stop their work. That city

---

3:9 Hebrew *sons of Judah* (i.e., *bene Yehudah*). *Bene* might also be read here as the proper name Binnui; *Yehudah* is probably another name for Hodaviah. Compare 2:40; Neh 7:43; 1 Esdras 5:58. 4:5 Darius reigned 521–486 B.C. 4:6 Hebrew *Ahasuerus*, another name for Xerxes. He reigned 486–465 B.C. 4:7 Artaxerxes reigned 465–424 B.C. 4:8 The original text of 4:8–6:18 is in Aramaic. 4:10a Aramaic *Osnappar*, another name for Ashurbanipal. 4:10b Aramaic *the province beyond the river;* also in 4:11, 16, 17, 20. 4:14 Aramaic *Since we eat the salt of the palace.*

must not be rebuilt except at my express command. ²²Be diligent, and don't neglect this matter, for we must not permit the situation to harm the king's interests."

²³When this letter from King Artaxerxes was read to Rehum, Shimshai, and their colleagues, they hurried to Jerusalem. Then, with a show of strength, they forced the Jews to stop building.

THE REBUILDING RESUMES

²⁴So the work on the Temple of God in Jerusalem had stopped, and it remained at a standstill until the second year of the reign of King Darius of Persia.*

5 At that time the prophets Haggai and Zechariah son of Iddo prophesied to the Jews in Judah and Jerusalem. They prophesied in the name of the God of Israel who was over them. ²Zerubbabel son of Shealtiel and Jeshua son of Jehozadak* responded by starting again to rebuild the Temple of God in Jerusalem. And the prophets of God were with them and helped them.

³But Tattenai, governor of the province west of the Euphrates River,* and Shethar-bozenai and their colleagues soon arrived in Jerusalem and asked, "Who gave you permission to rebuild this Temple and restore this structure?" ⁴They also asked for* the names of all the men working on the Temple. ⁵But because their God was watching over them, the leaders of the Jews were not prevented from building until a report was sent to Darius and he returned his decision.

TATTENAI'S LETTER TO KING DARIUS

⁶This is a copy of the letter that Tattenai the governor, Shethar-bozenai, and the other officials of the province west of the Euphrates River sent to King Darius:

⁷"To King Darius. Greetings.

⁸"The king should know that we went to the construction site of the Temple of the great God in the province of Judah. It is being rebuilt with specially prepared stones, and timber is being laid in its walls. The work is going forward with great energy and success.

⁹"We asked the leaders, 'Who gave you permission to rebuild this Temple and restore this structure?' ¹⁰And we demanded their names so that we could tell you who the leaders were.

¹¹"This was their answer: 'We are the servants of the God of heaven and earth, and we are rebuilding the Temple that was built here many years ago by a great king of Israel. ¹²But because our ancestors angered the God of heaven, he abandoned them to King Nebuchadnezzar of Babylon,* who

destroyed this Temple and exiled the people to Babylonia. ¹³However, King Cyrus of Babylon,* during the first year of his reign, issued a decree that the Temple of God should be rebuilt. ¹⁴King Cyrus returned the gold and silver cups that Nebuchadnezzar had taken from the Temple of God in Jerusalem and had placed in the temple of Babylon. These cups were taken from that temple and presented to a man named Sheshbazzar, whom King Cyrus appointed as governor of Judah. ¹⁵The king instructed him to return the cups to their place in Jerusalem and to rebuild the Temple of God there on its original site. ¹⁶So this Sheshbazzar came and laid the foundations of the Temple of God in Jerusalem. The people have been working on it ever since, though it is not yet completed.'

¹⁷"Therefore, if it pleases the king, we request that a search be made in the royal archives of Babylon to discover whether King Cyrus ever issued a decree to rebuild God's Temple in Jerusalem. And then let the king send us his decision in this matter."

DARIUS APPROVES THE REBUILDING

6 So King Darius issued orders that a search be made in the Babylonian archives, which were stored in the treasury. ²But it was at the fortress at Ecbatana in the province of Media that a scroll was found. This is what it said:

"Memorandum:

³"In the first year of King Cyrus's reign, a decree was sent out concerning the Temple of God at Jerusalem.

"Let the Temple be rebuilt on the site where Jews used to offer their sacrifices, using the original foundations. Its height will be ninety feet, and its width will be ninety feet.* ⁴Every three layers of specially prepared stones will be topped by a layer of timber. All expenses will be paid by the royal treasury. ⁵Furthermore, the gold and silver cups, which were taken to Babylon by Nebuchadnezzar from the Temple of God in Jerusalem, must be returned to Jerusalem and put back where they belong. Let them be taken back to the Temple of God."

4:24 The second year of Darius's reign was 520 B.C. The narrative started in 4:1-5 is resumed at verse 24. 5:2 Aramaic *Jozadak*, a variant spelling of Jehozadak. 5:3 Aramaic *the province beyond the river*; also in 5:6. 5:4 As in one Hebrew manuscript and Greek and Syriac versions; Masoretic Text reads *Then we told them.* 5:12 Aramaic *Nebuchadnezzar the Chaldean.* 5:13 King Cyrus of Persia is here identified as the king of Babylon because Persia had conquered the Babylonian Empire. 6:3 Aramaic *Its height will be 60 cubits* [27.6 meters], *and its width will be 60 cubits.* It is commonly held that this verse should be emended to read: "Its height will be 30 cubits [45 feet or 13.8 meters], its length will be 60 cubits [90 feet or 27.6 meters], and its width will be 20 cubits [30 feet or 9.2 meters]"; compare 1 Kgs 6:2. The emendation regarding the width is supported by the Syriac version.

⁶ So King Darius sent this message:

"Now therefore, Tattenai, governor of the province west of the Euphrates River,* and Shethar-bozenai, and your colleagues and other officials west of the Euphrates River— stay away from there! ⁷ Do not disturb the construction of the Temple of God. Let it be rebuilt on its original site, and do not hinder the governor of Judah and the elders of the Jews in their work.

⁸ "Moreover, I hereby decree that you are to help these elders of the Jews as they rebuild this Temple of God. You must pay the full construction costs, without delay, from my taxes collected in the province west of the Euphrates River so that the work will not be interrupted.

⁹ "Give the priests in Jerusalem whatever is needed in the way of young bulls, rams, and male lambs for the burnt offerings presented to the God of heaven. And without fail, provide them with as much wheat, salt, wine, and olive oil as they need each day. ¹⁰ Then they will be able to offer acceptable sacrifices to the God of heaven and pray for the welfare of the king and his sons.

¹¹ "Those who violate this decree in any way will have a beam pulled from their house. Then they will be lifted up and impaled on it, and their house will be reduced to a pile of rubble.* ¹² May the God who has chosen the city of Jerusalem as the place to honor his name destroy any king or nation that violates this command and destroys this Temple.

"I, Darius, have issued this decree. Let it be obeyed with all diligence."

THE TEMPLE'S DEDICATION

¹³ Tattenai, governor of the province west of the Euphrates River, and Shethar-bozenai and their colleagues complied at once with the command of King Darius. ¹⁴ So the Jewish elders continued their work, and they were greatly encouraged by the preaching of the prophets Haggai and Zechariah son of Iddo. The Temple was finally finished, as had been commanded by the God of Israel and decreed by Cyrus, Darius, and Artaxerxes, the kings of Persia. ¹⁵ The Temple was completed on March 12,* during the sixth year of King Darius's reign.

¹⁶ The Temple of God was then dedicated with great joy by the people of Israel, the priests, the Levites, and the rest of the people who had returned from exile. ¹⁷ During the dedication ceremony for the Temple of God, 100 young bulls, 200 rams, and 400 male lambs were sacrificed. And 12 male goats were presented as a sin offering for the twelve tribes of Israel. ¹⁸ Then the priests and Levites were divided into their various divisions to serve at the Temple

of God in Jerusalem, as prescribed in the Book of Moses.

CELEBRATION OF PASSOVER

¹⁹ On April 21* the returned exiles celebrated Passover. ²⁰ The priests and Levites had purified themselves and were ceremonially clean. So they slaughtered the Passover lamb for all the returned exiles, for their fellow priests, and for themselves. ²¹ The Passover meal was eaten by the people of Israel who had returned from exile and by the others in the land who had turned from their corrupt practices to worship the LORD, the God of Israel. ²² Then they celebrated the Festival of Unleavened Bread for seven days. There was great joy throughout the land because the LORD had caused the king of Assyria* to be favorable to them, so that he helped them to rebuild the Temple of God, the God of Israel.

EZRA ARRIVES IN JERUSALEM

7 Many years later, during the reign of King Artaxerxes of Persia,* there was a man named Ezra. He was the son* of Seraiah, son of Azariah, son of Hilkiah, ² son of Shallum, son of Zadok, son of Ahitub, ³ son of Amariah, son of Azariah, son* of Meraioth, ⁴ son of Zerahiah, son of Uzzi, son of Bukki, ⁵ son of Abishua, son of Phinehas, son of Eleazar, son of Aaron the high priest.* ⁶ This Ezra was a scribe who was well versed in the Law of Moses, which the LORD, the God of Israel, had given to the people of Israel. He came up to Jerusalem from Babylon, and the king gave him everything he asked for, because the gracious hand of the LORD his God was on him. ⁷ Some of the people of Israel, as well as some of the priests, Levites, singers, gatekeepers, and Temple servants, traveled up to Jerusalem with him in the seventh year of King Artaxerxes' reign.

⁸ Ezra arrived in Jerusalem in August* of that year. ⁹ He had arranged to leave Babylon on April 8, the first day of the new year,* and he arrived at Jerusalem on August 4,* for the gracious hand of his God was on him. ¹⁰ This was because Ezra had determined to study and obey the Law of the LORD and to teach those decrees and regulations to the people of Israel.

6:6 Aramaic *the province beyond the river;* also in 6:6b, 8, 13. 6:11 Aramaic *a dunghill.* 6:15 Aramaic *on the third day of the month Adar,* of the ancient Hebrew lunar calendar. A number of events in Ezra can be cross-checked with dates in surviving Persian records and related accurately to our modern calendar. This day was March 12, 515 B.C. 6:19 Hebrew *On the fourteenth day of the first month,* of the ancient Hebrew lunar calendar. This day was April 21, 515 B.C.; also see note on 6:15. 6:22 King Darius of Persia is here identified as the king of Assyria because Persia had conquered the Babylonian Empire, which included the earlier Assyrian Empire. 7:1a Artaxerxes reigned 465–424 B.C. 7:1b Or *descendant;* see 1 Chr 6:14. 7:3 Or *descendant;* see 1 Chr 6:6-10. 7:5 Or *the first priest.* 7:8 Hebrew *in the fifth month.* This month in the ancient Hebrew lunar calendar occurred within the months of August and September 458 B.C. 7:9a Hebrew *on the first day of the first month,* of the ancient Hebrew lunar calendar. This day was April 8, 458 B.C.; also see note on 6:15. 7:9b Hebrew *on the first day of the fifth month,* of the ancient Hebrew lunar calendar. This day was August 4, 458 B.C.; also see note on 6:15.

ARTAXERXES' LETTER TO EZRA

[11] King Artaxerxes had given a copy of the following letter to Ezra, the priest and scribe who studied and taught the commands and decrees of the LORD to Israel:

[12] "From Artaxerxes, the king of kings, to Ezra the priest, the teacher of the law of the God of heaven. Greetings.

[13] "I decree that any of the people of Israel in my kingdom, including the priests and Levites, may volunteer to return to Jerusalem with you. [14] I and my council of seven hereby instruct you to conduct an inquiry into the situation in Judah and Jerusalem, based on your God's law, which is in your hand. [15] We also commission you to take with you silver and gold, which we are freely presenting as an offering to the God of Israel who lives in Jerusalem.

[16] "Furthermore, you are to take any silver and gold that you may obtain from the province of Babylon, as well as the voluntary offerings of the people and the priests that are presented for the Temple of their God in Jerusalem. [17] These donations are to be used specifically for the purchase of bulls, rams, male lambs, and the appropriate grain offerings and liquid offerings, all of which will be offered on the altar of the Temple of your God in Jerusalem. [18] Any silver and gold that is left over may be used in whatever way you and your colleagues feel is the will of your God.

[19] "But as for the cups we are entrusting to you for the service of the Temple of your God, deliver them all to the God of Jerusalem. [20] If you need anything else for your God's Temple or for any similar needs, you may take it from the royal treasury.

[21] "I, Artaxerxes the king, hereby send this decree to all the treasurers in the province west of the Euphrates River*: 'You are to give Ezra, the priest and teacher of the law of the God of heaven, whatever he requests of you. [22] You are to give him up to 7,500 pounds* of silver, 500 bushels* of wheat, 550 gallons of wine, 550 gallons of olive oil,* and an unlimited supply of salt. [23] Be careful to provide whatever the God of heaven demands for his Temple, for why should we risk bringing God's anger against the realm of the king and his sons? [24] I also decree that no priest, Levite, singer, gatekeeper, Temple servant, or other worker in this Temple of God will be required to pay tribute, customs, or tolls of any kind.'

[25] "And you, Ezra, are to use the wisdom your God has given you to appoint magistrates and judges who know your God's laws to govern all the people in the province west of the Euphrates River. Teach the law to anyone who does not know it. [26] Anyone who refuses to obey the law of your God and the law of the king will be punished immediately, either by death, banishment, confiscation of goods, or imprisonment."

EZRA PRAISES THE LORD

[27] Praise the LORD, the God of our ancestors, who made the king want to beautify the Temple of the LORD in Jerusalem! [28] And praise him for demonstrating such unfailing love to me by honoring me before the king, his council, and all his mighty nobles! I felt encouraged because the gracious hand of the LORD my God was on me. And I gathered some of the leaders of Israel to return with me to Jerusalem.

EXILES WHO RETURNED WITH EZRA

8 Here is a list of the family leaders and the genealogies of those who came with me from Babylon during the reign of King Artaxerxes:

[2] From the family of Phinehas: Gershom.
From the family of Ithamar: Daniel.
From the family of David: Hattush, [3] a descendant of Shecaniah.
From the family of Parosh: Zechariah and 150 other men were registered.

[4] From the family of Pahath-moab: Eliehoenai son of Zerahiah and 200 other men.

[5] From the family of Zattu*: Shecaniah son of Jahaziel and 300 other men.

[6] From the family of Adin: Ebed son of Jonathan and 50 other men.

[7] From the family of Elam: Jeshaiah son of Athaliah and 70 other men.

[8] From the family of Shephatiah: Zebadiah son of Michael and 80 other men.

[9] From the family of Joab: Obadiah son of Jehiel and 218 other men.

[10] From the family of Bani*: Shelomith son of Josiphiah and 160 other men.

[11] From the family of Bebai: Zechariah son of Bebai and 28 other men.

[12] From the family of Azgad: Johanan son of Hakkatan and 110 other men.

[13] From the family of Adonikam, who came later*: Eliphelet, Jeuel, Shemaiah, and 60 other men.

[14] From the family of Bigvai: Uthai, Zaccur,* and 70 other men.

7:12 The original text of 7:12-26 is in Aramaic.   7:21 Aramaic *the province beyond the river;* also in 7:25.   7:22a Aramaic *100 talents* [3,400 kilograms].   7:22b Aramaic *100 cors* [22 kiloliters].
7:22c Aramaic *100 baths* [2.1 kiloliters] *of wine, 100 baths of olive oil.*   8:5 As in some Greek manuscripts (see also 1 Esdras 8:32); Hebrew lacks *Zattu.*   8:10 As in some Greek manuscripts (see also 1 Esdras 8:36); Hebrew lacks *Bani.*   8:13 Or *who were the last of his family.*   8:14 As in Greek and Syriac versions and an alternate reading of the Masoretic Text; the other alternate reads *Zabbud.*

EZRA'S JOURNEY TO JERUSALEM

15 I assembled the exiles at the Ahava Canal, and we camped there for three days while I went over the lists of the people and the priests who had arrived. I found that not one Levite had volunteered to come along. 16 So I sent for Eliezer, Ariel, Shemaiah, Elnathan, Jarib, Elnathan, Nathan, Zechariah, and Meshullam, who were leaders of the people. I also sent for Joiarib and Elnathan, who were men of discernment. 17 I sent them to Iddo, the leader of the Levites at Casiphia, to ask him and his relatives and the Temple servants to send us ministers for the Temple of God at Jerusalem.

18 Since the gracious hand of our God was on us, they sent us a man named Sherebiah, along with eighteen of his sons and brothers. He was a very astute man and a descendant of Mahli, who was a descendant of Levi son of Israel.* 19 They also sent Hashabiah, together with Jeshaiah from the descendants of Merari, and twenty of his sons and brothers, 20 and 220 Temple servants. The Temple servants were assistants to the Levites—a group of Temple workers first instituted by King David and his officials. They were all listed by name.

21 And there by the Ahava Canal, I gave orders for all of us to fast and humble ourselves before our God. We prayed that he would give us a safe journey and protect us, our children, and our goods as we traveled. 22 For I was ashamed to ask the king for soldiers and horsemen* to accompany us and protect us from enemies along the way. After all, we had told the king, "Our God's hand of protection is on all who worship him, but his fierce anger rages against those who abandon him." 23 So we fasted and earnestly prayed that our God would take care of us, and he heard our prayer.

24 I appointed twelve leaders of the priests—Sherebiah, Hashabiah, and ten other priests—25 to be in charge of transporting the silver, the gold, the gold bowls, and the other items that the king, his council, his officials, and all the people of Israel had presented for the Temple of God. 26 I weighed the treasure as I gave it to them and found the totals to be as follows:

24 tons* of silver,
7,500 pounds* of silver articles,
7,500 pounds of gold,
27 20 gold bowls, equal in value to 1,000 gold coins,*
2 fine articles of polished bronze, as precious as gold.

28 And I said to these priests, "You and these treasures have been set apart as holy to the LORD. This silver and gold is a voluntary offering to the LORD, the God of our ancestors. 29 Guard these treasures well until you present them to the leading priests, the Levites, and the leaders of Israel,

who will weigh them at the storerooms of the LORD's Temple in Jerusalem." 30 So the priests and the Levites accepted the task of transporting these treasures of silver and gold to the Temple of our God in Jerusalem.

31 We broke camp at the Ahava Canal on April 19* and started off to Jerusalem. And the gracious hand of our God protected us and saved us from enemies and bandits along the way. 32 So we arrived safely in Jerusalem, where we rested for three days.

33 On the fourth day after our arrival, the silver, gold, and other valuables were weighed at the Temple of our God and entrusted to Meremoth son of Uriah the priest and to Eleazar son of Phinehas, along with Jozabad son of Jeshua and Noadiah son of Binnui—both of whom were Levites. 34 Everything was accounted for by number and weight, and the total weight was officially recorded.

35 Then the exiles who had come out of captivity sacrificed burnt offerings to the God of Israel. They presented twelve bulls for all the people of Israel, as well as ninety-six rams and seventy-seven male lambs. They also offered twelve male goats as a sin offering. All this was given as a burnt offering to the LORD. 36 The king's decrees were delivered to his highest officers and the governors of the province west of the Euphrates River,* who then cooperated by supporting the people and the Temple of God.

EZRA'S PRAYER CONCERNING INTERMARRIAGE

9 When these things had been done, the Jewish leaders came to me and said, "Many of the people of Israel, and even some of the priests and Levites, have not kept themselves separate from the other peoples living in the land. They have taken up the detestable practices of the Canaanites, Hittites, Perizzites, Jebusites, Ammonites, Moabites, Egyptians, and Amorites. 2 For the men of Israel have married women from these people and have taken them as wives for their sons. So the holy race has become polluted by these mixed marriages. Worse yet, the leaders and officials have led the way in this outrage."

3 When I heard this, I tore my cloak and my shirt, pulled hair from my head and beard, and sat down utterly shocked. 4 Then all who trembled at the words of the God of Israel came and sat with me because of this outrage committed by the returned exiles. And I sat there utterly appalled until the time of the evening sacrifice.

5 At the time of the sacrifice, I stood up from where I had sat in mourning with my clothes

---

8:18 *Israel* is the name that God gave to Jacob. **8:22** Or *charioteers.* **8:26a** Hebrew *650 talents* [22 metric tons]. **8:26b** Hebrew *100 talents* [3,400 kilograms]; also in 8:26c. **8:27** Hebrew *1,000 darics*, about 19 pounds or 8.6 kilograms in weight. **8:31** Hebrew *on the twelfth day of the first month,* of the ancient Hebrew lunar calendar. This day was April 19, 458 B.C.; also see note on 6:15. **8:36** Hebrew *the province beyond the river.*

torn. I fell to my knees and lifted my hands to the LORD my God. ⁶ I prayed,

"O my God, I am utterly ashamed; I blush to lift up my face to you. For our sins are piled higher than our heads, and our guilt has reached to the heavens. ⁷ From the days of our ancestors until now, we have been steeped in sin. That is why we and our kings and our priests have been at the mercy of the pagan kings of the land. We have been killed, captured, robbed, and disgraced, just as we are today.

⁸ "But now we have been given a brief moment of grace, for the LORD our God has allowed a few of us to survive as a remnant. He has given us security in this holy place. Our God has brightened our eyes and granted us some relief from our slavery. ⁹ For we were slaves, but in his unfailing love our God did not abandon us in our slavery. Instead, he caused the kings of Persia to treat us favorably. He revived us so we could rebuild the Temple of our God and repair its ruins. He has given us a protective wall in Judah and Jerusalem.

¹⁰ "And now, O our God, what can we say after all of this? For once again we have abandoned your commands! ¹¹ Your servants the prophets warned us when they said, 'The land you are entering to possess is totally defiled by the detestable practices of the people living there. From one end to the other, the land is filled with corruption. ¹² Don't let your daughters marry their sons! Don't take their daughters as wives for your sons. Don't ever promote the peace and prosperity of those nations. If you follow these instructions, you will be strong and will enjoy the good things the land produces, and you will leave this prosperity to your children forever.'

¹³ "Now we are being punished because of our wickedness and our great guilt. But we have actually been punished far less than we deserve, for you, our God, have allowed some of us to survive as a remnant. ¹⁴ But even so, we are again breaking your commands and intermarrying with people who do these detestable things. Won't your anger be enough to destroy us, so that even this little remnant no longer survives? ¹⁵ O LORD, God of Israel, you are just. We come before you in our guilt as nothing but an escaped remnant, though in such a condition none of us can stand in your presence."

THE PEOPLE CONFESS THEIR SIN

10 While Ezra prayed and made this confession, weeping and lying face down on the ground in front of the Temple of God, a very large crowd of people from Israel—men, women, and children—gathered and wept bitterly with him. ² Then Shecaniah son of Jehiel, a descendant of Elam, said to Ezra, "We have been unfaithful to our God, for we have married these pagan women of the land. But in spite of this there is hope for Israel. ³ Let us now make a covenant with our God to divorce our pagan wives and to send them away with their children. We will follow the advice given by you and by the others who respect the commands of our God. Let it be done according to the Law of God. ⁴ Get up, for it is your duty to tell us how to proceed in setting things straight. We are behind you, so be strong and take action."

⁵ So Ezra stood up and demanded that the leaders of the priests and the Levites and all the people of Israel swear that they would do as Shecaniah had said. And they all swore a solemn oath. ⁶ Then Ezra left the front of the Temple of God and went to the room of Jehohanan son of Eliashib. He spent the night* there without eating or drinking anything. He was still in mourning because of the unfaithfulness of the returned exiles.

⁷ Then a proclamation was made throughout Judah and Jerusalem that all the exiles should come to Jerusalem. ⁸ Those who failed to come within three days would, if the leaders and elders so decided, forfeit all their property and be expelled from the assembly of the exiles.

⁹ Within three days, all the people of Judah and Benjamin had gathered in Jerusalem. This took place on December 19,* and all the people were sitting in the square before the Temple of God. They were trembling both because of the seriousness of the matter and because it was raining. ¹⁰ Then Ezra the priest stood and said to them: "You have committed a terrible sin. By marrying pagan women, you have increased Israel's guilt. ¹¹ So now confess your sin to the LORD, the God of your ancestors, and do what he demands. Separate yourselves from the people of the land and from these pagan women."

¹² Then the whole assembly raised their voices and answered, "Yes, you are right; we must do as you say!" ¹³ Then they added, "This isn't something that can be done in a day or two, for many of us are involved in this extremely sinful affair. And this is the rainy season, so we cannot stay out here much longer. ¹⁴ Let our leaders act on behalf of us all. Let everyone who has a pagan wife come at a scheduled time, accompanied by the leaders and judges of his city, so that the fierce anger of our God concerning this affair may be turned away from us."

¹⁵ Only Jonathan son of Asahel and Jahzeiah son of Tikvah opposed this course of action, and

_____
10:6 As in parallel text at 1 Esdras 9:2; Hebrew reads *He went.*
10:9 Hebrew *on the twentieth day of the ninth month,* of the ancient Hebrew lunar calendar. This day was December 19, 458 B.C.; also see note on 6:15.

they were supported by Meshullam and Shabbethai the Levite.

[16] So this was the plan they followed. Ezra selected leaders to represent their families, designating each of the representatives by name. On December 29,* the leaders sat down to investigate the matter. [17] By March 27, the first day of the new year,* they had finished dealing with all the men who had married pagan wives.

THOSE GUILTY OF INTERMARRIAGE

[18] These are the priests who had married pagan wives:

From the family of Jeshua son of Jehozadak* and his brothers: Maaseiah, Eliezer, Jarib, and Gedaliah. [19] They vowed to divorce their wives, and they each acknowledged their guilt by offering a ram as a guilt offering.
[20] From the family of Immer: Hanani and Zebadiah.
[21] From the family of Harim: Maaseiah, Elijah, Shemaiah, Jehiel, and Uzziah.
[22] From the family of Pashhur: Elioenai, Maaseiah, Ishmael, Nethanel, Jozabad, and Elasah.

[23] These are the Levites who were guilty: Jozabad, Shimei, Kelaiah (also called Kelita), Pethahiah, Judah, and Eliezer.

[24] This is the singer who was guilty: Eliashib.

These are the gatekeepers who were guilty: Shallum, Telem, and Uri.

[25] These are the other people of Israel who were guilty:

From the family of Parosh: Ramiah, Izziah, Malkijah, Mijamin, Eleazar, Hashabiah,* and Benaiah.

[26] From the family of Elam: Mattaniah, Zechariah, Jehiel, Abdi, Jeremoth, and Elijah.
[27] From the family of Zattu: Elioenai, Eliashib, Mattaniah, Jeremoth, Zabad, and Aziza.
[28] From the family of Bebai: Jehohanan, Hananiah, Zabbai, and Athlai.
[29] From the family of Bani: Meshullam, Malluch, Adaiah, Jashub, Sheal, and Jeremoth.
[30] From the family of Pahath-moab: Adna, Kelal, Benaiah, Maaseiah, Mattaniah, Bezalel, Binnui, and Manasseh.
[31] From the family of Harim: Eliezer, Ishijah, Malkijah, Shemaiah, Shimeon, [32] Benjamin, Malluch, and Shemariah.
[33] From the family of Hashum: Mattenai, Mattattah, Zabad, Eliphelet, Jeremai, Manasseh, and Shimei.
[34] From the family of Bani: Maadai, Amram, Uel, [35] Benaiah, Bedeiah, Keluhi, [36] Vaniah, Meremoth, Eliashib, [37] Mattaniah, Mattenai, and Jaasu.
[38] From the family of Binnui*: Shimei, [39] Shelemiah, Nathan, Adaiah, [40] Macnadebai, Shashai, Sharai, [41] Azarel, Shelemiah, Shemariah, [42] Shallum, Amariah, and Joseph.
[43] From the family of Nebo: Jeiel, Mattithiah, Zabad, Zebina, Jaddai, Joel, and Benaiah.

[44] Each of these men had a pagan wife, and some even had children by these wives.*

10:16 Hebrew On the first day of the tenth month, of the ancient Hebrew lunar calendar. This day was December 29, 458 B.C.; also see note on 6:15. 10:17 Hebrew By the first day of the first month, of the ancient Hebrew lunar calendar. This day was March 27, 457 B.C.; also see note on 6:15. 10:18 Hebrew Jozadak, a variant spelling of Jehozadak. 10:25 As in parallel text at 1 Esdras 9:26; Hebrew reads Malkijah. 10:37-38 As in Greek version; Hebrew reads Jaasu, [38]Bani, Binnui. 10:44 Or and they sent them away with their children. The meaning of the Hebrew is uncertain.

NEHEMIAH

1 These are the memoirs of Nehemiah son of Hacaliah.

NEHEMIAH'S CONCERN FOR JERUSALEM

In late autumn, in the month of Kislev, in the twentieth year of King Artaxerxes' reign,* I was at the fortress of Susa. [2] Hanani, one of my brothers, came to visit me with some other men who had just arrived from Judah. I asked them about the Jews who had returned there from captivity and about how things were going in Jerusalem.

[3] They said to me, "Things are not going well for those who returned to the province of Judah. They are in great trouble and disgrace. The wall of Jerusalem has been torn down, and the gates have been destroyed by fire."

[4] When I heard this, I sat down and wept. In fact, for days I mourned, fasted, and prayed to the God of heaven. [5] Then I said,

"O LORD, God of heaven, the great and awesome God who keeps his covenant of unfailing love with those who love him and obey his commands, [6] listen to my prayer! Look down and see me praying night and day for your people Israel. I confess that we have sinned against you. Yes, even my own family and I have sinned! [7] We have sinned terribly by not obeying the commands, decrees, and regulations that you gave us through your servant Moses.

[8] "Please remember what you told your servant Moses: 'If you are unfaithful to me, I will scatter you among the nations. [9] But if you return to me and obey my commands and live by them, then even if you are exiled to the ends of the earth,* I will bring you back to the place I have chosen for my name to be honored.'

[10] "The people you rescued by your great power and strong hand are your servants. [11] O Lord, please hear my prayer! Listen to the prayers of those of us who delight in honoring you. Please grant me success today by making the king favorable to me.* Put it into his heart to be kind to me."

In those days I was the king's cup-bearer.

NEHEMIAH GOES TO JERUSALEM

2 Early the following spring, in the month of Nisan,* during the twentieth year of King Artaxerxes' reign, I was serving the king his wine. I had never before appeared sad in his presence. [2] So the king asked me, "Why are you looking so sad? You don't look sick to me. You must be deeply troubled."

Then I was terrified, [3] but I replied, "Long live the king! How can I not be sad? For the city where my ancestors are buried is in ruins, and the gates have been destroyed by fire."

[4] The king asked, "Well, how can I help you?"

With a prayer to the God of heaven, [5] I replied, "If it please the king, and if you are pleased with me, your servant, send me to Judah to rebuild the city where my ancestors are buried."

[6] The king, with the queen sitting beside him, asked, "How long will you be gone? When will you return?" After I told him how long I would be gone, the king agreed to my request.

[7] I also said to the king, "If it please the king, let me have letters addressed to the governors of the province west of the Euphrates River,* instructing them to let me travel safely through their territories on my way to Judah. [8] And please give me a letter addressed to Asaph, the manager of the king's forest, instructing him to give me timber. I will need it to make beams for the gates of the Temple fortress, for the city walls, and for a house

---

NEHEMIAH: REBUILDER OF THE BROKEN
Nehemiah 1:3–4   TOM LANE

A hero is an ordinary person who does extraordinary things. The heroes of the Bible were ordinary people who said yes to God and changed the course of many lives (Hebrews 11:32-34).

Like many other Jews of his time, Nehemiah was exiled to a foreign city. When he heard about the trouble and shame of the people in Jerusalem, he felt stirred by God to do something about it. Four months passed before Nehemiah could execute his plan, but his unwavering resolve ultimately led him to a two-fold restoration. He helped rebuild the walls of Jerusalem, and he also helped renew the spiritual vitality of God's people who lived there.

We all know people who are in distress and living with the consequences of sin. Our faith may need to go through a maturing process, but like Nehemiah, we each have the potential to help rebuild broken lives.

1:1 Hebrew *In the month of Kislev of the twentieth year.* A number of dates in the book of Nehemiah can be cross-checked with dates in surviving Persian records and related accurately to our modern calendar. This month of the ancient Hebrew lunar calendar occurred within the months of November and December 446 B.C. The *twentieth year* probably refers to the reign of King Artaxerxes I; compare 2:1; 5:14. **1:9** Hebrew *of the heavens.* **1:11** Hebrew *today in the sight of this man.* **2:1** Hebrew *In the month of Nisan.* This month of the ancient Hebrew lunar calendar occurred within the months of April and May 445 B.C. **2:7** Hebrew *the province beyond the river;* also in 2:9.

for myself." And the king granted these requests, because the gracious hand of God was on me.

[9] When I came to the governors of the province west of the Euphrates River, I delivered the king's letters to them. The king, I should add, had sent along army officers and horsemen* to protect me. [10] But when Sanballat the Horonite and Tobiah the Ammonite official heard of my arrival, they were very displeased that someone had come to help the people of Israel.

NEHEMIAH INSPECTS JERUSALEM'S WALL

[11] So I arrived in Jerusalem. Three days later, [12] I slipped out during the night, taking only a few others with me. I had not told anyone about the plans God had put in my heart for Jerusalem. We took no pack animals with us except the donkey I was riding. [13] After dark I went out through the Valley Gate, past the Jackal's Well,* and over to the Dung Gate to inspect the broken walls and burned gates. [14] Then I went to the Fountain Gate and to the King's Pool, but my donkey couldn't get through the rubble. [15] So, though it was still dark, I went up the Kidron Valley* instead, inspecting the wall before I turned back and entered again at the Valley Gate.

[16] The city officials did not know I had been out there or what I was doing, for I had not yet said anything to anyone about my plans. I had not yet spoken to the Jewish leaders—the priests, the nobles, the officials, or anyone else in the administration. [17] But now I said to them, "You know very well what trouble we are in. Jerusalem lies in ruins, and its gates have been destroyed by fire. Let us rebuild the wall of Jerusalem and end this disgrace!" [18] Then I told them about how the gracious hand of God had been on me, and about my conversation with the king.

They replied at once, "Yes, let's rebuild the wall!" So they began the good work.

[19] But when Sanballat, Tobiah, and Geshem the Arab heard of our plan, they scoffed contemptuously. "What are you doing? Are you rebelling against the king?" they asked.

[20] I replied, "The God of heaven will help us succeed. We, his servants, will start rebuilding this wall. But you have no share, legal right, or historic claim in Jerusalem."

REBUILDING THE WALL OF JERUSALEM

3 Then Eliashib the high priest and the other priests started to rebuild at the Sheep Gate. They dedicated it and set up its doors, building the wall as far as the Tower of the Hundred, which they dedicated, and the Tower of Hananel. [2] People from the town of Jericho worked next to them, and beyond them was Zaccur son of Imri.

[3] The Fish Gate was built by the sons of Hassenaah. They laid the beams, set up its doors, and installed its bolts and bars. [4] Meremoth son of Uriah and grandson of Hakkoz repaired the next section of wall. Beside him were Meshullam son

of Berekiah and grandson of Meshezabel, and then Zadok son of Baana. [5] Next were the people from Tekoa, though their leaders refused to work with the construction supervisors.

[6] The Old City Gate* was repaired by Joiada son of Paseah and Meshullam son of Besodeiah. They laid the beams, set up its doors, and installed its bolts and bars. [7] Next to them were Melatiah from Gibeon, Jadon from Meronoth, people from Gibeon, and people from Mizpah, the headquarters of the governor of the province west of the Euphrates River.* [8] Next was Uzziel son of Harhaiah, a goldsmith by trade, who also worked on the wall. Beyond him was Hananiah, a manufacturer of perfumes. They left out a section of Jerusalem as they built the Broad Wall.*

[9] Rephaiah son of Hur, the leader of half the district of Jerusalem, was next to them on the wall. [10] Next Jedaiah son of Harumaph repaired the wall across from his own house, and next to him was Hattush son of Hashabneiah. [11] Then came Malkijah son of Harim and Hasshub son of Pahath-moab, who repaired another section of the wall and the Tower of the Ovens. [12] Shallum son of Hallohesh and his daughters repaired the next section. He was the leader of the other half of the district of Jerusalem.

[13] The Valley Gate was repaired by the people from Zanoah, led by Hanun. They set up its doors and installed its bolts and bars. They also repaired the 1,500 feet* of wall to the Dung Gate.

[14] The Dung Gate was repaired by Malkijah son of Recab, the leader of the Beth-hakkerem district. He rebuilt it, set up its doors, and installed its bolts and bars.

[15] The Fountain Gate was repaired by Shallum* son of Col-hozeh, the leader of the Mizpah district. He rebuilt it, roofed it, set up its doors, and installed its bolts and bars. Then he repaired the wall of the pool of Siloam* near the king's garden, and he rebuilt the wall as far as the stairs that descend from the City of David. [16] Next to him was Nehemiah son of Azbuk, the leader of half the district of Beth-zur. He rebuilt the wall from a place across from the tombs of David's family as far as the water reservoir and the House of the Warriors.

[17] Next to him, repairs were made by a group of Levites working under the supervision of Rehum son of Bani. Then came Hashabiah, the leader of half the district of Keilah, who supervised the building of the wall on behalf of his own district. [18] Next down the line were his countrymen led by Binnui* son of Henadad, the leader of the other half of the district of Keilah.

2:9 Or *chariboteers*.   2:13 Or *Serpent's Well*.   2:15 Hebrew *the valley*.   3:6 Or *The Mishneh Gate*, or *The Jeshanah Gate*.
3:7 Hebrew *the province beyond the river*.   3:8 Or *They fortified Jerusalem up to the Broad Wall*.   3:13 Hebrew *1,000 cubits* [460 meters].   3:15a As in Syriac version; Hebrew reads *Shallun*.   3:15b Hebrew *pool of Shelah*, another name for the pool of Siloam.   3:18 As in a few Hebrew manuscripts, some Greek manuscripts, and Syriac version (see also 3:24; 10:9); most Hebrew manuscripts read *Bavvai*.

¹⁹ Next to them, Ezer son of Jeshua, the leader of Mizpah, repaired another section of wall across from the ascent to the armory near the angle in the wall. ²⁰ Next to him was Baruch son of Zabbai, who zealously repaired an additional section from the angle to the door of the house of Eliashib the high priest. ²¹ Meremoth son of Uriah and grandson of Hakkoz rebuilt another section of the wall extending from the door of Eliashib's house to the end of the house.

²² The next repairs were made by the priests from the surrounding region. ²³ After them, Benjamin and Hasshub repaired the section across from their house, and Azariah son of Maaseiah and grandson of Ananiah repaired the section across from his house. ²⁴ Next was Binnui son of Henadad, who rebuilt another section of the wall from Azariah's house to the angle and the corner. ²⁵ Palal son of Uzai carried on the work from a point opposite the angle and the tower that projects up from the king's upper house beside the court of the guard. Next to him were Pedaiah son of Parosh, ²⁶ with the Temple servants living on the hill of Ophel, who repaired the wall as far as a point across from the Water Gate to the east and the projecting tower. ²⁷ Then came the people of Tekoa, who repaired another section across from the great projecting tower and over to the wall of Ophel.

²⁸ Above the Horse Gate, the priests repaired the wall. Each one repaired the section immediately across from his own house. ²⁹ Next Zadok son of Immer also rebuilt the wall across from his own house, and beyond him was Shemaiah son of Shecaniah, the gatekeeper of the East Gate. ³⁰ Next Hananiah son of Shelemiah and Hanun, the sixth son of Zalaph, repaired another section, while Meshullam son of Berekiah rebuilt the wall across from where he lived. ³¹ Malkijah, one of the goldsmiths, repaired the wall as far as the housing for the Temple servants and merchants, across from the Inspection Gate. Then he continued as far as the upper room at the corner. ³² The other goldsmiths and merchants repaired the wall from that corner to the Sheep Gate.

ENEMIES OPPOSE THE REBUILDING

4 ¹* Sanballat was very angry when he learned that we were rebuilding the wall. He flew into a rage and mocked the Jews, ² saying in front of his friends and the Samarian army officers, "What does this bunch of poor, feeble Jews think they're doing? Do they think they can build the wall in a single day by just offering a few sacrifices?* Do they actually think they can make something of stones from a rubbish heap—and charred ones at that?"

³ Tobiah the Ammonite, who was standing beside him, remarked, "That stone wall would collapse if even a fox walked along the top of it!"

⁴ Then I prayed, "Hear us, our God, for we are being mocked. May their scoffing fall back on their own heads, and may they themselves become captives in a foreign land! ⁵ Do not ignore their guilt. Do not blot out their sins, for they have provoked you to anger here in front of* the builders."

⁶ At last the wall was completed to half its height around the entire city, for the people had worked with enthusiasm.

⁷* But when Sanballat and Tobiah and the Arabs, Ammonites, and Ashdodites heard that the work was going ahead and that the gaps in the wall of Jerusalem were being repaired, they were furious. ⁸ They all made plans to come and fight against Jerusalem and throw us into confusion. ⁹ But we prayed to our God and guarded the city day and night to protect ourselves.

¹⁰ Then the people of Judah began to complain, "The workers are getting tired, and there is so much rubble to be moved. We will never be able to build the wall by ourselves."

¹¹ Meanwhile, our enemies were saying, "Before they know what's happening, we will swoop down on them and kill them and end their work."

¹² The Jews who lived near the enemy came and told us again and again, "They will come from all directions and attack us!"* ¹³ So I placed armed guards behind the lowest parts of the wall in the exposed areas. I stationed the people to stand guard by families, armed with swords, spears, and bows.

¹⁴ Then as I looked over the situation, I called together the nobles and the rest of the people and said to them, "Don't be afraid of the enemy! Remember the Lord, who is great and glorious, and fight for your brothers, your sons, your daughters, your wives, and your homes!"

¹⁵ When our enemies heard that we knew of their plans and that God had frustrated them, we all returned to our work on the wall. ¹⁶ But from then on, only half my men worked while the other half stood guard with spears, shields, bows, and coats of mail. The leaders stationed themselves behind the people of Judah ¹⁷ who were building the wall. The laborers carried on their work with one hand supporting their load and one hand holding a weapon. ¹⁸ All the builders had a sword belted to their side. The trumpeter stayed with me to sound the alarm.

¹⁹ Then I explained to the nobles and officials and all the people, "The work is very spread out, and we are widely separated from each other along the wall. ²⁰ When you hear the blast of the trumpet, rush to wherever it is sounding. Then our God will fight for us!"

²¹ We worked early and late, from sunrise to sunset. And half the men were always on guard. ²² I also told everyone living outside the walls to

4:1 Verses 4:1-6 are numbered 3:33-38 in Hebrew text. 4:2 The meaning of the Hebrew is uncertain. 4:5 Or *for they have thrown insults in the face of.* 4:7 Verses 4:7-23 are numbered 4:1-17 in Hebrew text. 4:12 The meaning of the Hebrew is uncertain.

stay in Jerusalem. That way they and their servants could help with guard duty at night and work during the day. ²³ During this time, none of us—not I, nor my relatives, nor my servants, nor the guards who were with me—ever took off our clothes. We carried our weapons with us at all times, even when we went for water.*

NEHEMIAH DEFENDS THE OPPRESSED

5 About this time some of the men and their wives raised a cry of protest against their fellow Jews. ² They were saying, "We have such large families. We need more food to survive."

³ Others said, "We have mortgaged our fields, vineyards, and homes to get food during the famine."

⁴ And others said, "We have had to borrow money on our fields and vineyards to pay our taxes. ⁵ We belong to the same family as those who are wealthy, and our children are just like theirs. Yet we must sell our children into slavery just to get enough money to live. We have already sold some of our daughters, and we are helpless to do anything about it, for our fields and vineyards are already mortgaged to others."

⁶ When I heard their complaints, I was very angry. ⁷ After thinking it over, I spoke out against these nobles and officials. I told them, "You are hurting your own relatives by charging interest when they borrow money!" Then I called a public meeting to deal with the problem.

⁸ At the meeting I said to them, "We are doing all we can to redeem our Jewish relatives who have had to sell themselves to pagan foreigners, but you are selling them back into slavery again. How often must we redeem them?" And they had nothing to say in their defense.

⁹ Then I pressed further, "What you are doing is not right! Should you not walk in the fear of our God in order to avoid being mocked by enemy nations? ¹⁰ I myself, as well as my brothers and my workers, have been lending the people money and grain, but now let us stop this business of charging interest. ¹¹ You must restore their fields, vineyards, olive groves, and homes to them this very day. And repay the interest you charged when you lent them money, grain, new wine, and olive oil."

¹² They replied, "We will give back everything and demand nothing more from the people. We will do as you say." Then I called the priests and made the nobles and officials swear to do what they had promised.

¹³ I shook out the folds of my robe and said, "If you fail to keep your promise, may God shake you like this from your homes and from your property!"

The whole assembly responded, "Amen," and they praised the LORD. And the people did as they had promised.

¹⁴ For the entire twelve years that I was governor of Judah—from the twentieth year to the thirty-second year of the reign of King Artaxerxes*—neither I nor my officials drew on our official food allowance. ¹⁵ The former governors, in contrast, had laid heavy burdens on the people, demanding a daily ration of food and wine, besides forty pieces* of silver. Even their assistants took advantage of the people. But because I feared God, I did not act that way.

¹⁶ I also devoted myself to working on the wall and refused to acquire any land. And I required all my servants to spend time working on the wall. ¹⁷ I asked for nothing, even though I regularly fed 150 Jewish officials at my table, besides all the visitors from other lands! ¹⁸ The provisions I paid for each day included one ox, six choice sheep or goats, and a large number of poultry. And every ten days we needed a large supply of all kinds of wine. Yet I refused to claim the governor's food allowance because the people already carried a heavy burden.

¹⁹ Remember, O my God, all that I have done for these people, and bless me for it.

CONTINUED OPPOSITION TO REBUILDING

6 Sanballat, Tobiah, Geshem the Arab, and the rest of our enemies found out that I had finished rebuilding the wall and that no gaps remained—though we had not yet set up the doors in the gates. ² So Sanballat and Geshem sent a message asking me to meet them at one of the villages* in the plain of Ono.

But I realized they were plotting to harm me, ³ so I replied by sending this message to them: "I am engaged in a great work, so I can't come. Why should I stop working to come and meet with you?"

⁴ Four times they sent the same message, and each time I gave the same reply. ⁵ The fifth time, Sanballat's servant came with an open letter in his hand, ⁶ and this is what it said:

"There is a rumor among the surrounding nations, and Geshem* tells me it is true, that you and the Jews are planning to rebel and that is why you are building the wall. According to his reports, you plan to be their king. ⁷ He also reports that you have appointed prophets in Jerusalem to proclaim about you, 'Look! There is a king in Judah!'

"You can be very sure that this report will get back to the king, so I suggest that you come and talk it over with me."

⁸ I replied, "There is no truth in any part of your story. You are making up the whole thing."

4:23 Or *Each carried his weapon in his right hand.* Hebrew reads *Each his weapon the water.* The meaning of the Hebrew is uncertain.   5:14 That is, 445–433 B.C.   5:15 Hebrew *40 shekels* [1 pound or 456 grams].   6:2 As in Greek version; Hebrew reads at *Kephirim.*   6:6 Hebrew *Gashmu,* a variant spelling of Geshem.

9 They were just trying to intimidate us, imagining that they could discourage us and stop the work. So I continued the work with even greater determination.*

10 Later I went to visit Shemaiah son of Delaiah and grandson of Mehetabel, who was confined to his home. He said, "Let us meet together inside the Temple of God and bolt the doors shut. Your enemies are coming to kill you tonight."

11 But I replied, "Should someone in my position run from danger? Should someone in my position enter the Temple to save his life? No, I won't do it!" 12 I realized that God had not spoken to him, but that he had uttered this prophecy against me because Tobiah and Sanballat had hired him. 13 They were hoping to intimidate me and make me sin. Then they would be able to accuse and discredit me.

14 Remember, O my God, all the evil things that Tobiah and Sanballat have done. And remember Noadiah the prophet and all the prophets like her who have tried to intimidate me.

THE BUILDERS COMPLETE THE WALL

15 So on October 2* the wall was finished—just fifty-two days after we had begun. 16 When our enemies and the surrounding nations heard about it, they were frightened and humiliated. They realized this work had been done with the help of our God.

17 During those fifty-two days, many letters went back and forth between Tobiah and the nobles of Judah. 18 For many in Judah had sworn allegiance to him because his father-in-law was Shecaniah son of Arah, and his son Jehohanan was married to the daughter of Meshullam son of Berekiah. 19 They kept telling me about Tobiah's good deeds, and then they told him everything I said. And Tobiah kept sending threatening letters to intimidate me.

7 After the wall was finished and I had set up the doors in the gates, the gatekeepers, singers, and Levites were appointed. 2 I gave the responsibility of governing Jerusalem to my brother Hanani, along with Hananiah, the commander of the fortress, for he was a faithful man who feared God more than most. 3 I said to them, "Do not leave the gates open during the hottest part of the day.* And even while the gatekeepers are on duty, have them shut and bar the doors. Appoint the residents of Jerusalem to act as guards, everyone on a regular watch. Some will serve at sentry posts and some in front of their own homes."

NEHEMIAH REGISTERS THE PEOPLE

4 At that time the city was large and spacious, but the population was small, and none of the houses had been rebuilt. 5 So my God gave me the idea to call together all the nobles and leaders of the city, along with the ordinary citizens, for registration. I had found the genealogical record of those who had first returned to Judah. This is what was written there:

6 Here is the list of the Jewish exiles of the provinces who returned from their captivity. King Nebuchadnezzar had deported them to Babylon, but now they returned to Jerusalem and the other towns in Judah where they originally lived. 7 Their leaders were Zerubbabel, Jeshua, Nehemiah, Seraiah,* Reelaiah,* Nahamani, Mordecai, Bilshan, Mispar,* Bigvai, Rehum,* and Baanah.

This is the number of the men of Israel who returned from exile:

8 The family of Parosh	2,172
9 The family of Shephatiah	372
10 The family of Arah	652
11 The family of Pahath-moab (descendants of Jeshua and Joab)	2,818
12 The family of Elam	1,254
13 The family of Zattu	845
14 The family of Zaccai	760
15 The family of Bani*	648
16 The family of Bebai	628
17 The family of Azgad	2,322
18 The family of Adonikam	667
19 The family of Bigvai	2,067
20 The family of Adin	655
21 The family of Ater (descendants of Hezekiah)	98
22 The family of Hashum	328
23 The family of Bezai	324
24 The family of Jorah*	112
25 The family of Gibbar*	95
26 The people of Bethlehem and Netophah	188
27 The people of Anathoth	128
28 The people of Beth-azmaveth	42
29 The people of Kiriath-jearim, Kephirah, and Beeroth	743
30 The people of Ramah and Geba	621
31 The people of Micmash	122
32 The people of Bethel and Ai	123
33 The people of West Nebo*	52
34 The citizens of West Elam*	1,254
35 The citizens of Harim	320
36 The citizens of Jericho	345

6:9 As in Greek version; Hebrew reads *But now to strengthen my hands.* 6:15 Hebrew *on the twenty-fifth day of the month Elul,* of the ancient Hebrew lunar calendar. This day was October 2, 445 B.C.; also see note on 1:1. 7:3 Or *Keep the gates of Jerusalem closed until the sun is hot.* 7:7a As in parallel text at Ezra 2:2; Hebrew reads *Azariah.* 7:7b As in parallel text at Ezra 2:2; Hebrew reads *Raamiah.* 7:7c As in parallel text at Ezra 2:2; Hebrew reads *Mispereth.* 7:7d As in parallel text at Ezra 2:2; Hebrew reads *Nehum.* 7:15 As in parallel text at Ezra 2:10; Hebrew reads *Binnui.* 7:24 As in parallel text at Ezra 2:18; Hebrew reads *Hariph.* 7:25 As in parallel text at Ezra 2:20; Hebrew reads *Gibeon.* 7:33 Or *of the other Nebo.* 7:34 Or *of the other Elam.*

³⁷ The citizens of Lod, Hadid, and Ono . . .721
³⁸ The citizens of Senaah 3,930

³⁹These are the priests who returned from exile:

The family of Jedaiah
(through the line of Jeshua) 973
⁴⁰ The family of Immer 1,052
⁴¹ The family of Pashhur 1,247
⁴² The family of Harim 1,017

⁴³These are the Levites who returned from exile:

The families of Jeshua and Kadmiel
(descendants of Hodaviah*) 74
⁴⁴ The singers of the family of Asaph. . . . 148
⁴⁵ The gatekeepers of the families of
Shallum, Ater, Talmon, Akkub,
Hatita, and Shobai 138

⁴⁶The descendants of the following Temple servants returned from exile:
Ziha, Hasupha, Tabbaoth,
⁴⁷ Keros, Siaha,* Padon,
⁴⁸ Lebanah, Hagabah, Shalmai,
⁴⁹ Hanan, Giddel, Gahar,
⁵⁰ Reaiah, Rezin, Nekoda,
⁵¹ Gazzam, Uzza, Paseah,
⁵² Besai, Meunim, Nephusim,*
⁵³ Bakbuk, Hakupha, Harhur,
⁵⁴ Bazluth,* Mehida, Harsha,
⁵⁵ Barkos, Sisera, Temah,
⁵⁶ Neziah, and Hatipha.

⁵⁷The descendants of these servants of King Solomon returned from exile:
Sotai, Hassophereth, Peruda,*
⁵⁸ Jaalah,* Darkon, Giddel,
⁵⁹ Shephatiah, Hattil, Pokereth-hazzebaim, and Ami.*

⁶⁰In all, the Temple servants and the descendants of Solomon's servants numbered 392.

⁶¹Another group returned at this time from the towns of Tel-melah, Tel-harsha, Kerub, Addan,* and Immer. However, they could not prove that they or their families were descendants of Israel. ⁶²This group included the families of Delaiah, Tobiah, and Nekoda—a total of 642 people.

⁶³Three families of priests—Hobaiah, Hakkoz, and Barzillai—also returned. (This Barzillai had married a woman who was a descendant of Barzillai of Gilead, and he had taken her family name.) ⁶⁴They searched for their names in the genealogical records, but they were not found, so they were disqualified from serving as priests. ⁶⁵The governor told them not to eat the priests' share of food from the sacrifices until a

priest could consult the LORD about the matter by using the Urim and Thummim—the sacred lots.

⁶⁶So a total of 42,360 people returned to Judah, ⁶⁷in addition to 7,337 servants and 245 singers, both men and women. ⁶⁸They took with them 736 horses, 245 mules,* ⁶⁹435 camels, and 6,720 donkeys.

⁷⁰Some of the family leaders gave gifts for the work. The governor gave to the treasury 1,000 gold coins,* 50 gold basins, and 530 robes for the priests. ⁷¹The other leaders gave to the treasury a total of 20,000 gold coins* and some 2,750 pounds* of silver for the work. ⁷²The rest of the people gave 20,000 gold coins, about 2,500 pounds* of silver, and 67 robes for the priests.

⁷³So the priests, the Levites, the gatekeepers, the singers, the Temple servants, and some of the common people settled near Jerusalem. The rest of the people returned to their own towns throughout Israel.

EZRA READS THE LAW

8 In October,* when the Israelites had settled in their towns, ⁸:¹all the people assembled with a unified purpose at the square just inside the Water Gate. They asked Ezra the scribe to bring out the Book of the Law of Moses, which the LORD had given for Israel to obey.

²So on October 8* Ezra the priest brought the Book of the Law before the assembly, which included the men and women and all the children old enough to understand. ³He faced the square just inside the Water Gate from early morning until noon and read aloud to everyone who could understand. All the people listened closely to the Book of the Law.

⁴Ezra the scribe stood on a high wooden platform that had been made for the occasion. To his right stood Mattithiah, Shema, Anaiah, Uriah, Hilkiah, and Maaseiah. To his left stood Pedaiah, Mishael, Malkijah, Hashum, Hashbaddanah, Zechariah, and Meshullam. ⁵Ezra stood on the platform in full view of all the people. When they saw him open the book, they all rose to their feet.

7:43 As in parallel text at Ezra 2:40; Hebrew reads *Hodevah*. 7:47 As in parallel text at Ezra 2:44; Hebrew reads *Sia*. 7:52 As in parallel text at Ezra 2:50; Hebrew reads *Nephusesim*. 7:54 As in parallel text at Ezra 2:52; Hebrew reads *Bazlith*. 7:57 As in parallel text at Ezra 2:55; Hebrew reads *Sotai, Sophereth, Perida*. 7:58 As in parallel text at Ezra 2:56; Hebrew reads *Jaala*. 7:59 As in parallel text at Ezra 2:57; Hebrew reads *Amon*. 7:61 As in parallel text at Ezra 2:59; Hebrew reads *Addon*. 7:68 As in some Hebrew manuscripts (see also Ezra 2:66); most Hebrew manuscripts lack this verse. Verses 7:69-73 are numbered 7:68-72 in Hebrew text. 7:70 Hebrew *1,000 darics of gold*, about 19 pounds or 8.6 kilograms in weight. 7:71a Hebrew *20,000 darics of gold*, about 375 pounds or 170 kilograms in weight; also in 7:72. 7:71b Hebrew *2,200 minas* [1,300 kilograms]. 7:72 Hebrew *2,000 minas* [1,200 kilograms]. 7:73 Hebrew *In the seventh month*. This month of the ancient Hebrew lunar calendar occurred within the months of October and November 445 B.C. 8:2 Hebrew *on the first day of the seventh month*, of the ancient Hebrew lunar calendar. This day was October 8, 445 B.C.; also see note on 1:1.

⁶Then Ezra praised the LORD, the great God, and all the people chanted, "Amen! Amen!" as they lifted their hands. Then they bowed down and worshiped the LORD with their faces to the ground.

⁷The Levites—Jeshua, Bani, Sherebiah, Jamin, Akkub, Shabbethai, Hodiah, Maaseiah, Kelita, Azariah, Jozabad, Hanan, and Pelaiah—then instructed the people in the Law while everyone remained in their places. ⁸They read from the Book of the Law of God and clearly explained the meaning of what was being read, helping the people understand each passage.

⁹Then Nehemiah the governor, Ezra the priest and scribe, and the Levites who were interpreting for the people said to them, "Don't mourn or weep on such a day as this! For today is a sacred day before the LORD your God." For the people had all been weeping as they listened to the words of the Law.

¹⁰And Nehemiah* continued, "Go and celebrate with a feast of rich foods and sweet drinks, and share gifts of food with people who have nothing prepared. This is a sacred day before our Lord. Don't be dejected and sad, for the joy of the LORD is your strength!"

¹¹And the Levites, too, quieted the people, telling them, "Hush! Don't weep! For this is a sacred day." ¹²So the people went away to eat and drink at a festive meal, to share gifts of food, and to celebrate with great joy because they had heard God's words and understood them.

THE FESTIVAL OF SHELTERS

¹³On October 9* the family leaders of all the people, together with the priests and Levites, met with Ezra the scribe to go over the Law in greater detail. ¹⁴As they studied the Law, they discovered that the LORD had commanded through Moses that the Israelites should live in shelters during the festival to be held that month.* ¹⁵He had said that a proclamation should be made throughout their towns and in Jerusalem, telling the people to go to the hills to get branches from olive, wild olive,* myrtle, palm, and other leafy trees. They were to use these branches to make shelters in which they would live during the festival, as prescribed in the Law.

¹⁶So the people went out and cut branches and used them to build shelters on the roofs of their houses, in their courtyards, in the courtyards of God's Temple, or in the squares just inside the Water Gate and the Ephraim Gate. ¹⁷So everyone who had returned from captivity lived in these shelters during the festival, and they were all filled with great joy! The Israelites had not celebrated like this since the days of Joshua* son of Nun.

¹⁸Ezra read from the Book of the Law of God on each of the seven days of the festival. Then on the eighth day they held a solemn assembly, as was required by law.

THE PEOPLE CONFESS THEIR SINS

9 On October 31* the people assembled again, and this time they fasted and dressed in burlap and sprinkled dust on their heads. ²Those of Israelite descent separated themselves from all foreigners as they confessed their own sins and the sins of their ancestors. ³They remained standing in place for three hours* while the Book of the Law of the LORD their God was read aloud to them. Then for three more hours they confessed their sins and worshiped the LORD their God. ⁴The Levites—Jeshua, Bani, Kadmiel, Shebaniah, Bunni, Sherebiah, Bani, and Kenani—stood on the stairway of the Levites and cried out to the LORD their God with loud voices.

⁵Then the leaders of the Levites—Jeshua, Kadmiel, Bani, Hashabneiah, Sherebiah, Hodiah, Shebaniah, and Pethahiah—called out to the people: "Stand up and praise the LORD your God, for he lives from everlasting to everlasting!" Then they prayed:

"May your glorious name be praised! May it be exalted above all blessing and praise!

⁶"You alone are the LORD. You made the skies and the heavens and all the stars. You made the earth and the seas and everything in them. You preserve them all, and the angels of heaven worship you.

⁷"You are the LORD God, who chose Abram and brought him from Ur of the Chaldeans and renamed him Abraham. ⁸When he had proved himself faithful, you made a covenant with him to give him and his descendants the land of the Canaanites, Hittites, Amorites, Perizzites, Jebusites, and Girgashites. And you have done what you promised, for you are always true to your word.

⁹"You saw the misery of our ancestors in Egypt, and you heard their cries from beside the Red Sea.* ¹⁰You displayed miraculous signs and wonders against Pharaoh, his officials, and all his people, for you knew how arrogantly they were treating our ancestors. You have a glorious reputation that has never been forgotten. ¹¹You divided the sea for your people so they could walk through on dry land! And then you hurled their enemies into the depths of the sea. They sank like stones beneath the mighty waters. ¹²You led our ancestors by a pillar of cloud during the day and a pillar of fire at night so that they could find their way.

8:10 Hebrew *he.* **8:13** Hebrew *On the second day,* of the seventh month of the ancient Hebrew lunar calendar. This day was October 9, 445 B.C.; also see notes on 1:1 and 8:2. **8:14** Hebrew *in the seventh month.* This month of the ancient Hebrew lunar calendar usually occurs within the months of September and October. See Lev 23:39-43. **8:15** Or *pine;* Hebrew reads *oil tree.* **8:17** Hebrew *Jeshua,* a variant spelling of Joshua. **9:1** Hebrew *On the twenty-fourth day of that same month,* the seventh month of the ancient Hebrew lunar calendar. This day was October 31, 445 B.C.; also see notes on 1:1 and 8:2. **9:3** Hebrew *for a quarter of a day.* **9:9** Hebrew *sea of reeds.*

¹³ "You came down at Mount Sinai and spoke to them from heaven. You gave them regulations and instructions that were just, and decrees and commands that were good. ¹⁴ You instructed them concerning your holy Sabbath. And you commanded them, through Moses your servant, to obey all your commands, decrees, and instructions.

¹⁵ "You gave them bread from heaven when they were hungry and water from the rock when they were thirsty. You commanded them to go and take possession of the land you had sworn to give them.

¹⁶ "But our ancestors were proud and stubborn, and they paid no attention to your commands. ¹⁷ They refused to obey and did not remember the miracles you had done for them. Instead, they became stubborn and appointed a leader to take them back to their slavery in Egypt.* But you are a God of forgiveness, gracious and merciful, slow to become angry, and rich in unfailing love. You did not abandon them, ¹⁸ even when they made an idol shaped like a calf and said, 'This is your god who brought you out of Egypt!' They committed terrible blasphemies.

¹⁹ "But in your great mercy you did not abandon them to die in the wilderness. The pillar of cloud still led them forward by day, and the pillar of fire showed them the way through the night. ²⁰ You sent your good Spirit to instruct them, and you did not stop giving them manna from heaven or water for their thirst. ²¹ For forty years you sustained them in the wilderness, and they lacked nothing. Their clothes did not wear out, and their feet did not swell!

²² "Then you helped our ancestors conquer kingdoms and nations, and you placed your people in every corner of the land.* They took over the land of King Sihon of Heshbon and the land of King Og of Bashan. ²³ You made their descendants as numerous as the stars in the sky and brought them into the land you had promised to their ancestors.

²⁴ "They went in and took possession of the land. You subdued whole nations before them. Even the Canaanites, who inhabited the land, were powerless! Your people could deal with these nations and their kings as they pleased. ²⁵ Our ancestors captured fortified cities and fertile land. They took over houses full of good things, with cisterns already dug and vineyards and olive groves and fruit trees in abundance. So they ate until they were full and grew fat and enjoyed themselves in all your blessings.

²⁶ "But despite all this, they were disobedient and rebelled against you. They turned their backs on your Law, they killed your prophets who warned them to return to you, and they committed terrible blasphemies. ²⁷ So you handed them over to their enemies, who made them suffer. But in their time of trouble they cried to you, and you heard them from heaven. In your great mercy, you sent them liberators who rescued them from their enemies.

²⁸ "But as soon as they were at peace, your people again committed evil in your sight, and once more you let their enemies conquer them. Yet whenever your people turned and cried to you again for help, you listened once more from heaven. In your wonderful mercy, you rescued them many times!

²⁹ "You warned them to return to your Law, but they became proud and obstinate and disobeyed your commands. They did not follow your regulations, by which people will find life if only they obey. They stubbornly turned their backs on you and refused to listen. ³⁰ In your love, you were patient with them for many years. You sent your Spirit, who warned them through the prophets. But still they wouldn't listen! So once again you allowed the peoples of the land to conquer them. ³¹ But in your great mercy, you did not destroy them completely or abandon them forever. What a gracious and merciful God you are!

³² "And now, our God, the great and mighty and awesome God, who keeps his covenant of unfailing love, do not let all the hardships we have suffered seem insignificant to you. Great trouble has come upon us and upon our kings and leaders and priests and prophets and ancestors—all of your people—from the days when the kings of Assyria first triumphed over us until now. ³³ Every time you punished us you were being just. We have sinned greatly, and you gave us only what we deserved. ³⁴ Our kings, leaders, priests, and ancestors did not obey your Law or listen to the warnings in your commands and laws. ³⁵ Even while they had their own kingdom, they did not serve you, though you showered your goodness on them. You gave them a large, fertile land, but they refused to turn from their wickedness.

³⁶ "So now today we are slaves in the land of plenty that you gave our ancestors for their enjoyment! We are slaves here in this good land. ³⁷ The lush produce of this land piles up in the hands of the kings whom you have set over us because of our sins. They have power over us and our livestock. We serve them at their pleasure, and we are in great misery."

9:17 As in Greek version; Hebrew reads *in their rebellion.*
9:22 The meaning of the Hebrew is uncertain.

THE PEOPLE AGREE TO OBEY

38*The people responded, "In view of all this,* we are making a solemn promise and putting it in writing. On this sealed document are the names of our leaders and Levites and priests."

10
1* The document was ratified and sealed with the following names:

The governor:
Nehemiah son of Hacaliah, and also Zedekiah.

2 The following priests:
Seraiah, Azariah, Jeremiah, 3 Pashhur, Amariah, Malkijah, 4 Hattush, Shebaniah, Malluch, 5 Harim, Meremoth, Obadiah, 6 Daniel, Ginnethon, Baruch, 7 Meshullam, Abijah, Mijamin, 8 Maaziah, Bilgai, and Shemaiah. These were the priests.

9 The following Levites:
Jeshua son of Azaniah, Binnui from the family of Henadad, Kadmiel, 10 and their fellow Levites: Shebaniah, Hodiah, Kelita, Pelaiah, Hanan, 11 Mica, Rehob, Hashabiah, 12 Zaccur, Sherebiah, Shebaniah, 13 Hodiah, Bani, and Beninu.

14 The following leaders:
Parosh, Pahath-moab, Elam, Zattu, Bani, 15 Bunni, Azgad, Bebai, 16 Adonijah, Bigvai, Adin, 17 Ater, Hezekiah, Azzur, 18 Hodiah, Hashum, Bezai, 19 Hariph, Anathoth, Nebai, 20 Magpiash, Meshullam, Hezir, 21 Meshezabel, Zadok, Jaddua, 22 Pelatiah, Hanan, Anaiah, 23 Hoshea, Hananiah, Hasshub, 24 Hallohesh, Pilha, Shobek, 25 Rehum, Hashabnah, Maaseiah, 26 Ahiah, Hanan, Anan, 27 Malluch, Harim, and Baanah.

THE VOW OF THE PEOPLE

28 Then the rest of the people—the priests, Levites, gatekeepers, singers, Temple servants, and all who had separated themselves from the pagan people of the land in order to obey the Law of God, together with their wives, sons, daughters, and all who were old enough to understand—29 joined their leaders and bound themselves with an oath. They swore a curse on themselves if they failed to obey the Law of God as issued by his servant Moses. They solemnly promised to carefully follow all the commands, regulations, and decrees of the LORD our Lord:

30 "We promise not to let our daughters marry the pagan people of the land, and not to let our sons marry their daughters.

31 "We also promise that if the people of the land should bring any merchandise or grain to be sold on the Sabbath or on any other holy day, we will refuse to buy it. Every seventh year we will let our land rest, and we will cancel all debts owed to us.

32 "In addition, we promise to obey the command to pay the annual Temple tax of one-eighth of an ounce of silver* for the care of the Temple of our God. 33 This will provide for the Bread of the Presence; for the regular grain offerings and burnt offerings; for the offerings on the Sabbaths, the new moon celebrations, and the annual festivals; for the holy offerings; and for the sin offerings to make atonement for Israel. It will provide for everything necessary for the work of the Temple of our God.

34 "We have cast sacred lots to determine when—at regular times each year—the families of the priests, Levites, and the common people should bring wood to God's Temple to be burned on the altar of the LORD our God, as is written in the Law.

35 "We promise to bring the first part of every harvest to the LORD's Temple year after year—whether it be a crop from the soil or from our fruit trees. 36 We agree to give God our oldest sons and the firstborn of all our herds and flocks, as prescribed in the Law. We will present them to the priests who minister in the Temple of our God. 37 We will store the produce in the storerooms of the Temple of our God. We will bring the best of our flour and other grain offerings, the best of our fruit, and the best of our new wine and olive oil. And we promise to bring to the Levites a tenth of everything our land produces, for it is the Levites who collect the tithes in all our rural towns.

38 "A priest—a descendant of Aaron—will be with the Levites as they receive these tithes. And a tenth of all that is collected as tithes will be delivered by the Levites to the Temple of our God and placed in the storerooms. 39 The people and the Levites must bring these offerings of grain, new wine, and olive oil to the storerooms and place them in the sacred containers near the ministering priests, the gatekeepers, and the singers.

"We promise together not to neglect the Temple of our God."

THE PEOPLE OCCUPY JERUSALEM

11
The leaders of the people were living in Jerusalem, the holy city. A tenth of the people from the other towns of Judah and Benjamin were chosen by sacred lots to live there, too, while the rest stayed where they were. 2 And the people commended everyone who volunteered to resettle in Jerusalem.

3 Here is a list of the names of the provincial officials who came to live in Jerusalem. (Most of the people, priests, Levites, Temple servants, and

9:38a Verse 9:38 is numbered 10:1 in Hebrew text. 9:38b Or *In spite of all this.* 10:1 Verses 10:1-39 are numbered 10:2-40 in Hebrew text. 10:32 Hebrew *tax of ⅓ of a shekel* [4 grams].

descendants of Solomon's servants continued to live in their own homes in the various towns of Judah, [4]but some of the people from Judah and Benjamin resettled in Jerusalem.)

From the tribe of Judah:
Athaiah son of Uzziah, son of Zechariah, son of Amariah, son of Shephatiah, son of Mahalalel, of the family of Perez. [5]Also Maaseiah son of Baruch, son of Col-hozeh, son of Hazaiah, son of Adaiah, son of Joiarib, son of Zechariah, of the family of Shelah.* [6]There were 468 descendants of Perez who lived in Jerusalem—all outstanding men.
[7]From the tribe of Benjamin:
Sallu son of Meshullam, son of Joed, son of Pedaiah, son of Kolaiah, son of Maaseiah, son of Ithiel, son of Jeshaiah. [8]After him were Gabbai and Sallai and a total of 928 relatives. [9]Their chief officer was Joel son of Zicri, who was assisted by Judah son of Hassenuah, second-in-command over the city.
[10]From the priests:
Jedaiah son of Joiarib; Jakin; [11]and Seraiah son of Hilkiah, son of Meshullam, son of Zadok, son of Meraioth, son of Ahitub, the supervisor of the Temple of God. [12]Also 822 of their associates, who worked at the Temple. Also Adaiah son of Jeroham, son of Pelaliah, son of Amzi, son of Zechariah, son of Pashhur, son of Malkijah, [13]along with 242 of his associates, who were heads of their families. Also Amashsai son of Azarel, son of Ahzai, son of Meshillemoth, son of Immer, [14]and 128 of his* outstanding associates. Their chief officer was Zabdiel son of Haggedolim.
[15]From the Levites:
Shemaiah son of Hasshub, son of Azrikam, son of Hashabiah, son of Bunni. [16]Also Shabbethai and Jozabad, who were in charge of the work outside the Temple of God. [17]Also Mattaniah son of Mica, son of Zabdi, a descendant of Asaph, who led in thanksgiving and prayer. Also Bakbukiah, who was Mattaniah's assistant, and Abda son of Shammua, son of Galal, son of Jeduthun. [18]In all, there were 284 Levites in the holy city.
[19]From the gatekeepers:
Akkub, Talmon, and 172 of their associates, who guarded the gates.

[20]The other priests, Levites, and the rest of the Israelites lived wherever their family inheritance was located in any of the towns of Judah. [21]The Temple servants, however, whose leaders were Ziha and Gishpa, all lived on the hill of Ophel.
[22]The chief officer of the Levites in Jerusalem was Uzzi son of Bani, son of Hashabiah, son of Mattaniah, son of Mica, a descendant of Asaph, whose family served as singers at God's Temple. [23]Their daily responsibilities were carried out according to the terms of a royal command.
[24]Pethahiah son of Meshezabel, a descendant of Zerah son of Judah, was the royal adviser in all matters of public administration.
[25]As for the surrounding villages with their open fields, some of the people of Judah lived in Kiriath-arba with its settlements, Dibon with its settlements, and Jekabzeel with its villages. [26]They also lived in Jeshua, Moladah, Beth-pelet, [27]Hazar-shual, Beersheba with its settlements, [28]Ziklag, and Meconah with its settlements. [29]They also lived in En-rimmon, Zorah, Jarmuth, [30]Zanoah, and Adullam with their surrounding villages. They also lived in Lachish with its nearby fields and Azekah with its surrounding villages. So the people of Judah were living all the way from Beersheba in the south to the valley of Hinnom.
[31]Some of the people of Benjamin lived at Geba, Micmash, Aija, and Bethel with its settlements. [32]They also lived in Anathoth, Nob, Ananiah, [33]Hazor, Ramah, Gittaim, [34]Hadid, Zeboim, Neballat, [35]Lod, Ono, and the Valley of Craftsmen.* [36]Some of the Levites who lived in Judah were sent to live with the tribe of Benjamin.

A HISTORY OF THE PRIESTS AND LEVITES

12 Here is the list of the priests and Levites who returned with Zerubbabel son of Shealtiel and Jeshua the high priest:

Seraiah, Jeremiah, Ezra,
[2] Amariah, Malluch, Hattush,
[3] Shecaniah, Harim,* Meremoth,
[4] Iddo, Ginnethon,* Abijah,
[5] Miniamin, Moadiah,* Bilgah,
[6] Shemaiah, Joiarib, Jedaiah,
[7] Sallu, Amok, Hilkiah, and Jedaiah.
These were the leaders of the priests and their associates in the days of Jeshua.

[8]The Levites who returned with them were Jeshua, Binnui, Kadmiel, Sherebiah, Judah, and Mattaniah, who with his associates was in charge of the songs of thanksgiving. [9]Their associates, Bakbukiah and Unni, stood opposite them during the service.

[10] Jeshua the high priest was the father of Joiakim.
Joiakim was the father of Eliashib.
Eliashib was the father of Joiada.
[11] Joiada was the father of Johanan.*
Johanan was the father of Jaddua.

11:5 Hebrew son of the Shilonite. 11:14 As in Greek version; Hebrew reads their. 11:35 Or and Ge-harashim. 12:3 Hebrew Rehum; compare 7:42; 12:15; Ezra 2:39. 12:4 As in some Hebrew manuscripts and Latin Vulgate (see also 12:16); most Hebrew manuscripts read Ginnethoi. 12:5 Hebrew Mijamin, Maadiah; compare 12:17. 12:11 Hebrew Jonathan; compare 12:22.

¹²Now when Joiakim was high priest, the family leaders of the priests were as follows:

Meraiah was leader of the family of Seraiah.
Hananiah was leader of the family of Jeremiah.
¹³ Meshullam was leader of the family of Ezra.
Jehohanan was leader of the family of Amariah.
¹⁴ Jonathan was leader of the family of Malluch.*
Joseph was leader of the family of Shecaniah.*
¹⁵ Adna was leader of the family of Harim.
Helkai was leader of the family of Meremoth.*
¹⁶ Zechariah was leader of the family of Iddo.
Meshullam was leader of the family of Ginnethon.
¹⁷ Zicri was leader of the family of Abijah.
There was also a* leader of the family of Miniamin.
Piltai was leader of the family of Moadiah.
¹⁸ Shammua was leader of the family of Bilgah.
Jehonathan was leader of the family of Shemaiah.
¹⁹ Mattenai was leader of the family of Joiarib.
Uzzi was leader of the family of Jedaiah.
²⁰ Kallai was leader of the family of Sallu.*
Eber was leader of the family of Amok.
²¹ Hashabiah was leader of the family of Hilkiah.
Nethanel was leader of the family of Jedaiah.

²²A record of the Levite families was kept during the years when Eliashib, Joiada, Johanan, and Jaddua served as high priest. Another record of the priests was kept during the reign of Darius the Persian.* ²³A record of the heads of the Levite families was kept in *The Book of History* down to the days of Johanan, the grandson* of Eliashib.

²⁴These were the family leaders of the Levites: Hashabiah, Sherebiah, Jeshua, Binnui,* Kadmiel, and other associates, who stood opposite them during the ceremonies of praise and thanksgiving, one section responding to the other, as commanded by David, the man of God. ²⁵This included Mattaniah, Bakbukiah, and Obadiah.

Meshullam, Talmon, and Akkub were the gatekeepers in charge of the storerooms at the gates. ²⁶These all served in the days of Joiakim son of Jeshua, son of Jehozadak,* and in the days of Nehemiah the governor and of Ezra the priest and scribe.

DEDICATION OF JERUSALEM'S WALL

²⁷For the dedication of the new wall of Jerusalem, the Levites throughout the land were asked to come to Jerusalem to assist in the ceremonies. They were to take part in the joyous occasion with their songs of thanksgiving and with the music of cymbals, harps, and lyres. ²⁸The singers were brought together from the region around Jerusalem and from the villages of the Netophathites. ²⁹They also came from Beth-gilgal and the rural areas near Geba and Azmaveth, for the singers had built their own settlements around Jerusalem. ³⁰The priests and Levites first purified themselves; then they purified the people, the gates, and the wall.

³¹I led the leaders of Judah to the top of the wall and organized two large choirs to give thanks. One of the choirs proceeded southward* along the top of the wall to the Dung Gate. ³²Hoshaiah and half the leaders of Judah followed them, ³³along with Azariah, Ezra, Meshullam, ³⁴Judah, Benjamin, Shemaiah, and Jeremiah. ³⁵Then came some priests who played trumpets, including Zechariah son of Jonathan, son of Shemaiah, son of Mattaniah, son of Micaiah, son of Zaccur, a descendant of Asaph. ³⁶And Zechariah's colleagues were Shemaiah, Azarel, Milalai, Gilalai, Maai, Nethanel, Judah, and Hanani. They used the musical instruments prescribed by David, the man of God. Ezra the scribe led this procession. ³⁷At the Fountain Gate they went straight up the steps on the ascent of the city wall toward the City of David. They passed the house of David and then proceeded to the Water Gate on the east.

³⁸The second choir giving thanks went northward* around the other way to meet them. I followed them, together with the other half of the people, along the top of the wall past the Tower of the Ovens to the Broad Wall, ³⁹then past the Ephraim Gate to the Old City Gate,* past the Fish Gate and the Tower of Hananel, and on to the Tower of the Hundred. Then we continued on to the Sheep Gate and stopped at the Guard Gate.

⁴⁰The two choirs that were giving thanks then proceeded to the Temple of God, where they took their places. So did I, together with the group of leaders who were with me. ⁴¹We went together with the trumpet-playing priests—Eliakim, Maaseiah, Miniamin, Micaiah, Elioenai, Zechariah, and Hananiah—⁴²and the singers—Maaseiah, Shemaiah, Eleazar, Uzzi, Jehohanan, Malkijah, Elam, and Ezer. They played and sang loudly under the direction of Jezrahiah the choir director.

⁴³Many sacrifices were offered on that joyous day, for God had given the people cause for great joy. The women and children also participated

---

12:14a As in Greek version (see also 10:4; 12:2); Hebrew reads *Malluchi*. **12:14b** As in many Hebrew manuscripts, some Greek manuscripts, and Syriac version (see also 12:3); most Hebrew manuscripts read *Shebaniah*. **12:15** As in some Greek manuscripts (see also 12:3); Hebrew reads *Meraioth*. **12:17** Hebrew lacks the name of this family leader. **12:20** Hebrew *Sallai;* compare 12:7. **12:22** *Darius the Persian* is probably Darius II, who reigned 423–404 B.C., or possibly Darius III, who reigned 336–331 B.C. **12:23** Hebrew *descendant;* compare 12:10-11. **12:24** Hebrew *son of* (i.e., *ben*), which should probably be read here as the proper name Binnui; compare Ezra 3:9 and the note there. **12:26** Hebrew *Jozadak,* a variant spelling of Jehozadak. **12:31** Hebrew *to the right.* **12:38** Hebrew *to the left.* **12:39** Or *the Mishneh Gate,* or *the Jeshanah Gate.*

in the celebration, and the joy of the people of Jerusalem could be heard far away.

PROVISIONS FOR TEMPLE WORSHIP

[44] On that day men were appointed to be in charge of the storerooms for the offerings, the first part of the harvest, and the tithes. They were responsible to collect from the fields outside the towns the portions required by the Law for the priests and Levites. For all the people of Judah took joy in the priests and Levites and their work. [45] They performed the service of their God and the service of purification, as commanded by David and his son Solomon, and so did the singers and the gatekeepers. [46] The custom of having choir directors to lead the choirs in hymns of praise and thanksgiving to God began long ago in the days of David and Asaph. [47] So now, in the days of Zerubbabel and of Nehemiah, all Israel brought a daily supply of food for the singers, the gatekeepers, and the Levites. The Levites, in turn, gave a portion of what they received to the priests, the descendants of Aaron.

NEHEMIAH'S VARIOUS REFORMS

13 On that same day, as the Book of Moses was being read to the people, the passage was found that said no Ammonite or Moabite should ever be permitted to enter the assembly of God.* [2] For they had not provided the Israelites with food and water in the wilderness. Instead, they hired Balaam to curse them, though our God turned the curse into a blessing. [3] When this passage of the Law was read, all those of foreign descent were immediately excluded from the assembly.

[4] Before this had happened, Eliashib the priest, who had been appointed as supervisor of the storerooms of the Temple of our God and who was also a relative of Tobiah, [5] had converted a large storage room and placed it at Tobiah's disposal. The room had previously been used for storing the grain offerings, the frankincense, various articles for the Temple, and the tithes of grain, new wine, and olive oil (which were prescribed for the Levites, the singers, and the gatekeepers), as well as the offerings for the priests.

[6] I was not in Jerusalem at that time, for I had returned to King Artaxerxes of Babylon in the thirty-second year of his reign,* though I later asked his permission to return. [7] When I arrived back in Jerusalem, I learned about Eliashib's evil deed in providing Tobiah with a room in the courtyards of the Temple of God. [8] I became very upset and threw all of Tobiah's belongings out of the room. [9] Then I demanded that the rooms be purified, and I brought back the articles for God's Temple, the grain offerings, and the frankincense.

[10] I also discovered that the Levites had not been given their prescribed portions of food, so

THE PRINCIPLE OF PROTECTION
Nehemiah 13:23-25   ROBERT MORRIS

When Nehemiah learned some of the Jews had married people from other nations, he was furious. God had specifically told His people not to marry foreigners (Deuteronomy 7:3-4). Some people may misapply or misinterpret this principle of protection to justify prejudice and racism. However, God's command was never about race. It was about protecting Israel's faith. God knew if the people of Israel intermarried with foreign nations, the people they married would draw their hearts away from Him.

You may be a bit romantic and think, Well, if they really loved each other . . . However, these marriages had nothing to do with love; instead, they were rooted in the fears of poverty and slavery. The Israelite men married pagan women to encourage other nations to do business with them and also to prevent them from attacking Israel. Through these marriages, Israel told God, "We don't trust You to protect or provide for us, so we are going to make a deal with the devil!" After all, these foreign women were not simply unbelievers. They were idol worshippers and thus devil worshippers. They even burned their children alive! They knew about the God of Israel and defiantly refused to believe in Him.

The principle of protection is not simply for marriage—it applies to anything that draws our hearts away from God. What about the books and magazines you read, the movies and television shows you watch, the business partners you choose, and the friends with whom you associate? Are any of these pulling you away from God? Remember, all God's principles are for our good. He wants to protect us, but we must choose to separate ourselves from ungodly influences.

they and the singers who were to conduct the worship services had all returned to work their fields. [11] I immediately confronted the leaders and demanded, "Why has the Temple of God been neglected?" Then I called all the Levites back again and restored them to their proper duties. [12] And once more all the people of Judah began bringing their tithes of grain, new wine, and olive oil to the Temple storerooms.

[13] I assigned supervisors for the storerooms: Shelemiah the priest, Zadok the scribe, and Pedaiah, one of the Levites. And I appointed Hanan son of Zaccur and grandson of Mattaniah as their assistant. These men had an excellent

13:1 See Deut 23:3-6.   13:6 King Artaxerxes of Persia is here identified as the king of Babylon because Persia had conquered the Babylonian Empire. The thirty-second year of Artaxerxes was 433 B.C.

reputation, and it was their job to make honest distributions to their fellow Levites.

¹⁴Remember this good deed, O my God, and do not forget all that I have faithfully done for the Temple of my God and its services.

¹⁵In those days I saw men of Judah treading out their winepresses on the Sabbath. They were also bringing in grain, loading it on donkeys, and bringing their wine, grapes, figs, and all sorts of produce to Jerusalem to sell on the Sabbath. So I rebuked them for selling their produce on that day. ¹⁶Some men from Tyre, who lived in Jerusalem, were bringing in fish and all kinds of merchandise. They were selling it on the Sabbath to the people of Judah—and in Jerusalem at that!

¹⁷So I confronted the nobles of Judah. "Why are you profaning the Sabbath in this evil way?" I asked. ¹⁸"Wasn't it just this sort of thing that your ancestors did that caused our God to bring all this trouble upon us and our city? Now you are bringing even more wrath upon Israel by permitting the Sabbath to be desecrated in this way!"

¹⁹Then I commanded that the gates of Jerusalem should be shut as darkness fell every Friday evening,* not to be opened until the Sabbath ended. I sent some of my own servants to guard the gates so that no merchandise could be brought in on the Sabbath day. ²⁰The merchants and tradesmen with a variety of wares camped outside Jerusalem once or twice. ²¹But I spoke sharply to them and said, "What are you doing out here, camping around the wall? If you do this again, I will arrest you!" And that was the last time they came on the Sabbath. ²²Then I commanded the Levites to purify themselves and to guard the gates in order to preserve the holiness of the Sabbath.

Remember this good deed also, O my God! Have compassion on me according to your great and unfailing love.

²³About the same time I realized that some of the men of Judah had married women from Ashdod, Ammon, and Moab. ²⁴Furthermore, half their children spoke the language of Ashdod or of some other people and could not speak the language of Judah at all. ²⁵So I confronted them and called down curses on them. I beat some of them and pulled out their hair. I made them swear in the name of God that they would not let their children intermarry with the pagan people of the land.

²⁶"Wasn't this exactly what led King Solomon of Israel into sin?" I demanded. "There was no king from any nation who could compare to him, and God loved him and made him king over all Israel. But even he was led into sin by his foreign wives. ²⁷How could you even think of committing this sinful deed and acting unfaithfully toward God by marrying foreign women?"

²⁸One of the sons of Joiada son of Eliashib the high priest had married a daughter of Sanballat the Horonite, so I banished him from my presence.

²⁹Remember them, O my God, for they have defiled the priesthood and the solemn vows of the priests and Levites.

³⁰So I purged out everything foreign and assigned tasks to the priests and Levites, making certain that each knew his work. ³¹I also made sure that the supply of wood for the altar and the first portions of the harvest were brought at the proper times.

Remember this in my favor, O my God.

13:19 Hebrew *on the day before the Sabbath.*

ESTHER

JON HUNTZINGER, PHD

The book of Esther tells the story of a Jewish woman who saves her people, the Jews, from destruction by risking her high position as queen in a foreign kingdom. Like the story of Daniel, which is set in far-off Babylon in the sixth century BC, this story is set far from Israel in Persia during the reign of Xerxes (486-465 BC) and gives insight into life at the palace of the Persian king. It was written a short time after the reign of Xerxes to describe the origins of the Jewish festival of Purim, which celebrates God's protection of His people from disaster. The word Purim is derived from the Hebrew word Pur, which means 'lot.' Haman, the antagonist of the story, threw lots, or dice, to determine his plans for destroying the Jewish people because of his hatred for them.

The plot of the book of Esther contains seven major events:

— Chapters 1:1-2:18 include the events that led to the appointment of Esther as queen.
— Chapter 2:19-23 tells how Mordecai, a Jew, discovered the plan to kill the king, and the plot is thwarted as a result.
— Chapter 3 reveals the plan by Haman, the king's chief administrator, to destroy Mordecai and the Jews because of Mordecai's refusal to bow to him.
— Chapters 4:1-5:8 tell about Esther's willingness to intervene to save the Jews and her preparation of a banquet to tell the king of the plot.
— Chapters 6-7 record the king's decision to honor Mordecai and execute Haman.
— Chapters 8:1-9:19 contain the king's decree to reverse Haman's plan, the promotion of Mordecai, and reprisals against the enemies of the Jews.
— Chapters 9:20-10:3 tell about the inauguration of the festival of Purim.

The most unusual feature of the book of Esther is that it does not mention God in the story. Neither is there any reference to His worship. Despite this, the writer shows through a series of events how the Jews are saved from Haman's intended destruction. In the writer's view, God is active in the life of His people in everyday occurrences through their own decisions and actions. The reader will see the providence of God, meaning the provision and guidance for His people according to His will, in all the coincidences that occur in the story. *For God's people, nothing is coincidental or accidental; everything is providential* because God oversees all the events of their lives, even as He is at work through their lives as well.

The story of Esther should be read against the backdrop of world history. Over the centuries, many people have plotted to persecute and even destroy the Jewish people. Ultimately, God will not allow it. These attempts include the Egyptian army's pursuit of Moses and the Israelites in the fifteenth century BC, the Inquisition in Spain and Portugal by the medieval church in the thirteenth century, and even the Holocaust, or *Shoah*, by the Nazis in the twentieth century. Still, the Jewish people remain under God's protective hand. Esther is a faith-filled story that holds out the perpetual hope for the Jewish people in their ultimate deliverance from their enemies (4:14).

THE KING'S BANQUET

1 These events happened in the days of King Xerxes,* who reigned over 127 provinces stretching from India to Ethiopia.* ²At that time Xerxes ruled his empire from his royal throne at the fortress of Susa. ³In the third year of his reign, he gave a banquet for all his nobles and officials. He invited all the military officers of Persia and Media as well as the princes and nobles of the provinces. ⁴The celebration lasted 180 days—a tremendous display of the opulent wealth of his empire and the pomp and splendor of his majesty.

⁵When it was all over, the king gave a banquet for all the people, from the greatest to the least, who were in the fortress of Susa. It lasted for seven days and was held in the courtyard of the palace garden. ⁶The courtyard was beautifully decorated with white cotton curtains and blue hangings, which were fastened with white linen cords and purple ribbons to silver rings embedded in marble pillars. Gold and silver couches stood on a mosaic pavement of porphyry, marble, mother-of-pearl, and other costly stones.

⁷Drinks were served in gold goblets of many designs, and there was an abundance of royal wine, reflecting the king's generosity. ⁸By edict of the king, no limits were placed on the drinking, for the king had instructed all his palace officials to serve each man as much as he wanted.

⁹At the same time, Queen Vashti gave a banquet for the women in the royal palace of King Xerxes.

QUEEN VASHTI DEPOSED

¹⁰On the seventh day of the feast, when King Xerxes was in high spirits because of the wine, he told the seven eunuchs who attended him—Mehuman, Biztha, Harbona, Bigtha, Abagtha, Zethar, and Carcas—¹¹to bring Queen Vashti to him with the royal crown on her head. He wanted the nobles and all the other men to gaze on her beauty, for she was a very beautiful woman. ¹²But when they conveyed the king's order to Queen Vashti, she refused to come. This made the king furious, and he burned with anger.

¹³He immediately consulted with his wise advisers, who knew all the Persian laws and customs, for he always asked their advice. ¹⁴The names of these men were Carshena, Shethar, Admatha, Tarshish, Meres, Marsena, and Memucan—seven nobles of Persia and Media. They met with the king regularly and held the highest positions in the empire.

¹⁵"What must be done to Queen Vashti?" the king demanded. "What penalty does the law provide for a queen who refuses to obey the king's orders, properly sent through her eunuchs?"

¹⁶Memucan answered the king and his nobles, "Queen Vashti has wronged not only the king but also every noble and citizen throughout your empire. ¹⁷Women everywhere will begin to despise their husbands when they learn that Queen Vashti has refused to appear before the king. ¹⁸Before this day is out, the wives of all the king's nobles throughout Persia and Media will hear what the queen did and will start treating their husbands the same way. There will be no end to their contempt and anger.

¹⁹"So if it please the king, we suggest that you issue a written decree, a law of the Persians and Medes that cannot be revoked. It should order that Queen Vashti be forever banished from the presence of King Xerxes, and that the king should choose another queen more worthy than she. ²⁰When this decree is published throughout the king's vast empire, husbands everywhere, whatever their rank, will receive proper respect from their wives!"

²¹The king and his nobles thought this made good sense, so he followed Memucan's counsel. ²²He sent letters to all parts of the empire, to each province in its own script and language, proclaiming that every man should be the ruler of his own home and should say whatever he pleases.*

ESTHER BECOMES QUEEN

2 But after Xerxes' anger had subsided, he began thinking about Vashti and what she had done and the decree he had made. ²So his personal attendants suggested, "Let us search the empire to find beautiful young virgins for the king. ³Let the king appoint agents in each province to bring these beautiful young women into the royal harem at the fortress of Susa. Hegai, the king's eunuch in charge of the harem, will see that they are all given beauty treatments. ⁴After that, the young woman who most pleases the king will be made queen instead of Vashti." This advice was very appealing to the king, so he put the plan into effect.

⁵At that time there was a Jewish man in the fortress of Susa whose name was Mordecai son of Jair. He was from the tribe of Benjamin and was a descendant of Kish and Shimei. ⁶His family* had been among those who, with King Jehoiachin* of Judah, had been exiled from Jerusalem to Babylon by King Nebuchadnezzar. ⁷This man had a very beautiful and lovely young cousin, Hadassah, who was also called Esther. When her father and mother died, Mordecai adopted her into his family and raised her as his own daughter.

⁸As a result of the king's decree, Esther, along with many other young women, was brought to the king's harem at the fortress of Susa and placed in Hegai's care. ⁹Hegai was very impressed with Esther and treated her kindly. He quickly ordered a special menu for her and provided her

1:1a Hebrew *Ahasuerus*, another name for Xerxes; also throughout the book of Esther. Xerxes reigned 486–465 B.C. 1:1b Hebrew *to Cush*. 1:22 Or *and should speak in the language of his own people*. 2:6a Hebrew *He*. 2:6b Hebrew *Jeconiah*, a variant spelling of Jehoiachin.

with beauty treatments. He also assigned her seven maids specially chosen from the king's palace, and he moved her and her maids into the best place in the harem.

[10] Esther had not told anyone of her nationality and family background, because Mordecai had directed her not to do so. [11] Every day Mordecai would take a walk near the courtyard of the harem to find out about Esther and what was happening to her.

[12] Before each young woman was taken to the king's bed, she was given the prescribed twelve months of beauty treatments—six months with oil of myrrh, followed by six months with special perfumes and ointments. [13] When it was time for her to go to the king's palace, she was given her choice of whatever clothing or jewelry she wanted to take from the harem. [14] That evening she was taken to the king's private rooms, and the next morning she was brought to the second harem,* where the king's wives lived. There she would be under the care of Shaashgaz, the king's eunuch in charge of the concubines. She would never go to the king again unless he had especially enjoyed her and requested her by name.

[15] Esther was the daughter of Abihail, who was Mordecai's uncle. (Mordecai had adopted his younger cousin Esther.) When it was Esther's turn to go to the king, she accepted the advice of Hegai, the eunuch in charge of the harem. She asked for nothing except what he suggested, and she was admired by everyone who saw her. [16] Esther was taken to King Xerxes at the royal palace in early winter* of the seventh year of his reign. [17] And the king loved Esther more than any of the other young women. He was so delighted with her that he set the royal crown on her head and declared her queen instead of Vashti. [18] To celebrate the occasion, he gave a great banquet in Esther's honor for all his nobles and officials, declaring a public holiday for the provinces and giving generous gifts to everyone.

[19] Even after all the young women had been transferred to the second harem* and Mordecai had become a palace official,* [20] Esther continued to keep her family background and nationality a secret. She was still following Mordecai's directions, just as she did when she lived in his home.

MORDECAI'S LOYALTY TO THE KING

[21] One day as Mordecai was on duty at the king's gate, two of the king's eunuchs, Bigthana* and Teresh—who were guards at the door of the king's private quarters—became angry at King Xerxes and plotted to assassinate him. [22] But Mordecai heard about the plot and gave the information to Queen Esther. She then told the king about it and gave Mordecai credit for the report. [23] When an investigation was made and Mordecai's story was found to be true, the two men were impaled on a sharpened pole. This was all recorded in *The Book of the History of King Xerxes' Reign.*

HAMAN'S PLOT AGAINST THE JEWS

3 Some time later King Xerxes promoted Haman son of Hammedatha the Agagite over all the other nobles, making him the most powerful official in the empire. [2] All the king's officials would bow down before Haman to show him respect whenever he passed by, for so the king had commanded. But Mordecai refused to bow down or show him respect.

[3] Then the palace officials at the king's gate asked Mordecai, "Why are you disobeying the king's command?" [4] They spoke to him day after day, but still he refused to comply with the order. So they spoke to Haman about this to see if he would tolerate Mordecai's conduct, since Mordecai had told them he was a Jew.

[5] When Haman saw that Mordecai would not bow down or show him respect, he was filled with rage. [6] He had learned of Mordecai's nationality, so he decided it was not enough to lay hands on Mordecai alone. Instead, he looked for a way to destroy all the Jews throughout the entire empire of Xerxes.

[7] So in the month of April,* during the twelfth year of King Xerxes' reign, lots were cast in Haman's presence (the lots were called *purim*) to determine the best day and month to take action. And the day selected was March 7, nearly a year later.*

[8] Then Haman approached King Xerxes and said, "There is a certain race of people scattered through all the provinces of your empire who keep themselves separate from everyone else. Their laws are different from those of any other people, and they refuse to obey the laws of the king. So it is not in the king's interest to let them live. [9] If it please the king, issue a decree that they be destroyed, and I will give 10,000 large sacks* of silver to the government administrators to be deposited in the royal treasury."

[10] The king agreed, confirming his decision by removing his signet ring from his finger and giving it to Haman son of Hammedatha the Agagite, the enemy of the Jews. [11] The king said, "The money and the people are both yours to do with as you see fit."

[12] So on April 17* the king's secretaries were summoned, and a decree was written exactly

2:14 Or *to another part of the harem.* 2:16 Hebrew *in the tenth month, the month of Tebeth.* A number of dates in the book of Esther can be cross-checked with dates in surviving Persian records and related accurately to our modern calendar. This month of the ancient Hebrew lunar calendar occurred within the months of December 479 B.C. and January 478 B.C. 2:19a The meaning of the Hebrew is uncertain. 2:19b Hebrew *and Mordecai was sitting in the gate of the king.* 2:21 Hebrew *Bigthan;* compare 6:2. 3:7a Hebrew *in the first month, the month of Nisan.* This month of the ancient Hebrew lunar calendar occurred within the months of April and May 474 B.C.; also see note on 2:16. 3:7b As in 3:13, which reads *the thirteenth day of the twelfth month, the month of Adar;* Hebrew reads *in the twelfth month,* of the ancient Hebrew lunar calendar. The date selected was March 7, 473 B.C.; also see note on 2:16. 3:9 Hebrew *10,000 talents,* about 375 tons or 340 metric tons in weight. 3:12 Hebrew *On the thirteenth day of the first month,* of the ancient Hebrew lunar calendar. This day was April 17, 474 B.C.; also see note on 2:16.

as Haman dictated. It was sent to the king's highest officers, the governors of the respective provinces, and the nobles of each province in their own scripts and languages. The decree was written in the name of King Xerxes and sealed with the king's signet ring. [13] Dispatches were sent by swift messengers into all the provinces of the empire, giving the order that all Jews—young and old, including women and children—must be killed, slaughtered, and annihilated on a single day. This was scheduled to happen on March 7 of the next year.* The property of the Jews would be given to those who killed them.

[14] A copy of this decree was to be issued as law in every province and proclaimed to all peoples, so that they would be ready to do their duty on the appointed day. [15] At the king's command, the decree went out by swift messengers, and it was also proclaimed in the fortress of Susa. Then the king and Haman sat down to drink, but the city of Susa fell into confusion.

MORDECAI REQUESTS ESTHER'S HELP

4 When Mordecai learned about all that had been done, he tore his clothes, put on burlap and ashes, and went out into the city, crying with a loud and bitter wail. [2] He went as far as the gate of the palace, for no one was allowed to enter the palace gate while wearing clothes of mourning. [3] And as news of the king's decree reached all the provinces, there was great mourning among the Jews. They fasted, wept, and wailed, and many people lay in burlap and ashes.

[4] When Queen Esther's maids and eunuchs came and told her about Mordecai, she was deeply distressed. She sent clothing to him to replace the burlap, but he refused it. [5] Then Esther sent for Hathach, one of the king's eunuchs who had been appointed as her attendant. She ordered him to go to Mordecai and find out what was troubling him and why he was in mourning. [6] So Hathach went out to Mordecai in the square in front of the palace gate.

[7] Mordecai told him the whole story, including the exact amount of money Haman had promised to pay into the royal treasury for the destruction of the Jews. [8] Mordecai gave Hathach a copy of the decree issued in Susa that called for the death of all Jews. He asked Hathach to show it to Esther and explain the situation to her. He also asked Hathach to direct her to go to the king to beg for mercy and plead for her people. [9] So Hathach returned to Esther with Mordecai's message.

[10] Then Esther told Hathach to go back and relay this message to Mordecai: [11] "All the king's officials and even the people in the provinces know that anyone who appears before the king in his inner court without being invited is doomed to die unless the king holds out his gold scepter. And the king has not called for me to come to him for thirty days." [12] So Hathach* gave Esther's message to Mordecai.

[13] Mordecai sent this reply to Esther: "Don't think for a moment that because you're in the palace you will escape when all other Jews are killed. [14] If you keep quiet at a time like this, deliverance and relief for the Jews will arise from some other place, but you and your relatives will die. Who knows if perhaps you were made queen for just such a time as this?"

[15] Then Esther sent this reply to Mordecai: [16] "Go and gather together all the Jews of Susa and fast for me. Do not eat or drink for three days, night or day. My maids and I will do the same. And then, though it is against the law, I will go in to see the king. If I must die, I must die." [17] So Mordecai went away and did everything as Esther had ordered him.

ESTHER'S REQUEST TO THE KING

5 On the third day of the fast, Esther put on her royal robes and entered the inner court of the palace, just across from the king's hall. The king was sitting on his royal throne, facing the entrance. [2] When he saw Queen Esther standing there in the inner court, he welcomed her and held out the gold scepter to her. So Esther approached and touched the end of the scepter.

[3] Then the king asked her, "What do you want, Queen Esther? What is your request? I will give it to you, even if it is half the kingdom!"

[4] And Esther replied, "If it please the king, let the king and Haman come today to a banquet I have prepared for the king."

[5] The king turned to his attendants and said, "Tell Haman to come quickly to a banquet, as Esther has requested." So the king and Haman went to Esther's banquet.

[6] And while they were drinking wine, the king said to Esther, "Now tell me what you really want. What is your request? I will give it to you, even if it is half the kingdom!"

[7] Esther replied, "This is my request and deepest wish. [8] If I have found favor with the king, and if it pleases the king to grant my request and do what I ask, please come with Haman tomorrow to the banquet I will prepare for you. Then I will explain what this is all about."

HAMAN'S PLAN TO KILL MORDECAI

[9] Haman was a happy man as he left the banquet! But when he saw Mordecai sitting at the palace gate, not standing up or trembling nervously before him, Haman became furious. [10] However, he restrained himself and went on home.

Then Haman gathered together his friends and Zeresh, his wife, [11] and boasted to them about his great wealth and his many children. He bragged about the honors the king had given

---

3:13 Hebrew *on the thirteenth day of the twelfth month, the month of Adar,* of the ancient Hebrew lunar calendar. The date selected was March 7, 473 B.C.; also see note on 2:16. 4:12 As in Greek version; Hebrew reads *they.*

him and how he had been promoted over all the other nobles and officials.

¹²Then Haman added, "And that's not all! Queen Esther invited only me and the king himself to the banquet she prepared for us. And she has invited me to dine with her and the king again tomorrow!" ¹³Then he added, "But this is all worth nothing as long as I see Mordecai the Jew just sitting there at the palace gate."

¹⁴So Haman's wife, Zeresh, and all his friends suggested, "Set up a sharpened pole that stands seventy-five feet* tall, and in the morning ask the king to impale Mordecai on it. When this is done, you can go on your merry way to the banquet with the king." This pleased Haman, and he ordered the pole set up.

THE KING HONORS MORDECAI

6 That night the king had trouble sleeping, so he ordered an attendant to bring the book of the history of his reign so it could be read to him. ²In those records he discovered an account of how Mordecai had exposed the plot of Bigthana and Teresh, two of the eunuchs who guarded the door to the king's private quarters. They had plotted to assassinate King Xerxes.

³"What reward or recognition did we ever give Mordecai for this?" the king asked.

His attendants replied, "Nothing has been done for him."

⁴"Who is that in the outer court?" the king inquired. As it happened, Haman had just arrived in the outer court of the palace to ask the king to impale Mordecai on the pole he had prepared.

⁵So the attendants replied to the king, "Haman is out in the court."

"Bring him in," the king ordered. ⁶So Haman came in, and the king said, "What should I do to honor a man who truly pleases me?"

Haman thought to himself, "Whom would the king wish to honor more than me?" ⁷So he replied, "If the king wishes to honor someone, ⁸he should bring out one of the king's own royal robes, as well as a horse that the king himself has ridden—one with a royal emblem on its head. ⁹Let the robes and the horse be handed over to one of the king's most noble officials. And let him see that the man whom the king wishes to honor is dressed in the king's robes and led through the city square on the king's horse. Have the official shout as they go, 'This is what the king does for someone he wishes to honor!'"

¹⁰"Excellent!" the king said to Haman. "Quick! Take the robes and my horse, and do just as you have said for Mordecai the Jew, who sits at the gate of the palace. Leave out nothing you have suggested!"

¹¹So Haman took the robes and put them on Mordecai, placed him on the king's own horse, and led him through the city square, shouting, "This is what the king does for someone he wishes to honor!" ¹²Afterward Mordecai returned

to the palace gate, but Haman hurried home dejected and completely humiliated.

¹³When Haman told his wife, Zeresh, and all his friends what had happened, his wise advisers and his wife said, "Since Mordecai—this man who has humiliated you—is of Jewish birth, you will never succeed in your plans against him. It will be fatal to continue opposing him."

¹⁴While they were still talking, the king's eunuchs arrived and quickly took Haman to the banquet Esther had prepared.

THE KING EXECUTES HAMAN

7 So the king and Haman went to Queen Esther's banquet. ²On this second occasion, while they were drinking wine, the king again said to Esther, "Tell me what you want, Queen Esther. What is your request? I will give it to you, even if it is half the kingdom!"

³Queen Esther replied, "If I have found favor with the king, and if it pleases the king to grant my request, I ask that my life and the lives of my people will be spared. ⁴For my people and I have been sold to those who would kill, slaughter, and annihilate us. If we had merely been sold as slaves, I could remain quiet, for that would be too trivial a matter to warrant disturbing the king."

⁵"Who would do such a thing?" King Xerxes demanded. "Who would be so presumptuous as to touch you?"

⁶Esther replied, "This wicked Haman is our adversary and our enemy." Haman grew pale with fright before the king and queen. ⁷Then the king jumped to his feet in a rage and went out into the palace garden.

Haman, however, stayed behind to plead for his life with Queen Esther, for he knew that the king intended to kill him. ⁸In despair he fell on the couch where Queen Esther was reclining, just as the king was returning from the palace garden.

The king exclaimed, "Will he even assault the queen right here in the palace, before my very eyes?" And as soon as the king spoke, his attendants covered Haman's face, signaling his doom.

⁹Then Harbona, one of the king's eunuchs, said, "Haman has set up a sharpened pole that stands seventy-five feet* tall in his own courtyard. He intended to use it to impale Mordecai, the man who saved the king from assassination."

"Then impale Haman on it!" the king ordered. ¹⁰So they impaled Haman on the pole he had set up for Mordecai, and the king's anger subsided.

A DECREE TO HELP THE JEWS

8 On that same day King Xerxes gave the property of Haman, the enemy of the Jews, to Queen Esther. Then Mordecai was brought before the king, for Esther had told the king how they

---

5:14 Hebrew *50 cubits* [23 meters].   7:9 Hebrew *50 cubits* [23 meters].

were related. [2]The king took off his signet ring—which he had taken back from Haman—and gave it to Mordecai. And Esther appointed Mordecai to be in charge of Haman's property.

[3]Then Esther went again before the king, falling down at his feet and begging him with tears to stop the evil plot devised by Haman the Agagite against the Jews. [4]Again the king held out the gold scepter to Esther. So she rose and stood before him.

[5]Esther said, "If it please the king, and if I have found favor with him, and if he thinks it is right, and if I am pleasing to him, let there be a decree that reverses the orders of Haman son of Hammedatha the Agagite, who ordered that Jews throughout all the king's provinces should be destroyed. [6]For how can I endure to see my people and my family slaughtered and destroyed?"

[7]Then King Xerxes said to Queen Esther and Mordecai the Jew, "I have given Esther the property of Haman, and he has been impaled on a pole because he tried to destroy the Jews. [8]Now go ahead and send a message to the Jews in the king's name, telling them whatever you want, and seal it with the king's signet ring. But remember that whatever has already been written in the king's name and sealed with his signet ring can never be revoked."

[9]So on June 25* the king's secretaries were summoned, and a decree was written exactly as Mordecai dictated. It was sent to the Jews and to the highest officers, the governors, and the nobles of all the 127 provinces stretching from India to Ethiopia.* The decree was written in the scripts and languages of all the peoples of the empire, including that of the Jews. [10]The decree was written in the name of King Xerxes and sealed with the king's signet ring. Mordecai sent the dispatches by swift messengers, who rode fast horses especially bred for the king's service.

[11]The king's decree gave the Jews in every city authority to unite to defend their lives. They were allowed to kill, slaughter, and annihilate anyone of any nationality or province who might attack them or their children and wives, and to take the property of their enemies. [12]The day chosen for this event throughout all the provinces of King Xerxes was March 7 of the next year.*

[13]A copy of this decree was to be issued as law in every province and proclaimed to all peoples, so that the Jews would be ready to take revenge on their enemies on the appointed day. [14]So urged on by the king's command, the messengers rode out swiftly on fast horses bred for the king's service. The same decree was also proclaimed in the fortress of Susa.

[15]Then Mordecai left the king's presence, wearing the royal robe of blue and white, the great crown of gold, and an outer cloak of fine linen and purple. And the people of Susa celebrated the new decree. [16]The Jews were filled with joy and gladness and were honored everywhere. [17]In every province and city, wherever the king's decree arrived, the Jews rejoiced and had a great celebration and declared a public festival and holiday. And many of the people of the land became Jews themselves, for they feared what the Jews might do to them.

THE VICTORY OF THE JEWS

9 So on March 7* the two decrees of the king were put into effect. On that day, the enemies of the Jews had hoped to overpower them, but quite the opposite happened. It was the Jews who overpowered their enemies. [2]The Jews gathered in their cities throughout all the king's provinces to attack anyone who tried to harm them. But no one could make a stand against them, for everyone was afraid of them. [3]And all the nobles of the provinces, the highest officers, the governors, and the royal officials helped the Jews for fear of Mordecai. [4]For Mordecai had been promoted in the king's palace, and his fame spread throughout all the provinces as he became more and more powerful.

[5]So the Jews went ahead on the appointed day and struck down their enemies with the sword. They killed and annihilated their enemies and did as they pleased with those who hated them. [6]In the fortress of Susa itself, the Jews killed 500 men. [7]They also killed Parshandatha, Dalphon, Aspatha, [8]Poratha, Adalia, Aridatha, [9]Parmashta, Arisai, Aridai, and Vaizatha—[10]the ten sons of Haman son of Hammedatha, the enemy of the Jews. But they did not take any plunder.

[11]That very day, when the king was informed of the number of people killed in the fortress of Susa, [12]he called for Queen Esther. He said, "The Jews have killed 500 men in the fortress of Susa alone, as well as Haman's ten sons. If they have done that here, what has happened in the rest of the provinces? But now, what more do you want? It will be granted to you; tell me and I will do it."

[13]Esther responded, "If it please the king, give the Jews in Susa permission to do again tomorrow as they have done today, and let the bodies of Haman's ten sons be impaled on a pole."

[14]So the king agreed, and the decree was announced in Susa. And they impaled the bodies of Haman's ten sons. [15]Then the Jews at Susa gathered together on March 8* and killed 300 more men, and again they took no plunder.

[16]Meanwhile, the other Jews throughout the king's provinces had gathered together to defend

---

8:9a Hebrew *on the twenty-third day of the third month, the month of Sivan,* of the ancient Hebrew lunar calendar. This day was June 25, 474 B.C.; also see note on 2:16.   8:9b Hebrew *to Cush.* 8:12 Hebrew *the thirteenth day of the twelfth month, the month of Adar,* of the ancient Hebrew lunar calendar. The date selected was March 7, 473 B.C.; also see note on 2:16.   9:1 Hebrew *on the thirteenth day of the twelfth month, the month of Adar,* of the ancient Hebrew lunar calendar. This day was March 7, 473 B.C.; also see note on 2:16.   9:15 Hebrew *the fourteenth day of the month of Adar,* of the ancient Hebrew lunar calendar. This day was March 8, 473 B.C.; also see note on 2:16.

their lives. They gained relief from all their enemies, killing 75,000 of those who hated them. But they did not take any plunder. ¹⁷This was done throughout the provinces on March 7, and on March 8 they rested,* celebrating their victory with a day of feasting and gladness. ¹⁸(The Jews at Susa killed their enemies on March 7 and again on March 8, then rested on March 9,* making that their day of feasting and gladness.) ¹⁹So to this day, rural Jews living in remote villages celebrate an annual festival and holiday on the appointed day in late winter,* when they rejoice and send gifts of food to each other.

THE FESTIVAL OF PURIM

²⁰Mordecai recorded these events and sent letters to the Jews near and far, throughout all the provinces of King Xerxes, ²¹calling on them to celebrate an annual festival on these two days.* ²²He told them to celebrate these days with feasting and gladness and by giving gifts of food to each other and presents to the poor. This would commemorate a time when the Jews gained relief from their enemies, when their sorrow was turned into gladness and their mourning into joy.

²³So the Jews accepted Mordecai's proposal and adopted this annual custom. ²⁴Haman son of Hammedatha the Agagite, the enemy of the Jews, had plotted to crush and destroy them on the date determined by casting lots (the lots were called *purim*). ²⁵But when Esther came before the king, he issued a decree causing Haman's evil plot to backfire, and Haman and his sons were impaled on a sharpened pole. ²⁶That is why this celebration is called Purim, because it is the ancient word for casting lots.

So because of Mordecai's letter and because of what they had experienced, ²⁷the Jews throughout the realm agreed to inaugurate this tradition and to pass it on to their descendants and to all who became Jews. They declared they would never fail to celebrate these two prescribed days at the appointed time each year. ²⁸These days would be remembered and kept from generation to generation and celebrated by every family throughout the provinces and cities of the empire. This Festival of Purim would never cease to be celebrated among the Jews, nor would the memory of what happened ever die out among their descendants.

²⁹Then Queen Esther, the daughter of Abihail, along with Mordecai the Jew, wrote another letter putting the queen's full authority behind Mordecai's letter to establish the Festival of Purim. ³⁰Letters wishing peace and security were sent to the Jews throughout the 127 provinces of the empire of Xerxes. ³¹These letters established the Festival of Purim—an annual celebration of these days at the appointed time, decreed by both Mordecai the Jew and Queen Esther. (The people decided to observe this festival, just as they had decided for themselves and their descendants to establish the times of fasting and mourning.) ³²So the command of Esther confirmed the practices of Purim, and it was all written down in the records.

THE GREATNESS OF XERXES AND MORDECAI

10 King Xerxes imposed a tribute throughout his empire, even to the distant coastlands. ²His great achievements and the full account of the greatness of Mordecai, whom the king had promoted, are recorded in *The Book of the History of the Kings of Media and Persia.* ³Mordecai the Jew became the prime minister, with authority next to that of King Xerxes himself. He was very great among the Jews, who held him in high esteem, because he continued to work for the good of his people and to speak up for the welfare of all their descendants.

9:17 Hebrew *on the thirteenth day of the month of Adar, and on the fourteenth day they rested.* These days were March 7 and 8, 473 B.C.; also see note on 2:16.   9:18 Hebrew *hilled their enemies on the thirteenth day and the fourteenth day, and then rested on the fifteenth day,* of the Hebrew month of Adar.   9:19 Hebrew *on the fourteenth day of the month of Adar.* This day of the ancient Hebrew lunar calendar occurs in February or March.   9:21 Hebrew *on the fourteenth and fifteenth days of Adar,* of the ancient Hebrew lunar calendar.

JOB

JON HUNTZINGER, PHD

The Bible contains two types of ancient wisdom literature. The first type, *proverbial wisdom literature*, is found in the book of Proverbs and is primarily instructional in nature. It originated in Egypt and provides insight into how to live daily life. The second type of wisdom literature originated in Mesopotamia and *looks at the large questions of life through stories and discourses*. The book of Job is an example of this second type and addresses the question, "Why do bad things happen to good people?" The technical term for this type of question is *theodicy*: If God is good, loving, and powerful, then why does He allow good, innocent people to suffer? This question is an old one, and men and women have asked it for thousands of years.

The book of Job is the story of one such person who asks that question. At the beginning of the book, the anonymous writer describes Job as blameless, and even God describes him in that way (1:1, 8; 2:3). This description does not mean Job is sinless or perfect in his life, but it does mean he lives in the right way given the understanding he has. The word *blameless* is the translation of a word that can also mean 'whole' or 'complete.' The writer introduces Job as a complete man who pleases God in the sacrifices that he gives, but he still undergoes a terrible ordeal when his property is stripped from him, his family taken from him, and his health afflicted by Satan. Satan asks God for permission to test Job to discover the sincerity of his worship to God (1:6–2:10). "Yes, but Job has good reason to fear God" (1:9). Satan makes the claim that Job only worships God because of the blessings God gave him rather than because he really loves God.

Most of the book of Job recounts the discourse—the difficult conversations—Job has with his friends. They try to help him make sense of the suffering and the tragedy that has fallen upon him (chapters 4–37). Job's friend Eliphaz explains that Job must have sinned against God, which accounts for his calamity. Innocent people do not experience loss or affliction as Job has, reasons Eliphaz. Another friend, Bildad, agrees with Eliphaz and tells Job he must repent. A third friend, Zophar, rebukes Job for defending himself and declaring his innocence. He says that Job deserves even greater judgment for whatever he has done

to bring on all of this suffering. All of Job's friends believe he is suffering because of his sin. Job strongly rejects their explanations and asserts that he is blameless.

Despite their differences, Job and his three friends all share a common understanding of the way God works. They all believe sin against God brings judgment and faithfulness to Him brings blessing. But Job has been faithful, yet he still suffers. Can anyone explain his suffering? Then a fourth friend, Elihu, rebukes Job's other friends because of their counsel as well as Job for his defense. Elihu simply says God is just, majestic, and beyond human understanding in all He does. After all this, God Himself speaks to Job and reminds him that there are things he simply cannot know (chapters 38–41). Was Job present at Creation? Did he form the animals? Does Job cause rain to fall? When Job acknowledges that there are things he does not know, such as the reason for his suffering, and repents for doubting God in the way that Satan doubts Him, God restores Job's life and fortunes (chapter 42).

The question asked in the book of Job is the one the disciples ask Jesus (John 9:1–7). One day they see a man who has been blind since birth. Since many people at that time saw blindness as a condition related to sin and judgment, they ask Jesus, "Why was this man born blind? Was it because of his own sins or his parents' sins?" (v. 2). By asking this question, the disciples reveal that they share the theology of Job and his friends. Jesus points them in a different direction with his answer: "It was not because of his sins or his parents' sins. . . . This happened so the power of God could be seen in him. We must quickly carry out the tasks assigned us by the one who sent us" (vv. 3–4). Jesus moves the question from "Why has this happened?" to "What can be done?" to show God's presence in such circumstances. The book of Job addresses the difficult question, "Why do bad things happen to blameless people?" by answering that some events and experiences in life do not have any easy answers. There is a limit to what theology can answer. God remains God despite the hard circumstances that people sometimes experience.

PROLOGUE

1 There once was a man named Job who lived in the land of Uz. He was blameless—a man of complete integrity. He feared God and stayed away from evil. ² He had seven sons and three daughters. ³ He owned 7,000 sheep, 3,000 camels, 500 teams of oxen, and 500 female donkeys. He also had many servants. He was, in fact, the richest person in that entire area.

⁴ Job's sons would take turns preparing feasts in their homes, and they would also invite their three sisters to celebrate with them. ⁵ When these celebrations ended—sometimes after several days—Job would purify his children. He would get up early in the morning and offer a burnt offering for each of them. For Job said to himself, "Perhaps my children have sinned and have cursed God in their hearts." This was Job's regular practice.

JOB'S FIRST TEST

⁶ One day the members of the heavenly court* came to present themselves before the LORD, and the Accuser, Satan,* came with them. ⁷ "Where have you come from?" the LORD asked Satan.

Satan answered the LORD, "I have been patrolling the earth, watching everything that's going on."

⁸ Then the LORD asked Satan, "Have you noticed my servant Job? He is the finest man in all the earth. He is blameless—a man of complete integrity. He fears God and stays away from evil."

⁹ Satan replied to the LORD, "Yes, but Job has good reason to fear God. ¹⁰ You have always put a wall of protection around him and his home and his property. You have made him prosper in everything he does. Look how rich he is! ¹¹ But reach out and take away everything he has, and he will surely curse you to your face!"

¹² "All right, you may test him," the LORD said to Satan. "Do whatever you want with everything he possesses, but don't harm him physically." So Satan left the LORD's presence.

¹³ One day when Job's sons and daughters were feasting at the oldest brother's house, ¹⁴ a messenger arrived at Job's home with this news: "Your oxen were plowing, with the donkeys feeding beside them, ¹⁵ when the Sabeans raided us. They stole all the animals and killed all the farmhands. I am the only one who escaped to tell you."

¹⁶ While he was still speaking, another messenger arrived with this news: "The fire of God has fallen from heaven and burned up your sheep and all the shepherds. I am the only one who escaped to tell you."

¹⁷ While he was still speaking, a third messenger arrived with this news: "Three bands of Chaldean raiders have stolen your camels and killed your servants. I am the only one who escaped to tell you."

¹⁸ While he was still speaking, another messenger arrived with this news: "Your sons and daughters were feasting in their oldest brother's home. ¹⁹ Suddenly, a powerful wind swept in from the wilderness and hit the house on all sides. The house collapsed, and all your children are dead. I am the only one who escaped to tell you."

²⁰ Job stood up and tore his robe in grief. Then he shaved his head and fell to the ground to worship. ²¹ He said,

"I came naked from my mother's womb,
    and I will be naked when I leave.
The LORD gave me what I had,
    and the LORD has taken it away.
Praise the name of the LORD!"

²² In all of this, Job did not sin by blaming God.

JOB'S SECOND TEST

2 One day the members of the heavenly court* came again to present themselves before the LORD, and the Accuser, Satan,* came with them. ² "Where have you come from?" the LORD asked Satan.

Satan answered the LORD, "I have been patrolling the earth, watching everything that's going on."

³ Then the LORD asked Satan, "Have you noticed my servant Job? He is the finest man in all the earth. He is blameless—a man of complete integrity. He fears God and stays away from evil. And he has maintained his integrity, even though you urged me to harm him without cause."

⁴ Satan replied to the LORD, "Skin for skin! A man will give up everything he has to save his life. ⁵ But reach out and take away his health, and he will surely curse you to your face!"

⁶ "All right, do with him as you please," the LORD said to Satan. "But spare his life." ⁷ So Satan left the LORD's presence, and he struck Job with terrible boils from head to foot.

⁸ Job scraped his skin with a piece of broken pottery as he sat among the ashes. ⁹ His wife said to him, "Are you still trying to maintain your integrity? Curse God and die."

¹⁰ But Job replied, "You talk like a foolish woman. Should we accept only good things from the hand of God and never anything bad?" So in all this, Job said nothing wrong.

JOB'S THREE FRIENDS SHARE HIS ANGUISH

¹¹ When three of Job's friends heard of the tragedy he had suffered, they got together and traveled from their homes to comfort and console him. Their names were Eliphaz the Temanite, Bildad the Shuhite, and Zophar the Naamathite. ¹² When they saw Job from a distance, they scarcely recognized him. Wailing loudly, they tore their

---

1:6a Hebrew *the sons of God.*   1:6b Hebrew *and the satan;* similarly throughout this chapter.   2:1a Hebrew *the sons of God.* 2:1b Hebrew *and the satan;* similarly throughout this chapter.

robes and threw dust into the air over their heads to show their grief. [13] Then they sat on the ground with him for seven days and nights. No one said a word to Job, for they saw that his suffering was too great for words.

JOB'S FIRST SPEECH

3 At last Job spoke, and he cursed the day of his birth. [2] He said:

[3] "Let the day of my birth be erased,
and the night I was conceived.
[4] Let that day be turned to darkness.
Let it be lost even to God on high,
and let no light shine on it.
[5] Let the darkness and utter gloom claim that
day for its own.
Let a black cloud overshadow it,
and let the darkness terrify it.
[6] Let that night be blotted off the calendar,
never again to be counted among the days
of the year,
never again to appear among the months.
[7] Let that night be childless.
Let it have no joy.
[8] Let those who are experts at cursing—
whose cursing could rouse Leviathan*—
curse that day.
[9] Let its morning stars remain dark.
Let it hope for light, but in vain;
may it never see the morning light.
[10] Curse that day for failing to shut my
mother's womb,
for letting me be born to see all this trouble.

[11] "Why wasn't I born dead?
Why didn't I die as I came from the womb?
[12] Why was I laid on my mother's lap?
Why did she nurse me at her breasts?
[13] Had I died at birth, I would now be at peace.
I would be asleep and at rest.
[14] I would rest with the world's kings and
prime ministers,
whose great buildings now lie in ruins.
[15] I would rest with princes, rich in gold,
whose palaces were filled with silver.
[16] Why wasn't I buried like a stillborn child,
like a baby who never lives to see the light?
[17] For in death the wicked cause no trouble,
and the weary are at rest.
[18] Even captives are at ease in death,
with no guards to curse them.
[19] Rich and poor are both there,
and the slave is free from his master.

[20] "Oh, why give light to those in misery,
and life to those who are bitter?
[21] They long for death, and it won't come.
They search for death more eagerly than
for hidden treasure.
[22] They're filled with joy when they finally die,
and rejoice when they find the grave.

[23] Why is life given to those with no future,
those God has surrounded with
difficulties?
[24] I cannot eat for sighing;
my groans pour out like water.
[25] What I always feared has happened to me.
What I dreaded has come true.
[26] I have no peace, no quietness.
I have no rest; only trouble comes."

ELIPHAZ'S FIRST RESPONSE TO JOB

4 Then Eliphaz the Temanite replied to Job:

[2] "Will you be patient and let me say a word?
For who could keep from speaking out?

[3] "In the past you have encouraged
many people;
you have strengthened those who
were weak.
[4] Your words have supported those who were
falling;
you encouraged those with shaky knees.
[5] But now when trouble strikes, you lose heart.
You are terrified when it touches you.
[6] Doesn't your reverence for God give you
confidence?
Doesn't your life of integrity give you
hope?

[7] "Stop and think! Do the innocent die?
When have the upright been destroyed?
[8] My experience shows that those who
plant trouble
and cultivate evil will harvest the same.
[9] A breath from God destroys them.
They vanish in a blast of his anger.
[10] The lion roars and the wildcat snarls,
but the teeth of strong lions will be
broken.
[11] The fierce lion will starve for lack of prey,
and the cubs of the lioness will be
scattered.

[12] "This truth was given to me in secret,
as though whispered in my ear.
[13] It came to me in a disturbing vision at night,
when people are in a deep sleep.
[14] Fear gripped me,
and my bones trembled.
[15] A spirit* swept past my face,
and my hair stood on end.*
[16] The spirit stopped, but I couldn't see
its shape.
There was a form before my eyes.
In the silence I heard a voice say,
[17] 'Can a mortal be innocent before God?
Can anyone be pure before the Creator?'

3:8 The identification of Leviathan is disputed, ranging from an earthly creature to a mythical sea monster in ancient literature. **4:15a** Or *wind;* also in 4:16. **4:15b** Or *its wind sent shivers up my spine.*

¹⁸ "If God does not trust his own angels
  and has charged his messengers with
    foolishness,
¹⁹ how much less will he trust people made
    of clay!
  They are made of dust, crushed as easily
    as a moth.
²⁰ They are alive in the morning but dead
    by evening,
  gone forever without a trace.
²¹ Their tent-cords are pulled and the tent
    collapses,
  and they die in ignorance.

ELIPHAZ'S RESPONSE CONTINUES

5 ¹ "Cry for help, but will anyone answer
    you?
  Which of the angels* will help you?
² Surely resentment destroys the fool,
  and jealousy kills the simple.
³ I have seen that fools may be successful for
    the moment,
  but then comes sudden disaster.
⁴ Their children are abandoned far from help;
  they are crushed in court with no one to
    defend them.
⁵ The hungry devour their harvest,
  even when it is guarded by brambles.*
  The thirsty pant after their wealth.*
⁶ But evil does not spring from the soil,
  and trouble does not sprout from the earth.
⁷ People are born for trouble
  as readily as sparks fly up from a fire.

⁸ "If I were you, I would go to God
  and present my case to him.
⁹ He does great things too marvelous to
    understand.
  He performs countless miracles.
¹⁰ He gives rain for the earth
  and water for the fields.
¹¹ He gives prosperity to the poor
  and protects those who suffer.
¹² He frustrates the plans of schemers
  so the work of their hands will not
    succeed.
¹³ He traps the wise in their own cleverness
  so their cunning schemes are thwarted.
¹⁴ They find it is dark in the daytime,
  and they grope at noon as if it were night.
¹⁵ He rescues the poor from the cutting words
    of the strong,
  and rescues them from the clutches of the
    powerful.
¹⁶ And so at last the poor have hope,
  and the snapping jaws of the wicked
    are shut.

¹⁷ "But consider the joy of those corrected
    by God!
  Do not despise the discipline of the
    Almighty when you sin.

¹⁸ For though he wounds, he also bandages.
  He strikes, but his hands also heal.
¹⁹ From six disasters he will rescue you;
  even in the seventh, he will keep you
    from evil.
²⁰ He will save you from death in time of
    famine,
  from the power of the sword in time of war.
²¹ You will be safe from slander
  and have no fear when destruction comes.
²² You will laugh at destruction and famine;
  wild animals will not terrify you.
²³ You will be at peace with the stones of
    the field,
  and its wild animals will be at peace
    with you.
²⁴ You will know that your home is safe.
  When you survey your possessions,
    nothing will be missing.
²⁵ You will have many children;
  your descendants will be as plentiful
    as grass!
²⁶ You will go to the grave at a ripe old age,
  like a sheaf of grain harvested at the
    proper time!

²⁷ "We have studied life and found all this
    to be true.
  Listen to my counsel, and apply it to
    yourself."

JOB'S SECOND SPEECH:
A RESPONSE TO ELIPHAZ

6 Then Job spoke again:

² "If my misery could be weighed
  and my troubles be put on the scales,
³ they would outweigh all the sands of the sea.
  That is why I spoke impulsively.
⁴ For the Almighty has struck me down with
    his arrows.
  Their poison infects my spirit.
  God's terrors are lined up against me.
⁵ Don't I have a right to complain?
  Don't wild donkeys bray when they find
    no grass,
  and oxen bellow when they have no food?
⁶ Don't people complain about unsalted food?
  Does anyone want the tasteless white
    of an egg?*
⁷ My appetite disappears when I look at it;
  I gag at the thought of eating it!

⁸ "Oh, that I might have my request,
  that God would grant my desire.
⁹ I wish he would crush me.
  I wish he would reach out his hand and
    kill me.

5:1 Hebrew *the holy ones.* 5:5a The meaning of the Hebrew for
this phrase is uncertain. 5:5b As in Greek and Syriac versions;
Hebrew reads *A snare snatches their wealth.* 6:6 Or *the tasteless
juice of the mallow plant?*

¹⁰ At least I can take comfort in this:
Despite the pain,
I have not denied the words of the
Holy One.
¹¹ But I don't have the strength to endure.
I have nothing to live for.
¹² Do I have the strength of a stone?
Is my body made of bronze?
¹³ No, I am utterly helpless,
without any chance of success.

¹⁴ "One should be kind to a fainting friend,
but you accuse me without any fear of
the Almighty.*
¹⁵ My brothers, you have proved as unreliable
as a seasonal brook
that overflows its banks in the spring
¹⁶ when it is swollen with ice and
melting snow.
¹⁷ But when the hot weather arrives,
the water disappears.
The brook vanishes in the heat.
¹⁸ The caravans turn aside to be refreshed,
but there is nothing to drink, so they die.
¹⁹ The caravans from Tema search for
this water;
the travelers from Sheba hope to find it.
²⁰ They count on it but are disappointed.
When they arrive, their hopes are dashed.
²¹ You, too, have given no help.
You have seen my calamity,
and you are afraid.
²² But why? Have I ever asked you for a gift?
Have I begged for anything of yours
for myself?
²³ Have I asked you to rescue me from
my enemies,
or to save me from ruthless people?
²⁴ Teach me, and I will keep quiet.
Show me what I have done wrong.
²⁵ Honest words can be painful,
but what do your criticisms amount to?
²⁶ Do you think your words are convincing
when you disregard my cry
of desperation?
²⁷ You would even send an orphan
into slavery*
or sell a friend.
²⁸ Look at me!
Would I lie to your face?
²⁹ Stop assuming my guilt,
for I have done no wrong.
³⁰ Do you think I am lying?
Don't I know the difference between
right and wrong?

7 ¹ "Is not all human life a struggle?
Our lives are like that of a hired hand,
² like a worker who longs for the shade,
like a servant waiting to be paid.
³ I, too, have been assigned months of futility,
long and weary nights of misery.

⁴ Lying in bed, I think,
'When will it be morning?'
But the night drags on, and I toss till dawn.
⁵ My body is covered with maggots and scabs.
My skin breaks open, oozing with pus.

JOB CRIES OUT TO GOD
⁶ "My days fly faster than a weaver's shuttle.
They end without hope.
⁷ O God, remember that my life is but a breath,
and I will never again feel happiness.
⁸ You see me now, but not for long.
You will look for me, but I will be gone.
⁹ Just as a cloud dissipates and vanishes,
those who die* will not come back.
¹⁰ They are gone forever from their home—
never to be seen again.

¹¹ "I cannot keep from speaking.
I must express my anguish.
My bitter soul must complain.
¹² Am I a sea monster or a dragon
that you must place me under guard?
¹³ I think, 'My bed will comfort me,
and sleep will ease my misery,'
¹⁴ but then you shatter me with dreams
and terrify me with visions.
¹⁵ I would rather be strangled—
rather than suffer like this.
¹⁶ I hate my life and don't want to go on living.
Oh, leave me alone for my few
remaining days.

¹⁷ "What are people, that you should make
so much of us,
that you should think of us so often?
¹⁸ For you examine us every morning
and test us every moment.
¹⁹ Why won't you leave me alone,
at least long enough for me to swallow!
²⁰ If I have sinned, what have I done to you,
O watcher of all humanity?
Why make me your target?
Am I a burden to you?*
²¹ Why not just forgive my sin
and take away my guilt?
For soon I will lie down in the dust and die.
When you look for me, I will be gone."

BILDAD'S FIRST RESPONSE TO JOB
8 Then Bildad the Shuhite replied to Job:

² "How long will you go on like this?
You sound like a blustering wind.
³ Does God twist justice?
Does the Almighty twist what is right?
⁴ Your children must have sinned against him,
so their punishment was well deserved.

6:14 Or friend, / or he might lose his fear of the Almighty.
6:27 Hebrew even gamble over an orphan. 7:9 Hebrew who go
down to Sheol. 7:20 As in Greek version; Hebrew reads target, so
that I am a burden to myself?

⁵ But if you pray to God
and seek the favor of the Almighty,
⁶ and if you are pure and live with integrity,
he will surely rise up and restore your
happy home.
⁷ And though you started with little,
you will end with much.

⁸ "Just ask the previous generation.
Pay attention to the experience of
our ancestors.
⁹ For we were born but yesterday and know
nothing.
Our days on earth are as fleeting
as a shadow.
¹⁰ But those who came before us will teach you.
They will teach you the wisdom of old.

¹¹ "Can papyrus reeds grow tall without
a marsh?
Can marsh grass flourish without water?
¹² While they are still flowering,
not ready to be cut,
they begin to wither more quickly
than grass.
¹³ The same happens to all who forget God.
The hopes of the godless evaporate.
¹⁴ Their confidence hangs by a thread.
They are leaning on a spider's web.
¹⁵ They cling to their home for security,
but it won't last.
They try to hold it tight,
but it will not endure.
¹⁶ The godless seem like a lush plant growing
in the sunshine,
its branches spreading across the garden.
¹⁷ Its roots grow down through a pile of stones;
it takes hold on a bed of rocks.
¹⁸ But when it is uprooted,
it's as though it never existed!
¹⁹ That's the end of its life,
and others spring up from the earth to
replace it.

²⁰ "But look, God will not reject a person
of integrity,
nor will he lend a hand to the wicked.
²¹ He will once again fill your mouth
with laughter
and your lips with shouts of joy.
²² Those who hate you will be clothed
with shame,
and the home of the wicked will be
destroyed."

JOB'S THIRD SPEECH:
A RESPONSE TO BILDAD

9 Then Job spoke again:

² "Yes, I know all this is true in principle.
But how can a person be declared
innocent in God's sight?

³ If someone wanted to take God to court,*
would it be possible to answer him even
once in a thousand times?
⁴ For God is so wise and so mighty.
Who has ever challenged him
successfully?

⁵ "Without warning,
he moves the mountains,
overturning them in his anger.
⁶ He shakes the earth from its place,
and its foundations tremble.
⁷ If he commands it, the sun won't rise
and the stars won't shine.
⁸ He alone has spread out the heavens
and marches on the waves of the sea.
⁹ He made all the stars—the Bear and Orion,
the Pleiades and the constellations
of the southern sky.
¹⁰ He does great things too marvelous to
understand.
He performs countless miracles.

¹¹ "Yet when he comes near, I cannot see him.
When he moves by, I do not see him go.
¹² If he snatches someone in death,
who can stop him?
Who dares to ask, 'What are you doing?'
¹³ And God does not restrain his anger.
Even the monsters of the sea* are crushed
beneath his feet.

¹⁴ "So who am I, that I should try to
answer God
or even reason with him?
¹⁵ Even if I were right, I would have no defense.
I could only plead for mercy.
¹⁶ And even if I summoned him and he
responded,
I'm not sure he would listen to me.
¹⁷ For he attacks me with a storm
and repeatedly wounds me
without cause.
¹⁸ He will not let me catch my breath,
but fills me instead with bitter sorrows.
¹⁹ If it's a question of strength, he's the
strong one.
If it's a matter of justice, who dares to
summon him* to court?
²⁰ Though I am innocent, my own mouth
would pronounce me guilty.
Though I am blameless, it* would prove
me wicked.

²¹ "I am innocent,
but it makes no difference to me—
I despise my life.
²² Innocent or wicked, it is all the same to God.

9:3 Or *If God wanted to take someone to court.* 9:13 Hebrew
the helpers of Rahab, the name of a mythical sea monster that
represents chaos in ancient literature. 9:19 As in Greek version;
Hebrew reads *me.* 9:20 Or *he.*

That's why I say, 'He destroys both the blameless and the wicked.'

²³ When a plague* sweeps through,
he laughs at the death of the innocent.
²⁴ The whole earth is in the hands of
the wicked,
and God blinds the eyes of the judges.
If he's not the one who does it, who is?

²⁵ "My life passes more swiftly than a runner.
It flees away without a glimpse
of happiness.
²⁶ It disappears like a swift papyrus boat,
like an eagle swooping down on
its prey.
²⁷ If I decided to forget my complaints,
to put away my sad face and be cheerful,
²⁸ I would still dread all the pain,
for I know you will not find me innocent,
O God.
²⁹ Whatever happens, I will be found guilty.
So what's the use of trying?
³⁰ Even if I were to wash myself with soap
and clean my hands with lye,
³¹ you would plunge me into a muddy ditch,
and my own filthy clothing would
hate me.

³² "God is not a mortal like me,
so I cannot argue with him or take him
to trial.
³³ If only there were a mediator between us,
someone who could bring us together.
³⁴ The mediator could make God stop
beating me,
and I would no longer live in terror of
his punishment.
³⁵ Then I could speak to him without fear,
but I cannot do that in my own
strength.

JOB FRAMES HIS PLEA TO GOD

10 ¹ "I am disgusted with my life.
Let me complain freely.
My bitter soul must complain.
² I will say to God,
'Don't simply condemn me—
tell me the charge you are bringing
against me.
³ What do you gain by oppressing me?
Why do you reject me, the work of your
own hands,
while smiling on the schemes of
the wicked?
⁴ Are your eyes like those of a human?
Do you see things only as people see them?
⁵ Is your lifetime only as long as ours?
Is your life so short
⁶ that you must quickly probe for my guilt
and search for my sin?
⁷ Although you know I am not guilty,
no one can rescue me from your hands.

⁸ "'You formed me with your hands;
you made me,
yet now you completely destroy me.
⁹ Remember that you made me from dust—
will you turn me back to dust so soon?
¹⁰ You guided my conception
and formed me in the womb.*
¹¹ You clothed me with skin and flesh,
and you knit my bones and sinews
together.
¹² You gave me life and showed me your
unfailing love.
My life was preserved by your care.

¹³ "'Yet your real motive—
your true intent—
¹⁴ was to watch me, and if I sinned,
you would not forgive my guilt.
¹⁵ If I am guilty, too bad for me;
and even if I'm innocent, I can't hold
my head high,
because I am filled with shame
and misery.
¹⁶ And if I hold my head high, you hunt me
like a lion
and display your awesome power
against me.
¹⁷ Again and again you witness against me.
You pour out your growing anger on me
and bring fresh armies against me.

¹⁸ "'Why, then, did you deliver me from my
mother's womb?
Why didn't you let me die at birth?
¹⁹ It would be as though I had never existed,
going directly from the womb to the grave.
²⁰ I have only a few days left, so leave me
alone,
that I may have a moment of comfort
²¹ before I leave—never to return—
for the land of darkness and utter gloom.
²² It is a land as dark as midnight,
a land of gloom and confusion,
where even the light is dark as midnight.'"

ZOPHAR'S FIRST RESPONSE TO JOB

11 Then Zophar the Naamathite replied to Job:

² "Shouldn't someone answer this torrent
of words?
Is a person proved innocent just by a lot
of talking?
³ Should I remain silent while you babble on?
When you mock God, shouldn't someone
make you ashamed?
⁴ You claim, 'My beliefs are pure,'
and 'I am clean in the sight of God.'
⁵ If only God would speak;
if only he would tell you what he thinks!

9:23 Or *disaster.* 10:10 Hebrew *You poured me out like milk / and
curdled me like cheese.*

6 If only he would tell you the secrets of
wisdom,
for true wisdom is not a simple matter.
Listen! God is doubtless punishing you
far less than you deserve!

7 "Can you solve the mysteries of God?
Can you discover everything about
the Almighty?
8 Such knowledge is higher than the
heavens—
and who are you?
It is deeper than the underworld*—
what do you know?
9 It is broader than the earth
and wider than the sea.
10 If God comes and puts a person in prison
or calls the court to order, who can
stop him?
11 For he knows those who are false,
and he takes note of all their sins.
12 An empty-headed person won't become wise
any more than a wild donkey can bear
a human child.*

13 "If only you would prepare your heart
and lift up your hands to him in prayer!
14 Get rid of your sins,
and leave all iniquity behind you.
15 Then your face will brighten with
innocence.
You will be strong and free of fear.
16 You will forget your misery;
it will be like water flowing away.
17 Your life will be brighter than the noonday.
Even darkness will be as bright as
morning.
18 Having hope will give you courage.
You will be protected and will rest in
safety.
19 You will lie down unafraid,
and many will look to you for help.
20 But the wicked will be blinded.
They will have no escape.
Their only hope is death."

JOB'S FOURTH SPEECH:
A RESPONSE TO ZOPHAR

12 Then Job spoke again:

2 "You people really know everything,
don't you?
And when you die, wisdom will die
with you!
3 Well, I know a few things myself—
and you're no better than I am.
Who doesn't know these things you've
been saying?
4 Yet my friends laugh at me,
for I call on God and expect an answer.
I am a just and blameless man,
yet they laugh at me.

5 People who are at ease mock those
in trouble.
They give a push to people who are
stumbling.
6 But robbers are left in peace,
and those who provoke God live
in safety—
though God keeps them in his power.*

7 "Just ask the animals, and they will
teach you.
Ask the birds of the sky, and they will
tell you.
8 Speak to the earth, and it will instruct you.
Let the fish in the sea speak to you.
9 For they all know
that my disaster* has come from the hand
of the LORD.
10 For the life of every living thing is
in his hand,
and the breath of every human being.
11 The ear tests the words it hears
just as the mouth distinguishes
between foods.
12 Wisdom belongs to the aged,
and understanding to the old.

13 "But true wisdom and power are found
in God;
counsel and understanding are his.
14 What he destroys cannot be rebuilt.
When he puts someone in prison,
there is no escape.
15 If he holds back the rain, the earth becomes
a desert.
If he releases the waters,
they flood the earth.
16 Yes, strength and wisdom are his;
deceivers and deceived are both
in his power.
17 He leads counselors away,
stripped of good judgment;
wise judges become fools.
18 He removes the royal robe of kings.
They are led away with ropes around
their waist.
19 He leads priests away, stripped of status;
he overthrows those with long years
in power.
20 He silences the trusted adviser
and removes the insight of the elders.
21 He pours disgrace upon princes
and disarms the strong.

22 "He uncovers mysteries hidden in darkness;
he brings light to the deepest gloom.
23 He builds up nations, and he destroys them.
He expands nations,
and he abandons them.

11:8 Hebrew than Sheol. 11:12 Or than a wild male donkey can bear
a tame colt. 12:6 Or safety—those who try to manipulate God. The
meaning of the Hebrew is uncertain. 12:9 Hebrew that this.

²⁴ He strips kings of understanding
and leaves them wandering in a pathless
wasteland.
²⁵ They grope in the darkness without
a light.
He makes them stagger like drunkards.

JOB WANTS TO ARGUE HIS CASE WITH GOD

13 ¹ "Look, I have seen all this with
my own eyes
and heard it with my own ears, and now
I understand.
² I know as much as you do.
You are no better than I am.
³ As for me, I would speak directly to
the Almighty.
I want to argue my case with
God himself.
⁴ As for you, you smear me with lies.
As physicians, you are worthless quacks.
⁵ If only you could be silent!
That's the wisest thing you could do.
⁶ Listen to my charge;
pay attention to my arguments.

⁷ "Are you defending God with lies?
Do you make your dishonest arguments
for his sake?
⁸ Will you slant your testimony in his favor?
Will you argue God's case for him?
⁹ What will happen when he finds out what
you are doing?
Can you fool him as easily as you fool
people?
¹⁰ No, you will be in trouble with him
if you secretly slant your testimony
in his favor.
¹¹ Doesn't his majesty terrify you?
Doesn't your fear of him overwhelm you?
¹² Your platitudes are as valuable as ashes.
Your defense is as fragile as a clay pot.

¹³ "Be silent now and leave me alone.
Let me speak, and I will face the
consequences.
¹⁴ Why should I put myself in mortal danger*
and take my life in my own hands?
¹⁵ God might kill me,
but I have no other hope.*
I am going to argue my case with him.
¹⁶ But this is what will save me—I am not
godless.
If I were, I could not stand before him.

¹⁷ "Listen closely to what I am about to say.
Hear me out.
¹⁸ I have prepared my case;
I will be proved innocent.
¹⁹ Who can argue with me over this?
And if you prove me wrong, I will remain
silent and die.

JOB ASKS HOW HE HAS SINNED

²⁰ "O God, grant me these two things,
and then I will be able to face you.
²¹ Remove your heavy hand from me,
and don't terrify me with your awesome
presence.
²² Now summon me, and I will answer!
Or let me speak to you, and you reply.
²³ Tell me, what have I done wrong?
Show me my rebellion and my sin.
²⁴ Why do you turn away from me?
Why do you treat me as your enemy?
²⁵ Would you terrify a leaf blown by the wind?
Would you chase dry straw?

²⁶ "You write bitter accusations against me
and bring up all the sins of my youth.
²⁷ You put my feet in stocks.
You examine all my paths.
You trace all my footprints.
²⁸ I waste away like rotting wood,
like a moth-eaten coat.

14 ¹ "How frail is humanity!
How short is life, how full of
trouble!
² We blossom like a flower and then wither.
Like a passing shadow, we quickly
disappear.
³ Must you keep an eye on such a frail
creature
and demand an accounting from me?
⁴ Who can bring purity out of an impure
person?
No one!
⁵ You have decided the length of our lives.
You know how many months we will live,
and we are not given a minute longer.
⁶ So leave us alone and let us rest!
We are like hired hands, so let us finish
our work in peace.

⁷ "Even a tree has more hope!
If it is cut down, it will sprout again
and grow new branches.
⁸ Though its roots have grown old in the earth
and its stump decays,
⁹ at the scent of water it will bud
and sprout again like a new seedling.

¹⁰ "But when people die, their strength is gone.
They breathe their last, and then where
are they?
¹¹ As water evaporates from a lake
and a river disappears in drought,
¹² people are laid to rest and do not rise again.
Until the heavens are no more, they will
not wake up
nor be roused from their sleep.

13:14 Hebrew *Why should I take my flesh in my teeth.* **13:15** An alternate reading in the Masoretic Text reads *God might kill me, but I hope in him.*

¹³ "I wish you would hide me in the grave*
and forget me there until your anger
has passed.
But mark your calendar to think of me
again!
¹⁴ Can the dead live again?
If so, this would give me hope through
all my years of struggle,
and I would eagerly await the release
of death.
¹⁵ You would call and I would answer,
and you would yearn for me, your
handiwork.
¹⁶ For then you would guard my steps,
instead of watching for my sins.
¹⁷ My sins would be sealed in a pouch,
and you would cover my guilt.

¹⁸ "But instead, as mountains fall
and crumble
and as rocks fall from a cliff,
¹⁹ as water wears away the stones
and floods wash away the soil,
so you destroy people's hope.
²⁰ You always overpower them, and they pass
from the scene.
You disfigure them in death and send
them away.
²¹ They never know if their children grow up
in honor
or sink to insignificance.
²² They suffer painfully;
their life is full of trouble."

ELIPHAZ'S SECOND RESPONSE TO JOB

15 Then Eliphaz the Temanite replied:

² "A wise man wouldn't answer with such
empty talk!
You are nothing but a windbag.
³ The wise don't engage in empty chatter.
What good are such words?
⁴ Have you no fear of God,
no reverence for him?
⁵ Your sins are telling your mouth what
to say.
Your words are based on clever deception.
⁶ Your own mouth condemns you, not I.
Your own lips testify against you.

⁷ "Were you the first person ever born?
Were you born before the hills
were made?
⁸ Were you listening at God's secret council?
Do you have a monopoly on wisdom?
⁹ What do you know that we don't?
What do you understand that we do not?
¹⁰ On our side are aged, gray-haired men
much older than your father!

¹¹ "Is God's comfort too little for you?
Is his gentle word not enough?

¹² What has taken away your reason?
What has weakened your vision,*
¹³ that you turn against God
and say all these evil things?
¹⁴ Can any mortal be pure?
Can anyone born of a woman be just?
¹⁵ Look, God does not even trust the angels.*
Even the heavens are not absolutely pure
in his sight.
¹⁶ How much less pure is a corrupt and
sinful person
with a thirst for wickedness!

¹⁷ "If you will listen, I will show you.
I will answer you from my own
experience.
¹⁸ And it is confirmed by the reports of
wise men
who have heard the same thing from
their fathers—
¹⁹ from those to whom the land was given
long before any foreigners arrived.

²⁰ "The wicked writhe in pain throughout
their lives.
Years of trouble are stored up for the
ruthless.
²¹ The sound of terror rings in their ears,
and even on good days they fear the
attack of the destroyer.
²² They dare not go out into the darkness
for fear they will be murdered.
²³ They wander around, saying,
'Where can I find bread?'*
They know their day of destruction is near.
²⁴ That dark day terrifies them.
They live in distress and anguish,
like a king preparing for battle.
²⁵ For they shake their fists at God,
defying the Almighty.
²⁶ Holding their strong shields,
they defiantly charge against him.

²⁷ "These wicked people are heavy and
prosperous;
their waists bulge with fat.
²⁸ But their cities will be ruined.
They will live in abandoned houses
that are ready to tumble down.
²⁹ Their riches will not last,
and their wealth will not endure.
Their possessions will no longer spread
across the horizon.

³⁰ "They will not escape the darkness.
The burning sun will wither their shoots,
and the breath of God will destroy them.
³¹ Let them no longer fool themselves by
trusting in empty riches,

14:13 Hebrew *in Sheol.*   15:12 Or *Why do your eyes flash with anger;*
Hebrew reads *Why do your eyes blink.*   15:15 Hebrew *the holy ones.*
15:23 Greek version reads *He is appointed to be food for a vulture.*

for emptiness will be their only reward.
³² They will be cut down in the prime of life;
their branches will never again
be green.
³³ They will be like a vine whose grapes are
harvested too early,
like an olive tree that loses its blossoms
before the fruit can form.
³⁴ For the godless are barren.
Their homes, enriched through bribery,
will burn.
³⁵ They conceive trouble and give
birth to evil.
Their womb produces deceit."

JOB'S FIFTH SPEECH:
A RESPONSE TO ELIPHAZ

16 Then Job spoke again:

² "I have heard all this before.
What miserable comforters you are!
³ Won't you ever stop blowing hot air?
What makes you keep on talking?
⁴ I could say the same things if you were
in my place.
I could spout off criticism and shake my
head at you.
⁵ But if it were me, I would encourage you.
I would try to take away your grief.
⁶ Instead, I suffer if I defend myself,
and I suffer no less if I refuse to speak.

⁷ "O God, you have ground me down
and devastated my family.
⁸ As if to prove I have sinned, you've reduced
me to skin and bones.
My gaunt flesh testifies against me.
⁹ God hates me and angrily tears me apart.
He snaps his teeth at me
and pierces me with his eyes.
¹⁰ People jeer and laugh at me.
They slap my cheek in contempt.
A mob gathers against me.
¹¹ God has handed me over to sinners.
He has tossed me into the hands
of the wicked.

¹² "I was living quietly until he shattered me.
He took me by the neck and broke me
in pieces.
Then he set me up as his target,
¹³ and now his archers surround me.
His arrows pierce me without mercy.
The ground is wet with my blood.*
¹⁴ Again and again he smashes against me,
charging at me like a warrior.
¹⁵ I wear burlap to show my grief.
My pride lies in the dust.
¹⁶ My eyes are red with weeping;
dark shadows circle my eyes.
¹⁷ Yet I have done no wrong,
and my prayer is pure.

¹⁸ "O earth, do not conceal my blood.
Let it cry out on my behalf.
¹⁹ Even now my witness is in heaven.
My advocate is there on high.
²⁰ My friends scorn me,
but I pour out my tears to God.
²¹ I need someone to mediate between God
and me,
as a person mediates between friends.
²² For soon I must go down that road
from which I will never return.

JOB CONTINUES TO DEFEND
HIS INNOCENCE

17 ¹ "My spirit is crushed,
and my life is nearly snuffed out.
The grave is ready to receive me.
² I am surrounded by mockers.
I watch how bitterly they taunt me.

³ "You must defend my innocence, O God,
since no one else will stand up for me.
⁴ You have closed their minds to
understanding,
but do not let them triumph.
⁵ They betray their friends for their own
advantage,
so let their children faint with hunger.

⁶ "God has made a mockery of me among
the people;
they spit in my face.
⁷ My eyes are swollen with weeping,
and I am but a shadow of my former self.
⁸ The virtuous are horrified when they
see me.
The innocent rise up against
the ungodly.
⁹ The righteous keep moving forward,
and those with clean hands become
stronger and stronger.

¹⁰ "As for all of you, come back with a better
argument,
though I still won't find a wise man
among you.
¹¹ My days are over.
My hopes have disappeared.
My heart's desires are broken.
¹² These men say that night is day;
they claim that the darkness is light.
¹³ What if I go to the grave*
and make my bed in darkness?
¹⁴ What if I call the grave my father,
and the maggot my mother or my sister?
¹⁵ Where then is my hope?
Can anyone find it?
¹⁶ No, my hope will go down with me
to the grave.
We will rest together in the dust!"

16:13 Hebrew *my gall*. **17:13** Hebrew *to Sheol;* also in 17:16.

BILDAD'S SECOND RESPONSE TO JOB

18 Then Bildad the Shuhite replied:

2 "How long before you stop talking?
  Speak sense if you want us to answer!
3 Do you think we are mere animals?
  Do you think we are stupid?
4 You may tear out your hair in anger,
  but will that destroy the earth?
  Will it make the rocks tremble?

5 "Surely the light of the wicked will be
    snuffed out.
  The sparks of their fire will not glow.
6 The light in their tent will grow dark.
  The lamp hanging above them will be
    quenched.
7 The confident stride of the wicked will be
    shortened.
  Their own schemes will be their downfall.
8 The wicked walk into a net.
  They fall into a pit.
9 A trap grabs them by the heel.
  A snare holds them tight.
10 A noose lies hidden on the ground.
  A rope is stretched across their path.

11 "Terrors surround the wicked
    and trouble them at every step.
12 Hunger depletes their strength,
    and calamity waits for them to stumble.
13 Disease eats their skin;
    death devours their limbs.
14 They are torn from the security of their homes
    and are brought down to the king of
    terrors.
15 The homes of the wicked will burn down;
    burning sulfur rains on their houses.
16 Their roots will dry up,
    and their branches will wither.
17 All memory of their existence will fade
    from the earth;
    no one will remember their names.
18 They will be thrust from light into darkness,
    driven from the world.
19 They will have neither children nor
    grandchildren,
    nor any survivor in the place where
    they lived.
20 People in the west are appalled at their fate;
    people in the east are horrified.
21 They will say, 'This was the home of a
    wicked person,
    the place of one who rejected God.'"

JOB'S SIXTH SPEECH:
A RESPONSE TO BILDAD

19 Then Job spoke again:

2 "How long will you torture me?
  How long will you try to crush me with
    your words?

3 You have already insulted me ten times.
  You should be ashamed of treating me
    so badly.
4 Even if I have sinned,
  that is my concern, not yours.
5 You think you're better than I am,
  using my humiliation as evidence of
    my sin.
6 But it is God who has wronged me,
  capturing me in his net.*

7 "I cry out, 'Help!' but no one answers me.
  I protest, but there is no justice.
8 God has blocked my way so I cannot move.
  He has plunged my path into darkness.
9 He has stripped me of my honor
  and removed the crown from my head.
10 He has demolished me on every side,
    and I am finished.
  He has uprooted my hope like a fallen tree.
11 His fury burns against me;
  he counts me as an enemy.
12 His troops advance.
  They build up roads to attack me.
  They camp all around my tent.

13 "My relatives stay far away,
    and my friends have turned against me.
14 My family is gone,
    and my close friends have forgotten me.
15 My servants and maids consider me a
    stranger.
  I am like a foreigner to them.
16 When I call my servant, he doesn't come;
  I have to plead with him!
17 My breath is repulsive to my wife.
  I am rejected by my own family.
18 Even young children despise me.
  When I stand to speak, they turn their
    backs on me.
19 My close friends detest me.
  Those I loved have turned against me.
20 I have been reduced to skin and bones
    and have escaped death by the skin of
    my teeth.

21 "Have mercy on me, my friends, have mercy,
    for the hand of God has struck me.
22 Must you also persecute me, like God does?
  Haven't you chewed me up enough?

23 "Oh, that my words could be recorded.
  Oh, that they could be inscribed on
    a monument,
24 carved with an iron chisel and filled with lead,
  engraved forever in the rock.

25 "But as for me, I know that
    my Redeemer lives,
  and he will stand upon the earth at last.

___
19:6 Or *for I am like a city under siege.*

²⁶ And after my body has decayed,
  yet in my body I will see God!*
²⁷ I will see him for myself.
  Yes, I will see him with my own eyes.
  I am overwhelmed at the thought!

²⁸ "How dare you go on persecuting me,
  saying, 'It's his own fault'?
²⁹ You should fear punishment yourselves,
  for your attitude deserves punishment.
  Then you will know that there is indeed a
    judgment."

ZOPHAR'S SECOND RESPONSE TO JOB

20 Then Zophar the Naamathite replied:

² "I must reply
  because I am greatly disturbed.
³ I've had to endure your insults,
  but now my spirit prompts me to reply.

⁴ "Don't you realize that from the beginning
    of time,
  ever since people were first placed on
    the earth,
⁵ the triumph of the wicked has been
    short lived
  and the joy of the godless has been only
    temporary?
⁶ Though the pride of the godless reaches
    to the heavens
  and their heads touch the clouds,
⁷ yet they will vanish forever,
  thrown away like their own dung.
  Those who knew them will ask,
    'Where are they?'
⁸ They will fade like a dream and not be found.
  They will vanish like a vision in the night.
⁹ Those who once saw them will see them
    no more.
  Their families will never see them again.
¹⁰ Their children will beg from the poor,
  for they must give back their stolen
    riches.
¹¹ Though they are young,
  their bones will lie in the dust.

¹² "They enjoyed the sweet taste of
    wickedness,
  letting it melt under their tongue.
¹³ They savored it,
  holding it long in their mouths.
¹⁴ But suddenly the food in their bellies
    turns sour,
  a poisonous venom in their stomach.
¹⁵ They will vomit the wealth they swallowed.
  God won't let them keep it down.
¹⁶ They will suck the poison of cobras.
  The viper will kill them.
¹⁷ They will never again enjoy streams of
    olive oil
  or rivers of milk and honey.

¹⁸ They will give back everything they
    worked for.
  Their wealth will bring them no joy.
¹⁹ For they oppressed the poor and left them
    destitute.
  They foreclosed on their homes.
²⁰ They were always greedy and never satisfied.
  Nothing remains of all the things they
    dreamed about.
²¹ Nothing is left after they finish gorging
    themselves.
  Therefore, their prosperity will
    not endure.

²² "In the midst of plenty, they will run into
    trouble
  and be overcome by misery.
²³ May God give them a bellyful of trouble.
  May God rain down his anger upon them.
²⁴ When they try to escape an iron weapon,
  a bronze-tipped arrow will pierce them.
²⁵ The arrow is pulled from their back,
  and the arrowhead glistens with blood.*
  The terrors of death are upon them.
²⁶   Their treasures will be thrown into
    deepest darkness.
  A wildfire will devour their goods,
    consuming all they have left.
²⁷ The heavens will reveal their guilt,
  and the earth will testify against them.
²⁸ A flood will sweep away their house.
  God's anger will descend on them
    in torrents.
²⁹ This is the reward that God gives the wicked.
  It is the inheritance decreed by God."

JOB'S SEVENTH SPEECH: A RESPONSE TO ZOPHAR

21 Then Job spoke again:

² "Listen closely to what I am saying.
  That's one consolation you can give me.
³ Bear with me, and let me speak.
  After I have spoken, you may resume
    mocking me.

⁴ "My complaint is with God, not with people.
  I have good reason to be so impatient.
⁵ Look at me and be stunned.
  Put your hand over your mouth in shock.
⁶ When I think about what I am saying,
    I shudder.
  My body trembles.

⁷ "Why do the wicked prosper,
  growing old and powerful?
⁸ They live to see their children grow up and
    settle down,
  and they enjoy their grandchildren.

19:26 Or *without my body I will see God*. The meaning of the
Hebrew is uncertain. 20:25 Hebrew *with gall*.

⁹ Their homes are safe from every fear,
  and God does not punish them.
¹⁰ Their bulls never fail to breed.
  Their cows bear calves and never miscarry.
¹¹ They let their children frisk about like
  lambs.
  Their little ones skip and dance.
¹² They sing with tambourine and harp.
  They celebrate to the sound of the flute.
¹³ They spend their days in prosperity,
  then go down to the grave* in peace.
¹⁴ And yet they say to God, 'Go away.
  We want no part of you and your ways.
¹⁵ Who is the Almighty, and why should we
  obey him?
  What good will it do us to pray?'
¹⁶ (They think their prosperity is of
  their own doing,
  but I will have nothing to do with that
  kind of thinking.)

¹⁷ "Yet the light of the wicked never seems to
  be extinguished.
  Do they ever have trouble?
  Does God distribute sorrows to them
  in anger?
¹⁸ Are they driven before the wind like straw?
  Are they carried away by the storm
  like chaff?
  Not at all!

¹⁹ "'Well,' you say, 'at least God will punish
  their children!'
  But I say he should punish the ones
  who sin,
  so that they understand his judgment.
²⁰ Let them see their destruction with their
  own eyes.
  Let them drink deeply of the anger of
  the Almighty.
²¹ For they will not care what happens to
  their family
  after they are dead.

²² "But who can teach a lesson to God,
  since he judges even the most powerful?
²³ One person dies in prosperity,
  completely comfortable and secure,
²⁴ the picture of good health,
  vigorous and fit.
²⁵ Another person dies in bitter poverty,
  never having tasted the good life.
²⁶ But both are buried in the same dust,
  both eaten by the same maggots.

²⁷ "Look, I know what you're thinking.
  I know the schemes you plot against me.
²⁸ You will tell me of rich and wicked people
  whose houses have vanished because of
  their sins.
²⁹ But ask those who have been around,
  and they will tell you the truth.

³⁰ Evil people are spared in times of calamity
  and are allowed to escape disaster.
³¹ No one criticizes them openly
  or pays them back for what they
  have done.
³² When they are carried to the grave,
  an honor guard keeps watch at
  their tomb.
³³ A great funeral procession goes to the
  cemetery.
  Many pay their respects as the body
  is laid to rest,
  and the earth gives sweet repose.

³⁴ "How can your empty clichés comfort me?
  All your explanations are lies!"

ELIPHAZ'S THIRD RESPONSE TO JOB

22 Then Eliphaz the Temanite replied:

² "Can a person do anything to help God?
  Can even a wise person be helpful to him?
³ Is it any advantage to the Almighty if you
  are righteous?
  Would it be any gain to him if you were
  perfect?
⁴ Is it because you're so pious that he
  accuses you
  and brings judgment against you?
⁵ No, it's because of your wickedness!
  There's no limit to your sins.

⁶ "For example, you must have lent money
  to your friend
  and demanded clothing as security.
  Yes, you stripped him to the bone.
⁷ You must have refused water for the thirsty
  and food for the hungry.
⁸ You probably think the land belongs to the
  powerful
  and only the privileged have a right
  to it!
⁹ You must have sent widows away
  empty-handed
  and crushed the hopes of orphans.
¹⁰ That is why you are surrounded by traps
  and tremble from sudden fears.
¹¹ That is why you cannot see in the darkness,
  and waves of water cover you.

¹² "God is so great—higher than the heavens,
  higher than the farthest stars.
¹³ But you reply, 'That's why God can't see
  what I am doing!
  How can he judge through the thick
  darkness?
¹⁴ For thick clouds swirl about him, and he
  cannot see us.
  He is way up there, walking on the vault
  of heaven.'

_____
21:13 Hebrew *to Sheol*.

¹⁵ "Will you continue on the old paths
  where evil people have walked?
¹⁶ They were snatched away in the prime of
    life,
  the foundations of their lives washed
    away.
¹⁷ For they said to God, 'Leave us alone!
  What can the Almighty do to us?'
¹⁸ Yet he was the one who filled their homes
    with good things,
  so I will have nothing to do with that kind
    of thinking.

¹⁹ "The righteous will be happy to see the
    wicked destroyed,
  and the innocent will laugh
    in contempt.
²⁰ They will say, 'See how our enemies have
    been destroyed.
  The last of them have been consumed
    in the fire.'

²¹ "Submit to God, and you will have peace;
  then things will go well for you.
²² Listen to his instructions,
  and store them in your heart.
²³ If you return to the Almighty,
  you will be restored—
  so clean up your life.
²⁴ If you give up your lust for money
    and throw your precious gold
  into the river,
²⁵ the Almighty himself will be your treasure.
  He will be your precious silver!

²⁶ "Then you will take delight in the Almighty
  and look up to God.
²⁷ You will pray to him, and he will hear you,
  and you will fulfill your vows to him.
²⁸ You will succeed in whatever you choose
    to do,
  and light will shine on the road ahead
    of you.
²⁹ If people are in trouble and you say,
    'Help them,'
  God will save them.
³⁰ Even sinners will be rescued;
  they will be rescued because your hands
    are pure."

JOB'S EIGHTH SPEECH:
A RESPONSE TO ELIPHAZ

23 Then Job spoke again:

² "My complaint today is still a bitter one,
  and I try hard not to groan aloud.
³ If only I knew where to find God,
  I would go to his court.
⁴ I would lay out my case
  and present my arguments.
⁵ Then I would listen to his reply
  and understand what he says to me.

⁶ Would he use his great power to argue
    with me?
  No, he would give me a fair hearing.
⁷ Honest people can reason with him,
  so I would be forever acquitted by
    my judge.
⁸ I go east, but he is not there.
  I go west, but I cannot find him.
⁹ I do not see him in the north,
    for he is hidden.
  I look to the south, but he is concealed.

¹⁰ "But he knows where I am going.
  And when he tests me, I will come out
    as pure as gold.
¹¹ For I have stayed on God's paths;
  I have followed his ways and not turned
    aside.
¹² I have not departed from his commands,
  but have treasured his words more than
    daily food.
¹³ But once he has made his decision,
    who can change his mind?
  Whatever he wants to do, he does.
¹⁴ So he will do to me whatever he has
    planned.
  He controls my destiny.
¹⁵ No wonder I am so terrified in his
    presence.
  When I think of it, terror grips me.
¹⁶ God has made me sick at heart;
  the Almighty has terrified me.
¹⁷ Darkness is all around me;
  thick, impenetrable darkness is
    everywhere.

JOB ASKS WHY THE WICKED
ARE NOT PUNISHED

24 ¹ "Why doesn't the Almighty bring
    the wicked to judgment?
  Why must the godly wait for him
    in vain?
² Evil people steal land by moving the
    boundary markers.
  They steal livestock and put them
    in their own pastures.
³ They take the orphan's donkey
  and demand the widow's ox as security
    for a loan.
⁴ The poor are pushed off the path;
  the needy must hide together
    for safety.
⁵ Like wild donkeys in the wilderness,
  the poor must spend all their time
    looking for food,
  searching even in the desert for food for
    their children.
⁶ They harvest a field they do not own,
  and they glean in the vineyards of
    the wicked.
⁷ All night they lie naked in the cold,
  without clothing or covering.

8 They are soaked by mountain showers,
    and they huddle against the rocks for
      want of a home.

9 "The wicked snatch a widow's child from
      her breast,
    taking the baby as security for a loan.
10 The poor must go about naked,
      without any clothing.
    They harvest food for others while they
      themselves are starving.
11 They press out olive oil without being
      allowed to taste it,
    and they tread in the winepress as they
      suffer from thirst.
12 The groans of the dying rise from the city,
      and the wounded cry for help,
    yet God ignores their moaning.

13 "Wicked people rebel against the light.
    They refuse to acknowledge its ways
      or stay in its paths.
14 The murderer rises in the early dawn
      to kill the poor and needy;
    at night he is a thief.
15 The adulterer waits for the twilight,
      saying, 'No one will see me then.'
    He hides his face so no one
      will know him.
16 Thieves break into houses at night
      and sleep in the daytime.
    They are not acquainted with the light.
17 The black night is their morning.
    They ally themselves with the terrors of
      the darkness.

18 "But they disappear like foam down a river.
    Everything they own is cursed,
    and they are afraid to enter
      their own vineyards.
19 The grave* consumes sinners
    just as drought and heat consume snow.
20 Their own mothers will forget them.
    Maggots will find them sweet to eat.
  No one will remember them.
    Wicked people are broken like a tree in
      the storm.
21 They cheat the woman who has no son
      to help her.
    They refuse to help the needy widow.

22 "God, in his power, drags away the rich.
    They may rise high, but they have no
      assurance of life.
23 They may be allowed to live in security,
    but God is always watching them.
24 And though they are great now,
    in a moment they will be gone
      like all others,
    cut off like heads of grain.
25 Can anyone claim otherwise?
    Who can prove me wrong?"

BILDAD'S THIRD RESPONSE TO JOB

25 Then Bildad the Shuhite replied:

2 "God is powerful and dreadful.
    He enforces peace in the heavens.
3 Who is able to count his heavenly army?
    Doesn't his light shine on all the earth?
4 How can a mortal be innocent before God?
    Can anyone born of a woman be pure?
5 God is more glorious than the moon;
    he shines brighter than the stars.
6 In comparison, people are maggots;
    we mortals are mere worms."

JOB'S NINTH SPEECH:
A RESPONSE TO BILDAD

26 Then Job spoke again:

2 "How you have helped the powerless!
    How you have saved the weak!
3 How you have enlightened my stupidity!
    What wise advice you have offered!
4 Where have you gotten all these wise sayings?
    Whose spirit speaks through you?

5 "The dead tremble—
    those who live beneath the waters.
6 The underworld* is naked in God's presence.
    The place of destruction* is uncovered.
7 God stretches the northern sky over
      empty space
    and hangs the earth on nothing.
8 He wraps the rain in his thick clouds,
    and the clouds don't burst with the weight.
9 He covers the face of the moon,*
    shrouding it with his clouds.
10 He created the horizon when he separated
      the waters;
    he set the boundary between day and night.
11 The foundations of heaven tremble;
    they shudder at his rebuke.
12 By his power the sea grew calm.
    By his skill he crushed the great sea
      monster.*
13 His Spirit made the heavens beautiful,
    and his power pierced the gliding serpent.
14 These are just the beginning of all that he does,
    merely a whisper of his power.
    Who, then, can comprehend the thunder
      of his power?"

JOB'S FINAL SPEECH

27 Job continued speaking:

2 "I vow by the living God, who has taken
      away my rights,
    by the Almighty who has embittered
      my soul—

24:19 Hebrew *Sheol*. 26:6a Hebrew *Sheol*. 26:6b Hebrew
Abaddon. 26:9 Or *covers his throne*. 26:12 Hebrew *Rahab*, the
name of a mythical sea monster that represents chaos in ancient
literature.

²⁴ for he looks throughout the whole earth
and sees everything under the heavens.
²⁵ He decided how hard the winds should blow
and how much rain should fall.
²⁶ He made the laws for the rain
and laid out a path for the lightning.
²⁷ Then he saw wisdom and evaluated it.
He set it in place and examined it
thoroughly.
²⁸ And this is what he says to all humanity:
'The fear of the Lord is true wisdom;
to forsake evil is real understanding.'"

JOB SPEAKS OF HIS FORMER BLESSINGS

29 Job continued speaking:

² "I long for the years gone by
when God took care of me,
³ when he lit up the way before me
and I walked safely through the darkness.
⁴ When I was in my prime,
God's friendship was felt in my home.
⁵ The Almighty was still with me,
and my children were around me.
⁶ My steps were awash in cream,
and the rocks gushed olive oil for me.

⁷ "Those were the days when I went to the
city gate
and took my place among the honored
leaders.
⁸ The young stepped aside when they saw me,
and even the aged rose in respect
at my coming.
⁹ The princes stood in silence
and put their hands over their mouths.
¹⁰ The highest officials of the city
stood quietly,
holding their tongues in respect.

¹¹ "All who heard me praised me.
All who saw me spoke well of me.
¹² For I assisted the poor in their need
and the orphans who required help.
¹³ I helped those without hope,
and they blessed me.
And I caused the widows' hearts to sing
for joy.
¹⁴ Everything I did was honest.
Righteousness covered me like a robe,
and I wore justice like a turban.
¹⁵ I served as eyes for the blind
and feet for the lame.
¹⁶ I was a father to the poor
and assisted strangers who needed help.
¹⁷ I broke the jaws of godless oppressors
and plucked their victims
from their teeth.

¹⁸ "I thought, 'Surely I will die surrounded
by my family
after a long, good life.*

¹⁹ For I am like a tree whose roots reach
the water,
whose branches are refreshed
with the dew.
²⁰ New honors are constantly bestowed on me,
and my strength is continually renewed.'

²¹ "Everyone listened to my advice.
They were silent as they waited for me
to speak.
²² And after I spoke, they had nothing to add,
for my counsel satisfied them.
²³ They longed for me to speak as people long
for rain.
They drank my words like a refreshing
spring rain.
²⁴ When they were discouraged, I smiled at
them.
My look of approval was precious to them.
²⁵ Like a chief, I told them what to do.
I lived like a king among his troops
and comforted those who mourned.

JOB SPEAKS OF HIS ANGUISH

30 ¹ "But now I am mocked by people
younger than I,
by young men whose fathers are not
worthy to run with my sheepdogs.
² A lot of good they are to me—
those worn-out wretches!
³ They are gaunt from poverty and hunger.
They claw the dry ground in desolate
wastelands.
⁴ They pluck wild greens from among
the bushes
and eat from the roots of broom trees.
⁵ They are driven from human society,
and people shout at them as if they were
thieves.
⁶ So now they live in frightening ravines,
in caves and among the rocks.
⁷ They sound like animals howling
among the bushes,
huddled together beneath the nettles.
⁸ They are nameless fools,
outcasts from society.

⁹ "And now they mock me with vulgar songs!
They taunt me!
¹⁰ They despise me and won't come near me,
except to spit in my face.
¹¹ For God has cut my bowstring.
He has humbled me,
so they have thrown off all restraint.
¹² These outcasts oppose me to my face.
They send me sprawling
and lay traps in my path.
¹³ They block my road
and do everything they can to destroy me.

29:18 Hebrew *after I have counted my days like sand.*

They know I have no one to help me.
14 They come at me from all directions.
They jump on me when I am down.
15 I live in terror now.
My honor has blown away in the wind,
and my prosperity has vanished like
a cloud.

16 "And now my life seeps away.
Depression haunts my days.
17 At night my bones are filled with pain,
which gnaws at me relentlessly.
18 With a strong hand, God grabs my shirt.*
He grips me by the collar of my coat.
19 He has thrown me into the mud.
I'm nothing more than dust and ashes.

20 "I cry to you, O God, but you don't answer.
I stand before you, but you don't even
look.
21 You have become cruel toward me.
You use your power to persecute me.
22 You throw me into the whirlwind
and destroy me in the storm.
23 And I know you are sending me to my
death—
the destination of all who live.

24 "Surely no one would turn against the needy
when they cry for help in their trouble.
25 Did I not weep for those in trouble?
Was I not deeply grieved for the needy?
26 So I looked for good, but evil came instead.
I waited for the light, but darkness fell.
27 My heart is troubled and restless.
Days of suffering torment me.
28 I walk in gloom, without sunlight.
I stand in the public square and cry
for help.
29 Instead, I am considered a brother to jackals
and a companion to owls.
30 My skin has turned dark,
and my bones burn with fever.
31 My harp plays sad music,
and my flute accompanies those who
weep.

JOB'S FINAL PROTEST OF INNOCENCE

31 1 "I made a covenant with my eyes
not to look with lust at a young
woman.
2 For what has God above chosen for us?
What is our inheritance from the
Almighty on high?
3 Isn't it calamity for the wicked
and misfortune for those who do evil?
4 Doesn't he see everything I do
and every step I take?

5 "Have I lied to anyone
or deceived anyone?
6 Let God weigh me on the scales of justice,

for he knows my integrity.
7 If I have strayed from his pathway,
or if my heart has lusted for what
my eyes have seen,
or if I am guilty of any other sin,
8 then let someone else eat the crops
I have planted.
Let all that I have planted be uprooted.

9 "If my heart has been seduced by a woman,
or if I have lusted for my neighbor's wife,
10 then let my wife serve* another man;
let other men sleep with her.
11 For lust is a shameful sin,
a crime that should be punished.
12 It is a fire that burns all the way to hell.*
It would wipe out everything I own.

13 "If I have been unfair to my male or female
servants
when they brought their complaints
to me,
14 how could I face God?
What could I say when he questioned me?
15 For God created both me and my servants.
He created us both in the womb.

16 "Have I refused to help the poor,
or crushed the hopes of widows?
17 Have I been stingy with my food
and refused to share it with orphans?
18 No, from childhood I have cared for orphans
like a father,
and all my life I have cared for widows.
19 Whenever I saw the homeless
without clothes
and the needy with nothing to wear,
20 did they not praise me
for providing wool clothing
to keep them warm?

21 "If I raised my hand against an orphan,
knowing the judges would take my side,
22 then let my shoulder be wrenched
out of place!
Let my arm be torn from its socket!
23 That would be better than facing God's
judgment.
For if the majesty of God opposes me,
what hope is there?

24 "Have I put my trust in money
or felt secure because of my gold?
25 Have I gloated about my wealth
and all that I own?
26 "Have I looked at the sun shining in the skies,
or the moon walking down its silver
pathway,

30:18 As in Greek version; Hebrew reads *hand, my garment is
disfigured.* 31:10 Hebrew *grind for.* 31:12 Hebrew *to Abaddon.*

27 and been secretly enticed in my heart
   to throw kisses at them in worship?
28 If so, I should be punished by the judges,
   for it would mean I had denied the God
      of heaven.

29 "Have I ever rejoiced when disaster struck
      my enemies,
   or become excited when harm came
      their way?
30 No, I have never sinned by cursing anyone
   or by asking for revenge.

31 "My servants have never said,
   'He let others go hungry.'
32 I have never turned away a stranger
   but have opened my doors to everyone.

33 "Have I tried to hide my sins like other
      people do,
   concealing my guilt in my heart?
34 Have I feared the crowd
   or the contempt of the masses,
   so that I kept quiet and stayed indoors?

35 "If only someone would listen to me!
   Look, I will sign my name to
      my defense.
   Let the Almighty answer me.
   Let my accuser write out the charges
      against me.
36 I would face the accusation proudly.
   I would wear it like a crown.
37 For I would tell him exactly what
      I have done.
   I would come before him like a prince.

38 "If my land accuses me
   and all its furrows cry out together,
39 or if I have stolen its crops
   or murdered its owners,
40 then let thistles grow on that land instead
      of wheat,
   and weeds instead of barley."

Job's words are ended.

ELIHU RESPONDS TO JOB'S FRIENDS

32 Job's three friends refused to reply further
to him because he kept insisting on his
innocence. 2 Then Elihu son of Barakel the Buzite, of
the clan of Ram, became angry. He was angry
because Job refused to admit that he had sinned
and that God was right in punishing him. 3 He
was also angry with Job's three friends, for they
made God* appear to be wrong by their inability
to answer Job's arguments. 4 Elihu had waited
for the others to speak to Job because they were
older than he. 5 But when he saw that they had
no further reply, he spoke out angrily. 6 Elihu son
of Barakel the Buzite said,

"I am young and you are old,
   so I held back from telling you
      what I think.
7 I thought, 'Those who are older should speak,
   for wisdom comes with age.'
8 But there is a spirit* within people,
   the breath of the Almighty within them,
   that makes them intelligent.
9 Sometimes the elders are not wise.
   Sometimes the aged do not understand
      justice.
10 So listen to me,
   and let me tell you what I think.

11 "I have waited all this time,
   listening very carefully to your
      arguments,
   listening to you grope for words.
12 I have listened,
   but not one of you has refuted Job
   or answered his arguments.
13 And don't tell me, 'He is too wise for us.
   Only God can convince him.'
14 If Job had been arguing with me,
   I would not answer with your kind of
      logic!
15 You sit there baffled,
   with nothing more to say.
16 Should I continue to wait, now that you
      are silent?
   Must I also remain silent?
17 No, I will say my piece.
   I will speak my mind.
18 For I am full of pent-up words,
   and the spirit within me urges me on.
19 I am like a cask of wine without a vent,
   like a new wineskin ready to burst!
20 I must speak to find relief,
   so let me give my answers.
21 I won't play favorites
   or try to flatter anyone.
22 For if I tried flattery,
   my Creator would soon destroy me.

ELIHU PRESENTS HIS CASE AGAINST JOB

33 1 "Listen to my words, Job;
      pay attention to what
         I have to say.
2 Now that I have begun to speak,
   let me continue.
3 I speak with all sincerity;
   I speak the truth.
4 For the Spirit of God has made me,
   and the breath of the Almighty
      gives me life.
5 Answer me, if you can;
   make your case and take your stand.
6 Look, you and I both belong to God.
   I, too, was formed from clay.

32:3 As in ancient Hebrew scribal tradition; the Masoretic Text
reads *Job*. 32:8 Or *Spirit;* also in 32:18.

7 So you don't need to be afraid of me.
I won't come down hard on you.

8 "You have spoken in my hearing,
and I have heard your very words.
9 You said, 'I am pure; I am without sin;
I am innocent; I have no guilt.
10 God is picking a quarrel with me,
and he considers me his enemy.
11 He puts my feet in the stocks
and watches my every move.'

12 "But you are wrong, and I will show you why.
For God is greater than any human being.
13 So why are you bringing a charge
against him?
Why say he does not respond to people's
complaints?
14 For God speaks again and again,
though people do not recognize it.
15 He speaks in dreams, in visions of the night,
when deep sleep falls on people
as they lie in their beds.
16 He whispers in their ears
and terrifies them with warnings.
17 He makes them turn from doing wrong;
he keeps them from pride.
18 He protects them from the grave,
from crossing over the river of death.

19 "Or God disciplines people with pain on
their sickbeds,
with ceaseless aching in their bones.
20 They lose their appetite
for even the most delicious food.
21 Their flesh wastes away,
and their bones stick out.
22 They are at death's door;
the angels of death wait for them.

23 "But if an angel from heaven appears—
a special messenger to intercede
for a person
and declare that he is upright—
24 he will be gracious and say,
'Rescue him from the grave,
for I have found a ransom for his life.'
25 Then his body will become as healthy
as a child's,
firm and youthful again.
26 When he prays to God,
he will be accepted.
And God will receive him with joy
and restore him to good standing.
27 He will declare to his friends,
'I sinned and twisted the truth,
but it was not worth it.*
28 God rescued me from the grave,
and now my life is filled with light.'

29 "Yes, God does these things
again and again for people.

30 He rescues them from the grave
so they may enjoy the light of life.
31 Mark this well, Job. Listen to me,
for I have more to say.
32 But if you have anything to say, go ahead.
Speak, for I am anxious to see you
justified.
33 But if not, then listen to me.
Keep silent and I will teach you wisdom!"

ELIHU ACCUSES JOB OF ARROGANCE

34 Then Elihu said:

2 "Listen to me, you wise men.
Pay attention, you who have knowledge.
3 Job said, 'The ear tests the words it hears
just as the mouth distinguishes
between foods.'
4 So let us discern for ourselves what is right;
let us learn together what is good.
5 For Job also said, 'I am innocent,
but God has taken away my rights.
6 I am innocent, but they call me a liar.
My suffering is incurable, though I have
not sinned.'

7 "Tell me, has there ever been
a man like Job,
with his thirst for irreverent talk?
8 He chooses evil people as companions.
He spends his time with wicked men.
9 He has even said, 'Why waste time
trying to please God?'

10 "Listen to me, you who have understanding.
Everyone knows that God doesn't sin!
The Almighty can do no wrong.
11 He repays people according to their deeds.
He treats people as they deserve.
12 Truly, God will not do wrong.
The Almighty will not twist justice.
13 Did someone else put the world in his care?
Who set the whole world in place?
14 If God were to take back his spirit
and withdraw his breath,
15 all life would cease,
and humanity would turn again to dust.

16 "Now listen to me if you are wise.
Pay attention to what I say.
17 Could God govern if he hated justice?
Are you going to condemn
the almighty judge?
18 For he says to kings, 'You are wicked,'
and to nobles, 'You are unjust.'
19 He doesn't care how great a person may be,
and he pays no more attention to the rich
than to the poor.
He made them all.

33:27 Greek version reads *but he* [God] *did not punish me as my sin
deserved.*

442 | JOB 34:20

In a moment they die.
In the middle of the night they pass away;
the mighty are removed without human
hand.

"For God watches how people live;
he sees everything they do.
No darkness is thick enough
to hide the wicked from his eyes.
We don't set the time
when we will come before God in
judgment.
He brings the mighty to ruin
without asking anyone,
and he sets up others in their place.
He knows what they do,
and in the night he overturns and
destroys them.
He strikes them down because they are
wicked,
doing it openly for all to see.
For they turned away from following him.
They have no respect for any of his ways.
They cause the poor to cry out, catching
God's attention.
He hears the cries of the needy.
But if he chooses to remain quiet,
who can criticize him?
When he hides his face, no one can find him,
whether an individual or a nation.
He prevents the godless from ruling
so they cannot be a snare to the people.

"Why don't people say to God, 'I have sinned,
but I will sin no more'?
Or 'I don't know what evil I have done—
tell me.
If I have done wrong, I will stop at once'?

"Must God tailor his justice to your
demands?
But you have rejected him!
The choice is yours, not mine.
Go ahead, share your wisdom with us.
After all, bright people will tell me,
and wise people will hear me say,
'Job speaks out of ignorance;
his words lack insight.'
Job, you deserve the maximum penalty
for the wicked way you have talked.
For you have added rebellion to your sin;
you show no respect,
and you speak many angry words
against God."

ELIHU REMINDS JOB OF GOD'S JUSTICE

35 Then Elihu said:

"Do you think it is right for you to claim,
'I am righteous before God'?
For you also ask, 'What's in it for me?
What's the use of living a righteous life?'

"I will answer you
and all your friends, too.
Look up into the sky,
and see the clouds high above you.
If you sin, how does that affect God?
Even if you sin again and again,
what effect will it have on him?
If you are good, is this some great gift
to him?
What could you possibly give him?
No, your sins affect only people like yourself,
and your good deeds also affect only
humans.

"People cry out when they are oppressed.
They groan beneath the power
of the mighty.
Yet they don't ask, 'Where is God my Creator,
the one who gives songs in the night?
Where is the one who makes us smarter
than the animals
and wiser than the birds of the sky?'
And when they cry out, God does not answer
because of their pride.
But it is wrong to say God doesn't listen,
to say the Almighty isn't concerned.
You say you can't see him,
but he will bring justice
if you will only wait.*
You say he does not respond to sinners
with anger
and is not greatly concerned
about wickedness.*
But you are talking nonsense, Job.
You have spoken like a fool."

36 Elihu continued speaking:

"Let me go on, and I will show you the truth.
For I have not finished defending God!
I will present profound arguments
for the righteousness of my Creator.
I am telling you nothing but the truth,
for I am a man of great knowledge.

"God is mighty,
but he does not despise anyone!
He is mighty in both power and
understanding.
He does not let the wicked live
but gives justice to the afflicted.
He never takes his eyes off the innocent,
but he sets them on thrones with kings
and exalts them forever.
If they are bound in chains
and caught up in a web of trouble,

35:13-14 These verses can also be translated as follows: 13Indeed,
God doesn't listen to their empty plea; / the Almighty is not concerned.
/ 14How much less will he listen when you say you don't see him, / and
that your case is before him and you're waiting for justice.   35:15 As
in Greek and Latin versions; the meaning of this Hebrew word
is uncertain.

9 he shows them the reason.
  He shows them their sins of pride.
10 He gets their attention
  and commands that they turn from evil.

11 "If they listen and obey God,
  they will be blessed with prosperity
    throughout their lives.
  All their years will be pleasant.
12 But if they refuse to listen to him,
  they will cross over the river of death,
    dying from lack of understanding.
13 For the godless are full of resentment.
  Even when he punishes them,
  they refuse to cry out to him for help.
14 They die when they are young,
  after wasting their lives in
    immoral living.
15 But by means of their suffering,
  he rescues those who suffer.
  For he gets their attention through
    adversity.

16 "God is leading you away from danger, Job,
  to a place free from distress.
  He is setting your table with
    the best food.
17 But you are obsessed with whether the
    godless will be judged.
  Don't worry, judgment and justice
    will be upheld.
18 But watch out, or you may be seduced
    by wealth.*
  Don't let yourself be bribed into sin.
19 Could all your wealth*
  or all your mighty efforts
  keep you from distress?
20 Do not long for the cover of night,
  for that is when people will be destroyed.*
21 Be on guard! Turn back from evil,
  for God sent this suffering
  to keep you from a life of evil.

ELIHU REMINDS JOB OF GOD'S POWER

22 "Look, God is all-powerful.
  Who is a teacher like him?
23 No one can tell him what to do,
  or say to him, 'You have done wrong.'
24 Instead, glorify his mighty works,
  singing songs of praise.
25 Everyone has seen these things,
  though only from a distance.

26 "Look, God is greater than we can
    understand.
  His years cannot be counted.
27 He draws up the water vapor
  and then distills it into rain.
28 The rain pours down from the clouds,
  and everyone benefits.
29 Who can understand the spreading
  of the clouds

and the thunder that rolls forth from
    heaven?
30 See how he spreads the lightning around him
  and how it lights up the depths of the sea.
31 By these mighty acts he nourishes* the
    people,
  giving them food in abundance.
32 He fills his hands with lightning bolts
  and hurls each at its target.
33 The thunder announces his presence;
  the storm announces his indignant
    anger.*

37 1 "My heart pounds as I think of this.
  It trembles within me.
2 Listen carefully to the thunder of God's voice
  as it rolls from his mouth.
3 It rolls across the heavens,
  and his lightning flashes
    in every direction.
4 Then comes the roaring of the thunder—
  the tremendous voice of his majesty.
  He does not restrain it when he speaks.
5 God's voice is glorious in the thunder.
  We can't even imagine the greatness of
    his power.

6 "He directs the snow to fall on the earth
  and tells the rain to pour down.
7 Then everyone stops working
  so they can watch his power.
8 The wild animals take cover
  and stay inside their dens.
9 The stormy wind comes from its chamber,
  and the driving winds bring the cold.
10 God's breath sends the ice,
  freezing wide expanses of water.
11 He loads the clouds with moisture,
  and they flash with his lightning.
12 The clouds churn about at his direction.
  They do whatever he commands
    throughout the earth.
13 He makes these things happen either to
    punish people
  or to show his unfailing love.

14 "Pay attention to this, Job.
  Stop and consider the wonderful
    miracles of God!
15 Do you know how God controls the storm
  and causes the lightning to flash
    from his clouds?
16 Do you understand how he moves the clouds
  with wonderful perfection and skill?
17 When you are sweltering in your clothes
  and the south wind dies down and
    everything is still,

36:18 Or But don't let your anger lead you to mockery. 36:19 Or
Could all your cries for help. 36:16-20 The meaning of the Hebrew
in this passage is uncertain. 36:31 Or he governs. 36:33 Or
even the cattle know when a storm is coming. The meaning of the
Hebrew is uncertain.

18 he makes the skies reflect the heat like a
    bronze mirror.
    Can you do that?

19 "So teach the rest of us what to say to God.
    We are too ignorant to make our own
    arguments.

20 Should God be notified that I want to speak?
    Can people even speak when they are
    confused?*

21 We cannot look at the sun,
    for it shines brightly in the sky
    when the wind clears away the clouds.

22 So also, golden splendor comes from the
    mountain of God.*
    He is clothed in dazzling splendor.

23 We cannot imagine the power of the
    Almighty;
    but even though he is just and righteous,
    he does not destroy us.

24 No wonder people everywhere fear him.
    All who are wise show him reverence.*"

THE LORD CHALLENGES JOB

38 Then the Lord answered Job from the
   whirlwind:

2 "Who is this that questions my wisdom
    with such ignorant words?

3 Brace yourself like a man,
    because I have some questions for you,
    and you must answer them.

4 "Where were you when I laid the
    foundations of the earth?
    Tell me, if you know so much.

5 Who determined its dimensions
    and stretched out the surveying line?

6 What supports its foundations,
    and who laid its cornerstone

7 as the morning stars sang together
    and all the angels* shouted for joy?

8 "Who kept the sea inside its boundaries
    as it burst from the womb,

9 and as I clothed it with clouds
    and wrapped it in thick darkness?

10 For I locked it behind barred gates,
    limiting its shores.

11 I said, 'This far and no farther will you come.
    Here your proud waves must stop!'

12 "Have you ever commanded the morning
    to appear
    and caused the dawn to rise in the east?

13 Have you made daylight spread to the ends
    of the earth,
    to bring an end to the night's wickedness?

14 As the light approaches,
    the earth takes shape like clay pressed
    beneath a seal;
    it is robed in brilliant colors.*

15 The light disturbs the wicked
    and stops the arm that is raised in
    violence.

16 "Have you explored the springs from which
    the seas come?
    Have you explored their depths?

17 Do you know where the gates of death
    are located?
    Have you seen the gates of utter gloom?

18 Do you realize the extent of the earth?
    Tell me about it if you know!

19 "Where does light come from,
    and where does darkness go?

20 Can you take each to its home?
    Do you know how to get there?

21 But of course you know all this!
    For you were born before it was all created,
    and you are so very experienced!

22 "Have you visited the storehouses of
    the snow
    or seen the storehouses of hail?

23 (I have reserved them as weapons for the
    time of trouble,
    for the day of battle and war.)

24 Where is the path to the source of light?
    Where is the home of the east wind?

25 "Who created a channel for the torrents
    of rain?
    Who laid out the path for the lightning?

26 Who makes the rain fall on barren land,
    in a desert where no one lives?

27 Who sends rain to satisfy the parched
    ground
    and make the tender grass spring up?

28 "Does the rain have a father?
    Who gives birth to the dew?

29 Who is the mother of the ice?
    Who gives birth to the frost from the
    heavens?

30 For the water turns to ice as hard as rock,
    and the surface of the water freezes.

31 "Can you direct the movement of
    the stars—
    binding the cluster of the Pleiades
    or loosening the cords of Orion?

32 Can you direct the constellations through
    the seasons
    or guide the Bear with her cubs across
    the heavens?

33 Do you know the laws of the universe?
    Can you use them to regulate the earth?

37:20 Or speak without being swallowed up? 37:22 Or from the
north; or from the abode. 37:24 As in Greek version; Hebrew
reads He is not impressed by the wise. 38:7 Hebrew the sons of
God. 38:14 Or its features stand out like folds in a robe.

34 "Can you shout to the clouds
and make it rain?
35 Can you make lightning appear
and cause it to strike as you direct?
36 Who gives intuition to the heart
and instinct to the mind?
37 Who is wise enough to count all the clouds?
Who can tilt the water jars of heaven
38 when the parched ground is dry
and the soil has hardened into clods?

39 "Can you stalk prey for a lioness
and satisfy the young lions' appetites
40 as they lie in their dens
or crouch in the thicket?
41 Who provides food for the ravens
when their young cry out to God
and wander about in hunger?

THE LORD'S CHALLENGE CONTINUES

39 1 "Do you know when the wild goats
give birth?
Have you watched as deer are born
in the wild?
2 Do you know how many months they carry
their young?
Are you aware of the time of their delivery?
3 They crouch down to give birth to
their young
and deliver their offspring.
4 Their young grow up in the open fields,
then leave home and never return.

5 "Who gives the wild donkey its freedom?
Who untied its ropes?
6 I have placed it in the wilderness;
its home is the wasteland.
7 It hates the noise of the city
and has no driver to shout at it.
8 The mountains are its pastureland,
where it searches for every blade of grass.

9 "Will the wild ox consent to being tamed?
Will it spend the night in your stall?
10 Can you hitch a wild ox to a plow?
Will it plow a field for you?
11 Given its strength, can you trust it?
Can you leave and trust the ox
to do your work?
12 Can you rely on it to bring home your grain
and deliver it to your threshing floor?

13 "The ostrich flaps her wings grandly,
but they are no match for the feathers
of the stork.
14 She lays her eggs on top of the earth,
letting them be warmed in the dust.
15 She doesn't worry that a foot might crush
them
or a wild animal might destroy them.
16 She is harsh toward her young,
as if they were not her own.

She doesn't care if they die.
17 For God has deprived her of wisdom.
He has given her no understanding.
18 But whenever she jumps up to run,
she passes the swiftest horse with its rider.

19 "Have you given the horse its strength
or clothed its neck with a flowing mane?
20 Did you give it the ability to leap
like a locust?
Its majestic snorting is terrifying!
21 It paws the earth and rejoices in
its strength
when it charges out to battle.
22 It laughs at fear and is unafraid.
It does not run from the sword.
23 The arrows rattle against it,
and the spear and javelin flash.
24 It paws the ground fiercely
and rushes forward into battle when the
ram's horn blows.
25 It snorts at the sound of the horn.
It senses the battle in the distance.
It quivers at the captain's commands and
the noise of battle.

26 "Is it your wisdom that makes
the hawk soar
and spread its wings toward the south?
27 Is it at your command that the eagle rises
to the heights to make its nest?
28 It lives on the cliffs,
making its home on a distant, rocky crag.
29 From there it hunts its prey,
keeping watch with piercing eyes.
30 Its young gulp down blood.
Where there's a carcass, there you'll
find it."

40 Then the LORD said to Job,

2 "Do you still want to argue with
the Almighty?
You are God's critic, but do you have
the answers?"

JOB RESPONDS TO THE LORD

3 Then Job replied to the LORD,

4 "I am nothing—how could I ever find
the answers?
I will cover my mouth with my hand.
5 I have said too much already.
I have nothing more to say."

THE LORD CHALLENGES JOB AGAIN

6 Then the LORD answered Job from the
whirlwind:

7 "Brace yourself like a man,
because I have some questions for you,
and you must answer them.

8 "Will you discredit my justice
    and condemn me just to prove
        you are right?
9 Are you as strong as God?
    Can you thunder with a voice like his?
10 All right, put on your glory and splendor,
    your honor and majesty.
11 Give vent to your anger.
    Let it overflow against the proud.
12 Humiliate the proud with a glance;
    walk on the wicked where they stand.
13 Bury them in the dust.
    Imprison them in the world of the dead.
14 Then even I would praise you,
    for your own strength would save you.

15 "Take a look at Behemoth,*
    which I made, just as I made you.
    It eats grass like an ox.
16 See its powerful loins
    and the muscles of its belly.
17 Its tail is as strong as a cedar.
    The sinews of its thighs are knit
        tightly together.
18 Its bones are tubes of bronze.
    Its limbs are bars of iron.
19 It is a prime example of God's handiwork,
    and only its Creator can threaten it.
20 The mountains offer it their best food,
    where all the wild animals play.
21 It lies under the lotus plants,*
    hidden by the reeds in the marsh.
22 The lotus plants give it shade
    among the willows beside the stream.
23 It is not disturbed by the raging river,
    not concerned when the swelling Jordan
        rushes around it.
24 No one can catch it off guard
    or put a ring in its nose and lead it away.

THE LORD'S CHALLENGE CONTINUES

41 1* "Can you catch Leviathan* with a hook
        or put a noose around its jaw?
2 Can you tie it with a rope through the nose
    or pierce its jaw with a spike?
3 Will it beg you for mercy
    or implore you for pity?
4 Will it agree to work for you,
    to be your slave for life?
5 Can you make it a pet like a bird,
    or give it to your little girls to play with?
6 Will merchants try to buy it
    to sell it in their shops?
7 Will its hide be hurt by spears
    or its head by a harpoon?
8 If you lay a hand on it,
    you will certainly remember the battle
        that follows.
    You won't try that again!
9* No, it is useless to try to capture it.
    The hunter who attempts it will be
        knocked down.

10 And since no one dares to disturb it,
    who then can stand up to me?
11 Who has given me anything that
    I need to pay back?
    Everything under heaven is mine.

12 "I want to emphasize Leviathan's limbs
    and its enormous strength and
        graceful form.
13 Who can strip off its hide,
    and who can penetrate its double layer
        of armor?*
14 Who could pry open its jaws?
    For its teeth are terrible!
15 The scales on its back are like*
        rows of shields
    tightly sealed together.
16 They are so close together
    that no air can get between them.
17 Each scale sticks tight to the next.
    They interlock and cannot be penetrated.

18 "When it sneezes, it flashes light!
    Its eyes are like the red of dawn.
19 Lightning leaps from its mouth;
    flames of fire flash out.
20 Smoke streams from its nostrils
    like steam from a pot heated over
        burning rushes.
21 Its breath would kindle coals,
    for flames shoot from its mouth.

22 "The tremendous strength in
        Leviathan's neck
    strikes terror wherever it goes.
23 Its flesh is hard and firm
    and cannot be penetrated.
24 Its heart is hard as rock,
    hard as a millstone.
25 When it rises, the mighty are afraid,
    gripped by terror.
26 No sword can stop it,
    no spear, dart, or javelin.
27 Iron is nothing but straw to that creature,
    and bronze is like rotten wood.
28 Arrows cannot make it flee.
    Stones shot from a sling are like
        bits of grass.
29 Clubs are like a blade of grass,
    and it laughs at the swish of javelins.
30 Its belly is covered with scales as sharp
        as glass.
    It plows up the ground as it drags through
        the mud.

40:15 The identification of Behemoth is disputed, ranging
from an earthly creature to a mythical sea monster in ancient
literature.   40:21 Or *bramble bushes;* also in 40:22.   41:1a Verses
41:1-8 are numbered 40:25-32 in Hebrew text.   41:1b The
identification of Leviathan is disputed, ranging from an earthly
creature to a mythical sea monster in ancient literature.
41:9 Verses 41:9-34 are numbered 41:1-26 in Hebrew text.
41:13 As in Greek version; Hebrew reads *its bridle?*   41:15 As in
some Greek manuscripts and Latin Vulgate; Hebrew reads *Its
pride is in its.*

31 "Leviathan makes the water boil with its
     commotion.
   It stirs the depths like a pot of ointment.
32 The water glistens in its wake,
     making the sea look white.
33 Nothing on earth is its equal,
     no other creature so fearless.
34 Of all the creatures, it is the proudest.
   It is the king of beasts."

JOB RESPONDS TO THE LORD

42 Then Job replied to the LORD:

2 "I know that you can do anything,
     and no one can stop you.
3 You asked, 'Who is this that questions my
     wisdom with such ignorance?'
   It is I—and I was talking about things
     I knew nothing about,
     things far too wonderful for me.
4 You said, 'Listen and I will speak!
     I have some questions for you,
     and you must answer them.'
5 I had only heard about you before,
     but now I have seen you
     with my own eyes.
6 I take back everything I said,
     and I sit in dust and ashes to show
       my repentance."

CONCLUSION: THE LORD BLESSES JOB

7 After the LORD had finished speaking to Job,
he said to Eliphaz the Temanite: "I am angry
with you and your two friends, for you have not
spoken accurately about me, as my servant Job
has. 8 So take seven bulls and seven rams and
go to my servant Job and offer a burnt offering
for yourselves. My servant Job will pray for you,
and I will accept his prayer on your behalf. I
will not treat you as you deserve, for you have
not spoken accurately about me, as my servant
Job has." 9 So Eliphaz the Temanite, Bildad the
Shuhite, and Zophar the Naamathite did as the
LORD commanded them, and the LORD accepted
Job's prayer.

10 When Job prayed for his friends, the LORD
restored his fortunes. In fact, the LORD gave him
twice as much as before! 11 Then all his brothers,
sisters, and former friends came and feasted
with him in his home. And they consoled him
and comforted him because of all the trials the
LORD had brought against him. And each of them
brought him a gift of money* and a gold ring.

12 So the LORD blessed Job in the second half of
his life even more than in the beginning. For now
he had 14,000 sheep, 6,000 camels, 1,000 teams
of oxen, and 1,000 female donkeys. 13 He also gave
Job seven more sons and three more daughters.
14 He named his first daughter Jemimah, the
second Keziah, and the third Keren-happuch.
15 In all the land no women were as lovely as the
daughters of Job. And their father put them into
his will along with their brothers.

16 Job lived 140 years after that, living to see
four generations of his children and grandchildren. 17 Then he died, an old man who had
lived a long, full life.

42:11 Hebrew a *kesitah;* the value or weight of the kesitah is no
longer known.

What Does the Bible Say About . . .

TITHING?

— Abraham gave Melchizedek a tenth of all his goods (Genesis 14:20; Hebrews 7:1-2).
— Jacob vowed to give God a tenth of everything God gave him (Genesis 28:22).
— Moses introduced the tithe as law (Leviticus 27:30-34).
— Offerings and tithes were to be given at the place of God's choosing (Deuteronomy 12:5-6).
— The people brought the first share of their fields' produce as a tithe (2 Chronicles 31:4-5).
— Nehemiah reestablished the tithe after the Exile (Nehemiah 10:35-37).
— Honoring the Lord with your firstfruits will bring blessings on your life (Proverbs 3:9-10).
— Giving the tithe does not mean you can ignore God's other laws (Amos 4:4-5; Matthew 23:23).
— Tithes were given before the Law of Moses (Hebrews 7:1-13).
— Do not cheat God of the tithe. Bring all the tithes into the storehouse, and God will open the windows of heaven for you (Malachi 3:8-12).

FASTING?

— Deny yourself by fasting (Psalm 35:13).
— Fast for guidance (2 Chronicles 20:3).
— Fast the way God wants (Isaiah 58).
— Fast in repentance (Joel 1:14).
— Fast in secret (Matthew 6:16).
— Fast and worship (Acts 13:2).
— Fast and pray when appointing elders (Acts 14:23).

MEDITATION?

— Meditate on the Scriptures day and night (Joshua 1:8).
— Meditate on the law of the Lord day and night (Psalm 1:2).
— Meditate on God through the night (Psalm 63:6).
— Meditate on God's mighty works (Psalm 77:12).
— May all your thoughts be pleasing to God (Psalm 104:34).
— Meditate on God's Word (Psalm 119:23, 48).
— Concentrate on God's commands (Psalm 119:78).
— Think about God's promises through the night (Psalm 119:148).
— Think about God's great works (Psalm 143:5).

What Does the Bible Say About . . .

PRAYER?

— Jesus gave us an example in the Lord's Prayer (Matthew 6:9–13).
— Jesus rose early to pray (Mark 1:35).
— Jesus went by Himself to pray (Matthew 14:23).
— Believe when you pray (Mark 11:24).
— Watch and pray (Mark 14:38).
— Pray for those who hurt you (Luke 6:28).
— Pray for workers in the field (Luke 10:2).
— Always pray and never give up (Luke 18:1).
— Unite with other believers in prayer (Acts 1:14).
— The Holy Spirit helps you pray (Romans 8:26).
— Never stop praying (1 Thessalonians 5:17).
— Pray with holy hands lifted to God (1 Timothy 2:8).
— Pray when you are suffering (James 5:13).
— You help God's servants by praying (2 Corinthians 1:11).

WORSHIP?

— Worship in the splendor of God's holiness (Psalm 29:2).
— Earnestly search for God (Psalm 63:1).
— Everything on earth will worship God (Psalm 66:4).
— Worship and bow down to God (Psalm 95:6).
— Worship the Lord with gladness (Psalm 100:2).
— Praise the Lord with your whole heart (Psalm 103:1).
— Sing unto the Lord (Isaiah 12:5).
— Worship God in spirit and truth (John 4:24).
— Sing in the spirit and in words you understand (1 Corinthians 14:15).
— Offer spiritual sacrifices (1 Peter 2:5).
— Offer a continual sacrifice of praise (Hebrews 13:15).

SINGING?

— Sing because the Lord has triumphed (Exodus 15:1).
— Sing God's praises (1 Chronicles 16:9).
— When we sing, God defeats our enemies (2 Chronicles 20:22).
— Sing and give praises (Psalm 30:4).
— Sing about God's power (Psalm 59:16).
— Sing of God's unfailing love (Psalm 89:1).
— Sing and shout joyfully to God (Psalm 95:1).
— Sing a new song to the Lord (Psalm 96:1).
— Sing praises to God with a harp (Psalm 147:7).
— Sing in the spirit and in words you understand (1 Corinthians 14:15).

PSALMS

JON HUNTZINGER, PHD

The book of Psalms is ancient Israel's hymn-book. It is an anthology of songs that gets its name from the Greek word *psalmos*, meaning 'song' or 'hymn.' The Hebrew title for the book is *tehillim*, which means 'praises.'

The practice of writing psalms predates the book of Psalms. For example, an early psalm is the "Song of the Sea" (Exodus 15), which commemorates God's deliverance of Israel through the Red Sea. Because the psalms in the book of Psalms reflect the experiences of people at different times, they do not provide new theological ideas but preserve preexisting ones shared by the Jewish people.

The book of Psalms contains five divisions: 1-41; 42-72; 73-89; 90-106; and 107-150. Each of the first four divisions concludes with a doxology, which means a song of praise (Psalm 41; 72; 89; 106), while Psalms 146-150 represent an extended doxology or five songs of praise to end the entire collection. The five divisions of Psalms correspond to the five books of the Torah, which itself was divided into 153 readings in the synagogue each year.

Most psalms in the first division name David as the writer and refer to God by His covenant name (*Yahweh*). Most of the psalms in division two are attributed to David as well (51-65; 68-70), with Korah (42-49) and Asaph (50) named as writers of the additional psalms. These psalms refer to God as *Elohim* (a Hebrew word that means 'God'). Korah (84-85; 87-88) and Asaph (73-83) are the writers of most of the psalms in division three. Only five of these psalms are attributed to David. Moses appears seven times in division four (90 [title]; 99:6; 103:7; 105:26; 106:16, 23, 32-33). Several of these psalms describe the rule of God (*Yahweh*) on behalf of the people (93, 97, 99). These were written after the time of David. Division five begins (107) and ends with a psalm of praise (150). This division of Psalms is divided into smaller sections: 108-110 (psalms sung about the dominion of the Hebrew king); 111-112 (acrostic psalms in which each verse or stanza begins with a different letter of the Hebrew alphabet, these are related to Psalm 110); 113-118 (psalms sung at Passover); 120-134 (psalms sung during pilgrimages to Jerusalem); 138-145 (psalms of David); and 146-150 (a five-part hallelujah).

Several psalms deserve special attention:
— Psalm 1, the very first in the book, introduces the basic theological outlook for all the psalms

that follow by identifying the two ways of life a person may choose to live. There is the way of God's Word (Torah), and there is the way of the scoffer who is dismissive of that Word. The way of Torah results in a life of purpose and fruitfulness, whereas the way of scoffing results in a barren life without meaning. God should be praised for giving His people the Torah as a way of blessing in their lives.
— Psalm 22 is one of the most dramatic and emotion-filled songs of the collection. It begins with the agonizing plea, "My God, my God, why have you abandoned me?" (v. 1). These are the words Jesus cried from the cross, revealing that this song was on His mind in the midst of His agony. It was typical for teachers at that time to cite the first few words of a passage of Scripture in place of the whole passage when talking about it, making it likely that Jesus was recalling the whole song and not just the first words of despair. The significance of this is that the song concludes with the promise that all nations will praise God due to the ministry of the forsaken one (Jesus).
— Psalm 23 is the best known of all the psalms. In it, David compares the essential nature of God to that of a shepherd who cares and provides for His people. This psalm affirms that God restores His people and shows honor to them.
— Psalm 109 is a very different psalm. It expresses the real and sometimes raw feelings of our natural human condition. This psalm reminds us of the feelings we might experience when other people take advantage of us or hurt us. The deep feelings of anger in this psalm speak of the consequences of sinful actions. The angry response may be wrong (Leviticus 19:17-18; Proverbs 24:17; 25:21), but it shows a high awareness of sin and a close relationship to God that allows for such a strong expression.
— Psalm 119 dramatically demonstrates the importance of the Torah in the longest song in the collection with 176 verses. Not only is this psalm the longest, but it is an acrostic divided into sections. Each section begins with one of the 22 letters of the Hebrew alphabet. The length and structure of the psalm is designed to show that the all of the people's language—even its most basic elements (letters)—should be used to praise God for the Word He Himself speaks.

BOOK ONE (Psalms 1–41)

1 ¹ Oh, the joys of those who do not
follow the advice of the wicked,
or stand around with sinners,
or join in with mockers.
² But they delight in the law of the LORD,
meditating on it day and night.
³ They are like trees planted along
the riverbank,
bearing fruit each season.
Their leaves never wither,
and they prosper in all they do.

⁴ But not the wicked!
They are like worthless chaff, scattered
by the wind.
⁵ They will be condemned at the time
of judgment.
Sinners will have no place among
the godly.
⁶ For the LORD watches over the path of
the godly,
but the path of the wicked leads to
destruction.

2 ¹ Why are the nations so angry?
Why do they waste their time with
futile plans?
² The kings of the earth prepare for battle;
the rulers plot together
against the LORD
and against his anointed one.
³ "Let us break their chains," they cry,
"and free ourselves from slavery to God."

⁴ But the one who rules in heaven laughs.
The Lord scoffs at them.
⁵ Then in anger he rebukes them,
terrifying them with his fierce fury.
⁶ For the Lord declares, "I have placed my
chosen king on the throne
in Jerusalem,* on my holy mountain."

⁷ The king proclaims the LORD's decree:
"The LORD said to me, 'You are my son.*
Today I have become your Father.*
⁸ Only ask, and I will give you the nations as
your inheritance,
the whole earth as your possession.
⁹ You will break* them with an iron rod
and smash them like clay pots.'"

¹⁰ Now then, you kings, act wisely!
Be warned, you rulers of the earth!
¹¹ Serve the LORD with reverent fear,
and rejoice with trembling.
¹² Submit to God's royal son,* or he will
become angry,
and you will be destroyed in the midst of
all your activities—
for his anger flares up in an instant.

But what joy for all who take refuge
in him!

3 *A psalm of David, regarding the time David fled
from his son Absalom.*

¹ O LORD, I have so many enemies;
so many are against me.
² So many are saying,
"God will never rescue him!"   *Interlude**

³ But you, O LORD, are a shield around me;
you are my glory, the one who holds
my head high.
⁴ I cried out to the LORD,
and he answered me from his
holy mountain.   *Interlude*

⁵ I lay down and slept,
yet I woke up in safety,
for the LORD was watching over me.
⁶ I am not afraid of ten thousand enemies
who surround me on every side.

⁷ Arise, O LORD!
Rescue me, my God!
Slap all my enemies in the face!
Shatter the teeth of the wicked!
⁸ Victory comes from you, O LORD.
May you bless your people.   *Interlude*

4 *For the choir director: A psalm of David,
to be accompanied by stringed instruments.*

¹ Answer me when I call to you,
O God who declares me innocent.
Free me from my troubles.
Have mercy on me and hear my prayer.

² How long will you people ruin my reputation?
How long will you make groundless
accusations?
How long will you continue
your lies?   *Interlude*
³ You can be sure of this:
The LORD set apart the godly for himself.
The LORD will answer when I call to him.

⁴ Don't sin by letting anger control you.
Think about it overnight and
remain silent.   *Interlude*
⁵ Offer sacrifices in the right spirit,
and trust the LORD.

⁶ Many people say, "Who will show us
better times?"
Let your face smile on us, LORD.

2:6 Hebrew *on Zion.* **2:7a** Or *Son;* also in 2:12. **2:7b** Or *Today
I reveal you as my son.* **2:9** Greek version reads *rule.* Compare
Rev 2:27. **2:12** The meaning of the Hebrew is uncertain.
3:2 Hebrew *Selah.* The meaning of this word is uncertain, though
it is probably a musical or literary term. It is rendered *Interlude*
throughout the Psalms.

7 You have given me greater joy
than those who have abundant harvests
of grain and new wine.
8 In peace I will lie down and sleep,
for you alone, O LORD, will keep me safe.

5 For the choir director: A psalm of David,
to be accompanied by the flute.

1 O LORD, hear me as I pray;
pay attention to my groaning.
2 Listen to my cry for help,
my King and my God,
for I pray to no one but you.
3 Listen to my voice in the morning, LORD.
Each morning I bring my requests to you
and wait expectantly.

4 O God, you take no pleasure in wickedness;
you cannot tolerate the sins of the wicked.
5 Therefore, the proud may not stand in
your presence,
for you hate all who do evil.
6 You will destroy those who tell lies.
The LORD detests murderers and
deceivers.

7 Because of your unfailing love,
I can enter your house;
I will worship at your Temple with
deepest awe.
8 Lead me in the right path, O LORD,
or my enemies will conquer me.
Make your way plain for me to follow.

9 My enemies cannot speak a truthful word.
Their deepest desire is to destroy others.
Their talk is foul, like the stench from an
open grave.
Their tongues are filled with flattery.*
10 O God, declare them guilty.
Let them be caught in their own traps.
Drive them away because of their many sins,
for they have rebelled against you.

11 But let all who take refuge in you rejoice;
let them sing joyful praises forever.
Spread your protection over them,
that all who love your name may be
filled with joy.
12 For you bless the godly, O LORD;
you surround them with your shield
of love.

6 For the choir director: A psalm of David, to be
accompanied by an eight-stringed instrument.*

1 O LORD, don't rebuke me in your anger
or discipline me in your rage.
2 Have compassion on me, LORD,
for I am weak.
Heal me, LORD, for my bones are in agony.

3 I am sick at heart.
How long, O LORD, until you restore me?
4 Return, O LORD, and rescue me.
Save me because of your unfailing love.
5 For the dead do not remember you.
Who can praise you from the grave?*

6 I am worn out from sobbing.
All night I flood my bed with weeping,
drenching it with my tears.
7 My vision is blurred by grief;
my eyes are worn out because of
all my enemies.

8 Go away, all you who do evil,
for the LORD has heard my weeping.
9 The LORD has heard my plea;
the LORD will answer my prayer.
10 May all my enemies be disgraced
and terrified.
May they suddenly turn back in shame.

7 A psalm* of David, which he sang to the LORD
concerning Cush of the tribe of Benjamin.

1 I come to you for protection,
O LORD my God.
Save me from my persecutors—rescue me!
2 If you don't, they will maul me like a lion,
tearing me to pieces with no one to
rescue me.
3 O LORD my God, if I have done wrong
or am guilty of injustice,
4 if I have betrayed a friend
or plundered my enemy without cause,
5 then let my enemies capture me.
Let them trample me into the ground
and drag my honor in the dust.   Interlude

6 Arise, O LORD, in anger!
Stand up against the fury of my enemies!
Wake up, my God, and bring justice!
7 Gather the nations before you.
Rule over them from on high.
8 The LORD judges the nations.
Declare me righteous, O LORD,
for I am innocent, O Most High!
9 End the evil of those who are wicked,
and defend the righteous.
For you look deep within the mind and heart,
O righteous God.

10 God is my shield,
saving those whose hearts are true
and right.
11 God is an honest judge.
He is angry with the wicked every day.

5:9 Greek version reads with lies. Compare Rom 3:13.
6:TITLE Hebrew with stringed instruments; according to the
sheminith.   6:5 Hebrew from Sheol?   7:TITLE Hebrew A shiggaion,
probably indicating a musical setting for the psalm.

12 If a person does not repent,
   God* will sharpen his sword;
   he will bend and string his bow.
13 He will prepare his deadly weapons
   and shoot his flaming arrows.

14 The wicked conceive evil;
   they are pregnant with trouble
   and give birth to lies.
15 They dig a deep pit to trap others,
   then fall into it themselves.
16 The trouble they make for others backfires
      on them.
   The violence they plan falls on their
      own heads.

17 I will thank the LORD because he is just;
   I will sing praise to the name of
   the LORD Most High.

8 *For the choir director: A psalm of David,
   to be accompanied by a stringed instrument.**

1 O LORD, our Lord, your majestic name fills
      the earth!
   Your glory is higher than the heavens.
2 You have taught children and infants
      to tell of your strength,*
   silencing your enemies
   and all who oppose you.

3 When I look at the night sky and see the
      work of your fingers—
   the moon and the stars you set in place—
4 what are mere mortals that you should
      think about them,
   human beings that you should care
      for them?*
5 Yet you made them only a little lower
      than God*
   and crowned them* with glory and honor.
6 You gave them charge of everything you
      made,
   putting all things under their authority—
7 the flocks and the herds
   and all the wild animals,
8 the birds in the sky, the fish in the sea,
   and everything that swims
      the ocean currents.

9 O LORD, our Lord, your majestic name
   fills the earth!

9 *For the choir director: A psalm of David,
   to be sung to the tune "Death of the Son."*

1 I will praise you, LORD, with all my heart;
   I will tell of all the marvelous things
      you have done.
2 I will be filled with joy because of you.
   I will sing praises to your name,
   O Most High.

3 My enemies retreated;
   they staggered and died when you
      appeared.
4 For you have judged in my favor;
   from your throne you have judged
      with fairness.
5 You have rebuked the nations and destroyed
      the wicked;
   you have erased their names forever.
6 The enemy is finished, in endless ruins;
   the cities you uprooted are now forgotten.

7 But the LORD reigns forever,
   executing judgment from his throne.
8 He will judge the world with justice
   and rule the nations with fairness.
9 The LORD is a shelter for the oppressed,
   a refuge in times of trouble.
10 Those who know your name trust in you,
   for you, O LORD, do not abandon those
      who search for you.

11 Sing praises to the LORD who reigns
      in Jerusalem.*
   Tell the world about his
      unforgettable deeds.
12 For he who avenges murder cares for
      the helpless.
   He does not ignore the cries of those
      who suffer.

13 LORD, have mercy on me.
   See how my enemies torment me.
   Snatch me back from the jaws of death.
14 Save me so I can praise you publicly at
      Jerusalem's gates,
   so I can rejoice that you have rescued me.

15 The nations have fallen into the pit they dug
      for others.
   Their own feet have been caught in the
      trap they set.
16 The LORD is known for his justice.
   The wicked are trapped by
      their own deeds.   *Quiet Interlude**

17 The wicked will go down to the grave.*
   This is the fate of all the nations who
      ignore God.
18 But the needy will not be ignored forever;
   the hopes of the poor will not always
      be crushed.

19 Arise, O LORD!
   Do not let mere mortals defy you!

7:12 Hebrew *he.*   **8:TITLE** Hebrew *according to the gittith.*
8:2 Greek version reads *to give you praise.* Compare Matt 21:16.
8:4 Hebrew *what is man that you should think of him, / the son of
man that you should care for him?*   **8:5a** Or *Yet you made them only
a little lower than the angels;* Hebrew reads *Yet you made him* [i.e.,
man] *a little lower than Elohim.*   **8:5b** Hebrew *him* [i.e., man];
similarly in 8:6.   **9:11** Hebrew *Zion;* also in 9:14.   **9:16** Hebrew
Higgaion Selah. The meaning of this phrase is uncertain.
9:17 Hebrew *to Sheol.*

Judge the nations!
²⁰ Make them tremble in fear, O LORD.
    Let the nations know they are
        merely human.   *Interlude*

10

¹ O LORD, why do you stand so far away?
    Why do you hide when I am in
        trouble?
² The wicked arrogantly hunt down the poor.
    Let them be caught in the evil they plan
        for others.
³ For they brag about their evil desires;
    they praise the greedy and curse the LORD.

⁴ The wicked are too proud to seek God.
    They seem to think that God is dead.
⁵ Yet they succeed in everything they do.
    They do not see your punishment
        awaiting them.
    They sneer at all their enemies.
⁶ They think, "Nothing bad will ever happen
        to us!
    We will be free of trouble forever!"

⁷ Their mouths are full of cursing, lies,
        and threats.*
    Trouble and evil are on the tips of
        their tongues.
⁸ They lurk in ambush in the villages,
    waiting to murder innocent people.
    They are always searching for
        helpless victims.
⁹ Like lions crouched in hiding,
    they wait to pounce on the helpless.
    Like hunters they capture the helpless
        and drag them away in nets.
¹⁰ Their helpless victims are crushed;
    they fall beneath the strength of
        the wicked.
¹¹ The wicked think, "God isn't watching us!
    He has closed his eyes and won't even see
        what we do!"

¹² Arise, O LORD!
    Punish the wicked, O God!
    Do not ignore the helpless!
¹³ Why do the wicked get away with
        despising God?
    They think, "God will never call us
        to account."
¹⁴ But you see the trouble and grief they cause.
    You take note of it and punish them.
    The helpless put their trust in you.
    You defend the orphans.

¹⁵ Break the arms of these wicked,
        evil people!
    Go after them until the last one
        is destroyed.
¹⁶ The LORD is king forever and ever!
    The godless nations will vanish from
        the land.

¹⁷ LORD, you know the hopes of the helpless.
    Surely you will hear their cries and
        comfort them.
¹⁸ You will bring justice to the orphans and
        the oppressed,
    so mere people can no longer terrify them.

11

For the choir director: A psalm of David.

¹ I trust in the LORD for protection.
    So why do you say to me,
    "Fly like a bird to the mountains
        for safety!
² The wicked are stringing their bows
    and fitting their arrows on the
        bowstrings.
    They shoot from the shadows
        at those whose hearts are right.
³ The foundations of law and order
        have collapsed.
    What can the righteous do?"

⁴ But the LORD is in his holy Temple;
    the LORD still rules from heaven.
    He watches everyone closely,
        examining every person on earth.
⁵ The LORD examines both the righteous and
        the wicked.
    He hates those who love violence.
⁶ He will rain down blazing coals and burning
        sulfur on the wicked,
    punishing them with scorching winds.
⁷ For the righteous LORD loves justice.
    The virtuous will see his face.

12

*For the choir director: A psalm of David,
    to be accompanied by an eight-stringed
instrument.**

¹ Help, O LORD, for the godly are fast
        disappearing!
    The faithful have vanished from the earth!
² Neighbors lie to each other,
    speaking with flattering lips and
        deceitful hearts.
³ May the LORD cut off their flattering lips
    and silence their boastful tongues.
⁴ They say, "We will lie to our hearts' content.
    Our lips are our own—who can stop us?"

⁵ The LORD replies, "I have seen violence done
        to the helpless,
    and I have heard the groans of the poor.
    Now I will rise up to rescue them,
        as they have longed for me to do."
⁶ The LORD's promises are pure,
    like silver refined in a furnace,
    purified seven times over.

10:7 Greek version reads *cursing and bitterness.* Compare Rom 3:14.
12:TITLE Hebrew *according to the sheminith.*

7 Therefore, LORD, we know you will protect
the oppressed,
preserving them forever from this lying
generation,
8 even though the wicked strut about,
and evil is praised throughout the land.

13 For the choir director: A psalm of David.

1 O LORD, how long will you forget me?
Forever?
How long will you look the other way?
2 How long must I struggle with anguish
in my soul,
with sorrow in my heart every day?
How long will my enemy have
the upper hand?

3 Turn and answer me, O LORD my God!
Restore the sparkle to my eyes,
or I will die.
4 Don't let my enemies gloat, saying,
"We have defeated him!"
Don't let them rejoice at my downfall.

5 But I trust in your unfailing love.
I will rejoice because you have rescued me.
6 I will sing to the LORD
because he is good to me.

14 For the choir director: A psalm of David.

1 Only fools say in their hearts,
"There is no God."
They are corrupt, and their actions are evil;
not one of them does good!

2 The LORD looks down from heaven
on the entire human race;
he looks to see if anyone is truly wise,
if anyone seeks God.
3 But no, all have turned away;
all have become corrupt.*
No one does good,
not a single one!

4 Will those who do evil never learn?
They eat up my people like bread
and wouldn't think of praying to the LORD.
5 Terror will grip them,
for God is with those who obey him.
6 The wicked frustrate the plans of
the oppressed,
but the LORD will protect his people.

7 Who will come from Mount Zion
to rescue Israel?
When the LORD restores his people,
Jacob will shout with joy,
and Israel will rejoice.

15 A psalm of David.

1 Who may worship in your sanctuary, LORD?
Who may enter your presence on your
holy hill?
2 Those who lead blameless lives and do what
is right,
speaking the truth from sincere hearts.
3 Those who refuse to gossip
or harm their neighbors
or speak evil of their friends.
4 Those who despise flagrant sinners,
and honor the faithful followers of
the LORD,
and keep their promises even
when it hurts.
5 Those who lend money without
charging interest,
and who cannot be bribed to lie about
the innocent.
Such people will stand firm forever.

16 A psalm* of David.

1 Keep me safe, O God,
for I have come to you for refuge.

2 I said to the LORD, "You are my Master!
Every good thing I have comes from you."
3 The godly people in the land
are my true heroes!
I take pleasure in them!
4 Troubles multiply for those who chase after
other gods.
I will not take part in their sacrifices
of blood
or even speak the names of their gods.

5 LORD, you alone are my inheritance,
my cup of blessing.
You guard all that is mine.
6 The land you have given me is
a pleasant land.
What a wonderful inheritance!

7 I will bless the LORD who guides me;
even at night my heart instructs me.
8 I know the LORD is always with me.
I will not be shaken,
for he is right beside me.

9 No wonder my heart is glad, and I rejoice.*
My body rests in safety.
10 For you will not leave my soul among
the dead*
or allow your holy one* to rot in the grave.

14:3 Greek version reads *have become useless.* Compare Rom 3:12.
16:TITLE Hebrew *miktam.* This may be a literary or musical term.
16:9 Greek version reads *and my tongue shouts his praises.* Compare
Acts 2:26. 16:10a Hebrew *in Sheol.* 16:10b Or *your Holy One.*

¹¹ You will show me the way of life,
 granting me the joy of your presence
 and the pleasures of living
  with you forever.*

17 A prayer of David.

¹ O LORD, hear my plea for justice.
 Listen to my cry for help.
Pay attention to my prayer,
 for it comes from honest lips.
² Declare me innocent,
 for you see those who do right.

³ You have tested my thoughts and examined
  my heart in the night.
 You have scrutinized me and found
  nothing wrong.
 I am determined not to sin in what I say.
⁴ I have followed your commands,
 which keep me from following cruel and
  evil people.
⁵ My steps have stayed on your path;
 I have not wavered from following you.

⁶ I am praying to you because I know
  you will answer, O God.
 Bend down and listen as I pray.
⁷ Show me your unfailing love
 in wonderful ways.
 By your mighty power you rescue
  those who seek refuge from their enemies.
⁸ Guard me as you would guard your own eyes.*
 Hide me in the shadow of your wings.
⁹ Protect me from wicked people who
  attack me,
 from murderous enemies who
  surround me.
¹⁰ They are without pity.
 Listen to their boasting!
¹¹ They track me down and surround me,
 watching for the chance to throw me
  to the ground.
¹² They are like hungry lions,
 eager to tear me apart—
 like young lions hiding in ambush.

¹³ Arise, O LORD!
 Stand against them, and bring them
  to their knees!
 Rescue me from the wicked
  with your sword!
¹⁴ By the power of your hand, O LORD,
 destroy those who look to this world for
  their reward.
 But satisfy the hunger of your
  treasured ones.
 May their children have plenty,
 leaving an inheritance for their
  descendants.
¹⁵ Because I am righteous, I will see you.

When I awake, I will see you face to face
 and be satisfied.

18 For the choir director: A psalm of David, the servant of the LORD. He sang this song to the LORD on the day the LORD rescued him from all his enemies and from Saul. He sang:

¹ I love you, LORD;
 you are my strength.
² The LORD is my rock, my fortress,
  and my savior;
 my God is my rock, in whom I find
  protection.
 He is my shield, the power that saves me,
  and my place of safety.
³ I called on the LORD,
  who is worthy of praise,
 and he saved me from my enemies.

⁴ The ropes of death entangled me;
 floods of destruction swept over me.
⁵ The grave* wrapped its ropes around me;
 death laid a trap in my path.
⁶ But in my distress I cried out to the LORD;
 yes, I prayed to my God for help.
 He heard me from his sanctuary;
  my cry to him reached his ears.

⁷ Then the earth quaked and trembled.
 The foundations of the mountains shook;
 they quaked because of his anger.
⁸ Smoke poured from his nostrils;
 fierce flames leaped from his mouth.
 Glowing coals blazed forth from him.
⁹ He opened the heavens and came down;
 dark storm clouds were beneath his feet.
¹⁰ Mounted on a mighty angelic being,* he
  flew,
 soaring on the wings of the wind.
¹¹ He shrouded himself in darkness,
 veiling his approach with dark
  rain clouds.
¹² Thick clouds shielded the brightness
  around him
 and rained down hail and burning coals.*
¹³ The LORD thundered from heaven;
 the voice of the Most High resounded
  amid the hail and burning coals.
¹⁴ He shot his arrows and scattered
  his enemies;
 great bolts of lightning flashed, and they
  were confused.
¹⁵ Then at your command, O LORD,
 at the blast of your breath,
 the bottom of the sea could be seen,
 and the foundations of the earth were
  laid bare.

16:11 Greek version reads *You have shown me the way of life, / and you will fill me with the joy of your presence.* Compare Acts 2:28. 17:8 Hebrew *as the pupil of your eye.* 18:5 Hebrew *Sheol.* 18:10 Hebrew *a cherub.* 18:12 Or *and lightning bolts;* also in 18:13.

16 He reached down from heaven
  and rescued me;
  he drew me out of deep waters.
17 He rescued me from my powerful enemies,
  from those who hated me and were too
    strong for me.
18 They attacked me at a moment when
    I was in distress,
  but the LORD supported me.
19 He led me to a place of safety;
  he rescued me because he delights in me.
20 The LORD rewarded me for doing right;
  he restored me because of my innocence.
21 For I have kept the ways of the LORD;
  I have not turned from my God
    to follow evil.
22 I have followed all his regulations;
  I have never abandoned his decrees.
23 I am blameless before God;
  I have kept myself from sin.
24 The LORD rewarded me for doing right.
  He has seen my innocence.

25 To the faithful you show yourself faithful;
  to those with integrity you show integrity.
26 To the pure you show yourself pure,
  but to the crooked you show yourself
    shrewd.
27 You rescue the humble,
  but you humiliate the proud.
28 You light a lamp for me.
  The LORD, my God, lights up my darkness.
29 In your strength I can crush an army;
  with my God I can scale any wall.

30 God's way is perfect.
  All the LORD's promises prove true.
  He is a shield for all who look to him for
    protection.
31 For who is God except the LORD?
  Who but our God is a solid rock?
32 God arms me with strength,
  and he makes my way perfect.
33 He makes me as surefooted as a deer,
  enabling me to stand on mountain heights.
34 He trains my hands for battle;
  he strengthens my arm to draw
    a bronze bow.
35 You have given me your shield of victory.
  Your right hand supports me;
  your help* has made me great.
36 You have made a wide path for my feet
  to keep them from slipping.

37 I chased my enemies and caught them;
  I did not stop until they were conquered.
38 I struck them down so they could not get up;
  they fell beneath my feet.
39 You have armed me with strength
    for the battle;
  you have subdued my enemies
    under my feet.

40 You placed my foot on their necks.
  I have destroyed all who hated me.
41 They called for help, but no one came to
    their rescue.
  They even cried to the LORD, but he
    refused to answer.
42 I ground them as fine as dust in the wind.
  I swept them into the gutter like dirt.
43 You gave me victory over my accusers.
  You appointed me ruler over nations;
  people I don't even know now serve me.
44 As soon as they hear of me, they submit;
  foreign nations cringe before me.
45 They all lose their courage
  and come trembling from their
    strongholds.

46 The LORD lives! Praise to my Rock!
  May the God of my salvation be exalted!
47 He is the God who pays back those who
    harm me;
  he subdues the nations under me
48 and rescues me from my enemies.
  You hold me safe beyond the reach of my
    enemies;
  you save me from violent opponents.
49 For this, O LORD, I will praise you among
    the nations;
  I will sing praises to your name.
50 You give great victories to your king;
  you show unfailing love to
    your anointed,
  to David and all his descendants forever.

19 For the choir director: A psalm of David.

1 The heavens proclaim the glory of God.
  The skies display his craftsmanship.
2 Day after day they continue to speak;
  night after night they make him known.
3 They speak without a sound or word;
  their voice is never heard.*
4 Yet their message has gone throughout
    the earth,
  and their words to all the world.

  God has made a home in the heavens
    for the sun.
5 It bursts forth like a radiant bridegroom
    after his wedding.
  It rejoices like a great athlete eager
    to run the race.
6 The sun rises at one end of the heavens
  and follows its course to the other end.
  Nothing can hide from its heat.

7 The instructions of the LORD are perfect,
  reviving the soul.

18:35 Hebrew your humility; compare 2 Sam 22:36. 19:3 Or There
is no speech or language where their voice is not heard.

The decrees of the LORD are trustworthy,
  making wise the simple.
8 The commandments of the LORD are right,
  bringing joy to the heart.
The commands of the LORD are clear,
  giving insight for living.
9 Reverence for the LORD is pure,
  lasting forever.
The laws of the LORD are true;
  each one is fair.
10 They are more desirable than gold,
  even the finest gold.
They are sweeter than honey,
  even honey dripping from the comb.
11 They are a warning to your servant,
  a great reward for those who obey them.

12 How can I know all the sins lurking
  in my heart?
Cleanse me from these hidden faults.
13 Keep your servant from deliberate sins!
  Don't let them control me.
Then I will be free of guilt
  and innocent of great sin.

14 May the words of my mouth
  and the meditation of my heart
be pleasing to you,
  O LORD, my rock and my redeemer.

20

For the choir director: A psalm of David.

1 In times of trouble,
    may the LORD answer your cry.
  May the name of the God of Jacob keep
  you safe from all harm.
2 May he send you help from his sanctuary
  and strengthen you from Jerusalem.*
3 May he remember all your gifts
  and look favorably on your burnt
    offerings.   *Interlude*

4 May he grant your heart's desires
  and make all your plans succeed.
5 May we shout for joy when we hear of
  your victory
  and raise a victory banner in the name of
    our God.
May the LORD answer all your prayers.

6 Now I know that the LORD rescues his
    anointed king.
  He will answer him from
    his holy heaven
  and rescue him by his great power.
7 Some nations boast of their chariots
    and horses,
  but we boast in the name of the LORD
    our God.
8 Those nations will fall down and collapse,
  but we will rise up and stand firm.

9 Give victory to our king, O LORD!
  Answer our cry for help.

21

For the choir director: A psalm of David.

1 How the king rejoices in your strength,
    O LORD!
  He shouts with joy because
    you give him victory.
2 For you have given him his heart's desire;
  you have withheld nothing
    he requested.   *Interlude*

3 You welcomed him back with success
    and prosperity.
  You placed a crown of finest gold
    on his head.
4 He asked you to preserve his life,
  and you granted his request.
  The days of his life stretch on forever.
5 Your victory brings him great honor,
  and you have clothed him with splendor
    and majesty.
6 You have endowed him with eternal
    blessings
  and given him the joy of your presence.
7 For the king trusts in the LORD.
  The unfailing love of the Most High will
    keep him from stumbling.

8 You will capture all your enemies.
  Your strong right hand will seize
    all who hate you.
9 You will throw them in a flaming furnace
    when you appear.
  The LORD will consume them in his anger;
    fire will devour them.
10 You will wipe their children from the face
    of the earth;
  they will never have descendants.
11 Although they plot against you,
  their evil schemes will never succeed.
12 For they will turn and run
  when they see your arrows aimed at them.
13 Rise up, O LORD, in all your power.
  With music and singing we celebrate
    your mighty acts.

22

*For the choir director: A psalm of David,
to be sung to the tune "Doe of the Dawn."*

1 My God, my God,
    why have you abandoned me?
  Why are you so far away when I groan
    for help?
2 Every day I call to you, my God, but you do
    not answer.
  Every night I lift my voice,
    but I find no relief.

___
20:2 Hebrew *Zion.*

³ Yet you are holy,
   enthroned on the praises of Israel.
⁴ Our ancestors trusted in you,
   and you rescued them.
⁵ They cried out to you and were saved.
   They trusted in you and were
   never disgraced.

⁶ But I am a worm and not a man.
   I am scorned and despised by all!
⁷ Everyone who sees me mocks me.
   They sneer and shake their heads, saying,
⁸ "Is this the one who relies on the LORD?
   Then let the LORD save him!
   If the LORD loves him so much,
   let the LORD rescue him!"

⁹ Yet you brought me safely from my
   mother's womb
   and led me to trust you
   at my mother's breast.
¹⁰ I was thrust into your arms at my birth.
   You have been my God from the moment
   I was born.

¹¹ Do not stay so far from me,
   for trouble is near,
   and no one else can help me.
¹² My enemies surround me
   like a herd of bulls;
   fierce bulls of Bashan
   have hemmed me in!
¹³ Like lions they open their jaws against me,
   roaring and tearing into their prey.
¹⁴ My life is poured out like water,
   and all my bones are out of joint.
   My heart is like wax,
   melting within me.
¹⁵ My strength has dried up like sunbaked clay.
   My tongue sticks to the roof of my mouth.
   You have laid me in the dust and left me
   for dead.
¹⁶ My enemies surround me like a pack of
   dogs;
   an evil gang closes in on me.
   They have pierced* my hands and feet.
¹⁷ I can count all my bones.
   My enemies stare at me and gloat.
¹⁸ They divide my garments among
   themselves
   and throw dice* for my clothing.

¹⁹ O LORD, do not stay far away!
   You are my strength;
   come quickly to my aid!
²⁰ Save me from the sword;
   spare my precious life from these dogs.
²¹ Snatch me from the lion's jaws
   and from the horns of these wild oxen.

²² I will proclaim your name to my brothers
   and sisters.*

I will praise you among your
   assembled people.
²³ Praise the LORD, all you who fear him!
   Honor him,
   all you descendants of Jacob!
   Show him reverence, all you descendants
   of Israel!
²⁴ For he has not ignored or belittled the
   suffering of the needy.
   He has not turned his back on them,
   but has listened to their cries for help.

²⁵ I will praise you in the great assembly.
   I will fulfill my vows in the presence of
   those who worship you.
²⁶ The poor will eat and be satisfied.
   All who seek the LORD will praise him.
   Their hearts will rejoice with
   everlasting joy.
²⁷ The whole earth will acknowledge the LORD
   and return to him.
   All the families of the nations will bow
   down before him.
²⁸ For royal power belongs to the LORD.
   He rules all the nations.

²⁹ Let the rich of the earth feast and worship.
   Bow before him, all who are mortal,
   all whose lives will end as dust.
³⁰ Our children will also serve him.
   Future generations will hear about the
   wonders of the Lord.
³¹ His righteous acts will be told to those
   not yet born.
   They will hear about everything
   he has done.

23 *A psalm of David.*

¹ The LORD is my shepherd;
   I have all that I need.
² He lets me rest in green meadows;
   he leads me beside peaceful streams.
³ He renews my strength.
   He guides me along right paths,
   bringing honor to his name.
⁴ Even when I walk
   through the darkest valley,*
   I will not be afraid,
   for you are close beside me.
   Your rod and your staff
   protect and comfort me.
⁵ You prepare a feast for me
   in the presence of my enemies.
   You honor me by anointing my head
   with oil.
   My cup overflows with blessings.

22:16 As in some Hebrew manuscripts and Greek and Syriac
versions; most Hebrew manuscripts read *They are like a lion at.*
22:18 Hebrew *cast lots.*   22:22 Hebrew *my brothers.*   23:4 Or *the
dark valley of death.*

⁶ Surely your goodness and unfailing love
    will pursue me
all the days of my life,
and I will live in the house of the LORD
    forever.

24 A psalm of David.

¹ The earth is the LORD's, and everything in it.
    The world and all its people belong to him.
² For he laid the earth's foundation on the seas
    and built it on the ocean depths.

³ Who may climb the mountain of the LORD?
    Who may stand in his holy place?
⁴ Only those whose hands and hearts are pure,
    who do not worship idols
    and never tell lies.
⁵ They will receive the LORD's blessing
    and have a right relationship with God
    their savior.
⁶ Such people may seek you
    and worship in your presence,
    O God of Jacob.*   *Interlude*

⁷ Open up, ancient gates!
    Open up, ancient doors,
    and let the King of glory enter.
⁸ Who is the King of glory?
    The LORD, strong and mighty;
    the LORD, invincible in battle.
⁹ Open up, ancient gates!
    Open up, ancient doors,
    and let the King of glory enter.
¹⁰ Who is the King of glory?
    The LORD of Heaven's Armies—
    he is the King of glory.   *Interlude*

25* A psalm of David.

¹ O LORD, I give my life to you.
²   I trust in you, my God!
Do not let me be disgraced,
    or let my enemies rejoice in my defeat.
³ No one who trusts in you will ever be
        disgraced,
    but disgrace comes to those who try to
        deceive others.

⁴ Show me the right path, O LORD;
    point out the road for me to follow.
⁵ Lead me by your truth and teach me,
    for you are the God who saves me.
    All day long I put my hope in you.
⁶ Remember, O LORD, your compassion and
        unfailing love,
    which you have shown from
        long ages past.
⁷ Do not remember the rebellious
    sins of my youth.

Remember me in the light of your
        unfailing love,
    for you are merciful, O LORD.

⁸ The LORD is good and does what is right;
    he shows the proper path to
        those who go astray.
⁹ He leads the humble in doing right,
    teaching them his way.
¹⁰ The LORD leads with unfailing love
        and faithfulness
    all who keep his covenant and obey
        his demands.

¹¹ For the honor of your name, O LORD,
    forgive my many, many sins.
¹² Who are those who fear the LORD?
    He will show them the path
        they should choose.
¹³ They will live in prosperity,
    and their children will inherit the land.
¹⁴ The LORD is a friend to those who fear him.
    He teaches them his covenant.
¹⁵ My eyes are always on the LORD,
    for he rescues me from the traps of my
        enemies.

¹⁶ Turn to me and have mercy,
    for I am alone and in deep distress.
¹⁷ My problems go from bad to worse.
    Oh, save me from them all!
¹⁸ Feel my pain and see my trouble.
    Forgive all my sins.
¹⁹ See how many enemies I have
    and how viciously they hate me!
²⁰ Protect me! Rescue my life from them!
    Do not let me be disgraced, for in you
        I take refuge.
²¹ May integrity and honesty protect me,
    for I put my hope in you.

²² O God, ransom Israel
    from all its troubles.

26 A psalm of David.

¹ Declare me innocent, O LORD,
    for I have acted with integrity;
    I have trusted in the LORD without
        wavering.
² Put me on trial, LORD, and cross-examine me.
    Test my motives and my heart.
³ For I am always aware of your
        unfailing love,
    and I have lived according to your truth.
⁴ I do not spend time with liars
    or go along with hypocrites.

24:6 As in two Hebrew manuscripts and Greek and Syriac
versions; most Hebrew manuscripts read *O Jacob*. 25 This
psalm is a Hebrew acrostic poem; each verse begins with a
successive letter of the Hebrew alphabet.

⁵ I hate the gatherings of those who do evil,
and I refuse to join in with the wicked.
⁶ I wash my hands to declare my innocence.
I come to your altar, O LORD,
⁷ singing a song of thanksgiving
and telling of all your wonders.
⁸ I love your sanctuary, LORD,
the place where your glorious
presence dwells.

⁹ Don't let me suffer the fate of sinners.
Don't condemn me along with
murderers.
¹⁰ Their hands are dirty with evil schemes,
and they constantly take bribes.
¹¹ But I am not like that; I live with integrity.
So redeem me and show me mercy.
¹² Now I stand on solid ground,
and I will publicly praise the LORD.

27 *A psalm of David.*

¹ The LORD is my light and my salvation—
so why should I be afraid?
The LORD is my fortress,
protecting me from danger,
so why should I tremble?
² When evil people come to devour me,
when my enemies and foes attack me,
they will stumble and fall.
³ Though a mighty army surrounds me,
my heart will not be afraid.
Even if I am attacked,
I will remain confident.

⁴ The one thing I ask of the LORD—
the thing I seek most—
is to live in the house of the LORD all the
days of my life,
delighting in the LORD's perfections
and meditating in his Temple.
⁵ For he will conceal me there
when troubles come;
he will hide me in his sanctuary.
He will place me out of reach on
a high rock.
⁶ Then I will hold my head high
above my enemies who surround me.
At his sanctuary I will offer sacrifices with
shouts of joy,
singing and praising the LORD
with music.

⁷ Hear me as I pray, O LORD.
Be merciful and answer me!
⁸ My heart has heard you say,
"Come and talk with me."
And my heart responds,
"LORD, I am coming."
⁹ Do not turn your back on me.
Do not reject your servant in anger.

You have always been my helper.
Don't leave me now; don't abandon me,
O God of my salvation!
¹⁰ Even if my father and mother abandon me,
the LORD will hold me close.

¹¹ Teach me how to live, O LORD.
Lead me along the right path,
for my enemies are waiting for me.
¹² Do not let me fall into their hands.
For they accuse me of things
I've never done;
with every breath they threaten me
with violence.
¹³ Yet I am confident I will see
the LORD's goodness
while I am here in the land of the living.

¹⁴ Wait patiently for the LORD.
Be brave and courageous.
Yes, wait patiently for the LORD.

28 *A psalm of David.*

¹ I pray to you, O LORD, my rock.
Do not turn a deaf ear to me.
For if you are silent,
I might as well give up and die.
² Listen to my prayer for mercy
as I cry out to you for help,
as I lift my hands toward
your holy sanctuary.

³ Do not drag me away with the wicked—
with those who do evil—
those who speak friendly words to
their neighbors
while planning evil in their hearts.
⁴ Give them the punishment they
so richly deserve!
Measure it out in proportion to their
wickedness.
Pay them back for all their evil deeds!
Give them a taste of what they have done
to others.
⁵ They care nothing for what the LORD
has done
or for what his hands have made.
So he will tear them down,
and they will never be rebuilt!

⁶ Praise the LORD!
For he has heard my cry for mercy.
⁷ The LORD is my strength and shield.
I trust him with all my heart.
He helps me,
and my heart is filled with joy.
I burst out in songs of thanksgiving.

⁸ The LORD gives his people strength.
He is a safe fortress for his anointed king.

⁹ Save your people!
Bless Israel, your special possession.*
Lead them like a shepherd,
and carry them in your arms forever.

29 A psalm of David.

¹ Honor the LORD, you heavenly beings*;
honor the LORD for his glory
and strength.
² Honor the LORD for the glory of his name.
Worship the LORD in the splendor
of his holiness.

³ The voice of the LORD echoes above the sea.
The God of glory thunders.
The LORD thunders over the mighty sea.
⁴ The voice of the LORD is powerful;
the voice of the LORD is majestic.
⁵ The voice of the LORD splits the mighty
cedars;
the LORD shatters the cedars of Lebanon.
⁶ He makes Lebanon's mountains skip
like a calf;
he makes Mount Hermon* leap like
a young wild ox.
⁷ The voice of the LORD strikes
with bolts of lightning.
⁸ The voice of the LORD makes the barren
wilderness quake;
the LORD shakes the wilderness of Kadesh.
⁹ The voice of the LORD twists mighty oaks*
and strips the forests bare.
In his Temple everyone shouts, "Glory!"

¹⁰ The LORD rules over the floodwaters.
The LORD reigns as king forever.
¹¹ The LORD gives his people strength.
The LORD blesses them with peace.

30 A psalm of David. A song for the dedication of the Temple.

¹ I will exalt you, LORD, for you rescued me.
You refused to let my enemies triumph
over me.
² O LORD my God, I cried to you for help,
and you restored my health.
³ You brought me up from the grave,* O LORD.
You kept me from falling into the pit
of death.

⁴ Sing to the LORD, all you godly ones!
Praise his holy name.
⁵ For his anger lasts only a moment,
but his favor lasts a lifetime!
Weeping may last through the night,
but joy comes with the morning.

⁶ When I was prosperous, I said,
"Nothing can stop me now!"

⁷ Your favor, O LORD, made me as secure
as a mountain.
Then you turned away from me,
and I was shattered.

⁸ I cried out to you, O LORD.
I begged the Lord for mercy, saying,
⁹ "What will you gain if I die,
if I sink into the grave?
Can my dust praise you?
Can it tell of your faithfulness?
¹⁰ Hear me, LORD, and have mercy on me.
Help me, O LORD."

¹¹ You have turned my mourning into
joyful dancing.
You have taken away my clothes of
mourning and clothed me with joy,
¹² that I might sing praises to you and
not be silent.
O LORD my God, I will give you thanks
forever!

31 For the choir director: A psalm of David.

¹ O LORD, I have come to you for protection;
don't let me be disgraced.
Save me, for you do what is right.
² Turn your ear to listen to me;
rescue me quickly.
Be my rock of protection,
a fortress where I will be safe.
³ You are my rock and my fortress.
For the honor of your name, lead me out
of this danger.
⁴ Pull me from the trap my enemies
set for me,
for I find protection in you alone.
⁵ I entrust my spirit into your hand.
Rescue me, LORD, for you are
a faithful God.

⁶ I hate those who worship worthless idols.
I trust in the LORD.
⁷ I will be glad and rejoice in your
unfailing love,
for you have seen my troubles,
and you care about the anguish of
my soul.
⁸ You have not handed me over to my enemies
but have set me in a safe place.

⁹ Have mercy on me, LORD,
for I am in distress.
Tears blur my eyes.
My body and soul are withering away.
¹⁰ I am dying from grief;
my years are shortened by sadness.

28:9 Hebrew *Bless your inheritance.* 29:1 Hebrew *you sons of God.*
29:6 Hebrew *Sirion,* another name for Mount Hermon. 29:9 Or
causes the deer to writhe in labor. 30:3 Hebrew *from Sheol.*

Sin has drained my strength;
 I am wasting away from within.
[11] I am scorned by all my enemies
 and despised by my neighbors—
 even my friends are afraid to come near me.
When they see me on the street,
 they run the other way.
[12] I am ignored as if I were dead,
 as if I were a broken pot.
[13] I have heard the many rumors about me,
 and I am surrounded by terror.
My enemies conspire against me,
 plotting to take my life.

[14] But I am trusting you, O LORD,
 saying, "You are my God!"
[15] My future is in your hands.
 Rescue me from those who hunt me
 down relentlessly.
[16] Let your favor shine on your servant.
 In your unfailing love, rescue me.
[17] Don't let me be disgraced, O LORD,
 for I call out to you for help.
Let the wicked be disgraced;
 let them lie silent in the grave.*
[18] Silence their lying lips—
 those proud and arrogant lips that accuse
 the godly.

[19] How great is the goodness
 you have stored up for those who fear you.
You lavish it on those who come to you for
 protection,
 blessing them before the watching world.
[20] You hide them in the shelter of your presence,
 safe from those who conspire against them.
You shelter them in your presence,
 far from accusing tongues.

[21] Praise the LORD,
 for he has shown me the wonders of his
 unfailing love.
 He kept me safe when my city was under
 attack.
[22] In panic I cried out,
 "I am cut off from the LORD!"
But you heard my cry for mercy
 and answered my call for help.

[23] Love the LORD, all you godly ones!
 For the LORD protects those who are loyal
 to him,
 but he harshly punishes the arrogant.
[24] So be strong and courageous,
 all you who put your hope in the LORD!

32 *A psalm* of David.

[1] Oh, what joy for those
 whose disobedience is forgiven,
 whose sin is put out of sight!

[2] Yes, what joy for those
 whose record the LORD has cleared
 of guilt,*
 whose lives are lived in complete honesty!
[3] When I refused to confess my sin,
 my body wasted away,
 and I groaned all day long.
[4] Day and night your hand of discipline was
 heavy on me.
 My strength evaporated like water in the
 summer heat. *Interlude*

[5] Finally, I confessed all my sins to you
 and stopped trying to hide my guilt.
I said to myself, "I will confess my rebellion
 to the LORD."
 And you forgave me!
 All my guilt is gone. *Interlude*

[6] Therefore, let all the godly pray to you while
 there is still time,
 that they may not drown in the
 floodwaters of judgment.
[7] For you are my hiding place;
 you protect me from trouble.
You surround me with songs
 of victory. *Interlude*

[8] The LORD says, "I will guide you along the
 best pathway for your life.
 I will advise you and watch over you.
[9] Do not be like a senseless horse or mule
 that needs a bit and bridle to keep it
 under control."

[10] Many sorrows come to the wicked,
 but unfailing love surrounds those who
 trust the LORD.
[11] So rejoice in the LORD and be glad, all you
 who obey him!
Shout for joy, all you whose hearts
 are pure!

33

[1] Let the godly sing for joy to the LORD;
 it is fitting for the pure to praise him.
[2] Praise the LORD with melodies on the lyre;
 make music for him on the ten-stringed
 harp.
[3] Sing a new song of praise to him;
 play skillfully on the harp,
 and sing with joy.
[4] For the word of the LORD holds true,
 and we can trust everything he does.
[5] He loves whatever is just and good;
 the unfailing love of the LORD fills
 the earth.
[6] The LORD merely spoke,
 and the heavens were created.

31:17 Hebrew *in Sheol.* 32:TITLE Hebrew *maskil.* This may be
a literary or musical term. 32:2 Greek version reads *of sin.*
Compare Rom 4:8.

He breathed the word,
and all the stars were born.
7 He assigned the sea its boundaries
and locked the oceans in vast reservoirs.
8 Let the whole world fear the LORD,
and let everyone stand in awe of him.
9 For when he spoke, the world began!
It appeared at his command.

10 The LORD frustrates the plans of the nations
and thwarts all their schemes.
11 But the LORD's plans stand firm forever;
his intentions can never be shaken.

12 What joy for the nation whose God is
the LORD,
whose people he has chosen as his
inheritance.

13 The LORD looks down from heaven
and sees the whole human race.
14 From his throne he observes
all who live on the earth.
15 He made their hearts,
so he understands everything they do.
16 The best-equipped army cannot save a king,
nor is great strength enough to save
a warrior.
17 Don't count on your warhorse
to give you victory—
for all its strength, it cannot save you.

18 But the LORD watches over those who
fear him,
those who rely on his unfailing love.
19 He rescues them from death
and keeps them alive in times of famine.

20 We put our hope in the LORD.
He is our help and our shield.
21 In him our hearts rejoice,
for we trust in his holy name.
22 Let your unfailing love surround us, LORD,
for our hope is in you alone.

34 * *A psalm of David, regarding the time he
pretended to be insane in front of Abimelech,
who sent him away.*

1 I will praise the LORD at all times.
I will constantly speak his praises.
2 I will boast only in the LORD;
let all who are helpless take heart.
3 Come, let us tell of the LORD's greatness;
let us exalt his name together.

4 I prayed to the LORD, and he answered me.
He freed me from all my fears.
5 Those who look to him for help will be
radiant with joy;
no shadow of shame will darken
their faces.

6 In my desperation I prayed, and the LORD
listened;
he saved me from all my troubles.
7 For the angel of the LORD is a guard;
he surrounds and defends all who fear him.

8 Taste and see that the LORD is good.
Oh, the joys of those who take refuge
in him!
9 Fear the LORD, you his godly people,
for those who fear him will have
all they need.
10 Even strong young lions sometimes
go hungry,
but those who trust in the LORD will lack
no good thing.

11 Come, my children, and listen to me,
and I will teach you to fear the LORD.
12 Does anyone want to live a life
that is long and prosperous?
13 Then keep your tongue from speaking evil
and your lips from telling lies!
14 Turn away from evil and do good.
Search for peace, and work to maintain it.

15 The eyes of the LORD watch over those who
do right;
his ears are open to their cries for help.
16 But the LORD turns his face against those
who do evil;
he will erase their memory from the earth.
17 The LORD hears his people when they call
to him for help.
He rescues them from all their troubles.
18 The LORD is close to the brokenhearted;
he rescues those whose spirits are
crushed.

19 The righteous person faces many troubles,
but the LORD comes to the rescue
each time.
20 For the LORD protects the bones of
the righteous;
not one of them is broken!

21 Calamity will surely destroy the wicked,
and those who hate the righteous will be
punished.
22 But the LORD will redeem those who
serve him.
No one who takes refuge in him will be
condemned.

35 *A psalm of David.*

1 O LORD, oppose those who oppose me.
Fight those who fight against me.

---

34 This psalm is a Hebrew acrostic poem; each verse begins with
a successive letter of the Hebrew alphabet.

² Put on your armor, and take up your shield.
Prepare for battle, and come to my aid.
³ Lift up your spear and javelin
against those who pursue me.
Let me hear you say,
"I will give you victory!"
⁴ Bring shame and disgrace on those trying
to kill me;
turn them back and humiliate those who
want to harm me.
⁵ Blow them away like chaff in the wind—
a wind sent by the angel of the LORD.
⁶ Make their path dark and slippery,
with the angel of the LORD pursuing them.
⁷ I did them no wrong, but they laid a trap
for me.
I did them no wrong, but they dug a pit
to catch me.
⁸ So let sudden ruin come upon them!
Let them be caught in the trap they set
for me!
Let them be destroyed in the pit they dug
for me.

⁹ Then I will rejoice in the LORD.
I will be glad because he rescues me.
¹⁰ With every bone in my body I will praise him:
"LORD, who can compare with you?
Who else rescues the helpless from
the strong?
Who else protects the helpless and poor
from those who rob them?"

¹¹ Malicious witnesses testify against me.
They accuse me of crimes I know
nothing about.
¹² They repay me evil for good.
I am sick with despair.
¹³ Yet when they were ill, I grieved for them.
I denied myself by fasting for them,
but my prayers returned unanswered.
¹⁴ I was sad, as though they were my friends
or family,
as if I were grieving for my own mother.
¹⁵ But they are glad now that I am in trouble;
they gleefully join together against me.
I am attacked by people I don't even know;
they slander me constantly.
¹⁶ They mock me and call me names;
they snarl at me.

¹⁷ How long, O Lord, will you look on and
do nothing?
Rescue me from their fierce attacks.
Protect my life from these lions!
¹⁸ Then I will thank you in front of the
great assembly.
I will praise you before all the people.
¹⁹ Don't let my treacherous enemies rejoice
over my defeat.
Don't let those who hate me without
cause gloat over my sorrow.

²⁰ They don't talk of peace;
they plot against innocent people who
mind their own business.
²¹ They shout, "Aha! Aha!
With our own eyes we saw him do it!"

²² O LORD, you know all about this.
Do not stay silent.
Do not abandon me now, O Lord.
²³ Wake up! Rise to my defense!
Take up my case, my God and my Lord.
²⁴ Declare me not guilty, O LORD my God,
for you give justice.
Don't let my enemies laugh about me in
my troubles.
²⁵ Don't let them say, "Look, we got what
we wanted!
Now we will eat him alive!"

²⁶ May those who rejoice at my troubles
be humiliated and disgraced.
May those who triumph over me
be covered with shame and dishonor.
²⁷ But give great joy to those who came to
my defense.
Let them continually say,
"Great is the LORD,
who delights in blessing his servant
with peace!"
²⁸ Then I will proclaim your justice,
and I will praise you all day long.

36

*For the choir director: A psalm of David,
the servant of the LORD.*

¹ Sin whispers to the wicked, deep within
their hearts.*
They have no fear of God at all.
² In their blind conceit,
they cannot see how wicked
they really are.
³ Everything they say is crooked and deceitful.
They refuse to act wisely or do good.
⁴ They lie awake at night,
hatching sinful plots.
Their actions are never good.
They make no attempt to turn from evil.

⁵ Your unfailing love, O LORD, is as vast as
the heavens;
your faithfulness reaches beyond
the clouds.
⁶ Your righteousness is like the mighty
mountains,
your justice like the ocean depths.
You care for people and animals alike,
O LORD.
⁷ How precious is your unfailing love,
O God!

36:1 As in some Hebrew manuscripts and Syriac version, which
read *in his heart*. Masoretic Text reads *in my heart*.

All humanity finds shelter
    in the shadow of your wings.
8 You feed them from the abundance of your
    own house,
    letting them drink from your river of
    delights.
9 For you are the fountain of life,
    the light by which we see.

10 Pour out your unfailing love on those who
    love you;
    give justice to those with honest hearts.
11 Don't let the proud trample me
    or the wicked push me around.
12 Look! Those who do evil have fallen!
    They are thrown down,
    never to rise again.

37 *

A psalm of David.

1 Don't worry about the wicked
    or envy those who do wrong.
2 For like grass, they soon fade away.
    Like spring flowers, they soon wither.

3 Trust in the LORD and do good.
    Then you will live safely in the land
    and prosper.
4 Take delight in the LORD,
    and he will give you your heart's desires.

5 Commit everything you do to the LORD.
    Trust him, and he will help you.
6 He will make your innocence radiate like
    the dawn,
    and the justice of your cause will shine
    like the noonday sun.

7 Be still in the presence of the LORD,
    and wait patiently for him to act.
Don't worry about evil people who prosper
    or fret about their wicked schemes.

8 Stop being angry!
    Turn from your rage!
Do not lose your temper—
    it only leads to harm.
9 For the wicked will be destroyed,
    but those who trust in the LORD will
    possess the land.

10 Soon the wicked will disappear.
    Though you look for them,
    they will be gone.
11 The lowly will possess the land
    and will live in peace and prosperity.

12 The wicked plot against the godly;
    they snarl at them in defiance.
13 But the Lord just laughs,
    for he sees their day of judgment coming.

14 The wicked draw their swords
    and string their bows
to kill the poor and the oppressed,
    to slaughter those who do right.
15 But their swords will stab their own hearts,
    and their bows will be broken.

16 It is better to be godly and have little
    than to be evil and rich.
17 For the strength of the wicked will be
    shattered,
    but the LORD takes care of the godly.

18 Day by day the LORD takes care of the
    innocent,
    and they will receive an inheritance that
    lasts forever.
19 They will not be disgraced in hard times;
    even in famine they will have
    more than enough.

20 But the wicked will die.
    The LORD's enemies are like flowers
    in a field—
    they will disappear like smoke.

21 The wicked borrow and never repay,
    but the godly are generous givers.
22 Those the LORD blesses will possess
    the land,
    but those he curses will die.

23 The LORD directs the steps of the godly.
    He delights in every detail of their lives.
24 Though they stumble, they will never fall,
    for the LORD holds them by the hand.

25 Once I was young, and now I am old.
    Yet I have never seen the godly
    abandoned
    or their children begging for bread.
26 The godly always give generous loans
    to others,
    and their children are a blessing.

27 Turn from evil and do good,
    and you will live in the land forever.
28 For the LORD loves justice,
    and he will never abandon the godly.

He will keep them safe forever,
    but the children of the wicked will die.
29 The godly will possess the land
    and will live there forever.

30 The godly offer good counsel;
    they teach right from wrong.
31 They have made God's law their own,
    so they will never slip from his path.

---

37 This psalm is a Hebrew acrostic poem; each stanza begins
with a successive letter of the Hebrew alphabet.

³² The wicked wait in ambush for the godly,
 looking for an excuse to kill them.
³³ But the LORD will not let the wicked succeed
 or let the godly be condemned when they
  are put on trial.

³⁴ Put your hope in the LORD.
 Travel steadily along his path.
He will honor you by giving you the land.
 You will see the wicked destroyed.

³⁵ I have seen wicked and ruthless people
 flourishing like a tree in its native soil.
³⁶ But when I looked again, they were gone!
 Though I searched for them,
  I could not find them!

³⁷ Look at those who are honest and good,
 for a wonderful future awaits those who
  love peace.
³⁸ But the rebellious will be destroyed;
 they have no future.

³⁹ The LORD rescues the godly;
 he is their fortress in times of trouble.
⁴⁰ The LORD helps them,
 rescuing them from the wicked.
He saves them,
 and they find shelter in him.

38

*A psalm of David,
asking God to remember him.*

¹ O LORD, don't rebuke me in your anger
 or discipline me in your rage!
² Your arrows have struck deep,
 and your blows are crushing me.
³ Because of your anger,
 my whole body is sick;
 my health is broken because of my sins.
⁴ My guilt overwhelms me—
 it is a burden too heavy to bear.
⁵ My wounds fester and stink
 because of my foolish sins.
⁶ I am bent over and racked with pain.
 All day long I walk around filled with grief.
⁷ A raging fever burns within me,
 and my health is broken.
⁸ I am exhausted and completely crushed.
 My groans come from an anguished heart.

⁹ You know what I long for, Lord;
 you hear my every sigh.
¹⁰ My heart beats wildly, my strength fails,
 and I am going blind.
¹¹ My loved ones and friends stay away,
 fearing my disease.
 Even my own family stands at a distance.
¹² Meanwhile, my enemies lay traps to kill me.
 Those who wish me harm make plans to
  ruin me.
 All day long they plan their treachery.

¹³ But I am deaf to all their threats.
 I am silent before them as one who
  cannot speak.
¹⁴ I choose to hear nothing,
 and I make no reply.
¹⁵ For I am waiting for you, O LORD.
 You must answer for me,
  O Lord my God.
¹⁶ I prayed, "Don't let my enemies gloat
  over me
  or rejoice at my downfall."

¹⁷ I am on the verge of collapse,
 facing constant pain.
¹⁸ But I confess my sins;
 I am deeply sorry for what I have done.
¹⁹ I have many aggressive enemies;
 they hate me without reason.
²⁰ They repay me evil for good
 and oppose me for pursuing good.
²¹ Do not abandon me, O LORD.
 Do not stand at a distance, my God.
²² Come quickly to help me,
 O Lord my savior.

39

*For Jeduthun, the choir director:
A psalm of David.*

¹ I said to myself, "I will watch what I do
 and not sin in what I say.
I will hold my tongue
 when the ungodly are around me."
² But as I stood there in silence—
 not even speaking of good things—
 the turmoil within me grew worse.
³ The more I thought about it,
 the hotter I got,
 igniting a fire of words:
⁴ "LORD, remind me how brief my time on
  earth will be.
 Remind me that my days are numbered—
 how fleeting my life is.
⁵ You have made my life no longer than the
  width of my hand.
 My entire lifetime is just a moment
  to you;
 at best, each of us is but
  a breath."   *Interlude*

⁶ We are merely moving shadows,
 and all our busy rushing ends in nothing.
We heap up wealth,
 not knowing who will spend it.
⁷ And so, Lord, where do I put my hope?
 My only hope is in you.
⁸ Rescue me from my rebellion.
 Do not let fools mock me.
⁹ I am silent before you; I won't say a word,
 for my punishment is from you.
¹⁰ But please stop striking me!
 I am exhausted by the blows from
  your hand.

¹¹ When you discipline us for our sins,
you consume like a moth what is precious
to us.
Each of us is but a breath.   *Interlude*

¹² Hear my prayer, O LORD!
Listen to my cries for help!
Don't ignore my tears.
For I am your guest—
a traveler passing through,
as my ancestors were before me.
¹³ Leave me alone so I can smile again
before I am gone and exist no more.

40
For the choir director: A psalm of David.

¹ I waited patiently for the LORD to help me,
and he turned to me and heard my cry.
² He lifted me out of the pit of despair,
out of the mud and the mire.
He set my feet on solid ground
and steadied me as I walked along.
³ He has given me a new song to sing,
a hymn of praise to our God.
Many will see what he has done and be
amazed.
They will put their trust in the LORD.

⁴ Oh, the joys of those who trust the LORD,
who have no confidence in the proud
or in those who worship idols.
⁵ O LORD my God, you have performed many
wonders for us.
Your plans for us are too numerous
to list.
You have no equal.
If I tried to recite all your wonderful deeds,
I would never come to the end of them.

⁶ You take no delight in sacrifices or
offerings.
Now that you have made me listen,
I finally understand*—
you don't require burnt offerings or sin
offerings.
⁷ Then I said, "Look, I have come.
As is written about me in the Scriptures:
⁸ I take joy in doing your will, my God,
for your instructions are written on
my heart."

⁹ I have told all your people about your
justice.
I have not been afraid to speak out,
as you, O LORD, well know.
¹⁰ I have not kept the good news of your justice
hidden in my heart;
I have talked about your faithfulness and
saving power.
I have told everyone in the great assembly
of your unfailing love and faithfulness.

¹¹ LORD, don't hold back your tender mercies
from me.
Let your unfailing love and faithfulness
always protect me.
¹² For troubles surround me—
too many to count!
My sins pile up so high
I can't see my way out.
They outnumber the hairs on my head.
I have lost all courage.

¹³ Please, LORD, rescue me!
Come quickly, LORD, and help me.
¹⁴ May those who try to destroy me
be humiliated and put to shame.
May those who take delight in my trouble
be turned back in disgrace.
¹⁵ Let them be horrified by their shame,
for they said, "Aha! We've got him now!"

¹⁶ But may all who search for you
be filled with joy and gladness in you.
May those who love your salvation
repeatedly shout, "The LORD is great!"
¹⁷ As for me, since I am poor and needy,
let the Lord keep me in his thoughts.
You are my helper and my savior.
O my God, do not delay.

41
For the choir director: A psalm of David.

¹ Oh, the joys of those who are kind to
the poor!
The LORD rescues them when they are
in trouble.
² The LORD protects them
and keeps them alive.
He gives them prosperity in the land
and rescues them from their enemies.
³ The LORD nurses them when they are sick
and restores them to health.

⁴ "O LORD," I prayed, "have mercy on me.
Heal me, for I have sinned against you."
⁵ But my enemies say nothing but evil
about me.
"How soon will he die and be forgotten?"
they ask.
⁶ They visit me as if they were my friends,
but all the while they gather gossip,
and when they leave, they spread it
everywhere.
⁷ All who hate me whisper about me,
imagining the worst.
⁸ "He has some fatal disease," they say.
"He will never get out of that bed!"
⁹ Even my best friend, the one I trusted
completely,

40:6 Greek version reads *You have given me a body.* Compare
Heb 10:5.

UNDER ATTACK
Psalm 42:5   ROBERT MORRIS

The enemy often attacks us by flooding us with sad memories or hijacking our thoughts with past tragedies. However, there is a way to stop Satan in his tracks. Freedom begins with four power-packed words: the Lord rebuke you!

When you are beaten down emotionally, mentally, or spiritually, understand that you're in a real battle. Satan will take advantage of situations and attack you when you are down, but you have to attack back. When the enemy accuses you, you are empowered to say, "The Lord rebuke you!" (Jude 9).

Learn to talk about your feelings in the right way. Surround yourself with people who will support you and minister to you. You can also encourage yourself, as the psalmist did in Psalm 42:5. Most importantly, go before God. The atmosphere will become different when you listen to worship music and enter His presence. When God shows up, He changes things!

    the one who shared my food,
      has turned against me.

10 LORD, have mercy on me.
    Make me well again,
      so I can pay them back!
11 I know you are pleased with me,
    for you have not let my enemies
      triumph over me.
12 You have preserved my life because
    I am innocent;
    you have brought me into your presence
      forever.

13 Praise the LORD, the God of Israel,
    who lives from everlasting
      to everlasting.
    Amen and amen!

BOOK TWO (Psalms 42–72)

42 *For the choir director: A psalm* of the descendants of Korah.*

1 As the deer longs for streams of water,
    so I long for you, O God.
2 I thirst for God, the living God.
    When can I go and stand before him?
3 Day and night I have only tears for food,
    while my enemies continually
      taunt me, saying,
    "Where is this God of yours?"

4 My heart is breaking
    as I remember how it used to be:
I walked among the crowds
    of worshipers,
    leading a great procession to
      the house of God,
singing for joy and giving thanks
    amid the sound of a great celebration!

5 Why am I discouraged?
    Why is my heart so sad?
I will put my hope in God!
    I will praise him again—
    my Savior and 6 my God!

Now I am deeply discouraged,
    but I will remember you—
even from distant Mount Hermon,
    the source of the Jordan,
    from the land of Mount Mizar.
7 I hear the tumult of the raging seas
    as your waves and surging tides sweep
      over me.
8 But each day the LORD pours his unfailing
    love upon me,
    and through each night I sing his songs,
    praying to God who gives me life.

9 "O God my rock," I cry,
    "why have you forgotten me?
Why must I wander around in grief,
    oppressed by my enemies?"
10 Their taunts break my bones.
    They scoff, "Where is this God of yours?"

11 Why am I discouraged?
    Why is my heart so sad?
I will put my hope in God!
    I will praise him again—
    my Savior and my God!

43 1 Declare me innocent, O God!
    Defend me against these ungodly
      people.
    Rescue me from these unjust liars.
2 For you are God, my only safe haven.
    Why have you tossed me aside?
Why must I wander around in grief,
    oppressed by my enemies?
3 Send out your light and your truth;
    let them guide me.
Let them lead me to your holy mountain,
    to the place where you live.
4 There I will go to the altar of God,
    to God—the source of all my joy.
I will praise you with my harp,
    O God, my God!

5 Why am I discouraged?
    Why is my heart so sad?

42:TITLE Hebrew *mashil*. This may be a literary or musical term.

I will put my hope in God!
I will praise him again—
my Savior and my God!

44

For the choir director: A psalm* of the descendants of Korah.

¹ O God, we have heard it with our own ears—
our ancestors have told us
of all you did in their day,
in days long ago:
² You drove out the pagan nations by
your power
and gave all the land to our ancestors.
You crushed their enemies
and set our ancestors free.
³ They did not conquer the land with
their swords;
it was not their own strong arm that gave
them victory.
It was your right hand and strong arm
and the blinding light from your face
that helped them,
for you loved them.

⁴ You are my King and my God.
You command victories for Israel.*
⁵ Only by your power can we push back
our enemies;
only in your name can we trample
our foes.
⁶ I do not trust in my bow;
I do not count on my sword to save me.
⁷ You are the one who gives us victory over
our enemies;
you disgrace those who hate us.
⁸ O God, we give glory to you all day long
and constantly praise your name.
Interlude

⁹ But now you have tossed us aside in dishonor.
You no longer lead our armies to battle.
¹⁰ You make us retreat from our enemies
and allow those who hate us to plunder
our land.
¹¹ You have butchered us like sheep
and scattered us among the nations.
¹² You sold your precious people for a pittance,
making nothing on the sale.
¹³ You let our neighbors mock us.
We are an object of scorn and derision to
those around us.
¹⁴ You have made us the butt of their jokes;
they shake their heads at us in scorn.
¹⁵ We can't escape the constant humiliation;
shame is written across our faces.
¹⁶ All we hear are the taunts of our mockers.
All we see are our vengeful enemies.

¹⁷ All this has happened though we have not
forgotten you.
We have not violated your covenant.

¹⁸ Our hearts have not deserted you.
We have not strayed from your path.
¹⁹ Yet you have crushed us in the jackal's
desert home.
You have covered us with darkness
and death.
²⁰ If we had forgotten the name of our God
or spread our hands in prayer to
foreign gods,
²¹ God would surely have known it,
for he knows the secrets of every heart.
²² But for your sake we are killed every day;
we are being slaughtered like sheep.

²³ Wake up, O Lord! Why do you sleep?
Get up! Do not reject us forever.
²⁴ Why do you look the other way?
Why do you ignore our suffering
and oppression?
²⁵ We collapse in the dust,
lying face down in the dirt.
²⁶ Rise up! Help us!
Ransom us because of your unfailing love.

45

For the choir director: A love song to be sung to the tune "Lilies." A psalm* of the descendants of Korah.

¹ Beautiful words stir my heart.
I will recite a lovely poem about the king,
for my tongue is like the pen of
a skillful poet.

² You are the most handsome of all.
Gracious words stream from your lips.
God himself has blessed you forever.
³ Put on your sword, O mighty warrior!
You are so glorious, so majestic!
⁴ In your majesty, ride out to victory,
defending truth, humility, and justice.
Go forth to perform awe-inspiring deeds!
⁵ Your arrows are sharp, piercing your
enemies' hearts.
The nations fall beneath your feet.

⁶ Your throne, O God,* endures forever and ever.
You rule with a scepter of justice.
⁷ You love justice and hate evil.
Therefore God, your God,
has anointed you,
pouring out the oil of joy on you more
than on anyone else.
⁸ Myrrh, aloes, and cassia perfume your robes.
In ivory palaces the music of strings
entertains you.
⁹ Kings' daughters are among your noble
women.

44:TITLE Hebrew *mashil*. This may be a literary or musical
term.   44:4 Hebrew *for Jacob*. The names "Jacob" and "Israel"
are often interchanged throughout the Old Testament, referring
sometimes to the individual patriarch and sometimes to the
nation.   45:TITLE Hebrew *mashil*. This may be a literary or
musical term.   45:6 Or *Your divine throne*.

THE RESULTS OF REFUGE
Psalm 46:1-3

ROBERT MORRIS

There is so much fear and anxiety in the world today. Everyone is looking for a refuge, a safe place. Thankfully, as believers, we have a refuge—God! In Psalm 46:1-3, David calls God his *refuge*, a word translated from the Hebrew, which means an 'elevated fortress.' It's a high place that's guarded and completely protected from all enemies. When God is our refuge, we will have no fear.

Sadly, many people choose the *wrong* refuge in times of trouble with these devastating results:

1. Distance

    The first commandment is to have no other gods before the Lord (Exodus 20:3). If you have the wrong refuge, you put it before God, which creates distance between you and Him.

2. Disappointment

    Satan is a false comforter. He tells us we can receive comfort from somewhere, someone, or something other than God. However, when we listen to him, we find only disappointment and hopelessness.

3. Destruction

    The wrong refuge will take over your life and become your prison. If you choose pornography, gambling, drugs, alcohol, or anything else as your refuge, you'll move closer to destruction each day.

So what are the results of choosing the *right* refuge?

1. Strength

    God can help you through whatever you're going through. No other refuge can give you strength. In fact, any refuge other than God actually takes away strength.

2. Help

    Psalm 46:1 says God is "always ready to help in times of trouble." As believers, we have the Holy Spirit living inside us. He is with us wherever we go, and He wants to help us.

3. No fear

    God created us to live inside His refuge where there is no fear. He is our Friend and our Redeemer. God loves us even when we do the wrong thing, and when we run to Him, His "perfect love expels all fear" (1 John 4:18).

At your right side stands the queen,
    wearing jewelry of finest gold from Ophir!

10 Listen to me, O royal daughter; take to heart
    what I say.
    Forget your people and your family
    far away.
11 For your royal husband delights in your
    beauty;
    honor him, for he is your lord.
12 The princess of Tyre* will shower you with
    gifts.
    The wealthy will beg your favor.
13 The bride, a princess, looks glorious
    in her golden gown.
14 In her beautiful robes, she is led to the king,
    accompanied by her bridesmaids.
15 What a joyful and enthusiastic procession
    as they enter the king's palace!

16 Your sons will become kings like their father.
    You will make them rulers over many lands.
17 I will bring honor to your name in every
    generation.
    Therefore, the nations will praise you
    forever and ever.

46 *For the choir director: A song of the descendants of Korah, to be sung by soprano voices.**

1 God is our refuge and strength,
    always ready to help in times of trouble.

2 So we will not fear when earthquakes come
    and the mountains crumble into the sea.
3 Let the oceans roar and foam.
    Let the mountains tremble
        as the waters surge!   *Interlude*

4 A river brings joy to the city of our God,
    the sacred home of the Most High.
5 God dwells in that city;
        it cannot be destroyed.
    From the very break of day,
        God will protect it.
6 The nations are in chaos,
    and their kingdoms crumble!
    God's voice thunders,
    and the earth melts!
7 The LORD of Heaven's Armies is here
        among us;
        the God of Israel* is our fortress.   *Interlude*

8 Come, see the glorious works of the LORD:
    See how he brings destruction upon
        the world.
9 He causes wars to end throughout the earth.
    He breaks the bow and snaps the spear;
    he burns the shields with fire.

10 "Be still, and know that I am God!
    I will be honored by every nation.
    I will be honored throughout the world."

45:12 Hebrew *The daughter of Tyre*.   46:TITLE Hebrew *according to alamoth*.   46:7 Hebrew *of Jacob*; also in 46:11. See note on 44:4.

¹¹ The LORD of Heaven's Armies is here
among us;
the God of Israel is our fortress.   *Interlude*

47

*For the choir director: A psalm of the
descendants of Korah.*

¹ Come, everyone! Clap your hands!
Shout to God with joyful praise!
² For the LORD Most High is awesome.
He is the great King of all the earth.
³ He subdues the nations before us,
putting our enemies beneath our feet.
⁴ He chose the Promised Land as our
inheritance,
the proud possession of Jacob's
descendants, whom he loves.   *Interlude*

⁵ God has ascended with a mighty shout.
The LORD has ascended with trumpets
blaring.
⁶ Sing praises to God, sing praises;
sing praises to our King, sing praises!
⁷ For God is the King over all the earth.
Praise him with a psalm.*
⁸ God reigns above the nations,
sitting on his holy throne.
⁹ The rulers of the world have
gathered together
with the people of the God of Abraham.
For all the kings of the earth belong to God.
He is highly honored everywhere.

48

A song. A psalm of the descendants of Korah.

¹ How great is the LORD,
how deserving of praise,
in the city of our God,
which sits on his holy mountain!
² It is high and magnificent;
the whole earth rejoices to see it!
Mount Zion, the holy mountain,*
is the city of the great King!
³ God himself is in Jerusalem's towers,
revealing himself as its defender.

⁴ The kings of the earth joined forces
and advanced against the city.
⁵ But when they saw it, they were stunned;
they were terrified and ran away.
⁶ They were gripped with terror
and writhed in pain like a woman in labor.
⁷ You destroyed them like the mighty ships
of Tarshish
shattered by a powerful east wind.

⁸ We had heard of the city's glory,
but now we have seen it ourselves—
the city of the LORD of Heaven's Armies.
It is the city of our God;
he will make it safe forever.   *Interlude*

⁹ O God, we meditate on your unfailing love
as we worship in your Temple.
¹⁰ As your name deserves, O God,
you will be praised to the ends of the earth.
Your strong right hand is
filled with victory.
¹¹ Let the people on Mount Zion rejoice.
Let all the towns of Judah be glad
because of your justice.

¹² Go, inspect the city of Jerusalem.*
Walk around and count the many towers.
¹³ Take note of the fortified walls,
and tour all the citadels,
that you may describe them
to future generations.
¹⁴ For that is what God is like.
He is our God forever and ever,
and he will guide us until we die.

49

*For the choir director: A psalm of the
descendants of Korah.*

¹ Listen to this, all you people!
Pay attention, everyone in the world!
² High and low,
rich and poor—listen!
³ For my words are wise,
and my thoughts are filled with insight.
⁴ I listen carefully to many proverbs
and solve riddles with inspiration
from a harp.

⁵ Why should I fear when trouble comes,
when enemies surround me?
⁶ They trust in their wealth
and boast of great riches.
⁷ Yet they cannot redeem themselves
from death*
by paying a ransom to God.
⁸ Redemption does not come so easily,
for no one can ever pay enough
⁹ to live forever
and never see the grave.

¹⁰ Those who are wise must finally die,
just like the foolish and senseless,
leaving all their wealth behind.
¹¹ The grave* is their eternal home,
where they will stay forever.
They may name their estates after
themselves,
¹² but their fame will not last.
They will die, just like animals.
¹³ This is the fate of fools,
though they are remembered as
being wise.*   *Interlude*

47:7 Hebrew *maskil*. This may be a literary or musical term.
48:2 Or *Mount Zion, in the far north;* Hebrew reads *Mount Zion,
the heights of Zaphon.*   48:12 Hebrew *Zion.*   49:7 Some Hebrew
manuscripts read *no one can redeem the life of another.*   49:11 As in
Greek and Syriac versions; Hebrew reads *Their inward [thought].*
49:13 The meaning of the Hebrew is uncertain.

¹⁴ Like sheep, they are led to the grave,*
    where death will be their shepherd.
In the morning the godly will rule
        over them.
    Their bodies will rot in the grave,
        far from their grand estates.
¹⁵ But as for me, God will redeem my life.
    He will snatch me from the power of
        the grave.   *Interlude*

¹⁶ So don't be dismayed when the wicked
        grow rich
    and their homes become
        ever more splendid.
¹⁷ For when they die, they take nothing
        with them.
    Their wealth will not follow them
        into the grave.
¹⁸ In this life they consider themselves
        fortunate
    and are applauded for their success.
¹⁹ But they will die like all before them
    and never again see the light of day.
²⁰ People who boast of their wealth don't
        understand;
    they will die, just like animals.

50 *A psalm of Asaph.*

¹ The LORD, the Mighty One, is God,
    and he has spoken;
he has summoned all humanity
    from where the sun rises to where
        it sets.
² From Mount Zion, the perfection of beauty,
    God shines in glorious radiance.
³ Our God approaches,
    and he is not silent.
Fire devours everything in his way,
    and a great storm rages around him.
⁴ He calls on the heavens above and
        earth below
    to witness the judgment of his people.
⁵ "Bring my faithful people to me—
    those who made a covenant with me by
        giving sacrifices."
⁶ Then let the heavens proclaim his justice,
    for God himself will be the judge.
                                Interlude

⁷ "O my people, listen as I speak.
    Here are my charges against you, O Israel:
    I am God, your God!
⁸ I have no complaint about your sacrifices
    or the burnt offerings you constantly offer.
⁹ But I do not need the bulls from your barns
    or the goats from your pens.
¹⁰ For all the animals of the forest are mine,
    and I own the cattle on a thousand hills.
¹¹ I know every bird on the mountains,
    and all the animals of the field are mine.

¹² If I were hungry, I would not tell you,
    for all the world is mine and
        everything in it.
¹³ Do I eat the meat of bulls?
    Do I drink the blood of goats?
¹⁴ Make thankfulness your sacrifice to God,
    and keep the vows you made to
        the Most High.
¹⁵ Then call on me when you are in trouble,
    and I will rescue you,
    and you will give me glory."

¹⁶ But God says to the wicked:
"Why bother reciting my decrees
    and pretending to obey my covenant?
¹⁷ For you refuse my discipline
    and treat my words like trash.
¹⁸ When you see thieves,
    you approve of them,
    and you spend your time with adulterers.
¹⁹ Your mouth is filled with wickedness,
    and your tongue is full of lies.
²⁰ You sit around and slander your brother—
    your own mother's son.
²¹ While you did all this, I remained silent,
    and you thought I didn't care.
But now I will rebuke you,
    listing all my charges against you.
²² Repent, all of you who forget me,
    or I will tear you apart,
    and no one will help you.
²³ But giving thanks is a sacrifice that truly
        honors me.
    If you keep to my path,
    I will reveal to you the salvation of God."

51 *For the choir director: A psalm of David, regarding the time Nathan the prophet came to him after David had committed adultery with Bathsheba.*

¹ Have mercy on me, O God,
    because of your unfailing love.
Because of your great compassion,
    blot out the stain of my sins.
² Wash me clean from my guilt.
    Purify me from my sin.
³ For I recognize my rebellion;
    it haunts me day and night.
⁴ Against you, and you alone, have I sinned;
    I have done what is evil in your sight.
You will be proved right in what you say,
    and your judgment against me is just.*
⁵ For I was born a sinner—
    yes, from the moment my mother
        conceived me.
⁶ But you desire honesty from the womb,*
    teaching me wisdom even there.

49:14 Hebrew *Sheol;* also in 49:14b, 15.   51:4 Greek version reads
and you will win your case in court. Compare Rom 3:4.   51:6 Or
from the heart; Hebrew reads *in the inward parts.*

⁷ Purify me from my sins,* and I will be clean;
  wash me, and I will be whiter than snow.
⁸ Oh, give me back my joy again;
  you have broken me—
    now let me rejoice.
⁹ Don't keep looking at my sins.
  Remove the stain of my guilt.
¹⁰ Create in me a clean heart, O God.
  Renew a loyal spirit within me.
¹¹ Do not banish me from your presence,
  and don't take your Holy Spirit* from me.

¹² Restore to me the joy of your salvation,
  and make me willing to obey you.
¹³ Then I will teach your ways to rebels,
  and they will return to you.
¹⁴ Forgive me for shedding blood,
  O God who saves;
    then I will joyfully sing of your
      forgiveness.
¹⁵ Unseal my lips, O Lord,
  that my mouth may praise you.

¹⁶ You do not desire a sacrifice, or I would
    offer one.
  You do not want a burnt offering.
¹⁷ The sacrifice you desire is a broken spirit.
  You will not reject a broken and repentant
    heart, O God.
¹⁸ Look with favor on Zion and help her;
  rebuild the walls of Jerusalem.
¹⁹ Then you will be pleased with sacrifices
    offered in the right spirit—
  with burnt offerings and whole
    burnt offerings.
  Then bulls will again be sacrificed
    on your altar.

52 For the choir director: A psalm* of David,
regarding the time Doeg the Edomite said to
Saul, "David has gone to see Ahimelech."

¹ Why do you boast about your crimes,
    great warrior?
  Don't you realize God's justice continues
    forever?
² All day long you plot destruction.
  Your tongue cuts like a sharp razor;
  you're an expert at telling lies.
³ You love evil more than good
  and lies more than truth.   *Interlude*

⁴ You love to destroy others with your words,
  you liar!
⁵ But God will strike you down once
    and for all.
  He will pull you from your home
  and uproot you from the land of the
    living.   *Interlude*

⁶ The righteous will see it and be amazed.
  They will laugh and say,

⁷ "Look what happens to mighty warriors
    who do not trust in God.
  They trust their wealth instead
    and grow more and more bold in their
      wickedness."

⁸ But I am like an olive tree, thriving in the
    house of God.
  I will always trust in God's unfailing love.
⁹ I will praise you forever, O God,
  for what you have done.
  I will trust in your good name
    in the presence of your faithful people.

53 For the choir director: A meditation;
a psalm* of David.

¹ Only fools say in their hearts,
    "There is no God."
  They are corrupt, and their actions are evil;
    not one of them does good!

² God looks down from heaven
    on the entire human race;
  he looks to see if anyone is truly wise,
    if anyone seeks God.
³ But no, all have turned away;
    all have become corrupt.*
  No one does good,
    not a single one!

⁴ Will those who do evil never learn?
  They eat up my people like bread
  and wouldn't think of praying to God.
⁵ Terror will grip them,
    terror like they have never known before.
  God will scatter the bones of your enemies.
  You will put them to shame, for God has
    rejected them.

⁶ Who will come from Mount Zion
    to rescue Israel?
  When God restores his people,
  Jacob will shout with joy, and Israel will
    rejoice.

54 For the choir director: A psalm* of David,
regarding the time the Ziphites came and
said to Saul, "We know where David is hiding."
To be accompanied by stringed instruments.

¹ Come with great power, O God,
    and rescue me!
  Defend me with your might.
² Listen to my prayer, O God.
  Pay attention to my plea.

51:7 Hebrew *Purify me with the hyssop branch.*   **51:11** Or *your spirit of holiness.*   **52:TITLE** Hebrew *mashil.* This may be a literary or musical term.   **53:TITLE** Hebrew *According to mahalath; a mashil.* These may be literary or musical terms.   **53:3** Greek version reads *have become useless.* Compare Rom 3:12.   **54:TITLE** Hebrew *mashil.* This may be a literary or musical term.

³ For strangers are attacking me;
    violent people are trying to kill me.
    They care nothing for God. *Interlude*

⁴ But God is my helper.
    The Lord keeps me alive!
⁵ May the evil plans of my enemies be turned
    against them.
    Do as you promised and put an end
    to them.

⁶ I will sacrifice a voluntary offering to you;
    I will praise your name, O LORD,
    for it is good.
⁷ For you have rescued me from my troubles
    and helped me to triumph over
    my enemies.

55 *For the choir director: A psalm* of David,*
to be accompanied by stringed instruments.

¹ Listen to my prayer, O God.
    Do not ignore my cry for help!
² Please listen and answer me,
    for I am overwhelmed by my troubles.
³ My enemies shout at me,
    making loud and wicked threats.
They bring trouble on me
    and angrily hunt me down.

⁴ My heart pounds in my chest.
    The terror of death assaults me.
⁵ Fear and trembling overwhelm me,
    and I can't stop shaking.
⁶ Oh, that I had wings like a dove;
    then I would fly away and rest!
⁷ I would fly far away
    to the quiet of the wilderness. *Interlude*
⁸ How quickly I would escape—
    far from this wild storm of hatred.

⁹ Confuse them, Lord, and frustrate
    their plans,
    for I see violence and conflict in the city.
¹⁰ Its walls are patrolled day and night
    against invaders,
    but the real danger is wickedness within
    the city.
¹¹ Everything is falling apart;
    threats and cheating are rampant
    in the streets.

¹² It is not an enemy who taunts me—
    I could bear that.
It is not my foes who so arrogantly
    insult me—
    I could have hidden from them.
¹³ Instead, it is you—my equal,
    my companion and close friend.
¹⁴ What good fellowship we once enjoyed
    as we walked together to the house
    of God.

¹⁵ Let death stalk my enemies;
    let the grave* swallow them alive,
    for evil makes its home within them.

¹⁶ But I will call on God,
    and the LORD will rescue me.
¹⁷ Morning, noon, and night
    I cry out in my distress,
    and the LORD hears my voice.
¹⁸ He ransoms me and keeps me safe
    from the battle waged against me,
    though many still oppose me.
¹⁹ God, who has ruled forever,
    will hear me and humble them. *Interlude*
For my enemies refuse to change their ways;
    they do not fear God.

²⁰ As for my companion, he betrayed his
    friends;
    he broke his promises.
²¹ His words are as smooth as butter,
    but in his heart is war.
His words are as soothing as lotion,
    but underneath are daggers!

²² Give your burdens to the LORD,
    and he will take care of you.
    He will not permit the godly to slip and fall.

²³ But you, O God, will send the wicked
    down to the pit of destruction.
Murderers and liars will die young,
    but I am trusting you to save me.

56 *For the choir director: A psalm* of David,*
regarding the time the Philistines seized
him in Gath. To be sung to the tune "Dove on
Distant Oaks."

¹ O God, have mercy on me,
    for people are hounding me.
    My foes attack me all day long.
² I am constantly hounded by those who
    slander me,
    and many are boldly attacking me.
³ But when I am afraid,
    I will put my trust in you.
⁴ I praise God for what he has promised.
    I trust in God, so why should I be afraid?
    What can mere mortals do to me?

⁵ They are always twisting what I say;
    they spend their days plotting to harm me.
⁶ They come together to spy on me—
    watching my every step, eager to kill me.
⁷ Don't let them get away with their
    wickedness;
    in your anger, O God, bring them down.

55:TITLE Hebrew *mashil.* This may be a literary or musical term.
55:15 Hebrew *let Sheol.*   56:TITLE Hebrew *mihtam.* This may be a
literary or musical term.

8 You keep track of all my sorrows.*
  You have collected all my tears in
    your bottle.
  You have recorded each one in your book.

9 My enemies will retreat when I call to you
    for help.
  This I know: God is on my side!
10 I praise God for what he has promised;
  yes, I praise the LORD for what he
    has promised.
11 I trust in God, so why should I be afraid?
  What can mere mortals do to me?

12 I will fulfill my vows to you, O God,
  and will offer a sacrifice of thanks for
    your help.
13 For you have rescued me from death;
  you have kept my feet from slipping.
  So now I can walk in your presence, O God,
  in your life-giving light.

57 For the choir director: A psalm* of David,
regarding the time he fled from Saul and
went into the cave. To be sung to the tune "Do Not
Destroy!"

1 Have mercy on me, O God, have mercy!
  I look to you for protection.
  I will hide beneath the shadow of your wings
  until the danger passes by.
2 I cry out to God Most High,*
  to God who will fulfill his purpose for me.
3 He will send help from heaven
    to rescue me,
  disgracing those who hound me. *Interlude*
  My God will send forth his unfailing love
    and faithfulness.

4 I am surrounded by fierce lions
  who greedily devour human prey—
  whose teeth pierce like spears and arrows,
  and whose tongues cut like swords.

5 Be exalted, O God,
  above the highest heavens!
  May your glory shine over all the earth.

6 My enemies have set a trap for me.
  I am weary from distress.
  They have dug a deep pit in my path,
  but they themselves have fallen
    into it. *Interlude*

7 My heart is confident in you, O God;
  my heart is confident.
  No wonder I can sing your praises!
8 Wake up, my heart!
  Wake up, O lyre and harp!
  I will wake the dawn with my song.

9 I will thank you, Lord, among all the people.
  I will sing your praises among the nations.

10 For your unfailing love is as high as
    the heavens.
  Your faithfulness reaches to the clouds.

11 Be exalted, O God,
  above the highest heavens.
  May your glory shine over all the earth.

58 For the choir director: A psalm* of David,
to be sung to the tune "Do Not Destroy!"

1 Justice—do you rulers* know the meaning
    of the word?
  Do you judge the people fairly?
2 No! You plot injustice in your hearts.
  You spread violence throughout the land.
3 These wicked people are born sinners;
  even from birth they have lied and gone
    their own way.
4 They spit venom like deadly snakes;
  they are like cobras that refuse to listen,
5 ignoring the tunes of the snake charmers,
  no matter how skillfully they play.

6 Break off their fangs, O God!
  Smash the jaws of these lions, O LORD!
7 May they disappear like water into
    thirsty ground.
  Make their weapons useless
    in their hands.*
8 May they be like snails that dissolve
    into slime,
  like a stillborn child who will never see
    the sun.
9 God will sweep them away,
    both young and old,
  faster than a pot heats over
    burning thorns.

10 The godly will rejoice when they see
    injustice avenged.
  They will wash their feet in the blood of
    the wicked.
11 Then at last everyone will say,
  "There truly is a reward for those who live
    for God;
  surely there is a God who judges justly
    here on earth."

59 For the choir director: A psalm* of David,
regarding the time Saul sent soldiers to watch
David's house in order to kill him. To be sung to the
tune "Do Not Destroy!"

1 Rescue me from my enemies, O God.
  Protect me from those who have come
    to destroy me.

56:8 Or *my wanderings.*   57:TITLE Hebrew *miktam.* This may
be a literary or musical term.   57:2 Hebrew *Elohim-Elyon.*
58:TITLE Hebrew *miktam.* This may be a literary or musical term.
58:1 Or *you gods.*   58:7 Or *Let them be trodden down and wither like
grass.* The meaning of the Hebrew is uncertain.   59:TITLE Hebrew
miktam. This may be a literary or musical term.

² Rescue me from these criminals;
  save me from these murderers.
³ They have set an ambush for me.
    Fierce enemies are out there waiting,
    Lord,
  though I have not sinned or
    offended them.
⁴ I have done nothing wrong,
  yet they prepare to attack me.
  Wake up! See what is happening
    and help me!
⁵ O Lord God of Heaven's Armies,
    the God of Israel,
  wake up and punish those hostile nations.
  Show no mercy to
    wicked traitors.   *Interlude*

⁶ They come out at night,
  snarling like vicious dogs
  as they prowl the streets.
⁷ Listen to the filth that comes from
    their mouths;
  their words cut like swords.
  "After all, who can hear us?" they sneer.
⁸ But Lord, you laugh at them.
  You scoff at all the hostile nations.
⁹ You are my strength;
    I wait for you to rescue me,
  for you, O God, are my fortress.
¹⁰ In his unfailing love, my God will stand
    with me.
  He will let me look down in triumph on
    all my enemies.

¹¹ Don't kill them, for my people soon forget
    such lessons;
  stagger them with your power, and bring
    them to their knees,
  O Lord our shield.
¹² Because of the sinful things they say,
  because of the evil that is on their lips,
  let them be captured by their pride,
    their curses, and their lies.
¹³ Destroy them in your anger!
    Wipe them out completely!
  Then the whole world will know
    that God reigns in Israel.*   *Interlude*

¹⁴ My enemies come out at night,
  snarling like vicious dogs
  as they prowl the streets.
¹⁵ They scavenge for food
  but go to sleep unsatisfied.*

¹⁶ But as for me, I will sing about your power.
  Each morning I will sing with joy about
    your unfailing love.
  For you have been my refuge,
    a place of safety when I am in distress.
¹⁷ O my Strength, to you I sing praises,
  for you, O God, are my refuge,
  the God who shows me unfailing love.

60 *For the choir director: A psalm* of David
  *useful for teaching, regarding the time David
  fought Aram-naharaim and Aram-zobah, and Joab
  returned and killed 12,000 Edomites in the Valley of
  Salt. To be sung to the tune "Lily of the Testimony."*

¹ You have rejected us, O God, and broken
    our defenses.
  You have been angry with us; now restore
    us to your favor.
² You have shaken our land and split it open.
  Seal the cracks, for the land trembles.
³ You have been very hard on us,
  making us drink wine that sent us reeling.
⁴ But you have raised a banner for those who
    fear you—
  a rallying point in the face
    of attack.   *Interlude*

⁵ Now rescue your beloved people.
  Answer and save us by your power.
⁶ God has promised this by his holiness*:
  "I will divide up Shechem with joy.
  I will measure out the valley of Succoth.
⁷ Gilead is mine,
    and Manasseh, too.
  Ephraim, my helmet,
    will produce my warriors,
  and Judah, my scepter,
    will produce my kings.
⁸ But Moab, my washbasin,
    will become my servant,
  and I will wipe my feet on Edom
    and shout in triumph over Philistia."

⁹ Who will bring me into the fortified city?
  Who will bring me victory over Edom?
¹⁰ Have you rejected us, O God?
  Will you no longer march with our armies?
¹¹ Oh, please help us against our enemies,
  for all human help is useless.
¹² With God's help we will do mighty things,
  for he will trample down our foes.

61 *For the choir director: A psalm of David,
  to be accompanied by stringed instruments.*

¹ O God, listen to my cry!
  Hear my prayer!
² From the ends of the earth,
  I cry to you for help
  when my heart is overwhelmed.
  Lead me to the towering rock of safety,
³   for you are my safe refuge,
  a fortress where my enemies cannot
    reach me.
⁴ Let me live forever in your sanctuary,
  safe beneath the shelter of
    your wings!   *Interlude*

59:13 Hebrew *in Jacob*. See note on 44:4.   **59:15** Or *and growl if
they don't get enough.*   **60:TITLE** Hebrew *miktam.* This may be a
literary or musical term.   **60:6** Or *in his sanctuary.*

5 For you have heard my vows, O God.
    You have given me an inheritance
        reserved for those who fear
        your name.
6 Add many years to the life of the king!
    May his years span the generations!
7 May he reign under God's protection forever.
    May your unfailing love and faithfulness
        watch over him.
8 Then I will sing praises to your name forever
    as I fulfill my vows each day.

62

For Jeduthun, the choir director:
A psalm of David.

1 I wait quietly before God,
    for my victory comes from him.
2 He alone is my rock and my salvation,
    my fortress where I will never
        be shaken.

3 So many enemies against one man—
    all of them trying to kill me.
To them I'm just a broken-down wall
    or a tottering fence.
4 They plan to topple me from my
        high position.
    They delight in telling lies about me.
They praise me to my face
    but curse me in their hearts.   *Interlude*

5 Let all that I am wait quietly before God,
    for my hope is in him.
6 He alone is my rock and my salvation,
    my fortress where I will not be shaken.
7 My victory and honor come
        from God alone.
    He is my refuge, a rock where no enemy
        can reach me.
8 O my people, trust in him at all times.
    Pour out your heart to him,
    for God is our refuge.   *Interlude*

9 Common people are as worthless as
        a puff of wind,
    and the powerful are not what they
        appear to be.
If you weigh them on the scales,
    together they are lighter than
        a breath of air.

10 Don't make your living by extortion
    or put your hope in stealing.
And if your wealth increases,
    don't make it the center of your life.

11 God has spoken plainly,
    and I have heard it many times:
Power, O God, belongs to you;
12   unfailing love, O Lord, is yours.
Surely you repay all people
    according to what they have done.

63

A psalm of David, regarding a time when
David was in the wilderness of Judah.

1 O God, you are my God;
    I earnestly search for you.
My soul thirsts for you;
    my whole body longs for you
in this parched and weary land
    where there is no water.
2 I have seen you in your sanctuary
    and gazed upon your power and glory.
3 Your unfailing love is better than life itself;
    how I praise you!
4 I will praise you as long as I live,
    lifting up my hands to you in prayer.
5 You satisfy me more than the richest feast.
    I will praise you with songs of joy.

6 I lie awake thinking of you,
    meditating on you through the night.
7 Because you are my helper,
    I sing for joy in the shadow of
        your wings.
8 I cling to you;
    your strong right hand
        holds me securely.

9 But those plotting to destroy me will
        come to ruin.
    They will go down into the depths of
        the earth.
10 They will die by the sword
    and become the food of jackals.
11 But the king will rejoice in God.
    All who swear to tell the truth
        will praise him,
    while liars will be silenced.

64

For the choir director: A psalm of David.

1 O God, listen to my complaint.
    Protect my life from my enemies'
        threats.
2 Hide me from the plots of this evil mob,
    from this gang of wrongdoers.
3 They sharpen their tongues like swords
    and aim their bitter words like arrows.
4 They shoot from ambush at the innocent,
    attacking suddenly and fearlessly.
5 They encourage each other to do evil
    and plan how to set their traps
        in secret.
    "Who will ever notice?" they ask.
6 As they plot their crimes, they say,
    "We have devised the perfect plan!"
    Yes, the human heart and mind
        are cunning.

7 But God himself will shoot them with
        his arrows,
    suddenly striking them down.

8 Their own tongues will ruin them,
  and all who see them will shake their
    heads in scorn.
9 Then everyone will be afraid;
  they will proclaim the mighty acts of God
  and realize all the amazing things
    he does.
10 The godly will rejoice in the LORD
  and find shelter in him.
  And those who do what is right
    will praise him.

65 For the choir director:
   A song. A psalm of David.

1 What mighty praise, O God,
  belongs to you in Zion.
  We will fulfill our vows to you,
2   for you answer our prayers.
  All of us must come to you.
3 Though we are overwhelmed by our sins,
  you forgive them all.
4 What joy for those you choose to bring near,
  those who live in your holy courts.
  What festivities await us
    inside your holy Temple.

5 You faithfully answer our prayers with
    awesome deeds,
  O God our savior.
  You are the hope of everyone on earth,
  even those who sail on distant seas.
6 You formed the mountains by your power
  and armed yourself with
    mighty strength.
7 You quieted the raging oceans
  with their pounding waves
  and silenced the shouting of the nations.
8 Those who live at the ends of the earth
  stand in awe of your wonders.
  From where the sun rises to where it sets,
  you inspire shouts of joy.

9 You take care of the earth and water it,
  making it rich and fertile.
  The river of God has plenty of water;
  it provides a bountiful harvest of grain,
  for you have ordered it so.
10 You drench the plowed ground with rain,
  melting the clods and leveling the ridges.
  You soften the earth with showers
  and bless its abundant crops.
11 You crown the year with a bountiful harvest;
  even the hard pathways overflow
    with abundance.
12 The grasslands of the wilderness become
    a lush pasture,
  and the hillsides blossom with joy.
13 The meadows are clothed with
    flocks of sheep,
  and the valleys are carpeted with grain.
  They all shout and sing for joy!

66 For the choir director: A song. A psalm.

1 Shout joyful praises to God, all the earth!
2   Sing about the glory of his name!
  Tell the world how glorious he is.
3 Say to God, "How awesome are your deeds!
  Your enemies cringe before your
    mighty power.
4 Everything on earth will worship you;
  they will sing your praises,
  shouting your name in
    glorious songs."   Interlude

5 Come and see what our God has done,
  what awesome miracles he performs for
    people!
6 He made a dry path through the Red Sea,*
  and his people went across on foot.
  There we rejoiced in him.
7 For by his great power he rules forever.
  He watches every movement of
    the nations;
  let no rebel rise in defiance.   Interlude

8 Let the whole world bless our God
  and loudly sing his praises.
9 Our lives are in his hands,
  and he keeps our feet from stumbling.
10 You have tested us, O God;
  you have purified us like silver.
11 You captured us in your net
  and laid the burden of slavery on our backs.
12 Then you put a leader over us.*
  We went through fire and flood,
  but you brought us to a place of great
    abundance.

13 Now I come to your Temple with
    burnt offerings
  to fulfill the vows I made to you—
14 yes, the sacred vows that I made
  when I was in deep trouble.
15 That is why I am sacrificing burnt offerings
    to you—
  the best of my rams as a pleasing aroma,
  and a sacrifice of bulls and
    male goats.   Interlude

16 Come and listen, all you who fear God,
  and I will tell you what he did for me.
17 For I cried out to him for help,
  praising him as I spoke.
18 If I had not confessed the sin in my heart,
  the Lord would not have listened.
19 But God did listen!
  He paid attention to my prayer.
20 Praise God, who did not ignore my prayer
  or withdraw his unfailing love from me.

66:6 Hebrew the sea.   66:12 Or You made people ride over our
heads.

67

For the choir director: A song. A psalm, to be accompanied by stringed instruments.

¹ May God be merciful and bless us.
May his face smile with favor
on us.   *Interlude*

² May your ways be known throughout
the earth,
your saving power among people
everywhere.
³ May the nations praise you, O God.
Yes, may all the nations praise you.
⁴ Let the whole world sing for joy,
because you govern the nations
with justice
and guide the people of
the whole world.   *Interlude*

⁵ May the nations praise you, O God.
Yes, may all the nations praise you.
⁶ Then the earth will yield its harvests,
and God, our God, will richly bless us.
⁷ Yes, God will bless us,
and people all over the world will fear him.

68

For the choir director: A song. A psalm of David.

¹ Rise up, O God, and scatter your enemies.
Let those who hate God run for their lives.
² Blow them away like smoke.
Melt them like wax in a fire.
Let the wicked perish in
the presence of God.
³ But let the godly rejoice.
Let them be glad in God's presence.
Let them be filled with joy.
⁴ Sing praises to God and to his name!
Sing loud praises to him who rides
the clouds.*
His name is the LORD—
rejoice in his presence!

⁵ Father to the fatherless, defender of widows—
this is God, whose dwelling is holy.
⁶ God places the lonely in families;
he sets the prisoners free and gives
them joy.
But he makes the rebellious live in a
sun-scorched land.

⁷ O God, when you led your people
out from Egypt,
when you marched through the dry
wasteland,   *Interlude*
⁸ the earth trembled, and the heavens poured
down rain
before you, the God of Sinai,
before God, the God of Israel.
⁹ You sent abundant rain, O God,
to refresh the weary land.

¹⁰ There your people finally settled,
and with a bountiful harvest, O God,
you provided for your needy people.

¹¹ The Lord gives the word,
and a great army* brings the good news.
¹² Enemy kings and their armies flee,
while the women of Israel divide
the plunder.
¹³ Even those who lived among the sheepfolds
found treasures—
doves with wings of silver
and feathers of gold.
¹⁴ The Almighty scattered the enemy kings
like a blowing snowstorm
on Mount Zalmon.

¹⁵ The mountains of Bashan are majestic,
with many peaks stretching high
into the sky.
¹⁶ Why do you look with envy,
O rugged mountains,
at Mount Zion,
where God has chosen to live,
where the LORD himself will live forever?

¹⁷ Surrounded by unnumbered
thousands of chariots,
the Lord came from Mount Sinai into
his sanctuary.
¹⁸ When you ascended to the heights,
you led a crowd of captives.
You received gifts from the people,
even from those who rebelled against you.
Now the LORD God will live among us there.

¹⁹ Praise the Lord; praise God our savior!
For each day he carries us
in his arms.   *Interlude*
²⁰ Our God is a God who saves!
The Sovereign LORD rescues us from death.

²¹ But God will smash the heads of his enemies,
crushing the skulls of those who love
their guilty ways.
²² The Lord says, "I will bring my enemies
down from Bashan;
I will bring them up from the depths of
the sea.
²³ You, my people, will wash* your feet in
their blood,
and even your dogs will get their share!"

²⁴ Your procession has come into view, O God—
the procession of my God and King as he
goes into the sanctuary.
²⁵ Singers are in front, musicians behind;
between them are young women playing
tambourines.

68:4 Or *rides through the deserts.*   68:11 Or *a host of women.*
68:23 As in Greek and Syriac versions; Hebrew reads *shatter.*

²⁶ Praise God, all you people of Israel;
    praise the LORD, the source of Israel's life.
²⁷ Look, the little tribe of Benjamin leads
    the way.
    Then comes a great throng of rulers
    from Judah
    and all the rulers of Zebulun and Naphtali.

²⁸ Summon your might, O God.*
    Display your power, O God, as you have in
    the past.
²⁹ The kings of the earth are bringing tribute
    to your Temple in Jerusalem.
³⁰ Rebuke these enemy nations—
    these wild animals lurking in the reeds,
    this herd of bulls among the weaker calves.
    Make them bring bars of silver in
    humble tribute.
    Scatter the nations that delight in war.
³¹ Let Egypt come with gifts of
    precious metals*;
    let Ethiopia* bring tribute to God.
³² Sing to God, you kingdoms of the earth.
    Sing praises to the Lord.   *Interlude*
³³ Sing to the one who rides across the
    ancient heavens,
    his mighty voice thundering from the sky.
³⁴ Tell everyone about God's power.
    His majesty shines down on Israel;
    his strength is mighty in the heavens.
³⁵ God is awesome in his sanctuary.
    The God of Israel gives power and
    strength to his people.

Praise be to God!

69

*For the choir director: A psalm of David,
to be sung to the tune "Lilies."*

¹ Save me, O God,
    for the floodwaters are up to my neck.
² Deeper and deeper I sink into the mire;
    I can't find a foothold.
    I am in deep water,
    and the floods overwhelm me.
³ I am exhausted from crying for help;
    my throat is parched.
    My eyes are swollen with weeping,
    waiting for my God to help me.
⁴ Those who hate me without cause
    outnumber the hairs on my head.
    Many enemies try to destroy me with lies,
    demanding that I give back what
    I didn't steal.

⁵ O God, you know how foolish I am;
    my sins cannot be hidden from you.
⁶ Don't let those who trust in you be ashamed
    because of me,
    O Sovereign LORD of Heaven's Armies.
    Don't let me cause them to be humiliated,
    O God of Israel.

⁷ For I endure insults for your sake;
    humiliation is written all over my face.
⁸ Even my own brothers pretend they don't
    know me;
    they treat me like a stranger.

⁹ Passion for your house has consumed me,
    and the insults of those who insult you
    have fallen on me.
¹⁰ When I weep and fast,
    they scoff at me.
¹¹ When I dress in burlap to show sorrow,
    they make fun of me.
¹² I am the favorite topic of town gossip,
    and all the drunks sing about me.

¹³ But I keep praying to you, LORD,
    hoping this time you will show me favor.
    In your unfailing love, O God,
    answer my prayer with your sure
    salvation.
¹⁴ Rescue me from the mud;
    don't let me sink any deeper!
    Save me from those who hate me,
    and pull me from these deep waters.
¹⁵ Don't let the floods overwhelm me,
    or the deep waters swallow me,
    or the pit of death devour me.

¹⁶ Answer my prayers, O LORD,
    for your unfailing love is wonderful.
    Take care of me,
    for your mercy is so plentiful.
¹⁷ Don't hide from your servant;
    answer me quickly, for I am in deep
    trouble!
¹⁸ Come and redeem me;
    free me from my enemies.

¹⁹ You know of my shame, scorn, and disgrace.
    You see all that my enemies are doing.
²⁰ Their insults have broken my heart,
    and I am in despair.
    If only one person would show some pity;
    if only one would turn and comfort me.
²¹ But instead, they give me poison* for food;
    they offer me sour wine for my thirst.

²² Let the bountiful table set before them
    become a snare
    and their prosperity become a trap.*
²³ Let their eyes go blind so they cannot see,
    and make their bodies shake continually.*
²⁴ Pour out your fury on them;
    consume them with your burning anger.

68:28 As in some Hebrew manuscripts and Greek and Syriac
versions; most Hebrew manuscripts read *Your God has commanded
your strength.*   68:31a Or *of rich cloth.*   68:31b Hebrew *Cush.*
69:21 Or *gall.*   69:22 Greek version reads *Let their bountiful table
set before them become a snare, / a trap that makes them think all is
well. / Let their blessings cause them to stumble, / and let them get
what they deserve.* Compare Rom 11:9.   69:23 Greek version reads
and let their backs be bent forever. Compare Rom 11:10.

25 Let their homes become desolate
    and their tents be deserted.
26 To the one you have punished,
    they add insult to injury;
    they add to the pain of those you have hurt.
27 Pile their sins up high,
    and don't let them go free.
28 Erase their names from the Book of Life;
    don't let them be counted among
    the righteous.

29 I am suffering and in pain.
    Rescue me, O God, by your saving power.

30 Then I will praise God's name with singing,
    and I will honor him with thanksgiving.
31 For this will please the LORD more than
    sacrificing cattle,
    more than presenting a bull with its
    horns and hooves.
32 The humble will see their God at work and
    be glad.
    Let all who seek God's help be encouraged.
33 For the LORD hears the cries of the needy;
    he does not despise his imprisoned people.

34 Praise him, O heaven and earth,
    the seas and all that move in them.
35 For God will save Jerusalem*
    and rebuild the towns of Judah.
    His people will live there
    and settle in their own land.
36 The descendants of those who obey him will
    inherit the land,
    and those who love him will live there
    in safety.

70 *For the choir director: A psalm of David,
    asking God to remember him.*

1 Please, God, rescue me!
    Come quickly, LORD, and help me.
2 May those who try to kill me
    be humiliated and put to shame.
    May those who take delight in my trouble
    be turned back in disgrace.
3 Let them be horrified by their shame,
    for they said, "Aha! We've got him now!"
4 But may all who search for you
    be filled with joy and gladness in you.
    May those who love your salvation
    repeatedly shout, "God is great!"
5 But as for me, I am poor and needy;
    please hurry to my aid, O God.
    You are my helper and my savior;
    O LORD, do not delay.

71 1 O LORD, I have come to you for
    protection;
    don't let me be disgraced.
2 Save me and rescue me,
    for you do what is right.

Turn your ear to listen to me,
    and set me free.
3 Be my rock of safety
    where I can always hide.
    Give the order to save me,
    for you are my rock and my fortress.
4 My God, rescue me from the power of
    the wicked,
    from the clutches of cruel oppressors.
5 O Lord, you alone are my hope.
    I've trusted you, O LORD, from childhood.
6 Yes, you have been with me from birth;
    from my mother's womb you have cared
    for me.
    No wonder I am always praising you!

7 My life is an example to many,
    because you have been my strength
    and protection.
8 That is why I can never stop praising you;
    I declare your glory all day long.
9 And now, in my old age, don't set me aside.
    Don't abandon me when my strength
    is failing.
10 For my enemies are whispering against me.
    They are plotting together to kill me.
11 They say, "God has abandoned him.
    Let's go and get him,
    for no one will help him now."

12 O God, don't stay away.
    My God, please hurry to help me.
13 Bring disgrace and destruction on
    my accusers.
    Humiliate and shame those who want to
    harm me.
14 But I will keep on hoping for your help;
    I will praise you more and more.
15 I will tell everyone about your
    righteousness.
    All day long I will proclaim your saving
    power,
    though I am not skilled with words.*
16 I will praise your mighty deeds,
    O Sovereign LORD.
    I will tell everyone that you alone are just.

17 O God, you have taught me from
    my earliest childhood,
    and I constantly tell others about the
    wonderful things you do.
18 Now that I am old and gray,
    do not abandon me, O God.
    Let me proclaim your power to this
    new generation,
    your mighty miracles to all who come
    after me.
19 Your righteousness, O God, reaches to the
    highest heavens.

_____
69:35 Hebrew *Zion.*   71:15 Or *though I cannot count it.*

You have done such wonderful things.
Who can compare with you, O God?
²⁰ You have allowed me to suffer
 much hardship,
 but you will restore me to life again
 and lift me up from the depths of the earth.
²¹ You will restore me to even greater honor
 and comfort me once again.

²² Then I will praise you with music on the
 harp,
 because you are faithful to your promises,
 O my God.
 I will sing praises to you with a lyre,
 O Holy One of Israel.
²³ I will shout for joy and sing your praises,
 for you have ransomed me.
²⁴ I will tell about your righteous deeds
 all day long,
 for everyone who tried to hurt me
 has been shamed and humiliated.

72 *A psalm of Solomon.*

¹ Give your love of justice to the king, O God,
 and righteousness to the king's son.
² Help him judge your people in the right way;
 let the poor always be treated fairly.
³ May the mountains yield prosperity for all,
 and may the hills be fruitful.
⁴ Help him to defend the poor,
 to rescue the children of the needy,
 and to crush their oppressors.
⁵ May they fear you* as long as the sun shines,
 as long as the moon remains in the sky.
 Yes, forever!

⁶ May the king's rule be refreshing like spring
 rain on freshly cut grass,
 like the showers that water the earth.
⁷ May all the godly flourish during his reign.
 May there be abundant prosperity until
 the moon is no more.
⁸ May he reign from sea to sea,
 and from the Euphrates River* to the ends
 of the earth.
⁹ Desert nomads will bow before him;
 his enemies will fall before him in the dust.
¹⁰ The western kings of Tarshish and other
 distant lands
 will bring him tribute.
 The eastern kings of Sheba and Seba
 will bring him gifts.
¹¹ All kings will bow before him,
 and all nations will serve him.

¹² He will rescue the poor when they cry to him;
 he will help the oppressed, who have no
 one to defend them.
¹³ He feels pity for the weak and the needy,
 and he will rescue them.

¹⁴ He will redeem them from oppression
 and violence,
 for their lives are precious to him.

¹⁵ Long live the king!
 May the gold of Sheba be given to him.
 May the people always pray for him
 and bless him all day long.
¹⁶ May there be abundant grain throughout
 the land,
 flourishing even on the hilltops.
 May the fruit trees flourish like the trees
 of Lebanon,
 and may the people thrive like grass
 in a field.
¹⁷ May the king's name endure forever;
 may it continue as long as the sun shines.
 May all nations be blessed through him
 and bring him praise.

¹⁸ Praise the LORD God, the God of Israel,
 who alone does such wonderful things.
¹⁹ Praise his glorious name forever!
 Let the whole earth be filled with his glory.
 Amen and amen!

²⁰ (This ends the prayers of David son of Jesse.)

BOOK THREE (Psalms 73–89)

73 *A psalm of Asaph.*

¹ Truly God is good to Israel,
 to those whose hearts are pure.
² But as for me, I almost lost my footing.
 My feet were slipping,
 and I was almost gone.
³ For I envied the proud
 when I saw them prosper despite their
 wickedness.
⁴ They seem to live such painless lives;
 their bodies are so healthy and strong.
⁵ They don't have troubles like other people;
 they're not plagued with problems like
 everyone else.
⁶ They wear pride like a jeweled necklace
 and clothe themselves with cruelty.
⁷ These fat cats have everything
 their hearts could ever wish for!
⁸ They scoff and speak only evil;
 in their pride they seek to crush others.
⁹ They boast against the very heavens,
 and their words strut throughout the earth.
¹⁰ And so the people are dismayed and
 confused,
 drinking in all their words.
¹¹ "What does God know?" they ask.
 "Does the Most High even know what's
 happening?"

72:5 Greek version reads *May they endure.*   72:8 Hebrew *the river.*

¹² Look at these wicked people—
  enjoying a life of ease while their
    riches multiply.

¹³ Did I keep my heart pure for nothing?
  Did I keep myself innocent for no reason?
¹⁴ I get nothing but trouble all day long;
  every morning brings me pain.

¹⁵ If I had really spoken this way to others,
  I would have been a traitor to your people.
¹⁶ So I tried to understand why the wicked
    prosper.
  But what a difficult task it is!
¹⁷ Then I went into your sanctuary, O God,
  and I finally understood the destiny of
    the wicked.
¹⁸ Truly, you put them on a slippery path
  and send them sliding over the cliff to
    destruction.
¹⁹ In an instant they are destroyed,
  completely swept away by terrors.
²⁰ When you arise, O Lord,
  you will laugh at their silly ideas
  as a person laughs at dreams in the
    morning.

²¹ Then I realized that my heart was bitter,
  and I was all torn up inside.
²² I was so foolish and ignorant—
  I must have seemed like a senseless
    animal to you.
²³ Yet I still belong to you;
  you hold my right hand.
²⁴ You guide me with your counsel,
  leading me to a glorious destiny.
²⁵ Whom have I in heaven but you?
  I desire you more than anything on earth.
²⁶ My health may fail, and my spirit may
    grow weak,
  but God remains the strength of my heart;
  he is mine forever.

²⁷ Those who desert him will perish,
  for you destroy those who abandon you.
²⁸ But as for me, how good it is to be near God!
  I have made the Sovereign LORD my shelter,
  and I will tell everyone about the
    wonderful things you do.

74 A psalm* of Asaph.

¹ O God, why have you rejected us so long?
  Why is your anger so intense against the
    sheep of your own pasture?
² Remember that we are the people you chose
    long ago,
  the tribe you redeemed as your own
    special possession!
  And remember Jerusalem,* your home
    here on earth.

³ Walk through the awful ruins of the city;
  see how the enemy has destroyed your
    sanctuary.

⁴ There your enemies shouted their victorious
    battle cries;
  there they set up their battle standards.
⁵ They swung their axes
  like woodcutters in a forest.
⁶ With axes and picks,
  they smashed the carved paneling.
⁷ They burned your sanctuary to the ground.
  They defiled the place that bears
    your name.
⁸ Then they thought,
  "Let's destroy everything!"
  So they burned down all the places where
    God was worshiped.

⁹ We no longer see your miraculous signs.
  All the prophets are gone,
  and no one can tell us when it will end.
¹⁰ How long, O God, will you allow our enemies
    to insult you?
  Will you let them dishonor
    your name forever?
¹¹ Why do you hold back your strong right hand?
  Unleash your powerful fist and
    destroy them.

¹² You, O God, are my king from ages past,
  bringing salvation to the earth.
¹³ You split the sea by your strength
  and smashed the heads of
    the sea monsters.
¹⁴ You crushed the heads of Leviathan*
  and let the desert animals eat him.
¹⁵ You caused the springs and streams
    to gush forth,
  and you dried up rivers that never run dry.
¹⁶ Both day and night belong to you;
  you made the starlight* and the sun.
¹⁷ You set the boundaries of the earth,
  and you made both summer and winter.

¹⁸ See how these enemies insult you, LORD.
  A foolish nation has dishonored
    your name.
¹⁹ Don't let these wild beasts destroy
    your turtledoves.
  Don't forget your suffering people forever.

²⁰ Remember your covenant promises,
  for the land is full of darkness and violence!
²¹ Don't let the downtrodden be
    humiliated again.
  Instead, let the poor and needy praise
    your name.

74:TITLE Hebrew *maskil.* This may be a literary or musical term.
74:2 Hebrew *Mount Zion.* 74:14 The identification of Leviathan
is disputed, ranging from an earthly creature to a mythical sea
monster in ancient literature. 74:16 Or *moon;* Hebrew reads *light.*

²² Arise, O God, and defend your cause.
   Remember how these fools insult you
      all day long.
²³ Don't overlook what your enemies have said
   or their growing uproar.

75 *For the choir director: A psalm of Asaph.*
   A song to be sung to the tune "Do Not Destroy!"

¹ We thank you, O God!
   We give thanks because you are near.
   People everywhere tell of your
      wonderful deeds.

² God says, "At the time I have planned,
   I will bring justice against the wicked.
³ When the earth quakes and its people
      live in turmoil,
   I am the one who keeps its
      foundations firm.   *Interlude*

⁴ "I warned the proud, 'Stop your boasting!'
   I told the wicked, 'Don't raise your fists!
⁵ Don't raise your fists in defiance at the
      heavens
   or speak with such arrogance.'"
⁶ For no one on earth—from east or west,
   or even from the wilderness—
   should raise a defiant fist.*
⁷ It is God alone who judges;
   he decides who will rise and who will fall.
⁸ For the LORD holds a cup in his hand
   that is full of foaming wine mixed
      with spices.
   He pours out the wine in judgment,
   and all the wicked must drink it,
      draining it to the dregs.

⁹ But as for me, I will always proclaim what
      God has done;
   I will sing praises to the God of Jacob.
¹⁰ For God says, "I will break the strength of
      the wicked,
   but I will increase the power of the godly."

76 *For the choir director: A psalm of Asaph.*
   A song to be accompanied by stringed
instruments.

¹ God is honored in Judah;
   his name is great in Israel.
² Jerusalem* is where he lives;
   Mount Zion is his home.
³ There he has broken the fiery arrows of
      the enemy,
   the shields and swords and
      weapons of war.   *Interlude*

⁴ You are glorious and more majestic
   than the everlasting mountains.*
⁵ Our boldest enemies have been plundered.
   They lie before us in the sleep of death.

No warrior could lift a hand against us.
⁶ At the blast of your breath,
      O God of Jacob,
   their horses and chariots lay still.

⁷ No wonder you are greatly feared!
   Who can stand before you when your
      anger explodes?
⁸ From heaven you sentenced your enemies;
   the earth trembled and stood silent
      before you.
⁹ You stand up to judge those who do evil,
      O God,
   and to rescue the oppressed
      of the earth.   *Interlude*
¹⁰ Human defiance only enhances your glory,
   for you use it as a weapon.*

¹¹ Make vows to the LORD your God,
   and keep them.
   Let everyone bring tribute to the
      Awesome One.
¹² For he breaks the pride of princes,
   and the kings of the earth fear him.

77 *For Jeduthun, the choir director:*
   A psalm of Asaph.

¹ I cry out to God; yes, I shout.
   Oh, that God would listen to me!
² When I was in deep trouble,
   I searched for the Lord.
   All night long I prayed, with hands lifted
      toward heaven,
   but my soul was not comforted.
³ I think of God, and I moan,
   overwhelmed with longing
      for his help.   *Interlude*

⁴ You don't let me sleep.
   I am too distressed even to pray!
⁵ I think of the good old days,
   long since ended,
⁶ when my nights were filled with
      joyful songs.
   I search my soul and ponder the
      difference now.
⁷ Has the Lord rejected me forever?
   Will he never again be kind to me?
⁸ Is his unfailing love gone forever?
   Have his promises permanently failed?
⁹ Has God forgotten to be gracious?
   Has he slammed the door on his
      compassion?   *Interlude*

¹⁰ And I said, "This is my fate;
   the Most High has turned his hand
      against me."

75:6 Hebrew *should lift.*   76:2 Hebrew *Salem,* another name
for Jerusalem.   76:4 As in Greek version; Hebrew reads *than
mountains filled with beasts of prey.*   76:10 The meaning of the
Hebrew is uncertain.

¹¹ But then I recall all you have done,
O LORD;
I remember your wonderful deeds
of long ago.
¹² They are constantly in my thoughts.
I cannot stop thinking about your
mighty works.

¹³ O God, your ways are holy.
Is there any god as mighty as you?
¹⁴ You are the God of great wonders!
You demonstrate your awesome power
among the nations.
¹⁵ By your strong arm,
you redeemed your people,
the descendants of Jacob
and Joseph.   *Interlude*

¹⁶ When the Red Sea* saw you, O God,
its waters looked and trembled!
The sea quaked to its very depths.
¹⁷ The clouds poured down rain;
the thunder rumbled in the sky.
Your arrows of lightning flashed.
¹⁸ Your thunder roared from the whirlwind;
the lightning lit up the world!
The earth trembled and shook.
¹⁹ Your road led through the sea,
your pathway through the mighty
waters—
a pathway no one knew was there!
²⁰ You led your people along that road like
a flock of sheep,
with Moses and Aaron as their shepherds.

78 *A psalm* of Asaph.*

¹ O my people, listen to my instructions.
Open your ears to what I am saying,
² for I will speak to you in a parable.
I will teach you hidden lessons from
our past—
³ stories we have heard and known,
stories our ancestors handed down to us.
⁴ We will not hide these truths from
our children;
we will tell the next generation
about the glorious deeds of the LORD,
about his power and his mighty wonders.
⁵ For he issued his laws to Jacob;
he gave his instructions to Israel.
He commanded our ancestors
to teach them to their children,
⁶ so the next generation might know them—
even the children not yet born—
and they in turn will teach their own
children.
⁷ So each generation should set its hope anew
on God,
not forgetting his glorious miracles
and obeying his commands.

⁸ Then they will not be like their ancestors—
stubborn, rebellious, and unfaithful,
refusing to give their hearts to God.

⁹ The warriors of Ephraim, though armed
with bows,
turned their backs and fled on the day
of battle.
¹⁰ They did not keep God's covenant
and refused to live by his instructions.
¹¹ They forgot what he had done—
the great wonders he had shown them,
¹² the miracles he did for their ancestors
on the plain of Zoan in the land of Egypt.
¹³ For he divided the sea and led them through,
making the water stand up like walls!
¹⁴ In the daytime he led them by a cloud,
and all night by a pillar of fire.
¹⁵ He split open the rocks in the wilderness
to give them water, as from a gushing
spring.
¹⁶ He made streams pour from the rock,
making the waters flow down like a river!

¹⁷ Yet they kept on sinning against him,
rebelling against the Most High
in the desert.
¹⁸ They stubbornly tested God in their hearts,
demanding the foods they craved.
¹⁹ They even spoke against God himself,
saying,
"God can't give us food in the wilderness.
²⁰ Yes, he can strike a rock so water gushes out,
but he can't give his people bread
and meat."
²¹ When the LORD heard them, he was furious.
The fire of his wrath burned against
Jacob.
Yes, his anger rose against Israel,
²² for they did not believe God
or trust him to care for them.
²³ But he commanded the skies to open;
he opened the doors of heaven.
²⁴ He rained down manna for them to eat;
he gave them bread from heaven.
²⁵ They ate the food of angels!
God gave them all they could hold.
²⁶ He released the east wind in the heavens
and guided the south wind by
his mighty power.
²⁷ He rained down meat as thick as dust—
birds as plentiful as the sand on the
seashore!
²⁸ He caused the birds to fall within their camp
and all around their tents.
²⁹ The people ate their fill.
He gave them what they craved.
³⁰ But before they satisfied their craving,
while the meat was yet in their mouths,

77:16 Hebrew *the waters.* 78:TITLE Hebrew *mashil.* This may be a
literary or musical term.

³¹ the anger of God rose against them,
and he killed their strongest men.
He struck down the finest of Israel's
young men.

³² But in spite of this, the people kept sinning.
Despite his wonders, they refused to
trust him.
³³ So he ended their lives in failure,
their years in terror.
³⁴ When God began killing them,
they finally sought him.
They repented and took God seriously.
³⁵ Then they remembered that God was
their rock,
that God Most High* was their redeemer.
³⁶ But all they gave him was lip service;
they lied to him with their tongues.
³⁷ Their hearts were not loyal to him.
They did not keep his covenant.
³⁸ Yet he was merciful and forgave their sins
and did not destroy them all.
Many times he held back his anger
and did not unleash his fury!
³⁹ For he remembered that they were
merely mortal,
gone like a breath of wind that never
returns.

⁴⁰ Oh, how often they rebelled against him
in the wilderness
and grieved his heart in that dry wasteland.
⁴¹ Again and again they tested God's patience
and provoked the Holy One of Israel.
⁴² They did not remember his power
and how he rescued them from
their enemies.
⁴³ They did not remember his miraculous
signs in Egypt,
his wonders on the plain of Zoan.
⁴⁴ For he turned their rivers into blood,
so no one could drink from the streams.
⁴⁵ He sent vast swarms of flies to consume them
and hordes of frogs to ruin them.
⁴⁶ He gave their crops to caterpillars;
their harvest was consumed by locusts.
⁴⁷ He destroyed their grapevines with hail
and shattered their sycamore-figs
with sleet.
⁴⁸ He abandoned their cattle to the hail,
their livestock to bolts of lightning.
⁴⁹ He loosed on them his fierce anger—
all his fury, rage, and hostility.
He dispatched against them
a band of destroying angels.
⁵⁰ He turned his anger against them;
he did not spare the Egyptians' lives
but ravaged them with the plague.
⁵¹ He killed the oldest son in each
Egyptian family,
the flower of youth throughout the land
of Egypt.*

⁵² But he led his own people like a flock
of sheep,
guiding them safely through
the wilderness.
⁵³ He kept them safe so they were not afraid;
but the sea covered their enemies.
⁵⁴ He brought them to the border of
his holy land,
to this land of hills he had won for them.
⁵⁵ He drove out the nations before them;
he gave them their inheritance by lot.
He settled the tribes of Israel into
their homes.

⁵⁶ But they kept testing and rebelling against
God Most High.
They did not obey his laws.
⁵⁷ They turned back and were as faithless as
their parents.
They were as undependable as
a crooked bow.
⁵⁸ They angered God by building shrines to
other gods;
they made him jealous with their idols.
⁵⁹ When God heard them, he was very angry,
and he completely rejected Israel.
⁶⁰ Then he abandoned his dwelling at Shiloh,
the Tabernacle where he had lived
among the people.
⁶¹ He allowed the Ark of his might to be
captured;
he surrendered his glory into enemy
hands.
⁶² He gave his people over to be butchered by
the sword,
because he was so angry with his own
people—his special possession.
⁶³ Their young men were killed by fire;
their young women died before singing
their wedding songs.
⁶⁴ Their priests were slaughtered,
and their widows could not mourn
their deaths.

⁶⁵ Then the Lord rose up as though waking
from sleep,
like a warrior aroused from a drunken
stupor.
⁶⁶ He routed his enemies
and sent them to eternal shame.
⁶⁷ But he rejected Joseph's descendants;
he did not choose the tribe of Ephraim.
⁶⁸ He chose instead the tribe of Judah,
and Mount Zion, which he loved.
⁶⁹ There he built his sanctuary as high
as the heavens,
as solid and enduring as the earth.
⁷⁰ He chose his servant David,
calling him from the sheep pens.

___
78:35 Hebrew *El-Elyon.*   78:51 Hebrew *in the tents of Ham.*

⁷¹ He took David from tending the ewes
and lambs
and made him the shepherd of Jacob's
descendants—
God's own people, Israel.
⁷² He cared for them with a true heart
and led them with skillful hands.

79

A psalm of Asaph.

¹ O God, pagan nations have conquered
your land,
your special possession.
They have defiled your holy Temple
and made Jerusalem a heap of ruins.
² They have left the bodies of your servants
as food for the birds of heaven.
The flesh of your godly ones
has become food for the wild animals.
³ Blood has flowed like water all around
Jerusalem;
no one is left to bury the dead.
⁴ We are mocked by our neighbors,
an object of scorn and derision to
those around us.

⁵ O LORD, how long will you be angry with us?
Forever?
How long will your jealousy burn like fire?
⁶ Pour out your wrath on the nations that
refuse to acknowledge you—
on kingdoms that do not call upon
your name.
⁷ For they have devoured your people Israel,*
making the land a desolate wilderness.
⁸ Do not hold us guilty for the sins of
our ancestors!
Let your compassion quickly meet
our needs,
for we are on the brink of despair.

⁹ Help us, O God of our salvation!
Help us for the glory of your name.
Save us and forgive our sins
for the honor of your name.
¹⁰ Why should pagan nations be allowed to scoff,
asking, "Where is their God?"
Show us your vengeance against the nations,
for they have spilled the blood of
your servants.
¹¹ Listen to the moaning of the prisoners.
Demonstrate your great power by saving
those condemned to die.

¹² O Lord, pay back our neighbors seven times
for the scorn they have hurled at you.
¹³ Then we your people,
the sheep of your pasture,
will thank you forever and ever,
praising your greatness from generation
to generation.

80

*For the choir director: A psalm of Asaph,
to be sung to the tune "Lilies of the Covenant."*

¹ Please listen, O Shepherd of Israel,
you who lead Joseph's descendants like
a flock.
O God, enthroned above the cherubim,
display your radiant glory
² to Ephraim, Benjamin, and Manasseh.
Show us your mighty power.
Come to rescue us!

³ Turn us again to yourself, O God.
Make your face shine down upon us.
Only then will we be saved.
⁴ O LORD God of Heaven's Armies,
how long will you be angry with
our prayers?
⁵ You have fed us with sorrow
and made us drink tears by the bucketful.
⁶ You have made us the scorn* of
neighboring nations.
Our enemies treat us as a joke.

⁷ Turn us again to yourself,
O God of Heaven's Armies.
Make your face shine down upon us.
Only then will we be saved.
⁸ You brought us from Egypt like a grapevine;
you drove away the pagan nations and
transplanted us into your land.
⁹ You cleared the ground for us,
and we took root and filled the land.
¹⁰ Our shade covered the mountains;
our branches covered the mighty cedars.
¹¹ We spread our branches west to the
Mediterranean Sea;
our shoots spread east to the
Euphrates River.*
¹² But now, why have you broken down
our walls
so that all who pass by may steal our fruit?
¹³ The wild boar from the forest devours it,
and the wild animals feed on it.

¹⁴ Come back, we beg you, O God of
Heaven's Armies.
Look down from heaven and see our plight.
Take care of this grapevine
¹⁵ that you yourself have planted,
this son you have raised for yourself.
¹⁶ For we are chopped up and burned by
our enemies.
May they perish at the sight of your frown.
¹⁷ Strengthen the man you love,
the son of your choice.
¹⁸ Then we will never abandon you again.
Revive us so we can call on your name
once more.

79:7 Hebrew *devoured Jacob.* See note on 44:4.   80:6 As in Syriac
version; Hebrew reads *the strife.*   80:11 Hebrew *west to the
sea, . . . east to the river.*

19 Turn us again to yourself,
   O LORD God of Heaven's Armies.
   Make your face shine down upon us.
   Only then will we be saved.

81

*For the choir director: A psalm of Asaph,
to be accompanied by a stringed instrument.**

1 Sing praises to God, our strength.
   Sing to the God of Jacob.
2 Sing! Beat the tambourine.
   Play the sweet lyre and the harp.
3 Blow the ram's horn at new moon,
   and again at full moon to call
   a festival!
4 For this is required by the decrees
   of Israel;
   it is a regulation of the God of Jacob.
5 He made it a law for Israel*
   when he attacked Egypt to set us free.

   I heard an unknown voice say,
6 "Now I will take the load from your
   shoulders;
   I will free your hands from their heavy
   tasks.
7 You cried to me in trouble, and
   I saved you;
   I answered out of the thundercloud
   and tested your faith when there was no
   water at Meribah.   *Interlude*

8 "Listen to me, O my people,
   while I give you stern warnings.
   O Israel, if you would only listen to me!
9 You must never have a foreign god;
   you must not bow down before
   a false god.
10 For it was I, the LORD your God,
   who rescued you from the land
   of Egypt.
   Open your mouth wide,
   and I will fill it with good things.

11 "But no, my people wouldn't listen.
   Israel did not want me around.
12 So I let them follow their own stubborn
   desires,
   living according to their own ideas.
13 Oh, that my people would listen to me!
   Oh, that Israel would follow me,
   walking in my paths!
14 How quickly I would then subdue
   their enemies!
   How soon my hands would be upon
   their foes!
15 Those who hate the LORD would cringe
   before him;
   they would be doomed forever.
16 But I would feed you with the finest wheat.
   I would satisfy you with wild honey from
   the rock."

82

A psalm of Asaph.

1 God presides over heaven's court;
   he pronounces judgment on the
   heavenly beings:
2 "How long will you hand down
   unjust decisions
   by favoring the wicked?   *Interlude*

3 "Give justice to the poor and the orphan;
   uphold the rights of the oppressed and
   the destitute.
4 Rescue the poor and helpless;
   deliver them from the grasp of evil people.
5 But these oppressors know nothing;
   they are so ignorant!
They wander about in darkness,
   while the whole world is shaken to
   the core.
6 I say, 'You are gods;
   you are all children of the Most High.
7 But you will die like mere mortals
   and fall like every other ruler.'"

8 Rise up, O God, and judge the earth,
   for all the nations belong to you.

83

A song. A psalm of Asaph.

1 O God, do not be silent!
   Do not be deaf.
   Do not be quiet, O God.
2 Don't you hear the uproar of your enemies?
   Don't you see that your arrogant enemies
   are rising up?
3 They devise crafty schemes against your
   people;
   they conspire against your precious ones.
4 "Come," they say,
   "let us wipe out Israel as a nation.
   We will destroy the very memory of
   its existence."
5 Yes, this was their unanimous decision.
   They signed a treaty as allies against you—
6 these Edomites and Ishmaelites;
   Moabites and Hagrites;
7 Gebalites, Ammonites, and Amalekites;
   and people from Philistia and Tyre.
8 Assyria has joined them, too,
   and is allied with the descendants
   of Lot.   *Interlude*

9 Do to them as you did to the Midianites
   and as you did to Sisera and Jabin at the
   Kishon River.
10 They were destroyed at Endor,
   and their decaying corpses fertilized
   the soil.

_____
81:TITLE Hebrew *according to the gittith.*   81:5 Hebrew *for Joseph.*

11 Let their mighty nobles die as Oreb
     and Zeeb did.
   Let all their princes die like Zebah
     and Zalmunna.
12 for they said, "Let us seize for our own use
     these pasturelands of God!"
13 O my God, scatter them like tumbleweed,
     like chaff before the wind!
14 As a fire burns a forest
     and as a flame sets mountains ablaze,
15 chase them with your fierce storm;
     terrify them with your tempest.
16 Utterly disgrace them
     until they submit to your name, O LORD.
17 Let them be ashamed and terrified forever.
   Let them die in disgrace.
18 Then they will learn that you alone are
     called the LORD,
   that you alone are the Most High,
   supreme over all the earth.

84 For the choir director: A psalm of the descendants of Korah, to be accompanied by a stringed instrument.*

1 How lovely is your dwelling place,
   O LORD of Heaven's Armies.
2 I long, yes, I faint with longing
   to enter the courts of the LORD.
   With my whole being, body and soul,
   I will shout joyfully to the living God.
3 Even the sparrow finds a home,
     and the swallow builds her nest and
     raises her young
   at a place near your altar,
   O LORD of Heaven's Armies,
     my King and my God!
4 What joy for those who can live
     in your house,
   always singing your praises.   Interlude

5 What joy for those whose strength comes
     from the LORD,
   who have set their minds on a pilgrimage
     to Jerusalem.
6 When they walk through the
     Valley of Weeping,*
   it will become a place of
     refreshing springs.
   The autumn rains will clothe it with
     blessings.
7 They will continue to grow stronger,
     and each of them will appear before God
     in Jerusalem.*

8 O LORD God of Heaven's Armies,
     hear my prayer.
   Listen, O God of Jacob.   Interlude

9 O God, look with favor upon the king,
     our shield!
   Show favor to the one you have anointed.

10 A single day in your courts
     is better than a thousand anywhere else!
   I would rather be a gatekeeper in the house
     of my God
   than live the good life in the homes of
     the wicked.
11 For the LORD God is our sun and our shield.
   He gives us grace and glory.
   The LORD will withhold no good thing
     from those who do what is right.
12 O LORD of Heaven's Armies,
   what joy for those who trust in you.

85 For the choir director: A psalm of the descendants of Korah.

1 LORD, you poured out blessings on
     your land!
   You restored the fortunes of Israel.*
2 You forgave the guilt of your people—
     yes, you covered all their sins.   Interlude
3 You held back your fury.
   You kept back your blazing anger.

4 Now restore us again, O God of our salvation.
   Put aside your anger against us
     once more.
5 Will you be angry with us always?
   Will you prolong your wrath to all
     generations?
6 Won't you revive us again,
     so your people can rejoice in you?
7 Show us your unfailing love, O LORD,
     and grant us your salvation.

8 I listen carefully to what God the LORD
     is saying,
   for he speaks peace to his faithful people.
   But let them not return to their
     foolish ways.
9 Surely his salvation is near to those who
     fear him,
   so our land will be filled with his glory.

10 Unfailing love and truth have met together.
   Righteousness and peace have kissed!
11 Truth springs up from the earth,
     and righteousness smiles down
     from heaven.
12 Yes, the LORD pours down his blessings.
   Our land will yield its bountiful harvest.
13 Righteousness goes as a herald before him,
     preparing the way for his steps.

86 A prayer of David.

1 Bend down, O LORD, and hear my prayer;
     answer me, for I need your help.

84:TITLE Hebrew according to the gittith.   84:6 Or Valley of Poplars;
Hebrew reads valley of Baca.   84:7 Hebrew Zion.   85:1 Hebrew of
Jacob. See note on 44:4.

² Protect me, for I am devoted to you.
    Save me, for I serve you and trust you.
    You are my God.
³ Be merciful to me, O Lord,
    for I am calling on you constantly.
⁴ Give me happiness, O Lord,
    for I give myself to you.
⁵ O Lord, you are so good,
    so ready to forgive,
    so full of unfailing love for all who ask for
    your help.
⁶ Listen closely to my prayer, O Lord;
    hear my urgent cry.
⁷ I will call to you whenever I'm in trouble,
    and you will answer me.

⁸ No pagan god is like you, O Lord.
    None can do what you do!
⁹ All the nations you made
    will come and bow before you, Lord;
    they will praise your holy name.
¹⁰ For you are great and perform
    wonderful deeds.
    You alone are God.

¹¹ Teach me your ways, O Lord,
    that I may live according to your truth!
    Grant me purity of heart,
    so that I may honor you.
¹² With all my heart I will praise you,
    O Lord my God.
    I will give glory to your name forever,
¹³ for your love for me is very great.
    You have rescued me from the depths
    of death.*

¹⁴ O God, insolent people rise up against me;
    a violent gang is trying to kill me.
    You mean nothing to them.
¹⁵ But you, O Lord,
    are a God of compassion and mercy,
    slow to get angry
    and filled with unfailing love and
    faithfulness.
¹⁶ Look down and have mercy on me.
    Give your strength to your servant;
    save me, the son of your servant.
¹⁷ Send me a sign of your favor.
    Then those who hate me will be put
    to shame,
    for you, O Lord, help and comfort me.

87 *A song. A psalm of the descendants of Korah.*

¹ On the holy mountain
    stands the city founded by the Lord.
² He loves the city of Jerusalem
    more than any other city in Israel.*
³ O city of God,
    what glorious things are said
    of you!   *Interlude*

⁴ I will count Egypt* and Babylon among
    those who know me—
    also Philistia and Tyre, and even
    distant Ethiopia.*
    They have all become citizens of
    Jerusalem!
⁵ Regarding Jerusalem* it will be said,
    "Everyone enjoys the rights of
    citizenship there."
    And the Most High will personally bless
    this city.
⁶ When the Lord registers the nations,
    he will say,
    "They have all become citizens of
    Jerusalem."   *Interlude*

⁷ The people will play flutes* and sing,
    "The source of my life springs from
    Jerusalem!"

88 *For the choir director: A psalm of the descendants of Korah. A song to be sung to the tune "The Suffering of Affliction." A psalm* of Heman the Ezrahite.*

¹ O Lord, God of my salvation,
    I cry out to you by day.
    I come to you at night.
² Now hear my prayer;
    listen to my cry.
³ For my life is full of troubles,
    and death* draws near.
⁴ I am as good as dead,
    like a strong man with
    no strength left.
⁵ They have left me among the dead,
    and I lie like a corpse in a grave.
    I am forgotten,
    cut off from your care.
⁶ You have thrown me into the lowest pit,
    into the darkest depths.
⁷ Your anger weighs me down;
    with wave after wave you have
    engulfed me.   *Interlude*

⁸ You have driven my friends away
    by making me repulsive to them.
    I am in a trap with no way of escape.
⁹ My eyes are blinded by my tears.
    Each day I beg for your help, O Lord;
    I lift my hands to you for mercy.
¹⁰ Are your wonderful deeds of any use to
    the dead?
    Do the dead rise up and
    praise you?   *Interlude*

11 Can those in the grave declare your
    unfailing love?
    Can they proclaim your faithfulness in
    the place of destruction?*
12 Can the darkness speak of your
    wonderful deeds?
    Can anyone in the land of forgetfulness
    talk about your righteousness?
13 O Lord, I cry out to you.
    I will keep on pleading day by day.
14 O Lord, why do you reject me?
    Why do you turn your face from me?

15 I have been sick and close to death since
    my youth.
    I stand helpless and desperate before
    your terrors.
16 Your fierce anger has overwhelmed me.
    Your terrors have paralyzed me.
17 They swirl around me like floodwaters
    all day long.
    They have engulfed me completely.
18 You have taken away my companions and
    loved ones.
    Darkness is my closest friend.

89 *A psalm* of Ethan the Ezrahite.

1 I will sing of the Lord's unfailing love
    forever!
    Young and old will hear of your faithfulness.
2 Your unfailing love will last forever.
    Your faithfulness is as enduring as
    the heavens.

3 The Lord said, "I have made a covenant
    with David, my chosen servant.
    I have sworn this oath to him:
4 'I will establish your descendants as
    kings forever;
    they will sit on your throne from now
    until eternity.'"   *Interlude*
5 All heaven will praise your great wonders,
    Lord;
    myriads of angels will praise you for
    your faithfulness.
6 For who in all of heaven can compare with
    the Lord?
    What mightiest angel is anything like
    the Lord?
7 The highest angelic powers stand in
    awe of God.
    He is far more awesome than all who
    surround his throne.
8 O Lord God of Heaven's Armies!
    Where is there anyone as mighty as you,
    O Lord?
    You are entirely faithful.

9 You rule the oceans.
    You subdue their storm-tossed waves.

10 You crushed the great sea monster.*
    You scattered your enemies with your
    mighty arm.
11 The heavens are yours, and the earth is yours;
    everything in the world is yours—you
    created it all.
12 You created north and south.
    Mount Tabor and Mount Hermon praise
    your name.
13 Powerful is your arm!
    Strong is your hand!
    Your right hand is lifted high in
    glorious strength.
14 Righteousness and justice are the
    foundation of your throne.
    Unfailing love and truth walk before you
    as attendants.
15 Happy are those who hear the joyful
    call to worship,
    for they will walk in the light of your
    presence, Lord.
16 They rejoice all day long in your wonderful
    reputation.
    They exult in your righteousness.
17 You are their glorious strength.
    It pleases you to make us strong.
18 Yes, our protection comes from the Lord,
    and he, the Holy One of Israel, has given
    us our king.

19 Long ago you spoke in a vision to your
    faithful people.
    You said, "I have raised up a warrior.
    I have selected him from the common
    people to be king.
20 I have found my servant David.
    I have anointed him with my holy oil.
21 I will steady him with my hand;
    with my powerful arm I will
    make him strong.
22 His enemies will not defeat him,
    nor will the wicked overpower him.
23 I will beat down his adversaries before him
    and destroy those who hate him.
24 My faithfulness and unfailing love will be
    with him,
    and by my authority he will grow in power.
25 I will extend his rule over the sea,
    his dominion over the rivers.
26 And he will call out to me,
    'You are my Father,
    my God, and the Rock of my salvation.'
27 I will make him my firstborn son,
    the mightiest king on earth.
28 I will love him and be kind to him forever;
    my covenant with him will never end.
29 I will preserve an heir for him;
    his throne will be as endless as the days
    of heaven.

88:11 Hebrew *in Abaddon?*   **89:TITLE** Hebrew *mashil.* This may be
a literary or musical term.   **89:10** Hebrew *Rahab,* the name of a
mythical sea monster that represents chaos in ancient literature.

30 But if his descendants forsake
        my instructions
    and fail to obey my regulations,
31 if they do not obey my decrees
    and fail to keep my commands,
32 then I will punish their sin with the rod,
    and their disobedience with beating.
33 But I will never stop loving him
    nor fail to keep my promise to him.
34 No, I will not break my covenant;
    I will not take back a single word I said.
35 I have sworn an oath to David,
    and in my holiness I cannot lie:
36 His dynasty will go on forever;
    his kingdom will endure as the sun.
37 It will be as eternal as the moon,
    my faithful witness in the sky!"   *Interlude*

38 But now you have rejected him and
        cast him off.
    You are angry with your anointed king.
39 You have renounced your covenant
        with him;
    you have thrown his crown in the dust.
40 You have broken down the walls
        protecting him
    and ruined every fort defending him.
41 Everyone who comes along has robbed him,
    and he has become a joke to his
        neighbors.
42 You have strengthened his enemies
    and made them all rejoice.
43 You have made his sword useless
    and refused to help him in battle.
44 You have ended his splendor
    and overturned his throne.
45 You have made him old before his time
    and publicly disgraced him.   *Interlude*

46 O Lord, how long will this go on?
    Will you hide yourself forever?
    How long will your anger burn like fire?
47 Remember how short my life is,
    how empty and futile this human
        existence!
48 No one can live forever; all will die.
    No one can escape the power of
        the grave.*   *Interlude*

49 Lord, where is your unfailing love?
    You promised it to David with a faithful
        pledge.
50 Consider, Lord, how your servants
        are disgraced!
    I carry in my heart the insults of so
        many people.
51 Your enemies have mocked me, O Lord;
    they mock your anointed king wherever
        he goes.

52 Praise the Lord forever!
    Amen and amen!

BOOK FOUR (Psalms 90–106)

90 *A prayer of Moses, the man of God.*

1 Lord, through all the generations
    you have been our home!
2 Before the mountains were born,
    before you gave birth to the earth and
        the world,
    from beginning to end, you are God.

3 You turn people back to dust, saying,
    "Return to dust, you mortals!"
4 For you, a thousand years are as a
        passing day,
    as brief as a few night hours.
5 You sweep people away like dreams that
        disappear.
    They are like grass that springs up in
        the morning.
6 In the morning it blooms and flourishes,
    but by evening it is dry and withered.
7 We wither beneath your anger;
    we are overwhelmed by your fury.
8 You spread out our sins before you—
    our secret sins—and you see them all.
9 We live our lives beneath your wrath,
    ending our years with a groan.

10 Seventy years are given to us!
    Some even live to eighty.
    But even the best years are filled with pain
        and trouble;
    soon they disappear, and we fly away.
11 Who can comprehend the power of
        your anger?
    Your wrath is as awesome as the fear
        you deserve.
12 Teach us to realize the brevity of life,
    so that we may grow in wisdom.

13 O Lord, come back to us!
    How long will you delay?
    Take pity on your servants!
14 Satisfy us each morning with your
        unfailing love,
    so we may sing for joy to the end of
        our lives.
15 Give us gladness in proportion to our
        former misery!
    Replace the evil years with good.
16 Let us, your servants,
        see you work again;
    let our children see your glory.
17 And may the Lord our God show us
        his approval
    and make our efforts successful.
    Yes, make our efforts successful!

_____
89:48 Hebrew *of Sheol.*

91

¹ Those who live in the shelter of
   the Most High
will find rest in the shadow of
   the Almighty.
² This I declare about the LORD:
   He alone is my refuge, my place of safety;
   he is my God, and I trust him.
³ For he will rescue you from every trap
   and protect you from deadly disease.
⁴ He will cover you with his feathers.
   He will shelter you with his wings.
   His faithful promises are your armor
   and protection.
⁵ Do not be afraid of the terrors of the night,
   nor the arrow that flies in the day.
⁶ Do not dread the disease that stalks
   in darkness,
   nor the disaster that strikes at midday.
⁷ Though a thousand fall at your side,
   though ten thousand are dying around you,
   these evils will not touch you.
⁸ Just open your eyes,
   and see how the wicked are punished.

⁹ If you make the LORD your refuge,
   if you make the Most High your shelter,
¹⁰ no evil will conquer you;
   no plague will come near your home.
¹¹ For he will order his angels
   to protect you wherever you go.
¹² They will hold you up with their hands
   so you won't even hurt your foot on
   a stone.
¹³ You will trample upon lions and cobras;
   you will crush fierce lions and serpents
   under your feet!

¹⁴ The LORD says, "I will rescue those
   who love me.
   I will protect those who trust in my name.
¹⁵ When they call on me, I will answer;
   I will be with them in trouble.
   I will rescue and honor them.
¹⁶ I will reward them with a long life
   and give them my salvation."

92

A psalm. A song to be sung on the
Sabbath Day.

¹ It is good to give thanks to the LORD,
   to sing praises to the Most High.
² It is good to proclaim your unfailing love
   in the morning,
   your faithfulness in the evening,
³ accompanied by a ten-stringed instrument,
   a harp,
   and the melody of a lyre.

⁴ You thrill me, LORD, with all you have done
   for me!
   I sing for joy because of what
   you have done.

ANOINTED TO REST
Psalm 92   ROBERT MORRIS

Many believers live right on the verge of total exhaustion. If we know the fourth commandment is rest (Exodus 20:8–11), then why do many of us treat it as optional?

Rest is refreshing and refueling. Observing the Sabbath allows you to stop and breathe—to restart your mind, body, emotions, and spirit. It's a command, a blessing, and a benefit!

Psalm 92 identifies itself as "a song to be sung on the Sabbath Day." Verse 10 says, "You have anointed me with the finest oil." In other words, the psalmist is saying, "Because I took a day to rest and honor the Lord, I've received new anointing." Is it possible that the degree of our anointing is affected by whether or not we honor God's principle of rest? If we set aside one day for the Lord every week, we will be more anointed, refueled, and refreshed.

⁵ O LORD, what great works you do!
   And how deep are your thoughts.
⁶ Only a simpleton would not know,
   and only a fool would not understand this:
⁷ Though the wicked sprout like weeds
   and evildoers flourish,
   they will be destroyed forever.

⁸ But you, O LORD, will be exalted forever.
⁹ Your enemies, LORD, will surely perish;
   all evildoers will be scattered.
¹⁰ But you have made me as strong as a wild ox.
   You have anointed me with the finest oil.
¹¹ My eyes have seen the downfall of
   my enemies;
   my ears have heard the defeat of my
   wicked opponents.

¹² But the godly will flourish like palm trees
   and grow strong like the cedars of Lebanon.
¹³ For they are transplanted to the LORD's
   own house.
   They flourish in the courts of our God.
¹⁴ Even in old age they will still produce fruit;
   they will remain vital and green.
¹⁵ They will declare, "The LORD is just!
   He is my rock!
   There is no evil in him!"

93

¹ The LORD is king!
   He is robed in majesty.
Indeed, the LORD is robed in majesty and
   armed with strength.
The world stands firm
   and cannot be shaken.

² Your throne, O LORD, has stood from time
   immemorial.
   You yourself are from the everlasting past.

³ The floods have risen up, O LORD.
The floods have roared like thunder;
the floods have lifted their
pounding waves.
⁴ But mightier than the violent raging of
the seas,
mightier than the breakers on the shore—
the LORD above is mightier than these!
⁵ Your royal laws cannot be changed.
Your reign, O LORD,
is holy forever and ever.

94 ¹ O LORD, the God of vengeance,
O God of vengeance, let your glorious
justice shine forth!
² Arise, O Judge of the earth.
Give the proud what they deserve.
³ How long, O LORD?
How long will the wicked be allowed
to gloat?
⁴ How long will they speak with arrogance?
How long will these evil people boast?
⁵ They crush your people, LORD,
hurting those you claim as your own.
⁶ They kill widows and foreigners
and murder orphans.
⁷ "The LORD isn't looking," they say,
"and besides, the God of Israel*
doesn't care."

⁸ Think again, you fools!
When will you finally catch on?
⁹ Is he deaf—the one who made your ears?
Is he blind—the one who formed
your eyes?
¹⁰ He punishes the nations—won't he also
punish you?
He knows everything—doesn't he also
know what you are doing?
¹¹ The LORD knows people's thoughts;
he knows they are worthless!

¹² Joyful are those you discipline, LORD,
those you teach with your instructions.
¹³ You give them relief from troubled times
until a pit is dug to capture the wicked.
¹⁴ The LORD will not reject his people;
he will not abandon his special
possession.
¹⁵ Judgment will again be founded on justice,
and those with virtuous hearts will
pursue it.

¹⁶ Who will protect me from the wicked?
Who will stand up for me against
evildoers?
¹⁷ Unless the LORD had helped me,
I would soon have settled in the silence
of the grave.
¹⁸ I cried out, "I am slipping!"
but your unfailing love, O LORD,
supported me.

¹⁹ When doubts filled my mind,
your comfort gave me renewed
hope and cheer.
²⁰ Can unjust leaders claim that God is on
their side—
leaders whose decrees permit injustice?
²¹ They gang up against the righteous
and condemn the innocent to death.
²² But the LORD is my fortress;
my God is the mighty rock where I hide.
²³ God will turn the sins of evil people back
on them.
He will destroy them for their sins.
The LORD our God will destroy them.

95 ¹ Come, let us sing to the LORD!
Let us shout joyfully to
the Rock of our salvation.
² Let us come to him with thanksgiving.
Let us sing psalms of praise to him.
³ For the LORD is a great God,
a great King above all gods.
⁴ He holds in his hands the depths of
the earth
and the mightiest mountains.
⁵ The sea belongs to him, for he made it.
His hands formed the dry land, too.

⁶ Come, let us worship and bow down.
Let us kneel before the LORD our maker,
⁷ for he is our God.
We are the people he watches over,
the flock under his care.

If only you would listen to his voice today!
⁸ The LORD says, "Don't harden your hearts
as Israel did at Meribah,
as they did at Massah in the wilderness.
⁹ For there your ancestors tested and tried
my patience,
even though they saw everything I did.
¹⁰ For forty years I was angry with them,
and I said,
'They are a people whose hearts turn away
from me.
They refuse to do what I tell them.'
¹¹ So in my anger I took an oath:
'They will never enter my place of rest.'"

96 ¹ Sing a new song to the LORD!
Let the whole earth sing to
the LORD!
² Sing to the LORD; praise his name.
Each day proclaim the good news that
he saves.
³ Publish his glorious deeds among
the nations.
Tell everyone about the amazing things
he does.

⁴ Great is the LORD! He is most worthy
   of praise!
He is to be feared above all gods.
⁵ The gods of other nations are mere idols,
   but the LORD made the heavens!
⁶ Honor and majesty surround him;
   strength and beauty fill his sanctuary.

⁷ O nations of the world, recognize the LORD;
   recognize that the LORD is glorious
      and strong.
⁸ Give to the LORD the glory he deserves!
   Bring your offering and come into
      his courts.
⁹ Worship the LORD in all his holy splendor.
   Let all the earth tremble before him.
¹⁰ Tell all the nations, "The LORD reigns!"
   The world stands firm and cannot
      be shaken.
   He will judge all peoples fairly.

¹¹ Let the heavens be glad,
   and the earth rejoice!
Let the sea and everything in it shout
   his praise!
¹² Let the fields and their crops burst out
   with joy!
Let the trees of the forest sing for joy
¹³ before the LORD, for he is coming!
   He is coming to judge the earth.
He will judge the world with justice,
   and the nations with his truth.

97 ¹ The LORD is king!
   Let the earth rejoice!
Let the farthest coastlands be glad.
² Dark clouds surround him.
   Righteousness and justice are the
      foundation of his throne.
³ Fire spreads ahead of him
   and burns up all his foes.
⁴ His lightning flashes out across the world.
   The earth sees and trembles.
⁵ The mountains melt like wax before
      the LORD,
   before the Lord of all the earth.
⁶ The heavens proclaim his righteousness;
   every nation sees his glory.
⁷ Those who worship idols are disgraced—
   all who brag about their worthless gods—
for every god must bow to him.
⁸ Jerusalem* has heard and rejoiced,
   and all the towns of Judah are glad
because of your justice, O LORD!
⁹ For you, O LORD, are supreme over
      all the earth;
   you are exalted far above all gods.

¹⁰ You who love the LORD, hate evil!
   He protects the lives of his godly people
   and rescues them from the power of
      the wicked.

¹¹ Light shines on the godly,
   and joy on those whose hearts are right.
¹² May all who are godly rejoice in the LORD
   and praise his holy name!

98 *A psalm.*

¹ Sing a new song to the LORD,
   for he has done wonderful deeds.
His right hand has won a mighty victory;
   his holy arm has shown his saving power!
² The LORD has announced his victory
   and has revealed his righteousness to
      every nation!
³ He has remembered his promise to love and
      be faithful to Israel.
   The ends of the earth have seen the
      victory of our God.

⁴ Shout to the LORD, all the earth;
   break out in praise and sing for joy!
⁵ Sing your praise to the LORD with the harp,
   with the harp and melodious song,
⁶ with trumpets and the sound of
      the ram's horn.
   Make a joyful symphony before the LORD,
      the King!

⁷ Let the sea and everything in it shout
      his praise!
   Let the earth and all living things join in.
⁸ Let the rivers clap their hands in glee!
   Let the hills sing out their songs of joy
⁹ before the LORD,
   for he is coming to judge the earth.
He will judge the world with justice,
   and the nations with fairness.

99 ¹ The LORD is king!
   Let the nations tremble!
He sits on his throne between the cherubim.
   Let the whole earth quake!
² The LORD sits in majesty in Jerusalem,*
   exalted above all the nations.
³ Let them praise your great and
      awesome name.
   Your name is holy!
⁴ Mighty King, lover of justice,
   you have established fairness.
You have acted with justice
   and righteousness throughout Israel.*
⁵ Exalt the LORD our God!
   Bow low before his feet, for he is holy!

⁶ Moses and Aaron were among his priests;
   Samuel also called on his name.
They cried to the LORD for help,
   and he answered them.

97:8 Hebrew *Zion.* **99:2** Hebrew *Zion.* **99:4** Hebrew *Jacob.* See note on 44:4.

⁷ He spoke to Israel from the pillar of cloud,
and they followed the laws and decrees
he gave them.
⁸ O LORD our God, you answered them.
You were a forgiving God to them,
but you punished them when they
went wrong.

⁹ Exalt the LORD our God,
and worship at his holy mountain
in Jerusalem,
for the LORD our God is holy!

100 *A psalm of thanksgiving.*

¹ Shout with joy to the LORD,
all the earth!
² Worship the LORD with gladness.
Come before him, singing with joy.
³ Acknowledge that the LORD is God!
He made us, and we are his.*
We are his people,
the sheep of his pasture.
⁴ Enter his gates with thanksgiving;
go into his courts with praise.
Give thanks to him and praise his name.
⁵ For the LORD is good.
His unfailing love continues forever,
and his faithfulness continues to each
generation.

101 *A psalm of David.*

¹ I will sing of your love and justice, LORD.
I will praise you with songs.
² I will be careful to live a blameless life—
when will you come to help me?
I will lead a life of integrity
in my own home.
³ I will refuse to look at
anything vile and vulgar.
I hate all who deal crookedly;
I will have nothing to do with them.
⁴ I will reject perverse ideas
and stay away from every evil.
⁵ I will not tolerate people who slander
their neighbors.
I will not endure conceit and pride.

⁶ I will search for faithful people
to be my companions.
Only those who are above reproach
will be allowed to serve me.
⁷ I will not allow deceivers to serve in
my house,
and liars will not stay in my presence.
⁸ My daily task will be to ferret out
the wicked
and free the city of the LORD from
their grip.

102 *A prayer of one overwhelmed with trouble, pouring out problems before the LORD.*

¹ LORD, hear my prayer!
Listen to my plea!
² Don't turn away from me
in my time of distress.
Bend down to listen,
and answer me quickly when I call to you.
³ For my days disappear like smoke,
and my bones burn like red-hot coals.
⁴ My heart is sick, withered like grass,
and I have lost my appetite.
⁵ Because of my groaning,
I am reduced to skin and bones.
⁶ I am like an owl in the desert,
like a little owl in a far-off wilderness.
⁷ I lie awake,
lonely as a solitary bird on the roof.
⁸ My enemies taunt me day after day.
They mock and curse me.
⁹ I eat ashes for food.
My tears run down into my drink
¹⁰ because of your anger and wrath.
For you have picked me up and thrown
me out.
¹¹ My life passes as swiftly as the evening
shadows.
I am withering away like grass.

¹² But you, O LORD,
will sit on your throne forever.
Your fame will endure to every
generation.
¹³ You will arise and have mercy on Jerusalem*—
and now is the time to pity her,
now is the time you promised to help.
¹⁴ For your people love every stone in her walls
and cherish even the dust in her streets.
¹⁵ Then the nations will tremble before
the LORD.
The kings of the earth will tremble before
his glory.
¹⁶ For the LORD will rebuild Jerusalem.
He will appear in his glory.
¹⁷ He will listen to the prayers of the destitute.
He will not reject their pleas.

¹⁸ Let this be recorded for future generations,
so that a people not yet born will praise
the LORD.
¹⁹ Tell them the LORD looked down
from his heavenly sanctuary.
He looked down to earth from heaven
²⁰ to hear the groans of the prisoners,
to release those condemned to die.
²¹ And so the LORD's fame will be celebrated
in Zion,
his praises in Jerusalem,

100:3 As in an alternate reading in the Masoretic Text; the other
alternate and some ancient versions read *and not we ourselves.*
102:13 Hebrew *Zion;* also in 102:16.

²² when multitudes gather together
 and kingdoms come to worship the LORD.

²³ He broke my strength in midlife,
 cutting short my days.
²⁴ But I cried to him, "O my God, who lives
 forever,
 don't take my life while I am so young!
²⁵ Long ago you laid the foundation of the earth
 and made the heavens with your hands.
²⁶ They will perish, but you remain forever;
 they will wear out like old clothing.
 You will change them like a garment
 and discard them.
²⁷ But you are always the same;
 you will live forever.
²⁸ The children of your people
 will live in security.
 Their children's children
 will thrive in your presence."

103 *A psalm of David.*

¹ Let all that I am praise the LORD;
 with my whole heart,
 I will praise his holy name.
² Let all that I am praise the LORD;
 may I never forget the good things
 he does for me.
³ He forgives all my sins
 and heals all my diseases.
⁴ He redeems me from death
 and crowns me with love and
 tender mercies.
⁵ He fills my life with good things.
 My youth is renewed like the eagle's!

⁶ The LORD gives righteousness
 and justice to all who are treated unfairly.

⁷ He revealed his character to Moses
 and his deeds to the people of Israel.
⁸ The LORD is compassionate and merciful,
 slow to get angry and filled with
 unfailing love.
⁹ He will not constantly accuse us,
 nor remain angry forever.
¹⁰ He does not punish us for all our sins;
 he does not deal harshly with us, as we
 deserve.
¹¹ For his unfailing love toward those
 who fear him
 is as great as the height of the heavens
 above the earth.
¹² He has removed our sins as far from us
 as the east is from the west.
¹³ The LORD is like a father to his children,
 tender and compassionate to those
 who fear him.
¹⁴ For he knows how weak we are;
 he remembers we are only dust.

¹⁵ Our days on earth are like grass;
 like wildflowers, we bloom and die.
¹⁶ The wind blows, and we are gone—
 as though we had never been here.
¹⁷ But the love of the LORD remains forever
 with those who fear him.
 His salvation extends to the children's
 children
¹⁸ of those who are faithful to his covenant,
 of those who obey his commandments!

¹⁹ The LORD has made the heavens his throne;
 from there he rules over everything.

²⁰ Praise the LORD, you angels,
 you mighty ones who carry out his plans,
 listening for each of his commands.
²¹ Yes, praise the LORD, you armies of angels
 who serve him and do his will!
²² Praise the LORD, everything he has created,
 everything in all his kingdom.

 Let all that I am praise the LORD.

104 ¹ Let all that I am praise the LORD.

 O LORD my God, how great you are!
 You are robed with honor and majesty.
² You are dressed in a robe of light.
 You stretch out the starry curtain of the
 heavens;
³ you lay out the rafters of your home
 in the rain clouds.
 You make the clouds your chariot;
 you ride upon the wings of the wind.
⁴ The winds are your messengers;
 flames of fire are your servants.*

⁵ You placed the world on its foundation
 so it would never be moved.
⁶ You clothed the earth with floods of water,
 water that covered even the mountains.
⁷ At your command, the water fled;
 at the sound of your thunder,
 it hurried away.
⁸ Mountains rose and valleys sank
 to the levels you decreed.
⁹ Then you set a firm boundary for the seas,
 so they would never again cover
 the earth.

¹⁰ You make springs pour water into
 the ravines,
 so streams gush down from the
 mountains.
¹¹ They provide water for all the animals,
 and the wild donkeys quench their thirst.
¹² The birds nest beside the streams
 and sing among the branches of the trees.

104:4 Greek version reads *He sends his angels like the winds, / his servants like flames of fire.* Compare Heb 1:7.

13 You send rain on the mountains from your
  heavenly home,
   and you fill the earth with the fruit of
   your labor.
14 You cause grass to grow for the livestock
   and plants for people to use.
 You allow them to produce food from
   the earth—
15 wine to make them glad,
 olive oil to soothe their skin,
   and bread to give them strength.
16 The trees of the LORD are well cared for—
   the cedars of Lebanon that he planted.
17 There the birds make their nests,
   and the storks make their homes in
   the cypresses.
18 High in the mountains live the wild goats,
   and the rocks form a refuge for
   the hyraxes.*
19 You made the moon to mark the seasons,
   and the sun knows when to set.
20 You send the darkness, and it becomes night,
   when all the forest animals prowl about.
21 Then the young lions roar for their prey,
   stalking the food provided by God.
22 At dawn they slink back
   into their dens to rest.
23 Then people go off to their work,
   where they labor until evening.
24 O LORD, what a variety of things you
   have made!
 In wisdom you have made them all.
   The earth is full of your creatures.
25 Here is the ocean, vast and wide,
   teeming with life of every kind,
   both large and small.
26 See the ships sailing along,
   and Leviathan,* which you made to play
   in the sea.
27 They all depend on you
   to give them food as they need it.
28 When you supply it, they gather it.
   You open your hand to feed them,
   and they are richly satisfied.
29 But if you turn away from them, they panic.
   When you take away their breath,
   they die and turn again to dust.
30 When you give them your breath,*
   life is created,
   and you renew the face of the earth.
31 May the glory of the LORD continue forever!
   The LORD takes pleasure in all
   he has made!
32 The earth trembles at his glance;
   the mountains smoke at his touch.
33 I will sing to the LORD as long as I live.
   I will praise my God to my last breath!

34 May all my thoughts be pleasing to him,
   for I rejoice in the LORD.
35 Let all sinners vanish from the face
   of the earth;
   let the wicked disappear forever.

 Let all that I am praise the LORD.

 Praise the LORD!

105 ¹ Give thanks to the LORD and
   proclaim his greatness.
 Let the whole world know what
   he has done.
2 Sing to him; yes, sing his praises.
   Tell everyone about his wonderful deeds.
3 Exult in his holy name;
   rejoice, you who worship the LORD.
4 Search for the LORD and for his strength;
   continually seek him.
5 Remember the wonders he has performed,
   his miracles, and the rulings he has given,
6 you children of his servant Abraham,
   you descendants of Jacob,
   his chosen ones.

7 He is the LORD our God.
   His justice is seen throughout the land.
8 He always stands by his covenant—
   the commitment he made to a thousand
   generations.
9 This is the covenant he made with Abraham
   and the oath he swore to Isaac.
10 He confirmed it to Jacob as a decree,
   and to the people of Israel as a
   never-ending covenant:
11 "I will give you the land of Canaan
   as your special possession."

12 He said this when they were few in number,
   a tiny group of strangers in Canaan.
13 They wandered from nation to nation,
   from one kingdom to another.
14 Yet he did not let anyone oppress them.
   He warned kings on their behalf:
15 "Do not touch my chosen people,
   and do not hurt my prophets."

16 He called for a famine on
   the land of Canaan,
   cutting off its food supply.
17 Then he sent someone to Egypt
   ahead of them—
   Joseph, who was sold as a slave.
18 They bruised his feet with fetters
   and placed his neck in an iron collar.
19 Until the time came to fulfill his dreams,*
   the LORD tested Joseph's character.

104:18 Or coneys, or rock badgers. 104:26 The identification of
Leviathan is disputed, ranging from an earthly creature to a
mythical sea monster in ancient literature. 104:30 Or When you
send your Spirit. 105:19 Hebrew his word.

20 Then Pharaoh sent for him and set him free;
   the ruler of the nation opened his
      prison door.
21 Joseph was put in charge of all
      the king's household;
   he became ruler over all
      the king's possessions.
22 He could instruct* the king's aides
      as he pleased
   and teach the king's advisers.

23 Then Israel arrived in Egypt;
   Jacob lived as a foreigner in the land
      of Ham.
24 And the LORD multiplied the people of Israel
   until they became too mighty for
      their enemies.
25 Then he turned the Egyptians against
      the Israelites,
   and they plotted against
      the LORD's servants.

26 But the LORD sent his servant Moses,
   along with Aaron, whom he had chosen.
27 They performed miraculous signs among
      the Egyptians,
   and wonders in the land of Ham.
28 The LORD blanketed Egypt in darkness,
   for they had defied* his commands to let
      his people go.
29 He turned their water into blood,
   poisoning all the fish.
30 Then frogs overran the land
   and even invaded the king's bedrooms.
31 When the LORD spoke, flies descended on
      the Egyptians,
   and gnats swarmed across Egypt.
32 He sent them hail instead of rain,
   and lightning flashed over the land.
33 He ruined their grapevines and fig trees
   and shattered all the trees.
34 He spoke, and hordes of locusts came—
   young locusts beyond number.
35 They ate up everything green in the land,
   destroying all the crops in their fields.
36 Then he killed the oldest son in each
      Egyptian home,
   the pride and joy of each family.

37 The LORD brought his people out of Egypt,
   loaded with silver and gold;
   and not one among the tribes of Israel
      even stumbled.
38 Egypt was glad when they were gone,
   for they feared them greatly.
39 The LORD spread a cloud above them
      as a covering
   and gave them a great fire to light the
      darkness.
40 They asked for meat, and he sent them quail;
   he satisfied their hunger with manna—
      bread from heaven.

41 He split open a rock, and water gushed out
   to form a river through the dry wasteland.
42 For he remembered his sacred promise
   to his servant Abraham.
43 So he brought his people out of Egypt with joy,
   his chosen ones with rejoicing.
44 He gave his people the lands of pagan nations,
   and they harvested crops that others had
      planted.
45 All this happened so they would follow his
      decrees
   and obey his instructions.

Praise the LORD!

106
1 Praise the LORD!

Give thanks to the LORD, for he is good!
   His faithful love endures forever.
2 Who can list the glorious miracles of
      the LORD?
   Who can ever praise him enough?
3 There is joy for those who deal justly
      with others
   and always do what is right.

4 Remember me, LORD, when you show favor
      to your people;
   come near and rescue me.
5 Let me share in the prosperity of your
      chosen ones.
   Let me rejoice in the joy of your people;
   let me praise you with those who are your
      heritage.

6 Like our ancestors, we have sinned.
   We have done wrong!
   We have acted wickedly!
7 Our ancestors in Egypt
   were not impressed by the LORD's
      miraculous deeds.
   They soon forgot his many acts of kindness
      to them.
   Instead, they rebelled against him at
      the Red Sea.*
8 Even so, he saved them—
   to defend the honor of his name
   and to demonstrate his mighty power.
9 He commanded the Red Sea* to dry up.
   He led Israel across the sea as if it were
      a desert.
10 So he rescued them from their enemies
   and redeemed them from their foes.
11 Then the water returned and covered
      their enemies;
   not one of them survived.
12 Then his people believed his promises.
   Then they sang his praise.

105:22 As in Greek and Syriac versions; Hebrew reads *bind* or
imprison.   105:28 As in Greek and Syriac versions; Hebrew
reads *had not defied.*   106:7 Hebrew *at the sea, the sea of reeds.*
106:9 Hebrew *sea of reeds;* also in 106:22.

¹³ Yet how quickly they forgot what he
      had done!
   They wouldn't wait for his counsel!
¹⁴ In the wilderness their desires ran wild,
      testing God's patience in that
      dry wasteland.
¹⁵ So he gave them what they asked for,
      but he sent a plague along with it.
¹⁶ The people in the camp were jealous of Moses
      and envious of Aaron,
      the LORD's holy priest.
¹⁷ Because of this, the earth opened up;
      it swallowed Dathan
      and buried Abiram and the other rebels.
¹⁸ Fire fell upon their followers;
      a flame consumed the wicked.

¹⁹ The people made a calf at Mount Sinai*;
      they bowed before an image made of gold.
²⁰ They traded their glorious God
      for a statue of a grass-eating bull.
²¹ They forgot God, their savior,
      who had done such great things in Egypt—
²² such wonderful things in the land of Ham,
      such awesome deeds at the Red Sea.
²³ So he declared he would destroy them.
      But Moses, his chosen one, stepped
         between the LORD and the people.
      He begged him to turn from his anger
         and not destroy them.

²⁴ The people refused to enter the pleasant land,
      for they wouldn't believe his promise to
      care for them.
²⁵ Instead, they grumbled in their tents
      and refused to obey the LORD.
²⁶ Therefore, he solemnly swore
      that he would kill them in the wilderness,
²⁷ that he would scatter their descendants*
      among the nations,
      exiling them to distant lands.

²⁸ Then our ancestors joined in the worship of
      Baal at Peor;
      they even ate sacrifices offered to the dead!
²⁹ They angered the LORD with all these things,
      so a plague broke out among them.
³⁰ But Phinehas had the courage to intervene,
      and the plague was stopped.
³¹ So he has been regarded as a righteous man
      ever since that time.

³² At Meribah, too, they angered the LORD,
      causing Moses serious trouble.
³³ They made Moses angry,*
      and he spoke foolishly.

³⁴ Israel failed to destroy the nations in
      the land,
      as the LORD had commanded them.
³⁵ Instead, they mingled among the pagans
      and adopted their evil customs.

³⁶ They worshiped their idols,
      which led to their downfall.
³⁷ They even sacrificed their sons
      and their daughters to the demons.
³⁸ They shed innocent blood,
      the blood of their sons and daughters.
   By sacrificing them to the idols of Canaan,
      they polluted the land with murder.
³⁹ They defiled themselves by their evil deeds,
      and their love of idols was adultery in the
      LORD's sight.

⁴⁰ That is why the LORD's anger burned
      against his people,
   and he abhorred his own special
      possession.
⁴¹ He handed them over to pagan nations,
      and they were ruled by those who
      hated them.
⁴² Their enemies crushed them
      and brought them under their cruel power.
⁴³ Again and again he rescued them,
      but they chose to rebel against him,
      and they were finally destroyed by their sin.
⁴⁴ Even so, he pitied them in their distress
      and listened to their cries.
⁴⁵ He remembered his covenant with them
      and relented because of his unfailing love.
⁴⁶ He even caused their captors
      to treat them with kindness.

⁴⁷ Save us, O LORD our God!
      Gather us back from among the nations,
   so we can thank your holy name
      and rejoice and praise you.

⁴⁸ Praise the LORD, the God of Israel,
      who lives from everlasting to everlasting!
   Let all the people say, "Amen!"

   Praise the LORD!

BOOK FIVE (Psalms 107–150)

107 ¹ Give thanks to the LORD,
         for he is good!
      His faithful love endures forever.
   ² Has the LORD redeemed you?
         Then speak out!
      Tell others he has redeemed you from
         your enemies.
   ³ For he has gathered the exiles from
         many lands,
      from east and west,
      from north and south.*

   ⁴ Some wandered in the wilderness,
         lost and homeless.

106:19 Hebrew at Horeb, another name for Sinai.   106:27 As in
Syriac version; Hebrew reads he would cause their descendants to
fall.   106:33 Hebrew They embittered his spirit.   107:3 Hebrew
and sea.

5 Hungry and thirsty,
     they nearly died.
6 "LORD, help!" they cried in their trouble,
     and he rescued them from their distress.
7 He led them straight to safety,
     to a city where they could live.
8 Let them praise the LORD for his great love
     and for the wonderful things he has done
       for them.
9 For he satisfies the thirsty
     and fills the hungry with good things.

10 Some sat in darkness and deepest gloom,
     imprisoned in iron chains of misery.
11 They rebelled against the words of God,
     scorning the counsel of the Most High.
12 That is why he broke them with hard labor;
     they fell, and no one was there to help them.
13 "LORD, help!" they cried in their trouble,
     and he saved them from their distress.
14 He led them from the darkness and
       deepest gloom;
     he snapped their chains.
15 Let them praise the LORD for his great love
     and for the wonderful things he has done
       for them.
16 For he broke down their prison gates
       of bronze;
     he cut apart their bars of iron.

17 Some were fools; they rebelled
     and suffered for their sins.
18 They couldn't stand the thought of food,
     and they were knocking on death's door.
19 "LORD, help!" they cried in their trouble,
     and he saved them from their distress.
20 He sent out his word and healed them,
     snatching them from the door of death.
21 Let them praise the LORD for his great love
     and for the wonderful things he has done
       for them.
22 Let them offer sacrifices of thanksgiving
     and sing joyfully about his glorious acts.

23 Some went off to sea in ships,
     plying the trade routes of the world.
24 They, too, observed the LORD's power in action,
     his impressive works on
       the deepest seas.
25 He spoke, and the winds rose,
     stirring up the waves.
26 Their ships were tossed to the heavens
     and plunged again to the depths;
     the sailors cringed in terror.
27 They reeled and staggered like drunkards
     and were at their wits' end.
28 "LORD, help!" they cried in their trouble,
     and he saved them from their distress.
29 He calmed the storm to a whisper
     and stilled the waves.
30 What a blessing was that stillness
     as he brought them safely into harbor!

31 Let them praise the LORD for his great love
     and for the wonderful things he has done
       for them.
32 Let them exalt him publicly before the
       congregation
     and before the leaders of the nation.

33 He changes rivers into deserts,
     and springs of water into dry, thirsty land.
34 He turns the fruitful land into salty
       wastelands,
     because of the wickedness of those who
       live there.
35 But he also turns deserts into pools of water,
     the dry land into springs of water.
36 He brings the hungry to settle there
     and to build their cities.
37 They sow their fields, plant their vineyards,
     and harvest their bumper crops.
38 How he blesses them!
     They raise large families there,
     and their herds of livestock increase.

39 When they decrease in number and become
       impoverished
     through oppression, trouble, and sorrow,
40 the LORD pours contempt on their princes,
     causing them to wander in trackless
       wastelands.
41 But he rescues the poor from trouble
     and increases their families like flocks of
       sheep.
42 The godly will see these things and be glad,
     while the wicked are struck silent.
43 Those who are wise will take all this
       to heart;
     they will see in our history the faithful
       love of the LORD.

108 *A song. A psalm of David.*

1 My heart is confident in you, O God;
     no wonder I can sing your praises
       with all my heart!
2 Wake up, lyre and harp!
     I will wake the dawn with my song.
3 I will thank you, LORD,
     among all the people.
     I will sing your praises among the
       nations.
4 For your unfailing love is higher than
       the heavens.
     Your faithfulness reaches to the clouds.
5 Be exalted, O God, above the highest heavens.
     May your glory shine over all the earth.

6 Now rescue your beloved people.
     Answer and save us by your power.
7 God has promised this by his holiness*:

108:7 Or *in his sanctuary.*

"I will divide up Shechem with joy.
I will measure out the valley of Succoth.
[8] Gilead is mine,
and Manasseh, too.
Ephraim, my helmet,
will produce my warriors,
and Judah, my scepter,
will produce my kings.
[9] But Moab, my washbasin,
will become my servant,
and I will wipe my feet on Edom
and shout in triumph over Philistia."

[10] Who will bring me into the fortified city?
Who will bring me victory over Edom?
[11] Have you rejected us, O God?
Will you no longer march with
our armies?
[12] Oh, please help us against our enemies,
for all human help is useless.
[13] With God's help we will do mighty things,
for he will trample down our foes.

109

For the choir director: A psalm of David.

[1] O God, whom I praise,
don't stand silent and aloof
[2] while the wicked slander me
and tell lies about me.
[3] They surround me with hateful words
and fight against me for no reason.
[4] I love them, but they try to destroy me
with accusations
even as I am praying for them!
[5] They repay evil for good,
and hatred for my love.

[6] They say,* "Get an evil person to turn
against him.
Send an accuser to bring him to trial.
[7] When his case comes up for judgment,
let him be pronounced guilty.
Count his prayers as sins.
[8] Let his years be few;
let someone else take his position.
[9] May his children become fatherless,
and his wife a widow.
[10] May his children wander as beggars
and be driven from* their ruined homes.
[11] May creditors seize his entire estate,
and strangers take all he has earned.
[12] Let no one be kind to him;
let no one pity his fatherless children.
[13] May all his offspring die.
May his family name be blotted out in the
next generation.
[14] May the LORD never forget the sins of
his fathers;
may his mother's sins never be erased
from the record.
[15] May the LORD always remember these sins,

and may his name disappear from
human memory.
[16] For he refused all kindness to others;
he persecuted the poor and needy,
and he hounded the brokenhearted
to death.
[17] He loved to curse others;
now you curse him.
He never blessed others;
now don't you bless him.
[18] Cursing is as natural to him as his clothing,
or the water he drinks,
or the rich food he eats.
[19] Now may his curses return and cling to him
like clothing;
may they be tied around him like a belt."

[20] May those curses become the LORD's
punishment
for my accusers who speak evil of me.
[21] But deal well with me, O Sovereign LORD,
for the sake of your own reputation!
Rescue me
because you are so faithful and good.
[22] For I am poor and needy,
and my heart is full of pain.
[23] I am fading like a shadow at dusk;
I am brushed off like a locust.
[24] My knees are weak from fasting,
and I am skin and bones.
[25] I am a joke to people everywhere;
when they see me,
they shake their heads in scorn.

[26] Help me, O LORD my God!
Save me because of your unfailing love.
[27] Let them see that this is your doing,
that you yourself have done it, LORD.
[28] Then let them curse me if they like,
but you will bless me!
When they attack me, they will be disgraced!
But I, your servant, will go right on
rejoicing!
[29] May my accusers be clothed with disgrace;
may their humiliation cover them like
a cloak.
[30] But I will give repeated thanks to the LORD,
praising him to everyone.
[31] For he stands beside the needy,
ready to save them from those who
condemn them.

110

A psalm of David.

[1] The LORD said to my Lord,*
"Sit in the place of honor at my right hand
until I humble your enemies,
making them a footstool under your feet."

109:6 Hebrew lacks *They say.*   109:10 As in Greek version;
Hebrew reads *and seek.*   110:1 Or *my lord.*

2 The LORD will extend your powerful
  kingdom from Jerusalem*;
  you will rule over your enemies.
3 When you go to war,
  your people will serve you willingly.
You are arrayed in holy garments,
  and your strength will be renewed each
  day like the morning dew.

4 The LORD has taken an oath and will not
  break his vow:
  "You are a priest forever in the order of
  Melchizedek."

5 The Lord stands at your right hand to
  protect you.
  He will strike down many kings when his
  anger erupts.
6 He will punish the nations
  and fill their lands with corpses;
  he will shatter heads over the whole
  earth.
7 But he himself will be refreshed from
  brooks along the way.
  He will be victorious.

111* ¹ Praise the LORD!

I will thank the LORD with all my heart
  as I meet with his godly people.
2 How amazing are the deeds of the LORD!
  All who delight in him should
  ponder them.
3 Everything he does reveals his glory and
  majesty.
  His righteousness never fails.
4 He causes us to remember his wonderful
  works.
  How gracious and merciful is our LORD!
5 He gives food to those who fear him;
  he always remembers his covenant.
6 He has shown his great power
  to his people
  by giving them the lands of
  other nations.
7 All he does is just and good,
  and all his commandments are
  trustworthy.
8 They are forever true,
  to be obeyed faithfully and
  with integrity.
9 He has paid a full ransom for his people.
  He has guaranteed his covenant with
  them forever.
  What a holy, awe-inspiring name
  he has!
10 Fear of the LORD is the foundation of
  true wisdom.
  All who obey his commandments will
  grow in wisdom.

Praise him forever!

112* ¹ Praise the LORD!

How joyful are those who fear the LORD
  and delight in obeying his commands.
2 Their children will be successful everywhere;
  an entire generation of godly people will
  be blessed.
3 They themselves will be wealthy,
  and their good deeds will last forever.
4 Light shines in the darkness for the godly.
  They are generous, compassionate,
  and righteous.
5 Good comes to those who lend money
  generously
  and conduct their business fairly.
6 Such people will not be overcome by evil.
  Those who are righteous will be long
  remembered.
7 They do not fear bad news;
  they confidently trust the LORD to care
  for them.
8 They are confident and fearless
  and can face their foes triumphantly.
9 They share freely and give generously to
  those in need.
  Their good deeds will be remembered
  forever.
  They will have influence and honor.
10 The wicked will see this and be infuriated.
  They will grind their teeth in anger;
  they will slink away,
  their hopes thwarted.

113 ¹ Praise the LORD!

Yes, give praise, O servants of the LORD.
  Praise the name of the LORD!
2 Blessed be the name of the LORD
  now and forever.
3 Everywhere—from east to west—
  praise the name of the LORD.
4 For the LORD is high above the nations;
  his glory is higher than the heavens.

5 Who can be compared with the LORD
  our God,
  who is enthroned on high?
6 He stoops to look down
  on heaven and on earth.
7 He lifts the poor from the dust
  and the needy from the garbage dump.
8 He sets them among princes,
  even the princes of his own people!
9 He gives the childless woman a family,
  making her a happy mother.

Praise the LORD!

110:2 Hebrew *Zion*. 111 This psalm is a Hebrew acrostic poem;
after the introductory note of praise, each line begins with a
successive letter of the Hebrew alphabet. 112 This psalm is a
Hebrew acrostic poem; after the introductory note of praise,
each line begins with a successive letter of the Hebrew alphabet.

114

¹ When the Israelites escaped
from Egypt—
when the family of Jacob left that
foreign land—
² the land of Judah became God's sanctuary,
and Israel became his kingdom.

³ The Red Sea* saw them coming and hurried
out of their way!
The water of the Jordan River turned away.
⁴ The mountains skipped like rams,
the hills like lambs!

⁵ What's wrong, Red Sea, that made you hurry
out of their way?
What happened, Jordan River,
that you turned away?
⁶ Why, mountains, did you skip like rams?
Why, hills, like lambs?

⁷ Tremble, O earth, at the presence of the Lord,
at the presence of the God of Jacob.
⁸ He turned the rock into a pool of water;
yes, a spring of water flowed from
solid rock.

115

¹ Not to us, O Lord, not to us,
but to your name goes all the glory
for your unfailing love and faithfulness.
² Why let the nations say,
"Where is their God?"
³ Our God is in the heavens,
and he does as he wishes.
⁴ Their idols are merely things of silver
and gold,
shaped by human hands.
⁵ They have mouths but cannot speak,
and eyes but cannot see.
⁶ They have ears but cannot hear,
and noses but cannot smell.
⁷ They have hands but cannot feel,
and feet but cannot walk,
and throats but cannot make a sound.
⁸ And those who make idols are just like them,
as are all who trust in them.

⁹ O Israel, trust the Lord!
He is your helper and your shield.
¹⁰ O priests, descendants of Aaron,
trust the Lord!
He is your helper and your shield.
¹¹ All you who fear the Lord, trust the Lord!
He is your helper and your shield.

¹² The Lord remembers us and will bless us.
He will bless the people of Israel
and bless the priests, the descendants
of Aaron.
¹³ He will bless those who fear the Lord,
both great and lowly.

¹⁴ May the Lord richly bless
both you and your children.

¹⁵ May you be blessed by the Lord,
who made heaven and earth.
¹⁶ The heavens belong to the Lord,
but he has given the earth to
all humanity.
¹⁷ The dead cannot sing praises to the Lord,
for they have gone into the silence of
the grave.
¹⁸ But we can praise the Lord
both now and forever!

Praise the Lord!

116

¹ I love the Lord because he hears
my voice
and my prayer for mercy.
² Because he bends down to listen,
I will pray as long as I have breath!
³ Death wrapped its ropes around me;
the terrors of the grave* overtook me.
I saw only trouble and sorrow.
⁴ Then I called on the name of the Lord:
"Please, Lord, save me!"
⁵ How kind the Lord is! How good he is!
So merciful, this God of ours!
⁶ The Lord protects those of childlike faith;
I was facing death, and he saved me.
⁷ Let my soul be at rest again,
for the Lord has been good to me.
⁸ He has saved me from death,
my eyes from tears,
my feet from stumbling.
⁹ And so I walk in the Lord's presence
as I live here on earth!
¹⁰ I believed in you, so I said,
"I am deeply troubled, Lord."
¹¹ In my anxiety I cried out to you,
"These people are all liars!"
¹² What can I offer the Lord
for all he has done for me?
¹³ I will lift up the cup of salvation
and praise the Lord's name
for saving me.
¹⁴ I will keep my promises to the Lord
in the presence of all his people.

¹⁵ The Lord cares deeply
when his loved ones die.
¹⁶ O Lord, I am your servant;
yes, I am your servant,
born into your household;
you have freed me from my chains.
¹⁷ I will offer you a sacrifice of thanksgiving
and call on the name of the Lord.
¹⁸ I will fulfill my vows to the Lord
in the presence of all his people—
¹⁹ in the house of the Lord
in the heart of Jerusalem.

Praise the Lord!

114:3 Hebrew *the sea;* also in 114:5.   116:3 Hebrew *of Sheol.*

117

¹ Praise the LORD, all you nations.
Praise him, all you people of the earth.
² For his unfailing love for us is powerful;
the LORD's faithfulness endures forever.

Praise the LORD!

118

¹ Give thanks to the LORD,
for he is good!
His faithful love endures forever.

² Let all Israel repeat:
"His faithful love endures forever."
³ Let Aaron's descendants, the priests, repeat:
"His faithful love endures forever."
⁴ Let all who fear the LORD repeat:
"His faithful love endures forever."

⁵ In my distress I prayed to the LORD,
and the LORD answered me and
set me free.
⁶ The LORD is for me, so I will have no fear.
What can mere people do to me?
⁷ Yes, the LORD is for me; he will help me.
I will look in triumph at those who
hate me.
⁸ It is better to take refuge in the LORD
than to trust in people.
⁹ It is better to take refuge in the LORD
than to trust in princes.

¹⁰ Though hostile nations surrounded me,
I destroyed them all with the authority
of the LORD.
¹¹ Yes, they surrounded and attacked me,
but I destroyed them all with the
authority of the LORD.
¹² They swarmed around me like bees;
they blazed against me like
a crackling fire.
But I destroyed them all with the
authority of the LORD.
¹³ My enemies did their best to kill me,
but the LORD rescued me.
¹⁴ The LORD is my strength and my song;
he has given me victory.
¹⁵ Songs of joy and victory are sung in the
camp of the godly.
The strong right arm of the LORD has
done glorious things!
¹⁶ The strong right arm of the LORD is raised
in triumph.
The strong right arm of the LORD has
done glorious things!
¹⁷ I will not die; instead, I will live
to tell what the LORD has done.
¹⁸ The LORD has punished me severely,
but he did not let me die.

¹⁹ Open for me the gates where
the righteous enter,
and I will go in and thank the LORD.

²⁰ These gates lead to the presence of the LORD,
and the godly enter there.
²¹ I thank you for answering my prayer
and giving me victory!

²² The stone that the builders rejected
has now become the cornerstone.
²³ This is the LORD's doing,
and it is wonderful to see.
²⁴ This is the day the LORD has made.
We will rejoice and be glad in it.
²⁵ Please, LORD, please save us.
Please, LORD, please give us success.
²⁶ Bless the one who comes in the name
of the LORD.
We bless you from the house of the LORD.
²⁷ The LORD is God, shining upon us.
Take the sacrifice and bind it with cords
on the altar.
²⁸ You are my God, and I will praise you!
You are my God, and I will exalt you!

²⁹ Give thanks to the LORD, for he is good!
His faithful love endures forever.

Aleph

119

¹ Joyful are people of integrity,
who follow the instructions
of the LORD.
² Joyful are those who obey his laws
and search for him with all their hearts.
³ They do not compromise with evil,
and they walk only in his paths.
⁴ You have charged us
to keep your commandments carefully.
⁵ Oh, that my actions would consistently
reflect your decrees!
⁶ Then I will not be ashamed
when I compare my life with
your commands.
⁷ As I learn your righteous regulations,
I will thank you by living as I should!
⁸ I will obey your decrees.
Please don't give up on me!

Beth

⁹ How can a young person stay pure?
By obeying your word.
¹⁰ I have tried hard to find you—
don't let me wander from your commands.
¹¹ I have hidden your word in my heart,
that I might not sin against you.
¹² I praise you, O LORD;
teach me your decrees.
¹³ I have recited aloud
all the regulations you have given us.
¹⁴ I have rejoiced in your laws
as much as in riches.

---

119 This psalm is a Hebrew acrostic poem; there are twenty-two stanzas, one for each successive letter of the Hebrew alphabet. Each of the eight verses within each stanza begins with the Hebrew letter named in its heading.

15 I will study your commandments
    and reflect on your ways.
16 I will delight in your decrees
    and not forget your word.

Gimel
17 Be good to your servant,
    that I may live and obey your word.
18 Open my eyes to see
    the wonderful truths in your instructions.
19 I am only a foreigner in the land.
    Don't hide your commands from me!
20 I am always overwhelmed
    with a desire for your regulations.
21 You rebuke the arrogant;
    those who wander from your commands
    are cursed.
22 Don't let them scorn and insult me,
    for I have obeyed your laws.
23 Even princes sit and speak against me,
    but I will meditate on your decrees.
24 Your laws please me;
    they give me wise advice.

Daleth
25 I lie in the dust;
    revive me by your word.
26 I told you my plans, and you answered.
    Now teach me your decrees.
27 Help me understand the meaning of your
    commandments,
    and I will meditate on your
    wonderful deeds.
28 I weep with sorrow;
    encourage me by your word.
29 Keep me from lying to myself;
    give me the privilege of knowing your
    instructions.
30 I have chosen to be faithful;
    I have determined to live by your
    regulations.
31 I cling to your laws.
    LORD, don't let me be put to shame!
32 I will pursue your commands,
    for you expand my understanding.

He
33 Teach me your decrees, O LORD;
    I will keep them to the end.
34 Give me understanding and I will obey your
    instructions;
    I will put them into practice with
    all my heart.
35 Make me walk along the path of your
    commands,
    for that is where my happiness is found.
36 Give me an eagerness for your laws
    rather than a love for money!
37 Turn my eyes from worthless things,
    and give me life through your word.*
38 Reassure me of your promise,
    made to those who fear you.

39 Help me abandon my shameful ways;
    for your regulations are good.
40 I long to obey your commandments!
    Renew my life with your goodness.

Waw
41 LORD, give me your unfailing love,
    the salvation that you promised me.
42 Then I can answer those who taunt me,
    for I trust in your word.
43 Do not snatch your word of truth from me,
    for your regulations are my only hope.
44 I will keep on obeying your instructions
    forever and ever.
45 I will walk in freedom,
    for I have devoted myself to your
    commandments.
46 I will speak to kings about your laws,
    and I will not be ashamed.
47 How I delight in your commands!
    How I love them!
48 I honor and love your commands.
    I meditate on your decrees.

Zayin
49 Remember your promise to me;
    it is my only hope.
50 Your promise revives me;
    it comforts me in all my troubles.
51 The proud hold me in utter contempt,
    but I do not turn away from your
    instructions.
52 I meditate on your age-old regulations;
    O LORD, they comfort me.
53 I become furious with the wicked,
    because they reject your instructions.
54 Your decrees have been the theme of
    my songs
    wherever I have lived.
55 I reflect at night on who you are, O LORD;
    therefore, I obey your instructions.
56 This is how I spend my life:
    obeying your commandments.

Heth
57 LORD, you are mine!
    I promise to obey your words!
58 With all my heart I want your blessings.
    Be merciful as you promised.
59 I pondered the direction of my life,
    and I turned to follow your laws.
60 I will hurry, without delay,
    to obey your commands.
61 Evil people try to drag me into sin,
    but I am firmly anchored to your
    instructions.
62 I rise at midnight to thank you
    for your just regulations.
63 I am a friend to anyone who fears you—
    anyone who obeys your commandments.

119:37 Some manuscripts read *in your ways.*

64 O Lord, your unfailing love fills the earth;
teach me your decrees.

Teth

65 You have done many good things for me,
Lord,
just as you promised.
66 I believe in your commands;
now teach me good judgment and
knowledge.
67 I used to wander off until you disciplined me;
but now I closely follow your word.
68 You are good and do only good;
teach me your decrees.
69 Arrogant people smear me with lies,
but in truth I obey your commandments
with all my heart.
70 Their hearts are dull and stupid,
but I delight in your instructions.
71 My suffering was good for me,
for it taught me to pay attention to your
decrees.
72 Your instructions are more valuable to me
than millions in gold and silver.

Yodh

73 You made me; you created me.
Now give me the sense to follow your
commands.
74 May all who fear you find in me a cause for joy,
for I have put my hope in your word.
75 I know, O Lord, that your regulations are fair;
you disciplined me because I needed it.
76 Now let your unfailing love comfort me,
just as you promised me, your servant.
77 Surround me with your tender mercies so
I may live,
for your instructions are my delight.
78 Bring disgrace upon the arrogant people
who lied about me;
meanwhile, I will concentrate on your
commandments.
79 Let me be united with all who fear you,
with those who know your laws.
80 May I be blameless in keeping your decrees;
then I will never be ashamed.

Kaph

81 I am worn out waiting for your rescue,
but I have put my hope in your word.
82 My eyes are straining to see your promises
come true.
When will you comfort me?
83 I am shriveled like a wineskin in the smoke,
but I have not forgotten to obey your
decrees.
84 How long must I wait?
When will you punish those who
persecute me?
85 These arrogant people who hate your
instructions
have dug deep pits to trap me.

86 All your commands are trustworthy.
Protect me from those who hunt me
down without cause.
87 They almost finished me off,
but I refused to abandon your
commandments.
88 In your unfailing love, spare my life;
then I can continue to obey your laws.

Lamedh

89 Your eternal word, O Lord,
stands firm in heaven.
90 Your faithfulness extends to
every generation,
as enduring as the earth you created.
91 Your regulations remain true to this day,
for everything serves your plans.
92 If your instructions hadn't sustained me
with joy,
I would have died in my misery.
93 I will never forget your commandments,
for by them you give me life.
94 I am yours; rescue me!
For I have worked hard at obeying your
commandments.
95 Though the wicked hide along the way
to kill me,
I will quietly keep my mind on
your laws.
96 Even perfection has its limits,
but your commands have no limit.

Mem

97 Oh, how I love your instructions!
I think about them all day long.
98 Your commands make me wiser than
my enemies,
for they are my constant guide.
99 Yes, I have more insight than my teachers,
for I am always thinking of your laws.
100 I am even wiser than my elders,
for I have kept your commandments.
101 I have refused to walk on any evil path,
so that I may remain obedient to
your word.
102 I haven't turned away from
your regulations,
for you have taught me well.
103 How sweet your words taste to me;
they are sweeter than honey.
104 Your commandments give me
understanding;
no wonder I hate every false way of life.

Nun

105 Your word is a lamp to guide my feet
and a light for my path.
106 I've promised it once,
and I'll promise it again:
I will obey your righteous regulations.
107 I have suffered much, O Lord;
restore my life again as you promised.

LIGHTING THE LAMP
Psalm 119:105   ROBERT MORRIS

Maybe things seem pretty good in your life right now. Perhaps it doesn't feel like you need to spend time in the Word to get through your day. Let me tell you something, though: God's Word doesn't just drive out the darkness; it can also keep you from it.

Psalm 119:105 says,

Your word is a lamp to guide my feet
and a light for my path.

We need to spend time letting God's lamp light our paths every day. If there's always light, we won't have the chance to stumble. We will be able to walk in the light of God's guidance.

Are there any areas in your life where you need God's Word to drive out darkness? Are you working in a dark environment where you need His light to shine? Spend time in God's Word and clothe yourself with it. His lamp will always overcome the darkness.

108 LORD, accept my offering of praise,
    and teach me your regulations.
109 My life constantly hangs in the balance,
    but I will not stop obeying your instructions.
110 The wicked have set their traps for me,
    but I will not turn from your commandments.
111 Your laws are my treasure;
    they are my heart's delight.
112 I am determined to keep your decrees
    to the very end.

Samekh

113 I hate those with divided loyalties,
    but I love your instructions.
114 You are my refuge and my shield;
    your word is my source of hope.
115 Get out of my life, you evil-minded people,
    for I intend to obey the commands
    of my God.
116 LORD, sustain me as you promised, that I
    may live!
    Do not let my hope be crushed.
117 Sustain me, and I will be rescued;
    then I will meditate continually on
    your decrees.
118 But you have rejected all who stray from
    your decrees.
    They are only fooling themselves.
119 You skim off the wicked of the earth
    like scum;
    no wonder I love to obey your laws!
120 I tremble in fear of you;
    I stand in awe of your regulations.

Ayin

121 Don't leave me to the mercy of my enemies,
    for I have done what is just and right.
122 Please guarantee a blessing for me.
    Don't let the arrogant oppress me!
123 My eyes strain to see your rescue,
    to see the truth of your promise fulfilled.
124 I am your servant; deal with me in
    unfailing love,
    and teach me your decrees.
125 Give discernment to me, your servant;
    then I will understand your laws.
126 LORD, it is time for you to act,
    for these evil people have violated your
    instructions.
127 Truly, I love your commands
    more than gold, even the finest gold.
128 Each of your commandments is right.
    That is why I hate every false way.

Pe

129 Your laws are wonderful.
    No wonder I obey them!
130 The teaching of your word gives light,
    so even the simple can understand.
131 I pant with expectation,
    longing for your commands.
132 Come and show me your mercy,
    as you do for all who love your name.
133 Guide my steps by your word,
    so I will not be overcome by evil.
134 Ransom me from the oppression of
    evil people;
    then I can obey your commandments.
135 Look upon me with love;
    teach me your decrees.
136 Rivers of tears gush from my eyes
    because people disobey your instructions.

Tsadhe

137 O LORD, you are righteous,
    and your regulations are fair.
138 Your laws are perfect
    and completely trustworthy.
139 I am overwhelmed with indignation,
    for my enemies have disregarded your
    words.
140 Your promises have been thoroughly
    tested;
    that is why I love them so much.
141 I am insignificant and despised,
    but I don't forget your commandments.
142 Your justice is eternal,
    and your instructions are perfectly true.
143 As pressure and stress bear down on me,
    I find joy in your commands.
144 Your laws are always right;
    help me to understand them so I may live.

Qoph

145 I pray with all my heart; answer me, LORD!
    I will obey your decrees.

¹⁴⁶ I cry out to you; rescue me,
    that I may obey your laws.
¹⁴⁷ I rise early, before the sun is up;
    I cry out for help and put my hope in
        your words.
¹⁴⁸ I stay awake through the night,
    thinking about your promise.
¹⁴⁹ In your faithful love, O Lord, hear my cry;
    let me be revived by following your
        regulations.
¹⁵⁰ Lawless people are coming to attack me;
    they live far from your instructions.
¹⁵¹ But you are near, O Lord,
    and all your commands are true.
¹⁵² I have known from my earliest days
    that your laws will last forever.

Resh

¹⁵³ Look upon my suffering and rescue me,
    for I have not forgotten your instructions.
¹⁵⁴ Argue my case; take my side!
    Protect my life as you promised.
¹⁵⁵ The wicked are far from rescue,
    for they do not bother with your decrees.
¹⁵⁶ Lord, how great is your mercy;
    let me be revived by following your
        regulations.
¹⁵⁷ Many persecute and trouble me,
    yet I have not swerved from your laws.
¹⁵⁸ Seeing these traitors makes me sick at heart,
    because they care nothing for your word.
¹⁵⁹ See how I love your commandments, Lord.
    Give back my life because of your
        unfailing love.
¹⁶⁰ The very essence of your words is truth;
    all your just regulations will stand forever.

Shin

¹⁶¹ Powerful people harass me without cause,
    but my heart trembles only at your word.
¹⁶² I rejoice in your word
    like one who discovers a great treasure.
¹⁶³ I hate and abhor all falsehood,
    but I love your instructions.
¹⁶⁴ I will praise you seven times a day
    because all your regulations are just.
¹⁶⁵ Those who love your instructions have
        great peace
    and do not stumble.
¹⁶⁶ I long for your rescue, Lord,
    so I have obeyed your commands.
¹⁶⁷ I have obeyed your laws,
    for I love them very much.
¹⁶⁸ Yes, I obey your commandments and laws
    because you know everything I do.

Taw

¹⁶⁹ O Lord, listen to my cry;
    give me the discerning mind
        you promised.
¹⁷⁰ Listen to my prayer;
    rescue me as you promised.

¹⁷¹ Let praise flow from my lips,
    for you have taught me your decrees.
¹⁷² Let my tongue sing about your word,
    for all your commands are right.
¹⁷³ Give me a helping hand,
    for I have chosen to follow
        your commandments.
¹⁷⁴ O Lord, I have longed for your rescue,
    and your instructions are my delight.
¹⁷⁵ Let me live so I can praise you,
    and may your regulations help me.
¹⁷⁶ I have wandered away like a lost sheep;
    come and find me,
    for I have not forgotten your commands.

120

A song for pilgrims ascending to Jerusalem.

¹ I took my troubles to the Lord;
    I cried out to him, and he answered
        my prayer.
² Rescue me, O Lord, from liars
    and from all deceitful people.
³ O deceptive tongue,
    what will God do to you?
    How will he increase your punishment?
⁴ You will be pierced with sharp arrows
    and burned with glowing coals.

⁵ How I suffer in far-off Meshech.
    It pains me to live in distant Kedar.
⁶ I am tired of living
    among people who hate peace.
⁷ I search for peace;
    but when I speak of peace,
        they want war!

121

A song for pilgrims ascending to Jerusalem.

¹ I look up to the mountains—
    does my help come from there?
² My help comes from the Lord,
    who made heaven and earth!

³ He will not let you stumble;
    the one who watches over you will not
        slumber.
⁴ Indeed, he who watches over Israel
    never slumbers or sleeps.

⁵ The Lord himself watches over you!
    The Lord stands beside you as your
        protective shade.
⁶ The sun will not harm you by day,
    nor the moon at night.

⁷ The Lord keeps you from all harm
    and watches over your life.
⁸ The Lord keeps watch over you as you
        come and go,
    both now and forever.

122

A song for pilgrims ascending to Jerusalem. A psalm of David.

1 I was glad when they said to me,
  "Let us go to the house of the LORD."
2 And now here we are,
  standing inside your gates, O Jerusalem.
3 Jerusalem is a well-built city;
  its seamless walls cannot be breached.
4 All the tribes of Israel—the LORD's people—
  make their pilgrimage here.
  They come to give thanks to the name of
  the LORD,
  as the law requires of Israel.
5 Here stand the thrones where judgment
  is given,
  the thrones of the dynasty of David.

6 Pray for peace in Jerusalem.
  May all who love this city prosper.
7 O Jerusalem, may there be peace within
  your walls
  and prosperity in your palaces.
8 For the sake of my family and friends,
  I will say,
  "May you have peace."
9 For the sake of the house of the LORD our God,
  I will seek what is best for you, O Jerusalem.

123

A song for pilgrims ascending to Jerusalem.

1 I lift my eyes to you,
  O God, enthroned in heaven.
2 We keep looking to the LORD our God for
  his mercy,
  just as servants keep their eyes on their
  master,
  as a slave girl watches her mistress for the
  slightest signal.
3 Have mercy on us, LORD, have mercy,
  for we have had our fill of contempt.
4 We have had more than our fill of the
  scoffing of the proud
  and the contempt of the arrogant.

124

A song for pilgrims ascending to Jerusalem. A psalm of David.

1 What if the LORD had not been on our side?
  Let all Israel repeat:
2 What if the LORD had not been on our side
  when people attacked us?
3 They would have swallowed us alive
  in their burning anger.
4 The waters would have engulfed us;
  a torrent would have overwhelmed us.
5 Yes, the raging waters of their fury
  would have overwhelmed our very lives.

6 Praise the LORD,
  who did not let their teeth tear us apart!

7 We escaped like a bird from a hunter's trap.
  The trap is broken, and we are free!
8 Our help is from the LORD,
  who made heaven and earth.

125

A song for pilgrims ascending to Jerusalem.

1 Those who trust in the LORD are as secure as
  Mount Zion;
  they will not be defeated but will endure
  forever.
2 Just as the mountains surround Jerusalem,
  so the LORD surrounds his people, both
  now and forever.
3 The wicked will not rule the land of the godly,
  for then the godly might be tempted
  to do wrong.
4 O LORD, do good to those who are good,
  whose hearts are in tune with you.
5 But banish those who turn to crooked ways,
  O LORD.
  Take them away with those who do evil.

May Israel have peace!

126

A song for pilgrims ascending to Jerusalem.

1 When the LORD brought back his exiles
  to Jerusalem,*
  it was like a dream!
2 We were filled with laughter,
  and we sang for joy.
  And the other nations said,
  "What amazing things the LORD has done
  for them."
3 Yes, the LORD has done amazing things
  for us!
  What joy!

4 Restore our fortunes, LORD,
  as streams renew the desert.
5 Those who plant in tears
  will harvest with shouts of joy.
6 They weep as they go to plant their seed,
  but they sing as they return with the
  harvest.

127

A song for pilgrims ascending to Jerusalem. A psalm of Solomon.

1 Unless the LORD builds a house,
  the work of the builders is wasted.
  Unless the LORD protects a city,
  guarding it with sentries will do no good.
2 It is useless for you to work so hard
  from early morning until late at night,
  anxiously working for food to eat;
  for God gives rest to his loved ones.

126:1 Hebrew *Zion*.

3 Children are a gift from the LORD;
  they are a reward from him.
4 Children born to a young man
  are like arrows in a warrior's hands.
5 How joyful is the man whose quiver
    is full of them!
  He will not be put to shame when he
    confronts his accusers at the city gates.

128

A song for pilgrims ascending to Jerusalem.

1 How joyful are those who fear the LORD—
  all who follow his ways!
2 You will enjoy the fruit of your labor.
  How joyful and prosperous you will be!
3 Your wife will be like a fruitful grapevine,
    flourishing within your home.
  Your children will be like vigorous young
    olive trees
    as they sit around your table.
4 That is the LORD's blessing
  for those who fear him.

5 May the LORD continually bless you
    from Zion.
  May you see Jerusalem prosper as long
    as you live.
6 May you live to enjoy your grandchildren.
  May Israel have peace!

129

A song for pilgrims ascending to Jerusalem.

1 From my earliest youth my enemies have
    persecuted me.
  Let all Israel repeat this:
2 From my earliest youth my enemies have
    persecuted me,
  but they have never defeated me.
3 My back is covered with cuts,
  as if a farmer had plowed long furrows.
4 But the LORD is good;
  he has cut me free from the ropes of the
    ungodly.

5 May all who hate Jerusalem*
  be turned back in shameful defeat.
6 May they be as useless as grass on a rooftop,
  turning yellow when only half grown,
7 ignored by the harvester,
  despised by the binder.
8 And may those who pass by
    refuse to give them this blessing:
  "The LORD bless you;
  we bless you in the LORD's name."

130

A song for pilgrims ascending to Jerusalem.

1 From the depths of despair, O LORD,
  I call for your help.

2 Hear my cry, O Lord.
  Pay attention to my prayer.

3 LORD, if you kept a record of our sins,
  who, O Lord, could ever survive?
4 But you offer forgiveness,
  that we might learn to fear you.

5 I am counting on the LORD;
  yes, I am counting on him.
  I have put my hope in his word.
6 I long for the Lord
  more than sentries long for the dawn,
  yes, more than sentries long for the dawn.

7 O Israel, hope in the LORD;
  for with the LORD there is unfailing love.
  His redemption overflows.
8 He himself will redeem Israel
  from every kind of sin.

131

A song for pilgrims ascending to Jerusalem. A psalm of David.

1 LORD, my heart is not proud;
  my eyes are not haughty.
I don't concern myself with matters
    too great
  or too awesome for me to grasp.
2 Instead, I have calmed and quieted myself,
  like a weaned child who no longer cries
    for its mother's milk.
  Yes, like a weaned child is my soul
    within me.

3 O Israel, put your hope in the LORD—
  now and always.

132

A song for pilgrims ascending to Jerusalem.

1 LORD, remember David
  and all that he suffered.
2 He made a solemn promise to the LORD.
  He vowed to the Mighty One of Israel,*
3 "I will not go home;
  I will not let myself rest.
4 I will not let my eyes sleep
  nor close my eyelids in slumber
5 until I find a place to build a house for
    the LORD,
  a sanctuary for the Mighty One of Israel."

6 We heard that the Ark was in Ephrathah;
  then we found it in the distant
    countryside of Jaar.
7 Let us go to the sanctuary of the LORD;
  let us worship at the footstool of
    his throne.

129:5 Hebrew *Zion.* 132:2 Hebrew *of Jacob;* also in 132:5.
See note on 44:4.

⁸ Arise, O LORD, and enter your resting place,
along with the Ark, the symbol of your
power.
⁹ May your priests be clothed in godliness;
may your loyal servants sing for joy.
¹⁰ For the sake of your servant David,
do not reject the king you have anointed.
¹¹ The LORD swore an oath to David
with a promise he will never take back:
"I will place one of your descendants
on your throne.
¹² If your descendants obey the terms of
my covenant
and the laws that I teach them,
then your royal line
will continue forever and ever."

¹³ For the LORD has chosen Jerusalem*;
he has desired it for his home.
¹⁴ "This is my resting place forever," he said.
"I will live here, for this is the home
I desired.
¹⁵ I will bless this city and make it prosperous;
I will satisfy its poor with food.
¹⁶ I will clothe its priests with godliness;
its faithful servants will sing for joy.
¹⁷ Here I will increase the power of David;
my anointed one will be a light for my
people.
¹⁸ I will clothe his enemies with shame,
but he will be a glorious king."

133

*A song for pilgrims ascending to Jerusalem.
A psalm of David.*

¹ How wonderful and pleasant it is
when brothers live together
in harmony!
² For harmony is as precious as the
anointing oil
that was poured over Aaron's head,
that ran down his beard
and onto the border of his robe.
³ Harmony is as refreshing as the dew from
Mount Hermon
that falls on the mountains of Zion.
And there the LORD has pronounced his
blessing,
even life everlasting.

134

*A song for pilgrims ascending to
Jerusalem.*

¹ Oh, praise the LORD, all you servants of
the LORD,
you who serve at night in the house of
the LORD.
² Lift your hands toward the sanctuary,
and praise the LORD.

³ May the LORD, who made heaven and earth,
bless you from Jerusalem.*

135

¹ Praise the LORD!

Praise the name of the LORD!
Praise him, you who serve the LORD,
² you who serve in the house of the LORD,
in the courts of the house of our God.

³ Praise the LORD, for the LORD is good;
celebrate his lovely name with music.
⁴ For the LORD has chosen Jacob for himself,
Israel for his own special treasure.

⁵ I know the greatness of the LORD—
that our Lord is greater than
any other god.
⁶ The LORD does whatever pleases him
throughout all heaven and earth,
and on the seas and in their depths.
⁷ He causes the clouds to rise over
the whole earth.
He sends the lightning with the rain
and releases the wind from his
storehouses.

⁸ He destroyed the firstborn in each
Egyptian home,
both people and animals.
⁹ He performed miraculous signs and
wonders in Egypt
against Pharaoh and all his people.
¹⁰ He struck down great nations
and slaughtered mighty kings—
¹¹ Sihon king of the Amorites,
Og king of Bashan,
and all the kings of Canaan.
¹² He gave their land as an inheritance,
a special possession to his people Israel.

¹³ Your name, O LORD, endures forever;
your fame, O LORD, is known to every
generation.
¹⁴ For the LORD will give justice to his people
and have compassion on his servants.

¹⁵ The idols of the nations are merely things
of silver and gold,
shaped by human hands.
¹⁶ They have mouths but cannot speak,
and eyes but cannot see.
¹⁷ They have ears but cannot hear,
and mouths but cannot breathe.
¹⁸ And those who make idols are just like them,
as are all who trust in them.

¹⁹ O Israel, praise the LORD!
O priests—descendants of Aaron—praise
the LORD!
²⁰ O Levites, praise the LORD!
All you who fear the LORD,
praise the LORD!

132:13 Hebrew *Zion.*   134:3 Hebrew *Zion.*

²¹ The Lord be praised from Zion,
   for he lives here in Jerusalem.

Praise the Lord!

136

¹ Give thanks to the Lord,
   for he is good!
   His faithful love endures forever.
² Give thanks to the God of gods.
   His faithful love endures forever.
³ Give thanks to the Lord of lords.
   His faithful love endures forever.

⁴ Give thanks to him who alone does mighty
   miracles.
   His faithful love endures forever.
⁵ Give thanks to him who made the heavens
   so skillfully.
   His faithful love endures forever.
⁶ Give thanks to him who placed the earth
   among the waters.
   His faithful love endures forever.
⁷ Give thanks to him who made the heavenly
   lights—
   His faithful love endures forever.
⁸ the sun to rule the day,
   His faithful love endures forever.
⁹ and the moon and stars to rule the night.
   His faithful love endures forever.

¹⁰ Give thanks to him who killed the firstborn
   of Egypt.
   His faithful love endures forever.
¹¹ He brought Israel out of Egypt.
   His faithful love endures forever.
¹² He acted with a strong hand
   and powerful arm.
   His faithful love endures forever.
¹³ Give thanks to him who parted
   the Red Sea.*
   His faithful love endures forever.
¹⁴ He led Israel safely through,
   His faithful love endures forever.
¹⁵ but he hurled Pharaoh and his army
   into the Red Sea.
   His faithful love endures forever.
¹⁶ Give thanks to him who led his people
   through the wilderness.
   His faithful love endures forever.

¹⁷ Give thanks to him who struck down
   mighty kings.
   His faithful love endures forever.
¹⁸ He killed powerful kings—
   His faithful love endures forever.
¹⁹ Sihon king of the Amorites,
   His faithful love endures forever.
²⁰ and Og king of Bashan.
   His faithful love endures forever.
²¹ God gave the land of these kings
   as an inheritance—
   His faithful love endures forever.

²² a special possession to his servant Israel.
   His faithful love endures forever.

²³ He remembered us in our weakness.
   His faithful love endures forever.
²⁴ He saved us from our enemies.
   His faithful love endures forever.
²⁵ He gives food to every living thing.
   His faithful love endures forever.
²⁶ Give thanks to the God of heaven.
   His faithful love endures forever.

137

¹ Beside the rivers of Babylon,
   we sat and wept
   as we thought of Jerusalem.*
² We put away our harps,
   hanging them on the branches of
   poplar trees.
³ For our captors demanded a song from us.
   Our tormentors insisted on
   a joyful hymn:
   "Sing us one of those songs of
   Jerusalem!"
⁴ But how can we sing the songs of the Lord
   while in a pagan land?

⁵ If I forget you, O Jerusalem,
   let my right hand forget how to play
   the harp.
⁶ May my tongue stick to the roof
   of my mouth
   if I fail to remember you,
   if I don't make Jerusalem
   my greatest joy.

⁷ O Lord, remember what the Edomites did
   on the day the armies of Babylon captured
   Jerusalem.
   "Destroy it!" they yelled.
   "Level it to the ground!"
⁸ O Babylon, you will be destroyed.
   Happy is the one who pays you back
   for what you have done to us.
⁹ Happy is the one who takes your babies
   and smashes them against the rocks!

138

A psalm of David.

¹ I give you thanks, O Lord, with all my
   heart;
   I will sing your praises before the gods.
² I bow before your holy Temple as I worship.
   I praise your name for your unfailing love
   and faithfulness;
   for your promises are backed
   by all the honor of your name.
³ As soon as I pray, you answer me;
   you encourage me by giving me strength.

136:13 Hebrew *sea of reeds;* also in 136:15.   137:1 Hebrew *Zion;*
also in 137:3.

4 Every king in all the earth will
    thank you, LORD,
  for all of them will hear your words.
5 Yes, they will sing about the LORD's ways,
    for the glory of the LORD is very great.
6 Though the LORD is great, he cares for
    the humble,
  but he keeps his distance from the proud.

7 Though I am surrounded by troubles,
    you will protect me from the anger of
    my enemies.
  You reach out your hand,
    and the power of your right hand saves me.
8 The LORD will work out his plans for
    my life—
  for your faithful love, O LORD, endures
    forever.
  Don't abandon me, for you made me.

139

For the choir director: A psalm of David.

1 O LORD, you have examined my heart
    and know everything about me.
2 You know when I sit down or stand up.
  You know my thoughts even when
    I'm far away.
3 You see me when I travel
    and when I rest at home.
  You know everything I do.
4 You know what I am going to say
    even before I say it, LORD.
5 You go before me and follow me.
  You place your hand of blessing on my
    head.
6 Such knowledge is too wonderful for me,
    too great for me to understand!

7 I can never escape from your Spirit!
  I can never get away from your presence!
8 If I go up to heaven, you are there;
  if I go down to the grave,* you are there.
9 If I ride the wings of the morning,
  if I dwell by the farthest oceans,
10 even there your hand will guide me,
  and your strength will support me.
11 I could ask the darkness to hide me
  and the light around me to become night—
12   but even in darkness I cannot hide
    from you.
  To you the night shines as bright as day.
  Darkness and light are the same to you.

13 You made all the delicate, inner parts of
    my body
  and knit me together in
    my mother's womb.
14 Thank you for making me so wonderfully
    complex!
  Your workmanship is marvelous—how
    well I know it.

15 You watched me as I was being formed in
    utter seclusion,
  as I was woven together in the dark of
    the womb.
16 You saw me before I was born.
  Every day of my life was recorded
    in your book.
  Every moment was laid out
    before a single day had passed.

17 How precious are your thoughts about me,*
    O God.
  They cannot be numbered!
18 I can't even count them;
  they outnumber the grains of sand!
  And when I wake up,
    you are still with me!

19 O God, if only you would destroy the wicked!
  Get out of my life, you murderers!
20 They blaspheme you;
  your enemies misuse your name.
21 O LORD, shouldn't I hate those who
    hate you?
  Shouldn't I despise those who oppose you?
22 Yes, I hate them with total hatred,
  for your enemies are my enemies.

23 Search me, O God, and know my heart;
  test me and know my anxious thoughts.
24 Point out anything in me that offends you,
  and lead me along the path of everlasting
    life.

140

For the choir director: A psalm of David.

1 O LORD, rescue me from evil people.
  Protect me from those who are violent,
2 those who plot evil in their hearts
  and stir up trouble all day long.
3 Their tongues sting like a snake;
  the venom of a viper drips from
    their lips.   *Interlude*

4 O LORD, keep me out of the hands of
    the wicked.
  Protect me from those who are violent,
  for they are plotting against me.
5 The proud have set a trap to catch me;
  they have stretched out a net;
  they have placed traps
    all along the way.   *Interlude*

6 I said to the LORD, "You are my God!"
  Listen, O LORD, to my cries for mercy!
7 O Sovereign LORD, the strong one who
    rescued me,
  you protected me on the day of battle.

139:8 Hebrew *to Sheol.*   139:17 Or *How precious to me are your thoughts.*

8 LORD, do not let evil people have their way.
  Do not let their evil schemes succeed,
  or they will become proud.   *Interlude*

9 Let my enemies be destroyed
  by the very evil they have planned
    for me.
10 Let burning coals fall down on
    their heads.
  Let them be thrown into the fire
  or into watery pits from which
    they can't escape.
11 Don't let liars prosper here in our land.
  Cause great disasters to fall
    on the violent.
12 But I know the LORD will help those they
    persecute;
  he will give justice to the poor.
13 Surely righteous people are praising
    your name;
  the godly will live in your presence.

141 A psalm of David.

1 O LORD, I am calling to you. Please hurry!
  Listen when I cry to you for help!
2 Accept my prayer as incense offered
    to you,
  and my upraised hands as an
    evening offering.

3 Take control of what I say, O LORD,
  and guard my lips.
4 Don't let me drift toward evil
  or take part in acts of wickedness.
  Don't let me share in the delicacies
  of those who do wrong.

5 Let the godly strike me!
  It will be a kindness!
  If they correct me, it is soothing medicine.
  Don't let me refuse it.

But I pray constantly
  against the wicked and their deeds.
6 When their leaders are thrown down
    from a cliff,
  the wicked will listen to my words and
    find them true.
7 Like rocks brought up by a plow,
  the bones of the wicked will lie scattered
    without burial.*

8 I look to you for help, O Sovereign LORD.
  You are my refuge; don't let them kill me.
9 Keep me from the traps they have set
    for me,
  from the snares of those who do wrong.
10 Let the wicked fall into their own nets,
  but let me escape.

142 A psalm* of David, regarding his experience in the cave. A prayer.

1 I cry out to the LORD;
  I plead for the LORD's mercy.
2 I pour out my complaints before him
  and tell him all my troubles.
3 When I am overwhelmed,
  you alone know the way I should turn.
Wherever I go,
  my enemies have set traps for me.
4 I look for someone to come and help me,
  but no one gives me
    a passing thought!
No one will help me;
  no one cares a bit what happens to me.
5 Then I pray to you, O LORD.
  I say, "You are my place of refuge.
  You are all I really want in life.
6 Hear my cry,
  for I am very low.
Rescue me from my persecutors,
  for they are too strong for me.
7 Bring me out of prison
  so I can thank you.
The godly will crowd around me,
  for you are good to me."

143 A psalm of David.

1 Hear my prayer, O LORD;
  listen to my plea!
  Answer me because you are faithful
    and righteous.
2 Don't put your servant on trial,
  for no one is innocent before you.
3 My enemy has chased me.
  He has knocked me to the ground
  and forces me to live in darkness like
    those in the grave.
4 I am losing all hope;
  I am paralyzed with fear.
5 I remember the days of old.
  I ponder all your great works
  and think about what you have done.
6 I lift my hands to you in prayer.
  I thirst for you as parched land thirsts
    for rain.   *Interlude*

7 Come quickly, LORD, and answer me,
  for my depression deepens.
Don't turn away from me,
  or I will die.
8 Let me hear of your unfailing love
    each morning,
  for I am trusting you.
Show me where to walk,
  for I give myself to you.

141:7 Hebrew *our bones will be scattered at the mouth of Sheol.*
142:TITLE Hebrew *maskil.* This may be a literary or musical term.

9 Rescue me from my enemies, LORD;
   I run to you to hide me.
10 Teach me to do your will,
   for you are my God.
   May your gracious Spirit lead me forward
   on a firm footing.
11 For the glory of your name, O LORD,
   preserve my life.
   Because of your faithfulness, bring me out
   of this distress.
12 In your unfailing love, silence all my enemies
   and destroy all my foes,
   for I am your servant.

144 *A psalm of David.*

1 Praise the LORD, who is my rock.
   He trains my hands for war
   and gives my fingers skill for battle.
2 He is my loving ally and my fortress,
   my tower of safety, my rescuer.
   He is my shield, and I take refuge in him.
   He makes the nations* submit to me.

3 O LORD, what are human beings that you
   should notice them,
   mere mortals that you should think
   about them?
4 For they are like a breath of air;
   their days are like a passing shadow.

5 Open the heavens, LORD, and come down.
   Touch the mountains so they billow smoke.
6 Hurl your lightning bolts and scatter
   your enemies!
   Shoot your arrows and confuse them!
7 Reach down from heaven and rescue me;
   rescue me from deep waters,
   from the power of my enemies.
8 Their mouths are full of lies;
   they swear to tell the truth,
   but they lie instead.

9 I will sing a new song to you, O God!
   I will sing your praises with
   a ten-stringed harp.
10 For you grant victory to kings!
   You rescued your servant David from
   the fatal sword.
11 Save me!
   Rescue me from the power of my enemies.
   Their mouths are full of lies;
   they swear to tell the truth,
   but they lie instead.

12 May our sons flourish in their youth
   like well-nurtured plants.
   May our daughters be like graceful pillars,
   carved to beautify a palace.
13 May our barns be filled
   with crops of every kind.

May the flocks in our fields multiply
   by the thousands,
   even tens of thousands,
14 and may our oxen be loaded down
   with produce.
   May there be no enemy breaking through
   our walls,
   no going into captivity,
   no cries of alarm in our town squares.
15 Yes, joyful are those who live like this!
   Joyful indeed are those whose God is
   the LORD.

145 * *A psalm of praise of David.*

1 I will exalt you, my God and King,
   and praise your name forever and ever.
2 I will praise you every day;
   yes, I will praise you forever.
3 Great is the LORD! He is most worthy
   of praise!
   No one can measure his greatness.

4 Let each generation tell its children of
   your mighty acts;
   let them proclaim your power.
5 I will meditate on your majestic,
   glorious splendor
   and your wonderful miracles.
6 Your awe-inspiring deeds will be
   on every tongue;
   I will proclaim your greatness.
7 Everyone will share the story of your
   wonderful goodness;
   they will sing with joy about your
   righteousness.

8 The LORD is merciful and compassionate,
   slow to get angry and filled with
   unfailing love.
9 The LORD is good to everyone.
   He showers compassion on all
   his creation.
10 All of your works will thank you, LORD,
   and your faithful followers
   will praise you.
11 They will speak of the glory of your kingdom;
   they will give examples of your power.
12 They will tell about your mighty deeds
   and about the majesty and glory of
   your reign.
13 For your kingdom is an everlasting kingdom.
   You rule throughout all generations.

The LORD always keeps his promises;
   he is gracious in all he does.*

144:2 Some manuscripts read *my people.*   145 This psalm is a
Hebrew acrostic poem; each verse (including 13b) begins with a
successive letter of the Hebrew alphabet.   145:13 As in Dead Sea
Scrolls and Greek and Syriac versions; the Masoretic Text lacks
the final two lines of this verse.

¹⁴ The LORD helps the fallen
    and lifts those bent beneath
        their loads.
¹⁵ The eyes of all look to you in hope;
    you give them their food as they need it.
¹⁶ When you open your hand,
    you satisfy the hunger and thirst of every
        living thing.
¹⁷ The LORD is righteous in everything
        he does;
    he is filled with kindness.
¹⁸ The LORD is close to all who call on him,
    yes, to all who call on him in truth.
¹⁹ He grants the desires of those
        who fear him;
    he hears their cries for help and
        rescues them.
²⁰ The LORD protects all those who love him,
    but he destroys the wicked.

²¹ I will praise the LORD,
    and may everyone on earth bless
        his holy name
    forever and ever.

146

¹ Praise the LORD!

Let all that I am praise the LORD.
²   I will praise the LORD as long as I live.
    I will sing praises to my God with my
        dying breath.

³ Don't put your confidence in
        powerful people;
    there is no help for you there.
⁴ When they breathe their last, they return
        to the earth,
    and all their plans die with them.
⁵ But joyful are those who have the God of
        Israel* as their helper,
    whose hope is in the LORD their God.
⁶ He made heaven and earth,
    the sea, and everything in them.
    He keeps every promise forever.
⁷ He gives justice to the oppressed
        and food to the hungry.
    The LORD frees the prisoners.
⁸ The LORD opens the eyes of the blind.
    The LORD lifts up those who are
        weighed down.
    The LORD loves the godly.
⁹ The LORD protects the foreigners
        among us.
    He cares for the orphans and widows,
    but he frustrates the plans
        of the wicked.

¹⁰ The LORD will reign forever.
    He will be your God, O Jerusalem,*
        throughout the generations.

Praise the LORD!

147

¹ Praise the LORD!

How good to sing praises to our God!
    How delightful and how fitting!
² The LORD is rebuilding Jerusalem
    and bringing the exiles back to Israel.
³ He heals the brokenhearted
    and bandages their wounds.
⁴ He counts the stars
    and calls them all by name.
⁵ How great is our Lord! His power
        is absolute!
    His understanding is beyond
        comprehension!
⁶ The LORD supports the humble,
    but he brings the wicked down into
        the dust.

⁷ Sing out your thanks to the LORD;
    sing praises to our God with a harp.
⁸ He covers the heavens with clouds,
    provides rain for the earth,
    and makes the grass grow in mountain
        pastures.
⁹ He gives food to the wild animals
    and feeds the young ravens when they cry.
¹⁰ He takes no pleasure in the strength of
        a horse
    or in human might.
¹¹ No, the LORD's delight is in those who
        fear him,
    those who put their hope in his
        unfailing love.

¹² Glorify the LORD, O Jerusalem!
    Praise your God, O Zion!
¹³ For he has strengthened the bars of
        your gates
    and blessed your children within
        your walls.
¹⁴ He sends peace across your nation
    and satisfies your hunger with the finest
        wheat.
¹⁵ He sends his orders to the world—
    how swiftly his word flies!
¹⁶ He sends the snow like white wool;
    he scatters frost upon the ground
        like ashes.
¹⁷ He hurls the hail like stones.*
    Who can stand against his
        freezing cold?
¹⁸ Then, at his command, it all melts.
    He sends his winds, and the ice thaws.
¹⁹ He has revealed his words to Jacob,
    his decrees and regulations to Israel.
²⁰ He has not done this for any other nation;
    they do not know his regulations.

Praise the LORD!

146:5 Hebrew *of Jacob.* See note on 44:4.   146:10 Hebrew *Zion.*
147:17 Hebrew *like bread crumbs.*

148

¹ Praise the LORD!

Praise the LORD from the heavens!
  Praise him from the skies!
² Praise him, all his angels!
  Praise him, all the armies of heaven!
³ Praise him, sun and moon!
  Praise him, all you twinkling stars!
⁴ Praise him, skies above!
  Praise him, vapors high above the clouds!
⁵ Let every created thing give praise
    to the LORD,
  for he issued his command, and they
    came into being.
⁶ He set them in place forever and ever.
  His decree will never be revoked.

⁷ Praise the LORD from the earth,
  you creatures of the ocean depths,
⁸ fire and hail, snow and clouds,*
  wind and weather that obey him,
⁹ mountains and all hills,
  fruit trees and all cedars,
¹⁰ wild animals and all livestock,
  small scurrying animals and birds,
¹¹ kings of the earth and all people,
  rulers and judges of the earth,
¹² young men and young women,
  old men and children.

¹³ Let them all praise the name of the LORD.
  For his name is very great;
  his glory towers over the earth and heaven!
¹⁴ He has made his people strong,
  honoring his faithful ones—
  the people of Israel who are close to him.

Praise the LORD!

149

¹ Praise the LORD!

Sing to the LORD a new song.
  Sing his praises in the assembly
    of the faithful.

² O Israel, rejoice in your Maker.
  O people of Jerusalem,*
    exult in your King.
³ Praise his name with dancing,
  accompanied by tambourine and harp.
⁴ For the LORD delights in his people;
  he crowns the humble with victory.
⁵ Let the faithful rejoice that he honors them.
  Let them sing for joy as they lie on
    their beds.

⁶ Let the praises of God be in their mouths,
  and a sharp sword in their hands—
⁷ to execute vengeance on the nations
  and punishment on the peoples,
⁸ to bind their kings with shackles
  and their leaders with iron chains,
⁹ to execute the judgment written
  against them.
  This is the glorious privilege of his
    faithful ones.

Praise the LORD!

150

¹ Praise the LORD!

Praise God in his sanctuary;
  praise him in his mighty heaven!
² Praise him for his mighty works;
  praise his unequaled greatness!
³ Praise him with a blast of the ram's horn;
  praise him with the lyre and harp!
⁴ Praise him with the tambourine and
    dancing;
  praise him with strings and flutes!
⁵ Praise him with a clash of cymbals;
  praise him with loud clanging cymbals.
⁶ Let everything that breathes sing praises
    to the LORD!

Praise the LORD!

148:8 Or *mist*, or *smoke*. 149:2 Hebrew *Zion*.

What Does the Bible Say About . . .

FEELING SAD OR DEPRESSED?

— You should think about excellent things (Philippians 4:8).
— The Lord will never abandon you (Deuteronomy 31:8).
— God will lift you out of the pit of despair (Psalm 40:1-3).
— God comforts you (2 Corinthians 1:3-4).
— Your trials make you a partner with Christ (1 Peter 4:12-13).
— Enduring trials makes you complete (James 1:2-4).
— You are not alone when you are in deep distress (Psalm 25:16-17).
— You have no more shadow of shame (Psalm 34:4-6).
— Jesus was despised for us (Isaiah 53:3-4).
— You can trust in God's unfailing love (Psalm 13).
— You will feast in the presence of your enemies (Psalm 23).
— Your hope is in God (Psalm 43:3-5).
— Your sorrow and mourning will disappear (Isaiah 35:10; 51:11).
— God will give you a crown of beauty for ashes and a joyous blessing instead of mourning (Isaiah 61:1-3).
— Godly sorrow will lead you away from sin (2 Corinthians 7:10).
— God will wipe away all your tears (Revelation 21:4).

MY DOUBTS AND FEARS?

— You can do everything through Christ (Philippians 4:13).
— Don't be afraid, for God is with you (Isaiah 41:10, 13).
— You do not fear bad news (Psalm 112:7).
— The Lord frees you from all your fears (Psalm 34:4).
— You live untroubled by fear (Proverbs 1:33).
— God has not given you a spirit of fear and timidity (2 Timothy 1:7).

MY ANXIETY AND WORRY?

— God's peace guards your heart and mind (Philippians 4:6-7).
— Give all your worries and cares to God (1 Peter 5:7).
— Your strength is in quietness and confidence (Isaiah 30:15).
— God calms the storm and stills the waves (Psalm 107:28-30).
— God's people live in safety (Isaiah 32:18).
— Be still in the presence of the Lord (Psalm 37:7).
— God will give your soul rest (Matthew 11:28-29).
— Jesus went to a quiet place to rest (Mark 6:31).
— A special rest awaits the people of God (Hebrews 4:9).
— Jesus gives you peace of mind and heart (John 14:27).
— God's comfort gives you renewed hope (Psalm 94:19).
— God will never abandon you or let you be destroyed (2 Corinthians 4:9).

GOD'S JOY FOR ME?

— God will grant you the joy of His presence (Psalm 16:11).
— Even though you weep at night, joy will come in the morning (Psalm 30:5).
— God will restore the joy of your salvation (Psalm 51:12).

What Does the Bible Say About . . .

— You may plant in tears, but you will harvest in joy (Psalm 126:5).
— As a faithful servant, you will sing for joy (Psalm 132:16).
— With joy, you will drink from the fountain of salvation (Isaiah 12:3).
— If you are humble, you will be filled with fresh joy (Isaiah 29:19).
— You will be crowned with everlasting joy (Isaiah 35:10).
— You will have joyous blessing instead of mourning (Isaiah 61:3).
— You can be joyful in the God of your salvation (Habakkuk 3:18).
— God rejoices over you with joyful songs (Zephaniah 3:17).
— Your joy will overflow (John 15:11).
— You will have abundant joy (John 16:24).
— You will be filled with joy and the Holy Spirit (Acts 13:52).
— The Kingdom of God is joy in the Holy Spirit (Romans 14:17).
— You will be filled completely with joy and peace (Romans 15:13).
— The Holy Spirit produces joy (Galatians 5:22).
— Troubles are an opportunity for great joy (James 1:2).
— God gives glorious, inexpressible joy (1 Peter 1:8).

GOD'S PEACE FOR ME?

— God's peace guards you (Philippians 4:7).
— God speaks peace to His people (Psalm 85:8).
— Jesus leaves a gift of peace (John 14:27).
— You can lie down in peace and sleep (Psalm 4:8).
— God blesses you with peace (Psalm 29:11).
— God gives peace to those who love His instructions (Psalm 119:165).
— God gives perfect peace to those who trust Him (Isaiah 26:3).
— You will live in joy and peace (Isaiah 55:12).
— Spirit-controlled minds have peace (Romans 8:6).
— You have peace in Jesus (John 16:33).
— Because of Jesus, you have peace with God (Romans 5:1).
— The Holy Spirit produces peace (Galatians 5:22).
— The Kingdom of God is peace (Romans 14:17).

GOD'S HOPE FOR ME?

— Your only hope is in God (Psalm 39:7; 71:5).
— God's Word is your hope (Psalm 119:114).
— The hopes of the godly result in happiness (Proverbs 10:28).
— You are blessed to hope in the Lord (Jeremiah 17:7).
— Your hope is in the Lord (Lamentations 3:24).
— God's hope will not disappoint you (Romans 5:5).
— You were given hope when you were saved (Romans 8:24).
— You can rejoice in confident hope (Romans 12:12).
— The Scriptures give you hope and encouragement (Romans 15:4).
— You have confident hope for what God has reserved for you in heaven
  (Colossians 1:5).
— God gave you an eternal comfort and a wonderful hope
  (2 Thessalonians 2:16).
— As part of God's house, you remain confident in your hope (Hebrews 3:6).
— Hope is a strong and trustworthy anchor (Hebrews 6:19).

PROVERBS

JON HUNTZINGER, PHD

The wisdom presented in the book of Proverbs, from its beginning to its end, is grounded in the fear of the Lord (1:7; 31:30) and should be read from the perspective of God's covenant with Israel preserved in the Torah. The book is a collection of sayings initiated by King Solomon (1:1), who is responsible for the largest parts of the collection. It also includes contributions from other people over time. A later editor put it into its final form.

An outline of the book of Proverbs is as follows:
— Proverbs 1:1-7 begins the book with an introduction, which joins wisdom to the fear or reverence of God.
— Proverbs 1:8-9:18 follows the introduction with a long discourse about wisdom and foolishness, which are portrayed as two different women: one represents God's covenant with His people, and the other represents idolatry.
— Proverbs 10:1-22:16 and 25:1-29:27 contain numerous individual proverbs from King Solomon.
— Proverbs 22:17-24:34 includes shorter collections of proverbs known as the Sayings of the Wise.
— Proverbs 30 is a collection of the Sayings of Agur.
— Proverbs 31 contains two sections of the Sayings of King Lemuel as spoken to him by his mother. Verses 1-9 are various wise sayings from Lemuel highlighting the life (covenantal) and death (idolatrous) significance of the things people do in life. Verses 10-31 conclude the book with the description of a wise woman.

A primary theological theme of the books of Job and Psalms is also present in Proverbs. A young person can choose one of two paths to walk—the way of righteousness and light in the covenant or the way of foolishness and darkness in idolatry (4:18-19). The metaphor or image of walking draws from the book of Deuteronomy (5:31-33; 8:2-6) where the Israelites are exhorted to walk with God by obeying His commandments. To walk in God's way means to live by the words He has given. Thus,

Follow the steps of the good,
    and stay on the paths of the righteous
        (Proverbs 2:20)

is an exhortation to live by God's Word. When people apply God's Word to their lives, they walk in God's way and show wisdom.

Proverbs was originally compiled as instruction for young men preparing for service to the king. The book concludes with a description of the most excellent woman (31:10-31). The Proverbs woman represents the test of wisdom for these young men. The proof of their understanding of the teaching given throughout Proverbs is found in the kind of women they will choose for their wives. They show they are ready to serve the king by choosing wise women to be their wives, such as the one described in chapter 31.

Jesus employed the wisdom teaching found in the book of Proverbs and throughout the rest of the Old Testament in many of His parables or teachings. When he says, "Wisdom is shown to be right by its results" (Matthew 11:19), He means that the works of His ministry manifest the wisdom of God.

THE PURPOSE OF PROVERBS

1 These are the proverbs of Solomon, David's son, king of Israel.

2 Their purpose is to teach people wisdom and discipline,
   to help them understand the insights of the wise.
3 Their purpose is to teach people to live disciplined and successful lives,
   to help them do what is right, just, and fair.
4 These proverbs will give insight to the simple,
   knowledge and discernment to the young.

5 Let the wise listen to these proverbs and become even wiser.
   Let those with understanding receive guidance
6 by exploring the meaning in these proverbs and parables,
   the words of the wise and their riddles.

7 Fear of the LORD is the foundation of true knowledge,
   but fools despise wisdom and discipline.

A FATHER'S EXHORTATION: ACQUIRE WISDOM

8 My child,* listen when your father corrects you.
   Don't neglect your mother's instruction.
9 What you learn from them will crown you with grace
   and be a chain of honor around your neck.

10 My child, if sinners entice you,
   turn your back on them!
11 They may say, "Come and join us.
   Let's hide and kill someone!
   Just for fun, let's ambush the innocent!
12 Let's swallow them alive, like the grave*;
   let's swallow them whole, like those who go down to the pit of death.
13 Think of the great things we'll get!
   We'll fill our houses with all the stuff we take.
14 Come, throw in your lot with us;
   we'll all share the loot."

15 My child, don't go along with them!
   Stay far away from their paths.
16 They rush to commit evil deeds.
   They hurry to commit murder.
17 If a bird sees a trap being set,
   it knows to stay away.
18 But these people set an ambush for themselves;
   they are trying to get themselves killed.
19 Such is the fate of all who are greedy for money;
   it robs them of life.

WISDOM SHOUTS IN THE STREETS

20 Wisdom shouts in the streets.
   She cries out in the public square.
21 She calls to the crowds along the main street,
   to those gathered in front of the city gate:
22 "How long, you simpletons,
   will you insist on being simpleminded?
   How long will you mockers relish your mocking?
   How long will you fools hate knowledge?
23 Come and listen to my counsel.
   I'll share my heart with you
   and make you wise.

24 "I called you so often, but you wouldn't come.
   I reached out to you, but you paid no attention.
25 You ignored my advice
   and rejected the correction I offered.
26 So I will laugh when you are in trouble!
   I will mock you when disaster overtakes you—
27 when calamity overtakes you like a storm,
   when disaster engulfs you like a cyclone,
   and anguish and distress overwhelm you.

28 "When they cry for help, I will not answer.
   Though they anxiously search for me,
   they will not find me.
29 For they hated knowledge
   and chose not to fear the LORD.
30 They rejected my advice
   and paid no attention when I corrected them.
31 Therefore, they must eat the bitter fruit of living their own way,
   choking on their own schemes.
32 For simpletons turn away from me—to death.
   Fools are destroyed by their own complacency.
33 But all who listen to me will live in peace,
   untroubled by fear of harm."

THE BENEFITS OF WISDOM

2 1 My child,* listen to what I say,
   and treasure my commands.
2 Tune your ears to wisdom,
   and concentrate on understanding.
3 Cry out for insight,
   and ask for understanding.
4 Search for them as you would for silver;
   seek them like hidden treasures.
5 Then you will understand what it means to fear the LORD,
   and you will gain knowledge of God.
6 For the LORD grants wisdom!
   From his mouth come knowledge and understanding.

1:8 Hebrew My son; also in 1:10, 15.   1:12 Hebrew like Sheol.
2:1 Hebrew My son.

⁷ He grants a treasure of common sense to
the honest.
He is a shield to those who walk with
integrity.
⁸ He guards the paths of the just
and protects those who are faithful to him.

⁹ Then you will understand what is right,
just, and fair,
and you will find the right way to go.
¹⁰ For wisdom will enter your heart,
and knowledge will fill you with joy.
¹¹ Wise choices will watch over you.
Understanding will keep you safe.

¹² Wisdom will save you from evil people,
from those whose words are twisted.
¹³ These men turn from the right way
to walk down dark paths.
¹⁴ They take pleasure in doing wrong,
and they enjoy the twisted ways of evil.
¹⁵ Their actions are crooked,
and their ways are wrong.

¹⁶ Wisdom will save you from the immoral
woman,
from the seductive words of the
promiscuous woman.
¹⁷ She has abandoned her husband
and ignores the covenant she made
before God.
¹⁸ Entering her house leads to death;
it is the road to the grave.*
¹⁹ The man who visits her is doomed.
He will never reach the paths of life.

²⁰ So follow the steps of the good,
and stay on the paths of the righteous.
²¹ For only the godly will live in the land,
and those with integrity will remain in it.
²² But the wicked will be removed from
the land,
and the treacherous will be uprooted.

TRUSTING IN THE LORD

3 ¹ My child,* never forget the things
I have taught you.
Store my commands in your heart.
² If you do this, you will live many years,
and your life will be satisfying.
³ Never let loyalty and kindness leave you!
Tie them around your neck as a reminder.
Write them deep within your heart.
⁴ Then you will find favor with both God
and people,
and you will earn a good reputation.

⁵ Trust in the LORD with all your heart;
do not depend on your own
understanding.
⁶ Seek his will in all you do,
and he will show you which path to take.

⁷ Don't be impressed with your own wisdom.
Instead, fear the LORD and turn away
from evil.
⁸ Then you will have healing for your body
and strength for your bones.

⁹ Honor the LORD with your wealth
and with the best part of everything
you produce.
¹⁰ Then he will fill your barns with grain,
and your vats will overflow with
good wine.

¹¹ My child, don't reject the LORD's discipline,
and don't be upset when he corrects you.
¹² For the LORD corrects those he loves,
just as a father corrects a child in whom
he delights.*

¹³ Joyful is the person who finds wisdom,
the one who gains understanding.
¹⁴ For wisdom is more profitable than silver,
and her wages are better than gold.
¹⁵ Wisdom is more precious than rubies;
nothing you desire can compare with her.
¹⁶ She offers you long life in her right hand,
and riches and honor in her left.
¹⁷ She will guide you down delightful paths;
all her ways are satisfying.
¹⁸ Wisdom is a tree of life to those who
embrace her;
happy are those who hold her tightly.

¹⁹ By wisdom the LORD founded the earth;
by understanding he created the heavens.
²⁰ By his knowledge the deep fountains of the
earth burst forth,
and the dew settles beneath
the night sky.

²¹ My child, don't lose sight of common sense
and discernment.
Hang on to them,
²² for they will refresh your soul.
They are like jewels on a necklace.
²³ They keep you safe on your way,
and your feet will not stumble.
²⁴ You can go to bed without fear;
you will lie down and sleep soundly.
²⁵ You need not be afraid of sudden disaster
or the destruction that comes upon
the wicked,
²⁶ for the LORD is your security.
He will keep your foot from being caught
in a trap.

²⁷ Do not withhold good from those who
deserve it
when it's in your power to help them.

2:18 Hebrew *to the spirits of the dead.* 3:1 Hebrew *My son;* also in
3:11, 21. 3:12 Greek version reads *loves, / and he punishes those he
accepts as his children.* Compare Heb 12:6.

²⁸ If you can help your neighbor now, don't say,
"Come back tomorrow, and then
I'll help you."

²⁹ Don't plot harm against your neighbor,
for those who live nearby trust you.

³⁰ Don't pick a fight without reason,
when no one has done you harm.

³¹ Don't envy violent people
or copy their ways.

³² Such wicked people are detestable to
the LORD,
but he offers his friendship to the godly.

³³ The LORD curses the house of the wicked,
but he blesses the home of the upright.

³⁴ The LORD mocks the mockers
but is gracious to the humble.*

³⁵ The wise inherit honor,
but fools are put to shame!

A FATHER'S WISE ADVICE

4 ¹ My children,* listen when your father
corrects you.
Pay attention and learn good judgment,
² for I am giving you good guidance.
Don't turn away from my instructions.
³ For I, too, was once my father's son,
tenderly loved as my mother's only child.

⁴ My father taught me,
"Take my words to heart.
Follow my commands, and you will live.
⁵ Get wisdom; develop good judgment.
Don't forget my words or turn away
from them.
⁶ Don't turn your back on wisdom,
for she will protect you.
Love her, and she will guard you.
⁷ Getting wisdom is the wisest thing
you can do!
And whatever else you do,
develop good judgment.
⁸ If you prize wisdom,
she will make you great.
Embrace her, and she will honor you.
⁹ She will place a lovely wreath on your head;
she will present you with
a beautiful crown."

¹⁰ My child,* listen to me and do as I say,
and you will have a long, good life.
¹¹ I will teach you wisdom's ways
and lead you in straight paths.
¹² When you walk, you won't be held back;
when you run, you won't stumble.
¹³ Take hold of my instructions; don't let
them go.
Guard them, for they are the key to life.

¹⁴ Don't do as the wicked do,
and don't follow the path of evildoers.
¹⁵ Don't even think about it; don't go that way.
Turn away and keep moving.
¹⁶ For evil people can't sleep until they've done
their evil deed for the day.
They can't rest until they've caused
someone to stumble.
¹⁷ They eat the food of wickedness
and drink the wine of violence!

¹⁸ The way of the righteous is like the first
gleam of dawn,
which shines ever brighter until the full
light of day.
¹⁹ But the way of the wicked is like
total darkness.
They have no idea what they are
stumbling over.

²⁰ My child, pay attention to what I say.
Listen carefully to my words.
²¹ Don't lose sight of them.
Let them penetrate deep into your heart,
²² for they bring life to those who find them,
and healing to their whole body.

²³ Guard your heart above all else,
for it determines the course of your life.

²⁴ Avoid all perverse talk;
stay away from corrupt speech.

²⁵ Look straight ahead,
and fix your eyes on what lies
before you.
²⁶ Mark out a straight path for your feet;
stay on the safe path.
²⁷ Don't get sidetracked;
keep your feet from following evil.

AVOID IMMORAL WOMEN

5 ¹ My son, pay attention to my wisdom;
listen carefully to my wise counsel.
² Then you will show discernment,
and your lips will express what
you've learned.
³ For the lips of an immoral woman are as
sweet as honey,
and her mouth is smoother than oil.
⁴ But in the end she is as bitter as poison,
as dangerous as a double-edged sword.
⁵ Her feet go down to death;
her steps lead straight to the grave.*
⁶ For she cares nothing about the path
to life.
She staggers down a crooked trail and
doesn't realize it.

3:34 Greek version reads *The LORD opposes the proud / but gives
grace to the humble.* Compare Jas 4:6; 1 Pet 5:5. **4:1** Hebrew *My
sons.* **4:10** Hebrew *My son;* also in 4:20. **5:5** Hebrew *to Sheol.*

HEALTHY SEXUALITY
Proverbs 5   JACK HAYFORD

The subject of sexuality captures the attention of believers and nonbelievers alike. It is at the heart of our identity, creativity, and personality. Sadly, it is also a topic the world has demeaned and degraded until it barely resembles God's intent. Those who reject God's truth regarding sex are ever searching but never satisfied.

Sexual fulfillment is found in the marital relationship, which Scripture defines as a lifelong covenant between one man and one woman (Matthew 19:3–9). In marriage, spouses should have a loving and healthy physical relationship. This relationship grows as they learn to be tenderhearted and sensitive to one another's needs. Sex is not strange, nor is it filled with worldly pursuits. God designed sex to be physically safe, personally satisfying, and part of a fulfilling private life between a husband and wife.

7 So now, my sons, listen to me.
Never stray from what I am about to say:
8 Stay away from her!
Don't go near the door of her house!
9 If you do, you will lose your honor
and will lose to merciless people all you
have achieved.
10 Strangers will consume your wealth,
and someone else will enjoy the fruit of
your labor.
11 In the end you will groan in anguish
when disease consumes your body.
12 You will say, "How I hated discipline!
If only I had not ignored all the warnings!
13 Oh, why didn't I listen to my teachers?
Why didn't I pay attention to my
instructors?
14 I have come to the brink of utter ruin,
and now I must face public disgrace."

15 Drink water from your own well—
share your love only with your wife.*
16 Why spill the water of your springs
in the streets,
having sex with just anyone?*
17 You should reserve it for yourselves.
Never share it with strangers.
18 Let your wife be a fountain of blessing for you.
Rejoice in the wife of your youth.
19 She is a loving deer, a graceful doe.
Let her breasts satisfy you always.
May you always be captivated by her love.
20 Why be captivated, my son,
by an immoral woman,
or fondle the breasts of a promiscuous
woman?

21 For the LORD sees clearly what a man does,
examining every path he takes.
22 An evil man is held captive by his own sins;
they are ropes that catch and hold him.
23 He will die for lack of self-control;
he will be lost because of his great
foolishness.

LESSONS FOR DAILY LIFE

6 1 My child,* if you have put up security
for a friend's debt
or agreed to guarantee the debt of
a stranger—
2 if you have trapped yourself by
your agreement
and are caught by what you said—
3 follow my advice and save yourself,
for you have placed yourself at your
friend's mercy.
Now swallow your pride;
go and beg to have your name erased.
4 Don't put it off; do it now!
Don't rest until you do.
5 Save yourself like a gazelle escaping
from a hunter,
like a bird fleeing from a net.

6 Take a lesson from the ants, you lazybones.
Learn from their ways and become wise!
7 Though they have no prince
or governor or ruler to make them work,
8 they labor hard all summer,
gathering food for the winter.
9 But you, lazybones, how long will you sleep?
When will you wake up?
10 A little extra sleep, a little more slumber,
a little folding of the hands to rest—
11 then poverty will pounce on you like a bandit;
scarcity will attack you like an
armed robber.

12 What are worthless and wicked people like?
They are constant liars,
13 signaling their deceit with a wink of the eye,
a nudge of the foot, or the wiggle of fingers.
14 Their perverted hearts plot evil,
and they constantly stir up trouble.
15 But they will be destroyed suddenly,
broken in an instant beyond all hope
of healing.

16 There are six things the LORD hates—
no, seven things he detests:
17 haughty eyes,
a lying tongue,
hands that kill the innocent,
18 a heart that plots evil,
feet that race to do wrong,

5:15 Hebrew *Drink water from your own cistern, / flowing water from your own well.* 5:16 Hebrew *Why spill your springs in the streets, / your streams in the city squares?* 6:1 Hebrew *My son.*

¹⁹ a false witness who pours out lies,
a person who sows discord in a family.

²⁰ My son, obey your father's commands,
and don't neglect your mother's instruction.
²¹ Keep their words always in your heart.
Tie them around your neck.
²² When you walk, their counsel will lead you.
When you sleep, they will protect you.
When you wake up, they will advise you.
²³ For their command is a lamp
and their instruction a light;
their corrective discipline
is the way to life.
²⁴ It will keep you from the immoral woman,
from the smooth tongue of
a promiscuous woman.
²⁵ Don't lust for her beauty.
Don't let her coy glances seduce you.
²⁶ For a prostitute will bring you to poverty,*
but sleeping with another man's wife
will cost you your life.
²⁷ Can a man scoop a flame into his lap
and not have his clothes catch on fire?
²⁸ Can he walk on hot coals
and not blister his feet?
²⁹ So it is with the man who sleeps with
another man's wife.
He who embraces her will not go
unpunished.

³⁰ Excuses might be found for a thief
who steals because he is starving.
³¹ But if he is caught, he must pay back seven
times what he stole,
even if he has to sell everything in his
house.
³² But the man who commits adultery is
an utter fool,
for he destroys himself.
³³ He will be wounded and disgraced.
His shame will never be erased.
³⁴ For the woman's jealous husband will be
furious,
and he will show no mercy when he
takes revenge.
³⁵ He will accept no compensation,
nor be satisfied with a payoff of any size.

ANOTHER WARNING ABOUT IMMORAL WOMEN

7 ¹ Follow my advice, my son;
always treasure my commands.
² Obey my commands and live!
Guard my instructions as you guard
your own eyes.*
³ Tie them on your fingers as a reminder.
Write them deep within your heart.

⁴ Love wisdom like a sister;
make insight a beloved member of
your family.

⁵ Let them protect you from an affair with
an immoral woman,
from listening to the flattery of
a promiscuous woman.

⁶ While I was at the window of my house,
looking through the curtain,
⁷ I saw some naive young men,
and one in particular who lacked
common sense.
⁸ He was crossing the street near the house of
an immoral woman,
strolling down the path by her house.
⁹ It was at twilight, in the evening,
as deep darkness fell.
¹⁰ The woman approached him,
seductively dressed and sly of heart.
¹¹ She was the brash, rebellious type,
never content to stay at home.
¹² She is often in the streets and markets,
soliciting at every corner.
¹³ She threw her arms around him
and kissed him,
and with a brazen look she said,
¹⁴ "I've just made my peace offerings
and fulfilled my vows.
¹⁵ You're the one I was looking for!
I came out to find you, and here you are!
¹⁶ My bed is spread with beautiful blankets,
with colored sheets of Egyptian linen.
¹⁷ I've perfumed my bed
with myrrh, aloes, and cinnamon.
¹⁸ Come, let's drink our fill of love
until morning.
Let's enjoy each other's caresses,
¹⁹ for my husband is not home.
He's away on a long trip.
²⁰ He has taken a wallet full of money with him
and won't return until later this month.*"

²¹ So she seduced him with her pretty speech
and enticed him with her flattery.
²² He followed her at once,
like an ox going to the slaughter.
He was like a stag caught in a trap,*
²³ awaiting the arrow that would pierce its
heart.
He was like a bird flying into a snare,
little knowing it would cost him his life.

²⁴ So listen to me, my sons,
and pay attention to my words.
²⁵ Don't let your hearts stray away toward her.
Don't wander down her wayward path.
²⁶ For she has been the ruin of many;
many men have been her victims.
²⁷ Her house is the road to the grave.*
Her bedroom is the den of death.

6:26 Hebrew *to a loaf of bread.* **7:2** Hebrew *as the pupil of your eye.* **7:20** Hebrew *until the moon is full.* **7:22** As in Greek and Syriac versions; Hebrew reads *slaughter,* as shackles are for the discipline of a fool. **7:27** Hebrew *to Sheol.*

FIGHTING FOR YOUR LIFE
Proverbs 7

ROBERT MORRIS

Immorality is rampant today in our culture and even in our churches. Why? Because lust is one of the most subtle and deceiving spirits there is. It had a huge stronghold in me before I became a believer and even a few years afterward. Proverbs 7 describes how the spirit of lust operates:

1. **Desire**
   The word *lust* actually means 'desire.' Every person has a God-given, natural, and healthy desire for sex. However, Satan takes this pure desire and turns it into the lust of the flesh, which is evil and deceitful. First John 2:16 says, "The world offers only a craving for physical pleasure, a craving for everything we see."

2. **Deception**
   Lust is a liar. It says we will be happy if we give in to temptation, but it just makes our cravings worse. Lust promises to satisfy us, but it never does (Proverbs 27:20).

3. **Death**
   Proverbs 7:27 describes the immoral woman's house as "the road to the grave" and her bedroom as "the den of death." Love brings life, but lust always results in death. How many marriages have died due to lust? How many families have been sacrificed because desires

went the wrong way? Satan is a thief, and the spirit of lust will always rob you of life.

If lust is such a serious problem, what is the solution? Deliverance and discipleship.

Demons cannot be discipled; they have to be cast out. Jesus spent a third of His ministry casting demons out and told His disciples to do the same (Matthew 10:8).

In 2 Corinthians 10:4, the apostle Paul writes, "We use God's mighty weapons, not worldly weapons, to knock down the strongholds of human reasoning and to destroy false arguments." In this passage, a *stronghold* represents a way of thinking. Our minds are like Grand Central Station with trains of thought pulling in and out every few seconds. Godly thoughts lead to freedom, life, and creativity. Lustful thoughts, however, lead to bondage and death. Your destiny depends on which train you board.

To overcome lust, you must discipline your mind and fill it with the Word of God. Capture rebellious thoughts and make them obedient to Christ (2 Corinthians 10:5; 1 Peter 2:11). And as Paul instructs, "Fix your thoughts on what is true, and honorable, and right, and pure, and lovely, and admirable. Think about things that are excellent and worthy of praise" (Philippians 4:8).

WISDOM CALLS FOR A HEARING

8 ¹ Listen as Wisdom calls out!
　　Hear as understanding raises
　　　her voice!
² On the hilltop along the road,
　　she takes her stand at the crossroads.
³ By the gates at the entrance to the town,
　　on the road leading in, she cries aloud,
⁴ "I call to you, to all of you!
　　I raise my voice to all people.
⁵ You simple people, use good judgment.
　　You foolish people,
　　　show some understanding.
⁶ Listen to me! For I have important things
　　to tell you.
　　Everything I say is right,
⁷ for I speak the truth
　　and detest every kind of deception.
⁸ My advice is wholesome.
　　There is nothing devious or crooked in it.
⁹ My words are plain to anyone
　　with understanding,
　　clear to those with knowledge.
¹⁰ Choose my instruction rather than silver,
　　and knowledge rather than pure gold.
¹¹ For wisdom is far more valuable
　　than rubies.
　　Nothing you desire can compare with it.

¹² "I, Wisdom, live together with
　　good judgment.
　　I know where to discover knowledge and
　　discernment.
¹³ All who fear the LORD will hate evil.
　　Therefore, I hate pride and arrogance,
　　corruption and perverse speech.
¹⁴ Common sense and success belong to me.
　　Insight and strength are mine.
¹⁵ Because of me, kings reign,
　　and rulers make just decrees.
¹⁶ Rulers lead with my help,
　　and nobles make righteous judgments.*
¹⁷ "I love all who love me.
　　Those who search will surely find me.
¹⁸ I have riches and honor,
　　as well as enduring wealth and justice.
¹⁹ My gifts are better than gold, even the
　　purest gold,
　　my wages better than sterling silver!
²⁰ I walk in righteousness,
　　in paths of justice.
²¹ Those who love me inherit wealth.
　　I will fill their treasuries.

8:16 Some Hebrew manuscripts and Greek version read *and nobles are judges over the earth.*

²² "The LORD formed me from the beginning,
    before he created anything else.
²³ I was appointed in ages past,
    at the very first, before the earth began.
²⁴ I was born before the oceans were created,
    before the springs bubbled forth
        their waters.
²⁵ Before the mountains were formed,
    before the hills, I was born—
²⁶ before he had made the earth and fields
    and the first handfuls of soil.
²⁷ I was there when he established the heavens,
    when he drew the horizon on the oceans.
²⁸ I was there when he set the clouds above,
    when he established springs deep in
        the earth.
²⁹ I was there when he set the limits of the seas,
    so they would not spread beyond their
        boundaries.
    And when he marked off the earth's
        foundations,
³⁰   I was the architect at his side.
    I was his constant delight,
    rejoicing always in his presence.
³¹ And how happy I was with the world
        he created;
    how I rejoiced with the human family!

³² "And so, my children,* listen to me,
    for all who follow my ways are joyful.
³³ Listen to my instruction and be wise.
    Don't ignore it.
³⁴ Joyful are those who listen to me,
    watching for me daily at my gates,
    waiting for me outside my home!
³⁵ For whoever finds me finds life
    and receives favor from the LORD.
³⁶ But those who miss me injure themselves.
    All who hate me love death."

9
¹ Wisdom has built her house;
    she has carved its seven columns.
² She has prepared a great banquet,
    mixed the wines, and set the table.
³ She has sent her servants to invite everyone
        to come.
    She calls out from the heights overlooking
        the city.
⁴ "Come in with me," she urges the simple.
    To those who lack good judgment, she says,
⁵ "Come, eat my food,
    and drink the wine I have mixed.
⁶ Leave your simple ways behind,
        and begin to live;
    learn to use good judgment."

⁷ Anyone who rebukes a mocker will get
        an insult in return.
    Anyone who corrects the wicked
        will get hurt.
⁸ So don't bother correcting mockers;
    they will only hate you.

But correct the wise,
    and they will love you.
⁹ Instruct the wise,
    and they will be even wiser.
Teach the righteous,
    and they will learn even more.

¹⁰ Fear of the LORD is the foundation of wisdom.
    Knowledge of the Holy One results in
        good judgment.

¹¹ Wisdom will multiply your days
    and add years to your life.
¹² If you become wise, you will be the one
        to benefit.
    If you scorn wisdom, you will be the one
        to suffer.

FOLLY CALLS FOR A HEARING

¹³ The woman named Folly is brash.
    She is ignorant and doesn't know it.
¹⁴ She sits in her doorway
    on the heights overlooking the city.
¹⁵ She calls out to men going by
    who are minding their own business.
¹⁶ "Come in with me," she urges the simple.
    To those who lack good judgment, she says,
¹⁷ "Stolen water is refreshing;
    food eaten in secret tastes the best!"
¹⁸ But little do they know that the dead
        are there.
    Her guests are in the depths of the grave.*

THE PROVERBS OF SOLOMON

10 The proverbs of Solomon:

A wise child* brings joy to a father;
    a foolish child brings grief to a mother.

² Tainted wealth has no lasting value,
    but right living can save your life.

³ The LORD will not let the godly go hungry,
    but he refuses to satisfy the craving of
        the wicked.

⁴ Lazy people are soon poor;
    hard workers get rich.

⁵ A wise youth harvests in the summer,
    but one who sleeps during harvest
        is a disgrace.

⁶ The godly are showered with blessings;
    the words of the wicked conceal
        violent intentions.

⁷ We have happy memories of the godly,
    but the name of a wicked person rots away.

8:32 Hebrew *my sons.* 9:18 Hebrew *in Sheol.* 10:1 Hebrew *son;*
also in 10:1b.

8 The wise are glad to be instructed,
  but babbling fools fall flat on their faces.

9 People with integrity walk safely,
  but those who follow crooked paths will
    be exposed.

10 People who wink at wrong cause trouble,
  but a bold reproof promotes peace.*

11 The words of the godly are a life-giving
    fountain;
  the words of the wicked conceal violent
    intentions.

12 Hatred stirs up quarrels,
  but love makes up for all offenses.

13 Wise words come from the lips of people
    with understanding,
  but those lacking sense will be beaten
    with a rod.

14 Wise people treasure knowledge,
  but the babbling of a fool invites disaster.

15 The wealth of the rich is their fortress;
  the poverty of the poor is their
    destruction.

16 The earnings of the godly enhance their lives,
  but evil people squander their money
    on sin.

17 People who accept discipline are on the
    pathway to life,
  but those who ignore correction will
    go astray.

18 Hiding hatred makes you a liar;
  slandering others makes you a fool.

19 Too much talk leads to sin.
  Be sensible and keep your mouth shut.

20 The words of the godly are like sterling silver;
  the heart of a fool is worthless.

21 The words of the godly encourage many,
  but fools are destroyed by their lack of
    common sense.

22 The blessing of the LORD makes
    a person rich,
  and he adds no sorrow with it.

23 Doing wrong is fun for a fool,
  but living wisely brings pleasure to the
    sensible.

24 The fears of the wicked will be fulfilled;
  the hopes of the godly will be granted.

25 When the storms of life come, the wicked
    are whirled away,
  but the godly have a lasting foundation.

26 Lazy people irritate their employers,
  like vinegar to the teeth or smoke in
    the eyes.

27 Fear of the LORD lengthens one's life,
  but the years of the wicked are cut short.

28 The hopes of the godly result in happiness,
  but the expectations of the wicked come
    to nothing.

29 The way of the LORD is a stronghold to those
    with integrity,
  but it destroys the wicked.

30 The godly will never be disturbed,
  but the wicked will be removed from
    the land.

31 The mouth of the godly person gives
    wise advice,
  but the tongue that deceives will be
    cut off.

32 The lips of the godly speak helpful words,
  but the mouth of the wicked speaks
    perverse words.

11 1 The LORD detests the use of
    dishonest scales,
  but he delights in accurate weights.

2 Pride leads to disgrace,
  but with humility comes wisdom.

3 Honesty guides good people;
  dishonesty destroys treacherous people.

4 Riches won't help on the day of judgment,
  but right living can save you from death.

5 The godly are directed by honesty;
  the wicked fall beneath their load of sin.

6 The godliness of good people rescues them;
  the ambition of treacherous people
    traps them.

7 When the wicked die,
  their hopes die with them,
  for they rely on their own feeble strength.

8 The godly are rescued from trouble,
  and it falls on the wicked instead.

10:10 As in Greek version; Hebrew reads *but babbling fools fall flat on their faces.*

⁹ With their words, the godless destroy
their friends,
but knowledge will rescue the righteous.

¹⁰ The whole city celebrates when the
godly succeed;
they shout for joy when the wicked die.

¹¹ Upright citizens are good for a city and
make it prosper,
but the talk of the wicked tears it apart.

¹² It is foolish to belittle one's neighbor;
a sensible person keeps quiet.

¹³ A gossip goes around telling secrets,
but those who are trustworthy can keep a
confidence.

¹⁴ Without wise leadership, a nation falls;
there is safety in having many advisers.

¹⁵ There's danger in putting up security
for a stranger's debt;
it's safer not to guarantee another
person's debt.

¹⁶ A gracious woman gains respect,
but ruthless men gain only wealth.

¹⁷ Your kindness will reward you,
but your cruelty will destroy you.

¹⁸ Evil people get rich for the moment,
but the reward of the godly will last.

¹⁹ Godly people find life;
evil people find death.

²⁰ The LORD detests people with crooked hearts,
but he delights in those with integrity.

²¹ Evil people will surely be punished,
but the children of the godly will go free.

²² A beautiful woman who lacks discretion
is like a gold ring in a pig's snout.

²³ The godly can look forward to a reward,
while the wicked can expect only
judgment.

²⁴ Give freely and become more wealthy;
be stingy and lose everything.

²⁵ The generous will prosper;
those who refresh others will themselves
be refreshed.

²⁶ People curse those who hoard their grain,
but they bless the one who sells in time
of need.

²⁷ If you search for good, you will find favor;
but if you search for evil, it will find you!

²⁸ Trust in your money and down you go!
But the godly flourish like leaves in
spring.

²⁹ Those who bring trouble on their families
inherit the wind.
The fool will be a servant to the wise.

³⁰ The seeds of good deeds become
a tree of life;
a wise person wins friends.*

³¹ If the righteous are rewarded here on earth,
what will happen to wicked sinners?*

12 ¹ To learn, you must love discipline;
it is stupid to hate correction.

² The LORD approves of those who are good,
but he condemns those who plan
wickedness.

³ Wickedness never brings stability,
but the godly have deep roots.

⁴ A worthy wife is a crown for her husband,
but a disgraceful woman is like cancer
in his bones.

⁵ The plans of the godly are just;
the advice of the wicked is treacherous.

⁶ The words of the wicked are like a
murderous ambush,
but the words of the godly save lives.

⁷ The wicked die and disappear,
but the family of the godly stands firm.

⁸ A sensible person wins admiration,
but a warped mind is despised.

⁹ Better to be an ordinary person with
a servant
than to be self-important but have no food.

¹⁰ The godly care for their animals,
but the wicked are always cruel.

¹¹ A hard worker has plenty of food,
but a person who chases fantasies has
no sense.

¹² Thieves are jealous of each other's loot,
but the godly are well rooted and bear
their own fruit.

11:30 Or *and those who win souls are wise.*   11:31 Greek version
reads *If the righteous are barely saved, / what will happen to godless
sinners?* Compare 1 Pet 4:18.

¹³ The wicked are trapped by their own words,
   but the godly escape such trouble.

¹⁴ Wise words bring many benefits,
   and hard work brings rewards.

¹⁵ Fools think their own way is right,
   but the wise listen to others.

¹⁶ A fool is quick-tempered,
   but a wise person stays calm when insulted.

¹⁷ An honest witness tells the truth;
   a false witness tells lies.

¹⁸ Some people make cutting remarks,
   but the words of the wise bring healing.

¹⁹ Truthful words stand the test of time,
   but lies are soon exposed.

²⁰ Deceit fills hearts that are plotting evil;
   joy fills hearts that are planning peace!

²¹ No harm comes to the godly,
   but the wicked have their fill of trouble.

²² The LORD detests lying lips,
   but he delights in those who tell the truth.

²³ The wise don't make a show of their
      knowledge,
   but fools broadcast their foolishness.

²⁴ Work hard and become a leader;
   be lazy and become a slave.

²⁵ Worry weighs a person down;
   an encouraging word cheers a person up.

²⁶ The godly give good advice to their friends;*
   the wicked lead them astray.

²⁷ Lazy people don't even cook the game
      they catch,
   but the diligent make use of everything
      they find.

²⁸ The way of the godly leads to life;
   that path does not lead to death.

13 ¹ A wise child accepts a parent's
      discipline;*
   a mocker refuses to listen to correction.

² Wise words will win you a good meal,
   but treacherous people have an appetite
      for violence.

³ Those who control their tongue will have
      a long life;
   opening your mouth can ruin everything.

⁴ Lazy people want much but get little,
   but those who work hard will prosper.

⁵ The godly hate lies;
   the wicked cause shame and disgrace.

⁶ Godliness guards the path of the blameless,
   but the evil are misled by sin.

⁷ Some who are poor pretend to be rich;
   others who are rich pretend to be poor.

⁸ The rich can pay a ransom for their lives,
   but the poor won't even get threatened.

⁹ The life of the godly is full of light and joy,
   but the light of the wicked will be
      snuffed out.

¹⁰ Pride leads to conflict;
   those who take advice are wise.

¹¹ Wealth from get-rich-quick schemes
      quickly disappears;
   wealth from hard work grows over time.

¹² Hope deferred makes the heart sick,
   but a dream fulfilled is a tree of life.

¹³ People who despise advice are asking for
      trouble;
   those who respect a command will succeed.

¹⁴ The instruction of the wise is like a
      life-giving fountain;
   those who accept it avoid the snares
      of death.

¹⁵ A person with good sense is respected;
   a treacherous person is headed for
      destruction.*

¹⁶ Wise people think before they act;
   fools don't—and even brag about their
      foolishness.

¹⁷ An unreliable messenger stumbles
      into trouble,
   but a reliable messenger brings healing.

¹⁸ If you ignore criticism, you will end in
      poverty and disgrace;
   if you accept correction,
      you will be honored.

¹⁹ It is pleasant to see dreams come true,
   but fools refuse to turn from evil to
      attain them.

12:26 Or *The godly are cautious in friendship;* or *The godly are freed from evil.* The meaning of the Hebrew is uncertain.   13:1 Hebrew *A wise son accepts his father's discipline.*   13:15 As in Greek version; Hebrew reads *the way of the treacherous is lasting.*

²⁰ Walk with the wise and become wise;
    associate with fools and get in trouble.

²¹ Trouble chases sinners,
    while blessings reward the righteous.

²² Good people leave an inheritance to their
    grandchildren,
    but the sinner's wealth passes to the godly.

²³ A poor person's farm may produce much
    food,
    but injustice sweeps it all away.

²⁴ Those who spare the rod of discipline hate
    their children.
    Those who love their children care
    enough to discipline them.

²⁵ The godly eat to their hearts' content,
    but the belly of the wicked goes hungry.

14

¹ A wise woman builds her home,
    but a foolish woman tears it down
    with her own hands.

² Those who follow the right path fear
    the LORD;
    those who take the wrong path
    despise him.

³ A fool's proud talk becomes a rod that beats
    him,
    but the words of the wise keep them safe.

⁴ Without oxen a stable stays clean,
    but you need a strong ox for
    a large harvest.

⁵ An honest witness does not lie;
    a false witness breathes lies.

⁶ A mocker seeks wisdom and never finds it,
    but knowledge comes easily to those with
    understanding.

⁷ Stay away from fools,
    for you won't find knowledge on their lips.

⁸ The prudent understand where they
    are going,
    but fools deceive themselves.

⁹ Fools make fun of guilt,
    but the godly acknowledge it and seek
    reconciliation.

¹⁰ Each heart knows its own bitterness,
    and no one else can fully share its joy.

¹¹ The house of the wicked will be destroyed,
    but the tent of the godly will flourish.

¹² There is a path before each person that
    seems right,
    but it ends in death.

¹³ Laughter can conceal a heavy heart,
    but when the laughter ends,
    the grief remains.

¹⁴ Backsliders get what they deserve;
    good people receive their reward.

¹⁵ Only simpletons believe everything
    they're told!
    The prudent carefully consider
    their steps.

¹⁶ The wise are cautious* and avoid danger;
    fools plunge ahead with reckless
    confidence.

¹⁷ Short-tempered people do foolish things,
    and schemers are hated.

¹⁸ Simpletons are clothed with foolishness,*
    but the prudent are crowned with
    knowledge.

¹⁹ Evil people will bow before good people;
    the wicked will bow at the gates of
    the godly.

²⁰ The poor are despised even by their
    neighbors,
    while the rich have many "friends."

²¹ It is a sin to belittle one's neighbor;
    blessed are those who help the poor.

²² If you plan to do evil, you will be lost;
    if you plan to do good, you will receive
    unfailing love and faithfulness.

²³ Work brings profit,
    but mere talk leads to poverty!

²⁴ Wealth is a crown for the wise;
    the effort of fools yields only foolishness.

²⁵ A truthful witness saves lives,
    but a false witness is a traitor.

²⁶ Those who fear the LORD are secure;
    he will be a refuge for their children.

²⁷ Fear of the LORD is a life-giving fountain;
    it offers escape from the snares of death.

²⁸ A growing population is a king's glory;
    a prince without subjects has nothing.

14:16 Hebrew *The wise fear.*   14:18 Or *inherit foolishness.*

²⁹ People with understanding control
  their anger;
  a hot temper shows great foolishness.

³⁰ A peaceful heart leads to a healthy body;
  jealousy is like cancer in the bones.

³¹ Those who oppress the poor insult
  their Maker,
  but helping the poor honors him.

³² The wicked are crushed by disaster,
  but the godly have a refuge when they die.

³³ Wisdom is enshrined in
  an understanding heart;
  wisdom is not* found among fools.

³⁴ Godliness makes a nation great,
  but sin is a disgrace to any people.

³⁵ A king rejoices in wise servants
  but is angry with those who disgrace him.

15

¹ A gentle answer deflects anger,
  but harsh words make tempers flare.

² The tongue of the wise makes knowledge
  appealing,
  but the mouth of a fool belches out
  foolishness.

³ The LORD is watching everywhere,
  keeping his eye on both the evil and
  the good.

⁴ Gentle words are a tree of life;
  a deceitful tongue crushes the spirit.

⁵ Only a fool despises a parent's* discipline;
  whoever learns from correction is wise.

⁶ There is treasure in the house of the godly,
  but the earnings of the wicked bring
  trouble.

⁷ The lips of the wise give good advice;
  the heart of a fool has none to give.

⁸ The LORD detests the sacrifice of the wicked,
  but he delights in the prayers of
  the upright.

⁹ The LORD detests the way of the wicked,
  but he loves those who pursue godliness.

¹⁰ Whoever abandons the right path will be
  severely disciplined;
  whoever hates correction will die.

¹¹ Even Death and Destruction* hold no secrets
  from the LORD.

How much more does he know
  the human heart!

¹² Mockers hate to be corrected,
  so they stay away from the wise.

¹³ A glad heart makes a happy face;
  a broken heart crushes the spirit.

¹⁴ A wise person is hungry for knowledge,
  while the fool feeds on trash.

¹⁵ For the despondent,
  every day brings trouble;
  for the happy heart,
  life is a continual feast.

¹⁶ Better to have little, with fear for the LORD,
  than to have great treasure and inner
  turmoil.

¹⁷ A bowl of vegetables with someone you love
  is better than steak with someone
  you hate.

¹⁸ A hot-tempered person starts fights;
  a cool-tempered person stops them.

¹⁹ A lazy person's way is blocked with briers,
  but the path of the upright is an open
  highway.

²⁰ Sensible children bring joy to their father;
  foolish children despise their mother.

²¹ Foolishness brings joy to those with
  no sense;
  a sensible person stays on the right path.

²² Plans go wrong for lack of advice;
  many advisers bring success.

²³ Everyone enjoys a fitting reply;
  it is wonderful to say the right thing at
  the right time!

²⁴ The path of life leads upward for the wise;
  they leave the grave* behind.

²⁵ The LORD tears down the house of
  the proud,
  but he protects the property of widows.

²⁶ The LORD detests evil plans,
  but he delights in pure words.

²⁷ Greed brings grief to the whole family,
  but those who hate bribes will live.

14:33 As in Greek and Syriac versions; Hebrew lacks *not*.
15:5 Hebrew *father's*.   15:11 Hebrew *Sheol and Abaddon*.
15:24 Hebrew *Sheol*.

28 The heart of the godly thinks carefully
    before speaking;
    the mouth of the wicked overflows with
    evil words.

29 The LORD is far from the wicked,
    but he hears the prayers of
    the righteous.

30 A cheerful look brings joy to the heart;
    good news makes for good health.

31 If you listen to constructive criticism,
    you will be at home among the wise.

32 If you reject discipline,
    you only harm yourself;
    but if you listen to correction,
    you grow in understanding.

33 Fear of the LORD teaches wisdom;
    humility precedes honor.

16 ¹ We can make our own plans,
    but the LORD gives the right answer.

² People may be pure in their own eyes,
    but the LORD examines their motives.

³ Commit your actions to the LORD,
    and your plans will succeed.

⁴ The LORD has made everything for
    his own purposes,
    even the wicked for a day of disaster.

⁵ The LORD detests the proud;
    they will surely be punished.

⁶ Unfailing love and faithfulness make
    atonement for sin.
    By fearing the LORD, people avoid evil.

⁷ When people's lives please the LORD,
    even their enemies are at peace
    with them.

⁸ Better to have little, with godliness,
    than to be rich and dishonest.

⁹ We can make our plans,
    but the LORD determines our steps.

¹⁰ The king speaks with divine wisdom;
    he must never judge unfairly.

¹¹ The LORD demands accurate scales
    and balances;
    he sets the standards for fairness.

¹² A king detests wrongdoing,
    for his rule is built on justice.

¹³ The king is pleased with words from
    righteous lips;
    he loves those who speak honestly.

¹⁴ The anger of the king is a deadly threat;
    the wise will try to appease it.

¹⁵ When the king smiles, there is life;
    his favor refreshes like a spring rain.

¹⁶ How much better to get wisdom than gold,
    and good judgment than silver!

¹⁷ The path of the virtuous leads away
    from evil;
    whoever follows that path is safe.

¹⁸ Pride goes before destruction,
    and haughtiness before a fall.

¹⁹ Better to live humbly with the poor
    than to share plunder with the proud.

²⁰ Those who listen to instruction
    will prosper;
    those who trust the LORD will be joyful.

²¹ The wise are known for their understanding,
    and pleasant words are persuasive.

²² Discretion is a life-giving fountain to those
    who possess it,
    but discipline is wasted on fools.

²³ From a wise mind comes wise speech;
    the words of the wise are persuasive.

²⁴ Kind words are like honey—
    sweet to the soul and healthy
    for the body.

²⁵ There is a path before each person that
    seems right,
    but it ends in death.

²⁶ It is good for workers to have an appetite;
    an empty stomach drives them on.

²⁷ Scoundrels create trouble;
    their words are a destructive blaze.

²⁸ A troublemaker plants seeds of strife;
    gossip separates the best of friends.

²⁹ Violent people mislead their companions,
    leading them down a harmful path.

³⁰ With narrowed eyes, people plot evil;
    with a smirk, they plan their mischief.

³¹ Gray hair is a crown of glory;
    it is gained by living a godly life.

³² Better to be patient than powerful;
    better to have self-control than to
        conquer a city.

³³ We may throw the dice,*
    but the LORD determines how they fall.

17

¹ Better a dry crust eaten in peace
    than a house filled with feasting—
        and conflict.

² A wise servant will rule over the master's
        disgraceful son
    and will share the inheritance of the
        master's children.

³ Fire tests the purity of silver and gold,
    but the LORD tests the heart.

⁴ Wrongdoers eagerly listen to gossip;
    liars pay close attention to slander.

⁵ Those who mock the poor insult their Maker;
    those who rejoice at the misfortune of
        others will be punished.

⁶ Grandchildren are the crowning glory of
        the aged;
    parents* are the pride of their children.

⁷ Eloquent words are not fitting for a fool;
    even less are lies fitting for a ruler.

⁸ A bribe is like a lucky charm;
    whoever gives one will prosper!

⁹ Love prospers when a fault is forgiven,
    but dwelling on it separates close friends.

¹⁰ A single rebuke does more for a person of
        understanding
    than a hundred lashes on the back of a fool.

¹¹ Evil people are eager for rebellion,
    but they will be severely punished.

¹² It is safer to meet a bear robbed of her cubs
    than to confront a fool caught in
        foolishness.

¹³ If you repay good with evil,
    evil will never leave your house.

¹⁴ Starting a quarrel is like opening a floodgate,
    so stop before a dispute breaks out.

¹⁵ Acquitting the guilty and condemning the
        innocent—
    both are detestable to the LORD.

¹⁶ It is senseless to pay to educate a fool,
    since he has no heart for learning.

¹⁷ A friend is always loyal,
    and a brother is born to help in time
        of need.

¹⁸ It's poor judgment to guarantee another
        person's debt
    or put up security for a friend.

¹⁹ Anyone who loves to quarrel loves sin;
    anyone who trusts in high walls invites
        disaster.

²⁰ The crooked heart will not prosper;
    the lying tongue tumbles into trouble.

²¹ It is painful to be the parent of a fool;
    there is no joy for the father of a rebel.

²² A cheerful heart is good medicine,
    but a broken spirit saps a person's
        strength.

²³ The wicked take secret bribes
    to pervert the course of justice.

²⁴ Sensible people keep their eyes glued on
        wisdom,
    but a fool's eyes wander to the ends of
        the earth.

²⁵ Foolish children* bring grief to their father
    and bitterness to the one who gave
        them birth.

²⁶ It is wrong to punish the godly for being good
    or to flog leaders for being honest.

²⁷ A truly wise person uses few words;
    a person with understanding is
        even-tempered.

²⁸ Even fools are thought wise when they
        keep silent;
    with their mouths shut, they seem
        intelligent.

18

¹ Unfriendly people care only about
        themselves;
    they lash out at common sense.

² Fools have no interest in understanding;
    they only want to air their own opinions.

³ Doing wrong leads to disgrace,
    and scandalous behavior brings contempt.

⁴ Wise words are like deep waters;
    wisdom flows from the wise like a
        bubbling brook.

16:33 Hebrew *We may cast lots.*   17:6 Hebrew *fathers.*
17:25 Hebrew *A foolish son.*

THE VALUE OF WORDS
Proverbs 18:20–21

ROBERT MORRIS

The quality of your life often depends upon the words you speak. Proverbs 18:21 says, "The tongue can bring death or life." Some people try to make God agree with their words, but if we want our words to bring life, we must make them agree with God.

Here are two truths about the value of our words:

1. Words connect us to God.

   When God created the universe, He *spoke* everything into existence (Genesis 1). Words are the way God connects from the spiritual realm where He lives to the natural realm where we live. John 1 says Jesus is "the Word" who "became human and made his home among us" (v. 14). Words are also how we connect to God. Throughout the Bible, the mouth and the heart are connected many times.

Why? Because whatever is in our hearts will come out of our mouths. That is why Romans 10:9 says, "If you openly declare that Jesus is Lord and believe in your heart that God raised him from the dead, you will be saved."

2. Words connect us to each other.

   As humans, we can't simply speak and make things happen in the same way God did when He said, "Let there be light" (Genesis 1:3). However, our words do have power. Everything we say releases either death or life into our lives. Many people speak death over their marriage, family, finances, and health, and then they wonder why they aren't blessed. If you want to have great relationships, you have to make them with your words. Decide today that everything coming out of your mouth is going to agree with God's Word. I guarantee this will change your life!

---

⁵ It is not right to acquit the guilty
   or deny justice to the innocent.

⁶ Fools' words get them into constant
      quarrels;
   they are asking for a beating.

⁷ The mouths of fools are their ruin;
   they trap themselves with their lips.

⁸ Rumors are dainty morsels
   that sink deep into one's heart.

⁹ A lazy person is as bad as
   someone who destroys things.

¹⁰ The name of the LORD is a strong fortress;
   the godly run to him and are safe.

¹¹ The rich think of their wealth as a strong
      defense;
   they imagine it to be a high wall of safety.

¹² Haughtiness goes before destruction;
   humility precedes honor.

¹³ Spouting off before listening to the facts
   is both shameful and foolish.

¹⁴ The human spirit can endure a sick body,
   but who can bear a crushed spirit?

¹⁵ Intelligent people are always
      ready to learn.
   Their ears are open for knowledge.

¹⁶ Giving a gift can open doors;
   it gives access to important people!

¹⁷ The first to speak in court sounds right—
   until the cross-examination begins.

¹⁸ Flipping a coin* can end arguments;
   it settles disputes between powerful
      opponents.

¹⁹ An offended friend is harder to win back
      than a fortified city.
   Arguments separate friends like a gate
      locked with bars.

²⁰ Wise words satisfy like a good meal;
   the right words bring satisfaction.

²¹ The tongue can bring death or life;
   those who love to talk will reap the
      consequences.

²² The man who finds a wife finds a treasure,
   and he receives favor from the LORD.

²³ The poor plead for mercy;
   the rich answer with insults.

²⁴ There are "friends" who destroy
      each other,
   but a real friend sticks closer than
      a brother.

19 ¹ Better to be poor and honest
         than to be dishonest and a fool.

² Enthusiasm without knowledge is no good;
   haste makes mistakes.

18:18 Hebrew *Casting lots.*

3 People ruin their lives by their own
 foolishness
 and then are angry at the LORD.

4 Wealth makes many "friends";
 poverty drives them all away.

5 A false witness will not go unpunished,
 nor will a liar escape.

6 Many seek favors from a ruler;
 everyone is the friend of a person who
 gives gifts!

7 The relatives of the poor despise them;
 how much more will their friends
 avoid them!
Though the poor plead with them,
 their friends are gone.

8 To acquire wisdom is to love yourself;
 people who cherish understanding
 will prosper.

9 A false witness will not go unpunished,
 and a liar will be destroyed.

10 It isn't right for a fool to live in luxury
 or for a slave to rule over princes!

11 Sensible people control their temper;
 they earn respect by overlooking wrongs.

12 The king's anger is like a lion's roar,
 but his favor is like dew on the grass.

13 A foolish child* is a calamity to a father;
 a quarrelsome wife is as annoying as
 constant dripping.

14 Fathers can give their sons an inheritance
 of houses and wealth,
 but only the LORD can give an
 understanding wife.

15 Lazy people sleep soundly,
 but idleness leaves them hungry.

16 Keep the commandments and keep
 your life;
 despising them leads to death.

17 If you help the poor, you are lending to
 the LORD—
 and he will repay you!

18 Discipline your children while there is hope.
 Otherwise you will ruin their lives.

19 Hot-tempered people must pay the penalty.
 If you rescue them once,
 you will have to do it again.

20 Get all the advice and instruction you can,
 so you will be wise the rest of your life.

21 You can make many plans,
 but the LORD's purpose will prevail.

22 Loyalty makes a person attractive.
 It is better to be poor than dishonest.

23 Fear of the LORD leads to life,
 bringing security and protection
 from harm.

24 Lazy people take food in their hand
 but don't even lift it to their mouth.

25 If you punish a mocker, the simpleminded
 will learn a lesson;
 if you correct the wise, they will be
 all the wiser.

26 Children who mistreat their father or chase
 away their mother
 are an embarrassment and
 a public disgrace.

27 If you stop listening to instruction, my child,
 you will turn your back on knowledge.

28 A corrupt witness makes a mockery
 of justice;
 the mouth of the wicked gulps down evil.

29 Punishment is made for mockers,
 and the backs of fools are made to
 be beaten.

20 1 Wine produces mockers; alcohol
 leads to brawls.
 Those led astray by drink cannot be wise.

2 The king's fury is like a lion's roar;
 to rouse his anger is to risk your life.

3 Avoiding a fight is a mark of honor;
 only fools insist on quarreling.

4 Those too lazy to plow in the right season
 will have no food at the harvest.

5 Though good advice lies deep within
 the heart,
 a person with understanding will draw
 it out.

6 Many will say they are loyal friends,
 but who can find one who is truly reliable?

7 The godly walk with integrity;
 blessed are their children who follow them.

19:13 Hebrew *son;* also in 19:27.

8 When a king sits in judgment, he weighs
    all the evidence,
    distinguishing the bad from the good.

9 Who can say, "I have cleansed my heart;
    I am pure and free from sin"?

10 False weights and unequal measures*—
    the LORD detests double standards of
    every kind.

11 Even children are known by the way they act,
    whether their conduct is pure, and
    whether it is right.

12 Ears to hear and eyes to see—
    both are gifts from the LORD.

13 If you love sleep, you will end in poverty.
    Keep your eyes open, and there will be
    plenty to eat!

14 The buyer haggles over the price, saying,
    "It's worthless,"
    then brags about getting a bargain!

15 Wise words are more valuable
    than much gold and many rubies.

16 Get security from someone who guarantees
    a stranger's debt.
    Get a deposit if he does it for foreigners.*

17 Stolen bread tastes sweet,
    but it turns to gravel in the mouth.

18 Plans succeed through good counsel;
    don't go to war without wise advice.

19 A gossip goes around telling secrets,
    so don't hang around with chatterers.

20 If you insult your father or mother,
    your light will be snuffed out in total
    darkness.

21 An inheritance obtained too early in life
    is not a blessing in the end.

22 Don't say, "I will get even for this wrong."
    Wait for the LORD to handle the matter.

23 The LORD detests double standards;
    he is not pleased by dishonest scales.

24 The LORD directs our steps,
    so why try to understand everything
    along the way?

25 Don't trap yourself by making a rash
    promise to God
    and only later counting the cost.

26 A wise king scatters the wicked like wheat,
    then runs his threshing wheel over them.

27 The LORD's light penetrates
    the human spirit,*
    exposing every hidden motive.

28 Unfailing love and faithfulness protect
    the king;
    his throne is made secure through love.

29 The glory of the young is their strength;
    the gray hair of experience is the splendor
    of the old.

30 Physical punishment cleanses away evil;*
    such discipline purifies the heart.

21 1 The king's heart is like a stream of
    water directed by the LORD;
    he guides it wherever he pleases.

2 People may be right in their own eyes,
    but the LORD examines their heart.

3 The LORD is more pleased when we do what
    is right and just
    than when we offer him sacrifices.

4 Haughty eyes, a proud heart,
    and evil actions are all sin.

5 Good planning and hard work
    lead to prosperity,
    but hasty shortcuts lead to poverty.

6 Wealth created by a lying tongue
    is a vanishing mist and a deadly trap.*

7 The violence of the wicked sweeps
    them away,
    because they refuse to do what is just.

8 The guilty walk a crooked path;
    the innocent travel a straight road.

9 It's better to live alone in the corner of an attic
    than with a quarrelsome wife in
    a lovely home.

10 Evil people desire evil;
    their neighbors get no mercy from them.

11 If you punish a mocker, the simpleminded
    become wise;
    if you instruct the wise,
    they will be all the wiser.

20:10 Hebrew *A stone and a stone, an ephah and an ephah.*
20:16 An alternate reading in the Masoretic Text is *for a promiscuous woman.*   20:27 Or *The human spirit is the LORD's light.*
20:30 The meaning of the Hebrew is uncertain.   21:6 As in Greek version; Hebrew reads *mist for those who seek death.*

¹² The Righteous One* knows what is going on
in the homes of the wicked;
he will bring disaster on them.

¹³ Those who shut their ears to the cries of
the poor
will be ignored in their own time of need.

¹⁴ A secret gift calms anger;
a bribe under the table pacifies fury.

¹⁵ Justice is a joy to the godly,
but it terrifies evildoers.

¹⁶ The person who strays from common sense
will end up in the company of the dead.

¹⁷ Those who love pleasure become poor;
those who love wine and luxury will
never be rich.

¹⁸ The wicked are punished in place of the godly,
and traitors in place of the honest.

¹⁹ It's better to live alone in the desert
than with a quarrelsome,
complaining wife.

²⁰ The wise have wealth and luxury,
but fools spend whatever they get.

²¹ Whoever pursues righteousness and
unfailing love
will find life, righteousness, and honor.

²² The wise conquer the city of the strong
and level the fortress in which they trust.

²³ Watch your tongue and keep your
mouth shut,
and you will stay out of trouble.

²⁴ Mockers are proud and haughty;
they act with boundless arrogance.

²⁵ Despite their desires, the lazy will come
to ruin,
for their hands refuse to work.

²⁶ Some people are always greedy for more,
but the godly love to give!

²⁷ The sacrifice of an evil person is detestable,
especially when it is offered with wrong
motives.

²⁸ A false witness will be cut off,
but a credible witness will be allowed
to speak.

²⁹ The wicked bluff their way through,
but the virtuous think before they act.

³⁰ No human wisdom or understanding or plan
can stand against the LORD.

³¹ The horse is prepared for the day of battle,
but the victory belongs to the LORD.

22 ¹ Choose a good reputation over
great riches;
being held in high esteem is better than
silver or gold.

² The rich and poor have this in common:
The LORD made them both.

³ A prudent person foresees danger and takes
precautions.
The simpleton goes blindly on and suffers
the consequences.

⁴ True humility and fear of the LORD
lead to riches, honor, and long life.

⁵ Corrupt people walk a thorny,
treacherous road;
whoever values life will avoid it.

⁶ Direct your children onto the right path,
and when they are older,
they will not leave it.

⁷ Just as the rich rule the poor,
so the borrower is servant to the lender.

⁸ Those who plant injustice will harvest
disaster,
and their reign of terror will come to
an end.*

⁹ Blessed are those who are generous,
because they feed the poor.

¹⁰ Throw out the mocker, and fighting goes, too.
Quarrels and insults will disappear.

¹¹ Whoever loves a pure heart and gracious
speech
will have the king as a friend.

¹² The LORD preserves those with knowledge,
but he ruins the plans of the treacherous.

¹³ The lazy person claims,
"There's a lion out there!
If I go outside, I might be killed!"

¹⁴ The mouth of an immoral woman is
a dangerous trap;
those who make the LORD angry will
fall into it.

21:12 Or *The righteous man.*   22:8 The Greek version includes an
additional proverb: *God blesses a man who gives cheerfully, / but his
worthless deeds will come to an end.* Compare 2 Cor 9:7.

¹⁵ A youngster's heart is filled with
foolishness,
but physical discipline will drive it
far away.

¹⁶ A person who gets ahead by oppressing
the poor
or by showering gifts on the rich will
end in poverty.

SAYINGS OF THE WISE

¹⁷ Listen to the words of the wise;
apply your heart to my instruction.
¹⁸ For it is good to keep these sayings in
your heart
and always ready on your lips.
¹⁹ I am teaching you today—yes, you—
so you will trust in the LORD.
²⁰ I have written thirty sayings* for you,
filled with advice and knowledge.
²¹ In this way, you may know the truth
and take an accurate report to those
who sent you.

²² Don't rob the poor just because you can,
or exploit the needy in court.
²³ For the LORD is their defender.
He will ruin anyone who ruins them.

²⁴ Don't befriend angry people
or associate with hot-tempered people,
²⁵ or you will learn to be like them
and endanger your soul.

²⁶ Don't agree to guarantee another
person's debt
or put up security for someone else.
²⁷ If you can't pay it,
even your bed will be snatched from
under you.

²⁸ Don't cheat your neighbor by moving the
ancient boundary markers
set up by previous generations.

²⁹ Do you see any truly competent workers?
They will serve kings
rather than working for ordinary people.

23

¹ While dining with a ruler,
pay attention to what is put
before you.
² If you are a big eater,
put a knife to your throat;
³ don't desire all the delicacies,
for he might be trying to trick you.

⁴ Don't wear yourself out trying to get rich.
Be wise enough to know when to quit.
⁵ In the blink of an eye wealth disappears,
for it will sprout wings
and fly away like an eagle.

⁶ Don't eat with people who are stingy;
don't desire their delicacies.
⁷ They are always thinking about
how much it costs.*
"Eat and drink," they say,
but they don't mean it.
⁸ You will throw up what little you've eaten,
and your compliments will be wasted.

⁹ Don't waste your breath on fools,
for they will despise the wisest advice.

¹⁰ Don't cheat your neighbor by moving
the ancient boundary markers;
don't take the land of
defenseless orphans.
¹¹ For their Redeemer* is strong;
he himself will bring their charges
against you.

¹² Commit yourself to instruction;
listen carefully to words of knowledge.

¹³ Don't fail to discipline your children.
The rod of punishment won't kill them.
¹⁴ Physical discipline
may well save them from death.*

¹⁵ My child,* if your heart is wise,
my own heart will rejoice!
¹⁶ Everything in me will celebrate
when you speak what is right.

¹⁷ Don't envy sinners,
but always continue to fear the LORD.
¹⁸ You will be rewarded for this;
your hope will not be disappointed.

¹⁹ My child, listen and be wise:
Keep your heart on the right course.
²⁰ Do not carouse with drunkards
or feast with gluttons,
²¹ for they are on their way to poverty,
and too much sleep clothes them in rags.

²² Listen to your father, who gave you life,
and don't despise your mother when
she is old.
²³ Get the truth and never sell it;
also get wisdom, discipline,
and good judgment.
²⁴ The father of godly children has cause
for joy.
What a pleasure to have children who
are wise.*
²⁵ So give your father and mother joy!
May she who gave you birth be happy.

22:20 Or *excellent sayings;* the meaning of the Hebrew is
uncertain.   23:7 The meaning of the Hebrew is uncertain.
23:11 Or *redeemer.*   23:14 Hebrew *from Sheol.*   23:15 Hebrew *My
son;* also in 23:19.   23:24 Hebrew *to have a wise son.*

26 O my son, give me your heart.
   May your eyes take delight in following
      my ways.
27 A prostitute is a dangerous trap;
   a promiscuous woman is as dangerous as
      falling into a narrow well.
28 She hides and waits like a robber,
   eager to make more men unfaithful.

29 Who has anguish? Who has sorrow?
   Who is always fighting? Who is always
      complaining?
   Who has unnecessary bruises? Who has
      bloodshot eyes?
30 It is the one who spends long hours in
      the taverns,
   trying out new drinks.
31 Don't gaze at the wine, seeing how red it is,
   how it sparkles in the cup, how smoothly
      it goes down.
32 For in the end it bites like
      a poisonous snake;
   it stings like a viper.
33 You will see hallucinations,
   and you will say crazy things.
34 You will stagger like a sailor tossed at sea,
   clinging to a swaying mast.
35 And you will say, "They hit me,
   but I didn't feel it.
   I didn't even know it when they
      beat me up.
   When will I wake up
      so I can look for another drink?"

24 ¹ Don't envy evil people
      or desire their company.
² For their hearts plot violence,
   and their words always stir up trouble.

³ A house is built by wisdom
   and becomes strong through good sense.
⁴ Through knowledge its rooms are filled
   with all sorts of precious riches and
      valuables.

⁵ The wise are mightier than the strong,*
   and those with knowledge grow stronger
      and stronger.
⁶ So don't go to war without wise guidance;
   victory depends on having many advisers.

⁷ Wisdom is too lofty for fools.
   Among leaders at the city gate, they have
      nothing to say.

⁸ A person who plans evil
   will get a reputation as a troublemaker.
⁹ The schemes of a fool are sinful;
   everyone detests a mocker.

10 If you fail under pressure,
   your strength is too small.

11 Rescue those who are unjustly sentenced
      to die;
   save them as they stagger to their death.
12 Don't excuse yourself by saying,
   "Look, we didn't know."
   For God understands all hearts,
      and he sees you.
   He who guards your soul knows you knew.
   He will repay all people as
      their actions deserve.

13 My child,* eat honey, for it is good,
   and the honeycomb is sweet to the taste.
14 In the same way, wisdom is sweet to
      your soul.
   If you find it, you will have a bright future,
   and your hopes will not be cut short.

15 Don't wait in ambush at the home of
      the godly,
   and don't raid the house where
      the godly live.
16 The godly may trip seven times, but they
      will get up again.
   But one disaster is enough to overthrow
      the wicked.

17 Don't rejoice when your enemies fall;
   don't be happy when they stumble.
18 For the LORD will be displeased with you
   and will turn his anger away from them.

19 Don't fret because of evildoers;
   don't envy the wicked.
20 For evil people have no future;
   the light of the wicked will be
      snuffed out.

21 My child, fear the LORD and the king.
   Don't associate with rebels,
22 for disaster will hit them suddenly.
   Who knows what punishment will come
      from the LORD and the king?

MORE SAYINGS OF THE WISE

23 Here are some further sayings of the wise:

   It is wrong to show favoritism when
      passing judgment.
24 A judge who says to the wicked,
   "You are innocent,"
   will be cursed by many people and
      denounced by the nations.
25 But it will go well for those who convict
      the guilty;
   rich blessings will be showered on them.

26 An honest answer
   is like a kiss of friendship.

24:5 As in Greek version; Hebrew reads *A wise man is strength.*
24:13 Hebrew *My son;* also in 24:21.

²⁷ Do your planning and prepare your fields
    before building your house.

²⁸ Don't testify against your neighbors
        without cause;
    don't lie about them.
²⁹ And don't say, "Now I can pay them back
        for what they've done to me!
    I'll get even with them!"

³⁰ I walked by the field of a lazy person,
    the vineyard of one with no common sense.
³¹ I saw that it was overgrown with nettles.
    It was covered with weeds,
    and its walls were broken down.
³² Then, as I looked and thought about it,
    I learned this lesson:
³³ A little extra sleep, a little more slumber,
    a little folding of the hands to rest—
³⁴ then poverty will pounce on you like a bandit;
    scarcity will attack you like
        an armed robber.

MORE PROVERBS OF SOLOMON

25 These are more proverbs of Solomon, col-
    lected by the advisers of King Hezekiah
of Judah.

² It is God's privilege to conceal things
    and the king's privilege to discover them.

³ No one can comprehend the height of
        heaven, the depth of the earth,
    or all that goes on in the king's mind!

⁴ Remove the impurities from silver,
    and the sterling will be ready for
        the silversmith.
⁵ Remove the wicked from the king's court,
    and his reign will be made secure by
        justice.

⁶ Don't demand an audience with the king
    or push for a place among the great.
⁷ It's better to wait for an invitation to
        the head table
    than to be sent away in public disgrace.

    Just because you've seen something,
⁸   don't be in a hurry to go to court.
    For what will you do in the end
    if your neighbor deals you
        a shameful defeat?

⁹ When arguing with your neighbor,
    don't betray another person's secret.
¹⁰ Others may accuse you of gossip,
    and you will never regain your
        good reputation.

¹¹ Timely advice is lovely,
    like golden apples in a silver basket.

¹² To one who listens, valid criticism
    is like a gold earring or other gold jewelry.

¹³ Trustworthy messengers refresh like snow
        in summer.
    They revive the spirit of their employer.

¹⁴ A person who promises a gift but doesn't
        give it
    is like clouds and wind that bring no rain.

¹⁵ Patience can persuade a prince,
    and soft speech can break bones.

¹⁶ Do you like honey?
    Don't eat too much,
    or it will make you sick!

¹⁷ Don't visit your neighbors too often,
    or you will wear out your welcome.

¹⁸ Telling lies about others
    is as harmful as hitting them with
        an ax,
    wounding them with a sword,
    or shooting them with a sharp arrow.

¹⁹ Putting confidence in an unreliable person
        in times of trouble
    is like chewing with a broken tooth or
        walking on a lame foot.

²⁰ Singing cheerful songs to a person with
        a heavy heart
    is like taking someone's coat in cold
        weather
    or pouring vinegar in a wound.*

²¹ If your enemies are hungry,
        give them food to eat.
    If they are thirsty, give them water
        to drink.
²² You will heap burning coals of shame on
        their heads,
    and the LORD will reward you.

²³ As surely as a north wind brings rain,
    so a gossiping tongue causes anger!

²⁴ It's better to live alone in the corner of
        an attic
    than with a quarrelsome wife in
        a lovely home.

²⁵ Good news from far away
    is like cold water to the thirsty.

²⁶ If the godly give in to the wicked,
    it's like polluting a fountain or muddying
        a spring.

25:20 As in Greek version; Hebrew reads *pouring vinegar on soda.*

²⁷ It's not good to eat too much honey,
    and it's not good to seek honors
        for yourself.

²⁸ A person without self-control
    is like a city with broken-down walls.

26

¹ Honor is no more associated
    with fools
than snow with summer or rain with
    harvest.

² Like a fluttering sparrow or a darting
        swallow,
    an undeserved curse will not land on its
        intended victim.

³ Guide a horse with a whip,
    a donkey with a bridle,
    and a fool with a rod to his back!

⁴ Don't answer the foolish arguments of fools,
    or you will become as foolish as they are.

⁵ Be sure to answer the foolish arguments
        of fools,
    or they will become wise in their own
        estimation.

⁶ Trusting a fool to convey a message
    is like cutting off one's feet or
        drinking poison!

⁷ A proverb in the mouth of a fool
    is as useless as a paralyzed leg.

⁸ Honoring a fool
    is as foolish as tying a stone to a slingshot.

⁹ A proverb in the mouth of a fool
    is like a thorny branch brandished by
        a drunk.

¹⁰ An employer who hires a fool or a bystander
    is like an archer who shoots at random.

¹¹ As a dog returns to its vomit,
    so a fool repeats his foolishness.

¹² There is more hope for fools
    than for people who think they are wise.

¹³ The lazy person claims,
    "There's a lion on the road!
    Yes, I'm sure there's a lion out there!"

¹⁴ As a door swings back and forth on
        its hinges,
    so the lazy person turns over in bed.

¹⁵ Lazy people take food in their hand
    but don't even lift it to their mouth.

¹⁶ Lazy people consider themselves smarter
    than seven wise counselors.

¹⁷ Interfering in someone else's argument
    is as foolish as yanking a dog's ears.

¹⁸ Just as damaging
    as a madman shooting a deadly weapon
¹⁹ is someone who lies to a friend
    and then says, "I was only joking."

²⁰ Fire goes out without wood,
    and quarrels disappear when
        gossip stops.

²¹ A quarrelsome person starts fights
    as easily as hot embers light charcoal or
        fire lights wood.

²² Rumors are dainty morsels
    that sink deep into one's heart.

²³ Smooth* words may hide a wicked heart,
    just as a pretty glaze covers a clay pot.

²⁴ People may cover their hatred with
        pleasant words,
    but they're deceiving you.
²⁵ They pretend to be kind, but don't
        believe them.
    Their hearts are full of many evils.*
²⁶ While their hatred may be concealed
        by trickery,
    their wrongdoing will be exposed
        in public.

²⁷ If you set a trap for others,
    you will get caught in it yourself.
    If you roll a boulder down on others,
        it will crush you instead.

²⁸ A lying tongue hates its victims,
    and flattering words cause ruin.

27

¹ Don't brag about tomorrow,
    since you don't know what
        the day will bring.

² Let someone else praise you,
    not your own mouth—
    a stranger, not your own lips.

³ A stone is heavy and sand is weighty,
    but the resentment caused by a fool is
        even heavier.

⁴ Anger is cruel, and wrath is like a flood,
    but jealousy is even more dangerous.

26:23 As in Greek version; Hebrew reads *Burning*. 26:25 Hebrew
seven evils.

CHANGING YOUR MIND ABOUT YOUR ATTITUDE
Proverbs 27:19   TOM LANE

When it comes to success, your attitude is more important than your aptitude. Good attitudes open us to God's transforming work. Bad attitudes open us to the devil's influence.

Attitudes are the birthplace of behavior; your attitude will always show through your actions. This is why God rewards our good attitudes and disciplines us for bad ones (Hebrews 12:7, 11). Your attitude will also influence your perspective (Philippians 4:11-13). Some people choose to be happy and thankful. As a result, they influence others to have the same perspective. Other people choose to be unhappy, and they infect those around them with their discontent.

The devil wants us to believe the lie that if our circumstances were different, our attitudes would change. God's truth is that we can overcome any circumstance by choosing the right attitude. We do this by finding God's perspective on our situation and letting that determine our attitude.

⁵ An open rebuke
    is better than hidden love!

⁶ Wounds from a sincere friend
    are better than many kisses from an enemy.

⁷ A person who is full refuses honey,
    but even bitter food tastes sweet to
    the hungry.

⁸ A person who strays from home
    is like a bird that strays from its nest.

⁹ The heartfelt counsel of a friend
    is as sweet as perfume and incense.

¹⁰ Never abandon a friend—
    either yours or your father's.
    When disaster strikes, you won't have to ask
    your brother for assistance.
    It's better to go to a neighbor than to a
    brother who lives far away.

¹¹ Be wise, my child,* and make my heart glad.
    Then I will be able to answer my critics.

¹² A prudent person foresees danger and
    takes precautions.
    The simpleton goes blindly on and suffers
    the consequences.

¹³ Get security from someone who
    guarantees a stranger's debt.
    Get a deposit if he does it for foreigners.*

¹⁴ A loud and cheerful greeting early in
    the morning
    will be taken as a curse!

¹⁵ A quarrelsome wife is as annoying
    as constant dripping on a rainy day.

¹⁶ Stopping her complaints is like trying to
    stop the wind
    or trying to hold something with
    greased hands.

¹⁷ As iron sharpens iron,
    so a friend sharpens a friend.

¹⁸ As workers who tend a fig tree are allowed
    to eat the fruit,
    so workers who protect their employer's
    interests will be rewarded.

¹⁹ As a face is reflected in water,
    so the heart reflects the real person.

²⁰ Just as Death and Destruction* are
    never satisfied,
    so human desire is never satisfied.

²¹ Fire tests the purity of silver and gold,
    but a person is tested by being
    praised.*

²² You cannot separate fools from their
    foolishness,
    even though you grind them like grain
    with mortar and pestle.

²³ Know the state of your flocks,
    and put your heart into caring for
    your herds,
²⁴ for riches don't last forever,
    and the crown might not be passed to the
    next generation.
²⁵ After the hay is harvested and
    the new crop appears
    and the mountain grasses are
    gathered in,
²⁶ your sheep will provide wool for clothing,
    and your goats will provide the price of
    a field.
²⁷ And you will have enough goats' milk
    for yourself,
    your family, and your servant girls.

28

¹ The wicked run away when no one
    is chasing them,
    but the godly are as bold as lions.

² When there is moral rot within a nation,
    its government topples easily.

27:11 Hebrew *my son.*   27:13 As in Greek and Latin versions (see also 20:16); Hebrew reads *for a promiscuous woman.* 27:20 Hebrew *Sheol and Abaddon.*   27:21 Or *by flattery.*

But wise and knowledgeable leaders
  bring stability.

³ A poor person who oppresses the poor
  is like a pounding rain that destroys
    the crops.

⁴ To reject the law is to praise the wicked;
  to obey the law is to fight them.

⁵ Evil people don't understand justice,
  but those who follow the LORD
    understand completely.

⁶ Better to be poor and honest
  than to be dishonest and rich.

⁷ Young people who obey the law are wise;
  those with wild friends bring shame to
    their parents.*

⁸ Income from charging high interest rates
  will end up in the pocket of someone who
    is kind to the poor.

⁹ God detests the prayers
  of a person who ignores the law.

¹⁰ Those who lead good people along an evil path
  will fall into their own trap,
    but the honest will inherit good things.

¹¹ Rich people may think they are wise,
  but a poor person with discernment can
    see right through them.

¹² When the godly succeed, everyone is glad.
  When the wicked take charge, people go
    into hiding.

¹³ People who conceal their sins will not prosper,
  but if they confess and turn from them,
    they will receive mercy.

¹⁴ Blessed are those who fear to do wrong,*
  but the stubborn are headed for
    serious trouble.

¹⁵ A wicked ruler is as dangerous to the poor
  as a roaring lion or an attacking bear.

¹⁶ A ruler with no understanding will oppress
    his people,
  but one who hates corruption will have
    a long life.

¹⁷ A murderer's tormented conscience will
    drive him into the grave.
  Don't protect him!

¹⁸ The blameless will be rescued from harm,
  but the crooked will be suddenly destroyed.

¹⁹ A hard worker has plenty of food,
  but a person who chases fantasies
    ends up in poverty.

²⁰ The trustworthy person will get
    a rich reward,
  but a person who wants quick riches
    will get into trouble.

²¹ Showing partiality is never good,
  yet some will do wrong for a mere piece
    of bread.

²² Greedy people try to get rich quick
  but don't realize they're headed
    for poverty.

²³ In the end, people appreciate
    honest criticism
  far more than flattery.

²⁴ Anyone who steals from his father
    and mother
  and says, "What's wrong with that?"
    is no better than a murderer.

²⁵ Greed causes fighting;
  trusting the LORD leads to prosperity.

²⁶ Those who trust their own insight
    are foolish,
  but anyone who walks in wisdom is safe.

²⁷ Whoever gives to the poor will lack nothing,
  but those who close their eyes to poverty
    will be cursed.

²⁸ When the wicked take charge, people go
    into hiding.
  When the wicked meet disaster,
    the godly flourish.

29

¹ Whoever stubbornly refuses to
    accept criticism
  will suddenly be destroyed
    beyond recovery.

² When the godly are in authority,
    the people rejoice.
  But when the wicked are in power,
    they groan.

³ The man who loves wisdom brings joy
    to his father,
  but if he hangs around with prostitutes,
    his wealth is wasted.

⁴ A just king gives stability to his nation,
  but one who demands bribes destroys it.

28:7 Hebrew *their father.*   28:14 Or *those who fear the LORD;*
Hebrew reads *those who fear.*

⁵ To flatter friends
    is to lay a trap for their feet.

⁶ Evil people are trapped by sin,
    but the righteous escape, shouting for joy.

⁷ The godly care about the rights of the poor;
    the wicked don't care at all.

⁸ Mockers can get a whole town agitated,
    but the wise will calm anger.

⁹ If a wise person takes a fool to court,
    there will be ranting and ridicule but no
        satisfaction.

¹⁰ The bloodthirsty hate blameless people,
    but the upright seek to help them.*

¹¹ Fools vent their anger,
    but the wise quietly hold it back.

¹² If a ruler pays attention to liars,
    all his advisers will be wicked.

¹³ The poor and the oppressor have this in
        common—
    the LORD gives sight to the eyes of both.

¹⁴ If a king judges the poor fairly,
    his throne will last forever.

¹⁵ To discipline a child produces wisdom,
    but a mother is disgraced by an
        undisciplined child.

¹⁶ When the wicked are in authority, sin
        flourishes,
    but the godly will live to see their downfall.

¹⁷ Discipline your children, and they will give
        you peace of mind
    and will make your heart glad.

¹⁸ When people do not accept divine guidance,
        they run wild.
    But whoever obeys the law is joyful.

¹⁹ Words alone will not discipline a servant;
    the words may be understood, but they
        are not heeded.

²⁰ There is more hope for a fool
    than for someone who speaks without
        thinking.

²¹ A servant pampered from childhood
    will become a rebel.

²² An angry person starts fights;
    a hot-tempered person commits
        all kinds of sin.

²³ Pride ends in humiliation,
    while humility brings honor.

²⁴ If you assist a thief, you only hurt yourself.
    You are sworn to tell the truth,
        but you dare not testify.

²⁵ Fearing people is a dangerous trap,
    but trusting the LORD means safety.

²⁶ Many seek the ruler's favor,
    but justice comes from the LORD.

²⁷ The righteous despise the unjust;
    the wicked despise the godly.

THE SAYINGS OF AGUR

30 The sayings of Agur son of Jakeh contain
    this message.*

    I am weary, O God;
        I am weary and worn out, O God.*
² I am too stupid to be human,
        and I lack common sense.
³ I have not mastered human wisdom,
        nor do I know the Holy One.

⁴ Who but God goes up to heaven and comes
        back down?
    Who holds the wind in his fists?
    Who wraps up the oceans in his cloak?
    Who has created the whole wide world?
    What is his name—and his son's name?
    Tell me if you know!

⁵ Every word of God proves true.
    He is a shield to all who come to him
        for protection.
⁶ Do not add to his words,
    or he may rebuke you and expose you
        as a liar.

⁷ O God, I beg two favors from you;
    let me have them before I die.
⁸ First, help me never to tell a lie.
    Second, give me neither poverty
        nor riches!
    Give me just enough to satisfy my needs.
⁹ For if I grow rich, I may deny you and say,
        "Who is the LORD?"
    And if I am too poor, I may steal and thus
        insult God's holy name.

¹⁰ Never slander a worker to the employer,
    or the person will curse you,
        and you will pay for it.

29:10 Or *The bloodthirsty hate blameless people, / and they seek to
kill the upright;* Hebrew reads *The bloodthirsty hate blameless people;
/ as for the upright, they seek their life.*   **30:1a** Or *son of Jakeh from
Massa;* or *son of Jakeh, an oracle.*   **30:1b** The Hebrew can also be
translated *The man declares this to Ithiel, / to Ithiel and to Ucal.*

11 Some people curse their father
    and do not thank their mother.
12 They are pure in their own eyes,
    but they are filthy and unwashed.
13 They look proudly around,
    casting disdainful glances.
14 They have teeth like swords
    and fangs like knives.
  They devour the poor from the earth
    and the needy from among humanity.

15 The leech has two suckers
    that cry out, "More, more!"*

  There are three things that are never
      satisfied—
    no, four that never say, "Enough!":
16 the grave,*
    the barren womb,
    the thirsty desert,
    the blazing fire.

17 The eye that mocks a father
    and despises a mother's instructions
  will be plucked out by ravens of the valley
    and eaten by vultures.

18 There are three things that amaze me—
    no, four things that I don't understand:
19 how an eagle glides through the sky,
    how a snake slithers on a rock,
    how a ship navigates the ocean,
    how a man loves a woman.

20 An adulterous woman consumes a man,
    then wipes her mouth and says,
    "What's wrong with that?"

21 There are three things that make
      the earth tremble—
    no, four it cannot endure:
22 a slave who becomes a king,
    an overbearing fool who prospers,
23   a bitter woman who finally gets a
      husband,
    a servant girl who supplants her mistress.

24 There are four things on earth that are small
    but unusually wise:
25 Ants—they aren't strong,
    but they store up food all summer.
26 Hyraxes*—they aren't powerful,
    but they make their homes among
      the rocks.
27 Locusts—they have no king,
    but they march in formation.
28 Lizards—they are easy to catch,
    but they are found even in kings' palaces.

29 There are three things that walk with
      stately stride—
    no, four that strut about:

30 the lion, king of animals,
    who won't turn aside for anything,
31 the strutting rooster,
    the male goat,
    a king as he leads his army.

32 If you have been a fool by being proud or
      plotting evil,
    cover your mouth in shame.

33 As the beating of cream yields butter
    and striking the nose causes bleeding,
    so stirring up anger causes quarrels.

THE SAYINGS OF KING LEMUEL

31 The sayings of King Lemuel contain this
    message,* which his mother taught him.

2 O my son, O son of my womb,
    O son of my vows,
3 do not waste your strength on women,
    on those who ruin kings.

4 It is not for kings, O Lemuel,
    to guzzle wine.
  Rulers should not crave alcohol.
5 For if they drink, they may forget the law
    and not give justice to the oppressed.
6 Alcohol is for the dying,
    and wine for those in bitter distress.
7 Let them drink to forget their poverty
    and remember their troubles no more.

8 Speak up for those who cannot speak
      for themselves;
    ensure justice for those being crushed.
9 Yes, speak up for the poor and helpless,
    and see that they get justice.

A WIFE OF NOBLE CHARACTER

10*Who can find a virtuous and
      capable wife?
    She is more precious than rubies.
11 Her husband can trust her,
    and she will greatly enrich his life.
12 She brings him good, not harm,
    all the days of her life.

13 She finds wool and flax
    and busily spins it.
14 She is like a merchant's ship,
    bringing her food from afar.
15 She gets up before dawn to prepare
      breakfast for her household
    and plan the day's work for her
      servant girls.

30:15 Hebrew *two daughters who cry out, "Give, give!"*
30:16 Hebrew *Sheol.*   30:26 Or *Coneys,* or *Rock badgers.*   31:1 Or
of Lemuel, king of Massa; or *of King Lemuel, an oracle.*   31:10 Verses
10-31 comprise a Hebrew acrostic poem; each verse begins with
a successive letter of the Hebrew alphabet.

16 She goes to inspect a field and buys it;
    with her earnings she plants a vineyard.
17 She is energetic and strong,
    a hard worker.
18 She makes sure her dealings are profitable;
    her lamp burns late into the night.

19 Her hands are busy spinning thread,
    her fingers twisting fiber.
20 She extends a helping hand to the poor
    and opens her arms to the needy.
21 She has no fear of winter for her household,
    for everyone has warm* clothes.

22 She makes her own bedspreads.
    She dresses in fine linen and
        purple gowns.
23 Her husband is well known at the city gates,
    where he sits with the other civic leaders.
24 She makes belted linen garments
    and sashes to sell to the merchants.

25 She is clothed with strength and dignity,
    and she laughs without fear of the future.
26 When she speaks, her words are wise,
    and she gives instructions with kindness.
27 She carefully watches everything in
        her household
    and suffers nothing from laziness.

28 Her children stand and bless her.
    Her husband praises her:
29 "There are many virtuous and capable
        women in the world,
    but you surpass them all!"

30 Charm is deceptive, and beauty does not last;
    but a woman who fears the LORD will be
        greatly praised.
31 Reward her for all she has done.
    Let her deeds publicly declare her praise.

_____

31:21 As in Greek and Latin versions; Hebrew reads *scarlet*.

ECCLESIASTES

JON HUNTZINGER, PHD

The book of Ecclesiastes is attributed to King Solomon, even though the book does not mention him by name. However, the first line of the book reads, "These are the words of the Teacher, King David's son, who ruled in Jerusalem," and 1:12 states, "I, the Teacher, was king of Israel, and I lived in Jerusalem." Throughout history, many people have considered that the "Teacher" refers to Solomon, a son of David and king in Jerusalem. This thought is further supported by the reflections in the book given from the perspective of someone who has experienced much in life and is conflicted by what he has gone through, which could well describe Solomon.

The word *Teacher* translates the Hebrew word *Qohelet*. Since *Qohelet* is based upon the Hebrew word that means 'congregation' or 'assembly,' "Teacher" is often used because it is thought that someone related to the assembly of the people of Israel gave the book's instruction. Since Ecclesiastes refers to David's son (Solomon) within the first 12 verses, it was compiled sometime after his kingship in 930 BC.

The book begins with its primary themes in chapter 1, continues with a long teaching by *Qohelet* based on his life experiences (chapters 2-11), and concludes with an epilogue in chapter 12.

A primary teaching in Ecclesiastes is balance in life. In chapter 3, for example, the writer says that there is a time for everything. Then he names some of the experiences people have in life. There is a time for birth and a time for death (3:2), there is a time to cry and a time to laugh (3:4), and there is a time to keep and a time to throw away (3:6). Following the two distinct ways delineated in other books of the Bible (Deuteronomy, Psalms, Proverbs), the writer of Ecclesiastes contrasts wisdom and foolishness and exhorts his readers to seek wisdom and to act wisely (7:1-13; 9:13-10:20). The writer encourages people to enjoy their work and the fruit that comes from it (2:24; 3:12-13).

Another major theme in Ecclesiastes is meaninglessness. The word itself means *ephemeral* or passing like vapor. The book describes many things of life as meaningless. For instance, life is meaningless because it ends in death. Work can be meaningless, and even wisdom can be meaningless! Life passes, work passes, and wisdom passes. For this reason, Ecclesiastes is unusual among the books of the Bible for some of its exhortations. Not only does the writer declare that "everything is meaningless" (2:17), but he also advises, "Don't be too good or too wise!" (7:16). Because there are many such statements in the book, it is important to read all of it in view of the final chapter where the reader is encouraged to "fear God and obey His commands" (12:13). What ultimately gives meaning in life is cultivating a relationship with God by living according to the Word He has given to His people, which reveals His heart and desire for them.

Ecclesiastes has an important place in the canon, the collection of the accepted books of the Bible. It preserves the feelings and outlook on life that many people have from time to time. It recognizes that people struggle with questions of meaning, feelings of despair, and the need for security. The answer is as simple as it is profound: "Fear God instead" (5:7). He is the one with whom you must live in relationship.

1 These are the words of the Teacher,* King David's son, who ruled in Jerusalem.

EVERYTHING IS MEANINGLESS

2 "Everything is meaningless," says the Teacher, "completely meaningless!"

3 What do people get for all their hard work under the sun? 4 Generations come and generations go, but the earth never changes. 5 The sun rises and the sun sets, then hurries around to rise again. 6 The wind blows south, and then turns north. Around and around it goes, blowing in circles. 7 Rivers run into the sea, but the sea is never full. Then the water returns again to the rivers and flows out again to the sea. 8 Everything is wearisome beyond description. No matter how much we see, we are never satisfied. No matter how much we hear, we are not content.

9 History merely repeats itself. It has all been done before. Nothing under the sun is truly new. 10 Sometimes people say, "Here is something new!" But actually it is old; nothing is ever truly new. 11 We don't remember what happened in the past, and in future generations, no one will remember what we are doing now.

THE TEACHER SPEAKS: THE FUTILITY OF WISDOM

12 I, the Teacher, was king of Israel, and I lived in Jerusalem. 13 I devoted myself to search for understanding and to explore by wisdom everything being done under heaven. I soon discovered that God has dealt a tragic existence to the human race. 14 I observed everything going on under the sun, and really, it is all meaningless—like chasing the wind.

15 What is wrong cannot be made right.
　　What is missing cannot be recovered.

16 I said to myself, "Look, I am wiser than any of the kings who ruled in Jerusalem before me. I have greater wisdom and knowledge than any of them." 17 So I set out to learn everything from wisdom to madness and folly. But I learned firsthand that pursuing all this is like chasing the wind.

18 The greater my wisdom,
　　the greater my grief.
　　To increase knowledge only increases
　　　sorrow.

THE FUTILITY OF PLEASURE

2 I said to myself, "Come on, let's try pleasure. Let's look for the 'good things' in life." But I found that this, too, was meaningless. 2 So I said, "Laughter is silly. What good does it do to seek pleasure?" 3 After much thought, I decided to cheer myself with wine. And while still seeking wisdom, I clutched at foolishness. In this way, I tried to experience the only happiness most people find during their brief life in this world.

4 I also tried to find meaning by building huge homes for myself and by planting beautiful vineyards. 5 I made gardens and parks, filling them with all kinds of fruit trees. 6 I built reservoirs to collect the water to irrigate my many flourishing groves. 7 I bought slaves, both men and women, and others were born into my household. I also owned large herds and flocks, more than any of the kings who had lived in Jerusalem before me. 8 I collected great sums of silver and gold, the treasure of many kings and provinces. I hired wonderful singers, both men and women, and had many beautiful concubines. I had everything a man could desire!

9 So I became greater than all who had lived in Jerusalem before me, and my wisdom never failed me. 10 Anything I wanted, I would take. I denied myself no pleasure. I even found great pleasure in hard work, a reward for all my labors. 11 But as I looked at everything I had worked so hard to accomplish, it was all so meaningless—like chasing the wind. There was nothing really worthwhile anywhere.

THE WISE AND THE FOOLISH

12 So I decided to compare wisdom with foolishness and madness (for who can do this better than I, the king?*). 13 I thought, "Wisdom is better than foolishness, just as light is better than darkness. 14 For the wise can see where they are going, but fools walk in the dark." Yet I saw that the wise and the foolish share the same fate. 15 Both will die. So I said to myself, "Since I will end up the same as the fool, what's the value of all my wisdom? This is all so meaningless!" 16 For the wise and the foolish both die. The wise will not be remembered any longer than the fool. In the days to come, both will be forgotten.

17 So I came to hate life because everything done here under the sun is so troubling. Everything is meaningless—like chasing the wind.

THE FUTILITY OF WORK

18 I came to hate all my hard work here on earth, for I must leave to others everything I have earned. 19 And who can tell whether my successors will be wise or foolish? Yet they will control everything I have gained by my skill and hard work under the sun. How meaningless! 20 So I gave up in despair, questioning the value of all my hard work in this world.

21 Some people work wisely with knowledge and skill, then must leave the fruit of their efforts to someone who hasn't worked for it. This, too, is meaningless, a great tragedy. 22 So what do people get in this life for all their hard work and anxiety? 23 Their days of labor are filled with pain and grief; even at night their minds cannot rest. It is all meaningless.

1:1 Hebrew *Qoheleth;* this term is rendered "the Teacher" throughout this book. 2:12 The meaning of the Hebrew is uncertain.

²⁴So I decided there is nothing better than to enjoy food and drink and to find satisfaction in work. Then I realized that these pleasures are from the hand of God. ²⁵For who can eat or enjoy anything apart from him?* ²⁶God gives wisdom, knowledge, and joy to those who please him. But if a sinner becomes wealthy, God takes the wealth away and gives it to those who please him. This, too, is meaningless—like chasing the wind.

A TIME FOR EVERYTHING

3 ¹ For everything there is a season,
a time for every activity under heaven.
² A time to be born and a time to die.
A time to plant and a time to harvest.
³ A time to kill and a time to heal.
A time to tear down and a time to build up.
⁴ A time to cry and a time to laugh.
A time to grieve and a time to dance.
⁵ A time to scatter stones and a time to gather stones.
A time to embrace and a time to turn away.
⁶ A time to search and a time to quit searching.
A time to keep and a time to throw away.
⁷ A time to tear and a time to mend.
A time to be quiet and a time to speak.
⁸ A time to love and a time to hate.
A time for war and a time for peace.

⁹What do people really get for all their hard work? ¹⁰I have seen the burden God has placed on us all. ¹¹Yet God has made everything beautiful for its own time. He has planted eternity in the human heart, but even so, people cannot see the whole scope of God's work from beginning to end. ¹²So I concluded there is nothing better than to be happy and enjoy ourselves as long as we can. ¹³And people should eat and drink and enjoy the fruits of their labor, for these are gifts from God.

¹⁴And I know that whatever God does is final. Nothing can be added to it or taken from it. God's purpose is that people should fear him. ¹⁵What is happening now has happened before, and what will happen in the future has happened before, because God makes the same things happen over and over again.

THE INJUSTICES OF LIFE

¹⁶I also noticed that under the sun there is evil in the courtroom. Yes, even the courts of law are corrupt! ¹⁷I said to myself, "In due season God will judge everyone, both good and bad, for all their deeds."

¹⁸I also thought about the human condition—how God proves to people that they are like animals. ¹⁹For people and animals share the same fate—both breathe* and both must die. So people have no real advantage over the animals. How meaningless! ²⁰Both go to the same place—they came from dust and they return to dust. ²¹For who can prove that the human spirit goes up and the spirit of animals goes down into the earth? ²²So I saw that there is nothing better for people than to be happy in their work. That is our lot in life. And no one can bring us back to see what happens after we die.

4 Again, I observed all the oppression that takes place under the sun. I saw the tears of the oppressed, with no one to comfort them. The oppressors have great power, and their victims are helpless. ²So I concluded that the dead are better off than the living. ³But most fortunate of all are those who are not yet born. For they have not seen all the evil that is done under the sun.

⁴Then I observed that most people are motivated to success because they envy their neighbors. But this, too, is meaningless—like chasing the wind.

⁵ "Fools fold their idle hands,
leading them to ruin."

⁶And yet,

"Better to have one handful with quietness
than two handfuls with hard work
and chasing the wind."

THE ADVANTAGES OF COMPANIONSHIP

⁷I observed yet another example of something meaningless under the sun. ⁸This is the case of a man who is all alone, without a child or a brother, yet who works hard to gain as much wealth as he can. But then he asks himself, "Who am I working for? Why am I giving up so much pleasure now?" It is all so meaningless and depressing.

⁹Two people are better off than one, for they can help each other succeed. ¹⁰If one person falls, the other can reach out and help. But someone who falls alone is in real trouble. ¹¹Likewise, two people lying close together can keep each other warm. But how can one be warm alone? ¹²A person standing alone can be attacked and defeated, but two can stand back-to-back and conquer. Three are even better, for a triple-braided cord is not easily broken.

THE FUTILITY OF POLITICAL POWER

¹³It is better to be a poor but wise youth than an old and foolish king who refuses all advice. ¹⁴Such a youth could rise from poverty and succeed. He might even become king, though he has been in prison. ¹⁵But then everyone rushes to the side of yet another youth* who replaces him. ¹⁶Endless crowds stand around him,* but then another generation grows up and rejects him, too. So it is all meaningless—like chasing the wind.

2:25 As in Greek and Syriac versions; Hebrew reads *apart from me?* 3:19 Or *both have the same spirit.* 4:15 Hebrew *the second youth.* 4:16 Hebrew *There is no end to all the people, to all those who are before them.*

APPROACHING GOD WITH CARE

5 [1]*As you enter the house of God, keep your ears open and your mouth shut. It is evil to make mindless offerings to God. [2]*Don't make rash promises, and don't be hasty in bringing matters before God. After all, God is in heaven, and you are here on earth. So let your words be few.

[3] Too much activity gives you restless dreams; too many words make you a fool.

[4] When you make a promise to God, don't delay in following through, for God takes no pleasure in fools. Keep all the promises you make to him. [5] It is better to say nothing than to make a promise and not keep it. [6] Don't let your mouth make you sin. And don't defend yourself by telling the Temple messenger that the promise you made was a mistake. That would make God angry, and he might wipe out everything you have achieved.

[7] Talk is cheap, like daydreams and other useless activities. Fear God instead.

THE FUTILITY OF WEALTH

[8] Don't be surprised if you see a poor person being oppressed by the powerful and if justice is being miscarried throughout the land. For every official is under orders from higher up, and matters of justice get lost in red tape and bureaucracy. [9] Even the king milks the land for his own profit!*

[10] Those who love money will never have enough. How meaningless to think that wealth brings true happiness! [11] The more you have, the more people come to help you spend it. So what good is wealth—except perhaps to watch it slip through your fingers!

[12] People who work hard sleep well, whether they eat little or much. But the rich seldom get a good night's sleep.

[13] There is another serious problem I have seen under the sun. Hoarding riches harms the saver. [14] Money is put into risky investments that turn sour, and everything is lost. In the end, there is nothing left to pass on to one's children. [15] We all come to the end of our lives as naked and empty-handed as on the day we were born. We can't take our riches with us.

[16] And this, too, is a very serious problem. People leave this world no better off than when they came. All their hard work is for nothing— like working for the wind. [17] Throughout their lives, they live under a cloud—frustrated, discouraged, and angry.

[18] Even so, I have noticed one thing, at least, that is good. It is good for people to eat, drink, and enjoy their work under the sun during the short life God has given them, and to accept their lot in life. [19] And it is a good thing to receive wealth from God and the good health to enjoy it. To enjoy your work and accept your lot in life—this is indeed a gift from God. [20] God keeps such people so busy enjoying life that they take no time to brood over the past.

6 There is another serious tragedy I have seen under the sun, and it weighs heavily on humanity. [2] God gives some people great wealth and honor and everything they could ever want, but then he doesn't give them the chance to enjoy these things. They die, and someone else, even a stranger, ends up enjoying their wealth! This is meaningless—a sickening tragedy.

[3] A man might have a hundred children and live to be very old. But if he finds no satisfaction in life and doesn't even get a decent burial, it would have been better for him to be born dead. [4] His birth would have been meaningless, and he would have ended in darkness. He wouldn't even have had a name, [5] and he would never have seen the sun or known of its existence. Yet he would have had more peace than in growing up to be an unhappy man. [6] He might live a thousand years twice over but still not find contentment. And since he must die like everyone else—well, what's the use?

[7] All people spend their lives scratching for food, but they never seem to have enough. [8] So are wise people really better off than fools? Do poor people gain anything by being wise and knowing how to act in front of others?

[9] Enjoy what you have rather than desiring what you don't have. Just dreaming about nice things is meaningless—like chasing the wind.

THE FUTURE—DETERMINED AND UNKNOWN

[10] Everything has already been decided. It was known long ago what each person would be. So there's no use arguing with God about your destiny.

[11] The more words you speak, the less they mean. So what good are they?

[12] In the few days of our meaningless lives, who knows how our days can best be spent? Our lives are like a shadow. Who can tell what will happen on this earth after we are gone?

WISDOM FOR LIFE

7 [1] A good reputation is more valuable than costly perfume.
And the day you die is better than the day you are born.
[2] Better to spend your time at funerals than at parties.
After all, everyone dies—
so the living should take this to heart.
[3] Sorrow is better than laughter,
for sadness has a refining influence on us.
[4] A wise person thinks a lot about death,
while a fool thinks only about having a good time.

[5] Better to be criticized by a wise person
than to be praised by a fool.

5:1 Verse 5:1 is numbered 4:17 in Hebrew text.   5:2 Verses 5:2-20 are numbered 5:1-19 in Hebrew text.   5:9 The meaning of the Hebrew in verses 8 and 9 is uncertain.

⁶ A fool's laughter is quickly gone,
    like thorns crackling in a fire.
    This also is meaningless.

⁷ Extortion turns wise people into fools,
    and bribes corrupt the heart.

⁸ Finishing is better than starting.
    Patience is better than pride.

⁹ Control your temper,
    for anger labels you a fool.

¹⁰ Don't long for "the good old days."
    This is not wise.

¹¹ Wisdom is even better when you have money.
    Both are a benefit as you go through life.
¹² Wisdom and money can get you almost
    anything,
    but only wisdom can save your life.

¹³ Accept the way God does things,
    for who can straighten what he has
    made crooked?
¹⁴ Enjoy prosperity while you can,
    but when hard times strike, realize that
    both come from God.
    Remember that nothing is certain in
    this life.

THE LIMITS OF HUMAN WISDOM

¹⁵ I have seen everything in this meaningless life, including the death of good young people and the long life of wicked people. ¹⁶ So don't be too good or too wise! Why destroy yourself? ¹⁷ On the other hand, don't be too wicked either. Don't be a fool! Why die before your time? ¹⁸ Pay attention to these instructions, for anyone who fears God will avoid both extremes.*

¹⁹ One wise person is stronger than ten leading citizens of a town!

²⁰ Not a single person on earth is always good and never sins.

²¹ Don't eavesdrop on others—you may hear your servant curse you. ²² For you know how often you yourself have cursed others.

²³ I have always tried my best to let wisdom guide my thoughts and actions. I said to myself, "I am determined to be wise." But it didn't work. ²⁴ Wisdom is always distant and difficult to find. ²⁵ I searched everywhere, determined to find wisdom and to understand the reason for things. I was determined to prove to myself that wickedness is stupid and that foolishness is madness. ²⁶ I discovered that a seductive woman* is a trap more bitter than death. Her passion is a snare, and her soft hands are chains. Those who are pleasing to God will escape her, but sinners will be caught in her snare. ²⁷ "This is my conclusion," says the Teacher. "I discovered this after looking at the matter from every possible angle. ²⁸ Though I have searched repeatedly, I have not found what I was looking for. Only one out of a thousand men is virtuous, but not one woman! ²⁹ But I did find this: God created people to be virtuous, but they have each turned to follow their own downward path."

8 ¹ How wonderful to be wise,
    to analyze and interpret things.
Wisdom lights up a person's face,
    softening its harshness.

OBEDIENCE TO THE KING

² Obey the king since you vowed to God that you would. ³ Don't try to avoid doing your duty, and don't stand with those who plot evil, for the king can do whatever he wants. ⁴ His command is backed by great power. No one can resist or question it. ⁵ Those who obey him will not be punished. Those who are wise will find a time and a way to do what is right, ⁶ for there is a time and a way for everything, even when a person is in trouble.

⁷ Indeed, how can people avoid what they don't know is going to happen? ⁸ None of us can hold back our spirit from departing. None of us has the power to prevent the day of our death. There is no escaping that obligation, that dark battle. And in the face of death, wickedness will certainly not rescue the wicked.

THE WICKED AND THE RIGHTEOUS

⁹ I have thought deeply about all that goes on here under the sun, where people have the power to hurt each other. ¹⁰ I have seen wicked people buried with honor. Yet they were the very ones who frequented the Temple and are now praised* in the same city where they committed their crimes! This, too, is meaningless. ¹¹ When a crime is not punished quickly, people feel it is safe to do wrong. ¹² But even though a person sins a hundred times and still lives a long time, I know that those who fear God will be better off. ¹³ The wicked will not prosper, for they do not fear God. Their days will never grow long like the evening shadows.

¹⁴ And this is not all that is meaningless in our world. In this life, good people are often treated as though they were wicked, and wicked people are often treated as though they were good. This is so meaningless!

¹⁵ So I recommend having fun, because there is nothing better for people in this world than to eat, drink, and enjoy life. That way they will experience some happiness along with all the hard work God gives them under the sun.

¹⁶ In my search for wisdom and in my observation of people's burdens here on earth, I discovered that there is ceaseless activity, day and

7:18 Or will follow them both. 7:26 Hebrew a woman. 8:10 As in some Hebrew manuscripts and Greek version; many Hebrew manuscripts read and are forgotten.

night. ¹⁷I realized that no one can discover everything God is doing under the sun. Not even the wisest people discover everything, no matter what they claim.

DEATH COMES TO ALL

9 This, too, I carefully explored: Even though the actions of godly and wise people are in God's hands, no one knows whether God will show them favor. ²The same destiny ultimately awaits everyone, whether righteous or wicked, good or bad,* ceremonially clean or unclean, religious or irreligious. Good people receive the same treatment as sinners, and people who make promises to God are treated like people who don't.

³It seems so wrong that everyone under the sun suffers the same fate. Already twisted by evil, people choose their own mad course, for they have no hope. There is nothing ahead but death anyway. ⁴There is hope only for the living. As they say, "It's better to be a live dog than a dead lion!"

⁵The living at least know they will die, but the dead know nothing. They have no further reward, nor are they remembered. ⁶Whatever they did in their lifetime—loving, hating, envying—is all long gone. They no longer play a part in anything here on earth. ⁷So go ahead. Eat your food with joy, and drink your wine with a happy heart, for God approves of this! ⁸Wear fine clothes, with a splash of cologne!

⁹Live happily with the woman you love through all the meaningless days of life that God has given you under the sun. The wife God gives you is your reward for all your earthly toil. ¹⁰Whatever you do, do well. For when you go to the grave,* there will be no work or planning or knowledge or wisdom.

¹¹I have observed something else under the sun. The fastest runner doesn't always win the race, and the strongest warrior doesn't always win the battle. The wise sometimes go hungry, and the skillful are not necessarily wealthy. And those who are educated don't always lead successful lives. It is all decided by chance, by being in the right place at the right time.

¹²People can never predict when hard times might come. Like fish in a net or birds in a trap, people are caught by sudden tragedy.

THOUGHTS ON WISDOM AND FOLLY

¹³Here is another bit of wisdom that has impressed me as I have watched the way our world works. ¹⁴There was a small town with only a few people, and a great king came with his army and besieged it. ¹⁵A poor, wise man knew how to save the town, and so it was rescued. But afterward no one thought to thank him. ¹⁶So even though wisdom is better than strength, those who are wise will be despised if they are poor. What they say will not be appreciated for long.

¹⁷ Better to hear the quiet words of
a wise person
than the shouts of a foolish king.
¹⁸ Better to have wisdom than weapons
of war,
but one sinner can destroy much
that is good.

10 ¹ As dead flies cause even a bottle of
perfume to stink,
so a little foolishness spoils great wisdom
and honor.

² A wise person chooses the right road;
a fool takes the wrong one.

³ You can identify fools
just by the way they walk down
the street!

⁴ If your boss is angry at you, don't quit!
A quiet spirit can overcome even great
mistakes.

THE IRONIES OF LIFE

⁵There is another evil I have seen under the sun. Kings and rulers make a grave mistake ⁶when they give great authority to foolish people and low positions to people of proven worth. ⁷I have even seen servants riding horseback like princes—and princes walking like servants!

⁸ When you dig a well,
you might fall in.
When you demolish an old wall,
you could be bitten by a snake.
⁹ When you work in a quarry,
stones might fall and crush you.
When you chop wood,
there is danger with each stroke
of your ax.

¹⁰ Using a dull ax requires great strength,
so sharpen the blade.
That's the value of wisdom;
it helps you succeed.

¹¹ If a snake bites before you charm it,
what's the use of being a snake charmer?

¹² Wise words bring approval,
but fools are destroyed by their
own words.

¹³ Fools base their thoughts on foolish
assumptions,
so their conclusions will be wicked
madness;
¹⁴ they chatter on and on.

9:2 As in Greek and Syriac versions and Latin Vulgate; Hebrew lacks *or bad.* 9:10 Hebrew *to Sheol.*

No one really knows what is going
 to happen;
 no one can predict the future.

¹⁵ Fools are so exhausted by a little work
 that they can't even find their way home.

¹⁶ What sorrow for the land ruled by a servant,*
 the land whose leaders feast in the
 morning.
¹⁷ Happy is the land whose king is
 a noble leader
 and whose leaders feast at
 the proper time
 to gain strength for their work,
 not to get drunk.

¹⁸ Laziness leads to a sagging roof;
 idleness leads to a leaky house.

¹⁹ A party gives laughter,
 wine gives happiness,
 and money gives everything!

²⁰ Never make light of the king,
 even in your thoughts.
 And don't make fun of the powerful,
 even in your own bedroom.
 For a little bird might deliver your message
 and tell them what you said.

THE UNCERTAINTIES OF LIFE

11 ¹ Send your grain across the seas,
 and in time, profits will flow back
 to you.*
² But divide your investments among
 many places,*
 for you do not know what risks might
 lie ahead.

³ When clouds are heavy,
 the rains come down.
 Whether a tree falls north or south,
 it stays where it falls.

⁴ Farmers who wait for perfect weather
 never plant.
 If they watch every cloud,
 they never harvest.

⁵ Just as you cannot understand the path of the wind or the mystery of a tiny baby growing in its mother's womb,* so you cannot understand the activity of God, who does all things.
⁶ Plant your seed in the morning and keep busy all afternoon, for you don't know if profit will come from one activity or another—or maybe both.

ADVICE FOR YOUNG AND OLD

⁷ Light is sweet; how pleasant to see a new day dawning.

⁸ When people live to be very old, let them rejoice in every day of life. But let them also remember there will be many dark days. Everything still to come is meaningless.
⁹ Young people,* it's wonderful to be young! Enjoy every minute of it. Do everything you want to do; take it all in. But remember that you must give an account to God for everything you do. ¹⁰ So refuse to worry, and keep your body healthy. But remember that youth, with a whole life before you, is meaningless.

12 Don't let the excitement of youth cause you to forget your Creator. Honor him in your youth before you grow old and say, "Life is not pleasant anymore." ² Remember him before the light of the sun, moon, and stars is dim to your old eyes, and rain clouds continually darken your sky. ³ Remember him before your legs—the guards of your house—start to tremble; and before your shoulders—the strong men—stoop. Remember him before your teeth—your few remaining servants—stop grinding; and before your eyes—the women looking through the windows—see dimly.

⁴ Remember him before the door to life's opportunities is closed and the sound of work fades. Now you rise at the first chirping of the birds, but then all their sounds will grow faint.

⁵ Remember him before you become fearful of falling and worry about danger in the streets; before your hair turns white like an almond tree in bloom, and you drag along without energy like a dying grasshopper, and the caperberry no longer inspires sexual desire. Remember him before you near the grave, your everlasting home, when the mourners will weep at your funeral.

⁶ Yes, remember your Creator now while you are young, before the silver cord of life snaps and the golden bowl is broken. Don't wait until the water jar is smashed at the spring and the pulley is broken at the well. ⁷ For then the dust will return to the earth, and the spirit will return to God who gave it.

CONCLUDING THOUGHTS ABOUT THE TEACHER

⁸ "Everything is meaningless," says the Teacher, "completely meaningless."

⁹ Keep this in mind: The Teacher was considered wise, and he taught the people everything he knew. He listened carefully to many proverbs, studying and classifying them. ¹⁰ The Teacher sought to find just the right words to express truths clearly.*

10:16 Or *a child.* **11:1** Or *Give generously, / for your gifts will return to you later.* Hebrew reads *Throw your bread on the waters, / for after many days you will find it again.* **11:2** Hebrew *among seven or even eight.* **11:5** Some manuscripts read *Just as you cannot understand how breath comes to a tiny baby in its mother's womb.* **11:9** Hebrew *Young man.* **12:10** Or *sought to write what was upright and true.*

11 The words of the wise are like cattle prods—painful but helpful. Their collected sayings are like a nail-studded stick with which a shepherd* drives the sheep.

12 But, my child,* let me give you some further advice: Be careful, for writing books is endless, and much study wears you out.

13 That's the whole story. Here now is my final conclusion: Fear God and obey his commands, for this is everyone's duty. 14 God will judge us for everything we do, including every secret thing, whether good or bad.

____

12:11 Or *one shepherd.*   12:12 Hebrew *my son.*

SONG OF SONGS

JON HUNTZINGER, PHD

Song of Songs identifies King Solomon as the author or compiler of the material in the first verse. The book is also known as the Song of Solomon. The title *Song of Songs* is a translation of the superlative in Hebrew, meaning the greatest of all songs.

At one time, Song of Songs was read either as an allegory of God's love for Israel or, within Christian circles, as Christ's love for His Church. All of these allegorical interpretations avoided direct references to human sexual love. Today, Bible scholars usually regard the book as either a written drama of a man and woman's love for one another or as a collection of love poems that give lyrical expression to human sexual love. The New Living Translation adds the words "Young Woman," "Young Man," and "Young Women of Jerusalem" in the fashion of a script to identify who is speaking in the drama, though these words were not part of the original Hebrew.

Most people who read the book as a drama see Solomon and a young Shulammite woman as the two main characters in the story, who are joined in places by a chorus of young women. The book describes the couple throughout as "the lover" and "the beloved." The drama progresses from their expressions of desire for each other to their marriage and then to trouble in their marriage, which they ultimately overcome due to their deep love for each other. Others who read the book as a drama see three main characters. They see Solomon, a young Shulammite woman, and a young shepherd with whom she is in love. According to this reading, even after Solomon takes the young woman and places her in his harem, she remains passionately in love with the young shepherd.

Not everyone reads the book as a drama. Some see it as a collection of love poems similar to other love poetry from the ancient world that describe the strong feelings of love a man and a woman share. The wisdom of such poetry is the affirmation and celebration of human sexual love and identity within marriage and the honest recognition that even the most intimate and close human relationships at times are tested.

1

This is Solomon's song of songs, more wonderful than any other.

Young Woman*

² Kiss me and kiss me again,
for your love is sweeter than wine.
³ How pleasing is your fragrance;
your name is like the spreading fragrance
of scented oils.
No wonder all the young women love you!
⁴ Take me with you; come, let's run!
The king has brought me into
his bedroom.

Young Women of Jerusalem

How happy we are for you, O king.
We praise your love even more
than wine.

Young Woman

How right they are to adore you.

⁵ I am dark but beautiful,
O women of Jerusalem—
dark as the tents of Kedar,
dark as the curtains of Solomon's tents.
⁶ Don't stare at me because I am dark—
the sun has darkened my skin.
My brothers were angry with me;
they forced me to care for their vineyards,
so I couldn't care for myself—my own
vineyard.

⁷ Tell me, my love, where are you leading your
flock today?
Where will you rest your sheep at noon?
For why should I wander like a prostitute*
among your friends and their flocks?

Young Man

⁸ If you don't know, O most beautiful woman,
follow the trail of my flock,
and graze your young goats by the
shepherds' tents.
⁹ You are as exciting, my darling,
as a mare among Pharaoh's stallions.
¹⁰ How lovely are your cheeks;
your earrings set them afire!
How lovely is your neck,
enhanced by a string of jewels.
¹¹ We will make for you earrings of gold
and beads of silver.

Young Woman

¹² The king is lying on his couch,
enchanted by the fragrance of my
perfume.
¹³ My lover is like a sachet of myrrh
lying between my breasts.
¹⁴ He is like a bouquet of sweet henna
blossoms
from the vineyards of En-gedi.

Young Man

¹⁵ How beautiful you are, my darling,
how beautiful!
Your eyes are like doves.

Young Woman

¹⁶ You are so handsome, my love,
pleasing beyond words!
The soft grass is our bed;
¹⁷ fragrant cedar branches are the beams of
our house,
and pleasant smelling firs are the rafters.

Young Woman

2

¹ I am the spring crocus blooming on
the Sharon Plain,*
the lily of the valley.

Young Man

² Like a lily among thistles
is my darling among young women.

Young Woman

³ Like the finest apple tree in the orchard
is my lover among other young men.
I sit in his delightful shade
and taste his delicious fruit.
⁴ He escorts me to the banquet hall;
it's obvious how much he loves me.
⁵ Strengthen me with raisin cakes,
refresh me with apples,
for I am weak with love.
⁶ His left arm is under my head,
and his right arm embraces me.

⁷ Promise me, O women of Jerusalem,
by the gazelles and wild deer,
not to awaken love until the time is right.*

⁸ Ah, I hear my lover coming!
He is leaping over the mountains,
bounding over the hills.
⁹ My lover is like a swift gazelle
or a young stag.
Look, there he is behind the wall,
looking through the window,
peering into the room.

¹⁰ My lover said to me,
"Rise up, my darling!
Come away with me, my fair one!
¹¹ Look, the winter is past,
and the rains are over and gone.
¹² The flowers are springing up,
the season of singing birds* has come,
and the cooing of turtledoves fills the air.

1:1 The headings identifying the speakers are not in the original text, though the Hebrew usually gives clues by means of the gender of the person speaking. 1:7 Hebrew *like a veiled woman.* 2:1 Traditionally rendered *I am the rose of Sharon.* Sharon Plain is a region in the coastal plain of Palestine. 2:7 Or *not to awaken love until it is ready.* 2:12 Or *the season of pruning vines.*

¹³ The fig trees are forming young fruit,
    and the fragrant grapevines are
        blossoming.
Rise up, my darling!
    Come away with me, my fair one!"

Young Man
¹⁴ My dove is hiding behind the rocks,
    behind an outcrop on the cliff.
Let me see your face;
    let me hear your voice.
For your voice is pleasant,
    and your face is lovely.

Young Women of Jerusalem
¹⁵ Catch all the foxes,
    those little foxes,
before they ruin the vineyard of love,
    for the grapevines are blossoming!

Young Woman
¹⁶ My lover is mine, and I am his.
    He browses among the lilies.
¹⁷ Before the dawn breezes blow
    and the night shadows flee,
return to me, my love, like a gazelle
    or a young stag on the rugged
        mountains.*

Young Woman
3 ¹ One night as I lay in bed,
    I yearned for my lover.
I yearned for him, but he did not come.
² So I said to myself,
    "I will get up and roam the city,
searching in all its streets and squares.
    I will search for the one I love."
So I searched everywhere but did not
    find him.
³ The watchmen stopped me as they made
    their rounds,
and I asked, "Have you seen the one
    I love?"
⁴ Then scarcely had I left them
    when I found my love!
I caught and held him tightly,
    then I brought him to my mother's house,
    into my mother's bed,
        where I had been conceived.

⁵ Promise me, O women of Jerusalem,
    by the gazelles and wild deer,
not to awaken love until the time
    is right.*

Young Women of Jerusalem
⁶ Who is this sweeping in from
    the wilderness
like a cloud of smoke?
Who is it, fragrant with myrrh
    and frankincense
        and every kind of spice?

⁷ Look, it is Solomon's carriage,
    surrounded by sixty heroic men,
    the best of Israel's soldiers.
⁸ They are all skilled swordsmen,
    experienced warriors.
Each wears a sword on his thigh,
    ready to defend the king against an attack
        in the night.
⁹ King Solomon's carriage is built
    of wood imported from Lebanon.
¹⁰ Its posts are silver,
    its canopy gold;
    its cushions are purple.
It was decorated with love
    by the young women of Jerusalem.

Young Woman
¹¹ Come out to see King Solomon,
    young women of Jerusalem.*
He wears the crown his mother gave him on
    his wedding day,
    his most joyous day.

Young Man
4 ¹ You are beautiful, my darling,
    beautiful beyond words.
Your eyes are like doves
    behind your veil.
Your hair falls in waves,
    like a flock of goats winding down the
        slopes of Gilead.
² Your teeth are as white as sheep,
    recently shorn and freshly washed.
Your smile is flawless,
    each tooth matched with its twin.*
³ Your lips are like scarlet ribbon;
    your mouth is inviting.
Your cheeks are like rosy pomegranates
    behind your veil.
⁴ Your neck is as beautiful as the tower of
    David,
    jeweled with the shields of a thousand
        heroes.
⁵ Your breasts are like two fawns,
    twin fawns of a gazelle grazing among
        the lilies.
⁶ Before the dawn breezes blow
    and the night shadows flee,
I will hurry to the mountain of myrrh
    and to the hill of frankincense.
⁷ You are altogether beautiful, my darling,
    beautiful in every way.

⁸ Come with me from Lebanon, my bride,
    come with me from Lebanon.
Come down* from Mount Amana,
    from the peaks of Senir and Hermon,
where the lions have their dens
    and leopards live among the hills.

2:17 Or *on the hills of Bether.* 3:5 Or *not to awaken love until it is ready.* 3:11 Hebrew *of Zion.* 4:2 Hebrew *Not one is missing; each has a twin.* 4:8 Or *Look down.*

9 You have captured my heart,
  my treasure,* my bride.
You hold it hostage with one glance of
  your eyes,
  with a single jewel of your necklace.
10 Your love delights me,
  my treasure, my bride.
Your love is better than wine,
  your perfume more fragrant than spices.
11 Your lips are as sweet as nectar, my bride.
  Honey and milk are under your tongue.
Your clothes are scented
  like the cedars of Lebanon.

12 You are my private garden, my treasure,
  my bride,
  a secluded spring, a hidden fountain.
13 Your thighs shelter a paradise of
  pomegranates
  with rare spices—
henna with nard,
14   nard and saffron,
  fragrant calamus and cinnamon,
with all the trees of frankincense,
  myrrh, and aloes,
  and every other lovely spice.
15 You are a garden fountain,
  a well of fresh water
  streaming down from Lebanon's
  mountains.

Young Woman
16 Awake, north wind!
  Rise up, south wind!
Blow on my garden
  and spread its fragrance all around.
Come into your garden, my love;
  taste its finest fruits.

Young Man
5 1 I have entered my garden,
  my treasure,* my bride!
I gather myrrh with my spices
and eat honeycomb with my honey.
  I drink wine with my milk.

Young Women of Jerusalem
Oh, lover and beloved, eat and drink!
  Yes, drink deeply of your love!

Young Woman
2 I slept, but my heart was awake,
  when I heard my lover knocking
  and calling:
"Open to me, my treasure, my darling,
  my dove, my perfect one.
My head is drenched with dew,
  my hair with the dampness of the night."

3 But I responded,
"I have taken off my robe.
  Should I get dressed again?

I have washed my feet.
  Should I get them soiled?"

4 My lover tried to unlatch the door,
  and my heart thrilled within me.
5 I jumped up to open the door for my love,
  and my hands dripped with perfume.
My fingers dripped with lovely myrrh
  as I pulled back the bolt.
6 I opened to my lover,
  but he was gone!
  My heart sank.
I searched for him
  but could not find him anywhere.
I called to him,
  but there was no reply.
7 The night watchmen found me
  as they made their rounds.
They beat and bruised me
  and stripped off my veil,
  those watchmen on the walls.

8 Make this promise,
  O women of Jerusalem—
If you find my lover,
  tell him I am weak with love.

Young Women of Jerusalem
9 Why is your lover better than all others,
  O woman of rare beauty?
What makes your lover so special
  that we must promise this?

Young Woman
10 My lover is dark and dazzling,
  better than ten thousand others!
11 His head is finest gold,
  his wavy hair is black as a raven.
12 His eyes sparkle like doves
  beside springs of water;
they are set like jewels
  washed in milk.
13 His cheeks are like gardens of spices
  giving off fragrance.
His lips are like lilies,
  perfumed with myrrh.
14 His arms are like rounded bars of gold,
  set with beryl.
His body is like bright ivory,
  glowing with lapis lazuli.
15 His legs are like marble pillars
  set in sockets of finest gold.
His posture is stately,
  like the noble cedars of Lebanon.
16 His mouth is sweetness itself;
  he is desirable in every way.
Such, O women of Jerusalem,
  is my lover, my friend.

4:9 Hebrew *my sister;* also in 4:10, 12.　5:1 Hebrew *my sister;*
also in 5:2.

Young Women of Jerusalem

6 ¹ Where has your lover gone,
O woman of rare beauty?
Which way did he turn
so we can help you find him?

Young Woman

² My lover has gone down to his garden,
to his spice beds,
to browse in the gardens
and gather the lilies.
³ I am my lover's, and my lover is mine.
He browses among the lilies.

Young Man

⁴ You are beautiful, my darling,
like the lovely city of Tirzah.
Yes, as beautiful as Jerusalem,
as majestic as an army with
billowing banners.
⁵ Turn your eyes away,
for they overpower me.
Your hair falls in waves,
like a flock of goats winding down
the slopes of Gilead.
⁶ Your teeth are as white as sheep
that are freshly washed.
Your smile is flawless,
each tooth matched with its twin.*
⁷ Your cheeks are like rosy pomegranates
behind your veil.

⁸ Even among sixty queens
and eighty concubines
and countless young women,
⁹ I would still choose my dove,
my perfect one—
the favorite of her mother,
dearly loved by the one who bore her.
The young women see her and praise her;
even queens and royal concubines sing
her praises:
¹⁰ "Who is this, arising like the dawn,
as fair as the moon,
as bright as the sun,
as majestic as an army with billowing
banners?"

Young Woman

¹¹ I went down to the grove of walnut trees
and out to the valley to see the new
spring growth,
to see whether the grapevines had budded
or the pomegranates were in bloom.
¹² Before I realized it,
my strong desires had taken me to the
chariot of a noble man.*

Young Women of Jerusalem

¹³*Return, return to us, O maid of Shulam.
Come back, come back,
that we may see you again.

Young Man

Why do you stare at this young woman
of Shulam,
as she moves so gracefully between two
lines of dancers?*

7 ¹*How beautiful are your sandaled feet,
O queenly maiden.
Your rounded thighs are like jewels,
the work of a skilled craftsman.
² Your navel is perfectly formed
like a goblet filled with mixed wine.
Between your thighs lies a mound of wheat
bordered with lilies.
³ Your breasts are like two fawns,
twin fawns of a gazelle.
⁴ Your neck is as beautiful as an ivory tower.
Your eyes are like the sparkling pools
in Heshbon
by the gate of Bath-rabbim.
Your nose is as fine as the tower of Lebanon
overlooking Damascus.
⁵ Your head is as majestic as Mount Carmel,
and the sheen of your hair radiates
royalty.
The king is held captive by its tresses.
⁶ Oh, how beautiful you are!
How pleasing, my love,
how full of delights!
⁷ You are slender like a palm tree,
and your breasts are like its clusters
of fruit.
⁸ I said, "I will climb the palm tree
and take hold of its fruit."
May your breasts be like grape clusters,
and the fragrance of your breath
like apples.
⁹ May your kisses be as exciting as
the best wine—

Young Woman

Yes, wine that goes down smoothly
for my lover,
flowing gently over lips and teeth.*
¹⁰ I am my lover's,
and he claims me as his own.
¹¹ Come, my love, let us go out to the fields
and spend the night among the
wildflowers.*
¹² Let us get up early and go to the vineyards
to see if the grapevines have budded,
if the blossoms have opened,
and if the pomegranates have bloomed.
There I will give you my love.

6:6 Hebrew *Not one is missing; each has a twin.* 6:12 Or *to the royal chariots of my people,* or *to the chariots of Amminadab.* The meaning of the Hebrew is uncertain. 6:13a Verse 6:13 is numbered 7:1 in Hebrew text. 6:13b Or *as you would at the movements of two armies?* or *as you would at the dance of Mahanaim?* The meaning of the Hebrew is uncertain. 7:1 Verses 7:1-13 are numbered 7:2-14 in Hebrew text. 7:9 As in Greek and Syriac versions and Latin Vulgate; Hebrew reads *over lips of sleepers.* 7:11 Or *in the villages.*

¹³ There the mandrakes give off
 their fragrance,
 and the finest fruits are at our door,
new delights as well as old,
 which I have saved for you, my lover.

Young Woman

8 ¹ Oh, I wish you were my brother,
 who nursed at my mother's breasts.
Then I could kiss you no matter
 who was watching,
 and no one would criticize me.
² I would bring you to my childhood home,
 and there you would teach me.*
I would give you spiced wine to drink,
 my sweet pomegranate wine.
³ Your left arm would be under my head,
 and your right arm would embrace me.

⁴ Promise me, O women of Jerusalem,
 not to awaken love until the time is right.*

Young Women of Jerusalem
⁵ Who is this sweeping in from the desert,
 leaning on her lover?

Young Woman
I aroused you under the apple tree,
 where your mother gave you birth,
 where in great pain she delivered you.
⁶ Place me like a seal over your heart,
 like a seal on your arm.
For love is as strong as death,
 its jealousy* as enduring as the grave.*
Love flashes like fire,
 the brightest kind of flame.
⁷ Many waters cannot quench love,
 nor can rivers drown it.
If a man tried to buy love
 with all his wealth,
 his offer would be utterly scorned.

The Young Woman's Brothers
⁸ We have a little sister
 too young to have breasts.
What will we do for our sister
 if someone asks to marry her?
⁹ If she is a virgin, like a wall,
 we will protect her with a silver tower.
But if she is promiscuous,
 like a swinging door,
 we will block her door with a cedar bar.

Young Woman
¹⁰ I was a virgin, like a wall;
 now my breasts are like towers.
When my lover looks at me,
 he is delighted with what he sees.

¹¹ Solomon has a vineyard at Baal-hamon,
 which he leases out to tenant farmers.
Each of them pays a thousand pieces
 of silver
 for harvesting its fruit.
¹² But my vineyard is mine to give,
 and Solomon need not pay a thousand
 pieces of silver.
But I will give two hundred pieces
 to those who care for its vines.

Young Man
¹³ O my darling, lingering in the gardens,
 your companions are fortunate to hear
 your voice.
 Let me hear it, too!

Young Woman
¹⁴ Come away, my love! Be like a gazelle
 or a young stag on the mountains
 of spices.

8:2 Or *there she will teach me.*   **8:4** Or *not to awaken love until it is ready.*   **8:6a** Or *its passion.*   **8:6b** Hebrew as *Sheol.*

— THE HISTORICAL CONTEXT — OF THE PROPHETS

JON HUNTZINGER, PHD

B eginning in the eighth century BC with Assyria, the people of Israel and their prophets were affected by the different foreign policy initiatives of the nations who controlled Israel's affairs. Assyria practiced a policy that may be described as assimilation. They forcibly removed many of the Israelites from their land to other regions Assyria had previously conquered, and they brought in other conquered peoples from those regions to Israel. The purpose of this practice was to encourage intermarriage and assimilation of the people, with their languages, cultures, and religions and, in the process, weaken the nationalistic feelings and allegiances they would naturally have for their individual languages, cultures, and religions.

The Babylonians rose to power in the late seventh century BC and followed a different foreign policy. Rather than moving large numbers of people around, the Babylonians identified the most valuable resources in a province and then took possession of them. They did this with people as well. They identified the best and the brightest and took them to Babylon, where they would learn the language of the Babylonians, eat their foods, wear their clothing, become familiar with their culture, and be trained to serve in the government. The Babylonians were not interested in common laborers or unskilled workers, but they were interested in educated people and those with specific skills. Thus, Daniel and the Hebrew young men described in the book of Daniel represent those who were deported to Babylon because they were useful and valuable to the Babylonians. This policy may be described as one of acquisition and removal.

The Persians practiced yet another form of foreign policy. Beginning in the sixth century BC, when they overthrew the Babylonians, the Persians allowed the people in conquered provinces some degree of self-government and religious freedom. By doing this, they promoted goodwill among the people for their policies and ensured the people's support against other empires such as Egypt and Greece. Cyrus and Artaxerxes demonstrated this type of initiative when they allowed Ezra and Nehemiah to return to the land to reinstate traditional worship and rebuild the walls of the city of Jerusalem and the Temple.

THE TEMPLE IN JERUSALEM

JON HUNTZINGER, PHD

Israel's Temple was located in Jerusalem. King David founded Jerusalem as the capital in 930 BC on the site of the ancient Jebusite town of Salem. Though David founded the city, he did not build the Temple. That privilege was reserved for his son Solomon, a brilliant and accomplished ruler who wrote 3,000 proverbs, composed more than 1,000 songs, studied botany and zoology, and established peaceful relations with numerous tribes and nations. He was also a builder who oversaw the construction of the Temple, the palace, the walls of Jerusalem, and the gates of the cities of Hazor, Megiddo, and Gezer. He accomplished all of these with forced labor from foreigners living in Israel: 30,000 men worked on Solomon's building projects, an additional 70,000 men carried burdens, and 80,000 men worked in the stone quarries.

Solomon paid for the Temple and his other building projects by collecting taxes from the people in the form of produce, animals, goods, and money. The Temple was expensive to build, especially given that Solomon used the finest raw materials, including cypress and cedar wood, quarried stones, gold, and silver. Many of the materials came from King Hiram of Tyre, a wealthy city-state on the Mediterranean coast, which prospered because of its trade with cities throughout the Mediterranean world. The tax burden on the people was heavy, but it allowed Solomon to complete the Temple seven years after he started.

The Temple included three main areas: the outside court, the Holy Place inside, and the Most Holy Place. The walls of the Most Holy Place were covered with gold plating because it was the place where the people believed God sat on His throne, the Ark of the Covenant. To enter this place was to come into a divine dimension. The only person allowed in the Most Holy Place was the high priest. There was no statue of God there. There was no representation of any kind. The priests came from chosen families and did the work of the Temple. They called people to worship by blowing the shofar (a sacred ram's horn), sang songs, killed the animals for sacrifices, cleaned up, and kept the altar fires burning. They determined who was "in" and who was "out" with respect to community life.

The priests offered seven types of sacrifices at the Temple, including the whole burnt offering (a year-old male sheep or bull) given for the sin of all the people, the grain offering (a cake of grain) given for thankfulness, and the peace offering (an animal) given for blessing. They offered the fat of the sacrifices to God, and the meat went to the priests (and sometimes to the man who brought the sacrifice). The worst thing to happen at the Temple was its destruction in 586 BC. The Babylonian army under Nebuchadnezzar marched across the desert, overthrew Jerusalem, destroyed the Temple, carried away all the gold and silver utensils, and sent many of the gifted and talented people in the city into exile.

THE BIBLICAL PROPHETS AND THE TEMPLE

JON HUNTZINGER, PHD

Great differences existed among the biblical prophets. For example, Isaiah served in the court of the king in Jerusalem in the eighth century BC while Malachi spoke on behalf of God to the returned exiles in the fifth century BC. Even so, there were certain convictions all the prophets shared. They all urged the people to be faithful to God's covenant that He made with Israel through Moses and later confirmed through David. They all believed in justice for orphans, widows, immigrants, and foreigners. And they all spoke out against idolatry and indifferent worship. One other significant matter concerned all of them—the Temple in Jerusalem. Since the Temple was the architectural symbol of the worship of Israel, what the prophets said about it and their experience of it was of primary importance.

Each of the three major biblical prophets (Isaiah, Jeremiah, and Ezekiel) had that close connection to the Temple. Isaiah receives his prophetic commission while he worships God there (Isaiah 6:1-13). He sees God upon His throne, hears angels shout "Holy!" and feels the earth shake beneath his feet, all while he is in God's house, the Temple. For Isaiah, it is the place of revelation where he becomes aware of God's holy nature, humanity's fallen nature, and the need to proclaim God's word to His people. God does not exclude anyone from coming to Him and having a relationship with Him. He says, therefore, "My Temple will be called a house of prayer for all nations" (Isaiah 56:7).

Jeremiah condemns the people for misunderstanding what the Temple represented. In his view, the people do not regard the Temple as a place of worship and prayer for everyone, where they receive revelation as they call to God, but only as a place where they fulfill their duties and religious obligations (Jeremiah 7:11). The people sing, "The LORD's Temple is here! The LORD's Temple is here!" and think that by giving offerings and observing holy days there, they will continue to experience God's favor even while they fail to live by the covenant He made with them (Jeremiah 7:4).

As a priest, Ezekiel may have expressed the strongest feelings for the Temple of all the prophets. He sees everything in terms of purity and impurity. Not only does he see God's throne while in worship, as did Isaiah (Ezekiel 1:26-28), but he also has a vision of God's glory leaving the Temple because the people mixed their worship of God with that of other gods (Ezekiel 10-11). God's glory cannot abide in the Temple if it is tainted with impurity and filled with idols and false rituals. Not only does Ezekiel see God's glory leave the Temple, but he also sees a plain scattered with dry bones (Ezekiel 37:1-14). He was filled with horror as he looked upon Israel's graveyard! How he must have closed his eyes when he saw the awfulness of their impurity! And yet, to this valley of dead people, Ezekiel speaks a resurrection word over their dried bones. Where will resurrected Israel worship? They will worship in a new and greater Temple flowing with fresh water and bringing new life to the driest places of the earth (Ezekiel 40-43; 47:1-12).

Among the prophets who lived after the Exile in the sixth century BC, Zechariah, Haggai, and Malachi all give special attention to the Temple. This is to be expected since the Babylonian destruction of it was such a catastrophe that forever changed the way the people viewed their past and looked ahead to their future. Zechariah and Haggai prophesy at the same time in the late 500s BC, about 20 years after some of the exiles had returned to the land. Not all of them returned, and those who did experienced opposition from the people who had remained behind. They also experienced the hardships of rebuilding homes, restarting businesses, and replanting crops. It was difficult, time-consuming work, which caused them to set aside other matters, such as the rebuilding of the Temple. Still, despite the real reasons the people had for not rebuilding the Temple, its neglect caused them to lose sight of their divine purpose. The people had lost sight of their primary calling to be men and women of worship. Because of the people's loss of vision, God gives vision to Zechariah. If they can't see for themselves, then He will help them by giving sight to the prophet. One of the things God shows Zechariah is a vision of the high priest Jeshua (Joshua) with a clean turban on his head, rebuilding the Temple and ruling on a throne (Zechariah 3:1-10). This vision is about God's ambition for all His people as represented in Jeshua. God intends for them to be a priestly, royal people—a kingdom of priests (Exodus 19:6)—who lead nations in worship. The joining of turban and Temple is a picture of Israel's calling and what God desired for all His people from the time of their deliverance from Egypt almost 1,000 years earlier.

At the same time that God gives Zechariah this vision of the turban and the Temple, Haggai is urging the people to make the rebuilding of the Temple their top priority (Haggai 1:7-8). He tells them that when they do, God will be with them by His Spirit and bless them with the wealth of the nations. He will shake treasure from the nations and cause His glory to be upon them (Haggai 2:6–9). God's people are hungry and experiencing poverty because they have made the construction of their own houses and businesses a priority over rebuilding God's house (Haggai 1:4). Rather than rebuild their own houses, Haggai exhorts them to rebuild God's Temple.

A generation later, the situation still had not changed. Malachi quotes God in a series of charges that take the form of lawsuits. God says His people have dishonored Him in their worship. They bring crippled and sick animals to the Temple as sacrifices and complain when He desires something more (Malachi 1:6–14). They do this because they are disappointed in the recently rebuilt temple as the people described by Haggai were (Haggai 2:2–3). They wonder what happened to the magnificent Temple envisioned by Ezekiel more than a century earlier. They also wonder, *Where is God's glory?* They question the truth of God's Word and have become lethargic toward the Temple and its rituals. Then they wonder why God is displeased with them.

Malachi says God will purify His people in order for them to worship Him with their offerings. When they "bring all the tithes into the storehouse," He "will open the windows of heaven" to them and bless them. The blessing will be so great that the nations will take notice and call Israel "blessed, for [their] land will be such a delight" (Malachi 3:6–15). For Malachi, the Temple is the place for the people to give God the best of their lives in worship.

— ISAIAH

The book of Isaiah records the messages God gave to the people of Judah and Jerusalem through a prophet who lived at the king's court during the second half of the eighth century (740–690s BC). The name *Isaiah* means 'Yahweh saves,' and since biblical names often express the character and identity of the person, place, or thing to which they are attached, the messages contained in this book of Isaiah center on God's salvation. This is why many people have referred to Isaiah as the "Gospel (Good News) of the Old Testament." In Isaiah, God promises to save Judah and Jerusalem from both present and future enemies, even as He promises ultimately to save the nations of the earth.

The book of Isaiah may be divided into two primary sections:
— Chapters 1–39 record messages directed to the people and leadership of Judah, as well as the surrounding countries, during the 700s BC. This was the time when Assyria was growing as a world power.
— Chapters 40–66 contain messages directed toward the people during the period of the Babylonian Exile (500s BC).

Since the book of Isaiah directs its messages to people at different times in history, some Bible scholars have concluded different people wrote these two parts. They say that the original prophet Isaiah wrote the first part while a later prophet wrote the second part. These scholars believe this later prophet so closely identified with Isaiah that he prophesied and wrote under Isaiah's name. Though this is possible, it is not necessary to hold this position. The book itself presents one prophet as the source for all of its messages, and no manuscript evidence exists to show Isaiah was ever divided into two books. Furthermore, the language and the message of the two sections are unified. Isaiah the prophet heard from God and delivered messages relevant to His people in the 700s BC as well as messages important for their descendants at a later time during the 500s BC.

The first section of Isaiah is divided into three smaller parts:
— Chapters 1–12 survey domestic issues, such as the need for justice, and foreign issues, such as the growth of Assyria. These are the matters facing the people during Isaiah's lifetime. God's judgment is soon going to come because of their failure to live according to His covenant.
— Chapters 13–35 recount the judgments against the surrounding nations.

— Chapters 36–39 describe the rule of King Hezekiah and shift the focus from the Assyrian period during which Isaiah lived to the Babylonian period he only envisioned.

The second section of the book of Isaiah includes four messages for the people at a future time:
— Chapters 40–45 speak of a time when the people would find themselves in exile under Babylonian rule and promise God's ultimate deliverance from the Exile.
— Chapters 46–47 continue with judgments against Babylon.
— Chapters 49–55 tell about the ministry of God's servant.
— Chapters 56–66 conclude the messages with an extended description of the salvation of the nations and the restoration of creation.

The Bible's prophecies, like those of Isaiah, are messages from God to His people. These prophets heard Him due to their faithfulness to His covenant and their willingness to speak what they heard Him say. They spoke on God's behalf despite the rejection they received. His messages were always meant to influence the people who heard them in the present, even if they spoke of future events. Though a particular message might be for a later time, the people who first heard were affected by it because they were forced to consider the future consequences of their present actions. They had to think about their responsibility to their sons, daughters, and later descendants who would ultimately experience the results of the message.

Isaiah's experience of God in the Temple (6:1–13), where he hears angels cry,

> "Holy, holy, holy is the LORD of Heaven's Armies! The whole earth is filled with his glory!"

points to the primary depiction of God in the book. God is "the Holy One of Israel" (1:4; 5:19–24; 10:17–20; 12:6; 17:7; 29:19–23; 30:11–15; 31:1; 37:23; 40:25; 41:14–20; 43:3, 14–15; 45:11; 47:4; 48:17; 49:7; 54:5; 55:5; 60:9). He will save His people from their Assyrian enemies (17:1–3; 11:10–12:3) and Babylonian enemies (45:17; 48:14–20; 49:25–26). He is the Father to His people, who will redeem them from the Babylonians (29:22; 35:9; 41:14; 44:6, 22–24; 47:4; 48:17–20; 49:7, 26; 52:3; 54:5; 63:16).

Isaiah also describes a servant who will participate in God's saving and redemptive work among His people. Several passages in the second section of Isaiah specifically describe this servant

(42:1-9; 49:1-7; 50:4-11; 52:13-53:12). Some readers think these passages describe the prophet Isaiah himself or even the nation of Israel as a whole. New Testament writers, however, link the servant to Jesus and His ministry. For example, Matthew 12:18-21 quotes Isaiah 42:1-9 to connect Jesus with the servant who ushers in God's Kingdom, and Peter quotes from Isaiah 52:13-53:12 to show that Jesus gave His disciples an example of humility in the midst of persecution (1 Peter 2:21-25).

The following describes the content of those servant passages:

— Isaiah 42:1-9: The servant receives God's Spirit for the special purpose of establishing justice among the nations and to be a light of knowledge for those nations.
— Isaiah 49:1-7: The servant is called from the womb to speak God's word to His people and restore their relationship with Him.
— Isaiah 50:4-11: The servant teaches God's people what He hears even though He is beaten and opposed, because God is with Him.
— Isaiah 52:13-53:12: Finally, God's servant is brutally treated but then exalted by God, and in His marred appearance, He testifies to the nations.

The servant suffers on behalf of others and bears their griefs, sorrows, sins, and iniquities (53:1-6). He accepts His fate as part of God's plan and receives God's reward as a result of His obedience (53:7-12). These passages show the servant as one who possesses God's Spirit to teach His people and bring justice to the nations. He will be opposed and even beaten as He bears the burdens of others, but God will ultimately honor Him for this reason.

---

1 These are the visions that Isaiah son of Amoz saw concerning Judah and Jerusalem. He saw these visions during the years when Uzziah, Jotham, Ahaz, and Hezekiah were kings of Judah.*

A MESSAGE FOR REBELLIOUS JUDAH

2 Listen, O heavens! Pay attention, earth!
This is what the LORD says:
"The children I raised and cared for
have rebelled against me.
3 Even an ox knows its owner,
and a donkey recognizes its master's care—
but Israel doesn't know its master.
My people don't recognize my care
for them."
4 Oh, what a sinful nation they are—
loaded down with a burden of guilt.
They are evil people,
corrupt children who have rejected
the LORD.
They have despised the Holy One of Israel
and turned their backs on him.

5 Why do you continue to invite punishment?
Must you rebel forever?
Your head is injured,
and your heart is sick.
6 You are battered from head to foot—
covered with bruises, welts,
and infected wounds—
without any soothing ointments
or bandages.
7 Your country lies in ruins,
and your towns are burned.
Foreigners plunder your fields before
your eyes
and destroy everything they see.

8 Beautiful Jerusalem* stands abandoned
like a watchman's shelter in a vineyard,
like a lean-to in a cucumber field after
the harvest,
like a helpless city under siege.
9 If the LORD of Heaven's Armies
had not spared a few of us,*
we would have been wiped out like Sodom,
destroyed like Gomorrah.

10 Listen to the LORD, you leaders of "Sodom."
Listen to the law of our God,
people of "Gomorrah."
11 "What makes you think I want all
your sacrifices?"
says the LORD.
"I am sick of your burnt offerings of rams
and the fat of fattened cattle.
I get no pleasure from the blood
of bulls and lambs and goats.
12 When you come to worship me,
who asked you to parade through my
courts with all your ceremony?
13 Stop bringing me your meaningless gifts;
the incense of your offerings
disgusts me!
As for your celebrations of the new moon
and the Sabbath
and your special days for fasting—
they are all sinful and false.
I want no more of your pious meetings.
14 I hate your new moon celebrations and
your annual festivals.
They are a burden to me.
I cannot stand them!

1:1 These kings reigned from 792 to 686 B.C. 1:8 Hebrew *The daughter of Zion.* 1:9 Greek version reads *a few of our children.* Compare Rom 9:29.

15 When you lift up your hands in prayer,
  I will not look.
Though you offer many prayers,
  I will not listen,
for your hands are covered with the blood
  of innocent victims.
16 Wash yourselves and be clean!
  Get your sins out of my sight.
  Give up your evil ways.
17 Learn to do good.
  Seek justice.
  Help the oppressed.
  Defend the cause of orphans.
  Fight for the rights of widows.

18 "Come now, let's settle this,"
  says the LORD.
"Though your sins are like scarlet,
  I will make them as white as snow.
Though they are red like crimson,
  I will make them as white as wool.
19 If you will only obey me,
  you will have plenty to eat.
20 But if you turn away and refuse to listen,
  you will be devoured by the sword of
    your enemies.
  I, the LORD, have spoken!"

UNFAITHFUL JERUSALEM

21 See how Jerusalem, once so faithful,
  has become a prostitute.
Once the home of justice and righteousness,
  she is now filled with murderers.
22 Once like pure silver,
  you have become like worthless slag.
Once so pure,
  you are now like watered-down wine.
23 Your leaders are rebels,
  the companions of thieves.
All of them love bribes
  and demand payoffs,
but they refuse to defend the cause of orphans
  or fight for the rights of widows.

24 Therefore, the Lord, the LORD of
    Heaven's Armies,
  the Mighty One of Israel, says,
"I will take revenge on my enemies
  and pay back my foes!
25 I will raise my fist against you.
  I will melt you down and skim off your slag.
  I will remove all your impurities.
26 Then I will give you good judges again
  and wise counselors like you used
    to have.
Then Jerusalem will again be called the
  Home of Justice
  and the Faithful City."

27 Zion will be restored by justice;
  those who repent will be revived by
    righteousness.

28 But rebels and sinners will be
    completely destroyed,
  and those who desert the LORD will
    be consumed.

29 You will be ashamed of your idol worship
  in groves of sacred oaks.
You will blush because you worshiped
  in gardens dedicated to idols.
30 You will be like a great tree with
    withered leaves,
  like a garden without water.
31 The strongest among you will disappear
    like straw;
  their evil deeds will be the spark that
    sets it on fire.
They and their evil works will
    burn up together,
  and no one will be able to put out the fire.

THE LORD'S FUTURE REIGN

2 This is a vision that Isaiah son of Amoz saw
  concerning Judah and Jerusalem:

2 In the last days, the mountain of
    the LORD's house
  will be the highest of all—
  the most important place on earth.
It will be raised above the other hills,
  and people from all over the world will
    stream there to worship.
3 People from many nations will
    come and say,
"Come, let us go up to the mountain
    of the LORD,
  to the house of Jacob's God.
There he will teach us his ways,
  and we will walk in his paths."
For the LORD's teaching will go out
    from Zion;
  his word will go out from Jerusalem.
4 The LORD will mediate between nations
  and will settle international disputes.
They will hammer their swords
    into plowshares
  and their spears into pruning hooks.
Nation will no longer fight against nation,
  nor train for war anymore.

A WARNING OF JUDGMENT

5 Come, descendants of Jacob,
  let us walk in the light of the LORD!
6 For the LORD has rejected his people,
  the descendants of Jacob,
because they have filled their land with
    practices from the East
  and with sorcerers, as the Philistines do.
  They have made alliances with pagans.
7 Israel is full of silver and gold;
  there is no end to its treasures.
Their land is full of warhorses;
  there is no end to its chariots.

ISAIAH 3:15 | 571

8 Their land is full of idols;
  the people worship things they have made
    with their own hands.
9 So now they will be humbled,
  and all will be brought low—
    do not forgive them.
10 Crawl into caves in the rocks.
  Hide in the dust
from the terror of the LORD
  and the glory of his majesty.
11 Human pride will be brought down,
  and human arrogance will be humbled.
Only the LORD will be exalted
  on that day of judgment.

12 For the LORD of Heaven's Armies
  has a day of reckoning.
He will punish the proud and mighty
  and bring down everything that is exalted.
13 He will cut down the tall cedars of Lebanon
  and all the mighty oaks of Bashan.
14 He will level all the high mountains
  and all the lofty hills.
15 He will break down every high tower
  and every fortified wall.
16 He will destroy all the great trading ships*
  and every magnificent vessel.
17 Human pride will be humbled,
  and human arrogance will be
    brought down.
Only the LORD will be exalted
  on that day of judgment.

18 Idols will completely disappear.
19 When the LORD rises to shake the earth,
  his enemies will crawl into holes
    in the ground.
They will hide in caves in the rocks
  from the terror of the LORD
  and the glory of his majesty.
20 On that day of judgment they will abandon
  the gold and silver idols
  they made for themselves to worship.
They will leave their gods to the rodents
  and bats,
21 while they crawl away into caverns
  and hide among the jagged rocks
    in the cliffs.
They will try to escape the terror of the LORD
  and the glory of his majesty
  as he rises to shake the earth.
22 Don't put your trust in mere humans.
  They are as frail as breath.
  What good are they?

JUDGMENT AGAINST JUDAH

3 ¹ The Lord, the LORD of Heaven's Armies,
    will take away from Jerusalem and
      Judah
everything they depend on:
  every bit of bread
  and every drop of water,

2 all their heroes and soldiers,
  judges and prophets,
  fortune-tellers and elders,
3 army officers and high officials,
  advisers, skilled sorcerers,
    and astrologers.

4 I will make boys their leaders,
  and toddlers their rulers.
5 People will oppress each other—
  man against man,
  neighbor against neighbor.
Young people will insult their elders,
  and vulgar people will sneer at the
    honorable.

6 In those days a man will say to his brother,
"Since you have a coat, you be our leader!
  Take charge of this heap of ruins!"
7 But he will reply,
  "No! I can't help.
I don't have any extra food or clothes.
  Don't put me in charge!"

8 For Jerusalem will stumble,
  and Judah will fall,
because they speak out against the LORD
  and refuse to obey him.
  They provoke him to his face.
9 The very look on their faces gives them away.
  They display their sin like the people
  of Sodom
  and don't even try to hide it.
They are doomed!
  They have brought destruction upon
    themselves.

10 Tell the godly that all will be well for them.
  They will enjoy the rich reward they
    have earned!
11 But the wicked are doomed,
  for they will get exactly what they deserve.

12 Childish leaders oppress my people,
  and women rule over them.
O my people, your leaders mislead you;
  they send you down the wrong road.

13 The LORD takes his place in court
  and presents his case against his people.*
14 The LORD comes forward to pronounce
    judgment
  on the elders and rulers of his people:
"You have ruined Israel, my vineyard.
  Your houses are filled with things stolen
    from the poor.
15 How dare you crush my people,
  grinding the faces of the poor into
    the dust?"

3:16 Hebrew *every ship of Tarshish.* 3:13 As in Greek and Syriac
versions; Hebrew reads *against the peoples.*

demands the Lord, the LORD of
Heaven's Armies.

A WARNING TO JERUSALEM

[16] The LORD says, "Beautiful Zion* is haughty:
craning her elegant neck,
flirting with her eyes,
walking with dainty steps,
tinkling her ankle bracelets.
[17] So the Lord will send scabs on her head;
the LORD will make beautiful Zion bald."

[18] On that day of judgment
the Lord will strip away everything that
makes her beautiful:
ornaments, headbands, crescent necklaces,
[19] earrings, bracelets, and veils;
[20] scarves, ankle bracelets, sashes,
perfumes, and charms;
[21] rings, jewels,
[22] party clothes, gowns, capes, and purses;
[23] mirrors, fine linen garments,
head ornaments, and shawls.

[24] Instead of smelling of sweet perfume,
she will stink.
She will wear a rope for a sash,
and her elegant hair will fall out.
She will wear rough burlap instead of
rich robes.
Shame will replace her beauty.*
[25] The men of the city will be killed with
the sword,
and her warriors will die in battle.
[26] The gates of Zion will weep and mourn.
The city will be like a ravaged woman,
huddled on the ground.

4 In that day so few men will be left that seven
women will fight for each man, saying, "Let
us all marry you! We will provide our own food
and clothing. Only let us take your name so we
won't be mocked as old maids."

A PROMISE OF RESTORATION

[2] But in that day, the branch* of the LORD
will be beautiful and glorious;
the fruit of the land will be the pride
and glory
of all who survive in Israel.
[3] All who remain in Zion
will be a holy people—
those who survive the destruction
of Jerusalem
and are recorded among the living.
[4] The Lord will wash the filth from
beautiful Zion*
and cleanse Jerusalem of its bloodstains
with the hot breath of fiery judgment.
[5] Then the LORD will provide shade for
Mount Zion
and all who assemble there.

He will provide a canopy of cloud during
the day
and smoke and flaming fire at night,
covering the glorious land.
[6] It will be a shelter from daytime heat
and a hiding place from storms and rain.

A SONG ABOUT THE LORD'S VINEYARD

5 [1] Now I will sing for the one I love
a song about his vineyard:
My beloved had a vineyard
on a rich and fertile hill.
[2] He plowed the land, cleared its stones,
and planted it with the best vines.
In the middle he built a watchtower
and carved a winepress in the nearby rocks.
Then he waited for a harvest of sweet grapes,
but the grapes that grew were bitter.

[3] Now, you people of Jerusalem and Judah,
you judge between me and my vineyard.
[4] What more could I have done for my vineyard
that I have not already done?
When I expected sweet grapes,
why did my vineyard give me bitter
grapes?

[5] Now let me tell you
what I will do to my vineyard:
I will tear down its hedges
and let it be destroyed.
I will break down its walls
and let the animals trample it.
[6] I will make it a wild place
where the vines are not pruned and
the ground is not hoed,
a place overgrown with briers
and thorns.
I will command the clouds
to drop no rain on it.

[7] The nation of Israel is the vineyard of the
LORD of Heaven's Armies.
The people of Judah are his
pleasant garden.
He expected a crop of justice,
but instead he found oppression.
He expected to find righteousness,
but instead he heard cries of violence.

JUDAH'S GUILT AND JUDGMENT

[8] What sorrow for you who buy up house
after house and field after field,
until everyone is evicted and you live
alone in the land.
[9] But I have heard the LORD of
Heaven's Armies

3:16 Or *The women of Zion* (with corresponding changes to plural
forms through verse 24); Hebrew reads *The daughters of Zion;* also
in 3:17.   3:24 As in Dead Sea Scrolls; Masoretic Text reads *robes
/ because instead of beauty.*   4:2 Or *the Branch.*   4:4 Or *from the
women of Zion;* Hebrew reads *from the daughters of Zion.*

swear a solemn oath:
"Many houses will stand deserted;
even beautiful mansions will be empty.
10 Ten acres* of vineyard will not produce even
six gallons* of wine.
Ten baskets of seed will yield only one
basket* of grain."

11 What sorrow for those who get up early in
the morning
looking for a drink of alcohol
and spend long evenings drinking wine
to make themselves flaming drunk.
12 They furnish wine and lovely music at their
grand parties—
lyre and harp, tambourine and flute—
but they never think about the LORD
or notice what he is doing.

13 So my people will go into exile far away
because they do not know me.
Those who are great and honored will
starve,
and the common people will die
of thirst.
14 The grave* is licking its lips in anticipation,
opening its mouth wide.
The great and the lowly
and all the drunken mob will be
swallowed up.
15 Humanity will be destroyed, and people
brought down;
even the arrogant will lower their eyes in
humiliation.
16 But the LORD of Heaven's Armies will be
exalted by his justice.
The holiness of God will be displayed by
his righteousness.
17 In that day lambs will find good pastures,
and fattened sheep and young goats* will
feed among the ruins.

18 What sorrow for those who drag their sins
behind them
with ropes made of lies,
who drag wickedness behind them
like a cart!
19 They even mock God and say,
"Hurry up and do something!
We want to see what you can do.
Let the Holy One of Israel carry out his plan,
for we want to know what it is."

20 What sorrow for those who say
that evil is good and good is evil,
that dark is light and light is dark,
that bitter is sweet and sweet is bitter.
21 What sorrow for those who are wise in
their own eyes
and think themselves so clever.
22 What sorrow for those who are heroes at
drinking wine

and boast about all the alcohol they
can hold.
23 They take bribes to let the wicked go free,
and they punish the innocent.

24 Therefore, just as fire licks up stubble
and dry grass shrivels in the flame,
so their roots will rot
and their flowers wither.
For they have rejected the law of the LORD
of Heaven's Armies;
they have despised the word of
the Holy One of Israel.
25 That is why the LORD's anger burns against
his people,
and why he has raised his fist
to crush them.
The mountains tremble,
and the corpses of his people litter the
streets like garbage.
But even then the LORD's anger is not
satisfied.
His fist is still poised to strike!

26 He will send a signal to distant nations
far away
and whistle to those at the ends of
the earth.
They will come racing toward Jerusalem.
27 They will not get tired or stumble.
They will not stop for rest or sleep.
Not a belt will be loose,
not a sandal strap broken.
28 Their arrows will be sharp
and their bows ready for battle.
Sparks will fly from their horses' hooves,
and the wheels of their chariots will spin
like a whirlwind.
29 They will roar like lions,
like the strongest of lions.
Growling, they will pounce on their victims
and carry them off,
and no one will be there to rescue them.
30 They will roar over their victims on that day
of destruction
like the roaring of the sea.
If someone looks across the land,
only darkness and distress will be seen;
even the light will be darkened by clouds.

ISAIAH'S CLEANSING AND CALL

6 It was in the year King Uzziah died* that
I saw the Lord. He was sitting on a lofty
throne, and the train of his robe filled the
Temple. 2Attending him were mighty seraphim,
each having six wings. With two wings they
covered their faces, with two they covered their

5:10a Hebrew *A ten yoke,* that is, the area of land plowed by
ten teams of oxen in one day.   5:10b Hebrew *a bath* [21 liters].
5:10c Hebrew *A homer* [5 bushels or 220 liters] *of seed will yield
only an ephah* [20 quarts or 22 liters].   5:14 Hebrew *Sheol.*
5:17 As in Greek version; Hebrew reads *and strangers.*
6:1 King Uzziah died in 740 B.C.

GIVING UP; GIVING IN; GIVING OUT
Isaiah 6:1–8 ROBERT MORRIS

When the prophet Isaiah went to worship in the Temple, he had a vision of God. There were three aspects to this vision:

1. An upward vision—Isaiah saw the Lord.
2. An inward vision—Isaiah saw himself.
3. An outward vision—Isaiah saw others.

We have the opportunity to have a vision every time we have a quiet time or participate in a worship service. God wants us to look upward and see Him, look inward and see what He wants to put in or take out of our lives, and look outward and see what He wants us to do. Another way to describe these three steps is giving up, giving in, and giving out.

1. Giving Up

Many people don't understand how powerful and loving God really is. They don't want to give up control of their lives because they don't fully understand His ability and desire to bless them. God controls everything in the entire universe, but He has given you a free will. This means He won't take control of your life until you give it to Him. To do this, we must have an encounter with God. Isaiah wasn't cleansed until he saw his own sin, and he didn't see his own sin until he saw God's holiness. Every day we have the opportunity to have an encounter with God and give Him control over every part of our lives.

2. Giving In

Isaiah saw himself in two ways. He saw how unclean he was, but after he confessed his sin, God did a work in his heart. Then Isaiah saw himself as cleansed. This is what God wants to do every time we meet with Him. You can't see God's holiness and perfection without seeing your unholiness and imperfection. However, if you confess your sins, He promises to cleanse you from them and remove them as far away "as the east is from the west" (Psalm 103:12). God wants you to have an abundant life, but you must be willing to give Him control.

3. Giving Out

As soon as Isaiah received God's word in his own life, he wanted to tell others about it. Giving out is a natural result of having an encounter with God—we want to share with others what we have freely received. The enemy wants to silence us by making us think others are more qualified to share the Good News. However, Jesus said, "As the Father has sent me, so I am sending you" (John 20:21). God wants to use *you*!

---

feet, and with two they flew. ³ They were calling out to each other,

"Holy, holy, holy is the LORD of
    Heaven's Armies!
The whole earth is filled with his glory!"

⁴ Their voices shook the Temple to its foundations, and the entire building was filled with smoke.

⁵ Then I said, "It's all over! I am doomed, for I am a sinful man. I have filthy lips, and I live among a people with filthy lips. Yet I have seen the King, the LORD of Heaven's Armies."

⁶ Then one of the seraphim flew to me with a burning coal he had taken from the altar with a pair of tongs. ⁷ He touched my lips with it and said, "See, this coal has touched your lips. Now your guilt is removed, and your sins are forgiven."

⁸ Then I heard the Lord asking, "Whom should I send as a messenger to this people? Who will go for us?"

I said, "Here I am. Send me."

⁹ And he said, "Yes, go, and say to this people,

'Listen carefully, but do not understand.
    Watch closely, but learn nothing.'
¹⁰ Harden the hearts of these people.
    Plug their ears and shut their eyes.

That way, they will not see with their eyes,
    nor hear with their ears,
nor understand with their hearts
    and turn to me for healing."*

¹¹ Then I said, "Lord, how long will this go on?" And he replied,

"Until their towns are empty,
    their houses are deserted,
    and the whole country is a wasteland;
¹² until the LORD has sent everyone away,
    and the entire land of Israel lies deserted.
¹³ If even a tenth—a remnant—survive,
    it will be invaded again and burned.
But as a terebinth or oak tree leaves a stump
        when it is cut down,
    so Israel's stump will be a holy seed."

A MESSAGE FOR AHAZ

7 When Ahaz, son of Jotham and grandson of Uzziah, was king of Judah, King Rezin of Syria* and Pekah son of Remaliah, the king of

---

6:9-10 Greek version reads *And he said, "Go and say to this people, / 'When you hear what I say, you will not understand. / When you see what I do, you will not comprehend.' / For the hearts of these people are hardened, / and their ears cannot hear, and they have closed their eyes— / so their eyes cannot see, / and their ears cannot hear, / and their hearts cannot understand, / and they cannot turn to me and let me heal them."* Compare Matt 13:14-15; Mark 4:12; Luke 8:10; Acts 28:26-27.   7:1 Hebrew *Aram*; also in 7:2, 4, 5, 8.

Israel, set out to attack Jerusalem. However, they were unable to carry out their plan.

[2] The news had come to the royal court of Judah: "Syria is allied with Israel* against us!" So the hearts of the king and his people trembled with fear, like trees shaking in a storm.

[3] Then the LORD said to Isaiah, "Take your son Shear-jashub* and go out to meet King Ahaz. You will find him at the end of the aqueduct that feeds water into the upper pool, near the road leading to the field where cloth is washed.* [4] Tell him to stop worrying. Tell him he doesn't need to fear the fierce anger of those two burned-out embers, King Rezin of Syria and Pekah son of Remaliah. [5] Yes, the kings of Syria and Israel are plotting against him, saying, [6] 'We will attack Judah and capture it for ourselves. Then we will install the son of Tabeel as Judah's king.' [7] But this is what the Sovereign LORD says:

"This invasion will never happen;
    it will never take place;
[8] for Syria is no stronger than its capital,
        Damascus,
    and Damascus is no stronger than its
        king, Rezin.
As for Israel, within sixty-five years
    it will be crushed and completely
        destroyed.
[9] Israel is no stronger than its capital, Samaria,
    and Samaria is no stronger than its king,
        Pekah son of Remaliah.
Unless your faith is firm,
    I cannot make you stand firm."

THE SIGN OF IMMANUEL

[10] Later, the LORD sent this message to King Ahaz: [11] "Ask the LORD your God for a sign of confirmation, Ahaz. Make it as difficult as you want—as high as heaven or as deep as the place of the dead.*"

[12] But the king refused. "No," he said, "I will not test the LORD like that."

[13] Then Isaiah said, "Listen well, you royal family of David! Isn't it enough to exhaust human patience? Must you exhaust the patience of my God as well? [14] All right then, the Lord himself will give you the sign. Look! The virgin* will conceive a child! She will give birth to a son and will call him Immanuel (which means 'God is with us'). [15] By the time this child is old enough to choose what is right and reject what is wrong, he will be eating yogurt* and honey. [16] For before the child is that old, the lands of the two kings you fear so much will both be deserted.

[17] "Then the LORD will bring things on you, your nation, and your family unlike anything since Israel broke away from Judah. He will bring the king of Assyria upon you!"

[18] In that day the LORD will whistle for the army of southern Egypt and for the army of Assyria. They will swarm around you like flies and bees. [19] They will come in vast hordes and settle in the fertile areas and also in the desolate valleys, caves, and thorny places. [20] In that day the Lord will hire a "razor" from beyond the Euphrates River*—the king of Assyria—and use it to shave off everything: your land, your crops, and your people.*

[21] In that day a farmer will be fortunate to have a cow and two sheep or goats left. [22] Nevertheless, there will be enough milk for everyone because so few people will be left in the land. They will eat their fill of yogurt and honey. [23] In that day the lush vineyards, now worth 1,000 pieces of silver,* will become patches of briers and thorns. [24] The entire land will become a vast expanse of briers and thorns, a hunting ground overrun by wildlife. [25] No one will go to the fertile hillsides where the gardens once grew, for briers and thorns will cover them. Cattle, sheep, and goats will graze there.

THE COMING ASSYRIAN INVASION

8 Then the LORD said to me, "Make a large signboard and clearly write this name on it: Maher-shalal-hash-baz.*" [2] I asked Uriah the priest and Zechariah son of Jeberekiah, both known as honest men, to witness my doing this.

[3] Then I slept with my wife, and she became pregnant and gave birth to a son. And the LORD said, "Call him Maher-shalal-hash-baz. [4] For before this child is old enough to say 'Papa' or 'Mama,' the king of Assyria will carry away both the abundance of Damascus and the riches of Samaria."

[5] Then the LORD spoke to me again and said, [6] "My care for the people of Judah is like the gently flowing waters of Shiloah, but they have rejected it. They are rejoicing over what will happen to* King Rezin and King Pekah.* [7] Therefore, the Lord will overwhelm them with a mighty flood from the Euphrates River*—the king of Assyria and all his glory. This flood will overflow all its channels [8] and sweep into Judah until it is chin deep. It will spread its wings, submerging your land from one end to the other, O Immanuel.

[9] "Huddle together, you nations,
        and be terrified.
    Listen, all you distant lands.
    Prepare for battle, but you will be crushed!
        Yes, prepare for battle,
            but you will be crushed!
[10] Call your councils of war,
        but they will be worthless.
    Develop your strategies,
        but they will not succeed.
    For God is with us!*"

7:2 Hebrew *Ephraim,* referring to the northern kingdom of Israel; also in 7:5, 8, 9, 17. 7:3a *Shear-jashub* means "A remnant will return." 7:3b Or *bleached.* 7:11 Hebrew *as deep as Sheol.* 7:14 Or *young woman.* 7:15 Or *curds;* also in 7:22. 7:20a Hebrew *the river.* 7:20b Hebrew *shave off the head, the hair of the legs, and the beard.* 7:23 Hebrew *1,000 [shekels] of silver,* about 25 pounds or 11.4 kilograms in weight. 8:1 *Maher-shalal-hash-baz* means "Swift to plunder and quick to carry away." 8:6a Or *They are rejoicing because of.* 8:6b Hebrew *and the son of Remaliah.* 8:7 Hebrew *the river.* 8:10 Hebrew *Immanuel!*

A CALL TO TRUST THE LORD

¹¹The LORD has given me a strong warning not to think like everyone else does. He said,

¹² "Don't call everything a conspiracy,
like they do,
and don't live in dread of what
frightens them.
¹³ Make the LORD of Heaven's Armies holy
in your life.
He is the one you should fear.
He is the one who should make you tremble.
¹⁴ He will keep you safe.
But to Israel and Judah
he will be a stone that makes
people stumble,
a rock that makes them fall.
And for the people of Jerusalem
he will be a trap and a snare.
¹⁵ Many will stumble and fall,
never to rise again.
They will be snared and captured."

¹⁶ Preserve the teaching of God;
entrust his instructions to those who
follow me.
¹⁷ I will wait for the LORD,
who has turned away from the
descendants of Jacob.
I will put my hope in him.

¹⁸I and the children the LORD has given me serve as signs and warnings to Israel from the LORD of Heaven's Armies who dwells in his Temple on Mount Zion.

¹⁹Someone may say to you, "Let's ask the mediums and those who consult the spirits of the dead. With their whisperings and mutterings, they will tell us what to do." But shouldn't people ask God for guidance? Should the living seek guidance from the dead?

²⁰Look to God's instructions and teachings! People who contradict his word are completely in the dark. ²¹They will go from one place to another, weary and hungry. And because they are hungry, they will rage and curse their king and their God. They will look up to heaven ²²and down at the earth, but wherever they look, there will be trouble and anguish and dark despair. They will be thrown out into the darkness.

HOPE IN THE MESSIAH

9 ¹*Nevertheless, that time of darkness and despair will not go on forever. The land of Zebulun and Naphtali will be humbled, but there will be a time in the future when Galilee of the Gentiles, which lies along the road that runs between the Jordan and the sea, will be filled with glory.

²*The people who walk in darkness
will see a great light.

For those who live in a land of
deep darkness,*
a light will shine.
³ You will enlarge the nation of Israel,
and its people will rejoice.
They will rejoice before you
as people rejoice at the harvest
and like warriors dividing the plunder.
⁴ For you will break the yoke of their slavery
and lift the heavy burden from their
shoulders.
You will break the oppressor's rod,
just as you did when you destroyed
the army of Midian.
⁵ The boots of the warrior
and the uniforms bloodstained by war
will all be burned.
They will be fuel for the fire.

⁶ For a child is born to us,
a son is given to us.
The government will rest on his shoulders.
And he will be called:
Wonderful Counselor,* Mighty God,
Everlasting Father, Prince of Peace.
⁷ His government and its peace
will never end.
He will rule with fairness and justice from
the throne of his ancestor David
for all eternity.
The passionate commitment of the LORD of
Heaven's Armies
will make this happen!

THE LORD'S ANGER AGAINST ISRAEL

⁸ The Lord has spoken out against Jacob;
his judgment has fallen upon Israel.
⁹ And the people of Israel* and Samaria,
who spoke with such pride and arrogance,
will soon know it.
¹⁰ They said, "We will replace the broken
bricks of our ruins with finished stone,
and replant the felled sycamore-fig trees
with cedars."

¹¹ But the LORD will bring Rezin's enemies
against Israel
and stir up all their foes.
¹² The Syrians* from the east and the
Philistines from the west
will bare their fangs and devour Israel.
But even then the LORD's anger will not
be satisfied.
His fist is still poised to strike.

¹³ For after all this punishment, the people
will still not repent.

9:1 Verse 9:1 is numbered 8:23 in Hebrew text. 9:2a Verses 9:2-21 are numbered 9:1-20 in Hebrew text. 9:2b Greek version reads *a land where death casts its shadow*. Compare Matt 4:16. 9:6 Or *Wonderful, Counselor*. 9:9 Hebrew *of Ephraim*, referring to the northern kingdom of Israel. 9:12 Hebrew *Arameans*.

They will not seek the LORD of
Heaven's Armies.
14 Therefore, in a single day the LORD will
destroy both the head and the tail,
the noble palm branch and
the lowly reed.
15 The leaders of Israel are the head,
and the lying prophets are the tail.
16 For the leaders of the people have
misled them.
They have led them down the path
of destruction.
17 That is why the Lord takes no pleasure in
the young men
and shows no mercy even to the widows
and orphans.
For they are all wicked hypocrites,
and they all speak foolishness.
But even then the LORD's anger will not
be satisfied.
His fist is still poised to strike.

18 This wickedness is like a brushfire.
It burns not only briers and thorns
but also sets the forests ablaze.
Its burning sends up clouds of smoke.
19 The land will be blackened
by the fury of the LORD of
Heaven's Armies.
The people will be fuel for the fire,
and no one will spare even his own
brother.
20 They will attack their neighbor on the right
but will still be hungry.
They will devour their neighbor on the left
but will not be satisfied.
In the end they will even eat
their own children.*
21 Manasseh will feed on Ephraim,
Ephraim will feed on Manasseh,
and both will devour Judah.
But even then the LORD's anger will not
be satisfied.
His fist is still poised to strike.

10 ¹ What sorrow awaits the unjust judges
and those who issue unfair laws.
² They deprive the poor of justice
and deny the rights of the needy among
my people.
They prey on widows
and take advantage of orphans.
³ What will you do when I punish you,
when I send disaster upon you from
a distant land?
To whom will you turn for help?
Where will your treasures be safe?
⁴ You will stumble along as prisoners
or lie among the dead.
But even then the LORD's anger will not
be satisfied.
His fist is still poised to strike.

JUDGMENT AGAINST ASSYRIA

⁵ "What sorrow awaits Assyria, the rod of
my anger.
I use it as a club to express my anger.
⁶ I am sending Assyria against
a godless nation,
against a people with whom I am angry.
Assyria will plunder them,
trampling them like dirt beneath its feet.
⁷ But the king of Assyria will not understand
that he is my tool;
his mind does not work that way.
His plan is simply to destroy,
to cut down nation after nation.
⁸ He will say,
'Each of my princes will soon be a king.
⁹ We destroyed Calno just as we did
Carchemish.
Hamath fell before us as Arpad did.
And we destroyed Samaria just as
we did Damascus.
¹⁰ Yes, we have finished off many a kingdom
whose gods were greater than those in
Jerusalem and Samaria.
¹¹ So we will defeat Jerusalem and her gods,
just as we destroyed Samaria with hers.'"

¹²After the Lord has used the king of Assyria
to accomplish his purposes on Mount Zion and
in Jerusalem, he will turn against the king of
Assyria and punish him—for he is proud and
arrogant. ¹³He boasts,

"By my own powerful arm I have done this.
With my own shrewd wisdom
I planned it.
I have broken down the defenses of nations
and carried off their treasures.
I have knocked down their kings
like a bull.
¹⁴ I have robbed their nests of riches
and gathered up kingdoms as a farmer
gathers eggs.
No one can even flap a wing against me
or utter a peep of protest."

¹⁵ But can the ax boast greater power than the
person who uses it?
Is the saw greater than the person who
saws?
Can a rod strike unless a hand moves it?
Can a wooden cane walk by itself?
¹⁶ Therefore, the Lord,
the LORD of Heaven's Armies,
will send a plague among Assyria's
proud troops,
and a flaming fire will consume
its glory.
¹⁷ The LORD, the Light of Israel, will be a fire;
the Holy One will be a flame.

9:20 Or eat their own arms.

He will devour the thorns and briers
with fire,
burning up the enemy in a single night.
[18] The LORD will consume Assyria's glory
like a fire consumes a forest in
a fruitful land;
it will waste away like sick people in
a plague.
[19] Of all that glorious forest, only a few trees
will survive—
so few that a child could count them!

HOPE FOR THE LORD'S PEOPLE

[20] In that day the remnant left in Israel,
the survivors in the house of Jacob,
will no longer depend on allies
who seek to destroy them.
But they will faithfully trust the LORD,
the Holy One of Israel.
[21] A remnant will return;*
yes, the remnant of Jacob will return to
the Mighty God.
[22] But though the people of Israel are
as numerous
as the sand of the seashore,
only a remnant of them will return.
The LORD has rightly decided to destroy
his people.
[23] Yes, the Lord, the LORD of Heaven's Armies,
has already decided to destroy
the entire land.*

[24] So this is what the Lord, the LORD of Heaven's Armies, says: "O my people in Zion, do not be afraid of the Assyrians when they oppress you with rod and club as the Egyptians did long ago. [25] In a little while my anger against you will end, and then my anger will rise up to destroy them." [26] The LORD of Heaven's Armies will lash them with his whip, as he did when Gideon triumphed over the Midianites at the rock of Oreb, or when the LORD's staff was raised to drown the Egyptian army in the sea.

[27] In that day the LORD will end the bondage
of his people.
He will break the yoke of slavery
and lift it from their shoulders.*

[28] Look, the Assyrians are now at Aiath.
They are passing through Migron
and are storing their equipment
at Micmash.
[29] They are crossing the pass
and are camping at Geba.
Fear strikes the town of Ramah.
All the people of Gibeah,
the hometown of Saul,
are running for their lives.
[30] Scream in terror,
you people of Gallim!
Shout out a warning to Laishah.

Oh, poor Anathoth!
[31] There go the people of Madmenah,
all fleeing.
The citizens of Gebim are trying to hide.
[32] The enemy stops at Nob for the rest of
that day.
He shakes his fist at beautiful
Mount Zion, the mountain of
Jerusalem.

[33] But look! The Lord,
the LORD of Heaven's Armies,
will chop down the mighty tree of Assyria
with great power!
He will cut down the proud.
That lofty tree will be brought down.
[34] He will cut down the forest trees with an ax.
Lebanon will fall to the Mighty One.*

A BRANCH FROM DAVID'S LINE

11 [1] Out of the stump of David's family*
will grow a shoot—
yes, a new Branch bearing fruit from the
old root.
[2] And the Spirit of the LORD will rest on him—
the Spirit of wisdom and understanding,
the Spirit of counsel and might,
the Spirit of knowledge and the fear of the
LORD.
[3] He will delight in obeying the LORD.
He will not judge by appearance
nor make a decision based on hearsay.
[4] He will give justice to the poor
and make fair decisions for the exploited.
The earth will shake at the force of his word,
and one breath from his mouth will
destroy the wicked.
[5] He will wear righteousness like a belt
and truth like an undergarment.

[6] In that day the wolf and the lamb will
live together;
the leopard will lie down with
the baby goat.
The calf and the yearling will be safe with
the lion,
and a little child will lead them all.
[7] The cow will graze near the bear.
The cub and the calf will lie down
together.
The lion will eat hay like a cow.
[8] The baby will play safely near the hole
of a cobra.
Yes, a little child will put its hand in a
nest of deadly snakes without harm.

10:21 Hebrew *Shear-jashub*; see 7:3; 8:18. 10:22-23 Greek version reads *only a remnant of them will be saved. / For he will carry out his sentence quickly and with finality and righteousness; / for God will carry out his sentence upon all the world with finality.* Compare Rom 9:27-28. 10:27 As in Greek version; Hebrew reads *The yoke will be broken, / for you have grown so fat.* 10:34 Or *with an ax / as even the mighty trees of Lebanon fall.* 11:1 Hebrew *the stump of the line of Jesse.* Jesse was King David's father.

⁹ Nothing will hurt or destroy in all my
      holy mountain,
   for as the waters fill the sea,
      so the earth will be filled with people who
      know the LORD.

¹⁰ In that day the heir to David's throne*
      will be a banner of salvation to
      all the world.
   The nations will rally to him,
      and the land where he lives will be
      a glorious place.*
¹¹ In that day the Lord will reach out his hand
      a second time
   to bring back the remnant of his people—
      those who remain in Assyria and
      northern Egypt;
   in southern Egypt, Ethiopia,* and Elam;
      in Babylonia,* Hamath, and all the distant
      coastlands.
¹² He will raise a flag among the nations
      and assemble the exiles of Israel.
   He will gather the scattered people of Judah
      from the ends of the earth.

¹³ Then at last the jealousy between Israel*
      and Judah will end.
   They will not be rivals anymore.
¹⁴ They will join forces to swoop down on
      Philistia to the west.
   Together they will attack and plunder the
      nations to the east.
   They will occupy the lands of Edom
      and Moab,
      and Ammon will obey them.
¹⁵ The LORD will make a dry path through
      the gulf of the Red Sea.*
   He will wave his hand over
      the Euphrates River,*
   sending a mighty wind to divide it into
      seven streams
      so it can easily be crossed on foot.
¹⁶ He will make a highway for the remnant
      of his people,
      the remnant coming from Assyria,
   just as he did for Israel long ago
      when they returned from Egypt.

SONGS OF PRAISE FOR SALVATION

12 ¹ In that day you will sing:
      "I will praise you, O LORD!
   You were angry with me, but not anymore.
      Now you comfort me.
² See, God has come to save me.
      I will trust in him and not be afraid.
   The LORD GOD is my strength and my song;
      he has given me victory."

³ With joy you will drink deeply
      from the fountain of salvation!
⁴ In that wonderful day you will sing:
      "Thank the LORD! Praise his name!

Tell the nations what he has done.
      Let them know how mighty he is!
⁵ Sing to the LORD, for he has done
      wonderful things.
   Make known his praise around the world.
⁶ Let all the people of Jerusalem* shout his
      praise with joy!
   For great is the Holy One of Israel who
      lives among you."

A MESSAGE ABOUT BABYLON

13 Isaiah son of Amoz received this message
      concerning the destruction of Babylon:

² "Raise a signal flag on a bare hilltop.
      Call up an army against Babylon.
   Wave your hand to encourage them
      as they march into the palaces of the high
      and mighty.
³ I, the LORD, have dedicated these soldiers
      for this task.
   Yes, I have called mighty warriors to
      express my anger,
      and they will rejoice when I am exalted."

⁴ Hear the noise on the mountains!
      Listen, as the vast armies march!
   It is the noise and shouting of many nations.
   The LORD of Heaven's Armies has called
      this army together.
⁵ They come from distant countries,
      from beyond the farthest horizons.
   They are the LORD's weapons to carry out
      his anger.
   With them he will destroy the whole land.

⁶ Scream in terror, for the day of the LORD has
      arrived—
      the time for the Almighty to destroy.
⁷ Every arm is paralyzed with fear.
      Every heart melts,
⁸ and people are terrified.
   Pangs of anguish grip them,
      like those of a woman in labor.
   They look helplessly at one another,
      their faces aflame with fear.

⁹ For see, the day of the LORD is coming—
      the terrible day of his fury and fierce
      anger.
   The land will be made desolate,
      and all the sinners destroyed with it.
¹⁰ The heavens will be black above them;
      the stars will give no light.
   The sun will be dark when it rises,
      and the moon will provide no light.

11:10a Hebrew *the root of Jesse.*   11:10b Greek version reads *In
that day the heir to David's throne* [literally *the root of Jesse*] *will
come,* / *and he will rule over the Gentiles.* / *They will place their hopes
on him.* Compare Rom 15:12.   11:11a Hebrew *in Pathros, Cush.*
11:11b Hebrew *in Shinar.*   11:13 Hebrew *Ephraim,* referring to the
northern kingdom of Israel.   11:15a Hebrew *will destroy the tongue
of the sea of Egypt.*   11:15b Hebrew *the river.*   12:6 Hebrew *Zion.*

11 "I, the LORD, will punish the world for its evil
        and the wicked for their sin.
    I will crush the arrogance of the proud
        and humble the pride of the mighty.
12 I will make people scarcer than gold—
        more rare than the fine gold of Ophir.
13 For I will shake the heavens.
        The earth will move from its place
    when the LORD of Heaven's Armies
            displays his wrath
            in the day of his fierce anger."

14 Everyone in Babylon will run about like a
            hunted gazelle,
        like sheep without a shepherd.
    They will try to find their own people
        and flee to their own land.
15 Anyone who is captured will be cut down—
        run through with a sword.
16 Their little children will be dashed
        to death before their eyes.
    Their homes will be sacked,
        and their wives will be raped.

17 "Look, I will stir up the Medes against
            Babylon.
    They cannot be tempted by silver
        or bribed with gold.
18 The attacking armies will shoot down
        the young men with arrows.
    They will have no mercy on
        helpless babies
        and will show no compassion for
        children."

19 Babylon, the most glorious of kingdoms,
        the flower of Chaldean pride,
    will be devastated like Sodom and Gomorrah
        when God destroyed them.
20 Babylon will never be inhabited again.
        It will remain empty for generation
        after generation.
    Nomads will refuse to camp there,
        and shepherds will not bed down
            their sheep.
21 Desert animals will move into the ruined city,
        and the houses will be haunted by
            howling creatures.
    Owls will live among the ruins,
        and wild goats will go there to dance.
22 Hyenas will howl in its fortresses,
        and jackals will make dens in its
            luxurious palaces.
    Babylon's days are numbered;
        its time of destruction will soon arrive.

A TAUNT FOR BABYLON'S KING

14 But the LORD will have mercy on the
    descendants of Jacob. He will choose Israel
as his special people once again. He will bring
them back to settle once again in their own land.
And people from many different nations will
come and join them there and unite with the
people of Israel.* 2 The nations of the world will
help the people of Israel to return, and those who
come to live in the LORD's land will serve them.
Those who captured Israel will themselves be
captured, and Israel will rule over its enemies.

3 In that wonderful day when the LORD gives
his people rest from sorrow and fear, from slavery
and chains, 4 you will taunt the king of Babylon.
You will say,

"The mighty man has been destroyed.
        Yes, your insolence* is ended.
5 For the LORD has crushed your wicked power
        and broken your evil rule.
6 You struck the people with endless blows
            of rage
        and held the nations in your angry grip
        with unrelenting tyranny.
7 But finally the earth is at rest and quiet.
        Now it can sing again!
8 Even the trees of the forest—
        the cypress trees and the cedars
            of Lebanon—
    sing out this joyous song:
    'Since you have been cut down,
        no one will come now to cut us down!'

9 "In the place of the dead* there is
            excitement
        over your arrival.
    The spirits of world leaders and mighty
            kings long dead
        stand up to see you.
10 With one voice they all cry out,
        'Now you are as weak as we are!
11 Your might and power were buried with you.*
        The sound of the harp in your palace
            has ceased.
    Now maggots are your sheet,
        and worms your blanket.'

12 "How you are fallen from heaven,
        O shining star, son of the morning!
    You have been thrown down to the earth,
        you who destroyed the nations of the world.
13 For you said to yourself,
        'I will ascend to heaven and set my throne
            above God's stars.
    I will preside on the mountain of the gods
        far away in the north.*
14 I will climb to the highest heavens
        and be like the Most High.'
15 Instead, you will be brought down to
            the place of the dead,
        down to its lowest depths.

14:1 Hebrew *the house of Jacob.* The names "Jacob" and "Israel"
are often interchanged throughout the Old Testament, referring
sometimes to the individual patriarch and sometimes to the
nation.   14:4 As in Dead Sea Scrolls; the meaning of the
Masoretic Text is uncertain.   14:9 Hebrew *Sheol;* also in 14:15.
14:11 Hebrew *were brought down to Sheol.*   14:13 Or *on the heights
of Zaphon.*

16 Everyone there will stare at you and ask, 'Can this be the one who shook the earth and made the kingdoms of the world tremble?

17 Is this the one who destroyed the world and made it into a wasteland? Is this the king who demolished the world's greatest cities and had no mercy on his prisoners?'

18 "The kings of the nations lie in stately glory, each in his own tomb,

19 but you will be thrown out of your grave like a worthless branch. Like a corpse trampled underfoot, you will be dumped into a mass grave with those killed in battle. You will descend to the pit.

20 You will not be given a proper burial, for you have destroyed your nation and slaughtered your people.

The descendants of such an evil person will never again receive honor.

21 Kill this man's children! Let them die because of their father's sins! They must not rise and conquer the earth, filling the world with their cities."

22 This is what the LORD of Heaven's Armies says: "I, myself, have risen against Babylon! I will destroy its children and its children's children," says the LORD.

23 "I will make Babylon a desolate place of owls, filled with swamps and marshes. I will sweep the land with the broom of destruction. I, the LORD of Heaven's Armies, have spoken!"

A MESSAGE ABOUT ASSYRIA

24 The LORD of Heaven's Armies has sworn this oath:

"It will all happen as I have planned. It will be as I have decided.

25 I will break the Assyrians when they are in Israel; I will trample them on my mountains. My people will no longer be their slaves nor bow down under their heavy loads.

26 I have a plan for the whole earth, a hand of judgment upon all the nations.

27 The LORD of Heaven's Armies has spoken— who can change his plans? When his hand is raised, who can stop him?"

A MESSAGE ABOUT PHILISTIA

28 This message came to me the year King Ahaz died:*

29 Do not rejoice, you Philistines, that the rod that struck you is broken— that the king who attacked you is dead. For from that snake a more poisonous snake will be born, a fiery serpent to destroy you!

30 I will feed the poor in my pasture; the needy will lie down in peace. But as for you, I will wipe you out with famine and destroy the few who remain.

31 Wail at the gates! Weep in the cities! Melt with fear, you Philistines! A powerful army comes like smoke from the north. Each soldier rushes forward eager to fight.

14:28 King Ahaz died in 715 B.C.

³² What should we tell the Philistine messengers? Tell them,

"The LORD has built Jerusalem*;
 its walls will give refuge to his oppressed
 people."

A MESSAGE ABOUT MOAB

15 This message came to me concerning Moab:

In one night the town of Ar will be leveled,
 and the city of Kir will be destroyed.
² Your people will go to their temple in Dibon
 to mourn.
They will go to their sacred shrines to weep.
They will wail for the fate of Nebo
 and Medeba,
 shaving their heads in sorrow and cutting
 off their beards.
³ They will wear burlap as they wander
 the streets.
From every home and public square will
 come the sound of wailing.
⁴ The people of Heshbon and Elealeh will
 cry out;
 their voices will be heard as far away
 as Jahaz!
The bravest warriors of Moab will cry out
 in utter terror.
They will be helpless with fear.
⁵ My heart weeps for Moab.
Its people flee to Zoar and
 Eglath-shelishiyah.
Weeping, they climb the road to Luhith.
Their cries of distress can be heard all
 along the road to Horonaim.
⁶ Even the waters of Nimrim are dried up!
The grassy banks are scorched.
The tender plants are gone;
 nothing green remains.
⁷ The people grab their possessions
 and carry them across
 the Ravine of Willows.
⁸ A cry of distress echoes through the land
 of Moab
 from one end to the other—
 from Eglaim to Beer-elim.
⁹ The stream near Dibon* runs red with blood,
 but I am still not finished with Dibon!
Lions will hunt down the survivors—
 both those who try to escape
 and those who remain behind.

16 ¹ Send lambs from Sela as tribute
 to the ruler of the land.
Send them through the desert
 to the mountain of beautiful Zion.
² The women of Moab are left
 like homeless birds
 at the shallow crossings of the Arnon River.

³ "Help us," they cry.
"Defend us against our enemies.
Protect us from their relentless attack.
Do not betray us now that we have escaped.
⁴ Let our refugees stay among you.
Hide them from our enemies until the
 terror is past."

When oppression and destruction
 have ended
 and enemy raiders have disappeared,
⁵ then God will establish one of David's
 descendants as king.
He will rule with mercy and truth.
He will always do what is just
 and be eager to do what is right.

⁶ We have heard about proud Moab—
 about its pride and arrogance and rage.
But all that boasting has disappeared.
⁷ The entire land of Moab weeps.
Yes, everyone in Moab mourns
for the cakes of raisins from Kir-hareseth.
They are all gone now.
⁸ The farms of Heshbon are abandoned;
 the vineyards at Sibmah are deserted.
The rulers of the nations have
 broken down Moab—
 that beautiful grapevine.
Its tendrils spread north as far as the town
 of Jazer
 and trailed eastward into the wilderness.
Its shoots reached so far west
 that they crossed over the Dead Sea.*
⁹ So now I weep for Jazer and the vineyards
 of Sibmah;
 my tears will flow for Heshbon and
 Elealeh.
There are no more shouts of joy
 over your summer fruits and harvest.
¹⁰ Gone now is the gladness,
 gone the joy of harvest.
There will be no singing in the vineyards,
 no more happy shouts,
 no treading of grapes in the winepresses.
I have ended all their harvest joys.
¹¹ My heart's cry for Moab is like a lament
 on a harp.
I am filled with anguish for Kir-hareseth.*
¹² The people of Moab will worship at their
 pagan shrines,
 but it will do them no good.
They will cry to the gods in their temples,
 but no one will be able to save them.

¹³ The LORD has already said these things about Moab in the past. ¹⁴ But now the LORD

14:32 Hebrew *Zion.* 15:9 As in Dead Sea Scrolls, some Greek manuscripts, and Latin Vulgate; Masoretic Text reads *Dimon;* also in 15:9b. 16:8 Hebrew *the sea.* 16:11 Hebrew *Kir-heres,* a variant spelling of Kir-hareseth.

says, "Within three years, counting each day,* the glory of Moab will be ended. From its great population, only a feeble few will be left alive."

A MESSAGE ABOUT DAMASCUS AND ISRAEL

17 This message came to me concerning Damascus:

"Look, the city of Damascus will disappear!
It will become a heap of ruins.
2 The towns of Aroer will be deserted.
Flocks will graze in the streets and lie
down undisturbed,
with no one to chase them away.
3 The fortified towns of Israel* will also
be destroyed,
and the royal power of Damascus will end.
All that remains of Syria*
will share the fate of Israel's
departed glory,"
declares the LORD of Heaven's Armies.

4 "In that day Israel's* glory will grow dim;
its robust body will waste away.
5 The whole land will look like a grainfield
after the harvesters have gathered the
grain.
It will be desolate,
like the fields in the valley of Rephaim
after the harvest.
6 Only a few of its people will be left,
like stray olives left on a tree after the
harvest.
Only two or three remain in the highest
branches,
four or five scattered here and there on
the limbs,"
declares the LORD, the God of Israel.

7 Then at last the people will look to their
Creator
and turn their eyes to the Holy One
of Israel.
8 They will no longer look to their idols for help
or worship what their own hands
have made.
They will never again bow down to their
Asherah poles
or worship at the pagan shrines they
have built.
9 Their largest cities will be like a deserted
forest,
like the land the Hivites and Amorites
abandoned*
when the Israelites came here so long ago.
It will be utterly desolate.
10 Why? Because you have turned from the God
who can save you.
You have forgotten the Rock who can
hide you.
So you may plant the finest grapevines
and import the most expensive seedlings.

11 They may sprout on the day you set
them out;
yes, they may blossom on the very
morning you plant them,
but you will never pick any grapes from them.
Your only harvest will be a load of grief
and unrelieved pain.

12 Listen! The armies of many nations
roar like the roaring of the sea.
Hear the thunder of the mighty forces
as they rush forward like thundering
waves.
13 But though they thunder like breakers on
a beach,
God will silence them, and they will
run away.
They will flee like chaff scattered by the wind,
like a tumbleweed whirling before
a storm.
14 In the evening Israel waits in terror,
but by dawn its enemies are dead.
This is the just reward of those who
plunder us,
a fitting end for those who destroy us.

A MESSAGE ABOUT ETHIOPIA

18 1 Listen, Ethiopia*—land of fluttering
sails*
that lies at the headwaters of the Nile,
2 that sends ambassadors
in swift boats down the river.

Go, swift messengers!
Take a message to a tall,
smooth-skinned people,
who are feared far and wide
for their conquests and destruction,
and whose land is divided by rivers.

3 All you people of the world,
everyone who lives on the earth—
when I raise my battle flag on
the mountain, look!
When I blow the ram's horn, listen!
4 For the LORD has told me this:
"I will watch quietly from
my dwelling place—
as quietly as the heat rises on
a summer day,
or as the morning dew forms during
the harvest."
5 Even before you begin your attack,
while your plans are ripening like grapes,
the LORD will cut off your new growth with
pruning shears.

16:14 Hebrew *Within three years, as a servant bound by contract would count them.* 17:3a Hebrew *of Ephraim,* referring to the northern kingdom of Israel. 17:3b Hebrew *Aram.* 17:4 Hebrew *Jacob's.* See note on 14:1. 17:9 As in Greek version; Hebrew reads *like places of the wood and the highest bough.* 18:1a Hebrew *Cush.* 18:1b Or *land of many locusts;* Hebrew reads *land of whirring wings.*

He will snip off and discard your
spreading branches.
⁶ Your mighty army will be left dead
in the fields
for the mountain vultures and
wild animals.
The vultures will tear at the corpses
all summer.
The wild animals will gnaw at the bones
all winter.

⁷ At that time the LORD of Heaven's Armies
will receive gifts
from this land divided by rivers,
from this tall, smooth-skinned people,
who are feared far and wide for their
conquests and destruction.
They will bring the gifts to Jerusalem,*
where the LORD of Heaven's Armies
dwells.

A MESSAGE ABOUT EGYPT

19 This message came to me concerning
Egypt:

Look! The LORD is advancing against Egypt,
riding on a swift cloud.
The idols of Egypt tremble.
The hearts of the Egyptians melt with fear.

² "I will make Egyptian fight
against Egyptian—
brother against brother,
neighbor against neighbor,
city against city,
province against province.
³ The Egyptians will lose heart,
and I will confuse their plans.
They will plead with their idols for wisdom
and call on spirits, mediums, and those
who consult the spirits of the dead.
⁴ I will hand Egypt over
to a hard, cruel master.
A fierce king will rule them,"
says the Lord, the LORD of
Heaven's Armies.

⁵ The waters of the Nile will fail to rise and
flood the fields.
The riverbed will be parched and dry.
⁶ The canals of the Nile will dry up,
and the streams of Egypt will stink
with rotting reeds and rushes.
⁷ All the greenery along the riverbank
and all the crops along the river
will dry up and blow away.
⁸ The fishermen will lament for lack of work.
Those who cast hooks into the Nile
will groan,
and those who use nets will lose heart.
⁹ There will be no flax for the harvesters,
no thread for the weavers.

¹⁰ They will be in despair,
and all the workers will be sick at heart.

¹¹ What fools are the officials of Zoan!
Their best counsel to the king of Egypt is
stupid and wrong.
Will they still boast to Pharaoh of
their wisdom?
Will they dare brag about all their
wise ancestors?
¹² Where are your wise counselors, Pharaoh?
Let them tell you what God plans,
what the LORD of Heaven's Armies is
going to do to Egypt.
¹³ The officials of Zoan are fools,
and the officials of Memphis* are deluded.
The leaders of the people
have led Egypt astray.
¹⁴ The LORD has sent a spirit of foolishness
on them,
so all their suggestions are wrong.
They cause Egypt to stagger
like a drunk in his vomit.
¹⁵ There is nothing Egypt can do.
All are helpless—
the head and the tail,
the noble palm branch and the lowly reed.

¹⁶ In that day the Egyptians will be as weak
as women. They will cower in fear beneath the
upraised fist of the LORD of Heaven's Armies.
¹⁷ Just to speak the name of Israel will terrorize
them, for the LORD of Heaven's Armies has laid
out his plans against them.

¹⁸ In that day five of Egypt's cities will follow
the LORD of Heaven's Armies. They will even
begin to speak Hebrew, the language of Canaan.
One of these cities will be Heliopolis, the City
of the Sun.*

¹⁹ In that day there will be an altar to the LORD
in the heart of Egypt, and there will be a monument to the LORD at its border. ²⁰ It will be a sign
and a witness that the LORD of Heaven's Armies
is worshiped in the land of Egypt. When the
people cry to the LORD for help against those who
oppress them, he will send them a savior who
will rescue them. ²¹ The LORD will make himself
known to the Egyptians. Yes, they will know the
LORD and will give their sacrifices and offerings
to him. They will make a vow to the LORD and
will keep it. ²² The LORD will strike Egypt, and
then he will bring healing. For the Egyptians
will turn to the LORD, and he will listen to their
pleas and heal them.

²³ In that day Egypt and Assyria will be connected by a highway. The Egyptians and Assyrians will move freely between their lands, and
they will both worship God. ²⁴ In that day Israel
will be the third, along with Egypt and Assyria, a

18:7 Hebrew *to Mount Zion.*   19:13 Hebrew *Noph.*   19:18 Or *will
be the City of Destruction.*

blessing in the midst of the earth. [25] For the LORD of Heaven's Armies will say, "Blessed be Egypt, my people. Blessed be Assyria, the land I have made. Blessed be Israel, my special possession!"

A MESSAGE ABOUT EGYPT AND ETHIOPIA

20 In the year when King Sargon of Assyria sent his commander in chief to capture the Philistine city of Ashdod,* [2] the LORD told Isaiah son of Amoz, "Take off the burlap you have been wearing, and remove your sandals." Isaiah did as he was told and walked around naked and barefoot.

[3] Then the LORD said, "My servant Isaiah has been walking around naked and barefoot for the last three years. This is a sign—a symbol of the terrible troubles I will bring upon Egypt and Ethiopia.* [4] For the king of Assyria will take away the Egyptians and Ethiopians* as prisoners. He will make them walk naked and barefoot, both young and old, their buttocks bared, to the shame of Egypt. [5] Then the Philistines will be thrown into panic, for they counted on the power of Ethiopia and boasted of their allies in Egypt! [6] They will say, 'If this can happen to Egypt, what chance do we have? We were counting on Egypt to protect us from the king of Assyria.'"

A MESSAGE ABOUT BABYLON

21 This message came to me concerning Babylon—the desert by the sea*:

Disaster is roaring down on you from
    the desert,
    like a whirlwind sweeping in from
    the Negev.
[2] I see a terrifying vision:
    I see the betrayer betraying,
    the destroyer destroying.
Go ahead, you Elamites and Medes,
    attack and lay siege.
I will make an end
    to all the groaning Babylon caused.
[3] My stomach aches and burns with pain.
    Sharp pangs of anguish are upon me,
    like those of a woman in labor.
I grow faint when I hear what God
    is planning;
    I am too afraid to look.
[4] My mind reels and my heart races.
    I longed for evening to come,
    but now I am terrified of the dark.

[5] Look! They are preparing a great feast.
    They are spreading rugs for people to sit on.
    Everyone is eating and drinking.
But quick! Grab your shields and prepare
    for battle.
    You are being attacked!

[6] Meanwhile, the Lord said to me,
    "Put a watchman on the city wall.

Let him shout out what he sees.
[7] He should look for chariots
    drawn by pairs of horses,
and for riders on donkeys and camels.
    Let the watchman be fully alert."

[8] Then the watchman* called out,
    "Day after day I have stood on the
    watchtower, my lord.
    Night after night I have remained
    at my post.
[9] Now at last—look!
Here comes a man in a chariot
    with a pair of horses!"
Then the watchman said,
    "Babylon is fallen, fallen!
All the idols of Babylon
    lie broken on the ground!"
[10] O my people, threshed and winnowed,
    I have told you everything the LORD of
    Heaven's Armies has said,
    everything the God of Israel has told me.

A MESSAGE ABOUT EDOM

[11] This message came to me concerning Edom*:

Someone from Edom* keeps calling to me,
    "Watchman, how much longer until
    morning?
    When will the night be over?"
[12] The watchman replies,
    "Morning is coming,
    but night will soon return.
If you wish to ask again, then come back
    and ask."

A MESSAGE ABOUT ARABIA

[13] This message came to me concerning Arabia:

O caravans from Dedan,
    hide in the deserts of Arabia.
[14] O people of Tema,
    bring water to these thirsty people,
    food to these weary refugees.
[15] They have fled from the sword,
    from the drawn sword,
from the bent bow
    and the terrors of battle.

[16] The Lord said to me, "Within a year, counting each day,* all the glory of Kedar will come to an end. [17] Only a few of its courageous archers will survive. I, the LORD, the God of Israel, have spoken!"

20:1 Ashdod was captured by Assyria in 711 B.C.   20:3 Hebrew *Cush;* also in 20:5.   20:4 Hebrew *Cushites.*   21:1 Hebrew *concerning the desert by the sea.*   21:8 As in Dead Sea Scrolls and Syriac version; Masoretic Text reads *a lion.*   21:11a Hebrew *Dumah,* which means "silence" or "stillness." It is a wordplay on the word *Edom.*   21:11b Hebrew *Seir,* another name for Edom.   21:16 Hebrew *Within a year, as a servant bound by contract would count it.* Some ancient manuscripts read *Within three years,* as in 16:14.

A MESSAGE ABOUT JERUSALEM

22 This message came to me concerning Jerusalem—the Valley of Vision*:

What is happening?
   Why is everyone running to the rooftops?
2 The whole city is in a terrible uproar.
   What do I see in this reveling city?
Bodies are lying everywhere,
   killed not in battle but by famine
      and disease.
3 All your leaders have fled.
   They surrendered without resistance.
The people tried to slip away,
   but they were captured, too.
4 That's why I said, "Leave me alone to weep;
   do not try to comfort me.
Let me cry for my people
   as I watch them being destroyed."

5 Oh, what a day of crushing defeat!
   What a day of confusion and terror
brought by the Lord,
   the Lord of Heaven's Armies,
upon the Valley of Vision!
The walls of Jerusalem have been broken,
   and cries of death echo from the
      mountainsides.
6 Elamites are the archers,
   with their chariots and charioteers.
   The men of Kir hold up the shields.
7 Chariots fill your beautiful valleys,
   and charioteers storm your gates.
8 Judah's defenses have been stripped away.
   You run to the armory* for your weapons.
9 You inspect the breaks in the walls of
      Jerusalem.*
   You store up water in the lower pool.
10 You survey the houses and tear some down
      for stone to strengthen the walls.
11 Between the city walls, you build a reservoir
      for water from the old pool.
But you never ask for help from the One
      who did all this.
   You never considered the One who
      planned this long ago.

12 At that time the Lord,
   the Lord of Heaven's Armies,
called you to weep and mourn.
He told you to shave your heads in sorrow
      for your sins
   and to wear clothes of burlap to show
      your remorse.
13 But instead, you dance and play;
   you slaughter cattle and kill sheep.
You feast on meat and drink wine.
You say, "Let's feast and drink,
   for tomorrow we die!"

14 The Lord of Heaven's Armies has revealed this to me: "Till the day you die, you will never be forgiven for this sin." That is the judgment of the Lord, the Lord of Heaven's Armies.

A MESSAGE FOR SHEBNA

15 This is what the Lord, the Lord of Heaven's Armies, said to me: "Confront Shebna, the palace administrator, and give him this message:

16 "Who do you think you are,
   and what are you doing here,
   building a beautiful tomb for yourself—
      a monument high up in the rock?
17 For the Lord is about to hurl you away,
      mighty man.
   He is going to grab you,
18 crumple you into a ball,
   and toss you away into a distant,
      barren land.
There you will die,
   and your glorious chariots will be broken
      and useless.
   You are a disgrace to your master!

19 "Yes, I will drive you out of office," says the Lord. "I will pull you down from your high position. 20 And then I will call my servant Eliakim son of Hilkiah to replace you. 21 I will dress him in your royal robes and will give him your title and your authority. And he will be a father to the people of Jerusalem and Judah. 22 I will give him the key to the house of David—the highest position in the royal court. When he opens doors, no one will be able to close them; when he closes doors, no one will be able to open them. 23 He will bring honor to his family name, for I will drive him firmly in place like a nail in the wall. 24 They will give him great responsibility, and he will bring honor to even the lowliest members of his family.*"

25 But the Lord of Heaven's Armies also says: "The time will come when I will pull out the nail that seemed so firm. It will come out and fall to the ground. Everything it supports will fall with it. I, the Lord, have spoken!"

A MESSAGE ABOUT TYRE

23 This message came to me concerning Tyre:

Wail, you trading ships of Tarshish,
   for the harbor and houses of Tyre are gone!
The rumors you heard in Cyprus*
   are all true.
2 Mourn in silence, you people of the coast
   and you merchants of Sidon.
Your traders crossed the sea,*
3   sailing over deep waters.

22:1 Hebrew *concerning the Valley of Vision.*   22:8 Hebrew *to the House of the Forest;* see 1 Kgs 7:2-5.   22:9 Hebrew *the city of David.*   22:24 Hebrew *They will hang on him all the glory of his father's house: its offspring and offshoots, all its lesser vessels, from the bowls to all the jars.*   23:1 Hebrew *Kittim;* also in 23:12.   23:2 As in Dead Sea Scrolls and Greek version; Masoretic Text reads *Those who have gone over the sea have filled you.*

They brought you grain from Egypt*
and harvests from along the Nile.
You were the marketplace of the world.

4 But now you are put to shame, city of Sidon,
for Tyre, the fortress of the sea, says,*
"Now I am childless;
I have no sons or daughters."

5 When Egypt hears the news about Tyre,
there will be great sorrow.

6 Send word now to Tarshish!
Wail, you people who live in
distant lands!

7 Is this silent ruin all that is left of your once
joyous city?
What a long history was yours!
Think of all the colonists you sent to
distant places.

8 Who has brought this disaster on Tyre,
that great creator of kingdoms?
Her traders were all princes,
her merchants were nobles.

9 The LORD of Heaven's Armies has done it
to destroy your pride
and bring low all earth's nobility.

10 Come, people of Tarshish,
sweep over the land like the flooding Nile,
for Tyre is defenseless.*

11 The LORD held out his hand over the sea
and shook the kingdoms of the earth.
He has spoken out against Phoenicia,*
ordering that her fortresses be destroyed.

12 He says, "Never again will you rejoice,
O daughter of Sidon,
for you have been crushed.
Even if you flee to Cyprus,
you will find no rest."

13 Look at the land of Babylonia*—
the people of that land are gone!
The Assyrians have handed Babylon over
to the wild animals of the desert.
They have built siege ramps against its walls,
torn down its palaces,
and turned it to a heap of rubble.

14 Wail, you ships of Tarshish,
for your harbor is destroyed!

15 For seventy years, the length of a king's
life, Tyre will be forgotten. But then the city
will come back to life as in the song about the
prostitute:

16 Take a harp and walk the streets,
you forgotten harlot.
Make sweet melody and sing your songs
so you will be remembered again.

17 Yes, after seventy years the LORD will revive
Tyre. But she will be no different than she was

before. She will again be a prostitute to all kingdoms around the world. 18 But in the end her
profits will be given to the LORD. Her wealth will
not be hoarded but will provide good food and
fine clothing for the LORD's priests.

DESTRUCTION OF THE EARTH

24 1 Look! The LORD is about to destroy
the earth
and make it a vast wasteland.
He devastates the surface of the earth
and scatters the people.

2 Priests and laypeople,
servants and masters,
maids and mistresses,
buyers and sellers,
lenders and borrowers,
bankers and debtors—none will be spared.

3 The earth will be completely emptied
and looted.
The LORD has spoken!

4 The earth mourns and dries up,
and the land wastes away and withers.
Even the greatest people on earth
waste away.

5 The earth suffers for the sins of its people,
for they have twisted God's instructions,
violated his laws,
and broken his everlasting covenant.

6 Therefore, a curse consumes the earth.
Its people must pay the price for their sin.
They are destroyed by fire,
and only a few are left alive.

7 The grapevines waste away,
and there is no new wine.
All the merrymakers sigh and mourn.

8 The cheerful sound of tambourines is stilled;
the happy cries of celebration are heard
no more.
The melodious chords of the harp
are silent.

9 Gone are the joys of wine and song;
alcoholic drink turns bitter in the mouth.

10 The city writhes in chaos;
every home is locked to keep out intruders.

11 Mobs gather in the streets, crying out for
wine.
Joy has turned to gloom.
Gladness has been banished from
the land.

12 The city is left in ruins,
its gates battered down.

13 Throughout the earth the story is the same—
only a remnant is left,
like the stray olives left on the tree
or the few grapes left on the vine
after harvest.

23:3 Hebrew *from Shihor,* a branch of the Nile River.   23:4 Or
for the god of the sea says; Hebrew reads *for the sea, the fortress of
the sea, says.*   23:10 The meaning of the Hebrew in this verse is
uncertain.   23:11 Hebrew *Canaan.*   23:13 Or *Chaldea.*

14 But all who are left shout and sing for joy.
    Those in the west praise the LORD's majesty.
15 In eastern lands, give glory to the LORD.
    In the lands beyond the sea, praise the
        name of the LORD, the God of Israel.
16 We hear songs of praise from the ends
        of the earth,
    songs that give glory to the Righteous One!

But my heart is heavy with grief.
    Weep for me, for I wither away.
Deceit still prevails,
    and treachery is everywhere.
17 Terror and traps and snares will be your lot,
    you people of the earth.
18 Those who flee in terror will fall into a trap,
    and those who escape the trap will be
        caught in a snare.

Destruction falls like rain from the heavens;
    the foundations of the earth shake.
19 The earth has broken up.
    It has utterly collapsed;
    it is violently shaken.
20 The earth staggers like a drunk.
    It trembles like a tent in a storm.
    It falls and will not rise again,
        for the guilt of its rebellion is very heavy.

21 In that day the LORD will punish the gods
        in the heavens
    and the proud rulers of the nations
        on earth.
22 They will be rounded up and put in prison.
    They will be shut up in prison
    and will finally be punished.
23 Then the glory of the moon will wane,
    and the brightness of the sun will fade,
    for the LORD of Heaven's Armies will rule
        on Mount Zion.
    He will rule in great glory in Jerusalem,
        in the sight of all the leaders of his people.

PRAISE FOR JUDGMENT AND SALVATION

25 1 O LORD, I will honor and praise
        your name,
    for you are my God.
    You do such wonderful things!
    You planned them long ago,
    and now you have accomplished them.
2 You turn mighty cities into heaps of ruins.
    Cities with strong walls are turned
        to rubble.
    Beautiful palaces in distant lands disappear
        and will never be rebuilt.
3 Therefore, strong nations will declare
        your glory;
    ruthless nations will fear you.

4 But you are a tower of refuge to the poor,
        O LORD,
    a tower of refuge to the needy in distress.

You are a refuge from the storm
    and a shelter from the heat.
For the oppressive acts of ruthless people
    are like a storm beating against a wall,
5   or like the relentless heat of the desert.
But you silence the roar of foreign nations.
    As the shade of a cloud cools
        relentless heat,
    so the boastful songs of ruthless people
        are stilled.

6 In Jerusalem,* the LORD of Heaven's Armies
    will spread a wonderful feast
    for all the people of the world.
    It will be a delicious banquet
    with clear, well-aged wine and choice meat.
7 There he will remove the cloud of gloom,
    the shadow of death that hangs over
        the earth.
8 He will swallow up death forever!
    The Sovereign LORD will wipe away
        all tears.
    He will remove forever all insults
        and mockery
    against his land and people.
    The LORD has spoken!

9 In that day the people will proclaim,
    "This is our God!
    We trusted in him, and he saved us!
    This is the LORD, in whom we trusted.
    Let us rejoice in the salvation he brings!"
10 For the LORD's hand of blessing will rest
        on Jerusalem.
    But Moab will be crushed.
    It will be like straw trampled down and
        left to rot.
11 God will push down Moab's people
    as a swimmer pushes down water with
        his hands.
    He will end their pride
    and all their evil works.
12 The high walls of Moab will be demolished.
    They will be brought down to the ground,
        down into the dust.

A SONG OF PRAISE TO THE LORD

26 In that day, everyone in the land of Judah
    will sing this song:

Our city is strong!
    We are surrounded by the walls of
        God's salvation.
2 Open the gates to all who are righteous;
    allow the faithful to enter.
3 You will keep in perfect peace
    all who trust in you,
    all whose thoughts are fixed on you!
4 Trust in the LORD always,
    for the LORD GOD is the eternal Rock.

―――――――――
25:6 Hebrew On this mountain; also in 25:10.

⁵ He humbles the proud
and brings down the arrogant city.
He brings it down to the dust.
⁶ The poor and oppressed trample
it underfoot,
and the needy walk all over it.

⁷ But for those who are righteous,
the way is not steep and rough.
You are a God who does what is right,
and you smooth out the path ahead
of them.
⁸ LORD, we show our trust in you by obeying
your laws;
our heart's desire is to glorify your name.
⁹ In the night I search for you;
in the morning* I earnestly seek you.
For only when you come to judge the earth
will people learn what is right.
¹⁰ Your kindness to the wicked
does not make them do good.
Although others do right, the wicked keep
doing wrong
and take no notice of the LORD's majesty.
¹¹ O LORD, they pay no attention to your
upraised fist.
Show them your eagerness to defend
your people.
Then they will be ashamed.
Let your fire consume your enemies.

¹² LORD, you will grant us peace;
all we have accomplished is really
from you.
¹³ O LORD our God, others have ruled us,
but you alone are the one we worship.
¹⁴ Those we served before are dead and gone.
Their departed spirits will never return!
You attacked them and destroyed them,
and they are long forgotten.
¹⁵ O LORD, you have made our nation great;
yes, you have made us great.
You have extended our borders,
and we give you the glory!

¹⁶ LORD, in distress we searched for you.
We prayed beneath the burden of your
discipline.
¹⁷ Just as a pregnant woman
writhes and cries out in pain as
she gives birth,
so were we in your presence, LORD.
¹⁸ We, too, writhe in agony,
but nothing comes of our suffering.
We have not given salvation to the earth,
nor brought life into the world.
¹⁹ But those who die in the LORD will live;
their bodies will rise again!
Those who sleep in the earth
will rise up and sing for joy!
For your life-giving light will fall like dew
on your people in the place of the dead!

RESTORATION FOR ISRAEL

²⁰ Go home, my people,
and lock your doors!
Hide yourselves for a little while
until the LORD's anger has passed.
²¹ Look! The LORD is coming from heaven
to punish the people of the earth for
their sins.
The earth will no longer hide those who
have been killed.
They will be brought out for all to see.

27 In that day the LORD will take his terrible,
swift sword and punish Leviathan,* the
swiftly moving serpent, the coiling, writhing
serpent. He will kill the dragon of the sea.

² "In that day,
sing about the fruitful vineyard.
³ I, the LORD, will watch over it,
watering it carefully.
Day and night I will watch so no one can
harm it.
⁴ My anger will be gone.
If I find briers and thorns growing,
I will attack them;
I will burn them up—
⁵ unless they turn to me for help.
Let them make peace with me;
yes, let them make peace with me."
⁶ The time is coming when Jacob's
descendants will take root.
Israel will bud and blossom
and fill the whole earth with fruit!

⁷ Has the LORD struck Israel
as he struck her enemies?
Has he punished her
as he punished them?
⁸ No, but he exiled Israel to call her
to account.
She was exiled from her land
as though blown away in a storm from
the east.
⁹ The LORD did this to purge Israel's*
wickedness,
to take away all her sin.
As a result, all the pagan altars will be
crushed to dust.
No Asherah pole or pagan shrine will be
left standing.
¹⁰ The fortified towns will be silent and empty,
the houses abandoned, the streets
overgrown with weeds.
Calves will graze there,
chewing on twigs and branches.
¹¹ The people are like the dead branches
of a tree,

26:9 Hebrew *within me.* 27:1 The identification of Leviathan
is disputed, ranging from an earthly creature to a mythical sea
monster in ancient literature. 27:9 Hebrew *Jacob's.* See note
on 14:1.

broken off and used for kindling beneath
the cooking pots.
Israel is a foolish and stupid nation,
for its people have turned away from God.
Therefore, the one who made them
will show them no pity or mercy.

¹² Yet the time will come when the LORD will
gather them together like handpicked grain. One
by one he will gather them—from the Euphrates
River* in the east to the Brook of Egypt in the
west. ¹³ In that day the great trumpet will sound.
Many who were dying in exile in Assyria and
Egypt will return to Jerusalem to worship the
LORD on his holy mountain.

A MESSAGE ABOUT SAMARIA

28 ¹ What sorrow awaits the proud city
of Samaria—
the glorious crown of the drunks
of Israel.*
It sits at the head of a fertile valley,
but its glorious beauty will fade like
a flower.
It is the pride of a people
brought down by wine.
² For the Lord will send a mighty army
against it.
Like a mighty hailstorm and
a torrential rain,
they will burst upon it like a surging flood
and smash it to the ground.
³ The proud city of Samaria—
the glorious crown of the drunks
of Israel*—
will be trampled beneath its enemies' feet.
⁴ It sits at the head of a fertile valley,
but its glorious beauty will fade like
a flower.
Whoever sees it will snatch it up,
as an early fig is quickly picked and eaten.

⁵ Then at last the LORD of Heaven's Armies
will himself be Israel's glorious crown.
He will be the pride and joy
of the remnant of his people.
⁶ He will give a longing for justice
to their judges.
He will give great courage
to their warriors who stand at the gates.

⁷ Now, however, Israel is led by drunks
who reel with wine and stagger
with alcohol.
The priests and prophets stagger with alcohol
and lose themselves in wine.
They reel when they see visions
and stagger as they render decisions.
⁸ Their tables are covered with vomit;
filth is everywhere.
⁹ "Who does the LORD think we are?" they ask.
"Why does he speak to us like this?

Are we little children,
just recently weaned?
¹⁰ He tells us everything over and over—
one line at a time,
one line at a time,
a little here,
and a little there!"

¹¹ So now God will have to speak to his people
through foreign oppressors who speak a
strange language!
¹² God has told his people,
"Here is a place of rest;
let the weary rest here.
This is a place of quiet rest."
But they would not listen.
¹³ So the LORD will spell out his message for
them again,
one line at a time,
one line at a time,
a little here,
and a little there,
so that they will stumble and fall.
They will be injured, trapped,
and captured.

¹⁴ Therefore, listen to this message from
the LORD,
you scoffing rulers in Jerusalem.
¹⁵ You boast, "We have struck a bargain to
cheat death
and have made a deal to dodge the grave.*
The coming destruction can never touch us,
for we have built a strong refuge made of
lies and deception."

¹⁶ Therefore, this is what the Sovereign LORD
says:
"Look! I am placing a foundation stone in
Jerusalem,*
a firm and tested stone.
It is a precious cornerstone that is safe to
build on.
Whoever believes need never be shaken.*
¹⁷ I will test you with the measuring line
of justice
and the plumb line of righteousness.
Since your refuge is made of lies,
a hailstorm will knock it down.
Since it is made of deception,
a flood will sweep it away.
¹⁸ I will cancel the bargain you made to
cheat death,
and I will overturn your deal to dodge
the grave.

27:12 Hebrew *the river.* 28:1 Hebrew *What sorrow awaits the
crowning glory of the drunks of Ephraim,* referring to Samaria,
capital of the northern kingdom of Israel. 28:3 Hebrew
The crowning glory of the drunks of Ephraim; see note on 28:1.
28:15 Hebrew *Sheol;* also in 28:18. 28:16a Hebrew *in Zion.*
28:16b Greek version reads *Look! I am placing a stone in the
foundation of Jerusalem* [literally *Zion*], / *a precious cornerstone for
its foundation, chosen for great honor.* / *Anyone who trusts in him will
never be disgraced.* Compare Rom 9:33; 1 Pet 2:6.

When the terrible enemy sweeps through,
    you will be trampled into the ground.
19 Again and again that flood will come,
    morning after morning,
day and night,
    until you are carried away."

This message will bring terror to
    your people.
20 The bed you have made is too short to lie on.
    The blankets are too narrow to cover you.
21 The LORD will come as he did against the
    Philistines at Mount Perazim
    and against the Amorites at Gibeon.
He will come to do a strange thing;
    he will come to do an unusual deed:
22 For the Lord, the LORD of Heaven's Armies,
    has plainly said that he is determined to
    crush the whole land.
So scoff no more,
    or your punishment will be even greater.

23 Listen to me;
    listen, and pay close attention.
24 Does a farmer always plow and never sow?
    Is he forever cultivating the soil and
    never planting?
25 Does he not finally plant his seeds—
    black cumin, cumin, wheat, barley,
    and emmer wheat—
each in its proper way,
    and each in its proper place?
26 The farmer knows just what to do,
    for God has given him understanding.
27 A heavy sledge is never used to thresh
    black cumin;
rather, it is beaten with a light stick.
A threshing wheel is never rolled on cumin;
    instead, it is beaten lightly with a flail.
28 Grain for bread is easily crushed,
    so he doesn't keep on pounding it.
He threshes it under the wheels of a cart,
    but he doesn't pulverize it.
29 The LORD of Heaven's Armies is
    a wonderful teacher,
    and he gives the farmer great wisdom.

A MESSAGE ABOUT JERUSALEM

29 ¹ "What sorrow awaits Ariel,* the City
    of David.
    Year after year you celebrate your feasts.
² Yet I will bring disaster upon you,
    and there will be much weeping
    and sorrow.
For Jerusalem will become what her name
    Ariel means—
    an altar covered with blood.
³ I will be your enemy,
    surrounding Jerusalem and attacking
    its walls.
I will build siege towers
    and destroy it.

⁴ Then deep from the earth you will speak;
    from low in the dust your words will come.
Your voice will whisper from the ground
    like a ghost conjured up from the grave.

⁵ "But suddenly, your ruthless enemies
    will be crushed
    like the finest of dust.
Your many attackers will be driven away
    like chaff before the wind.
Suddenly, in an instant,
⁶   I, the LORD of Heaven's Armies,
    will act for you
with thunder and earthquake and great noise,
    with whirlwind and storm and
    consuming fire.
⁷ All the nations fighting against Jerusalem*
    will vanish like a dream!
Those who are attacking her walls
    will vanish like a vision in the night.
⁸ A hungry person dreams of eating
    but wakes up still hungry.
A thirsty person dreams of drinking
    but is still faint from thirst when
    morning comes.
So it will be with your enemies,
    with those who attack Mount Zion."

⁹ Are you amazed and incredulous?
    Don't you believe it?
Then go ahead and be blind.
    You are stupid, but not from wine!
    You stagger, but not from liquor!
¹⁰ For the LORD has poured out on you a spirit
    of deep sleep.
He has closed the eyes of your prophets
    and visionaries.

¹¹All the future events in this vision are like a
sealed book to them. When you give it to those
who can read, they will say, "We can't read it
because it is sealed." ¹²When you give it to those
who cannot read, they will say, "We don't know
how to read."

¹³ And so the Lord says,
    "These people say they are mine.
They honor me with their lips,
    but their hearts are far from me.
And their worship of me
    is nothing but man-made rules learned
    by rote.*
¹⁴ Because of this, I will once again astound
    these hypocrites
    with amazing wonders.
The wisdom of the wise will pass away,
    and the intelligence of the intelligent will
    disappear."

29:1 *Ariel* sounds like a Hebrew term that means "hearth" or
"altar."   **29:7** Hebrew *Ariel.*   **29:13** Greek version reads *Their
worship is a farce, / for they teach man-made ideas as commands from
God.* Compare Mark 7:7.

¹⁵ What sorrow awaits those who try to hide
their plans from the LORD,
who do their evil deeds in the dark!
"The LORD can't see us," they say.
"He doesn't know what's going on!"
¹⁶ How foolish can you be?
He is the Potter, and he is certainly
greater than you, the clay!
Should the created thing say of the one
who made it,
"He didn't make me"?
Does a jar ever say,
"The potter who made me is stupid"?

¹⁷ Soon—and it will not be very long—
the forests of Lebanon will become a
fertile field,
and the fertile field will yield
bountiful crops.
¹⁸ In that day the deaf will hear words read
from a book,
and the blind will see through the gloom
and darkness.
¹⁹ The humble will be filled with fresh joy
from the LORD.
The poor will rejoice in the Holy One
of Israel.
²⁰ The scoffer will be gone,
the arrogant will disappear,
and those who plot evil will be killed.
²¹ Those who convict the innocent
by their false testimony will disappear.
A similar fate awaits those who use trickery
to pervert justice
and who tell lies to destroy the innocent.

²² That is why the LORD, who redeemed Abraham,
says to the people of Israel,*

"My people will no longer be ashamed
or turn pale with fear.
²³ For when they see their many children
and all the blessings I have given them,
they will recognize the holiness of
the Holy One of Jacob.
They will stand in awe of the God of Israel.
²⁴ Then the wayward will gain understanding,
and complainers will accept instruction.

JUDAH'S WORTHLESS TREATY WITH EGYPT

30 ¹ "What sorrow awaits my rebellious
children,"
says the LORD.
"You make plans that are contrary to mine.
You make alliances not directed by
my Spirit,
thus piling up your sins.
² For without consulting me,
you have gone down to Egypt for help.
You have put your trust in Pharaoh's
protection.
You have tried to hide in his shade.

³ But by trusting Pharaoh,
you will be humiliated,
and by depending on him,
you will be disgraced.
⁴ For though his power extends to Zoan
and his officials have arrived in Hanes,
⁵ all who trust in him will be ashamed.
He will not help you.
Instead, he will disgrace you."

⁶ This message came to me concerning the
animals in the Negev:

The caravan moves slowly
across the terrible desert to Egypt—
donkeys weighed down with riches
and camels loaded with treasure—
all to pay for Egypt's protection.
They travel through the wilderness,
a place of lionesses and lions,
a place where vipers and poisonous
snakes live.
All this, and Egypt will give you nothing
in return.
⁷ Egypt's promises are worthless!
Therefore, I call her Rahab—
the Harmless Dragon.*

A WARNING FOR REBELLIOUS JUDAH

⁸ Now go and write down these words.
Write them in a book.
They will stand until the end of time
as a witness
⁹ that these people are stubborn rebels
who refuse to pay attention to
the LORD's instructions.
¹⁰ They tell the seers,
"Stop seeing visions!"
They tell the prophets,
"Don't tell us what is right.
Tell us nice things.
Tell us lies.
¹¹ Forget all this gloom.
Get off your narrow path.
Stop telling us about your
'Holy One of Israel.'"

¹² This is the reply of the Holy One of Israel:

"Because you despise what I tell you
and trust instead in oppression and lies,
¹³ calamity will come upon you suddenly—
like a bulging wall that bursts and falls.
In an instant it will collapse
and come crashing down.
¹⁴ You will be smashed like a piece of pottery—
shattered so completely that
there won't be a piece big enough

29:22 Hebrew *of Jacob.* See note on 14:1. **30:7** Hebrew *Rahab who sits still.* Rahab is the name of a mythical sea monster that represents chaos in ancient literature. The name is used here as a poetic name for Egypt.

to carry coals from a fireplace
or a little water from the well."

¹⁵ This is what the Sovereign LORD,
the Holy One of Israel, says:
"Only in returning to me
and resting in me will you be saved.
In quietness and confidence is your strength.
But you would have none of it.
¹⁶ You said, 'No, we will get our help
from Egypt.
They will give us swift horses for riding
into battle.'
But the only swiftness you are going to see
is the swiftness of your enemies
chasing you!
¹⁷ One of them will chase a thousand of you.
Five of them will make all of you flee.
You will be left like a lonely flagpole on a hill
or a tattered banner on a distant
mountaintop."

BLESSINGS FOR THE LORD'S PEOPLE

¹⁸ So the LORD must wait for you to come
to him
so he can show you his love
and compassion.
For the LORD is a faithful God.
Blessed are those who wait for his help.

¹⁹ O people of Zion, who live in Jerusalem,
you will weep no more.
He will be gracious if you ask for help.
He will surely respond to the sound of
your cries.
²⁰ Though the Lord gave you adversity for food
and suffering for drink,
he will still be with you to teach you.
You will see your teacher with your
own eyes.
²¹ Your own ears will hear him.
Right behind you a voice will say,
"This is the way you should go,"
whether to the right or to the left.
²² Then you will destroy all your silver idols
and your precious gold images.
You will throw them out like filthy rags,
saying to them, "Good riddance!"

²³ Then the LORD will bless you with rain at
planting time. There will be wonderful harvests
and plenty of pastureland for your livestock.
²⁴ The oxen and donkeys that till the ground will
eat good grain, its chaff blown away by the wind.
²⁵ In that day, when your enemies are slaughtered
and the towers fall, there will be streams of water
flowing down every mountain and hill. ²⁶ The
moon will be as bright as the sun, and the sun
will be seven times brighter—like the light of
seven days in one! So it will be when the LORD
begins to heal his people and cure the wounds
he gave them.

²⁷ Look! The LORD is coming from far away,
burning with anger,
surrounded by thick, rising smoke.
His lips are filled with fury;
his words consume like fire.
²⁸ His hot breath pours out like a flood
up to the neck of his enemies.
He will sift out the proud nations
for destruction.
He will bridle them and lead them away
to ruin.

²⁹ But the people of God will sing a song of joy,
like the songs at the holy festivals.
You will be filled with joy,
as when a flutist leads a group
of pilgrims
to Jerusalem, the mountain of the LORD—
to the Rock of Israel.
³⁰ And the LORD will make his majestic
voice heard.
He will display the strength of his
mighty arm.
It will descend with devouring flames,
with cloudbursts, thunderstorms,
and huge hailstones.
³¹ At the LORD's command,
the Assyrians will be shattered.
He will strike them down with
his royal scepter.
³² And as the LORD strikes them with his rod
of punishment,*
his people will celebrate with
tambourines and harps.
Lifting his mighty arm, he will fight
the Assyrians.
³³ Topheth—the place of burning—
has long been ready for the Assyrian king;
the pyre is piled high with wood.
The breath of the LORD, like fire from
a volcano,
will set it ablaze.

THE FUTILITY OF RELYING ON EGYPT

31 ¹ What sorrow awaits those who look
to Egypt for help,
trusting their horses, chariots, and
charioteers
and depending on the strength of human
armies
instead of looking to the LORD,
the Holy One of Israel.
² In his wisdom, the LORD will send
great disaster;
he will not change his mind.
He will rise against the wicked
and against their helpers.
³ For these Egyptians are mere humans,
not God!

30:32 As in some Hebrew manuscripts and Syriac version;
Masoretic Text reads *with the founded rod.*

Their horses are puny flesh,
  not mighty spirits!
When the LORD raises his fist against them,
  those who help will stumble,
and those being helped will fall.
  They will all fall down and die together.

4 But this is what the LORD has told me:

"When a strong young lion
  stands growling over a sheep it has killed,
it is not frightened by the shouts and noise
  of a whole crowd of shepherds.
In the same way, the LORD of Heaven's Armies
  will come down and fight on Mount Zion.
5 The LORD of Heaven's Armies will hover
    over Jerusalem
  and protect it like a bird protecting its nest.
He will defend and save the city;
  he will pass over it and rescue it."

6 Though you are such wicked rebels, my people, come and return to the LORD. 7 I know the glorious day will come when each of you will throw away the gold idols and silver images your sinful hands have made.

8 "The Assyrians will be destroyed,
  but not by the swords of men.
The sword of God will strike them,
  and they will panic and flee.
The strong young Assyrians
  will be taken away as captives.
9 Even the strongest will quake with terror,
  and princes will flee when they see your
    battle flags,"
says the LORD, whose fire burns in Zion,
  whose flame blazes from Jerusalem.

ISRAEL'S ULTIMATE DELIVERANCE

32 ¹ Look, a righteous king is coming!
    And honest princes will rule under
    him.
2 Each one will be like a shelter from the wind
  and a refuge from the storm,
like streams of water in the desert
  and the shadow of a great rock in a
    parched land.

3 Then everyone who has eyes will be able to
    see the truth,
  and everyone who has ears will be able to
    hear it.
4 Even the hotheads will be full of sense and
    understanding.
  Those who stammer will speak out plainly.
5 In that day ungodly fools will not be heroes.
  Scoundrels will not be respected.
6 For fools speak foolishness
  and make evil plans.
They practice ungodliness
  and spread false teachings about the LORD.

They deprive the hungry of food
  and give no water to the thirsty.
7 The smooth tricks of scoundrels are evil.
  They plot crooked schemes.
They lie to convict the poor,
  even when the cause of the poor is just.
8 But generous people plan to do what
    is generous,
  and they stand firm in their generosity.

9 Listen, you women who lie around in ease.
  Listen to me, you who are so smug.
10 In a short time—just a little more than
    a year—
  you careless ones will suddenly begin
    to care.
For your fruit crops will fail,
  and the harvest will never take place.
11 Tremble, you women of ease;
  throw off your complacency.
Strip off your pretty clothes,
  and put on burlap to show your grief.
12 Beat your breasts in sorrow for your
    bountiful farms
  and your fruitful grapevines.
13 For your land will be overgrown with thorns
    and briers.
  Your joyful homes and happy towns will
    be gone.
14 The palace and the city will be deserted,
  and busy towns will be empty.
Wild donkeys will frolic and flocks will graze
  in the empty forts* and watchtowers
15 until at last the Spirit is poured out
  on us from heaven.
Then the wilderness will become a fertile
    field,
  and the fertile field will yield bountiful
    crops.

16 Justice will rule in the wilderness
  and righteousness in the fertile field.
17 And this righteousness will bring peace.
  Yes, it will bring quietness and
    confidence forever.
18 My people will live in safety, quietly
    at home.
  They will be at rest.
19 Even if the forest should be destroyed
  and the city torn down,
20 the LORD will greatly bless his people.
  Wherever they plant seed, bountiful crops
    will spring up.
  Their cattle and donkeys will graze freely.

A MESSAGE ABOUT ASSYRIA

33 ¹ What sorrow awaits you Assyrians,
    who have destroyed others*
  but have never been destroyed yourselves.

32:14 Hebrew *the Ophel.* 33:1 Hebrew *What sorrow awaits you, O destroyer.* The Hebrew text does not specifically name Assyria as the object of the prophecy in this chapter.

You betray others,
but you have never been betrayed.
When you are done destroying,
you will be destroyed.
When you are done betraying,
you will be betrayed.

2 But LORD, be merciful to us,
for we have waited for you.
Be our strong arm each day
and our salvation in times of trouble.

3 The enemy runs at the sound of your voice.
When you stand up, the nations flee!

4 Just as caterpillars and locusts strip the
fields and vines,
so the fallen army of Assyria will
be stripped!

5 Though the LORD is very great and lives
in heaven,
he will make Jerusalem* his home of
justice and righteousness.

6 In that day he will be your sure foundation,
providing a rich store of salvation,
wisdom, and knowledge.
The fear of the LORD will be your treasure.

7 But now your brave warriors weep in public.
Your ambassadors of peace cry in bitter
disappointment.

8 Your roads are deserted;
no one travels them anymore.
The Assyrians have broken their peace treaty
and care nothing for the promises they
made before witnesses.*
They have no respect for anyone.

9 The land of Israel wilts in mourning.
Lebanon withers with shame.
The plain of Sharon is now a wilderness.
Bashan and Carmel have been plundered.

10 But the LORD says: "Now I will stand up.
Now I will show my power and might.

11 You Assyrians produce nothing but
dry grass and stubble.
Your own breath will turn to fire and
consume you.

12 Your people will be burned up completely,
like thornbushes cut down and tossed in
a fire.

13 Listen to what I have done,
you nations far away!
And you that are near,
acknowledge my might!"

14 The sinners in Jerusalem shake with fear.
Terror seizes the godless.
"Who can live with this devouring fire?"
they cry.
"Who can survive this all-consuming fire?"

15 Those who are honest and fair,
who refuse to profit by fraud,
who stay far away from bribes,

who refuse to listen to those who plot murder,
who shut their eyes to all enticement to
do wrong—

16 these are the ones who will dwell on high.
The rocks of the mountains will be their
fortress.
Food will be supplied to them,
and they will have water in abundance.

17 Your eyes will see the king in all his splendor,
and you will see a land that stretches into
the distance.

18 You will think back to this time of terror,
asking,
"Where are the Assyrian officers
who counted our towers?
Where are the bookkeepers
who recorded the plunder taken from our
fallen city?"

19 You will no longer see these fierce,
violent people
with their strange, unknown language.

20 Instead, you will see Zion as a place of
holy festivals.
You will see Jerusalem,
a city quiet and secure.
It will be like a tent whose ropes are taut
and whose stakes are firmly fixed.

21 The LORD will be our Mighty One.
He will be like a wide river of protection
that no enemy can cross,
that no enemy ship can sail upon.

22 For the LORD is our judge,
our lawgiver, and our king.
He will care for us and save us.

23 The enemies' sails hang loose
on broken masts with useless tackle.
Their treasure will be divided by
the people of God.
Even the lame will take their share!

24 The people of Israel will no longer say,
"We are sick and helpless,"
for the LORD will forgive their sins.

A MESSAGE FOR THE NATIONS

34 1 Come here and listen,
O nations of the earth.
Let the world and everything in it hear
my words.

2 For the LORD is enraged against the nations.
His fury is against all their armies.
He will completely destroy* them,
dooming them to slaughter.

3 Their dead will be left unburied,
and the stench of rotting bodies will
fill the land.

33:5 Hebrew *Zion;* also in 33:14. 33:8 As in Dead Sea Scrolls;
Masoretic Text reads *care nothing for the cities.* 34:2 The Hebrew
term used here refers to the complete consecration of things or
people to the LORD, either by destroying them or by giving them
as an offering; similarly in 34:5.

The mountains will flow with their blood.
4 The heavens above will melt away
and disappear like a rolled-up scroll.
The stars will fall from the sky
like withered leaves from a grapevine,
or shriveled figs from a fig tree.

5 And when my sword has finished its work
in the heavens,
it will fall upon Edom,
the nation I have marked for destruction.
6 The sword of the LORD is drenched with blood
and covered with fat—
with the blood of lambs and goats,
with the fat of rams prepared for
sacrifice.
Yes, the LORD will offer a sacrifice in the
city of Bozrah.
He will make a mighty slaughter in Edom.
7 Even men as strong as wild oxen will die—
the young men alongside the veterans.
The land will be soaked with blood
and the soil enriched with fat.

8 For it is the day of the LORD's revenge,
the year when Edom will be paid back for
all it did to Israel.*
9 The streams of Edom will be filled with
burning pitch,
and the ground will be covered with fire.
10 This judgment on Edom will never end;
the smoke of its burning will rise forever.
The land will lie deserted from generation to
generation.
No one will live there anymore.
11 It will be haunted by the desert owl and the
screech owl,
the great owl and the raven.*
For God will measure that land carefully;
he will measure it for chaos and
destruction.
12 It will be called the Land of Nothing,
and all its nobles will soon be gone.*
13 Thorns will overrun its palaces;
nettles and thistles will grow in its forts.
The ruins will become a haunt for jackals
and a home for owls.
14 Desert animals will mingle there with hyenas,
their howls filling the night.
Wild goats will bleat at one another among
the ruins,
and night creatures* will come there
to rest.
15 There the owl will make her nest and lay
her eggs.
She will hatch her young and cover them
with her wings.
And the buzzards will come,
each one with its mate.

16 Search the book of the LORD,
and see what he will do.

Not one of these birds and animals
will be missing,
and none will lack a mate,
for the LORD has promised this.
His Spirit will make it all come true.
17 He has surveyed and divided the land
and deeded it over to those creatures.
They will possess it forever,
from generation to generation.

HOPE FOR RESTORATION

35 1 Even the wilderness and desert
will be glad in those days.
The wasteland will rejoice and blossom
with spring crocuses.
2 Yes, there will be an abundance of flowers
and singing and joy!
The deserts will become as green as the
mountains of Lebanon,
as lovely as Mount Carmel or the plain
of Sharon.
There the LORD will display his glory,
the splendor of our God.

3 With this news, strengthen those who have
tired hands,
and encourage those who have weak knees.
4 Say to those with fearful hearts,
"Be strong, and do not fear,
for your God is coming to destroy
your enemies.
He is coming to save you."

5 And when he comes, he will open the eyes
of the blind
and unplug the ears of the deaf.
6 The lame will leap like a deer,
and those who cannot speak will sing
for joy!
Springs will gush forth in the wilderness,
and streams will water the wasteland.
7 The parched ground will become a pool,
and springs of water will satisfy the
thirsty land.
Marsh grass and reeds and rushes
will flourish
where desert jackals once lived.

8 And a great road will go through that once
deserted land.
It will be named the Highway of Holiness.
Evil-minded people will never travel on it.
It will be only for those who walk in
God's ways;
fools will never walk there.
9 Lions will not lurk along its course,
nor any other ferocious beasts.
There will be no other dangers.
Only the redeemed will walk on it.

34:8 Hebrew to Zion.　34:11 The identification of some of
these birds is uncertain.　34:12 The meaning of the Hebrew
is uncertain.　34:14 Hebrew Lilith, possibly a reference to a
mythical demon of the night.

[10] Those who have been ransomed by the LORD
will return.
They will enter Jerusalem* singing,
crowned with everlasting joy.
Sorrow and mourning will disappear,
and they will be filled with joy and
gladness.

ASSYRIA INVADES JUDAH

36 In the fourteenth year of King Hezekiah's reign,* King Sennacherib of Assyria came to attack the fortified towns of Judah and conquered them. [2] Then the king of Assyria sent his chief of staff* from Lachish with a huge army to confront King Hezekiah in Jerusalem. The Assyrians took up a position beside the aqueduct that feeds water into the upper pool, near the road leading to the field where cloth is washed.* [3] These are the officials who went out to meet with them: Eliakim son of Hilkiah, the palace administrator; Shebna the court secretary; and Joah son of Asaph, the royal historian.

SENNACHERIB THREATENS JERUSALEM

[4] Then the Assyrian king's chief of staff told them to give this message to Hezekiah:

"This is what the great king of Assyria says: What are you trusting in that makes you so confident? [5] Do you think* that mere words can substitute for military skill and strength? Who are you counting on, that you have rebelled against me? [6] On Egypt? If you lean on Egypt, it will be like a reed that splinters beneath your weight and pierces your hand. Pharaoh, the king of Egypt, is completely unreliable!

[7] "But perhaps you will say to me, 'We are trusting in the LORD our God!' But isn't he the one who was insulted by Hezekiah? Didn't Hezekiah tear down his shrines and altars and make everyone in Judah and Jerusalem worship only at the altar here in Jerusalem?

[8] "I'll tell you what! Strike a bargain with my master, the king of Assyria. I will give you 2,000 horses if you can find that many men to ride on them! [9] With your tiny army, how can you think of challenging even the weakest contingent of my master's troops, even with the help of Egypt's chariots and charioteers? [10] What's more, do you think we have invaded your land without the LORD's direction? The LORD himself told us, 'Attack this land and destroy it!'"

[11] Then Eliakim, Shebna, and Joah said to the Assyrian chief of staff, "Please speak to us in Aramaic, for we understand it well. Don't speak in Hebrew,* for the people on the wall will hear."
[12] But Sennacherib's chief of staff replied, "Do you think my master sent this message only to

you and your master? He wants all the people to hear it, for when we put this city under siege, they will suffer along with you. They will be so hungry and thirsty that they will eat their own dung and drink their own urine."

[13] Then the chief of staff stood and shouted in Hebrew to the people on the wall, "Listen to this message from the great king of Assyria! [14] This is what the king says: Don't let Hezekiah deceive you. He will never be able to rescue you. [15] Don't let him fool you into trusting in the LORD by saying, 'The LORD will surely rescue us. This city will never fall into the hands of the Assyrian king!'

[16] "Don't listen to Hezekiah! These are the terms the king of Assyria is offering: Make peace with me—open the gates and come out. Then each of you can continue eating from your own grapevine and fig tree and drinking from your own well. [17] Then I will arrange to take you to another land like this one—a land of grain and new wine, bread and vineyards.

[18] "Don't let Hezekiah mislead you by saying, 'The LORD will rescue us!' Have the gods of any other nations ever saved their people from the king of Assyria? [19] What happened to the gods of Hamath and Arpad? And what about the gods of Sepharvaim? Did any god rescue Samaria from my power? [20] What god of any nation has ever been able to save its people from my power? So what makes you think that the LORD can rescue Jerusalem from me?"

[21] But the people were silent and did not utter a word because Hezekiah had commanded them, "Do not answer him."

[22] Then Eliakim son of Hilkiah, the palace administrator; Shebna the court secretary; and Joah son of Asaph, the royal historian, went back to Hezekiah. They tore their clothes in despair, and they went in to see the king and told him what the Assyrian chief of staff had said.

HEZEKIAH SEEKS THE LORD'S HELP

37 When King Hezekiah heard their report, he tore his clothes and put on burlap and went into the Temple of the LORD. [2] And he sent Eliakim the palace administrator, Shebna the court secretary, and the leading priests, all dressed in burlap, to the prophet Isaiah son of Amoz. [3] They told him, "This is what King Hezekiah says: Today is a day of trouble, insults, and disgrace. It is like when a child is ready to be born, but the mother has no strength to deliver the baby. [4] But perhaps the LORD your God has heard the Assyrian chief of staff,* sent by the king to defy the living God, and will punish him for his words. Oh, pray for those of us who are left!"

35:10 Hebrew *Zion*. 36:1 The fourteenth year of Hezekiah's reign was 701 B.C. 36:2a Or *the rabshakeh*; also in 36:4, 11, 12, 22. 36:2b Or *bleached*. 36:5 As in Dead Sea Scrolls (see also 2 Kgs 18:20); Masoretic Text reads *Do I think*. 36:11 Hebrew in the dialect of Judah; also in 36:13. 37:4 Or *the rabshakeh*; also in 37:8.

[5]After King Hezekiah's officials delivered the king's message to Isaiah, [6]the prophet replied, "Say to your master, 'This is what the LORD says: Do not be disturbed by this blasphemous speech against me from the Assyrian king's messengers. [7]Listen! I myself will move against him,* and the king will receive a message that he is needed at home. So he will return to his land, where I will have him killed with a sword.'"

[8]Meanwhile, the Assyrian chief of staff left Jerusalem and went to consult the king of Assyria, who had left Lachish and was attacking Libnah.

[9]Soon afterward King Sennacherib received word that King Tirhakah of Ethiopia* was leading an army to fight against him. Before leaving to meet the attack, he sent messengers back to Hezekiah in Jerusalem with this message:

[10]"This message is for King Hezekiah of Judah. Don't let your God, in whom you trust, deceive you with promises that Jerusalem will not be captured by the king of Assyria. [11]You know perfectly well what the kings of Assyria have done wherever they have gone. They have completely destroyed everyone who stood in their way! Why should you be any different? [12]Have the gods of other nations rescued them—such nations as Gozan, Haran, Rezeph, and the people of Eden who were in Tel-assar? My predecessors destroyed them all! [13]What happened to the king of Hamath and the king of Arpad? What happened to the kings of Sepharvaim, Hena, and Ivvah?"

[14]After Hezekiah received the letter from the messengers and read it, he went up to the LORD's Temple and spread it out before the LORD. [15]And Hezekiah prayed this prayer before the LORD: [16]"O LORD of Heaven's Armies, God of Israel, you are enthroned between the mighty cherubim! You alone are God of all the kingdoms of the earth. You alone created the heavens and the earth. [17]Bend down, O LORD, and listen! Open your eyes, O LORD, and see! Listen to Sennacherib's words of defiance against the living God.

[18]"It is true, LORD, that the kings of Assyria have destroyed all these nations. [19]And they have thrown the gods of these nations into the fire and burned them. But of course the Assyrians could destroy them! They were not gods at all—only idols of wood and stone shaped by human hands. [20]Now, O LORD our God, rescue us from his power; then all the kingdoms of the earth will know that you alone, O LORD, are God.*"

ISAIAH PREDICTS JUDAH'S DELIVERANCE

[21]Then Isaiah son of Amoz sent this message to Hezekiah: "This is what the LORD, the God of Israel, says: Because you prayed about King Sennacherib of Assyria, [22]the LORD has spoken this word against him:

"The virgin daughter of Zion
    despises you and laughs at you.
The daughter of Jerusalem
    shakes her head in derision as you flee.

[23] "Whom have you been defying and
        ridiculing?
    Against whom did you raise your voice?
At whom did you look with such haughty
        eyes?
    It was the Holy One of Israel!
[24] By your messengers you have defied
        the Lord.
    You have said, 'With my many chariots
I have conquered the highest mountains—
    yes, the remotest peaks of Lebanon.
I have cut down its tallest cedars
    and its finest cypress trees.
I have reached its farthest heights
    and explored its deepest forests.
[25] I have dug wells in many foreign lands*
    and refreshed myself with their water.
With the sole of my foot,
    I stopped up all the rivers of Egypt!'

[26] "But have you not heard?
    I decided this long ago.
Long ago I planned it,
    and now I am making it happen.
I planned for you to crush fortified cities
    into heaps of rubble.
[27] That is why their people have so little power
    and are so frightened and confused.
They are as weak as grass,
    as easily trampled as tender green shoots.
They are like grass sprouting on a housetop,
    scorched* before it can grow lush and tall.

[28] "But I know you well—
    where you stay
and when you come and go.
    I know the way you have raged
        against me.
[29] And because of your raging against me
    and your arrogance, which I have heard
        for myself,
I will put my hook in your nose
    and my bit in your mouth.
I will make you return
    by the same road on which you came."

[30]Then Isaiah said to Hezekiah, "Here is the proof that what I say is true:

"This year you will eat only what grows up
    by itself,

37:7 Hebrew *I will put a spirit in him.*   37:9 Hebrew *of Cush.*   37:20 As in Dead Sea Scrolls (see also 2 Kgs 19:19); Masoretic Text reads *you alone are the LORD.*   37:25 As in Dead Sea Scrolls (see also 2 Kgs 19:24); Masoretic Text lacks *in many foreign lands.*   37:27 As in Dead Sea Scrolls and some Greek manuscripts (see also 2 Kgs 19:26); most Hebrew manuscripts read *like a terraced field.*

and next year you will eat what springs
    up from that.
But in the third year you will plant crops
    and harvest them;
    you will tend vineyards and eat their fruit.
³¹ And you who are left in Judah,
    who have escaped the ravages of the siege,
will put roots down in your own soil
    and grow up and flourish.
³² For a remnant of my people will spread out
    from Jerusalem,
    a group of survivors from Mount Zion.
The passionate commitment of the LORD of
    Heaven's Armies
    will make this happen!

³³ "And this is what the LORD says about the king
of Assyria:

"'His armies will not enter Jerusalem.
    They will not even shoot an arrow at it.
They will not march outside its gates with
    their shields
    nor build banks of earth against its walls.
³⁴ The king will return to his own country
    by the same road on which he came.
He will not enter this city,'
    says the LORD.
³⁵ 'For my own honor and for the sake of my
    servant David,
    I will defend this city and protect it.'"

³⁶ That night the angel of the LORD went out to
the Assyrian camp and killed 185,000 Assyrian
soldiers. When the surviving Assyrians* woke
up the next morning, they found corpses everywhere. ³⁷ Then King Sennacherib of Assyria broke
camp and returned to his own land. He went
home to his capital of Nineveh and stayed there.
³⁸ One day while he was worshiping in the
temple of his god Nisroch, his sons Adrammelech and Sharezer killed him with their swords.
They then escaped to the land of Ararat, and
another son, Esarhaddon, became the next king
of Assyria.

HEZEKIAH'S SICKNESS AND RECOVERY

38 About that time Hezekiah became deathly
ill, and the prophet Isaiah son of Amoz
went to visit him. He gave the king this message:
"This is what the LORD says: 'Set your affairs
in order, for you are going to die. You will not
recover from this illness.'"

² When Hezekiah heard this, he turned his face
to the wall and prayed to the LORD, ³ "Remember,
O LORD, how I have always been faithful to you
and have served you single-mindedly, always
doing what pleases you." Then he broke down
and wept bitterly.

⁴ Then this message came to Isaiah from the
LORD: ⁵ "Go back to Hezekiah and tell him, 'This
is what the LORD, the God of your ancestor David,

says: I have heard your prayer and seen your
tears. I will add fifteen years to your life, ⁶ and
I will rescue you and this city from the king of
Assyria. Yes, I will defend this city.

⁷ "'And this is the sign from the LORD to prove
that he will do as he promised: ⁸ I will cause the
sun's shadow to move ten steps backward on the
sundial* of Ahaz!'" So the shadow on the sundial
moved backward ten steps.

HEZEKIAH'S POEM OF PRAISE

⁹ When King Hezekiah was well again, he wrote
this poem:

¹⁰ I said, "In the prime of my life,
    must I now enter the place of the dead?*
    Am I to be robbed of the rest of my years?"
¹¹ I said, "Never again will I see the LORD GOD
    while still in the land of the living.
Never again will I see my friends
    or be with those who live in this world.
¹² My life has been blown away
    like a shepherd's tent in a storm.
It has been cut short,
    as when a weaver cuts cloth from a loom.
    Suddenly, my life was over.
¹³ I waited patiently all night,
    but I was torn apart as though by lions.
    Suddenly, my life was over.
¹⁴ Delirious, I chattered like a swallow or
    a crane,
    and then I moaned like a mourning dove.
My eyes grew tired of looking to heaven
    for help.
    I am in trouble, Lord. Help me!"

¹⁵ But what could I say?
    For he himself sent this sickness.
Now I will walk humbly throughout my years
    because of this anguish I have felt.
¹⁶ Lord, your discipline is good,
    for it leads to life and health.
You restore my health
    and allow me to live!
¹⁷ Yes, this anguish was good for me,
    for you have rescued me from death
    and forgiven all my sins.
¹⁸ For the dead* cannot praise you;
    they cannot raise their voices in praise.
Those who go down to the grave
    can no longer hope in your faithfulness.
¹⁹ Only the living can praise you as
    I do today.
    Each generation tells of your faithfulness
    to the next.
²⁰ Think of it—the LORD is ready to heal me!
    I will sing his praises with instruments
every day of my life
    in the Temple of the LORD.

37:36 Hebrew *When they.*   38:8 Hebrew *the steps.*
38:10 Hebrew *enter the gates of Sheol?*   38:18 Hebrew *Sheol.*

²¹Isaiah had said to Hezekiah's servants, "Make an ointment from figs and spread it over the boil, and Hezekiah will recover."

²²And Hezekiah had asked, "What sign will prove that I will go to the Temple of the LORD?"

ENVOYS FROM BABYLON

39 Soon after this, Merodach-baladan son of Baladan, king of Babylon, sent Hezekiah his best wishes and a gift. He had heard that Hezekiah had been very sick and that he had recovered. ²Hezekiah was delighted with the Babylonian envoys and showed them everything in his treasure-houses—the silver, the gold, the spices, and the aromatic oils. He also took them to see his armory and showed them everything in his royal treasuries! There was nothing in his palace or kingdom that Hezekiah did not show them.

³Then Isaiah the prophet went to King Hezekiah and asked him, "What did those men want? Where were they from?"

Hezekiah replied, "They came from the distant land of Babylon."

⁴"What did they see in your palace?" asked Isaiah.

"They saw everything," Hezekiah replied. "I showed them everything I own—all my royal treasuries."

⁵Then Isaiah said to Hezekiah, "Listen to this message from the LORD of Heaven's Armies: ⁶'The time is coming when everything in your palace—all the treasures stored up by your ancestors until now—will be carried off to Babylon. Nothing will be left,' says the LORD. ⁷'Some of your very own sons will be taken away into exile. They will become eunuchs who will serve in the palace of Babylon's king.'"

⁸Then Hezekiah said to Isaiah, "This message you have given me from the LORD is good." For the king was thinking, "At least there will be peace and security during my lifetime."

COMFORT FOR GOD'S PEOPLE

40 ¹ "Comfort, comfort my people," says your God.
² "Speak tenderly to Jerusalem.
Tell her that her sad days are gone
    and her sins are pardoned.
Yes, the LORD has punished her twice over
    for all her sins."

³ Listen! It's the voice of someone shouting,
"Clear the way through the wilderness
    for the LORD!
Make a straight highway through the
    wasteland
    for our God!
⁴ Fill in the valleys,
    and level the mountains and hills.
Straighten the curves,
    and smooth out the rough places.

⁵ Then the glory of the LORD will be revealed,
    and all people will see it together.
The LORD has spoken!"*

⁶ A voice said, "Shout!"
    I asked, "What should I shout?"

"Shout that people are like the grass.
    Their beauty fades as quickly
    as the flowers in a field.
⁷ The grass withers and the flowers fade
    beneath the breath of the LORD.
    And so it is with people.
⁸ The grass withers and the flowers fade,
    but the word of our God stands forever."

⁹ O Zion, messenger of good news,
    shout from the mountaintops!
Shout it louder, O Jerusalem.*
    Shout, and do not be afraid.
Tell the towns of Judah,
    "Your God is coming!"
¹⁰ Yes, the Sovereign LORD is coming in power.
    He will rule with a powerful arm.
    See, he brings his reward with him as
    he comes.
¹¹ He will feed his flock like a shepherd.
    He will carry the lambs in his arms,
holding them close to his heart.
    He will gently lead the mother sheep
    with their young.

THE LORD HAS NO EQUAL

¹² Who else has held the oceans in his hand?
    Who has measured off the heavens with
    his fingers?
Who else knows the weight of the earth
    or has weighed the mountains and hills
    on a scale?
¹³ Who is able to advise the Spirit of the LORD?*
    Who knows enough to give him advice
    or teach him?
¹⁴ Has the LORD ever needed anyone's advice?
    Does he need instruction about what is
    good?
Did someone teach him what is right
    or show him the path of justice?

¹⁵ No, for all the nations of the world
    are but a drop in the bucket.
They are nothing more
    than dust on the scales.
He picks up the whole earth
    as though it were a grain of sand.
¹⁶ All the wood in Lebanon's forests

40:3-5 Greek version reads *He is a voice shouting in the wilderness,* / *"Prepare the way for the LORD's coming!* / *Clear a road for our God!* / *Fill in the valleys,* / *and level the mountains and hills.* / *And then the glory of the LORD will be revealed,* / *and all people will see the salvation sent from God.* / *The LORD has spoken!"* Compare Matt 3:3; Mark 1:3; Luke 3:4-6.   **40:9** Or *O messenger of good news, shout to Zion from the mountaintops! Shout it louder to Jerusalem.*   **40:13** Greek version reads *Who can know the LORD's thoughts?* Compare Rom 11:34; 1 Cor 2:16.

and all Lebanon's animals would not
be enough
to make a burnt offering worthy of our God.
17 The nations of the world are worth nothing
to him.
In his eyes they count for less than
nothing—
mere emptiness and froth.

18 To whom can you compare God?
What image can you find to resemble him?
19 Can he be compared to an idol formed in
a mold,
overlaid with gold, and decorated with
silver chains?
20 Or if people are too poor for that,
they might at least choose wood that
won't decay
and a skilled craftsman
to carve an image that won't fall down!

21 Haven't you heard? Don't you understand?
Are you deaf to the words of God—
the words he gave before the world began?
Are you so ignorant?
22 God sits above the circle of the earth.
The people below seem like grasshoppers
to him!
He spreads out the heavens like a curtain
and makes his tent from them.
23 He judges the great people of the world
and brings them all to nothing.
24 They hardly get started, barely taking root,
when he blows on them and they wither.
The wind carries them off like chaff.

25 "To whom will you compare me?
Who is my equal?" asks the Holy One.

26 Look up into the heavens.
Who created all the stars?
He brings them out like an army,
one after another,
calling each by its name.
Because of his great power and
incomparable strength,
not a single one is missing.
27 O Jacob, how can you say the LORD does not
see your troubles?
O Israel, how can you say God ignores
your rights?
28 Have you never heard?
Have you never understood?
The LORD is the everlasting God,
the Creator of all the earth.
He never grows weak or weary.
No one can measure the depths of his
understanding.
29 He gives power to the weak
and strength to the powerless.
30 Even youths will become weak and tired,
and young men will fall in exhaustion.

31 But those who trust in the LORD will find
new strength.
They will soar high on wings like eagles.
They will run and not grow weary.
They will walk and not faint.

GOD'S HELP FOR ISRAEL

41 ¹ "Listen in silence before me, you
lands beyond the sea.
Bring your strongest arguments.
Come now and speak.
The court is ready for your case.

2 "Who has stirred up this king from the east,
rightly calling him to God's service?
Who gives this man victory over many
nations
and permits him to trample their kings
underfoot?
With his sword, he reduces armies to dust.
With his bow, he scatters them like chaff
before the wind.
3 He chases them away and goes on safely,
though he is walking over unfamiliar
ground.
4 Who has done such mighty deeds,
summoning each new generation from
the beginning of time?
It is I, the LORD, the First and the Last.
I alone am he."

5 The lands beyond the sea watch in fear.
Remote lands tremble and mobilize for war.
6 The idol makers encourage one another,
saying to each other, "Be strong!"
7 The carver encourages the goldsmith,
and the molder helps at the anvil.
"Good," they say. "It's coming along fine."
Carefully they join the parts together,
then fasten the thing in place so it won't
fall over.

8 "But as for you, Israel my servant,
Jacob my chosen one,
descended from Abraham my friend,
9 I have called you back from the ends of
the earth,
saying, 'You are my servant.'
For I have chosen you
and will not throw you away.
10 Don't be afraid, for I am with you.
Don't be discouraged, for I am your God.
I will strengthen you and help you.
I will hold you up with my victorious
right hand.

11 "See, all your angry enemies lie there,
confused and humiliated.
Anyone who opposes you will die
and come to nothing.
12 You will look in vain
for those who tried to conquer you.

Those who attack you
    will come to nothing.
¹³ For I hold you by your right hand—
    I, the LORD your God.
And I say to you,
    'Don't be afraid. I am here to help you.
¹⁴ Though you are a lowly worm, O Jacob,
    don't be afraid, people of Israel,
      for I will help you.
I am the LORD, your Redeemer.
    I am the Holy One of Israel.'
¹⁵ You will be a new threshing instrument
    with many sharp teeth.
You will tear your enemies apart,
    making chaff of mountains.
¹⁶ You will toss them into the air,
    and the wind will blow them all away;
    a whirlwind will scatter them.
Then you will rejoice in the LORD.
    You will glory in the Holy One of Israel.

¹⁷ "When the poor and needy search for water
    and there is none,
    and their tongues are parched from thirst,
then I, the LORD, will answer them.
    I, the God of Israel,
      will never abandon them.
¹⁸ I will open up rivers for them on
    the high plateaus.
I will give them fountains of water in
    the valleys.
I will fill the desert with pools of water.
    Rivers fed by springs will flow across
      the parched ground.
¹⁹ I will plant trees in the barren desert—
    cedar, acacia, myrtle, olive, cypress, fir,
      and pine.
²⁰ I am doing this so all who see this miracle
    will understand what it means—
that it is the LORD who has done this,
    the Holy One of Israel who created it.

²¹ "Present the case for your idols,"
    says the LORD.
"Let them show what they can do,"
    says the King of Israel.*
²² "Let them try to tell us what happened
    long ago
    so that we may consider the evidence.
Or let them tell us what the future holds,
    so we can know what's going to happen.
²³ Yes, tell us what will occur in the days ahead.
    Then we will know you are gods.
In fact, do anything—good or bad!
    Do something that will amaze and
      frighten us.
²⁴ But no! You are less than nothing and can do
    nothing at all.
    Those who choose you pollute themselves.

²⁵ "But I have stirred up a leader who will
    approach from the north.

From the east he will call on my name.
    I will give him victory over kings and princes.
He will trample them as a potter treads
    on clay.

²⁶ "Who told you from the beginning
    that this would happen?
Who predicted this,
    making you admit that he was right?
    No one said a word!
²⁷ I was the first to tell Zion,
    'Look! Help is on the way!'*
    I will send Jerusalem a messenger with
      good news.
²⁸ Not one of your idols told you this.
    Not one gave any answer when I asked.
²⁹ See, they are all foolish, worthless things.
    All your idols are as empty as the wind.

THE LORD'S CHOSEN SERVANT

42 ¹ "Look at my servant,
    whom I strengthen.
He is my chosen one, who pleases me.
    I have put my Spirit upon him.
    He will bring justice to the nations.
² He will not shout
    or raise his voice in public.
³ He will not crush the weakest reed
    or put out a flickering candle.
He will bring justice to all who have
      been wronged.
⁴ He will not falter or lose heart
    until justice prevails throughout the earth.
Even distant lands beyond the sea will
    wait for his instruction.*"

⁵ God, the LORD, created the heavens and
    stretched them out.
He created the earth and everything in it.
    He gives breath to everyone,
    life to everyone who walks the earth.
And it is he who says,
⁶ "I, the LORD, have called you to demonstrate
    my righteousness.
I will take you by the hand and guard you,
and I will give you to my people, Israel,
    as a symbol of my covenant with them.
And you will be a light to guide the nations.
⁷   You will open the eyes of the blind.
You will free the captives from prison,
    releasing those who sit in dark dungeons.

⁸ "I am the LORD; that is my name!
    I will not give my glory to anyone else,
    nor share my praise with carved idols.
⁹ Everything I prophesied has come true,
    and now I will prophesy again.
I will tell you the future before it happens."

41:21 Hebrew *the King of Jacob.* See note on 14:1. 41:27 Or *'Look!
They are coming home.'* 42:4 Greek version reads *And his name will
be the hope of all the world.* Compare Matt 12:21.

A SONG OF PRAISE TO THE LORD

¹⁰ Sing a new song to the LORD!
    Sing his praises from the ends of
        the earth!
Sing, all you who sail the seas,
    all you who live in distant coastlands.
¹¹ Join in the chorus, you desert towns;
    let the villages of Kedar rejoice!
Let the people of Sela sing for joy;
    shout praises from the mountaintops!
¹² Let the whole world glorify the LORD;
    let it sing his praise.
¹³ The LORD will march forth like
        a mighty hero;
    he will come out like a warrior,
        full of fury.
He will shout his battle cry
    and crush all his enemies.

¹⁴ He will say, "I have long been silent;
    yes, I have restrained myself.
But now, like a woman in labor,
    I will cry and groan and pant.
¹⁵ I will level the mountains and hills
    and blight all their greenery.
I will turn the rivers into dry land
    and will dry up all the pools.
¹⁶ I will lead blind Israel down a new path,
    guiding them along an unfamiliar way.
I will brighten the darkness before them
    and smooth out the road ahead of them.
Yes, I will indeed do these things;
    I will not forsake them.
¹⁷ But those who trust in idols,
    who say, 'You are our gods,'
    will be turned away in shame.

ISRAEL'S FAILURE TO LISTEN AND SEE

¹⁸ "Listen, you who are deaf!
    Look and see, you blind!
¹⁹ Who is as blind as my own people,
    my servant?
Who is as deaf as my messenger?
Who is as blind as my chosen people,
    the servant of the LORD?
²⁰ You see and recognize what is right
    but refuse to act on it.
You hear with your ears,
    but you don't really listen."

²¹ Because he is righteous,
    the LORD has exalted his glorious law.
²² But his own people have been robbed and
        plundered,
    enslaved, imprisoned, and trapped.
They are fair game for anyone
    and have no one to protect them,
    no one to take them back home.

²³ Who will hear these lessons from the past
    and see the ruin that awaits you
        in the future?
²⁴ Who allowed Israel to be robbed and hurt?
    It was the LORD,
        against whom we sinned,
for the people would not walk in his path,
    nor would they obey his law.
²⁵ Therefore, he poured out his fury on them
    and destroyed them in battle.
They were enveloped in flames,
    but they still refused to understand.
They were consumed by fire,
    but they did not learn their lesson.

THE SAVIOR OF ISRAEL

43 ¹ But now, O Jacob, listen to the LORD
    who created you.
O Israel, the one who formed you says,
"Do not be afraid, for I have ransomed you.
    I have called you by name; you are mine.
² When you go through deep waters,
    I will be with you.
When you go through rivers of difficulty,
    you will not drown.
When you walk through the fire of
        oppression,
    you will not be burned up;
    the flames will not consume you.
³ For I am the LORD, your God,
    the Holy One of Israel, your Savior.
I gave Egypt as a ransom for
    your freedom;
    I gave Ethiopia* and Seba in your place.
⁴ Others were given in exchange for you.
    I traded their lives for yours
because you are precious to me.
    You are honored, and I love you.

43:3 Hebrew *Cush.*

5 "Do not be afraid, for I am with you.
 I will gather you and your children from
   east and west.
6 I will say to the north and south,
 'Bring my sons and daughters back to Israel
   from the distant corners of the earth.
7 Bring all who claim me as their God,
   for I have made them for my glory.
   It was I who created them.'"

8 Bring out the people who have eyes
     but are blind,
   who have ears but are deaf.
9 Gather the nations together!
   Assemble the peoples of the world!
 Which of their idols has ever foretold
     such things?
   Which can predict what will happen
     tomorrow?
 Where are the witnesses of such predictions?
   Who can verify that they spoke the truth?

10 "But you are my witnesses,
     O Israel!" says the LORD.
 "You are my servant.
 You have been chosen to know me,
     believe in me,
   and understand that I alone am God.
 There is no other God—
   there never has been, and there never
     will be.
11 I, yes I, am the LORD,
   and there is no other Savior.
12 First I predicted your rescue,
   then I saved you and proclaimed it to
     the world.
 No foreign god has ever done this.
   You are witnesses that I am the only God,"
   says the LORD.
13 "From eternity to eternity I am God.
   No one can snatch anyone out of my hand.
   No one can undo what I have done."

THE LORD'S PROMISE OF VICTORY

14 This is what the LORD says—your Redeemer,
the Holy One of Israel:

 "For your sakes I will send an army
     against Babylon,
   forcing the Babylonians* to flee in those
     ships they are so proud of.
15 I am the LORD, your Holy One,
   Israel's Creator and King.
16 I am the LORD, who opened a way through
     the waters,
   making a dry path through the sea.
17 I called forth the mighty army of Egypt
   with all its chariots and horses.
 I drew them beneath the waves,
     and they drowned,
   their lives snuffed out like a smoldering
     candlewick.

18 "But forget all that—
   it is nothing compared to what I am going
     to do.
19 For I am about to do something new.
   See, I have already begun!
     Do you not see it?
 I will make a pathway through
     the wilderness.
   I will create rivers in the dry wasteland.
20 The wild animals in the fields will thank me,
   the jackals and owls, too,
     for giving them water in the desert.
 Yes, I will make rivers in the dry wasteland
   so my chosen people can be refreshed.
21 I have made Israel for myself,
   and they will someday honor me before
     the whole world.

22 "But, dear family of Jacob, you refuse to ask
     for my help.
   You have grown tired of me, O Israel!
23 You have not brought me sheep or goats for
     burnt offerings.
   You have not honored me with sacrifices,
 though I have not burdened and wearied you
   with requests for grain offerings and
     frankincense.
24 You have not brought me fragrant calamus
   or pleased me with the fat from
     sacrifices.
 Instead, you have burdened me with your sins
   and wearied me with your faults.

25 "I—yes, I alone—will blot out your sins for
     my own sake
   and will never think of them again.
26 Let us review the situation together,
   and you can present your case to prove
     your innocence.
27 From the very beginning, your first ancestor
     sinned against me;
   all your leaders broke my laws.
28 That is why I have disgraced your priests;
   I have decreed complete destruction*
     for Jacob
   and shame for Israel.

44 ¹ "But now, listen to me,
       Jacob my servant,
   Israel my chosen one.
² The LORD who made you and helps you says:
   Do not be afraid, O Jacob, my servant,
   O dear Israel,* my chosen one.
³ For I will pour out water to quench your thirst
   and to irrigate your parched fields.
 And I will pour out my Spirit on your
     descendants,
   and my blessing on your children.

43:14 Or *Chaldeans.* 43:28 The Hebrew term used here refers
to the complete consecration of things or people to the LORD,
either by destroying them or by giving them as an offering.
44:2 Hebrew *Jeshurun,* a term of endearment for Israel.

⁴ They will thrive like watered grass,
    like willows on a riverbank.
⁵ Some will proudly claim,
        'I belong to the LORD.'
    Others will say,
        'I am a descendant of Jacob.'
    Some will write the LORD's name on
        their hands
    and will take the name of Israel
        as their own."

THE FOOLISHNESS OF IDOLS

⁶ This is what the LORD says—Israel's King and Redeemer, the LORD of Heaven's Armies:

    "I am the First and the Last;
        there is no other God.
⁷ Who is like me?
    Let him step forward and prove to you
        his power.
    Let him do as I have done since
        ancient times
    when I established a people and
        explained its future.
⁸ Do not tremble; do not be afraid.
    Did I not proclaim my purposes for you
        long ago?
    You are my witnesses—is there
        any other God?
    No! There is no other Rock—not one!"

⁹ How foolish are those who manufacture idols.
    These prized objects are really worthless.
    The people who worship idols don't
        know this,
    so they are all put to shame.
¹⁰ Who but a fool would make his own god—
    an idol that cannot help him one bit?
¹¹ All who worship idols will be disgraced
    along with all these craftsmen—mere
        humans—
    who claim they can make a god.
    They may all stand together,
        but they will stand in terror and shame.

¹² The blacksmith stands at his forge to make
        a sharp tool,
    pounding and shaping it with
        all his might.
    His work makes him hungry and weak.
    It makes him thirsty and faint.
¹³ Then the wood-carver measures
        a block of wood
    and draws a pattern on it.
    He works with chisel and plane
    and carves it into a human figure.
    He gives it human beauty
    and puts it in a little shrine.
¹⁴ He cuts down cedars;
        he selects the cypress and the oak;
    he plants the pine in the forest
        to be nourished by the rain.

¹⁵ Then he uses part of the wood to make a fire.
    With it he warms himself and bakes
        his bread.
    Then—yes, it's true—he takes the rest of it
    and makes himself a god to worship!
    He makes an idol
        and bows down in front of it!
¹⁶ He burns part of the tree to roast his meat
        and to keep himself warm.
    He says, "Ah, that fire feels good."
¹⁷ Then he takes what's left
        and makes his god: a carved idol!
    He falls down in front of it,
        worshiping and praying to it.
    "Rescue me!" he says.
        "You are my god!"

¹⁸ Such stupidity and ignorance!
    Their eyes are closed, and they cannot see.
    Their minds are shut,
        and they cannot think.
¹⁹ The person who made the idol never stops
        to reflect,
    "Why, it's just a block of wood!
    I burned half of it for heat
        and used it to bake my bread and roast
        my meat.
    How can the rest of it be a god?
    Should I bow down to worship
        a piece of wood?"
²⁰ The poor, deluded fool feeds on ashes.
    He trusts something that can't help him
        at all.
    Yet he cannot bring himself to ask,
    "Is this idol that I'm holding in my hand
        a lie?"

RESTORATION FOR JERUSALEM

²¹ "Pay attention, O Jacob,
        for you are my servant, O Israel.
    I, the LORD, made you,
        and I will not forget you.
²² I have swept away your sins like a cloud.
    I have scattered your offenses like the
        morning mist.
    Oh, return to me,
        for I have paid the price to set you free."

²³ Sing, O heavens, for the LORD has done
        this wondrous thing.
    Shout for joy, O depths of the earth!
    Break into song,
        O mountains and forests and every tree!
    For the LORD has redeemed Jacob
        and is glorified in Israel.

²⁴ This is what the LORD says—
        your Redeemer and Creator:
    "I am the LORD, who made all things.
    I alone stretched out the heavens.
    Who was with me
        when I made the earth?

25 I expose the false prophets as liars
   and make fools of fortune-tellers.
I cause the wise to give bad advice,
   thus proving them to be fools.
26 But I carry out the predictions of
      my prophets!
   By them I say to Jerusalem,
      'People will live here again,'
   and to the towns of Judah,
      'You will be rebuilt;
      I will restore all your ruins!'
27 When I speak to the rivers and say,
      'Dry up!'
   they will be dry.
28 When I say of Cyrus, 'He is my shepherd,'
      he will certainly do as I say.
   He will command,
      'Rebuild Jerusalem';
   he will say, 'Restore the Temple.'"

CYRUS, THE LORD'S CHOSEN ONE

45 ¹ This is what the LORD says to Cyrus,
      his anointed one,
   whose right hand he will empower.
Before him, mighty kings will be
      paralyzed with fear.
   Their fortress gates will be opened,
      never to shut again.
2 This is what the LORD says:

"I will go before you, Cyrus,
   and level the mountains.*
I will smash down gates of bronze
   and cut through bars of iron.
3 And I will give you treasures hidden in
      the darkness—
   secret riches.
I will do this so you may know that I am
      the LORD,
   the God of Israel,
      the one who calls you by name.
4 "And why have I called you for this work?
   Why did I call you by name when you did
      not know me?
It is for the sake of Jacob my servant,
   Israel my chosen one.
5 I am the LORD;
   there is no other God.
I have equipped you for battle,
   though you don't even know me,
6 so all the world from east to west
   will know there is no other God.
I am the LORD, and there is no other.
7   I create the light and make
      the darkness.
I send good times and bad times.
   I, the LORD, am the one who does
      these things.

8 "Open up, O heavens,
   and pour out your righteousness.

Let the earth open wide
   so salvation and righteousness can sprout
      up together.
   I, the LORD, created them.

9 "What sorrow awaits those who argue with
      their Creator.
   Does a clay pot argue with its maker?
Does the clay dispute with the one who
      shapes it, saying,
   'Stop, you're doing it wrong!'
Does the pot exclaim,
   'How clumsy can you be?'
10 How terrible it would be if a newborn baby
      said to its father,
   'Why was I born?'
or if it said to its mother,
   'Why did you make me this way?'"

11 This is what the LORD says—
   the Holy One of Israel and your Creator:
"Do you question what I do for
      my children?
   Do you give me orders about the work of
      my hands?
12 I am the one who made the earth
   and created people to live on it.
With my hands I stretched out the heavens.
   All the stars are at my command.
13 I will raise up Cyrus to fulfill my
      righteous purpose,
   and I will guide his actions.
He will restore my city and free my
      captive people—
   without seeking a reward!
   I, the LORD of Heaven's Armies,
      have spoken!"

FUTURE CONVERSION OF GENTILES

14 This is what the LORD says:

"You will rule the Egyptians,
   the Ethiopians,* and the Sabeans.
They will come to you with all their
      merchandise,
   and it will all be yours.
They will follow you as prisoners in chains.
   They will fall to their knees
      in front of you and say,
'God is with you, and he is the only God.
   There is no other.'"

15 Truly, O God of Israel, our Savior,
   you work in mysterious ways.
16 All craftsmen who make idols will
      be humiliated.
   They will all be disgraced together.
17 But the LORD will save the people of Israel
   with eternal salvation.

45:2 As in Dead Sea Scrolls and Greek version; Masoretic Text
reads the swellings. 45:14 Hebrew Cushites.

Throughout everlasting ages,
they will never again be humiliated
and disgraced.

¹⁸ For the LORD is God,
and he created the heavens and earth
and put everything in place.
He made the world to be lived in,
not to be a place of empty chaos.
"I am the LORD," he says,
"and there is no other.

¹⁹ I publicly proclaim bold promises.
I do not whisper obscurities in some dark
corner.
I would not have told the people of Israel*
to seek me
if I could not be found.
I, the LORD, speak only what is true
and declare only what is right.

²⁰ "Gather together and come,
you fugitives from surrounding nations.
What fools they are who carry around their
wooden idols
and pray to gods that cannot save!

²¹ Consult together, argue your case.
Get together and decide what to say.
Who made these things known so long ago?
What idol ever told you they would
happen?
Was it not I, the LORD?
For there is no other God but me,
a righteous God and Savior.
There is none but me.

²² Let all the world look to me for salvation!
For I am God; there is no other.

²³ I have sworn by my own name;
I have spoken the truth,
and I will never go back on my word:
Every knee will bend to me,
and every tongue will declare allegiance
to me.*"

²⁴ The people will declare,
"The LORD is the source of all my
righteousness and strength."
And all who were angry with him
will come to him and be ashamed.

²⁵ In the LORD all the generations of Israel will
be justified,
and in him they will boast.

BABYLON'S FALSE GODS

46

¹ Bel and Nebo, the gods of Babylon,
bow as they are lowered to the
ground.
They are being hauled away on ox carts.
The poor beasts stagger under the weight.

² Both the idols and their owners are
bowed down.
The gods cannot protect the people,
and the people cannot protect the gods.
They go off into captivity together.

SOVEREIGN RULER
Isaiah 46:9-10   ROBERT MORRIS

Every decade, our world seems to get darker
and darker. The news is filled with political
scandals, corporate corruption, civil unrest,
and wars. However, that's only one part of
the story. As believers, we are the light of the
world because we have the eternal Light—
Jesus Christ—living inside us (Matthew 5:14).
Regardless of what we hear or see, Jesus is
still the answer, and God is still in control.

Whenever there's an election, we never
ever get to vote for the best candidate. I don't
know who or what you voted for, but the best
candidate didn't run for that office. And it's
because the best candidate has already been
nominated *and* appointed as the "King of all
kings and Lord of all lords" (Revelation 19:16).
During troubling times, it gives me so much
peace to know that God is still on the throne.
He is still in control, and He is still sovereign.

³ "Listen to me, descendants of Jacob,
all you who remain in Israel.
I have cared for you since you were born.
Yes, I carried you before you were born.

⁴ I will be your God throughout your
lifetime—
until your hair is white with age.
I made you, and I will care for you.
I will carry you along and save you.

⁵ "To whom will you compare me?
Who is my equal?

⁶ Some people pour out their silver and gold
and hire a craftsman to make a god
from it.
Then they bow down and worship it!

⁷ They carry it around on their shoulders,
and when they set it down, it stays there.
It can't even move!
And when someone prays to it, there is
no answer.
It can't rescue anyone from trouble.

⁸ "Do not forget this! Keep it in mind!
Remember this, you guilty ones.

⁹ Remember the things I have done in
the past.
For I alone am God!
I am God, and there is none like me.

¹⁰ Only I can tell you the future
before it even happens.
Everything I plan will come to pass,
for I do whatever I wish.

¹¹ I will call a swift bird of prey from the east—

45:19 Hebrew *of Jacob.* See note on 14:1.   45:23 Hebrew *will
confess;* Greek version reads *will declare allegiance to God.* Compare
Rom 14:11.

a leader from a distant land to come and
do my bidding.
I have said what I would do,
and I will do it.

¹² "Listen to me, you stubborn people
who are so far from doing right.
¹³ For I am ready to set things right,
not in the distant future, but right now!
I am ready to save Jerusalem*
and show my glory to Israel.

PREDICTION OF BABYLON'S FALL

47 ¹ "Come down, virgin daughter of
Babylon, and sit in the dust.
For your days of sitting on a throne
have ended.
O daughter of Babylonia,* never again
will you be
the lovely princess, tender and delicate.
² Take heavy millstones and grind flour.
Remove your veil, and strip off your robe.
Expose yourself to public view.*
³ You will be naked and burdened
with shame.
I will take vengeance against you
without pity."

⁴ Our Redeemer, whose name is the LORD of
Heaven's Armies,
is the Holy One of Israel.

⁵ "O beautiful Babylon, sit now in darkness
and silence.
Never again will you be known as the
queen of kingdoms.
⁶ For I was angry with my chosen people
and punished them by letting them fall
into your hands.
But you, Babylon, showed them no mercy.
You oppressed even the elderly.
⁷ You said, 'I will reign forever as queen of
the world!'
You did not reflect on your actions
or think about their consequences.

⁸ "Listen to this, you pleasure-loving kingdom,
living at ease and feeling secure.
You say, 'I am the only one,
and there is no other.
I will never be a widow or lose my
children.'
⁹ Well, both these things will come upon you
in a moment:
widowhood and the loss of your children.
Yes, these calamities will come upon you,
despite all your witchcraft and magic.

¹⁰ "You felt secure in your wickedness.
'No one sees me,' you said.
But your 'wisdom' and 'knowledge' have led
you astray,

and you said, 'I am the only one, and
there is no other.'
¹¹ So disaster will overtake you,
and you won't be able to charm it away.
Calamity will fall upon you,
and you won't be able to buy your way out.
A catastrophe will strike you suddenly,
one for which you are not prepared.

¹² "Now use your magical charms!
Use the spells you have worked at all
these years!
Maybe they will do you some good.
Maybe they can make someone
afraid of you.
¹³ All the advice you receive has made you tired.
Where are all your astrologers,
those stargazers who make predictions
each month?
Let them stand up and save you from
what the future holds.
¹⁴ But they are like straw burning in a fire;
they cannot save themselves from
the flame.
You will get no help from them at all;
their hearth is no place to sit for warmth.
¹⁵ And all your friends,
those with whom you've done business
since childhood,
will go their own ways,
turning a deaf ear to your cries.

GOD'S STUBBORN PEOPLE

48 ¹ "Listen to me, O family of Jacob,
you who are called by the name of
Israel
and born into the family of Judah.
Listen, you who take oaths in the name of
the LORD
and call on the God of Israel.
You don't keep your promises,
² even though you call yourself the holy city
and talk about depending on
the God of Israel,
whose name is the LORD of Heaven's
Armies.
³ Long ago I told you what was going to happen.
Then suddenly I took action,
and all my predictions came true.
⁴ For I know how stubborn and obstinate
you are.
Your necks are as unbending as iron.
Your heads are as hard as bronze.
⁵ That is why I told you what would happen;
I told you beforehand what I was going
to do.
Then you could never say, 'My idols did it.
My wooden image and metal god
commanded it to happen!'

46:13 Hebrew *Zion.* 47:1 Or *Chaldea;* also in 47:5. 47:2 Hebrew
Bare your legs; pass through the rivers.

6 You have heard my predictions and seen
   them fulfilled,
      but you refuse to admit it.
   Now I will tell you new things,
      secrets you have not yet heard.
7 They are brand new, not things from
   the past.
      So you cannot say, 'We knew that
      all the time!'

8 "Yes, I will tell you of things that are
   entirely new,
      things you never heard of before.
   For I know so well what traitors you are.
      You have been rebels from birth.
9 Yet for my own sake and for the honor of
   my name,
      I will hold back my anger and not wipe
      you out.
10 I have refined you, but not as silver is
   refined.
      Rather, I have refined you in the furnace
      of suffering.
11 I will rescue you for my sake—
      yes, for my own sake!
   I will not let my reputation be tarnished,
      and I will not share my glory with idols!

FREEDOM FROM BABYLON

12 "Listen to me, O family of Jacob,
      Israel my chosen one!
   I alone am God,
      the First and the Last.
13 It was my hand that laid the foundations
   of the earth,
      my right hand that spread out
      the heavens above.
   When I call out the stars,
      they all appear in order."

14 Have any of your idols ever told you this?
      Come, all of you, and listen:
   The Lord has chosen Cyrus as his ally.
      He will use him to put an end to the
      empire of Babylon
      and to destroy the Babylonian* armies.

15 "I have said it: I am calling Cyrus!
      I will send him on this errand and will
      help him succeed.
16 Come closer, and listen to this.
      From the beginning I have told you
      plainly what would happen."

And now the Sovereign Lord and his Spirit
   have sent me with this message.
17 This is what the Lord says—
      your Redeemer, the Holy One of Israel:
   "I am the Lord your God,
      who teaches you what is good for you
      and leads you along the paths you
      should follow.

18 Oh, that you had listened to my commands!
      Then you would have had peace flowing
      like a gentle river
      and righteousness rolling over you like
      waves in the sea.
19 Your descendants would have been like
      the sands along the seashore—
      too many to count!
   There would have been no need for your
      destruction,
      or for cutting off your family name."

20 Yet even now, be free from your captivity!
      Leave Babylon and the Babylonians.*
   Sing out this message!
      Shout it to the ends of the earth!
   The Lord has redeemed his servants,
      the people of Israel.*
21 They were not thirsty
      when he led them through the desert.
   He divided the rock,
      and water gushed out for them to drink.
22 "But there is no peace for the wicked,"
      says the Lord.

THE LORD'S SERVANT COMMISSIONED

49 1 Listen to me, all you in
      distant lands!
   Pay attention, you who are far away!
   The Lord called me before my birth;
      from within the womb he called me
      by name.
2 He made my words of judgment as sharp
      as a sword.
   He has hidden me in the shadow of
      his hand.
   I am like a sharp arrow in his quiver.

3 He said to me, "You are my servant, Israel,
      and you will bring me glory."

4 I replied, "But my work seems so useless!
      I have spent my strength for nothing and
      to no purpose.
   Yet I leave it all in the Lord's hand;
      I will trust God for my reward."

5 And now the Lord speaks—
      the one who formed me in my mother's
      womb to be his servant,
   who commissioned me to bring Israel
      back to him.
   The Lord has honored me,
      and my God has given me strength.
6 He says, "You will do more than restore
      the people of Israel to me.
   I will make you a light to the Gentiles,
      and you will bring my salvation to the
      ends of the earth."

48:14 Or *Chaldean.* 48:20a Or *the Chaldeans.* 48:20b Hebrew
his servant, Jacob. See note on 14:1.

⁷ The LORD, the Redeemer
and Holy One of Israel,
says to the one who is despised and rejected
by the nations,
to the one who is the servant of rulers:
"Kings will stand at attention when you
pass by.
Princes will also bow low
because of the LORD, the faithful one,
the Holy One of Israel,
who has chosen you."

PROMISES OF ISRAEL'S RESTORATION

⁸ This is what the LORD says:

"At just the right time,
I will respond to you.*
On the day of salvation I will help you.
I will protect you and give you to the people
as my covenant with them.
Through you I will reestablish the land
of Israel
and assign it to its own people again.
⁹ I will say to the prisoners,
'Come out in freedom,'
and to those in darkness,
'Come into the light.'
They will be my sheep, grazing in green
pastures
and on hills that were previously bare.
¹⁰ They will neither hunger nor thirst.
The searing sun will not reach them
anymore.
For the LORD in his mercy will lead them;
he will lead them beside cool waters.
¹¹ And I will make my mountains into level
paths for them.
The highways will be raised above the
valleys.
¹² See, my people will return from far away,
from lands to the north and west,
and from as far south as Egypt.*"

¹³ Sing for joy, O heavens!
Rejoice, O earth!
Burst into song, O mountains!
For the LORD has comforted his people
and will have compassion on them in
their suffering.

¹⁴ Yet Jerusalem* says,
"The LORD has deserted us;
the Lord has forgotten us."

¹⁵ "Never! Can a mother forget her nursing
child?
Can she feel no love for the child she
has borne?
But even if that were possible,
I would not forget you!
¹⁶ See, I have written your name on the palms
of my hands.

Always in my mind is a picture of
Jerusalem's walls in ruins.
¹⁷ Soon your descendants will come back,
and all who are trying to destroy you
will go away.
¹⁸ Look around you and see,
for all your children will come back to you.
As surely as I live," says the LORD,
"they will be like jewels or bridal
ornaments for you to display.

¹⁹ "Even the most desolate parts of your
abandoned land
will soon be crowded with your people.
Your enemies who enslaved you
will be far away.
²⁰ The generations born in exile will return
and say,
'We need more room! It's crowded here!'
²¹ Then you will think to yourself,
'Who has given me all these descendants?
For most of my children were killed,
and the rest were carried away into exile.
I was left here all alone.
Where did all these people come from?
Who bore these children?
Who raised them for me?'"

²² This is what the Sovereign LORD says:
"See, I will give a signal to the godless
nations.
They will carry your little sons back to you
in their arms;
they will bring your daughters on their
shoulders.
²³ Kings and queens will serve you
and care for all your needs.
They will bow to the earth before you
and lick the dust from your feet.
Then you will know that I am the LORD.
Those who trust in me will never be
put to shame."

²⁴ Who can snatch the plunder of war from the
hands of a warrior?
Who can demand that a tyrant* let his
captives go?
²⁵ But the LORD says,
"The captives of warriors will be released,
and the plunder of tyrants will
be retrieved.
For I will fight those who fight you,
and I will save your children.
²⁶ I will feed your enemies with their own
flesh.
They will be drunk with rivers of their
own blood.

49:8 Greek version reads *I heard you.* Compare 2 Cor 6:2.
49:12 As in Dead Sea Scrolls, which read *from the region of Aswan,*
which is in southern Egypt. Masoretic Text reads *from the region
of Sinim.* 49:14 Hebrew *Zion.* 49:24 As in Dead Sea Scrolls,
Syriac version, and Latin Vulgate (also see 49:25); Masoretic Text
reads *a righteous person.*

All the world will know that I, the LORD,
  am your Savior and your Redeemer,
  the Mighty One of Israel.*"

50

This is what the LORD says:

"Was your mother sent away because
    I divorced her?
  Did I sell you as slaves to my creditors?
No, you were sold because of your sins.
    And your mother, too, was taken because
    of your sins.
² Why was no one there when I came?
    Why didn't anyone answer when I called?
Is it because I have no power to rescue?
    No, that is not the reason!
For I can speak to the sea and make it dry up!
    I can turn rivers into deserts covered with
    dying fish.
³ I dress the skies in darkness,
    covering them with clothes of mourning."

THE LORD'S OBEDIENT SERVANT

⁴ The Sovereign LORD has given me his words
    of wisdom,
  so that I know how to comfort the weary.
Morning by morning he wakens me
    and opens my understanding to his will.
⁵ The Sovereign LORD has spoken to me,
    and I have listened.
  I have not rebelled or turned away.
⁶ I offered my back to those who beat me
    and my cheeks to those who pulled out
    my beard.
I did not hide my face
    from mockery and spitting.

⁷ Because the Sovereign LORD helps me,
    I will not be disgraced.
Therefore, I have set my face like a stone,
    determined to do his will.
    And I know that I will not be put to shame.
⁸ He who gives me justice is near.
    Who will dare to bring charges against
    me now?
Where are my accusers?
    Let them appear!
⁹ See, the Sovereign LORD is on my side!
    Who will declare me guilty?
All my enemies will be destroyed
    like old clothes that have been eaten
    by moths!

¹⁰ Who among you fears the LORD
    and obeys his servant?
If you are walking in darkness,
    without a ray of light,
trust in the LORD
    and rely on your God.
¹¹ But watch out, you who live in your own
    light
    and warm yourselves by your own fires.

This is the reward you will receive from me:
    You will soon fall down in great torment.

A CALL TO TRUST THE LORD

51

¹ "Listen to me, all who hope for
    deliverance—
  all who seek the LORD!
Consider the rock from which you were cut,
    the quarry from which you were mined.
² Yes, think about Abraham, your ancestor,
    and Sarah, who gave birth to your nation.
Abraham was only one man when I called
    him.
But when I blessed him, he became a
    great nation."

³ The LORD will comfort Israel* again
    and have pity on her ruins.
Her desert will blossom like Eden,
    her barren wilderness like the garden of
    the LORD.
Joy and gladness will be found there.
    Songs of thanksgiving will fill the air.

⁴ "Listen to me, my people.
    Hear me, Israel,
for my law will be proclaimed,
    and my justice will become a light to
    the nations.
⁵ My mercy and justice are coming soon.
    My salvation is on the way.
My strong arm will bring justice to the
    nations.
All distant lands will look to me
    and wait in hope for my powerful arm.
⁶ Look up to the skies above,
    and gaze down on the earth below.
For the skies will disappear like smoke,
    and the earth will wear out like a piece
    of clothing.
The people of the earth will die like flies,
    but my salvation lasts forever.
    My righteous rule will never end!

⁷ "Listen to me, you who know right
    from wrong,
    you who cherish my law in your hearts.
Do not be afraid of people's scorn,
    nor fear their insults.
⁸ For the moth will devour them as it
    devours clothing.
    The worm will eat at them as it eats wool.
But my righteousness will last forever.
    My salvation will continue from
    generation to generation."

⁹ Wake up, wake up, O LORD! Clothe yourself
    with strength!
    Flex your mighty right arm!

49:26 Hebrew *of Jacob.* See note on 14:1.   **51:3** Hebrew *Zion;* also in 51:16.

Rouse yourself as in the days of old
when you slew Egypt, the dragon of
the Nile.*
[10] Are you not the same today,
the one who dried up the sea,
making a path of escape through the depths
so that your people could cross over?
[11] Those who have been ransomed by the LORD
will return.
They will enter Jerusalem* singing,
crowned with everlasting joy.
Sorrow and mourning will disappear,
and they will be filled with joy and
gladness.

[12] "I, yes I, am the one who comforts you.
So why are you afraid of mere humans,
who wither like the grass and disappear?
[13] Yet you have forgotten the LORD, your Creator,
the one who stretched out the sky like a
canopy
and laid the foundations of the earth.
Will you remain in constant dread of
human oppressors?
Will you continue to fear the anger of
your enemies?
Where is their fury and anger now?
It is gone!
[14] Soon all you captives will be released!
Imprisonment, starvation, and death will
not be your fate!
[15] For I am the LORD your God,
who stirs up the sea, causing its waves
to roar.
My name is the LORD of Heaven's Armies.
[16] And I have put my words in your mouth
and hidden you safely in my hand.
I stretched out* the sky like a canopy
and laid the foundations of the earth.
I am the one who says to Israel,
'You are my people!'"

[17] Wake up, wake up, O Jerusalem!
You have drunk the cup of the LORD's fury.
You have drunk the cup of terror,
tipping out its last drops.
[18] Not one of your children is left alive
to take your hand and guide you.
[19] These two calamities have fallen on you:
desolation and destruction,
famine and war.
And who is left to sympathize with you?
Who is left to comfort you?*
[20] For your children have fainted and lie in
the streets,
helpless as antelopes caught in a net.
The LORD has poured out his fury;
God has rebuked them.

[21] But now listen to this, you afflicted ones
who sit in a drunken stupor,
though not from drinking wine.

[22] This is what the Sovereign LORD,
your God and Defender, says:
"See, I have taken the terrible cup from
your hands.
You will drink no more of my fury.
[23] Instead, I will hand that cup to your
tormentors,
those who said, 'We will trample you into
the dust
and walk on your backs.'"

DELIVERANCE FOR JERUSALEM

52 [1] Wake up, wake up, O Zion!
Clothe yourself with strength.
Put on your beautiful clothes, O holy city
of Jerusalem,
for unclean and godless people will enter
your gates no longer.
[2] Rise from the dust, O Jerusalem.
Sit in a place of honor.
Remove the chains of slavery from
your neck,
O captive daughter of Zion.
[3] For this is what the LORD says:
"When I sold you into exile,
I received no payment.
Now I can redeem you
without having to pay for you."

[4] This is what the Sovereign LORD says: "Long
ago my people chose to live in Egypt. Now they
are oppressed by Assyria. [5] What is this?" asks the
LORD. "Why are my people enslaved again? Those
who rule them shout in exultation.* My name is
blasphemed all day long.* [6] But I will reveal my
name to my people, and they will come to know
its power. Then at last they will recognize that I
am the one who speaks to them."

[7] How beautiful on the mountains
are the feet of the messenger who brings
good news,
the good news of peace and salvation,
the news that the God of Israel* reigns!
[8] The watchmen shout and sing with joy,
for before their very eyes
they see the LORD returning to
Jerusalem.*
[9] Let the ruins of Jerusalem break into
joyful song,
for the LORD has comforted his people.
He has redeemed Jerusalem.
[10] The LORD has demonstrated his holy power
before the eyes of all the nations.

51:9 Hebrew *You slew Rahab; you pierced the dragon.* Rahab is
the name of a mythical sea monster that represents chaos in
ancient literature. The name is used here as a poetic name for
Egypt. 51:11 Hebrew *Zion.* 51:16 As in Syriac version (see also
51:13); Hebrew reads *planted.* 51:19 As in Dead Sea Scrolls and
Greek, Latin, and Syriac versions; Masoretic Text reads *How can I
comfort you?* 52:5a As in Dead Sea Scrolls; Masoretic Text reads
Those who rule them wail. 52:5b Greek version reads *The Gentiles
continually blaspheme my name because of you.* Compare Rom 2:24.
52:7 Hebrew *of Zion.* 52:8 Hebrew *to Zion.*

All the ends of the earth will see
  the victory of our God.

¹¹ Get out! Get out and leave your captivity,
  where everything you touch is unclean.
Get out of there and purify yourselves,
  you who carry home the sacred objects
  of the LORD.
¹² You will not leave in a hurry,
  running for your lives.
For the LORD will go ahead of you;
  yes, the God of Israel will protect you
  from behind.

THE LORD'S SUFFERING SERVANT

¹³ See, my servant will prosper;
  he will be highly exalted.
¹⁴ But many were amazed when they saw him.*
  His face was so disfigured he seemed
  hardly human,
  and from his appearance, one would
  scarcely know he was a man.
¹⁵ And he will startle* many nations.
  Kings will stand speechless in
  his presence.
For they will see what they had not been told;
  they will understand what they had not
  heard about.*

53 ¹ Who has believed our message?
  To whom has the LORD revealed
  his powerful arm?
² My servant grew up in the LORD's presence
  like a tender green shoot,
  like a root in dry ground.
There was nothing beautiful or majestic
  about his appearance,
  nothing to attract us to him.
³ He was despised and rejected—
  a man of sorrows, acquainted with
  deepest grief.
We turned our backs on him and looked
  the other way.
  He was despised, and we did not care.

⁴ Yet it was our weaknesses he carried;
  it was our sorrows* that weighed
  him down.
And we thought his troubles were a
  punishment from God,
  a punishment for his own sins!
⁵ But he was pierced for our rebellion,
  crushed for our sins.
He was beaten so we could be whole.
  He was whipped so we could be healed.
⁶ All of us, like sheep, have strayed away.
  We have left God's paths to follow our own.
Yet the LORD laid on him
  the sins of us all.

⁷ He was oppressed and treated harshly,
  yet he never said a word.

DOES JESUS STILL HEAL?
Isaiah 53:4-5   ROBERT MORRIS

While Jesus walked on earth, He healed many people of sickness and disease (Matthew 4:23-24). But does He still heal today? Because of the sacrifice Jesus made on the cross, God gives us access to the forgiveness of sin *and* healing by His grace even today. Isaiah 53:5 says:

He was pierced for our rebellion,
  crushed for our sins.
He was beaten so we could be whole.
  He was whipped so we could be healed.

Even though Jesus bore our sins on the cross, we still sin. And we still become sick even though He bore our sicknesses. So how can we receive healing today? It's the same way we receive forgiveness of sin: by grace through faith. Healing, like salvation, happens because of God's great grace.

He was led like a lamb to the slaughter.
  And as a sheep is silent before
  the shearers,
  he did not open his mouth.
⁸ Unjustly condemned,
  he was led away.*
No one cared that he died without
  descendants,
  that his life was cut short in midstream.*
But he was struck down
  for the rebellion of my people.
⁹ He had done no wrong
  and had never deceived anyone.
But he was buried like a criminal;
  he was put in a rich man's grave.

¹⁰ But it was the LORD's good plan to crush him
  and cause him grief.
Yet when his life is made an offering for sin,
  he will have many descendants.
He will enjoy a long life,
  and the LORD's good plan will prosper in
  his hands.
¹¹ When he sees all that is accomplished
  by his anguish,
  he will be satisfied.
And because of his experience,
  my righteous servant will make it possible

52:14 As in Syriac version; Hebrew reads *you.* 52:15a Or *cleanse.*
52:15b Greek version reads *Those who have never been told about him will see, / and those who have never heard of him will understand.* Compare Rom 15:21. 53:4 Or *Yet it was our sicknesses he carried; / it was our diseases.* 53:8a Greek version reads *He was humiliated and received no justice.* Compare Acts 8:33. 53:8b Or *As for his contemporaries, / who cared that his life was cut short in midstream?* Greek version reads *Who can speak of his descendants? / For his life was taken from the earth.* Compare Acts 8:33.

for many to be counted righteous,
for he will bear all their sins.
¹² I will give him the honors of a victorious
soldier,
because he exposed himself to death.
He was counted among the rebels.
He bore the sins of many and interceded
for rebels.

FUTURE GLORY FOR JERUSALEM

54 ¹ "Sing, O childless woman,
you who have never given birth!
Break into loud and joyful song,
O Jerusalem,
you who have never been in labor.
For the desolate woman now has more
children
than the woman who lives with
her husband,"
says the LORD.
² "Enlarge your house; build an addition.
Spread out your home,
and spare no expense!
³ For you will soon be bursting at the seams.
Your descendants will occupy other
nations
and resettle the ruined cities.

⁴ "Fear not; you will no longer live in shame.
Don't be afraid; there is no more disgrace
for you.
You will no longer remember the shame of
your youth
and the sorrows of widowhood.
⁵ For your Creator will be your husband;
the LORD of Heaven's Armies is his name!
He is your Redeemer, the Holy One of Israel,
the God of all the earth.
⁶ For the LORD has called you back from
your grief—
as though you were a young wife
abandoned by her husband,"
says your God.
⁷ "For a brief moment I abandoned you,
but with great compassion I will take
you back.
⁸ In a burst of anger I turned my face away for
a little while.
But with everlasting love I will have
compassion on you,"
says the LORD, your Redeemer.

⁹ "Just as I swore in the time of Noah
that I would never again let a flood cover
the earth,
so now I swear
that I will never again be angry and
punish you.
¹⁰ For the mountains may move
and the hills disappear,
but even then my faithful love for you
will remain.

My covenant of blessing will never
be broken,"
says the LORD, who has mercy on you.

¹¹ "O storm-battered city,
troubled and desolate!
I will rebuild you with precious jewels
and make your foundations from
lapis lazuli.
¹² I will make your towers of sparkling rubies,
your gates of shining gems,
and your walls of precious stones.
¹³ I will teach all your children,
and they will enjoy great peace.
¹⁴ You will be secure under a government
that is just and fair.
Your enemies will stay far away.
You will live in peace,
and terror will not come near.
¹⁵ If any nation comes to fight you,
it is not because I sent them.
Whoever attacks you will go down
in defeat.

¹⁶ "I have created the blacksmith
who fans the coals beneath the forge
and makes the weapons of destruction.
And I have created the armies that
destroy.
¹⁷ But in that coming day
no weapon turned against you will
succeed.
You will silence every voice
raised up to accuse you.
These benefits are enjoyed by the servants
of the LORD;
their vindication will come from me.
I, the LORD, have spoken!

INVITATION TO THE LORD'S SALVATION

55 ¹ "Is anyone thirsty?
Come and drink—
even if you have no money!
Come, take your choice of wine or milk—
it's all free!
² Why spend your money on food that does
not give you strength?
Why pay for food that does you no good?
Listen to me, and you will eat what is good.
You will enjoy the finest food.

³ "Come to me with your ears wide open.
Listen, and you will find life.
I will make an everlasting covenant
with you.
I will give you all the unfailing love
I promised to David.
⁴ See how I used him to display my power
among the peoples.
I made him a leader among the nations.
⁵ You also will command nations you do
not know,

and peoples unknown to you will come
    running to obey,
because I, the LORD your God,
    the Holy One of Israel, have made you
    glorious."

⁶ Seek the LORD while you can find him.
    Call on him now while he is near.
⁷ Let the wicked change their ways
    and banish the very thought of
    doing wrong.
Let them turn to the LORD that he may
    have mercy on them.
    Yes, turn to our God, for he will forgive
    generously.

⁸ "My thoughts are nothing like your
    thoughts," says the LORD.
    "And my ways are far beyond anything
    you could imagine.
⁹ For just as the heavens are higher than
    the earth,
    so my ways are higher than your ways
    and my thoughts higher than
    your thoughts.

¹⁰ "The rain and snow come down from
    the heavens
    and stay on the ground to water the earth.
They cause the grain to grow,
    producing seed for the farmer
    and bread for the hungry.
¹¹ It is the same with my word.
    I send it out, and it always produces fruit.
It will accomplish all I want it to,
    and it will prosper everywhere I send it.
¹² You will live in joy and peace.
    The mountains and hills will burst
    into song,
and the trees of the field will clap
    their hands!
¹³ Where once there were thorns, cypress trees
    will grow.
    Where nettles grew, myrtles will sprout up.
These events will bring great honor to the
    LORD's name;
    they will be an everlasting sign of his
    power and love."

BLESSINGS FOR ALL NATIONS

56 This is what the LORD says:

"Be just and fair to all.
    Do what is right and good,
for I am coming soon to rescue you
    and to display my righteousness
    among you.
² Blessed are all those
    who are careful to do this.
Blessed are those who honor my
    Sabbath days of rest
    and keep themselves from doing wrong.

³ "Don't let foreigners who commit
    themselves to the LORD say,
    'The LORD will never let me be part of
    his people.'
And don't let the eunuchs say,
    'I'm a dried-up tree with no children
    and no future.'
⁴ For this is what the LORD says:
I will bless those eunuchs
    who keep my Sabbath days holy
and who choose to do what pleases me
    and commit their lives to me.
⁵ I will give them—within the walls of
    my house—
    a memorial and a name
    far greater than sons and daughters
    could give.
For the name I give them is an
    everlasting one.
    It will never disappear!

⁶ "I will also bless the foreigners who
    commit themselves to the LORD,
    who serve him and love his name,
    who worship him and do not desecrate the
    Sabbath day of rest,
    and who hold fast to my covenant.
⁷ I will bring them to my holy mountain
    of Jerusalem
    and will fill them with joy in
    my house of prayer.
I will accept their burnt offerings and
    sacrifices,
    because my Temple will be called
    a house of prayer for all nations.
⁸ For the Sovereign LORD,
    who brings back the outcasts
    of Israel, says:
I will bring others, too,
    besides my people Israel."

SINFUL LEADERS CONDEMNED

⁹ Come, wild animals of the field!
    Come, wild animals of the forest!
    Come and devour my people!
¹⁰ For the leaders of my people—
    the LORD's watchmen, his shepherds—
    are blind and ignorant.
They are like silent watchdogs
    that give no warning
    when danger comes.
They love to lie around,
    sleeping and dreaming.
¹¹   Like greedy dogs, they are never satisfied.
They are ignorant shepherds,
    all following their own path
    and intent on personal gain.
¹² "Come," they say,
    "let's get some wine and have a party.
    Let's all get drunk.
Then tomorrow we'll do it again
    and have an even bigger party!"

57

¹ Good people pass away;
the godly often die before
their time.
But no one seems to care or wonder why.
No one seems to understand
that God is protecting them from the evil
to come.
² For those who follow godly paths
will rest in peace when they die.

IDOLATROUS WORSHIP CONDEMNED

³ "But you—come here, you witches' children,
you offspring of adulterers and
prostitutes!
⁴ Whom do you mock,
making faces and sticking out
your tongues?
You children of sinners and liars!
⁵ You worship your idols with great passion
beneath the oaks and under every
green tree.
You sacrifice your children down in
the valleys,
among the jagged rocks in the cliffs.
⁶ Your gods are the smooth stones in
the valleys.
You worship them with liquid offerings
and grain offerings.
They, not I, are your inheritance.
Do you think all this makes me happy?
⁷ You have committed adultery on every
high mountain.
There you have worshiped idols
and have been unfaithful to me.
⁸ You have put pagan symbols
on your doorposts and behind your doors.
You have left me
and climbed into bed with these
detestable gods.
You have committed yourselves to them.
You love to look at their naked bodies.
⁹ You have gone to Molech*
with olive oil and many perfumes,
sending your agents far and wide,
even to the world of the dead.*
¹⁰ You grew weary in your search,
but you never gave up.
Desire gave you renewed strength,
and you did not grow weary.

¹¹ "Are you afraid of these idols?
Do they terrify you?
Is that why you have lied to me
and forgotten me and my words?
Is it because of my long silence
that you no longer fear me?
¹² Now I will expose your so-called good deeds.
None of them will help you.
¹³ Let's see if your idols can save you
when you cry to them for help.
Why, a puff of wind can knock them down!
If you just breathe on them, they fall over!

But whoever trusts in me will inherit
the land
and possess my holy mountain."

GOD FORGIVES THE REPENTANT

¹⁴ God says, "Rebuild the road!
Clear away the rocks and stones
so my people can return from captivity."
¹⁵ The high and lofty one who lives
in eternity,
the Holy One, says this:
"I live in the high and holy place
with those whose spirits are contrite
and humble.
I restore the crushed spirit of the humble
and revive the courage of those with
repentant hearts.
¹⁶ For I will not fight against you forever;
I will not always be angry.
If I were, all people would pass away—
all the souls I have made.
¹⁷ I was angry,
so I punished these greedy people.
I withdrew from them,
but they kept going on their own
stubborn way.
¹⁸ I have seen what they do,
but I will heal them anyway!
I will lead them.
I will comfort those who mourn,
¹⁹ bringing words of praise to their lips.
May they have abundant peace,
both near and far,"
says the LORD, who heals them.
²⁰ "But those who still reject me are like the
restless sea,
which is never still
but continually churns up mud and dirt.
²¹ There is no peace for the wicked,"
says my God.

TRUE AND FALSE WORSHIP

58

¹ "Shout with the voice of
a trumpet blast.
Shout aloud! Don't be timid.
Tell my people Israel* of their sins!
² Yet they act so pious!
They come to the Temple every day
and seem delighted to learn
all about me.
They act like a righteous nation
that would never abandon the laws of
its God.
They ask me to take action on their behalf,
pretending they want to be near me.
³ 'We have fasted before you!' they say.
'Why aren't you impressed?
We have been very hard on ourselves,
and you don't even notice it!'

57:9a Or to the king. **57:9b** Hebrew to Sheol. **58:1** Hebrew Jacob.
See note on 14:1.

"I will tell you why!" I respond.
"It's because you are fasting to please
yourselves.
Even while you fast,
you keep oppressing your workers.
⁴ What good is fasting
when you keep on fighting and quarreling?
This kind of fasting
will never get you anywhere with me.
⁵ You humble yourselves
by going through the motions of penance,
bowing your heads
like reeds bending in the wind.
You dress in burlap
and cover yourselves with ashes.
Is this what you call fasting?
Do you really think this will please
the LORD?

⁶ "No, this is the kind of fasting I want:
Free those who are wrongly imprisoned;
lighten the burden of those who work
for you.
Let the oppressed go free,
and remove the chains that bind people.
⁷ Share your food with the hungry,
and give shelter to the homeless.
Give clothes to those who need them,
and do not hide from relatives who need
your help.

⁸ "Then your salvation will come like the dawn,
and your wounds will quickly heal.
Your godliness will lead you forward,
and the glory of the LORD will protect you
from behind.
⁹ Then when you call, the LORD will answer.
'Yes, I am here,' he will quickly reply.

"Remove the heavy yoke of oppression.
Stop pointing your finger and spreading
vicious rumors!
¹⁰ Feed the hungry,
and help those in trouble.
Then your light will shine out from the
darkness,
and the darkness around you will be as
bright as noon.
¹¹ The LORD will guide you continually,
giving you water when you are dry
and restoring your strength.
You will be like a well-watered garden,
like an ever-flowing spring.
¹² Some of you will rebuild the deserted ruins
of your cities.
Then you will be known as a rebuilder
of walls
and a restorer of homes.

¹³ "Keep the Sabbath day holy.
Don't pursue your own interests on
that day,
but enjoy the Sabbath
and speak of it with delight as the LORD's
holy day.
Honor the Sabbath in everything you do
on that day,
and don't follow your own desires or
talk idly.
¹⁴ Then the LORD will be your delight.
I will give you great honor
and satisfy you with the inheritance I
promised to your ancestor Jacob.
I, the LORD, have spoken!"

WARNINGS AGAINST SIN

59 ¹ Listen! The LORD's arm is not too
weak to save you,
nor is his ear too deaf to hear you call.
² It's your sins that have cut you off from God.
Because of your sins, he has turned away
and will not listen anymore.
³ Your hands are the hands of murderers,
and your fingers are filthy with sin.
Your lips are full of lies,
and your mouth spews corruption.

⁴ No one cares about being fair and honest.
The people's lawsuits are based on lies.
They conceive evil deeds
and then give birth to sin.
⁵ They hatch deadly snakes
and weave spiders' webs.
Whoever eats their eggs will die;
whoever cracks them will hatch a viper.
⁶ Their webs can't be made into clothing,
and nothing they do is productive.
All their activity is filled with sin,
and violence is their trademark.
⁷ Their feet run to do evil,
and they rush to commit murder.
They think only about sinning.
Misery and destruction always follow
them.
⁸ They don't know where to find peace
or what it means to be just and good.
They have mapped out crooked roads,
and no one who follows them knows a
moment's peace.

⁹ So there is no justice among us,
and we know nothing about right living.
We look for light but find only darkness.
We look for bright skies but walk
in gloom.
¹⁰ We grope like the blind along a wall,
feeling our way like people without eyes.
Even at brightest noontime,
we stumble as though it were dark.
Among the living,
we are like the dead.
¹¹ We growl like hungry bears;
we moan like mournful doves.
We look for justice, but it never comes.

TEN DEADLY SINS
Isaiah 59:1-3

ROBERT MORRIS

In Isaiah 59, Isaiah tells the people of Israel they have destroyed their closeness with God by what they have done and what they have *said*. Here are the 10 most deadly sins we commit with our words:

1. **Lying**
A "lying tongue" (Proverbs 6:17) is detestable to God because lying is the opposite of His nature. Not only does God speak truth, but He also *is* truth (John 14:6). Satan, on the other hand, is the "father of lies" (John 8:44).

2. **Sowing Discord**
Many people have a habit of sowing discord (Proverbs 6:19). They think they're guardians of the truth, but instead of being peacemakers (Matthew 5:9), they're troublemakers. People who sow discord will reap calamity, disharmony, and disunity in their lives.

3. **Gossip**
Whether a secret is a rumor or a fact, it's still gossip (Proverbs 20:19). People often try to disguise gossip by sharing it as a "prayer request," even though they're not actually praying about the situation. We need to examine our hearts and get into the habit of *not* listening to or spreading gossip.

4. **Slander**
Slander is a false and malicious statement or report about someone. Whether we get our information from a person, the internet, or another source, we can slander others without even realizing it. Slander is foolish and dangerous (Proverbs 10:18), and we need to stop spreading bad reports about others.

5. **Tale-bearing**
Like those who gossip, talebearers reveal secrets and break confidences with others (Proverbs 11:13). We confess our faults to God to be forgiven, but James 5:16 tells us to confess our faults to each other to be healed. How many people are not healed because they're afraid of their secrets being spread all over the church?

6. **Cursing**
Romans 3:13-14 links cursing with bitterness. When you curse, you are speaking a curse over someone or something. Why would you curse your marriage, your business, or your finances? Blessing and cursing do not mix (Psalm 109:17-18), and a person who curses is not blessed.

7. **Blasphemy**
Blasphemy means to use God's name in an unsacred or self-serving way. The third commandment says a person who misuses God's name will not go unpunished (Exodus 20:7). There are two ways to misuse God's name: using it as a curse word and saying, "God told me . . ." in an effort to manipulate others. We should never use God's name to get our way—it's blasphemy.

8. **Dirty Language**
In Colossians 3:8, the apostle Paul warns believers to get rid of "dirty language." Dirty language comes out of your mouth because it's in your heart. It stirs up lust and leads to unclean thoughts. Don't listen to dirty language and don't participate in it either.

9. **Contentious Speech**
Contentious (or quarrelsome) speech is words that are hurtful, hateful, malicious, disagreeable, or argumentative. Proverbs 26:21 says that quarreling is like adding wood to a fire. Some people love to argue or stir up strife because they think it's fun, but no one wants to spend time with a person who is always picking a fight.

10. **Unbelief**
Unbelief is a heart issue (Hebrews 3:12-13) that shows itself through negativity. If unbelief is in your heart, negative words will come out of your mouth. The opposite of negativity is faith. Faith does not mean you don't see a problem; it means you see the problem *and* the answer. Faith is believing God is bigger than any problem you'll ever face.

We look for rescue, but it is far away
from us.
¹² For our sins are piled up before God
and testify against us.
Yes, we know what sinners we are.
¹³ We know we have rebelled and have
denied the LORD.
We have turned our backs on our God.
We know how unfair and oppressive we
have been,
carefully planning our deceitful lies.
¹⁴ Our courts oppose the righteous,
and justice is nowhere to be found.

Truth stumbles in the streets,
and honesty has been outlawed.
¹⁵ Yes, truth is gone,
and anyone who renounces evil is
attacked.

The LORD looked and was displeased
to find there was no justice.
¹⁶ He was amazed to see that no one intervened
to help the oppressed.
So he himself stepped in to save them with
his strong arm,
and his justice sustained him.

BUILDING A HOUSE OF WORSHIP: THE WALLS
Isaiah 60:1-18
JACK HAYFORD

During the destruction of Jerusalem, neither the walls of the city nor the efforts of the people inside had been enough to save it. Through the prophet Isaiah, God now promises,

"Salvation will surround you like city walls, and praise will be on the lips of all who enter there" (Isaiah 60:18).

The Lord speaks about what He wants to do for His people, not only then but also today. With worship comes the building up of our lives. Capture a sense of God's promise, lay hold of it, and stand firm in it, praising the Lord. No matter where you are on the recovery scale, God is building your walls of salvation. His salvation permeates everything from the forgiveness of sins, to justification, to bodily, relational, and vocational health. As surely as God's glory visited Solomon's Temple, He will visit the place where you live too.

BUILDING A HOUSE OF WORSHIP: THE GATES
Isaiah 60:19-22
JACK HAYFORD

Isaiah prophesies about a temple that will surpass the glory of Solomon's Temple, namely Jesus Christ. John 1:14 says, "The Word became human and made his home among us. . . . And we have seen his glory, the glory of the Father's one and only Son" (John 1:14). Jesus came to display the glory of God to humanity. He died, rose again, and poured out His Spirit on the Church, His body (Ephesians 1:22-23).

Within the global Church, there are local churches. These local bodies are called to worship the Lord in spirit and in truth (John 4:23-24). Worship provides a place for God to display His glory. As God filled the Tabernacle, as He filled the Temple, and as He filled the person of Jesus Christ, so also He wants to fill the Church. When believers gather together in worship, we open the gates for God's presence to enter and fill each of us with His glory.

17 He put on righteousness as his body armor
    and placed the helmet of salvation on
      his head.
He clothed himself with a robe of vengeance
    and wrapped himself in a cloak of divine
      passion.
18 He will repay his enemies for their evil deeds.
    His fury will fall on his foes.
He will pay them back even to the ends of
      the earth.
19 In the west, people will respect the name of
      the LORD;
    in the east, they will glorify him.
For he will come like a raging flood tide
    driven by the breath of the LORD.*

20 "The Redeemer will come to Jerusalem
to buy back those in Israel
who have turned from their sins,"*
says the LORD.

21"And this is my covenant with them," says the LORD. "My Spirit will not leave them, and neither will these words I have given you. They will be on your lips and on the lips of your children and your children's children forever. I, the LORD, have spoken!

FUTURE GLORY FOR JERUSALEM

60 1 "Arise, Jerusalem! Let your light
      shine for all to see.
For the glory of the LORD rises to shine
    on you.
2 Darkness as black as night covers all the
    nations of the earth,

but the glory of the LORD rises and
    appears over you.
3 All nations will come to your light;
    mighty kings will come to see your
      radiance.

4 "Look and see, for everyone is coming home!
    Your sons are coming from distant lands;
    your little daughters will be carried home.
5 Your eyes will shine,
    and your heart will thrill with joy,
for merchants from around the world will
      come to you.
They will bring you the wealth of
      many lands.
6 Vast caravans of camels will converge on you,
    the camels of Midian and Ephah.
The people of Sheba will bring gold and
      frankincense
    and will come worshiping the LORD.
7 The flocks of Kedar will be given to you,
    and the rams of Nebaioth will be brought
      for my altars.
I will accept their offerings,
    and I will make my Temple glorious.

8 "And what do I see flying like clouds
    to Israel,
    like doves to their nests?

59:19 Or *When the enemy comes like a raging flood tide, / the Spirit of the LORD will drive him back.* 59:20 Hebrew *The Redeemer will come to Zion / to buy back those in Jacob / who have turned from their sins.* Greek version reads *The one who rescues will come on behalf of Zion, / and he will turn Jacob away from ungodliness.* Compare Rom 11:26.

9 They are ships from the ends of the earth,
    from lands that trust in me,
    led by the great ships of Tarshish.
They are bringing the people of Israel home
        from far away,
    carrying their silver and gold.
They will honor the LORD your God,
    the Holy One of Israel,
    for he has filled you with splendor.

10 "Foreigners will come to rebuild your towns,
    and their kings will serve you.
For though I have destroyed you in
        my anger,
    I will now have mercy on you through
        my grace.
11 Your gates will stay open day and night
    to receive the wealth of many lands.
The kings of the world will be led as captives
    in a victory procession.
12 For the nations that refuse to serve you
    will be destroyed.

13 "The glory of Lebanon will be yours—
    the forests of cypress, fir, and pine—
to beautify my sanctuary.
    My Temple will be glorious!
14 The descendants of your tormentors
    will come and bow before you.
Those who despised you
    will kiss your feet.
They will call you the City of the LORD,
    and Zion of the Holy One of Israel.

15 "Though you were once despised and hated,
    with no one traveling through you,
I will make you beautiful forever,
    a joy to all generations.
16 Powerful kings and mighty nations
    will satisfy your every need,
as though you were a child
    nursing at the breast of a queen.
You will know at last that I, the LORD,
    am your Savior and your Redeemer,
    the Mighty One of Israel.*
17 I will exchange your bronze for gold,
    your iron for silver,
your wood for bronze,
    and your stones for iron.
I will make peace your leader
    and righteousness your ruler.
18 Violence will disappear from your land;
    the desolation and destruction of war
        will end.
Salvation will surround you like
        city walls,
    and praise will be on the lips of all who
        enter there.

19 "No longer will you need the sun to shine
        by day,
    nor the moon to give its light by night,
for the LORD your God will be your
        everlasting light,
    and your God will be your glory.
20 Your sun will never set;
    your moon will not go down.
For the LORD will be your everlasting light.
    Your days of mourning will come to
        an end.
21 All your people will be righteous.
    They will possess their land forever,
for I will plant them there with my own
        hands
    in order to bring myself glory.
22 The smallest family will become
        a thousand people,
    and the tiniest group will become a
        mighty nation.
At the right time, I, the LORD, will make
    it happen."

GOOD NEWS FOR THE OPPRESSED

61 1 The Spirit of the Sovereign LORD
        is upon me,
    for the LORD has anointed me
        to bring good news to the poor.
He has sent me to comfort the
        brokenhearted
    and to proclaim that captives will be
        released
    and prisoners will be freed.*
2 He has sent me to tell those who mourn
    that the time of the LORD's favor has
        come,*
    and with it, the day of God's anger against
        their enemies.
3 To all who mourn in Israel,*
    he will give a crown of beauty for ashes,
a joyous blessing instead of mourning,
    festive praise instead of despair.
In their righteousness, they will be like
        great oaks
    that the LORD has planted for
        his own glory.

4 They will rebuild the ancient ruins,
    repairing cities destroyed long ago.
They will revive them,
    though they have been deserted for many
        generations.
5 Foreigners will be your servants.
    They will feed your flocks
and plow your fields
    and tend your vineyards.
6 You will be called priests of the LORD,
    ministers of our God.
You will feed on the treasures of the nations
    and boast in their riches.
7 Instead of shame and dishonor,
    you will enjoy a double share of honor.

60:16 Hebrew *of Jacob.* See note on 14:1.   61:1 Greek version
reads *and the blind will see.* Compare Luke 4:18.   61:2 Or *to
proclaim the acceptable year of the LORD.*   61:3 Hebrew *in Zion.*

You will possess a double portion of
    prosperity in your land,
    and everlasting joy will be yours.

8 "For I, the LORD, love justice.
    I hate robbery and wrongdoing.
I will faithfully reward my people for their
    suffering
    and make an everlasting covenant with
    them.
9 Their descendants will be recognized
    and honored among the nations.
Everyone will realize that they are a people
    the LORD has blessed."

10 I am overwhelmed with joy in the LORD
    my God!
For he has dressed me with the clothing
    of salvation
    and draped me in a robe of righteousness.
I am like a bridegroom dressed for his
    wedding
    or a bride with her jewels.
11 The Sovereign LORD will show his justice to
    the nations of the world.
Everyone will praise him!
His righteousness will be like a garden in
    early spring,
    with plants springing up everywhere.

ISAIAH'S PRAYER FOR JERUSALEM

62 1 Because I love Zion,
    I will not keep still.
Because my heart yearns for Jerusalem,
    I cannot remain silent.
I will not stop praying for her
    until her righteousness shines like the
    dawn,
    and her salvation blazes like a burning
    torch.
2 The nations will see your righteousness.
    World leaders will be blinded by
    your glory.
And you will be given a new name
    by the LORD's own mouth.
3 The LORD will hold you in his hand for all
    to see—
    a splendid crown in the hand of God.
4 Never again will you be called
    "The Forsaken City"*
    or "The Desolate Land."*
Your new name will be "The City of God's
    Delight"*
    and "The Bride of God,"*
for the LORD delights in you
    and will claim you as his bride.
5 Your children will commit themselves to
    you, O Jerusalem,
    just as a young man commits himself
    to his bride.
Then God will rejoice over you
    as a bridegroom rejoices over his bride.

6 O Jerusalem, I have posted watchmen on
    your walls;
    they will pray day and night, continually.
Take no rest, all you who pray to the LORD.
7 Give the LORD no rest until he completes
    his work,
    until he makes Jerusalem the pride of
    the earth.
8 The LORD has sworn to Jerusalem by
    his own strength:
    "I will never again hand you over to
    your enemies.
Never again will foreign warriors come
    and take away your grain and new wine.
9 You raised the grain, and you will eat it,
    praising the LORD.
Within the courtyards of the Temple,
    you yourselves will drink the wine you
    have pressed."

10 Go out through the gates!
    Prepare the highway for my people
    to return!
Smooth out the road; pull out the boulders;
    raise a flag for all the nations to see.
11 The LORD has sent this message to
    every land:
    "Tell the people of Israel,*
'Look, your Savior is coming.
    See, he brings his reward with him as he
    comes.'"
12 They will be called "The Holy People"
    and "The People Redeemed by the LORD."
And Jerusalem will be known as "The
    Desirable Place"
    and "The City No Longer Forsaken."

JUDGMENT AGAINST THE LORD'S ENEMIES

63 1 Who is this who comes from Edom,
    from the city of Bozrah,
    with his clothing stained red?
Who is this in royal robes,
    marching in his great strength?

"It is I, the LORD, announcing your
    salvation!
It is I, the LORD, who has the power to
    save!"

2 Why are your clothes so red,
    as if you have been treading out grapes?

3 "I have been treading the winepress alone;
    no one was there to help me.
In my anger I have trampled my enemies
    as if they were grapes.
In my fury I have trampled my foes.
    Their blood has stained my clothes.

62:4a Hebrew *Azubah*, which means "forsaken."   62:4b Hebrew
Shemamah, which means "desolate."   62:4c Hebrew *Hephzibah*,
which means "my delight is in her."   62:4d Hebrew *Beulah*,
which means "married."   62:11 Hebrew *Tell the daughter of Zion.*

⁴ For the time has come for me to avenge
   my people,
   to ransom them from their oppressors.
⁵ I was amazed to see that no one intervened
   to help the oppressed.
So I myself stepped in to save them with my
   strong arm,
   and my wrath sustained me.
⁶ I crushed the nations in my anger
   and made them stagger and fall to
   the ground,
   spilling their blood upon the earth."

PRAISE FOR DELIVERANCE

⁷ I will tell of the LORD's unfailing love.
   I will praise the LORD for all he has done.
I will rejoice in his great goodness to Israel,
   which he has granted according to his
   mercy and love.
⁸ He said, "They are my very own people.
   Surely they will not betray me again."
   And he became their Savior.
⁹ In all their suffering he also suffered,
   and he personally* rescued them.
In his love and mercy he redeemed them.
   He lifted them up and carried them
   through all the years.
¹⁰ But they rebelled against him
   and grieved his Holy Spirit.
So he became their enemy
   and fought against them.

¹¹ Then they remembered those days of old
   when Moses led his people out of Egypt.
They cried out, "Where is the one who
   brought Israel through the sea,
   with Moses as their shepherd?
Where is the one who sent his Holy Spirit
   to be among his people?
¹² Where is the one whose power was displayed
   when Moses lifted up his hand—
the one who divided the sea before them,
   making himself famous forever?
¹³ Where is the one who led them through the
   bottom of the sea?
They were like fine stallions
   racing through the desert, never
   stumbling.
¹⁴ As with cattle going down into a peaceful
   valley,
   the Spirit of the LORD gave them rest.
You led your people, LORD,
   and gained a magnificent reputation."

PRAYER FOR MERCY AND PARDON

¹⁵ LORD, look down from heaven;
   look from your holy, glorious home,
   and see us.
Where is the passion and the might
   you used to show on our behalf?
Where are your mercy and
   compassion now?

¹⁶ Surely you are still our Father!
   Even if Abraham and Jacob* would
   disown us,
   LORD, you would still be our Father.
You are our Redeemer from ages past.
¹⁷ LORD, why have you allowed us to turn
   from your path?
Why have you given us stubborn hearts so
   we no longer fear you?
Return and help us, for we are your servants,
   the tribes that are your special possession.
¹⁸ How briefly your holy people possessed your
   holy place,
   and now our enemies have destroyed it.
¹⁹ Sometimes it seems as though we never
   belonged to you,
   as though we had never been known as
   your people.

64 ¹*Oh, that you would burst from
      the heavens and come down!
How the mountains would quake in
   your presence!
²*As fire causes wood to burn
   and water to boil,
your coming would make the nations tremble.
   Then your enemies would learn the
   reason for your fame!
³ When you came down long ago,
   you did awesome deeds beyond our
   highest expectations.
And oh, how the mountains quaked!
⁴ For since the world began,
   no ear has heard
and no eye has seen a God like you,
   who works for those who wait for him!
⁵ You welcome those who gladly do good,
   who follow godly ways.
But you have been very angry with us,
   for we are not godly.
We are constant sinners;
   how can people like us be saved?
⁶ We are all infected and impure with sin.
   When we display our righteous deeds,
   they are nothing but filthy rags.
Like autumn leaves, we wither and fall,
   and our sins sweep us away like the wind.
⁷ Yet no one calls on your name
   or pleads with you for mercy.
Therefore, you have turned away from us
   and turned us over* to our sins.
⁸ And yet, O LORD, you are our Father.
   We are the clay, and you are the potter.
   We all are formed by your hand.
⁹ Don't be so angry with us, LORD.
   Please don't remember our sins forever.

63:9 Hebrew *and the angel of his presence.*   63:16 Hebrew *Israel.*
See note on 14:1.   64:1 In the Hebrew text this verse is included
in 63:19.   64:2 Verses 64:2-12 are numbered 64:1-11 in Hebrew
text.   64:7 As in Greek, Syriac, and Aramaic versions; Hebrew
reads *melted us.*

Look at us, we pray,
    and see that we are all your people.
[10] Your holy cities are destroyed.
    Zion is a wilderness;
    yes, Jerusalem is a desolate ruin.
[11] The holy and beautiful Temple
    where our ancestors praised you
has been burned down,
    and all the things of beauty are destroyed.
[12] After all this, LORD, must you still refuse
    to help us?
Will you continue to be silent and
    punish us?

JUDGMENT AND FINAL SALVATION

65 The LORD says,

"I was ready to respond,
    but no one asked for help.
I was ready to be found,
    but no one was looking for me.
I said, 'Here I am, here I am!'
    to a nation that did not call on my name.*
[2] All day long I opened my arms to a
    rebellious people.*
But they follow their own evil paths
    and their own crooked schemes.
[3] All day long they insult me to my face
    by worshiping idols in their sacred gardens.
    They burn incense on pagan altars.
[4] At night they go out among the graves,
    worshiping the dead.
They eat the flesh of pigs
    and make stews with other
      forbidden foods.
[5] Yet they say to each other,
    'Don't come too close or you will defile me!
    I am holier than you!'
These people are a stench in my nostrils,
    an acrid smell that never goes away.

[6] "Look, my decree is written out* in front
    of me:
I will not stand silent;
    I will repay them in full!
Yes, I will repay them—
[7] both for their own sins
    and for those of their ancestors,"
    says the LORD.
"For they also burned incense on
    the mountains
and insulted me on the hills.
    I will pay them back in full!

[8] "But I will not destroy them all,"
    says the LORD.
"For just as good grapes are found among a
    cluster of bad ones
(and someone will say,
    'Don't throw them all away—
    some of those grapes are good!'),
so I will not destroy all Israel.

For I still have true servants there.
[9] I will preserve a remnant of the people
    of Israel*
and of Judah to possess my land.
Those I choose will inherit it,
    and my servants will live there.
[10] The plain of Sharon will again be filled
    with flocks
for my people who have searched for me,
    and the valley of Achor will be a place to
      pasture herds.

[11] "But because the rest of you have forsaken
    the LORD
and have forgotten his Temple,
and because you have prepared feasts to
    honor the god of Fate
and have offered mixed wine to the god
    of Destiny,
[12] now I will 'destine' you for the sword.
    All of you will bow down before the
      executioner.
For when I called, you did not answer.
    When I spoke, you did not listen.
You deliberately sinned—before my
    very eyes—
    and chose to do what you know I despise."

[13] Therefore, this is what the Sovereign
    LORD says:
"My servants will eat,
    but you will starve.
My servants will drink,
    but you will be thirsty.
My servants will rejoice,
    but you will be sad and ashamed.
[14] My servants will sing for joy,
    but you will cry in sorrow and despair.
[15] Your name will be a curse word among
    my people,
for the Sovereign LORD will destroy you
    and will call his true servants by
    another name.
[16] All who invoke a blessing or take an oath
    will do so by the God of truth.
For I will put aside my anger
    and forget the evil of earlier days.

[17] "Look! I am creating new heavens and
    a new earth,
and no one will even think about the old
    ones anymore.
[18] Be glad; rejoice forever in my creation!
    And look! I will create Jerusalem as a
    place of happiness.
Her people will be a source of joy.

65:1 Or *to a nation that did not bear my name.*   65:1-2 Greek
version reads *I was found by people who were not looking for me. /
I showed myself to those who were not asking for me. / All day long I
opened my arms to them, / but they were disobedient and rebellious.*
Compare Rom 10:20-21.   65:6 Or *their sins are written out;*
Hebrew reads *it stands written.*   65:9 Hebrew *remnant of Jacob.*
See note on 14:1.

¹⁹ I will rejoice over Jerusalem
　　and delight in my people.
And the sound of weeping and crying
　　will be heard in it no more.

²⁰ "No longer will babies die when only
　　a few days old.
No longer will adults die before they have
　　lived a full life.
No longer will people be considered old at
　　one hundred!
Only the cursed will die that young!
²¹ In those days people will live in the houses
　　they build
　　and eat the fruit of their own vineyards.
²² Unlike the past, invaders will not take
　　their houses
　　and confiscate their vineyards.
For my people will live as long as trees,
　　and my chosen ones will have time to
　　enjoy their hard-won gains.
²³ They will not work in vain,
　　and their children will not be doomed
　　to misfortune.
For they are people blessed by the LORD,
　　and their children, too, will be blessed.
²⁴ I will answer them before they even call
　　to me.
While they are still talking about
　　their needs,
I will go ahead and answer their prayers!
²⁵ The wolf and the lamb will feed together.
　　The lion will eat hay like a cow.
　　But the snakes will eat dust.
In those days no one will be hurt or
　　destroyed on my holy mountain.
I, the LORD, have spoken!"

66

This is what the LORD says:

"Heaven is my throne,
　　and the earth is my footstool.
Could you build me a temple as good as that?
　　Could you build me such a resting place?
² My hands have made both heaven
　　and earth;
　　they and everything in them are mine.*
I, the LORD, have spoken!

"I will bless those who have humble and
　　contrite hearts,
　　who tremble at my word.
³ But those who choose their own ways—
　　delighting in their detestable sins—
　　will not have their offerings accepted.
When such people sacrifice a bull,
　　it is no more acceptable than a human
　　sacrifice.
When they sacrifice a lamb,
　　it's as though they had sacrificed a dog!
When they bring an offering of grain,
　　they might as well offer the blood of a pig.

When they burn frankincense,
　　it's as if they had blessed an idol.
⁴ I will send them great trouble—
　　all the things they feared.
For when I called, they did not answer.
　　When I spoke, they did not listen.
They deliberately sinned before
　　my very eyes
　　and chose to do what they know
　　I despise."

⁵ Hear this message from the LORD,
　　all you who tremble at his words:
"Your own people hate you
　　and throw you out for being loyal to my
　　name.
'Let the LORD be honored!' they scoff.
　　'Be joyful in him!'
But they will be put to shame.
⁶ What is all the commotion in the city?
　　What is that terrible noise from
　　the Temple?
It is the voice of the LORD
　　taking vengeance against his enemies.

⁷ "Before the birth pains even begin,
　　Jerusalem gives birth to a son.
⁸ Who has ever seen anything as strange
　　as this?
　　Who ever heard of such a thing?
Has a nation ever been born in a single day?
　　Has a country ever come forth in
　　a mere moment?
But by the time Jerusalem's*
　　birth pains begin,
　　her children will be born.
⁹ Would I ever bring this nation to
　　the point of birth
　　and then not deliver it?" asks the LORD.
"No! I would never keep this nation from
　　being born,"
　　says your God.

¹⁰ "Rejoice with Jerusalem!
　　Be glad with her, all you who love her
　　and all you who mourn for her.
¹¹ Drink deeply of her glory
　　even as an infant drinks at its mother's
　　comforting breasts."

¹² This is what the LORD says:
"I will give Jerusalem a river of peace and
　　prosperity.
　　The wealth of the nations will flow
　　to her.
Her children will be nursed at her breasts,
　　carried in her arms, and held on her lap.
¹³ I will comfort you there in Jerusalem
　　as a mother comforts her child."

66:2 As in Greek, Latin, and Syriac versions; Hebrew reads *these
things are.*　66:8 Hebrew *Zion's.*

¹⁴ When you see these things,
    your heart will rejoice.
You will flourish like the grass!
Everyone will see the LORD's hand of
    blessing on his servants—
    and his anger against his enemies.
¹⁵ See, the LORD is coming with fire,
    and his swift chariots roar like
    a whirlwind.
He will bring punishment with the fury
    of his anger
    and the flaming fire of his hot rebuke.
¹⁶ The LORD will punish the world by fire
    and by his sword.
He will judge the earth,
    and many will be killed by him.

¹⁷ "Those who 'consecrate' and 'purify' themselves in a sacred garden with its idol in the center—feasting on pork and rats and other detestable meats—will come to a terrible end," says the LORD.

¹⁸ "I can see what they are doing, and I know what they are thinking. So I will gather all nations and peoples together, and they will see my glory. ¹⁹ I will perform a sign among them. And I will send those who survive to be messengers to the nations—to Tarshish, to the Libyans* and Lydians* (who are famous as archers), to Tubal and Greece,* and to all the lands beyond the sea that have not heard of my fame or seen my glory. There they will declare my glory to the nations. ²⁰ They will bring the remnant of your people back from every nation. They will bring them to my holy mountain in Jerusalem as an offering to the LORD. They will ride on horses, in chariots and wagons, and on mules and camels," says the LORD. ²¹ "And I will appoint some of them to be my priests and Levites. I, the LORD, have spoken!

²² "As surely as my new heavens and earth
    will remain,
    so will you always be my people,
with a name that will never disappear,"
    says the LORD.
²³ "All humanity will come to worship me
    from week to week
    and from month to month.
²⁴ And as they go out, they will see
    the dead bodies of those who have
    rebelled against me.
For the worms that devour them
    will never die,
    and the fire that burns them
    will never go out.
All who pass by
    will view them with utter horror."

66:19a As in some Greek manuscripts, which read *Put* [that is, *Libya*]; Hebrew reads *Pul.*   **66:19b** Hebrew *Lud.*   **66:19c** Hebrew *Javan.*

JEREMIAH

JON HUNTZINGER, PHD

The book of Jeremiah is the longest in the Bible. It is named after the prophet who is called to speak God's words to the people of Judah beginning in the year 626 BC (the thirteenth year of King Josiah's rule in Judah). He continues in that ministry until the beginning of the Babylonian Exile in 586 BC. The book of Jeremiah contains more personal information about this man than any other book from a biblical prophet. For example, the book reveals Jeremiah came from a priestly family living in the village of Anathoth just outside Jerusalem (1:1). He grew tired of the messages God gave him to speak due to the opposition he received (20:7-18). He was thrown into a deep well by royal officials who wanted him to die (38:1-6).

The book of Jeremiah recounts messages related to events in Judah at the end of Assyrian rule and the beginning of Babylonian rule in the late seventh century BC. Thus, it covers the period of King Josiah and his reforms (639-609 BC) down to the time of his son Zedekiah's rule and the collapse of Jerusalem (597-586 BC). The Babylonians were a strong nation known for confiscating the valuable assets and resources of the peoples they conquered. They laid siege to Jerusalem in 598 BC and eventually overthrew the city and destroyed the Temple in 586 BC, carting away the silver and gold of the Temple and sending thousands of people into exile. Jeremiah's message to Judah throughout these events was not one of resistance. He did not promise God's deliverance from the ungodly Babylonians. Rather, Jeremiah delivered a message of accusation. He accuses the people of not keeping faith with God by not living according to His covenant (2:1-5:31) and by refusing to repent for their faithlessness. For these sins, Jeremiah says, God will judge them at the hands of the Babylonians (6:1-11:23). No one in Jerusalem wanted to hear such a message. They wanted to hear about God's deliverance and the judgment He would bring upon the Babylonians, not about the judgment they would experience at the hands of the Babylonians.

Jeremiah delivered these messages over a long period. Jeremiah or his secretary, Baruch, ultimately collected and arranged them according to a topical rather than chronological order. Identifiable collections within the book include the following:

— Jeremiah 1-25 include judgments against Judah and Jerusalem.
— Jeremiah 30-33 offer words of hope in God's restoration of Jerusalem, also known as the "Book of Comfort," which includes God's well-known promise to write His covenant on the hearts of His people (31:31-34).
— Jeremiah 46-51 contain pronouncements against foreign nations.
— Jeremiah 26-29 and 34-45 are interspersed with biographical information on Jeremiah.

A primary theme of the book is the supreme authority of God's Word. God places His words in Jeremiah's mouth (1:9). Jeremiah cannot resist speaking them, even though others ridicule and reject him for it (20:7-9). In fact, many people in the book of Jeremiah consistently reject God's word, including the king, the priests, the prophets, and even Jeremiah's family and friends. King Jehoiakim tears up the scroll on which God's word through Jeremiah is written and throws it into the fire of his winter palace (36:1-32). Pashhur the Temple priest has Jeremiah beaten and placed in stocks when he hears the message Jeremiah gives (20:1-6). And Hananiah the prophet contradicts God's word spoken by Jeremiah when he promises victory over the Babylonians and the soon return of the first exiles (28:1-17). Even Jeremiah's friends turn upon him for speaking God's word of judgment (20:10-12). All of these responses represent the negative attitude that the people of Jerusalem have toward God's word through Jeremiah. Nonetheless, that word is proven true when the people are sent into the Exile (52:24-30).

According to Jeremiah, the God of Israel is the God of all nations. In fact, God calls Jeremiah as a prophet to the nations (1:5), to "uproot and tear down, destroy and overthrow," and "build up and plant" (1:10). Jeremiah will do this through the words of God that he speaks. The specific prophecies Jeremiah makes concerning the nations of Egypt, Gaza, Moab, Ammon, Edom, Syria, and Babylon are evidence of God's rule over the nations as well as Israel (chapters 46-51).

Though much of Jeremiah's message is about judgment for the faithlessness and sin of the people, it is not the total message. Jeremiah also speaks of future hope, and he declares God's providential word, "For I know the plans I have for you . . . to give you a future and a hope" (29:11). It is a plan that will be accomplished by a "righteous descendant" of David (23:5-8; 33:14-18), and in order to help the people hold on to this plan and have hope for the future, Jeremiah buys a field to signify that they will once again inherit the land of promise after the Exile (32:1-15).

The writers of the Gospels saw Jeremiah as a forerunner to Jesus. Matthew reports that when

Jesus asked His disciples what people were saying about Him, they replied that some thought He was Jeremiah who had come back to them (Matthew 16:13–14). The people thought this for several reasons:
— The stories of Jesus' birth reminded them of Jeremiah. Those stories included angels who announced His birth to Mary by the Spirit of God (Matthew 1:18–21; Luke 1:31–35).
— God knew Jesus before He was born, even as God knew Jeremiah when he was in his mother's womb (Jeremiah 1:5).
— Jesus preached a message of repentance (Matthew 4:17; Mark 1:14–15), just as Jeremiah called the people to repent of their sin and return to the covenant God had made with them (Jeremiah 3:6–4:4; 7:1–15; 26:1–15).
— Jesus was critical of leaders who had compromised the pure ministry of the Temple for all people (Mark 11:15–19), not unlike Jeremiah's criticism of people who worshipped at the Temple, thinking that their mere participation protected

them from judgment for their worship of other gods at the same time (Jeremiah 7:1–11).
— The persecution of Jesus by certain leaders reminded many people of the persecution of Jeremiah. People wanted to destroy Jesus for His teaching and actions (Mark 3:1–6; John 8:31–59), even as King Jehoiakim, the priest Pashhur, and others attempted to put Jeremiah to death (Jeremiah 38:1–6).
— Many people close to Jesus misunderstood Him, said that He was "out of his mind," and ultimately rejected Him (Mark 3:20–21; John 6:60–71). His disciples and family were confused and alarmed by His teaching and ministry, just as many who were close to Jeremiah were confused by his messages and rejected them as well (Jeremiah 11:18–12:6; 17:14–18; 18:18–23; 20:7–12).

For all of these reasons, many people at the time of Jesus viewed Him as another Jeremiah-type prophet.

1 These are the words of Jeremiah son of Hilkiah, one of the priests from the town of Anathoth in the land of Benjamin. ²The LORD first gave messages to Jeremiah during the thirteenth year of the reign of Josiah son of Amon, king of Judah.* ³The LORD's messages continued throughout the reign of King Jehoiakim, Josiah's son, until the eleventh year of the reign of King Zedekiah, another of Josiah's sons. In August* of that eleventh year the people of Jerusalem were taken away as captives.

JEREMIAH'S CALL AND FIRST VISIONS
⁴The LORD gave me this message:

⁵ "I knew you before I formed you in your
mother's womb.
Before you were born I set you apart
and appointed you as my prophet to
the nations."

⁶"O Sovereign LORD," I said, "I can't speak for you! I'm too young!"
⁷The LORD replied, "Don't say, 'I'm too young,' for you must go wherever I send you and say whatever I tell you. ⁸And don't be afraid of the people, for I will be with you and will protect you. I, the LORD, have spoken!" ⁹Then the LORD reached out and touched my mouth and said,

"Look, I have put my words in your mouth!
¹⁰ Today I appoint you to stand up
against nations and kingdoms.
Some you must uproot and tear down,
destroy and overthrow.

Others you must build up
and plant."

¹¹Then the LORD said to me, "Look, Jeremiah! What do you see?"
And I replied, "I see a branch from an almond tree."
¹²And the LORD said, "That's right, and it means that I am watching,* and I will certainly carry out all my plans."
¹³Then the LORD spoke to me again and asked, "What do you see now?"
And I replied, "I see a pot of boiling water, spilling from the north."
¹⁴"Yes," the LORD said, "for terror from the north will boil out on the people of this land. ¹⁵Listen! I am calling the armies of the kingdoms of the north to come to Jerusalem. I, the LORD, have spoken!

"They will set their thrones
at the gates of the city.
They will attack its walls
and all the other towns of Judah.
¹⁶ I will pronounce judgment
on my people for all their evil—
for deserting me and burning incense to
other gods.

1:2 The thirteenth year of Josiah's reign was 627 B.C.
1:3 Hebrew In the fifth month, of the ancient Hebrew lunar calendar. A number of events in Jeremiah can be cross-checked with dates in surviving Babylonian records and related accurately to our modern calendar. The fifth month in the eleventh year of Zedekiah's reign occurred within the months of August and September 586 B.C. Also see 52:12 and the note there. 1:12 The Hebrew word for "watching" (shoqed) sounds like the word for "almond tree" (shaqed).

SPIRITUAL DNA
Jeremiah 1:4-5

ROBERT MORRIS

If you have a physical DNA that determines your physical characteristics, then is it possible that you also have a spiritual DNA that determines your spiritual characteristics? The answer is yes!

God put spiritual DNA in you before you were even born (Jeremiah 1:4-5). When Jeremiah was still in his mother's womb, God gave him the spiritual genes to prophesy. God also gave John the Baptist a special spiritual calling before he was born (Luke 1:13-17). Neither man was forced to fulfill his calling, but both had the God-given ability to do so if they chose.

How do you unlock your spiritual DNA? First, I will tell you what *not* to do:

1. Don't have distorted vision.
   You become what you look at, so it is important to avoid negative role models.
2. Don't manipulate to control your destiny.
   Sometimes people look at other members of the body of Christ and think, *That person seems to get a lot of attention and praise for their gift. I want their gift too!* Then they try to manipulate their destiny rather than serving God's Kingdom.

3. Don't go near spiritual disease.
   Spiritual disease includes bad doctrine, bad relationships, and bad attitudes. Satan wants you to absorb the wrong teachings, hang out with the wrong people, and adopt the wrong attitudes.

Now that you know what not to do, here's what you *should* do:

1. Find good spiritual parents.
   All of us need mentors, no matter how old we are. Find mature, trustworthy believers who will be your spiritual oversight and encourage you to use the gifts God's given you.
2. Take in the proper nourishment.
   God's Word is the best place for you to find food. Get in the habit of reading it every day.
3. Put yourself in the right environment.
   A local church is where you'll unlock and fulfill your spiritual DNA. Paul and Barnabas were members of the church at Antioch for 13 years before the elders sent them out. Every time they returned from a missionary journey, they reported back to the elders. They were in constant relationship with their local church.

Yes, they worship idols made with their
   own hands!

[17] "Get up and prepare for action.
   Go out and tell them everything
      I tell you to say.
   Do not be afraid of them,
      or I will make you look foolish in front
         of them.
[18] For see, today I have made you strong
      like a fortified city that cannot be captured,
      like an iron pillar or a bronze wall.
   You will stand against the whole land—
      the kings, officials, priests, and people
         of Judah.
[19] They will fight you, but they will fail.
   For I am with you, and I will take care
      of you.
   I, the LORD, have spoken!"

THE LORD'S CASE AGAINST HIS PEOPLE

2 The LORD gave me another message. He said,
[2] "Go and shout this message to Jerusalem.
This is what the LORD says:

"I remember how eager you were
      to please me
   as a young bride long ago,
how you loved me and followed me
   even through the barren wilderness.
[3] In those days Israel was holy to the LORD,
   the first of his children.*

All who harmed his people were
      declared guilty,
   and disaster fell on them.
   I, the LORD, have spoken!"

[4] Listen to the word of the LORD, people of Jacob—all you families of Israel! [5] This is what the LORD says:

"What did your ancestors find wrong
      with me
   that led them to stray so far from me?
They worshiped worthless idols,
   only to become worthless themselves.
[6] They did not ask, 'Where is the LORD
   who brought us safely out of Egypt
and led us through the
      barren wilderness—
   a land of deserts and pits,
a land of drought and death,
   where no one lives or even travels?'

[7] "And when I brought you into
      a fruitful land
   to enjoy its bounty and goodness,
you defiled my land
   and corrupted the possession I had
      promised you.
[8] The priests did not ask,
   'Where is the LORD?'

2:3 Hebrew *the firstfruits of his harvest*.

Those who taught my word ignored me,
the rulers turned against me,
and the prophets spoke in the name of Baal,
wasting their time on worthless idols.
⁹ Therefore, I will bring my case against you,"
says the LORD.
"I will even bring charges against your
children's children
in the years to come.

¹⁰ "Go west and look in the land of Cyprus*;
go east and search through the land
of Kedar.
Has anyone ever heard of anything
as strange as this?
¹¹ Has any nation ever traded its gods for
new ones,
even though they are not gods at all?
Yet my people have exchanged
their glorious God*
for worthless idols!
¹² The heavens are shocked at such a thing
and shrink back in horror and dismay,"
says the LORD.
¹³ "For my people have done two evil things:
They have abandoned me—
the fountain of living water.
And they have dug for themselves
cracked cisterns
that can hold no water at all!

THE RESULTS OF ISRAEL'S SIN

¹⁴ "Why has Israel become a slave?
Why has he been carried away as plunder?
¹⁵ Strong lions have roared against him,
and the land has been destroyed.
The towns are now in ruins,
and no one lives in them anymore.
¹⁶ Egyptians, marching from their cities of
Memphis* and Tahpanhes,
have destroyed Israel's glory and power.
¹⁷ And you have brought this upon yourselves
by rebelling against the LORD your God,
even though he was leading you
on the way!

¹⁸ "What have you gained by your alliances
with Egypt
and your covenants with Assyria?
What good to you are the streams of the Nile*
or the waters of the Euphrates River?*
¹⁹ Your wickedness will bring its own
punishment.
Your turning from me will shame you.
You will see what an evil, bitter thing it is
to abandon the LORD your God and not to
fear him.
I, the Lord, the LORD of Heaven's Armies,
have spoken!

²⁰ "Long ago I broke the yoke that oppressed you
and tore away the chains of your slavery,

but still you said,
'I will not serve you.'
On every hill and under every green tree,
you have prostituted yourselves by
bowing down to idols.
²¹ But I was the one who planted you,
choosing a vine of the purest stock—the
very best.
How did you grow into this corrupt
wild vine?
²² No amount of soap or lye can make you clean.
I still see the stain of your guilt.
I, the Sovereign LORD, have spoken!

ISRAEL, AN UNFAITHFUL WIFE

²³ "You say, 'That's not true!
I haven't worshiped the images of Baal!'
But how can you say that?
Go and look in any valley in the land!
Face the awful sins you have done.
You are like a restless female camel
desperately searching for a mate.
²⁴ You are like a wild donkey,
sniffing the wind at mating time.
Who can restrain her lust?
Those who desire her don't need to search,
for she goes running to them!
²⁵ When will you stop running?
When will you stop panting after
other gods?
But you say, 'Save your breath.
I'm in love with these foreign gods,
and I can't stop loving them now!'

²⁶ "Israel is like a thief
who feels shame only when he gets caught.
They, their kings, officials, priests,
and prophets—
all are alike in this.
²⁷ To an image carved from a piece of wood
they say,
'You are my father.'
To an idol chiseled from a block of stone
they say,
'You are my mother.'
They turn their backs on me,
but in times of trouble they cry out to me,
'Come and save us!'
²⁸ But why not call on these gods you
have made?
When trouble comes, let them save you if
they can!
For you have as many gods
as there are towns in Judah.
²⁹ Why do you accuse me of doing wrong?
You are the ones who have rebelled,"
says the LORD.
³⁰ "I have punished your children,
but they did not respond to my discipline.

2:10 Hebrew *Kittim.* 2:11 Hebrew *their glory.* 2:16 Hebrew
Noph. 2:18a Hebrew *of Shihor,* a branch of the Nile River.
2:18b Hebrew *the river?*

You yourselves have killed your prophets
  as a lion kills its prey.

31 "O my people, listen to the words of
    the Lord!
Have I been like a desert to Israel?
Have I been to them a land of darkness?
Why then do my people say, 'At last we are
    free from God!
We don't need him anymore!'
32 Does a young woman forget her jewelry,
  or a bride her wedding dress?
Yet for years on end
  my people have forgotten me.

33 "How you plot and scheme to win
    your lovers.
Even an experienced prostitute could
    learn from you!
34 Your clothing is stained with the blood of
    the innocent and the poor,
though you didn't catch them breaking
    into your houses!
35 And yet you say,
  'I have done nothing wrong.
  Surely God isn't angry with me!'
But now I will punish you severely
  because you claim you have not sinned.
36 First here, then there—
  you flit from one ally to another asking
    for help.
But your new friends in Egypt will let
    you down,
just as Assyria did before.
37 In despair, you will be led into exile
  with your hands on your heads,
for the Lord has rejected the nations
    you trust.
They will not help you at all.

3 1 "If a man divorces a woman
    and she goes and marries someone else,
he will not take her back again,
  for that would surely corrupt the land.
But you have prostituted yourself with
    many lovers,
so why are you trying to come back
    to me?"
says the Lord.
2 "Look at the shrines on every hilltop.
Is there any place you have not been
    defiled
by your adultery with other gods?
You sit like a prostitute beside the road
    waiting for a customer.
You sit alone like a nomad in the desert.
You have polluted the land with your
    prostitution
and your wickedness.
3 That's why even the spring rains have failed.
For you are a brazen prostitute and
    completely shameless.

4 Yet you say to me,
  'Father, you have been my guide since
    my youth.
5 Surely you won't be angry forever!
  Surely you can forget about it!'
So you talk,
  but you keep on doing all the evil
    you can."

JUDAH FOLLOWS ISRAEL'S EXAMPLE

6 During the reign of King Josiah, the Lord said to me, "Have you seen what fickle Israel has done? Like a wife who commits adultery, Israel has worshiped other gods on every hill and under every green tree. 7 I thought, 'After she has done all this, she will return to me.' But she did not return, and her faithless sister Judah saw this. 8 She saw* that I divorced faithless Israel because of her adultery. But that treacherous sister Judah had no fear, and now she, too, has left me and given herself to prostitution. 9 Israel treated it all so lightly—she thought nothing of committing adultery by worshiping idols made of wood and stone. So now the land has been polluted. 10 But despite all this, her faithless sister Judah has never sincerely returned to me. She has only pretended to be sorry. I, the Lord, have spoken!"

HOPE FOR WAYWARD ISRAEL

11 Then the Lord said to me, "Even faithless Israel is less guilty than treacherous Judah! 12 Therefore, go and give this message to Israel.* This is what the Lord says:

"O Israel, my faithless people,
  come home to me again,
for I am merciful.
  I will not be angry with you forever.
13 Only acknowledge your guilt.
  Admit that you rebelled against the Lord
    your God
and committed adultery against him
  by worshiping idols under every
    green tree.
Confess that you refused to listen to
    my voice.
I, the Lord, have spoken!

14 "Return home, you wayward children,"
  says the Lord,
  "for I am your master.
I will bring you back to the land of Israel*—
  one from this town and two from
    that family—
from wherever you are scattered.
15 And I will give you shepherds after my
    own heart,
who will guide you with knowledge and
    understanding.

3:8 As in Dead Sea Scrolls, one Greek manuscript, and Syriac version; Masoretic Text reads *I saw*.   3:12 Hebrew *toward the north*.   3:14 Hebrew *to Zion*.

¹⁶ "And when your land is once more filled with people," says the LORD, "you will no longer wish for 'the good old days' when you possessed the Ark of the LORD's Covenant. You will not miss those days or even remember them, and there will be no need to rebuild the Ark. ¹⁷ In that day Jerusalem will be known as 'The Throne of the LORD.' All nations will come there to honor the LORD. They will no longer stubbornly follow their own evil desires. ¹⁸ In those days the people of Judah and Israel will return together from exile in the north. They will return to the land I gave your ancestors as an inheritance forever.

¹⁹ "I thought to myself,
  'I would love to treat you as
    my own children!'
I wanted nothing more than to give you
  this beautiful land—
  the finest possession in the world.
I looked forward to your calling me 'Father,'
  and I wanted you never to turn from me.
²⁰ But you have been unfaithful to me, you
  people of Israel!
You have been like a faithless wife who
  leaves her husband.
  I, the LORD, have spoken."

²¹ Voices are heard high on the windswept
  mountains,
  the weeping and pleading of Israel's people.
For they have chosen crooked paths
  and have forgotten the LORD their God.

²² "My wayward children," says the LORD,
  "come back to me, and I will heal your
    wayward hearts."

"Yes, we're coming," the people reply,
  "for you are the LORD our God.
²³ Our worship of idols on the hills
  and our religious orgies on the mountains
  are a delusion.
Only in the LORD our God
  will Israel ever find salvation.
²⁴ From childhood we have watched
  as everything our ancestors worked for—
their flocks and herds, their sons and
  daughters—
  was squandered on a delusion.
²⁵ Let us now lie down in shame
  and cover ourselves with dishonor,
for we and our ancestors have sinned
  against the LORD our God.
From our childhood to this day
  we have never obeyed him."

4 ¹ "O Israel," says the LORD,
  "if you wanted to return to me,
    you could.
You could throw away your detestable idols
  and stray away no more.

² Then when you swear by my name, saying,
  'As surely as the LORD lives,'
you could do so
  with truth, justice, and righteousness.
Then you would be a blessing to the nations
  of the world,
  and all people would come and praise
    my name."

COMING JUDGMENT AGAINST JUDAH

³ This is what the LORD says to the people of Judah and Jerusalem:

"Plow up the hard ground of your hearts!
  Do not waste your good seed
    among thorns.
⁴ O people of Judah and Jerusalem,
  surrender your pride and power.
Change your hearts before the LORD,*
  or my anger will burn like an
    unquenchable fire
  because of all your sins.

⁵ "Shout to Judah, and broadcast to
  Jerusalem!
Tell them to sound the alarm
  throughout the land:
'Run for your lives!
  Flee to the fortified cities!'
⁶ Raise a signal flag as a warning
  for Jerusalem*:
  'Flee now! Do not delay!'
For I am bringing terrible destruction
  upon you
  from the north."

⁷ A lion stalks from its den,
  a destroyer of nations.
It has left its lair and is headed your way.
  It's going to devastate your land!
Your towns will lie in ruins,
  with no one living in them anymore.
⁸ So put on clothes of mourning
  and weep with broken hearts,
for the fierce anger of the LORD
  is still upon us.

⁹ "In that day," says the LORD,
  "the king and the officials will tremble
    in fear.
The priests will be struck with horror,
  and the prophets will be appalled."

¹⁰ Then I said, "O Sovereign LORD,
  the people have been deceived by what
    you said,
for you promised peace for Jerusalem.
  But the sword is held at their throats!"

4:4 Hebrew *Circumcise yourselves to the LORD, and take away the foreskins of your heart.* 4:6 Hebrew *Zion.*

¹¹ The time is coming when the LORD will say
to the people of Jerusalem,
"My dear people, a burning wind is blowing
in from the desert,
and it's not a gentle breeze useful for
winnowing grain.
¹² It is a roaring blast sent by me!
Now I will pronounce your destruction!"

¹³ Our enemy rushes down on us like
storm clouds!
His chariots are like whirlwinds.
His horses are swifter than eagles.
How terrible it will be, for we are doomed!
¹⁴ O Jerusalem, cleanse your heart
that you may be saved.
How long will you harbor
your evil thoughts?
¹⁵ Your destruction has been announced
from Dan and the hill country of Ephraim.

¹⁶ "Warn the surrounding nations
and announce this to Jerusalem:
The enemy is coming from a distant land,
raising a battle cry against the towns
of Judah.
¹⁷ They surround Jerusalem like watchmen
around a field,
for my people have rebelled against me,"
says the LORD.
¹⁸ "Your own actions have brought this
upon you.
This punishment is bitter, piercing you to
the heart!"

JEREMIAH WEEPS FOR HIS PEOPLE

¹⁹ My heart, my heart—I writhe in pain!
My heart pounds within me!
I cannot be still.
For I have heard the blast of enemy trumpets
and the roar of their battle cries.
²⁰ Waves of destruction roll over the land,
until it lies in complete desolation.
Suddenly my tents are destroyed;
in a moment my shelters are crushed.
²¹ How long must I see the battle flags
and hear the trumpets of war?

²² "My people are foolish
and do not know me," says the LORD.
"They are stupid children
who have no understanding.
They are clever enough at doing wrong,
but they have no idea how to do right!"

JEREMIAH'S VISION OF COMING DISASTER

²³ I looked at the earth, and it was empty and
formless.
I looked at the heavens,
and there was no light.
²⁴ I looked at the mountains and hills,
and they trembled and shook.

²⁵ I looked, and all the people were gone.
All the birds of the sky had flown away.
²⁶ I looked, and the fertile fields had become
a wilderness.
The towns lay in ruins,
crushed by the LORD's fierce anger.

²⁷ This is what the LORD says:
"The whole land will be ruined,
but I will not destroy it completely.
²⁸ The earth will mourn
and the heavens will be draped in black
because of my decree against my people.
I have made up my mind and will not
change it."

²⁹ At the noise of charioteers and archers,
the people flee in terror.
They hide in the bushes
and run for the mountains.
All the towns have been abandoned—
not a person remains!
³⁰ What are you doing,
you who have been plundered?
Why do you dress up in beautiful clothing
and put on gold jewelry?
Why do you brighten your eyes
with mascara?
Your primping will do you no good!
The allies who were your lovers
despise you and seek to kill you.

³¹ I hear a cry, like that of a woman in labor,
the groans of a woman giving birth to
her first child.
It is beautiful Jerusalem*
gasping for breath and crying out,
"Help! I'm being murdered!"

THE SINS OF JUDAH

5 ¹ "Run up and down every street in
Jerusalem," says the LORD.
"Look high and low;
search throughout the city!
If you can find even one just and
honest person,
I will not destroy the city.
² But even when they are under oath,
saying, 'As surely as the LORD lives,'
they are still telling lies!"

³ LORD, you are searching for honesty.
You struck your people,
but they paid no attention.
You crushed them,
but they refused to be corrected.
They are determined,
with faces set like stone;
they have refused to repent.

4:31 Hebrew *the daughter of Zion.*

⁴ Then I said, "But what can we expect
   from the poor?
   They are ignorant.
They don't know the ways of the LORD.
   They don't understand God's laws.
⁵ So I will go and speak to their leaders.
   Surely they know the ways of the LORD
   and understand God's laws."
But the leaders, too, as one man,
   had thrown off God's yoke
   and broken his chains.
⁶ So now a lion from the forest will
   attack them;
   a wolf from the desert will pounce
   on them.
A leopard will lurk near their towns,
   tearing apart any who dare to venture out.
For their rebellion is great,
   and their sins are many.

⁷ "How can I pardon you?
   For even your children have turned
   from me.
They have sworn by gods that are not gods
   at all!
I fed my people until they were full.
But they thanked me by committing
   adultery
   and lining up at the brothels.
⁸ They are well-fed, lusty stallions,
   each neighing for his neighbor's wife.
⁹ Should I not punish them for this?"
      says the LORD.
   "Should I not avenge myself against
   such a nation?

¹⁰ "Go down the rows of the vineyards and
   destroy the grapevines,
   leaving a scattered few alive.
Strip the branches from the vines,
   for these people do not belong to the LORD.
¹¹ The people of Israel and Judah
   are full of treachery against me,"
      says the LORD.
¹² "They have lied about the LORD
   and said, 'He won't bother us!
No disasters will come upon us.
   There will be no war or famine.
¹³ God's prophets are all windbags
   who don't really speak for him.
   Let their predictions of disaster fall on
   themselves!'"

¹⁴ Therefore, this is what the LORD God of Heaven's
Armies says:

"Because the people are talking like this,
   my messages will flame out of your mouth
   and burn the people like kindling wood.
¹⁵ O Israel, I will bring a distant nation
   against you,"
      says the LORD.

"It is a mighty nation,
   an ancient nation,
a people whose language you do not know,
   whose speech you cannot understand.
¹⁶ Their weapons are deadly;
   their warriors are mighty.
¹⁷ They will devour the food of your harvest;
   they will devour your sons and daughters.
They will devour your flocks and herds;
   they will devour your grapes and figs.
And they will destroy your fortified towns,
   which you think are so safe.

¹⁸ "Yet even in those days I will not blot you
out completely," says the LORD. ¹⁹ "And when
your people ask, 'Why did the LORD our God do
all this to us?' you must reply, 'You rejected him
and gave yourselves to foreign gods in your own
land. Now you will serve foreigners in a land that
is not your own.'

A WARNING FOR GOD'S PEOPLE

²⁰ "Make this announcement to Israel,*
   and say this to Judah:
²¹ Listen, you foolish and senseless people,
   with eyes that do not see
   and ears that do not hear.
²² Have you no respect for me?
   Why don't you tremble in my presence?
I, the LORD, define the ocean's sandy
   shoreline
   as an everlasting boundary that the
   waters cannot cross.
The waves may toss and roar,
   but they can never pass the boundaries
   I set.
²³ But my people have stubborn and
   rebellious hearts.
   They have turned away and
   abandoned me.
²⁴ They do not say from the heart,
   'Let us live in awe of the LORD our God,
for he gives us rain each spring and fall,
   assuring us of a harvest when the time
   is right.'
²⁵ Your wickedness has deprived you of these
   wonderful blessings.
   Your sin has robbed you of all these good
   things.

²⁶ "Among my people are wicked men
   who lie in wait for victims like a hunter
   hiding in a blind.
They continually set traps
   to catch people.
²⁷ Like a cage filled with birds,
   their homes are filled with evil plots.
   And now they are great and rich.

5:20 Hebrew *to the house of Jacob.* The names "Jacob" and "Israel"
are often interchanged throughout the Old Testament, referring
sometimes to the individual patriarch and sometimes to the
nation.

28 They are fat and sleek,
  and there is no limit to their wicked deeds.
They refuse to provide justice to orphans
  and deny the rights of the poor.
29 Should I not punish them for this?"
     says the LORD.
  "Should I not avenge myself against
    such a nation?
30 A horrible and shocking thing
  has happened in this land—
31 the prophets give false prophecies,
  and the priests rule with an iron hand.
Worse yet, my people like it that way!
But what will you do when
  the end comes?

JERUSALEM'S LAST WARNING

6 ¹ "Run for your lives,
     you people of Benjamin!
Get out of Jerusalem!
Sound the alarm in Tekoa!
Send up a signal at Beth-hakkerem!
A powerful army is coming from the north,
  coming with disaster and destruction.
² O Jerusalem,* you are my beautiful and
     delicate daughter—
  but I will destroy you!
³ Enemies will surround you, like shepherds
     camped around the city.
  Each chooses a place for his troops
     to devour.
⁴ They shout, 'Prepare for battle!
  Attack at noon!'
'No, it's too late; the day is fading,
  and the evening shadows are falling.'
⁵ 'Well then, let's attack at night
  and destroy her palaces!'"
⁶ This is what the LORD of
     Heaven's Armies says:
"Cut down the trees for battering rams.
  Build siege ramps against the walls of
     Jerusalem.
This is the city to be punished,
  for she is wicked through and through.
⁷ She spouts evil like a fountain.
  Her streets echo with the sounds of
     violence and destruction.
  I always see her sickness and sores.
⁸ Listen to this warning, Jerusalem,
  or I will turn from you in disgust.
Listen, or I will turn you into a heap
  of ruins,
  a land where no one lives."

⁹ This is what the LORD of
     Heaven's Armies says:
"Even the few who remain in Israel
  will be picked over again,
as when a harvester checks each vine
  a second time
  to pick the grapes that were missed."

JUDAH'S CONSTANT REBELLION

10 To whom can I give warning?
  Who will listen when I speak?
Their ears are closed,
  and they cannot hear.
They scorn the word of the LORD.
  They don't want to listen at all.
11 So now I am filled with the LORD's fury.
  Yes, I am tired of holding it in!

"I will pour out my fury on children
     playing in the streets
  and on gatherings of young men,
on husbands and wives
  and on those who are old and gray.
12 Their homes will be turned over to
     their enemies,
  as will their fields and their wives.
For I will raise my powerful fist
  against the people of this land,"
  says the LORD.
13 "From the least to the greatest,
  their lives are ruled by greed.
From prophets to priests,
  they are all frauds.
14 They offer superficial treatments
  for my people's mortal wound.
They give assurances of peace
  when there is no peace.
15 Are they ashamed of their disgusting
     actions?
  Not at all—they don't even know
     how to blush!
Therefore, they will lie among
     the slaughtered.
They will be brought down when
  I punish them,"
  says the LORD.

JUDAH REJECTS THE LORD'S WAY

16 This is what the LORD says:
"Stop at the crossroads and look around.
  Ask for the old, godly way, and walk in it.
Travel its path, and you will find rest for
  your souls.
  But you reply, 'No, that's not the road we
     want!'
17 I posted watchmen over you who said,
  'Listen for the sound of the alarm.'
But you replied,
  'No! We won't pay attention!'

18 "Therefore, listen to this,
  all you nations.
Take note of my people's situation.
19 Listen, all the earth!
  I will bring disaster on my people.
It is the fruit of their own schemes,
  because they refuse to listen to me.
  They have rejected my word.

6:2 Hebrew *Daughter of Zion*.

20 There's no use offering me sweet
frankincense from Sheba.
Keep your fragrant calamus imported
from distant lands!
I will not accept your burnt offerings.
Your sacrifices have no pleasing aroma
for me."

21 Therefore, this is what the LORD says:
"I will put obstacles in my people's path.
Fathers and sons will both fall over them.
Neighbors and friends will die together."

AN INVASION FROM THE NORTH

22 This is what the LORD says:
"Look! A great army coming from the north!
A great nation is rising against you from
far-off lands.
23 They are armed with bows and spears.
They are cruel and show no mercy.
They sound like a roaring sea
as they ride forward on horses.
They are coming in battle formation,
planning to destroy you,
beautiful Jerusalem.*"

24 We have heard reports about the enemy,
and we wring our hands in fright.
Pangs of anguish have gripped us,
like those of a woman in labor.
25 Don't go out to the fields!
Don't travel on the roads!
The enemy's sword is everywhere
and terrorizes us at every turn!
26 Oh, my people, dress yourselves in burlap
and sit among the ashes.
Mourn and weep bitterly,
as for the loss of an only son.
For suddenly the destroying armies will
be upon you!

27 "Jeremiah, I have made you a tester
of metals,*
that you may determine the quality of
my people.
28 They are the worst kind of rebel,
full of slander.
They are as hard as bronze and iron,
and they lead others into corruption.
29 The bellows fiercely fan the flames
to burn out the corruption.
But it does not purify them,
for the wickedness remains.
30 I will label them 'Rejected Silver,'
for I, the LORD, am discarding them."

JEREMIAH SPEAKS AT THE TEMPLE

7 The LORD gave another message to Jeremiah.
He said, 2 "Go to the entrance of the LORD's
Temple, and give this message to the people:
'O Judah, listen to this message from the LORD!
Listen to it, all of you who worship here! 3 This
is what the LORD of Heaven's Armies, the God
of Israel, says:

"'Even now, if you quit your evil ways, I will
let you stay in your own land. 4 But don't be
fooled by those who promise you safety simply
because the LORD's Temple is here. They chant,
"The LORD's Temple is here! The LORD's Temple is
here!" 5 But I will be merciful only if you stop your
evil thoughts and deeds and start treating each
other with justice; 6 only if you stop exploiting
foreigners, orphans, and widows; only if you stop
your murdering; and only if you stop harming
yourselves by worshiping idols. 7 Then I will let
you stay in this land that I gave to your ancestors
to keep forever.

8 "'Don't be fooled into thinking that you will
never suffer because the Temple is here. It's a
lie! 9 Do you really think you can steal, murder,
commit adultery, lie, and burn incense to Baal
and all those other new gods of yours, 10 and then
come here and stand before me in my Temple
and chant, "We are safe!"—only to go right back
to all those evils again? 11 Don't you yourselves
admit that this Temple, which bears my name,
has become a den of thieves? Surely I see all the
evil going on there. I, the LORD, have spoken!

12 "'Go now to the place at Shiloh where I once
put the Tabernacle that bore my name. See what
I did there because of all the wickedness of my
people, the Israelites. 13 While you were doing
these wicked things, says the LORD, I spoke to
you about it repeatedly, but you would not listen.
I called out to you, but you refused to answer. 14 So
just as I destroyed Shiloh, I will now destroy this
Temple that bears my name, this Temple that you
trust in for help, this place that I gave to you and
your ancestors. 15 And I will send you out of my
sight into exile, just as I did your relatives, the
people of Israel.*'

JUDAH'S PERSISTENT IDOLATRY

16 "Pray no more for these people, Jeremiah. Do
not weep or pray for them, and don't beg me to
help them, for I will not listen to you. 17 Don't you
see what they are doing throughout the towns of
Judah and in the streets of Jerusalem? 18 No wonder I am so angry! Watch how the children gather
wood and the fathers build sacrificial fires. See
how the women knead dough and make cakes to
offer to the Queen of Heaven. And they pour out
liquid offerings to their other idol gods! 19 Am I
the one they are hurting?" asks the LORD. "Most
of all, they hurt themselves, to their own shame."

20 So this is what the Sovereign LORD says: "I
will pour out my terrible fury on this place. Its
people, animals, trees, and crops will be consumed by the unquenchable fire of my anger."

21 This is what the LORD of Heaven's Armies,
the God of Israel, says: "Take your burnt offerings

6:23 Hebrew *daughter of Zion.*   6:27 As in Greek version; Hebrew
reads *a tester of my people a fortress.*   7:15 Hebrew *of Ephraim,*
referring to the northern kingdom of Israel.

and your other sacrifices and eat them yourselves! ²² When I led your ancestors out of Egypt, it was not burnt offerings and sacrifices I wanted from them. ²³ This is what I told them: 'Obey me, and I will be your God, and you will be my people. Do everything as I say, and all will be well!'

²⁴ "But my people would not listen to me. They kept doing whatever they wanted, following the stubborn desires of their evil hearts. They went backward instead of forward. ²⁵ From the day your ancestors left Egypt until now, I have continued to send my servants, the prophets—day in and day out. ²⁶ But my people have not listened to me or even tried to hear. They have been stubborn and sinful—even worse than their ancestors.

²⁷ "Tell them all this, but do not expect them to listen. Shout out your warnings, but do not expect them to respond. ²⁸ Say to them, 'This is the nation whose people will not obey the LORD their God and who refuse to be taught. Truth has vanished from among them; it is no longer heard on their lips. ²⁹ Shave your head in mourning, and weep alone on the mountains. For the LORD has rejected and forsaken this generation that has provoked his fury.'

THE VALLEY OF SLAUGHTER

³⁰ "The people of Judah have sinned before my very eyes," says the LORD. "They have set up their abominable idols right in the Temple that bears my name, defiling it. ³¹ They have built pagan shrines at Topheth, the garbage dump in the valley of Ben-Hinnom, and there they burn their sons and daughters in the fire. I have never commanded such a horrible deed; it never even crossed my mind to command such a thing! ³² So beware, for the time is coming," says the LORD, "when that garbage dump will no longer be called Topheth or the valley of Ben-Hinnom, but the Valley of Slaughter. They will bury the bodies in Topheth until there is no more room for them. ³³ The bodies of my people will be food for the vultures and wild animals, and no one will be left to scare them away. ³⁴ I will put an end to the happy singing and laughter in the streets of Jerusalem. The joyful voices of bridegrooms and brides will no longer be heard in the towns of Judah. The land will lie in complete desolation.

8 "In that day," says the LORD, "the enemy will break open the graves of the kings and officials of Judah, and the graves of the priests, prophets, and common people of Jerusalem. ² They will spread out their bones on the ground before the sun, moon, and stars—the gods my people have loved, served, and worshiped. Their bones will not be gathered up again or buried but will be scattered on the ground like manure. ³ And the people of this evil nation who survive will wish to die rather than live where I will send them. I, the LORD of Heaven's Armies, have spoken!

DECEPTION BY FALSE PROPHETS

⁴ "Jeremiah, say to the people, 'This is what the LORD says:

"'When people fall down,
    don't they get up again?
When they discover they're on the wrong
    road, don't they turn back?
⁵ Then why do these people stay on their
    self-destructive path?
Why do the people of Jerusalem refuse
    to turn back?
They cling tightly to their lies
    and will not turn around.
⁶ I listen to their conversations
    and don't hear a word of truth.
Is anyone sorry for doing wrong?
    Does anyone say, "What a terrible thing I
    have done"?
No! All are running down the path of sin
    as swiftly as a horse galloping into battle!
⁷ Even the stork that flies across the sky
    knows the time of her migration,
as do the turtledove, the swallow,
    and the crane.*
They all return at the proper time each year.
But not my people!
    They do not know the LORD's laws.

⁸ "'How can you say, "We are wise because we
    have the word of the LORD,"
when your teachers have twisted it by
    writing lies?
⁹ These wise teachers will fall
    into the trap of their own foolishness,
for they have rejected the word of the LORD.
    Are they so wise after all?
¹⁰ I will give their wives to others
    and their farms to strangers.
From the least to the greatest,
    their lives are ruled by greed.
Yes, even my prophets and priests are
    like that.
    They are all frauds.
¹¹ They offer superficial treatments
    for my people's mortal wound.
They give assurances of peace
    when there is no peace.
¹² Are they ashamed of these disgusting actions?
    Not at all—they don't even know how
    to blush!
Therefore, they will lie among the
    slaughtered.
    They will be brought down when I
    punish them,
    says the LORD.
¹³ I will surely consume them.
    There will be no more harvests of figs
    and grapes.
Their fruit trees will all die.

8:7 The identification of some of these birds is uncertain.

Whatever I gave them will soon be gone.
I, the LORD, have spoken!'

14 "Then the people will say,
'Why should we wait here to die?
Come, let's go to the fortified towns and
die there.
For the LORD our God has decreed our
destruction
and has given us a cup of poison to drink
because we sinned against the LORD.
15 We hoped for peace, but no peace came.
We hoped for a time of healing,
but found only terror.'

16 "The snorting of the enemies' warhorses
can be heard
all the way from the land of Dan in the
north!
The neighing of their stallions makes the
whole land tremble.
They are coming to devour the land and
everything in it—
cities and people alike.

17 I will send these enemy troops among you
like poisonous snakes you cannot charm.
They will bite you, and you will die.
I, the LORD, have spoken!"

JEREMIAH WEEPS FOR SINFUL JUDAH

18 My grief is beyond healing;
my heart is broken.
19 Listen to the weeping of my people;
it can be heard all across the land.
"Has the LORD abandoned Jerusalem?*"
the people ask.
"Is her King no longer there?"

"Oh, why have they provoked my anger with
their carved idols
and their worthless foreign gods?"
says the LORD.

20 "The harvest is finished,
and the summer is gone," the people cry,
"yet we are not saved!"

21 I hurt with the hurt of my people.
I mourn and am overcome with grief.
22 Is there no medicine in Gilead?
Is there no physician there?
Why is there no healing
for the wounds of my people?

9 1*If only my head were a pool of water
and my eyes a fountain of tears,
I would weep day and night
for all my people who have been
slaughtered.
2*Oh, that I could go away and forget
my people
and live in a travelers' shack in the desert.

For they are all adulterers—
a pack of treacherous liars.

JUDGMENT FOR DISOBEDIENCE

3 "My people bend their tongues like bows
to shoot out lies.
They refuse to stand up for the truth.
They only go from bad to worse.
They do not know me,"
says the LORD.

4 "Beware of your neighbor!
Don't even trust your brother!
For brother takes advantage of brother,
and friend slanders friend.
5 They all fool and defraud each other;
no one tells the truth.
With practiced tongues they tell lies;
they wear themselves out with all
their sinning.
6 They pile lie upon lie
and utterly refuse to acknowledge me,"
says the LORD.

7 Therefore, this is what the LORD of Heaven's
Armies says:
"See, I will melt them down in a crucible
and test them like metal.
What else can I do with my people?*
8 For their tongues shoot lies like poisoned
arrows.
They speak friendly words to their neighbors
while scheming in their heart to kill them.
9 Should I not punish them for this?" says the
LORD.
"Should I not avenge myself against such
a nation?"

10 I will weep for the mountains
and wail for the wilderness pastures.
For they are desolate and empty of life;
the lowing of cattle is heard no more;
the birds and wild animals have all fled.

11 "I will make Jerusalem into a heap of ruins,"
says the LORD.
"It will be a place haunted by jackals.
The towns of Judah will be ghost towns,
with no one living in them."

12Who is wise enough to understand all this?
Who has been instructed by the LORD and can
explain it to others? Why has the land been so
ruined that no one dares to travel through it?
13The LORD replies, "This has happened
because my people have abandoned my instructions; they have refused to obey what I said.
14Instead, they have stubbornly followed their

8:19 Hebrew Zion?   9:1 Verse 9:1 is numbered 8:23 in Hebrew
text.   9:2 Verses 9:2-26 are numbered 9:1-25 in Hebrew text.
9:7 Hebrew with the daughter of my people? Greek version reads
with the evil daughter of my people?

own desires and worshiped the images of Baal, as their ancestors taught them. ¹⁵ So now, this is what the Lord of Heaven's Armies, the God of Israel, says: Look! I will feed them with bitterness and give them poison to drink. ¹⁶ I will scatter them around the world, in places they and their ancestors never heard of, and even there I will chase them with the sword until I have destroyed them completely."

WEEPING IN JERUSALEM

¹⁷ This is what the Lord of Heaven's
        Armies says:
"Consider all this, and call for the mourners.
    Send for the women who mourn
        at funerals.
¹⁸ Quick! Begin your weeping!
    Let the tears flow from your eyes.
¹⁹ Hear the people of Jerusalem* crying
        in despair,
    'We are ruined! We are completely
        humiliated!
We must leave our land,
    because our homes have been torn down.'"

²⁰ Listen, you women, to the words of the Lord;
    open your ears to what he has to say.
Teach your daughters to wail;
    teach one another how to lament.
²¹ For death has crept in through our windows
    and has entered our mansions.
It has killed off the flower of our youth:
    Children no longer play in the streets,
    and young men no longer gather in
        the squares.

²² This is what the Lord says:
"Bodies will be scattered across the fields
        like clumps of manure,
    like bundles of grain after the harvest.
No one will be left to bury them."

²³ This is what the Lord says:
"Don't let the wise boast in their wisdom,
    or the powerful boast in their power,
    or the rich boast in their riches.
²⁴ But those who wish to boast
        should boast in this alone:
that they truly know me and understand
        that I am the Lord
    who demonstrates unfailing love
    and who brings justice and righteousness
        to the earth,
    and that I delight in these things.
    I, the Lord, have spoken!

²⁵ "A time is coming," says the Lord, "when I will punish all those who are circumcised in body but not in spirit—²⁶ the Egyptians, Edomites, Ammonites, Moabites, the people who live in the desert in remote places,* and yes, even the people of Judah. And like all these pagan nations, the people of Israel also have uncircumcised hearts."

IDOLATRY BRINGS DESTRUCTION

10 Hear the word that the Lord speaks to you, O Israel! ² This is what the Lord says:

"Do not act like the other nations,
    who try to read their future in the stars.
Do not be afraid of their predictions,
    even though other nations are terrified
        by them.
³ Their ways are futile and foolish.
    They cut down a tree, and a craftsman
        carves an idol.
⁴ They decorate it with gold and silver
    and then fasten it securely with hammer
        and nails
    so it won't fall over.
⁵ Their gods are like
    helpless scarecrows in a cucumber field!
They cannot speak,
    and they need to be carried because they
        cannot walk.
Do not be afraid of such gods,
    for they can neither harm you nor do you
        any good."

⁶ Lord, there is no one like you!
    For you are great, and your name is
        full of power.
⁷ Who would not fear you, O King of nations?
    That title belongs to you alone!
Among all the wise people of the earth
    and in all the kingdoms of the world,
    there is no one like you.

⁸ People who worship idols are stupid and
        foolish.
    The things they worship are made of wood!
⁹ They bring beaten sheets of silver from
        Tarshish
    and gold from Uphaz,
and they give these materials to skillful
        craftsmen
    who make their idols.
Then they dress these gods in royal blue and
        purple robes
    made by expert tailors.
¹⁰ But the Lord is the only true God.
    He is the living God and the everlasting
        King!
The whole earth trembles at his anger.
    The nations cannot stand up to his wrath.

¹¹ Say this to those who worship other gods: "Your so-called gods, who did not make the heavens and earth, will vanish from the earth and from under the heavens."*

9:19 Hebrew *Zion.*   9:26 Or *in the desert and clip the corners of their hair.*   10:11 The original text of this verse is in Aramaic.

¹² But the Lord made the earth by his power,
    and he preserves it by his wisdom.
With his own understanding
    he stretched out the heavens.
¹³ When he speaks in the thunder,
    the heavens roar with rain.
He causes the clouds to rise over the earth.
    He sends the lightning with the rain
    and releases the wind from
        his storehouses.
¹⁴ The whole human race is foolish and has
        no knowledge!
    The craftsmen are disgraced by the idols
        they make,
for their carefully shaped works are a fraud.
    These idols have no breath or power.
¹⁵ Idols are worthless; they are ridiculous lies!
    On the day of reckoning they will all
        be destroyed.
¹⁶ But the God of Israel* is no idol!
    He is the Creator of everything that exists,
including Israel, his own special possession.
    The Lord of Heaven's Armies is his name!

THE COMING DESTRUCTION

¹⁷ Pack your bags and prepare to leave;
    the siege is about to begin.
¹⁸ For this is what the Lord says:
    "Suddenly, I will fling out
    all you who live in this land.
I will pour great troubles upon you,
    and at last you will feel my anger."

¹⁹ My wound is severe,
    and my grief is great.
My sickness is incurable,
    but I must bear it.
²⁰ My home is gone,
    and no one is left to help me rebuild it.
My children have been taken away,
    and I will never see them again.
²¹ The shepherds of my people have lost
        their senses.
    They no longer seek wisdom from the
        Lord.
Therefore, they fail completely,
    and their flocks are scattered.
²² Listen! Hear the terrifying roar of
        great armies
    as they roll down from the north.
The towns of Judah will be destroyed
    and become a haunt for jackals.

JEREMIAH'S PRAYER

²³ I know, Lord, that our lives are not our own.
    We are not able to plan our own course.
²⁴ So correct me, Lord, but please be gentle.
    Do not correct me in anger, for I would die.
²⁵ Pour out your wrath on the nations that
        refuse to acknowledge you—
    on the peoples that do not call upon
        your name.

For they have devoured your people Israel*;
    they have devoured and consumed them,
    making the land a desolate wilderness.

JUDAH'S BROKEN COVENANT

11 The Lord gave another message to Jeremiah. He said, ²"Remind the people of Judah and Jerusalem about the terms of my covenant with them. ³Say to them, 'This is what the Lord, the God of Israel, says: Cursed is anyone who does not obey the terms of my covenant! ⁴For I said to your ancestors when I brought them out of the iron-smelting furnace of Egypt, "If you obey me and do whatever I command you, then you will be my people, and I will be your God." ⁵I said this so I could keep my promise to your ancestors to give you a land flowing with milk and honey—the land you live in today.'"

Then I replied, "Amen, Lord! May it be so."

⁶Then the Lord said, "Broadcast this message in the streets of Jerusalem. Go from town to town throughout the land and say, 'Remember the ancient covenant, and do everything it requires. ⁷For I solemnly warned your ancestors when I brought them out of Egypt, "Obey me!" I have repeated this warning over and over to this day, ⁸but your ancestors did not listen or even pay attention. Instead, they stubbornly followed their own evil desires. And because they refused to obey, I brought upon them all the curses described in this covenant.'"

⁹Again the Lord spoke to me and said, "I have discovered a conspiracy against me among the people of Judah and Jerusalem. ¹⁰They have returned to the sins of their ancestors. They have refused to listen to me and are worshiping other gods. Israel and Judah have both broken the covenant I made with their ancestors. ¹¹Therefore, this is what the Lord says: I am going to bring calamity upon them, and they will not escape. Though they beg for mercy, I will not listen to their cries. ¹²Then the people of Judah and Jerusalem will pray to their idols and burn incense before them. But the idols will not save them when disaster strikes! ¹³Look now, people of Judah; you have as many gods as you have towns. You have as many altars of shame—altars for burning incense to your god Baal—as there are streets in Jerusalem.

¹⁴"Pray no more for these people, Jeremiah. Do not weep or pray for them, for I will not listen to them when they cry out to me in distress.

¹⁵ "What right do my beloved people have to
        come to my Temple,
    when they have done so many
        immoral things?

10:16 Hebrew *the Portion of Jacob.* See note on 5:20.
10:25 Hebrew *devoured Jacob.* See note on 5:20.

Can their vows and sacrifices prevent their
   destruction?
They actually rejoice in doing evil!
[16] I, the LORD, once called them a thriving
   olive tree,
beautiful to see and full of good fruit.
But now I have sent the fury of
   their enemies
to burn them with fire,
   leaving them charred and broken.

[17] "I, the LORD of Heaven's Armies, who planted
this olive tree, have ordered it destroyed. For
the people of Israel and Judah have done evil,
arousing my anger by burning incense to Baal."

A PLOT AGAINST JEREMIAH

[18] Then the LORD told me about the plots my enemies were making against me. [19] I was like a lamb
being led to the slaughter. I had no idea that they
were planning to kill me! "Let's destroy this man
and all his words," they said. "Let's cut him down,
so his name will be forgotten forever."

[20] O LORD of Heaven's Armies,
   you make righteous judgments,
   and you examine the deepest thoughts
      and secrets.
Let me see your vengeance against them,
   for I have committed my cause to you.

[21] This is what the LORD says about the men of
Anathoth who wanted me dead. They had said,
"We will kill you if you do not stop prophesying
in the LORD's name." [22] So this is what the LORD of
Heaven's Armies says about them: "I will punish
them! Their young men will die in battle, and
their boys and girls will starve to death. [23] Not
one of these plotters from Anathoth will survive,
for I will bring disaster upon them when their
time of punishment comes."

JEREMIAH QUESTIONS THE LORD'S JUSTICE

12 [1] LORD, you always give me justice
      when I bring a case before you.
So let me bring you this complaint:
Why are the wicked so prosperous?
   Why are evil people so happy?
[2] You have planted them,
   and they have taken root and prospered.
Your name is on their lips,
   but you are far from their hearts.
[3] But as for me, LORD, you know my heart.
   You see me and test my thoughts.
Drag these people away like sheep to be
   butchered!
Set them aside to be slaughtered!

[4] How long must this land mourn?
   Even the grass in the fields has withered.
The wild animals and birds have disappeared
   because of the evil in the land.

For the people have said,
   "The LORD doesn't see what's ahead
      for us!"

THE LORD'S REPLY TO JEREMIAH

[5] "If racing against mere men makes
      you tired,
   how will you race against horses?
If you stumble and fall on open ground,
   what will you do in the thickets near
      the Jordan?
[6] Even your brothers, members of your own
      family,
   have turned against you.
They plot and raise complaints against you.
Do not trust them,
   no matter how pleasantly they speak.

[7] "I have abandoned my people, my special
      possession.
   I have surrendered my dearest ones to
      their enemies.
[8] My chosen people have roared at me like
      a lion of the forest,
   so I have treated them with contempt.
[9] My chosen people act like speckled
      vultures,*
   but they themselves are surrounded
      by vultures.
Bring on the wild animals to pick their
      corpses clean!

[10] "Many rulers have ravaged my vineyard,
      trampling down the vines
   and turning all its beauty into
      a barren wilderness.
[11] They have made it an empty wasteland;
   I hear its mournful cry.
The whole land is desolate,
   and no one even cares.
[12] On all the bare hilltops,
   destroying armies can be seen.
The sword of the LORD devours people
   from one end of the nation to the other.
No one will escape!
[13] My people have planted wheat
   but are harvesting thorns.
They have worn themselves out,
   but it has done them no good.
They will harvest a crop of shame
   because of the fierce anger of the LORD."

A MESSAGE FOR ISRAEL'S NEIGHBORS

[14] Now this is what the LORD says: "I will uproot
from their land all the evil nations reaching out
for the possession I gave my people Israel. And I
will uproot Judah from among them. [15] But afterward I will return and have compassion on all of
them. I will bring them home to their own lands
again, each nation to its own possession. [16] And if

12:9 Or *speckled hyenas.*

these nations truly learn the ways of my people, and if they learn to swear by my name, saying, 'As surely as the LORD lives' (just as they taught my people to swear by the name of Baal), then they will be given a place among my people. ¹⁷ But any nation who refuses to obey me will be uprooted and destroyed. I, the LORD, have spoken!"

JEREMIAH'S LINEN LOINCLOTH

13 This is what the LORD said to me: "Go and buy a linen loincloth and put it on, but do not wash it." ² So I bought the loincloth as the LORD directed me, and I put it on.

³ Then the LORD gave me another message: ⁴ "Take the linen loincloth you are wearing, and go to the Euphrates River.* Hide it there in a hole in the rocks." ⁵ So I went and hid it by the Euphrates as the LORD had instructed me.

⁶ A long time afterward the LORD said to me, "Go back to the Euphrates and get the loincloth I told you to hide there." ⁷ So I went to the Euphrates and dug it out of the hole where I had hidden it. But now it was rotting and falling apart. The loincloth was good for nothing.

⁸ Then I received this message from the LORD: ⁹ "This is what the LORD says: This shows how I will rot away the pride of Judah and Jerusalem. ¹⁰ These wicked people refuse to listen to me. They stubbornly follow their own desires and worship other gods. Therefore, they will become like this loincloth—good for nothing! ¹¹ As a loincloth clings to a man's waist, so I created Judah and Israel to cling to me, says the LORD. They were to be my people, my pride, my glory—an honor to my name. But they would not listen to me.

¹² "So tell them, 'This is what the LORD, the God of Israel, says: May all your jars be filled with wine.' And they will reply, 'Of course! Jars are made to be filled with wine!'

¹³ "Then tell them, 'No, this is what the LORD means: I will fill everyone in this land with drunkenness—from the king sitting on David's throne to the priests and the prophets, right down to the common people of Jerusalem. ¹⁴ I will smash them against each other, even parents against children, says the LORD. I will not let my pity or mercy or compassion keep me from destroying them.'"

A WARNING AGAINST PRIDE

¹⁵ Listen and pay attention!
  Do not be arrogant,
    for the LORD has spoken.
¹⁶ Give glory to the LORD your God
    before it is too late.
  Acknowledge him before he brings darkness
    upon you,
  causing you to stumble and fall on the
    darkening mountains.
  For then, when you look for light,
    you will find only terrible darkness
    and gloom.

¹⁷ And if you still refuse to listen,
    I will weep alone because of your pride.
  My eyes will overflow with tears,
    because the LORD's flock will be led away
    into exile.

¹⁸ Say to the king and his mother,
  "Come down from your thrones
    and sit in the dust,
  for your glorious crowns
    will soon be snatched from your heads."
¹⁹ The towns of the Negev will close their gates,
    and no one will be able to open them.
  The people of Judah will be taken away
    as captives.
  All will be carried into exile.

²⁰ Open up your eyes and see
    the armies marching down from the north!
  Where is your flock—
    your beautiful flock—
    that he gave you to care for?
²¹ What will you say when the LORD takes the
      allies you have cultivated
    and appoints them as your rulers?
  Pangs of anguish will grip you,
    like those of a woman in labor!
²² You may ask yourself,
  "Why is all this happening to me?"
    It is because of your many sins!
  That is why you have been stripped
    and raped by invading armies.
²³ Can an Ethiopian* change the color of
      his skin?
  Can a leopard take away its spots?
  Neither can you start doing good,
    for you have always done evil.

²⁴ "I will scatter you like chaff
    that is blown away by the desert winds.
²⁵ This is your allotment,
    the portion I have assigned to you,"
      says the LORD,
  "for you have forgotten me,
    putting your trust in false gods.
²⁶ I myself will strip you
    and expose you to shame.
²⁷ I have seen your adultery and lust,
    and your disgusting idol worship out in
      the fields and on the hills.
  What sorrow awaits you, Jerusalem!
    How long before you are pure?"

JUDAH'S TERRIBLE DROUGHT

14 This message came to Jeremiah from the LORD, explaining why he was holding back the rain:

² "Judah wilts;
    commerce at the city gates grinds to a halt.

13:4 Hebrew *Perath;* also in 13:5, 6, 7. 13:23 Hebrew *a Cushite.*

All the people sit on the ground
in mourning,
and a great cry rises from Jerusalem.
3 The nobles send servants to get water,
but all the wells are dry.
The servants return with empty pitchers,
confused and desperate,
covering their heads in grief.
4 The ground is parched
and cracked for lack of rain.
The farmers are deeply troubled;
they, too, cover their heads.
5 Even the doe abandons her newborn fawn
because there is no grass in the field.
6 The wild donkeys stand on the bare hills
panting like thirsty jackals.
They strain their eyes looking for grass,
but there is none to be found."

7 The people say, "Our wickedness has caught
up with us, LORD,
but help us for the sake of your own
reputation.
We have turned away from you
and sinned against you again and again.
8 O Hope of Israel, our Savior in times of
trouble,
why are you like a stranger to us?
Why are you like a traveler passing through
the land,
stopping only for the night?
9 Are you also confused?
Is our champion helpless to save us?
You are right here among us, LORD.
We are known as your people.
Please don't abandon us now!"

10 So this is what the LORD says to his people:
"You love to wander far from me
and do not restrain yourselves.
Therefore, I will no longer accept you as
my people.
Now I will remember all your wickedness
and will punish you for your sins."

THE LORD FORBIDS JEREMIAH TO INTERCEDE

11 Then the LORD said to me, "Do not pray for these people anymore. 12 When they fast, I will pay no attention. When they present their burnt offerings and grain offerings to me, I will not accept them. Instead, I will devour them with war, famine, and disease."

13 Then I said, "O Sovereign LORD, their prophets are telling them, 'All is well—no war or famine will come. The LORD will surely send you peace.'"

14 Then the LORD said, "These prophets are telling lies in my name. I did not send them or tell them to speak. I did not give them any messages. They prophesy of visions and revelations they have never seen or heard. They speak foolishness

made up in their own lying hearts. 15 Therefore, this is what the LORD says: I will punish these lying prophets, for they have spoken in my name even though I never sent them. They say that no war or famine will come, but they themselves will die by war and famine! 16 As for the people to whom they prophesy—their bodies will be thrown out into the streets of Jerusalem, victims of famine and war. There will be no one left to bury them. Husbands, wives, sons, and daughters—all will be gone. For I will pour out their own wickedness on them. 17 Now, Jeremiah, say this to them:

"Night and day my eyes overflow with tears.
I cannot stop weeping,
for my virgin daughter—my precious
people—
has been struck down
and lies mortally wounded.
18 If I go out into the fields,
I see the bodies of people slaughtered by
the enemy.
If I walk the city streets,
I see people who have died of starvation.
The prophets and priests continue with
their work,
but they don't know what they're doing."

A PRAYER FOR HEALING

19 LORD, have you completely rejected Judah?
Do you really hate Jerusalem?*
Why have you wounded us past all hope of
healing?
We hoped for peace, but no peace came.
We hoped for a time of healing, but found
only terror.
20 LORD, we confess our wickedness
and that of our ancestors, too.
We all have sinned against you.
21 For the sake of your reputation, LORD, do
not abandon us.
Do not disgrace your own glorious throne.
Please remember us,
and do not break your covenant with us.
22 Can any of the worthless foreign gods send
us rain?
Does it fall from the sky by itself?
No, you are the one, O LORD our God!
Only you can do such things.
So we will wait for you to help us.

JUDAH'S INEVITABLE DOOM

15 Then the LORD said to me, "Even if Moses and Samuel stood before me pleading for these people, I wouldn't help them. Away with them! Get them out of my sight! 2 And if they say to you, 'But where can we go?' tell them, 'This is what the LORD says:

14:19 Hebrew *Zion?*

"'Those who are destined for death, to death;
those who are destined for war, to war;
those who are destined for famine, to famine;
those who are destined for captivity,
to captivity.'

³"I will send four kinds of destroyers against them," says the LORD. "I will send the sword to kill, the dogs to drag away, the vultures to devour, and the wild animals to finish up what is left. ⁴ Because of the wicked things Manasseh son of Hezekiah, king of Judah, did in Jerusalem, I will make my people an object of horror to all the kingdoms of the earth.

⁵ "Who will feel sorry for you, Jerusalem?
Who will weep for you?
Who will even bother to ask how you are?
⁶ You have abandoned me
and turned your back on me,"
says the LORD.
"Therefore, I will raise my fist to destroy you.
I am tired of always giving you
another chance.
⁷ I will winnow you like grain at the gates of
your cities
and take away the children you hold dear.
I will destroy my own people,
because they refuse to change their
evil ways.
⁸ There will be more widows
than the grains of sand on the seashore.
At noontime I will bring a destroyer
against the mothers of young men.
I will cause anguish and terror
to come upon them suddenly.
⁹ The mother of seven grows faint and
gasps for breath;
her sun has gone down while it is still day.
She sits childless now,
disgraced and humiliated.
And I will hand over those who are left
to be killed by the enemy.
I, the LORD, have spoken!"

JEREMIAH'S COMPLAINT

¹⁰ Then I said,

"What sorrow is mine, my mother.
Oh, that I had died at birth!
I am hated everywhere I go.
I am neither a lender who threatens
to foreclose
nor a borrower who refuses to pay—
yet they all curse me."

¹¹ The LORD replied,

"I will take care of you, Jeremiah.
Your enemies will ask you to plead on
their behalf
in times of trouble and distress.

¹² Can a man break a bar of iron from the north,
or a bar of bronze?
¹³ At no cost to them,
I will hand over your wealth and
treasures
as plunder to your enemies,
for sin runs rampant in your land.
¹⁴ I will tell your enemies to take you
as captives to a foreign land.
For my anger blazes like a fire
that will burn forever.*"

¹⁵ Then I said,

"LORD, you know what's happening to me.
Please step in and help me.
Punish my persecutors!
Please give me time; don't let me die young.
It's for your sake that I am suffering.
¹⁶ When I discovered your words,
I devoured them.
They are my joy and my heart's delight,
for I bear your name,
O LORD God of Heaven's Armies.
¹⁷ I never joined the people in their merry feasts.
I sat alone because your hand was on me.
I was filled with indignation at their sins.
¹⁸ Why then does my suffering continue?
Why is my wound so incurable?
Your help seems as uncertain as
a seasonal brook,
like a spring that has gone dry."

¹⁹ This is how the LORD responds:

"If you return to me, I will restore you
so you can continue to serve me.
If you speak good words rather than
worthless ones,
you will be my spokesman.
You must influence them;
do not let them influence you!
²⁰ They will fight against you like
an attacking army,
but I will make you as secure as a fortified
wall of bronze.
They will not conquer you,
for I am with you to protect and rescue you.
I, the LORD, have spoken!
²¹ Yes, I will certainly keep you safe from these
wicked men.
I will rescue you from their cruel hands."

JEREMIAH FORBIDDEN TO MARRY

16 The LORD gave me another message. He said, ²"Do not get married or have children in this place. ³For this is what the LORD says about the children born here in this city and about their mothers and fathers: ⁴They will die

---

15:14 As in some Hebrew manuscripts (see also 17:4); most Hebrew manuscripts read *will burn against you.*

from terrible diseases. No one will mourn for them or bury them, and they will lie scattered on the ground like manure. They will die from war and famine, and their bodies will be food for the vultures and wild animals."

JUDAH'S COMING PUNISHMENT

5 This is what the LORD says: "Do not go to funerals to mourn and show sympathy for these people, for I have removed my protection and peace from them. I have taken away my unfailing love and my mercy. 6 Both the great and the lowly will die in this land. No one will bury them or mourn for them. Their friends will not cut themselves in sorrow or shave their heads in sadness. 7 No one will offer a meal to comfort those who mourn for the dead—not even at the death of a mother or father. No one will send a cup of wine to console them.

8 "And do not go to their feasts and parties. Do not eat and drink with them at all. 9 For this is what the LORD of Heaven's Armies, the God of Israel, says: In your own lifetime, before your very eyes, I will put an end to the happy singing and laughter in this land. The joyful voices of bridegrooms and brides will no longer be heard.

10 "When you tell the people all these things, they will ask, 'Why has the LORD decreed such terrible things against us? What have we done to deserve such treatment? What is our sin against the LORD our God?'

11 "Then you will give them the LORD's reply: 'It is because your ancestors were unfaithful to me. They worshiped other gods and served them. They abandoned me and did not obey my word. 12 And you are even worse than your ancestors! You stubbornly follow your own evil desires and refuse to listen to me. 13 So I will throw you out of this land and send you into a foreign land where you and your ancestors have never been. There you can worship idols day and night—and I will grant you no favors!'

HOPE DESPITE THE DISASTER

14 "But the time is coming," says the LORD, "when people who are taking an oath will no longer say, 'As surely as the LORD lives, who rescued the people of Israel from the land of Egypt.' 15 Instead, they will say, 'As surely as the LORD lives, who brought the people of Israel back to their own land from the land of the north and from all the countries to which he had exiled them.' For I will bring them back to this land that I gave their ancestors.

16 "But now I am sending for many fishermen who will catch them," says the LORD. "I am sending for hunters who will hunt them down in the mountains, hills, and caves. 17 I am watching them closely, and I see every sin. They cannot hope to hide from me. 18 I will double their punishment for all their sins, because they have defiled my land with lifeless images of their detestable gods and have filled my territory with their evil deeds."

JEREMIAH'S PRAYER OF CONFIDENCE

19 LORD, you are my strength and fortress,
my refuge in the day of trouble!
Nations from around the world
will come to you and say,
"Our ancestors left us a foolish heritage,
for they worshiped worthless idols.
20 Can people make their own gods?
These are not real gods at all!"

21 The LORD says,
"Now I will show them my power;
now I will show them my might.
At last they will know and understand
that I am the LORD.

JUDAH'S SIN AND PUNISHMENT

17 1 "The sin of Judah
is inscribed with an iron chisel—
engraved with a diamond point on their
stony hearts
and on the corners of their altars.
2 Even their children go to worship
at their pagan altars and Asherah poles,
beneath every green tree
and on every high hill.
3 So I will hand over my holy mountain—
along with all your wealth and treasures
and your pagan shrines—
as plunder to your enemies,
for sin runs rampant in your land.
4 The wonderful possession I have reserved
for you
will slip from your hands.
I will tell your enemies to take you
as captives to a foreign land.
For my anger blazes like a fire
that will burn forever."

WISDOM FROM THE LORD

5 This is what the LORD says:
"Cursed are those who put their trust in
mere humans,
who rely on human strength
and turn their hearts away from the LORD.
6 They are like stunted shrubs in the desert,
with no hope for the future.
They will live in the barren wilderness,
in an uninhabited salty land.

7 "But blessed are those who trust in the LORD
and have made the LORD their hope and
confidence.
8 They are like trees planted along a riverbank,
with roots that reach deep into the water.
Such trees are not bothered by the heat
or worried by long months of drought.
Their leaves stay green,
and they never stop producing fruit.

9 "The human heart is the most deceitful of
all things,
and desperately wicked.
Who really knows how bad it is?
10 But I, the LORD, search all hearts
and examine secret motives.
I give all people their due rewards,
according to what their actions deserve."

JEREMIAH'S TRUST IN THE LORD

11 Like a partridge that hatches eggs
she has not laid,
so are those who get their wealth by
unjust means.
At midlife they will lose their riches;
in the end, they will become poor
old fools.
12 But we worship at your throne—
eternal, high, and glorious!
13 O LORD, the hope of Israel,
all who turn away from you will
be disgraced.
They will be buried in the dust of the earth,
for they have abandoned the LORD, the
fountain of living water.

14 O LORD, if you heal me, I will be truly healed;
if you save me, I will be truly saved.
My praises are for you alone!
15 People scoff at me and say,
"What is this 'message from the LORD' you
talk about?
Why don't your predictions come true?"
16 LORD, I have not abandoned my job
as a shepherd for your people.
I have not urged you to send disaster.
You have heard everything I've said.
17 LORD, don't terrorize me!
You alone are my hope in the day
of disaster.
18 Bring shame and dismay on all who
persecute me,
but don't let me experience shame
and dismay.
Bring a day of terror on them.
Yes, bring double destruction upon them!

OBSERVING THE SABBATH

19 This is what the LORD said to me: "Go and stand
in the gates of Jerusalem, first in the gate where
the king goes in and out, and then in each of the
other gates. 20 Say to all the people, 'Listen to this
message from the LORD, you kings of Judah and
all you people of Judah and everyone living in
Jerusalem. 21 This is what the LORD says: Listen to
my warning! Stop carrying on your trade at Jerusalem's gates on the Sabbath day. 22 Do not do your
work on the Sabbath, but make it a holy day. I
gave this command to your ancestors, 23 but they
did not listen or obey. They stubbornly refused to
pay attention or accept my discipline.

24 "'But if you obey me, says the LORD, and do
not carry on your trade at the gates or work on the
Sabbath day, and if you keep it holy, 25 then kings
and their officials will go in and out of these gates
forever. There will always be a descendant of David
sitting on the throne here in Jerusalem. Kings and
their officials will always ride in and out among
the people of Judah in chariots and on horses,
and this city will remain forever. 26 And from all
around Jerusalem, from the towns of Judah and
Benjamin, from the western foothills* and the
hill country and the Negev, the people will come
with their burnt offerings and sacrifices. They
will bring their grain offerings, frankincense,
and thanksgiving offerings to the LORD's Temple.

27 "'But if you do not listen to me and refuse
to keep the Sabbath holy, and if on the Sabbath
day you bring loads of merchandise through the
gates of Jerusalem just as on other days, then I
will set fire to these gates. The fire will spread
to the palaces, and no one will be able to put out
the roaring flames.'"

THE POTTER AND THE CLAY

18 The LORD gave another message to Jeremiah. He said, 2 "Go down to the potter's
shop, and I will speak to you there." 3 So I did as
he told me and found the potter working at his
wheel. 4 But the jar he was making did not turn
out as he had hoped, so he crushed it into a lump
of clay again and started over.

5 Then the LORD gave me this message:
6 "O Israel, can I not do to you as this potter has
done to his clay? As the clay is in the potter's
hand, so are you in my hand. 7 If I announce that
a certain nation or kingdom is to be uprooted,
torn down, and destroyed, 8 but then that nation
renounces its evil ways, I will not destroy it as I
had planned. 9 And if I announce that I will plant
and build up a certain nation or kingdom, 10 but
then that nation turns to evil and refuses to obey
me, I will not bless it as I said I would.

11 "Therefore, Jeremiah, go and warn all Judah
and Jerusalem. Say to them, 'This is what the
LORD says: I am planning disaster for you instead
of good. So turn from your evil ways, each of you,
and do what is right.'"

12 But the people replied, "Don't waste your
breath. We will continue to live as we want to,
stubbornly following our own evil desires."

13 So this is what the LORD says:

"Has anyone ever heard of such a thing,
even among the pagan nations?
My virgin daughter Israel
has done something terrible!
14 Does the snow ever disappear from the
mountaintops of Lebanon?
Do the cold streams flowing from those
distant mountains ever run dry?

17:26 Hebrew the Shephelah.

15 But my people are not so reliable, for they
    have deserted me;
   they burn incense to worthless idols.
They have stumbled off the ancient highways
    and walk in muddy paths.
16 Therefore, their land will become desolate,
    a monument to their stupidity.
All who pass by will be astonished
    and will shake their heads in amazement.
17 I will scatter my people before their enemies
    as the east wind scatters dust.
And in all their trouble I will turn my back
    on them
    and refuse to notice their distress."

A PLOT AGAINST JEREMIAH

18 Then the people said, "Come on, let's plot a way
to stop Jeremiah. We have plenty of priests and
wise men and prophets. We don't need him to
teach the word and give us advice and prophecies. Let's spread rumors about him and ignore
what he says."

19 LORD, hear me and help me!
    Listen to what my enemies are saying.
20 Should they repay evil for good?
    They have dug a pit to kill me,
though I pleaded for them
    and tried to protect them from your anger.
21 So let their children starve!
    Let them die by the sword!
Let their wives become childless widows.
    Let their old men die in a plague,
    and let their young men be killed in battle!
22 Let screaming be heard from their homes
    as warriors come suddenly upon them.
For they have dug a pit for me
    and have hidden traps along my path.
23 LORD, you know all about their murderous
    plots against me.
Don't forgive their crimes and blot out
    their sins.
Let them die before you.
    Deal with them in your anger.

JEREMIAH'S SHATTERED JAR

19 This is what the LORD said to me: "Go and
buy a clay jar. Then ask some of the leaders
of the people and of the priests to follow you.
2 Go out through the Gate of Broken Pots to the
garbage dump in the valley of Ben-Hinnom, and
give them this message. 3 Say to them, 'Listen to
this message from the LORD, you kings of Judah
and citizens of Jerusalem! This is what the LORD
of Heaven's Armies, the God of Israel, says: I will
bring a terrible disaster on this place, and the
ears of those who hear about it will ring!

4 "'For Israel has forsaken me and turned this
valley into a place of wickedness. The people
burn incense to foreign gods—idols never before
acknowledged by this generation, by their ancestors, or by the kings of Judah. And they have

filled this place with the blood of innocent children. 5 They have built pagan shrines to Baal, and
there they burn their sons as sacrifices to Baal. I
have never commanded such a horrible deed; it
never even crossed my mind to command such
a thing! 6 So beware, for the time is coming, says
the LORD, when this garbage dump will no longer
be called Topheth or the valley of Ben-Hinnom,
but the Valley of Slaughter.

7 "'For I will upset the careful plans of Judah
and Jerusalem. I will allow the people to be
slaughtered by invading armies, and I will leave
their dead bodies as food for the vultures and
wild animals. 8 I will reduce Jerusalem to ruins,
making it a monument to their stupidity. All who
pass by will be astonished and will gasp at the
destruction they see there. 9 I will see to it that
your enemies lay siege to the city until all the
food is gone. Then those trapped inside will eat
their own sons and daughters and friends. They
will be driven to utter despair.'

10 "As these men watch you, Jeremiah, smash
the jar you brought. 11 Then say to them, 'This is
what the LORD of Heaven's Armies says: As this
jar lies shattered, so I will shatter the people of
Judah and Jerusalem beyond all hope of repair.
They will bury the bodies here in Topheth, the
garbage dump, until there is no more room for
them. 12 This is what I will do to this place and
its people, says the LORD. I will cause this city to
become defiled like Topheth. 13 Yes, all the houses
in Jerusalem, including the palace of Judah's
kings, will become like Topheth—all the houses
where you burned incense on the rooftops to
your star gods, and where liquid offerings were
poured out to your idols.'"

14 Then Jeremiah returned from Topheth, the
garbage dump where he had delivered this message, and he stopped in front of the Temple of the
LORD. He said to the people there, 15 "This is what
the LORD of Heaven's Armies, the God of Israel,
says: 'I will bring disaster upon this city and its
surrounding towns as I promised, because you
have stubbornly refused to listen to me.'"

JEREMIAH AND PASHHUR

20 Now Pashhur son of Immer, the priest in
charge of the Temple of the LORD, heard
what Jeremiah was prophesying. 2 So he arrested
Jeremiah the prophet and had him whipped
and put in stocks at the Benjamin Gate of the
LORD's Temple.

3 The next day, when Pashhur finally released
him, Jeremiah said, "Pashhur, the LORD has
changed your name. From now on you are to be
called 'The Man Who Lives in Terror.'* 4 For this
is what the LORD says: 'I will send terror upon
you and all your friends, and you will watch as
they are slaughtered by the swords of the enemy.

20:3 Hebrew *Magor-missabib*, which means "surrounded by
terror"; also in 20:10.

I will hand the people of Judah over to the king of Babylon. He will take them captive to Babylon or run them through with the sword. ⁵And I will let your enemies plunder Jerusalem. All the famed treasures of the city—the precious jewels and gold and silver of your kings—will be carried off to Babylon. ⁶As for you, Pashhur, you and all your household will go as captives to Babylon. There you will die and be buried, you and all your friends to whom you prophesied that everything would be all right.'"

JEREMIAH'S COMPLAINT

⁷ O LORD, you misled me,
  and I allowed myself to be misled.
  You are stronger than I am,
  and you overpowered me.
  Now I am mocked every day;
  everyone laughs at me.
⁸ When I speak, the words burst out.
  "Violence and destruction!" I shout.
  So these messages from the LORD
  have made me a household joke.
⁹ But if I say I'll never mention the LORD
  or speak in his name,
  his word burns in my heart like a fire.
  It's like a fire in my bones!
  I am worn out trying to hold it in!
  I can't do it!
¹⁰ I have heard the many rumors about me.
  They call me "The Man Who Lives
    in Terror."
  They threaten, "If you say anything,
    we will report it."
  Even my old friends are watching me,
    waiting for a fatal slip.
  "He will trap himself," they say,
    "and then we will get our revenge on him."

¹¹ But the LORD stands beside me like
    a great warrior.
  Before him my persecutors will stumble.
  They cannot defeat me.
  They will fail and be thoroughly humiliated.
  Their dishonor will never be forgotten.
¹² O LORD of Heaven's Armies,
  you test those who are righteous,
  and you examine the deepest thoughts
    and secrets.
  Let me see your vengeance against them,
  for I have committed my cause to you.
¹³ Sing to the LORD!
  Praise the LORD!
  For though I was poor and needy,
  he rescued me from my oppressors.

¹⁴ Yet I curse the day I was born!
  May no one celebrate the day of my birth.
¹⁵ I curse the messenger who told my father,
  "Good news—you have a son!"
¹⁶ Let him be destroyed like the cities of old
  that the LORD overthrew without mercy.

Terrify him all day long with battle shouts,
¹⁷   because he did not kill me at birth.
  Oh, that I had died in my mother's womb,
    that her body had been my grave!
¹⁸ Why was I ever born?
  My entire life has been filled
    with trouble, sorrow, and shame.

NO DELIVERANCE FROM BABYLON

21 The LORD spoke through Jeremiah when King Zedekiah sent Pashhur son of Malkijah and Zephaniah son of Maaseiah, the priest, to speak with him. They begged Jeremiah, ²"Please speak to the LORD for us and ask him to help us. King Nebuchadnezzar* of Babylon is attacking Judah. Perhaps the LORD will be gracious and do a mighty miracle as he has done in the past. Perhaps he will force Nebuchadnezzar to withdraw his armies."

³Jeremiah replied, "Go back to King Zedekiah and tell him, ⁴'This is what the LORD, the God of Israel, says: I will make your weapons useless against the king of Babylon and the Babylonians* who are outside your walls attacking you. In fact, I will bring your enemies right into the heart of this city. ⁵I myself will fight against you with a strong hand and a powerful arm, for I am very angry. You have made me furious! ⁶I will send a terrible plague upon this city, and both people and animals will die. ⁷And after all that, says the LORD, I will hand over King Zedekiah, his staff, and everyone else in the city who survives the disease, war, and famine. I will hand them over to King Nebuchadnezzar of Babylon and to their other enemies. He will slaughter them and show them no mercy, pity, or compassion.'

⁸"Tell all the people, 'This is what the LORD says: Take your choice of life or death! ⁹Everyone who stays in Jerusalem will die from war, famine, or disease, but those who go out and surrender to the Babylonians will live. Their reward will be life! ¹⁰For I have decided to bring disaster and not good upon this city, says the LORD. It will be handed over to the king of Babylon, and he will reduce it to ashes.'

JUDGMENT ON JUDAH'S KINGS

¹¹"Say to the royal family of Judah, 'Listen to this message from the LORD! ¹²This is what the LORD says to the dynasty of David:

"'Give justice each morning to the people
    you judge!
  Help those who have been robbed;
    rescue them from their oppressors.
  Otherwise, my anger will burn like an
    unquenchable fire
  because of all your sins.

21:2 Hebrew *Nebuchadrezzar*, a variant spelling of Nebuchadnezzar; also in 21:7. 21:4 Or *Chaldeans;* also in 21:9.

13 I will personally fight against the people
in Jerusalem,
that mighty fortress—
the people who boast, "No one can touch us
here.
No one can break in here."
14 And I myself will punish you for
your sinfulness,
says the LORD.
I will light a fire in your forests
that will burn up everything
around you.'"

A MESSAGE FOR JUDAH'S KINGS

22 This is what the LORD said to me: "Go over and speak directly to the king of Judah. Say to him, 2 'Listen to this message from the LORD, you king of Judah, sitting on David's throne. Let your attendants and your people listen, too. 3 This is what the LORD says: Be fair-minded and just. Do what is right! Help those who have been robbed; rescue them from their oppressors. Quit your evil deeds! Do not mistreat foreigners, orphans, and widows. Stop murdering the innocent! 4 If you obey me, there will always be a descendant of David sitting on the throne here in Jerusalem. The king will ride through the palace gates in chariots and on horses, with his parade of attendants and subjects. 5 But if you refuse to pay attention to this warning, I swear by my own name, says the LORD, that this palace will become a pile of rubble.'"

A MESSAGE ABOUT THE PALACE

6 Now this is what the LORD says concerning Judah's royal palace:

"I love you as much as fruitful Gilead
and the green forests of Lebanon.
But I will turn you into a desert,
with no one living within your walls.
7 I will call for wreckers,
who will bring out their tools to
dismantle you.
They will tear out all your fine cedar beams
and throw them on the fire.

8 "People from many nations will pass by the ruins of this city and say to one another, 'Why did the LORD destroy such a great city?' 9 And the answer will be, 'Because they violated their covenant with the LORD their God by worshiping other gods.'"

A MESSAGE ABOUT JEHOAHAZ

10 Do not weep for the dead king or mourn
his loss.
Instead, weep for the captive king
being led away!
For he will never return to see his native
land again.

11 For this is what the LORD says about Jehoahaz,* who succeeded his father, King Josiah, and was taken away as a captive: "He will never return. 12 He will die in a distant land and will never again see his own country."

A MESSAGE ABOUT JEHOIAKIM

13 And the LORD says, "What sorrow awaits
Jehoiakim,*
who builds his palace with forced labor.*
He builds injustice into its walls,
for he makes his neighbors work
for nothing.
He does not pay them for their labor.
14 He says, 'I will build a magnificent palace
with huge rooms and many windows.
I will panel it throughout with fragrant cedar
and paint it a lovely red.'
15 But a beautiful cedar palace does not make
a great king!
Your father, Josiah, also had plenty to eat
and drink.
But he was just and right in all his dealings.
That is why God blessed him.
16 He gave justice and help to the poor
and needy,
and everything went well for him.
Isn't that what it means to know me?"
says the LORD.
17 "But you! You have eyes only for greed
and dishonesty!
You murder the innocent,
oppress the poor, and reign ruthlessly."

18 Therefore, this is what the LORD says about Jehoiakim, son of King Josiah:

"The people will not mourn for him,
crying to one another,
'Alas, my brother! Alas, my sister!'
His subjects will not mourn for him, crying,
'Alas, our master is dead! Alas,
his splendor is gone!'
19 He will be buried like a dead donkey—
dragged out of Jerusalem and dumped
outside the gates!
20 Weep for your allies in Lebanon.
Shout for them in Bashan.
Search for them in the regions east of
the river.*
See, they are all destroyed.
Not one is left to help you.
21 I warned you when you were prosperous,
but you replied, 'Don't bother me.'
You have been that way since childhood—
you simply will not obey me!
22 And now the wind will blow away your allies.
All your friends will be taken away
as captives.

22:11 Hebrew *Shallum*, another name for Jehoahaz.   22:13a The
brother and successor of the exiled Jehoahaz. See 22:18.
22:13b Hebrew *by unrighteousness*.   22:20 Or *in Abarim*.

Surely then you will see your wickedness
and be ashamed.
23 It may be nice to live in a beautiful palace
paneled with wood from the cedars
of Lebanon,
but soon you will groan with pangs
of anguish—
anguish like that of a woman in labor.

A MESSAGE FOR JEHOIACHIN

24 "As surely as I live," says the LORD, "I will abandon you, Jehoiachin* son of Jehoiakim, king of Judah. Even if you were the signet ring on my right hand, I would pull you off. 25 I will hand you over to those who seek to kill you, those you so desperately fear—to King Nebuchadnezzar* of Babylon and the mighty Babylonian* army. 26 I will expel you and your mother from this land, and you will die in a foreign country, not in your native land. 27 You will never again return to the land you yearn for.

28 "Why is this man Jehoiachin like a
discarded, broken jar?
Why are he and his children to be exiled
to a foreign land?
29 O earth, earth, earth!
Listen to this message from the LORD!
30 This is what the LORD says:
'Let the record show that this man
Jehoiachin was childless.
He is a failure,
for none of his children will succeed him on
the throne of David
to rule over Judah.'

THE RIGHTEOUS DESCENDANT

23 "What sorrow awaits the leaders of my people—the shepherds of my sheep—for they have destroyed and scattered the very ones they were expected to care for," says the LORD. 2 Therefore, this is what the LORD, the God of Israel, says to these shepherds: "Instead of caring for my flock and leading them to safety, you have deserted them and driven them to destruction. Now I will pour out judgment on you for the evil you have done to them. 3 But I will gather together the remnant of my flock from the countries where I have driven them. I will bring them back to their own sheepfold, and they will be fruitful and increase in number. 4 Then I will appoint responsible shepherds who will care for them, and they will never be afraid again. Not a single one will be lost or missing. I, the LORD, have spoken!

5 "For the time is coming,"
says the LORD,
"when I will raise up a righteous
descendant*
from King David's line.
He will be a King who rules with wisdom.

He will do what is just and right
throughout the land.
6 And this will be his name:
'The LORD Is Our Righteousness.'*
In that day Judah will be saved,
and Israel will live in safety.

7 "In that day," says the LORD, "when people are taking an oath, they will no longer say, 'As surely as the LORD lives, who rescued the people of Israel from the land of Egypt.' 8 Instead, they will say, 'As surely as the LORD lives, who brought the people of Israel back to their own land from the land of the north and from all the countries to which he had exiled them.' Then they will live in their own land."

JUDGMENT ON FALSE PROPHETS

9 My heart is broken because of
the false prophets,
and my bones tremble.
I stagger like a drunkard,
like someone overcome by wine,
because of the holy words
the LORD has spoken against them.
10 For the land is full of adultery,
and it lies under a curse.
The land itself is in mourning—
its wilderness pastures are dried up.
For they all do evil
and abuse what power they have.

11 "Even the priests and prophets
are ungodly, wicked men.
I have seen their despicable acts
right here in my own Temple,"
says the LORD.
12 "Therefore, the paths they take
will become slippery.
They will be chased through the dark,
and there they will fall.
For I will bring disaster upon them
at the time fixed for their punishment.
I, the LORD, have spoken!

13 "I saw that the prophets of Samaria were
terribly evil,
for they prophesied in the name of Baal
and led my people of Israel into sin.
14 But now I see that the prophets of Jerusalem
are even worse!
They commit adultery and love
dishonesty.
They encourage those who are doing evil
so that no one turns away from their sins.
These prophets are as wicked
as the people of Sodom and Gomorrah
once were."

22:24 Hebrew *Coniah*, a variant spelling of Jehoiachin; also in 22:28.   22:25a Hebrew *Nebuchadrezzar*, a variant spelling of Nebuchadnezzar.   22:25b Or *Chaldean*.   23:5 Hebrew *a righteous branch*.   23:6 Hebrew *Yahweh Tsidqenu*.

¹⁵ Therefore, this is what the LORD of Heaven's Armies says concerning the prophets:

"I will feed them with bitterness
  and give them poison to drink.
For it is because of Jerusalem's prophets
  that wickedness has filled this land."

¹⁶ This is what the LORD of Heaven's Armies says to his people:

"Do not listen to these prophets when they
    prophesy to you,
  filling you with futile hopes.
They are making up everything they say.
  They do not speak for the LORD!
¹⁷ They keep saying to those who despise
    my word,
  'Don't worry! The LORD says you will
    have peace!'
And to those who stubbornly follow their
    own desires,
  they say, 'No harm will come your way!'

¹⁸ "Have any of these prophets been in the
    LORD's presence
  to hear what he is really saying?
  Has even one of them cared enough
    to listen?
¹⁹ Look! The LORD's anger bursts out
    like a storm,
  a whirlwind that swirls down on the
    heads of the wicked.
²⁰ The anger of the LORD will not diminish
  until it has finished all he has planned.
In the days to come
  you will understand all this very clearly.

²¹ "I have not sent these prophets,
  yet they run around claiming to speak
    for me.
I have given them no message,
  yet they go on prophesying.
²² If they had stood before me and listened
    to me,
  they would have spoken my words,
and they would have turned my people
  from their evil ways and deeds.
²³ Am I a God who is only close at hand?"
  says the LORD.
"No, I am far away at the same time.
²⁴ Can anyone hide from me in a secret place?
  Am I not everywhere in all the heavens
    and earth?"
  says the LORD.

²⁵ "I have heard these prophets say, 'Listen to the dream I had from God last night.' And then they proceed to tell lies in my name. ²⁶ How long will this go on? If they are prophets, they are prophets of deceit, inventing everything they say. ²⁷ By telling these false dreams, they are trying to get my people to forget me, just as their ancestors did by worshiping the idols of Baal.

²⁸ "Let these false prophets tell their dreams,
  but let my true messengers faithfully
    proclaim my every word.
There is a difference between straw
    and grain!
²⁹ Does not my word burn like fire?"
  says the LORD.
"Is it not like a mighty hammer
  that smashes a rock to pieces?

³⁰ "Therefore," says the LORD, "I am against these prophets who steal messages from each other and claim they are from me. ³¹ I am against these smooth-tongued prophets who say, 'This prophecy is from the LORD!' ³² I am against these false prophets. Their imaginary dreams are flagrant lies that lead my people into sin. I did not send or appoint them, and they have no message at all for my people. I, the LORD, have spoken!

FALSE PROPHECIES AND FALSE PROPHETS

³³ "Suppose one of the people or one of the prophets or priests asks you, 'What prophecy has the LORD burdened you with now?' You must reply, 'You are the burden!* The LORD says he will abandon you!'

³⁴ "If any prophet, priest, or anyone else says, 'I have a prophecy from the LORD,' I will punish that person along with his entire family. ³⁵ You should keep asking each other, 'What is the LORD's answer?' or 'What is the LORD saying?' ³⁶ But stop using this phrase, 'prophecy from the LORD.' For people are using it to give authority to their own ideas, turning upside down the words of our God, the living God, the LORD of Heaven's Armies.

³⁷ "This is what you should say to the prophets: 'What is the LORD's answer?' or 'What is the LORD saying?' ³⁸ But suppose they respond, 'This is a prophecy from the LORD!' Then you should say, 'This is what the LORD says: Because you have used this phrase, "prophecy from the LORD," even though I warned you not to use it, ³⁹ I will forget you completely.* I will expel you from my presence, along with this city that I gave to you and your ancestors. ⁴⁰ And I will make you an object of ridicule, and your name will be infamous throughout the ages.'"

GOOD AND BAD FIGS

24 After King Nebuchadnezzar* of Babylon exiled Jehoiachin* son of Jehoiakim, king of Judah, to Babylon along with the officials of Judah and all the craftsmen and artisans, the

---

23:33 As in Greek version and Latin Vulgate; Hebrew reads *What burden?* 23:39 Some Hebrew manuscripts and Greek version read *I will surely lift you up.* 24:1a Hebrew *Nebuchadrezzar,* a variant spelling of Nebuchadnezzar. 24:1b Hebrew *Jeconiah,* a variant spelling of Jehoiachin.

LORD gave me this vision. I saw two baskets of figs placed in front of the LORD's Temple in Jerusalem. ² One basket was filled with fresh, ripe figs, while the other was filled with bad figs that were too rotten to eat.

³ Then the LORD said to me, "What do you see, Jeremiah?"

I replied, "Figs, some very good and some very bad, too rotten to eat."

⁴ Then the LORD gave me this message: ⁵ "This is what the LORD, the God of Israel, says: The good figs represent the exiles I sent from Judah to the land of the Babylonians.* ⁶ I will watch over and care for them, and I will bring them back here again. I will build them up and not tear them down. I will plant them and not uproot them. ⁷ I will give them hearts that recognize me as the LORD. They will be my people, and I will be their God, for they will return to me wholeheartedly.

⁸ "But the bad figs," the LORD said, "represent King Zedekiah of Judah, his officials, all the people left in Jerusalem, and those who live in Egypt. I will treat them like bad figs, too rotten to eat. ⁹ I will make them an object of horror and a symbol of evil to every nation on earth. They will be disgraced and mocked, taunted and cursed, wherever I scatter them. ¹⁰ And I will send war, famine, and disease until they have vanished from the land of Israel, which I gave to them and their ancestors."

SEVENTY YEARS OF CAPTIVITY

25 This message for all the people of Judah came to Jeremiah from the LORD during the fourth year of Jehoiakim's reign over Judah.* This was the year when King Nebuchadnezzar* of Babylon began his reign.

² Jeremiah the prophet said to all the people in Judah and Jerusalem, ³ "For the past twenty-three years—from the thirteenth year of the reign of Josiah son of Amon,* king of Judah, until now—the LORD has been giving me his messages. I have faithfully passed them on to you, but you have not listened.

⁴ "Again and again the LORD has sent you his servants, the prophets, but you have not listened or even paid attention. ⁵ Each time the message was this: 'Turn from the evil road you are traveling and from the evil things you are doing. Only then will I let you live in this land that the LORD gave to you and your ancestors forever. ⁶ Do not provoke my anger by worshiping idols you made with your own hands. Then I will not harm you.'

⁷ "But you would not listen to me," says the LORD. "You made me furious by worshiping idols you made with your own hands, bringing on yourselves all the disasters you now suffer. ⁸ And now the LORD of Heaven's Armies says: Because you have not listened to me, ⁹ I will gather together all the armies of the north under King Nebuchadnezzar of Babylon, whom I have appointed

as my deputy. I will bring them all against this land and its people and against the surrounding nations. I will completely destroy* you and make you an object of horror and contempt and a ruin forever. ¹⁰ I will take away your happy singing and laughter. The joyful voices of bridegrooms and brides will no longer be heard. Your millstones will fall silent, and the lights in your homes will go out. ¹¹ This entire land will become a desolate wasteland. Israel and her neighboring lands will serve the king of Babylon for seventy years.

¹² "Then, after the seventy years of captivity are over, I will punish the king of Babylon and his people for their sins," says the LORD. "I will make the country of the Babylonians* a wasteland forever. ¹³ I will bring upon them all the terrors I have promised in this book—all the penalties announced by Jeremiah against the nations. ¹⁴ Many nations and great kings will enslave the Babylonians, just as they enslaved my people. I will punish them in proportion to the suffering they cause my people."

THE CUP OF THE LORD'S ANGER

¹⁵ This is what the LORD, the God of Israel, said to me: "Take from my hand this cup filled to the brim with my anger, and make all the nations to whom I send you drink from it. ¹⁶ When they drink from it, they will stagger, crazed by the warfare I will send against them."

¹⁷ So I took the cup of anger from the LORD and made all the nations drink from it—every nation to which the LORD sent me. ¹⁸ I went to Jerusalem and the other towns of Judah, and their kings and officials drank from the cup. From that day until this, they have been a desolate ruin, an object of horror, contempt, and cursing. ¹⁹ I gave the cup to Pharaoh, king of Egypt, his attendants, his officials, and all his people, ²⁰ along with all the foreigners living in that land. I also gave it to all the kings of the land of Uz and the kings of the Philistine cities of Ashkelon, Gaza, Ekron, and what remains of Ashdod. ²¹ Then I gave the cup to the nations of Edom, Moab, and Ammon, ²² and the kings of Tyre and Sidon, and the kings of the regions across the sea. ²³ I gave it to Dedan, Tema, and Buz, and to the people who live in distant places.* ²⁴ I gave it to the kings of Arabia, the kings of the nomadic tribes of the desert, ²⁵ and to the kings of Zimri, Elam, and Media. ²⁶ And I gave it to the kings of the northern countries, far and near, one after the other—all the kingdoms of the world. And finally, the king of Babylon* himself drank from the cup of the LORD's anger.

24:5 Or *Chaldeans.* 25:1a The fourth year of Jehoiakim's reign and the accession year of Nebuchadnezzar's reign was 605 B.C. 25:1b Hebrew *Nebuchadrezzar,* a variant spelling of Nebuchadnezzar; also in 25:9. 25:3 The thirteenth year of Josiah's reign was 627 B.C. 25:9 The Hebrew term used here refers to the complete consecration of things or people to the LORD, either by destroying them or by giving them as an offering. 25:12 Or *Chaldeans.* 25:23 Or *who clip the corners of their hair.* 25:26 Hebrew *of Sheshach,* a code name for Babylon.

[27] Then the LORD said to me, "Now tell them, 'This is what the LORD of Heaven's Armies, the God of Israel, says: Drink from this cup of my anger. Get drunk and vomit; fall to rise no more, for I am sending terrible wars against you.' [28] And if they refuse to accept the cup, tell them, 'The LORD of Heaven's Armies says: You have no choice but to drink from it. [29] I have begun to punish Jerusalem, the city that bears my name. Now should I let you go unpunished? No, you will not escape disaster. I will call for war against all the nations of the earth. I, the LORD of Heaven's Armies, have spoken!'

[30] "Now prophesy all these things, and say to them,

"'The LORD will roar against his own land
from his holy dwelling in heaven.
He will shout like those who tread grapes;
he will shout against everyone on earth.
[31] His cry of judgment will reach the ends of
the earth,
for the LORD will bring his case against
all the nations.
He will judge all the people of the earth,
slaughtering the wicked with the sword.
I, the LORD, have spoken!'"

[32] This is what the LORD of Heaven's
Armies says:
"Look! Disaster will fall upon nation
after nation!
A great whirlwind of fury is rising
from the most distant corners
of the earth!"

[33] In that day those the LORD has slaughtered will fill the earth from one end to the other. No one will mourn for them or gather up their bodies to bury them. They will be scattered on the ground like manure.

[34] Weep and moan, you evil shepherds!
Roll in the dust, you leaders of the flock!
The time of your slaughter has arrived;
you will fall and shatter like
a fragile vase.
[35] You will find no place to hide;
there will be no way to escape.
[36] Listen to the frantic cries of
the shepherds.
The leaders of the flock are wailing
in despair,
for the LORD is ruining their pastures.
[37] Peaceful meadows will be turned into
a wasteland
by the LORD's fierce anger.
[38] He has left his den like a strong lion seeking
its prey,
and their land will be made desolate
by the sword* of the enemy
and the LORD's fierce anger.

JEREMIAH'S ESCAPE FROM DEATH

26 This message came to Jeremiah from the LORD early in the reign of Jehoiakim son of Josiah,* king of Judah. [2] "This is what the LORD says: Stand in the courtyard in front of the Temple of the LORD, and make an announcement to the people who have come there to worship from all over Judah. Give them my entire message; include every word. [3] Perhaps they will listen and turn from their evil ways. Then I will change my mind about the disaster I am ready to pour out on them because of their sins.

[4] "Say to them, 'This is what the LORD says: If you will not listen to me and obey my word I have given you, [5] and if you will not listen to my servants, the prophets—for I sent them again and again to warn you, but you would not listen to them—[6] then I will destroy this Temple as I destroyed Shiloh, the place where the Tabernacle was located. And I will make Jerusalem an object of cursing in every nation on earth.'"

[7] The priests, the prophets, and all the people listened to Jeremiah as he spoke in front of the LORD's Temple. [8] But when Jeremiah had finished his message, saying everything the LORD had told him to say, the priests and prophets and all the people at the Temple mobbed him. "Kill him!" they shouted. [9] "What right do you have to prophesy in the LORD's name that this Temple will be destroyed like Shiloh? What do you mean, saying that Jerusalem will be destroyed and left with no inhabitants?" And all the people threatened him as he stood in front of the Temple.

[10] When the officials of Judah heard what was happening, they rushed over from the palace and sat down at the New Gate of the Temple to hold court. [11] The priests and prophets presented their accusations to the officials and the people. "This man should die!" they said. "You have heard with your own ears what a traitor he is, for he has prophesied against this city."

[12] Then Jeremiah spoke to the officials and the people in his own defense. "The LORD sent me to prophesy against this Temple and this city," he said. "The LORD gave me every word that I have spoken. [13] But if you stop your sinning and begin to obey the LORD your God, he will change his mind about this disaster that he has announced against you. [14] As for me, I am in your hands—do with me as you think best. [15] But if you kill me, rest assured that you will be killing an innocent man! The responsibility for such a deed will lie on you, on this city, and on every person living in it. For it is absolutely true that the LORD sent me to speak every word you have heard."

[16] Then the officials and the people said to the priests and prophets, "This man does not deserve the death sentence, for he has spoken to us in the name of the LORD our God."

25:38 As in some Hebrew manuscripts and Greek version; Masoretic Text reads by the anger. 26:1 The first year of Jehoiakim's reign was 608 B.C.

[17] Then some of the wise old men stood and spoke to all the people assembled there. [18] They said, "Remember when Micah of Moresheth prophesied during the reign of King Hezekiah of Judah. He told the people of Judah,

'This is what the LORD of Heaven's
Armies says:
Mount Zion will be plowed like an
open field;
Jerusalem will be reduced to ruins!
A thicket will grow on the heights
where the Temple now stands.'*

[19] But did King Hezekiah and the people kill him for saying this? No, they turned from their sins and worshiped the LORD. They begged him for mercy. Then the LORD changed his mind about the terrible disaster he had pronounced against them. So we are about to do ourselves great harm."

[20] At this time Uriah son of Shemaiah from Kiriath-jearim was also prophesying for the LORD. And he predicted the same terrible disaster against the city and nation as Jeremiah did. [21] When King Jehoiakim and the army officers and officials heard what he was saying, the king sent someone to kill him. But Uriah heard about the plan and escaped in fear to Egypt. [22] Then King Jehoiakim sent Elnathan son of Acbor to Egypt along with several other men to capture Uriah. [23] They took him prisoner and brought him back to King Jehoiakim. The king then killed Uriah with a sword and had him buried in an unmarked grave.

[24] Nevertheless, Ahikam son of Shaphan stood up for Jeremiah and persuaded the court not to turn him over to the mob to be killed.

JEREMIAH WEARS AN OX YOKE

27 This message came to Jeremiah from the LORD early in the reign of Zedekiah* son of Josiah, king of Judah.

[2] This is what the LORD said to me: "Make a yoke, and fasten it on your neck with leather straps. [3] Then send messages to the kings of Edom, Moab, Ammon, Tyre, and Sidon through their ambassadors who have come to see King Zedekiah in Jerusalem. [4] Give them this message for their masters: 'This is what the LORD of Heaven's Armies, the God of Israel, says: [5] With my great strength and powerful arm I made the earth and all its people and every animal. I can give these things of mine to anyone I choose. [6] Now I will give your countries to King Nebuchadnezzar of Babylon, who is my servant. I have put everything, even the wild animals, under his control. [7] All the nations will serve him, his son, and his grandson until his time is up. Then many nations and great kings will conquer and rule over Babylon. [8] So you must submit to Babylon's king and serve him; put your neck under Babylon's yoke! I will punish any nation that refuses to be his slave, says the LORD. I will send war, famine, and disease upon that nation until Babylon has conquered it.

[9] "'Do not listen to your false prophets, fortune-tellers, interpreters of dreams, mediums, and sorcerers who say, "The king of Babylon will not conquer you." [10] They are all liars, and their lies will lead to your being driven out of your land. I will drive you out and send you far away to die. [11] But the people of any nation that submits to the king of Babylon will be allowed to stay in their own country to farm the land as usual. I, the LORD, have spoken!'"

[12] Then I repeated this same message to King Zedekiah of Judah. "If you want to live, submit to the yoke of the king of Babylon and his people. [13] Why do you insist on dying—you and your people? Why should you choose war, famine, and disease, which the LORD will bring against every nation that refuses to submit to Babylon's king? [14] Do not listen to the false prophets who keep telling you, 'The king of Babylon will not conquer you.' They are liars. [15] This is what the LORD says: 'I have not sent these prophets! They are telling you lies in my name, so I will drive you from this land. You will all die—you and all these prophets, too.'"

[16] Then I spoke to the priests and the people and said, "This is what the LORD says: 'Do not listen to your prophets who claim that soon the gold articles taken from my Temple will be returned from Babylon. It is all a lie! [17] Do not listen to them. Surrender to the king of Babylon, and you will live. Why should this whole city be destroyed? [18] If they really are prophets and speak the LORD's messages, let them pray to the LORD of Heaven's Armies. Let them pray that the articles remaining in the LORD's Temple and in the king's palace and in the palaces of Jerusalem will not be carried away to Babylon!'

[19] "For the LORD of Heaven's Armies has spoken about the pillars in front of the Temple, the great bronze basin called the Sea, the water carts, and all the other ceremonial articles. [20] King Nebuchadnezzar of Babylon left them here when he exiled Jehoiachin* son of Jehoiakim, king of Judah, to Babylon, along with all the other nobles of Judah and Jerusalem. [21] Yes, this is what the LORD of Heaven's Armies, the God of Israel, says about the precious things still in the Temple, in the palace of Judah's king, and in Jerusalem: [22] 'They will all be carried away to Babylon and will stay there until I send for them,' says the LORD. 'Then I will bring them back to Jerusalem again.'"

26:18 Mic 3:12.   27:1 As in some Hebrew manuscripts and Syriac version (see also 27:3, 12); most Hebrew manuscripts read *Jehoiakim*.   27:20 Hebrew *Jeconiah*, a variant spelling of Jehoiachin.

JEREMIAH CONDEMNS HANANIAH

28 One day in late summer* of that same year—the fourth year of the reign of Zedekiah, king of Judah—Hananiah son of Azzur, a prophet from Gibeon, addressed me publicly in the Temple while all the priests and people listened. He said, ²"This is what the Lord of Heaven's Armies, the God of Israel, says: 'I will remove the yoke of the king of Babylon from your necks. ³Within two years I will bring back all the Temple treasures that King Nebuchadnezzar carried off to Babylon. ⁴And I will bring back Jehoiachin* son of Jehoiakim, king of Judah, and all the other captives that were taken to Babylon. I will surely break the yoke that the king of Babylon has put on your necks. I, the Lord, have spoken!'"

⁵Jeremiah responded to Hananiah as they stood in front of all the priests and people at the Temple. ⁶He said, "Amen! May your prophecies come true! I hope the Lord does everything you say. I hope he does bring back from Babylon the treasures of this Temple and all the captives. ⁷But listen now to the solemn words I speak to you in the presence of all these people. ⁸The ancient prophets who preceded you and me spoke against many nations, always warning of war, disaster, and disease. ⁹So a prophet who predicts peace must show he is right. Only when his predictions come true can we know that he is really from the Lord."

¹⁰Then Hananiah the prophet took the yoke off Jeremiah's neck and broke it in pieces. ¹¹And Hananiah said again to the crowd that had gathered, "This is what the Lord says: 'Just as this yoke has been broken, within two years I will break the yoke of oppression from all the nations now subject to King Nebuchadnezzar of Babylon.'" With that, Jeremiah left the Temple area.

¹²Soon after this confrontation with Hananiah, the Lord gave this message to Jeremiah: ¹³"Go and tell Hananiah, 'This is what the Lord says: You have broken a wooden yoke, but you have replaced it with a yoke of iron. ¹⁴The Lord of Heaven's Armies, the God of Israel, says: I have put a yoke of iron on the necks of all these nations, forcing them into slavery under King Nebuchadnezzar of Babylon. I have put everything, even the wild animals, under his control.'"

¹⁵Then Jeremiah the prophet said to Hananiah, "Listen, Hananiah! The Lord has not sent you, but the people believe your lies. ¹⁶Therefore, this is what the Lord says: 'You must die. Your life will end this very year because you have rebelled against the Lord.'"

¹⁷Two months later* the prophet Hananiah died.

A LETTER TO THE EXILES

29 Jeremiah wrote a letter from Jerusalem to the elders, priests, prophets, and all the people who had been exiled to Babylon by King Nebuchadnezzar. ²This was after King Jehoiachin,* the queen mother, the court officials, the other officials of Judah, and all the craftsmen and artisans had been deported from Jerusalem. ³He sent the letter with Elasah son of Shaphan and Gemariah son of Hilkiah when they went to Babylon as King Zedekiah's ambassadors to Nebuchadnezzar. This is what Jeremiah's letter said:

⁴This is what the Lord of Heaven's Armies, the God of Israel, says to all the captives he has exiled to Babylon from Jerusalem: ⁵"Build homes, and plan to stay. Plant gardens, and eat the food they produce. ⁶Marry and have children. Then find spouses for them so that you may have many grandchildren. Multiply! Do not dwindle away! ⁷And work for the peace and prosperity of the city where I sent you into exile. Pray to the Lord for it, for its welfare will determine your welfare."

⁸This is what the Lord of Heaven's Armies, the God of Israel, says: "Do not let your prophets and fortune-tellers who are with you in the land of Babylon trick you. Do not listen to their dreams, ⁹because they are telling you lies in my name. I have not sent them," says the Lord.

¹⁰This is what the Lord says: "You will be in Babylon for seventy years. But then I will come and do for you all the good things I have promised, and I will bring you home again. ¹¹For I know the plans I have for you," says the Lord. "They are plans for good and not for disaster, to give you a future and a hope. ¹²In those days when you pray, I will listen. ¹³If you look for me wholeheartedly, you will find me. ¹⁴I will be found by you," says the Lord. "I will end your captivity and restore your fortunes. I will gather you out of the nations where I sent you and will bring you home again to your own land."

¹⁵You claim that the Lord has raised up prophets for you in Babylon. ¹⁶But this is what the Lord says about the king who sits on David's throne and all those still living here in Jerusalem—your relatives who were not exiled to Babylon. ¹⁷This is what the Lord of Heaven's Armies says: "I will send war, famine, and disease upon them and make them like bad figs, too rotten to eat. ¹⁸Yes, I will pursue them with war, famine, and disease, and I will scatter them around the world. In every nation where I send them, I will make them an object of damnation, horror, contempt, and mockery.

28:1 Hebrew *In the fifth month,* of the ancient Hebrew lunar calendar. The fifth month in the fourth year of Zedekiah's reign occurred within the months of August and September 593 B.C. Also see note on 1:3.   **28:4** Hebrew *Jeconiah,* a variant spelling of Jehoiachin.   **28:17** Hebrew *In the seventh month of that same year.* See 28:1 and the note there.   **29:2** Hebrew *Jeconiah,* a variant spelling of Jehoiachin.

KNOWING GOD'S WILL FOR YOUR LIFE
Jeremiah 29:11-13   JIMMY EVANS

If you want to know God's will for your life, you must first have a correct concept of God. Many people struggle to understand God's will because they mistakenly believe He is harsh or punishing. In reality, God wants to bless us, but we need to understand who we are in Him and surrender to His divine plan.

God's will for your life does not change based on how well or how poorly you perform. Romans 11:29 says, "God's gifts and his call can never be withdrawn." The enemy tries to use failures, sins, and tragedies to convince you that God is not faithful. Satan will taunt you with lies, trying to make you harden your heart. But the Bible shows us what God's thoughts and intentions for us really are. When you diligently seek Him with a yielded heart, He promises you will find Him *and* His will (Jeremiah 29:13).

¹⁹ For they refuse to listen to me, though I have spoken to them repeatedly through the prophets I sent. And you who are in exile have not listened either," says the LORD.

²⁰ Therefore, listen to this message from the LORD, all you captives there in Babylon. ²¹ This is what the LORD of Heaven's Armies, the God of Israel, says about your prophets—Ahab son of Kolaiah and Zedekiah son of Maaseiah—who are telling you lies in my name: "I will turn them over to Nebuchadnezzar* for execution before your eyes. ²² Their terrible fate will become proverbial, so that the Judean exiles will curse someone by saying, 'May the LORD make you like Zedekiah and Ahab, whom the king of Babylon burned alive!' ²³ For these men have done terrible things among my people. They have committed adultery with their neighbors' wives and have lied in my name, saying things I did not command. I am a witness to this. I, the LORD, have spoken."

A MESSAGE FOR SHEMAIAH

²⁴ The LORD sent this message to Shemaiah the Nehelamite in Babylon: ²⁵ "This is what the LORD of Heaven's Armies, the God of Israel, says: You wrote a letter on your own authority to Zephaniah son of Maaseiah, the priest, and you sent copies to the other priests and people in Jerusalem. You wrote to Zephaniah,

²⁶ "The LORD has appointed you to replace Jehoiada as the priest in charge of the house of the LORD. You are responsible to put into stocks and neck irons any crazy man who claims to be a prophet. ²⁷ So why have

you done nothing to stop Jeremiah from Anathoth, who pretends to be a prophet among you? ²⁸ Jeremiah sent a letter here to Babylon, predicting that our captivity will be a long one. He said, 'Build homes, and plan to stay. Plant gardens, and eat the food they produce.'"

²⁹ But when Zephaniah the priest received Shemaiah's letter, he took it to Jeremiah and read it to him. ³⁰ Then the LORD gave this message to Jeremiah: ³¹ "Send an open letter to all the exiles in Babylon. Tell them, 'This is what the LORD says concerning Shemaiah the Nehelamite: Since he has prophesied to you when I did not send him and has tricked you into believing his lies, ³² I will punish him and his family. None of his descendants will see the good things I will do for my people, for he has incited you to rebel against me. I, the LORD, have spoken!'"

PROMISES OF DELIVERANCE

30 The LORD gave another message to Jeremiah. He said, ² "This is what the LORD, the God of Israel, says: Write down for the record everything I have said to you, Jeremiah. ³ For the time is coming when I will restore the fortunes of my people of Israel and Judah. I will bring them home to this land that I gave to their ancestors, and they will possess it again. I, the LORD, have spoken!"

⁴ This is the message the LORD gave concerning Israel and Judah. ⁵ This is what the LORD says:

"I hear cries of fear;
    there is terror and no peace.
⁶ Now let me ask you a question:
    Do men give birth to babies?
Then why do they stand there, ashen-faced,
    hands pressed against their sides
    like a woman in labor?
⁷ In all history there has never been such
        a time of terror.
    It will be a time of trouble for my people
        Israel.*
    Yet in the end they will be saved!
⁸ For in that day,"
        says the LORD of Heaven's Armies,
"I will break the yoke from their necks
        and snap their chains.
Foreigners will no longer be their masters.
⁹   For my people will serve the LORD
            their God
    and their king descended from David—
        the king I will raise up for them.

¹⁰ "So do not be afraid, Jacob, my servant;
        do not be dismayed, Israel,"
    says the LORD.

29:21 Hebrew *Nebuchadrezzar*, a variant spelling of Nebuchadnezzar.   30:7 Hebrew *Jacob;* also in 30:10b, 18. See note on 5:20.

"For I will bring you home again from
distant lands,
and your children will return from
their exile.
Israel will return to a life of peace and quiet,
and no one will terrorize them.
[11] For I am with you and will save you,"
says the LORD.
"I will completely destroy the nations where
I have scattered you,
but I will not completely destroy you.
I will discipline you, but with justice;
I cannot let you go unpunished."

[12] This is what the LORD says:
"Your injury is incurable—
a terrible wound.
[13] There is no one to help you
or to bind up your injury.
No medicine can heal you.
[14] All your lovers—your allies—have left you
and do not care about you anymore.
I have wounded you cruelly,
as though I were your enemy.
For your sins are many,
and your guilt is great.
[15] Why do you protest your punishment—
this wound that has no cure?
I have had to punish you
because your sins are many
and your guilt is great.

[16] "But all who devour you will be devoured,
and all your enemies will be sent
into exile.
All who plunder you will be plundered,
and all who attack you will be attacked.
[17] I will give you back your health
and heal your wounds," says the LORD.
"For you are called an outcast—
'Jerusalem* for whom no one cares.'"

[18] This is what the LORD says:
"When I bring Israel home again
from captivity
and restore their fortunes,
Jerusalem will be rebuilt on its ruins,
and the palace reconstructed as before.
[19] There will be joy and songs of thanksgiving,
and I will multiply my people,
not diminish them;
I will honor them, not despise them.
[20] Their children will prosper as they did
long ago.
I will establish them as a nation before me,
and I will punish anyone who hurts them.
[21] They will have their own ruler again,
and he will come from their own people.
I will invite him to approach me,"
says the LORD,
"for who would dare to come
unless invited?

[22] You will be my people,
and I will be your God."

[23] Look! The LORD's anger bursts out like
a storm,
a driving wind that swirls down on the
heads of the wicked.
[24] The fierce anger of the LORD will not
diminish
until it has finished all he has planned.
In the days to come
you will understand all this.

HOPE FOR RESTORATION

31 "In that day," says the LORD, "I will be the
God of all the families of Israel, and they
will be my people. [2] This is what the LORD says:

"Those who survive the coming destruction
will find blessings even in the barren
land,
for I will give rest to the people of Israel."

[3] Long ago the LORD said to Israel:
"I have loved you, my people, with an
everlasting love.
With unfailing love I have drawn you
to myself.
[4] I will rebuild you, my virgin Israel.
You will again be happy
and dance merrily with your tambourines.
[5] Again you will plant your vineyards on the
mountains of Samaria
and eat from your own gardens there.
[6] The day will come when watchmen will
shout
from the hill country of Ephraim,
'Come, let us go up to Jerusalem*
to worship the LORD our God.'"

[7] Now this is what the LORD says:
"Sing with joy for Israel.*
Shout for the greatest of nations!
Shout out with praise and joy:
'Save your people, O LORD,
the remnant of Israel!'
[8] For I will bring them from the north
and from the distant corners of the earth.
I will not forget the blind and lame,
the expectant mothers and women
in labor.
A great company will return!
[9] Tears of joy will stream down their faces,
and I will lead them home with great care.
They will walk beside quiet streams
and on smooth paths where they will not
stumble.
For I am Israel's father,
and Ephraim is my oldest child.

30:17 Hebrew *Zion*. 31:6 Hebrew *Zion;* also in 31:12.
31:7 Hebrew *Jacob;* also in 31:11. See note on 5:20.

¹⁰ "Listen to this message from the LORD,
  you nations of the world;
    proclaim it in distant coastlands:
The LORD, who scattered his people,
  will gather them and watch over them
  as a shepherd does his flock.
¹¹ For the LORD has redeemed Israel
  from those too strong for them.
¹² They will come home and sing songs of joy
  on the heights of Jerusalem.
They will be radiant because of
    the LORD's good gifts—
  the abundant crops of grain, new wine,
    and olive oil,
  and the healthy flocks and herds.
Their life will be like a watered garden,
  and all their sorrows will be gone.
¹³ The young women will dance for joy,
  and the men—old and young—will join in
    the celebration.
I will turn their mourning into joy.
  I will comfort them and exchange their
    sorrow for rejoicing.
¹⁴ The priests will enjoy abundance,
  and my people will feast on my good gifts.
  I, the LORD, have spoken!"

RACHEL'S SADNESS TURNS TO JOY

¹⁵ This is what the LORD says:

"A cry is heard in Ramah—
  deep anguish and bitter weeping.
Rachel weeps for her children,
  refusing to be comforted—
  for her children are gone."

¹⁶ But now this is what the LORD says:
"Do not weep any longer,
  for I will reward you," says the LORD.
"Your children will come back to you
  from the distant land of the enemy.
¹⁷ There is hope for your future,"
    says the LORD.
"Your children will come again to their
    own land.
¹⁸ I have heard Israel* saying,
'You disciplined me severely,
  like a calf that needs training for the yoke.
Turn me again to you and restore me,
  for you alone are the LORD my God.
¹⁹ I turned away from God,
  but then I was sorry.
I kicked myself for my stupidity!
  I was thoroughly ashamed of all I did in
    my younger days.'
²⁰ "Is not Israel still my son,
  my darling child?" says the LORD.
"I often have to punish him,
  but I still love him.
That's why I long for him
  and surely will have mercy on him.

²¹ Set up road signs;
  put up guideposts.
Mark well the path
  by which you came.
Come back again, my virgin Israel;
  return to your towns here.
²² How long will you wander,
  my wayward daughter?
For the LORD will cause something new to
    happen—
  Israel will embrace her God.*"

²³ This is what the LORD of Heaven's Armies, the God of Israel, says: "When I bring them back from captivity, the people of Judah and its towns will again say, 'The LORD bless you, O righteous home, O holy mountain!' ²⁴ Townspeople and farmers and shepherds alike will live together in peace and happiness. ²⁵ For I have given rest to the weary and joy to the sorrowing."

²⁶ At this, I woke up and looked around. My sleep had been very sweet.

²⁷ "The day is coming," says the LORD, "when I will greatly increase the human population and the number of animals here in Israel and Judah. ²⁸ In the past I deliberately uprooted and tore down this nation. I overthrew it, destroyed it, and brought disaster upon it. But in the future I will just as deliberately plant it and build it up. I, the LORD, have spoken!

²⁹ "The people will no longer quote this proverb:

'The parents have eaten sour grapes,
  but their children's mouths pucker at
    the taste.'

³⁰ All people will die for their own sins—those who eat the sour grapes will be the ones whose mouths will pucker.

³¹ "The day is coming," says the LORD, "when I will make a new covenant with the people of Israel and Judah. ³² This covenant will not be like the one I made with their ancestors when I took them by the hand and brought them out of the land of Egypt. They broke that covenant, though I loved them as a husband loves his wife," says the LORD.

³³ "But this is the new covenant I will make with the people of Israel after those days," says the LORD. "I will put my instructions deep within them, and I will write them on their hearts. I will be their God, and they will be my people. ³⁴ And they will not need to teach their neighbors, nor will they need to teach their relatives, saying, 'You should know the LORD.' For everyone, from the least to the greatest, will know me already," says the LORD. "And I will forgive their wickedness, and I will never again remember their sins."

31:18 Hebrew *Ephraim*, referring to the northern kingdom of Israel; also in 31:20. 31:22 Hebrew *a woman will surround a man*.

35 It is the LORD who provides the sun
　　to light the day
　and the moon and stars to light the night,
　and who stirs the sea into roaring waves.
His name is the LORD of Heaven's Armies,
　and this is what he says:
36 "I am as likely to reject my people Israel
　as I am to abolish the laws of nature!"
37 This is what the LORD says:
"Just as the heavens cannot be measured
　and the foundations of the earth cannot
　be explored,
so I will not consider casting them away
　for the evil they have done.
I, the LORD, have spoken!

38 "The day is coming," says the LORD, "when all Jerusalem will be rebuilt for me, from the Tower of Hananel to the Corner Gate. 39 A measuring line will be stretched out over the hill of Gareb and across to Goah. 40 And the entire area—including the graveyard and ash dump in the valley, and all the fields out to the Kidron Valley on the east as far as the Horse Gate—will be holy to the LORD. The city will never again be captured or destroyed."

JEREMIAH'S LAND PURCHASE

32 The following message came to Jeremiah from the LORD in the tenth year of the reign of Zedekiah,* king of Judah. This was also the eighteenth year of the reign of King Nebuchadnezzar.* 2 Jerusalem was then under siege from the Babylonian army, and Jeremiah was imprisoned in the courtyard of the guard in the royal palace. 3 King Zedekiah had put him there, asking why he kept giving this prophecy: "This is what the LORD says: 'I am about to hand this city over to the king of Babylon, and he will take it. 4 King Zedekiah will be captured by the Babylonians* and taken to meet the king of Babylon face to face. 5 He will take Zedekiah to Babylon, and I will deal with him there,' says the LORD. 'If you fight against the Babylonians, you will never succeed.'"

6 At that time the LORD sent me a message. He said, 7 "Your cousin Hanamel son of Shallum will come and say to you, 'Buy my field at Anathoth. By law you have the right to buy it before it is offered to anyone else.'"

8 Then, just as the LORD had said he would, my cousin Hanamel came and visited me in the prison. He said, "Please buy my field at Anathoth in the land of Benjamin. By law you have the right to buy it before it is offered to anyone else, so buy it for yourself." Then I knew that the message I had heard was from the LORD.

9 So I bought the field at Anathoth, paying Hanamel seventeen pieces* of silver for it. 10 I signed and sealed the deed of purchase before witnesses, weighed out the silver, and paid him. 11 Then I took the sealed deed and an unsealed copy of the deed, which contained the terms and conditions of the purchase, 12 and I handed them to Baruch son of Neriah and grandson of Mahseiah. I did all this in the presence of my cousin Hanamel, the witnesses who had signed the deed, and all the men of Judah who were there in the courtyard of the guardhouse.

13 Then I said to Baruch as they all listened, 14 "This is what the LORD of Heaven's Armies, the God of Israel, says: 'Take both this sealed deed and the unsealed copy, and put them into a pottery jar to preserve them for a long time.' 15 For this is what the LORD of Heaven's Armies, the God of Israel, says: 'Someday people will again own property here in this land and will buy and sell houses and vineyards and fields.'"

JEREMIAH'S PRAYER

16 Then after I had given the papers to Baruch, I prayed to the LORD:

17 "O Sovereign LORD! You made the heavens and earth by your strong hand and powerful arm. Nothing is too hard for you! 18 You show unfailing love to thousands, but you also bring the consequences of one generation's sin upon the next. You are the great and powerful God, the LORD of Heaven's Armies. 19 You have all wisdom and do great and mighty miracles. You see the conduct of all people, and you give them what they deserve. 20 You performed miraculous signs and wonders in the land of Egypt—things still remembered to this day! And you have continued to do great miracles in Israel and all around the world. You have made your name famous to this day.

21 "You brought Israel out of Egypt with mighty signs and wonders, with a strong hand and powerful arm, and with overwhelming terror. 22 You gave the people of Israel this land that you had promised their ancestors long before—a land flowing with milk and honey. 23 Our ancestors came and conquered it and lived in it, but they refused to obey you or follow your word. They have not done anything you commanded. That is why you have sent this terrible disaster upon them.

24 "See how the siege ramps have been built against the city walls! Through war, famine, and disease, the city will be handed over to the Babylonians, who will conquer it. Everything has happened just as you said. 25 And yet, O Sovereign LORD, you have told me to buy the field—paying good money for it before these witnesses—even though

---

32:1a The tenth year of Zedekiah's reign and the eighteenth year of Nebuchadnezzar's reign was 587 B.C. 　32:1b Hebrew *Nebuchadrezzar*, a variant spelling of Nebuchadnezzar; also in 32:28. 　32:4 Or *Chaldeans;* also in 32:5, 24, 25, 28, 29, 43. 　32:9 Hebrew *17 shekels*, about 7 ounces or 194 grams in weight.

the city will soon be handed over to the Babylonians."

A PREDICTION OF JERUSALEM'S FALL

²⁶ Then this message came to Jeremiah from the LORD: ²⁷ "I am the LORD, the God of all the peoples of the world. Is anything too hard for me? ²⁸ Therefore, this is what the LORD says: I will hand this city over to the Babylonians and to Nebuchadnezzar, king of Babylon, and he will capture it. ²⁹ The Babylonians outside the walls will come in and set fire to the city. They will burn down all these houses where the people provoked my anger by burning incense to Baal on the rooftops and by pouring out liquid offerings to other gods. ³⁰ Israel and Judah have done nothing but wrong since their earliest days. They have infuriated me with all their evil deeds," says the LORD. ³¹ "From the time this city was built until now, it has done nothing but anger me, so I am determined to get rid of it.

³² "The sins of Israel and Judah—the sins of the people of Jerusalem, the kings, the officials, the priests, and the prophets—have stirred up my anger. ³³ My people have turned their backs on me and have refused to return. Even though I diligently taught them, they would not receive instruction or obey. ³⁴ They have set up their abominable idols right in my own Temple, defiling it. ³⁵ They have built pagan shrines to Baal in the valley of Ben-Hinnom, and there they sacrifice their sons and daughters to Molech. I have never commanded such a horrible deed; it never even crossed my mind to command such a thing. What an incredible evil, causing Judah to sin so greatly!

A PROMISE OF RESTORATION

³⁶ "Now I want to say something more about this city. You have been saying, 'It will fall to the king of Babylon through war, famine, and disease.' But this is what the LORD, the God of Israel, says: ³⁷ I will certainly bring my people back again from all the countries where I will scatter them in my fury. I will bring them back to this very city and let them live in peace and safety. ³⁸ They will be my people, and I will be their God. ³⁹ And I will give them one heart and one purpose: to worship me forever, for their own good and for the good of all their descendants. ⁴⁰ And I will make an everlasting covenant with them: I will never stop doing good for them. I will put a desire in their hearts to worship me, and they will never leave me. ⁴¹ I will find joy doing good for them and will faithfully and wholeheartedly replant them in this land.

⁴² "This is what the LORD says: Just as I have brought all these calamities on them, so I will do all the good I have promised them. ⁴³ Fields will again be bought and sold in this land about which you now say, 'It has been ravaged by the Babylonians, a desolate land where people and animals have all disappeared.' ⁴⁴ Yes, fields will once again be bought and sold—deeds signed and sealed and witnessed—in the land of Benjamin and here in Jerusalem, in the towns of Judah and in the hill country, in the foothills of Judah* and in the Negev, too. For someday I will restore prosperity to them. I, the LORD, have spoken!"

PROMISES OF PEACE AND PROSPERITY

33 While Jeremiah was still confined in the courtyard of the guard, the LORD gave him this second message: ² "This is what the LORD says—the LORD who made the earth, who formed and established it, whose name is the LORD: ³ Ask me and I will tell you remarkable secrets you do not know about things to come. ⁴ For this is what the LORD, the God of Israel, says: You have torn down the houses of this city and even the king's palace to get materials to strengthen the walls against the siege ramps and swords of the enemy. ⁵ You expect to fight the Babylonians,* but the men of this city are already as good as dead, for I have determined to destroy them in my terrible anger. I have abandoned them because of all their wickedness.

⁶ "Nevertheless, the time will come when I will heal Jerusalem's wounds and give it prosperity and true peace. ⁷ I will restore the fortunes of Judah and Israel and rebuild their towns. ⁸ I will cleanse them of their sins against me and forgive all their sins of rebellion. ⁹ Then this city will bring me joy, glory, and honor before all the nations of the earth! The people of the world will see all the good I do for my people, and they will tremble with awe at the peace and prosperity I provide for them.

¹⁰ "This is what the LORD says: You have said, 'This is a desolate land where people and animals have all disappeared.' Yet in the empty streets of Jerusalem and Judah's other towns, there will be heard once more ¹¹ the sounds of joy and laughter. The joyful voices of bridegrooms and brides will be heard again, along with the joyous songs of people bringing thanksgiving offerings to the LORD. They will sing,

'Give thanks to the LORD of Heaven's Armies,
    for the LORD is good.
His faithful love endures forever!'

For I will restore the prosperity of this land to what it was in the past, says the LORD.

¹² "This is what the LORD of Heaven's Armies says: This land—though it is now desolate and has no people and animals—will once more have pastures where shepherds can lead their flocks. ¹³ Once again shepherds will count their flocks in the towns of the hill country, the foothills of Judah,* the Negev, the land of Benjamin, the

vicinity of Jerusalem, and all the towns of Judah. I, the LORD, have spoken!

14 "The day will come, says the LORD, when I will do for Israel and Judah all the good things I have promised them.

15 "In those days and at that time
I will raise up a righteous descendant*
from King David's line.
He will do what is just and right
throughout the land.
16 In that day Judah will be saved,
and Jerusalem will live in safety.
And this will be its name:
'The LORD Is Our Righteousness.'*

17 For this is what the LORD says: David will have a descendant sitting on the throne of Israel forever. 18 And there will always be Levitical priests to offer burnt offerings and grain offerings and sacrifices to me."

19 Then this message came to Jeremiah from the LORD: 20 "This is what the LORD says: If you can break my covenant with the day and the night so that one does not follow the other, 21 only then will my covenant with my servant David be broken. Only then will he no longer have a descendant to reign on his throne. The same is true for my covenant with the Levitical priests who minister before me. 22 And as the stars of the sky cannot be counted and the sand on the seashore cannot be measured, so I will multiply the descendants of my servant David and the Levites who minister before me."

23 The LORD gave another message to Jeremiah. He said, 24 "Have you noticed what people are saying?—'The LORD chose Judah and Israel and then abandoned them!' They are sneering and saying that Israel is not worthy to be counted as a nation. 25 But this is what the LORD says: I would no more reject my people than I would change my laws that govern night and day, earth and sky. 26 I will never abandon the descendants of Jacob or David, my servant, or change the plan that David's descendants will rule the descendants of Abraham, Isaac, and Jacob. Instead, I will restore them to their land and have mercy on them."

A WARNING FOR ZEDEKIAH

34 King Nebuchadnezzar* of Babylon came with all the armies from the kingdoms he ruled, and he fought against Jerusalem and the towns of Judah. At that time this message came to Jeremiah from the LORD: 2 "Go to King Zedekiah of Judah, and tell him, 'This is what the LORD, the God of Israel, says: I am about to hand this city over to the king of Babylon, and he will burn it down. 3 You will not escape his grasp but will be captured and taken to meet the king of Babylon face to face. Then you will be exiled to Babylon.

4 "'But listen to this promise from the LORD, O Zedekiah, king of Judah. This is what the LORD says: You will not be killed in war 5 but will die peacefully. People will burn incense in your memory, just as they did for your ancestors, the kings who preceded you. They will mourn for you, crying, "Alas, our master is dead!" This I have decreed, says the LORD.'"

6 So Jeremiah the prophet delivered the message to King Zedekiah of Judah. 7 At this time the Babylonian army was besieging Jerusalem, Lachish, and Azekah—the only fortified cities of Judah not yet captured.

FREEDOM FOR HEBREW SLAVES

8 This message came to Jeremiah from the LORD after King Zedekiah made a covenant with the people, proclaiming freedom for the slaves. 9 He had ordered all the people to free their Hebrew slaves—both men and women. No one was to keep a fellow Judean in bondage. 10 The officials and all the people had obeyed the king's command, 11 but later they changed their minds. They took back the men and women they had freed, forcing them to be slaves again.

12 So the LORD gave them this message through Jeremiah: 13 "This is what the LORD, the God of Israel, says: I made a covenant with your ancestors long ago when I rescued them from their slavery in Egypt. 14 I told them that every Hebrew slave must be freed after serving six years. But your ancestors paid no attention to me. 15 Recently you repented and did what was right, following my command. You freed your slaves and made a solemn covenant with me in the Temple that bears my name. 16 But now you have shrugged off your oath and defiled my name by taking back the men and women you had freed, forcing them to be slaves once again.

17 "Therefore, this is what the LORD says: Since you have not obeyed me by setting your countrymen free, I will set you free to be destroyed by war, disease, and famine. You will be an object of horror to all the nations of the earth. 18 Because you have broken the terms of our covenant, I will cut you apart just as you cut apart the calf when you walked between its halves to solemnize your vows. 19 Yes, I will cut you apart, whether you are officials of Judah or Jerusalem, court officials, priests, or common people—for you have broken your oath. 20 I will give you to your enemies, and they will kill you. Your bodies will be food for the vultures and wild animals.

21 "I will hand over King Zedekiah of Judah and his officials to the army of the king of Babylon. And although they have left Jerusalem for a while, 22 I will call the Babylonian armies back again. They will fight against this city and will capture it and burn it down. I will see to it that all the towns of Judah are destroyed, with no one living there."

33:15 Hebrew *a righteous branch.* 33:16 Hebrew *Yahweh Tsidqenu.* 34:1 Hebrew *Nebuchadrezzar,* a variant spelling of Nebuchadnezzar.

THE FAITHFUL RECABITES

35 This is the message the LORD gave Jeremiah when Jehoiakim son of Josiah was king of Judah: [2] "Go to the settlement where the families of the Recabites live, and invite them to the LORD's Temple. Take them into one of the inner rooms, and offer them some wine."

[3] So I went to see Jaazaniah son of Jeremiah and grandson of Habazziniah and all his brothers and sons—representing all the Recabite families. [4] I took them to the Temple, and we went into the room assigned to the sons of Hanan son of Igdaliah, a man of God. This room was located next to the one used by the Temple officials, directly above the room of Maaseiah son of Shallum, the Temple gatekeeper.

[5] I set cups and jugs of wine before them and invited them to have a drink, [6] but they refused. "No," they said, "we don't drink wine, because our ancestor Jehonadab* son of Recab gave us this command: 'You and your descendants must never drink wine. [7] And do not build houses or plant crops or vineyards, but always live in tents. If you follow these commands, you will live long, good lives in the land.' [8] So we have obeyed him in all these things. We have never had a drink of wine to this day, nor have our wives, our sons, or our daughters. [9] We haven't built houses or owned vineyards or farms or planted crops. [10] We have lived in tents and have fully obeyed all the commands of Jehonadab, our ancestor. [11] But when King Nebuchadnezzar* of Babylon attacked this country, we were afraid of the Babylonian and Syrian* armies. So we decided to move to Jerusalem. That is why we are here."

[12] Then the LORD gave this message to Jeremiah: [13] "This is what the LORD of Heaven's Armies, the God of Israel, says: Go and say to the people in Judah and Jerusalem, 'Come and learn a lesson about how to obey me. [14] The Recabites do not drink wine to this day because their ancestor Jehonadab told them not to. But I have spoken to you again and again, and you refuse to obey me. [15] Time after time I sent you prophets, who told you, "Turn from your wicked ways, and start doing things right. Stop worshiping other gods so that you might live in peace here in the land I have given to you and your ancestors." But you would not listen to me or obey me. [16] The descendants of Jehonadab son of Recab have obeyed their ancestor completely, but you have refused to listen to me.'

[17] "Therefore, this is what the LORD God of Heaven's Armies, the God of Israel, says: 'Because you refuse to listen or answer when I call, I will send upon Judah and Jerusalem all the disasters I have threatened.'"

[18] Then Jeremiah turned to the Recabites and said, "This is what the LORD of Heaven's Armies, the God of Israel, says: 'You have obeyed your ancestor Jehonadab in every respect, following all his instructions.' [19] Therefore, this is what the LORD of Heaven's Armies, the God of Israel, says: 'Jehonadab son of Recab will always have descendants who serve me.'"

BARUCH READS THE LORD'S MESSAGES

36 During the fourth year that Jehoiakim son of Josiah was king in Judah,* the LORD gave this message to Jeremiah: [2] "Get a scroll, and write down all my messages against Israel, Judah, and the other nations. Begin with the first message back in the days of Josiah, and write down every message, right up to the present time. [3] Perhaps the people of Judah will repent when they hear again all the terrible things I have planned for them. Then I will be able to forgive their sins and wrongdoings."

[4] So Jeremiah sent for Baruch son of Neriah, and as Jeremiah dictated all the prophecies that the LORD had given him, Baruch wrote them on a scroll. [5] Then Jeremiah said to Baruch, "I am a prisoner here and unable to go to the Temple. [6] So you go to the Temple on the next day of fasting, and read the messages from the LORD that I have had you write on this scroll. Read them so the people who are there from all over Judah will hear them. [7] Perhaps even yet they will turn from their evil ways and ask the LORD's forgiveness before it is too late. For the LORD has threatened them with his terrible anger."

[8] Baruch did as Jeremiah told him and read these messages from the LORD to the people at the Temple. [9] He did this on a day of sacred fasting held in late autumn,* during the fifth year of the reign of Jehoiakim son of Josiah. People from all over Judah had come to Jerusalem to attend the services at the Temple on that day. [10] Baruch read Jeremiah's words on the scroll to all the people. He stood in front of the Temple room of Gemariah, son of Shaphan the secretary. This room was just off the upper courtyard of the Temple, near the New Gate entrance.

[11] When Micaiah son of Gemariah and grandson of Shaphan heard the messages from the LORD, [12] he went down to the secretary's room in the palace where the administrative officials were meeting. Elishama the secretary was there, along with Delaiah son of Shemaiah, Elnathan son of Acbor, Gemariah son of Shaphan, Zedekiah son of Hananiah, and all the other officials. [13] When Micaiah told them about the messages Baruch was reading to the people, [14] the officials sent Jehudi son of Nethaniah, grandson of Shelemiah and great-grandson of Cushi, to ask Baruch to come and read the messages to them, too. So

35:6 Hebrew *Jonadab,* a variant spelling of Jehonadab; also in 35:10, 19. See 2 Kgs 10:15.   35:11a Hebrew *Nebuchadrezzar,* a variant spelling of Nebuchadnezzar.   35:11b Or *Chaldean and Aramean.*   36:1 The fourth year of Jehoiakim's reign was 605 B.C.   36:9 Hebrew *in the ninth month,* of the ancient Hebrew lunar calendar (also in 36:22). The ninth month in the fifth year of Jehoiakim's reign occurred within the months of November and December 604 B.C. Also see note on 1:3.

Baruch took the scroll and went to them. ¹⁵"Sit down and read the scroll to us," the officials said, and Baruch did as they requested.

¹⁶When they heard all the messages, they looked at one another in alarm. "We must tell the king what we have heard," they said to Baruch. ¹⁷"But first, tell us how you got these messages. Did they come directly from Jeremiah?"

¹⁸So Baruch explained, "Jeremiah dictated them, and I wrote them down in ink, word for word, on this scroll."

¹⁹"You and Jeremiah should both hide," the officials told Baruch. "Don't tell anyone where you are!" ²⁰Then the officials left the scroll for safekeeping in the room of Elishama the secretary and went to tell the king what had happened.

KING JEHOIAKIM BURNS THE SCROLL

²¹The king sent Jehudi to get the scroll. Jehudi brought it from Elishama's room and read it to the king as all his officials stood by. ²²It was late autumn, and the king was in a winterized part of the palace, sitting in front of a fire to keep warm. ²³Each time Jehudi finished reading three or four columns, the king took a knife and cut off that section of the scroll. He then threw it into the fire, section by section, until the whole scroll was burned up. ²⁴Neither the king nor his attendants showed any signs of fear or repentance at what they heard. ²⁵Even when Elnathan, Delaiah, and Gemariah begged the king not to burn the scroll, he wouldn't listen.

²⁶Then the king commanded his son Jerahmeel, Seraiah son of Azriel, and Shelemiah son of Abdeel to arrest Baruch and Jeremiah. But the LORD had hidden them.

JEREMIAH REWRITES THE SCROLL

²⁷After the king had burned the scroll on which Baruch had written Jeremiah's words, the LORD gave Jeremiah another message. He said, ²⁸"Get another scroll, and write everything again just as you did on the scroll King Jehoiakim burned. ²⁹Then say to the king, 'This is what the LORD says: You burned the scroll because it said the king of Babylon would destroy this land and empty it of people and animals. ³⁰Now this is what the LORD says about King Jehoiakim of Judah: He will have no heirs to sit on the throne of David. His dead body will be thrown out to lie unburied—exposed to the heat of the day and the frost of the night. ³¹I will punish him and his family and his attendants for their sins. I will pour out on them and on all the people of Jerusalem and Judah all the disasters I promised, for they would not listen to my warnings.'"

³²So Jeremiah took another scroll and dictated again to his secretary, Baruch. He wrote everything that had been on the scroll King Jehoiakim had burned in the fire. Only this time he added much more!

ZEDEKIAH CALLS FOR JEREMIAH

37 Zedekiah son of Josiah succeeded Jehoiachin* son of Jehoiakim as the king of Judah. He was appointed by King Nebuchadnezzar* of Babylon. ²But neither King Zedekiah nor his attendants nor the people who were left in the land listened to what the LORD said through Jeremiah.

³Nevertheless, King Zedekiah sent Jehucal son of Shelemiah, and Zephaniah the priest, son of Maaseiah, to ask Jeremiah, "Please pray to the LORD our God for us." ⁴Jeremiah had not yet been imprisoned, so he could come and go among the people as he pleased.

⁵At this time the army of Pharaoh Hophra* of Egypt appeared at the southern border of Judah. When the Babylonian* army heard about it, they withdrew from their siege of Jerusalem.

⁶Then the LORD gave this message to Jeremiah: ⁷"This is what the LORD, the God of Israel, says: The king of Judah sent you to ask me what is going to happen. Tell him, 'Pharaoh's army is about to return to Egypt, though he came here to help you. ⁸Then the Babylonians* will come back and capture this city and burn it to the ground.' ⁹This is what the LORD says: Do not fool yourselves into thinking that the Babylonians are gone for good. They aren't! ¹⁰Even if you were to destroy the entire Babylonian army, leaving only a handful of wounded survivors, they would still stagger from their tents and burn this city to the ground!"

JEREMIAH IS IMPRISONED

¹¹When the Babylonian army left Jerusalem because of Pharaoh's approaching army, ¹²Jeremiah started to leave the city on his way to the territory of Benjamin, to claim his share of the property among his relatives there.* ¹³But as he was walking through the Benjamin Gate, a sentry arrested him and said, "You are defecting to the Babylonians!" The sentry making the arrest was Irijah son of Shelemiah, grandson of Hananiah.

¹⁴"That's not true!" Jeremiah protested. "I had no intention of doing any such thing." But Irijah wouldn't listen, and he took Jeremiah before the officials. ¹⁵They were furious with Jeremiah and had him flogged and imprisoned in the house of Jonathan the secretary. Jonathan's house had been converted into a prison. ¹⁶Jeremiah was put into a dungeon cell, where he remained for many days.

¹⁷Later King Zedekiah secretly requested that Jeremiah come to the palace, where the king asked him, "Do you have any messages from the LORD?"

37:1a Hebrew *Coniah*, a variant spelling of Jehoiachin.
37:1b Hebrew *Nebuchadrezzar*, a variant spelling of Nebuchadnezzar.   37:5a Hebrew *army of Pharaoh*; see 44:30.
37:5b Or *Chaldean*; also in 37:10, 11.   37:8 Or *Chaldeans*; also in 37:9, 13.   37:12 Hebrew *to separate from there in the midst of the people.*

"Yes, I do!" said Jeremiah. "You will be defeated by the king of Babylon."

[18] Then Jeremiah asked the king, "What crime have I committed? What have I done against you, your attendants, or the people that I should be imprisoned like this? [19] Where are your prophets now who told you the king of Babylon would not attack you or this land? [20] Listen, my lord the king, I beg you. Don't send me back to the dungeon in the house of Jonathan the secretary, for I will die there."

[21] So King Zedekiah commanded that Jeremiah not be returned to the dungeon. Instead, he was imprisoned in the courtyard of the guard in the royal palace. The king also commanded that Jeremiah be given a loaf of fresh bread every day as long as there was any left in the city. So Jeremiah was put in the palace prison.

JEREMIAH IN A CISTERN

38 Now Shephatiah son of Mattan, Gedaliah son of Pashhur, Jehucal* son of Shelemiah, and Pashhur son of Malkijah heard what Jeremiah had been telling the people. He had been saying, [2] "This is what the LORD says: 'Everyone who stays in Jerusalem will die from war, famine, or disease, but those who surrender to the Babylonians* will live. Their reward will be life. They will live!' [3] The LORD also says: 'The city of Jerusalem will certainly be handed over to the army of the king of Babylon, who will capture it.'"

[4] So these officials went to the king and said, "Sir, this man must die! That kind of talk will undermine the morale of the few fighting men we have left, as well as that of all the people. This man is a traitor!"

[5] King Zedekiah agreed. "All right," he said. "Do as you like. I can't stop you."

[6] So the officials took Jeremiah from his cell and lowered him by ropes into an empty cistern in the prison yard. It belonged to Malkijah, a member of the royal family. There was no water in the cistern, but there was a thick layer of mud at the bottom, and Jeremiah sank down into it.

[7] But Ebed-melech the Ethiopian,* an important court official, heard that Jeremiah was in the cistern. At that time the king was holding court at the Benjamin Gate, [8] so Ebed-melech rushed from the palace to speak with him. [9] "My lord the king," he said, "these men have done a very evil thing in putting Jeremiah the prophet into the cistern. He will soon die of hunger, for almost all the bread in the city is gone."

[10] So the king told Ebed-melech, "Take thirty of my men with you, and pull Jeremiah out of the cistern before he dies."

[11] So Ebed-melech took the men with him and went to a room in the palace beneath the treasury, where he found some old rags and discarded clothing. He carried these to the cistern and lowered them to Jeremiah on a rope. [12] Ebed-melech called down to Jeremiah, "Put these rags under your armpits to protect you from the ropes." Then when Jeremiah was ready, [13] they pulled him out. So Jeremiah was returned to the courtyard of the guard—the palace prison—where he remained.

ZEDEKIAH QUESTIONS JEREMIAH

[14] One day King Zedekiah sent for Jeremiah and had him brought to the third entrance of the LORD's Temple. "I want to ask you something," the king said. "And don't try to hide the truth."

[15] Jeremiah said, "If I tell you the truth, you will kill me. And if I give you advice, you won't listen to me anyway."

[16] So King Zedekiah secretly promised him, "As surely as the LORD our Creator lives, I will not kill you or hand you over to the men who want you dead."

[17] Then Jeremiah said to Zedekiah, "This is what the LORD God of Heaven's Armies, the God of Israel, says: 'If you surrender to the Babylonian officers, you and your family will live, and the city will not be burned down. [18] But if you refuse to surrender, you will not escape! This city will be handed over to the Babylonians, and they will burn it to the ground.'"

[19] "But I am afraid to surrender," the king said, "for the Babylonians may hand me over to the Judeans who have defected to them. And who knows what they will do to me!"

[20] Jeremiah replied, "You won't be handed over to them if you choose to obey the LORD. Your life will be spared, and all will go well for you. [21] But if you refuse to surrender, this is what the LORD has revealed to me: [22] All the women left in your palace will be brought out and given to the officers of the Babylonian army. Then the women will taunt you, saying,

'What fine friends you have!
    They have betrayed and misled you.
When your feet sank in the mud,
    they left you to your fate!'

[23] All your wives and children will be led out to the Babylonians, and you will not escape. You will be seized by the king of Babylon, and this city will be burned down."

[24] Then Zedekiah said to Jeremiah, "Don't tell anyone you told me this, or you will die! [25] My officials may hear that I spoke to you, and they may say, 'Tell us what you and the king were talking about. If you don't tell us, we will kill you.' [26] If this happens, just tell them you begged me not to send you back to Jonathan's dungeon, for fear you would die there."

[27] Sure enough, it wasn't long before the king's officials came to Jeremiah and asked him why the king had called for him. But Jeremiah followed the king's instructions, and they left

---

38:1 Hebrew *Jucal,* a variant spelling of Jehucal; see 37:3.
38:2 Or *Chaldeans;* also in 38:18, 19, 23.   38:7 Hebrew *the Cushite.*

without finding out the truth. No one had overheard the conversation between Jeremiah and the king. 28And Jeremiah remained a prisoner in the courtyard of the guard until the day Jerusalem was captured.

THE FALL OF JERUSALEM

39 In January* of the ninth year of King Zedekiah's reign, King Nebuchadnezzar* of Babylon came with his entire army to besiege Jerusalem. 2Two and a half years later, on July 18* in the eleventh year of Zedekiah's reign, a section of the city wall was broken down. 3All the officers of the Babylonian army came in and sat in triumph at the Middle Gate: Nergal-sharezer of Samgar, and Nebo-sarsekim,* a chief officer, and Nergal-sharezer, the king's adviser, and all the other officers of the king of Babylon.

4When King Zedekiah of Judah and all the soldiers saw that the Babylonians had broken into the city, they fled. They waited for nightfall and then slipped through the gate between the two walls behind the king's garden and headed toward the Jordan Valley.* 5But the Babylonian* troops chased them and overtook Zedekiah on the plains of Jericho. They captured him and took him to King Nebuchadnezzar of Babylon, who was at Riblah in the land of Hamath. There the king of Babylon pronounced judgment upon Zedekiah. 6The king of Babylon made Zedekiah watch as he slaughtered his sons at Riblah. The king of Babylon also slaughtered all the nobles of Judah. 7Then he gouged out Zedekiah's eyes and bound him in bronze chains to lead him away to Babylon.

8Meanwhile, the Babylonians burned Jerusalem, including the royal palace and the houses of the people, and they tore down the walls of the city. 9Then Nebuzaradan, the captain of the guard, took as exiles to Babylon the rest of the people who remained in the city, those who had defected to him, and everyone else who remained. 10But Nebuzaradan allowed some of the poorest people to stay behind in the land of Judah, and he assigned them to care for the vineyards and fields.

JEREMIAH REMAINS IN JUDAH

11King Nebuchadnezzar had told Nebuzaradan, the captain of the guard, to find Jeremiah. 12"See that he isn't hurt," he said. "Look after him well, and give him anything he wants." 13So Nebuzaradan, the captain of the guard; Nebushazban, a chief officer; Nergal-sharezer, the king's adviser; and the other officers of Babylon's king 14sent messengers to bring Jeremiah out of the prison. They put him under the care of Gedaliah son of Ahikam and grandson of Shaphan, who took him back to his home. So Jeremiah stayed in Judah among his own people.

15The LORD had given the following message to Jeremiah while he was still in prison: 16"Say to Ebed-melech the Ethiopian,* 'This is what the LORD of Heaven's Armies, the God of Israel, says: I will do to this city everything I have threatened. I will send disaster, not prosperity. You will see its destruction, 17but I will rescue you from those you fear so much. 18Because you trusted me, I will give you your life as a reward. I will rescue you and keep you safe. I, the LORD, have spoken!'"

40 The LORD gave a message to Jeremiah after Nebuzaradan, the captain of the guard, had released him at Ramah. He had found Jeremiah bound in chains among all the other captives of Jerusalem and Judah who were being sent to exile in Babylon.

2The captain of the guard called for Jeremiah and said, "The LORD your God has brought this disaster on this land, 3just as he said he would. For these people have sinned against the LORD and disobeyed him. That is why it happened. 4But I am going to take off your chains and let you go. If you want to come with me to Babylon, you are welcome. I will see that you are well cared for. But if you don't want to come, you may stay here. The whole land is before you—go wherever you like. 5If you decide to stay, then return to Gedaliah son of Ahikam and grandson of Shaphan. He has been appointed governor of Judah by the king of Babylon. Stay there with the people he rules. But it's up to you; go wherever you like."

Then Nebuzaradan, the captain of the guard, gave Jeremiah some food and money and let him go. 6So Jeremiah returned to Gedaliah son of Ahikam at Mizpah, and he lived in Judah with the few who were still left in the land.

GEDALIAH GOVERNS IN JUDAH

7The leaders of the Judean military groups in the countryside heard that the king of Babylon had appointed Gedaliah son of Ahikam as governor over the poor people who were left behind in Judah—the men, women, and children who hadn't been exiled to Babylon. 8So they went to see Gedaliah at Mizpah. These included: Ishmael son of Nethaniah, Johanan and Jonathan sons of Kareah, Seraiah son of Tanhumeth, the sons of Ephai the Netophathite, Jezaniah son of the Maacathite, and all their men. 9Gedaliah vowed to them that the Babylonians* meant them no harm. "Don't be afraid to serve them. Live in the land and serve the king of Babylon, and all will go well for you," he promised. 10"As for me, I will stay at Mizpah to represent

---

39:1a Hebrew *In the tenth month,* of the ancient Hebrew lunar calendar. A number of events in Jeremiah can be cross-checked with dates in surviving Babylonian records and related accurately to our modern calendar. This event occurred on January 15, 588 B.C.; see 52:4a and the note there. 39:1b Hebrew *Nebuchadrezzar,* a variant spelling of Nebuchadnezzar; also in 39:5, 11. 39:2 Hebrew *On the ninth day of the fourth month.* This day was July 18, 586 B.C.; also see note on 39:1a. 39:3 Or *Nergal-sharezer, Samgar-nebo, Sarsekim.* 39:4 Hebrew *the Arabah.* 39:5 Or *Chaldean;* similarly in 39:8. 39:16 Hebrew *the Cushite.* 40:9 Or *Chaldeans;* also in 40:10.

you before the Babylonians who come to meet with us. Settle in the towns you have taken, and live off the land. Harvest the grapes and summer fruits and olives, and store them away."

[11] When the Judeans in Moab, Ammon, Edom, and the other nearby countries heard that the king of Babylon had left a few people in Judah and that Gedaliah was the governor, [12] they began to return to Judah from the places to which they had fled. They stopped at Mizpah to meet with Gedaliah and then went into the Judean countryside to gather a great harvest of grapes and other crops.

A PLOT AGAINST GEDALIAH

[13] Soon after this, Johanan son of Kareah and the other military leaders came to Gedaliah at Mizpah. [14] They said to him, "Did you know that Baalis, king of Ammon, has sent Ishmael son of Nethaniah to assassinate you?" But Gedaliah refused to believe them.

[15] Later Johanan had a private conference with Gedaliah and volunteered to kill Ishmael secretly. "Why should we let him come and murder you?" Johanan asked. "What will happen then to the Judeans who have returned? Why should the few of us who are still left be scattered and lost?"

[16] But Gedaliah said to Johanan, "I forbid you to do any such thing, for you are lying about Ishmael."

THE MURDER OF GEDALIAH

41 But in midautumn of that year,* Ishmael son of Nethaniah and grandson of Elishama, who was a member of the king's high officials, went to Mizpah with ten men to meet Gedaliah. While they were eating together, [2] Ishmael and his ten men suddenly jumped up, drew their swords, and killed Gedaliah, whom the king of Babylon had appointed governor. [3] Ishmael also killed all the Judeans and the Babylonian* soldiers who were with Gedaliah at Mizpah.

[4] The next day, before anyone had heard about Gedaliah's murder, [5] eighty men arrived from Shechem, Shiloh, and Samaria to worship at the Temple of the LORD. They had shaved off their beards, torn their clothes, and cut themselves, and had brought along grain offerings and frankincense. [6] Ishmael left Mizpah to meet them, weeping as he went. When he reached them, he said, "Oh, come and see what has happened to Gedaliah!"

[7] But as soon as they were all inside the town, Ishmael and his men killed all but ten of them and threw their bodies into a cistern. [8] The other ten had talked Ishmael into letting them go by promising to bring him their stores of wheat, barley, olive oil, and honey that they had hidden away. [9] The cistern where Ishmael dumped the bodies of the men he murdered was the large one* dug by King Asa when he fortified Mizpah

to protect himself against King Baasha of Israel. Ishmael son of Nethaniah filled it with corpses.

[10] Then Ishmael made captives of the king's daughters and the other people who had been left under Gedaliah's care in Mizpah by Nebuzaradan, the captain of the guard. Taking them with him, he started back toward the land of Ammon.

[11] But when Johanan son of Kareah and the other military leaders heard about Ishmael's crimes, [12] they took all their men and set out to stop him. They caught up with him at the large pool near Gibeon. [13] The people Ishmael had captured shouted for joy when they saw Johanan and the other military leaders. [14] And all the captives from Mizpah escaped and began to help Johanan. [15] Meanwhile, Ishmael and eight of his men escaped from Johanan into the land of Ammon.

[16] Then Johanan son of Kareah and the other military leaders took all the people they had rescued in Gibeon—the soldiers, women, children, and court officials* whom Ishmael had captured after he killed Gedaliah. [17] They took them all to the village of Geruth-kimham near Bethlehem, where they prepared to leave for Egypt. [18] They were afraid of what the Babylonians* would do when they heard that Ishmael had killed Gedaliah, the governor appointed by the Babylonian king.

WARNING TO STAY IN JUDAH

42 Then all the military leaders, including Johanan son of Kareah and Jezaniah* son of Hoshaiah, and all the people, from the least to the greatest, approached [2] Jeremiah the prophet. They said, "Please pray to the LORD your God for us. As you can see, we are only a tiny remnant compared to what we were before. [3] Pray that the LORD your God will show us what to do and where to go."

[4] "All right," Jeremiah replied. "I will pray to the LORD your God, as you have asked, and I will tell you everything he says. I will hide nothing from you."

[5] Then they said to Jeremiah, "May the LORD your God be a faithful witness against us if we refuse to obey whatever he tells us to do! [6] Whether we like it or not, we will obey the LORD our God to whom we are sending you with our plea. For if we obey him, everything will turn out well for us."

[7] Ten days later the LORD gave his reply to Jeremiah. [8] So he called for Johanan son of Kareah and the other military leaders, and for all the people, from the least to the greatest. [9] He said to them, "You sent me to the LORD, the God of

---

41:1 Hebrew *in the seventh month,* of the ancient Hebrew lunar calendar. This month occurred within the months of October and November 586 B.C.; also see note on 39:1a.   41:3 Or *Chaldean.*
41:9 As in Greek version; Hebrew reads *murdered because of Gedaliah was one.*   41:16 Or *eunuchs.*   41:18 Or *Chaldeans.*
42:1 Greek version reads *Azariah;* compare 43:2.

Israel, with your request, and this is his reply: [10] 'Stay here in this land. If you do, I will build you up and not tear you down; I will plant you and not uproot you. For I am sorry about all the punishment I have had to bring upon you. [11] Do not fear the king of Babylon anymore,' says the Lord. 'For I am with you and will save you and rescue you from his power. [12] I will be merciful to you by making him kind, so he will let you stay here in your land.'

[13] "But if you refuse to obey the Lord your God, and if you say, 'We will not stay here; [14] instead, we will go to Egypt where we will be free from war, the call to arms, and hunger,' [15] then hear the Lord's message to the remnant of Judah. This is what the Lord of Heaven's Armies, the God of Israel, says: 'If you are determined to go to Egypt and live there, [16] the very war and famine you fear will catch up to you, and you will die there. [17] That is the fate awaiting every one of you who insists on going to live in Egypt. Yes, you will die from war, famine, and disease. None of you will escape the disaster I will bring upon you there.'

[18] "This is what the Lord of Heaven's Armies, the God of Israel, says: 'Just as my anger and fury have been poured out on the people of Jerusalem, so they will be poured out on you when you enter Egypt. You will be an object of damnation, horror, cursing, and mockery. And you will never see your homeland again.'

[19] "Listen, you remnant of Judah. The Lord has told you: 'Do not go to Egypt!' Don't forget this warning I have given you today. [20] For you were not being honest when you sent me to pray to the Lord your God for you. You said, 'Just tell us what the Lord our God says, and we will do it!' [21] And today I have told you exactly what he said, but you will not obey the Lord your God any better now than you have in the past. [22] So you can be sure that you will die from war, famine, and disease in Egypt, where you insist on going."

JEREMIAH TAKEN TO EGYPT

43 When Jeremiah had finished giving this message from the Lord their God to all the people, [2] Azariah son of Hoshaiah and Johanan son of Kareah and all the other proud men said to Jeremiah, "You lie! The Lord our God hasn't forbidden us to go to Egypt! [3] Baruch son of Neriah has convinced you to say this, because he wants us to stay here and be killed by the Babylonians* or be carried off into exile."

[4] So Johanan and the other military leaders and all the people refused to obey the Lord's command to stay in Judah. [5] Johanan and the other leaders took with them all the people who had returned from the nearby countries to which they had fled. [6] In the crowd were men, women, and children, the king's daughters, and all those whom Nebuzaradan, the captain of the guard, had left with Gedaliah. The prophet Jeremiah and Baruch were also included. [7] The people refused to obey the voice of the Lord and went to Egypt, going as far as the city of Tahpanhes.

[8] Then at Tahpanhes, the Lord gave another message to Jeremiah. He said, [9] "While the people of Judah are watching, take some large rocks and bury them under the pavement stones at the entrance of Pharaoh's palace here in Tahpanhes. [10] Then say to the people of Judah, 'This is what the Lord of Heaven's Armies, the God of Israel, says: I will certainly bring my servant Nebuchadnezzar,* king of Babylon, here to Egypt. I will set his throne over these stones that I have hidden. He will spread his royal canopy over them. [11] And when he comes, he will destroy the land of Egypt. He will bring death to those destined for death, captivity to those destined for captivity, and war to those destined for war. [12] He will set fire to the temples of Egypt's gods; he will burn the temples and carry the idols away as plunder. He will pick clean the land of Egypt as a shepherd picks fleas from his cloak. And he himself will leave unharmed. [13] He will break down the sacred pillars standing in the temple of the sun* in Egypt, and he will burn down the temples of Egypt's gods.'"

JUDGMENT FOR IDOLATRY

44 This is the message Jeremiah received concerning the Judeans living in northern Egypt in the cities of Migdol, Tahpanhes, and Memphis,* and in southern Egypt* as well: [2] "This is what the Lord of Heaven's Armies, the God of Israel, says: You saw the calamity I brought on Jerusalem and all the towns of Judah. They now lie deserted and in ruins. [3] They provoked my anger with all their wickedness. They burned incense and worshiped other gods—gods that neither they nor you nor any of your ancestors had ever even known.

[4] "Again and again I sent my servants, the prophets, to plead with them, 'Don't do these horrible things that I hate so much.' [5] But my people would not listen or turn back from their wicked ways. They kept on burning incense to these gods. [6] And so my fury boiled over and fell like fire on the towns of Judah and into the streets of Jerusalem, and they are still a desolate ruin today.

[7] "And now the Lord God of Heaven's Armies, the God of Israel, asks you: Why are you destroying yourselves? For not one of you will survive—not a man, woman, or child among you who has come here from Judah, not even the babies in your arms. [8] Why provoke my anger by burning incense to the idols you have made here in Egypt? You will only destroy yourselves and make yourselves an object of cursing and mockery for all the nations of the earth. [9] Have you forgotten

---

43:3 Or *Chaldeans.*   43:10 Hebrew *Nebuchadrezzar,* a variant spelling of Nebuchadnezzar.   43:13 Or in *Heliopolis.*   44:1a Hebrew *Noph.*   44:1b Hebrew *in Pathros.*

the sins of your ancestors, the sins of the kings and queens of Judah, and the sins you and your wives committed in Judah and Jerusalem? [10] To this very hour you have shown no remorse or reverence. No one has chosen to follow my word and the decrees I gave to you and your ancestors before you.

[11] "Therefore, this is what the LORD of Heaven's Armies, the God of Israel, says: I am determined to destroy every one of you! [12] I will take this remnant of Judah—those who were determined to come here and live in Egypt—and I will consume them. They will fall here in Egypt, killed by war and famine. All will die, from the least to the greatest. They will be an object of damnation, horror, cursing, and mockery. [13] I will punish them in Egypt just as I punished them in Jerusalem, by war, famine, and disease. [14] Of that remnant who fled to Egypt, hoping someday to return to Judah, there will be no survivors. Even though they long to return home, only a handful will do so."

[15] Then all the women present and all the men who knew that their wives had burned incense to idols—a great crowd of all the Judeans living in northern Egypt and southern Egypt*—answered Jeremiah, [16] "We will not listen to your messages from the LORD! [17] We will do whatever we want. We will burn incense and pour out liquid offerings to the Queen of Heaven just as much as we like—just as we, and our ancestors, and our kings and officials have always done in the towns of Judah and in the streets of Jerusalem. For in those days we had plenty to eat, and we were well off and had no troubles! [18] But ever since we quit burning incense to the Queen of Heaven and stopped worshiping her with liquid offerings, we have been in great trouble and have been dying from war and famine."

[19] "Besides," the women added, "do you suppose that we were burning incense and pouring out liquid offerings to the Queen of Heaven, and making cakes marked with her image, without our husbands knowing it and helping us? Of course not!"

[20] Then Jeremiah said to all of them, men and women alike, who had given him that answer, [21] "Do you think the LORD did not know that you and your ancestors, your kings and officials, and all the people were burning incense to idols in the towns of Judah and in the streets of Jerusalem? [22] It was because the LORD could no longer bear all the disgusting things you were doing that he made your land an object of cursing—a desolate ruin without inhabitants—as it is today. [23] All these terrible things happened to you because you have burned incense to idols and sinned against the LORD. You have refused to obey him and have not followed his instructions, his decrees, and his laws."

[24] Then Jeremiah said to them all, including the women, "Listen to this message from the LORD, all you citizens of Judah who live in Egypt. [25] This is what the LORD of Heaven's Armies, the God of Israel, says: 'You and your wives have said, "We will keep our promises to burn incense and pour out liquid offerings to the Queen of Heaven," and you have proved by your actions that you meant it. So go ahead and carry out your promises and vows to her!'

[26] "But listen to this message from the LORD, all you Judeans now living in Egypt: 'I have sworn by my great name,' says the LORD, 'that my name will no longer be spoken by any of the Judeans in the land of Egypt. None of you may invoke my name or use this oath: "As surely as the Sovereign LORD lives." [27] For I will watch over you to bring you disaster and not good. Everyone from Judah who is now living in Egypt will suffer war and famine until all of you are dead. [28] Only a small number will escape death and return to Judah from Egypt. Then all those who came to Egypt will find out whose words are true—mine or theirs!

[29] "'And this is the proof I give you,' says the LORD, 'that all I have threatened will happen to you and that I will punish you here.' [30] This is what the LORD says: 'I will turn Pharaoh Hophra, king of Egypt, over to his enemies who want to kill him, just as I turned King Zedekiah of Judah over to King Nebuchadnezzar* of Babylon.'"

A MESSAGE FOR BARUCH

45 The prophet Jeremiah gave a message to Baruch son of Neriah in the fourth year of the reign of Jehoiakim son of Josiah,* after Baruch had written down everything Jeremiah had dictated to him. He said, [2] "This is what the LORD, the God of Israel, says to you, Baruch: [3] You have said, 'I am overwhelmed with trouble! Haven't I had enough pain already? And now the LORD has added more! I am worn out from sighing and can find no rest.'

[4] "Baruch, this is what the LORD says: 'I will destroy this nation that I built. I will uproot what I planted. [5] Are you seeking great things for yourself? Don't do it! I will bring great disaster upon all these people; but I will give you your life as a reward wherever you go. I, the LORD, have spoken!'"

MESSAGES FOR THE NATIONS

46 The following messages were given to Jeremiah the prophet from the LORD concerning foreign nations.

MESSAGES ABOUT EGYPT

[2] This message concerning Egypt was given in the fourth year of the reign of Jehoiakim son of Josiah, the king of Judah, on the occasion of

---

44:15 Hebrew *in Egypt, in Pathros.* 44:30 Hebrew *Nebuchadrezzar,* a variant spelling of Nebuchadnezzar. 45:1 The fourth year of Jehoiakim's reign was 605 B.C.

the battle of Carchemish* when Pharaoh Neco, king of Egypt, and his army were defeated beside the Euphrates River by King Nebuchadnezzar* of Babylon.

³ "Prepare your shields,
  and advance into battle!
⁴ Harness the horses,
  and mount the stallions.
Take your positions.
  Put on your helmets.
Sharpen your spears,
  and prepare your armor.
⁵ But what do I see?
The Egyptian army flees in terror.
The bravest of its fighting men run
  without a backward glance.
They are terrorized at every turn,"
  says the LORD.
⁶ "The swiftest runners cannot flee;
  the mightiest warriors cannot escape.
By the Euphrates River to the north,
  they stumble and fall.

⁷ "Who is this, rising like the Nile at
    floodtime,
  overflowing all the land?
⁸ It is the Egyptian army,
  overflowing all the land,
boasting that it will cover the earth like
    a flood,
  destroying cities and their people.
⁹ Charge, you horses and chariots;
  attack, you mighty warriors of Egypt!
Come, all you allies from Ethiopia, Libya,
    and Lydia*
who are skilled with the shield
    and bow!
¹⁰ For this is the day of the Lord, the LORD of
    Heaven's Armies,
  a day of vengeance on his enemies.
The sword will devour until it is satisfied,
  yes, until it is drunk with your blood!
The Lord, the LORD of Heaven's Armies,
  will receive a sacrifice today
  in the north country beside
    the Euphrates River.

¹¹ "Go up to Gilead to get medicine,
    O virgin daughter of Egypt!
But your many treatments
  will bring you no healing.
¹² The nations have heard of your shame.
  The earth is filled with your cries
    of despair.
Your mightiest warriors will run into
    each other
  and fall down together."

¹³ Then the LORD gave the prophet Jeremiah this message about King Nebuchadnezzar's plans to attack Egypt.

¹⁴ "Shout it out in Egypt!
  Publish it in the cities of Migdol,
    Memphis,* and Tahpanhes!
Mobilize for battle,
  for the sword will devour everyone
    around you.
¹⁵ Why have your warriors fallen?
  They cannot stand, for the LORD has
    knocked them down.
¹⁶ They stumble and fall over each other
  and say among themselves,
'Come, let's go back to our people,
  to the land of our birth.
Let's get away from the sword of
    the enemy!'
¹⁷ There they will say,
  'Pharaoh, the king of Egypt, is a
    loudmouth
  who missed his opportunity!'

¹⁸ "As surely as I live," says the King,
  whose name is the LORD of
    Heaven's Armies,
"one is coming against Egypt
  who is as tall as Mount Tabor,
  or as Mount Carmel by the sea!
¹⁹ Pack up! Get ready to leave for exile,
  you citizens of Egypt!
The city of Memphis will be destroyed,
  without a single inhabitant.
²⁰ Egypt is as sleek as a beautiful heifer,
  but a horsefly from the north is on
    its way!
²¹ Egypt's mercenaries have become like
    fattened calves.
  They, too, will turn and run,
for it is a day of great disaster for Egypt,
  a time of great punishment.
²² Egypt flees, silent as a serpent gliding away.
  The invading army marches in;
they come against her with axes
  like woodsmen.
²³ They will cut down her people like trees,"
  says the LORD,
"for they are more numerous than locusts.
²⁴ Egypt will be humiliated;
  she will be handed over to people from
    the north."

²⁵ The LORD of Heaven's Armies, the God of Israel, says: "I will punish Amon, the god of Thebes,* and all the other gods of Egypt. I will punish its rulers and Pharaoh, too, and all who trust in him. ²⁶ I will hand them over to those who want them killed—to King Nebuchadnezzar of Babylon and his army. But afterward the

---

46:2a This event occurred in 605 B.C., during the fourth year of Jehoiakim's reign (according to the calendar system in which the new year begins in the spring).   46:2b Hebrew *Nebuchadrezzar*, a variant spelling of Nebuchadnezzar; also in 46:13, 26.
46:9 Hebrew *from Cush, Put, and Lud.*   46:14 Hebrew *Noph;* also in 46:19.   46:25 Hebrew *of No.*

land will recover from the ravages of war. I, the LORD, have spoken!

²⁷ "But do not be afraid, Jacob, my servant;
     do not be dismayed, Israel.
For I will bring you home again from
          distant lands,
     and your children will return from
          their exile.
Israel* will return to a life of peace and quiet,
     and no one will terrorize them.
²⁸ Do not be afraid, Jacob, my servant,
     for I am with you," says the LORD.
"I will completely destroy the nations to
          which I have exiled you,
     but I will not completely destroy you.
I will discipline you, but with justice;
     I cannot let you go unpunished."

A MESSAGE ABOUT PHILISTIA

47 This is the LORD's message to the prophet Jeremiah concerning the Philistines of Gaza, before it was captured by the Egyptian army. ² This is what the LORD says:

"A flood is coming from the north
     to overflow the land.
It will destroy the land and everything
          in it—
     cities and people alike.
People will scream in terror,
     and everyone in the land will wail.
³ Hear the clatter of stallions' hooves
     and the rumble of wheels as the chariots
          rush by.
Terrified fathers run madly,
     without a backward glance at their
          helpless children.

⁴ "The time has come for the Philistines
     to be destroyed,
     along with their allies from Tyre
          and Sidon.
Yes, the LORD is destroying the remnant of
     the Philistines,
     those colonists from the island of Crete.*
⁵ Gaza will be humiliated, its head shaved bald;
     Ashkelon will lie silent.
You remnant from the Mediterranean coast,*
     how long will you cut yourselves in
          mourning?

⁶ "Now, O sword of the LORD,
     when will you be at rest again?
Go back into your sheath;
     rest and be still.

⁷ "But how can it be still
     when the LORD has sent it on a mission?
For the city of Ashkelon
     and the people living along the sea
     must be destroyed."

A MESSAGE ABOUT MOAB

48 This message was given concerning Moab. This is what the LORD of Heaven's Armies, the God of Israel, says:

"What sorrow awaits the city of Nebo;
     it will soon lie in ruins.
The city of Kiriathaim will be humiliated
          and captured;
     the fortress will be humiliated and
          broken down.
² No one will ever brag about Moab again,
     for in Heshbon there is a plot to destroy her.
'Come,' they say, 'we will cut her off from
          being a nation.'
     The town of Madmen,* too, will be
          silenced;
     the sword will follow you there.
³ Listen to the cries from Horonaim,
     cries of devastation and great destruction.
⁴ All Moab is destroyed.
     Her little ones will cry out.*
⁵ Her refugees weep bitterly,
     climbing the slope to Luhith.
They cry out in terror,
     descending the slope to Horonaim.
⁶ Flee for your lives!
     Hide* in the wilderness!
⁷ Because you have trusted in your wealth
          and skill,
     you will be taken captive.
Your god Chemosh, with his priests and
          officials,
     will be hauled off to distant lands!

⁸ "All the towns will be destroyed,
     and no one will escape—
either on the plateaus or in the valleys,
     for the LORD has spoken.
⁹ Oh, that Moab had wings
     so she could fly away,*
for her towns will be left empty,
     with no one living in them.
¹⁰ Cursed are those who refuse to do the
          LORD's work,
     who hold back their swords from
          shedding blood!

¹¹ "From his earliest history,
     Moab has lived in peace,
     never going into exile.
He is like wine that has been allowed
          to settle.
He has not been poured from flask to flask,
     and he is now fragrant and smooth.

46:27 Hebrew *Jacob*. See note on 5:20.   47:4 Hebrew *from Caphtor*.   47:5 Hebrew *the plain*.   48:2 *Madmen* sounds like the Hebrew word for "silence"; it should not be confused with the English word *madmen*.   48:4 Greek version reads *Her cries are heard as far away as Zoar*.   48:6 Or *Hide like a wild donkey;* or *Hide like a juniper shrub;* or *Be like* [the town of] *Aroer*. The meaning of the Hebrew is uncertain.   48:9 Or *Put salt on Moab, / for she will be laid waste*.

¹² But the time is coming soon," says the LORD,
  "when I will send men to pour him from
    his jar.
They will pour him out,
  then shatter the jar!
¹³ At last Moab will be ashamed of his idol
    Chemosh,
  as the people of Israel were ashamed of
    their gold calf at Bethel.*
¹⁴ "You used to boast, 'We are heroes,
    mighty men of war.'
¹⁵ But now Moab and his towns will
    be destroyed.
  His most promising youth are doomed
    to slaughter,"
  says the King, whose name is the LORD of
    Heaven's Armies.
¹⁶ "Destruction is coming fast for Moab;
    calamity threatens ominously.
¹⁷ You friends of Moab,
    weep for him and cry!
  See how the strong scepter is broken,
    how the beautiful staff is shattered!
¹⁸ "Come down from your glory
    and sit in the dust, you people of Dibon,
  for those who destroy Moab will shatter
    Dibon, too.
  They will tear down all your towers.
¹⁹ You people of Aroer,
    stand beside the road and watch.
  Shout to those who flee from Moab,
    'What has happened there?'

²⁰ "And the reply comes back,
    'Moab lies in ruins, disgraced;
    weep and wail!
  Tell it by the banks of the Arnon River:
    Moab has been destroyed!'
²¹ Judgment has been poured out on the towns
    of the plateau—
  on Holon and Jahaz* and Mephaath,
²² on Dibon and Nebo and Beth-diblathaim,
²³   on Kiriathaim and Beth-gamul and
    Beth-meon,
²⁴ on Kerioth and Bozrah—
    all the towns of Moab, far and near.

²⁵ "The strength of Moab has ended.
    His arm has been broken," says the LORD.
²⁶ "Let him stagger and fall like a drunkard,
    for he has rebelled against the LORD.
  Moab will wallow in his own vomit,
    ridiculed by all.
²⁷ Did you not ridicule the people of Israel?
  Were they caught in the company
    of thieves
    that you should despise them as you do?

²⁸ "You people of Moab,
    flee from your towns and live in the caves.

Hide like doves that nest
  in the clefts of the rocks.
²⁹ We have all heard of the pride of Moab,
    for his pride is very great.
  We know of his lofty pride,
    his arrogance, and his haughty heart.
³⁰ I know about his insolence,"
    says the LORD,
  "but his boasts are empty—
    as empty as his deeds.
³¹ So now I wail for Moab;
    yes, I will mourn for Moab.
  My heart is broken for the men of
    Kir-hareseth.*

³² "You people of Sibmah, rich in vineyards,
    I will weep for you even more than I did
      for Jazer.
  Your spreading vines once reached as far as
    the Dead Sea,*
  but the destroyer has stripped you bare!
  He has harvested your grapes and
    summer fruits.
³³ Joy and gladness are gone from
    fruitful Moab.
  The presses yield no wine.
  No one treads the grapes with shouts of joy.
    There is shouting, yes, but not of joy.

³⁴ "Instead, their awful cries of terror can be heard from Heshbon clear across to Elealeh and Jahaz; from Zoar all the way to Horonaim and Eglath-shelishiyah. Even the waters of Nimrim are dried up now.

³⁵ "I will put an end to Moab," says the LORD, "for the people offer sacrifices to the pagan shrines and burn incense to their false gods. ³⁶ My heart moans like a flute for Moab and Kir-hareseth, for all their wealth has disappeared. ³⁷ The people shave their heads and beards in mourning. They slash their hands and put on clothes made of burlap. ³⁸ There is crying and sorrow in every Moabite home and on every street. For I have smashed Moab like an old, unwanted jar. ³⁹ How it is shattered! Hear the wailing! See the shame of Moab! It has become an object of ridicule, an example of ruin to all its neighbors."

⁴⁰ This is what the LORD says:

"Look! The enemy swoops down like an eagle,
    spreading his wings over Moab.
⁴¹ Its cities will fall,
    and its strongholds will be seized.
  Even the mightiest warriors will be in
    anguish
    like a woman in labor.
⁴² Moab will no longer be a nation,
    for it has boasted against the LORD.

48:13 Hebrew *ashamed when they trusted in Bethel.*   48:21 Hebrew *Jahzah,* a variant spelling of Jahaz.   48:31 Hebrew *Kir-heres,* a variant spelling of Kir-hareseth; also in 48:36.   48:32 Hebrew *the sea of Jazer.*

⁴³ "Terror and traps and snares will be your lot,
   O Moab," says the LORD.
⁴⁴ "Those who flee in terror will fall into a trap,
   and those who escape the trap will step
      into a snare.
I will see to it that you do not get away,
   for the time of your judgment has come,"
says the LORD.
⁴⁵ "The people flee as far as Heshbon
   but are unable to go on.
For a fire comes from Heshbon,
   King Sihon's ancient home,
to devour the entire land
   with all its rebellious people.

⁴⁶ "What sorrow awaits you, O people of Moab!
   The people of the god Chemosh are
      destroyed!
Your sons and your daughters
   have been taken away as captives.
⁴⁷ But I will restore the fortunes of Moab
   in days to come.
   I, the LORD, have spoken!"

This is the end of Jeremiah's prophecy concerning Moab.

A MESSAGE ABOUT AMMON

49 This message was given concerning the
Ammonites. This is what the LORD says:

"Are there no descendants of Israel
   to inherit the land of Gad?
Why are you, who worship Molech,*
   living in its towns?
² In the days to come," says the LORD,
   "I will sound the battle cry against your
      city of Rabbah.
It will become a desolate heap of ruins,
   and the neighboring towns will
      be burned.
Then Israel will take back the land
   you took from her," says the LORD.

³ "Cry out, O Heshbon,
   for the town of Ai is destroyed.
Weep, O people of Rabbah!
   Put on your clothes of mourning.
Weep and wail, hiding in the hedges,
   for your god Molech, with his priests and
      officials,
   will be hauled off to distant lands.
⁴ You are proud of your fertile valleys,
   but they will soon be ruined.
You trusted in your wealth,
   you rebellious daughter,
   and thought no one could ever harm you.
⁵ But look! I will bring terror upon you,"
   says the Lord, the LORD of
      Heaven's Armies.
"Your neighbors will chase you from
   your land,

and no one will help your exiles
   as they flee.
⁶ But I will restore the fortunes of
   the Ammonites
   in days to come.
   I, the LORD, have spoken."

MESSAGES ABOUT EDOM

⁷This message was given concerning Edom. This
is what the LORD of Heaven's Armies says:

"Is there no wisdom in Teman?
   Is no one left to give wise counsel?
⁸ Turn and flee!
   Hide in deep caves, you people of Dedan!
For when I bring disaster on Edom,*
   I will punish you, too!
⁹ Those who harvest grapes
   always leave a few for the poor.
If thieves came at night,
   they would not take everything.
¹⁰ But I will strip bare the land of Edom,
   and there will be no place left to hide.
Its children, its brothers, and its neighbors
   will all be destroyed,
   and Edom itself will be no more.
¹¹ But I will protect the orphans who remain
      among you.
   Your widows, too, can depend on me
      for help."

¹²And this is what the LORD says: "If the innocent must suffer, how much more must you! You
will not go unpunished! You must drink this
cup of judgment! ¹³ For I have sworn by my own
name," says the LORD, "that Bozrah will become
an object of horror and a heap of ruins; it will be
mocked and cursed. All its towns and villages
will be desolate forever."

¹⁴ I have heard a message from the LORD
   that an ambassador was sent to the
      nations to say,
"Form a coalition against Edom,
   and prepare for battle!"

¹⁵ The LORD says to Edom,
"I will cut you down to size among
   the nations.
You will be despised by all.
¹⁶ You have been deceived
   by the fear you inspire in others
   and by your own pride.
You live in a rock fortress
   and control the mountain heights.
But even if you make your nest among the
      peaks with the eagles,
   I will bring you crashing down,"
   says the LORD.

49:1 Hebrew *Malcam*, a variant spelling of Molech; also in 49:3.
49:8 Hebrew *Esau*; also in 49:10.

¹⁷ "Edom will be an object of horror.
  All who pass by will be appalled
    and will gasp at the destruction
      they see there.
¹⁸ It will be like the destruction of Sodom
    and Gomorrah
  and their neighboring towns,"
    says the LORD.
"No one will live there;
  no one will inhabit it.
¹⁹ I will come like a lion from the thickets of
    the Jordan,
  leaping on the sheep in the pasture.
I will chase Edom from its land,
  and I will appoint the leader of my choice.
For who is like me, and who can challenge
    me?
  What ruler can oppose my will?"

²⁰ Listen to the LORD's plans against Edom
    and the people of Teman.
Even the little children will be dragged off
    like sheep,
  and their homes will be destroyed.
²¹ The earth will shake with the noise of
    Edom's fall,
  and its cry of despair will be heard all
    the way to the Red Sea.*
²² Look! The enemy swoops down like
    an eagle,
  spreading his wings over Bozrah.
Even the mightiest warriors will be
    in anguish
  like a woman in labor.

A MESSAGE ABOUT DAMASCUS

²³ This message was given concerning Damascus.
This is what the LORD says:

"The towns of Hamath and Arpad are
    struck with fear,
  for they have heard the news of their
    destruction.
Their hearts are troubled
  like a wild sea in a raging storm.
²⁴ Damascus has become feeble,
  and all her people turn to flee.
Fear, anguish, and pain have gripped her
  as they grip a woman in labor.
²⁵ That famous city, a city of joy,
  will be forsaken!
²⁶ Her young men will fall in the streets
    and die.
  Her soldiers will all be killed,"
    says the LORD of Heaven's Armies.
²⁷ "And I will set fire to the walls of Damascus
  that will burn up the palaces of
    Ben-hadad."

A MESSAGE ABOUT KEDAR AND HAZOR

²⁸ This message was given concerning Kedar and
the kingdoms of Hazor, which were attacked by
King Nebuchadnezzar* of Babylon. This is what
the LORD says:

"Advance against Kedar!
  Destroy the warriors from the East!
²⁹ Their flocks and tents will be captured,
  and their household goods and camels
    will be taken away.
Everywhere shouts of panic will be heard:
  'We are terrorized at every turn!'
³⁰ Run for your lives," says the LORD.
  "Hide yourselves in deep caves, you
    people of Hazor,
for King Nebuchadnezzar of Babylon has
    plotted against you
  and is preparing to destroy you.

³¹ "Go up and attack that complacent nation,"
    says the LORD.
"Its people live alone in the desert
  without walls or gates.
³² Their camels and other livestock will all
    be yours.
  I will scatter to the winds these people
    who live in remote places.*
I will bring calamity upon them
  from every direction," says the LORD.
³³ "Hazor will be inhabited by jackals,
  and it will be desolate forever.
No one will live there;
  no one will inhabit it."

A MESSAGE ABOUT ELAM

³⁴ This message concerning Elam came to the
prophet Jeremiah from the LORD at the beginning of the reign of King Zedekiah of Judah.
³⁵ This is what the LORD of Heaven's Armies says:

"I will destroy the archers of Elam—
  the best of their forces.
³⁶ I will bring enemies from all directions,
  and I will scatter the people of Elam to
    the four winds.
They will be exiled to countries around
    the world.
³⁷ I myself will go with Elam's enemies to
    shatter it.
  In my fierce anger, I will bring great
    disaster
  upon the people of Elam," says the LORD.
"Their enemies will chase them with the
    sword
  until I have destroyed them completely.
³⁸ I will set my throne in Elam," says the LORD,
  "and I will destroy its king and officials.
³⁹ But I will restore the fortunes of Elam
  in days to come.
    I, the LORD, have spoken!"

49:21 Hebrew *sea of reeds*. 49:28 Hebrew *Nebuchadrezzar*, a
variant spelling of Nebuchadnezzar; also in 49:30. 49:32 Or *who
clip the corners of their hair*.

A MESSAGE ABOUT BABYLON

50 The LORD gave Jeremiah the prophet this message concerning Babylon and the land of the Babylonians.* 2 This is what the LORD says:

"Tell the whole world,
  and keep nothing back.
Raise a signal flag
  to tell everyone that Babylon will fall!
Her images and idols* will be shattered.
  Her gods Bel and Marduk will be utterly
    disgraced.
3 For a nation will attack her from the north
  and bring such destruction that no one
    will live there again.
Everything will be gone;
  both people and animals will flee.

HOPE FOR ISRAEL AND JUDAH

4 "In those coming days,"
  says the LORD,
"the people of Israel will return home
  together with the people of Judah.
They will come weeping
  and seeking the LORD their God.
5 They will ask the way to Jerusalem*
  and will start back home again.
They will bind themselves to the LORD
  with an eternal covenant that will never
    be forgotten.

6 "My people have been lost sheep.
  Their shepherds have led them astray
  and turned them loose in the mountains.
They have lost their way
  and can't remember how to get back to
    the sheepfold.
7 All who found them devoured them.
  Their enemies said,
'We did nothing wrong in attacking them,
  for they sinned against the LORD,
their true place of rest,
  and the hope of their ancestors.'

8 "But now, flee from Babylon!
  Leave the land of the Babylonians.
Like male goats at the head of the flock,
  lead my people home again.
9 For I am raising up an army
  of great nations from the north.
They will join forces to attack Babylon,
  and she will be captured.
The enemies' arrows will go straight to
    the mark;
  they will not miss!
10 Babylonia* will be looted
  until the attackers are glutted with loot.
I, the LORD, have spoken!

BABYLON'S SURE FALL

11 "You rejoice and are glad,
  you who plundered my chosen people.

You frisk about like a calf in a meadow
  and neigh like a stallion.
12 But your homeland* will be overwhelmed
  with shame and disgrace.
You will become the least of nations—
  a wilderness, a dry and desolate land.
13 Because of the LORD's anger,
  Babylon will become a deserted wasteland.
All who pass by will be horrified
  and will gasp at the destruction they
    see there.

14 "Yes, prepare to attack Babylon,
  all you surrounding nations.
Let your archers shoot at her; spare no arrows.
  For she has sinned against the LORD.
15 Shout war cries against her from every side.
  Look! She surrenders!
  Her walls have fallen.
It is the LORD's vengeance,
  so take vengeance on her.
  Do to her as she has done to others!
16 Take from Babylon all those who plant crops;
  send all the harvesters away.
Because of the sword of the enemy,
  everyone will run away and rush back to
    their own lands.

HOPE FOR GOD'S PEOPLE

17 "The Israelites are like sheep
  that have been scattered by lions.
First the king of Assyria ate them up.
  Then King Nebuchadnezzar* of Babylon
    cracked their bones."
18 Therefore, this is what the LORD of
    Heaven's Armies,
  the God of Israel, says:
"Now I will punish the king of Babylon and
    his land,
  just as I punished the king of Assyria.
19 And I will bring Israel home again to its
    own land,
  to feed in the fields of Carmel and Bashan,
and to be satisfied once more
  in the hill country of Ephraim and Gilead.
20 In those days," says the LORD,
  "no sin will be found in Israel or in Judah,
  for I will forgive the remnant I preserve.

THE LORD'S JUDGMENT ON BABYLON

21 "Go up, my warriors, against the land of
    Merathaim
  and against the people of Pekod.
Pursue, kill, and completely destroy* them,
  as I have commanded you," says the LORD.

50:1 Or *Chaldeans;* also in 50:8, 25, 35, 45. 50:2 The Hebrew term (literally *round things*) probably alludes to dung. 50:5 Hebrew *Zion;* also in 50:28. 50:10 Or *Chaldea.* 50:12 Hebrew *your mother.* 50:17 Hebrew *Nebuchadrezzar,* a variant spelling of Nebuchadnezzar. 50:21 The Hebrew term used here refers to the complete consecration of things or people to the LORD, either by destroying them or by giving them as an offering.

²² "Let the battle cry be heard in the land,
a shout of great destruction.
²³ Babylon, the mightiest hammer in
all the earth,
lies broken and shattered.
Babylon is desolate among the nations!
²⁴ Listen, Babylon, for I have set a trap for you.
You are caught, for you have fought
against the Lord.
²⁵ The Lord has opened his armory
and brought out weapons to vent his fury.
The terror that falls upon the Babylonians
will be the work of the Sovereign Lord of
Heaven's Armies.
²⁶ Yes, come against her from distant lands.
Break open her granaries.
Crush her walls and houses into
heaps of rubble.
Destroy her completely, and leave nothing!
²⁷ Destroy even her young bulls—
it will be terrible for them, too!
Slaughter them all!
For Babylon's day of reckoning has come.
²⁸ Listen to the people who have escaped
from Babylon,
as they tell in Jerusalem
how the Lord our God has taken vengeance
against those who destroyed his Temple.

²⁹ "Send out a call for archers to come to
Babylon.
Surround the city so none can escape.
Do to her as she has done to others,
for she has defied the Lord,
the Holy One of Israel.
³⁰ Her young men will fall in the streets and die.
Her soldiers will all be killed,"
says the Lord.

³¹ "See, I am your enemy, you arrogant people,"
says the Lord, the Lord of Heaven's
Armies.
"Your day of reckoning has arrived—
the day when I will punish you.
³² O land of arrogance, you will stumble and
fall,
and no one will raise you up.
For I will light a fire in the cities of Babylon
that will burn up everything around them."

³³ This is what the Lord of Heaven's
Armies says:
"The people of Israel and Judah have been
wronged.
Their captors hold them and refuse to let
them go.
³⁴ But the one who redeems them is strong.
His name is the Lord of Heaven's Armies.
He will defend them
and give them rest again in Israel.
But for the people of Babylon
there will be no rest!

³⁵ "The sword of destruction will strike
the Babylonians,"
says the Lord.
"It will strike the people of Babylon—
her officials and wise men, too.
³⁶ The sword will strike her wise counselors,
and they will become fools.
The sword will strike her mightiest warriors,
and panic will seize them.
³⁷ The sword will strike her horses and chariots
and her allies from other lands,
and they will all become like women.
The sword will strike her treasures,
and they all will be plundered.
³⁸ A drought* will strike her water supply,
causing it to dry up.
And why? Because the whole land is filled
with idols,
and the people are madly in love with them.

³⁹ "Soon Babylon will be inhabited by desert
animals and hyenas.
It will be a home for owls.
Never again will people live there;
it will lie desolate forever.
⁴⁰ I will destroy it as I* destroyed Sodom
and Gomorrah
and their neighboring towns,"
says the Lord.
"No one will live there;
no one will inhabit it.

⁴¹ "Look! A great army is coming from the
north.
A great nation and many kings
are rising against you from far-off lands.
⁴² They are armed with bows and spears.
They are cruel and show no mercy.
As they ride forward on horses,
they sound like a roaring sea.
They are coming in battle formation,
planning to destroy you, Babylon.
⁴³ The king of Babylon has heard reports about
the enemy,
and he is weak with fright.
Pangs of anguish have gripped him,
like those of a woman in labor.

⁴⁴ "I will come like a lion from the thickets of
the Jordan,
leaping on the sheep in the pasture.
I will chase Babylon from its land,
and I will appoint the leader of my choice.
For who is like me, and who can challenge
me?
What ruler can oppose my will?"

⁴⁵ Listen to the Lord's plans against Babylon
and the land of the Babylonians.

50:38 Or *sword;* the Hebrew words for *drought* and *sword* are very
similar.   50:40 Hebrew *as God.*

Even the little children will be dragged off
  like sheep,
and their homes will be destroyed.
⁴⁶ The earth will shake with the shout,
  "Babylon has been taken!"
and its cry of despair will be heard around
  the world.

51 ¹ This is what the LORD says:
  "I will stir up a destroyer against
    Babylon
  and the people of Babylonia.*
² Foreigners will come and winnow her,
  blowing her away as chaff.
They will come from every side
  to rise against her in her day of trouble.
³ Don't let the archers put on their armor
  or draw their bows.
Don't spare even her best soldiers!
  Let her army be completely destroyed.*
⁴ They will fall dead in the land of the
    Babylonians,*
  slashed to death in her streets.
⁵ For the LORD of Heaven's Armies
  has not abandoned Israel and Judah.
He is still their God,
  even though their land was filled with sin
    against the Holy One of Israel."

⁶ Flee from Babylon! Save yourselves!
  Don't get trapped in her punishment!
It is the LORD's time for vengeance;
  he will repay her in full.
⁷ Babylon has been a gold cup in
    the LORD's hands,
  a cup that made the whole earth drunk.
The nations drank Babylon's wine,
  and it drove them all mad.
⁸ But suddenly Babylon, too, has fallen.
  Weep for her.
Give her medicine.
  Perhaps she can yet be healed.
⁹ We would have helped her if we could,
  but nothing can save her now.
Let her go; abandon her.
  Return now to your own land.
For her punishment reaches to the heavens;
  it is so great it cannot be measured.
¹⁰ The LORD has vindicated us.
  Come, let us announce in Jerusalem*
  everything the LORD our God has done.

¹¹ Sharpen the arrows!
  Lift up the shields!*
For the LORD has inspired the kings of
    the Medes
  to march against Babylon and destroy her.
This is his vengeance against those
  who desecrated his Temple.
¹² Raise the battle flag against Babylon!
  Reinforce the guard and station the
    watchmen.

Prepare an ambush,
  for the LORD will fulfill all his plans
    against Babylon.
¹³ You are a city by a great river,
  a great center of commerce,
but your end has come.
  The thread of your life is cut.
¹⁴ The LORD of Heaven's Armies has taken
    this vow
  and has sworn to it by his own name:
"Your cities will be filled with enemies,
  like fields swarming with locusts,
  and they will shout in triumph over you."

A HYMN OF PRAISE TO THE LORD
¹⁵ The LORD made the earth by his power,
  and he preserves it by his wisdom.
With his own understanding
  he stretched out the heavens.
¹⁶ When he speaks in the thunder,
  the heavens roar with rain.
He causes the clouds to rise over the earth.
  He sends the lightning with the rain
  and releases the wind from his
    storehouses.

¹⁷ The whole human race is foolish and
    has no knowledge!
  The craftsmen are disgraced by the idols
    they make,
for their carefully shaped works are a fraud.
  These idols have no breath or power.
¹⁸ Idols are worthless; they are ridiculous lies!
  On the day of reckoning they will all be
    destroyed.
¹⁹ But the God of Israel* is no idol!
  He is the Creator of everything that exists,
including his people, his own special
    possession.
  The LORD of Heaven's Armies is his name!

BABYLON'S GREAT PUNISHMENT
²⁰ "You* are my battle-ax and sword,"
    says the LORD.
  "With you I will shatter nations
  and destroy many kingdoms.
²¹ With you I will shatter armies—
  destroying the horse and rider,
  the chariot and charioteer.
²² With you I will shatter men and women,
  old people and children,
  young men and young women.
²³ With you I will shatter shepherds and flocks,
  farmers and oxen,
  captains and officers.

51:1 Hebrew *of Leb-kamai*, a code name for Babylonia.   51:3 The
Hebrew term used here refers to the complete consecration
of things or people to the LORD, either by destroying them or
by giving them as an offering.   51:4 Or *Chaldeans;* also in 51:54.
51:10 Hebrew *Zion;* also in 51:24.   51:11 Greek version reads *Fill up
the quivers.*   51:19 Hebrew *the Portion of Jacob.* See note on 5:20.
51:20 Possibly Cyrus, whom God used to conquer Babylon.
Compare Isa 44:28; 45:1.

²⁴ "I will repay Babylon
    and the people of Babylonia*
for all the wrong they have done
    to my people in Jerusalem," says the LORD.

²⁵ "Look, O mighty mountain, destroyer of
      the earth!
    I am your enemy," says the LORD.
"I will raise my fist against you,
    to knock you down from the heights.
When I am finished,
    you will be nothing but a heap of burnt
      rubble.
²⁶ You will be desolate forever.
    Even your stones will never again be used
      for building.
You will be completely wiped out,"
    says the LORD.

²⁷ Raise a signal flag to the nations.
    Sound the battle cry!
Mobilize them all against Babylon.
    Prepare them to fight against her!
Bring out the armies of Ararat, Minni, and
      Ashkenaz.
    Appoint a commander,
    and bring a multitude of horses like
      swarming locusts!
²⁸ Bring against her the armies of the
      nations—
    led by the kings of the Medes
    and all their captains and officers.

²⁹ The earth trembles and writhes in pain,
    for everything the LORD has planned
      against Babylon stands unchanged.
Babylon will be left desolate without a
      single inhabitant.
³⁰   Her mightiest warriors no longer fight.
They stay in their barracks, their courage
      gone.
    They have become like women.
The invaders have burned the houses
    and broken down the city gates.
³¹ The news is passed from one runner to
      the next
    as the messengers hurry to tell the king
    that his city has been captured.
³² All the escape routes are blocked.
    The marshes have been set aflame,
    and the army is in a panic.

³³ This is what the LORD of Heaven's Armies,
    the God of Israel, says:
"Babylon is like wheat on a threshing floor,
    about to be trampled.
In just a little while
    her harvest will begin."

³⁴ "King Nebuchadnezzar* of Babylon has
      eaten and crushed us
    and drained us of strength.

He has swallowed us like a great monster
    and filled his belly with our riches.
He has thrown us out of our own country.
³⁵ Make Babylon suffer as she made us suffer,"
    say the people of Zion.
"Make the people of Babylonia pay for
      spilling our blood,"
    says Jerusalem.

THE LORD'S VENGEANCE ON BABYLON

³⁶ This is what the LORD says to Jerusalem:

"I will be your lawyer to plead your case,
    and I will avenge you.
I will dry up her river,
    as well as her springs,
³⁷ and Babylon will become a heap of ruins,
    haunted by jackals.
She will be an object of horror and contempt,
    a place where no one lives.
³⁸ Her people will roar together like
      strong lions.
    They will growl like lion cubs.
³⁹ And while they lie inflamed with all
      their wine,
    I will prepare a different kind of feast
      for them.
I will make them drink until they fall asleep,
    and they will never wake up again,"
    says the LORD.
⁴⁰ "I will bring them down
    like lambs to the slaughter,
    like rams and goats to be sacrificed.

⁴¹ "How Babylon* is fallen—
    great Babylon, praised throughout
      the earth!
Now she has become an object of horror
    among the nations.
⁴² The sea has risen over Babylon;
    she is covered by its crashing waves.
⁴³ Her cities now lie in ruins;
    she is a dry wasteland
    where no one lives or even passes by.
⁴⁴ And I will punish Bel, the god of Babylon,
    and make him vomit up all he has eaten.
The nations will no longer come and
      worship him.
    The wall of Babylon has fallen!

A MESSAGE FOR THE EXILES

⁴⁵ "Come out, my people, flee from Babylon.
    Save yourselves! Run from the LORD's
      fierce anger.
⁴⁶ But do not panic; don't be afraid
    when you hear the first rumor of
      approaching forces.
    For rumors will keep coming year by year.

51:24 Or *Chaldea*; also in 51:35.　**51:34** Hebrew *Nebuchadrezzar*, a variant spelling of Nebuchadnezzar.　**51:41** Hebrew *Sheshach*, a code name for Babylon.

Violence will erupt in the land
  as the leaders fight against each other.

⁴⁷ For the time is surely coming
  when I will punish this great city and
    all her idols.
Her whole land will be disgraced,
  and her dead will lie in the streets.

⁴⁸ Then the heavens and earth will rejoice,
  for out of the north will come
    destroying armies
  against Babylon," says the LORD.

⁴⁹ "Just as Babylon killed the people of Israel
  and others throughout the world,
    so must her people be killed.

⁵⁰ Get out, all you who have escaped
    the sword!
  Do not stand and watch—flee while
    you can!
  Remember the LORD, though you are in a
    far-off land,
  and think about your home
    in Jerusalem."

⁵¹ "We are ashamed," the people say.
  "We are insulted and disgraced
  because the LORD's Temple
    has been defiled by foreigners."

⁵² "Yes," says the LORD, "but the time is
    coming
  when I will destroy Babylon's idols.
  The groans of her wounded people
    will be heard throughout the land.

⁵³ Though Babylon reaches as high as the
    heavens
  and makes her fortifications incredibly
    strong,
  I will still send enemies to plunder her.
  I, the LORD, have spoken!

BABYLON'S COMPLETE DESTRUCTION

⁵⁴ "Listen! Hear the cry of Babylon,
  the sound of great destruction from the
    land of the Babylonians.

⁵⁵ For the LORD is destroying Babylon.
  He will silence her loud voice.
  Waves of enemies pound against her;
    the noise of battle rings through the city.

⁵⁶ Destroying armies come against Babylon.
  Her mighty men are captured,
    and their weapons break in their hands.
  For the LORD is a God who gives just
    punishment;
  he always repays in full.

⁵⁷ I will make her officials and wise men
    drunk,
  along with her captains, officers, and
    warriors.
  They will fall asleep
    and never wake up again!"
says the King, whose name is
  the LORD of Heaven's Armies.

⁵⁸ This is what the LORD of Heaven's
    Armies says:
  "The thick walls of Babylon will be leveled
    to the ground,
  and her massive gates will be burned.
  The builders from many lands have worked
    in vain,
  for their work will be destroyed by fire!"

JEREMIAH'S MESSAGE SENT TO BABYLON

⁵⁹The prophet Jeremiah gave this message to Seraiah son of Neriah and grandson of Mahseiah, a staff officer, when Seraiah went to Babylon with King Zedekiah of Judah. This was during the fourth year of Zedekiah's reign.* ⁶⁰Jeremiah had recorded on a scroll all the terrible disasters that would soon come upon Babylon—all the words written here. ⁶¹He said to Seraiah, "When you get to Babylon, read aloud everything on this scroll. ⁶²Then say, 'LORD, you have said that you will destroy Babylon so that neither people nor animals will remain here. She will lie empty and abandoned forever.' ⁶³When you have finished reading the scroll, tie it to a stone and throw it into the Euphrates River. ⁶⁴Then say, 'In this same way Babylon and her people will sink, never again to rise, because of the disasters I will bring upon her.'"

This is the end of Jeremiah's messages.

THE FALL OF JERUSALEM

52 Zedekiah was twenty-one years old when he became king, and he reigned in Jerusalem eleven years. His mother was Hamutal, the daughter of Jeremiah from Libnah. ²But Zedekiah did what was evil in the LORD's sight, just as Jehoiakim had done. ³These things happened because of the LORD's anger against the people of Jerusalem and Judah, until he finally banished them from his presence and sent them into exile.

Zedekiah rebelled against the king of Babylon. ⁴So on January 15,* during the ninth year of Zedekiah's reign, King Nebuchadnezzar* of Babylon led his entire army against Jerusalem. They surrounded the city and built siege ramps against its walls. ⁵Jerusalem was kept under siege until the eleventh year of King Zedekiah's reign.

⁶By July 18 in the eleventh year of Zedekiah's reign,* the famine in the city had become very severe, and the last of the food was entirely gone. ⁷Then a section of the city wall was broken down, and all the soldiers fled. Since the city was surrounded by the Babylonians,* they waited for

---

51:59 The fourth year of Zedekiah's reign was 593 B.C.
52:4a Hebrew *on the tenth day of the tenth month,* of the ancient Hebrew lunar calendar. A number of events in Jeremiah can be cross-checked with dates in surviving Babylonian records and related accurately to our modern calendar. This day was January 15, 588 B.C. 52:4b Hebrew *Nebuchadrezzar,* a variant spelling of Nebuchadnezzar; also in 52:12, 28, 29, 30. 52:6 Hebrew *By the ninth day of the fourth month* [in the eleventh year of Zedekiah's reign]. This day was July 18, 586 B.C.; also see note on 52:4a. 52:7a Or *the Chaldeans;* similarly in 52:8, 17.

nightfall. Then they slipped through the gate between the two walls behind the king's garden and headed toward the Jordan Valley.*

8 But the Babylonian troops chased King Zedekiah and overtook him on the plains of Jericho, for his men had all deserted him and scattered. 9 They captured the king and took him to the king of Babylon at Riblah in the land of Hamath. There the king of Babylon pronounced judgment upon Zedekiah. 10 The king of Babylon made Zedekiah watch as he slaughtered his sons. He also slaughtered all the officials of Judah at Riblah. 11 Then he gouged out Zedekiah's eyes and bound him in bronze chains, and the king of Babylon led him away to Babylon. Zedekiah remained there in prison until the day of his death.

THE TEMPLE DESTROYED

12 On August 17 of that year,* which was the nineteenth year of King Nebuchadnezzar's reign, Nebuzaradan, the captain of the guard and an official of the Babylonian king, arrived in Jerusalem. 13 He burned down the Temple of the LORD, the royal palace, and all the houses of Jerusalem. He destroyed all the important buildings* in the city. 14 Then he supervised the entire Babylonian* army as they tore down the walls of Jerusalem on every side. 15 Then Nebuzaradan, the captain of the guard, took as exiles some of the poorest of the people, the rest of the people who remained in the city, the defectors who had declared their allegiance to the king of Babylon, and the rest of the craftsmen. 16 But Nebuzaradan allowed some of the poorest people to stay behind to care for the vineyards and fields.

17 The Babylonians broke up the bronze pillars in front of the LORD's Temple, the bronze water carts, and the great bronze basin called the Sea, and they carried all the bronze away to Babylon. 18 They also took all the ash buckets, shovels, lamp snuffers, basins, dishes, and all the other bronze articles used for making sacrifices at the Temple. 19 The captain of the guard also took the small bowls, incense burners, basins, pots, lampstands, ladles, bowls used for liquid offerings, and all the other articles made of pure gold or silver.

20 The weight of the bronze from the two pillars, the Sea with the twelve bronze oxen beneath it, and the water carts was too great to be measured. These things had been made for the LORD's Temple in the days of King Solomon. 21 Each of the pillars was 27 feet tall and 18 feet in circumference.* They were hollow, with walls 3 inches thick.* 22 The bronze capital on top of each pillar was 7½ feet* high and was decorated with a network of bronze pomegranates all the way around. 23 There were 96 pomegranates on the sides, and a total of 100 pomegranates on the network around the top.

24 Nebuzaradan, the captain of the guard, took with him as prisoners Seraiah the high priest, Zephaniah the priest of the second rank, and the three chief gatekeepers. 25 And from among the people still hiding in the city, he took an officer who had been in charge of the Judean army; seven of the king's personal advisers; the army commander's chief secretary, who was in charge of recruitment; and sixty other citizens. 26 Nebuzaradan, the captain of the guard, took them all to the king of Babylon at Riblah. 27 And there at Riblah, in the land of Hamath, the king of Babylon had them all put to death. So the people of Judah were sent into exile from their land.

28 The number of captives taken to Babylon in the seventh year of Nebuchadnezzar's reign* was 3,023. 29 Then in Nebuchadnezzar's eighteenth year* he took 832 more. 30 In Nebuchadnezzar's twenty-third year* he sent Nebuzaradan, the captain of the guard, who took 745 more—a total of 4,600 captives in all.

HOPE FOR ISRAEL'S ROYAL LINE

31 In the thirty-seventh year of the exile of King Jehoiachin of Judah, Evil-merodach ascended to the Babylonian throne. He was kind to* Jehoiachin and released him from prison on March 31 of that year.* 32 He spoke kindly to Jehoiachin and gave him a higher place than all the other exiled kings in Babylon. 33 He supplied Jehoiachin with new clothes to replace his prison garb and allowed him to dine in the king's presence for the rest of his life. 34 So the Babylonian king gave him a regular food allowance as long as he lived. This continued until the day of his death.

52:7b Hebrew the Arabah. 52:12 Hebrew On the tenth day of the fifth month, of the ancient Hebrew lunar calendar. This day was August 17, 586 B.C.; also see note on 52:4a. 52:13 Or destroyed the houses of all the important people. 52:14 Or Chaldean. 52:21a Hebrew 18 cubits [8.3 meters] tall and 12 cubits [5.5 meters] in circumference. 52:21b Hebrew 4 fingers thick [8 centimeters]. 52:22 Hebrew 5 cubits [2.3 meters]. 52:28 This exile in the seventh year of Nebuchadnezzar's reign occurred in 597 B.C. 52:29 This exile in the eighteenth year of Nebuchadnezzar's reign occurred in 586 B.C. 52:30 This exile in the twenty-third year of Nebuchadnezzar's reign occurred in 581 B.C. 52:31a Hebrew He raised the head of. 52:31b Hebrew on the twenty-fifth day of the twelfth month, of the ancient Hebrew lunar calendar. This day was March 31, 561 B.C.; also see note on 52:4a.

LAMENTATIONS

JON HUNTZINGER, PHD

A lament is an expression of mourning or sorrow. The book of Lamentations contains five poems of lament that give expression to the pathos of heartache, confusion, and loss that followed the final destruction of Jerusalem in 586 BC by the Babylonians. Jewish tradition identifies Jeremiah as the writer of these poems, and it is certain that they were written sometime after the fall of the city and the dismantling of the Temple.

The writer carefully composed and constructed these poems. The first four are acrostic poems, meaning each verse in the poem begins with a different letter of the Hebrew alphabet in sequential order. The first and second poems (chapters 1–2) each contain 22 verses, corresponding to the 22 letters of the Hebrew alphabet. Each verse is made up of three lines. The fourth poem (chapter 4) has 22 verses of two lines each, while the fifth poem (chapter 5) has 22 verses but is not an acrostic and, for that reason, is emphatic. The change in the writer's pattern is certainly deliberate. The third, or middle, poem (chapter 3) represents the center and climax of the book. It is an acrostic poem with three verses for each letter of the alphabet, totaling 66 verses in all.

Altogether, the poems represent a lament for the entire Jerusalem community, though each one has its own theme:

— The first compares Jerusalem to a forsaken woman and repeats the phrase (or a variation), "There is no one to comfort me" five times (1:2, 9, 16, 17, 21). There is no comfort for the city and its people.
— The second accuses God for being the One who destroyed Zion and who has acted like a warrior against His own people.
— The third urges the people to be patient because God is compassionate. The middle verses

(3:21–42) of the middle poem speak of God's mercies and goodness.
— The fourth places the guilt for the destruction of the city and Temple on everyone, especially the leaders.
— The fifth poem is a long prayer for restoration even though the people do not deserve it.

The writer preserved the people's shock at the destruction of Jerusalem and the Exile from different perspectives. Sometimes the view is from a first-person singular perspective:

"The LORD is right," Jerusalem says,
    "for I rebelled against him.
Listen, people everywhere;
    look upon my anguish and despair,
for my sons and daughters
    have been taken captive to distant lands"
    (1:18).

Sometimes the view is from a first-person plural perspective:

"LORD, remember what has happened to us.
    See how we have been disgraced!" (5:1).

At other times, the perspective is from a narrator third-person perspective:

"But now their faces are blacker than soot.
    No one recognizes them in the streets.
Their skin sticks to their bones;
    it is as dry and hard as wood" (4:8).

Regardless of the perspective, the poems preserve the cries and anguish of the people of Judah in the sixth century BC out of the ruins of Jerusalem's fall.

SORROW IN JERUSALEM

1 * ¹ Jerusalem, once so full of people,
    is now deserted.
She who was once great among
    the nations
    now sits alone like a widow.
Once the queen of all the earth,
    she is now a slave.

² She sobs through the night;
    tears stream down her cheeks.
Among all her lovers,
    there is no one left to comfort her.
All her friends have betrayed her
    and become her enemies.

³ Judah has been led away into captivity,
    oppressed with cruel slavery.
She lives among foreign nations
    and has no place of rest.
Her enemies have chased her down,
    and she has nowhere to turn.

⁴ The roads to Jerusalem* are in mourning,
    for crowds no longer come to celebrate
    the festivals.
The city gates are silent,
    her priests groan,
her young women are crying—
    how bitter is her fate!

⁵ Her oppressors have become her masters,
    and her enemies prosper,
for the LORD has punished Jerusalem
    for her many sins.
Her children have been captured
    and taken away to distant lands.

⁶ All the majesty of beautiful Jerusalem*
    has been stripped away.
Her princes are like starving deer
    searching for pasture.
They are too weak to run
    from the pursuing enemy.

⁷ In the midst of her sadness and
    wandering,
Jerusalem remembers her ancient
    splendor.
But now she has fallen to her enemy,
    and there is no one to help her.
Her enemy struck her down
    and laughed as she fell.

⁸ Jerusalem has sinned greatly,
    so she has been tossed away like a
    filthy rag.
All who once honored her now despise her,
    for they have seen her stripped naked and
    humiliated.
All she can do is groan
    and hide her face.

⁹ She defiled herself with immorality
    and gave no thought to her future.
Now she lies in the gutter
    with no one to lift her out.
"LORD, see my misery," she cries.
    "The enemy has triumphed."

¹⁰ The enemy has plundered her completely,
    taking every precious thing she owns.
She has seen foreigners violate her
    sacred Temple,
    the place the LORD had forbidden them
    to enter.

¹¹ Her people groan as they search for bread.
    They have sold their treasures for food to
    stay alive.
"O LORD, look," she mourns,
    "and see how I am despised.

¹² "Does it mean nothing to you,
    all you who pass by?
Look around and see if there is any
    suffering like mine,
which the LORD brought on me
    when he erupted in fierce anger.

¹³ "He has sent fire from heaven that burns in
    my bones.
He has placed a trap in my path and
    turned me back.
He has left me devastated,
    racked with sickness all day long.

¹⁴ "He wove my sins into ropes
    to hitch me to a yoke of captivity.
The Lord sapped my strength and turned me
    over to my enemies;
    I am helpless in their hands.

¹⁵ "The Lord has treated my mighty men
    with contempt.
At his command a great army has come
    to crush my young warriors.
The Lord has trampled his beloved city*
    like grapes are trampled in a winepress.

¹⁶ "For all these things I weep;
    tears flow down my cheeks.
No one is here to comfort me;
    any who might encourage me are
    far away.
My children have no future,
    for the enemy has conquered us."

---

1 Each of the first four chapters of this book is an acrostic, laid out in the order of the Hebrew alphabet. The first word of each verse begins with a successive Hebrew letter. Chapters 1, 2, and 4 have one verse for each of the 22 Hebrew letters. Chapter 3 contains 22 stanzas of three verses each. Though chapter 5 has 22 verses, it is not an acrostic. **1:4** Hebrew *Zion;* also in 1:17. **1:6** Hebrew *of the daughter of Zion.* **1:15** Hebrew *the virgin daughter of Judah.*

¹⁷ Jerusalem reaches out for help,
but no one comforts her.
Regarding his people Israel,*
the LORD has said,
"Let their neighbors be their enemies!
Let them be thrown away like a
filthy rag!"

¹⁸ "The LORD is right," Jerusalem says,
"for I rebelled against him.
Listen, people everywhere;
look upon my anguish and despair,
for my sons and daughters
have been taken captive to distant lands.

¹⁹ "I begged my allies for help,
but they betrayed me.
My priests and leaders
starved to death in the city,
even as they searched for food
to save their lives.

²⁰ "LORD, see my anguish!
My heart is broken
and my soul despairs,
for I have rebelled against you.
In the streets the sword kills,
and at home there is only death.

²¹ "Others heard my groans,
but no one turned to comfort me.
When my enemies heard about my troubles,
they were happy to see what you had done.
Oh, bring the day you promised,
when they will suffer as I have suffered.

²² "Look at all their evil deeds, LORD.
Punish them,
as you have punished me
for all my sins.
My groans are many,
and I am sick at heart."

GOD'S ANGER AT SIN

2 ¹ The Lord in his anger
has cast a dark shadow over beautiful
Jerusalem.*
The fairest of Israel's cities lies in the dust,
thrown down from the heights of heaven.
In his day of great anger,
the Lord has shown no mercy even
to his Temple.*

² Without mercy the Lord has destroyed
every home in Israel.*
In his anger he has broken down
the fortress walls of beautiful Jerusalem.*
He has brought them to the ground,
dishonoring the kingdom and its rulers.

³ All the strength of Israel
vanishes beneath his fierce anger.

The Lord has withdrawn his protection
as the enemy attacks.
He consumes the whole land of Israel
like a raging fire.

⁴ He bends his bow against his people,
as though he were their enemy.
His strength is used against them
to kill their finest youth.
His fury is poured out like fire
on beautiful Jerusalem.*

⁵ Yes, the Lord has vanquished Israel
like an enemy.
He has destroyed her palaces
and demolished her fortresses.
He has brought unending sorrow and tears
upon beautiful Jerusalem.

⁶ He has broken down his Temple
as though it were merely a garden shelter.
The LORD has blotted out all memory
of the holy festivals and Sabbath days.
Kings and priests fall together
before his fierce anger.

⁷ The Lord has rejected his own altar;
he despises his own sanctuary.
He has given Jerusalem's palaces
to her enemies.
They shout in the LORD's Temple
as though it were a day of celebration.

⁸ The LORD was determined
to destroy the walls of beautiful
Jerusalem.
He made careful plans for their destruction,
then did what he had planned.
Therefore, the ramparts and walls
have fallen down before him.

⁹ Jerusalem's gates have sunk into
the ground.
He has smashed their locks and bars.
Her kings and princes have been exiled to
distant lands;
her law has ceased to exist.
Her prophets receive
no more visions from the LORD.

¹⁰ The leaders of beautiful Jerusalem
sit on the ground in silence.
They are clothed in burlap
and throw dust on their heads.
The young women of Jerusalem
hang their heads in shame.

1:17 Hebrew *Jacob.* The names "Jacob" and "Israel" are often interchanged throughout the Old Testament, referring sometimes to the individual patriarch and sometimes to the nation. **2:1a** Hebrew *the daughter of Zion;* also in 2:8, 10, 18. **2:1b** Hebrew *his footstool.* **2:2a** Hebrew *Jacob;* also in 2:3b. See note on 1:17. **2:2b** Hebrew *the daughter of Judah;* also in 2:5. **2:4** Hebrew *on the tent of the daughter of Zion.*

¹¹ I have cried until the tears no longer come;
   my heart is broken.
My spirit is poured out in agony
   as I see the desperate plight of my people.
Little children and tiny babies
   are fainting and dying in the streets.

¹² They cry out to their mothers,
   "We need food and drink!"
Their lives ebb away in the streets
   like the life of a warrior wounded in battle.
They gasp for life
   as they collapse in their mothers' arms.

¹³ What can I say about you?
   Who has ever seen such sorrow?
O daughter of Jerusalem,
   to what can I compare your anguish?
O virgin daughter of Zion,
   how can I comfort you?
For your wound is as deep as the sea.
   Who can heal you?

¹⁴ Your prophets have said
   so many foolish things, false to the core.
They did not save you from exile
   by pointing out your sins.
Instead, they painted false pictures,
   filling you with false hope.

¹⁵ All who pass by jeer at you.
   They scoff and insult beautiful
      Jerusalem,* saying,
"Is this the city called
   'Most Beautiful in All the World'
   and 'Joy of All the Earth'?"

¹⁶ All your enemies mock you.
   They scoff and snarl and say,
"We have destroyed her at last!
   We have long waited for this day,
   and it is finally here!"

¹⁷ But it is the LORD who did just as he
      planned.
   He has fulfilled the promises of disaster
   he made long ago.
He has destroyed Jerusalem without mercy.
   He has caused her enemies to gloat
      over her
   and has given them power over her.

¹⁸ Cry aloud* before the Lord,
   O walls of beautiful Jerusalem!
Let your tears flow like a river
   day and night.
Give yourselves no rest;
   give your eyes no relief.

¹⁹ Rise during the night and cry out.
   Pour out your hearts like water to
      the Lord.

Lift up your hands to him in prayer,
   pleading for your children,
for in every street
   they are faint with hunger.

²⁰ "O LORD, think about this!
   Should you treat your own people
      this way?
Should mothers eat their own children,
   those they once bounced on
      their knees?
Should priests and prophets be killed
   within the Lord's Temple?

²¹ "See them lying in the streets—
   young and old,
boys and girls,
   killed by the swords of the enemy.
You have killed them in your anger,
   slaughtering them without mercy.

²² "You have invited terrors from all around,
   as though you were calling them to
      a day of feasting.
In the day of the LORD's anger,
   no one has escaped or survived.
The enemy has killed all the children
   whom I carried and raised."

HOPE IN THE LORD'S FAITHFULNESS

3 ¹ I am the one who has seen
      the afflictions
   that come from the rod of
      the LORD's anger.
² He has led me into darkness,
   shutting out all light.
³ He has turned his hand against me
   again and again, all day long.

⁴ He has made my skin and flesh grow old.
   He has broken my bones.
⁵ He has besieged and surrounded me
   with anguish and distress.
⁶ He has buried me in a dark place,
   like those long dead.

⁷ He has walled me in, and I cannot escape.
   He has bound me in heavy chains.
⁸ And though I cry and shout,
   he has shut out my prayers.
⁹ He has blocked my way with a high
      stone wall;
   he has made my road crooked.

¹⁰ He has hidden like a bear or a lion,
   waiting to attack me.
¹¹ He has dragged me off the path and torn me
      in pieces,
   leaving me helpless and devastated.

2:15 Hebrew *the daughter of Jerusalem.*   2:18 Hebrew *Their heart cried.*

¹² He has drawn his bow
 and made me the target for his arrows.
¹³ He shot his arrows
 deep into my heart.
¹⁴ My own people laugh at me.
 All day long they sing their mocking songs.
¹⁵ He has filled me with bitterness
 and given me a bitter cup of sorrow
 to drink.
¹⁶ He has made me chew on gravel.
 He has rolled me in the dust.
¹⁷ Peace has been stripped away,
 and I have forgotten what prosperity is.
¹⁸ I cry out, "My splendor is gone!
 Everything I had hoped for from the LORD
 is lost!"

¹⁹ The thought of my suffering and
 homelessness
 is bitter beyond words.*
²⁰ I will never forget this awful time,
 as I grieve over my loss.
²¹ Yet I still dare to hope
 when I remember this:

²² The faithful love of the LORD never ends!*
 His mercies never cease.
²³ Great is his faithfulness;
 his mercies begin afresh each morning.
²⁴ I say to myself, "The LORD is my inheritance;
 therefore, I will hope in him!"

²⁵ The LORD is good to those who depend
 on him,
 to those who search for him.
²⁶ So it is good to wait quietly
 for salvation from the LORD.
²⁷ And it is good for people to submit at an
 early age
 to the yoke of his discipline:

²⁸ Let them sit alone in silence
 beneath the LORD's demands.
²⁹ Let them lie face down in the dust,
 for there may be hope at last.
³⁰ Let them turn the other cheek to those
 who strike them
 and accept the insults of their enemies.

³¹ For no one is abandoned
 by the Lord forever.
³² Though he brings grief, he also shows
 compassion
 because of the greatness of his
 unfailing love.
³³ For he does not enjoy hurting people
 or causing them sorrow.

³⁴ If people crush underfoot
 all the prisoners of the land,

³⁵ if they deprive others of their rights
 in defiance of the Most High,
³⁶ if they twist justice in the courts—
 doesn't the Lord see all these things?
³⁷ Who can command things to happen
 without the Lord's permission?
³⁸ Does not the Most High
 send both calamity and good?
³⁹ Then why should we, mere humans,
 complain
 when we are punished for our sins?

⁴⁰ Instead, let us test and examine our ways.
 Let us turn back to the LORD.
⁴¹ Let us lift our hearts and hands
 to God in heaven and say,
⁴² "We have sinned and rebelled,
 and you have not forgiven us.

⁴³ "You have engulfed us with your anger,
 chased us down,
 and slaughtered us without mercy.
⁴⁴ You have hidden yourself in a cloud
 so our prayers cannot reach you.
⁴⁵ You have discarded us as refuse and garbage
 among the nations.

⁴⁶ "All our enemies
 have spoken out against us.
⁴⁷ We are filled with fear,
 for we are trapped, devastated,
 and ruined."
⁴⁸ Tears stream from my eyes
 because of the destruction of
 my people!

⁴⁹ My tears flow endlessly;
 they will not stop
⁵⁰ until the LORD looks down
 from heaven and sees.
⁵¹ My heart is breaking
 over the fate of all the women of
 Jerusalem.

⁵² My enemies, whom I have never harmed,
 hunted me down like a bird.
⁵³ They threw me into a pit
 and dropped stones on me.
⁵⁴ The water rose over my head,
 and I cried out, "This is the end!"

⁵⁵ But I called on your name, LORD,
 from deep within the pit.
⁵⁶ You heard me when I cried,
 "Listen to my pleading!
 Hear my cry for help!"
⁵⁷ Yes, you came when I called;
 you told me, "Do not fear."

3:19 Or *is wormwood and gall.* 3:22 As in Syriac version; Hebrew
reads *of the LORD keeps us from destruction.*

⁵⁸ Lord, you have come to my defense;
 you have redeemed my life.
⁵⁹ You have seen the wrong they have done
 to me, LORD.
 Be my judge, and prove me right.
⁶⁰ You have seen the vengeful plots
 my enemies have laid against me.

⁶¹ LORD, you have heard the vile names
 they call me.
 You know all about the plans
 they have made.
⁶² My enemies whisper and mutter
 as they plot against me all day long.
⁶³ Look at them! Whether they sit or stand,
 I am the object of their mocking songs.

⁶⁴ Pay them back, LORD,
 for all the evil they have done.
⁶⁵ Give them hard and stubborn hearts,
 and then let your curse fall on them!
⁶⁶ Chase them down in your anger,
 destroying them beneath the LORD's
 heavens.

GOD'S ANGER SATISFIED

4 ¹ How the gold has lost its luster!
 Even the finest gold has become dull.
The sacred gemstones
 lie scattered in the streets!

² See how the precious children of
 Jerusalem,*
 worth their weight in fine gold,
are now treated like pots of clay
 made by a common potter.

³ Even the jackals feed their young,
 but not my people Israel.
They ignore their children's cries,
 like ostriches in the desert.

⁴ The parched tongues of their little ones
 stick to the roofs of their mouths in thirst.
The children cry for bread,
 but no one has any to give them.

⁵ The people who once ate the richest foods
 now beg in the streets for anything they
 can get.
Those who once wore the finest clothes
 now search the garbage dumps for food.

⁶ The guilt* of my people
 is greater than that of Sodom,
where utter disaster struck in a moment
 and no hand offered help.

⁷ Our princes once glowed with health—
 brighter than snow, whiter than milk.
Their faces were as ruddy as rubies,
 their appearance like fine jewels.*

⁸ But now their faces are blacker than soot.
 No one recognizes them in the streets.
Their skin sticks to their bones;
 it is as dry and hard as wood.

⁹ Those killed by the sword are better off
 than those who die of hunger.
Starving, they waste away
 for lack of food from the fields.

¹⁰ Tenderhearted women
 have cooked their own children.
They have eaten them
 to survive the siege.

¹¹ But now the anger of the LORD is satisfied.
 His fierce anger has been poured out.
He started a fire in Jerusalem*
 that burned the city to its foundations.

¹² Not a king in all the earth—
 no one in all the world—
would have believed that an enemy
 could march through the gates of
 Jerusalem.

¹³ Yet it happened because of the sins of
 her prophets
 and the sins of her priests,
who defiled the city
 by shedding innocent blood.

¹⁴ They wandered blindly
 through the streets,
so defiled by blood
 that no one dared touch them.

¹⁵ "Get away!" the people shouted at them.
 "You're defiled! Don't touch us!"
So they fled to distant lands
 and wandered among foreign nations,
 but none would let them stay.

¹⁶ The LORD himself has scattered them,
 and he no longer helps them.
People show no respect for the priests
 and no longer honor the leaders.

¹⁷ We looked in vain for our allies
 to come and save us,
but we were looking to nations
 that could not help us.

¹⁸ We couldn't go into the streets
 without danger to our lives.
Our end was near; our days were numbered.
 We were doomed!

4:2 Hebrew *precious sons of Zion.* 4:6 Or *punishment.*
4:7 Hebrew *like lapis lazuli.* 4:11 Hebrew *in Zion.*

¹⁹ Our enemies were swifter than eagles
in flight.
If we fled to the mountains,
they found us.
If we hid in the wilderness,
they were waiting for us there.

²⁰ Our king—the LORD's anointed, the very life
of our nation—
was caught in their snares.
We had thought that his shadow
would protect us against any nation
on earth!

²¹ Are you rejoicing in the land of Uz,
O people of Edom?
But you, too, must drink from the cup of
the LORD's anger.
You, too, will be stripped naked in your
drunkenness.

²² O beautiful Jerusalem,* your punishment
will end;
you will soon return from exile.
But Edom, your punishment is just
beginning;
soon your many sins will be exposed.

PRAYER FOR RESTORATION

5 ¹ LORD, remember what has happened
to us.
See how we have been disgraced!
² Our inheritance has been turned over
to strangers,
our homes to foreigners.
³ We are orphaned and fatherless.
Our mothers are widowed.
⁴ We have to pay for water to drink,
and even firewood is expensive.
⁵ Those who pursue us are at our heels;
we are exhausted but are given no rest.
⁶ We submitted to Egypt and Assyria
to get enough food to survive.

⁷ Our ancestors sinned, but they have died—
and we are suffering the punishment
they deserved!

⁸ Slaves have now become our masters;
there is no one left to rescue us.
⁹ We hunt for food at the risk of our lives,
for violence rules the countryside.
¹⁰ The famine has blackened our skin
as though baked in an oven.
¹¹ Our enemies rape the women in Jerusalem*
and the young girls in all the towns
of Judah.
¹² Our princes are being hanged by
their thumbs,
and our elders are treated with contempt.
¹³ Young men are led away to work at millstones,
and boys stagger under heavy loads
of wood.
¹⁴ The elders no longer sit in the city gates;
the young men no longer dance and sing.
¹⁵ Joy has left our hearts;
our dancing has turned to mourning.
¹⁶ The garlands have* fallen from our heads.
Weep for us because we have sinned.
¹⁷ Our hearts are sick and weary,
and our eyes grow dim with tears.
¹⁸ For Jerusalem* is empty and desolate,
a place haunted by jackals.

¹⁹ But LORD, you remain the same forever!
Your throne continues from generation
to generation.
²⁰ Why do you continue to forget us?
Why have you abandoned us for so long?
²¹ Restore us, O LORD, and bring us back to
you again!
Give us back the joys we once had!
²² Or have you utterly rejected us?
Are you angry with us still?

4:22 Hebrew *O daughter of Zion.*   5:11 Hebrew *in Zion.*
5:16 Or *The crown has.*   5:18 Hebrew *Mount Zion.*

EZEKIEL

JON HUNTZINGER, PHD

The book of Ezekiel records messages spoken by the prophet Ezekiel in Babylon during the Babylonian Exile. It contains 13 dates that help to establish the years of his ministry. The Babylonians forcibly removed people from Judah on three separate occasions in the late seventh century BC and early sixth century BC, with the last deportation occurring in 586 BC. Ezekiel went into exile in 597 BC and prophesied after he arrived in Babylon (593 BC) until 571 BC.

The book of Ezekiel contains three major sections:
— Chapters 1-24 constitute the first half of the book and recall Ezekiel's call to prophesy to Judah and Jerusalem and report his messages (given in words and deeds) about the current judgment of the Exile.
— Chapters 25-32 continue with messages of judgment against foreign nations.
— Chapters 33-48 conclude the book with prophecies of future blessing upon Judah and Jerusalem, including a vision of a new Temple and rebuilt city.

Solomon completed the construction of the Temple in Jerusalem in 959 BC. It contained three parts: the outside court, the Holy Place, and the Most Holy Place (also known as the inner sanctuary or Holy of Holies.) The building was 60 cubits long (90 feet or 27 meters), 20 cubits wide (30 feet or 9 meters), and 25 cubits high (45 feet or 13 meters). A complete description of the Temple is recorded in 1 Kings 6:1-38 and 2 Chronicles 3:1-17. The Most Holy Place contained the Ark of the Covenant, and the people of Israel regarded it as the holiest place on earth. Three facts within the book support the fact that Ezekiel was a priest called by God to prophesy to the exiles (1:1-2):
— He possesses specific knowledge of the Temple precincts.
— He has a vision of the Spirit of God departing from the Temple because of idolatry (10:1-11:13).
— He envisions a glorious future Temple (40:1-46:24).

The book of Ezekiel records several visions given to the prophet by God, meaning Ezekiel sees what God sees.
— In his first vision (1:4-28), Ezekiel sees God's throne, which appears as wheels within wheels, and the creatures who give God praise around it.
— In a later vision, Ezekiel sees idolatry practiced in the Temple and the glory of God departing from it as a result. He sees an idol in the north gate, idols in the court of the priests, another idol being worshipped in the court of the women, and the sun being worshipped at the entrance to the sanctuary (8:1-11:25).
— In yet another vision, Ezekiel sees human bones, scattered across a valley, given new life by the breath of God through the prophet (37:1-14).
— In a final grand vision, Ezekiel sees a rebuilt, enlarged, and glorious Temple from which water flows into the desert and empties into the Dead Sea to grow groves and orchards and to replenish the life of the salty water (chapters 40-48).

The first idol Ezekiel sees in the north gate of the Temple represents the Phoenician goddess Asherah (8:3). King Josiah abolished this idol during his reforms, and when the people reinstalled it, it made God angry. In the court of the priests, Ezekiel sees engravings that were prohibited by God (Deuteronomy 4:17-18; Ezekiel 8:7-10; 11). In the court of the women, he sees an idol to the god Tammuz (8:14), a popular Babylonian god with women. Finally, at the entrance to the sanctuary, Ezekiel sees the worship of the sun god, which Josiah had attempted to stop (8:16; 2 Kings 23:11-12). People in Syria commonly worshipped the sun at that time. All of these idols made God furious.

All of Ezekiel's visions relate to the Temple:
— Ezekiel's first vision reveals the worship around God's throne as a sign of the worship the people should give at the Temple in Jerusalem. Not only does the worship of the Temple not reflect the worship of the throne room of God, but it also reflects the profane worship of idols.
— In Ezekiel's vision of the dry bones, the prophet finds himself in the midst of an unclean graveyard surrounded by the uncovered bones of dead people. What has happened to the people of God is a desecration, but God will give life to that which has died and make holy that which has become unholy. In doing this, He will renew their worship and establish a glorious new and holy place for them to rejoice in Him.

Although Ezekiel eats a scroll God places in his mouth (3:1-3), he does not rely only upon the spoken word to communicate God's message to His people. Like the eating of the scroll, Ezekiel dramatizes God's word for the people in order to intensify its impact and make it memorable for them. The book records seven minidramas Ezekiel performs to focus the people's attention on what God is doing in their midst. In the first (4:1-17), he takes a stone and attacks it to enact the siege of

Jerusalem. He then lies upon his left side for 390 days to represent the number of years the northern kingdom of Israel sinned against God, and he lies upon his right side for 40 days to represent the number of years that the southern kingdom of Judah has sinned. He eats meals of barley, beans, and lentils cooked with fuel from cow manure. This entire drama describes the siege of Jerusalem, the reason for the siege, and the hardship experienced by the people.

In a second drama (5:1-17), Ezekiel uses a sword to cut his hair. He burns one part of his hair, strikes a second part with the sword, and scatters a third part to the wind. This signifies the threefold manner by which God will judge the people for worshipping idols. In his third drama (6:1-14), Ezekiel shouts a message of judgment to the mountains. He does this because the mountains represented the high places where many shrines to various idols were located. God will judge those who engage in idolatry. In a following drama (12:1-27), Ezekiel digs through the walls of his house and carries his luggage through the hole he digs to indicate the nearness of the time for the Exile. In yet a later drama (24:1-14),

Ezekiel cooks bones in a pot to represent the time of judgment (24:1-14).

In one of Ezekiel's most difficult dramas, he acts with indifference to the death of his wife (24:15-27). Through this act, he shows God's reaction to the Exile of His people for worshipping idols. In a final drama (37:15-23), Ezekiel writes the names of Ephraim and Judah on a couple of sticks and binds them together to signify the unity of God's people. Even as God judges them, He will also save them.

Throughout the book, God addresses Ezekiel as "son of man," which identifies him with God's people who went into exile. Unlike the prophet Jeremiah, who remained in Judah during the Exile, the Babylonians took Ezekiel to Babylon. There he experienced what the people experienced. The visions he received in exile allowed him to see events from God's perspective, which he translated into messages and dramatic events so that the people could see and experience for themselves what was happening and how to understand those things. As a son of man, Ezekiel shared in both the people's experience of the Exile as well as God's knowledge of the Exile through the visions he was given.

A VISION OF LIVING BEINGS

1 On July 31* of my thirtieth year,* while I was with the Judean exiles beside the Kebar River in Babylon, the heavens were opened and I saw visions of God. ²This happened during the fifth year of King Jehoiachin's captivity. ³(The LORD gave this message to Ezekiel son of Buzi, a priest, beside the Kebar River in the land of the Babylonians,* and he felt the hand of the LORD take hold of him.)

⁴As I looked, I saw a great storm coming from the north, driving before it a huge cloud that flashed with lightning and shone with brilliant light. There was fire inside the cloud, and in the middle of the fire glowed something like gleaming amber.* ⁵From the center of the cloud came four living beings that looked human, ⁶except that each had four faces and four wings. ⁷Their legs were straight, and their feet had hooves like those of a calf and shone like burnished bronze. ⁸Under each of their four wings I could see human hands. So each of the four beings had four faces and four wings. ⁹The wings of each living being touched the wings of the beings beside it. Each one moved straight forward in any direction without turning around.

¹⁰Each had a human face in the front, the face of a lion on the right side, the face of an ox on the left side, and the face of an eagle at the back. ¹¹Each had two pairs of outstretched wings—one pair stretched out to touch the wings of the living beings on either side of it, and the other pair

covered its body. ¹²They went in whatever direction the spirit chose, and they moved straight forward in any direction without turning around.

¹³The living beings looked like bright coals of fire or brilliant torches, and lightning seemed to flash back and forth among them. ¹⁴And the living beings darted to and fro like flashes of lightning.

¹⁵As I looked at these beings, I saw four wheels touching the ground beside them, one wheel belonging to each. ¹⁶The wheels sparkled as if made of beryl. All four wheels looked alike and were made the same; each wheel had a second wheel turning crosswise within it. ¹⁷The beings could move in any of the four directions they faced, without turning as they moved. ¹⁸The rims of the four wheels were tall and frightening, and they were covered with eyes all around.

¹⁹When the living beings moved, the wheels moved with them. When they flew upward, the wheels went up, too. ²⁰The spirit of the living beings was in the wheels. So wherever the spirit went, the wheels and the living beings also went. ²¹When the beings moved, the wheels moved. When the beings stopped, the wheels stopped. When the beings flew upward, the wheels rose up, for the spirit of the living beings was in the wheels.

1:1a Hebrew *On the fifth day of the fourth month,* of the ancient Hebrew lunar calendar. A number of dates in Ezekiel can be cross-checked with dates in surviving Babylonian records and related accurately to our modern calendar. This event occurred on July 31, 593 B.C.   1:1b Or *in the thirtieth year.*   1:3 Or *Chaldeans.*   1:4 Or *like burnished metal;* also in 1:27.

²²Spread out above them was a surface like the sky, glittering like crystal. ²³Beneath this surface the wings of each living being stretched out to touch the others' wings, and each had two wings covering its body. ²⁴As they flew, their wings sounded to me like waves crashing against the shore or like the voice of the Almighty* or like the shouting of a mighty army. When they stopped, they let down their wings. ²⁵As they stood with wings lowered, a voice spoke from beyond the crystal surface above them.

²⁶Above this surface was something that looked like a throne made of blue lapis lazuli. And on this throne high above was a figure whose appearance resembled a man. ²⁷From what appeared to be his waist up, he looked like gleaming amber, flickering like a fire. And from his waist down, he looked like a burning flame, shining with splendor. ²⁸All around him was a glowing halo, like a rainbow shining in the clouds on a rainy day. This is what the glory of the LORD looked like to me. When I saw it, I fell face down on the ground, and I heard someone's voice speaking to me.

EZEKIEL'S CALL AND COMMISSION

2 "Stand up, son of man," said the voice. "I want to speak with you." ²The Spirit came into me as he spoke, and he set me on my feet. I listened carefully to his words. ³"Son of man," he said, "I am sending you to the nation of Israel, a rebellious nation that has rebelled against me. They and their ancestors have been rebelling against me to this very day. ⁴They are a stubborn and hard-hearted people. But I am sending you to say to them, 'This is what the Sovereign LORD says!' ⁵And whether they listen or refuse to listen—for remember, they are rebels—at least they will know they have had a prophet among them.

⁶"Son of man, do not fear them or their words. Don't be afraid even though their threats surround you like nettles and briers and stinging scorpions. Do not be dismayed by their dark scowls, even though they are rebels. ⁷You must give them my messages whether they listen or not. But they won't listen, for they are completely rebellious! ⁸Son of man, listen to what I say to you. Do not join them in their rebellion. Open your mouth, and eat what I give you."

⁹Then I looked and saw a hand reaching out to me. It held a scroll, ¹⁰which he unrolled. And I saw that both sides were covered with funeral songs, words of sorrow, and pronouncements of doom.

3 The voice said to me, "Son of man, eat what I am giving you—eat this scroll! Then go and give its message to the people of Israel." ²So I opened my mouth, and he fed me the scroll. ³"Fill your stomach with this," he said. And when I ate it, it tasted as sweet as honey in my mouth.

⁴Then he said, "Son of man, go to the people of Israel and give them my messages. ⁵I am not sending you to a foreign people whose language you cannot understand. ⁶No, I am not sending you to people with strange and difficult speech. If I did, they would listen! ⁷But the people of Israel won't listen to you any more than they listen to me! For the whole lot of them are hard-hearted and stubborn. ⁸But look, I have made you as obstinate and hard-hearted as they are. ⁹I have made your forehead as hard as the hardest rock! So don't be afraid of them or fear their angry looks, even though they are rebels."

¹⁰Then he added, "Son of man, let all my words sink deep into your own heart first. Listen to them carefully for yourself. ¹¹Then go to your people in exile and say to them, 'This is what the Sovereign LORD says!' Do this whether they listen to you or not."

¹²Then the Spirit lifted me up, and I heard a loud rumbling sound behind me. (May the glory of the LORD be praised in his place!)* ¹³It was the sound of the wings of the living beings as they brushed against each other and the rumbling of their wheels beneath them.

¹⁴The Spirit lifted me up and took me away. I went in bitterness and turmoil, but the LORD's hold on me was strong. ¹⁵Then I came to the colony of Judean exiles in Tel-abib, beside the Kebar River. I was overwhelmed and sat among them for seven days.

A WATCHMAN FOR ISRAEL

¹⁶After seven days the LORD gave me a message. He said, ¹⁷"Son of man, I have appointed you as a watchman for Israel. Whenever you receive a message from me, warn people immediately. ¹⁸If I warn the wicked, saying, 'You are under the penalty of death,' but you fail to deliver the warning, they will die in their sins. And I will hold you responsible for their deaths. ¹⁹If you warn them and they refuse to repent and keep on sinning, they will die in their sins. But you will have saved yourself because you obeyed me.

²⁰"If righteous people turn away from their righteous behavior and ignore the obstacles I put in their way, they will die. And if you do not warn them, they will die in their sins. None of their righteous acts will be remembered, and I will hold you responsible for their deaths. ²¹But if you warn righteous people not to sin and they listen to you and do not sin, they will live, and you will have saved yourself, too."

²²Then the LORD took hold of me and said, "Get up and go out into the valley, and I will speak to you there." ²³So I got up and went, and there I saw the glory of the LORD, just as I had seen in my first vision by the Kebar River. And I fell face down on the ground.

1:24 Hebrew *Shaddai.* 3:12 A possible reading for this verse is *Then the Spirit lifted me up, and as the glory of the LORD rose from its place, I heard a loud rumbling sound behind me.*

²⁴ Then the Spirit came into me and set me on my feet. He spoke to me and said, "Go to your house and shut yourself in. ²⁵ There, son of man, you will be tied with ropes so you cannot go out among the people. ²⁶ And I will make your tongue stick to the roof of your mouth so that you will be speechless and unable to rebuke them, for they are rebels. ²⁷ But when I give you a message, I will loosen your tongue and let you speak. Then you will say to them, 'This is what the Sovereign LORD says!' Those who choose to listen will listen, but those who refuse will refuse, for they are rebels.

A SIGN OF THE COMING SIEGE

4 "And now, son of man, take a large clay brick and set it down in front of you. Then draw a map of the city of Jerusalem on it. ² Show the city under siege. Build a wall around it so no one can escape. Set up the enemy camp, and surround the city with siege ramps and battering rams. ³ Then take an iron griddle and place it between you and the city. Turn toward the city and demonstrate how harsh the siege will be against Jerusalem. This will be a warning to the people of Israel.

⁴ "Now lie on your left side and place the sins of Israel on yourself. You are to bear their sins for the number of days you lie there on your side. ⁵ I am requiring you to bear Israel's sins for 390 days—one day for each year of their sin. ⁶ After that, turn over and lie on your right side for 40 days—one day for each year of Judah's sin.

⁷ "Meanwhile, keep staring at the siege of Jerusalem. Lie there with your arm bared and prophesy her destruction. ⁸ I will tie you up with ropes so you won't be able to turn from side to side until the days of your siege have been completed.

⁹ "Now go and get some wheat, barley, beans, lentils, millet, and emmer wheat, and mix them together in a storage jar. Use them to make bread for yourself during the 390 days you will be lying on your side. ¹⁰ Ration this out to yourself, eight ounces* of food for each day, and eat it at set times. ¹¹ Then measure out a jar* of water for each day, and drink it at set times. ¹² Prepare and eat this food as you would barley cakes. While all the people are watching, bake it over a fire using dried human dung as fuel and then eat the bread." ¹³ Then the LORD said, "This is how Israel will eat defiled bread in the Gentile lands to which I will banish them!"

¹⁴ Then I said, "O Sovereign LORD, must I be defiled by using human dung? For I have never been defiled before. From the time I was a child until now I have never eaten any animal that died of sickness or was killed by other animals. I have never eaten any meat forbidden by the law."

¹⁵ "All right," the LORD said. "You may bake your bread with cow dung instead of human dung." ¹⁶ Then he told me, "Son of man, I will make food very scarce in Jerusalem. It will be weighed out with great care and eaten fearfully. The water will be rationed out drop by drop, and the people will drink it with dismay. ¹⁷ Lacking food and water, people will look at one another in terror, and they will waste away under their punishment.

A SIGN OF THE COMING JUDGMENT

5 "Son of man, take a sharp sword and use it as a razor to shave your head and beard. Use a scale to weigh the hair into three equal parts. ² Place a third of it at the center of your map of Jerusalem. After acting out the siege, burn it there. Scatter another third across your map and chop it with a sword. Scatter the last third to the wind, for I will scatter my people with the sword. ³ Keep just a bit of the hair and tie it up in your robe. ⁴ Then take some of these hairs out and throw them into the fire, burning them up. A fire will then spread from this remnant and destroy all of Israel.

⁵ "This is what the Sovereign LORD says: This is an illustration of what will happen to Jerusalem. I placed her at the center of the nations, ⁶ but she has rebelled against my regulations and decrees and has been even more wicked than the surrounding nations. She has refused to obey the regulations and decrees I gave her to follow.

⁷ "Therefore, this is what the Sovereign LORD says: You people have behaved worse than your neighbors and have refused to obey my decrees and regulations. You have not even lived up to the standards of the nations around you. ⁸ Therefore, I myself, the Sovereign LORD, am now your enemy. I will punish you publicly while all the nations watch. ⁹ Because of your detestable idols, I will punish you like I have never punished anyone before or ever will again. ¹⁰ Parents will eat their own children, and children will eat their parents. I will punish you and scatter to the winds the few who survive.

¹¹ "As surely as I live, says the Sovereign LORD, I will cut you off completely. I will show you no pity at all because you have defiled my Temple with your vile images and detestable sins. ¹² A third of your people will die in the city from disease and famine. A third of them will be slaughtered by the enemy outside the city walls. And I will scatter a third to the winds, chasing them with my sword. ¹³ Then at last my anger will be spent, and I will be satisfied. And when my fury against them has subsided, all Israel will know that I, the LORD, have spoken to them in my jealous anger.

¹⁴ "So I will turn you into a ruin, a mockery in the eyes of the surrounding nations and to all who pass by. ¹⁵ You will become an object of

4:10 Hebrew *20 shekels* [228 grams]. 4:11 Hebrew *⅙ of a hin* [about 1 pint or 0.6 liters].

mockery and taunting and horror. You will be a warning to all the nations around you. They will see what happens when the LORD punishes a nation in anger and rebukes it, says the LORD.

16 "I will shower you with the deadly arrows of famine to destroy you. The famine will become more and more severe until every crumb of food is gone. 17 And along with the famine, wild animals will attack you and rob you of your children. Disease and war will stalk your land, and I will bring the sword of the enemy against you. I, the LORD, have spoken!"

JUDGMENT AGAINST ISRAEL'S MOUNTAINS

6 Again a message came to me from the LORD: 2 "Son of man, turn and face the mountains of Israel and prophesy against them. 3 Proclaim this message from the Sovereign LORD against the mountains of Israel. This is what the Sovereign LORD says to the mountains and hills and to the ravines and valleys: I am about to bring war upon you, and I will smash your pagan shrines. 4 All your altars will be demolished, and your places of worship will be destroyed. I will kill your people in front of your idols.* 5 I will lay your corpses in front of your idols and scatter your bones around your altars. 6 Wherever you live there will be desolation, and I will destroy your pagan shrines. Your altars will be demolished, your idols will be smashed, your places of worship will be torn down, and all the religious objects you have made will be destroyed. 7 The place will be littered with corpses, and you will know that I alone am the LORD.

8 "But I will let a few of my people escape destruction, and they will be scattered among the nations of the world. 9 Then when they are exiled among the nations, they will remember me. They will recognize how hurt I am by their unfaithful hearts and lustful eyes that long for their idols. Then at last they will hate themselves for all their detestable sins. 10 They will know that I alone am the LORD and that I was serious when I said I would bring this calamity on them.

11 "This is what the Sovereign LORD says: Clap your hands in horror, and stamp your feet. Cry out because of all the detestable sins the people of Israel have committed. Now they are going to die from war and famine and disease. 12 Disease will strike down those who are far away in exile. War will destroy those who are nearby. And anyone who survives will be killed by famine. So at last I will spend my fury on them. 13 They will know that I am the LORD when their dead lie scattered among their idols and altars on every hill and mountain and under every green tree and every great shade tree—the places where they offered sacrifices to their idols. 14 I will crush them and make their cities desolate from the wilderness in the south to Riblah* in the north. Then they will know that I am the LORD."

THE COMING OF THE END

7 Then this message came to me from the LORD: 2 "Son of man, this is what the Sovereign LORD says to Israel:

"The end is here!
Wherever you look—
east, west, north, or south—
your land is finished.
3 No hope remains,
for I will unleash my anger against you.
I will call you to account
for all your detestable sins.
4 I will turn my eyes away and show no pity.
I will repay you for all your detestable sins.
Then you will know that I am the LORD.

5 "This is what the Sovereign LORD says:
Disaster after disaster
is coming your way!
6 The end has come.
It has finally arrived.
Your final doom is waiting!
7 O people of Israel, the day of your
destruction is dawning.
The time has come; the day of trouble
is near.
Shouts of anguish will be heard on the
mountains,
not shouts of joy.
8 Soon I will pour out my fury on you
and unleash my anger against you.
I will call you to account
for all your detestable sins.
9 I will turn my eyes away and show no pity.
I will repay you for all your detestable sins.
Then you will know that it is I, the LORD,
who is striking the blow.

10 "The day of judgment is here;
your destruction awaits!
The people's wickedness and pride
have blossomed to full flower.
11 Their violence has grown into a rod
that will beat them for their wickedness.
None of these proud and wicked people
will survive.
All their wealth and prestige will be
swept away.
12 Yes, the time has come;
the day is here!
Buyers should not rejoice over bargains,
nor sellers grieve over losses,
for all of them will fall
under my terrible anger.
13 Even if the merchants survive,
they will never return to their business.
For what God has said applies to everyone—
it will not be changed!

6:4 The Hebrew term (literally round things) probably alludes to dung; also in 6:5, 6, 9, 13.   6:14 As in some Hebrew manuscripts; most Hebrew manuscripts read Diblah.

Not one person whose life is twisted by sin
will ever recover.

THE DESOLATION OF ISRAEL

14 "The trumpet calls Israel's army to mobilize,
but no one listens,
for my fury is against them all.
15 There is war outside the city
and disease and famine within.
Those outside the city walls
will be killed by enemy swords.
Those inside the city
will die of famine and disease.
16 The survivors who escape to the mountains
will moan like doves, weeping for
their sins.
17 Their hands will hang limp,
their knees will be weak as water.
18 They will dress themselves in burlap;
horror and shame will cover them.
They will shave their heads
in sorrow and remorse.
19 "They will throw their money in the streets,
tossing it out like worthless trash.
Their silver and gold won't save them
on that day of the LORD's anger.
It will neither satisfy nor feed them,
for their greed can only trip them up.
20 They were proud of their beautiful jewelry
and used it to make detestable idols and
vile images.
Therefore, I will make all their wealth
disgusting to them.
21 I will give it as plunder to foreigners,
to the most wicked of nations,
and they will defile it.
22 I will turn my eyes from them
as these robbers invade and defile my
treasured land.
23 "Prepare chains for my people,
for the land is bloodied by terrible crimes.
Jerusalem is filled with violence.
24 I will bring the most ruthless of nations
to occupy their homes.
I will break down their proud fortresses
and defile their sanctuaries.
25 Terror and trembling will overcome
my people.
They will look for peace but not find it.
26 Calamity will follow calamity;
rumor will follow rumor.
They will look in vain
for a vision from the prophets.
They will receive no teaching from
the priests
and no counsel from the leaders.
27 The king and the prince will stand helpless,
weeping in despair,
and the people's hands
will tremble with fear.

I will bring on them
the evil they have done to others,
and they will receive the punishment
they so richly deserve.
Then they will know that I am the LORD."

IDOLATRY IN THE TEMPLE

8 Then on September 17,* during the sixth year of King Jehoiachin's captivity, while the leaders of Judah were in my home, the Sovereign LORD took hold of me. 2I saw a figure that appeared to be a man.* From what appeared to be his waist down, he looked like a burning flame. From the waist up he looked like gleaming amber.* 3He reached out what seemed to be a hand and took me by the hair. Then the Spirit lifted me up into the sky and transported me to Jerusalem in a vision from God. I was taken to the north gate of the inner courtyard of the Temple, where there is a large idol that has made the LORD very jealous. 4Suddenly, the glory of the God of Israel was there, just as I had seen it before in the valley.

5Then the LORD said to me, "Son of man, look toward the north." So I looked, and there to the north, beside the entrance to the gate near the altar, stood the idol that had made the LORD so jealous.

6"Son of man," he said, "do you see what they are doing? Do you see the detestable sins the people of Israel are committing to drive me from my Temple? But come, and you will see even more detestable sins than these!" 7Then he brought me to the door of the Temple courtyard, where I could see a hole in the wall. 8He said to me, "Now, son of man, dig into the wall." So I dug into the wall and found a hidden doorway.

9"Go in," he said, "and see the wicked and detestable sins they are committing in there!" 10So I went in and saw the walls covered with engravings of all kinds of crawling animals and detestable creatures. I also saw the various idols* worshiped by the people of Israel. 11Seventy leaders of Israel were standing there with Jaazaniah son of Shaphan in the center. Each of them held an incense burner, from which a cloud of incense rose above their heads.

12Then the LORD said to me, "Son of man, have you seen what the leaders of Israel are doing with their idols in dark rooms? They are saying, 'The LORD doesn't see us; he has deserted our land!'" 13Then the LORD added, "Come, and I will show you even more detestable sins than these!"

14He brought me to the north gate of the LORD's Temple, and some women were sitting there, weeping for the god Tammuz. 15"Have you

---

8:1 Hebrew *on the fifth [day] of the sixth month,* of the ancient Hebrew lunar calendar. This event occurred on September 17, 592 B.C.; also see note on 1:1. 8:2a As in Greek version; Hebrew reads *appeared to be fire.* 8:2b Or *like burnished metal.* 8:10 The Hebrew term (literally *round things*) probably alludes to dung.

seen this?" he asked. "But I will show you even more detestable sins than these!"

¹⁶ Then he brought me into the inner courtyard of the LORD's Temple. At the entrance to the sanctuary, between the entry room and the bronze altar, there were about twenty-five men with their backs to the sanctuary of the LORD. They were facing east, bowing low to the ground, worshiping the sun!

¹⁷ "Have you seen this, son of man?" he asked. "Is it nothing to the people of Judah that they commit these detestable sins, leading the whole nation into violence, thumbing their noses at me, and provoking my anger? ¹⁸ Therefore, I will respond in fury. I will neither pity nor spare them. And though they cry for mercy, I will not listen."

THE SLAUGHTER OF IDOLATERS

9 Then the LORD thundered, "Bring on the men appointed to punish the city! Tell them to bring their weapons with them!" ² Six men soon appeared from the upper gate that faces north, each carrying a deadly weapon in his hand. With them was a man dressed in linen, who carried a writer's case at his side. They all went into the Temple courtyard and stood beside the bronze altar.

³ Then the glory of the God of Israel rose up from between the cherubim, where it had rested, and moved to the entrance of the Temple. And the LORD called to the man dressed in linen who was carrying the writer's case. ⁴ He said to him, "Walk through the streets of Jerusalem and put a mark on the foreheads of all who weep and sigh because of the detestable sins being committed in their city."

⁵ Then I heard the LORD say to the other men, "Follow him through the city and kill everyone whose forehead is not marked. Show no mercy; have no pity! ⁶ Kill them all—old and young, girls and women and little children. But do not touch anyone with the mark. Begin right here at the Temple." So they began by killing the seventy leaders.

⁷ "Defile the Temple!" the LORD commanded. "Fill its courtyards with corpses. Go!" So they went and began killing throughout the city.

⁸ While they were out killing, I was all alone. I fell face down on the ground and cried out, "O Sovereign LORD! Will your fury against Jerusalem wipe out everyone left in Israel?"

⁹ Then he said to me, "The sins of the people of Israel and Judah are very, very great. The entire land is full of murder; the city is filled with injustice. They are saying, 'The LORD doesn't see it! The LORD has abandoned the land!' ¹⁰ So I will not spare them or have any pity on them. I will fully repay them for all they have done."

¹¹ Then the man in linen clothing, who carried the writer's case, reported back and said, "I have done as you commanded."

THE LORD'S GLORY LEAVES THE TEMPLE

10 In my vision I saw what appeared to be a throne of blue lapis lazuli above the crystal surface over the heads of the cherubim. ² Then the LORD spoke to the man in linen clothing and said, "Go between the whirling wheels beneath the cherubim, and take a handful of burning coals and scatter them over the city." He did this as I watched.

³ The cherubim were standing at the south end of the Temple when the man went in, and the cloud of glory filled the inner courtyard. ⁴ Then the glory of the LORD rose up from above the cherubim and went over to the entrance of the Temple. The Temple was filled with this cloud of glory, and the courtyard glowed brightly with the glory of the LORD. ⁵ The moving wings of the cherubim sounded like the voice of God Almighty* and could be heard even in the outer courtyard.

⁶ The LORD said to the man in linen clothing, "Go between the cherubim and take some burning coals from between the wheels." So the man went in and stood beside one of the wheels. ⁷ Then one of the cherubim reached out his hand and took some live coals from the fire burning among them. He put the coals into the hands of the man in linen clothing, and the man took them and went out. ⁸ (All the cherubim had what looked like human hands under their wings.)

⁹ I looked, and each of the four cherubim had a wheel beside him, and the wheels sparkled like beryl. ¹⁰ All four wheels looked alike and were made the same; each wheel had a second wheel turning crosswise within it. ¹¹ The cherubim could move in any of the four directions they faced, without turning as they moved. They went straight in the direction they faced, never turning aside. ¹² Both the cherubim and the wheels were covered with eyes. The cherubim had eyes all over their bodies, including their hands, their backs, and their wings. ¹³ I heard someone refer to the wheels as "the whirling wheels." ¹⁴ Each of the four cherubim had four faces: the first was the face of an ox,* the second was a human face, the third was the face of a lion, and the fourth was the face of an eagle.

¹⁵ Then the cherubim rose upward. These were the same living beings I had seen beside the Kebar River. ¹⁶ When the cherubim moved, the wheels moved with them. When they lifted their wings to fly, the wheels stayed beside them. ¹⁷ When the cherubim stopped, the wheels stopped. When they flew upward, the wheels rose up, for the spirit of the living beings was in the wheels.

¹⁸ Then the glory of the LORD moved out from the entrance of the Temple and hovered above the cherubim. ¹⁹ And as I watched, the cherubim flew with their wheels to the east gate of the

---

10:5 Hebrew *El-Shaddai*.   10:14 Hebrew *the face of a cherub;* compare 1:10.

LORD's Temple. And the glory of the God of Israel hovered above them.

²⁰These were the same living beings I had seen beneath the God of Israel when I was by the Kebar River. I knew they were cherubim, ²¹for each had four faces and four wings and what looked like human hands under their wings. ²²And their faces were just like the faces of the beings I had seen at the Kebar, and they traveled straight ahead, just as the others had.

JUDGMENT ON ISRAEL'S LEADERS

11 Then the Spirit lifted me and brought me to the east gateway of the LORD's Temple, where I saw twenty-five prominent men of the city. Among them were Jaazaniah son of Azzur and Pelatiah son of Benaiah, who were leaders among the people.

²The Spirit said to me, "Son of man, these are the men who are planning evil and giving wicked counsel in this city. ³They say to the people, 'Is it not a good time to build houses? This city is like an iron pot. We are safe inside it like meat in a pot.*' ⁴Therefore, son of man, prophesy against them loudly and clearly."

⁵Then the Spirit of the LORD came upon me, and he told me to say, "This is what the LORD says to the people of Israel: I know what you are saying, for I know every thought that comes into your minds. ⁶You have murdered many in this city and filled its streets with the dead.

⁷"Therefore, this is what the Sovereign LORD says: This city is an iron pot all right, but the pieces of meat are the victims of your injustice. As for you, I will soon drag you from this pot. ⁸I will bring on you the sword of war you so greatly fear, says the Sovereign LORD. ⁹I will drive you out of Jerusalem and hand you over to foreigners, who will carry out my judgments against you. ¹⁰You will be slaughtered all the way to the borders of Israel. I will execute judgment on you, and you will know that I am the LORD. ¹¹No, this city will not be an iron pot for you, and you will not be like meat safe inside it. I will judge you even to the borders of Israel, ¹²and you will know that I am the LORD. For you have refused to obey my decrees and regulations; instead, you have copied the standards of the nations around you."

¹³While I was still prophesying, Pelatiah son of Benaiah suddenly died. Then I fell face down on the ground and cried out, "O Sovereign LORD, are you going to kill everyone in Israel?"

HOPE FOR EXILED ISRAEL

¹⁴Then this message came to me from the LORD: ¹⁵"Son of man, the people still left in Jerusalem are talking about you and your relatives and all the people of Israel who are in exile. They are saying, 'Those people are far away from the LORD, so now he has given their land to us!'

¹⁶"Therefore, tell the exiles, 'This is what the Sovereign LORD says: Although I have scattered you in the countries of the world, I will be a sanctuary to you during your time in exile. ¹⁷I, the Sovereign LORD, will gather you back from the nations where you have been scattered, and I will give you the land of Israel once again.'

¹⁸"When the people return to their homeland, they will remove every trace of their vile images and detestable idols. ¹⁹And I will give them singleness of heart and put a new spirit within them. I will take away their stony, stubborn heart and give them a tender, responsive heart,* ²⁰so they will obey my decrees and regulations. Then they will truly be my people, and I will be their God. ²¹But as for those who long for vile images and detestable idols, I will repay them fully for their sins. I, the Sovereign LORD, have spoken!"

THE LORD'S GLORY LEAVES JERUSALEM

²²Then the cherubim lifted their wings and rose into the air with their wheels beside them, and the glory of the God of Israel hovered above them. ²³Then the glory of the LORD went up from the city and stopped above the mountain to the east. ²⁴Afterward the Spirit of God carried me back again to Babylonia,* to the people in exile there. And so ended the vision of my visit to Jerusalem. ²⁵And I told the exiles everything the LORD had shown me.

SIGNS OF THE COMING EXILE

12 Again a message came to me from the LORD: ²"Son of man, you live among rebels who have eyes but refuse to see. They have ears but refuse to hear. For they are a rebellious people.

³"So now, son of man, pretend you are being sent into exile. Pack the few items an exile could carry, and leave your home to go somewhere else. Do this right in front of the people so they can see you. For perhaps they will pay attention to this, even though they are such rebels. ⁴Bring your baggage outside during the day so they can watch you. Then in the evening, as they are watching, leave your house as captives do when they begin a long march to distant lands. ⁵Dig a hole through the wall while they are watching and go out through it. ⁶As they watch, lift your pack to your shoulders and walk away into the night. Cover your face so you cannot see the land you are leaving. For I have made you a sign for the people of Israel."

⁷So I did as I was told. In broad daylight I brought my pack outside, filled with the things I might carry into exile. Then in the evening while the people looked on, I dug through the wall with my hands and went out into the night with my pack on my shoulder.

⁸The next morning this message came to me from the LORD: ⁹"Son of man, these rebels, the

---

11:3 Hebrew This city is the pot, and we are the meat.
11:19 Hebrew a heart of flesh.　11:24 Or Chaldea.

people of Israel, have asked you what all this means. ¹⁰ Say to them, 'This is what the Sovereign Lord says: These actions contain a message for King Zedekiah in Jerusalem* and for all the people of Israel.' ¹¹ Explain that your actions are a sign to show what will soon happen to them, for they will be driven into exile as captives.

¹² "Even Zedekiah will leave Jerusalem at night through a hole in the wall, taking only what he can carry with him. He will cover his face, and his eyes will not see the land he is leaving. ¹³ Then I will throw my net over him and capture him in my snare. I will bring him to Babylon, the land of the Babylonians,* though he will never see it, and he will die there. ¹⁴ I will scatter his servants and warriors to the four winds and send the sword after them. ¹⁵ And when I scatter them among the nations, they will know that I am the Lord. ¹⁶ But I will spare a few of them from death by war, famine, or disease, so they can confess all their detestable sins to their captors. Then they will know that I am the Lord."

¹⁷ Then this message came to me from the Lord: ¹⁸ "Son of man, tremble as you eat your food. Shake with fear as you drink your water. ¹⁹ Tell the people, 'This is what the Sovereign Lord says concerning those living in Israel and Jerusalem: They will eat their food with trembling and sip their water in despair, for their land will be stripped bare because of their violence. ²⁰ The cities will be destroyed and the farmland made desolate. Then you will know that I am the Lord.'"

A NEW PROVERB FOR ISRAEL

²¹ Again a message came to me from the Lord: ²² "Son of man, you've heard that proverb they quote in Israel: 'Time passes, and prophecies come to nothing.' ²³ Tell the people, 'This is what the Sovereign Lord says: I will put an end to this proverb, and you will soon stop quoting it.' Now give them this new proverb to replace the old one: 'The time has come for every prophecy to be fulfilled!'

²⁴ "There will be no more false visions and flattering predictions in Israel. ²⁵ For I am the Lord! If I say it, it will happen. There will be no more delays, you rebels of Israel. I will fulfill my threat of destruction in your own lifetime. I, the Sovereign Lord, have spoken!"

²⁶ Then this message came to me from the Lord: ²⁷ "Son of man, the people of Israel are saying, 'He's talking about the distant future. His visions won't come true for a long, long time.' ²⁸ Therefore, tell them, 'This is what the Sovereign Lord says: No more delay! I will now do everything I have threatened. I, the Sovereign Lord, have spoken!'"

JUDGMENT AGAINST FALSE PROPHETS

13 Then this message came to me from the Lord: ² "Son of man, prophesy against the false prophets of Israel who are inventing their own prophecies. Say to them, 'Listen to the word of the Lord. ³ This is what the Sovereign Lord says: What sorrow awaits the false prophets who are following their own imaginations and have seen nothing at all!'

⁴ "O people of Israel, these prophets of yours are like jackals digging in the ruins. ⁵ They have done nothing to repair the breaks in the walls around the nation. They have not helped it to stand firm in battle on the day of the Lord. ⁶ Instead, they have told lies and made false predictions. They say, 'This message is from the Lord,' even though the Lord never sent them. And yet they expect him to fulfill their prophecies! ⁷ Can your visions be anything but false if you claim, 'This message is from the Lord,' when I have not even spoken to you?

⁸ "Therefore, this is what the Sovereign Lord says: Because what you say is false and your visions are a lie, I will stand against you, says the Sovereign Lord. ⁹ I will raise my fist against all the prophets who see false visions and make lying predictions, and they will be banished from the community of Israel. I will blot their names from Israel's record books, and they will never again set foot in their own land. Then you will know that I am the Sovereign Lord.

¹⁰ "This will happen because these evil prophets deceive my people by saying, 'All is peaceful' when there is no peace at all! It's as if the people have built a flimsy wall, and these prophets are trying to reinforce it by covering it with whitewash! ¹¹ Tell these whitewashers that their wall will soon fall down. A heavy rainstorm will undermine it; great hailstones and mighty winds will knock it down. ¹² And when the wall falls, the people will cry out, 'What happened to your whitewash?'

¹³ "Therefore, this is what the Sovereign Lord says: I will sweep away your whitewashed wall with a storm of indignation, with a great flood of anger, and with hailstones of fury. ¹⁴ I will break down your wall right to its foundation, and when it falls, it will crush you. Then you will know that I am the Lord. ¹⁵ At last my anger against the wall and those who covered it with whitewash will be satisfied. Then I will say to you: 'The wall and those who whitewashed it are both gone. ¹⁶ They were lying prophets who claimed peace would come to Jerusalem when there was no peace. I, the Sovereign Lord, have spoken!'

JUDGMENT AGAINST FALSE WOMEN PROPHETS

¹⁷ "Now, son of man, speak out against the women who prophesy from their own imaginations. ¹⁸ This is what the Sovereign Lord says: What sorrow awaits you women who are ensnaring the souls of my people, young and old alike. You tie

---

12:10 Hebrew *the prince in Jerusalem;* similarly in 12:12.   12:13 Or *Chaldeans.*

IDOLATRY OF THE HEART
Ezekiel 14:1-11   ROBERT MORRIS

The word *idol* means 'image,' which is the root word of *imagination*. If you think about something more than you think about God, it's very possible you have an idol in your heart. In Ezekiel 14:3, God tells the prophet, "These leaders have set up idols in their hearts."

Here are four ways to determine if you have an idol in your heart:

1. Presumption

   If you have an idol, you'll start catering to it and making plans to sin. The apostle Paul tells us not to think about ways to indulge our evil desires (Romans 13:14), yet we often do this very thing. We make up stories to cover up our actions, and we even make plans to ask God for forgiveness later. This is *presumption*—presuming on the grace of God—which is a sin.

2. Estrangement

   An idol causes you to be estranged from God. In Ezekiel 14:5, the prophet says the elders of Israel have turned their hearts and minds away from God and toward idols. In Hebrew, this verse uses the same term as a woman who is married but living with another man in an adulterous relationship. The people of Israel built altars and made sacrifices to other gods, and in doing so, they committed adultery against God and estranged themselves from Him.

3. Spiritual Deafness

   Sin brings a separation to our intimacy with God (Isaiah 59:2). The elders went to the prophet to find out what God was saying because they couldn't hear Him for themselves. Why? They had an idol in their hearts. We can live in constant communion with the Holy Spirit, but if we have an idol in our hearts, we turn down the volume on the Holy Spirit and turn up the voice of the idol. As we begin to move away from God, we can no longer hear Him as clearly.

4. Consequences

   God loves people, and He takes a stand against sin because He knows its consequences. In Ezekiel 14:10, God says the false prophets will face the same punishment as those who asked them to justify their sins. He wants these leaders to understand that if they didn't take a stand against sin, they would have the same consequences as the original sinners.

magic charms on their wrists and furnish them with magic veils. Do you think you can trap others without bringing destruction on yourselves? [19] You bring shame on me among my people for a few handfuls of barley or a piece of bread. By lying to my people who love to listen to lies, you kill those who should not die, and you promise life to those who should not live.

[20] "This is what the Sovereign LORD says: I am against all your magic charms, which you use to ensnare my people like birds. I will tear them from your arms, setting my people free like birds set free from a cage. [21] I will tear off the magic veils and save my people from your grasp. They will no longer be your victims. Then you will know that I am the LORD. [22] You have discouraged the righteous with your lies, but I didn't want them to be sad. And you have encouraged the wicked by promising them life, even though they continue in their sins. [23] Because of all this, you will no longer talk of seeing visions that you never saw, nor will you make predictions. For I will rescue my people from your grasp. Then you will know that I am the LORD."

THE IDOLATRY OF ISRAEL'S LEADERS

14 Then some of the leaders of Israel visited me, and while they were sitting with me, [2] this message came to me from the LORD: [3] "Son of man, these leaders have set up idols* in their hearts. They have embraced things that will make them fall into sin. Why should I listen to their requests? [4] Tell them, 'This is what the Sovereign LORD says: The people of Israel have set up idols in their hearts and fallen into sin, and then they go to a prophet asking for a message. So I, the LORD, will give them the kind of answer their great idolatry deserves. [5] I will do this to capture the minds and hearts of all my people who have turned from me to worship their detestable idols.'

[6] "Therefore, tell the people of Israel, 'This is what the Sovereign LORD says: Repent and turn away from your idols, and stop all your detestable sins. [7] I, the LORD, will answer all those, both Israelites and foreigners, who reject me and set up idols in their hearts and so fall into sin, and who then come to a prophet asking for my advice. [8] I will turn against such people and make a terrible example of them, eliminating them from among my people. Then you will know that I am the LORD.

[9] "'And if a prophet is deceived into giving a message, it is because I, the LORD, have deceived that prophet. I will lift my fist against such prophets and cut them off from the community of Israel. [10] False prophets and those who seek their guidance will all be punished for their sins. [11] In this way, the people of Israel will learn not to stray from me, polluting themselves with sin. They will be my people, and I will be their God. I, the Sovereign LORD, have spoken!'"

14:3 The Hebrew term (literally *round things*) probably alludes to dung; also in 14:4, 5, 6, 7.

THE CERTAINTY OF THE LORD'S JUDGMENT

¹²Then this message came to me from the LORD: ¹³"Son of man, suppose the people of a country were to sin against me, and I lifted my fist to crush them, cutting off their food supply and sending a famine to destroy both people and animals. ¹⁴Even if Noah, Daniel, and Job were there, their righteousness would save no one but themselves, says the Sovereign LORD.

¹⁵"Or suppose I were to send wild animals to invade the country, kill the people, and make the land too desolate and dangerous to pass through. ¹⁶As surely as I live, says the Sovereign LORD, even if those three men were there, they wouldn't be able to save their own sons or daughters. They alone would be saved, but the land would be made desolate.

¹⁷"Or suppose I were to bring war against the land, and I sent enemy armies to destroy both people and animals. ¹⁸As surely as I live, says the Sovereign LORD, even if those three men were there, they wouldn't be able to save their own sons or daughters. They alone would be saved.

¹⁹"Or suppose I were to pour out my fury by sending an epidemic into the land, and the disease killed people and animals alike. ²⁰As surely as I live, says the Sovereign LORD, even if Noah, Daniel, and Job were there, they wouldn't be able to save their own sons or daughters. They alone would be saved by their righteousness.

²¹"Now this is what the Sovereign LORD says: How terrible it will be when all four of these dreadful punishments fall upon Jerusalem—war, famine, wild animals, and disease—destroying all her people and animals. ²²Yet there will be survivors, and they will come here to join you as exiles in Babylon. You will see with your own eyes how wicked they are, and then you will feel better about what I have done to Jerusalem. ²³When you meet them and see their behavior, you will understand that these things are not being done to Israel without cause. I, the Sovereign LORD, have spoken!"

JERUSALEM—A USELESS VINE

15 Then this message came to me from the LORD: ²"Son of man, how does a grapevine compare to a tree? Is a vine's wood as useful as the wood of a tree? ³Can its wood be used for making things, like pegs to hang up pots and pans? ⁴No, it can only be used for fuel, and even as fuel, it burns too quickly. ⁵Vines are useless both before and after being put into the fire!

⁶"And this is what the Sovereign LORD says: The people of Jerusalem are like grapevines growing among the trees of the forest. Since they are useless, I have thrown them on the fire to be burned. ⁷And I will see to it that if they escape from one fire, they will fall into another. When I turn against them, you will know that I am the LORD. ⁸And I will make the land desolate because my people have been unfaithful to me. I, the Sovereign LORD, have spoken!"

JERUSALEM—AN UNFAITHFUL WIFE

16 Then another message came to me from the LORD: ²"Son of man, confront Jerusalem with her detestable sins. ³Give her this message from the Sovereign LORD: You are nothing but a Canaanite! Your father was an Amorite and your mother a Hittite. ⁴On the day you were born, no one cared about you. Your umbilical cord was not cut, and you were never washed, rubbed with salt, and wrapped in cloth. ⁵No one had the slightest interest in you; no one pitied you or cared for you. On the day you were born, you were unwanted, dumped in a field and left to die.

⁶"But I came by and saw you there, helplessly kicking about in your own blood. As you lay there, I said, 'Live!' ⁷And I helped you to thrive like a plant in the field. You grew up and became a beautiful jewel. Your breasts became full, and your body hair grew, but you were still naked. ⁸And when I passed by again, I saw that you were old enough for love. So I wrapped my cloak around you to cover your nakedness and declared my marriage vows. I made a covenant with you, says the Sovereign LORD, and you became mine.

⁹"Then I bathed you and washed off your blood, and I rubbed fragrant oils into your skin. ¹⁰I gave you expensive clothing of fine linen and silk, beautifully embroidered, and sandals made of fine goatskin leather. ¹¹I gave you lovely jewelry, bracelets, beautiful necklaces, ¹²a ring for your nose, earrings for your ears, and a lovely crown for your head. ¹³And so you were adorned with gold and silver. Your clothes were made of fine linen and costly fabric and were beautifully embroidered. You ate the finest foods—choice flour, honey, and olive oil—and became more beautiful than ever. You looked like a queen, and so you were! ¹⁴Your fame soon spread throughout the world because of your beauty. I dressed you in my splendor and perfected your beauty, says the Sovereign LORD.

¹⁵"But you thought your fame and beauty were your own. So you gave yourself as a prostitute to every man who came along. Your beauty was theirs for the asking. ¹⁶You used the lovely things I gave you to make shrines for idols, where you played the prostitute. Unbelievable! How could such a thing ever happen? ¹⁷You took the very jewels and gold and silver ornaments I had given you and made statues of men and worshiped them. This is adultery against me! ¹⁸You used the beautifully embroidered clothes I gave you to dress your idols. Then you used my special oil and my incense to worship them. ¹⁹Imagine it! You set before them as a sacrifice the choice flour, olive oil, and honey I had given you, says the Sovereign LORD.

²⁰"Then you took your sons and daughters—the children you had borne to me—and sacrificed

them to your gods. Was your prostitution not enough? ²¹ Must you also slaughter my children by sacrificing them to idols? ²² In all your years of adultery and detestable sin, you have not once remembered the days long ago when you lay naked in a field, kicking about in your own blood.

²³ "What sorrow awaits you, says the Sovereign LORD. In addition to all your other wickedness, ²⁴ you built a pagan shrine and put altars to idols in every town square. ²⁵ On every street corner you defiled your beauty, offering your body to every passerby in an endless stream of prostitution. ²⁶ Then you added lustful Egypt to your lovers, provoking my anger with your increasing promiscuity. ²⁷ That is why I struck you with my fist and reduced your boundaries. I handed you over to your enemies, the Philistines, and even they were shocked by your lewd conduct. ²⁸ You have prostituted yourself with the Assyrians, too. It seems you can never find enough new lovers! And after your prostitution there, you still were not satisfied. ²⁹ You added to your lovers by embracing Babylonia,* the land of merchants, but you still weren't satisfied.

³⁰ "What a sick heart you have, says the Sovereign LORD, to do such things as these, acting like a shameless prostitute. ³¹ You build your pagan shrines on every street corner and your altars to idols in every square. In fact, you have been worse than a prostitute, so eager for sin that you have not even demanded payment. ³² Yes, you are an adulterous wife who takes in strangers instead of her own husband. ³³ Prostitutes charge for their services—but not you! You give gifts to your lovers, bribing them to come and have sex with you. ³⁴ So you are the opposite of other prostitutes. You pay your lovers instead of their paying you!

JUDGMENT ON JERUSALEM'S PROSTITUTION

³⁵ "Therefore, you prostitute, listen to this message from the LORD! ³⁶ This is what the Sovereign LORD says: Because you have poured out your lust and exposed yourself in prostitution to all your lovers, and because you have worshiped detestable idols,* and because you have slaughtered your children as sacrifices to your gods, ³⁷ this is what I am going to do. I will gather together all your allies—the lovers with whom you have sinned, both those you loved and those you hated—and I will strip you naked in front of them so they can stare at you. ³⁸ I will punish you for your murder and adultery. I will cover you with blood in my jealous fury. ³⁹ Then I will give you to these many nations who are your lovers, and they will destroy you. They will knock down your pagan shrines and the altars to your idols. They will strip you and take your beautiful jewels, leaving you stark naked. ⁴⁰ They will band together in a mob to stone you and cut you up with swords. ⁴¹ They will burn your homes and

punish you in front of many women. I will stop your prostitution and end your payments to your many lovers.

⁴² "Then at last my fury against you will be spent, and my jealous anger will subside. I will be calm and will not be angry with you anymore. ⁴³ But first, because you have not remembered your youth but have angered me by doing all these evil things, I will fully repay you for all of your sins, says the Sovereign LORD. For you have added lewd acts to all your detestable sins. ⁴⁴ Everyone who makes up proverbs will say of you, 'Like mother, like daughter.' ⁴⁵ For your mother loathed her husband and her children, and so do you. And you are exactly like your sisters, for they despised their husbands and their children. Truly your mother was a Hittite and your father an Amorite.

⁴⁶ "Your older sister was Samaria, who lived with her daughters in the north. Your younger sister was Sodom, who lived with her daughters in the south. ⁴⁷ But you have not merely sinned as they did. You quickly surpassed them in corruption. ⁴⁸ As surely as I live, says the Sovereign LORD, Sodom and her daughters were never as wicked as you and your daughters. ⁴⁹ Sodom's sins were pride, gluttony, and laziness, while the poor and needy suffered outside her door. ⁵⁰ She was proud and committed detestable sins, so I wiped her out, as you have seen.*

⁵¹ "Even Samaria did not commit half your sins. You have done far more detestable things than your sisters ever did. They seem righteous compared to you. ⁵² Shame on you! Your sins are so terrible that you make your sisters seem righteous, even virtuous.

⁵³ "But someday I will restore the fortunes of Sodom and Samaria, and I will restore you, too. ⁵⁴ Then you will be truly ashamed of everything you have done, for your sins make them feel good in comparison. ⁵⁵ Yes, your sisters, Sodom and Samaria, and all their people will be restored, and at that time you also will be restored. ⁵⁶ In your proud days you held Sodom in contempt. ⁵⁷ But now your greater wickedness has been exposed to all the world, and you are the one who is scorned—by Edom* and all her neighbors and by Philistia. ⁵⁸ This is your punishment for all your lewdness and detestable sins, says the LORD.

⁵⁹ "Now this is what the Sovereign LORD says: I will give you what you deserve, for you have taken your solemn vows lightly by breaking your covenant. ⁶⁰ Yet I will remember the covenant I made with you when you were young, and I will establish an everlasting covenant with you. ⁶¹ Then you will remember with shame all the evil you have done. I will make your sisters, Samaria

---

16:29 Or *Chaldea.*   **16:36** The Hebrew term (literally *round things*) probably alludes to dung.   **16:50** As in a few Hebrew manuscripts and Greek version; Masoretic Text reads *as I have seen.*   **16:57** As in many Hebrew manuscripts and Syriac version; Masoretic Text reads *Aram.*

and Sodom, to be your daughters, even though they are not part of our covenant. ⁶²And I will reaffirm my covenant with you, and you will know that I am the LORD. ⁶³You will remember your sins and cover your mouth in silent shame when I forgive you of all that you have done. I, the Sovereign LORD, have spoken!"

A STORY OF TWO EAGLES

17 Then this message came to me from the LORD: ²"Son of man, give this riddle, and tell this story to the people of Israel. ³Give them this message from the Sovereign LORD:

"A great eagle with broad wings and long
    feathers,
    covered with many-colored plumage,
    came to Lebanon.
He seized the top of a cedar tree
⁴   and plucked off its highest branch.
He carried it away to a city filled with
    merchants.
    He planted it in a city of traders.
⁵ He also took a seedling from the land
    and planted it in fertile soil.
He placed it beside a broad river,
    where it could grow like a willow tree.
⁶ It took root there
    and grew into a low, spreading vine.
Its branches turned up toward the eagle,
    and its roots grew down into the ground.
It produced strong branches
    and put out shoots.
⁷ But then another great eagle came
    with broad wings and full plumage.
So the vine now sent its roots and branches
    toward him for water,
⁸ even though it was already planted
    in good soil
    and had plenty of water
so it could grow into a splendid vine
    and produce rich leaves and luscious fruit.

⁹ "So now the Sovereign LORD asks:
Will this vine grow and prosper?
    No! I will pull it up, roots and all!
I will cut off its fruit
    and let its leaves wither and die.
I will pull it up easily
    without a strong arm or a large army.
¹⁰ But when the vine is transplanted,
    will it thrive?
No, it will wither away
    when the east wind blows against it.
It will die in the same good soil
    where it had grown so well."

THE RIDDLE EXPLAINED

¹¹ Then this message came to me from the LORD: ¹²"Say to these rebels of Israel: Don't you understand the meaning of this riddle of the eagles? The king of Babylon came to Jerusalem, took

away her king and princes, and brought them to Babylon. ¹³He made a treaty with a member of the royal family and forced him to take an oath of loyalty. He also exiled Israel's most influential leaders, ¹⁴so Israel would not become strong again and revolt. Only by keeping her treaty with Babylon could Israel survive.

¹⁵"Nevertheless, this man of Israel's royal family rebelled against Babylon, sending ambassadors to Egypt to request a great army and many horses. Can Israel break her sworn treaties like that and get away with it? ¹⁶No! For as surely as I live, says the Sovereign LORD, the king of Israel will die in Babylon, the land of the king who put him in power and whose treaty he disregarded and broke. ¹⁷Pharaoh and all his mighty army will fail to help Israel when the king of Babylon lays siege to Jerusalem again and destroys many lives. ¹⁸For the king of Israel disregarded his treaty and broke it after swearing to obey; therefore, he will not escape.

¹⁹"So this is what the Sovereign LORD says: As surely as I live, I will punish him for breaking my covenant and disregarding the solemn oath he made in my name. ²⁰I will throw my net over him and capture him in my snare. I will bring him to Babylon and put him on trial for this treason against me. ²¹And all his best warriors* will be killed in battle, and those who survive will be scattered to the four winds. Then you will know that I, the LORD, have spoken.

²²"This is what the Sovereign LORD says: I will take a branch from the top of a tall cedar, and I will plant it on the top of Israel's highest mountain. ²³It will become a majestic cedar, sending forth its branches and producing seed. Birds of every sort will nest in it, finding shelter in the shade of its branches. ²⁴And all the trees will know that it is I, the LORD, who cuts the tall tree down and makes the short tree grow tall. It is I who makes the green tree wither and gives the dead tree new life. I, the LORD, have spoken, and I will do what I said!"

THE JUSTICE OF A RIGHTEOUS GOD

18 Then another message came to me from the LORD: ²"Why do you quote this proverb concerning the land of Israel: 'The parents have eaten sour grapes, but their children's mouths pucker at the taste'? ³As surely as I live, says the Sovereign LORD, you will not quote this proverb anymore in Israel. ⁴For all people are mine to judge—both parents and children alike. And this is my rule: The person who sins is the one who will die.

⁵"Suppose a certain man is righteous and does what is just and right. ⁶He does not feast in the mountains before Israel's idols* or worship them.

17:21 As in many Hebrew manuscripts; Masoretic Text reads *his fleeing warriors*. The meaning is uncertain. 18:6 The Hebrew term (literally *round things*) probably alludes to dung; also in 18:12, 15.

He does not commit adultery or have intercourse with a woman during her menstrual period. [7]He is a merciful creditor, not keeping the items given as security by poor debtors. He does not rob the poor but instead gives food to the hungry and provides clothes for the needy. [8]He grants loans without interest, stays away from injustice, is honest and fair when judging others, [9]and faithfully obeys my decrees and regulations. Anyone who does these things is just and will surely live, says the Sovereign Lord.

[10]"But suppose that man has a son who grows up to be a robber or murderer and refuses to do what is right. [11]And that son does all the evil things his father would never do—he worships idols on the mountains, commits adultery, [12]oppresses the poor and helpless, steals from debtors by refusing to let them redeem their security, worships idols, commits detestable sins, [13]and lends money at excessive interest. Should such a sinful person live? No! He must die and must take full blame.

[14]"But suppose that sinful son, in turn, has a son who sees his father's wickedness and decides against that kind of life. [15]This son refuses to worship idols on the mountains and does not commit adultery. [16]He does not exploit the poor, but instead is fair to debtors and does not rob them. He gives food to the hungry and provides clothes for the needy. [17]He helps the poor,* does not lend money at interest, and obeys all my regulations and decrees. Such a person will not die because of his father's sins; he will surely live. [18]But the father will die for his many sins—for being cruel, robbing people, and doing what was clearly wrong among his people.

[19]"'What?' you ask. 'Doesn't the child pay for the parent's sins?' No! For if the child does what is just and right and keeps my decrees, that child will surely live. [20]The person who sins is the one who will die. The child will not be punished for the parent's sins, and the parent will not be punished for the child's sins. Righteous people will be rewarded for their own righteous behavior, and wicked people will be punished for their own wickedness. [21]But if wicked people turn away from all their sins and begin to obey my decrees and do what is just and right, they will surely live and not die. [22]All their past sins will be forgotten, and they will live because of the righteous things they have done.

[23]"Do you think that I like to see wicked people die? says the Sovereign Lord. Of course not! I want them to turn from their wicked ways and live. [24]However, if righteous people turn from their righteous behavior and start doing sinful things and act like other sinners, should they be allowed to live? No, of course not! All their righteous acts will be forgotten, and they will die for their sins.

[25]"Yet you say, 'The Lord isn't doing what's right!' Listen to me, O people of Israel. Am I the one not doing what's right, or is it you? [26]When righteous people turn from their righteous behavior and start doing sinful things, they will die for it. Yes, they will die because of their sinful deeds. [27]And if wicked people turn from their wickedness, obey the law, and do what is just and right, they will save their lives. [28]They will live because they thought it over and decided to turn from their sins. Such people will not die. [29]And yet the people of Israel keep saying, 'The Lord isn't doing what's right!' O people of Israel, it is you who are not doing what's right, not I.

[30]"Therefore, I will judge each of you, O people of Israel, according to your actions, says the Sovereign Lord. Repent, and turn from your sins. Don't let them destroy you! [31]Put all your rebellion behind you, and find yourselves a new heart and a new spirit. For why should you die, O people of Israel? [32]I don't want you to die, says the Sovereign Lord. Turn back and live!

A FUNERAL SONG FOR ISRAEL'S KINGS

19 "Sing this funeral song for the princes of Israel:

[2] "What is your mother?
    A lioness among lions!
She lay down among the young lions
    and reared her cubs.
[3] She raised one of her cubs
    to become a strong young lion.
He learned to hunt and devour prey,
    and he became a man-eater.
[4] Then the nations heard about him,
    and he was trapped in their pit.
They led him away with hooks
    to the land of Egypt.

[5] "When the lioness saw
    that her hopes for him were gone,
she took another of her cubs
    and taught him to be a strong young lion.
[6] He prowled among the other lions
    and stood out among them in his strength.
He learned to hunt and devour prey,
    and he, too, became a man-eater.
[7] He demolished fortresses*
    and destroyed their towns and cities.
Their farms were desolated,
    and their crops were destroyed.
The land and its people trembled in fear
    when they heard him roar.
[8] Then the armies of the nations attacked him,
    surrounding him from every direction.
They threw a net over him
    and captured him in their pit.
[9] With hooks, they dragged him into a cage
    and brought him before the king of Babylon.

18:17 Greek version reads *He refuses to do evil.*   19:7 As in Greek version; Hebrew reads *He knew widows.*

They held him in captivity,
    so his voice could never again be heard
    on the mountains of Israel.

¹⁰ "Your mother was like a vine
    planted by the water's edge.
It had lush, green foliage
    because of the abundant water.
¹¹ Its branches became strong—
    strong enough to be a ruler's scepter.
It grew very tall,
    towering above all others.
It stood out because of its height
    and its many lush branches.
¹² But the vine was uprooted in fury
    and thrown down to the ground.
The desert wind dried up its fruit
    and tore off its strong branches,
so that it withered
    and was destroyed by fire.
¹³ Now the vine is transplanted to
    the wilderness,
    where the ground is hard and dry.
¹⁴ A fire has burst out from its branches
    and devoured its fruit.
Its remaining limbs are not
    strong enough to be a ruler's scepter.

"This is a funeral song, and it will be used in a funeral."

THE REBELLION OF ISRAEL

20 On August 14,* during the seventh year of King Jehoiachin's captivity, some of the leaders of Israel came to request a message from the LORD. They sat down in front of me to wait for his reply. ² Then this message came to me from the LORD: ³ "Son of man, tell the leaders of Israel, 'This is what the Sovereign LORD says: How dare you come to ask me for a message? As surely as I live, says the Sovereign LORD, I will tell you nothing!'

⁴ "Son of man, bring charges against them and condemn them. Make them realize how detestable the sins of their ancestors really were. ⁵ Give them this message from the Sovereign LORD: When I chose Israel—when I revealed myself to the descendants of Jacob in Egypt—I took a solemn oath that I, the LORD, would be their God. ⁶ I took a solemn oath that day that I would bring them out of Egypt to a land I had discovered and explored for them—a good land, a land flowing with milk and honey, the best of all lands anywhere. ⁷ Then I said to them, 'Each of you, get rid of the vile images you are so obsessed with. Do not defile yourselves with the idols* of Egypt, for I am the LORD your God.'

⁸ "But they rebelled against me and would not listen. They did not get rid of the vile images they were obsessed with, or forsake the idols of Egypt. Then I threatened to pour out my fury on them to satisfy my anger while they were still in Egypt. ⁹ But I didn't do it, for I acted to protect the honor of my name. I would not allow shame to be brought on my name among the surrounding nations who saw me reveal myself by bringing the Israelites out of Egypt. ¹⁰ So I brought them out of Egypt and led them into the wilderness. ¹¹ There I gave them my decrees and regulations so they could find life by keeping them. ¹² And I gave them my Sabbath days of rest as a sign between them and me. It was to remind them that I am the LORD, who had set them apart to be holy.

¹³ "But the people of Israel rebelled against me, and they refused to obey my decrees there in the wilderness. They wouldn't obey my regulations even though obedience would have given them life. They also violated my Sabbath days. So I threatened to pour out my fury on them, and I made plans to utterly consume them in the wilderness. ¹⁴ But again I held back in order to protect the honor of my name before the nations who had seen my power in bringing Israel out of Egypt. ¹⁵ But I took a solemn oath against them in the wilderness. I swore I would not bring them into the land I had given them, a land flowing with milk and honey, the most beautiful place on earth. ¹⁶ For they had rejected my regulations, refused to follow my decrees, and violated my Sabbath days. Their hearts were given to their idols. ¹⁷ Nevertheless, I took pity on them and held back from destroying them in the wilderness.

¹⁸ "Then I warned their children not to follow in their parents' footsteps, defiling themselves with their idols. ¹⁹ 'I am the LORD your God,' I told them. 'Follow my decrees, pay attention to my regulations, ²⁰ and keep my Sabbath days holy, for they are a sign to remind you that I am the LORD your God.'

²¹ "But their children, too, rebelled against me. They refused to keep my decrees and follow my regulations, even though obedience would have given them life. And they also violated my Sabbath days. So again I threatened to pour out my fury on them in the wilderness. ²² Nevertheless, I withdrew my judgment against them to protect the honor of my name before the nations that had seen my power in bringing them out of Egypt. ²³ But I took a solemn oath against them in the wilderness. I swore I would scatter them among all the nations ²⁴ because they did not obey my regulations. They scorned my decrees by violating my Sabbath days and longing for the idols of their ancestors. ²⁵ I gave them over to worthless decrees and regulations that would not lead to life. ²⁶ I let them pollute themselves* with the very gifts I had given them, and I allowed them to give their firstborn children as offerings to their gods—so I might devastate them and remind them that I alone am the LORD.

20:1 Hebrew *In the fifth month, on the tenth day,* of the ancient Hebrew lunar calendar. This day was August 14, 591 B.C.; also see note on 1:1.   20:7 The Hebrew term (literally *round things*) probably alludes to dung; also in 20:8, 16, 18, 24, 31, 39.
20:25-26 Or *I gave them worthless decrees and regulations. . . . I polluted them.*

JUDGMENT AND RESTORATION

27 "Therefore, son of man, give the people of Israel this message from the Sovereign LORD: Your ancestors continued to blaspheme and betray me, 28 for when I brought them into the land I had promised them, they offered sacrifices on every high hill and under every green tree they saw! They roused my fury as they offered up sacrifices to their gods. They brought their perfumes and incense and poured out their liquid offerings to them. 29 I said to them, 'What is this high place where you are going?' (This kind of pagan shrine has been called Bamah—'high place'—ever since.)

30 "Therefore, give the people of Israel this message from the Sovereign LORD: Do you plan to pollute yourselves just as your ancestors did? Do you intend to keep prostituting yourselves by worshiping vile images? 31 For when you offer gifts to them and give your little children to be burned as sacrifices,* you continue to pollute yourselves with idols to this day. Should I allow you to ask for a message from me, O people of Israel? As surely as I live, says the Sovereign LORD, I will tell you nothing.

32 "You say, 'We want to be like the nations all around us, who serve idols of wood and stone.' But what you have in mind will never happen. 33 As surely as I live, says the Sovereign LORD, I will rule over you with an iron fist in great anger and with awesome power. 34 And in anger I will reach out with my strong hand and powerful arm, and I will bring you back* from the lands where you are scattered. 35 I will bring you into the wilderness of the nations, and there I will judge you face to face. 36 I will judge you there just as I did your ancestors in the wilderness after bringing them out of Egypt, says the Sovereign LORD. 37 I will examine you carefully and hold you to the terms of the covenant. 38 I will purge you of all those who rebel and revolt against me. I will bring them out of the countries where they are in exile, but they will never enter the land of Israel. Then you will know that I am the LORD.

39 "As for you, O people of Israel, this is what the Sovereign LORD says: Go right ahead and worship your idols, but sooner or later you will obey me and will stop bringing shame on my holy name by worshiping idols. 40 For on my holy mountain, the great mountain of Israel, says the Sovereign LORD, the people of Israel will someday worship me, and I will accept them. There I will require that you bring me all your offerings and choice gifts and sacrifices. 41 When I bring you home from exile, you will be like a pleasing sacrifice to me. And I will display my holiness through you as all the nations watch. 42 Then when I have brought you home to the land I promised with a solemn oath to give to your ancestors, you will know that I am the LORD. 43 You will look back on all the ways you defiled yourselves and will hate yourselves because of the evil you have done. 44 You will know that I am the LORD, O people of Israel, when I have honored my name by treating you mercifully in spite of your wickedness. I, the Sovereign LORD, have spoken!"

JUDGMENT AGAINST THE NEGEV

45 *Then this message came to me from the LORD: 46 "Son of man, turn and face the south* and speak out against it; prophesy against the brushlands of the Negev. 47 Tell the southern wilderness, 'This is what the Sovereign LORD says: Hear the word of the LORD! I will set you on fire, and every tree, both green and dry, will be burned. The terrible flames will not be quenched and will scorch everything from south to north. 48 And everyone in the world will see that I, the LORD, have set this fire. It will not be put out.'"

49 Then I said, "O Sovereign LORD, they are saying of me, 'He only talks in riddles!'"

THE LORD'S SWORD OF JUDGMENT

21 1 *Then this message came to me from the LORD: 2 "Son of man, turn and face Jerusalem and prophesy against Israel and her sanctuaries. 3 Tell her, 'This is what the LORD says: I am your enemy, O Israel, and I am about to unsheath my sword to destroy your people—the righteous and the wicked alike. 4 Yes, I will cut off both the righteous and the wicked! I will draw my sword against everyone in the land from south to north. 5 Everyone in the world will know that I am the LORD. My sword is in my hand, and it will not return to its sheath until its work is finished.'

6 "Son of man, groan before the people! Groan before them with bitter anguish and a broken heart. 7 When they ask why you are groaning, tell them, 'I groan because of the terrifying news I have heard. When it comes true, the boldest heart will melt with fear; all strength will disappear. Every spirit will faint; strong knees will become as weak as water. And the Sovereign LORD says: It is coming! It's on its way!'"

8 Then the LORD said to me, 9 "Son of man, give the people this message from the Lord:

"A sword, a sword
    is being sharpened and polished.
10 It is sharpened for terrible slaughter
    and polished to flash like lightning!
Now will you laugh?
    Those far stronger than you have fallen
        beneath its power!*
11 Yes, the sword is now being sharpened
        and polished;
    it is being prepared for the executioner.

---

¹² "Son of man, cry out and wail;
    pound your thighs in anguish,
for that sword will slaughter my people
        and their leaders—
    everyone will die!
¹³ It will put them all to the test.
    What chance do they have?*
    says the Sovereign LORD.

¹⁴ "Son of man, prophesy to them
    and clap your hands.
Then take the sword and brandish it twice,
    even three times,
to symbolize the great massacre,
    the great massacre facing them on
        every side.
¹⁵ Let their hearts melt with terror,
    for the sword glitters at every gate.
It flashes like lightning
    and is polished for slaughter!
¹⁶ O sword, slash to the right,
    then slash to the left,
wherever you will,
    wherever you want.
¹⁷ I, too, will clap my hands,
    and I will satisfy my fury.
I, the LORD, have spoken!"

OMENS FOR BABYLON'S KING

¹⁸ Then this message came to me from the LORD:
¹⁹ "Son of man, make a map and trace two routes
on it for the sword of Babylon's king to follow.
Put a signpost on the road that comes out of
Babylon where the road forks into two—²⁰ one
road going to Ammon and its capital, Rabbah,
and the other to Judah and fortified Jerusalem. ²¹ The king of Babylon now stands at the
fork, uncertain whether to attack Jerusalem
or Rabbah. He calls his magicians to look for
omens. They cast lots by shaking arrows from
the quiver. They inspect the livers of animal
sacrifices. ²² The omen in his right hand says,
'Jerusalem!' With battering rams his soldiers
will go against the gates, shouting for the kill.
They will put up siege towers and build ramps
against the walls. ²³ The people of Jerusalem will
think it is a false omen, because of their treaty
with the Babylonians. But the king of Babylon
will remind the people of their rebellion. Then
he will attack and capture them.

²⁴ "Therefore, this is what the Sovereign LORD
says: Again and again you remind me of your
sin and your guilt. You don't even try to hide it!
In everything you do, your sins are obvious for
all to see. So now the time of your punishment
has come!

²⁵ "O you corrupt and wicked prince of Israel,
your final day of reckoning is here! ²⁶ This is what
the Sovereign LORD says:

"Take off your jeweled crown,
    for the old order changes.

Now the lowly will be exalted,
    and the mighty will be brought down.
²⁷ Destruction! Destruction!
    I will surely destroy the kingdom.
And it will not be restored until
        the one appears
    who has the right to judge it.
Then I will hand it over to him.

A MESSAGE FOR THE AMMONITES

²⁸ "And now, son of man, prophesy concerning
the Ammonites and their mockery. Give them
this message from the Sovereign LORD:

"A sword, a sword
    is drawn for your slaughter.
It is polished to destroy,
    flashing like lightning!
²⁹ Your prophets have given false visions,
    and your fortune-tellers have told lies.
The sword will fall on the necks
        of the wicked
    for whom the day of final reckoning
        has come.

³⁰ "Now return the sword to its sheath,
    for in your own country,
the land of your birth,
    I will pass judgment upon you.
³¹ I will pour out my fury on you
    and blow on you with the fire of my anger.
I will hand you over to cruel men
    who are skilled in destruction.
³² You will be fuel for the fire,
    and your blood will be spilled in your
        own land.
You will be utterly wiped out,
    your memory lost to history,
for I, the LORD, have spoken!"

THE SINS OF JERUSALEM

22 Now this message came to me from the
LORD: ² "Son of man, are you ready to judge
Jerusalem? Are you ready to judge this city of
murderers? Publicly denounce her detestable
sins, ³ and give her this message from the Sovereign LORD: O city of murderers, doomed and
damned—city of idols,* filthy and foul—⁴ you are
guilty because of the blood you have shed. You are
defiled because of the idols you have made. Your
day of destruction has come! You have reached
the end of your years. I will make you an object
of mockery throughout the world. ⁵ O infamous
city, filled with confusion, you will be mocked
by people far and near.

⁶ "Every leader in Israel who lives within your
walls is bent on murder. ⁷ Fathers and mothers
are treated with contempt. Foreigners are forced

21:13 The meaning of the Hebrew is uncertain.   22:3 The
Hebrew term (literally *round things*) probably alludes to dung;
also in 22:4.

to pay for protection. Orphans and widows are wronged and oppressed among you. ⁸ You despise my holy things and violate my Sabbath days of rest. ⁹ People accuse others falsely and send them to their death. You are filled with idol worshipers and people who do obscene things. ¹⁰ Men sleep with their fathers' wives and force themselves on women who are menstruating. ¹¹ Within your walls live men who commit adultery with their neighbors' wives, who defile their daughters-in-law, or who rape their own sisters. ¹² There are hired murderers, loan racketeers, and extortioners everywhere. They never even think of me and my commands, says the Sovereign LORD.

¹³ "But now I clap my hands in indignation over your dishonest gain and bloodshed. ¹⁴ How strong and courageous will you be in my day of reckoning? I, the LORD, have spoken, and I will do what I said. ¹⁵ I will scatter you among the nations and purge you of your wickedness. ¹⁶ And when I have been dishonored among the nations because of you,* you will know that I am the LORD."

THE LORD'S REFINING FURNACE

¹⁷ Then this message came to me from the LORD: ¹⁸ "Son of man, the people of Israel are the worthless slag that remains after silver is smelted. They are the dross that is left over—a useless mixture of copper, tin, iron, and lead. ¹⁹ So tell them, 'This is what the Sovereign LORD says: Because you are all worthless slag, I will bring you to my crucible in Jerusalem. ²⁰ Just as silver, copper, iron, lead, and tin are melted down in a furnace, I will melt you down in the heat of my fury. ²¹ I will gather you together and blow the fire of my anger upon you, ²² and you will melt like silver in fierce heat. Then you will know that I, the LORD, have poured out my fury on you.'"

THE SINS OF ISRAEL'S LEADERS

²³ Again a message came to me from the LORD: ²⁴ "Son of man, give the people of Israel this message: In the day of my indignation, you will be like a polluted land, a land without rain. ²⁵ Your princes* plot conspiracies just as lions stalk their prey. They devour innocent people, seizing treasures and extorting wealth. They make many widows in the land. ²⁶ Your priests have violated my instructions and defiled my holy things. They make no distinction between what is holy and what is not. And they do not teach my people the difference between what is ceremonially clean and unclean. They disregard my Sabbath days so that I am dishonored among them. ²⁷ Your leaders are like wolves who tear apart their victims. They actually destroy people's lives for money! ²⁸ And your prophets cover up for them by announcing false visions and making lying predictions. They say, 'My message is from the Sovereign LORD,' when the LORD hasn't spoken a single word to them.

²⁹ Even common people oppress the poor, rob the needy, and deprive foreigners of justice.

³⁰ "I looked for someone who might rebuild the wall of righteousness that guards the land. I searched for someone to stand in the gap in the wall so I wouldn't have to destroy the land, but I found no one. ³¹ So now I will pour out my fury on them, consuming them with the fire of my anger. I will heap on their heads the full penalty for all their sins. I, the Sovereign LORD, have spoken!"

THE ADULTERY OF TWO SISTERS

23 This message came to me from the LORD: ² "Son of man, once there were two sisters who were daughters of the same mother. ³ They became prostitutes in Egypt. Even as young girls, they allowed men to fondle their breasts. ⁴ The older girl was named Oholah, and her sister was Oholibah. I married them, and they bore me sons and daughters. I am speaking of Samaria and Jerusalem, for Oholah is Samaria and Oholibah is Jerusalem.

⁵ "Then Oholah lusted after other lovers instead of me, and she gave her love to the Assyrian officers. ⁶ They were all attractive young men, captains and commanders dressed in handsome blue, charioteers driving their horses. ⁷ And so she prostituted herself with the most desirable men of Assyria, worshiping their idols* and defiling herself. ⁸ For when she left Egypt, she did not leave her spirit of prostitution behind. She was still as lewd as in her youth, when the Egyptians slept with her, fondled her breasts, and used her as a prostitute.

⁹ "And so I handed her over to her Assyrian lovers, whom she desired so much. ¹⁰ They stripped her, took away her children as their slaves, and then killed her. After she received her punishment, her reputation was known to every woman in the land.

¹¹ "Yet even though Oholibah saw what had happened to Oholah, her sister, she followed right in her footsteps. And she was even more depraved, abandoning herself to her lust and prostitution. ¹² She fawned over all the Assyrian officers—those captains and commanders in handsome uniforms, those charioteers driving their horses—all of them attractive young men. ¹³ I saw the way she was going, defiling herself just like her older sister.

¹⁴ "Then she carried her prostitution even further. She fell in love with pictures that were painted on a wall—pictures of Babylonian* military officers, outfitted in striking red uniforms. ¹⁵ Handsome belts encircled their waists, and flowing turbans crowned their heads. They were

---

22:16 As in one Hebrew manuscript and Greek and Syriac versions; Masoretic Text reads *when you have been dishonored among the nations.*   22:25 As in Greek version; Hebrew reads *prophets.*   23:7 The Hebrew term (literally *round pieces*) probably alludes to dung; also in 23:30, 37, 39, 49.   23:14 Or *Chaldean.*

dressed like chariot officers from the land of Babylonia.* ¹⁶ When she saw these paintings, she longed to give herself to them, so she sent messengers to Babylonia to invite them to come to her. ¹⁷ So they came and committed adultery with her, defiling her in the bed of love. After being defiled, however, she rejected them in disgust.

¹⁸ "In the same way, I became disgusted with Oholibah and rejected her, just as I had rejected her sister, because she flaunted herself before them and gave herself to satisfy their lusts. ¹⁹ Yet she turned to even greater prostitution, remembering her youth when she was a prostitute in Egypt. ²⁰ She lusted after lovers with genitals as large as a donkey's and emissions like those of a horse. ²¹ And so, Oholibah, you relived your former days as a young girl in Egypt, when you first allowed your breasts to be fondled.

THE LORD'S JUDGMENT OF OHOLIBAH

²² "Therefore, Oholibah, this is what the Sovereign LORD says: I will send your lovers against you from every direction—those very nations from which you turned away in disgust. ²³ For the Babylonians will come with all the Chaldeans from Pekod and Shoa and Koa. And all the Assyrians will come with them—handsome young captains, commanders, chariot officers, and other high-ranking officers, all riding their horses. ²⁴ They will all come against you from the north* with chariots, wagons, and a great army prepared for attack. They will take up positions on every side, surrounding you with men armed with shields and helmets. And I will hand you over to them for punishment so they can do with you as they please. ²⁵ I will turn my jealous anger against you, and they will deal harshly with you. They will cut off your nose and ears, and any survivors will then be slaughtered by the sword. Your children will be taken away as captives, and everything that is left will be burned. ²⁶ They will strip you of your beautiful clothes and jewels. ²⁷ In this way, I will put a stop to the lewdness and prostitution you brought from Egypt. You will never again cast longing eyes on those things or fondly remember your time in Egypt.

²⁸ "For this is what the Sovereign LORD says: I will surely hand you over to your enemies, to those you loathe, those you rejected. ²⁹ They will treat you with hatred and rob you of all you own, leaving you stark naked. The shame of your prostitution will be exposed to all the world. ³⁰ You brought all this on yourself by prostituting yourself to other nations, defiling yourself with all their idols. ³¹ Because you have followed in your sister's footsteps, I will force you to drink the same cup of terror she drank.

³² "Yes, this is what the Sovereign LORD says:

"You will drink from your sister's cup
    of terror,
  a cup that is large and deep.

It is filled to the brim
  with scorn and derision.
³³ Drunkenness and anguish will fill you,
  for your cup is filled to the brim with
    distress and desolation,
  the same cup your sister Samaria drank.
³⁴ You will drain that cup of terror
  to the very bottom.
Then you will smash it to pieces
  and beat your breast in anguish.
  I, the Sovereign LORD, have spoken!

³⁵ "And because you have forgotten me and turned your back on me, this is what the Sovereign LORD says: You must bear the consequences of all your lewdness and prostitution."

THE LORD'S JUDGMENT ON BOTH SISTERS

³⁶ The LORD said to me, "Son of man, you must accuse Oholah and Oholibah of all their detestable sins. ³⁷ They have committed both adultery and murder—adultery by worshiping idols and murder by burning as sacrifices the children they bore to me. ³⁸ Furthermore, they have defiled my Temple and violated my Sabbath day! ³⁹ On the very day that they sacrificed their children to their idols, they boldly came into my Temple to worship! They came in and defiled my house.

⁴⁰ "You sisters sent messengers to distant lands to get men. Then when they arrived, you bathed yourselves, painted your eyelids, and put on your finest jewels for them. ⁴¹ You sat with them on a beautifully embroidered couch and put my incense and my special oil on a table that was spread before you. ⁴² From your room came the sound of many men carousing. They were lustful men and drunkards* from the wilderness, who put bracelets on your wrists and beautiful crowns on your heads. ⁴³ Then I said, 'If they really want to have sex with old worn-out prostitutes like these, let them!' ⁴⁴ And that is what they did. They had sex with Oholah and Oholibah, these shameless prostitutes. ⁴⁵ But righteous people will judge these sister cities for what they really are—adulterers and murderers.

⁴⁶ "Now this is what the Sovereign LORD says: Bring an army against them and hand them over to be terrorized and plundered. ⁴⁷ For their enemies will stone them and kill them with swords. They will butcher their sons and daughters and burn their homes. ⁴⁸ In this way, I will put an end to lewdness and idolatry in the land, and my judgment will be a warning to all women not to follow your wicked example. ⁴⁹ You will be fully repaid for all your prostitution—your worship of idols. Yes, you will suffer the full penalty. Then you will know that I am the Sovereign LORD."

23:15 Or *Chaldea;* also in 23:16.   23:24 As in Greek version; the meaning of the Hebrew is uncertain.   23:42 Or *Sabeans.*

THE SIGN OF THE COOKING POT

24 On January 15,* during the ninth year of King Jehoiachin's captivity, this message came to me from the LORD: 2"Son of man, write down today's date, because on this very day the king of Babylon is beginning his attack against Jerusalem. 3Then give these rebels an illustration with this message from the Sovereign LORD:

"Put a pot on the fire,
　and pour in some water.
4 Fill it with choice pieces of meat—
　the rump and the shoulder
　and all the most tender cuts.
5 Use only the best sheep from the flock,
　and heap fuel on the fire beneath the pot.
Bring the pot to a boil,
　and cook the bones along with the meat.

6 "Now this is what the Sovereign LORD says:
What sorrow awaits Jerusalem,
　the city of murderers!
She is a cooking pot
　whose corruption can't be cleaned out.
Take the meat out in random order,
　for no piece is better than another.
7 For the blood of her murders
　is splashed on the rocks.
It isn't even spilled on the ground,
　where the dust could cover it!
8 So I will splash her blood on a rock
　for all to see,
an expression of my anger
　and vengeance against her.

9 "This is what the Sovereign LORD says:
What sorrow awaits Jerusalem,
　the city of murderers!
　I myself will pile up the fuel beneath her.
10 Yes, heap on the wood!
Let the fire roar to make the pot boil.
Cook the meat with many spices,
　and afterward burn the bones.
11 Now set the empty pot on the coals.
　Heat it red hot!
　Burn away the filth and corruption.
12 But it's hopeless;
　the corruption can't be cleaned out.
　So throw it into the fire.
13 Your impurity is your lewdness
　and the corruption of your idolatry.
I tried to cleanse you,
　but you refused.
So now you will remain in your filth
　until my fury against you has been
　　satisfied.

14 "I, the LORD, have spoken! The time has come, and I won't hold back. I will not change my mind, and I will have no pity on you. You will be judged on the basis of all your wicked actions, says the Sovereign LORD."

THE DEATH OF EZEKIEL'S WIFE

15Then this message came to me from the LORD: 16"Son of man, with one blow I will take away your dearest treasure. Yet you must not show any sorrow at her death. Do not weep; let there be no tears. 17Groan silently, but let there be no wailing at her grave. Do not uncover your head or take off your sandals. Do not perform the usual rituals of mourning or accept any food brought to you by consoling friends."

18So I proclaimed this to the people the next morning, and in the evening my wife died. The next morning I did everything I had been told to do. 19Then the people asked, "What does all this mean? What are you trying to tell us?"

20So I said to them, "A message came to me from the LORD, 21and I was told to give this message to the people of Israel. This is what the Sovereign LORD says: I will defile my Temple, the source of your security and pride, the place your heart delights in. Your sons and daughters whom you left behind in Judah will be slaughtered by the sword. 22Then you will do as Ezekiel has done. You will not mourn in public or console yourselves by eating the food brought by friends. 23Your heads will remain covered, and your sandals will not be taken off. You will not mourn or weep, but you will waste away because of your sins. You will groan among yourselves for all the evil you have done. 24Ezekiel is an example for you; you will do just as he has done. And when that time comes, you will know that I am the Sovereign LORD."

25Then the LORD said to me, "Son of man, on the day I take away their stronghold—their joy and glory, their heart's desire, their dearest treasure—I will also take away their sons and daughters. 26And on that day a survivor from Jerusalem will come to you in Babylon and tell you what has happened. 27And when he arrives, your voice will suddenly return so you can talk to him, and you will be a symbol for these people. Then they will know that I am the LORD."

A MESSAGE FOR AMMON

25 Then this message came to me from the LORD: 2"Son of man, turn and face the land of Ammon and prophesy against its people. 3Give the Ammonites this message from the Sovereign LORD: Hear the word of the Sovereign LORD! Because you cheered when my Temple was defiled, mocked Israel in her desolation, and laughed at Judah as she went away into exile, 4I will allow nomads from the eastern deserts to overrun your country. They will set up their camps among you and pitch their tents on your land. They will harvest all your fruit and drink the milk from your livestock. 5And I will turn the city of Rabbah into a pasture for camels, and all the land of the Ammonites into a resting place for sheep and goats. Then you will know that I am the LORD.

⁶"This is what the Sovereign LORD says: Because you clapped and danced and cheered with glee at the destruction of my people, ⁷I will raise my fist of judgment against you. I will give you as plunder to many nations. I will cut you off from being a nation and destroy you completely. Then you will know that I am the LORD.

A MESSAGE FOR MOAB

⁸"This is what the Sovereign LORD says: Because the people of Moab* have said that Judah is just like all the other nations, ⁹I will open up their eastern flank and wipe out their glorious frontier towns—Beth-jeshimoth, Baal-meon, and Kiriathaim. ¹⁰And I will hand Moab over to nomads from the eastern deserts, just as I handed over Ammon. Yes, the Ammonites will no longer be counted among the nations. ¹¹In the same way, I will bring my judgment down on the Moabites. Then they will know that I am the LORD.

A MESSAGE FOR EDOM

¹²"This is what the Sovereign LORD says: The people of Edom have sinned greatly by avenging themselves against the people of Judah. ¹³Therefore, says the Sovereign LORD, I will raise my fist of judgment against Edom. I will wipe out its people and animals with the sword. I will make a wasteland of everything from Teman to Dedan. ¹⁴I will accomplish this by the hand of my people of Israel. They will carry out my vengeance with anger, and Edom will know that this vengeance is from me. I, the Sovereign LORD, have spoken!

A MESSAGE FOR PHILISTIA

¹⁵"This is what the Sovereign LORD says: The people of Philistia have acted against Judah out of bitter revenge and long-standing contempt. ¹⁶Therefore, this is what the Sovereign LORD says: I will raise my fist of judgment against the land of the Philistines. I will wipe out the Kerethites and utterly destroy the people who live by the sea. ¹⁷I will execute terrible vengeance against them to punish them for what they have done. And when I have inflicted my revenge, they will know that I am the LORD."

A MESSAGE FOR TYRE

26 On February 3, during the twelfth year of King Jehoiachin's captivity,* this message came to me from the LORD: ²"Son of man, Tyre has rejoiced over the fall of Jerusalem, saying, 'Ha! She who was the gateway to the rich trade routes to the east has been broken, and I am the heir! Because she has been made desolate, I will become wealthy!'

³"Therefore, this is what the Sovereign LORD says: I am your enemy, O Tyre, and I will bring many nations against you, like the waves of the sea crashing against your shoreline. ⁴They will destroy the walls of Tyre and tear down its towers. I will scrape away its soil and make it a bare rock! ⁵It will be just a rock in the sea, a place for fishermen to spread their nets, for I have spoken, says the Sovereign LORD. Tyre will become the prey of many nations, ⁶and its mainland villages will be destroyed by the sword. Then they will know that I am the LORD.

⁷"This is what the Sovereign LORD says: From the north I will bring King Nebuchadnezzar* of Babylon against Tyre. He is king of kings and brings his horses, chariots, charioteers, and great army. ⁸First he will destroy your mainland villages. Then he will attack you by building a siege wall, constructing a ramp, and raising a roof of shields against you. ⁹He will pound your walls with battering rams and demolish your towers with sledgehammers. ¹⁰The hooves of his horses will choke the city with dust, and the noise of the charioteers and chariot wheels will shake your walls as they storm through your broken gates. ¹¹His horsemen will trample through every street in the city. They will butcher your people, and your strong pillars will topple.

¹²"They will plunder all your riches and merchandise and break down your walls. They will destroy your lovely homes and dump your stones and timbers and even your dust into the sea. ¹³I will stop the music of your songs. No more will the sound of harps be heard among your people. ¹⁴I will make your island a bare rock, a place for fishermen to spread their nets. You will never be rebuilt, for I, the LORD, have spoken. Yes, the Sovereign LORD has spoken!

THE EFFECT OF TYRE'S DESTRUCTION

¹⁵"This is what the Sovereign LORD says to Tyre: The whole coastline will tremble at the sound of your fall, as the screams of the wounded echo in the continuing slaughter. ¹⁶All the seaport rulers will step down from their thrones and take off their royal robes and beautiful clothing. They will sit on the ground trembling with horror at your destruction. ¹⁷Then they will wail for you, singing this funeral song:

"O famous island city,
  once ruler of the sea,
how you have been destroyed!
Your people, with their naval power,
  once spread fear around the world.
¹⁸ Now the coastlands tremble at your fall.
  The islands are dismayed as you
    disappear.

25:8 As in Greek version; Hebrew reads Moab and Seir. 26:1 Hebrew In the eleventh year, on the first day of the month, of the ancient Hebrew lunar calendar year. Since an element is missing in the date formula here, scholars have reconstructed this probable reading: In the eleventh [month of the twelfth] year, on the first day of the month. This reading would put this message on February 3, 585 B.C.; also see note on 1:1. 26:7 Hebrew Nebuchadrezzar, a variant spelling of Nebuchadnezzar.

¹⁹"This is what the Sovereign LORD says: I will make Tyre an uninhabited ruin, like many others. I will bury you beneath the terrible waves of enemy attack. Great seas will swallow you. ²⁰I will send you to the pit to join those who descended there long ago. Your city will lie in ruins, buried beneath the earth, like those in the pit who have entered the world of the dead. You will have no place of respect here in the land of the living. ²¹I will bring you to a terrible end, and you will exist no more. You will be looked for, but you will never again be found. I, the Sovereign LORD, have spoken!"

THE END OF TYRE'S GLORY

27 Then this message came to me from the LORD: ²"Son of man, sing a funeral song for Tyre, ³that mighty gateway to the sea, the trading center of the world. Give Tyre this message from the Sovereign LORD:

"You boasted, O Tyre,
  'My beauty is perfect!'
⁴ You extended your boundaries into the sea.
  Your builders made your beauty perfect.
⁵ You were like a great ship
  built of the finest cypress from Senir.*
They took a cedar from Lebanon
  to make a mast for you.
⁶ They carved your oars
  from the oaks of Bashan.
Your deck of pine from the coasts of Cyprus*
  was inlaid with ivory.
⁷ Your sails were made of Egypt's finest linen,
  and they flew as a banner above you.
You stood beneath blue and purple awnings
  made bright with dyes from the coasts
  of Elishah.
⁸ Your oarsmen came from Sidon and Arvad;
  your helmsmen were skilled men from
  Tyre itself.
⁹ Wise old craftsmen from Gebal did
  the caulking.
  Ships from every land came with goods to
  barter for your trade.

¹⁰"Men from distant Persia, Lydia, and Libya* served in your great army. They hung their shields and helmets on your walls, giving you great honor. ¹¹Men from Arvad and Helech stood on your walls. Your towers were manned by men from Gammad. Their shields hung on your walls, completing your beauty.

¹²"Tarshish sent merchants to buy your wares in exchange for silver, iron, tin, and lead. ¹³Merchants from Greece,* Tubal, and Meshech brought slaves and articles of bronze to trade with you. ¹⁴"From Beth-togarmah came riding horses, chariot horses, and mules, all in exchange for your goods. ¹⁵Merchants came to you from Dedan.* Numerous coastlands were your captive markets; they brought payment in ivory tusks and ebony wood.

¹⁶"Syria* sent merchants to buy your rich variety of goods. They traded turquoise, purple dyes, embroidery, fine linen, and jewelry of coral and rubies. ¹⁷Judah and Israel traded for your wares, offering wheat from Minnith, figs,* honey, olive oil, and balm.

¹⁸"Damascus sent merchants to buy your rich variety of goods, bringing wine from Helbon and white wool from Zahar. ¹⁹Greeks from Uzal* came to trade for your merchandise. Wrought iron, cassia, and fragrant calamus were bartered for your wares.

²⁰"Dedan sent merchants to trade their expensive saddle blankets with you. ²¹The Arabians and the princes of Kedar sent merchants to trade lambs and rams and male goats in exchange for your goods. ²²The merchants of Sheba and Raamah came with all kinds of spices, jewels, and gold in exchange for your wares.

²³"Haran, Canneh, Eden, Sheba, Asshur, and Kilmad came with their merchandise, too. ²⁴They brought choice fabrics to trade—blue cloth, embroidery, and multicolored carpets rolled up and bound with cords. ²⁵The ships of Tarshish were your ocean caravans. Your island warehouse was filled to the brim!

THE DESTRUCTION OF TYRE

²⁶ "But look! Your oarsmen
  have taken you into stormy seas!
A mighty eastern gale
  has wrecked you in the heart of the sea!
²⁷ Everything is lost—
  your riches and wares,
  your sailors and pilots,
  your ship builders, merchants,
  and warriors.
On the day of your ruin,
  everyone on board sinks into the depths
  of the sea.
²⁸ Your cities by the sea tremble
  as your pilots cry out in terror.
²⁹ All the oarsmen abandon their ships;
  the sailors and pilots stand
  on the shore.
³⁰ They cry aloud over you
  and weep bitterly.
They throw dust on their heads
  and roll in ashes.
³¹ They shave their heads in grief for you
  and dress themselves in burlap.
They weep for you with bitter anguish
  and deep mourning.
³² As they wail and mourn over you,
  they sing this sad funeral song:
'Was there ever such a city as Tyre,
  now silent at the bottom of the sea?

27:5 Or Hermon. 27:6 Hebrew Kittim. 27:10 Hebrew Paras, Lud, and Put. 27:13 Hebrew Javan. 27:15 Greek version reads Rhodes. 27:16 Hebrew Aram; some manuscripts read Edom. 27:17 The meaning of the Hebrew is uncertain. 27:19 Hebrew Vedan and Javan from Uzal. The meaning of the Hebrew is uncertain.

33 The merchandise you traded
 satisfied the desires of many nations.
Kings at the ends of the earth
 were enriched by your trade.
34 Now you are a wrecked ship,
 broken at the bottom of the sea.
All your merchandise and crew
 have gone down with you.
35 All who live along the coastlands
 are appalled at your terrible fate.
Their kings are filled with horror
 and look on with twisted faces.
36 The merchants among the nations
 shake their heads at the sight of you,*
for you have come to a horrible end
 and will exist no more.'"

A MESSAGE FOR TYRE'S KING

28 Then this message came to me from the LORD: 2 "Son of man, give the prince of Tyre this message from the Sovereign LORD:

"In your great pride you claim, 'I am a god!
 I sit on a divine throne in the heart of
 the sea.'
But you are only a man and not a god,
 though you boast that you are a god.
3 You regard yourself as wiser than Daniel
 and think no secret is hidden from you.
4 With your wisdom and understanding you
 have amassed great wealth—
 gold and silver for your treasuries.
5 Yes, your wisdom has made you very rich,
 and your riches have made you very proud.

6 "Therefore, this is what the Sovereign LORD
 says:
Because you think you are as wise as a god,
7 I will now bring against you a foreign
 army,
 the terror of the nations.
They will draw their swords against your
 marvelous wisdom
 and defile your splendor!
8 They will bring you down to the pit,
 and you will die in the heart of the sea,
 pierced with many wounds.
9 Will you then boast, 'I am a god!'
 to those who kill you?
To them you will be no god
 but merely a man!
10 You will die like an outcast*
 at the hands of foreigners.
 I, the Sovereign LORD, have spoken!"

11 Then this further message came to me from the LORD: 12 "Son of man, sing this funeral song for the king of Tyre. Give him this message from the Sovereign LORD:

"You were the model of perfection,
 full of wisdom and exquisite in beauty.

EXPOSING PRIDE
Ezekiel 28:12-17   JIMMY EVANS

Satan was originally an angel created to reflect God's glory. However, his heart "was filled with pride" (Ezekiel 28:17), and he said, "I will climb to the highest heavens and be like the Most High" (Isaiah 14:14). Satan wanted the glory for himself, and he immediately fell from heaven as a result. Today, the enemy uses pride as a weapon to try to take our focus off God and place it on ourselves.

God loves us too much to let us succeed when we are walking in pride. Pride exposes us to spiritual attacks and weakens our spiritual authority. However, God has given us the key to overcome it—genuine worship. Pride and worship cannot coexist because worship takes our focus off ourselves and puts it directly on God. When you magnify the Lord, you strengthen your faith and allow God to work through you to defeat the devil's schemes.

13 You were in Eden,
 the garden of God.
Your clothing was adorned with every
 precious stone*—
 red carnelian, pale-green peridot,
 white moonstone,
 blue-green beryl, onyx, green jasper,
 blue lapis lazuli, turquoise,
 and emerald—
all beautifully crafted for you
 and set in the finest gold.
They were given to you
 on the day you were created.
14 I ordained and anointed you
 as the mighty angelic guardian.*
You had access to the holy mountain of God
 and walked among the stones of fire.

15 "You were blameless in all you did
 from the day you were created
 until the day evil was found in you.
16 Your rich commerce led you to violence,
 and you sinned.
So I banished you in disgrace
 from the mountain of God.
I expelled you, O mighty guardian,
 from your place among the stones of fire.
17 Your heart was filled with pride
 because of all your beauty.
Your wisdom was corrupted
 by your love of splendor.
So I threw you to the ground
 and exposed you to the curious gaze
 of kings.

27:36 Hebrew hiss at you. 28:10 Hebrew will die the death of the uncircumcised. 28:13 The identification of some of these gemstones is uncertain. 28:14 Hebrew guardian cherub; similarly in 28:16.

18 You defiled your sanctuaries
    with your many sins and your
        dishonest trade.
So I brought fire out from within you,
    and it consumed you.
I reduced you to ashes on the ground
    in the sight of all who were watching.
19 All who knew you are appalled at your fate.
    You have come to a terrible end,
    and you will exist no more."

A MESSAGE FOR SIDON

20 Then another message came to me from the
LORD: 21 "Son of man, turn and face the city of
Sidon and prophesy against it. 22 Give the people
of Sidon this message from the Sovereign LORD:

"I am your enemy, O Sidon,
    and I will reveal my glory by
        what I do to you.
When I bring judgment against you
    and reveal my holiness among you,
everyone watching will know
    that I am the LORD.
23 I will send a plague against you,
    and blood will be spilled in your streets.
The attack will come from every direction,
    and your people will lie slaughtered
        within your walls.
Then everyone will know
    that I am the LORD.
24 No longer will Israel's scornful neighbors
    prick and tear at her like briers and thorns.
For then they will know
    that I am the Sovereign LORD.

RESTORATION FOR ISRAEL

25 "This is what the Sovereign LORD says: The
people of Israel will again live in their own land,
the land I gave my servant Jacob. For I will gather
them from the distant lands where I have scattered them. I will reveal to the nations of the
world my holiness among my people. 26 They will
live safely in Israel and build homes and plant
vineyards. And when I punish the neighboring
nations that treated them with contempt, they
will know that I am the LORD their God."

A MESSAGE FOR EGYPT

29 On January 7,* during the tenth year of
King Jehoiachin's captivity, this message
came to me from the LORD: 2 "Son of man, turn
and face Egypt and prophesy against Pharaoh
the king and all the people of Egypt. 3 Give them
this message from the Sovereign LORD:

"I am your enemy, O Pharaoh,
    king of Egypt—
you great monster, lurking in the streams
    of the Nile.
For you have said, 'The Nile River is mine;
    I made it for myself.'

4 I will put hooks in your jaws
    and drag you out on the land
    with fish sticking to your scales.
5 I will leave you and all your fish
    stranded in the wilderness to die.
You will lie unburied on the open ground,
    for I have given you as food to the wild
        animals and birds.
6 All the people of Egypt will know that
        I am the LORD,
    for to Israel you were just a staff made
        of reeds.
7 When Israel leaned on you,
    you splintered and broke
    and stabbed her in the armpit.
When she put her weight on you,
    you collapsed, and her legs gave way.

8 "Therefore, this is what the Sovereign LORD
says: I will bring an army against you, O Egypt,
and destroy both people and animals. 9 The land
of Egypt will become a desolate wasteland, and
the Egyptians will know that I am the LORD.

"Because you said, 'The Nile River is mine;
I made it,' 10 I am now the enemy of both you
and your river. I will make the land of Egypt
a totally desolate wasteland, from Migdol to
Aswan, as far south as the border of Ethiopia.* 11 For forty years not a soul will pass that
way, neither people nor animals. It will be
completely uninhabited. 12 I will make Egypt
desolate, and it will be surrounded by other
desolate nations. Its cities will be empty and
desolate for forty years, surrounded by other
ruined cities. I will scatter the Egyptians to
distant lands.

13 "But this is what the Sovereign LORD also
says: At the end of the forty years I will bring the
Egyptians home again from the nations to which
they have been scattered. 14 I will restore the prosperity of Egypt and bring its people back to the
land of Pathros in southern Egypt from which
they came. But Egypt will remain an unimportant, minor kingdom. 15 It will be the lowliest of
all the nations, never again great enough to rise
above its neighbors.

16 "Then Israel will no longer be tempted to
trust in Egypt for help. Egypt's shattered condition will remind Israel of how sinful she was
to trust Egypt in earlier days. Then Israel will
know that I am the Sovereign LORD."

NEBUCHADNEZZAR TO CONQUER EGYPT

17 On April 26, the first day of the new year,*
during the twenty-seventh year of King Jehoiachin's captivity, this message came to me from

---

29:1 Hebrew *On the twelfth day of the tenth month,* of the ancient
Hebrew lunar calendar. This event occurred on January 7,
587 B.C.; also see note on 1:1.   29:10 Hebrew *from Migdol to Syene
as far as the border of Cush.*   29:17 Hebrew *On the first day of the
first month,* of the ancient Hebrew lunar calendar. This event
occurred on April 26, 571 B.C.; also see note on 1:1.

the LORD: [18] "Son of man, the army of King Nebuchadnezzar* of Babylon fought so hard against Tyre that the warriors' heads were rubbed bare and their shoulders were raw and blistered. Yet Nebuchadnezzar and his army won no plunder to compensate them for all their work. [19] Therefore, this is what the Sovereign LORD says: I will give the land of Egypt to Nebuchadnezzar, king of Babylon. He will carry off its wealth, plundering everything it has so he can pay his army. [20] Yes, I have given him the land of Egypt as a reward for his work, says the Sovereign LORD, because he was working for me when he destroyed Tyre.

[21] "And the day will come when I will cause the ancient glory of Israel to revive,* and then, Ezekiel, your words will be respected. Then they will know that I am the LORD."

A SAD DAY FOR EGYPT

30 This is another message that came to me from the LORD: [2] "Son of man, prophesy and give this message from the Sovereign LORD:

"Weep and wail
    for that day,
[3] for the terrible day is almost here—
    the day of the LORD!
It is a day of clouds and gloom,
    a day of despair for the nations.
[4] A sword will come against Egypt,
    and those who are slaughtered will cover
        the ground.
Its wealth will be carried away
    and its foundations destroyed.
The land of Ethiopia* will be ravished.
[5] Ethiopia, Libya, Lydia, all Arabia,*
    and all their other allies
    will be destroyed in that war.

[6] "For this is what the LORD says:
All of Egypt's allies will fall,
    and the pride of her power will end.
From Migdol to Aswan*
    they will be slaughtered by the sword,
    says the Sovereign LORD.
[7] Egypt will be desolate,
    surrounded by desolate nations,
and its cities will be in ruins,
    surrounded by other ruined cities.
[8] And the people of Egypt will know that
        I am the LORD
    when I have set Egypt on fire
    and destroyed all their allies.
[9] At that time I will send swift messengers
        in ships
    to terrify the complacent Ethiopians.
Great panic will come upon them
    on that day of Egypt's certain
        destruction.
Watch for it!
    It is sure to come!

[10] "For this is what the Sovereign LORD says:
By the power of King Nebuchadnezzar* of
        Babylon,
    I will destroy the hordes of Egypt.
[11] He and his armies—the most ruthless of all—
    will be sent to demolish the land.
They will make war against Egypt
    until slaughtered Egyptians cover the
        ground.
[12] I will dry up the Nile River
    and sell the land to wicked men.
I will destroy the land of Egypt and
        everything in it
    by the hands of foreigners.
    I, the LORD, have spoken!

[13] "This is what the Sovereign LORD says:
I will smash the idols* of Egypt
    and the images at Memphis.*
There will be no rulers left in Egypt;
    terror will sweep the land.
[14] I will destroy southern Egypt,*
    set fire to Zoan,
    and bring judgment against Thebes.*
[15] I will pour out my fury on Pelusium,*
    the strongest fortress of Egypt,
and I will stamp out
    the hordes of Thebes.
[16] Yes, I will set fire to all Egypt!
Pelusium will be racked with pain;
Thebes will be torn apart;
Memphis will live in constant terror.
[17] The young men of Heliopolis and Bubastis*
    will die in battle,
    and the women* will be taken away
        as slaves.
[18] When I come to break the proud strength
        of Egypt,
    it will be a dark day for Tahpanhes, too.
A dark cloud will cover Tahpanhes,
    and its daughters will be led away
        as captives.
[19] And so I will greatly punish Egypt,
    and they will know that I am the LORD."

THE BROKEN ARMS OF PHARAOH

[20] On April 29,* during the eleventh year of King Jehoiachin's captivity, this message came to me from the LORD: [21] "Son of man, I have broken the arm of Pharaoh, the king of Egypt. His arm has not been put in a cast so that it may heal. Neither

---

29:18 Hebrew *Nebuchadrezzar*, a variant spelling of Nebuchadnezzar; also in 29:19.   29:21 Hebrew *I will cause a horn to sprout for the house of Israel.*   30:4 Hebrew *Cush*; similarly in 30:9.   30:5 Hebrew *Cush, Put, Lud, all Arabia, Cub. Cub* is otherwise unknown and may be another spelling for *Lub* (Libya).   30:6 Hebrew *to Syene.*   30:10 Hebrew *Nebuchadrezzar*, a variant spelling of Nebuchadnezzar.   30:13a The Hebrew term (literally *round things*) probably alludes to dung.   30:13b Hebrew *Noph*; also in 30:16.   30:14a Hebrew *Pathros.*   30:14b Hebrew *No*; also in 30:15, 16.   30:15 Hebrew *Sin*; also in 30:16.   30:17a Hebrew *of Awen and Pi-beseth.*   30:17b Or *and her cities.*   30:20 Hebrew *On the seventh day of the first month*, of the ancient Hebrew lunar calendar. This event occurred on April 29, 587 B.C.; also see note on 1:1.

has it been bound up with a splint to make it strong enough to hold a sword. 22 Therefore, this is what the Sovereign LORD says: I am the enemy of Pharaoh, the king of Egypt! I will break both of his arms—the good arm along with the broken one—and I will make his sword clatter to the ground. 23 I will scatter the Egyptians to many lands throughout the world. 24 I will strengthen the arms of Babylon's king and put my sword in his hand. But I will break the arms of Pharaoh, king of Egypt, and he will lie there mortally wounded, groaning in pain. 25 I will strengthen the arms of the king of Babylon, while the arms of Pharaoh fall useless to his sides. And when I put my sword in the hand of Babylon's king and he brings it against the land of Egypt, Egypt will know that I am the LORD. 26 I will scatter the Egyptians among the nations, dispersing them throughout the earth. Then they will know that I am the LORD."

EGYPT COMPARED TO FALLEN ASSYRIA

31 On June 21,* during the eleventh year of King Jehoiachin's captivity, this message came to me from the LORD: 2 "Son of man, give this message to Pharaoh, king of Egypt, and all his hordes:

"To whom would you compare your
    greatness?
3 You are like mighty Assyria,
    which was once like a cedar of Lebanon,
with beautiful branches that cast deep
        forest shade
    and with its top high among the clouds.
4 Deep springs watered it
    and helped it to grow tall and luxuriant.
The water flowed around it like a river,
    streaming to all the trees nearby.
5 This great tree towered high,
    higher than all the other trees around it.
It prospered and grew long thick branches
    because of all the water at its roots.
6 The birds nested in its branches,
    and in its shade all the wild animals
        gave birth.
All the great nations of the world
    lived in its shadow.
7 It was strong and beautiful,
    with wide-spreading branches,
for its roots went deep
    into abundant water.
8 No other cedar in the garden of God
    could rival it.
No cypress had branches to equal it;
    no plane tree had boughs to compare.
No tree in the garden of God
    came close to it in beauty.
9 Because I made this tree so beautiful,
    and gave it such magnificent foliage,
it was the envy of all the other trees of Eden,
    the garden of God.

10 "Therefore, this is what the Sovereign LORD says: Because Egypt* became proud and arrogant, and because it set itself so high above the others, with its top reaching to the clouds, 11 I will hand it over to a mighty nation that will destroy it as its wickedness deserves. I have already discarded it. 12 A foreign army—the terror of the nations—has cut it down and left it fallen on the ground. Its branches are scattered across the mountains and valleys and ravines of the land. All those who lived in its shadow have gone away and left it lying there.

13 "The birds roost on its fallen trunk,
    and the wild animals lie among its
        branches.
14 Let the tree of no other nation
    proudly exult in its own prosperity,
though it be higher than the clouds
    and it be watered from the depths.
For all are doomed to die,
    to go down to the depths of the earth.
They will land in the pit
    along with everyone else on earth.

15 "This is what the Sovereign LORD says: When Assyria went down to the grave,* I made the deep springs mourn. I stopped its rivers and dried up its abundant water. I clothed Lebanon in black and caused the trees of the field to wilt. 16 I made the nations shake with fear at the sound of its fall, for I sent it down to the grave with all the others who descend to the pit. And all the other proud trees of Eden, the most beautiful and the best of Lebanon, the ones whose roots went deep into the water, took comfort to find it there with them in the depths of the earth. 17 Its allies, too, were all destroyed and had passed away. They had gone down to the grave—all those nations that had lived in its shade.

18 "O Egypt, to which of the trees of Eden will you compare your strength and glory? You, too, will be brought down to the depths with all these other nations. You will lie there among the outcasts* who have died by the sword. This will be the fate of Pharaoh and all his hordes. I, the Sovereign LORD, have spoken!"

A WARNING FOR PHARAOH

32 On March 3,* during the twelfth year of King Jehoiachin's captivity, this message came to me from the LORD: 2 "Son of man, mourn for Pharaoh, king of Egypt, and give him this message:

"You think of yourself as a strong young lion
   among the nations,
   but you are really just a sea monster,
heaving around in your own rivers,
   stirring up mud with your feet.
³ Therefore, this is what the Sovereign
   Lord says:
I will send many people
   to catch you in my net
   and haul you out of the water.
⁴ I will leave you stranded on the land to die.
   All the birds of the heavens will land
      on you,
and the wild animals of the whole earth
   will gorge themselves on you.
⁵ I will scatter your flesh on the hills
   and fill the valleys with your bones.
⁶ I will drench the earth with your
      gushing blood
   all the way to the mountains,
   filling the ravines to the brim.
⁷ When I blot you out,
   I will veil the heavens and darken
      the stars.
I will cover the sun with a cloud,
   and the moon will not give you its light.
⁸ I will darken the bright stars overhead
   and cover your land in darkness.
   I, the Sovereign Lord, have spoken!

⁹ "I will disturb many hearts when I bring
news of your downfall to distant nations you
have never seen. ¹⁰ Yes, I will shock many lands,
and their kings will be terrified at your fate. They
will shudder in fear for their lives as I brandish
my sword before them on the day of your fall.
¹¹ For this is what the Sovereign Lord says:

"The sword of the king of Babylon
   will come against you.
¹² I will destroy your hordes with the swords
      of mighty warriors—
   the terror of the nations.
They will shatter the pride of Egypt,
   and all its hordes will be destroyed.
¹³ I will destroy all your flocks and herds
   that graze beside the streams.
Never again will people or animals
   muddy those waters with their feet.
¹⁴ Then I will let the waters of Egypt become
      calm again,
   and they will flow as smoothly as olive oil,
   says the Sovereign Lord.
¹⁵ And when I destroy Egypt
   and strip you of everything you own
and strike down all your people,
   then you will know that I am the Lord.
¹⁶ Yes, this is the funeral song
   they will sing for Egypt.
Let all the nations mourn.
   Let them mourn for Egypt and its hordes.
   I, the Sovereign Lord, have spoken!"

EGYPT FALLS INTO THE PIT

¹⁷ On March 17,* during the twelfth year, another
message came to me from the Lord: ¹⁸ "Son of
man, weep for the hordes of Egypt and for the
other mighty nations.* For I will send them
down to the world below in company with those
who descend to the pit. ¹⁹ Say to them,

'O Egypt, are you lovelier than the other
      nations?
   No! So go down to the pit and lie there
      among the outcasts.*'

²⁰ The Egyptians will fall with the many who have
died by the sword, for the sword is drawn against
them. Egypt and its hordes will be dragged away
to their judgment. ²¹ Down in the grave* mighty
leaders will mockingly welcome Egypt and its
allies, saying, 'They have come down; they lie
among the outcasts, hordes slaughtered by the
sword.'

²² "Assyria lies there surrounded by the graves
of its army, those who were slaughtered by the
sword. ²³ Their graves are in the depths of the
pit, and they are surrounded by their allies.
They struck terror in the hearts of people everywhere, but now they have been slaughtered by
the sword.

²⁴ "Elam lies there surrounded by the graves of
all its hordes, those who were slaughtered by the
sword. They struck terror in the hearts of people
everywhere, but now they have descended as
outcasts to the world below. Now they lie in the
pit and share the shame of those who have gone
before them. ²⁵ They have a resting place among
the slaughtered, surrounded by the graves of all
their hordes. Yes, they terrorized the nations
while they lived, but now they lie in shame with
others in the pit, all of them outcasts, slaughtered by the sword.

²⁶ "Meshech and Tubal are there, surrounded
by the graves of all their hordes. They once struck
terror in the hearts of people everywhere. But
now they are outcasts, all slaughtered by the
sword. ²⁷ They are not buried in honor like their
fallen heroes, who went down to the grave* with
their weapons—their shields covering their bodies* and their swords beneath their heads. Their
guilt rests upon them because they brought terror to everyone while they were still alive.

²⁸ "You too, Egypt, will lie crushed and broken
among the outcasts, all slaughtered by the sword.

32:17 Hebrew On the fifteenth day of the month, presumably in the
twelfth month of the ancient Hebrew lunar calendar (see 32:1).
This would put this message at the end of the King Jehoiachin's
twelfth year of captivity, on March 17, 585 b.c.; also see note
on 1:1. Greek version reads On the fifteenth day of the first month,
which would put this message on April 27, 586 b.c., at the
beginning of Jehoiachin's twelfth year. 32:18 The meaning
of the Hebrew is uncertain. 32:19 Hebrew the uncircumcised;
also in 32:21, 24, 25, 26, 28, 29, 30, 32. 32:21 Hebrew in Sheol.
32:27a Hebrew to Sheol. 32:27b The meaning of the Hebrew is
uncertain.

²⁹ "Edom is there with its kings and princes. Mighty as they were, they also lie among those slaughtered by the sword, with the outcasts who have gone down to the pit.

³⁰ "All the princes of the north and the Sidonians are there with others who have died. Once a terror, they have been put to shame. They lie there as outcasts with others who were slaughtered by the sword. They share the shame of all who have descended to the pit.

³¹ "When Pharaoh and his entire army arrive, he will take comfort that he is not alone in having his hordes killed, says the Sovereign LORD. ³² Although I have caused his terror to fall upon all the living, Pharaoh and his hordes will lie there among the outcasts who were slaughtered by the sword. I, the Sovereign LORD, have spoken!"

EZEKIEL AS ISRAEL'S WATCHMAN

33 Once again a message came to me from the LORD: ² "Son of man, give your people this message: 'When I bring an army against a country, the people of that land choose one of their own to be a watchman. ³ When the watchman sees the enemy coming, he sounds the alarm to warn the people. ⁴ Then if those who hear the alarm refuse to take action, it is their own fault if they die. ⁵ They heard the alarm but ignored it, so the responsibility is theirs. If they had listened to the warning, they could have saved their lives. ⁶ But if the watchman sees the enemy coming and doesn't sound the alarm to warn the people, he is responsible for their captivity. They will die in their sins, but I will hold the watchman responsible for their deaths.'

⁷ "Now, son of man, I am making you a watchman for the people of Israel. Therefore, listen to what I say and warn them for me. ⁸ If I announce that some wicked people are sure to die and you fail to tell them to change their ways, then they will die in their sins, and I will hold you responsible for their deaths. ⁹ But if you warn them to repent and they don't repent, they will die in their sins, but you will have saved yourself.

THE WATCHMAN'S MESSAGE

¹⁰ "Son of man, give the people of Israel this message: You are saying, 'Our sins are heavy upon us; we are wasting away! How can we survive?' ¹¹ As surely as I live, says the Sovereign LORD, I take no pleasure in the death of wicked people. I only want them to turn from their wicked ways so they can live. Turn! Turn from your wickedness, O people of Israel! Why should you die?

¹² "Son of man, give your people this message: The righteous behavior of righteous people will not save them if they turn to sin, nor will the wicked behavior of wicked people destroy them if they repent and turn from their sins. ¹³ When I tell righteous people that they will live, but then they sin, expecting their past righteousness to save them, then none of their righteous acts will be remembered. I will destroy them for their sins. ¹⁴ And suppose I tell some wicked people that they will surely die, but then they turn from their sins and do what is just and right. ¹⁵ For instance, they might give back a debtor's security, return what they have stolen, and obey my life-giving laws, no longer doing what is evil. If they do this, then they will surely live and not die. ¹⁶ None of their past sins will be brought up again, for they have done what is just and right, and they will surely live.

¹⁷ "Your people are saying, 'The Lord isn't doing what's right,' but it is they who are not doing what's right. ¹⁸ For again I say, when righteous people turn away from their righteous behavior and turn to evil, they will die. ¹⁹ But if wicked people turn from their wickedness and do what is just and right, they will live. ²⁰ O people of Israel, you are saying, 'The Lord isn't doing what's right.' But I judge each of you according to your deeds."

EXPLANATION OF JERUSALEM'S FALL

²¹ On January 8,* during the twelfth year of our captivity, a survivor from Jerusalem came to me and said, "The city has fallen!" ²² The previous evening the LORD had taken hold of me and given me back my voice. So I was able to speak when this man arrived the next morning.

²³ Then this message came to me from the LORD: ²⁴ "Son of man, the scattered remnants of Israel living among the ruined cities keep saying, 'Abraham was only one man, yet he gained possession of the entire land. We are many; surely the land has been given to us as a possession.' ²⁵ So tell these people, 'This is what the Sovereign LORD says: You eat meat with blood in it, you worship idols,* and you murder the innocent. Do you really think the land should be yours? ²⁶ Murderers! Idolaters! Adulterers! Should the land belong to you?'

²⁷ "Say to them, 'This is what the Sovereign LORD says: As surely as I live, those living in the ruins will die by the sword. And I will send wild animals to eat those living in the open fields. Those hiding in the forts and caves will die of disease. ²⁸ I will completely destroy the land and demolish her pride. Her arrogant power will come to an end. The mountains of Israel will be so desolate that no one will even travel through them. ²⁹ When I have completely destroyed the land because of their detestable sins, then they will know that I am the LORD.'

³⁰ "Son of man, your people talk about you in their houses and whisper about you at the doors. They say to each other, 'Come on, let's go hear the prophet tell us what the LORD is saying!' ³¹ So my people come pretending to be sincere

---

33:21 Hebrew *On the fifth day of the tenth month,* of the ancient Hebrew lunar calendar. This event occurred on January 8, 585 b.c.; also see note on 1:1. 33:25 The Hebrew term (literally *round things*) probably alludes to dung.

and sit before you. They listen to your words, but they have no intention of doing what you say. Their mouths are full of lustful words, and their hearts seek only after money. 32 You are very entertaining to them, like someone who sings love songs with a beautiful voice or plays fine music on an instrument. They hear what you say, but they don't act on it! 33 But when all these terrible things happen to them—as they certainly will—then they will know a prophet has been among them."

THE SHEPHERDS OF ISRAEL

34 Then this message came to me from the LORD: 2 "Son of man, prophesy against the shepherds, the leaders of Israel. Give them this message from the Sovereign LORD: What sorrow awaits you shepherds who feed yourselves instead of your flocks. Shouldn't shepherds feed their sheep? 3 You drink the milk, wear the wool, and butcher the best animals, but you let your flocks starve. 4 You have not taken care of the weak. You have not tended the sick or bound up the injured. You have not gone looking for those who have wandered away and are lost. Instead, you have ruled them with harshness and cruelty. 5 So my sheep have been scattered without a shepherd, and they are easy prey for any wild animal. 6 They have wandered through all the mountains and all the hills, across the face of the earth, yet no one has gone to search for them.

7 "Therefore, you shepherds, hear the word of the LORD: 8 As surely as I live, says the Sovereign LORD, you abandoned my flock and left them to be attacked by every wild animal. And though you were my shepherds, you didn't search for my sheep when they were lost. You took care of yourselves and left the sheep to starve. 9 Therefore, you shepherds, hear the word of the LORD. 10 This is what the Sovereign LORD says: I now consider these shepherds my enemies, and I will hold them responsible for what has happened to my flock. I will take away their right to feed the flock, and I will stop them from feeding themselves. I will rescue my flock from their mouths; the sheep will no longer be their prey.

THE GOOD SHEPHERD

11 "For this is what the Sovereign LORD says: I myself will search and find my sheep. 12 I will be like a shepherd looking for his scattered flock. I will find my sheep and rescue them from all the places where they were scattered on that dark and cloudy day. 13 I will bring them back home to their own land of Israel from among the peoples and nations. I will feed them on the mountains of Israel and by the rivers and in all the places where people live. 14 Yes, I will give them good pastureland on the high hills of Israel. There they will lie down in pleasant places and feed in the lush pastures of the hills. 15 I myself will tend my sheep and give them a place to lie down in

peace, says the Sovereign LORD. 16 I will search for my lost ones who strayed away, and I will bring them safely home again. I will bandage the injured and strengthen the weak. But I will destroy those who are fat and powerful. I will feed them, yes—feed them justice!

17 "And as for you, my flock, this is what the Sovereign LORD says to his people: I will judge between one animal of the flock and another, separating the sheep from the goats. 18 Isn't it enough for you to keep the best of the pastures for yourselves? Must you also trample down the rest? Isn't it enough for you to drink clear water for yourselves? Must you also muddy the rest with your feet? 19 Why must my flock eat what you have trampled down and drink water you have fouled?

20 "Therefore, this is what the Sovereign LORD says: I will surely judge between the fat sheep and the scrawny sheep. 21 For you fat sheep pushed and butted and crowded my sick and hungry flock until you scattered them to distant lands. 22 So I will rescue my flock, and they will no longer be abused. I will judge between one animal of the flock and another. 23 And I will set over them one shepherd, my servant David. He will feed them and be a shepherd to them. 24 And I, the LORD, will be their God, and my servant David will be a prince among my people. I, the LORD, have spoken!

THE LORD'S COVENANT OF PEACE

25 "I will make a covenant of peace with my people and drive away the dangerous animals from the land. Then they will be able to camp safely in the wildest places and sleep in the woods without fear. 26 I will bless my people and their homes around my holy hill. And in the proper season I will send the showers they need. There will be showers of blessing. 27 The orchards and fields of my people will yield bumper crops, and everyone will live in safety. When I have broken their chains of slavery and rescued them from those who enslaved them, then they will know that I am the LORD. 28 They will no longer be prey for other nations, and wild animals will no longer devour them. They will live in safety, and no one will frighten them.

29 "And I will make their land famous for its crops, so my people will never again suffer from famines or the insults of foreign nations. 30 In this way, they will know that I, the LORD their God, am with them. And they will know that they, the people of Israel, are my people, says the Sovereign LORD. 31 You are my flock, the sheep of my pasture. You are my people, and I am your God. I, the Sovereign LORD, have spoken!"

A MESSAGE FOR EDOM

35 Again a message came to me from the LORD: 2 "Son of man, turn and face Mount Seir, and prophesy against its people. 3 Give them this message from the Sovereign LORD:

"I am your enemy, O Mount Seir,
    and I will raise my fist against you
    to destroy you completely.
⁴ I will demolish your cities
    and make you desolate.
Then you will know that I am the LORD.

⁵ "Your eternal hatred for the people of Israel led you to butcher them when they were helpless, when I had already punished them for all their sins. ⁶ As surely as I live, says the Sovereign LORD, since you show no distaste for blood, I will give you a bloodbath of your own. Your turn has come! ⁷ I will make Mount Seir utterly desolate, killing off all who try to escape and any who return. ⁸ I will fill your mountains with the dead. Your hills, your valleys, and your ravines will be filled with people slaughtered by the sword. ⁹ I will make you desolate forever. Your cities will never be rebuilt. Then you will know that I am the LORD.

¹⁰ "For you said, 'The lands of Israel and Judah will be ours. We will take possession of them. What do we care that the LORD is there!' ¹¹ Therefore, as surely as I live, says the Sovereign LORD, I will pay back your angry deeds with my own. I will punish you for all your acts of anger, envy, and hatred. And I will make myself known to Israel* by what I do to you. ¹² Then you will know that I, the LORD, have heard every contemptuous word you spoke against the mountains of Israel. For you said, 'They are desolate; they have been given to us as food to eat!' ¹³ In saying that, you boasted proudly against me, and I have heard it all!

¹⁴ "This is what the Sovereign LORD says: The whole world will rejoice when I make you desolate. ¹⁵ You rejoiced at the desolation of Israel's territory. Now I will rejoice at yours! You will be wiped out, you people of Mount Seir and all who live in Edom! Then you will know that I am the LORD.

RESTORATION FOR ISRAEL

36 "Son of man, prophesy to Israel's mountains. Give them this message: O mountains of Israel, hear the word of the LORD! ² This is what the Sovereign LORD says: Your enemies have taunted you, saying, 'Aha! Now the ancient heights belong to us!' ³ Therefore, son of man, give the mountains of Israel this message from the Sovereign LORD: Your enemies have attacked you from all directions, making you the property of many nations and the object of much mocking and slander. ⁴ Therefore, O mountains of Israel, hear the word of the Sovereign LORD. He speaks to the hills and mountains, ravines and valleys, and to ruined wastes and long-deserted cities that have been destroyed and mocked by the surrounding nations. ⁵ This is what the Sovereign LORD says: My jealous anger burns against these nations, especially Edom, because they have shown utter contempt for me by gleefully taking my land for themselves as plunder.

⁶ "Therefore, prophesy to the hills and mountains, the ravines and valleys of Israel. This is what the Sovereign LORD says: I am furious that you have suffered shame before the surrounding nations. ⁷ Therefore, this is what the Sovereign LORD says: I have taken a solemn oath that those nations will soon have their own shame to endure.

⁸ "But the mountains of Israel will produce heavy crops of fruit for my people—for they will be coming home again soon! ⁹ See, I care about you, and I will pay attention to you. Your ground will be plowed and your crops planted. ¹⁰ I will greatly increase the population of Israel, and the ruined cities will be rebuilt and filled with people. ¹¹ I will increase not only the people, but also your animals. O mountains of Israel, I will bring people to live on you once again. I will make you even more prosperous than you were before. Then you will know that I am the LORD. ¹² I will cause my people to walk on you once again, and you will be their territory. You will never again rob them of their children.

¹³ "This is what the Sovereign LORD says: The other nations taunt you, saying, 'Israel is a land that devours its own people and robs them of their children!' ¹⁴ But you will never again devour your people or rob them of their children, says the Sovereign LORD. ¹⁵ I will not let you hear those other nations insult you, and you will no longer be mocked by them. You will not be a land that causes its nation to fall, says the Sovereign LORD."

¹⁶ Then this further message came to me from the LORD: ¹⁷ "Son of man, when the people of Israel were living in their own land, they defiled it by the evil way they lived. To me their conduct was as unclean as a woman's menstrual cloth. ¹⁸ They polluted the land with murder and the worship of idols,* so I poured out my fury on them. ¹⁹ I scattered them to many lands to punish them for the evil way they had lived. ²⁰ But when they were scattered among the nations, they brought shame on my holy name. For the nations said, 'These are the people of the LORD, but he couldn't keep them safe in his own land!' ²¹ Then I was concerned for my holy name, on which my people brought shame among the nations.

²² "Therefore, give the people of Israel this message from the Sovereign LORD: I am bringing you back, but not because you deserve it. I am doing it to protect my holy name, on which you brought shame while you were scattered among the nations. ²³ I will show how holy my great name is—the name on which you brought shame among the nations. And when I reveal my holiness through you before their very eyes, says the Sovereign LORD, then the nations will know that I am the LORD. ²⁴ For I will gather you

---

35:11 Hebrew *to them;* Greek version reads *to you.*   36:18 The Hebrew term (literally *round things*) probably alludes to dung; also in 36:25.

KEEPING A HUMBLE HEART
Ezekiel 36:26   ROBERT MORRIS

One of the best ways you can protect your heart from becoming hardened is by keeping it humble. In Isaiah 57:15, God says,

> "I restore the crushed spirit of the humble and revive the courage of those with repentant hearts."

What happens if we don't humble our hearts? We become like the Pharisees. They were the religious leaders who thought they knew everything about God, but they weren't willing to learn anything new, not even from God's own Son! Their pride hardened their hearts and kept them from receiving the Good News Jesus came to share with everyone who was willing to listen.

How is your heart today? Humble yourself before the Lord and ask Him to remove any pride in your heart. God promises, "I will give you a new heart, and I will put a new spirit in you. I will take out your stony, stubborn heart and give you a tender, responsive heart" (Ezekiel 36:26).

---

up from all the nations and bring you home again to your land.

²⁵ "Then I will sprinkle clean water on you, and you will be clean. Your filth will be washed away, and you will no longer worship idols. ²⁶ And I will give you a new heart, and I will put a new spirit in you. I will take out your stony, stubborn heart and give you a tender, responsive heart.* ²⁷ And I will put my Spirit in you so that you will follow my decrees and be careful to obey my regulations.

²⁸ "And you will live in Israel, the land I gave your ancestors long ago. You will be my people, and I will be your God. ²⁹ I will cleanse you of your filthy behavior. I will give you good crops of grain, and I will send no more famines on the land. ³⁰ I will give you great harvests from your fruit trees and fields, and never again will the surrounding nations be able to scoff at your land for its famines. ³¹ Then you will remember your past sins and despise yourselves for all the detestable things you did. ³² But remember, says the Sovereign LORD, I am not doing this because you deserve it. O my people of Israel, you should be utterly ashamed of all you have done!

³³ "This is what the Sovereign LORD says: When I cleanse you from your sins, I will repopulate your cities, and the ruins will be rebuilt. ³⁴ The fields that used to lie empty and desolate in plain view of everyone will again be farmed. ³⁵ And when I bring you back, people will say, 'This former wasteland is now like the Garden of Eden! The abandoned and ruined cities now have strong walls and are filled with people!'

³⁶ Then the surrounding nations that survive will know that I, the LORD, have rebuilt the ruins and replanted the wasteland. For I, the LORD, have spoken, and I will do what I say.

³⁷ "This is what the Sovereign LORD says: I am ready to hear Israel's prayers and to increase their numbers like a flock. ³⁸ They will be as numerous as the sacred flocks that fill Jerusalem's streets at the time of her festivals. The ruined cities will be crowded with people once more, and everyone will know that I am the LORD."

A VALLEY OF DRY BONES

37 The LORD took hold of me, and I was carried away by the Spirit of the LORD to a valley filled with bones. ² He led me all around among the bones that covered the valley floor. They were scattered everywhere across the ground and were completely dried out. ³ Then he asked me, "Son of man, can these bones become living people again?"

"O Sovereign LORD," I replied, "you alone know the answer to that."

⁴ Then he said to me, "Speak a prophetic message to these bones and say, 'Dry bones, listen to the word of the LORD! ⁵ This is what the Sovereign LORD says: Look! I am going to put breath into you and make you live again! ⁶ I will put flesh and muscles on you and cover you with skin. I will put breath into you, and you will come to life. Then you will know that I am the LORD.'"

⁷ So I spoke this message, just as he told me. Suddenly as I spoke, there was a rattling noise all across the valley. The bones of each body came together and attached themselves as complete skeletons. ⁸ Then as I watched, muscles and flesh formed over the bones. Then skin formed to cover their bodies, but they still had no breath in them.

⁹ Then he said to me, "Speak a prophetic message to the winds, son of man. Speak a prophetic message and say, 'This is what the Sovereign LORD says: Come, O breath, from the four winds! Breathe into these dead bodies so they may live again.'"

¹⁰ So I spoke the message as he commanded me, and breath came into their bodies. They all came to life and stood up on their feet—a great army.

¹¹ Then he said to me, "Son of man, these bones represent the people of Israel. They are saying, 'We have become old, dry bones—all hope is gone. Our nation is finished.' ¹² Therefore, prophesy to them and say, 'This is what the Sovereign LORD says: O my people, I will open your graves of exile and cause you to rise again. Then I will bring you back to the land of Israel. ¹³ When this happens, O my people, you will know that I am the LORD. ¹⁴ I will put my Spirit in you, and you will live again and return home to your own land. Then you will know that I, the LORD, have spoken, and I have done what I said. Yes, the LORD has spoken!'"

36:26 Hebrew *a heart of flesh.*

PUTTING THE PIECES TOGETHER
Ezekiel 37:7   ROBERT MORRIS

God led Ezekiel to a valley of dry bones and told him to prophesy over the bones. When Ezekiel obeyed, "there was a rattling noise all across the valley. The bones of each body came together and attached themselves as complete skeletons" (Ezekiel 37:7). When people read this story, they often miss that the valley was full of *bones,* not *skeletons.* The bones did not come together until Ezekiel prophesied the word of God.

The Bible is not just a book of words. God's Word is His breath, and it has the power to bring order to any situation. Genesis 1:2-3 says God spoke and formed the earth out of *nothing.* His breath came out and created what His word said. If God can create the universe from nothing, how much more do you think He can put pieces of your life back together?

HIS WORD HAS POWER
Ezekiel 37:8-10   ROBERT MORRIS

In Ezekiel 37:8, God's breath causes muscles and flesh to cover bones that have just come together as skeletons. God's Word literally brings strength to the body and allows it to function.

God's breath has all the power you need, and it can breathe life into any situation you're facing. In verse 10, Ezekiel prophesies over the now fully formed bodies, and "breath came into their bodies. They all came to life and stood up on their feet—a great army."

Keep in mind that Ezekiel did not speak his own words; he spoke God's word. We can do the same in our own lives. We need to eat, drink, and breathe in the Word of God every day. When you speak the Word of God, His breath is released into your situation. Whether it's your marriage, your family, your health, or your business, God's Word brings life to it.

REUNION OF ISRAEL AND JUDAH

[15] Again a message came to me from the LORD: [16] "Son of man, take a piece of wood and carve on it these words: 'This represents Judah and its allied tribes.' Then take another piece and carve these words on it: 'This represents Ephraim and the northern tribes of Israel.'* [17] Now hold them together in your hand as if they were one piece of wood. [18] When your people ask you what your actions mean, [19] say to them, 'This is what the Sovereign LORD says: I will take Ephraim and the northern tribes and join them to Judah. I will make them one piece of wood in my hand.'

[20] "Then hold out the pieces of wood you have inscribed, so the people can see them. [21] And give them this message from the Sovereign LORD: I will gather the people of Israel from among the nations. I will bring them home to their own land from the places where they have been scattered. [22] I will unify them into one nation on the mountains of Israel. One king will rule them all; no longer will they be divided into two nations or into two kingdoms. [23] They will never again pollute themselves with their idols* and vile images and rebellion, for I will save them from their sinful apostasy.* I will cleanse them. Then they will truly be my people, and I will be their God.

[24] "My servant David will be their king, and they will have only one shepherd. They will obey my regulations and be careful to keep my decrees. [25] They will live in the land I gave my servant Jacob, the land where their ancestors lived. They and their children and their grandchildren after them will live there forever, generation after generation. And my servant David will be their prince forever. [26] And I will make a covenant of peace with them, an everlasting covenant. I will give them their land and increase their

numbers,* and I will put my Temple among them forever. [27] I will make my home among them. I will be their God, and they will be my people. [28] And when my Temple is among them forever, the nations will know that I am the LORD, who makes Israel holy."

A MESSAGE FOR GOG

38 This is another message that came to me from the LORD: [2] "Son of man, turn and face Gog of the land of Magog, the prince who rules over the nations of Meshech and Tubal, and prophesy against him. [3] Give him this message from the Sovereign LORD: Gog, I am your enemy! [4] I will turn you around and put hooks in your jaws to lead you out with your whole army—your horses and charioteers in full armor and a great horde armed with shields and swords. [5] Persia, Ethiopia, and Libya* will join you, too, with all their weapons. [6] Gomer and all its armies will also join you, along with the armies of Beth-togarmah from the distant north, and many others.

[7] "Get ready; be prepared! Keep all the armies around you mobilized, and take command of them. [8] A long time from now you will be called into action. In the distant future you will swoop down on the land of Israel, which will be enjoying peace after recovering from war and after its people have returned from many lands to the mountains of Israel. [9] You and all your allies—a vast and awesome army—will roll down on them like a storm and cover the land like a cloud.

37:16 Hebrew *This is Ephraim's wood, representing Joseph and all the house of Israel;* similarly in 37:19.   37:23a The Hebrew term (literally *round things*) probably alludes to dung.   37:23b As in many Hebrew manuscripts and Greek version; Masoretic Text reads *from all their dwelling places where they sinned.*   37:26 Hebrew reads *I will give them and increase their numbers;* Greek version lacks the entire phrase.   38:5 Hebrew *Paras, Cush, and Put.*

¹⁰ "This is what the Sovereign LORD says: At that time evil thoughts will come to your mind, and you will devise a wicked scheme. ¹¹ You will say, 'Israel is an unprotected land filled with unwalled villages! I will march against her and destroy these people who live in such confidence! ¹² I will go to those formerly desolate cities that are now filled with people who have returned from exile in many nations. I will capture vast amounts of plunder, for the people are rich with livestock and other possessions now. They think the whole world revolves around them!' ¹³ But Sheba and Dedan and the merchants of Tarshish will ask, 'Do you really think the armies you have gathered can rob them of silver and gold? Do you think you can drive away their livestock and seize their goods and carry off plunder?'

¹⁴ "Therefore, son of man, prophesy against Gog. Give him this message from the Sovereign LORD: When my people are living in peace in their land, then you will rouse yourself.* ¹⁵ You will come from your homeland in the distant north with your vast cavalry and your mighty army, ¹⁶ and you will attack my people Israel, covering their land like a cloud. At that time in the distant future, I will bring you against my land as everyone watches, and my holiness will be displayed by what happens to you, Gog. Then all the nations will know that I am the LORD.

¹⁷ "This is what the Sovereign LORD asks: Are you the one I was talking about long ago, when I announced through Israel's prophets that in the future I would bring you against my people? ¹⁸ But this is what the Sovereign LORD says: When Gog invades the land of Israel, my fury will boil over! ¹⁹ In my jealousy and blazing anger, I promise a mighty shaking in the land of Israel on that day. ²⁰ All living things—the fish in the sea, the birds of the sky, the animals of the field, the small animals that scurry along the ground, and all the people on earth—will quake in terror at my presence. Mountains will be thrown down; cliffs will crumble; walls will fall to the earth. ²¹ I will summon the sword against you on all the hills of Israel, says the Sovereign LORD. Your men will turn their swords against each other. ²² I will punish you and your armies with disease and bloodshed; I will send torrential rain, hailstones, fire, and burning sulfur! ²³ In this way, I will show my greatness and holiness, and I will make myself known to all the nations of the world. Then they will know that I am the LORD.

THE SLAUGHTER OF GOG'S HORDES

39 "Son of man, prophesy against Gog. Give him this message from the Sovereign LORD: I am your enemy, O Gog, ruler of the nations of Meshech and Tubal. ² I will turn you around and drive you toward the mountains of Israel, bringing you from the distant north. ³ I will knock the bow from your left hand and the arrows from your right hand, and I will leave you

helpless. ⁴ You and your army and your allies will all die on the mountains. I will feed you to the vultures and wild animals. ⁵ You will fall in the open fields, for I have spoken, says the Sovereign LORD. ⁶ And I will rain down fire on Magog and on all your allies who live safely on the coasts. Then they will know that I am the LORD.

⁷ "In this way, I will make known my holy name among my people of Israel. I will not let anyone bring shame on it. And the nations, too, will know that I am the LORD, the Holy One of Israel. ⁸ That day of judgment will come, says the Sovereign LORD. Everything will happen just as I have declared it.

⁹ "Then the people in the towns of Israel will go out and pick up your small and large shields, bows and arrows, javelins and spears, and they will use them for fuel. There will be enough to last them seven years! ¹⁰ They won't need to cut wood from the fields or forests, for these weapons will give them all the fuel they need. They will plunder those who planned to plunder them, and they will rob those who planned to rob them, says the Sovereign LORD.

¹¹ "And I will make a vast graveyard for Gog and his hordes in the Valley of the Travelers, east of the Dead Sea.* It will block the way of those who travel there, and they will change the name of the place to the Valley of Gog's Hordes. ¹² It will take seven months for the people of Israel to bury the bodies and cleanse the land. ¹³ Everyone in Israel will help, for it will be a glorious victory for Israel when I demonstrate my glory on that day, says the Sovereign LORD.

¹⁴ "After seven months, teams of men will be appointed to search the land for skeletons to bury, so the land will be made clean again. ¹⁵ Whenever bones are found, a marker will be set up so the burial crews will take them to be buried in the Valley of Gog's Hordes. ¹⁶ (There will be a town there named Hamonah, which means 'horde.') And so the land will finally be cleansed.

¹⁷ "And now, son of man, this is what the Sovereign LORD says: Call all the birds and wild animals. Say to them: Gather together for my great sacrificial feast. Come from far and near to the mountains of Israel, and there eat flesh and drink blood! ¹⁸ Eat the flesh of mighty men and drink the blood of princes as though they were rams, lambs, goats, and bulls—all fattened animals from Bashan! ¹⁹ Gorge yourselves with flesh until you are glutted; drink blood until you are drunk. This is the sacrificial feast I have prepared for you. ²⁰ Feast at my banquet table—feast on horses and charioteers, on mighty men and all kinds of valiant warriors, says the Sovereign LORD.

²¹ "In this way, I will demonstrate my glory to the nations. Everyone will see the punishment I have inflicted on them and the power of my

---

38:14 As in Greek version; Hebrew reads *then you will know.*
39:11 Hebrew *the sea.*

fist when I strike. [22] And from that time on the people of Israel will know that I am the LORD their God. [23] The nations will then know why Israel was sent away to exile—it was punishment for sin, for they were unfaithful to their God. Therefore, I turned away from them and let their enemies destroy them. [24] I turned my face away and punished them because of their defilement and their sins.

RESTORATION FOR GOD'S PEOPLE

[25] "So now, this is what the Sovereign LORD says: I will end the captivity of my people*; I will have mercy on all Israel, for I jealously guard my holy reputation! [26] They will accept responsibility for* their past shame and unfaithfulness after they come home to live in peace in their own land, with no one to bother them. [27] When I bring them home from the lands of their enemies, I will display my holiness among them for all the nations to see. [28] Then my people will know that I am the LORD their God, because I sent them away to exile and brought them home again. I will leave none of my people behind. [29] And I will never again turn my face from them, for I will pour out my Spirit upon the people of Israel. I, the Sovereign LORD, have spoken!"

THE NEW TEMPLE AREA

40 On April 28,* during the twenty-fifth year of our captivity—fourteen years after the fall of Jerusalem—the LORD took hold of me. [2] In a vision from God he took me to the land of Israel and set me down on a very high mountain. From there I could see toward the south what appeared to be a city. [3] As he brought me nearer, I saw a man whose face shone like bronze standing beside a gateway entrance. He was holding in his hand a linen measuring cord and a measuring rod.

[4] He said to me, "Son of man, watch and listen. Pay close attention to everything I show you. You have been brought here so I can show you many things. Then you will return to the people of Israel and tell them everything you have seen."

THE EAST GATEWAY

[5] I could see a wall completely surrounding the Temple area. The man took a measuring rod that was 10½ feet* long and measured the wall, and the wall was 10½ feet* thick and 10½ feet high.

[6] Then he went over to the eastern gateway. He climbed the steps and measured the threshold of the gateway; it was 10½ feet front to back.* [7] There were guard alcoves on each side built into the gateway passage. Each of these alcoves were 10½ feet square, with a distance between them of 8¾ feet* along the passage wall. The gateway's inner threshold, which led to the entry room at the inner end of the gateway passage, was 10½ feet front to back. [8] He also measured the entry room of the gateway.* [9] It was 14 feet* across, with supporting columns 3½ feet* thick. This

entry room was at the inner end of the gateway structure, facing toward the Temple.

[10] There were three guard alcoves on each side of the gateway passage. Each had the same measurements, and the dividing walls separating them were also identical. [11] The man measured the gateway entrance, which was 17½ feet* wide at the opening and 22¾ feet* wide in the gateway passage. [12] In front of each of the guard alcoves was a 21-inch* curb. The alcoves themselves were 10½ feet* on each side.

[13] Then he measured the entire width of the gateway, measuring the distance between the back walls of facing guard alcoves; this distance was 43¾ feet.* [14] He measured the dividing walls all along the inside of the gateway up to the entry room of the gateway; this distance was 105 feet.* [15] The full length of the gateway passage was 87½ feet* from one end to the other. [16] There were recessed windows that narrowed inward through the walls of the guard alcoves and their dividing walls. There were also windows in the entry room. The surfaces of the dividing walls were decorated with carved palm trees.

THE OUTER COURTYARD

[17] Then the man brought me through the gateway into the outer courtyard of the Temple. A stone pavement ran along the walls of the courtyard, and thirty rooms were built against the walls, opening onto the pavement. [18] This pavement flanked the gates and extended out from the walls into the courtyard the same distance as the gateway entrance. This was the lower pavement. [19] Then the man measured across the Temple's outer courtyard between the outer and inner gateways; the distance was 175 feet.*

THE NORTH GATEWAY

[20] The man measured the gateway on the north just like the one on the east. [21] Here, too, there were three guard alcoves on each side, with dividing walls and an entry room. All the measurements matched those of the east gateway. The gateway passage was 87½ feet long and 43¾

39:25 Hebrew *of Jacob.* 39:26 A few Hebrew manuscripts read *They will forget.* 40:1 Hebrew *At the beginning of the year, on the tenth day of the month,* of the ancient Hebrew lunar calendar. This event occurred on April 28, 573 B.C.; also see note on 1:1. 40:5a Hebrew *6 long cubits* [3.2 meters], *each being a cubit* [18 inches or 45 centimeters] *and a handbreadth* [3 inches or 8 centimeters] *in length.* 40:5b Hebrew *1 rod* [3.2 meters]; also in 40:5c, 7. 40:6 As in Greek version, which reads *1 rod* [3.2 meters] *deep;* Hebrew reads *1 rod deep, and 1 threshold, 1 rod deep.* 40:7 Hebrew *5 cubits* [2.7 meters]; also in 40:48. 40:8 As in many Hebrew manuscripts and Syriac version; other Hebrew manuscripts add *which faced inward toward the Temple; it was 1 rod* [10.5 feet or 3.2 meters] *deep.* 40:9a Hebrew *the measured the entry room of the gateway.* 40:9a Hebrew *8 cubits* [4.2 meters]. 40:9b Hebrew *2 cubits* [1.1 meters]. 40:11a Hebrew *10 cubits* [5.3 meters]. 40:11b Hebrew *13 cubits* [6.9 meters]. 40:12a Hebrew *1 cubit* [53 centimeters]. 40:12b Hebrew *6 cubits* [3.2 meters]. 40:13 Hebrew *25 cubits* [13.3 meters]; also in 40:21, 25, 29, 30, 33, 36. 40:14 Hebrew *60 cubits* [31.8 meters]. Greek version reads *20 cubits* [35 feet or 10.6 meters]. The meaning of the Hebrew in this verse is uncertain. 40:15 Hebrew *50 cubits* [26.5 meters]; also in 40:21, 25, 29, 33, 36. 40:19 Hebrew *100 cubits* [53 meters]; also in 40:23, 27, 47.

feet wide between the back walls of facing guard alcoves. ²²The windows, the entry room, and the palm tree decorations were identical to those in the east gateway. There were seven steps leading up to the gateway entrance, and the entry room was at the inner end of the gateway passage. ²³Here on the north side, just as on the east, there was another gateway leading to the Temple's inner courtyard directly opposite this outer gateway. The distance between the two gateways was 175 feet.

THE SOUTH GATEWAY

²⁴Then the man took me around to the south gateway and measured its various parts, and they were exactly the same as in the others. ²⁵It had windows along the walls as the others did, and there was an entry room where the gateway passage opened into the outer courtyard. And like the others, the gateway passage was 87½ feet long and 43¾ feet wide between the back walls of facing guard alcoves. ²⁶This gateway also had a stairway of seven steps leading up to it, and an entry room at the inner end, and palm tree decorations along the dividing walls. ²⁷And here again, directly opposite the outer gateway, was another gateway that led into the inner courtyard. The distance between the two gateways was 175 feet.

GATEWAYS TO THE INNER COURTYARD

²⁸Then the man took me to the south gateway leading into the inner courtyard. He measured it, and it had the same measurements as the other gateways. ²⁹Its guard alcoves, dividing walls, and entry room were the same size as those in the others. It also had windows along its walls and in the entry room. And like the others, the gateway passage was 87½ feet long and 43¾ feet wide. ³⁰(The entry rooms of the gateways leading into the inner courtyard were 14 feet* across and 43¾ feet wide.) ³¹The entry room to the south gateway faced into the outer courtyard. It had palm tree decorations on its columns, and there were eight steps leading to its entrance.

³²Then he took me to the east gateway leading to the inner courtyard. He measured it, and it had the same measurements as the other gateways. ³³Its guard alcoves, dividing walls, and entry room were the same size as those of the others, and there were windows along the walls and in the entry room. The gateway passage measured 87½ feet long and 43¾ feet wide. ³⁴Its entry room faced into the outer courtyard. It had palm tree decorations on its columns, and there were eight steps leading to its entrance.

³⁵Then he took me around to the north gateway leading to the inner courtyard. He measured it, and it had the same measurements as the other gateways. ³⁶The guard alcoves, dividing walls, and entry room of this gateway had the same measurements as in the others and the same window arrangements. The gateway passage measured 87½ feet long and 43¾ feet wide. ³⁷Its entry room* faced into the outer courtyard, and it had palm tree decorations on the columns. There were eight steps leading to its entrance.

ROOMS FOR PREPARING SACRIFICES

³⁸A door led from the entry room of one of the inner gateways into a side room, where the meat for sacrifices was washed. ³⁹On each side of this entry room were two tables, where the sacrificial animals were slaughtered for the burnt offerings, sin offerings, and guilt offerings. ⁴⁰Outside the entry room, on each side of the stairs going up to the north entrance, were two more tables. ⁴¹So there were eight tables in all—four inside and four outside—where the sacrifices were cut up and prepared. ⁴²There were also four tables of finished stone for preparation of the burnt offerings, each 31½ inches square and 21 inches high.* On these tables were placed the butchering knives and other implements for slaughtering the sacrificial animals. ⁴³There were hooks, each 3 inches* long, fastened all around the foyer walls. The sacrificial meat was laid on the tables.

ROOMS FOR THE PRIESTS

⁴⁴Inside the inner courtyard were two rooms,* one beside the north gateway, facing south, and the other beside the south* gateway, facing north. ⁴⁵And the man said to me, "The room beside the north inner gate is for the priests who supervise the Temple maintenance. ⁴⁶The room beside the south inner gate is for the priests in charge of the altar—the descendants of Zadok— for they alone of all the Levites may approach the LORD to minister to him."

THE INNER COURTYARD AND TEMPLE

⁴⁷Then the man measured the inner courtyard, and it was a square, 175 feet wide and 175 feet across. The altar stood in the courtyard in front of the Temple. ⁴⁸Then he brought me to the entry room of the Temple. He measured the walls on either side of the opening to the entry room, and they were 8¾ feet thick. The entrance itself was 24½ feet wide, and the walls on each side of the entrance were an additional 5¼ feet long.* ⁴⁹The entry room was 35 feet* wide and 21 feet* deep. There were ten steps* leading up to it, with a column on each side.

40:30 As in 40:9, which reads 8 cubits [14 feet or 4.2 meters]; here the Hebrew reads 5 cubits [8¾ feet or 2.7 meters]. Some Hebrew manuscripts and the Greek version lack this entire verse. 40:37 As in Greek version (compare parallels at 40:26, 31, 34); Hebrew reads Its dividing wall. 40:42 Hebrew 1½ cubits [80 centimeters] long and 1½ cubits wide and 1 cubit [53 centimeters] high. 40:44a As in Greek version; Hebrew reads rooms for singers. 40:44b As in Greek version; Hebrew reads east. 40:48 As in Greek version, which reads The entrance was 14 cubits [7.4 meters] wide, and the walls of the entrance were 3 cubits [1.6 meters] on each side; Hebrew lacks 14 cubits wide, and the walls of the entrance were. 40:49a Hebrew 20 cubits [10.6 meters]. 40:49b As in Greek version, which reads 12 cubits [21 feet or 6.4 meters]; Hebrew reads 11 cubits [19¼ feet or 5.8 meters]. 40:49c As in Greek version; Hebrew reads There were steps that were.

41

After that, the man brought me into the sanctuary of the Temple. He measured the walls on either side of its doorway,* and they were 10½ feet* thick. ²The doorway was 17½ feet* wide, and the walls on each side of it were 8¾ feet* long. The sanctuary itself was 70 feet long and 35 feet wide.*

³Then he went beyond the sanctuary into the inner room. He measured the walls on either side of its entrance, and they were 3½ feet* thick. The entrance was 10½ feet wide, and the walls on each side of the entrance were 12¼ feet* long. ⁴The inner room of the sanctuary was 35 feet* long and 35 feet wide. "This," he told me, "is the Most Holy Place."

⁵Then he measured the wall of the Temple, and it was 10½ feet thick. There was a row of rooms along the outside wall; each room was 7 feet* wide. ⁶These side rooms were built in three levels, one above the other, with thirty rooms on each level. The supports for these side rooms rested on exterior ledges on the Temple wall; they did not extend into the wall. ⁷Each level was wider than the one below it, corresponding to the narrowing of the Temple wall as it rose higher. A stairway led up from the bottom level through the middle level to the top level.

⁸I saw that the Temple was built on a terrace, which provided a foundation for the side rooms. This terrace was 10½ feet* high. ⁹The outer wall of the Temple's side rooms was 8¾ feet thick. This left an open area between these side rooms ¹⁰and the row of rooms along the outer wall of the inner courtyard. This open area was 35 feet wide, and it went all the way around the Temple. ¹¹Two doors opened from the side rooms into the terrace yard, which was 8¾ feet wide. One door faced north and the other south.

¹²A large building stood on the west, facing the Temple courtyard. It was 122½ feet wide and 157½ feet long, and its walls were 8¾ feet* thick. ¹³Then the man measured the Temple, and it was 175 feet* long. The courtyard around the building, including its walls, was an additional 175 feet in length. ¹⁴The inner courtyard to the east of the Temple was also 175 feet wide. ¹⁵The building to the west, including its two walls, was also 175 feet wide.

The sanctuary, the inner room, and the entry room of the Temple ¹⁶were all paneled with wood, as were the frames of the recessed windows. The inner walls of the Temple were paneled with wood above and below the windows. ¹⁷The space above the door leading into the inner room, and its walls inside and out, were also paneled. ¹⁸All the walls were decorated with carvings of cherubim, each with two faces, and there was a carving of a palm tree between each of the cherubim. ¹⁹One face—that of a man—looked toward the palm tree on one side. The other face—that of a young lion—looked toward the palm tree on the other side. The figures were carved all along the inside

of the Temple, ²⁰from the floor to the top of the walls, including the outer wall of the sanctuary.

²¹There were square columns at the entrance to the sanctuary, and the ones at the entrance of the Most Holy Place were similar. ²²There was an altar made of wood, 5¼ feet high and 3½ feet across.* Its corners, base, and sides were all made of wood. "This," the man told me, "is the table that stands in the LORD's presence."

²³Both the sanctuary and the Most Holy Place had double doorways, ²⁴each with two swinging doors. ²⁵The doors leading into the sanctuary were decorated with carved cherubim and palm trees, just as on the walls. And there was a wooden roof at the front of the entry room to the Temple. ²⁶On both sides of the entry room were recessed windows decorated with carved palm trees. The side rooms along the outside wall also had roofs.

ROOMS FOR THE PRIESTS

42

Then the man led me out of the Temple courtyard by way of the north gateway. We entered the outer courtyard and came to a group of rooms against the north wall of the inner courtyard. ²This structure, whose entrance opened toward the north, was 175 feet* long and 87½ feet* wide. ³One block of rooms overlooked the 35-foot* width of the inner courtyard. Another block of rooms looked out onto the pavement of the outer courtyard. The two blocks were built three levels high and stood across from each other. ⁴Between the two blocks of rooms ran a walkway 17½ feet* wide. It extended the entire 175 feet of the complex,* and all the doors faced north. ⁵Each of the two upper levels of rooms was narrower than the one beneath it because the upper levels had to allow space for walkways in front of them. ⁶Since there were three levels and they did not have supporting columns as in the courtyards, each of the upper levels was set back from the level beneath it. ⁷There was an outer wall that separated the rooms from the outer courtyard; it was 87½ feet long. ⁸This wall added length to the outer block of rooms, which extended for only 87½ feet, while the inner block—the rooms toward the Temple—extended for 175 feet. ⁹There was an eastern entrance from the outer courtyard to these rooms.

41:1a As in Greek version; the meaning of the Hebrew is uncertain. 41:1b Hebrew 6 cubits [3.2 meters]; also in 41:3, 5. 41:2a Hebrew 10 cubits [5.3 meters]. 41:2b Hebrew 5 cubits [2.7 meters]; also in 41:9, 11. 41:2c Hebrew 40 cubits [21.2 meters] long and 20 cubits [10.6 meters] wide. 41:3a Hebrew 2 cubits [1.1 meters]. 41:3b Hebrew 7 cubits [3.7 meters]. 41:4 Hebrew 20 cubits [10.6 meters]; also in 41:4b, 10. 41:5 Hebrew 4 cubits [2.1 meters]. 41:8 Hebrew 1 rod, 6 cubits [3.2 meters]. 41:12 Hebrew 70 cubits [37.1 meters] wide and 90 cubits [47.7 meters] long, and its walls were 5 cubits [2.7 meters] thick. 41:13 Hebrew 100 cubits [53 meters]; also in 41:13b, 14, 15. 41:22 Hebrew 3 cubits [1.6 meters] high and 2 cubits [1.1 meters] across. 42:2a Hebrew 100 cubits [53 meters]; also in 42:8. 42:2b Hebrew 50 cubits [26.5 meters]; also in 42:7, 8. 42:3 Hebrew 20[-cubit] [10.6-meter]. 42:4a Hebrew 10 cubits [5.3 meters]. 42:4b As in Greek and Syriac versions, which read Its length was 100 cubits [53 meters]; Hebrew reads and a passage 1 cubit [21 inches or 53 centimeters] wide.

¹⁰On the south* side of the Temple there were two blocks of rooms just south of the inner courtyard between the Temple and the outer courtyard. These rooms were arranged just like the rooms on the north. ¹¹There was a walkway between the two blocks of rooms just like the complex on the north side of the Temple. This complex of rooms was the same length and width as the other one, and it had the same entrances and doors. The dimensions of each were identical. ¹²So there was an entrance in the wall facing the doors of the inner block of rooms, and another on the east at the end of the interior walkway.

¹³Then the man told me, "These rooms that overlook the Temple from the north and south are holy. Here the priests who offer sacrifices to the LORD will eat the most holy offerings. And because these rooms are holy, they will be used to store the sacred offerings—the grain offerings, sin offerings, and guilt offerings. ¹⁴When the priests leave the sanctuary, they must not go directly to the outer courtyard. They must first take off the clothes they wore while ministering, because these clothes are holy. They must put on other clothes before entering the parts of the building complex open to the public."

¹⁵When the man had finished measuring the inside of the Temple area, he led me out through the east gateway to measure the entire perimeter. ¹⁶He measured the east side with his measuring rod, and it was 875 feet long.* ¹⁷Then he measured the north side, and it was also 875 feet. ¹⁸The south side was also 875 feet, ¹⁹and the west side was also 875 feet. ²⁰So the area was 875 feet on each side with a wall all around it to separate what was holy from what was common.

THE LORD'S GLORY RETURNS

43 After this, the man brought me back around to the east gateway. ²Suddenly, the glory of the God of Israel appeared from the east. The sound of his coming was like the roar of rushing waters, and the whole landscape shone with his glory. ³This vision was just like the others I had seen, first by the Kebar River and then when he came* to destroy Jerusalem. I fell face down on the ground. ⁴And the glory of the LORD came into the Temple through the east gateway.

⁵Then the Spirit took me up and brought me into the inner courtyard, and the glory of the LORD filled the Temple. ⁶And I heard someone speaking to me from within the Temple, while the man who had been measuring stood beside me. ⁷The LORD said to me, "Son of man, this is the place of my throne and the place where I will rest my feet. I will live here forever among the people of Israel. They and their kings will not defile my holy name any longer by their adulterous worship of other gods or by honoring the relics of their kings who have died.* ⁸They put their idol altars right next to mine with only a wall between them and me. They defiled my holy name by such detestable sin, so I consumed them in my anger. ⁹Now let them stop worshiping other gods and honoring the relics of their kings, and I will live among them forever.

¹⁰"Son of man, describe to the people of Israel the Temple I have shown you, so they will be ashamed of all their sins. Let them study its plan, ¹¹and they will be ashamed* of what they have done. Describe to them all the specifications of the Temple—including its entrances and exits—and everything else about it. Tell them about its decrees and laws. Write down all these specifications and decrees as they watch so they will be sure to remember and follow them. ¹²And this is the basic law of the Temple: absolute holiness! The entire top of the mountain where the Temple is built is holy. Yes, this is the basic law of the Temple.

THE ALTAR

¹³"These are the measurements of the altar*: There is a gutter all around the altar 21 inches deep and 21 inches wide,* with a curb 9 inches* wide around its edge. And this is the height* of the altar: ¹⁴From the gutter the altar rises 3½ feet* to a lower ledge that surrounds the altar and is 21 inches* wide. From the lower ledge the altar rises 7 feet* to the upper ledge that is also 21 inches wide. ¹⁵The top of the altar, the hearth, rises another 7 feet higher, with a horn rising up from each of the four corners. ¹⁶The top of the altar is square, measuring 21 feet by 21 feet.* ¹⁷The upper ledge also forms a square, measuring 24½ feet by 24½ feet,* with a 21-inch gutter and a 10½-inch curb* all around the edge. There are steps going up the east side of the altar."

¹⁸Then he said to me, "Son of man, this is what the Sovereign LORD says: These will be the regulations for the burning of offerings and the sprinkling of blood when the altar is built. ¹⁹At that time, the Levitical priests of the family of Zadok, who minister before me, are to be given a young bull for a sin offering, says the Sovereign LORD. ²⁰You will take some of its blood and smear it on the four horns of the altar, the four corners of the upper ledge, and the curb that runs around that ledge. This will cleanse and make atonement for the altar. ²¹Then take the young bull for the

---

42:10 As in Greek version; Hebrew reads *east.*   42:16 As in 45:2 and in Greek version at 42:17, which reads *500 cubits* [265 meters]; Hebrew reads *500 rods* [5,250 feet or 1,590 meters]; similarly in 42:17, 18, 19, 20.   43:3 As in some Hebrew manuscripts and Latin Vulgate; Masoretic Text reads *I came.*   43:7 Or *kings on their high places.*   43:11 As in Greek version; Hebrew reads *if they are ashamed.*   43:13a Hebrew *measurements of the altar in long cubits, each being a cubit* [18 inches or 45 centimeters] *and a handbreadth* [3 inches or 8 centimeters] *in length.*   43:13b Hebrew *a cubit* [53 centimeters] *deep and a cubit wide.*   43:13c Hebrew *1 span* [23 centimeters].   43:13d As in Greek version; Hebrew reads *base.*   43:14a Hebrew *2 cubits* [1.1 meters].   43:14b Hebrew *1 cubit* [53 centimeters]; also in 43:14d.   43:14c Hebrew *4 cubits* [2.1 meters]; also in 43:15.   43:16 Hebrew *12 [cubits]* [6.4 meters] *long and 12 [cubits] wide.*   43:17a Hebrew *14 [cubits]* [7.4 meters] *long and 14 [cubits] wide.*   43:17b Hebrew *a gutter of 1 cubit* [53 centimeters] *and a curb of 1/2 a cubit* [27 centimeters].

sin offering and burn it at the appointed place outside the Temple area.

22 "On the second day, sacrifice as a sin offering a young male goat that has no physical defects. Then cleanse and make atonement for the altar again, just as you did with the young bull. 23 When you have finished the cleansing ceremony, offer another young bull that has no defects and a perfect ram from the flock. 24 You are to present them to the LORD, and the priests are to sprinkle salt on them and offer them as a burnt offering to the LORD.

25 "Every day for seven days a male goat, a young bull, and a ram from the flock will be sacrificed as a sin offering. None of these animals may have physical defects of any kind. 26 Do this each day for seven days to cleanse and make atonement for the altar, thus setting it apart for holy use. 27 On the eighth day, and on each day afterward, the priests will sacrifice on the altar the burnt offerings and peace offerings of the people. Then I will accept you. I, the Sovereign LORD, have spoken!"

THE PRINCE, LEVITES, AND PRIESTS

44 Then the man brought me back to the east gateway in the outer wall of the Temple area, but it was closed. 2 And the LORD said to me, "This gate must remain closed; it will never again be opened. No one will ever open it and pass through, for the LORD, the God of Israel, has entered here. Therefore, it must always remain shut. 3 Only the prince himself may sit inside this gateway to feast in the LORD's presence. But he may come and go only through the entry room of the gateway."

4 Then the man brought me through the north gateway to the front of the Temple. I looked and saw that the glory of the LORD filled the Temple of the LORD, and I fell face down on the ground.

5 And the LORD said to me, "Son of man, take careful notice. Use your eyes and ears, and listen to everything I tell you about the regulations concerning the LORD's Temple. Take careful note of the procedures for using the Temple's entrances and exits. 6 And give these rebels, the people of Israel, this message from the Sovereign LORD: O people of Israel, enough of your detestable sins! 7 You have brought uncircumcised foreigners into my sanctuary—people who have no heart for God. In this way, you defiled my Temple even as you offered me my food, the fat and blood of sacrifices. In addition to all your other detestable sins, you have broken my covenant. 8 Instead of safeguarding my sacred rituals, you have hired foreigners to take charge of my sanctuary.

9 "So this is what the Sovereign LORD says: No foreigners, including those who live among the people of Israel, will enter my sanctuary if they have not been circumcised and have not surrendered themselves to the LORD. 10 And the men of the tribe of Levi who abandoned me when

Israel strayed away from me to worship idols* must bear the consequences of their unfaithfulness. 11 They may still be Temple guards and gatekeepers, and they may slaughter the animals brought for burnt offerings and be present to help the people. 12 But they encouraged my people to worship idols, causing Israel to fall into deep sin. So I have taken a solemn oath that they must bear the consequences for their sins, says the Sovereign LORD. 13 They may not approach me to minister as priests. They may not touch any of my holy things or the holy offerings, for they must bear the shame of all the detestable sins they have committed. 14 They are to serve as the Temple caretakers, taking charge of the maintenance work and performing general duties.

15 "However, the Levitical priests of the family of Zadok continued to minister faithfully in the Temple when Israel abandoned me for idols. These men will serve as my ministers. They will stand in my presence and offer the fat and blood of the sacrifices, says the Sovereign LORD. 16 They alone will enter my sanctuary and approach my table to serve me. They will fulfill all my requirements.

17 "When they enter the gateway to the inner courtyard, they must wear only linen clothing. They must wear no wool while on duty in the inner courtyard or in the Temple itself. 18 They must wear linen turbans and linen undergarments. They must not wear anything that would cause them to perspire. 19 When they return to the outer courtyard where the people are, they must take off the clothes they wear while ministering to me. They must leave them in the sacred rooms and put on other clothes so they do not endanger anyone by transmitting holiness to them through this clothing.

20 "They must neither shave their heads nor let their hair grow too long. Instead, they must trim it regularly. 21 The priests must not drink wine before entering the inner courtyard. 22 They may choose their wives only from among the virgins of Israel or the widows of the priests. They may not marry other widows or divorced women. 23 They will teach my people the difference between what is holy and what is common, what is ceremonially clean and unclean.

24 "They will serve as judges to resolve any disagreements among my people. Their decisions must be based on my regulations. And the priests themselves must obey my instructions and decrees at all the sacred festivals, and see to it that the Sabbaths are set apart as holy days.

25 "A priest must not defile himself by being in the presence of a dead person unless it is his father, mother, child, brother, or unmarried sister. In such cases it is permitted. 26 Even then, he can return to his Temple duties only after

being ceremonially cleansed and then waiting for seven days. ²⁷The first day he returns to work and enters the inner courtyard and the sanctuary, he must offer a sin offering for himself, says the Sovereign LORD.

²⁸"The priests will not have any property or possession of land, for I alone am their special possession. ²⁹Their food will come from the gifts and sacrifices brought to the Temple by the people—the grain offerings, the sin offerings, and the guilt offerings. Whatever anyone sets apart* for the LORD will belong to the priests. ³⁰The first of the ripe fruits and all the gifts brought to the LORD will go to the priests. The first batch of dough must also be given to the priests so the LORD will bless your homes. ³¹The priests may not eat meat from any bird or animal that dies a natural death or that dies after being attacked by another animal.

DIVISION OF THE LAND

45 "When you divide the land among the tribes of Israel, you must set aside a section for the LORD as his holy portion. This piece of land will be 8⅓ miles long and 6⅔ miles wide.* The entire area will be holy. ²A section of this land, measuring 875 feet by 875 feet,* will be set aside for the Temple. An additional strip of land 87½ feet* wide is to be left empty all around it. ³Within the larger sacred area, measure out a portion of land 8⅓ miles long and 3⅓ miles wide.* Within it the sanctuary of the Most Holy Place will be located. ⁴This area will be holy, set aside for the priests who minister to the LORD in the sanctuary. They will use it for their homes, and my Temple will be located within it. ⁵The strip of sacred land next to it, also 8⅓ miles long and 3⅓ miles wide, will be a living area for the Levites who work at the Temple. It will be their possession and a place for their towns.*

⁶"Adjacent to the larger sacred area will be a section of land 8⅓ miles long and 1⅔ miles wide.* This will be set aside for a city where anyone in Israel can live.

⁷"Two special sections of land will be set apart for the prince. One section will share a border with the east side of the sacred lands and city, and the second section will share a border on the west side. Then the far eastern and western borders of the prince's lands will line up with the eastern and western boundaries of the tribal areas. ⁸These sections of land will be the prince's allotment. Then my princes will no longer oppress and rob my people; they will assign the rest of the land to the people, giving an allotment to each tribe.

RULES FOR THE PRINCES

⁹"For this is what the Sovereign LORD says: Enough, you princes of Israel! Stop your violence and oppression and do what is just and right. Quit robbing and cheating my people out of their land. Stop expelling them from their homes, says the Sovereign LORD. ¹⁰Use only honest weights and scales and honest measures, both dry and liquid.* ¹¹The homer* will be your standard unit for measuring volume. The ephah and the bath* will each measure one-tenth of a homer. ¹²The standard unit for weight will be the silver shekel.* One shekel will consist of twenty gerahs, and sixty shekels will be equal to one mina.*

SPECIAL OFFERINGS AND CELEBRATIONS

¹³"You must give this tax to the prince: one bushel of wheat or barley for every 60* you harvest, ¹⁴one percent of your olive oil,* ¹⁵and one sheep or goat for every 200 in your flocks in Israel. These will be the grain offerings, burnt offerings, and peace offerings that will make atonement for the people who bring them, says the Sovereign LORD. ¹⁶All the people of Israel must join in bringing these offerings to the prince. ¹⁷The prince will be required to provide offerings that are given at the religious festivals, the new moon celebrations, the Sabbath days, and all other similar occasions. He will provide the sin offerings, burnt offerings, grain offerings, liquid offerings, and peace offerings to purify the people of Israel, making them right with the LORD.*

¹⁸"This is what the Sovereign LORD says: In early spring, on the first day of each new year,* sacrifice a young bull with no defects to purify the Temple. ¹⁹The priest will take blood from this sin offering and put it on the doorposts of the Temple, the four corners of the upper ledge of the altar, and the gateposts at the entrance to the inner courtyard. ²⁰Do this also on the seventh day of the new year for anyone who has sinned through error or ignorance. In this way, you will purify* the Temple.

²¹"On the fourteenth day of the first month,* you must celebrate the Passover. This festival will last for seven days. The bread you eat during that time must be made without yeast. ²²On the

44:29 The Hebrew term used here refers to the complete consecration of things or people to the LORD, either by destroying them or by giving them as an offering. 45:1 As in Greek version, which reads 25,000 [cubits] [13.3 kilometers] long and 20,000 [cubits] [10.6 kilometers] wide; Hebrew reads 25,000 [cubits] long and 10,000 [cubits] [3⅓ miles or 5.3 kilometers] wide. Compare 45:3, 5; 48:9. 45:2a Hebrew 500 [cubits] [265 meters] by 500 [cubits], a square. 45:2b Hebrew 50 cubits [26.5 meters]. 45:3 Hebrew 25,000 [cubits] [13.3 kilometers] long and 10,000 [cubits] [5.3 kilometers] wide; also in 45:5. 45:5 As in Greek version; Hebrew reads They will have as their possession 20 rooms. 45:6 Hebrew 25,000 [cubits] [13.3 kilometers] long and 5,000 [cubits] [2.65 kilometers] wide. 45:10 Hebrew Use honest scales, an honest ephah, and an honest bath. 45:11a The homer measures about 50 gallons or 220 liters. 45:11b The ephah is a dry measure; the bath is a liquid measure. 45:12a The shekel weighs about 0.4 ounces or 11 grams. 45:12b Elsewhere the mina is equated to 50 shekels. 45:13 Hebrew ⅙ of an ephah from each homer of wheat and ⅙ of an ephah from each homer of barley. 45:14 Hebrew the portion of oil, measured by the bath, is ⅒ of a bath from each cor, which consists of 10 baths or 1 homer, for 10 baths are equivalent to a homer. 45:17 Or to make atonement for the people of Israel. 45:18 Hebrew On the first day of the first month, of the Hebrew calendar. This day in the ancient Hebrew lunar calendar occurred in March or April. 45:20 Or will make atonement for. 45:21 This day in the ancient Hebrew lunar calendar occurred in late March, April, or early May.

day of Passover the prince will provide a young bull as a sin offering for himself and the people of Israel. [23] On each of the seven days of the feast he will prepare a burnt offering to the LORD, consisting of seven young bulls and seven rams without defects. A male goat will also be given each day for a sin offering. [24] The prince will provide a basket of flour as a grain offering and a gallon of olive oil* with each young bull and ram.

[25] "During the seven days of the Festival of Shelters, which occurs every year in early autumn,* the prince will provide these same sacrifices for the sin offering, the burnt offering, and the grain offering, along with the required olive oil.

46

"This is what the Sovereign LORD says: The east gateway of the inner courtyard will be closed during the six workdays each week, but it will be open on Sabbath days and the days of new moon celebrations. [2] The prince will enter the entry room of the gateway from the outside. Then he will stand by the gatepost while the priest offers his burnt offering and peace offering. He will bow down in worship inside the gateway passage and then go back out the way he came. The gateway will not be closed until evening. [3] The common people will bow down and worship the LORD in front of this gateway on Sabbath days and the days of new moon celebrations.

[4] "Each Sabbath day the prince will present to the LORD a burnt offering of six lambs and one ram, all with no defects. [5] He will present a grain offering of a basket of choice flour to go with the ram and whatever amount of flour he chooses to go with each lamb, and he is to offer one gallon of olive oil* for each basket of flour. [6] At the new moon celebrations, he will bring one young bull, six lambs, and one ram, all with no defects. [7] With the young bull he must bring a basket of choice flour for a grain offering. With the ram he must bring another basket of flour. And with each lamb he is to bring whatever amount of flour he chooses to give. With each basket of flour he must offer one gallon of olive oil.

[8] "The prince must enter the gateway through the entry room, and he must leave the same way. [9] But when the people come in through the north gateway to worship the LORD during the religious festivals, they must leave by the south gateway. And those who entered through the south gateway must leave by the north gateway. They must never leave by the same gateway they came in, but must always use the opposite gateway. [10] The prince will enter and leave with the people on these occasions.

[11] "So at the special feasts and sacred festivals, the grain offering will be a basket of choice flour with each young bull, another basket of flour with each ram, and as much flour as the worshiper chooses to give with each lamb. Give

one gallon of olive oil with each basket of flour. [12] When the prince offers a voluntary burnt offering or peace offering to the LORD, the east gateway to the inner courtyard will be opened for him, and he will offer his sacrifices as he does on Sabbath days. Then he will leave, and the gateway will be shut behind him.

[13] "Each morning you must sacrifice a one-year-old lamb with no defects as a burnt offering to the LORD. [14] With the lamb, a grain offering must also be given to the LORD—about three quarts of flour with a third of a gallon of olive oil* to moisten the choice flour. This will be a permanent law for you. [15] The lamb, the grain offering, and the olive oil must be given as a daily sacrifice every morning without fail.

[16] "This is what the Sovereign LORD says: If the prince gives a gift of land to one of his sons as his inheritance, it will belong to him and his descendants forever. [17] But if the prince gives a gift of land from his inheritance to one of his servants, the servant may keep it only until the Year of Jubilee, which comes every fiftieth year.* At that time the land will return to the prince. But when the prince gives gifts to his sons, those gifts will be permanent. [18] And the prince may never take anyone's property by force. If he gives property to his sons, it must be from his own land, for I do not want any of my people unjustly evicted from their property."

THE TEMPLE KITCHENS

[19] In my vision, the man brought me through the entrance beside the gateway and led me to the sacred rooms assigned to the priests, which faced toward the north. He showed me a place at the extreme west end of these rooms. [20] He explained, "This is where the priests will cook the meat from the guilt offerings and sin offerings and bake the flour from the grain offerings into bread. They will do it here to avoid carrying the sacrifices through the outer courtyard and endangering the people by transmitting holiness to them."

[21] Then he brought me back to the outer courtyard and led me to each of its four corners. In each corner I saw an enclosure. [22] Each of these enclosures was 70 feet long and 52½ feet wide,* surrounded by walls. [23] Along the inside of these walls was a ledge of stone with fireplaces under the ledge all the way around. [24] The man said to me, "These are the kitchens to be used by the Temple assistants to boil the sacrifices offered by the people."

45:24 Hebrew an ephah [20 quarts or 22 liters] of flour . . . and a hin [3.8 liters] of olive oil. 45:25 Hebrew the festival which begins on the fifteenth day of the seventh month (see Lev 23:34). This day in the ancient Hebrew lunar calendar occurred in late September, October, or early November. 46:5 Hebrew an ephah [20 quarts or 22 liters] of choice flour . . . a hin [3.8 liters] of olive oil; similarly in 46:7, 11. 46:14 Hebrew ⅙ of an ephah [3.7 liters] of flour with ⅓ of a hin [1.3 liters] of olive oil. 46:17 Hebrew until the Year of Release; see Lev 25:8-17. 46:22 Hebrew 40 [cubits] [21.2 meters] long and 30 [cubits] [15.9 meters] wide.

THE RIVER OF HEALING

47 In my vision, the man brought me back to the entrance of the Temple. There I saw a stream flowing east from beneath the door of the Temple and passing to the right of the altar on its south side. ²The man brought me outside the wall through the north gateway and led me around to the eastern entrance. There I could see the water flowing out through the south side of the east gateway.

³Measuring as he went, he took me along the stream for 1,750 feet* and then led me across. The water was up to my ankles. ⁴He measured off another 1,750 feet and led me across again. This time the water was up to my knees. After another 1,750 feet, it was up to my waist. ⁵Then he measured another 1,750 feet, and the river was too deep to walk across. It was deep enough to swim in, but too deep to walk through.

⁶He asked me, "Have you been watching, son of man?" Then he led me back along the riverbank. ⁷When I returned, I was surprised by the sight of many trees growing on both sides of the river. ⁸Then he said to me, "This river flows east through the desert into the valley of the Dead Sea.* The waters of this stream will make the salty waters of the Dead Sea fresh and pure. ⁹There will be swarms of living things wherever the water of this river flows.* Fish will abound in the Dead Sea, for its waters will become fresh. Life will flourish wherever this water flows. ¹⁰Fishermen will stand along the shores of the Dead Sea. All the way from En-gedi to En-eglaim, the shores will be covered with nets drying in the sun. Fish of every kind will fill the Dead Sea, just as they fill the Mediterranean.* ¹¹But the marshes and swamps will not be purified; they will still be salty. ¹²Fruit trees of all kinds will grow along both sides of the river. The leaves of these trees will never turn brown and fall, and there will always be fruit on their branches. There will be a new crop every month, for they are watered by the river flowing from the Temple. The fruit will be for food and the leaves for healing."

BOUNDARIES FOR THE LAND

¹³This is what the Sovereign LORD says: "Divide the land in this way for the twelve tribes of Israel: The descendants of Joseph will be given two shares of land.* ¹⁴Otherwise each tribe will receive an equal share. I took a solemn oath and swore that I would give this land to your ancestors, and it will now come to you as your possession.

¹⁵"These are the boundaries of the land: The northern border will run from the Mediterranean toward Hethlon, then on through Lebo-hamath to Zedad; ¹⁶then it will run to Berothah and Sibraim,* which are on the border between Damascus and Hamath, and finally to Hazer-hatticon, on the border of Hauran. ¹⁷So the northern border will run from the Mediterranean to Hazar-enan, on the border between Hamath to the north and Damascus to the south.

¹⁸"The eastern border starts at a point between Hauran and Damascus and runs south along the Jordan River between Israel and Gilead, past the Dead Sea* and as far south as Tamar.* This will be the eastern border.

¹⁹"The southern border will go west from Tamar to the waters of Meribah at Kadesh* and then follow the course of the Brook of Egypt to the Mediterranean. This will be the southern border.

²⁰"On the west side, the Mediterranean itself will be your border from the southern border to the point where the northern border begins, opposite Lebo-hamath.

²¹"Divide the land within these boundaries among the tribes of Israel. ²²Distribute the land as an allotment for yourselves and for the foreigners who have joined you and are raising their families among you. They will be like native-born Israelites to you and will receive an allotment among the tribes. ²³These foreigners are to be given land within the territory of the tribe with whom they now live. I, the Sovereign LORD, have spoken!

DIVISION OF THE LAND

48 "Here is the list of the tribes of Israel and the territory each is to receive. The territory of Dan is in the extreme north. Its boundary line follows the Hethlon road to Lebo-hamath and then runs on to Hazar-enan on the border of Damascus, with Hamath to the north. Dan's territory extends all the way across the land of Israel from east to west.

²"Asher's territory lies south of Dan's and also extends from east to west. ³Naphtali's land lies south of Asher's, also extending from east to west. ⁴Then comes Manasseh south of Naphtali, and its territory also extends from east to west. ⁵South of Manasseh is Ephraim, ⁶and then Reuben, ⁷and then Judah, all of whose boundaries extend from east to west.

⁸"South of Judah is the land set aside for a special purpose. It will be 8⅓ miles* wide and will extend as far east and west as the tribal territories, with the Temple at the center.

47:3 Hebrew *1,000 cubits* [530 meters]; also in 47:4, 5.
47:8 Hebrew *the sea.* 47:9 As in Greek and Syriac versions; Hebrew reads *of these two rivers flow.* 47:10 Hebrew *the Great Sea*; also in 47:15, 17, 19, 20. 47:13 It was important to retain twelve portions of land. Since Levi had no portion, the descendants of Joseph's sons, Ephraim and Manasseh, received land as two tribes. 47:15-16 As in Greek version; Masoretic Text reads *then on through Lebo to Zedad;* *then it will run to Hamath, Berothah, and Sibraim.* 47:18a Hebrew *the eastern sea.* 47:18b As in Greek version; Hebrew reads *you will measure.* 47:19 Hebrew *waters of Meribath-kadesh.* 48:8 Hebrew *25,000* [cubits] [13.3 kilometers].

⁹"The area set aside for the LORD's Temple will be 8⅓ miles long and 6⅔ miles wide.* ¹⁰For the priests there will be a strip of land measuring 8⅓ miles long by 3⅓ miles wide,* with the LORD's Temple at the center. ¹¹This area is set aside for the ordained priests, the descendants of Zadok who served me faithfully and did not go astray with the people of Israel and the rest of the Levites. ¹²It will be their special portion when the land is distributed, the most sacred land of all. Next to the priests' territory will lie the land where the other Levites will live.

¹³"The land allotted to the Levites will be the same size and shape as that belonging to the priests—8⅓ miles long and 3⅓ miles wide. Together these portions of land will measure 8⅓ miles long by 6⅔ miles wide.* ¹⁴None of this special land may ever be sold or traded or used by others, for it belongs to the LORD; it is set apart as holy.

¹⁵"An additional strip of land 8⅓ miles long by 1⅔ miles wide,* south of the sacred Temple area, will be allotted for public use—homes, pasturelands, and common lands, with a city at the center. ¹⁶The city will measure 1½ miles* on each side—north, south, east, and west. ¹⁷Open lands will surround the city for 150 yards* in every direction. ¹⁸Outside the city there will be a farming area that stretches 3⅓ miles to the east and 3⅓ miles to the west* along the border of the sacred area. This farmland will produce food for the people working in the city. ¹⁹Those who come from the various tribes to work in the city may farm it. ²⁰This entire area—including the sacred lands and the city—is a square that measures 8⅓ miles* on each side.

²¹"The areas that remain, to the east and to the west of the sacred lands and the city, will belong to the prince. Each of these areas will be 8⅓ miles wide, extending in opposite directions to the eastern and western borders of Israel, with the sacred lands and the sanctuary of the Temple in the center. ²²So the prince's land will include everything between the territories allotted to Judah and Benjamin, except for the areas set aside for the sacred lands and the city.

²³"These are the territories allotted to the rest of the tribes. Benjamin's territory lies just south of the prince's lands, and it extends across the entire land of Israel from east to west. ²⁴South of Benjamin's territory lies that of Simeon, also extending across the land from east to west. ²⁵Next is the territory of Issachar with the same eastern and western boundaries.

²⁶"Then comes the territory of Zebulun, which also extends across the land from east to west. ²⁷The territory of Gad is just south of Zebulun with the same borders to the east and west. ²⁸The southern border of Gad runs from Tamar to the waters of Meribah at Kadesh* and then follows the Brook of Egypt to the Mediterranean.*

²⁹"These are the allotments that will be set aside for each tribe's exclusive possession. I, the Sovereign LORD, have spoken!

THE GATES OF THE CITY

³⁰"These will be the exits to the city: On the north wall, which is 1½ miles long, ³¹there will be three gates, each one named after a tribe of Israel. The first will be named for Reuben, the second for Judah, and the third for Levi. ³²On the east wall, also 1½ miles long, the gates will be named for Joseph, Benjamin, and Dan. ³³The south wall, also 1½ miles long, will have gates named for Simeon, Issachar, and Zebulun. ³⁴And on the west wall, also 1½ miles long, the gates will be named for Gad, Asher, and Naphtali.

³⁵"The distance around the entire city will be 6 miles.* And from that day the name of the city will be 'The LORD Is There.'*"

48:9 As in one Greek manuscript and the Greek reading in 45:1; 25,000 [cubits] [13.3 kilometers] long and 20,000 [cubits] [10.6 kilometers] wide; Hebrew reads 25,000 [cubits] long and 10,000 [cubits] [3⅓ miles or 5.3 kilometers] wide. Similarly in 48:13b. Compare 45:1-5; 48:10-13. 48:10 Hebrew 25,000 [cubits] [13.3 kilometers] long by 10,000 [cubits] [5.3 kilometers] wide; also in 48:13a. 48:13 See note on 48:9. 48:15 Hebrew 25,000 [cubits] [13.3 kilometers] long by 5,000 [cubits] [2.65 kilometers] wide. 48:16 Hebrew 4,500 [cubits] [2.4 kilometers]; also in 48:30, 32, 33, 34. 48:17 Hebrew 250 [cubits] [133 meters]. 48:18 Hebrew 10,000 [cubits] [5.3 kilometers] to the east and 10,000 [cubits] to the west. 48:20 Hebrew 25,000 [cubits] [13.3 kilometers]; also in 48:21. 48:28a Hebrew waters of Meribath-kadesh. 48:28b Hebrew the Great Sea. 48:35a Hebrew 18,000 [cubits] [9.6 kilometers]. 48:35b Hebrew Yahweh Shammah.

DANIEL

JON HUNTZINGER, PHD

The book of Daniel is named for its central character, a public official in service to the king of Babylon and a prophet to the people of Israel. The name *Daniel* means 'God is my judge,' and connects him to how God is depicted in the book as a judge who discerns and acts with authority in the life of the prophet and the present and future events of His people. Daniel was among the exiles taken from Judah to Babylon by King Nebuchadnezzar, where he remained for the rest of his life. He did not return to Judah when the Persian king Cyrus allowed the people to return in 539 BC.

The book of Daniel is historical in that it recounts stories from the sixth century BC, and at the same time, it reports visions given to Daniel that describe future events. Because of the historical stories, the Hebrew Bible does not include this book among the prophets, such as it is listed in English versions. The Hebrew text places it among the books known as "Writings," which include Esther, Ezra, and Nehemiah. One unusual feature of the book is that it is written in both Hebrew and Aramaic. Daniel 1:1–2:4 and 8:1–12:13 are written in Hebrew, and 2:5–7:28 is given in Aramaic, which looks and sounds like Hebrew and was the common language of many people in the ancient Near East.

The book was written after the end of the Exile in 539 BC when Cyrus overthrew the Babylonian king Belshazzar, a descendant of Nebuchadnezzar. Because some of the visions recorded in chapters 7–12 seem to describe events that relate to the third century BC, some Bible scholars date the book to that time. However, God knows past, present, and future, so such foreknowledge shared with one of His faithful people does not require such a late date.

The book is best known for its stories of Daniel in the lions' den and the three Hebrew young men in the furnace as well as the visions God gave to Daniel. It may be divided into two parts:

Part one contains six stories that recount Daniel's experience in Nebuchadnezzar's court and show his ability to interpret dreams during the years 586–539 BC.

Part two describes several visions God gives to Daniel about future events. Because of these visions, Bible scholars identify that part of the book as apocalyptic, which means it is literature that reports visions of future events with extraordinary imagery so that God's people may share in the knowledge only God possesses. The word derives from the Greek *apokalypsis*, which means 'revelation.' This word is used to describe the book because in it God reveals the mystery of Israel's future and that of all the nations of the world.

In part one, Daniel is in exile and has the ability to interpret King Nebuchadnezzar's dreams (chapters 2, 4). Next, God saves three Hebrew exiles after they are put into a blazing furnace (chapter 3). Years later, God brings judgment on King Belshazzar and brings about the end of Babylonian rule (chapter 5). The last story of part one is the salvation of Daniel in the lions' den. He is thrown into the den for not worshipping Darius, the newly appointed king of Persia (chapter 6).

These stories show the Hebrew people how to live under the power of foreign nations. God oversees the present and knows the future. He is not surprised by what is happening or what will happen. Consequently, His people should not be anxious or worried. They should live in confidence that God is involved in all of their affairs from small matters to great ones.

The visions that make up part two include one in which four beasts are placed in contrast with the Ancient One and the son of man (chapter 7). This vision is followed by one of a ram and a goat (chapter 8). As a result of prayer on behalf of the people, God gives Daniel a vision of 70 weeks (chapter 9) and then one of a man of glory, who describes the rise of four future kings (chapters 10–11). The book concludes with a promise of resurrection (chapter 12). These visions show that God is the God of all the nations, which are represented in the images of beasts, animals, and kings. He knows who they are, and He will raise them up and bring them down as He patiently works out His plans for all.

God knows the past, present, and future of His people because He is the Ancient One. He is from the beginning, and He is eternal. He can reveal the future because He is the foundation of the past, and as a result, He can make known to prophets like Daniel what He will do. For his part, Daniel is an example of a righteous servant of God who is able to receive God's revelation because of his righteousness. Because Daniel honors God and is faithful to Him, God honors His servant with insight and understanding.

DANIEL IN NEBUCHADNEZZAR'S COURT

1 During the third year of King Jehoiakim's reign in Judah,* King Nebuchadnezzar of Babylon came to Jerusalem and besieged it. ² The Lord gave him victory over King Jehoiakim of Judah and permitted him to take some of the sacred objects from the Temple of God. So Nebuchadnezzar took them back to the land of Babylonia* and placed them in the treasure-house of his god.

³ Then the king ordered Ashpenaz, his chief of staff, to bring to the palace some of the young men of Judah's royal family and other noble families, who had been brought to Babylon as captives. ⁴ "Select only strong, healthy, and good-looking young men," he said. "Make sure they are well versed in every branch of learning, are gifted with knowledge and good judgment, and are suited to serve in the royal palace. Train these young men in the language and literature of Babylon.*" ⁵ The king assigned them a daily ration of food and wine from his own kitchens. They were to be trained for three years, and then they would enter the royal service.

⁶ Daniel, Hananiah, Mishael, and Azariah were four of the young men chosen, all from the tribe of Judah. ⁷ The chief of staff renamed them with these Babylonian names:

Daniel was called Belteshazzar.
Hananiah was called Shadrach.
Mishael was called Meshach.
Azariah was called Abednego.

⁸ But Daniel was determined not to defile himself by eating the food and wine given to them by the king. He asked the chief of staff for permission not to eat these unacceptable foods. ⁹ Now God had given the chief of staff both respect and affection for Daniel. ¹⁰ But he responded, "I am afraid of my lord the king, who has ordered that you eat this food and wine. If you become pale and thin compared to the other youths your age, I am afraid the king will have me beheaded."

¹¹ Daniel spoke with the attendant who had been appointed by the chief of staff to look after Daniel, Hananiah, Mishael, and Azariah. ¹² "Please test us for ten days on a diet of vegetables and water," Daniel said. ¹³ "At the end of the ten days, see how we look compared to the other young men who are eating the king's food. Then make your decision in light of what you see." ¹⁴ The attendant agreed to Daniel's suggestion and tested them for ten days.

¹⁵ At the end of the ten days, Daniel and his three friends looked healthier and better nourished than the young men who had been eating the food assigned by the king. ¹⁶ So after that, the attendant fed them only vegetables instead of the food and wine provided for the others.

¹⁷ God gave these four young men an unusual aptitude for understanding every aspect of literature and wisdom. And God gave Daniel the special ability to interpret the meanings of visions and dreams.

¹⁸ When the training period ordered by the king was completed, the chief of staff brought all the young men to King Nebuchadnezzar. ¹⁹ The king talked with them, and no one impressed him as much as Daniel, Hananiah, Mishael, and Azariah. So they entered the royal service. ²⁰ Whenever the king consulted them in any matter requiring wisdom and balanced judgment, he found them ten times more capable than any of the magicians and enchanters in his entire kingdom.

²¹ Daniel remained in the royal service until the first year of the reign of King Cyrus.*

NEBUCHADNEZZAR'S DREAM

2 One night during the second year of his reign,* Nebuchadnezzar had such disturbing dreams that he couldn't sleep. ² He called in his magicians, enchanters, sorcerers, and astrologers,* and he demanded that they tell him what he had dreamed. As they stood before the king, ³ he said, "I have had a dream that deeply troubles me, and I must know what it means."

⁴ Then the astrologers answered the king in Aramaic,* "Long live the king! Tell us the dream, and we will tell you what it means."

⁵ But the king said to the astrologers, "I am serious about this. If you don't tell me what my dream was and what it means, you will be torn

---

FUELED BY PURPOSE
Daniel 1:8   MARCUS BRECHEEN

We all go through seasons when our walk with God feels dry. Sometimes we settle into a habit of working for God but not really connecting with Him. Sometimes we distance ourselves because we feel as if He has not followed through on something we think He should have. Thankfully, God uses even our difficult seasons to bring about His purpose in and through our lives.

The life of Daniel teaches us that every one of us has a purpose. Daniel experienced great difficulty as a Jewish captive in Babylon, but God was weaving the circumstances of his life to accomplish His purpose in and through Daniel. God did not forget Daniel, and He hasn't forgotten you either. Not a single moment or experience in your life is without purpose if you choose to keep your faith in God in spite of your circumstances.

1:1 This event occurred in 605 B.C., during the third year of Jehoiakim's reign (according to the calendar system in which the new year begins in the spring). 1:2 Hebrew *the land of Shinar.* 1:4 Or *of the Chaldeans.* 1:21 Cyrus began his reign (over Babylon) in 539 B.C. 2:1 The second year of Nebuchadnezzar's reign was 603 B.C. 2:2 Or *Chaldeans;* also in 2:4, 5, 10. 2:4 The original text from this point through chapter 7 is in Aramaic.

limb from limb, and your houses will be turned into heaps of rubble! [6]But if you tell me what I dreamed and what the dream means, I will give you many wonderful gifts and honors. Just tell me the dream and what it means!"

[7]They said again, "Please, Your Majesty. Tell us the dream, and we will tell you what it means."

[8]The king replied, "I know what you are doing! You're stalling for time because you know I am serious when I say, [9]'If you don't tell me the dream, you are doomed.' So you have conspired to tell me lies, hoping I will change my mind. But tell me the dream, and then I'll know that you can tell me what it means."

[10]The astrologers replied to the king, "No one on earth can tell the king his dream! And no king, however great and powerful, has ever asked such a thing of any magician, enchanter, or astrologer! [11]The king's demand is impossible. No one except the gods can tell you your dream, and they do not live here among people."

[12]The king was furious when he heard this, and he ordered that all the wise men of Babylon be executed. [13]And because of the king's decree, men were sent to find and kill Daniel and his friends.

[14]When Arioch, the commander of the king's guard, came to kill them, Daniel handled the situation with wisdom and discretion. [15]He asked Arioch, "Why has the king issued such a harsh decree?" So Arioch told him all that had happened. [16]Daniel went at once to see the king and requested more time to tell the king what the dream meant.

[17]Then Daniel went home and told his friends Hananiah, Mishael, and Azariah what had happened. [18]He urged them to ask the God of heaven to show them his mercy by telling them the secret, so they would not be executed along with the other wise men of Babylon. [19]That night the secret was revealed to Daniel in a vision. Then Daniel praised the God of heaven. [20]He said,

"Praise the name of God forever and ever,
    for he has all wisdom and power.
[21] He controls the course of world events;
    he removes kings and sets up other kings.
He gives wisdom to the wise
    and knowledge to the scholars.
[22] He reveals deep and mysterious things
    and knows what lies hidden in darkness,
    though he is surrounded by light.
[23] I thank and praise you, God of my ancestors,
    for you have given me wisdom and
        strength.
You have told me what we asked of you
    and revealed to us what the king
        demanded."

DANIEL INTERPRETS THE DREAM

[24]Then Daniel went in to see Arioch, whom the king had ordered to execute the wise men of Babylon. Daniel said to him, "Don't kill the wise men. Take me to the king, and I will tell him the meaning of his dream."

[25]Arioch quickly took Daniel to the king and said, "I have found one of the captives from Judah who will tell the king the meaning of his dream!"

[26]The king said to Daniel (also known as Belteshazzar), "Is this true? Can you tell me what my dream was and what it means?"

[27]Daniel replied, "There are no wise men, enchanters, magicians, or fortune-tellers who can reveal the king's secret. [28]But there is a God in heaven who reveals secrets, and he has shown King Nebuchadnezzar what will happen in the future. Now I will tell you your dream and the visions you saw as you lay on your bed.

[29]"While Your Majesty was sleeping, you dreamed about coming events. He who reveals secrets has shown you what is going to happen. [30]And it is not because I am wiser than anyone else that I know the secret of your dream, but because God wants you to understand what was in your heart.

[31]"In your vision, Your Majesty, you saw standing before you a huge, shining statue of a man. It was a frightening sight. [32]The head of the statue was made of fine gold. Its chest and arms were silver, its belly and thighs were bronze, [33]its legs were iron, and its feet were a combination of iron and baked clay. [34]As you watched, a rock was cut from a mountain,* but not by human hands. It struck the feet of iron and clay, smashing them to bits. [35]The whole statue was crushed into small pieces of iron, clay, bronze, silver, and gold. Then the wind blew them away without a trace, like chaff on a threshing floor. But the rock that knocked the statue down became a great mountain that covered the whole earth.

[36]"That was the dream. Now we will tell the king what it means. [37]Your Majesty, you are the greatest of kings. The God of heaven has given you sovereignty, power, strength, and honor. [38]He has made you the ruler over all the inhabited world and has put even the wild animals and birds under your control. You are the head of gold.

[39]"But after your kingdom comes to an end, another kingdom, inferior to yours, will rise to take your place. After that kingdom has fallen, yet a third kingdom, represented by bronze, will rise to rule the world. [40]Following that kingdom, there will be a fourth one, as strong as iron. That kingdom will smash and crush all previous empires, just as iron smashes and crushes everything it strikes. [41]The feet and toes you saw were a combination of iron and baked clay, showing that this kingdom will be divided. Like iron mixed with clay, it will have some of the strength of iron. [42]But while some parts of it will be as strong as iron, other parts will be as weak as clay. [43]This mixture of iron and clay also shows that these

---

2:34 As in Greek version (see also 2:45); Hebrew lacks *from a mountain*.

kingdoms will try to strengthen themselves by forming alliances with each other through intermarriage. But they will not hold together, just as iron and clay do not mix.

⁴⁴"During the reigns of those kings, the God of heaven will set up a kingdom that will never be destroyed or conquered. It will crush all these kingdoms into nothingness, and it will stand forever. ⁴⁵That is the meaning of the rock cut from the mountain, though not by human hands, that crushed to pieces the statue of iron, bronze, clay, silver, and gold. The great God was showing the king what will happen in the future. The dream is true, and its meaning is certain."

NEBUCHADNEZZAR REWARDS DANIEL

⁴⁶Then King Nebuchadnezzar threw himself down before Daniel and worshiped him, and he commanded his people to offer sacrifices and burn sweet incense before him. ⁴⁷The king said to Daniel, "Truly, your God is the greatest of gods, the Lord over kings, a revealer of mysteries, for you have been able to reveal this secret."

⁴⁸Then the king appointed Daniel to a high position and gave him many valuable gifts. He made Daniel ruler over the whole province of Babylon, as well as chief over all his wise men. ⁴⁹At Daniel's request, the king appointed Shadrach, Meshach, and Abednego to be in charge of all the affairs of the province of Babylon, while Daniel remained in the king's court.

NEBUCHADNEZZAR'S GOLD STATUE

3 King Nebuchadnezzar made a gold statue ninety feet tall and nine feet wide* and set it up on the plain of Dura in the province of Babylon. ²Then he sent messages to the high officers, officials, governors, advisers, treasurers, judges, magistrates, and all the provincial officials to come to the dedication of the statue he had set up. ³So all these officials* came and stood before the statue King Nebuchadnezzar had set up.

⁴Then a herald shouted out, "People of all races and nations and languages, listen to the king's command! ⁵When you hear the sound of the horn, flute, zither, lyre, harp, pipes, and other musical instruments,* bow to the ground to worship King Nebuchadnezzar's gold statue. ⁶Anyone who refuses to obey will immediately be thrown into a blazing furnace."

⁷So at the sound of the musical instruments,* all the people, whatever their race or nation or language, bowed to the ground and worshiped the gold statue that King Nebuchadnezzar had set up.

⁸But some of the astrologers* went to the king and informed on the Jews. ⁹They said to King Nebuchadnezzar, "Long live the king! ¹⁰You issued a decree requiring all the people to bow down and worship the gold statue when they hear the sound of the horn, flute, zither, lyre, harp, pipes, and other musical instruments.

¹¹That decree also states that those who refuse to obey must be thrown into a blazing furnace. ¹²But there are some Jews—Shadrach, Meshach, and Abednego—whom you have put in charge of the province of Babylon. They pay no attention to you, Your Majesty. They refuse to serve your gods and do not worship the gold statue you have set up."

¹³Then Nebuchadnezzar flew into a rage and ordered that Shadrach, Meshach, and Abednego be brought before him. When they were brought in, ¹⁴Nebuchadnezzar said to them, "Is it true, Shadrach, Meshach, and Abednego, that you refuse to serve my gods or to worship the gold statue I have set up? ¹⁵I will give you one more chance to bow down and worship the statue I have made when you hear the sound of the musical instruments.* But if you refuse, you will be thrown immediately into the blazing furnace. And then what god will be able to rescue you from my power?"

¹⁶Shadrach, Meshach, and Abednego replied, "O Nebuchadnezzar, we do not need to defend ourselves before you. ¹⁷If we are thrown into the blazing furnace, the God whom we serve is able to save us. He will rescue us from your power, Your Majesty. ¹⁸But even if he doesn't, we want to make it clear to you, Your Majesty, that we will never serve your gods or worship the gold statue you have set up."

THE BLAZING FURNACE

¹⁹Nebuchadnezzar was so furious with Shadrach, Meshach, and Abednego that his face became distorted with rage. He commanded that the furnace be heated seven times hotter than usual. ²⁰Then he ordered some of the strongest men of his army to bind Shadrach, Meshach, and Abednego and throw them into the blazing furnace. ²¹So they tied them up and threw them into the furnace, fully dressed in their pants, turbans, robes, and other garments. ²²And because the king, in his anger, had demanded such a hot fire in the furnace, the flames killed the soldiers as they threw the three men in. ²³So Shadrach, Meshach, and Abednego, securely tied, fell into the roaring flames.

²⁴But suddenly, Nebuchadnezzar jumped up in amazement and exclaimed to his advisers, "Didn't we tie up three men and throw them into the furnace?"

"Yes, Your Majesty, we certainly did," they replied.

²⁵"Look!" Nebuchadnezzar shouted. "I see four men, unbound, walking around in the fire unharmed! And the fourth looks like a god*!"

3:1 Aramaic 60 cubits [27 meters] tall and 6 cubits [2.7 meters] wide. 3:3 Aramaic the high officers, officials, governors, advisers, treasurers, judges, magistrates, and all the provincial officials. 3:5 The identification of some of these musical instruments is uncertain. 3:7 Aramaic the horn, flute, zither, lyre, harp, and other musical instruments. 3:8 Aramaic Chaldeans. 3:15 Aramaic the horn, flute, zither, lyre, harp, pipes, and other musical instruments. 3:25 Aramaic like a son of the gods.

²⁶ Then Nebuchadnezzar came as close as he could to the door of the flaming furnace and shouted: "Shadrach, Meshach, and Abednego, servants of the Most High God, come out! Come here!"

So Shadrach, Meshach, and Abednego stepped out of the fire. ²⁷ Then the high officers, officials, governors, and advisers crowded around them and saw that the fire had not touched them. Not a hair on their heads was singed, and their clothing was not scorched. They didn't even smell of smoke!

²⁸ Then Nebuchadnezzar said, "Praise to the God of Shadrach, Meshach, and Abednego! He sent his angel to rescue his servants who trusted in him. They defied the king's command and were willing to die rather than serve or worship any god except their own God. ²⁹ Therefore, I make this decree: If any people, whatever their race or nation or language, speak a word against the God of Shadrach, Meshach, and Abednego, they will be torn limb from limb, and their houses will be turned into heaps of rubble. There is no other god who can rescue like this!"

³⁰ Then the king promoted Shadrach, Meshach, and Abednego to even higher positions in the province of Babylon.

NEBUCHADNEZZAR'S DREAM ABOUT A TREE

4 ¹*King Nebuchadnezzar sent this message to the people of every race and nation and language throughout the world:

"Peace and prosperity to you!

² "I want you all to know about the miraculous signs and wonders the Most High God has performed for me.

³ How great are his signs,
  how powerful his wonders!
His kingdom will last forever,
  his rule through all generations.

⁴*"I, Nebuchadnezzar, was living in my palace in comfort and prosperity. ⁵ But one night I had a dream that frightened me; I saw visions that terrified me as I lay in my bed. ⁶ So I issued an order calling in all the wise men of Babylon, so they could tell me what my dream meant. ⁷ When all the magicians, enchanters, astrologers,* and fortune-tellers came in, I told them the dream, but they could not tell me what it meant. ⁸ At last Daniel came in before me, and I told him the dream. (He was named Belteshazzar after my god, and the spirit of the holy gods is in him.)

⁹ "I said to him, 'Belteshazzar, chief of the magicians, I know that the spirit of the holy gods is in you and that no mystery is too great for you to solve. Now tell me what my dream means.

¹⁰ "'While I was lying in my bed, this is what I dreamed. I saw a large tree in the middle of the earth. ¹¹ The tree grew very tall and strong, reaching high into the heavens for all the world to see. ¹² It had fresh green leaves, and it was loaded with fruit for all to eat. Wild animals lived in its shade, and birds nested in its branches. All the world was fed from this tree.

¹³ "'Then as I lay there dreaming, I saw a messenger,* a holy one, coming down from heaven. ¹⁴ The messenger shouted,

"Cut down the tree and lop off
   its branches!
  Shake off its leaves and scatter its fruit!
Chase the wild animals from its shade
   and the birds from its branches.
¹⁵ But leave the stump and the roots
   in the ground,
  bound with a band of iron and bronze
   and surrounded by tender grass.
Now let him be drenched with the dew
   of heaven,
  and let him live with the wild animals
   among the plants of the field.
¹⁶ For seven periods of time,
  let him have the mind of a wild animal
   instead of the mind of a human.
¹⁷ For this has been decreed by the
   messengers*;
  it is commanded by the holy ones,
so that everyone may know
  that the Most High rules over the
   kingdoms of the world.
He gives them to anyone he chooses—
  even to the lowliest of people."

¹⁸ "'Belteshazzar, that was the dream that I, King Nebuchadnezzar, had. Now tell me what it means, for none of the wise men of my kingdom can do so. But you can tell me because the spirit of the holy gods is in you.'

DANIEL EXPLAINS THE DREAM

¹⁹ "Upon hearing this, Daniel (also known as Belteshazzar) was overcome for a time, frightened by the meaning of the dream. Then the king said to him, 'Belteshazzar, don't be alarmed by the dream and what it means.'

"Belteshazzar replied, 'I wish the events foreshadowed in this dream would happen to your enemies, my lord, and not to you! ²⁰ The tree you saw was growing very tall and strong, reaching high into the heavens for all the world to see. ²¹ It had fresh green leaves and was loaded with fruit for all to eat. Wild

---

4:1 Verses 4:1-3 are numbered 3:31-33 in Aramaic text. 4:4 Verses 4:4-37 are numbered 4:1-34 in Aramaic text. 4:7 Or Chaldeans. 4:13 Aramaic *a watcher;* also in 4:23. 4:17 Aramaic *the watchers.*

animals lived in its shade, and birds nested in its branches. [22] That tree, Your Majesty, is you. For you have grown strong and great; your greatness reaches up to heaven, and your rule to the ends of the earth.

[23] "'Then you saw a messenger, a holy one, coming down from heaven and saying, "Cut down the tree and destroy it. But leave the stump and the roots in the ground, bound with a band of iron and bronze and surrounded by tender grass. Let him be drenched with the dew of heaven. Let him live with the animals of the field for seven periods of time."

[24] "'This is what the dream means, Your Majesty, and what the Most High has declared will happen to my lord the king. [25] You will be driven from human society, and you will live in the fields with the wild animals. You will eat grass like a cow, and you will be drenched with the dew of heaven. Seven periods of time will pass while you live this way, until you learn that the Most High rules over the kingdoms of the world and gives them to anyone he chooses. [26] But the stump and roots of the tree were left in the ground. This means that you will receive your kingdom back again when you have learned that heaven rules.

[27] "'King Nebuchadnezzar, please accept my advice. Stop sinning and do what is right. Break from your wicked past and be merciful to the poor. Perhaps then you will continue to prosper.'

THE DREAM'S FULFILLMENT

[28] "But all these things did happen to King Nebuchadnezzar. [29] Twelve months later he was taking a walk on the flat roof of the royal palace in Babylon. [30] As he looked out across the city, he said, 'Look at this great city of Babylon! By my own mighty power, I have built this beautiful city as my royal residence to display my majestic splendor.'

[31] "While these words were still in his mouth, a voice called down from heaven, 'O King Nebuchadnezzar, this message is for you! You are no longer ruler of this kingdom. [32] You will be driven from human society. You will live in the fields with the wild animals, and you will eat grass like a cow. Seven periods of time will pass while you live this way, until you learn that the Most High rules over the kingdoms of the world and gives them to anyone he chooses.'

[33] "That same hour the judgment was fulfilled, and Nebuchadnezzar was driven from human society. He ate grass like a cow, and he was drenched with the dew of heaven. He lived this way until his hair was as long as eagles' feathers and his nails were like birds' claws.

NEBUCHADNEZZAR PRAISES GOD

[34] "After this time had passed, I, Nebuchadnezzar, looked up to heaven. My sanity returned, and I praised and worshiped the Most High and honored the one who lives forever.

> His rule is everlasting,
>   and his kingdom is eternal.
[35] All the people of the earth
>   are nothing compared to him.
> He does as he pleases
>   among the angels of heaven
>   and among the people of the earth.
> No one can stop him or say to him,
>   'What do you mean by doing these
>   things?'

[36] "When my sanity returned to me, so did my honor and glory and kingdom. My advisers and nobles sought me out, and I was restored as head of my kingdom, with even greater honor than before. [37] Now I, Nebuchadnezzar, praise and glorify and honor the King of heaven. All his acts are just and true, and he is able to humble the proud."

THE WRITING ON THE WALL

5 Many years later King Belshazzar gave a great feast for 1,000 of his nobles, and he drank wine with them. [2] While Belshazzar was drinking the wine, he gave orders to bring in the gold and silver cups that his predecessor,* Nebuchadnezzar, had taken from the Temple in Jerusalem. He wanted to drink from them with his nobles, his wives, and his concubines. [3] So they brought these gold cups taken from the Temple, the house of God in Jerusalem, and the king and his nobles, his wives, and his concubines drank from them. [4] While they drank from them they praised their idols made of gold, silver, bronze, iron, wood, and stone.

[5] Suddenly, they saw the fingers of a human hand writing on the plaster wall of the king's palace, near the lampstand. The king himself saw the hand as it wrote, [6] and his face turned pale with fright. His knees knocked together in fear and his legs gave way beneath him.

[7] The king shouted for the enchanters, astrologers,* and fortune-tellers to be brought before him. He said to these wise men of Babylon, "Whoever can read this writing and tell me what it means will be dressed in purple robes of royal honor and will have a gold chain placed around his neck. He will become the third highest ruler in the kingdom!"

[8] But when all the king's wise men had come in, none of them could read the writing or tell him what it meant. [9] So the king grew even more

---

5:2 Aramaic *father;* also in 5:11, 13, 18.   5:7 Or *Chaldeans;* also in 5:11.

alarmed, and his face turned pale. His nobles, too, were shaken.

[10] But when the queen mother heard what was happening, she hurried to the banquet hall. She said to Belshazzar, "Long live the king! Don't be so pale and frightened. [11] There is a man in your kingdom who has within him the spirit of the holy gods. During Nebuchadnezzar's reign, this man was found to have insight, understanding, and wisdom like that of the gods. Your predecessor, the king—your predecessor King Nebuchadnezzar—made him chief over all the magicians, enchanters, astrologers, and fortune-tellers of Babylon. [12] This man Daniel, whom the king named Belteshazzar, has exceptional ability and is filled with divine knowledge and understanding. He can interpret dreams, explain riddles, and solve difficult problems. Call for Daniel, and he will tell you what the writing means."

DANIEL EXPLAINS THE WRITING

[13] So Daniel was brought in before the king. The king asked him, "Are you Daniel, one of the exiles brought from Judah by my predecessor, King Nebuchadnezzar? [14] I have heard that you have the spirit of the gods within you and that you are filled with insight, understanding, and wisdom. [15] My wise men and enchanters have tried to read the words on the wall and tell me their meaning, but they cannot do it. [16] I am told that you can give interpretations and solve difficult problems. If you can read these words and tell me their meaning, you will be clothed in purple robes of royal honor, and you will have a gold chain placed around your neck. You will become the third highest ruler in the kingdom."

[17] Daniel answered the king, "Keep your gifts or give them to someone else, but I will tell you what the writing means. [18] Your Majesty, the Most High God gave sovereignty, majesty, glory, and honor to your predecessor, Nebuchadnezzar. [19] He made him so great that people of all races and nations and languages trembled before him in fear. He killed those he wanted to kill and spared those he wanted to spare. He honored those he wanted to honor and disgraced those he wanted to disgrace. [20] But when his heart and mind were puffed up with arrogance, he was brought down from his royal throne and stripped of his glory. [21] He was driven from human society. He was given the mind of a wild animal, and he lived among the wild donkeys. He ate grass like a cow, and he was drenched with the dew of heaven, until he learned that the Most High God rules over the kingdoms of the world and appoints anyone he desires to rule over them.

[22] "You are his successor,* O Belshazzar, and you knew all this, yet you have not humbled yourself. [23] For you have proudly defied the Lord of heaven and have had these cups from his Temple brought before you. You and your nobles and your wives and concubines have been drinking wine from them while praising gods of silver, gold, bronze, iron, wood, and stone—gods that neither see nor hear nor know anything at all. But you have not honored the God who gives you the breath of life and controls your destiny! [24] So God has sent this hand to write this message.

[25] "This is the message that was written: Mene, Mene, Tekel, and Parsin. [26] This is what these words mean:

Mene means 'numbered'—God has numbered the days of your reign and has brought it to an end.
[27] Tekel means 'weighed'—you have been weighed on the balances and have not measured up.
[28] Parsin* means 'divided'—your kingdom has been divided and given to the Medes and Persians."

[29] Then at Belshazzar's command, Daniel was dressed in purple robes, a gold chain was hung around his neck, and he was proclaimed the third highest ruler in the kingdom.

[30] That very night Belshazzar, the Babylonian* king, was killed.*

[31]* And Darius the Mede took over the kingdom at the age of sixty-two.

DANIEL IN THE LIONS' DEN

6 [1]* Darius the Mede decided to divide the kingdom into 120 provinces, and he appointed a high officer to rule over each province. [2] The king also chose Daniel and two others as administrators to supervise the high officers and protect the king's interests. [3] Daniel soon proved himself more capable than all the other administrators and high officers. Because of Daniel's great ability, the king made plans to place him over the entire empire.

[4] Then the other administrators and high officers began searching for some fault in the way Daniel was handling government affairs, but they couldn't find anything to criticize or condemn. He was faithful, always responsible, and completely trustworthy. [5] So they concluded, "Our only chance of finding grounds for accusing Daniel will be in connection with the rules of his religion."

[6] So the administrators and high officers went to the king and said, "Long live King Darius! [7] We are all in agreement—we administrators, officials, high officers, advisers, and governors—that the king should make a law that will be strictly enforced. Give orders that for the next thirty days any person who prays to anyone, divine or human—except to you, Your Majesty—will be thrown into the den of lions. [8] And now, Your

---

5:22 Aramaic son.   5:28 Aramaic Peres, the singular of Parsin.
5:30a Or Chaldean.   5:30b The Persians and Medes conquered Babylon in October 539 B.C.   5:31 Verse 5:31 is numbered 6:1 in Aramaic text.   6:1 Verses 6:1-28 are numbered 6:2-29 in Aramaic text.

Majesty, issue and sign this law so it cannot be changed, an official law of the Medes and Persians that cannot be revoked." ⁹So King Darius signed the law.

¹⁰But when Daniel learned that the law had been signed, he went home and knelt down as usual in his upstairs room, with its windows open toward Jerusalem. He prayed three times a day, just as he had always done, giving thanks to his God. ¹¹Then the officials went together to Daniel's house and found him praying and asking for God's help. ¹²So they went straight to the king and reminded him about his law. "Did you not sign a law that for the next thirty days any person who prays to anyone, divine or human—except to you, Your Majesty—will be thrown into the den of lions?"

"Yes," the king replied, "that decision stands; it is an official law of the Medes and Persians that cannot be revoked."

¹³Then they told the king, "That man Daniel, one of the captives from Judah, is ignoring you and your law. He still prays to his God three times a day."

¹⁴Hearing this, the king was deeply troubled, and he tried to think of a way to save Daniel. He spent the rest of the day looking for a way to get Daniel out of this predicament.

¹⁵In the evening the men went together to the king and said, "Your Majesty, you know that according to the law of the Medes and the Persians, no law that the king signs can be changed."

¹⁶So at last the king gave orders for Daniel to be arrested and thrown into the den of lions. The king said to him, "May your God, whom you serve so faithfully, rescue you."

¹⁷A stone was brought and placed over the mouth of the den. The king sealed the stone with his own royal seal and the seals of his nobles, so that no one could rescue Daniel. ¹⁸Then the king returned to his palace and spent the night fasting. He refused his usual entertainment and couldn't sleep at all that night.

¹⁹Very early the next morning, the king got up and hurried out to the lions' den. ²⁰When he got there, he called out in anguish, "Daniel, servant of the living God! Was your God, whom you serve so faithfully, able to rescue you from the lions?"

²¹Daniel answered, "Long live the king! ²²My God sent his angel to shut the lions' mouths so that they would not hurt me, for I have been found innocent in his sight. And I have not wronged you, Your Majesty."

²³The king was overjoyed and ordered that Daniel be lifted from the den. Not a scratch was found on him, for he had trusted in his God.

²⁴Then the king gave orders to arrest the men who had maliciously accused Daniel. He had them thrown into the lions' den, along with their wives and children. The lions leaped on them and tore them apart before they even hit the floor of the den.

²⁵Then King Darius sent this message to the people of every race and nation and language throughout the world:

"Peace and prosperity to you!

²⁶"I decree that everyone throughout my kingdom should tremble with fear before the God of Daniel.

For he is the living God,
and he will endure forever.
His kingdom will never be destroyed,
and his rule will never end.
²⁷He rescues and saves his people;
he performs miraculous signs and
wonders
in the heavens and on earth.
He has rescued Daniel
from the power of the lions."

²⁸So Daniel prospered during the reign of Darius and the reign of Cyrus the Persian.*

DANIEL'S VISION OF FOUR BEASTS

7 Earlier, during the first year of King Belshazzar's reign in Babylon,* Daniel had a dream and saw visions as he lay in his bed. He wrote down the dream, and this is what he saw.

²In my vision that night, I, Daniel, saw a great storm churning the surface of a great sea, with strong winds blowing from every direction. ³Then four huge beasts came up out of the water, each different from the others.

⁴The first beast was like a lion with eagles' wings. As I watched, its wings were pulled off, and it was left standing with its two hind feet on the ground, like a human being. And it was given a human mind.

⁵Then I saw a second beast, and it looked like a bear. It was rearing up on one side, and it had three ribs in its mouth between its teeth. And I heard a voice saying to it, "Get up! Devour the flesh of many people!"

⁶Then the third of these strange beasts appeared, and it looked like a leopard. It had four bird's wings on its back, and it had four heads. Great authority was given to this beast.

⁷Then in my vision that night, I saw a fourth beast—terrifying, dreadful, and very strong. It devoured and crushed its victims with huge iron teeth and trampled their remains beneath its feet. It was different from any of the other beasts, and it had ten horns.

⁸As I was looking at the horns, suddenly another small horn appeared among them. Three of the first horns were torn out by the roots to make room for it. This little horn had eyes like human eyes and a mouth that was boasting arrogantly.

6:28 Or *of Darius, that is, the reign of Cyrus the Persian.* 7:1 The first year of Belshazzar's reign (who was co-regent with his father, Nabonidus) was 556 B.C. (or perhaps as late as 553 B.C.).

⁹ I watched as thrones were put in place
   and the Ancient One* sat down to judge.
His clothing was as white as snow,
   his hair like purest wool.
He sat on a fiery throne
   with wheels of blazing fire,
¹⁰ and a river of fire was pouring out,
   flowing from his presence.
Millions of angels ministered to him;
   many millions stood to attend him.
Then the court began its session,
   and the books were opened.

¹¹ I continued to watch because I could hear the little horn's boastful speech. I kept watching until the fourth beast was killed and its body was destroyed by fire. ¹² The other three beasts had their authority taken from them, but they were allowed to live a while longer.*

¹³ As my vision continued that night, I saw someone like a son of man* coming with the clouds of heaven. He approached the Ancient One and was led into his presence. ¹⁴ He was given authority, honor, and sovereignty over all the nations of the world, so that people of every race and nation and language would obey him. His rule is eternal—it will never end. His kingdom will never be destroyed.

THE VISION IS EXPLAINED

¹⁵ I, Daniel, was troubled by all I had seen, and my visions terrified me. ¹⁶ So I approached one of those standing beside the throne and asked him what it all meant. He explained it to me like this: ¹⁷ "These four huge beasts represent four kingdoms that will arise from the earth. ¹⁸ But in the end, the holy people of the Most High will be given the kingdom, and they will rule forever and ever."

¹⁹ Then I wanted to know the true meaning of the fourth beast, the one so different from the others and so terrifying. It had devoured and crushed its victims with iron teeth and bronze claws, trampling their remains beneath its feet. ²⁰ I also asked about the ten horns on the fourth beast's head and the little horn that came up afterward and destroyed three of the other horns. This horn had seemed greater than the others, and it had human eyes and a mouth that was boasting arrogantly. ²¹ As I watched, this horn was waging war against God's holy people and was defeating them, ²² until the Ancient One— the Most High—came and judged in favor of his holy people. Then the time arrived for the holy people to take over the kingdom.

²³ Then he said to me, "This fourth beast is the fourth world power that will rule the earth. It will be different from all the others. It will devour the whole world, trampling and crushing everything in its path. ²⁴ Its ten horns are ten kings who will rule that empire. Then another king will arise, different from the other ten, who will subdue three of them. ²⁵ He will defy the Most High and oppress the holy people of the Most High. He will try to change their sacred festivals and laws, and they will be placed under his control for a time, times, and half a time.

²⁶ "But then the court will pass judgment, and all his power will be taken away and completely destroyed. ²⁷ Then the sovereignty, power, and greatness of all the kingdoms under heaven will be given to the holy people of the Most High. His kingdom will last forever, and all rulers will serve and obey him."

²⁸ That was the end of the vision. I, Daniel, was terrified by my thoughts and my face was pale with fear, but I kept these things to myself.

DANIEL'S VISION OF A RAM AND GOAT

8 ¹*During the third year of King Belshazzar's reign, I, Daniel, saw another vision, following the one that had already appeared to me. ² In this vision I was at the fortress of Susa, in the province of Elam, standing beside the Ulai River.*

³ As I looked up, I saw a ram with two long horns standing beside the river.* One of the horns was longer than the other, even though it had grown later than the other one. ⁴ The ram butted everything out of his way to the west, to the north, and to the south, and no one could stand against him or help his victims. He did as he pleased and became very great.

⁵ While I was watching, suddenly a male goat appeared from the west, crossing the land so swiftly that he didn't even touch the ground. This goat, which had one very large horn between its eyes, ⁶ headed toward the two-horned ram that I had seen standing beside the river, rushing at him in a rage. ⁷ The goat charged furiously at the ram and struck him, breaking off both his horns. Now the ram was helpless, and the goat knocked him down and trampled him. No one could rescue the ram from the goat's power.

⁸ The goat became very powerful. But at the height of his power, his large horn was broken off. In the large horn's place grew four prominent horns pointing in the four directions of the earth. ⁹ Then from one of the prominent horns came a small horn whose power grew very great. It extended toward the south and the east and toward the glorious land of Israel. ¹⁰ Its power reached to the heavens, where it attacked the heavenly army, throwing some of the heavenly beings and some of the stars to the ground and trampling them. ¹¹ It even challenged the Commander of heaven's army by canceling the daily sacrifices offered to him and by destroying his Temple. ¹² The army of heaven was restrained from responding to this rebellion. So the daily

---

7:9 Aramaic *an Ancient of Days;* also in 7:13, 22.   7:12 Aramaic *for a season and a time.*   7:13 Or *like a Son of Man.*   8:1 The original text from this point through chapter 12 is in Hebrew. See note at 2:4.   8:2 Or *the Ulai Gate;* also in 8:16.
8:3 Or *the gate;* also in 8:6.

sacrifice was halted, and truth was overthrown. The horn succeeded in everything it did.*

[13] Then I heard two holy ones talking to each other. One of them asked, "How long will the events of this vision last? How long will the rebellion that causes desecration stop the daily sacrifices? How long will the Temple and heaven's army be trampled on?"

[14] The other replied, "It will take 2,300 evenings and mornings; then the Temple will be made right again."

GABRIEL EXPLAINS THE VISION

[15] As I, Daniel, was trying to understand the meaning of this vision, someone who looked like a man stood in front of me. [16] And I heard a human voice calling out from the Ulai River, "Gabriel, tell this man the meaning of his vision."

[17] As Gabriel approached the place where I was standing, I became so terrified that I fell with my face to the ground. "Son of man," he said, "you must understand that the events you have seen in your vision relate to the time of the end."

[18] While he was speaking, I fainted and lay there with my face to the ground. But Gabriel roused me with a touch and helped me to my feet.

[19] Then he said, "I am here to tell you what will happen later in the time of wrath. What you have seen pertains to the very end of time. [20] The two-horned ram represents the kings of Media and Persia. [21] The shaggy male goat represents the king of Greece,* and the large horn between his eyes represents the first king of the Greek Empire. [22] The four prominent horns that replaced the one large horn show that the Greek Empire will break into four kingdoms, but none as great as the first.

[23] "At the end of their rule, when their sin is at its height, a fierce king, a master of intrigue, will rise to power. [24] He will become very strong, but not by his own power. He will cause a shocking amount of destruction and succeed in everything he does. He will destroy powerful leaders and devastate the holy people. [25] He will be a master of deception and will become arrogant; he will destroy many without warning. He will even take on the Prince of princes in battle, but he will be broken, though not by human power.

[26] "This vision about the 2,300 evenings and mornings* is true. But none of these things will happen for a long time, so keep this vision a secret."

[27] Then I, Daniel, was overcome and lay sick for several days. Afterward I got up and performed my duties for the king, but I was greatly troubled by the vision and could not understand it.

DANIEL'S PRAYER FOR HIS PEOPLE

9 It was the first year of the reign of Darius the Mede, the son of Ahasuerus, who became king of the Babylonians.* [2] During the first year of his reign, I, Daniel, learned from reading the word of the LORD, as revealed to Jeremiah the prophet, that Jerusalem must lie desolate for seventy years.* [3] So I turned to the Lord God and pleaded with him in prayer and fasting. I also wore rough burlap and sprinkled myself with ashes.

[4] I prayed to the LORD my God and confessed:

"O Lord, you are a great and awesome God! You always fulfill your covenant and keep your promises of unfailing love to those who love you and obey your commands. [5] But we have sinned and done wrong. We have rebelled against you and scorned your commands and regulations. [6] We have refused to listen to your servants the prophets, who spoke on your authority to our kings and princes and ancestors and to all the people of the land.

[7] "Lord, you are in the right; but as you see, our faces are covered with shame. This is true of all of us, including the people of Judah and Jerusalem and all Israel, scattered near and far, wherever you have driven us because of our disloyalty to you. [8] O LORD, we and our kings, princes, and ancestors are covered with shame because we have sinned against you. [9] But the Lord our God is merciful and forgiving, even though we have rebelled against him. [10] We have not obeyed the LORD our God, for we have not followed the instructions he gave us through his servants the prophets. [11] All Israel has disobeyed your instruction and turned away, refusing to listen to your voice.

"So now the solemn curses and judgments written in the Law of Moses, the servant of God, have been poured down on us because of our sin. [12] You have kept your word and done to us and our rulers exactly as you warned. Never has there been such a disaster as happened in Jerusalem. [13] Every curse written against us in the Law of Moses has come true. Yet we have refused to seek mercy from the LORD our God by turning from our sins and recognizing his truth. [14] Therefore, the LORD has brought upon us the disaster he prepared. The LORD our God was right to do all of these things, for we did not obey him.

[15] "O Lord our God, you brought lasting honor to your name by rescuing your people from Egypt in a great display of power. But we have sinned and are full of wickedness. [16] In view of all your faithful mercies, Lord, please turn your furious anger away from your city Jerusalem, your holy mountain.

8:11-12 The meaning of the Hebrew for these verses is uncertain. 8:21 Hebrew of Javan. 8:26 Hebrew about the evenings and mornings; compare 8:14. 9:1 Or the Chaldeans. 9:2 See Jer 25:11-12; 29:10.

All the neighboring nations mock Jerusalem and your people because of our sins and the sins of our ancestors. [17]"O our God, hear your servant's prayer! Listen as I plead. For your own sake, Lord, smile again on your desolate sanctuary. [18]"O my God, lean down and listen to me. Open your eyes and see our despair. See how your city—the city that bears your name—lies in ruins. We make this plea, not because we deserve help, but because of your mercy. [19]"O Lord, hear. O Lord, forgive. O Lord, listen and act! For your own sake, do not delay, O my God, for your people and your city bear your name."

GABRIEL'S MESSAGE ABOUT THE ANOINTED ONE

[20]I went on praying and confessing my sin and the sin of my people, pleading with the LORD my God for Jerusalem, his holy mountain. [21]As I was praying, Gabriel, whom I had seen in the earlier vision, came swiftly to me at the time of the evening sacrifice. [22]He explained to me, "Daniel, I have come here to give you insight and understanding. [23]The moment you began praying, a command was given. And now I am here to tell you what it was, for you are very precious to God. Listen carefully so that you can understand the meaning of your vision.

[24]"A period of seventy sets of seven* has been decreed for your people and your holy city to finish their rebellion, to put an end to their sin, to atone for their guilt, to bring in everlasting righteousness, to confirm the prophetic vision, and to anoint the Most Holy Place.* [25]Now listen and understand! Seven sets of seven plus sixty-two sets of seven* will pass from the time the command is given to rebuild Jerusalem until a ruler—the Anointed One*—comes. Jerusalem will be rebuilt with streets and strong defenses,* despite the perilous times.

[26]"After this period of sixty-two sets of seven,* the Anointed One will be killed, appearing to have accomplished nothing, and a ruler will arise whose armies will destroy the city and the Temple. The end will come with a flood, and war and its miseries are decreed from that time to the very end. [27]The ruler will make a treaty with the people for a period of one set of seven,* but after half this time, he will put an end to the sacrifices and offerings. And as a climax to all his terrible deeds,* he will set up a sacrilegious object that causes desecration,* until the fate decreed for this defiler is finally poured out on him."

DANIEL'S VISION OF A MESSENGER

10 In the third year of the reign of King Cyrus of Persia,* Daniel (also known as Belteshazzar) had another vision. He understood that the vision concerned events certain to happen in the future—times of war and great hardship.

[2]When this vision came to me, I, Daniel, had been in mourning for three whole weeks. [3]All that time I had eaten no rich food. No meat or wine crossed my lips, and I used no fragrant lotions until those three weeks had passed.

[4]On April 23,* as I was standing on the bank of the great Tigris River, [5]I looked up and saw a man dressed in linen clothing, with a belt of pure gold around his waist. [6]His body looked like a precious gem. His face flashed like lightning, and his eyes flamed like torches. His arms and feet shone like polished bronze, and his voice roared like a vast multitude of people.

[7]Only I, Daniel, saw this vision. The men with me saw nothing, but they were suddenly terrified and ran away to hide. [8]So I was left there all alone to see this amazing vision. My strength left me, my face grew deathly pale, and I felt very weak. [9]Then I heard the man speak, and when I heard the sound of his voice, I fainted and lay there with my face to the ground.

[10]Just then a hand touched me and lifted me, still trembling, to my hands and knees. [11]And the man said to me, "Daniel, you are very precious to God, so listen carefully to what I have to say to you. Stand up, for I have been sent to you." When he said this to me, I stood up, still trembling.

[12]Then he said, "Don't be afraid, Daniel. Since the first day you began to pray for understanding and to humble yourself before your God, your request has been heard in heaven. I have come in answer to your prayer. [13]But for twenty-one days the spirit prince* of the kingdom of Persia blocked my way. Then Michael, one of the archangels,* came to help me, and I left him there with the spirit prince of the kingdom of Persia.* [14]Now I am here to explain what will happen to your people in the future, for this vision concerns a time yet to come."

[15]While he was speaking to me, I looked down at the ground, unable to say a word. [16]Then the one who looked like a man* touched my lips, and I opened my mouth and began to speak. I said to the one standing in front of me, "I am filled with anguish because of the vision I have seen, my lord, and I am very weak. [17]How can someone like me, your servant, talk to you, my lord? My strength is gone, and I can hardly breathe."

9:24a Hebrew *seventy sevens.* 9:24b Or *the Most Holy One.*
9:25a Hebrew *Seven sevens plus sixty-two sevens.* 9:25b Or *an anointed one;* similarly in 9:26. Hebrew reads *a messiah.* 9:25c Or *and a moat, or and trenches.* 9:26 Hebrew *After sixty-two sevens.* 9:27a Hebrew *for one seven.* 9:27b Hebrew *And on the wing;* the meaning of the Hebrew is uncertain. 9:27c Hebrew *an abomination of desolation.* 10:1 The third year of Cyrus's reign was 536 B.C. 10:4 Hebrew *On the twenty-fourth day of the first month,* of the ancient Hebrew lunar calendar. This date in the book of Daniel can be cross-checked with dates in surviving Persian records and can be related accurately to our modern calendar. This event occurred on April 23, 536 B.C. 10:13a Hebrew *the prince;* also in 10:13c, 20. 10:13b Hebrew *the chief princes.* 10:13c As in one Greek version; Hebrew reads *and I was left there with the kings of Persia.* The meaning of the Hebrew is uncertain. 10:16 As in most manuscripts of the Masoretic Text; one manuscript of the Masoretic Text and one Greek version read *Then something that looked like a human hand.*

¹⁸ Then the one who looked like a man touched me again, and I felt my strength returning. ¹⁹ "Don't be afraid," he said, "for you are very precious to God. Peace! Be encouraged! Be strong!"

As he spoke these words to me, I suddenly felt stronger and said to him, "Please speak to me, my lord, for you have strengthened me."

²⁰ He replied, "Do you know why I have come? Soon I must return to fight against the spirit prince of the kingdom of Persia, and after that the spirit prince of the kingdom of Greece* will come. ²¹ Meanwhile, I will tell you what is written in the Book of Truth. (No one helps me against these spirit princes except Michael, your spirit prince.* ^{11:1} I have been standing beside Michael* to support and strengthen him since the first year of the reign of Darius the Mede.)

KINGS OF THE SOUTH AND NORTH

11 ² "Now then, I will reveal the truth to you. Three more Persian kings will reign, to be succeeded by a fourth, far richer than the others. He will use his wealth to stir up everyone to fight against the kingdom of Greece.*

³ "Then a mighty king will rise to power who will rule with great authority and accomplish everything he sets out to do. ⁴ But at the height of his power, his kingdom will be broken apart and divided into four parts. It will not be ruled by the king's descendants, nor will the kingdom hold the authority it once had. For his empire will be uprooted and given to others.

⁵ "The king of the south will increase in power, but one of his own officials will become more powerful than he and will rule his kingdom with great strength.

⁶ "Some years later an alliance will be formed between the king of the north and the king of the south. The daughter of the king of the south will be given in marriage to the king of the north to secure the alliance, but she will lose her influence over him, and so will her father. She will be abandoned along with her supporters. ⁷ But when one of her relatives* becomes king of the south, he will raise an army and enter the fortress of the king of the north and defeat him. ⁸ When he returns to Egypt, he will carry back their idols with him, along with priceless articles of gold and silver. For some years afterward he will leave the king of the north alone.

⁹ "Later the king of the north will invade the realm of the king of the south but will soon return to his own land. ¹⁰ However, the sons of the king of the north will assemble a mighty army that will advance like a flood and carry the battle as far as the enemy's fortress.

¹¹ "Then, in a rage, the king of the south will rally against the vast forces assembled by the king of the north and will defeat them. ¹² After the enemy army is swept away, the king of the south will be filled with pride and will execute many thousands of his enemies. But his success will be short lived.

¹³ "A few years later the king of the north will return with a fully equipped army far greater than before. ¹⁴ At that time there will be a general uprising against the king of the south. Violent men among your own people will join them in fulfillment of this vision, but they will not succeed. ¹⁵ Then the king of the north will come and lay siege to a fortified city and capture it. The best troops of the south will not be able to stand in the face of the onslaught.

¹⁶ "The king of the north will march onward unopposed; none will be able to stop him. He will pause in the glorious land of Israel,* intent on destroying it. ¹⁷ He will make plans to come with the might of his entire kingdom and will form an alliance with the king of the south. He will give him a daughter in marriage in order to overthrow the kingdom from within, but his plan will fail.

¹⁸ "After this, he will turn his attention to the coastland and conquer many cities. But a commander from another land will put an end to his insolence and cause him to retreat in shame. ¹⁹ He will take refuge in his own fortresses but will stumble and fall and be seen no more.

²⁰ "His successor will send out a tax collector to maintain the royal splendor. But after a very brief reign, he will die, though not from anger or in battle.

²¹ "The next to come to power will be a despicable man who is not in line for royal succession. He will slip in when least expected and take over the kingdom by flattery and intrigue. ²² Before him great armies will be swept away, including a covenant prince. ²³ With deceitful promises, he will make various alliances. He will become strong despite having only a handful of followers. ²⁴ Without warning he will enter the richest areas of the land. Then he will distribute among his followers the plunder and wealth of the rich— something his predecessors had never done. He will plot the overthrow of strongholds, but this will last for only a short while.

²⁵ "Then he will stir up his courage and raise a great army against the king of the south. The king of the south will go to battle with a mighty army, but to no avail, for there will be plots against him. ²⁶ His own household will cause his downfall. His army will be swept away, and many will be killed. ²⁷ Seeking nothing but each other's harm, these kings will plot against each other at the conference table, attempting to deceive each other. But it will make no difference, for the end will come at the appointed time.

²⁸ "The king of the north will then return home with great riches. On the way he will set himself against the people of the holy covenant, doing much damage before continuing his journey.

10:20 Hebrew *of Javan.* 10:21 Hebrew *against these except Michael, your prince.* 11:1 Hebrew *him.* 11:2 Hebrew *of Javan.* 11:7 Hebrew *a branch from her roots.* 11:16 Hebrew *the glorious land.*

²⁹ "Then at the appointed time he will once again invade the south, but this time the result will be different. ³⁰ For warships from western coastlands* will scare him off, and he will withdraw and return home. But he will vent his anger against the people of the holy covenant and reward those who forsake the covenant.

³¹ "His army will take over the Temple fortress, pollute the sanctuary, put a stop to the daily sacrifices, and set up the sacrilegious object that causes desecration.* ³² He will flatter and win over those who have violated the covenant. But the people who know their God will be strong and will resist him.

³³ "Wise leaders will give instruction to many, but these teachers will die by fire and sword, or they will be jailed and robbed. ³⁴ During these persecutions, little help will arrive, and many who join them will not be sincere. ³⁵ And some of the wise will fall victim to persecution. In this way, they will be refined and cleansed and made pure until the time of the end, for the appointed time is still to come.

³⁶ "The king will do as he pleases, exalting himself and claiming to be greater than every god, even blaspheming the God of gods. He will succeed, but only until the time of wrath is completed. For what has been determined will surely take place. ³⁷ He will have no respect for the gods of his ancestors, or for the god loved by women, or for any other god, for he will boast that he is greater than them all. ³⁸ Instead of these, he will worship the god of fortresses—a god his ancestors never knew—and lavish on him gold, silver, precious stones, and expensive gifts. ³⁹ Claiming this foreign god's help, he will attack the strongest fortresses. He will honor those who submit to him, appointing them to positions of authority and dividing the land among them as their reward.*

⁴⁰ "Then at the time of the end, the king of the south will attack the king of the north. The king of the north will storm out with chariots, charioteers, and a vast navy. He will invade various lands and sweep through them like a flood. ⁴¹ He will enter the glorious land of Israel,* and many nations will fall, but Moab, Edom, and the best part of Ammon will escape. ⁴² He will conquer many countries, and even Egypt will not escape. ⁴³ He will gain control over the gold, silver, and treasures of Egypt, and the Libyans and Ethiopians* will be his servants.

⁴⁴ "But then news from the east and the north will alarm him, and he will set out in great anger to destroy and obliterate many. ⁴⁵ He will stop between the glorious holy mountain and the sea and will pitch his royal tents. But while he is there, his time will suddenly run out, and no one will help him.

THE TIME OF THE END

12 "At that time Michael, the archangel* who stands guard over your nation, will arise. Then there will be a time of anguish greater than any since nations first came into existence. But at that time every one of your people whose name is written in the book will be rescued. ² Many of those whose bodies lie dead and buried will rise up, some to everlasting life and some to shame and everlasting disgrace. ³ Those who are wise will shine as bright as the sky, and those who lead many to righteousness will shine like the stars forever. ⁴ But you, Daniel, keep this prophecy a secret; seal up the book until the time of the end, when many will rush here and there, and knowledge will increase."

⁵ Then I, Daniel, looked and saw two others standing on opposite banks of the river. ⁶ One of them asked the man dressed in linen, who was now standing above the river, "How long will it be until these shocking events are over?"

⁷ The man dressed in linen, who was standing above the river, raised both his hands toward heaven and took a solemn oath by the One who lives forever, saying, "It will go on for a time, times, and half a time. When the shattering of the holy people has finally come to an end, all these things will have happened."

⁸ I heard what he said, but I did not understand what he meant. So I asked, "How will all this finally end, my lord?"

⁹ But he said, "Go now, Daniel, for what I have said is kept secret and sealed until the time of the end. ¹⁰ Many will be purified, cleansed, and refined by these trials. But the wicked will continue in their wickedness, and none of them will understand. Only those who are wise will know what it means.

¹¹ "From the time the daily sacrifice is stopped and the sacrilegious object that causes desecration* is set up to be worshiped, there will be 1,290 days. ¹² And blessed are those who wait and remain until the end of the 1,335 days!

¹³ "As for you, go your way until the end. You will rest, and then at the end of the days, you will rise again to receive the inheritance set aside for you."

_____

11:30 Hebrew *from Kittim.*   11:31 Hebrew *the abomination of desolation.*   11:39 Or *at a price.*   11:41 Hebrew *the glorious land.*   11:43 Hebrew *Cushites.*   12:1 Hebrew *the great prince.*   12:11 Hebrew *the abomination of desolation.*

— THE BOOK OF THE TWELVE —

The Old Testament concludes with twelve prophetic books, beginning with Hosea and concluding with Malachi. These books are usually called The Twelve Minor Prophets because they are much shorter in length than the prophetic books of Isaiah, Jeremiah, and Ezekiel (also known as The Major Prophets). In fact, the book of Obadiah contains only 21 verses. However, these books should not be seen as less significant because they are shorter. Instead, they should be seen as a collection that is equal to The Major Prophets. Many Bible scholars refer to these books as The Book of the Twelve, which recognizes their significance to be as great as that of Isaiah, Jeremiah, and Ezekiel. The length of the books when added up and the importance of the issues they address certainly make them as significant as Isaiah, Jeremiah, or Ezekiel.

In the Bible, these books are not in chronological order but represent prophets who spoke God's word to His people over several hundred years from the eighth century (700s BC) to the fifth century (400s BC). The messages contained in these books come from the pre-Exilic (before the Babylonian Exile) period, the Exilic (during the Babylonian Exile) period, and post-Exilic (after the Babylonian Exile) period.

— The books from the period before the Exile include Hosea, Joel, Amos, Jonah, Micah, Nahum, and Zephaniah.
— The books from the Exile itself include Obadiah and Habakkuk.
— The books from after the Exile include Haggai, Zechariah, and Malachi.

HOSEA

JON HUNTZINGER, PHD

H osea is the only *literary* prophet (a prophet who has a biblical book named for him unlike, for example, Elijah, who does not have such a book) from the northern kingdom of Israel. He prophesied during the years 750–715 BC.

Most readers remember Hosea as the prophet God commanded to marry an unfaithful woman (Gomer). She represents the people of Israel as a whole. The term "prostitute" is used several times to describe the attitude and behavior of the people and to emphasize their ignorance of God (4:12; 5:4), which is revealed in their worship of idols (4:7).

The book of Hosea comprises two major sections:
— Part one includes the prophet's messages and describes his difficult marriage (chapters 1–3).
— Part two contains a series of passages describing the unfaithfulness of God's people, God's judgment for their unfaithfulness, and God's ultimate forgiveness and blessing (chapters 4–14). This section contains a series of negative metaphorical depictions of the people to show the creative way the prophet attempted to get them to think about their condition in a new way. Hosea jostles their understanding of the desperate nature of their condition by describing the people as "an oven that is kept hot" (7:4–7), "half-baked cake" (7:8), "silly, witless doves" (7:11), "crooked bow" (7:16), "wild donkey" (8:9), "grapes in the desert" (9:10), "vine loaded with fruit" (10:1), and a "stubborn heifer" (4:16).

The book of Hosea shows the influence of Hebrew wisdom writing by depicting Hosea's wife to resemble the "immoral" woman of Proverbs 5–7, which is an example of wisdom literature. At the same time, she represents the people of Israel. Like the woman of Proverbs 5–7 who leads unthinking and unknowing young men astray along her "wayward path" (a metaphor for ignorance), she (as in Israel) leads others astray by giving them a false understanding of God. By worshiping idols and displaying a lack knowledge of Him, Israel fails in her calling to the nations, who are dependent on her for instruction about God and His ways. Hosea's remarriage to Gomer shows God's willingness to take Israel back to Himself for Israel's sake and for the sake of the other nations. They need to know God but cannot as long as Israel is separated from Him and living in ignorance.

The connection between the book of Hosea and wisdom literature with its focus on the knowledge of God is sealed in the last verses of the book. There Hosea says knowledge comes from listening to and obeying God's word, which is the prophetic word given by Hosea:

Let those who are wise understand these things.
Let those with discernment listen carefully.
The paths of the LORD are true and right,
and righteous people live by walking in them
(14:9).

1 The LORD gave this message to Hosea son of Beeri during the years when Uzziah, Jotham, Ahaz, and Hezekiah were kings of Judah, and Jeroboam son of Jehoash* was king of Israel.

HOSEA'S WIFE AND CHILDREN

[2] When the LORD first began speaking to Israel through Hosea, he said to him, "Go and marry a prostitute,* so that some of her children will be conceived in prostitution. This will illustrate how Israel has acted like a prostitute by turning against the LORD and worshiping other gods."

[3] So Hosea married Gomer, the daughter of Diblaim, and she became pregnant and gave Hosea a son. [4] And the LORD said, "Name the child Jezreel, for I am about to punish King Jehu's dynasty to avenge the murders he committed at Jezreel. In fact, I will bring an end to Israel's independence. [5] I will break its military power in the Jezreel Valley."

[6] Soon Gomer became pregnant again and gave birth to a daughter. And the LORD said to Hosea, "Name your daughter Lo-ruhamah—'Not loved'—for I will no longer show love to the people of Israel or forgive them. [7] But I will show love to the people of Judah. I will free them from their enemies—not with weapons and armies or horses and charioteers, but by my power as the LORD their God."

[8] After Gomer had weaned Lo-ruhamah, she again became pregnant and gave birth to a second son. [9] And the LORD said, "Name him Lo-ammi—'Not my people'—for Israel is not my people, and I am not their God.

[10]*"Yet the time will come when Israel's people will be like the sands of the seashore—too many to count! Then, at the place where they were told, 'You are not my people,' it will be said, 'You are children of the living God.' [11] Then the people of Judah and Israel will unite together. They will choose one leader for themselves, and they will return from exile together. What a day that will be—the day of Jezreel*—when God will again plant his people in his land.

[2:1]*"In that day you will call your brothers Ammi—'My people.' And you will call your sisters Ruhamah—'The ones I love.'

CHARGES AGAINST AN UNFAITHFUL WIFE

2 [2] "But now bring charges against Israel—your mother—
for she is no longer my wife,
and I am no longer her husband.
Tell her to remove the prostitute's makeup from her face
and the clothing that exposes her breasts.
[3] Otherwise, I will strip her as naked
as she was on the day she was born.
I will leave her to die of thirst,
as in a dry and barren wilderness.
[4] And I will not love her children,
for they were conceived in prostitution.

[5] Their mother is a shameless prostitute
and became pregnant in a shameful way.
She said, 'I'll run after other lovers
and sell myself to them for food and water,
for clothing of wool and linen,
and for olive oil and drinks.'

[6] "For this reason I will fence her in with thornbushes.
I will block her path with a wall
to make her lose her way.
[7] When she runs after her lovers,
she won't be able to catch them.
She will search for them
but not find them.
Then she will think,
'I might as well return to my husband,
for I was better off with him than
I am now.'
[8] She doesn't realize it was I who gave her everything she has—
the grain, the new wine, the olive oil;
I even gave her silver and gold.
But she gave all my gifts to Baal.

[9] "But now I will take back the ripened grain and new wine
I generously provided each harvest season.
I will take away the wool and linen clothing
I gave her to cover her nakedness.
[10] I will strip her naked in public,
while all her lovers look on.
No one will be able
to rescue her from my hands.
[11] I will put an end to her annual festivals,
her new moon celebrations, and her Sabbath days—
all her appointed festivals.
[12] I will destroy her grapevines and fig trees,
things she claims her lovers gave her.
I will let them grow into tangled thickets,
where only wild animals will eat the fruit.
[13] I will punish her for all those times
when she burned incense to her images of Baal,
when she put on her earrings and jewels
and went out to look for her lovers
but forgot all about me,"
says the LORD.

THE LORD'S LOVE FOR UNFAITHFUL ISRAEL

[14] "But then I will win her back once again.
I will lead her into the desert
and speak tenderly to her there.
[15] I will return her vineyards to her
and transform the Valley of Trouble* into a gateway of hope.

1:1 Hebrew *Joash*, a variant spelling of Jehoash.   1:2 Or *a promiscuous woman*.   1:10 Verses 1:10-11 are numbered 2:1-2 in Hebrew text.   1:11 *Jezreel* means "God plants."   2:1 Verses 2:1-23 are numbered 2:3-25 in Hebrew text.   2:15 Hebrew *valley of Achor*.

She will give herself to me there,
    as she did long ago when she was young,
    when I freed her from her captivity
      in Egypt.
¹⁶ When that day comes," says the LORD,
    "you will call me 'my husband'
    instead of 'my master.'*
¹⁷ O Israel, I will wipe the many names of Baal
      from your lips,
    and you will never mention them again.
¹⁸ On that day I will make a covenant
    with all the wild animals and the birds
      of the sky
    and the animals that scurry along
      the ground
    so they will not harm you.
    I will remove all weapons of war from
      the land,
    all swords and bows,
    so you can live unafraid
      in peace and safety.
¹⁹ I will make you my wife forever,
    showing you righteousness and justice,
    unfailing love and compassion.
²⁰ I will be faithful to you and make you mine,
    and you will finally know me as the LORD.

²¹ "In that day, I will answer,"
    says the LORD.
    "I will answer the sky as it pleads for clouds.
    And the sky will answer the earth with rain.
²² Then the earth will answer the thirsty cries
    of the grain, the grapevines,
      and the olive trees.
    And they in turn will answer,
    'Jezreel'—'God plants!'
²³ At that time I will plant a crop of Israelites
    and raise them for myself.
    I will show love
      to those I called 'Not loved.'*
    And to those I called 'Not my people,'*
    I will say, 'Now you are my people.'
    And they will reply, 'You are our God!'"

HOSEA'S WIFE IS REDEEMED

3 Then the LORD said to me, "Go and love your wife again, even though she* commits adultery with another lover. This will illustrate that the LORD still loves Israel, even though the people have turned to other gods and love to worship them.*"

²So I bought her back for fifteen pieces of silver* and five bushels of barley and a measure of wine.* ³Then I said to her, "You must live in my house for many days and stop your prostitution. During this time, you will not have sexual relations with anyone, not even with me.*"

⁴This shows that Israel will go a long time without a king or prince, and without sacrifices, sacred pillars, priests,* or even idols! ⁵But afterward the people will return and devote themselves to the LORD their God and to David's

descendant, their king.* In the last days, they will tremble in awe of the LORD and of his goodness.

THE LORD'S CASE AGAINST ISRAEL

4 ¹ Hear the word of the LORD, O people of Israel!
    The LORD has brought charges against
      you, saying:
"There is no faithfulness, no kindness,
    no knowledge of God in your land.
² You make vows and break them;
    you kill and steal and commit adultery.
There is violence everywhere—
    one murder after another.
³ That is why your land is in mourning,
    and everyone is wasting away.
Even the wild animals, the birds of the sky,
    and the fish of the sea are disappearing.

⁴ "Don't point your finger at someone else
    and try to pass the blame!
My complaint, you priests,
    is with you.*
⁵ So you will stumble in broad daylight,
    and your false prophets will fall with you
      in the night.
    And I will destroy Israel, your mother.
⁶ My people are being destroyed
    because they don't know me.
Since you priests refuse to know me,
    I refuse to recognize you as my priests.
Since you have forgotten the laws
      of your God,
    I will forget to bless your children.
⁷ The more priests there are,
    the more they sin against me.
They have exchanged the glory of God
    for the shame of idols.*

⁸ "When the people bring their sin offerings,
    the priests get fed.
    So the priests are glad when the people sin!
⁹ 'And what the priests do, the people also do.'
    So now I will punish both priests
      and people
    for their wicked deeds.
¹⁰ They will eat and still be hungry.
    They will play the prostitute and gain
      nothing from it,
for they have deserted the LORD
¹¹   to worship other gods.

2:16 Hebrew *my baal.*   2:23a Hebrew *Lo-ruhamah*; see 1:6.   2:23b Hebrew *Lo-ammi*; see 1:9.   3:1a Or *Go and love a woman who.*   3:1b Hebrew *love their raisin cakes.*   3:2a Hebrew 15 [*shekels*] *of silver*, about 6 ounces or 171 grams in weight. 3:2b As in Greek version, which reads *a homer of barley and a wineskin full of wine*; Hebrew reads *a homer* [5 bushels or 220 liters] *of barley and a lethek* [2.5 bushels or 110 liters] *of barley.* 3:3 Or *and I will live with you.*   3:4 Hebrew *ephod*, the vest worn by the priest.   3:5 Hebrew *to David their king.*   4:4 Hebrew *Your people are like those with a complaint against the priests.*   4:7 As in Syriac version and an ancient Hebrew tradition; Masoretic Text reads *I will turn their glory into shame.*

"Wine has robbed my people
of their understanding.
¹² They ask a piece of wood for advice!
They think a stick can tell them the future!
Longing after idols
has made them foolish.
They have played the prostitute,
serving other gods and deserting their God.
¹³ They offer sacrifices to idols on the
mountaintops.
They go up into the hills to burn incense
in the pleasant shade of oaks, poplars,
and terebinth trees.

"That is why your daughters turn to
prostitution,
and your daughters-in-law commit
adultery.
¹⁴ But why should I punish them
for their prostitution and adultery?
For your men are doing the same thing,
sinning with whores and
shrine prostitutes.
O foolish people! You refuse to understand,
so you will be destroyed.

¹⁵ "Though you, Israel, are a prostitute,
may Judah not be guilty of such things.
Do not join the false worship at Gilgal
or Beth-aven,*
and do not take oaths there in
the LORD's name.
¹⁶ Israel is stubborn,
like a stubborn heifer.
So should the LORD feed her
like a lamb in a lush pasture?
¹⁷ Leave Israel* alone,
because she is married to idolatry.
¹⁸ When the rulers of Israel finish
their drinking,
off they go to find some prostitutes.
They love shame more than honor.*
¹⁹ So a mighty wind will sweep them away.
Their sacrifices to idols will bring
them shame.

THE FAILURE OF ISRAEL'S LEADERS

5 ¹ "Hear this, you priests.
Pay attention, you leaders of Israel.
Listen, you members of the royal family.
Judgment has been handed down
against you.
For you have led the people into a snare
by worshiping the idols at Mizpah
and Tabor.
² You have dug a deep pit to trap them at
Acacia Grove.*
But I will settle with you for what you
have done.
³ I know what you are like, O Ephraim.
You cannot hide yourself from me,
O Israel.

You have left me as a prostitute leaves
her husband;
you are utterly defiled.
⁴ Your deeds won't let you return to your God.
You are a prostitute through and through,
and you do not know the LORD.

⁵ "The arrogance of Israel testifies against her;
Israel and Ephraim will stumble under
their load of guilt.
Judah, too, will fall with them.
⁶ When they come with their flocks and herds
to offer sacrifices to the LORD,
they will not find him,
because he has withdrawn from them.
⁷ They have betrayed the honor of the LORD,
bearing children that are not his.
Now their false religion will devour them
along with their wealth.*

⁸ "Sound the alarm in Gibeah!
Blow the trumpet in Ramah!
Raise the battle cry in Beth-aven*!
Lead on into battle, O warriors of
Benjamin!
⁹ One thing is certain, Israel*:
On your day of punishment,
you will become a heap of rubble.

¹⁰ "The leaders of Judah have become
like thieves.*
So I will pour my anger on them
like a waterfall.
¹¹ The people of Israel will be crushed and
broken by my judgment
because they are determined to
worship idols.*
¹² I will destroy Israel as a moth consumes wool.
I will make Judah as weak as rotten wood.

¹³ "When Israel and Judah saw how sick
they were,
Israel turned to Assyria—
to the great king there—
but he could neither help nor cure them.
¹⁴ I will be like a lion to Israel,
like a strong young lion to Judah.
I will tear them to pieces!
I will carry them off,
and no one will be left to rescue them.
¹⁵ Then I will return to my place
until they admit their guilt and turn to me.

4:15 Beth-aven means "house of wickedness"; it is being used as another name for Bethel, which means "house of God." 4:17 Hebrew Ephraim, referring to the northern kingdom of Israel. 4:18 As in Greek version; the meaning of the Hebrew is uncertain. 5:2 Hebrew at Shittim. The meaning of the Hebrew for this sentence is uncertain. 5:7 The meaning of the Hebrew is uncertain. 5:8 Beth-aven means "house of wickedness"; it is being used as another name for Bethel, which means "house of God." 5:9 Hebrew Ephraim, referring to the northern kingdom of Israel; also in 5:11, 12, 13, 14. 5:10 Hebrew like those who move a boundary marker. 5:11 Or determined to follow human commands. The meaning of the Hebrew is uncertain.

For as soon as trouble comes,
  they will earnestly search for me."

A CALL TO REPENTANCE

6 ¹ "Come, let us return to the LORD.
    He has torn us to pieces;
  now he will heal us.
He has injured us;
  now he will bandage our wounds.
² In just a short time he will restore us,
  so that we may live in his presence.
³ Oh, that we might know the LORD!
  Let us press on to know him.
He will respond to us as surely as
    the arrival of dawn
  or the coming of rains in early spring."

⁴ "O Israel* and Judah,
  what should I do with you?" asks the LORD.
"For your love vanishes like the
    morning mist
  and disappears like dew in the sunlight.
⁵ I sent my prophets to cut you to pieces—
  to slaughter you with my words,
  with judgments as inescapable as light.
⁶ I want you to show love,*
  not offer sacrifices.
I want you to know me*
  more than I want burnt offerings.
⁷ But like Adam,* you broke my covenant
  and betrayed my trust.

⁸ "Gilead is a city of sinners,
  tracked with footprints of blood.
⁹ Priests form bands of robbers,
  waiting in ambush for their victims.
They murder travelers along the road
    to Shechem
  and practice every kind of sin.
¹⁰ Yes, I have seen something horrible in
    Ephraim and Israel:
My people are defiled by prostituting
  themselves with other gods!

¹¹ "O Judah, a harvest of punishment is also
    waiting for you,
  though I wanted to restore the fortunes
    of my people.

ISRAEL'S LOVE FOR WICKEDNESS

7 ¹ "I want to heal Israel, but its* sins
    are too great.
  Samaria is filled with liars.
Thieves are on the inside
  and bandits on the outside!
² Its people don't realize
  that I am watching them.
Their sinful deeds are all around them,
  and I see them all.

³ "The people entertain the king
  with their wickedness,

and the princes laugh at their lies.
⁴ They are all adulterers,
  always aflame with lust.
They are like an oven that is kept hot
  while the baker is kneading the dough.
⁵ On royal holidays, the princes get drunk
    with wine,
  carousing with those who mock them.
⁶ Their hearts are like an oven
  blazing with intrigue.
Their plot smolders* through the night,
  and in the morning it breaks out like
    a raging fire.
⁷ Burning like an oven,
  they consume their leaders.
They kill their kings one after another,
  and no one cries to me for help.

⁸ "The people of Israel mingle with godless
    foreigners,
  making themselves as worthless as a
    half-baked cake!
⁹ Worshiping foreign gods has sapped their
    strength,
  but they don't even know it.
Their hair is gray,
  but they don't realize they're old
    and weak.
¹⁰ Their arrogance testifies against them,
  yet they don't return to the LORD
    their God
  or even try to find him.

¹¹ "The people of Israel have become like silly,
    witless doves,
  first calling to Egypt, then flying to
    Assyria for help.
¹² But as they fly about,
  I will throw my net over them
and bring them down like a bird
    from the sky.
  I will punish them for all the evil they do.*

¹³ "What sorrow awaits those who have
    deserted me!
  Let them die, for they have rebelled
    against me.
I wanted to redeem them,
  but they have told lies about me.
¹⁴ They do not cry out to me with
    sincere hearts.
  Instead, they sit on their couches and wail.
They cut themselves,* begging foreign gods
    for grain and new wine,
  and they turn away from me.

6:4 Hebrew *Ephraim*, referring to the northern kingdom of Israel. 6:6a Greek version translates this Hebrew term as *to show mercy.* Compare Matt 9:13; 12:7. 6:6b Hebrew *to know God.* 6:7 Or *But at Adam.* 7:1 Hebrew *Ephraim's*, referring to the northern kingdom of Israel; similarly in 7:8, 11. 7:6 Hebrew *Their baker sleeps.* 7:12 Hebrew *I will punish them because of what was reported against them in the assembly.* 7:14 As in Greek version; Hebrew reads *They gather together.*

15 I trained them and made them strong,
  yet now they plot evil against me.
16 They look everywhere except to
    the Most High.
  They are as useless as a crooked bow.
  Their leaders will be killed by
    their enemies
  because of their insolence toward me.
  Then the people of Egypt
    will laugh at them.

ISRAEL HARVESTS THE WHIRLWIND

8 1 "Sound the alarm!
    The enemy descends like an eagle on
      the people of the LORD,
  for they have broken my covenant
    and revolted against my law.
2 Now Israel pleads with me,
  'Help us, for you are our God!'
3 But it is too late.
  The people of Israel have rejected
    what is good,
  and now their enemies will chase
    after them.
4 The people have appointed kings without
    my consent,
  and princes without my approval.
  By making idols for themselves from their
    silver and gold,
  they have brought about their own
    destruction.
5 "O Samaria, I reject this calf—
    this idol you have made.
  My fury burns against you.
    How long will you be incapable of
      innocence?
6 This calf you worship, O Israel,
    was crafted by your own hands!
  It is not God!
    Therefore, it must be smashed to bits.

7 "They have planted the wind
    and will harvest the whirlwind.
  The stalks of grain wither
    and produce nothing to eat.
  And even if there is any grain,
    foreigners will eat it.
8 The people of Israel have been
    swallowed up;
  they lie among the nations like an old
    discarded pot.
9 Like a wild donkey looking for a mate,
    they have gone up to Assyria.
  The people of Israel* have sold themselves—
    sold themselves to many lovers.
10 But though they have sold themselves
    to many allies,
  I will now gather them together
    for judgment.
  Then they will writhe
    under the burden of the great king.

11 "Israel has built many altars to
    take away sin,
  but these very altars became places for
    sinning!
12 Even though I gave them all my laws,
    they act as if those laws don't apply
      to them.
13 The people love to offer sacrifices to me,
    feasting on the meat,
  but I do not accept their sacrifices.
  I will hold my people accountable for
    their sins,
  and I will punish them.
    They will return to Egypt.
14 Israel has forgotten its Maker and built
    great palaces,
  and Judah has fortified its cities.
  Therefore, I will send down fire on
    their cities
  and will burn up their fortresses."

HOSEA ANNOUNCES ISRAEL'S PUNISHMENT

9 1 O people of Israel,
    do not rejoice as other nations do.
  For you have been unfaithful to your God,
    hiring yourselves out like prostitutes,
    worshiping other gods on every
      threshing floor.
2 So now your harvests will be too small
    to feed you.
  There will be no grapes for making new
    wine.
3 You may no longer stay here in
    the LORD's land.
  Instead, you will return to Egypt,
  and in Assyria you will eat food
    that is ceremonially unclean.
4 There you will make no offerings of wine
    to the LORD.
  None of your sacrifices there will please
    him.
  They will be unclean, like food touched by
    a person in mourning.
  All who present such sacrifices will be
    defiled.
  They may eat this food themselves,
    but they may not offer it to the LORD.
5 What then will you do on festival days?
    How will you observe the LORD's festivals?
6 Even if you escape destruction from Assyria,
    Egypt will conquer you, and Memphis*
      will bury you.
  Nettles will take over your treasures
    of silver;
    thistles will invade your ruined homes.

7 The time of Israel's punishment has come;
    the day of payment is here.
  Soon Israel will know this all too well.

8:9 Hebrew *Ephraim*, referring to the northern kingdom of Israel;
also in 8:11. 9:6 Memphis was the capital of northern Egypt.

Because of your great sin and hostility,
you say, "The prophets are crazy
and the inspired men are fools!"
[8] The prophet is a watchman over Israel*
for my God,
yet traps are laid for him wherever
he goes.
He faces hostility even in
the house of God.
[9] The things my people do are as depraved
as what they did in Gibeah long ago.
God will not forget.
He will surely punish them for their sins.

[10] The LORD says, "O Israel,
when I first found you,
it was like finding fresh grapes
in the desert.
When I saw your ancestors,
it was like seeing the first ripe figs of the
season.
But then they deserted me for Baal-peor,
giving themselves to that shameful idol.
Soon they became vile,
as vile as the god they worshiped.
[11] The glory of Israel will fly away
like a bird,
for your children will not be born
or grow in the womb
or even be conceived.
[12] Even if you do have children who grow up,
I will take them from you.
It will be a terrible day when I turn away
and leave you alone.
[13] I have watched Israel become
as beautiful as Tyre.
But now Israel will bring out her children
for slaughter."

[14] O LORD, what should I request for
your people?
I will ask for wombs that don't
give birth
and breasts that give no milk.

[15] The LORD says, "All their wickedness
began at Gilgal;
there I began to hate them.
I will drive them from my land
because of their evil actions.
I will love them no more
because all their leaders are rebels.
[16] The people of Israel are struck down.
Their roots are dried up,
and they will bear no more fruit.
And if they give birth,
I will slaughter their beloved children."

[17] My God will reject the people of Israel
because they will not listen or obey.
They will be wanderers,
homeless among the nations.

THE LORD'S JUDGMENT AGAINST ISRAEL

10 [1] How prosperous Israel is—
a luxuriant vine loaded with fruit.
But the richer the people get,
the more pagan altars they build.
The more bountiful their harvests,
the more beautiful their sacred pillars.
[2] The hearts of the people are fickle;
they are guilty and must be punished.
The LORD will break down their altars
and smash their sacred pillars.
[3] Then they will say, "We have no king
because we didn't fear the LORD.
But even if we had a king,
what could he do for us anyway?"
[4] They spout empty words
and make covenants they don't intend
to keep.
So injustice springs up among them
like poisonous weeds in a farmer's field.
[5] The people of Samaria tremble in fear
for their calf idol at Beth-aven,*
and they mourn for it.
Though its priests rejoice over it,
its glory will be stripped away.*
[6] This idol will be carted away to Assyria,
a gift to the great king there.
Ephraim will be ridiculed and Israel will
be shamed,
because its people have trusted in this idol.
[7] Samaria and its king will be cut off;
they will float away like driftwood on
an ocean wave.
[8] And the pagan shrines of Aven,*
the place of Israel's sin, will crumble.
Thorns and thistles will grow up around
their altars.
They will beg the mountains, "Bury us!"
and plead with the hills, "Fall on us!"
[9] The LORD says, "O Israel, ever since Gibeah,
there has been only sin and more sin!
You have made no progress whatsoever.
Was it not right that the wicked men of
Gibeah were attacked?
[10] Now whenever it fits my plan,
I will attack you, too.
I will call out the armies of the nations
to punish you for your multiplied sins.

[11] "Israel* is like a trained heifer treading out
the grain—
an easy job she loves.
But I will put a heavy yoke on her
tender neck.

9:8 Hebrew *Ephraim*, referring to the northern kingdom of Israel; also in 9:11, 13, 16. 10:5a *Beth-aven* means "house of wickedness"; it is being used as another name for Bethel, which means "house of God." 10:5b Or *will be taken away into exile.* 10:8 *Aven* is a reference to Beth-aven; see 10:5a and the note there. 10:11a Hebrew *Ephraim*, referring to the northern kingdom of Israel.

I will force Judah to pull the plow
and Israel* to break up the hard ground.
¹² I said, 'Plant the good seeds of righteousness,
and you will harvest a crop of love.
Plow up the hard ground of your hearts,
for now is the time to seek the LORD,
that he may come
and shower righteousness upon you.'

¹³ "But you have cultivated wickedness
and harvested a thriving crop of sins.
You have eaten the fruit of lies—
trusting in your military might,
believing that great armies
could make your nation safe.
¹⁴ Now the terrors of war
will rise among your people.
All your fortifications will fall,
just as when Shalman destroyed
Beth-arbel.
Even mothers and children
were dashed to death there.
¹⁵ You will share that fate, Bethel,
because of your great wickedness.
When the day of judgment dawns,
the king of Israel will be completely
destroyed.

THE LORD'S LOVE FOR ISRAEL

11 ¹ "When Israel was a child, I loved him,
and I called my son out of Egypt.
² But the more I called to him,
the farther he moved from me,*
offering sacrifices to the images of Baal
and burning incense to idols.
³ I myself taught Israel* how to walk,
leading him along by the hand.
But he doesn't know or even care
that it was I who took care of him.
⁴ I led Israel along
with my ropes of kindness and love.
I lifted the yoke from his neck,
and I myself stooped to feed him.

⁵ "But since my people refuse to return to me,
they will return to Egypt
and will be forced to serve Assyria.
⁶ War will swirl through their cities;
their enemies will crash through
their gates.
They will destroy them,
trapping them in their own evil plans.
⁷ For my people are determined to desert me.
They call me the Most High,
but they don't truly honor me.

⁸ "Oh, how can I give you up, Israel?
How can I let you go?
How can I destroy you like Admah
or demolish you like Zeboiim?
My heart is torn within me,
and my compassion overflows.

⁹ No, I will not unleash my fierce anger.
I will not completely destroy Israel,
for I am God and not a mere mortal.
I am the Holy One living among you,
and I will not come to destroy.
¹⁰ For someday the people will follow me.
I, the LORD, will roar like a lion.
And when I roar,
my people will return trembling
from the west.
¹¹ Like a flock of birds,
they will come from Egypt.
Trembling like doves,
they will return from Assyria.
And I will bring them home again,"
says the LORD.

CHARGES AGAINST ISRAEL AND JUDAH

¹²*Israel surrounds me with lies and deceit,
but Judah still obeys God
and is faithful to the Holy One.*

12 ¹* The people of Israel* feed on
the wind;
they chase after the east wind
all day long.
They pile up lies and violence;
they are making an alliance with Assyria
while sending olive oil to buy support
from Egypt.

² Now the LORD is bringing charges
against Judah.
He is about to punish Jacob* for all his
deceitful ways,
and pay him back for all he has done.
³ Even in the womb,
Jacob struggled with his brother;
when he became a man,
he even fought with God.
⁴ Yes, he wrestled with the angel and won.
He wept and pleaded for a blessing
from him.
There at Bethel he met God face to face,
and God spoke to him*—
⁵ the LORD God of Heaven's Armies,
the LORD is his name!
⁶ So now, come back to your God.
Act with love and justice,
and always depend on him.

10:11b Hebrew *Jacob*. The names "Jacob" and "Israel" are
often interchanged throughout the Old Testament, referring
sometimes to the individual patriarch and sometimes to the
nation.   11:2 As in Greek version; Hebrew reads *the more they
called to him, the farther he moved from them.*   11:3 Hebrew
Ephraim, referring to the northern kingdom of Israel; also in
11:8, 9, 12.   11:12a Verse 11:12 is numbered 12:1 in Hebrew text.
11:12b Or *and Judah is unruly against God, the faithful Holy One.*
The meaning of the Hebrew is uncertain.   12:1a Verses 12:1-14
are numbered 12:2-15 in Hebrew text.   12:1b Hebrew *Ephraim*,
referring to the northern kingdom of Israel; also in 12:8, 14.
12:2 *Jacob* sounds like the Hebrew word for "deceiver."
12:4 As in Greek and Syriac versions; Hebrew reads *to us.*

⁷ But no, the people are like
crafty merchants
selling from dishonest scales—
they love to cheat.
⁸ Israel boasts, "I am rich!
I've made a fortune all by myself!
No one has caught me cheating!
My record is spotless!"

⁹ "But I am the LORD your God,
who rescued you from slavery in Egypt.
And I will make you live in tents again,
as you do each year at the
Festival of Shelters.*
¹⁰ I sent my prophets to warn you
with many visions and parables."

¹¹ But the people of Gilead are worthless
because of their idol worship.
And in Gilgal, too, they sacrifice bulls;
their altars are lined up like the heaps
of stone
along the edges of a plowed field.
¹² Jacob fled to the land of Aram,
and there he* earned a wife by
tending sheep.
¹³ Then by a prophet
the LORD brought Jacob's descendants*
out of Egypt;
and by that prophet
they were protected.
¹⁴ But the people of Israel
have bitterly provoked the LORD,
so their Lord will now sentence them
to death
in payment for their sins.

THE LORD'S ANGER AGAINST ISRAEL

13 ¹ When the tribe of Ephraim spoke,
the people shook with fear,
for that tribe was important in Israel.
But the people of Ephraim sinned by
worshiping Baal
and thus sealed their destruction.
² Now they continue to sin by making
silver idols,
images shaped skillfully with
human hands.
"Sacrifice to these," they cry,
"and kiss the calf idols!"
³ Therefore, they will disappear like
the morning mist,
like dew in the morning sun,
like chaff blown by the wind,
like smoke from a chimney.

⁴ "I have been the LORD your God
ever since I brought you out of Egypt.
You must acknowledge no God but me,
for there is no other savior.
⁵ I took care of you in the wilderness,
in that dry and thirsty land.

⁶ But when you had eaten and were satisfied,
you became proud and forgot me.
⁷ So now I will attack you like a lion,
like a leopard that lurks along the road.
⁸ Like a bear whose cubs have been taken away,
I will tear out your heart.
I will devour you like a hungry lioness
and mangle you like a wild animal.

⁹ "You are about to be destroyed, O Israel—
yes, by me, your only helper.
¹⁰ Now where is* your king?
Let him save you!
Where are all the leaders of the land,
the king and the officials you demanded
of me?
¹¹ In my anger I gave you kings,
and in my fury I took them away.

¹² "Ephraim's guilt has been collected,
and his sin has been stored up for
punishment.
¹³ Pain has come to the people
like the pain of childbirth,
but they are like a child
who resists being born.
The moment of birth has arrived,
but they stay in the womb!

¹⁴ "Should I ransom them from the grave*?
Should I redeem them from death?
O death, bring on your terrors!
O grave, bring on your plagues!*
For I will not take pity on them.
¹⁵ Ephraim was the most fruitful of all
his brothers,
but the east wind—a blast from the LORD—
will arise in the desert.
All their flowing springs will run dry,
and all their wells will disappear.
Every precious thing they own
will be plundered and carried away.
¹⁶*The people of Samaria
must bear the consequences of their guilt
because they rebelled against their God.
They will be killed by an invading army,
their little ones dashed to death against
the ground,
their pregnant women ripped open
by swords."

HEALING FOR THE REPENTANT

14 ¹* Return, O Israel,
to the LORD your God,
for your sins have brought you down.

12:9 Hebrew *as in the days of your appointed feast.*
12:12 Hebrew *Israel.* See note on 10:11b.   12:13 Hebrew *brought Israel.* See note on 10:11b.   13:10 As in Greek and Syriac versions and Latin Vulgate; Hebrew reads *I will be.*   13:14a Hebrew *Sheol;* also in 13:14b.   13:14b Greek version reads *O death, where is your punishment? / O grave* [Hades]*, where is your sting?* Compare 1 Cor 15:55.   13:16 Verse 16 is numbered 14:1 in Hebrew text.   14:1 Verses 14:1-9 are numbered 14:2-10 in Hebrew text.

² Bring your confessions,
and return to the LORD.
Say to him,
"Forgive all our sins and graciously receive us,
so that we may offer you our praises.*
³ Assyria cannot save us,
nor can our warhorses.
Never again will we say to the idols
we have made,
'You are our gods.'
No, in you alone
do the orphans find mercy."

⁴ The LORD says,
"Then I will heal you of your faithlessness;
my love will know no bounds,
for my anger will be gone forever.
⁵ I will be to Israel
like a refreshing dew from heaven.
Israel will blossom like the lily;
it will send roots deep into the soil
like the cedars in Lebanon.
⁶ Its branches will spread out like beautiful
olive trees,
as fragrant as the cedars of Lebanon.

⁷ My people will again live under my shade.
They will flourish like grain and blossom
like grapevines.
They will be as fragrant as the wines of
Lebanon.

⁸ "O Israel,* stay away from idols!
I am the one who answers your prayers
and cares for you.
I am like a tree that is always green;
all your fruit comes from me."

⁹ Let those who are wise understand
these things.
Let those with discernment listen
carefully.
The paths of the LORD are true and right,
and righteous people live by walking
in them.
But in those paths sinners stumble
and fall.

14:2 As in Greek and Syriac versions, which read *may repay
the fruit of our lips*; Hebrew reads *may repay the bulls of our lips.*
14:8 Hebrew *Ephraim*, referring to the northern kingdom of Israel.

JOEL

JON HUNTZINGER, PHD

L ittle is known about the prophet Joel or the circumstances of his prophetic ministry. His name means 'Yahweh is God.' Because of the lack of historical information about the prophet or his book, Bible scholars remain divided about when to date its writing. Some date it to 835–805 BC, before the Assyrian period. Others date it sometime in the late 500s BC, after the Babylonian period ended in 539 BC. They date it to one of these two time periods because neither the Assyrians nor the Babylonians are mentioned among the nations in the book, which is unusual given that they were the two dominant powers in the ancient Near East at that time. This lack of mention means the book was likely written prior to the Assyrians or after the Babylonians. Other scholars think the book represents a lament that was part of the worship at the Temple and used to call people to be faithful to the covenant and repent of sin in view of future judgment, which is why it is so hard to date.

Scholars who date Joel to the 800s BC, prior to the Assyrians, point to a couple of sayings in the book that are found in Amos and Isaiah and say that those prophets drew upon Joel for their own messages. (Compare Joel 3:16 with Amos 1:2 and Joel 1:15 with Isaiah 13:6, for example.) Since Amos and Isaiah prophesied in the 700s BC, these scholars think that Joel must have been written prior to that time. In addition, they say that the brief references to Temple worship in the book reflect the renewal of worship begun by King Joash, who ruled 835–796 BC, and the high priest Jehoiada (2 Kings 11–12).

The book of Joel contains three major sections:

— Chapter 1 describes the approaching invasion and destruction of Judah as a locust plague coming in judgment for Judah's sin. The people are called to repent for "the day of the LORD is near."

— Chapter 2:1-27 expands upon the first section by saying the day of the Lord is not only near, but it is a day of darkness and fire. The people are called to return to the Lord because when they do, He will show compassion on them and bless them greatly.

— Chapters 2:28–3:16 forecast the judgment of the nations for "the day of the Lord will soon arrive" (3:14). Just as God will judge Judah, so also He will judge the nations. This time of judgment of the nations, however, is also a time when God will give His Spirit to His people so they will know what He is saying by being able to prophesy and see what He is doing through dreams and visions (2:28–29).

The book concludes with a vision of God's presence and provision for His people "in that day," even while their enemies experience barrenness. Thus, the book of Joel casts the life of Judah and the nations in the light of the day of the Lord. That day is near and will reveal God in all of His holiness and compassion.

1

The LORD gave this message to Joel son of Pethuel.

MOURNING OVER THE LOCUST PLAGUE

2 Hear this, you leaders of the people.
   Listen, all who live in the land.
In all your history,
   has anything like this happened before?
3 Tell your children about it in the years
      to come,
   and let your children tell their children.
   Pass the story down from generation to
      generation.
4 After the cutting locusts finished eating
      the crops,
   the swarming locusts took what was left!
After them came the hopping locusts,
   and then the stripping locusts,* too!

5 Wake up, you drunkards, and weep!
   Wail, all you wine-drinkers!
All the grapes are ruined,
   and all your sweet wine is gone.
6 A vast army of locusts* has invaded
      my land,
   a terrible army too numerous to count.
Its teeth are like lions' teeth,
   its fangs like those of a lioness.
7 It has destroyed my grapevines
   and ruined my fig trees,
   stripping their bark and destroying it,
      leaving the branches white and bare.

8 Weep like a bride dressed in black,
   mourning the death of her husband.
9 For there is no grain or wine
   to offer at the Temple of the LORD.
So the priests are in mourning.
   The ministers of the LORD are weeping.
10 The fields are ruined,
   the land is stripped bare.
The grain is destroyed,
   the grapes have shriveled,
   and the olive oil is gone.

11 Despair, all you farmers!
   Wail, all you vine growers!
Weep, because the wheat and barley—
   all the crops of the field—are ruined.
12 The grapevines have dried up,
   and the fig trees have withered.
The pomegranate trees, palm trees,
      and apple trees—
   all the fruit trees—have dried up.
   And the people's joy has dried up with
      them.

13 Dress yourselves in burlap and weep,
      you priests!
   Wail, you who serve before the altar!
Come, spend the night in burlap,
   you ministers of my God.

For there is no grain or wine
   to offer at the Temple of your God.
14 Announce a time of fasting;
   call the people together for a solemn
      meeting.
Bring the leaders
   and all the people of the land
into the Temple of the LORD your God,
   and cry out to him there.
15 The day of the LORD is near,
   the day when destruction comes from
      the Almighty.
   How terrible that day will be!

16 Our food disappears before our very eyes.
   No joyful celebrations are held in the
      house of our God.
17 The seeds die in the parched ground,
   and the grain crops fail.
The barns stand empty,
   and granaries are abandoned.
18 How the animals moan with hunger!
   The herds of cattle wander about
      confused,
because they have no pasture.
   The flocks of sheep and goats bleat
      in misery.

19 LORD, help us!
The fire has consumed the wilderness
      pastures,
   and flames have burned up all the trees.
20 Even the wild animals cry out to you
   because the streams have dried up,
   and fire has consumed the wilderness
      pastures.

LOCUSTS INVADE LIKE AN ARMY

2

1 Sound the trumpet in Jerusalem*!
   Raise the alarm on my holy mountain!
Let everyone tremble in fear
   because the day of the LORD is upon us.
2 It is a day of darkness and gloom,
   a day of thick clouds and deep blackness.
Suddenly, like dawn spreading across the
      mountains,
   a great and mighty army appears.
Nothing like it has been seen before
   or will ever be seen again.

3 Fire burns in front of them,
   and flames follow after them.
Ahead of them the land lies
   as beautiful as the Garden of Eden.
Behind them is nothing but desolation;
   not one thing escapes.
4 They look like horses;
   they charge forward like warhorses.*

1:4 The precise identification of the four kinds of locusts
mentioned here is uncertain. 1:6 Hebrew *A nation.* 2:1 Hebrew
Zion; also in 2:15, 23. 2:4 Or *like charioteers.*

⁵ Look at them as they leap along the
mountaintops.
Listen to the noise they make—like the
rumbling of chariots,
like the roar of fire sweeping across a field
of stubble,
or like a mighty army moving
into battle.

⁶ Fear grips all the people;
every face grows pale with terror.
⁷ The attackers march like warriors
and scale city walls like soldiers.
Straight forward they march,
never breaking rank.
⁸ They never jostle each other;
each moves in exactly the right position.
They break through defenses
without missing a step.
⁹ They swarm over the city
and run along its walls.
They enter all the houses,
climbing like thieves through
the windows.
¹⁰ The earth quakes as they advance,
and the heavens tremble.
The sun and moon grow dark,
and the stars no longer shine.

¹¹ The LORD is at the head of the column.
He leads them with a shout.
This is his mighty army,
and they follow his orders.
The day of the LORD is an awesome,
terrible thing.
Who can possibly survive?

A CALL TO REPENTANCE

¹² That is why the LORD says,
"Turn to me now, while there is time.
Give me your hearts.
Come with fasting, weeping,
and mourning.
¹³ Don't tear your clothing in your grief,
but tear your hearts instead."
Return to the LORD your God,
for he is merciful and compassionate,
slow to get angry and filled with
unfailing love.
He is eager to relent and not punish.
¹⁴ Who knows? Perhaps he will give you
a reprieve,
sending you a blessing instead of
this curse.
Perhaps you will be able to offer grain
and wine
to the LORD your God as before.

¹⁵ Blow the ram's horn in Jerusalem!
Announce a time of fasting;
call the people together
for a solemn meeting.

¹⁶ Gather all the people—
the elders, the children,
and even the babies.
Call the bridegroom from his quarters
and the bride from her private room.
¹⁷ Let the priests, who minister in
the LORD's presence,
stand and weep between the entry room
to the Temple and the altar.
Let them pray, "Spare your people, LORD!
Don't let your special possession become
an object of mockery.
Don't let them become a joke for
unbelieving foreigners who say,
'Has the God of Israel left them?'"

THE LORD'S PROMISE OF RESTORATION

¹⁸ Then the LORD will pity his people
and jealously guard the honor of his land.
¹⁹ The LORD will reply,
"Look! I am sending you grain and new wine
and olive oil,
enough to satisfy your needs.
You will no longer be an object of mockery
among the surrounding nations.
²⁰ I will drive away these armies from the north.
I will send them into the parched
wastelands.
Those in the front will be driven into
the Dead Sea,
and those at the rear into
the Mediterranean.*
The stench of their rotting bodies will rise
over the land."

Surely the LORD has done great things!
²¹   Don't be afraid, O land.
Be glad now and rejoice,
for the LORD has done great things.
²² Don't be afraid, you animals of the field,
for the wilderness pastures will soon
be green.
The trees will again be filled with fruit;
fig trees and grapevines will be loaded
down once more.
²³ Rejoice, you people of Jerusalem!
Rejoice in the LORD your God!
For the rain he sends demonstrates his
faithfulness.
Once more the autumn rains will come,
as well as the rains of spring.
²⁴ The threshing floors will again be piled
high with grain,
and the presses will overflow with new
wine and olive oil.

²⁵ The LORD says, "I will give you back what
you lost
to the swarming locusts,
the hopping locusts,

2:20 Hebrew *into the eastern sea, . . . into the western sea.*

the stripping locusts,
and the cutting locusts.*
It was I who sent this great destroying
army against you.
²⁶ Once again you will have all the food
you want,
and you will praise the LORD your God,
who does these miracles for you.
Never again will my people be disgraced.
²⁷ Then you will know that I am among my
people Israel,
that I am the LORD your God,
and there is no other.
Never again will my people be disgraced.

THE LORD'S PROMISE OF HIS SPIRIT

²⁸*"Then, after doing all those things,
I will pour out my Spirit upon all people.
Your sons and daughters will prophesy.
Your old men will dream dreams,
and your young men will see visions.
²⁹ In those days I will pour out my Spirit
even on servants—men and
women alike.
³⁰ And I will cause wonders in the heavens
and on the earth—
blood and fire and columns of smoke.
³¹ The sun will become dark,
and the moon will turn blood red
before that great and terrible*
day of the LORD arrives.
³² But everyone who calls on the name of
the LORD
will be saved,
for some on Mount Zion in Jerusalem
will escape,
just as the LORD has said.
These will be among the survivors
whom the LORD has called.

JUDGMENT AGAINST ENEMY NATIONS

3 ¹*"At the time of those events,"
says the LORD,
"when I restore the prosperity of Judah
and Jerusalem,
² I will gather the armies of the world
into the valley of Jehoshaphat.*
There I will judge them
for harming my people,
my special possession,
for scattering my people among the nations,
and for dividing up my land.
³ They threw dice* to decide which of
my people
would be their slaves.
They traded boys to obtain prostitutes
and sold girls for enough wine
to get drunk.

⁴ "What do you have against me, Tyre and
Sidon and you cities of Philistia? Are you trying
to take revenge on me? If you are, then watch

out! I will strike swiftly and pay you back for
everything you have done. ⁵ You have taken my
silver and gold and all my precious treasures,
and have carried them off to your pagan temples.
⁶ You have sold the people of Judah and Jerusalem
to the Greeks,* so they could take them far from
their homeland.
⁷ "But I will bring them back from all the places
to which you sold them, and I will pay you back
for everything you have done. ⁸ I will sell your
sons and daughters to the people of Judah, and
they will sell them to the people of Arabia,* a
nation far away. I, the LORD, have spoken!"

⁹ Say to the nations far and wide:
"Get ready for war!
Call out your best warriors.
Let all your fighting men advance for
the attack.
¹⁰ Hammer your plowshares into swords
and your pruning hooks into spears.
Train even your weaklings to
be warriors.
¹¹ Come quickly, all you nations everywhere.
Gather together in the valley."

And now, O LORD, call out your warriors!

¹² "Let the nations be called to arms.
Let them march to the valley of
Jehoshaphat.
There I, the LORD, will sit
to pronounce judgment on them all.
¹³ Swing the sickle,
for the harvest is ripe.*
Come, tread the grapes,
for the winepress is full.
The storage vats are overflowing
with the wickedness of these people."

¹⁴ Thousands upon thousands are waiting
in the valley of decision.
There the day of the LORD will
soon arrive.
¹⁵ The sun and moon will grow dark,
and the stars will no longer shine.
¹⁶ The LORD's voice will roar from Zion
and thunder from Jerusalem,
and the heavens and the earth
will shake.
But the LORD will be a refuge for
his people,
a strong fortress for the people
of Israel.

2:25 The precise identification of the four kinds of locusts
mentioned here is uncertain.   2:28 Verses 2:28-32 are
numbered 3:1-5 in Hebrew text.   2:31 Greek version reads
glorious.   3:1 Verses 3:1-21 are numbered 4:1-21 in Hebrew text.
3:2 *Jehoshaphat* means "the LORD judges."   3:3 Hebrew *They
cast lots.*   3:6 Hebrew *to the peoples of Javan.*   3:8 Hebrew *to the
Sabeans.*   3:13 Greek version reads *for the harvest time has come.*
Compare Mark 4:29.

BLESSINGS FOR GOD'S PEOPLE

17 "Then you will know that I, the LORD
      your God,
    live in Zion, my holy mountain.
  Jerusalem will be holy forever,
    and foreign armies will never conquer
      her again.
18 In that day the mountains will drip with
      sweet wine,
    and the hills will flow with milk.
  Water will fill the streambeds of Judah,
    and a fountain will burst forth from
      the LORD's Temple,
    watering the arid valley of acacias.*

19 But Egypt will become a wasteland
    and Edom will become a wilderness,
  because they attacked the people of Judah
    and killed innocent people in their land.

20 "But Judah will be filled with people forever,
    and Jerusalem will endure through
      all generations.
21 I will pardon my people's crimes,
    which I have not yet pardoned;
  and I, the LORD, will make my home
    in Jerusalem* with my people."

_____

3:18 Hebrew *valley of Shittim.*   **3:21** Hebrew *Zion.*

AMOS

JON HUNTZINGER, PHD

The prophet Amos is an angry man. He is angry over the exploitation of poor people (*dallim*) by Israel's royal and religious leaders. Amos was a shepherd from the southern kingdom of Judah and lived in the first half of the eighth century BC. This was a period of growth and prosperity in both the northern kingdom of Israel and the southern kingdom of Judah, but he is unhappy nonetheless.

The book of Amos has three major parts:
— Chapters 1-2 contain judgments against the surrounding nations.
— Chapters 3-6 contain messages against Israel.
— Chapters 7-9 report five visions that conclude with a proclamation of salvation—the last being a vision of the Lord himself (9:1-15).

The book of Amos is carefully crafted and contains distinctive literary elements. For example, in the first part Amos uses the expression, "have sinned again and again" (1:3, 6, 9, 13; 2:1, 4, 6) to indicate God's patience in judging the nations. In the second part, Amos uses a lawsuit form to judge Israel for her sins. A command for the people to listen begins each of the judgments (3:1; 4:1; 5:1), followed by a listing of past relationship, a call of witnesses, a formal indictment, a cross-examination, and an offer of repentance. These elements are common to this type of literature.

Amos traveled to Samaria in the north to denounce practices that confiscated the land of small farmers. Prophets did not usually speak to people outside their own communities. Almost all biblical prophets delivered their messages to the people among whom they lived. This is not so with Amos. He was so angered by the exploitation of small farmers in the northern kingdom that he went there to condemn those who were exploiting them. He used the word *pesha* (transgression) to describe this exploitation. Because of high taxes, these small farmers were forced to sell their goods, their lands, and even their family members into slavery to pay off debts. Without the land, they could not serve in the militia. They were excluded from the gates of their cities and could not participate in city decisions. They were also barred from Temple worship. Wealthy people used the money gained from these taxes to build houses of hewn stone (specially crafted stone) and for Temple offerings. Amos's message is that God does not want offerings that come from wealthy people who paid for them with the money extracted from small farmers! God wants justice (*mishpat*) and righteousness (*zedekah*) instead. He wants the people to deal fairly with each other (justice) and faithfully with His covenant (righteousness). Amos says God will not tolerate the current behaviors, and the "fat cows living in Samaria" (wealthy women who are compared to the pampered and fattened cows of Samaria) will be led away like "fish on a hook" (4:1-2), which symbolizes Assyria and its fishing industry, anticipating the Assyrian Exile that occurred in 722 BC.

1 This message was given to Amos, a shepherd from the town of Tekoa in Judah. He received this message in visions two years before the earthquake, when Uzziah was king of Judah and Jeroboam II, the son of Jehoash,* was king of Israel.

² This is what he saw and heard:

"The LORD's voice will roar from Zion
    and thunder from Jerusalem!
The lush pastures of the shepherds will
        dry up;
    the grass on Mount Carmel will wither
        and die."

GOD'S JUDGMENT ON ISRAEL'S NEIGHBORS

³ This is what the LORD says:

"The people of Damascus have sinned again
        and again,*
    and I will not let them go unpunished!
They beat down my people in Gilead
    as grain is threshed with iron sledges.
⁴ So I will send down fire on King Hazael's
        palace,
    and the fortresses of King Ben-hadad will
        be destroyed.
⁵ I will break down the gates of Damascus
    and slaughter the people in the valley
        of Aven.
I will destroy the ruler in Beth-eden,
    and the people of Aram will go as captives
        to Kir,"
    says the LORD.

⁶ This is what the LORD says:

"The people of Gaza have sinned again
        and again,
    and I will not let them go unpunished!
They sent whole villages into exile,
    selling them as slaves to Edom.
⁷ So I will send down fire on the walls of Gaza,
    and all its fortresses will be destroyed.
⁸ I will slaughter the people of Ashdod
    and destroy the king of Ashkelon.
Then I will turn to attack Ekron,
    and the few Philistines still left
        will be killed,"
    says the Sovereign LORD.

⁹ This is what the LORD says:

"The people of Tyre have sinned again
        and again,
    and I will not let them go unpunished!
They broke their treaty of brotherhood
        with Israel,
    selling whole villages as slaves to Edom.
¹⁰ So I will send down fire on the walls
        of Tyre,
    and all its fortresses will be destroyed."

¹¹ This is what the LORD says:

"The people of Edom have sinned again
        and again,
    and I will not let them go unpunished!
They chased down their relatives,
        the Israelites, with swords,
    showing them no mercy.
In their rage, they slashed them continually
    and were unrelenting in their anger.
¹² So I will send down fire on Teman,
    and the fortresses of Bozrah will be
        destroyed."

¹³ This is what the LORD says:

"The people of Ammon have sinned again
        and again,
    and I will not let them go unpunished!
When they attacked Gilead to extend
        their borders,
    they ripped open pregnant women with
        their swords.
¹⁴ So I will send down fire on the walls
        of Rabbah,
    and all its fortresses will be destroyed.
The battle will come upon them with shouts,
    like a whirlwind in a mighty storm.
¹⁵ And their king* and his princes will go into
        exile together,"
    says the LORD.

2 This is what the LORD says:

"The people of Moab have sinned again
        and again,*
    and I will not let them go unpunished!
They desecrated the bones of Edom's king,
    burning them to ashes.
² So I will send down fire on the land of Moab,
    and all the fortresses in Kerioth will
        be destroyed.
The people will fall in the noise of battle,
    as the warriors shout and
        the ram's horn sounds.
³ And I will destroy their king
    and slaughter all their princes,"
    says the LORD.

GOD'S JUDGMENT ON JUDAH AND ISRAEL

⁴ This is what the LORD says:

"The people of Judah have sinned again
        and again,
    and I will not let them go unpunished!
They have rejected the instruction of
        the LORD,
    refusing to obey his decrees.

1:1 Hebrew *Joash,* a variant spelling of Jehoash.   1:3 Hebrew *have committed three sins, even four;* also in 1:6, 9, 11, 13.   1:15 Hebrew *malcam,* possibly referring to their god Molech.   2:1 Hebrew *have committed three sins, even four;* also in 2:4, 6.

They have been led astray by the same lies
that deceived their ancestors.
⁵ So I will send down fire on Judah,
and all the fortresses of Jerusalem will
be destroyed."

⁶ This is what the LORD says:

"The people of Israel have sinned again
and again,
and I will not let them go unpunished!
They sell honorable people for silver
and poor people for a pair of sandals.
⁷ They trample helpless people in the dust
and shove the oppressed out of the way.
Both father and son sleep with
the same woman,
corrupting my holy name.
⁸ At their religious festivals,
they lounge in clothing their debtors put
up as security.
In the house of their gods,*
they drink wine bought with
unjust fines.

⁹ "But as my people watched,
I destroyed the Amorites,
though they were as tall as cedars
and as strong as oaks.
I destroyed the fruit on their branches
and dug out their roots.
¹⁰ It was I who rescued you from Egypt
and led you through the desert
for forty years,
so you could possess the land of
the Amorites.
¹¹ I chose some of your sons to be prophets
and others to be Nazirites.
Can you deny this, my people of Israel?"
asks the LORD.
¹² "But you caused the Nazirites to sin by
making them drink wine,
and you commanded the prophets,
'Shut up!'

¹³ "So I will make you groan
like a wagon loaded down with sheaves
of grain.
¹⁴ Your fastest runners will not get away.
The strongest among you will become weak.
Even mighty warriors will be unable to save
themselves.
¹⁵ The archers will not stand their ground.
The swiftest runners won't be fast enough
to escape.
Even those riding horses won't be able to
save themselves.
¹⁶ On that day the most courageous of your
fighting men
will drop their weapons and run for
their lives,"
says the LORD.

3 Listen to this message that the LORD has
spoken against you, O people of Israel—
against the entire family I rescued from Egypt:

² "From among all the families on the earth,
I have been intimate with you alone.
That is why I must punish you
for all your sins."

WITNESSES AGAINST GUILTY ISRAEL
³ Can two people walk together
without agreeing on the direction?
⁴ Does a lion ever roar in a thicket
without first finding a victim?
Does a young lion growl in its den
without first catching its prey?
⁵ Does a bird ever get caught in a trap
that has no bait?
Does a trap spring shut
when there's nothing to catch?
⁶ When the ram's horn blows a warning,
shouldn't the people be alarmed?
Does disaster come to a city
unless the LORD has planned it?

⁷ Indeed, the Sovereign LORD never
does anything
until he reveals his plans to his servants
the prophets.

⁸ The lion has roared—
so who isn't frightened?
The Sovereign LORD has spoken—
so who can refuse to proclaim
his message?
⁹ Announce this to the leaders of Philistia*
and to the great ones of Egypt:
"Take your seats now on the hills around
Samaria,
and witness the chaos and oppression
in Israel."

¹⁰ "My people have forgotten how
to do right,"
says the LORD.
"Their fortresses are filled with wealth
taken by theft and violence.
¹¹ Therefore," says the Sovereign LORD,
"an enemy is coming!
He will surround them and shatter their
defenses.
Then he will plunder all
their fortresses."

¹² This is what the LORD says:

"A shepherd who tries to rescue a sheep
from a lion's mouth
will recover only two legs or a piece of
an ear.

So it will be for the Israelites in Samaria
    lying on luxurious beds,
and for the people of Damascus reclining
    on couches.*

13 "Now listen to this, and announce it throughout all Israel,*" says the Lord, the LORD God of
Heaven's Armies.

14 "On the very day I punish Israel for its sins,
    I will destroy the pagan altars at Bethel.
The horns of the altar will be cut off
    and fall to the ground.
15 And I will destroy the beautiful homes of
    the wealthy—
    their winter mansions and their summer
      houses, too—
all their palaces filled with ivory,"
    says the LORD.

ISRAEL'S FAILURE TO LEARN

4 ¹ Listen to me, you fat cows*
    living in Samaria,
you women who oppress the poor
    and crush the needy,
and who are always calling to
    your husbands,
    "Bring us another drink!"
² The Sovereign LORD has sworn this by his
    holiness:
"The time will come when you will
    be led away
    with hooks in your noses.
Every last one of you will be dragged away
    like a fish on a hook!
³ You will be led out through the ruins of
    the wall;
    you will be thrown from your fortresses,*"
    says the LORD.

⁴ "Go ahead and offer sacrifices to the idols
    at Bethel.
    Keep on disobeying at Gilgal.
Offer sacrifices each morning,
    and bring your tithes every three days.
⁵ Present your bread made with yeast
    as an offering of thanksgiving.
Then give your extra voluntary offerings
    so you can brag about it everywhere!
This is the kind of thing you Israelites
    love to do,"
    says the Sovereign LORD.

⁶ "I brought hunger to every city
    and famine to every town.
But still you would not return to me,"
    says the LORD.

⁷ "I kept the rain from falling
    when your crops needed it the most.
I sent rain on one town
    but withheld it from another.

Rain fell on one field,
    while another field withered away.
⁸ People staggered from town to town
    looking for water,
    but there was never enough.
But still you would not return to me,"
    says the LORD.

⁹ "I struck your farms and vineyards with
    blight and mildew.
Locusts devoured all your fig and
    olive trees.
But still you would not return to me,"
    says the LORD.

¹⁰ "I sent plagues on you
    like the plagues I sent on Egypt long ago.
I killed your young men in war
    and led all your horses away.*
    The stench of death filled the air!
But still you would not return to me,"
    says the LORD.

¹¹ "I destroyed some of your cities,
    as I destroyed* Sodom and Gomorrah.
Those of you who survived
    were like charred sticks pulled
    from a fire.
But still you would not return to me,"
    says the LORD.

¹² "Therefore, I will bring upon you all the
    disasters I have announced.
Prepare to meet your God in judgment,
    you people of Israel!"

¹³ For the LORD is the one who shaped
    the mountains,
stirs up the winds, and reveals his
    thoughts to mankind.
He turns the light of dawn into darkness
    and treads on the heights of the earth.
The LORD God of Heaven's Armies is
    his name!

A CALL TO REPENTANCE

5 Listen, you people of Israel! Listen to this
  funeral song I am singing:

² "The virgin Israel has fallen,
    never to rise again!
She lies abandoned on the ground,
    with no one to help her up."

³ The Sovereign LORD says:

3:12 The meaning of the Hebrew in this sentence is uncertain.
3:13 Hebrew *the house of Jacob*. The names "Jacob" and "Israel"
are often interchanged throughout the Old Testament, referring
sometimes to the individual patriarch and sometimes to the
nation. 4:1 Hebrew *you cows of Bashan*. 4:3 Or *thrown out
toward Harmon*, possibly a reference to Mount Hermon. 4:10 Or
and slaughtered your captured horses. 4:11 Hebrew *as when God
destroyed*.

"When a city sends a thousand men
to battle,
only a hundred will return.
When a town sends a hundred,
only ten will come back alive."

⁴Now this is what the LORD says to the family of Israel:

"Come back to me and live!
⁵ Don't worship at the pagan altars at Bethel;
don't go to the shrines at Gilgal or
Beersheba.
For the people of Gilgal will be dragged off
into exile,
and the people of Bethel will be reduced
to nothing."
⁶ Come back to the LORD and live!
Otherwise, he will roar through Israel*
like a fire,
devouring you completely.
Your gods in Bethel
won't be able to quench the flames.
⁷ You twist justice, making it a bitter pill for
the oppressed.
You treat the righteous like dirt.

⁸ It is the LORD who created the stars,
the Pleiades and Orion.
He turns darkness into morning
and day into night.
He draws up water from the oceans
and pours it down as rain on the land.
The LORD is his name!
⁹ With blinding speed and power he destroys
the strong,
crushing all their defenses.

¹⁰ How you hate honest judges!
How you despise people who tell the truth!
¹¹ You trample the poor,
stealing their grain through taxes and
unfair rent.
Therefore, though you build beautiful
stone houses,
you will never live in them.
Though you plant lush vineyards,
you will never drink wine from them.
¹² For I know the vast number of your sins
and the depth of your rebellions.
You oppress good people by taking bribes
and deprive the poor of justice in
the courts.
¹³ So those who are smart keep their
mouths shut,
for it is an evil time.

¹⁴ Do what is good and run from evil
so that you may live!
Then the LORD God of Heaven's Armies will
be your helper,
just as you have claimed.

¹⁵ Hate evil and love what is good;
turn your courts into true halls of justice.
Perhaps even yet the LORD God of
Heaven's Armies
will have mercy on the remnant of his
people.*

¹⁶ Therefore, this is what the Lord, the LORD God
of Heaven's Armies, says:

"There will be crying in all the
public squares
and mourning in every street.
Call for the farmers to weep with you,
and summon professional mourners
to wail.
¹⁷ There will be wailing in every vineyard,
for I will destroy them all,"
says the LORD.

WARNING OF COMING JUDGMENT

¹⁸ What sorrow awaits you who say,
"If only the day of the LORD were here!"
You have no idea what you are wishing for.
That day will bring darkness, not light.
¹⁹ In that day you will be like a man who runs
from a lion—
only to meet a bear.
Escaping from the bear, he leans his hand
against a wall in his house—
and he's bitten by a snake.
²⁰ Yes, the day of the LORD will be dark
and hopeless,
without a ray of joy or hope.

²¹ "I hate all your show and pretense—
the hypocrisy of your religious festivals
and solemn assemblies.
²² I will not accept your burnt offerings and
grain offerings.
I won't even notice all your choice
peace offerings.
²³ Away with your noisy hymns of praise!
I will not listen to the music of
your harps.
²⁴ Instead, I want to see a mighty flood
of justice,
an endless river of righteous living.

²⁵"Was it to me you were bringing sacrifices and offerings during the forty years in the wilderness, Israel? ²⁶No, you served your pagan gods—Sakkuth your king god and Kaiwan your star god—the images you made for yourselves. ²⁷So I will send you into exile, to a land east of Damascus,*" says the LORD, whose name is the God of Heaven's Armies.

5:6 Hebrew *the house of Joseph.* 5:15 Hebrew *the remnant of Joseph.* 5:26-27 Greek version reads *No, you carried your pagan gods—the shrine of Molech, the star of your god Rephan, and the images you made for yourselves. So I will send you into exile, to a land east of Damascus.* Compare Acts 7:43.

6

¹ What sorrow awaits you who lounge in
  luxury in Jerusalem,*
  and you who feel secure in Samaria!
You are famous and popular in Israel,
  and people go to you for help.
² But go over to Calneh
  and see what happened there.
Then go to the great city of Hamath
  and down to the Philistine city of Gath.
You are no better than they were,
  and look at how they were destroyed.
³ You push away every thought of coming
  disaster,
  but your actions only bring the day of
  judgment closer.
⁴ How terrible for you who sprawl
  on ivory beds
  and lounge on your couches,
eating the meat of tender lambs from
  the flock
  and of choice calves fattened in the stall.
⁵ You sing trivial songs to the sound of
  the harp
  and fancy yourselves to be great
  musicians like David.
⁶ You drink wine by the bowlful
  and perfume yourselves with fragrant
  lotions.
  You care nothing about the ruin of
  your nation.*
⁷ Therefore, you will be the first to be led
  away as captives.
  Suddenly, all your parties will end.

⁸ The Sovereign LORD has sworn by his own
name, and this is what he, the LORD God of
Heaven's Armies, says:

"I despise the arrogance of Israel,*
  and I hate their fortresses.
I will give this city
  and everything in it to their enemies."

⁹ (If there are ten men left in one house, they will
all die. ¹⁰ And when a relative who is responsible
to dispose of the dead* goes into the house to
carry out the bodies, he will ask the last survivor, "Is anyone else with you?" When the person
begins to swear, "No, by . . . ," he will interrupt
and say, "Stop! Don't even mention the name
of the LORD.")

¹¹ When the LORD gives the command,
  homes both great and small will be
  smashed to pieces.

¹² Can horses gallop over boulders?
  Can oxen be used to plow them?
But that's how foolish you are when you
  turn justice into poison
  and the sweet fruit of righteousness into
  bitterness.

¹³ And you brag about your conquest of
  Lo-debar.*
  You boast, "Didn't we take Karnaim*
  by our own strength?"

¹⁴ "O people of Israel, I am about to bring an
  enemy nation against you,"
  says the LORD God of Heaven's Armies.
"They will oppress you throughout
  your land—
  from Lebo-hamath in the north
  to the Arabah Valley in the south."

A VISION OF LOCUSTS

7

The Sovereign LORD showed me a vision. I
saw him preparing to send a vast swarm of
locusts over the land. This was after the king's
share had been harvested from the fields and as
the main crop was coming up. ² In my vision the
locusts ate every green plant in sight. Then I said,
"O Sovereign LORD, please forgive us or we will
not survive, for Israel* is so small."

³ So the LORD relented from this plan. "I will
not do it," he said.

A VISION OF FIRE

⁴ Then the Sovereign LORD showed me another
vision. I saw him preparing to punish his people
with a great fire. The fire had burned up the
depths of the sea and was devouring the entire
land. ⁵ Then I said, "O Sovereign LORD, please
stop or we will not survive, for Israel is so small."

⁶ Then the LORD relented from this plan, too. "I
will not do that either," said the Sovereign LORD.

A VISION OF A PLUMB LINE

⁷ Then he showed me another vision. I saw the
Lord standing beside a wall that had been built
using a plumb line. He was using a plumb line
to see if it was still straight. ⁸ And the LORD said
to me, "Amos, what do you see?"

I answered, "A plumb line."

And the Lord replied, "I will test my people
with this plumb line. I will no longer ignore all
their sins. ⁹ The pagan shrines of your ancestors*
will be ruined, and the temples of Israel will be
destroyed; I will bring the dynasty of King Jeroboam to a sudden end."

AMOS AND AMAZIAH

¹⁰ Then Amaziah, the priest of Bethel, sent a
message to Jeroboam, king of Israel: "Amos is
hatching a plot against you right here on your
very doorstep! What he is saying is intolerable.
¹¹ He is saying, 'Jeroboam will soon be killed, and
the people of Israel will be sent away into exile.'"

6:1 Hebrew *in Zion.* 6:6 Hebrew *of Joseph.* 6:8 Hebrew *Jacob.*
See note on 3:13. 6:10 Or *to burn the dead.* The meaning of
the Hebrew is uncertain. 6:13a *Lo-debar* means "nothing."
6:13b *Karnaim* means "horns," a term that symbolizes strength.
7:2 Hebrew *Jacob;* also in 7:5. See note on 3:13. 7:9 Hebrew *of
Isaac.*

¹²Then Amaziah sent orders to Amos: "Get out of here, you prophet! Go on back to the land of Judah, and earn your living by prophesying there! ¹³Don't bother us with your prophecies here in Bethel. This is the king's sanctuary and the national place of worship!"

¹⁴But Amos replied, "I'm not a professional prophet, and I was never trained to be one.* I'm just a shepherd, and I take care of sycamore-fig trees. ¹⁵But the LORD called me away from my flock and told me, 'Go and prophesy to my people in Israel.' ¹⁶Now then, listen to this message from the LORD:

"You say,
'Don't prophesy against Israel.
  Stop preaching against my people.*'
¹⁷But this is what the LORD says:
'Your wife will become a prostitute in
    this city,
  and your sons and daughters will be killed.
Your land will be divided up,
  and you yourself will die in a foreign land.
And the people of Israel will certainly
    become captives in exile,
  far from their homeland.'"

A VISION OF RIPE FRUIT

8 Then the Sovereign LORD showed me another vision. In it I saw a basket filled with ripe fruit. ²"What do you see, Amos?" he asked.

I replied, "A basket full of ripe fruit."

Then the LORD said, "Like this fruit, Israel is ripe for punishment! I will not delay their punishment again. ³In that day the singing in the temple will turn to wailing. Dead bodies will be scattered everywhere. They will be carried out of the city in silence. I, the Sovereign LORD, have spoken!"

⁴Listen to this, you who rob the poor
  and trample down the needy!
⁵You can't wait for the Sabbath day to be over
  and the religious festivals to end
  so you can get back to cheating the helpless.
You measure out grain with dishonest
    measures
  and cheat the buyer with dishonest scales.*
⁶And you mix the grain you sell
  with chaff swept from the floor.
Then you enslave poor people
  for one piece of silver or a pair of sandals.

⁷Now the LORD has sworn this oath
  by his own name, the Pride of Israel*:
"I will never forget
  the wicked things you have done!
⁸The earth will tremble for your deeds,
  and everyone will mourn.
The ground will rise like the Nile River
    at floodtime;
  it will heave up, then sink again.

⁹"In that day," says the Sovereign LORD,
"I will make the sun go down at noon
  and darken the earth while it is still day.
¹⁰I will turn your celebrations into times
    of mourning
  and your singing into weeping.
You will wear funeral clothes
  and shave your heads to show your
    sorrow—
as if your only son had died.
  How very bitter that day will be!

¹¹"The time is surely coming," says the
    Sovereign LORD,
"when I will send a famine on the land—
not a famine of bread or water
  but of hearing the words of the LORD.
¹²People will stagger from sea to sea
  and wander from border to border*
searching for the word of the LORD,
  but they will not find it.
¹³Beautiful girls and strong young men
  will grow faint in that day,
  thirsting for the LORD's word.
¹⁴And those who swear by the shameful idols
    of Samaria—
who take oaths in the name of the god
    of Dan
  and make vows in the name of the god
    of Beersheba*—
they will all fall down,
  never to rise again."

A VISION OF GOD AT THE ALTAR

9 Then I saw a vision of the Lord standing beside the altar. He said,

"Strike the tops of the Temple columns,
  so that the foundation will shake.
Bring down the roof
  on the heads of the people below.
I will kill with the sword those who survive.
  No one will escape!

²"Even if they dig down to the place of
    the dead,*
  I will reach down and pull them up.
Even if they climb up into the heavens,
  I will bring them down.
³Even if they hide at the very top of
    Mount Carmel,
  I will search them out and capture them.
Even if they hide at the bottom of
    the ocean,
  I will send the sea serpent after them to
    bite them.

7:14 Or I'm not a prophet nor the son of a prophet.   7:16 Hebrew against the house of Isaac.   8:5 Hebrew You make the ephah [a unit for measuring grain] small and the shekel [a unit of weight] great, and you deal falsely by using deceitful balances.   8:7 Hebrew the pride of Jacob. See note on 3:13.   8:12 Hebrew from north to east.   8:14 Hebrew the way of Beersheba.   9:2 Hebrew to Sheol.

4 Even if their enemies drive them
   into exile,
   I will command the sword to kill
   them there.
I am determined to bring disaster upon them
   and not to help them."

5 The Lord, the LORD of Heaven's Armies,
   touches the land and it melts,
   and all its people mourn.
   The ground rises like the Nile River
      at floodtime,
   and then it sinks again.
6 The LORD's home reaches up to the heavens,
   while its foundation is on the earth.
He draws up water from the oceans
   and pours it down as rain on the land.
The LORD is his name!

7 "Are you Israelites more important to me
   than the Ethiopians?*" asks the LORD.
"I brought Israel out of Egypt,
   but I also brought the Philistines
      from Crete*
   and led the Arameans out of Kir.

8 "I, the Sovereign LORD,
   am watching this sinful nation of Israel.
I will destroy it
   from the face of the earth.
But I will never completely destroy the
      family of Israel,*"
says the LORD.
9 "For I will give the command
   and will shake Israel along with
      the other nations
as grain is shaken in a sieve,
   yet not one true kernel will be lost.
10 But all the sinners will die by the sword—
   all those who say, 'Nothing bad will
      happen to us.'

A PROMISE OF RESTORATION

11 "In that day I will restore the fallen house*
   of David.
I will repair its damaged walls.
From the ruins I will rebuild it
   and restore its former glory.
12 And Israel will possess what is left of Edom
   and all the nations I have called to
      be mine.*"

GOD'S DWELLING AT YOUR HOUSE
Amos 9:11   JACK HAYFORD

God can be worshipped anywhere a believer
creates an atmosphere of praise and worship in spirit and in truth. As a priest in your
home, you entertain the presence of the Lord.
Focus your attention on preparing a place
where God can dwell in your home. Fill your
tabernacle with the breath of praise.

God is calling you to integrate the power
of the Spirit, the truth of the Word, and the
love of the Lord Jesus into your house. The
challenge is not only to become a person of
worship but also a person who welcomes the
presence and glory of God into your home.
If you feel discouraged by past failures, take
heart because there is hope. God will raise
up the tabernacle in your house as you follow
His directives. As He promised through the
prophet Amos, God will rebuild the ruins and
restore His glory in you.

The LORD has spoken,
   and he will do these things.

13 "The time will come," says the LORD,
"when the grain and grapes will
      grow faster
   than they can be harvested.
Then the terraced vineyards on the hills
   of Israel
   will drip with sweet wine!
14 I will bring my exiled people of Israel
   back from distant lands,
and they will rebuild their ruined cities
   and live in them again.
They will plant vineyards and gardens;
   they will eat their crops and drink
      their wine.
15 I will firmly plant them there
   in their own land.
They will never again be uprooted
   from the land I have given them,"
   says the LORD your God.

9:7a Hebrew *the Cushites?* 9:7b Hebrew *Caphtor.* 9:8 Hebrew
the house of Jacob. See note on 3:13. 9:11a Or *kingdom;* Hebrew
reads *tent.* 9:11b-12 Greek version reads *and restore its former
glory, / so that the rest of humanity, including the Gentiles— / all those
I have called to be mine—might seek me.* Compare Acts 15:16-17.

OBADIAH

JON HUNTZINGER, PHD

O badiah, whose name means 'Servant of Yahweh,' prophesied around 587 BC, when the Babylonians overran Judah and destroyed the city of Jerusalem. The book of Obadiah is the shortest in the Old Testament with only 21 verses. In his denunciation of the nation of Edom, Obadiah may be grouped with Isaiah (34:5-15), Jeremiah (49:7-22), Ezekiel (25:12-14), Amos (1:11-12), and Malachi (1:2-5). Edom was located to the south and east of the Dead Sea. In the Old Testament, Edom is also known as Seir, meaning 'hairy,' because of its shrub lands. The people who lived there were the descendants of Esau, the brother of Jacob. The Edomites had taken advantage of the Babylonian destruction of Jerusalem to invade Judah at that time. Their invasion of Judah was only the most recent conflict over the centuries. After the Exodus, for example, the Edomites had denied the Israelites passage through their land into Canaan (Numbers 20:14-21), and during the unified kingdom of David and Solomon, they had fought against Israel (2 Samuel 8:13-14; 1 Kings 9:26-28; 11:14-22).

Obadiah's short prophecy reveals the outrage he feels toward the Edomites for their violence against Judah. In his view, God is the God of all people, including the people of Edom, and He will judge them for their exploitation of His people. His view is informed by God's promise to Abraham that He would bless those who blessed Abraham's descendants and curse those who cursed them (Genesis 12:2-3). Since Edom had historically battled (or cursed) Abraham's descendants in the people of Judah and had taken advantage of their most recent struggle with the Babylonians, the nation would be judged (cursed) by God in return as He had said He would do to the enemies of His people.

This is the vision that the Sovereign LORD revealed to Obadiah concerning the land of Edom.

EDOM'S JUDGMENT ANNOUNCED

We have heard a message from the LORD
    that an ambassador was sent to the
        nations to say,
"Get ready, everyone!
    Let's assemble our armies and
        attack Edom!"

2 The LORD says to Edom,
"I will cut you down to size among the
        nations;
    you will be greatly despised.
3 You have been deceived by your own pride
    because you live in a rock fortress
    and make your home high in the
        mountains.
'Who can ever reach us way up here?'
    you ask boastfully.
4 But even if you soar as high as eagles
    and build your nest among the stars,
I will bring you crashing down,"
    says the LORD.

5 "If thieves came at night and robbed you
    (what a disaster awaits you!),
    they would not take everything.
Those who harvest grapes
    always leave a few for the poor.
But your enemies will wipe you out
        completely!
6 Every nook and cranny of Edom*
    will be searched and looted.
    Every treasure will be found and taken.

7 "All your allies will turn against you.
    They will help to chase you from
        your land.
They will promise you peace
    while plotting to deceive and destroy you.
Your trusted friends will set traps for you,
    and you won't even know about it.
8 At that time not a single wise person
    will be left in the whole land of Edom,"
    says the LORD.
"For on the mountains of Edom
    I will destroy everyone who has
        understanding.
9 The mightiest warriors of Teman
    will be terrified,
and everyone on the mountains of Edom
    will be cut down in the slaughter.

REASONS FOR EDOM'S PUNISHMENT

10 "Because of the violence you did
    to your close relatives in Israel,*
you will be filled with shame
    and destroyed forever.
11 When they were invaded,
    you stood aloof, refusing to help them.

Foreign invaders carried off their wealth
    and cast lots to divide up Jerusalem,
    but you acted like one of Israel's
        enemies.

12 "You should not have gloated
    when they exiled your relatives to
        distant lands.
You should not have rejoiced
    when the people of Judah suffered such
        misfortune.
You should not have spoken arrogantly
    in that terrible time of trouble.
13 You should not have plundered the land
        of Israel
    when they were suffering such calamity.
You should not have gloated over their
        destruction
    when they were suffering such calamity.
You should not have seized their wealth
    when they were suffering such calamity.
14 You should not have stood at
        the crossroads,
    killing those who tried to escape.
You should not have captured
        the survivors
    and handed them over in their terrible
        time of trouble.

EDOM DESTROYED, ISRAEL RESTORED

15 "The day is near when I, the LORD,
    will judge all godless nations!
As you have done to Israel,
    so it will be done to you.
All your evil deeds
    will fall back on your own heads.
16 Just as you swallowed up my people
    on my holy mountain,
so you and the surrounding nations
    will swallow the punishment I pour out
        on you.
Yes, all you nations will drink and stagger
    and disappear from history.

17 "But Jerusalem* will become a refuge for
        those who escape;
    it will be a holy place.
And the people of Israel* will come back
    to reclaim their inheritance.
18 The people of Israel will be a raging fire,
    and Edom a field of dry stubble.
The descendants of Joseph will be a flame
    roaring across the field, devouring
        everything.
There will be no survivors in Edom.
    I, the LORD, have spoken!

6 Hebrew *Esau;* also in 8b, 9, 18, 19, 21.   10 Hebrew *your brother Jacob.* The names "Jacob" and "Israel" are often interchanged throughout the Old Testament, referring sometimes to the individual patriarch and sometimes to the nation.   17a Hebrew *Mount Zion.*   17b Hebrew *house of Jacob;* also in 18. See note on 10.

¹⁹ "Then my people living in the Negev
   will occupy the mountains of Edom.
Those living in the foothills of Judah*
   will possess the Philistine plains
and take over the fields of Ephraim
   and Samaria.
And the people of Benjamin
   will occupy the land of Gilead.
²⁰ The exiles of Israel will return to their land
   and occupy the Phoenician coast as far
   north as Zarephath.

The captives from Jerusalem exiled in
   the north*
will return home and resettle the towns
   of the Negev.
²¹ Those who have been rescued* will go up to*
   Mount Zion in Jerusalem
to rule over the mountains of Edom.
And the LORD himself will be king!"

---

19 Hebrew *the Shephelah*. **20** Hebrew *in Sepharad*. **21a** As in Greek and Syriac versions; Hebrew reads *Rescuers*. **21b** Or *from*.

JONAH

The story of Jonah and the great fish is one of the best known in the Bible, along with Noah's boat (ark), David and Goliath, and Daniel in the lions' den. The book is unusual because, unlike other prophetic books that preserve the messages of the prophets, this one preserves the story of the prophet himself rather than the details of his message.

Jonah lived during the reign of King Jeroboam II (786-746 BC) and was from the town of Gath-hepher in the northern kingdom of Israel (2 Kings 14:25), which would be overrun by the Assyrians less than a generation later in 722 BC. This historical background is important for understanding Jonah's initial refusal to go to Nineveh, the capital of Assyria, as described in the book.

Jonah boards a ship heading away from Nineveh when God commands him to preach repentance to the people there. He refuses to go to Nineveh because he knows the people are hard and cruel. God then sends a storm that threatens to sink the ship until the sailors throw him overboard, where a large fish swallows him and spits him onto the land after three days. Jonah then obeys God and goes to the capital, where he warns the people of God's judgment unless they repent of their sin. When the people respond with sackcloth and ashes, God saves them, to Jonah's unhappiness. At that time, Nineveh was one of the largest cities in the ancient Near East with 120,000 people, according to the book, making the salvation of its people extraordinary. In response to Jonah's displeasure at the conclusion of the story, God asks His prophet, "Shouldn't I feel sorry for such a great city?" (4:11).

A major question that readers have about the story concerns the historicity of the events it describes. Did all of these events really happen? Did God really send a storm? Did a large fish swallow Jonah and then expel him onto dry land? Some scholars think that the story is fiction and that ancient readers were more susceptible than modern ones to believe such accounts as historical. Of course, ancient readers were no more prone to reading fictitious stories as real history than people today and would have asked the same questions. The writer of the story would have known about such questions, too, as would those in the community who preserved the story. This means that when they upheld the story and added it to the other prophetic books, they did so because they were convinced that it was just as historical as those books, despite the incredible nature of the miracles it reports. Moreover, the fact that Jesus and His disciples (Matthew 12:38-42; 16:1-4) accepted the story as historical points to its authenticity. The book of Jonah is a true story.

The story of Jonah is the story of God's great compassion for all people and all nations, including the idolatrous people of Nineveh. Should God not feel sorry for the Ninevites? (4:11). Moreover, it depicts God's will and word as irresistible—they cannot be stopped. Because He has determined that the people of Nineveh should hear His word and be given a chance to repent, nothing will prevent that goal from being fulfilled. He will even use a great fish to do so. And when the people hear God's word, they do repent (3:6-10).

JONAH RUNS FROM THE LORD

1 The LORD gave this message to Jonah son of Amittai: ²"Get up and go to the great city of Nineveh. Announce my judgment against it because I have seen how wicked its people are."

³But Jonah got up and went in the opposite direction to get away from the LORD. He went down to the port of Joppa, where he found a ship leaving for Tarshish. He bought a ticket and went on board, hoping to escape from the LORD by sailing to Tarshish.

⁴But the LORD hurled a powerful wind over the sea, causing a violent storm that threatened to break the ship apart. ⁵Fearing for their lives, the desperate sailors shouted to their gods for help and threw the cargo overboard to lighten the ship.

But all this time Jonah was sound asleep down in the hold. ⁶So the captain went down after him. "How can you sleep at a time like this?" he shouted. "Get up and pray to your god! Maybe he will pay attention to us and spare our lives."

⁷Then the crew cast lots to see which of them had offended the gods and caused the terrible storm. When they did this, the lots identified Jonah as the culprit. ⁸"Why has this awful storm come down on us?" they demanded. "Who are you? What is your line of work? What country are you from? What is your nationality?"

⁹Jonah answered, "I am a Hebrew, and I worship the LORD, the God of heaven, who made the sea and the land."

¹⁰The sailors were terrified when they heard this, for he had already told them he was running away from the LORD. "Oh, why did you do it?" they groaned. ¹¹And since the storm was getting worse all the time, they asked him, "What should we do to you to stop this storm?"

¹²"Throw me into the sea," Jonah said, "and it will become calm again. I know that this terrible storm is all my fault."

¹³Instead, the sailors rowed even harder to get the ship to the land. But the stormy sea was too violent for them, and they couldn't make it. ¹⁴Then they cried out to the LORD, Jonah's God. "O LORD," they pleaded, "don't make us die for this man's sin. And don't hold us responsible for his death. O LORD, you have sent this storm upon him for your own good reasons."

¹⁵Then the sailors picked Jonah up and threw him into the raging sea, and the storm stopped at once! ¹⁶The sailors were awestruck by the LORD's great power, and they offered him a sacrifice and vowed to serve him.

¹⁷*Now the LORD had arranged for a great fish to swallow Jonah. And Jonah was inside the fish for three days and three nights.

JONAH'S PRAYER

2 ¹*Then Jonah prayed to the LORD his God from inside the fish. ²He said,

"I cried out to the LORD in my great trouble,
    and he answered me.
I called to you from the land of the dead,*
    and LORD, you heard me!
³ You threw me into the ocean depths,
    and I sank down to the heart of the sea.
The mighty waters engulfed me;
    I was buried beneath your wild and
        stormy waves.
⁴ Then I said, 'O LORD, you have driven me
        from your presence.
    Yet I will look once more toward your
        holy Temple.'

⁵ "I sank beneath the waves,
    and the waters closed over me.
    Seaweed wrapped itself around my head.
⁶ I sank down to the very roots of the
        mountains.
    I was imprisoned in the earth,
        whose gates lock shut forever.
But you, O LORD my God,
    snatched me from the jaws of death!
⁷ As my life was slipping away,
    I remembered the LORD.
And my earnest prayer went out to you
    in your holy Temple.
⁸ Those who worship false gods
    turn their backs on all God's mercies.
⁹ But I will offer sacrifices to you with
        songs of praise,
    and I will fulfill all my vows.
For my salvation comes from
    the LORD alone."

¹⁰Then the LORD ordered the fish to spit Jonah out onto the beach.

JONAH GOES TO NINEVEH

3 Then the LORD spoke to Jonah a second time: ²"Get up and go to the great city of Nineveh, and deliver the message I have given you."

³This time Jonah obeyed the LORD's command and went to Nineveh, a city so large that it took three days to see it all.* ⁴On the day Jonah entered the city, he shouted to the crowds: "Forty days from now Nineveh will be destroyed!" ⁵The people of Nineveh believed God's message, and from the greatest to the least, they declared a fast and put on burlap to show their sorrow.

⁶When the king of Nineveh heard what Jonah was saying, he stepped down from his throne and took off his royal robes. He dressed himself in burlap and sat on a heap of ashes. ⁷Then the

---

1:17 Verse 1:17 is numbered 2:1 in Hebrew text.   2:1 Verses 2:1-10
are numbered 2:2-11 in Hebrew text.   2:2 Hebrew *from Sheol.*
3:3 Hebrew *a great city to God, of three days' journey.*

king and his nobles sent this decree throughout the city:

"No one, not even the animals from your herds and flocks, may eat or drink anything at all. ⁸ People and animals alike must wear garments of mourning, and everyone must pray earnestly to God. They must turn from their evil ways and stop all their violence. ⁹ Who can tell? Perhaps even yet God will change his mind and hold back his fierce anger from destroying us."

¹⁰ When God saw what they had done and how they had put a stop to their evil ways, he changed his mind and did not carry out the destruction he had threatened.

JONAH'S ANGER AT THE LORD'S MERCY

4 This change of plans greatly upset Jonah, and he became very angry. ² So he complained to the LORD about it: "Didn't I say before I left home that you would do this, LORD? That is why I ran away to Tarshish! I knew that you are a merciful and compassionate God, slow to get angry and filled with unfailing love. You are eager to turn back from destroying people. ³ Just kill me now, LORD! I'd rather be dead than alive if what I predicted will not happen."

⁴ The LORD replied, "Is it right for you to be angry about this?"

⁵ Then Jonah went out to the east side of the city and made a shelter to sit under as he waited to see what would happen to the city. ⁶ And the LORD God arranged for a leafy plant to grow there, and soon it spread its broad leaves over Jonah's head, shading him from the sun. This eased his discomfort, and Jonah was very grateful for the plant.

⁷ But God also arranged for a worm! The next morning at dawn the worm ate through the stem of the plant so that it withered away. ⁸ And as the sun grew hot, God arranged for a scorching east wind to blow on Jonah. The sun beat down on his head until he grew faint and wished to die. "Death is certainly better than living like this!" he exclaimed.

⁹ Then God said to Jonah, "Is it right for you to be angry because the plant died?"

"Yes," Jonah retorted, "even angry enough to die!"

¹⁰ Then the LORD said, "You feel sorry about the plant, though you did nothing to put it there. It came quickly and died quickly. ¹¹ But Nineveh has more than 120,000 people living in spiritual darkness,* not to mention all the animals. Shouldn't I feel sorry for such a great city?"

_____
4:11 Hebrew *people who don't know their right hand from their left.*

MICAH

JON HUNTZINGER, PHD

The name *Micah* is an abbreviation of the Hebrew word that means 'Who is like Yahweh?' The prophet lived in the town of Moresheth, which is about 25 miles from Jerusalem. Micah also may have been a small farmer like the prophet Amos. He attributes his strength to proclaim God's judgment against the people of Israel and Judah to the Spirit of God and the sense of justice and power that the Spirit gives (3:8).

Micah is identified with the Judean kings Jotham (750-732 BC), Ahaz (732-716 BC), and Hezekiah (715-686 BC). He prophesied from the latter part of Jotham's reign to the beginning years of Hezekiah's. Micah was identified by Jeremiah's supporters (about 100 years later) when they defended Jeremiah's messages of judgment against Judah and Jerusalem by recalling Micah's oracles against Israel and Judah during his time (Jeremiah 26:16-19). The threat to Jerusalem (Micah 3:12) and the description of Assyria as a major enemy (5:5-6) point to the period 722-701 BC (when the Assyrian king threatened Jerusalem but could not overthrow the city) for the prime years of his ministry, during which he spoke God's oracles.

Micah has been described as "the doomsayer prophet" because the oracles he delivers switch back and forth between doom and hope. He begins (1:2-2:11) by announcing the impending destruction of Samaria for idolatry and oppression (doom) and then declares (2:12-13) God will come and lead His people like a shepherd (hope). Micah continues (3:1-12) by denouncing the rulers and prophets of that time for leading the people astray (doom), only to say (4:1-5:15) that "in the last days" God will teach the people His laws, and they along with Zion will be restored by a king from Bethlehem (hope). Finally, he issues a courtroom-like indictment (6:1-7:7) against the people for injustice (doom), which he follows by saying (7:8-20) that despite sin God will show compassion and faithfulness (hope).

Many people best remember Micah for his prophecy of a ruler who will come from Bethlehem and shepherd God's flock (5:2-5), which Matthew quotes and relates to the birth of Jesus (Matthew 2:5-6).

Micah is also known for his definition of goodness:

> to do what is right, to love mercy,
> and to walk humbly with your God (6:8).

Like Amos, who condemns those who take advantage of others, causing them to lose their homes, farms, and possessions (see the introduction to the book of Amos), Micah is upset by unjust practices that are causing people to lose their fields and houses (2:1-2). For this reason, he condemns bribery and the influence of money among administrative and religious leaders (3:9-11; 6:10-12; 7:3). The Spirit of God that fills Micah revolts against injustice and desires for justice to be done among His people (3:8).

1 The LORD gave this message to Micah of Moresheth during the years when Jotham, Ahaz, and Hezekiah were kings of Judah. The visions he saw concerned both Samaria and Jerusalem.

GRIEF OVER SAMARIA AND JERUSALEM

2 Attention! Let all the people of the world listen!
    Let the earth and everything in it hear.
The Sovereign LORD is making accusations against you;
    the Lord speaks from his holy Temple.
3 Look! The LORD is coming!
    He leaves his throne in heaven
    and tramples the heights of the earth.
4 The mountains melt beneath his feet
    and flow into the valleys
like wax in a fire,
    like water pouring down a hill.
5 And why is this happening?
    Because of the rebellion of Israel*—
    yes, the sins of the whole nation.
Who is to blame for Israel's rebellion?
    Samaria, its capital city!
Where is the center of idolatry in Judah?
    In Jerusalem, its capital!

6 "So I, the LORD, will make the city of Samaria
    a heap of ruins.
Her streets will be plowed up
    for planting vineyards.
I will roll the stones of her walls into the valley below,
    exposing her foundations.
7 All her carved images will be smashed.
    All her sacred treasures will be burned.
These things were bought with the money
    earned by her prostitution,
and they will now be carried away
    to pay prostitutes elsewhere."

8 Therefore, I will mourn and lament.
    I will walk around barefoot and naked.
I will howl like a jackal
    and moan like an owl.
9 For my people's wound
    is too deep to heal.
It has reached into Judah,
    even to the gates of Jerusalem.

10 Don't tell our enemies in Gath*;
    don't weep at all.
You people in Beth-leaphrah,*
    roll in the dust to show your despair.
11 You people in Shaphir,*
    go as captives into exile—naked and ashamed.
The people of Zaanan*
    dare not come outside their walls.

The people of Beth-ezel* mourn,
    for their house has no support.
12 The people of Maroth* anxiously wait for relief,
    but only bitterness awaits them
as the LORD's judgment reaches
    even to the gates of Jerusalem.

13 Harness your chariot horses and flee,
    you people of Lachish.*
You were the first city in Judah
    to follow Israel in her rebellion,
    and you led Jerusalem* into sin.
14 Send farewell gifts to Moresheth-gath*;
    there is no hope of saving it.
The town of Aczib*
    has deceived the kings of Israel.
15 O people of Mareshah,*
    I will bring a conqueror to capture your town.
And the leaders* of Israel
    will go to Adullam.

16 Oh, people of Judah, shave your heads in sorrow,
    for the children you love will be snatched away.
Make yourselves as bald as a vulture,
    for your little ones will be exiled to distant lands.

JUDGMENT AGAINST WEALTHY OPPRESSORS

2 What sorrow awaits you who lie awake at night,
    thinking up evil plans.
You rise at dawn and hurry to carry them out,
    simply because you have the power to do so.
2 When you want a piece of land,
    you find a way to seize it.
When you want someone's house,
    you take it by fraud and violence.
You cheat a man of his property,
    stealing his family's inheritance.

3 But this is what the LORD says:
"I will reward your evil with evil;
    you won't be able to pull your neck out of the noose.
You will no longer walk around proudly,
    for it will be a terrible time."

1:5 Hebrew *Jacob*; also in 1:5b. The names "Jacob" and "Israel" are often interchanged throughout the Old Testament, referring sometimes to the individual patriarch and sometimes to the nation. 1:10a *Gath* sounds like the Hebrew term for "tell." 1:10b *Beth-leaphrah* means "house of dust." 1:11a *Shaphir* means "pleasant." 1:11b *Zaanan* sounds like the Hebrew term for "come out." 1:11c *Beth-ezel* means "adjoining house." 1:12 *Maroth* sounds like the Hebrew term for "bitter." 1:13a *Lachish* sounds like the Hebrew term for "team of horses." 1:13b Hebrew *the daughter of Zion*. 1:14a *Moresheth* sounds like the Hebrew term for "gift" or "dowry." 1:14b *Aczib* means "deception." 1:15a *Mareshah* sounds like the Hebrew term for "conqueror." 1:15b Hebrew *the glory*.

⁴ In that day your enemies will make fun
of you
by singing this song of despair about you:
"We are finished,
completely ruined!
God has confiscated our land,
taking it from us.
He has given our fields
to those who betrayed us.*"
⁵ Others will set your boundaries then,
and the LORD's people will have no say
in how the land is divided.

TRUE AND FALSE PROPHETS

⁶ "Don't say such things,"
the people respond.*
"Don't prophesy like that.
Such disasters will never come our way!"

⁷ Should you talk that way,
O family of Israel?*
Will the LORD's Spirit have patience with
such behavior?
If you would do what is right,
you would find my words comforting.
⁸ Yet to this very hour
my people rise against me
like an enemy!
You steal the shirts right off the backs
of those who trusted you,
making them as ragged as men
returning from battle.
⁹ You have evicted women from their
pleasant homes
and forever stripped their children of all
that God would give them.
¹⁰ Up! Begone!
This is no longer your land and home,
for you have filled it with sin
and ruined it completely.

¹¹ Suppose a prophet full of lies would say
to you,
"I'll preach to you the joys of wine
and alcohol!"
That's just the kind of prophet you
would like!

HOPE FOR RESTORATION

¹² "Someday, O Israel, I will gather you;
I will gather the remnant who are left.
I will bring you together again like sheep
in a pen,
like a flock in its pasture.
Yes, your land will again
be filled with noisy crowds!
¹³ Your leader will break out
and lead you out of exile,
out through the gates of the enemy cities,
back to your own land.
Your king will lead you;
the LORD himself will guide you."

JUDGMENT AGAINST ISRAEL'S LEADERS

3 ¹ I said, "Listen, you leaders of Israel!
You are supposed to know right
from wrong,
² but you are the very ones
who hate good and love evil.
You skin my people alive
and tear the flesh from their bones.
³ Yes, you eat my people's flesh,
strip off their skin,
and break their bones.
You chop them up
like meat for the cooking pot.
⁴ Then you beg the LORD for help in times
of trouble!
Do you really expect him to answer?
After all the evil you have done,
he won't even look at you!"

⁵ This is what the LORD says:
"You false prophets are leading
my people astray!
You promise peace for those who
give you food,
but you declare war on those who refuse
to feed you.
⁶ Now the night will close around you,
cutting off all your visions.
Darkness will cover you,
putting an end to your predictions.
The sun will set for you prophets,
and your day will come to an end.
⁷ Then you seers will be put to shame,
and you fortune-tellers will be disgraced.
And you will cover your faces
because there is no answer from God."

⁸ But as for me, I am filled with power—
with the Spirit of the LORD.
I am filled with justice and strength
to boldly declare Israel's sin and rebellion.
⁹ Listen to me, you leaders of Israel!
You hate justice and twist all that is right.
¹⁰ You are building Jerusalem
on a foundation of murder and corruption.
¹¹ You rulers make decisions based on bribes;
you priests teach God's laws only for
a price;
you prophets won't prophesy unless you
are paid.
Yet all of you claim to depend on the LORD.
"No harm can come to us," you say,
"for the LORD is here among us."
¹² Because of you, Mount Zion will be plowed
like an open field;
Jerusalem will be reduced to ruins!
A thicket will grow on the heights
where the Temple now stands.

2:4 Or *to those who took us captive.* **2:6** Or *the prophets respond;*
Hebrew reads *they prophesy.* **2:7** Hebrew *O house of Jacob?* See
note on 1:5a.

THE LORD'S FUTURE REIGN

4 ¹ In the last days, the mountain of
the LORD's house
will be the highest of all—
the most important place on earth.
It will be raised above the other hills,
and people from all over the world will
stream there to worship.
² People from many nations will come and say,
"Come, let us go up to the mountain of
the LORD,
to the house of Jacob's God.
There he will teach us his ways,
and we will walk in his paths."
For the LORD's teaching will go out
from Zion;
his word will go out from Jerusalem.
³ The LORD will mediate between peoples
and will settle disputes between strong
nations far away.
They will hammer their swords
into plowshares
and their spears into pruning hooks.
Nation will no longer fight against nation,
nor train for war anymore.
⁴ Everyone will live in peace and prosperity,
enjoying their own grapevines and
fig trees,
for there will be nothing to fear.
The LORD of Heaven's Armies
has made this promise!
⁵ Though the nations around us follow
their idols,
we will follow the LORD our God forever
and ever.

ISRAEL'S RETURN FROM EXILE

⁶ "In that coming day," says the LORD,
"I will gather together those who are lame,
those who have been exiles,
and those whom I have filled with grief.
⁷ Those who are weak will survive as
a remnant;
those who were exiles will become
a strong nation.
Then I, the LORD, will rule from Jerusalem*
as their king forever."
⁸ As for you, Jerusalem,
the citadel of God's people,*
your royal might and power
will come back to you again.
The kingship will be restored
to my precious Jerusalem.

⁹ But why are you now screaming in terror?
Have you no king to lead you?
Have your wise people all died?
Pain has gripped you like a woman
in childbirth.
¹⁰ Writhe and groan like a woman in labor,
you people of Jerusalem,*
for now you must leave this city

to live in the open country.
You will soon be sent in exile
to distant Babylon.
But the LORD will rescue you there;
he will redeem you from the grip of
your enemies.

¹¹ Now many nations have gathered
against you.
"Let her be desecrated," they say.
"Let us see the destruction of Jerusalem.*"
¹² But they do not know the LORD's thoughts
or understand his plan.
These nations don't know
that he is gathering them together
to be beaten and trampled
like sheaves of grain on a threshing floor.
¹³ "Rise up and crush the nations,
O Jerusalem!"*
says the LORD.
"For I will give you iron horns and
bronze hooves,
so you can trample many nations
to pieces.
You will present their stolen riches to
the LORD,
their wealth to the Lord of all the earth."

5 ¹* Mobilize! Marshal your troops!
The enemy is laying siege
to Jerusalem.
They will strike Israel's leader
in the face with a rod.

A RULER FROM BETHLEHEM

²*But you, O Bethlehem Ephrathah,
are only a small village among all
the people of Judah.
Yet a ruler of Israel,
whose origins are in the distant past,
will come from you on my behalf.
³ The people of Israel will be abandoned to
their enemies
until the woman in labor gives birth.
Then at last his fellow countrymen
will return from exile to their own land.
⁴ And he will stand to lead his flock with the
LORD's strength,
in the majesty of the name of the LORD
his God.
Then his people will live there undisturbed,
for he will be highly honored around
the world.
⁵ And he will be the source of peace.

When the Assyrians invade our land
and break through our defenses,

4:7 Hebrew *Mount Zion.* 4:8 Hebrew *As for you, Migdal-eder, /
the Ophel of the daughter of Zion.* 4:10 Hebrew *O daughter of
Zion.* 4:11 Hebrew *of Zion.* 4:13 Hebrew *"Rise up and thresh,
O daughter of Zion."* 5:1 Verse 5:1 is numbered 4:14 in Hebrew
text. 5:2 Verses 5:2-15 are numbered 5:1-14 in Hebrew text.

we will appoint seven rulers to watch
over us,
eight princes to lead us.
[6] They will rule Assyria with drawn swords
and enter the gates of the land of Nimrod.
He will rescue us from the Assyrians
when they pour over the borders to
invade our land.

THE REMNANT PURIFIED

[7] Then the remnant left in Israel*
will take their place among the nations.
They will be like dew sent by the LORD
or like rain falling on the grass,
which no one can hold back
and no one can restrain.
[8] The remnant left in Israel
will take their place among the nations.
They will be like a lion among the animals
of the forest,
like a strong young lion among flocks of
sheep and goats,
pouncing and tearing as they go
with no rescuer in sight.
[9] The people of Israel will stand up to
their foes,
and all their enemies will be wiped out.

[10] "In that day," says the LORD,
"I will slaughter your horses
and destroy your chariots.
[11] I will tear down your walls
and demolish your defenses.
[12] I will put an end to all witchcraft,
and there will be no more fortune-tellers.
[13] I will destroy all your idols and sacred pillars,
so you will never again worship the work
of your own hands.
[14] I will abolish your idol shrines with their
Asherah poles
and destroy your pagan cities.
[15] I will pour out my vengeance
on all the nations that refuse to obey me."

THE LORD'S CASE AGAINST ISRAEL

6 Listen to what the LORD is saying:

"Stand up and state your case against me.
Let the mountains and hills be called to
witness your complaints.
[2] And now, O mountains,
listen to the LORD's complaint!
He has a case against his people.
He will bring charges against Israel.

[3] "O my people, what have I done to you?
What have I done to make you tired of me?
Answer me!
[4] For I brought you out of Egypt
and redeemed you from slavery.
I sent Moses, Aaron, and Miriam to
help you.

[5] Don't you remember, my people,
how King Balak of Moab tried to
have you cursed
and how Balaam son of Beor
blessed you instead?
And remember your journey from Acacia
Grove* to Gilgal,
when I, the LORD, did everything I could
to teach you about my faithfulness."

[6] What can we bring to the LORD?
Should we bring him burnt offerings?
Should we bow before God Most High
with offerings of yearling calves?
[7] Should we offer him thousands of rams
and ten thousand rivers of olive oil?
Should we sacrifice our firstborn children
to pay for our sins?

[8] No, O people, the LORD has told you what
is good,
and this is what he requires of you:
to do what is right, to love mercy,
and to walk humbly with your God.

ISRAEL'S GUILT AND PUNISHMENT

[9] Fear the LORD if you are wise!
His voice calls to everyone in Jerusalem:
"The armies of destruction are coming;
the LORD is sending them.*
[10] What shall I say about the homes of
the wicked
filled with treasures gained by cheating?
What about the disgusting practice
of measuring out grain with dishonest
measures?*
[11] How can I tolerate your merchants
who use dishonest scales and weights?
[12] The rich among you have become wealthy
through extortion and violence.
Your citizens are so used to lying
that their tongues can no longer tell
the truth.

[13] "Therefore, I will wound you!
I will bring you to ruin for all your sins.
[14] You will eat but never have enough.
Your hunger pangs and emptiness
will remain.
And though you try to save your money,
it will come to nothing in the end.
You will save a little,
but I will give it to those who conquer you.
[15] You will plant crops
but not harvest them.
You will press your olives
but not get enough oil to anoint
yourselves.

5:7 Hebrew *in Jacob;* also in 5:8. See note on 1:5a.   6:5 Hebrew *Shittim.*   6:9 Hebrew *"Listen to the rod. / Who appointed it?"*
6:10 Hebrew *of using the short ephah?* The ephah was a unit for measuring grain.

You will trample the grapes
    but get no juice to make your wine.
[16] You keep only the laws of evil King Omri;
    you follow only the example of wicked
        King Ahab!
Therefore, I will make an example of you,
    bringing you to complete ruin.
You will be treated with contempt,
    mocked by all who see you."

MISERY TURNED TO HOPE

7 [1] How miserable I am!
    I feel like the fruit picker after the harvest
    who can find nothing to eat.
Not a cluster of grapes or a single early fig
    can be found to satisfy my hunger.
[2] The godly people have all disappeared;
    not one honest person is left on the earth.
They are all murderers,
    setting traps even for their own brothers.
[3] Both their hands are equally skilled at
        doing evil!
Officials and judges alike demand bribes.
The people with influence get what
    they want,
and together they scheme to twist justice.
[4] Even the best of them is like a brier;
    the most honest is as dangerous as
        a hedge of thorns.
But your judgment day is coming
    swiftly now.
    Your time of punishment is here,
        a time of confusion.
[5] Don't trust anyone—
    not your best friend or even your wife!
[6] For the son despises his father.
    The daughter defies her mother.
The daughter-in-law defies her
        mother-in-law.
    Your enemies are right in your own
        household!

[7] As for me, I look to the LORD for help.
    I wait confidently for God to save me,
    and my God will certainly hear me.
[8] Do not gloat over me, my enemies!
    For though I fall, I will rise again.
Though I sit in darkness,
    the LORD will be my light.
[9] I will be patient as the LORD punishes me,
    for I have sinned against him.
But after that, he will take up my case
    and give me justice for all I have suffered
        from my enemies.
The LORD will bring me into the light,
    and I will see his righteousness.
[10] Then my enemies will see that the LORD is
    on my side.
They will be ashamed that they taunted
    me, saying,
"So where is the LORD—
    that God of yours?"

With my own eyes I will see their downfall;
    they will be trampled like mud in
        the streets.

[11] In that day, Israel, your cities will be rebuilt,
    and your borders will be extended.
[12] People from many lands will come and
        honor you—
from Assyria all the way to the towns
    of Egypt,
from Egypt all the way to the Euphrates
    River,*
and from distant seas and mountains.
[13] But the land* will become empty and desolate
    because of the wickedness of those who
    live there.

THE LORD'S COMPASSION ON ISRAEL

[14] O LORD, protect your people with your
        shepherd's staff;
    lead your flock, your special possession.
Though they live alone in a thicket
    on the heights of Mount Carmel,*
let them graze in the fertile pastures of
        Bashan and Gilead
    as they did long ago.

[15] "Yes," says the LORD,
    "I will do mighty miracles for you,
like those I did when I rescued you
    from slavery in Egypt."

[16] All the nations of the world will stand amazed
    at what the LORD will do for you.
They will be embarrassed
    at their feeble power.
They will cover their mouths in silent awe,
    deaf to everything around them.
[17] Like snakes crawling from their holes,
    they will come out to meet the LORD
        our God.
They will fear him greatly,
    trembling in terror at his presence.

[18] Where is another God like you,
    who pardons the guilt of the remnant,
    overlooking the sins of his special people?
You will not stay angry with your
    people forever,
    because you delight in showing
        unfailing love.
[19] Once again you will have compassion on us.
    You will trample our sins under your feet
    and throw them into the depths of
        the ocean!
[20] You will show us your faithfulness and
    unfailing love
    as you promised to our ancestors
        Abraham and Jacob long ago.

7:12 Hebrew *the river.* 7:13 Or *earth.* 7:14 Or *surrounded by a fruitful land.*

NAHUM

JON HUNTZINGER, PHD

The name *Nahum* means 'compassion' which is ironic given the harsh message of rebuke the prophet makes against the Assyrian capital of Nineveh. The prophecies of this book occurred sometime after the destruction of the Egyptian city of Thebes by the Assyrians in 664 BC (which is recounted in 3:8-10) and before the destruction of the Assyrian city of Nineveh by the Medes in 612 BC.

This book is a vision that sees and describes the future destruction of Nineveh in striking images. Its primary theme is that the enemies of Israel are God's enemies as well, and He will overthrow any nation that exploits and does violence to them. Nahum depicts God as the avenger of His people Israel who fights on their behalf.

The book moves from a general description of God as an avenger who will save His people (1:2-2:2) to a specific description of Nineveh's destruction (2:3-10). Then it makes a series of gibes that the city of Nineveh is like a leaking reservoir (2:8), lions in their den that no longer incite fear (2:10-12), a mistress of deadly charms (3:4-7), an overrun city like Thebes (3:8-10), and swarming locusts (3:15-17). The movement in the book from the general to the specific is designed to show that Nineveh's days are numbered because of the city's violence against God's people. Nahum clearly sees the divine hand of God at work in the downfall of Assyria as an international power.

The books of Nahum and Jonah are connected in three ways:

— The city of Nineveh is central to both books. In Jonah, the prophet goes to the city to preach repentance; in Nahum, the prophet foretells judgment against the city.
— Both books emphasize God's compassion. Jonah highlights God's compassion for all people, including Nineveh, by describing the extraordinary measures He takes to have His Word preached to them. Nahum (again, whose name means 'compassion') shows God's compassion on behalf of His people by coming *against* Nineveh. This does not mean God's compassion is capricious or unpredictable. It means that God's nature is compassionate, and He will respond with compassion to all people, but He will also act with justice toward those who are exploited.
— Jonah and Nahum are the only two prophetic books that conclude with a rhetorical question. Jonah ends with God asking, "Shouldn't I feel sorry for such a great city?" (4:11) while Nahum ends with God asking,

"Where can anyone be found
  who has not suffered from your [Nineveh's]
    continual cruelty?" (3:19).

The answer to Jonah's question is that, yes, God should show compassion to Nineveh, even as the answer to Nahum's question is that everyone has suffered under Nineveh's violence, and Nineveh must be judged for its actions. From Jonah and Nahum, we learn that God can be both compassionate and just to His people Israel as well as to the nations.

1

This message concerning Nineveh came as a vision to Nahum, who lived in Elkosh.

THE LORD'S ANGER AGAINST NINEVEH

2 The LORD is a jealous God,
   filled with vengeance and rage.
He takes revenge on all who oppose him
   and continues to rage against
      his enemies!
3 The LORD is slow to get angry, but his power
      is great,
   and he never lets the guilty go
      unpunished.
He displays his power in the whirlwind and
      the storm.
   The billowing clouds are the dust beneath
      his feet.
4 At his command the oceans dry up,
   and the rivers disappear.
The lush pastures of Bashan and
      Carmel fade,
   and the green forests of Lebanon wither.
5 In his presence the mountains quake,
   and the hills melt away;
the earth trembles,
   and its people are destroyed.
6 Who can stand before his fierce anger?
   Who can survive his burning fury?
His rage blazes forth like fire,
   and the mountains crumble to dust in
      his presence.

7 The LORD is good,
   a strong refuge when trouble comes.
   He is close to those who trust in him.
8 But he will sweep away his enemies*
   in an overwhelming flood.
He will pursue his foes
   into the darkness of night.

9 Why are you scheming against the LORD?
   He will destroy you with one blow;
   he won't need to strike twice!
10 His enemies, tangled like thornbushes
   and staggering like drunks,
   will be burned up like dry stubble
      in a field.

11 Who is this wicked counselor of yours
   who plots evil against the LORD?

12 This is what the LORD says:
"Though the Assyrians have many allies,
   they will be destroyed and disappear.
O my people, I have punished you before,
   but I will not punish you again.
13 Now I will break the yoke of bondage from
      your neck
   and tear off the chains of Assyrian
      oppression."

14 And this is what the LORD says concerning
   the Assyrians in Nineveh:

"You will have no more children to carry on
      your name.
   I will destroy all the idols in the temples
      of your gods.
I am preparing a grave for you
   because you are despicable!"

15*Look! A messenger is coming over
      the mountains with good news!
   He is bringing a message of peace.
Celebrate your festivals,
   O people of Judah,
   and fulfill all your vows,
for your wicked enemies will never invade
      your land again.
   They will be completely destroyed!

THE FALL OF NINEVEH

2

1*Your enemy is coming to crush you,
      Nineveh.
   Man the ramparts! Watch the roads!
   Prepare your defenses!
   Call out your forces!

2 Even though the destroyer has destroyed
      Judah,
   the LORD will restore its honor.
Israel's vine has been stripped of branches,
   but he will restore its splendor.

3 Shields flash red in the sunlight!
   See the scarlet uniforms of the
      valiant troops!
Watch as their glittering chariots move
      into position,
   with a forest of spears waving
      above them.*
4 The chariots race recklessly along
      the streets
   and rush wildly through the squares.
They flash like firelight
   and move as swiftly as lightning.
5 The king shouts to his officers;
   they stumble in their haste,
   rushing to the walls to set up their
      defenses.
6 The river gates have been torn open!
   The palace is about to collapse!
7 Nineveh's exile has been decreed,
   and all the servant girls mourn
      its capture.
They moan like doves
   and beat their breasts in sorrow.
8 Nineveh is like a leaking water reservoir!
   The people are slipping away.
"Stop, stop!" someone shouts,
   but no one even looks back.

1:8 As in Greek version; Hebrew reads sweep away her place.
1:15 Verse 1:15 is numbered 2:1 in Hebrew text.   2:1 Verses 2:1-13
are numbered 2:2-14 in Hebrew text.   2:3 Greek and Syriac
versions read into position, / the horses whipped into a frenzy.

⁹ Loot the silver!
   Plunder the gold!
There's no end to Nineveh's treasures—
   its vast, uncounted wealth.
¹⁰ Soon the city is plundered, empty,
      and ruined.
   Hearts melt and knees shake.
The people stand aghast,
   their faces pale and trembling.

¹¹ Where now is that great Nineveh,
   that den filled with young lions?
It was a place where people—like lions and
      their cubs—
   walked freely and without fear.
¹² The lion tore up meat for his cubs
   and strangled prey for his mate.
He filled his den with prey,
   his caverns with his plunder.

¹³ "I am your enemy!"
   says the LORD of Heaven's Armies.
"Your chariots will soon go up in smoke.
   Your young men* will be killed in battle.
Never again will you plunder conquered
      nations.
   The voices of your proud messengers will
      be heard no more."

THE LORD'S JUDGMENT AGAINST NINEVEH

3 ¹ What sorrow awaits Nineveh,
      the city of murder and lies!
She is crammed with wealth
   and is never without victims.
² Hear the crack of whips,
   the rumble of wheels!
Horses' hooves pound,
   and chariots clatter wildly.
³ See the flashing swords and glittering spears
   as the charioteers charge past!
There are countless casualties,
   heaps of bodies—
so many bodies that
   people stumble over them.
⁴ All this because Nineveh,
   the beautiful and faithless city,
mistress of deadly charms,
   enticed the nations with her beauty.
She taught them all her magic,
   enchanting people everywhere.

⁵ "I am your enemy!"
   says the LORD of Heaven's Armies.
"And now I will lift your skirts
   and show all the earth your nakedness
      and shame.
⁶ I will cover you with filth
   and show the world how vile you really are.
⁷ All who see you will shrink back and say,
   'Nineveh lies in ruins.
Where are the mourners?'
   Does anyone regret your destruction?"

⁸ Are you any better than the city of Thebes,*
   situated on the Nile River, surrounded
      by water?
She was protected by the river on all sides,
   walled in by water.
⁹ Ethiopia* and the land of Egypt
   gave unlimited assistance.
The nations of Put and Libya
   were among her allies.
¹⁰ Yet Thebes fell,
   and her people were led away
      as captives.
Her babies were dashed to death
   against the stones of the streets.
Soldiers threw dice* to get Egyptian officers
   as servants.
   All their leaders were bound in chains.

¹¹ And you, Nineveh, will also stagger like
      a drunkard.
   You will hide for fear of the
      attacking enemy.
¹² All your fortresses will fall.
   They will be devoured like the ripe figs
that fall into the mouths
   of those who shake the trees.
¹³ Your troops will be as weak
   and helpless as women.
The gates of your land will be opened wide
      to the enemy
   and set on fire and burned.
¹⁴ Get ready for the siege!
   Store up water!
   Strengthen the defenses!
Go into the pits to trample clay,
   and pack it into molds,
      making bricks to repair the walls.

¹⁵ But the fire will devour you;
   the sword will cut you down.
The enemy will consume you like locusts,
   devouring everything they see.
There will be no escape,
   even if you multiply like swarming
      locusts.
¹⁶ Your merchants have multiplied
   until they outnumber the stars.
But like a swarm of locusts,
   they strip the land and fly away.
¹⁷ Your guards* and officials are also like
      swarming locusts
   that crowd together in the hedges on
      a cold day.
But like locusts that fly away when the sun
      comes up,
   all of them will fly away and disappear.

¹⁸ Your shepherds are asleep, O Assyrian king;
   your princes lie dead in the dust.

2:13 Hebrew *young lions.*   3:8 Hebrew *No-amon;* also in 3:10.
3:9 Hebrew *Cush.*   3:10 Hebrew *They cast lots.*   3:17 Or *princes.*

Your people are scattered across the
    mountains
    with no one to gather them together.
19 There is no healing for your wound;
    your injury is fatal.

All who hear of your destruction
    will clap their hands for joy.
Where can anyone be found
    who has not suffered from your
    continual cruelty?

HABAKKUK

JON HUNTZINGER, PHD

Of the many prophets who prophesied to the people of Judah in the seventh century BC when Assyria was in steep decline and Babylon on the rise, Jeremiah, Ezekiel, and Habakkuk stand out. Though not much is known about Habakkuk the person, he prophesied during the years 608-587 BC in the final days of Judah before its fall to the Babylonians and the destruction of Jerusalem and the Temple. This means that he prophesied during a hard and difficult time in Judah's history. Early Jewish literature identifies Habakkuk as a Levite, which means he would have had some priestly responsibilities connected to the Temple.

The book of Habakkuk has four major sections:
— Chapter 1:1-11 records Habakkuk's complaint over the unrighteousness he sees among the people of Judah and his question of why God does not do something about it. God responds by saying He plans to judge the people through the Babylonians.
— Chapters 1:12-2:5 follow by reporting Habakkuk's confusion about God's judgment by the Babylonians and ask how God can use the unrighteous Babylonians to judge the unrighteousness of Judah. God responds by saying He knows who the Babylonians are, and thus, He knows what He is doing.
— Chapter 2:6-20 lists a series of "woes" against the Babylonians, revealing that even though God has chosen to use them to judge His people, they themselves will not go unjudged.
— Chapter 3 contains a psalm in which God is depicted in power to save His people, concluding with a beautiful expression of hope in the trustworthiness of God Himself.

An important issue addressed in the book, as in the book of Job, is theodicy: If God is good, loving, and powerful, then why does He allow good, innocent people to suffer? Habakkuk addresses the same question, yet on a different level. Why would God use the profane, arrogant, and unrighteous Babylonians to judge His people? At first, it does not make sense to Habakkuk, and he

struggles with God's purposes (1:2; 1:12-2:1). When the prophet directs these questions to God, the divine response is unyielding. God knows who the Babylonians are and has chosen them to carry out His will even so:

> "Look at the proud [the Babylonians]!
> They trust in themselves, and their lives
> are crooked.
> But the righteous [God's people] will live
> by their faithfulness to God" (2:4).

This declaration means that God knows the nature of the people He has chosen to judge Israel. They may be proud and puffed up; they may be unrighteous and not upright. Yet He will use them to see His ultimate plans for Israel accomplished. Will the people trust God's words and ways? They will show righteousness by believing God's words based on what He has done for them in the past. "But the righteous will live by their faithfulness to God" (2:4) means that God's people will trust Him because He has proven Himself to be trustworthy in the past.

Habakkuk's message resonated over the centuries, and he is quoted by both Paul (Romans 1:17) and the writer of Hebrews (Hebrews 10:38). What is the response of faith to the words God speaks, which at times are hard to comprehend? We find the answer in Habakkuk's final affirmation:

> Even though the fig trees have no blossoms . . .
> yet I will rejoice in the LORD!
> I will be joyful in the God of my salvation!"
> (3:17-18).

Even when there is no evidence for belief in the present moment—when there is no blossom on the tree—the prophet says that he "will rejoice in the LORD" because God has proven to be faithful in the past. God's provision in the past gives Habakkuk confidence in the present and hope for the future. This is the faith of Habakkuk at the time of the Exile, and it is why he is known as God's faith-filled prophet.

1

This is the message that the prophet Habakkuk received in a vision.

HABAKKUK'S COMPLAINT

² How long, O Lord, must I call for help?
　But you do not listen!
"Violence is everywhere!" I cry,
　but you do not come to save.
³ Must I forever see these evil deeds?
　Why must I watch all this misery?
Wherever I look,
　I see destruction and violence.
I am surrounded by people
　who love to argue and fight.
⁴ The law has become paralyzed,
　and there is no justice in the courts.
The wicked far outnumber the righteous,
　so that justice has become perverted.

THE LORD'S REPLY

⁵ The Lord replied,

"Look around at the nations;
　look and be amazed!*
For I am doing something in your own day,
　something you wouldn't believe
　even if someone told you about it.
⁶ I am raising up the Babylonians,*
　a cruel and violent people.
They will march across the world
　and conquer other lands.
⁷ They are notorious for their cruelty
　and do whatever they like.
⁸ Their horses are swifter than cheetahs*
　and fiercer than wolves at dusk.
Their charioteers charge from far away.
　Like eagles, they swoop down to devour
　their prey.
⁹ "On they come, all bent on violence.
　Their hordes advance like a desert wind,
　sweeping captives ahead of them
　like sand.
¹⁰ They scoff at kings and princes
　and scorn all their fortresses.
They simply pile ramps of earth
　against their walls and capture them!
¹¹ They sweep past like the wind
　and are gone.
But they are deeply guilty,
　for their own strength is their god."

HABAKKUK'S SECOND COMPLAINT

¹² O Lord my God, my Holy One, you who are eternal—
　surely you do not plan to wipe us out?
O Lord, our Rock, you have sent these
　Babylonians to correct us,
　to punish us for our many sins.
¹³ But you are pure and cannot stand
　the sight of evil.
　Will you wink at their treachery?

Should you be silent while the wicked
　swallow up people more righteous
　than they?
¹⁴ Are we only fish to be caught and killed?
　Are we only sea creatures that have
　no leader?
¹⁵ Must we be strung up on their hooks
　and caught in their nets while they
　rejoice and celebrate?
¹⁶ Then they will worship their nets
　and burn incense in front of them.
"These nets are the gods who have made
　us rich!"
　they will claim.
¹⁷ Will you let them get away with this
　forever?
　Will they succeed forever in their
　heartless conquests?

2

¹ I will climb up to my watchtower
　and stand at my guardpost.
There I will wait to see what the Lord says
　and how he* will answer my complaint.

THE LORD'S SECOND REPLY

² Then the Lord said to me,

"Write my answer plainly on tablets,
　so that a runner can carry the correct
　message to others.
³ This vision is for a future time.
　It describes the end, and it will be fulfilled.
If it seems slow in coming, wait patiently,
　for it will surely take place.
　It will not be delayed.

⁴ "Look at the proud!
　They trust in themselves,
　and their lives are crooked.
But the righteous will live by their
　faithfulness to God.*
⁵ Wealth* is treacherous,
　and the arrogant are never at rest.
They open their mouths as wide as
　the grave,*
　and like death, they are never satisfied.
In their greed they have gathered up many
　nations
　and swallowed many peoples.

⁶ "But soon their captives will taunt them.
　They will mock them, saying,
'What sorrow awaits you thieves!
　Now you will get what you deserve!

1:5 Greek version reads Look, you mockers; / look and be amazed and die. Compare Acts 13:41.   1:6 Or Chaldeans.   1:8 Or leopards.   2:1 As in Syriac version; Hebrew reads I.   2:3b-4 Greek version reads If the vision is delayed, wait patiently, / for it will surely come and not delay. / *I will take no pleasure in anyone who turns away. / But the righteous person will live by my faith. Compare Rom 1:17; Gal 3:11; Heb 10:37-38.   2:5a As in Dead Sea Scroll 1QpHab; other Hebrew manuscripts read Wine.   2:5b Hebrew as Sheol.

TESTIMONIES
Habakkuk 2:2   ROBERT MORRIS

Stories about God's work in your life are not *just* stories; they are testimonies. And testimonies are memorials to God's faithfulness and goodness in our lives. In Habakkuk 2:2, God says,

"Write my answer plainly on tablets
    so that a runner can carry the correct
        message to others."

When a person hears your testimony, it can encourage them and accelerate their walk with God.

The Bible is full of testimonies, such as the woman whom Jesus healed after 18 years of sickness (Luke 13:10-12), the 5,000 people Jesus fed (Matthew 14:13-21), and the entire nation of Israel that God set free from bondage in Egypt (Exodus 12:31-42). When you read these stories of God's goodness, you begin to think, *If God did it for them, He can do it for me too.* Your stories are really just testimonies of God's miraculous work in your life and the lives of others.

You've become rich by extortion,
    but how much longer can this go on?'
⁷ Suddenly, your debtors will take action.
    They will turn on you and take
        all you have,
    while you stand trembling and helpless.
⁸ Because you have plundered many nations,
    now all the survivors will plunder you.
You committed murder throughout the
        countryside
    and filled the towns with violence.

⁹ "What sorrow awaits you who build big
        houses
    with money gained dishonestly!
You believe your wealth will buy security,
    putting your family's nest beyond the
        reach of danger.
¹⁰ But by the murders you committed,
    you have shamed your name and forfeited
        your lives.
¹¹ The very stones in the walls cry out
        against you,
    and the beams in the ceilings echo the
        complaint.

¹² "What sorrow awaits you who build cities
    with money gained through murder and
        corruption!
¹³ Has not the LORD of Heaven's Armies
        promised
    that the wealth of nations will turn
        to ashes?

They work so hard,
    but all in vain!
¹⁴ For as the waters fill the sea,
    the earth will be filled with an awareness
        of the glory of the LORD.

¹⁵ "What sorrow awaits you who make your
        neighbors drunk!
    You force your cup on them
    so you can gloat over their shameful
        nakedness.
¹⁶ But soon it will be your turn to be disgraced.
    Come, drink and be exposed!*
Drink from the cup of the LORD's judgment,
    and all your glory will be turned
        to shame.
¹⁷ You cut down the forests of Lebanon.
    Now you will be cut down.
You destroyed the wild animals,
    so now their terror will be yours.
You committed murder throughout the
        countryside
    and filled the towns with violence.

¹⁸ "What good is an idol carved by man,
    or a cast image that deceives you?
How foolish to trust in your own creation—
    a god that can't even talk!
¹⁹ What sorrow awaits you who say to
        wooden idols,
    'Wake up and save us!'
To speechless stone images you say,
    'Rise up and teach us!'
Can an idol tell you what to do?
They may be overlaid with gold and silver,
    but they are lifeless inside.
²⁰ But the LORD is in his holy Temple.
    Let all the earth be silent before him."

HABAKKUK'S PRAYER

3 This prayer was sung by the prophet
Habakkuk*:

² I have heard all about you, LORD.
    I am filled with awe by your
        amazing works.
In this time of our deep need,
    help us again as you did in years gone by.
And in your anger,
    remember your mercy.

³ I see God moving across the deserts
        from Edom,*
    the Holy One coming from Mount Paran.*
His brilliant splendor fills the heavens,
    and the earth is filled with his praise.

2:16 Dead Sea Scrolls and Greek and Syriac versions read *and stagger!* 3:1 Hebrew adds *according to shigionoth,* probably indicating the musical setting for the prayer. 3:3a Hebrew *Teman.* 3:3b Hebrew adds *selah;* also in 3:9, 13. The meaning of this Hebrew term is uncertain; it is probably a musical or literary term.

⁴ His coming is as brilliant as the sunrise.
   Rays of light flash from his hands,
      where his awesome power is hidden.
⁵ Pestilence marches before him;
   plague follows close behind.
⁶ When he stops, the earth shakes.
   When he looks, the nations tremble.
He shatters the everlasting mountains
   and levels the eternal hills.
He is the Eternal One!*
⁷ I see the people of Cushan in distress,
   and the nation of Midian trembling
      in terror.

⁸ Was it in anger, LORD, that you struck
      the rivers
   and parted the sea?
Were you displeased with them?
   No, you were sending your chariots
      of salvation!
⁹ You brandished your bow
   and your quiver of arrows.
   You split open the earth with flowing
      rivers.
¹⁰ The mountains watched and trembled.
   Onward swept the raging waters.
The mighty deep cried out,
   lifting its hands in submission.
¹¹ The sun and moon stood still in the sky
   as your brilliant arrows flew
   and your glittering spear flashed.

¹² You marched across the land in anger
   and trampled the nations in your fury.
¹³ You went out to rescue your chosen people,
   to save your anointed ones.

You crushed the heads of the wicked
   and stripped their bones from head
      to toe.
¹⁴ With his own weapons,
   you destroyed the chief of those
who rushed out like a whirlwind,
   thinking Israel would be easy prey.
¹⁵ You trampled the sea with your horses,
   and the mighty waters piled high.

¹⁶ I trembled inside when I heard this;
   my lips quivered with fear.
My legs gave way beneath me,*
   and I shook in terror.
I will wait quietly for the coming day
   when disaster will strike the people who
      invade us.
¹⁷ Even though the fig trees have
      no blossoms,
   and there are no grapes on the vines;
even though the olive crop fails,
   and the fields lie empty and barren;
even though the flocks die in the fields,
   and the cattle barns are empty,
¹⁸ yet I will rejoice in the LORD!
   I will be joyful in the God of
      my salvation!
¹⁹ The Sovereign LORD is my strength!
   He makes me as surefooted as a deer,*
   able to tread upon the heights.

(For the choir director: This prayer is to be accompanied by stringed instruments.)

3:6 Or *The ancient paths belong to him.*   3:16 Hebrew *Decay entered my bones.*   3:19 Or *He gives me the speed of a deer.*

ZEPHANIAH

JON HUNTZINGER, PHD

The book of Zephaniah begins by tracing the prophet's lineage back to King Hezekiah, who was a descendant of King David. It also links his prophetic ministry to the time of King Josiah (640-609 BC), who discovered the Book of the Law in the Temple (2 Kings 22:1-23:3). These two facts mean Zephaniah would have had access to the court of the king because of his ancestry and would have witnessed the rapid decline of Assyria in the late seventh century BC because of the time he prophesied.

The book of Zephaniah has three parts:

— Chapters 1:2-2:3 describe God's sweeping judgment upon Judah for idolatry (1:17). This time of judgment is described as the day of the Lord (1:7, 14).

— Chapters 2:4-3:8 tell about God's judgment of the nations around Judah, particularly the cities of Gaza, Ashkelon, Ashdod, and Ekron to the west, the countries of Moab and Ammon to the east, and the countries of Ethiopia to the south and Assyria to the north (chapter 2). If God will judge His people, He will also judge the surrounding nations.

— Chapter 3:9-20 promises a time after judgment when God will save the nations and also be present in the midst of His people as the King of Israel.

Zephaniah joins other prophets like Amos (Amos 5:18-20) and Isaiah (Isaiah 13:9-22) in describing "the day of the Lord," when God will establish His justice among His people, the nations, and all of creation. Though the prophets often describe that day as one of darkness and despair, it primarily involves God's justice. His justice results in punishment for sin but also features the promotion of humility. Zephaniah depicts the God of Judah as a God of justice.

The judgment of which Zephaniah prophesies is related to the pride of Judah (and that of the nations) as it is expressed in the practice of idolatry (1:4-6). The people of Judah had imitated the worship of Assyria (1:8-9) and engaged in idolatry, which influenced how they lived with one another. This is why the prophet calls the people of Judah to seek humility (2:3). At the heart of idolatry is the pride of people who want to form their own idols and arrange their own religious rituals. According to the prophet, the humble person (like Moses, according to Numbers 12:3) recognizes the power of God and submits to the form of worship He has given in His covenant. The reforms to Temple worship instituted by King Josiah during the time of Zephaniah (see 2 Kings 22-23 listed above) point to the kind of humility that the prophet encourages. God desires offerings of worship from humble people who live justly with one another (Zepheniah 3:11-13).

1 The LORD gave this message to Zephaniah when Josiah son of Amon was king of Judah. Zephaniah was the son of Cushi, son of Gedaliah, son of Amariah, son of Hezekiah.

COMING JUDGMENT AGAINST JUDAH

2 "I will sweep away everything
from the face of the earth," says the LORD.
3 "I will sweep away people and animals alike.
I will sweep away the birds of the sky and
the fish in the sea.
I will reduce the wicked to heaps of rubble,*
and I will wipe humanity from the face of
the earth," says the LORD.
4 "I will crush Judah and Jerusalem with
my fist
and destroy every last trace of their Baal
worship.
I will put an end to all the idolatrous priests,
so that even the memory of them will
disappear.
5 For they go up to their roofs
and bow down to the sun, moon, and stars.
They claim to follow the LORD,
but then they worship Molech,* too.
6 And I will destroy those who used to
worship me
but now no longer do.
They no longer ask for the LORD's guidance
or seek my blessings."

7 Stand in silence in the presence of the
Sovereign LORD,
for the awesome day of the LORD's
judgment is near.
The LORD has prepared his people for
a great slaughter
and has chosen their executioners.*
8 "On that day of judgment,"
says the LORD,
"I will punish the leaders and princes
of Judah
and all those following pagan customs.
9 Yes, I will punish those who participate in
pagan worship ceremonies,
and those who fill their masters' houses
with violence and deceit.

10 "On that day," says the LORD,
"a cry of alarm will come from the Fish Gate
and echo throughout the New Quarter of
the city.*
And a great crash will sound from the hills.
11 Wail in sorrow, all you who live in the
market area,*
for all the merchants and traders will be
destroyed.

12 "I will search with lanterns in Jerusalem's
darkest corners
to punish those who sit complacent in
their sins.

They think the LORD will do nothing
to them,
either good or bad.
13 So their property will be plundered,
their homes will be ransacked.
They will build new homes
but never live in them.
They will plant vineyards
but never drink wine from them.

14 "That terrible day of the LORD is near.
Swiftly it comes—
a day of bitter tears,
a day when even strong men will cry out.
15 It will be a day when the LORD's anger is
poured out—
a day of terrible distress and anguish,
a day of ruin and desolation,
a day of darkness and gloom,
a day of clouds and blackness,
16 a day of trumpet calls and battle cries.
Down go the walled cities
and the strongest battlements!

17 "Because you have sinned against the LORD,
I will make you grope around like
the blind.
Your blood will be poured into the dust,
and your bodies will lie rotting on
the ground."

18 Your silver and gold will not save you
on that day of the LORD's anger.
For the whole land will be devoured
by the fire of his jealousy.
He will make a terrifying end
of all the people on earth.*

A CALL TO REPENTANCE

2 1 Gather together—yes, gather together,
you shameless nation.
2 Gather before judgment begins,
before your time to repent is blown away
like chaff.
Act now, before the fierce fury of
the LORD falls
and the terrible day of the LORD's
anger begins.
3 Seek the LORD, all who are humble,
and follow his commands.
Seek to do what is right
and to live humbly.
Perhaps even yet the LORD will
protect you—
protect you from his anger on that day of
destruction.

1:3 The meaning of the Hebrew is uncertain.   1:5 Hebrew *Malcam*, a variant spelling of Molech; or it could possibly mean *their king*.   1:7 Hebrew *has prepared a sacrifice and sanctified his guests*.   1:10 Or *the Second Quarter*, a newer section of Jerusalem. Hebrew reads *the Mishneh*.   1:11 Or *in the valley*, a lower section of Jerusalem. Hebrew reads *the Maktesh*.   1:18 Or *the people living in the land*.

JUDGMENT AGAINST PHILISTIA

4 Gaza and Ashkelon will be abandoned,
    Ashdod and Ekron torn down.
5 And what sorrow awaits you Philistines*
    who live along the coast and in the land
        of Canaan,
    for this judgment is against you, too!
  The LORD will destroy you
    until not one of you is left.
6 The Philistine coast will become a
        wilderness pasture,
    a place of shepherd camps
    and enclosures for sheep and goats.
7 The remnant of the tribe of Judah will
        pasture there.
    They will rest at night in the abandoned
        houses in Ashkelon.
  For the LORD their God will visit his people
        in kindness
    and restore their prosperity again.

JUDGMENT AGAINST MOAB AND AMMON

8 "I have heard the taunts of the Moabites
        and the insults of the Ammonites,
  mocking my people
    and invading their borders.
9 Now, as surely as I live,"
    says the LORD of Heaven's Armies, the
        God of Israel,
  "Moab and Ammon will be destroyed—
    destroyed as completely as Sodom and
        Gomorrah.
  Their land will become a place of stinging
        nettles,
    salt pits, and eternal desolation.
  The remnant of my people will plunder them
    and take their land."

10 They will receive the wages of their pride,
    for they have scoffed at the people of the
        LORD of Heaven's Armies.
11 The LORD will terrify them
    as he destroys all the gods in the land.
  Then nations around the world will worship
        the LORD,
    each in their own land.

JUDGMENT AGAINST ETHIOPIA
AND ASSYRIA

12 "You Ethiopians* will also be slaughtered
    by my sword," says the LORD.

13 And the LORD will strike the lands of the
        north with his fist,
    destroying the land of Assyria.
  He will make its great capital, Nineveh,
    a desolate wasteland,
    parched like a desert.
14 The proud city will become a pasture for
        flocks and herds,
    and all sorts of wild animals will settle
        there.

The desert owl and screech owl will roost
    on its ruined columns,
  their calls echoing through the gaping
        windows.
Rubble will block all the doorways,
    and the cedar paneling will be exposed
        to the weather.
15 This is the boisterous city,
    once so secure.
  "I am the greatest!" it boasted.
    "No other city can compare with me!"
  But now, look how it has become an utter
        ruin,
    a haven for wild animals.
  Everyone passing by will laugh
        in derision
    and shake a defiant fist.

JERUSALEM'S REBELLION
AND REDEMPTION

3 ¹ What sorrow awaits rebellious,
        polluted Jerusalem,
    the city of violence and crime!
2 No one can tell it anything;
    it refuses all correction.
  It does not trust in the LORD
    or draw near to its God.
3 Its leaders are like roaring lions
    hunting for their victims.
  Its judges are like ravenous wolves at
        evening time,
    who by dawn have left no trace of
        their prey.
4 Its prophets are arrogant liars seeking their
        own gain.
    Its priests defile the Temple by
        disobeying God's instructions.
5 But the LORD is still there in the city,
    and he does no wrong.
  Day by day he hands down justice,
    and he does not fail.
  But the wicked know no shame.

6 "I have wiped out many nations,
    devastating their fortress walls
        and towers.
  Their streets are now deserted;
    their cities lie in silent ruin.
  There are no survivors—
    none at all.
7 I thought, 'Surely they will have reverence
        for me now!
  Surely they will listen to my warnings.
  Then I won't need to strike again,
    destroying their homes.'
  But no, they get up early
    to continue their evil deeds.
8 Therefore, be patient," says the LORD.
    "Soon I will stand and accuse these
        evil nations.

2:5 Hebrew *Kerethites*.   **2:12** Hebrew *Cushites*.

For I have decided to gather the kingdoms
  of the earth
and pour out my fiercest anger and fury
  on them.
All the earth will be devoured
  by the fire of my jealousy.

⁹ "Then I will purify the speech of all people,
  so that everyone can worship the LORD
  together.
¹⁰ My scattered people who live beyond the
  rivers of Ethiopia*
  will come to present their offerings.
¹¹ On that day you will no longer need to
  be ashamed,
  for you will no longer be rebels
  against me.
I will remove all proud and arrogant people
  from among you.
There will be no more haughtiness on
  my holy mountain.
¹² Those who are left will be the lowly and
  humble,
  for it is they who trust in the name of
  the LORD.
¹³ The remnant of Israel will do no wrong;
  they will never tell lies or deceive
  one another.
They will eat and sleep in safety,
  and no one will make them afraid."

¹⁴ Sing, O daughter of Zion;
  shout aloud, O Israel!
Be glad and rejoice with all your heart,
  O daughter of Jerusalem!
¹⁵ For the LORD will remove his hand of
  judgment
  and will disperse the armies of your enemy.

And the LORD himself, the King of Israel,
  will live among you!
At last your troubles will be over,
  and you will never again fear disaster.
¹⁶ On that day the announcement to
  Jerusalem will be,
  "Cheer up, Zion! Don't be afraid!
¹⁷ For the LORD your God is living among you.
  He is a mighty savior.
He will take delight in you with gladness.
  With his love, he will calm all your fears.*
  He will rejoice over you with
  joyful songs."

¹⁸ "I will gather you who mourn for the
  appointed festivals;
  you will be disgraced no more.*
¹⁹ And I will deal severely with all who have
  oppressed you.
  I will save the weak and helpless ones;
I will bring together
  those who were chased away.
I will give glory and fame to my
  former exiles,
  wherever they have been mocked and
  shamed.
²⁰ On that day I will gather you together
  and bring you home again.
I will give you a good name, a name of
  distinction,
  among all the nations of the earth,
as I restore your fortunes before their
  very eyes.
  I, the LORD, have spoken!"

3:10 Hebrew *Cush.*   3:17 Or *He will be silent in his love.* Greek and
Syriac versions read *He will renew you with his love.*   3:18 The
meaning of the Hebrew for this verse is uncertain.

HAGGAI

JON HUNTZINGER, PHD

The prophet Haggai prophesied in Jerusalem in 520 BC at the same time as Zechariah. He is known simply as "the prophet," which indicates he was well known at that time, and his name comes from the Hebrew word *hag*, meaning 'festival,' suggesting he was born on a holy day. Many of the people who had been taken into exile in 587 BC were permitted to return in 539 BC by Cyrus, the king of Persia (2 Chronicles 36:23; Ezra 1:2-4). They began rebuilding the Temple when they arrived back in the land. However, the work that started so quickly soon stopped when local opposition to the project arose from those who did not want to see the Temple rebuilt and Judah returned to its former power (Ezra 4:1-5; 5:3-5). When a new king (Darius, 521-486 BC) rose to the throne in Persia, God inspired Haggai to exhort the people to recommit themselves to rebuilding the Temple (Haggai 1:1-2).

The book of Haggai can be divided by four dated prophecies (1:1; 2:1; 2:10; 2:20), all of which occur within a four-month period during the second year of King Darius in 520 BC:

— The first prophecy (1:1-11) was given at the end of August when Haggai declares that the hardship the people had experienced after their return to the land was because they had put their own interests before those of God. They had devoted time and resources to rebuilding their homes and fields and had neglected the Temple.

— The second prophecy (2:1-9) was delivered in October on the last day of the Festival of Shelters. It encouraged people to rejoice in the Temple that was being rebuilt because, even if it might not appear as great as Solomon's Temple to those who had seen the previous one, its glory would be greater (2:3; Ezra 3:12-13; Zechariah 4:10).

— The third prophecy (2:10-19) was given in December during the growing season. It reminded the people to pursue holiness in their offerings and that time away from their own interests like farming would result in greater harvests.

— The fourth prophecy (2:20-23) immediately followed the third and happened on that same day. It declared that Zerubbabel, the Jewish governor who served under Darius, would be God's "signet ring" to accomplish His purposes. This word was fulfilled when work on the Temple was completed in 515 BC under his supervision.

The book of Haggai emphasizes the priority of worship in the lives of God's people. The prophet declares that when people give their time, energy, and resources to God's worship by rebuilding the Temple, then God will be present to them and provide for their needs.

A CALL TO REBUILD THE TEMPLE

1 On August 29* of the second year of King Darius's reign, the LORD gave a message through the prophet Haggai to Zerubbabel son of Shealtiel, governor of Judah, and to Jeshua* son of Jehozadak, the high priest.

[2] "This is what the LORD of Heaven's Armies says: The people are saying, 'The time has not yet come to rebuild the house of the LORD.'"

[3] Then the LORD sent this message through the prophet Haggai: [4] "Why are you living in luxurious houses while my house lies in ruins? [5] This is what the LORD of Heaven's Armies says: Look at what's happening to you! [6] You have planted much but harvest little. You eat but are not satisfied. You drink but are still thirsty. You put on clothes but cannot keep warm. Your wages disappear as though you were putting them in pockets filled with holes!

[7] "This is what the LORD of Heaven's Armies says: Look at what's happening to you! [8] Now go up into the hills, bring down timber, and rebuild my house. Then I will take pleasure in it and be honored, says the LORD. [9] You hoped for rich harvests, but they were poor. And when you brought your harvest home, I blew it away. Why? Because my house lies in ruins, says the LORD of Heaven's Armies, while all of you are busy building your own fine houses. [10] It's because of you that the heavens withhold the dew and the earth produces no crops. [11] I have called for a drought on your fields and hills—a drought to wither the grain and grapes and olive trees and all your other crops, a drought to starve you and your livestock and to ruin everything you have worked so hard to get."

OBEDIENCE TO GOD'S CALL

[12] Then Zerubbabel son of Shealtiel, and Jeshua son of Jehozadak, the high priest, and the whole remnant of God's people began to obey the message from the LORD their God. When they heard the words of the prophet Haggai, whom the LORD their God had sent, the people feared the LORD. [13] Then Haggai, the LORD's messenger, gave the people this message from the LORD: "I am with you, says the LORD!"

[14] So the LORD sparked the enthusiasm of Zerubbabel son of Shealtiel, governor of Judah, and the enthusiasm of Jeshua son of Jehozadak, the high priest, and the enthusiasm of the whole remnant of God's people. They began to work on the house of their God, the LORD of Heaven's Armies, [15] on September 21* of the second year of King Darius's reign.

THE NEW TEMPLE'S DIMINISHED SPLENDOR

2 Then on October 17 of that same year,* the LORD sent another message through the prophet Haggai. [2] "Say this to Zerubbabel son of Shealtiel, governor of Judah, and to Jeshua* son of Jehozadak, the high priest, and to the remnant of God's people there in the land: [3] 'Does anyone remember this house—this Temple—in its former splendor? How, in comparison, does it look to you now? It must seem like nothing at all! [4] But now the LORD says: Be strong, Zerubbabel. Be strong, Jeshua son of Jehozadak, the high priest. Be strong, all you people still left in the land. And now get to work, for I am with you, says the LORD of Heaven's Armies. [5] My Spirit remains among you, just as I promised when you came out of Egypt. So do not be afraid.'

[6] "For this is what the LORD of Heaven's Armies says: In just a little while I will again shake the heavens and the earth, the oceans and the dry land. [7] I will shake all the nations, and the treasures of all the nations will be brought to this Temple. I will fill this place with glory, says the LORD of Heaven's Armies. [8] The silver is mine, and the gold is mine, says the LORD of Heaven's Armies. [9] The future glory of this Temple will be greater than its past glory, says the LORD of Heaven's Armies. And in this place I will bring peace. I, the LORD of Heaven's Armies, have spoken!"

BLESSINGS PROMISED FOR OBEDIENCE

[10] On December 18* of the second year of King Darius's reign, the LORD sent this message to the prophet Haggai: [11] "This is what the LORD of Heaven's Armies says. Ask the priests this question about the law: [12] 'If one of you is carrying some meat from a holy sacrifice in his robes and his robe happens to brush against some bread or stew, wine or olive oil, or any other kind of food, will it also become holy?'"

The priests replied, "No."

[13] Then Haggai asked, "If someone becomes ceremonially unclean by touching a dead person and then touches any of these foods, will the food be defiled?"

And the priests answered, "Yes."

[14] Then Haggai responded, "That is how it is with this people and this nation, says the LORD. Everything they do and everything they offer is defiled by their sin. [15] Look at what was happening to you before you began to lay the foundation of the LORD's Temple. [16] When you hoped for a twenty-bushel crop, you harvested only ten. When you expected to draw fifty gallons from the winepress, you found only twenty. [17] I sent blight and mildew and hail to destroy everything you

---

1:1a Hebrew *On the first day of the sixth month,* of the ancient Hebrew lunar calendar. A number of dates in Haggai can be cross-checked with dates in surviving Persian records and related accurately to our modern calendar. This event occurred on August 29, 520 B.C. 1:1b Hebrew *Joshua,* a variant spelling of Jeshua; also in 1:12, 14. 1:15 Hebrew *on the twenty-fourth day of the sixth month,* of the ancient Hebrew lunar calendar. This event occurred on September 21, 520 B.C.; also see note on 1:1a. 2:1 Hebrew *on the twenty-first day of the seventh month,* of the ancient Hebrew lunar calendar. This event (in the second year of Darius's reign) occurred on October 17, 520 B.C.; also see note on 1:1a. 2:2 Hebrew *Joshua,* a variant spelling of Jeshua; also in 2:4. 2:10 Hebrew *On the twenty-fourth day of the ninth month,* of the ancient Hebrew lunar calendar (similarly in 2:18). This event occurred on December 18, 520 B.C.; also see note on 1:1a.

worked so hard to produce. Even so, you refused to return to me, says the Lord.

[18] "Think about this eighteenth day of December, the day* when the foundation of the Lord's Temple was laid. Think carefully. [19] I am giving you a promise now while the seed is still in the barn.* You have not yet harvested your grain, and your grapevines, fig trees, pomegranates, and olive trees have not yet produced their crops. But from this day onward I will bless you."

PROMISES FOR ZERUBBABEL

[20] On that same day, December 18,* the Lord sent this second message to Haggai: [21] "Tell Zerubbabel, the governor of Judah, that I am about to shake the heavens and the earth. [22] I will overthrow royal thrones and destroy the power of foreign kingdoms. I will overturn their chariots and riders. The horses will fall, and their riders will kill each other.

[23] "But when this happens, says the Lord of Heaven's Armies, I will honor you, Zerubbabel son of Shealtiel, my servant. I will make you like a signet ring on my finger, says the Lord, for I have chosen you. I, the Lord of Heaven's Armies, have spoken!"

2:18 Or *On this eighteenth day of December, think about the day.*
2:19 Hebrew *Is the seed yet in the barn?* 2:20 Hebrew *On the twenty-fourth day of the [ninth] month;* see note on 2:10.

ZECHARIAH

JON HUNTZINGER, PHD

There are more than 25 people in the Bible named Zechariah, which means 'Yahweh has remembered.' The particular Zechariah for whom the book is named prophesied in Jerusalem during the years 520-518 BC at the same time as Haggai (Ezra 5:1). He came from a priestly family and had returned to Judah from the Exile with the Jewish governor Zerubbabel (Nehemiah 12:16). The writers of the New Testament Gospels quote Zechariah more than any other Old Testament book in relation to Jesus' passion (His arrest, trial, and crucifixion).

Like Ezekiel, who prophesied 50 years earlier, Zechariah was a priest concerned about the worship of God. That is why his book is filled with visions and oracles related to worship. A primary message of the book is that God's people are called to worship Him, and God will do what is necessary to make that possible.

The book of Zechariah contains two major sections:
— Chapters 1-8 feature eight visions that address the current situation of Judah (1:7-6:8), followed by a series of messages that are described as coming from the Lord.
— Chapters 9-14 are divided into two prophecies. The first is poetic and condemns the enemies of God's people even as it promises to restore Judah and Israel (chapters 9-11). The second is narrative and describes what the people should expect in their future "on that day," a phrase that is used 16 times (chapters 12-14).

Zechariah receives his visions at night (1:7-8). This fact highlights the type of revelation they give. Since night not only represents time but also ignorance or lack of understanding, the visions God gives to Zechariah represent the knowledge He possesses and is now sharing with His prophet in contrast to surrounding ignorance. God does not want His people to live in ignorance but with understanding. And the imagery of the visions is intended to guarantee that the knowledge given is remembered. It would be hard to forget a vision of a man on a red horse, the high priest with filthy clothes, a flying scroll, a woman in a basket, or four chariots with different colored horses. God gives understanding to His people and helps them remember the knowledge that He gives.

Altogether, the visions center on the renewal of worship in the life of God's people. This can be seen in that the prophet has arranged the visions in the form of a chiasm. A chiasm was a popular way of writing used at that time to emphasize the main point of a passage or teaching by linking the first and last elements of the passage or teaching together, then the second and next-to-last elements, and so on, down to the two central elements side-by-side. The two elements of the central pair represented the core of the passage or teaching. For example:

A
  B
    C
    C
  B
A

Thus, the vision of a horseman is paired with the vision of horse-drawn chariots (1:7-17; 6:1-8). The vision of scattered horns is paired with vision of a woman in a basket being taken away (1:18-21; 5:5-11). The vision of a man who measures Jerusalem is matched with that of a flying scroll that judges or "measures" falsehood (2:1-13; 5:1-4). At the center of the chiasm, the vision of the high priest is matched with that of a golden lampstand (3:1-10; 4:1-14). In these visions, Zechariah sees Jeshua is given clean garments (he is purified), even as he sees a lampstand and hears that Zerubbabel will complete the rebuilding of the Temple through the power of the Spirit of the Lord (4:6). According to the book, these visions were given in February 519 BC, four years prior to the completion of the Temple in 515 BC (Ezra 6:13-15).

The second part of the book of Zechariah contains two messages given by the prophet that shift the focus from the near present to the more distant future. The first message (chapters 9-11) is poetic. It begins with judgment against the nations that have fought against Judah and continues with a vision of a coming king who will save the people. Despite the certainty of their salvation, the people will suffer much. The second message (chapters 12-14) is a narrative that describes what will happen "on that day" (12:3, 4, 6, 8, 9, 11; 13:1, 2, 4; 14:4, 6, 8, 9, 13, 20, 21), which culminates in the Festival of Shelters and the worship of God as King in Jerusalem by all nations (14:16-21). Just as the first major part of Zechariah (chapters 1-8) emphasizes the worship of God at the Temple by placing the two visions of the high priest and the lampstand in the middle of all the visions, so also the second major part (chapters 9-14) emphasizes worship by concluding with the promise of all nations joining God's people in worship in Jerusalem. The book of Zechariah sees God's present activity as well as His future ministry in terms of the restoration of His people, along with the nations, to worship Him.

A CALL TO RETURN TO THE LORD

1 In November* of the second year of King Darius's reign, the LORD gave this message to the prophet Zechariah son of Berekiah and grandson of Iddo:

2 "I, the LORD, was very angry with your ancestors. 3 Therefore, say to the people, 'This is what the LORD of Heaven's Armies says: Return to me, and I will return to you, says the LORD of Heaven's Armies.' 4 Don't be like your ancestors who would not listen or pay attention when the earlier prophets said to them, 'This is what the LORD of Heaven's Armies says: Turn from your evil ways, and stop all your evil practices.'

5 "Where are your ancestors now? They and the prophets are long dead. 6 But everything I said through my servants the prophets happened to your ancestors, just as I said. As a result, they repented and said, 'We have received what we deserved from the LORD of Heaven's Armies. He has done what he said he would do.'"

A MAN AMONG THE MYRTLE TREES

7 Three months later, on February 15,* the LORD sent another message to the prophet Zechariah son of Berekiah and grandson of Iddo.

8 In a vision during the night, I saw a man sitting on a red horse that was standing among some myrtle trees in a small valley. Behind him were riders on red, brown, and white horses. 9 I asked the angel who was talking with me, "My lord, what do these horses mean?"

"I will show you," the angel replied.

10 The rider standing among the myrtle trees then explained, "They are the ones the LORD has sent out to patrol the earth."

11 Then the other riders reported to the angel of the LORD, who was standing among the myrtle trees, "We have been patrolling the earth, and the whole earth is at peace."

12 Upon hearing this, the angel of the LORD prayed this prayer: "O LORD of Heaven's Armies, for seventy years now you have been angry with Jerusalem and the towns of Judah. How long until you again show mercy to them?" 13 And the LORD spoke kind and comforting words to the angel who talked with me.

14 Then the angel said to me, "Shout this message for all to hear: 'This is what the LORD of Heaven's Armies says: My love for Jerusalem and Mount Zion is passionate and strong. 15 But I am very angry with the other nations that are now enjoying peace and security. I was only a little angry with my people, but the nations inflicted harm on them far beyond my intentions.

16 "'Therefore, this is what the LORD says: I have returned to show mercy to Jerusalem. My Temple will be rebuilt, says the LORD of Heaven's Armies, and measurements will be taken for the reconstruction of Jerusalem.*'

17 "Say this also: 'This is what the LORD of Heaven's Armies says: The towns of Israel will again overflow with prosperity, and the LORD will again comfort Zion and choose Jerusalem as his own.'"

FOUR HORNS AND FOUR BLACKSMITHS

18* Then I looked up and saw four animal horns. 19 "What are these?" I asked the angel who was talking with me.

He replied, "These horns represent the nations that scattered Judah, Israel, and Jerusalem."

20 Then the LORD showed me four blacksmiths. 21 "What are these men coming to do?" I asked.

The angel replied, "These four horns—these nations—scattered and humbled Judah. Now these blacksmiths have come to terrify those nations and throw them down and destroy them."

FUTURE PROSPERITY OF JERUSALEM

2 1* When I looked again, I saw a man with a measuring line in his hand. 2 "Where are you going?" I asked.

He replied, "I am going to measure Jerusalem, to see how wide and how long it is."

3 Then the angel who was with me went to meet a second angel who was coming toward him. 4 The other angel said, "Hurry, and say to that young man, 'Jerusalem will someday be so full of people and livestock that there won't be room enough for everyone! Many will live outside the city walls. 5 Then I, myself, will be a protective wall of fire around Jerusalem, says the LORD. And I will be the glory inside the city!'"

THE EXILES ARE CALLED HOME

6 The LORD says, "Come away! Flee from Babylon in the land of the north, for I have scattered you to the four winds. 7 Come away, people of Zion, you who are exiled in Babylon!"

8 After a period of glory, the LORD of Heaven's Armies sent me* against the nations who plundered you. For he said, "Anyone who harms you harms my most precious possession.* 9 I will raise my fist to crush them, and their own slaves will plunder them." Then you will know that the LORD of Heaven's Armies has sent me.

10 The LORD says, "Shout and rejoice, O beautiful Jerusalem,* for I am coming to live among you. 11 Many nations will join themselves to the LORD on that day, and they, too, will be my people. I will live among you, and you will know

---

1:1 Hebrew *In the eighth month.* A number of dates in Zechariah can be cross-checked with dates in surviving Persian records and related accurately to our modern calendar. This month of the ancient Hebrew lunar calendar occurred within the months of October and November 520 B.C. 1:7 Hebrew *On the twenty-fourth day of the eleventh month, the month of Shebat, in the second year of Darius.* This event occurred on February 15, 519 B.C.; also see note on 1:1. 1:16 Hebrew *and the measuring line will be stretched out over Jerusalem.* 1:18 Verses 1:18-21 are numbered 2:1-4 in Hebrew text. 2:1 Verses 2:1-13 are numbered 2:5-17 in Hebrew text. 2:8a The meaning of the Hebrew is uncertain. 2:8b Hebrew *Anyone who touches you touches the pupil of his eye.* 2:10 Hebrew *O daughter of Zion.*

that the Lord of Heaven's Armies sent me to you. [12]The land of Judah will be the Lord's special possession in the holy land, and he will once again choose Jerusalem to be his own city. [13]Be silent before the Lord, all humanity, for he is springing into action from his holy dwelling."

CLEANSING FOR THE HIGH PRIEST

3 Then the angel showed me Jeshua* the high priest standing before the angel of the Lord. The Accuser, Satan,* was there at the angel's right hand, making accusations against Jeshua. [2]And the Lord said to Satan, "I, the Lord, reject your accusations, Satan. Yes, the Lord, who has chosen Jerusalem, rebukes you. This man is like a burning stick that has been snatched from the fire."

[3]Jeshua's clothing was filthy as he stood there before the angel. [4]So the angel said to the others standing there, "Take off his filthy clothes." And turning to Jeshua he said, "See, I have taken away your sins, and now I am giving you these fine new clothes."

[5]Then I said, "They should also place a clean turban on his head." So they put a clean priestly turban on his head and dressed him in new clothes while the angel of the Lord stood by.

[6]Then the angel of the Lord spoke very solemnly to Jeshua and said, [7]"This is what the Lord of Heaven's Armies says: If you follow my ways and carefully serve me, then you will be given authority over my Temple and its courtyards. I will let you walk among these others standing here.

[8]"Listen to me, O Jeshua the high priest, and all you other priests. You are symbols of things to come. Soon I am going to bring my servant, the Branch. [9]Now look at the jewel I have set before Jeshua, a single stone with seven facets.* I will engrave an inscription on it, says the Lord of Heaven's Armies, and I will remove the sins of this land in a single day.

[10]"And on that day, says the Lord of Heaven's Armies, each of you will invite your neighbor to sit with you peacefully under your own grapevine and fig tree."

A LAMPSTAND AND TWO OLIVE TREES

4 Then the angel who had been talking with me returned and woke me, as though I had been asleep. [2]"What do you see now?" he asked.

I answered, "I see a solid gold lampstand with a bowl of oil on top of it. Around the bowl are seven lamps, each having seven spouts with wicks. [3]And I see two olive trees, one on each side of the bowl." [4]Then I asked the angel, "What are these, my lord? What do they mean?"

[5]"Don't you know?" the angel asked.

"No, my lord," I replied.

[6]Then he said to me, "This is what the Lord says to Zerubbabel: It is not by force nor by strength, but by my Spirit, says the Lord of Heaven's Armies. [7]Nothing, not even a mighty mountain, will stand in Zerubbabel's way; it will become a level plain before him! And when Zerubbabel sets the final stone of the Temple in place, the people will shout: 'May God bless it! May God bless it!'*"

[8]Then another message came to me from the Lord: [9]"Zerubbabel is the one who laid the foundation of this Temple, and he will complete it. Then you will know that the Lord of Heaven's Armies has sent me. [10]Do not despise these small beginnings, for the Lord rejoices to see the work begin, to see the plumb line in Zerubbabel's hand."

(The seven lamps* represent the eyes of the Lord that search all around the world.)

[11]Then I asked the angel, "What are these two olive trees on each side of the lampstand, [12]and what are the two olive branches that pour out golden oil through two gold tubes?"

[13]"Don't you know?" he asked.

"No, my lord," I replied.

[14]Then he said to me, "They represent the two anointed ones* who stand in the court of the Lord of all the earth."

A FLYING SCROLL

5 I looked up again and saw a scroll flying through the air.

[2]"What do you see?" the angel asked.

"I see a flying scroll," I replied. "It appears to be about 30 feet long and 15 feet wide.*"

[3]Then he said to me, "This scroll contains the curse that is going out over the entire land. One side of the scroll says that those who steal will be banished from the land; the other side says that those who swear falsely will be banished from the land. [4]And this is what the Lord of Heaven's Armies says: I am sending this curse into the house of every thief and into the house of everyone who swears falsely using my name. And my curse will remain in that house and completely destroy it—even its timbers and stones."

A WOMAN IN A BASKET

[5]Then the angel who was talking with me came forward and said, "Look up and see what's coming."

[6]"What is it?" I asked.

He replied, "It is a basket for measuring grain,* and it's filled with the sins* of everyone throughout the land."

[7]Then the heavy lead cover was lifted off the basket, and there was a woman sitting inside it. [8]The angel said, "The woman's name is Wickedness,"

3:1a Hebrew *Joshua,* a variant spelling of Jeshua; also in 3:3, 4, 6, 8, 9.   3:1b Hebrew *The satan;* similarly in 3:2.   3:9 Hebrew *seven eyes.*   4:7 Hebrew *'Grace, grace to it.'*   4:10 Or *The seven facets* (see 3:9); Hebrew reads *These seven.*   4:14 Or *two heavenly beings;* Hebrew reads *two sons of fresh oil.*   5:2 Hebrew *20 cubits* [9.2 meters] *long and 10 cubits* [4.6 meters] *wide.*   5:6a Hebrew *an ephah* [20 quarts or 22 liters]; also in 5:7, 8, 9, 10, 11.   5:6b As in Greek version; Hebrew reads *the appearance.*

and he pushed her back into the basket and closed the heavy lid again.

⁹Then I looked up and saw two women flying toward us, gliding on the wind. They had wings like a stork, and they picked up the basket and flew into the sky.

¹⁰"Where are they taking the basket?" I asked the angel.

¹¹He replied, "To the land of Babylonia,* where they will build a temple for the basket. And when the temple is ready, they will set the basket there on its pedestal."

FOUR CHARIOTS

6 Then I looked up again and saw four chariots coming from between two bronze mountains. ²The first chariot was pulled by red horses, the second by black horses, ³the third by white horses, and the fourth by powerful dappled-gray horses. ⁴"And what are these, my lord?" I asked the angel who was talking with me.

⁵The angel replied, "These are the four spirits* of heaven who stand before the Lord of all the earth. They are going out to do his work. ⁶The chariot with black horses is going north, the chariot with white horses is going west,* and the chariot with dappled-gray horses is going south."

⁷The powerful horses were eager to set out to patrol the earth. And the LORD said, "Go and patrol the earth!" So they left at once on their patrol.

⁸Then the LORD summoned me and said, "Look, those who went north have vented the anger of my Spirit* there in the land of the north."

THE CROWNING OF JESHUA

⁹Then I received another message from the LORD: ¹⁰"Heldai, Tobijah, and Jedaiah will bring gifts of silver and gold from the Jews exiled in Babylon. As soon as they arrive, meet them at the home of Josiah son of Zephaniah. ¹¹Accept their gifts, and make a crown from the silver and gold. Then put the crown on the head of Jeshua* son of Jehozadak, the high priest. ¹²Tell him, 'This is what the LORD of Heaven's Armies says: Here is the man called the Branch. He will branch out from where he is and build the Temple of the LORD. ¹³Yes, he will build the Temple of the LORD. Then he will receive royal honor and will rule as king from his throne. He will also serve as priest from his throne,* and there will be perfect harmony between his two roles.'

¹⁴"The crown will be a memorial in the Temple of the LORD to honor those who gave it—Heldai,* Tobijah, Jedaiah, and Josiah* son of Zephaniah."

¹⁵People will come from distant lands to rebuild the Temple of the LORD. And when this happens, you will know that my messages have been from the LORD of Heaven's Armies. All this will happen if you carefully obey what the LORD your God says.

A CALL TO JUSTICE AND MERCY

7 On December 7* of the fourth year of King Darius's reign, another message came to Zechariah from the LORD. ²The people of Bethel had sent Sharezer and Regemmelech,* along with their attendants, to seek the LORD's favor. ³They were to ask this question of the prophets and the priests at the Temple of the LORD of Heaven's Armies: "Should we continue to mourn and fast each summer on the anniversary of the Temple's destruction,* as we have done for so many years?"

⁴The LORD of Heaven's Armies sent me this message in reply: ⁵"Say to all your people and your priests, 'During these seventy years of exile, when you fasted and mourned in the summer and in early autumn,* was it really for me that you were fasting? ⁶And even now in your holy festivals, aren't you eating and drinking just to please yourselves? ⁷Isn't this the same message the LORD proclaimed through the prophets in years past when Jerusalem and the towns of Judah were bustling with people, and the Negev and the foothills of Judah* were well populated?'"

⁸Then this message came to Zechariah from the LORD: ⁹"This is what the LORD of Heaven's Armies says: Judge fairly, and show mercy and kindness to one another. ¹⁰Do not oppress widows, orphans, foreigners, and the poor. And do not scheme against each other.

¹¹"Your ancestors refused to listen to this message. They stubbornly turned away and put their fingers in their ears to keep from hearing. ¹²They made their hearts as hard as stone, so they could not hear the instructions or the messages that the LORD of Heaven's Armies had sent them by his Spirit through the earlier prophets. That is why the LORD of Heaven's Armies was so angry with them.

¹³"Since they refused to listen when I called to them, I would not listen when they called to me, says the LORD of Heaven's Armies. ¹⁴As with a whirlwind, I scattered them among the distant nations, where they lived as strangers. Their land became so desolate that no one even traveled through it. They turned their pleasant land into a desert."

5:11 Hebrew *the land of Shinar.* 6:5 Or *the four winds.* 6:6 Hebrew *is going after them.* 6:8 Hebrew *have given my Spirit rest.* 6:11 Hebrew *Joshua,* a variant spelling of Jeshua. 6:13 Or *There will be a priest by his throne.* 6:14a As in Syriac version (compare 6:10); Hebrew reads *Helem.* 6:14b As in Syriac version (compare 6:10); Hebrew reads *Hen.* 7:1 Hebrew *On the fourth day of the ninth month, the month of Kislev,* of the ancient Hebrew lunar calendar. This event occurred on December 7, 518 B.C.; also see note on 1:1. 7:2 Or *Bethel-sharezer had sent Regemmelech.* 7:3 Hebrew *mourn and fast in the fifth month.* The Temple had been destroyed in the fifth month of the ancient Hebrew lunar calendar (August 586 B.C.); see 2 Kgs 25:8. 7:5 Hebrew *fasted and mourned in the fifth and seventh months.* The fifth month of the ancient Hebrew lunar calendar usually occurs within the months of July and August. The seventh month usually occurs within the months of September and October; both the Day of Atonement and the Festival of Shelters were celebrated in the seventh month. 7:7 Hebrew *the Shephelah.*

PROMISED BLESSINGS FOR JERUSALEM

8 Then another message came to me from the LORD of Heaven's Armies: ² "This is what the LORD of Heaven's Armies says: My love for Mount Zion is passionate and strong; I am consumed with passion for Jerusalem!

³ "And now the LORD says: I am returning to Mount Zion, and I will live in Jerusalem. Then Jerusalem will be called the Faithful City; the mountain of the LORD of Heaven's Armies will be called the Holy Mountain.

⁴ "This is what the LORD of Heaven's Armies says: Once again old men and women will walk Jerusalem's streets with their canes and will sit together in the city squares. ⁵ And the streets of the city will be filled with boys and girls at play.

⁶ "This is what the LORD of Heaven's Armies says: All this may seem impossible to you now, a small remnant of God's people. But is it impossible for me? says the LORD of Heaven's Armies.

⁷ "This is what the LORD of Heaven's Armies says: You can be sure that I will rescue my people from the east and from the west. ⁸ I will bring them home again to live safely in Jerusalem. They will be my people, and I will be faithful and just toward them as their God.

⁹ "This is what the LORD of Heaven's Armies says: Be strong and finish the task! Ever since the laying of the foundation of the Temple of the LORD of Heaven's Armies, you have heard what the prophets have been saying about completing the building. ¹⁰ Before the work on the Temple began, there were no jobs and no money to hire people or animals. No traveler was safe from the enemy, for there were enemies on all sides. I had turned everyone against each other.

¹¹ "But now I will not treat the remnant of my people as I treated them before, says the LORD of Heaven's Armies. ¹² For I am planting seeds of peace and prosperity among you. The grapevines will be heavy with fruit. The earth will produce its crops, and the heavens will release the dew. Once more I will cause the remnant in Judah and Israel to inherit these blessings. ¹³ Among the other nations, Judah and Israel became symbols of a cursed nation. But no longer! Now I will rescue you and make you both a symbol and a source of blessing. So don't be afraid. Be strong, and get on with rebuilding the Temple!

¹⁴ "For this is what the LORD of Heaven's Armies says: I was determined to punish you when your ancestors angered me, and I did not change my mind, says the LORD of Heaven's Armies. ¹⁵ But now I am determined to bless Jerusalem and the people of Judah. So don't be afraid. ¹⁶ But this is what you must do: Tell the truth to each other. Render verdicts in your courts that are just and that lead to peace. ¹⁷ Don't scheme against each other. Stop your love of telling lies that you swear are the truth. I hate all these things, says the LORD."

¹⁸ Here is another message that came to me from the LORD of Heaven's Armies. ¹⁹ "This is what the LORD of Heaven's Armies says: The traditional fasts and times of mourning you have kept in early summer, midsummer, autumn, and winter* are now ended. They will become festivals of joy and celebration for the people of Judah. So love truth and peace.

²⁰ "This is what the LORD of Heaven's Armies says: People from nations and cities around the world will travel to Jerusalem. ²¹ The people of one city will say to the people of another, 'Come with us to Jerusalem to ask the LORD to bless us. Let's worship the LORD of Heaven's Armies. I'm determined to go.' ²² Many peoples and powerful nations will come to Jerusalem to seek the LORD of Heaven's Armies and to ask for his blessing.

²³ "This is what the LORD of Heaven's Armies says: In those days ten men from different nations and languages of the world will clutch at the sleeve of one Jew. And they will say, 'Please let us walk with you, for we have heard that God is with you.'"

JUDGMENT AGAINST ISRAEL'S ENEMIES

9 This is the message* from the LORD against the land of Aram* and the city of Damascus, for the eyes of humanity, including all the tribes of Israel, are on the LORD.

² Doom is certain for Hamath,
     near Damascus,
and for the cities of Tyre and Sidon,
     though they are so clever.
³ Tyre has built a strong fortress
     and has made silver and gold
     as plentiful as dust in the streets!
⁴ But now the Lord will strip away Tyre's
     possessions
     and hurl its fortifications into the sea,
     and it will be burned to the ground.
⁵ The city of Ashkelon will see Tyre fall
     and will be filled with fear.
Gaza will shake with terror,
     as will Ekron, for their hopes will
     be dashed.
Gaza's king will be killed,
     and Ashkelon will be deserted.
⁶ Foreigners will occupy the city of Ashdod.
     I will destroy the pride of the Philistines.
⁷ I will grab the bloody meat from
     their mouths
     and snatch the detestable sacrifices from
     their teeth.
Then the surviving Philistines will worship
     our God
     and become like a clan in Judah.*

8:19 Hebrew *in the fourth, fifth, seventh, and tenth months.* The fourth month of the ancient Hebrew lunar calendar usually occurs within the months of June and July. The fifth month usually occurs within the months of July and August. The seventh month usually occurs within the months of September and October. The tenth month usually occurs within the months of December and January.   9:1a Hebrew *An Oracle: The message.*   9:1b Hebrew *land of Hadrach.*   9:7 Hebrew *like a leader in Judah.*

PRISONERS WHO STILL HAVE HOPE
Zechariah 9:11–12   OLEN GRIFFING

We all have seasons in our lives that we like and others that we do not. Because we live in a fallen world, we sometimes find ourselves in a dry pit. A dry pit is a season or situation that causes us to fall into a place where we lose hope. People find themselves in a dry pit because they either misunderstand God's ways, or they become strangers to His covenant promise of hope. We cannot get out of a dry pit on our own; we need God's help.

God wants us to return to His stronghold as "prisoners who still have hope" (Zechariah 9:12). He can draw us out of the dry pit, but we must agree with Him by declaring His truth. We enter God's stronghold of hope when we worship and align our attitudes with His Word. God promises to restore hope to our lives if we will put our trust in Him.

The Philistines of Ekron will join my people,
  as the ancient Jebusites once did.
⁸ I will guard my Temple
  and protect it from invading armies.
I am watching closely to ensure
  that no more foreign oppressors overrun
  my people's land.

ZION'S COMING KING

⁹ Rejoice, O people of Zion!*
  Shout in triumph, O people of
  Jerusalem!
Look, your king is coming to you.
  He is righteous and victorious,*
yet he is humble, riding on a donkey—
  riding on a donkey's colt.
¹⁰ I will remove the battle chariots from Israel*
  and the warhorses from Jerusalem.
I will destroy all the weapons used
  in battle,
  and your king will bring peace to the
  nations.
His realm will stretch from sea to sea
  and from the Euphrates River*
  to the ends of the earth.*
¹¹ Because of the covenant I made with you,
  sealed with blood,
I will free your prisoners
  from death in a waterless dungeon.
¹² Come back to the place of safety,
  all you prisoners who still have hope!
I promise this very day
  that I will repay two blessings for each
  of your troubles.
¹³ Judah is my bow,
  and Israel is my arrow.
Jerusalem* is my sword,
  and like a warrior, I will brandish it
  against the Greeks.*

¹⁴ The Lord will appear above his people;
  his arrows will fly like lightning!
The Sovereign Lord will sound the
  ram's horn
  and attack like a whirlwind from the
  southern desert.
¹⁵ The Lord of Heaven's Armies will protect
  his people,
  and they will defeat their enemies by
  hurling great stones.
They will shout in battle as though drunk
  with wine.
  They will be filled with blood
  like a bowl,
  drenched with blood like the corners of
  the altar.
¹⁶ On that day the Lord their God will rescue
  his people,
  just as a shepherd rescues his sheep.
They will sparkle in his land
  like jewels in a crown.
¹⁷ How wonderful and beautiful they will be!
  The young men will thrive on
  abundant grain,
  and the young women will flourish on
  new wine.

THE LORD WILL RESTORE HIS PEOPLE

10 ¹ Ask the Lord for rain in the spring,
  for he makes the storm clouds.
And he will send showers of rain
  so every field becomes a lush pasture.
² Household gods give worthless advice,
  fortune-tellers predict only lies,
and interpreters of dreams pronounce
  falsehoods that give no comfort.
So my people are wandering like
  lost sheep;
  they are attacked because they have
  no shepherd.

³ "My anger burns against your shepherds,
  and I will punish these leaders.*
For the Lord of Heaven's Armies has arrived
  to look after Judah, his flock.
He will make them strong and glorious,
  like a proud warhorse in battle.
⁴ From Judah will come the cornerstone,
  the tent peg,
the bow for battle,
  and all the rulers.
⁵ They will be like mighty warriors in battle,
  trampling their enemies in the mud
  under their feet.
Since the Lord is with them as they fight,
  they will overthrow even the enemy's
  horsemen.

9:9a Hebrew *O daughter of Zion!* **9:9b** Hebrew *and is being
vindicated.* **9:10a** Hebrew *Ephraim,* referring to the northern
kingdom of Israel; also in 9:13. **9:10b** Hebrew *the river.*
9:10c Or *the end of the land.* **9:13a** Hebrew *Zion.* **9:13b** Hebrew
the sons of Javan. **10:3** Or *these male goats.*

6 "I will strengthen Judah and save Israel*;
   I will restore them because of my
      compassion.
It will be as though I had never
   rejected them,
   for I am the LORD their God, who will
      hear their cries.
7 The people of Israel* will become like
      mighty warriors,
   and their hearts will be made happy as if
      by wine.
Their children, too, will see it and be glad;
   their hearts will rejoice in the LORD.
8 When I whistle to them, they will come
      running,
   for I have redeemed them.
From the few who are left,
   they will grow as numerous as they were
      before.
9 Though I have scattered them like seeds
      among the nations,
   they will still remember me in
      distant lands.
They and their children will survive
   and return again to Israel.
10 I will bring them back from Egypt
   and gather them from Assyria.
I will resettle them in Gilead and Lebanon
   until there is no more room for them all.
11 They will pass safely through the sea of
      distress,*
   for the waves of the sea will be
      held back,
   and the waters of the Nile will dry up.
The pride of Assyria will be crushed,
   and the rule of Egypt will end.
12 By my power* I will make my people strong,
   and by my authority they will go
      wherever they wish.
   I, the LORD, have spoken!"

11 ¹ Open your doors, Lebanon,
      so that fire may devour your
         cedar forests.
² Weep, you cypress trees, for all the ruined
      cedars;
   the most majestic ones have fallen.
Weep, you oaks of Bashan,
   for the thick forests have been cut down.
³ Listen to the wailing of the shepherds,
   for their rich pastures are destroyed.
Hear the young lions roaring,
   for their thickets in the Jordan Valley
      are ruined.

THE GOOD AND EVIL SHEPHERDS

⁴ This is what the LORD my God says: "Go and
care for the flock that is intended for slaughter. ⁵ The buyers slaughter their sheep without
remorse. The sellers say, 'Praise the LORD! Now
I'm rich!' Even the shepherds have no compassion for them. ⁶ Likewise, I will no longer have

pity on the people of the land," says the LORD.
"I will let them fall into each other's hands and
into the hands of their king. They will turn the
land into a wilderness, and I will not rescue
them."

⁷ So I cared for the flock intended for slaughter—the flock that was oppressed. Then I took
two shepherd's staffs and named one Favor and
the other Union. ⁸ I got rid of their three evil
shepherds in a single month.

But I became impatient with these sheep, and
they hated me, too. ⁹ So I told them, "I won't be
your shepherd any longer. If you die, you die. If
you are killed, you are killed. And let those who
remain devour each other!"

¹⁰ Then I took my staff called Favor and cut it
in two, showing that I had revoked the covenant
I had made with all the nations. ¹¹ That was the
end of my covenant with them. The suffering
flock was watching me, and they knew that the
LORD was speaking through my actions.

¹² And I said to them, "If you like, give me my
wages, whatever I am worth; but only if you
want to." So they counted out for my wages thirty
pieces of silver.

¹³ And the LORD said to me, "Throw it to the
potter*"—this magnificent sum at which they
valued me! So I took the thirty coins and threw
them to the potter in the Temple of the LORD.

¹⁴ Then I took my other staff, Union, and cut it
in two, showing that the bond of unity between
Judah and Israel was broken.

¹⁵ Then the LORD said to me, "Go again and
play the part of a worthless shepherd. ¹⁶ This
illustrates how I will give this nation a shepherd
who will not care for those who are dying, nor
look after the young, nor heal the injured, nor
feed the healthy. Instead, this shepherd will
eat the meat of the fattest sheep and tear off
their hooves.

¹⁷ "What sorrow awaits this worthless
      shepherd
   who abandons the flock!
The sword will cut his arm
   and pierce his right eye.
His arm will become useless,
   and his right eye completely blind."

FUTURE DELIVERANCE FOR JERUSALEM

12 This* message concerning the fate of Israel
   came from the LORD: "This message is
from the LORD, who stretched out the heavens,
laid the foundations of the earth, and formed
the human spirit. ² I will make Jerusalem like an
intoxicating drink that makes the nearby nations
stagger when they send their armies to besiege
Jerusalem and Judah. ³ On that day I will make

10:6 Hebrew save the house of Joseph.   10:7 Hebrew of Ephraim.
10:11 Or the sea of Egypt, referring to the Red Sea.   10:12 Hebrew
In the LORD.   11:13 Syriac version reads into the treasury; also in
11:13b. Compare Matt 27:6-10.   12:1 Hebrew An Oracle: This.

Jerusalem an immovable rock. All the nations will gather against it to try to move it, but they will only hurt themselves.

4 "On that day," says the LORD, "I will cause every horse to panic and every rider to lose his nerve. I will watch over the people of Judah, but I will blind all the horses of their enemies. 5 And the clans of Judah will say to themselves, 'The people of Jerusalem have found strength in the LORD of Heaven's Armies, their God.'

6 "On that day I will make the clans of Judah like a flame that sets a woodpile ablaze or like a burning torch among sheaves of grain. They will burn up all the neighboring nations right and left, while the people living in Jerusalem remain secure.

7 "The LORD will give victory to the rest of Judah first, before Jerusalem, so that the people of Jerusalem and the royal line of David will not have greater honor than the rest of Judah. 8 On that day the LORD will defend the people of Jerusalem; the weakest among them will be as mighty as King David! And the royal descendants will be like God, like the angel of the LORD who goes before them! 9 For on that day I will begin to destroy all the nations that come against Jerusalem.

10 "Then I will pour out a spirit* of grace and prayer on the family of David and on the people of Jerusalem. They will look on me whom they have pierced and mourn for him as for an only son. They will grieve bitterly for him as for a firstborn son who has died. 11 The sorrow and mourning in Jerusalem on that day will be like the great mourning for Hadad-rimmon in the valley of Megiddo.

12 "All Israel will mourn, each clan by itself, and with the husbands separate from their wives. The clan of David will mourn alone, as will the clan of Nathan, 13 the clan of Levi, and the clan of Shimei. 14 Each of the surviving clans from Judah will mourn separately, and with the husbands separate from their wives.

A FOUNTAIN OF CLEANSING

13 "On that day a fountain will be opened for the dynasty of David and for the people of Jerusalem, a fountain to cleanse them from all their sins and impurity.

2 "And on that day," says the LORD of Heaven's Armies, "I will erase idol worship throughout the land, so that even the names of the idols will be forgotten. I will remove from the land both the false prophets and the spirit of impurity that came with them. 3 If anyone continues to prophesy, his own father and mother will tell him, 'You must die, for you have prophesied lies in the name of the LORD.' And as he prophesies, his own father and mother will stab him.

4 "On that day people will be ashamed to claim the prophetic gift. No one will pretend to be a prophet by wearing prophet's clothes. 5 He will

say, 'I'm no prophet; I'm a farmer. I began working for a farmer as a boy.' 6 And if someone asks, 'Then what about those wounds on your chest?*' he will say, 'I was wounded at my friends' house!'

THE SCATTERING OF THE SHEEP

7 "Awake, O sword, against my shepherd,
   the man who is my partner,"
   says the LORD of Heaven's Armies.
"Strike down the shepherd,
   and the sheep will be scattered,
   and I will turn against the lambs.
8 Two-thirds of the people in the land
   will be cut off and die," says the LORD.
"But one-third will be left in the land.
9 I will bring that group through the fire
   and make them pure.
I will refine them like silver
   and purify them like gold.
They will call on my name,
   and I will answer them.
I will say, 'These are my people,'
   and they will say, 'The LORD is our God.'"

THE LORD WILL RULE THE EARTH

14 Watch, for the day of the LORD is coming when your possessions will be plundered right in front of you! 2 I will gather all the nations to fight against Jerusalem. The city will be taken, the houses looted, and the women raped. Half the population will be taken into captivity, and the rest will be left among the ruins of the city.

3 Then the LORD will go out to fight against those nations, as he has fought in times past. 4 On that day his feet will stand on the Mount of Olives, east of Jerusalem. And the Mount of Olives will split apart, making a wide valley running from east to west. Half the mountain will move toward the north and half toward the south. 5 You will flee through this valley, for it will reach across to Azal.* Yes, you will flee as you did from the earthquake in the days of King Uzziah of Judah. Then the LORD my God will come, and all his holy ones with him.*

6 On that day the sources of light will no longer shine,* 7 yet there will be continuous day! Only the LORD knows how this could happen. There will be no normal day and night, for at evening time it will still be light.

8 On that day life-giving waters will flow out from Jerusalem, half toward the Dead Sea and half toward the Mediterranean,* flowing continuously in both summer and winter.

9 And the LORD will be king over all the earth. On that day there will be one LORD—his name alone will be worshiped.

12:10 Or the Spirit. 13:6 Hebrew wounds between your hands? 14:5a The meaning of the Hebrew is uncertain. 14:5b As in Greek version; Hebrew reads with you. 14:6 Hebrew the precious ones shall diminish; or the precious ones and frost. The meaning of the Hebrew is uncertain. 14:8 Hebrew half toward the eastern sea and half toward the western sea.

¹⁰All the land from Geba, north of Judah, to Rimmon, south of Jerusalem, will become one vast plain. But Jerusalem will be raised up in its original place and will be inhabited all the way from the Benjamin Gate over to the site of the old gate, then to the Corner Gate, and from the Tower of Hananel to the king's winepresses. ¹¹And Jerusalem will be filled, safe at last, never again to be cursed and destroyed.

¹²And the LORD will send a plague on all the nations that fought against Jerusalem. Their people will become like walking corpses, their flesh rotting away. Their eyes will rot in their sockets, and their tongues will rot in their mouths. ¹³On that day they will be terrified, stricken by the LORD with great panic. They will fight their neighbors hand to hand. ¹⁴Judah, too, will be fighting at Jerusalem. The wealth of all the neighboring nations will be captured—great quantities of gold and silver and fine clothing. ¹⁵This same plague will strike the horses, mules, camels, donkeys, and all the other animals in the enemy camps.

¹⁶In the end, the enemies of Jerusalem who survive the plague will go up to Jerusalem each year to worship the King, the LORD of Heaven's Armies, and to celebrate the Festival of Shelters. ¹⁷Any nation in the world that refuses to come to Jerusalem to worship the King, the LORD of Heaven's Armies, will have no rain. ¹⁸If the people of Egypt refuse to attend the festival, the LORD will punish* them with the same plague that he sends on the other nations who refuse to go. ¹⁹Egypt and the other nations will all be punished if they don't go to celebrate the Festival of Shelters.

²⁰On that day even the harness bells of the horses will be inscribed with these words: HOLY TO THE LORD. And the cooking pots in the Temple of the LORD will be as sacred as the basins used beside the altar. ²¹In fact, every cooking pot in Jerusalem and Judah will be holy to the LORD of Heaven's Armies. All who come to worship will be free to use any of these pots to boil their sacrifices. And on that day there will no longer be traders* in the Temple of the LORD of Heaven's Armies.

14:18 As in some Hebrew manuscripts and Greek and Syriac versions; Masoretic Text reads *will not punish*.   14:21 Hebrew *Canaanites*.

MALACHI

JON HUNTZINGER, PHD

Malachi, whose name means 'My messenger,' prophesied during the fifth century BC prior to the time of Ezra and Nehemiah. He prophesied after the people had returned to the land after the Exile and had begun to rebuild their lives. Not all the people who went into exile returned. Because they had put down roots in Babylon, they followed Jeremiah's advice (Jeremiah 29:5-6) and decided to remain and continue to live their lives where they had started businesses, had children, and embraced parts of the culture.

However, for those who returned, the work was hard, and the reality of their circumstances left many disappointed. They responded by giving offerings at the Temple that would have been unacceptable if they had been given to the governor (1:6-14). Malachi denounced the apathetic worship that the priests and people were giving to God at that time and the general lack of honor they were showing to His name in their behavior.

The book of Malachi is organized by several disputation speeches or arguments in which God and His people dispute or argue with each other (1:2; 1:6-9; 2:17; 3:7-8; 3:13-14). In these passages, God makes a claim, and the people question the validity or truthfulness of the claim that He makes:

— When God says He loves them, the people wonder if He truly does (1:2).

— When God says that His people do not honor Him, they ask how they have despised Him (1:6).
— When God says that His people have made Him weary, the people wonder how (2:17).
— When God says the people have cheated Him, they ask how they have cheated Him (3:8).
— When God says the people have said terrible things about Him, they say, "What have we said against you?" (3:13).

The people constantly argued with God and attempted to refute the words He spoke, revealing their disbelief. Malachi shows that the post-Exilic period (the period after the Exile) was difficult for the people of Judah. They had to make sense of their current circumstances in view of earlier prophecies that declared a glorious future (Ezekiel 40-48). Because of their disappointment, the people and priests had begun to disbelieve those earlier prophecies and the word that God spoke to them.

Malachi holds out hope and declares that God will personally appear to His people to purify their hearts so that they might once again offer worthy praise to Him and receive the blessings He wants them to enjoy as a result of their worship (3:10-12). Malachi says that day will bring healing like a warm sun ("the Sun of Righteousness") for those who respond with worship or destruction "burning like a furnace" (4:1-2) to those who remain in their disbelief.

1

This is the message* that the LORD gave to Israel through the prophet Malachi.*

THE LORD'S LOVE FOR ISRAEL

²"I have always loved you," says the LORD.

But you retort, "Really? How have you loved us?"

And the LORD replies, "This is how I showed my love for you: I loved your ancestor Jacob, ³but I rejected his brother, Esau, and devastated his hill country. I turned Esau's inheritance into a desert for jackals."

⁴Esau's descendants in Edom may say, "We have been shattered, but we will rebuild the ruins."

But the LORD of Heaven's Armies replies, "They may try to rebuild, but I will demolish them again. Their country will be known as 'The Land of Wickedness,' and their people will be called 'The People with Whom the LORD Is Forever Angry.' ⁵When you see the destruction for yourselves, you will say, 'Truly, the LORD's greatness reaches far beyond Israel's borders!'"

UNWORTHY SACRIFICES

⁶The LORD of Heaven's Armies says to the priests: "A son honors his father, and a servant respects his master. If I am your father and master, where are the honor and respect I deserve? You have shown contempt for my name!

"But you ask, 'How have we ever shown contempt for your name?'

⁷"You have shown contempt by offering defiled sacrifices on my altar.

"Then you ask, 'How have we defiled the sacrifices?'*

"You defile them by saying the altar of the LORD deserves no respect. ⁸When you give blind animals as sacrifices, isn't that wrong? And isn't it wrong to offer animals that are crippled and diseased? Try giving gifts like that to your governor, and see how pleased he is!" says the LORD of Heaven's Armies.

⁹"Go ahead, beg God to be merciful to you! But when you bring that kind of offering, why should he show you any favor at all?" asks the LORD of Heaven's Armies.

¹⁰"How I wish one of you would shut the Temple doors so that these worthless sacrifices could not be offered! I am not pleased with you," says the LORD of Heaven's Armies, "and I will not accept your offerings. ¹¹But my name is honored* by people of other nations from morning till night. All around the world they offer* sweet incense and pure offerings in honor of my name. For my name is great among the nations," says the LORD of Heaven's Armies.

¹²"But you dishonor my name with your actions. By bringing contemptible food, you are saying it's all right to defile the Lord's table. ¹³You say, 'It's too hard to serve the LORD,' and you turn up your noses at my commands," says the LORD of Heaven's Armies. "Think of it! Animals that are stolen and crippled and sick are being presented as offerings! Should I accept from you such offerings as these?" asks the LORD.

¹⁴"Cursed is the cheat who promises to give a fine ram from his flock but then sacrifices a defective one to the Lord. For I am a great king," says the LORD of Heaven's Armies, "and my name is feared among the nations!

A WARNING TO THE PRIESTS

2

"Listen, you priests—this command is for you! ²Listen to me and make up your minds to honor my name," says the LORD of Heaven's Armies, "or I will bring a terrible curse against you. I will curse even the blessings you receive. Indeed, I have already cursed them, because you have not taken my warning to heart. ³I will punish your descendants and splatter your faces with the manure from your festival sacrifices, and I will throw you on the manure pile. ⁴Then at last you will know it was I who sent you this warning so that my covenant with the Levites can continue," says the LORD of Heaven's Armies.

⁵"The purpose of my covenant with the Levites was to bring life and peace, and that is what I gave them. This required reverence from them, and they greatly revered me and stood in awe of my name. ⁶They passed on to the people the truth of the instructions they received from me. They did not lie or cheat; they walked with me, living good and righteous lives, and they turned many from lives of sin.

⁷"The words of a priest's lips should preserve knowledge of God, and people should go to him for instruction, for the priest is the messenger of the LORD of Heaven's Armies. ⁸But you priests have left God's paths. Your instructions have caused many to stumble into sin. You have corrupted the covenant I made with the Levites," says the LORD of Heaven's Armies. ⁹"So I have made you despised and humiliated in the eyes of all the people. For you have not obeyed me but have shown favoritism in the way you carry out my instructions."

A CALL TO FAITHFULNESS

¹⁰Are we not all children of the same Father? Are we not all created by the same God? Then why do we betray each other, violating the covenant of our ancestors?

¹¹Judah has been unfaithful, and a detestable thing has been done in Israel and in Jerusalem. The men of Judah have defiled the LORD's beloved sanctuary by marrying women who worship idols. ¹²May the LORD cut off from the nation of Israel* every last man who has done

---

1:1a Hebrew *An Oracle: The message.*   1:1b *Malachi* means "my messenger."   1:7 As in Greek version; Hebrew reads *defiled you?*   1:11a Or *will be honored.*   1:11b Or *will offer.*   2:12 Hebrew *from the tents of Jacob.* The names "Jacob" and "Israel" are often interchanged throughout the Old Testament, referring sometimes to the individual patriarch and sometimes to the nation.

this and yet brings an offering to the LORD of Heaven's Armies.

¹³Here is another thing you do. You cover the LORD's altar with tears, weeping and groaning because he pays no attention to your offerings and doesn't accept them with pleasure. ¹⁴You cry out, "Why doesn't the LORD accept my worship?" I'll tell you why! Because the LORD witnessed the vows you and your wife made when you were young. But you have been unfaithful to her, though she remained your faithful partner, the wife of your marriage vows.

¹⁵Didn't the LORD make you one with your wife? In body and spirit you are his.* And what does he want? Godly children from your union. So guard your heart; remain loyal to the wife of your youth. ¹⁶"For I hate divorce!"* says the LORD, the God of Israel. "To divorce your wife is to overwhelm her with cruelty,*" says the LORD of Heaven's Armies. "So guard your heart; do not be unfaithful to your wife."

¹⁷You have wearied the LORD with your words. "How have we wearied him?" you ask.

You have wearied him by saying that all who do evil are good in the LORD's sight, and he is pleased with them. You have wearied him by asking, "Where is the God of justice?"

THE COMING DAY OF JUDGMENT

3 "Look! I am sending my messenger, and he will prepare the way before me. Then the Lord you are seeking will suddenly come to his Temple. The messenger of the covenant, whom you look for so eagerly, is surely coming," says the LORD of Heaven's Armies.

²"But who will be able to endure it when he comes? Who will be able to stand and face him when he appears? For he will be like a blazing fire that refines metal, or like a strong soap that bleaches clothes. ³He will sit like a refiner of silver, burning away the dross. He will purify the Levites, refining them like gold and silver, so that they may once again offer acceptable sacrifices to the LORD. ⁴Then once more the LORD will accept the offerings brought to him by the people of Judah and Jerusalem, as he did in the past.

⁵"At that time I will put you on trial. I am eager to witness against all sorcerers and adulterers and liars. I will speak against those who cheat employees of their wages, who oppress widows and orphans, or who deprive the foreigners living among you of justice, for these people do not fear me," says the LORD of Heaven's Armies.

A CALL TO REPENTANCE

⁶"I am the LORD, and I do not change. That is why you descendants of Jacob are not already destroyed. ⁷Ever since the days of your ancestors, you have scorned my decrees and failed to obey them. Now return to me, and I will return to you," says the LORD of Heaven's Armies.

WHAT TEST?
Malachi 3:6–12   ROBERT MORRIS

Most people know they're not supposed to test God. However, when it comes to tithing, God makes an exception. He says, "Try it! Put me to the test!" (Malachi 3:10). Tithing is a test of the heart. In fact, the word *tithe* means a "tenth part." Throughout Scripture, the number 10 represents testing. God tests our hearts through the tithe, and it's the only area where He says we can test Him too.

God wants His children to bring their tithes and offerings into the storehouse of the church. If we don't, we are under a curse. But the good news is if we do, we are under a blessing. Giving the firstfruits to God should be ordinary behavior for redeemed people. When we do this, God says He will pour out His blessings upon us, and "all the nations will call you blessed, for your land will be such a delight" (Malachi 3:12).

THE POWER OF OFFERINGS
Malachi 3:8   ROBERT MORRIS

In Malachi 3:8, God tells the people of Israel, "You have cheated me of the tithes and *offerings* due to me" (emphasis added). Because the firstfruits actually belong to the Lord, tithing isn't really giving—it's *returning*. To truly give to God, we have to go beyond our tithe.

In Matthew 14:13–21, Jesus feeds a crowd of 5,000 men plus their families with only five loaves of bread and two fish. In the same way, God can cause our finances to go further than we could ever imagine. I know this is true; I've seen it happen in my own life over and over again. However, if we want to see the multiplication of our finances, we must understand two principles:
— We give to the Lord first so that our finances are blessed.
— We give over and above our tithes because only that which is shared can be multiplied.

"But you ask, 'How can we return when we have never gone away?'

⁸"Should people cheat God? Yet you have cheated me!

"But you ask, 'What do you mean? When did we ever cheat you?'

2:15 Or *Didn't the one LORD make us and preserve our life and breath?* or *Didn't the one LORD make her, both flesh and spirit?* The meaning of the Hebrew is uncertain. 2:16a Hebrew *For he hates divorcing.* 2:16b Hebrew *to cover one's garment with violence.*

"You have cheated me of the tithes and offerings due to me. 9 You are under a curse, for your whole nation has been cheating me. 10 Bring all the tithes into the storehouse so there will be enough food in my Temple. If you do," says the LORD of Heaven's Armies, "I will open the windows of heaven for you. I will pour out a blessing so great you won't have enough room to take it in! Try it! Put me to the test! 11 Your crops will be abundant, for I will guard them from insects and disease.* Your grapes will not fall from the vine before they are ripe," says the LORD of Heaven's Armies. 12 "Then all nations will call you blessed, for your land will be such a delight," says the LORD of Heaven's Armies.

13 "You have said terrible things about me," says the LORD.

"But you say, 'What do you mean? What have we said against you?'

14 "You have said, 'What's the use of serving God? What have we gained by obeying his commands or by trying to show the LORD of Heaven's Armies that we are sorry for our sins? 15 From now on we will call the arrogant blessed. For those who do evil get rich, and those who dare God to punish them suffer no harm.'"

THE LORD'S PROMISE OF MERCY

16 Then those who feared the LORD spoke with each other, and the LORD listened to what they said. In his presence, a scroll of remembrance was written to record the names of those who feared him and always thought about the honor of his name.

17 "They will be my people," says the LORD of Heaven's Armies. "On the day when I act in judgment, they will be my own special treasure. I will spare them as a father spares an obedient child. 18 Then you will again see the difference between the righteous and the wicked, between those who serve God and those who do not."

THE COMING DAY OF JUDGMENT

4 1* The LORD of Heaven's Armies says, "The day of judgment is coming, burning like a furnace. On that day the arrogant and the wicked will be burned up like straw. They will be consumed—roots, branches, and all.

2 "But for you who fear my name, the Sun of Righteousness will rise with healing in his wings.* And you will go free, leaping with joy like calves let out to pasture. 3 On the day when I act, you will tread upon the wicked as if they were dust under your feet," says the LORD of Heaven's Armies.

4 "Remember to obey the Law of Moses, my servant—all the decrees and regulations that I gave him on Mount Sinai* for all Israel.

5 "Look, I am sending you the prophet Elijah before the great and dreadful day of the LORD arrives. 6 His preaching will turn the hearts of fathers to their children, and the hearts of children to their fathers. Otherwise I will come and strike the land with a curse."

3:11 Hebrew from the devourer.   4:1 Verses 4:1-6 are numbered 3:19-24 in Hebrew text.   4:2 Or the sun of righteousness will rise with healing in its wings.   4:4 Hebrew Horeb, another name for Sinai.

THE PROBLEM OF SIN?

— When Adam disobeyed God, sin and death entered the world (Romans 5:12).
— Sin infects every person (Isaiah 64:6).
— Every person is born a sinner (Psalm 51:5).
— No person is free from sin (Ecclesiastes 7:20).
— If we claim not to sin, we are lying and calling God a liar (1 John 1:8-10).
— Nothing good comes from a sinful nature (Romans 7:18).
— Sin cuts us off from God (Isaiah 59:2).
— Sin makes us fall short of God's standard (Romans 3:23).
— Sin subjects us to God's anger (Ephesians 2:3).
— Sinful behavior originates in the heart (Mark 7:20-23).
— The human heart is deceitful and wicked (Jeremiah 17:9).
— The payment for sin is death (Romans 6:23).
— If you live by your sinful nature, you will not inherit the Kingdom of God (Galatians 5:19-21).

TEMPTATION?

— Joseph ran away from a woman who tried to seduce him (Genesis 39:7-12).
— Job made a covenant with his eyes not to look with lust (Job 31:1).
— Be on guard. Stand firm in faith (1 Corinthians 16:13).
— God's love supported the psalmist when he cried out, "I am slipping!" (Psalm 94:18).
— Jesus taught us to ask the Father to keep us from yielding to temptation (Matthew 6:13).
— Stay alert because the devil prowls like a lion (1 Peter 5:8-9).
— Jesus told His followers to watch and pray so that they would not give in to temptation (Mark 14:38).
— We should gently and humbly help other believers who are struggling with temptation (Galatians 6:1).
— Humble yourself before God and resist the devil (James 4:7).
— Believers defeat Satan by their testimony and the blood of the Lamb (Revelation 12:11).

THE FORGIVENESS OF SINS?

— God sent His Son to save the world, not to judge it (John 3:17).
— God purchased your freedom with the blood of Jesus (Ephesians 1:7).
— God saves you by His grace when you believe (Ephesians 2:8).
— If you confess your sins, God will forgive and cleanse you (1 John 1:9).
— God makes you right with Him through Christ (2 Corinthians 5:21).
— God makes you alive with Christ and forgives all your sins (Colossians 2:13).
— If you belong to Christ, you have become a new person (2 Corinthians 5:17).
— There is no condemnation when you belong to Christ (Romans 8:1).
— God will make your sins as white as snow (Isaiah 1:18).
— God no longer counts our sins against us (2 Corinthians 5:19).
— God will never again remember your sins (Hebrews 8:12).
— God removes your sins as far as the east is from the west (Psalm 103:12).
— God puts our sins out of sight (Romans 4:7).
— Jesus saves us and intercedes with God on our behalf forever (Hebrews 7:25).
— Jesus is our advocate before God the Father when we sin (1 John 2:1).
— We should forgive one another as God through Christ forgave us (Ephesians 4:32).

What Does the Bible Say About . . .

ETERNAL LIFE?

— Whoever believes in Jesus has eternal life (John 3:16).
— Whoever believes in Jesus will live after dying (John 11:23–25).
— The Lord will swallow up death forever (Isaiah 25:8).
— Everyone who follows Jesus will inherit eternal life (Matthew 19:29).
— John wrote to believers so they would know they have eternal life (1 John 5:11–13).
— Believers will be with the Lord forever (1 Thessalonians 4:13–18).
— Jesus' followers are children of the resurrection (Luke 20:36).
— The dead will hear the voice of Jesus and live (John 5:25).
— The free gift of God is eternal life through Jesus (Romans 6:23).
— Believers will have an eternal body made by God (2 Corinthians 5:1).
— We are buried in natural bodies but raised in spiritual bodies (1 Corinthians 15:42–44).

HEALING?

— God says He is the Lord who heals you (Exodus 15:26).
— The Lord restored David's health when he cried for help (Psalm 30:2).
— God sent out His Word and healed those who were at death's door (Psalm 107:20).
— Jesus was whipped so we could be healed (Isaiah 53:5).
— If the Lord heals you, you are truly healed (Jeremiah 17:14).
— Jesus said, "I am willing. . . . Be healed!" (Matthew 8:3).
— Jesus healed every kind of disease and illness (Matthew 4:23).
— Jesus took our sicknesses and removed our diseases (Matthew 8:17).
— By His wounds you are healed (1 Peter 2:24).
— Confess your sins to one another and pray for one another to be healed (James 5:16).
— Jesus preached the Good News and healed the sick (Luke 9:6).
— Jesus taught about the Kingdom of God and healed the sick (Luke 9:11).
— God healed a man who had been lame for more than 40 years (Acts 4:22).
— Jesus went about doing good and healing the sick (Acts 10:38).
— The Holy Spirit gives the gift of healing (1 Corinthians 12:9).
— Paul realized a man born with crippled feet had faith to be healed (Acts 14:9).

THE TRINITY?

— "Let us make human beings in our image" (Genesis 1:26).
— The Lord said, "Look, the human beings have become like us" (Genesis 3:22).
— God said, "Come, let's go down and confuse the people with different languages" (Genesis 11:6-7).
— The Lord said, "Who will go for us?" (Isaiah 6:8).
— The Father, Son, and Holy Spirit were present at Jesus' baptism (Matthew 3:16-17).
— Jesus said, "The Spirit of the LORD is upon me" (Luke 4:18).
— Jesus says He will ask the Father to send the Advocate—the Holy Spirit (John 14:16-17).
— Jesus told His followers to baptize disciples in the name of the Father, Son, and Holy Spirit (Matthew 28:19).
— God anointed Jesus with the Holy Spirit and power (Acts 10:38).
— God raised Jesus from death by the Holy Spirit's power (Romans 1:2-4).
— God enables us to stand firm for Christ and places the Holy Spirit in our hearts (2 Corinthians 1:21-22).
— The Father knew and chose you, the Holy Spirit made you holy, and Jesus' blood cleansed you (2 Peter 1:2).

What Does the Bible Say About . . .

THE CHURCH?

— Jesus builds His Church, and hell will not conquer it (Matthew 16:18).
— Jesus is present where two or three of His followers gather (Matthew 18:20).
— All the believers were meeting in one place when the Holy Spirit came (Acts 2:1-4).
— The believers were devoted to teaching, fellowship, sharing meals, and prayer (Acts 2:42-47).
— The Church gathered to pray in times of trouble (Acts 12:5, 12).
— God calls prophets and teachers in the Church (Acts 13:1).
— The Church worshipped, fasted, and prayed (Acts 13:2-3).
— Elders were appointed in every church (every city) (Acts 14:23).
— The churches were strengthened in their faith and grew larger (Acts 16:5).
— The Spirit speaks to the churches (Revelation 2-3).
— The Church is a body made up of different parts, and each part does its own special work (Ephesians 4:1-16).
— The Church is God's flock, purchased by Jesus' blood (Acts 20:28).
— The Lord's Supper should be taken in an orderly way (1 Corinthians 11:17-34).
— We should not neglect meeting together but should encourage one another (Hebrews 10:25).
— We are living stones for God's temple and His holy priests (1 Peter 2:4-9).

NEW TESTAMENT

GOOD NEWS COMES IN JESUS CHRIST

JON HUNTZINGER, PHD

THE MESSAGE OF GOOD NEWS

An angel from heaven announced the birth of Jesus as "good news that will bring great joy" (Luke 2:10). What does the angel mean by "good news"? This proclamation is about God's salvation for all people. It is also about freedom from fear and ignorance and, ultimately, freedom from death. This "good news" is about healing for shattered hearts, deliverance from captivity, and the restoration of lost things (Isaiah 61:1–3). Therefore, when the angel says "good news" to simple shepherds, these aren't mere words. The angel is promising good news of freedom, healing, deliverance, and restoration, which will all come from this newborn baby.

The New Testament is more than a collection of books. It is a message of good news! It further develops the message of the Old Testament in which people first encountered God's good news. Seven hundred years before the birth of Jesus, the prophet Isaiah declared God's salvation and deliverance to a people living far away from their homeland in the Babylonian Exile. He exclaimed, "O Zion, messenger of good news, shout from the mountaintops! Shout it louder, O Jerusalem. Shout, and do not be afraid. Tell the towns of Judah, 'Your God is coming!'" (Isaiah 40:9). The four men God chose to record the Good News about Jesus are, in fact, Good News-casters. They describe God's salvation through Jesus to a world in need of freedom, deliverance, healing, and understanding. The apostle Paul picks up this theme of good news in his letters. He writes that there is only one gospel, only one declaration of Good News, and if anyone, including angels from heaven, announces a different one, the believers in Jesus should resist and reject them (Galatians 1:6–9).

THE NEW TESTMENT RECORD OF GOOD NEWS

The New Testament consists of 27 books, including Gospels, letters, a history, a sermon or exhortation, wisdom literature, and one book of prophecy. Together, all of these books proclaim the Good News of God's salvation through Jesus. It took about 50 years for all the writers of the New Testament to finish their work. They wrote from the late 40s to the 90s. As many as nine different men had the God-given task of writing these books.

The subject matter holds this collection of books together. That subject is Jesus of Nazareth. He is the focus of every book from Matthew to Revelation. The four Gospels record Jesus' ministry, death, and resurrection. The letters of Paul, Peter, John, and others provide instruction for the churches that have accepted the Good News message about the truth of God's salvation coming through Jesus. All of these churches see Jesus as Messiah and Savior. The history of the book of Acts reports the spread of the Good News from Jerusalem to Rome through the ministry of the Holy Spirit in the lives of the followers of Jesus. The sermon of Hebrews proclaims the Good News that Jesus is God's great High Priest, who is also the acceptable sacrifice for the sins of all people. The wisdom literature, represented by the book of James, shows that the proper response to the Good News is to live in faithfulness to the Word of God (who is Jesus). The prophetic book of Revelation speaks of the rule of Jesus as the risen Messiah over His Church and the world in the present as well as in the future.

God inspired these writers, who developed these books of Good News from eyewitness accounts, oral and written sources, and through revelation from the Holy Spirit (Luke 1:1–4; Galatians 1:6–20; 2 Timothy 3:16). Why did the writers compose these books during this specific period? The answer includes several reasons:
— By the end of the first century, firsthand eye-witnesses were dying, so the writers surely sensed the urgency.
— The Church needed a permanent record of Jesus' ministry in written form.
— Some false documents began to spring up, including false gospels. Churches began to circulate them, so the writers needed to create an authoritative record and correct false teaching.
— The early followers of Jesus saw these books as vital for preserving the message of Good News and for establishing the basics of belief and the manner in which they should live together.
— The Holy Spirit moved in a special way to inspire the writers at this time.

So how did the early Church leaders decide which books were inspired by God and should be included in the collection? They used the following three criteria:

1. Apostolic—each book had to have a relationship to an apostle.
   They began by tracing each book to an apostle. The New Testament contains writings the early Church saw as having a connection with the apostles, each of whom had a personal connection with Jesus. Apostolicity represents the relational center of every book to Jesus Himself.
2. Universal—each book had to be meant for all churches.
   The books had to speak to all people, in all places, and at all times. Another term for this criterion is *catholicity*, which means "universal." Universality represents the global nature of the collection for the Church throughout the entire world.
3. Orthodox—each book had to have the right beliefs, especially about Jesus.
   They also saw books that conformed to the basic Good News about Jesus as acceptable. These books are orthodox, which means they have the right beliefs or the true theological standard.

If everyone in the early Church's leadership agreed that a book contained these three important criteria, then they included it in the Canon. The word *canon* means "measuring stick," which in relation to these books means they had to measure up to the right standards for the leaders to include them in the Bible. The books that make up the New Testament, then, are "canonical." The Church's leadership officially accepted them into the collection because they are directly related to Jesus Himself, developed with all of God's people in mind, and devoted to the true proclamation of the Good News of God's salvation in Jesus Christ.

EARLY NEW TESTAMENT DEVELOPMENT

JON HUNTZINGER, PHD

Jesus Himself began the development of the New Testament, meaning that without Him there would be no need for it to exist. Though Jesus could write (John 8:6), He did not leave any personal writings behind. Instead, He passed on that responsibility to His followers. Contrary to what many people may think, literacy was common in Israel during the time of Jesus. Consequently, at least some of Jesus' followers would have easily memorized His sayings and also have written them down.

Very likely, the first written stages occurred during the time of Jesus' own ministry. The ability to write in shorthand (tachygraphy) had already developed in the Greco-Roman world and in Israel before the time of Jesus. Since writing materials were scarce, shards of pottery and wax tablets were often used for writing, and because of their small size, shorthand was a way to record information efficiently within a small space. Government officials and business people quickly learned this skill. The apostle Matthew, for example, would have possessed the ability to do shorthand as a tax collector.

In the prologue to his Gospel, Luke writes that he has used many written sources to compile his book. He also notes that specific people among Jesus' followers were entrusted with telling about the events in Jesus' life. Luke's Gospel refers to eyewitnesses and servants of the word. More than likely, he was referring to specific people who saw and heard Jesus firsthand and had followed Him from the beginning of His ministry. The early Church entrusted these witnesses with the accurate recounting of Jesus' life because of their personal and long-term perspective. A ruler of a synagogue had the responsibility to remove the scroll of the Torah from a replica of the Ark of the Covenant, make it available for reading and study, and return it to its case. This great care preserved the integrity of the scroll. In the same way, some followers of Jesus who were servants of the Word had the responsibility for the precise preservation of the story of Jesus' teachings and ministry. Undoubtedly, these people would have been disciples whom Jesus called at the beginning of His ministry. They heard His teachings, saw His miracles, and even witnessed His suffering, death, and resurrection.

Some theories exist of a long and slow development of the Gospels, beginning with oral accounts of Jesus' teaching and healing ministry and evolving over a long time. According to these theories, the writers relaxed the standards of accountability and accuracy to meet the particular needs of local churches. Consequently, these theorists believe the messages in the New Testament may not be factual.

However, *none of these theories are true*. Instead, the writers carefully developed the New Testament under the watchful supervision of the followers of Jesus—the apostles—who had been with Him from the beginning. They knew what He said and did, and they reported the truth as it actually happened. They referred humorously to the many things Jesus did (John 21:25), mentioned writing materials (2 Timothy 4:13), and even wrote themselves (Revelation 1:11). Moreover, they collected texts and developed archives. Early Christian letters were among the first documents to be distributed as collections (2 Peter 3:15–16). Very likely, a collection of Paul's letters was gathered and distributed by the churches by the early 60s.

THE NEW TESTAMENT GOSPELS

JON HUNTZINGER, PHD

The English word *gospel* is a translation of the Greek word *evangelion*, meaning 'good news.' When referring to the books of the Bible, it applies to the Gospels of Matthew, Mark, Luke, and John. Each book records the Good News story of God's redemptive work in His Son, Jesus, as well as the Good News message itself.

Even though the Gospels bear some similarities to the biographies of famous people in the Greco-Roman world, they are not exactly like them. A primary similarity is that both record remarkable events and achievements in the lives of their main subjects. For instance, Matthew and Luke tell about the amazing circumstances surrounding Jesus' birth—including angelic visitations and dreams. In addition, all the Gospels describe healings performed by Jesus for blindness, deafness, lameness, leprosy, epilepsy, deliverance from spiritual powers and death, and miracles such as the feeding of more than 5,000 people. A major difference, however, is that the Gospels also report opposition to Jesus and criticism of Him by numerous people. Pharisees are critical of His words and actions; scribes say He is possessed by a demon; Temple leaders, like Caiaphas, plot His death; Romans, like Pontius Pilate, are unimpressed with Him; and God His Father seemingly turns His back on Him. Whereas ancient biographies only included events that highlighted the positive traits of their heroes, such as virtue, courage, and fidelity, the Gospels reach the moment when Jesus is beaten and then executed outside the walls of Jerusalem by Roman soldiers. All four Gospels give detailed attention to His humiliating and shameful death on a cross. Unlike most biographies of the time, the Gospels represent personal eyewitness testimony to Jesus' life and ministry.

New Testament scholars also see the Gospels as works of theology and not simply bare records of facts. They interpret Jesus as much as they give information about Him. This feature of the Gospels raises an important question: If they are theological as well as historical, can readers trust the historical information given in them? To answer, no ancient histories simply told the facts from an objective point of view. Writers of those histories always tried to teach lessons and sway readers to a particular point of view. The Gospels also follow this pattern. The Gospel writers never intended to give play-by-play accounts, such as a court stenographer might do. They gave factual accounts, but they also designed a portrait of Jesus to educate their readers, so they would know He is the Messiah, the Son of God who has come to save the world. Those who knew Him best intended these Gospels to assist their churches in worship and proclamation.

Nonetheless, the Gospel writers composed their accounts to give a true and accurate understanding of Jesus' ministry (Luke 1:1-4). We can trust the truthfulness of the Gospels because these eyewitnesses, including those who opposed Jesus and His message, were alive when they were written. These eyewitnesses could either confirm or contradict the portrayal of Jesus and the information about Him provided by the Gospels. So important was the goal of truthfulness that they recorded information about Him that many would view as embarrassing or difficult to explain otherwise. Thus, they report Jesus' baptism by John at the Jordan River; they recount His rejection by the religious leaders; they tell of His abandonment by some of His followers (John 6:66-71); and they describe the failure of the other disciples to stand alongside Him during His trial and crucifixion. The Gospel writers were so careful to give an accurate report of Jesus' ministry that they do not try to exaggerate or overstate His miracles. For example, Mark says Jesus could do few miracles in Nazareth, and a blind man required a second touch by Jesus before he could see clearly (Mark 6:5-6; 8:22-26). In the final analysis, these men wrote the Gospels to strengthen people in their belief and to assure them that what eyewitnesses had heard and experienced was true (John 20:30-31). To summarize, the Gospels' fourfold witness to Jesus is biographical, theological, and historical. Most of all, it is truthful testimony to the saving work of God in Jesus, His Son and Messiah.

THE MIRACLES AND HEALINGS OF JESUS

MIRACLE OR HEALING	MATTHEW	MARK	LUKE	JOHN
Jesus Turns Water into Wine				2:1-11
Jesus Heals an Official's Son				4:43-54
Jesus Casts Out a Demon		1:21-27	4:31-36	
Jesus Heals Simon Peter's Mother-in-Law	8:14-15	1:29-31	4:38-39	
Jesus Heals Many People	8:16-17	1:32-34	4:40-41	
The First Miraculous Catch of Fish			5:1-11	
Jesus Heals a Man with Leprosy	8:1-4	1:40-45	5:12-14	
Jesus Heals a Roman Officer's Servant	8:5-13		7:1-10	
Jesus Heals a Paralyzed Man	9:1-8	2:1-12	5:17-26	
Jesus Heals a Man with a Deformed Hand	12:9-14	3:1-6	6:6-11	
Jesus Raises a Widow's Son from Death			7:11-17	
Jesus Calms the Storm	8:23-27	4:35-41	8:22-25	
Jesus Heals a Demon-Possessed Man (Men)	8:28-33	5:1-20	8:26-39	
Jesus Heals a Woman with Twelve Years of Bleeding	9:20-22	5:25-34	8:43-48	
Jesus Raises Jairus's Daughter from Death	9:18, 23-26	5:21-24, 35-43	8:41-42, 49-56	
Jesus Heals the Blind	9:27-31			
Jesus Heals a Demon-Possessed Man Who Could Not Speak	9:32-34			
Jesus Heals a Lame Man				5:1-15
Jesus Feeds 5,000	14:13-21	6:30-44	9:10-17	6:1-15
Jesus Walks on Water	14:22-33	6:45-52		6:16-21
Jesus Heals Many Sick People at Gennesaret	14:34-36	6:53-56		
Jesus Heals the Demon-Possessed Daughter of a Gentile Woman	15:21-28	7:24-30		
Jesus Heals a Deaf Man		7:31-37		
Jesus Heals Many People at the Sea of Galilee	15:29-31			
Jesus Feeds 4,000	15:32-39	8:1-9		
Jesus Heals a Blind Man at Bethsaida		8:22-26		
Jesus Heals a Man Born Blind				9:1-7
Jesus Heals a Demon-Possessed Boy	17:14-20	9:14-27	9:37-43	
Miraculous Payment for the Temple Tax	17:24-27			
Jesus Heals a Blind and Mute Demon-Possessed Man	12:22-23		11:14-23	
Jesus Heals a Woman Crippled by an Evil Spirit			13:10-17	
Jesus Heals a Man with Swollen Legs and Arms			14:1-6	
Jesus Heals 10 Men of Leprosy			17:11-19	
Jesus Raises Lazarus from Death				11:1-44
Jesus Heals Two Blind Men (Bartimaeus)	20:29-34	10:46-52	18:35-43	
Jesus Curses the Fig Tree	21:18-22	11:12-14, 20-21		
Jesus Heals a Slave with His Ear Slashed Off			22:50-51	
The Second Miraculous Catch of Fish				21:1-14

SPECIAL FEATURES OF THE SYNOPTIC GOSPELS

JON HUNTZINGER, PHD

The books of Matthew, Mark, and Luke are called the Synoptic Gospels from the Greek word *synoptic*, which means 'with the same vision or to see with the same eye.' These three Gospels all present a shared view of Jesus' teaching and miracle ministry, whereas the Gospel of John records teachings and miracles of Jesus that are different from, yet complementary to, those in the other Gospels. While the Synoptic Gospels share common structure, content, and vocabulary, each also contains unique information about Jesus. Each of these three writers had a special motivation and intention behind his Gospel.

MATTHEW'S SPECIAL GOSPEL MATERIAL

Much of the unique material in Matthew is found in Jesus' teachings. Matthew gave priority to teachings over miracles, such as Jesus' teachings in the Sermon on the Mount (Matthew 5-7) and the Great Commission (Matthew 28:18-20). Matthew's genealogy of Jesus stretches back to Abraham and is only found in this Gospel. He alone gave unique emphasis to Joseph's role in Jesus' birth.

MATTHEW	EVENT	MIRACLE	TEACHING
Genealogy 1:1-17	Begins with Abraham and includes David		
Birth of Jesus 1:18-2:23	Emphasizes Joseph's role; includes Herod and wise men; Jesus taken to Egypt		
Sermon on the Mount 5-7			Beatitudes; Jesus' word as new law; Lord's Prayer; fruit tree
Parable 13:24-30			Field of weeds and wheat
Miracle 17:24-27		Coin from fish used to pay Temple tax	
Teaching 18:15-22		Forbid and permit; gathering of two or three; forgiveness and 70 times 7	
Parable 18:23-35			Unforgiving servant
Parable 21:28-32			Two sons
Lament 23:1-36			Woe concerning scribes and Pharisees
Parable 25:1-13			10 bridesmaids
Last Judgment 25:31-46			Jesus' teaching on judgment
Passion 27:3-10	30 pieces of silver; Judas hangs himself		
Passion 27:51-53, 62-66	Tombs break open; guards posted at tomb		
Passion 28:11-15	False report about the Resurrection		
Great Commission 28:16-20			Jesus commissions His disciples

MARK'S SPECIAL GOSPEL MATERIAL

Because much of the Gospel of Mark is found in Matthew and Luke, this book does not contain as much unique material as the other two. In fact, Mark is distinctive for what he does not record. For example, he does not provide a genealogy for Jesus like Matthew and Luke do, nor does he present a birth narrative. Moreover, he does not record anything like Matthew's Sermon on the Mount (Matthew 5–7) or Luke's three lost-and-found parables (Luke 15).

Most surprising, according to the earliest manuscripts of the Gospel, Mark does not include an account of Jesus' followers encountering Him after the Resurrection. Instead, he concludes his Gospel with a description of an empty tomb (16:8).

MARK	EVENT	MIRACLE	TEACHING
Introduction	No genealogy or birth narrative		
Temptation 1:12–13	Reference to wild animals and angels		
Event 3:20–21	Family thinks Jesus is "out of his mind"		
Parable 4:26–29			Growing seed
Event 6:1–3	Community refers to Jesus as "son of Mary"		
Miracle 8:22–26		Blind man healed; spit shows Jesus' willingness to accommodate man's lack of faith; difficulty of healing underscores sub-theme of resistance in Mark	
Passion 14:51–52	Young man flees; autobiographical note; Mark identifies himself with the other disciples whom he portrayed as weak and fearful		
Resurrection 16:19–20		Missing from earliest manuscripts	

LUKE'S SPECIAL GOSPEL MATERIAL

Other than the Gospel of John, Luke has the most unique material of the four Gospels. Much of this content is in the form of stories and teachings recorded nowhere else. For example, only Luke tells the stories of the Good Samaritan, the Rich Fool, and the Lost Son. And only Luke tells the famous story of Zacchaeus and the resurrection day account of Jesus on the road to Emmaus.

LUKE	EVENT	MIRACLE	TEACHING
Introduction 1:1–80	Birth of John		
Birth of Jesus 2:1–38, 41–52	Birth and circumcision of Jesus		
Event 3:10–14	John's response to the people		
Preaching 4:16–30	Jesus preaches in Nazareth		
Teaching 6:20–26			Beatitudes and sorrows
Healing 7:11–17		Widow of Nain's son healed	
Event 9:52–56	Rejection by Samaritans		
Parable 10:29–37			Good Samaritan
Parable 11:5–8			Friend at midnight
Teaching 12:13–15			Beware of greed
Parable 12:16–21			Rich fool
Healing 13:10–17		Crippled woman healed	
Comment 13:31–33			Warning about Herod
Healing 14:1–6		Man with swollen arms and legs healed	
Teaching 14:7–14			Humility
Teaching 14:25–33			Cost of being a disciple
Parable 15:3–32			Lost coin; lost son; lost sheep
Parable 16:1–9			Shrewd manger
Teaching 16:10–12			Faithful in little things
Parable 16:19–31			Rich man and Lazarus
Teaching 17:7–10			Servants' duty
Healing 17:11–19		10 lepers healed	
Parable 18:1–8			Persistent widow and unjust judge
Visit 19:1–10	Zacchaeus		
Passion 19:41–44	Jesus weeps over Jerusalem		
Passion 23:6–12	Herod questions Jesus		
Passion 23:39–43	Two criminals beside Jesus		
Resurrection 24:13–35	Jesus on road to Emmaus		
Resurrection 24:44–53	Jesus ascends to heaven		

People have long wondered about the literary relationship among the Gospels of Matthew, Mark, and Luke, given their common chronology of Jesus' life and ministry and the similarities of the vocabulary they use. How do these three Gospels relate to one another? Bible scholars have offered various theories about their relationship. The most popular theory is that Mark wrote his Gospel first, in part because it is the shortest of the three. Then Matthew and Luke used another common source to develop their Gospels. However it happened, from the very beginning, Jesus' followers preserved and ensured the accuracy of His teaching and the accounts of His miracles in writing and in memory as servants of the Word (Luke 1:2).

PARABLES OF JESUS IN CHRONOLOGICAL ORDER

PARABLE	MATTHEW	MARK	LUKE
New Cloth on Old Clothing	9:16	2:21	5:36
New Wine into Old Wineskins	9:17	2:22	5:37-38
Lamp on a Stand	5:14-15		
Wise and Foolish Builders	7:24-27		6:47-49
Moneylender Forgives Unequal Debts			7:41-43
Lamp on a Stand (2nd time)		4:21-22	8:16; 11:33
Rich Fool Builds Bigger Barns			12:16-21
Servants Must Remain Watchful			12:35-40
Faithful and Evil Servants			12:42-48
Unfruitful Fig Tree			13:6-9
Farmer Scattering Seed	13:3-8, 18-23	4:2-8, 14-20	8:4-8, 11-15
Wheat and Weeds (Kingdom of Heaven)	13:24-30, 36-43		
Growing Seed (Kingdom of God)		4:26-29	
Mustard Seed (Kingdom of Heaven/God)	13:31-32	4:30-32	13:18-19
Yeast (Kingdom of Heaven/God)	13:33		13:20-21
Hidden Treasure (Kingdom of Heaven)	13:44		
Valuable Pearl (Kingdom of Heaven)	13:45-46		
Fishing Net (Kingdom of Heaven)	13:47-50		
Homeowner (Kingdom of Heaven)	13:52		
Lost Sheep (sheep as children)	18:12-14		
Master and His Servant			17:7-10
Unforgiving Debtor (Kingdom of Heaven)	18:23-34		
Good Samaritan			10:30-37
Friend at Midnight			11:5-8
Lowest Seat at the Feast			14:7-14
Invitation to a Great Banquet			14:16-24
Cost of Being a Disciple			14:28-33
Lost Sheep (Sheep as Sinners)			15:4-7
Lost Coin			15:8-10
Lost (Prodigal) Son			15:11-32
Shrewd Manager			16:1-9
Rich Man and Lazarus			16:19-31
First and Last Vineyard Workers	20:1-16		
Persistent Widow and Unjust Judge			18:2-8
Pharisee and Tax Collector			18:10-14
King's 10 Servants Given Silver			19:12-27
Two sons, One Obeys and One Does Not	21:28-32		
Evil Tenant Farmers	21:33-44	12:1-11	20:9-18
The Great Feast (Kingdom of Heaven)	22:2-14		
Signs of the Future from a Fig Tree	24:32-35	13:28-31	21:29-33
Faithful and Evil Servants (2nd time)	24:45-51		
Wise and Foolish Bridesmaids	25:1-13		
Servants Must Remain Watchful (2nd time)		13:35-37	
Three Servants Given Silver (talents)	25:14-30		
Sheep and Goats Will Be Separated	25:31-46		

MATTHEW

JON HUNTZINGER, PHD

Early church tradition links the Gospel of Matthew to Jesus' disciple by that name. Matthew was a tax collector (Matthew 10:3; 9:9-13; Mark 2:14-17). As such, he would have had connections with King Herod's administration and would have assumed responsibility for collecting various fees and taxes from local people. Since Matthew worked in the area around Capernaum, along the shore of the Sea of Galilee, he would have issued commercial fishing licenses, which means he likely collected fishing fees from fishermen like Simon (Peter), Andrew, James, and John.

Matthew's Gospel contains five major sections centered on five major teachings of Jesus and their supporting stories:
— The Sermon on the Mount (Chapters 5-7)
— The disciples' mission to Israel (Chapter 10)
— Parables about the Kingdom of Heaven (Chapter 13)
— Teaching about humility and forgiveness (Chapter 18)
— Teaching about judgment and future events (Chapters 23-25)

Each of these teachings concludes with "When Jesus had finished saying . . . " or similar words (7:28; 11:1; 13:53; 19:1; 26:1).

A NEW MOSES

Matthew records these teachings to show Jesus to be like Moses, the great teacher of Israel. Jesus is like Moses in other ways too. For instance, Matthew reports the escape of the young Jesus with His parents to Egypt when King Herod attempted to kill all young boys Jesus' age (2:13-23). This event recalls Moses' rescue from Pharaoh, who had ordered the killing of all male Israelite babies at that time (Exodus 1:15-16; 2:1-10). Matthew tells about Jesus' temptations in the wilderness (Matthew 4:1-11), which are like Moses' struggle with the Israelites during their journey to Canaan. Matthew records Jesus' teaching on the mountain (5-7), which recalls God's words to Moses on Mount Sinai. He also relates how Jesus often referred to the disciples as having little faith (8:23-27; 14:28-32; 16:5-12; 17:14-21), which recalls the Israelites' struggle with faith during their deliverance from Egypt (for example, Exodus 16; 17:1-7).

SON OF DAVID

Matthew not only shows the relationship of Jesus to Moses but also to King David. Nine times, Matthew describes Jesus as "a descendant of David." He introduces Jesus as a son of David in His genealogy (1:1) and says His earthly father, Joseph, is a "son of David" too (1:20). Matthew reports wise men search for "the newborn king of the Jews" (2:1-12), meaning they were looking for a "Son of David"; a Canaanite woman calls Jesus "Son of David" and asks Him to deliver her daughter from a demon (15:21-28); and two blind men call Jesus "Son of David" as they ask Him to restore their sight (20:29-34). Matthew also reports Simon Peter's declaration that Jesus is "the Messiah, the Son of the living God" (16:16), an insight that recalls 2 Samuel 7 where God's covenant with David is described. And, finally, Matthew says the people of Jerusalem proclaim Jesus to be the "Son of David" upon His entry into the city (21:9). Jesus is crucified a week later as "King of the Jews" (27:29, 42).

Matthew likely wrote first to Jewish followers of Jesus. He alluded to Moses and David. Matthew also used the phrase "Kingdom of Heaven" (33 times) rather than "Kingdom of God" to refer to God's will. By making this reference, he showed honor to God by not referring to Him directly. Jewish readers would have recognized these associations and this style of writing and would have found them particularly meaningful.

Matthew's writing shows he had a strong and comprehensive understanding of the Hebrew Scriptures. In addition to his allusions to Moses and David, he quotes from the Old Testament 14 times and begins each quote with the word "fulfill." For Matthew, Jesus "fulfills" the Scriptures. Matthew shows what life looks like for God's people in relationship to His covenant and demonstrated through the teachings and miracles of Jesus.

THE ANCESTORS OF JESUS THE MESSIAH

1 This is a record of the ancestors of Jesus the Messiah, a descendant of David and of Abraham*:

2 Abraham was the father of Isaac.
  Isaac was the father of Jacob.
  Jacob was the father of Judah and
    his brothers.
3 Judah was the father of Perez and Zerah
    (whose mother was Tamar).
  Perez was the father of Hezron.
  Hezron was the father of Ram.*
4 Ram was the father of Amminadab.
  Amminadab was the father of Nahshon.
  Nahshon was the father of Salmon.
5 Salmon was the father of Boaz
    (whose mother was Rahab).
  Boaz was the father of Obed
    (whose mother was Ruth).
  Obed was the father of Jesse.
6 Jesse was the father of King David.
  David was the father of Solomon
    (whose mother was Bathsheba,
    the widow of Uriah).
7 Solomon was the father of Rehoboam.
  Rehoboam was the father of Abijah.
  Abijah was the father of Asa.*
8 Asa was the father of Jehoshaphat.
  Jehoshaphat was the father of Jehoram.*
  Jehoram was the father* of Uzziah.
9 Uzziah was the father of Jotham.
  Jotham was the father of Ahaz.
  Ahaz was the father of Hezekiah.
10 Hezekiah was the father of Manasseh.
  Manasseh was the father of Amon.*
  Amon was the father of Josiah.
11 Josiah was the father of Jehoiachin*
    and his brothers (born at the time of
    the exile to Babylon).

12 After the Babylonian exile:
  Jehoiachin was the father of Shealtiel.
  Shealtiel was the father of Zerubbabel.
13 Zerubbabel was the father of Abiud.
  Abiud was the father of Eliakim.
  Eliakim was the father of Azor.
14 Azor was the father of Zadok.
  Zadok was the father of Akim.
  Akim was the father of Eliud.
15 Eliud was the father of Eleazar.
  Eleazar was the father of Matthan.
  Matthan was the father of Jacob.
16 Jacob was the father of Joseph,
    the husband of Mary.
  Mary gave birth to Jesus,
    who is called the Messiah.

17 All those listed above include fourteen generations from Abraham to David, fourteen from David to the Babylonian exile, and fourteen from the Babylonian exile to the Messiah.

THE BIRTH OF JESUS THE MESSIAH

18 This is how Jesus the Messiah was born. His mother, Mary, was engaged to be married to Joseph. But before the marriage took place, while she was still a virgin, she became pregnant through the power of the Holy Spirit. 19 Joseph, to whom she was engaged, was a righteous man and did not want to disgrace her publicly, so he decided to break the engagement* quietly.

20 As he considered this, an angel of the Lord appeared to him in a dream. "Joseph, son of David," the angel said, "do not be afraid to take Mary as your wife. For the child within her was conceived by the Holy Spirit. 21 And she will have a son, and you are to name him Jesus,* for he will save his people from their sins."

22 All of this occurred to fulfill the Lord's message through his prophet:

23 "Look! The virgin will conceive a child!
  She will give birth to a son,
  and they will call him Immanuel,*
    which means 'God is with us.'"

24 When Joseph woke up, he did as the angel of the Lord commanded and took Mary as his wife. 25 But he did not have sexual relations with her until her son was born. And Joseph named him Jesus.

AMAZING SAVIOR
Matthew 1:21   ROBERT MORRIS

The name *Jesus* is the same name as *Joshua* in the Old Testament. *Joshua* means 'God is salvation,' and *Jesus* means 'Savior.' After Moses died, God used Joshua to lead His people into the Promised Land. Similarly, God used His Son, Jesus, to bring us out from under the law and place us under grace. Jesus Christ is the only One who can save us. There's nothing we can do to earn our salvation. We just have to receive it by God's mercy and grace. And once we receive salvation by submitting to Jesus, God mercifully removes our sins as far "as the east is from the west" (Psalm 103:12). Just as Joshua led his people out of the wilderness and into the Promised Land, Jesus leads us out of sin and into restoration. He truly is an amazing Savior!

1:1 Greek *Jesus the Messiah, Son of David and son of Abraham.*
1:3 Greek *Aram,* a variant spelling of Ram; also in 1:4. See 1 Chr 2:9-10.   1:7 Greek *Asaph,* a variant spelling of Asa; also in 1:8. See 1 Chr 3:10.   1:8a Greek *Joram,* a variant spelling of Jehoram; also in 1:8b. See 1 Kgs 22:50 and note at 1 Chr 3:11.   1:8b Or *ancestor;* also in 1:11.   1:10 Greek *Amos,* a variant spelling of Amon; also in 1:10b. See 1 Chr 3:14.   1:11 Greek *Jeconiah,* a variant spelling of Jehoiachin; also in 1:12. See 2 Kgs 24:6 and note at 1 Chr 3:16.   1:19 Greek *to divorce her.*   1:21 *Jesus* means "The LORD saves."   1:23 Isa 7:14; 8:8, 10 (Greek version).

WE THREE KINGS
Matthew 2:1-12
ROBERT MORRIS

When you think about the first Christmas, do you picture shepherds and wise men kneeling by a manger? Many people do. However, the wise men actually weren't present at the birth of Jesus. They had to travel 1,000 miles from Persia to Bethlehem, a journey that probably took six to nine months. It may also surprise you to learn the wise men are not the only kings in the Christmas story. Matthew 2 mentions three: the wise men, King Herod, and Jesus.

1. The Joyous Kings
The wise men were men of science, the wealthy intelligentsia of the day. Yet they rejoiced unashamedly when the star finally stopped. When they entered the house and saw Jesus, the wise men "bowed down and worshiped him" (v. 11). They were completely undone in the presence of this Child! Overwhelmed, they "opened their treasure chests" (v. 11) and presented extravagant gifts. Why did the wise men behave this way? Because they knew they were in the presence of the King of all kings.

2. The Jealous King
From the moment he spoke with the wise men, Herod began plotting to kill the "newborn king of the Jews" (v. 2). He likely wanted to kill any witnesses, too, which is why he told the wise men to come back to see him. "When he realized that the wise men had outwitted him" (v. 16), Herod ordered the death of every boy in Bethlehem two years old or younger. This king was a ruthless leader with an insecure, manipulative spirit, and this same spirit drives people today, seeking to suffocate the life and rule of God's spirit in us.

3. The Just King
The King of all kings and Lord of all lords came into this world as a vulnerable, helpless baby. The Creator became dependent upon His creation. Jesus could have come in splendor, but in direct contrast to the Herod spirit, He chose to be the ultimate example of humility and mercy. Many women died during childbirth at that time, so the strips of cloth in which Mary wrapped Jesus were probably first intended as burial cloths. Those cloths were certainly symbolic for Jesus—Revelation 13:8 says He is "the Lamb who was slaughtered before the world was made." The message of Christmas is not simply that Jesus was born but that He came for a purpose: to give His life for humanity.

VISITORS FROM THE EAST

2 Jesus was born in Bethlehem in Judea, during the reign of King Herod. About that time some wise men* from eastern lands arrived in Jerusalem, asking, [2] "Where is the newborn king of the Jews? We saw his star as it rose,* and we have come to worship him."

[3] King Herod was deeply disturbed when he heard this, as was everyone in Jerusalem. [4] He called a meeting of the leading priests and teachers of religious law and asked, "Where is the Messiah supposed to be born?"

[5] "In Bethlehem in Judea," they said, "for this is what the prophet wrote:

[6] 'And you, O Bethlehem in the land of Judah,
are not least among the ruling cities*
of Judah,
for a ruler will come from you
who will be the shepherd for
my people Israel.'*"

[7] Then Herod called for a private meeting with the wise men, and he learned from them the time when the star first appeared. [8] Then he told them, "Go to Bethlehem and search carefully for the child. And when you find him, come back and tell me so that I can go and worship him, too!"

[9] After this interview the wise men went their way. And the star they had seen in the east guided them to Bethlehem. It went ahead of them and stopped over the place where the child was. [10] When they saw the star, they were filled with joy! [11] They entered the house and saw the child with his mother, Mary, and they bowed down and worshiped him. Then they opened their treasure chests and gave him gifts of gold, frankincense, and myrrh.

[12] When it was time to leave, they returned to their own country by another route, for God had warned them in a dream not to return to Herod.

THE ESCAPE TO EGYPT

[13] After the wise men were gone, an angel of the Lord appeared to Joseph in a dream. "Get up! Flee to Egypt with the child and his mother," the angel said. "Stay there until I tell you to return, because Herod is going to search for the child to kill him."

[14] That night Joseph left for Egypt with the child and Mary, his mother, [15] and they stayed there until Herod's death. This fulfilled what the Lord had spoken through the prophet: "I called my Son out of Egypt."*

[16] Herod was furious when he realized that the wise men had outwitted him. He sent soldiers to kill all the boys in and around Bethlehem who were two years old and under, based on the wise men's report of the star's first appearance.

2:1 Or *royal astrologers;* Greek reads *magi;* also in 2:7, 16.　2:2 Or *star in the east.*　2:6a Greek *the rulers.*　2:6b Mic 5:2; 2 Sam 5:2.　2:15 Hos 11:1.

GETTING FROM PROMISE TO PURPOSE
Matthew 2:13   TODD LANE

When God gives us a promise, we often have to wait to see the fulfillment of His purpose. In Matthew 2:13, God tells Joseph in a dream to take Mary and Jesus to Egypt. God may call you to your own "Egypt," a place that feels off course from your calling or destiny. What seems like a detour, however, may be a divine arrangement for you to be a blessing to someone else.

Some people think God is slow, but He has the timing of everything in His hands. Jesus had to wait 30 years to begin His ministry, and when He did, He certainly did not meet the Jewish people's expectations. They were expecting the Messiah to be a part of the priestly elite or from a kingly family, neither of which applied to Jesus. God's purpose for the Messiah was bigger than their expectations. Jesus was not just for the Jews but also for the whole world.

[17] Herod's brutal action fulfilled what God had spoken through the prophet Jeremiah:

[18] "A cry was heard in Ramah—
weeping and great mourning.
Rachel weeps for her children,
refusing to be comforted,
for they are dead."*

THE RETURN TO NAZARETH

[19] When Herod died, an angel of the Lord appeared in a dream to Joseph in Egypt. [20] "Get up!" the angel said. "Take the child and his mother back to the land of Israel, because those who were trying to kill the child are dead."

[21] So Joseph got up and returned to the land of Israel with Jesus and his mother. [22] But when he learned that the new ruler of Judea was Herod's son Archelaus, he was afraid to go there. Then, after being warned in a dream, he left for the region of Galilee. [23] So the family went and lived in a town called Nazareth. This fulfilled what the prophets had said: "He will be called a Nazarene."

JOHN THE BAPTIST PREPARES THE WAY

3 In those days John the Baptist came to the Judean wilderness and began preaching. His message was, [2] "Repent of your sins and turn to God, for the Kingdom of Heaven is near.*" [3] The prophet Isaiah was speaking about John when he said,

"He is a voice shouting in the wilderness,
'Prepare the way for the LORD's coming!
Clear the road for him!'"*

[4] John's clothes were woven from coarse camel hair, and he wore a leather belt around his waist.

For food he ate locusts and wild honey. [5] People from Jerusalem and from all of Judea and all over the Jordan Valley went out to see and hear John. [6] And when they confessed their sins, he baptized them in the Jordan River.

[7] But when he saw many Pharisees and Sadducees coming to watch him baptize,* he denounced them. "You brood of snakes!" he exclaimed. "Who warned you to flee the coming wrath? [8] Prove by the way you live that you have repented of your sins and turned to God. [9] Don't just say to each other, 'We're safe, for we are descendants of Abraham.' That means nothing, for I tell you, God can create children of Abraham from these very stones. [10] Even now the ax of God's judgment is poised, ready to sever the roots of the trees. Yes, every tree that does not produce good fruit will be chopped down and thrown into the fire.

[11] "I baptize with* water those who repent of their sins and turn to God. But someone is coming soon who is greater than I am—so much greater that I'm not worthy even to be his slave and carry his sandals. He will baptize you with the Holy Spirit and with fire.* [12] He is ready to separate the chaff from the wheat with his winnowing fork. Then he will clean up the threshing area, gathering the wheat into his barn but burning the chaff with never-ending fire."

THE BAPTISM OF JESUS

[13] Then Jesus went from Galilee to the Jordan River to be baptized by John. [14] But John tried to talk him out of it. "I am the one who needs to be baptized by you," he said, "so why are you coming to me?"

[15] But Jesus said, "It should be done, for we must carry out all that God requires.*" So John agreed to baptize him.

[16] After his baptism, as Jesus came up out of the water, the heavens were opened* and he saw the Spirit of God descending like a dove and settling on him. [17] And a voice from heaven said, "This is my dearly loved Son, who brings me great joy."

THE TEMPTATION OF JESUS

4 Then Jesus was led by the Spirit into the wilderness to be tempted there by the devil. [2] For forty days and forty nights he fasted and became very hungry.

[3] During that time the devil* came and said to him, "If you are the Son of God, tell these stones to become loaves of bread."

[4] But Jesus told him, "No! The Scriptures say,

'People do not live by bread alone,
but by every word that comes from the
mouth of God.'*"

2:18 Jer 31:15.   3:2 Or *has come, or is coming soon.*   3:3 Isa 40:3 (Greek version).   3:7 Or *coming to be baptized.*   3:11a Or *in.* 3:11b Or *in the Holy Spirit and in fire.*   3:15 Or *for we must fulfill all righteousness.*   3:16 Some manuscripts read *opened* to him. 4:3 Greek *the tempter.*   4:4 Deut 8:3.

THE BREAD OF HEAVEN
Matthew 4:4   ROBERT MORRIS

In Matthew 4, Jesus fasts and prays in the wilderness for 40 days. Knowing Jesus is hungry, Satan arrives to tempt Him, saying, "If you are the Son of God, tell these stones to become loaves of bread" (v. 3). Instead of giving into temptation, Jesus replies,

"No! The Scriptures say,

'People do not live by bread alone,
    but by every word that comes from
    the mouth of God'" (v. 4).

There is nothing more important we can do than feed our spirits with God's Word. The more we allow ourselves to be sustained and nourished by the Word of God, the more we are equipped to resist temptation. When we know His Word, we'll be able to respond, *No! The Scriptures say . . .* No matter what comes against us, God's Word will sustain us.

RELEVANT FISHERMEN
Matthew 4:18-19   ROBERT MORRIS

Why did Jesus choose fishermen to be His disciples? A more obvious choice might have been to choose preachers or even politicians. Instead, He chose rugged, everyday men who knew how to go after something and catch it. He gave the work of the ministry to normal, working, and imperfect people.

Jesus calls all believers to be fishers of men, and it's surprisingly simple to do. All you need is the right bait and to cast your line in the right location. And the good news is you already have your bait! Bait is any story about God's goodness. It could be your salvation experience or a story about how God changed your life.

Every Christian can be like the disciples and learn how to "fish for people" (Matthew 4:19). People are hungry for the Good News, and you have what they're craving. So start "fishing" today!

⁵Then the devil took him to the holy city, Jerusalem, to the highest point of the Temple, ⁶and said, "If you are the Son of God, jump off! For the Scriptures say,

'He will order his angels to protect you.
And they will hold you up with their hands
    so you won't even hurt your foot on a
    stone.'*"

⁷Jesus responded, "The Scriptures also say, 'You must not test the LORD your God.'*"

⁸Next the devil took him to the peak of a very high mountain and showed him all the kingdoms of the world and their glory. ⁹"I will give it all to you," he said, "if you will kneel down and worship me."

¹⁰"Get out of here, Satan," Jesus told him. "For the Scriptures say,

'You must worship the LORD your God
    and serve only him.'*"

¹¹Then the devil went away, and angels came and took care of Jesus.

THE MINISTRY OF JESUS BEGINS
¹²When Jesus heard that John had been arrested, he left Judea and returned to Galilee. ¹³He went first to Nazareth, then left there and moved to Capernaum, beside the Sea of Galilee, in the region of Zebulun and Naphtali. ¹⁴This fulfilled what God said through the prophet Isaiah:

¹⁵ "In the land of Zebulun and of Naphtali,
    beside the sea, beyond the Jordan River,
    in Galilee where so many Gentiles live,
¹⁶ the people who sat in darkness
    have seen a great light.
And for those who lived in the land where
    death casts its shadow,
    a light has shined."*

¹⁷From then on Jesus began to preach, "Repent of your sins and turn to God, for the Kingdom of Heaven is near.*"

THE FIRST DISCIPLES
¹⁸One day as Jesus was walking along the shore of the Sea of Galilee, he saw two brothers—Simon, also called Peter, and Andrew—throwing a net into the water, for they fished for a living. ¹⁹Jesus called out to them, "Come, follow me, and I will show you how to fish for people!" ²⁰And they left their nets at once and followed him.

²¹A little farther up the shore he saw two other brothers, James and John, sitting in a boat with their father, Zebedee, repairing their nets. And he called them to come, too. ²²They immediately followed him, leaving the boat and their father behind.

CROWDS FOLLOW JESUS
²³Jesus traveled throughout the region of Galilee, teaching in the synagogues and announcing the Good News about the Kingdom. And he healed every kind of disease and illness. ²⁴News about him spread as far as Syria, and people soon began bringing to him all who were sick. And whatever

4:6 Ps 91:11-12.   4:7 Deut 6:16.   4:10 Deut 6:13.   4:15-16 Isa 9:1-2 (Greek version).   4:17 Or *has come,* or *is coming soon.*

HAPPINESS REDEFINED
Matthew 5:1–12

ROBERT MORRIS

You serve a happy God. Perhaps you've never thought about that. Sadly, religion often portrays God as angry. But the truth is God is happy, and He wants you to be happy too!

Matthew 5 contains one of Jesus' most famous teachings, the Beatitudes, in which He describes people whom God blesses. The Greek word for blessed is *makarios*, which means 'happy.' Jesus wants us to understand that God's version of happiness does not depend on emotions or possessions. Instead, it is an inner joy that remains constant in every situation.

1. "God blesses those who are poor and realize their need for him" (v. 3).

Jesus is not referring to the state of our bank accounts but to the state of our *hearts*. To enter the Kingdom of Heaven, we must see ourselves as spiritually bankrupt, unable to pay anything toward the overwhelming debt of sin. Our only hope is God, who is "rich in mercy" (Ephesians 2:4). When we enter His presence, we can't help but recognize His richness and our poverty.

2. "God blesses those who mourn" (v. 4).

When we think about a mourning person, we usually picture someone who has suffered a great loss. However, the mourning Jesus refers to is what we should feel about sin, especially when we realize that our sin put Jesus on the cross. This kind of godly sorrow produces repentance—a change in our hearts and minds. When we repent, the Holy Spirit comes to comfort us, and we experience the joy of salvation (Psalm 32:1–5; 51:1–4, 12).

3. "God blesses those who are humble" (v. 5).

Humility is not weakness—it's strength under control. Jesus was strong and still completely submissive and obedient to His Father. None of us are born with humility. Instead, it's a work of the Holy Spirit in our lives. Humility brings our strength under His control and harnesses it in the right direction. James 4:10 says, "Humble yourselves before the Lord, and he will lift you up in honor."

4. "God blesses those who hunger and thirst for justice" (v. 6).

The word translated *justice* is sometimes translated as *righteousness*, which means 'right standing with a perfect and holy God.' Jesus uses the terms *hunger* and *thirst* because these are the two strongest impulses we experience; food and water are absolute necessities for physical life. In the same way, righteousness is an absolute necessity for spiritual life, and the only one who can satisfy our need for true righteousness is Jesus.

5. "God blesses those who are merciful" (v. 7).

In Jesus' day, *mercy* meant showing compassion on the poor or guilty. As sinful humans, we are both poor *and* guilty! The greatest need in our lives is the *continuing* mercy of God. Thankfully, "His mercies never cease"; they "begin afresh each morning" (Lamentations 3:22–23). Because we have received God's mercy, we can be merciful to others and receive even more of His mercy in return.

6. "God blesses those whose hearts are pure" (v. 8).

The word translated *pure* means 'free from any impure mixture.' How can we ever have pure hearts and see God? Jesus said, "You must be born again" (John 3:7). Attending church, reading the Bible, and tithing are all good things, but they do not save you. Eternal life comes only through believing in Jesus (John 3:36). If you want to know if you've been born again, ask yourself, *When did I stop going my way and start going God's way?*

7. "God blesses those who work for peace" (v. 9).

Jesus is the Prince of Peace (Isaiah 9:6), and He calls His followers to work for peace in a world that's filled with war. Peace is not the absence of conflict; it's the presence of righteousness. James 3:18 says, "Those who are peacemakers will plant seeds of peace and reap a harvest of righteousness." We can't be peacemakers if we aren't at peace. We must stay focused on the Lord and His Word because perfect peace comes only from Him (Isaiah 26:3).

8. "God blesses those who are persecuted for doing right" (vv. 10–12).

The word translated *persecute* means 'to drive someone away in a hostile manner.' People often believe everything will be easy once they get saved, but "everyone who wants to live a godly life in Christ Jesus will suffer persecution" (2 Timothy 3:12). Persecution comes through people, but it's a spiritual attack. The world hates righteousness just as darkness hates light. However, when we are persecuted, Jesus instructs us to "be happy about it!" Why? Because "a great reward awaits you in heaven" (v. 12). There is a deep joy that comes from building the Kingdom of Heaven, and like Stephen in Acts 7:55, we too will see the glory of God.

---

their sickness or disease, or if they were demon possessed or epileptic or paralyzed—he healed them all. ²⁵ Large crowds followed him wherever he went—people from Galilee, the Ten Towns,* Jerusalem, from all over Judea, and from east of the Jordan River.

4:25 Greek *Decapolis*.

THE SERMON ON THE MOUNT

5 One day as he saw the crowds gathering, Jesus went up on the mountainside and sat down. His disciples gathered around him, [2] and he began to teach them.

THE BEATITUDES

[3] "God blesses those who are poor and realize their need for him,*
for the Kingdom of Heaven is theirs.
[4] God blesses those who mourn,
for they will be comforted.
[5] God blesses those who are humble,
for they will inherit the whole earth.
[6] God blesses those who hunger and thirst for justice,*
for they will be satisfied.
[7] God blesses those who are merciful,
for they will be shown mercy.
[8] God blesses those whose hearts are pure,
for they will see God.
[9] God blesses those who work for peace,
for they will be called the children of God.
[10] God blesses those who are persecuted for doing right,
for the Kingdom of Heaven is theirs.

[11] "God blesses you when people mock you and persecute you and lie about you and say all sorts of evil things against you because you are my followers. [12] Be happy about it! Be very glad! For a great reward awaits you in heaven. And remember, the ancient prophets were persecuted in the same way.

TEACHING ABOUT SALT AND LIGHT

[13] "You are the salt of the earth. But what good is salt if it has lost its flavor? Can you make it salty again? It will be thrown out and trampled underfoot as worthless.

[14] "You are the light of the world—like a city on a hilltop that cannot be hidden. [15] No one lights a lamp and then puts it under a basket. Instead, a lamp is placed on a stand, where it gives light to everyone in the house. [16] In the same way, let your good deeds shine out for all to see, so that everyone will praise your heavenly Father.

TEACHING ABOUT THE LAW

[17] "Don't misunderstand why I have come. I did not come to abolish the law of Moses or the writings of the prophets. No, I came to accomplish their purpose. [18] I tell you the truth, until heaven and earth disappear, not even the smallest detail of God's law will disappear until its purpose is achieved. [19] So if you ignore the least commandment and teach others to do the same, you will be called the least in the Kingdom of Heaven. But anyone who obeys God's laws and teaches them will be called great in the Kingdom of Heaven.

[20] "But I warn you—unless your righteousness is better than the righteousness of the teachers

ENGAGING INFLUENCERS
Matthew 5:13-15   ROBERT MORRIS

In Matthew 5:13, Jesus calls believers the "salt of the earth." Salt is a preservative, and it also makes food taste better. In the natural, salt remains pure by staying close to the rock and by being washed by water. In the same way, to stay pure as believers, we must remain close to our Rock (1 Corinthians 10:4) and wash ourselves with God's Word (Ephesians 5:26).

Then in Matthew 5:14, Jesus also calls believers the "light of the world." Jesus is the Light who shines through us, the body of Christ. If we hide our light under a basket (Matthew 5:15), darkness will overtake the world.

Everywhere we go, we have the opportunity and responsibility to influence others for the Lord. We need to shine our light so the world can see Jesus. If people are going to be influenced toward God, it has to be through us—His salt and light.

UNDER GRACE
Matthew 5:17   ROBERT MORRIS

I hear many different excuses for not tithing, but the one I hear the most is, "I'm under grace, not law." Some believers think that because Jesus fulfilled the Old Testament Law, they are off the hook from tithing. They somehow miss that every time Jesus pointed to an old covenant law, He then set a higher standard under new covenant grace. For example, the Law of Moses says not to commit adultery (Exodus 20:14 and Deuteronomy 5:18). However, in Matthew 5:27, Jesus says you should not even look at a woman lustfully. In other words, the righteousness that grace demands goes further than that which law demands.

I smile when someone tells me they give according to grace, not law. Then I reply, "Great! That means you give much more than 10 percent, because the righteousness of grace is a higher standard and always exceeds the righteousness of law."

of religious law and the Pharisees, you will never enter the Kingdom of Heaven!

TEACHING ABOUT ANGER

[21] "You have heard that our ancestors were told, 'You must not murder. If you commit murder, you are subject to judgment.'* [22] But I say, if you are even angry with someone,* you are subject to judgment! If you call someone an idiot,* you are in danger of

5:3 Greek *poor in spirit.* 5:6 Or *for righteousness.* 5:21 Exod 20:13; Deut 5:17. 5:22a Some manuscripts add *without cause.* 5:22b Greek uses an Aramaic term of contempt: *If you say to your brother, 'Raca.'*

THE GOSPEL AND MORALITY
Matthew 5:17–20　　　　　　　JACK HAYFORD

People often try to find fulfillment in life by grasping at what the world has to offer. We will not win those people to Christ by confronting them. We have to recognize they are living the way they do because they are blinded, bound, and in the dark.

So how can we reconcile the joy of the gospel with the call to discipleship? *Love*. The Christian faith becomes convincing when it's demonstrated, not when it's demanded. When we approach people based on love, we spread the power of the gospel. Jesus calls us to live morally consistent and joyously vibrant lives. Make your home and church inviting places. Show you care for your neighborhood, your city, and your nation by trying to help people. We need to bring people to Jesus, not control the system. You cannot disciple darkened minds. Jesus brought people first into life and then into discipleship.

THE ANATOMY OF ADULTERY
Matthew 5:27–30　　　　　　　JACK HAYFORD

Adultery is first spiritual. It starts when you give your heart to another person through your attitude. What begins in your mind then seeps into your heart and nourishes and feeds your eyes. As your eyes view pornography or look at another person with lust, an adulterous act forms.

How can you resist temptation?
— Avoid and discern.
— Don't be alone with a person when you know you shouldn't.
— Don't compliment in ways you know you shouldn't.
— Don't accept a protective role. It is not your job to be the protector of someone who is not your spouse.

Your body is the temple of the Holy Spirit (1 Corinthians 6:19). God is not against sexual fulfillment, but He doesn't want anything to defile its beauty. We should not taint intimacy with something that is inappropriate to God's divine order. Scripture prohibits adultery, warns against it, and assures that judgment will inevitably follow.

being brought before the court. And if you curse someone,* you are in danger of the fires of hell.*

²³ "So if you are presenting a sacrifice* at the altar in the Temple and you suddenly remember that someone has something against you, ²⁴ leave your sacrifice there at the altar. Go and be reconciled to that person. Then come and offer your sacrifice to God.

²⁵ "When you are on the way to court with your adversary, settle your differences quickly. Otherwise, your accuser may hand you over to the judge, who will hand you over to an officer, and you will be thrown into prison. ²⁶ And if that happens, you surely won't be free again until you have paid the last penny.*

TEACHING ABOUT ADULTERY
²⁷ "You have heard the commandment that says, 'You must not commit adultery.'* ²⁸ But I say, anyone who even looks at a woman with lust has already committed adultery with her in his heart. ²⁹ So if your eye—even your good eye*—causes you to lust, gouge it out and throw it away. It is better for you to lose one part of your body than for your whole body to be thrown into hell. ³⁰ And if your hand—even your stronger hand*—causes you to sin, cut it off and throw it away. It is better for you to lose one part of your body than for your whole body to be thrown into hell.

TEACHING ABOUT DIVORCE
³¹ "You have heard the law that says, 'A man can divorce his wife by merely giving her a written notice of divorce.'* ³² But I say that a man who divorces his wife, unless she has been unfaithful, causes her to commit adultery. And anyone who marries a divorced woman also commits adultery.

TEACHING ABOUT VOWS
³³ "You have also heard that our ancestors were told, 'You must not break your vows; you must carry out the vows you make to the LORD.'* ³⁴ But I say, do not make any vows! Do not say, 'By heaven!' because heaven is God's throne. ³⁵ And do not say, 'By the earth!' because the earth is his footstool. And do not say, 'By Jerusalem!' for Jerusalem is the city of the great King. ³⁶ Do not even say, 'By my head!' for you can't turn one hair white or black. ³⁷ Just say a simple, 'Yes, I will,' or 'No, I won't.' Anything beyond this is from the evil one.

TEACHING ABOUT REVENGE
³⁸ "You have heard the law that says the punishment must match the injury: 'An eye for an eye, and a tooth for a tooth.'* ³⁹ But I say, do not resist an evil person! If someone slaps you on the right cheek, offer the other cheek also. ⁴⁰ If you are sued in court and your shirt is taken from you, give your coat, too. ⁴¹ If a soldier demands that you carry his gear for a mile,* carry it two miles. ⁴² Give to those who ask, and don't turn away from those who want to borrow.

5:22c Greek *if you say, 'You fool.'*　5:22d Greek *Gehenna;* also in 5:29, 30.　5:23 Greek *gift;* also in 5:24.　5:26 Greek *the last hodrantes* [i.e., quadrans].　5:27 Exod 20:14; Deut 5:18.　5:29 Greek *your right eye.*　5:30 Greek *your right hand.*　5:31 Deut 24:1.　5:33 Num 30:2.　5:38 Greek *the law that says: 'An eye for an eye and a tooth for a tooth.'* Exod 21:24; Lev 24:20; Deut 19:21.　5:41 Greek *milion* [4,854 feet or 1,478 meters].

TEACHING ABOUT LOVE FOR ENEMIES

⁴³"You have heard the law that says, 'Love your neighbor'* and hate your enemy. ⁴⁴But I say, love your enemies!* Pray for those who persecute you! ⁴⁵In that way, you will be acting as true children of your Father in heaven. For he gives his sunlight to both the evil and the good, and he sends rain on the just and the unjust alike. ⁴⁶If you love only those who love you, what reward is there for that? Even corrupt tax collectors do that much. ⁴⁷If you are kind only to your friends,* how are you different from anyone else? Even pagans do that. ⁴⁸But you are to be perfect, even as your Father in heaven is perfect.

TEACHING ABOUT GIVING TO THE NEEDY

6 "Watch out! Don't do your good deeds publicly, to be admired by others, for you will lose the reward from your Father in heaven. ²When you give to someone in need, don't do as the hypocrites do—blowing trumpets in the synagogues and streets to call attention to their acts of charity! I tell you the truth, they have received all the reward they will ever get. ³But when you give to someone in need, don't let your left hand know what your right hand is doing. ⁴Give your gifts in private, and your Father, who sees everything, will reward you.

TEACHING ABOUT PRAYER AND FASTING

⁵"When you pray, don't be like the hypocrites who love to pray publicly on street corners and in the synagogues where everyone can see them. I tell you the truth, that is all the reward they will ever get. ⁶But when you pray, go away by yourself, shut the door behind you, and pray to your Father in private. Then your Father, who sees everything, will reward you.

⁷"When you pray, don't babble on and on as the Gentiles do. They think their prayers are answered merely by repeating their words again and again. ⁸Don't be like them, for your Father knows exactly what you need even before you ask him! ⁹Pray like this:

Our Father in heaven,
    may your name be kept holy.
¹⁰ May your Kingdom come soon.
May your will be done on earth,
    as it is in heaven.
¹¹ Give us today the food we need,*
¹² and forgive us our sins,
    as we have forgiven those who sin
        against us.
¹³ And don't let us yield to temptation,*
    but rescue us from the evil one.*

¹⁴"If you forgive those who sin against you, your heavenly Father will forgive you. ¹⁵But if you refuse to forgive others, your Father will not forgive your sins.

HOW TO HAVE A DAILY, DYNAMIC PRAYER LIFE
Matthew 6:5-15   JIMMY EVANS

God never intended the Christian life to be dull or boring. He wants every person to have a dynamic, fulfilling relationship with Him, but this requires communication going both ways. We cannot know someone without talking and listening, and the same is true for our relationship with God. Because we have a free will, He comes only by invitation.

Prayer is an intimate conversation with God. We pray to build a personal relationship with Him. In Matthew 6:5-15, Jesus gives the disciples a model for prayer. We should always begin by acknowledging God and His greatness. We worship and honor God for who He is and what He has done in our lives. Our prayers should be private and relational, not for showing off our "spirituality." Prayer recognizes our need for God's help and guidance, and it surrenders to His lordship and authority in every area of our lives.

TRUE RICHES
Matthew 6:19-20   ROBERT MORRIS

How can we obey Jesus' command to store our treasures in heaven (Matthew 6:20)? By being good stewards and using our money for righteous purposes. The human soul is eternal, and the only things that last are *people*. This is why I want to invest my money in churches and ministries that invest in people. I know God loves people more than anything, so I want my money to be used in helping people, loving people, feeding people, and caring for people.

You may be thinking, *I don't have a lot of money to give.* That's okay! Having only a little bit of money gives us a great opportunity for blessing. In Luke 16:10, Jesus tells us, "If you are faithful in little things, you will be faithful in large ones. But if you are dishonest in little things, you won't be honest with greater responsibilities."

¹⁶"And when you fast, don't make it obvious, as the hypocrites do, for they try to look miserable and disheveled so people will admire them for their fasting. I tell you the truth, that is the only reward they will ever get. ¹⁷But when you fast,

5:43 Lev 19:18.   5:44 Some manuscripts add *Bless those who curse you. Do good to those who hate you.* Compare Luke 6:27-28.   5:47 Greek *your brothers.*   6:11 Or *Give us today our food for the day;* or *Give us today our food for tomorrow.*   6:13a Or *And keep us from being tested.*   6:13b Or *from evil.* Some manuscripts add *For yours is the kingdom and the power and the glory forever. Amen.*

PASSING THE TEST
Matthew 6:21   ROBERT MORRIS

Many people think Matthew 6:21 says, "Where your heart is, there your treasure will also be." However, the verse actually says your heart follows your treasure. God knows where your heart is by where your treasure is. If you say, "My heart is in the Kingdom of God," your bank account will either validate or refute that claim.

Jesus spent 30 percent of His time teaching on money for a reason. Tithing represents the ultimate heart test for every believer. The test is how we handle our money, and the outcome of this test determines whether God can trust us with true riches or not. In Malachi 3:10, He says, "Bring all the tithes into the storehouse . . . I will open the windows of heaven for you. I will pour out a blessing so great you won't have enough room to take it in. Try it! Put me to the test!"

comb your hair* and wash your face. ¹⁸ Then no one will notice that you are fasting, except your Father, who knows what you do in private. And your Father, who sees everything, will reward you.

TEACHING ABOUT MONEY AND POSSESSIONS

¹⁹ "Don't store up treasures here on earth, where moths eat them and rust destroys them, and where thieves break in and steal. ²⁰ Store your treasures in heaven, where moths and rust cannot destroy, and thieves do not break in and steal. ²¹ Wherever your treasure is, there the desires of your heart will also be.

²² "Your eye is like a lamp that provides light for your body. When your eye is healthy, your whole body is filled with light. ²³ But when your eye is unhealthy, your whole body is filled with darkness. And if the light you think you have is actually darkness, how deep that darkness is!

²⁴ "No one can serve two masters. For you will hate one and love the other; you will be devoted to one and despise the other. You cannot serve God and be enslaved to money.

²⁵ "That is why I tell you not to worry about everyday life—whether you have enough food and drink, or enough clothes to wear. Isn't life more than food, and your body more than clothing? ²⁶ Look at the birds. They don't plant or harvest or store food in barns, for your heavenly Father feeds them. And aren't you far more valuable to him than they are? ²⁷ Can all your worries add a single moment to your life?

²⁸ "And why worry about your clothing? Look at the lilies of the field and how they grow. They don't work or make their clothing, ²⁹ yet Solomon in all his glory was not dressed as beautifully as

they are. ³⁰ And if God cares so wonderfully for wildflowers that are here today and thrown into the fire tomorrow, he will certainly care for you. Why do you have so little faith?

³¹ "So don't worry about these things, saying, 'What will we eat? What will we drink? What will we wear?' ³² These things dominate the thoughts of unbelievers, but your heavenly Father already knows all your needs. ³³ Seek the Kingdom of God* above all else, and live righteously, and he will give you everything you need.

³⁴ "So don't worry about tomorrow, for tomorrow will bring its own worries. Today's trouble is enough for today.

DO NOT JUDGE OTHERS

7 "Do not judge others, and you will not be judged. ² For you will be treated as you treat others.* The standard you use in judging is the standard by which you will be judged.*

³ "And why worry about a speck in your friend's eye* when you have a log in your own? ⁴ How can you think of saying to your friend,* 'Let me help you get rid of that speck in your eye,' when you can't see past the log in your own eye? ⁵ Hypocrite! First get rid of the log in your own eye; then you will see well enough to deal with the speck in your friend's eye.

⁶ "Don't waste what is holy on people who are unholy.* Don't throw your pearls to pigs! They will trample the pearls, then turn and attack you.

EFFECTIVE PRAYER

⁷ "Keep on asking, and you will receive what you ask for. Keep on seeking, and you will find. Keep on knocking, and the door will be opened to you. ⁸ For everyone who asks, receives. Everyone who seeks, finds. And to everyone who knocks, the door will be opened.

⁹ "You parents—if your children ask for a loaf of bread, do you give them a stone instead? ¹⁰ Or if they ask for a fish, do you give them a snake? Of course not! ¹¹ So if you sinful people know how to give good gifts to your children, how much more will your heavenly Father give good gifts to those who ask him.

THE GOLDEN RULE

¹² "Do to others whatever you would like them to do to you. This is the essence of all that is taught in the law and the prophets.

THE NARROW GATE

¹³ "You can enter God's Kingdom only through the narrow gate. The highway to hell* is broad, and its gate is wide for the many who choose that

---

6:17 Greek *anoint your head.*   **6:33** Some manuscripts do not include *of God.*   **7:2a** Or *For God will judge you as you judge others.*   **7:2b** Or *The measure you give will be the measure you get back.*   **7:3** Greek *your brother's eye;* also in 7:5.   **7:4** Greek *your brother.*   **7:6** Greek *Don't give the sacred to dogs.*   **7:13** Greek *The road that leads to destruction.*

way. ¹⁴ But the gateway to life is very narrow and the road is difficult, and only a few ever find it.

THE TREE AND ITS FRUIT

¹⁵ "Beware of false prophets who come disguised as harmless sheep but are really vicious wolves. ¹⁶ You can identify them by their fruit, that is, by the way they act. Can you pick grapes from thornbushes, or figs from thistles? ¹⁷ A good tree produces good fruit, and a bad tree produces bad fruit. ¹⁸ A good tree can't produce bad fruit, and a bad tree can't produce good fruit. ¹⁹ So every tree that does not produce good fruit is chopped down and thrown into the fire. ²⁰ Yes, just as you can identify a tree by its fruit, so you can identify people by their actions.

TRUE DISCIPLES

²¹ "Not everyone who calls out to me, 'Lord! Lord!' will enter the Kingdom of Heaven. Only those who actually do the will of my Father in heaven will enter. ²² On judgment day many will say to me, 'Lord! Lord! We prophesied in your name and cast out demons in your name and performed many miracles in your name.' ²³ But I will reply, 'I never knew you. Get away from me, you who break God's laws.'

BUILDING ON A SOLID FOUNDATION

²⁴ "Anyone who listens to my teaching and follows it is wise, like a person who builds a house on solid rock. ²⁵ Though the rain comes in torrents and the floodwaters rise and the winds beat against that house, it won't collapse because it is built on bedrock. ²⁶ But anyone who hears my teaching and doesn't obey it is foolish, like a person who builds a house on sand. ²⁷ When the rains and floods come and the winds beat against that house, it will collapse with a mighty crash."

STAND FIRM
Matthew 7:24-25   ROBERT MORRIS

Satan's first priority is not to get you to sin; it's to get you to believe a lie. The serpent lied to Eve in the Garden of Eden, and he continues to lie to us today. The way to defeat the words of the enemy and stand against him is to position ourselves firmly in God's Word.

In Matthew 7:24, Jesus says, "Anyone who listens to my teaching and follows it is wise, like a person who builds a house on solid rock." (Remember, 1 Corinthians 10:4 tells us that Jesus is the rock.) Jesus continues, "Though the rain comes in torrents and the floodwaters rise and the winds beat against that house, it won't collapse because it is built on bedrock" (v. 25).

The next time the enemy comes against you, it will be his word versus God's Word, and we already know who wins that battle!

THE FOUNDATION OF HEALING
Matthew 8:1-17   JACK HAYFORD

Healing is not arbitrary or an afterthought to salvation. Healing is tied up in the same package of total release for humanity, which comes through the cross of Jesus Christ. It is a historical fact that Jesus' healing ministry has been transmitted to the Church. There is a biblical basis for God's provision of health, healing, and deliverance. Jesus cast out demonic spirits and healed those who were sick as a fulfillment of the prophet Isaiah's words:

He was pierced for our rebellion,
    crushed for our sins.
He was beaten so we could be whole.
    He was whipped so we could be healed
    (Isaiah 53:5).

---

²⁸ When Jesus had finished saying these things, the crowds were amazed at his teaching, ²⁹ for he taught with real authority—quite unlike their teachers of religious law.

JESUS HEALS A MAN WITH LEPROSY

8 Large crowds followed Jesus as he came down the mountainside. ² Suddenly, a man with leprosy approached him and knelt before him. "Lord," the man said, "if you are willing, you can heal me and make me clean."

³ Jesus reached out and touched him. "I am willing," he said. "Be healed!" And instantly the leprosy disappeared. ⁴ Then Jesus said to him, "Don't tell anyone about this. Instead, go to the priest and let him examine you. Take along the offering required in the law of Moses for those who have been healed of leprosy.* This will be a public testimony that you have been cleansed."

THE FAITH OF A ROMAN OFFICER

⁵ When Jesus returned to Capernaum, a Roman officer* came and pleaded with him, ⁶ "Lord, my young servant* lies in bed, paralyzed and in terrible pain."

⁷ Jesus said, "I will come and heal him."

⁸ But the officer said, "Lord, I am not worthy to have you come into my home. Just say the word from where you are, and my servant will be healed. ⁹ I know this because I am under the authority of my superior officers, and I have authority over my soldiers. I only need to say, 'Go,' and they go, or 'Come,' and they come. And if I say to my slaves, 'Do this,' they do it."

¹⁰ When Jesus heard this, he was amazed. Turning to those who were following him, he said, "I tell you the truth, I haven't seen faith like

---

8:4 See Lev 14:2-32.   8:5 Greek *a centurion;* similarly in 8:8, 13.
8:6 Or *child;* also in 8:13.

this in all Israel! ¹¹And I tell you this, that many Gentiles will come from all over the world—from east and west—and sit down with Abraham, Isaac, and Jacob at the feast in the Kingdom of Heaven. ¹²But many Israelites—those for whom the Kingdom was prepared—will be thrown into outer darkness, where there will be weeping and gnashing of teeth."

¹³Then Jesus said to the Roman officer, "Go back home. Because you believed, it has happened." And the young servant was healed that same hour.

JESUS HEALS MANY PEOPLE

¹⁴When Jesus arrived at Peter's house, Peter's mother-in-law was sick in bed with a high fever. ¹⁵But when Jesus touched her hand, the fever left her. Then she got up and prepared a meal for him.

¹⁶That evening many demon-possessed people were brought to Jesus. He cast out the evil spirits with a simple command, and he healed all the sick. ¹⁷This fulfilled the word of the Lord through the prophet Isaiah, who said,

"He took our sicknesses
and removed our diseases."*

THE COST OF FOLLOWING JESUS

¹⁸When Jesus saw the crowd around him, he instructed his disciples to cross to the other side of the lake.

¹⁹Then one of the teachers of religious law said to him, "Teacher, I will follow you wherever you go."

²⁰But Jesus replied, "Foxes have dens to live in, and birds have nests, but the Son of Man* has no place even to lay his head."

²¹Another of his disciples said, "Lord, first let me return home and bury my father."

²²But Jesus told him, "Follow me now. Let the spiritually dead bury their own dead.*"

JESUS CALMS THE STORM

²³Then Jesus got into the boat and started across the lake with his disciples. ²⁴Suddenly, a fierce storm struck the lake, with waves breaking into the boat. But Jesus was sleeping. ²⁵The disciples went and woke him up, shouting, "Lord, save us! We're going to drown!"

²⁶Jesus responded, "Why are you afraid? You have so little faith!" Then he got up and rebuked the wind and waves, and suddenly there was a great calm.

²⁷The disciples were amazed. "Who is this man?" they asked. "Even the winds and waves obey him!"

JESUS HEALS TWO DEMON-POSSESSED MEN

²⁸When Jesus arrived on the other side of the lake, in the region of the Gadarenes,* two men who were possessed by demons met him. They came out of the tombs and were so violent that no one could go through that area.

²⁹They began screaming at him, "Why are you interfering with us, Son of God? Have you come here to torture us before God's appointed time?"

³⁰There happened to be a large herd of pigs feeding in the distance. ³¹So the demons begged, "If you cast us out, send us into that herd of pigs."

³²"All right, go!" Jesus commanded them. So the demons came out of the men and entered the pigs, and the whole herd plunged down the steep hillside into the lake and drowned in the water.

³³The herdsmen fled to the nearby town, telling everyone what happened to the demon-possessed men. ³⁴Then the entire town came out to meet Jesus, but they begged him to go away and leave them alone.

JESUS HEALS A PARALYZED MAN

9 Jesus climbed into a boat and went back across the lake to his own town. ²Some people brought to him a paralyzed man on a mat. Seeing their faith, Jesus said to the paralyzed man, "Be encouraged, my child! Your sins are forgiven."

³But some of the teachers of religious law said to themselves, "That's blasphemy! Does he think he's God?"

⁴Jesus knew* what they were thinking, so he asked them, "Why do you have such evil thoughts in your hearts? ⁵Is it easier to say 'Your sins are forgiven,' or 'Stand up and walk'? ⁶So I will prove to you that the Son of Man* has the authority on earth to forgive sins." Then Jesus turned to the paralyzed man and said, "Stand up, pick up your mat, and go home!"

⁷And the man jumped up and went home! ⁸Fear swept through the crowd as they saw this happen. And they praised God for giving humans such authority.

JESUS CALLS MATTHEW

⁹As Jesus was walking along, he saw a man named Matthew sitting at his tax collector's booth. "Follow me and be my disciple," Jesus said to him. So Matthew got up and followed him.

¹⁰Later, Matthew invited Jesus and his disciples to his home as dinner guests, along with many tax collectors and other disreputable sinners. ¹¹But when the Pharisees saw this, they asked his disciples, "Why does your teacher eat with such scum?*"

¹²When Jesus heard this, he said, "Healthy people don't need a doctor—sick people do." ¹³Then he added, "Now go and learn the meaning of this Scripture: 'I want you to show mercy, not offer sacrifices.'* For I have come to call not

---

8:17 Isa 53:4. 8:20 "Son of Man" is a title Jesus used for himself. 8:22 Greek *Let the dead bury their own dead.* 8:28 Other manuscripts read *Gerasenes;* still others read *Gergesenes.* Compare Mark 5:1; Luke 8:26. 9:4 Some manuscripts read *saw.* 9:6 "Son of Man" is a title Jesus used for himself. 9:11 Greek *with tax collectors and sinners?* 9:13 Hos 6:6 (Greek version).

LET'S BE FRIENDS
Matthew 9:9-13

ROBERT MORRIS

Matthew (also known as Levi) was a tax collector until he answered Jesus' call in Matthew 9 to "Follow me and be my disciple" (v. 9). He invited Jesus and the other disciples to come to dinner at his home, and "many tax collectors and other disreputable sinners" joined them (v. 10). The Pharisees saw this and asked Jesus' disciples, "Why does your teacher eat with such scum?" (v. 11). Jesus heard and responded, "I have come to call not those who think they are righteous, but those who know they are sinners" (v. 13).

Jesus is the best friend a sinner could ever have, and we are *all* sinners (Romans 3:23). You may wonder, *What makes Him such a good friend?* Here are three reasons:

1. A friend like Jesus isn't condemning.
Jesus was perfect and holy, yet sinners loved being around Him. Why? They knew He loved them. Yes, Jesus hates sin, but the reason He hates sin is because He loves sinners! He knows sin destroys people and separates them from God. John 3:17 says, "God sent His Son into the world not to judge the world, but to save the world through him." Jesus was not surprised when sinners sinned, and we shouldn't be either. They usually don't know there is a line they have crossed, and you wouldn't either if it weren't for the grace of God in your life.

2. A friend like Jesus isn't compromising.
In John 8, Jesus tells the woman caught in adultery two things: He doesn't condemn her, and "Go and sin no more" (v. 11). When faced with others' sin, we tend either to compromise our faith by "being a good friend," or we withdraw completely to "be separate from the world." However, Jesus is the perfect example of being both a friend of sinners and separate from them. He understands what it feels like to be tempted, but He never sinned (Hebrews 4:15). Jesus wasn't even curious about sin; He knows that sin always destroys people. He did not compromise in order to gain favor with sinners. Instead, sinners followed Him because they knew He spoke the truth! If we want to be in the world but not of it, we have no better example than Jesus.

3. A friend like Jesus is compassionate.
The woman caught in adultery was brought before the most important spiritual leader in all of history. According to the Law of Moses, Jesus could have stoned her for her immorality. Instead, He had compassion on her. The woman knew Jesus did not approve of her lifestyle, but she also knew that He loved her. Everyone Jesus met knew He loved them. How can we show this same love to others? The only way is to meet with the Compassionate One—Jesus. The more time we spend with Him, the more we will have His heart for people.

those who think they are righteous, but those who know they are sinners."

A DISCUSSION ABOUT FASTING

¹⁴ One day the disciples of John the Baptist came to Jesus and asked him, "Why don't your disciples fast* like we do and the Pharisees do?"

¹⁵ Jesus replied, "Do wedding guests mourn while celebrating with the groom? Of course not. But someday the groom will be taken away from them, and then they will fast.

¹⁶ "Besides, who would patch old clothing with new cloth? For the new patch would shrink and rip away from the old cloth, leaving an even bigger tear than before.

¹⁷ "And no one puts new wine into old wineskins. For the old skins would burst from the pressure, spilling the wine and ruining the skins. New wine is stored in new wineskins so that both are preserved."

JESUS HEALS IN RESPONSE TO FAITH

¹⁸ As Jesus was saying this, the leader of a synagogue came and knelt before him. "My daughter has just died," he said, "but you can bring her back to life again if you just come and lay your hand on her."

¹⁹ So Jesus and his disciples got up and went with him. ²⁰ Just then a woman who had suffered for twelve years with constant bleeding came up behind him. She touched the fringe of his robe, ²¹ for she thought, "If I can just touch his robe, I will be healed."

²² Jesus turned around, and when he saw her he said, "Daughter, be encouraged! Your faith has made you well." And the woman was healed at that moment.

²³ When Jesus arrived at the official's home, he saw the noisy crowd and heard the funeral music. ²⁴ "Get out!" he told them. "The girl isn't dead; she's only asleep." But the crowd laughed at him. ²⁵ After the crowd was put outside, however, Jesus went in and took the girl by the hand, and she stood up! ²⁶ The report of this miracle swept through the entire countryside.

JESUS HEALS THE BLIND

²⁷ After Jesus left the girl's home, two blind men followed along behind him, shouting, "Son of David, have mercy on us!"

9:14 Some manuscripts read *fast often.*

[28] They went right into the house where he was staying, and Jesus asked them, "Do you believe I can make you see?"

"Yes, Lord," they told him, "we do."

[29] Then he touched their eyes and said, "Because of your faith, it will happen." [30] Then their eyes were opened, and they could see! Jesus sternly warned them, "Don't tell anyone about this." [31] But instead, they went out and spread his fame all over the region.

[32] When they left, a demon-possessed man who couldn't speak was brought to Jesus. [33] So Jesus cast out the demon, and then the man began to speak. The crowds were amazed. "Nothing like this has ever happened in Israel!" they exclaimed.

[34] But the Pharisees said, "He can cast out demons because he is empowered by the prince of demons."

THE NEED FOR WORKERS

[35] Jesus traveled through all the towns and villages of that area, teaching in the synagogues and announcing the Good News about the Kingdom. And he healed every kind of disease and illness. [36] When he saw the crowds, he had compassion on them because they were confused and helpless, like sheep without a shepherd. [37] He said to his disciples, "The harvest is great, but the workers are few. [38] So pray to the Lord who is in charge of the harvest; ask him to send more workers into his fields."

JESUS SENDS OUT THE TWELVE APOSTLES

10 Jesus called his twelve disciples together and gave them authority to cast out evil* spirits and to heal every kind of disease and illness. [2] Here are the names of the twelve apostles:

first, Simon (also called Peter),
then Andrew (Peter's brother),
James (son of Zebedee),
John (James's brother),
[3] Philip,
Bartholomew,
Thomas,
Matthew (the tax collector),
James (son of Alphaeus),
Thaddaeus,*
[4] Simon (the zealot*),
Judas Iscariot (who later betrayed him).

[5] Jesus sent out the twelve apostles with these instructions: "Don't go to the Gentiles or the Samaritans, [6] but only to the people of Israel—God's lost sheep. [7] Go and announce to them that the Kingdom of Heaven is near.* [8] Heal the sick, raise the dead, cure those with leprosy, and cast out demons. Give as freely as you have received!

[9] "Don't take any money in your money belts—no gold, silver, or even copper coins. [10] Don't carry a traveler's bag with a change of clothes and sandals or even a walking stick. Don't hesitate

to accept hospitality, because those who work deserve to be fed.

[11] "Whenever you enter a city or village, search for a worthy person and stay in his home until you leave town. [12] When you enter the home, give it your blessing. [13] If it turns out to be a worthy home, let your blessing stand; if it is not, take back the blessing. [14] If any household or town refuses to welcome you or listen to your message, shake its dust from your feet as you leave. [15] I tell you the truth, the wicked cities of Sodom and Gomorrah will be better off than such a town on the judgment day.

[16] "Look, I am sending you out as sheep among wolves. So be as shrewd as snakes and harmless as doves. [17] But beware! For you will be handed over to the courts and will be flogged with whips in the synagogues. [18] You will stand trial before governors and kings because you are my followers. But this will be your opportunity to tell the rulers and other unbelievers about me.* [19] When you are arrested, don't worry about how to respond or what to say. God will give you the right words at the right time. [20] For it is not you who will be speaking—it will be the Spirit of your Father speaking through you.

[21] "A brother will betray his brother to death, a father will betray his own child, and children will rebel against their parents and cause them to be killed. [22] And all nations will hate you because you are my followers.* But everyone who endures to the end will be saved. [23] When you are persecuted in one town, flee to the next. I tell you

---

9:1 Greek *unclean*. 9:3 Other manuscripts read *Lebbaeus;* still others read *Lebbaeus who is called Thaddaeus.* 9:4 Greek *the Cananean,* an Aramaic term for Jewish nationalists. 9:7 Or *has come,* or *is coming soon.* 9:18 Or *But this will be your testimony against the rulers and other unbelievers.* 9:22 Greek *on account of my name.*

the truth, the Son of Man* will return before you have reached all the towns of Israel.

²⁴ "Students* are not greater than their teacher, and slaves are not greater than their master. ²⁵ Students are to be like their teacher, and slaves are to be like their master. And since I, the master of the household, have been called the prince of demons,* the members of my household will be called by even worse names!

²⁶ "But don't be afraid of those who threaten you. For the time is coming when everything that is covered will be revealed, and all that is secret will be made known to all. ²⁷ What I tell you now in the darkness, shout abroad when daybreak comes. What I whisper in your ear, shout from the housetops for all to hear! ²⁸ "Don't be afraid of those who want to kill your body; they cannot touch your soul. Fear only God, who can destroy both soul and body in hell.* ²⁹ What is the price of two sparrows—one copper coin*? But not a single sparrow can fall to the ground without your Father knowing it. ³⁰ And the very hairs on your head are all numbered. ³¹ So don't be afraid; you are more valuable to God than a whole flock of sparrows.

³² "Everyone who acknowledges me publicly here on earth, I will also acknowledge before my Father in heaven. ³³ But everyone who denies me here on earth, I will also deny before my Father in heaven. ³⁴ "Don't imagine that I came to bring peace to the earth! I came not to bring peace, but a sword.

³⁵ 'I have come to set a man against his father,
    a daughter against her mother,
 and a daughter-in-law against her
    mother-in-law.
³⁶   Your enemies will be right in your own
    household!'*

³⁷ "If you love your father or mother more than you love me, you are not worthy of being mine; or if you love your son or daughter more than me, you are not worthy of being mine. ³⁸ If you refuse to take up your cross and follow me, you are not worthy of being mine. ³⁹ If you cling to your life, you will lose it; but if you give up your life for me, you will find it.

⁴⁰ "Anyone who receives you receives me, and anyone who receives me receives the Father who sent me. ⁴¹ If you receive a prophet as one who speaks for God,* you will be given the same reward as a prophet. And if you receive righteous people because of their righteousness, you will be given a reward like theirs. ⁴² And if you give even a cup of cold water to one of the least of my followers, you will surely be rewarded."

JESUS AND JOHN THE BAPTIST

11 When Jesus had finished giving these instructions to his twelve disciples, he went out to teach and preach in towns throughout the region.

² John the Baptist, who was in prison, heard about all the things the Messiah was doing. So he sent his disciples to ask Jesus, ³ "Are you the Messiah we've been expecting,* or should we keep looking for someone else?"

⁴ Jesus told them, "Go back to John and tell him what you have heard and seen—⁵ the blind see, the lame walk, those with leprosy are cured, the deaf hear, the dead are raised to life, and the Good News is being preached to the poor." ⁶ And he added, "God blesses those who do not fall away because of me.*"

⁷ As John's disciples were leaving, Jesus began talking about him to the crowds. "What kind of man did you go into the wilderness to see? Was he a weak reed, swayed by every breath of wind? ⁸ Or were you expecting to see a man dressed in expensive clothes? No, people with expensive clothes live in palaces. ⁹ Were you looking for a prophet? Yes, and he is more than a prophet. ¹⁰ John is the man to whom the Scriptures refer when they say,

'Look, I am sending my messenger ahead
    of you,
    and he will prepare your way before you.'*

¹¹ "I tell you the truth, of all who have ever lived, none is greater than John the Baptist. Yet even the least person in the Kingdom of Heaven is greater than he is! ¹² And from the time John the Baptist began preaching until now, the Kingdom of Heaven has been forcefully advancing,* and violent people are attacking it. ¹³ For before John came, all the prophets and the law of Moses looked forward to this present time. ¹⁴ And if you are willing to accept what I say, he is Elijah, the one the prophets said would come.* ¹⁵ Anyone with ears to hear should listen and understand!

¹⁶ "To what can I compare this generation? It is like children playing a game in the public square. They complain to their friends,

¹⁷ 'We played wedding songs,
    and you didn't dance,
 so we played funeral songs,
    and you didn't mourn.'

¹⁸ For John didn't spend his time eating and drinking, and you say, 'He's possessed by a demon.' ¹⁹ The Son of Man,* on the other hand, feasts and drinks, and you say, 'He's a glutton and a drunkard, and a friend of tax collectors and other sinners!' But wisdom is shown to be right by its results."

10:23 "Son of Man" is a title Jesus used for himself. 10:24 Or *Disciples.* 10:25 Greek *Beelzeboul;* other manuscripts read *Beezeboul;* Latin version reads *Beelzebub.* 10:28 Greek *Gehenna.* 10:29 Greek *one assarion* [i.e., one "as," a Roman coin equal to ¹⁄₁₆ of a denarius]. 10:35-36 Mic 7:6. 10:41 Greek *receive a prophet in the name of a prophet.* 11:3 Greek *Are you the one who is coming?* 11:6 Or *who are not offended by me.* 11:10 Mal 3:1. 11:12 Or *the Kingdom of Heaven has suffered from violence.* 11:14 See Mal 4:5. 11:19 "Son of Man" is a title Jesus used for himself.

JUDGMENT FOR THE UNBELIEVERS

²⁰Then Jesus began to denounce the towns where he had done so many of his miracles, because they hadn't repented of their sins and turned to God. ²¹"What sorrow awaits you, Korazin and Bethsaida! For if the miracles I did in you had been done in wicked Tyre and Sidon, their people would have repented of their sins long ago, clothing themselves in burlap and throwing ashes on their heads to show their remorse. ²²I tell you, Tyre and Sidon will be better off on judgment day than you.

²³"And you people of Capernaum, will you be honored in heaven? No, you will go down to the place of the dead.* For if the miracles I did for you had been done in wicked Sodom, it would still be here today. ²⁴I tell you, even Sodom will be better off on judgment day than you."

JESUS' PRAYER OF THANKSGIVING

²⁵At that time Jesus prayed this prayer: "O Father, Lord of heaven and earth, thank you for hiding these things from those who think themselves wise and clever, and for revealing them to the childlike. ²⁶Yes, Father, it pleased you to do it this way!

²⁷"My Father has entrusted everything to me. No one truly knows the Son except the Father, and no one truly knows the Father except the Son and those to whom the Son chooses to reveal him."

²⁸Then Jesus said, "Come to me, all of you who are weary and carry heavy burdens, and I will give you rest. ²⁹Take my yoke upon you. Let me teach you, because I am humble and gentle at heart, and you will find rest for your souls. ³⁰For my yoke is easy to bear, and the burden I give you is light."

A DISCUSSION ABOUT THE SABBATH

12 At about that time Jesus was walking through some grainfields on the Sabbath. His disciples were hungry, so they began breaking off some heads of grain and eating them. ²But some Pharisees saw them do it and protested, "Look, your disciples are breaking the law by harvesting grain on the Sabbath."

³Jesus said to them, "Haven't you read in the Scriptures what David did when he and his companions were hungry? ⁴He went into the house of God, and he and his companions broke the law by eating the sacred loaves of bread that only the priests are allowed to eat. ⁵And haven't you read in the law of Moses that the priests on duty in the Temple may work on the Sabbath? ⁶I tell you, there is one here who is even greater than the Temple! ⁷But you would not have condemned my innocent disciples if you knew the meaning of this Scripture: 'I want you to show mercy, not offer sacrifices.'* ⁸For the Son of Man* is Lord, even over the Sabbath!"

JESUS HEALS ON THE SABBATH

⁹Then Jesus went over to their synagogue, ¹⁰where he noticed a man with a deformed hand.

The Pharisees asked Jesus, "Does the law permit a person to work by healing on the Sabbath?" (They were hoping he would say yes, so they could bring charges against him.)

¹¹And he answered, "If you had a sheep that fell into a well on the Sabbath, wouldn't you work to pull it out? Of course you would. ¹²And how much more valuable is a person than a sheep! Yes, the law permits a person to do good on the Sabbath."

¹³Then he said to the man, "Hold out your hand." So the man held out his hand, and it was restored, just like the other one! ¹⁴Then the Pharisees called a meeting to plot how to kill Jesus.

JESUS, GOD'S CHOSEN SERVANT

¹⁵But Jesus knew what they were planning. So he left that area, and many people followed him. He healed all the sick among them, ¹⁶but he warned them not to reveal who he was. ¹⁷This fulfilled the prophecy of Isaiah concerning him:

¹⁸ "Look at my Servant, whom I have chosen.
He is my Beloved, who pleases me.
I will put my Spirit upon him,
and he will proclaim justice to
the nations.
¹⁹ He will not fight or shout
or raise his voice in public.
²⁰ He will not crush the weakest reed
or put out a flickering candle.
Finally he will cause justice to
be victorious.
²¹ And his name will be the hope
of all the world."*

JESUS AND THE PRINCE OF DEMONS

²²Then a demon-possessed man, who was blind and couldn't speak, was brought to Jesus. He healed the man so that he could both speak and see. ²³The crowd was amazed and asked, "Could it be that Jesus is the Son of David, the Messiah?"

²⁴But when the Pharisees heard about the miracle, they said, "No wonder he can cast out demons. He gets his power from Satan,* the prince of demons."

²⁵Jesus knew their thoughts and replied, "Any kingdom divided by civil war is doomed. A town or family splintered by feuding will fall apart. ²⁶And if Satan is casting out Satan, he is divided and fighting against himself. His own kingdom will not survive. ²⁷And if I am empowered by Satan, what about your own exorcists? They cast out demons, too, so they will condemn you for what you have said. ²⁸But if I am casting out demons by the Spirit of God, then the Kingdom of God has arrived among you. ²⁹For who is powerful enough to enter the house of a strong man and plunder his goods? Only someone even

THE TRUTH ABOUT WORDS
Matthew 12:33-37   ROBERT MORRIS

In Matthew 12:33, Jesus speaks to the Pharisees about their words by comparing their hearts to a tree and their words to the tree's fruit. Just as its fruit reveals if a tree is good or bad, a person's words reveal the state of their heart. People who have experienced God's grace have a true heart change, and this should be reflected in the way they speak. If your mouth hasn't changed, it's possible your heart hasn't either.

Here are three truths about the words that come out of your mouth:

1. Words cost.

Can a person ever speak freely? The answer may surprise you. The truth is words are never free—they always cost something. Freedom of speech is an important right for which we should be grateful, but God's law is higher than any human law. According to Matthew 12:36-37, we are accountable to God for every word we speak. When we speak hurtful words over someone, the cost can be diminished trust, decreased intimacy, or even the loss of the relationship itself. If you find yourself saying, "I probably shouldn't say this," then it is either the Holy Spirit or common sense (or both!) telling you not to say something.

2. Words hurt.

Words don't hurt if you're just joking, right? Actually, they do. We try to convince ourselves that humor removes the sting of hurtful words, but this is simply not true. The writer of Proverbs says a person who lies and then claims to be joking is as destructive as "a madman shooting a deadly weapon" (Proverbs 26:18-19). Even if we aren't lying, we often put little jabs in our comments that hurt people. You may say you don't mean it, but Jesus says you do: "Whatever is in your heart determines what you say" (Matthew 12:34). When evil words come out of your mouth, it's time to examine your heart, repent, and ask for forgiveness. If someone has spoken hurtful words to you, the only way to break free is to forgive that person.

3. Words last.

Words don't evaporate or disappear into the air. On the contrary, James 3:5-6 says the tongue can start a forest fire. Hurtful words don't go away; instead, they can and do damage the people around us. Thankfully, good words last as well. They can build people up and heal old wounds. When we pray, we may not see an immediate answer, but we can rest assured that our prayers have no expiration date before God.

---

stronger—someone who could tie him up and then plunder his house.

³⁰ "Anyone who isn't with me opposes me, and anyone who isn't working with me is actually working against me.

³¹ "So I tell you, every sin and blasphemy can be forgiven—except blasphemy against the Holy Spirit, which will never be forgiven. ³² Anyone who speaks against the Son of Man can be forgiven, but anyone who speaks against the Holy Spirit will never be forgiven, either in this world or in the world to come.

³³ "A tree is identified by its fruit. If a tree is good, its fruit will be good. If a tree is bad, its fruit will be bad. ³⁴ You brood of snakes! How could evil men like you speak what is good and right? For whatever is in your heart determines what you say. ³⁵ A good person produces good things from the treasury of a good heart, and an evil person produces evil things from the treasury of an evil heart. ³⁶ And I tell you this, you must give an account on judgment day for every idle word you speak. ³⁷ The words you say will either acquit you or condemn you."

THE SIGN OF JONAH

³⁸ One day some teachers of religious law and Pharisees came to Jesus and said, "Teacher, we want you to show us a miraculous sign to prove your authority."

FILL YOUR HOUSE WITH THE WORD
Matthew 12:43-45   ROBERT MORRIS

Did you know Christians can be in bondage to demons? I used to think this was impossible, but God's Word says:

> "When an evil spirit leaves a person, it goes into the desert, seeking rest but finding none. Then it says, 'I will return to the person I came from.' So it returns and finds its former home empty, swept, and in order. Then the spirit finds seven other spirits more evil than itself, and they all enter the person and live there. And so that person is worse off than before" (Matthew 12:43-45).

The key word in this passage is *empty*. If a demonic spirit is driven out of you, then it will come back with others. Your house may be clean and in order, but you cannot afford to leave it empty and unguarded. You need to fill it with the power and protection of God's Word.

³⁹ But Jesus replied, "Only an evil, adulterous generation would demand a miraculous sign; but the only sign I will give them is the sign of the prophet Jonah. ⁴⁰ For as Jonah was in the belly of

the great fish for three days and three nights, so will the Son of Man be in the heart of the earth for three days and three nights.

[41] "The people of Nineveh will stand up against this generation on judgment day and condemn it, for they repented of their sins at the preaching of Jonah. Now someone greater than Jonah is here—but you refuse to repent. [42] The queen of Sheba* will also stand up against this generation on judgment day and condemn it, for she came from a distant land to hear the wisdom of Solomon. Now someone greater than Solomon is here—but you refuse to listen.

[43] "When an evil* spirit leaves a person, it goes into the desert, seeking rest but finding none. [44] Then it says, 'I will return to the person I came from.' So it returns and finds its former home empty, swept, and in order. [45] Then the spirit finds seven other spirits more evil than itself, and they all enter the person and live there. And so that person is worse off than before. That will be the experience of this evil generation."

THE TRUE FAMILY OF JESUS

[46] As Jesus was speaking to the crowd, his mother and brothers stood outside, asking to speak to him. [47] Someone told Jesus, "Your mother and your brothers are standing outside, and they want to speak to you."*

[48] Jesus asked, "Who is my mother? Who are my brothers?" [49] Then he pointed to his disciples and said, "Look, these are my mother and brothers. [50] Anyone who does the will of my Father in heaven is my brother and sister and mother!"

PARABLE OF THE FARMER SCATTERING SEED

13 Later that same day Jesus left the house and sat beside the lake. [2] A large crowd soon gathered around him, so he got into a boat. Then he sat there and taught as the people stood on the shore. [3] He told many stories in the form of parables, such as this one:

"Listen! A farmer went out to plant some seeds. [4] As he scattered them across his field, some seeds fell on a footpath, and the birds came and ate them. [5] Other seeds fell on shallow soil with underlying rock. The seeds sprouted quickly because the soil was shallow. [6] But the plants soon wilted under the hot sun, and since they didn't have deep roots, they died. [7] Other seeds fell among thorns that grew up and choked out the tender plants. [8] Still other seeds fell on fertile soil, and they produced a crop that was thirty, sixty, and even a hundred times as much as had been planted! [9] Anyone with ears to hear should listen and understand."

[10] His disciples came and asked him, "Why do you use parables when you talk to the people?"

[11] He replied, "You are permitted to understand the secrets* of the Kingdom of Heaven, but others are not. [12] To those who listen to my teaching, more understanding will be given, and they will have an abundance of knowledge. But for those who are not listening, even what little understanding they have will be taken away from them. [13] That is why I use these parables,

For they look, but they don't really see.
They hear, but they don't really listen or understand.

[14] This fulfills the prophecy of Isaiah that says,

'When you hear what I say,
you will not understand.
When you see what I do,
you will not comprehend.
[15] For the hearts of these people are hardened,
and their ears cannot hear,
and they have closed their eyes—
so their eyes cannot see,
and their ears cannot hear,
and their hearts cannot understand,
and they cannot turn to me
and let me heal them.'*

[16] "But blessed are your eyes, because they see; and your ears, because they hear. [17] I tell you the truth, many prophets and righteous people longed to see what you see, but they didn't see it. And they longed to hear what you hear, but they didn't hear it.

[18] "Now listen to the explanation of the parable about the farmer planting seeds: [19] The seed that fell on the footpath represents those who hear the message about the Kingdom and don't understand it. Then the evil one comes and snatches away the seed that was planted in their hearts. [20] The seed on the rocky soil represents those who hear the message and immediately receive it with joy. [21] But since they don't have deep roots, they don't last long. They fall away as soon as they have problems or are persecuted for believing God's word. [22] The seed that fell among the thorns represents those who hear God's word, but all too quickly the message is crowded out by the worries of this life and the lure of wealth, so no fruit is produced. [23] The seed that fell on good soil represents those who truly hear and understand God's word and produce a harvest of thirty, sixty, or even a hundred times as much as had been planted!"

PARABLE OF THE WHEAT AND WEEDS

[24] Here is another story Jesus told: "The Kingdom of Heaven is like a farmer who planted good seed in his field. [25] But that night as the workers slept, his enemy came and planted weeds among the wheat, then slipped away. [26] When the crop began to grow and produce grain, the weeds also grew.

12:42 Greek *The queen of the south.*   **12:43** Greek *unclean.*
12:47 Some manuscripts do not include verse 47. Compare Mark 3:32 and Luke 8:20.   **13:11** Greek *the mysteries.*   **13:14-15** Isa 6:9-10 (Greek version).

PRAYING LOVED ONES INTO THE FAMILY
Matthew 13:31-34
JACK HAYFORD

In Matthew 13:31-34, Jesus talks about the introduction of God's rule into places where His Kingdom was not before. He speaks about seeds planted in a field and yeast used in a kitchen. Both of these are everyday places in people's lives. The Kingdom enters and eventually takes over where people simply do the little bit they need to do. God says, "It is not by force nor by strength, but by my Spirit" (Zechariah 4:6).

In all of your family relationships, don't be typecast as the weird religious person. Be sensitive for the right timing. Ask the Holy Spirit to give you grace and wisdom, and let your presence communicate that to others. Be sensitive and sensible. Show an interest in the members of your family; love and care about them as people, as well as about their eternal souls. God is working. You have to trust that, even when you can't see it.

---

27 "The farmer's workers went to him and said, 'Sir, the field where you planted that good seed is full of weeds! Where did they come from?'

28 "'An enemy has done this!' the farmer exclaimed.

"'Should we pull out the weeds?' they asked.

29 "'No,' he replied, 'you'll uproot the wheat if you do. 30 Let both grow together until the harvest. Then I will tell the harvesters to sort out the weeds, tie them into bundles, and burn them, and to put the wheat in the barn.'"

PARABLE OF THE MUSTARD SEED

31 Here is another illustration Jesus used: "The Kingdom of Heaven is like a mustard seed planted in a field. 32 It is the smallest of all seeds, but it becomes the largest of garden plants; it grows into a tree, and birds come and make nests in its branches."

PARABLE OF THE YEAST

33 Jesus also used this illustration: "The Kingdom of Heaven is like the yeast a woman used in making bread. Even though she put only a little yeast in three measures of flour, it permeated every part of the dough."

34 Jesus always used stories and illustrations like these when speaking to the crowds. In fact, he never spoke to them without using such parables. 35 This fulfilled what God had spoken through the prophet:

"I will speak to you in parables.
I will explain things hidden since
the creation of the world.*"

PARABLE OF THE WHEAT AND WEEDS EXPLAINED

36 Then, leaving the crowds outside, Jesus went into the house. His disciples said, "Please explain to us the story of the weeds in the field."

37 Jesus replied, "The Son of Man* is the farmer who plants the good seed. 38 The field is the world, and the good seed represents the people of the Kingdom. The weeds are the people who belong to the evil one. 39 The enemy who planted the weeds among the wheat is the devil. The harvest is the end of the world,* and the harvesters are the angels.

40 "Just as the weeds are sorted out and burned in the fire, so it will be at the end of the world. 41 The Son of Man will send his angels, and they will remove from his Kingdom everything that causes sin and all who do evil. 42 And the angels will throw them into the fiery furnace, where there will be weeping and gnashing of teeth. 43 Then the righteous will shine like the sun in their Father's Kingdom. Anyone with ears to hear should listen and understand!

PARABLES OF THE HIDDEN TREASURE AND THE PEARL

44 "The Kingdom of Heaven is like a treasure that a man discovered hidden in a field. In his excitement, he hid it again and sold everything he owned to get enough money to buy the field.

45 "Again, the Kingdom of Heaven is like a merchant on the lookout for choice pearls. 46 When he discovered a pearl of great value, he sold everything he owned and bought it!

PARABLE OF THE FISHING NET

47 "Again, the Kingdom of Heaven is like a fishing net that was thrown into the water and caught fish of every kind. 48 When the net was full, they dragged it up onto the shore, sat down, and sorted the good fish into crates, but threw the bad ones away. 49 That is the way it will be at the end of the world. The angels will come and separate the wicked people from the righteous, 50 throwing the wicked into the fiery furnace, where there will be weeping and gnashing of teeth. 51 Do you understand all these things?"

"Yes," they said, "we do."

52 Then he added, "Every teacher of religious law who becomes a disciple in the Kingdom of Heaven is like a homeowner who brings from his storeroom new gems of truth as well as old."

JESUS REJECTED AT NAZARETH

53 When Jesus had finished telling these stories and illustrations, he left that part of the country. 54 He returned to Nazareth, his hometown. When he taught there in the synagogue, everyone was amazed and said, "Where does he get

---

13:35 Some manuscripts do not include *of the world*. Ps 78:2. 13:37 "Son of Man" is a title Jesus used for himself. 13:39 Or *the age;* also in 13:40, 49.

this wisdom and the power to do miracles?" [55]Then they scoffed, "He's just the carpenter's son, and we know Mary, his mother, and his brothers—James, Joseph,* Simon, and Judas. [56]All his sisters live right here among us. Where did he learn all these things?" [57]And they were deeply offended and refused to believe in him.

Then Jesus told them, "A prophet is honored everywhere except in his own hometown and among his own family." [58]And so he did only a few miracles there because of their unbelief.

THE DEATH OF JOHN THE BAPTIST

14 When Herod Antipas, the ruler of Galilee,* heard about Jesus, [2]he said to his advisers, "This must be John the Baptist raised from the dead! That is why he can do such miracles."

[3]For Herod had arrested and imprisoned John as a favor to his wife Herodias (the former wife of Herod's brother Philip). [4]John had been telling Herod, "It is against God's law for you to marry her." [5]Herod wanted to kill John, but he was afraid of a riot, because all the people believed John was a prophet.

[6]But at a birthday party for Herod, Herodias's daughter performed a dance that greatly pleased him, [7]so he promised with a vow to give her anything she wanted. [8]At her mother's urging, the girl said, "I want the head of John the Baptist on a tray!" [9]Then the king regretted what he had said; but because of the vow he had made in front of his guests, he issued the necessary orders. [10]So John was beheaded in the prison, [11]and his head was brought on a tray and given to the girl, who took it to her mother. [12]Later, John's disciples came for his body and buried it. Then they went and told Jesus what had happened.

THE EYE OF THE STORM
Matthew 14:22-33   DEBBIE MORRIS

Sometimes we think we won't face difficult situations if we're obediently following God. The disciples followed Jesus, but they still found themselves in the middle of a storm on the Sea of Galilee. And when they saw Jesus walking on the water toward the boat, they thought He was a ghost. Jesus reassured them, "Don't be afraid. . . . Take courage. I am here!" (Matthew 14:27).

All of us have "storms" in our lives. We all experience difficulties, whether in relationships, health, finances, work, or ministry. These storms test our faith and expose our fears. Sometimes the winds and waves of life are so strong that they threaten to capsize us. But we have a promise from the One whom "even the winds and waves obey" (Matthew 8:27): *I am here.* The disciples were not alone in their storm, and neither are we. Our Savior is with us, and He will not let us drown.

JESUS FEEDS FIVE THOUSAND

[13]As soon as Jesus heard the news, he left in a boat to a remote area to be alone. But the crowds heard where he was headed and followed on foot from many towns. [14]Jesus saw the huge crowd as he stepped from the boat, and he had compassion on them and healed their sick.

[15]That evening the disciples came to him and said, "This is a remote place, and it's already getting late. Send the crowds away so they can go to the villages and buy food for themselves."

[16]But Jesus said, "That isn't necessary—you feed them."

[17]"But we have only five loaves of bread and two fish!" they answered.

[18]"Bring them here," he said. [19]Then he told the people to sit down on the grass. Jesus took the five loaves and two fish, looked up toward heaven, and blessed them. Then, breaking the loaves into pieces, he gave the bread to the disciples, who distributed it to the people. [20]They all ate as much as they wanted, and afterward, the disciples picked up twelve baskets of leftovers. [21]About 5,000 men were fed that day, in addition to all the women and children!

JESUS WALKS ON WATER

[22]Immediately after this, Jesus insisted that his disciples get back into the boat and cross to the other side of the lake, while he sent the people home. [23]After sending them home, he went up into the hills by himself to pray. Night fell while he was there alone.

[24]Meanwhile, the disciples were in trouble far away from land, for a strong wind had risen, and they were fighting heavy waves. [25]About three o'clock in the morning* Jesus came toward them, walking on the water. [26]When the disciples saw him walking on the water, they were terrified. In their fear, they cried out, "It's a ghost!"

[27]But Jesus spoke to them at once. "Don't be afraid," he said. "Take courage. I am here!*"

[28]Then Peter called to him, "Lord, if it's really you, tell me to come to you, walking on the water."

[29]"Yes, come," Jesus said.

So Peter went over the side of the boat and walked on the water toward Jesus. [30]But when he saw the strong* wind and the waves, he was terrified and began to sink. "Save me, Lord!" he shouted.

[31]Jesus immediately reached out and grabbed him. "You have so little faith," Jesus said. "Why did you doubt me?"

[32]When they climbed back into the boat, the wind stopped. [33]Then the disciples worshiped him. "You really are the Son of God!" they exclaimed.

13:55 Other manuscripts read *Joses;* still others read *John.*
14:1 Greek *Herod the tetrarch.* Herod Antipas was a son of King Herod and was ruler over Galilee.   14:25 Greek *In the fourth watch of the night.*   14:27 Or *The 'I Am' is here;* Greek reads *I am.* See Exod 3:14.   14:30 Some manuscripts do not include *strong.*

34After they had crossed the lake, they landed at Gennesaret. 35When the people recognized Jesus, the news of his arrival spread quickly throughout the whole area, and soon people were bringing all their sick to be healed. 36They begged him to let the sick touch at least the fringe of his robe, and all who touched him were healed.

JESUS TEACHES ABOUT INNER PURITY

15 Some Pharisees and teachers of religious law now arrived from Jerusalem to see Jesus. They asked him, 2"Why do your disciples disobey our age-old tradition? For they ignore our tradition of ceremonial hand washing before they eat."

3Jesus replied, "And why do you, by your traditions, violate the direct commandments of God? 4For instance, God says, 'Honor your father and mother,'* and 'Anyone who speaks disrespectfully of father or mother must be put to death.'* 5But you say it is all right for people to say to their parents, 'Sorry, I can't help you. For I have vowed to give to God what I would have given to you.' 6In this way, you say they don't need to honor their parents.* And so you cancel the word of God for the sake of your own tradition. 7You hypocrites! Isaiah was right when he prophesied about you, for he wrote,

8 'These people honor me with their lips,
     but their hearts are far from me.
9 Their worship is a farce,
     for they teach man-made ideas as
         commands from God.'*"

10Then Jesus called to the crowd to come and hear. "Listen," he said, "and try to understand. 11It's not what goes into your mouth that defiles you; you are defiled by the words that come out of your mouth."

12Then the disciples came to him and asked, "Do you realize you offended the Pharisees by what you just said?"

13Jesus replied, "Every plant not planted by my heavenly Father will be uprooted, 14so ignore them. They are blind guides leading the blind, and if one blind person guides another, they will both fall into a ditch."

15Then Peter said to Jesus, "Explain to us the parable that says people aren't defiled by what they eat."

16"Don't you understand yet?" Jesus asked. 17"Anything you eat passes through the stomach and then goes into the sewer. 18But the words you speak come from the heart—that's what defiles you. 19For from the heart come evil thoughts, murder, adultery, all sexual immorality, theft, lying, and slander. 20These are what defile you. Eating with unwashed hands will never defile you."

THE FAITH OF A GENTILE WOMAN

21Then Jesus left Galilee and went north to the region of Tyre and Sidon. 22A Gentile* woman who lived there came to him, pleading, "Have mercy on me, O Lord, Son of David! For my daughter is possessed by a demon that torments her severely."

23But Jesus gave her no reply, not even a word. Then his disciples urged him to send her away. "Tell her to go away," they said. "She is bothering us with all her begging."

24Then Jesus said to the woman, "I was sent only to help God's lost sheep—the people of Israel."

25But she came and worshiped him, pleading again, "Lord, help me!"

26Jesus responded, "It isn't right to take food from the children and throw it to the dogs."

27She replied, "That's true, Lord, but even dogs are allowed to eat the scraps that fall beneath their masters' table."

28"Dear woman," Jesus said to her, "your faith is great. Your request is granted." And her daughter was instantly healed.

JESUS HEALS MANY PEOPLE

29Jesus returned to the Sea of Galilee and climbed a hill and sat down. 30A vast crowd brought to him people who were lame, blind, crippled, those who couldn't speak, and many others. They laid them before Jesus, and he healed them all. 31The crowd was amazed! Those who hadn't been able to speak were talking, the crippled were made well, the lame were walking, and the blind could see again! And they praised the God of Israel.

JESUS FEEDS FOUR THOUSAND

32Then Jesus called his disciples and told them, "I feel sorry for these people. They have been here with me for three days, and they have nothing left to eat. I don't want to send them away hungry, or they will faint along the way."

33The disciples replied, "Where would we get enough food here in the wilderness for such a huge crowd?"

34Jesus asked, "How much bread do you have?"

They replied, "Seven loaves, and a few small fish."

35So Jesus told all the people to sit down on the ground. 36Then he took the seven loaves and the fish, thanked God for them, and broke them into pieces. He gave them to the disciples, who distributed the food to the crowd. 37They all ate as much as they wanted. Afterward, the disciples picked up seven large baskets of leftover food. 38There were 4,000 men who were fed that day, in addition to all the women and children. 39Then Jesus sent the people home, and he got into a boat and crossed over to the region of Magadan.

15:4a Exod 20:12; Deut 5:16.   15:4b Exod 21:17 (Greek version); Lev 20:9 (Greek version).   15:6 Greek *their father;* other manuscripts read *their father or their mother.*   15:8-9 Isa 29:13 (Greek version).   15:22 Greek *Canaanite.*

LEADERS DEMAND A MIRACULOUS SIGN

16 One day the Pharisees and Sadducees came to test Jesus, demanding that he show them a miraculous sign from heaven to prove his authority.

² He replied, "You know the saying, 'Red sky at night means fair weather tomorrow; ³ red sky in the morning means foul weather all day.' You know how to interpret the weather signs in the sky, but you don't know how to interpret the signs of the times!* ⁴ Only an evil, adulterous generation would demand a miraculous sign, but the only sign I will give them is the sign of the prophet Jonah.*" Then Jesus left them and went away.

YEAST OF THE PHARISEES AND SADDUCEES

⁵ Later, after they crossed to the other side of the lake, the disciples discovered they had forgotten to bring any bread. ⁶ "Watch out!" Jesus warned them. "Beware of the yeast of the Pharisees and Sadducees."

⁷ At this they began to argue with each other because they hadn't brought any bread. ⁸ Jesus knew what they were saying, so he said, "You have so little faith! Why are you arguing with each other about having no bread? ⁹ Don't you understand even yet? Don't you remember the 5,000 I fed with five loaves, and the baskets of leftovers you picked up? ¹⁰ Or the 4,000 I fed with seven loaves, and the large baskets of leftovers you picked up? ¹¹ Why can't you understand that I'm not talking about bread? So again I say, 'Beware of the yeast of the Pharisees and Sadducees.'"

¹² Then at last they understood that he wasn't speaking about the yeast in bread, but about the deceptive teaching of the Pharisees and Sadducees.

PETER'S DECLARATION ABOUT JESUS

¹³ When Jesus came to the region of Caesarea Philippi, he asked his disciples, "Who do people say that the Son of Man is?"*

¹⁴ "Well," they replied, "some say John the Baptist, some say Elijah, and others say Jeremiah or one of the other prophets."

¹⁵ Then he asked them, "But who do you say I am?"

¹⁶ Simon Peter answered, "You are the Messiah,* the Son of the living God."

¹⁷ Jesus replied, "You are blessed, Simon son of John,* because my Father in heaven has revealed this to you. You did not learn this from any human being. ¹⁸ Now I say to you that you are Peter (which means 'rock'),* and upon this rock I will build my church, and all the powers of hell* will not conquer it. ¹⁹ And I will give you the keys of the Kingdom of Heaven. Whatever you forbid* on earth will be forbidden in heaven, and whatever you permit* on earth will be permitted in heaven."

GOD WILL BUILD HIS CHURCH
Matthew 16:18 ROBERT MORRIS

Three months after we planted Gateway Church, I was having my quiet time. I had forgotten about the Scripture the Lord used to confirm the dream He gave me seven years earlier, but then I got to 1 Samuel 11:8. Once again, I read about God numbering the men of Israel at 300,000 and the men of Judah at 30,000. Then the Lord said to me, "I'm going to remind you what I've called you to do. I'm going to confirm these numbers to you again." Right then, I remembered that Trinity Fellowship gave us $30,000 to start when we planted Gateway Church.

Later that same day, I had lunch with a man who had visited our church twice. He said, "My family and I are going to join the church, and we're excited about it! Every now and then, we have some resources we can sow into the Kingdom. The Lord put an amount on my heart, and I want to give this to the church." He handed me a check and said, "God told me to tell you that this amount is going to confirm something to you." I thanked him and told him how grateful we were. We said goodbye, and after I got in my car, I reached into my pocket and pulled out the check. It was for $300,000! In just one day, the Lord had confirmed both numbers He had given me in a dream seven years before!

I have no doubt in my mind these numbers are from God. He wants to do something, and my part is to serve Him passionately with all my heart. It's up to God to accomplish His Word, and it's up to me to obey!

Jesus says, "I will build my church" (Matthew 16:18). Another way of reading this verse is, "I—*Jesus*—will—*meaning there's no doubt*—build—*He's the One doing the building, not me*—my—*it belongs to Him*—church—*meaning it's a body, which is all of us and takes all of us to do.*"

I knew God was telling me that if I would take care of the depth of my relationship with Him by having an intimate and thriving relationship with Jesus Christ, He would take care of the width of my ministry. *He would take care of the numbers.* And all these years later, God is still the One who makes the difference at Gateway Church.

²⁰ Then he sternly warned the disciples not to tell anyone that he was the Messiah.

16:2-3 Several manuscripts do not include any of the words in 16:2-3 after *He replied.* 16:4 Greek *the sign of Jonah.* 16:13 "Son of Man" is a title Jesus used for himself. 16:16 Or *the Christ. Messiah* (a Hebrew term) and *Christ* (a Greek term) both mean "anointed one." 16:17 Greek *Simon bar-Jonah;* see John 1:42; 21:15-17. 16:18a Greek *that you are Peter.* 16:18b Greek *and the gates of Hades.* 16:19a Or *bind,* or *lock.* 16:19b Or *loose,* or *open.*

JESUS PREDICTS HIS DEATH

²¹From then on Jesus* began to tell his disciples plainly that it was necessary for him to go to Jerusalem, and that he would suffer many terrible things at the hands of the elders, the leading priests, and the teachers of religious law. He would be killed, but on the third day he would be raised from the dead.

²²But Peter took him aside and began to reprimand him* for saying such things. "Heaven forbid, Lord," he said. "This will never happen to you!"

²³Jesus turned to Peter and said, "Get away from me, Satan! You are a dangerous trap to me. You are seeing things merely from a human point of view, not from God's."

²⁴Then Jesus said to his disciples, "If any of you wants to be my follower, you must give up your own way, take up your cross, and follow me. ²⁵If you try to hang on to your life, you will lose it. But if you give up your life for my sake, you will save it. ²⁶And what do you benefit if you gain the whole world but lose your own soul?* Is anything worth more than your soul? ²⁷For the Son of Man will come with his angels in the glory of his Father and will judge all people according to their deeds. ²⁸And I tell you the truth, some standing here right now will not die before they see the Son of Man coming in his Kingdom."

THE TRANSFIGURATION

17 Six days later Jesus took Peter and the two brothers, James and John, and led them up a high mountain to be alone. ²As the men watched, Jesus' appearance was transformed so that his face shone like the sun, and his clothes became as white as light. ³Suddenly, Moses and Elijah appeared and began talking with Jesus.

⁴Peter exclaimed, "Lord, it's wonderful for us to be here! If you want, I'll make three shelters as memorials*—one for you, one for Moses, and one for Elijah."

⁵But even as he spoke, a bright cloud overshadowed them, and a voice from the cloud said, "This is my dearly loved Son, who brings me great joy. Listen to him." ⁶The disciples were terrified and fell face down on the ground.

⁷Then Jesus came over and touched them. "Get up," he said. "Don't be afraid." ⁸And when they looked up, Moses and Elijah were gone, and they saw only Jesus.

⁹As they went back down the mountain, Jesus commanded them, "Don't tell anyone what you have seen until the Son of Man* has been raised from the dead."

¹⁰Then his disciples asked him, "Why do the teachers of religious law insist that Elijah must return before the Messiah comes?*"

¹¹Jesus replied, "Elijah is indeed coming first to get everything ready. ¹²But I tell you, Elijah has already come, but he wasn't recognized, and they chose to abuse him. And in the same way they will also make the Son of Man suffer." ¹³Then the disciples realized he was talking about John the Baptist.

JESUS HEALS A DEMON-POSSESSED BOY

¹⁴At the foot of the mountain, a large crowd was waiting for them. A man came and knelt before Jesus and said, ¹⁵"Lord, have mercy on my son. He has seizures and suffers terribly. He often falls into the fire or into the water. ¹⁶So I brought him to your disciples, but they couldn't heal him."

¹⁷Jesus said, "You faithless and corrupt people! How long must I be with you? How long must I put up with you? Bring the boy here to me." ¹⁸Then Jesus rebuked the demon in the boy, and it left him. From that moment the boy was well.

¹⁹Afterward the disciples asked Jesus privately, "Why couldn't we cast out that demon?"

²⁰"You don't have enough faith," Jesus told them. "I tell you the truth, if you had faith even as small as a mustard seed, you could say to this mountain, 'Move from here to there,' and it would move. Nothing would be impossible.*"

JESUS AGAIN PREDICTS HIS DEATH

²²After they gathered again in Galilee, Jesus told them, "The Son of Man is going to be betrayed into the hands of his enemies. ²³He will be killed, but on the third day he will be raised from the dead." And the disciples were filled with grief.

PAYMENT OF THE TEMPLE TAX

²⁴On their arrival in Capernaum, the collectors of the Temple tax* came to Peter and asked him, "Doesn't your teacher pay the Temple tax?"

²⁵"Yes, he does," Peter replied. Then he went into the house.

But before he had a chance to speak, Jesus asked him, "What do you think, Peter?* Do kings tax their own people or the people they have conquered?*"

²⁶"They tax the people they have conquered," Peter replied.

"Well, then," Jesus said, "the citizens are free! ²⁷However, we don't want to offend them, so go down to the lake and throw in a line. Open the mouth of the first fish you catch, and you will find a large silver coin.* Take it and pay the tax for both of us."

THE GREATEST IN THE KINGDOM

18 About that time the disciples came to Jesus and asked, "Who is greatest in the Kingdom of Heaven?"

16:21 Some manuscripts read *Jesus the Messiah.*   16:22 Or *began to correct him.*   16:26 Or *your self?* also in 16:26b.   17:4 Greek *three tabernacles.*   17:9 "Son of Man" is a title Jesus used for himself. 17:10 Greek *that Elijah must come first?*   17:20 Some manuscripts add verse 21, *But this kind of demon won't leave except by prayer and fasting.* Compare Mark 9:29.   17:24 Greek *the two-drachma [tax];* also in 17:24b. See Exod 30:13-16; Neh 10:32-33.   17:25a Greek *Simon?*   17:25b Greek *their sons or others?*   17:27 Greek *a stater* [a Greek coin equivalent to four drachmas].

² Jesus called a little child to him and put the child among them. ³ Then he said, "I tell you the truth, unless you turn from your sins and become like little children, you will never get into the Kingdom of Heaven. ⁴ So anyone who becomes as humble as this little child is the greatest in the Kingdom of Heaven.

⁵ "And anyone who welcomes a little child like this on my behalf* is welcoming me. ⁶ But if you cause one of these little ones who trusts in me to fall into sin, it would be better for you to have a large millstone tied around your neck and be drowned in the depths of the sea.

⁷ "What sorrow awaits the world, because it tempts people to sin. Temptations are inevitable, but what sorrow awaits the person who does the tempting. ⁸ So if your hand or foot causes you to sin, cut it off and throw it away. It's better to enter eternal life with only one hand or one foot than to be thrown into eternal fire with both of your hands and feet. ⁹ And if your eye causes you to sin, gouge it out and throw it away. It's better to enter eternal life with only one eye than to have two eyes and be thrown into the fire of hell.*

¹⁰ "Beware that you don't look down on any of these little ones. For I tell you that in heaven their angels are always in the presence of my heavenly Father.*

PARABLE OF THE LOST SHEEP

¹² "If a man has a hundred sheep and one of them wanders away, what will he do? Won't he leave the ninety-nine others on the hills and go out to search for the one that is lost? ¹³ And if he finds it, I tell you the truth, he will rejoice over it more than over the ninety-nine that didn't wander away! ¹⁴ In the same way, it is not my heavenly Father's will that even one of these little ones should perish.

CORRECTING ANOTHER BELIEVER

¹⁵ "If another believer* sins against you,* go privately and point out the offense. If the other person listens and confesses it, you have won that person back. ¹⁶ But if you are unsuccessful, take one or two others with you and go back again, so that everything you say may be confirmed by two or three witnesses. ¹⁷ If the person still refuses to listen, take your case to the church. Then if he or she won't accept the church's decision, treat that person as a pagan or a corrupt tax collector.

¹⁸ "I tell you the truth, whatever you forbid* on earth will be forbidden in heaven, and whatever you permit* on earth will be permitted in heaven.

¹⁹ "I also tell you this: If two of you agree here on earth concerning anything you ask, my Father in heaven will do it for you. ²⁰ For where two or three gather together as my followers,* I am there among them."

PARABLE OF THE UNFORGIVING DEBTOR

²¹ Then Peter came to him and asked, "Lord, how often should I forgive someone* who sins against me? Seven times?"

²² "No, not seven times," Jesus replied, "but seventy times seven!*

²³ "Therefore, the Kingdom of Heaven can be compared to a king who decided to bring his accounts up to date with servants who had borrowed money from him. ²⁴ In the process, one of his debtors was brought in who owed him millions of dollars.* ²⁵ He couldn't pay, so his master ordered that he be sold—along with his wife, his children, and everything he owned—to pay the debt.

²⁶ "But the man fell down before his master and begged him, 'Please, be patient with me, and I will pay it all.' ²⁷ Then his master was filled with pity for him, and he released him and forgave his debt.

²⁸ "But when the man left the king, he went to a fellow servant who owed him a few thousand dollars.* He grabbed him by the throat and demanded instant payment.

²⁹ "His fellow servant fell down before him and begged for a little more time. 'Be patient with me, and I will pay it,' he pleaded. ³⁰ But his creditor wouldn't wait. He had the man arrested and put in prison until the debt could be paid in full.

³¹ "When some of the other servants saw this, they were very upset. They went to the king and told him everything that had happened. ³² Then the king called in the man he had forgiven and said, 'You evil servant! I forgave you that tremendous debt because you pleaded with me. ³³ Shouldn't you have mercy on your fellow servant, just as I had mercy on you?' ³⁴ Then the angry king sent the man to prison to be tortured until he had paid his entire debt.

³⁵ "That's what my heavenly Father will do to you if you refuse to forgive your brothers and sisters* from your heart."

DISCUSSION ABOUT DIVORCE AND MARRIAGE

19 When Jesus had finished saying these things, he left Galilee and went down to the region of Judea east of the Jordan River. ² Large crowds followed him there, and he healed their sick.

³ Some Pharisees came and tried to trap him with this question: "Should a man be allowed to divorce his wife for just any reason?"

18:5 Greek *in my name.* 18:9 Greek *the Gehenna of fire.* 18:10 Some manuscripts add verse 11, *And the Son of Man came to save those who are lost.* Compare Luke 19:10. 18:15a Greek *If your brother.* 18:15b Some manuscripts do not include *against you.* 18:18a Or *bind,* or *lock.* 18:18b Or *loose,* or *open.* 18:20 Greek *gather together in my name.* 18:21 Greek *my brother.* 18:22 Or *seventy-seven times.* 18:24 Greek *10,000 talents* [375 tons or 340 metric tons of silver]. 18:28 Greek *100 denarii.* A denarius was equivalent to a laborer's full day's wage. 18:35 Greek *your brother.*

⁴"Haven't you read the Scriptures?" **Jesus** replied. "They record that from the beginning 'God made them male and female.'*" ⁵**And he said,** "'This explains why a man leaves his father and mother and is joined to his wife, and the two are united into one.'* ⁶Since they are no longer two but one, let no one split apart what God has joined together."

⁷"Then why did Moses say in the law that a man could give his wife a written notice of divorce and send her away?"* they asked.

⁸**Jesus replied,** "Moses permitted divorce only as a concession to your hard hearts, but it was not what God had originally intended. ⁹And I tell you this, whoever divorces his wife and marries someone else commits adultery—unless his wife has been unfaithful.*"

¹⁰Jesus' disciples then said to him, "If this is the case, it is better not to marry!"

¹¹"Not everyone can accept this statement," Jesus said. "Only those whom God helps. ¹²Some are born as eunuchs, some have been made eunuchs by others, and some choose not to marry* for the sake of the Kingdom of Heaven. Let anyone accept this who can."

JESUS BLESSES THE CHILDREN

¹³One day some parents brought their children to Jesus so he could lay his hands on them and pray for them. But the disciples scolded the parents for bothering him.

¹⁴But Jesus said, "Let the children come to me. Don't stop them! For the Kingdom of Heaven belongs to those who are like these children." ¹⁵And he placed his hands on their heads and blessed them before he left.

THE RICH MAN

¹⁶Someone came to Jesus with this question: "Teacher,* what good deed must I do to have eternal life?"

¹⁷"Why ask me about what is good?" **Jesus** replied. "There is only One who is good. But to answer your question—if you want to receive eternal life, keep* the commandments."

¹⁸"Which ones?" the man asked.

And Jesus replied: "'You must not murder. You must not commit adultery. You must not steal. You must not testify falsely. ¹⁹Honor your father and mother. Love your neighbor as yourself.'*"

²⁰"I've obeyed all these commandments," the young man replied. "What else must I do?"

²¹Jesus told him, "If you want to be perfect, go and sell all your possessions and give the money to the poor, and you will have treasure in heaven. Then come, follow me."

²²But when the young man heard this, he went away sad, for he had many possessions.

²³Then Jesus said to his disciples, "I tell you the truth, it is very hard for a rich person to enter the Kingdom of Heaven. ²⁴I'll say it again—it is easier for a camel to go through the eye of a needle than for a rich person to enter the Kingdom of God!"

²⁵The disciples were astounded. "Then who in the world can be saved?" they asked.

²⁶Jesus looked at them intently and said, "Humanly speaking, it is impossible. But with God everything is possible."

²⁷Then Peter said to him, "We've given up everything to follow you. What will we get?"

²⁸Jesus replied, "I assure you that when the world is made new* and the Son of Man* sits upon his glorious throne, you who have been my followers will also sit on twelve thrones, judging the twelve tribes of Israel. ²⁹And everyone who has given up houses or brothers or sisters or father or mother or children or property, for my sake, will receive a hundred times as much in return and will inherit eternal life. ³⁰But many who are the greatest now will be least important then, and those who seem least important now will be the greatest then.*

PARABLE OF THE VINEYARD WORKERS

20 "For the Kingdom of Heaven is like the landowner who went out early one morning to hire workers for his vineyard. ²He agreed to pay the normal daily wage* and sent them out to work.

³"At nine o'clock in the morning he was passing through the marketplace and saw some people standing around doing nothing. ⁴So he hired them, telling them he would pay them whatever was right at the end of the day. ⁵So they went to work in the vineyard. At noon and again at three o'clock he did the same thing.

⁶"At five o'clock that afternoon he was in town again and saw some more people standing around. He asked them, 'Why haven't you been working today?'

⁷"They replied, 'Because no one hired us.'

"The landowner told them, 'Then go out and join the others in my vineyard.'

⁸"That evening he told the foreman to call the workers in and pay them, beginning with the last workers first. ⁹When those hired at five o'clock were paid, each received a full day's wage. ¹⁰When those hired first came to get their pay, they assumed they would receive more. But they, too, were paid a day's wage. ¹¹When they received their pay, they protested to the owner, ¹²'Those people worked only one hour, and yet you've paid them just as much as you paid us who worked all day in the scorching heat.'

19:4 Gen 1:27; 5:2.　19:5 Gen 2:24.　19:7 See Deut 24:1.
19:9 Some manuscripts add *And anyone who marries a divorced woman commits adultery. Compare Matt 5:32.*　19:12 Greek *and some make themselves eunuchs.*　19:16 Some manuscripts read *Good Teacher.*　19:17 Some manuscripts read *continue to keep.*
19:18-19 Exod 20:12-16; Deut 5:16-20; Lev 19:18.　19:28a Or *in the regeneration.*　19:28b "Son of Man" is a title Jesus used for himself.　19:30 Greek *But many who are first will be last; and the last, first.*　20:2 Greek *a denarius,* the payment for a full day's labor; similarly in 20:9, 10, 13.

[13] "He answered one of them, 'Friend, I haven't been unfair! Didn't you agree to work all day for the usual wage? [14] Take your money and go. I wanted to pay this last worker the same as you. [15] Is it against the law for me to do what I want with my money? Should you be jealous because I am kind to others?'

[16] "So those who are last now will be first then, and those who are first will be last."

JESUS AGAIN PREDICTS HIS DEATH

[17] As Jesus was going up to Jerusalem, he took the twelve disciples aside privately and told them what was going to happen to him. [18] "Listen," he said, "we're going up to Jerusalem, where the Son of Man* will be betrayed to the leading priests and the teachers of religious law. They will sentence him to die. [19] Then they will hand him over to the Romans* to be mocked, flogged with a whip, and crucified. But on the third day he will be raised from the dead."

JESUS TEACHES ABOUT SERVING OTHERS

[20] Then the mother of James and John, the sons of Zebedee, came to Jesus with her sons. She knelt respectfully to ask a favor. [21] "What is your request?" he asked.

She replied, "In your Kingdom, please let my two sons sit in places of honor next to you, one on your right and the other on your left."

[22] But Jesus answered by saying to them, "You don't know what you are asking! Are you able to drink from the bitter cup of suffering I am about to drink?"

"Oh yes," they replied, "we are able!"

[23] Jesus told them, "You will indeed drink from my bitter cup. But I have no right to say who will sit on my right or my left. My Father has prepared those places for the ones he has chosen."

[24] When the ten other disciples heard what James and John had asked, they were indignant. [25] But Jesus called them together and said, "You know that the rulers in this world lord it over their people, and officials flaunt their authority over those under them. [26] But among you it will be different. Whoever wants to be a leader among you must be your servant, [27] and whoever wants to be first among you must become your slave. [28] For even the Son of Man came not to be served but to serve others and to give his life as a ransom for many."

JESUS HEALS TWO BLIND MEN

[29] As Jesus and the disciples left the town of Jericho, a large crowd followed behind. [30] Two blind men were sitting beside the road. When they heard that Jesus was coming that way, they began shouting, "Lord, Son of David, have mercy on us!"

[31] "Be quiet!" the crowd yelled at them.

But they only shouted louder, "Lord, Son of David, have mercy on us!"

[32] When Jesus heard them, he stopped and called, "What do you want me to do for you?"

[33] "Lord," they said, "we want to see!" [34] Jesus felt sorry for them and touched their eyes. Instantly they could see! Then they followed him.

JESUS' TRIUMPHANT ENTRY

21 As Jesus and the disciples approached Jerusalem, they came to the town of Bethphage on the Mount of Olives. Jesus sent two of them on ahead. [2] "Go into the village over there," he said. "As soon as you enter it, you will see a donkey tied there, with its colt beside it. Untie them and bring them to me. [3] If anyone asks what you are doing, just say, 'The Lord needs them,' and he will immediately let you take them."

[4] This took place to fulfill the prophecy that said,

[5] "Tell the people of Jerusalem,*
   'Look, your King is coming to you.
He is humble, riding on a donkey—
   riding on a donkey's colt.'"*

[6] The two disciples did as Jesus commanded. [7] They brought the donkey and the colt to him and threw their garments over the colt, and he sat on it.* [8] Most of the crowd spread their garments on the road ahead of him, and others cut branches from the trees and spread them on the road. [9] Jesus was in the center of the procession, and the people all around him were shouting,

"Praise God* for the Son of David!
   Blessings on the one who comes in the
      name of the LORD!
   Praise God in highest heaven!"*

[10] The entire city of Jerusalem was in an uproar as he entered. "Who is this?" they asked.

[11] And the crowds replied, "It's Jesus, the prophet from Nazareth in Galilee."

JESUS CLEARS THE TEMPLE

[12] Jesus entered the Temple and began to drive out all the people buying and selling animals for sacrifice. He knocked over the tables of the money changers and the chairs of those selling doves. [13] He said to them, "The Scriptures declare, 'My Temple will be called a house of prayer,' but you have turned it into a den of thieves!"*

[14] The blind and the lame came to him in the Temple, and he healed them. [15] The leading priests and the teachers of religious law saw these wonderful miracles and heard even the

---

20:18 "Son of Man" is a title Jesus used for himself.   20:19 Greek the Gentiles.   21:5a Greek Tell the daughter of Zion. Isa 62:11.
21:5b Zech 9:9.   21:7 Greek over them, and he sat on them.
21:9a Greek Hosanna, an exclamation of praise that literally means "save now"; also in 21:9b, 15.   21:9b Pss 118:25-26; 148:1.
21:13 Isa 56:7; Jer 7:11.

children in the Temple shouting, "Praise God for the Son of David."

But the leaders were indignant. [16] They asked Jesus, "Do you hear what these children are saying?"

"Yes," Jesus replied. "Haven't you ever read the Scriptures? For they say, 'You have taught children and infants to give you praise.'*" [17] Then he returned to Bethany, where he stayed overnight.

JESUS CURSES THE FIG TREE

[18] In the morning, as Jesus was returning to Jerusalem, he was hungry, [19] and he noticed a fig tree beside the road. He went over to see if there were any figs, but there were only leaves. Then he said to it, "May you never bear fruit again!" And immediately the fig tree withered up.

[20] The disciples were amazed when they saw this and asked, "How did the fig tree wither so quickly?"

[21] Then Jesus told them, "I tell you the truth, if you have faith and don't doubt, you can do things like this and much more. You can even say to this mountain, 'May you be lifted up and thrown into the sea,' and it will happen. [22] You can pray for anything, and if you have faith, you will receive it."

THE AUTHORITY OF JESUS CHALLENGED

[23] When Jesus returned to the Temple and began teaching, the leading priests and elders came up to him. They demanded, "By what authority are you doing all these things? Who gave you the right?"

[24] "I'll tell you by what authority I do these things if you answer one question," Jesus replied. [25] "Did John's authority to baptize come from heaven, or was it merely human?"

They talked it over among themselves. "If we say it was from heaven, he will ask us why we didn't believe John. [26] But if we say it was merely human, we'll be mobbed because the people believe John was a prophet." [27] So they finally replied, "We don't know."

And Jesus responded, "Then I won't tell you by what authority I do these things.

PARABLE OF THE TWO SONS

[28] "But what do you think about this? A man with two sons told the older boy, 'Son, go out and work in the vineyard today.' [29] The son answered, 'No, I won't go,' but later he changed his mind and went anyway. [30] Then the father told the other son, 'You go,' and he said, 'Yes, sir, I will.' But he didn't go.

[31] "Which of the two obeyed his father?"

They replied, "The first."*

Then Jesus explained his meaning: "I tell you the truth, corrupt tax collectors and prostitutes will get into the Kingdom of God before you do. [32] For John the Baptist came and showed you the right way to live, but you didn't believe him, while tax collectors and prostitutes did. And even when you saw this happening, you refused to believe him and repent of your sins.

PARABLE OF THE EVIL FARMERS

[33] "Now listen to another story. A certain landowner planted a vineyard, built a wall around it, dug a pit for pressing out the grape juice, and built a lookout tower. Then he leased the vineyard to tenant farmers and moved to another country. [34] At the time of the grape harvest, he sent his servants to collect his share of the crop. [35] But the farmers grabbed his servants, beat one, killed one, and stoned another. [36] So the landowner sent a larger group of his servants to collect for him, but the results were the same.

[37] "Finally, the owner sent his son, thinking, 'Surely they will respect my son.'

[38] "But when the tenant farmers saw his son coming, they said to one another, 'Here comes the heir to this estate. Come on, let's kill him and get the estate for ourselves!' [39] So they grabbed him, dragged him out of the vineyard, and murdered him.

[40] "When the owner of the vineyard returns," Jesus asked, "what do you think he will do to those farmers?"

[41] The religious leaders replied, "He will put the wicked men to a horrible death and lease the vineyard to others who will give him his share of the crop after each harvest."

[42] Then Jesus asked them, "Didn't you ever read this in the Scriptures?

'The stone that the builders rejected
    has now become the cornerstone.
This is the LORD's doing,
    and it is wonderful to see.'*

[43] I tell you, the Kingdom of God will be taken away from you and given to a nation that will produce the proper fruit. [44] Anyone who stumbles over that stone will be broken to pieces, and it will crush anyone it falls on.*"

[45] When the leading priests and Pharisees heard this parable, they realized he was telling the story against them—they were the wicked farmers. [46] They wanted to arrest him, but they were afraid of the crowds, who considered Jesus to be a prophet.

PARABLE OF THE GREAT FEAST

22 Jesus also told them other parables. He said, [2] "The Kingdom of Heaven can be illustrated by the story of a king who prepared a great wedding feast for his son. [3] When the

---

21:16 Ps 8:2 (Greek version). 21:29-31 Other manuscripts read *"The second."* In still other manuscripts the first son says "Yes" but does nothing, the second son says "No" but then repents and goes, and the answer to Jesus' question is that the second son obeyed his father. 21:42 Ps 118:22-23. 21:44 This verse is not included in some early manuscripts. Compare Luke 20:18.

banquet was ready, he sent his servants to notify those who were invited. But they all refused to come!

⁴"So he sent other servants to tell them, 'The feast has been prepared. The bulls and fattened cattle have been killed, and everything is ready. Come to the banquet!' ⁵But the guests he had invited ignored them and went their own way, one to his farm, another to his business. ⁶Others seized his messengers and insulted them and killed them.

⁷"The king was furious, and he sent out his army to destroy the murderers and burn their town. ⁸And he said to his servants, 'The wedding feast is ready, and the guests I invited aren't worthy of the honor. ⁹Now go out to the street corners and invite everyone you see.' ¹⁰So the servants brought in everyone they could find, good and bad alike, and the banquet hall was filled with guests.

¹¹"But when the king came in to meet the guests, he noticed a man who wasn't wearing the proper clothes for a wedding. ¹²'Friend,' he asked, 'how is it that you are here without wedding clothes?' But the man had no reply. ¹³Then the king said to his aides, 'Bind his hands and feet and throw him into the outer darkness, where there will be weeping and gnashing of teeth.'

¹⁴"For many are called, but few are chosen."

TAXES FOR CAESAR

¹⁵Then the Pharisees met together to plot how to trap Jesus into saying something for which he could be arrested. ¹⁶They sent some of their disciples, along with the supporters of Herod, to meet with him. "Teacher," they said, "we know how honest you are. You teach the way of God truthfully. You are impartial and don't play favorites. ¹⁷Now tell us what you think about this: Is it right to pay taxes to Caesar or not?"

¹⁸But Jesus knew their evil motives. "You hypocrites!" he said. "Why are you trying to trap me? ¹⁹Here, show me the coin used for the tax." When they handed him a Roman coin,* ²⁰he asked, "Whose picture and title are stamped on it?"

²¹"Caesar's," they replied.

"Well, then," he said, "give to Caesar what belongs to Caesar, and give to God what belongs to God."

²²His reply amazed them, and they went away.

DISCUSSION ABOUT RESURRECTION

²³That same day Jesus was approached by some Sadducees—religious leaders who say there is no resurrection from the dead. They posed this question: ²⁴"Teacher, Moses said, 'If a man dies without children, his brother should marry the widow and have a child who will carry on the brother's name.'* ²⁵Well, suppose there were seven brothers. The oldest one married and then died without children, so his brother married the widow. ²⁶But the second brother also died, and the

THE TEACHER
Matthew 22:33   ROBERT MORRIS

Many people believe Jesus is the greatest teacher who ever lived. In fact, He is referred to as "teacher" 48 times in the four Gospels. Huge crowds would follow Him everywhere He went, even to deserted places where there was little or no food, just to hear Him teach. Whenever Jesus taught, "the people were amazed at his teaching, for he taught with real authority—quite unlike the teachers of religious law" (Mark 1:22).

Jesus taught authoritatively, practically, and graphically. He never spoke the truth in a dull or boring lecture. He painted pictures and told stories. Jesus was a master teacher who knew that using visuals and illustrations would help the people learn and retain what He was teaching them.

third brother married her. This continued with all seven of them. ²⁷Last of all, the woman also died. ²⁸So tell us, whose wife will she be in the resurrection? For all seven were married to her."

²⁹Jesus replied, "Your mistake is that you don't know the Scriptures, and you don't know the power of God. ³⁰For when the dead rise, they will neither marry nor be given in marriage. In this respect they will be like the angels in heaven.

³¹"But now, as to whether there will be a resurrection of the dead—haven't you ever read about this in the Scriptures? Long after Abraham, Isaac, and Jacob had died, God said,* ³²'I am the God of Abraham, the God of Isaac, and the God of Jacob.'* So he is the God of the living, not the dead."

³³When the crowds heard him, they were astounded at his teaching.

THE MOST IMPORTANT COMMANDMENT

³⁴But when the Pharisees heard that he had silenced the Sadducees with his reply, they met together to question him again. ³⁵One of them, an expert in religious law, tried to trap him with this question: ³⁶"Teacher, which is the most important commandment in the law of Moses?"

³⁷Jesus replied, "'You must love the Lord your God with all your heart, all your soul, and all your mind.'* ³⁸This is the first and greatest commandment. ³⁹A second is equally important: 'Love your neighbor as yourself.'* ⁴⁰The entire law and all the demands of the prophets are based on these two commandments."

WHOSE SON IS THE MESSIAH?

⁴¹Then, surrounded by the Pharisees, Jesus asked them a question: ⁴²"What do you think about the Messiah? Whose son is he?"

22:19 Greek *a denarius.*   22:24 Deut 25:5-6.   22:31 Greek *read about this? God said.*   22:32 Exod 3:6.   22:37 Deut 6:5.
22:39 Lev 19:18.

They replied, "He is the son of David."

⁴³ Jesus responded, "Then why does David, speaking under the inspiration of the Spirit, call the Messiah 'my Lord'? For David said,

⁴⁴ 'The LORD said to my Lord,
　Sit in the place of honor at my right hand
　　until I humble your enemies beneath
　　　your feet.'*

⁴⁵ Since David called the Messiah 'my Lord,' how can the Messiah be his son?"

⁴⁶ No one could answer him. And after that, no one dared to ask him any more questions.

JESUS CRITICIZES THE RELIGIOUS LEADERS

23 Then Jesus said to the crowds and to his disciples, ² "The teachers of religious law and the Pharisees are the official interpreters of the law of Moses.* ³ So practice and obey whatever they tell you, but don't follow their example. For they don't practice what they teach. ⁴ They crush people with unbearable religious demands and never lift a finger to ease the burden.

⁵ "Everything they do is for show. On their arms they wear extra wide prayer boxes with Scripture verses inside, and they wear robes with extra long tassels.* ⁶ And they love to sit at the head table at banquets and in the seats of honor in the synagogues. ⁷ They love to receive respectful greetings as they walk in the marketplaces, and to be called 'Rabbi.'*

⁸ "Don't let anyone call you 'Rabbi,' for you have only one teacher, and all of you are equal as brothers and sisters.* ⁹ And don't address anyone here on earth as 'Father,' for only God in heaven is your Father. ¹⁰ And don't let anyone call you 'Teacher,' for you have only one teacher, the Messiah. ¹¹ The greatest among you must be a servant. ¹² But those who exalt themselves will be humbled, and those who humble themselves will be exalted.

¹³ "What sorrow awaits you teachers of religious law and you Pharisees. Hypocrites! For you shut the door of the Kingdom of Heaven in people's faces. You won't go in yourselves, and you don't let others enter either.*

¹⁵ "What sorrow awaits you teachers of religious law and you Pharisees. Hypocrites! For you cross land and sea to make one convert, and then you turn that person into twice the child of hell* you yourselves are!

¹⁶ "Blind guides! What sorrow awaits you! For you say that it means nothing to swear 'by God's Temple,' but that it is binding to swear 'by the gold in the Temple.' ¹⁷ Blind fools! Which is more important—the gold or the Temple that makes the gold sacred? ¹⁸ And you say that to swear 'by the altar' is not binding, but to swear 'by the gifts on the altar' is binding. ¹⁹ How blind! For which is more important—the gift on the altar or the altar that makes the gift sacred? ²⁰ When you swear 'by the altar,' you are swearing by it and by everything on it. ²¹ And when you swear 'by the Temple,' you are swearing by it and by God, who lives in it. ²² And when you swear 'by heaven,' you are swearing by the throne of God and by God, who sits on the throne.

²³ "What sorrow awaits you teachers of religious law and you Pharisees. Hypocrites! For you are careful to tithe even the tiniest income from your herb gardens,* but you ignore the more important aspects of the law—justice, mercy, and faith. You should tithe, yes, but do not neglect the more important things. ²⁴ Blind guides! You strain your water so you won't accidentally swallow a gnat, but you swallow a camel!*

²⁵ "What sorrow awaits you teachers of religious law and you Pharisees. Hypocrites! For you are so careful to clean the outside of the cup and the dish, but inside you are filthy—full of greed and self-indulgence! ²⁶ You blind Pharisee! First wash the inside of the cup and the dish,* and then the outside will become clean, too.

²⁷ "What sorrow awaits you teachers of religious law and you Pharisees. Hypocrites! For you are like whitewashed tombs—beautiful on the outside but filled on the inside with dead people's bones and all sorts of impurity. ²⁸ Outwardly you look like righteous people, but inwardly your hearts are filled with hypocrisy and lawlessness.

²⁹ "What sorrow awaits you teachers of religious law and you Pharisees. Hypocrites! For you build tombs for the prophets your ancestors killed, and you decorate the monuments of the godly people your ancestors destroyed. ³⁰ Then you say, 'If we had lived in the days of our ancestors, we would never have joined them in killing the prophets.'

³¹ "But in saying that, you testify against yourselves that you are indeed the descendants of those who murdered the prophets. ³² Go ahead and finish what your ancestors started. ³³ Snakes! Sons of vipers! How will you escape the judgment of hell?

³⁴ "Therefore, I am sending you prophets and wise men and teachers of religious law. But you will kill some by crucifixion, and you will flog others with whips in your synagogues, chasing them from city to city. ³⁵ As a result, you will be held responsible for the murder of all godly people of all time—from the murder of righteous Abel to the murder of Zechariah son of Berekiah, whom you killed in the Temple

22:44 Ps 110:1. 23:2 Greek and the Pharisees sit in the seat of Moses. 23:5 Greek They enlarge their phylacteries and lengthen their tassels. 23:7 Rabbi, from Aramaic, means "master" or "teacher." 23:8 Greek brothers. 23:13 Some manuscripts add verse 14, What sorrow awaits you teachers of religious law and you Pharisees. Hypocrites! You shamelessly cheat widows out of their property and then pretend to be pious by making long prayers in public. Because of this, you will be severely punished. Compare Mark 12:40 and Luke 20:47. 23:15 Greek of Gehenna; also in 23:33. 23:23 Greek tithe the mint, the dill, and the cumin. 23:24 See Lev 11:4, 23, where gnats and camels are both forbidden as food. 23:26 Some manuscripts do not include and the dish.

850 | MATTHEW 23:36

between the sanctuary and the altar. ³⁶ I tell you the truth, this judgment will fall on this very generation.

JESUS GRIEVES OVER JERUSALEM

³⁷ "O Jerusalem, Jerusalem, the city that kills the prophets and stones God's messengers! How often I have wanted to gather your children together as a hen protects her chicks beneath her wings, but you wouldn't let me. ³⁸ And now, look, your house is abandoned and desolate.* ³⁹ For I tell you this, you will never see me again until you say, 'Blessings on the one who comes in the name of the Lᴏʀᴅ!'*"

JESUS SPEAKS ABOUT THE FUTURE

24 As Jesus was leaving the Temple grounds, his disciples pointed out to him the various Temple buildings. ² But he responded, "Do you see all these buildings? I tell you the truth, they will be completely demolished. Not one stone will be left on top of another!"

³ Later, Jesus sat on the Mount of Olives. His disciples came to him privately and said, "Tell us, when will all this happen? What sign will signal your return and the end of the world?*"

⁴ Jesus told them, "Don't let anyone mislead you, ⁵ for many will come in my name, claiming, 'I am the Messiah.' They will deceive many. ⁶ And you will hear of wars and threats of wars, but don't panic. Yes, these things must take place, but the end won't follow immediately. ⁷ Nation will go to war against nation, and kingdom against kingdom. There will be famines and earthquakes in many parts of the world. ⁸ But all this is only the first of the birth pains, with more to come.

⁹ "Then you will be arrested, persecuted, and killed. You will be hated all over the world because you are my followers.* ¹⁰ And many will turn away from me and betray and hate each other. ¹¹ And many false prophets will appear and will deceive many people. ¹² Sin will be rampant everywhere, and the love of many will grow cold. ¹³ But the one who endures to the end will be saved. ¹⁴ And the Good News about the Kingdom will be preached throughout the whole world, so that all nations* will hear it; and then the end will come.

¹⁵ "The day is coming when you will see what Daniel the prophet spoke about—the sacrilegious object that causes desecration* standing in the Holy Place." (Reader, pay attention!) ¹⁶ "Then those in Judea must flee to the hills. ¹⁷ A person out on the deck of a roof must not go down into the house to pack. ¹⁸ A person out in the field must not return even to get a coat. ¹⁹ How terrible it will be for pregnant women and for nursing mothers in those days. ²⁰ And pray that your flight will not be in winter or on the Sabbath. ²¹ For there will be greater anguish than at any time since the world began. And it will never

be so great again. ²² In fact, unless that time of calamity is shortened, not a single person will survive. But it will be shortened for the sake of God's chosen ones.

²³ "Then if anyone tells you, 'Look, here is the Messiah,' or 'There he is,' don't believe it. ²⁴ For false messiahs and false prophets will rise up and perform great signs and wonders so as to deceive, if possible, even God's chosen ones. ²⁵ See, I have warned you about this ahead of time.

²⁶ "So if someone tells you, 'Look, the Messiah is out in the desert,' don't bother to go and look. Or, 'Look, he is hiding here,' don't believe it! ²⁷ For as the lightning flashes in the east and shines to the west, so it will be when the Son of Man* comes. ²⁸ Just as the gathering of vultures shows there is a carcass nearby, so these signs indicate that the end is near.*

²⁹ "Immediately after the anguish of those days,

the sun will be darkened,
    the moon will give no light,
the stars will fall from the sky,
    and the powers in the heavens will be
        shaken.*

³⁰ And then at last, the sign that the Son of Man is coming will appear in the heavens, and there will be deep mourning among all the peoples of the earth. And they will see the Son of Man coming on the clouds of heaven with power and great glory.* ³¹ And he will send out his angels with the mighty blast of a trumpet, and they will gather his chosen ones from all over the world*—from the farthest ends of the earth and heaven.

³² "Now learn a lesson from the fig tree. When its branches bud and its leaves begin to sprout, you know that summer is near. ³³ In the same way, when you see all these things, you can know his return is very near, right at the door. ³⁴ I tell you the truth, this generation* will not pass from the scene until all these things take place. ³⁵ Heaven and earth will disappear, but my words will never disappear.

³⁶ "However, no one knows the day or hour when these things will happen, not even the angels in heaven or the Son himself.* Only the Father knows.

³⁷ "When the Son of Man returns, it will be like it was in Noah's day. ³⁸ In those days before the flood, the people were enjoying banquets and parties and weddings right up to the time Noah entered his boat. ³⁹ People didn't realize what was going to happen until the flood came and swept

23:38 Some manuscripts do not include *and desolate.*   23:39 Ps 118:26.   24:3 Or *the age?*   24:9 Greek *on account of my name.* 24:14 Or *all peoples.*   24:15 Greek *the abomination of desolation.* See Dan 9:27; 11:31; 12:11.   24:27 "Son of Man" is a title Jesus used for himself.   24:28 Greek *Wherever the carcass is, the vultures gather.*   24:29 See Isa 13:10; 34:4; Joel 2:10.   24:30 See Dan 7:13. 24:31 Greek *from the four winds.*   24:34 Or *this age,* or *this nation.* 24:36 Some manuscripts do not include *or the Son himself.*

them all away. That is the way it will be when the Son of Man comes.

40 "Two men will be working together in the field; one will be taken, the other left. 41 Two women will be grinding flour at the mill; one will be taken, the other left.

42 "So you, too, must keep watch! For you don't know what day your Lord is coming. 43 Understand this: If a homeowner knew exactly when a burglar was coming, he would keep watch and not permit his house to be broken into. 44 You also must be ready all the time, for the Son of Man will come when least expected.

45 "A faithful, sensible servant is one to whom the master can give the responsibility of managing his other household servants and feeding them. 46 If the master returns and finds that the servant has done a good job, there will be a reward. 47 I tell you the truth, the master will put that servant in charge of all he owns. 48 But what if the servant is evil and thinks, 'My master won't be back for a while,' 49 and he begins beating the other servants, partying, and getting drunk? 50 The master will return unannounced and unexpected, 51 and he will cut the servant to pieces and assign him a place with the hypocrites. In that place there will be weeping and gnashing of teeth.

PARABLE OF THE TEN BRIDESMAIDS

25 "Then the Kingdom of Heaven will be like ten bridesmaids* who took their lamps and went to meet the bridegroom. 2 Five of them were foolish, and five were wise. 3 The five who were foolish didn't take enough olive oil for their lamps, 4 but the other five were wise enough to take along extra oil. 5 When the bridegroom was delayed, they all became drowsy and fell asleep.

6 "At midnight they were roused by the shout, 'Look, the bridegroom is coming! Come out and meet him!'

7 "All the bridesmaids got up and prepared their lamps. 8 Then the five foolish ones asked the others, 'Please give us some of your oil because our lamps are going out.'

9 "But the others replied, 'We don't have enough for all of us. Go to a shop and buy some for yourselves.'

10 "But while they were gone to buy oil, the bridegroom came. Then those who were ready went in with him to the marriage feast, and the door was locked. 11 Later, when the other five bridesmaids returned, they stood outside, calling, 'Lord! Lord! Open the door for us!'

12 "But he called back, 'Believe me, I don't know you!'

13 "So you, too, must keep watch! For you do not know the day or hour of my return.

PARABLE OF THE THREE SERVANTS

14 "Again, the Kingdom of Heaven can be illustrated by the story of a man going on a long trip. He called together his servants and entrusted his money to them while he was gone. 15 He gave five bags of silver* to one, two bags of silver to another, and one bag of silver to the last—dividing it in proportion to their abilities. He then left on his trip.

16 "The servant who received the five bags of silver began to invest the money and earned five more. 17 The servant with two bags of silver also went to work and earned two more. 18 But the servant who received the one bag of silver dug a hole in the ground and hid the master's money.

19 "After a long time their master returned from his trip and called them to give an account of how they had used his money. 20 The servant to whom he had entrusted the five bags of silver came forward with five more and said, 'Master, you gave me five bags of silver to invest, and I have earned five more.'

21 "The master was full of praise. 'Well done, my good and faithful servant. You have been faithful in handling this small amount, so now I will give you many more responsibilities. Let's celebrate together!*'

22 "The servant who had received the two bags of silver came forward and said, 'Master, you gave me two bags of silver to invest, and I have earned two more.'

23 "The master said, 'Well done, my good and faithful servant. You have been faithful in handling this small amount, so now I will give you many more responsibilities. Let's celebrate together!'

24 "Then the servant with the one bag of silver came and said, 'Master, I knew you were a harsh man, harvesting crops you didn't plant and gathering crops you didn't cultivate. 25 I was afraid I would lose your money, so I hid it in the earth. Look, here is your money back.'

26 "But the master replied, 'You wicked and lazy servant! If you knew I harvested crops I didn't plant and gathered crops I didn't cultivate, 27 why didn't you deposit my money in the bank? At least I could have gotten some interest on it.'

28 "Then he ordered, 'Take the money from this servant, and give it to the one with the ten bags of silver. 29 To those who use well what they are given, even more will be given, and they will have an abundance. But from those who do nothing, even what little they have will be taken away. 30 Now throw this useless servant into outer darkness, where there will be weeping and gnashing of teeth.'

THE FINAL JUDGMENT

31 "But when the Son of Man* comes in his glory, and all the angels with him, then he will sit upon

25:1 Or virgins; also in 25:7, 11.   25:15 Greek talents; also throughout the story. A talent is equal to 75 pounds or 34 kilograms.   25:21 Greek Enter into the joy of your master [or your Lord]; also in 25:23.   25:31 "Son of Man" is a title Jesus used for himself.

CARING FOR GOD'S BRIDE
Matthew 25:29   ROBERT MORRIS

I love my bride, Debbie, with all my heart. If I had to go away on an extended trip, I would ensure that all her needs would be met and that she would lack nothing until I returned.

Did you know that the Church is also called a bride? It's the bride of Christ, and Jesus has gone away for a season, but He left instructions for us to follow until His return. He says, "I want you to take care of My bride (the Church) while I am away by giving 10 percent of what I have given you to My house. You can spend the remaining 90 percent as you desire."

Matthew 25:29 promises, "To those who use well what they are given, even more will be given, and they will have an abundance." It also warns, "But from those who do nothing, even what little they have will be taken away."

his glorious throne. [32] All the nations* will be gathered in his presence, and he will separate the people as a shepherd separates the sheep from the goats. [33] He will place the sheep at his right hand and the goats at his left.

[34] "Then the King will say to those on his right, 'Come, you who are blessed by my Father, inherit the Kingdom prepared for you from the creation of the world. [35] For I was hungry, and you fed me. I was thirsty, and you gave me a drink. I was a stranger, and you invited me into your home. [36] I was naked, and you gave me clothing. I was sick, and you cared for me. I was in prison, and you visited me.'

[37] "Then these righteous ones will reply, 'Lord, when did we ever see you hungry and feed you? Or thirsty and give you something to drink? [38] Or a stranger and show you hospitality? Or naked and give you clothing? [39] When did we ever see you sick or in prison and visit you?'

[40] "And the King will say, 'I tell you the truth, when you did it to one of the least of these my brothers and sisters,* you were doing it to me!'

[41] "Then the King will turn to those on the left and say, 'Away with you, you cursed ones, into the eternal fire prepared for the devil and his demons.* [42] For I was hungry, and you didn't feed me. I was thirsty, and you didn't give me a drink. [43] I was a stranger, and you didn't invite me into your home. I was naked, and you didn't give me clothing. I was sick and in prison, and you didn't visit me.'

[44] "Then they will reply, 'Lord, when did we ever see you hungry or thirsty or a stranger or naked or sick or in prison, and not help you?'

[45] "And he will answer, 'I tell you the truth, when you refused to help the least of these my brothers and sisters, you were refusing to help me.'

[46] "And they will go away into eternal punishment, but the righteous will go into eternal life."

THE PLOT TO KILL JESUS

26 When Jesus had finished saying all these things, he said to his disciples, [2] "As you know, Passover begins in two days, and the Son of Man* will be handed over to be crucified."

[3] At that same time the leading priests and elders were meeting at the residence of Caiaphas, the high priest, [4] plotting how to capture Jesus secretly and kill him. [5] "But not during the Passover celebration," they agreed, "or the people may riot."

JESUS ANOINTED AT BETHANY

[6] Meanwhile, Jesus was in Bethany at the home of Simon, a man who had previously had leprosy. [7] While he was eating,* a woman came in with a beautiful alabaster jar of expensive perfume and poured it over his head.

[8] The disciples were indignant when they saw this. "What a waste!" they said. [9] "It could have been sold for a high price and the money given to the poor."

[10] But Jesus, aware of this, replied, "Why criticize this woman for doing such a good thing to me? [11] You will always have the poor among you, but you will not always have me. [12] She has poured this perfume on me to prepare my body for burial. [13] I tell you the truth, wherever the Good News is preached throughout the world, this woman's deed will be remembered and discussed."

JUDAS AGREES TO BETRAY JESUS

[14] Then Judas Iscariot, one of the twelve disciples, went to the leading priests [15] and asked, "How much will you pay me to betray Jesus to you?" And they gave him thirty pieces of silver. [16] From that time on, Judas began looking for an opportunity to betray Jesus.

THE LAST SUPPER

[17] On the first day of the Festival of Unleavened Bread, the disciples came to Jesus and asked, "Where do you want us to prepare the Passover meal for you?"

[18] "As you go into the city," he told them, "you will see a certain man. Tell him, 'The Teacher says: My time has come, and I will eat the Passover meal with my disciples at your house.'" [19] So the disciples did as Jesus told them and prepared the Passover meal there.

[20] When it was evening, Jesus sat down at the table* with the Twelve. [21] While they were eating, he said, "I tell you the truth, one of you will betray me."

25:32 Or *peoples.*   25:40 Greek *my brothers.*   25:41 Greek *his angels.*   26:2 "Son of Man" is a title Jesus used for himself.   26:7 Or *reclining.*   26:20 Or *Jesus reclined.*

WHAT DIFFERENCE DOES THE RESURRECTION MAKE?
Matthew 26

ROBERT MORRIS

Some people *think* Jesus is the Messiah, but because of the Resurrection, we *know* He is the Messiah. This knowing makes a difference in our behavior. We don't just think Jesus is Lord—we know He's Lord. The apostle Peter thought Jesus was the Messiah, so he left everything to follow Him (Matthew 4:18). However, it took three years and three significant events in Peter's life before he *knew* Jesus was the Messiah.

1. The Declaration (Matthew 26:31-35)
Before His arrest, Jesus warned the disciples, "All of you will desert me" (v. 31) He even detailed how Peter would deny Him: "Before the rooster crows, you will deny three times that you even know me" (v. 34). However, Peter emphatically declared that even if he faced death, he would never deny Jesus.

2. The Denial (Matthew 26:69-75)
Peter not only denied Jesus, but he also cursed and swore in an attempt to prove he wasn't one of Jesus' disciples. Can you imagine how Peter felt when he heard the rooster crow and realized Jesus' words had come true? Even worse, Jesus turned and looked at Peter the moment it happened (Luke 22:60-61). You may think, *Well, I've never denied Jesus with my words*, but have you ever denied Him by the way you live (Titus 1:16)? We've all done it.

3. The Decision (John 21)
In John 21, Peter encounters the newly-risen Jesus after the Resurrection. Like the first time he met the Savior (Luke 5:1-7), the disciple was tired from fishing all night and catching nothing. Once again, Jesus tells him to throw his net over the other side of the boat, and the same miracle happens as before—the net instantly fills with fish! Why does Jesus do the same miracle? I think He wants Peter to know, *You can start again. I died for your failures, and I rose again. Every time you make a mistake, you can start over.* Then Jesus repeatedly asks Peter, "Do you love me?" (John 21:15-17). I think He is saying, *Peter, I know you love Me, but I want you to know you love Me. You're the one who is having doubts right now. You feel bad because you messed up, but My resurrection takes care of that. It takes care of all your failures.*

Peter knew the cross meant death, but until the Resurrection, he didn't know it also meant life after death. He started following Jesus three years earlier, but there by the Sea of Galilee, he makes a commitment to follow Him again. Peter is a man who goes from denying Jesus to preaching about Him in a matter of weeks. What could make such a drastic difference? Only one thing: the Resurrection.

---

²² Greatly distressed, each one asked in turn, "Am I the one, Lord?"

²³ He replied, "One of you who has just eaten from this bowl with me will betray me. ²⁴ For the Son of Man must die, as the Scriptures declared long ago. But how terrible it will be for the one who betrays him. It would be far better for that man if he had never been born!"

²⁵ Judas, the one who would betray him, also asked, "Rabbi, am I the one?"

And Jesus told him, "You have said it."

²⁶ As they were eating, Jesus took some bread and blessed it. Then he broke it in pieces and gave it to the disciples, saying, "Take this and eat it, for this is my body."

²⁷ And he took a cup of wine and gave thanks to God for it. He gave it to them and said, "Each of you drink from it, ²⁸ for this is my blood, which confirms the covenant* between God and his people. It is poured out as a sacrifice to forgive the sins of many. ²⁹ Mark my words—I will not drink wine again until the day I drink it new with you in my Father's Kingdom."

³⁰ Then they sang a hymn and went out to the Mount of Olives.

JESUS PREDICTS PETER'S DENIAL
³¹ On the way, Jesus told them, "Tonight all of you will desert me. For the Scriptures say,

'God will strike* the Shepherd,
    and the sheep of the flock will be
        scattered.'

³² But after I have been raised from the dead, I will go ahead of you to Galilee and meet you there."

³³ Peter declared, "Even if everyone else deserts you, I will never desert you."

³⁴ Jesus replied, "I tell you the truth, Peter—this very night, before the rooster crows, you will deny three times that you even know me."

³⁵ "No!" Peter insisted. "Even if I have to die with you, I will never deny you!" And all the other disciples vowed the same.

JESUS PRAYS IN GETHSEMANE
³⁶ Then Jesus went with them to the olive grove called Gethsemane, and he said, "Sit here while I go over there to pray." ³⁷ He took Peter and Zebedee's two sons, James and John, and he became anguished and distressed. ³⁸ He told them, "My soul is crushed with grief to the point of death. Stay here and keep watch with me."

³⁹ He went on a little farther and bowed with his face to the ground, praying, "My Father! If it is possible, let this cup of suffering be taken

---

26:28 Some manuscripts read *the new covenant.* 26:31 Greek *I will strike.* Zech 13:7.

away from me. Yet I want your will to be done, not mine."

⁴⁰ Then he returned to the disciples and found them asleep. He said to Peter, "Couldn't you watch with me even one hour? ⁴¹ Keep watch and pray, so that you will not give in to temptation. For the spirit is willing, but the body is weak!"

⁴² Then Jesus left them a second time and prayed, "My Father! If this cup cannot be taken away* unless I drink it, your will be done." ⁴³ When he returned to them again, he found them sleeping, for they couldn't keep their eyes open.

⁴⁴ So he went to pray a third time, saying the same things again. ⁴⁵ Then he came to the disciples and said, "Go ahead and sleep. Have your rest. But look—the time has come. The Son of Man is betrayed into the hands of sinners. ⁴⁶ Up, let's be going. Look, my betrayer is here!"

JESUS IS BETRAYED AND ARRESTED

⁴⁷ And even as Jesus said this, Judas, one of the twelve disciples, arrived with a crowd of men armed with swords and clubs. They had been sent by the leading priests and elders of the people. ⁴⁸ The traitor, Judas, had given them a prearranged signal: "You will know which one to arrest when I greet him with a kiss." ⁴⁹ So Judas came straight to Jesus. "Greetings, Rabbi!" he exclaimed and gave him the kiss.

⁵⁰ Jesus said, "My friend, go ahead and do what you have come for."

Then the others grabbed Jesus and arrested him. ⁵¹ But one of the men with Jesus pulled out his sword and struck the high priest's slave, slashing off his ear.

⁵² "Put away your sword," Jesus told him. "Those who use the sword will die by the sword. ⁵³ Don't you realize that I could ask my Father for thousands* of angels to protect us, and he would send them instantly? ⁵⁴ But if I did, how would the Scriptures be fulfilled that describe what must happen now?"

⁵⁵ Then Jesus said to the crowd, "Am I some dangerous revolutionary, that you come with swords and clubs to arrest me? Why didn't you arrest me in the Temple? I was there teaching every day. ⁵⁶ But this is all happening to fulfill the words of the prophets as recorded in the Scriptures." At that point, all the disciples deserted him and fled.

JESUS BEFORE THE COUNCIL

⁵⁷ Then the people who had arrested Jesus led him to the home of Caiaphas, the high priest, where the teachers of religious law and the elders had gathered. ⁵⁸ Meanwhile, Peter followed him at a distance and came to the high priest's courtyard. He went in and sat with the guards and waited to see how it would all end.

⁵⁹ Inside, the leading priests and the entire high council* were trying to find witnesses who would lie about Jesus, so they could put him to death. ⁶⁰ But even though they found many who agreed to give false witness, they could not use anyone's testimony. Finally, two men came forward ⁶¹ who declared, "This man said, 'I am able to destroy the Temple of God and rebuild it in three days.'"

⁶² Then the high priest stood up and said to Jesus, "Well, aren't you going to answer these charges? What do you have to say for yourself?" ⁶³ But Jesus remained silent. Then the high priest said to him, "I demand in the name of the living God—tell us if you are the Messiah, the Son of God."

⁶⁴ Jesus replied, "You have said it. And in the future you will see the Son of Man seated in the place of power at God's right hand* and coming on the clouds of heaven."*

⁶⁵ Then the high priest tore his clothing to show his horror and said, "Blasphemy! Why do we need other witnesses? You have all heard his blasphemy. ⁶⁶ What is your verdict?"

"Guilty!" they shouted. "He deserves to die!"

⁶⁷ Then they began to spit in Jesus' face and beat him with their fists. And some slapped him, ⁶⁸ jeering, "Prophesy to us, you Messiah! Who hit you that time?"

PETER DENIES JESUS

⁶⁹ Meanwhile, Peter was sitting outside in the courtyard. A servant girl came over and said to him, "You were one of those with Jesus the Galilean."

⁷⁰ But Peter denied it in front of everyone. "I don't know what you're talking about," he said.

⁷¹ Later, out by the gate, another servant girl noticed him and said to those standing around, "This man was with Jesus of Nazareth.*"

⁷² Again Peter denied it, this time with an oath. "I don't even know the man," he said.

⁷³ A little later some of the other bystanders came over to Peter and said, "You must be one of them; we can tell by your Galilean accent."

⁷⁴ Peter swore, "A curse on me if I'm lying—I don't know the man!" And immediately the rooster crowed.

⁷⁵ Suddenly, Jesus' words flashed through Peter's mind: "Before the rooster crows, you will deny three times that you even know me." And he went away, weeping bitterly.

JUDAS HANGS HIMSELF

27 Very early in the morning the leading priests and the elders of the people met again to lay plans for putting Jesus to death. ² Then they bound him, led him away, and took him to Pilate, the Roman governor.

³ When Judas, who had betrayed him, realized that Jesus had been condemned to die, he

---

26:42 Greek *If this cannot pass.*   26:53 Greek *twelve legions.*
26:59 Greek *the Sanhedrin.*   26:64a Greek *seated at the right hand of the power.* See Ps 110:1.   26:64b See Dan 7:13.   26:71 Or *Jesus the Nazarene.*

was filled with remorse. So he took the thirty pieces of silver back to the leading priests and the elders. [4] "I have sinned," he declared, "for I have betrayed an innocent man."

"What do we care?" they retorted. "That's your problem."

[5] Then Judas threw the silver coins down in the Temple and went out and hanged himself.

[6] The leading priests picked up the coins. "It wouldn't be right to put this money in the Temple treasury," they said, "since it was payment for murder."* [7] After some discussion they finally decided to buy the potter's field, and they made it into a cemetery for foreigners. [8] That is why the field is still called the Field of Blood. [9] This fulfilled the prophecy of Jeremiah that says,

"They took* the thirty pieces of silver—
the price at which he was valued by
the people of Israel,
[10] and purchased the potter's field,
as the Lord directed.*"

JESUS' TRIAL BEFORE PILATE

[11] Now Jesus was standing before Pilate, the Roman governor. "Are you the king of the Jews?" the governor asked him.

Jesus replied, "You have said it."

[12] But when the leading priests and the elders made their accusations against him, Jesus remained silent. [13] "Don't you hear all these charges they are bringing against you?" Pilate demanded. [14] But Jesus made no response to any of the charges, much to the governor's surprise.

[15] Now it was the governor's custom each year during the Passover celebration to release one prisoner to the crowd—anyone they wanted. [16] This year there was a notorious prisoner, a man named Barabbas.* [17] As the crowds gathered before Pilate's house that morning, he asked them, "Which one do you want me to release to you—Barabbas, or Jesus who is called the Messiah?" [18] (He knew very well that the religious leaders had arrested Jesus out of envy.)

[19] Just then, as Pilate was sitting on the judgment seat, his wife sent him this message: "Leave that innocent man alone. I suffered through a terrible nightmare about him last night."

[20] Meanwhile, the leading priests and the elders persuaded the crowd to ask for Barabbas to be released and for Jesus to be put to death. [21] So the governor asked again, "Which of these two do you want me to release to you?"

The crowd shouted back, "Barabbas!"

[22] Pilate responded, "Then what should I do with Jesus who is called the Messiah?"

They shouted back, "Crucify him!"

[23] "Why?" Pilate demanded. "What crime has he committed?"

But the mob roared even louder, "Crucify him!"

[24] Pilate saw that he wasn't getting anywhere and that a riot was developing. So he sent for a bowl of water and washed his hands before the crowd, saying, "I am innocent of this man's blood. The responsibility is yours!"

[25] And all the people yelled back, "We will take responsibility for his death—we and our children!"*

[26] So Pilate released Barabbas to them. He ordered Jesus flogged with a lead-tipped whip, then turned him over to the Roman soldiers to be crucified.

THE SOLDIERS MOCK JESUS

[27] Some of the governor's soldiers took Jesus into their headquarters* and called out the entire regiment. [28] They stripped him and put a scarlet robe on him. [29] They wove thorn branches into a crown and put it on his head, and they placed a reed stick in his right hand as a scepter. Then they knelt before him in mockery and taunted, "Hail! King of the Jews!" [30] And they spit on him and grabbed the stick and struck him on the head with it. [31] When they were finally tired of mocking him, they took off the robe and put his own clothes on him again. Then they led him away to be crucified.

THE CRUCIFIXION

[32] Along the way, they came across a man named Simon, who was from Cyrene,* and the soldiers forced him to carry Jesus' cross. [33] And they went out to a place called Golgotha (which means "Place of the Skull"). [34] The soldiers gave Jesus wine mixed with bitter gall, but when he had tasted it, he refused to drink it.

[35] After they had nailed him to the cross, the soldiers gambled for his clothes by throwing dice.* [36] Then they sat around and kept guard as he hung there. [37] A sign was fastened above Jesus' head, announcing the charge against him. It read: "This is Jesus, the King of the Jews." [38] Two revolutionaries* were crucified with him, one on his right and one on his left.

[39] The people passing by shouted abuse, shaking their heads in mockery. [40] "Look at you now!" they yelled at him. "You said you were going to destroy the Temple and rebuild it in three days. Well then, if you are the Son of God, save yourself and come down from the cross!"

[41] The leading priests, the teachers of religious law, and the elders also mocked Jesus. [42] "He saved others," they scoffed, "but he can't save himself! So he is the King of Israel, is he? Let him come down from the cross right now, and we will believe in him! [43] He trusted God, so let God rescue him now if he wants him! For he said,

---

27:6 Greek *since it is the price for blood.*   27:9 Or *I took.*
27:9-10 Greek *as the Lord directed me.* Zech 11:12-13; Jer 32:6-9.   27:16 Some manuscripts read *Jesus Barabbas;* also in 27:17.
27:25 Greek *"His blood be on us and on our children."*   27:27 Or *into the Praetorium.*   27:32 *Cyrene* was a city in northern Africa.
27:35 Greek *by casting lots.* A few late manuscripts add *This fulfilled the word of the prophet: "They divided my garments among themselves and cast lots for my robe."* See Ps 22:18.   27:38 Or *criminals;* also in 27:44.

'I am the Son of God.'" ⁴⁴Even the revolutionaries who were crucified with him ridiculed him in the same way.

THE DEATH OF JESUS

⁴⁵At noon, darkness fell across the whole land until three o'clock. ⁴⁶At about three o'clock, Jesus called out with a loud voice, *"Eli, Eli,* lema sabach-thani?"* which means "My God, my God, why have you abandoned me?"*

⁴⁷Some of the bystanders misunderstood and thought he was calling for the prophet Elijah. ⁴⁸One of them ran and filled a sponge with sour wine, holding it up to him on a reed stick so he could drink. ⁴⁹But the rest said, "Wait! Let's see whether Elijah comes to save him."*

⁵⁰Then Jesus shouted out again, and he released his spirit. ⁵¹At that moment the curtain in the sanctuary of the Temple was torn in two, from top to bottom. The earth shook, rocks split apart, ⁵²and tombs opened. The bodies of many godly men and women who had died were raised from the dead. ⁵³They left the cemetery after Jesus' resurrection, went into the holy city of Jerusalem, and appeared to many people.

⁵⁴The Roman officer* and the other soldiers at the crucifixion were terrified by the earthquake and all that had happened. They said, "This man truly was the Son of God!"

⁵⁵And many women who had come from Galilee with Jesus to care for him were watching from a distance. ⁵⁶Among them were Mary Magdalene, Mary (the mother of James and Joseph), and the mother of James and John, the sons of Zebedee.

THE BURIAL OF JESUS

⁵⁷As evening approached, Joseph, a rich man from Arimathea who had become a follower of Jesus, ⁵⁸went to Pilate and asked for Jesus' body. And Pilate issued an order to release it to him. ⁵⁹Joseph took the body and wrapped it in a long sheet of clean linen cloth. ⁶⁰He placed it in his own new tomb, which had been carved out of the rock. Then he rolled a great stone across the entrance and left. ⁶¹Both Mary Magdalene and the other Mary were sitting across from the tomb and watching.

THE GUARD AT THE TOMB

⁶²The next day, on the Sabbath,* the leading priests and Pharisees went to see Pilate. ⁶³They told him, "Sir, we remember what that deceiver once said while he was still alive: 'After three days I will rise from the dead.' ⁶⁴So we request that you seal the tomb until the third day. This will prevent his disciples from coming and stealing his body and then telling everyone he was raised from the dead! If that happens, we'll be worse off than we were at first."

⁶⁵Pilate replied, "Take guards and secure it the best you can." ⁶⁶So they sealed the tomb and posted guards to protect it.

THE RESURRECTION

28 Early on Sunday morning,* as the new day was dawning, Mary Magdalene and the other Mary went out to visit the tomb.

²Suddenly there was a great earthquake! For an angel of the Lord came down from heaven, rolled aside the stone, and sat on it. ³His face shone like lightning, and his clothing was as white as snow. ⁴The guards shook with fear when they saw him, and they fell into a dead faint.

⁵Then the angel spoke to the women. "Don't be afraid!" he said. "I know you are looking for Jesus, who was crucified. ⁶He isn't here! He is risen from the dead, just as he said would happen. Come, see where his body was lying. ⁷And now, go quickly and tell his disciples that he has risen from the dead, and he is going ahead of you to Galilee. You will see him there. Remember what I have told you."

⁸The women ran quickly from the tomb. They were very frightened but also filled with great joy, and they rushed to give the disciples the angel's message. ⁹And as they went, Jesus met them and greeted them. And they ran to him, grasped his feet, and worshiped him. ¹⁰Then Jesus said to them, "Don't be afraid! Go tell my brothers to leave for Galilee, and they will see me there."

THE REPORT OF THE GUARD

¹¹As the women were on their way, some of the guards went into the city and told the leading priests what had happened. ¹²A meeting with the elders was called, and they decided to give the soldiers a large bribe. ¹³They told the soldiers, "You must say, 'Jesus' disciples came during the night while we were sleeping, and they stole his body.' ¹⁴If the governor hears about it, we'll stand up for you so you won't get in trouble." ¹⁵So the guards accepted the bribe and said what they were told to say. Their story spread widely among the Jews, and they still tell it today.

THE GREAT COMMISSION

¹⁶Then the eleven disciples left for Galilee, going to the mountain where Jesus had told them to go. ¹⁷When they saw him, they worshiped him—but some of them doubted!

¹⁸Jesus came and told his disciples, "I have been given all authority in heaven and on earth. ¹⁹Therefore, go and make disciples of all the nations,* baptizing them in the name of the Father and the Son and the Holy Spirit. ²⁰Teach these new disciples to obey all the commands I have given you. And be sure of this: I am with you always, even to the end of the age."

27:46a Some manuscripts read *Eloi, Eloi.* 27:46b Ps 22:1.
27:49 Some manuscripts add *And another took a spear and pierced his side, and out flowed water and blood.* Compare John 19:34.
27:54 Greek *The centurion.* 27:62 Or *On the next day, which is after the Preparation.* 28:1 Greek *After the Sabbath, on the first day of the week.* 28:19 Or *all peoples.*

MARK

JON HUNTZINGER, PHD

O f the four Gospels in the New Testament, Mark's is the shortest. Most Bible scholars believe it was also the first Gospel written, composed by John Mark from Jerusalem in the early 60s (Acts 12:12). He assisted both Peter and Paul in their ministries (Acts 13:5, 13; 15:36-40; Philemon 24; Colossians 4:10; 2 Timothy 4:11; and 1 Peter 5:13). →

Since the fourth century, readers of Mark's Gospel have noticed that his depiction of Jesus and His ministry closely follows the outline of Peter's sermon to the Roman centurion Cornelius (Acts 10:36-41). For that reason and others, readers throughout history have traced this Gospel's origins to the teachings of Peter about Jesus.

PETER'S SERMON (ACTS 10)	PRIMARY SECTIONS IN MARK'S GOSPEL
Peter preaches the "Good News" (v. 36).	Mark begins his account with "This is the Good News" (1:1).
"God anointed Jesus of Nazareth with the Holy Spirit" (v. 38).	The Holy Spirit descends upon Jesus at the outset of His ministry (1:10).
Peter says that Jesus began His ministry in Galilee (v. 37).	Mark centers Jesus' ministry in Galilee in chapters 1-8.
Peter summarizes Jesus' ministry by saying that He "went around doing good and healing all who were oppressed by the devil" (v. 38).	Mark depicts Jesus' ministry as one of healing and exorcism. Though he describes Jesus as a teacher, Mark does not record much of His teaching.
Peter says he is a "[witness] of all [Jesus] did throughout Judea and in Jerusalem" (v. 39).	Mark shifts the location of Jesus' ministry from Galilee to Jerusalem in chapters 11-16.
Peter says, "They put [Jesus] to death by hanging him on a cross" (v. 39).	Mark gives a detailed description of Jesus' death in chapter 15.
Peter concludes his sermon by proclaiming, "God raised [Jesus] to life on the third day" (v. 40).	Mark concludes his Gospel with the announcement of the angel to the women, "He isn't here! He is risen from the dead!" (16:6).

Mark's Gospel may be divided into seven parts, which supports the outline given above:

Part one introduces John the Baptist and reports Jesus' baptism (1:1-15).

Part two recounts the calling of the first disciples and the beginning of Jesus' ministry in the synagogues of Galilee (1:16-3:12).

Part three follows Jesus' teaching and miracle ministry to the crowds in and around Galilee (3:13-5:43).

Part four reports the sending of the disciples to continue Jesus' ministry and Jesus' two feeding miracles by the Sea of Galilee (6:1-8:26).

Part five tracks Jesus as He makes His "way" to Jerusalem (8:27-10:52; in particular, see 8:27; 10:17, 32, 46, 52; 11:1, 11).

Part six reports Jesus' entry into Jerusalem and the Temple (11:1-13:37).

Part seven describes Jesus' final meal with His disciples, His crucifixion, and the empty tomb (14:1-16:8).

Mark depicts Jesus as the Son of God at the beginning of his Gospel and near its conclusion (1:1; 15:39). In between, he uses the word *immediately* 40 times to show Jesus as a man of action. Jesus acts decisively in everything He does because the Holy Spirit is with Him as God's Son (1:10-11) to teach, heal, deliver, and cleanse people of their sin and impurity.

Thus, a particular focus in Mark is Jesus' ministry of purity. At different times in His ministry, Jesus delivers people from unclean spirits (1:21-28; 5:1-20; 9:14-29); He cleanses a leper of his skin disease (1:40-44); He heals a woman who is unclean because of a "constant bleeding" (5:21-34); He teaches about the nature of uncleanness (7:14-23); and He prophetically "cleanses" the Temple (11:15-19). By delivering and healing these people through the Holy Spirit, Jesus restores them so they might live their lives in wholeness and purity. And His actions in the Temple speak of His desire to revitalize worship for all people.

JOHN THE BAPTIST PREPARES THE WAY

1 This is the Good News about Jesus the Messiah, the Son of God.* It began ²just as the prophet Isaiah had written:

"Look, I am sending my messenger ahead
    of you,
    and he will prepare your way.*
³ He is a voice shouting in the wilderness,
'Prepare the way for the LORD's coming!
    Clear the road for him!'*"

⁴This messenger was John the Baptist. He was in the wilderness and preached that people should be baptized to show that they had repented of their sins and turned to God to be forgiven. ⁵All of Judea, including all the people of Jerusalem, went out to see and hear John. And when they confessed their sins, he baptized them in the Jordan River. ⁶His clothes were woven from coarse camel hair, and he wore a leather belt around his waist. For food he ate locusts and wild honey.

⁷John announced: "Someone is coming soon who is greater than I am—so much greater that I'm not even worthy to stoop down like a slave and untie the straps of his sandals. ⁸I baptize you with* water, but he will baptize you with the Holy Spirit!"

THE BAPTISM AND TEMPTATION OF JESUS

⁹One day Jesus came from Nazareth in Galilee, and John baptized him in the Jordan River. ¹⁰As Jesus came up out of the water, he saw the heavens splitting apart and the Holy Spirit descending on him* like a dove. ¹¹And a voice from heaven said, "You are my dearly loved Son, and you bring me great joy."

¹²The Spirit then compelled Jesus to go into the wilderness, ¹³where he was tempted by Satan for forty days. He was out among the wild animals, and angels took care of him.

¹⁴Later on, after John was arrested, Jesus went into Galilee, where he preached God's Good News.* ¹⁵"The time promised by God has come at last!" he announced. "The Kingdom of God is near! Repent of your sins and believe the Good News!"

THE FIRST DISCIPLES

¹⁶One day as Jesus was walking along the shore of the Sea of Galilee, he saw Simon* and his brother Andrew throwing a net into the water, for they fished for a living. ¹⁷Jesus called out to them, "Come, follow me, and I will show you how to fish for people!" ¹⁸And they left their nets at once and followed him.

¹⁹A little farther up the shore Jesus saw Zebedee's sons, James and John, in a boat repairing their nets. ²⁰He called them at once, and they also followed him, leaving their father, Zebedee, in the boat with the hired men.

THE BENEFITS OF BAPTISM
Mark 1:9-11   JACK HAYFORD

Three things happened at Jesus' baptism, and these same things also happen in the baptism of all believers.

1. The Father pronounced His approval of His Son.

For believers, God declares that sin is removed, and our faith in Jesus Christ brings Him great joy. We are His sons and daughters now.

2. The heavens parted.

For believers, the spiritual realm is opened, enabling them to see beyond the limits of human sight. God's Word becomes alive and powerful, like a sword.

3. Jesus received the fullness of the Holy Spirit for the ministry set before Him.

For believers, baptism opens the way to the overflowing of the Holy Spirit. God sent His Son and gave Him the unlimited power of the Holy Spirit (John 3:34). Jesus later sent His disciples and gave them the same unlimited power of the Holy Spirit (John 20:22).

JESUS CASTS OUT AN EVIL SPIRIT

²¹Jesus and his companions went to the town of Capernaum. When the Sabbath day came, he went into the synagogue and began to teach. ²²The people were amazed at his teaching, for he taught with real authority—quite unlike the teachers of religious law.

²³Suddenly, a man in the synagogue who was possessed by an evil* spirit cried out, ²⁴"Why are you interfering with us, Jesus of Nazareth? Have you come to destroy us? I know who you are—the Holy One of God!"

²⁵But Jesus reprimanded him. "Be quiet! Come out of the man," he ordered. ²⁶At that, the evil spirit screamed, threw the man into a convulsion, and then came out of him.

²⁷Amazement gripped the audience, and they began to discuss what had happened. "What sort of new teaching is this?" they asked excitedly. "It has such authority! Even evil spirits obey his orders!" ²⁸The news about Jesus spread quickly throughout the entire region of Galilee.

JESUS HEALS MANY PEOPLE

²⁹After Jesus left the synagogue with James and John, they went to Simon and Andrew's home. ³⁰Now Simon's mother-in-law was sick in bed with a high fever. They told Jesus about her right away. ³¹So he went to her bedside, took her by the hand, and helped her sit up. Then the fever left her, and she prepared a meal for them.

1:1 Some manuscripts do not include *the Son of God.* 1:2 Mal 3:1.
1:3 Isa 40:3 (Greek version). 1:8 Or *in;* also in 1:8b. 1:10 Or *toward him,* or *into him.* 1:14 Some manuscripts read *the Good News of the Kingdom of God.* 1:16 *Simon* is called "Peter" in 3:16 and thereafter. 1:23 Greek *unclean;* also in 1:26, 27.

³²That evening after sunset, many sick and demon-possessed people were brought to Jesus. ³³The whole town gathered at the door to watch. ³⁴So Jesus healed many people who were sick with various diseases, and he cast out many demons. But because the demons knew who he was, he did not allow them to speak.

JESUS PREACHES IN GALILEE

³⁵Before daybreak the next morning, Jesus got up and went out to an isolated place to pray. ³⁶Later Simon and the others went out to find him. ³⁷When they found him, they said, "Everyone is looking for you."

³⁸But Jesus replied, "We must go on to other towns as well, and I will preach to them, too. That is why I came." ³⁹So he traveled throughout the region of Galilee, preaching in the synagogues and casting out demons.

JESUS HEALS A MAN WITH LEPROSY

⁴⁰A man with leprosy came and knelt in front of Jesus, begging to be healed. "If you are willing, you can heal me and make me clean," he said.

⁴¹Moved with compassion,* Jesus reached out and touched him. "I am willing," he said. "Be healed!" ⁴²Instantly the leprosy disappeared, and the man was healed. ⁴³Then Jesus sent him on his way with a stern warning: ⁴⁴"Don't tell anyone about this. Instead, go to the priest and let him examine you. Take along the offering required in the law of Moses for those who have been healed of leprosy.* This will be a public testimony that you have been cleansed."

⁴⁵But the man went and spread the word, proclaiming to everyone what had happened. As a result, large crowds soon surrounded Jesus, and he couldn't publicly enter a town anywhere. He had to stay out in the secluded places, but people from everywhere kept coming to him.

JESUS HEALS A PARALYZED MAN

2 When Jesus returned to Capernaum several days later, the news spread quickly that he was back home. ²Soon the house where he was staying was so packed with visitors that there was no more room, even outside the door. While he was preaching God's word to them, ³four men arrived carrying a paralyzed man on a mat. ⁴They couldn't bring him to Jesus because of the crowd, so they dug a hole through the roof above his head. Then they lowered the man on his mat, right down in front of Jesus. ⁵Seeing their faith, Jesus said to the paralyzed man, "My child, your sins are forgiven."

⁶But some of the teachers of religious law who were sitting there thought to themselves, ⁷"What is he saying? This is blasphemy! Only God can forgive sins!"

⁸Jesus knew immediately what they were thinking, so he asked them, "Why do you question this in your hearts? ⁹Is it easier to say to the paralyzed man 'Your sins are forgiven,' or 'Stand up, pick up your mat, and walk'? ¹⁰So I will prove to you that the Son of Man* has the authority on earth to forgive sins." Then Jesus turned to the paralyzed man and said, ¹¹"Stand up, pick up your mat, and go home!"

¹²And the man jumped up, grabbed his mat, and walked out through the stunned onlookers. They were all amazed and praised God, exclaiming, "We've never seen anything like this before!"

JESUS CALLS LEVI (MATTHEW)

¹³Then Jesus went out to the lakeshore again and taught the crowds that were coming to him. ¹⁴As he walked along, he saw Levi son of Alphaeus sitting at his tax collector's booth. "Follow me and be my disciple," Jesus said to him. So Levi got up and followed him.

¹⁵Later, Levi invited Jesus and his disciples to his home as dinner guests, along with many tax collectors and other disreputable sinners. (There were many people of this kind among Jesus' followers.) ¹⁶But when the teachers of religious law who were Pharisees* saw him eating with tax collectors and other sinners, they asked his disciples, "Why does he eat with such scum?*"

¹⁷When Jesus heard this, he told them, "Healthy people don't need a doctor—sick people do. I have come to call not those who think they are righteous, but those who know they are sinners."

A DISCUSSION ABOUT FASTING

¹⁸Once when John's disciples and the Pharisees were fasting, some people came to Jesus and asked, "Why don't your disciples fast like John's disciples and the Pharisees do?"

¹⁹Jesus replied, "Do wedding guests fast while celebrating with the groom? Of course not. They can't fast while the groom is with them. ²⁰But someday the groom will be taken away from them, and then they will fast.

²¹"Besides, who would patch old clothing with new cloth? For the new patch would shrink and rip away from the old cloth, leaving an even bigger tear than before.

²²"And no one puts new wine into old wineskins. For the wine would burst the wineskins, and the wine and the skins would both be lost. New wine calls for new wineskins."

A DISCUSSION ABOUT THE SABBATH

²³One Sabbath day as Jesus was walking through some grainfields, his disciples began breaking off heads of grain to eat. ²⁴But the Pharisees said to Jesus, "Look, why are they breaking the law by harvesting grain on the Sabbath?"

²⁵Jesus said to them, "Haven't you ever read in the Scriptures what David did when he and

1:41 Some manuscripts read *Moved with anger.* 1:44 See Lev 14:2-32. 2:10 "Son of Man" is a title Jesus used for himself. 2:16a Greek *the scribes of the Pharisees.* 2:16b Greek *with tax collectors and sinners?*

his companions were hungry? ²⁶He went into the house of God (during the days when Abiathar was high priest) and broke the law by eating the sacred loaves of bread that only the priests are allowed to eat. He also gave some to his companions."

²⁷Then Jesus said to them, "The Sabbath was made to meet the needs of people, and not people to meet the requirements of the Sabbath. ²⁸So the Son of Man is Lord, even over the Sabbath!"

JESUS HEALS ON THE SABBATH

3 Jesus went into the synagogue again and noticed a man with a deformed hand. ²Since it was the Sabbath, Jesus' enemies watched him closely. If he healed the man's hand, they planned to accuse him of working on the Sabbath.

³Jesus said to the man with the deformed hand, "Come and stand in front of everyone." ⁴Then he turned to his critics and asked, "Does the law permit good deeds on the Sabbath, or is it a day for doing evil? Is this a day to save life or to destroy it?" But they wouldn't answer him.

⁵He looked around at them angrily and was deeply saddened by their hard hearts. Then he said to the man, "Hold out your hand." So the man held out his hand, and it was restored! ⁶At once the Pharisees went away and met with the supporters of Herod to plot how to kill Jesus.

CROWDS FOLLOW JESUS

⁷Jesus went out to the lake with his disciples, and a large crowd followed him. They came from all over Galilee, Judea, ⁸Jerusalem, Idumea, from east of the Jordan River, and even from as far north as Tyre and Sidon. The news about his miracles had spread far and wide, and vast numbers of people came to see him.

⁹Jesus instructed his disciples to have a boat ready so the crowd would not crush him. ¹⁰He had healed many people that day, so all the sick people eagerly pushed forward to touch him. ¹¹And whenever those possessed by evil* spirits caught sight of him, the spirits would throw them to the ground in front of him shrieking, "You are the Son of God!" ¹²But Jesus sternly commanded the spirits not to reveal who he was.

JESUS CHOOSES THE TWELVE APOSTLES

¹³Afterward Jesus went up on a mountain and called out the ones he wanted to go with him. And they came to him. ¹⁴Then he appointed twelve of them and called them his apostles.* They were to accompany him, and he would send them out to preach, ¹⁵giving them authority to cast out demons. ¹⁶These are the twelve he chose:

Simon (whom he named Peter),
¹⁷ James and John (the sons of Zebedee, but Jesus nicknamed them "Sons of Thunder"*),

¹⁸ Andrew,
Philip,
Bartholomew,
Matthew,
Thomas,
James (son of Alphaeus),
Thaddaeus,
Simon (the zealot*),
¹⁹ Judas Iscariot (who later betrayed him).

JESUS AND THE PRINCE OF DEMONS

²⁰One time Jesus entered a house, and the crowds began to gather again. Soon he and his disciples couldn't even find time to eat. ²¹When his family heard what was happening, they tried to take him away. "He's out of his mind," they said.

²²But the teachers of religious law who had arrived from Jerusalem said, "He's possessed by Satan,* the prince of demons. That's where he gets the power to cast out demons."

²³Jesus called them over and responded with an illustration. "How can Satan cast out Satan?" he asked. ²⁴"A kingdom divided by civil war will collapse. ²⁵Similarly, a family splintered by feuding will fall apart. ²⁶And if Satan is divided and fights against himself, how can he stand? He would never survive. ²⁷Let me illustrate this further. Who is powerful enough to enter the house of a strong man and plunder his goods? Only someone even stronger—someone who could tie him up and then plunder his house.

²⁸"I tell you the truth, all sin and blasphemy can be forgiven, ²⁹but anyone who blasphemes the Holy Spirit will never be forgiven. This is a sin with eternal consequences." ³⁰He told them this because they were saying, "He's possessed by an evil spirit."

THE TRUE FAMILY OF JESUS

³¹Then Jesus' mother and brothers came to see him. They stood outside and sent word for him to come out and talk with them. ³²There was a crowd sitting around Jesus, and someone said, "Your mother and your brothers* are outside asking for you."

³³Jesus replied, "Who is my mother? Who are my brothers?" ³⁴Then he looked at those around him and said, "Look, these are my mother and brothers. ³⁵Anyone who does God's will is my brother and sister and mother."

PARABLE OF THE FARMER SCATTERING SEED

4 Once again Jesus began teaching by the lakeshore. A very large crowd soon gathered around him, so he got into a boat. Then he sat

---

3:11 Greek *unclean;* also in 3:30.   3:14 Some manuscripts do not include *and called them his apostles.*   3:17 Greek *whom he named Boanerges, which means Sons of Thunder.*   3:18 Greek *the Cananean,* an Aramaic term for Jewish nationalists.   3:22 Greek *Beelzeboul;* other manuscripts read *Beezeboul;* Latin version reads *Beelzebub.*   3:32 Some manuscripts add *and sisters.*

DRIVING OUT THE ENEMY
Mark 4:7   ROBERT MORRIS

In Mark 4, Jesus tells the parable of the farmer scattering seed. The seed represents God's Word. Some seeds fell "among thorns that grew up and choked out the tender plants so they produced no grain" (v. 7). Jesus later explains that the thorns in this parable are symbolic of "the worries of this life, the lure of wealth, and the desire for other things" (v. 19).

Even the apostle Paul, who wrote a third of the New Testament, wrote about having "a thorn in my flesh" (2 Corinthians 12:7). No matter who you are or where you are in your walk with God, thorns will always try to choke the Word of God out of your life.

What does a thorn look like in your life? Maybe it's bitterness, unforgiveness, lust, pride, or anger. God's Word is the only tool that can defeat thorns and allow us to walk in freedom.

in the boat while all the people remained on the shore. ²He taught them by telling many stories in the form of parables, such as this one:

³"Listen! A farmer went out to plant some seed. ⁴As he scattered it across his field, some of the seed fell on a footpath, and the birds came and ate it. ⁵Other seed fell on shallow soil with underlying rock. The seed sprouted quickly because the soil was shallow. ⁶But the plant soon wilted under the hot sun, and since it didn't have deep roots, it died. ⁷Other seed fell among thorns that grew up and choked out the tender plants so they produced no grain. ⁸Still other seeds fell on fertile soil, and they sprouted, grew, and produced a crop that was thirty, sixty, and even a hundred times as much as had been planted!" ⁹Then he said, "Anyone with ears to hear should listen and understand."

¹⁰Later, when Jesus was alone with the twelve disciples and with the others who were gathered around, they asked him what the parables meant.

¹¹He replied, "You are permitted to understand the secret* of the Kingdom of God. But I use parables for everything I say to outsiders, ¹²so that the Scriptures might be fulfilled:

'When they see what I do,
    they will learn nothing.
When they hear what I say,
    they will not understand.
Otherwise, they will turn to me
    and be forgiven.'*"

¹³Then Jesus said to them, "If you can't understand the meaning of this parable, how will you understand all the other parables? ¹⁴The farmer plants seed by taking God's word to others. ¹⁵The seed that fell on the footpath represents those who hear the message, only to have Satan come

at once and take it away. ¹⁶The seed on the rocky soil represents those who hear the message and immediately receive it with joy. ¹⁷But since they don't have deep roots, they don't last long. They fall away as soon as they have problems or are persecuted for believing God's word. ¹⁸The seed that fell among the thorns represents others who hear God's word, ¹⁹but all too quickly the message is crowded out by the worries of this life, the lure of wealth, and the desire for other things, so no fruit is produced. ²⁰And the seed that fell on good soil represents those who hear and accept God's word and produce a harvest of thirty, sixty, or even a hundred times as much as had been planted!"

PARABLE OF THE LAMP

²¹Then Jesus asked them, "Would anyone light a lamp and then put it under a basket or under a bed? Of course not! A lamp is placed on a stand, where its light will shine. ²²For everything that is hidden will eventually be brought into the open, and every secret will be brought to light. ²³Anyone with ears to hear should listen and understand."

²⁴Then he added, "Pay close attention to what you hear. The closer you listen, the more understanding you will be given*—and you will receive even more. ²⁵To those who listen to my teaching, more understanding will be given. But for those who are not listening, even what little understanding they have will be taken away from them."

PARABLE OF THE GROWING SEED

²⁶Jesus also said, "The Kingdom of God is like a farmer who scatters seed on the ground. ²⁷Night and day, while he's asleep or awake, the seed sprouts and grows, but he does not understand how it happens. ²⁸The earth produces the crops on its own. First a leaf blade pushes through, then the heads of wheat are formed, and finally the grain ripens. ²⁹And as soon as the grain is ready, the farmer comes and harvests it with a sickle, for the harvest time has come."

PARABLE OF THE MUSTARD SEED

³⁰Jesus said, "How can I describe the Kingdom of God? What story should I use to illustrate it? ³¹It is like a mustard seed planted in the ground. It is the smallest of all seeds, ³²but it becomes the largest of all garden plants; it grows long branches, and birds can make nests in its shade."

³³Jesus used many similar stories and illustrations to teach the people as much as they could understand. ³⁴In fact, in his public ministry he never taught without using parables; but afterward, when he was alone with his disciples, he explained everything to them.

4:11 Greek *mystery.*   4:12 Isa 6:9-10 (Greek version).   4:24 Or *The measure you give will be the measure you get back.*

STEWARD HIS SPOKEN WORD
Mark 4:24-25　　　　　　ROBERT MORRIS

When God speaks something to your heart, what do you do with it? Many people know it's important to steward their finances, but the principle of stewardship applies to all of God's resources, including His words! Here are three ways to steward the words God speaks to you:

1. Steward what you hear.
Jesus said, "Pay close attention to what you hear. The closer you listen, the more understanding you will be given . . . But for those who are not listening, even what little understanding they have will be taken away from them" (Mark 4:24-25). God speaks all the time and in many different ways, such as dreams, circumstances, and people. We just need to listen.

2. Steward how you hear.
How do you know God is speaking to you? Ask yourself, *Does this word put the emphasis on others or on me?* Leadership in God's Kingdom is not about how many people you can get to serve you—it's about how many people you can serve. If a word causes you to become prideful, it's not God. God will resist our pride, and we cannot resist the devil when God is resisting us (James 4:6-7).

3. Heed what you hear.
Another word for heed is *obey*. When you don't obey what God has spoken to you, you leave His presence. The prophet Jonah refused to obey God's voice, so God spoke to him through circumstances—wind, waves, and a "great fish" (Jonah 1:17). If you're having trouble hearing God's voice, look at your circumstances. Has God told you to do something you still haven't done? If so, go and do it!

JESUS CALMS THE STORM

[35] As evening came, Jesus said to his disciples, "Let's cross to the other side of the lake." [36] So they took Jesus in the boat and started out, leaving the crowds behind (although other boats followed). [37] But soon a fierce storm came up. High waves were breaking into the boat, and it began to fill with water. [38] Jesus was sleeping at the back of the boat with his head on a cushion. The disciples woke him up, shouting, "Teacher, don't you care that we're going to drown?"

[39] When Jesus woke up, he rebuked the wind and said to the waves, "Silence! Be still!" Suddenly the wind stopped, and there was a great calm. [40] Then he asked them, "Why are you afraid? Do you still have no faith?"

[41] The disciples were absolutely terrified. "Who is this man?" they asked each other. "Even the wind and waves obey him!"

SOWING AND REAPING
Mark 4:26-29　　　　　　ROBERT MORRIS

There are three principles of sowing and reaping:

1. You reap what you sow.
Can you imagine a farmer planting wheat seeds and expecting corn to grow? That would be foolishness! Yet many believers expect a harvest of something they've never planted. If you want to reap financial blessings, you first have to sow your tithe.

2. You reap after you sow.
Many people say, "When I have more money, I'll start giving." The problem is you can't reap *before* you sow. Luke 16:10 says, "If you are faithful in little things, you will be faithful in large ones." You have to start right where you are.

3. You reap more than you sow.
Just a few kernels of planted corn will produce a stalk with several ears, and each ear will contain hundreds of seed kernels. That's a pretty good return, isn't it? You always get more when you sow God's way, but it starts with faithfully planting the first seed.

JESUS HEALS A DEMON-POSSESSED MAN

5 So they arrived at the other side of the lake, in the region of the Gerasenes.* [2] When Jesus climbed out of the boat, a man possessed by an evil* spirit came out from the tombs to meet him. [3] This man lived in the burial caves and could no longer be restrained, even with a chain. [4] Whenever he was put into chains and shackles—as he often was—he snapped the chains from his wrists and smashed the shackles. No one was strong enough to subdue him. [5] Day and night he wandered among the burial caves and in the hills, howling and cutting himself with sharp stones.

[6] When Jesus was still some distance away, the man saw him, ran to meet him, and bowed low before him. [7] With a shriek, he screamed, "Why are you interfering with me, Jesus, Son of the Most High God? In the name of God, I beg you, don't torture me!" [8] For Jesus had already said to the spirit, "Come out of the man, you evil spirit."

[9] Then Jesus demanded, "What is your name?"

And he replied, "My name is Legion, because there are many of us inside this man." [10] Then the evil spirits begged him again and again not to send them to some distant place.

[11] There happened to be a large herd of pigs feeding on the hillside nearby. [12] "Send us into those pigs," the spirits begged. "Let us enter them."

[13] So Jesus gave them permission. The evil spirits came out of the man and entered the pigs, and

---

5:1 Other manuscripts read *Gadarenes;* still others read *Gergesenes.* See Matt 8:28; Luke 8:26.　　5:2 Greek *unclean;* also in 5:8, 13.

RUN TO JESUS
Mark 5:6   ROBERT MORRIS

In Mark 5, Jesus and His disciples encounter a demon-possessed man. Even though this man was under Satan's power, the enemy couldn't stop him from running to Jesus. And that's just what we need to do when we're under attack. When we run to Jesus and allow Him to set us free, we "strip off every weight that slows us down" (Hebrews 12:1).

People often try to clean out the junk in their lives on their own, even though all the resolutions and promises in the world rarely seem to work. As a believer, you can decide to leave behind the things that are holding you back. You don't do this by making resolutions and promises to anyone. You simply need to run to Jesus, trust God, and allow the Holy Spirit to set you free! Then you can freely pursue God and experience a deeper level of His presence.

the entire herd of about 2,000 pigs plunged down the steep hillside into the lake and drowned in the water.

¹⁴ The herdsmen fled to the nearby town and the surrounding countryside, spreading the news as they ran. People rushed out to see what had happened. ¹⁵ A crowd soon gathered around Jesus, and they saw the man who had been possessed by the legion of demons. He was sitting there fully clothed and perfectly sane, and they were all afraid. ¹⁶ Then those who had seen what happened told the others about the demon-possessed man and the pigs. ¹⁷ And the crowd began pleading with Jesus to go away and leave them alone.

¹⁸ As Jesus was getting into the boat, the man who had been demon possessed begged to go with him. ¹⁹ But Jesus said, "No, go home to your family, and tell them everything the Lord has done for you and how merciful he has been." ²⁰ So the man started off to visit the Ten Towns* of that region and began to proclaim the great things Jesus had done for him; and everyone was amazed at what he told them.

JESUS HEALS IN RESPONSE TO FAITH

²¹ Jesus got into the boat again and went back to the other side of the lake, where a large crowd gathered around him on the shore. ²² Then a leader of the local synagogue, whose name was Jairus, arrived. When he saw Jesus, he fell at his feet, ²³ pleading fervently with him. "My little daughter is dying," he said. "Please come and lay your hands on her; heal her so she can live."

²⁴ Jesus went with him, and all the people followed, crowding around him. ²⁵ A woman in the crowd had suffered for twelve years with constant bleeding. ²⁶ She had suffered a great deal from

many doctors, and over the years she had spent everything she had to pay them, but she had gotten no better. In fact, she had gotten worse. ²⁷ She had heard about Jesus, so she came up behind him through the crowd and touched his robe. ²⁸ For she thought to herself, "If I can just touch his robe, I will be healed." ²⁹ Immediately the bleeding stopped, and she could feel in her body that she had been healed of her terrible condition.

³⁰ Jesus realized at once that healing power had gone out from him, so he turned around in the crowd and asked, "Who touched my robe?"

³¹ His disciples said to him, "Look at this crowd pressing around you. How can you ask, 'Who touched me?'"

³² But he kept on looking around to see who had done it. ³³ Then the frightened woman, trembling at the realization of what had happened to her, came and fell to her knees in front of him and told him what she had done. ³⁴ And he said to her, "Daughter, your faith has made you well. Go in peace. Your suffering is over."

³⁵ While he was still speaking to her, messengers arrived from the home of Jairus, the leader of the synagogue. They told him, "Your daughter is dead. There's no use troubling the Teacher now."

³⁶ But Jesus overheard* them and said to Jairus, "Don't be afraid. Just have faith."

³⁷ Then Jesus stopped the crowd and wouldn't let anyone go with him except Peter, James, and John (the brother of James). ³⁸ When they came to the home of the synagogue leader, Jesus saw much commotion and weeping and wailing. ³⁹ He went inside and asked, "Why all this commotion and weeping? The child isn't dead; she's only asleep."

⁴⁰ The crowd laughed at him. But he made them all leave, and he took the girl's father and mother and his three disciples into the room where the girl was lying. ⁴¹ Holding her hand, he said to her, "Talitha koum," which means "Little girl, get up!" ⁴² And the girl, who was twelve years old, immediately stood up and walked around! They were overwhelmed and totally amazed. ⁴³ Jesus gave them strict orders not to tell anyone what had happened, and then he told them to give her something to eat.

JESUS REJECTED AT NAZARETH

6 Jesus left that part of the country and returned with his disciples to Nazareth, his hometown. ² The next Sabbath he began teaching in the synagogue, and many who heard him were amazed. They asked, "Where did he get all this wisdom and the power to perform such miracles?" ³ Then they scoffed, "He's just a carpenter, the son of Mary* and the brother of James, Joseph,* Judas, and Simon. And his sisters live

---

5:20 Greek *Decapolis.*   5:36 Or *ignored.*   6:3a Some manuscripts read *He's just the son of the carpenter and of Mary.*   6:3b Most manuscripts read *Joses;* see Matt 13:55.

right here among us." They were deeply offended and refused to believe in him.

⁴Then Jesus told them, "A prophet is honored everywhere except in his own hometown and among his relatives and his own family." ⁵And because of their unbelief, he couldn't do any miracles among them except to place his hands on a few sick people and heal them. ⁶And he was amazed at their unbelief.

JESUS SENDS OUT THE TWELVE DISCIPLES

Then Jesus went from village to village, teaching the people. ⁷And he called his twelve disciples together and began sending them out two by two, giving them authority to cast out evil* spirits. ⁸He told them to take nothing for their journey except a walking stick—no food, no traveler's bag, no money.* ⁹He allowed them to wear sandals but not to take a change of clothes.

¹⁰"Wherever you go," he said, "stay in the same house until you leave town. ¹¹But if any place refuses to welcome you or listen to you, shake its dust from your feet as you leave to show that you have abandoned those people to their fate."

¹²So the disciples went out, telling everyone they met to repent of their sins and turn to God. ¹³And they cast out many demons and healed many sick people, anointing them with olive oil.

THE DEATH OF JOHN THE BAPTIST

¹⁴Herod Antipas, the king, soon heard about Jesus, because everyone was talking about him. Some were saying,* "This must be John the Baptist raised from the dead. That is why he can do such miracles." ¹⁵Others said, "He's the prophet Elijah." Still others said, "He's a prophet like the other great prophets of the past."

¹⁶When Herod heard about Jesus, he said, "John, the man I beheaded, has come back from the dead."

¹⁷For Herod had sent soldiers to arrest and imprison John as a favor to Herodias. She had been his brother Philip's wife, but Herod had married her. ¹⁸John had been telling Herod, "It is against God's law for you to marry your brother's wife." ¹⁹So Herodias bore a grudge against John and wanted to kill him. But without Herod's approval she was powerless, ²⁰for Herod respected John; and knowing that he was a good and holy man, he protected him. Herod was greatly disturbed whenever he talked with John, but even so, he liked to listen to him.

²¹Herodias's chance finally came on Herod's birthday. He gave a party for his high government officials, army officers, and the leading citizens of Galilee. ²²Then his daughter, also named Herodias,* came in and performed a dance that greatly pleased Herod and his guests. "Ask me for anything you like," the king said to the girl, "and I will give it to you." ²³He even vowed, "I will give you whatever you ask, up to half my kingdom!"

²⁴She went out and asked her mother, "What should I ask for?"

Her mother told her, "Ask for the head of John the Baptist!"

²⁵So the girl hurried back to the king and told him, "I want the head of John the Baptist, right now, on a tray!"

²⁶Then the king deeply regretted what he had said; but because of the vows he had made in front of his guests, he couldn't refuse her. ²⁷So he immediately sent an executioner to the prison to cut off John's head and bring it to him. The soldier beheaded John in the prison, ²⁸brought his head on a tray, and gave it to the girl, who took it to her mother. ²⁹When John's disciples heard what had happened, they came to get his body and buried it in a tomb.

JESUS FEEDS FIVE THOUSAND

³⁰The apostles returned to Jesus from their ministry tour and told him all they had done and taught. ³¹Then Jesus said, "Let's go off by ourselves to a quiet place and rest awhile." He said this because there were so many people coming and going that Jesus and his apostles didn't even have time to eat.

³²So they left by boat for a quiet place, where they could be alone. ³³But many people recognized them and saw them leaving, and people from many towns ran ahead along the shore and got there ahead of them. ³⁴Jesus saw the huge crowd as he stepped from the boat, and he had compassion on them because they were like sheep without a shepherd. So he began teaching them many things.

³⁵Late in the afternoon his disciples came to him and said, "This is a remote place, and it's already getting late. ³⁶Send the crowds away so they can go to the nearby farms and villages and buy something to eat."

³⁷But Jesus said, "You feed them."

"With what?" they asked. "We'd have to work for months to earn enough money* to buy food for all these people!"

³⁸"How much bread do you have?" he asked. "Go and find out."

They came back and reported, "We have five loaves of bread and two fish."

³⁹Then Jesus told the disciples to have the people sit down in groups on the green grass. ⁴⁰So they sat down in groups of fifty or a hundred.

⁴¹Jesus took the five loaves and two fish, looked up toward heaven, and blessed them. Then, breaking the loaves into pieces, he kept giving the bread to the disciples so they could distribute it to the people. He also divided the fish for everyone to share. ⁴²They all ate as much as they

---

6:7 Greek *unclean.* 6:8 Greek *no copper coins in their money belts.* 6:14 Some manuscripts read *He was saying.* 6:22 Some manuscripts read *the daughter of Herodias herself.* 6:37 Greek *It would take 200 denarii.* A denarius was equivalent to a laborer's full day's wage.

THE PRIORITY OF PEOPLE
Mark 6:34

ROBERT MORRIS

If we could point a video camera at Jesus' mind and show the footage on a big screen, what would we see? *People.* People were always on His mind. When Jesus called the fishermen Peter and Andrew to be His disciples, He said, "Follow me, and I will show you how to fish for people!" (Matthew 4:19). Even as He hung on the cross, Jesus thought about people. He thought about his mother's welfare and asked John to take care of her (John 19:26–27). He thought about the criminal hanging beside Him and promised, "Today you will be with me in paradise" (Luke 23:43). And He thought about the people who nailed Him to the cross as He prayed, "Father, forgive them . . ." (Luke 23:34).

Why did Jesus have people on His mind so much? Here are three reasons:

1. He knew the Father's heart.

Jesus knew the heart of the Father better than anyone. The Father loves people, so Jesus tried to reach people everywhere He went. At Gateway Church, our motto is "we're all about people." Some people ask, "Shouldn't we be all about God?" and I reply, "Yes! But if we're all about God, then we should be all about what God's all about. And God's all about people."

2. He knew the reality of eternity.

More than any other religious leader ever, Jesus talked about the absolute certainty of an impending eternal destination. Every person will spend eternity in one of two ways: communion with God or perpetual torment. Jesus knew that only *people* last forever, which is why He placed such a high value on human souls.

3. He knew the potential of people.

In Luke 19, Jesus meets a rich tax collector named Zacchaeus and goes to his house. This is an unpopular decision with many people, and they complain, "He has gone to be the guest of a notorious sinner" (v. 7). Jesus was the only one able to see the generous potential in Zacchaeus, and He can see your potential too. It doesn't matter where you come from, what you've gone through, or how many wounds you have. Jesus never gets bogged down by a person's past—He knows His power is *always* greater! He is radically inclusive of all people: young, old, rich, poor, popular, forgotten, saved, lost, healed, and hurting!

---

wanted, [43] and afterward, the disciples picked up twelve baskets of leftover bread and fish. [44] A total of 5,000 men and their families were fed.*

JESUS WALKS ON WATER

[45] Immediately after this, Jesus insisted that his disciples get back into the boat and head across the lake to Bethsaida, while he sent the people home. [46] After telling everyone good-bye, he went up into the hills by himself to pray.

[47] Late that night, the disciples were in their boat in the middle of the lake, and Jesus was alone on land. [48] He saw that they were in serious trouble, rowing hard and struggling against the wind and waves. About three o'clock in the morning* Jesus came toward them, walking on the water. He intended to go past them, [49] but when they saw him walking on the water, they cried out in terror, thinking he was a ghost. [50] They were all terrified when they saw him.

But Jesus spoke to them at once. "Don't be afraid," he said. "Take courage! I am here!*" [51] Then he climbed into the boat, and the wind stopped. They were totally amazed, [52] for they still didn't understand the significance of the miracle of the loaves. Their hearts were too hard to take it in.

[53] After they had crossed the lake, they landed at Gennesaret. They brought the boat to shore [54] and climbed out. The people recognized Jesus at once, [55] and they ran throughout the whole area, carrying sick people on mats to wherever they

THE PHYSICIAN
Mark 6:55-56

ROBERT MORRIS

Jesus is the Great Physician. When He walked on earth, He healed people because He was moved with compassion for them (Matthew 14:14). Hebrews 13:8 says, "Jesus Christ is the same yesterday, today, and forever," which means He still has compassion and heals people today.

Sometimes people believe Jesus took our sins on the cross, but they have a hard time believing Matthew 8:17:

"He took our sicknesses
and removed our diseases."

It is God's will for all to be saved *and* all to be healed. Jesus is willing and wants to heal you. Yet some people still feel as if they aren't good enough or deserving enough to be healed. The truth is, similar to salvation, no one is deserving. This is why we all need God's grace. The grace we need to be saved is the same grace we need to be healed. And the great news is that it's available to everyone!

6:44 Some manuscripts read *fed from the loaves.* **6:48** Greek *About the fourth watch of the night.* **6:50** Or *The 'I AM' is here;* Greek reads *I am.* See Exod 3:14.

heard he was. 56 Wherever he went—in villages, cities, or the countryside—they brought the sick out to the marketplaces. They begged him to let the sick touch at least the fringe of his robe, and all who touched him were healed.

JESUS TEACHES ABOUT INNER PURITY

7 One day some Pharisees and teachers of religious law arrived from Jerusalem to see Jesus. 2 They noticed that some of his disciples failed to follow the Jewish ritual of hand washing before eating. 3 (The Jews, especially the Pharisees, do not eat until they have poured water over their cupped hands,* as required by their ancient traditions. 4 Similarly, they don't eat anything from the market until they immerse their hands* in water. This is but one of many traditions they have clung to—such as their ceremonial washing of cups, pitchers, and kettles.*)

5 So the Pharisees and teachers of religious law asked him, "Why don't your disciples follow our age-old tradition? They eat without first performing the hand-washing ceremony."

6 Jesus replied, "You hypocrites! Isaiah was right when he prophesied about you, for he wrote,

'These people honor me with their lips,
    but their hearts are far from me.
7 Their worship is a farce,
    for they teach man-made ideas as
        commands from God.'*

8 For you ignore God's law and substitute your own tradition." 9 Then he said, "You skillfully sidestep God's law in order to hold on to your own tradition. 10 For instance, Moses gave you this law from God: 'Honor your father and mother,'* and 'Anyone who speaks disrespectfully of father or mother must be put to death.'* 11 But you say it is all right for people to say to their parents, 'Sorry, I can't help you. For I have vowed to give to God what I would have given to you.'* 12 In this way, you let them disregard their needy parents. 13 And so you cancel the word of God in order to hand down your own tradition. And this is only one example among many others."

14 Then Jesus called to the crowd to come and hear. "All of you listen," he said, "and try to understand. 15 It's not what goes into your body that defiles you; you are defiled by what comes from your heart.*"

17 Then Jesus went into a house to get away from the crowd, and his disciples asked him what he meant by the parable he had just used. 18 "Don't you understand either?" he asked. "Can't you see that the food you put into your body cannot defile you? 19 Food doesn't go into your heart, but only passes through the stomach and then goes into the sewer." (By saying this, he

declared that every kind of food is acceptable in God's eyes.)

20 And then he added, "It is what comes from inside that defiles you. 21 For from within, out of a person's heart, come evil thoughts, sexual immorality, theft, murder, 22 adultery, greed, wickedness, deceit, lustful desires, envy, slander, pride, and foolishness. 23 All these vile things come from within; they are what defile you."

THE FAITH OF A GENTILE WOMAN

24 Then Jesus left Galilee and went north to the region of Tyre.* He didn't want anyone to know which house he was staying in, but he couldn't keep it a secret. 25 Right away a woman who had heard about him came and fell at his feet. Her little girl was possessed by an evil* spirit, 26 and she begged him to cast out the demon from her daughter.

Since she was a Gentile, born in Syrian Phoenicia, 27 Jesus told her, "First I should feed the children—my own family, the Jews.* It isn't right to take food from the children and throw it to the dogs."

28 She replied, "That's true, Lord, but even the dogs under the table are allowed to eat the scraps from the children's plates."

29 "Good answer!" he said. "Now go home, for the demon has left your daughter." 30 And when she arrived home, she found her little girl lying quietly in bed, and the demon was gone.

JESUS HEALS A DEAF MAN

31 Jesus left Tyre and went up to Sidon before going back to the Sea of Galilee and the region of the Ten Towns.* 32 A deaf man with a speech impediment was brought to him, and the people begged Jesus to lay his hands on the man to heal him.

33 Jesus led him away from the crowd so they could be alone. He put his fingers into the man's ears. Then, spitting on his own fingers, he touched the man's tongue. 34 Looking up to heaven, he sighed and said, "Ephphatha," which means, "Be opened!" 35 Instantly the man could hear perfectly, and his tongue was freed so he could speak plainly!

36 Jesus told the crowd not to tell anyone, but the more he told them not to, the more they spread the news. 37 They were completely amazed and said again and again, "Everything he does is wonderful. He even makes the deaf to hear and gives speech to those who cannot speak."

7:3 Greek have washed with the fist.   7:4a Some manuscripts read sprinkle themselves.   7:4b Some manuscripts add and dining couches.   7:7 Isa 29:13 (Greek version).   7:10a Exod 20:12; Deut 5:16.   7:10b Exod 21:17 (Greek version); Lev 20:9 (Greek version). 7:11 Greek 'What I would have given to you is Corban' (that is, a gift).   7:15 Some manuscripts add verse 16, Anyone with ears to hear should listen and understand. Compare 4:9, 23.   7:24 Some manuscripts add and Sidon.   7:25 Greek unclean.   7:27 Greek Let the children eat first.   7:31 Greek Decapolis.

JESUS FEEDS FOUR THOUSAND

8 About this time another large crowd had gathered, and the people ran out of food again. Jesus called his disciples and told them, ²"I feel sorry for these people. They have been here with me for three days, and they have nothing left to eat. ³If I send them home hungry, they will faint along the way. For some of them have come a long distance."

⁴His disciples replied, "How are we supposed to find enough food to feed them out here in the wilderness?"

⁵Jesus asked, "How much bread do you have?"

"Seven loaves," they replied.

⁶So Jesus told all the people to sit down on the ground. Then he took the seven loaves, thanked God for them, and broke them into pieces. He gave them to his disciples, who distributed the bread to the crowd. ⁷A few small fish were found, too, so Jesus also blessed these and told the disciples to distribute them.

⁸They ate as much as they wanted. Afterward, the disciples picked up seven large baskets of leftover food. ⁹There were about 4,000 men in the crowd that day, and Jesus sent them home after they had eaten. ¹⁰Immediately after this, he got into a boat with his disciples and crossed over to the region of Dalmanutha.

PHARISEES DEMAND A MIRACULOUS SIGN

¹¹When the Pharisees heard that Jesus had arrived, they came and started to argue with him. Testing him, they demanded that he show them a miraculous sign from heaven to prove his authority.

¹²When he heard this, he sighed deeply in his spirit and said, "Why do these people keep demanding a miraculous sign? I tell you the truth, I will not give this generation any such sign." ¹³So he got back into the boat and left them, and he crossed to the other side of the lake.

YEAST OF THE PHARISEES AND HEROD

¹⁴But the disciples had forgotten to bring any food. They had only one loaf of bread with them in the boat. ¹⁵As they were crossing the lake, Jesus warned them, "Watch out! Beware of the yeast of the Pharisees and of Herod."

¹⁶At this they began to argue with each other because they hadn't brought any bread. ¹⁷Jesus knew what they were saying, so he said, "Why are you arguing about having no bread? Don't you know or understand even yet? Are your hearts too hard to take it in? ¹⁸'You have eyes—can't you see? You have ears—can't you hear?'* Don't you remember anything at all? ¹⁹When I fed the 5,000 with five loaves of bread, how many baskets of leftovers did you pick up afterward?"

"Twelve," they said.

²⁰"And when I fed the 4,000 with seven loaves, how many large baskets of leftovers did you pick up?"

"Seven," they said.

²¹"Don't you understand yet?" he asked them.

JESUS HEALS A BLIND MAN

²²When they arrived at Bethsaida, some people brought a blind man to Jesus, and they begged him to touch the man and heal him. ²³Jesus took the blind man by the hand and led him out of the village. Then, spitting on the man's eyes, he laid his hands on him and asked, "Can you see anything now?"

²⁴The man looked around. "Yes," he said, "I see people, but I can't see them very clearly. They look like trees walking around."

²⁵Then Jesus placed his hands on the man's eyes again, and his eyes were opened. His sight was completely restored, and he could see everything clearly. ²⁶Jesus sent him away, saying, "Don't go back into the village on your way home."

PETER'S DECLARATION ABOUT JESUS

²⁷Jesus and his disciples left Galilee and went up to the villages near Caesarea Philippi. As they were walking along, he asked them, "Who do people say I am?"

²⁸"Well," they replied, "some say John the Baptist, some say Elijah, and others say you are one of the other prophets."

²⁹Then he asked them, "But who do you say I am?"

Peter replied, "You are the Messiah.*"

8:18 Jer 5:21.   8:29 Or *the Christ. Messiah* (a Hebrew term) and *Christ* (a Greek term) both mean "anointed one."

[30] But Jesus warned them not to tell anyone about him.

JESUS PREDICTS HIS DEATH

[31] Then Jesus began to tell them that the Son of Man* must suffer many terrible things and be rejected by the elders, the leading priests, and the teachers of religious law. He would be killed, but three days later he would rise from the dead. [32] As he talked about this openly with his disciples, Peter took him aside and began to reprimand him for saying such things.*

[33] Jesus turned around and looked at his disciples, then reprimanded Peter. "Get away from me, Satan!" he said. "You are seeing things merely from a human point of view, not from God's."

[34] Then, calling the crowd to join his disciples, he said, "If any of you wants to be my follower, you must give up your own way, take up your cross, and follow me. [35] If you try to hang on to your life, you will lose it. But if you give up your life for my sake and for the sake of the Good News, you will save it. [36] And what do you benefit if you gain the whole world but lose your own soul?* [37] Is anything worth more than your soul? [38] If anyone is ashamed of me and my message in these adulterous and sinful days, the Son of Man will be ashamed of that person when he returns in the glory of his Father with the holy angels."

9 Jesus went on to say, "I tell you the truth, some standing here right now will not die before they see the Kingdom of God arrive in great power!"

THE TRANSFIGURATION

[2] Six days later Jesus took Peter, James, and John, and led them up a high mountain to be alone. As the men watched, Jesus' appearance was transformed, [3] and his clothes became dazzling white, far whiter than any earthly bleach could ever make them. [4] Then Elijah and Moses appeared and began talking with Jesus.

[5] Peter exclaimed, "Rabbi, it's wonderful for us to be here! Let's make three shelters as memorials*—one for you, one for Moses, and one for Elijah." [6] He said this because he didn't really know what else to say, for they were all terrified. [7] Then a cloud overshadowed them, and a voice from the cloud said, "This is my dearly loved Son. Listen to him." [8] Suddenly, when they looked around, Moses and Elijah were gone, and they saw only Jesus with them.

[9] As they went back down the mountain, he told them not to tell anyone what they had seen until the Son of Man* had risen from the dead. [10] So they kept it to themselves, but they often asked each other what he meant by "rising from the dead."

[11] Then they asked him, "Why do the teachers of religious law insist that Elijah must return before the Messiah comes?*"

[12] Jesus responded, "Elijah is indeed coming first to get everything ready. Yet why do the Scriptures say that the Son of Man must suffer greatly and be treated with utter contempt? [13] But I tell you, Elijah has already come, and they chose to abuse him, just as the Scriptures predicted."

JESUS HEALS A DEMON-POSSESSED BOY

[14] When they returned to the other disciples, they saw a large crowd surrounding them, and some teachers of religious law were arguing with them. [15] When the crowd saw Jesus, they were overwhelmed with awe, and they ran to greet him.

[16] "What is all this arguing about?" Jesus asked.

[17] One of the men in the crowd spoke up and said, "Teacher, I brought my son so you could heal him. He is possessed by an evil spirit that won't let him talk. [18] And whenever this spirit seizes him, it throws him violently to the ground. Then he foams at the mouth and grinds his teeth and becomes rigid.* So I asked your disciples to cast out the evil spirit, but they couldn't do it."

[19] Jesus said to them,* "You faithless people! How long must I be with you? How long must I put up with you? Bring the boy to me."

[20] So they brought the boy. But when the evil spirit saw Jesus, it threw the child into a violent convulsion, and he fell to the ground, writhing and foaming at the mouth.

[21] "How long has this been happening?" Jesus asked the boy's father.

He replied, "Since he was a little boy. [22] The spirit often throws him into the fire or into water, trying to kill him. Have mercy on us and help us, if you can."

[23] "What do you mean, 'If I can'?" Jesus asked. "Anything is possible if a person believes."

[24] The father instantly cried out, "I do believe, but help me overcome my unbelief!"

[25] When Jesus saw that the crowd of onlookers was growing, he rebuked the evil* spirit. "Listen, you spirit that makes this boy unable to hear and speak," he said. "I command you to come out of this child and never enter him again!"

[26] Then the spirit screamed and threw the boy into another violent convulsion and left him. The boy appeared to be dead. A murmur ran through the crowd as people said, "He's dead." [27] But Jesus took him by the hand and helped him to his feet, and he stood up.

[28] Afterward, when Jesus was alone in the house with his disciples, they asked him, "Why couldn't we cast out that evil spirit?"

[29] Jesus replied, "This kind can be cast out only by prayer.*"

8:31 "Son of Man" is a title Jesus used for himself.   8:32 Or *began to correct him.*   8:36 Or *your self?* also in 8:37.   9:5 Greek *three tabernacles.*   9:9 "Son of Man" is a title Jesus used for himself.   9:11 Greek *that Elijah must come first?*   9:18 Or *becomes weak.*   9:19 Or *said to his disciples.*   9:25 Greek *unclean.*   9:29 Some manuscripts read *by prayer and fasting.*

JESUS AGAIN PREDICTS HIS DEATH

[30] Leaving that region, they traveled through Galilee. Jesus didn't want anyone to know he was there, [31] for he wanted to spend more time with his disciples and teach them. He said to them, "The Son of Man is going to be betrayed into the hands of his enemies. He will be killed, but three days later he will rise from the dead." [32] They didn't understand what he was saying, however, and they were afraid to ask him what he meant.

THE GREATEST IN THE KINGDOM

[33] After they arrived at Capernaum and settled in a house, Jesus asked his disciples, "What were you discussing out on the road?" [34] But they didn't answer, because they had been arguing about which of them was the greatest. [35] He sat down, called the twelve disciples over to him, and said, "Whoever wants to be first must take last place and be the servant of everyone else."

[36] Then he put a little child among them. Taking the child in his arms, he said to them, [37] "Anyone who welcomes a little child like this on my behalf* welcomes me, and anyone who welcomes me welcomes not only me but also my Father who sent me."

USING THE NAME OF JESUS

[38] John said to Jesus, "Teacher, we saw someone using your name to cast out demons, but we told him to stop because he wasn't in our group."

[39] "Don't stop him!" Jesus said. "No one who performs a miracle in my name will soon be able to speak evil of me. [40] Anyone who is not against us is for us. [41] If anyone gives you even a cup of water because you belong to the Messiah, I tell you the truth, that person will surely be rewarded.

[42] "But if you cause one of these little ones who trusts in me to fall into sin, it would be better for you to be thrown into the sea with a large millstone hung around your neck. [43] If your hand causes you to sin, cut it off. It's better to enter eternal life with only one hand than to go into the unquenchable fires of hell* with two hands.* [45] If your foot causes you to sin, cut it off. It's better to enter eternal life with only one foot than to be thrown into hell with two feet.* [47] And if your eye causes you to sin, gouge it out. It's better to enter the Kingdom of God with only one eye than to have two eyes and be thrown into hell, [48] 'where the maggots never die and the fire never goes out.'*

[49] "For everyone will be tested with fire.* [50] Salt is good for seasoning. But if it loses its flavor, how do you make it salty again? You must have the qualities of salt among yourselves and live in peace with each other."

DISCUSSION ABOUT DIVORCE AND MARRIAGE

10 Then Jesus left Capernaum and went down to the region of Judea and into the area east of the Jordan River. Once again crowds gathered around him, and as usual he was teaching them.

[2] Some Pharisees came and tried to trap him with this question: "Should a man be allowed to divorce his wife?"

[3] Jesus answered them with a question: "What did Moses say in the law about divorce?"

[4] "Well, he permitted it," they replied. "He said a man can give his wife a written notice of divorce and send her away."*

[5] But Jesus responded, "He wrote this commandment only as a concession to your hard hearts. [6] But 'God made them male and female'* from the beginning of creation. [7] 'This explains why a man leaves his father and mother and is joined to his wife,* [8] and the two are united into one.'* Since they are no longer two but one, [9] let no one split apart what God has joined together."

[10] Later, when he was alone with his disciples in the house, they brought up the subject again. [11] He told them, "Whoever divorces his wife and marries someone else commits adultery against her. [12] And if a woman divorces her husband and marries someone else, she commits adultery."

JESUS BLESSES THE CHILDREN

[13] One day some parents brought their children to Jesus so he could touch and bless them. But the disciples scolded the parents for bothering him.

[14] When Jesus saw what was happening, he was angry with his disciples. He said to them, "Let the children come to me. Don't stop them! For the Kingdom of God belongs to those who are like these children. [15] I tell you the truth, anyone who doesn't receive the Kingdom of God like a child will never enter it." [16] Then he took the children in his arms and placed his hands on their heads and blessed them.

THE RICH MAN

[17] As Jesus was starting out on his way to Jerusalem, a man came running up to him, knelt down, and asked, "Good Teacher, what must I do to inherit eternal life?"

[18] "Why do you call me good?" Jesus asked. "Only God is truly good. [19] But to answer your question, you know the commandments: 'You must not murder. You must not commit adultery. You must not steal. You must not testify falsely. You must not cheat anyone. Honor your father and mother.'*"

[20] "Teacher," the man replied, "I've obeyed all these commandments since I was young."

9:37 Greek *in my name.*   9:43a Greek *Gehenna;* also in 9:45, 47.   9:43b Some manuscripts add verse 44, *'where the maggots never die and the fire never goes out.'* See 9:48.   9:45 Some manuscripts add verse 46, *'where the maggots never die and the fire never goes out.'* See 9:48.   9:48 Isa 66:24.   9:49 Greek *salted with fire;* other manuscripts add *and every sacrifice will be salted with salt.*   10:4 See Deut 24:1.   10:6 Gen 1:27; 5:2.   10:7 Some manuscripts do not include *and is joined to his wife.*   10:7-8 Gen 2:24.   10:19 Exod 20:12-16; Deut 5:16-20.

WHAT'S IN YOUR HEART?

Mark 10:17-27   ROBERT MORRIS

In Mark 10, Jesus tells the rich man to sell his possessions and give the proceeds to the poor because his wealth is keeping him from making a total commitment to the Lord. God requires the same from each of us: to take up our cross, deny ourselves, and follow Jesus.

Ask yourself if anything, like pride, fear, money, or a relationship, is keeping you from totally committing everything to the Lord. Then pray and ask Him to reveal to you what's in your heart. Just as He showed the rich man that he couldn't save himself and the truth about what was in his heart—that he loved his wealth more than he loved God— He'll do the same for you. Jesus loves you this much too. He wants to bless you, but first you must deny yourself, take up your cross, and follow Him.

²¹ Looking at the man, Jesus felt genuine love for him. "There is still one thing you haven't done," he told him. "Go and sell all your possessions and give the money to the poor, and you will have treasure in heaven. Then come, follow me."

²² At this the man's face fell, and he went away sad, for he had many possessions.

²³ Jesus looked around and said to his disciples, "How hard it is for the rich to enter the Kingdom of God!" ²⁴ This amazed them. But Jesus said again, "Dear children, it is very hard* to enter the Kingdom of God. ²⁵ In fact, it is easier for a camel to go through the eye of a needle than for a rich person to enter the Kingdom of God!"

²⁶ The disciples were astounded. "Then who in the world can be saved?" they asked.

²⁷ Jesus looked at them intently and said, "Humanly speaking, it is impossible. But not with God. Everything is possible with God."

²⁸ Then Peter began to speak up. "We've given up everything to follow you," he said.

²⁹ "Yes," Jesus replied, "and I assure you that everyone who has given up house or brothers or sisters or mother or father or children or property, for my sake and for the Good News, ³⁰ will receive now in return a hundred times as many houses, brothers, sisters, mothers, children, and property—along with persecution. And in the world to come that person will have eternal life. ³¹ But many who are the greatest now will be least important then, and those who seem least important now will be the greatest then.*"

JESUS AGAIN PREDICTS HIS DEATH

³² They were now on the way up to Jerusalem, and Jesus was walking ahead of them. The disciples were filled with awe, and the people following behind were overwhelmed with fear. Taking the twelve disciples aside, Jesus once more began to describe everything that was about to happen to him. ³³ "Listen," he said, "we're going up to Jerusalem, where the Son of Man* will be betrayed to the leading priests and the teachers of religious law. They will sentence him to die and hand him over to the Romans.* ³⁴ They will mock him, spit on him, flog him with a whip, and kill him, but after three days he will rise again."

JESUS TEACHES ABOUT SERVING OTHERS

³⁵ Then James and John, the sons of Zebedee, came over and spoke to him. "Teacher," they said, "we want you to do us a favor."

³⁶ "What is your request?" he asked.

³⁷ They replied, "When you sit on your glorious throne, we want to sit in places of honor next to you, one on your right and the other on your left."

³⁸ But Jesus said to them, "You don't know what you are asking! Are you able to drink from the bitter cup of suffering I am about to drink? Are you able to be baptized with the baptism of suffering I must be baptized with?"

³⁹ "Oh yes," they replied, "we are able!"

Then Jesus told them, "You will indeed drink from my bitter cup and be baptized with my baptism of suffering. ⁴⁰ But I have no right to say who will sit on my right or my left. God has prepared those places for the ones he has chosen."

⁴¹ When the ten other disciples heard what James and John had asked, they were indignant. ⁴² So Jesus called them together and said, "You know that the rulers in this world lord it over their people, and officials flaunt their authority over those under them. ⁴³ But among you it will be different. Whoever wants to be a leader among you must be your servant, ⁴⁴ and whoever wants to be first among you must be the slave of everyone else. ⁴⁵ For even the Son of Man came not to be served but to serve others and to give his life as a ransom for many."

JESUS HEALS BLIND BARTIMAEUS

⁴⁶ Then they reached Jericho, and as Jesus and his disciples left town, a large crowd followed him. A blind beggar named Bartimaeus (son of Timaeus) was sitting beside the road. ⁴⁷ When Bartimaeus heard that Jesus of Nazareth was nearby, he began to shout, "Jesus, Son of David, have mercy on me!"

⁴⁸ "Be quiet!" many of the people yelled at him.

But he only shouted louder, "Son of David, have mercy on me!"

⁴⁹ When Jesus heard him, he stopped and said, "Tell him to come here."

So they called the blind man. "Cheer up," they said. "Come on, he's calling you!" ⁵⁰ Bartimaeus threw aside his coat, jumped up, and came to Jesus.

10:24 Some manuscripts read *very hard for those who trust in riches.*   **10:31** Greek *But many who are first will be last; and the last, first.*   **10:33a** "Son of Man" is a title Jesus used for himself.   **10:33b** Greek *the Gentiles.*

⁵¹"What do you want me to do for you?" Jesus asked.

"My Rabbi,*" the blind man said, "I want to see!"

⁵²And Jesus said to him, "Go, for your faith has healed you." Instantly the man could see, and he followed Jesus down the road.*

JESUS' TRIUMPHANT ENTRY

11 As Jesus and his disciples approached Jerusalem, they came to the towns of Bethphage and Bethany on the Mount of Olives. Jesus sent two of them on ahead. ²"Go into that village over there," he told them. "As soon as you enter it, you will see a young donkey tied there that no one has ever ridden. Untie it and bring it here. ³If anyone asks, 'What are you doing?' just say, 'The Lord needs it and will return it soon.'"

⁴The two disciples left and found the colt standing in the street, tied outside the front door. ⁵As they were untying it, some bystanders demanded, "What are you doing, untying that colt?" ⁶They said what Jesus had told them to say, and they were permitted to take it. ⁷Then they brought the colt to Jesus and threw their garments over it, and he sat on it.

⁸Many in the crowd spread their garments on the road ahead of him, and others spread leafy branches they had cut in the fields. ⁹Jesus was in the center of the procession, and the people all around him were shouting,

"Praise God!*
Blessings on the one who comes in the
  name of the LORD!
¹⁰ Blessings on the coming Kingdom of our
  ancestor David!
Praise God in highest heaven!"*

¹¹So Jesus came to Jerusalem and went into the Temple. After looking around carefully at everything, he left because it was late in the afternoon. Then he returned to Bethany with the twelve disciples.

JESUS CURSES THE FIG TREE

¹²The next morning as they were leaving Bethany, Jesus was hungry. ¹³He noticed a fig tree in full leaf a little way off, so he went over to see if he could find any figs. But there were only leaves because it was too early in the season for fruit. ¹⁴Then Jesus said to the tree, "May no one ever eat your fruit again!" And the disciples heard him say it.

JESUS CLEARS THE TEMPLE

¹⁵When they arrived back in Jerusalem, Jesus entered the Temple and began to drive out the people buying and selling animals for sacrifices. He knocked over the tables of the money changers and the chairs of those selling doves, ¹⁶and he stopped everyone from using the Temple as a marketplace.* ¹⁷He said to them, "The Scriptures declare, 'My Temple will be called a house of prayer for all nations,' but you have turned it into a den of thieves."*

¹⁸When the leading priests and teachers of religious law heard what Jesus had done, they began planning how to kill him. But they were afraid of him because the people were so amazed at his teaching.

¹⁹That evening Jesus and the disciples left* the city.

²⁰The next morning as they passed by the fig tree he had cursed, the disciples noticed it had withered from the roots up. ²¹Peter remembered what Jesus had said to the tree on the previous day and exclaimed, "Look, Rabbi! The fig tree you cursed has withered and died!"

²²Then Jesus said to the disciples, "Have faith in God. ²³I tell you the truth, you can say to this mountain, 'May you be lifted up and thrown into the sea,' and it will happen. But you must really believe it will happen and have no doubt in your heart. ²⁴I tell you, you can pray for anything, and if you believe that you've received it, it will be yours. ²⁵But when you are praying, first forgive anyone you are holding a grudge against, so that your Father in heaven will forgive your sins, too.*"

THE AUTHORITY OF JESUS CHALLENGED

²⁷Again they entered Jerusalem. As Jesus was walking through the Temple area, the leading priests, the teachers of religious law, and the elders came up to him. ²⁸They demanded, "By what authority are you doing all these things? Who gave you the right to do them?"

²⁹"I'll tell you by what authority I do these things if you answer one question," Jesus replied. ³⁰"Did John's authority to baptize come from heaven, or was it merely human? Answer me!"

³¹They talked it over among themselves. "If we say it was from heaven, he will ask why we didn't believe John. ³²But do we dare say it was merely human?" For they were afraid of what the people would do, because everyone believed that John was a prophet. ³³So they finally replied, "We don't know."

And Jesus responded, "Then I won't tell you by what authority I do these things."

PARABLE OF THE EVIL FARMERS

12 Then Jesus began teaching them with stories: "A man planted a vineyard. He built a wall around it, dug a pit for pressing out the grape juice, and built a lookout tower. Then he leased the vineyard to tenant farmers and moved

---

10:51 Greek uses the Hebrew term *Rabboni.* 10:52 Or *on the way.* 11:9 Greek *Hosanna,* an exclamation of praise that literally means "save now"; also in 11:10. 11:9-10 Pss 118:25-26; 148:1. 11:16 Or *from carrying merchandise through the Temple.* 11:17 Isa 56:7; Jer 7:11. 11:19 Greek *they left;* other manuscripts read *he left.* 11:25 Some manuscripts add verse 26, *But if you refuse to forgive, your Father in heaven will not forgive your sins.* Compare Matt 6:15.

to another country. ²At the time of the grape harvest, he sent one of his servants to collect his share of the crop. ³But the farmers grabbed the servant, beat him up, and sent him back empty-handed. ⁴The owner then sent another servant, but they insulted him and beat him over the head. ⁵The next servant he sent was killed. Others he sent were either beaten or killed, ⁶until there was only one left—his son whom he loved dearly. The owner finally sent him, thinking, 'Surely they will respect my son.'

⁷"But the tenant farmers said to one another, 'Here comes the heir to this estate. Let's kill him and get the estate for ourselves!' ⁸So they grabbed him and murdered him and threw his body out of the vineyard.

⁹"What do you suppose the owner of the vineyard will do?" Jesus asked. "I'll tell you—he will come and kill those farmers and lease the vineyard to others. ¹⁰Didn't you ever read this in the Scriptures?

'The stone that the builders rejected
    has now become the cornerstone.
¹¹ This is the LORD's doing,
    and it is wonderful to see.'*"

¹²The religious leaders* wanted to arrest Jesus because they realized he was telling the story against them—they were the wicked farmers. But they were afraid of the crowd, so they left him and went away.

TAXES FOR CAESAR

¹³Later the leaders sent some Pharisees and supporters of Herod to trap Jesus into saying something for which he could be arrested. ¹⁴"Teacher," they said, "we know how honest you are. You are impartial and don't play favorites. You teach the way of God truthfully. Now tell us—is it right to pay taxes to Caesar or not? ¹⁵Should we pay them, or shouldn't we?"

Jesus saw through their hypocrisy and said, "Why are you trying to trap me? Show me a Roman coin,* and I'll tell you." ¹⁶When they handed it to him, he asked, "Whose picture and title are stamped on it?"

"Caesar's," they replied.

¹⁷"Well, then," Jesus said, "give to Caesar what belongs to Caesar, and give to God what belongs to God."

His reply completely amazed them.

DISCUSSION ABOUT RESURRECTION

¹⁸Then Jesus was approached by some Sadducees—religious leaders who say there is no resurrection from the dead. They posed this question: ¹⁹"Teacher, Moses gave us a law that if a man dies, leaving a wife without children, his brother should marry the widow and have a child who will carry on the brother's name.* ²⁰Well, suppose there were seven brothers. The oldest one

CREATED FOR LOVE
Mark 12:28-30
ROBERT MORRIS

Have you ever looked at a person and thought, *I just don't love God as much as they do, but I wish I did*? For many years, I felt this way about my wife, Debbie. When I got saved at age 19, she had already been walking and talking with God for 10 years. She already knew Him so well. Then I learned that love grows. The longer you know God, the more you're going to love Him.

Love also leaks. The apostle Paul says Satan is always trying to shoot arrows at you (Ephesians 6:16). He wants you to feel discouraged, depressed, hard, and bitter. He wants your love for God to leak out of your heart.

So how do you stop the leaks and grow in the Lord? By expressing your love to God through *worship*. Worship is simply communicating your love to God and God communicating His love to you. He created you to love and be loved.

married and then died without children. ²¹So the second brother married the widow, but he also died without children. Then the third brother married her. ²²This continued with all seven of them, and still there were no children. Last of all, the woman also died. ²³So tell us, whose wife will she be in the resurrection? For all seven were married to her."

²⁴Jesus replied, "Your mistake is that you don't know the Scriptures, and you don't know the power of God. ²⁵For when the dead rise, they will neither marry nor be given in marriage. In this respect they will be like the angels in heaven.

²⁶"But now, as to whether the dead will be raised—haven't you ever read about this in the writings of Moses, in the story of the burning bush? Long after Abraham, Isaac, and Jacob had died, God said to Moses,* 'I am the God of Abraham, the God of Isaac, and the God of Jacob.'* ²⁷So he is the God of the living, not the dead. You have made a serious error."

THE MOST IMPORTANT COMMANDMENT

²⁸One of the teachers of religious law was standing there listening to the debate. He realized that Jesus had answered well, so he asked, "Of all the commandments, which is the most important?"

²⁹Jesus replied, "The most important commandment is this: 'Listen, O Israel! The LORD our God is the one and only LORD. ³⁰And you must love the LORD your God with all your heart, all your soul, all your mind, and all your strength.'* ³¹The second is equally important: 'Love your

12:10-11 Ps 118:22-23.   12:12 Greek *They.*   12:15 Greek *a denarius.*   12:19 See Deut 25:5-6.   12:26a Greek *in the story of the bush? God said to him.*   12:26b Exod 3:6.   12:29-30 Deut 6:4-5.

neighbor as yourself.'* No other commandment is greater than these."

³²The teacher of religious law replied, "Well said, Teacher. You have spoken the truth by saying that there is only one God and no other. ³³And I know it is important to love him with all my heart and all my understanding and all my strength, and to love my neighbor as myself. This is more important than to offer all of the burnt offerings and sacrifices required in the law."

³⁴Realizing how much the man understood, Jesus said to him, "You are not far from the Kingdom of God." And after that, no one dared to ask him any more questions.

WHOSE SON IS THE MESSIAH?

³⁵Later, as Jesus was teaching the people in the Temple, he asked, "Why do the teachers of religious law claim that the Messiah is the son of David? ³⁶For David himself, speaking under the inspiration of the Holy Spirit, said,

'The LORD said to my Lord,
    Sit in the place of honor at my right hand
        until I humble your enemies beneath
            your feet.'*

³⁷Since David himself called the Messiah 'my Lord,' how can the Messiah be his son?" The large crowd listened to him with great delight.

³⁸Jesus also taught: "Beware of these teachers of religious law! For they like to parade around in flowing robes and receive respectful greetings as they walk in the marketplaces. ³⁹And how they love the seats of honor in the synagogues and the head table at banquets. ⁴⁰Yet they shamelessly cheat widows out of their property and then pretend to be pious by making long prayers in public. Because of this, they will be more severely punished."

THE WIDOW'S OFFERING

⁴¹Jesus sat down near the collection box in the Temple and watched as the crowds dropped in their money. Many rich people put in large amounts. ⁴²Then a poor widow came and dropped in two small coins.*

⁴³Jesus called his disciples to him and said, "I tell you the truth, this poor widow has given more than all the others who are making contributions. ⁴⁴For they gave a tiny part of their surplus, but she, poor as she is, has given everything she had to live on."

JESUS SPEAKS ABOUT THE FUTURE

13 As Jesus was leaving the Temple that day, one of his disciples said, "Teacher, look at these magnificent buildings! Look at the impressive stones in the walls."

²Jesus replied, "Yes, look at these great buildings. But they will be completely demolished. Not one stone will be left on top of another!"

³Later, Jesus sat on the Mount of Olives across the valley from the Temple. Peter, James, John, and Andrew came to him privately and asked him, ⁴"Tell us, when will all this happen? What sign will show us that these things are about to be fulfilled?"

⁵Jesus replied, "Don't let anyone mislead you, ⁶for many will come in my name, claiming, 'I am the Messiah.'* They will deceive many. ⁷And you will hear of wars and threats of wars, but don't panic. Yes, these things must take place, but the end won't follow immediately. ⁸Nation will go to war against nation, and kingdom against kingdom. There will be earthquakes in many parts of the world, as well as famines. But this is only the first of the birth pains, with more to come.

⁹"When these things begin to happen, watch out! You will be handed over to the local councils and beaten in the synagogues. You will stand trial before governors and kings because you are my followers. But this will be your opportunity to tell them about me.* ¹⁰For the Good News must first be preached to all nations.* ¹¹But when you are arrested and stand trial, don't worry in advance about what to say. Just say what God tells you at that time, for it is not you who will be speaking, but the Holy Spirit.

¹²"A brother will betray his brother to death, a father will betray his own child, and children will rebel against their parents and cause them to be killed. ¹³And everyone will hate you because you are my followers.* But the one who endures to the end will be saved.

¹⁴"The day is coming when you will see the sacrilegious object that causes desecration* standing where he* should not be." (Reader, pay attention!) "Then those in Judea must flee to the hills. ¹⁵A person out on the deck of a roof must not go down into the house to pack. ¹⁶A person out in the field must not return even to get a coat. ¹⁷How terrible it will be for pregnant women and for nursing mothers in those days. ¹⁸And pray that your flight will not be in winter. ¹⁹For there will be greater anguish in those days than at any time since God created the world. And it will never be so great again. ²⁰In fact, unless the Lord shortens that time of calamity, not a single person will survive. But for the sake of his chosen ones he has shortened those days.

²¹"Then if anyone tells you, 'Look, here is the Messiah,' or 'There he is,' don't believe it. ²²For false messiahs and false prophets will rise up and perform signs and wonders so as to deceive, if possible, even God's chosen ones. ²³Watch out! I have warned you about this ahead of time!

13:31 Lev 19:18.   12:36 Ps 110:1.   12:42 Greek *two lepta, which is a kodrantes* [i.e., a quadrans].   13:6 Greek *claiming, 'I am.'*   13:9 Or *But this will be your testimony against them.*   13:10 Or *all peoples.*   13:13 Greek *on account of my name.*   13:14a Greek *the abomination of desolation.* See Dan 9:27; 11:31; 12:11.   13:14b Or *it.*

²⁴"At that time, after the anguish of those days,

the sun will be darkened,
the moon will give no light,
²⁵ the stars will fall from the sky,
and the powers in the heavens
will be shaken.*

²⁶Then everyone will see the Son of Man* coming on the clouds with great power and glory.* ²⁷And he will send out his angels to gather his chosen ones from all over the world*—from the farthest ends of the earth and heaven.

²⁸"Now learn a lesson from the fig tree. When its branches bud and its leaves begin to sprout, you know that summer is near. ²⁹In the same way, when you see all these things taking place, you can know that his return is very near, right at the door. ³⁰I tell you the truth, this generation* will not pass from the scene before all these things take place. ³¹Heaven and earth will disappear, but my words will never disappear.

³²"However, no one knows the day or hour when these things will happen, not even the angels in heaven or the Son himself. Only the Father knows. ³³And since you don't know when that time will come, be on guard! Stay alert*!

³⁴"The coming of the Son of Man can be illustrated by the story of a man going on a long trip. When he left home, he gave each of his slaves instructions about the work they were to do, and he told the gatekeeper to watch for his return. ³⁵You, too, must keep watch! For you don't know when the master of the household will return— in the evening, at midnight, before dawn, or at daybreak. ³⁶Don't let him find you sleeping when he arrives without warning. ³⁷I say to you what I say to everyone: Watch for him!"

JESUS ANOINTED AT BETHANY

14 It was now two days before Passover and the Festival of Unleavened Bread. The leading priests and the teachers of religious law were still looking for an opportunity to capture Jesus secretly and kill him. ²"But not during the Passover celebration," they agreed, "or the people may riot."

³Meanwhile, Jesus was in Bethany at the home of Simon, a man who had previously had leprosy. While he was eating,* a woman came in with a beautiful alabaster jar of expensive perfume made from essence of nard. She broke open the jar and poured the perfume over his head.

⁴Some of those at the table were indignant. "Why waste such expensive perfume?" they asked. ⁵"It could have been sold for a year's wages* and the money given to the poor!" So they scolded her harshly.

⁶But Jesus replied, "Leave her alone. Why criticize her for doing such a good thing to me? ⁷You will always have the poor among you, and you can help them whenever you want to. But you

will not always have me. ⁸She has done what she could and has anointed my body for burial ahead of time. ⁹I tell you the truth, wherever the Good News is preached throughout the world, this woman's deed will be remembered and discussed."

JUDAS AGREES TO BETRAY JESUS

¹⁰Then Judas Iscariot, one of the twelve disciples, went to the leading priests to arrange to betray Jesus to them. ¹¹They were delighted when they heard why he had come, and they promised to give him money. So he began looking for an opportunity to betray Jesus.

THE LAST SUPPER

¹²On the first day of the Festival of Unleavened Bread, when the Passover lamb is sacrificed, Jesus' disciples asked him, "Where do you want us to go to prepare the Passover meal for you?"

¹³So Jesus sent two of them into Jerusalem with these instructions: "As you go into the city, a man carrying a pitcher of water will meet you. Follow him. ¹⁴At the house he enters, say to the owner, 'The Teacher asks: Where is the guest room where I can eat the Passover meal with my disciples?' ¹⁵He will take you upstairs to a large room that is already set up. That is where you should prepare our meal." ¹⁶So the two disciples went into the city and found everything just as Jesus had said, and they prepared the Passover meal there.

¹⁷In the evening Jesus arrived with the Twelve. ¹⁸As they were at the table* eating, Jesus said, "I tell you the truth, one of you eating with me here will betray me."

¹⁹Greatly distressed, each one asked in turn, "Am I the one?"

²⁰He replied, "It is one of you twelve who is eating from this bowl with me. ²¹For the Son of Man* must die, as the Scriptures declared long ago. But how terrible it will be for the one who betrays him. It would be far better for that man if he had never been born!"

²²As they were eating, Jesus took some bread and blessed it. Then he broke it in pieces and gave it to the disciples, saying, "Take it, for this is my body."

²³And he took a cup of wine and gave thanks to God for it. He gave it to them, and they all drank from it. ²⁴And he said to them, "This is my blood, which confirms the covenant* between God and his people. It is poured out as a sacrifice for many. ²⁵I tell you the truth, I will not drink wine again until the day I drink it new in the Kingdom of God."

13:24-25 See Isa 13:10; 34:4; Joel 2:10. **13:26a** "Son of Man" is a title Jesus used for himself. **13:26b** See Dan 7:13. **13:27** Greek *from the four winds.* **13:30** Or *this age,* or *this nation.* **13:33** Some manuscripts add *and pray.* **14:3** Or *reclining.* **14:5** Greek *for 300 denarii.* A denarius was equivalent to a laborer's full day's wage. **14:18** Or *As they reclined.* **14:21** "Son of Man" is a title Jesus used for himself. **14:24** Some manuscripts read *the new covenant.*

26 Then they sang a hymn and went out to the Mount of Olives.

JESUS PREDICTS PETER'S DENIAL

27 On the way, Jesus told them, "All of you will desert me. For the Scriptures say,

'God will strike* the Shepherd,
  and the sheep will be scattered.'

28 But after I am raised from the dead, I will go ahead of you to Galilee and meet you there."

29 Peter said to him, "Even if everyone else deserts you, I never will."

30 Jesus replied, "I tell you the truth, Peter—this very night, before the rooster crows twice, you will deny three times that you even know me."

31 "No!" Peter declared emphatically. "Even if I have to die with you, I will never deny you!" And all the others vowed the same.

JESUS PRAYS IN GETHSEMANE

32 They went to the olive grove called Gethsemane, and Jesus said, "Sit here while I go and pray." 33 He took Peter, James, and John with him, and he became deeply troubled and distressed. 34 He told them, "My soul is crushed with grief to the point of death. Stay here and keep watch with me."

35 He went on a little farther and fell to the ground. He prayed that, if it were possible, the awful hour awaiting him might pass him by. 36 "Abba, Father,"* he cried out, "everything is possible for you. Please take this cup of suffering away from me. Yet I want your will to be done, not mine."

37 Then he returned and found the disciples asleep. He said to Peter, "Simon, are you asleep? Couldn't you watch with me even one hour? 38 Keep watch and pray, so that you will not give in to temptation. For the spirit is willing, but the body is weak."

39 Then Jesus left them again and prayed the same prayer as before. 40 When he returned to them again, he found them sleeping, for they couldn't keep their eyes open. And they didn't know what to say.

41 When he returned to them the third time, he said, "Go ahead and sleep. Have your rest. But no—the time has come. The Son of Man is betrayed into the hands of sinners. 42 Up, let's be going. Look, my betrayer is here!"

JESUS IS BETRAYED AND ARRESTED

43 And immediately, even as Jesus said this, Judas, one of the twelve disciples, arrived with a crowd of men armed with swords and clubs. They had been sent by the leading priests, the teachers of religious law, and the elders. 44 The traitor, Judas, had given them a prearranged signal: "You will know which one to arrest when I greet him with a kiss. Then you can take him away under guard." 45 As soon as they arrived, Judas walked up to Jesus. "Rabbi!" he exclaimed, and gave him the kiss.

46 Then the others grabbed Jesus and arrested him. 47 But one of the men with Jesus pulled out his sword and struck the high priest's slave, slashing off his ear.

48 Jesus asked them, "Am I some dangerous revolutionary, that you come with swords and clubs to arrest me? 49 Why didn't you arrest me in the Temple? I was there among you teaching every day. But these things are happening to fulfill what the Scriptures say about me."

50 Then all his disciples deserted him and ran away. 51 One young man following behind was clothed only in a long linen shirt. When the mob tried to grab him, 52 he slipped out of his shirt and ran away naked.

JESUS BEFORE THE COUNCIL

53 They took Jesus to the high priest's home where the leading priests, the elders, and the teachers of religious law had gathered. 54 Meanwhile, Peter followed him at a distance and went right into the high priest's courtyard. There he sat with the guards, warming himself by the fire.

55 Inside, the leading priests and the entire high council* were trying to find evidence against Jesus, so they could put him to death. But they couldn't find any. 56 Many false witnesses spoke against him, but they contradicted each other. 57 Finally, some men stood up and gave this false testimony: 58 "We heard him say, 'I will destroy this Temple made with human hands, and in three days I will build another, made without human hands.'" 59 But even then they didn't get their stories straight!

60 Then the high priest stood up before the others and asked Jesus, "Well, aren't you going to answer these charges? What do you have to say for yourself?" 61 But Jesus was silent and made no reply. Then the high priest asked him, "Are you the Messiah, the Son of the Blessed One?"

62 Jesus said, "I AM.* And you will see the Son of Man seated in the place of power at God's right hand* and coming on the clouds of heaven.*"

63 Then the high priest tore his clothing to show his horror and said, "Why do we need other witnesses? 64 You have all heard his blasphemy. What is your verdict?"

"Guilty!" they all cried. "He deserves to die!"

65 Then some of them began to spit at him, and they blindfolded him and beat him with their fists. "Prophesy to us," they jeered. And the guards slapped him as they took him away.

14:27 Greek *I will strike.* Zech 13:7. 14:36 *Abba* is an Aramaic term for "father." 14:55 Greek *the Sanhedrin.* 14:62a Or *The 'I AM' is here;* or *I am the LORD.* See Exod 3:14. 14:62b Greek *seated at the right hand of the power.* See Ps 110:1. 14:62c See Dan 7:13.

PETER DENIES JESUS

66 Meanwhile, Peter was in the courtyard below. One of the servant girls who worked for the high priest came by 67 and noticed Peter warming himself at the fire. She looked at him closely and said, "You were one of those with Jesus of Nazareth.*"

68 But Peter denied it. "I don't know what you're talking about," he said, and he went out into the entryway. Just then, a rooster crowed.*

69 When the servant girl saw him standing there, she began telling the others, "This man is definitely one of them!" 70 But Peter denied it again.

A little later some of the other bystanders confronted Peter and said, "You must be one of them, because you are a Galilean."

71 Peter swore, "A curse on me if I'm lying—I don't know this man you're talking about!" 72 And immediately the rooster crowed the second time. Suddenly, Jesus' words flashed through Peter's mind: "Before the rooster crows twice, you will deny three times that you even know me." And he broke down and wept.

JESUS' TRIAL BEFORE PILATE

15 Very early in the morning the leading priests, the elders, and the teachers of religious law—the entire high council*—met to discuss their next step. They bound Jesus, led him away, and took him to Pilate, the Roman governor.

2 Pilate asked Jesus, "Are you the king of the Jews?"

Jesus replied, "You have said it."

3 Then the leading priests kept accusing him of many crimes, 4 and Pilate asked him, "Aren't you going to answer them? What about all these charges they are bringing against you?" 5 But Jesus said nothing, much to Pilate's surprise.

6 Now it was the governor's custom each year during the Passover celebration to release one prisoner—anyone the people requested. 7 One of the prisoners at that time was Barabbas, a revolutionary who had committed murder in an uprising. 8 The crowd went to Pilate and asked him to release a prisoner as usual.

9 "Would you like me to release to you this 'King of the Jews'?" Pilate asked. 10 (For he realized by now that the leading priests had arrested Jesus out of envy.) 11 But at this point the leading priests stirred up the crowd to demand the release of Barabbas instead of Jesus. 12 Pilate asked them, "Then what should I do with this man you call the king of the Jews?"

13 They shouted back, "Crucify him!"

14 "Why?" Pilate demanded. "What crime has he committed?"

But the mob roared even louder, "Crucify him!"

15 So to pacify the crowd, Pilate released Barabbas to them. He ordered Jesus flogged with a lead-tipped whip, then turned him over to the Roman soldiers to be crucified.

THE SOLDIERS MOCK JESUS

16 The soldiers took Jesus into the courtyard of the governor's headquarters (called the Praetorium) and called out the entire regiment. 17 They dressed him in a purple robe, and they wove thorn branches into a crown and put it on his head. 18 Then they saluted him and taunted, "Hail! King of the Jews!" 19 And they struck him on the head with a reed stick, spit on him, and dropped to their knees in mock worship. 20 When they were finally tired of mocking him, they took off the purple robe and put his own clothes on him again. Then they led him away to be crucified.

THE CRUCIFIXION

21 A passerby named Simon, who was from Cyrene,* was coming in from the countryside just then, and the soldiers forced him to carry Jesus' cross. (Simon was the father of Alexander and Rufus.) 22 And they brought Jesus to a place called Golgotha (which means "Place of the Skull"). 23 They offered him wine drugged with myrrh, but he refused it.

24 Then the soldiers nailed him to the cross. They divided his clothes and threw dice* to decide who would get each piece. 25 It was nine o'clock in the morning when they crucified him. 26 A sign announced the charge against him. It read, "The King of the Jews." 27 Two revolutionaries* were crucified with him, one on his right and one on his left.*

29 The people passing by shouted abuse, shaking their heads in mockery. "Ha! Look at you now!" they yelled at him. "You said you were going to destroy the Temple and rebuild it in three days. 30 Well then, save yourself and come down from the cross!"

31 The leading priests and teachers of religious law also mocked Jesus. "He saved others," they scoffed, "but he can't save himself! 32 Let this Messiah, this King of Israel, come down from the cross so we can see it and believe him!" Even the men who were crucified with Jesus ridiculed him.

THE DEATH OF JESUS

33 At noon, darkness fell across the whole land until three o'clock. 34 Then at three o'clock Jesus called out with a loud voice, "Eloi, Eloi, lema sabachthani?" which means "My God, my God, why have you abandoned me?"*

35 Some of the bystanders misunderstood and thought he was calling for the prophet Elijah. 36 One of them ran and filled a sponge with sour wine, holding it up to him on a reed stick so he could drink. "Wait!" he said. "Let's see whether Elijah comes to take him down!"

14:67 Or Jesus the Nazarene. 14:68 Some manuscripts do not include Just then, a rooster crowed. 15:1 Greek the Sanhedrin; also in 15:43. 15:21 Cyrene was a city in northern Africa. 15:24 Greek cast lots. See Ps 22:18. 15:27a Or Two criminals. 15:27b Some manuscripts add verse 28, And the Scripture was fulfilled that said, "He was counted among those who were rebels." See Isa 53:12; also compare Luke 22:37. 15:34 Ps 22:1.

³⁷Then Jesus uttered another loud cry and breathed his last. ³⁸And the curtain in the sanctuary of the Temple was torn in two, from top to bottom.

³⁹When the Roman officer* who stood facing him* saw how he had died, he exclaimed, "This man truly was the Son of God!"

⁴⁰Some women were there, watching from a distance, including Mary Magdalene, Mary (the mother of James the younger and of Joseph*), and Salome. ⁴¹They had been followers of Jesus and had cared for him while he was in Galilee. Many other women who had come with him to Jerusalem were also there.

THE BURIAL OF JESUS

⁴²This all happened on Friday, the day of preparation,* the day before the Sabbath. As evening approached, ⁴³Joseph of Arimathea took a risk and went to Pilate and asked for Jesus' body. (Joseph was an honored member of the high council, and he was waiting for the Kingdom of God to come.) ⁴⁴Pilate couldn't believe that Jesus was already dead, so he called for the Roman officer and asked if he had died yet. ⁴⁵The officer confirmed that Jesus was dead, so Pilate told Joseph he could have the body. ⁴⁶Joseph bought a long sheet of linen cloth. Then he took Jesus' body down from the cross, wrapped it in the cloth, and laid it in a tomb that had been carved out of the rock. Then he rolled a stone in front of the entrance. ⁴⁷Mary Magdalene and Mary the mother of Joseph saw where Jesus' body was laid.

THE RESURRECTION

16 Saturday evening, when the Sabbath ended, Mary Magdalene, Mary the mother of James, and Salome went out and purchased burial spices so they could anoint Jesus' body. ²Very early on Sunday morning,* just at sunrise, they went to the tomb. ³On the way they were asking each other, "Who will roll away the stone for us from the entrance to the tomb?" ⁴But as they arrived, they looked up and saw that the stone, which was very large, had already been rolled aside.

⁵When they entered the tomb, they saw a young man clothed in a white robe sitting on the right side. The women were shocked, ⁶but the angel said, "Don't be alarmed. You are looking for Jesus of Nazareth,* who was crucified. He isn't here! He is risen from the dead! Look, this is where they laid his body. ⁷Now go and tell his disciples, including Peter, that Jesus is going ahead of you to Galilee. You will see him there, just as he told you before he died."

⁸The women fled from the tomb, trembling and bewildered, and they said nothing to anyone because they were too frightened.*

[*The most ancient manuscripts of Mark conclude with verse 16:8. Later manuscripts add one or both of the following endings.*]

[*Shorter Ending of Mark*]

Then they briefly reported all this to Peter and his companions. Afterward Jesus himself sent them out from east to west with the sacred and unfailing message of salvation that gives eternal life. Amen.

[*Longer Ending of Mark*]

⁹After Jesus rose from the dead early on Sunday morning, the first person who saw him was Mary Magdalene, the woman from whom he had cast out seven demons. ¹⁰She went to the disciples, who were grieving and weeping, and told them what had happened. ¹¹But when she told them that Jesus was alive and she had seen him, they didn't believe her.

¹²Afterward he appeared in a different form to two of his followers who were walking from Jerusalem into the country. ¹³They rushed back to tell the others, but no one believed them.

¹⁴Still later he appeared to the eleven disciples as they were eating together. He rebuked them for their stubborn unbelief because they refused to believe those who had seen him after he had been raised from the dead.*

¹⁵And then he told them, "Go into all the world and preach the Good News to everyone. ¹⁶Anyone who believes and is baptized will be saved. But anyone who refuses to believe will be condemned. ¹⁷These miraculous signs will accompany those who believe: They will cast out demons in my name, and they will speak in new languages.* ¹⁸They will be able to handle snakes with safety, and if they drink anything poisonous, it won't hurt them. They will be able to place their hands on the sick, and they will be healed."

¹⁹When the Lord Jesus had finished talking with them, he was taken up into heaven and sat down in the place of honor at God's right hand. ²⁰And the disciples went everywhere and preached, and the Lord worked through them, confirming what they said by many miraculous signs.

15:39a Greek *the centurion;* similarly in 15:44, 45. **15:39b** Some manuscripts add *heard his cry and.* **15:40** Greek *Joses;* also in 15:47. See Matt 27:56. **15:42** Greek *It was the day of preparation.* **16:2** Greek *on the first day of the week;* also in 16:9. **16:6** Or *Jesus the Nazarene.* **16:8** The most reliable early manuscripts of the Gospel of Mark end at verse 8. Other manuscripts include various endings to the Gospel. A few include both the "shorter ending" and the "longer ending." The majority of manuscripts include the "longer ending" immediately after verse 8. **16:14** Some early manuscripts add: *And they excused themselves, saying, "This age of lawlessness and unbelief is under Satan, who does not permit God's truth and power to conquer the evil [unclean] spirits. Therefore, reveal your justice now." This is what they said to Christ. And Christ replied to them, "The period of years of Satan's power has been fulfilled, but other dreadful things will happen soon. And I was handed over to death for those who have sinned, so that they may return to the truth and sin no more, and so they may inherit the spiritual, incorruptible, and righteous glory in heaven."* **16:17** Or *new tongues;* some manuscripts do not include *new.*

LUKE

JON HUNTZINGER, PHD

The Gospel of Luke is the longest book in the New Testament. It was written by Paul's traveling companion by that name, who was also a physician (Colossians 4:14). It is the first part of a two-part work, which also includes the book of Acts. Together, they make up about a quarter of the New Testament. Since Acts concludes with a description of Paul in Rome awaiting his legal hearing before Caesar, which occurred sometime in the mid-60s, many believe Luke wrote both books prior to that time but after Mark wrote his Gospel.

Luke begins his Gospel by telling Theophilus (meaning 'friend of God'), the recipient of the book, that he has written an "accurate account" of the Good News of Jesus (1:1-3). Luke proceeds by giving attention to Jesus' ministry among humble and poor people (1:52-53; 4:16-19; 6:20-23; 10:29-37; 14:12-14; 16:19-23; 18:35-43; 21:1-4), as well as women (1:26-56; 2:17-19, 36-38; 7:11-17, 36-50; 8:1-3; 10:38-42; 18:1-8; 21:1-4; 23:27-31, 49; 23:55-24:11). He also shows Jesus in relation to those who, for one reason or another (such as impurity), stand on the margins of society (4:16-19; 17:11-19; 23:39-43).

Luke's Gospel may be divided into four primary parts:
— Jesus' birth and preparation for ministry (1:1-4:13)
— Jesus' ministry in Galilee (4:14-9:50)
— Jesus' movement toward Jerusalem (9:51-19:44)
— Jesus' arrival in Jerusalem, where He is put to death and raised to life (19:45-24:53)

Though the structure of Luke's Gospel is similar to that of Matthew and Mark, it is notable for the very long section describing Jesus' travel from Galilee to Jerusalem (10 chapters), which Matthew does not emphasize and Mark, though he does draw attention to it by describing Jesus "on his way," only gives a chapter (chapter 10) to that journey.

A primary theme in Luke's Gospel is God's salvation for all people. That is why he begins the Gospel by describing the angel Gabriel's appearance to Mary. Gabriel declares she is favored by God and will give birth to a son whose name will be *Jesus* (1:26-33). The name *Jesus* is the English form of the Greek *Iēsous*, which, in turn, comes from the Hebrew name *Yeshua*. Yeshua is derived from the Hebrew word *yašah*, meaning 'to save.' The name *Jesus* means 'salvation,' and Luke develops this important truth throughout his Gospel. Mary will give birth to a son who will bring salvation to God's people.

After Mary hears the angel's words, she sings that God is her Savior (1:47). Then the angels announce the birth of Jesus to the shepherds, saying the Savior has been born (2:11). Later, Luke describes the ministry of John the Baptist as preparation for Jesus' ministry by quoting from the prophet Isaiah, who looked forward to the day of God's salvation (3:4-6). Luke also shows that people experience salvation from Jesus in many ways: a woman is forgiven of her sins (7:47-50); a man is delivered from demons (8:26-36); another woman is healed of sickness in her body (8:43-48); and a rich man is restored to the people of his community (19:1-10). In all these stories, Luke uses a word meaning 'to save' to describe what Jesus has done.

According to Luke, Jesus ministers God's salvation among His people through prayer and the power of the Holy Spirit. Jesus is dependent on His relationship with His Father, which He cultivates through prayer, for understanding when and how He should minister, and He relies upon God's Spirit for the performance of that ministry. Luke shows Jesus as a man of prayer in numerous passages (5:16; 6:12; 9:18, 28-29; 10:21; 11:1, 5-13; 18:1-8; 22:31-32, 39-46; 23:34, 46;), even as He is shown to be a man of the Spirit (1:35; 3:21-22; 4:1, 14; 10:21; 24:49). He speaks with God His Father and enjoys the immediate presence of the Holy Spirit.

INTRODUCTION

1 Many people have set out to write accounts about the events that have been fulfilled among us. [2] They used the eyewitness reports circulating among us from the early disciples.* [3] Having carefully investigated everything from the beginning, I also have decided to write an accurate account for you, most honorable Theophilus, [4] so you can be certain of the truth of everything you were taught.

THE BIRTH OF JOHN THE BAPTIST FORETOLD

[5] When Herod was king of Judea, there was a Jewish priest named Zechariah. He was a member of the priestly order of Abijah, and his wife, Elizabeth, was also from the priestly line of Aaron. [6] Zechariah and Elizabeth were righteous in God's eyes, careful to obey all of the Lord's commandments and regulations. [7] They had no children because Elizabeth was unable to conceive, and they were both very old.

[8] One day Zechariah was serving God in the Temple, for his order was on duty that week. [9] As was the custom of the priests, he was chosen by lot to enter the sanctuary of the Lord and burn incense. [10] While the incense was being burned, a great crowd stood outside, praying.

[11] While Zechariah was in the sanctuary, an angel of the Lord appeared to him, standing to the right of the incense altar. [12] Zechariah was shaken and overwhelmed with fear when he saw him. [13] But the angel said, "Don't be afraid, Zechariah! God has heard your prayer. Your wife, Elizabeth, will give you a son, and you are to name him John. [14] You will have great joy and gladness, and many will rejoice at his birth, [15] for he will be great in the eyes of the Lord. He must never touch wine or other alcoholic drinks. He will be filled with the Holy Spirit, even before his birth.* [16] And he will turn many Israelites to the Lord their God. [17] He will be a man with the spirit and power of Elijah. He will prepare the people for the coming of the Lord. He will turn the hearts of the fathers to their children,* and he will cause those who are rebellious to accept the wisdom of the godly."

[18] Zechariah said to the angel, "How can I be sure this will happen? I'm an old man now, and my wife is also well along in years."

[19] Then the angel said, "I am Gabriel! I stand in the very presence of God. It was he who sent me to bring you this good news! [20] But now, since you didn't believe what I said, you will be silent and unable to speak until the child is born. For my words will certainly be fulfilled at the proper time."

[21] Meanwhile, the people were waiting for Zechariah to come out of the sanctuary, wondering why he was taking so long. [22] When he finally did come out, he couldn't speak to them. Then they realized from his gestures and his silence that he must have seen a vision in the sanctuary.

[23] When Zechariah's week of service in the Temple was over, he returned home. [24] Soon afterward his wife, Elizabeth, became pregnant and went into seclusion for five months. [25] "How kind the Lord is!" she exclaimed. "He has taken away my disgrace of having no children."

THE BIRTH OF JESUS FORETOLD

[26] In the sixth month of Elizabeth's pregnancy, God sent the angel Gabriel to Nazareth, a village in Galilee, [27] to a virgin named Mary. She was engaged to be married to a man named Joseph, a descendant of King David. [28] Gabriel appeared to her and said, "Greetings,* favored woman! The Lord is with you!*"

[29] Confused and disturbed, Mary tried to think what the angel could mean. [30] "Don't be afraid, Mary," the angel told her, "for you have found favor with God! [31] You will conceive and give birth to a son, and you will name him Jesus. [32] He will be very great and will be called the Son of the Most High. The Lord God will give him the throne of his ancestor David. [33] And he will reign over Israel* forever; his Kingdom will never end!"

[34] Mary asked the angel, "But how can this happen? I am a virgin."

[35] The angel replied, "The Holy Spirit will come upon you, and the power of the Most High will overshadow you. So the baby to be born will be holy, and he will be called the Son of God. [36] What's more, your relative Elizabeth has become pregnant in her old age! People used to say she was barren, but she has conceived a son and is now in her sixth month. [37] For the word of God will never fail.*"

[38] Mary responded, "I am the Lord's servant. May everything you have said about me come true." And then the angel left her.

MARY VISITS ELIZABETH

[39] A few days later Mary hurried to the hill country of Judea, to the town [40] where Zechariah lived. She entered the house and greeted Elizabeth. [41] At the sound of Mary's greeting, Elizabeth's child leaped within her, and Elizabeth was filled with the Holy Spirit.

[42] Elizabeth gave a glad cry and exclaimed to Mary, "God has blessed you above all women, and your child is blessed. [43] Why am I so honored, that the mother of my Lord should visit me? [44] When I heard your greeting, the baby in my womb jumped for joy. [45] You are blessed because you believed that the Lord would do what he said."

1:2 Greek *from those who from the beginning were servants of the word.* 1:15 Or *even from birth.* 1:17 See Mal 4:5-6. 1:28a Or *Rejoice.* 1:28b Some manuscripts add *Blessed are you among women.* 1:33 Greek *over the house of Jacob.* 1:37 Some manuscripts read *For nothing is impossible with God.*

THE MAGNIFICAT: MARY'S SONG OF PRAISE

⁴⁶ Mary responded,

"Oh, how my soul praises the Lord.
⁴⁷   How my spirit rejoices in God my Savior!
⁴⁸ For he took notice of his lowly servant girl,
     and from now on all generations
        will call me blessed.
⁴⁹ For the Mighty One is holy,
     and he has done great things for me.
⁵⁰ He shows mercy from generation to
        generation
     to all who fear him.
⁵¹ His mighty arm has done tremendous
        things!
     He has scattered the proud and
        haughty ones.
⁵² He has brought down princes from their
        thrones
     and exalted the humble.
⁵³ He has filled the hungry with good things
     and sent the rich away with
        empty hands.
⁵⁴ He has helped his servant Israel
     and remembered to be merciful.
⁵⁵ For he made this promise to our ancestors,
     to Abraham and his children forever."

⁵⁶ Mary stayed with Elizabeth about three months and then went back to her own home.

THE BIRTH OF JOHN THE BAPTIST

⁵⁷ When it was time for Elizabeth's baby to be born, she gave birth to a son. ⁵⁸ And when her neighbors and relatives heard that the Lord had been very merciful to her, everyone rejoiced with her.

⁵⁹ When the baby was eight days old, they all came for the circumcision ceremony. They wanted to name him Zechariah, after his father. ⁶⁰ But Elizabeth said, "No! His name is John!"

⁶¹ "What?" they exclaimed. "There is no one in all your family by that name." ⁶² So they used gestures to ask the baby's father what he wanted to name him. ⁶³ He motioned for a writing tablet, and to everyone's surprise he wrote, "His name is John." ⁶⁴ Instantly Zechariah could speak again, and he began praising God.

⁶⁵ Awe fell upon the whole neighborhood, and the news of what had happened spread throughout the Judean hills. ⁶⁶ Everyone who heard about it reflected on these events and asked, "What will this child turn out to be?" For the hand of the Lord was surely upon him in a special way.

ZECHARIAH'S PROPHECY

⁶⁷ Then his father, Zechariah, was filled with the Holy Spirit and gave this prophecy:

⁶⁸ "Praise the Lord, the God of Israel,
     because he has visited and redeemed
        his people.

⁶⁹ He has sent us a mighty Savior*
     from the royal line of his servant David,
⁷⁰ just as he promised
     through his holy prophets long ago.
⁷¹ Now we will be saved from our enemies
     and from all who hate us.
⁷² He has been merciful to our ancestors
     by remembering his sacred covenant—
⁷³ the covenant he swore with an oath
     to our ancestor Abraham.
⁷⁴ We have been rescued from our enemies
     so we can serve God without fear,
⁷⁵ in holiness and righteousness
     for as long as we live.

⁷⁶ "And you, my little son,
     will be called the prophet of the Most High,
     because you will prepare the way for
        the Lord.
⁷⁷ You will tell his people how to find salvation
     through forgiveness of their sins.
⁷⁸ Because of God's tender mercy,
     the morning light from heaven is about to
        break upon us,*
⁷⁹ to give light to those who sit in darkness
     and in the shadow of death,
     and to guide us to the path of peace."

⁸⁰ John grew up and became strong in spirit. And he lived in the wilderness until he began his public ministry to Israel.

THE BIRTH OF JESUS

2 At that time the Roman emperor, Augustus, decreed that a census should be taken throughout the Roman Empire. ² (This was the first census taken when Quirinius was governor of Syria.) ³ All returned to their own ancestral towns to register for this census. ⁴ And because Joseph was a descendant of King David, he had to go to Bethlehem in Judea, David's ancient home. He traveled there from the village of Nazareth in Galilee. ⁵ He took with him Mary, to whom he was engaged, who was now expecting a child.

⁶ And while they were there, the time came for her baby to be born. ⁷ She gave birth to her firstborn son. She wrapped him snugly in strips of cloth and laid him in a manger, because there was no lodging available for them.

THE SHEPHERDS AND ANGELS

⁸ That night there were shepherds staying in the fields nearby, guarding their flocks of sheep. ⁹ Suddenly, an angel of the Lord appeared among them, and the radiance of the Lord's glory surrounded them. They were terrified, ¹⁰ but the angel reassured them. "Don't be afraid!" he said. "I bring you good news that will bring great joy to all people. ¹¹ The Savior—yes, the Messiah, the

---

1:69 Greek has raised up a horn of salvation for us.   1:78 Or the Morning Light from Heaven is about to visit us.

THE CHRIST
Luke 2:8-12   ROBERT MORRIS

The word *Christ*, also translated *Messiah*, comes from the Greek word *Christos* and means 'anointed.' In the Old Testament, only three groups of people were anointed: prophets, priests, and kings. In the New Testament, Jesus is the Anointed One. That means He's our Prophet, Priest, *and* King.

In the Old Testament, God usually spoke through prophets. Jesus is now our Prophet, and we can hear God. The Holy Spirit lives within every believer and can speak to us at any time.

In the Old Testament, only the high priests could enter the presence of God. When Jesus came, He became our eternal High Priest, and now we can personally enter the presence of God.

Because Jesus is our King, He rules and reigns over everything in our lives—every situation, family issue, job problem, financial difficulty, emotional struggle, etc. *Everything*. We can live victoriously in every area of our lives!

PEACE ON EARTH
Luke 2:14   ROBERT MORRIS

The angels declared, "Peace on earth" as they announced Jesus' birth to frightened shepherds in the fields. But how can we have peace on our earth today?

1. Recognize you're in a battle.
Satan never takes a break, not even at Christmas. He's constantly reminding us of bad memories and the people we've lost. We need to remember that the battle is real. It's taking place in the spiritual realm, and it must also be fought in the spiritual realm.

2. Stop listening to yourself and start talking to yourself.
You have to quiet your soul (your mind, will, and emotions) and allow your spirit to start talking and rebuking the enemy.

3. Get with God.
You can have peace on your earth because you know the Prince of Peace (Isaiah 9:6). No matter what battle or struggle you're facing, spend time in His presence, and you will have peace in your heart.

Lord—has been born today in Bethlehem, the city of David! [12]And you will recognize him by this sign: You will find a baby wrapped snugly in strips of cloth, lying in a manger."

[13]Suddenly, the angel was joined by a vast host of others—the armies of heaven—praising God and saying,

[14] "Glory to God in highest heaven,
     and peace on earth to those with whom
       God is pleased."

[15]When the angels had returned to heaven, the shepherds said to each other, "Let's go to Bethlehem! Let's see this thing that has happened, which the Lord has told us about."

[16]They hurried to the village and found Mary and Joseph. And there was the baby, lying in the manger. [17]After seeing him, the shepherds told everyone what had happened and what the angel had said to them about this child. [18]All who heard the shepherds' story were astonished, [19]but Mary kept all these things in her heart and thought about them often. [20]The shepherds went back to their flocks, glorifying and praising God for all they had heard and seen. It was just as the angel had told them.

JESUS IS PRESENTED IN THE TEMPLE

[21]Eight days later, when the baby was circumcised, he was named Jesus, the name given him by the angel even before he was conceived.

[22]Then it was time for their purification offering, as required by the law of Moses after the birth of a child; so his parents took him to Jerusalem to present him to the Lord. [23]The law of the Lord says, "If a woman's first child is a boy, he must be dedicated to the LORD."* [24]So they offered the sacrifice required in the law of the Lord—"either a pair of turtledoves or two young pigeons."*

THE PROPHECY OF SIMEON

[25]At that time there was a man in Jerusalem named Simeon. He was righteous and devout and was eagerly waiting for the Messiah to come and rescue Israel. The Holy Spirit was upon him [26]and had revealed to him that he would not die until he had seen the Lord's Messiah. [27]That day the Spirit led him to the Temple. So when Mary and Joseph came to present the baby Jesus to the Lord as the law required, [28]Simeon was there. He took the child in his arms and praised God, saying,

[29] "Sovereign Lord, now let your servant
     die in peace,
     as you have promised.
[30] I have seen your salvation,
[31]   which you have prepared for all people.
[32] He is a light to reveal God to the nations,
     and he is the glory of your people Israel!"

[33]Jesus' parents were amazed at what was being said about him. [34]Then Simeon blessed them, and he said to Mary, the baby's mother, "This child is destined to cause many in Israel to fall, and many others to rise. He has been

sent as a sign from God, but many will oppose him. ³⁵As a result, the deepest thoughts of many hearts will be revealed. And a sword will pierce your very soul."

THE PROPHECY OF ANNA

³⁶Anna, a prophet, was also there in the Temple. She was the daughter of Phanuel from the tribe of Asher, and she was very old. Her husband died when they had been married only seven years. ³⁷Then she lived as a widow to the age of eighty-four.* She never left the Temple but stayed there day and night, worshiping God with fasting and prayer. ³⁸She came along just as Simeon was talking with Mary and Joseph, and she began praising God. She talked about the child to everyone who had been waiting expectantly for God to rescue Jerusalem.

³⁹When Jesus' parents had fulfilled all the requirements of the law of the Lord, they returned home to Nazareth in Galilee. ⁴⁰There the child grew up healthy and strong. He was filled with wisdom, and God's favor was on him.

JESUS SPEAKS WITH THE TEACHERS

⁴¹Every year Jesus' parents went to Jerusalem for the Passover festival. ⁴²When Jesus was twelve years old, they attended the festival as usual. ⁴³After the celebration was over, they started home to Nazareth, but Jesus stayed behind in Jerusalem. His parents didn't miss him at first, ⁴⁴because they assumed he was among the other travelers. But when he didn't show up that evening, they started looking for him among their relatives and friends.

⁴⁵When they couldn't find him, they went back to Jerusalem to search for him there. ⁴⁶Three days later they finally discovered him in the Temple, sitting among the religious teachers, listening to them and asking questions. ⁴⁷All who heard him were amazed at his understanding and his answers.

⁴⁸His parents didn't know what to think. "Son," his mother said to him, "why have you done this to us? Your father and I have been frantic, searching for you everywhere."

⁴⁹"But why did you need to search?" he asked. "Didn't you know that I must be in my Father's house?"* ⁵⁰But they didn't understand what he meant.

⁵¹Then he returned to Nazareth with them and was obedient to them. And his mother stored all these things in her heart.

⁵²Jesus grew in wisdom and in stature and in favor with God and all the people.

JOHN THE BAPTIST PREPARES THE WAY

3 It was now the fifteenth year of the reign of Tiberius, the Roman emperor. Pontius Pilate was governor over Judea; Herod Antipas was ruler* over Galilee; his brother Philip was ruler* over Iturea and Traconitis; Lysanias was ruler

THE EDGE OF REPENTANCE
Luke 3:1-14 JACK HAYFORD

Your spiritual life is like a garden. When you come under God's rule and make Jesus your Lord and King, you till the soil and plant the seed. Over time, though, weeds try to grow between the rows. Jesus will guide you by saying, "You're going to have to stop doing that." He wants you to acknowledge His words of warning and act immediately—cut the weeds.

John the Baptist preached the baptism of repentance in the wilderness. He said, "Every tree that does not produce good fruit will be chopped down and thrown into the fire" (Luke 3:9).

Repentance is the antidote to stop the weeds. There are specific issues in our hearts that need to be cut and rooted out, like lust, unforgiveness, pride, etc. Repentance stops the spread of spiritual disease and cuts down root beliefs and attitudes so we can become more and more like Christ.

over Abilene. ²Annas and Caiaphas were the high priests. At this time a message from God came to John son of Zechariah, who was living in the wilderness. ³Then John went from place to place on both sides of the Jordan River, preaching that people should be baptized to show that they had repented of their sins and turned to God to be forgiven. ⁴Isaiah had spoken of John when he said,

"He is a voice shouting in the wilderness,
'Prepare the way for the Lord's coming!
   Clear the road for him!
⁵ The valleys will be filled,
   and the mountains and hills made level.
The curves will be straightened,
   and the rough places made smooth.
⁶ And then all people will see
   the salvation sent from God.'"*

⁷When the crowds came to John for baptism, he said, "You brood of snakes! Who warned you to flee the coming wrath? ⁸Prove by the way you live that you have repented of your sins and turned to God. Don't just say to each other, 'We're safe, for we are descendants of Abraham.' That means nothing, for I tell you, God can create children of Abraham from these very stones. ⁹Even now the ax of God's judgment is poised, ready to sever the roots of the trees. Yes, every tree that does not produce good fruit will be chopped down and thrown into the fire."

2:37 Or *She had been a widow for eighty-four years.* 2:49 Or *"Didn't you realize that I should be involved with my Father's affairs?"* 3:1a Greek *Herod was tetrarch.* Herod Antipas was a son of King Herod. 3:1b Greek *tetrarch;* also in 3:1c. 3:4-6 Isa 40:3-5 (Greek version).

¹⁰ The crowds asked, "What should we do?"

¹¹ John replied, "If you have two shirts, give one to the poor. If you have food, share it with those who are hungry."

¹² Even corrupt tax collectors came to be baptized and asked, "Teacher, what should we do?"

¹³ He replied, "Collect no more taxes than the government requires."

¹⁴ "What should we do?" asked some soldiers.

John replied, "Don't extort money or make false accusations. And be content with your pay."

¹⁵ Everyone was expecting the Messiah to come soon, and they were eager to know whether John might be the Messiah. ¹⁶ John answered their questions by saying, "I baptize you with* water; but someone is coming soon who is greater than I am—so much greater that I'm not even worthy to be his slave and untie the straps of his sandals. He will baptize you with the Holy Spirit and with fire.* ¹⁷ He is ready to separate the chaff from the wheat with his winnowing fork. Then he will clean up the threshing area, gathering the wheat into his barn but burning the chaff with never-ending fire." ¹⁸ John used many such warnings as he announced the Good News to the people.

¹⁹ John also publicly criticized Herod Antipas, the ruler of Galilee,* for marrying Herodias, his brother's wife, and for many other wrongs he had done. ²⁰ So Herod put John in prison, adding this sin to his many others.

THE BAPTISM OF JESUS

²¹ One day when the crowds were being baptized, Jesus himself was baptized. As he was praying, the heavens opened, ²² and the Holy Spirit, in bodily form, descended on him like a dove. And a voice from heaven said, "You are my dearly loved Son, and you bring me great joy.*"

THE ANCESTORS OF JESUS

²³ Jesus was about thirty years old when he began his public ministry.

Jesus was known as the son of Joseph.
Joseph was the son of Heli.
²⁴ Heli was the son of Matthat.
Matthat was the son of Levi.
Levi was the son of Melki.
Melki was the son of Jannai.
Jannai was the son of Joseph.
²⁵ Joseph was the son of Mattathias.
Mattathias was the son of Amos.
Amos was the son of Nahum.
Nahum was the son of Esli.
Esli was the son of Naggai.
²⁶ Naggai was the son of Maath.
Maath was the son of Mattathias.
Mattathias was the son of Semein.
Semein was the son of Josech.
Josech was the son of Joda.

²⁷ Joda was the son of Joanan.
Joanan was the son of Rhesa.
Rhesa was the son of Zerubbabel.
Zerubbabel was the son of Shealtiel.
Shealtiel was the son of Neri.
²⁸ Neri was the son of Melki.
Melki was the son of Addi.
Addi was the son of Cosam.
Cosam was the son of Elmadam.
Elmadam was the son of Er.
²⁹ Er was the son of Joshua.
Joshua was the son of Eliezer.
Eliezer was the son of Jorim.
Jorim was the son of Matthat.
Matthat was the son of Levi.
³⁰ Levi was the son of Simeon.
Simeon was the son of Judah.
Judah was the son of Joseph.
Joseph was the son of Jonam.
Jonam was the son of Eliakim.
³¹ Eliakim was the son of Melea.
Melea was the son of Menna.
Menna was the son of Mattatha.
Mattatha was the son of Nathan.
Nathan was the son of David.
³² David was the son of Jesse.
Jesse was the son of Obed.
Obed was the son of Boaz.
Boaz was the son of Salmon.*
Salmon was the son of Nahshon.
³³ Nahshon was the son of Amminadab.
Amminadab was the son of Admin.
Admin was the son of Arni.*
Arni was the son of Hezron.
Hezron was the son of Perez.
Perez was the son of Judah.
³⁴ Judah was the son of Jacob.
Jacob was the son of Isaac.
Isaac was the son of Abraham.
Abraham was the son of Terah.
Terah was the son of Nahor.
³⁵ Nahor was the son of Serug.
Serug was the son of Reu.
Reu was the son of Peleg.
Peleg was the son of Eber.
Eber was the son of Shelah.
³⁶ Shelah was the son of Cainan.
Cainan was the son of Arphaxad.
Arphaxad was the son of Shem.
Shem was the son of Noah.
Noah was the son of Lamech.
³⁷ Lamech was the son of Methuselah.
Methuselah was the son of Enoch.
Enoch was the son of Jared.
Jared was the son of Mahalalel.
Mahalalel was the son of Kenan.

3:16a Or in. **3:16b** Or in the Holy Spirit and in fire. **3:19** Greek Herod the tetrarch. **3:22** Some manuscripts read my Son, and today I have become your Father. **3:32** Greek Sala, a variant spelling of Salmon; also in 3:32b. See Ruth 4:20-21. **3:33** Some manuscripts read Amminadab was the son of Aram. Arni and Aram are alternate spellings of Ram. See 1 Chr 2:9-10.

38 Kenan was the son of Enosh.*
Enosh was the son of Seth.
Seth was the son of Adam.
Adam was the son of God.

THE TEMPTATION OF JESUS

4 Then Jesus, full of the Holy Spirit, returned from the Jordan River. He was led by the Spirit in the wilderness,* 2 where he was tempted by the devil for forty days. Jesus ate nothing all that time and became very hungry.

3 Then the devil said to him, "If you are the Son of God, tell this stone to become a loaf of bread."

4 But Jesus told him, "No! The Scriptures say, 'People do not live by bread alone.'*"

5 Then the devil took him up and revealed to him all the kingdoms of the world in a moment of time. 6 "I will give you the glory of these kingdoms and authority over them," the devil said, "because they are mine to give to anyone I please. 7 I will give it all to you if you will worship me."

8 Jesus replied, "The Scriptures say,

'You must worship the LORD your God
    and serve only him.'*"

9 Then the devil took him to Jerusalem, to the highest point of the Temple, and said, "If you are the Son of God, jump off! 10 For the Scriptures say,

'He will order his angels to protect and
    guard you.
11 And they will hold you up with their hands
    so you won't even hurt your foot on
    a stone.'*"

12 Jesus responded, "The Scriptures also say, 'You must not test the LORD your God.'*"

13 When the devil had finished tempting Jesus, he left him until the next opportunity came.

JESUS REJECTED AT NAZARETH

14 Then Jesus returned to Galilee, filled with the Holy Spirit's power. Reports about him spread quickly through the whole region. 15 He taught regularly in their synagogues and was praised by everyone.

16 When he came to the village of Nazareth, his boyhood home, he went as usual to the synagogue on the Sabbath and stood up to read the Scriptures. 17 The scroll of Isaiah the prophet was handed to him. He unrolled the scroll and found the place where this was written:

18 "The Spirit of the LORD is upon me,
    for he has anointed me to bring Good
        News to the poor.
He has sent me to proclaim that captives
        will be released,
    that the blind will see,
    that the oppressed will be set free,

HEALED
Luke 4:14–30   ROBERT MORRIS

If you're saved, then God has healed your spirit. He has made your spirit whole. But what about your soul and body? Does God want to make them whole too? According to the Bible, yes! He does!

1. Physical Healing

In Exodus 15:26, God not only says what He does (heals) but also who He is—*Jehovah Rapha*, the Lord who heals. Over and over again in Scripture, God heals people who have physical sicknesses and diseases. For a few examples, see Exodus 23:25; Deuteronomy 7:15; Psalm 103:2–3; Isaiah 53:4; Matthew 4:23; and John 6:28. Hebrews 13:8 says God never changes, so since He healed in the Old and New Testaments, then He still heals today. Jesus never healed people to draw attention to Himself or to prove He was the Messiah. He healed people because He cared about them, and He cares about you too!

2. Emotional Healing

We wouldn't tell someone with a broken arm to "Get over it!" and we can't say that to someone with a broken heart either. Many people have deep emotional wounds that have never healed. Their hearts have been broken through harsh words, disappointments, and tragedies. The most common and longest lasting wound is *rejection*. Every single person has experienced rejection at some point in life, and this wound can hold us in terrible bondage. But here is the Good News: Jesus came to set you free! He doesn't want you just to cope with your problems—He wants to heal you from them! Will you let Him make you whole in your body, soul, and spirit?

---

19 and that the time of the LORD's favor
        has come.*"

20 He rolled up the scroll, handed it back to the attendant, and sat down. All eyes in the synagogue looked at him intently. 21 Then he began to speak to them. "The Scripture you've just heard has been fulfilled this very day!"

22 Everyone spoke well of him and was amazed by the gracious words that came from his lips. "How can this be?" they asked. "Isn't this Joseph's son?"

23 Then he said, "You will undoubtedly quote me this proverb: 'Physician, heal yourself'—meaning, 'Do miracles here in your hometown like those you did in Capernaum.' 24 But I tell

---

3:38 Greek *Enos*, a variant spelling of Enosh; also in 3:38b. See Gen 5:6. 4:1 Some manuscripts read *into the wilderness.* 4:4 Deut 8:3. 4:8 Deut 6:13. 4:10-11 Ps 91:11-12. 4:12 Deut 6:16. 4:18-19 Or *and to proclaim the acceptable year of the LORD.* Isa 61:1-2 (Greek version); 58:6.

THE MINISTRY OF JESUS
Luke 4:16-19

ROBERT MORRIS

In Luke 4, Jesus tells the people who He really is and what He came to do. Hebrews 13:8 says, "Jesus Christ is the same yesterday, today, and forever," but many churches today preach about a different Jesus. This "Jesus" can save you and get you to heaven, but He doesn't have any power to help you on this earth. Let me be clear—the real Jesus can help you. That's why God sent Him to earth!

Here are the five foundational ministries of Jesus:

1. Salvation
Jesus came to preach the gospel—the Good News—which is this: All people are sinners and completely lost. We cannot do anything to change our situation, so God sent Jesus to die on the cross and redeem us from our sins. Christianity is different from every other religion because it doesn't require you to work your way into heaven. Instead, salvation is by grace through faith. Salvation was the first and primary ministry of Jesus, and it must be ours as well.

2. Healing
Jesus came so "the blind will see" (Luke 4:18). This recovery of sight applies both to spiritual *and* physical healing. Yes, we want to see people healed physically, but we also want to see them no longer oppressed by the devil. Acts 10:38 says, "Jesus went around doing good and healing all who were oppressed by the devil, for God was

with him." Since Jesus doesn't change, He still heals people today.

3. Inner healing
Jesus came to heal broken-hearted people. How many times has your heart been hurt, bruised, or even shattered in a relationship? If your heart and emotions don't get healed properly, they will affect how much you can do on this earth and how you relate to other people. Jesus doesn't teach people how to cope; He sets them free. He wants to heal our hearts completely so we can love and trust again.

4. Deliverance
Jesus came not only to save us from our sins but also to free us from our sins. Demons still exist today, and even believers can be in bondage to spirits of unforgiveness, anger, envy, pride, lying, lust, etc. Demons tried to talk to Jesus, and they will try to speak with you too. It doesn't mean you're a bad person; you just need deliverance. Jesus came to set us free from every evil spirit.

5. Baptism in the Holy Spirit
Jesus did not begin His ministry until He was baptized in the Holy Spirit (Luke 3:21-22). And the last instruction He gave His followers before returning to heaven was to stay in Jerusalem and "receive power when the Holy Spirit comes upon you" (Acts 1:8). If Jesus and His disciples needed the power of the Holy Spirit on earth, how much more do we need that same power?

you the truth, no prophet is accepted in his own hometown.

²⁵"Certainly there were many needy widows in Israel in Elijah's time, when the heavens were closed for three and a half years, and a severe famine devastated the land. ²⁶Yet Elijah was not sent to any of them. He was sent instead to a foreigner—a widow of Zarephath in the land of Sidon. ²⁷And many in Israel had leprosy in the time of the prophet Elisha, but the only one healed was Naaman, a Syrian."

²⁸When they heard this, the people in the synagogue were furious. ²⁹Jumping up, they mobbed him and forced him to the edge of the hill on which the town was built. They intended to push him over the cliff, ³⁰but he passed right through the crowd and went on his way.

JESUS CASTS OUT A DEMON
³¹Then Jesus went to Capernaum, a town in Galilee, and taught there in the synagogue every Sabbath day. ³²There, too, the people were amazed at his teaching, for he spoke with authority.

³³Once when he was in the synagogue, a man possessed by a demon—an evil* spirit—cried out, shouting, ³⁴"Go away! Why are you interfering with us, Jesus of Nazareth? Have you come to

destroy us? I know who you are—the Holy One of God!"

³⁵But Jesus reprimanded him. "Be quiet! Come out of the man," he ordered. At that, the demon threw the man to the floor as the crowd watched; then it came out of him without hurting him further.

³⁶Amazed, the people exclaimed, "What authority and power this man's words possess! Even evil spirits obey him, and they flee at his command!" ³⁷The news about Jesus spread through every village in the entire region.

JESUS HEALS MANY PEOPLE
³⁸After leaving the synagogue that day, Jesus went to Simon's home, where he found Simon's mother-in-law very sick with a high fever. "Please heal her," everyone begged. ³⁹Standing at her bedside, he rebuked the fever, and it left her. And she got up at once and prepared a meal for them.

⁴⁰As the sun went down that evening, people throughout the village brought sick family members to Jesus. No matter what their diseases were, the touch of his hand healed every one.

4:33 Greek *unclean;* also in 4:36.

[41] Many were possessed by demons; and the demons came out at his command, shouting, "You are the Son of God!" But because they knew he was the Messiah, he rebuked them and refused to let them speak.

JESUS CONTINUES TO PREACH

[42] Early the next morning Jesus went out to an isolated place. The crowds searched everywhere for him, and when they finally found him, they begged him not to leave them. [43] But he replied, "I must preach the Good News of the Kingdom of God in other towns, too, because that is why I was sent." [44] So he continued to travel around, preaching in synagogues throughout Judea.*

THE FIRST DISCIPLES

5 One day as Jesus was preaching on the shore of the Sea of Galilee,* great crowds pressed in on him to listen to the word of God. [2] He noticed two empty boats at the water's edge, for the fishermen had left them and were washing their nets. [3] Stepping into one of the boats, Jesus asked Simon,* its owner, to push it out into the water. So he sat in the boat and taught the crowds from there.

[4] When he had finished speaking, he said to Simon, "Now go out where it is deeper, and let down your nets to catch some fish."

[5] "Master," Simon replied, "we worked hard all last night and didn't catch a thing. But if you say so, I'll let the nets down again." [6] And this time their nets were so full of fish they began to tear! [7] A shout for help brought their partners in the other boat, and soon both boats were filled with fish and on the verge of sinking.

[8] When Simon Peter realized what had happened, he fell to his knees before Jesus and said, "Oh, Lord, please leave me—I'm such a sinful man." [9] For he was awestruck by the number of fish they had caught, as were the others with him. [10] His partners, James and John, the sons of Zebedee, were also amazed.

Jesus replied to Simon, "Don't be afraid! From now on you'll be fishing for people!" [11] And as soon as they landed, they left everything and followed Jesus.

JESUS HEALS A MAN WITH LEPROSY

[12] In one of the villages, Jesus met a man with an advanced case of leprosy. When the man saw Jesus, he bowed with his face to the ground, begging to be healed. "Lord," he said, "if you are willing, you can heal me and make me clean." [13] Jesus reached out and touched him. "I am willing," he said. "Be healed!" And instantly the leprosy disappeared. [14] Then Jesus instructed him not to tell anyone what had happened. He said, "Go to the priest and let him examine you. Take along the offering required in the law of Moses for those who have been healed of leprosy.* This will be a public testimony that you have been cleansed."

CHOSEN FOR HIS PURPOSE
Luke 5:1–11   JACK HAYFORD

In Luke 5:8, Peter falls to his knees and says to Jesus, "Oh, Lord, please leave me—I'm such a sinful man." God wants us to see what happens when people seek Him on their knees at His feet. It is there at Jesus' feet that things begin to happen and transformation takes place.

God does not want you to be afraid because of your limitations. As with Peter, He can handle you with all your weaknesses if you give Him everything you have. Don't let anything obstruct the full flow of God's purpose in your life. The biggest miracles happen when a person's whole life is forever changed. The enemy would like to stop you from getting on your knees, but you cannot be afraid to expect God to do great things. Come to Jesus' feet and allow Him to work bigger things than you can ever imagine.

---

[15] But despite Jesus' instructions, the report of his power spread even faster, and vast crowds came to hear him preach and to be healed of their diseases. [16] But Jesus often withdrew to the wilderness for prayer.

JESUS HEALS A PARALYZED MAN

[17] One day while Jesus was teaching, some Pharisees and teachers of religious law were sitting nearby. (It seemed that these men showed up from every village in all Galilee and Judea, as well as from Jerusalem.) And the Lord's healing power was strongly with Jesus. [18] Some men came carrying a paralyzed man on a sleeping mat. They tried to take him inside to Jesus, [19] but they couldn't reach him because of the crowd. So they went up to the roof and took off some tiles. Then they lowered the sick man on his mat down into the crowd, right in front of Jesus. [20] Seeing their faith, Jesus said to the man, "Young man, your sins are forgiven."

[21] But the Pharisees and teachers of religious law said to themselves, "Who does he think he is? That's blasphemy! Only God can forgive sins!"

[22] Jesus knew what they were thinking, so he asked them, "Why do you question this in your hearts? [23] Is it easier to say 'Your sins are forgiven,' or 'Stand up and walk'? [24] So I will prove to you that the Son of Man* has the authority on earth to forgive sins." Then Jesus turned to the paralyzed man and said, "Stand up, pick up your mat, and go home!"

[25] And immediately, as everyone watched, the man jumped up, picked up his mat, and went home praising God. [26] Everyone was gripped

---

4:44 Some manuscripts read *Galilee*. 5:1 Greek *Lake Gennesaret*, another name for the Sea of Galilee. 5:3 *Simon* is called "Peter" in 6:14 and thereafter. 5:14 See Lev 14:2-32. 5:24 "Son of Man" is a title Jesus used for himself.

with great wonder and awe, and they praised God, exclaiming, "We have seen amazing things today!"

JESUS CALLS LEVI (MATTHEW)

[27] Later, as Jesus left the town, he saw a tax collector named Levi sitting at his tax collector's booth. "Follow me and be my disciple," Jesus said to him. [28] So Levi got up, left everything, and followed him.

[29] Later, Levi held a banquet in his home with Jesus as the guest of honor. Many of Levi's fellow tax collectors and other guests also ate with them. [30] But the Pharisees and their teachers of religious law complained bitterly to Jesus' disciples, "Why do you eat and drink with such scum?*"

[31] Jesus answered them, "Healthy people don't need a doctor—sick people do. [32] I have come to call not those who think they are righteous, but those who know they are sinners and need to repent."

A DISCUSSION ABOUT FASTING

[33] One day some people said to Jesus, "John the Baptist's disciples fast and pray regularly, and so do the disciples of the Pharisees. Why are your disciples always eating and drinking?"

[34] Jesus responded, "Do wedding guests fast while celebrating with the groom? Of course not. [35] But someday the groom will be taken away from them, and then they will fast."

[36] Then Jesus gave them this illustration: "No one tears a piece of cloth from a new garment and uses it to patch an old garment. For then the new garment would be ruined, and the new patch wouldn't even match the old garment. [37] "And no one puts new wine into old wineskins. For the new wine would burst the wineskins, spilling the wine and ruining the skins. [38] New wine must be stored in new wineskins. [39] But no one who drinks the old wine seems to want the new wine. 'The old is just fine,' they say."

A DISCUSSION ABOUT THE SABBATH

6 One Sabbath day as Jesus was walking through some grainfields, his disciples broke off heads of grain, rubbed off the husks in their hands, and ate the grain. [2] But some Pharisees said, "Why are you breaking the law by harvesting grain on the Sabbath?"

[3] Jesus replied, "Haven't you read in the Scriptures what David did when he and his companions were hungry? [4] He went into the house of God and broke the law by eating the sacred loaves of bread that only the priests can eat. He also gave some to his companions." [5] And Jesus added, "The Son of Man* is Lord, even over the Sabbath."

JESUS HEALS ON THE SABBATH

[6] On another Sabbath day, a man with a deformed right hand was in the synagogue while Jesus was teaching. [7] The teachers of religious law and the Pharisees watched Jesus closely. If he healed the man's hand, they planned to accuse him of working on the Sabbath.

[8] But Jesus knew their thoughts. He said to the man with the deformed hand, "Come and stand in front of everyone." So the man came forward. [9] Then Jesus said to his critics, "I have a question for you. Does the law permit good deeds on the Sabbath, or is it a day for doing evil? Is this a day to save life or to destroy it?"

[10] He looked around at them one by one and then said to the man, "Hold out your hand." So the man held out his hand, and it was restored! [11] At this, the enemies of Jesus were wild with rage and began to discuss what to do with him.

JESUS CHOOSES THE TWELVE APOSTLES

[12] One day soon afterward Jesus went up on a mountain to pray, and he prayed to God all night. [13] At daybreak he called together all of his disciples and chose twelve of them to be apostles. Here are their names:

[14] Simon (whom he named Peter),
Andrew (Peter's brother),
James,
John,
Philip,
Bartholomew,
[15] Matthew,
Thomas,
James (son of Alphaeus),
Simon (who was called the zealot),
[16] Judas (son of James),
Judas Iscariot (who later betrayed him).

CROWDS FOLLOW JESUS

[17] When they came down from the mountain, the disciples stood with Jesus on a large, level area, surrounded by many of his followers and by the crowds. There were people from all over Judea and from Jerusalem and from as far north as the seacoasts of Tyre and Sidon. [18] They had come to hear him and to be healed of their diseases; and those troubled by evil* spirits were healed. [19] Everyone tried to touch him, because healing power went out from him, and he healed everyone.

THE BEATITUDES

[20] Then Jesus turned to his disciples and said,

"God blesses you who are poor,
	for the Kingdom of God is yours.
[21] God blesses you who are hungry now,
	for you will be satisfied.
God blesses you who weep now,
	for in due time you will laugh.

5:30 Greek *with tax collectors and sinners?*   6:5 "Son of Man" is a title Jesus used for himself.   6:18 Greek *unclean.*

22 What blessings await you when people hate you and exclude you and mock you and curse you as evil because you follow the Son of Man. 23 When that happens, be happy! Yes, leap for joy! For a great reward awaits you in heaven. And remember, their ancestors treated the ancient prophets that same way.

SORROWS FORETOLD

24 "What sorrow awaits you who are rich,
for you have your only happiness now.
25 What sorrow awaits you who are fat and
prosperous now,
for a time of awful hunger awaits you.
What sorrow awaits you who laugh now,
for your laughing will turn to mourning
and sorrow.
26 What sorrow awaits you who are praised
by the crowds,
for their ancestors also praised false
prophets.

LOVE FOR ENEMIES

27 "But to you who are willing to listen, I say, love your enemies! Do good to those who hate you. 28 Bless those who curse you. Pray for those who hurt you. 29 If someone slaps you on one cheek, offer the other cheek also. If someone demands your coat, offer your shirt also. 30 Give to anyone who asks; and when things are taken away from you, don't try to get them back. 31 Do to others as you would like them to do to you.

32 "If you love only those who love you, why should you get credit for that? Even sinners love those who love them! 33 And if you do good only to those who do good to you, why should you get credit? Even sinners do that much! 34 And if you lend money only to those who can repay you, why should you get credit? Even sinners will lend to other sinners for a full return.

35 "Love your enemies! Do good to them. Lend to them without expecting to be repaid. Then your reward from heaven will be very great, and you will truly be acting as children of the Most High, for he is kind to those who are unthankful and wicked. 36 You must be compassionate, just as your Father is compassionate.

DO NOT JUDGE OTHERS

37 "Do not judge others, and you will not be judged. Do not condemn others, or it will all come back against you. Forgive others, and you will be forgiven. 38 Give, and you will receive. Your gift will return to you in full—pressed down, shaken together to make room for more, running over, and poured into your lap. The amount you give will determine the amount you get back.*"

39 Then Jesus gave the following illustration: "Can one blind person lead another? Won't they both fall into a ditch? 40 Students* are not greater than their teacher. But the student who is fully trained will become like the teacher.

41 "And why worry about a speck in your friend's eye* when you have a log in your own? 42 How can you think of saying, 'Friend,* let me help you get rid of that speck in your eye,' when you can't see past the log in your own eye? Hypocrite! First get rid of the log in your own eye; then you will see well enough to deal with the speck in your friend's eye.

THE TREE AND ITS FRUIT

43 "A good tree can't produce bad fruit, and a bad tree can't produce good fruit. 44 A tree is identified by its fruit. Figs are never gathered from thornbushes, and grapes are not picked from bramble bushes. 45 A good person produces good things from the treasury of a good heart, and an evil person produces evil things from the treasury of an evil heart. What you say flows from what is in your heart.

BUILDING ON A SOLID FOUNDATION

46 "So why do you keep calling me 'Lord, Lord!' when you don't do what I say? 47 I will show you what it's like when someone comes to me, listens to my teaching, and then follows it. 48 It is like a person building a house who digs deep and lays the foundation on solid rock. When the floodwaters rise and break against that house, it stands firm because it is well built. 49 But anyone who hears and doesn't obey is like a person who builds a house right on the ground, without a foundation. When the floods sweep down against that house, it will collapse into a heap of ruins."

IT'S ALL ABOUT THE HEART
Luke 6:38   ROBERT MORRIS

Many people read Luke 6:38 and think Jesus is talking only about money: "Give, and you will receive. Your gift will return to you in full—pressed down, shaken together to make room for more, running over, and poured into your lap." While this verse does apply to our finances, it also applies to forgiveness, mercy, understanding, and patience.

We must remember that God does not bless the mere act of giving; rather, He blesses giving from a right heart attitude. Personal gain should not be our motivation. When you were born in the natural, you were born selfish. But when you were born again into God's family, you were born generous. Genuine gratitude is powerful, and a heart of gratitude is vital for creating a lifestyle of generosity. Joy-filled giving is what God desires from us. God wants us to be generous in our giving because He is generous in His.

6:38 Or *The measure you give will be the measure you get back.*
6:40 Or *Disciples.* 6:41 Greek *your brother's eye;* also in 6:42.
6:42 Greek *Brother.*

THE FAITH OF A ROMAN OFFICER

7 When Jesus had finished saying all this to the people, he returned to Capernaum. ²At that time the highly valued slave of a Roman officer* was sick and near death. ³When the officer heard about Jesus, he sent some respected Jewish elders to ask him to come and heal his slave. ⁴So they earnestly begged Jesus to help the man. "If anyone deserves your help, he does," they said, ⁵"for he loves the Jewish people and even built a synagogue for us."

⁶So Jesus went with them. But just before they arrived at the house, the officer sent some friends to say, "Lord, don't trouble yourself by coming to my home, for I am not worthy of such an honor. ⁷I am not even worthy to come and meet you. Just say the word from where you are, and my servant will be healed. ⁸I know this because I am under the authority of my superior officers, and I have authority over my soldiers. I only need to say, 'Go,' and they go, or 'Come,' and they come. And if I say to my slaves, 'Do this,' they do it."

⁹When Jesus heard this, he was amazed. Turning to the crowd that was following him, he said, "I tell you, I haven't seen faith like this in all Israel!" ¹⁰And when the officer's friends returned to his house, they found the slave completely healed.

JESUS RAISES A WIDOW'S SON

¹¹Soon afterward Jesus went with his disciples to the village of Nain, and a large crowd followed him. ¹²A funeral procession was coming out as he approached the village gate. The young man who had died was a widow's only son, and a large crowd from the village was with her. ¹³When the Lord saw her, his heart overflowed with compassion. "Don't cry!" he said. ¹⁴Then he walked over to the coffin and touched it, and the bearers stopped. "Young man," he said, "I tell you, get up." ¹⁵Then the dead boy sat up and began to talk! And Jesus gave him back to his mother.

¹⁶Great fear swept the crowd, and they praised God, saying, "A mighty prophet has risen among us," and "God has visited his people today." ¹⁷And the news about Jesus spread throughout Judea and the surrounding countryside.

JESUS AND JOHN THE BAPTIST

¹⁸The disciples of John the Baptist told John about everything Jesus was doing. So John called for two of his disciples, ¹⁹and he sent them to the Lord to ask him, "Are you the Messiah we've been expecting,* or should we keep looking for someone else?"

²⁰John's two disciples found Jesus and said to him, "John the Baptist sent us to ask, 'Are you the Messiah we've been expecting, or should we keep looking for someone else?'"

²¹At that very time, Jesus cured many people of their diseases, illnesses, and evil spirits, and he restored sight to many who were blind. ²²Then he told John's disciples, "Go back to John and tell him what you have seen and heard—the blind see, the lame walk, those with leprosy are cured, the deaf hear, the dead are raised to life, and the Good News is being preached to the poor." ²³And he added, "God blesses those who do not fall away because of me.*"

²⁴After John's disciples left, Jesus began talking about him to the crowds. "What kind of man did you go into the wilderness to see? Was he a weak reed, swayed by every breath of wind? ²⁵Or were you expecting to see a man dressed in expensive clothes? No, people who wear beautiful clothes and live in luxury are found in palaces. ²⁶Were you looking for a prophet? Yes, and he is more than a prophet. ²⁷John is the man to whom the Scriptures refer when they say,

'Look, I am sending my messenger ahead of you,
    and he will prepare your way before you.'*

²⁸I tell you, of all who have ever lived, none is greater than John. Yet even the least person in the Kingdom of God is greater than he is!"

²⁹When they heard this, all the people—even the tax collectors—agreed that God's way was right,* for they had been baptized by John. ³⁰But the Pharisees and experts in religious law rejected God's plan for them, for they had refused John's baptism.

³¹"To what can I compare the people of this generation?" Jesus asked. "How can I describe them? ³²They are like children playing a game in the public square. They complain to their friends,

'We played wedding songs,
    and you didn't dance,
so we played funeral songs,
    and you didn't weep.'

³³For John the Baptist didn't spend his time eating bread or drinking wine, and you say, 'He's possessed by a demon.' ³⁴The Son of Man,* on the other hand, feasts and drinks, and you say, 'He's a glutton and a drunkard, and a friend of tax collectors and other sinners!' ³⁵But wisdom is shown to be right by the lives of those who follow it.*"

JESUS ANOINTED BY A SINFUL WOMAN

³⁶One of the Pharisees asked Jesus to have dinner with him, so Jesus went to his home and sat down to eat.* ³⁷When a certain immoral woman from that city heard he was eating there, she brought a beautiful alabaster jar filled with expensive perfume. ³⁸Then she knelt behind him

at his feet, weeping. Her tears fell on his feet, and she wiped them off with her hair. Then she kept kissing his feet and putting perfume on them.

[39] When the Pharisee who had invited him saw this, he said to himself, "If this man were a prophet, he would know what kind of woman is touching him. She's a sinner!"

[40] Then Jesus answered his thoughts. "Simon," he said to the Pharisee, "I have something to say to you."

"Go ahead, Teacher," Simon replied.

[41] Then Jesus told him this story: "A man loaned money to two people—500 pieces of silver* to one and 50 pieces to the other. [42] But neither of them could repay him, so he kindly forgave them both, canceling their debts. Who do you suppose loved him more after that?"

[43] Simon answered, "I suppose the one for whom he canceled the larger debt."

"That's right," Jesus said. [44] Then he turned to the woman and said to Simon, "Look at this woman kneeling here. When I entered your home, you didn't offer me water to wash the dust from my feet, but she has washed them with her tears and wiped them with her hair. [45] You didn't greet me with a kiss, but from the time I first came in, she has not stopped kissing my feet. [46] You neglected the courtesy of olive oil to anoint my head, but she has anointed my feet with rare perfume.

[47] "I tell you, her sins—and they are many—have been forgiven, so she has shown me much love. But a person who is forgiven little shows only little love." [48] Then Jesus said to the woman, "Your sins are forgiven."

[49] The men at the table said among themselves, "Who is this man, that he goes around forgiving sins?"

[50] And Jesus said to the woman, "Your faith has saved you; go in peace."

WOMEN WHO FOLLOWED JESUS

8 Soon afterward Jesus began a tour of the nearby towns and villages, preaching and announcing the Good News about the Kingdom of God. He took his twelve disciples with him, [2] along with some women who had been cured of evil spirits and diseases. Among them were Mary Magdalene, from whom he had cast out seven demons; [3] Joanna, the wife of Chuza, Herod's business manager; Susanna; and many others who were contributing from their own resources to support Jesus and his disciples.

PARABLE OF THE FARMER SCATTERING SEED

[4] One day Jesus told a story in the form of a parable to a large crowd that had gathered from many towns to hear him: [5] "A farmer went out to plant his seed. As he scattered it across his field, some seed fell on a footpath, where it was stepped on, and the birds ate it. [6] Other seed fell among

---

PREPARING THE SOIL
Luke 8:4-15　　　ROBERT MORRIS

What kind of soil do you have? This may sound like a question about gardening, but it's actually a question about your heart. In the parable of the farmer scattering seed, Jesus says, "The seeds that fell on the good soil represent honest, good-hearted people who hear God's word, cling to it, and patiently produce a huge harvest" (Luke 8:15). The soil in this parable is a metaphor for the heart. When we have a good heart, God's Word can do its work in us, and we can bear fruit.

We have to be careful to protect our hearts from becoming hardened. When we enter God's presence through praise and worship, pride and pain are stripped away, and our hearts begin to soften. Telling God how much we love Him opens our hearts so we can receive what His Word has to say.

---

rocks. It began to grow, but the plant soon wilted and died for lack of moisture. [7] Other seed fell among thorns that grew up with it and choked out the tender plants. [8] Still other seed fell on fertile soil. This seed grew and produced a crop that was a hundred times as much as had been planted!" When he had said this, he called out, "Anyone with ears to hear should listen and understand."

[9] His disciples asked him what this parable meant. [10] He replied, "You are permitted to understand the secrets* of the Kingdom of God. But I use parables to teach the others so that the Scriptures might be fulfilled:

'When they look, they won't really see.
When they hear, they won't understand.'*

[11] "This is the meaning of the parable: The seed is God's word. [12] The seeds that fell on the footpath represent those who hear the message, only to have the devil come and take it away from their hearts and prevent them from believing and being saved. [13] The seeds on the rocky soil represent those who hear the message and receive it with joy. But since they don't have deep roots, they believe for a while, then they fall away when they face temptation. [14] The seeds that fell among the thorns represent those who hear the message, but all too quickly the message is crowded out by the cares and riches and pleasures of this life. And so they never grow into maturity. [15] And the seeds that fell on the good soil represent honest, good-hearted people who hear God's word, cling to it, and patiently produce a huge harvest.

7:41 Greek *500 denarii.* A denarius was equivalent to a laborer's full day's wage.　**8:10a** Greek *mysteries.*　**8:10b** Isa 6:9 (Greek version).

LUKE 8:41 | 891

PARABLE OF THE LAMP

¹⁶ "No one lights a lamp and then covers it with a bowl or hides it under a bed. A lamp is placed on a stand, where its light can be seen by all who enter the house. ¹⁷ For all that is secret will eventually be brought into the open, and everything that is concealed will be brought to light and made known to all.

¹⁸ "So pay attention to how you hear. To those who listen to my teaching, more understanding will be given. But for those who are not listening, even what they think they understand will be taken away from them."

THE TRUE FAMILY OF JESUS

¹⁹ Then Jesus' mother and brothers came to see him, but they couldn't get to him because of the crowd. ²⁰ Someone told Jesus, "Your mother and your brothers are standing outside, and they want to see you."

²¹ Jesus replied, "My mother and my brothers are all those who hear God's word and obey it."

JESUS CALMS THE STORM

²² One day Jesus said to his disciples, "Let's cross to the other side of the lake." So they got into a boat and started out. ²³ As they sailed across, Jesus settled down for a nap. But soon a fierce storm came down on the lake. The boat was filling with water, and they were in real danger.

²⁴ The disciples went and woke him up, shouting, "Master, Master, we're going to drown!"

When Jesus woke up, he rebuked the wind and the raging waves. Suddenly the storm stopped and all was calm. ²⁵ Then he asked them, "Where is your faith?"

The disciples were terrified and amazed. "Who is this man?" they asked each other.

WHAT'S IN A TOUCH?
Luke 8:41-47   OLEN GRIFFING

If you have a problem, you are a candidate for a miracle. God wants to set us free for His glorious purpose, and this happens when we touch Jesus.

The woman with constant bleeding had a strategy. She heard about the power of Jesus, and she was determined to touch Him. In the same way, God wants you to determine a strategy through prayer for your own needs and then press forward. That is exactly what this woman did, and she received her miracle. Begin to pursue God's touch in your life, and you will find yourself on the road to a miracle.

God has a solution for every problem you face. His power is able to do the miraculous in your life. When you intentionally connect to God's power, you will experience complete wholeness—in body, soul, and spirit. Press into Jesus for His touch and never give up.

"When he gives a command, even the wind and waves obey him!"

JESUS HEALS A DEMON-POSSESSED MAN

²⁶ So they arrived in the region of the Gerasenes,* across the lake from Galilee. ²⁷ As Jesus was climbing out of the boat, a man who was possessed by demons came out to meet him. For a long time he had been homeless and naked, living in the tombs outside the town.

²⁸ As soon as he saw Jesus, he shrieked and fell down in front of him. Then he screamed, "Why are you interfering with me, Jesus, Son of the Most High God? Please, I beg you, don't torture me!" ²⁹ For Jesus had already commanded the evil* spirit to come out of him. This spirit had often taken control of the man. Even when he was placed under guard and put in chains and shackles, he simply broke them and rushed out into the wilderness, completely under the demon's power.

³⁰ Jesus demanded, "What is your name?"

"Legion," he replied, for he was filled with many demons. ³¹ The demons kept begging Jesus not to send them into the bottomless pit.*

³² There happened to be a large herd of pigs feeding on the hillside nearby, and the demons begged him to let them enter into the pigs.

So Jesus gave them permission. ³³ Then the demons came out of the man and entered the pigs, and the entire herd plunged down the steep hillside into the lake and drowned.

³⁴ When the herdsmen saw it, they fled to the nearby town and the surrounding countryside, spreading the news as they ran. ³⁵ People rushed out to see what had happened. A crowd soon gathered around Jesus, and they saw the man who had been freed from the demons. He was sitting at Jesus' feet, fully clothed and perfectly sane, and they were all afraid. ³⁶ Then those who had seen what happened told the others how the demon-possessed man had been healed. ³⁷ And all the people in the region of the Gerasenes begged Jesus to go away and leave them alone, for a great wave of fear swept over them.

So Jesus returned to the boat and left, crossing back to the other side of the lake. ³⁸ The man who had been freed from the demons begged to go with him. But Jesus sent him home, saying, ³⁹ "No, go back to your family, and tell them everything God has done for you." So he went all through the town proclaiming the great things Jesus had done for him.

JESUS HEALS IN RESPONSE TO FAITH

⁴⁰ On the other side of the lake the crowds welcomed Jesus, because they had been waiting for him. ⁴¹ Then a man named Jairus, a leader of

8:26 Other manuscripts read *Gadarenes;* still others read *Gergesenes;* also in 8:37. See Matt 8:28; Mark 5:1. 8:29 Greek *unclean.* 8:31 Or *the abyss,* or *the underworld.*

MY CHRISTIAN CALLING
Luke 9:1   ROBERT MORRIS

When I think of *calling*, I think of Jesus calling the disciples. He called 12 men to be His followers, and He also calls you and me. Here are three words to help us better understand what it means to follow Jesus:

1. Knowing
Jesus called the disciples to preach the gospel, cast out demons, and heal the sick (Luke 9:1-2). But before He called them to do those things, Jesus called the men to "accompany him"—to *be with* Him (Mark 3:14). Being with Jesus was their number one priority, and as Christians, this is our first and primary calling too. We have no power to preach, heal, or cast anything out without Him. Like extension cords, we have no power within ourselves. We are only effective when we are plugged into the Source.

2. Growing
In John 15:5, Jesus says, "I am the vine; you are the branches." Branches can only grow and bear fruit if they are connected to a living source. Second Peter 3:18 says, "You must grow in the grace and knowledge of our Lord and Savior Jesus Christ." As believers, growing is part of our calling, no matter how long we have been saved. We should all desire God's Word in the same way a new baby desires milk (1 Peter 2:2).

3. Glowing
We are not the light, but we know the Light—Jesus (John 8:12). The more we know Him, the more He shines through us and the more we reflect Him, just as the moon reflects the sun. All Christians have been called to bring light to this dark world. But we will only glow when we grow, and we will only grow when we know Jesus.

the local synagogue, came and fell at Jesus' feet, pleading with him to come home with him. ⁴²His only daughter,* who was about twelve years old, was dying.

As Jesus went with him, he was surrounded by the crowds. ⁴³A woman in the crowd had suffered for twelve years with constant bleeding,* and she could find no cure. ⁴⁴Coming up behind Jesus, she touched the fringe of his robe. Immediately, the bleeding stopped.

⁴⁵"Who touched me?" Jesus asked.

Everyone denied it, and Peter said, "Master, this whole crowd is pressing up against you."

⁴⁶But Jesus said, "Someone deliberately touched me, for I felt healing power go out from me." ⁴⁷When the woman realized that she could not stay hidden, she began to tremble and fell to her knees in front of him. The whole crowd heard her explain why she had touched him and that

she had been immediately healed. ⁴⁸"Daughter," he said to her, "your faith has made you well. Go in peace."

⁴⁹While he was still speaking to her, a messenger arrived from the home of Jairus, the leader of the synagogue. He told him, "Your daughter is dead. There's no use troubling the Teacher now."

⁵⁰But when Jesus heard what had happened, he said to Jairus, "Don't be afraid. Just have faith, and she will be healed."

⁵¹When they arrived at the house, Jesus wouldn't let anyone go in with him except Peter, John, James, and the little girl's father and mother. ⁵²The house was filled with people weeping and wailing, but he said, "Stop the weeping! She isn't dead; she's only asleep."

⁵³But the crowd laughed at him because they all knew she had died. ⁵⁴Then Jesus took her by the hand and said in a loud voice, "My child, get up!" ⁵⁵And at that moment her life* returned, and she immediately stood up! Then Jesus told them to give her something to eat. ⁵⁶Her parents were overwhelmed, but Jesus insisted that they not tell anyone what had happened.

JESUS SENDS OUT THE TWELVE DISCIPLES

9 One day Jesus called together his twelve disciples* and gave them power and authority to cast out all demons and to heal all diseases. ²Then he sent them out to tell everyone about the Kingdom of God and to heal the sick. ³"Take nothing for your journey," he instructed them. "Don't take a walking stick, a traveler's bag, food, money,* or even a change of clothes. ⁴Wherever you go, stay in the same house until you leave town. ⁵And if a town refuses to welcome you, shake its dust from your feet as you leave to show that you have abandoned those people to their fate."

⁶So they began their circuit of the villages, preaching the Good News and healing the sick.

HEROD'S CONFUSION

⁷When Herod Antipas, the ruler of Galilee,* heard about everything Jesus was doing, he was puzzled. Some were saying that John the Baptist had been raised from the dead. ⁸Others thought Jesus was Elijah or one of the other prophets risen from the dead.

⁹"I beheaded John," Herod said, "so who is this man about whom I hear such stories?" And he kept trying to see him.

JESUS FEEDS FIVE THOUSAND

¹⁰When the apostles returned, they told Jesus everything they had done. Then he slipped quietly away with them toward the town of

---

8:42 Or *His only child, a daughter.*   8:43 Some manuscripts add *having spent everything she had on doctors.*   8:55 Or *her spirit.*   9:1 Greek *the Twelve;* other manuscripts read *the twelve apostles.*   9:3 Or *silver coins.*   9:7 Greek *Herod the tetrarch.* Herod Antipas was a son of King Herod and was ruler over Galilee.

THE PRINCIPLE OF MULTIPLICATION
Luke 9:10-17 ROBERT MORRIS

Have you ever watched 12 guys try to organize 5,000 men plus women and children into groups of 50? Herding cats across Texas would be a breeze by comparison. Even more miraculously, Jesus used two fish and five loaves of bread to satisfy the entire crowd, and there were enough leftovers to fill 12 baskets.

The principle of multiplication requires that *something must be blessed before it can multiply*. The way our money is blessed and redeemed is by giving our firstfruits (the tithe). Jesus receives our tithes, and He is the only One with the power to bless them so they can multiply.

Additionally, *only what is given away can multiply*. If the disciples had simply kept the food for themselves, it would never have multiplied. It's when we give over and above our tithe that our finances have the potential to multiply.

Bethsaida. [11] But the crowds found out where he was going, and they followed him. He welcomed them and taught them about the Kingdom of God, and he healed those who were sick.

[12] Late in the afternoon the twelve disciples came to him and said, "Send the crowds away to the nearby villages and farms, so they can find food and lodging for the night. There is nothing to eat here in this remote place."

[13] But Jesus said, "You feed them."

"But we have only five loaves of bread and two fish," they answered. "Or are you expecting us to go and buy enough food for this whole crowd?" [14] For there were about 5,000 men there.

Jesus replied, "Tell them to sit down in groups of about fifty each." [15] So the people all sat down. [16] Jesus took the five loaves and two fish, looked up toward heaven, and blessed them. Then, breaking the loaves into pieces, he kept giving the bread and fish to the disciples so they could distribute it to the people. [17] They all ate as much as they wanted, and afterward, the disciples picked up twelve baskets of leftovers!

PETER'S DECLARATION ABOUT JESUS
[18] One day Jesus left the crowds to pray alone. Only his disciples were with him, and he asked them, "Who do people say I am?"

[19] "Well," they replied, "some say John the Baptist, some say Elijah, and others say you are one of the other ancient prophets risen from the dead."

[20] Then he asked them, "But who do you say I am?"

Peter replied, "You are the Messiah* sent from God!"

JESUS PREDICTS HIS DEATH
[21] Jesus warned his disciples not to tell anyone who he was. [22] "The Son of Man* must suffer many terrible things," he said. "He will be rejected by the elders, the leading priests, and the teachers of religious law. He will be killed, but on the third day he will be raised from the dead."

[23] Then he said to the crowd, "If any of you wants to be my follower, you must give up your own way, take up your cross daily, and follow me. [24] If you try to hang on to your life, you will lose it. But if you give up your life for my sake, you will save it. [25] And what do you benefit if you gain the whole world but are yourself lost or destroyed? [26] If anyone is ashamed of me and my message, the Son of Man will be ashamed of that person when he returns in his glory and in the glory of the Father and the holy angels. [27] I tell you the truth, some standing here right now will not die before they see the Kingdom of God."

THE TRANSFIGURATION
[28] About eight days later Jesus took Peter, John, and James up on a mountain to pray. [29] And as he was praying, the appearance of his face was transformed, and his clothes became dazzling white. [30] Suddenly, two men, Moses and Elijah, appeared and began talking with Jesus. [31] They were glorious to see. And they were speaking about his exodus from this world, which was about to be fulfilled in Jerusalem.

[32] Peter and the others had fallen asleep. When they woke up, they saw Jesus' glory and the two men standing with him. [33] As Moses and Elijah were starting to leave, Peter, not even knowing what he was saying, blurted out, "Master, it's wonderful for us to be here! Let's make three shelters as memorials*—one for you, one for Moses, and one for Elijah." [34] But even as he was saying this, a cloud overshadowed them, and terror gripped them as the cloud covered them.

[35] Then a voice from the cloud said, "This is my Son, my Chosen One.* Listen to him." [36] When the voice finished, Jesus was there alone. They didn't tell anyone at that time what they had seen.

JESUS HEALS A DEMON-POSSESSED BOY
[37] The next day, after they had come down the mountain, a large crowd met Jesus. [38] A man in the crowd called out to him, "Teacher, I beg you to look at my son, my only child. [39] An evil spirit keeps seizing him, making him scream. It throws him into convulsions so that he foams at the mouth. It batters him and hardly ever leaves him alone. [40] I begged your disciples to cast out the spirit, but they couldn't do it."

9:20 Or *the Christ. Messiah* (a Hebrew term) and *Christ* (a Greek term) both mean "anointed one." 9:22 "Son of Man" is a title Jesus used for himself. 9:33 Greek *three tabernacles.* 9:35 Some manuscripts read *This is my dearly loved Son.*

⁴¹Jesus said, "You faithless and corrupt people! How long must I be with you and put up with you?" Then he said to the man, "Bring your son here."

⁴²As the boy came forward, the demon knocked him to the ground and threw him into a violent convulsion. But Jesus rebuked the evil* spirit and healed the boy. Then he gave him back to his father. ⁴³Awe gripped the people as they saw this majestic display of God's power.

JESUS AGAIN PREDICTS HIS DEATH

While everyone was marveling at everything he was doing, Jesus said to his disciples, ⁴⁴"Listen to me and remember what I say. The Son of Man is going to be betrayed into the hands of his enemies." ⁴⁵But they didn't know what he meant. Its significance was hidden from them, so they couldn't understand it, and they were afraid to ask him about it.

THE GREATEST IN THE KINGDOM

⁴⁶Then his disciples began arguing about which of them was the greatest. ⁴⁷But Jesus knew their thoughts, so he brought a little child to his side. ⁴⁸Then he said to them, "Anyone who welcomes a little child like this on my behalf* welcomes me, and anyone who welcomes me also welcomes my Father who sent me. Whoever is the least among you is the greatest."

USING THE NAME OF JESUS

⁴⁹John said to Jesus, "Master, we saw someone using your name to cast out demons, but we told him to stop because he isn't in our group."

⁵⁰But Jesus said, "Don't stop him! Anyone who is not against you is for you."

OPPOSITION FROM SAMARITANS

⁵¹As the time drew near for him to ascend to heaven, Jesus resolutely set out for Jerusalem. ⁵²He sent messengers ahead to a Samaritan village to prepare for his arrival. ⁵³But the people of the village did not welcome Jesus because he was on his way to Jerusalem. ⁵⁴When James and John saw this, they said to Jesus, "Lord, should we call down fire from heaven to burn them up*?" ⁵⁵But Jesus turned and rebuked them.* ⁵⁶So they went on to another village.

THE COST OF FOLLOWING JESUS

⁵⁷As they were walking along, someone said to Jesus, "I will follow you wherever you go."

⁵⁸But Jesus replied, "Foxes have dens to live in, and birds have nests, but the Son of Man has no place even to lay his head."

⁵⁹He said to another person, "Come, follow me." The man agreed, but he said, "Lord, first let me return home and bury my father."

⁶⁰But Jesus told him, "Let the spiritually dead bury their own dead!* Your duty is to go and preach about the Kingdom of God."

⁶¹Another said, "Yes, Lord, I will follow you, but first let me say good-bye to my family."

⁶²But Jesus told him, "Anyone who puts a hand to the plow and then looks back is not fit for the Kingdom of God."

JESUS SENDS OUT HIS DISCIPLES

10 The Lord now chose seventy-two* other disciples and sent them ahead in pairs to all the towns and places he planned to visit. ²These were his instructions to them: "The harvest is great, but the workers are few. So pray to the Lord who is in charge of the harvest; ask him to send more workers into his fields. ³Now go, and remember that I am sending you out as lambs among wolves. ⁴Don't take any money with you, nor a traveler's bag, nor an extra pair of sandals. And don't stop to greet anyone on the road.

⁵"Whenever you enter someone's home, first say, 'May God's peace be on this house.' ⁶If those who live there are peaceful, the blessing will stand; if they are not, the blessing will return to you. ⁷Don't move around from home to home. Stay in one place, eating and drinking what they provide. Don't hesitate to accept hospitality, because those who work deserve their pay.

⁸"If you enter a town and it welcomes you, eat whatever is set before you. ⁹Heal the sick, and tell them, 'The Kingdom of God is near you now.' ¹⁰But if a town refuses to welcome you, go out into its streets and say, ¹¹'We wipe even the dust of your town from our feet to show that we have abandoned you to your fate. And know this—the Kingdom of God is near!' ¹²I assure you, even wicked Sodom will be better off than such a town on judgment day.

¹³"What sorrow awaits you, Korazin and Bethsaida! For if the miracles I did in you had been done in wicked Tyre and Sidon, their people would have repented of their sins long ago, clothing themselves in burlap and throwing ashes on their heads to show their remorse. ¹⁴Yes, Tyre and Sidon will be better off on judgment day than you. ¹⁵And you people of Capernaum, will you be honored in heaven? No, you will go down to the place of the dead.*"

¹⁶Then he said to the disciples, "Anyone who accepts your message is also accepting me. And anyone who rejects you is rejecting me. And anyone who rejects me is rejecting God, who sent me."

¹⁷When the seventy-two disciples returned, they joyfully reported to him, "Lord, even the demons obey us when we use your name!"

¹⁸"Yes," he told them, "I saw Satan fall from heaven like lightning! ¹⁹Look, I have given you

9:42 Greek *unclean.* 9:48 Greek *in my name.* 9:54 Some manuscripts add *as Elijah did.* 9:55 Some manuscripts add an expanded conclusion to verse 55 and an additional sentence in verse 56: *And he said, "You don't realize what your hearts are like.* ⁵⁶*For the Son of Man has not come to destroy people's lives, but to save them."* 9:60 Greek *Let the dead bury their own dead.* 10:1 Some manuscripts read *seventy;* also in 10:17. 10:15 Greek *to Hades.*

UNDER THE INFLUENCE
Luke 10:17-20 ROBERT MORRIS

To be free as God intends us to be, we must understand three things:

1. There really are demons.

When Satan rebelled against God, he was cast out of heaven, and one-third of the angels fell with him. These fallen angels are called demons. Mark 5 tells about a man under the influence of a multitude of demons and how this bondage affected him.

2. Demons really do enter people.

Demons have one purpose: to steal, kill, and destroy (John 10:10). A Christian cannot be possessed by a demon in the sense of being *owned*, but a Christian can be under the control or influence of a demon.

3. Jesus really does cast demons out.

Jesus cast out demons when He ministered to people, and He has empowered us to do the same. He declares, "I have given you authority over all the power of the enemy" (Luke 10:19).

BECOMING ONE SOUL
Luke 10:25-28 JIMMY EVANS

If you are married, God wants you and your spouse to become soul mates. True love is not just an emotion. It flows out of your total being—body, soul, and spirit. Becoming soul mates is based on choices, such as demonstrating empathy, being generous, and making your spouse a priority.

Don't believe soul mate lies that set you up for disappointment and failure. Some of these lies include:
— Your soul mate will be just like you.
— If you marry your soul mate, you won't have any big problems and will always be in love.
— Your soul mate will always make you happy and meet all of your needs.

God wants you to enjoy a lifelong marriage with your soul mate. Basic compatibility—in terms of shared faith and values—is important, but in the long run, it will be your choices that will determine the success of your marriage.

authority over all the power of the enemy, and you can walk among snakes and scorpions and crush them. Nothing will injure you. ²⁰But don't rejoice because evil spirits obey you; rejoice because your names are registered in heaven."

JESUS' PRAYER OF THANKSGIVING
²¹At that same time Jesus was filled with the joy of the Holy Spirit, and he said, "O Father, Lord of heaven and earth, thank you for hiding these things from those who think themselves wise and clever, and for revealing them to the childlike. Yes, Father, it pleased you to do it this way. ²²My Father has entrusted everything to me. No one truly knows the Son except the Father, and no one truly knows the Father except the Son and those to whom the Son chooses to reveal him."

²³Then when they were alone, he turned to the disciples and said, "Blessed are the eyes that see what you have seen. ²⁴I tell you, many prophets and kings longed to see what you see, but they didn't see it. And they longed to hear what you hear, but they didn't hear it."

THE MOST IMPORTANT COMMANDMENT
²⁵One day an expert in religious law stood up to test Jesus by asking him this question: "Teacher, what should I do to inherit eternal life?"

²⁶Jesus replied, "What does the law of Moses say? How do you read it?"

²⁷The man answered, "'You must love the LORD your God with all your heart, all your soul, all your strength, and all your mind.' And, 'Love your neighbor as yourself.'"*

²⁸"Right!" Jesus told him. "Do this and you will live!"

²⁹The man wanted to justify his actions, so he asked Jesus, "And who is my neighbor?"

PARABLE OF THE GOOD SAMARITAN
³⁰Jesus replied with a story: "A Jewish man was traveling from Jerusalem down to Jericho, and he was attacked by bandits. They stripped him of his clothes, beat him up, and left him half dead beside the road.

³¹"By chance a priest came along. But when he saw the man lying there, he crossed to the other side of the road and passed him by. ³²A Temple assistant* walked over and looked at him lying there, but he also passed by on the other side.

³³"Then a despised Samaritan came along, and when he saw the man, he felt compassion for him. ³⁴Going over to him, the Samaritan soothed his wounds with olive oil and wine and bandaged them. Then he put the man on his own donkey and took him to an inn, where he took care of him. ³⁵The next day he handed the innkeeper two silver coins,* telling him, 'Take care of this man. If his bill runs higher than this, I'll pay you the next time I'm here.'

³⁶"Now which of these three would you say was a neighbor to the man who was attacked by bandits?" Jesus asked.

³⁷The man replied, "The one who showed him mercy."

Then Jesus said, "Yes, now go and do the same."

10:27 Deut 6:5; Lev 19:18. 10:32 Greek *A Levite*. 10:35 Greek *two denarii*. A denarius was equivalent to a laborer's full day's wage.

JESUS VISITS MARTHA AND MARY

38 As Jesus and the disciples continued on their way to Jerusalem, they came to a certain village where a woman named Martha welcomed him into her home. 39 Her sister, Mary, sat at the Lord's feet, listening to what he taught. 40 But Martha was distracted by the big dinner she was preparing. She came to Jesus and said, "Lord, doesn't it seem unfair to you that my sister just sits here while I do all the work? Tell her to come and help me."

41 But the Lord said to her, "My dear Martha, you are worried and upset over all these details! 42 There is only one thing worth being concerned about. Mary has discovered it, and it will not be taken away from her."

TEACHING ABOUT PRAYER

11 Once Jesus was in a certain place praying. As he finished, one of his disciples came to him and said, "Lord, teach us to pray, just as John taught his disciples."

2 Jesus said, "This is how you should pray:*

"Father, may your name be kept holy.
    May your Kingdom come soon.
3 Give us each day the food we need,*
4 and forgive us our sins,
    as we forgive those who sin against us.
And don't let us yield to temptation.*"

5 Then, teaching them more about prayer, he used this story: "Suppose you went to a friend's house at midnight, wanting to borrow three loaves of bread. You say to him, 6 'A friend of mine has just arrived for a visit, and I have nothing for him to eat.' 7 And suppose he calls out from his bedroom, 'Don't bother me. The door is locked for the night, and my family and I are all in bed. I can't help you.' 8 But I tell you this—though he won't do it for friendship's sake, if you keep knocking long enough, he will get up and give you whatever you need because of your shameless persistence.*

9 "And so I tell you, keep on asking, and you will receive what you ask for. Keep on seeking, and you will find. Keep on knocking, and the door will be opened to you. 10 For everyone who asks, receives. Everyone who seeks, finds. And to everyone who knocks, the door will be opened.

11 "You fathers—if your children ask* for a fish, do you give them a snake instead? 12 Or if they ask for an egg, do you give them a scorpion? Of course not! 13 So if you sinful people know how to give good gifts to your children, how much more will your heavenly Father give the Holy Spirit to those who ask him."

JESUS AND THE PRINCE OF DEMONS

14 One day Jesus cast out a demon from a man who couldn't speak, and when the demon was gone, the man began to speak. The crowds were amazed, 15 but some of them said, "No wonder he can cast out demons. He gets his power from Satan,* the prince of demons." 16 Others, trying to test Jesus, demanded that he show them a miraculous sign from heaven to prove his authority.

17 He knew their thoughts, so he said, "Any kingdom divided by civil war is doomed. A family splintered by feuding will fall apart. 18 You say I am empowered by Satan. But if Satan is divided and fighting against himself, how can his kingdom survive? 19 And if I am empowered by Satan, what about your own exorcists? They cast out demons, too, so they will condemn you for what you have said. 20 But if I am casting out demons by the power of God,* then the Kingdom of God has arrived among you. 21 For when a strong man is fully armed and guards his palace, his possessions are safe—22 until someone even stronger attacks and overpowers him, strips him of his weapons, and carries off his belongings.

23 "Anyone who isn't with me opposes me, and anyone who isn't working with me is actually working against me.

24 "When an evil* spirit leaves a person, it goes into the desert, searching for rest. But when it finds none, it says, 'I will return to the person I came from.' 25 So it returns and finds that its former home is all swept and in order. 26 Then

THE PURPOSE OF PRAYER
Luke 11   ROBERT MORRIS

As followers of Jesus Christ, we all experience spiritual warfare. However, if we focus only on the attacks against us, we give the devil too much credit. When spiritual warfare increases in our lives, we need to go to a new level of prayer so we can release God's power and will.

You must take prayer seriously. You are in a war, and your enemy wants to kill you (John 10:10; Ephesians 6:12). One type of demon that comes against us is called a *principality*, which is a spirit prince over a geographic region. In the Old Testament, the prophet Daniel battled principalities (Daniel 10:12-13, 20-21). Jesus' healing of the demon-possessed man in Mark 5 also shows the reality of territorial principalities (Mark 5:9-10). We fight principalities every time souls are saved, every time we plant a new church in a new city, and every time we stand for righteousness in our nation.

11:2 Some manuscripts add additional phrases from the Lord's Prayer as it reads in Matt 6:9-13. 11:3 Or *Give us each day our food for the day;* or *Give us each day our food for tomorrow.* 11:4 Or *And keep us from being tested.* 11:8 Or *in order to avoid shame,* or *so his reputation won't be damaged.* 11:11 Some manuscripts add *for bread, do you give them a stone? Or [if they ask].* 11:15 Greek *Beelzeboul;* also in 11:18, 19. Other manuscripts read *Beezeboul;* Latin version reads *Beelzebub.* 11:20 Greek *by the finger of God.* 11:24 Greek *unclean.*

LISTEN AND OBEY
Luke 11:28   TOM LANE

Our society is filled with clutter. We often risk ignoring God because we cannot hear Him over the noise of life.

Every person is responsible for hearing from God for themselves, but we do not live in a vacuum. When God speaks and we believe and obey, our actions ripple outward, joining with the actions of other believers who are also listening to His voice. When I see everything God is doing through His Church around the world, I think, *Wow! This is what happens when people live with a passion for His presence and voice!*

When you listen to God, you can act on what He says and join the multitude of voices proclaiming His name in every nation. Together, we are the symphony of God's Kingdom on the earth. Let us link arms and pursue Him. One day we'll look back together and say, "Can you believe what God has done?! It's incredible!"

the spirit finds seven other spirits more evil than itself, and they all enter the person and live there. And so that person is worse off than before."

27 As he was speaking, a woman in the crowd called out, "God bless your mother—the womb from which you came, and the breasts that nursed you!"

28 Jesus replied, "But even more blessed are all who hear the word of God and put it into practice."

THE SIGN OF JONAH

29 As the crowd pressed in on Jesus, he said, "This evil generation keeps asking me to show them a miraculous sign. But the only sign I will give them is the sign of Jonah. 30 What happened to him was a sign to the people of Nineveh that God had sent him. What happens to the Son of Man* will be a sign to these people that he was sent by God.

31 "The queen of Sheba* will stand up against this generation on judgment day and condemn it, for she came from a distant land to hear the wisdom of Solomon. Now someone greater than Solomon is here—but you refuse to listen. 32 The people of Nineveh will also stand up against this generation on judgment day and condemn it, for they repented of their sins at the preaching of Jonah. Now someone greater than Jonah is here—but you refuse to repent.

RECEIVING THE LIGHT

33 "No one lights a lamp and then hides it or puts it under a basket.* Instead, a lamp is placed on a stand, where its light can be seen by all who enter the house.

34 "Your eye is like a lamp that provides light for your body. When your eye is healthy, your whole body is filled with light. But when it is unhealthy, your body is filled with darkness. 35 Make sure that the light you think you have is not actually darkness. 36 If you are filled with light, with no dark corners, then your whole life will be radiant, as though a floodlight were filling you with light."

JESUS CRITICIZES THE RELIGIOUS LEADERS

37 As Jesus was speaking, one of the Pharisees invited him home for a meal. So he went in and took his place at the table.* 38 His host was amazed to see that he sat down to eat without first performing the hand-washing ceremony required by Jewish custom. 39 Then the Lord said to him, "You Pharisees are so careful to clean the outside of the cup and the dish, but inside you are filthy—full of greed and wickedness! 40 Fools! Didn't God make the inside as well as the outside? 41 So clean the inside by giving gifts to the poor, and you will be clean all over.

42 "What sorrow awaits you Pharisees! For you are careful to tithe even the tiniest income from your herb gardens,* but you ignore justice and the love of God. You should tithe, yes, but do not neglect the more important things.

43 "What sorrow awaits you Pharisees! For you love to sit in the seats of honor in the synagogues and receive respectful greetings as you walk in the marketplaces. 44 Yes, what sorrow awaits you! For you are like hidden graves in a field. People walk over them without knowing the corruption they are stepping on."

45 "Teacher," said an expert in religious law, "you have insulted us, too, in what you just said."

46 "Yes," said Jesus, "what sorrow also awaits you experts in religious law! For you crush people with unbearable religious demands, and you never lift a finger to ease the burden. 47 What sorrow awaits you! For you build monuments for the prophets your own ancestors killed long ago. 48 But in fact, you stand as witnesses who agree with what your ancestors did. They killed the prophets, and you join in their crime by building the monuments! 49 This is what God in his wisdom said about you:* 'I will send prophets and apostles to them, but they will kill some and persecute the others.'

50 "As a result, this generation will be held responsible for the murder of all God's prophets from the creation of the world—51 from the murder of Abel to the murder of Zechariah, who was killed between the altar and the sanctuary. Yes, it will certainly be charged against this generation.

11:30 "Son of Man" is a title Jesus used for himself.   11:31 Greek *The queen of the south.*   11:33 Some manuscripts do not include *or puts it under a basket.*   11:37 Or *and reclined.*   11:42 Greek *tithe the mint, the rue, and every herb.*   11:49 Greek *Therefore, the wisdom of God said.*

⁵²"What sorrow awaits you experts in religious law! For you remove the key to knowledge from the people. You don't enter the Kingdom yourselves, and you prevent others from entering."

⁵³As Jesus was leaving, the teachers of religious law and the Pharisees became hostile and tried to provoke him with many questions. ⁵⁴They wanted to trap him into saying something they could use against him.

A WARNING AGAINST HYPOCRISY

12 Meanwhile, the crowds grew until thousands were milling about and stepping on each other. Jesus turned first to his disciples and warned them, "Beware of the yeast of the Pharisees—their hypocrisy. ²The time is coming when everything that is covered up will be revealed, and all that is secret will be made known to all. ³Whatever you have said in the dark will be heard in the light, and what you have whispered behind closed doors will be shouted from the housetops for all to hear!

⁴"Dear friends, don't be afraid of those who want to kill your body; they cannot do any more to you after that. ⁵But I'll tell you whom to fear. Fear God, who has the power to kill you and then throw you into hell.* Yes, he's the one to fear.

⁶"What is the price of five sparrows—two copper coins*? Yet God does not forget a single one of them. ⁷And the very hairs on your head are all numbered. So don't be afraid; you are more valuable to God than a whole flock of sparrows.

⁸"I tell you the truth, everyone who acknowledges me publicly here on earth, the Son of Man* will also acknowledge in the presence of God's angels. ⁹But anyone who denies me here on earth will be denied before God's angels. ¹⁰Anyone who speaks against the Son of Man can be forgiven, but anyone who blasphemes the Holy Spirit will not be forgiven.

¹¹"And when you are brought to trial in the synagogues and before rulers and authorities, don't worry about how to defend yourself or what to say, ¹²for the Holy Spirit will teach you at that time what needs to be said."

PARABLE OF THE RICH FOOL

¹³Then someone called from the crowd, "Teacher, please tell my brother to divide our father's estate with me."

¹⁴Jesus replied, "Friend, who made me a judge over you to decide such things as that?" ¹⁵Then he said, "Beware! Guard against every kind of greed. Life is not measured by how much you own."

¹⁶Then he told them a story: "A rich man had a fertile farm that produced fine crops. ¹⁷He said to himself, 'What should I do? I don't have room for all my crops.' ¹⁸Then he said, 'I know! I'll tear down my barns and build bigger ones. Then I'll have room enough to store all my wheat and other goods. ¹⁹And I'll sit back and say to myself, "My friend, you have enough stored away for

ABUNDANCE AND GENEROSITY
Luke 12:13-21   JACK HAYFORD

Financial management is every bit as important as other dimensions of life management. In fact, God sees money management not simply as materially but also as spiritually rooted. Some churches create a false dichotomy between godliness and wealth, leading to the belief that godliness equates with poverty. However, as believers, one of our primary calls in the Kingdom is becoming God's distributors of abundance.

We often fail to realize our accountability before God for the way we handle our resources. This is the rich fool's problem in Luke 12. The man is not in error for being rich, nor in his desire to enjoy his wealth. Verse 21 explains, "A person is a fool to store up earthly wealth but not have a rich relationship with God." Abundance and generosity can and should be embraced together; however, abundance without generosity is placing too much value on material things.

years to come. Now take it easy! Eat, drink, and be merry!'"

²⁰"But God said to him, 'You fool! You will die this very night. Then who will get everything you worked for?'

²¹"Yes, a person is a fool to store up earthly wealth but not have a rich relationship with God."

TEACHING ABOUT MONEY AND POSSESSIONS

²²Then, turning to his disciples, Jesus said, "That is why I tell you not to worry about everyday life—whether you have enough food to eat or enough clothes to wear. ²³For life is more than food, and your body more than clothing. ²⁴Look at the ravens. They don't plant or harvest or store food in barns, for God feeds them. And you are far more valuable to him than any birds! ²⁵Can all your worries add a single moment to your life? ²⁶And if worry can't accomplish a little thing like that, what's the use of worrying over bigger things?

²⁷"Look at the lilies and how they grow. They don't work or make their clothing, yet Solomon in all his glory was not dressed as beautifully as they are. ²⁸And if God cares so wonderfully for flowers that are here today and thrown into the fire tomorrow, he will certainly care for you. Why do you have so little faith?

²⁹"And don't be concerned about what to eat and what to drink. Don't worry about such things. ³⁰These things dominate the thoughts of

---

12:5 Greek *Gehenna.*   12:6 Greek *two assaria* [Roman coins equal to ¼₆ of a denarius].   12:8 "Son of Man" is a title Jesus used for himself.

unbelievers all over the world, but your Father already knows your needs. [31]Seek the Kingdom of God above all else, and he will give you everything you need.

[32]"So don't be afraid, little flock. For it gives your Father great happiness to give you the Kingdom.

[33]"Sell your possessions and give to those in need. This will store up treasure for you in heaven! And the purses of heaven never get old or develop holes. Your treasure will be safe; no thief can steal it and no moth can destroy it. [34]Wherever your treasure is, there the desires of your heart will also be.

BE READY FOR THE LORD'S COMING

[35]"Be dressed for service and keep your lamps burning, [36]as though you were waiting for your master to return from the wedding feast. Then you will be ready to open the door and let him in the moment he arrives and knocks. [37]The servants who are ready and waiting for his return will be rewarded. I tell you the truth, he himself will seat them, put on an apron, and serve them as they sit and eat! [38]He may come in the middle of the night or just before dawn.* But whenever he comes, he will reward the servants who are ready.

[39]"Understand this: If a homeowner knew exactly when a burglar was coming, he would not permit his house to be broken into. [40]You also must be ready all the time, for the Son of Man will come when least expected."

[41]Peter asked, "Lord, is that illustration just for us or for everyone?"

[42]And the Lord replied, "A faithful, sensible servant is one to whom the master can give the responsibility of managing his other household servants and feeding them. [43]If the master returns and finds that the servant has done a good job, there will be a reward. [44]I tell you the truth, the master will put that servant in charge of all he owns. [45]But what if the servant thinks, 'My master won't be back for a while,' and he begins beating the other servants, partying, and getting drunk? [46]The master will return unannounced and unexpected, and he will cut the servant in pieces and banish him with the unfaithful.

[47]"And a servant who knows what the master wants, but isn't prepared and doesn't carry out those instructions, will be severely punished. [48]But someone who does not know, and then does something wrong, will be punished only lightly. When someone has been given much, much will be required in return; and when someone has been entrusted with much, even more will be required.

JESUS CAUSES DIVISION

[49]"I have come to set the world on fire, and I wish it were already burning! [50]I have a terrible baptism of suffering ahead of me, and I am under a heavy burden until it is accomplished. [51]Do you think I have come to bring peace to the earth? No, I have come to divide people against each other! [52]From now on families will be split apart, three in favor of me, and two against—or two in favor and three against.

[53] 'Father will be divided against son
and son against father;
mother against daughter
and daughter against mother;
and mother-in-law against daughter-in-law
and daughter-in-law against
mother-in-law.'*"

[54]Then Jesus turned to the crowd and said, "When you see clouds beginning to form in the west, you say, 'Here comes a shower.' And you are right. [55]When the south wind blows, you say, 'Today will be a scorcher.' And it is. [56]You fools! You know how to interpret the weather signs of the earth and sky, but you don't know how to interpret the present times.

[57]"Why can't you decide for yourselves what is right? [58]When you are on the way to court with your accuser, try to settle the matter before you get there. Otherwise, your accuser may drag you before the judge, who will hand you over to an officer, who will throw you into prison. [59]And if that happens, you won't be free again until you have paid the very last penny.*"

A CALL TO REPENTANCE

13 About this time Jesus was informed that Pilate had murdered some people from Galilee as they were offering sacrifices at the Temple. [2]"Do you think those Galileans were worse sinners than all the other people from Galilee?" Jesus asked. "Is that why they suffered? [3]Not at all! And you will perish, too, unless you repent of your sins and turn to God. [4]And what about the eighteen people who died when the tower in Siloam fell on them? Were they the worst sinners in Jerusalem? [5]No, and I tell you again that unless you repent, you will perish, too."

PARABLE OF THE BARREN FIG TREE

[6]Then Jesus told this story: "A man planted a fig tree in his garden and came again and again to see if there was any fruit on it, but he was always disappointed. [7]Finally, he said to his gardener, 'I've waited three years, and there hasn't been a single fig! Cut it down. It's just taking up space in the garden.'

[8]"The gardener answered, 'Sir, give it one more chance. Leave it another year, and I'll give it special attention and plenty of fertilizer. [9]If we get figs next year, fine. If not, then you can cut it down.'"

12:38 Greek *in the second or third watch.*   **12:53** Mic 7:6.
12:59 Greek *last lepton* [the smallest Jewish coin].

BELIEVERS IN BONDAGE
Luke 13:10–16   ROBERT MORRIS

Believers can be in bondage to Satan through sin, sickness, and demonic influences allowed into their lives. Like the believers Jesus speaks to in John 8:31-36, we can be blind to our own bondage. Sometimes we view continued sin in our lives as merely weakness, not bondage that leads to death. But we can't be set free until we realize we're in bondage.

In Luke 13, Jesus heals a woman of a sickness caused by a spirit of infirmity. Not all sickness is demonic, but some sicknesses do have spiritual roots. Continued illness can be a sign that there is an open door to the enemy in our lives.

In Mark 7, Jesus casts an evil spirit out of the Syro-Phoenician woman's daughter. This woman's cultural heritage included significant instances of Jewish beliefs mixed with the occult. Many Christians today arrogantly believe that dabbling in the occult will not affect them. However, when we expose ourselves to the occult, we open the door to the enemy.

Jesus can set you free from *all* bondage. If you need freedom, be honest with yourself and with God. Then ask Him for help. God wants you to be completely free!

JESUS HEALS ON THE SABBATH

¹⁰ One Sabbath day as Jesus was teaching in a synagogue, ¹¹ he saw a woman who had been crippled by an evil spirit. She had been bent double for eighteen years and was unable to stand up straight. ¹² When Jesus saw her, he called her over and said, "Dear woman, you are healed of your sickness!" ¹³ Then he touched her, and instantly she could stand straight. How she praised God!

¹⁴ But the leader in charge of the synagogue was indignant that Jesus had healed her on the Sabbath day. "There are six days of the week for working," he said to the crowd. "Come on those days to be healed, not on the Sabbath."

¹⁵ But the Lord replied, "You hypocrites! Each of you works on the Sabbath day! Don't you untie your ox or your donkey from its stall on the Sabbath and lead it out for water? ¹⁶ This dear woman, a daughter of Abraham, has been held in bondage by Satan for eighteen years. Isn't it right that she be released, even on the Sabbath?"

¹⁷ This shamed his enemies, but all the people rejoiced at the wonderful things he did.

PARABLE OF THE MUSTARD SEED

¹⁸ Then Jesus said, "What is the Kingdom of God like? How can I illustrate it? ¹⁹ It is like a tiny mustard seed that a man planted in a garden; it grows and becomes a tree, and the birds make nests in its branches."

PARABLE OF THE YEAST

²⁰ He also asked, "What else is the Kingdom of God like? ²¹ It is like the yeast a woman used in making bread. Even though she put only a little yeast in three measures of flour, it permeated every part of the dough."

THE NARROW DOOR

²² Jesus went through the towns and villages, teaching as he went, always pressing on toward Jerusalem. ²³ Someone asked him, "Lord, will only a few be saved?"

He replied, ²⁴ "Work hard to enter the narrow door to God's Kingdom, for many will try to enter but will fail. ²⁵ When the master of the house has locked the door, it will be too late. You will stand outside knocking and pleading, 'Lord, open the door for us!' But he will reply, 'I don't know you or where you come from.' ²⁶ Then you will say, 'But we ate and drank with you, and you taught in our streets.' ²⁷ And he will reply, 'I tell you, I don't know you or where you come from. Get away from me, all you who do evil.'

²⁸ "There will be weeping and gnashing of teeth, for you will see Abraham, Isaac, Jacob, and all the prophets in the Kingdom of God, but you will be thrown out. ²⁹ And people will come from all over the world—from east and west, north and south—to take their places in the Kingdom of God. ³⁰ And note this: Some who seem least important now will be the greatest then, and some who are the greatest now will be least important then.*"

JESUS GRIEVES OVER JERUSALEM

³¹ At that time some Pharisees said to him, "Get away from here if you want to live! Herod Antipas wants to kill you!"

³² Jesus replied, "Go tell that fox that I will keep on casting out demons and healing people today and tomorrow; and the third day I will accomplish my purpose. ³³ Yes, today, tomorrow, and the next day I must proceed on my way. For it wouldn't do for a prophet of God to be killed except in Jerusalem!

³⁴ "O Jerusalem, Jerusalem, the city that kills the prophets and stones God's messengers! How often I have wanted to gather your children together as a hen protects her chicks beneath her wings, but you wouldn't let me. ³⁵ And now, look, your house is abandoned. And you will never see me again until you say, 'Blessings on the one who comes in the name of the LORD!'*"

JESUS HEALS ON THE SABBATH

14 One Sabbath day Jesus went to eat dinner in the home of a leader of the Pharisees, and the people were watching him closely.

13:30 Greek *Some are last who will be first, and some are first who will be last.*   13:35 Ps 118:26.

[2] There was a man there whose arms and legs were swollen.* [3] Jesus asked the Pharisees and experts in religious law, "Is it permitted in the law to heal people on the Sabbath day, or not?" [4] When they refused to answer, Jesus touched the sick man and healed him and sent him away. [5] Then he turned to them and said, "Which of you doesn't work on the Sabbath? If your son* or your cow falls into a pit, don't you rush to get him out?" [6] Again they could not answer.

JESUS TEACHES ABOUT HUMILITY

[7] When Jesus noticed that all who had come to the dinner were trying to sit in the seats of honor near the head of the table, he gave them this advice: [8] "When you are invited to a wedding feast, don't sit in the seat of honor. What if someone who is more distinguished than you has also been invited? [9] The host will come and say, 'Give this person your seat.' Then you will be embarrassed, and you will have to take whatever seat is left at the foot of the table!

[10] "Instead, take the lowest place at the foot of the table. Then when your host sees you, he will come and say, 'Friend, we have a better place for you!' Then you will be honored in front of all the other guests. [11] For those who exalt themselves will be humbled, and those who humble themselves will be exalted."

[12] Then he turned to his host. "When you put on a luncheon or a banquet," he said, "don't invite your friends, brothers, relatives, and rich neighbors. For they will invite you back, and that will be your only reward. [13] Instead, invite the poor, the crippled, the lame, and the blind. [14] Then at the resurrection of the righteous, God will reward you for inviting those who could not repay you."

PARABLE OF THE GREAT FEAST

[15] Hearing this, a man sitting at the table with Jesus exclaimed, "What a blessing it will be to attend a banquet* in the Kingdom of God!"

[16] Jesus replied with this story: "A man prepared a great feast and sent out many invitations. [17] When the banquet was ready, he sent his servant to tell the guests, 'Come, the banquet is ready.' [18] But they all began making excuses. One said, 'I have just bought a field and must inspect it. Please excuse me.' [19] Another said, 'I have just bought five pairs of oxen, and I want to try them out. Please excuse me.' [20] Another said, 'I just got married, so I can't come.'

[21] "The servant returned and told his master what they had said. His master was furious and said, 'Go quickly into the streets and alleys of the town and invite the poor, the crippled, the blind, and the lame.' [22] After the servant had done this, he reported, 'There is still room for more.' [23] So his master said, 'Go out into the country lanes and behind the hedges and urge anyone you find to come, so that the house will be full. [24] For none of those I first invited will get even the smallest taste of my banquet.'"

THE COST OF BEING A DISCIPLE

[25] A large crowd was following Jesus. He turned around and said to them, [26] "If you want to be my disciple, you must, by comparison, hate everyone else—your father and mother, wife and children, brothers and sisters—yes, even your own life. Otherwise, you cannot be my disciple. [27] And if you do not carry your own cross and follow me, you cannot be my disciple.

[28] "But don't begin until you count the cost. For who would begin construction of a building without first calculating the cost to see if there is enough money to finish it? [29] Otherwise, you might complete only the foundation before running out of money, and then everyone would laugh at you. [30] They would say, 'There's the person who started that building and couldn't afford to finish it!'

[31] "Or what king would go to war against another king without first sitting down with his counselors to discuss whether his army of 10,000 could defeat the 20,000 soldiers marching against him? [32] And if he can't, he will send a delegation to discuss terms of peace while the enemy is still far away. [33] So you cannot become my disciple without giving up everything you own.

[34] "Salt is good for seasoning. But if it loses its flavor, how do you make it salty again? [35] Flavorless salt is good neither for the soil nor for the manure pile. It is thrown away. Anyone with ears to hear should listen and understand!"

PARABLE OF THE LOST SHEEP

15 Tax collectors and other notorious sinners often came to listen to Jesus teach. [2] This made the Pharisees and teachers of religious law complain that he was associating with such sinful people—even eating with them!

[3] So Jesus told them this story: [4] "If a man has a hundred sheep and one of them gets lost, what will he do? Won't he leave the ninety-nine others in the wilderness and go to search for the one that is lost until he finds it? [5] And when he has found it, he will joyfully carry it home on his shoulders. [6] When he arrives, he will call together his friends and neighbors, saying, 'Rejoice with me because I have found my lost sheep.' [7] In the same way, there is more joy in heaven over one lost sinner who repents and returns to God than over ninety-nine others who are righteous and haven't strayed away!

PARABLE OF THE LOST COIN

[8] "Or suppose a woman has ten silver coins* and loses one. Won't she light a lamp and sweep the

---

14:2 Or *who had dropsy.*   14:5 Some manuscripts read *donkey.*
14:15 Greek *to eat bread.*   15:8 Greek *ten drachmas.* A drachma was the equivalent of a full day's wage.

FULL RESTORATION
Luke 15:8-9   ROBERT MORRIS

It's always good to read God's Word when you've lost something or someone precious to you. In Luke 15:8-9, Jesus tells the parable of the lost coin.

> "Suppose a woman has ten silver coins and loses one. Won't she light a lamp and sweep the entire house and search carefully until she finds it? And when she finds it, she will call in her friends and neighbors and say, 'Rejoice with me because I have found my lost coin.'"

The woman in the parable lights a lamp because she lost something precious. You too can "light a lamp" by allowing God's Word to be a lamp to your feet (Psalm 119:105). No matter what you've lost, God wants to bring restoration to your life. Start lighting a lamp every day so He can speak to you, heal you, and restore you through His Word.

entire house and search carefully until she finds it? ⁹ And when she finds it, she will call in her friends and neighbors and say, 'Rejoice with me because I have found my lost coin.' ¹⁰ In the same way, there is joy in the presence of God's angels when even one sinner repents.'"

PARABLE OF THE LOST SON
¹¹ To illustrate the point further, Jesus told them this story: "A man had two sons. ¹² The younger son told his father, 'I want my share of your estate now before you die.' So his father agreed to divide his wealth between his sons.

¹³ "A few days later this younger son packed all his belongings and moved to a distant land, and there he wasted all his money in wild living. ¹⁴ About the time his money ran out, a great famine swept over the land, and he began to starve. ¹⁵ He persuaded a local farmer to hire him, and the man sent him into his fields to feed the pigs. ¹⁶ The young man became so hungry that even the pods he was feeding the pigs looked good to him. But no one gave him anything.

¹⁷ "When he finally came to his senses, he said to himself, 'At home even the hired servants have food enough to spare, and here I am dying of hunger! ¹⁸ I will go home to my father and say, "Father, I have sinned against both heaven and you, ¹⁹ and I am no longer worthy of being called your son. Please take me on as a hired servant."'

²⁰ "So he returned home to his father. And while he was still a long way off, his father saw

HOW TO COME HOME
Luke 15:11-19   ROBERT MORRIS

Do you ever have trouble restraining yourself? The lost son (often called the "prodigal son") in Luke 15 certainly did. Demanding an early inheritance, he rejected his family and "wasted all his money in wild living" (v. 13). The son soon found himself penniless, and he had to make a choice: starve to death or return home. But how could he face his father after what he had done?

You may have asked yourself a similar question about your heavenly Father—*How could God ever forgive me for what I've done?* I've got great news for you: His grace is more powerful than your worst sin. You can come home to your Father today, and it's as simple as these three steps:

1. Come clean in your heart.
Verse 17 says the lost son "finally came to his senses." In other words, he stopped lying to himself. When his money ran out and his circumstances caught up with him, the lost son had to face the truth: sin will always catch you. Every person is born with a sinful heart, but when you have an encounter with God, He gives you a new, pure heart (Ezekiel 36:26). We must guard our new hearts against becoming cold or hard and remind ourselves that we are no longer sinners—we are children of the King!

2. Come clean with the Father.
Have you ever confessed a sin so many times that you worried God's grace was going to run out? Sin makes us want to hide from God, but the only way to overcome sin is to bring it to the Father. When the lost son returned home, his father could have demanded an account of his foolish behavior; instead, he simply forgave him. Our heavenly Father knows everything you've ever done or ever will do wrong, and guess what? He's forgiven you! If you're a believer, Jesus' blood covers *all* your sins—past, present, and future. First John 1:9 says, "If we confess our sins to him, he is faithful and just to forgive us our sins and to cleanse us from all wickedness."

3. Come clean from the pigs.
When his money ran out, the lost son took a job feeding pigs. This was not a glamorous job, and by the time he came home, he was probably dirty from head to toe. The lost son's body certainly needed a bath, but what about his spirit and soul? Past sins can still affect us today, and issues such as emotional wounds, generational curses, and habitual sins can keep believers in bondage. The only way to get free is to bring everything to Jesus. Deliverance is the birthright of every believer, and God wants to set you free today.

THE OLDER BROTHER SYNDROME
Luke 15:25-32   ROBERT MORRIS

When the lost son returned home, his father was so happy to see him that he threw a party. However, one family member was not in the mood to celebrate: the lost son's older brother. He refused to attend the party and angrily scolded the father, "When this son of yours comes back after squandering your money on prostitutes, you celebrate by killing the fattened calf!" (v. 30).

Have you ever felt that way about other believers? Have you ever thought, *That's not fair! I've been much more faithful to God, so why are they getting all the blessings?* I call this the older brother syndrome—seeing others as worse than yourself and despising them for it. I could also call it the Pharisaic syndrome, because all three parables in Luke 15 address how the Pharisees looked down on other people.

So what causes this syndrome? *Pride.* And pride has three major effects on our lives:

1. Pride affects the way we see ourselves. The older brother was prideful about his obedience—"I've slaved for you and never once refused to do a single thing you told me to" (v. 29). The root of pride is self-righteousness, which means we think we can attain righteousness on our own without Christ. However, no one is perfect; everyone sins (Romans 3:23). The Pharisees were self-righteous, and Jesus rebuked them for it (Luke 18:9-14).

2. Pride affects the way we see others. Some people think their sins are less "bad" than other people's sins. But Jesus never said there are better or worse sinners. Instead, we each owe the same amount—everything! The older brother saw himself as better than the lost son, but compared to God, no one is perfect. That is why we *all* need Jesus!

3. Pride affects the way we see the Father. When we allow self-righteousness to come into our lives, we not only look down on other believers, but we also begin to judge God. Have you ever responded to someone else's blessing like the older brother: "You never gave me even one young goat for a feast with my friends" (v. 29)? How many "mature" believers miss out on the presence and provision of the Father because they allow bitterness and envy to harden their hearts? The only way to avoid the older brother syndrome is to keep our focus on the cross. Like the apostle Paul, we must "forget everything except Jesus Christ, the one who was crucified" (1 Corinthians 2:2). We all are sinners, and we all need God's incredible grace.

him coming. Filled with love and compassion, he ran to his son, embraced him, and kissed him. [21] His son said to him, 'Father, I have sinned against both heaven and you, and I am no longer worthy of being called your son.*'

[22] "But his father said to the servants, 'Quick! Bring the finest robe in the house and put it on him. Get a ring for his finger and sandals for his feet. [23] And kill the calf we have been fattening. We must celebrate with a feast, [24] for this son of mine was dead and has now returned to life. He was lost, but now he is found.' So the party began.

[25] "Meanwhile, the older son was in the fields working. When he returned home, he heard music and dancing in the house, [26] and he asked one of the servants what was going on. [27] 'Your brother is back,' he was told, 'and your father has killed the fattened calf. We are celebrating because of his safe return.'

[28] "The older brother was angry and wouldn't go in. His father came out and begged him, [29] but he replied, 'All these years I've slaved for you and never once refused to do a single thing you told me to. And in all that time you never gave me even one young goat for a feast with my friends. [30] Yet when this son of yours comes back after squandering your money on prostitutes, you celebrate by killing the fattened calf!'

[31] "His father said to him, 'Look, dear son, you have always stayed by me, and everything I have is yours. [32] We had to celebrate this happy day. For your brother was dead and has come back to life! He was lost, but now he is found!'"

PARABLE OF THE SHREWD MANAGER

16 Jesus told this story to his disciples: "There was a certain rich man who had a manager handling his affairs. One day a report came that the manager was wasting his employer's money. [2] So the employer called him in and said, 'What's this I hear about you? Get your report in order, because you are going to be fired.'

[3] "The manager thought to himself, 'Now what? My boss has fired me. I don't have the strength to dig ditches, and I'm too proud to beg. [4] Ah, I know how to ensure that I'll have plenty of friends who will give me a home when I am fired.'

[5] "So he invited each person who owed money to his employer to come and discuss the situation. He asked the first one, 'How much do you owe him?' [6] The man replied, 'I owe him 800 gallons of olive oil.' So the manager told him, 'Take the bill and quickly change it to 400 gallons.*'

[7] "'And how much do you owe my employer?' he asked the next man. 'I owe him 1,000 bushels of wheat,' was the reply. 'Here,' the manager said, 'take the bill and change it to 800 bushels.*'

15:21 Some manuscripts add *Please take me on as a hired servant.* 16:6 Greek *100 baths . . . 50 [baths].* 16:7 Greek *100 horous . . . 80 [horous].*

BREAKING THE SPIRIT OF MAMMON
Luke 16:10–13   ROBERT MORRIS

Did you know that all money has a spirit on it? Money that has been redeemed through tithing has the Spirit of God on it, but unredeemed money has the spirit of mammon on it. *Mammon* is an Aramaic word that means 'riches.' The spirit of mammon stands in direct contrast to the Spirit of God and says that money is the answer to every problem.

Money is not inherently evil. It can be used for righteous or unrighteous purposes. However, Jesus plainly says, "You cannot serve God and be enslaved to money" (Luke 16:13). The first 10 percent of our income belongs to God. When we are faithful through tithing, we will be entrusted with "the true riches of heaven," meaning the souls of people (Luke 16:11). When we tithe, we submit our money to the Spirit of God and break the curse of the spirit of mammon.

⁸"The rich man had to admire the dishonest rascal for being so shrewd. And it is true that the children of this world are more shrewd in dealing with the world around them than are the children of the light. ⁹Here's the lesson: Use your worldly resources to benefit others and make friends. Then, when your possessions are gone, they will welcome you to an eternal home.*

¹⁰"If you are faithful in little things, you will be faithful in large ones. But if you are dishonest in little things, you won't be honest with greater responsibilities. ¹¹And if you are untrustworthy about worldly wealth, who will trust you with the true riches of heaven? ¹²And if you are not faithful with other people's things, why should you be trusted with things of your own?

¹³"No one can serve two masters. For you will hate one and love the other; you will be devoted to one and despise the other. You cannot serve God and be enslaved to money."

¹⁴The Pharisees, who dearly loved their money, heard all this and scoffed at him. ¹⁵Then he said to them, "You like to appear righteous in public, but God knows your hearts. What this world honors is detestable in the sight of God.

¹⁶"Until John the Baptist, the law of Moses and the messages of the prophets were your guides. But now the Good News of the Kingdom of God is preached, and everyone is eager to get in.* ¹⁷But that doesn't mean that the law has lost its force. It is easier for heaven and earth to disappear than for the smallest point of God's law to be overturned.

¹⁸"For example, a man who divorces his wife and marries someone else commits adultery. And anyone who marries a woman divorced from her husband commits adultery."

PARABLE OF THE RICH MAN AND LAZARUS

¹⁹**Jesus said,** "There was a certain rich man who was splendidly clothed in purple and fine linen and who lived each day in luxury. ²⁰At his gate lay a poor man named Lazarus who was covered with sores. ²¹As Lazarus lay there longing for scraps from the rich man's table, the dogs would come and lick his open sores.

²²"Finally, the poor man died and was carried by the angels to sit beside Abraham at the heavenly banquet.* The rich man also died and was buried, ²³and he went to the place of the dead.* There, in torment, he saw Abraham in the far distance with Lazarus at his side.

²⁴"The rich man shouted, 'Father Abraham, have some pity! Send Lazarus over here to dip the tip of his finger in water and cool my tongue. I am in anguish in these flames.'

²⁵"But Abraham said to him, 'Son, remember that during your lifetime you had everything you wanted, and Lazarus had nothing. So now he is here being comforted, and you are in anguish. ²⁶And besides, there is a great chasm separating us. No one can cross over to you from here, and no one can cross over to us from there.'

²⁷"Then the rich man said, 'Please, Father Abraham, at least send him to my father's home. ²⁸For I have five brothers, and I want him to warn them so they don't end up in this place of torment.'

²⁹"But Abraham said, 'Moses and the prophets have warned them. Your brothers can read what they wrote.'

³⁰"The rich man replied, 'No, Father Abraham! But if someone is sent to them from the dead, then they will repent of their sins and turn to God.'

³¹"But Abraham said, 'If they won't listen to Moses and the prophets, they won't be persuaded even if someone rises from the dead.'"

TEACHINGS ABOUT FORGIVENESS AND FAITH

17 One day Jesus said to his disciples, "There will always be temptations to sin, but what sorrow awaits the person who does the tempting! ²It would be better to be thrown into the sea with a millstone hung around your neck than to cause one of these little ones to fall into sin. ³So watch yourselves!

"If another believer* sins, rebuke that person; then if there is repentance, forgive. ⁴Even if that person wrongs you seven times a day and each time turns again and asks forgiveness, you must forgive."

⁵The apostles said to the Lord, "Show us how to increase our faith."

⁶The Lord answered, "If you had faith even as small as a mustard seed, you could say to this

---

16:9 Or *you will be welcomed into eternal homes.* 16:16 Or *everyone is urged to enter in.* 16:22 Greek *to Abraham's bosom.* 16:23 Greek *to Hades.* 17:3 Greek *If your brother.*

HIS THANKSGIVING
Luke 17:11–19   ROBERT MORRIS

We can live continually in God's presence by developing a life of thanksgiving. We are grateful to God as He blesses us with His miraculous provision, and we express our gratitude and love in worship.

1. Worship is giving thanks.

Worship is about thanking someone after you've received something. It's showing your gratitude and love. True, genuine love is always expressed. Perhaps you did not always see this in your family growing up, but you are in a new family now—the body of Christ. You have a good Father, and you can express your love to Him because you have received something good from Him.

2. Miracles precede gratitude.

If you had a disease and Jesus healed you, would it be appropriate to express your thanks? Of course it would be! Well, if you're a believer, God has healed you from the worst disease—sin! Romans 6:23 says, "For the wages of sin is death, but the free gift of God is eternal life through Christ Jesus our Lord." Salvation is a miracle, and it is definitely okay to express your gratitude to God through worship.

3. Obedience precedes miracles.

Miracles are not earned, but the Bible shows us an unmistakable pattern of obedience leading to miracles. Is it possible that we don't feel as though we have anything to be grateful for because we're not walking in daily obedience to God? If we obey, we'll experience miracles, and when we experience miracles, we'll be grateful and express our love to God through worship.

mulberry tree, 'May you be uprooted and be planted in the sea,' and it would obey you!

⁷ "When a servant comes in from plowing or taking care of sheep, does his master say, 'Come in and eat with me'? ⁸ No, he says, 'Prepare my meal, put on your apron, and serve me while I eat. Then you can eat later.' ⁹ And does the master thank the servant for doing what he was told to do? Of course not. ¹⁰ In the same way, when you obey me you should say, 'We are unworthy servants who have simply done our duty.'"

TEN HEALED OF LEPROSY

¹¹ As Jesus continued on toward Jerusalem, he reached the border between Galilee and Samaria. ¹² As he entered a village there, ten men with leprosy stood at a distance, ¹³ crying out, "Jesus, Master, have mercy on us!"

¹⁴ He looked at them and said, "Go show yourselves to the priests."* And as they went, they were cleansed of their leprosy.

¹⁵ One of them, when he saw that he was healed, came back to Jesus, shouting, "Praise God!" ¹⁶ He fell to the ground at Jesus' feet, thanking him for what he had done. This man was a Samaritan.

¹⁷ Jesus asked, "Didn't I heal ten men? Where are the other nine? ¹⁸ Has no one returned to give glory to God except this foreigner?" ¹⁹ And Jesus said to the man, "Stand up and go. Your faith has healed you.*"

THE COMING OF THE KINGDOM

²⁰ One day the Pharisees asked Jesus, "When will the Kingdom of God come?"

Jesus replied, "The Kingdom of God can't be detected by visible signs.* ²¹ You won't be able to say, 'Here it is!' or 'It's over there!' For the Kingdom of God is already among you.*"

²² Then he said to his disciples, "The time is coming when you will long to see the day when the Son of Man returns,* but you won't see it. ²³ People will tell you, 'Look, there is the Son of Man,' or 'Here he is,' but don't go out and follow them. ²⁴ For as the lightning flashes and lights up the sky from one end to the other, so it will be on the day* when the Son of Man comes. ²⁵ But first the Son of Man must suffer terribly* and be rejected by this generation.

²⁶ "When the Son of Man returns, it will be like it was in Noah's day. ²⁷ In those days, the people enjoyed banquets and parties and weddings right up to the time Noah entered his boat and the flood came and destroyed them all.

²⁸ "And the world will be as it was in the days of Lot. People went about their daily business—eating and drinking, buying and selling, farming and building—²⁹ until the morning Lot left Sodom. Then fire and burning sulfur rained down from heaven and destroyed them all. ³⁰ Yes, it will be 'business as usual' right up to the day when the Son of Man is revealed. ³¹ On that day a person out on the deck of a roof must not go down into the house to pack. A person out in the field must not return home. ³² Remember what happened to Lot's wife! ³³ If you cling to your life, you will lose it, and if you let your life go, you will save it. ³⁴ That night two people will be asleep in one bed; one will be taken, the other left. ³⁵ Two women will be grinding flour together at the mill; one will be taken, the other left.*"

³⁷ "Where will this happen, Lord?"* the disciples asked.

Jesus replied, "Just as the gathering of vultures shows there is a carcass nearby, so these signs indicate that the end is near."*

17:14 See Lev 14:2-32.   17:19 Or *Your faith has saved you.*
17:20 Or *by your speculations.*   17:21 Or *is within you,* or *is in your grasp.*   17:22 Or *long for even one day with the Son of Man.* "Son of Man" is a title Jesus used for himself.   17:24 Some manuscripts do not include *on the day.*   17:25 Or *suffer many things.*   17:35 Some manuscripts add verse 36, *Two men will be working in the field; one will be taken, the other left.* Compare Matt 24:40.   17:37a Greek *"Where, Lord?"*   17:37b Greek *"Wherever the carcass is, the vultures gather."*

PARABLE OF THE PERSISTENT WIDOW

18 One day Jesus told his disciples a story to show that they should always pray and never give up. ² "There was a judge in a certain city," he said, "who neither feared God nor cared about people. ³ A widow of that city came to him repeatedly, saying, 'Give me justice in this dispute with my enemy.' ⁴ The judge ignored her for a while, but finally he said to himself, 'I don't fear God or care about people, ⁵ but this woman is driving me crazy. I'm going to see that she gets justice, because she is wearing me out with her constant requests!'"

⁶ Then the Lord said, "Learn a lesson from this unjust judge. ⁷ Even he rendered a just decision in the end. So don't you think God will surely give justice to his chosen people who cry out to him day and night? Will he keep putting them off? ⁸ I tell you, he will grant justice to them quickly! But when the Son of Man* returns, how many will he find on the earth who have faith?"

PARABLE OF THE PHARISEE AND TAX COLLECTOR

⁹ Then Jesus told this story to some who had great confidence in their own righteousness and scorned everyone else: ¹⁰ "Two men went to the Temple to pray. One was a Pharisee, and the other was a despised tax collector. ¹¹ The Pharisee stood by himself and prayed this prayer*: 'I thank you, God, that I am not like other people—cheaters, sinners, adulterers. I'm certainly not like that tax collector! ¹² I fast twice a week, and I give you a tenth of my income.'

¹³ "But the tax collector stood at a distance and dared not even lift his eyes to heaven as he prayed. Instead, he beat his chest in sorrow, saying, 'O God, be merciful to me, for I am a sinner.' ¹⁴ I tell you, this sinner, not the Pharisee, returned home justified before God. For those who exalt themselves will be humbled, and those who humble themselves will be exalted."

JESUS BLESSES THE CHILDREN

¹⁵ One day some parents brought their little children to Jesus so he could touch and bless them. But when the disciples saw this, they scolded the parents for bothering him.

¹⁶ Then Jesus called for the children and said to the disciples, "Let the children come to me. Don't stop them! For the Kingdom of God belongs to those who are like these children. ¹⁷ I tell you the truth, anyone who doesn't receive the Kingdom of God like a child will never enter it."

THE RICH MAN

¹⁸ Once a religious leader asked Jesus this question: "Good Teacher, what should I do to inherit eternal life?"

¹⁹ "Why do you call me good?" Jesus asked him. "Only God is truly good. ²⁰ But to answer your question, you know the commandments: 'You must not commit adultery. You must not murder.

You must not steal. You must not testify falsely. Honor your father and mother.'*"

²¹ The man replied, "I've obeyed all these commandments since I was young."

²² When Jesus heard his answer, he said, "There is still one thing you haven't done. Sell all your possessions and give the money to the poor, and you will have treasure in heaven. Then come, follow me."

²³ But when the man heard this he became very sad, for he was very rich.

²⁴ When Jesus saw this,* he said, "How hard it is for the rich to enter the Kingdom of God! ²⁵ In fact, it is easier for a camel to go through the eye of a needle than for a rich person to enter the Kingdom of God!"

²⁶ Those who heard this said, "Then who in the world can be saved?"

²⁷ He replied, "What is impossible for people is possible with God."

²⁸ Peter said, "We've left our homes to follow you."

²⁹ "Yes," Jesus replied, "and I assure you that everyone who has given up house or wife or brothers or parents or children, for the sake of the Kingdom of God, ³⁰ will be repaid many times over in this life, and will have eternal life in the world to come."

JESUS AGAIN PREDICTS HIS DEATH

³¹ Taking the twelve disciples aside, Jesus said, "Listen, we're going up to Jerusalem, where all the predictions of the prophets concerning the Son of Man will come true. ³² He will be handed over to the Romans,* and he will be mocked, treated shamefully, and spit upon. ³³ They will flog him with a whip and kill him, but on the third day he will rise again."

³⁴ But they didn't understand any of this. The significance of his words was hidden from them, and they failed to grasp what he was talking about.

JESUS HEALS A BLIND BEGGAR

³⁵ As Jesus approached Jericho, a blind beggar was sitting beside the road. ³⁶ When he heard the noise of a crowd going past, he asked what was happening. ³⁷ They told him that Jesus the Nazarene* was going by. ³⁸ So he began shouting, "Jesus, Son of David, have mercy on me!"

³⁹ "Be quiet!" the people in front yelled at him.

But he only shouted louder, "Son of David, have mercy on me!"

⁴⁰ When Jesus heard him, he stopped and ordered that the man be brought to him. As the man came near, Jesus asked him, ⁴¹ "What do you want me to do for you?"

18:8 "Son of Man" is a title Jesus used for himself.   18:11 Some manuscripts read *stood and prayed this prayer to himself*.   18:20 Exod 20:12-16; Deut 5:16-20.   18:24 Some manuscripts read *When Jesus saw how sad the man was*.   18:32 Greek *the Gentiles*.   18:37 Or *Jesus of Nazareth*.

"Lord," he said, "I want to see!"

⁴²And Jesus said, "All right, receive your sight! Your faith has healed you." ⁴³Instantly the man could see, and he followed Jesus, praising God. And all who saw it praised God, too.

JESUS AND ZACCHAEUS

19 Jesus entered Jericho and made his way through the town. ²There was a man there named Zacchaeus. He was the chief tax collector in the region, and he had become very rich. ³He tried to get a look at Jesus, but he was too short to see over the crowd. ⁴So he ran ahead and climbed a sycamore-fig tree beside the road, for Jesus was going to pass that way.

⁵When Jesus came by, he looked up at Zacchaeus and called him by name. "Zacchaeus!" he said. "Quick, come down! I must be a guest in your home today."

⁶Zacchaeus quickly climbed down and took Jesus to his house in great excitement and joy. ⁷But the people were displeased. "He has gone to be the guest of a notorious sinner," they grumbled.

⁸Meanwhile, Zacchaeus stood before the Lord and said, "I will give half my wealth to the poor, Lord, and if I have cheated people on their taxes, I will give them back four times as much!"

⁹Jesus responded, "Salvation has come to this home today, for this man has shown himself to be a true son of Abraham. ¹⁰For the Son of Man* came to seek and save those who are lost."

PARABLE OF THE TEN SERVANTS

¹¹The crowd was listening to everything Jesus said. And because he was nearing Jerusalem, he told them a story to correct the impression that the Kingdom of God would begin right away. ¹²He said, "A nobleman was called away to a distant empire to be crowned king and then return. ¹³Before he left, he called together ten of his servants and divided among them ten pounds of silver,* saying, 'Invest this for me while I am gone.' ¹⁴But his people hated him and sent a delegation after him to say, 'We do not want him to be our king.'

¹⁵"After he was crowned king, he returned and called in the servants to whom he had given the money. He wanted to find out what their profits were. ¹⁶The first servant reported, 'Master, I invested your money and made ten times the original amount!'

¹⁷"'Well done!' the king exclaimed. 'You are a good servant. You have been faithful with the little I entrusted to you, so you will be governor of ten cities as your reward.'

¹⁸"The next servant reported, 'Master, I invested your money and made five times the original amount.'

¹⁹"'Well done!' the king said. 'You will be governor over five cities.'

²⁰"But the third servant brought back only the original amount of money and said, 'Master,

A GLORIOUS DAY
Luke 19:11-27   ROBERT MORRIS

Many people are obsessed with figuring out the details and the date of the second coming of Christ. They constantly argue over interpretations of prophecy and current events. Others have a lethargic, complacent attitude; they've heard the rapture is near, so they are content to sit and wait for it. Both of these extremes are tactics of the enemy to keep the body of Christ from its purpose: sharing the Gospel.

I can give you Gateway Church's doctrine of the end times in three words: *Jesus is coming.* That's it! Perhaps you were expecting more—a possible date or two—but instead of concentrating on speculative views, I believe we need to focus on scripturally irrefutable facts, such as Jesus Himself is coming again (1 Thessalonians 4:16), He will come with power and great glory (Matthew 24:30), and He will destroy the antichrist (2 Thessalonians 2:8).

No one knows the exact time or day when Jesus will return (Matthew 24:36), but He has given us clear instructions to follow while we wait:

1. Do business until I come.
In Jesus' parable of the 10 servants, the king gives money to his servants and says, "Invest this for me while I am gone" (Luke 19:13). Those who invest wisely receive even more, but the servant who does nothing with his money loses everything. Why did Jesus tell this story? He wants His followers—including you and me—to do more than just believe He will return. He wants us to do the work of the Kingdom of God: loving, serving, and witnessing to others.

2. Don't get sidetracked.
In Matthew 24, Jesus describes many things that will happen before His return. It may surprise you to learn that every generation has experienced some of these signs. But Jesus says, "Don't let anyone mislead you" (v. 4). In other words, *don't get sidetracked.* And then He reminds us of our purpose: "The Good News about the Kingdom will be preached throughout the whole world, so that all nations will hear it; and then the end will come" (v. 14). I don't mind talking about the Second Coming, but I do have a problem with believers becoming argumentative and divisive over it. We cannot focus on the end times so much that we stop doing the job at hand: spreading the gospel throughout the earth until He comes.

19:10 "Son of Man" is a title Jesus used for himself.   **19:13** Greek *ten minas;* one mina was worth about three months' wages.

I hid your money and kept it safe. ²¹ I was afraid because you are a hard man to deal with, taking what isn't yours and harvesting crops you didn't plant.'

²² "'You wicked servant!' the king roared. 'Your own words condemn you. If you knew that I'm a hard man who takes what isn't mine and harvests crops I didn't plant, ²³ why didn't you deposit my money in the bank? At least I could have gotten some interest on it.'

²⁴ "Then, turning to the others standing nearby, the king ordered, 'Take the money from this servant, and give it to the one who has ten pounds.'

²⁵ "'But, master,' they said, 'he already has ten pounds!'

²⁶ "'Yes,' the king replied, 'and to those who use well what they are given, even more will be given. But from those who do nothing, even what little they have will be taken away. ²⁷ And as for these enemies of mine who didn't want me to be their king—bring them in and execute them right here in front of me.'"

JESUS' TRIUMPHANT ENTRY

²⁸ After telling this story, Jesus went on toward Jerusalem, walking ahead of his disciples. ²⁹ As he came to the towns of Bethphage and Bethany on the Mount of Olives, he sent two disciples ahead. ³⁰ "Go into that village over there," he told them. "As you enter it, you will see a young donkey tied there that no one has ever ridden. Untie it and bring it here. ³¹ If anyone asks, 'Why are you untying that colt?' just say, 'The Lord needs it.'"

³² So they went and found the colt, just as Jesus had said. ³³ And sure enough, as they were untying it, the owners asked them, "Why are you untying that colt?"

³⁴ And the disciples simply replied, "The Lord needs it." ³⁵ So they brought the colt to Jesus and threw their garments over it for him to ride on.

³⁶ As he rode along, the crowds spread out their garments on the road ahead of him. ³⁷ When he reached the place where the road started down the Mount of Olives, all of his followers began to shout and sing as they walked along, praising God for all the wonderful miracles they had seen.

³⁸ "Blessings on the King who comes in the name of the LORD!
Peace in heaven, and glory in highest heaven!"*

³⁹ But some of the Pharisees among the crowd said, "Teacher, rebuke your followers for saying things like that!"

⁴⁰ He replied, "If they kept quiet, the stones along the road would burst into cheers!"

JESUS WEEPS OVER JERUSALEM

⁴¹ But as he came closer to Jerusalem and saw the city ahead, he began to weep. ⁴² "How I wish today that you of all people would understand the way to peace. But now it is too late, and peace is hidden from your eyes. ⁴³ Before long your enemies will build ramparts against your walls and encircle you and close in on you from every side. ⁴⁴ They will crush you into the ground, and your children with you. Your enemies will not leave a single stone in place, because you did not recognize it when God visited you.*"

JESUS CLEARS THE TEMPLE

⁴⁵ Then Jesus entered the Temple and began to drive out the people selling animals for sacrifices. ⁴⁶ He said to them, "The Scriptures declare, 'My Temple will be a house of prayer,' but you have turned it into a den of thieves."*

⁴⁷ After that, he taught daily in the Temple, but the leading priests, the teachers of religious law, and the other leaders of the people began planning how to kill him. ⁴⁸ But they could think of nothing, because all the people hung on every word he said.

THE AUTHORITY OF JESUS CHALLENGED

20 One day as Jesus was teaching the people and preaching the Good News in the Temple, the leading priests, the teachers of religious law, and the elders came up to him. ² They demanded, "By what authority are you doing all these things? Who gave you the right?"

³ "Let me ask you a question first," he replied. ⁴ "Did John's authority to baptize come from heaven, or was it merely human?"

⁵ They talked it over among themselves. "If we say it was from heaven, he will ask why we didn't believe John. ⁶ But if we say it was merely human, the people will stone us because they are convinced John was a prophet." ⁷ So they finally replied that they didn't know.

⁸ And Jesus responded, "Then I won't tell you by what authority I do these things."

PARABLE OF THE EVIL FARMERS

⁹ Now Jesus turned to the people again and told them this story: "A man planted a vineyard, leased it to tenant farmers, and moved to another country to live for several years. ¹⁰ At the time of the grape harvest, he sent one of his servants to collect his share of the crop. But the farmers attacked the servant, beat him up, and sent him back empty-handed. ¹¹ So the owner sent another servant, but they also insulted him, beat him up, and sent him away empty-handed. ¹² A third man was sent, and they wounded him and chased him away.

¹³ "'What will I do?' the owner asked himself. 'I know! I'll send my cherished son. Surely they will respect him.'

19:38 Pss 118:26; 148:1.   19:44 Greek *did not recognize the time of your visitation*, a reference to the Messiah's coming.   19:46 Isa 56:7; Jer 7:11.

¹⁴"But when the tenant farmers saw his son, they said to each other, 'Here comes the heir to this estate. Let's kill him and get the estate for ourselves!' ¹⁵So they dragged him out of the vineyard and murdered him.

"What do you suppose the owner of the vineyard will do to them?" Jesus asked. ¹⁶"I'll tell you—he will come and kill those farmers and lease the vineyard to others."

"How terrible that such a thing should ever happen," his listeners protested.

¹⁷Jesus looked at them and said, "Then what does this Scripture mean?

'The stone that the builders rejected
has now become the cornerstone.'*

¹⁸Everyone who stumbles over that stone will be broken to pieces, and it will crush anyone it falls on."

¹⁹The teachers of religious law and the leading priests wanted to arrest Jesus immediately because they realized he was telling the story against them—they were the wicked farmers. But they were afraid of the people's reaction.

TAXES FOR CAESAR

²⁰Watching for their opportunity, the leaders sent spies pretending to be honest men. They tried to get Jesus to say something that could be reported to the Roman governor so he would arrest Jesus. ²¹"Teacher," they said, "we know that you speak and teach what is right and are not influenced by what others think. You teach the way of God truthfully. ²²Now tell us—is it right for us to pay taxes to Caesar or not?"

²³He saw through their trickery and said, ²⁴"Show me a Roman coin.* Whose picture and title are stamped on it?"

"Caesar's," they replied.

²⁵"Well then," he said, "give to Caesar what belongs to Caesar, and give to God what belongs to God."

²⁶So they failed to trap him by what he said in front of the people. Instead, they were amazed by his answer, and they became silent.

DISCUSSION ABOUT RESURRECTION

²⁷Then Jesus was approached by some Sadducees—religious leaders who say there is no resurrection from the dead. ²⁸They posed this question: "Teacher, Moses gave us a law that if a man dies, leaving a wife but no children, his brother should marry the widow and have a child who will carry on the brother's name.* ²⁹Well, suppose there were seven brothers. The oldest one married and then died without children. ³⁰So the second brother married the widow, but he also died. ³¹Then the third brother married her. This continued with all seven of them, who died without children. ³²Finally, the woman also died. ³³So tell us, whose wife will she be in the resurrection? For all seven were married to her!"

³⁴Jesus replied, "Marriage is for people here on earth. ³⁵But in the age to come, those worthy of being raised from the dead will neither marry nor be given in marriage. ³⁶And they will never die again. In this respect they will be like angels. They are children of God and children of the resurrection.

³⁷"But now, as to whether the dead will be raised—even Moses proved this when he wrote about the burning bush. Long after Abraham, Isaac, and Jacob had died, he referred to the Lord* as 'the God of Abraham, the God of Isaac, and the God of Jacob.'* ³⁸So he is the God of the living, not the dead, for they are all alive to him."

³⁹"Well said, Teacher!" remarked some of the teachers of religious law who were standing there. ⁴⁰And then no one dared to ask him any more questions.

WHOSE SON IS THE MESSIAH?

⁴¹Then Jesus presented them with a question. "Why is it," he asked, "that the Messiah is said to be the son of David? ⁴²For David himself wrote in the book of Psalms:

'The LORD said to my Lord,
Sit in the place of honor at my right hand
⁴³ until I humble your enemies,
making them a footstool under your feet.'*

⁴⁴Since David called the Messiah 'Lord,' how can the Messiah be his son?"

⁴⁵Then, with the crowds listening, he turned to his disciples and said, ⁴⁶"Beware of these teachers of religious law! For they like to parade around in flowing robes and love to receive respectful greetings as they walk in the marketplaces. And how they love the seats of honor in the synagogues and the head table at banquets. ⁴⁷Yet they shamelessly cheat widows out of their property and then pretend to be pious by making long prayers in public. Because of this, they will be severely punished."

THE WIDOW'S OFFERING

21 While Jesus was in the Temple, he watched the rich people dropping their gifts in the collection box. ²Then a poor widow came by and dropped in two small coins.*

³"I tell you the truth," Jesus said, "this poor widow has given more than all the rest of them. ⁴For they have given a tiny part of their surplus, but she, poor as she is, has given everything she has."

20:17 Ps 118:22. 20:24 Greek a denarius. 20:28 See Deut 25:5-6. 20:37a Greek when he wrote about the bush. He referred to the Lord. 20:37b Exod 3:6. 20:42-43 Ps 110:1. 21:2 Greek two lepta [the smallest of Jewish coins].

JESUS SPEAKS ABOUT THE FUTURE

⁵ Some of his disciples began talking about the majestic stonework of the Temple and the memorial decorations on the walls. But Jesus said, ⁶ "The time is coming when all these things will be completely demolished. Not one stone will be left on top of another!"

⁷ "Teacher," they asked, "when will all this happen? What sign will show us that these things are about to take place?"

⁸ He replied, "Don't let anyone mislead you, for many will come in my name, claiming, 'I am the Messiah,'* and saying, 'The time has come!' But don't believe them. ⁹ And when you hear of wars and insurrections, don't panic. Yes, these things must take place first, but the end won't follow immediately." ¹⁰ Then he added, "Nation will go to war against nation, and kingdom against kingdom. ¹¹ There will be great earthquakes, and there will be famines and plagues in many lands, and there will be terrifying things and great miraculous signs from heaven.

¹² "But before all this occurs, there will be a time of great persecution. You will be dragged into synagogues and prisons, and you will stand trial before kings and governors because you are my followers. ¹³ But this will be your opportunity to tell them about me.* ¹⁴ So don't worry in advance about how to answer the charges against you, ¹⁵ for I will give you the right words and such wisdom that none of your opponents will be able to reply or refute you! ¹⁶ Even those closest to you—your parents, brothers, relatives, and friends—will betray you. They will even kill some of you. ¹⁷ And everyone will hate you because you are my followers.* ¹⁸ But not a hair of your head will perish! ¹⁹ By standing firm, you will win your souls.

²⁰ "And when you see Jerusalem surrounded by armies, then you will know that the time of its destruction has arrived. ²¹ Then those in Judea must flee to the hills. Those in Jerusalem must get out, and those out in the country should not return to the city. ²² For those will be days of God's vengeance, and the prophetic words of the Scriptures will be fulfilled. ²³ How terrible it will be for pregnant women and for nursing mothers in those days. For there will be disaster in the land and great anger against this people. ²⁴ They will be killed by the sword or sent away as captives to all the nations of the world. And Jerusalem will be trampled down by the Gentiles until the period of the Gentiles comes to an end.

²⁵ "And there will be strange signs in the sun, moon, and stars. And here on earth the nations will be in turmoil, perplexed by the roaring seas and strange tides. ²⁶ People will be terrified at what they see coming upon the earth, for the powers in the heavens will be shaken. ²⁷ Then everyone will see the Son of Man* coming on a cloud with power and great glory.* ²⁸ So when all these things begin to happen, stand and look up, for your salvation is near!"

²⁹ Then he gave them this illustration: "Notice the fig tree, or any other tree. ³⁰ When the leaves come out, you know without being told that summer is near. ³¹ In the same way, when you see all these things taking place, you can know that the Kingdom of God is near. ³² I tell you the truth, this generation will not pass from the scene until all these things have taken place. ³³ Heaven and earth will disappear, but my words will never disappear.

³⁴ "Watch out! Don't let your hearts be dulled by carousing and drunkenness, and by the worries of this life. Don't let that day catch you unaware, ³⁵ like a trap. For that day will come upon everyone living on the earth. ³⁶ Keep alert at all times. And pray that you might be strong enough to escape these coming horrors and stand before the Son of Man."

³⁷ Every day Jesus went to the Temple to teach, and each evening he returned to spend the night on the Mount of Olives. ³⁸ The crowds gathered at the Temple early each morning to hear him.

JUDAS AGREES TO BETRAY JESUS

22 The Festival of Unleavened Bread, which is also called Passover, was approaching. ² The leading priests and teachers of religious law were plotting how to kill Jesus, but they were afraid of the people's reaction.

³ Then Satan entered into Judas Iscariot, who was one of the twelve disciples, ⁴ and he went to the leading priests and captains of the Temple guard to discuss the best way to betray Jesus to them. ⁵ They were delighted, and they promised to give him money. ⁶ So he agreed and began looking for an opportunity to betray Jesus so they could arrest him when the crowds weren't around.

THE LAST SUPPER

⁷ Now the Festival of Unleavened Bread arrived, when the Passover lamb is sacrificed. ⁸ Jesus sent Peter and John ahead and said, "Go and prepare the Passover meal, so we can eat it together."

⁹ "Where do you want us to prepare it?" they asked him.

¹⁰ He replied, "As soon as you enter Jerusalem, a man carrying a pitcher of water will meet you. Follow him. At the house he enters, ¹¹ say to the owner, 'The Teacher asks: Where is the guest room where I can eat the Passover meal with my disciples?' ¹² He will take you upstairs to a large room that is already set up. That is where you should prepare our meal." ¹³ They went off to the city and found everything just as Jesus had said, and they prepared the Passover meal there.

21:8 Greek claiming, 'I am.' 21:13 Or This will be your testimony against them. 21:17 Greek on account of my name. 21:27a "Son of Man" is a title Jesus used for himself. 21:27b See Dan 7:13.

PERMISSION GRANTED
Luke 22:31-38

ROBERT MORRIS

Would you ever give Satan permission to come against you? You're probably thinking, *Of course not!* However, unaddressed sin in our lives opens the door to the enemy. Throughout the Old Testament, God's people sinned, and God granted Satan permission to take His people into bondage. Why? So they would cry out and return to the Lord.

Satan is a thief who is always trying to get into our lives in any way he can (John 10:10). He constantly searches for open windows and doors, and one of the biggest open doors he finds is *pride.* Here are three definitions of pride to help us identify and overcome it:

1. Pride is trusting in your own strength.

In Luke 22:31, Jesus tells Simon Peter that Satan has asked permission to sift him like wheat. Jesus warns him that there is an open door in his life, and I believe this open door is pride. When Jesus says all the disciples will desert Him, Peter pridefully responds, "I never will" (Mark 14:29). Peter trusts in his own strength, a trap into which even mature believers fall. When we rely on our own strength to resist temptation, we will always fail, as Peter did when he denied Jesus in Matthew 26:69-75.

2. Pride is trusting in your own righteousness.

If you think you're righteous for what you do rather than Whom you know, you have pride. In Job 1:12 and 2:6, God gives Satan permission to come against Job, a man whom God Himself calls "blameless" (Job 2:3). Another word for blameless is *righteous*. But why would God allow a righteous person to suffer? Job asks the same question. The problem is that his defense is in how he lives, not in Whom he trusts. Can any of us live righteously enough to meet God's standard? No! When we compare ourselves to God, none of us measure up. Yes, we should live righteously, but we must remember that our righteousness comes from the blood of Jesus, not our works.

3. Pride is trusting in your own wisdom.

Pride will destroy your life (Proverbs 16:18). If you believe you are smarter than anyone else and refuse correction, you don't have God's wisdom; instead, you open the door to the enemy who brings "disorder and evil of every kind" (James 3:16). The only way to close pride's door is to cry out to God and repent. He alone has the power to free you from bondage and restore your life.

---

[14] When the time came, Jesus and the apostles sat down together at the table.* [15] Jesus said, "I have been very eager to eat this Passover meal with you before my suffering begins. [16] For I tell you now that I won't eat this meal again until its meaning is fulfilled in the Kingdom of God."

[17] Then he took a cup of wine and gave thanks to God for it. Then he said, "Take this and share it among yourselves. [18] For I will not drink wine again until the Kingdom of God has come."

[19] He took some bread and gave thanks to God for it. Then he broke it in pieces and gave it to the disciples, saying, "This is my body, which is given for you. Do this in remembrance of me."

[20] After supper he took another cup of wine and said, "This cup is the new covenant between God and his people—an agreement confirmed with my blood, which is poured out as a sacrifice for you.*

[21] "But here at this table, sitting among us as a friend, is the man who will betray me. [22] For it has been determined that the Son of Man* must die. But what sorrow awaits the one who betrays him." [23] The disciples began to ask each other which of them would ever do such a thing.

[24] Then they began to argue among themselves about who would be the greatest among them. [25] Jesus told them, "In this world the kings and great men lord it over their people, yet they are called 'friends of the people.' [26] But among you it will be different. Those who are the greatest among you should take the lowest rank, and the leader should be like a servant. [27] Who is more important, the one who sits at the table or the one who serves? The one who sits at the table, of course. But not here! For I am among you as one who serves.

[28] "You have stayed with me in my time of trial. [29] And just as my Father has granted me a Kingdom, I now grant you the right [30] to eat and drink at my table in my Kingdom. And you will sit on thrones, judging the twelve tribes of Israel.

JESUS PREDICTS PETER'S DENIAL

[31] "Simon, Simon, Satan has asked to sift each of you like wheat. [32] But I have pleaded in prayer for you, Simon, that your faith should not fail. So when you have repented and turned to me again, strengthen your brothers."

[33] Peter said, "Lord, I am ready to go to prison with you, and even to die with you."

[34] But Jesus said, "Peter, let me tell you something. Before the rooster crows tomorrow morning, you will deny three times that you even know me."

[35] Then Jesus asked them, "When I sent you out to preach the Good News and you did not

---

22:14 Or *reclined together.* 22:19-20 Some manuscripts do not include 22:19b-20, *which is given for you . . . which is poured out as a sacrifice for you.* 22:22 "Son of Man" is a title Jesus used for himself.

have money, a traveler's bag, or an extra pair of sandals, did you need anything?"

"No," they replied.

36 "But now," he said, "take your money and a traveler's bag. And if you don't have a sword, sell your cloak and buy one! 37 For the time has come for this prophecy about me to be fulfilled: 'He was counted among the rebels.'* Yes, everything written about me by the prophets will come true."

38 "Look, Lord," they replied, "we have two swords among us."

"That's enough," he said.

JESUS PRAYS ON THE MOUNT OF OLIVES

39 Then, accompanied by the disciples, Jesus left the upstairs room and went as usual to the Mount of Olives. 40 There he told them, "Pray that you will not give in to temptation."

41 He walked away, about a stone's throw, and knelt down and prayed, 42 "Father, if you are willing, please take this cup of suffering away from me. Yet I want your will to be done, not mine." 43 Then an angel from heaven appeared and strengthened him. 44 He prayed more fervently, and he was in such agony of spirit that his sweat fell to the ground like great drops of blood.*

45 At last he stood up again and returned to the disciples, only to find them asleep, exhausted from grief. 46 "Why are you sleeping?" he asked them. "Get up and pray, so that you will not give in to temptation."

JESUS IS BETRAYED AND ARRESTED

47 But even as Jesus said this, a crowd approached, led by Judas, one of the twelve disciples. Judas walked over to Jesus to greet him with a kiss. 48 But Jesus said, "Judas, would you betray the Son of Man with a kiss?"

49 When the other disciples saw what was about to happen, they exclaimed, "Lord, should we fight? We brought the swords!" 50 And one of them struck at the high priest's slave, slashing off his right ear.

51 But Jesus said, "No more of this." And he touched the man's ear and healed him.

52 Then Jesus spoke to the leading priests, the captains of the Temple guard, and the elders who had come for him. "Am I some dangerous revolutionary," he asked, "that you come with swords and clubs to arrest me? 53 Why didn't you arrest me in the Temple? I was there every day. But this is your moment, the time when the power of darkness reigns."

PETER DENIES JESUS

54 So they arrested him and led him to the high priest's home. And Peter followed at a distance. 55 The guards lit a fire in the middle of the courtyard and sat around it, and Peter joined them there. 56 A servant girl noticed him in the firelight and began staring at him. Finally she said, "This man was one of Jesus' followers!"

57 But Peter denied it. "Woman," he said, "I don't even know him!"

58 After a while someone else looked at him and said, "You must be one of them!"

"No, man, I'm not!" Peter retorted.

59 About an hour later someone else insisted, "This must be one of them, because he is a Galilean, too."

60 But Peter said, "Man, I don't know what you are talking about." And immediately, while he was still speaking, the rooster crowed. 61 At that moment the Lord turned and looked at Peter. Suddenly, the Lord's words flashed through Peter's mind: "Before the rooster crows tomorrow morning, you will deny three times that you even know me." 62 And Peter left the courtyard, weeping bitterly.

63 The guards in charge of Jesus began mocking and beating him. 64 They blindfolded him and said, "Prophesy to us! Who hit you that time?" 65 And they hurled all sorts of terrible insults at him.

JESUS BEFORE THE COUNCIL

66 At daybreak all the elders of the people assembled, including the leading priests and the teachers of religious law. Jesus was led before this high council,* 67 and they said, "Tell us, are you the Messiah?"

But he replied, "If I tell you, you won't believe me. 68 And if I ask you a question, you won't answer. 69 But from now on the Son of Man will be seated in the place of power at God's right hand.*"

70 They all shouted, "So, are you claiming to be the Son of God?"

And he replied, "You say that I am."

71 "Why do we need other witnesses?" they said. "We ourselves heard him say it."

JESUS' TRIAL BEFORE PILATE

23 Then the entire council took Jesus to Pilate, the Roman governor. 2 They began to state their case: "This man has been leading our people astray by telling them not to pay their taxes to the Roman government and by claiming he is the Messiah, a king."

3 So Pilate asked him, "Are you the king of the Jews?"

Jesus replied, "You have said it."

4 Pilate turned to the leading priests and to the crowd and said, "I find nothing wrong with this man!"

5 Then they became insistent. "But he is causing riots by his teaching wherever he goes—all over Judea, from Galilee to Jerusalem!"

6 "Oh, is he a Galilean?" Pilate asked. 7 When they said that he was, Pilate sent him to Herod Antipas, because Galilee was under Herod's

---

22:37 Isa 53:12.   22:43-44 Verses 43 and 44 are not included in the most ancient manuscripts.   22:66 Greek before their Sanhedrin.   22:69 See Ps 110:1.

jurisdiction, and Herod happened to be in Jerusalem at the time.

8 Herod was delighted at the opportunity to see Jesus, because he had heard about him and had been hoping for a long time to see him perform a miracle. 9 He asked Jesus question after question, but Jesus refused to answer. 10 Meanwhile, the leading priests and the teachers of religious law stood there shouting their accusations. 11 Then Herod and his soldiers began mocking and ridiculing Jesus. Finally, they put a royal robe on him and sent him back to Pilate. 12 (Herod and Pilate, who had been enemies before, became friends that day.)

13 Then Pilate called together the leading priests and other religious leaders, along with the people, 14 and he announced his verdict. "You brought this man to me, accusing him of leading a revolt. I have examined him thoroughly on this point in your presence and find him innocent. 15 Herod came to the same conclusion and sent him back to us. Nothing this man has done calls for the death penalty. 16 So I will have him flogged, and then I will release him."*

18 Then a mighty roar rose from the crowd, and with one voice they shouted, "Kill him, and release Barabbas to us!" 19 (Barabbas was in prison for taking part in an insurrection in Jerusalem against the government, and for murder.) 20 Pilate argued with them, because he wanted to release Jesus. 21 But they kept shouting, "Crucify him! Crucify him!"

22 For the third time he demanded, "Why? What crime has he committed? I have found no reason to sentence him to death. So I will have him flogged, and then I will release him."

23 But the mob shouted louder and louder, demanding that Jesus be crucified, and their voices prevailed. 24 So Pilate sentenced Jesus to die as they demanded. 25 As they had requested, he released Barabbas, the man in prison for insurrection and murder. But he turned Jesus over to them to do as they wished.

THE CRUCIFIXION

26 As they led Jesus away, a man named Simon, who was from Cyrene,* happened to be coming in from the countryside. The soldiers seized him and put the cross on him and made him carry it behind Jesus. 27 A large crowd trailed behind, including many grief-stricken women. 28 But Jesus turned and said to them, "Daughters of Jerusalem, don't weep for me, but weep for yourselves and for your children. 29 For the days are coming when they will say, 'Fortunate indeed are the women who are childless, the wombs that have not borne a child and the breasts that have never nursed.' 30 People will beg the mountains, 'Fall on us,' and plead with the hills, 'Bury us.'* 31 For if these things are done when the tree is green, what will happen when it is dry?*"

32 Two others, both criminals, were led out to be executed with him. 33 When they came to a place called The Skull,* they nailed him to the cross. And the criminals were also crucified—one on his right and one on his left. 34 Jesus said, "Father, forgive them, for they don't know what they are doing."* And the soldiers gambled for his clothes by throwing dice.* 35 The crowd watched and the leaders scoffed. "He saved others," they said, "let him save himself if he is really God's Messiah, the Chosen One." 36 The soldiers mocked him, too, by offering him a drink of sour wine. 37 They called out to him, "If you are the King of the Jews, save yourself!" 38 A sign was fastened above him with these words: "This is the King of the Jews."

39 One of the criminals hanging beside him scoffed, "So you're the Messiah, are you? Prove it by saving yourself—and us, too, while you're at it!"

40 But the other criminal protested, "Don't you fear God even when you have been sentenced to die? 41 We deserve to die for our crimes, but this man hasn't done anything wrong." 42 Then he said, "Jesus, remember me when you come into your Kingdom."

43 And Jesus replied, "I assure you, today you will be with me in paradise."

THE DEATH OF JESUS

44 By this time it was about noon, and darkness fell across the whole land until three o'clock. 45 The light from the sun was gone. And suddenly, the curtain in the sanctuary of the Temple was torn down the middle. 46 Then Jesus shouted, "Father, I entrust my spirit into your hands!"* And with those words he breathed his last.

47 When the Roman officer* overseeing the execution saw what had happened, he worshiped God and said, "Surely this man was innocent.*" 48 And when all the crowd that came to see the crucifixion saw what had happened, they went home in deep sorrow.* 49 But Jesus' friends, including the women who had followed him from Galilee, stood at a distance watching.

THE BURIAL OF JESUS

50 Now there was a good and righteous man named Joseph. He was a member of the Jewish high council, 51 but he had not agreed with the decision and actions of the other religious leaders. He was from the town of Arimathea in Judea, and he was waiting for the Kingdom of God to come. 52 He went to Pilate and asked for

23:16 Some manuscripts add verse 17, Now it was necessary for him to release one prisoner to them during the Passover celebration. Compare Matt 27:15; Mark 15:6; John 18:39. 23:26 Cyrene was a city in northern Africa. 23:30 Hos 10:8. 23:31 Or If these things are done to me, the living tree, what will happen to you, the dry tree? 23:33 Sometimes rendered Calvary, which comes from the Latin word for "skull." 23:34a This sentence is not included in many ancient manuscripts. 23:34b Greek by casting lots. See Ps 22:18. 23:46 Ps 31:5. 23:47a Greek the centurion. 23:47b Or righteous. 23:48 Greek went home beating their breasts.

Jesus' body. [53] Then he took the body down from the cross and wrapped it in a long sheet of linen cloth and laid it in a new tomb that had been carved out of rock. [54] This was done late on Friday afternoon, the day of preparation,* as the Sabbath was about to begin.

[55] As his body was taken away, the women from Galilee followed and saw the tomb where his body was placed. [56] Then they went home and prepared spices and ointments to anoint his body. But by the time they were finished the Sabbath had begun, so they rested as required by the law.

THE RESURRECTION

24 But very early on Sunday morning* the women went to the tomb, taking the spices they had prepared. [2] They found that the stone had been rolled away from the entrance. [3] So they went in, but they didn't find the body of the Lord Jesus. [4] As they stood there puzzled, two men suddenly appeared to them, clothed in dazzling robes.

[5] The women were terrified and bowed with their faces to the ground. Then the men asked, "Why are you looking among the dead for someone who is alive? [6] He isn't here! He is risen from the dead! Remember what he told you back in Galilee, [7] that the Son of Man* must be betrayed into the hands of sinful men and be crucified, and that he would rise again on the third day."

[8] Then they remembered that he had said this. [9] So they rushed back from the tomb to tell his eleven disciples—and everyone else—what had happened. [10] It was Mary Magdalene, Joanna, Mary the mother of James, and several other women who told the apostles what had happened. [11] But the story sounded like nonsense to the men, so they didn't believe it. [12] However, Peter jumped up and ran to the tomb to look. Stooping, he peered in and saw the empty linen wrappings; then he went home again, wondering what had happened.

THE WALK TO EMMAUS

[13] That same day two of Jesus' followers were walking to the village of Emmaus, seven miles* from Jerusalem. [14] As they walked along they were talking about everything that had happened. [15] As they talked and discussed these things, Jesus himself suddenly came and began walking with them. [16] But God kept them from recognizing him.

[17] He asked them, "What are you discussing so intently as you walk along?"

They stopped short, sadness written across their faces. [18] Then one of them, Cleopas, replied, "You must be the only person in Jerusalem who hasn't heard about all the things that have happened there the last few days."

[19] "What things?" Jesus asked.

"The things that happened to Jesus, the man from Nazareth," they said. "He was a prophet who did powerful miracles, and he was a mighty teacher in the eyes of God and all the people. [20] But our leading priests and other religious leaders handed him over to be condemned to death, and they crucified him. [21] We had hoped he was the Messiah who had come to rescue Israel. This all happened three days ago.

[22] "Then some women from our group of his followers were at his tomb early this morning, and they came back with an amazing report. [23] They said his body was missing, and they had seen angels who told them Jesus is alive! [24] Some of our men ran out to see, and sure enough, his body was gone, just as the women had said."

[25] Then Jesus said to them, "You foolish people! You find it so hard to believe all that the prophets wrote in the Scriptures. [26] Wasn't it clearly predicted that the Messiah would have to suffer all these things before entering his glory?" [27] Then Jesus took them through the writings of Moses and all the prophets, explaining from all the Scriptures the things concerning himself.

[28] By this time they were nearing Emmaus and the end of their journey. Jesus acted as if he were going on, [29] but they begged him, "Stay the night with us, since it is getting late." So he went home with them. [30] As they sat down to eat,* he took the bread and blessed it. Then he broke it and gave it to them. [31] Suddenly, their eyes were opened, and they recognized him. And at that moment he disappeared!

[32] They said to each other, "Didn't our hearts burn within us as he talked with us on the road and explained the Scriptures to us?" [33] And within the hour they were on their way back to Jerusalem. There they found the eleven disciples and the others who had gathered with them, [34] who said, "The Lord has really risen! He appeared to Peter.*"

JESUS APPEARS TO THE DISCIPLES

[35] Then the two from Emmaus told their story of how Jesus had appeared to them as they were walking along the road, and how they had recognized him as he was breaking the bread. [36] And just as they were telling about it, Jesus himself was suddenly standing there among them. "Peace be with you," he said. [37] But the whole group was startled and frightened, thinking they were seeing a ghost!

[38] "Why are you frightened?" he asked. "Why are your hearts filled with doubt? [39] Look at my hands. Look at my feet. You can see that it's really me. Touch me and make sure that I am not a ghost, because ghosts don't have bodies, as you see that I do." [40] As he spoke, he showed them his hands and his feet.

23:54 Greek *It was the day of preparation.* 24:1 Greek *But on the first day of the week, very early in the morning.* 24:7 "Son of Man" is a title Jesus used for himself. 24:13 Greek *60 stadia* [11.1 kilometers]. 24:30 Or *As they reclined.* 24:34 Greek *Simon.*

UNDERSTANDING GOD'S WORD
Luke 24:45   ROBERT MORRIS

As Christians, sometimes when we turn to God's Word for understanding, we feel overwhelmed or confused. How many times do we say things like "If I could just understand what I'm going through" or "I don't know what God is trying to teach me right now, but I know He's trying to teach me *something*"?

When the disciples couldn't grasp Jesus' resurrection, He "opened their minds to understand the Scriptures" (Luke 24:45). Not only has God given us His Word, but He also wants to give us an understanding of it. The Word of God is the *only* way we can make sense of what's happening in our lives. The more you read it, the more you'll understand what's going on in your circumstances.

⁴¹ Still they stood there in disbelief, filled with joy and wonder. Then he asked them, "Do you have anything here to eat?" ⁴² They gave him a piece of broiled fish, ⁴³ and he ate it as they watched.

⁴⁴ Then he said, "When I was with you before, I told you that everything written about me in the law of Moses and the prophets and in the Psalms must be fulfilled." ⁴⁵ Then he opened their minds to understand the Scriptures. ⁴⁶ And he said, "Yes, it was written long ago that the Messiah would suffer and die and rise from the dead on the third day. ⁴⁷ It was also written that this message would be proclaimed in the authority of his name to all the nations,* beginning in Jerusalem: 'There is forgiveness of sins for all who repent.' ⁴⁸ You are witnesses of all these things.

⁴⁹ "And now I will send the Holy Spirit, just as my Father promised. But stay here in the city until the Holy Spirit comes and fills you with power from heaven."

THE ASCENSION

⁵⁰ Then Jesus led them to Bethany, and lifting his hands to heaven, he blessed them. ⁵¹ While he was blessing them, he left them and was taken up to heaven. ⁵² So they worshiped him and then returned to Jerusalem filled with great joy. ⁵³ And they spent all of their time in the Temple, praising God.

24:47 Or *all peoples.*

JOHN

JON HUNTZINGER, PHD

The Gospel of John gives a portrait of Jesus that complements the other Gospels but is different from them in several ways. In the three Synoptic Gospels (Matthew, Mark, and Luke), for example, Jesus teaches in stories, with occasional long discourses (such as those in Matthew). In John, however, Jesus primarily teaches in long discourses, and when He teaches, He talks about eternal life (3:16; 4:14, 36; 5:24-25, 39-40; 6:47, 54; 10:28; 11:25-26; 12:25, 49-50) and not the "Kingdom of God" or "Kingdom of Heaven" as in the other Gospels. In the Synoptic Gospels, Jesus performs healings and miracles. John calls Jesus' healings and miracles "signs" (2:11; 4:48, 54; 6:30; 20:30-31). These signs contain different content from the miracles in Matthew, Mark, and Luke. They include the miracle of water turned to wine (2:1-11), the healing of an official's son (4:46-54), the healing of the lame man by the pool of Bethesda (5:1-15), the restoration of sight to a man born blind (9:1-7), and the raising of Lazarus (11:38-44). No other Gospel includes these stories.

Additionally, in the Synoptic Gospels, Jesus ministers in and around Galilee before He goes to Jerusalem, where He overturns tables in the Temple, eats a Passover meal with His disciples, and is arrested and eventually put to death. In John, Jesus moves back and forth between Galilee and Jerusalem. He overturns tables in the Temple early in His ministry (2:13-17). John clearly intends to complement the depiction of Jesus given by the other Gospel writers by adding his own eyewitness knowledge and insight. For this reason, the Gospel of John was the last of the four Gospels, written sometime during the years after the destruction of the Temple in AD 70.

John, a son of Zebedee and brother of James, wrote this Gospel. He was with Jesus from the beginning of His public ministry and observed firsthand important moments throughout those years. Thus, John saw Jesus' restoration to life of Jairus's daughter (Mark 5:35-43; Luke 8:49-56), Jesus' transfiguration on the mountain (Mark 9:2-8; Matthew 17:1-8), and Jesus' agony in the Garden of Gethsemane before His crucifixion (Mark 14:32-34; Matthew 26:36-38). John refers to himself as "the disciple Jesus loved" in his accounts of Jesus' Last Supper (13:23), his place at the cross with Jesus' mother (19:26-27), and the empty tomb (20:2-9). And he says that he ("this disciple") is the one who has written the Gospel (21:24). The fact that he refers to himself in this way points to the great love he had personally experienced from Jesus. It explains why he emphasizes God's love throughout his Gospel. John uses the word *love* almost 60 times, including 3:16; 13:34-35; 14:15-24; 15:12-17; 21:15-19.

John's emphasis on God's love and the love the disciples are to have for one another is a key theme for him. Another theme is the ministry of the Holy Spirit. John reports the Spirit moved upon Jesus at His baptism and remained with Him (1:32-34), meaning everything Jesus said and did from that moment was done with the help of the Spirit. The same Holy Spirit will be with the disciples (14:15-17, 25-27; 15:26) as well as with the world (16:5-15).

Yet another theme is John's understanding of Jesus' identity. Just as Matthew sees Jesus in relation to Moses and David, Mark shows Him to be the Son of God, and Luke reveals Him to be the Savior of the world, John adds that Jesus is the Word of God (1:1-3, 14), the Light of the World (1:5, 9; 8:12), and the Lamb of God (1:29). Moreover, he presents Jesus in relation to the God of Israel who delivered His people from Egypt as "I Am Who I Am" (Exodus 3:13-14). Seven times Jesus uses the verbal expression "I Am" with different nouns to name Himself. Who is Jesus, according to John? He is the one God has sent to deliver people from bondage and give them eternal life just as God delivered Israel and led them into the rich land of Canaan. John shows that Jesus reprises God's great miracle of deliverance and manifests God's great act of love and faithfulness (Deuteronomy 4; 7; Hosea 11:1-4) to the people of His own day.

Thus, when Jesus says He is the "bread of life" (6:22-59), He means that He has come to provide

JOHN	"I AM"	EXODUS CONNECTION
6:22-59	Bread of Life	Manna
8:12-20; 9:1-7	Light of the World	Light in tabernacle
8:48-59	Before Abraham	Covenant
10:1-30	Gate for the Sheep/Good Shepherd	Moses
11:17-27	Resurrection and Life	New beginning in Canaan
14:1-6	Way, Truth, and Life	Commandments/Torah
15:1-8	The Vine	Bear fruit

what people need most in their lives, just as God provided manna for the Israelites in the wilderness (Exodus 16). When He says He is the "light of the world" (8:12-20; 9:1-7), He means He has come to give understanding (light) about what God is like. In the same way God was present to the Israelites in the form of fire (light) above the Tabernacle, they would know Jesus was with them (Exodus 40:34-38). When He says He is the "I Am" before Abraham (John 8:48-59), He means He has come to remind the people of the importance of belief for their relationship with God through the covenant He first made with Abraham (Genesis 15:1-6; Exodus 3:6, 13-16) and then with Moses (Exodus 19-20). When Jesus says He is the "gate for the sheep" and "the good shepherd" (John 10:1-30), He means He has come to care for God's people in the same way God cared for the Israelites as their Shepherd during the Exodus (Psalm 78:52). When He says He is "the resurrection and the life" (John 11:17-27), He means He has come to offer a new beginning, just as God gave a new beginning to the Israelites who had virtually died in slavery in Egypt. When Jesus says He is "the way, the truth, and the life" (14:1-6), He means He has come to

show what life looks like when lived in obedience to God's commandments, just as God gave the commandments to the Israelites at Mount Sinai to bless them (Deuteronomy 5-8). And when Jesus says He is the vine (John 15:1-8), He means He has come to make people fruitful in their lives when they are in relation to Him, just as the Israelites were to be fruitful when they lived in covenant relationship with God through His commandments.

According to John, not only does Jesus identify Himself with the God of the Exodus who delivered the Israelites from Egypt, but Jesus also performs seven signs to back up what He was saying about Himself. As noted above, John uses the word "sign" rather than "miracle" because, according to him, the miracles Jesus performed have special meaning. They prove He is qualified to talk to people about the love of God, and He is able to do all the things that His "I Am" names suggest.

Altogether, the signs performed by Jesus recall the Exodus story and reveal God's continued blessing upon His people through Jesus. God is with Jesus to heal them, deliver them, provide for their needs, give understanding to them, and empower them to experience new life.

JOHN	SIGNS	EXODUS CONNECTION
2:1-11	Water turned into wine	Water turned to blood is a sign to Pharaoh to release the Hebrews
4:46-54	Official's son healed	God's son Israel is restored (Hosea 11:1-4)
5:1-14	Lame man healed after 38 years	Israelites wander for 38 years in wilderness
6:1-15	5,000 fed bread	God provides manna in the wilderness
6:16-24	Walks on water	Red Sea is parted
9:1-41	Blind man healed	Moses sees God's glory
11:1-44	Lazarus raised	Israelites given new life by God

WISE SAYINGS OF JESUS IN JOHN IN CHRONOLOGICAL ORDER

TEACHING	VERSES
Blowing wind	3:8
Bridegroom and best man	3:29
Fields ripe for harvest	4:35-38
Father and Son	5:19-20
The slave and the son	8:35
The Good Shepherd	10:1-5
Twelve hours of daylight	11:9-10
Kernel of wheat	12:24
Walking in the light	12:35
Preparing a place	14:2-4
The vine and the branches	15:1-8
Woman suffering the pains of labor	16:20-21

Unlike the Synoptic Gospels, John's Gospel does not contain any parables. Instead, John records many of Jesus' teachings in the form of allegories or wise sayings.

PROLOGUE: CHRIST, THE ETERNAL WORD

1 [1] In the beginning the Word already
existed.
The Word was with God,
and the Word was God.
[2] He existed in the beginning with God.
[3] God created everything through him,
and nothing was created except through
him.
[4] The Word gave life to everything that
was created,*
and his life brought light to everyone.
[5] The light shines in the darkness,
and the darkness can never extinguish it.*

[6] God sent a man, John the Baptist,* [7] to tell
about the light so that everyone might believe
because of his testimony. [8] John himself was not
the light; he was simply a witness to tell about
the light. [9] The one who is the true light, who
gives light to everyone, was coming into the
world.

[10] He came into the very world he created, but
the world didn't recognize him. [11] He came to his
own people, and even they rejected him. [12] But
to all who believed him and accepted him, he
gave the right to become children of God. [13] They
are reborn—not with a physical birth resulting
from human passion or plan, but a birth that
comes from God.

[14] So the Word became human* and made his
home among us. He was full of unfailing love
and faithfulness.* And we have seen his glory,
the glory of the Father's one and only Son.

[15] John testified about him when he shouted to
the crowds, "This is the one I was talking about
when I said, 'Someone is coming after me who is
far greater than I am, for he existed long before
me.'"

[16] From his abundance we have all received one
gracious blessing after another.* [17] For the law
was given through Moses, but God's unfailing
love and faithfulness came through Jesus Christ.
[18] No one has ever seen God. But the unique One,
who is himself God,* is near to the Father's heart.
He has revealed God to us.

THE TESTIMONY OF JOHN THE BAPTIST

[19] This was John's testimony when the Jewish
leaders sent priests and Temple assistants* from
Jerusalem to ask John, "Who are you?" [20] He came
right out and said, "I am not the Messiah."

[21] "Well then, who are you?" they asked. "Are
you Elijah?"
"No," he replied.
"Are you the Prophet we are expecting?"*
"No."
[22] "Then who are you? We need an answer for
those who sent us. What do you have to say about
yourself?"
[23] John replied in the words of the prophet
Isaiah:

"I am a voice shouting in the wilderness,
'Clear the way for the LORD's coming!'"*

[24] Then the Pharisees who had been sent
[25] asked him, "If you aren't the Messiah or Elijah or the Prophet, what right do you have to
baptize?"

[26] John told them, "I baptize with* water, but
right here in the crowd is someone you do not
recognize. [27] Though his ministry follows mine,
I'm not even worthy to be his slave and untie the
straps of his sandal."

[28] This encounter took place in Bethany, an
area east of the Jordan River, where John was
baptizing.

JESUS, THE LAMB OF GOD

[29] The next day John saw Jesus coming toward
him and said, "Look! The Lamb of God who takes
away the sin of the world! [30] He is the one I was
talking about when I said, 'A man is coming after
me who is far greater than I am, for he existed
long before me.' [31] I did not recognize him as the
Messiah, but I have been baptizing with water
so that he might be revealed to Israel."

[32] Then John testified, "I saw the Holy Spirit
descending like a dove from heaven and resting
upon him. [33] I didn't know he was the one, but
when God sent me to baptize with water, he told
me, 'The one on whom you see the Spirit descend
and rest is the one who will baptize with the Holy
Spirit.' [34] I saw this happen to Jesus, so I testify
that he is the Chosen One of God.*"

THE FIRST DISCIPLES

[35] The following day John was again standing
with two of his disciples. [36] As Jesus walked by,
John looked at him and declared, "Look! There
is the Lamb of God!" [37] When John's two disciples
heard this, they followed Jesus.

[38] Jesus looked around and saw them following.
"What do you want?" he asked them.
They replied, "Rabbi" (which means "Teacher"),
"where are you staying?"
[39] "Come and see," he said. It was about four
o'clock in the afternoon when they went with
him to the place where he was staying, and they
remained with him the rest of the day.

[40] Andrew, Simon Peter's brother, was one of
these men who heard what John said and then
followed Jesus. [41] Andrew went to find his brother,
Simon, and told him, "We have found the Messiah" (which means "Christ"*).

1:3-4 Or *and nothing that was created was created except through
him. The Word gave life to everything.* 1:5 Or *and the darkness has
not understood it.* 1:6 Greek *a man named John.* 1:14a Greek
became flesh. 1:14b Or *grace and truth;* also in 1:17. 1:16 Or
received the grace of Christ rather than the grace of the law; Greek
reads *received grace upon grace.* 1:18 Some manuscripts read
But the one and only Son. 1:19 Greek *and Levites.* 1:21 Greek
Are you the Prophet? See Deut 18:15, 18; Mal 4:5-6. 1:23 Isa 40:3.
1:26 Or *in;* also in 1:31, 33. 1:34 Some manuscripts read *the Son
of God.* 1:41 *Messiah* (a Hebrew term) and *Christ* (a Greek term)
both mean "anointed one."

⁴²Then Andrew brought Simon to meet Jesus. Looking intently at Simon, Jesus said, "Your name is Simon, son of John—but you will be called Cephas" (which means "Peter"*).

⁴³The next day Jesus decided to go to Galilee. He found Philip and said to him, "Come, follow me." ⁴⁴Philip was from Bethsaida, Andrew and Peter's hometown.

⁴⁵Philip went to look for Nathanael and told him, "We have found the very person Moses* and the prophets wrote about! His name is Jesus, the son of Joseph from Nazareth."

⁴⁶"Nazareth!" exclaimed Nathanael. "Can anything good come from Nazareth?"

"Come and see for yourself," Philip replied.

⁴⁷As they approached, Jesus said, "Now here is a genuine son of Israel—a man of complete integrity."

⁴⁸"How do you know about me?" Nathanael asked.

Jesus replied, "I could see you under the fig tree before Philip found you."

⁴⁹Then Nathanael exclaimed, "Rabbi, you are the Son of God—the King of Israel!"

⁵⁰Jesus asked him, "Do you believe this just because I told you I had seen you under the fig tree? You will see greater things than this." ⁵¹Then he said, "I tell you the truth, you will all see heaven open and the angels of God going up and down on the Son of Man, the one who is the stairway between heaven and earth.*"

THE WEDDING AT CANA

2 The next day* there was a wedding celebration in the village of Cana in Galilee. Jesus' mother was there, ²and Jesus and his disciples were also invited to the celebration. ³The wine supply ran out during the festivities, so Jesus' mother told him, "They have no more wine."

⁴"Dear woman, that's not our problem," Jesus replied. "My time has not yet come."

⁵But his mother told the servants, "Do whatever he tells you."

⁶Standing nearby were six stone water jars, used for Jewish ceremonial washing. Each could hold twenty to thirty gallons.* ⁷Jesus told the servants, "Fill the jars with water." When the jars had been filled, ⁸he said, "Now dip some out, and take it to the master of ceremonies." So the servants followed his instructions.

⁹When the master of ceremonies tasted the water that was now wine, not knowing where it had come from (though, of course, the servants knew), he called the bridegroom over. ¹⁰"A host always serves the best wine first," he said. "Then, when everyone has had a lot to drink, he brings out the less expensive wine. But you have kept the best until now!"

¹¹This miraculous sign at Cana in Galilee was the first time Jesus revealed his glory. And his disciples believed in him.

¹²After the wedding he went to Capernaum for a few days with his mother, his brothers, and his disciples.

JESUS CLEARS THE TEMPLE

¹³It was nearly time for the Jewish Passover celebration, so Jesus went to Jerusalem. ¹⁴In the Temple area he saw merchants selling cattle, sheep, and doves for sacrifices; he also saw dealers at tables exchanging foreign money. ¹⁵Jesus made a whip from some ropes and chased them all out of the Temple. He drove out the sheep and cattle, scattered the money changers' coins over the floor, and turned over their tables. ¹⁶Then, going over to the people who sold doves, he told them, "Get these things out of here. Stop turning my Father's house into a marketplace!"

¹⁷Then his disciples remembered this prophecy from the Scriptures: "Passion for God's house will consume me."*

¹⁸But the Jewish leaders demanded, "What are you doing? If God gave you authority to do this, show us a miraculous sign to prove it."

¹⁹"All right," Jesus replied. "Destroy this temple, and in three days I will raise it up."

²⁰"What!" they exclaimed. "It has taken forty-six years to build this Temple, and you can rebuild it in three days?" ²¹But when Jesus said "this temple," he meant his own body. ²²After he was raised from the dead, his disciples remembered he had said this, and they believed both the Scriptures and what Jesus had said.

JESUS AND NICODEMUS

²³Because of the miraculous signs Jesus did in Jerusalem at the Passover celebration, many began to trust in him. ²⁴But Jesus didn't trust them, because he knew all about people. ²⁵No one needed to tell him about human nature, for he knew what was in each person's heart.

3 There was a man named Nicodemus, a Jewish religious leader who was a Pharisee. ²After dark one evening, he came to speak with Jesus. "Rabbi," he said, "we all know that God has sent you to teach us. Your miraculous signs are evidence that God is with you."

³Jesus replied, "I tell you the truth, unless you are born again,* you cannot see the Kingdom of God."

⁴"What do you mean?" exclaimed Nicodemus. "How can an old man go back into his mother's womb and be born again?"

1:42 The names Cephas (from Aramaic) and Peter (from Greek) both mean "rock." 1:45 Greek Moses in the law. 1:51 Greek going up and down on the Son of Man; see Gen 28:10-17. "Son of Man" is a title Jesus used for himself. 2:1 Greek On the third day; see 1:35, 43. 2:6 Greek 2 or 3 measures [75 to 113 liters]. 2:17 Or "Concern for God's house will be my undoing." Ps 69:9. 3:3 Or born from above; also in 3:7.

MUST-MANY-KNOW

John 3:1-21   ROBERT MORRIS

Think about when you first got saved. The apostle Paul said to the believers in Corinth, "Examine yourselves to see if your faith is genuine" (2 Corinthians 13:5). I'm not trying to get you to question your salvation; I just want you to think about on what you're basing your eternal destination. Attending church or giving money to a church does not save you. You only go to heaven if you truly accept Jesus Christ as your Lord and Savior.

Here is what Jesus says about salvation:

1. **You must be born again.**

In John 3, Jesus tells Nicodemus, "You must be born again" (v. 7). He doesn't say, "I think this is something you should strongly consider." Nicodemus was a Pharisee, which means he would have memorized the first five books of the Bible, tithed, fasted, prayed, and attended the Temple. He believed in the God of Abraham, Isaac, and Jacob. He even believed God was with Jesus. However, none of these things saved him. Jesus tells Nicodemus, "Unless you are born again, you cannot see the Kingdom of God" (v. 3).

2. **Many people have not been born again.**

In Matthew 7:21-22, Jesus says there are many people who prophesy, cast out demons, and do miracles in His name, but they will not enter heaven. Why? Because "I never knew you" (v. 23). It's possible to do good things without being born again. And if many people who are actively engaged in the work of God are not saved, how many more are not saved who just attend church? You can't change yourself; only Jesus can change you.

3. **How can you know if you've been born again?**

The apostle John says you can *know* you have eternal life (1 John 5:13). When you come to Jesus, you can't say, "Please save me *if* I'm a sinner." You have to say and believe, "I *am* a sinner, and I need You." When you submit your will to God's will, He changes you, and you begin to desire His way instead of your own way. God reverses the direction of where you were headed (hell) to the destination He provided for you from the very beginning (heaven). My life totally and radically changed when Jesus came into my heart. If you have never experienced this, or if you are doubting that you are truly saved, be honest with God and yourself. You can give your life to Jesus today, and He will change you!

WHAT IT MEANS TO BE SAVED

John 3:14-17   JACK HAYFORD

We enter a new world when we accept Jesus. By grace, through faith, we are regenerated, redeemed, and justified.

Regeneration brings the newness every human being needs. Sin makes us wither up and die on the inside, and we all need to be born again. God gives us a breath of spiritual life by His Holy Spirit.

Redemption refers to paying a price. We have no ability to pay the price for sin, which is death, so Jesus came and did this for us. He shed His own blood to make us right with God.

Justification has to do with being given a perfect record. As a judge, God is always honest, fair, and right. When we put our faith in the Lord Jesus, God gives us His Son's record. We are now legally right with Him.

Jesus has come to give us new life, redeem what's broken, and give us right standing before God.

---

spiritual life.* [7] So don't be surprised when I say, 'You* must be born again.' [8] The wind blows wherever it wants. Just as you can hear the wind but can't tell where it comes from or where it is going, so you can't explain how people are born of the Spirit."

[9] **"How are these things possible?" Nicodemus asked.**

[10] **Jesus replied,** "You are a respected Jewish teacher, and yet you don't understand these things? [11] I assure you, we tell you what we know and have seen, and yet you won't believe our testimony. [12] But if you don't believe me when I tell you about earthly things, how can you possibly believe if I tell you about heavenly things? [13] No one has ever gone to heaven and returned. But the Son of Man* has come down from heaven. [14] And as Moses lifted up the bronze snake on a pole in the wilderness, so the Son of Man must be lifted up, [15] so that everyone who believes in him will have eternal life.*

[16] "For this is how God loved the world: He gave* his one and only Son, so that everyone who believes in him will not perish but have eternal life. [17] God sent his Son into the world not to judge the world, but to save the world through him.

[18] "There is no judgment against anyone who believes in him. But anyone who does not believe in him has already been judged for not believing in God's one and only Son. [19] And the judgment is based on this fact: God's light came into the

---

[5] **Jesus replied,** "I assure you, no one can enter the Kingdom of God without being born of water and the Spirit.* [6] Humans can reproduce only human life, but the Holy Spirit gives birth to

3:5 Or *and spirit.* The Greek word for *Spirit* can also be translated *wind;* see 3:8.   **3:6** Greek *what is born of the Spirit is spirit.*   **3:7** The Greek word for *you* is plural; also in 3:12.   **3:13** Some manuscripts add *who lives in heaven.* "Son of Man" is a title Jesus used for himself.   **3:15** Or *everyone who believes will have eternal life in him.*   **3:16** Or *For God loved the world so much that he gave.*

THE SON
John 3:16
ROBERT MORRIS

God created us to exist in perfect relationship with Him, but when Adam and Eve disobeyed in the Garden of Eden, sin entered the world. Sin separates us from God, and we can never do enough "good" things to undo sin. However, God loves us so much that He gave His Son, Jesus, to save us and restore our relationship with Him.

When Jesus died on the cross, He stood in our place and took the punishment for our sins. Because Jesus never sinned, He was the perfect sacrifice and removed the barrier between God and us.

But after three days, God raised Jesus from the dead! More than 500 people saw Him during the next 40 days, and then He ascended to heaven. If you ask Jesus to forgive you for your sins and receive Him as your Lord and Savior, you can join Him one day for all eternity!

HE GAVE
John 3:16
ROBERT MORRIS

The entire Bible can be summarized in two words: *He gave*. Giving is the active expression of God's love. John 3:16 says, "For this is how God loved the world: He gave his one and only Son, so that everyone who believes in him will not perish but have eternal life." When we receive Jesus as our Lord and Savior, we also receive His giving nature.

A magazine reporter once asked me, "How often do you preach on giving?" Without even thinking, I replied, "Every week!" The reporter seemed surprised, so I explained, "I think you asked me the wrong question. I think you meant to ask me how often I preach on giving *money*, which is about every two to three years. But I can't preach on prayer, marriage, grace, or faith without giving!" Giving is the theme of the Bible, and it's the only reason we're here. God gave His Son for us, and we have eternal security when we give our lives to Him in return.

world, but people loved the darkness more than the light, for their actions were evil. ²⁰All who do evil hate the light and refuse to go near it for fear their sins will be exposed. ²¹But those who do what is right come to the light so others can see that they are doing what God wants.*"

JOHN THE BAPTIST EXALTS JESUS
²²Then Jesus and his disciples left Jerusalem and went into the Judean countryside. Jesus spent some time with them there, baptizing people.

²³At this time John the Baptist was baptizing at Aenon, near Salim, because there was plenty of water there; and people kept coming to him for baptism. ²⁴(This was before John was thrown into prison.) ²⁵A debate broke out between John's disciples and a certain Jew* over ceremonial cleansing. ²⁶So John's disciples came to him and said, "Rabbi, the man you met on the other side of the Jordan River, the one you identified as the Messiah, is also baptizing people. And everybody is going to him instead of coming to us."

²⁷John replied, "No one can receive anything unless God gives it from heaven. ²⁸You yourselves know how plainly I told you, 'I am not the Messiah. I am only here to prepare the way for him.' ²⁹It is the bridegroom who marries the bride, and the bridegroom's friend is simply glad to stand with him and hear his vows. Therefore, I am filled with joy at his success. ³⁰He must become greater and greater, and I must become less and less.

³¹"He has come from above and is greater than anyone else. We are of the earth, and we speak of earthly things, but he has come from heaven and is greater than anyone else.* ³²He testifies about what he has seen and heard, but how few believe what he tells them! ³³Anyone who accepts his testimony can affirm that God is true. ³⁴For

he is sent by God. He speaks God's words, for God gives him the Spirit without limit. ³⁵The Father loves his Son and has put everything into his hands. ³⁶And anyone who believes in God's Son has eternal life. Anyone who doesn't obey the Son will never experience eternal life but remains under God's angry judgment."

JESUS AND THE SAMARITAN WOMAN
4 Jesus* knew the Pharisees had heard that he was baptizing and making more disciples than John ²(though Jesus himself didn't baptize them—his disciples did). ³So he left Judea and returned to Galilee.

⁴He had to go through Samaria on the way. ⁵Eventually he came to the Samaritan village of Sychar, near the field that Jacob gave to his son Joseph. ⁶Jacob's well was there; and Jesus, tired from the long walk, sat wearily beside the well about noontime. ⁷Soon a Samaritan woman came to draw water, and Jesus said to her, "Please give me a drink." ⁸He was alone at the time because his disciples had gone into the village to buy some food.

⁹The woman was surprised, for Jews refuse to have anything to do with Samaritans.* She said to Jesus, "You are a Jew, and I am a Samaritan woman. Why are you asking me for a drink?"

¹⁰Jesus replied, "If you only knew the gift God has for you and who you are speaking to, you would ask me, and I would give you living water."

3:21 Or *can see God at work in what he is doing.* 3:25 Some manuscripts read *some Jews.* 3:31 Some manuscripts do not include *and is greater than anyone else.* 4:1 Some manuscripts read *The Lord.* 4:9 Some manuscripts do not include this sentence.

11 "But sir, you don't have a rope or a bucket," she said, "and this well is very deep. Where would you get this living water? 12 And besides, do you think you're greater than our ancestor Jacob, who gave us this well? How can you offer better water than he and his sons and his animals enjoyed?"

13 Jesus replied, "Anyone who drinks this water will soon become thirsty again. 14 But those who drink the water I give will never be thirsty again. It becomes a fresh, bubbling spring within them, giving them eternal life."

15 "Please, sir," the woman said, "give me this water! Then I'll never be thirsty again, and I won't have to come here to get water."

16 "Go and get your husband," Jesus told her.

17 "I don't have a husband," the woman replied.

Jesus said, "You're right! You don't have a husband— 18 for you have had five husbands, and you aren't even married to the man you're living with now. You certainly spoke the truth!"

19 "Sir," the woman said, "you must be a prophet. 20 So tell me, why is it that you Jews insist that Jerusalem is the only place of worship, while we Samaritans claim it is here at Mount Gerizim,* where our ancestors worshiped?"

21 Jesus replied, "Believe me, dear woman, the time is coming when it will no longer matter whether you worship the Father on this mountain or in Jerusalem. 22 You Samaritans know very little about the one you worship, while we Jews know all about him, for salvation comes through the Jews. 23 But the time is coming—indeed it's here now—when true worshipers will worship the Father in spirit and in truth. The Father is looking for those who will worship him that way. 24 For God is Spirit, so those who worship him must worship in spirit and in truth."

25 The woman said, "I know the Messiah is coming—the one who is called Christ. When he comes, he will explain everything to us."

26 Then Jesus told her, "I AM the Messiah!"*

27 Just then his disciples came back. They were shocked to find him talking to a woman, but none of them had the nerve to ask, "What do you want with her?" or "Why are you talking to her?" 28 The woman left her water jar beside the well and ran back to the village, telling everyone, 29 "Come and see a man who told me everything I ever did! Could he possibly be the Messiah?" 30 So the people came streaming from the village to see him.

31 Meanwhile, the disciples were urging Jesus, "Rabbi, eat something."

32 But Jesus replied, "I have a kind of food you know nothing about."

33 "Did someone bring him food while we were gone?" the disciples asked each other.

34 Then Jesus explained: "My nourishment comes from doing the will of God, who sent me, and from finishing his work. 35 You know the saying, 'Four months between planting and harvest.'

SHARING THE GOOD NEWS
John 4:27-38   ROBERT MORRIS

In John 4, Jesus is traveling to Galilee when He stops to rest at a well in a Samaritan village. A Samaritan woman comes to the well, and Jesus shares the good news of His "living water" (v. 10) with her. When the disciples return from buying food, they encourage Jesus to eat, but He replies, "I have a kind of food you know nothing about" (v. 32). The disciples wonder if their Master received food from someone else. They are also silently bewildered as to why Jesus (a Jewish man) would speak to a Samaritan woman— "for Jews refuse to have anything to do with Samaritans" (v. 9). Jesus' answer addresses both questions: "My nourishment comes from doing the will of God, who sent me, and from finishing his work" (v. 34).

Sharing the gospel nourishes us. There is a spiritual refreshing and replenishing that happens when we follow God's command to share the Good News.

But I say, wake up and look around. The fields are already ripe* for harvest. 36 The harvesters are paid good wages, and the fruit they harvest is people brought to eternal life. What joy awaits both the planter and the harvester alike! 37 You know the saying, 'One plants and another harvests.' And it's true. 38 I sent you to harvest where you didn't plant; others had already done the work, and now you will get to gather the harvest."

MANY SAMARITANS BELIEVE

39 Many Samaritans from the village believed in Jesus because the woman had said, "He told me everything I ever did!" 40 When they came out to see him, they begged him to stay in their village. So he stayed for two days, 41 long enough for many more to hear his message and believe. 42 Then they said to the woman, "Now we believe, not just because of what you told us, but because we have heard him ourselves. Now we know that he is indeed the Savior of the world."

JESUS HEALS AN OFFICIAL'S SON

43 At the end of the two days, Jesus went on to Galilee. 44 He himself had said that a prophet is not honored in his own hometown. 45 Yet the Galileans welcomed him, for they had been in Jerusalem at the Passover celebration and had seen everything he did there.

46 As he traveled through Galilee, he came to Cana, where he had turned the water into wine. There was a government official in nearby

4:20 Greek on this mountain. 4:26 Or "The 'I AM' is here"; or "I am the LORD"; Greek reads "I am, the one speaking to you." See Exod 3:14. 4:35 Greek white.

Capernaum whose son was very sick. ⁴⁷When he heard that Jesus had come from Judea to Galilee, he went and begged Jesus to come to Capernaum to heal his son, who was about to die.

⁴⁸Jesus asked, "Will you never believe in me unless you see miraculous signs and wonders?"

⁴⁹The official pleaded, "Lord, please come now before my little boy dies."

⁵⁰Then Jesus told him, "Go back home. Your son will live!" And the man believed what Jesus said and started home.

⁵¹While the man was on his way, some of his servants met him with the news that his son was alive and well. ⁵²He asked them when the boy had begun to get better, and they replied, "Yesterday afternoon at one o'clock his fever suddenly disappeared!" ⁵³Then the father realized that that was the very time Jesus had told him, "Your son will live." And he and his entire household believed in Jesus. ⁵⁴This was the second miraculous sign Jesus did in Galilee after coming from Judea.

JESUS HEALS A LAME MAN

5 Afterward Jesus returned to Jerusalem for one of the Jewish holy days. ²Inside the city, near the Sheep Gate, was the pool of Bethesda,* with five covered porches. ³Crowds of sick people—blind, lame, or paralyzed—lay on the porches.* ⁵One of the men lying there had been sick for thirty-eight years. ⁶When Jesus saw him and knew he had been ill for a long time, he asked him, "Would you like to get well?"

⁷"I can't, sir," the sick man said, "for I have no one to put me into the pool when the water bubbles up. Someone else always gets there ahead of me."

⁸Jesus told him, "Stand up, pick up your mat, and walk!"

⁹Instantly, the man was healed! He rolled up his sleeping mat and began walking! But this miracle happened on the Sabbath, ¹⁰so the Jewish leaders objected. They said to the man who was cured, "You can't work on the Sabbath! The law doesn't allow you to carry that sleeping mat!"

¹¹But he replied, "The man who healed me told me, 'Pick up your mat and walk.'"

¹²"Who said such a thing as that?" they demanded.

¹³The man didn't know, for Jesus had disappeared into the crowd. ¹⁴But afterward Jesus found him in the Temple and told him, "Now you are well; so stop sinning, or something even worse may happen to you." ¹⁵Then the man went and told the Jewish leaders that it was Jesus who had healed him.

JESUS CLAIMS TO BE THE SON OF GOD

¹⁶So the Jewish leaders began harassing* Jesus for breaking the Sabbath rules. ¹⁷But Jesus replied, "My Father is always working, and so am I." ¹⁸So the Jewish leaders tried all the harder to find a way to kill him. For he not only broke

THE LAME MAN'S STORY
John 5:1-30   ROBERT MORRIS

In John 5, we read the story of the lame man's encounter with Jesus at the pool of Bethesda. Jesus asks, "Would you like to get well?" (v. 6). Surprisingly, the man does not respond, "Yes!" But why wouldn't he want to be healed? And why do we often respond to God the same way?

1. Excuses
We often make excuses to explain why we're "different" and why God's healing won't work for us. The lame man said there was no one to help him into the pool (v. 7), which is the same as saying, "It's not my fault." This is the number one excuse in society for our problems—*someone else did something to me.* It is also one of the top lies of the enemy. No one can stop God's plans for us except us. People often tell me, "Pastor, you just don't understand my situation." I may not understand all the details, but I understand Jesus. He is the same yesterday, today, and forever (Hebrews 13:8), and no situation is beyond His power to redeem and overcome.

2. Effort
Jesus didn't tell the lame man, "Be healed!" Instead, He said, "Stand up, pick up your mat, and walk!" (v. 8). After being sick for 38 years, the man had to put some effort into his healing. It's easy for us to become comfortable in our weakness, so when Jesus says, "Would you like to get well?" He is really asking, "Are you willing to change your thinking and actions?" Are you willing to give up whatever is holding you down, such as bitterness, rejection, or self-pity?

3. Experience
Sometimes we miss God's healing because it looks different from our previous experiences. The lame man expected an angel to come down and stir the water, so he didn't recognize that Jesus was God. Jesus also told him to carry his bed on the Sabbath, which went against the man's religious upbringing. It is possible that for you to be healed, you will have to step out of your comfort zone. God may not come in the way you expect, so ask the Holy Spirit to show you what He wants you to do to pursue healing. Then obey whatever He asks you to do.

the Sabbath, he called God his Father, thereby making himself equal with God.

5:2 Other manuscripts read *Beth-zatha;* still others read *Bethsaida.* 5:3 Some manuscripts add an expanded conclusion to verse 3 and all of verse 4: *waiting for a certain movement of the water, "for an angel of the Lord came from time to time and stirred up the water. And the first person to step in after the water was stirred was healed of whatever disease he had.* 5:16 Or *persecuting.*

[19] So Jesus explained, "I tell you the truth, the Son can do nothing by himself. He does only what he sees the Father doing. Whatever the Father does, the Son also does. [20] For the Father loves the Son and shows him everything he is doing. In fact, the Father will show him how to do even greater works than healing this man. Then you will truly be astonished. [21] For just as the Father gives life to those he raises from the dead, so the Son gives life to anyone he wants. [22] In addition, the Father judges no one. Instead, he has given the Son absolute authority to judge, [23] so that everyone will honor the Son, just as they honor the Father. Anyone who does not honor the Son is certainly not honoring the Father who sent him.

[24] "I tell you the truth, those who listen to my message and believe in God who sent me have eternal life. They will never be condemned for their sins, but they have already passed from death into life.

[25] "And I assure you that the time is coming, indeed it's here now, when the dead will hear my voice—the voice of the Son of God. And those who listen will live. [26] The Father has life in himself, and he has granted that same life-giving power to his Son. [27] And he has given him authority to judge everyone because he is the Son of Man.* [28] Don't be so surprised! Indeed, the time is coming when all the dead in their graves will hear the voice of God's Son, [29] and they will rise again. Those who have done good will rise to experience eternal life, and those who have continued in evil will rise to experience judgment. [30] I can do nothing on my own. I judge as God tells me. Therefore, my judgment is just, because I carry out the will of the one who sent me, not my own will.

WITNESSES TO JESUS

[31] "If I were to testify on my own behalf, my testimony would not be valid. [32] But someone else is also testifying about me, and I assure you that everything he says about me is true. [33] In fact, you sent investigators to listen to John the Baptist, and his testimony about me was true. [34] Of course, I have no need of human witnesses, but I say these things so you might be saved. [35] John was like a burning and shining lamp, and you were excited for a while about his message. [36] But I have a greater witness than John—my teachings and my miracles. The Father gave me these works to accomplish, and they prove that he sent me. [37] And the Father who sent me has testified about me himself. You have never heard his voice or seen him face to face, [38] and you do not have his message in your hearts, because you do not believe me—the one he sent to you.

[39] "You search the Scriptures because you think they give you eternal life. But the Scriptures point to me! [40] Yet you refuse to come to me to receive this life.

[41] "Your approval means nothing to me, [42] because I know you don't have God's love within you. [43] For I have come to you in my Father's name, and you have rejected me. Yet if others come in their own name, you gladly welcome them. [44] No wonder you can't believe! For you gladly honor each other, but you don't care about the honor that comes from the one who alone is God.*

[45] "Yet it isn't I who will accuse you before the Father. Moses will accuse you! Yes, Moses, in whom you put your hopes. [46] If you really believed Moses, you would believe me, because he wrote about me. [47] But since you don't believe what he wrote, how will you believe what I say?"

JESUS FEEDS FIVE THOUSAND

6 After this, Jesus crossed over to the far side of the Sea of Galilee, also known as the Sea of Tiberias. [2] A huge crowd kept following him wherever he went, because they saw his miraculous signs as he healed the sick. [3] Then Jesus climbed a hill and sat down with his disciples around him. [4] (It was nearly time for the Jewish Passover celebration.) [5] Jesus soon saw a huge crowd of people coming to look for him. Turning to Philip, he asked, "Where can we buy bread to feed all these people?" [6] He was testing Philip, for he already knew what he was going to do.

[7] Philip replied, "Even if we worked for months, we wouldn't have enough money* to feed them!"

[8] Then Andrew, Simon Peter's brother, spoke up. [9] "There's a young boy here with five barley loaves and two fish. But what good is that with this huge crowd?"

[10] "Tell everyone to sit down," Jesus said. So they all sat down on the grassy slopes. (The men alone numbered about 5,000.) [11] Then Jesus took the loaves, gave thanks to God, and distributed them to the people. Afterward he did the same with the fish. And they all ate as much as they wanted. [12] After everyone was full, Jesus told his disciples, "Now gather the leftovers, so that nothing is wasted." [13] So they picked up the pieces and filled twelve baskets with scraps left by the people who had eaten from the five barley loaves.

[14] When the people saw him* do this miraculous sign, they exclaimed, "Surely, he is the Prophet we have been expecting!"* [15] When Jesus saw that they were ready to force him to be their king, he slipped away into the hills by himself.

JESUS WALKS ON WATER

[16] That evening Jesus' disciples went down to the shore to wait for him. [17] But as darkness fell and Jesus still hadn't come back, they got into the

---

5:27 "Son of Man" is a title Jesus used for himself.   5:44 Some manuscripts read *from the only One.*   6:7 Greek *Two hundred denarii would not be enough.* A denarius was equivalent to a laborer's full day's wage.   6:14a Some manuscripts read *Jesus.* 6:14b See Deut 18:15, 18; Mal 4:5-6.

boat and headed across the lake toward Capernaum. [18] Soon a gale swept down upon them, and the sea grew very rough. [19] They had rowed three or four miles* when suddenly they saw Jesus walking on the water toward the boat. They were terrified, [20] but he called out to them, "Don't be afraid. I am here!*" [21] Then they were eager to let him in the boat, and immediately they arrived at their destination!

JESUS, THE BREAD OF LIFE

[22] The next day the crowd that had stayed on the far shore saw that the disciples had taken the only boat, and they realized Jesus had not gone with them. [23] Several boats from Tiberias landed near the place where the Lord had blessed the bread and the people had eaten. [24] So when the crowd saw that neither Jesus nor his disciples were there, they got into the boats and went across to Capernaum to look for him. [25] They found him on the other side of the lake and asked, "Rabbi, when did you get here?"

[26] Jesus replied, "I tell you the truth, you want to be with me because I fed you, not because you understood the miraculous signs. [27] But don't be so concerned about perishable things like food. Spend your energy seeking the eternal life that the Son of Man* can give you. For God the Father has given me the seal of his approval."

[28] They replied, "We want to perform God's works, too. What should we do?"

[29] Jesus told them, "This is the only work God wants from you: Believe in the one he has sent."

[30] They answered, "Show us a miraculous sign if you want us to believe in you. What can you do? [31] After all, our ancestors ate manna while they journeyed through the wilderness! The Scriptures say, 'Moses gave them bread from heaven to eat.'*"

[32] Jesus said, "I tell you the truth, Moses didn't give you bread from heaven. My Father did. And now he offers you the true bread from heaven. [33] The true bread of God is the one who comes down from heaven and gives life to the world."

[34] "Sir," they said, "give us that bread every day."

[35] Jesus replied, "I am the bread of life. Whoever comes to me will never be hungry again. Whoever believes in me will never be thirsty. [36] But you haven't believed in me even though you have seen me. [37] However, those the Father has given me will come to me, and I will never reject them. [38] For I have come down from heaven to do the will of God who sent me, not to do my own will. [39] And this is the will of God, that I should not lose even one of all those he has given me, but that I should raise them up at the last day. [40] For it is my Father's will that all who see his Son and believe in him should have eternal life. I will raise them up at the last day."

[41] Then the people* began to murmur in disagreement because he had said, "I am the bread that came down from heaven." [42] They said, "Isn't this Jesus, the son of Joseph? We know his father and mother. How can he say, 'I came down from heaven'?"

[43] But Jesus replied, "Stop complaining about what I said. [44] For no one can come to me unless the Father who sent me draws them to me, and at the last day I will raise them up. [45] As it is written in the Scriptures,* 'They will all be taught by God.' Everyone who listens to the Father and learns from him comes to me. [46] (Not that anyone has ever seen the Father; only I, who was sent from God, have seen him.)

[47] "I tell you the truth, anyone who believes has eternal life. [48] Yes, I am the bread of life! [49] Your ancestors ate manna in the wilderness, but they all died. [50] Anyone who eats the bread from heaven, however, will never die. [51] I am the living bread that came down from heaven. Anyone who eats this bread will live forever; and this bread, which I will offer so the world may live, is my flesh."

[52] Then the people began arguing with each other about what he meant. "How can this man give us his flesh to eat?" they asked.

[53] So Jesus said again, "I tell you the truth, unless you eat the flesh of the Son of Man and drink his blood, you cannot have eternal life within you. [54] But anyone who eats my flesh and drinks my blood has eternal life, and I will raise that person at the last day. [55] For my flesh is true food, and my blood is true drink. [56] Anyone who eats my flesh and drinks my blood remains in me, and I in him. [57] I live because of the living Father who sent me; in the same way, anyone who feeds on me will live because of me. [58] I am the true bread that came down from heaven. Anyone who eats this bread will not die as your ancestors did (even though they ate the manna) but will live forever."

[59] He said these things while he was teaching in the synagogue in Capernaum.

MANY DISCIPLES DESERT JESUS

[60] Many of his disciples said, "This is very hard to understand. How can anyone accept it?"

[61] Jesus was aware that his disciples were complaining, so he said to them, "Does this offend you? [62] Then what will you think if you see the Son of Man ascend to heaven again? [63] The Spirit alone gives eternal life. Human effort accomplishes nothing. And the very words I have spoken to you are spirit and life. [64] But some of you do not believe me." (For Jesus knew from the beginning which ones didn't believe, and he knew who would betray him.) [65] Then he said, "That is why I said that people can't come to me unless the Father gives them to me."

6:19 Greek 25 or 30 stadia [4.6 or 5.5 kilometers]. 6:20 Or The 'I AM' is here; Greek reads I am. See Exod 3:14. 6:27 "Son of Man" is a title Jesus used for himself. 6:31 Exod 16:4; Ps 78:24. 6:41 Greek Jewish people; also in 6:52. 6:45 Greek in the prophets. Isa 54:13.

66 At this point many of his disciples turned away and deserted him. 67 Then Jesus turned to the Twelve and asked, "Are you also going to leave?"

68 Simon Peter replied, "Lord, to whom would we go? You have the words that give eternal life. 69 We believe, and we know you are the Holy One of God.*"

70 Then Jesus said, "I chose the twelve of you, but one is a devil." 71 He was speaking of Judas, son of Simon Iscariot, one of the Twelve, who would later betray him.

JESUS AND HIS BROTHERS

7 After this, Jesus traveled around Galilee. He wanted to stay out of Judea, where the Jewish leaders were plotting his death. 2 But soon it was time for the Jewish Festival of Shelters, 3 and Jesus' brothers said to him, "Leave here and go to Judea, where your followers can see your miracles! 4 You can't become famous if you hide like this! If you can do such wonderful things, show yourself to the world!" 5 For even his brothers didn't believe in him.

6 Jesus replied, "Now is not the right time for me to go, but you can go anytime. 7 The world can't hate you, but it does hate me because I accuse it of doing evil. 8 You go on. I'm not going* to this festival, because my time has not yet come." 9 After saying these things, Jesus remained in Galilee.

JESUS TEACHES OPENLY AT THE TEMPLE

10 But after his brothers left for the festival, Jesus also went, though secretly, staying out of public view. 11 The Jewish leaders tried to find him at the festival and kept asking if anyone had seen him. 12 There was a lot of grumbling about him among the crowds. Some argued, "He's a good man," but others said, "He's nothing but a fraud who deceives the people." 13 But no one had the courage to speak favorably about him in public, for they were afraid of getting in trouble with the Jewish leaders.

14 Then, midway through the festival, Jesus went up to the Temple and began to teach. 15 The people* were surprised when they heard him. "How does he know so much when he hasn't been trained?" they asked.

16 So Jesus told them, "My message is not my own; it comes from God who sent me. 17 Anyone who wants to do the will of God will know whether my teaching is from God or is merely my own. 18 Those who speak for themselves want glory only for themselves, but a person who seeks to honor the one who sent him speaks truth, not lies. 19 Moses gave you the law, but none of you obeys it! In fact, you are trying to kill me."

20 The crowd replied, "You're demon possessed! Who's trying to kill you?"

21 Jesus replied, "I did one miracle on the Sabbath, and you were amazed. 22 But you work on the Sabbath, too, when you obey Moses' law of circumcision. (Actually, this tradition of circumcision began with the patriarchs, long before the law of Moses.) 23 For if the correct time for circumcising your son falls on the Sabbath, you go ahead and do it so as not to break the law of Moses. So why should you be angry with me for healing a man on the Sabbath? 24 Look beneath the surface so you can judge correctly."

IS JESUS THE MESSIAH?

25 Some of the people who lived in Jerusalem started to ask each other, "Isn't this the man they are trying to kill? 26 But here he is, speaking in public, and they say nothing to him. Could our leaders possibly believe that he is the Messiah? 27 But how could he be? For we know where this man comes from. When the Messiah comes, he will simply appear; no one will know where he comes from."

28 While Jesus was teaching in the Temple, he called out, "Yes, you know me, and you know where I come from. But I'm not here on my own. The one who sent me is true, and you don't know him. 29 But I know him because I come from him, and he sent me to you." 30 Then the leaders tried to arrest him; but no one laid a hand on him, because his time* had not yet come.

31 Many among the crowds at the Temple believed in him. "After all," they said, "would you expect the Messiah to do more miraculous signs than this man has done?"

32 When the Pharisees heard that the crowds were whispering such things, they and the leading priests sent Temple guards to arrest Jesus. 33 But Jesus told them, "I will be with you only a little longer. Then I will return to the one who sent me. 34 You will search for me but not find me. And you cannot go where I am going."

35 The Jewish leaders were puzzled by this statement. "Where is he planning to go?" they asked. "Is he thinking of leaving the country and going to the Jews in other lands?* Maybe he will even teach the Greeks! 36 What does he mean when he says, 'You will search for me but not find me,' and 'You cannot go where I am going'?"

JESUS PROMISES LIVING WATER

37 On the last day, the climax of the festival, Jesus stood and shouted to the crowds, "Anyone who is thirsty may come to me! 38 Anyone who believes in me may come and drink! For the Scriptures declare, 'Rivers of living water will flow from his heart.'* 39 (When he said "living water," he was speaking of the Spirit, who would be given

6:69 Other manuscripts read you are the Christ, the Holy One of God; still others read you are the Christ, the Son of God; and still others read you are the Christ, the Son of the living God. 7:8 Some manuscripts read not yet going. 7:15 Greek Jewish people. 7:30 Greek his hour. 7:35 Or the Jews who live among the Greeks? 7:37-38 Or "Let anyone who is thirsty come to me and drink. 38 For the Scriptures declare, 'Rivers of living water will flow from the heart of anyone who believes in me.'"

to everyone believing in him. But the Spirit had not yet been given,* because Jesus had not yet entered into his glory.)

DIVISION AND UNBELIEF

⁴⁰ When the crowds heard him say this, some of them declared, "Surely this man is the Prophet we've been expecting."* ⁴¹ Others said, "He is the Messiah." Still others said, "But he can't be! Will the Messiah come from Galilee? ⁴² For the Scriptures clearly state that the Messiah will be born of the royal line of David, in Bethlehem, the village where King David was born."* ⁴³ So the crowd was divided about him. ⁴⁴ Some even wanted him arrested, but no one laid a hand on him.

⁴⁵ When the Temple guards returned without having arrested Jesus, the leading priests and Pharisees demanded, "Why didn't you bring him in?"

⁴⁶ "We have never heard anyone speak like this!" the guards responded.

⁴⁷ "Have you been led astray, too?" the Pharisees mocked. ⁴⁸ "Is there a single one of us rulers or Pharisees who believes in him? ⁴⁹ This foolish crowd follows him, but they are ignorant of the law. God's curse is on them!"

⁵⁰ Then Nicodemus, the leader who had met with Jesus earlier, spoke up. ⁵¹ "Is it legal to convict a man before he is given a hearing?" he asked.

⁵² They replied, "Are you from Galilee, too? Search the Scriptures and see for yourself—no prophet ever comes* from Galilee!"

[The most ancient Greek manuscripts do not include John 7:53–8:11.]

⁵³ Then the meeting broke up, and everybody went home.

A WOMAN CAUGHT IN ADULTERY

8 Jesus returned to the Mount of Olives, ²but early the next morning he was back again at the Temple. A crowd soon gathered, and he sat down and taught them. ³As he was speaking, the teachers of religious law and the Pharisees brought a woman who had been caught in the act of adultery. They put her in front of the crowd.

⁴ "Teacher," they said to Jesus, "this woman was caught in the act of adultery. ⁵ The law of Moses says to stone her. What do you say?"

⁶ They were trying to trap him into saying something they could use against him, but Jesus stooped down and wrote in the dust with his finger. ⁷ They kept demanding an answer, so he stood up again and said, "All right, but let the one who has never sinned throw the first stone!" ⁸ Then he stooped down again and wrote in the dust.

⁹ When the accusers heard this, they slipped away one by one, beginning with the oldest, until only Jesus was left in the middle of the crowd with the woman. ¹⁰ Then Jesus stood up again and said to the woman, "Where are your accusers? Didn't even one of them condemn you?"

¹¹ "No, Lord," she said.

And Jesus said, "Neither do I. Go and sin no more."

JESUS, THE LIGHT OF THE WORLD

¹² Jesus spoke to the people once more and said, "I am the light of the world. If you follow me, you won't have to walk in darkness, because you will have the light that leads to life."

¹³ The Pharisees replied, "You are making those claims about yourself! Such testimony is not valid."

¹⁴ Jesus told them, "These claims are valid even though I make them about myself. For I know where I came from and where I am going, but you don't know this about me. ¹⁵ You judge me by human standards, but I do not judge anyone. ¹⁶ And if I did, my judgment would be correct in every respect because I am not alone. The Father* who sent me is with me. ¹⁷ Your own law says that if two people agree about something, their witness is accepted as fact.* ¹⁸ I am one witness, and my Father who sent me is the other."

¹⁹ "Where is your father?" they asked.

Jesus answered, "Since you don't know who I am, you don't know who my Father is. If you knew me, you would also know my Father." ²⁰ Jesus made these statements while he was teaching in the section of the Temple known as the Treasury. But he was not arrested, because his time* had not yet come.

THE UNBELIEVING PEOPLE WARNED

²¹ Later Jesus said to them again, "I am going away. You will search for me but will die in your sin. You cannot come where I am going."

²² The people* asked, "Is he planning to commit suicide? What does he mean, 'You cannot come where I am going'?"

²³ Jesus continued, "You are from below; I am from above. You belong to this world; I do not. ²⁴ That is why I said that you will die in your sins; for unless you believe that I AM who I claim to be,* you will die in your sins."

²⁵ "Who are you?" they demanded.

Jesus replied, "The one I have always claimed to be.* ²⁶ I have much to say about you and much to condemn, but I won't. For I say only what I have heard from the one who sent me, and he is completely truthful." ²⁷ But they still didn't understand that he was talking about his Father.

7:39 Several early manuscripts read *But as yet there was no Spirit.* Still others read *But as yet there was no Holy Spirit.* **7:40** See Deut 18:15, 18; Mal 4:5-6. **7:42** See Mic 5:2. **7:52** Some manuscripts read *the prophet does not come.* **8:16** Some manuscripts read *The One.* **8:17** See Deut 19:15. **8:20** Greek *his hour.* **8:22** Greek *Jewish people;* also in 8:31, 48, 52, 57. **8:24** Greek *unless you believe that I am.* See Exod 3:14. **8:25** Or *Why do I speak to you at all?*

[28] So Jesus said, "When you have lifted up the Son of Man on the cross, then you will understand that I AM he.* I do nothing on my own but say only what the Father taught me. [29] And the one who sent me is with me—he has not deserted me. For I always do what pleases him." [30] Then many who heard him say these things believed in him.

JESUS AND ABRAHAM

[31] Jesus said to the people who believed in him, "You are truly my disciples if you remain faithful to my teachings. [32] And you will know the truth, and the truth will set you free."

[33] "But we are descendants of Abraham," they said. "We have never been slaves to anyone. What do you mean, 'You will be set free'?"

[34] Jesus replied, "I tell you the truth, everyone who sins is a slave of sin. [35] A slave is not a permanent member of the family, but a son is part of the family forever. [36] So if the Son sets you free, you are truly free. [37] Yes, I realize that you are descendants of Abraham. And yet some of you are trying to kill me because there's no room in your hearts for my message. [38] I am telling you what I saw when I was with my Father. But you are following the advice of your father."

[39] "Our father is Abraham!" they declared.

"No," Jesus replied, "for if you were really the children of Abraham, you would follow his example.* [40] Instead, you are trying to kill me because I told you the truth, which I heard from God. Abraham never did such a thing. [41] No, you are imitating your real father."

They replied, "We aren't illegitimate children! God himself is our true Father."

[42] Jesus told them, "If God were your Father, you would love me, because I have come to you from God. I am not here on my own, but he sent me. [43] Why can't you understand what I am saying? It's because you can't even hear me! [44] For you are the children of your father the devil, and you love to do the evil things he does. He was a murderer from the beginning. He has always hated the truth, because there is no truth in him. When he lies, it is consistent with his character; for he is a liar and the father of lies. [45] So when I tell the truth, you just naturally don't believe me! [46] Which of you can truthfully accuse me of sin? And since I am telling you the truth, why don't you believe me? [47] Anyone who belongs to God listens gladly to the words of God. But you don't listen because you don't belong to God."

[48] The people retorted, "You Samaritan devil! Didn't we say all along that you were possessed by a demon?"

[49] "No," Jesus said, "I have no demon in me. For I honor my Father—and you dishonor me. [50] And though I have no wish to glorify myself, God is going to glorify me. He is the true judge. [51] I tell you the truth, anyone who obeys my teaching will never die!"

[52] The people said, "Now we know you are possessed by a demon. Even Abraham and the prophets died, but you say, 'Anyone who obeys my teaching will never die!' [53] Are you greater than our father Abraham? He died, and so did the prophets. Who do you think you are?"

[54] Jesus answered, "If I want glory for myself, it doesn't count. But it is my Father who will glorify me. You say, 'He is our God,'* [55] but you don't even know him. I know him. If I said otherwise, I would be as great a liar as you! But I do know him and obey him. [56] Your father Abraham rejoiced as he looked forward to my coming. He saw it and was glad."

SET FREE
John 8:31-36   ROBERT MORRIS

At Gateway Church, one of our core values is to see every believer set free. In John 8:31-32, Jesus says those who faithfully follow His teachings "will know the truth, and the truth will set you free." Here are three key truths about being set free:

1. It's possible for believers to be in bondage. You may ask, *What is bondage?* Bondage is any impulsive or compulsive behavior that restricts us from walking in freedom and enjoying the blessings Jesus died to give us.

Jesus wasn't talking to unbelievers in John 8—He was talking to believers! We become free from the penalty of sin when we are saved, but we still need to be set free from the *power* of sin. It's possible to be saved and still have bondage in our lives.

2. It's difficult to admit you're in bondage. When Jesus told the Jews the truth would set them free, they argued, "We have never been slaves to anyone" (John 8:33). Apparently, these people had forgotten their own history; they had been in bondage to the Egyptians, Chaldeans, and Babylonians, not to mention their current bondage to the Romans! I encounter believers every week who say, "I'm a Christian, so I can't be in bondage." But if you keep struggling with sin in a certain area, you don't have a "weakness"—you have a bondage.

3. It's easy to be set free from bondage. Here's the good news about being set free: it doesn't depend on you! First John 3:8 says, "The Son of God came to destroy the works of the devil." Satan wants believers to think freedom is impossible. Here's the truth, though: it's not your responsibility to get set free. It's your responsibility to come to Jesus. If you come, He will set you free!

8:28 Greek *When you have lifted up the Son of Man, then you will know that I am.* "Son of Man" is a title Jesus used for himself. **8:39** Some manuscripts read *if you are really the children of Abraham, follow his example.* **8:54** Some manuscripts read *You say he is your God.*

[57] The people said, "You aren't even fifty years old. How can you say you have seen Abraham?*"

[58] Jesus answered, "I tell you the truth, before Abraham was even born, I Am!*" [59] At that point they picked up stones to throw at him. But Jesus was hidden from them and left the Temple.

JESUS HEALS A MAN BORN BLIND

9 As Jesus was walking along, he saw a man who had been blind from birth. [2] "Rabbi," his disciples asked him, "why was this man born blind? Was it because of his own sins or his parents' sins?"

[3] "It was not because of his sins or his parents' sins," Jesus answered. "This happened so the power of God could be seen in him. [4] We must quickly carry out the tasks assigned us by the one who sent us.* The night is coming, and then no one can work. [5] But while I am here in the world, I am the light of the world."

[6] Then he spit on the ground, made mud with the saliva, and spread the mud over the blind man's eyes. [7] He told him, "Go wash yourself in the pool of Siloam" (Siloam means "sent"). So the man went and washed and came back seeing!

[8] His neighbors and others who knew him as a blind beggar asked each other, "Isn't this the man who used to sit and beg?" [9] Some said he was, and others said, "No, he just looks like him!"

But the beggar kept saying, "Yes, I am the same one!"

[10] They asked, "Who healed you? What happened?"

[11] He told them, "The man they call Jesus made mud and spread it over my eyes and told me, 'Go to the pool of Siloam and wash yourself.' So I went and washed, and now I can see!"

[12] "Where is he now?" they asked.

"I don't know," he replied.

[13] Then they took the man who had been blind to the Pharisees, [14] because it was on the Sabbath that Jesus had made the mud and healed him. [15] The Pharisees asked the man all about it. So he told them, "He put the mud over my eyes, and when I washed it away, I could see!"

[16] Some of the Pharisees said, "This man Jesus is not from God, for he is working on the Sabbath." Others said, "But how could an ordinary sinner do such miraculous signs?" So there was a deep division of opinion among them.

[17] Then the Pharisees again questioned the man who had been blind and demanded, "What's your opinion about this man who healed you?"

The man replied, "I think he must be a prophet."

[18] The Jewish leaders still refused to believe the man had been blind and could now see, so they called in his parents. [19] They asked them, "Is this your son? Was he born blind? If so, how can he now see?"

[20] His parents replied, "We know this is our son and that he was born blind, [21] but we don't know how he can see or who healed him. Ask him. He is old enough to speak for himself." [22] His parents said this because they were afraid of the Jewish leaders, who had announced that anyone saying Jesus was the Messiah would be expelled from the synagogue. [23] That's why they said, "He is old enough. Ask him."

[24] So for the second time they called in the man who had been blind and told him, "God should get the glory for this,* because we know this man Jesus is a sinner."

[25] "I don't know whether he is a sinner," the man replied. "But I know this: I was blind, and now I can see!"

[26] "But what did he do?" they asked. "How did he heal you?"

[27] "Look!" the man exclaimed. "I told you once. Didn't you listen? Why do you want to hear it again? Do you want to become his disciples, too?"

[28] Then they cursed him and said, "You are his disciple, but we are disciples of Moses! [29] We know God spoke to Moses, but we don't even know where this man comes from."

[30] "Why, that's very strange!" the man replied. "He healed my eyes, and yet you don't know where he comes from? [31] We know that God doesn't listen to sinners, but he is ready to hear those who worship him and do his will. [32] Ever since the world began, no one has been able to open the eyes of someone born blind. [33] If this man were not from God, he couldn't have done it."

[34] "You were born a total sinner!" they answered. "Are you trying to teach us?" And they threw him out of the synagogue.

SPIRITUAL BLINDNESS

[35] When Jesus heard what had happened, he found the man and asked, "Do you believe in the Son of Man?*"

[36] The man answered, "Who is he, sir? I want to believe in him."

[37] "You have seen him," Jesus said, "and he is speaking to you!"

[38] "Yes, Lord, I believe!" the man said. And he worshiped Jesus.

[39] Then Jesus told him,* "I entered this world to render judgment—to give sight to the blind and to show those who think they see* that they are blind."

[40] Some Pharisees who were standing nearby heard him and asked, "Are you saying we're blind?"

[41] "If you were blind, you wouldn't be guilty," Jesus replied. "But you remain guilty because you claim you can see.

8:57 Some manuscripts read How can you say Abraham has seen you? 8:58 Or before Abraham was even born, I have always been alive; Greek reads before Abraham was, I am. See Exod 3:14. 9:4 Other manuscripts read I must quickly carry out the tasks assigned me by the one who sent me; still others read We must quickly carry out the tasks assigned us by the one who sent me. 9:24 Or Give glory to God, not to Jesus; Greek reads Give glory to God. 9:35 Some manuscripts read the Son of God? "Son of Man" is a title Jesus used for himself. 9:38-39a Some manuscripts do not include "Yes, Lord, I believe!" the man said. And he worshiped Jesus. Then Jesus told him. 9:39b Greek those who see.

THE GOOD SHEPHERD AND HIS SHEEP

10 "I tell you the truth, anyone who sneaks over the wall of a sheepfold, rather than going through the gate, must surely be a thief and a robber! ²But the one who enters through the gate is the shepherd of the sheep. ³The gatekeeper opens the gate for him, and the sheep recognize his voice and come to him. He calls his own sheep by name and leads them out. ⁴After he has gathered his own flock, he walks ahead of them, and they follow him because they know his voice. ⁵They won't follow a stranger; they will run from him because they don't know his voice."

⁶Those who heard Jesus use this illustration didn't understand what he meant, ⁷so he explained it to them: "I tell you the truth, I am the gate for the sheep. ⁸All who came before me* were thieves and robbers. But the true sheep did not listen to them. ⁹Yes, I am the gate. Those who come in through me will be saved.* They will come and go freely and will find good pastures. ¹⁰The thief's purpose is to steal and kill and destroy. My purpose is to give them a rich and satisfying life.

¹¹"I am the good shepherd. The good shepherd sacrifices his life for the sheep. ¹²A hired hand will run when he sees a wolf coming. He will abandon the sheep because they don't belong to him and he isn't their shepherd. And so the wolf attacks them and scatters the flock. ¹³The hired hand runs away because he's working only for the money and doesn't really care about the sheep.

¹⁴"I am the good shepherd; I know my own sheep, and they know me, ¹⁵just as my Father knows me and I know the Father. So I sacrifice my life for the sheep. ¹⁶I have other sheep, too, that are not in this sheepfold. I must bring them also. They will listen to my voice, and there will be one flock with one shepherd.

¹⁷"The Father loves me because I sacrifice my life so I may take it back again. ¹⁸No one can take my life from me. I sacrifice it voluntarily. For I have the authority to lay it down when I want to and also to take it up again. For this is what my Father has commanded."

¹⁹When he said these things, the people* were again divided in their opinions about him. ²⁰Some said, "He's demon possessed and out of his mind. Why listen to a man like that?" ²¹Others said, "This doesn't sound like a man possessed by a demon! Can a demon open the eyes of the blind?"

JESUS CLAIMS TO BE THE SON OF GOD

²²It was now winter, and Jesus was in Jerusalem at the time of Hanukkah, the Festival of Dedication. ²³He was in the Temple, walking through the section known as Solomon's Colonnade. ²⁴The people surrounded him and asked, "How long are you going to keep us in suspense? If you are the Messiah, tell us plainly."

WHO IS OUR SHEPHERD?
John 10:1–21   ROBERT MORRIS

Jesus is our Shepherd, and we are His sheep. A shepherd never drives his sheep; instead, "the sheep recognize his voice and come to him" (John 10:3). The more time we spend with Jesus, the better we will recognize His voice.

A shepherd's job is to protect and provide for his sheep. As our Good Shepherd, Jesus destroyed the enemy we fear most—death. Through His sacrifice on the cross, He made a way for us to have a right relationship with God. Sheep sometimes get into trouble, but Jesus protects us even in "the darkest valley" (Psalm 23:4). He offers goodness, mercy, and eternal life to everyone who follows Him.

²⁵Jesus replied, "I have already told you, and you don't believe me. The proof is the work I do in my Father's name. ²⁶But you don't believe me because you are not my sheep. ²⁷My sheep listen to my voice; I know them, and they follow me. ²⁸I give them eternal life, and they will never perish. No one can snatch them away from me, ²⁹for my Father has given them to me, and he is more powerful than anyone else.* No one can snatch them from the Father's hand. ³⁰The Father and I are one."

³¹Once again the people picked up stones to kill him. ³²Jesus said, "At my Father's direction I have done many good works. For which one are you going to stone me?"

³³They replied, "We're stoning you not for any good work, but for blasphemy! You, a mere man, claim to be God."

³⁴Jesus replied, "It is written in your own Scriptures* that God said to certain leaders of the people, 'I say, you are gods!'* ³⁵And you know that the Scriptures cannot be altered. So if those people who received God's message were called 'gods,' ³⁶why do you call it blasphemy when I say, 'I am the Son of God'? After all, the Father set me apart and sent me into the world. ³⁷Don't believe me unless I carry out my Father's work. ³⁸But if I do his work, believe in the evidence of the miraculous works I have done, even if you don't believe me. Then you will know and understand that the Father is in me, and I am in the Father."

³⁹Once again they tried to arrest him, but he got away and left them. ⁴⁰He went beyond the Jordan River near the place where John was first baptizing and stayed there awhile. ⁴¹And many followed him. "John didn't perform miraculous

---

10:8 Some manuscripts do not include *before me.* 10:9 Or *will find safety.* 10:19 Greek *Jewish people;* also in 10:24, 31. 10:29 Other manuscripts read *for what my Father has given me is more powerful than anything;* still others read *for regarding that which my Father has given me, he is greater than all.* 10:34a Greek *your own law.* 10:34b Ps 82:6.

signs," they remarked to one another, "but everything he said about this man has come true." [42]And many who were there believed in Jesus.

THE RAISING OF LAZARUS

11 A man named Lazarus was sick. He lived in Bethany with his sisters, Mary and Martha. [2]This is the Mary who later poured the expensive perfume on the Lord's feet and wiped them with her hair.* Her brother, Lazarus, was sick. [3]So the two sisters sent a message to Jesus telling him, "Lord, your dear friend is very sick."

[4]But when Jesus heard about it he said, "Lazarus's sickness will not end in death. No, it happened for the glory of God so that the Son of God will receive glory from this." [5]So although Jesus loved Martha, Mary, and Lazarus, [6]he stayed where he was for the next two days. [7]Finally, he said to his disciples, "Let's go back to Judea."

[8]But his disciples objected. "Rabbi," they said, "only a few days ago the people* in Judea were trying to stone you. Are you going there again?" [9]Jesus replied, "There are twelve hours of daylight every day. During the day people can walk safely. They can see because they have the light of this world. [10]But at night there is danger of stumbling because they have no light." [11]Then he said, "Our friend Lazarus has fallen asleep, but now I will go and wake him up."

[12]The disciples said, "Lord, if he is sleeping, he will soon get better!" [13]They thought Jesus meant Lazarus was simply sleeping, but Jesus meant Lazarus had died.

[14]So he told them plainly, "Lazarus is dead. [15]And for your sakes, I'm glad I wasn't there, for now you will really believe. Come, let's go see him."

[16]Thomas, nicknamed the Twin,* said to his fellow disciples, "Let's go, too—and die with Jesus."

[17]When Jesus arrived at Bethany, he was told that Lazarus had already been in his grave for four days. [18]Bethany was only a few miles* down the road from Jerusalem, [19]and many of the people had come to console Martha and Mary in their loss. [20]When Martha got word that Jesus was coming, she went to meet him. But Mary stayed in the house. [21]Martha said to Jesus, "Lord, if only you had been here, my brother would not have died. [22]But even now I know that God will give you whatever you ask."

[23]Jesus told her, "Your brother will rise again."

[24]"Yes," Martha said, "he will rise when everyone else rises, at the last day."

[25]Jesus told her, "I am the resurrection and the life.* Anyone who believes in me will live, even after dying. [26]Everyone who lives in me and believes in me will never ever die. Do you believe this, Martha?"

[27]"Yes, Lord," she told him. "I have always believed you are the Messiah, the Son of God, the one who has come into the world from God."

BECAUSE I LOVE YOU
John 11:1-44

ROBERT MORRIS

By the time Jesus arrived in Bethany, Lazarus had been dead for four days. His body had started to deteriorate, and even his sister objected to opening the tomb—"The smell will be terrible" (v. 39). Jesus raised Lazarus from the dead, but why did He wait so long to do it?

You may wonder why God does many of the things He does. Let's look at three tough questions people often have about God:

1. Why did God create pain?
God loves us, and He created pain to keep us from hurting ourselves. Many times when we have physical pain, we take medicine or try to ignore it and fight through it. However, pain can be a good thing—it warns us to stop what we're doing before we hurt ourselves even more. This applies not only to our bodies but also to our souls and spirits. I believe God uses pain to get our attention and help us change direction.

2. Why did God create suffering?
Actually, He didn't. *God created a perfect world, but humans ruined it by sinning.* Now we live in a fallen world dominated by sin, and sin opens the door to disease, poverty, violence, and injustice. Society's problems are because of sin, *not* because of God. He doesn't do anything evil, so we cannot blame suffering on Him.

3. Why did Jesus suffer and die?
This is the most amazing truth I know: the Creator became the creation, and He didn't exempt Himself from suffering or pain (Matthew 16:21). Jesus subjected Himself to everything we go through, even anguish and death. Hebrews 4:15 says, "He faced all of the same testings we do." Christians are the only people in the world who can truly say, "Our God knows how we feel." God identifies with us and does good things for us for one reason: He loves us.

[28]Then she returned to Mary. She called Mary aside from the mourners and told her, "The Teacher is here and wants to see you." [29]So Mary immediately went to him.

[30]Jesus had stayed outside the village, at the place where Martha met him. [31]When the people who were at the house consoling Mary saw her leave so hastily, they assumed she was going to Lazarus's grave to weep. So they followed her there. [32]When Mary arrived and saw Jesus, she

---

11:2 This incident is recorded in chapter 12. 11:8 Greek *Jewish people;* also in 11:19, 31, 33, 36, 45, 54. 11:16 Greek *Thomas, who was called Didymus.* 11:18 Greek *was about 15 stadia* [about 2.8 kilometers]. 11:25 Some manuscripts do not include *and the life.*

fell at his feet and said, "Lord, if only you had been here, my brother would not have died."

[33] When Jesus saw her weeping and saw the other people wailing with her, a deep anger welled up within him,* and he was deeply troubled. [34] "Where have you put him?" he asked them.

They told him, "Lord, come and see." [35] Then Jesus wept. [36] The people who were standing nearby said, "See how much he loved him!" [37] But some said, "This man healed a blind man. Couldn't he have kept Lazarus from dying?"

[38] Jesus was still angry as he arrived at the tomb, a cave with a stone rolled across its entrance. [39] "Roll the stone aside," Jesus told them.

But Martha, the dead man's sister, protested, "Lord, he has been dead for four days. The smell will be terrible."

[40] Jesus responded, "Didn't I tell you that you would see God's glory if you believe?" [41] So they rolled the stone aside. Then Jesus looked up to heaven and said, "Father, thank you for hearing me. [42] You always hear me, but I said it out loud for the sake of all these people standing here, so that they will believe you sent me." [43] Then Jesus shouted, "Lazarus, come out!" [44] And the dead man came out, his hands and feet bound in graveclothes, his face wrapped in a headcloth. Jesus told them, "Unwrap him and let him go!"

THE PLOT TO KILL JESUS

[45] Many of the people who were with Mary believed in Jesus when they saw this happen. [46] But some went to the Pharisees and told them what Jesus had done. [47] Then the leading priests and Pharisees called the high council* together. "What are we going to do?" they asked each other. "This man certainly performs many miraculous signs. [48] If we allow him to go on like this, soon everyone will believe in him. Then the Roman army will come and destroy both our Temple* and our nation."

[49] Caiaphas, who was high priest at that time,* said, "You don't know what you're talking about! [50] You don't realize that it's better for you that one man should die for the people than for the whole nation to be destroyed."

[51] He did not say this on his own; as high priest at that time he was led to prophesy that Jesus would die for the entire nation. [52] And not only for that nation, but to bring together and unite all the children of God scattered around the world.

[53] So from that time on, the Jewish leaders began to plot Jesus' death. [54] As a result, Jesus stopped his public ministry among the people and left Jerusalem. He went to a place near the wilderness, to the village of Ephraim, and stayed there with his disciples.

[55] It was now almost time for the Jewish Passover celebration, and many people from all over the country arrived in Jerusalem several days early so they could go through the purification ceremony before Passover began. [56] They kept looking for Jesus, but as they stood around in the Temple, they said to each other, "What do you think? He won't come for Passover, will he?" [57] Meanwhile, the leading priests and Pharisees had publicly ordered that anyone seeing Jesus must report it immediately so they could arrest him.

JESUS ANOINTED AT BETHANY

12 Six days before the Passover celebration began, Jesus arrived in Bethany, the home of Lazarus—the man he had raised from the dead. [2] A dinner was prepared in Jesus' honor. Martha served, and Lazarus was among those who ate* with him. [3] Then Mary took a twelve-ounce jar* of expensive perfume made from essence of nard, and she anointed Jesus' feet with it, wiping his feet with her hair. The house was filled with the fragrance.

[4] But Judas Iscariot, the disciple who would soon betray him, said, [5] "That perfume was worth a year's wages.* It should have been sold and the money given to the poor." [6] Not that he cared for the poor—he was a thief, and since he was in charge of the disciples' money, he often stole some for himself.

[7] Jesus replied, "Leave her alone. She did this in preparation for my burial. [8] You will always have the poor among you, but you will not always have me."

[9] When all the people* heard of Jesus' arrival, they flocked to see him and also to see Lazarus, the man Jesus had raised from the dead. [10] Then the leading priests decided to kill Lazarus, too, [11] for it was because of him that many of the people had deserted them* and believed in Jesus.

JESUS' TRIUMPHANT ENTRY

[12] The next day, the news that Jesus was on the way to Jerusalem swept through the city. A large crowd of Passover visitors [13] took palm branches and went down the road to meet him. They shouted,

"Praise God!*
Blessings on the one who comes in the
     name of the Lord!
Hail to the King of Israel!"*

[14] Jesus found a young donkey and rode on it, fulfilling the prophecy that said:

11:33 Or he was angry in his spirit.   11:47 Greek the Sanhedrin.
11:48 Or our position; Greek reads our place.   11:49 Greek that
year; also in 11:51.   12:2 Or who reclined.   12:3 Greek took 1 litra
[327 grams].   12:5 Greek worth 300 denarii. A denarius was
equivalent to a laborer's full day's wage.   12:9 Greek Jewish
people; also in 12:11.   12:11 Or had deserted their traditions; Greek
reads had deserted.   12:13a Greek Hosanna, an exclamation of
praise adapted from a Hebrew expression that means "save
now."   12:13b Ps 118:25-26; Zeph 3:15.

DREAM GIVERS
John 12:1–3   JIMMY EVANS

We all have dreams, but it is important to know that God has a dream too. He doesn't need anything outside of Himself to exist, but He does want a family.

Mary, a sister of Lazarus, had a dream. Her dream was to get married and have a family. That is why she planned and saved the perfume; it was probably her dowry. So when she poured the perfume over Jesus' feet, she was pouring out her dream on Jesus. Mary gave up her dream so that God could have His dream, and that is the spirit of the gospel. The gospel can only be successfully promoted by believers who value God's dream over their own.

Greed and selfishness blind us to the gospel and the importance of God's dream. The greatest threat to God's dream of building a family through the preaching of the gospel is our un-surrendered dreams.

¹⁵ "Don't be afraid, people of Jerusalem.*
Look, your King is coming,
    riding on a donkey's colt."*

¹⁶ His disciples didn't understand at the time that this was a fulfillment of prophecy. But after Jesus entered into his glory, they remembered what had happened and realized that these things had been written about him.

¹⁷ Many in the crowd had seen Jesus call Lazarus from the tomb, raising him from the dead, and they were telling others* about it. ¹⁸ That was the reason so many went out to meet him—because they had heard about this miraculous sign. ¹⁹ Then the Pharisees said to each other, "There's nothing we can do. Look, everyone* has gone after him!"

JESUS PREDICTS HIS DEATH
²⁰ Some Greeks who had come to Jerusalem for the Passover celebration ²¹ paid a visit to Philip, who was from Bethsaida in Galilee. They said, "Sir, we want to meet Jesus." ²² Philip told Andrew about it, and they went together to ask Jesus.

²³ Jesus replied, "Now the time has come for the Son of Man* to enter into his glory. ²⁴ I tell you the truth, unless a kernel of wheat is planted in the soil and dies, it remains alone. But its death will produce many new kernels—a plentiful harvest of new lives. ²⁵ Those who love their life in this world will lose it. Those who care nothing for their life in this world will keep it for eternity. ²⁶ Anyone who wants to serve me must follow me, because my servants must be where I am. And the Father will honor anyone who serves me.

²⁷ "Now my soul is deeply troubled. Should I pray, 'Father, save me from this hour'? But this is the very reason I came! ²⁸ Father, bring glory to your name."

Then a voice spoke from heaven, saying, "I have already brought glory to my name, and I will do so again." ²⁹ When the crowd heard the voice, some thought it was thunder, while others declared an angel had spoken to him.

³⁰ Then Jesus told them, "The voice was for your benefit, not mine. ³¹ The time for judging this world has come, when Satan, the ruler of this world, will be cast out. ³² And when I am lifted up from the earth, I will draw everyone to myself." ³³ He said this to indicate how he was going to die.

³⁴ The crowd responded, "We understood from Scripture* that the Messiah would live forever. How can you say the Son of Man will die? Just who is this Son of Man, anyway?"

³⁵ Jesus replied, "My light will shine for you just a little longer. Walk in the light while you can, so the darkness will not overtake you. Those who walk in the darkness cannot see where they are going. ³⁶ Put your trust in the light while there is still time; then you will become children of the light."

After saying these things, Jesus went away and was hidden from them.

THE UNBELIEF OF THE PEOPLE
³⁷ But despite all the miraculous signs Jesus had done, most of the people still did not believe in him. ³⁸ This is exactly what Isaiah the prophet had predicted:

"LORD, who has believed our message?
    To whom has the LORD revealed his
        powerful arm?"*

³⁹ But the people couldn't believe, for as Isaiah also said,

⁴⁰ "The Lord has blinded their eyes
    and hardened their hearts—
so that their eyes cannot see,
    and their hearts cannot understand,
and they cannot turn to me
    and have me heal them."*

⁴¹ Isaiah was referring to Jesus when he said this, because he saw the future and spoke of the Messiah's glory. ⁴² Many people did believe in him, however, including some of the Jewish leaders. But they wouldn't admit it for fear that the Pharisees would expel them from the synagogue. ⁴³ For they loved human praise more than the praise of God.

12:15a Greek *daughter of Zion.*   12:15b Zech 9:9.   12:17 Greek *were testifying.*   12:19 Greek *the world.*   12:23 "Son of Man" is a title Jesus used for himself.   12:34 Greek *from the law.*   12:38 Isa 53:1.   12:40 Isa 6:10.

[44]Jesus shouted to the crowds, "If you trust me, you are trusting not only me, but also God who sent me. [45]For when you see me, you are seeing the one who sent me. [46]I have come as a light to shine in this dark world, so that all who put their trust in me will no longer remain in the dark. [47]I will not judge those who hear me but don't obey me, for I have come to save the world and not to judge it. [48]But all who reject me and my message will be judged on the day of judgment by the truth I have spoken. [49]I don't speak on my own authority. The Father who sent me has commanded me what to say and how to say it. [50]And I know his commands lead to eternal life; so I say whatever the Father tells me to say."

JESUS WASHES HIS DISCIPLES' FEET

13 Before the Passover celebration, Jesus knew that his hour had come to leave this world and return to his Father. He had loved his disciples during his ministry on earth, and now he loved them to the very end.* [2]It was time for supper, and the devil had already prompted Judas,* son of Simon Iscariot, to betray Jesus. [3]Jesus knew that the Father had given him authority over everything and that he had come from God and would return to God. [4]So he got up from the table, took off his robe, wrapped a towel around his waist, [5]and poured water into a basin. Then he began to wash the disciples' feet, drying them with the towel he had around him.

[6]When Jesus came to Simon Peter, Peter said to him, "Lord, are you going to wash my feet?"

[7]Jesus replied, "You don't understand now what I am doing, but someday you will."

[8]"No," Peter protested, "you will never ever wash my feet!"

Jesus replied, "Unless I wash you, you won't belong to me."

[9]Simon Peter exclaimed, "Then wash my hands and head as well, Lord, not just my feet!"

[10]Jesus replied, "A person who has bathed all over does not need to wash, except for the feet,* to be entirely clean. And you disciples are clean, but not all of you." [11]For Jesus knew who would betray him. That is what he meant when he said, "Not all of you are clean."

[12]After washing their feet, he put on his robe again and sat down and asked, "Do you understand what I was doing? [13]You call me 'Teacher' and 'Lord,' and you are right, because that's what I am. [14]And since I, your Lord and Teacher, have washed your feet, you ought to wash each other's feet. [15]I have given you an example to follow. Do as I have done to you. [16]I tell you the truth, slaves are not greater than their master. Nor is the messenger more important than the one who sends the message. [17]Now that you know these things, God will bless you for doing them.

THE WIN

John 13:1-15   THOMAS MILLER

We only have one life to live—one life to win. As believers, we win by serving people, pursuing God's presence, knowing who we are in Christ, and focusing on unity.

To win, we must love people. Foot washing was the lowest task of a slave in ancient Jewish culture. Jesus took on the form of a servant when He washed the disciples' feet. He even washed the feet of both Peter, who would deny Him, and Judas, who would betray Him. Jesus used His power to love and serve others. We must love and serve as Jesus did to win as a church.

To win, we must pursue God's presence. We need the presence of God more than we need anything else. Even Moses did not want to go if God was not with Him (Exodus 33:15-16). As we come together, expect God to do great things in our lives, families, cities, and churches.

To win, we must find our significance in God. Jesus knew who He was and Whose He was. He was able to gird Himself with a towel and wash His disciples' feet because He found His significance in His relationship with His Father.

To win, we must focus on unity. Unity and the presence of God are reciprocal in nature. The more we forgive, the more God showers us with His presence. The more we experience God's presence, the more love we have for one another, which allows us to walk in forgiveness and unity.

JESUS PREDICTS HIS BETRAYAL

[18]"I am not saying these things to all of you; I know the ones I have chosen. But this fulfills the Scripture that says, 'The one who eats my food has turned against me.'* [19]I tell you this beforehand, so that when it happens you will believe that I Am the Messiah.* [20]I tell you the truth, anyone who welcomes my messenger is welcoming me, and anyone who welcomes me is welcoming the Father who sent me."

[21]Now Jesus was deeply troubled,* and he exclaimed, "I tell you the truth, one of you will betray me!"

[22]The disciples looked at each other, wondering whom he could mean. [23]The disciple Jesus loved was sitting next to Jesus at the table.* [24]Simon Peter motioned to him to ask, "Who's he talking about?" [25]So that disciple leaned over to Jesus and asked, "Lord, who is it?"

13:1 Or he showed them the full extent of his love.   13:2 Or the devil had already intended for Judas.   13:10 Some manuscripts do not include except for the feet.   13:18 Ps 41:9.   13:19 Or that the 'I AM' has come; or that I am the LORD; Greek reads that I am. See Exod 3:14.   13:21 Greek was troubled in his spirit.   13:23 Greek was reclining on Jesus' bosom. The "disciple Jesus loved" was probably John.

²⁶Jesus responded, "It is the one to whom I give the bread I dip in the bowl." And when he had dipped it, he gave it to Judas, son of Simon Iscariot. ²⁷When Judas had eaten the bread, Satan entered into him. Then Jesus told him, "Hurry and do what you're going to do." ²⁸None of the others at the table knew what Jesus meant. ²⁹Since Judas was their treasurer, some thought Jesus was telling him to go and pay for the food or to give some money to the poor. ³⁰So Judas left at once, going out into the night.

JESUS PREDICTS PETER'S DENIAL

³¹As soon as Judas left the room, Jesus said, "The time has come for the Son of Man* to enter into his glory, and God will be glorified because of him. ³²And since God receives glory because of the Son,* he will give his own glory to the Son, and he will do so at once. ³³Dear children, I will be with you only a little longer. And as I told the Jewish leaders, you will search for me, but you can't come where I am going. ³⁴So now I am giving you a new commandment: Love each other. Just as I have loved you, you should love each other. ³⁵Your love for one another will prove to the world that you are my disciples."

³⁶Simon Peter asked, "Lord, where are you going?"

And Jesus replied, "You can't go with me now, but you will follow me later."

³⁷"But why can't I come now, Lord?" he asked. "I'm ready to die for you."

³⁸Jesus answered, "Die for me? I tell you the truth, Peter—before the rooster crows tomorrow morning, you will deny three times that you even know me.

JESUS, THE WAY TO THE FATHER

14 "Don't let your hearts be troubled. Trust in God, and trust also in me. ²There is more than enough room in my Father's home.* If this were not so, would I have told you that I am going to prepare a place for you?* ³When everything is ready, I will come and get you, so that you will always be with me where I am. ⁴And you know the way to where I am going."

⁵"No, we don't know, Lord," Thomas said. "We have no idea where you are going, so how can we know the way?"

⁶Jesus told him, "I am the way, the truth, and the life. No one can come to the Father except through me. ⁷If you had really known me, you would know who my Father is.* From now on, you do know him and have seen him!"

⁸Philip said, "Lord, show us the Father, and we will be satisfied."

⁹Jesus replied, "Have I been with you all this time, Philip, and yet you still don't know who I am? Anyone who has seen me has seen the Father! So why are you asking me to show him to you? ¹⁰Don't you believe that I am in the Father and the Father is in me? The words I speak are

---

WHO IS THE HOLY SPIRIT?
John 14:16-18   ROBERT MORRIS

The Bible never refers to the Holy Spirit as "It" because *He* is a person. The Holy Spirit is the third person of the Trinity, along with God the Father and God the Son. He is the Advocate Jesus promised the Father would send in John 14:16-18.

The Holy Spirit is our Helper and our Friend who enables us to live in a way that is pleasing to God. He convicts (or convinces) us of our sins, and He also convinces us that we are forgiven by grace through faith. The Holy Spirit brings many incredible benefits to believers, including power and the fruit of the Spirit (Galatians 5:22-23).

The Holy Spirit is also our God. He is a full and equal member of the Trinity. The Holy Spirit hears, speaks, teaches, and guides us into all truth. He is the only One who can empower us to win the world to Jesus.

---

not my own, but my Father who lives in me does his work through me. ¹¹Just believe that I am in the Father and the Father is in me. Or at least believe because of the work you have seen me do. ¹²"I tell you the truth, anyone who believes in me will do the same works I have done, and even greater works, because I am going to be with the Father. ¹³You can ask for anything in my name, and I will do it, so that the Son can bring glory to the Father. ¹⁴Yes, ask me for anything in my name, and I will do it!

JESUS PROMISES THE HOLY SPIRIT

¹⁵"If you love me, obey* my commandments. ¹⁶And I will ask the Father, and he will give you another Advocate,* who will never leave you. ¹⁷He is the Holy Spirit, who leads into all truth. The world cannot receive him, because it isn't looking for him and doesn't recognize him. But you know him, because he lives with you now and later will be in you.* ¹⁸No, I will not abandon you as orphans—I will come to you. ¹⁹Soon the world will no longer see me, but you will see me. Since I live, you also will live. ²⁰When I am raised to life again, you will know that I am in my Father, and you are in me, and I am in you. ²¹Those who accept my commandments and obey them are the ones who love me. And because they love me, my Father will love them.

13:31 "Son of Man" is a title Jesus used for himself. **13:32** Several early manuscripts do not include *And since God receives glory because of the Son.* **14:2a** Or *There are many rooms in my Father's house.* **14:2b** Or *If this were not so, I would have told you that I am going to prepare a place for you.* Some manuscripts read *if this were not so, I would have told you. I am going to prepare a place for you.* **14:7** Some manuscripts read *If you have really known me, you will know who my Father is.* **14:15** Other manuscripts read *you will obey;* still others read *you should obey.* **14:16** Or *Comforter,* or *Encourager,* or *Counselor.* Greek reads *Paraclete;* also in 14:26. **14:17** Some manuscripts read *and is in you.*

THE SPIRIT OF MARRIAGE
John 14:16-18   JIMMY EVANS

God created us to be filled with His Holy Spirit, and He made marriage to be filled with His Holy Spirit too. The Holy Spirit meets our deepest needs. He brings unity that is from the heart, not just the mind, and He binds us together spirit-to-spirit in the closest intimacy possible.

True love isn't something—it's *Someone*. Human love can fail, but God's love never fails. He loves us with an everlasting love. The Holy Spirit nurtures and comforts us, and He offers every kind of grace—spiritual, emotional, physical, and mental. The best prayer any of us can pray is "Holy Spirit, I need You."

When God created man and breathed life into him, He gave him the Holy Spirit. When Adam and Eve sinned, they died spiritually and lost the Holy Spirit. But Jesus restored life, and if we ask, He will gladly fill us with the Holy Spirit today.

And I will love them and reveal myself to each of them."

²²Judas (not Judas Iscariot, but the other disciple with that name) said to him, "Lord, why are you going to reveal yourself only to us and not to the world at large?"

²³Jesus replied, "All who love me will do what I say. My Father will love them, and we will come and make our home with each of them. ²⁴Anyone who doesn't love me will not obey me. And remember, my words are not my own. What I am telling you is from the Father who sent me. ²⁵I am telling you these things now while I am still with you. ²⁶But when the Father sends the Advocate as my representative—that is, the Holy Spirit—he will teach you everything and will remind you of everything I have told you.

²⁷"I am leaving you with a gift—peace of mind and heart. And the peace I give is a gift the world cannot give. So don't be troubled or afraid. ²⁸Remember what I told you: I am going away, but I will come back to you again. If you really loved me, you would be happy that I am going to the Father, who is greater than I am. ²⁹I have told you these things before they happen so that when they do happen, you will believe.

³⁰"I don't have much more time to talk to you, because the ruler of this world approaches. He has no power over me, ³¹but I will do what the Father requires of me, so that the world will know that I love the Father. Come, let's be going.

JESUS, THE TRUE VINE

15 "I am the true grapevine, and my Father is the gardener. ²He cuts off every branch of mine that doesn't produce fruit, and he prunes the branches that do bear fruit so they will produce even more. ³You have already been pruned

ROOTS AND FRUIT
John 15:1-17   ROBERT MORRIS

What is the root cause of success in our lives? What is the root cause of failure? Every person has areas of life that seem to flourish and other areas that seem to struggle constantly. You could also call these areas *good fruit* and *bad fruit*. Matthew 7:17 says, "A good tree produces good fruit, and a bad tree produces bad fruit." As with any tree, the fruit of our lives depends on the root. Here are three important things to know about roots and fruit in your life:

1. Jesus is the Vine.

In John 15:1, Jesus says, "I am the true grapevine." *Grapevine* means 'a vine that produces fruit.' In verse 5, He continues, "Those who remain in me, and I in them, will produce much fruit. For apart from me you can do nothing." In other words, Jesus is the root. When we remain in Jesus by reading and obeying God's Word, He produces good fruit in us.

2. We are the branches.

John 15:4 says, "A branch cannot produce fruit if it is severed from the vine." As a believer, I want to have good fruit, but I can't do it if I'm not connected to God. Galatians 5:22-23 says, "The Holy Spirit produces this kind of fruit in our lives: love, joy, peace, patience, kindness, goodness, faithfulness, gentleness, and self-control." When we stay close to the Root, we will have good fruit. When we disconnect from Him, our fruit instantly spoils.

3. The Father is the Gardener.

God is the owner of the vineyard, and He takes care of His property. Jesus says, "He cuts off every branch of mine that doesn't produce fruit, and he prunes the branches that do bear fruit so they will produce even more" (John 15:2). God planted His Son, Jesus, as the best vine in the vineyard (our world), and He gives us a choice every day. Will we accept Jesus and remain connected to Him? If we want to have good fruit in our lives, the answer must be *yes*.

and purified by the message I have given you. ⁴Remain in me, and I will remain in you. For a branch cannot produce fruit if it is severed from the vine, and you cannot be fruitful unless you remain in me.

⁵"Yes, I am the vine; you are the branches. Those who remain in me, and I in them, will produce much fruit. For apart from me you can do nothing. ⁶Anyone who does not remain in me is thrown away like a useless branch and withers. Such branches are gathered into a pile to be burned. ⁷But if you remain in me and my words remain in you, you may ask for anything you want, and it will be granted! ⁸When you

GOD WANTS TO TALK TO YOU
John 15:15   ROBERT MORRIS

Did you know God wants to talk to you? Yes, *you*. John 15:15 says He calls us His friends. Friends talk to each other! You may have heard that God doesn't speak anymore, but I guarantee He still does. Here are three truths about how God speaks to us today:

1. God does not speak to robots.

As humans, we communicate in two ways: mechanically to machines and personally to people. God does not want to communicate mechanically with us. He wants to communicate personally, so He created us with minds, hearts, and wills. He loves us and wants to talk *with* us, not just give us directions.

2. God speaks to people.

The Bible records many times when God speaks to people, both in the Old and New Testaments. God never changes (Hebrews 13:8), so why would we think He speaks less frequently now? Hearing God requires faith, and Romans 10:17 says faith comes from "hearing the Good News about Christ." No matter who you are, you can hear God today.

3. God speaks to friends.

Exodus 33:11 says God talked to Moses "as one speaks to a friend." God does not want to input information into us like a computer. He wants to walk and talk with us and be our Friend. John 15:13 says, "There is no greater love than to lay down one's life for one's friends." Jesus gave His life for you and me. He is the best Friend we will ever have, and He wants to talk to us every day.

own if you belonged to it, but you are no longer part of the world. I chose you to come out of the world, so it hates you. ²⁰ Do you remember what I told you? 'A slave is not greater than the master.' Since they persecuted me, naturally they will persecute you. And if they had listened to me, they would listen to you. ²¹ They will do all this to you because of me, for they have rejected the one who sent me. ²² They would not be guilty if I had not come and spoken to them. But now they have no excuse for their sin. ²³ Anyone who hates me also hates my Father. ²⁴ If I hadn't done such miraculous signs among them that no one else could do, they would not be guilty. But as it is, they have seen everything I did, yet they still hate me and my Father. ²⁵ This fulfills what is written in their Scriptures*: 'They hated me without cause.'

²⁶ "But I will send you the Advocate*—the Spirit of truth. He will come to you from the Father and will testify all about me. ²⁷ And you must also testify about me because you have been with me from the beginning of my ministry.

16 "I have told you these things so that you won't abandon your faith. ² For you will be expelled from the synagogues, and the time is coming when those who kill you will think they are doing a holy service for God. ³ This is because they have never known the Father or me. ⁴ Yes, I'm telling you these things now, so that when they happen, you will remember my warning. I didn't tell you earlier because I was going to be with you for a while longer.

THE WORK OF THE HOLY SPIRIT

⁵ "But now I am going away to the one who sent me, and not one of you is asking where I am going. ⁶ Instead, you grieve because of what I've told you. ⁷ But in fact, it is best for you that I go away, because if I don't, the Advocate* won't come. If I do go away, then I will send him to you. ⁸ And when he comes, he will convict the world of its sin, and of God's righteousness, and of the coming judgment. ⁹ The world's sin is that it refuses to believe in me. ¹⁰ Righteousness is available because I go to the Father, and you will see me no more. ¹¹ Judgment will come because the ruler of this world has already been judged.

¹² "There is so much more I want to tell you, but you can't bear it now. ¹³ When the Spirit of truth comes, he will guide you into all truth. He will not speak on his own but will tell you what he has heard. He will tell you about the future. ¹⁴ He will bring me glory by telling you whatever he receives from me. ¹⁵ All that belongs to the Father is mine; this is why I said, 'The Spirit will tell you whatever he receives from me.'

produce much fruit, you are my true disciples. This brings great glory to my Father.

⁹ "I have loved you even as the Father has loved me. Remain in my love. ¹⁰ When you obey my commandments, you remain in my love, just as I obey my Father's commandments and remain in his love. ¹¹ I have told you these things so that you will be filled with my joy. Yes, your joy will overflow! ¹² This is my commandment: Love each other in the same way I have loved you. ¹³ There is no greater love than to lay down one's life for one's friends. ¹⁴ You are my friends if you do what I command. ¹⁵ I no longer call you slaves, because a master doesn't confide in his slaves. Now you are my friends, since I have told you everything the Father told me. ¹⁶ You didn't choose me. I chose you. I appointed you to go and produce lasting fruit, so that the Father will give you whatever you ask for, using my name. ¹⁷ This is my command: Love each other.

THE WORLD'S HATRED

¹⁸ "If the world hates you, remember that it hated me first. ¹⁹ The world would love you as one of its

IS THE HOLY SPIRIT A PERSON?
John 16:13   ROBERT MORRIS

The Holy Spirit is a person with a mind, will, and emotions. He can tell us what God thinks, desires, and feels because He *is* God.

The Holy Spirit is omniscient. He can guide us into all truth because He knows all truth. One of the benefits of being a Christian is that you have someone living inside of you who knows everything about everything and has committed Himself to be your Teacher.

The Holy Spirit has emotions. He feels joy when believers live godly lives, and He feels grief when we sin. The Holy Spirit loves us, and He knows that sin hurts our intimacy with God and destroys our lives.

The Holy Spirit teaches us what to pray. The Bible teaches us about God's general will for our lives, but the Holy Spirit tells us God's specific will for our lives. Because the Holy Spirit is God, He will never contradict His own written Word.

SADNESS WILL BE TURNED TO JOY

16 "In a little while you won't see me anymore. But a little while after that, you will see me again."

17 Some of the disciples asked each other, "What does he mean when he says, 'In a little while you won't see me, but then you will see me,' and 'I am going to the Father'? 18 And what does he mean by 'a little while'? We don't understand."

19 Jesus realized they wanted to ask him about it, so he said, "Are you asking yourselves what I meant? I said in a little while you won't see me, but a little while after that you will see me again. 20 I tell you the truth, you will weep and mourn over what is going to happen to me, but the world will rejoice. You will grieve, but your grief will suddenly turn to wonderful joy. 21 It will be like a woman suffering the pains of labor. When her child is born, her anguish gives way to joy because she has brought a new baby into the world. 22 So you have sorrow now, but I will see you again; then you will rejoice, and no one can rob you of that joy. 23 At that time you won't need to ask me for anything. I tell you the truth, you will ask the Father directly, and he will grant your request because you use my name. 24 You haven't done this before. Ask, using my name, and you will receive, and you will have abundant joy.

25 "I have spoken of these matters in figures of speech, but soon I will stop speaking figuratively and will tell you plainly all about the Father. 26 Then you will ask in my name. I'm not saying I will ask the Father on your behalf, 27 for the Father himself loves you dearly because you love me and believe that I came from God.* 28 Yes, I came from the Father into the world, and now I will leave the world and return to the Father."

29 Then his disciples said, "At last you are speaking plainly and not figuratively. 30 Now we understand that you know everything, and there's no need to question you. From this we believe that you came from God."

31 Jesus asked, "Do you finally believe? 32 But the time is coming—indeed it's here now—when you will be scattered, each one going his own way, leaving me alone. Yet I am not alone because the Father is with me. 33 I have told you all this so that you may have peace in me. Here on earth you will have many trials and sorrows. But take heart, because I have overcome the world."

THE PRAYER OF JESUS

17 After saying all these things, Jesus looked up to heaven and said, "Father, the hour has come. Glorify your Son so he can give glory back to you. 2 For you have given him authority over everyone. He gives eternal life to each one you have given him. 3 And this is the way to have eternal life—to know you, the only true God, and Jesus Christ, the one you sent to earth. 4 I brought glory to you here on earth by completing the work you gave me to do. 5 Now, Father, bring me into the glory we shared before the world began.

6 "I have revealed you* to the ones you gave me from this world. They were always yours. You gave them to me, and they have kept your word. 7 Now they know that everything I have is a gift from you, 8 for I have passed on to them the message you gave me. They accepted it and know that I came from you, and they believe you sent me.

9 "My prayer is not for the world, but for those you have given me, because they belong to you. 10 All who are mine belong to you, and you have given them to me, so they bring me glory. 11 Now I am departing from the world; they are staying in this world, but I am coming to you. Holy Father, you have given me your name;* now protect them by the power of your name so that they will be united just as we are. 12 During my time here, I protected them by the power of the name you gave me.* I guarded them so that not one was lost, except the one headed for destruction, as the Scriptures foretold.

13 "Now I am coming to you. I told them many things while I was with them in this world so they would be filled with my joy. 14 I have given them your word. And the world hates them because they do not belong to the world, just as I do not belong to the world. 15 I'm not asking you to take them out of the world, but to keep them safe from the evil one. 16 They do not belong to this world any more than I do. 17 Make them holy by your truth; teach them your word, which is truth. 18 Just as you sent me into the world, I am

---

16:27 Some manuscripts read *from the Father.*   17:6 Greek *have revealed your name;* also in 17:26.   17:11 Some manuscripts read *you have given me these [disciples].*   17:12 Some manuscripts read *I protected those you gave me, by the power of your name.*

sending them into the world. ¹⁹ And I give myself as a holy sacrifice for them so they can be made holy by your truth.

²⁰ "I am praying not only for these disciples but also for all who will ever believe in me through their message. ²¹ I pray that they will all be one, just as you and I are one—as you are in me, Father, and I am in you. And may they be in us so that the world will believe you sent me.

²² "I have given them the glory you gave me, so they may be one as we are one. ²³ I am in them and you are in me. May they experience such perfect unity that the world will know that you sent me and that you love them as much as you love me. ²⁴ Father, I want these whom you have given me to be with me where I am. Then they can see all the glory you gave me because you loved me even before the world began!

²⁵ "O righteous Father, the world doesn't know you, but I do; and these disciples know you sent me. ²⁶ I have revealed you to them, and I will continue to do so. Then your love for me will be in them, and I will be in them."

JESUS IS BETRAYED AND ARRESTED

18 After saying these things, Jesus crossed the Kidron Valley with his disciples and entered a grove of olive trees. ² Judas, the betrayer, knew this place, because Jesus had often gone there with his disciples. ³ The leading priests and Pharisees had given Judas a contingent of Roman soldiers and Temple guards to accompany him. Now with blazing torches, lanterns, and weapons, they arrived at the olive grove.

⁴ Jesus fully realized all that was going to happen to him, so he stepped forward to meet them. "Who are you looking for?" he asked.

⁵ "Jesus the Nazarene,"* they replied.

"I AM he,"* Jesus said. (Judas, who betrayed him, was standing with them.) ⁶ As Jesus said "I AM he," they all drew back and fell to the ground! ⁷ Once more he asked them, "Who are you looking for?"

And again they replied, "Jesus the Nazarene."

⁸ "I told you that I AM he," Jesus said. "And since I am the one you want, let these others go." ⁹ He did this to fulfill his own statement: "I did not lose a single one of those you have given me."*

¹⁰ Then Simon Peter drew a sword and slashed off the right ear of Malchus, the high priest's slave. ¹¹ But Jesus said to Peter, "Put your sword back into its sheath. Shall I not drink from the cup of suffering the Father has given me?"

JESUS AT THE HIGH PRIEST'S HOUSE

¹² So the soldiers, their commanding officer, and the Temple guards arrested Jesus and tied him up. ¹³ First they took him to Annas, since he was the father-in-law of Caiaphas, the high priest at that time.* ¹⁴ Caiaphas was the one who had told the other Jewish leaders, "It's better that one man should die for the people."

PETER'S FIRST DENIAL

¹⁵ Simon Peter followed Jesus, as did another of the disciples. That other disciple was acquainted with the high priest, so he was allowed to enter the high priest's courtyard with Jesus. ¹⁶ Peter had to stay outside the gate. Then the disciple who knew the high priest spoke to the woman watching at the gate, and she let Peter in. ¹⁷ The woman asked Peter, "You're not one of that man's disciples, are you?"

"No," he said, "I am not."

¹⁸ Because it was cold, the household servants and the guards had made a charcoal fire. They stood around it, warming themselves, and Peter stood with them, warming himself.

THE HIGH PRIEST QUESTIONS JESUS

¹⁹ Inside, the high priest began asking Jesus about his followers and what he had been teaching them. ²⁰ Jesus replied, "Everyone knows what I teach. I have preached regularly in the synagogues and the Temple, where the people* gather. I have not spoken in secret. ²¹ Why are you asking me this question? Ask those who heard me. They know what I said."

²² Then one of the Temple guards standing nearby slapped Jesus across the face. "Is that the way to answer the high priest?" he demanded.

²³ Jesus replied, "If I said anything wrong, you must prove it. But if I'm speaking the truth, why are you beating me?"

²⁴ Then Annas bound Jesus and sent him to Caiaphas, the high priest.

PETER'S SECOND AND THIRD DENIALS

²⁵ Meanwhile, as Simon Peter was standing by the fire warming himself, they asked him again, "You're not one of his disciples, are you?"

He denied it, saying, "No, I am not."

²⁶ But one of the household slaves of the high priest, a relative of the man whose ear Peter had cut off, asked, "Didn't I see you out there in the olive grove with Jesus?" ²⁷ Again Peter denied it. And immediately a rooster crowed.

JESUS' TRIAL BEFORE PILATE

²⁸ Jesus' trial before Caiaphas ended in the early hours of the morning. Then he was taken to the headquarters of the Roman governor.* His accusers didn't go inside because it would defile them, and they wouldn't be allowed to celebrate the Passover. ²⁹ So Pilate, the governor, went out to them and asked, "What is your charge against this man?"

³⁰ "We wouldn't have handed him over to you if he weren't a criminal!" they retorted.

18:5a Or *Jesus of Nazareth;* also in 18:7.   18:5b Or *"The 'I AM' is here";* or *"I am the LORD";* Greek reads *I am;* also in 18:6, 8. See Exod 3:14.   18:9 See John 6:39 and 17:12.   18:13 Greek *that year.*   18:20 Greek *Jewish people;* also in 18:38.   18:28 Greek *to the Praetorium;* also in 18:33.

³¹"Then take him away and judge him by your own law," Pilate told them.

"Only the Romans are permitted to execute someone," the Jewish leaders replied. ³²(This fulfilled Jesus' prediction about the way he would die.*)

³³Then Pilate went back into his headquarters and called for Jesus to be brought to him. "Are you the king of the Jews?" he asked him.

³⁴Jesus replied, "Is this your own question, or did others tell you about me?"

³⁵"Am I a Jew?" Pilate retorted. "Your own people and their leading priests brought you to me for trial. Why? What have you done?"

³⁶Jesus answered, "My Kingdom is not an earthly kingdom. If it were, my followers would fight to keep me from being handed over to the Jewish leaders. But my Kingdom is not of this world."

³⁷Pilate said, "So you are a king?"

Jesus responded, "You say I am a king. Actually, I was born and came into the world to testify to the truth. All who love the truth recognize that what I say is true."

³⁸"What is truth?" Pilate asked. Then he went out again to the people and told them, "He is not guilty of any crime. ³⁹But you have a custom of asking me to release one prisoner each year at Passover. Would you like me to release this 'King of the Jews'?"

⁴⁰But they shouted back, "No! Not this man. We want Barabbas!" (Barabbas was a revolutionary.)

JESUS SENTENCED TO DEATH

19 Then Pilate had Jesus flogged with a lead-tipped whip. ²The soldiers wove a crown of thorns and put it on his head, and they put a purple robe on him. ³"Hail! King of the Jews!" they mocked, as they slapped him across the face.

⁴Pilate went outside again and said to the people, "I am going to bring him out to you now, but understand clearly that I find him not guilty." ⁵Then Jesus came out wearing the crown of thorns and the purple robe. And Pilate said, "Look, here is the man!"

⁶When they saw him, the leading priests and Temple guards began shouting, "Crucify him! Crucify him!"

"Take him yourselves and crucify him," Pilate said. "I find him not guilty."

⁷The Jewish leaders replied, "By our law he ought to die because he called himself the Son of God."

⁸When Pilate heard this, he was more frightened than ever. ⁹He took Jesus back into the headquarters* again and asked him, "Where are you from?" But Jesus gave no answer. ¹⁰"Why don't you talk to me?" Pilate demanded. "Don't you realize that I have the power to release you or crucify you?"

¹¹Then Jesus said, "You would have no power over me at all unless it were given to you from above. So the one who handed me over to you has the greater sin."

¹²Then Pilate tried to release him, but the Jewish leaders shouted, "If you release this man, you are no 'friend of Caesar.'* Anyone who declares himself a king is a rebel against Caesar."

¹³When they said this, Pilate brought Jesus out to them again. Then Pilate sat down on the judgment seat on the platform that is called the Stone Pavement (in Hebrew, *Gabbatha*). ¹⁴It was now about noon on the day of preparation for the Passover. And Pilate said to the people,* "Look, here is your king!"

¹⁵"Away with him," they yelled. "Away with him! Crucify him!"

"What? Crucify your king?" Pilate asked.

"We have no king but Caesar," the leading priests shouted back.

¹⁶Then Pilate turned Jesus over to them to be crucified.

THE CRUCIFIXION

So they took Jesus away. ¹⁷Carrying the cross by himself, he went to the place called Place of the Skull (in Hebrew, *Golgotha*). ¹⁸There they nailed him to the cross. Two others were crucified with him, one on either side, with Jesus between them. ¹⁹And Pilate posted a sign on the cross that read, "Jesus of Nazareth,* the King of the Jews." ²⁰The place where Jesus was crucified was near the city, and the sign was written in Hebrew, Latin, and Greek, so that many people could read it.

²¹Then the leading priests objected and said to Pilate, "Change it from 'The King of the Jews' to 'He said, I am King of the Jews.'"

²²Pilate replied, "No, what I have written, I have written."

²³When the soldiers had crucified Jesus, they divided his clothes among the four of them. They also took his robe, but it was seamless, woven in one piece from top to bottom. ²⁴So they said, "Rather than tearing it apart, let's throw dice* for it." This fulfilled the Scripture that says, "They divided my garments among themselves and threw dice for my clothing."* So that is what they did.

²⁵Standing near the cross were Jesus' mother, and his mother's sister, Mary (the wife of Clopas), and Mary Magdalene. ²⁶When Jesus saw his mother standing there beside the disciple he loved, he said to her, "Dear woman, here is your son." ²⁷And he said to this disciple, "Here is your mother." And from then on this disciple took her into his home.

18:32 See John 12:32-33.   19:9 Greek *the Praetorium*.
19:12 "Friend of Caesar" is a technical term that refers to an ally of the emperor.   19:14 Greek *Jewish people;* also in 19:20.
19:19 Or *Jesus the Nazarene*.   19:24a Greek *cast lots*.
19:24b Ps 22:18.

THE DEATH OF JESUS

[28] Jesus knew that his mission was now finished, and to fulfill Scripture he said, "I am thirsty."* [29] A jar of sour wine was sitting there, so they soaked a sponge in it, put it on a hyssop branch, and held it up to his lips. [30] When Jesus had tasted it, he said, "It is finished!" Then he bowed his head and gave up his spirit.

[31] It was the day of preparation, and the Jewish leaders didn't want the bodies hanging there the next day, which was the Sabbath (and a very special Sabbath, because it was Passover week). So they asked Pilate to hasten their deaths by ordering that their legs be broken. Then their bodies could be taken down. [32] So the soldiers came and broke the legs of the two men crucified with Jesus. [33] But when they came to Jesus, they saw that he was already dead, so they didn't break his legs. [34] One of the soldiers, however, pierced his side with a spear, and immediately blood and water flowed out. [35] (This report is from an eyewitness giving an accurate account. He speaks the truth so that you also may continue to believe.*) [36] These things happened in fulfillment of the Scriptures that say, "Not one of his bones will be broken,"* [37] and "They will look on the one they pierced."*

THE BURIAL OF JESUS

[38] Afterward Joseph of Arimathea, who had been a secret disciple of Jesus (because he feared the Jewish leaders), asked Pilate for permission to take down Jesus' body. When Pilate gave permission, Joseph came and took the body away. [39] With him came Nicodemus, the man who had come to Jesus at night. He brought about seventy-five pounds* of perfumed ointment made from myrrh and aloes. [40] Following Jewish burial custom, they wrapped Jesus' body with the spices in long sheets of linen cloth. [41] The place of crucifixion was near a garden, where there was a new tomb, never used before. [42] And so, because it was the day of preparation for the Jewish Passover* and since the tomb was close at hand, they laid Jesus there.

THE RESURRECTION

20 Early on Sunday morning,* while it was still dark, Mary Magdalene came to the tomb and found that the stone had been rolled away from the entrance. [2] She ran and found Simon Peter and the other disciple, the one whom Jesus loved. She said, "They have taken the Lord's body out of the tomb, and we don't know where they have put him!"

[3] Peter and the other disciple started out for the tomb. [4] They were both running, but the other disciple outran Peter and reached the tomb first. [5] He stooped and looked in and saw the linen wrappings lying there, but he didn't go in. [6] Then Simon Peter arrived and went inside. He also noticed the linen wrappings

lying there, [7] while the cloth that had covered Jesus' head was folded up and lying apart from the other wrappings. [8] Then the disciple who had reached the tomb first also went in, and he saw and believed— [9] for until then they still hadn't understood the Scriptures that said Jesus must rise from the dead. [10] Then they went home.

JESUS APPEARS TO MARY MAGDALENE

[11] Mary was standing outside the tomb crying, and as she wept, she stooped and looked in. [12] She saw two white-robed angels, one sitting at the head and the other at the foot of the place where the body of Jesus had been lying. [13] "Dear woman, why are you crying?" the angels asked her.

"Because they have taken away my Lord," she replied, "and I don't know where they have put him."

[14] She turned to leave and saw someone standing there. It was Jesus, but she didn't recognize him. [15] "Dear woman, why are you crying?" Jesus asked her. "Who are you looking for?"

She thought he was the gardener. "Sir," she said, "if you have taken him away, tell me where you have put him, and I will go and get him."

[16] "Mary!" Jesus said.

She turned to him and cried out, "Rabboni!" (which is Hebrew for "Teacher").

19:28 See Pss 22:15; 69:21. 19:35 Some manuscripts read *that you also may believe.* 19:36 Exod 12:46; Num 9:12; Ps 34:20. 19:37 Zech 12:10. 19:39 Greek *100 litras* [32.7 kilograms]. 19:42 Greek *because of the Jewish day of preparation.* 20:1 Greek *On the first day of the week.*

PREPARING TO BE SENT
John 20:21   ROBERT MORRIS

What has God called you to do? Whatever it is, He wants to put His anointing and authority on you *before* He sends you. Even Jesus had to go through a process between the *call* and the *send*—He didn't begin His ministry until He was 30 years old. Many great men of the Bible, such as Abraham, Moses, Joseph, and David, also waited years and years between being called and being sent.

So what do you do while you are waiting? You work on developing a commitment to:

— Relationships—Find people who will help you go further in your walk with Christ.
— Friendships—Friendships are deeper than relationships; friendships are for life.
— Stewardship—Be a good steward with your finances, time, energy, and resources.
— Fellowship—Commit yourself to the local church by serving and tithing.
— Spiritual leadership—Submit to the leadership of the elders and spiritual authority of the church.

17 "Don't cling to me," Jesus said, "for I haven't yet ascended to the Father. But go find my brothers and tell them, 'I am ascending to my Father and your Father, to my God and your God.'"

18 Mary Magdalene found the disciples and told them, "I have seen the Lord!" Then she gave them his message.

JESUS APPEARS TO HIS DISCIPLES

19 That Sunday evening* the disciples were meeting behind locked doors because they were afraid of the Jewish leaders. Suddenly, Jesus was standing there among them! "Peace be with you," he said. 20 As he spoke, he showed them the wounds in his hands and his side. They were filled with joy when they saw the Lord! 21 Again he said, "Peace be with you. As the Father has sent me, so I am sending you." 22 Then he breathed on them and said, "Receive the Holy Spirit. 23 If you forgive anyone's sins, they are forgiven. If you do not forgive them, they are not forgiven."

JESUS APPEARS TO THOMAS

24 One of the twelve disciples, Thomas (nicknamed the Twin),* was not with the others when Jesus came. 25 They told him, "We have seen the Lord!"

But he replied, "I won't believe it unless I see the nail wounds in his hands, put my fingers into them, and place my hand into the wound in his side."

26 Eight days later the disciples were together again, and this time Thomas was with them. The doors were locked; but suddenly, as before, Jesus was standing among them. "Peace be with you," he said. 27 Then he said to Thomas, "Put your finger here, and look at my hands. Put your hand into the wound in my side. Don't be faithless any longer. Believe!"

28 "My Lord and my God!" Thomas exclaimed.

29 Then Jesus told him, "You believe because you have seen me. Blessed are those who believe without seeing me."

PURPOSE OF THE BOOK

30 The disciples saw Jesus do many other miraculous signs in addition to the ones recorded in this book. 31 But these are written so that you may continue to believe* that Jesus is the Messiah, the Son of God, and that by believing in him you will have life by the power of his name.

EPILOGUE: JESUS APPEARS TO SEVEN DISCIPLES

21 Later, Jesus appeared again to the disciples beside the Sea of Galilee.* This is how it happened. 2 Several of the disciples were there—Simon Peter, Thomas (nicknamed the Twin),* Nathanael from Cana in Galilee, the sons of Zebedee, and two other disciples. 3 Simon Peter said, "I'm going fishing."

THE SIN OF COMPARISON
John 21:18-23
ROBERT MORRIS

In John 21, the resurrected Jesus forgives Peter for denying Him and tells the disciple to "feed my sheep" (v. 17). But then the conversation takes an unexpected turn: Jesus tells Peter that one day he will die a terrible death. Peter looks at John, "the disciple Jesus loved," and asks, "What about him, Lord?" (v. 21). Peter is probably thinking, *Encourage me by saying John's death will be worse than mine.* Instead, Jesus replies, "If I want him to remain alive until I return, what is that to you?" (v. 22). In other words, *Stop comparing, Peter!* Jesus has no sympathy for comparison because it blocks our ability to relate to and receive from God. Let's look at the curse, cause, and cure for comparison.

1. The Curse
Comparison produces an attitude of inferiority or superiority in our hearts. When we see ourselves as better than others, we become prideful, and when we see ourselves as worse than others, we wonder, *Why doesn't God love me as much as He loves them?* Resenting the blessings of others produces anger toward God and opens the door for Satan to work in our lives (James 3:16).

2. The Cause
Comparison comes from not accepting or understanding who God has made each of us to be. God gives different gifts to every person because He has a unique calling for every person. Together, we make up the body of Christ (1 Corinthians 12:12). Comparison is a deadly spiritual disease that stems from *covetousness*: wanting what others have and not appreciating what God has given us. Covetousness is really idolatry because it places someone or something in the place of God.

3. The Cure
We can overcome comparison by choosing to glorify God. Trust that He has made you perfectly and has a great plan for your life. Develop a habit of thankfulness and gratitude by reminding yourself that if it weren't for God's grace, you wouldn't have anything at all. Finally, "let God transform you into a new person by changing the way you think" (Romans 12:2). This transformation comes by reading and meditating on God's Word every day. By doing so, "you will learn to know God's will for you, which is good and pleasing and perfect" (Romans 12:2).

20:19 Greek *In the evening of that day, the first day of the week.* 20:24 Greek *Thomas, who was called Didymus.* 20:31 Some manuscripts read *that you may believe.* 21:1 Greek *Sea of Tiberias,* another name for the Sea of Galilee. 21:2 Greek *Thomas, who was called Didymus.*

"We'll come, too," they all said. So they went out in the boat, but they caught nothing all night.

⁴At dawn Jesus was standing on the beach, but the disciples couldn't see who he was. ⁵He called out, "Fellows,* have you caught any fish?"

"No," they replied.

⁶Then he said, "Throw out your net on the right-hand side of the boat, and you'll get some!" So they did, and they couldn't haul in the net because there were so many fish in it.

⁷Then the disciple Jesus loved said to Peter, "It's the Lord!" When Simon Peter heard that it was the Lord, he put on his tunic (for he had stripped for work), jumped into the water, and headed to shore. ⁸The others stayed with the boat and pulled the loaded net to the shore, for they were only about a hundred yards* from shore. ⁹When they got there, they found breakfast waiting for them—fish cooking over a charcoal fire, and some bread.

¹⁰"Bring some of the fish you've just caught," Jesus said. ¹¹So Simon Peter went aboard and dragged the net to the shore. There were 153 large fish, and yet the net hadn't torn.

¹²"Now come and have some breakfast!" Jesus said. None of the disciples dared to ask him, "Who are you?" They knew it was the Lord. ¹³Then Jesus served them the bread and the fish. ¹⁴This was the third time Jesus had appeared to his disciples since he had been raised from the dead.

¹⁵After breakfast Jesus asked Simon Peter, "Simon son of John, do you love me more than these?*"

"Yes, Lord," Peter replied, "you know I love you."

"Then feed my lambs," Jesus told him.

¹⁶Jesus repeated the question: "Simon son of John, do you love me?"

"Yes, Lord," Peter said, "you know I love you."

"Then take care of my sheep," Jesus said.

¹⁷A third time he asked him, "Simon son of John, do you love me?"

Peter was hurt that Jesus asked the question a third time. He said, "Lord, you know everything. You know that I love you."

Jesus said, "Then feed my sheep.

¹⁸"I tell you the truth, when you were young, you were able to do as you liked; you dressed yourself and went wherever you wanted to go. But when you are old, you will stretch out your hands, and others* will dress you and take you where you don't want to go." ¹⁹Jesus said this to let him know by what kind of death he would glorify God. Then Jesus told him, "Follow me."

²⁰Peter turned around and saw behind them the disciple Jesus loved—the one who had leaned over to Jesus during supper and asked, "Lord, who will betray you?" ²¹Peter asked Jesus, "What about him, Lord?"

²²Jesus replied, "If I want him to remain alive until I return, what is that to you? As for you, follow me." ²³So the rumor spread among the community of believers* that this disciple wouldn't die. But that isn't what Jesus said at all. He only said, "If I want him to remain alive until I return, what is that to you?"

²⁴This disciple is the one who testifies to these events and has recorded them here. And we know that his account of these things is accurate.

²⁵Jesus also did many other things. If they were all written down, I suppose the whole world could not contain the books that would be written.

21:5 Greek *Children.*   21:8 Greek *200 cubits* [90 meters].   21:15 Or *more than these others do?*   21:18 Some manuscripts read *and another one.*   21:23 Greek *the brothers.*

The Holy Spirit at Work in . . .

THE OLD TESTAMENT

— The Spirit of God was hovering over the waters (Genesis 1:2).
— Joseph was filled with the Spirit of God (Genesis 41:38).
— Bezalel was filled with the Spirit of God (Exodus 31:3).
— The Holy Spirit rested upon the seventy elders of Israel, and they prophesied (Numbers 11:25).
— The Spirit of the Lord came upon Othniel (Judges 3:10).
— The Spirit of the Lord clothed Gideon with power (Judges 6:34).
— The Spirit of the Lord began to stir Samson (Judges 13:25).
— The Spirit of the God came powerfully upon Saul, and he prophesied (1 Samuel 10:10).
— The Spirit of the Lord came powerfully upon David (1 Samuel 16:13).
— Jesus credited the Holy Spirit for something David said (Mark 12:36).
— The Spirit of the Lord came upon Ezekiel and told him to speak (Ezekiel 11:5).
— David said the Spirit of the Lord spoke through him (2 Samuel 23:2).
— God promises to pour out His Spirit on all people (Joel 2:28).
— Victory is by God's Spirit, not by human force or strength (Zechariah 4:6).

THE LIFE OF JESUS

— Mary became pregnant through the power of the Holy Spirit (Matthew 1:18).
— The Holy Spirit came upon Mary and conceived Jesus in her (Luke 1:35).
— John the Baptist predicted Jesus would baptize with the Holy Spirit and with fire (Matthew 3:11).
— The Holy Spirit descended like a dove upon Jesus (Luke 3:22).
— John the Baptist saw the Holy Spirit descending like a dove from heaven and resting on Jesus (John 1:32).
— The Holy Spirit compelled Jesus to go into the wilderness to be tempted (Mark 1:12–13).
— Jesus returned to Galilee, filled with the Holy Spirit's power (Luke 4:14).
— Jesus said the Holy Spirit anointed Him to bring the Good News (Luke 4:18).
— Jesus cast out demons by the power of the Holy Spirit (Matthew 12:28).
— God gave Jesus the Spirit without limit (John 3:34).

THE NEW TESTAMENT BEFORE PENTECOST

— Elizabeth was filled with the Holy Spirit at the sound of Mary's voice (Luke 1:41).
— Zechariah was filled with the Holy Spirit and prophesied (Luke 1:67).
— The Holy Spirit was upon Simeon and had revealed to him about the Messiah (Luke 2:25–26).
— John the Baptist was filled with the Holy Spirit before his birth (Luke 1:15).
— Jesus promises that the Father will give the Holy Spirit to those who ask Him (Luke 11:13).
— You can only enter the Kingdom of God by being born of water and the Spirit (John 3:5).
— Jesus says that the Spirit will be given to everyone who believes in Him (John 7:39).
— The Holy Spirit will lead believers into all truth (John 14:17; 16:13).
— Jesus commands His disciples to baptize new believers in the name of the Father, Son, and Holy Spirit (Matthew 28:19).
— Jesus promises that the Holy Spirit will give words to His followers in times of duress (Mark 13:11).

The Baptism in the Holy Spirit . . .

PENTECOST AND BEYOND

— At Pentecost, all the believers were filled with the Holy Spirit and began speaking in other languages (Acts 2:1-4).
— Samaritan believers were filled with the Holy Spirit (Acts 8:14-17).
— The apostle Paul was filled with the Spirit (Acts 9:17).
— The gift of the Holy Spirit was poured out on the Gentiles (Acts 10:44-48).
— The Holy Spirit came upon several people in Ephesus, and they spoke in tongues and prophesied (Acts 19:1-7).

The Holy Spirit at Work in . . .

THE NEW TESTAMENT AFTER PENTECOST

— Seven men full of the Holy Spirit and wisdom were selected as deacons (Acts 6:3).
— Stephen was a man full of faith and the Holy Spirit (Acts 6:5).
— The Holy Spirit miraculously transported Philip (Acts 8:39).
— Through the Holy Spirit, Agabus predicted a coming famine (Acts 11:28).
— The requirement of the law is fully satisfied for those who follow the Spirit (Romans 8:4).
— Believers put the deeds of their sinful nature to death by the Spirit's power (Romans 8:13).
— The Holy Spirit joins our spirit to affirm that we are God's children (Romans 8:16).
— The Holy Spirit helps us in our weakness and prays for us with groanings (Romans 8:26).
— The Holy Spirit shows us God's deep secrets (1 Corinthians 2:10).
— The Spirit of God lives in believers (1 Corinthians 3:16).
— The Holy Spirit decides which spiritual gift each believer should have (1 Corinthians 12:3-11).
— Barnabas and Saul were sent out by the Holy Spirit (Acts 13:4).
— The believers were filled with joy and the Holy Spirit (Acts 13:52).
— The fellowship of the Holy Spirit is with believers (2 Corinthians 13:14).

The Holy Spirit Gives . . .

SPECIFIC INSTRUCTIONS

— The Holy Spirit gave Philip specific instructions (Acts 8:29).
— The Holy Spirit gave Peter specific instructions (Acts 11:12).
— The Holy Spirit specifically said, "Appoint Barnabas and Saul" (Acts 13:2).
— The Holy Spirit did not allow Paul and Silas to preach in Asia at that time (Acts 16:6-7).
— It seemed good to the Holy Spirit and the church's leaders (Acts 15:28).
— The Holy Spirit has appointed specific people as leaders over the Church (Acts 20:28).

THE GIFT OF TONGUES?

— Jesus said those who believe in Him will speak in new languages (Mark 16:17).
— All the believers were filled with the Holy Spirit and spoke in other languages on the Day of Pentecost (Acts 2:1–4).
— Jewish believers were amazed that the Gentiles prayed in other tongues (Acts 10:44–48).
— The believers at Ephesus spoke in other tongues and prophesied (Acts 19:1–7).
— Speaking in tongues is talking directly to God (1 Corinthians 14:2).
— Speaking in tongues strengthens the person who is praying (1 Corinthians 14:4).
— Paul spoke in tongues more than anyone else (1 Corinthians 14:18).
— Speaking in tongues is a sign for unbelievers (1 Corinthians 14:22).
— Tongues must be used with wisdom (1 Corinthians 14:6–11).
— Do not forbid others to speak in tongues (1 Corinthians 14:39).
— The Holy Spirit prays for us in harmony with God's will (Romans 8:26–27).
— Pray in the power of the Holy Spirit (Jude 20).

— ACTS OF THE APOSTLES —

JON HUNTZINGER, PhD

The book of Acts continues the account of Jesus' ministry begun in Luke's Gospel. Just as the Gospel traces Jesus' ministry from Galilee to Jerusalem, the center of the Jewish world, Acts traces Jesus' ministry through His followers from Jerusalem to Rome, the center of the Mediterranean world. The book spans a period of about 30 years, from the time of Jesus' crucifixion and resurrection (in the year 30/33) up to the time of Paul's house arrest in Rome in the mid-60's. Luke wrote Acts along with his Gospel shortly after that time. Just as he drew upon eyewitness reports for his Gospel portrait of Jesus (Luke 1:1-4), he relied on similar testimony for Acts. Luke also supplements the account with his own firsthand experiences during his travels with the apostle Paul, which he indicates with his first person plural use of we in the passages recounting those parts of Paul's ministry (16:10-18; 20:5-17; 21:1-18; 27:1-28:16).

Luke's Gospel and Acts share a strong connection. Luke addressed both to the same recipient, Theophilus (Luke 1:3; Acts 1:1), and he created a seamless storyline between the two books. He concludes the Gospel with Jesus' ascension and the return of the disciples to Jerusalem (Luke 24:50-53). Then Luke begins the book of Acts by recounting Jesus' ascension and placing the same disciples in Jerusalem waiting for the promise of the Father (Acts 1:4-11). In addition, he continues to highlight the saving work of Jesus through the Holy Spirit in Acts that he had started in the Gospel.

The book of Acts may be called the book of sermons since it records or alludes to as many as 15 messages preached by Peter, Paul, and others, everywhere from Jerusalem to Ephesus to Athens to Rome. These early church leaders preached sermons to people as different as the Jewish Sanhedrin, an Ethiopian eunuch, a Roman centurion, a Philippian jailer, philosophers at the Greek Areopagus, and Roman governors. (See 2:14-39; 3:11-26; 4:8-12; 5:29-32; 7:1-53; 8:30-38; 10:34-43; 13:16-39; 15:12; 16:31; 17:3, 22-31; 20:25-35; 22:1-21; 23:6; 24:10-21.)

The content of these sermons is the gospel, the Good News, which makes important and specific claims about Jesus:
— Jesus was from Nazareth, which means He was a real human being who came from a real town and whose life God's prophets had predicted.
— He was anointed with the Holy Spirit and performed good works, including miracles.
— He was put to death on a cross but then raised to life on the third day after His death.
— Jesus ascended to heaven, from where He will return one day to His followers.

Aspects of this gospel message are found in all the sermons recorded in Acts, the most complete example being Peter's sermon to the Roman Cornelius and his household (Acts 10:34-43).

The book of Acts may be divided by the movement of this gospel message from Jerusalem to Rome:
— After an introduction emphasizing Jesus' instructions to the disciples and the gift of the Holy Spirit (1:1-2:41), Luke describes events in Jerusalem and the proclamation of the gospel there (2:42-7:60).
— The gospel then is proclaimed in Samaria and in Caesarea to the Gentile household of Cornelius, even as Jesus confronts Paul on the way to Damascus and tells him he will go to the Gentiles and the people of Israel with the gospel (8:1-11:18).
— Persecution follows in Jerusalem while Paul begins his first gospel mission with Barnabas to cities in Asia Minor (Cyprus, Pisidia, Iconium, and Lystra) and returns to report to the leaders in Jerusalem (13:1-15:35).
— Paul begins his second gospel mission, this time with Silas, which takes him to the cities of Philippi, Thessalonica, Corinth, and Ephesus in Europe (16:1-20:38).
— Paul returns to Jerusalem, where he proclaims the gospel to Jewish leaders as well as Roman officials before he is jailed and ultimately sent to Rome (21:1-26:38).

At the heart of the gospel message preached by Peter, Paul, and others in the book of Acts is that God's salvation comes from having a relationship with Jesus. For Luke, salvation means "forgiveness of sins and wholeness in a person's life." It includes deliverance from bondage, cleansing from impurity, healing in body, and restoration in relationships that comes through the power of the Holy Spirit.

Luke draws attention to this salvation at the beginning of the book and at its conclusion. Thus, on the Day of Pentecost, Peter preaches about salvation and says, "Everyone who calls on the name of the LORD will be saved" (2:21). He says the presence of the Holy Spirit that they have experienced in the form of tongues of fire is a sign that the days of God's salvation for all people have now arrived. Then Peter finishes his sermon by urging everyone to "save yourselves from this crooked generation" (2:40) by repenting and being baptized. Luke reports that many were saved that day, and "each day the Lord added to their fellowship those who were being saved" (2:47). The book concludes as it began with a word about salvation when Paul declares to Roman Jewish leaders that any rejection of the gospel will result in the blessing of the nations: "I want you to know that this salvation from God has also been offered to the Gentiles, and they will accept it" (28:28).

One other way Acts resembles Luke's Gospel is the importance of prayer in the lives of Jesus' followers, just as it is in Jesus' own life. Luke says the disciples devoted themselves to prayer (1:14; 2:42; 6:4). They pray when making important decisions, such as when they chose a disciple to replace Judas (1:24-25) or when they needed courage (4:24-31). Luke reports that Peter received a vision from God, which prepared him for his ministry to Gentiles, while he was in prayer (10:9) even as the Gentile Cornelius heard God during prayer tell him to call for Peter to share the gospel with him and his family (10:30-33). Paul and Barnabas are sent by the church in Antioch on their mission to the Gentiles after fasting and prayer (13:2-3), and they pray and fast as they appoint leaders for the churches they start (14:23).

THE PROMISE OF THE HOLY SPIRIT

1 In my first book* I told you, Theophilus, about everything Jesus began to do and teach ² until the day he was taken up to heaven after giving his chosen apostles further instructions through the Holy Spirit. ³ During the forty days after he suffered and died, he appeared to the apostles from time to time, and he proved to them in many ways that he was actually alive. And he talked to them about the Kingdom of God.

⁴ Once when he was eating with them, he commanded them, "Do not leave Jerusalem until the Father sends you the gift he promised, as I told you before. ⁵ John baptized with* water, but in just a few days you will be baptized with the Holy Spirit."

THE ASCENSION OF JESUS

⁶ So when the apostles were with Jesus, they kept asking him, "Lord, has the time come for you to free Israel and restore our kingdom?"

⁷ He replied, "The Father alone has the authority to set those dates and times, and they are not for you to know. ⁸ But you will receive power when the Holy Spirit comes upon you. And you will be my witnesses, telling people about me everywhere—in Jerusalem, throughout Judea, in Samaria, and to the ends of the earth."

⁹ After saying this, he was taken up into a cloud while they were watching, and they could no longer see him. ¹⁰ As they strained to see him rising into heaven, two white-robed men suddenly stood among them. ¹¹ "Men of Galilee," they said, "why are you standing here staring into heaven? Jesus has been taken from you into heaven, but someday he will return from heaven in the same way you saw him go!"

MATTHIAS REPLACES JUDAS

¹² Then the apostles returned to Jerusalem from the Mount of Olives, a distance of half a mile.* ¹³ When they arrived, they went to the upstairs room of the house where they were staying.

Here are the names of those who were present: Peter, John, James, Andrew, Philip, Thomas, Bartholomew, Matthew, James (son of Alphaeus), Simon (the zealot), and Judas (son of James).

EMPOWERED
Acts 1:4-5   ROBERT MORRIS

To *empower* means 'to put power into.'
God wants us to live our lives to the fullest—
He wants us to be all He created us to be.
Wouldn't it be amazing to see every believer empowered and serving in his or her gift?
But how can we be empowered?

1. Believe and accept Jesus.
Jesus is the Savior of the world, but He's not your Savior until you believe and accept Him. John 1:12 says, "To all who believed him and accepted him, he gave the right to become children of God." Accepting Jesus is more than a mental agreement that He is the Son of God. It's submitting your will to Him. When we believe and accept Jesus, we release Him to be all God intended Him to be in our lives.

2. Receive the Holy Spirit.
When you believe and accept Jesus, the Holy Spirit comes to dwell within you. However, according to Acts 1:8, the Holy Spirit also "comes upon you" to give you power to witness. Many people have difficulty witnessing because they haven't received the person or the power of the Holy Spirit. We receive the Holy Spirit the same way we receive Jesus— by submitting ourselves to Him.

3. Receive spiritual authority.
We also receive power by submitting ourselves to the leadership of our local church. Many believers don't understand how important this is, but here's the truth: the only way to have spiritual authority is to submit to spiritual authority. Understanding and submitting to authority produces great faith, which is essential for winning the battle against the enemy.

¹⁴ They all met together and were constantly united in prayer, along with Mary the mother

1:1 The reference is to the Gospel of Luke.   1:5 Or *in;* also in 1:5b.
1:12 Greek *a Sabbath day's journey.*

POWER TO OBEY
Acts 1:8   STEVE DULIN

My wife, Melody, and I waited at the airport counter with our two-year-old daughter Kristin. After checking in, Melody turned to me and asked, "Where's Kristin?" I looked down and realized our daughter was gone. Praying silently, I sprinted toward the gift shop, but then I heard Melody scream, "My baby has been kidnapped!" This was completely out of character for my wife. She had worked as an emergency room nurse and was trained to handle crises quickly and calmly. I knew something was very wrong.

An announcement came over the loudspeaker, asking anyone who saw Kristin to alert the nearest authority. After several minutes of frantic searching, there was a second announcement: "Steve and Melody Dulin, please come to the security area. Your daughter has been found." Kristin later told us that a woman had picked her up while my back was turned and taken her through security. They were about to board a plane, but the announcement came over the loudspeaker, and the woman put Kristin down and disappeared. If Melody had not screamed when she did, the kidnapper likely would have escaped with our daughter.

Acts 1:8 says the Holy Spirit gives us power. This power is not only for witnessing but also for obeying in a way that witnesses to others. Melody said that as she prayed, the Holy Spirit strongly impressed upon her that Kristin had been kidnapped and everyone needed to be alerted right away. Melody believed what the Holy Spirit said, so she started screaming!

The Holy Spirit empowered my wife to do something contrary to her personality and experience. Melody heard His voice, believed what He said, and obeyed His instructions. Ask the Holy Spirit to speak to you today. He will give you the power to obey.

IS THE HOLY SPIRIT PENTECOSTAL?
Acts 2:1-41   ROBERT MORRIS

One of the three major feasts in ancient Jewish tradition, Pentecost celebrated the giving of the Law on Mount Sinai that took place 50 days after Passover. The word *Pentecost* means 'fiftieth.' Fifty days after Jesus' resurrection, the Holy Spirit was poured out on the believers in Jerusalem. They began speaking in other tongues, and people from many different nations heard about "the wonderful things God has done" (Acts 2:11). Three thousand people heard the gospel and were saved that day.

The apostle Peter said the "gift of the Holy Spirit" is for "all who have been called by the Lord our God" (Acts 2:38-39). That means us! We cannot keep God's commands by relying on our own strength. However, the Holy Spirit writes God's righteous standard on our hearts. Jesus came to give us right standing with God, and the Holy Spirit came to empower us to live righteously.

---

²⁰Peter continued, "This was written in the book of Psalms, where it says, 'Let his home become desolate, with no one living in it.' It also says, 'Let someone else take his position.'*

²¹"So now we must choose a replacement for Judas from among the men who were with us the entire time we were traveling with the Lord Jesus—²²from the time he was baptized by John until the day he was taken from us. Whoever is chosen will join us as a witness of Jesus' resurrection."

²³So they nominated two men: Joseph called Barsabbas (also known as Justus) and Matthias. ²⁴Then they all prayed, "O Lord, you know every heart. Show us which of these men you have chosen ²⁵as an apostle to replace Judas in this ministry, for he has deserted us and gone where he belongs." ²⁶Then they cast lots, and Matthias was selected to become an apostle with the other eleven.

THE HOLY SPIRIT COMES

2 On the day of Pentecost* all the believers were meeting together in one place. ²Suddenly, there was a sound from heaven like the roaring of a mighty windstorm, and it filled the house where they were sitting. ³Then, what looked like flames or tongues of fire appeared and settled on each of them. ⁴And everyone present was filled with the Holy Spirit and began speaking in other languages,* as the Holy Spirit gave them this ability.

---

of Jesus, several other women, and the brothers of Jesus.

¹⁵During this time, when about 120 believers* were together in one place, Peter stood up and addressed them. ¹⁶"Brothers," he said, "the Scriptures had to be fulfilled concerning Judas, who guided those who arrested Jesus. This was predicted long ago by the Holy Spirit, speaking through King David. ¹⁷Judas was one of us and shared in the ministry with us."

¹⁸(Judas had bought a field with the money he received for his treachery. Falling headfirst there, his body split open, spilling out all his intestines. ¹⁹The news of his death spread to all the people of Jerusalem, and they gave the place the Aramaic name *Akeldama,* which means "Field of Blood.")

1:15 Greek *brothers.*   1:20 Pss 69:25; 109:8.   2:1 The Festival of Pentecost came 50 days after Passover (when Jesus was crucified).   2:4 Or *in other tongues.*

[5] At that time there were devout Jews from every nation living in Jerusalem. [6] When they heard the loud noise, everyone came running, and they were bewildered to hear their own languages being spoken by the believers.

[7] They were completely amazed. "How can this be?" they exclaimed. "These people are all from Galilee, [8] and yet we hear them speaking in our own native languages! [9] Here we are—Parthians, Medes, Elamites, people from Mesopotamia, Judea, Cappadocia, Pontus, the province of Asia, [10] Phrygia, Pamphylia, Egypt, and the areas of Libya around Cyrene, visitors from Rome [11] (both Jews and converts to Judaism), Cretans, and Arabs. And we all hear these people speaking in our own languages about the wonderful things God has done!" [12] They stood there amazed and perplexed. "What can this mean?" they asked each other.

[13] But others in the crowd ridiculed them, saying, "They're just drunk, that's all!"

PETER PREACHES TO THE CROWD

[14] Then Peter stepped forward with the eleven other apostles and shouted to the crowd, "Listen carefully, all of you, fellow Jews and residents of Jerusalem! Make no mistake about this. [15] These people are not drunk, as some of you are assuming. Nine o'clock in the morning is much too early for that. [16] No, what you see was predicted long ago by the prophet Joel:

[17] 'In the last days,' God says,
  'I will pour out my Spirit upon all people.
  Your sons and daughters will prophesy.
  Your young men will see visions,
  and your old men will dream dreams.
[18] In those days I will pour out my Spirit
  even on my servants—men and
    women alike—
  and they will prophesy.
[19] And I will cause wonders in
    the heavens above
  and signs on the earth below—
  blood and fire and clouds of smoke.
[20] The sun will become dark,
  and the moon will turn blood red
  before that great and glorious day of
    the LORD arrives.
[21] But everyone who calls on the name of
    the LORD
  will be saved.'*

[22] "People of Israel, listen! God publicly endorsed Jesus the Nazarene* by doing powerful miracles, wonders, and signs through him, as you well know. [23] But God knew what would happen, and his prearranged plan was carried out when Jesus was betrayed. With the help of lawless Gentiles, you nailed him to a cross and killed him. [24] But God released him from the horrors of death and raised him back to life, for death could not keep him in its grip. [25] King David said this about him:

'I see that the LORD is always with me.
  I will not be shaken, for he is right
    beside me.
[26] No wonder my heart is glad,
  and my tongue shouts his praises!
  My body rests in hope.
[27] For you will not leave my soul among
    the dead*
  or allow your Holy One to rot in the grave.
[28] You have shown me the way of life,
  and you will fill me with the joy of
    your presence.'*

[29] "Dear brothers, think about this! You can be sure that the patriarch David wasn't referring to himself, for he died and was buried, and his tomb is still here among us. [30] But he was a prophet, and he knew God had promised with an oath that one of David's own descendants would sit on his throne. [31] David was looking into the future and speaking of the Messiah's resurrection. He was saying that God would not leave him among the dead or allow his body to rot in the grave.

[32] "God raised Jesus from the dead, and we are all witnesses of this. [33] Now he is exalted to the place of highest honor in heaven, at God's right hand. And the Father, as he had promised, gave him the Holy Spirit to pour out upon us, just as you see and hear today. [34] For David himself never ascended into heaven, yet he said,

'The LORD said to my Lord,
  "Sit in the place of honor at my right hand
[35] until I humble your enemies,
  making them a footstool under your feet."'*

[36] "So let everyone in Israel know for certain that God has made this Jesus, whom you crucified, to be both Lord and Messiah!"

[37] Peter's words pierced their hearts, and they said to him and to the other apostles, "Brothers, what should we do?"

[38] Peter replied, "Each of you must repent of your sins and turn to God, and be baptized in the name of Jesus Christ for the forgiveness of your sins. Then you will receive the gift of the Holy Spirit. [39] This promise is to you, to your children, and to those far away*—all who have been called by the Lord our God." [40] Then Peter continued preaching for a long time, strongly urging all his listeners, "Save yourselves from this crooked generation!"

[41] Those who believed what Peter said were baptized and added to the church that day—about 3,000 in all.

2:17-21 Joel 2:28-32. 2:22 Or *Jesus of Nazareth.* 2:27 Greek in *Hades;* also in 2:31. 2:25-28 Ps 16:8-11 (Greek version). 2:34-35 Ps 110:1. 2:39 Or *and to people far in the future,* or *and to the Gentiles.*

THE PERFECT SIZE CHURCH
Acts 2:42-47   ROBERT MORRIS

Debbie and I once saw a sign that said, "The Perfect Size Church." I thought, *What would be the perfect size church?* And if it's a certain number of people, then what do you do when you reach that number?

Nothing in Scripture tells us what the "perfect size church" is. However, I realize that many people believe "big churches" are just too big. They have the misconception that big churches are impersonal and difficult places in which to meet people. They believe this until they come, get involved, and build relationships.

Over the years, I've heard so many stories about people who've been through tough circumstances. Again and again, they say, "The way the Gateway Church family rallied around me and helped me through that time was phenomenal!" This is just one of the many reasons why I think being big gives us more opportunities to serve and help others. We may not be perfect, but we try very hard to follow the model of the early church in Acts 2.

THE BELIEVERS FORM A COMMUNITY

⁴²All the believers devoted themselves to the apostles' teaching, and to fellowship, and to sharing in meals (including the Lord's Supper*), and to prayer.

⁴³A deep sense of awe came over them all, and the apostles performed many miraculous signs and wonders. ⁴⁴And all the believers met together in one place and shared everything they had. ⁴⁵They sold their property and possessions and shared the money with those in need. ⁴⁶They worshiped together at the Temple each day, met in homes for the Lord's Supper, and shared their meals with great joy and generosity*—⁴⁷all the while praising God and enjoying the goodwill of all the people. And each day the Lord added to their fellowship those who were being saved.

PETER HEALS A CRIPPLED BEGGAR

3 Peter and John went to the Temple one afternoon to take part in the three o'clock prayer service. ²As they approached the Temple, a man lame from birth was being carried in. Each day he was put beside the Temple gate, the one called the Beautiful Gate, so he could beg from the people going into the Temple. ³When he saw Peter and John about to enter, he asked them for some money.

⁴Peter and John looked at him intently, and Peter said, "Look at us!" ⁵The lame man looked at them eagerly, expecting some money. ⁶But Peter said, "I don't have any silver or gold for you. But I'll give you what I have. In the name of Jesus Christ the Nazarene,* get up and* walk!"

⁷Then Peter took the lame man by the right hand and helped him up. And as he did, the man's feet and ankles were instantly healed and strengthened. ⁸He jumped up, stood on his feet, and began to walk! Then, walking, leaping, and praising God, he went into the Temple with them.

⁹All the people saw him walking and heard him praising God. ¹⁰When they realized he was the lame beggar they had seen so often at the Beautiful Gate, they were absolutely astounded! ¹¹They all rushed out in amazement to Solomon's Colonnade, where the man was holding tightly to Peter and John.

PETER PREACHES IN THE TEMPLE

¹²Peter saw his opportunity and addressed the crowd. "People of Israel," he said, "what is so surprising about this? And why stare at us as though we had made this man walk by our own power or godliness? ¹³For it is the God of Abraham, Isaac, and Jacob—the God of all our ancestors—who has brought glory to his servant Jesus by doing this. This is the same Jesus whom you handed over and rejected before Pilate, despite Pilate's decision to release him. ¹⁴You rejected this holy, righteous one and instead demanded the release of a murderer. ¹⁵You killed the author of life, but God raised him from the dead. And we are witnesses of this fact!

¹⁶"Through faith in the name of Jesus, this man was healed—and you know how crippled he was before. Faith in Jesus' name has healed him before your very eyes.

¹⁷"Friends,* I realize that what you and your leaders did to Jesus was done in ignorance. ¹⁸But God was fulfilling what all the prophets had foretold about the Messiah—that he must suffer these things. ¹⁹Now repent of your sins and turn to God, so that your sins may be wiped away. ²⁰Then times of refreshment will come from the presence of the Lord, and he will again send you Jesus, your appointed Messiah. ²¹For he must remain in heaven until the time for the final restoration of all things, as God promised long ago through his holy prophets. ²²Moses said, 'The LORD your God will raise up for you a Prophet like me from among your own people. Listen carefully to everything he tells you.'* ²³Then Moses said, 'Anyone who will not listen to that Prophet will be completely cut off from God's people.'*

²⁴"Starting with Samuel, every prophet spoke about what is happening today. ²⁵You are the children of those prophets, and you are included in the covenant God promised to your ancestors. For God said to Abraham, 'Through your descendants* all the families on earth will be blessed.'

2:42 Greek *the breaking of bread;* also in 2:46.   2:46 Or *and sincere hearts.*   3:6a Or *Jesus Christ of Nazareth.*   3:6b Some manuscripts do not include *get up and.*   3:17 Greek *Brothers.*   3:22 Deut 18:15.   3:23 Deut 18:19; Lev 23:29.   3:25 Greek *your seed;* see Gen 12:3; 22:18.

26 When God raised up his servant, Jesus, he sent him first to you people of Israel, to bless you by turning each of you back from your sinful ways."

PETER AND JOHN BEFORE THE COUNCIL

4 While Peter and John were speaking to the people, they were confronted by the priests, the captain of the Temple guard, and some of the Sadducees. ²These leaders were very disturbed that Peter and John were teaching the people that through Jesus there is a resurrection of the dead. ³They arrested them and, since it was already evening, put them in jail until morning. ⁴But many of the people who heard their message believed it, so the number of men who believed now totaled about 5,000.

⁵The next day the council of all the rulers and elders and teachers of religious law met in Jerusalem. ⁶Annas the high priest was there, along with Caiaphas, John, Alexander, and other relatives of the high priest. ⁷They brought in the two disciples and demanded, "By what power, or in whose name, have you done this?"

⁸Then Peter, filled with the Holy Spirit, said to them, "Rulers and elders of our people, ⁹are we being questioned today because we've done a good deed for a crippled man? Do you want to know how he was healed? ¹⁰Let me clearly state to all of you and to all the people of Israel that he was healed by the powerful name of Jesus Christ the Nazarene,* the man you crucified but whom God raised from the dead. ¹¹For Jesus is the one referred to in the Scriptures, where it says,

'The stone that you builders rejected
    has now become the cornerstone.'*

¹²There is salvation in no one else! God has given no other name under heaven by which we must be saved."

¹³The members of the council were amazed when they saw the boldness of Peter and John, for they could see that they were ordinary men with no special training in the Scriptures. They also recognized them as men who had been with Jesus. ¹⁴But since they could see the man who had been healed standing right there among them, there was nothing the council could say. ¹⁵So they ordered Peter and John out of the council chamber* and conferred among themselves.

¹⁶"What should we do with these men?" they asked each other. "We can't deny that they have performed a miraculous sign, and everybody in Jerusalem knows about it. ¹⁷But to keep them from spreading their propaganda any further, we must warn them not to speak to anyone in Jesus' name again." ¹⁸So they called the apostles back in and commanded them never again to speak or teach in the name of Jesus.

¹⁹But Peter and John replied, "Do you think God wants us to obey you rather than him? ²⁰We

HOW TO TELL OTHERS ABOUT JESUS
Acts 4:20   ROBERT MORRIS

Does telling others about Jesus feel intimidating? Are you worried you will say the wrong thing or sound too "religious"? Here are three practical steps you can take to tell others about Jesus:

1. Just talk to people.
Maybe you're not ready to talk about theology, ecclesiology, eschatology, or any other "ology." Maybe you don't know how to explain the Bible, and you're too nervous to invite someone to church. It's okay! Just start by saying, "Hi!" Look for opportunities to interact with people. Open doors for them. Smile. I can talk to anyone, anywhere, anytime. Why? Because I know every person's favorite subject: themselves! Ask people questions about their work, children, grandchildren, hobbies, etc. Everywhere Jesus went, He *talked* to people.

2. Just invite people.
Jesus not only talked to people, but He also invited them. When two of John the Baptist's disciples asked Jesus where He was staying, Jesus replied, "Come and see" (John 1:39). Someone may ask you questions such as "Where do you go to church?" or "What's your pastor like?" Here's an easy response you can use every time: "Come and see!"

3. Just witness to people.
I want to take the religiosity out of witnessing; in other words, you can act *normal*. You don't have to speak in King James English, use religious terms, or wave your hands and raise your voice. Remember, a witness is simply someone who shares what they have seen and heard. Just tell your story! I learned to tell my story in one sentence: "Growing up, I went to church, but I was really messed up until I gave God control of my life." It's that simple!

cannot stop telling about everything we have seen and heard."

²¹The council then threatened them further, but they finally let them go because they didn't know how to punish them without starting a riot. For everyone was praising God ²²for this miraculous sign—the healing of a man who had been lame for more than forty years.

THE BELIEVERS PRAY FOR COURAGE

²³As soon as they were freed, Peter and John returned to the other believers and told them what the leading priests and elders had said. ²⁴When they heard the report, all the believers lifted their voices together in prayer to God: "O Sovereign Lord, Creator of heaven and earth,

4:10 Or *Jesus Christ of Nazareth.*   4:11 Ps 118:22.   4:15 Greek *the Sanhedrin.*

GATHERED FOR POWER
Acts 4:24-31   JACK HAYFORD

One of the most prominent characteristics of the early church was their spiritual power. The disciples fasted and prayed often, and their faith released the miracle-working power of God. There were physical and spiritual demonstrations of the Holy Spirit's presence and power, which were experienced by all. Some people were filled with the Holy Spirit while others experienced a fresh energizing of the Spirit's power to proclaim and witness boldly.

Both the public ministry of Jesus in the Gospels and the public ministry of the early church in Acts began with a life-changing encounter with the Holy Spirit. In the Old Testament, only those who were uniquely called or anointed by God received the Holy Spirit. Under the New Covenant, every believer is offered the promise of the Father, the seal of Christ, and the active presence of the Holy Spirit. The Spirit's fullness in the life of every believer continues today.

the sea, and everything in them—²⁵you spoke long ago by the Holy Spirit through our ancestor David, your servant, saying,

'Why were the nations so angry?
Why did they waste their time with
    futile plans?
²⁶ The kings of the earth prepared for battle;
    the rulers gathered together
against the LORD
    and against his Messiah.'*

²⁷"In fact, this has happened here in this very city! For Herod Antipas, Pontius Pilate the governor, the Gentiles, and the people of Israel were all united against Jesus, your holy servant, whom you anointed. ²⁸But everything they did was determined beforehand according to your will. ²⁹And now, O Lord, hear their threats, and give us, your servants, great boldness in preaching your word. ³⁰Stretch out your hand with healing power; may miraculous signs and wonders be done through the name of your holy servant Jesus." ³¹After this prayer, the meeting place shook, and they were all filled with the Holy Spirit. Then they preached the word of God with boldness.

THE BELIEVERS SHARE THEIR POSSESSIONS
³²All the believers were united in heart and mind. And they felt that what they owned was not their own, so they shared everything they had. ³³The apostles testified powerfully to the resurrection of the Lord Jesus, and God's great blessing was upon them all. ³⁴There were no needy people among them, because those who owned land or

houses would sell them ³⁵and bring the money to the apostles to give to those in need.

³⁶For instance, there was Joseph, the one the apostles nicknamed Barnabas (which means "Son of Encouragement"). He was from the tribe of Levi and came from the island of Cyprus. ³⁷He sold a field he owned and brought the money to the apostles.

ANANIAS AND SAPPHIRA
5 But there was a certain man named Ananias who, with his wife, Sapphira, sold some property. ²He brought part of the money to the apostles, claiming it was the full amount. With his wife's consent, he kept the rest.

³Then Peter said, "Ananias, why have you let Satan fill your heart? You lied to the Holy Spirit, and you kept some of the money for yourself. ⁴The property was yours to sell or not sell, as you wished. And after selling it, the money was also yours to give away. How could you do a thing like this? You weren't lying to us but to God!"

⁵As soon as Ananias heard these words, he fell to the floor and died. Everyone who heard about it was terrified. ⁶Then some young men got up, wrapped him in a sheet, and took him out and buried him.

⁷About three hours later his wife came in, not knowing what had happened. ⁸Peter asked her, "Was this the price you and your husband received for your land?"

"Yes," she replied, "that was the price."

⁹And Peter said, "How could the two of you even think of conspiring to test the Spirit of the Lord like this? The young men who buried your husband are just outside the door, and they will carry you out, too."

¹⁰Instantly, she fell to the floor and died. When the young men came in and saw that she was dead, they carried her out and buried her beside her husband. ¹¹Great fear gripped the entire church and everyone else who heard what had happened.

THE APOSTLES HEAL MANY
¹²The apostles were performing many miraculous signs and wonders among the people. And all the believers were meeting regularly at the Temple in the area known as Solomon's Colonnade. ¹³But no one else dared to join them, even though all the people had high regard for them. ¹⁴Yet more and more people believed and were brought to the Lord—crowds of both men and women. ¹⁵As a result of the apostles' work, sick people were brought out into the streets on beds and mats so that Peter's shadow might fall across some of them as he went by. ¹⁶Crowds came from the villages around Jerusalem, bringing their sick and those possessed by evil* spirits, and they were all healed.

4:25-26 Or *his anointed one; or his Christ.* Ps 2:1-2. 5:16 Greek *unclean.*

THE APOSTLES MEET OPPOSITION

[17] The high priest and his officials, who were Sadducees, were filled with jealousy. [18] They arrested the apostles and put them in the public jail. [19] But an angel of the Lord came at night, opened the gates of the jail, and brought them out. Then he told them, [20] "Go to the Temple and give the people this message of life!"

[21] So at daybreak the apostles entered the Temple, as they were told, and immediately began teaching.

When the high priest and his officials arrived, they convened the high council*—the full assembly of the elders of Israel. Then they sent for the apostles to be brought from the jail for trial. [22] But when the Temple guards went to the jail, the men were gone. So they returned to the council and reported, [23] "The jail was securely locked, with the guards standing outside, but when we opened the gates, no one was there!"

[24] When the captain of the Temple guard and the leading priests heard this, they were perplexed, wondering where it would all end. [25] Then someone arrived with startling news: "The men you put in jail are standing in the Temple, teaching the people!"

[26] The captain went with his Temple guards and arrested the apostles, but without violence, for they were afraid the people would stone them. [27] Then they brought the apostles before the high council, where the high priest confronted them. [28] "We gave you strict orders never again to teach in this man's name!" he said. "Instead, you have filled all Jerusalem with your teaching about

him, and you want to make us responsible for his death!"

[29] But Peter and the apostles replied, "We must obey God rather than any human authority. [30] The God of our ancestors raised Jesus from the dead after you killed him by hanging him on a cross.* [31] Then God put him in the place of honor at his right hand as Prince and Savior. He did this so the people of Israel would repent of their sins and be forgiven. [32] We are witnesses of these things and so is the Holy Spirit, who is given by God to those who obey him."

[33] When they heard this, the high council was furious and decided to kill them. [34] But one member, a Pharisee named Gamaliel, who was an expert in religious law and respected by all the people, stood up and ordered that the men be sent outside the council chamber for a while. [35] Then he said to his colleagues, "Men of Israel, take care what you are planning to do to these men! [36] Some time ago there was that fellow Theudas, who pretended to be someone great. About 400 others joined him, but he was killed, and all his followers went their various ways. The whole movement came to nothing. [37] After him, at the time of the census, there was Judas of Galilee. He got people to follow him, but he was killed, too, and all his followers were scattered.

[38] "So my advice is, leave these men alone. Let them go. If they are planning and doing these things merely on their own, it will soon be overthrown. [39] But if it is from God, you will not be able to overthrow them. You may even find yourselves fighting against God!"

[40] The others accepted his advice. They called in the apostles and had them flogged. Then they ordered them never again to speak in the name of Jesus, and they let them go.

[41] The apostles left the high council rejoicing that God had counted them worthy to suffer disgrace for the name of Jesus.* [42] And every day, in the Temple and from house to house, they continued to teach and preach this message: "Jesus is the Messiah."

SEVEN MEN CHOSEN TO SERVE

6 But as the believers* rapidly multiplied, there were rumblings of discontent. The Greek-speaking believers complained about the Hebrew-speaking believers, saying that their widows were being discriminated against in the daily distribution of food.

[2] So the Twelve called a meeting of all the believers. They said, "We apostles should spend our time teaching the word of God, not running a food program. [3] And so, brothers, select seven men who are well respected and are full of the Spirit and wisdom. We will give them this

---

AUTHENTIC WITNESSES
Acts 5:32   ROBERT MORRIS

Imagine that you and I are coworkers. One day I tell you about a new medicine that helped me recover from an incurable disease. Would you think I was trying to shove my beliefs down your throat? Of course not! It would not be offensive because I was merely sharing my story with you.

Witnessing to people is much the same. You don't need to persuade or argue with people; you just need to share your story. Witnesses are people who accurately communicate their experiences—what they have personally seen and heard. And every Christian should be a witness. In fact, every Christian *is* a witness. There's just one question: are you a good witness or a bad one?

The disciples' testimonies were so powerful because they were *personal*. These men walked with Jesus and watched Him change lives everywhere He went. If you're a Christian, Jesus has changed your life too. Whom will you share your story with today?

5:21 Greek *Sanhedrin;* also in 5:27, 41.   5:30 Greek *on a tree.*
5:41 Greek *for the name.*   6:1 Greek *disciples;* also in 6:2, 7.

responsibility. [4] Then we apostles can spend our time in prayer and teaching the word."

[5] Everyone liked this idea, and they chose the following: Stephen (a man full of faith and the Holy Spirit), Philip, Procorus, Nicanor, Timon, Parmenas, and Nicolas of Antioch (an earlier convert to the Jewish faith). [6] These seven were presented to the apostles, who prayed for them as they laid their hands on them.

[7] So God's message continued to spread. The number of believers greatly increased in Jerusalem, and many of the Jewish priests were converted, too.

STEPHEN IS ARRESTED

[8] Stephen, a man full of God's grace and power, performed amazing miracles and signs among the people. [9] But one day some men from the Synagogue of Freed Slaves, as it was called, started to debate with him. They were Jews from Cyrene, Alexandria, Cilicia, and the province of Asia. [10] None of them could stand against the wisdom and the Spirit with which Stephen spoke.

[11] So they persuaded some men to lie about Stephen, saying, "We heard him blaspheme Moses, and even God." [12] This roused the people, the elders, and the teachers of religious law. So they arrested Stephen and brought him before the high council.*

[13] The lying witnesses said, "This man is always speaking against the holy Temple and against the law of Moses. [14] We have heard him say that this Jesus of Nazareth* will destroy the Temple and change the customs Moses handed down to us."

[15] At this point everyone in the high council stared at Stephen, because his face became as bright as an angel's.

STEPHEN ADDRESSES THE COUNCIL

7 Then the high priest asked Stephen, "Are these accusations true?"

[2] This was Stephen's reply: "Brothers and fathers, listen to me. Our glorious God appeared to our ancestor Abraham in Mesopotamia before he settled in Haran.* [3] God told him, 'Leave your native land and your relatives, and come into the land that I will show you.'* [4] So Abraham left the land of the Chaldeans and lived in Haran until his father died. Then God brought him here to the land where you now live.

[5] "But God gave him no inheritance here, not even one square foot of land. God did promise, however, that eventually the whole land would belong to Abraham and his descendants—even though he had no children yet. [6] God also told him that his descendants would live in a foreign land, where they would be oppressed as slaves for 400 years. [7] 'But I will punish the nation that enslaves them,' God said, 'and in the end they will come out and worship me here in this place.'*

[8] "God also gave Abraham the covenant of circumcision at that time. So when Abraham became the father of Isaac, he circumcised him on the eighth day. And the practice was continued when Isaac became the father of Jacob, and when Jacob became the father of the twelve patriarchs of the Israelite nation.

[9] "These patriarchs were jealous of their brother Joseph, and they sold him to be a slave in Egypt. But God was with him [10] and rescued him from all his troubles. And God gave him favor before Pharaoh, king of Egypt. God also gave Joseph unusual wisdom, so that Pharaoh appointed him governor over all of Egypt and put him in charge of the palace.

[11] "But a famine came upon Egypt and Canaan. There was great misery, and our ancestors ran out of food. [12] Jacob heard that there was still grain in Egypt, so he sent his sons—our ancestors—to buy some. [13] The second time they went, Joseph revealed his identity to his brothers,* and they were introduced to Pharaoh. [14] Then Joseph sent for his father, Jacob, and all his relatives to come to Egypt, seventy-five persons in all. [15] So Jacob went to Egypt. He died there, as did our ancestors. [16] Their bodies were taken to Shechem and buried in the tomb Abraham had bought for a certain price from Hamor's sons in Shechem.

[17] "As the time drew near when God would fulfill his promise to Abraham, the number of our people in Egypt greatly increased. [18] But then a new king came to the throne of Egypt who knew nothing about Joseph. [19] This king exploited our people and oppressed them, forcing parents to abandon their newborn babies so they would die.

[20] "At that time Moses was born—a beautiful child in God's eyes. His parents cared for him at home for three months. [21] When they had to abandon him, Pharaoh's daughter adopted him and raised him as her own son. [22] Moses was taught all the wisdom of the Egyptians, and he was powerful in both speech and action.

[23] "One day when Moses was forty years old, he decided to visit his relatives, the people of Israel. [24] He saw an Egyptian mistreating an Israelite. So Moses came to the man's defense and avenged him, killing the Egyptian. [25] Moses assumed his fellow Israelites would realize that God had sent him to rescue them, but they didn't.

[26] "The next day he visited them again and saw two men of Israel fighting. He tried to be a peacemaker. 'Men,' he said, 'you are brothers. Why are you fighting each other?'

[27] "But the man in the wrong pushed Moses aside. 'Who made you a ruler and judge over us?' he asked. [28] 'Are you going to kill me as you killed that Egyptian yesterday?' [29] When Moses

---

6:12 Greek *Sanhedrin;* also in 6:15.   6:14 Or *Jesus the Nazarene.*
7:2 *Mesopotamia* was the region now called Iraq. *Haran* was a city in what is now called Syria.   7:3 Gen 12:1.   7:5-7 Gen 12:7; 15:13-14; Exod 3:12.   7:13 Other manuscripts read *Joseph was recognized by his brothers.*

heard that, he fled the country and lived as a foreigner in the land of Midian. There his two sons were born.

³⁰ "Forty years later, in the desert near Mount Sinai, an angel appeared to Moses in the flame of a burning bush. ³¹ When Moses saw it, he was amazed at the sight. As he went to take a closer look, the voice of the LORD called out to him, ³² 'I am the God of your ancestors—the God of Abraham, Isaac, and Jacob.' Moses shook with terror and did not dare to look.

³³ "Then the LORD said to him, 'Take off your sandals, for you are standing on holy ground. ³⁴ I have certainly seen the oppression of my people in Egypt. I have heard their groans and have come down to rescue them. Now go, for I am sending you back to Egypt.'*

³⁵ "So God sent back the same man his people had previously rejected when they demanded, 'Who made you a ruler and judge over us?' Through the angel who appeared to him in the burning bush, God sent Moses to be their ruler and savior. ³⁶ And by means of many wonders and miraculous signs, he led them out of Egypt, through the Red Sea, and through the wilderness for forty years.

³⁷ "Moses himself told the people of Israel, 'God will raise up for you a Prophet like me from among your own people.'* ³⁸ Moses was with our ancestors, the assembly of God's people in the wilderness, when the angel spoke to him at Mount Sinai. And there Moses received life-giving words to pass on to us.*

³⁹ "But our ancestors refused to listen to Moses. They rejected him and wanted to return to Egypt. ⁴⁰ They told Aaron, 'Make us some gods who can lead us, for we don't know what has become of this Moses, who brought us out of Egypt.' ⁴¹ So they made an idol shaped like a calf, and they sacrificed to it and celebrated over this thing they had made. ⁴² Then God turned away from them and abandoned them to serve the stars of heaven as their gods! In the book of the prophets it is written,

'Was it to me you were bringing sacrifices
    and offerings
    during those forty years in the wilderness,
    Israel?

⁴³ No, you carried your pagan gods—
    the shrine of Molech,
    the star of your god Rephan,
    and the images you made to worship them.
So I will send you into exile
    as far away as Babylon.'*

⁴⁴ "Our ancestors carried the Tabernacle* with them through the wilderness. It was constructed according to the plan God had shown to Moses. ⁴⁵ Years later, when Joshua led our ancestors in battle against the nations that God drove out of this land, the Tabernacle was taken with them into their new territory. And it stayed there until the time of King David.

⁴⁶ "David found favor with God and asked for the privilege of building a permanent Temple for the God of Jacob.* ⁴⁷ But it was Solomon who actually built it. ⁴⁸ However, the Most High doesn't live in temples made by human hands. As the prophet says,

⁴⁹ 'Heaven is my throne,
    and the earth is my footstool.
Could you build me a temple as good as
        that?'
    asks the LORD.
'Could you build me such a resting place?
⁵⁰   Didn't my hands make both heaven and
        earth?'*

⁵¹ "You stubborn people! You are heathen* at heart and deaf to the truth. Must you forever resist the Holy Spirit? That's what your ancestors did, and so do you! ⁵² Name one prophet your ancestors didn't persecute! They even killed the ones who predicted the coming of the Righteous One—the Messiah whom you betrayed and murdered. ⁵³ You deliberately disobeyed God's law, even though you received it from the hands of angels."

⁵⁴ The Jewish leaders were infuriated by Stephen's accusation, and they shook their fists at him in rage.* ⁵⁵ But Stephen, full of the Holy Spirit, gazed steadily into heaven and saw the glory of God, and he saw Jesus standing in the place of honor at God's right hand. ⁵⁶ And he told them, "Look, I see the heavens opened and the Son of Man standing in the place of honor at God's right hand!"

⁵⁷ Then they put their hands over their ears and began shouting. They rushed at him ⁵⁸ and dragged him out of the city and began to stone him. His accusers took off their coats and laid them at the feet of a young man named Saul.*

⁵⁹ As they stoned him, Stephen prayed, "Lord Jesus, receive my spirit." ⁶⁰ He fell to his knees, shouting, "Lord, don't charge them with this sin!" And with that, he died.

8 Saul was one of the witnesses, and he agreed completely with the killing of Stephen.

PERSECUTION SCATTERS THE BELIEVERS

A great wave of persecution began that day, sweeping over the church in Jerusalem; and all the believers except the apostles were scattered through the regions of Judea and Samaria. ² (Some devout men came and buried Stephen

---

7:31-34 Exod 3:5-10.   7:37 Deut 18:15.   7:38 Some manuscripts read *to you.*   7:42-43 Amos 5:25-27 (Greek version).   7:44 Greek *the tent of witness.*   7:46 Some manuscripts read *the house of Jacob.*   7:49-50 Isa 66:1-2.   7:51 Greek *uncircumcised.*   7:54 Greek *they were grinding their teeth against him.*   7:58 *Saul* is later called Paul; see 13:9.

ENJOYING LIFE
Acts 8:9-24

ROBERT MORRIS

God wants you to enjoy life. According to Galatians 5:22-23, joy is part of the fruit of the Spirit. If you're a believer and you don't have joy, there is likely a blockage in your life. Let's identify three main blockages so they can be removed and you can enjoy life as God intended.

1. Actions
In Acts 8, a new believer named Simon tries to buy and manipulate the gift of the Holy Spirit. Peter responds, "You can have no part in this, for your heart is not right with God. . . . I can see that you are full of bitter jealousy and are held captive by sin" (v. 21). I'm not saying you must be perfect; we all make mistakes. However, if you have recurring sin in your life, it will rob you of your joy. Sin grieves the Holy Spirit and causes you to feel dirty, condemned, and ashamed. The only way to restore joy is to repent and turn to God.

2. Attitudes
Our attitudes are formed by our thoughts. Good attitudes come from good thoughts, and bad attitudes come from bad thoughts. Instead of being happy that other people were getting blessed, Simon was jealous and bitter. Bitterness is a poison that steals your joy and holds you in bondage. In 2 Corinthians 10:5, Paul says we must "capture [our] rebellious thoughts and teach them to obey Christ."

3. Attacks
Our actions and attitudes can leave an open door for the enemy to enter and attack us. Is it possible to be a Christian and still be in bondage? Yes. When Peter pointed out this problem, Simon didn't argue; instead, he begged Peter to pray for him (Acts 8:24). This should be our first response too. The best way to defeat the enemy's attacks is to come into the presence of God.

with great mourning.) ³But Saul was going everywhere to destroy the church. He went from house to house, dragging out both men and women to throw them into prison.

PHILIP PREACHES IN SAMARIA

⁴But the believers who were scattered preached the Good News about Jesus wherever they went. ⁵Philip, for example, went to the city of Samaria and told the people there about the Messiah. ⁶Crowds listened intently to Philip because they were eager to hear his message and see the miraculous signs he did. ⁷Many evil* spirits were cast out, screaming as they left their victims. And many who had been paralyzed or lame were healed. ⁸So there was great joy in that city.

⁹A man named Simon had been a sorcerer there for many years, amazing the people of Samaria and claiming to be someone great. ¹⁰Everyone, from the least to the greatest, often spoke of him as "the Great One—the Power of God." ¹¹They listened closely to him because for a long time he had astounded them with his magic.

¹²But now the people believed Philip's message of Good News concerning the Kingdom of God and the name of Jesus Christ. As a result, many men and women were baptized. ¹³Then Simon himself believed and was baptized. He began following Philip wherever he went, and he was amazed by the signs and great miracles Philip performed.

¹⁴When the apostles in Jerusalem heard that the people of Samaria had accepted God's message, they sent Peter and John there. ¹⁵As soon as they arrived, they prayed for these new believers to receive the Holy Spirit. ¹⁶The Holy Spirit had not yet come upon any of them, for they had only been baptized in the name of the Lord Jesus.

¹⁷Then Peter and John laid their hands upon these believers, and they received the Holy Spirit.

¹⁸When Simon saw that the Spirit was given when the apostles laid their hands on people, he offered them money to buy this power. ¹⁹"Let me have this power, too," he exclaimed, "so that when I lay my hands on people, they will receive the Holy Spirit!"

²⁰But Peter replied, "May your money be destroyed with you for thinking God's gift can be bought! ²¹You can have no part in this, for your heart is not right with God. ²²Repent of your wickedness and pray to the Lord. Perhaps he will forgive your evil thoughts, ²³for I can see that you are full of bitter jealousy and are held captive by sin."

²⁴"Pray to the Lord for me," Simon exclaimed, "that these terrible things you've said won't happen to me!"

²⁵After testifying and preaching the word of the Lord in Samaria, Peter and John returned to Jerusalem. And they stopped in many Samaritan villages along the way to preach the Good News.

PHILIP AND THE ETHIOPIAN EUNUCH

²⁶As for Philip, an angel of the Lord said to him, "Go south* down the desert road that runs from Jerusalem to Gaza." ²⁷So he started out, and he met the treasurer of Ethiopia, a eunuch of great authority under the Kandake, the queen of Ethiopia. The eunuch had gone to Jerusalem to worship, ²⁸and he was now returning. Seated in his carriage, he was reading aloud from the book of the prophet Isaiah. ²⁹The Holy Spirit said to Philip, "Go over and walk along beside the carriage."

8:7 Greek unclean. 8:26 Or Go at noon.

³⁰ Philip ran over and heard the man reading from the prophet Isaiah. Philip asked, "Do you understand what you are reading?"

³¹ The man replied, "How can I, unless someone instructs me?" And he urged Philip to come up into the carriage and sit with him.

³² The passage of Scripture he had been reading was this:

"He was led like a sheep to the slaughter.
    And as a lamb is silent before the
        shearers,
    he did not open his mouth.
³³ He was humiliated and received no justice.
    Who can speak of his descendants?
    For his life was taken from the earth."*

³⁴ The eunuch asked Philip, "Tell me, was the prophet talking about himself or someone else?" ³⁵ So beginning with this same Scripture, Philip told him the Good News about Jesus.

³⁶ As they rode along, they came to some water, and the eunuch said, "Look! There's some water! Why can't I be baptized?"* ³⁸ He ordered the carriage to stop, and they went down into the water, and Philip baptized him.

³⁹ When they came up out of the water, the Spirit of the Lord snatched Philip away. The eunuch never saw him again but went on his way rejoicing. ⁴⁰ Meanwhile, Philip found himself farther north at the town of Azotus. He preached the Good News there and in every town along the way until he came to Caesarea.

SAUL'S CONVERSION

9 Meanwhile, Saul was uttering threats with every breath and was eager to kill the Lord's followers.* So he went to the high priest. ² He requested letters addressed to the synagogues in Damascus, asking for their cooperation in the arrest of any followers of the Way he found there. He wanted to bring them—both men and women—back to Jerusalem in chains.

³ As he was approaching Damascus on this mission, a light from heaven suddenly shone down around him. ⁴ He fell to the ground and heard a voice saying to him, "Saul! Saul! Why are you persecuting me?"

⁵ "Who are you, lord?" Saul asked.

And the voice replied, "I am Jesus, the one you are persecuting! ⁶ Now get up and go into the city, and you will be told what you must do."

⁷ The men with Saul stood speechless, for they heard the sound of someone's voice but saw no one! ⁸ Saul picked himself up off the ground, but when he opened his eyes he was blind. So his companions led him by the hand to Damascus. ⁹ He remained there blind for three days and did not eat or drink.

¹⁰ Now there was a believer* in Damascus named Ananias. The Lord spoke to him in a vision, calling, "Ananias!"

ANANIAS: THE HIDDEN HERO
Acts 9:10-19   TIM ROSS

After Saul (also called Paul) met Jesus on the road to Damascus, God sent a believer named Ananias to pray for him. Scripture mentions nothing about Ananias before or after his encounter with Paul in Acts 9:10-18, but this believer made three heroic decisions:

1. He followed the voice of God into an uncertain and uncomfortable situation.
2. He chose obedience and fellowshipped with Paul, a former enemy.
3. He allowed God's power to flow through him to do God's work.

Ananias chose to be obedient and embrace someone with a dark past. He humbly chose to do what God asked of him, never seeking personal recognition. Like many Christians, Ananias was not a prominent leader. He was simply a person who was filled with the Holy Spirit and responded to God's voice.

At any given moment, God may call on you to be a hero to your spouse, your children, your coworkers, your friends, or even your enemies. You too can be one of God's hidden heroes.

"Yes, Lord!" he replied.

¹¹ The Lord said, "Go over to Straight Street, to the house of Judas. When you get there, ask for a man from Tarsus named Saul. He is praying to me right now. ¹² I have shown him a vision of a man named Ananias coming in and laying hands on him so he can see again."

¹³ "But Lord," exclaimed Ananias, "I've heard many people talk about the terrible things this man has done to the believers* in Jerusalem! ¹⁴ And he is authorized by the leading priests to arrest everyone who calls upon your name."

¹⁵ But the Lord said, "Go, for Saul is my chosen instrument to take my message to the Gentiles and to kings, as well as to the people of Israel. ¹⁶ And I will show him how much he must suffer for my name's sake."

¹⁷ So Ananias went and found Saul. He laid his hands on him and said, "Brother Saul, the Lord Jesus, who appeared to you on the road, has sent me so that you might regain your sight and be filled with the Holy Spirit." ¹⁸ Instantly something like scales fell from Saul's eyes, and he regained his sight. Then he got up and was baptized. ¹⁹ Afterward he ate some food and regained his strength.

8:32-33 Isa 53:7-8 (Greek version).   8:36 Some manuscripts add verse 37, *"You can," Philip answered, "if you believe with all your heart." And the eunuch replied, "I believe that Jesus Christ is the Son of God."*   9:1 Greek *disciples.*   9:10 Greek *disciple;* also in 9:26, 36.   9:13 Greek *God's holy people;* also in 9:32, 41.

SAUL IN DAMASCUS AND JERUSALEM

Saul stayed with the believers* in Damascus for a few days. ²⁰And immediately he began preaching about Jesus in the synagogues, saying, "He is indeed the Son of God!"

²¹All who heard him were amazed. "Isn't this the same man who caused such devastation among Jesus' followers in Jerusalem?" they asked. "And didn't he come here to arrest them and take them in chains to the leading priests?"

²²Saul's preaching became more and more powerful, and the Jews in Damascus couldn't refute his proofs that Jesus was indeed the Messiah. ²³After a while some of the Jews plotted together to kill him. ²⁴They were watching for him day and night at the city gate so they could murder him, but Saul was told about their plot. ²⁵So during the night, some of the other believers* lowered him in a large basket through an opening in the city wall.

²⁶When Saul arrived in Jerusalem, he tried to meet with the believers, but they were all afraid of him. They did not believe he had truly become a believer! ²⁷Then Barnabas brought him to the apostles and told them how Saul had seen the Lord on the way to Damascus and how the Lord had spoken to Saul. He also told them that Saul had preached boldly in the name of Jesus in Damascus.

²⁸So Saul stayed with the apostles and went all around Jerusalem with them, preaching boldly in the name of the Lord. ²⁹He debated with some Greek-speaking Jews, but they tried to murder him. ³⁰When the believers* heard about this, they took him down to Caesarea and sent him away to Tarsus, his hometown.

³¹The church then had peace throughout Judea, Galilee, and Samaria, and it became stronger as the believers lived in the fear of the Lord. And with the encouragement of the Holy Spirit, it also grew in numbers.

PETER HEALS AENEAS AND RAISES DORCAS

³²Meanwhile, Peter traveled from place to place, and he came down to visit the believers in the town of Lydda. ³³There he met a man named Aeneas, who had been paralyzed and bedridden for eight years. ³⁴Peter said to him, "Aeneas, Jesus Christ heals you! Get up, and roll up your sleeping mat!" And he was healed instantly. ³⁵Then the whole population of Lydda and Sharon saw Aeneas walking around, and they turned to the Lord.

³⁶There was a believer in Joppa named Tabitha (which in Greek is Dorcas*). She was always doing kind things for others and helping the poor. ³⁷About this time she became ill and died. Her body was washed for burial and laid in an upstairs room. ³⁸But the believers had heard that Peter was nearby at Lydda, so they sent two men to beg him, "Please come as soon as possible!"

³⁹So Peter returned with them; and as soon as he arrived, they took him to the upstairs room.

The room was filled with widows who were weeping and showing him the coats and other clothes Dorcas had made for them. ⁴⁰But Peter asked them all to leave the room; then he knelt and prayed. Turning to the body he said, "Get up, Tabitha." And she opened her eyes! When she saw Peter, she sat up! ⁴¹He gave her his hand and helped her up. Then he called in the widows and all the believers, and he presented her to them alive.

⁴²The news spread through the whole town, and many believed in the Lord. ⁴³And Peter stayed a long time in Joppa, living with Simon, a tanner of hides.

CORNELIUS CALLS FOR PETER

10 In Caesarea there lived a Roman army officer* named Cornelius, who was a captain of the Italian Regiment. ²He was a devout, God-fearing man, as was everyone in his household. He gave generously to the poor and prayed regularly to God. ³One afternoon about three o'clock, he had a vision in which he saw an angel of God coming toward him. "Cornelius!" the angel said.

⁴Cornelius stared at him in terror. "What is it, sir?" he asked the angel.

And the angel replied, "Your prayers and gifts to the poor have been received by God as an offering! ⁵Now send some men to Joppa, and summon a man named Simon Peter. ⁶He is staying with Simon, a tanner who lives near the seashore."

⁷As soon as the angel was gone, Cornelius called two of his household servants and a devout soldier, one of his personal attendants. ⁸He told them what had happened and sent them off to Joppa.

PETER VISITS CORNELIUS

⁹The next day as Cornelius's messengers were nearing the town, Peter went up on the flat roof to pray. It was about noon, ¹⁰and he was hungry. But while a meal was being prepared, he fell into a trance. ¹¹He saw the sky open, and something like a large sheet was let down by its four corners. ¹²In the sheet were all sorts of animals, reptiles, and birds. ¹³Then a voice said to him, "Get up, Peter; kill and eat them."

¹⁴"No, Lord," Peter declared. "I have never eaten anything that our Jewish laws have declared impure and unclean.*"

¹⁵But the voice spoke again: "Do not call something unclean if God has made it clean." ¹⁶The same vision was repeated three times. Then the sheet was suddenly pulled up to heaven.

¹⁷Peter was very perplexed. What could the vision mean? Just then the men sent by Cornelius found Simon's house. Standing outside the

---

9:19 Greek *disciples;* also in 9:26, 38. 9:25 Greek *his disciples.*
9:30 Greek *brothers.* 9:36 The names *Tabitha* in Aramaic and *Dorcas* in Greek both mean "gazelle." 10:1 Greek *a centurion;* similarly in 10:22. 10:14 Greek *anything common and unclean.*

gate, [18] they asked if a man named Simon Peter was staying there.

[19] Meanwhile, as Peter was puzzling over the vision, the Holy Spirit said to him, "Three men have come looking for you. [20] Get up, go downstairs, and go with them without hesitation. Don't worry, for I have sent them."

[21] So Peter went down and said, "I'm the man you are looking for. Why have you come?"

[22] They said, "We were sent by Cornelius, a Roman officer. He is a devout and God-fearing man, well respected by all the Jews. A holy angel instructed him to summon you to his house so that he can hear your message." [23] So Peter invited the men to stay for the night. The next day he went with them, accompanied by some of the brothers from Joppa.

[24] They arrived in Caesarea the following day. Cornelius was waiting for them and had called together his relatives and close friends. [25] As Peter entered his home, Cornelius fell at his feet and worshiped him. [26] But Peter pulled him up and said, "Stand up! I'm a human being just like you!" [27] So they talked together and went inside, where many others were assembled.

[28] Peter told them, "You know it is against our laws for a Jewish man to enter a Gentile home like this or to associate with you. But God has shown me that I should no longer think of anyone as impure or unclean. [29] So I came without objection as soon as I was sent for. Now tell me why you sent for me."

[30] Cornelius replied, "Four days ago I was praying in my house about this same time, three o'clock in the afternoon. Suddenly, a man in dazzling clothes was standing in front of me. [31] He told me, 'Cornelius, your prayer has been heard, and your gifts to the poor have been noticed by God! [32] Now send messengers to Joppa, and summon a man named Simon Peter. He is staying in the home of Simon, a tanner who lives near the seashore.' [33] So I sent for you at once, and it was good of you to come. Now we are all here, waiting before God to hear the message the Lord has given you."

THE GENTILES HEAR THE GOOD NEWS

[34] Then Peter replied, "I see very clearly that God shows no favoritism. [35] In every nation he accepts those who fear him and do what is right. [36] This is the message of Good News for the people of Israel—that there is peace with God through Jesus Christ, who is Lord of all. [37] You know what happened throughout Judea, beginning in Galilee, after John began preaching his message of baptism. [38] And you know that God anointed Jesus of Nazareth with the Holy Spirit and with power. Then Jesus went around doing good and healing all who were oppressed by the devil, for God was with him.

[39] "And we apostles are witnesses of all he did throughout Judea and in Jerusalem. They put

him to death by hanging him on a cross,* [40] but God raised him to life on the third day. Then God allowed him to appear, [41] not to the general public,* but to us whom God had chosen in advance to be his witnesses. We were those who ate and drank with him after he rose from the dead. [42] And he ordered us to preach everywhere and to testify that Jesus is the one appointed by God to be the judge of all—the living and the dead. [43] He is the one all the prophets testified about, saying that everyone who believes in him will have their sins forgiven through his name."

THE GENTILES RECEIVE THE HOLY SPIRIT

[44] Even as Peter was saying these things, the Holy Spirit fell upon all who were listening to the message. [45] The Jewish believers* who came with Peter were amazed that the gift of the Holy Spirit had been poured out on the Gentiles, too. [46] For they heard them speaking in other tongues* and praising God.

Then Peter asked, [47] "Can anyone object to their being baptized, now that they have received the Holy Spirit just as we did?" [48] So he gave orders for them to be baptized in the name of Jesus Christ. Afterward Cornelius asked him to stay with them for several days.

PETER EXPLAINS HIS ACTIONS

11 Soon the news reached the apostles and other believers* in Judea that the Gentiles had received the word of God. [2] But when Peter arrived back in Jerusalem, the Jewish believers* criticized him. [3] "You entered the home of Gentiles* and even ate with them!" they said.

[4] Then Peter told them exactly what had happened. [5] "I was in the town of Joppa," he said, "and while I was praying, I went into a trance and saw a vision. Something like a large sheet was let down by its four corners from the sky. And it came right down to me. [6] When I looked inside the sheet, I saw all sorts of tame and wild animals, reptiles, and birds. [7] And I heard a voice say, 'Get up, Peter; kill and eat them.'

[8] "'No, Lord,' I replied. 'I have never eaten anything that our Jewish laws have declared impure or unclean.*'

[9] "But the voice from heaven spoke again: 'Do not call something unclean if God has made it clean.' [10] This happened three times before the sheet and all it contained was pulled back up to heaven.

[11] "Just then three men who had been sent from Caesarea arrived at the house where we were staying. [12] The Holy Spirit told me to go with them and not to worry that they were Gentiles. These six brothers here accompanied me, and we soon entered the home of the man who had sent for us.

10:39 Greek *on a tree.*   10:41 Greek *the people.*   10:45 Greek *The faithful ones of the circumcision.*   10:46 Or *in other languages.*   11:1 Greek *brothers.*   11:2 Greek *those of the circumcision.*   11:3 Greek *of uncircumcised men.*   11:8 Greek *anything common or unclean.*

¹³ He told us how an angel had appeared to him in his home and had told him, 'Send messengers to Joppa, and summon a man named Simon Peter. ¹⁴ He will tell you how you and everyone in your household can be saved!'

¹⁵ "As I began to speak," Peter continued, "the Holy Spirit fell on them, just as he fell on us at the beginning. ¹⁶ Then I thought of the Lord's words when he said, 'John baptized with* water, but you will be baptized with the Holy Spirit.' ¹⁷ And since God gave these Gentiles the same gift he gave us when we believed in the Lord Jesus Christ, who was I to stand in God's way?"

¹⁸ When the others heard this, they stopped objecting and began praising God. They said, "We can see that God has also given the Gentiles the privilege of repenting of their sins and receiving eternal life."

THE CHURCH IN ANTIOCH OF SYRIA

¹⁹ Meanwhile, the believers who had been scattered during the persecution after Stephen's death traveled as far as Phoenicia, Cyprus, and Antioch of Syria. They preached the word of God, but only to Jews. ²⁰ However, some of the believers who went to Antioch from Cyprus and Cyrene began preaching to the Gentiles* about the Lord Jesus. ²¹ The power of the Lord was with them, and a large number of these Gentiles believed and turned to the Lord.

²² When the church at Jerusalem heard what had happened, they sent Barnabas to Antioch. ²³ When he arrived and saw this evidence of God's blessing, he was filled with joy, and he encouraged the believers to stay true to the Lord. ²⁴ Barnabas was a good man, full of the Holy Spirit and strong in faith. And many people were brought to the Lord.

²⁵ Then Barnabas went on to Tarsus to look for Saul. ²⁶ When he found him, he brought him back to Antioch. Both of them stayed there with the church for a full year, teaching large crowds of people. (It was at Antioch that the believers* were first called Christians.)

²⁷ During this time some prophets traveled from Jerusalem to Antioch. ²⁸ One of them named Agabus stood up in one of the meetings and predicted by the Spirit that a great famine was coming upon the entire Roman world. (This was fulfilled during the reign of Claudius.) ²⁹ So the believers in Antioch decided to send relief to the brothers and sisters* in Judea, everyone giving as much as they could. ³⁰ This they did, entrusting their gifts to Barnabas and Saul to take to the elders of the church in Jerusalem.

JAMES IS KILLED AND PETER IS IMPRISONED

12 About that time King Herod Agrippa* began to persecute some believers in the church. ² He had the apostle James (John's brother) killed with a sword. ³ When Herod saw how much this pleased the Jewish people, he also arrested Peter. (This took place during the Passover celebration.*) ⁴ Then he imprisoned him, placing him under the guard of four squads of four soldiers each. Herod intended to bring Peter out for public trial after the Passover. ⁵ But while Peter was in prison, the church prayed very earnestly for him.

PETER'S MIRACULOUS ESCAPE FROM PRISON

⁶ The night before Peter was to be placed on trial, he was asleep, fastened with two chains between two soldiers. Others stood guard at the prison gate. ⁷ Suddenly, there was a bright light in the cell, and an angel of the Lord stood before Peter. The angel struck him on the side to awaken him and said, "Quick! Get up!" And the chains fell off his wrists. ⁸ Then the angel told him, "Get dressed and put on your sandals." And he did. "Now put on your coat and follow me," the angel ordered.

⁹ So Peter left the cell, following the angel. But all the time he thought it was a vision. He didn't realize it was actually happening. ¹⁰ They passed the first and second guard posts and came to the iron gate leading to the city, and this opened for them all by itself. So they passed through and started walking down the street, and then the angel suddenly left him.

¹¹ Peter finally came to his senses. "It's really true!" he said. "The Lord has sent his angel and saved me from Herod and from what the Jewish leaders* had planned to do to me!"

¹² When he realized this, he went to the home of Mary, the mother of John Mark, where many were gathered for prayer. ¹³ He knocked at the door in the gate, and a servant girl named Rhoda came to open it. ¹⁴ When she recognized Peter's voice, she was so overjoyed that, instead of opening the door, she ran back inside and told everyone, "Peter is standing at the door!"

¹⁵ "You're out of your mind!" they said. When she insisted, they decided, "It must be his angel."

¹⁶ Meanwhile, Peter continued knocking. When they finally opened the door and saw him, they were amazed. ¹⁷ He motioned for them to quiet down and told them how the Lord had led him out of prison. "Tell James and the other brothers what happened," he said. And then he went to another place.

¹⁸ At dawn there was a great commotion among the soldiers about what had happened to Peter. ¹⁹ Herod Agrippa ordered a thorough search for him. When he couldn't be found, Herod interrogated the guards and sentenced them to death. Afterward Herod left Judea to stay in Caesarea for a while.

11:16 Or *in*; also in 11:16b. 11:20 Greek *the Hellenists* (i.e., those who speak Greek); other manuscripts read *the Greeks*. 11:26 Greek *disciples*; also in 11:29. 11:29 Greek *the brothers*. 12:1 Greek *Herod the king*. He was the nephew of Herod Antipas and a grandson of Herod the Great. 12:3 Greek *the days of unleavened bread*. 12:11 Or *the Jewish people*.

THE DEATH OF HEROD AGRIPPA

²⁰ Now Herod was very angry with the people of Tyre and Sidon. So they sent a delegation to make peace with him because their cities were dependent upon Herod's country for food. The delegates won the support of Blastus, Herod's personal assistant, ²¹ and an appointment with Herod was granted. When the day arrived, Herod put on his royal robes, sat on his throne, and made a speech to them. ²² The people gave him a great ovation, shouting, "It's the voice of a god, not of a man!"

²³ Instantly, an angel of the Lord struck Herod with a sickness, because he accepted the people's worship instead of giving the glory to God. So he was consumed with worms and died.

²⁴ Meanwhile, the word of God continued to spread, and there were many new believers.

²⁵ When Barnabas and Saul had finished their mission to Jerusalem, they returned,* taking John Mark with them.

BARNABAS AND SAUL ARE COMMISSIONED

13 Among the prophets and teachers of the church at Antioch of Syria were Barnabas, Simeon (called "the black man"*), Lucius (from Cyrene), Manaen (the childhood companion of King Herod Antipas*), and Saul. ² One day as these men were worshiping the Lord and fasting, the Holy Spirit said, "Appoint Barnabas and Saul for the special work to which I have called them." ³ So after more fasting and prayer, the men laid their hands on them and sent them on their way.

PAUL'S FIRST MISSIONARY JOURNEY

⁴ So Barnabas and Saul were sent out by the Holy Spirit. They went down to the seaport of Seleucia and then sailed for the island of Cyprus. ⁵ There, in the town of Salamis, they went to the Jewish synagogues and preached the word of God. John Mark went with them as their assistant.

⁶ Afterward they traveled from town to town across the entire island until finally they reached Paphos, where they met a Jewish sorcerer, a false prophet named Bar-Jesus. ⁷ He had attached himself to the governor, Sergius Paulus, who was an intelligent man. The governor invited Barnabas and Saul to visit him, for he wanted to hear the word of God. ⁸ But Elymas, the sorcerer (as his name means in Greek), interfered and urged the governor to pay no attention to what Barnabas and Saul said. He was trying to keep the governor from believing.

⁹ Saul, also known as Paul, was filled with the Holy Spirit, and he looked the sorcerer in the eye. ¹⁰ Then he said, "You son of the devil, full of every sort of deceit and fraud, and enemy of all that is good! Will you never stop perverting the true ways of the Lord? ¹¹ Watch now, for the Lord has laid his hand of punishment upon you, and you will be struck blind. You will not see the sunlight for some time." Instantly mist and darkness came over the man's eyes, and he began groping around begging for someone to take his hand and lead him.

¹² When the governor saw what had happened, he became a believer, for he was astonished at the teaching about the Lord.

PAUL PREACHES IN ANTIOCH OF PISIDIA

¹³ Paul and his companions then left Paphos by ship for Pamphylia, landing at the port town of Perga. There John Mark left them and returned to Jerusalem. ¹⁴ But Paul and Barnabas traveled inland to Antioch of Pisidia.*

On the Sabbath they went to the synagogue for the services. ¹⁵ After the usual readings from the books of Moses* and the prophets, those in charge of the service sent them this message: "Brothers, if you have any word of encouragement for the people, come and give it."

¹⁶ So Paul stood, lifted his hand to quiet them, and started speaking. "Men of Israel," he said, "and you God-fearing Gentiles, listen to me. ¹⁷ The God of this nation of Israel chose our ancestors and made them multiply and grow strong during their stay in Egypt. Then with a powerful arm he led them out of their slavery. ¹⁸ He put up with them* through forty years of wandering in the wilderness. ¹⁹ Then he destroyed seven nations in Canaan and gave their land to Israel as an inheritance. ²⁰ All this took about 450 years.

"After that, God gave them judges to rule until the time of Samuel the prophet. ²¹ Then the people begged for a king, and God gave them Saul son of Kish, a man of the tribe of Benjamin, who reigned for forty years. ²² But God removed Saul and replaced him with David, a man about whom God said, 'I have found David son of Jesse, a man after my own heart. He will do everything I want him to do.'*

²³ "And it is one of King David's descendants, Jesus, who is God's promised Savior of Israel! ²⁴ Before he came, John the Baptist preached that all the people of Israel needed to repent of their sins and turn to God and be baptized. ²⁵ As John was finishing his ministry he asked, 'Do you think I am the Messiah? No, I am not! But he is coming soon—and I'm not even worthy to be his slave and untie the sandals on his feet.'

²⁶ "Brothers—you sons of Abraham, and also you God-fearing Gentiles—this message of salvation has been sent to us! ²⁷ The people in Jerusalem and their leaders did not recognize Jesus as the one the prophets had spoken about. Instead, they condemned him, and in doing this they fulfilled the prophets' words that are read

---

12:25 Or *mission, they returned to Jerusalem.* Other manuscripts read *mission, they returned from Jerusalem;* still others read *mission, they returned from Jerusalem to Antioch.* 13:1a Greek *who was called Niger.* 13:1b Greek *Herod the tetrarch.* 13:13-14 *Pamphylia* and *Pisidia* were districts in what is now Turkey. 13:15 Greek *from the law.* 13:18 Some manuscripts read *He cared for them;* compare Deut 1:31. 13:22 1 Sam 13:14.

every Sabbath. [28] They found no legal reason to execute him, but they asked Pilate to have him killed anyway.

[29] "When they had done all that the prophecies said about him, they took him down from the cross* and placed him in a tomb. [30] But God raised him from the dead! [31] And over a period of many days he appeared to those who had gone with him from Galilee to Jerusalem. They are now his witnesses to the people of Israel.

[32] "And now we are here to bring you this Good News. The promise was made to our ancestors, [33] and God has now fulfilled it for us, their descendants, by raising Jesus. This is what the second psalm says about Jesus:

'You are my Son.
    Today I have become your Father.'*

[34] For God had promised to raise him from the dead, not leaving him to rot in the grave. He said, 'I will give you the sacred blessings I promised to David.'* [35] Another psalm explains it more fully: 'You will not allow your Holy One to rot in the grave.'* [36] This is not a reference to David, for after David had done the will of God in his own generation, he died and was buried with his ancestors, and his body decayed. [37] No, it was a reference to someone else—someone whom God raised and whose body did not decay.

[38] "Brothers, listen! We are here to proclaim that through this man Jesus there is forgiveness for your sins. [39] Everyone who believes in him is made right in God's sight—something the law of Moses could never do. [40] Be careful! Don't let the prophets' words apply to you. For they said,

[41] 'Look, you mockers,
    be amazed and die!
For I am doing something in your own day,
    something you wouldn't believe
    even if someone told you about it.'*"

[42] As Paul and Barnabas left the synagogue that day, the people begged them to speak about these things again the next week. [43] Many Jews and devout converts to Judaism followed Paul and Barnabas, and the two men urged them to continue to rely on the grace of God.

PAUL TURNS TO THE GENTILES

[44] The following week almost the entire city turned out to hear them preach the word of the Lord. [45] But when some of the Jews saw the crowds, they were jealous; so they slandered Paul and argued against whatever he said.

[46] Then Paul and Barnabas spoke out boldly and declared, "It was necessary that we first preach the word of God to you Jews. But since you have rejected it and judged yourselves unworthy of eternal life, we will offer it to the Gentiles. [47] For the Lord gave us this command when he said,

'I have made you a light to the Gentiles,
    to bring salvation to the farthest corners
        of the earth.'*"

[48] When the Gentiles heard this, they were very glad and thanked the Lord for his message; and all who were chosen for eternal life became believers. [49] So the Lord's message spread throughout that region.

[50] Then the Jews stirred up the influential religious women and the leaders of the city, and they incited a mob against Paul and Barnabas and ran them out of town. [51] So they shook the dust from their feet as a sign of rejection and went to the town of Iconium. [52] And the believers* were filled with joy and with the Holy Spirit.

PAUL AND BARNABAS IN ICONIUM

14 The same thing happened in Iconium.* Paul and Barnabas went to the Jewish synagogue and preached with such power that a great number of both Jews and Greeks became believers. [2] Some of the Jews, however, spurned God's message and poisoned the minds of the Gentiles against Paul and Barnabas. [3] But the apostles stayed there a long time, preaching boldly about the grace of the Lord. And the Lord proved their message was true by giving them power to do miraculous signs and wonders. [4] But the people of the town were divided in their opinion about them. Some sided with the Jews, and some with the apostles.

[5] Then a mob of Gentiles and Jews, along with their leaders, decided to attack and stone them. [6] When the apostles learned of it, they fled to the region of Lycaonia—to the towns of Lystra and Derbe and the surrounding area. [7] And there they preached the Good News.

PAUL AND BARNABAS IN LYSTRA AND DERBE

[8] While they were at Lystra, Paul and Barnabas came upon a man with crippled feet. He had been that way from birth, so he had never walked. He was sitting [9] and listening as Paul preached. Looking straight at him, Paul realized he had faith to be healed. [10] So Paul called to him in a loud voice, "Stand up!" And the man jumped to his feet and started walking.

[11] When the crowd saw what Paul had done, they shouted in their local dialect, "These men are gods in human form!" [12] They decided that Barnabas was the Greek god Zeus and that Paul was Hermes, since he was the chief speaker. [13] Now the temple of Zeus was located just outside the town. So the priest of the temple and

---

13:29 Greek *from the tree.* **13:33** Or *Today I reveal you as my Son.* Ps 2:7. **13:34** Isa 55:3. **13:35** Ps 16:10. **13:38** English translations divide verses 38 and 39 in various ways. **13:41** Hab 1:5 (Greek version). **13:47** Isa 49:6. **13:52** Greek *the disciples.* **14:1** *Iconium,* as well as *Lystra* and *Derbe* (14:6), were towns in what is now Turkey.

the crowd brought bulls and wreaths of flowers to the town gates, and they prepared to offer sacrifices to the apostles.

[14] But when the apostles Barnabas and Paul heard what was happening, they tore their clothing in dismay and ran out among the people, shouting, [15] "Friends,* why are you doing this? We are merely human beings—just like you! We have come to bring you the Good News that you should turn from these worthless things and turn to the living God, who made heaven and earth, the sea, and everything in them. [16] In the past he permitted all the nations to go their own ways, [17] but he never left them without evidence of himself and his goodness. For instance, he sends you rain and good crops and gives you food and joyful hearts." [18] But even with these words, Paul and Barnabas could scarcely restrain the people from sacrificing to them.

[19] Then some Jews arrived from Antioch and Iconium and won the crowds to their side. They stoned Paul and dragged him out of town, thinking he was dead. [20] But as the believers* gathered around him, he got up and went back into the town. The next day he left with Barnabas for Derbe.

PAUL AND BARNABAS RETURN TO ANTIOCH OF SYRIA

[21] After preaching the Good News in Derbe and making many disciples, Paul and Barnabas returned to Lystra, Iconium, and Antioch of Pisidia, [22] where they strengthened the believers. They encouraged them to continue in the faith, reminding them that we must suffer many hardships to enter the Kingdom of God. [23] Paul and Barnabas also appointed elders in every church. With prayer and fasting, they turned the elders over to the care of the Lord, in whom they had put their trust. [24] Then they traveled back through Pisidia to Pamphylia. [25] They preached the word in Perga, then went down to Attalia.

[26] Finally, they returned by ship to Antioch of Syria, where their journey had begun. The believers there had entrusted them to the grace of God to do the work they had now completed. [27] Upon arriving in Antioch, they called the church together and reported everything God had done through them and how he had opened the door of faith to the Gentiles, too. [28] And they stayed there with the believers for a long time.

THE COUNCIL AT JERUSALEM

15 While Paul and Barnabas were at Antioch of Syria, some men from Judea arrived and began to teach the believers*: "Unless you are circumcised as required by the law of Moses, you cannot be saved." [2] Paul and Barnabas disagreed with them, arguing vehemently. Finally, the church decided to send Paul and Barnabas to Jerusalem, accompanied by some local believers, to talk to the apostles and elders about this question. [3] The church sent the delegates to Jerusalem, and they stopped along the way in Phoenicia and Samaria to visit the believers. They told them—much to everyone's joy—that the Gentiles, too, were being converted.

[4] When they arrived in Jerusalem, Barnabas and Paul were welcomed by the whole church, including the apostles and elders. They reported everything God had done through them. [5] But then some of the believers who belonged to the sect of the Pharisees stood up and insisted, "The Gentile converts must be circumcised and required to follow the law of Moses."

[6] So the apostles and elders met together to resolve this issue. [7] At the meeting, after a long discussion, Peter stood and addressed them as follows: "Brothers, you all know that God chose me from among you some time ago to preach to the Gentiles so that they could hear the Good News and believe. [8] God knows people's hearts, and he confirmed that he accepts Gentiles by giving them the Holy Spirit, just as he did to us. [9] He made no distinction between us and them, for he cleansed their hearts through faith. [10] So why are you now challenging God by burdening the Gentile believers* with a yoke that neither we nor our ancestors were able to bear? [11] We believe that we are all saved the same way, by the undeserved grace of the Lord Jesus."

[12] Everyone listened quietly as Barnabas and Paul told about the miraculous signs and wonders God had done through them among the Gentiles.

[13] When they had finished, James stood and said, "Brothers, listen to me. [14] Peter* has told you about the time God first visited the Gentiles to take from them a people for himself. [15] And this conversion of Gentiles is exactly what the prophets predicted. As it is written:

[16] 'Afterward I will return
   and restore the fallen house* of David.
I will rebuild its ruins
   and restore it,
[17] so that the rest of humanity might seek
      the LORD,
   including the Gentiles—
   all those I have called to be mine.
The LORD has spoken—
[18]   he who made these things known
      so long ago.'*

[19] "And so my judgment is that we should not make it difficult for the Gentiles who are turning to God. [20] Instead, we should write and tell them to abstain from eating food offered to idols, from sexual immorality, from eating the meat of

---

14:15 Greek *Men.*   14:20 Greek *disciples;* also in 14:22, 28.
15:1 Greek *brothers;* also in 15:3, 23, 32, 33, 36, 40.   15:10 Greek
disciples.   15:14 Greek *Simeon.*   15:16 Or *kingdom;* Greek reads
tent.   15:16-18 Amos 9:11-12 (Greek version); Isa 45:21.

ISRAEL AND THE JEWS THROUGH GOD'S EYES
Acts 15:6–31   JACK HAYFORD

Many people in the early church thought Gentiles needed to become Jews to be saved. Today, many people believe Jews need to become Christians (in the cultural sense) to be saved. However, doctrine is not what determines a person's salvation.

Early Gentile believers faced pressure to be circumcised in order to be considered truly saved. Modern Christian traditions also tend to promote cultural requirements for acceptance. However, the apostle Peter argued, "God knows people's hearts. . . . We believe that we are all saved the same way, by the undeserved grace of the Lord Jesus" (Acts 15:8, 11).

The term *Christian* is not essential to acknowledging Jesus as Messiah. We must be sensitive to what the Holy Spirit is doing in the Jewish culture and not become fixated on doctrine. Just as the early church decided that Gentiles didn't need to become Jews to follow Christ, we must decide that Jews don't need to become "Christians" to follow the Messiah.

---

strangled animals, and from consuming blood. 21 For these laws of Moses have been preached in Jewish synagogues in every city on every Sabbath for many generations."

THE LETTER FOR GENTILE BELIEVERS
22 Then the apostles and elders together with the whole church in Jerusalem chose delegates, and they sent them to Antioch of Syria with Paul and Barnabas to report on this decision. The men chosen were two of the church leaders*—Judas (also called Barsabbas) and Silas. 23 This is the letter they took with them:

"This letter is from the apostles and elders, your brothers in Jerusalem. It is written to the Gentile believers in Antioch, Syria, and Cilicia. Greetings!

24 "We understand that some men from here have troubled you and upset you with their teaching, but we did not send them! 25 So we decided, having come to complete agreement, to send you official representatives, along with our beloved Barnabas and Paul, 26 who have risked their lives for the name of our Lord Jesus Christ. 27 We are sending Judas and Silas to confirm what we have decided concerning your question.

28 "For it seemed good to the Holy Spirit and to us to lay no greater burden on you than these few requirements: 29 You must abstain from eating food offered to idols, from consuming blood or the meat of strangled animals, and from sexual immorality. If you do this, you will do well. Farewell."

30 The messengers went at once to Antioch, where they called a general meeting of the believers and delivered the letter. 31 And there was great joy throughout the church that day as they read this encouraging message.

32 Then Judas and Silas, both being prophets, spoke at length to the believers, encouraging and strengthening their faith. 33 They stayed for a while, and then the believers sent them back to the church in Jerusalem with a blessing of peace.* 35 Paul and Barnabas stayed in Antioch. They and many others taught and preached the word of the Lord there.

PAUL AND BARNABAS SEPARATE
36 After some time Paul said to Barnabas, "Let's go back and visit each city where we previously preached the word of the Lord, to see how the new believers are doing." 37 Barnabas agreed and wanted to take along John Mark. 38 But Paul disagreed strongly, since John Mark had deserted them in Pamphylia and had not continued with them in their work. 39 Their disagreement was so sharp that they separated. Barnabas took John Mark with him and sailed for Cyprus. 40 Paul chose Silas, and as he left, the believers entrusted him to the Lord's gracious care. 41 Then he traveled throughout Syria and Cilicia, strengthening the churches there.

PAUL'S SECOND MISSIONARY JOURNEY
16 Paul went first to Derbe and then to Lystra, where there was a young disciple named Timothy. His mother was a Jewish believer, but his father was a Greek. 2 Timothy was well thought of by the believers* in Lystra and Iconium, 3 so Paul wanted him to join them on their journey. In deference to the Jews of the area, he arranged for Timothy to be circumcised before they left, for everyone knew that his father was a Greek. 4 Then they went from town to town, instructing the believers to follow the decisions made by the apostles and elders in Jerusalem. 5 So the churches were strengthened in their faith and grew larger every day.

A CALL FROM MACEDONIA
6 Next Paul and Silas traveled through the area of Phrygia and Galatia, because the Holy Spirit had prevented them from preaching the word in the province of Asia at that time. 7 Then coming to the borders of Mysia, they headed north for

---

15:22 Greek *were leaders among the brothers.*   15:33 Some manuscripts add verse 34, *But Silas decided to stay there.*
16:2 Greek *brothers;* also in 16:40.   16:6-7 *Phrygia, Galatia, Asia, Mysia,* and *Bithynia* were all districts in what is now Turkey.

THE GIFTS OF GRACE
Acts 16:22–40 ROBERT MORRIS

Many people feel they have to earn salvation or somehow pay it back later. But that's impossible! Salvation is completely, totally, 100 percent *free*! It comes only by grace through faith in Jesus Christ. It can't be earned, and there are no additional conditions to receive it. In other words, there's no fine print! Romans 11:6 calls God's grace "free and undeserved," and with salvation, we receive three incredible gifts:

1. Justification (Romans 3:24)
Justification means "true justice has been served and a wrong situation has been made right." We're all sinners who deserve death and hell, but Jesus died in our place. He paid the full price for our sins. When we put our faith in Jesus, we are justified in God's sight. He declares us *not guilty*!

2. Eternal Life (1 John 2:25; 5:13; Romans 6:23)
If you have received Jesus, you have received the gift of eternal life. A gift, by definition, is something you don't pay for, but many believers still think God's grace is a gift for which He expects to be paid back. They work hard to try to please Him and earn His grace. Here's the truth: you will *never* be able to earn God's grace. That's why it's a gift!

3. Redemption (1 Corinthians 6:19-20)
To *redeem* something means to "buy it back." God created us, but sin separated us from Him. So God sent Jesus to redeem us—to purchase us with His precious blood. If you're a believer, you don't belong to yourself anymore. You belong to God! I've heard some believers say, "What I do on my own time is my business." They're mistaken, though. If you're saved, everything in your life—including your time—belongs to God.

DETOUR TO YOUR DREAM
Acts 16:9–26 MARK JOBE

Have you ever felt as if you were in a spiritual or emotional prison? Maybe you didn't do anything wrong, but your life isn't going the way you planned, and you wonder, *Why is God mad at me?*

Even God-given dreams get detoured sometimes. Paul and Silas knew God had called them to minister in Macedonia, but shortly after arriving, they were beaten, imprisoned, and put in chains. While most of us would focus solely on getting out of such an uncomfortable situation, God focuses on changing us in it. He confronts our selfishness and challenges our shallow, "religious" living. He forces us to examine our character and discover what really matters.

At midnight, Paul and Silas began to pray and worship. A sudden earthquake shook the prison, and "the chains of every prisoner fell off" (Acts 16:26). During the darkest times of our lives, we need to pray and worship because the presence of God is the only thing that will set us free.

the province of Bithynia,* but again the Spirit of Jesus did not allow them to go there. [8] So instead, they went on through Mysia to the seaport of Troas. [9] That night Paul had a vision: A man from Macedonia in northern Greece was standing there, pleading with him, "Come over to Macedonia and help us!" [10] So we* decided to leave for Macedonia at once, having concluded that God was calling us to preach the Good News there.

LYDIA OF PHILIPPI BELIEVES IN JESUS
[11] We boarded a boat at Troas and sailed straight across to the island of Samothrace, and the next day we landed at Neapolis. [12] From there we reached Philippi, a major city of that district of Macedonia and a Roman colony. And we stayed there several days.

[13] On the Sabbath we went a little way outside the city to a riverbank, where we thought people would be meeting for prayer, and we sat down to speak with some women who had gathered there. [14] One of them was Lydia from Thyatira, a merchant of expensive purple cloth, who worshiped God. As she listened to us, the Lord opened her heart, and she accepted what Paul was saying. [15] She and her household were baptized, and she asked us to be her guests. "If you agree that I am a true believer in the Lord," she said, "come and stay at my home." And she urged us until we agreed.

PAUL AND SILAS IN PRISON
[16] One day as we were going down to the place of prayer, we met a slave girl who had a spirit that enabled her to tell the future. She earned a lot of money for her masters by telling fortunes. [17] She followed Paul and the rest of us, shouting, "These men are servants of the Most High God, and they have come to tell you how to be saved." [18] This went on day after day until Paul got so exasperated that he turned and said to the demon within her, "I command you in the name of Jesus Christ to come out of her." And instantly it left her.

[19] Her masters' hopes of wealth were now shattered, so they grabbed Paul and Silas and dragged

---
16:10 Luke, the writer of this book, here joined Paul and accompanied him on his journey.

them before the authorities at the marketplace. ²⁰ "The whole city is in an uproar because of these Jews!" they shouted to the city officials. ²¹ "They are teaching customs that are illegal for us Romans to practice."

²² A mob quickly formed against Paul and Silas, and the city officials ordered them stripped and beaten with wooden rods. ²³ They were severely beaten, and then they were thrown into prison. The jailer was ordered to make sure they didn't escape. ²⁴ So the jailer put them into the inner dungeon and clamped their feet in the stocks.

²⁵ Around midnight Paul and Silas were praying and singing hymns to God, and the other prisoners were listening. ²⁶ Suddenly, there was a massive earthquake, and the prison was shaken to its foundations. All the doors immediately flew open, and the chains of every prisoner fell off! ²⁷ The jailer woke up to see the prison doors wide open. He assumed the prisoners had escaped, so he drew his sword to kill himself. ²⁸ But Paul shouted to him, "Stop! Don't kill yourself! We are all here!"

²⁹ The jailer called for lights and ran to the dungeon and fell down trembling before Paul and Silas. ³⁰ Then he brought them out and asked, "Sirs, what must I do to be saved?"

³¹ They replied, "Believe in the Lord Jesus and you will be saved, along with everyone in your household." ³² And they shared the word of the Lord with him and with all who lived in his household. ³³ Even at that hour of the night, the jailer cared for them and washed their wounds. Then he and everyone in his household was immediately baptized. ³⁴ He brought them into his house and set a meal before them, and he and his entire household rejoiced because they all believed in God.

³⁵ The next morning the city officials sent the police to tell the jailer, "Let those men go!" ³⁶ So the jailer told Paul, "The city officials have said you and Silas are free to leave. Go in peace."

³⁷ But Paul replied, "They have publicly beaten us without a trial and put us in prison—and we are Roman citizens. So now they want us to leave secretly? Certainly not! Let them come themselves to release us!"

³⁸ When the police reported this, the city officials were alarmed to learn that Paul and Silas were Roman citizens. ³⁹ So they came to the jail and apologized to them. Then they brought them out and begged them to leave the city. ⁴⁰ When Paul and Silas left the prison, they returned to the home of Lydia. There they met with the believers and encouraged them once more. Then they left town.

PAUL PREACHES IN THESSALONICA

17 Paul and Silas then traveled through the towns of Amphipolis and Apollonia and came to Thessalonica, where there was a Jewish synagogue. ² As was Paul's custom, he went to the synagogue service, and for three Sabbaths in a row he used the Scriptures to reason with the

people. ³ He explained the prophecies and proved that the Messiah must suffer and rise from the dead. He said, "This Jesus I'm telling you about is the Messiah." ⁴ Some of the Jews who listened were persuaded and joined Paul and Silas, along with many God-fearing Greek men and quite a few prominent women.*

⁵ But some of the Jews were jealous, so they gathered some troublemakers from the marketplace to form a mob and start a riot. They attacked the home of Jason, searching for Paul and Silas so they could drag them out to the crowd.* ⁶ Not finding them there, they dragged out Jason and some of the other believers* instead and took them before the city council. "Paul and Silas have caused trouble all over the world," they shouted, "and now they are here disturbing our city, too. ⁷ And Jason has welcomed them into his home. They are all guilty of treason against Caesar, for they profess allegiance to another king, named Jesus."

⁸ The people of the city, as well as the city council, were thrown into turmoil by these reports. ⁹ So the officials forced Jason and the other believers to post bond, and then they released them.

PAUL AND SILAS IN BEREA

¹⁰ That very night the believers sent Paul and Silas to Berea. When they arrived there, they went to the Jewish synagogue. ¹¹ And the people of Berea were more open-minded than those in Thessalonica, and they listened eagerly to Paul's message. They searched the Scriptures day after day to see if Paul and Silas were teaching the truth. ¹² As a result, many Jews believed, as did many of the prominent Greek women and men.

¹³ But when some Jews in Thessalonica learned that Paul was preaching the word of God in Berea, they went there and stirred up trouble. ¹⁴ The believers acted at once, sending Paul on to the coast, while Silas and Timothy remained behind. ¹⁵ Those escorting Paul went with him all the way to Athens; then they returned to Berea with instructions for Silas and Timothy to hurry and join him.

PAUL PREACHES IN ATHENS

¹⁶ While Paul was waiting for them in Athens, he was deeply troubled by all the idols he saw everywhere in the city. ¹⁷ He went to the synagogue to reason with the Jews and the God-fearing Gentiles, and he spoke daily in the public square to all who happened to be there.

¹⁸ He also had a debate with some of the Epicurean and Stoic philosophers. When he told them about Jesus and his resurrection, they said, "What's this babbler trying to say with these strange ideas he's picked up?" Others said, "He seems to be preaching about some foreign gods."

17:4 Some manuscripts read *quite a few of the wives of the leading men.* 17:5 Or *the city council.* 17:6 Greek *brothers;* also in 17:10, 14.

What Does the Bible Say About . . .

RACISM?

ROBERT MORRIS

Racism and prejudice have no place in the Kingdom of God. Every single person, no matter their skin color, is made in His image. You may ask, "Does the Bible really talk about racism?" It absolutely does.

1. Racism is pure evil (Romans 12:9).
The apostle Paul writes, "Don't just pretend to love others. Really love them. Hate what is wrong. Hold tightly to what is good." You can't love some people and not love others. This is hypocritical love, and it's evil.

2. Racism is pure self-righteousness (Luke 18:11).
Jesus tells a story about a Pharisee who prayed, "I thank you, God, that I am not like other people." In other words, *Thank You for making me better than them!* However, Jesus said, "Those who exalt themselves will be humbled" (Luke 18:14). It's pride and self-righteousness for one race to think of itself as superior to others.

3. Racism violates the Great Commission (Matthew 28:19).
Jesus says to "make disciples of all the nations." The word *nations* is a translation of the Greek word *ethnos*, from which we get the English word *ethnicity*. We are supposed to make disciples of *all* ethnicities, not just a few.

4. Racism violates the Great Commandment (John 13:34–35).
Jesus says, "Just as I have loved you, you should love each other. Your love for one another will prove to the world that you are my disciples." People should know we're believers because we love everyone.

5. Racism questions God's creation (Acts 17:26).
Luke writes, "From one man he created all the nations throughout the whole earth." God made every nation—every *ethnos* or ethnic group—from one blood. No matter what color you are on the outside, all of us are red on the inside because we all come from one blood.

6. Racism questions God's plan (Revelation 5:9).
Jesus' blood is not meant to save only a few. It is for those "from every tribe and language and people and nation." God's plan is to redeem people from every ethnic group.

7. Racism questions God (John 3:16).
Racism defies God's Word: "For this is how God loved the *world*: He gave His one and only Son, so that *everyone* who believes in him will not perish but have eternal life" (emphasis added). God doesn't love just one race. He loves the entire world!

GOD NEEDS YOU
Acts 17:25   ROBERT MORRIS

God is completely self-existent, self-sufficient, and self-sustaining. He doesn't need anything, but He has chosen to need us. God chose to partner with Adam to name the animals of His new creation (Genesis 2:19), and He chose to partner with David to kill the Philistine giant Goliath (1 Samuel 17:32–49). God wants to partner with us today, and our responsibility is to step out in faith.

Many times we ask God to do things that He has given us the responsibility and the ability to do. We need to understand that God will never do our part for us, nor will He ever ask us to do His. God's responsibility is the supernatural part, which He did when He sent Jesus to reconcile the world back to Himself. Our responsibility is the natural part: we must decide to need Jesus and partner with God in every area of our lives.

---

¹⁹ Then they took him to the high council of the city.* "Come and tell us about this new teaching," they said. ²⁰ "You are saying some rather strange things, and we want to know what it's all about." ²¹ (It should be explained that all the Athenians as well as the foreigners in Athens seemed to spend all their time discussing the latest ideas.)

²² So Paul, standing before the council,* addressed them as follows: "Men of Athens, I notice that you are very religious in every way, ²³ for as I was walking along I saw your many shrines. And one of your altars had this inscription on it: 'To an Unknown God.' This God, whom you worship without knowing, is the one I'm telling you about.

²⁴ "He is the God who made the world and everything in it. Since he is Lord of heaven and earth, he doesn't live in man-made temples, ²⁵ and human hands can't serve his needs—for he has no needs. He himself gives life and breath to everything, and he satisfies every need. ²⁶ From one man* he created all the nations throughout the whole earth. He decided beforehand when they should rise and fall, and he determined their boundaries.

²⁷ "His purpose was for the nations to seek after God and perhaps feel their way toward him and find him—though he is not far from any one of us. ²⁸ For in him we live and move and exist. As some of your* own poets have said, 'We are his offspring.' ²⁹ And since this is true, we shouldn't think of God as an idol designed by craftsmen from gold or silver or stone.

³⁰ "God overlooked people's ignorance about these things in earlier times, but now he commands everyone everywhere to repent of their sins and turn to him. ³¹ For he has set a day for judging the world with justice by the man he has appointed, and he proved to everyone who this is by raising him from the dead."

³² When they heard Paul speak about the resurrection of the dead, some laughed in contempt, but others said, "We want to hear more about this later." ³³ That ended Paul's discussion with them, ³⁴ but some joined him and became believers. Among them were Dionysius, a member of the council,* a woman named Damaris, and others with them.

PAUL MEETS PRISCILLA AND AQUILA IN CORINTH

18 Then Paul left Athens and went to Corinth.* ² There he became acquainted with a Jew named Aquila, born in Pontus, who had recently arrived from Italy with his wife, Priscilla. They had left Italy when Claudius Caesar deported all Jews from Rome. ³ Paul lived and worked with them, for they were tentmakers* just as he was.

⁴ Each Sabbath found Paul at the synagogue, trying to convince the Jews and Greeks alike. ⁵ And after Silas and Timothy came down from Macedonia, Paul spent all his time preaching the word. He testified to the Jews that Jesus was the Messiah. ⁶ But when they opposed and insulted him, Paul shook the dust from his clothes and said, "Your blood is upon your own heads—I am innocent. From now on I will go preach to the Gentiles."

⁷ Then he left and went to the home of Titius Justus, a Gentile who worshiped God and lived next door to the synagogue. ⁸ Crispus, the leader of the synagogue, and everyone in his household believed in the Lord. Many others in Corinth also heard Paul, became believers, and were baptized.

⁹ One night the Lord spoke to Paul in a vision and told him, "Don't be afraid! Speak out! Don't be silent! ¹⁰ For I am with you, and no one will attack and harm you, for many people in this city belong to me." ¹¹ So Paul stayed there for the next year and a half, teaching the word of God.

¹² But when Gallio became governor of Achaia, some Jews rose up together against Paul and brought him before the governor for judgment. ¹³ They accused Paul of "persuading people to worship God in ways that are contrary to our law."

¹⁴ But just as Paul started to make his defense, Gallio turned to Paul's accusers and said, "Listen, you Jews, if this were a case involving some wrongdoing or a serious crime, I would have a reason to accept your case. ¹⁵ But since it is merely a question of words and names and your Jewish law, take care of it yourselves. I refuse to judge such matters." ¹⁶ And he threw them out of the courtroom.

17:19 Or *the most learned society of philosophers in the city.* Greek reads *the Areopagus.* 17:22 Traditionally rendered *standing in the middle of Mars Hill;* Greek reads *standing in the middle of the Areopagus.* 17:26 Greek *From one;* other manuscripts read *From one blood.* 17:28 Some manuscripts read *our.* 17:34 Greek *an Areopagite.* 18:1 *Athens* and *Corinth* were major cities in Achaia, the region in the southern portion of the Greek peninsula. 18:3 Or *leatherworkers.*

[17] The crowd* then grabbed Sosthenes, the leader of the synagogue, and beat him right there in the courtroom. But Gallio paid no attention.

PAUL RETURNS TO ANTIOCH OF SYRIA

[18] Paul stayed in Corinth for some time after that, then said good-bye to the brothers and sisters* and went to nearby Cenchrea. There he shaved his head according to Jewish custom, marking the end of a vow. Then he set sail for Syria, taking Priscilla and Aquila with him.

[19] They stopped first at the port of Ephesus, where Paul left the others behind. While he was there, he went to the synagogue to reason with the Jews. [20] They asked him to stay longer, but he declined. [21] As he left, however, he said, "I will come back later,* God willing." Then he set sail from Ephesus. [22] The next stop was at the port of Caesarea. From there he went up and visited the church at Jerusalem* and then went back to Antioch.

[23] After spending some time in Antioch, Paul went back through Galatia and Phrygia, visiting and strengthening all the believers.*

APOLLOS INSTRUCTED AT EPHESUS

[24] Meanwhile, a Jew named Apollos, an eloquent speaker who knew the Scriptures well, had arrived in Ephesus from Alexandria in Egypt. [25] He had been taught the way of the Lord, and he taught others about Jesus with an enthusiastic spirit* and with accuracy. However, he knew only about John's baptism. [26] When Priscilla and Aquila heard him preaching boldly in the synagogue, they took him aside and explained the way of God even more accurately.

[27] Apollos had been thinking about going to Achaia, and the brothers and sisters in Ephesus encouraged him to go. They wrote to the believers in Achaia, asking them to welcome him. When he arrived there, he proved to be of great benefit to those who, by God's grace, had believed. [28] He refuted the Jews with powerful arguments in public debate. Using the Scriptures, he explained to them that Jesus was the Messiah.

PAUL'S THIRD MISSIONARY JOURNEY

19 While Apollos was in Corinth, Paul traveled through the interior regions until he reached Ephesus, on the coast, where he found several believers.* [2] "Did you receive the Holy Spirit when you believed?" he asked them.

"No," they replied, "we haven't even heard that there is a Holy Spirit."

[3] "Then what baptism did you experience?" he asked.

And they replied, "The baptism of John."

[4] Paul said, "John's baptism called for repentance from sin. But John himself told the people to believe in the one who would come later, meaning Jesus."

[5] As soon as they heard this, they were baptized in the name of the Lord Jesus. [6] Then when Paul laid his hands on them, the Holy Spirit came on them, and they spoke in other tongues* and prophesied. [7] There were about twelve men in all.

PAUL MINISTERS IN EPHESUS

[8] Then Paul went to the synagogue and preached boldly for the next three months, arguing persuasively about the Kingdom of God. [9] But some became stubborn, rejecting his message and publicly speaking against the Way. So Paul left the synagogue and took the believers with him. Then he held daily discussions at the lecture hall of Tyrannus. [10] This went on for the next two years, so that people throughout the province of Asia—both Jews and Greeks—heard the word of the Lord.

[11] God gave Paul the power to perform unusual miracles. [12] When handkerchiefs or aprons that had merely touched his skin were placed on sick people, they were healed of their diseases, and evil spirits were expelled.

[13] A group of Jews was traveling from town to town casting out evil spirits. They tried to use the name of the Lord Jesus in their incantation, saying, "I command you in the name of Jesus, whom Paul preaches, to come out!" [14] Seven sons of Sceva, a leading priest, were doing this. [15] But one time when they tried it, the evil spirit replied, "I know Jesus, and I know Paul, but who are you?" [16] Then the man with the evil spirit leaped on them, overpowered them, and attacked them with such violence that they fled from the house, naked and battered.

[17] The story of what happened spread quickly all through Ephesus, to Jews and Greeks alike. A solemn fear descended on the city, and the name of the Lord Jesus was greatly honored. [18] Many who became believers confessed their sinful practices. [19] A number of them who had been practicing sorcery brought their incantation books and burned them at a public bonfire. The value of the books was several million dollars.* [20] So the message about the Lord spread widely and had a powerful effect.

[21] Afterward Paul felt compelled by the Spirit* to go over to Macedonia and Achaia before going to Jerusalem. "And after that," he said, "I must go on to Rome!" [22] He sent his two assistants, Timothy and Erastus, ahead to Macedonia while he stayed awhile longer in the province of Asia.

THE RIOT IN EPHESUS

[23] About that time, serious trouble developed in Ephesus concerning the Way. [24] It began with

---

18:17 Greek *Everyone;* other manuscripts read *All the Greeks.*
18:18 Greek *brothers;* also in 18:27. 18:21 Some manuscripts read *"I must by all means be at Jerusalem for the upcoming festival, but I will come back later."* 18:22 Greek *the church.* 18:23 Greek *disciples;* also in 18:27. 18:25 Or *with enthusiasm in the Spirit.* 19:1 Greek *disciples;* also in 19:9, 30. 19:6 Or *in other languages.* 19:19 Greek *50,000 pieces of silver,* each of which was the equivalent of a day's wage. 19:21 Or *decided in his spirit.*

Demetrius, a silversmith who had a large business manufacturing silver shrines of the Greek goddess Artemis.* He kept many craftsmen busy. ²⁵ He called them together, along with others employed in similar trades, and addressed them as follows:

"Gentlemen, you know that our wealth comes from this business. ²⁶ But as you have seen and heard, this man Paul has persuaded many people that handmade gods aren't really gods at all. And he's done this not only here in Ephesus but throughout the entire province! ²⁷ Of course, I'm not just talking about the loss of public respect for our business. I'm also concerned that the temple of the great goddess Artemis will lose its influence and that Artemis—this magnificent goddess worshiped throughout the province of Asia and all around the world—will be robbed of her great prestige!"

²⁸ At this their anger boiled, and they began shouting, "Great is Artemis of the Ephesians!" ²⁹ Soon the whole city was filled with confusion. Everyone rushed to the amphitheater, dragging along Gaius and Aristarchus, who were Paul's traveling companions from Macedonia. ³⁰ Paul wanted to go in, too, but the believers wouldn't let him. ³¹ Some of the officials of the province, friends of Paul, also sent a message to him, begging him not to risk his life by entering the amphitheater.

³² Inside, the people were all shouting, some one thing and some another. Everything was in confusion. In fact, most of them didn't even know why they were there. ³³ The Jews in the crowd pushed Alexander forward and told him to explain the situation. He motioned for silence and tried to speak. ³⁴ But when the crowd realized he was a Jew, they started shouting again and kept it up for about two hours: "Great is Artemis of the Ephesians! Great is Artemis of the Ephesians!"

³⁵ At last the mayor was able to quiet them down enough to speak. "Citizens of Ephesus," he said. "Everyone knows that Ephesus is the official guardian of the temple of the great Artemis, whose image fell down to us from heaven. ³⁶ Since this is an undeniable fact, you should stay calm and not do anything rash. ³⁷ You have brought these men here, but they have stolen nothing from the temple and have not spoken against our goddess.

³⁸ "If Demetrius and the craftsmen have a case against them, the courts are in session and the officials can hear the case at once. Let them make formal charges. ³⁹ And if there are complaints about other matters, they can be settled in a legal assembly. ⁴⁰ I am afraid we are in danger of being charged with rioting by the Roman government, since there is no cause for all this commotion. And if Rome demands an explanation, we won't know what to say." ⁴¹* Then he dismissed them, and they dispersed.

PAUL GOES TO MACEDONIA AND GREECE

20 When the uproar was over, Paul sent for the believers* and encouraged them. Then he said good-bye and left for Macedonia. ² While there, he encouraged the believers in all the towns he passed through. Then he traveled down to Greece, ³ where he stayed for three months. He was preparing to sail back to Syria when he discovered a plot by some Jews against his life, so he decided to return through Macedonia.

⁴ Several men were traveling with him. They were Sopater son of Pyrrhus from Berea; Aristarchus and Secundus from Thessalonica; Gaius from Derbe; Timothy; and Tychicus and Trophimus from the province of Asia. ⁵ They went on ahead and waited for us at Troas. ⁶ After the Passover* ended, we boarded a ship at Philippi in Macedonia and five days later joined them in Troas, where we stayed a week.

PAUL'S FINAL VISIT TO TROAS

⁷ On the first day of the week, we gathered with the local believers to share in the Lord's Supper.* Paul was preaching to them, and since he was leaving the next day, he kept talking until midnight. ⁸ The upstairs room where we met was lighted with many flickering lamps. ⁹ As Paul spoke on and on, a young man named Eutychus, sitting on the windowsill, became very drowsy. Finally, he fell sound asleep and dropped three stories to his death below. ¹⁰ Paul went down, bent over him, and took him into his arms. "Don't worry," he said, "he's alive!" ¹¹ Then they all went back upstairs, shared in the Lord's Supper,* and ate together. Paul continued talking to them until dawn, and then he left. ¹² Meanwhile, the young man was taken home alive and well, and everyone was greatly relieved.

PAUL MEETS THE EPHESIAN ELDERS

¹³ Paul went by land to Assos, where he had arranged for us to join him, while we traveled by ship. ¹⁴ He joined us there, and we sailed together to Mitylene. ¹⁵ The next day we sailed past the island of Kios. The following day we crossed to the island of Samos, and* a day later we arrived at Miletus.

¹⁶ Paul had decided to sail on past Ephesus, for he didn't want to spend any more time in the province of Asia. He was hurrying to get to Jerusalem, if possible, in time for the Festival of Pentecost. ¹⁷ But when we landed at Miletus, he sent a message to the elders of the church at Ephesus, asking them to come and meet him. ¹⁸ When they arrived he declared, "You know that from the day I set foot in the province of Asia until now ¹⁹ I have done the Lord's work

19:24 Artemis is otherwise known as Diana. 19:41 Some translations include verse 41 as part of verse 40. 20:1 Greek disciples. 20:6 Greek the days of unleavened bread. 20:7 Greek to break bread. 20:11 Greek broke the bread. 20:15 Some manuscripts read and having stayed at Trogyllium.

humbly and with many tears. I have endured the trials that came to me from the plots of the Jews. 20 I never shrank back from telling you what you needed to hear, either publicly or in your homes. 21 I have had one message for Jews and Greeks alike—the necessity of repenting from sin and turning to God, and of having faith in our Lord Jesus.

22 "And now I am bound by the Spirit* to go to Jerusalem. I don't know what awaits me, 23 except that the Holy Spirit tells me in city after city that jail and suffering lie ahead. 24 But my life is worth nothing to me unless I use it for finishing the work assigned me by the Lord Jesus—the work of telling others the Good News about the wonderful grace of God.

25 "And now I know that none of you to whom I have preached the Kingdom will ever see me again. 26 I declare today that I have been faithful. If anyone suffers eternal death, it's not my fault,* 27 for I didn't shrink from declaring all that God wants you to know.

28 "So guard yourselves and God's people. Feed and shepherd God's flock—his church, purchased with his own blood*—over which the Holy Spirit has appointed you as leaders.* 29 I know that false teachers, like vicious wolves, will come in among you after I leave, not sparing the flock. 30 Even some men from your own group will rise up and distort the truth in order to draw a following. 31 Watch out! Remember the three years I was with you—my constant watch and care over you night and day, and my many tears for you.

32 "And now I entrust you to God and the message of his grace that is able to build you up and give you an inheritance with all those he has set apart for himself.

33 "I have never coveted anyone's silver or gold or fine clothes. 34 You know that these hands of mine have worked to supply my own needs and even the needs of those who were with me. 35 And I have been a constant example of how you can help those in need by working hard. You should remember the words of the Lord Jesus: 'It is more blessed to give than to receive.'"

36 When he had finished speaking, he knelt and prayed with them. 37 They all cried as they embraced and kissed him good-bye. 38 They were sad most of all because he had said that they would never see him again. Then they escorted him down to the ship.

PAUL'S JOURNEY TO JERUSALEM

21 After saying farewell to the Ephesian elders, we sailed straight to the island of Cos. The next day we reached Rhodes and then went to Patara. 2 There we boarded a ship sailing for Phoenicia. 3 We sighted the island of Cyprus, passed it on our left, and landed at the harbor of Tyre, in Syria, where the ship was to unload its cargo.

4 We went ashore, found the local believers,* and stayed with them a week. These believers prophesied through the Holy Spirit that Paul should not go on to Jerusalem. 5 When we returned to the ship at the end of the week, the entire congregation, including women* and children, left the city and came down to the shore with us. There we knelt, prayed, 6 and said our farewells. Then we went aboard, and they returned home.

7 The next stop after leaving Tyre was Ptolemais, where we greeted the brothers and sisters* and stayed for one day. 8 The next day we went on to Caesarea and stayed at the home of Philip the Evangelist, one of the seven men who had been chosen to distribute food. 9 He had four unmarried daughters who had the gift of prophecy.

10 Several days later a man named Agabus, who also had the gift of prophecy, arrived from Judea. 11 He came over, took Paul's belt, and bound his own feet and hands with it. Then he said, "The Holy Spirit declares, 'So shall the owner of this belt be bound by the Jewish leaders in Jerusalem and turned over to the Gentiles.'" 12 When we heard this, we and the local believers all begged Paul not to go on to Jerusalem.

13 But he said, "Why all this weeping? You are breaking my heart! I am ready not only to be jailed at Jerusalem but even to die for the sake of the Lord Jesus." 14 When it was clear that we couldn't persuade him, we gave up and said, "The Lord's will be done."

PAUL ARRIVES AT JERUSALEM

15 After this we packed our things and left for Jerusalem. 16 Some believers from Caesarea accompanied us, and they took us to the home of Mnason, a man originally from Cyprus and one of the early believers. 17 When we arrived, the brothers and sisters in Jerusalem welcomed us warmly.

18 The next day Paul went with us to meet with James, and all the elders of the Jerusalem church were present. 19 After greeting them, Paul gave a detailed account of the things God had accomplished among the Gentiles through his ministry.

20 After hearing this, they praised God. And then they said, "You know, dear brother, how many thousands of Jews have also believed, and they all follow the law of Moses very seriously. 21 But the Jewish believers here in Jerusalem have been told that you are teaching all the Jews who live among the Gentiles to turn their backs on the laws of Moses. They've heard that you teach them not to circumcise their children or follow other Jewish customs. 22 What should we do? They will certainly hear that you have come.

²³ "Here's what we want you to do. We have four men here who have completed their vow. ²⁴ Go with them to the Temple and join them in the purification ceremony, paying for them to have their heads ritually shaved. Then everyone will know that the rumors are all false and that you yourself observe the Jewish laws.

²⁵ "As for the Gentile believers, they should do what we already told them in a letter: They should abstain from eating food offered to idols, from consuming blood or the meat of strangled animals, and from sexual immorality."

PAUL IS ARRESTED

²⁶ So Paul went to the Temple the next day with the other men. They had already started the purification ritual, so he publicly announced the date when their vows would end and sacrifices would be offered for each of them.

²⁷ The seven days were almost ended when some Jews from the province of Asia saw Paul in the Temple and roused a mob against him. They grabbed him, ²⁸ yelling, "Men of Israel, help us! This is the man who preaches against our people everywhere and tells everybody to disobey the Jewish laws. He speaks against the Temple—and even defiles this holy place by bringing in Gentiles.*" ²⁹ (For earlier that day they had seen him in the city with Trophimus, a Gentile from Ephesus,* and they assumed Paul had taken him into the Temple.)

³⁰ The whole city was rocked by these accusations, and a great riot followed. Paul was grabbed and dragged out of the Temple, and immediately the gates were closed behind him. ³¹ As they were trying to kill him, word reached the commander of the Roman regiment that all Jerusalem was in an uproar. ³² He immediately called out his soldiers and officers* and ran down among the crowd. When the mob saw the commander and the troops coming, they stopped beating Paul. ³³ Then the commander arrested him and ordered him bound with two chains. He asked the crowd who he was and what he had done. ³⁴ Some shouted one thing and some another. Since he couldn't find out the truth in all the uproar and confusion, he ordered that Paul be taken to the fortress. ³⁵ As Paul reached the stairs, the mob grew so violent the soldiers had to lift him to their shoulders to protect him. ³⁶ And the crowd followed behind, shouting, "Kill him, kill him!"

PAUL SPEAKS TO THE CROWD

³⁷ As Paul was about to be taken inside, he said to the commander, "May I have a word with you?"

"Do you know Greek?" the commander asked, surprised. ³⁸ "Aren't you the Egyptian who led a rebellion some time ago and took 4,000 members of the Assassins out into the desert?"

³⁹ "No," Paul replied, "I am a Jew and a citizen of Tarsus in Cilicia, which is an important city.

Please, let me talk to these people." ⁴⁰ The commander agreed, so Paul stood on the stairs and motioned to the people to be quiet. Soon a deep silence enveloped the crowd, and he addressed them in their own language, Aramaic.*

22 "Brothers and esteemed fathers," Paul said, "listen to me as I offer my defense." ² When they heard him speaking in their own language,* the silence was even greater.

³ Then Paul said, "I am a Jew, born in Tarsus, a city in Cilicia, and I was brought up and educated here in Jerusalem under Gamaliel. As his student, I was carefully trained in our Jewish laws and customs. I became very zealous to honor God in everything I did, just like all of you today. ⁴ And I persecuted the followers of the Way, hounding some to death, arresting both men and women and throwing them in prison. ⁵ The high priest and the whole council of elders can testify that this is so. For I received letters from them to our Jewish brothers in Damascus, authorizing me to bring the followers of the Way from there to Jerusalem, in chains, to be punished.

⁶ "As I was on the road, approaching Damascus about noon, a very bright light from heaven suddenly shone down around me. ⁷ I fell to the ground and heard a voice saying to me, 'Saul, Saul, why are you persecuting me?'

⁸ "'Who are you, lord?' I asked.

"And the voice replied, 'I am Jesus the Nazarene,* the one you are persecuting.' ⁹ The people with me saw the light but didn't understand the voice speaking to me.

¹⁰ "I asked, 'What should I do, Lord?'

"And the Lord told me, 'Get up and go into Damascus, and there you will be told everything you are to do.'

¹¹ "I was blinded by the intense light and had to be led by the hand to Damascus by my companions. ¹² A man named Ananias lived there. He was a godly man, deeply devoted to the law, and well regarded by all the Jews of Damascus. ¹³ He came and stood beside me and said, 'Brother Saul, regain your sight.' And that very moment I could see him!

¹⁴ "Then he told me, 'The God of our ancestors has chosen you to know his will and to see the Righteous One and hear him speak. ¹⁵ For you are to be his witness, telling everyone what you have seen and heard. ¹⁶ What are you waiting for? Get up and be baptized. Have your sins washed away by calling on the name of the Lord.'

¹⁷ "After I returned to Jerusalem, I was praying in the Temple and fell into a trance. ¹⁸ I saw a vision of Jesus* saying to me, 'Hurry! Leave Jerusalem, for the people here won't accept your testimony about me.'

21:28 Greek *Greeks.* 21:29 Greek *Trophimus, the Ephesian.* 21:32 Greek *centurions.* 21:40 Or *Hebrew.* 22:2 Greek *in Aramaic,* or *in Hebrew.* 22:8 Or *Jesus of Nazareth.* 22:18 Greek *him.*

[19] "'But Lord,' I argued, 'they certainly know that in every synagogue I imprisoned and beat those who believed in you. [20] And I was in complete agreement when your witness Stephen was killed. I stood by and kept the coats they took off when they stoned him.'

[21] "But the Lord said to me, 'Go, for I will send you far away to the Gentiles!'"

[22] The crowd listened until Paul said that word. Then they all began to shout, "Away with such a fellow! He isn't fit to live!" [23] They yelled, threw off their coats, and tossed handfuls of dust into the air.

PAUL REVEALS HIS ROMAN CITIZENSHIP

[24] The commander brought Paul inside and ordered him lashed with whips to make him confess his crime. He wanted to find out why the crowd had become so furious. [25] When they tied Paul down to lash him, Paul said to the officer* standing there, "Is it legal for you to whip a Roman citizen who hasn't even been tried?"

[26] When the officer heard this, he went to the commander and asked, "What are you doing? This man is a Roman citizen!"

[27] So the commander went over and asked Paul, "Tell me, are you a Roman citizen?"

"Yes, I certainly am," Paul replied.

[28] "I am, too," the commander muttered, "and it cost me plenty!"

Paul answered, "But I am a citizen by birth!"

[29] The soldiers who were about to interrogate Paul quickly withdrew when they heard he was a Roman citizen, and the commander was frightened because he had ordered him bound and whipped.

PAUL BEFORE THE HIGH COUNCIL

[30] The next day the commander ordered the leading priests into session with the Jewish high council.* He wanted to find out what the trouble was all about, so he released Paul to have him stand before them.

23 Gazing intently at the high council,* Paul began: "Brothers, I have always lived before God with a clear conscience!"

[2] Instantly Ananias the high priest commanded those close to Paul to slap him on the mouth. [3] But Paul said to him, "God will slap you, you corrupt hypocrite!* What kind of judge are you to break the law yourself by ordering me struck like that?"

[4] Those standing near Paul said to him, "Do you dare to insult God's high priest?"

[5] "I'm sorry, brothers, I didn't realize he was the high priest," Paul replied, "for the Scriptures say, 'You must not speak evil of any of your rulers.'*"

[6] Paul realized that some members of the high council were Sadducees and some were Pharisees, so he shouted, "Brothers, I am a Pharisee, as were my ancestors! And I am on trial because my hope is in the resurrection of the dead!"

[7] This divided the council—the Pharisees against the Sadducees—[8] for the Sadducees say there is no resurrection or angels or spirits, but the Pharisees believe in all of these. [9] So there was a great uproar. Some of the teachers of religious law who were Pharisees jumped up and began to argue forcefully. "We see nothing wrong with him," they shouted. "Perhaps a spirit or an angel spoke to him." [10] As the conflict grew more violent, the commander was afraid they would tear Paul apart. So he ordered his soldiers to go and rescue him by force and take him back to the fortress.

[11] That night the Lord appeared to Paul and said, "Be encouraged, Paul. Just as you have been a witness to me here in Jerusalem, you must preach the Good News in Rome as well."

THE PLAN TO KILL PAUL

[12] The next morning a group of Jews* got together and bound themselves with an oath not to eat or drink until they had killed Paul. [13] There were more than forty of them in the conspiracy. [14] They went to the leading priests and elders and told them, "We have bound ourselves with an oath to eat nothing until we have killed Paul. [15] So you and the high council should ask the commander to bring Paul back to the council again. Pretend you want to examine his case more fully. We will kill him on the way."

[16] But Paul's nephew—his sister's son—heard of their plan and went to the fortress and told Paul. [17] Paul called for one of the Roman officers* and said, "Take this young man to the commander. He has something important to tell him."

[18] So the officer did, explaining, "Paul, the prisoner, called me over and asked me to bring this young man to you because he has something to tell you."

[19] The commander took his hand, led him aside, and asked, "What is it you want to tell me?"

[20] Paul's nephew told him, "Some Jews are going to ask you to bring Paul before the high council tomorrow, pretending they want to get some more information. [21] But don't do it! There are more than forty men hiding along the way ready to ambush him. They have vowed not to eat or drink anything until they have killed him. They are ready now, just waiting for your consent."

[22] "Don't let anyone know you told me this," the commander warned the young man.

PAUL IS SENT TO CAESAREA

[23] Then the commander called two of his officers and ordered, "Get 200 soldiers ready to leave for Caesarea at nine o'clock tonight. Also take 200 spearmen and 70 mounted troops. [24] Provide

22:25 Greek *the centurion;* also in 22:26.   22:30 Greek *Sanhedrin.*
23:1 Greek *Sanhedrin;* also in 23:6, 15, 20, 28.   23:3 Greek *you whitewashed wall.*   23:5 Exod 22:28.   23:12 Greek *the Jews.*
23:17 Greek *centurions;* also in 23:23.

horses for Paul to ride, and get him safely to Governor Felix." [25] Then he wrote this letter to the governor:

[26] "From Claudius Lysias, to his Excellency, Governor Felix: Greetings!

[27] "This man was seized by some Jews, and they were about to kill him when I arrived with the troops. When I learned that he was a Roman citizen, I removed him to safety. [28] Then I took him to their high council to try to learn the basis of the accusations against him. [29] I soon discovered the charge was something regarding their religious law—certainly nothing worthy of imprisonment or death. [30] But when I was informed of a plot to kill him, I immediately sent him on to you. I have told his accusers to bring their charges before you."

[31] So that night, as ordered, the soldiers took Paul as far as Antipatris. [32] They returned to the fortress the next morning, while the mounted troops took him on to Caesarea. [33] When they arrived in Caesarea, they presented Paul and the letter to Governor Felix. [34] He read it and then asked Paul what province he was from. "Cilicia," Paul answered.

[35] "I will hear your case myself when your accusers arrive," the governor told him. Then the governor ordered him kept in the prison at Herod's headquarters.*

PAUL APPEARS BEFORE FELIX

24 Five days later Ananias, the high priest, arrived with some of the Jewish elders and the lawyer* Tertullus, to present their case against Paul to the governor. [2] When Paul was called in, Tertullus presented the charges against Paul in the following address to the governor:

"You have provided a long period of peace for us Jews and with foresight have enacted reforms for us. [3] For all of this, Your Excellency, we are very grateful to you. [4] But I don't want to bore you, so please give me your attention for only a moment. [5] We have found this man to be a troublemaker who is constantly stirring up riots among the Jews all over the world. He is a ringleader of the cult known as the Nazarenes. [6] Furthermore, he was trying to desecrate the Temple when we arrested him.* [8] You can find out the truth of our accusations by examining him yourself." [9] Then the other Jews chimed in, declaring that everything Tertullus said was true.

[10] The governor then motioned for Paul to speak. Paul said, "I know, sir, that you have been a judge of Jewish affairs for many years, so I gladly present my defense before you. [11] You can quickly discover that I arrived in Jerusalem no more than twelve days ago to worship at the Temple. [12] My accusers never found me arguing with anyone in the Temple, nor stirring up a riot in any synagogue or on the streets of the city. [13] These men cannot prove the things they accuse me of doing.

[14] "But I admit that I follow the Way, which they call a cult. I worship the God of our ancestors, and I firmly believe the Jewish law and everything written in the prophets. [15] I have the same hope in God that these men have, that he will raise both the righteous and the unrighteous. [16] Because of this, I always try to maintain a clear conscience before God and all people.

[17] "After several years away, I returned to Jerusalem with money to aid my people and to offer sacrifices to God. [18] My accusers saw me in the Temple as I was completing a purification ceremony. There was no crowd around me and no rioting. [19] But some Jews from the province of Asia were there—and they ought to be here to bring charges if they have anything against me! [20] Ask these men here what crime the Jewish high council* found me guilty of, [21] except for the one time I shouted out, 'I am on trial before you today because I believe in the resurrection of the dead!'"

[22] At that point Felix, who was quite familiar with the Way, adjourned the hearing and said, "Wait until Lysias, the garrison commander, arrives. Then I will decide the case." [23] He ordered an officer* to keep Paul in custody but to give him some freedom and allow his friends to visit him and take care of his needs.

[24] A few days later Felix came back with his wife, Drusilla, who was Jewish. Sending for Paul, they listened as he told them about faith in Christ Jesus. [25] As he reasoned with them about righteousness and self-control and the coming day of judgment, Felix became frightened. "Go away for now," he replied. "When it is more convenient, I'll call for you again." [26] He also hoped that Paul would bribe him, so he sent for him quite often and talked with him.

[27] After two years went by in this way, Felix was succeeded by Porcius Festus. And because Felix wanted to gain favor with the Jewish people, he left Paul in prison.

PAUL APPEARS BEFORE FESTUS

25 Three days after Festus arrived in Caesarea to take over his new responsibilities, he left for Jerusalem, [2] where the leading priests and other Jewish leaders met with him and made their accusations against Paul. [3] They asked Festus as a favor to transfer Paul to Jerusalem (planning to ambush and kill him on the way). [4] But Festus replied that Paul was at Caesarea and he himself would be returning there soon.

23:35 Greek *Herod's Praetorium.* 24:1 Greek *some elders and an orator.* 24:6 Some manuscripts add an expanded conclusion to verse 6, all of verse 7, and an additional phrase in verse 8: *We would have judged him by our law,* [7]*but Lysias, the commander of the garrison, came and violently took him away from us,* [8]*commanding his accusers to come before you.* 24:20 Greek *Sanhedrin.* 24:23 Greek *a centurion.*

5 So he said, "Those of you in authority can return with me. If Paul has done anything wrong, you can make your accusations."

6 About eight or ten days later Festus returned to Caesarea, and on the following day he took his seat in court and ordered that Paul be brought in. 7 When Paul arrived, the Jewish leaders from Jerusalem gathered around and made many serious accusations they couldn't prove.

8 Paul denied the charges. "I am not guilty of any crime against the Jewish laws or the Temple or the Roman government," he said.

9 Then Festus, wanting to please the Jews, asked him, "Are you willing to go to Jerusalem and stand trial before me there?"

10 But Paul replied, "No! This is the official Roman court, so I ought to be tried right here. You know very well I am not guilty of harming the Jews. 11 If I have done something worthy of death, I don't refuse to die. But if I am innocent, no one has a right to turn me over to these men to kill me. I appeal to Caesar!"

12 Festus conferred with his advisers and then replied, "Very well! You have appealed to Caesar, and to Caesar you will go!"

13 A few days later King Agrippa arrived with his sister, Bernice,* to pay their respects to Festus. 14 During their stay of several days, Festus discussed Paul's case with the king. "There is a prisoner here," he told him, "whose case was left for me by Felix. 15 When I was in Jerusalem, the leading priests and Jewish elders pressed charges against him and asked me to condemn him. 16 I pointed out to them that Roman law does not convict people without a trial. They must be given an opportunity to confront their accusers and defend themselves.

17 "When his accusers came here for the trial, I didn't delay. I called the case the very next day and ordered Paul brought in. 18 But the accusations made against him weren't any of the crimes I expected. 19 Instead, it was something about their religion and a dead man named Jesus, who Paul insists is alive. 20 I was at a loss to know how to investigate these things, so I asked him whether he would be willing to stand trial on these charges in Jerusalem. 21 But Paul appealed to have his case decided by the emperor. So I ordered that he be held in custody until I could arrange to send him to Caesar."

22 "I'd like to hear the man myself," Agrippa said.

And Festus replied, "You will—tomorrow!"

PAUL SPEAKS TO AGRIPPA

23 So the next day Agrippa and Bernice arrived at the auditorium with great pomp, accompanied by military officers and prominent men of the city. Festus ordered that Paul be brought in. 24 Then Festus said, "King Agrippa and all who are here, this is the man whose death is demanded by all the Jews, both here and in Jerusalem. 25 But in my opinion he has done nothing deserving death. However, since he appealed his case to the emperor, I have decided to send him to Rome. 26 But what shall I write the emperor? For there is no clear charge against him. So I have brought him before all of you, and especially you, King Agrippa, so that after we examine him, I might have something to write. 27 For it makes no sense to send a prisoner to the emperor without specifying the charges against him!"

26 Then Agrippa said to Paul, "You may speak in your defense."

So Paul, gesturing with his hand, started his defense: 2 "I am fortunate, King Agrippa, that you are the one hearing my defense today against all these accusations made by the Jewish leaders, 3 for I know you are an expert on all Jewish customs and controversies. Now please listen to me patiently!

4 "As the Jewish leaders are well aware, I was given a thorough Jewish training from my earliest childhood among my own people and in Jerusalem. 5 If they would admit it, they know that I have been a member of the Pharisees, the strictest sect of our religion. 6 Now I am on trial because of my hope in the fulfillment of God's promise made to our ancestors. 7 In fact, that is why the twelve tribes of Israel zealously worship God night and day, and they share the same hope I have. Yet, Your Majesty, they accuse me for having this hope! 8 Why does it seem incredible to any of you that God can raise the dead?

9 "I used to believe that I ought to do everything I could to oppose the very name of Jesus the Nazarene.* 10 Indeed, I did just that in Jerusalem. Authorized by the leading priests, I caused many believers* there to be sent to prison. And I cast my vote against them when they were condemned to death. 11 Many times I had them punished in the synagogues to get them to curse Jesus.* I was so violently opposed to them that I even chased them down in foreign cities.

12 "One day I was on such a mission to Damascus, armed with the authority and commission of the leading priests. 13 About noon, Your Majesty, as I was on the road, a light from heaven brighter than the sun shone down on me and my companions. 14 We all fell down, and I heard a voice saying to me in Aramaic,* 'Saul, Saul, why are you persecuting me? It is useless for you to fight against my will.*'

15 "'Who are you, lord?' I asked.

"And the Lord replied, 'I am Jesus, the one you are persecuting. 16 Now get to your feet! For I have appeared to you to appoint you as my servant and witness. Tell people that you have seen me, and tell them what I will show you in the future.

25:13 Greek Agrippa the king and Bernice arrived. 26:9 Or Jesus of Nazareth. 26:10 Greek many of God's holy people. 26:11 Greek to blaspheme. 26:14a Or Hebrew. 26:14b Greek It is hard for you to kick against the oxgoads.

¹⁷ And I will rescue you from both your own people and the Gentiles. Yes, I am sending you to the Gentiles ¹⁸ to open their eyes, so they may turn from darkness to light and from the power of Satan to God. Then they will receive forgiveness for their sins and be given a place among God's people, who are set apart by faith in me.'

¹⁹ "And so, King Agrippa, I obeyed that vision from heaven. ²⁰ I preached first to those in Damascus, then in Jerusalem and throughout all Judea, and also to the Gentiles, that all must repent of their sins and turn to God—and prove they have changed by the good things they do. ²¹ Some Jews arrested me in the Temple for preaching this, and they tried to kill me. ²² But God has protected me right up to this present time so I can testify to everyone, from the least to the greatest. I teach nothing except what the prophets and Moses said would happen—²³ that the Messiah would suffer and be the first to rise from the dead, and in this way announce God's light to Jews and Gentiles alike."

²⁴ Suddenly, Festus shouted, "Paul, you are insane. Too much study has made you crazy!"

²⁵ But Paul replied, "I am not insane, Most Excellent Festus. What I am saying is the sober truth. ²⁶ And King Agrippa knows about these things. I speak boldly, for I am sure these events are all familiar to him, for they were not done in a corner! ²⁷ King Agrippa, do you believe the prophets? I know you do—"

²⁸ Agrippa interrupted him. "Do you think you can persuade me to become a Christian so quickly?"*

²⁹ Paul replied, "Whether quickly or not, I pray to God that both you and everyone here in this audience might become the same as I am, except for these chains."

³⁰ Then the king, the governor, Bernice, and all the others stood and left. ³¹ As they went out, they talked it over and agreed, "This man hasn't done anything to deserve death or imprisonment."

³² And Agrippa said to Festus, "He could have been set free if he hadn't appealed to Caesar."

PAUL SAILS FOR ROME

27 When the time came, we set sail for Italy. Paul and several other prisoners were placed in the custody of a Roman officer* named Julius, a captain of the Imperial Regiment. ² Aristarchus, a Macedonian from Thessalonica, was also with us. We left on a ship whose home port was Adramyttium on the northwest coast of the province of Asia;* it was scheduled to make several stops at ports along the coast of the province.

³ The next day when we docked at Sidon, Julius was very kind to Paul and let him go ashore to visit with friends so they could provide for his needs. ⁴ Putting out to sea from there, we encountered strong headwinds that made it difficult to keep the ship on course, so we sailed

north of Cyprus between the island and the mainland. ⁵ Keeping to the open sea, we passed along the coast of Cilicia and Pamphylia, landing at Myra, in the province of Lycia. ⁶ There the commanding officer found an Egyptian ship from Alexandria that was bound for Italy, and he put us on board.

⁷ We had several days of slow sailing, and after great difficulty we finally neared Cnidus. But the wind was against us, so we sailed across to Crete and along the sheltered coast of the island, past the cape of Salmone. ⁸ We struggled along the coast with great difficulty and finally arrived at Fair Havens, near the town of Lasea. ⁹ We had lost a lot of time. The weather was becoming dangerous for sea travel because it was so late in the fall,* and Paul spoke to the ship's officers about it.

¹⁰ "Men," he said, "I believe there is trouble ahead if we go on—shipwreck, loss of cargo, and danger to our lives as well." ¹¹ But the officer in charge of the prisoners listened more to the ship's captain and the owner than to Paul. ¹² And since Fair Havens was an exposed harbor—a poor place to spend the winter—most of the crew wanted to go on to Phoenix, farther up the coast of Crete, and spend the winter there. Phoenix was a good harbor with only a southwest and northwest exposure.

THE STORM AT SEA

¹³ When a light wind began blowing from the south, the sailors thought they could make it. So they pulled up anchor and sailed close to the shore of Crete. ¹⁴ But the weather changed abruptly, and a wind of typhoon strength (called a "northeaster") burst across the island and blew us out to sea. ¹⁵ The sailors couldn't turn the ship into the wind, so they gave up and let it run before the gale.

¹⁶ We sailed along the sheltered side of a small island named Cauda,* where with great difficulty we hoisted aboard the lifeboat being towed behind us. ¹⁷ Then the sailors bound ropes around the hull of the ship to strengthen it. They were afraid of being driven across to the sandbars of Syrtis off the African coast, so they lowered the sea anchor to slow the ship and were driven before the wind.

¹⁸ The next day, as gale-force winds continued to batter the ship, the crew began throwing the cargo overboard. ¹⁹ The following day they even took some of the ship's gear and threw it overboard. ²⁰ The terrible storm raged for many days, blotting out the sun and the stars, until at last all hope was gone.

26:28 Or "A little more, and your arguments would make me a Christian." 27:1 Greek *centurion;* similarly in 27:6, 11, 31, 43. 27:2 *Asia* was a Roman province in what is now western Turkey. 27:9 Greek *because the fast was now already gone by.* This fast was associated with the Day of Atonement (*Yom Kippur*), which occurred in late September or early October. 27:16 Some manuscripts read *Clauda.*

[21] No one had eaten for a long time. Finally, Paul called the crew together and said, "Men, you should have listened to me in the first place and not left Crete. You would have avoided all this damage and loss. [22] But take courage! None of you will lose your lives, even though the ship will go down. [23] For last night an angel of the God to whom I belong and whom I serve stood beside me, [24] and he said, 'Don't be afraid, Paul, for you will surely stand trial before Caesar! What's more, God in his goodness has granted safety to everyone sailing with you.' [25] So take courage! For I believe God. It will be just as he said. [26] But we will be shipwrecked on an island."

THE SHIPWRECK

[27] About midnight on the fourteenth night of the storm, as we were being driven across the Sea of Adria,* the sailors sensed land was near. [28] They dropped a weighted line and found that the water was 120 feet deep. But a little later they measured again and found it was only 90 feet deep.* [29] At this rate they were afraid we would soon be driven against the rocks along the shore, so they threw out four anchors from the back of the ship and prayed for daylight.

[30] Then the sailors tried to abandon the ship; they lowered the lifeboat as though they were going to put out anchors from the front of the ship. [31] But Paul said to the commanding officer and the soldiers, "You will all die unless the sailors stay aboard." [32] So the soldiers cut the ropes to the lifeboat and let it drift away.

[33] Just as day was dawning, Paul urged everyone to eat. "You have been so worried that you haven't touched food for two weeks," he said. [34] "Please eat something now for your own good. For not a hair of your heads will perish." [35] Then he took some bread, gave thanks to God before them all, and broke off a piece and ate it. [36] Then everyone was encouraged and began to eat—[37] all 276 of us who were on board. [38] After eating, the crew lightened the ship further by throwing the cargo of wheat overboard.

[39] When morning dawned, they didn't recognize the coastline, but they saw a bay with a beach and wondered if they could get to shore by running the ship aground. [40] So they cut off the anchors and left them in the sea. Then they lowered the rudders, raised the foresail, and headed toward shore. [41] But they hit a shoal and ran the ship aground too soon. The bow of the ship stuck fast, while the stern was repeatedly smashed by the force of the waves and began to break apart.

[42] The soldiers wanted to kill the prisoners to make sure they didn't swim ashore and escape. [43] But the commanding officer wanted to spare Paul, so he didn't let them carry out their plan. Then he ordered all who could swim to jump overboard first and make for land. [44] The others held on to planks or debris from the broken ship.* So everyone escaped safely to shore.

PAUL ON THE ISLAND OF MALTA

28 Once we were safe on shore, we learned that we were on the island of Malta. [2] The people of the island were very kind to us. It was cold and rainy, so they built a fire on the shore to welcome us.

[3] As Paul gathered an armful of sticks and was laying them on the fire, a poisonous snake, driven out by the heat, bit him on the hand. [4] The people of the island saw it hanging from his hand and said to each other, "A murderer, no doubt! Though he escaped the sea, justice will not permit him to live." [5] But Paul shook off the snake into the fire and was unharmed. [6] The people waited for him to swell up or suddenly drop dead. But when they had waited a long time and saw that he wasn't harmed, they changed their minds and decided he was a god.

[7] Near the shore where we landed was an estate belonging to Publius, the chief official of the island. He welcomed us and treated us kindly for three days. [8] As it happened, Publius's father was ill with fever and dysentery. Paul went in and prayed for him, and laying his hands on him, he healed him. [9] Then all the other sick people on the island came and were healed. [10] As a result we were showered with honors, and when the time came to sail, people supplied us with everything we would need for the trip.

PAUL ARRIVES AT ROME

[11] It was three months after the shipwreck that we set sail on another ship that had wintered at the island—an Alexandrian ship with the twin gods* as its figurehead. [12] Our first stop was Syracuse,* where we stayed three days. [13] From there we sailed across to Rhegium.* A day later a south wind began blowing, so the following day we sailed up the coast to Puteoli. [14] There we found some believers,* who invited us to spend a week with them. And so we came to Rome.

[15] The brothers and sisters* in Rome had heard we were coming, and they came to meet us at the Forum* on the Appian Way. Others joined us at The Three Taverns.* When Paul saw them, he was encouraged and thanked God.

[16] When we arrived in Rome, Paul was permitted to have his own private lodging, though he was guarded by a soldier.

PAUL PREACHES AT ROME UNDER GUARD

[17] Three days after Paul's arrival, he called together the local Jewish leaders. He said to them, "Brothers, I was arrested in Jerusalem

---

27:27 The *Sea of Adria* includes the central portion of the Mediterranean.　27:28 Greek *20 fathoms . . . 15 fathoms* [37 meters . . . 27 meters].　27:44 Or *were helped by members of the ship's crew.*　28:11 The *twin gods* were the Roman gods Castor and Pollux.　28:12 *Syracuse* was on the island of Sicily.　28:13 *Rhegium* was on the southern tip of Italy.　28:14 Greek *brothers.*　28:15a Greek *brothers.*　28:15b *The Forum* was about 43 miles (70 kilometers) from Rome.　28:15c *The Three Taverns* was about 35 miles (57 kilometers) from Rome.

and handed over to the Roman government, even though I had done nothing against our people or the customs of our ancestors. ¹⁸ The Romans tried me and wanted to release me, because they found no cause for the death sentence. ¹⁹ But when the Jewish leaders protested the decision, I felt it necessary to appeal to Caesar, even though I had no desire to press charges against my own people. ²⁰ I asked you to come here today so we could get acquainted and so I could explain to you that I am bound with this chain because I believe that the hope of Israel—the Messiah—has already come."

²¹ They replied, "We have had no letters from Judea or reports against you from anyone who has come here. ²² But we want to hear what you believe, for the only thing we know about this movement is that it is denounced everywhere."

²³ So a time was set, and on that day a large number of people came to Paul's lodging. He explained and testified about the Kingdom of God and tried to persuade them about Jesus from the Scriptures. Using the law of Moses and the books of the prophets, he spoke to them from morning until evening. ²⁴ Some were persuaded by the things he said, but others did not believe. ²⁵ And after they had argued back and forth among themselves, they left with this final word from Paul: "The Holy Spirit was right

when he said to your ancestors through Isaiah the prophet,

²⁶ 'Go and say to this people:
When you hear what I say,
  you will not understand.
When you see what I do,
  you will not comprehend.
²⁷ For the hearts of these people are hardened,
  and their ears cannot hear,
  and they have closed their eyes—
so their eyes cannot see,
  and their ears cannot hear,
  and their hearts cannot understand,
and they cannot turn to me
  and let me heal them.'*

²⁸ So I want you to know that this salvation from God has also been offered to the Gentiles, and they will accept it."*

³⁰ For the next two years, Paul lived in Rome at his own expense.* He welcomed all who visited him, ³¹ boldly proclaiming the Kingdom of God and teaching about the Lord Jesus Christ. And no one tried to stop him.

_____

28:26-27 Isa 6:9-10 (Greek version).   28:28 Some manuscripts add verse 29, *And when he had said these words, the Jews departed, greatly disagreeing with each other.*   28:30 Or *in his own rented quarters.*

AN INTRODUCTION TO PAUL

JON HUNTZINGER, PHD

A WORLD IN NEED OF THE GOSPEL

This gospel message about Jesus, which is preserved in the four Gospels, goes out to a Roman world that stretched from Mesopotamia to Scotland. This was a world ruled by Caesar (Augustus). He created an autocracy (one-man rule) that had the appearance of a republic. Caesar controlled the army and navy, oversaw all foreign and domestic policy, and appointed administrators who represented the government before the people. His face was on all the coins of the empire, his name on all public buildings, and there were temples dedicated to his *genius* or spirit in all major cities. He was called the *princeps* or "First Citizen." Not all citizens were equal, and freedom of speech and political freedom did not exist. Yet there was more social and economic freedom than ever before.

The Roman Family

The head of every family was the *paterfamilias* or 'the father of the family.' The oldest male family member served this role. He was the undisputed master, with the power of life and death over all other members. For example, he determined whether a newborn child would live or die. He arranged marriages when a child reached adulthood. He was also the sole owner of the family property.

Childhood was short-lived, meaning even pre-adolescents sometimes had adult responsibilities. There was no public education, but private instruction was available when a teacher established a school and charged a fee to those who could afford it. Wax tablets were used for writing and doing calculations. Male tutors accompanied boys to school while nurses attended to the girls. Secondary education continued to the age of about 13 and emphasized grammar, syntax, rhetoric, and literature in both Latin and Greek, including Homer, Aeschylus, Sophocles, Euripides, Menander, Virgil, and Horace.

Girls typically married at 12–15 years old, and boys married when they were slightly older. Marriage was a serious legal bond among the Romans. Still, men and women often lived together without a formal ceremony. A dowry was an important part of Roman marriage since it represented the girl or woman's insurance. Rings were exchanged and worn on the index finger because the people believed a nerve connected the finger with the heart, hands were held, and the couple would say, "Where you go, I go."

In the first century, childbirth was in decline, so Augustus granted special privileges to women who had children, such as acting with legal authority for themselves. He imposed penalties on bachelors and childless couples, preventing them from being named in wills. Unwanted children were abandoned and left to exposure, and people would search the city dumps to find and raise such children as slaves.

Slavery in the Roman Empire

Slavery was practiced throughout the ancient world. Instead of killing the people of a conquered territory or city, the victorious armies would take them as slaves to serve as maids, cooks, gardeners, and house servants. The Greeks expanded slavery and established their entire economy upon it. Slaves worked in mines, fields, shops, and offices; they worked in both low-skilled and high-skilled positions. Often, business owners relied upon slaves to run their operations. Slaves also worked for the government. When slaves performed their work well, they were sometimes given their freedom, which led to citizenship. They would then continue in their work as freedmen.

Some ex-slaves succeeded in business and government and moved into Rome's middle class. During the reign of Claudius, for example, a freedman named Pallas served as the emperor's Secretary of the Treasury and became wealthy. His brother was Felix, the governor of Judea who threw Paul into prison (Acts 23:23–24:27).

Slavery was not based on race. Instead, its practice in the ancient world was based on power. People defeated in war were put into servitude rather than put to death. The victors became the masters. People who fell into debt were forced into slavery to repay their creditors. Debt bondage reinforced the privileges of those with money over those without. (Several passages in the Bible, such as Exodus 21, Leviticus 25, and Deuteronomy 15, show how the Hebrews put laws in place to protect those who fell into debt.)

So common was slavery in the ancient world that the Israelites also practiced it. In fact, slaves built Solomon's Temple (1 Kings 9:20–22; 2 Chronicles 8:10–18).

The New Testament identifies several slaves, including the Ethiopian eunuch (Acts 8), the maid Rhoda (Acts 12), the clairvoyant slave girl (Acts 16), and the Roman centurion's slave (Luke 7). In addition, the high priest Caiaphas owned slaves, and Jesus even included slaves in the parables He told, recognizing the reality of the institution.

The Roman Army

Military service lasted 20-25 years and offered decent pay, promotion, and the promise of freedom to slaves upon the completion of their duty. The imperial army consisted of 300,000 men, half of whom belonged to the famous Roman legions. They were made up of Roman citizens who carried standards embossed with images of eagles. Their army included 28-30 legions or divisions. In addition to these, the army contained auxiliaries made up of recruits from different people throughout the empire. The Praetorian Guard was the emperor's personal legion stationed in Rome.

A recruit had to be at least 5'8" tall (1.73 meters) and able to hike 15 miles (24 km) in 5 hours with a full pack. Often, the army worked on public projects when not engaged in training or warfare. The army did not allow soldiers to marry, but many lived with women from local areas where they were stationed since they were not frequently transferred.

Religion in the Roman Empire

Rome encouraged many gods from different areas. Over time, gods with similar characteristics were considered as one god. Two of the most popular were Isis and Cybele.

Isis was an Egyptian goddess who was especially popular with women. Priests dressed in linen, had shaved heads, offered prayers twice a day to the sound of a rattle, and sprinkled water from the Nile during ceremonies. They took a vow not to have physical relations with another person, drink wine, or eat pork or fish. Priests opened a veil so worshippers could see her image holding her infant son Horus.

Cybele was a goddess of Asia Minor. Her image was carried in a carriage while her devotees danced to drums, cymbals, and pipes. Her priests would periodically fast for a week and sometimes cut themselves. By the second century, followers of Cybele practiced baptism in blood. The worshippers would stand in a pit under a grating over which a bull was sacrificed so that its blood would fall upon their heads and renew them forever. Only wealthy followers could afford this practice.

Entertainment in the Roman Empire

Public baths were built in every Roman city and included courts for games, wrestling, and track and field. Most major festivals were marked by athletic games, which sometimes lasted numerous days and were paid for by the government. Romans also enjoyed the theatre and the circus, but horseracing was their favorite, which included both bareback and chariot races.

The Roman government operated gladiatorial fighting, a fearsome form of entertainment. When the Colosseum opened in AD 80, the occasion was marked by 100 days of fighting. The state acquired gladiators in a variety of ways: some slaves were purchased from slave markets, masters sold others to get rid of them, and free men signed up to pay off debts. Gladiatorial schools trained three types of fighters: men who fought with armor; men who fought with light armor; and men who fought in a tunic with a dagger and a net. The word *arena* means 'sand' and was the name given to the places where the gladiatorial contests took place because sand was used to cover the blood shed during fights. Not all matches ended in death; the crowd would wave handkerchiefs or place their thumbs against their chest to vote whether a fighter should live or die.

AN OVERVIEW OF PAUL'S LIFE

Other than the apostles Peter and John, no man stands out more than the apostle Paul in the proclamation of the gospel throughout the Roman world. Jesus charged each of the 12 disciples to take the Good News of salvation to the ends of the earth (Acts 1:8), along with the 70 He chose to go throughout Galilee. He also gave this responsibility to His other followers. Yet it remained for a man who was not Jesus' follower during His earthly ministry to take the gospel to the height of human power by going before Caesar in Rome. The apostle Paul is the man whom Jesus confronted on his way to Damascus and then re-directed to Rome with the Good News of God's salvation. Who was this man before Jesus apprehended him?

Paul was born in Tarsus in the Roman province of Cilicia, a city with a long history dating back to the eighth century BC. Prior to Roman rule, the Seleucids governed, and Antiochus Epiphanes made it a free city in 170 BC. Tarsus retained that designation under the Romans in 64 BC. It was a university city and renowned for Stoic philosophy and rhetoric (Acts 21:39). Paul was a Roman citizen by birth (Acts 22:28), though the New Testament doesn't record how his family obtained their citizenship. One popular theory is that his family made tents and supplied them to the Roman army. Thus, the army could have awarded them citizenship when it was camped in the region at that time.

Every Roman citizen had three names: a *praenomen* (first name), a *nomen* (family name), and a *cognomen* (surname). The New Testament only records Paul's *cognomen*, which was Paullus. If records existed for his *nomen*, then we would have some knowledge of how he obtained his citizenship. For example, if Paul's father had received his citizenship from Antony, his name would have been Marcus Antonius Paullus.

Since Paul was a Roman citizen by birth, his father or a family representative would have registered his birth within 30 days at the city record office, which would have entered Paul's name in the city's official register. His father then received a certified copy in the form of a hinged tablet. This certificate stood as legal evidence a person had Roman citizenship. Paul would have needed this tablet as evidence to back up his claims of citizenship because it is unlikely others would simply take his word for it (Acts 16:35-40; 22:22-29).

Paul's Jewish name was Saul, and likely he was called this in honor of Israel's first king, who came from the tribe of Benjamin, just as Paul did (Romans 11:1; Philippians 3:5). This fact raises the questions: How did Paul's family end up in Tarsus, and how did he eventually settle in Jerusalem? Jerome, a Patristic church father, says Paul's family originated in Gischala in Galilee and then immigrated to Tarsus at the time of the Roman conquest in the first century BC. Since Paul identifies his family as Hebrew, it means they spoke Aramaic and Hebrew in addition to Greek. They did not simply blend into the culture, as did some other Jewish people in Asia Minor. When Paul appeared before the Sanhedrin (Acts 23:6), his family is identified as Pharisaic, which explains why he was sent to Jerusalem to study under Gamaliel, the most distinguished disciple of the famous rabbi, Hillel.

Paul's family likely sent him to Jerusalem at an early age, and he was only later influenced by the city of Tarsus. Luke gives this information in Acts 22:3. Paul says he is a Jew, born at Tarsus in Cilicia, brought up "here" (in Jerusalem), and educated at the feet of Gamaliel. Paul learned his lessons well. He writes that he was an advanced student in the traditions of his people (Galatians 1:14), meaning he had mastered written and oral law, observed it in detail, and had not intentionally or consciously violated any part of it (Philippians 3:6).

The Jewish Talmud may refer to Paul when it remarks that an unnamed pupil had exhibited "impudence in matters of learning" (Shabbat 30b). If this reference is to Paul, then it views him as possessing an inadequate understanding of the law (as evident in his gospel teaching) despite his early studies. Such a reference also points to Paul's broad influence. Likely, he was ordained as a rabbi prior to his ministry of the gospel since he received authority to extradite Jewish followers of Jesus in Damascus back to Jerusalem. To qualify for such a position, Paul would have had to show a comprehensive knowledge of the written and oral law, understand the "disciples of the wise," and be at least 40 years old (Acts 7:58).

Paul's experience on the road to Damascus is critical for understanding his letters. This event was so important that Luke retells it three times in Acts: once in his own third-person description of Paul's encounter with the risen and glorified Jesus (9:1-19); once in Paul's first person account when confronted by the crowd in Jerusalem (22:2-16);

and once in Paul's first person account during his legal proceeding before King Agrippa (26:1-24).

Jesus had died by crucifixion and, thus, was under the curse of God (Deuteronomy 21:23). To Paul prior to his conversion, this meant Jesus could not be the Messiah upon whom God's blessing rested. Therefore, to say that Jesus was Messiah was blasphemous. Yet Jesus, the Crucified One, had appeared to him. How then could he be both cursed and raised from the dead?

After Paul's experience on the road to Damascus, he went to Arabia (Galatians 1:17). Possibly, this means Paul went to Mount Sinai, the place where God made His great revelation to Moses and the Israelites. Though tradition places the location of Mount Sinai in Egypt, some scholars believe it could be in Arabia. When Paul returned from Mount Sinai, he hid from the Arabian King Aretas in Damascus and later escaped by climbing over the wall of the city (2 Corinthians 11:32-33). Paul had become a fugitive because he began to preach that Jesus was the "Son of God" who was crucified and raised to life (Acts 9:20-22). He then traveled to Jerusalem to meet with Peter and eventually returned to Tarsus. For the next several years, the Bible does not record Paul's activities, but it would be a mistake to think he was inactive. He continued to preach the gospel (Galatians 1:22-24), and it was during this time that Paul had a vision of the "third heaven" (2 Corinthians 12:1-10). Apparently, some of his hardships occurred during this period (2 Corinthians 11:23-27), probably resulting from his confrontation with Hellenistic culture and, in particular, Stoicism.

Paul was not only a traveler but also a letter writer. During this time period, private letters averaged less than 100 words, and literary letters like those written by Cicero and Seneca averaged 200 words. Papyrus (ancient paper) sheets were 9½ by 11½ inches (approximately 24 by 29 cm) in size and provided space for about 150-200 words. Thus, most letters were about one page long. The average length of Paul's letters, however, is 1,300 words, which represented a new literary form: they were longer than most letters, theological in content with an emphasis on the gospel, and addressed to communities rather than individuals. To say Paul was a letter writer, however, is not to say that he wrote every word of every letter. Usually, letters were dictated to a person called an amanuensis or "secretary" who used shorthand to capture the contents of the letters. This would have been true for Paul. For example, he names Tertius as a personal scribe for his letter to the Romans (16:22) and concludes most letters with final greetings in his own hand, indicating assistants wrote the remainder of the letters (1 Corinthians 16:21; Galatians 6:11; Colossians 4:18; 2 Thessalonians 3:17). This practice accounts for Paul's distinctive but varied vocabulary and style. It also explains some incomplete sentences and sudden breaks in thought, both of which indicate that his dictation was sometimes rapid and not easy to follow, and he would sometimes break off his dictation for reasons unknown to us.

Paul's letters reveal a flexible use of language in the service of the gospel. Several things can be said about the language of Paul's letters:

— *His language is figurative and creative.*
For example, he describes the church as a family (Ephesians 1:3-6), body (1 Corinthians 12:12-26), temple (1 Corinthians 3:16-17; Ephesians 2:20-21), and soldier (Ephesians 6:10-20). Not only does he use metaphor, but he also uses allegory (Galatians 4).

— *His language is biblical.*
Paul makes numerous biblical allusions and references throughout his letters, especially to the stories of Adam and the Exodus.

— *His language is personal.*
He writes out of his own experience and knowledge (2 Corinthians 13; Romans 7).

— *His language is forceful.*
He writes with emotion and declares at different times, "Of course not!" (Romans 7:7). To the Galatians, he writes, "I just wish that those troublemakers . . . would mutilate themselves" (Galatians 5:12).

PAUL'S MINISTRY IN SEVEN STAGES

JON HUNTZINGER, PHD

Paul's ministry of the gospel as described in the book of Acts and in his own letters may be organized into seven stages:

1. **Zealotry:** Birth–AD 35 (Galatians 1; Philippians 3)
— Born into an observant Jewish family
— Trained by Rabbi Gamaliel in Jerusalem
— Opposed early church preaching about Jesus

2. **Revelation:** AD 35-45 (Acts 9; Galatians 1; 2 Corinthians 12)
— Has a vision of Jesus on the way to Damascus
— Commissioned with the gospel to the Gentiles and Israel
— Goes into Arabia to reflect on his experience
— Returns to Jerusalem as a follower of Jesus
— Returns to his birthplace in Tarsus

3. **Transition:** AD 45-46 (Acts 11; 13-15)
— Joins church in Antioch
— Visits Jerusalem with famine relief

4. **Proclamation:** AD 47-57 (Acts 13-20)
— Travels throughout Asia Minor and preaches the gospel
— Writes letters to the churches in Galatia (Galatians; 1-2 Thessalonians)
— Defends and describes his gospel to the apostles in Jerusalem
— Plants churches in Corinth and Ephesus
— Writes letters to Rome from Corinth and to Corinth from Ephesus
— Returns to Greece and Ephesus

5. **Incarceration:** AD 57-62 (Acts 21-28; Philippians 1:12-14; Ephesians 3:1; 2 Timothy 4:6-18)
— Travels to Jerusalem and testifies before the Jewish and Roman leaders
— Imprisoned in Caesarea
— Sails to Rome and is placed under house arrest
— Writes Ephesians, Colossians, Philippians, and Philemon

6. **Instruction:** AD 62-65
— Ministry in Asia Minor and Greece
— Writes 1 Timothy and Titus

7. **Exhortation:** AD 65 (2 Timothy 4:6-8)
— Writes 2 Timothy
— Martyred in Rome

PAUL THE APOSTLE

Ten perspectives on the "least of all the apostles," Paul's own self-description (1 Corinthians 15:9), may be drawn from autobiographical comments he makes in his letters and in those made by Luke in the book of Acts.

A Pupil of Scripture

Paul quoted from Scripture, interpreted Scripture, and applied Scripture to the real-life situations of the churches he founded based on his education (Acts 22).

A Proper Hebrew

Paul was blameless toward the law and its traditions. He followed the traditions of his ancestors and remained orthodox in his Jewish faith (Galatians 1:14; Philippians 3:4-6).

He Peered into Heaven

Paul saw God's glory and the glorified Jesus (Acts 9; 18:9-10; 22; 26:19) as well as the glories of heaven (2 Corinthians 12:1-10). He also received divine direction (Acts 16:6-10). Paul's visions of Jesus, a beckoning man, and the third heaven link him with biblical figures like Isaiah, Ezekiel, Zechariah, and Daniel.

A Proud Apostle

Paul's pride was not in his own accomplishments. He boasted only in the Lord Jesus (2 Corinthians 11:16–12:10) and preached "Christ was crucified" throughout his ministry (1 Corinthians 1:18-25).

He Planted God's Word

Paul planted the Word of God in the middle of God's field (1 Corinthians 3:5-9), and the Holy Spirit validated the Good News he proclaimed (Romans 8).

A Man of Prayer

Paul persistently prayed for God's people (2 Timothy 1:3; 1 Thessalonians 1:2; Colossians 1:3, 9; Philippians 1:4; Ephesians 1:16; 1 Corinthians 1:4; Romans 1:10), and he encouraged them to pray as well (1 Timothy 2; 1 Thessalonians 5:17; Colossians 4:2; Ephesians 6:18).

A Persecuted Apostle

Paul encountered opposition to the gospel in the same way he opposed it before his encounter with the glorified Jesus on the Road to

Damascus (Galatians 1:13; Philippians 3:6; Acts 9:1; 2 Corinthians 6:3-13; 11:16-29; 2 Timothy 4:6).

A Prisoner of Christ

Paul was placed in chains for preaching the Good News of Jesus (Philemon; Philippians 1:7, 12-14; Ephesians 3:1, 13; 4:1).

He Pressed Towards the Prize

Paul did not give up despite the hardships he experienced (Philippians 3:12-16; 2 Timothy 4:7).

A Man Content with God's Provision

Paul trusted God to provide for his life (2 Corinthians 12:7-10; Philippians 4:11-13).

BOTH PERSECUTOR AND PERSECUTED

The initial words the glorified Jesus spoke to Paul concerned persecution: "Why are you persecuting me?" (Acts 9:4-5). The Greek word *diōkō* is the same word Paul uses to identify himself as one who persecuted the church and thereby Jesus in several of his letters. In four different letters, he describes himself as a persecutor of the church. It was a primary way Paul viewed his former life (Galatians 1:13; Philippians 3:6; 1 Timothy 1:13; 1 Corinthians 15:9).

Paul understood Jesus to say that any actions against the Church represent actions against Jesus Himself. Jesus personally and directly identified with His persecuted followers. As the Son of Man, Jesus identified with men and women in the same manner as Ezekiel, who lived among the Judean exiles in Babylon. Ezekiel identified with them as "son of man." Jesus anticipated this eventuality when He exhorted the disciples to rejoice in suffering for the sake of His name (Matthew 5:10-11). How are the disciples blessed, according to Jesus' Beatitudes? They are blessed because they are in unity with Jesus. Persecution is part of the disciples' experience (Matthew 10:23).

Jesus' followers will experience persecution just as Paul does. They will receive the same rejection as the prophets. Prophets such as Jeremiah and Amos were persecuted because they proclaimed the message of God to people who did not want to hear it. Jeremiah announced God's judgment against Judah, and Amos did so earlier against Israel. Often, persecution takes the form of a negative response by people to the word God speaks to them.

Paul experienced persecution as a disciple of Jesus even as Jesus experienced persecution (Galatians 5:11; 2 Timothy 3:11), but to experience persecution also means to experience Jesus' strength and power (2 Corinthians 4:7-18; 12:10; Romans 8:35-39). For Paul, persecution often resulted in imprisonment. The Greek word for prison is *desmos,* and a prisoner is a *desmios*. These words refer to chains. To be in prison was to be bound with chains, and to be a prisoner meant to wear chains. Paul repeatedly used these terms in his letter to Philemon, as well as to the Philippians, Ephesians (3:1, 13; 4:1), and Timothy. During much of his ministry, Paul lived with chains on his body. Yet he never referred to himself as a prisoner of Rome but always as a prisoner of the Lord Jesus. The gospel, not Rome, chained Paul.

THE GOSPEL IN PAUL'S WRITINGS

JON HUNTZINGER, PHD

Paul's gospel, or his theology of the Good News, flows through all his letters. It is deeply rooted in both the soil of Scripture and Paul's own experience. He emphasizes the love of God, fulfillment by the Spirit of God, and the ultimate goal of the new creation through Jesus, the Son of God.

THE LOVE OF GOD

Jesus says the first commandment is to love God with all of your heart, soul, and mind. The second commandment, which completes the first, is to love your neighbor as yourself. In Jesus' estimation, loving God and loving your neighbor represent the totality of God's law. When a Temple scribe publicly agreed with Jesus' teaching that loving God and neighbor is better than whole burnt offerings and sacrifices, Jesus said the scribe was wise. He said the man was not far from the Kingdom of God (Mark 12:28-34).

Jesus' response to the scribe draws upon two passages in the Old Testament. The first, to love God with all of yourself, is found in Deuteronomy 6. This portion of Scripture is known as the *Shema*, which means 'listen,' and is the first Hebrew word in this passage. It also represents the foundation statement of Israel's religious faith. Because God is One, His people must respond to Him with one purpose and one focus. They must love Him with all of their beings, even as He has loved them. The second passage, to love your neighbor, is found in Leviticus 19. This chapter lists a series of moral laws and for the most part, repeats the Ten Commandments. Not only are people required to love their neighbors, but they also must love the stranger who comes into the community (Leviticus 19:18, 34).

Paul's writings reaffirm Jesus' understanding of the law. In Galatians 5, Paul upholds the relationship of law and love. Concerned that the Galatians are giving in to others' teaching on circumcision, Paul admonishes them to live in the freedom of the cross. This freedom comes as a result of Jesus' death and resurrection. Jesus gave it to them so they may serve and love one another. This is the gospel, and it represents the very essence of the law (Galatians 5:14). Paul continues by saying that the "law of Christ" is fulfilled when people bear one another's burdens (6:2). Paul's comment helps us see Jesus through Paul's own eyes. Jesus' life of obedience and sacrifice on behalf of others represents the embodiment of the law. This law,

according to Paul, can be fulfilled only as believers share the burdens of others, which is another way of showing love for them.

Paul's first letter to the Corinthians contains his most extensive remarks on love (1 Corinthians 13). Paul notes that love must be the attitude believers have in their speech, understanding, and actions (13:1-3). He then defines love as being directed to the other person and not toward yourself (13:4-5). It anticipates the continuing work of God among His people (13:6-7). At the end of all things, only love will remain. Thus, love is just as necessary to the ministry gifts of the Spirit as it is vital to the life found in God's law.

THE SPIRIT

Paul is not only a man of Scripture, but he also is a man of the Spirit. He was first filled with the Holy Spirit when Ananias prayed for him: "Brother Saul, the Lord Jesus, who appeared to you on the road, has sent me so that you might regain your sight and be filled with the Holy Spirit" (Acts 9:17). Because of the Spirit's presence, what appear to be scales fall from Paul's eyes, and he sees again, though truly for the first time. His renewed sight represents a transformation in Paul's understanding of God's purpose and ways. With the help of the Spirit, Paul will now be able to understand the mystery of God—joining Jews and Gentiles in relationship to one another as one new man (Ephesians 2:11-3:13).

While Paul *is filled* with the Spirit, the Roman centurion Cornelius experiences *the falling* of the Spirit (Acts 10:45). Being filled with the Spirit and experiencing the fall of the Spirit are equivalent events. The filling and falling of the Spirit has to do with the power of the gospel. For Paul, to be filled with the Spirit means God has enabled him to go to Jews and Gentiles in the knowledge and power of the gospel, despite the suffering that it will bring (Acts 9:16). For Cornelius, to have the Spirit fall means he experiences the power of the gospel to worship God with understanding (Acts 10:1-2).

Paul's instruction on "spiritual matters" in 1 Corinthians 12 relates the Holy Spirit to Jesus:
— First, the Spirit is linked to the Lord and to God. Paul identifies the Holy Spirit with Jesus (the Son) and God (the Father).
— Second, the Holy Spirit declares Jesus. A primary responsibility of the Spirit is to make Jesus known.

— Third, Paul uses the image of a human body for describing God's people as the present manifestation of Jesus in the power of the Spirit. Charismata or spiritual gifts are given for the common good of the whole body (12:7).

Whenever Paul describes *the Church as the body of Christ*, he also describes *the gifts the body possesses* (Ephesians 4; Romans 12; 1 Corinthians 12). The Spirit energizes the body to serve in the same way Jesus served when He ministered among His disciples. For Paul, this means that the Spirit is given to proclaim the Good News of the Kingdom of God and to serve others. This is a common theme in Paul's writing. In Philippians, for example, the people are to look to the interests of others by having the mind of Christ in the Holy Spirit. The mind of Christ is one of service, and such a mind and life gives glory to God (Philippians 2). The ministry of members of the body of Christ represents the ministry of Jesus Himself and is done for the benefit of other people.

THE NEW CREATION

Paul's gospel begins and ends with the death and resurrection of Jesus. It also places Jesus at the beginning of all things and looks forward to His work at the end. In several of his letters, Paul places Jesus and His ministry against the background of the Creation story of Genesis 1-3. Paul insists that Jesus was in the beginning and was involved in creation as God's Word (Colossians 1:15-20). For this reason, Jesus brings about the new creation by reconciling people to God (2 Corinthians 5:11-21). He is able to do this because He was obedient to God and through such obedience, He was able to take His place over the creation. He fulfilled what Adam did not (Philippians 2:5-11).

Paul writes that the problem of sin is age-old, and people today are faced with the same temptation as Adam. The antidote is the law of the Spirit of life in Christ Jesus. Life in harmony with this law enables people to reveal the new man for which all creation longs (Romans 7:6-8:30). Jesus is the Second Adam, who provides hope through His resurrection from the dead. When we are "in" Him, we share in His death to the old man and in His resurrection of the new (1 Corinthians 15:20-28).

The Scripture passages listed above speak of reconciliation and transformation. The work of new creation brings people into relationship with God as they were in the beginning, as well as in relationship with one another and with all of creation. This creation includes the angelic beings who serve God. All creation cries out for Adam to be restored to his original place so that God's original intention may be completed. What is God's intention? He desires the unification of all things under the benevolent rule of the Second Adam (Jesus) to the glory and majesty of God Himself (Psalm 8).

ROMANS

JON HUNTZINGER, PHD

Those who study Paul's letter to the Romans have seen it as Paul's sermon on righteousness by faith. However, a better description might be *Paul's sermon on the gospel* because he emphasizes God's love, life in God's Spirit, and the new creation ministry of Jesus. Paul wrote the letter about AD 56 from Corinth to introduce himself and his message of Good News to the church at Rome. Meanwhile, he collected funds for the church in Jerusalem in anticipation of a trip there afterward.

Paul's letter to the Romans includes the following sections:

— An introduction and a summary of his gospel as God's righteousness or means of relationship with Him (1:1–17)
— A discussion of the gospel as righteousness that comes through faith (1:18–4:25)
— A discussion of the gospel as power that results in salvation (5:1–8:39)
— A discussion of the gospel and Israel (9:1–11:36)
— Practical advice on how to show the gospel in one's life (12:1–15:14)
— A brief description of his own plans, personal greetings, and a benediction or closing prayer for his readers (15:16–16:27)

NOT ASHAMED OF THE GOSPEL

In Paul's introduction (1:1–17), he recalls several key elements of the gospel's message, including the fact that Jesus was descended from David in the flesh (emphasizing Jesus' humanity), that Jesus was resurrected from the dead by God, and that the prophets foretold this saving work of God through Jesus. At the conclusion of these verses, Paul says he is not ashamed of the gospel because it is God's power to save (1:16). When he says this, he alludes to Jesus' crucifixion, which would have been a difficult teaching for Jewish and Gentile Romans, for whom crucifixion was a sign of shame and criminality. Paul then adds, "It is through faith that a righteous person has life" (1:17). He takes this phrase from the book of Habakkuk, where God tells His prophet to trust in His ways, even though those ways are often difficult to understand. Specifically, the prophet refers to God's choice of the Babylonians, an idolatrous and hard people, to bring judgment to Israel. This word from Habakkuk was as inconceivable to the Judeans at that time as the use of the cross to bring salvation was to the Romans during Paul's time. Nonetheless, Paul says the Romans must hold on to this truth because the cross is at the heart of the gospel.

GOSPEL AND LAW

The Roman people were a people of laws. They were proud of the roads, aqueducts, and public buildings they had built throughout the empire, which gave physical shape to their environment and served their material needs. However, they were also proud of the society they had built upon a system of laws that gave order to their lives and met their intellectual, emotional, and social needs. Paul understood this pride, so he expounds upon the gospel by focusing on the law (*nomos*)—the commandments God gave to Moses for the people to live in relationship with Him. He also addresses the disruptive nature of sin and Jesus, who has made a way to God possible through His death. In all, the letter to the Romans represents a brief outline of the history of gospel and law from Adam to Abraham to Moses to the present.

In tracing this history, Paul writes about the *law* of faith (3:27), the *law* of the mind (7:23), the *law* of sin (7:23), and the *law* of the Spirit of life (8:2). By using the vocabulary of law, Paul gripped the imagination of the Romans, for whom law was the definitive way they understood their culture. It was a reality for them and governed all aspects of their lives. To describe faith as a law was a way for Paul to help Roman readers (Jewish and Gentile) see faith as not merely conceptual or subjective but also as a spiritual reality. For Paul to write about the law of the mind is to show that the mind is real and operates in specific ways. When he writes about the law of sin, he asserts that it, too, is real and operates according to patterns. And to write about the law of the Spirit is to declare that the Spirit of God is real and moves and ministers in specific ways related to who He is.

NO CONDEMNATION

Early in his letter, Paul describes the need for the gospel. Though God has revealed Himself in creation to people created in His image, they have turned away from His revelation to pursue their own desires (1:18–32). Nonetheless, Paul later says, "there is no condemnation for those who belong to Christ Jesus" (8:1). The removal of condemnation is the central blessing of the gospel. People do not need to live in fear of death and God's judgment due to the power of sin in their lives—condemnation—because Jesus has delivered them. "Who will free me from this life that is dominated by sin and death?" Paul asks. Then he answers,

"Thank God! The answer is in Jesus Christ our Lord" (7:24-25). By submitting to death and being raised to life, Jesus has secured victory for those who join themselves to Him.

THE POWER OF THE SPIRIT

Even though Paul affirms the positive place of the law in the life of God's people throughout the letter, he observes that sin seized an opportunity when the law was given to "arouse all kinds of covetous desires within me!" (7:8). He says, "Sin took advantage of those commands and deceived me; it used the commands to kill me" (7:11). Paul recalls the story of Eve when the serpent enticed her to eat the fruit of the tree of knowledge. God's commandment to Adam and Eve was that they *not* eat the fruit of that tree. To do so would result in death. The serpent encouraged a desire in Eve to eat from the tree, which she later describes as deception. She was deceived into eating from the tree and thus experienced death. By referring to sin in a way that alludes to the serpent of the garden, Paul indicates that he views sin more as a personified power than an abstract concept.

Paul says that sin (a personified power) took what was good (the commandment meant for Adam's welfare) and used it to bring death into the life of Adam and his descendants. Paul then says that as a descendant, he has been "a slave to sin," meaning he lives under the rule of a power to which he has submitted. He has become a slave, and his only hope is deliverance by a stronger power. This stronger power is the Spirit who raised Jesus from the dead and gives life in place of death to His followers (8:1-11). The Spirit pours God's love into their hearts and fills them with joy, peace, and hope by His power (5:5; 14:17; 15:13, 30), even as He purifies them and makes them holy (2:29; 7:6; 8:2, 13; 15:13, 16).

GREETINGS FROM PAUL

1 This letter is from Paul, a slave of Christ Jesus, chosen by God to be an apostle and sent out to preach his Good News. [2] God promised this Good News long ago through his prophets in the holy Scriptures. [3] The Good News is about his Son. In his earthly life he was born into King David's family line, [4] and he was shown to be* the Son of God when he was raised from the dead by the power of the Holy Spirit.* He is Jesus Christ our Lord. [5] Through Christ, God has given us the privilege* and authority as apostles to tell Gentiles everywhere what God has done for them, so that they will believe and obey him, bringing glory to his name.

[6] And you are included among those Gentiles who have been called to belong to Jesus Christ. [7] I am writing to all of you in Rome who are loved by God and are called to be his own holy people.

May God our Father and the Lord Jesus Christ give you grace and peace.

GOD'S GOOD NEWS

[8] Let me say first that I thank my God through Jesus Christ for all of you, because your faith in him is being talked about all over the world. [9] God knows how often I pray for you. Day and night I bring you and your needs in prayer to God, whom I serve with all my heart* by spreading the Good News about his Son. [10] One of the things I always pray for is the opportunity, God willing, to come at last to see you. [11] For I long to visit you so I can bring you some spiritual gift that will help you grow strong in the Lord. [12] When we get together, I want to encourage you in your faith, but I also want to be encouraged by yours.

[13] I want you to know, dear brothers and sisters,* that I planned many times to visit you, but I was prevented until now. I want to work among you and see spiritual fruit, just as I have seen among other Gentiles. [14] For I have a great sense of obligation to people in both the civilized world and the rest of the world,* to the educated and uneducated alike. [15] So I am eager to come to you in Rome, too, to preach the Good News.

[16] For I am not ashamed of this Good News about Christ. It is the power of God at work, saving everyone who believes—the Jew first and also the Gentile.* [17] This Good News tells us how God makes us right in his sight. This is accomplished from start to finish by faith. As the Scriptures say, "It is through faith that a righteous person has life."*

GOD'S ANGER AT SIN

[18] But God shows his anger from heaven against all sinful, wicked people who suppress the truth by their wickedness.* [19] They know the truth about God because he has made it obvious to them. [20] For ever since the world was created, people have seen the earth and sky. Through everything God made, they can clearly see his invisible qualities—his eternal power and divine nature. So they have no excuse for not knowing God.

[21] Yes, they knew God, but they wouldn't worship him as God or even give him thanks. And they began to think up foolish ideas of what God

1:4a Or *and was designated.* 1:4b Or *by the Spirit of holiness;* or *in the new realm of the Spirit.* 1:5 Or *the grace.* 1:9 Or *in my spirit.* 1:13 Greek *brothers.* 1:14 Greek *to Greeks and barbarians.* 1:16 Greek *also the Greek.* 1:17 Or *"The righteous will live by faith."* Hab 2:4. 1:18 Or *who, by their wickedness, prevent the truth from being known.*

TO THE JEW FIRST
Romans 1:16   ROBERT MORRIS

God's heart is for world evangelism. He wants to see the whole world saved. At Gateway Church, we take the gospel to the world by taking it *to the Jew first.* Even in our first year as a church, we began sowing very heavily into Jewish evangelism. And by God's grace, we have been able to take the gospel all over the world.

Our Shabbat Service is the first service we have every month, even before our weekend services. Paul writes, "For I am not ashamed of this Good News about Christ. It is the power of God at work, saving everyone who believes—*the Jew first* and also the Gentile" (Romans 1:16, emphasis added). This is a principle on which Gateway Church is built.

Even Jesus made it a priority to take the gospel to the Jew first (Matthew 15:24). Everywhere Paul traveled, he always took the gospel to the Jew first. He spent the first three months in Ephesus preaching in the synagogue before he went to the rest of the city (Acts 19:8). All throughout the book of Acts, Paul *never* stopped going to the Jews. He knew that *this* was God's order. God wants the whole world saved, and He has a specific way to do it—by taking the gospel to the Jew first.

A TOUGH QUESTION
Romans 1:18-20   ROBERT MORRIS

People often ask, "How could a loving God send a person to hell?" Some ask this in an accusatory way, but other people simply want to understand. To answer this tough question, we must first understand two aspects of God's character:

1. He is always just.

There will never be any injustice in God or any of His judgments. Since the beginning of time, God has revealed Himself to every person, both internally and externally (Romans 1:19-20). Every person is born with a God-given conscience, which gives them guidance about right and wrong. Scripture says creation itself is proof of God's existence. No one can ever say, "Well, no one told me about God" because God will say, "*I* told you." Every person who makes an effort to seek God will find Him (Proverbs 8:17; Jeremiah 29:13; Matthew 7:7-8).

2. He is always loving.

God did not create hell for people. Hell was created for Satan and the fallen angels who rebelled with him (Matthew 25:41). However, like Satan, Adam and Eve rebelled against God. This rebellion was an inexcusable rejection of a perfect, loving God, and sadly, this rebellion has affected all humanity! God sent Jesus to pay for our sins so no one else would have to go to hell, but He still gives us a free will. We can choose to love God and spend eternity with Him, or we can choose to reject God and spend eternity away from Him. The real question isn't "Why would a loving God send a person to hell?" Instead, it's "Why would anyone reject a loving God?"

was like. As a result, their minds became dark and confused. ²²Claiming to be wise, they instead became utter fools. ²³And instead of worshiping the glorious, ever-living God, they worshiped idols made to look like mere people and birds and animals and reptiles.

²⁴So God abandoned them to do whatever shameful things their hearts desired. As a result, they did vile and degrading things with each other's bodies. ²⁵They traded the truth about God for a lie. So they worshiped and served the things God created instead of the Creator himself, who is worthy of eternal praise! Amen. ²⁶That is why God abandoned them to their shameful desires. Even the women turned against the natural way to have sex and instead indulged in sex with each other. ²⁷And the men, instead of having normal sexual relations with women, burned with lust for each other. Men did shameful things with other men, and as a result of this sin, they suffered within themselves the penalty they deserved.

²⁸Since they thought it foolish to acknowledge God, he abandoned them to their foolish thinking and let them do things that should never be done. ²⁹Their lives became full of every kind of wickedness, sin, greed, hate, envy, murder, quarreling, deception, malicious behavior, and gossip. ³⁰They are backstabbers, haters of God, insolent, proud, and boastful. They invent new ways of

sinning, and they disobey their parents. ³¹They refuse to understand, break their promises, are heartless, and have no mercy. ³²They know God's justice requires that those who do these things deserve to die, yet they do them anyway. Worse yet, they encourage others to do them, too.

GOD'S JUDGMENT OF SIN

2 You may think you can condemn such people, but you are just as bad, and you have no excuse! When you say they are wicked and should be punished, you are condemning yourself, for you who judge others do these very same things. ²And we know that God, in his justice, will punish anyone who does such things. ³Since you judge others for doing these things, why do you think you can avoid God's judgment when you do the same things? ⁴Don't you see how wonderfully kind, tolerant, and patient God is with you? Does this mean nothing to you? Can't you see that his kindness is intended to turn you from your sin?

⁵But because you are stubborn and refuse to turn from your sin, you are storing up terrible punishment for yourself. For a day of anger is coming, when God's righteous judgment will be revealed. ⁶He will judge everyone according to what they have done. ⁷He will give eternal life to those who keep on doing good, seeking after the glory and honor and immortality that God offers. ⁸But he will pour out his anger and wrath on those who live for themselves, who refuse to obey the truth and instead live lives of wickedness. ⁹There will be trouble and calamity for everyone who keeps on doing what is evil—for the Jew first and also for the Gentile.* ¹⁰But there will be glory and honor and peace from God for all who do good—for the Jew first and also for the Gentile. ¹¹For God does not show favoritism.

¹²When the Gentiles sin, they will be destroyed, even though they never had God's written law. And the Jews, who do have God's law, will be judged by that law when they fail to obey it. ¹³For merely listening to the law doesn't make us right with God. It is obeying the law that makes us right in his sight. ¹⁴Even Gentiles, who do not have God's written law, show that they know his law when they instinctively obey it, even without having heard it. ¹⁵They demonstrate that God's law is written in their hearts, for their own conscience and thoughts either accuse them or tell them they are doing right. ¹⁶And this is the message I proclaim—that the day is coming when God, through Christ Jesus, will judge everyone's secret life.

THE JEWS AND THE LAW

¹⁷You who call yourselves Jews are relying on God's law, and you boast about your special relationship with him. ¹⁸You know what he wants; you know what is right because you have been taught his law. ¹⁹You are convinced that you are a guide for the blind and a light for people who are lost in darkness. ²⁰You think you can instruct the ignorant and teach children the ways of God. For you are certain that God's law gives you complete knowledge and truth.

²¹Well then, if you teach others, why don't you teach yourself? You tell others not to steal, but do you steal? ²²You say it is wrong to commit adultery, but do you commit adultery? You condemn idolatry, but do you use items stolen from pagan temples?* ²³You are so proud of knowing the law, but you dishonor God by breaking it. ²⁴No wonder the Scriptures say, "The Gentiles blaspheme the name of God because of you."*

²⁵The Jewish ceremony of circumcision has value only if you obey God's law. But if you don't obey God's law, you are no better off than an uncircumcised Gentile. ²⁶And if the Gentiles obey God's law, won't God declare them to be his own people? ²⁷In fact, uncircumcised Gentiles who keep God's law will condemn you Jews who are circumcised and possess God's law but don't obey it.

²⁸For you are not a true Jew just because you were born of Jewish parents or because you have gone through the ceremony of circumcision. ²⁹No, a true Jew is one whose heart is right with God. And true circumcision is not merely obeying the letter of the law; rather, it is a change of heart produced by the Spirit. And a person with a changed heart seeks praise* from God, not from people.

GOD REMAINS FAITHFUL

3 Then what's the advantage of being a Jew? Is there any value in the ceremony of circumcision? ²Yes, there are great benefits! First of all, the Jews were entrusted with the whole revelation of God.*

³True, some of them were unfaithful; but just because they were unfaithful, does that mean God will be unfaithful? ⁴Of course not! Even if everyone else is a liar, God is true. As the Scriptures say about him,

"You will be proved right in what you say,
and you will win your case in court."*

⁵"But," some might say, "our sinfulness serves a good purpose, for it helps people see how righteous God is. Isn't it unfair, then, for him to punish us?" (This is merely a human point of view.) ⁶Of course not! If God were not entirely fair, how would he be qualified to judge the world? ⁷"But," someone might still argue, "how can God condemn me as a sinner if my dishonesty highlights his truthfulness and brings him more glory?" ⁸And some people even slander us by claiming that we say, "The more we sin, the better it is!" Those who say such things deserve to be condemned.

ALL PEOPLE ARE SINNERS

⁹Well then, should we conclude that we Jews are better than others? No, not at all, for we have already shown that all people, whether Jews or Gentiles,* are under the power of sin. ¹⁰As the Scriptures say,

"No one is righteous—
not even one.
¹¹ No one is truly wise;
no one is seeking God.
¹² All have turned away;
all have become useless.
No one does good,
not a single one."*
¹³ "Their talk is foul, like the stench from an
open grave.
Their tongues are filled with lies."

2:9 Greek also for the Greek; also in 2:10.   2:22 Greek do you steal from temples?   2:24 Isa 52:5 (Greek version).   2:29 Or receives praise.   3:2 Greek the oracles of God.   3:4 Ps 51:4 (Greek version). 3:9 Greek or Greeks.   3:10-12 Pss 14:1-3; 53:1-3 (Greek version).

"Snake venom drips from their lips."*
14 "Their mouths are full of cursing and
bitterness."*
15 "They rush to commit murder.
16 Destruction and misery always
follow them.
17 They don't know where to find peace."*
18 "They have no fear of God at all."*

19 Obviously, the law applies to those to whom it was given, for its purpose is to keep people from having excuses, and to show that the entire world is guilty before God. 20 For no one can ever be made right with God by doing what the law commands. The law simply shows us how sinful we are.

CHRIST TOOK OUR PUNISHMENT

21 But now God has shown us a way to be made right with him without keeping the requirements of the law, as was promised in the writings of Moses* and the prophets long ago. 22 We are made right with God by placing our faith in Jesus Christ. And this is true for everyone who believes, no matter who we are.

23 For everyone has sinned; we all fall short of God's glorious standard. 24 Yet God, in his grace, freely makes us right in his sight. He did this through Christ Jesus when he freed us from the penalty for our sins. 25 For God presented Jesus as the sacrifice for sin. People are made right with God when they believe that Jesus sacrificed his life, shedding his blood. This sacrifice shows that God was being fair when he held back and did not punish those who sinned in times past, 26 for he was looking ahead and including them in what he would do in this present time. God did this to demonstrate his righteousness, for he himself is fair and just, and he makes sinners right in his sight when they believe in Jesus.

27 Can we boast, then, that we have done anything to be accepted by God? No, because our acquittal is not based on obeying the law. It is based on faith. 28 So we are made right with God through faith and not by obeying the law.

29 After all, is God the God of the Jews only? Isn't he also the God of the Gentiles? Of course he is. 30 There is only one God, and he makes people right with himself only by faith, whether they are Jews or Gentiles.* 31 Well then, if we emphasize faith, does this mean that we can forget about the law? Of course not! In fact, only when we have faith do we truly fulfill the law.

THE FAITH OF ABRAHAM

4 Abraham was, humanly speaking, the founder of our Jewish nation. What did he discover about being made right with God? 2 If his good deeds had made him acceptable to God, he would have had something to boast about. But that was not God's way. 3 For the Scriptures tell us, "Abraham believed God, and God counted him as righteous because of his faith."*

THE RIGHTEOUSNESS OF GRACE
Romans 4:1-5   ROBERT MORRIS

Many believers fall prey to *legalism*, which puts our focus on what we do, how we perform, and how those around us perform. However, God's grace is not just for salvation. It's for each and every day of our lives.

In Romans 4, the apostle Paul shares Abraham's secret to being made right with God: "Abraham believed God, and God counted him as righteous because of his faith" (v. 3).

1. What is righteousness?
Is a man righteous because he does righteous things, or does he do righteous things because he is righteous? *Righteousness* is "right standing with God." Romans 5:17 calls righteousness a "gift" from God, and "all who receive it will live in triumph over sin and death." I can never do enough "right" things to be righteous; it's just impossible. However, I do have right standing with God because I believe in Jesus. He alone is righteous.

2. Did Abraham earn it?
Romans 4:5 says, "People are counted as righteous, not because of their work, but because of their faith in God who forgives sinners." Abraham didn't earn righteousness, and neither can we. Romans 3:10 clearly says, "No one is righteous." The only way to receive the gift of righteousness is to believe and accept Jesus. When we do, God deposits His righteousness into our account.

3. What did Abraham have to do?
Abraham only had to do one thing: *believe*. Jesus told His followers, "This is the only work God wants from you: Believe in the one he has sent" (John 6:29). Abraham did not come from a "Christian" background when God called him, but he believed God. No matter what has happened in your life, you can believe God too.

---

4 When people work, their wages are not a gift, but something they have earned. 5 But people are counted as righteous, not because of their work, but because of their faith in God who forgives sinners. 6 David also spoke of this when he described the happiness of those who are declared righteous without working for it:

7 "Oh, what joy for those
    whose disobedience is forgiven,
    whose sins are put out of sight.
8 Yes, what joy for those
    whose record the LORD has cleared
    of sin."*

3:13 Pss 5:9 (Greek version); 140:3.   3:14 Ps 10:7 (Greek version).
3:15-17 Isa 59:7-8.   3:18 Ps 36:1.   3:21 Greek *in the law.*
3:30 Greek *whether they are circumcised or uncircumcised.*
4:3 Gen 15:6.   4:7-8 Ps 32:1-2 (Greek version).

⁹Now, is this blessing only for the Jews, or is it also for uncircumcised Gentiles?* Well, we have been saying that Abraham was counted as righteous by God because of his faith. ¹⁰But how did this happen? Was he counted as righteous only after he was circumcised, or was it before he was circumcised? Clearly, God accepted Abraham before he was circumcised!

¹¹Circumcision was a sign that Abraham already had faith and that God had already accepted him and declared him to be righteous— even before he was circumcised. So Abraham is the spiritual father of those who have faith but have not been circumcised. They are counted as righteous because of their faith. ¹²And Abraham is also the spiritual father of those who have been circumcised, but only if they have the same kind of faith Abraham had before he was circumcised.

¹³Clearly, God's promise to give the whole earth to Abraham and his descendants was based not on his obedience to God's law, but on a right relationship with God that comes by faith. ¹⁴If God's promise is only for those who obey the law, then faith is not necessary and the promise is pointless. ¹⁵For the law always brings punishment on those who try to obey it. (The only way to avoid breaking the law is to have no law to break!)

¹⁶So the promise is received by faith. It is given as a free gift. And we are all certain to receive it, whether or not we live according to the law of Moses, if we have faith like Abraham's. For Abraham is the father of all who believe. ¹⁷That is what the Scriptures mean when God told him, "I have made you the father of many nations."* This happened because Abraham believed in the God who brings the dead back to life and who creates new things out of nothing.

¹⁸Even when there was no reason for hope, Abraham kept hoping—believing that he would become the father of many nations. For God had said to him, "That's how many descendants you will have!"* ¹⁹And Abraham's faith did not weaken, even though, at about 100 years of age, he figured his body was as good as dead—and so was Sarah's womb.

²⁰Abraham never wavered in believing God's promise. In fact, his faith grew stronger, and in this he brought glory to God. ²¹He was fully convinced that God is able to do whatever he promises. ²²And because of Abraham's faith, God counted him as righteous. ²³And when God counted him as righteous, it wasn't just for Abraham's benefit. It was recorded ²⁴for our benefit, too, assuring us that God will also count us as righteous if we believe in him, the one who raised Jesus our Lord from the dead. ²⁵He was handed over to die because of our sins, and he was raised to life to make us right with God.

FAITH BRINGS JOY

5 Therefore, since we have been made right in God's sight by faith, we have peace* with God because of what Jesus Christ our Lord has done for us. ²Because of our faith, Christ has brought us into this place of undeserved privilege where we now stand, and we confidently and joyfully look forward to sharing God's glory.

³We can rejoice, too, when we run into problems and trials, for we know that they help us develop endurance. ⁴And endurance develops strength of character, and character strengthens our confident hope of salvation. ⁵And this hope will not lead to disappointment. For we know how dearly God loves us, because he has given us the Holy Spirit to fill our hearts with his love.

⁶When we were utterly helpless, Christ came at just the right time and died for us sinners. ⁷Now, most people would not be willing to die for an upright person, though someone might perhaps be willing to die for a person who is especially good. ⁸But God showed his great love for us by sending Christ to die for us while we were still sinners. ⁹And since we have been made right in God's sight by the blood of Christ, he will certainly save us from God's condemnation. ¹⁰For since our friendship with God was restored by the death of his Son while we were still his enemies, we will certainly be saved through the life of his Son. ¹¹So now we can rejoice in our wonderful new relationship with God because our Lord Jesus Christ has made us friends of God.

ADAM AND CHRIST CONTRASTED

¹²When Adam sinned, sin entered the world. Adam's sin brought death, so death spread to everyone, for everyone sinned. ¹³Yes, people sinned even before the law was given. But it was not counted as sin because there was not yet any law to break. ¹⁴Still, everyone died—from the time of Adam to the time of Moses—even those who did not disobey an explicit commandment of God, as Adam did. Now Adam is a symbol, a representation of Christ, who was yet to come.

¹⁵But there is a great difference between Adam's sin and God's gracious gift. For the sin of this one man, Adam, brought death to many. But even greater is God's wonderful grace and his gift of forgiveness to many through this other man, Jesus Christ. ¹⁶And the result of God's gracious gift is very different from the result of that one man's sin. For Adam's sin led to condemnation, but God's free gift leads to our being made right with God, even though we are guilty of many sins. ¹⁷For the sin of this one man, Adam, caused death to rule over many. But even greater is God's wonderful grace and his gift of righteousness, for all who receive it will live in triumph

---

4:9 Greek *is this blessing only for the circumcised, or is it also for the uncircumcised?* **4:17** Gen 17:5. **4:18** Gen 15:5. **5:1** Some manuscripts read *let us have peace.*

over sin and death through this one man, Jesus Christ.

[18] Yes, Adam's one sin brings condemnation for everyone, but Christ's one act of righteousness brings a right relationship with God and new life for everyone. [19] Because one person disobeyed God, many became sinners. But because one other person obeyed God, many will be made righteous.

[20] God's law was given so that all people could see how sinful they were. But as people sinned more and more, God's wonderful grace became more abundant. [21] So just as sin ruled over all people and brought them to death, now God's wonderful grace rules instead, giving us right standing with God and resulting in eternal life through Jesus Christ our Lord.

SIN'S POWER IS BROKEN

6 Well then, should we keep on sinning so that God can show us more and more of his wonderful grace? [2] Of course not! Since we have died to sin, how can we continue to live in it? [3] Or have you forgotten that when we were joined with Christ Jesus in baptism, we joined him in his death? [4] For we died and were buried with Christ by baptism. And just as Christ was raised from the dead by the glorious power of the Father, now we also may live new lives.

[5] Since we have been united with him in his death, we will also be raised to life as he was. [6] We know that our old sinful selves were crucified with Christ so that sin might lose its power in our lives. We are no longer slaves to sin. [7] For when we died with Christ we were set free from the power of sin. [8] And since we died with Christ, we know we will also live with him. [9] We are sure of this because Christ was raised from the dead, and

he will never die again. Death no longer has any power over him. [10] When he died, he died once to break the power of sin. But now that he lives, he lives for the glory of God. [11] So you also should consider yourselves to be dead to the power of sin and alive to God through Christ Jesus.

[12] Do not let sin control the way you live;* do not give in to sinful desires. [13] Do not let any part of your body become an instrument of evil to serve sin. Instead, give yourselves completely to God, for you were dead, but now you have new life. So use your whole body as an instrument to do what is right for the glory of God. [14] Sin is no longer your master, for you no longer live under the requirements of the law. Instead, you live under the freedom of God's grace.

[15] Well then, since God's grace has set us free from the law, does that mean we can go on sinning? Of course not! [16] Don't you realize that you become the slave of whatever you choose to obey? You can be a slave to sin, which leads to death, or you can choose to obey God, which leads to righteous living. [17] Thank God! Once you were slaves of sin, but now you wholeheartedly obey this teaching we have given you. [18] Now you are free from your slavery to sin, and you have become slaves to righteous living.

[19] Because of the weakness of your human nature, I am using the illustration of slavery to help you understand all this. Previously, you let yourselves be slaves to impurity and lawlessness, which led ever deeper into sin. Now you must give yourselves to be slaves to righteous living so that you will become holy. [20] When you were slaves to sin, you were free from the obligation to do right. [21] And what was the result? You are now ashamed of the things you used to do, things that end in eternal doom. [22] But now you are free from the power of sin and have become slaves of God. Now you do those things that lead to holiness and result in eternal life. [23] For the wages of sin is death, but the free gift of God is eternal life through Christ Jesus our Lord.

NO LONGER BOUND TO THE LAW

7 Now, dear brothers and sisters*—you who are familiar with the law—don't you know that the law applies only while a person is living? [2] For example, when a woman marries, the law binds her to her husband as long as he is alive. But if he dies, the laws of marriage no longer apply to her. [3] So while her husband is alive, she would be committing adultery if she married another man. But if her husband dies, she is free from that law and does not commit adultery when she remarries.

[4] So, my dear brothers and sisters, this is the point: You died to the power of the law when you died with Christ. And now you are united with

---

DELIVERANCE
Romans 6:6-23   JACK HAYFORD

Romans 6:23 says, "The wages of sin is death." Sin is the reason we need deliverance. Because all have sinned and come short of God's standard, there is no hope for humanity outside of Jesus. The name *Jesus* means 'Savior and Deliverer.' The whole message of the cross is that He delivered us from the penalty of sin.

In our world, sin manifests in the works of the flesh ("self"), the works of Satan, and sickness. You cannot cast your "self" out, but you can "put to death the sinful, earthly things lurking within you" (Colossians 3:5) and be crucified with Christ (Galatians 2:20). Though certainly not always the case, some sickness is the manifestation of a demonic presence. In every situation, we must ask the Holy Spirit for wisdom. We need to move with compassion as we diligently open God's Word and allow Jesus to be our final authority.

6:12 Or *Do not let sin reign in your body, which is subject to death.*
7:1 Greek *brothers;* also in 7:4.

the one who was raised from the dead. As a result, we can produce a harvest of good deeds for God. [5]When we were controlled by our old nature,* sinful desires were at work within us, and the law aroused these evil desires that produced a harvest of sinful deeds, resulting in death. [6]But now we have been released from the law, for we died to it and are no longer captive to its power. Now we can serve God, not in the old way of obeying the letter of the law, but in the new way of living in the Spirit.

GOD'S LAW REVEALS OUR SIN

[7]Well then, am I suggesting that the law of God is sinful? Of course not! In fact, it was the law that showed me my sin. I would never have known that coveting is wrong if the law had not said, "You must not covet."* [8]But sin used this command to arouse all kinds of covetous desires within me! If there were no law, sin would not have that power. [9]At one time I lived without understanding the law. But when I learned the command not to covet, for instance, the power of sin came to life, [10]and I died. So I discovered that the law's commands, which were supposed to bring life, brought spiritual death instead. [11]Sin took advantage of those commands and deceived me; it used the commands to kill me. [12]But still, the law itself is holy, and its commands are holy and right and good.

[13]But how can that be? Did the law, which is good, cause my death? Of course not! Sin used what was good to bring about my condemnation to death. So we can see how terrible sin really is. It uses God's good commands for its own evil purposes.

STRUGGLING WITH SIN

[14]So the trouble is not with the law, for it is spiritual and good. The trouble is with me, for I am all too human, a slave to sin. [15]I don't really understand myself, for I want to do what is right, but I don't do it. Instead, I do what I hate. [16]But if I know that what I am doing is wrong, this shows that I agree that the law is good. [17]So I am not the one doing wrong; it is sin living in me that does it.

[18]And I know that nothing good lives in me, that is, in my sinful nature.* I want to do what is right, but I can't. [19]I want to do what is good, but I don't. I don't want to do what is wrong, but I do it anyway. [20]But if I do what I don't want to do, I am not really the one doing wrong; it is sin living in me that does it.

[21]I have discovered this principle of life—that when I want to do what is right, I inevitably do what is wrong. [22]I love God's law with all my heart. [23]But there is another power* within me that is at war with my mind. This power makes me a slave to the sin that is still within me. [24]Oh, what a miserable person I am! Who will free me from this life that is dominated by sin and death?

[25]Thank God! The answer is in Jesus Christ our Lord. So you see how it is: In my mind I really want to obey God's law, but because of my sinful nature I am a slave to sin.

LIFE IN THE SPIRIT

8 So now there is no condemnation for those who belong to Christ Jesus. [2]And because you belong to him, the power* of the life-giving Spirit has freed you* from the power of sin that leads to death. [3]The law of Moses was unable to save us because of the weakness of our sinful nature.* So God did what the law could not do. He sent his own Son in a body like the bodies we sinners have. And in that body God declared an end to sin's control over us by giving his Son as a sacrifice for our sins. [4]He did this so that the just requirement of the law would be fully satisfied for us, who no longer follow our sinful nature but instead follow the Spirit.

[5]Those who are dominated by the sinful nature think about sinful things, but those who are controlled by the Holy Spirit think about things that please the Spirit. [6]So letting your sinful nature control your mind leads to death. But letting the Spirit control your mind leads to life and peace. [7]For the sinful nature is always hostile to God. It never did obey God's laws, and it never will. [8]That's why those who are still under the control of their sinful nature can never please God.

[9]But you are not controlled by your sinful nature. You are controlled by the Spirit if you have the Spirit of God living in you. (And remember that those who do not have the Spirit of Christ living in them do not belong to him at all.) [10]And Christ lives within you, so even though your body will die because of sin, the Spirit gives you life* because you have been made right with God. [11]The Spirit of God, who raised Jesus from the dead, lives in you. And just as God raised Christ Jesus from the dead, he will give life to your mortal bodies by this same Spirit living within you.

[12]Therefore, dear brothers and sisters,* you have no obligation to do what your sinful nature urges you to do. [13]For if you live by its dictates, you will die. But if through the power of the Spirit you put to death the deeds of your sinful nature,* you will live. [14]For all who are led by the Spirit of God are children* of God.

[15]So you have not received a spirit that makes you fearful slaves. Instead, you received God's Spirit when he adopted you as his own children.* Now we call him, "Abba, Father."* [16]For his Spirit joins with our spirit to affirm that we are God's

---

7:5 Greek *When we were in the flesh.*   7:7 Exod 20:17; Deut 5:21.
7:18 Greek *my flesh;* also in 7:25.   7:23 Greek *law;* also in 7:23b.
8:2a Greek *the law;* also in 8:2b.   8:2b Some manuscripts read *me.*   8:3 Greek *our flesh;* similarly in 8:4, 5, 6, 7, 8, 9, 12.   8:10 Or *your spirit is alive.*   8:12 Greek *brothers;* also in 8:29.   8:13 Greek *deeds of the body.*   8:14 Greek *sons;* also in 8:19.   8:15a Greek *you received a spirit of sonship.*   8:15b *Abba* is an Aramaic term for "father."

WHAT DOES "NO" MEAN?
Romans 8:1-3, 38-39   ROBERT MORRIS

When we say "no," we don't always mean it. I might say, "No dessert for me," but if someone mentions ice cream, my answer quickly changes to "Yes, I'll take two scoops!" Words are often relative to us, but when God says "no," He really means *no*!

In Romans 8, the apostle Paul makes two bold "no" statements. First, he says, "There is no condemnation for those who belong to Christ Jesus" (v. 1). Then he concludes the chapter by saying, "Nothing can ever separate us from God's love" (v. 38). No condemnation. No separation. Do you realize how different our lives would be if we actually believed this deep down in our hearts?

I've talked to many believers who respond to these verses with "Yeah, but . . ." They think they are somehow an exception to God's incredible, unending grace. If we're going to overcome the hurts, fears, and doubts that try to control our lives, we must decide we are going to believe God's Word. So how much condemnation and separation? None! When the devil lies to you, stand firm and declare, *No condemnation. No separation.*

FUELED BY HEAVEN
Romans 8:18-28   MARCUS BRECHEEN

To *hope* is "to anticipate (with pleasure) something better." Hope is not based on conjecture or fantasy but upon the knowledge of the truth. In Romans 8:18-28, Paul encourages believers to live on earth with the hope of heaven clearly in focus. The Bible has a lot to say about heaven—not to threaten us with missing it but to deepen the hopeful excitement God intends for it to produce within us.

Glory is "the honor that results from a good opinion." In heaven, God's glory and who we are in Christ will be fully revealed. Misery, suffering, and sickness will be swallowed up in victory, and the people of God will live in the glorious freedom of Christ. God wants us to live each day on earth focused on this hope, understanding that He currently sees us as the beautiful, sanctified children whom we will fully become in heaven.

children. ¹⁷And since we are his children, we are his heirs. In fact, together with Christ we are heirs of God's glory. But if we are to share his glory, we must also share his suffering.

THE FUTURE GLORY

¹⁸Yet what we suffer now is nothing compared to the glory he will reveal to us later. ¹⁹For all creation is waiting eagerly for that future day when God will reveal who his children really are. ²⁰Against its will, all creation was subjected to God's curse. But with eager hope, ²¹the creation looks forward to the day when it will join God's children in glorious freedom from death and decay. ²²For we know that all creation has been groaning as in the pains of childbirth right up to the present time. ²³And we believers also groan, even though we have the Holy Spirit within us as a foretaste of future glory, for we long for our bodies to be released from sin and suffering. We, too, wait with eager hope for the day when God will give us our full rights as his adopted children,* including the new bodies he has promised us. ²⁴We were given this hope when we were saved. (If we already have something, we don't need to hope* for it. ²⁵But if we look forward to something we don't yet have, we must wait patiently and confidently.)

²⁶And the Holy Spirit helps us in our weakness. For example, we don't know what God wants us to pray for. But the Holy Spirit prays for us with groanings that cannot be expressed in words.

²⁷And the Father who knows all hearts knows what the Spirit is saying, for the Spirit pleads for us believers* in harmony with God's own will. ²⁸And we know that God causes everything to work together* for the good of those who love God and are called according to his purpose for them. ²⁹For God knew his people in advance, and he chose them to become like his Son, so that his Son would be the firstborn* among many brothers and sisters. ³⁰And having chosen them, he called them to come to him. And having called them, he gave them right standing with himself. And having given them right standing, he gave them his glory.

NOTHING CAN SEPARATE US FROM GOD'S LOVE

³¹What shall we say about such wonderful things as these? If God is for us, who can ever be against us? ³²Since he did not spare even his own Son but gave him up for us all, won't he also give us everything else? ³³Who dares accuse us whom God has chosen for his own? No one—for God himself has given us right standing with himself. ³⁴Who then will condemn us? No one—for Christ Jesus died for us and was raised to life for us, and he is sitting in the place of honor at God's right hand, pleading for us.

³⁵Can anything ever separate us from Christ's love? Does it mean he no longer loves us if we have trouble or calamity, or are persecuted, or hungry, or destitute, or in danger, or threatened with death? ³⁶(As the Scriptures say, "For your sake we are killed every day; we are being slaughtered like sheep."*) ³⁷No, despite all these

8:23 Greek *wait anxiously for sonship.*   8:24 Some manuscripts read *wait.*   8:27 Greek *for God's holy people.*   8:28 Some manuscripts read *And we know that everything works together.*   8:29 Or *would be supreme.*   8:36 Ps 44:22.

things, overwhelming victory is ours through Christ, who loved us.

[38] And I am convinced that nothing can ever separate us from God's love. Neither death nor life, neither angels nor demons,* neither our fears for today nor our worries about tomorrow—not even the powers of hell can separate us from God's love. [39] No power in the sky above or in the earth below—indeed, nothing in all creation will ever be able to separate us from the love of God that is revealed in Christ Jesus our Lord.

GOD'S SELECTION OF ISRAEL

9 With Christ as my witness, I speak with utter truthfulness. My conscience and the Holy Spirit confirm it. [2] My heart is filled with bitter sorrow and unending grief [3] for my people, my Jewish brothers and sisters.* I would be willing to be forever cursed—cut off from Christ!—if that would save them. [4] They are the people of Israel, chosen to be God's adopted children.* God revealed his glory to them. He made covenants with them and gave them his law. He gave them the privilege of worshiping him and receiving his wonderful promises. [5] Abraham, Isaac, and Jacob are their ancestors, and Christ himself was an Israelite as far as his human nature is concerned. And he is God, the one who rules over everything and is worthy of eternal praise! Amen.*

[6] Well then, has God failed to fulfill his promise to Israel? No, for not all who are born into the nation of Israel are truly members of God's people! [7] Being descendants of Abraham doesn't make them truly Abraham's children. For the Scriptures say, "Isaac is the son through whom your descendants will be counted,"* though Abraham had other children, too. [8] This means that Abraham's physical descendants are not necessarily children of God. Only the children of the promise are considered to be Abraham's children. [9] For God had promised, "I will return about this time next year, and Sarah will have a son."*

[10] This son was our ancestor Isaac. When he married Rebekah, she gave birth to twins.* [11] But before they were born, before they had done anything good or bad, she received a message from God. (This message shows that God chooses people according to his own purposes; [12] he calls people, but not according to their good or bad works.) She was told, "Your older son will serve your younger son."* [13] In the words of the Scriptures, "I loved Jacob, but I rejected Esau."*

[14] Are we saying, then, that God was unfair? Of course not! [15] For God said to Moses,

"I will show mercy to anyone I choose,
    and I will show compassion to anyone
        I choose."*

[16] So it is God who decides to show mercy. We can neither choose it nor work for it.

[17] For the Scriptures say that God told Pharaoh, "I have appointed you for the very purpose of displaying my power in you and to spread my fame throughout the earth."* [18] So you see, God chooses to show mercy to some, and he chooses to harden the hearts of others so they refuse to listen.

[19] Well then, you might say, "Why does God blame people for not responding? Haven't they simply done what he makes them do?"

[20] No, don't say that. Who are you, a mere human being, to argue with God? Should the thing that was created say to the one who created it, "Why have you made me like this?" [21] When a potter makes jars out of clay, doesn't he have a right to use the same lump of clay to make one jar for decoration and another to throw garbage into? [22] In the same way, even though God has the right to show his anger and his power, he is very patient with those on whom his anger falls, who are destined for destruction. [23] He does this to make the riches of his glory shine even brighter on those to whom he shows mercy, who were prepared in advance for glory. [24] And we are among those whom he selected, both from the Jews and from the Gentiles.

8:38 Greek *nor rulers*.   9:3 Greek *my brothers*.   9:4 Greek *chosen for sonship*.   9:5 Or *May God, the one who rules over everything, be praised forever. Amen*.   9:7 Gen 21:12.   9:9 Gen 18:10, 14.   9:10 Greek *she conceived children through this one man*.   9:12 Gen 25:23.   9:13 Mal 1:2-3.   9:15 Exod 33:19.   9:17 Exod 9:16 (Greek version).

25 Concerning the Gentiles, God says in the prophecy of Hosea,

"Those who were not my people,
   I will now call my people.
And I will love those
   whom I did not love before."*

26 And,

"Then, at the place where they were told,
   'You are not my people,'
there they will be called
   'children of the living God.'"*

27 And concerning Israel, Isaiah the prophet cried out,

"Though the people of Israel are as
   numerous as the sand of the seashore,
only a remnant will be saved.
28 For the LORD will carry out his sentence
   upon the earth
quickly and with finality."*

29 And Isaiah said the same thing in another place:

"If the LORD of Heaven's Armies
   had not spared a few of our children,
we would have been wiped out like Sodom,
   destroyed like Gomorrah."*

ISRAEL'S UNBELIEF

30 What does all this mean? Even though the Gentiles were not trying to follow God's standards, they were made right with God. And it was by faith that this took place. 31 But the people of Israel, who tried so hard to get right with God by keeping the law, never succeeded. 32 Why not? Because they were trying to get right with God by keeping the law* instead of by trusting in him. They stumbled over the great rock in their path. 33 God warned them of this in the Scriptures when he said,

"I am placing a stone in Jerusalem* that
   makes people stumble,
   a rock that makes them fall.
But anyone who trusts in him
   will never be disgraced."*

10 Dear brothers and sisters,* the longing of my heart and my prayer to God is for the people of Israel to be saved. 2 I know what enthusiasm they have for God, but it is misdirected zeal. 3 For they don't understand God's way of making people right with himself. Refusing to accept God's way, they cling to their own way of getting right with God by trying to keep the law. 4 For Christ has already accomplished the purpose for which the law was given.* As a result, all who believe in him are made right with God.

WHY STAND WITH ISRAEL TODAY?
Romans 9–11   JACK HAYFORD

In Romans 9–11, the apostle Paul addresses the question of the Jews in God's providence and purpose. The Jews were the firstfruit— the first people, through Abraham, to understand a covenant God. They then relayed the riches of that truth to the world, and through them, the Messiah came. Scripture calls Jews the "root" and Gentiles the "branches."

We are living in a sobering moment in history that calls us, as believers in Jesus Christ, to take a stand with Israel. We could be the people of the world's last hour. God calls us to pray with passion, to intercede, and to minister according to the words of the Savior, who said it is not our task to speculate when the end will come. However, it is our responsibility to do Kingdom business until He comes (Luke 19:13). This is not about politics; this is about the Word of God.

SALVATION IS FOR EVERYONE

5 For Moses writes that the law's way of making a person right with God requires obedience to all of its commands.* 6 But faith's way of getting right with God says, "Don't say in your heart, 'Who will go up to heaven?' (to bring Christ down to earth). 7 And don't say, 'Who will go down to the place of the dead?' (to bring Christ back to life again)." 8 In fact, it says,

"The message is very close at hand;
   it is on your lips and in your heart."*

And that message is the very message about faith that we preach: 9 If you openly declare that Jesus is Lord and believe in your heart that God raised him from the dead, you will be saved. 10 For it is by believing in your heart that you are made right with God, and it is by openly declaring your faith that you are saved. 11 As the Scriptures tell us, "Anyone who trusts in him will never be disgraced."* 12 Jew and Gentile* are the same in this respect. They have the same Lord, who gives generously to all who call on him. 13 For "Everyone who calls on the name of the LORD will be saved."*

14 But how can they call on him to save them unless they believe in him? And how can they believe in him if they have never heard about him? And how can they hear about him unless someone tells them? 15 And how will anyone go and tell them without being sent? That is why

---

9:25 Hos 2:23.   9:26 Greek *sons of the living God.* Hos 1:10. 9:27-28 Isa 10:22-23 (Greek version).   9:29 Isa 1:9 (Greek version).   9:32 Greek *by works.*   9:33a Greek *in Zion.*   9:33b Isa 8:14; 28:16 (Greek version).   10:1 Greek *Brothers.*   10:4 Or *For Christ is the end of the law.*   10:5 See Lev 18:5.   10:6-8 Deut 30:12-14.   10:11 Isa 28:16 (Greek version).   10:12 Greek *and Greek.* 10:13 Joel 2:32.

the Scriptures say, "How beautiful are the feet of messengers who bring good news!"*

¹⁶But not everyone welcomes the Good News, for Isaiah the prophet said, "Lord, who has believed our message?"* ¹⁷So faith comes from hearing, that is, hearing the Good News about Christ. ¹⁸But I ask, have the people of Israel actually heard the message? Yes, they have:

"The message has gone throughout the earth, and the words to all the world."*

¹⁹But I ask, did the people of Israel really understand? Yes, they did, for even in the time of Moses, God said,

"I will rouse your jealousy through people who are not even a nation. I will provoke your anger through the foolish Gentiles."*

²⁰And later Isaiah spoke boldly for God, saying,

"I was found by people who were not looking for me. I showed myself to those who were not asking for me."*

²¹But regarding Israel, God said,

"All day long I opened my arms to them, but they were disobedient and rebellious."*

GOD'S MERCY ON ISRAEL

11 I ask, then, has God rejected his own people, the nation of Israel? Of course not! I myself am an Israelite, a descendant of Abraham and a member of the tribe of Benjamin.

²No, God has not rejected his own people, whom he chose from the very beginning. Do you realize what the Scriptures say about this? Elijah the prophet complained to God about the people of Israel and said, ³"Lord, they have killed your prophets and torn down your altars. I am the only one left, and now they are trying to kill me, too."*

⁴And do you remember God's reply? He said, "No, I have 7,000 others who have never bowed down to Baal!"*

⁵It is the same today, for a few of the people of Israel* have remained faithful because of God's grace—his undeserved kindness in choosing them. ⁶And since it is through God's kindness, then it is not by their good works. For in that case, God's grace would not be what it really is—free and undeserved.

⁷So this is the situation: Most of the people of Israel have not found the favor of God they are looking for so earnestly. A few have—the ones God has chosen—but the hearts of the rest were hardened. ⁸As the Scriptures say,

"God has put them into a deep sleep. To this day he has shut their eyes so they do not see, and closed their ears so they do not hear."*

⁹Likewise, David said,

"Let their bountiful table become a snare, a trap that makes them think all is well. Let their blessings cause them to stumble, and let them get what they deserve. ¹⁰ Let their eyes go blind so they cannot see, and let their backs be bent forever."*

¹¹Did God's people stumble and fall beyond recovery? Of course not! They were disobedient, so God made salvation available to the Gentiles. But he wanted his own people to become jealous and claim it for themselves. ¹²Now if the Gentiles were enriched because the people of Israel turned down God's offer of salvation, think how much greater a blessing the world will share when they finally accept it.

¹³I am saying all this especially for you Gentiles. God has appointed me as the apostle to the Gentiles. I stress this, ¹⁴for I want somehow to make the people of Israel jealous of what you Gentiles have, so I might save some of them. ¹⁵For since their rejection meant that God offered salvation to the rest of the world, their acceptance will be even more wonderful. It will be life for those who were dead! ¹⁶And since Abraham and the other patriarchs were holy, their descendants will also be holy—just as the entire batch of dough is holy because the portion given as an offering is holy. For if the roots of the tree are holy, the branches will be, too.

¹⁷But some of these branches from Abraham's tree—some of the people of Israel—have been broken off. And you Gentiles, who were branches from a wild olive tree, have been grafted in. So now you also receive the blessing God has promised Abraham and his children, sharing in the rich nourishment from the root of God's special olive tree. ¹⁸But you must not brag about being grafted in to replace the branches that were broken off. You are just a branch, not the root.

¹⁹"Well," you may say, "those branches were broken off to make room for me." ²⁰Yes, but remember—those branches were broken off because they didn't believe in Christ, and you are there because you do believe. So don't think highly of yourself, but fear what could happen. ²¹For if God did not spare the original branches, he won't* spare you either.

²²Notice how God is both kind and severe. He is severe toward those who disobeyed, but kind to

11:15 Isa 52:7.   11:16 Isa 53:1.   11:18 Ps 19:4.   11:19 Deut 32:21.
11:20 Isa 65:1 (Greek version).   11:21 Isa 65:2 (Greek version).
11:3 1 Kgs 19:10, 14.   11:4 1 Kgs 19:18.   11:5 Greek for a remnant.
11:8 Isa 29:10; Deut 29:4.   11:9-10 Ps 69:22-23 (Greek version).
11:21 Some manuscripts read perhaps he won't.

MORE THAN MONEY
Romans 11:16   ROBERT MORRIS

When most people hear the word *tithe*, they think of money. For God, however, tithing is actually a heart issue. Tithing is giving God the first in faith. Many people *say* they're putting God first, but it takes a lot of faith to pay God before we pay our rent, utilities, and taxes.

There was much more at stake than money when God told Abraham to sacrifice his son Isaac (Genesis 22). God had promised to make a great nation through Isaac, so it took great faith for Abraham to obey. This kind of faith is precisely what tithing requires.

Tithing is also one of the ways God blesses and protects us. When Satan comes against you with fear and doubt, you can firmly reply, "No! I'm a tither. I've trusted God with my firstfruits, and He is going to redeem and protect everything else in my life!"

THE WAY WE WORSHIP
Romans 12:1-2   JACK HAYFORD

We worship because of two foundational truths: God deserves it, and we need it. Romans 12 tells us how to worship and what we can expect to happen in response to worshipping God's way. The apostle Paul writes, "Give your bodies to God because of all he has done for you. Let them be a living and holy sacrifice . . . This is truly the way to worship him" (vv. 1-2).

Worship sets us apart from the world and unlocks the discovery of God's purpose in our lives. We give our total selves as spiritual sacrifices to the Lord. We worship Him with our words, our bodies, our hearts, and our spirits (Psalm 51:17; Hebrew 13:15; 1 Peter 2:5).

Worship conquers the human will and prevents it from asserting its false authority. When we enter the presence of the King with worship, we create a place for His glory to dwell with us.

you if you continue to trust in his kindness. But if you stop trusting, you also will be cut off. [23] And if the people of Israel turn from their unbelief, they will be grafted in again, for God has the power to graft them back into the tree. [24] You, by nature, were a branch cut from a wild olive tree. So if God was willing to do something contrary to nature by grafting you into his cultivated tree, he will be far more eager to graft the original branches back into the tree where they belong.

GOD'S MERCY IS FOR EVERYONE

[25] I want you to understand this mystery, dear brothers and sisters,* so that you will not feel proud about yourselves. Some of the people of Israel have hard hearts, but this will last only until the full number of Gentiles comes to Christ. [26] And so all Israel will be saved. As the Scriptures say,

"The one who rescues will come from
    Jerusalem,*
and he will turn Israel* away from
    ungodliness.
[27] And this is my covenant with them,
    that I will take away their sins."*

[28] Many of the people of Israel are now enemies of the Good News, and this benefits you Gentiles. Yet they are still the people he loves because he chose their ancestors Abraham, Isaac, and Jacob. [29] For God's gifts and his call can never be withdrawn. [30] Once, you Gentiles were rebels against God, but when the people of Israel rebelled against him, God was merciful to you instead. [31] Now they are the rebels, and God's mercy has come to you so that they, too, will share* in God's mercy. [32] For God has imprisoned everyone in disobedience so he could have mercy on everyone.

[33] Oh, how great are God's riches and wisdom and knowledge! How impossible it is for us to understand his decisions and his ways!

[34] For who can know the LORD's thoughts?
    Who knows enough to give him advice?*
[35] And who has given him so much
    that he needs to pay it back?*

[36] For everything comes from him and exists by his power and is intended for his glory. All glory to him forever! Amen.

A LIVING SACRIFICE TO GOD

12 And so, dear brothers and sisters,* I plead with you to give your bodies to God because of all he has done for you. Let them be a living and holy sacrifice—the kind he will find acceptable. This is truly the way to worship him.* [2] Don't copy the behavior and customs of this world, but let God transform you into a new person by changing the way you think. Then you will learn to know God's will for you, which is good and pleasing and perfect.

[3] Because of the privilege and authority* God has given me, I give each of you this warning: Don't think you are better than you really are. Be honest in your evaluation of yourselves, measuring yourselves by the faith God has given us.* [4] Just as our bodies have many parts and each

---

11:25 Greek *brothers.*   11:26a Greek *from Zion.*   11:26b Greek *Jacob.*   11:26-27 Isa 59:20-21; 27:9 (Greek version).   11:31 Other manuscripts read *will now share;* still others read *will someday share.*   11:34 Isa 40:13 (Greek version).   11:35 See Job 41:11.   12:1a Greek *brothers.*   12:1b Or *This is your spiritual worship;* or *This is your reasonable service.*   12:3a Or *Because of the grace;* compare 1:5.   12:3b Or *By the faith God has given you;* or *by the standard of our God-given faith.*

part has a special function, ⁵so it is with Christ's body. We are many parts of one body, and we all belong to each other.

⁶In his grace, God has given us different gifts for doing certain things well. So if God has given you the ability to prophesy, speak out with as much faith as God has given you. ⁷If your gift is serving others, serve them well. If you are a teacher, teach well. ⁸If your gift is to encourage others, be encouraging. If it is giving, give generously. If God has given you leadership ability, take the responsibility seriously. And if you have a gift for showing kindness to others, do it gladly.

⁹Don't just pretend to love others. Really love them. Hate what is wrong. Hold tightly to what is good. ¹⁰Love each other with genuine affection,* and take delight in honoring each other. ¹¹Never be lazy, but work hard and serve the Lord enthusiastically.* ¹²Rejoice in our confident hope. Be patient in trouble, and keep on praying. ¹³When God's people are in need, be ready to help them. Always be eager to practice hospitality.

¹⁴Bless those who persecute you. Don't curse them; pray that God will bless them. ¹⁵Be happy with those who are happy, and weep with those who weep. ¹⁶Live in harmony with each other. Don't be too proud to enjoy the company of ordinary people. And don't think you know it all!

¹⁷Never pay back evil with more evil. Do things in such a way that everyone can see you are honorable. ¹⁸Do all that you can to live in peace with everyone.

¹⁹Dear friends, never take revenge. Leave that to the righteous anger of God. For the Scriptures say,

"I will take revenge;
    I will pay them back,"*
    says the LORD.

²⁰Instead,

"If your enemies are hungry, feed them.
    If they are thirsty, give them something
        to drink.
    In doing this, you will heap
        burning coals of shame on their heads."*

²¹Don't let evil conquer you, but conquer evil by doing good.

RESPECT FOR AUTHORITY

13 Everyone must submit to governing authorities. For all authority comes from God, and those in positions of authority have been placed there by God. ²So anyone who rebels against authority is rebelling against what God has instituted, and they will be punished. ³For the authorities do not strike fear in people who are doing right, but in those who are doing wrong. Would you like to live without fear of the authorities? Do what is right, and they will

honor you. ⁴The authorities are God's servants, sent for your good. But if you are doing wrong, of course you should be afraid, for they have the power to punish you. They are God's servants, sent for the very purpose of punishing those who do what is wrong. ⁵So you must submit to them, not only to avoid punishment, but also to keep a clear conscience.

⁶Pay your taxes, too, for these same reasons. For government workers need to be paid. They are serving God in what they do. ⁷Give to everyone what you owe them: Pay your taxes and government fees to those who collect them, and give respect and honor to those who are in authority.

LOVE FULFILLS GOD'S REQUIREMENTS

⁸Owe nothing to anyone—except for your obligation to love one another. If you love your neighbor, you will fulfill the requirements of God's law. ⁹For the commandments say, "You must not commit adultery. You must not murder. You must not steal. You must not covet."* These—and other such commandments—are summed up in this one commandment: "Love your neighbor as yourself."* ¹⁰Love does no wrong to others, so love fulfills the requirements of God's law.

¹¹This is all the more urgent, for you know how late it is; time is running out. Wake up, for our salvation is nearer now than when we first believed. ¹²The night is almost gone; the day of salvation will soon be here. So remove your dark deeds like dirty clothes, and put on the shining armor of right living. ¹³Because we belong to the day, we must live decent lives for all to see. Don't participate in the darkness of wild parties and drunkenness, or in sexual promiscuity and immoral living, or in quarreling and jealousy. ¹⁴Instead, clothe yourself with the presence of the Lord Jesus Christ. And don't let yourself think about ways to indulge your evil desires.

THE DANGER OF CRITICISM

14 Accept other believers who are weak in faith, and don't argue with them about what they think is right or wrong. ²For instance, one person believes it's all right to eat anything. But another believer with a sensitive conscience will eat only vegetables. ³Those who feel free to eat anything must not look down on those who don't. And those who don't eat certain foods must not condemn those who do, for God has accepted them. ⁴Who are you to condemn someone else's servants? Their own master will judge whether they stand or fall. And with the Lord's help, they will stand and receive his approval.

⁵In the same way, some think one day is more holy than another day, while others think every day is alike. You should each be fully convinced

---

12:10 Greek with brotherly love.　12:11 Or but serve the Lord with a zealous spirit; or but let the Spirit excite you as you serve the Lord.　12:19 Deut 32:35.　12:20 Prov 25:21-22.　13:9a Exod 20:13-15, 17.　13:9b Lev 19:18.

MAMMON HAS FRIENDS
Romans 14:22   ROBERT MORRIS

Just as the spirit of mammon will keep you from experiencing the fullness of God's blessings, so will the spirits of poverty and pride.

The spirit of poverty causes you to be ashamed of the blessings of God. It makes you feel uncomfortable when receiving blessings from others or owning nice things.

The spirit of pride causes you to be overly proud of the blessings you have received. While seemingly opposite from the spirit of poverty, the two share a common root—they are both things-focused rather than God-focused.

The keys to staying God-focused with your finances are tithing and being a good steward of what God has given you. Don't worry about explaining your blessings to others. Once the spirits of pride and poverty no longer influence your life, you will be free to recognize and enjoy the blessings God has given you.

that whichever day you choose is acceptable. 6 Those who worship the Lord on a special day do it to honor him. Those who eat any kind of food do so to honor the Lord, since they give thanks to God before eating. And those who refuse to eat certain foods also want to please the Lord and give thanks to God. 7 For we don't live for ourselves or die for ourselves. 8 If we live, it's to honor the Lord. And if we die, it's to honor the Lord. So whether we live or die, we belong to the Lord. 9 Christ died and rose again for this very purpose—to be Lord both of the living and of the dead.

10 So why do you condemn another believer*? Why do you look down on another believer? Remember, we will all stand before the judgment seat of God. 11 For the Scriptures say,

"'As surely as I live,' says the LORD,
  'every knee will bend to me,
  and every tongue will declare allegiance
  to God.*'"

12 Yes, each of us will give a personal account to God. 13 So let's stop condemning each other. Decide instead to live in such a way that you will not cause another believer to stumble and fall.

14 I know and am convinced on the authority of the Lord Jesus that no food, in and of itself, is wrong to eat. But if someone believes it is wrong, then for that person it is wrong. 15 And if another believer is distressed by what you eat, you are not acting in love if you eat it. Don't let your eating ruin someone for whom Christ died. 16 Then you will not be criticized for doing something you believe is good. 17 For the Kingdom of God is not a matter of what we eat or drink, but of living a life

of goodness and peace and joy in the Holy Spirit. 18 If you serve Christ with this attitude, you will please God, and others will approve of you, too. 19 So then, let us aim for harmony in the church and try to build each other up.

20 Don't tear apart the work of God over what you eat. Remember, all foods are acceptable, but it is wrong to eat something if it makes another person stumble. 21 It is better not to eat meat or drink wine or do anything else if it might cause another believer to stumble.* 22 You may believe there's nothing wrong with what you are doing, but keep it between yourself and God. Blessed are those who don't feel guilty for doing something they have decided is right. 23 But if you have doubts about whether or not you should eat something, you are sinning if you go ahead and do it. For you are not following your convictions. If you do anything you believe is not right, you are sinning.*

LIVING TO PLEASE OTHERS

15 We who are strong must be considerate of those who are sensitive about things like this. We must not just please ourselves. 2 We should help others do what is right and build them up in the Lord. 3 For even Christ didn't live to please himself. As the Scriptures say, "The insults of those who insult you, O God, have fallen on me."* 4 Such things were written in the Scriptures long ago to teach us. And the Scriptures give us hope and encouragement as we wait patiently for God's promises to be fulfilled.

5 May God, who gives this patience and encouragement, help you live in complete harmony with each other, as is fitting for followers of Christ Jesus. 6 Then all of you can join together with one voice, giving praise and glory to God, the Father of our Lord Jesus Christ.

7 Therefore, accept each other just as Christ has accepted you so that God will be given glory. 8 Remember that Christ came as a servant to the Jews* to show that God is true to the promises he made to their ancestors. 9 He also came so that the Gentiles might give glory to God for his mercies to them. That is what the psalmist meant when he wrote:

"For this, I will praise you among
  the Gentiles;
  I will sing praises to your name."*

10 And in another place it is written,

"Rejoice with his people,
  you Gentiles."*

14:10 Greek your brother; also in 14:10b, 13, 15, 21. 14:11 Or declare praise for God. Isa 49:18; 45:23 (Greek version). 14:21 Some manuscripts read to stumble or be offended or be weakened. 14:23 Some manuscripts place the text of 16:25-27 here. 15:3 Greek who insult you have fallen on me. Ps 69:9. 15:8 Greek servant of circumcision. 15:9 Ps 18:49. 15:10 Deut 32:43.

[11]And yet again,

"Praise the LORD, all you Gentiles.
    Praise him, all you people of the earth."*

[12]And in another place Isaiah said,

"The heir to David's throne* will come,
    and he will rule over the Gentiles.
They will place their hope on him."*

[13]I pray that God, the source of hope, will fill you completely with joy and peace because you trust in him. Then you will overflow with confident hope through the power of the Holy Spirit.

PAUL'S REASON FOR WRITING

[14]I am fully convinced, my dear brothers and sisters,* that you are full of goodness. You know these things so well you can teach each other all about them. [15]Even so, I have been bold enough to write about some of these points, knowing that all you need is this reminder. For by God's grace, [16]I am a special messenger from Christ Jesus to you Gentiles. I bring you the Good News so that I might present you as an acceptable offering to God, made holy by the Holy Spirit. [17]So I have reason to be enthusiastic about all Christ Jesus has done through me in my service to God. [18]Yet I dare not boast about anything except what Christ has done through me, bringing the Gentiles to God by my message and by the way I worked among them. [19]They were convinced by the power of miraculous signs and wonders and by the power of God's Spirit.* In this way, I have fully presented the Good News of Christ from Jerusalem all the way to Illyricum.*

[20]My ambition has always been to preach the Good News where the name of Christ has never been heard, rather than where a church has already been started by someone else. [21]I have been following the plan spoken of in the Scriptures, where it says,

"Those who have never been told about him
    will see,
and those who have never heard of him
    will understand."*

[22]In fact, my visit to you has been delayed so long because I have been preaching in these places.

PAUL'S TRAVEL PLANS

[23]But now I have finished my work in these regions, and after all these long years of waiting, I am eager to visit you. [24]I am planning to go to Spain, and when I do, I will stop off in Rome. And after I have enjoyed your fellowship for a little while, you can provide for my journey.

[25]But before I come, I must go to Jerusalem to take a gift to the believers* there. [26]For you see, the believers in Macedonia and Achaia* have eagerly taken up an offering for the poor among the believers in Jerusalem. [27]They were glad to do this because they feel they owe a real debt to them. Since the Gentiles received the spiritual blessings of the Good News from the believers in Jerusalem, they feel the least they can do in return is to help them financially. [28]As soon as I have delivered this money and completed this good deed of theirs, I will come to see you on my way to Spain. [29]And I am sure that when I come, Christ will richly bless our time together.

[30]Dear brothers and sisters, I urge you in the name of our Lord Jesus Christ to join in my struggle by praying to God for me. Do this because of your love for me, given to you by the Holy Spirit. [31]Pray that I will be rescued from those in Judea who refuse to obey God. Pray also that the believers there will be willing to accept the donation* I am taking to Jerusalem. [32]Then, by the will of God, I will be able to come to you with a joyful heart, and we will be an encouragement to each other.

[33]And now may God, who gives us his peace, be with you all. Amen.*

PAUL GREETS HIS FRIENDS

16 I commend to you our sister Phoebe, who is a deacon in the church in Cenchrea. [2]Welcome her in the Lord as one who is worthy of honor among God's people. Help her in whatever she needs, for she has been helpful to many, and especially to me.

[3]Give my greetings to Priscilla and Aquila, my co-workers in the ministry of Christ Jesus. [4]In fact, they once risked their lives for me. I am thankful to them, and so are all the Gentile churches. [5]Also give my greetings to the church that meets in their home.

Greet my dear friend Epenetus. He was the first person from the province of Asia to become a follower of Christ. [6]Give my greetings to Mary, who has worked so hard for your benefit. [7]Greet Andronicus and Junia,* my fellow Jews,* who were in prison with me. They are highly respected among the apostles and became followers of Christ before I did. [8]Greet Ampliatus, my dear friend in the Lord. [9]Greet Urbanus, our co-worker in Christ, and my dear friend Stachys.

[10]Greet Apelles, a good man whom Christ approves. And give my greetings to the believers from the household of Aristobulus. [11]Greet Herodion, my fellow Jew.* Greet the Lord's people

15:11 Ps 117:1.   15:12a Greek *The root of Jesse.* David was the son of Jesse.   15:12b Isa 11:10 (Greek version).   15:14 Greek *brothers;* also in 15:30.   15:19a Other manuscripts read *the Spirit;* still others read *the Holy Spirit.*   15:19b *Illyricum* was a region northeast of Italy.   15:21 Isa 52:15 (Greek version).   15:25 Greek *God's holy people;* also in 15:26, 31.   15:26 *Macedonia* and *Achaia* were the northern and southern regions of Greece.   15:31 Greek *the ministry;* other manuscripts read *the gift.*   15:33 Some manuscripts do not include *Amen.* One very early manuscript places 16:25-27 here.   16:7a *Junia* is a feminine name. Some late manuscripts accent the word so it reads *Junias,* a masculine name; still others read *Julia* (feminine).   16:7b Or *compatriots;* also in 16:21.   16:11 Or *compatriot.*

from the household of Narcissus. [12] Give my greetings to Tryphena and Tryphosa, the Lord's workers, and to dear Persis, who has worked so hard for the Lord. [13] Greet Rufus, whom the Lord picked out to be his very own; and also his dear mother, who has been a mother to me.

[14] Give my greetings to Asyncritus, Phlegon, Hermes, Patrobas, Hermas, and the brothers and sisters* who meet with them. [15] Give my greetings to Philologus, Julia, Nereus and his sister, and to Olympas and all the believers* who meet with them. [16] Greet each other with a sacred kiss. All the churches of Christ send you their greetings.

PAUL'S FINAL INSTRUCTIONS

[17] And now I make one more appeal, my dear brothers and sisters. Watch out for people who cause divisions and upset people's faith by teaching things contrary to what you have been taught. Stay away from them. [18] Such people are not serving Christ our Lord; they are serving their own personal interests. By smooth talk and glowing words they deceive innocent people. [19] But everyone knows that you are obedient to the Lord. This makes me very happy. I want you to be wise in doing right and to stay innocent of any wrong. [20] The God of peace will soon crush Satan under your feet. May the grace of our Lord Jesus* be with you.

[21] Timothy, my fellow worker, sends you his greetings, as do Lucius, Jason, and Sosipater, my fellow Jews.

[22] I, Tertius, the one writing this letter for Paul, send my greetings, too, as one of the Lord's followers.

[23] Gaius says hello to you. He is my host and also serves as host to the whole church. Erastus, the city treasurer, sends you his greetings, and so does our brother Quartus.*

[25] Now all glory to God, who is able to make you strong, just as my Good News says. This message about Jesus Christ has revealed his plan for you Gentiles, a plan kept secret from the beginning of time. [26] But now as the prophets* foretold and as the eternal God has commanded, this message is made known to all Gentiles everywhere, so that they too might believe and obey him. [27] All glory to the only wise God, through Jesus Christ, forever. Amen.*

16:14 Greek brothers; also in 16:17. 16:15 Greek all of God's holy people. 16:20 Some manuscripts read Lord Jesus Christ. 16:23 Some manuscripts add verse 24, May the grace of our Lord Jesus Christ be with you all. Amen. Still others add this sentence after verse 27. 16:26 Greek the prophetic writings. 16:25-27 Various manuscripts place the doxology (shown here as 16:25-27) after 14:23 or after 15:33 or after 16:23.

PAUL'S MINISTRY AND LETTERS FROM CORINTH

JON HUNTZINGER, PHD

The following list outlines Paul's ministry in Corinth and the letters that he writes to the church there:

— After a difficult time of ministry (Acts 16–17), "in weakness—timid and trembling" (1 Corinthians 2:3), Paul founds the church in Corinth and lives there for 18 months in AD 50–51 (Acts 18:1–17).

— He leaves Corinth with Priscilla and Aquila and goes to Ephesus. He later leaves Ephesus and travels to Jerusalem for Passover and Pentecost (Acts 18:21–22).

— Paul leaves Jerusalem, travels to Antioch, and then returns to Ephesus, where he ministers for more than two years (AD 52–55) (Acts 18:22; 19:1–20).

— He hears of immorality in the Corinthian church and writes a letter to them that is now lost (1 Corinthians 5:9–11).

— Paul later hears from members of Chloe's household about divisions that have formed in the church (1 Corinthians 1:11) and writes 1 Corinthians in response.

— He plans to visit churches in Macedonia and afterward spend some time in Corinth (1 Corinthians 16:5–8).

— The situation in Corinth is worse than Paul imagined, so he changes his plans and visits the Corinthians on his way to Macedonia (2 Corinthians 1:15–16). The book of Acts does not record this visit.

— He describes his visit as "painful" (2 Corinthians 2:1; 13:2) because it results in a difficult confrontation (2 Corinthians 2:5–10; 7:12).

— Paul returns to Ephesus, where he writes a harsh letter that Titus then delivers. This letter has been lost.

— Titus takes the letter while Paul goes to Troas after a riot erupts in Ephesus (Acts 19:23–30) to wait for a report (2 Corinthians 2:12–13).

— Paul later meets Titus in Macedonia and rejoices at the news he brings (2 Corinthians 7:6–7).

— Paul writes 2 Corinthians from Macedonia around AD 56, where he (1) expresses relief to their response, (2) discusses the collection for Jerusalem believers, and (3) defends his authority to those who are holdouts.

— He continues to Corinth for a final visit (Acts 20), where he writes his letter to the Romans.

1 AND 2 CORINTHIANS

JON HUNTZINGER, PHD

O f the two existing letters from Paul to the church he founded in Corinth, he wrote the one designated 1 Corinthians from Ephesus around AD 55 in response to problems he had received in a report.

The church in Corinth was splitting apart over a host of issues:

— Members divided over their loyalties to individual leaders and likely gave preference to whatever individual baptized them into the faith (1:10–17).
— They divided over their response to immoral behavior, with some tolerating the behavior and others finding it scandalous (5:1–13; 6:12–20).
— They divided because of lawsuits, with some members suing others in civil court rather than settling matters amicably within the church (6:1–8).
— They divided over meat offered to idols, with some willing to eat such meat and others finding the practice offensive (8:1–13).
— They divided over the proper approach to the Lord's Table (11:20–34).
— They also experienced some confusion about the exercise of spiritual matters (*pneumatika*) and the appropriate form of worship when they gathered together (chapters 12–14).

What is Paul's answer to these problems? How does he address the division present in the church? The opening passage of the letter contains his answer. In this prologue, Paul makes reference to Jesus (Christ Jesus, Lord Jesus Christ, Jesus Christ our Lord, Christ) ten times in the first 10 verses.

These references show that before Paul addressed the various issues brought to him by members of the church, he wanted to establish the basic fact that Jesus is the foundation for their fellowship. Jesus called Paul to be an apostle (1:1); Jesus called the Corinthians into relationship with God (1:2; 1:9); Jesus drew the people into relationship with one another and gave them grace (1:3–4); and Jesus will be revealed on a future day (1:7–8). Paul's conviction is that Jesus is the essence of their existence, and their division is due to their failure to remember this important fact. Jesus is the unity of the Church, and the fractures in their fellowship are happening because they are not building upon Him. Since the gospel features Jesus—His life, death, and resurrection—the division of the church shows that they have lost sight of the gospel.

The importance of the gospel is apparent as Paul begins and ends his letter with extended discussions of the *two primary elements of the gospel: Jesus' crucifixion and His resurrection*. After he reminds the Corinthians of their foundation in Jesus (1:1–10), Paul asserts that the gospel he preached to them when he first visited them featured the cross (1:18–2:5) and was delivered through the power of the Spirit (2:5–16). He then addresses the various forms of division in the Corinthian church (chapters 3–11) and concludes his letter with an extended discussion on the Resurrection (chapter 15). In doing this, he frames the issues tearing at the church with the two essential elements of the gospel and draws their attention to what binds them together and upon which they must be in full agreement. There is only one gospel, and it features the crucifixion and resurrection of Jesus.

VERSE	TITLE	MEANING TO THE CORINTHIANS
1	Christ Jesus	The one for whom Paul is an apostle
2	Christ Jesus	The one who has sanctified them
2	Lord Jesus Christ	The name that binds them together
3	Lord Jesus Christ	The one who gives them grace and peace
4	Christ Jesus	The one who gives them the grace of God
6	Christ	Jesus should be the subject of their testimony
7	Lord Jesus Christ	The one who will be revealed
8	Lord Jesus Christ	The one who will return on "that day"
9	Jesus Christ our Lord	The one who gives them fellowship
10	Lord Jesus Christ	The name by which Paul appeals to them

The letter known as 2 Corinthians represents Paul's response to the continuing situation in the Corinthian church in AD 56. Even as Paul's focus in 1 Corinthians is Jesus as the foundation for the people's faith and the gospel as the answer to their division, his focus in 2 Corinthians is on his ministry among them. This letter is one of his most personal.

This letter contains three major sections:
— In chapters 1-7, Paul defends his actions and his ministry.
— In chapters 8-9, he discusses an offering he is collecting for poor believers in Jerusalem.
— In chapters 10-13, he responds to critics of his ministry.

After discussing his plans and recommending forgiveness for someone who has opposed him (2:3-11), Paul expounds upon the ministry he has among them by the Holy Spirit. He writes, "It is not that we think we are qualified to do anything on our own. Our qualification comes from God.

He has enabled us to be ministers of his new covenant. This is a covenant not of written laws, but of the Spirit" (3:5-6). He continues by saying this ministry of the gospel is one of glory, even though some have had a veil pulled over their eyes to keep them from seeing its truth (4:3-4). Jesus

is the subject of the gospel that Paul preaches out of love: "Christ's love controls us. Since we believe that Christ died for all, we also believe that we have all died to our old life" (5:14). In sum, Paul's ministry of the gospel concerning Jesus' death and resurrection is one of reconciliation with God (5:18-21) and fellowship with one another.

Paul's collection for the poor believers in Jerusalem is an example of what unity and reconciliation look like in a practical way. The Corinthian believers (most of whom are Gentiles) can show unity with their Jewish brothers and sisters in Judea by contributing to the gift that Paul is raising for them. Generosity toward others is a tangible manifestation of the gospel (9:1-14).

The gospel Paul preached has demanded much from him. It has involved affliction (1:3-11) and personal opposition from some inside the church (2:3-11). It has involved personal sacrifice as he has provided for his own needs so as not to burden others (12:14-18). It has involved spiritual struggle and warfare (10:1-6). It has involved everything from scourging to hunger to a thorn in the flesh (11:23-27; 12:7-10). Paul has willingly endured much because the gospel offers much. It offers unity with God through the Spirit on account of Jesus' death, resurrection, and present ministry.

1 CORINTHIANS

GREETINGS FROM PAUL

1 This letter is from Paul, chosen by the will of God to be an apostle of Christ Jesus, and from our brother Sosthenes.

² I am writing to God's church in Corinth,* to you who have been called by God to be his own holy people. He made you holy by means of Christ Jesus,* just as he did for all people everywhere who call on the name of our Lord Jesus Christ, their Lord and ours.

³ May God our Father and the Lord Jesus Christ give you grace and peace.

PAUL GIVES THANKS TO GOD

⁴ I always thank my God for you and for the gracious gifts he has given you, now that you belong to Christ Jesus. ⁵ Through him, God has enriched your church in every way—with all of your eloquent words and all of your knowledge. ⁶ This confirms that what I told you about Christ is true. ⁷ Now you have every spiritual gift you need as you eagerly wait for the return of our Lord Jesus Christ. ⁸ He will keep you strong to the end so that

you will be free from all blame on the day when our Lord Jesus Christ returns. ⁹ God will do this, for he is faithful to do what he says, and he has invited you into partnership with his Son, Jesus Christ our Lord.

DIVISIONS IN THE CHURCH

¹⁰ I appeal to you, dear brothers and sisters,* by the authority of our Lord Jesus Christ, to live in harmony with each other. Let there be no divisions in the church. Rather, be of one mind, united in thought and purpose. ¹¹ For some members of Chloe's household have told me about your quarrels, my dear brothers and sisters. ¹² Some of you are saying, "I am a follower of Paul." Others are saying, "I follow Apollos," or "I follow Peter,*" or "I follow only Christ."

¹³ Has Christ been divided into factions? Was I, Paul, crucified for you? Were any of you baptized

1:2a *Corinth* was the capital city of Achaia, the southern region of the Greek peninsula.   1:2b Or *because you belong to Christ Jesus.*   1:10 Greek *brothers;* also in 1:11, 26.   1:12 Greek *Cephas.*

in the name of Paul? Of course not! [14] I thank God that I did not baptize any of you except Crispus and Gaius, [15] for now no one can say they were baptized in my name. [16] (Oh yes, I also baptized the household of Stephanas, but I don't remember baptizing anyone else.) [17] For Christ didn't send me to baptize, but to preach the Good News—and not with clever speech, for fear that the cross of Christ would lose its power.

THE WISDOM OF GOD

[18] The message of the cross is foolish to those who are headed for destruction! But we who are being saved know it is the very power of God. [19] As the Scriptures say,

"I will destroy the wisdom of the wise
    and discard the intelligence of the
    intelligent."*

[20] So where does this leave the philosophers, the scholars, and the world's brilliant debaters? God has made the wisdom of this world look foolish. [21] Since God in his wisdom saw to it that the world would never know him through human wisdom, he has used our foolish preaching to save those who believe. [22] It is foolish to the Jews, who ask for signs from heaven. And it is foolish to the Greeks, who seek human wisdom. [23] So when we preach that Christ was crucified, the Jews are offended and the Gentiles say it's all nonsense.

[24] But to those called by God to salvation, both Jews and Gentiles,* Christ is the power of God and the wisdom of God. [25] This foolish plan of God is wiser than the wisest of human plans, and God's weakness is stronger than the greatest of human strength.

[26] Remember, dear brothers and sisters, that few of you were wise in the world's eyes or powerful or wealthy* when God called you. [27] Instead, God chose things the world considers foolish in order to shame those who think they are wise. And he chose things that are powerless to shame those who are powerful. [28] God chose things despised by the world,* things counted as nothing at all, and used them to bring to nothing what the world considers important. [29] As a result, no one can ever boast in the presence of God.

[30] God has united you with Christ Jesus. For our benefit God made him to be wisdom itself. Christ made us right with God; he made us pure and holy, and he freed us from sin. [31] Therefore, as the Scriptures say, "If you want to boast, boast only about the LORD."*

PAUL'S MESSAGE OF WISDOM

2 When I first came to you, dear brothers and sisters,* I didn't use lofty words and impressive wisdom to tell you God's secret plan.* [2] For I decided that while I was with you I would forget everything except Jesus Christ, the one who was crucified. [3] I came to you in weakness—timid and

trembling. [4] And my message and my preaching were very plain. Rather than using clever and persuasive speeches, I relied only on the power of the Holy Spirit. [5] I did this so you would trust not in human wisdom but in the power of God.

[6] Yet when I am among mature believers, I do speak with words of wisdom, but not the kind of wisdom that belongs to this world or to the rulers of this world, who are soon forgotten. [7] No, the wisdom we speak of is the mystery of God*—his plan that was previously hidden, even though he made it for our ultimate glory before the world began. [8] But the rulers of this world have not understood it; if they had, they would not have crucified our glorious Lord. [9] That is what the Scriptures mean when they say,

"No eye has seen, no ear has heard,
    and no mind has imagined
what God has prepared
    for those who love him."*

[10] But* it was to us that God revealed these things by his Spirit. For his Spirit searches out everything and shows us God's deep secrets. [11] No one can know a person's thoughts except that person's own spirit, and no one can know God's thoughts except God's own Spirit. [12] And we have received God's Spirit (not the world's spirit), so we can know the wonderful things God has freely given us.

[13] When we tell you these things, we do not use words that come from human wisdom. Instead, we speak words given to us by the Spirit, using the Spirit's words to explain spiritual truths.* [14] But people who aren't spiritual* can't receive these truths from God's Spirit. It all sounds foolish to them and they can't understand it, for only those who are spiritual can understand what the Spirit means. [15] Those who are spiritual can evaluate all things, but they themselves cannot be evaluated by others. [16] For,

"Who can know the LORD's thoughts?
    Who knows enough to teach him?"*

But we understand these things, for we have the mind of Christ.

PAUL AND APOLLOS, SERVANTS OF CHRIST

3 Dear brothers and sisters,* when I was with you I couldn't talk to you as I would to spiritual people.* I had to talk as though you belonged to this world or as though you were infants in

1:19 Isa 29:14.   1:24 Greek and Greeks.   1:26 Or high born.
1:28 Or God chose those who are low born.   1:31 Jer 9:24.
2:1a Greek brothers.   2:1b Greek God's mystery; other manuscripts read God's testimony.   2:7 Greek But we speak God's wisdom in a mystery.   2:9 Isa 64:4.   2:10 Some manuscripts read For.
2:13 Or explaining spiritual truths in spiritual language, or explaining spiritual truths to spiritual people.   2:14 Or who don't have the Spirit; or who have only physical life.   2:16 Isa 40:13 (Greek version).
3:1a Greek Brothers.   3:1b Or to people who have the Spirit.

Christ. [2] I had to feed you with milk, not with solid food, because you weren't ready for anything stronger. And you still aren't ready, [3] for you are still controlled by your sinful nature. You are jealous of one another and quarrel with each other. Doesn't that prove you are controlled by your sinful nature? Aren't you living like people of the world? [4] When one of you says, "I am a follower of Paul," and another says, "I follow Apollos," aren't you acting just like people of the world?

[5] After all, who is Apollos? Who is Paul? We are only God's servants through whom you believed the Good News. Each of us did the work the Lord gave us. [6] I planted the seed in your hearts, and Apollos watered it, but it was God who made it grow. [7] It's not important who does the planting, or who does the watering. What's important is that God makes the seed grow. [8] The one who plants and the one who waters work together with the same purpose. And both will be rewarded for their own hard work. [9] For we are both God's workers. And you are God's field. You are God's building.

[10] Because of God's grace to me, I have laid the foundation like an expert builder. Now others are building on it. But whoever is building on this foundation must be very careful. [11] For no one can lay any foundation other than the one we already have—Jesus Christ.

[12] Anyone who builds on that foundation may use a variety of materials—gold, silver, jewels, wood, hay, or straw. [13] But on the judgment day, fire will reveal what kind of work each builder has done. The fire will show if a person's work has any value. [14] If the work survives, that builder will receive a reward. [15] But if the work is burned up, the builder will suffer great loss. The builder will be saved, but like someone barely escaping through a wall of flames.

[16] Don't you realize that all of you together are the temple of God and that the Spirit of God lives in[*] you? [17] God will destroy anyone who destroys this temple. For God's temple is holy, and you are that temple.

[18] Stop deceiving yourselves. If you think you are wise by this world's standards, you need to become a fool to be truly wise. [19] For the wisdom of this world is foolishness to God. As the Scriptures say,

"He traps the wise
   in the snare of their own cleverness."[*]

[20] And again,

"The LORD knows the thoughts of the wise;
   he knows they are worthless."[*]

[21] So don't boast about following a particular human leader. For everything belongs to you— [22] whether Paul or Apollos or Peter,[*] or the world, or life and death, or the present and the future.

Everything belongs to you, [23] and you belong to Christ, and Christ belongs to God.

PAUL'S RELATIONSHIP WITH THE CORINTHIANS

4 So look at Apollos and me as mere servants of Christ who have been put in charge of explaining God's mysteries. [2] Now, a person who is put in charge as a manager must be faithful. [3] As for me, it matters very little how I might be evaluated by you or by any human authority. I don't even trust my own judgment on this point. [4] My conscience is clear, but that doesn't prove I'm right. It is the Lord himself who will examine me and decide.

[5] So don't make judgments about anyone ahead of time—before the Lord returns. For he will bring our darkest secrets to light and will reveal our private motives. Then God will give to each one whatever praise is due.

[6] Dear brothers and sisters,[*] I have used Apollos and myself to illustrate what I've been saying. If you pay attention to what I have quoted from the Scriptures,[*] you won't be proud of one of your leaders at the expense of another. [7] For what gives you the right to make such a judgment? What do you have that God hasn't given you? And if everything you have is from God, why boast as though it were not a gift?

[8] You think you already have everything you need. You think you are already rich. You have begun to reign in God's kingdom without us! I wish you really were reigning already, for then we would be reigning with you. [9] Instead, I sometimes think God has put us apostles on display, like prisoners of war at the end of a victor's parade, condemned to die. We have become a spectacle to the entire world—to people and angels alike.

[10] Our dedication to Christ makes us look like fools, but you claim to be so wise in Christ! We are weak, but you are so powerful! You are honored, but we are ridiculed. [11] Even now we go hungry and thirsty, and we don't have enough clothes to keep warm. We are often beaten and have no home. [12] We work wearily with our own hands to earn our living. We bless those who curse us. We are patient with those who abuse us. [13] We appeal gently when evil things are said about us. Yet we are treated like the world's garbage, like everybody's trash—right up to the present moment.

[14] I am not writing these things to shame you, but to warn you as my beloved children. [15] For even if you had ten thousand others to teach you about Christ, you have only one spiritual father. For I became your father in Christ Jesus when I preached the Good News to you. [16] So I urge you to imitate me.

3:16 Or among. 3:19 Job 5:13. 3:20 Ps 94:11. 3:22 Greek Cephas. 4:6a Greek Brothers. 4:6b Or If you learn not to go beyond "what is written."

¹⁷ That's why I have sent Timothy, my beloved and faithful child in the Lord. He will remind you of how I follow Christ Jesus, just as I teach in all the churches wherever I go.

¹⁸ Some of you have become arrogant, thinking I will not visit you again. ¹⁹ But I will come—and soon—if the Lord lets me, and then I'll find out whether these arrogant people just give pretentious speeches or whether they really have God's power. ²⁰ For the Kingdom of God is not just a lot of talk; it is living by God's power. ²¹ Which do you choose? Should I come with a rod to punish you, or should I come with love and a gentle spirit?

PAUL CONDEMNS SPIRITUAL PRIDE

5 I can hardly believe the report about the sexual immorality going on among you—something that even pagans don't do. I am told that a man in your church is living in sin with his stepmother.* ² You are so proud of yourselves, but you should be mourning in sorrow and shame. And you should remove this man from your fellowship.

³ Even though I am not with you in person, I am with you in the Spirit.* And as though I were there, I have already passed judgment on this man ⁴ in the name of the Lord Jesus. You must call a meeting of the church.* I will be present with you in spirit, and so will the power of our Lord Jesus. ⁵ Then you must throw this man out and hand him over to Satan so that his sinful nature will be destroyed* and he himself* will be saved on the day the Lord* returns.

⁶ Your boasting about this is terrible. Don't you realize that this sin is like a little yeast that spreads through the whole batch of dough? ⁷ Get rid of the old "yeast" by removing this wicked person from among you. Then you will be like a fresh batch of dough made without yeast, which is what you really are. Christ, our Passover Lamb, has been sacrificed for us.* ⁸ So let us celebrate the festival, not with the old bread* of wickedness and evil, but with the new bread* of sincerity and truth.

⁹ When I wrote to you before, I told you not to associate with people who indulge in sexual sin. ¹⁰ But I wasn't talking about unbelievers who indulge in sexual sin, or are greedy, or cheat people, or worship idols. You would have to leave this world to avoid people like that. ¹¹ I meant that you are not to associate with anyone who claims to be a believer* yet indulges in sexual sin, or is greedy, or worships idols, or is abusive, or is a drunkard, or cheats people. Don't even eat with such people.

¹² It isn't my responsibility to judge outsiders, but it certainly is your responsibility to judge those inside the church who are sinning. ¹³ God will judge those on the outside; but as the Scriptures say, "You must remove the evil person from among you."*

AVOIDING LAWSUITS WITH CHRISTIANS

6 When one of you has a dispute with another believer, how dare you file a lawsuit and ask a secular court to decide the matter instead of taking it to other believers*! ² Don't you realize that someday we believers will judge the world? And since you are going to judge the world, can't you decide even these little things among yourselves? ³ Don't you realize that we will judge angels? So you should surely be able to resolve ordinary disputes in this life. ⁴ If you have legal disputes about such matters, why go to outside judges who are not respected by the church? ⁵ I am saying this to shame you. Isn't there anyone in all the church who is wise enough to decide these issues? ⁶ But instead, one believer* sues another—right in front of unbelievers!

⁷ Even to have such lawsuits with one another is a defeat for you. Why not just accept the injustice and leave it at that? Why not let yourselves be cheated? ⁸ Instead, you yourselves are the ones who do wrong and cheat even your fellow believers.*

⁹ Don't you realize that those who do wrong will not inherit the Kingdom of God? Don't fool yourselves. Those who indulge in sexual sin, or who worship idols, or commit adultery, or are male prostitutes, or practice homosexuality, ¹⁰ or

---

RESISTING THE WORLD'S SPIRIT
1 Corinthians 5:1-8   JACK HAYFORD

In 1 Corinthians 5, Paul establishes that sin is serious and must be addressed. The Corinthians have a misguided sense of mercy, and the form of sexual immorality permitted in their church is one that even the surrounding pagan culture rejects. Grace is available to deliver us, but it is not intended to enable careless living and sinful accommodation to the spirit of the world.

Paul's point is clear: every believer is to engage in holy living. Rooting out the spirit of this world from our hearts, homes, jobs, and other relationships is necessary for disciples of Jesus Christ. The world's spirit confuses us with compromised choices and destroys authentic spiritual living.

Salvation is not just "fire insurance" to save us from hell. Instead, it's an invitation to sanctification—to purify our lives. Jesus died to grant us a rich and abundant life, and now we must contend for it.

5:1 Greek *his father's wife.* 5:3 Or *in spirit.* 5:4 Or *In the name of the Lord Jesus, you must call a meeting of the church.* 5:5a Or *so that his body will be destroyed;* Greek reads *for the destruction of the flesh.* 5:5b Greek *and the spirit.* 5:5c Other manuscripts read *the Lord Jesus;* still others read *our Lord Jesus Christ.* 5:7 Greek *has been sacrificed.* 5:8a Greek *not with old leaven.* 5:8b Greek *but with unleavened [bread].* 5:11 Greek *a brother.* 5:13 Deut 17:7. 6:1 Greek *God's holy people;* also in 6:2. 6:6 Greek *one brother.* 6:8 Greek *even the brothers.*

GLORIFY GOD IN YOUR BODY
1 Corinthians 6:12-20   ROBERT MORRIS

The way you care for your body is similar to the way you manage your bank account. When you steward your finances well and tithe regularly, you glorify God. You also glorify Him when you honor your body as the temple of the Holy Spirit through healthy eating and regular exercise.

The Bible says gluttony is a sin (Ezekiel 16:49). Contrary to what you may think, however, gluttony is not a weight issue. It's a thought issue—it's the way we *think* about food. We should not allow food or anything else in this world to have power over us. Self-control is part of the fruit of the Spirit that should be evident in every believer's life (Galatians 5:22-23). God wants the appetites of our flesh to be under the control of His Spirit. He asks each of us to make a conscious choice to give Him our bodies and to care for them well.

TAKING CARE OF THE TEMPLE
1 Corinthians 6:18-20   ROBERT MORRIS

Are there things you don't like about your body? I think almost every person has something they'd like to change. Growing up, I was ashamed of my body because I was very skinny, and I really wanted to be big and strong. Even after I became a believer (and wasn't quite so skinny anymore), I still didn't appreciate my body. I knew it was "the temple of the Holy Spirit" (1 Corinthians 6:19), but it took a near-death experience in 2013 for me to realize that my negative thoughts about my body had opened a door for the enemy to attack me.

Are you taking care of your temple "as Christ cares for the church" (Ephesians 5:29)? If you aren't, the Holy Spirit's expression through you will be limited, and you won't be able to accomplish all God wants you to accomplish. There were several times in my life when I could have died because I wasn't taking care of my body. However, I don't want to leave this earth prematurely and miss fulfilling God's purpose for me. I know He has a purpose for you too. No matter how you've felt about your body in the past, decide today to take care of your temple and begin thanking God as King David did:

> "Thank you for making me so
> wonderfully complex!
> Your workmanship is marvelous—how
> well I know it" (Psalm 139:14).

are thieves, or greedy people, or drunkards, or are abusive, or cheat people—none of these will inherit the Kingdom of God. ¹¹Some of you were once like that. But you were cleansed; you were made holy; you were made right with God by calling on the name of the Lord Jesus Christ and by the Spirit of our God.

AVOIDING SEXUAL SIN

¹²You say, "I am allowed to do anything"—but not everything is good for you. And even though "I am allowed to do anything," I must not become a slave to anything. ¹³You say, "Food was made for the stomach, and the stomach for food." (This is true, though someday God will do away with both of them.) But you can't say that our bodies were made for sexual immorality. They were made for the Lord, and the Lord cares about our bodies. ¹⁴And God will raise us from the dead by his power, just as he raised our Lord from the dead.

¹⁵Don't you realize that your bodies are actually parts of Christ? Should a man take his body, which is part of Christ, and join it to a prostitute? Never! ¹⁶And don't you realize that if a man joins himself to a prostitute, he becomes one body with her? For the Scriptures say, "The two are united into one."* ¹⁷But the person who is joined to the Lord is one spirit with him.

¹⁸Run from sexual sin! No other sin so clearly affects the body as this one does. For sexual immorality is a sin against your own body. ¹⁹Don't you realize that your body is the temple of the Holy Spirit, who lives in you and was given to you by God? You do not belong to yourself, ²⁰for God bought you with a high price. So you must honor God with your body.

INSTRUCTION ON MARRIAGE

7 Now regarding the questions you asked in your letter. Yes, it is good to abstain from sexual relations.* ²But because there is so much sexual immorality, each man should have his own wife, and each woman should have her own husband.

³The husband should fulfill his wife's sexual needs, and the wife should fulfill her husband's needs. ⁴The wife gives authority over her body to her husband, and the husband gives authority over his body to his wife. ⁵Do not deprive each other of sexual relations, unless you both agree to refrain from sexual intimacy for a limited time so you can give yourselves more completely to prayer. Afterward, you should come together again so that Satan won't be able to tempt you because of your lack of self-control. ⁶I say this as a concession, not as a command. ⁷But I wish everyone were single, just as I am. Yet each person has a special gift from God, of one kind or another.

6:16 Gen 2:24.   **7:1** Or *to live a celibate life;* Greek reads *It is good for a man not to touch a woman.*

8 So I say to those who aren't married and to widows—it's better to stay unmarried, just as I am. 9 But if they can't control themselves, they should go ahead and marry. It's better to marry than to burn with lust.

10 But for those who are married, I have a command that comes not from me, but from the Lord.* A wife must not leave her husband. 11 But if she does leave him, let her remain single or else be reconciled to him. And the husband must not leave his wife.

12 Now, I will speak to the rest of you, though I do not have a direct command from the Lord. If a fellow believer* has a wife who is not a believer and she is willing to continue living with him, he must not leave her. 13 And if a believing woman has a husband who is not a believer and he is willing to continue living with her, she must not leave him. 14 For the believing wife brings holiness to her marriage, and the believing husband* brings holiness to his marriage. Otherwise, your children would not be holy, but now they are holy. 15 (But if the husband or wife who isn't a believer insists on leaving, let them go. In such cases the believing husband or wife* is no longer bound to the other, for God has called you* to live in peace.) 16 Don't you wives realize that your husbands might be saved because of you? And don't you husbands realize that your wives might be saved because of you?

17 Each of you should continue to live in whatever situation the Lord has placed you, and remain as you were when God first called you. This is my rule for all the churches. 18 For instance, a man who was circumcised before he became a believer should not try to reverse it. And the man who was uncircumcised when he became a believer should not be circumcised now. 19 For it makes no difference whether or not a man has been circumcised. The important thing is to keep God's commandments.

20 Yes, each of you should remain as you were when God called you. 21 Are you a slave? Don't let that worry you—but if you get a chance to be free, take it. 22 And remember, if you were a slave when the Lord called you, you are now free in the Lord. And if you were free when the Lord called you, you are now a slave of Christ. 23 God paid a high price for you, so don't be enslaved by the world.* 24 Each of you, dear brothers and sisters,* should remain as you were when God first called you.

25 Now regarding your question about the young women who are not yet married. I do not have a command from the Lord for them. But the Lord in his mercy has given me wisdom that can be trusted, and I will share it with you. 26 Because of the present crisis,* I think it is best to remain as you are. 27 If you have a wife, do not seek to end the marriage. If you do not have a wife, do not seek to get married. 28 But if you do get married, it is not a sin. And if a young woman gets married, it is not a sin. However, those who get married at this time will have troubles, and I am trying to spare you those problems.

29 But let me say this, dear brothers and sisters: The time that remains is very short. So from now on, those with wives should not focus only on their marriage. 30 Those who weep or who rejoice or who buy things should not be absorbed by their weeping or their joy or their possessions. 31 Those who use the things of the world should not become attached to them. For this world as we know it will soon pass away.

32 I want you to be free from the concerns of this life. An unmarried man can spend his time doing the Lord's work and thinking how to please him. 33 But a married man has to think about his earthly responsibilities and how to please his wife. 34 His interests are divided. In the same way, a woman who is no longer married or has never been married can be devoted to the Lord and holy in body and in spirit. But a married woman has to think about her earthly responsibilities and how to please her husband. 35 I am saying this for your benefit, not to place restrictions on you. I want you to do whatever will help you serve the Lord best, with as few distractions as possible.

36 But if a man thinks that he's treating his fiancée improperly and will inevitably give in to his passion, let him marry her as he wishes. It is not a sin. 37 But if he has decided firmly not to marry and there is no urgency and he can control his passion, he does well not to marry. 38 So the person who marries his fiancée does well, and the person who doesn't marry does even better.

39 A wife is bound to her husband as long as he lives. If her husband dies, she is free to marry anyone she wishes, but only if he loves the Lord.* 40 But in my opinion it would be better for her to stay single, and I think I am giving you counsel from God's Spirit when I say this.

FOOD SACRIFICED TO IDOLS

8 Now regarding your question about food that has been offered to idols. Yes, we know that "we all have knowledge" about this issue. But while knowledge makes us feel important, it is love that strengthens the church. 2 Anyone who claims to know all the answers doesn't really know very much. 3 But the person who loves God is the one whom God recognizes.*

4 So, what about eating meat that has been offered to idols? Well, we all know that an idol is not really a god and that there is only one God. 5 There may be so-called gods both in heaven and on earth, and some people actually worship many gods and many lords. 6 But for us,

7:10 See Matt 5:32; 19:9; Mark 10:11-12; Luke 16:18.   7:12 Greek a brother.   7:14 Greek the brother.   7:15a Greek the brother or sister.   7:15b Some manuscripts read us.   7:23 Greek don't become slaves of people.   7:24 Greek brothers; also in 7:29.   7:26 Or the pressures of life.   7:39 Greek but only in the Lord.   8:3 Some manuscripts read the person who loves has full knowledge.

There is one God, the Father,
by whom all things were created,
and for whom we live.
And there is one Lord, Jesus Christ,
through whom all things were created,
and through whom we live.

[7] However, not all believers know this. Some are accustomed to thinking of idols as being real, so when they eat food that has been offered to idols, they think of it as the worship of real gods, and their weak consciences are violated. [8] It's true that we can't win God's approval by what we eat. We don't lose anything if we don't eat it, and we don't gain anything if we do.

[9] But you must be careful so that your freedom does not cause others with a weaker conscience to stumble. [10] For if others see you—with your "superior knowledge"—eating in the temple of an idol, won't they be encouraged to violate their conscience by eating food that has been offered to an idol? [11] So because of your superior knowledge, a weak believer* for whom Christ died will be destroyed. [12] And when you sin against other believers* by encouraging them to do something they believe is wrong, you are sinning against Christ. [13] So if what I eat causes another believer to sin, I will never eat meat again as long as I live—for I don't want to cause another believer to stumble.

PAUL GIVES UP HIS RIGHTS

9 Am I not as free as anyone else? Am I not an apostle? Haven't I seen Jesus our Lord with my own eyes? Isn't it because of my work that you belong to the Lord? [2] Even if others think I am not an apostle, I certainly am to you. You yourselves are proof that I am the Lord's apostle.

[3] This is my answer to those who question my authority.* [4] Don't we have the right to live in your homes and share your meals? [5] Don't we have the right to bring a believing wife* with us as the other apostles and the Lord's brothers do, and as Peter* does? [6] Or is it only Barnabas and I who have to work to support ourselves?

[7] What soldier has to pay his own expenses? What farmer plants a vineyard and doesn't have the right to eat some of its fruit? What shepherd cares for a flock of sheep and isn't allowed to drink some of the milk? [8] Am I expressing merely a human opinion, or does the law say the same thing? [9] For the law of Moses says, "You must not muzzle an ox to keep it from eating as it treads out the grain."* Was God thinking only about oxen when he said this? [10] Wasn't he actually speaking to us? Yes, it was written for us, so that the one who plows and the one who threshes the grain might both expect a share of the harvest.

[11] Since we have planted spiritual seed among you, aren't we entitled to a harvest of physical food and drink? [12] If you support others who preach to you, shouldn't we have an even greater

right to be supported? But we have never used this right. We would rather put up with anything than be an obstacle to the Good News about Christ.

[13] Don't you realize that those who work in the temple get their meals from the offerings brought to the temple? And those who serve at the altar get a share of the sacrificial offerings. [14] In the same way, the Lord ordered that those who preach the Good News should be supported by those who benefit from it. [15] Yet I have never used any of these rights. And I am not writing this to suggest that I want to start now. In fact, I would rather die than lose my right to boast about preaching without charge. [16] Yet preaching the Good News is not something I can boast about. I am compelled by God to do it. How terrible for me if I didn't preach the Good News!

[17] If I were doing this on my own initiative, I would deserve payment. But I have no choice, for God has given me this sacred trust. [18] What then is my pay? It is the opportunity to preach the Good News without charging anyone. That's why I never demand my rights when I preach the Good News.

[19] Even though I am a free man with no master, I have become a slave to all people to bring many to Christ. [20] When I was with the Jews, I lived like a Jew to bring the Jews to Christ. When I was with those who follow the Jewish law, I too lived under that law. Even though I am not subject to the law, I did this so I could bring to Christ those who are under the law. [21] When I am with the Gentiles who do not follow the Jewish law,* I too live apart from that law so I can bring them to Christ. But I do not ignore the law of God; I obey the law of Christ.

[22] When I am with those who are weak, I share their weakness, for I want to bring the weak to Christ. Yes, I try to find common ground with everyone, doing everything I can to save some. [23] I do everything to spread the Good News and share in its blessings.

[24] Don't you realize that in a race everyone runs, but only one person gets the prize? So run to win! [25] All athletes are disciplined in their training. They do it to win a prize that will fade away, but we do it for an eternal prize. [26] So I run with purpose in every step. I am not just shadowboxing. [27] I discipline my body like an athlete, training it to do what it should. Otherwise, I fear that after preaching to others I myself might be disqualified.

LESSONS FROM ISRAEL'S IDOLATRY

10 I don't want you to forget, dear brothers and sisters,* about our ancestors in the wilderness long ago. All of them were guided

---

8:11 Greek *brother;* also in 8:13.   8:12 Greek *brothers.*   9:3 Greek *those who examine me.*   9:5a Greek *a sister a wife.*   9:5b Greek *Cephas.*   9:9 Deut 25:4.   9:21 Greek *those without the law.*
10:1 Greek *brothers.*

HYDRATE YOUR SPIRIT
1 Corinthians 10:3-4   ROBERT MORRIS

In addition to the bread of heaven, the Word of God is also the water of life. Writing about the people of Israel, the apostle Paul says, "All of them drank the same spiritual water. For they drank from the spiritual rock that traveled with them, and that rock was Christ" (1 Corinthians 10:4).

Jesus is the rock, and the water is God's Word. There is something about reading Scripture that hydrates your spirit. Psalm 1:2-3 says that people who constantly meditate on God's Word are like fruit-bearing trees. Think about the fruit of the Spirit: love, joy, peace, patience, kindness, goodness, faithfulness, gentleness, and self-control (Galatians 5:22-23). Meditating on the Word of God will bring forth this *spiritual* fruit in your life and cause you to prosper.

What are some habits you can change in order to make reading God's Word a part of your daily life?

TEMPTATION
1 Corinthians 10:6-14   MARCUS BRECHEEN

A *temptation* is a promise that doesn't come from God and is, therefore, a lie. Temptations stem from idolatry in our lives—any areas of our hearts in which we love something else more than we love God (James 1:13-15).

There are several common temptations every person faces. Any type of sexual immorality is idolatry because we're placing our desires above what God says is best for us. We are also tempted to "put Christ to the test" when we believe what God has done for us is not good enough (1 Corinthians 10:9). And when we see someone else receive what we want, we are tempted to complain as we disregard the promises of God.

When temptation comes, our flesh wants to indulge in the pleasure of sin. Our only way to escape is to choose, through a conscious act of our wills, to believe what God has for us is better than sin and its consequences.

[6] These things happened as a warning to us, so that we would not crave evil things as they did, [7] or worship idols as some of them did. As the Scriptures say, "The people celebrated with feasting and drinking, and they indulged in pagan revelry."* [8] And we must not engage in sexual immorality as some of them did, causing 23,000 of them to die in one day.

[9] Nor should we put Christ* to the test, as some of them did and then died from snakebites. [10] And don't grumble as some of them did, and then were destroyed by the angel of death. [11] These things happened to them as examples for us. They were written down to warn us who live at the end of the age.

[12] If you think you are standing strong, be careful not to fall. [13] The temptations in your life are no different from what others experience. And God is faithful. He will not allow the temptation to be more than you can stand. When you are tempted, he will show you a way out so that you can endure.

[14] So, my dear friends, flee from the worship of idols. [15] You are reasonable people. Decide for yourselves if what I am saying is true. [16] When we bless the cup at the Lord's Table, aren't we sharing in the blood of Christ? And when we break the bread, aren't we sharing in the body of Christ? [17] And though we are many, we all eat from one loaf of bread, showing that we are one body. [18] Think about the people of Israel. Weren't they united by eating the sacrifices at the altar? [19] What am I trying to say? Am I saying that food offered to idols has some significance, or that idols are real gods? [20] No, not at all. I am saying that these sacrifices are offered to demons, not to God. And I don't want you to participate with demons. [21] You cannot drink from the cup of the Lord and from the cup of demons, too. You cannot eat at the Lord's Table and at the table of demons, too. [22] What? Do we dare to rouse the Lord's jealousy? Do you think we are stronger than he is?

[23] You say, "I am allowed to do anything"*—but not everything is good for you. You say, "I am allowed to do anything"—but not everything is beneficial. [24] Don't be concerned for your own good but for the good of others.

[25] So you may eat any meat that is sold in the marketplace without raising questions of conscience. [26] For "the earth is the LORD's, and everything in it."*

[27] If someone who isn't a believer asks you home for dinner, accept the invitation if you want to. Eat whatever is offered to you without raising questions of conscience. [28] (But suppose someone tells you, "This meat was offered to an idol." Don't eat it, out of consideration for the conscience of the one who told you. [29] It might

by a cloud that moved ahead of them, and all of them walked through the sea on dry ground. [2] In the cloud and in the sea, all of them were baptized as followers of Moses. [3] All of them ate the same spiritual food, [4] and all of them drank the same spiritual water. For they drank from the spiritual rock that traveled with them, and that rock was Christ. [5] Yet God was not pleased with most of them, and their bodies were scattered in the wilderness.

10:7 Exod 32:6.   10:9 Some manuscripts read *the Lord.*
10:23 Greek *All things are lawful;* also in 10:23b.   10:26 Ps 24:1.

not be a matter of conscience for you, but it is for the other person.) For why should my freedom be limited by what someone else thinks? ³⁰ If I can thank God for the food and enjoy it, why should I be condemned for eating it?

³¹ So whether you eat or drink, or whatever you do, do it all for the glory of God. ³² Don't give offense to Jews or Gentiles* or the church of God. ³³ I, too, try to please everyone in everything I do. I don't just do what is best for me; I do what is best for others so that many may be saved. ¹¹:¹ And you should imitate me, just as I imitate Christ.

INSTRUCTIONS FOR PUBLIC WORSHIP

11 ² I am so glad that you always keep me in your thoughts, and that you are following the teachings I passed on to you. ³ But there is one thing I want you to know: The head of every man is Christ, the head of woman is man, and the head of Christ is God.* ⁴ A man dishonors his head* if he covers his head while praying or prophesying. ⁵ But a woman dishonors her head* if she prays or prophesies without a covering on her head, for this is the same as shaving her head. ⁶ Yes, if she refuses to wear a head covering, she should cut off all her hair! But since it is shameful for a woman to have her hair cut or her head shaved, she should wear a covering.*

⁷ A man should not wear anything on his head when worshiping, for man is made in God's image and reflects God's glory. And woman reflects man's glory. ⁸ For the first man didn't come from woman, but the first woman came from man. ⁹ And man was not made for woman, but woman was made for man. ¹⁰ For this reason, and because the angels are watching, a woman should wear a covering on her head to show she is under authority.*

¹¹ But among the Lord's people, women are not independent of men, and men are not independent of women. ¹² For although the first woman came from man, every other man was born from a woman, and everything comes from God.

¹³ Judge for yourselves. Is it right for a woman to pray to God in public without covering her head? ¹⁴ Isn't it obvious that it's disgraceful for a man to have long hair? ¹⁵ And isn't long hair a woman's pride and joy? For it has been given to her as a covering. ¹⁶ But if anyone wants to argue about this, I simply say that we have no other custom than this, and neither do God's other churches.

ORDER AT THE LORD'S SUPPER

¹⁷ But in the following instructions, I cannot praise you. For it sounds as if more harm than good is done when you meet together. ¹⁸ First, I hear that there are divisions among you when you meet as a church, and to some extent I believe it. ¹⁹ But, of course, there must be divisions among you so that you who have God's approval will be recognized!

²⁰ When you meet together, you are not really interested in the Lord's Supper. ²¹ For some of you hurry to eat your own meal without sharing with others. As a result, some go hungry while others get drunk. ²² What? Don't you have your own homes for eating and drinking? Or do you really want to disgrace God's church and shame the poor? What am I supposed to say? Do you want me to praise you? Well, I certainly will not praise you for this!

²³ For I pass on to you what I received from the Lord himself. On the night when he was betrayed, the Lord Jesus took some bread ²⁴ and gave thanks to God for it. Then he broke it in pieces and said, "This is my body, which is given for you.* Do this in remembrance of me." ²⁵ In the same way, he took the cup of wine after supper, saying, "This cup is the new covenant between God and his people—an agreement confirmed with my blood. Do this in remembrance of me as often as you drink it." ²⁶ For every time you eat this bread and drink this cup, you are announcing the Lord's death until he comes again.

²⁷ So anyone who eats this bread or drinks this cup of the Lord unworthily is guilty of sinning against* the body and blood of the Lord. ²⁸ That is why you should examine yourself before eating the bread and drinking the cup. ²⁹ For if you eat the bread or drink the cup without honoring the body of Christ,* you are eating and drinking God's judgment upon yourself. ³⁰ That is why many of you are weak and sick and some have even died. ³¹ But if we would examine ourselves, we would not be judged by God in this way. ³² Yet when we are judged by the Lord, we are being disciplined so that we will not be condemned along with the world.

³³ So, my dear brothers and sisters,* when you gather for the Lord's Supper, wait for each other. ³⁴ If you are really hungry, eat at home so you won't bring judgment upon yourselves when you meet together. I'll give you instructions about the other matters after I arrive.

SPIRITUAL GIFTS

12 Now, dear brothers and sisters,* regarding your question about the special abilities the Spirit gives us. I don't want you to misunderstand this. ² You know that when you were still pagans, you were led astray and swept along in worshiping speechless idols. ³ So I want you to know that no one speaking by the Spirit of God will curse Jesus, and no one can say Jesus is Lord, except by the Holy Spirit.

10:32 Greek or Greeks. 11:3 Or to know: The source of every man is Christ, the source of woman is man, and the source of Christ is God. Or to know: Every man is responsible to Christ, a woman is responsible to her husband, and Christ is responsible to God. 11:4 Or dishonors Christ. 11:5 Or dishonors her husband. 11:6 Or should have long hair. 11:10 Greek should have an authority on her head. 11:24 Greek which is for you; other manuscripts read which is broken for you. 11:27 Or is responsible for. 11:29 Greek the body; other manuscripts read the Lord's body. 11:33 Greek brothers. 12:1 Greek brothers.

THE FATHER IS OMNI
1 Corinthians 10:12-13 ROBERT MORRIS

Understanding who God is will change your life. The word *omni* means 'all,' and the only person this word truly applies to is God. He isn't just powerful—He has *all* power. He isn't just wise—He has *all* knowledge. And He isn't just present with a few special pastors or teachers—He's present with *all* people.

1. The Father is omnipotent.

Potent means 'powerful,' and *omnipotent* means 'all-powerful.' God has all power and all ability to perform all of His decrees. Yes, God is good, but if He weren't also all-powerful, then He couldn't effectively act on His goodness. God has supreme and absolute power, which means He has the right and the ability to act. Because God is omnipotent, we can have peace even when there is chaos around us. We can overcome sin (1 Corinthians 10:13), sickness (Romans 8:11), and Satan (1 John 4:4).

2. The Father is omniscient.

The suffix of this word has the same root as *science*—meaning "knowledge." God is all-knowing. He knows everything actual and everything possible, including all events and creatures, past, present, and future. Nothing has ever "occurred" to God. He can't learn anything because He already knows everything and He cannot change—He is *immutable*. God is never bewildered or confused; He never has to figure something out. Nothing can ever happen to you that God did not already know, plan, or provide. Our knowledge can never compare to His (see Job 38).

3. The Father is omnipresent.

God is all-present; He is in all places at all times. If there were any place that He could not go, then He would have limits. However, God has no limits because He is infinite (Psalm 139:7-12). He doesn't travel because He is already everywhere. No matter where you go or what you walk through, God is with you at all times.

MY COMMITTED CALLING
1 Corinthians 12:1-31 ROBERT MORRIS

Every believer is called to ministry. Now I'm not saying every person is meant to be a pastor or missionary—those are *vocational* ministry callings. But every believer has been given a gift to use for the Kingdom of God.

As a pastor, I can't win everyone to Jesus, but together, *we* can. Most of the great people in the Bible were not in vocational ministry. Instead, they were farmers, shepherds, fishermen, government employees, etc. They had ordinary jobs, but they still did great things for God. You can do great things for God too. Here are three steps to find your committed calling:

1. Draw near to God (Psalm 73:28).

Sometimes we don't feel like "drawing near," especially if we've had a bad day or even a bad life. However, we *can* draw near because we come by grace (Hebrews 7:19; 10:22). You may think, *I just can't seem to stop this particular sin.* In Mark 5, a man was full of demons, but they couldn't stop him from running to Jesus. Whether you're in bondage, depression, or have been away from God for a long time, it's *always* a good time to draw near to God. You're never going to discover and minister in the calling God has for you without drawing near to Him.

2. Discover and develop your gifts (1 Corinthians 12).

We're all members of the body of Christ, and every member is important. You may see another believer and think, *I wish I had his gift*, but 1 Corinthians 12:18 says, "God has put each part just where he wants it." God has given every person specific gifts. It's our responsibility to discover and develop our gifts and use them for the Kingdom of God (Romans 12:4-6).

3. Just do something.

You might not start off doing what you think you're called to do, and you may not start at the top. Just start somewhere. I knew I was called to preach, but I spent years developing my gift before Gateway Church ever existed. Whatever you hear God telling you to do, start developing your gift today.

[4] There are different kinds of spiritual gifts, but the same Spirit is the source of them all. [5] There are different kinds of service, but we serve the same Lord. [6] God works in different ways, but it is the same God who does the work in all of us.

[7] A spiritual gift is given to each of us so we can help each other. [8] To one person the Spirit gives the ability to give wise advice*; to another the same Spirit gives a message of special knowledge.* [9] The same Spirit gives great faith to another, and to someone else the one Spirit gives the gift of healing. [10] He gives one person the power to perform miracles, and another the ability to prophesy. He gives someone else the ability to discern whether a message is from the Spirit of God or from another spirit. Still another person is given the ability to speak in unknown languages,* while another is given the ability to interpret what is being said. [11] It is the one and only Spirit who distributes all these gifts. He alone decides which gift each person should have.

12:8a Or *gives a word of wisdom.* 12:8b Or *gives a word of knowledge.* 12:10 Or *in various tongues;* also in 12:28, 30.

IS THE HOLY SPIRIT CHARISMATIC?
1 Corinthians 12:7-11　　　ROBERT MORRIS

The word *charismatic* comes from the Greek word *charisma*, which means 'grace gift.' Charisma is the instantaneous enablement of the Holy Spirit in the life of any believer to exercise a gift for the edification of others. According to Scripture, if you have a gift given to you by God's grace, you are charismatic.

The apostle Paul writes about nine manifestational gifts in 1 Corinthians 12:7-11. These gifts are divided into three categories. The discerning gifts include a word of knowledge, a word of wisdom, and discerning of spirits. The declarative gifts include prophecy, tongues, and interpretation of tongues. The dynamic gifts include faith, gifts of healings, and working of miracles.

No one "has" any of these gifts. Instead, they are given to each person as the Holy Spirit desires. Any believer can minister in any of these gifts as the Holy Spirit empowers them to do so.

DOES THE HOLY SPIRIT BAPTIZE?
1 Corinthians 12:13　　　ROBERT MORRIS

Just as the Trinity is one God in three persons, there are also three distinct forms of baptism:
1. The Holy Spirit baptizes us in Jesus when we receive salvation.
The Holy Spirit comes to live inside us, and we become part of the body of Christ.
2. A fellow believer (disciple) baptizes us in water.
Water baptism is when our old, sinful selves are cut off.
3. Jesus baptizes us in the Holy Spirit.
When we receive this baptism, we are empowered to walk in our new lives in Christ.

Many believers live defeated lives because they only experience the first two baptisms, but all three steps are essential to living a victorious Christian life.

ONE BODY WITH MANY PARTS

[12] The human body has many parts, but the many parts make up one whole body. So it is with the body of Christ. [13] Some of us are Jews, some are Gentiles,* some are slaves, and some are free. But we have all been baptized into one body by one Spirit, and we all share the same Spirit.* [14] Yes, the body has many different parts, not just one part. [15] If the foot says, "I am not a part of the body because I am not a hand," that does not make it any less a part of the body. [16] And if the ear says, "I am not part of the body because I am not an eye," would that make it any less a part of the body? [17] If the whole body were an eye, how would you hear? Or if your whole body were an ear, how would you smell anything?

[18] But our bodies have many parts, and God has put each part just where he wants it. [19] How strange a body would be if it had only one part! [20] Yes, there are many parts, but only one body. [21] The eye can never say to the hand, "I don't need you." The head can't say to the feet, "I don't need you."

[22] In fact, some parts of the body that seem weakest and least important are actually the most necessary. [23] And the parts we regard as less honorable are those we clothe with the greatest care. So we carefully protect those parts that should not be seen, [24] while the more honorable parts do not require this special care. So God has put the body together such that extra honor and care are given to those parts that have less dignity. [25] This makes for harmony among the members, so that all the members care for each other. [26] If one part suffers, all the parts suffer with it, and if one part is honored, all the parts are glad.

[27] All of you together are Christ's body, and each of you is a part of it. [28] Here are some of the parts God has appointed for the church:

first are apostles,
second are prophets,
third are teachers,
then those who do miracles,
those who have the gift of healing,
those who can help others,
those who have the gift of leadership,
those who speak in unknown languages.

[29] Are we all apostles? Are we all prophets? Are we all teachers? Do we all have the power to do miracles? [30] Do we all have the gift of healing? Do we all have the ability to speak in unknown languages? Do we all have the ability to interpret unknown languages? Of course not! [31] So you should earnestly desire the most helpful gifts.

But now let me show you a way of life that is best of all.

LOVE IS THE GREATEST

13 If I could speak all the languages of earth and of angels, but didn't love others, I would only be a noisy gong or a clanging cymbal. [2] If I had the gift of prophecy, and if I understood all of God's secret plans and possessed all knowledge, and if I had such faith that I could move mountains, but didn't love others, I would be nothing. [3] If I gave everything I have to the poor and even sacrificed my body, I could boast about it;* but if I didn't love others, I would have gained nothing.

12:13a Greek *some are Greeks.*　**12:13b** Greek *we were all given one Spirit to drink.*　**13:3** Some manuscripts read *sacrificed my body to be burned.*

[4] Love is patient and kind. Love is not jealous or boastful or proud [5] or rude. It does not demand its own way. It is not irritable, and it keeps no record of being wronged. [6] It does not rejoice about injustice but rejoices whenever the truth wins out. [7] Love never gives up, never loses faith, is always hopeful, and endures through every circumstance.

[8] Prophecy and speaking in unknown languages* and special knowledge will become useless. But love will last forever! [9] Now our knowledge is partial and incomplete, and even the gift of prophecy reveals only part of the whole picture! [10] But when the time of perfection comes, these partial things will become useless.

[11] When I was a child, I spoke and thought and reasoned as a child. But when I grew up, I put away childish things. [12] Now we see things imperfectly, like puzzling reflections in a mirror, but then we will see everything with perfect clarity.* All that I know now is partial and incomplete, but then I will know everything completely, just as God now knows me completely.

[13] Three things will last forever—faith, hope, and love—and the greatest of these is love.

TONGUES AND PROPHECY

14 Let love be your highest goal! But you should also desire the special abilities the Spirit gives—especially the ability to prophesy. [2] For if you have the ability to speak in tongues,* you will be talking only to God, since people won't be able to understand you. You will be speaking by the power of the Spirit,* but it will all be mysterious. [3] But one who prophesies strengthens others, encourages them, and comforts them. [4] A person who speaks in tongues is strengthened personally, but one who speaks a word of prophecy strengthens the entire church.

[5] I wish you could all speak in tongues, but even more I wish you could all prophesy. For prophecy is greater than speaking in tongues, unless someone interprets what you are saying so that the whole church will be strengthened.

[6] Dear brothers and sisters,* if I should come to you speaking in an unknown language,* how would that help you? But if I bring you a revelation or some special knowledge or prophecy or teaching, that will be helpful. [7] Even lifeless instruments like the flute or the harp must play the notes clearly, or no one will recognize the melody. [8] And if the bugler doesn't sound a clear call, how will the soldiers know they are being called to battle?

[9] It's the same for you. If you speak to people in words they don't understand, how will they know what you are saying? You might as well be talking into empty space.

[10] There are many different languages in the world, and every language has meaning. [11] But if I don't understand a language, I will be a foreigner to someone who speaks it, and the one who speaks it will be a foreigner to me. [12] And the same is true for you. Since you are so eager to have the special abilities the Spirit gives, seek those that will strengthen the whole church.

[13] So anyone who speaks in tongues should pray also for the ability to interpret what has been said. [14] For if I pray in tongues, my spirit is praying, but I don't understand what I am saying.

[15] Well then, what shall I do? I will pray in the spirit,* and I will also pray in words I understand. I will sing in the spirit, and I will also sing in words I understand. [16] For if you praise God only in the spirit, how can those who don't understand you praise God along with you? How can they join you in giving thanks when they don't understand what you are saying? [17] You will be giving thanks very well, but it won't strengthen the people who hear you.

[18] I thank God that I speak in tongues more than any of you. [19] But in a church meeting I would rather speak five understandable words to help others than ten thousand words in an unknown language.

[20] Dear brothers and sisters, don't be childish in your understanding of these things. Be innocent as babies when it comes to evil, but be mature in understanding matters of this kind. [21] It is written in the Scriptures*:

"I will speak to my own people
  through strange languages
  and through the lips of foreigners.

DOES THE HOLY SPIRIT SPEAK IN TONGUES?
1 Corinthians 14:2   ROBERT MORRIS

Speaking in tongues is biblical. The manifestational gift of tongues is a message from God that needs to be interpreted for edification. There is also a grace gift of tongues—a prayer language not from God but *to* God.

Praying in tongues is a choice available to every believer. It is an act of your will that requires faith. When you pray in tongues, your spirit prays even though your mind does not understand what you're saying. The apostle Paul says it is beneficial to pray in the spirit *and* in words you understand (1 Corinthians 14:14-18).

Praying in the spirit is also the final piece of the armor of God (Ephesians 6:18). It will build you up and help you control the most unruly member of your body—your tongue. As believers, we need all the building up we can get!

13:8 Or *in tongues.*   13:12 Greek *see face to face.*   14:2a Or *in unknown languages;* also in 14:4, 5, 13, 14, 18, 22, 26, 27, 28, 39. 14:2b Or *speaking in your spirit.*   14:6a Greek *brothers;* also in 14:20, 26, 39.   14:6b Or *in tongues;* also in 14:19, 23.   14:15 Or *in the Spirit;* also in 14:15b, 16.   14:21a Greek *in the law.*

But even then, they will not listen to me,"* says the LORD.

²²So you see that speaking in tongues is a sign, not for believers, but for unbelievers. Prophecy, however, is for the benefit of believers, not unbelievers. ²³Even so, if unbelievers or people who don't understand these things come into your church meeting and hear everyone speaking in an unknown language, they will think you are crazy. ²⁴But if all of you are prophesying, and unbelievers or people who don't understand these things come into your meeting, they will be convicted of sin and judged by what you say. ²⁵As they listen, their secret thoughts will be exposed, and they will fall to their knees and worship God, declaring, "God is truly here among you."

A CALL TO ORDERLY WORSHIP

²⁶Well, my brothers and sisters, let's summarize. When you meet together, one will sing, another will teach, another will tell some special revelation God has given, one will speak in tongues, and another will interpret what is said. But everything that is done must strengthen all of you.

²⁷No more than two or three should speak in tongues. They must speak one at a time, and someone must interpret what they say. ²⁸But if no one is present who can interpret, they must be silent in your church meeting and speak in tongues to God privately.

²⁹Let two or three people prophesy, and let the others evaluate what is said. ³⁰But if someone is prophesying and another person receives a revelation from the Lord, the one who is speaking must stop. ³¹In this way, all who prophesy will have a turn to speak, one after the other, so that everyone will learn and be encouraged. ³²Remember that people who prophesy are in control of their spirit and can take turns. ³³For God is not a God of disorder but of peace, as in all the meetings of God's holy people.*

³⁴Women should be silent during the church meetings. It is not proper for them to speak. They should be submissive, just as the law says. ³⁵If they have any questions, they should ask their husbands at home, for it is improper for women to speak in church meetings.*

³⁶Or do you think God's word originated with you Corinthians? Are you the only ones to whom it was given? ³⁷If you claim to be a prophet or think you are spiritual, you should recognize that what I am saying is a command from the Lord himself. ³⁸But if you do not recognize this, you yourself will not be recognized.*

³⁹So, my dear brothers and sisters, be eager to prophesy, and don't forbid speaking in tongues. ⁴⁰But be sure that everything is done properly and in order.

THE RESURRECTION OF CHRIST

15 Let me now remind you, dear brothers and sisters,* of the Good News I preached to you before. You welcomed it then, and you still stand firm in it. ²It is this Good News that saves you if you continue to believe the message I told you—unless, of course, you believed something that was never true in the first place.*

³I passed on to you what was most important and what had also been passed on to me. Christ died for our sins, just as the Scriptures said. ⁴He was buried, and he was raised from the dead on the third day, just as the Scriptures said. ⁵He was seen by Peter* and then by the Twelve. ⁶After that, he was seen by more than 500 of his followers* at one time, most of whom are still alive, though some have died. ⁷Then he was seen by James and later by all the apostles. ⁸Last of all, as though I had been born at the wrong time, I also saw him. ⁹For I am the least of all the apostles. In fact, I'm not even worthy to be called an apostle after the way I persecuted God's church.

¹⁰But whatever I am now, it is all because God poured out his special favor on me—and not without results. For I have worked harder than any of the other apostles; yet it was not I but God who was working through me by his grace. ¹¹So it makes no difference whether I preach or they preach, for we all preach the same message you have already believed.

THE RESURRECTION OF THE DEAD

¹²But tell me this—since we preach that Christ rose from the dead, why are some of you saying there will be no resurrection of the dead? ¹³For if there is no resurrection of the dead, then Christ has not been raised either. ¹⁴And if Christ has not been raised, then all our preaching is useless, and your faith is useless. ¹⁵And we apostles would all be lying about God—for we have said that God raised Christ from the grave. But that can't be true if there is no resurrection of the dead. ¹⁶And if there is no resurrection of the dead, then Christ has not been raised. ¹⁷And if Christ has not been raised, then your faith is useless and you are still guilty of your sins. ¹⁸In that case, all who have died believing in Christ are lost! ¹⁹And if our hope in Christ is only for this life, we are more to be pitied than anyone in the world.

²⁰But in fact, Christ has been raised from the dead. He is the first of a great harvest of all who have died.

²¹So you see, just as death came into the world through a man, now the resurrection from the dead has begun through another man. ²²Just as everyone dies because we all belong to Adam,

---

14:21b Isa 28:11-12. 14:33 The phrase *as in all the meetings of God's holy people* could instead be joined to the beginning of 14:34. 14:35 Some manuscripts place verses 34-35 after 14:40. 14:38 Some manuscripts read *If you are ignorant of this, stay in your ignorance.* 15:1 Greek *brothers;* also in 15:31, 50, 58. 15:2 Or *unless you never believed it in the first place.* 15:5 Greek *Cephas.* 15:6 Greek *the brothers.*

everyone who belongs to Christ will be given new life. ²³ But there is an order to this resurrection: Christ was raised as the first of the harvest; then all who belong to Christ will be raised when he comes back.

²⁴ After that the end will come, when he will turn the Kingdom over to God the Father, having destroyed every ruler and authority and power. ²⁵ For Christ must reign until he humbles all his enemies beneath his feet. ²⁶ And the last enemy to be destroyed is death. ²⁷ For the Scriptures say, "God has put all things under his authority."* (Of course, when it says "all things are under his authority," that does not include God himself, who gave Christ his authority.) ²⁸ Then, when all things are under his authority, the Son will put himself under God's authority, so that God, who gave his Son authority over all things, will be utterly supreme over everything everywhere.

²⁹ If the dead will not be raised, what point is there in people being baptized for those who are dead? Why do it unless the dead will someday rise again?

³⁰ And why should we ourselves risk our lives hour by hour? ³¹ For I swear, dear brothers and sisters, that I face death daily. This is as certain as my pride in what Christ Jesus our Lord has done in you. ³² And what value was there in fighting wild beasts—those people of Ephesus*—if there will be no resurrection from the dead? And if there is no resurrection, "Let's feast and drink, for tomorrow we die!"* ³³ Don't be fooled by those who say such things, for "bad company corrupts good character." ³⁴ Think carefully about what is right, and stop sinning. For to your shame I say that some of you don't know God at all.

THE RESURRECTION BODY

³⁵ But someone may ask, "How will the dead be raised? What kind of bodies will they have?" ³⁶ What a foolish question! When you put a seed into the ground, it doesn't grow into a plant unless it dies first. ³⁷ And what you put in the ground is not the plant that will grow, but only a bare seed of wheat or whatever you are planting. ³⁸ Then God gives it the new body he wants it to have. A different plant grows from each kind of seed. ³⁹ Similarly there are different kinds of flesh—one kind for humans, another for animals, another for birds, and another for fish.

⁴⁰ There are also bodies in the heavens and bodies on the earth. The glory of the heavenly bodies is different from the glory of the earthly bodies. ⁴¹ The sun has one kind of glory, while the moon and stars each have another kind. And even the stars differ from each other in their glory.

⁴² It is the same way with the resurrection of the dead. Our earthly bodies are planted in the ground when we die, but they will be raised to live forever. ⁴³ Our bodies are buried in brokenness, but they will be raised in glory. They are buried in weakness, but they will be raised in strength. ⁴⁴ They are buried as natural human bodies, but they will be raised as spiritual bodies. For just as there are natural bodies, there are also spiritual bodies.

⁴⁵ The Scriptures tell us, "The first man, Adam, became a living person."* But the last Adam—that is, Christ—is a life-giving Spirit. ⁴⁶ What comes first is the natural body, then the spiritual body comes later. ⁴⁷ Adam, the first man, was made from the dust of the earth, while Christ, the second man, came from heaven. ⁴⁸ Earthly people are like the earthly man, and heavenly people are like the heavenly man. ⁴⁹ Just as we are now like the earthly man, we will someday be like* the heavenly man.

⁵⁰ What I am saying, dear brothers and sisters, is that our physical bodies cannot inherit the Kingdom of God. These dying bodies cannot inherit what will last forever.

⁵¹ But let me reveal to you a wonderful secret. We will not all die, but we will all be transformed! ⁵² It will happen in a moment, in the blink of an eye, when the last trumpet is blown. For when the trumpet sounds, those who have died will be raised to live forever. And we who are living will also be transformed. ⁵³ For our dying bodies must be transformed into bodies that will never die; our mortal bodies must be transformed into immortal bodies.

⁵⁴ Then, when our dying bodies have been transformed into bodies that will never die,* this Scripture will be fulfilled:

"Death is swallowed up in victory.*
⁵⁵ O death, where is your victory?
O death, where is your sting?*"

⁵⁶ For sin is the sting that results in death, and the law gives sin its power. ⁵⁷ But thank God! He gives us victory over sin and death through our Lord Jesus Christ.

⁵⁸ So, my dear brothers and sisters, be strong and immovable. Always work enthusiastically for the Lord, for you know that nothing you do for the Lord is ever useless.

THE COLLECTION FOR JERUSALEM

16 Now regarding your question about the money being collected for God's people in Jerusalem. You should follow the same procedure I gave to the churches in Galatia. ² On the first day of each week, you should each put aside a portion of the money you have earned. Don't wait until I get there and then try to collect it all at once. ³ When I come, I will write letters of recommendation for the messengers you choose

---

15:27 Ps 8:6.   15:32a Greek *fighting wild beasts in Ephesus.*
15:32b Isa 22:13.   15:45 Gen 2:7.   15:49 Some manuscripts
read *let us be like.*   15:54a Some manuscripts add *and our mortal
bodies have been transformed into immortal bodies.*   15:54b Isa 25:8.
15:55 Hos 13:14 (Greek version).

to deliver your gift to Jerusalem. ⁴And if it seems appropriate for me to go along, they can travel with me.

PAUL'S FINAL INSTRUCTIONS

⁵I am coming to visit you after I have been to Macedonia,* for I am planning to travel through Macedonia. ⁶Perhaps I will stay awhile with you, possibly all winter, and then you can send me on my way to my next destination. ⁷This time I don't want to make just a short visit and then go right on. I want to come and stay awhile, if the Lord will let me. ⁸In the meantime, I will be staying here at Ephesus until the Festival of Pentecost. ⁹There is a wide-open door for a great work here, although many oppose me.

¹⁰When Timothy comes, don't intimidate him. He is doing the Lord's work, just as I am. ¹¹Don't let anyone treat him with contempt. Send him on his way with your blessing when he returns to me. I expect him to come with the other believers.*

¹²Now about our brother Apollos—I urged him to visit you with the other believers, but he was not willing to go right now. He will see you later when he has the opportunity.

¹³Be on guard. Stand firm in the faith. Be courageous.* Be strong. ¹⁴And do everything with love.

¹⁵You know that Stephanas and his household were the first of the harvest of believers in Greece,* and they are spending their lives in service to God's people. I urge you, dear brothers and sisters,* ¹⁶to submit to them and others like them who serve with such devotion. ¹⁷I am very glad that Stephanas, Fortunatus, and Achaicus have come here. They have been providing the help you weren't here to give me. ¹⁸They have been a wonderful encouragement to me, as they have been to you. You must show your appreciation to all who serve so well.

PAUL'S FINAL GREETINGS

¹⁹The churches here in the province of Asia* send greetings in the Lord, as do Aquila and Priscilla* and all the others who gather in their home for church meetings. ²⁰All the brothers and sisters here send greetings to you. Greet each other with a sacred kiss.

²¹HERE IS MY GREETING IN MY OWN HANDWRITING—PAUL.

²²If anyone does not love the Lord, that person is cursed. Our Lord, come!*

²³May the grace of the Lord Jesus be with you. ²⁴My love to all of you in Christ Jesus.*

16:5 *Macedonia* was in the northern region of Greece. 16:11 Greek *with the brothers;* also in 16:12.   16:13 Greek *Be men.* 16:15a Greek *in Achaia,* the southern region of the Greek peninsula.   16:15b Greek *brothers;* also in 16:20.   16:19a *Asia* was a Roman province in what is now western Turkey.   16:19b Greek *Prisca.*   16:22 From Aramaic, *Marana tha.* Some manuscripts read *Maran atha,* "Our Lord has come."   16:24 Some manuscripts add *Amen.*

2 CORINTHIANS

GREETINGS FROM PAUL

1 This letter is from Paul, chosen by the will of God to be an apostle of Christ Jesus, and from our brother Timothy.

I am writing to God's church in Corinth and to all of his holy people throughout Greece.* ² May God our Father and the Lord Jesus Christ give you grace and peace.

GOD OFFERS COMFORT TO ALL

³ All praise to God, the Father of our Lord Jesus Christ. God is our merciful Father and the source of all comfort. ⁴ He comforts us in all our troubles so that we can comfort others. When they are troubled, we will be able to give them the same comfort God has given us. ⁵ For the more we suffer for Christ, the more God will shower us with his comfort through Christ. ⁶ Even when we are weighed down with troubles, it is for your comfort and salvation! For when we ourselves are comforted, we will certainly comfort you. Then you can patiently endure the same things we suffer. ⁷ We are confident that as you share in our sufferings, you will also share in the comfort God gives us.

⁸ We think you ought to know, dear brothers and sisters,* about the trouble we went through in the province of Asia. We were crushed and overwhelmed beyond our ability to endure, and we thought we would never live through it. ⁹ In fact, we expected to die. But as a result, we stopped relying on ourselves and learned to rely only on God, who raises the dead. ¹⁰ And he did rescue us from mortal danger, and he will rescue us again. We have placed our confidence in him, and he will continue to rescue us. ¹¹ And you are helping us by praying for us. Then many people will give thanks because God has graciously answered so many prayers for our safety.

PAUL'S CHANGE OF PLANS

¹² We can say with confidence and a clear conscience that we have lived with a God-given holiness* and sincerity in all our dealings. We have depended on God's grace, not on our own human wisdom. That is how we have conducted ourselves before the world, and especially toward you. ¹³ Our letters have been straightforward, and there is nothing written between the lines and nothing you can't understand. I hope someday you will fully understand us, ¹⁴ even if you don't understand us now. Then on the day when the Lord Jesus* returns, you will be proud of us in the same way we are proud of you.

¹⁵ Since I was so sure of your understanding and trust, I wanted to give you a double blessing by visiting you twice—¹⁶ first on my way to Macedonia and again when I returned from Macedonia.* Then you could send me on my way to Judea.

¹⁷ You may be asking why I changed my plan. Do you think I make my plans carelessly? Do you think I am like people of the world who say "Yes" when they really mean "No"? ¹⁸ As surely as God is faithful, our word to you does not waver between "Yes" and "No." ¹⁹ For Jesus Christ, the Son of God, does not waver between "Yes" and "No." He is the one whom Silas,* Timothy, and I preached to you, and as God's ultimate "Yes," he always does what he says. ²⁰ For all of God's promises have been fulfilled in Christ with a resounding "Yes!" And through Christ, our "Amen" (which means "Yes") ascends to God for his glory.

²¹ It is God who enables us, along with you, to stand firm for Christ. He has commissioned us, ²² and he has identified us as his own by placing the Holy Spirit in our hearts as the first installment that guarantees everything he has promised us.

²³ Now I call upon God as my witness that I am telling the truth. The reason I didn't return to Corinth was to spare you from a severe rebuke. ²⁴ But that does not mean we want to dominate you by telling you how to put your faith into practice. We want to work together with you so you will be full of joy, for it is by your own faith that you stand firm.

2 So I decided that I would not bring you grief with another painful visit. ² For if I cause you grief, who will make me glad? Certainly not someone I have grieved. ³ That is why I wrote to you as I did, so that when I do come, I won't be grieved by the very ones who ought to give me the greatest joy. Surely you all know that my joy comes from your being joyful. ⁴ I wrote that letter in great anguish, with a troubled heart and many tears. I didn't want to grieve you, but I wanted to let you know how much love I have for you.

FORGIVENESS FOR THE SINNER

⁵ I am not overstating it when I say that the man who caused all the trouble hurt all of you more than he hurt me. ⁶ Most of you opposed him, and that was punishment enough. ⁷ Now, however, it is time to forgive and comfort him. Otherwise he may be overcome by discouragement. ⁸ So I urge you now to reaffirm your love for him.

⁹ I wrote to you as I did to test you and see if you would fully comply with my instructions.

1:1 Greek *Achaia*, the southern region of the Greek peninsula. 1:8 Greek *brothers.* 1:12 Some manuscripts read *honesty.* 1:14 Some manuscripts read *our Lord Jesus.* 1:16 *Macedonia* was in the northern region of Greece. 1:19 Greek *Silvanus.*

¹⁰When you forgive this man, I forgive him, too. And when I forgive whatever needs to be forgiven, I do so with Christ's authority for your benefit, ¹¹so that Satan will not outsmart us. For we are familiar with his evil schemes.

¹²When I came to the city of Troas to preach the Good News of Christ, the Lord opened a door of opportunity for me. ¹³But I had no peace of mind because my dear brother Titus hadn't yet arrived with a report from you. So I said good-bye and went on to Macedonia to find him.

MINISTERS OF THE NEW COVENANT

¹⁴But thank God! He has made us his captives and continues to lead us along in Christ's triumphal procession. Now he uses us to spread the knowledge of Christ everywhere, like a sweet perfume. ¹⁵Our lives are a Christ-like fragrance rising up to God. But this fragrance is perceived differently by those who are being saved and by those who are perishing. ¹⁶To those who are perishing, we are a dreadful smell of death and doom. But to those who are being saved, we are a life-giving perfume. And who is adequate for such a task as this?

¹⁷You see, we are not like the many hucksters* who preach for personal profit. We preach the word of God with sincerity and with Christ's authority, knowing that God is watching us.

3 Are we beginning to praise ourselves again? Are we like others, who need to bring you letters of recommendation, or who ask you to write such letters on their behalf? Surely not! ²The only letter of recommendation we need is you yourselves. Your lives are a letter written in our* hearts; everyone can read it and recognize our good work among you. ³Clearly, you are a letter from Christ showing the result of our ministry among you. This "letter" is written not with pen and ink, but with the Spirit of the living God. It is carved not on tablets of stone, but on human hearts.

⁴We are confident of all this because of our great trust in God through Christ. ⁵It is not that we think we are qualified to do anything on our own. Our qualification comes from God. ⁶He has enabled us to be ministers of his new covenant. This is a covenant not of written laws, but of the Spirit. The old written covenant ends in death; but under the new covenant, the Spirit gives life.

THE GLORY OF THE NEW COVENANT

⁷The old way,* with laws etched in stone, led to death, though it began with such glory that the people of Israel could not bear to look at Moses' face. For his face shone with the glory of God, even though the brightness was already fading away. ⁸Shouldn't we expect far greater glory under the new way, now that the Holy Spirit is giving life? ⁹If the old way, which brings condemnation, was glorious, how much more

glorious is the new way, which makes us right with God! ¹⁰In fact, that first glory was not glorious at all compared with the overwhelming glory of the new way. ¹¹So if the old way, which has been replaced, was glorious, how much more glorious is the new, which remains forever!

¹²Since this new way gives us such confidence, we can be very bold. ¹³We are not like Moses, who put a veil over his face so the people of Israel would not see the glory, even though it was destined to fade away. ¹⁴But the people's minds were hardened, and to this day whenever the old covenant is being read, the same veil covers their minds so they cannot understand the truth. And this veil can be removed only by believing in Christ. ¹⁵Yes, even today when they read Moses' writings, their hearts are covered with that veil, and they do not understand.

¹⁶But whenever someone turns to the Lord, the veil is taken away. ¹⁷For the Lord is the Spirit, and wherever the Spirit of the Lord is, there is freedom. ¹⁸So all of us who have had that veil removed can see and reflect the glory of the Lord. And the Lord—who is the Spirit—makes us more and more like him as we are changed into his glorious image.

TREASURE IN FRAGILE CLAY JARS

4 Therefore, since God in his mercy has given us this new way,* we never give up. ²We reject all shameful deeds and underhanded methods. We don't try to trick anyone or distort the word of God. We tell the truth before God, and all who are honest know this.

³If the Good News we preach is hidden behind a veil, it is hidden only from people who are perishing. ⁴Satan, who is the god of this world, has blinded the minds of those who don't believe. They are unable to see the glorious light of the Good News. They don't understand this message about the glory of Christ, who is the exact likeness of God.

⁵You see, we don't go around preaching about ourselves. We preach that Jesus Christ is Lord, and we ourselves are your servants for Jesus' sake. ⁶For God, who said, "Let there be light in the darkness," has made this light shine in our hearts so we could know the glory of God that is seen in the face of Jesus Christ.

⁷We now have this light shining in our hearts, but we ourselves are like fragile clay jars containing this great treasure.* This makes it clear that our great power is from God, not from ourselves.

⁸We are pressed on every side by troubles, but we are not crushed. We are perplexed, but not driven to despair. ⁹We are hunted down, but never abandoned by God. We get knocked down, but we are not destroyed. ¹⁰Through suffering,

---

2:17 Some manuscripts read *the rest of the hucksters.* 3:2 Some manuscripts read *your.* 3:7 Or *ministry;* also in 3:8, 9, 10, 11, 12. 4:1 Or *ministry.* 4:7 Greek *We now have this treasure in clay jars.*

our bodies continue to share in the death of Jesus so that the life of Jesus may also be seen in our bodies. [11] Yes, we live under constant danger of death because we serve Jesus, so that the life of Jesus will be evident in our dying bodies. [12] So we live in the face of death, but this has resulted in eternal life for you.

[13] But we continue to preach because we have the same kind of faith the psalmist had when he said, "I believed in God, so I spoke."* [14] We know that God, who raised the Lord Jesus,* will also raise us with Jesus and present us to himself together with you. [15] All of this is for your benefit. And as God's grace reaches more and more people, there will be great thanksgiving, and God will receive more and more glory.

[16] That is why we never give up. Though our bodies are dying, our spirits are* being renewed every day. [17] For our present troubles are small and won't last very long. Yet they produce for us a glory that vastly outweighs them and will last forever! [18] So we don't look at the troubles we can see now; rather, we fix our gaze on things that cannot be seen. For the things we see now will soon be gone, but the things we cannot see will last forever.

NEW BODIES

5 For we know that when this earthly tent we live in is taken down (that is, when we die and leave this earthly body), we will have a house in heaven, an eternal body made for us by God himself and not by human hands. [2] We grow weary in our present bodies, and we long to put on our heavenly bodies like new clothing. [3] For we will put on heavenly bodies; we will not be spirits without bodies.* [4] While we live in these earthly bodies, we groan and sigh, but it's not that we want to die and get rid of these bodies that clothe us. Rather, we want to put on our new bodies so that these dying bodies will be swallowed up by life. [5] God himself has prepared us for this, and as a guarantee he has given us his Holy Spirit.

[6] So we are always confident, even though we know that as long as we live in these bodies we are not at home with the Lord. [7] For we live by believing and not by seeing. [8] Yes, we are fully confident, and we would rather be away from these earthly bodies, for then we will be at home with the Lord. [9] So whether we are here in this body or away from this body, our goal is to please him. [10] For we must all stand before Christ to be judged. We will each receive whatever we deserve for the good or evil we have done in this earthly body.

WE ARE GOD'S AMBASSADORS

[11] Because we understand our fearful responsibility to the Lord, we work hard to persuade others. God knows we are sincere, and I hope you know this, too. [12] Are we commending ourselves to you again? No, we are giving you a reason to be proud of us,* so you can answer those who brag about having a spectacular ministry rather than having a sincere heart. [13] If it seems we are crazy, it is to bring glory to God. And if we are in our right minds, it is for your benefit. [14] Either way, Christ's love controls us.* Since we believe that Christ died for all, we also believe that we have all died to our old life.* [15] He died for everyone so that those who receive his new life will no longer live for themselves. Instead, they will live for Christ, who died and was raised for them.

[16] So we have stopped evaluating others from a human point of view. At one time we thought of Christ merely from a human point of view. How differently we know him now! [17] This means that anyone who belongs to Christ has become a new person. The old life is gone; a new life has begun!

[18] And all of this is a gift from God, who brought us back to himself through Christ. And God has given us this task of reconciling people to him. [19] For God was in Christ, reconciling the world to himself, no longer counting people's sins against them. And he gave us this wonderful message of reconciliation. [20] So we are Christ's ambassadors; God is making his appeal through us. We speak for Christ when we plead, "Come back to God!" [21] For God made Christ, who never sinned, to be the offering for our sin,* so that we could be made right with God through Christ.

WHY CAN'T WE ALL JUST GET ALONG?
2 Corinthians 5:14-21　　　　　　JACK HAYFORD

Our relationship with God dictates our relationship with other people. God brought us out of a deep pit and showed us mercy and kindness. His grace should mirror through us to the world.

You have to make the decision that you *want* to be reconciled to other people. You have to believe that Jesus can help you love a person for His sake. Human kindness will only get us so far, but the blood of Jesus has the power to transform us and bring new life to our relationships.

We should approach people as Jesus did, as a servant who loves and cares for them. We can't do this by ourselves; we need His Spirit. The life of Jesus comes through us by the ministry of reconciliation. When God reconciled us to Himself, He did not label us with our failures. He welcomed and accepted us despite all our shortcomings.

4:13 Ps 116:10.　4:14 Some manuscripts read *who raised Jesus.*
4:16 Greek *our inner being is.*　5:3 Greek *we will not be naked.*
5:12 Some manuscripts read *proud of yourselves.*　5:14a Or *urges us on.*　5:14b Greek *Since one died for all, then all died.*　5:21 Or *to become sin itself.*

6

As God's partners,* we beg you not to accept this marvelous gift of God's kindness and then ignore it. ² For God says,

"At just the right time, I heard you.
On the day of salvation, I helped you."*

Indeed, the "right time" is now. Today is the day of salvation.

PAUL'S HARDSHIPS

³ We live in such a way that no one will stumble because of us, and no one will find fault with our ministry. ⁴ In everything we do, we show that we are true ministers of God. We patiently endure troubles and hardships and calamities of every kind. ⁵ We have been beaten, been put in prison, faced angry mobs, worked to exhaustion, endured sleepless nights, and gone without food. ⁶ We prove ourselves by our purity, our understanding, our patience, our kindness, by the Holy Spirit within us,* and by our sincere love. ⁷ We faithfully preach the truth. God's power is working in us. We use the weapons of righteousness in the right hand for attack and the left hand for defense. ⁸ We serve God whether people honor us or despise us, whether they slander us or praise us. We are honest, but they call us impostors. ⁹ We are ignored, even though we are well known. We live close to death, but we are still alive. We have been beaten, but we have not been killed. ¹⁰ Our hearts ache, but we always have joy. We are poor, but we give spiritual riches to others. We own nothing, and yet we have everything.

¹¹ Oh, dear Corinthian friends! We have spoken honestly with you, and our hearts are open to you. ¹² There is no lack of love on our part, but you have withheld your love from us. ¹³ I am asking you to respond as if you were my own children. Open your hearts to us!

THE TEMPLE OF THE LIVING GOD

¹⁴ Don't team up with those who are unbelievers. How can righteousness be a partner with wickedness? How can light live with darkness? ¹⁵ What harmony can there be between Christ and the devil*? How can a believer be a partner with an unbeliever? ¹⁶ And what union can there be between God's temple and idols? For we are the temple of the living God. As God said:

"I will live in them
and walk among them.
I will be their God,
and they will be my people.*
¹⁷ Therefore, come out from among
unbelievers,
and separate yourselves from them,
says the LORD.
Don't touch their filthy things,
and I will welcome you.*

THE ESSENCE OF REPENTANCE
2 Corinthians 7:8-10   JACK HAYFORD

Repentance is the action that follows a specific moment of perception about God's purpose for our lives. There are two stages of repentance. First, there is repentance to new birth (salvation), after which there is continuous repentance to growth (spiritual life). For believers, repentance is not a quick and cheap way out of a tight spot. It is an everyday process in which we seek God's light on all areas of our lives.

In 2 Corinthians 7:10, the apostle Paul refers to repentance when he writes, "The kind of sorrow God wants us to experience leads us away from sin and results in salvation." God is constantly working to shape our lives to mold us into His likeness. Repentance is a directional choice the Lord desires in our hearts, where we open ourselves to His searchlight, readily and regularly confessing our wrongdoings and turning to embrace His ways.

---

¹⁸ And I will be your Father,
and you will be my sons and daughters,
says the LORD Almighty.*"

7

Because we have these promises, dear friends, let us cleanse ourselves from everything that can defile our body or spirit. And let us work toward complete holiness because we fear God.

² Please open your hearts to us. We have not done wrong to anyone, nor led anyone astray, nor taken advantage of anyone. ³ I'm not saying this to condemn you. I said before that you are in our hearts, and we live or die together with you. ⁴ I have the highest confidence in you, and I take great pride in you. You have greatly encouraged me and made me happy despite all our troubles.

PAUL'S JOY AT THE CHURCH'S REPENTANCE

⁵ When we arrived in Macedonia, there was no rest for us. We faced conflict from every direction, with battles on the outside and fear on the inside. ⁶ But God, who encourages those who are discouraged, encouraged us by the arrival of Titus. ⁷ His presence was a joy, but so was the news he brought of the encouragement he received from you. When he told us how much you long to see me, and how sorry you are for what happened, and how loyal you are to me, I was filled with joy!

⁸ I am not sorry that I sent that severe letter to you, though I was sorry at first, for I know it was painful to you for a little while. ⁹ Now I am

---

6:1 Or *As we work together.*　6:2 Isa 49:8 (Greek version).
6:6 Or *by our holiness of spirit.*　6:15 Greek *Beliar;* various other manuscripts render this proper name of the devil as *Belian, Beliab,* or *Belial.*　6:16 Lev 26:12; Ezek 37:27.　6:17 Isa 52:11; Ezek 20:34 (Greek version).　6:18 2 Sam 7:14.

glad I sent it, not because it hurt you, but because the pain caused you to repent and change your ways. It was the kind of sorrow God wants his people to have, so you were not harmed by us in any way. ¹⁰For the kind of sorrow God wants us to experience leads us away from sin and results in salvation. There's no regret for that kind of sorrow. But worldly sorrow, which lacks repentance, results in spiritual death.

¹¹Just see what this godly sorrow produced in you! Such earnestness, such concern to clear yourselves, such indignation, such alarm, such longing to see me, such zeal, and such a readiness to punish wrong. You showed that you have done everything necessary to make things right. ¹²My purpose, then, was not to write about who did the wrong or who was wronged. I wrote to you so that in the sight of God you could see for yourselves how loyal you are to us. ¹³We have been greatly encouraged by this.

In addition to our own encouragement, we were especially delighted to see how happy Titus was about the way all of you welcomed him and set his mind* at ease. ¹⁴I had told him how proud I was of you—and you didn't disappoint me. I have always told you the truth, and now my boasting to Titus has also proved true! ¹⁵Now he cares for you more than ever when he remembers the way all of you obeyed him and welcomed him with such fear and deep respect. ¹⁶I am very happy now because I have complete confidence in you.

A CALL TO GENEROUS GIVING

8 Now I want you to know, dear brothers and sisters,* what God in his kindness has done through the churches in Macedonia. ²They are being tested by many troubles, and they are very poor. But they are also filled with abundant joy, which has overflowed in rich generosity.

³For I can testify that they gave not only what they could afford, but far more. And they did it of their own free will. ⁴They begged us again and again for the privilege of sharing in the gift for the believers in Jerusalem.* ⁵They even did more than we had hoped, for their first action was to give themselves to the Lord and to us, just as God wanted them to do.

⁶So we have urged Titus, who encouraged your giving in the first place, to return to you and encourage you to finish this ministry of giving. ⁷Since you excel in so many ways—in your faith, your gifted speakers, your knowledge, your enthusiasm, and your love from us*—I want you to excel also in this gracious act of giving.

⁸I am not commanding you to do this. But I am testing how genuine your love is by comparing it with the eagerness of the other churches. ⁹You know the generous grace of our Lord Jesus Christ. Though he was rich, yet for your sakes he became poor, so that by his poverty he could make you rich.

¹⁰Here is my advice: It would be good for you to finish what you started a year ago. Last year you were the first who wanted to give, and you were the first to begin doing it. ¹¹Now you should finish what you started. Let the eagerness you showed in the beginning be matched now by your giving. Give in proportion to what you have. ¹²Whatever you give is acceptable if you give it eagerly. And give according to what you have, not what you don't have. ¹³Of course, I don't mean your giving should make life easy for others and hard for yourselves. I only mean that there should be some equality. ¹⁴Right now you have plenty and can help those who are in need. Later, they will have plenty and can share with you when you need it. In this way, things will be equal. ¹⁵As the Scriptures say,

"Those who gathered a lot had nothing
    left over,
  and those who gathered only a little
    had enough."*

TITUS AND HIS COMPANIONS

¹⁶But thank God! He has given Titus the same enthusiasm for you that I have. ¹⁷Titus welcomed our request that he visit you again. In fact, he himself was very eager to go and see you. ¹⁸We are also sending another brother with Titus. All the churches praise him as a preacher of the Good News. ¹⁹He was appointed by the churches to accompany us as we take the offering to Jerusalem*—a service that glorifies the Lord and shows our eagerness to help.

²⁰We are traveling together to guard against any criticism for the way we are handling this generous gift. ²¹We are careful to be honorable before the Lord, but we also want everyone else to see that we are honorable.

²²We are also sending with them another of our brothers who has proven himself many times and has shown on many occasions how eager he is. He is now even more enthusiastic because of his great confidence in you. ²³If anyone asks about Titus, say that he is my partner who works with me to help you. And the brothers with him have been sent by the churches,* and they bring honor to Christ. ²⁴So show them your love, and prove to all the churches that our boasting about you is justified.

THE COLLECTION FOR CHRISTIANS IN JERUSALEM

9 I really don't need to write to you about this ministry of giving for the believers in Jerusalem.* ²For I know how eager you are to help, and I have been boasting to the churches in Macedonia that you in Greece* were ready to

7:13 Greek *his spirit.* 8:1 Greek *brothers.* 8:4 Greek *for God's holy people.* 8:7 Some manuscripts read *your love for us.* 8:15 Exod 16:18. 8:19 See 1 Cor 16:3-4. 8:23 Greek *are apostles of the churches.* 9:1 Greek *about the offering for God's holy people.* 9:2 Greek *in Achaia,* the southern region of the Greek peninsula. *Macedonia* was in the northern region of Greece.

LIFE-GIVING FARMERS
2 Corinthians 9:6   ROBERT MORRIS

When a farmer plants a single kernel of corn, the kernel grows into a stalk that will produce hundreds of individual kernels. Second Corinthians 9:6 says, "A farmer who plants only a few seeds will get a small crop. But the one who plants generously will get a generous crop." It's astonishing to me that some people expect to reap a huge harvest of souls when they haven't sown the gospel.

As believers, we exist on this earth as ambassadors for Christ. We are called to plant and water seeds of the gospel, and there are people everywhere who need to hear it. We may not always win someone to Christ when we witness, but that doesn't mean we've failed. Our responsibility is to sow the gospel; winning souls is God's job. When we share our stories of God's goodness with others, God takes care of the results.

GIVE CHEERFULLY
2 Corinthians 9:7-8   ROBERT MORRIS

In 2 Corinthians 9:7, Paul writes, "You must each decide in your heart how much to give. And don't give reluctantly or in response to pressure. 'For God loves a person who gives cheerfully.'" God isn't looking for tithes, offerings, and gifts that are given because we feel forced or obligated. He wants you to give from a place of love. You are the only person on earth who knows what God has called you to give.

So how do you learn to give cheerfully? There's only one way: God must do a work in your heart. You must allow God to replace your selfish heart with generosity. When you do, "God will generously provide all you need. Then you will have everything you need and plenty left over to share with others" (v. 8).

send an offering a year ago. In fact, it was your enthusiasm that stirred up many of the Macedonian believers to begin giving.

³ But I am sending these brothers to be sure you really are ready, as I have been telling them, and that your money is all collected. I don't want to be wrong in my boasting about you. ⁴ We would be embarrassed—not to mention your own embarrassment—if some Macedonian believers came with me and found that you weren't ready after all I had told them! ⁵ So I thought I should send these brothers ahead of me to make sure the gift you promised is ready. But I want it to be a willing gift, not one given grudgingly.

⁶ Remember this—a farmer who plants only a few seeds will get a small crop. But the one who plants generously will get a generous crop. ⁷ You must each decide in your heart how much to give. And don't give reluctantly or in response to pressure. "For God loves a person who gives cheerfully."* ⁸ And God will generously provide all you need. Then you will always have everything you need and plenty left over to share with others. ⁹ As the Scriptures say,

"They share freely and give generously
    to the poor.
Their good deeds will be remembered
    forever."*

¹⁰ For God is the one who provides seed for the farmer and then bread to eat. In the same way, he will provide and increase your resources and then produce a great harvest of generosity* in you. ¹¹ Yes, you will be enriched in every way so that you can always be generous. And when we take your gifts to those who need them, they will thank God. ¹² So two good things will result from this ministry of giving—the needs of the believers in Jerusalem* will be met, and they will joyfully express their thanks to God.

¹³ As a result of your ministry, they will give glory to God. For your generosity to them and to all believers will prove that you are obedient to the Good News of Christ. ¹⁴ And they will pray for you with deep affection because of the overflowing grace God has given to you. ¹⁵ Thank God for this gift* too wonderful for words!

PAUL DEFENDS HIS AUTHORITY

10 Now I, Paul, appeal to you with the gentleness and kindness of Christ—though I realize you think I am timid in person and bold only when I write from far away. ² Well, I am begging you now so that when I come I won't have to be bold with those who think we act from human motives.

³ We are human, but we don't wage war as humans do. ⁴*We use God's mighty weapons, not worldly weapons, to knock down the strongholds of human reasoning and to destroy false arguments. ⁵ We destroy every proud obstacle that keeps people from knowing God. We capture their rebellious thoughts and teach them to obey Christ. ⁶ And after you have become fully obedient, we will punish everyone who remains disobedient.

⁷ Look at the obvious facts.* Those who say they belong to Christ must recognize that we belong to Christ as much as they do. ⁸ I may seem to be boasting too much about the authority given to

---

9:7 See footnote on Prov 22:8. 9:9 Ps 112:9. 9:10 Greek *righteousness.* 9:12 Greek *of God's holy people.* 9:15 Greek *his gift.* 10:4 English translations divide verses 4 and 5 in various ways. 10:7 Or *You look at things only on the basis of appearance.*

A MIND SET FREE
2 Corinthians 10:3-5   JIMMY EVANS

Satan introduces thoughts to our minds that are contrary to God's Word and uses them to hold us captive. However, we can fight the devil with truth and be free from every bondage.

Here are three keys we need to understand about freedom:

1. The mind is the main battlefield between good and evil (James 4:7).

Freedom in our minds begins with making Jesus the Lord of our thoughts.

2. God's Word is a spiritual weapon (Ephesians 6:10-17).

Every piece of spiritual armor God gives us is an application of His truth in our lives. We fight Satan with truth—God's Word.

3. Biblical meditation is spiritual warfare (Deuteronomy 6:6-9).

Biblical meditation is the practice of repeatedly reading and thinking about specific Scriptures. We reprogram our brains to think differently by replacing bondage-related thoughts with Scriptures that declare the truth of God's Word.

BREAKING STRONGHOLDS
2 Corinthians 10:3-5   MARCUS BRECHEEN

In 2 Corinthians 10:4, Paul writes, "We use God's mighty weapons, not worldly weapons, to knock down the strongholds of human reasoning and to destroy false arguments." A *stronghold* is anything you know to be against the will of God that you also believe is unchangeable. Only the Word of God has the power to destroy strongholds.

One day I was teaching a class at church when a storm came blowing in from the west. My wife was at home with our children, and she quickly ushered them into the safest room in the house. After about 15 minutes, my son Seth got tired of waiting for the tornado to pass. He stood up, lifted his finger, and said, "God, I command You, in Jesus' name, to move that tornado!"

Now, we obviously had to work on Seth's understanding of who the boss is, but I think God enjoys the spunk of someone who will stand up and say, "I've had enough of this! Here's what the Word of God says!"

us by the Lord. But our authority builds you up; it doesn't tear you down. So I will not be ashamed of using my authority.

⁹ I'm not trying to frighten you by my letters. ¹⁰ For some say, "Paul's letters are demanding and forceful, but in person he is weak, and his speeches are worthless!" ¹¹ Those people should realize that our actions when we arrive in person will be as forceful as what we say in our letters from far away.

¹² Oh, don't worry; we wouldn't dare say that we are as wonderful as these other men who tell you how important they are! But they are only comparing themselves with each other, using themselves as the standard of measurement. How ignorant!

¹³ We will not boast about things done outside our area of authority. We will boast only about what has happened within the boundaries of the work God has given us, which includes our working with you. ¹⁴ We are not reaching beyond these boundaries when we claim authority over you, as if we had never visited you. For we were the first to travel all the way to Corinth with the Good News of Christ.

¹⁵ Nor do we boast and claim credit for the work someone else has done. Instead, we hope that your faith will grow so that the boundaries of our work among you will be extended. ¹⁶ Then we will be able to go and preach the Good News in other places far beyond you, where no one else is working. Then there will be no question of our boasting about work done in someone else's territory. ¹⁷ As the Scriptures say, "If you want to boast, boast only about the LORD."*

¹⁸ When people commend themselves, it doesn't count for much. The important thing is for the Lord to commend them.

PAUL AND THE FALSE APOSTLES

11 I hope you will put up with a little more of my foolishness. Please bear with me. ² For I am jealous for you with the jealousy of God himself. I promised you as a pure bride* to one husband—Christ. ³ But I fear that somehow your pure and undivided devotion to Christ will be corrupted, just as Eve was deceived by the cunning ways of the serpent. ⁴ You happily put up with whatever anyone tells you, even if they preach a different Jesus than the one we preach, or a different kind of Spirit than the one you received, or a different kind of gospel than the one you believed.

⁵ But I don't consider myself inferior in any way to these "super apostles" who teach such things. ⁶ I may be unskilled as a speaker, but I'm not lacking in knowledge. We have made this clear to you in every possible way.

⁷ Was I wrong when I humbled myself and honored you by preaching God's Good News to you without expecting anything in return? ⁸ I "robbed" other churches by accepting their contributions so I could serve you at no cost. ⁹ And when I was with you and didn't have enough to live on, I did not become a financial burden to anyone. For the brothers who came from

10:17 Jer 9:24. 11:2 Greek *a virgin.*

THE HURT WHISPERER

2 Corinthians 11:14   JIMMY EVANS

In our vulnerable moments, the devil pounces on us and whispers lies to separate us from God and keep us in bondage. He uses subtlety and disguises to try to make us believe his words are our own thoughts or even the voice of God.

We can destroy the devil's lies that limit our lives by:

1. Exposing our thoughts to the light.
Whatever is in the light comes before God, and the devil has no power over what's in the light.

2. Expelling any thought that doesn't agree with God's Word.
Knowing that the devil wants to torment us, we must capture and reject every negative thought.

3. Expressing our agreement with God's Word.
Scripture declares how much God loves us and what He says about us. Instead of believing the devil's lies, we must learn to say what God says. His Word will change the way we live.

Macedonia brought me all that I needed. I have never been a burden to you, and I never will be. ¹⁰ As surely as the truth of Christ is in me, no one in all of Greece* will ever stop me from boasting about this. ¹¹ Why? Because I don't love you? God knows that I do.

¹² But I will continue doing what I have always done. This will undercut those who are looking for an opportunity to boast that their work is just like ours. ¹³ These people are false apostles. They are deceitful workers who disguise themselves as apostles of Christ. ¹⁴ But I am not surprised! Even Satan disguises himself as an angel of light. ¹⁵ So it is no wonder that his servants also disguise themselves as servants of righteousness. In the end they will get the punishment their wicked deeds deserve.

PAUL'S MANY TRIALS

¹⁶ Again I say, don't think that I am a fool to talk like this. But even if you do, listen to me, as you would to a foolish person, while I also boast a little. ¹⁷ Such boasting is not from the Lord, but I am acting like a fool. ¹⁸ And since others boast about their human achievements, I will, too. ¹⁹ After all, you think you are so wise, but you enjoy putting up with fools! ²⁰ You put up with it when someone enslaves you, takes everything you have, takes advantage of you, takes control of everything, and slaps you in the face. ²¹ I'm ashamed to say that we've been too "weak" to do that!

But whatever they dare to boast about—I'm talking like a fool again—I dare to boast about it, too. ²² Are they Hebrews? So am I. Are they Israelites? So am I. Are they descendants of Abraham? So am I. ²³ Are they servants of Christ? I know I sound like a madman, but I have served him far more! I have worked harder, been put in prison more often, been whipped times without number, and faced death again and again. ²⁴ Five different times the Jewish leaders gave me thirty-nine lashes. ²⁵ Three times I was beaten with rods. Once I was stoned. Three times I was shipwrecked. Once I spent a whole night and a day adrift at sea. ²⁶ I have traveled on many long journeys. I have faced danger from rivers and from robbers. I have faced danger from my own people, the Jews, as well as from the Gentiles. I have faced danger in the cities, in the deserts, and on the seas. And I have faced danger from men who claim to be believers but are not.* ²⁷ I have worked hard and long, enduring many sleepless nights. I have been hungry and thirsty and have often gone without food. I have shivered in the cold, without enough clothing to keep me warm.

²⁸ Then, besides all this, I have the daily burden of my concern for all the churches. ²⁹ Who is weak without my feeling that weakness? Who is led astray, and I do not burn with anger?

³⁰ If I must boast, I would rather boast about the things that show how weak I am. ³¹ God, the Father of our Lord Jesus, who is worthy of eternal praise, knows I am not lying. ³² When I was in Damascus, the governor under King Aretas kept guards at the city gates to catch me. ³³ I had to be lowered in a basket through a window in the city wall to escape from him.

PAUL'S VISION AND HIS THORN IN THE FLESH

12 This boasting will do no good, but I must go on. I will reluctantly tell about visions and revelations from the Lord. ² I* was caught up to the third heaven fourteen years ago. Whether I was in my body or out of my body, I don't know—only God knows. ³ Yes, only God knows whether I was in my body or outside my body. But I do know ⁴ that I was caught up* to paradise and heard things so astounding that they cannot be expressed in words, things no human is allowed to tell.

⁵ That experience is worth boasting about, but I'm not going to do it. I will boast only about my weaknesses. ⁶ If I wanted to boast, I would be no fool in doing so, because I would be telling the truth. But I won't do it, because I don't want anyone to give me credit beyond what they can see in my life or hear in my message, ⁷ even though I have received such wonderful revelations from God. So to keep me from becoming proud, I was

---

11:10 Greek Achaia, the southern region of the Greek peninsula.
11:26 Greek from false brothers.   12:2 Greek I know a man in Christ who.   12:3-4 Greek But I know such a man, ⁴that he was caught up.

WHEN THE ANSWER IS NO
2 Corinthians 12:1-12   TIM ROSS

What do we do when God's answer to us is *no*? In 2 Corinthians 12, Paul writes about the "thorn" in his flesh. He does not specify what his problem is, but he does admit to begging God to remove it three times. God always has the same answer, though: "My grace is all you need" (v. 9).

Hearing "no" from God does not mean something is wrong with us, nor is it a sign of His rejection or abandonment. Instead, a "no" from God gives us an opportunity to learn about who He is in a completely new way. It forces us to rely solely on His grace instead of our own strength. By surrendering to God's *no*, Paul allows the power of Christ to work through him and discovers, "When I am weak, then I am strong" (v. 10).

---

given a thorn in my flesh, a messenger from Satan to torment me and keep me from becoming proud. ⁸Three different times I begged the Lord to take it away. ⁹Each time he said, "My grace is all you need. My power works best in weakness." So now I am glad to boast about my weaknesses, so that the power of Christ can work through me. ¹⁰That's why I take pleasure in my weaknesses, and in the insults, hardships, persecutions, and troubles that I suffer for Christ. For when I am weak, then I am strong.

PAUL'S CONCERN FOR THE CORINTHIANS

¹¹You have made me act like a fool. You ought to be writing commendations for me, for I am not at all inferior to these "super apostles," even though I am nothing at all. ¹²When I was with you, I certainly gave you proof that I am an apostle. For I patiently did many signs and wonders and miracles among you. ¹³The only thing I failed to do, which I do in the other churches, was to become a financial burden to you. Please forgive me for this wrong!

¹⁴Now I am coming to you for the third time, and I will not be a burden to you. I don't want what you have—I want you. After all, children don't provide for their parents. Rather, parents provide for their children. ¹⁵I will gladly spend myself and all I have for you, even though it seems that the more I love you, the less you love me.

¹⁶Some of you admit I was not a burden to you. But others still think I was sneaky and took advantage of you by trickery. ¹⁷But how? Did any of the men I sent to you take advantage of you? ¹⁸When I urged Titus to visit you and sent our other brother with him, did Titus take advantage of you? No! For we have the same spirit and walk in each other's steps, doing things the same way.

¹⁹Perhaps you think we're saying these things just to defend ourselves. No, we tell you this as Christ's servants, and with God as our witness. Everything we do, dear friends, is to strengthen you. ²⁰For I am afraid that when I come I won't like what I find, and you won't like my response. I am afraid that I will find quarreling, jealousy, anger, selfishness, slander, gossip, arrogance, and disorderly behavior. ²¹Yes, I am afraid that when I come again, God will humble me in your presence. And I will be grieved because many of you have not given up your old sins. You have not repented of your impurity, sexual immorality, and eagerness for lustful pleasure.

PAUL'S FINAL ADVICE

13 This is the third time I am coming to visit you (and as the Scriptures say, "The facts of every case must be established by the testimony of two or three witnesses"*). ²I have already warned those who had been sinning when I was there on my second visit. Now I again warn them and all others, just as I did before, that next time I will not spare them.

³I will give you all the proof you want that Christ speaks through me. Christ is not weak when he deals with you; he is powerful among you. ⁴Although he was crucified in weakness, he now lives by the power of God. We, too, are weak, just as Christ was, but when we deal with you we will be alive with him and will have God's power.

⁵Examine yourselves to see if your faith is genuine. Test yourselves. Surely you know that Jesus Christ is among you*; if not, you have failed the test of genuine faith. ⁶As you test yourselves, I hope you will recognize that we have not failed the test of apostolic authority.

⁷We pray to God that you will not do what is wrong by refusing our correction. I hope we won't need to demonstrate our authority when we arrive. Do the right thing before we come— even if that makes it look like we have failed to demonstrate our authority. ⁸For we cannot oppose the truth, but must always stand for the truth. ⁹We are glad to seem weak if it helps show that you are actually strong. We pray that you will become mature.

¹⁰I am writing this to you before I come, hoping that I won't need to deal severely with you when I do come. For I want to use the authority the Lord has given me to strengthen you, not to tear you down.

PAUL'S FINAL GREETINGS

¹¹Dear brothers and sisters,* I close my letter with these last words: Be joyful. Grow to maturity. Encourage each other. Live in harmony and peace. Then the God of love and peace will be with you. ¹²Greet each other with a sacred kiss. ¹³All of God's people here send you their greetings.

13:1 Deut 19:15. 13:5 Or *in you.* 13:11 Greek *Brothers.*

HAVE YOU BEEN BORN AGAIN?
2 Corinthians 13:5

ROBERT MORRIS

The most important, game-changing question you can ask yourself is this: *"Have I been born again?"* Many people think they have been born again, but they really haven't (Matthew 7:13-14). Some people mentally believe in God while others believe growing up in church or being active in God's work is enough (Matthew 7:21-23). However, if you have not submitted your life to God, then you have not been born again.

The Bible says you *can know* if you have truly been born again (1 John 5:13). You are born again when you give God control of your life. He moves in and changes your heart. You want to follow Him and do what's right, and you no longer feel the need to try to change yourself. Some believers may not remember the exact date they were born again, but they remember the event because it was when their lives radically changed.

¹⁴*May the grace of the Lord Jesus Christ, the love of God, and the fellowship of the Holy Spirit be with you all.

13:14 Some English translations include verse 13 as part of verse 12, and then verse 14 becomes verse 13.

GALATIANS

JON HUNTZINGER, PHD

A primary theme of Paul's letter to the Galatians is the freedom of the gospel. However, Paul's idea of freedom is different from that of other people. It is *not only* deliverance from bondage, but it is *also* the power to help others. The gospel leads to freedom, which leads to service and doing good for other people.

In the late AD 40s, Paul wrote this letter to churches he had founded in Galatia during his first missionary journey. The letter contains seven parts:

— It includes a greeting to the churches (1:1–5).
— Paul claims there is no other gospel or "any other Good News" (1:6–10).
— He defends his calling and the acceptance of his message by the apostles (1:11–2:10).
— Paul retells the defense of his message to Peter (2:11–14).
— He teaches about faith and the example of Abraham (2:15–4:31).
— Paul exhorts the Galatians to live in freedom (5:1–6:10).
— He offers a final blessing (6:11–18).

THE GOSPEL AND FREEDOM

In the letter, the apostle responds to what he calls "a different kind of" gospel. Some people were saying Gentile believers should follow certain Jewish practices, such as circumcision. In Paul's mind, Jewish followers of Jesus should continue to live as Jews, but Gentile followers should live in freedom from their old pagan way of life and in a new freedom that God has given them in the gospel to love others. The importance of this gospel is evident in Paul's opening words. He says there is only one gospel, and it is the one he has preached to them: "Let God's curse fall on anyone, including us or even an angel from heaven, who preaches a different kind of Good News than the one we preached to you" (1:8). Paul's strong language points to the uncompromising nature of the gospel. Though Paul does not elaborate on the gospel's content in these verses, he identifies the subject of the gospel—Jesus. "Even before I was born, God chose me and called me by his marvelous grace. Then it pleased him to reveal his Son to me so that I would proclaim the Good News about Jesus to the Gentiles" (1:15–16). He affirms his responsibility to the Gentiles when he says that the leaders in Jerusalem "saw that God had given me the responsibility of preaching the gospel to the Gentiles" (2:7).

With this in mind, Paul writes, "Christ has truly set us free" (5:1). This freedom includes release from certain practices, such as circumcision. He warns, "This false teaching is like a little yeast that spreads through the whole batch of dough!" (5:9). Likely drawing on Jesus' own teaching about the "yeast of the Pharisees" (Mark 8:15), Paul observes that to give ground on this point will lead to others, and in any case, nothing needs to be added to the gospel, which is what keeping certain dietary practices or performing circumcision would mean to the Gentiles. Christ has given them their freedom, not to build these behaviors into their lives but to build service to others into their lives. "For you have been called to live in freedom. . . . But don't use your freedom to satisfy your sinful nature. Instead, use your freedom to serve one another in love" (5:13). This freedom is not for self-gratification, and he cites Leviticus 19:18 to emphasize this point: "Love your neighbor as yourself." Paul's gospel ethic is a freedom-oriented ethic focused on the welfare of others.

Paul clearly saw that people live in one of two ways. They either live by the flesh, or they live by the Spirit (5:13–24). To live by the flesh is to live focusing on oneself; to live by the Spirit is to live focusing on others. The flesh is "me-centered" while the Spirit is "us-centered." The Spirit bears fruit in our lives so that we may nourish and strengthen one another (5:22–23) and even bear each other's burdens (6:2) in imitation of Jesus who bore our burden of sin upon Himself on the cross.

THE GOSPEL AND ABRAHAM

The believers who argued for the Gentiles to practice circumcision as part of their commitment to God, in addition to their faith in Jesus, appealed to the Galatians' desire for security. As former pagans and followers of other Greco-Roman religious cults of the time, they were accustomed to rituals, recitations, sacrifices, and other such practices. They were used to processions, shrines, and priests. By describing circumcision as a practice that Abraham, the father of faith, introduced and followed, these believers could plausibly argue that the Galatians should follow his example. It was a powerful and persuasive message.

Paul is concerned that such practice would only lead back to the old Israelite malpractice of adding to their worship of the one true God. The Israelites were never polytheists who believed in many gods. Instead, they recognized the God of Israel as the greatest but added other lesser gods to their worship. They believed their God, the God of Abraham, Isaac, and David, was the Creator of all things, but they gave recognition to other gods for various reasons. Sometimes they were attempting to make peace with other tribes, and at others, they simply wanted to "cover all the bases." For Gentiles to practice circumcision would interfere with the singular power of the cross of Christ. Paul agreed that Abraham is an example to be followed but not with respect to circumcision. He is an example of one who left his former gods behind to live by faith in a new freedom. Likewise, the Gentile Galatians have left their old idols behind by accepting the gospel. Now they should live in new freedom by committing themselves to loving other people.

GREETINGS FROM PAUL

1 This letter is from Paul, an apostle. I was not appointed by any group of people or any human authority, but by Jesus Christ himself and by God the Father, who raised Jesus from the dead.

2 All the brothers and sisters* here join me in sending this letter to the churches of Galatia.

3 May God the Father and our Lord Jesus Christ* give you grace and peace. 4 Jesus gave his life for our sins, just as God our Father planned, in order to rescue us from this evil world in which we live. 5 All glory to God forever and ever! Amen.

THERE IS ONLY ONE GOOD NEWS

6 I am shocked that you are turning away so soon from God, who called you to himself through the loving mercy of Christ.* You are following a different way that pretends to be the Good News 7 but is not the Good News at all. You are being fooled by those who deliberately twist the truth concerning Christ.

8 Let God's curse fall on anyone, including us or even an angel from heaven, who preaches a different kind of Good News than the one we preached to you. 9 I say again what we have said before: If anyone preaches any other Good News than the one you welcomed, let that person be cursed.

10 Obviously, I'm not trying to win the approval of people, but of God. If pleasing people were my goal, I would not be Christ's servant.

PAUL'S MESSAGE COMES FROM CHRIST

11 Dear brothers and sisters, I want you to understand that the gospel message I preach is not based on mere human reasoning. 12 I received my message from no human source, and no one taught me. Instead, I received it by direct revelation from Jesus Christ.*

13 You know what I was like when I followed the Jewish religion—how I violently persecuted God's church. I did my best to destroy it. 14 I was far ahead of my fellow Jews in my zeal for the traditions of my ancestors.

15 But even before I was born, God chose me and called me by his marvelous grace. Then it pleased him 16 to reveal his Son to me* so that I would proclaim the Good News about Jesus to the Gentiles.

When this happened, I did not rush out to consult with any human being.* 17 Nor did I go up to Jerusalem to consult with those who were apostles before I was. Instead, I went away into Arabia, and later I returned to the city of Damascus.

18 Then three years later I went to Jerusalem to get to know Peter,* and I stayed with him for fifteen days. 19 The only other apostle I met at that time was James, the Lord's brother. 20 I declare before God that what I am writing to you is not a lie.

21 After that visit I went north into the provinces of Syria and Cilicia. 22 And still the churches in Christ that are in Judea didn't know me personally. 23 All they knew was that people were saying, "The one who used to persecute us is now preaching the very faith he tried to destroy!" 24 And they praised God because of me.

THE APOSTLES ACCEPT PAUL

2 Then fourteen years later I went back to Jerusalem again, this time with Barnabas; and Titus came along, too. 2 I went there because God revealed to me that I should go. While I was there I met privately with those considered to be leaders of the church and shared with them the message I had been preaching to the Gentiles. I wanted to make sure that we were in agreement, for fear that all my efforts had been wasted and I was running the race for nothing. 3 And they supported me and did not even demand that my companion Titus be circumcised, though he was a Gentile.*

4 Even that question came up only because of some so-called believers there—false ones, really*—who were secretly brought in. They sneaked in to spy on us and take away the freedom we have in Christ Jesus. They wanted to enslave us and force us to follow their Jewish regulations. 5 But we refused to give in to them for a single moment. We wanted to preserve the truth of the gospel message for you.

6 And the leaders of the church had nothing to add to what I was preaching. (By the way,

1:2 Greek brothers; also in 1:11.   1:3 Some manuscripts read God our Father and the Lord Jesus Christ.   1:6 Some manuscripts read through loving mercy.   1:12 Or by the revelation of Jesus Christ. 1:16a Or in me.   1:16b Greek with flesh and blood.   1:18 Greek Cephas.   2:3 Greek a Greek.   2:4 Greek some false brothers.

their reputation as great leaders made no difference to me, for God has no favorites.) [7] Instead, they saw that God had given me the responsibility of preaching the gospel to the Gentiles, just as he had given Peter the responsibility of preaching to the Jews. [8] For the same God who worked through Peter as the apostle to the Jews also worked through me as the apostle to the Gentiles.

[9] In fact, James, Peter,* and John, who were known as pillars of the church, recognized the gift God had given me, and they accepted Barnabas and me as their co-workers. They encouraged us to keep preaching to the Gentiles, while they continued their work with the Jews. [10] Their only suggestion was that we keep on helping the poor, which I have always been eager to do.

PAUL CONFRONTS PETER

[11] But when Peter came to Antioch, I had to oppose him to his face, for what he did was very wrong. [12] When he first arrived, he ate with the Gentile believers, who were not circumcised. But afterward, when some friends of James came, Peter wouldn't eat with the Gentiles anymore. He was afraid of criticism from these people who insisted on the necessity of circumcision. [13] As a result, other Jewish believers followed Peter's hypocrisy, and even Barnabas was led astray by their hypocrisy.

[14] When I saw that they were not following the truth of the gospel message, I said to Peter in front of all the others, "Since you, a Jew by birth, have discarded the Jewish laws and are living like a Gentile, why are you now trying to make these Gentiles follow the Jewish traditions?

[15] "You and I are Jews by birth, not 'sinners' like the Gentiles. [16] Yet we know that a person is made right with God by faith in Jesus Christ, not by obeying the law. And we have believed in Christ Jesus, so that we might be made right with God because of our faith in Christ, not because we have obeyed the law. For no one will ever be made right with God by obeying the law."*

[17] But suppose we seek to be made right with God through faith in Christ and then we are found guilty because we have abandoned the law. Would that mean Christ has led us into sin? Absolutely not! [18] Rather, I am a sinner if I rebuild the old system of law I already tore down. [19] For when I tried to keep the law, it condemned me. So I died to the law—I stopped trying to meet all its requirements—so that I might live for God. [20] My old self has been crucified with Christ.* It is no longer I who live, but Christ lives in me. So I live in this earthly body by trusting in the Son of God, who loved me and gave himself for me. [21] I do not treat the grace of God as meaningless. For if keeping the law could make us right with God, then there was no need for Christ to die.

THE LAW AND FAITH IN CHRIST

3 Oh, foolish Galatians! Who has cast an evil spell on you? For the meaning of Jesus Christ's death was made as clear to you as if you had seen a picture of his death on the cross. [2] Let me ask you this one question: Did you receive the Holy Spirit by obeying the law of Moses? Of course not! You received the Spirit because you believed the message you heard about Christ. [3] How foolish can you be? After starting your new lives in the Spirit, why are you now trying to become perfect by your own human effort? [4] Have you experienced* so much for nothing? Surely it was not in vain, was it?

[5] I ask you again, does God give you the Holy Spirit and work miracles among you because you obey the law? Of course not! It is because you believe the message you heard about Christ.

[6] In the same way, "Abraham believed God, and God counted him as righteous because of his faith."* [7] The real children of Abraham, then, are those who put their faith in God.

[8] What's more, the Scriptures looked forward to this time when God would make the Gentiles right in his sight because of their faith. God proclaimed this good news to Abraham long ago when he said, "All nations will be blessed through you."* [9] So all who put their faith in Christ share the same blessing Abraham received because of his faith.

[10] But those who depend on the law to make them right with God are under his curse, for the Scriptures say, "Cursed is everyone who does not observe and obey all the commands that are written in God's Book of the Law."* [11] So it is clear that no one can be made right with God by trying to keep the law. For the Scriptures say, "It is through faith that a righteous person has life."*
[12] This way of faith is very different from the way of law, which says, "It is through obeying the law that a person has life."*

[13] But Christ has rescued us from the curse pronounced by the law. When he was hung on the cross, he took upon himself the curse for our wrongdoing. For it is written in the Scriptures, "Cursed is everyone who is hung on a tree."*
[14] Through Christ Jesus, God has blessed the Gentiles with the same blessing he promised to Abraham, so that we who are believers might receive the promised* Holy Spirit through faith.

THE LAW AND GOD'S PROMISE

[15] Dear brothers and sisters,* here's an example from everyday life. Just as no one can set aside or amend an irrevocable agreement, so it is in this case. [16] God gave the promises to Abraham and

---

2:9 Greek *Cephas;* also in 2:11, 14. 2:16 Some translators hold that the quotation extends through verse 14; others through verse 16; and still others through verse 21. 2:20 Some English translations put this sentence in verse 19. 3:4 Or *Have you suffered.* 3:6 Gen 15:6. 3:8 Gen 12:3; 18:18; 22:18. 3:10 Deut 27:26. 3:11 Hab 2:4. 3:12 Lev 18:5. 3:13 Deut 21:23 (Greek version). 3:14 Some manuscripts read *the blessing of the.* 3:15 Greek *Brothers.*

his child.* And notice that the Scripture doesn't say "to his children,*" as if it meant many descendants. Rather, it says "to his child"—and that, of course, means Christ. [17] This is what I am trying to say: The agreement God made with Abraham could not be canceled 430 years later when God gave the law to Moses. God would be breaking his promise. [18] For if the inheritance could be received by keeping the law, then it would not be the result of accepting God's promise. But God graciously gave it to Abraham as a promise.

[19] Why, then, was the law given? It was given alongside the promise to show people their sins. But the law was designed to last only until the coming of the child who was promised. God gave his law through angels to Moses, who was the mediator between God and the people. [20] Now a mediator is helpful if more than one party must reach an agreement. But God, who is one, did not use a mediator when he gave his promise to Abraham.

[21] Is there a conflict, then, between God's law and God's promises?* Absolutely not! If the law could give us new life, we could be made right with God by obeying it. [22] But the Scriptures declare that we are all prisoners of sin, so we receive God's promise of freedom only by believing in Jesus Christ.

GOD'S CHILDREN THROUGH FAITH

[23] Before the way of faith in Christ was available to us, we were placed under guard by the law. We were kept in protective custody, so to speak, until the way of faith was revealed.

[24] Let me put it another way. The law was our guardian until Christ came; it protected us until we could be made right with God through faith. [25] And now that the way of faith has come, we no longer need the law as our guardian.

[26] For you are all children* of God through faith in Christ Jesus. [27] And all who have been united with Christ in baptism have put on Christ, like putting on new clothes.* [28] There is no longer Jew or Gentile,* slave or free, male and female. For you are all one in Christ Jesus. [29] And now that you belong to Christ, you are the true children* of Abraham. You are his heirs, and God's promise to Abraham belongs to you.

4 Think of it this way. If a father dies and leaves an inheritance for his young children, those children are not much better off than slaves until they grow up, even though they actually own everything their father had. [2] They have to obey their guardians until they reach whatever age their father set. [3] And that's the way it was with us before Christ came. We were like children; we were slaves to the basic spiritual principles* of this world.

[4] But when the right time came, God sent his Son, born of a woman, subject to the law. [5] God sent him to buy freedom for us who were slaves to the law, so that he could adopt us as his very own children.* [6] And because we* are his children, God has sent the Spirit of his Son into our hearts, prompting us to call out, "Abba, Father."* [7] Now you are no longer a slave but God's own child.* And since you are his child, God has made you his heir.

PAUL'S CONCERN FOR THE GALATIANS

[8] Before you Gentiles knew God, you were slaves to so-called gods that do not even exist. [9] So now that you know God (or should I say, now that God knows you), why do you want to go back again and become slaves once more to the weak and useless spiritual principles of this world? [10] You are trying to earn favor with God by observing certain days or months or seasons or years. [11] I fear for you. Perhaps all my hard work with you was for nothing. [12] Dear brothers and sisters,* I plead with you to live as I do in freedom from these things, for I have become like you Gentiles—free from those laws.

You did not mistreat me when I first preached to you. [13] Surely you remember that I was sick when I first brought you the Good News. [14] But even though my condition tempted you to reject me, you did not despise me or turn me away. No, you took me in and cared for me as though I were an angel from God or even Christ Jesus himself. [15] Where is that joyful and grateful spirit you felt then? I am sure you would have taken out your own eyes and given them to me if it had been possible. [16] Have I now become your enemy because I am telling you the truth?

[17] Those false teachers are so eager to win your favor, but their intentions are not good. They are trying to shut you off from me so that you will pay attention only to them. [18] If someone is eager to do good things for you, that's all right; but let them do it all the time, not just when I'm with you.

[19] Oh, my dear children! I feel as if I'm going through labor pains for you again, and they will continue until Christ is fully developed in your lives. [20] I wish I were with you right now so I could change my tone. But at this distance I don't know how else to help you.

ABRAHAM'S TWO CHILDREN

[21] Tell me, you who want to live under the law, do you know what the law actually says? [22] The Scriptures say that Abraham had two sons, one from his slave wife and one from his freeborn wife.* [23] The son of the slave wife was born in a human attempt to bring about the fulfillment of God's promise. But the son of the freeborn wife was born as God's own fulfillment of his promise.

3:16a Greek *seed;* also in 3:16c, 19. See notes on Gen 12:7 and 13:15.   3:16b Greek *seeds.*   3:21 Some manuscripts read *and the promises?*   3:26 Greek *sons.*   3:27 Greek *have put on Christ.* 3:28 Greek *Jew or Greek.*   3:29 Greek *seed.*   4:3 Or *powers;* also in 4:9.   4:5 Greek *sons;* also in 4:6.   4:6a Greek *you.*   4:6b *Abba* is an Aramaic term for "father."   4:7 Greek *son;* also in 4:7b. 4:12 Greek *brothers;* also in 4:28, 31.   4:22 See Gen 16:15; 21:2-3.

24 These two women serve as an illustration of God's two covenants. The first woman, Hagar, represents Mount Sinai where people received the law that enslaved them. 25 And now Jerusalem is just like Mount Sinai in Arabia,* because she and her children live in slavery to the law. 26 But the other woman, Sarah, represents the heavenly Jerusalem. She is the free woman, and she is our mother. 27 As Isaiah said,

"Rejoice, O childless woman,
    you who have never given birth!
Break into a joyful shout,
    you who have never been in labor!
For the desolate woman now has more
        children
    than the woman who lives with her
        husband!"*

28 And you, dear brothers and sisters, are children of the promise, just like Isaac. 29 But you are now being persecuted by those who want you to keep the law, just as Ishmael, the child born by human effort, persecuted Isaac, the child born by the power of the Spirit. 30 But what do the Scriptures say about that? "Get rid of the slave and her son, for the son of the slave woman will not share the inheritance with the free woman's son."* 31 So, dear brothers and sisters, we are not children of the slave woman; we are children of the free woman.

FREEDOM IN CHRIST

5 So Christ has truly set us free. Now make sure that you stay free, and don't get tied up again in slavery to the law.

2 Listen! I, Paul, tell you this: If you are counting on circumcision to make you right with God, then Christ will be of no benefit to you. 3 I'll say it again. If you are trying to find favor with God by being circumcised, you must obey every regulation in the whole law of Moses. 4 For if you are trying to make yourselves right with God by keeping the law, you have been cut off from Christ! You have fallen away from God's grace. 5 But we who live by the Spirit eagerly wait to receive by faith the righteousness God has promised to us. 6 For when we place our faith in Christ Jesus, there is no benefit in being circumcised or being uncircumcised. What is important is faith expressing itself in love.

7 You were running the race so well. Who has held you back from following the truth? 8 It certainly isn't God, for he is the one who called you to freedom. 9 This false teaching is like a little yeast that spreads through the whole batch of dough! 10 I am trusting the Lord to keep you from believing false teachings. God will judge that person, whoever he is, who has been confusing you.

11 Dear brothers and sisters,* if I were still preaching that you must be circumcised—as some say I do—why am I still being persecuted? If I were no longer preaching salvation through the cross of Christ, no one would be offended. 12 I just wish that those troublemakers who want to mutilate you by circumcision would mutilate themselves.*

13 For you have been called to live in freedom, my brothers and sisters. But don't use your freedom to satisfy your sinful nature. Instead, use your freedom to serve one another in love. 14 For the whole law can be summed up in this one command: "Love your neighbor as yourself."* 15 But if you are always biting and devouring one another, watch out! Beware of destroying one another.

LIVING BY THE SPIRIT'S POWER

16 So I say, let the Holy Spirit guide your lives. Then you won't be doing what your sinful nature craves. 17 The sinful nature wants to do evil, which is just the opposite of what the Spirit wants. And the Spirit gives us desires that are the opposite of what the sinful nature desires. These two forces are constantly fighting each other, so you are not free to carry out your good intentions. 18 But when you are directed by the Spirit, you are not under obligation to the law of Moses.

19 When you follow the desires of your sinful nature, the results are very clear: sexual immorality, impurity, lustful pleasures, 20 idolatry, sorcery, hostility, quarreling, jealousy, outbursts of anger, selfish ambition, dissension, division, 21 envy, drunkenness, wild parties, and other sins like these. Let me tell you again, as I have before, that anyone living that sort of life will not inherit the Kingdom of God.

22 But the Holy Spirit produces this kind of fruit in our lives: love, joy, peace, patience, kindness, goodness, faithfulness, 23 gentleness, and self-control. There is no law against these things! 24 Those who belong to Christ Jesus have nailed the passions and desires of their sinful nature to his cross and crucified them there. 25 Since we are living by the Spirit, let us follow the Spirit's leading in every part of our lives. 26 Let us not become conceited, or provoke one another, or be jealous of one another.

WE HARVEST WHAT WE PLANT

6 Dear brothers and sisters, if another believer* is overcome by some sin, you who are godly* should gently and humbly help that person back onto the right path. And be careful not to fall into the same temptation yourself. 2 Share each other's burdens, and in this way obey the law of Christ. 3 If you think you are too important to

---

4:25 Greek And Hagar, which is Mount Sinai in Arabia, is now like Jerusalem; other manuscripts read And Mount Sinai in Arabia is now like Jerusalem. 4:27 Isa 54:1. 4:30 Gen 21:10. 5:11 Greek Brothers; similarly in 5:13. 5:12 Or castrate themselves, or cut themselves off from you; Greek reads cut themselves off. 5:14 Lev 19:18. 6:1a Greek Brothers, if a man. 6:1b Greek spiritual.

help someone, you are only fooling yourself. You are not that important.

[4] Pay careful attention to your own work, for then you will get the satisfaction of a job well done, and you won't need to compare yourself to anyone else. [5] For we are each responsible for our own conduct.

[6] Those who are taught the word of God should provide for their teachers, sharing all good things with them.

[7] Don't be misled—you cannot mock the justice of God. You will always harvest what you plant. [8] Those who live only to satisfy their own sinful nature will harvest decay and death from that sinful nature. But those who live to please the Spirit will harvest everlasting life from the Spirit. [9] So let's not get tired of doing what is good. At just the right time we will reap a harvest of blessing if we don't give up. [10] Therefore, whenever we have the opportunity, we should do good to everyone—especially to those in the family of faith.

PAUL'S FINAL ADVICE

[11] NOTICE WHAT LARGE LETTERS I USE AS I WRITE THESE CLOSING WORDS IN MY OWN HANDWRITING.

[12] Those who are trying to force you to be circumcised want to look good to others. They don't want to be persecuted for teaching that the cross of Christ alone can save. [13] And even those who advocate circumcision don't keep the whole law themselves. They only want you to be circumcised so they can boast about it and claim you as their disciples.

[14] As for me, may I never boast about anything except the cross of our Lord Jesus Christ. Because of that cross,* my interest in this world has been crucified, and the world's interest in me has also died. [15] It doesn't matter whether we have been circumcised or not. What counts is whether we have been transformed into a new creation. [16] May God's peace and mercy be upon all who live by this principle; they are the new people of God.*

[17] From now on, don't let anyone trouble me with these things. For I bear on my body the scars that show I belong to Jesus.

[18] Dear brothers and sisters,* may the grace of our Lord Jesus Christ be with your spirit. Amen.

6:14 Or Because of him.   6:16 Greek this principle, and upon the Israel of God.   6:18 Greek Brothers.

THE MINISTRY OF THE HOLY SPIRIT IN EPHESIANS

JON HUNTZINGER, PHD

Not only does Paul refer to the Father and Son in his letter, but he also discusses the ministry of the Holy Spirit and uses several metaphors to describe His ministry. Paul begins by saying the Spirit is a "guarantee" of all God's future promises (1:13-14). The Ephesians were given the Spirit when they received the word of truth (the gospel) concerning Jesus. The image of the Spirit in this metaphor is of a notary who validates a word or promise and makes authentic God's adoption of the Ephesians as His sons and daughters.

The Spirit builds God's people into a dwelling place God can inhabit (2:21-22). The Spirit places Jews and Gentiles together in such a way that God can be present to them. He does this by fitting each together in relation to Jesus, who is the cornerstone. The image of the Spirit in the metaphor is of a contractor who builds up a people into a holy place where God can be present.

The Spirit unites God's people as they walk as children of God (4:3-4). The people are bound together in their hope of being sons and daughters and joined in relationship to Jesus and to God the Father. The gift of the Spirit is relationship with others and with God. The image of the Spirit here is of a bond that binds one person to another.

The Spirit fills God's people so they may walk in wisdom and worship God with all their hearts (5:15-20), know God's will, and submit to the way of life He offers. The image of the Spirit in these verses is of inspiration that moves people in the praises of God.

The Spirit arms God's people with His Word and enables them to pray. The Word of God and prayer is the means by which the Ephesians will fulfill their purpose as the body of Christ (6:17-18). The image of the Spirit in this passage is of an instrument of spiritual warfare.

Finally, the Spirit strengthens the inner man (2:18). Since the inner being is the place where we make decisions, the gift of the Spirit is that Jesus will dwell in our hearts and thus determine what we will and will not do. The image of the Spirit is of a trainer who makes the people strong in their resolve and commitment to God.

EPHESIANS

JON HUNTZINGER, PHD

BACKGROUND

Paul's ministry in Ephesus began during his third missionary journey in AD 55. According to the book of Acts, when Paul first arrived in the city, he baptized followers of John in the name of Jesus, laid hands on them to receive the Holy Spirit, taught them about the Kingdom of God, and was "held daily discussions" in Tyrannus's hall (Acts 19:9). Miracles supported his teaching, including the deliverance of an evil spirit that had overwhelmed the seven sons of Sceva (Acts 19:13-16).

Ephesus was the third largest city in the Roman world after Rome and Alexandria, with a population of 250,000 people. It was a center for the worship of Artemis (goddess of fertility), and its temple (the Artemisian) was one of the seven wonders of the ancient world. It measured 425 feet (130 m) long, 220 feet (67 m) wide, 60 feet (18 m) high, and had 127 pillars of marble inlaid with gold. Temple priestesses were called *bees*, and eunuch priests were called *drones*. So important was the cult of Artemis in Ephesus that the city was known as the guardian (*neokoros*) of Artemis. A festival celebrating the goddess was held every May when statues of her were carried along the main street with music and dancing to the theatre that seated 25,000-30,000 people. So successful was Paul's ministry of the gospel in the city that the silversmith Demetrius stirred up massive opposition to it because of the loss of business at the temple (Acts 19:23-20:1).

Paul wrote the letter to the Ephesians during his house arrest in Rome in the early AD 60s as he waited for his hearing before Caesar. Paul had been arrested in Jerusalem for causing a disturbance at the Temple (Acts 23-25), but he had requested that Caesar hear his case, which was his right as a Roman citizen. Consequently, this letter is identified as one of Paul's "prison epistles," letters written by him while under arrest. The other prison epistles include Colossians, Philippians, and Philemon, which he wrote around the same time. This letter to the Ephesians was a sermon addressed to Jewish and Gentile believers in and around Ephesus.

Paul's letter to the Ephesians includes seven major sections:
— The people receive their election and inheritance through love (1:1-14).
— God has revealed His purposes to His people (1:15-22).
— Paul discusses human sin and divine mercy (2:1-10).

— He expounds on the formation of a people for worship (2:11-22).
— Paul explains his calling to be a minister of God's mystery (3:1-13).
— He discusses walking as the people of God (4:1-6:9).
— Paul describes God's people as a fully-equipped soldier ready to stand and conquer (6:10-20).

ELECTION IN EPHESIANS

Paul begins his letter by saying that God has elected the Ephesian church to be His sons and daughters. For the apostle, election is not simply about individual salvation but also about witness and worship, as well as testimony, proclamation, and service. Therefore, Paul's idea of election is about the privilege God gives to people to be in relationship with Him and to tell others about Him. Election is another word for calling, and such calling involves human response. In the Old Testament, God chose the Israelites to be His people because He loved them—not because He did not love others (Deuteronomy 7). The Israelites had a choice about how they would respond. It is important to remember that the biblical teaching about election does not speak of divine damnation of those who are not elected. *God shows His mercy to all people through the election of one people.* Israel is the means by which all people can know God.

PAUL'S MINISTRY OF THE GOSPEL OF PEACE

The Ephesian church called by God consisted of Jews and Gentiles, and the gospel Paul preached among them included the mystery that they (Jews and Gentiles) had been joined together as one people according to God (3:8-9). Paul says this reconciliation was accomplished through the blood of Jesus, which (1) brought the Gentiles near to God the Father, (2) broke down the wall of hostility with the Jews, and (3) created a unified man in place of a divided man (2:13-17). For Paul, this is the promise of the gospel and the foundation upon which the church must stand. Consequently, the gospel is ultimately a message of peace and not hostility or division, which he compares to shoes that allow people to stand firmly on their two feet (6:15). For Paul, the gospel or Good News is that Jesus intends for His Church to stand on its two feet of Jews and

Gentiles in peace with one another. The gospel is ultimately a message about the reconciliation that comes through Jesus who has made peace through His cross—for all people with God and for Jews and Gentiles with one another.

FATHER, SON, CHILDREN

In the opening passage of Ephesians, Paul introduces God as a Father, Jesus as His Son, and the Ephesians as adopted children through the love of God by the Spirit. Throughout the remainder of the letter, Paul elaborates on who God is, who Jesus is, and who the Ephesian church is:

Who God Is
— God is the Father of the Lord Jesus, and He is the Father of the Ephesians who have become sons and daughters through adoption (1:3).
— He has an eternal plan for His children (1:9-10).
— God gives an inheritance to them (1:11, 18).
— He gives spiritual blessing to them by sealing them with His Spirit (1:3, 13).
— God is the Father of glory, who reveals His glory to others (1:17).
— He is rich in mercy (2:4).

Who Jesus Is
— Jesus is the Son of the Father (1:3).

— He is seated at the right hand of God in heaven far above all rule, authority, power, and dominion (1:20-21).
— Jesus' life is a fragrant offering to God since He gave His life for the Church (5:2).
— Because of His offering, Jesus is the head of the Church (1:22; 4:15; 5:23).
— Jesus' life, death, and resurrection—the essence of the gospel—cleanses the Church by His Word and makes the Church holy (5:26-27).

Who the (Ephesian) Church Is
— The Church is God's "masterpiece" (2:10).
— It has been brought near to God (2:13).
— The Church is a holy temple and dwelling place for the Holy Spirit (2:21-22).
— Members of the Church are children of the light (5:8).
— They are worshippers of God (5:19-20).
— The Church is a soldier for God (6:10-18).

Thus, Paul uses several different metaphors to describe the Church in his letter to the Ephesians. They are a family of adopted sons and daughters with the promise of an inheritance; a priceless work of art; a holy temple in which God's Spirit will dwell; the body of Christ blessed with gifts and with Jesus as the head (4:11-16); and a fully-equipped soldier called to stand in the vanguard against God's cosmic enemies.

GREETINGS FROM PAUL

1 This letter is from Paul, chosen by the will of God to be an apostle of Christ Jesus.

I am writing to God's holy people in Ephesus,* who are faithful followers of Christ Jesus. ² May God our Father and the Lord Jesus Christ give you grace and peace.

SPIRITUAL BLESSINGS

³ All praise to God, the Father of our Lord Jesus Christ, who has blessed us with every spiritual blessing in the heavenly realms because we are united with Christ. ⁴ Even before he made the world, God loved us and chose us in Christ to be holy and without fault in his eyes. ⁵ God decided in advance to adopt us into his own family by bringing us to himself through Jesus Christ. This is what he wanted to do, and it gave him great pleasure. ⁶ So we praise God for the glorious grace he has poured out on us who belong to his dear Son.* ⁷ He is so rich in kindness and grace that he purchased our freedom with the blood of his Son and forgave our sins. ⁸ He has showered his kindness on us, along with all wisdom and understanding. ⁹ God has now revealed to us his mysterious will regarding Christ—which is to fulfill his own good plan. ¹⁰ And this is the plan: At the right

time he will bring everything together under the authority of Christ—everything in heaven and on earth. ¹¹ Furthermore, because we are united with Christ, we have received an inheritance from God,* for he chose us in advance, and he makes everything work out according to his plan. ¹² God's purpose was that we Jews who were the first to trust in Christ would bring praise and glory to God. ¹³ And now you Gentiles have also heard the truth, the Good News that God saves you. And when you believed in Christ, he identified you as his own* by giving you the Holy Spirit, whom he promised long ago. ¹⁴ The Spirit is God's guarantee that he will give us the inheritance he promised and that he has purchased us to be his own people. He did this so we would praise and glorify him.

PAUL'S PRAYER FOR SPIRITUAL WISDOM

¹⁵ Ever since I first heard of your strong faith in the Lord Jesus and your love for God's people everywhere,* ¹⁶ I have not stopped thanking God

---

1:1 The most ancient manuscripts do not include *in Ephesus.* 1:6 Greek *to us in the beloved.* 1:11 Or *we have become God's inheritance.* 1:13 Or *he put his seal on you.* 1:15 Some manuscripts read *your faithfulness to the Lord Jesus and to God's people everywhere.*

SAVED
Ephesians 2:1-8   ROBERT MORRIS

At Gateway Church, our vision statement begins with seeing people saved. But what does *saved* really mean? The Greek word for saved is *sozo* (pronounced "sode-zo"), and it means 'to be made whole spirit, soul, and body.' Here are seven essential truths about being saved:

1. It's a gift.

We receive salvation by grace through faith in Jesus Christ. Salvation isn't a goal to be achieved; it's a gift to be received. A gift, by definition, is free, and the apostle Paul confirms that God's grace is "free and undeserved" (Romans 11:6).

2. It's eternal life.

Romans 6:23 says, "The wages of sin is death, but the free gift of God is eternal life through Christ Jesus our Lord."

3. It's forgiveness.

Salvation means "we receive God's forgiveness for all our sins"—past, present, and future. We are completely and totally released, and God promises never to remember them again (Psalm 103:12; Jeremiah 31:34).

4. It's justification.

Justification means "justice has been served and a wrong situation has been made right." Jesus took the punishment we deserved for our sins, and because of His sacrifice, we are now justified in God's sight (Romans 3:24; Galatians 2:16). God declares us *not guilty!*

5. It's righteousness.

Righteousness means "right standing with God." (Romans 4:3). We could never be good enough on our own, but when we get saved, God takes Jesus' righteousness and puts it into our account.

6. It's redemption.

Redeemed means "to be bought back." God gave the ownership of the world to Adam and Eve, but through sin, they lost it to Satan. Jesus came and legally bought us back "with a high price"—His own blood (1 Corinthians 6:19-20).

7. It's total commitment.

Salvation requires total commitment—the complete submission of our wills to the lordship of Christ. Many people think they are saved because they believe Jesus is God's Son and because they attend church. However, they aren't willing to give up control of their lives, so they are actually on their way to hell (Matthew 7:21; Luke 6:46). Ask yourself, *Who is in control of my life?* First John 5:13 says we can know that we have eternal life, and this only comes through total submission to Jesus.

WHAT'S SO AMAZING ABOUT GRACE?
Ephesians 2:8-9   ROBERT MORRIS

Salvation has nothing to do with human effort or works; it comes by *grace* through faith. The apostle Paul writes, "God saved you by his grace when you believed. And you can't take the credit for this; it is a gift from God" (Ephesians 2:8-9).

Grace is the unmerited, undeserved, and unearned kindness and favor of God. Nothing we could ever do or say would be enough to pay the price for our sins. So God paid it for us! In the most incredible demonstration of grace in history, He gave His own Son, Jesus, as a perfect sacrifice and "freed us from the penalty for our sins" (Romans 3:24).

When we put our faith in Jesus, His blood covers all our mistakes, problems, and failures and puts us in right standing with God forever. This kind of grace really is *amazing*!

you might grow in your knowledge of God. [18] I pray that your hearts will be flooded with light so that you can understand the confident hope he has given to those he called—his holy people who are his rich and glorious inheritance.*

[19] I also pray that you will understand the incredible greatness of God's power for us who believe him. This is the same mighty power [20] that raised Christ from the dead and seated him in the place of honor at God's right hand in the heavenly realms. [21] Now he is far above any ruler or authority or power or leader or anything else—not only in this world but also in the world to come. [22] God has put all things under the authority of Christ and has made him head over all things for the benefit of the church. [23] And the church is his body; it is made full and complete by Christ, who fills all things everywhere with himself.

MADE ALIVE WITH CHRIST

2 Once you were dead because of your disobedience and your many sins. [2] You used to live in sin, just like the rest of the world, obeying the devil—the commander of the powers in the unseen world.* He is the spirit at work in the hearts of those who refuse to obey God. [3] All of us used to live that way, following the passionate desires and inclinations of our sinful nature. By our very nature we were subject to God's anger, just like everyone else.

[4] But God is so rich in mercy, and he loved us so much, [5] that even though we were dead because of our sins, he gave us life when he raised Christ from the dead. (It is only by God's grace that you

for you. I pray for you constantly, [17] asking God, the glorious Father of our Lord Jesus Christ, to give you spiritual wisdom* and insight so that

---

1:17 Or *to give you the Spirit of wisdom.* 1:18 Or *called, and the rich and glorious inheritance he has given to his holy people.* 2:2 Greek *obeying the commander of the power of the air.*

LIVING TOGETHER GOD'S WAY
Ephesians 3   JACK HAYFORD

The open door for the Gentiles to receive salvation is something the Old Testament prophets did not see coming. Everyone thought the Kingdom of God would be fully in place immediately following the appearance of the Messiah. The revelation that Gentiles also had a place in this Kingdom required a significant shift in the minds of Jewish believers.

In Ephesians 3, Paul expresses deep gratitude for "the privilege of telling the Gentiles about the endless treasures available to them in Christ" (v. 8). He explains that both Jews *and* Gentiles are part of the body of Christ and heirs of God's promises. Together, as God's family, they are to spread the seeds of His love and plan to the entire world.

God cares more about people than cultural backgrounds or doctrines. He wants Jews and Gentiles to believe in Him, trust His purpose in them, and live together as a family in Him forever.

have been saved!) ⁶ For he raised us from the dead along with Christ and seated us with him in the heavenly realms because we are united with Christ Jesus. ⁷ So God can point to us in all future ages as examples of the incredible wealth of his grace and kindness toward us, as shown in all he has done for us who are united with Christ Jesus.

⁸ God saved you by his grace when you believed. And you can't take credit for this; it is a gift from God. ⁹ Salvation is not a reward for the good things we have done, so none of us can boast about it. ¹⁰ For we are God's masterpiece. He has created us anew in Christ Jesus, so we can do the good things he planned for us long ago.

ONENESS AND PEACE IN CHRIST

¹¹ Don't forget that you Gentiles used to be outsiders. You were called "uncircumcised heathens" by the Jews, who were proud of their circumcision, even though it affected only their bodies and not their hearts. ¹² In those days you were living apart from Christ. You were excluded from citizenship among the people of Israel, and you did not know the covenant promises God had made to them. You lived in this world without God and without hope. ¹³ But now you have been united with Christ Jesus. Once you were far away from God, but now you have been brought near to him through the blood of Christ.

¹⁴ For Christ himself has brought peace to us. He united Jews and Gentiles into one people when, in his own body on the cross, he broke down the wall of hostility that separated us. ¹⁵ He did this by ending the system of law with its commandments and regulations. He made peace

between Jews and Gentiles by creating in himself one new people from the two groups. ¹⁶ Together as one body, Christ reconciled both groups to God by means of his death on the cross, and our hostility toward each other was put to death.

¹⁷ He brought this Good News of peace to you Gentiles who were far away from him, and peace to the Jews who were near. ¹⁸ Now all of us can come to the Father through the same Holy Spirit because of what Christ has done for us.

A TEMPLE FOR THE LORD

¹⁹ So now you Gentiles are no longer strangers and foreigners. You are citizens along with all of God's holy people. You are members of God's family. ²⁰ Together, we are his house, built on the foundation of the apostles and the prophets. And the cornerstone is Christ Jesus himself. ²¹ We are carefully joined together in him, becoming a holy temple for the Lord. ²² Through him you Gentiles are also being made part of this dwelling where God lives by his Spirit.

GOD'S MYSTERIOUS PLAN REVEALED

3 When I think of all this, I, Paul, a prisoner of Christ Jesus for the benefit of you Gentiles* . . . ² assuming, by the way, that you know God gave me the special responsibility of extending his grace to you Gentiles. ³ As I briefly wrote earlier, God himself revealed his mysterious plan to me. ⁴ As you read what I have written, you will understand my insight into this plan regarding Christ. ⁵ God did not reveal it to previous generations, but now by his Spirit he has revealed it to his holy apostles and prophets.

⁶ And this is God's plan: Both Gentiles and Jews who believe the Good News share equally in the riches inherited by God's children. Both are part of the same body, and both enjoy the promise of blessings because they belong to Christ Jesus.* ⁷ By God's grace and mighty power, I have been given the privilege of serving him by spreading this Good News.

⁸ Though I am the least deserving of all God's people, he graciously gave me the privilege of telling the Gentiles about the endless treasures available to them in Christ. ⁹ I was chosen to explain to everyone* this mysterious plan that God, the Creator of all things, had kept secret from the beginning.

¹⁰ God's purpose in all this was to use the church to display his wisdom in its rich variety to all the unseen rulers and authorities in the heavenly places. ¹¹ This was his eternal plan, which he carried out through Christ Jesus our Lord.

¹² Because of Christ and our faith in him,* we can now come boldly and confidently into God's presence. ¹³ So please don't lose heart because

---

3:1 Paul resumes this thought in verse 14: "When I think of all this, I fall to my knees and pray to the Father." 3:6 Or *because they are united with Christ Jesus.* 3:9 Some manuscripts do not include *to everyone.* 3:12 Or *Because of Christ's faithfulness.*

of my trials here. I am suffering for you, so you should feel honored.

PAUL'S PRAYER FOR SPIRITUAL GROWTH

¹⁴ When I think of all this, I fall to my knees and pray to the Father,* ¹⁵ the Creator of everything in heaven and on earth.* ¹⁶ I pray that from his glorious, unlimited resources he will empower you with inner strength through his Spirit. ¹⁷ Then Christ will make his home in your hearts as you trust in him. Your roots will grow down into God's love and keep you strong. ¹⁸ And may you have the power to understand, as all God's people should, how wide, how long, how high, and how deep his love is. ¹⁹ May you experience the love of Christ, though it is too great to understand fully. Then you will be made complete with all the fullness of life and power that comes from God.

²⁰ Now all glory to God, who is able, through his mighty power at work within us, to accomplish infinitely more than we might ask or think. ²¹ Glory to him in the church and in Christ Jesus through all generations forever and ever! Amen.

UNITY IN THE BODY

4 Therefore I, a prisoner for serving the Lord, beg you to lead a life worthy of your calling, for you have been called by God. ² Always be humble and gentle. Be patient with each other, making allowance for each other's faults because of your love. ³ Make every effort to keep yourselves united in the Spirit, binding yourselves together with peace. ⁴ For there is one body and one Spirit, just as you have been called to one glorious hope for the future.

⁵ There is one Lord, one faith, one baptism,
⁶ one God and Father of all,
   who is over all, in all, and living through all.

⁷ However, he has given each one of us a special gift* through the generosity of Christ. ⁸ That is why the Scriptures say,

"When he ascended to the heights,
   he led a crowd of captives
   and gave gifts to his people."*

⁹ Notice that it says "he ascended." This clearly means that Christ also descended to our lowly world.* ¹⁰ And the same one who descended is the one who ascended higher than all the heavens, so that he might fill the entire universe with himself.

¹¹ Now these are the gifts Christ gave to the church: the apostles, the prophets, the evangelists, and the pastors and teachers. ¹² Their responsibility is to equip God's people to do his work and build up the church, the body of Christ. ¹³ This will continue until we all come to such unity in our faith and knowledge of God's Son

EQUIPPED
Ephesians 4:11-12   ROBERT MORRIS

One of my favorite things about our church is the way people do the work of the ministry by loving, caring, and reaching out to others. You may be thinking, *Isn't ministry the pastor's job?* However, Ephesians 4:12 says a pastor's job is to "equip God's people to do his work and build up the church." In other words, a pastor's purpose is to equip *you* for the work of the ministry.

No matter what your job title is, if you're a believer, God calls you to ministry. Here are three keys to being equipped to do God's work:

1. Be available.

God doesn't need people with ability; after all, He has all the ability in the universe. Instead, He looks for people with *availability*. Paul instructs Timothy to teach the truths of God's Word "to other trustworthy people who will be able to pass them on to others" (2 Timothy 2:2). Notice the order: you have to be trustworthy before God will make you able.

2. Be a servant.

The world measures success by how many people serve you. In the Kingdom of God, however, success is measured by how many people you serve. Jesus told His disciples, "Whoever wants to be first must take last place and be the servant of everyone else" (Mark 9:35). You may start by serving somewhere that's not your ultimate place of gifting, but as you faithfully serve, God will open the door for you to use your gifts.

3. Be a minister.

Some people are called to vocational ministry; being a pastor, evangelist, or missionary is their profession. However, *every* believer is called to full-time ministry. No one gets to be a part-time Christian. First Peter 3:15 says, "If someone asks about your hope as a believer, always be ready to explain it." No matter where we work, we should always be ready and available to minister to others.

that we will be mature in the Lord, measuring up to the full and complete standard of Christ. ¹⁴ Then we will no longer be immature like children. We won't be tossed and blown about by every wind of new teaching. We will not be influenced when people try to trick us with lies so clever they sound like the truth. ¹⁵ Instead, we will speak the truth in love, growing in every way more and more like Christ, who is the head of his body, the church. ¹⁶ He makes the whole body fit together perfectly. As each part does its

---

3:14 Some manuscripts read *the Father of our Lord Jesus Christ.*
3:15 Or *from whom every family in heaven and on earth takes its name.*   4:7 Greek *a grace.*   4:8 Ps 68:18.   4:9 Some manuscripts read *to the lower parts of the earth.*

BREAKING OLD MOLDS, BUILDING NEW PATTERNS
Ephesians 4:22-32   JACK HAYFORD

Today, the average believer thinks human nature can be reshaped and improved, but it really cannot. Human nature is corrupt and can only be transformed by the power of God's Word and the Holy Spirit. Ephesians 4 explains how God is calling us to come away from the world, the flesh, and the devil:

— "Stop telling lies" (v. 25).
  God desires us to live completely free of deceit, dishonesty, and compromising speech.
— "Don't sin by letting anger control you" (v. 26).
  We must deal with anger immediately and not allow it to become a foothold for the devil.
— "Quit stealing. Instead, use your hands for good hard work" (v. 28).
  God calls us to honor our commitments to our job.
— "Don't use foul or abusive language" (v. 29).
  Our words should build respect, not tear each other down.
— "Get rid of all bitterness, rage, anger, harsh words, and slander . . . Instead, be kind to each other" (vv. 31-32).
  All of these things flow out of bitterness. Bitterness infects our souls. When it pours out, it spreads infection to others.

CONFLICT RESOLUTION
Ephesians 4:25-27   TOM LANE

Conflict is a normal part of relationships. It is unrealistic to expect godly relationships not to have conflict. The absence of conflict does not necessarily determine or reflect the quality or depth of a relationship. However, godly relationships should not have violent interactions, stonewalling, withdrawal, rages, and unrighteous verbal assaults.

Ephesians 4:26 tells us not to "let the sun go down while you are still angry." We need to address conflict while it is fresh, or else it can become a root of bitterness and hurt that will damage our relationships. Some situations are easy to forgive while others are more complicated. Here is a simple but important question to ask in times of anger: *God, how should I respond?* Ask Him to come to your defense and bring the situation to a resolution. God's wisdom is greater than any human mediation, and He can bring peace to even the most troubled relationships.

own special work, it helps the other parts grow, so that the whole body is healthy and growing and full of love.

LIVING AS CHILDREN OF LIGHT
[17] With the Lord's authority I say this: Live no longer as the Gentiles do, for they are hopelessly confused. [18] Their minds are full of darkness; they wander far from the life God gives because they have closed their minds and hardened their hearts against him. [19] They have no sense of shame. They live for lustful pleasure and eagerly practice every kind of impurity.

[20] But that isn't what you learned about Christ. [21] Since you have heard about Jesus and have learned the truth that comes from him, [22] throw off your old sinful nature and your former way of life, which is corrupted by lust and deception. [23] Instead, let the Spirit renew your thoughts and attitudes. [24] Put on your new nature, created to be like God—truly righteous and holy.

[25] So stop telling lies. Let us tell our neighbors the truth, for we are all parts of the same body. [26] And "don't sin by letting anger control you."* Don't let the sun go down while you are still angry, [27] for anger gives a foothold to the devil. [28] If you are a thief, quit stealing. Instead, use your hands for good hard work, and then give generously to others in need. [29] Don't use foul or abusive language. Let everything you say be good and helpful, so that your words will be an encouragement to those who hear them.

[30] And do not bring sorrow to God's Holy Spirit by the way you live. Remember, he has identified you as his own,* guaranteeing that you will be saved on the day of redemption. [31] Get rid of all bitterness, rage, anger, harsh words, and slander, as well as all types of evil behavior. [32] Instead, be kind to each other, tenderhearted, forgiving one another, just as God through Christ has forgiven you.

LIVING IN THE LIGHT
5 Imitate God, therefore, in everything you do, because you are his dear children. [2] Live a life filled with love, following the example of Christ. He loved us* and offered himself as a sacrifice for us, a pleasing aroma to God.

[3] Let there be no sexual immorality, impurity, or greed among you. Such sins have no place among God's people. [4] Obscene stories, foolish talk, and coarse jokes—these are not for you. Instead, let there be thankfulness to God. [5] You can be sure that no immoral, impure, or greedy person will inherit the Kingdom of Christ and of God. For a greedy person is an idolater, worshiping the things of this world.

[6] Don't be fooled by those who try to excuse these sins, for the anger of God will fall on all

4:26 Ps 4:4.   4:30 Or *has put his seal on you.*   5:2 Some manuscripts read *loved you.*

HAPPY HUSBAND, HAPPY HOME
Ephesians 5:21-31   ROBERT MORRIS

In Ephesians 5:21, the apostle Paul tells us to "submit to one another out of reverence for Christ." Many people don't like the word *submit*, but as believers, we are called to live in submission to God and each other. If you're married, submission simply means taking your mission (i.e., your desires and dreams) in life and putting it under the Lord and under your spouse's mission.

God designed marriage to be a reflection of His image on earth, and a great marriage is one in which each spouse's needs are recognized and met by the other in a biblical way. Here are three of the greatest needs of every husband:

1. Companionship
God made Eve because Adam needed a helper—a companion (Genesis 2:18). I would even use the word "friend" or "playmate." Adam wanted someone with whom he could do things. Men love to have fun with their wives; it's the reason they fell in love in the first place!

2. Sex
Sex is not a dirty word. God created it for men and women to enjoy within the confines of marriage. Men connect with their emotions through sex. Sex is a valid need; however, it can only truly be met within the confines of marriage. When it's met in an impure way or outside of marriage, it will always bring destruction and death (James 1:14-15).

3. Honor
Honor is the number one need in a man's life—it's the key to his heart. A husband will never open up emotionally if his wife doesn't honor him. Men are much more sensitive to words than we often realize. The key to connecting to a man's heart is not *what* you say but *how* you say it.

WASHED BY THE WORD
Ephesians 5:25-26   ROBERT MORRIS

Do you take a bath every day? This question isn't about your body. It's about your soul—your mind, will, and emotions. Your soul is in a battle with Satan, who constantly tries to flood your thoughts, desires, and feelings with lies. Many Christians are losing this battle, and the reason is simple—they are not being washed by the Word (Ephesians 5:25-26). Simply put, they're not bathing in God's Word every day.

When you accept God's salvation through Jesus, your spirit is justified and completely cleansed. However, your soul is still being saved, which in the Greek means 'made whole.' For example, some believers continue to have impure and immoral thoughts because they are still copying the world's behavior. Romans 12:2 says, "Let God transform you into a new person by changing the way you think." Allow God's Word to wash you every day, and I guarantee your life will be transformed!

LIVING BY THE SPIRIT'S POWER

15 So be careful how you live. Don't live like fools, but like those who are wise. 16 Make the most of every opportunity in these evil days. 17 Don't act thoughtlessly, but understand what the Lord wants you to do. 18 Don't be drunk with wine, because that will ruin your life. Instead, be filled with the Holy Spirit, 19 singing psalms and hymns and spiritual songs among yourselves, and making music to the Lord in your hearts. 20 And give thanks for everything to God the Father in the name of our Lord Jesus Christ.

SPIRIT-GUIDED RELATIONSHIPS: WIVES AND HUSBANDS

21 And further, submit to one another out of reverence for Christ.

22 For wives, this means submit to your husbands as to the Lord. 23 For a husband is the head of his wife as Christ is the head of the church. He is the Savior of his body, the church. 24 As the church submits to Christ, so you wives should submit to your husbands in everything.

25 For husbands, this means love your wives, just as Christ loved the church. He gave up his life for her 26 to make her holy and clean, washed by the cleansing of God's word.* 27 He did this to present her to himself as a glorious church without a spot or wrinkle or any other blemish. Instead, she will be holy and without fault. 28 In the same way, husbands ought to love their wives as they love their own bodies. For a man who loves his wife actually shows love for himself.

who disobey him. 7 Don't participate in the things these people do. 8 For once you were full of darkness, but now you have light from the Lord. So live as people of light! 9 For this light within you produces only what is good and right and true. 10 Carefully determine what pleases the Lord. 11 Take no part in the worthless deeds of evil and darkness; instead, expose them. 12 It is shameful even to talk about the things that ungodly people do in secret. 13 But their evil intentions will be exposed when the light shines on them, 14 for the light makes everything visible. This is why it is said,

"Awake, O sleeper,
    rise up from the dead,
    and Christ will give you light."

5:26 Greek *washed by water with the word.*

HAPPY WIFE, HAPPY LIFE
Ephesians 5:25-30   ROBERT MORRIS

Ephesians 5:25 tells husbands to love their wives as Jesus loves the Church: "He gave up his life for her." Giving up your life for your spouse means recognizing and honoring his or her needs and desires, especially when they are different than yours. Here are three needs wives have that their husbands are designed to meet:

1. Communication
Women don't want the headlines or bottom lines—they want the full story with all the details. For wives, communication isn't simply talking; it's connecting on a heart-to-heart level.

2. Leadership
The number one complaint I've encountered from women in marriage counseling is "My husband won't lead." Wives don't want to be dominated, but they do want their husbands to take initiative, especially when it comes to spiritual matters, children, and romance. By the way, romance for a woman isn't just sex; it's thinking about her and meeting a need before it's spoken.

3. Security
Security is a woman's most important need. The number one thing that makes a woman feel secure is a selfless, sacrificial man. A wife wants to know her husband will do whatever it takes to take care of her for the rest of her life. When this need is met in a woman's life, it changes everything!

---

[29] No one hates his own body but feeds and cares for it, just as Christ cares for the church. [30] And we are members of his body.

[31] As the Scriptures say, "A man leaves his father and mother and is joined to his wife, and the two are united into one."* [32] This is a great mystery, but it is an illustration of the way Christ and the church are one. [33] So again I say, each man must love his wife as he loves himself, and the wife must respect her husband.

CHILDREN AND PARENTS

6 Children, obey your parents because you belong to the Lord,* for this is the right thing to do. [2] "Honor your father and mother." This is the first commandment with a promise: [3] If you honor your father and mother, "things will

go well for you, and you will have a long life on the earth."*

[4] Fathers,* do not provoke your children to anger by the way you treat them. Rather, bring them up with the discipline and instruction that comes from the Lord.

SLAVES AND MASTERS

[5] Slaves, obey your earthly masters with deep respect and fear. Serve them sincerely as you would serve Christ. [6] Try to please them all the time, not just when they are watching you. As slaves of Christ, do the will of God with all your heart. [7] Work with enthusiasm, as though you were working for the Lord rather than for people. [8] Remember that the Lord will reward each one of us for the good we do, whether we are slaves or free.

[9] Masters, treat your slaves in the same way. Don't threaten them; remember, you both have the same Master in heaven, and he has no favorites.

THE WHOLE ARMOR OF GOD

[10] A final word: Be strong in the Lord and in his mighty power. [11] Put on all of God's armor so that you will be able to stand firm against all strategies of the devil. [12] For we* are not fighting against flesh-and-blood enemies, but against evil rulers and authorities of the unseen world, against mighty powers in this dark world, and against evil spirits in the heavenly places.

[13] Therefore, put on every piece of God's armor so you will be able to resist the enemy in the time of evil. Then after the battle you will still be standing firm. [14] Stand your ground, putting on the belt of truth and the body armor of God's

HONORING OUR TWO FATHERS
Ephesians 6:1-3   JIMMY EVANS

We all have two fathers—an earthly father and a heavenly Father. Fathers provide protection, provision, affection, training, and guidance. Our two fathers were designed to operate as a team and bring blessings into our lives. Even if your earthly father had shortcomings, your heavenly Father is perfect.

In Ephesians 6:2, Paul tells us to honor our fathers and mothers. This command comes with a promise: if we do this, our lives will be long and blessed. There is no qualifier in this verse that says we only honor them if they are worthy or deserving. We are to honor them in obedience to God's Word.

Honor your earthly father by remembering what he did right and thanking him for it. Give him grace for his imperfections and mistakes. Honor your heavenly Father by believing in His love and putting your faith in Him.

5:31 Gen 2:24. 6:1 Or *Children, obey your parents who belong to the Lord;* some manuscripts read simply *Children, obey your parents.* 6:2-3 Exod 20:12; Deut 5:16. 6:4 Or *Parents.* 6:12 Some manuscripts read *you.*

READY FOR BATTLE
Ephesians 6:17   MARCUS BRECHEEN

Throughout Scripture, any reference to a *sword* could mean one of two things. The first is what we see when we think of medieval swords—weapons so huge and heavy that they require two hands just to lift. The other meaning is the one Paul uses in Ephesians 6:17: "Take the sword of the Spirit, which is the Word of God." The word Paul uses for *sword* refers to a dagger, between six and eighteen inches long and razor-sharp on both sides. Every soldier in the Roman army at that time carried one of these weapons. It was designed to do serious damage to the enemy.

The Word of God does serious damage to the enemy of your soul. To Satan, the sword of the Spirit is the most fearful weapon you can hold.

THE HELMET OF SALVATION
Ephesians 6:17   JACK HAYFORD

Paul says to "put on salvation as your helmet" to be able to stand against the war being waged on our minds (Ephesians 6:17). In the salvation of Jesus Christ, there is full provision for our minds to be totally secure within His saving grace.

During Paul's day, helmets were made of thick leather strips and had an imperial seal on the forehead to protect the soldier from any blows that passed the shield. The helmet of salvation believers wear also has a seal in the center of the forehead, in the shape of a cross imprinted on our minds. By the power of the cross, we bring every weapon, scheme, and strategy the enemy seeks to use against us to the feet of Jesus. Our Savior captures and defeats everything that ever dares to oppose us. Our responsibility is to put on His helmet of salvation and strap it on tightly.

righteousness. ¹⁵ For shoes, put on the peace that comes from the Good News so that you will be fully prepared.* ¹⁶ In addition to all of these, hold up the shield of faith to stop the fiery arrows of the devil.* ¹⁷ Put on salvation as your helmet, and take the sword of the Spirit, which is the word of God.

¹⁸ Pray in the Spirit at all times and on every occasion. Stay alert and be persistent in your prayers for all believers everywhere.*

¹⁹ And pray for me, too. Ask God to give me the right words so I can boldly explain God's mysterious plan that the Good News is for Jews and Gentiles alike.* ²⁰ I am in chains now, still preaching this message as God's ambassador. So pray that I will keep on speaking boldly for him, as I should.

FINAL GREETINGS

²¹ To bring you up to date, Tychicus will give you a full report about what I am doing and how I am getting along. He is a beloved brother and faithful helper in the Lord's work. ²² I have sent him to you for this very purpose—to let you know how we are doing and to encourage you.

²³ Peace be with you, dear brothers and sisters,* and may God the Father and the Lord Jesus Christ give you love with faithfulness. ²⁴ May God's grace be eternally upon all who love our Lord Jesus Christ.

6:15 Or *For shoes, put on the readiness to preach the Good News of peace with God.* 6:16 Greek *the evil one.* 6:18 Greek *all of God's holy people.* 6:19 Greek *explain the mystery of the Good News;* some manuscripts read simply *explain the mystery.* 6:23 Greek *brothers.*

What Does the Bible Say About . . .

FRIENDSHIP?

— A friend is always loyal (Proverbs 17:17).
— A real friend sticks closer than a brother (Proverbs 18:24).
— Friends sharpen each other like iron sharpens iron (Proverbs 27:17).
— Two are better than one (Ecclesiastes 4:9-10).
— David and Jonathan had an immediate bond and made a pact together (1 Samuel 18:1-4).
— Paul greeted his many friends (Romans 16).
— Humility is the key to true friendship (Philippians 2:1-4).
— Paul showed his true friendship with Timothy (Philippians 2:19-24).
— Jesus called us His friends (John 15:15).

MARRIAGE?

— God created the first woman from Adam's rib (Genesis 2:23).
— A man joins his wife, and the two become one (Genesis 2:24).
— They were naked with no shame (Genesis 2:25).
— Live happily with the woman you love. Your wife is God's reward (Ecclesiastes 9:9).
— Guard your heart and remain loyal to your wife (Malachi 2:15-16).
— Husbands and wives should fulfill each other's physical needs (1 Corinthians 7:3).
— A believing spouse can influence an unbelieving spouse (1 Corinthians 7:16).
— Husbands should love their wives like Christ loves the Church (Ephesians 5:25).
— A wife should respect her husband (Ephesians 5:33).
— Husbands should honor their wives as equal partners (1 Peter 3:7).
— We should give honor to marriage and remain faithful to one another (Hebrews 13:4).

PARENTING?

— Children are a gift and reward from the Lord (Psalm 127:3).
— Noah's righteousness saved his children (Genesis 6:9-10, 18).
— God chose Abraham to direct his descendants to follow the Lord (Genesis 18:19).
— Parents should teach God's commands to their children (Deuteronomy 6:1-9; 11:19).
— Tragedy occurs when parents fail to discipline their children (2 Samuel 13).
— Parents celebrate the significant events of their children's lives (Genesis 21:8).
— Parents risk their lives to protect their children (Exodus 2:2).
— Direct your child onto the right path (Proverbs 22:6).
— Don't fail to discipline your children (Proverbs 23:13).
— An undisciplined child brings disgrace (Proverbs 29:15).
— Fathers should bring up children with discipline and instruction from the Lord (Ephesians 6:4).
— Wise parents leave memorials for their children (Joshua 4:6-7).

PHILIPPIANS

JON HUNTZINGER, PHD

Paul wrote to the Philippians while under house arrest in Rome at the same time he wrote his other prison letters (Ephesians, Colossians, and Philemon) in the early AD 60s. He had founded the church in Philippi during his second missionary journey in AD 51 and maintained a close relationship with the people from that time. He thanks them for their continued prayers and financial support for his ministry (1:3–5; 4:15–19).

Paul's letter to the Philippians includes seven major sections:

— Paul offers thanksgiving and prayer for the Philippians (1:1–11).
— He remarks about his imprisonment because of his preaching about Jesus the Messiah (1:12–26).
— Paul exhorts the Philippians to live like Jesus (1:27–2:18).
— He tells of his plans concerning his coworkers, Timothy and Epaphroditus (2:19–30).
— Paul gives warnings against those who are "enemies of the cross" versus his own personal qualifications and example (3:1–21).
— He encourages the Philippians to rejoice and to think about what is worthy of praise (4:1–9).
— Paul leaves his final words about God's provision, thanksgiving for the Philippians' financial gift, and a farewell blessing (4:10–23).

JOY AND THE GOSPEL

A primary theme in Paul's letter is joy. The word itself (*chairo*) is found almost 75 times in the New Testament and describes the feeling believers have when they see God at work in particular situations (Matthew 2:10; Luke 19:37; 23:8; John 8:56; 20:20; Acts 8:39; 11:23; 15:31). This feeling is the one people have when they see God's will being done in their lives or the lives of others. As such, people can experience joy even in the midst of suffering or difficult circumstances. They are able to see that what God is doing is greater than their present hardship (John 11:15; 14:28; 1 Peter 4:13). That is why Paul, even though he is under arrest, uses the word repeatedly in his letter. In fact, he uses the verb *rejoice* six times and the noun *joy* four times. Paul views his circumstance as nothing in comparison to the work God is doing and the reward he will receive for sharing in it.

Joy also comes from living in unity with Jesus and following His example in serving others. Paul says, "Make me truly happy by agreeing wholeheartedly with each other, loving one another, and working together with one mind and purpose" (2:2). The following verses (2:5–11) are known as Paul's Christological Hymn, which means it is a song about the primary nature and work of Jesus. In it, he describes how believers are to follow Jesus' example, which stands in contrast to Adam's actions. God made Adam in His image, yet Adam gave in to the serpent's temptation (through Eve) to be like God and know good and evil (Genesis 1; 3) through eating of the tree of knowledge. Jesus did not think equality with God was something to be held onto tightly (*harpagmos*) but willingly. He became a servant and was born in the likeness of men. Jesus shows that to be truly human is to serve others. The word *harpagmos* that Paul uses also means 'rob' or 'grab' and describes what Jesus *did not do*. The use of this word suggests that what Adam did was rob God of what belonged to Him. The tree of knowledge was God's tree. By eating from this tree, Adam was robbing God. Jesus did not come to rob God! He came to give an example of who God created people to be and how He created them to live in joy by staying in relation with Him and His Word.

BLAMELESS PAUL

In his letter, Paul says he lived blameless under the law (3:6). The Greek word he uses is the same word used to describe Job's nature in the Greek Old Testament translation of the book of Job: "He was blameless—a man of complete integrity" (Job 1:1). In that story, God agrees with the narrator that Job is a blameless and upright man (Job 1:8; 2:3).

Both Paul and Job are blameless because they live faithfully with their God and the understanding they have of Him and His ways. Paul had not broken God's law in any way but had lived in harmony with it. He was confident in his theology. Job, too, lived in harmony with God and offered sacrifices to Him (Job 1:5). Yet he was confused and shaken to his core when he lost his property, family, and health (1:13–22; 2:7–10). In Job's understanding of God, since he is blameless, he should experience God's blessing.

God engages blameless Paul and Job in the same way—through revelation. The glorified Jesus appeared to Paul on the Damascus Road and showed Himself to be the way, truth, and life. Jesus asks, "Why are you persecuting me?" (Acts 9:4). In the case of Job, God came in a whirlwind and asked, "Who is this that questions my wisdom with such ignorant words?" (Job 38:2). Job eventually responds, "I know that you can do anything, and no one can stop you. . . . I had only heard about you before, but now I have seen you with my own eyes" (42:2, 5). Like Paul, who regains his sight after being blinded by the glory of Jesus on the road (Acts 9:3-19), Job sees and understands because of the revelation God gives. Only such revelation can increase Paul and Job's understanding of God to help them appreciate even more His mysterious and remarkable ways.

GREETINGS FROM PAUL

1 This letter is from Paul and Timothy, slaves of Christ Jesus.

I am writing to all of God's holy people in Philippi who belong to Christ Jesus, including the church leaders* and deacons.

[2] May God our Father and the Lord Jesus Christ give you grace and peace.

PAUL'S THANKSGIVING AND PRAYER

[3] Every time I think of you, I give thanks to my God. [4] Whenever I pray, I make my requests for all of you with joy, [5] for you have been my partners in spreading the Good News about Christ from the time you first heard it until now. [6] And I am certain that God, who began the good work within you, will continue his work until it is finally finished on the day when Christ Jesus returns.

[7] So it is right that I should feel as I do about all of you, for you have a special place in my heart. You share with me the special favor of God, both in my imprisonment and in defending and confirming the truth of the Good News. [8] God knows how much I love you and long for you with the tender compassion of Christ Jesus.

[9] I pray that your love will overflow more and more, and that you will keep on growing in knowledge and understanding. [10] For I want you to understand what really matters, so that you may live pure and blameless lives until the day of Christ's return. [11] May you always be filled with the fruit of your salvation—the righteous character produced in your life by Jesus Christ*— for this will bring much glory and praise to God.

PAUL'S JOY THAT CHRIST IS PREACHED

[12] And I want you to know, my dear brothers and sisters,* that everything that has happened to me here has helped to spread the Good News. [13] For everyone here, including the whole palace guard,* knows that I am in chains because of Christ. [14] And because of my imprisonment, most of the believers* here have gained confidence and boldly speak God's message* without fear.

[15] It's true that some are preaching out of jealousy and rivalry. But others preach about Christ with pure motives. [16] They preach because they love me, for they know I have been appointed to defend the Good News. [17] Those others do not have pure motives as they preach about Christ. They preach with selfish ambition, not sincerely, intending to make my chains more painful to me. [18] But that doesn't matter. Whether their motives are false or genuine, the message about Christ is being preached either way, so I rejoice. And I will continue to rejoice. [19] For I know that as you pray for me and the Spirit of Jesus Christ helps me, this will lead to my deliverance.

PAUL'S LIFE FOR CHRIST

[20] For I fully expect and hope that I will never be ashamed, but that I will continue to be bold for Christ, as I have been in the past. And I trust that my life will bring honor to Christ, whether I live or die. [21] For to me, living means living for Christ, and dying is even better. [22] But if I live, I can do more fruitful work for Christ. So I really don't know which is better. [23] I'm torn between two desires: I long to go and be with Christ, which would be far better for me. [24] But for your sakes, it is better that I continue to live.

[25] Knowing this, I am convinced that I will remain alive so I can continue to help all of you grow and experience the joy of your faith. [26] And when I come to you again, you will have even more reason to take pride in Christ Jesus because of what he is doing through me.

LIVE AS CITIZENS OF HEAVEN

[27] Above all, you must live as citizens of heaven, conducting yourselves in a manner worthy of the Good News about Christ. Then, whether I come and see you again or only hear about you, I will know that you are standing together with one spirit and one purpose, fighting together for the faith, which is the Good News. [28] Don't be intimidated in any way by your enemies. This will be a sign to them that they are going to be destroyed, but that you are going to be saved, even by God himself. [29] For you have been given not only the privilege of trusting in Christ but also the privilege of suffering for him. [30] We are in this struggle together. You have seen my struggle in the past, and you know that I am still in the midst of it.

HAVE THE ATTITUDE OF CHRIST

2 Is there any encouragement from belonging to Christ? Any comfort from his love? Any fellowship together in the Spirit? Are your hearts tender and compassionate? [2] Then make me truly happy by agreeing wholeheartedly with each other, loving one another, and working together with one mind and purpose.

1:1 Or *overseers,* or *bishops.* 1:11 Greek *with the fruit of righteousness through Jesus Christ.* 1:12 Greek *brothers.* 1:13 Greek *including all the Praetorium.* 1:14a Greek *brothers in the Lord.* 1:14b Some manuscripts read *speak the message.*

THE SECRET OF SUCCESS
Philippians 2:1-9

ROBERT MORRIS

Would you like to be successful in everything you do? In Philippians 2, the apostle Paul tells us how: "You must have the same attitude that Christ Jesus had" (v. 5). In other words, we need to think as Jesus thought when He was on this earth. Here are four practical ways we can think like Jesus:

1. Forget about your reputation.
Reputation is the way you appear to other people. Sometimes we become so worried about the way we appear to others that we compromise our Christian values. Jesus didn't focus on the fact that He was God; instead, He "gave up his divine privileges" and "was born as a human being" (v. 7). If you're going to succeed in marriage or any other area of life, you have to lay down your rights as Jesus did.

2. Become a slave.
Jesus "took the humble position of a slave" (v. 7). What position have you taken? Many believers like to talk about being kings and priests (Revelation 1:6), but they forget that Paul constantly referred to himself as "a slave" for Jesus

(Romans 1:1; Philippians 1:1; Titus 1:1). Do you realize how many relationship problems would be solved if Christians acted with this kind of humility?

3. Take the low road.
Jesus "humbled himself in obedience to God" (v. 8). Here is the best definition of *humility* I know: making yourself lower than others. There are only two times when you need to take the low road. First, take the low road when you're wrong. Just admit it! Second, take the low road when you're right. Jesus was *always* right, and He still took the low road.

4. Die.
Jesus willingly "died a criminal's death on a cross" (v. 8). We need to live with this same attitude. The only way you'll ever be truly successful (and happy) is to die to yourself. Matthew 16:25 says, "If you try to hang on to your life, you will lose it. But if you give up your life for my sake, you will save it." God lifted Jesus "to the place of highest honor" (Philippians 2:9), and if you'll lower yourself, He'll lift you up too.

---

³ Don't be selfish; don't try to impress others. Be humble, thinking of others as better than yourselves. ⁴ Don't look out only for your own interests, but take an interest in others, too. ⁵ You must have the same attitude that Christ Jesus had.

⁶ Though he was God,*
he did not think of equality with God
as something to cling to.
⁷ Instead, he gave up his divine privileges*;
he took the humble position of a slave*
and was born as a human being.
When he appeared in human form,*
⁸ he humbled himself in obedience to God
and died a criminal's death on a cross.

⁹ Therefore, God elevated him to the place of
highest honor
and gave him the name above all
other names,
¹⁰ that at the name of Jesus every knee
should bow,
in heaven and on earth and under the earth,
¹¹ and every tongue declare that Jesus Christ
is Lord,
to the glory of God the Father.

SHINE BRIGHTLY FOR CHRIST
¹² Dear friends, you always followed my instructions when I was with you. And now that I am away, it is even more important. Work hard to show the results of your salvation, obeying God with deep reverence and fear. ¹³ For God is

working in you, giving you the desire and the power to do what pleases him.

¹⁴ Do everything without complaining and arguing, ¹⁵ so that no one can criticize you. Live clean, innocent lives as children of God, shining like bright lights in a world full of crooked and perverse people. ¹⁶ Hold firmly to the word of life; then, on the day of Christ's return, I will be proud that I did not run the race in vain and that my work was not useless. ¹⁷ But I will rejoice even if I lose my life, pouring it out like a liquid offering to God,* just like your faithful service is an offering to God. And I want all of you to share that joy. ¹⁸ Yes, you should rejoice, and I will share your joy.

PAUL COMMENDS TIMOTHY
¹⁹ If the Lord Jesus is willing, I hope to send Timothy to you soon for a visit. Then he can cheer me up by telling me how you are getting along. ²⁰ I have no one else like Timothy, who genuinely cares about your welfare. ²¹ All the others care only for themselves and not for what matters to Jesus Christ. ²² But you know how Timothy has proved himself. Like a son with his father, he has served with me in preaching the Good News. ²³ I hope to send him to you just as soon as I find out what is going to happen to me here. ²⁴ And I have confidence from the Lord that I myself will come to see you soon.

2:6 Or *Being in the form of God.*   2:7a Greek *he emptied himself.*
2:7b Or *the form of a slave.*   2:7c Some English translations put this phrase in verse 8.   2:17 Greek *I will rejoice even if I am to be poured out as a liquid offering.*

WORSHIP EVEN WHEN YOU DON'T FEEL LIKE IT
Philippians 4:4   ROBERT MORRIS

Do you ever *not* feel like worshipping? If we're being honest, we've all felt this way at some point in our lives. Let me encourage you, though: worship isn't based on feelings. We can worship even when we don't feel like it, and here are the top five reasons why:

1. He is worthy.
Our circumstances may change, but God never does (Malachi 3:6). No matter what we're going through, He's still worthy of our worship.

2. Worship is being true to who we really are.
Satan tells us that if we worship when we don't feel like it, we're being hypocrites. A *hypocrite* is someone who pretends to be something they're not. However, if you're a believer, then you're a worshipper. You're only a hypocrite if you come to church and don't worship.

3. Praise is a command.
The Bible tells us to shout to the Lord and to clap and lift our hands (Psalm 47:1; 134:2). These are imperatives—commands, not suggestions.

4. Feelings shouldn't dictate our actions. Principles should!
Is God still worthy even if we get sick, have an argument with our spouse, or lose our job? Yes! Even when we don't feel like praying, we should pray. Even when we don't feel like tithing, we should tithe. And even when we don't feel like worshipping, we should worship.

5. We worship by faith.
Everything we do in the Christian life is by faith. We pray by faith, we give by faith, and we worship by faith.

PAUL COMMENDS EPAPHRODITUS
25 Meanwhile, I thought I should send Epaphroditus back to you. He is a true brother, co-worker, and fellow soldier. And he was your messenger to help me in my need. 26 I am sending him because he has been longing to see you, and he was very distressed that you heard he was ill. 27 And he certainly was ill; in fact, he almost died. But God had mercy on him—and also on me, so that I would not have one sorrow after another.

28 So I am all the more anxious to send him back to you, for I know you will be glad to see him, and then I will not be so worried about you. 29 Welcome him in the Lord's love* and with great joy, and give him the honor that people like him deserve. 30 For he risked his life for the work of Christ, and he was at the point of death while doing for me what you couldn't do from far away.

THE PRICELESS VALUE OF KNOWING CHRIST
3 Whatever happens, my dear brothers and sisters,* rejoice in the Lord. I never get tired of telling you these things, and I do it to safeguard your faith.

2 Watch out for those dogs, those people who do evil, those mutilators who say you must be circumcised to be saved. 3 For we who worship by the Spirit of God* are the ones who are truly circumcised. We rely on what Christ Jesus has done for us. We put no confidence in human effort, 4 though I could have confidence in my own effort if anyone could. Indeed, if others have reason for confidence in their own efforts, I have even more!

5 I was circumcised when I was eight days old. I am a pure-blooded citizen of Israel and a member of the tribe of Benjamin—a real Hebrew if there ever was one! I was a member of the Pharisees, who demand the strictest obedience to the Jewish law. 6 I was so zealous that I harshly persecuted the church. And as for righteousness, I obeyed the law without fault.

7 I once thought these things were valuable, but now I consider them worthless because of what Christ has done. 8 Yes, everything else is worthless when compared with the infinite value of knowing Christ Jesus my Lord. For his sake I have discarded everything else, counting it all as garbage, so that I could gain Christ 9 and become one with him. I no longer count on my own righteousness through obeying the law; rather, I become righteous through faith in Christ.* For God's way of making us right with himself depends on faith. 10 I want to know Christ and experience the mighty power that raised him from the dead. I want to suffer with him, sharing in his death, 11 so that one way or another I will experience the resurrection from the dead!

PRESSING TOWARD THE GOAL
12 I don't mean to say that I have already achieved these things or that I have already reached perfection. But I press on to possess that perfection for which Christ Jesus first possessed me. 13 No, dear brothers and sisters, I have not achieved it,* but I focus on this one thing: Forgetting the past and looking forward to what lies ahead, 14 I press on to reach the end of the race and receive the heavenly prize for which God, through Christ Jesus, is calling us.

15 Let all who are spiritually mature agree on these things. If you disagree on some point, I believe God will make it plain to you. 16 But we must hold on to the progress we have already made.

2:29 Greek *in the Lord.* 3:1 Greek *brothers;* also in 3:13, 17. 3:3 Some manuscripts read *worship God in spirit;* one early manuscript reads *worship in spirit.* 3:9 Or *through the faithfulness of Christ.* 3:13 Some manuscripts read *not yet achieved it.*

HOW TO GET A WORD
Philippians 4:6   ROBERT MORRIS

God's Word is eternal. If He spoke it 3,000 years ago, it's still true today. It's simple to hear a clear word from God by reading His Word. The first step is to enter His presence with praise (Psalm 100:4). Then you begin to pray. God invites us to make our requests known to Him: "Tell God what you need" (Philippians 4:6).

The next step is to open the Bible. If a particular story or Scripture comes to mind when you're spending time in God's presence and praying, read it. If you're going through a financial problem, read verses about finances and stewardship. If you're going through a health problem, read verses on health and healing. It helps to write down your prayers and what you hear God saying.

I encourage you to do this every day. You have a personal relationship with God, and He wants to talk to you.

JESUS IS THE WORD
Philippians 4:8   ROBERT MORRIS

Jesus is the Word, and all things were made through Him (John 1:1-4). All things in your life come from Him, and without Him, nothing happens.

When you accept Jesus, you determine how much of His life you're going to let flow through you. The more time you spend in His Word, the more you'll get to know Him and release His life in yours. That's when the supernatural happens. Why? Because we're actually meditating with Jesus when we study the Word.

Philippians 4:8 says, "Fix your thoughts on what is true, and honorable, and right, and pure, and lovely, and admirable." All of these words can be used to describe God's Word. How incredible is that? I encourage you to dive deeper into His Word. As you continue to read and meditate on it, the Lord will continue to prosper you in everything you do.

17 Dear brothers and sisters, pattern your lives after mine, and learn from those who follow our example. 18 For I have told you often before, and I say it again with tears in my eyes, that there are many whose conduct shows they are really enemies of the cross of Christ. 19 They are headed for destruction. Their god is their appetite, they brag about shameful things, and they think only about this life here on earth. 20 But we are citizens of heaven, where the Lord Jesus Christ lives. And we are eagerly waiting for him to return as our Savior. 21 He will take our weak mortal bodies and change them into glorious bodies like his own, using the same power with which he will bring everything under his control.

4 Therefore, my dear brothers and sisters,* stay true to the Lord. I love you and long to see you, dear friends, for you are my joy and the crown I receive for my work.

WORDS OF ENCOURAGEMENT
2 Now I appeal to Euodia and Syntyche. Please, because you belong to the Lord, settle your disagreement. 3 And I ask you, my true partner,* to help these two women, for they worked hard with me in telling others the Good News. They worked along with Clement and the rest of my co-workers, whose names are written in the Book of Life.

4 Always be full of joy in the Lord. I say it again—rejoice! 5 Let everyone see that you are considerate in all you do. Remember, the Lord is coming soon.*

6 Don't worry about anything; instead, pray about everything. Tell God what you need, and

thank him for all he has done. 7 Then you will experience God's peace, which exceeds anything we can understand. His peace will guard your hearts and minds as you live in Christ Jesus.

8 And now, dear brothers and sisters, one final thing. Fix your thoughts on what is true, and honorable, and right, and pure, and lovely, and admirable. Think about things that are excellent and worthy of praise. 9 Keep putting into practice all you learned and received from me—everything you heard from me and saw me doing. Then the God of peace will be with you.

PAUL'S THANKS FOR THEIR GIFTS
10 How I praise the Lord that you are concerned about me again. I know you have always been concerned for me, but you didn't have the chance to help me. 11 Not that I was ever in need, for I have learned how to be content with whatever I have. 12 I know how to live on almost nothing or with everything. I have learned the secret of living in every situation, whether it is with a full stomach or empty, with plenty or little. 13 For I can do everything through Christ,* who gives me strength. 14 Even so, you have done well to share with me in my present difficulty.

15 As you know, you Philippians were the only ones who gave me financial help when I first brought you the Good News and then traveled on from Macedonia. No other church did this. 16 Even when I was in Thessalonica you sent help more than once. 17 I don't say this because I want a gift from you. Rather, I want you to receive a reward for your kindness.

4:1 Greek *brothers;* also in 4:8.   4:3 Or *loyal Syzygus.*   4:5 Greek *the Lord is near.*   4:13 Greek *through the one.*

¹⁸At the moment I have all I need—and more! I am generously supplied with the gifts you sent me with Epaphroditus. They are a sweet-smelling sacrifice that is acceptable and pleasing to God. ¹⁹And this same God who takes care of me will supply all your needs from his glorious riches, which have been given to us in Christ Jesus.

²⁰Now all glory to God our Father forever and ever! Amen.

PAUL'S FINAL GREETINGS

²¹Give my greetings to each of God's holy people—all who belong to Christ Jesus. The brothers who are with me send you their greetings. ²²And all the rest of God's people send you greetings, too, especially those in Caesar's household.

²³May the grace of the Lord Jesus Christ be with your spirit.*

4:23 Some manuscripts add *Amen.*

COLOSSIANS

JON HUNTZINGER, PHD

Paul wrote to the Colossians while under house arrest in Rome in the early AD 60s at the same time he wrote Ephesians, Philippians, and Philemon. He had not met the believers in Colossae, which was a small town about 100 miles east of Ephesus. However, he did know of them through Epaphras, one of his coworkers in ministry who likely founded the church there (1:7–8; 4:12–13). In this letter, Paul confronts false teaching that is threatening the faith of the believers by emphasizing the gospel and the supremacy of Jesus. Because the content in several passages closely resembles what Paul writes to the Ephesians (for example, Colossians 3:18–4:1 and Ephesians 5:22–33; Colossians 3:12–17 and Ephesians 6:10–20), it is likely he wrote both letters near the same time and used one as a source for the other. It is not clear in which order he wrote the letters, however.

Paul's letter includes seven major sections:
— He gives a greeting and a prayer for the Colossians' faith and continued growth in knowledge (1:1–14).
— Paul describes Jesus' supremacy over creation and the Church (1:15–2:4).
— He writes about his sufferings for Christ (1:24–2:5).
— Paul issues warnings against deceitful teaching, human traditions, angel worship, and asceticism, which includes severe self-discipline and the avoidance of all forms of physical pleasure (2:6–23).
— He exhorts the Colossians to cultivate what he describes elsewhere as the fruit of the Spirit (Galatians 5:22–23) and for them to live with respect for one another (Colossians 3:1–4:6).
— Paul concludes with recognition of his fellow workers and final greetings (4:7–18).

WHO JESUS IS

As much as Paul's letter to the Ephesians highlights the identity and calling of believers, his letter to the Colossians highlights the identity of Jesus and His ministry to believers (1:13–20). As in his other letters, Paul reminds his readers of the gospel and says that Jesus has delivered them from darkness, offered forgiveness for sins, and reconciled everything to Himself through His cross (1:13–14, 20). He adds that Jesus brought creation into being and is now over all creation. Specifically, He is the head of the body over the people of God

as the resurrected one (1:15–18). Not only does Jesus reflect the invisible God, but also God fully dwells within Him (2:9). Since God dwells within Him—God is reconciled in Him—Jesus reconciles all things to God.

Paul commends the Colossians for their faith, love, and hope in his opening remarks (1:4–5). As he does elsewhere (Romans 5:1–5), Paul sees the previous work of God in Jesus (faith) and the anticipated future promise of God (hope) joining in the present love of God for "all of God's people."

COMPLETING CHRIST'S SUFFERINGS

Paul says he is "participating in the sufferings of Christ that continue for his body, the church" (1:24). What he means is that just as the followers of Jesus make up His body and continue His ministry in their own lives (and bodies), so also when they suffer (as Paul has suffered), Jesus suffers. When Jesus first appeared to Paul, he asked, "Why are you persecuting me?" (Acts 9:4). Jesus so closely identified with His followers that He was sharing in their experience. Now, in some way, Jesus shares in Paul's sufferings. When Paul is imprisoned, Jesus is imprisoned; when he is flogged, Jesus is flogged; when he is beaten, so is Jesus. It is a mystery how Jesus continues to experience affliction in His followers, such as Paul. Paul uses the metaphor of the body for the Church three times in this letter (Colossians 1:18; 2:19; 3:15), which speaks of Jesus' close identification with His people. Just as Jesus continues to intercede for God's people (Hebrews 7:23–25) and continues to minister salvation to all people, so also He continues to experience what His followers experience when they endure hardship and even persecution for His sake as they proclaim the gospel. Jesus' afflictions are filled up as His followers proclaim the gospel and, in the process, suffer resistance, rejection, and even persecution.

Thus, Paul's primary message in his letter is that through the death of Jesus, His followers have been reconciled to God. Paul uses the expression "in Him," which emphasizes the relation Jesus' followers have with Him. They are "in" Him, meaning they make up His body and share in His experience. To be "in" Jesus is to share in His death to sin, sickness, and death, and it is to participate with Him in new life through His resurrection.

GREETINGS FROM PAUL

1 This letter is from Paul, chosen by the will of God to be an apostle of Christ Jesus, and from our brother Timothy.

²We are writing to God's holy people in the city of Colosse, who are faithful brothers and sisters* in Christ.

May God our Father give you grace and peace.

PAUL'S THANKSGIVING AND PRAYER

³We always pray for you, and we give thanks to God, the Father of our Lord Jesus Christ. ⁴For we have heard of your faith in Christ Jesus and your love for all of God's people, ⁵which come from your confident hope of what God has reserved for you in heaven. You have had this expectation ever since you first heard the truth of the Good News.

⁶This same Good News that came to you is going out all over the world. It is bearing fruit everywhere by changing lives, just as it changed your lives from the day you first heard and understood the truth about God's wonderful grace.

⁷You learned about the Good News from Epaphras, our beloved co-worker. He is Christ's faithful servant, and he is helping us on your behalf.* ⁸He has told us about the love for others that the Holy Spirit has given you.

⁹So we have not stopped praying for you since we first heard about you. We ask God to give you complete knowledge of his will and to give you spiritual wisdom and understanding. ¹⁰Then the way you live will always honor and please the Lord, and your lives will produce every kind of good fruit. All the while, you will grow as you learn to know God better and better.

¹¹We also pray that you will be strengthened with all his glorious power so you will have all the endurance and patience you need. May you be filled with joy,* ¹²always thanking the Father. He has enabled you to share in the inheritance that belongs to his people, who live in the light. ¹³For he has rescued us from the kingdom of darkness and transferred us into the Kingdom of his dear Son, ¹⁴who purchased our freedom* and forgave our sins.

CHRIST IS SUPREME

¹⁵ Christ is the visible image of
the invisible God.
He existed before anything was created
and is supreme over all creation,*
¹⁶ for through him God created everything
in the heavenly realms and on earth.
He made the things we can see
and the things we can't see—
such as thrones, kingdoms, rulers, and
authorities in the unseen world.
Everything was created through him
and for him.
¹⁷ He existed before anything else,
and he holds all creation together.

¹⁸ Christ is also the head of the church,
which is his body.
He is the beginning,
supreme over all who rise from the dead.*
So he is first in everything.
¹⁹ For God in all his fullness
was pleased to live in Christ,
²⁰ and through him God reconciled
everything to himself.
He made peace with everything in heaven
and on earth
by means of Christ's blood on the cross.

²¹This includes you who were once far away from God. You were his enemies, separated from him by your evil thoughts and actions. ²²Yet now he has reconciled you to himself through the death of Christ in his physical body. As a result, he has brought you into his own presence, and you are holy and blameless as you stand before him without a single fault.

²³But you must continue to believe this truth and stand firmly in it. Don't drift away from the assurance you received when you heard the Good News. The Good News has been preached all over the world, and I, Paul, have been appointed as God's servant to proclaim it.

PAUL'S WORK FOR THE CHURCH

²⁴I am glad when I suffer for you in my body, for I am participating in the sufferings of Christ that continue for his body, the church. ²⁵God has given me the responsibility of serving his church by proclaiming his entire message to you. ²⁶This message was kept secret for centuries and generations past, but now it has been revealed to God's people. ²⁷For God wanted them to know that the riches and glory of Christ are for you Gentiles, too. And this is the secret: Christ lives in you. This gives you assurance of sharing his glory.

²⁸So we tell others about Christ, warning everyone and teaching everyone with all the wisdom God has given us. We want to present them to God, perfect* in their relationship to Christ. ²⁹That's why I work and struggle so hard, depending on Christ's mighty power that works within me.

2 I want you to know how much I have agonized for you and for the church at Laodicea, and for many other believers who have never met me personally. ²I want them to be encouraged and knit together by strong ties of love. I want them to have complete confidence that they understand God's mysterious plan, which is Christ himself. ³In him lie hidden all the treasures of wisdom and knowledge.

1:2 Greek *faithful brothers.*   1:7 Or *he is ministering on your behalf;* some manuscripts read *he is ministering on our behalf.*   1:11 Or *all the patience and endurance you need with joy.*   1:14 Some manuscripts add *with his blood.*   1:15 Or *He is the firstborn of all creation.*   1:18 Or *the firstborn from the dead.*   1:28 Or *mature.*

⁴I am telling you this so no one will deceive you with well-crafted arguments. ⁵For though I am far away from you, my heart is with you. And I rejoice that you are living as you should and that your faith in Christ is strong.

FREEDOM FROM RULES AND NEW LIFE IN CHRIST

⁶And now, just as you accepted Christ Jesus as your Lord, you must continue to follow him. ⁷Let your roots grow down into him, and let your lives be built on him. Then your faith will grow strong in the truth you were taught, and you will overflow with thankfulness.

⁸Don't let anyone capture you with empty philosophies and high-sounding nonsense that come from human thinking and from the spiritual powers* of this world, rather than from Christ. ⁹For in Christ lives all the fullness of God in a human body.* ¹⁰So you also are complete through your union with Christ, who is the head over every ruler and authority.

¹¹When you came to Christ, you were "circumcised," but not by a physical procedure. Christ performed a spiritual circumcision—the cutting away of your sinful nature.* ¹²For you were buried with Christ when you were baptized. And with him you were raised to new life because you trusted the mighty power of God, who raised Christ from the dead.

¹³You were dead because of your sins and because your sinful nature was not yet cut away. Then God made you alive with Christ, for he forgave all our sins. ¹⁴He canceled the record of the charges against us and took it away by nailing it to the cross. ¹⁵In this way, he disarmed* the spiritual rulers and authorities. He shamed them publicly by his victory over them on the cross.

¹⁶So don't let anyone condemn you for what you eat or drink, or for not celebrating certain holy days or new moon ceremonies or Sabbaths. ¹⁷For these rules are only shadows of the reality yet to come. And Christ himself is that reality. ¹⁸Don't let anyone condemn you by insisting on pious self-denial or the worship of angels,* saying they have had visions about these things. Their sinful minds have made them proud, ¹⁹and they are not connected to Christ, the head of the body. For he holds the whole body together with its joints and ligaments, and it grows as God nourishes it.

²⁰You have died with Christ, and he has set you free from the spiritual powers of this world. So why do you keep on following the rules of the world, such as, ²¹"Don't handle! Don't taste! Don't touch!"? ²²Such rules are mere human teachings about things that deteriorate as we use them. ²³These rules may seem wise because they require strong devotion, pious self-denial, and severe bodily discipline. But they provide no help in conquering a person's evil desires.

LIVING THE NEW LIFE

3 Since you have been raised to new life with Christ, set your sights on the realities of heaven, where Christ sits in the place of honor at God's right hand. ²Think about the things of heaven, not the things of earth. ³For you died to this life, and your real life is hidden with Christ in God. ⁴And when Christ, who is your* life, is revealed to the whole world, you will share in all his glory.

⁵So put to death the sinful, earthly things lurking within you. Have nothing to do with sexual immorality, impurity, lust, and evil desires. Don't be greedy, for a greedy person is an idolater, worshiping the things of this world. ⁶Because of these sins, the anger of God is coming.* ⁷You used to do these things when your life was still part of this world. ⁸But now is the time to get rid of anger, rage, malicious behavior, slander, and dirty language. ⁹Don't lie to each other, for you have stripped off your old sinful nature and all its wicked deeds. ¹⁰Put on your new nature, and be renewed as you learn to know your Creator and become like him. ¹¹In this new life, it doesn't matter if you are a Jew or a Gentile,* circumcised or uncircumcised, barbaric, uncivilized,* slave, or free. Christ is all that matters, and he lives in all of us.

¹²Since God chose you to be the holy people he loves, you must clothe yourselves with tenderhearted mercy, kindness, humility, gentleness, and patience. ¹³Make allowance for each other's faults, and forgive anyone who offends you. Remember, the Lord forgave you, so you must forgive others. ¹⁴Above all, clothe yourselves with love, which binds us all together in perfect harmony. ¹⁵And let the peace that comes from Christ rule in your hearts. For as members of one body you are called to live in peace. And always be thankful.

¹⁶Let the message about Christ, in all its richness, fill your lives. Teach and counsel each other with all the wisdom he gives. Sing psalms and hymns and spiritual songs to God with thankful hearts. ¹⁷And whatever you do or say, do it as a representative of the Lord Jesus, giving thanks through him to God the Father.

INSTRUCTIONS FOR CHRISTIAN HOUSEHOLDS

¹⁸Wives, submit to your husbands, as is fitting for those who belong to the Lord.

¹⁹Husbands, love your wives and never treat them harshly.

²⁰Children, always obey your parents, for this pleases the Lord. ²¹Fathers, do not aggravate your children, or they will become discouraged.

2:8 Or *the spiritual principles;* also in 2:20.   2:9 Or *in him dwells all the completeness of the Godhead bodily.*   2:11 Greek *the cutting away of the body of the flesh.*   2:15 Or *he stripped off.*   2:18 Or *or worshiping with angels.*   3:4 Some manuscripts read *our.*   3:6 Some manuscripts read *is coming on all who disobey him.*   3:11a Greek *a Greek.*   3:11b Greek *Barbarian, Scythian.*

[22] Slaves, obey your earthly masters in everything you do. Try to please them all the time, not just when they are watching you. Serve them sincerely because of your reverent fear of the Lord. [23] Work willingly at whatever you do, as though you were working for the Lord rather than for people. [24] Remember that the Lord will give you an inheritance as your reward, and that the Master you are serving is Christ.* [25] But if you do what is wrong, you will be paid back for the wrong you have done. For God has no favorites.

4 Masters, be just and fair to your slaves. Remember that you also have a Master—in heaven.

AN ENCOURAGEMENT FOR PRAYER

[2] Devote yourselves to prayer with an alert mind and a thankful heart. [3] Pray for us, too, that God will give us many opportunities to speak about his mysterious plan concerning Christ. That is why I am here in chains. [4] Pray that I will proclaim this message as clearly as I should.

[5] Live wisely among those who are not believers, and make the most of every opportunity. [6] Let your conversation be gracious and attractive* so that you will have the right response for everyone.

PAUL'S FINAL INSTRUCTIONS AND GREETINGS

[7] Tychicus will give you a full report about how I am getting along. He is a beloved brother and faithful helper who serves with me in the Lord's work. [8] I have sent him to you for this very purpose—to let you know how we are doing and to

encourage you. [9] I am also sending Onesimus, a faithful and beloved brother, one of your own people. He and Tychicus will tell you everything that's happening here.

[10] Aristarchus, who is in prison with me, sends you his greetings, and so does Mark, Barnabas's cousin. As you were instructed before, make Mark welcome if he comes your way. [11] Jesus (the one we call Justus) also sends his greetings. These are the only Jewish believers among my co-workers; they are working with me here for the Kingdom of God. And what a comfort they have been!

[12] Epaphras, a member of your own fellowship and a servant of Christ Jesus, sends you his greetings. He always prays earnestly for you, asking God to make you strong and perfect, fully confident that you are following the whole will of God. [13] I can assure you that he prays hard for you and also for the believers in Laodicea and Hierapolis.

[14] Luke, the beloved doctor, sends his greetings, and so does Demas. [15] Please give my greetings to our brothers and sisters* at Laodicea, and to Nympha and the church that meets in her house.

[16] After you have read this letter, pass it on to the church at Laodicea so they can read it, too. And you should read the letter I wrote to them. [17] And say to Archippus, "Be sure to carry out the ministry the Lord gave you."

[18] HERE IS MY GREETING IN MY OWN HAND-WRITING—PAUL.

Remember my chains.

May God's grace be with you.

3:24 Or *and serve Christ as your Master.*   **4:6** Greek *and seasoned with salt.*   **4:15** Greek *brothers.*

— 1 AND 2 THESSALONIANS —

JON HUNTZINGER, PHD

The city of Thessalonica was a business center in the region of Macedonia when Paul arrived there in the late AD 40s (Acts 17:1-9). His gospel stirred a strong response from some of the citizens. They threw him into jail as a result, and eventually, he had to leave the city. Paul wrote his letters of 1 and 2 Thessalonians after that time to both Jews and Gentiles who responded to his message. It seems from some of the letters' contents that the majority were Gentiles; for example, 1 Thessalonians 1:9 reports the people had turned away from idols.

The letter of 1 Thessalonians includes the following sections:

— Paul, along with his associates Silas and Timothy, greets the believers in Thessalonica (1:1-3).
— Paul gives thanks for their response to the gospel (1:4-10).
— He reviews his ministry to them and expresses his desire to see them again (2:1-3:13).
— Paul exhorts the Thessalonians to live in a way pleasing to God and teaches about the Day of the Lord and the return of the Lord Jesus (4:1-5:11).
— He offers final exhortations and a prayer that they remain blameless (5:12-28).

The letter of 2 Thessalonians includes the following sections:

— Paul greets the Thessalonians along with Silas and Timothy once again (1:1-2).
— He offers thanksgiving for their abundant faith and a word of encouragement for them to remain strong despite persecution (1:3-12).
— Paul gives additional teaching about the Day of the Lord (2:1-12).
— He exhorts them to stand firm in faith (2:13-17).
— Paul makes a request for prayer (3:1-5).
— He issues a command to do good works along with a final greeting written in his own hand (3:6-17).

The fact that Paul names Silas and Timothy in his greetings in both letters does not mean they coauthored them with him, but rather that they stood with him and supported what he wrote to the church. Moreover, the two letters contain similar vocabulary and teaching (1 Thessalonians 1:1 and 2 Thessalonians 1:1-2; 1 Thessalonians 1:2-3 and 2 Thessalonians 1:3; 1 Thessalonians 2:9 and 2 Thessalonians 3:8). Though some scholars credit different authors because they think Paul would not repeat himself when writing to the same group of people, these parallel passages speak to

a common manner and purpose by the apostle. Very likely, he wrote 2 Thessalonians soon after 1 Thessalonians in response to questions his initial teaching raised (2 Thessalonians 2:1, 15).

FAITH, HOPE, LOVE

In 1 Thessalonians, Paul commends the people for their faith, hope, and love, even while they suffer afflictions (1:3, 6; 2:14). He also talks about his blameless ministry of the gospel of God among them (2:9-10) before being "separated" from them and hindered by Satan from seeing them (2:17-18). Paul encourages them to live holy lives and to live in brotherly love with each other (4:1-12). He then offers comfort over the death of loved ones by reminding them that the risen Jesus will one day return for His followers, and all will be resurrected (4:13-18). In the meantime, the Thessalonians should live in faith, hope, and love (5:8), the second time in the letter he has emphasized these three virtues. Finally, Paul tells them to devote themselves to doing good for one another (5:15) and to be joyful at all times (5:16). For Paul, faith, hope, and love represent the defining attributes of a follower of Jesus, and he writes about them in other letters, such as Romans (5:1-5) and 1 Corinthians (13:13). Faith is confidence in God's words and promises because of what God has done in the past. Hope is confidence in those same words and promises for the future, and love is the present reality of God's words and promises regardless of circumstances. Despite affliction because of their faith, the Thessalonians can continue to live in the present with *love* toward one another (4:9-10), which came through the power and demonstration of the Holy Spirit (1:5), and *hope*, which they have based on their *faith*.

HARD WORK AND GOOD WORKS

In 2 Thessalonians, Paul continues to encourage the believers who are experiencing persecution (1:4-6) by reminding them that the Lord Jesus Christ will return one day, but only after someone Paul describes as the "man of lawlessness" is revealed (2:1-12). For this reason, they should stand firm in faith (2:15), pray for Paul (3:1-2), and devote themselves to hard work on the one hand and to good works on the other (3:6-15). Paul has given an example to the Thessalonians of both hard work and good works (3:7-9). He was not a burden to the people when he was with them but supported himself. He also showed good works in his teaching and ministry among them. To Paul's mind, followers of the Lord Jesus can testify of Him to others by working hard and blessing them through the hard work they do and by doing good works that show the love of God in their own lives.

1 THESSALONIANS

GREETINGS FROM PAUL

1 This letter is from Paul, Silas,* and Timothy. We are writing to the church in Thessalonica, to you who belong to God the Father and the Lord Jesus Christ.

May God give you grace and peace.

THE FAITH OF THE THESSALONIAN BELIEVERS

2 We always thank God for all of you and pray for you constantly. 3 As we pray to our God and Father about you, we think of your faithful work, your loving deeds, and the enduring hope you have because of our Lord Jesus Christ.

4 We know, dear brothers and sisters,* that God loves you and has chosen you to be his own people. 5 For when we brought you the Good News, it was not only with words but also with power, for the Holy Spirit gave you full assurance* that what we said was true. And you know of our concern for you from the way we lived when we were with you. 6 So you received the message with joy from the Holy Spirit in spite of the severe suffering it brought you. In this way, you imitated both us and the Lord. 7 As a result, you have become an example to all the believers in Greece—throughout both Macedonia and Achaia.*

8 And now the word of the Lord is ringing out from you to people everywhere, even beyond Macedonia and Achaia, for wherever we go we find people telling us about your faith in God. We don't need to tell them about it, 9 for they keep talking about the wonderful welcome you gave us and how you turned away from idols to serve the living and true God. 10 And they speak of how you are looking forward to the coming of God's Son from heaven—Jesus, whom God raised from the dead. He is the one who has rescued us from the terrors of the coming judgment.

PAUL REMEMBERS HIS VISIT

2 You yourselves know, dear brothers and sisters,* that our visit to you was not a failure. 2 You know how badly we had been treated at Philippi just before we came to you and how much we suffered there. Yet our God gave us the courage to declare his Good News to you boldly, in spite of great opposition. 3 So you can see we were not preaching with any deceit or impure motives or trickery.

4 For we speak as messengers approved by God to be entrusted with the Good News. Our purpose is to please God, not people. He alone examines the motives of our hearts. 5 Never once did we try to win you with flattery, as you well know. And God is our witness that we were not pretending to be your friends just to get your money! 6 As for human praise, we have never sought it from you or anyone else.

7 As apostles of Christ we certainly had a right to make some demands of you, but instead we were like children* among you. Or we were like a mother feeding and caring for her own children. 8 We loved you so much that we shared with you not only God's Good News but our own lives, too.

9 Don't you remember, dear brothers and sisters, how hard we worked among you? Night and day we toiled to earn a living so that we would not be a burden to any of you as we preached God's Good News to you. 10 You yourselves are our witnesses—and so is God—that we were devout and honest and faultless toward all of you believers. 11 And you know that we treated each of you as a father treats his own children. 12 We pleaded with you, encouraged you, and urged you to live your lives in a way that God would consider worthy. For he called you to share in his Kingdom and glory.

13 Therefore, we never stop thanking God that when you received his message from us, you didn't think of our words as mere human ideas. You accepted what we said as the very word of God—which, of course, it is. And this word continues to work in you who believe.

14 And then, dear brothers and sisters, you suffered persecution from your own countrymen. In this way, you imitated the believers in God's churches in Judea who, because of their belief in Christ Jesus, suffered from their own people, the Jews. 15 For some of the Jews killed the prophets,

---

1:1 Greek Silvanus, the Greek form of the name.   1:4 Greek brothers.   1:5 Or with the power of the Holy Spirit, so you can have full assurance.   1:7 Macedonia and Achaia were the northern and southern regions of Greece.   2:1 Greek brothers; also in 2:9, 14, 17.   2:7 Some manuscripts read we were gentle.

and some even killed the Lord Jesus. Now they have persecuted us, too. They fail to please God and work against all humanity [16]as they try to keep us from preaching the Good News of salvation to the Gentiles. By doing this, they continue to pile up their sins. But the anger of God has caught up with them at last.

TIMOTHY'S GOOD REPORT ABOUT THE CHURCH

[17]Dear brothers and sisters, after we were separated from you for a little while (though our hearts never left you), we tried very hard to come back because of our intense longing to see you again. [18]We wanted very much to come to you, and I, Paul, tried again and again, but Satan prevented us. [19]After all, what gives us hope and joy, and what will be our proud reward and crown as we stand before our Lord Jesus when he returns? It is you! [20]Yes, you are our pride and joy.

3 Finally, when we could stand it no longer, we decided to stay alone in Athens, [2]and we sent Timothy to visit you. He is our brother and God's co-worker* in proclaiming the Good News of Christ. We sent him to strengthen you, to encourage you in your faith, [3]and to keep you from being shaken by the troubles you were going through. But you know that we are destined for such troubles. [4]Even while we were with you, we warned you that troubles would soon come—and they did, as you well know. [5]That is why, when I could bear it no longer, I sent Timothy to find out whether your faith was still strong. I was afraid that the tempter had gotten the best of you and that our work had been useless.

[6]But now Timothy has just returned, bringing us good news about your faith and love. He reports that you always remember our visit with joy and that you want to see us as much as we want to see you. [7]So we have been greatly encouraged in the midst of our troubles and suffering, dear brothers and sisters,* because you have remained strong in your faith. [8]It gives us new life to know that you are standing firm in the Lord.

[9]How we thank God for you! Because of you we have great joy as we enter God's presence. [10]Night and day we pray earnestly for you, asking God to let us see you again to fill the gaps in your faith.

[11]May God our Father and our Lord Jesus bring us to you very soon. [12]And may the Lord make your love for one another and for all people grow and overflow, just as our love for you overflows. [13]May he, as a result, make your hearts strong, blameless, and holy as you stand before God our Father when our Lord Jesus comes again with all his holy people. Amen.

LIVE TO PLEASE GOD

4 Finally, dear brothers and sisters,* we urge you in the name of the Lord Jesus to live in a way that pleases God, as we have taught you.

You live this way already, and we encourage you to do so even more. [2]For you remember what we taught you by the authority of the Lord Jesus.

[3]God's will is for you to be holy, so stay away from all sexual sin. [4]Then each of you will control his own body* and live in holiness and honor—[5]not in lustful passion like the pagans who do not know God and his ways. [6]Never harm or cheat a fellow believer in this matter by violating his wife,* for the Lord avenges all such sins, as we have solemnly warned you before. [7]God has called us to live holy lives, not impure lives. [8]Therefore, anyone who refuses to live by these rules is not disobeying human teaching but is rejecting God, who gives his Holy Spirit to you.

[9]But we don't need to write to you about the importance of loving each other,* for God himself has taught you to love one another. [10]Indeed, you already show your love for all the believers* throughout Macedonia. Even so, dear brothers and sisters, we urge you to love them even more.

[11]Make it your goal to live a quiet life, minding your own business and working with your hands, just as we instructed you before. [12]Then people who are not believers will respect the way you live, and you will not need to depend on others.

THE HOPE OF THE RESURRECTION

[13]And now, dear brothers and sisters, we want you to know what will happen to the believers who have died* so you will not grieve like people who have no hope. [14]For since we believe that Jesus died and was raised to life again, we also believe that when Jesus returns, God will bring back with him the believers who have died.

[15]We tell you this directly from the Lord: We who are still living when the Lord returns will not meet him ahead of those who have died.* [16]For the Lord himself will come down from heaven with a commanding shout, with the voice of the archangel, and with the trumpet call of God. First, the believers who have died* will rise from their graves. [17]Then, together with them, we who are alive and remain on the earth will be caught up in the clouds to meet the Lord in the air. Then we will be with the Lord forever. [18]So encourage each other with these words.

5 Now concerning how and when all this will happen, dear brothers and sisters,* we don't really need to write you. [2]For you know quite well that the day of the Lord's return will come unexpectedly, like a thief in the night. [3]When people are saying, "Everything is peaceful and secure,"

3:2 Other manuscripts read *and God's servant;* still others read *and a co-worker,* or *and a servant and co-worker for God,* or *and God's servant and our co-worker.* 3:7 Greek *brothers.* 4:1 Greek *brothers;* also in 4:10, 13. 4:4 Or *will know how to take a wife for himself;* or *will learn to live with his own wife;* Greek reads *will know how to possess his own vessel.* 4:6 Greek *Never harm or cheat a brother in this matter.* 4:9 Greek *about brotherly love.* 4:10 Greek *the brothers.* 4:13 Greek *those who have fallen asleep;* also in 4:14. 4:15 Greek *those who have fallen asleep.* 4:16 Greek *the dead in Christ.* 5:1 Greek *brothers;* also in 5:4, 12, 14, 25, 26, 27.

HOW TO PRAY WITHOUT CEASING
1 Thessalonians 5:17   JACK HAYFORD

In 1 Thessalonians 5, Paul gives 17 ways for believers to "encourage each other and build each other up" (v. 11). Most of the apostle's list is easy to understand and implement. But how do we "never stop praying" (v. 17)?

One way is to pray and sing, either out loud or in the silence of your heart. Songs of joy express God's strength and defeat the enemy. In 2 Chronicles 20, God's people went into battle with the choir leading the way, "singing to the LORD and praising him for his holy splendor" (v. 21). The enemy fell, and the people returned victorious.

Our call as God's people today is to introduce the place for God to reign. Singing songs in our mind and heart, keeping praise upon our lips and Scripture under our breath, we make a place for the ongoing entry and display of His work and power.

ALWAYS THANKFUL
1 Thessalonians 5:18   ROBERT MORRIS

An attitude of gratitude isn't just a one-day-a-year celebration. It's a daily lifestyle that every believer should embrace.

Jesus is the perfect example of someone who had a lifestyle of thanksgiving. Every time He ate, He gave thanks. And when the disciples asked Him to teach them how to pray, He said, "Give us today the food we need" (Matthew 6:11). Jesus was trying to impart an attitude to His followers. He was essentially saying, "Guys, this is a miracle. I want you to understand that God provided this food for us today—and every day!"

God wants us to give Him thanks. If we remind ourselves every day that He has provided us with everything we have, our attitude will change to one of thanksgiving.

I encourage you to be thankful every day, and it starts with acknowledging that God is your provider.

then disaster will fall on them as suddenly as a pregnant woman's labor pains begin. And there will be no escape.

⁴ But you aren't in the dark about these things, dear brothers and sisters, and you won't be surprised when the day of the Lord comes like a thief.* ⁵ For you are all children of the light and of the day; we don't belong to darkness and night. ⁶ So be on your guard, not asleep like the others. Stay alert and be clearheaded. ⁷ Night is the time when people sleep and drinkers get drunk. ⁸ But let us who live in the light be clearheaded, protected by the armor of faith and love, and wearing as our helmet the confidence of our salvation.

⁹ For God chose to save us through our Lord Jesus Christ, not to pour out his anger on us. ¹⁰ Christ died for us so that, whether we are dead or alive when he returns, we can live with him forever. ¹¹ So encourage each other and build each other up, just as you are already doing.

PAUL'S FINAL ADVICE
¹² Dear brothers and sisters, honor those who are your leaders in the Lord's work. They work hard among you and give you spiritual guidance. ¹³ Show them great respect and wholehearted love because of their work. And live peacefully with each other.

¹⁴ Brothers and sisters, we urge you to warn those who are lazy. Encourage those who are timid. Take tender care of those who are weak. Be patient with everyone.

¹⁵ See that no one pays back evil for evil, but always try to do good to each other and to all people.

¹⁶ Always be joyful. ¹⁷ Never stop praying. ¹⁸ Be thankful in all circumstances, for this is God's will for you who belong to Christ Jesus.

¹⁹ Do not stifle the Holy Spirit. ²⁰ Do not scoff at prophecies, ²¹ but test everything that is said. Hold on to what is good. ²² Stay away from every kind of evil.

PAUL'S FINAL GREETINGS
²³ Now may the God of peace make you holy in every way, and may your whole spirit and soul and body be kept blameless until our Lord Jesus Christ comes again. ²⁴ God will make this happen, for he who calls you is faithful.

²⁵ Dear brothers and sisters, pray for us. ²⁶ Greet all the brothers and sisters with a sacred kiss.

²⁷ I command you in the name of the Lord to read this letter to all the brothers and sisters.

²⁸ May the grace of our Lord Jesus Christ be with you.

5:4 Some manuscripts read *comes upon you as if you were thieves.*

2 THESSALONIANS

GREETINGS FROM PAUL

1 This letter is from Paul, Silas,* and Timothy.
We are writing to the church in Thessalonica, to you who belong to God our Father and the Lord Jesus Christ.

² May God our Father* and the Lord Jesus Christ give you grace and peace.

ENCOURAGEMENT DURING PERSECUTION

³ Dear brothers and sisters,* we can't help but thank God for you, because your faith is flourishing and your love for one another is growing. ⁴ We proudly tell God's other churches about your endurance and faithfulness in all the persecutions and hardships you are suffering. ⁵ And God will use this persecution to show his justice and to make you worthy of his Kingdom, for which you are suffering. ⁶ In his justice he will pay back those who persecute you.

⁷ And God will provide rest for you who are being persecuted and also for us when the Lord Jesus appears from heaven. He will come with his mighty angels, ⁸ in flaming fire, bringing judgment on those who don't know God and on those who refuse to obey the Good News of our Lord Jesus. ⁹ They will be punished with eternal destruction, forever separated from the Lord and from his glorious power. ¹⁰ When he comes on that day, he will receive glory from his holy people—praise from all who believe. And this includes you, for you believed what we told you about him.

¹¹ So we keep on praying for you, asking our God to enable you to live a life worthy of his call. May he give you the power to accomplish all the good things your faith prompts you to do. ¹² Then the name of our Lord Jesus will be honored because of the way you live, and you will be honored along with him. This is all made possible because of the grace of our God and Lord, Jesus Christ.*

EVENTS PRIOR TO THE LORD'S SECOND COMING

2 Now, dear brothers and sisters,* let us clarify some things about the coming of our Lord Jesus Christ and how we will be gathered to meet him. ² Don't be so easily shaken or alarmed by those who say that the day of the Lord has already begun. Don't believe them, even if they claim to have had a spiritual vision, a revelation, or a letter supposedly from us. ³ Don't be fooled by what they say. For that day will not come until there is a great rebellion against God and the man of lawlessness* is revealed—the one who brings destruction.* ⁴ He will exalt himself and defy everything that people call god and every object of worship. He will even sit in the temple of God, claiming that he himself is God.

⁵ Don't you remember that I told you about all this when I was with you? ⁶ And you know what is holding him back, for he can be revealed only when his time comes. ⁷ For this lawlessness is already at work secretly, and it will remain secret until the one who is holding it back steps out of the way. ⁸ Then the man of lawlessness will be revealed, but the Lord Jesus will slay him with the breath of his mouth and destroy him by the splendor of his coming.

⁹ This man will come to do the work of Satan with counterfeit power and signs and miracles. ¹⁰ He will use every kind of evil deception to fool those on their way to destruction, because they refuse to love and accept the truth that would save them. ¹¹ So God will cause them to be greatly deceived, and they will believe these lies. ¹² Then they will be condemned for enjoying evil rather than believing the truth.

BELIEVERS SHOULD STAND FIRM

¹³ As for us, we can't help but thank God for you, dear brothers and sisters loved by the Lord. We are always thankful that God chose you to be among the first* to experience salvation—a salvation that came through the Spirit who makes you holy and through your belief in the truth. ¹⁴ He called you to salvation when we told you the Good News; now you can share in the glory of our Lord Jesus Christ.

¹⁵ With all these things in mind, dear brothers and sisters, stand firm and keep a strong grip on the teaching we passed on to you both in person and by letter.

¹⁶ Now may our Lord Jesus Christ himself and God our Father, who loved us and by his grace gave us eternal comfort and a wonderful hope, ¹⁷ comfort you and strengthen you in every good thing you do and say.

PAUL'S REQUEST FOR PRAYER

3 Finally, dear brothers and sisters,* we ask you to pray for us. Pray that the Lord's message will spread rapidly and be honored wherever it goes, just as when it came to you. ² Pray, too, that we will be rescued from wicked and evil people, for not everyone is a believer. ³ But the Lord is faithful; he will strengthen you and guard you from the evil one.* ⁴ And we are confident in the Lord that you are doing and will continue to do the things we commanded you. ⁵ May the Lord

---

1:1 Greek *Silvanus,* the Greek form of the name. 1:2 Some manuscripts read *God the Father.* 1:3 Greek *Brothers.* 1:12 Or *of our God and our Lord Jesus Christ.* 2:1 Greek *brothers;* also in 2:13, 15. 2:3a Some manuscripts read *the man of sin.* 2:3b Greek *the son of destruction.* 2:13 Some manuscripts read *chose you from the very beginning.* 3:1 Greek *brothers;* also in 3:6, 13. 3:3 Or *from evil.*

lead your hearts into a full understanding and expression of the love of God and the patient endurance that comes from Christ.

AN EXHORTATION TO PROPER LIVING

⁶And now, dear brothers and sisters, we give you this command in the name of our Lord Jesus Christ: Stay away from all believers* who live idle lives and don't follow the tradition they received* from us. ⁷For you know that you ought to imitate us. We were not idle when we were with you. ⁸We never accepted food from anyone without paying for it. We worked hard day and night so we would not be a burden to any of you. ⁹We certainly had the right to ask you to feed us, but we wanted to give you an example to follow. ¹⁰Even while we were with you, we gave you this command: "Those unwilling to work will not get to eat."

¹¹Yet we hear that some of you are living idle lives, refusing to work and meddling in other people's business. ¹²We command such people and urge them in the name of the Lord Jesus Christ to settle down and work to earn their own living. ¹³As for the rest of you, dear brothers and sisters, never get tired of doing good.

¹⁴Take note of those who refuse to obey what we say in this letter. Stay away from them so they will be ashamed. ¹⁵Don't think of them as enemies, but warn them as you would a brother or sister.*

PAUL'S FINAL GREETINGS

¹⁶Now may the Lord of peace himself give you his peace at all times and in every situation. The Lord be with you all.

¹⁷HERE IS MY GREETING IN MY OWN HAND-WRITING—PAUL. I DO THIS IN ALL MY LETTERS TO PROVE THEY ARE FROM ME.

¹⁸May the grace of our Lord Jesus Christ be with you all.

3:6a Greek *from every brother.*   3:6b Some manuscripts read *you received.*   3:15 Greek *as a brother.*

1 TIMOTHY

JON HUNTZINGER, PHD

Paul wrote the letter of 1 Timothy to his young associate Timothy in the early AD 60s to provide instruction for his pastoral leadership for the church at Ephesus, which Paul had founded about a decade earlier. Timothy likely came to faith through his mother and grandmother when they received the gospel from Paul in Asia Minor (Lystra) in the late AD 40s. In order for Timothy to serve alongside the apostle to both Jews and Gentiles, given the fact his mother was Jewish and his father a Gentile, Paul directs him to be circumcised. Jewish people would be more willing to hear the gospel from a young Jewish man who had been circumcised according to the teaching of Scripture than one who had not.

Paul's first letter to Timothy includes the following sections:

— Paul greets his "true son in the faith" and instructs him in the need to teach the goodness of the law (1:1-11).
— He gives thanks for the ministry of the gospel that God has given to him and encourages Timothy to remain faithful in that same ministry (1:12-20).
— Paul teaches about proper prayer and learning (2:1-15).
— He lists the qualifications for church leaders (3:1-13).
— Paul makes a statement on the mystery of the gospel (3:14-16).
— He gives a warning against false teaching and emphasizes the need for good doctrine (4:1-16).
— Paul gives instructions on the pastoral care of people in the church (5:1-6:10).
— He gives a final exhortation for Timothy to live a blameless life (6:11-21).

THE IMPORTANCE OF TEACHING

The word *gospel* or *Good News* only occurs one time in the letter: "We know that the law is good . . . from the glorious Good News entrusted to me by our blessed God" (1:8-11). This small amount of usage could indicate that Paul's attention is on other matters besides the gospel in this letter. However, that assumption would be a mistake. In the letter, Paul addresses the problem of "teaching [that] is contrary to the truth" (1:3) or unorthodox teaching that threatens the sound doctrine of the church at Ephesus. In fact, the thrust of the entire letter is primarily concerned with teaching. The word for *teaching* (*didasko*) is used eight times; the verb (*didasko*) is used six times; and the word *teacher* (*didashalos*) is used two times. Good or true teaching versus false teaching is the context in which the letter must be read. Good teaching is that which upholds the essential content of the gospel, and false teaching is that which would contradict it. Paul writes that he was appointed a teacher of the Gentiles (2:7) to make known the truth: "There is one God and one Mediator who can reconcile God and humanity—the man Christ Jesus. He gave his life to purchase freedom for everyone" (2:5-6). In this statement, he shows the close connection between good teaching and the gospel. Myths, genealogies, prohibitions against marriage, and abstaining from foods are all aspects of the false teaching Paul condemns. True teaching shows the practical consequences of the gospel in a person's life in the form of devotion to family, careful speech, and the right attitude toward money.

GREETINGS FROM PAUL

1 This letter is from Paul, an apostle of Christ Jesus, appointed by the command of God our Savior and Christ Jesus, who gives us hope.

[2] I am writing to Timothy, my true son in the faith.

May God the Father and Christ Jesus our Lord give you grace, mercy, and peace.

WARNINGS AGAINST FALSE TEACHINGS

[3] When I left for Macedonia, I urged you to stay there in Ephesus and stop those whose teaching is contrary to the truth. [4] Don't let them waste their time in endless discussion of myths and spiritual pedigrees. These things only lead to meaningless speculations,* which don't help people live a life of faith in God.*

[5] The purpose of my instruction is that all believers would be filled with love that comes from a pure heart, a clear conscience, and genuine faith. [6] But some people have missed this whole point. They have turned away from these things and spend their time in meaningless discussions. [7] They want to be known as teachers of the law of Moses, but they don't know what they are talking about, even though they speak so confidently.

[8] We know that the law is good when used correctly. [9] For the law was not intended for people who do what is right. It is for people who are lawless and rebellious, who are ungodly and sinful, who consider nothing sacred and defile what is holy, who kill their father or mother or commit other murders. [10] The law is for people who are sexually immoral, or who practice homosexuality, or are slave traders,* liars, promise breakers, or who do anything else that contradicts the wholesome teaching [11] that comes from the glorious Good News entrusted to me by our blessed God.

PAUL'S GRATITUDE FOR GOD'S MERCY

[12] I thank Christ Jesus our Lord, who has given me strength to do his work. He considered me trustworthy and appointed me to serve him, [13] even though I used to blaspheme the name of Christ. In my insolence, I persecuted his people. But God had mercy on me because I did it in ignorance and unbelief. [14] Oh, how generous and gracious our Lord was! He filled me with the faith and love that come from Christ Jesus.

[15] This is a trustworthy saying, and everyone should accept it: "Christ Jesus came into the world to save sinners"—and I am the worst of them all. [16] But God had mercy on me so that Christ Jesus could use me as a prime example of his great patience with even the worst sinners. Then others will realize that they, too, can believe in him and receive eternal life. [17] All honor and glory to God forever and ever! He is the eternal King, the unseen one who never dies; he alone is God. Amen.

BELIEVING YOUR PRAYERS ARE DECISIVE

1 Timothy 2:1-5   JACK HAYFORD

Some believers never learn to pray beyond personal or family needs. However, each of us has a responsibility to pray regularly for our neighborhoods and cities. We have the power to decide whether we will have a quiet and peaceful life where we live and then beyond that to our state, our nation, and the world. This is our starting place as believers if we expect to see social peace and justice (v. 2), as well as spiritual opportunities (v. 4). It is the will of God (v. 3).

Begin to pray with a passion for both personal and global needs. Because God has empowered you by His Spirit, you can have confidence that your prayers really do make a difference. If we, as the people of God, will stand in the gap, the power of God will accomplish His intended purpose in the world.

TIMOTHY'S RESPONSIBILITY

[18] Timothy, my son, here are my instructions for you, based on the prophetic words spoken about you earlier. May they help you fight well in the Lord's battles. [19] Cling to your faith in Christ, and keep your conscience clear. For some people have deliberately violated their consciences; as a result, their faith has been shipwrecked. [20] Hymenaeus and Alexander are two examples. I threw them out and handed them over to Satan so they might learn not to blaspheme God.

INSTRUCTIONS ABOUT WORSHIP

2 I urge you, first of all, to pray for all people. Ask God to help them; intercede on their behalf, and give thanks for them. [2] Pray this way for kings and all who are in authority so that we can live peaceful and quiet lives marked by godliness and dignity. [3] This is good and pleases God our Savior, [4] who wants everyone to be saved and to understand the truth. [5] For,

There is one God and one Mediator who can reconcile God and humanity—the man Christ Jesus. [6] He gave his life to purchase freedom for everyone.

This is the message God gave to the world at just the right time. [7] And I have been chosen as a preacher and apostle to teach the Gentiles this message about faith and truth. I'm not exaggerating—just telling the truth.

[8] In every place of worship, I want men to pray with holy hands lifted up to God, free from anger and controversy.

1:4a Greek *in myths and endless genealogies, which cause speculation.*
1:4b Greek *a stewardship of God in faith.*   1:10 Or *kidnappers.*

⁹And I want women to be modest in their appearance.* They should wear decent and appropriate clothing and not draw attention to themselves by the way they fix their hair or by wearing gold or pearls or expensive clothes. ¹⁰For women who claim to be devoted to God should make themselves attractive by the good things they do.

¹¹Women should learn quietly and submissively. ¹²I do not let women teach men or have authority over them.* Let them listen quietly. ¹³For God made Adam first, and afterward he made Eve. ¹⁴And it was not Adam who was deceived by Satan. The woman was deceived, and sin was the result. ¹⁵But women will be saved through childbearing,* assuming they continue to live in faith, love, holiness, and modesty.

LEADERS IN THE CHURCH

3 This is a trustworthy saying: "If someone aspires to be a church leader,* he desires an honorable position." ²So a church leader must be a man whose life is above reproach. He must be faithful to his wife.* He must exercise self-control, live wisely, and have a good reputation. He must enjoy having guests in his home, and he must be able to teach. ³He must not be a heavy drinker* or be violent. He must be gentle, not quarrelsome, and not love money. ⁴He must manage his own family well, having children who respect and obey him. ⁵For if a man cannot manage his own household, how can he take care of God's church?

⁶A church leader must not be a new believer, because he might become proud, and the devil would cause him to fall.* ⁷Also, people outside the church must speak well of him so that he will not be disgraced and fall into the devil's trap.

⁸In the same way, deacons must be well respected and have integrity. They must not be heavy drinkers or dishonest with money. ⁹They must be committed to the mystery of the faith now revealed and must live with a clear conscience. ¹⁰Before they are appointed as deacons, let them be closely examined. If they pass the test, then let them serve as deacons.

¹¹In the same way, their wives* must be respected and must not slander others. They must exercise self-control and be faithful in everything they do.

¹²A deacon must be faithful to his wife, and he must manage his children and household well. ¹³Those who do well as deacons will be rewarded with respect from others and will have increased confidence in their faith in Christ Jesus.

THE TRUTHS OF OUR FAITH

¹⁴I am writing these things to you now, even though I hope to be with you soon, ¹⁵so that if I am delayed, you will know how people must conduct themselves in the household of God.

This is the church of the living God, which is the pillar and foundation of the truth.

¹⁶Without question, this is the great mystery of our faith*:

Christ* was revealed in a human body
  and vindicated by the Spirit.*
He was seen by angels
  and announced to the nations.
He was believed in throughout the world
  and taken to heaven in glory.

WARNINGS AGAINST FALSE TEACHERS

4 Now the Holy Spirit tells us clearly that in the last times some will turn away from the true faith; they will follow deceptive spirits and teachings that come from demons. ²These people are hypocrites and liars, and their consciences are dead.* ³They will say it is wrong to be married and wrong to eat certain foods. But God created those foods to be eaten with thanks by faithful people who know the truth. ⁴Since everything God created is good, we should not reject any of it but receive it with thanks. ⁵For we know it is made acceptable* by the word of God and prayer.

A GOOD SERVANT OF CHRIST JESUS

⁶If you explain these things to the brothers and sisters,* Timothy, you will be a worthy servant of Christ Jesus, one who is nourished by the message of faith and the good teaching you have followed. ⁷Do not waste time arguing over godless ideas and old wives' tales. Instead, train yourself to be godly. ⁸"Physical training is good, but training for godliness is much better, promising benefits in this life and in the life to come." ⁹This is a trustworthy saying, and everyone should accept it. ¹⁰This is why we work hard and continue to struggle,* for our hope is in the living God, who is the Savior of all people and particularly of all believers.

¹¹Teach these things and insist that everyone learn them. ¹²Don't let anyone think less of you because you are young. Be an example to all believers in what you say, in the way you live, in your love, your faith, and your purity. ¹³Until I get there, focus on reading the Scriptures to the church, encouraging the believers, and teaching them.

¹⁴Do not neglect the spiritual gift you received through the prophecy spoken over you when

---

2:9 Or to pray in modest apparel. 2:12 Or teach men or usurp their authority. 2:15 Or will be saved by accepting their role as mothers, or will be saved by the birth of the Child. 3:1 Or an overseer, or a bishop; also in 3:2, 6. 3:2 Or must have only one wife, or must be married only once; Greek reads must be the husband of one wife; also in 3:12. 3:3 Greek must not drink too much wine; similarly in 3:8. 3:6 Or he might fall into the same judgment as the devil. 3:11 Or the women deacons. The Greek word can be translated women or wives. 3:16a Or of godliness. 3:16b Greek He who; other manuscripts read God. 3:16c Or in his spirit. 4:2 Greek are seared. 4:5 Or made holy. 4:6 Greek brothers. 4:10 Some manuscripts read continue to suffer.

PRESBYTERY AND PROPHECY
1 Timothy 4:14   ROBERT MORRIS

The word *presbytery* comes from the Greek word *presbuterion*, which means 'body of elders.' At Gateway Church, we bring in a group of elders (pastors and teachers) from both inside and outside our church to speak prophetic words to individuals and couples. The purpose of prophecy is to encourage and edify people, not to embarrass them or call out their past sins.

Here are a few important things to know about presbytery and prophecy:

1. It's God speaking.
God speaks through prophecy. I've seen many people give their lives to the Lord, and I've seen others turn their lives around based on a prophetic word spoken during a presbytery service.

2. It's an impartation.
When God wants something, He speaks. It's how He created the earth and everything in it. So when He wants you to do something, He's going to speak it. In other words, He's going to *impart* it to you. In 1 Timothy 4:14, Paul tells Timothy, "Do not neglect the spiritual gift you received through the prophecy spoken over you when the elders of the church laid their hands on you."

3. It's team ministry.
Paul says, "Let two or three people prophesy, and let the others evaluate what is said" (1 Corinthians 14:29). There's accountability when prophetic ministry is done as a team. The most accurate prophetic words I've heard have come through presbytery because God is speaking to multiple people. And it's incredible to hear similar words coming from different people. It's confirmation that the message truly came from the Lord.

the elders of the church laid their hands on you. [15] Give your complete attention to these matters. Throw yourself into your tasks so that everyone will see your progress. [16] Keep a close watch on how you live and on your teaching. Stay true to what is right for the sake of your own salvation and the salvation of those who hear you.

ADVICE ABOUT WIDOWS, ELDERS, AND SLAVES

5 Never speak harshly to an older man,* but appeal to him respectfully as you would to your own father. Talk to younger men as you would to your own brothers. [2] Treat older women as you would your mother, and treat younger women with all purity as you would your own sisters.

[3] Take care of* any widow who has no one else to care for her. [4] But if she has children or grandchildren, their first responsibility is to show godliness at home and repay their parents by taking care of them. This is something that pleases God.

[5] Now a true widow, a woman who is truly alone in this world, has placed her hope in God. She prays night and day, asking God for his help. [6] But the widow who lives only for pleasure is spiritually dead even while she lives. [7] Give these instructions to the church so that no one will be open to criticism.

[8] But those who won't care for their relatives, especially those in their own household, have denied the true faith. Such people are worse than unbelievers.

[9] A widow who is put on the list for support must be a woman who is at least sixty years old and was faithful to her husband.* [10] She must be well respected by everyone because of the good she has done. Has she brought up her children well? Has she been kind to strangers and served other believers humbly?* Has she helped those who are in trouble? Has she always been ready to do good?

[11] The younger widows should not be on the list, because their physical desires will overpower their devotion to Christ and they will want to remarry. [12] Then they would be guilty of breaking their previous pledge. [13] And if they are on the list, they will learn to be lazy and will spend their time gossiping from house to house, meddling in other people's business and talking about things they shouldn't. [14] So I advise these younger widows to marry again, have children, and take care of their own homes. Then the enemy will not be able to say anything against them. [15] For I am afraid that some of them have already gone astray and now follow Satan.

[16] If a woman who is a believer has relatives who are widows, she must take care of them and not put the responsibility on the church. Then the church can care for the widows who are truly alone.

[17] Elders who do their work well should be respected and paid well,* especially those who work hard at both preaching and teaching. [18] For the Scripture says, "You must not muzzle an ox to keep it from eating as it treads out the grain." And in another place, "Those who work deserve their pay!"*

[19] Do not listen to an accusation against an elder unless it is confirmed by two or three witnesses. [20] Those who sin should be reprimanded in front of the whole church; this will serve as a strong warning to others.

[21] I solemnly command you in the presence of God and Christ Jesus and the highest angels to obey these instructions without taking sides or showing favoritism to anyone.

5:1 Or *an elder.*   5:3 Or *Honor.*   5:9 Greek *was the wife of one husband.*   5:10 Greek *and washed the feet of God's holy people?*   5:17 Greek *should be worthy of double honor.*   5:18 Deut 25:4; Luke 10:7.

²²Never be in a hurry about appointing a church leader.* Do not share in the sins of others. Keep yourself pure.

²³Don't drink only water. You ought to drink a little wine for the sake of your stomach because you are sick so often.

²⁴Remember, the sins of some people are obvious, leading them to certain judgment. But there are others whose sins will not be revealed until later. ²⁵In the same way, the good deeds of some people are obvious. And the good deeds done in secret will someday come to light.

6 All slaves should show full respect for their masters so they will not bring shame on the name of God and his teaching. ²If the masters are believers, that is no excuse for being disrespectful. Those slaves should work all the harder because their efforts are helping other believers* who are well loved.

FALSE TEACHING AND TRUE RICHES

Teach these things, Timothy, and encourage everyone to obey them. ³Some people may contradict our teaching, but these are the wholesome teachings of the Lord Jesus Christ. These teachings promote a godly life. ⁴Anyone who teaches something different is arrogant and lacks understanding. Such a person has an unhealthy desire to quibble over the meaning of words. This stirs up arguments ending in jealousy, division, slander, and evil suspicions. ⁵These people always cause trouble. Their minds are corrupt, and they have turned their backs on the truth. To them, a show of godliness is just a way to become wealthy.

⁶Yet true godliness with contentment is itself great wealth. ⁷After all, we brought nothing with us when we came into the world, and we can't take anything with us when we leave it. ⁸So if we have enough food and clothing, let us be content. ⁹But people who long to be rich fall into temptation and are trapped by many foolish and harmful desires that plunge them into ruin and destruction. ¹⁰For the love of money is the root of all kinds of evil. And some people, craving money, have wandered from the true faith and pierced themselves with many sorrows.

PAUL'S FINAL INSTRUCTIONS

¹¹But you, Timothy, are a man of God; so run from all these evil things. Pursue righteousness and a godly life, along with faith, love, perseverance, and gentleness. ¹²Fight the good fight for the true faith. Hold tightly to the eternal life to which God has called you, which you have declared so well before many witnesses. ¹³And I charge you before God, who gives life to all, and before Christ Jesus,

---

THE DECEITFULNESS OF MONEY

1 Timothy 6:17   ROBERT MORRIS

In his first letter to Timothy, the apostle Paul tells us not to place our security or trust in money. Why is this so important? Because our identity and trust should only be in *God*. There's nothing wrong with wanting to provide for your family or have a successful career. However, if your focus is only on earthly things, the Word of God will be choked out of your life.

When you start looking to money to give you happiness and love, you will never be truly satisfied. Satan looks for moments to sneak in and whisper that your car isn't new enough or your house isn't big enough. He wants to make you forget that Jesus is your provider and security.

Remind yourself who your true Source is. When you allow Jesus to be your Supplier, you open yourself up to receive His Word and His blessings.

---

who gave a good testimony before Pontius Pilate, ¹⁴that you obey this command without wavering. Then no one can find fault with you from now until our Lord Jesus Christ comes again. ¹⁵For,

At just the right time Christ will be revealed from heaven by the blessed and only almighty God, the King of all kings and Lord of all lords. ¹⁶He alone can never die, and he lives in light so brilliant that no human can approach him. No human eye has ever seen him, nor ever will. All honor and power to him forever! Amen.

¹⁷Teach those who are rich in this world not to be proud and not to trust in their money, which is so unreliable. Their trust should be in God, who richly gives us all we need for our enjoyment. ¹⁸Tell them to use their money to do good. They should be rich in good works and generous to those in need, always being ready to share with others. ¹⁹By doing this they will be storing up their treasure as a good foundation for the future so that they may experience true life.

²⁰Timothy, guard what God has entrusted to you. Avoid godless, foolish discussions with those who oppose you with their so-called knowledge. ²¹Some people have wandered from the faith by following such foolishness.

May God's grace be with you all.

5:22 Greek *about the laying on of hands.*   **6:2** Greek *brothers.*

2 TIMOTHY

JON HUNTZINGER, PHD

The circumstances of Paul's second letter to Timothy seem different from the first. It is the most personal letter we have from Paul (along with 2 Corinthians). He wrote it shortly before his execution in AD 66-67. Because the vocabulary is different from 1 Timothy and the tone of the letter emotional, some people have questioned whether Paul wrote it. This concern can be answered by the fact that Paul used secretaries to write his letters and different secretaries sometimes wrote what Paul dictated to them in different ways. Also, his situation had changed. Whereas Paul wrote 1 Timothy as a free man (likely released after his hearing before Caesar, which the book of Acts anticipates), he wrote 2 Timothy later, having been rearrested and charged with a capital offense.

Paul's letter includes the following information:
— He greets Timothy, his "dear son," and expresses thanksgiving (1:1-5).
— Paul encourages Timothy to remain true to the gospel (1:6-18).
— He charges Timothy to be strong in faith (2:1-13).
— Paul tells him to teach the inspired Word of God (2:14-3:17).
— He also encourages Timothy to preach God's Word (4:1-5).
— Paul concludes with a final declaration that he has "fought the good fight" even though "everyone" deserted him at his defense (4:6-22).

THE GOSPEL AND PAUL'S SUFFERING

In this letter, Paul links the gospel and the power of God with his suffering. The ministry of the gospel has resulted in much hardship for Paul, so he encourages Timothy to "never be ashamed to tell others about our Lord. And don't be ashamed of me, either, even though I'm in prison for him" (1:8). Paul continues by saying that Jesus "broke

the power of death and illuminated the way to life and immortality through the Good News. . . . That is why I am suffering here in prison. But I am not ashamed of it" (1:10, 12). Later, Paul says, "Always remember that Jesus Christ, a descendant of King David, was raised from the dead. This is the Good News I preach. And because I preach this Good News, I am suffering and have been chained like a criminal" (2:8-9). Paul has paid a high price for preaching the Good News about Jesus' death and resurrection because not all want to hear it nor do they want others to hear it.

THE GOSPEL AND THE RESURRECTION

Paul suffers on account of the gospel, which he calls "truth," "the word of God," and "the Good News" in other parts of the letter (2:18; 4:2, 17). According to Paul, there is a right way and a wrong way to understand and interpret the gospel and its message of Good News. There is no middle way. The gospel must be correctly explained (2:15), he says, and must emphasize the resurrection of Jesus. The word of truth does not claim that the resurrection of the dead has already happened and is only a past event (2:18). Such teaching upsets the faith of people and causes them to doubt. It cannot be the word of truth or the gospel because the resurrection of the dead is at the heart of the gospel.

The Scriptures support Paul's understanding of the gospel, which for him would have been the books that make up the Hebrew Bible or Old Testament. Paul exhorts Timothy to continue to study these books because they contain the very breath and life of God. He says they are "inspired" or God-breathed (3:16), meaning they are filled with God's life and to the people who read them, provide wisdom and strength to do the good things God has always wanted them to do.

GREETINGS FROM PAUL

1 This letter is from Paul, chosen by the will of God to be an apostle of Christ Jesus. I have been sent out to tell others about the life he has promised through faith in Christ Jesus. ²I am writing to Timothy, my dear son.

May God the Father and Christ Jesus our Lord give you grace, mercy, and peace.

ENCOURAGEMENT TO BE FAITHFUL

³Timothy, I thank God for you—the God I serve with a clear conscience, just as my ancestors did. Night and day I constantly remember you in my prayers. ⁴I long to see you again, for I remember your tears as we parted. And I will be filled with joy when we are together again.

⁵I remember your genuine faith, for you share the faith that first filled your grandmother Lois and your mother, Eunice. And I know that same faith continues strong in you. ⁶This is why I remind you to fan into flames the spiritual gift God gave you when I laid my hands on you. ⁷For God has not given us a spirit of fear and timidity, but of power, love, and self-discipline.

⁸So never be ashamed to tell others about our Lord. And don't be ashamed of me, either, even though I'm in prison for him. With the strength God gives you, be ready to suffer with me for the sake of the Good News. ⁹For God saved us and called us to live a holy life. He did this, not because we deserved it, but because that was his plan from before the beginning of time—to show us his grace through Christ Jesus. ¹⁰And now he has made all of this plain to us by the appearing of Christ Jesus, our Savior. He broke the power of death and illuminated the way to life and immortality through the Good News. ¹¹And God chose me to be a preacher, an apostle, and a teacher of this Good News.

¹²That is why I am suffering here in prison. But I am not ashamed of it, for I know the one in whom I trust, and I am sure that he is able to guard what I have entrusted to him* until the day of his return.

¹³Hold on to the pattern of wholesome teaching you learned from me—a pattern shaped by the faith and love that you have in Christ Jesus. ¹⁴Through the power of the Holy Spirit who lives within us, carefully guard the precious truth that has been entrusted to you.

¹⁵As you know, everyone from the province of Asia has deserted me—even Phygelus and Hermogenes. ¹⁶May the Lord show special kindness to Onesiphorus and all his family because he often visited and encouraged me. He was never ashamed of me because I was in chains. ¹⁷When he came to Rome, he searched everywhere until he found me. ¹⁸May the Lord show him special kindness on the day of Christ's return. And you know very well how helpful he was in Ephesus.

A GOOD SOLDIER OF CHRIST JESUS

2 Timothy, my dear son, be strong through the grace that God gives you in Christ Jesus. ²You have heard me teach things that have been confirmed by many reliable witnesses. Now teach these truths to other trustworthy people who will be able to pass them on to others.

³Endure suffering along with me, as a good soldier of Christ Jesus. ⁴Soldiers don't get tied up in the affairs of civilian life, for then they cannot please the officer who enlisted them. ⁵And athletes cannot win the prize unless they follow the rules. ⁶And hardworking farmers should be the first to enjoy the fruit of their labor. ⁷Think about what I am saying. The Lord will help you understand all these things.

⁸Always remember that Jesus Christ, a descendant of King David, was raised from the dead. This is the Good News I preach. ⁹And because I preach this Good News, I am suffering and have been chained like a criminal. But the word of God cannot be chained. ¹⁰So I am willing to endure anything if it will bring salvation and eternal glory in Christ Jesus to those God has chosen.

¹¹This is a trustworthy saying:

If we die with him,
  we will also live with him.
¹² If we endure hardship,
  we will reign with him.
If we deny him,
  he will deny us.
¹³ If we are unfaithful,
  he remains faithful,
  for he cannot deny who he is.

¹⁴Remind everyone about these things, and command them in God's presence to stop fighting over words. Such arguments are useless, and they can ruin those who hear them.

AN APPROVED WORKER

¹⁵Work hard so you can present yourself to God and receive his approval. Be a good worker, one who does not need to be ashamed and who correctly explains the word of truth. ¹⁶Avoid worthless, foolish talk that only leads to more godless behavior. ¹⁷This kind of talk spreads like cancer,* as in the case of Hymenaeus and Philetus. ¹⁸They have left the path of truth, claiming that the resurrection of the dead has already occurred; in this way, they have turned some people away from the faith.

¹⁹But God's truth stands firm like a foundation stone with this inscription: "The LORD knows those who are his,"* and "All who belong to the LORD must turn away from evil."*

²⁰In a wealthy home some utensils are made of gold and silver, and some are made of wood

---

1:12 Or *what has been entrusted to me.*   2:17 Greek *gangrene.*
2:19a Num 16:5.   2:19b See Isa 52:11.

and clay. The expensive utensils are used for special occasions, and the cheap ones are for everyday use. ²¹If you keep yourself pure, you will be a special utensil for honorable use. Your life will be clean, and you will be ready for the Master to use you for every good work.

²²Run from anything that stimulates youthful lusts. Instead, pursue righteous living, faithfulness, love, and peace. Enjoy the companionship of those who call on the Lord with pure hearts.

²³Again I say, don't get involved in foolish, ignorant arguments that only start fights. ²⁴A servant of the Lord must not quarrel but must be kind to everyone, be able to teach, and be patient with difficult people. ²⁵Gently instruct those who oppose the truth. Perhaps God will change those people's hearts, and they will learn the truth. ²⁶Then they will come to their senses and escape from the devil's trap. For they have been held captive by him to do whatever he wants.

THE DANGERS OF THE LAST DAYS

3 You should know this, Timothy, that in the last days there will be very difficult times. ²For people will love only themselves and their money. They will be boastful and proud, scoffing at God, disobedient to their parents, and ungrateful. They will consider nothing sacred. ³They will be unloving and unforgiving; they will slander others and have no self-control. They will be cruel and hate what is good. ⁴They will betray their friends, be reckless, be puffed up with pride, and love pleasure rather than God. ⁵They will act religious, but they will reject the power that could make them godly. Stay away from people like that!

⁶They are the kind who work their way into people's homes and win the confidence of* vulnerable women who are burdened with the guilt of sin and controlled by various desires. ⁷(Such women are forever following new teachings, but they are never able to understand the truth.) ⁸These teachers oppose the truth just as Jannes and Jambres opposed Moses. They have depraved minds and a counterfeit faith. ⁹But they won't get away with this for long. Someday everyone will recognize what fools they are, just as with Jannes and Jambres.

PAUL'S CHARGE TO TIMOTHY

¹⁰But you, Timothy, certainly know what I teach, and how I live, and what my purpose in life is. You know my faith, my patience, my love, and my endurance. ¹¹You know how much persecution and suffering I have endured. You know all about how I was persecuted in Antioch, Iconium, and Lystra—but the Lord rescued me from all of it. ¹²Yes, and everyone who wants to live a godly life in Christ Jesus will suffer persecution. ¹³But evil people and impostors will flourish. They will deceive others and will themselves be deceived.

TAKE A BREATH
2 Timothy 3:16   ROBERT MORRIS

Paul writes, "All Scripture is inspired by God" (2 Timothy 3:16). The root of the Greek word for *inspiration* means 'breath.' In other words, all Scripture is the breath of God.

In Ezekiel 37, God tells Ezekiel to prophesy to a valley of dry bones. The bones come together and are covered with muscles and flesh; however, they are still breathless. I wonder how many people feel like those bodies—alive with no breath? Many of us live in a spiritually oxygen-depleted atmosphere because we're not breathing in God's Word.

Then God tells Ezekiel to prophesy again. Breath comes into the bodies, and they "all came to life and stood up on their feet—a great army" (Ezekiel 37:10). If God's breath can cause a valley of dry bones to become an army, think about the power it can have in your life! Take a breath today and see what God does.

---

¹⁴But you must remain faithful to the things you have been taught. You know they are true, for you know you can trust those who taught you. ¹⁵You have been taught the holy Scriptures from childhood, and they have given you the wisdom to receive the salvation that comes by trusting in Christ Jesus. ¹⁶All Scripture is inspired by God and is useful to teach us what is true and to make us realize what is wrong in our lives. It corrects us when we are wrong and teaches us to do what is right. ¹⁷God uses it to prepare and equip his people to do every good work.

4 I solemnly urge you in the presence of God and Christ Jesus, who will someday judge the living and the dead when he comes to set up his Kingdom: ²Preach the word of God. Be prepared, whether the time is favorable or not. Patiently correct, rebuke, and encourage your people with good teaching.

³For a time is coming when people will no longer listen to sound and wholesome teaching. They will follow their own desires and will look for teachers who will tell them whatever their itching ears want to hear. ⁴They will reject the truth and chase after myths.

⁵But you should keep a clear mind in every situation. Don't be afraid of suffering for the Lord. Work at telling others the Good News, and fully carry out the ministry God has given you.

⁶As for me, my life has already been poured out as an offering to God. The time of my death is near. ⁷I have fought the good fight, I have finished the race, and I have remained faithful. ⁸And now the prize awaits me—the crown of

---

3:6 Greek *and take captive.*

righteousness, which the Lord, the righteous Judge, will give me on the day of his return. And the prize is not just for me but for all who eagerly look forward to his appearing.

PAUL'S FINAL WORDS

⁹ Timothy, please come as soon as you can. ¹⁰ Demas has deserted me because he loves the things of this life and has gone to Thessalonica. Crescens has gone to Galatia, and Titus has gone to Dalmatia. ¹¹ Only Luke is with me. Bring Mark with you when you come, for he will be helpful to me in my ministry. ¹² I sent Tychicus to Ephesus. ¹³ When you come, be sure to bring the coat I left with Carpus at Troas. Also bring my books, and especially my papers.*

¹⁴ Alexander the coppersmith did me much harm, but the Lord will judge him for what he has done. ¹⁵ Be careful of him, for he fought against everything we said.

¹⁶ The first time I was brought before the judge, no one came with me. Everyone abandoned me.

May it not be counted against them. ¹⁷ But the Lord stood with me and gave me strength so that I might preach the Good News in its entirety for all the Gentiles to hear. And he rescued me from certain death.* ¹⁸ Yes, and the Lord will deliver me from every evil attack and will bring me safely into his heavenly Kingdom. All glory to God forever and ever! Amen.

PAUL'S FINAL GREETINGS

¹⁹ Give my greetings to Priscilla and Aquila and those living in the household of Onesiphorus. ²⁰ Erastus stayed at Corinth, and I left Trophimus sick at Miletus.

²¹ Do your best to get here before winter. Eubulus sends you greetings, and so do Pudens, Linus, Claudia, and all the brothers and sisters.*

²² May the Lord be with your spirit. And may his grace be with all of you.

4:13 Greek *especially the parchments.*   **4:17** Greek *from the mouth of a lion.*   **4:21** Greek *brothers.*

TITUS

JON HUNTZINGER, PHD

P aul's letter to Titus is one of three letters in the New Testament that he wrote to individual associates advising them on matters related to pastoral ministry. For that reason, they (Titus and 1-2 Timothy) are called the "pastoral epistles." Titus was a Gentile believer who had received the gospel from Paul and traveled with him to Jerusalem (Galatians 2:1-3) and later represented him to the Corinthian church (2 Corinthians 7:6-7; 8:6, 16-24). He also went to Dalmatia on Paul's behalf (2 Timothy 4:10). The letter advises Titus on the appointment of leaders in Crete and other matters after they had conducted ministry there (which is not recorded in the book of Acts). It is one of the last letters Paul wrote, sometime in the early AD 60s.

Paul's letter includes the following information:
— Paul gives a self-description and greets Titus as his "true son in the faith that we share" (1:1-4).
— He lists the qualifications for elders (1:5-16).
— Paul outlines proper behavior for men and women, young and old (2:1-15).
— He discusses the importance of good works (3:1-11).
— Paul gives his final instructions (3:12-15).

BELIEF AND BEHAVIOR

As with Paul's letters to Timothy, the letter to Titus is full of practical information. A common theme is the relationship between belief and behavior. Leaders must show in their lives the truth of the Word that they teach to others. The qualities of leadership—hospitality, goodness, self-control, uprightness, and holiness (1:8)—recall the fruit of the Spirit Paul writes about to the Galatians (Galatians 5:22-23). This means that, according to Paul, leaders must know God's Word and be filled with God's Spirit. For his part, Titus is to give "wholesome teaching" (Titus 2:1), do "good works" (2:7), and guard his speech (2:8).

GOOD WORKS

Good works is another theme that ties the letter together. Not only are leaders to show goodness in their personal lives (1:8), but Titus must match good works with his sound teaching (2:1, 7). Leaders are to follow the example of Jesus who gave His life so that people might be purified and able to do "good deeds" (2:14). In fact, Jesus' appearance was an example of God's goodness or good works (3:4) and made possible the ministry of the Holy Spirit, which leads to good works (3:5-8). In Paul's mind, good works are the best testimony to the gospel and the best defense of it. When people do good works, the gospel cannot be criticized, and "those who oppose us will be ashamed and have nothing bad to say about us" (2:8).

GREETINGS FROM PAUL

1 This letter is from Paul, a slave of God and an apostle of Jesus Christ. I have been sent to proclaim faith to* those God has chosen and to teach them to know the truth that shows them how to live godly lives. [2]This truth gives them confidence that they have eternal life, which God—who does not lie—promised them before the world began. [3]And now at just the right time he has revealed this message, which we announce to everyone. It is by the command of God our Savior that I have been entrusted with this work for him.

[4]I am writing to Titus, my true son in the faith that we share.

May God the Father and Christ Jesus our Savior give you grace and peace.

TITUS'S WORK IN CRETE

[5]I left you on the island of Crete so you could complete our work there and appoint elders in each town as I instructed you. [6]An elder must live a blameless life. He must be faithful to his wife,* and his children must be believers who don't have a reputation for being wild or rebellious. [7]A church leader* is a manager of God's household, so he must live a blameless life. He must not be arrogant or quick-tempered; he must not be a heavy drinker,* violent, or dishonest with money. [8]Rather, he must enjoy having guests in his home, and he must love what is good. He must live wisely and be just. He must live a devout and disciplined life. [9]He must have a strong belief in the trustworthy message he was taught; then he will be able to encourage others with wholesome teaching and show those who oppose it where they are wrong.

[10]For there are many rebellious people who engage in useless talk and deceive others. This is especially true of those who insist on circumcision for salvation. [11]They must be silenced, because they are turning whole families away from the truth by their false teaching. And they do it only for money. [12]Even one of their own men, a prophet from Crete, has said about them, "The people of Crete are all liars, cruel animals, and lazy gluttons."* [13]This is true. So reprimand them sternly to make them strong in the faith. [14]They must stop listening to Jewish myths and the commands of people who have turned away from the truth.

[15]Everything is pure to those whose hearts are pure. But nothing is pure to those who are corrupt and unbelieving, because their minds and consciences are corrupted. [16]Such people claim they know God, but they deny him by the way they live. They are detestable and disobedient, worthless for doing anything good.

PROMOTE RIGHT TEACHING

2 As for you, Titus, promote the kind of living that reflects wholesome teaching. [2]Teach the older men to exercise self-control, to be worthy of respect, and to live wisely. They must have sound faith and be filled with love and patience.

[3]Similarly, teach the older women to live in a way that honors God. They must not slander others or be heavy drinkers.* Instead, they should teach others what is good. [4]These older women must train the younger women to love their husbands and their children, [5]to live wisely and be pure, to work in their homes,* to do good, and to be submissive to their husbands. Then they will not bring shame on the word of God.

[6]In the same way, encourage the young men to live wisely. [7]And you yourself must be an example to them by doing good works of every kind. Let everything you do reflect the integrity and seriousness of your teaching. [8]Teach the truth so that your teaching can't be criticized. Then those who oppose us will be ashamed and have nothing bad to say about us.

[9]Slaves must always obey their masters and do their best to please them. They must not talk back [10]or steal, but must show themselves to be entirely trustworthy and good. Then they will make the teaching about God our Savior attractive in every way.

[11]For the grace of God has been revealed, bringing salvation to all people. [12]And we are instructed to turn from godless living and sinful pleasures. We should live in this evil world with wisdom, righteousness, and devotion to God, [13]while we look forward with hope to that wonderful day when the glory of our great God and Savior, Jesus Christ, will be revealed. [14]He gave his life to free us from every kind of sin, to cleanse us, and to make us his very own people, totally committed to doing good deeds.

[15]You must teach these things and encourage the believers to do them. You have the authority to correct them when necessary, so don't let anyone disregard what you say.

DO WHAT IS GOOD

3 Remind the believers to submit to the government and its officers. They should be obedient, always ready to do what is good. [2]They must not slander anyone and must avoid quarreling. Instead, they should be gentle and show true humility to everyone.

[3]Once we, too, were foolish and disobedient. We were misled and became slaves to many lusts and pleasures. Our lives were full of evil and envy, and we hated each other. [4]But—

When God our Savior revealed his kindness and love, [5]he saved us, not because of the

---

1:1 Or to strengthen the faith of.   1:6 Or must have only one wife, or must be married only once; Greek reads must be the husband of one wife.   1:7a Or An overseer, or A bishop.   1:7b Greek must not drink too much wine.   1:12 This quotation is from Epimenides of Knossos.   2:3 Greek be enslaved to much wine.   2:5 Some manuscripts read to care for their homes.

righteous things we had done, but because of his mercy. He washed away our sins, giving us a new birth and new life through the Holy Spirit.* ⁶ He generously poured out the Spirit upon us through Jesus Christ our Savior. ⁷ Because of his grace he made us right in his sight and gave us confidence that we will inherit eternal life.

⁸ This is a trustworthy saying, and I want you to insist on these teachings so that all who trust in God will devote themselves to doing good. These teachings are good and beneficial for everyone.

⁹ Do not get involved in foolish discussions about spiritual pedigrees* or in quarrels and fights about obedience to Jewish laws. These things are useless and a waste of time. ¹⁰ If people are causing divisions among you, give a first and second warning. After that, have nothing more to do with them. ¹¹ For people like that have turned away from the truth, and their own sins condemn them.

PAUL'S FINAL REMARKS AND GREETINGS

¹² I am planning to send either Artemas or Tychicus to you. As soon as one of them arrives, do your best to meet me at Nicopolis, for I have decided to stay there for the winter. ¹³ Do everything you can to help Zenas the lawyer and Apollos with their trip. See that they are given everything they need. ¹⁴ Our people must learn to do good by meeting the urgent needs of others; then they will not be unproductive.

¹⁵ Everybody here sends greetings. Please give my greetings to the believers—all who love us.

May God's grace be with you all.

3:5 Greek *He saved us through the washing of regeneration and renewing of the Holy Spirit.* 3:9 Or *spiritual genealogies.*

PHILEMON

JON HUNTZINGER, PHD

Paul's letter to Philemon is the only one we have from the apostle to an individual believer about a personal matter. His other letters are to churches (at Rome, Corinth, Philippi, and Thessalonica), groups of churches (in Galatia and possibly in or around Ephesus), or to individuals who are working in ministry with him (the letters to Timothy and Titus). Paul wrote this letter while he was under house arrest, waiting for a hearing before Caesar, at about the same time he wrote Ephesians, Colossians, and Philippians in the early AD 60s.

Paul makes a sincere, emotional appeal to Philemon to release his slave Onesimus from his legal servitude into Paul's care to help Paul and to serve in ministry with him. He recalls their own close relationship and expresses his personal appreciation for Philemon's good works. Thus, Paul calls Philemon his "beloved" (*agapetos*) fellow worker and recognizes that he has made a name for himself by showing love to others (vv. 5, 7). At the same time, Paul describes himself as a prisoner (vv. 1, 9), a soldier (v. 2), an old man (v. 9), a father (v. 10), a brother (v. 16), a partner (v. 17), and a worker (v. 24).

Moreover, as part of his appeal, Paul draws attention to his imprisonment. The first thing he says in the letter is that he is a prisoner (v. 1). He repeats this by writing that he is "a prisoner for the sake of Christ Jesus" (v. 9) and by referring to his imprisonment (vv. 10, 13). He concludes the letter by referring to his "fellow prisoner" Epaphras (v. 23). In this way, Paul juxtaposes his situation as a bound prisoner who cannot act on his own with Philemon's situation as a free man who can exercise his free will (v. 14) by releasing Onesimus to minister to Paul at that time.

GREETINGS FROM PAUL

This letter is from Paul, a prisoner for preaching the Good News about Christ Jesus, and from our brother Timothy.

I am writing to Philemon, our beloved co-worker, [2] and to our sister Apphia, and to our fellow soldier Archippus, and to the church that meets in your* house.

[3] May God our Father and the Lord Jesus Christ give you grace and peace.

PAUL'S THANKSGIVING AND PRAYER

[4] I always thank my God when I pray for you, Philemon, [5] because I keep hearing about your faith in the Lord Jesus and your love for all of God's people. [6] And I am praying that you will put into action the generosity that comes from your faith as you understand and experience all the good things we have in Christ. [7] Your love has given me much joy and comfort, my brother, for your kindness has often refreshed the hearts of God's people.

PAUL'S APPEAL FOR ONESIMUS

[8] That is why I am boldly asking a favor of you. I could demand it in the name of Christ because it is the right thing for you to do. [9] But because of our love, I prefer simply to ask you. Consider this as a request from me—Paul, an old man and now also a prisoner for the sake of Christ Jesus.*

[10] I appeal to you to show kindness to my child, Onesimus. I became his father in the faith while here in prison. [11] Onesimus* hasn't been of much use to you in the past, but now he is very useful to both of us. [12] I am sending him back to you, and with him comes my own heart.

[13] I wanted to keep him here with me while I am in these chains for preaching the Good News, and he would have helped me on your behalf. [14] But I didn't want to do anything without your consent. I wanted you to help because you were willing, not because you were forced. [15] It seems you lost Onesimus for a little while so that you could have him back forever. [16] He is no longer like a slave to you. He is more than a slave, for he is a beloved brother, especially to me. Now he will mean much more to you, both as a man and as a brother in the Lord.

[17] So if you consider me your partner, welcome him as you would welcome me. [18] If he has wronged you in any way or owes you anything, charge it to me. [19] I, PAUL, WRITE THIS WITH MY OWN HAND: I WILL REPAY IT. AND I WON'T MENTION THAT YOU OWE ME YOUR VERY SOUL!

[20] Yes, my brother, please do me this favor* for the Lord's sake. Give me this encouragement in Christ.

[21] I am confident as I write this letter that you will do what I ask and even more! [22] One more thing—please prepare a guest room for me, for I am hoping that God will answer your prayers and let me return to you soon.

PAUL'S FINAL GREETINGS

[23] Epaphras, my fellow prisoner in Christ Jesus, sends you his greetings. [24] So do Mark, Aristarchus, Demas, and Luke, my co-workers.

[25] May the grace of the Lord Jesus Christ be with your spirit.

---

2 Throughout this letter, you and your are singular except in verses 3, 22, and 25. 9 Or a prisoner of Christ Jesus.
11 Onesimus means "useful." 20 Greek onaimen, a play on the name Onesimus.

HEBREWS

JON HUNTZINGER, PHD

The book of Hebrews is a sermon about cour-age, in which the author seeks to build up his readers in their faith. The author is unknown, though some people have suggested Paul while others have suggested Barnabas, Apollos, or oth-ers. Whoever he was, he wrote to Jewish believers who had experienced hardship and persecution because of their commitment to Jesus as God's Messiah. References to the Temple and its sacri-fices throughout the book indicate it was written prior to its destruction in AD 70.

Though the book is often described as an epistle or a letter, it is better read as a long sermon about faith and fear, like the long multipart sermon series preached by many pastors today. The sermon addresses the fear of rejection, alienation, loss, and even imprisonment (10:32-36). The preacher of Hebrews reminds his people that Jesus is the source of their courage, and he uses numerous titles and descriptions to talk about Him and emphasize this point:
— Jesus is God's Son. Through Jesus, who reflects God's glory, all things were created (1:1-3).
— Jesus is greater than angels are. As God's Son, He is greater than any other being (1:4-14).
— Jesus is greater than Moses is (3:1-6).
— Jesus is "a perfect leader" (2:10).
— Jesus is a high priest from the order of Melchizedek (5:1-10; 7:1-28).
— Jesus is the One "who has entered heaven" (4:14).
— Jesus is seated at the right hand of majesty (8:1).
— Jesus is the perfect sacrifice (9:11-14, 28; 10:12).
— Jesus is the mediator of a new covenant (9:15).
— Jesus is the One who "initiates and perfects our faith" who endured the cross (12:2).
— Jesus is "the same yesterday, today, and forever" (13:8).
— Jesus is the "great Shepherd of the sheep" (13:20).

The writer gives all these descriptions and titles to build confidence in the people so they will be strong and have courage in the midst of diffi-cult circumstances. They should endure as Jesus endured the cross (12:2). They should stay in their faith and continue to embrace God's will during difficult times.

All the key elements of Jesus' story found in the four Gospels and preached by the early church (see the introduction to the book of Acts) are present in Hebrews:
— The preacher says that Jesus was a man (2:14).
— He obeyed God's will and performed signs by the Spirit (10:5-7).
— Jesus suffered and was crucified (2:9; 5:7-8; 6:6).
— He was raised to life (13:20).

— Jesus has ascended to His Father in glory (1:3; 4:14).

By presenting this Good News message, the preacher shows his broad understanding of the Hebrew Scriptures by quoting from them numerous times. In fact, he quotes from the prophet Jeremiah about the new covenant (Jeremiah 31:31-34), which is the longest single-passage quotation from the Hebrew Scriptures in the New Testament (Hebrews 8:8-12).

Faith is the key theme that unifies the sermon and defines the primary characteristic of the people of God. After an introduction that describes Jesus as the last and greatest word God has spoken to His people (1:1-2), the preacher identifies the primary characteristic of Jesus Himself as faithfulness. He says Jesus showed His faithfulness by serving as a high priest and offering himself as a sacrifice (2:17-3:3). The preacher then discusses Jesus' faith-fulness as high priest in chapters 7-10. He follows this description with another of what faith looked like in the lives of the biblical heroes who went before Jesus (chapter 11) and concludes with a final description of Jesus who provides the example of faith by following their example and pursuing joy. According to the preacher, even though God heard Jesus' "prayers and pleadings, with a loud cry and tears," He did not remove Jesus from those circum-stances and from giving His life as a sacrifice for others (5:7-8). Jesus endured and ran the race in which God placed Him (12:1-2). Thus, the preacher declares that faith is running the race in which God has placed us and living faithfully (enduring, 10:32-39; 12:1-11, 14-28) as Jesus did. The sermon concludes with practical advice and an encourage-ment for the Hebrews to be faithful. They should not grow weary nor neglect hospitality to one another but continue to live sacrificially because, he suggests, these are signs of faith (13:1-19).

The preacher of Hebrews famously describes faith as "the reality of what we hope for; it is the evidence of things we cannot see" (11:1). The key to understanding this definition is in the preceding passage (10:32-39). In those verses, the preacher urges the people to recall their earlier hardship and suffering and to respond to their present circum-stances with the same kind of determination and diligence as they did then. He reminds them that though they had been put in jail and even lost pos-sessions, they did not shift from their allegiance to the Lord. He then refers to Habakkuk 2:4: "The righteous will live by their faithfulness to God."

The passage from Habakkuk teaches that although God's people may not understand

God's ways—even in the most troubling and dire circumstances—they must trust in the word that He speaks to them. This truth comes to Habakkuk in Jerusalem in the sixth century BC as he watches the Babylonians prepare to overthrow the city. He confesses that the people have sinned against God and deserve His judgment, but Habakkuk cannot understand why God would use the Babylonians to bring that judgment. The prophet vows to wait for God's answer and watch for His action (Habakkuk 2:1). Against this background, God says, "Look at the proud! They trust in themselves, and their lives are crooked. But the righteous will live by their faithfulness to God" (2:4). God knows the Babylonians and says His people are to be different from such proud people and trust in His word, even though they cannot see it, and it may not seem as real to them as the Babylonians themselves. The writer of Hebrews draws on this passage to remind his readers that though their present experience may be hard to comprehend, they should trust the gospel they have received and the divine signs that came with it. They may not be able to see evidence of God's promise because of the greatness of their current needs, but they are to have faith based on what they have experienced in the past.

JESUS CHRIST IS GOD'S SON

1 Long ago God spoke many times and in many ways to our ancestors through the prophets. ²And now in these final days, he has spoken to us through his Son. God promised everything to the Son as an inheritance, and through the Son he created the universe. ³The Son radiates God's own glory and expresses the very character of God, and he sustains everything by the mighty power of his command. When he had cleansed us from our sins, he sat down in the place of honor at the right hand of the majestic God in heaven. ⁴This shows that the Son is far greater than the angels, just as the name God gave him is greater than their names.

THE SON IS GREATER THAN THE ANGELS

⁵For God never said to any angel what he said to Jesus:

"You are my Son.
Today I have become your Father.*"

God also said,

"I will be his Father,
and he will be my Son."*

⁶And when he brought his supreme* Son into the world, God said,*

"Let all of God's angels worship him."*

⁷Regarding the angels, he says,

"He sends his angels like the winds,
his servants like flames of fire."*

⁸But to the Son he says,

"Your throne, O God, endures forever
and ever.
You rule with a scepter of justice.

THE PERSON WE WORSHIP
Hebrews 1:1-4   JACK HAYFORD

Jesus is the essence and focus of our worship. In the opening words of Hebrews, the writer makes seven statements about our Savior:

1. He is the predestined heir of all things (v. 2).
2. He is the channel of God's operational power (v. 2).
3. He is the projection of the radiance of God's glory toward man (v. 3).
4. He is the expression of the ultimate reality, being the expressed image of the Almighty (v. 3).
5. He is the sustainer of the universe and the One who upholds all things by the Word of His power, having laid the foundation of the earth and erected all that we know of creation (v. 3).
6. He is the Redeemer of sinful humanity, for with Himself, He cleansed us of our sins. (v. 3).
7. He is the ascended Lord above all, who sat down at the right hand of the Majesty on high where He reigns even now (v. 3).

⁹ You love justice and hate evil.
Therefore, O God, your God has
anointed you,
pouring out the oil of joy on you more
than on anyone else."*

¹⁰ He also says to the Son,

"In the beginning, Lord, you laid the
foundation of the earth
and made the heavens with your hands.

1:5a Or *Today I reveal you as my Son.* Ps 2:7.   1:5b 2 Sam 7:14.
1:6a Or *firstborn.*   1:6b Or *when he again brings his supreme Son* [or *firstborn Son*] *into the world, God will say.*   1:6c Deut 32:43.
1:7 Ps 104:4 (Greek version).   1:8-9 Ps 45:6-7.

¹¹ They will perish, but you remain forever.
They will wear out like old clothing.
¹² You will fold them up like a cloak
and discard them like old clothing.
But you are always the same;
you will live forever."*

¹³ And God never said to any of the angels,

"Sit in the place of honor at my right hand
until I humble your enemies,
making them a footstool under
your feet."*

¹⁴ Therefore, angels are only servants—spirits sent to care for people who will inherit salvation.

A WARNING AGAINST DRIFTING AWAY

2 So we must listen very carefully to the truth we have heard, or we may drift away from it. ² For the message God delivered through angels has always stood firm, and every violation of the law and every act of disobedience was punished. ³ So what makes us think we can escape if we ignore this great salvation that was first announced by the Lord Jesus himself and then delivered to us by those who heard him speak? ⁴ And God confirmed the message by giving signs and wonders and various miracles and gifts of the Holy Spirit whenever he chose.

JESUS, THE MAN

⁵ And furthermore, it is not angels who will control the future world we are talking about. ⁶ For in one place the Scriptures say,

"What are mere mortals that you should
think about them,
or a son of man* that you should
care for him?
⁷ Yet for a little while you made them a little
lower than the angels
and crowned them with glory and honor.*
⁸ You gave them authority over all things."*

Now when it says "all things," it means nothing is left out. But we have not yet seen all things put under their authority. ⁹ What we do see is Jesus, who for a little while was given a position "a little lower than the angels"; and because he suffered death for us, he is now "crowned with glory and honor." Yes, by God's grace, Jesus tasted death for everyone. ¹⁰ God, for whom and through whom everything was made, chose to bring many children into glory. And it was only right that he should make Jesus, through his suffering, a perfect leader, fit to bring them into their salvation. ¹¹ So now Jesus and the ones he makes holy have the same Father. That is why Jesus is not ashamed to call them his brothers and sisters.* ¹² For he said to God,

"I will proclaim your name to my brothers
and sisters.
I will praise you among your assembled
people."*

¹³ He also said,

"I will put my trust in him,"
that is, "I and the children God has
given me."*

¹⁴ Because God's children are human beings—made of flesh and blood—the Son also became flesh and blood. For only as a human being could he die, and only by dying could he break the power of the devil, who had* the power of death. ¹⁵ Only in this way could he set free all who have lived their lives as slaves to the fear of dying. ¹⁶ We also know that the Son did not come to help angels; he came to help the descendants of Abraham. ¹⁷ Therefore, it was necessary for him to be made in every respect like us, his brothers and sisters,* so that he could be our merciful and faithful High Priest before God. Then he could offer a sacrifice that would take away the sins of the people. ¹⁸ Since he himself has gone through suffering and testing, he is able to help us when we are being tested.

JESUS IS GREATER THAN MOSES

3 And so, dear brothers and sisters who belong to God and* are partners with those called to heaven, think carefully about this Jesus whom we declare to be God's messenger* and High Priest. ² For he was faithful to God, who appointed him, just as Moses served faithfully when he was entrusted with God's entire* house. ³ But Jesus deserves far more glory than Moses, just as a person who builds a house deserves more praise than the house itself. ⁴ For every house has a builder, but the one who built everything is God. ⁵ Moses was certainly faithful in God's house as a servant. His work was an illustration of the truths God would reveal later. ⁶ But Christ, as the Son, is in charge of God's entire house. And we are God's house, if we keep our courage and remain confident in our hope in Christ.* ⁷ That is why the Holy Spirit says,

"Today when you hear his voice,
⁸ don't harden your hearts
as Israel did when they rebelled,
when they tested me in the wilderness.

1:10-12 Ps 102:25-27. 1:13 Ps 110:1. 2:6 Or the Son of Man. 2:7 Some manuscripts add You gave them charge of everything you made. 2:6-8 Ps 8:4-6 (Greek version). 2:11 Greek brothers; also in 2:12. 2:12 Ps 22:22. 2:13 Isa 8:17-18. 2:14 Or has. 2:17 Greek like the brothers. 3:1a Greek And so, holy brothers who. 3:1b Greek God's apostle. 3:2 Some manuscripts do not include entire. 3:6 Some manuscripts add faithful to the end.

JESUS THE CARPENTER
Hebrews 2:17

ROBERT MORRIS

Why did Jesus become a carpenter?

The answer is *identification*. Jesus didn't come to earth and merely pretend to understand us; instead, He became a real human being and was made "in every respect like us" (Hebrews 2:17). Jesus can identify with us because He knows how hard it is to live in a sinful world. Here are three things He understands especially well:

1. Relationships

Jesus understands what it's like to have a family. He had four brothers and at least two sisters (Mark 6:3) as well as aunts, uncles, and cousins. Jesus understands how it feels when your family doesn't support you or believe in you. At one point, his family even said He was "out of his mind" (Mark 3:21). Jesus also knows what it's like to have friends and to have those friends be angry with you or even betray you. Peter, James, and John were the three disciples who were closest to Jesus—they even witnessed incredible things the other disciples didn't get to see. Yet when the soldiers came to arrest Jesus, "*all* his disciples deserted him and ran away" (Mark 14:50, emphasis added). No matter what

kind of relationship problem you may have, you can talk to Jesus, and He understands.

2. Work

Jesus was a carpenter for many more years than He was a preacher and teacher. He knows what it's like to work hard and be exhausted at the end of a long day. He understands the frustrations of dealing with delays and setbacks and working with other people in business. You can talk to Jesus about your work problems. He understands, and He cares.

3. Pain

Jesus understands emotional and physical pain (Isaiah 53:3-5, 7). He was called illegitimate because of His miraculous birth. People rejected His teaching because He was "just a carpenter" (Mark 6:3). Jesus was ridiculed, mocked, and beaten, and then He was nailed to a cross and tortured to death. If you are struggling or hurting, you have a Friend who has endured more pain than any other person in the history of the world. He understands, and He invites you to come to His throne of grace where "we will receive his mercy, and we will find grace to help us when we need it most" (Hebrews 4:16).

⁹ There your ancestors tested and tried
    my patience,
  even though they saw my miracles
    for forty years.
¹⁰ So I was angry with them, and I said,
  'Their hearts always turn away from me.
    They refuse to do what I tell them.'
¹¹ So in my anger I took an oath:
  'They will never enter my place of rest.'"*

¹² Be careful then, dear brothers and sisters.* Make sure that your own hearts are not evil and unbelieving, turning you away from the living God. ¹³ You must warn each other every day, while it is still "today," so that none of you will be deceived by sin and hardened against God. ¹⁴ For if we are faithful to the end, trusting God just as firmly as when we first believed, we will share in all that belongs to Christ. ¹⁵ Remember what it says:

"Today when you hear his voice,
  don't harden your hearts
  as Israel did when they rebelled."*

¹⁶ And who was it who rebelled against God, even though they heard his voice? Wasn't it the people Moses led out of Egypt? ¹⁷ And who made God angry for forty years? Wasn't it the people who sinned, whose corpses lay in the wilderness? ¹⁸ And to whom was God speaking when he took an oath that they would never enter his rest?

Wasn't it the people who disobeyed him? ¹⁹ So we see that because of their unbelief they were not able to enter his rest.

PROMISED REST FOR GOD'S PEOPLE

4 God's promise of entering his rest still stands, so we ought to tremble with fear that some of you might fail to experience it. ² For this good news—that God has prepared this rest—has been announced to us just as it was to them. But it did them no good because they didn't share the faith of those who listened to God.* ³ For only we who believe can enter his rest. As for the others, God said,

"In my anger I took an oath:
  'They will never enter my place of rest,'"*

even though this rest has been ready since he made the world. ⁴ We know it is ready because of the place in the Scriptures where it mentions the seventh day: "On the seventh day God rested from all his work."* ⁵ But in the other passage God said, "They will never enter my place of rest."*

⁶ So God's rest is there for people to enter, but those who first heard this good news failed to enter because they disobeyed God. ⁷ So God set another time for entering his rest, and that time

---

3:7-11 Ps 95:7-11.   3:12 Greek *brothers.*   3:15 Ps 95:7-8.
4:2 Some manuscripts read *they didn't combine what they heard with faith.*   4:3 Ps 95:11.   4:4 Gen 2:2.   4:5 Ps 95:11.

FINDING FREEDOM
Hebrews 4:12   MARCUS BRECHEEN

Growing up, my biggest fear was that I would one day stand before God and still have some sin on my plate. It wasn't until years later that this internal battle ended, my fear defeated by the Word of God.

God created us in His own image with a spirit, soul, and body. Only one part can be in charge, though. Before sin, Adam and Eve had constant communion with God and were ruled by their spirits. After they sinned, however, they were ruled by their souls.

We too are ruled by our souls when we are born. When we receive salvation, our spirit comes alive and says, "I want God to rule in my life." The problem is that your soul is used to ruling, so a battle begins. Thankfully, the Word of God is a sharp weapon. It cuts us free from being controlled by the soul and allows us to live under the rule of the spirit.

is today. God announced this through David much later in the words already quoted:

"Today when you hear his voice,
    don't harden your hearts."*

⁸Now if Joshua had succeeded in giving them this rest, God would not have spoken about another day of rest still to come. ⁹So there is a special rest* still waiting for the people of God. ¹⁰For all who have entered into God's rest have rested from their labors, just as God did after creating the world. ¹¹So let us do our best to enter that rest. But if we disobey God, as the people of Israel did, we will fall.

¹²For the word of God is alive and powerful. It is sharper than the sharpest two-edged sword, cutting between soul and spirit, between joint and marrow. It exposes our innermost thoughts and desires. ¹³Nothing in all creation is hidden from God. Everything is naked and exposed before his eyes, and he is the one to whom we are accountable.

CHRIST IS OUR HIGH PRIEST
¹⁴So then, since we have a great High Priest who has entered heaven, Jesus the Son of God, let us hold firmly to what we believe. ¹⁵This High Priest of ours understands our weaknesses, for he faced all of the same testings we do, yet he did not sin. ¹⁶So let us come boldly to the throne of our gracious God. There we will receive his mercy, and we will find grace to help us when we need it most.

5 Every high priest is a man chosen to represent other people in their dealings with God. He presents their gifts to God and offers sacrifices for their sins. ²And he is able to deal gently

with ignorant and wayward people because he himself is subject to the same weaknesses. ³That is why he must offer sacrifices for his own sins as well as theirs.

⁴And no one can become a high priest simply because he wants such an honor. He must be called by God for this work, just as Aaron was. ⁵That is why Christ did not honor himself by assuming he could become High Priest. No, he was chosen by God, who said to him,

"You are my Son.
    Today I have become your Father.*"

⁶And in another passage God said to him,

"You are a priest forever in the order of
    Melchizedek."*

⁷While Jesus was here on earth, he offered prayers and pleadings, with a loud cry and tears, to the one who could rescue him from death. And God heard his prayers because of his deep reverence for God. ⁸Even though Jesus was God's Son, he learned obedience from the things he suffered. ⁹In this way, God qualified him as a perfect High Priest, and he became the source of eternal salvation for all those who obey him. ¹⁰And God designated him to be a High Priest in the order of Melchizedek.

A CALL TO SPIRITUAL GROWTH
¹¹There is much more we would like to say about this, but it is difficult to explain, especially since you are spiritually dull and don't seem to listen. ¹²You have been believers so long now that you ought to be teaching others. Instead, you need someone to teach you again the basic things about God's word.* You are like babies who need milk and cannot eat solid food. ¹³For someone who lives on milk is still an infant and doesn't know how to do what is right. ¹⁴Solid food is for those who are mature, who through training have the skill to recognize the difference between right and wrong.

6 So let us stop going over the basic teachings about Christ again and again. Let us go on instead and become mature in our understanding. Surely we don't need to start again with the fundamental importance of repenting from evil deeds* and placing our faith in God. ²You don't need further instruction about baptisms, the laying on of hands, the resurrection of the dead, and eternal judgment. ³And so, God willing, we will move forward to further understanding.

⁴For it is impossible to bring back to repentance those who were once enlightened—those

---

4:7 Ps 95:7-8.   4:9 Or *a Sabbath rest.*   5:5 Or *Today I reveal you as my Son.* Ps 2:7.   5:6 Ps 110:4.   5:12 Or *about the oracles of God.*
6:1 Greek *from dead works.*

who have experienced the good things of heaven and shared in the Holy Spirit, [5] who have tasted the goodness of the word of God and the power of the age to come—[6] and who then turn away from God. It is impossible to bring such people back to repentance; by rejecting the Son of God, they themselves are nailing him to the cross once again and holding him up to public shame.

[7] When the ground soaks up the falling rain and bears a good crop for the farmer, it has God's blessing. [8] But if a field bears thorns and thistles, it is useless. The farmer will soon condemn that field and burn it.

[9] Dear friends, even though we are talking this way, we really don't believe it applies to you. We are confident that you are meant for better things, things that come with salvation. [10] For God is not unjust. He will not forget how hard you have worked for him and how you have shown your love to him by caring for other believers,* as you still do. [11] Our great desire is that you will keep on loving others as long as life lasts, in order to make certain that what you hope for will come true. [12] Then you will not become spiritually dull and indifferent. Instead, you will follow the example of those who are going to inherit God's promises because of their faith and endurance.

GOD'S PROMISES BRING HOPE

[13] For example, there was God's promise to Abraham. Since there was no one greater to swear by, God took an oath in his own name, saying:

[14] "I will certainly bless you,
    and I will multiply your descendants
        beyond number."*

[15] Then Abraham waited patiently, and he received what God had promised.

[16] Now when people take an oath, they call on someone greater than themselves to hold them to it. And without any question that oath is binding. [17] God also bound himself with an oath, so that those who received the promise could be perfectly sure that he would never change his mind. [18] So God has given both his promise and his oath. These two things are unchangeable because it is impossible for God to lie. Therefore, we who have fled to him for refuge can have great confidence as we hold to the hope that lies before us. [19] This hope is a strong and trustworthy anchor for our souls. It leads us through the curtain into God's inner sanctuary. [20] Jesus has already gone in there for us. He has become our eternal High Priest in the order of Melchizedek.

MELCHIZEDEK IS GREATER THAN ABRAHAM

7 This Melchizedek was king of the city of Salem and also a priest of God Most High. When Abraham was returning home after winning a great battle against the kings, Melchizedek met him and blessed him. [2] Then Abraham took a tenth of all he had captured in battle and gave it to Melchizedek. The name Melchizedek means "king of justice," and king of Salem means "king of peace." [3] There is no record of his father or mother or any of his ancestors—no beginning or end to his life. He remains a priest forever, resembling the Son of God.

[4] Consider then how great this Melchizedek was. Even Abraham, the great patriarch of Israel, recognized this by giving him a tenth of what he had taken in battle. [5] Now the law of Moses required that the priests, who are descendants of Levi, must collect a tithe from the rest of the people of Israel,* who are also descendants of Abraham. [6] But Melchizedek, who was not a descendant of Levi, collected a tenth from Abraham. And Melchizedek placed a blessing upon Abraham, the one who had already received the promises of God. [7] And without question, the person who has the power to give a blessing is greater than the one who is blessed.

[8] The priests who collect tithes are men who die, so Melchizedek is greater than they are, because we are told that he lives on. [9] In addition, we might even say that these Levites—the ones who collect the tithe—paid a tithe to Melchizedek when their ancestor Abraham paid a tithe to him. [10] For although Levi wasn't born yet, the seed from which he came was in Abraham's body when Melchizedek collected the tithe from him.

[11] So if the priesthood of Levi, on which the law was based, could have achieved the perfection God intended, why did God need to establish a different priesthood, with a priest in the order of Melchizedek instead of the order of Levi and Aaron?*

[12] And if the priesthood is changed, the law must also be changed to permit it. [13] For the priest we are talking about belongs to a different tribe, whose members have never served at the altar as priests. [14] What I mean is, our Lord came from the tribe of Judah, and Moses never mentioned priests coming from that tribe.

JESUS IS LIKE MELCHIZEDEK

[15] This change has been made very clear since a different priest, who is like Melchizedek, has appeared. [16] Jesus became a priest, not by meeting the physical requirement of belonging to the tribe of Levi, but by the power of a life that cannot be destroyed. [17] And the psalmist pointed this out when he prophesied,

"You are a priest forever in the order of
    Melchizedek."*

[18] Yes, the old requirement about the priesthood was set aside because it was weak and useless. [19] For the law never made anything perfect.

6:10 Greek for God's holy people.   6:14 Gen 22:17.   7:5 Greek from their brothers.   7:11 Greek the order of Aaron?   7:17 Ps 110:4.

But now we have confidence in a better hope, through which we draw near to God. ²⁰This new system was established with a solemn oath. Aaron's descendants became priests without such an oath, ²¹but there was an oath regarding Jesus. For God said to him,

"The LORD has taken an oath and will not
   break his vow:
   'You are a priest forever.'"*

²²Because of this oath, Jesus is the one who guarantees this better covenant with God.

²³There were many priests under the old system, for death prevented them from remaining in office. ²⁴But because Jesus lives forever, his priesthood lasts forever. ²⁵Therefore he is able, once and forever, to save* those who come to God through him. He lives forever to intercede with God on their behalf.

²⁶He is the kind of high priest we need because he is holy and blameless, unstained by sin. He has been set apart from sinners and has been given the highest place of honor in heaven.* ²⁷Unlike those other high priests, he does not need to offer sacrifices every day. They did this for their own sins first and then for the sins of the people. But Jesus did this once for all when he offered himself as the sacrifice for the people's sins. ²⁸The law appointed high priests who were limited by human weakness. But after the law was given, God appointed his Son with an oath, and his Son has been made the perfect High Priest forever.

CHRIST IS OUR HIGH PRIEST

8 Here is the main point: We have a High Priest who sat down in the place of honor beside the throne of the majestic God in heaven. ²There he ministers in the heavenly Tabernacle,* the true place of worship that was built by the Lord and not by human hands.

³And since every high priest is required to offer gifts and sacrifices, our High Priest must make an offering, too. ⁴If he were here on earth, he would not even be a priest, since there already are priests who offer the gifts required by the law. ⁵They serve in a system of worship that is only a copy, a shadow of the real one in heaven. For when Moses was getting ready to build the Tabernacle, God gave him this warning: "Be sure that you make everything according to the pattern I have shown you here on the mountain."*

⁶But now Jesus, our High Priest, has been given a ministry that is far superior to the old priesthood, for he is the one who mediates for us a far better covenant with God, based on better promises.

⁷If the first covenant had been faultless, there would have been no need for a second covenant to replace it. ⁸But when God found fault with the people, he said:

"The day is coming, says the LORD,
   when I will make a new covenant
   with the people of Israel and Judah.
⁹ This covenant will not be like the one
   I made with their ancestors
   when I took them by the hand
   and led them out of the land of Egypt.
They did not remain faithful to my
   covenant,
   so I turned my back on them, says the
   LORD.
¹⁰ But this is the new covenant I will make
   with the people of Israel on that day,*
   says the LORD:
I will put my laws in their minds,
   and I will write them on their hearts.
I will be their God,
   and they will be my people.
¹¹ And they will not need to teach their
   neighbors,
   nor will they need to teach their
   relatives,*
   saying, 'You should know the LORD.'
For everyone, from the least to the greatest,
   will know me already.
¹² And I will forgive their wickedness,
   and I will never again remember their
   sins."*

¹³When God speaks of a "new" covenant, it means he has made the first one obsolete. It is now out of date and will soon disappear.

OLD RULES ABOUT WORSHIP

9 That first covenant between God and Israel had regulations for worship and a place of worship here on earth. ²There were two rooms in that Tabernacle.* In the first room were a lampstand, a table, and sacred loaves of bread on the table. This room was called the Holy Place. ³Then there was a curtain, and behind the curtain was the second room* called the Most Holy Place. ⁴In that room were a gold incense altar and a wooden chest called the Ark of the Covenant, which was covered with gold on all sides. Inside the Ark were a gold jar containing manna, Aaron's staff that sprouted leaves, and the stone tablets of the covenant. ⁵Above the Ark were the cherubim of divine glory, whose wings stretched out over the Ark's cover, the place of atonement. But we cannot explain these things in detail now.

⁶When these things were all in place, the priests regularly entered the first room* as they performed their religious duties. ⁷But only the high priest ever entered the Most Holy Place, and only once a year. And he always offered blood

---

7:21 Ps 110:4.   7:25 Or is able to save completely.   7:26 Or has been exalted higher than the heavens.   8:2 Or tent; also in 8:5. 8:5 Exod 25:40; 26:30.   8:10 Greek after those days.   8:11 Greek their brother.   8:8-12 Jer 31:31-34.   9:2 Or tent; also in 9:11, 21. 9:3 Greek second tent.   9:6 Greek first tent.

for his own sins and for the sins the people had committed in ignorance. ⁸ By these regulations the Holy Spirit revealed that the entrance to the Most Holy Place was not freely open as long as the Tabernacle* and the system it represented were still in use.

⁹ This is an illustration pointing to the present time. For the gifts and sacrifices that the priests offer are not able to cleanse the consciences of the people who bring them. ¹⁰ For that old system deals only with food and drink and various cleansing ceremonies—physical regulations that were in effect only until a better system could be established.

CHRIST IS THE PERFECT SACRIFICE

¹¹ So Christ has now become the High Priest over all the good things that have come.* He has entered that greater, more perfect Tabernacle in heaven, which was not made by human hands and is not part of this created world. ¹² With his own blood—not the blood of goats and calves—he entered the Most Holy Place once for all time and secured our redemption forever.

¹³ Under the old system, the blood of goats and bulls and the ashes of a heifer could cleanse people's bodies from ceremonial impurity. ¹⁴ Just think how much more the blood of Christ will purify our consciences from sinful deeds* so that we can worship the living God. For by the power of the eternal Spirit, Christ offered himself to God as a perfect sacrifice for our sins. ¹⁵ That is why he is the one who mediates a new covenant between God and people, so that all who are called can receive the eternal inheritance God has promised them. For Christ died to set them free from the penalty of the sins they had committed under that first covenant.

¹⁶ Now when someone leaves a will,* it is necessary to prove that the person who made it is dead.* ¹⁷ The will goes into effect only after the person's death. While the person who made it is still alive, the will cannot be put into effect.

¹⁸ That is why even the first covenant was put into effect with the blood of an animal. ¹⁹ For after Moses had read each of God's commandments to all the people, he took the blood of calves and goats,* along with water, and sprinkled both the book of God's law and all the people, using hyssop branches and scarlet wool. ²⁰ Then he said, "This blood confirms the covenant God has made with you."* ²¹ And in the same way, he sprinkled blood on the Tabernacle and on everything used for worship. ²² In fact, according to the law of Moses, nearly everything was purified with blood. For without the shedding of blood, there is no forgiveness.

²³ That is why the Tabernacle and everything in it, which were copies of things in heaven, had to be purified by the blood of animals. But the real things in heaven had to be purified with far better sacrifices than the blood of animals.

²⁴ For Christ did not enter into a holy place made with human hands, which was only a copy of the true one in heaven. He entered into heaven itself to appear now before God on our behalf. ²⁵ And he did not enter heaven to offer himself again and again, like the high priest here on earth who enters the Most Holy Place year after year with the blood of an animal. ²⁶ If that had been necessary, Christ would have had to die again and again, ever since the world began. But now, once for all time, he has appeared at the end of the age* to remove sin by his own death as a sacrifice.

²⁷ And just as each person is destined to die once and after that comes judgment, ²⁸ so also Christ was offered once for all time as a sacrifice to take away the sins of many people. He will come again, not to deal with our sins, but to bring salvation to all who are eagerly waiting for him.

CHRIST'S SACRIFICE ONCE FOR ALL

10 The old system under the law of Moses was only a shadow, a dim preview of the good things to come, not the good things themselves. The sacrifices under that system were repeated again and again, year after year, but they were never able to provide perfect cleansing for those who came to worship. ² If they could have provided perfect cleansing, the sacrifices would have stopped, for the worshipers would have been purified once for all time, and their feelings of guilt would have disappeared.

³ But instead, those sacrifices actually reminded them of their sins year after year. ⁴ For it is not possible for the blood of bulls and goats to take away sins. ⁵ That is why, when Christ* came into the world, he said to God,

"You did not want animal sacrifices or
    sin offerings.
But you have given me a body to offer.
⁶ You were not pleased with burnt offerings
    or other offerings for sin.
⁷ Then I said, 'Look, I have come to do your
    will, O God—
    as is written about me in the
    Scriptures.'"*

⁸ First, Christ said, "You did not want animal sacrifices or sin offerings or burnt offerings or other offerings for sin, nor were you pleased with them" (though they are required by the law of Moses). ⁹ Then he said, "Look, I have come to do your will." He cancels the first covenant in order to put the second into effect. ¹⁰ For God's will was

---

9:8 Or *the first room;* Greek reads *the first tent.*   9:11 Some manuscripts read *that are about to come.*   9:14 Greek *from dead works.*   9:16a Or *covenant;* also in 9:17.   9:16b Or *Now when someone makes a covenant, it is necessary to ratify it with the death of a sacrifice.*   9:19 Some manuscripts do not include *and goats.*   9:20 Exod 24:8.   9:26 Greek *the ages.*   10:5 Greek *he;* also in 10:8.   10:5-7 Ps 40:6-8 (Greek version).

for us to be made holy by the sacrifice of the body of Jesus Christ, once for all time.

[11] Under the old covenant, the priest stands and ministers before the altar day after day, offering the same sacrifices again and again, which can never take away sins. [12] But our High Priest offered himself to God as a single sacrifice for sins, good for all time. Then he sat down in the place of honor at God's right hand. [13] There he waits until his enemies are humbled and made a footstool under his feet. [14] For by that one offering he forever made perfect those who are being made holy.

[15] And the Holy Spirit also testifies that this is so. For he says,

[16] "This is the new covenant I will make
    with my people on that day,*
  says the LORD:
  I will put my laws in their hearts,
    and I will write them on their minds."*

[17] Then he says,

  "I will never again remember
    their sins and lawless deeds."*

[18] And when sins have been forgiven, there is no need to offer any more sacrifices.

A CALL TO PERSEVERE

[19] And so, dear brothers and sisters,* we can boldly enter heaven's Most Holy Place because of the blood of Jesus. [20] By his death,* Jesus opened a new and life-giving way through the curtain into the Most Holy Place. [21] And since we have a great High Priest who rules over God's house, [22] let us go right into the presence of God with sincere hearts fully trusting him. For our guilty consciences have been sprinkled with Christ's blood to make us clean, and our bodies have been washed with pure water.

[23] Let us hold tightly without wavering to the hope we affirm, for God can be trusted to keep his promise. [24] Let us think of ways to motivate one another to acts of love and good works. [25] And let us not neglect our meeting together, as some people do, but encourage one another, especially now that the day of his return is drawing near.

[26] Dear friends, if we deliberately continue sinning after we have received knowledge of the truth, there is no longer any sacrifice that will cover these sins. [27] There is only the terrible expectation of God's judgment and the raging fire that will consume his enemies. [28] For anyone who refused to obey the law of Moses was put to death without mercy on the testimony of two or three witnesses. [29] Just think how much worse the punishment will be for those who have trampled on the Son of God, and have treated the blood of the covenant, which made us holy, as if it were common and unholy, and

have insulted and disdained the Holy Spirit who brings God's mercy to us. [30] For we know the one who said,

  "I will take revenge.
    I will pay them back."*

He also said,

  "The LORD will judge his own people."*

[31] It is a terrible thing to fall into the hands of the living God.

[32] Think back on those early days when you first learned about Christ.* Remember how you remained faithful even though it meant terrible suffering. [33] Sometimes you were exposed to public ridicule and were beaten, and sometimes you helped others who were suffering the same things. [34] You suffered along with those who were thrown into jail, and when all you owned was taken from you, you accepted it with joy. You knew there were better things waiting for you that will last forever.

[35] So do not throw away this confident trust in the Lord. Remember the great reward it brings you! [36] Patient endurance is what you need now, so that you will continue to do God's will. Then you will receive all that he has promised.

[37] "For in just a little while,
    the Coming One will come and
    not delay.
[38] And my righteous ones will live by faith.*
    But I will take no pleasure in anyone
    who turns away."*

[39] But we are not like those who turn away from God to their own destruction. We are the faithful ones, whose souls will be saved.

GREAT EXAMPLES OF FAITH

11 Faith shows the reality of what we hope for; it is the evidence of things we cannot see. [2] Through their faith, the people in days of old earned a good reputation.

[3] By faith we understand that the entire universe was formed at God's command, that what we now see did not come from anything that can be seen.

[4] It was by faith that Abel brought a more acceptable offering to God than Cain did. Abel's offering gave evidence that he was a righteous man, and God showed his approval of his gifts. Although Abel is long dead, he still speaks to us by his example of faith.

10:16a Greek *after those days.* 10:16b Jer 31:33a. 10:17 Jer 31:34b. 10:19 Greek *brothers.* 10:20 Greek *Through his flesh.* 10:30a Deut 32:35. 10:30b Deut 32:36. 10:32 Greek *when you were first enlightened.* 10:38 Or *my righteous ones will live by their faithfulness;* Greek reads *my righteous one will live by faith.* 10:37-38 Hab 2:3-4.

HEAR. *BELIEVE.* OBEY.
Hebrews 11:6

STEVE DULIN

If you grew up going to church, you've probably heard the phrase "Hear and obey." This instruction is important for believers; we should all want to hear God's voice, and we should obey whatever He says. However, I believe there is an often overlooked but critical step between hearing and obey: *believing*.

Why is believing so important? Because you can *hear* God and not obey, as Jonah did when God told him to warn the people of Nineveh of their impending destruction (Jonah 1:2–3). You can also *obey* God but not hear Him. The Pharisees carefully followed all the Jewish religious laws and traditions, but they wouldn't listen to Jesus. They refused to believe He was the Son of God (Matthew 12:22–24). Their "obedience" (i.e., rule-following) lacked faith, which comes from "hearing the Good News about Christ" (Romans 10:17) and *believing* it.

So who are some biblical examples of people who heard, believed, and obeyed? Hebrews 11

has a great list. Noah heard and believed God's warning about the coming flood, so he obediently built a large boat that saved his family and many animals (v. 7). Moses heard God tell him to "lead my people Israel out of Egypt" (Exodus 3:10). Even though he did not think himself capable of the task, Moses believed and obeyed, ending Israel's centuries of captivity. Joshua heard God's command to march around Jericho and then shout. While this advice would seem strange to anyone leading a battle, Joshua believed and led the Israelites to obey God. Soon the city's walls crumbled.

I think many modern believers want to hear God. And they want to do the right thing. But we won't have the ability to obey God fully until we start believing what He says. Obeying God requires faith, so start building your faith today by meditating on "the Good News about Christ." *Hear. Believe. Obey.* It will change your life!

SAVING YOUR HOUSE
Hebrews 11:7

JACK HAYFORD

Noah had never seen rain, but when God warned him of the impending flood, he believed and built a large boat (or ark) as God instructed. Noah's respect for God's nature and reverence for God's Word allowed him to save his house (his family) from total destruction.

God gave Noah precise instructions on how to build the boat. Today, God seeks a people who will live according to His perfect order. This order requires us to be like Noah and build our lives according to God's blueprints. We allow the Holy Spirit to work in and through us, and we remain faithful even in the face of adversity.

Jesus says that people who hear His Word and obey are like a man who built his house on a rock. No matter how fiercely the storms of life rage, the house "won't collapse because it is built on bedrock" (Matthew 7:25).

⁵ It was by faith that Enoch was taken up to heaven without dying—"he disappeared, because God took him."* For before he was taken up, he was known as a person who pleased God. ⁶ And it is impossible to please God without faith. Anyone who wants to come to him must believe that God exists and that he rewards those who sincerely seek him.

⁷ It was by faith that Noah built a large boat to save his family from the flood. He obeyed God, who warned him about things that had never happened before. By his faith Noah condemned

the rest of the world, and he received the righteousness that comes by faith.

⁸ It was by faith that Abraham obeyed when God called him to leave home and go to another land that God would give him as his inheritance. He went without knowing where he was going. ⁹ And even when he reached the land God promised him, he lived there by faith—for he was like a foreigner, living in tents. And so did Isaac and Jacob, who inherited the same promise. ¹⁰ Abraham was confidently looking forward to a city with eternal foundations, a city designed and built by God.

¹¹ It was by faith that even Sarah was able to have a child, though she was barren and was too old. She believed* that God would keep his promise. ¹² And so a whole nation came from this one man who was as good as dead—a nation with so many people that, like the stars in the sky and the sand on the seashore, there is no way to count them.

¹³ All these people died still believing what God had promised them. They did not receive what was promised, but they saw it all from a distance and welcomed it. They agreed that they were foreigners and nomads here on earth. ¹⁴ Obviously people who say such things are looking forward to a country they can call their own. ¹⁵ If they had longed for the country they came from, they could have gone back. ¹⁶ But they were looking for a better place, a heavenly homeland. That is why God is not ashamed to be called their God, for he has prepared a city for them.

11:5 Gen 5:24.　11:11 Or *It was by faith that he [Abraham] was able to have a child, even though Sarah was barren and he was too old. He believed.*

¹⁷ It was by faith that Abraham offered Isaac as a sacrifice when God was testing him. Abraham, who had received God's promises, was ready to sacrifice his only son, Isaac, ¹⁸ even though God had told him, "Isaac is the son through whom your descendants will be counted."* ¹⁹ Abraham reasoned that if Isaac died, God was able to bring him back to life again. And in a sense, Abraham did receive his son back from the dead.

²⁰ It was by faith that Isaac promised blessings for the future to his sons, Jacob and Esau.

²¹ It was by faith that Jacob, when he was old and dying, blessed each of Joseph's sons and bowed in worship as he leaned on his staff.

²² It was by faith that Joseph, when he was about to die, said confidently that the people of Israel would leave Egypt. He even commanded them to take his bones with them when they left.

²³ It was by faith that Moses' parents hid him for three months when he was born. They saw that God had given them an unusual child, and they were not afraid to disobey the king's command.

²⁴ It was by faith that Moses, when he grew up, refused to be called the son of Pharaoh's daughter. ²⁵ He chose to share the oppression of God's people instead of enjoying the fleeting pleasures of sin. ²⁶ He thought it was better to suffer for the sake of Christ than to own the treasures of Egypt, for he was looking ahead to his great reward. ²⁷ It was by faith that Moses left the land of Egypt, not fearing the king's anger. He kept right on going because he kept his eyes on the one who is invisible. ²⁸ It was by faith that Moses commanded the people of Israel to keep the Passover and to sprinkle blood on the doorposts so that the angel of death would not kill their firstborn sons.

²⁹ It was by faith that the people of Israel went right through the Red Sea as though they were on dry ground. But when the Egyptians tried to follow, they were all drowned.

³⁰ It was by faith that the people of Israel marched around Jericho for seven days, and the walls came crashing down.

³¹ It was by faith that Rahab the prostitute was not destroyed with the people in her city who refused to obey God. For she had given a friendly welcome to the spies.

³² How much more do I need to say? It would take too long to recount the stories of the faith of Gideon, Barak, Samson, Jephthah, David, Samuel, and all the prophets. ³³ By faith these people overthrew kingdoms, ruled with justice, and received what God had promised them. They shut the mouths of lions, ³⁴ quenched the flames of fire, and escaped death by the edge of the sword. Their weakness was turned to strength. They became strong in battle and put whole armies to flight. ³⁵ Women received their loved ones back again from death.

But others were tortured, refusing to turn from God in order to be set free. They placed their hope in a better life after the resurrection. ³⁶ Some were jeered at, and their backs were cut open with whips. Others were chained in prisons. ³⁷ Some died by stoning, some were sawed in half,* and others were killed with the sword. Some went about wearing skins of sheep and goats, destitute and oppressed and mistreated. ³⁸ They were too good for this world, wandering over deserts and mountains, hiding in caves and holes in the ground.

³⁹ All these people earned a good reputation because of their faith, yet none of them received all that God had promised. ⁴⁰ For God had something better in mind for us, so that they would not reach perfection without us.

GOD'S DISCIPLINE PROVES HIS LOVE

12 Therefore, since we are surrounded by such a huge crowd of witnesses to the life of faith, let us strip off every weight that slows us down, especially the sin that so easily trips us up. And let us run with endurance the race God has set before us. ² We do this by keeping our eyes on Jesus, the champion who initiates and perfects our faith.* Because of the joy* awaiting him, he endured the cross, disregarding its shame. Now he is seated in the place of honor beside God's throne. ³ Think of all the hostility he endured from sinful people;* then you won't become weary and give up. ⁴ After all, you have not yet given your lives in your struggle against sin.

⁵ And have you forgotten the encouraging words God spoke to you as his children?* He said,

"My child,* don't make light of the LORD's discipline,
    and don't give up when he corrects you.
⁶ For the LORD disciplines those he loves,
    and he punishes each one he accepts as his child."*

⁷ As you endure this divine discipline, remember that God is treating you as his own children. Who ever heard of a child who is never disciplined by its father? ⁸ If God doesn't discipline you as he does all of his children, it means that you are illegitimate and are not really his children at all. ⁹ Since we respected our earthly fathers who disciplined us, shouldn't we submit even more to the discipline of the Father of our spirits, and live forever?* ¹⁰ For our earthly fathers disciplined us for a few years, doing the best they knew how. But God's discipline is always good for us, so that

---

11:18 Gen 21:12.   11:37 Some manuscripts add *some were tested.*
12:2a Or *Jesus, the originator and perfecter of our faith.*   12:2b Or
Instead of the joy.   12:3 Some manuscripts read *Think of how
people hurt themselves by opposing him.*   12:5a Greek *sons;* also
in 12:7, 8.   12:5b Greek *son;* also in 12:6, 7.   12:5-6 Prov 3:11-12
(Greek version).   12:9 Or *and really live?*

BITTER ROOTS
Hebrews 12:14–17   ROBERT MORRIS

When we've been hurt by another person or believe God has wronged us in some way, we can become angry and bitter. However, Hebrews 12:15 warns us against the "poisonous root of bitterness." Bitterness is a poison that will ruin our lives if we let it go unchecked.

1. Bitter roots deceive.
A bitter root always has a little bit of truth in it. Satan told Eve she would know "both good and evil" if she ate the forbidden fruit (Genesis 3:5). Adam and Eve already knew *good*—they walked and talked with God every day. But Satan convinced them that God was holding something back. The root of bitterness tells us there's something better than what God has already given us.

2. Bitter roots corrupt.
When bad things happen in our lives, they can change the way we see everything around us, even God. Most of us can trace any anger we have toward God to a root of bitterness. Bad things happen not because God doesn't love us or care about us, but because we live in a fallen world. God allows us to make our own choices, and the enemy always tries to corrupt our choices with sin.

3. Bitter roots depress.
The root of bitterness is envy, and the root of envy is hate. We can become angry with God when something good happens for someone but doesn't happen for us. Bitterness is a poison that produces deception, defilement, and depression. We all have difficult, even painful experiences, but we cannot afford to become bitter. We must choose to let Jesus heal these areas of our lives and remove any bitter roots in our hearts.

he was rejected. It was too late for repentance, even though he begged with bitter tears.

[18] You have not come to a physical mountain,* to a place of flaming fire, darkness, gloom, and whirlwind, as the Israelites did at Mount Sinai. [19] For they heard an awesome trumpet blast and a voice so terrible that they begged God to stop speaking. [20] They staggered back under God's command: "If even an animal touches the mountain, it must be stoned to death."* [21] Moses himself was so frightened at the sight that he said, "I am terrified and trembling."*

[22] No, you have come to Mount Zion, to the city of the living God, the heavenly Jerusalem, and to countless thousands of angels in a joyful gathering. [23] You have come to the assembly of God's firstborn children, whose names are written in heaven. You have come to God himself, who is the judge over all things. You have come to the spirits of the righteous ones in heaven who have now been made perfect. [24] You have come to Jesus, the one who mediates the new covenant between God and people, and to the sprinkled blood, which speaks of forgiveness instead of crying out for vengeance like the blood of Abel.

[25] Be careful that you do not refuse to listen to the One who is speaking. For if the people of Israel did not escape when they refused to listen to Moses, the earthly messenger, we will certainly not escape if we reject the One who speaks to us from heaven! [26] When God spoke from Mount Sinai his voice shook the earth, but now he makes another promise: "Once again I will shake not only the earth but the heavens also."* [27] This means that all of creation will be shaken and removed, so that only unshakable things will remain.

[28] Since we are receiving a Kingdom that is unshakable, let us be thankful and please God by worshiping him with holy fear and awe. [29] For our God is a devouring fire.

CONCLUDING WORDS

13 Keep on loving each other as brothers and sisters.* [2] Don't forget to show hospitality to strangers, for some who have done this have entertained angels without realizing it! [3] Remember those in prison, as if you were there yourself. Remember also those being mistreated, as if you felt their pain in your own bodies.

[4] Give honor to marriage, and remain faithful to one another in marriage. God will surely judge people who are immoral and those who commit adultery.

[5] Don't love money; be satisfied with what you have. For God has said,

"I will never fail you.
    I will never abandon you."*

we might share in his holiness. [11] No discipline is enjoyable while it is happening—it's painful! But afterward there will be a peaceful harvest of right living for those who are trained in this way. [12] So take a new grip with your tired hands and strengthen your weak knees. [13] Mark out a straight path for your feet so that those who are weak and lame will not fall but become strong.

A CALL TO LISTEN TO GOD

[14] Work at living in peace with everyone, and work at living a holy life, for those who are not holy will not see the Lord. [15] Look after each other so that none of you fails to receive the grace of God. Watch out that no poisonous root of bitterness grows up to trouble you, corrupting many. [16] Make sure that no one is immoral or godless like Esau, who traded his birthright as the firstborn son for a single meal. [17] You know that afterward, when he wanted his father's blessing,

---

12:18 Greek *to something that can be touched.* 12:20 Exod 19:13.
12:21 Deut 9:19. 12:26 Hag 2:6. 13:1 Greek *Continue in brotherly love.* 13:5 Deut 31:6, 8.

[6]So we can say with confidence,

"The LORD is my helper,
    so I will have no fear.
    What can mere people do to me?"*

[7]Remember your leaders who taught you the word of God. Think of all the good that has come from their lives, and follow the example of their faith.
[8]Jesus Christ is the same yesterday, today, and forever. [9]So do not be attracted by strange, new ideas. Your strength comes from God's grace, not from rules about food, which don't help those who follow them.
[10]We have an altar from which the priests in the Tabernacle* have no right to eat. [11]Under the old system, the high priest brought the blood of animals into the Holy Place as a sacrifice for sin, and the bodies of the animals were burned outside the camp. [12]So also Jesus suffered and died outside the city gates to make his people holy by means of his own blood. [13]So let us go out to him, outside the camp, and bear the disgrace he bore. [14]For this world is not our permanent home; we are looking forward to a home yet to come.
[15]Therefore, let us offer through Jesus a continual sacrifice of praise to God, proclaiming our allegiance to his name. [16]And don't forget to do good and to share with those in need. These are the sacrifices that please God.
[17]Obey your spiritual leaders, and do what they say. Their work is to watch over your souls, and they are accountable to God. Give them reason to do this with joy and not with sorrow. That would certainly not be for your benefit.
[18]Pray for us, for our conscience is clear and we want to live honorably in everything we do. [19]And especially pray that I will be able to come back to you soon.

[20] Now may the God of peace—
    who brought up from the dead
    our Lord Jesus,
    the great Shepherd of the sheep,

THE BUILDER
Hebrews 13:8   ROBERT MORRIS

Jesus is a builder, and everything He creates fits together perfectly. He expertly developed, framed, and constructed the foundation of our world. And He's still building today.

Jesus began building you in your mother's womb the moment you were conceived. When you accepted His free gift of salvation, you joined the body of Christ and became one of the "living stones that God is building into his spiritual temple" (1 Peter 2:4-6). Jesus is still building His Church, but if we don't obey His direction in our lives, the building process will come to a halt.

God is faithful. He always has been, and He always will be. Your past may include painful memories, but God has the power to redeem your past and bless your future. He can build or rebuild any area of your life, and His plans for you are good!

and ratified an eternal covenant
    with his blood—
[21] may he equip you with all you need
    for doing his will.
May he produce in you,*
    through the power of Jesus Christ,
every good thing that is pleasing to him.
    All glory to him forever and ever! Amen.

[22]I urge you, dear brothers and sisters,* to pay attention to what I have written in this brief exhortation.
[23]I want you to know that our brother Timothy has been released from jail. If he comes here soon, I will bring him with me to see you.
[24]Greet all your leaders and all the believers there.* The believers from Italy send you their greetings.
[25]May God's grace be with you all.

13:6 Ps 118:6.   13:10 Or *tent*.   13:21 Some manuscripts read *in us*.
13:22 Greek *brothers*.   13:24 Greek *all of God's holy people*.

JAMES

JON HUNTZINGER, PHD

The letter of James is a New Testament example of Hebrew wisdom literature in the tradition of the book of Proverbs. It begins, "If you need wisdom, ask our generous God, and he will give it to you" (1:5). Hebrew wisdom should not be thought of as mere learning or the accumulation of information. It was knowledge of God's Word and a commitment to living by that Word. The writers expressed such wisdom in short sayings, which were easy to remember. They encouraged people to act and live in specific ways before God and with others. This means that wisdom revealed itself in ethics or moral living.

A sampling of the proverbial sayings in James includes the following:
— "A person with divided loyalty is as unsettled as a wave of the sea that is blown and tossed by the wind" (1:6).
— "Just as the body is dead without breath, so also faith is dead without good works" (2:26).
— "Does a fig tree produce olives, or a grapevine produce figs? No, and you can't draw fresh water from a salty spring" (3:12).
— "Don't you realize that friendship with the world makes you an enemy of God?" (4:4).
— "Resist the devil, and he will flee from you. Come close to God, and God will come close to you" (4:7-8).
— "Your life is like the morning fog—it's here a little while, then it's gone" (4:14).
— "Never take an oath, by heaven or earth or anything else. Just say a simple yes or no" (5:12).

The book that contains these proverbs was written by the brother of Jesus who was a leader of the Jerusalem church (Galatians 1:19; Acts 12:17; 15:13; 21:18). Because of the emphasis he gives to such proverbial wisdom, it is likely that he wrote for Jewish believers.

James gives attention to the words people speak. Words reflect the heart of the speaker and influence how they act toward others. People should be "slow to speak" (1:19), and they should live out the word that God gives to them (1:22-25). They should be careful about what they say (1:26; 3:1-12), and they should never speak "evil" against one another (4:11). Instead, their words should be trustworthy and their "yes" be "yes" and their "no" be "no" (5:12). They should confess their sins to one another with words and also pray for one another (5:16). According to James, wisdom shows itself in the words people speak and the actions performed in connection with those words.

Throughout the letter, James emphasizes the works a person does and the ethics of the gospel. For him, wisdom is the appropriate expression of the gospel in a person's life, which shows itself in how a person lives with others. People should perform God's Word and not only think about it: "Don't just listen to God's word. You must do what it says" (1:22). Wisdom is the engagement of the gospel in our lives.

James continues, "If you are wise and understand God's ways, prove it by living an honorable life, doing good works with the humility that comes from wisdom" (3:13). What will such "good works" look like? James gives the following picture: "The wisdom from above is first of all pure. It is also peace loving, gentle at all times, and willing to yield to others. It is full of mercy and the fruit of good deeds. It shows no favoritism and is always sincere" (3:17). This view of wisdom recalls the fruit of the Spirit described by Paul ("love, joy, peace, patience, kindness, goodness, faithfulness, gentleness, and self-control") in Galatians 5:22-23 and Peter's description of the divine nature ("Supplement your faith with a generous provision of moral excellence, and moral excellence with knowledge, and knowledge with self-control, and self-control with patient endurance, and patient endurance with godliness, and godliness with brotherly affection, and brotherly affection with love for everyone") in 2 Peter 1:5-7. Wisdom, the fruit of the Spirit, and the divine nature all represent different ways by which James, Paul, and Peter talk about the same thing. They use different metaphors to describe what God does in a person's life in relation to Him: He gives wisdom; He grows fruit; He shares His nature. He does all these for the benefit of other people. Family, friends, coworkers, and others are blessed by the wisdom in a person's life, or the fruit of the Spirit that grows in them (to be eaten by others), or the nature of God being exhibited through them.

GREETINGS FROM JAMES

1 This letter is from James, a slave of God and of the Lord Jesus Christ.

I am writing to the "twelve tribes"—Jewish believers scattered abroad.

Greetings!

FAITH AND ENDURANCE

[2] Dear brothers and sisters,* when troubles of any kind come your way, consider it an opportunity for great joy. [3] For you know that when your faith is tested, your endurance has a chance to grow. [4] So let it grow, for when your endurance is fully developed, you will be perfect and complete, needing nothing.

[5] If you need wisdom, ask our generous God, and he will give it to you. He will not rebuke you for asking. [6] But when you ask him, be sure that your faith is in God alone. Do not waver, for a person with divided loyalty is as unsettled as a wave of the sea that is blown and tossed by the wind. [7] Such people should not expect to receive anything from the Lord. [8] Their loyalty is divided between God and the world, and they are unstable in everything they do.

[9] Believers who are* poor have something to boast about, for God has honored them. [10] And those who are rich should boast that God has humbled them. They will fade away like a little flower in the field. [11] The hot sun rises and the grass withers; the little flower droops and falls, and its beauty fades away. In the same way, the rich will fade away with all of their achievements.

[12] God blesses those who patiently endure testing and temptation. Afterward they will receive the crown of life that God has promised to those who love him. [13] And remember, when you are being tempted, do not say, "God is tempting me." God is never tempted to do wrong,* and he never tempts anyone else. [14] Temptation comes from our own desires, which entice us and drag us away. [15] These desires give birth to sinful actions. And when sin is allowed to grow, it gives birth to death.

[16] So don't be misled, my dear brothers and sisters. [17] Whatever is good and perfect is a gift coming down to us from God our Father, who created all the lights in the heavens.* He never changes or casts a shifting shadow.* [18] He chose to give birth to us by giving us his true word. And we, out of all creation, became his prized possession.*

LISTENING AND DOING

[19] Understand this, my dear brothers and sisters: You must all be quick to listen, slow to speak, and slow to get angry. [20] Human anger* does not produce the righteousness* God desires. [21] So get rid of all the filth and evil in your lives, and humbly accept the word God has planted in your hearts, for it has the power to save your souls.

THE FATHER IS GOOD

James 1:17-18   ROBERT MORRIS

Some people have the misconception that God the Father is mean. They think of Him as a cruel parent who can't wait to punish us for any mistakes we make. Let me tell you something: you may have had an earthly father like that, but our heavenly Father is different. He is *good*. Understanding God's goodness makes a huge difference in our relationship with Him.

1. The Father is completely good. When Moses asked to see God's glory in Exodus 33:18, he was really asking to see the best thing about God. God responded, "I will make all my goodness pass before you" (v. 19). God's goodness cannot be measured; it has no limits. God doesn't just *have* goodness, though; He *is* goodness! God cannot get "better" because He is already completely, perfectly, and infinitely good! There has never been and never will be a time when God isn't good.

2. We were created because the Father is good. James 1:17 says every good and perfect gift comes from God. But why were we created? Did we somehow deserve it? No, the only reason we were created is because God is good. And the only reason why we aren't immediately destroyed the first (or hundredth) time we sin is because God is good. God sent Jesus to save us because He loves us. He created us in His image (Genesis 1:26), and His image is good.

3. We must choose the Father's goodness. In Romans 11:22, Paul says God is "severe toward those who disobeyed, but kind to you if you continue to trust in his kindness." God gives us a choice: will we trust Him or not? Satan doesn't want us to believe God is good, so he points to every problem in the world and accuses God. Don't let him confuse you, though. God *is* good, and He has a *good* plan for your life.

[22] But don't just listen to God's word. You must do what it says. Otherwise, you are only fooling yourselves. [23] For if you listen to the word and don't obey, it is like glancing at your face in a mirror. [24] You see yourself, walk away, and forget what you look like. [25] But if you look carefully into the perfect law that sets you free, and if you do what it says and don't forget what you heard, then God will bless you for doing it.

1:2 Greek *brothers;* also in 1:16, 19. 1:9 Greek *The brother who is.* 1:13 Or *God should not be put to a test by evil people.* 1:17a Greek *from above, from the Father of lights.* 1:17b Some manuscripts read *He never changes, as a shifting shadow does.* 1:18 Greek *we became a kind of firstfruit of his creatures.* 1:20a Greek *A man's anger.* 1:20b Or *the justice.*

26 If you claim to be religious but don't control your tongue, you are fooling yourself, and your religion is worthless. 27 Pure and genuine religion in the sight of God the Father means caring for orphans and widows in their distress and refusing to let the world corrupt you.

A WARNING AGAINST PREJUDICE

2 My dear brothers and sisters,* how can you claim to have faith in our glorious Lord Jesus Christ if you favor some people over others?

2 For example, suppose someone comes into your meeting* dressed in fancy clothes and expensive jewelry, and another comes in who is poor and dressed in dirty clothes. 3 If you give special attention and a good seat to the rich person, but you say to the poor one, "You can stand over there, or else sit on the floor"—well, 4 doesn't this discrimination show that your judgments are guided by evil motives?

5 Listen to me, dear brothers and sisters. Hasn't God chosen the poor in this world to be rich in faith? Aren't they the ones who will inherit the Kingdom he promised to those who love him? 6 But you dishonor the poor! Isn't it the rich who oppress you and drag you into court? 7 Aren't they the ones who slander Jesus Christ, whose noble name* you bear?

8 Yes indeed, it is good when you obey the royal law as found in the Scriptures: "Love your neighbor as yourself."* 9 But if you favor some people over others, you are committing a sin. You are guilty of breaking the law.

10 For the person who keeps all of the laws except one is as guilty as a person who has broken all of God's laws. 11 For the same God who said, "You must not commit adultery," also said, "You must not murder."* So if you murder someone but do not commit adultery, you have still broken the law.

12 So whatever you say or whatever you do, remember that you will be judged by the law that sets you free. 13 There will be no mercy for those who have not shown mercy to others. But if you have been merciful, God will be merciful when he judges you.

FAITH WITHOUT GOOD DEEDS IS DEAD

14 What good is it, dear brothers and sisters, if you say you have faith but don't show it by your actions? Can that kind of faith save anyone? 15 Suppose you see a brother or sister who has no food or clothing, 16 and you say, "Good-bye and have a good day; stay warm and eat well"—but then you don't give that person any food or clothing. What good does that do?

17 So you see, faith by itself isn't enough. Unless it produces good deeds, it is dead and useless. 18 Now someone may argue, "Some people have faith; others have good deeds." But I say, "How can you show me your faith if you don't have good deeds? I will show you my faith by my good deeds."

19 You say you have faith, for you believe that there is one God.* Good for you! Even the demons believe this, and they tremble in terror. 20 How foolish! Can't you see that faith without good deeds is useless?

21 Don't you remember that our ancestor Abraham was shown to be right with God by his actions when he offered his son Isaac on the altar? 22 You see, his faith and his actions worked together. His actions made his faith complete. 23 And so it happened just as the Scriptures say: "Abraham believed God, and God counted him as righteous because of his faith."* He was even called the friend of God.* 24 So you see, we are shown to be right with God by what we do, not by faith alone.

25 Rahab the prostitute is another example. She was shown to be right with God by her actions when she hid those messengers and sent them safely away by a different road. 26 Just as the body is dead without breath,* so also faith is dead without good works.

CONTROLLING THE TONGUE

3 Dear brothers and sisters,* not many of you should become teachers in the church, for we who teach will be judged more strictly. 2 Indeed, we all make many mistakes. For if we could control our tongues, we would be perfect and could also control ourselves in every other way.

3 We can make a large horse go wherever we want by means of a small bit in its mouth. 4 And a small rudder makes a huge ship turn wherever the pilot chooses to go, even though the winds are strong. 5 In the same way, the tongue is a small thing that makes grand speeches.

But a tiny spark can set a great forest on fire. 6 And among all the parts of the body, the tongue is a flame of fire. It is a whole world of wickedness, corrupting your entire body. It can set your whole life on fire, for it is set on fire by hell itself.* 7 People can tame all kinds of animals, birds, reptiles, and fish, 8 but no one can tame the tongue. It is restless and evil, full of deadly poison. 9 Sometimes it praises our Lord and Father, and sometimes it curses those who have been made in the image of God. 10 And so blessing and cursing come pouring out of the same mouth. Surely, my brothers and sisters, this is not right! 11 Does a spring of water bubble out with both fresh water and bitter water? 12 Does a fig tree produce olives, or a grapevine produce figs? No, and you can't draw fresh water from a salty spring.*

TRUE WISDOM COMES FROM GOD

13 If you are wise and understand God's ways, prove it by living an honorable life, doing good

2:1 Greek brothers; also in 2:5, 14. 2:2 Greek your synagogue. 2:7 Greek slander the noble name. 2:8 Lev 19:18. 2:11 Exod 20:13-14; Deut 5:17-18. 2:19 Some manuscripts read that God is one; see Deut 6:4. 2:23a Gen 15:6. 2:23b See Isa 41:8. 2:26 Or without spirit. 3:1 Greek brothers; also in 3:10. 3:6 Or for it will burn in hell (Greek Gehenna). 3:12 Greek from salt.

AMAZING FACTS ABOUT THE TONGUE
James 3:1-12

ROBERT MORRIS

Did you know you produce life or death every time you speak? It's true. Your tongue is the most powerful part of your body. James 3:2 says, "If we could control our tongues, we would be perfect and could also control ourselves in every other way." Here are four amazing facts about the tongue:

1. It's disproportionately powerful (vv. 3-5).
I could just say the tongue is powerful, but that's not the amazing fact. It's *disproportionately* powerful, meaning it's very small but its effect is very large. James compares the tongue to a bit in a horse's mouth; it controls the strength and direction of our whole life. Like the rudder of a ship, the tongue determines whether we remain on course during both the storms and the calm times of life. And like a small spark that starts a large forest fire, our tongue can speak careless words that destroy ourselves and others.

2. It's inherently evil (vv. 6, 8).
Every person is born with an evil tongue, and I can prove it. Do you have to teach children to be rude or say mean things? No, we have to teach them to say nice things. The default setting on the tongue is to destroy, and unless we change this setting, we will always do more damage than good.

3. It's humanly untamable (vv. 7-8).
No person can tame the tongue—it's *humanly* untamable. That's the bad news. The good news is the tongue is divinely tamable. The One who made it can tame it. The first thing the Holy Spirit did for the believers on the Day of Pentecost was to change their tongues (Acts 2). The only way you can change your tongue is to submit it to the Holy Spirit.

4. It's contrastingly productive (vv. 9-12).
The tongue is *contrastingly* productive. It can produce life and death, good and bad. Why do we think it's okay to use our words to praise God but then curse other people? God certainly doesn't agree. The good news is that our tongue can produce good fruit. You can use it to bless your job, your finances, and your family.

---

works with the humility that comes from wisdom. ¹⁴But if you are bitterly jealous and there is selfish ambition in your heart, don't cover up the truth with boasting and lying. ¹⁵For jealousy and selfishness are not God's kind of wisdom. Such things are earthly, unspiritual, and demonic. ¹⁶For wherever there is jealousy and selfish ambition, there you will find disorder and evil of every kind.

¹⁷But the wisdom from above is first of all pure. It is also peace loving, gentle at all times, and willing to yield to others. It is full of mercy and the fruit of good deeds. It shows no favoritism and is always sincere. ¹⁸And those who are peacemakers will plant seeds of peace and reap a harvest of righteousness.*

DRAWING CLOSE TO GOD

4 What is causing the quarrels and fights among you? Don't they come from the evil desires at war within you? ²You want what you don't have, so you scheme and kill to get it. You are jealous of what others have, but you can't get it, so you fight and wage war to take it away from them. Yet you don't have what you want because you don't ask God for it. ³And even when you ask, you don't get it because your motives are all wrong—you want only what will give you pleasure.

⁴You adulterers!* Don't you realize that friendship with the world makes you an enemy of God? I say it again: If you want to be a friend of the world, you make yourself an enemy of God. ⁵Do you think the Scriptures have no meaning? They say that God is passionate that the spirit

THE MOTIVE OF GENEROSITY
James 4:3

ROBERT MORRIS

Are you proud of your children when they're unselfish? Are you blessed when they're generous without being bribed or threatened? Of course, we're pleased when our children help and prefer one another in love. And what's true for us as earthly parents is infinitely true for our heavenly Father.

James 4:3 explains why some believers don't receive what they pray for: "You don't get it because your motives are all wrong—you want only what will give you pleasure." God is the ultimate giver, but He doesn't bless us simply to satisfy our selfish desires. Blessings come when we allow Him to do a work inside us and realign our motives to match His. A properly focused heart is always more excited about giving than receiving. God gives to us so we can have the joy of imitating Him and giving to others.

---

he has placed within us should be faithful to him.* ⁶And he gives grace generously. As the Scriptures say,

"God opposes the proud
 but gives grace to the humble."*

---

7 So humble yourselves before God. Resist the devil, and he will flee from you. 8 Come close to God, and God will come close to you. Wash your hands, you sinners; purify your hearts, for your loyalty is divided between God and the world. 9 Let there be tears for what you have done. Let there be sorrow and deep grief. Let there be sadness instead of laughter, and gloom instead of joy. 10 Humble yourselves before the Lord, and he will lift you up in honor.

WARNING AGAINST JUDGING OTHERS

11 Don't speak evil against each other, dear brothers and sisters.* If you criticize and judge each other, then you are criticizing and judging God's law. But your job is to obey the law, not to judge whether it applies to you. 12 God alone, who gave the law, is the Judge. He alone has the power to save or to destroy. So what right do you have to judge your neighbor?

WARNING ABOUT SELF-CONFIDENCE

13 Look here, you who say, "Today or tomorrow we are going to a certain town and will stay there a year. We will do business there and make a profit." 14 How do you know what your life will be like tomorrow? Your life is like the morning fog—it's here a little while, then it's gone. 15 What you ought to say is, "If the Lord wants us to, we will live and do this or that." 16 Otherwise you are boasting about your own pretentious plans, and all such boasting is evil.

17 Remember, it is sin to know what you ought to do and then not do it.

WARNING TO THE RICH

5 Look here, you rich people: Weep and groan with anguish because of all the terrible troubles ahead of you. 2 Your wealth is rotting away, and your fine clothes are moth-eaten rags. 3 Your gold and silver are corroded. The very wealth you were counting on will eat away your flesh like fire. This corroded treasure you have hoarded will testify against you on the day of judgment. 4 For listen! Hear the cries of the field workers whom you have cheated of their pay. The cries of those who harvest your fields have reached the ears of the LORD of Heaven's Armies. 5 You have spent your years on earth in luxury, satisfying your every desire. You have fattened yourselves for the day of slaughter. 6 You have condemned and killed innocent people,* who do not resist you.*

PATIENCE AND ENDURANCE

7 Dear brothers and sisters,* be patient as you wait for the Lord's return. Consider the farmers who patiently wait for the rains in the fall and in the spring. They eagerly look for the valuable harvest to ripen. 8 You, too, must be patient. Take courage, for the coming of the Lord is near.

9 Don't grumble about each other, brothers and sisters, or you will be judged. For look—the Judge is standing at the door!

10 For examples of patience in suffering, dear brothers and sisters, look at the prophets who spoke in the name of the Lord. 11 We give great honor to those who endure under suffering. For instance, you know about Job, a man of great endurance. You can see how the Lord was kind to him at the end, for the Lord is full of tenderness and mercy.

12 But most of all, my brothers and sisters, never take an oath, by heaven or earth or anything else. Just say a simple yes or no, so that you will not sin and be condemned.

THE POWER OF PRAYER

13 Are any of you suffering hardships? You should pray. Are any of you happy? You should sing praises. 14 Are any of you sick? You should call for the elders of the church to come and pray over you, anointing you with oil in the name of the Lord. 15 Such a prayer offered in faith will heal the sick, and the Lord will make you well. And if you have committed any sins, you will be forgiven.

16 Confess your sins to each other and pray for each other so that you may be healed. The earnest prayer of a righteous person has great power and produces wonderful results. 17 Elijah was as human as we are, and yet when he prayed earnestly that no rain would fall, none fell for three and a half years! 18 Then, when he prayed again, the sky sent down rain and the earth began to yield its crops.

RESTORE WANDERING BELIEVERS

19 My dear brothers and sisters, if someone among you wanders away from the truth and is brought back, 20 you can be sure that whoever brings the sinner back from wandering will save that person from death and bring about the forgiveness of many sins.

4:11 Greek brothers. 5:6a Or killed the Righteous One. 5:6b Or Don't they resist you? or Doesn't God oppose you? or Aren't they now accusing you before God? 5:7 Greek brothers; also in 5:9, 10, 12, 19.

1 PETER

JON HUNTZINGER, PHD

The apostle Peter's influence in the New Testament is comparable to that of John (who wrote the Gospel of John, the letters of John, and Revelation), Paul (who wrote 13 letters), and Luke (who wrote the Gospel of Luke and the book of Acts). As discussed in the introduction to Mark's Gospel, many Bible scholars think Peter's preaching provided the basis and outline for that book. Two letters (1 and 2 Peter) are attributed to him, according to early church tradition. Though some people question his authorship of the letters (especially 2 Peter) based on their analysis of the theology, vocabulary, or style they contain, such opinions are subjective and cannot be supported since Peter, like Paul and other writers at that time, used secretaries to assist him in writing to his readers. Early church documents say he was put to death during the reign of the Roman emperor Nero, who himself died in AD 68. Consequently, Peter would have written his letters before then in the AD 60s.

Peter refers to the readers of his first letter as "God's chosen people who are living as foreigners" and, in this way, identifies them with the Israelites who had experienced hardship because of their calling to be God's people (1:1). Because they "had no identity as a people" (2:10) at one time and lived a life of idolatry (4:3), it is likely that the first intended audience were Gentiles who had come to proclaim Jesus as God's Messiah. Peter writes to encourage them and says that a life of righteousness and wholeness is possible because Jesus "personally carried our sins in his body on the cross so that we can be dead to sin and live for what is right. By his wounds you are healed" (2:24). He reminds them that they have been born again and have hope despite their circumstances because "God raised Jesus Christ from the dead" (1:3). Their hope is based in the fact they have been "ransom[ed]" through "the precious blood of Christ" who was raised by God from the dead and sits in glory (1:17-21) and even now exercises power at God's right hand (3:18-22).

Despite their circumstances, Peter exhorts these believers to serve one another in love. In a passage similar to Paul's message to the Galatians (Galatians 5:13-14), Peter says "you are free, yet you are God's slaves" (1 Peter 2:16). Just as Paul exhorted the Galatians to use their freedom to love one another rather than gratify their flesh, Peter encourages his readers to do the same. He then says they should "continue to show deep love for each other, for love covers a multitude of sins. . . . God has given each of you a gift from his great variety of spiritual gifts. Use them well to serve one another" (4:8-10). Here, again, Peter recalls Paul who tells the Galatians they should allow the Spirit to cultivate fruit in their lives for the purpose of giving strength and nourishment to one another (Galatians 5:22-23). *Hospitality* means to provide for the needs of others. Whether this is through the fruit the Spirit grows, according to Paul, or the gifts the Spirit gives, according to Peter, both apostles look to the Spirit to provide what the Church needs to be strong and healthy. Such a life is a witness to the world (1 Peter 2:12, 15; 3:1, 15-16; 4:4).

Peter was one of the twelve disciples and one of three who are depicted in the Gospels as particularly close to Jesus (Matthew 17:1; 26:36-37; Mark 5:37; 9:2; 14:32-33; Luke 8:51). It is not surprising that Peter leans heavily on the words of Jesus to write his first letter:

— He refers to God as "Father" (1:2, 3, 17) in the same way Jesus spoke of God as His Father (John 14-17).
— Peter tells his readers that they must be holy even as God is holy (1:15), just as Jesus taught His disciples to be perfect as God their Father is perfect (Matthew 5:48).
— He says God judges impartially, based on the deeds a person performs (1:17), recalling Jesus' words to Nicodemus that God's Son did not enter the world to judge it but to provide an opportunity for people to believe. The judgment is that people will show their belief through their deeds (John 3:16-21).
— Peter exhorts the believers to love one another from a pure heart (1:22), recalling Jesus' final command to the disciples to love one another "as I have loved you" (John 13:34-35; 15:17).
— He says the believers "have had a taste of the Lord's kindness" (2:3), which alludes to Jesus' remarks that His body and blood are food and drink for His disciples (John 6:53-58).
— When Peter says Jesus is the cornerstone of God's temple (2:6-8), he is repeating what Jesus said about himself being the cornerstone (Matthew 21:42-43).
— He urges the believers to do good works (2:15-17), much like Jesus told His disciples that their good works should shine before people (Matthew 5:16; Luke 6:27-33).
— Peter says the believers should be prepared to give a defense for the hope that resides in them (3:15), even as Jesus promised the disciples that the Holy Spirit would help them speak when they were brought before leaders (Mark 13:11).
— He says the believers should rejoice when they are insulted on account of Jesus because this means they are blessed (4:13-14), just as Jesus

promised the disciples they would experience rejection because of His name and should rejoice nevertheless (Matthew 5:11-12).

— Peter says elders should not be overbearing to God's flock (5:3), which recalls Jesus' remarks to the disciples that they should seek to serve rather than be served (Matthew 20:24-28).

Even as Peter relies upon the words of Jesus for his remarks to his readers, he draws on the words of the prophet Isaiah too. By referring to his readers as "foreigners" (1:1), Peter connects them to the time of the Exile addressed by Isaiah in chapters 40-66:

— He quotes from Isaiah 40:6-8 and says they have been born again by the "eternal, living word of God" (1 Peter 1:23-25). The verses he quotes are from a passage in which the prophet speaks comfort to the exiles and concludes by describing God as shepherd and creator (Isaiah 40:1-31). Peter wants his readers to be comforted by God's Word to them.

— Peter also says his readers are "living stones" (2:5), being built into a holy house for God with Jesus as its cornerstone and quotes from Isaiah 28:16-17 and 8:14 where the prophet speaks of a cornerstone that is the basis for justice and revokes the "bargain . . . made to cheat death." Peter wants his readers to know that they have been delivered from death due to the work of Jesus the cornerstone.

— He continues, saying his readers have been called out of darkness into the light of God (2:9), recalling the prophet's words: "The people who walk in darkness will see a great light. For those who live in a land of deep darkness, a light will shine" (Isaiah 9:2). Peter wants to confirm to his readers that God has given them knowledge through His Son and His Word.

— Peter recalls Jesus' suffering (2:21-25) and exhorts his readers to endure sorrow and suffering for good (4:12-19). He recalls those passages in Isaiah that describe the servant of the Lord, who suffers in this way (Isaiah 40; 42; 49; 52-53). Peter wants his readers to continue in faith, though it may be difficult for them to do so.

GREETINGS FROM PETER

1 This letter is from Peter, an apostle of Jesus Christ.

I am writing to God's chosen people who are living as foreigners in the provinces of Pontus, Galatia, Cappadocia, Asia, and Bithynia.* ²God the Father knew you and chose you long ago, and his Spirit has made you holy. As a result, you have obeyed him and have been cleansed by the blood of Jesus Christ.

May God give you more and more grace and peace.

THE HOPE OF ETERNAL LIFE

³All praise to God, the Father of our Lord Jesus Christ. It is by his great mercy that we have been born again, because God raised Jesus Christ from the dead. Now we live with great expectation, ⁴and we have a priceless inheritance—an inheritance that is kept in heaven for you, pure and undefiled, beyond the reach of change and decay. ⁵And through your faith, God is protecting you by his power until you receive this salvation, which is ready to be revealed on the last day for all to see.

⁶So be truly glad.* There is wonderful joy ahead, even though you must endure many trials for a little while. ⁷These trials will show that your faith is genuine. It is being tested as fire tests and purifies gold—though your faith is far more precious than mere gold. So when your faith remains strong through many trials, it will bring you much praise and glory and honor on the day when Jesus Christ is revealed to the whole world.

⁸You love him even though you have never seen him. Though you do not see him now, you trust him; and you rejoice with a glorious, inexpressible joy. ⁹The reward for trusting him will be the salvation of your souls.

¹⁰This salvation was something even the prophets wanted to know more about when they prophesied about this gracious salvation prepared for you. ¹¹They wondered what time or situation the Spirit of Christ within them was talking about when he told them in advance about Christ's suffering and his great glory afterward.

¹²They were told that their messages were not for themselves, but for you. And now this Good News has been announced to you by those who preached in the power of the Holy Spirit sent from heaven. It is all so wonderful that even the angels are eagerly watching these things happen.

A CALL TO HOLY LIVING

¹³So prepare your minds for action and exercise self-control. Put all your hope in the gracious salvation that will come to you when Jesus Christ is revealed to the world. ¹⁴So you must live as God's obedient children. Don't slip back into your old ways of living to satisfy your own desires. You didn't know any better then. ¹⁵But now you must be holy in everything you do, just as God who chose you is holy. ¹⁶For the Scriptures say, "You must be holy because I am holy."*

1:1 Pontus, Galatia, Cappadocia, Asia, and Bithynia were Roman provinces in what is now Turkey.   1:6 Or So you are truly glad.
1:16 Lev 11:44-45; 19:2; 20:7.

PLANTING THE SEED
1 Peter 1:23   ROBERT MORRIS

When you open a package of seeds, do they look anything like the pretty picture on the package? Of course not; they're just seeds. But if you put them in the ground, they have the potential to produce what's in the picture. It's the same way with God's Word. When I read God's Word and meditate on it, I'm actually putting a seed in my heart that's going to produce fruit.

We all meditate on things. When we're in bondage to something, it's easier to meditate on the lie that holds us captive than the truth that sets us free. If you spend your time meditating on lust, pride, or bitterness, you'll soon have a depressed and discouraged heart.

Instead, we need to plant the seed of God's Word in our lives. We may not see results right away, but we can know for sure that it will produce good fruit in us.

BELIEVERS' BASICS: WORSHIP
1 Peter 2:1-10   JACK HAYFORD

As a holy priesthood, God calls us to offer up spiritual sacrifices—worship (1 Peter 2:5). Worship is an intimate time with the Lord in which we recognize our unholiness compared to His holiness. We realize that we will never be whole without God's power.

We grow through an ongoing desire for the "pure spiritual milk" of God's Word (1 Peter 2:2). God's promise to believers who stay in the Word is that they can become what the Word teaches. Jesus said, "Heaven and earth will disappear, but my words will never disappear" (Luke 21:33).

Having received God's mercy, we are also able to minister to others (1 Peter 2:10). The ministry and power are in God, not us. We simply apply it as His people. We know God's mercy in our lives, and we now have the privilege of sharing it with those who have not yet started their lives with Jesus Christ.

[17] And remember that the heavenly Father to whom you pray has no favorites. He will judge or reward you according to what you do. So you must live in reverent fear of him during your time here as "temporary residents." [18] For you know that God paid a ransom to save you from the empty life you inherited from your ancestors. And it was not paid with mere gold or silver, which lose their value. [19] It was the precious blood of Christ, the sinless, spotless Lamb of God. [20] God chose him as your ransom long before the world began, but now in these last days he has been revealed for your sake.

[21] Through Christ you have come to trust in God. And you have placed your faith and hope in God because he raised Christ from the dead and gave him great glory.

[22] You were cleansed from your sins when you obeyed the truth, so now you must show sincere love to each other as brothers and sisters.* Love each other deeply with all your heart.*

[23] For you have been born again, but not to a life that will quickly end. Your new life will last forever because it comes from the eternal, living word of God. [24] As the Scriptures say,

"People are like grass;
    their beauty is like a flower in the field.
The grass withers and the flower fades.
[25]   But the word of the Lord remains forever."*

And that word is the Good News that was preached to you.

2 So get rid of all evil behavior. Be done with all deceit, hypocrisy, jealousy, and all unkind speech. [2] Like newborn babies, you must crave pure spiritual milk so that you will grow into a full experience of salvation. Cry out for this nourishment, [3] now that you have had a taste of the Lord's kindness.

LIVING STONES FOR GOD'S HOUSE

[4] You are coming to Christ, who is the living cornerstone of God's temple. He was rejected by people, but he was chosen by God for great honor.

[5] And you are living stones that God is building into his spiritual temple. What's more, you are his holy priests.* Through the mediation of Jesus Christ, you offer spiritual sacrifices that please God. [6] As the Scriptures say,

"I am placing a cornerstone in Jerusalem,*
    chosen for great honor,
and anyone who trusts in him
    will never be disgraced."*

[7] Yes, you who trust him recognize the honor God has given him.* But for those who reject him,

"The stone that the builders rejected
    has now become the cornerstone."*

[8] And,

"He is the stone that makes
    people stumble,
    the rock that makes them fall."*

1:22a Greek must have brotherly love. 1:22b Some manuscripts read with a pure heart. 1:24-25 Isa 40:6-8. 2:5 Greek holy priesthood. 2:6a Greek in Zion. 2:6b Isa 28:16 (Greek version). 2:7a Or Yes, for you who believe, there is honor. 2:7b Ps 118:22. 2:8 Isa 8:14.

They stumble because they do not obey God's word, and so they meet the fate that was planned for them.

⁹But you are not like that, for you are a chosen people. You are royal priests,* a holy nation, God's very own possession. As a result, you can show others the goodness of God, for he called you out of the darkness into his wonderful light.

¹⁰ "Once you had no identity as a people;
    now you are God's people.
Once you received no mercy;
    now you have received God's mercy."*

¹¹Dear friends, I warn you as "temporary residents and foreigners" to keep away from worldly desires that wage war against your very souls. ¹²Be careful to live properly among your unbelieving neighbors. Then even if they accuse you of doing wrong, they will see your honorable behavior, and they will give honor to God when he judges the world.*

RESPECTING PEOPLE IN AUTHORITY

¹³For the Lord's sake, submit to all human authority—whether the king as head of state, ¹⁴or the officials he has appointed. For the king has sent them to punish those who do wrong and to honor those who do right.

¹⁵It is God's will that your honorable lives should silence those ignorant people who make foolish accusations against you. ¹⁶For you are free, yet you are God's slaves, so don't use your freedom as an excuse to do evil. ¹⁷Respect everyone, and love the family of believers.* Fear God, and respect the king.

SLAVES

¹⁸You who are slaves must submit to your masters with all respect.* Do what they tell you—not only if they are kind and reasonable, but even if they

are cruel. ¹⁹For God is pleased when, conscious of his will, you patiently endure unjust treatment. ²⁰Of course, you get no credit for being patient if you are beaten for doing wrong. But if you suffer for doing good and endure it patiently, God is pleased with you.

²¹For God called you to do good, even if it means suffering, just as Christ suffered* for you. He is your example, and you must follow in his steps.

²² He never sinned,
    nor ever deceived anyone.*
²³ He did not retaliate when
        he was insulted,
    nor threaten revenge when
        he suffered.
He left his case in the hands of God,
    who always judges fairly.
²⁴ He personally carried our sins
    in his body on the cross
so that we can be dead to sin
    and live for what is right.
By his wounds
    you are healed.
²⁵ Once you were like sheep
    who wandered away.
But now you have turned to your Shepherd,
    the Guardian of your souls.

WIVES

3 In the same way, you wives must accept the authority of your husbands. Then, even if some refuse to obey the Good News, your godly lives will speak to them without any words. They will be won over ²by observing your pure and reverent lives.

³Don't be concerned about the outward beauty of fancy hairstyles, expensive jewelry, or beautiful clothes. ⁴You should clothe yourselves instead with the beauty that comes from within, the unfading beauty of a gentle and quiet spirit, which is so precious to God. ⁵This is how the holy women of old made themselves beautiful. They put their trust in God and accepted the authority of their husbands. ⁶For instance, Sarah obeyed her husband, Abraham, and called him her master. You are her daughters when you do what is right without fear of what your husbands might do.

HUSBANDS

⁷In the same way, you husbands must give honor to your wives. Treat your wife with understanding as you live together. She may be weaker than you are, but she is your equal partner in God's gift of new life. Treat her as you should so your prayers will not be hindered.

2:9 Greek *a royal priesthood.* **2:10** Hos 1:6, 9; 2:23. **2:12** Or *on the day of visitation.* **2:17** Greek *love the brotherhood.* **2:18** Or *because you fear God;* Greek reads *in all fear.* **2:21** Some manuscripts read *died.* **2:22** Isa 53:9.

ALL CHRISTIANS

[8] Finally, all of you should be of one mind. Sympathize with each other. Love each other as brothers and sisters.* Be tenderhearted, and keep a humble attitude. [9] Don't repay evil for evil. Don't retaliate with insults when people insult you. Instead, pay them back with a blessing. That is what God has called you to do, and he will grant you his blessing. [10] For the Scriptures say,

"If you want to enjoy life
 and see many happy days,
keep your tongue from speaking evil
 and your lips from telling lies.
[11] Turn away from evil and do good.
 Search for peace, and work to maintain it.
[12] The eyes of the LORD watch over those who
    do right,
 and his ears are open to their prayers.
But the LORD turns his face
 against those who do evil."*

SUFFERING FOR DOING GOOD

[13] Now, who will want to harm you if you are eager to do good? [14] But even if you suffer for doing what is right, God will reward you for it. So don't worry or be afraid of their threats. [15] Instead, you must worship Christ as Lord of your life. And if someone asks about your hope as a believer, always be ready to explain it. [16] But do this in a gentle and respectful way.* Keep your conscience clear. Then if people speak against you, they will be ashamed when they see what a good life you live because you belong to Christ. [17] Remember, it is better to suffer for doing good, if that is what God wants, than to suffer for doing wrong!

[18] Christ suffered* for our sins once for all time. He never sinned, but he died for sinners to bring you safely home to God. He suffered physical death, but he was raised to life in the Spirit.* [19] So he went and preached to the spirits in prison—[20] those who disobeyed God long ago when God waited patiently while Noah was building his boat. Only eight people were saved from drowning in that terrible flood.* [21] And that water is a picture of baptism, which now saves you, not by removing dirt from your body, but as a response to God from* a clean conscience. It is effective because of the resurrection of Jesus Christ.

[22] Now Christ has gone to heaven. He is seated in the place of honor next to God, and all the angels and authorities and powers accept his authority.

LIVING FOR GOD

4 So then, since Christ suffered physical pain, you must arm yourselves with the same attitude he had, and be ready to suffer, too. For if you have suffered physically for Christ, you have finished with sin.* [2] You won't spend the rest of your lives chasing your own desires, but you will be anxious to do the will of God. [3] You have had enough in the past of the evil things that godless people enjoy—their immorality and lust, their feasting and drunkenness and wild parties, and their terrible worship of idols.

[4] Of course, your former friends are surprised when you no longer plunge into the flood of wild and destructive things they do. So they slander you. [5] But remember that they will have to face God, who stands ready to judge everyone, both the living and the dead. [6] That is why the Good News was preached to those who are now dead*—so although they were destined to die like all people,* they now live forever with God in the Spirit.*

[7] The end of the world is coming soon. Therefore, be earnest and disciplined in your prayers. [8] Most important of all, continue to show deep love for each other, for love covers a multitude of sins. [9] Cheerfully share your home with those who need a meal or a place to stay.

[10] God has given each of you a gift from his great variety of spiritual gifts. Use them well to serve one another. [11] Do you have the gift of speaking? Then speak as though God himself were speaking through you. Do you have the gift of helping others? Do it with all the strength and energy that God supplies. Then everything you do will bring glory to God through Jesus Christ. All glory and power to him forever and ever! Amen.

SUFFERING FOR BEING A CHRISTIAN

[12] Dear friends, don't be surprised at the fiery trials you are going through, as if something strange were happening to you. [13] Instead, be very glad—for these trials make you partners with Christ in his suffering, so that you will have the wonderful joy of seeing his glory when it is revealed to all the world.

[14] If you are insulted because you bear the name of Christ, you will be blessed, for the glorious Spirit of God* rests upon you.* [15] If you suffer, however, it must not be for murder, stealing, making trouble, or prying into other people's affairs. [16] But it is no shame to suffer for being a Christian. Praise God for the privilege of being called by his name! [17] For the time has come for judgment, and it must begin with God's household. And if judgment begins with us, what terrible fate awaits those who have never obeyed God's Good News? [18] And also,

"If the righteous are barely saved,
 what will happen to godless sinners?"*

3:8 Greek Show brotherly love.   3:10-12 Ps 34:12-16.   3:16 Some English translations put this sentence in verse 15.   3:18a Some manuscripts read died.   3:18b Or in spirit.   3:20 Greek saved through water.   3:21 Or as an appeal to God for.   4:1 Or For the one [or One] who has suffered physically has finished with sin.   4:6a Greek preached even to the dead.   4:6b Or so although people had judged them worthy of death.   4:6c Or in spirit.   4:14a Or for the glory of God, which is his Spirit.   4:14b Some manuscripts add On their part he is blasphemed, but on your part he is glorified.   4:18 Prov 11:31 (Greek version).

[19] So if you are suffering in a manner that pleases God, keep on doing what is right, and trust your lives to the God who created you, for he will never fail you.

ADVICE FOR ELDERS AND YOUNG MEN

5 And now, a word to you who are elders in the churches. I, too, am an elder and a witness to the sufferings of Christ. And I, too, will share in his glory when he is revealed to the whole world. As a fellow elder, I appeal to you: [2] Care for the flock that God has entrusted to you. Watch over it willingly, not grudgingly—not for what you will get out of it, but because you are eager to serve God. [3] Don't lord it over the people assigned to your care, but lead them by your own good example. [4] And when the Great Shepherd appears, you will receive a crown of never-ending glory and honor.

[5] In the same way, you who are younger must accept the authority of the elders. And all of you, dress yourselves in humility as you relate to one another, for

"God opposes the proud
    but gives grace to the humble."*

[6] So humble yourselves under the mighty power of God, and at the right time he will lift you up in honor. [7] Give all your worries and cares to God, for he cares about you.

[8] Stay alert! Watch out for your great enemy, the devil. He prowls around like a roaring lion, looking for someone to devour. [9] Stand firm against him, and be strong in your faith. Remember that your family of believers* all over the world is going through the same kind of suffering you are.

[10] In his kindness God called you to share in his eternal glory by means of Christ Jesus. So after you have suffered a little while, he will restore, support, and strengthen you, and he will place you on a firm foundation. [11] All power to him forever! Amen.

PETER'S FINAL GREETINGS

[12] I have written and sent this short letter to you with the help of Silas,* whom I commend to you as a faithful brother. My purpose in writing is to encourage you and assure you that what you are experiencing is truly part of God's grace for you. Stand firm in this grace.

[13] Your sister church here in Babylon* sends you greetings, and so does my son Mark. [14] Greet each other with a kiss of love.

Peace be with all of you who are in Christ.

BELIEVERS' BASICS: INTERCESSION
1 Peter 5:6-9   JACK HAYFORD

Intercessory prayer is a resistance movement, which opposes the flow of hell and the works of darkness. Intercessors are vigilant in recognizing God-ordained situations where a need intersects their paths. They understand that our adversary, the devil, "prowls around like a roaring lion, looking for someone to devour" (1 Peter 5:8).

Intercessors step into situations and stand firm against the devil (1 Peter 5:9). The key to standing against the enemy is knowing *where* you stand—on holy ground. Our authority is found through the cross and the blood of Jesus Christ.

Because of what Jesus has already accomplished, God has given authority and victory to all believers. However, driving the enemy into the ground does not usually come easily or quickly. Instead, we must cry out to God, wrestle with the enemy, and pray in the Spirit until we see our divinely appointed victory come to pass.

GIVING ALL YOUR CARES
1 Peter 5:7   ROBERT MORRIS

Has worry ever caused your mind to wander while you're worshipping or reading the Word? Perhaps you just had a fight with your spouse. Or maybe you're having trouble with a friend, or you're worried about your finances.

First Peter 5:7 says, "Give all your worries and cares to God, for he cares about you." I've heard so many people say they give their cares to God over and over again. But how can you *keep* giving something to another person unless you're taking it back each time? When we do this, we're not actually giving our cares to God at all.

The cares of this world can choke out the Word of God in your life if you keep hanging on to them. No matter how strong you are, you are not meant to carry worry. God wants you to have peace, and He is ready to take *all* your cares right now. Just give them to Him.

5:5 Prov 3:34 (Greek version).   5:9 Greek *your brotherhood.*
5:12 Greek *Silvanus.*   5:13 Greek *The elect one in Babylon.* Babylon was probably symbolic for Rome.

2 PETER

JON HUNTZINGER, PHD

Second Peter teaches that behavior and lifestyle matter for followers of Jesus. The apostle writes to those who have received the Holy Spirit and will "share his divine nature" now that they have escaped from the corruption of the world and its sinful desires (1:4). At the same time, he warns them about false prophets who deny Jesus ("the Master," meaning "teacher"), gratify their own desires, and by doing this, blaspheme the way of truth (2:1-2). Peter says God will judge them for their "twisted sexual desires" and rejection of authority (2:10), and for tempting others to join them in their desires of the flesh (2:18). What Peter writes about false teachers and their message of self-gratification is very similar to what Jude writes, which means they both shared a common concern for the negative impact such teaching and behavior could have on the moral life of God's people. The Greek word for *desire* (*epithumia*), which Peter uses in these passages, indicates he is addressing false teaching that emphasizes a person's own individual gratification without regard for others or for God's design for people made in His image. In his second letter, Peter confronts the false teaching that claims such gratification is acceptable and appropriate.

In addition to confronting false teaching, Peter reminds his readers that he did not make up "clever stories" when he proclaimed Jesus to them (1:16). Rather, he reported what he himself had experienced and seen. More important than the stories taught by false teachers is God's word through His prophets, which shines like a lamp and rises like the morning star (Psalm 119:105). God's people can know how to live and what He desires because it has been revealed in the Word of Scripture (*logos*). The word of the prophets in Scripture came from the Spirit of God and not people's imaginations, even as Peter's own testimony is true and not made up.

Not only does God's Word provide understanding for God's people, but it is also the foundation for their faith. Scoffers might dismiss God's prophetic words (*rhēmata*) about Jesus' return from men like Peter, but he urges his readers to trust his words and testimony because they are comparable to the words that brought heaven and earth into existence and continues to sustain all creation (3:1-7). God's Word conveys His will and desire, and it is that desire the people should seek to fulfill as they live as His children and wait for Jesus' return.

GREETINGS FROM PETER

1 This letter is from Simon* Peter, a slave and apostle of Jesus Christ.

I am writing to you who share the same precious faith we have. This faith was given to you because of the justice and fairness* of Jesus Christ, our God and Savior.

[2] May God give you more and more grace and peace as you grow in your knowledge of God and Jesus our Lord.

GROWING IN FAITH

[3] By his divine power, God has given us everything we need for living a godly life. We have received all of this by coming to know him, the one who called us to himself by means of his marvelous glory and excellence. [4] And because of his glory and excellence, he has given us great and precious promises. These are the promises that enable you to share his divine nature and escape the world's corruption caused by human desires.

[5] In view of all this, make every effort to respond to God's promises. Supplement your faith with a generous provision of moral excellence, and moral excellence with knowledge, [6] and knowledge with self-control, and self-control with patient endurance, and patient endurance with godliness, [7] and godliness with brotherly affection, and brotherly affection with love for everyone.

[8] The more you grow like this, the more productive and useful you will be in your knowledge of our Lord Jesus Christ. [9] But those who fail to develop in this way are shortsighted or blind, forgetting that they have been cleansed from their old sins.

[10] So, dear brothers and sisters,* work hard to prove that you really are among those God has called and chosen. Do these things, and you will never fall away. [11] Then God will give you a grand entrance into the eternal Kingdom of our Lord and Savior Jesus Christ.

PAYING ATTENTION TO SCRIPTURE

[12] Therefore, I will always remind you about these things—even though you already know them and are standing firm in the truth you have been taught. [13] And it is only right that I should keep on reminding you as long as I live.* [14] For our Lord Jesus Christ has shown me that I must soon leave this earthly life,* [15] so I will work hard to make sure you always remember these things after I am gone.

[16] For we were not making up clever stories when we told you about the powerful coming of our Lord Jesus Christ. We saw his majestic splendor with our own eyes [17] when he received honor and glory from God the Father. The voice from the majestic glory of God said to him, "This is my dearly loved Son, who brings me great joy."* [18] We ourselves heard that voice from heaven when we were with him on the holy mountain.

[19] Because of that experience, we have even greater confidence in the message proclaimed by the prophets. You must pay close attention to what they wrote, for their words are like a lamp shining in a dark place—until the Day dawns, and Christ the Morning Star shines* in your hearts. [20] Above all, you must realize that no prophecy in Scripture ever came from the prophet's own understanding,* [21] or from human initiative. No, those prophets were moved by the Holy Spirit, and they spoke from God.

THE DANGER OF FALSE TEACHERS

2 But there were also false prophets in Israel, just as there will be false teachers among you. They will cleverly teach destructive heresies and even deny the Master who bought them. In this way, they will bring sudden destruction on themselves. [2] Many will follow their evil teaching and shameful immorality. And because of these teachers, the way of truth will be slandered. [3] In their greed they will make up clever lies to get hold of your money. But God condemned them long ago, and their destruction will not be delayed.

[4] For God did not spare even the angels who sinned. He threw them into hell,* in gloomy pits of darkness,* where they are being held until the day of judgment. [5] And God did not spare the ancient world—except for Noah and the seven others in his family. Noah warned the world of God's righteous judgment. So God protected Noah when he destroyed the world of ungodly people with a vast flood. [6] Later, God condemned the cities of Sodom and Gomorrah and turned them into heaps of ashes. He made them an example of what will happen to ungodly people. [7] But God also rescued Lot out of Sodom because he was a righteous man who was sick of the shameful immorality of the wicked people around him. [8] Yes, Lot was a righteous man who was tormented in his soul by the wickedness he saw and heard day after day. [9] So you see, the Lord knows how to rescue godly people from their trials, even while keeping the wicked under punishment until the day of final judgment. [10] He is especially hard on those who follow their own twisted sexual desire, and who despise authority.

These people are proud and arrogant, daring even to scoff at supernatural beings* without so much as trembling. [11] But the angels, who are far greater in power and strength, do not dare to bring from the Lord* a charge of blasphemy against those supernatural beings.

1:1a Greek *Simeon*. 1:1b Or *to you in the righteousness*. 1:10 Greek *brothers*. 1:13 Greek *as long as I am in this tent* [or *tabernacle*]. 1:14 Greek *I must soon put off my tent* [or *tabernacle*]. 1:17 Matt 17:5; Mark 9:7; Luke 9:35. 1:19 Or *rises*. 1:20 Or *is a matter of one's own interpretation*. 2:4a Greek *Tartarus*. 2:4b Some manuscripts read *in chains of gloom*. 2:10 Greek *at glorious ones*, which are probably evil angels. 2:11 Other manuscripts read *to the Lord;* still others do not include this phrase at all.

¹²These false teachers are like unthinking animals, creatures of instinct, born to be caught and destroyed. They scoff at things they do not understand, and like animals, they will be destroyed. ¹³Their destruction is their reward for the harm they have done. They love to indulge in evil pleasures in broad daylight. They are a disgrace and a stain among you. They delight in deception* even as they eat with you in your fellowship meals. ¹⁴They commit adultery with their eyes, and their desire for sin is never satisfied. They lure unstable people into sin, and they are well trained in greed. They live under God's curse. ¹⁵They have wandered off the right road and followed the footsteps of Balaam son of Beor,* who loved to earn money by doing wrong. ¹⁶But Balaam was stopped from his mad course when his donkey rebuked him with a human voice.

¹⁷These people are as useless as dried-up springs or as mist blown away by the wind. They are doomed to blackest darkness. ¹⁸They brag about themselves with empty, foolish boasting. With an appeal to twisted sexual desires, they lure back into sin those who have barely escaped from a lifestyle of deception. ¹⁹They promise freedom, but they themselves are slaves of sin and corruption. For you are a slave to whatever controls you. ²⁰And when people escape from the wickedness of the world by knowing our Lord and Savior Jesus Christ and then get tangled up and enslaved by sin again, they are worse off than before. ²¹It would be better if they had never known the way to righteousness than to know it and then reject the command they were given to live a holy life. ²²They prove the truth of this proverb: "A dog returns to its vomit."* And another says, "A washed pig returns to the mud."

THE DAY OF THE LORD IS COMING

3 This is my second letter to you, dear friends, and in both of them I have tried to stimulate your wholesome thinking and refresh your memory. ²I want you to remember what the holy prophets said long ago and what our Lord and Savior commanded through your apostles.

³Most importantly, I want to remind you that in the last days scoffers will come, mocking the truth and following their own desires. ⁴They will say, "What happened to the promise that Jesus is coming again? From before the times of our ancestors, everything has remained the same since the world was first created."

⁵They deliberately forget that God made the heavens long ago by the word of his command, and he brought the earth out from the water and surrounded it with water. ⁶Then he used the water to destroy the ancient world with a mighty flood. ⁷And by the same word, the present heavens and earth have been stored up for fire. They are being kept for the day of judgment, when ungodly people will be destroyed.

⁸But you must not forget this one thing, dear friends: A day is like a thousand years to the Lord, and a thousand years is like a day. ⁹The Lord isn't really being slow about his promise, as some people think. No, he is being patient for your sake. He does not want anyone to be destroyed, but wants everyone to repent. ¹⁰But the day of the Lord will come as unexpectedly as a thief. Then the heavens will pass away with a terrible noise, and the very elements themselves will disappear in fire, and the earth and everything on it will be found to deserve judgment.*

¹¹Since everything around us is going to be destroyed like this, what holy and godly lives you should live, ¹²looking forward to the day of God and hurrying it along. On that day, he will set the heavens on fire, and the elements will melt away in the flames. ¹³But we are looking forward to the new heavens and new earth he has promised, a world filled with God's righteousness.

¹⁴And so, dear friends, while you are waiting for these things to happen, make every effort to be found living peaceful lives that are pure and blameless in his sight.

¹⁵And remember, our Lord's patience gives people time to be saved. This is what our beloved brother Paul also wrote to you with the wisdom God gave him—¹⁶speaking of these things in all of his letters. Some of his comments are hard to understand, and those who are ignorant and unstable have twisted his letters to mean something quite different, just as they do with other parts of Scripture. And this will result in their destruction.

PETER'S FINAL WORDS

¹⁷You already know these things, dear friends. So be on guard; then you will not be carried away by the errors of these wicked people and lose your own secure footing. ¹⁸Rather, you must grow in the grace and knowledge of our Lord and Savior Jesus Christ.

All glory to him, both now and forever! Amen.

2:13 Some manuscripts read *in fellowship meals.* 2:15 Some manuscripts read *Bosor.* 2:22 Prov 26:11. 3:10 Other manuscripts read *will be burned up;* one early manuscript reads *will be found destroyed.*

THE LETTERS OF JOHN

JON HUNTZINGER, PHD

Early church tradition consistently identifies John, the disciple of Jesus and son of Zebedee, as the author of the three letters attributed to him in the New Testament. Given the connections between these letters and the Gospel of John, which he likely wrote, it is probable that he composed them about the same time as his Gospel in the years after the destruction of the Temple. The affection he has for his readers is apparent from his description of them as "dear children" (1 John 2:1, 18, 28; 3:7; 4:4; 5:21) and "dear friends" (1 John 2:7; 3:2, 21; 4:1, 7, 11; 3 John 2, 5, 11). John's designation of his readers as *dear friends* is especially significant since it recalls how he referred to himself in his Gospel as *the disciple loved by Jesus*. The words are the same in the Greek language in which the books were originally written. This designation shows that he sees them as he saw himself—as recipients of God's great love through His Son.

Though 2 and 3 John are letters addressed to specific people, 1 John is not addressed as a letter to anyone and is thought by some people to be a sermon John delivered to all of those under his spiritual care. Whether written originally as a letter or a sermon, the book shows a strong relationship with the Gospel of John:

— In both, Jesus is identified as the "Word" who came in physical form (1 John 1:1; John 1:1-2, 14).
— God gives His people "eternal life" through His Son (1 John 1:2; 5:11-13; John 3:16).
— Jesus laid down His life for them (1 John 3:16; John 10:11-18).
— God sent His son to save the world (1 John 4:14; John 3:17).
— People who believe in the Son are born of God and are His children (1 John 2:29; 3:9; 5:4; John 1:13).
— Life with God and life apart from Him are depicted through the imagery of light and darkness (1 John 1:5-7; 2:9-11; John 1:4-9; 8:12).
— Those who do not confess Jesus as the Son or show love in their life belong to the world (1 John 2:16; 4:2-5; John 8:23).
— Those kinds of people live in darkness (1 John 1:6, 2:11; John 8:12; 12:35).

John has been described as the "apostle of love" because of the emphasis he gives to love in the Gospel of John and in 1 John. If 1 John is a sermon, it is a message that is unified by the theme of love. John says God is love (4:8), and the first thing his people learned when they came to faith is the commandment to "love one another" (2:7-10; 3:11, 23-24; 4:7-12). Such love is defined as laying down one's life for others (3:16) and is based in the love

God demonstrated by sending His Son to forgive people of their sins (4:9-10). To live a life of devotion to others is to live or to abide in God and is confirmation of the life they have with Him (3:23-24). Anyone who does not love in this way does not know God and does not live in relationship with Him (2:9-11; 4:20). Thus, John exhorts the people to walk in the light of understanding who God is by loving as He loves. When they love in this way, they will be free from fear and condemnation (3:19-24; 4:18).

Not only is God love, but John writes God is light (1:5), which means God helps His people know how to live by giving them commandments by which they should live and follow. The new commandment John writes about is the old commandment to love one another, which they "have had from the very beginning" (2:7), meaning from the time they came to faith. This commandment goes back to Jesus' teaching the night before His crucifixion when He urged His disciples to keep His commandments, to love one another, and to abide in Him with the help of the Spirit (John 13-17). Thus, when John writes, "And this is his commandment: We must believe in the name of his Son, Jesus Christ, and love one another, just as he commanded us. Those who obey God's commandments remain in fellowship with him, and he with them. And we know he lives in us because the Spirit he gave us lives in us" (1 John 3:23-24), he is recalling Jesus' last teaching, which John recorded in his Gospel. Jesus' "last words" have become the beginning and definitive words that speak to John's followers.

The same connection exists between the short letters of 2 and 3 John and the Gospel of John. The letter of 2 John is addressed to "the chosen lady and to her children" (v. 1), a different congregation from that of 1 John. He urges them to walk in the commandment they have had from the beginning to love one another (vv. 5-6) and to remain in Jesus' teaching to love one another (vv. 9-10). John says to know the truth is to know that Jesus came in the flesh as a real human being (v. 7). As in 1 John, life with God is lived out in love for other people. Any other way of life, John says, is false and not the truth Jesus showed.

The letter of 3 John is written to an individual believer, Gaius, who is walking in the truth and showing love in his life (vv. 3-4). The help he shows to others (vv. 5-6) is an example of the commandment John writes about in his Gospel and in 1 and 2 John. The commandment to love one another that John emphasizes in those books is being challenged by a member, Diotrephes, who "loves to be the leader" (v. 9). He apparently is more interested in his own welfare than in that of others. This way of leading is the antithesis of the love for one another that John emphasizes in his writings and something he will confront when he meets with them the next time.

1 JOHN

INTRODUCTION

1 We proclaim to you the one who existed from the beginning,* whom we have heard and seen. We saw him with our own eyes and touched him with our own hands. He is the Word of life. ²This one who is life itself was revealed to us, and we have seen him. And now we testify and proclaim to you that he is the one who is eternal life. He was with the Father, and then he was revealed to us. ³We proclaim to you what we ourselves have actually seen and heard so that you may have fellowship with us. And our fellowship is with the Father and with his Son, Jesus Christ. ⁴We are writing these things so that you may fully share our joy.*

LIVING IN THE LIGHT

⁵This is the message we heard from Jesus* and now declare to you: God is light, and there is no darkness in him at all. ⁶So we are lying if we say we have fellowship with God but go on living in spiritual darkness; we are not practicing the truth. ⁷But if we are living in the light, as God is in the light, then we have fellowship with each other, and the blood of Jesus, his Son, cleanses us from all sin.

⁸If we claim we have no sin, we are only fooling ourselves and not living in the truth. ⁹But if we confess our sins to him, he is faithful and just to forgive us our sins and to cleanse us from all wickedness. ¹⁰If we claim we have not sinned, we are calling God a liar and showing that his word has no place in our hearts.

2 My dear children, I am writing this to you so that you will not sin. But if anyone does sin, we have an advocate who pleads our case before the Father. He is Jesus Christ, the one who is truly righteous. ²He himself is the sacrifice that atones for our sins—and not only our sins but the sins of all the world.

³And we can be sure that we know him if we obey his commandments. ⁴If someone claims, "I know God," but doesn't obey God's commandments, that person is a liar and is not living in the truth. ⁵But those who obey God's word truly show how completely they love him. That is how we know we are living in him. ⁶Those who say they live in God should live their lives as Jesus did.

A NEW COMMANDMENT

⁷Dear friends, I am not writing a new commandment for you; rather it is an old one you have had from the very beginning. This old commandment—to love one another—is the same message you heard before. ⁸Yet it is also new. Jesus lived the truth of this commandment, and you also are living it. For the darkness is disappearing, and the true light is already shining.

⁹If anyone claims, "I am living in the light," but hates a fellow believer,* that person is still living in darkness. ¹⁰Anyone who loves a fellow believer* is living in the light and does not cause others to stumble. ¹¹But anyone who hates a fellow believer is still living and walking in darkness. Such a person does not know the way to go, having been blinded by the darkness.

LIGHT DISPELS DARKNESS
1 John 1:5-7   ROBERT MORRIS

When you're in sin or running from God, the last thing you want to do is read the Bible. However, reading the Bible is actually the *first* thing you need to do. Why? Because light dispels darkness. First John 1:5-7 says,

God is light, and there is no darkness in him at all. So we are lying if we say we have fellowship with God but go on living in spiritual darkness . . . But if we are living in the light, as God is in the light, then we have fellowship with each other, and the blood of Jesus, his Son, cleanses us from all sin.

When you turn a light switch on, there's no argument between light and darkness. The light comes, and the darkness instantly leaves. If you want to get out of a dark place in your life, the best thing you can do is read God's Word.

1:1 Greek *What was from the beginning.* 1:4 Or *so that our joy may be complete;* some manuscripts read *your joy.* 1:5 Greek *from him.* 2:9 Greek *hates his brother;* also in 2:11. 2:10 Greek *loves his brother.*

¹² I am writing to you who are God's children
because your sins have been forgiven
through Jesus.*
¹³ I am writing to you who are mature
in the faith*
because you know Christ, who existed
from the beginning.
I am writing to you who are young
in the faith
because you have won your battle with
the evil one.
¹⁴ I have written to you who are
God's children
because you know the Father.
I have written to you who are mature
in the faith
because you know Christ, who existed
from the beginning.
I have written to you who are young
in the faith
because you are strong.
God's word lives in your hearts,
and you have won your battle with
the evil one.

DO NOT LOVE THIS WORLD

¹⁵ Do not love this world nor the things it offers you, for when you love the world, you do not have the love of the Father in you. ¹⁶ For the world offers only a craving for physical pleasure, a craving for everything we see, and pride in our achievements and possessions. These are not from the Father, but are from this world. ¹⁷ And this world is fading away, along with everything that people crave. But anyone who does what pleases God will live forever.

WARNING ABOUT ANTICHRISTS

¹⁸ Dear children, the last hour is here. You have heard that the Antichrist is coming, and already many such antichrists have appeared. From this we know that the last hour has come. ¹⁹ These people left our churches, but they never really belonged with us; otherwise they would have stayed with us. When they left, it proved that they did not belong with us. ²⁰ But you are not like that, for the Holy One has given you his Spirit,* and all of you know the truth. ²¹ So I am writing to you not because you don't know the truth but because you know the difference between truth and lies. ²² And who is a liar? Anyone who says that Jesus is not the Christ.* Anyone who denies the Father and the Son is an antichrist.* ²³ Anyone who denies the Son doesn't have the Father, either. But anyone who acknowledges the Son has the Father also. ²⁴ So you must remain faithful to what you have been taught from the beginning. If you do, you will remain in fellowship with the Son and with the Father. ²⁵ And in this fellowship we enjoy the eternal life he promised us.

CREATED FOR PASSION
1 John 2:16   ROBERT MORRIS

When I was in my 20s, I fell in love with God. I still had a lot of junk to deal with, though, because I had been a very immoral person before I got saved. I shared my struggles with my pastor, Olen Griffing, and asked for help. He looked at me, put his hands on my head, and prayed, "Father, I pray that You will cause Robert to fall *passionately* in love with You. In Jesus' name, Amen." Then he just walked away. That prayer changed my life.

The enemy often tries to choke us and keep us from the Word of God by giving us a desire for other things. However, the *only* thing that can satisfy the human soul is God. First John 2:16 says, "The world offers only a craving for physical pleasure, a craving for everything we see, and pride in our achievements and possessions. These are not from the Father, but are from the world." The word *craving* can also be translated as *lust*, which comes from the Greek word *epithumia*. This word actually means 'passion.' God created you with passion, but Satan twists it into lust. We're supposed to be passionate about God and people. Satan turns it to lust for the wrong people in the wrong way and for wrong things.

The morning after Pastor Olen prayed for me, the Lord spoke to me and said, "Son, it's a *passion* for Me that drives out lust for others." It's that simple. Pursue the Lord—not so you can check it off your list, but so you can fall passionately in love with the One who is passionate for you.

²⁶ I am writing these things to warn you about those who want to lead you astray. ²⁷ But you have received the Holy Spirit,* and he lives within you, so you don't need anyone to teach you what is true. For the Spirit* teaches you everything you need to know, and what he teaches is true—it is not a lie. So just as he has taught you, remain in fellowship with Christ.

LIVING AS CHILDREN OF GOD

²⁸ And now, dear children, remain in fellowship with Christ so that when he returns, you will be full of courage and not shrink back from him in shame.

²⁹ Since we know that Christ is righteous, we also know that all who do what is right are God's children.

2:12 Greek *through his name.*   2:13 Or *to you fathers;* also in 2:14.
2:20 Greek *But you have an anointing from the Holy One.*   2:22a Or *not the Messiah.*   2:22b Or *the antichrist.*   2:27a Greek *the anointing from him.*   2:27b Greek *the anointing.*

3 See how very much our Father loves us, for he calls us his children, and that is what we are! But the people who belong to this world don't recognize that we are God's children because they don't know him. ² Dear friends, we are already God's children, but he has not yet shown us what we will be like when Christ appears. But we do know that we will be like him, for we will see him as he really is. ³ And all who have this eager expectation will keep themselves pure, just as he is pure.

⁴ Everyone who sins is breaking God's law, for all sin is contrary to the law of God. ⁵ And you know that Jesus came to take away our sins, and there is no sin in him. ⁶ Anyone who continues to live in him will not sin. But anyone who keeps on sinning does not know him or understand who he is.

⁷ Dear children, don't let anyone deceive you about this: When people do what is right, it shows that they are righteous, even as Christ is righteous. ⁸ But when people keep on sinning, it shows that they belong to the devil, who has been sinning since the beginning. But the Son of God came to destroy the works of the devil. ⁹ Those who have been born into God's family do not make a practice of sinning, because God's life* is in them. So they can't keep on sinning, because they are children of God. ¹⁰ So now we can tell who are children of God and who are children of the devil. Anyone who does not live righteously and does not love other believers* does not belong to God.

LOVE ONE ANOTHER

¹¹ This is the message you have heard from the beginning: We should love one another. ¹² We must not be like Cain, who belonged to the evil one and killed his brother. And why did he kill him? Because Cain had been doing what was evil, and his brother had been doing what was righteous. ¹³ So don't be surprised, dear brothers and sisters,* if the world hates you.

¹⁴ If we love our brothers and sisters who are believers,* it proves that we have passed from death to life. But a person who has no love is still dead. ¹⁵ Anyone who hates another brother or sister* is really a murderer at heart. And you know that murderers don't have eternal life within them.

¹⁶ We know what real love is because Jesus gave up his life for us. So we also ought to give up our lives for our brothers and sisters. ¹⁷ If someone has enough money to live well and sees a brother or sister* in need but shows no compassion—how can God's love be in that person?

¹⁸ Dear children, let's not merely say that we love each other; let us show the truth by our actions. ¹⁹ Our actions will show that we belong to the truth, so we will be confident when we stand before God. ²⁰ Even if we feel guilty, God is greater than our feelings, and he knows everything.

²¹ Dear friends, if we don't feel guilty, we can come to God with bold confidence. ²² And we will receive from him whatever we ask because we obey him and do the things that please him.

²³ And this is his commandment: We must believe in the name of his Son, Jesus Christ, and love one another, just as he commanded us. ²⁴ Those who obey God's commandments remain in fellowship with him, and he with them. And we know he lives in us because the Spirit he gave us lives in us.

DISCERNING FALSE PROPHETS

4 Dear friends, do not believe everyone who claims to speak by the Spirit. You must test them to see if the spirit they have comes from God. For there are many false prophets in the world. ² This is how we know if they have the Spirit of God: If a person claiming to be a prophet* acknowledges that Jesus Christ came in a real body, that person has the Spirit of God. ³ But if someone claims to be a prophet and does not acknowledge the truth about Jesus, that person is not from God. Such a person has the spirit of the Antichrist, which you heard is coming into the world and indeed is already here.

⁴ But you belong to God, my dear children. You have already won a victory over those people, because the Spirit who lives in you is greater than the spirit who lives in the world. ⁵ Those people belong to this world, so they speak from the world's viewpoint, and the world listens to them. ⁶ But we belong to God, and those who know God listen to us. If they do not belong to God, they do not listen to us. That is how we know if someone has the Spirit of truth or the spirit of deception.

LOVING ONE ANOTHER

⁷ Dear friends, let us continue to love one another, for love comes from God. Anyone who loves is a child of God and knows God. ⁸ But anyone who does not love does not know God, for God is love.

⁹ God showed how much he loved us by sending his one and only Son into the world so that we might have eternal life through him. ¹⁰ This is real love—not that we loved God, but that he loved us and sent his Son as a sacrifice to take away our sins.

¹¹ Dear friends, since God loved us that much, we surely ought to love each other. ¹² No one has ever seen God. But if we love each other, God lives in us, and his love is brought to full expression in us.

¹³ And God has given us his Spirit as proof that we live in him and he in us. ¹⁴ Furthermore, we have seen with our own eyes and now testify that the Father sent his Son to be the Savior of

3:9 Greek because his seed. 3:10 Greek does not love his brother. 3:13 Greek brothers. 3:14 Greek the brothers; similarly in 3:16. 3:15 Greek hates his brother. 3:17 Greek sees his brother. 4:2 Greek If a spirit; similarly in 4:3.

the world. [15]All who declare that Jesus is the Son of God have God living in them, and they live in God. [16]We know how much God loves us, and we have put our trust in his love.

God is love, and all who live in love live in God, and God lives in them. [17]And as we live in God, our love grows more perfect. So we will not be afraid on the day of judgment, but we can face him with confidence because we live like Jesus here in this world.

[18]Such love has no fear, because perfect love expels all fear. If we are afraid, it is for fear of punishment, and this shows that we have not fully experienced his perfect love. [19]We love each other* because he loved us first.

[20]If someone says, "I love God," but hates a fellow believer,* that person is a liar; for if we don't love people we can see, how can we love God, whom we cannot see? [21]And he has given us this command: Those who love God must also love their fellow believers.*

FAITH IN THE SON OF GOD

5 Everyone who believes that Jesus is the Christ* has become a child of God. And everyone who loves the Father loves his children, too. [2]We know we love God's children if we love God and obey his commandments. [3]Loving God means keeping his commandments, and his commandments are not burdensome. [4]For every child of God defeats this evil world, and we achieve this victory through our faith. [5]And who can win this battle against the world? Only those who believe that Jesus is the Son of God.

[6]And Jesus Christ was revealed as God's Son by his baptism in water and by shedding his blood on the cross*—not by water only, but by water and blood. And the Spirit, who is truth, confirms it with his testimony. [7]So we have these three witnesses*—[8]the Spirit, the water, and the blood—and all three agree. [9]Since we believe human testimony, surely we can believe the greater testimony that comes from God. And God has testified about his Son. [10]All who believe

in the Son of God know in their hearts that this testimony is true. Those who don't believe this are actually calling God a liar because they don't believe what God has testified about his Son. [11]And this is what God has testified: He has given us eternal life, and this life is in his Son. [12]Whoever has the Son has life; whoever does not have God's Son does not have life.

CONCLUSION

[13]I have written this to you who believe in the name of the Son of God, so that you may know you have eternal life. [14]And we are confident that he hears us whenever we ask for anything that pleases him. [15]And since we know he hears us when we make our requests, we also know that he will give us what we ask for.

[16]If you see a fellow believer* sinning in a way that does not lead to death, you should pray, and God will give that person life. But there is a sin that leads to death, and I am not saying you should pray for those who commit it. [17]All wicked actions are sin, but not every sin leads to death.

[18]We know that God's children do not make a practice of sinning, for God's Son holds them securely, and the evil one cannot touch them. [19]We know that we are children of God and that the world around us is under the control of the evil one.

[20]And we know that the Son of God has come, and he has given us understanding so that we can know the true God.* And now we live in fellowship with the true God because we live in fellowship with his Son, Jesus Christ. He is the only true God, and he is eternal life.

[21]Dear children, keep away from anything that might take God's place in your hearts.*

4:19 Greek We love. Other manuscripts read We love God; still others read We love him.   4:20 Greek hates his brother.
4:21 Greek The one who loves God must also love his brother.
5:1 Or the Messiah.   5:6 Greek This is he who came by water and blood.   5:7 A few very late manuscripts add in heaven—the Father, the Word, and the Holy Spirit, and these three are one. And we have three witnesses on earth.   5:16 Greek a brother.   5:20 Greek the one who is true.   5:21 Greek keep yourselves from idols.

2 JOHN

GREETINGS

This letter is from John, the elder.*

I am writing to the chosen lady and to her children,* whom I love in the truth—as does everyone else who knows the truth—²because the truth lives in us and will be with us forever.

³Grace, mercy, and peace, which come from God the Father and from Jesus Christ—the Son of the Father—will continue to be with us who live in truth and love.

LIVE IN THE TRUTH

⁴How happy I was to meet some of your children and find them living according to the truth, just as the Father commanded.

⁵I am writing to remind you, dear friends,* that we should love one another. This is not a new commandment, but one we have had from the beginning. ⁶Love means doing what God has commanded us, and he has commanded us to love one another, just as you heard from the beginning.

⁷I say this because many deceivers have gone out into the world. They deny that Jesus Christ came* in a real body. Such a person is a deceiver and an antichrist. ⁸Watch out that you do not lose what we* have worked so hard to achieve. Be diligent so that you receive your full reward. ⁹Anyone who wanders away from this teaching has no relationship with God. But anyone who remains in the teaching of Christ has a relationship with both the Father and the Son.

¹⁰If anyone comes to your meeting and does not teach the truth about Christ, don't invite that person into your home or give any kind of encouragement. ¹¹Anyone who encourages such people becomes a partner in their evil work.

CONCLUSION

¹²I have much more to say to you, but I don't want to do it with paper and ink. For I hope to visit you soon and talk with you face to face. Then our joy will be complete.

¹³Greetings from the children of your sister,* chosen by God.

1a Greek *From the elder.*   **1b** Or *the church God has chosen and its members.*   **5** Greek *I urge you, lady.*   **7** Or *will come.*   **8** Some manuscripts read *you.*   **13** Or *from the members of your sister church.*

— 3 JOHN —

GREETINGS

This letter is from John, the elder.*

I am writing to Gaius, my dear friend, whom I love in the truth.

² Dear friend, I hope all is well with you and that you are as healthy in body as you are strong in spirit. ³ Some of the traveling teachers* recently returned and made me very happy by telling me about your faithfulness and that you are living according to the truth. ⁴ I could have no greater joy than to hear that my children are following the truth.

CARING FOR THE LORD'S WORKERS

⁵ Dear friend, you are being faithful to God when you care for the traveling teachers who pass through, even though they are strangers to you. ⁶ They have told the church here of your loving friendship. Please continue providing for such teachers in a manner that pleases God. ⁷ For they are traveling for the Lord,* and they accept nothing from people who are not believers.* ⁸ So we ourselves should support them so that we can be their partners as they teach the truth.

⁹ I wrote to the church about this, but Diotrephes, who loves to be the leader, refuses to have anything to do with us. ¹⁰ When I come, I will report some of the things he is doing and the evil accusations he is making against us. Not only does he refuse to welcome the traveling teachers, he also tells others not to help them. And when they do help, he puts them out of the church.

¹¹ Dear friend, don't let this bad example influence you. Follow only what is good. Remember that those who do good prove that they are God's children, and those who do evil prove that they do not know God.*

¹² Everyone speaks highly of Demetrius, as does the truth itself. We ourselves can say the same for him, and you know we speak the truth.

CONCLUSION

¹³ I have much more to say to you, but I don't want to write it with pen and ink. ¹⁴ For I hope to see you soon, and then we will talk face to face.

¹⁵*Peace be with you.

Your friends here send you their greetings. Please give my personal greetings to each of our friends there.

---

1 Greek *From the elder.*   3 Greek *the brothers;* also in verses 5 and 10.   7a Greek *They went out on behalf of the Name.*   7b Greek *from Gentiles.*   11 Greek *they have not seen God.*   15 Some English translations combine verses 14 and 15 into verse 14.

JUDE

JON HUNTZINGER, PHD

Though Jude is one of the shortest books in the New Testament, it is also one of the most fascinating with its references to angels bound by chains, its allusion to the fight over Moses' body by the archangel Michael and the devil, and its use of the book of Enoch to underscore the judgment of God through His Son, Jesus. Jude, a brother of James and Jesus, wrote the book. He does not identify himself as a brother of Jesus, but as "a slave of Jesus Christ and a brother of James" (v. 1) out of respect to his half-brother, who is also his Lord. The name *Jude* is an English version of 'Judas.' Most English translations use the name Jude to differentiate the writer of the letter from the other Judases in the New Testament, including the two disciples of Jesus named Judas.

Jude's brief letter is dense with biblical allusions as he warns his readers against teachers who argue God's grace means freedom from sexual restraint and fidelity. He refers to the story of the Exodus, the time before the great Flood (Genesis 6:1–8), and the story of Sodom and Gomorrah (Genesis 19:23–29). Jude says that God's grace did not spare the Israelites from judgment in the wilderness when they disbelieved His promise to give them a new land; nor did His grace keep Him from judging angels who abused their place of authority or the people of Sodom and Gomorrah for their sexual immorality. He reminds his readers that God expects His people to live by the standards He has given them, and He will judge them when they do not live by those standards.

Such teachers actually blaspheme, Jude says, which means they show disregard for God and the holy way He has given His people to live. The example he provides for this important point is taken from a Jewish writing not found in the Bible, which describes a fight between the devil and

God's angel over Moses' body after he died on Mount Nebo (Deuteronomy 34:7). In Jude's mind, it was blasphemous for the devil to try to take Moses' body after he died, and it is blasphemous for teachers to misrepresent God's grace as freedom to do anything they want.

The story of Moses' body alluded to by Jude reveals he believed it to be true. Many Jewish books written during the biblical period were not included in the Bible. However, that does not mean they were unimportant; rather, the people at that time did not think they were specially inspired by God in the same way as the Torah, the Psalms, or prophets like Isaiah were. The fact that Jude knows of this book and the book of Enoch that he quotes later in the letter means he found them important, even if he did not think they were inspired Scripture. Under the guidance of the Holy Spirit, Jude was able to discern what was useful and what was not for teaching his people from books such as these. The Holy Spirit knows what is true and what is false, and He helped Jude determine this when he wrote his letter.

Jude continues to draw on various biblical stories to support his points when he recalls Cain and the later story of Korah. Both of these men acted against God's Word, which was directly given in Cain's case (Genesis 4:1–16) and given through Moses in Korah's case (Numbers 16). Jude warns his readers that the blasphemous behavior he has described rejects the holy standard God gave to them, and it will lead to judgment (vv. 14–15).

Jude concludes his book with an exhilarating doxology or prayer of praise that speaks to the greatness of Jesus' ministry and the glory and power of God as eternal, "before all time, and in the present, and beyond all time" (vv. 24–25).

GREETINGS FROM JUDE

This letter is from Jude, a slave of Jesus Christ and a brother of James.

I am writing to all who have been called by God the Father, who loves you and keeps you safe in the care of Jesus Christ.*

[2] May God give you more and more mercy, peace, and love.

THE DANGER OF FALSE TEACHERS

[3] Dear friends, I had been eagerly planning to write to you about the salvation we all share. But now I find that I must write about something else, urging you to defend the faith that God has entrusted once for all time to his holy people. [4] I say this because some ungodly people have wormed their way into your churches, saying that God's marvelous grace allows us to live immoral lives. The condemnation of such people was recorded long ago, for they have denied our only Master and Lord, Jesus Christ.

[5] So I want to remind you, though you already know these things, that Jesus* first rescued the nation of Israel from Egypt, but later he destroyed those who did not remain faithful. [6] And I remind you of the angels who did not stay within the limits of authority God gave them but left the place where they belonged. God has kept them securely chained in prisons of darkness, waiting for the great day of judgment. [7] And don't forget Sodom and Gomorrah and their neighboring towns, which were filled with immorality and every kind of sexual perversion. Those cities were destroyed by fire and serve as a warning of the eternal fire of God's judgment.

[8] In the same way, these people—who claim authority from their dreams—live immoral lives, defy authority, and scoff at supernatural beings.* [9] But even Michael, one of the mightiest of the angels,* did not dare accuse the devil of blasphemy, but simply said, "The Lord rebuke you!" (This took place when Michael was arguing with the devil about Moses' body.) [10] But these people scoff at things they do not understand. Like unthinking animals, they do whatever their instincts tell them, and so they bring about their own destruction. [11] What sorrow awaits them! For they follow in the footsteps of Cain, who killed his brother. Like Balaam, they deceive people for money. And like Korah, they perish in their rebellion.

[12] When these people eat with you in your fellowship meals commemorating the Lord's love, they are like dangerous reefs that can shipwreck you.* They are like shameless shepherds who care only for themselves. They are like clouds blowing over the land without giving any rain. They are like trees in autumn that are doubly dead, for they bear no fruit and have been pulled up by the roots. [13] They are like wild waves of the sea, churning up the foam of their shameful deeds. They are like wandering stars, doomed forever to blackest darkness.

[14] Enoch, who lived in the seventh generation after Adam, prophesied about these people. He said, "Listen! The Lord is coming with countless thousands of his holy ones [15] to execute judgment on the people of the world. He will convict every person of all the ungodly things they have done and for all the insults that ungodly sinners have spoken against him."* [16] These people are grumblers and complainers, living only to satisfy their desires. They brag loudly about themselves, and they flatter others to get what they want.

A CALL TO REMAIN FAITHFUL

[17] But you, my dear friends, must remember what the apostles of our Lord Jesus Christ predicted. [18] They told you that in the last times there would be scoffers whose purpose in life is to satisfy their ungodly desires. [19] These people are the ones who are creating divisions among you. They follow their natural instincts because they do not have God's Spirit in them.

[20] But you, dear friends, must build each other up in your most holy faith, pray in the power of the Holy Spirit,* [21] and await the mercy of our Lord Jesus Christ, who will bring you eternal life. In this way, you will keep yourselves safe in God's love.

[22] And you must show mercy to* those whose faith is wavering. [23] Rescue others by snatching them from the flames of judgment. Show mercy to still others,* but do so with great caution, hating the sins that contaminate their lives.*

A PRAYER OF PRAISE

[24] Now all glory to God, who is able to keep you from falling away and will bring you with great joy into his glorious presence without a single fault. [25] All glory to him who alone is God, our Savior through Jesus Christ our Lord. All glory, majesty, power, and authority are his before all time, and in the present, and beyond all time! Amen.

---

1 Or *keeps you for Jesus Christ.*   5 Other manuscripts read *[the] Lord,* or *God,* or *God Christ.*   8 Greek *at glorious ones,* which are probably evil angels.   9 Greek *Michael, the archangel.*   12 Or *they are contaminants among you;* or *they are stains.*   14-15 The quotation comes from intertestamental literature: 1 Enoch 1:9.   20 Greek *pray in the Holy Spirit.*   22 Some manuscripts read *must reprove.*   22-23a Some manuscripts have only two categories of people: (1) those whose faith is wavering and therefore need to be snatched from the flames of judgment, and (2) those who need to be shown mercy.   23b Greek *with fear, hating even the clothing stained by the flesh.*

REVELATION

JON HUNTZINGER, PHD

From the time it was written in the late first century, Christians have attributed the book of Revelation to the apostle John. Revelation contains thematic similarities to John's Gospel:

— In the New Testament, only Revelation and John's Gospel refer to Jesus as "the Word" (John 1:14; Revelation 19:13). They also describe Him as "the Lamb" (John 1:29, 36; Revelation 5:6 and 28 times in other passages).

— Both Revelation and John's Gospel give an unusual number of titles to Jesus in addition to that of "Word" and "Lamb." In Revelation, Jesus is the Alpha and Omega (1:8; 22:13), the Almighty (1:8), the Lion of the tribe of Judah (5:5), the source of David (22:16), the King of all kings and Lord of all lords (19:16), and the bright morning star (22:16). In the Gospel of John, Jesus is the I Am (meaning He is the Bread of Life, the Light of the World, the Good Shepherd, the Resurrection and the Life, the Way, the Truth, and the Life, and the True Grapevine of the branches) (chapters 6; 8; 10; 11; 14; 15).

— Moreover, both Revelation and John describe Jesus as the One who quenches thirst by giving "living water" and who satisfies hunger by giving His own life (John 4:10; 6:35; Revelation 7:16–17).

— Both books predict the persecution of the Church (John 15:18–16:4; Revelation 3:10; 13:7) and the ultimate union of the Church with God (John 17:11, 20–26; Revelation 21:3; 22:3–5).

According to Revelation, John is not only an *apostle*, which means 'one who is sent,' but also a prophet (1:3; 22:9–10). He is conscious of his responsibility to speak God's message (22:18–19) and does so as someone who shares in the suffering of fellow believers as he writes from the island of Patmos in the Aegean Sea, where he lives in exile (1:9). John is familiar with the distinctive situations in each of the seven churches of Asia he addresses (2:1–3:22) and writes as one who exercises authority among them. He also possesses a broad knowledge of the Hebrew Scriptures, making more than 400 allusions to the Torah, Prophets, and Psalms. Thus, he reports the vision Jesus gave him as one who knows the people with whom he shares it. He sees his vision supported by the words of Scripture that God has given in the past.

The Greek word for revelation is *apokalypsis*, which means 'disclosure.' The vision the book preserves discloses what God is doing and will do in the life of His people and in the world. God knows His own plans and is bringing those plans to fulfillment. John's vision can be difficult to understand because of the fantastic imagery and many numbers John uses to report what he sees. What is the meaning of seals, trumpets, and bowls? Who are the dragon, the beast, and the woman dressed in purple and red? Why are there 144,000 people with the name of the Lamb on their foreheads? What is the meaning of 12 gates in the New Jerusalem? All of this may seem confusing, but the book is not intended to confuse or upset anyone who hears or reads it. It is not John's intention to cause misgiving or apprehension through this revelation from Jesus. It is his intention, however, for readers to interact thoughtfully with the vision he gives, which is why he reports that Jesus pronounces a blessing upon everyone who reads and hears its message (1:3; 22:7). This statement recalls what Jesus told His disciples when He taught them the parable of the farmer scattering seed: "Anyone with ears to hear should listen and understand" (Mark 4:9). In other words, those who heard His parables were responsible for thinking about their meaning. Revelation is like a parable in that it requires those who read or hear it to do so carefully and humbly.

Jesus is the subject of the book of Revelation. John sees Jesus walking in the midst of seven lampstands (1:12–16); he sees Jesus standing by the throne of God opening the seals of a scroll (5:6–14); and he sees Jesus riding a white horse (19:11–16). From beginning to end, Jesus is depicted as holy, powerful, and victorious. John hears Jesus say that He is "the Alpha and the Omega" (1:8; 22:13); he hears Jesus say to His churches, "I know . . ." (nine times in 2:1–3:22); and he hears Jesus say that He will soon return to His followers on earth (22:7, 12, 20). Jesus knows who He is, who His people are, and what He is doing. In addition to this, Jesus' appearance is mesmerizing. He radiates glory (1:14–16), wears a robe "dipped in blood" (19:13) with the name "King of all kings and Lord of all lords" on it (19:16), and even appears as a sacrificed lamb (5:6). When Jesus speaks, John sees a sword come out of His mouth (1:16; 19:15; also 2:16), and he hears a voice that sounds like "mighty ocean waves" (1:15). It is an appearance that reveals holiness, humility, and awesome authority. Finally, Jesus receives the worship of angels, elders, saints, and all creatures (5:6–14). He is worthy because He has ransomed people for God and made them a kingdom of priests for Him (5:10).

Bible scholars have outlined Revelation in many ways. The most helpful outline is based on the three times John says he was "in the Spirit" (1:10; 4:2; 21:10). For John to be "in the Spirit" means God's Spirit was with him in a special way to give knowledge and understanding (1 Corinthians 2:6–13).

— The first time he is in the Spirit (1:10), he sees the seven churches of Asia and delivers a message to each one on behalf of the glorified Jesus.
— The second time he is in the Spirit (4:2), he has a long, sweeping vision of the activity of heaven filled with seals, trumpets, bowls, angels, "beasts," plagues, natural upheavals, and even a marriage feast.
— The third time he is in the Spirit (21:10), John sees the new Jerusalem, the tree of life, and the worship of God by the nations.

Thus, the Spirit of God enables John to see what God sees among His churches, what He is doing in heaven and the significance of these things for the earth and its people, and what God's goal for creation and His people ultimately is.

Within this broad outline, John uses the number seven (a number in Hebrew that stands for completeness) to describe ultimate reality from God's point of view. In fact, the entirety of Revelation is organized according to the number seven with six series of seven listed in the book:

— John begins by writing to the seven churches on behalf of Jesus (2:1–3:22). God knows His people and what is happening in their midst.
— John sees seven seals of a scroll opened by Jesus the Lamb (4:1–8:5). The removal of the seals prepares for God's final word (as represented by the scroll) to be spoken.
— John hears seven trumpets blown by angels (8:6–11:19), which marks a time of judgment on the earth.
— John beholds seven signs in heaven (12:1–15:8), which depicts the warfare of angelic beings and the effects of a powerful beast on the earth (12:1; 13:1, 11; 14:1, 6, 14; 15:1).
— John looks on as seven bowls of wrath are poured on the earth (16:1–21), not unlike the plagues that afflicted Egypt when God delivered His people from slavery (Exodus 7–12).
— Finally, John sees a series of visions (17:1–18; 18:1–19:10; 19:11–21; 20:1–10; 20:11–15; 21:1–22:17) related to God's final goal of having a "home" among His people (21:3).

Taken together, these "sevens" reveal God's knowledge of all things in heaven and earth and of past, present, and future. What is done on earth matters in heaven, and the decisions made in heaven impact life on earth. The realms of heaven and earth are not as distant from each other as people think. In John's vision, they interact and are interconnected. The reason there is not a "seventh" series is because it will occur after everything else when God lives among His people and receives their worship in the new heaven and new earth.

PROLOGUE

1 This is a revelation from* Jesus Christ, which God gave him to show his servants the events that must soon* take place. He sent an angel to present this revelation to his servant John, ²who faithfully reported everything he saw. This is his report of the word of God and the testimony of Jesus Christ.

³God blesses the one who reads the words of this prophecy to the church, and he blesses all who listen to its message and obey what it says, for the time is near.

JOHN'S GREETING TO THE SEVEN CHURCHES

⁴This letter is from John to the seven churches in the province of Asia.*

Grace and peace to you from the one who is, who always was, and who is still to come; from the sevenfold Spirit* before his throne; ⁵and from Jesus Christ. He is the faithful witness to these things, the first to rise from the dead, and the ruler of all the kings of the world.

All glory to him who loves us and has freed us from our sins by shedding his blood for us. ⁶He has made us a Kingdom of priests for God

his Father. All glory and power to him forever and ever! Amen.

⁷ Look! He comes with the clouds
    of heaven.
  And everyone will see him—
    even those who pierced him.
  And all the nations of the world
    will mourn for him.
  Yes! Amen!

⁸ "I am the Alpha and the Omega—the beginning and the end,"* says the Lord God. "I am the one who is, who always was, and who is still to come—the Almighty One."

VISION OF THE SON OF MAN

⁹I, John, am your brother and your partner in suffering and in God's Kingdom and in the patient endurance to which Jesus calls us. I was exiled to the island of Patmos for preaching the word of God and for my testimony about Jesus.

1:1a Or of. 1:1b Or suddenly, or quickly. 1:4a Asia was a Roman province in what is now western Turkey. 1:4b Greek the seven spirits. 1:8 Greek I am the Alpha and the Omega, referring to the first and last letters of the Greek alphabet.

HE HOLDS THE KEYS
Revelation 1:17   ROBERT MORRIS

Have you ever lost your keys? Have you ever thought, *I know they'll be in the last place I look!* Unlike us, Jesus has never lost His keys. He gave the keys of this earth to Adam and Eve, but they lost them to Satan. Through His death and resurrection, Jesus reclaimed the master key to life. Let's look at several important "keys" in Scripture:

1. The Key of Death
Years after the Resurrection, the risen Jesus appeared to the apostle John and told him, "I hold the keys of death and the grave" (Revelation 1:18). The grave, or *Hades* in Greek, was the place of waiting for the people who died before Jesus came. When Jesus died on the cross, He went to Hades and took the keys away from Satan. He then led every Old Testament saint to heaven, though He stopped by the earth for a few moments to give Mary Magdalene a message for the disciples (John 20:17). Why is this key important? Because Jesus doesn't lock people up in hell. He leads them out to freedom!

2. The Key of David
Revelation 3:7 says Jesus has "the key of David." This is a quote from Isaiah 22:15-25, in which Isaiah tells a prophetic story about Shebna (a type of Satan), who sought to exalt himself by using the resources that were meant to build the kingdom for the people of Israel. Isaiah prophesied that Eliakim (a type of Jesus) would pull him down. In other words, Satan would be thrown down, and Jesus would be raised up. The key of David is the master key to the Kingdom of God. With it, Jesus can close and lock every door of fear, sin, and shame, and He can open every good door to freedom in our lives.

3. The Gate to Everlasting Life
Jesus not only has the keys to the gate, but He also *is* the Gate. In John 10:9, He says, "I am the gate. Those who come in through me will be saved." There is only one way to heaven and one gate to everlasting life: His name is Jesus.

[10] It was the Lord's Day, and I was worshiping in the Spirit.* Suddenly, I heard behind me a loud voice like a trumpet blast. [11] It said, "Write in a book* everything you see, and send it to the seven churches in the cities of Ephesus, Smyrna, Pergamum, Thyatira, Sardis, Philadelphia, and Laodicea."

[12] When I turned to see who was speaking to me, I saw seven gold lampstands. [13] And standing in the middle of the lampstands was someone like the Son of Man.* He was wearing a long robe with a gold sash across his chest. [14] His head

and his hair were white like wool, as white as snow. And his eyes were like flames of fire. [15] His feet were like polished bronze refined in a furnace, and his voice thundered like mighty ocean waves. [16] He held seven stars in his right hand, and a sharp two-edged sword came from his mouth. And his face was like the sun in all its brilliance.

[17] When I saw him, I fell at his feet as if I were dead. But he laid his right hand on me and said, "Don't be afraid! I am the First and the Last. [18] I am the living one. I died, but look—I am alive forever and ever! And I hold the keys of death and the grave.*

[19] "Write down what you have seen—both the things that are now happening and the things that will happen.* [20] This is the meaning of the mystery of the seven stars you saw in my right hand and the seven gold lampstands: The seven stars are the angels* of the seven churches, and the seven lampstands are the seven churches.

THE MESSAGE TO THE CHURCH IN EPHESUS

2 "Write this letter to the angel* of the church in Ephesus. This is the message from the one who holds the seven stars in his right hand, the one who walks among the seven gold lampstands:

[2] "I know all the things you do. I have seen your hard work and your patient endurance. I know you don't tolerate evil people. You have examined the claims of those who say they are apostles but are not. You have discovered they are liars. [3] You have patiently suffered for me without quitting.

[4] "But I have this complaint against you. You don't love me or each other as you did at first!* [5] Look how far you have fallen! Turn back to me and do the works you did at first. If you don't repent, I will come and remove your lampstand from its place among the churches. [6] But this is in your favor: You hate the evil deeds of the Nicolaitans, just as I do.

[7] "Anyone with ears to hear must listen to the Spirit and understand what he is saying to the churches. To everyone who is victorious I will give fruit from the tree of life in the paradise of God.

THE MESSAGE TO THE CHURCH IN SMYRNA

[8] "Write this letter to the angel of the church in Smyrna. This is the message from the one who is the First and the Last, who was dead but is now alive:

1:10 Or *in spirit.* 1:11 Or *on a scroll.* 1:13 Or *like a son of man.* See Dan 7:13. "Son of Man" is a title Jesus used for himself. 1:18 Greek *and Hades.* 1:19 Or *what you have seen and what they mean—the things that have already begun to happen.* 1:20 Or *the messengers.* 2:1 Or *the messenger;* also in 2:8, 12, 18. 2:4 Greek *You have lost your first love.*

9 "I know about your suffering and your poverty—but you are rich! I know the blasphemy of those opposing you. They say they are Jews, but they are not, because their synagogue belongs to Satan. 10 Don't be afraid of what you are about to suffer. The devil will throw some of you into prison to test you. You will suffer for ten days. But if you remain faithful even when facing death, I will give you the crown of life.

11 "Anyone with ears to hear must listen to the Spirit and understand what he is saying to the churches. Whoever is victorious will not be harmed by the second death.

THE MESSAGE TO THE CHURCH IN PERGAMUM

12 "Write this letter to the angel of the church in Pergamum. This is the message from the one with the sharp two-edged sword:

13 "I know that you live in the city where Satan has his throne, yet you have remained loyal to me. You refused to deny me even when Antipas, my faithful witness, was martyred among you there in Satan's city. 14 "But I have a few complaints against you. You tolerate some among you whose teaching is like that of Balaam, who showed Balak how to trip up the people of Israel. He taught them to sin by eating food offered to idols and by committing sexual sin. 15 In a similar way, you have some Nicolaitans among you who follow the same teaching. 16 Repent of your sin, or I will come to you suddenly and fight against them with the sword of my mouth.

17 "Anyone with ears to hear must listen to the Spirit and understand what he is saying to the churches. To everyone who is victorious I will give some of the manna that has been hidden away in heaven. And I will give to each one a white stone, and on the stone will be engraved a new name that no one understands except the one who receives it.

THE MESSAGE TO THE CHURCH IN THYATIRA

18 "Write this letter to the angel of the church in Thyatira. This is the message from the Son of God, whose eyes are like flames of fire, whose feet are like polished bronze:

19 "I know all the things you do. I have seen your love, your faith, your service, and your patient endurance. And I can see your constant improvement in all these things. 20 "But I have this complaint against you. You are permitting that woman—that Jezebel who calls herself a prophet—to lead my servants astray. She teaches them to commit sexual sin and to eat food offered to idols.

21 I gave her time to repent, but she does not want to turn away from her immorality. 22 "Therefore, I will throw her on a bed of suffering,* and those who commit adultery with her will suffer greatly unless they repent and turn away from her evil deeds. 23 I will strike her children dead. Then all the churches will know that I am the one who searches out the thoughts and intentions of every person. And I will give to each of you whatever you deserve.

24 "But I also have a message for the rest of you in Thyatira who have not followed this false teaching ('deeper truths,' as they call them—depths of Satan, actually). I will ask nothing more of you 25 except that you hold tightly to what you have until I come. 26 To all who are victorious, who obey me to the very end,

To them I will give authority over all the nations.
27 They will rule the nations with an iron rod and smash them like clay pots.*

28 They will have the same authority I received from my Father, and I will also give them the morning star!

29 "Anyone with ears to hear must listen to the Spirit and understand what he is saying to the churches.

THE MESSAGE TO THE CHURCH IN SARDIS

3 "Write this letter to the angel* of the church in Sardis. This is the message from the one who has the sevenfold Spirit* of God and the seven stars:

"I know all the things you do, and that you have a reputation for being alive—but you are dead. 2 Wake up! Strengthen what little remains, for even what is left is almost dead. I find that your actions do not meet the requirements of my God. 3 Go back to what you heard and believed at first; hold to it firmly. Repent and turn to me again. If you don't wake up, I will come to you suddenly, as unexpected as a thief.

4 "Yet there are some in the church in Sardis who have not soiled their clothes with evil. They will walk with me in white, for they are worthy. 5 All who are victorious will be clothed in white. I will never erase their names from the Book of Life, but I will announce before my Father and his angels that they are mine.

6 "Anyone with ears to hear must listen to the Spirit and understand what he is saying to the churches.

2:22 Greek *a bed.* 2:26-27 Ps 2:8-9 (Greek version). 3:1a Or *the messenger;* also in 3:7, 14. 3:1b Greek *the seven spirits.*

THE MESSAGE TO THE CHURCH IN PHILADELPHIA

7 "Write this letter to the angel of the church in Philadelphia.

This is the message from the one who is
holy and true,
the one who has the key of David.
What he opens, no one can close;
and what he closes, no one can open:*

8 "I know all the things you do, and I have opened a door for you that no one can close. You have little strength, yet you obeyed my word and did not deny me. 9 Look, I will force those who belong to Satan's synagogue—those liars who say they are Jews but are not—to come and bow down at your feet. They will acknowledge that you are the ones I love. 10 "Because you have obeyed my command to persevere, I will protect you from the great time of testing that will come upon the whole world to test those who belong to this world. 11 I am coming soon.* Hold on to what you have, so that no one will take away your crown. 12 All who are victorious will become pillars in the Temple of my God, and they will never have to leave it. And I will write on them the name of my God, and they will be citizens in the city of my God—the new Jerusalem that comes down from heaven from my God. And I will also write on them my new name. 13 "Anyone with ears to hear must listen to the Spirit and understand what he is saying to the churches.

THE MESSAGE TO THE CHURCH IN LAODICEA

14 "Write this letter to the angel of the church in Laodicea. This is the message from the one who is the Amen—the faithful and true witness, the beginning* of God's new creation:

15 "I know all the things you do, that you are neither hot nor cold. I wish that you were one or the other! 16 But since you are like lukewarm water, neither hot nor cold, I will spit you out of my mouth! 17 You say, 'I am rich. I have everything I want. I don't need a thing!' And you don't realize that you are wretched and miserable and poor and blind and naked. 18 So I advise you to buy gold from me—gold that has been purified by fire. Then you will be rich. Also buy white garments from me so you will not be shamed by your nakedness, and ointment for your eyes so you will be able to see. 19 I correct and discipline everyone I love. So be diligent and turn from your indifference.

20 "Look! I stand at the door and knock. If you hear my voice and open the door, I will come in, and we will share a meal together as friends. 21 Those who are victorious will sit with me on my throne, just as I was victorious and sat with my Father on his throne. 22 "Anyone with ears to hear must listen to the Spirit and understand what he is saying to the churches."

WORSHIP IN HEAVEN

4 Then as I looked, I saw a door standing open in heaven, and the same voice I had heard before spoke to me like a trumpet blast. The voice said, "Come up here, and I will show you what must happen after this." 2 And instantly I was in the Spirit,* and I saw a throne in heaven and someone sitting on it. 3 The one sitting on the throne was as brilliant as gemstones—like jasper and carnelian. And the glow of an emerald circled his throne like a rainbow. 4 Twenty-four thrones surrounded him, and twenty-four elders sat on them. They were all clothed in white and had gold crowns on their heads. 5 From the throne came flashes of lightning and the rumble of thunder. And in front of the throne were seven torches with burning flames. This is the sevenfold Spirit* of God. 6 In front of the throne was a shiny sea of glass, sparkling like crystal.

In the center and around the throne were four living beings, each covered with eyes, front and back. 7 The first of these living beings was like a lion; the second was like an ox; the third had a human face; and the fourth was like an eagle in flight. 8 Each of these living beings had six wings, and their wings were covered all over with eyes, inside and out. Day after day and night after night they keep on saying,

"Holy, holy, holy is the Lord God, the
Almighty—
the one who always was, who is, and who
is still to come."

9 Whenever the living beings give glory and honor and thanks to the one sitting on the throne (the one who lives forever and ever), 10 the twenty-four elders fall down and worship the one sitting on the throne (the one who lives forever and ever). And they lay their crowns before the throne and say,

11 "You are worthy, O Lord our God,
to receive glory and honor and power.
For you created all things,
and they exist because you created what
you pleased."

HEAVEN?

ROBERT MORRIS

Do you ever wonder about heaven? Many people do. Some answers will only come when we are face-to-face with God, but addressed here are 10 of the most common questions about heaven:

1. Will we have bodies in heaven?
Jesus had an earthly body that suffered and died, but after the Resurrection, He had a heavenly body. When Jesus returns, we too will have heavenly bodies. In 1 Corinthians 15:42, the apostle Paul writes, "Our earthly bodies are planted in the ground when we die, but they will be raised to live forever."

2. Will we go to heaven immediately?
Jesus told the thief on the cross next to Him, "Today you will be with me in paradise" (Luke 23:43). When we leave our earthly bodies, we will immediately be with the Lord in heaven. Paul writes, "We would rather be away from these earthly bodies, for then we will be at home with the Lord" (2 Corinthians 5:8).

3. Will we be able to communicate?
Revelation 6:10 says the martyrs in heaven "shouted to the Lord." They can communicate, and we will be able to as well.

4. Will we have emotions?
The martyrs care deeply about what is happening on earth (Revelation 6:9-11). Your emotions are part of your soul, which is going to heaven. Luke 15:7 speaks about joy in heaven "over one lost sinner who repents." This joy is far beyond anything we can experience on this earth.

5. Will we know everything?
No, we will not know everything. The martyrs don't know the future, so they ask God when He will avenge their deaths. However, we will have an eternal, heavenly perspective and will be constantly learning and discovering new things.

6. Will we know what's happening on earth?
Yes, we will. The martyrs know what's happening on earth—they know the people who killed them are still alive. According to Hebrews 12:1, people in heaven are able to witness the events on earth. This means you have people in heaven who are cheering you on right now!

7. Will we remember our lives on earth?
The martyrs in heaven remember they were murdered, and they remember their lives on earth. We too will remember our earthly lives when we are in heaven. These memories will make us grateful for God's incredible grace and mercy.

8. Will we know people?
In Matthew 8:11, Jesus says many people in heaven will sit down and talk with Abraham, Isaac, and Jacob. We will *know* and genuinely understand people for the first time in our lives.

9. Will it be boring?
Heaven is going to be the most spectacular place ever! It will be beautiful, pain-free, and completely satisfying (Revelation 21:1-7). The greatest thing about heaven is going to be our fellowship with God and other believers for all eternity.

10. Who will be there?
Jesus and His Bride (the Church) will be in heaven (Revelation 21:6; 22:17). Anyone who confesses Jesus as Lord and calls on His name will be there (Romans 10:9, 13).

THE LAMB OPENS THE SCROLL

5 Then I saw a scroll* in the right hand of the one who was sitting on the throne. There was writing on the inside and the outside of the scroll, and it was sealed with seven seals. ²And I saw a strong angel, who shouted with a loud voice: "Who is worthy to break the seals on this scroll and open it?" ³But no one in heaven or on earth or under the earth was able to open the scroll and read it.

⁴Then I began to weep bitterly because no one was found worthy to open the scroll and read it. ⁵But one of the twenty-four elders said to me, "Stop weeping! Look, the Lion of the tribe of Judah, the heir to David's throne,* has won the victory. He is worthy to open the scroll and its seven seals."

⁶Then I saw a Lamb that looked as if it had been slaughtered, but it was now standing between the throne and the four living beings and among the twenty-four elders. He had seven horns and seven eyes, which represent the sevenfold Spirit* of God that is sent out into every part of the earth. ⁷He stepped forward and took the scroll from the right hand of the one sitting on the throne. ⁸And when he took the scroll, the four living beings and the twenty-four elders fell down before the Lamb. Each one had a harp, and they held gold bowls filled with incense, which are the prayers of God's people. ⁹And they sang a new song with these words:

"You are worthy to take the scroll
    and break its seals and open it.
For you were slaughtered, and your blood
        has ransomed people for God
    from every tribe and language and people
        and nation.
¹⁰ And you have caused them to become
    a Kingdom of priests for our God.
And they will reign* on the earth."

¹¹Then I looked again, and I heard the voices of thousands and millions of angels around the throne and of the living beings and the elders. ¹²And they sang in a mighty chorus:

"Worthy is the Lamb who was slaughtered—
    to receive power and riches
    and wisdom and strength
    and honor and glory and blessing."

¹³And then I heard every creature in heaven and on earth and under the earth and in the sea. They sang:

"Blessing and honor and glory and power
    belong to the one sitting on the throne
    and to the Lamb forever and ever."

¹⁴And the four living beings said, "Amen!" And the twenty-four elders fell down and worshiped the Lamb.

THE LAMB BREAKS THE FIRST SIX SEALS

6 As I watched, the Lamb broke the first of the seven seals on the scroll.* Then I heard one of the four living beings say with a voice like thunder, "Come!" ²I looked up and saw a white horse standing there. Its rider carried a bow, and a crown was placed on his head. He rode out to win many battles and gain the victory.

³When the Lamb broke the second seal, I heard the second living being say, "Come!" ⁴Then another horse appeared, a red one. Its rider was given a mighty sword and the authority to take peace from the earth. And there was war and slaughter everywhere.

⁵When the Lamb broke the third seal, I heard the third living being say, "Come!" I looked up and saw a black horse, and its rider was holding a pair of scales in his hand. ⁶And I heard a voice from among the four living beings say, "A loaf of wheat bread or three loaves of barley will cost a day's pay.* And don't waste* the olive oil and wine."

⁷When the Lamb broke the fourth seal, I heard the fourth living being say, "Come!" ⁸I looked up and saw a horse whose color was pale green. Its rider was named Death, and his companion was the Grave.* These two were given authority over one-fourth of the earth, to kill with the sword and famine and disease* and wild animals.

⁹When the Lamb broke the fifth seal, I saw under the altar the souls of all who had been martyred for the word of God and for being faithful in their testimony. ¹⁰They shouted to the Lord and said, "O Sovereign Lord, holy and true, how long before you judge the people who belong to this world and avenge our blood for what they have done to us?" ¹¹Then a white robe was given to each of them. And they were told to rest a little longer until the full number of their brothers and sisters*—their fellow servants of Jesus who were to be martyred—had joined them.

¹²I watched as the Lamb broke the sixth seal, and there was a great earthquake. The sun became as dark as black cloth, and the moon became as red as blood. ¹³Then the stars of the sky fell to the earth like green figs falling from a tree shaken by a strong wind. ¹⁴The sky was rolled up like a scroll, and all of the mountains and islands were moved from their places.

¹⁵Then everyone—the kings of the earth, the rulers, the generals, the wealthy, the powerful, and every slave and free person—all hid themselves in the caves and among the rocks of the mountains. ¹⁶And they cried to the mountains and the rocks, "Fall on us and hide us from the

5:1 Or book; also in 5:2, 3, 4, 5, 7, 8, 9. 5:5 Greek the root of David. See Isa 11:10. 5:6 Greek which are the seven spirits. 5:10 Some manuscripts read they are reigning. 6:1 Or book. 6:6a Greek A choinix [1 quart or 1 liter] of wheat for a denarius, and 3 choinix of barley for a denarius. A denarius was equivalent to a laborer's full day's wage. 6:6b Or harm. 6:8a Greek was Hades. 6:8b Greek death. 6:11 Greek their brothers.

face of the one who sits on the throne and from the wrath of the Lamb. ¹⁷For the great day of their wrath has come, and who is able to survive?"

GOD'S PEOPLE WILL BE PRESERVED

7 Then I saw four angels standing at the four corners of the earth, holding back the four winds so they did not blow on the earth or the sea, or even on any tree. ²And I saw another angel coming up from the east, carrying the seal of the living God. And he shouted to those four angels, who had been given power to harm land and sea, ³"Wait! Don't harm the land or the sea or the trees until we have placed the seal of God on the foreheads of his servants."

⁴And I heard how many were marked with the seal of God—144,000 were sealed from all the tribes of Israel:

⁵ from Judah	12,000
from Reuben	12,000
from Gad	12,000
⁶ from Asher	12,000
from Naphtali	12,000
from Manasseh	12,000
⁷ from Simeon	12,000
from Levi	12,000
from Issachar	12,000
⁸ from Zebulun	12,000
from Joseph	12,000
from Benjamin	12,000

PRAISE FROM THE GREAT CROWD

⁹After this I saw a vast crowd, too great to count, from every nation and tribe and people and language, standing in front of the throne and before the Lamb. They were clothed in white robes and held palm branches in their hands. ¹⁰And they were shouting with a great roar,

"Salvation comes from our God who sits on
    the throne
    and from the Lamb!"

¹¹And all the angels were standing around the throne and around the elders and the four living beings. And they fell before the throne with their faces to the ground and worshiped God. ¹²They sang,

"Amen! Blessing and glory and wisdom
    and thanksgiving and honor
and power and strength belong to our God
    forever and ever! Amen."

¹³Then one of the twenty-four elders asked me, "Who are these who are clothed in white? Where did they come from?"

¹⁴And I said to him, "Sir, you are the one who knows."

Then he said to me, "These are the ones who died in* the great tribulation.* They have washed their robes in the blood of the Lamb and made them white.

¹⁵ "That is why they stand in front of
        God's throne
    and serve him day and night in his Temple.
And he who sits on the throne
    will give them shelter.
¹⁶ They will never again be hungry or thirsty;
    they will never be scorched by the heat of
        the sun.
¹⁷ For the Lamb on the throne*
    will be their Shepherd.
He will lead them to springs of
    life-giving water.
    And God will wipe every tear from
        their eyes."

THE LAMB BREAKS THE SEVENTH SEAL

8 When the Lamb broke the seventh seal on the scroll,* there was silence throughout heaven for about half an hour. ²I saw the seven angels who stand before God, and they were given seven trumpets.

³Then another angel with a gold incense burner came and stood at the altar. And a great amount of incense was given to him to mix with the prayers of God's people as an offering on the gold altar before the throne. ⁴The smoke of the incense, mixed with the prayers of God's holy people, ascended up to God from the altar where the angel had poured them out. ⁵Then the angel filled the incense burner with fire from the altar and threw it down upon the earth; and thunder crashed, lightning flashed, and there was a terrible earthquake.

THE FIRST FOUR TRUMPETS

⁶Then the seven angels with the seven trumpets prepared to blow their mighty blasts.

⁷The first angel blew his trumpet, and hail and fire mixed with blood were thrown down on the earth. One-third of the earth was set on fire, one-third of the trees were burned, and all the green grass was burned.

⁸Then the second angel blew his trumpet, and a great mountain of fire was thrown into the sea. One-third of the water in the sea became blood, ⁹one-third of all things living in the sea died, and one-third of all the ships on the sea were destroyed.

¹⁰Then the third angel blew his trumpet, and a great star fell from the sky, burning like a torch. It fell on one-third of the rivers and on the springs of water. ¹¹The name of the star was Bitterness.* It made one-third of the water bitter, and many people died from drinking the bitter water.

7:14a Greek *who came out of.*   **7:14b** Or *the great suffering.*
7:17 Greek *on the center of the throne.*   **8:1** Or *book.*   **8:11** Greek *Wormwood.*

¹²Then the fourth angel blew his trumpet, and one-third of the sun was struck, and one-third of the moon, and one-third of the stars, and they became dark. And one-third of the day was dark, and also one-third of the night. ¹³Then I looked, and I heard a single eagle crying loudly as it flew through the air, "Terror, terror, terror to all who belong to this world because of what will happen when the last three angels blow their trumpets."

THE FIFTH TRUMPET BRINGS THE FIRST TERROR

9 Then the fifth angel blew his trumpet, and I saw a star that had fallen to earth from the sky, and he was given the key to the shaft of the bottomless pit.* ²When he opened it, smoke poured out as though from a huge furnace, and the sunlight and air turned dark from the smoke. ³Then locusts came from the smoke and descended on the earth, and they were given power to sting like scorpions. ⁴They were told not to harm the grass or plants or trees, but only the people who did not have the seal of God on their foreheads. ⁵They were told not to kill them but to torture them for five months with pain like the pain of a scorpion sting. ⁶In those days people will seek death but will not find it. They will long to die, but death will flee from them! ⁷The locusts looked like horses prepared for battle. They had what looked like gold crowns on their heads, and their faces looked like human faces. ⁸They had hair like women's hair and teeth like the teeth of a lion. ⁹They wore armor made of iron, and their wings roared like an army of chariots rushing into battle. ¹⁰They had tails that stung like scorpions, and for five months they had the power to torment people. ¹¹Their king is the angel from the bottomless pit; his name in Hebrew is *Abaddon*, and in Greek, *Apollyon*—the Destroyer.

¹²The first terror is past, but look, two more terrors are coming!

THE SIXTH TRUMPET BRINGS THE SECOND TERROR

¹³Then the sixth angel blew his trumpet, and I heard a voice speaking from the four horns of the gold altar that stands in the presence of God. ¹⁴And the voice said to the sixth angel who held the trumpet, "Release the four angels who are bound at the great Euphrates River." ¹⁵Then the four angels who had been prepared for this hour and day and month and year were turned loose to kill one-third of all the people on earth. ¹⁶I heard the size of their army, which was 200 million mounted troops.

¹⁷And in my vision, I saw the horses and the riders sitting on them. The riders wore armor that was fiery red and dark blue and yellow. The horses had heads like lions, and fire and smoke and burning sulfur billowed from their mouths.

¹⁸One-third of all the people on earth were killed by these three plagues—by the fire and smoke and burning sulfur that came from the mouths of the horses. ¹⁹Their power was in their mouths and in their tails. For their tails had heads like snakes, with the power to injure people.

²⁰But the people who did not die in these plagues still refused to repent of their evil deeds and turn to God. They continued to worship demons and idols made of gold, silver, bronze, stone, and wood—idols that can neither see nor hear nor walk! ²¹And they did not repent of their murders or their witchcraft or their sexual immorality or their thefts.

THE ANGEL AND THE SMALL SCROLL

10 Then I saw another mighty angel coming down from heaven, surrounded by a cloud, with a rainbow over his head. His face shone like the sun, and his feet were like pillars of fire. ²And in his hand was a small scroll* that had been opened. He stood with his right foot on the sea and his left foot on the land. ³And he gave a great shout like the roar of a lion. And when he shouted, the seven thunders answered.

⁴When the seven thunders spoke, I was about to write. But I heard a voice from heaven saying, "Keep secret* what the seven thunders said, and do not write it down."

⁵Then the angel I saw standing on the sea and on the land raised his right hand toward heaven. ⁶He swore an oath in the name of the one who lives forever and ever, who created the heavens and everything in them, the earth and everything in it, and the sea and everything in it. He said, "There will be no more delay. ⁷When the seventh angel blows his trumpet, God's mysterious plan will be fulfilled. It will happen just as he announced it to his servants the prophets."

⁸Then the voice from heaven spoke to me again: "Go and take the open scroll from the hand of the angel who is standing on the sea and on the land."

⁹So I went to the angel and told him to give me the small scroll. "Yes, take it and eat it," he said. "It will be sweet as honey in your mouth, but it will turn sour in your stomach!" ¹⁰So I took the small scroll from the hand of the angel, and I ate it! It was sweet in my mouth, but when I swallowed it, it turned sour in my stomach.

¹¹Then I was told, "You must prophesy again about many peoples, nations, languages, and kings."

THE TWO WITNESSES

11 Then I was given a measuring stick, and I was told, "Go and measure the Temple of God and the altar, and count the number of worshipers. ²But do not measure the outer courtyard,

9:1 Or *the abyss,* or *the underworld;* also in 9:11.   10:2 Or *book;* also in 10:8, 9, 10.   10:4 Greek *Seal up.*

for it has been turned over to the nations. They will trample the holy city for 42 months. ³And I will give power to my two witnesses, and they will be clothed in burlap and will prophesy during those 1,260 days."

⁴These two prophets are the two olive trees and the two lampstands that stand before the Lord of all the earth. ⁵If anyone tries to harm them, fire flashes from their mouths and consumes their enemies. This is how anyone who tries to harm them must die. ⁶They have power to shut the sky so that no rain will fall for as long as they prophesy. And they have the power to turn the rivers and oceans into blood, and to strike the earth with every kind of plague as often as they wish.

⁷When they complete their testimony, the beast that comes up out of the bottomless pit* will declare war against them, and he will conquer them and kill them. ⁸And their bodies will lie in the main street of Jerusalem,* the city that is figuratively called "Sodom" and "Egypt," the city where their Lord was crucified. ⁹And for three and a half days, all peoples, tribes, languages, and nations will stare at their bodies. No one will be allowed to bury them. ¹⁰All the people who belong to this world will gloat over them and give presents to each other to celebrate the death of the two prophets who had tormented them.

¹¹But after three and a half days, God breathed life into them, and they stood up! Terror struck all who were staring at them. ¹²Then a loud voice from heaven called to the two prophets, "Come up here!" And they rose to heaven in a cloud as their enemies watched.

¹³At the same time there was a terrible earthquake that destroyed a tenth of the city. Seven thousand people died in that earthquake, and everyone else was terrified and gave glory to the God of heaven.

¹⁴The second terror is past, but look, the third terror is coming quickly.

THE SEVENTH TRUMPET BRINGS THE THIRD TERROR

¹⁵Then the seventh angel blew his trumpet, and there were loud voices shouting in heaven:

"The world has now become the Kingdom of
    our Lord and of his Christ,*
    and he will reign forever and ever."

¹⁶The twenty-four elders sitting on their thrones before God fell with their faces to the ground and worshiped him. ¹⁷And they said,

"We give thanks to you, Lord God,
    the Almighty,
the one who is and who always was,
for now you have assumed your great power
    and have begun to reign.

¹⁸ The nations were filled with wrath,
    but now the time of your wrath
        has come.
It is time to judge the dead
    and reward your servants the prophets,
        as well as your holy people,
and all who fear your name,
    from the least to the greatest.
It is time to destroy
    all who have caused destruction on
        the earth."

¹⁹Then, in heaven, the Temple of God was opened and the Ark of his covenant could be seen inside the Temple. Lightning flashed, thunder crashed and roared, and there was an earthquake and a terrible hailstorm.

THE WOMAN AND THE DRAGON

12 Then I witnessed in heaven an event of great significance. I saw a woman clothed with the sun, with the moon beneath her feet, and a crown of twelve stars on her head. ²She was pregnant, and she cried out because of her labor pains and the agony of giving birth.

³Then I witnessed in heaven another significant event. I saw a large red dragon with seven heads and ten horns, with seven crowns on his heads. ⁴His tail swept away one-third of the stars in the sky, and he threw them to the earth. He stood in front of the woman as she was about to give birth, ready to devour her baby as soon as it was born.

⁵She gave birth to a son who was to rule all nations with an iron rod. And her child was snatched away from the dragon and was caught up to God and to his throne. ⁶And the woman fled into the wilderness, where God had prepared a place to care for her for 1,260 days.

⁷Then there was war in heaven. Michael and his angels fought against the dragon and his angels. ⁸And the dragon lost the battle, and he and his angels were forced out of heaven. ⁹This great dragon—the ancient serpent called the devil, or Satan, the one deceiving the whole world—was thrown down to the earth with all his angels.

¹⁰Then I heard a loud voice shouting across the heavens,

"It has come at last—
    salvation and power
and the Kingdom of our God,
    and the authority of his Christ.*
For the accuser of our brothers and sisters*
    has been thrown down to earth—
the one who accuses them
    before our God day and night.

11:7 Or *the abyss,* or *the underworld.*   11:8 Greek *the great city.*
11:15 Or *his Messiah.*   12:10a Or *his Messiah.*   12:10b Greek
brothers.

11 And they have defeated him by the blood of
the Lamb
and by their testimony.
And they did not love their lives so much
that they were afraid to die.
12 Therefore, rejoice, O heavens!
And you who live in the heavens, rejoice!
But terror will come on the earth and the
sea,
for the devil has come down to you in
great anger,
knowing that he has little time."

13 When the dragon realized that he had been
thrown down to the earth, he pursued the
woman who had given birth to the male child.
14 But she was given two wings like those of a
great eagle so she could fly to the place prepared
for her in the wilderness. There she would be
cared for and protected from the dragon* for a
time, times, and half a time. 15 Then the dragon tried to drown the woman
with a flood of water that flowed from his mouth.
16 But the earth helped her by opening its mouth
and swallowing the river that gushed out from
the mouth of the dragon. 17 And the dragon was
angry at the woman and declared war against
the rest of her children—all who keep God's
commandments and maintain their testimony
for Jesus.

18 Then the dragon took his stand* on the shore
beside the sea.

THE BEAST OUT OF THE SEA

13 Then I saw a beast rising up out of the sea.
It had seven heads and ten horns, with
ten crowns on its horns. And written on each
head were names that blasphemed God. 2 This
beast looked like a leopard, but it had the feet of
a bear and the mouth of a lion! And the dragon
gave the beast his own power and throne and
great authority.

3 I saw that one of the heads of the beast
seemed wounded beyond recovery—but the fatal
wound was healed! The whole world marveled
at this miracle and gave allegiance to the beast.
4 They worshiped the dragon for giving the beast
such power, and they also worshiped the beast.
"Who is as great as the beast?" they exclaimed.
"Who is able to fight against him?"

5 Then the beast was allowed to speak great
blasphemies against God. And he was given
authority to do whatever he wanted for forty-two
months. 6 And he spoke terrible words of blasphemy against God, slandering his name and his
dwelling—that is, those who dwell in heaven.*
7 And the beast was allowed to wage war against
God's holy people and to conquer them. And he
was given authority to rule over every tribe and
people and language and nation. 8 And all the
people who belong to this world worshiped the
beast. They are the ones whose names were not

written in the Book of Life that belongs to the
Lamb who was slaughtered before the world was
made.*

9 Anyone with ears to hear
should listen and understand.
10 Anyone who is destined for prison
will be taken to prison.
Anyone destined to die by the sword
will die by the sword.

This means that God's holy people must endure
persecution patiently and remain faithful.

THE BEAST OUT OF THE EARTH

11 Then I saw another beast come up out of the
earth. He had two horns like those of a lamb,
but he spoke with the voice of a dragon. 12 He
exercised all the authority of the first beast.
And he required all the earth and its people to
worship the first beast, whose fatal wound had
been healed. 13 He did astounding miracles, even
making fire flash down to earth from the sky
while everyone was watching. 14 And with all the
miracles he was allowed to perform on behalf of
the first beast, he deceived all the people who
belong to this world. He ordered the people to
make a great statue of the first beast, who was
fatally wounded and then came back to life. 15 He
was then permitted to give life to this statue so
that it could speak. Then the statue of the beast
commanded that anyone refusing to worship
it must die.

16 He required everyone—small and great, rich
and poor, free and slave—to be given a mark on
the right hand or on the forehead. 17 And no one
could buy or sell anything without that mark,
which was either the name of the beast or the
number representing his name. 18 Wisdom is
needed here. Let the one with understanding
solve the meaning of the number of the beast, for
it is the number of a man.* His number is 666.*

THE LAMB AND THE 144,000

14 Then I saw the Lamb standing on Mount
Zion, and with him were 144,000 who had
his name and his Father's name written on their
foreheads. 2 And I heard a sound from heaven like
the roar of mighty ocean waves or the rolling
of loud thunder. It was like the sound of many
harpists playing together.

3 This great choir sang a wonderful new song
in front of the throne of God and before the four
living beings and the twenty-four elders. No one
could learn this song except the 144,000 who had
been redeemed from the earth. 4 They have kept

12:14 Greek the serpent; also in 12:15. See 12:9. 12:18 Greek Then
he took his stand; some manuscripts read Then I took my stand.
Some translations put this entire sentence into 13:1. 13:6 Some
manuscripts read and his dwelling and all who dwell in heaven.
13:8 Or not written in the Book of Life before the world was made—
the Book that belongs to the Lamb who was slaughtered. 13:18a Or
of humanity. 13:18b Some manuscripts read 616.

themselves as pure as virgins,* following the Lamb wherever he goes. They have been purchased from among the people on the earth as a special offering* to God and to the Lamb. ⁵They have told no lies; they are without blame.

THE THREE ANGELS

⁶And I saw another angel flying through the sky, carrying the eternal Good News to proclaim to the people who belong to this world—to every nation, tribe, language, and people. ⁷"Fear God," he shouted. "Give glory to him. For the time has come when he will sit as judge. Worship him who made the heavens, the earth, the sea, and all the springs of water."

⁸Then another angel followed him through the sky, shouting, "Babylon is fallen—that great city is fallen—because she made all the nations of the world drink the wine of her passionate immorality."

⁹Then a third angel followed them, shouting, "Anyone who worships the beast and his statue or who accepts his mark on the forehead or on the hand ¹⁰must drink the wine of God's anger. It has been poured full strength into God's cup of wrath. And they will be tormented with fire and burning sulfur in the presence of the holy angels and the Lamb. ¹¹The smoke of their torment will rise forever and ever, and they will have no relief day or night, for they have worshiped the beast and his statue and have accepted the mark of his name."

¹²This means that God's holy people must endure persecution patiently, obeying his commands and maintaining their faith in Jesus.

¹³And I heard a voice from heaven saying, "Write this down: Blessed are those who die in the Lord from now on. Yes, says the Spirit, they are blessed indeed, for they will rest from their hard work; for their good deeds follow them!"

THE HARVEST OF THE EARTH

¹⁴Then I saw a white cloud, and seated on the cloud was someone like the Son of Man.* He had a gold crown on his head and a sharp sickle in his hand.

¹⁵Then another angel came from the Temple and shouted to the one sitting on the cloud, "Swing the sickle, for the time of harvest has come; the crop on earth is ripe." ¹⁶So the one sitting on the cloud swung his sickle over the earth, and the whole earth was harvested.

¹⁷After that, another angel came from the Temple in heaven, and he also had a sharp sickle. ¹⁸Then another angel, who had power to destroy with fire, came from the altar. He shouted to the angel with the sharp sickle, "Swing your sickle now to gather the clusters of grapes from the vines of the earth, for they are ripe for judgment." ¹⁹So the angel swung his sickle over the earth and loaded the grapes into the great winepress of God's wrath. ²⁰The grapes were trampled in the winepress outside the city, and blood flowed from the winepress in a stream about 180 miles* long and as high as a horse's bridle.

THE SONG OF MOSES AND OF THE LAMB

15 Then I saw in heaven another marvelous event of great significance. Seven angels were holding the seven last plagues, which would bring God's wrath to completion. ²I saw before me what seemed to be a glass sea mixed with fire. And on it stood all the people who had been victorious over the beast and his statue and the number representing his name. They were all holding harps that God had given them. ³And they were singing the song of Moses, the servant of God, and the song of the Lamb:

> "Great and marvelous are your works,
>   O Lord God, the Almighty.
> Just and true are your ways,
>   O King of the nations.*
> ⁴ Who will not fear you, Lord,
>   and glorify your name?
>   For you alone are holy.
> All nations will come and worship before
>   you,
>   for your righteous deeds have been
>   revealed."

THE SEVEN BOWLS OF THE SEVEN PLAGUES

⁵Then I looked and saw that the Temple in heaven, God's Tabernacle, was thrown wide open. ⁶The seven angels who were holding the seven plagues came out of the Temple. They were clothed in spotless white linen* with gold sashes across their chests. ⁷Then one of the four living beings handed each of the seven angels a gold bowl filled with the wrath of God, who lives forever and ever. ⁸The Temple was filled with smoke from God's glory and power. No one could enter the Temple until the seven angels had completed pouring out the seven plagues.

16 Then I heard a mighty voice from the Temple say to the seven angels, "Go your ways and pour out on the earth the seven bowls containing God's wrath."

²So the first angel left the Temple and poured out his bowl on the earth, and horrible, malignant sores broke out on everyone who had the mark of the beast and who worshiped his statue.

³Then the second angel poured out his bowl on the sea, and it became like the blood of a corpse. And everything in the sea died.

14:4a Greek *They are virgins who have not defiled themselves with women.*   14:4b Greek *as firstfruits.*   14:14 Or *like a son of man.* See Dan 7:13. "Son of Man" is a title Jesus used for himself.   14:20 Greek *1,600 stadia* [300 kilometers].   15:3 Some manuscripts read *King of the ages.*   15:6 Other manuscripts read *white stone;* still others read *white [garments] made of linen.*

⁴ Then the third angel poured out his bowl on the rivers and springs, and they became blood. ⁵ And I heard the angel who had authority over all water saying,

"You are just, O Holy One, who is and who
  always was,
 because you have sent these judgments.
⁶ Since they shed the blood
  of your holy people and your prophets,
 you have given them blood to drink.
  It is their just reward."

⁷ And I heard a voice from the altar,* saying,

"Yes, O Lord God, the Almighty,
 your judgments are true and just."

⁸ Then the fourth angel poured out his bowl on the sun, causing it to scorch everyone with its fire. ⁹ Everyone was burned by this blast of heat, and they cursed the name of God, who had control over all these plagues. They did not repent of their sins and turn to God and give him glory. ¹⁰ Then the fifth angel poured out his bowl on the throne of the beast, and his kingdom was plunged into darkness. His subjects ground their teeth* in anguish, ¹¹ and they cursed the God of heaven for their pains and sores. But they did not repent of their evil deeds and turn to God.

¹² Then the sixth angel poured out his bowl on the great Euphrates River, and it dried up so that the kings from the east could march their armies toward the west without hindrance. ¹³ And I saw three evil* spirits that looked like frogs leap from the mouths of the dragon, the beast, and the false prophet. ¹⁴ They are demonic spirits who work miracles and go out to all the rulers of the world to gather them for battle against the Lord on that great judgment day of God the Almighty.

¹⁵ "Look, I will come as unexpectedly as a thief! Blessed are all who are watching for me, who keep their clothing ready so they will not have to walk around naked and ashamed."

¹⁶ And the demonic spirits gathered all the rulers and their armies to a place with the Hebrew name *Armageddon.**

¹⁷ Then the seventh angel poured out his bowl into the air. And a mighty shout came from the throne in the Temple, saying, "It is finished!" ¹⁸ Then the thunder crashed and rolled, and lightning flashed. And a great earthquake struck—the worst since people were placed on the earth. ¹⁹ The great city of Babylon split into three sections, and the cities of many nations fell into heaps of rubble. So God remembered all of Babylon's sins, and he made her drink the cup that was filled with the wine of his fierce wrath. ²⁰ And every island disappeared, and all the mountains were leveled. ²¹ There was a terrible hailstorm, and hailstones weighing as much as seventy-five pounds* fell from the sky onto the people below. They cursed God because of the terrible plague of the hailstorm.

THE GREAT PROSTITUTE

17 One of the seven angels who had poured out the seven bowls came over and spoke to me. "Come with me," he said, "and I will show you the judgment that is going to come on the great prostitute, who rules over many waters. ² The kings of the world have committed adultery with her, and the people who belong to this world have been made drunk by the wine of her immorality."

³ So the angel took me in the Spirit* into the wilderness. There I saw a woman sitting on a scarlet beast that had seven heads and ten horns, and blasphemies against God were written all over it. ⁴ The woman wore purple and scarlet clothing and beautiful jewelry made of gold and precious gems and pearls. In her hand she held a gold goblet full of obscenities and the impurities of her immorality. ⁵ A mysterious name was written on her forehead: "Babylon the Great, Mother of All Prostitutes and Obscenities in the World." ⁶ I could see that she was drunk—drunk with the blood of God's holy people who were witnesses for Jesus. I stared at her in complete amazement.

⁷ "Why are you so amazed?" the angel asked. "I will tell you the mystery of this woman and of the beast with seven heads and ten horns on which she sits. ⁸ The beast you saw was once alive but isn't now. And yet he will soon come up out of the bottomless pit* and go to eternal destruction. And the people who belong to this world, whose names were not written in the Book of Life before the world was made, will be amazed at the reappearance of this beast who had died.

⁹ "This calls for a mind with understanding: The seven heads of the beast represent the seven hills where the woman rules. They also represent seven kings. ¹⁰ Five kings have already fallen, the sixth now reigns, and the seventh is yet to come, but his reign will be brief.

¹¹ "The scarlet beast that was, but is no longer, is the eighth king. He is like the other seven, and he, too, is headed for destruction. ¹² The ten horns of the beast are ten kings who have not yet risen to power. They will be appointed to their kingdoms for one brief moment to reign with the beast. ¹³ They will all agree to give him their power and authority. ¹⁴ Together they will go to war against the Lamb, but the Lamb will defeat them because he is Lord of all lords and King of all kings. And his called and chosen and faithful ones will be with him."

16:7 Greek *I heard the altar.* 16:10 Greek *gnawed their tongues.* 16:13 Greek *unclean.* 16:16 Or *Harmagedon.* 16:21 Greek *1 talent* [34 kilograms]. 17:3 Or *in spirit.* 17:8 Or *the abyss,* or *the underworld.*

¹⁵Then the angel said to me, "The waters where the prostitute is ruling represent masses of people of every nation and language. ¹⁶The scarlet beast and his ten horns all hate the prostitute. They will strip her naked, eat her flesh, and burn her remains with fire. ¹⁷For God has put a plan into their minds, a plan that will carry out his purposes. They will agree to give their authority to the scarlet beast, and so the words of God will be fulfilled. ¹⁸And this woman you saw in your vision represents the great city that rules over the kings of the world."

THE FALL OF BABYLON

18 After all this I saw another angel come down from heaven with great authority, and the earth grew bright with his splendor. ²He gave a mighty shout:

"Babylon is fallen—that great city is fallen!
    She has become a home for demons.
She is a hideout for every foul* spirit,
    a hideout for every foul vulture
    and every foul and dreadful animal.*
³ For all the nations have fallen*
    because of the wine of her passionate
        immorality.
The kings of the world
    have committed adultery with her.
Because of her desires for extravagant luxury,
    the merchants of the world have
        grown rich."

⁴Then I heard another voice calling from heaven,

"Come away from her, my people.
    Do not take part in her sins,
    or you will be punished with her.
⁵ For her sins are piled as high as heaven,
    and God remembers her evil deeds.
⁶ Do to her as she has done to others.
    Double her penalty* for all her evil deeds.
She brewed a cup of terror for others,
    so brew twice as much* for her.
⁷ She glorified herself and lived in luxury,
    so match it now with torment and sorrow.
She boasted in her heart,
    'I am queen on my throne.
I am no helpless widow,
    and I have no reason to mourn.'
⁸ Therefore, these plagues will overtake her
    in a single day—
    death and mourning and famine.
She will be completely consumed by fire,
    for the Lord God who judges her is mighty."

⁹And the kings of the world who committed adultery with her and enjoyed her great luxury will mourn for her as they see the smoke rising from her charred remains. ¹⁰They will stand at a distance, terrified by her great torment. They will cry out,

"How terrible, how terrible for you,
    O Babylon, you great city!
In a single moment
    God's judgment came on you."

¹¹The merchants of the world will weep and mourn for her, for there is no one left to buy their goods. ¹²She bought great quantities of gold, silver, jewels, and pearls; fine linen, purple, silk, and scarlet cloth; things made of fragrant thyine wood, ivory goods, and objects made of expensive wood; and bronze, iron, and marble. ¹³She also bought cinnamon, spice, incense, myrrh, frankincense, wine, olive oil, fine flour, wheat, cattle, sheep, horses, wagons, and bodies—that is, human slaves.

¹⁴ "The fancy things you loved so much
    are gone," they cry.
"All your luxuries and splendor
    are gone forever,
    never to be yours again."

¹⁵The merchants who became wealthy by selling her these things will stand at a distance, terrified by her great torment. They will weep and cry out,

¹⁶ "How terrible, how terrible for that
        great city!
She was clothed in finest purple and
        scarlet linens,
    decked out with gold and precious stones
        and pearls!
¹⁷ In a single moment
    all the wealth of the city is gone!"

And all the captains of the merchant ships and their passengers and sailors and crews will stand at a distance. ¹⁸They will cry out as they watch the smoke ascend, and they will say, "Where is there another city as great as this?" ¹⁹And they will weep and throw dust on their heads to show their grief. And they will cry out,

"How terrible, how terrible for that
        great city!
The shipowners became wealthy
    by transporting her great wealth
        on the seas.
In a single moment it is all gone."

²⁰ Rejoice over her fate, O heaven
    and people of God and apostles
        and prophets!
For at last God has judged her
    for your sakes.

18:2a Greek *unclean;* also in each of the two following phrases.
18:2b Some manuscripts condense the last two lines to read *a hideout for every foul [unclean] and dreadful vulture.* 18:3 Some manuscripts read *have drunk.* 18:6a Or *Give her an equal penalty.*
18:6b Or *brew just as much.*

[21] Then a mighty angel picked up a boulder the size of a huge millstone. He threw it into the ocean and shouted,

"Just like this, the great city Babylon
    will be thrown down with violence
    and will never be found again.
[22] The sound of harps, singers, flutes,
        and trumpets
    will never be heard in you again.
No craftsmen and no trades
    will ever be found in you again.
The sound of the mill
    will never be heard in you again.
[23] The light of a lamp
    will never shine in you again.
The happy voices of brides and grooms
    will never be heard in you again.
For your merchants were the greatest
    in the world,
    and you deceived the nations with
        your sorceries.
[24] In your* streets flowed the blood of the
        prophets and of God's holy people
    and the blood of people slaughtered
        all over the world."

SONGS OF VICTORY IN HEAVEN

19 After this, I heard what sounded like a vast crowd in heaven shouting,

"Praise the LORD!*
    Salvation and glory and power belong to
        our God.
[2] His judgments are true and just.
    He has punished the great prostitute
who corrupted the earth with her immorality.
    He has avenged the murder of his servants."

[3] And again their voices rang out:

"Praise the LORD!
    The smoke from that city ascends forever
        and ever!"

[4] Then the twenty-four elders and the four living beings fell down and worshiped God, who was sitting on the throne. They cried out, "Amen! Praise the LORD!"
[5] And from the throne came a voice that said,

"Praise our God,
    all his servants,
    all who fear him,
        from the least to the greatest."

[6] Then I heard again what sounded like the shout of a vast crowd or the roar of mighty ocean waves or the crash of loud thunder:

"Praise the LORD!
    For the Lord our God,* the Almighty, reigns.

[7] Let us be glad and rejoice,
        and let us give honor to him.
    For the time has come for the wedding feast
        of the Lamb,
    and his bride has prepared herself.
[8] She has been given the finest of pure white
        linen to wear."
For the fine linen represents the good
        deeds of God's holy people.

[9] And the angel said to me, "Write this: Blessed are those who are invited to the wedding feast of the Lamb." And he added, "These are true words that come from God."

[10] Then I fell down at his feet to worship him, but he said, "No, don't worship me. I am a servant of God, just like you and your brothers and sisters* who testify about their faith in Jesus. Worship only God. For the essence of prophecy is to give a clear witness for Jesus.*"

THE RIDER ON THE WHITE HORSE

[11] Then I saw heaven opened, and a white horse was standing there. Its rider was named Faithful and True, for he judges fairly and wages a righteous war. [12] His eyes were like flames of fire, and on his head were many crowns. A name was written on him that no one understood except himself. [13] He wore a robe dipped in blood, and his title was the Word of God. [14] The armies of heaven, dressed in the finest of pure white linen, followed him on white horses. [15] From his mouth came a sharp sword to strike down the nations. He will rule them with an iron rod. He will release the fierce wrath of God, the Almighty, like juice flowing from a winepress. [16] On his robe at his thigh* was written this title: King of all kings and Lord of all lords.

[17] Then I saw an angel standing in the sun, shouting to the vultures flying high in the sky: "Come! Gather together for the great banquet God has prepared. [18] Come and eat the flesh of kings, generals, and strong warriors; of horses and their riders; and of all humanity, both free and slave, small and great."

[19] Then I saw the beast and the kings of the world and their armies gathered together to fight against the one sitting on the horse and his army. [20] And the beast was captured, and with him the false prophet who did mighty miracles on behalf of the beast—miracles that deceived all who had accepted the mark of the beast and who worshiped his statue. Both the beast and his false prophet were thrown alive into the fiery lake of burning sulfur. [21] Their entire army was killed by the sharp sword that came from the mouth of the one riding the white horse.

18:24 Greek *her.* 19:1 Greek *Hallelujah;* also in 19:3, 4, 6. *Hallelujah* is the transliteration of a Hebrew term that means "Praise the LORD." 19:6 Some manuscripts read *the Lord God.* 19:10a Greek *brothers.* 19:10b Or *is the message confirmed by Jesus.* 19:16 Or *On his robe and thigh.*

And the vultures all gorged themselves on the dead bodies.

THE THOUSAND YEARS

20 Then I saw an angel coming down from heaven with the key to the bottomless pit* and a heavy chain in his hand. ²He seized the dragon—that old serpent, who is the devil, Satan—and bound him in chains for a thousand years. ³The angel threw him into the bottomless pit, which he then shut and locked so Satan could not deceive the nations anymore until the thousand years were finished. Afterward he must be released for a little while.

⁴Then I saw thrones, and the people sitting on them had been given the authority to judge. And I saw the souls of those who had been beheaded for their testimony about Jesus and for proclaiming the word of God. They had not worshiped the beast or his statue, nor accepted his mark on their foreheads or their hands. They all came to life again, and they reigned with Christ for a thousand years.

⁵This is the first resurrection. (The rest of the dead did not come back to life until the thousand years had ended.) ⁶Blessed and holy are those who share in the first resurrection. For them the second death holds no power, but they will be priests of God and of Christ and will reign with him a thousand years.

THE DEFEAT OF SATAN

⁷When the thousand years come to an end, Satan will be let out of his prison. ⁸He will go out to deceive the nations—called Gog and Magog—in every corner of the earth. He will gather them together for battle—a mighty army, as numberless as sand along the seashore. ⁹And I saw them as they went up on the broad plain of the earth and surrounded God's people and the beloved city. But fire from heaven came down on the attacking armies and consumed them.

¹⁰Then the devil, who had deceived them, was thrown into the fiery lake of burning sulfur, joining the beast and the false prophet. There they will be tormented day and night forever and ever.

THE FINAL JUDGMENT

¹¹And I saw a great white throne and the one sitting on it. The earth and sky fled from his presence, but they found no place to hide. ¹²I saw the dead, both great and small, standing before God's throne. And the books were opened, including the Book of Life. And the dead were judged according to what they had done, as recorded in the books. ¹³The sea gave up its dead, and death and the grave* gave up their dead. And all were judged according to their deeds. ¹⁴Then death and the grave were thrown into the lake of fire. This lake of fire is the second death. ¹⁵And anyone whose name was not found recorded in the Book of Life was thrown into the lake of fire.

THE NEW JERUSALEM

21 Then I saw a new heaven and a new earth, for the old heaven and the old earth had disappeared. And the sea was also gone. ²And I saw the holy city, the new Jerusalem, coming down from God out of heaven like a bride beautifully dressed for her husband.

³I heard a loud shout from the throne, saying, "Look, God's home is now among his people! He will live with them, and they will be his people. God himself will be with them.* ⁴He will wipe every tear from their eyes, and there will be no more death or sorrow or crying or pain. All these things are gone forever."

⁵And the one sitting on the throne said, "Look, I am making everything new!" And then he said to me, "Write this down, for what I tell you is trustworthy and true." ⁶And he also said, "It is finished! I am the Alpha and the Omega—the Beginning and the End. To all who are thirsty I will give freely from the springs of the water of life. ⁷All who are victorious will inherit all these blessings, and I will be their God, and they will be my children. ⁸But cowards, unbelievers, the corrupt, murderers, the immoral, those who practice witchcraft, idol worshipers, and all liars—their fate is in the fiery lake of burning sulfur. This is the second death."

⁹Then one of the seven angels who held the seven bowls containing the seven last plagues came and said to me, "Come with me! I will show you the bride, the wife of the Lamb."

¹⁰So he took me in the Spirit* to a great, high mountain, and he showed me the holy city, Jerusalem, descending out of heaven from God. ¹¹It shone with the glory of God and sparkled like a precious stone—like jasper as clear as crystal. ¹²The city wall was broad and high, with twelve gates guarded by twelve angels. And the names of the twelve tribes of Israel were written on the gates. ¹³There were three gates on each side—east, north, south, and west. ¹⁴The wall of the city had twelve foundation stones, and on them were written the names of the twelve apostles of the Lamb.

¹⁵The angel who talked to me held in his hand a gold measuring stick to measure the city, its gates, and its wall. ¹⁶When he measured it, he found it was a square, as wide as it was long. In fact, its length and width and height were each 1,400 miles.* ¹⁷Then he measured the walls and found them to be 216 feet thick* (according to the human standard used by the angel).

¹⁸The wall was made of jasper, and the city was pure gold, as clear as glass. ¹⁹The wall of the city was built on foundation stones inlaid with twelve precious stones:* the first was jasper, the second sapphire, the third agate, the fourth

JESUS WANTS TO FILL US
Revelation 22:1   ROBERT MORRIS

In John 4, Jesus meets a Samaritan woman at a well and asks her for a drink. Then He speaks to her about living water. Jesus describes this living water as "a fresh, bubbling spring" that gives eternal life to whoever drinks it (v. 14).

Are you thirsty for living water? Maybe you have been feeling spiritually dehydrated. Wouldn't you like to have a fresh, bubbling spring of eternal life inside you every day? God wants to quench your thirst. He wants to fill you up and speak to you. All you have to do is meditate on His Word. Revelation 22:1 says a river "with the water of life, clear as crystal" flows from the throne of God. And verse 17 says, "Let anyone who is thirsty come. Let anyone who desires drink freely from the water of life."

emerald, ²⁰the fifth onyx, the sixth carnelian, the seventh chrysolite, the eighth beryl, the ninth topaz, the tenth chrysoprase, the eleventh jacinth, the twelfth amethyst. ²¹The twelve gates were made of pearls—each gate from a single pearl! And the main street was pure gold, as clear as glass.

²²I saw no temple in the city, for the Lord God Almighty and the Lamb are its temple. ²³And the city has no need of sun or moon, for the glory of God illuminates the city, and the Lamb is its light. ²⁴The nations will walk in its light, and the kings of the world will enter the city in all their glory. ²⁵Its gates will never be closed at the end of day because there is no night there. ²⁶And all the nations will bring their glory and honor into the city. ²⁷Nothing evil* will be allowed to enter, nor anyone who practices shameful idolatry and dishonesty—but only those whose names are written in the Lamb's Book of Life.

22 Then the angel showed me a river with the water of life, clear as crystal, flowing from the throne of God and of the Lamb. ²It flowed down the center of the main street. On each side of the river grew a tree of life, bearing twelve crops of fruit,* with a fresh crop each month. The leaves were used for medicine to heal the nations.

³No longer will there be a curse upon anything. For the throne of God and of the Lamb will be there, and his servants will worship him. ⁴And they will see his face, and his name will be written on their foreheads. ⁵And there will be no night there—no need for lamps or sun—for the Lord God will shine on them. And they will reign forever and ever.

⁶Then the angel said to me, "Everything you have heard and seen is trustworthy and true. The Lord God, who inspires his prophets,* has sent his angel to tell his servants what will happen soon.*"

JESUS IS COMING

⁷"Look, I am coming soon! Blessed are those who obey the words of prophecy written in this book.*"

⁸I, John, am the one who heard and saw all these things. And when I heard and saw them, I fell down to worship at the feet of the angel who showed them to me. ⁹But he said, "No, don't worship me. I am a servant of God, just like you and your brothers the prophets, as well as all who obey what is written in this book. Worship only God!"

¹⁰Then he instructed me, "Do not seal up the prophetic words in this book, for the time is near. ¹¹Let the one who is doing harm continue to do harm; let the one who is vile continue to be vile; let the one who is righteous continue to live righteously; let the one who is holy continue to be holy."

¹²"Look, I am coming soon, bringing my reward with me to repay all people according to their deeds. ¹³I am the Alpha and the Omega, the First and the Last, the Beginning and the End."

¹⁴Blessed are those who wash their robes. They will be permitted to enter through the gates of the city and eat the fruit from the tree of life. ¹⁵Outside the city are the dogs—the sorcerers, the sexually immoral, the murderers, the idol worshipers, and all who love to live a lie.

¹⁶"I, Jesus, have sent my angel to give you this message for the churches. I am both the source of David and the heir to his throne.* I am the bright morning star."

¹⁷The Spirit and the bride say, "Come." Let anyone who hears this say, "Come." Let anyone who is thirsty come. Let anyone who desires drink freely from the water of life. ¹⁸And I solemnly declare to everyone who hears the words of prophecy written in this book: If anyone adds anything to what is written here, God will add to that person the plagues described in this book. ¹⁹And if anyone removes any of the words from this book of prophecy, God will remove that person's share in the tree of life and in the holy city that are described in this book.

²⁰He who is the faithful witness to all these things says, "Yes, I am coming soon!"

Amen! Come, Lord Jesus!

²¹May the grace of the Lord Jesus be with God's holy people.*

21:27 Or *ceremonially unclean.*   22:2 Or *twelve kinds of fruit.*
22:6a Or *The Lord, the God of the spirits of the prophets.*   22:6b Or *suddenly*, or *quickly*; also in 22:7, 12, 20.   22:7 Or *scroll*; also in 22:9, 10, 18, 19.   22:16 Greek *I am the root and offspring of David.*
22:21 Other manuscripts read *be with all*; still others read *be with all of God's holy people.* Some manuscripts add *Amen.*

INTERSECTIONS

1 THE GOOD CREATOR
The Story of Creation

GENESIS 1–2

The Bible begins with these words: "In the beginning God created the heavens and the earth" (Genesis 1:1). These words lay the foundation for everything that follows and introduce the Bible's most important character:

God.

God is the source of every created thing. He made the planet on which we live. He also created everything else. Before Him, there was nothing.

God is.

If God did not exist, then nothing would exist. Nothing and no one can compare to Him. Everything God created has a beginning, but He is without beginning or end. He created the world with order and is not the source of confusion. Just as He brought order to the chaotic universe, He can also restructure our disordered lives. When we trust Him and allow the Holy Spirit to work freely within us, God takes away our confusion and chaos and restores order to our lives.

God created the world in six days and rested on the seventh (Genesis 2:2). This fact does not mean He grew tired from making the world; rather, God rested to show us there is a time for activity and a time for rest and reflection. Both of these are part of His order for us. Though we live in a busy world, God has given us an opportunity to rest from work, although we often ignore this gift to our own detriment.

God is holy.

No part of God's creation can be called "God." He is separate and distinct from everything else. One way to express this truth is to say He is holy. Although God is different from creation, He is not disconnected from it. Instead, He is very involved. He cares about all He created, and He cares especially for people like *you*.

God is good.

As God was in the process of creating, He said everything He made was "good" (Genesis 1:10, 12, 18, 21, 25). Then, as He finished His creation, He said it was "very good" (Genesis 1:31). The reason everything was good is God is good. *A good God made good things*.

God is love.

Although everything God made was good, He only created people in His image. He cared so much about us that He created us to be like Him. We are not God, but because He made us in His image, we can relate to Him and others in ways nothing else in creation can. The Bible says, "God is love" (1 John 4:8). He created us because He loves us. And God created us in His image so we could freely choose to love Him in return. Because of His love, we also have the ability to love others.

1. Why do you think there is evil in the world?
2. How does your belief about the world's origins affect the way you view God? How does it influence the way you see yourself?
3. Why do some people find it difficult to believe a good and loving God created the world?
4. How would you tell someone what it means to be created in the image of God?

Although God is holy, loving, and good, the world is not the same as when He first created it. Something very bad happened to change it, and every human has been affected as a result.

---

2 A BLAMELESS MAN
Job

The Bible opens with the creation of the world and the rest of the universe, but this is actually not the oldest event recorded in the Bible. Before He created the world, God created heavenly creatures called angels. The word *angel* means 'messenger' or 'agent.' God created angels to carry out His work (Psalm 103:20). These spiritual beings witnessed the creation of the world (Job 38:4–7), and although they are not visible to humans most of the time, angels are always working on God's behalf and protecting God's people (Psalm 91:11). Angels constantly surround God's throne, praising and communicating with Him.

Why would a being who has seen God and heard the secrets of heaven ever turn against Him? We will probably never understand in this life, but one of the angels did just that. Of all the beings God created, Lucifer once had the most intimate relationship with Him in heaven. *Lucifer* means 'shining one.' He directly reflected God's glory, similar to the way the moon reflects the sun.

The most beautiful of all the angels, Lucifer became filled with pride. He attempted a mutiny to take over heaven and rule in God's place. He then led one-third of the angels to join in his rebellion

(Revelation 12:4). So God kicked Lucifer and all the angels who followed him out of heaven.

The Bible often refers to Lucifer by a different name: *Satan*, which means 'the adversary,' 'the enemy,' or 'the one who resists.' Ezekiel compared the king of Tyre to Lucifer, and in this comparison, he explained what happened to Satan before the world began (Ezekiel 28:13-15). Isaiah also wrote about Satan's fall from heaven (Isaiah 14:12), and the apostle John seemed to have known about this story as well (Revelation 12:9). Jesus said, "I saw Satan fall from heaven like lightning!" (Luke 10:18). The enemy is very active in this world, but he will ultimately be condemned to eternal fire, separated from God (Matthew 25:41).

Satan stood in opposition to God, which was bad enough news. But the story only gets worse. Satan hated God so much he tried to destroy what God loves most—*people*. Satan focused all his attention on trying to put an end to humanity. The story of Job shows just how much Satan wants to do us harm.

JOB 1; 42

No one really knows when the story of Job was composed or who the writer was. However, it is a very ancient story, possibly written even before the book of Genesis. Job was a blameless man who "feared God and stayed away from evil" (Job 1:1). God blessed Job and made him very rich and happy, giving him thousands of animals and many servants. Job was a man of integrity, but he lost everything he had, even his children and his health. How could this happen?

Job's success caught Satan's attention. One day, Satan decided to challenge God regarding Job. Satan told God that Job only served Him because Job was so wealthy. If God did not protect and bless this man with so much wealth, then he would curse God. God responded by allowing Satan to take away everything Job had. In one day, Job lost his animals, his servants, and his 10 children. When Job learned of this tragedy, he still worshipped God rather than blaming Him.

Then Satan told God that Job would curse Him if God allowed Satan to take Job's health. Job contracted terrible boils, which covered his entire body. Rather than comforting him, Job's wife told him to curse God and die. Even so, Job refused to turn against God.

Job's three friends came to comfort him. However, when they saw Job's physical condition, they didn't even recognize him. Job's friends believed he must have done something very sinful for God to allow such tragedy. They reasoned that God would not permit a righteous person to suffer as Job did. The friends argued back and forth. They accused Job while he consistently justified himself and proclaimed his innocence.

Finally, Job asked God to explain his suffering. God responded by asking Job questions, such as where he was when God created the world and all of its complexities. Then Job realized the greatness of God and the foolishness of his questions. God also corrected Job's friends about the way they treated him. After this, God restored Job and "gave him twice as much as before!" (Job 42:10), including seven more sons and three more daughters. Job lived a long and full life before he died.

The story of Job provides two important lessons for us today:

It is dangerous to hold uninformed opinions about God and others.
— God is not the author of death and sickness; Satan is. God allowed Satan to inflict Job, but He did not initiate it. God returned to Job double what he had lost, showing that God can be trusted even when things appear to be unfair. Job's friends made assumptions about him. They thought he had done something to deserve what he experienced. Job was not a perfect person, but God described him as being "blameless." Job was foolish for complaining to God about what had happened to him, but his friends were wrong to accuse him of sin and deserving sin's consequences.

This world is a battleground between good and evil.
— Satan always tries to attack the true nature and character of God. He is the destroyer, but God is the restorer. Satan wants you to blame God for the sorrow and difficulty in the world. He wants you to believe God is not just, trustworthy, or good. Satan hopes you will look at the evil and tragedy in the world and curse God rather than worship Him. Satan was created to worship God, but he wanted to *be worshipped* instead. He will always try to convince us to believe lies about God.

God does good; Satan does evil. God is never the source of evil in the world. We also cannot assume those who have trouble are wicked or sinful and those who don't are righteous. Yes, we live in a world that experiences the effects of sin and Satan, but God is good and can be trusted. By His goodness, He will right all wrongs. Job said,

> "But as for me, I know that my Redeemer lives,
>   and he will stand upon the earth at last.
> And after my body has decayed,
>   yet in my body I will see God!
> I will see him for myself.
>   Yes, I will see him with my own eyes.
>   I am overwhelmed at the thought!" (Job 19:25-27).

1. What tragedy did Job experience in Job 1:18-19? Do you know anyone who has had this experience in their own life? Why is this kind of heartbreak so difficult for people to bear?

2. What can you learn about Satan from the story of Job? What can you learn about God?
3. Did Job sin as Satan predicted? What did Job do?
4. How can you respond to tragedies and difficulties in a way that pleases God?

Satan was unsuccessful in getting Job to turn away from God. Job is an example of a person who follows God and stays away from evil. However, not all people have been able to follow Job's model. In fact, the very first humans did not. They disobeyed God, and we have paid for their mistakes ever since.

3 THE FIRST PEOPLE
Adam and Eve

Satan could not get Job to disobey God, but this failed attempt did not stop him. Like a lion, the "great enemy" is always on the prowl, looking for people to destroy (1 Peter 5:8). Sadly, he has found many willing victims. The first two were Adam and Eve.

GENESIS 3

People are very special to God. Of all the things He made, humans were the last—the crown of His creation. The first two humans were Adam and Eve. God formed Adam from the dust of the earth and breathed life into him. Then He placed Adam in the beautiful Garden of Eden to tend and care for it. God decided it was not good for Adam to be alone; the man needed a companion. God caused Adam to fall into a deep sleep and then formed a woman from the man's rib (Genesis 2:21-22). Adam named this woman *Eve* (Genesis 3:20).

Of all God's creation, only Adam and Eve were made in His image. They were able to relate to God and each other on a higher level than any other created being. God placed the man and woman in a perfect environment. The Garden of Eden had no pain, sickness, or suffering. It was very different from our present world.

One day, Adam and Eve made a choice that changed everything—for the worse. God had placed many trees in the Garden of Eden and told Adam and Eve they could eat from all of them, with one important exception. God specifically told them not to eat from a single tree in the middle of Eden: the tree of the knowledge of good and evil. He said if they ate from it, they would die. Sadly, both the man and the woman disobeyed God and ate from the tree. This decision changed the course of all creation, including the entire human race.

Those first two humans made a terrible choice because they believed something false—the serpent's lie. Later revealed to be Satan (Revelation 12:9; 20:2), the serpent had approached Eve and caused her to question God. Then he deceived her and convinced her that God was not good and could not be trusted. Adam also believed this lie. Next, the serpent persuaded the couple that if they ate from the forbidden tree, they could become

like God. If they could be like God, then why would they need Him? Adam and Eve believed they would become wise enough to make their own choices apart from God.

Those two lies have been the root causes of sin ever since. We don't trust God or believe He is good, so we take matters into our own hands. We try to be the gods of our own lives and the lives of others.

Long ago, Satan rebelled against God. Then he convinced Adam and Eve to do the same. Although God created Satan as a special angel to serve and worship Him, Satan decided he wanted to *be* God. Pride entered his heart, and he no longer wanted to do things God's way (Ezekiel 28:14-15). This pride and rebellion against God cost Satan everything. No wonder he tempted Adam and Eve to oppose God as well. He deceived them into believing God was not good and that doing things their own way would be better than following God's way. However, they quickly found out how tragic it is to ignore God's way.

The saddest part of this story is that people have been turning from God's way ever since. We still have much to learn, and God wants to teach us these truths:

God is good.
— We know about His goodness from the very beginning of Genesis—a good God created good things. He does not try to keep anything good from us. God is always working for our best interests.

God's commands are good.
— God gives us instructions for living because He wants to help us. Sometimes children view their parents' instructions as unnecessary roadblocks, but good parents simply want to protect their children. God gives commands for the same reason. Sometimes we think we know better than God does. But we do not. When God's children fail to do things God's way, they get hurt and soon realize how wrong they were.

God loves us.
— God wants us to have a loving relationship with Him. But love cannot be forced—it always involves a choice. Adam and Eve made theirs.

They could eat from all the trees except one. They could choose to love and obey God or decide to disobey. Sadly, they chose disobedience. God could have forced them to obey, but that is not the way God works. We cannot really love Him without obeying Him. And most of us will not obey God if we do not believe He is good. Satan knew this from his own experience, so he persuaded Adam and Eve to disobey God, just as he had done. He will try to tempt you to do the same. Believe God is good. Believe God is love.

Pride is the disease. Humility is the cure.

— Pride is dangerous. It was for Adam and Eve, and it is for you too. It can destroy you (Proverbs 16:18). It will lead you to believe that your way is better than God's way. When we follow our way, we act as if we are gods. But we are not God. Unlike pride, humility will lift you up (1 Peter 5:6). When you love God and obey Him, you humble yourself by saying His way is better

than your own. When you love and obey God, blessings follow.

1. The story of Adam and Eve's sin is also every person's story. How has it been your story?
2. What have been the results of Adam and Eve's sin? How can you see those results in the world today?
3. What other examples can you think of that show the dangers of pride?
4. Do you know someone whom you consider to be humble? How does that person show humility? How could you follow that person's example?
5. How did Jesus do things differently than Adam and Eve?

Bad choices did not end with Adam and Eve. God removed them from the perfect garden, and soon they had children. They named their first two children Cain and Abel. Before long, these sons followed in their parents' footsteps.

4 THE FIRST MURDER
Cain and Abel

Adam and Eve disobeyed God, so He made them leave the perfect garden He had given them to manage. Not long after, Adam and Eve began having children.

GENESIS 4:1–16

Adam and Eve's first son was Cain, and the second was Abel. As the brothers grew, they selected separate professions; Cain became a farmer while Abel chose to be a shepherd. Because Adam and Eve had sinned against God, they could not come into His presence. Therefore, God established a way for people to give sacrifices and offerings to honor Him and make payment for their sins. Cain and Abel both offered some of the product of their work to God. Cain brought some of his crops, and Abel brought the best parts of the firstborn (or firstfruits) of his animals.

God accepted Abel's offering, but He did not accept Cain's. The writer of Hebrews says Abel's offering was "more acceptable" (Hebrews 11:4). Cain became very angry when his offering was rejected, and of course, God saw this anger. When He asked Cain about it, though, Cain did not reply. Then God told Cain to beware of sin because it was so close—"crouching at the door, eager to control you" (Genesis 4:7). If Cain would follow the Lord and do what was right, God would bless him. But if Cain refused, sin would take over his life and bring destruction.

Cain made his choice. He was the first human born in the world, but he also became the first

human to kill. One day in the field, while he thought God was not watching, Cain murdered his brother. Later, God asked him where Abel was. Cain tried to deflect God's question with another question: "Am I my brother's guardian?" (Genesis 4:9). However, God already knew the answer; He knew Cain had his brother's blood on his hands. As a result, God cursed Cain and banished him from the land, making Cain a wanderer for the rest of his life.

Humans had a very sad and tragic beginning, but it did not have to be that way. God gave Cain a choice: do what is right, or sin will take over your life. Cain thought God was unfair, so he took matters into his own hands and killed his brother. Jesus may have had Abel's murder in mind when He told His followers to be reconciled to each other before offering sacrifices (Matthew 5:23-24).

As a believer, you will sometimes feel as if life is unfair. Occasionally, you may think it is God's fault. Even if you believe you are right, ask God to show you if there is any sin in your life. Remember, no matter the situation, you can choose God's way to live, or you can choose your own path. Your own way will ultimately lead to destruction. Still, God is always good, and He wants to forgive you and bring you back to Him. Even though God punished Cain, He also protected him with a special mark so others would not kill him. God shows mercy and grace even when we don't deserve it.

The Bible does not remember Cain in a positive way. In three other verses, it reminds us not to act like him (Hebrews 11:4; 1 John 3:12; Jude 1). Even when life seems unfair or when your disobedience has made a mess of things, God wants the best for you. He always wants to give you mercy and grace.

1. Think of a time when you thought life was unfair. How did you respond? What could you have done differently?
2. Why did God accept Abel's offering but not Cain's? What was the difference between the two?
3. We should still honor God with our firstfruits and our offerings, but God made another way for us to deal with the problem of sin. What has He done? How would you tell someone else about it?

4. Can you remember a time when God showed grace and mercy to you, even though you did not deserve it?
5. If you have something in your life that is keeping you from following God's way, ask the Holy Spirit to show you what you need to change.

The death of Abel was a very high cost to pay for the disobedience of Adam, Eve, and Cain. Sadly, humans continued to turn from God's way to follow their own. Sin corrupted people's hearts so thoroughly that God decided to start over. Only one man "found favor with the LORD" (Genesis 6:8). His name was Noah.

5 THE GREAT RESCUE
Noah and the Flood

When left untended, weeds will soon overtake a beautiful garden. During times of drought and intense heat, many plants will die, but weeds seem to grow anyway. When they fully take over a garden, the only solution is to remove all the plants, till the soil, and begin again.

After Cain killed Abel, Adam and Eve had other children. People began to increase in number and inhabit the earth. However, they continued to disobey God. People became so bad that "everything they thought or imagined was consistently and totally evil" (Genesis 6:5). The effects of sin that began with Adam and Eve had spread to everyone. The world was so corrupt that God decided to make a fresh start.

GENESIS 6-8

Humanity's disobedience broke God's heart, but He did not become bitter. God is always good. He is full of mercy and grace, and He was unwilling to give up on the human race entirely. In such an evil world, one man "found favor with the LORD" (Genesis 6:8). His name was Noah. As God prepared to start over, He laid out a plan to rescue Noah and his family.

God told Noah He was going to send a flood that would destroy every living thing on the earth. He instructed Noah to make a large boat (or ark) to shelter Noah and his family from the water to come. The flood would cover the whole earth, but by His grace, God would protect Noah. So God's rescue operation began.

It took many years for Noah to build the boat, but he obeyed everything God told him to do. The Lord brought Noah one pair (male and female) of every kind of animal and seven pairs of every kind of bird to fill the earth after the flood. God also told Noah to bring seven pairs of the animals the Bible calls "clean" (Genesis 7:2-3) for food and

sacrifices. As the rain was about to begin, God told Noah and his family to get inside the boat. When they were all safely inside, God closed the boat's door with His own hand and released the flood.

For 40 days and 40 nights, rain fell upon the earth, and water came up from the ground until the earth was completely under water. Even after the floodwaters began to recede, it took many months for the earth to become dry again. Noah, his family, and the animals finally left the boat over a year after the flood first began. Because Noah was faithful and obedient to God's commands, he and his family were saved, and through them, the human race was rescued as well.

Even in the very worst of situations, God is always working for our good. The Bible contains many stories of God using just one man or woman to make a fresh start. Although you are only one person, God can make that kind of fresh start for you as well.

As you think about your past experiences, do you wonder if God can change your life? Perhaps you have done many things you know are wrong. You may have experienced some terrible situations. Nevertheless, God alone is able to give you a fresh start. The rescue begins when you put your faith in Him. The apostle Paul says, "Anyone who belongs to Christ has become a new person. The old life is gone; a new life has begun!" (2 Corinthians 5:17).

Baptism is a necessary picture of this fresh start for us. Just as the world was covered with water, we are placed under water as a sign that our old life is over. Much like the fresh start God made through Noah, we declare the new life we have in Jesus as we come out of the water. Paul says when we place our faith in Christ, it is as if we died with Him. Just as God rescued Jesus from death through the Resurrection, we also receive new life by the work of the Holy Spirit (Romans 6:1-11).

God told Noah He would never again destroy the earth with a flood, and as a reminder of this promise, He put a rainbow in the sky (Genesis 9:13-16). God has given us a promise as well: whoever believes in Jesus will not perish but have eternal life (John 3:16). If Noah ever feared that the world would again be flooded, he could look to the rainbow and remember God's promise. Likewise, if you ever doubt God's love and forgiveness, remember He rescued you through the blood of Jesus. It is the promise of your salvation—your rescue.

God made a fresh start when He rescued Noah, and He will do the same for you. Regardless of your past, God has never given up on you. When you change your heart and mind and put your faith in Jesus, your old life comes to an end, and your new

life begins in Him. Through Jesus, you can have a fresh start too.

1. Have you ever thought God had given up on you? What was that experience like?
2. How can you know what God really thinks about you?
3. Has God ever rescued you from destruction? How has He helped you remember that experience?
4. What is one thing God needs to rescue you from today? Ask Him for His help right now.
5. If someone told you, "God has given up on me," what would you say?

The human race had a fresh start, but it didn't last long. People soon fell back into old habits. They even built the Tower of Babel as a monument to their disobedience and pride.

6 A MONUMENT TO PRIDE
The Tower of Babel

During the days of Noah, people had become so wicked and cruel that God allowed a flood to cover the whole earth. Only Noah, his family, and the animals on the boat were saved. After this fresh start, you might think people would have learned to obey God. Sadly, they did not.

Adam and Eve sinned because they believed Satan's lies that God could not be trusted and they could be like God. Every time we sin against God, these two ideas are at the root of our disobedience. They were certainly the reasons the people of Babel rebelled against God. As a demonstration of their pride and disobedience, they built a tower in an attempt to reach heaven.

GENESIS 11:1-9

Some years after the great flood, there lived a man named Nimrod. He was "the greatest hunter in the world" (Genesis 10:9), and he founded the city of Babylonia. At that time, the people spoke one language. They decided to build a tower that reached into the sky, believing it would make them famous (Genesis 11:4). Rather than serving God, they wanted to lift up themselves.

God saw what they were doing and recognized what they could accomplish if the people worked together in pride. So He confused them by causing the people to speak in many different languages. As a result, they could no longer communicate with each other. God stopped their prideful plan and scattered them throughout the world.

Humanity was so evil in Noah's day that God saved only eight people from death. At the Tower of Babel, human wickedness showed itself again. Just two generations after Noah, these rebellious

and prideful people tried to build a tower to reach heaven. The tower showed they did not want God to rule them. Instead, they wanted to rise to the place they believed God lived.

The people of Babel had the same pride that led Satan to try to be like God. Satan said,

"I will climb to the highest heavens
and be like the Most High" (Isaiah 14:14).

Adam and Eve followed Satan's example, and so did the people of Babel. They tried to build the tower because they were motivated by the same rebellion as Satan, the originator of the sin of pride.

When Jesus does not control people's lives, they tend toward the sins of pride and self-will. Rather than submitting to God, they try to be like God so they can control their own destinies. They want to make their own decisions apart from God. People who continue to live in pride and rebellion against God suffer disastrous consequences for their decisions—their "tower" will ultimately fall.

Unlike the people at Babel, who wanted to exalt themselves, God came down to us! Jesus, the Son of God, was willing to humble Himself and become a man (Philippians 2:6-7). He lived in obedient submission to His Father. Jesus said He came to serve, not to be served (Matthew 20:28). He demonstrated His humility when He was even willing to wash His disciples' feet (John 13:1-17).

Pride, rebellion, and self-promotion may lead to temporary fame and fortune on earth, but they will not lift a person up in the Kingdom of God. Jesus taught that the way to greatness is through serving others. When His disciples argued about who would be the greatest among them, Jesus said, "Whoever wants to be a leader among you must be your servant" (Matthew 20:26). There is no higher place than under the lordship of Jesus Christ.

> "God opposes the proud
>   but gives grace to the humble."
>
> So humble yourselves under the mighty power of God, and at the right time he will lift you up in honor (1 Peter 5:5-6).

1. Have you ever let pride control your actions? What were the results?
2. In what ways can you practice humility as you follow Jesus?

3. Ask God what He wants to say to you about submission to His authority and to the authority of those He has placed over you.

The people of Babel did not trust God's character. They did not believe in His goodness, nor would they submit to His authority. Instead, they tried to become *like God*, and the sin of pride took over the whole city. In the end, their pride caused their destruction. The story of Babel ends badly. The whole world is in confusion, and people have become enemies of each other and God. There is hope, though, because God still loves people. And through one special person, He will once again launch His rescue plan for humanity. This person is Abraham.

7 THE FATHER OF FAITH
Abraham

The Bible begins with some tragic stories: Adam and Eve's sin, Cain's murder of Abel, and Noah and the great Flood. Although there are terrible parts to each of these stories, God was always working for the good of humanity. Adam and Eve disobeyed God and were punished, but God also gave them protection, food, and children. Cain killed his brother, but God put a special mark of protection on Cain. The world was evil, and God chose to destroy it with a flood, but He rescued Noah and his family, thereby saving humanity. Yes, even in the bad times, God was always working for good.

GENESIS 12; 15-16; 18:1-15; 21:1-7; 22

The story of the Tower of Babel seems to disrupt this pattern. Because of their pride, the people built a great tower to lift themselves up to the level of God. God then brought judgment, confusing their language and scattering them all over the earth. It might look like this story ends without God doing anything good. But that interpretation would be a mistake. God answered the story of Babel in a most wonderful way: He chose Abraham.

Through Abraham, God also chose a people—a nation—through whom He would show His true self to the whole world. God told Abraham to leave his home and travel to a place God would show him. Then God promised, "I will make you into a great nation. I will bless you and make you famous, and you will be a blessing to others" (Genesis 12:2). From this one man, God would build a special and blessed nation that would then bless all other nations.

Abraham obeyed God and left his home. However, Abraham knew he would need more than land to become a great nation—he would need a son. One day, God made another promise to him. He told Abraham, "Look up into the sky and count the stars if you can. That's how many descendants

you will have!" (Genesis 15:5). At the time, Abraham had no children, but he believed God would do as He promised.

Many years passed, but Abraham and his wife, Sarah, still had no children. So Sarah told Abraham to have a baby with her servant, Hagar. Hagar became pregnant and gave birth to a son named Ishmael. Abraham and Sarah thought God would keep His promises through Ishmael, but that was never God's plan. Abraham and Sarah grew older still and were past the age for most people to have children. God spoke to Abraham again and reminded him of the promise that he and Sarah would have a son. This time, Abraham laughed, and when Sarah heard about God's promise, she laughed too.

Not long after, a miracle happened: Sarah gave birth to the promised son. They named him *Isaac*, which means 'laughter.' Abraham and Sarah had laughed when they heard they would have a son in their old age, but when Isaac was born, God had the last laugh! He promised to bless Abraham, and He also said many nations would be blessed through him.

This blessing began with Isaac. One day, however, it looked as if God had changed His mind. As a test of faith, God told Abraham to sacrifice Isaac as a burnt offering. Abraham obeyed God and took his son to the mountain where God had instructed him to go. When they arrived, Abraham built an altar and placed Isaac on it. Just as the father was about to kill his son, God's angel called out to him, saying, "Do not hurt him in any way, for now I know that you truly fear God" (Genesis 22:12).

At that moment, Abraham saw a ram caught by his horns in a bush. He offered the ram to God in place of his son. God, and not Abraham, had provided a sacrifice. Sometimes people read this story through modern eyes and forget that the nations surrounding Abraham often killed their children as offerings to their gods. Abraham's God had the power and right to demand the life of his son, but God only wanted to test the father's faith. Abraham served a good God.

This event paints the picture of God's willingness to sacrifice Jesus in our place. Like the ram He provided for Abraham, God the Father sent His own Son into the world to die for our sins. What may be the most famous verse in the Bible tells us:

"For this is how God loved the world: He gave his one and only Son, so that everyone who believes in him will not perish but have eternal life" (John 3:16).

1. Have you ever felt like God had forgotten you or forgotten His promises to you? What did you do during that time? What will you do differently if it happens again?
2. Abraham obeyed God's directions and traveled to a land he had never seen before. He also made some mistakes, such as having a child with Hagar. Still, God blessed him. How has God blessed you even when you have not obeyed Him as you should?
3. How would you explain to someone that Jesus is our sacrifice?
4. How has God blessed all the nations of the world through Abraham?
5. God still loves the nation of Israel, although Gentile believers have been brought into that family as well. Take a moment now to pray for peace and salvation for God's people, Israel.

Abraham became the father of Isaac and, eventually, of the nation of Israel. Through this nation, God sent Jesus into the world. When John the Baptist saw Jesus, he exclaimed, "Look! The Lamb of God who takes away the sin of the world!" (John 1:29). Through Abraham and then through Jesus, all the nations of the earth were blessed.

8 THE PROMISED SON
Isaac

Although Abraham and Sarah doubted God's promise, God fulfilled it by giving them a son named Isaac. *Isaac* means 'laughter.' Abraham and Sarah laughed for two reasons. They first laughed because they did not believe they would have a son in their old age, and then they laughed for joy at God's gift of Isaac. God made the same promises to Isaac that He made to his father, Abraham.

GENESIS 21:1-7; 22; 24; 26:25

When Abraham was very old, he received the fulfillment of the Lord's promise: his son Isaac. When Isaac was still a child, God tested Abraham's faith by telling the father to sacrifice his son as a burnt offering. Abraham was willing to obey, but just as he was about to kill Isaac, the Lord told him to stop. Abraham had proven he was willing to obey God, no matter the cost. God provided a ram, which Abraham offered as a sacrifice in Isaac's place.

When Isaac became a man, he married a woman named Rebekah. He loved her very much (Genesis 24:67). After Abraham's death, God made the same promises to Isaac that He made to Isaac's father: "I will give all these lands to you and your descendants. . . . I will cause your descendants to be as numerous as the stars of the sky" (Genesis 26:3-4). The Lord said this would happen not because of anything Isaac had done but because of Abraham's obedience.

Isaac was God's promised son to Abraham. His birth was nothing short of miraculous. All the promises God made to Abraham continued through Isaac and his descendants. Isaac had two sons, Esau and Jacob. Jacob eventually had 12 sons of his own, and from these sons came the 12 tribes of Israel.

In many ways, Isaac's life points to Jesus:
— Both came through a miraculous birth.
— Many people received the promises of God because of them (2 Corinthians 1:20).
— Both were willing to lay down their lives: Isaac submitted to Abraham, and Jesus submitted to His Father's will by dying on the cross for us.

Isaac's life also demonstrates the blessings of sonship. He received the promises God made to his father, Abraham, and he enjoyed a blessed life. All of this happened because of whose son he was. In the same way, we share in the blessings of the Father because He has called us His sons. We were once separated from God, but now through faith in Jesus Christ, we have become His adopted children. God is now our Father (Romans 8:15-16). Like Isaac, every Christian has experienced a miraculous birth (John 3:3-5). As a result, we also have become heirs of God (Romans 8:17). And we receive all the promises God made to Abraham (Galatians 3:29).

Have you had a difficult past? Perhaps your family was broken. No matter what, God wants to adopt you and give you a fresh start. When you put your faith in Christ, you become God's child. The apostle John wrote, "See how very much our Father loves us, for he calls us his children, and that is what we are!" (1 John 3:1). As Isaac was, you too are a blessed child of your Father!

1. What does it mean to you to know you are God's child?
2. What inheritance have you received from other believers who have gone before you?
3. Have you ever had difficulty believing God loves you and wants you to be His child? Why or why not?

4. What does it mean to you when you hear that Abraham is also your father?

Isaac's wife, Rebecca, gave birth to twin boys. God stated that the older son, Esau, would serve the younger. In time, the younger son would have 12 sons of his own who would then become the 12 tribes of Israel. The younger son's name was Jacob.

9 A CHANGED MAN
Jacob/Israel

God gave Isaac two sons. They both became the fathers of great nations. A conflict developed between the two sons while they were still in their mother's womb, and it has lasted even until today.

GENESIS 25:19-34; 27-33; 35:1-15

When Isaac and Rebekah's twin sons were born, the younger son, Jacob, was holding onto the heel of his older brother, Esau. As they grew, Esau loved being outdoors and became a skilled hunter. Jacob had a quieter temperament and preferred staying at home (Genesis 25:27). Isaac favored Esau, but Rebekah preferred Jacob.

One day, Esau returned from hunting while Jacob was cooking some stew. Esau was very hungry and asked his brother for some of the food. Jacob told Esau he would give him some stew in exchange for Esau's rights as the firstborn. In his great hunger, Esau agreed to do what Jacob wanted.

Nearing the end of his life, Isaac told Esau he wanted to bless him before dying. Rebekah overheard this conversation and came up with a plan to have her husband bless Jacob instead. Due to his old age, Isaac could not see well. He could only distinguish his sons by touch—Esau was very hairy while Jacob had smooth skin. Rebekah covered Jacob's arms and neck with goat skin so he would feel like Esau when Isaac touched him.

Rebekah's plan worked. Isaac mistook Jacob for Esau and gave him the blessing that belonged to the firstborn son. When Esau discovered what happened, he was furious; he plotted to kill Jacob after their father's death. When Rebekah learned of Esau's plan, she sent Jacob away.

On the run, Jacob went to Haran, where his uncle Laban lived. Upon arrival, Jacob fell in love with Laban's younger daughter, Rachel. Jacob agreed to work seven years for Laban to gain the privilege of marrying her. After the seven years, however, Laban tricked Jacob into marrying Rachel's older sister, Leah. Jacob was angry with his uncle but agreed to work another seven years for Laban in exchange for marrying Rachel.

God blessed and multiplied everything Jacob owned. This blessing angered his uncle, however. Aware of this jealousy, Jacob began to feel it was time to get away from Laban and return to his homeland. On the journey back, Jacob worried about what his brother, Esau, might do to him. The night before he was to reunite with Esau, Jacob was alone in his camp when "a man came and wrestled with him until the dawn began to break" (Genesis 32:24). This "man" gave Jacob a new name—Israel. To Israel's great surprise, the reunion with his brother was peaceful, and Esau forgave him.

During his lifetime, Jacob had 12 sons who became the founders of the 12 tribes of Israel. God promised him the same blessings He had promised to Jacob's father, Isaac, and his grandfather Abraham (Genesis 28:12-14). Jacob blessed all his sons before he died at an old age.

Jacob received God's blessings and promises by grace, not through his own efforts. Before the twin brothers were even born, the Lord had said the older (Esau) would serve the younger (Jacob). In spite of this promise, Jacob chose to take things into his own hands. He took his brother's firstborn rights in exchange for stew, and with the help of Rebekah, deceived Isaac and stole Esau's blessing. Jacob's trickery outraged Esau, forcing the younger brother to flee to his uncle's home. There Jacob met his match. Laban not only tricked Jacob into marrying Leah before giving him Rachel, but he also changed Jacob's wages 10 times (Genesis 31:41).

Jacob was humbled as he finally learned God was the source of his provision and blessing. While wrestling with the "man," Jacob had his hip pulled out of its socket, but his heart was corrected. His faith was strengthened too. His name was changed from Jacob, which means 'to take the place of another through force, scheming, or strategy,' to Israel, which means 'he struggles with God, and God prevails.'

God has called us to a life of faith and obedience. This does not include looking to gain an advantage over others for selfish reasons. As Jacob encountered God, he learned of God's plan to bless him. However, God had to humble him before he could fully experience those blessings. God has a plan for your life. He may have to humble you to reveal it, but He will give it to you by grace.

1. What blessings has God promised you? Have you done things that help or prevent you from receiving them?
2. Have you experienced "wrestling" with God? If so, what was that experience like?
3. Have you ever felt God was slow in keeping His promises to you? How can someone hold onto faith during these times?

10 THE FAITHFUL DREAMER
Joseph the Patriarch

The story goes that a man got lost trying to travel to a place he had never been. Then he noticed another man who might be able to help him with directions. The lost traveler asked how to get to where he was going, and the other man replied, "If that's where I was going, I sure wouldn't start from here!"

The story of Joseph is very much like the one of the lost traveler. By the end of Genesis, Joseph is a powerful ruler in Egypt, but his story starts in a dramatically different way. At different points in his life, Joseph is kidnapped, sold into slavery, and eventually imprisoned. Through all these trials, God remains faithful to him, and in the same way, God will remain faithful to you.

GENESIS 37; 39–47; 50

As a young man, Joseph had two dreams. Both revealed that God would one day place him in a position of high authority, and even his family would bow down to him. Joseph's brothers found these dreams offensive, not only because Joseph was their brother, but also because he was the second youngest of Jacob's sons. Who did Joseph think he was to tell his brothers they would bow to him? Their father had always favored Joseph, and these dreams only made the brothers more jealous and angry. So they plotted to get rid of the dreamer. At first, they planned to kill Joseph and blame his death on a wild animal attack. Then they decided it would be easier to sell him to slave traders. To cover up their actions, the brothers led Jacob to believe that a wild animal had killed his favorite son.

The slave traders took Joseph to Egypt and sold him to a powerful man named Potiphar. God blessed Joseph in all he did, and the young man's hard work and success caught Potiphar's attention. However, Joseph also caught the attention of his master's wife. She was very attracted to Joseph and repeatedly propositioned him. Joseph refused her advances, saying, "How could I do such a wicked thing? It would be a great sin against God" (Genesis 39:9). Potiphar's wife became angry, so

Jacob had 12 sons. He loved them all, but he had a special relationship with one of them—Joseph. Joseph was the first son of Jacob's wife Rachel. Jacob had a special love for Rachel (Genesis 29:18, 30), which may have influenced his special love for Joseph. Jacob's other sons noticed the attention and affection their father had for Joseph. Ultimately, jealousy grew in their hearts, and they wanted to destroy him.

she accused Joseph of trying to take advantage of her. Potiphar believed this lie and had Joseph thrown into prison.

Even while in prison, Joseph continued to experience God's blessings. The prison warden was fond of Joseph and soon put him in charge of the other prisoners. One night, two of the prisoners had dreams. With God's help, Joseph told these men what their dreams meant. One would be released from prison and allowed to resume his position working for Pharaoh (Egypt's ruler). The other man, however, would be killed. Before the first man was released, Joseph asked him to speak to Pharaoh on his behalf. He asked him to tell the ruler that Joseph did not deserve to be in prison. However, the man "forgot all about Joseph, never giving him another thought" (Genesis 40:23).

Two years passed, and Joseph remained in prison. Then Pharaoh had two dreams that greatly disturbed him. He was desperate for someone to interpret the dreams, but no one could do so. Finally, the man who had been in prison with Joseph remembered that Joseph could interpret dreams. Pharaoh sent for Joseph, and God immediately gave him the interpretation of the dreams. Egypt would experience seven years of great harvests followed seven years of extreme famine. The famine would be so terrible that no one would remember the good years. Joseph recommended that Pharaoh should assign someone to begin storing food so the people of Egypt would not starve.

When the ruler heard Joseph's words, he replied, "Clearly no one else is as intelligent or wise as you are. . . . I hereby put you in charge of the entire land of Egypt" (Genesis 41:39, 41). In an instant, Joseph went from being a lowly prisoner to the second in command over a nation. Only Pharaoh had more power than Joseph had.

Joseph's predictions came true. After seven bountiful years, a famine hit Egypt and all the surrounding countries. Even Joseph's family in Canaan suffered. The famine became so bad that Jacob sent his sons to Egypt to buy food. When they arrived, Joseph recognized them right away, but the brothers did not recognize him. As they bowed before him, Joseph remembered the dreams he had as a young man. God was fulfilling them at last!

The brothers took the food home, but when it ran out, they returned to Egypt once again. This time, Joseph revealed his identity to his brothers. They couldn't believe it! Joseph quickly reassured them, "Don't be angry with yourselves for selling me to this place. . . . God has sent me ahead of you to keep you and your families alive and to preserve many survivors" (Genesis 45:5, 7). The brothers returned home to tell their father the wonderful news that his son was alive. Jacob, his sons, and their entire family moved to Egypt, where Joseph took care of them.

After Jacob died at the old age of 147, the brothers feared Joseph might finally seek revenge. However, he continued to show them kindness:

"Don't be afraid of me. Am I God, that I can punish you? You intended to harm me, but God intended it all for good. He brought me to this position so I could save the lives of many people" (Genesis 50:19-20).

Joseph could have been angry and bitter with his brothers. He could have scolded them and said, "I told you so!" Instead, he showed them honor and love. Because Joseph maintained a humble heart, God was able to use him in a miraculous way to save his family, the nation of Egypt, and every person who bought food from Egypt during the famine.

The story of Joseph is about an amazingly good God who keeps His promises and rescues His people. God will bring about His plans in ways no one expects. You may have been placed in a humbling position, but God will have His way. Joseph did not become a ruler through traditional methods, but it was God's way, and it saved God's people.

You cannot control everything, but you can be faithful. Like Joseph, you can trust God and obey His commands in every situation. God did not make Joseph a ruler so he could shame his family. God lifted Joseph up so he could *save* his family.

God will give you dreams and promises to hold onto when life gets hard. Be faithful in everything you do and trust Him to bring it to pass. While Joseph was interpreting the dreams of others, God was working to fulfill the dream He gave Joseph! Be willing to serve others, and God will put you in places you never dreamed possible.

1. What would you have thought if Joseph told you about his dreams? How can you have confidence in God's promises even when others don't understand?
2. Have you ever experienced rejection or persecution even when you knew you were doing the right thing? If so, how did you respond?
3. How would you tell someone who is going through a difficult time that God has a plan and is in control?
4. When we experience difficult times, we often cannot see the bigger picture. Thinking about your own life, in what ways can you see that God has been working all along?

When Joseph died, things changed over time. Several centuries years later, Egypt had a new ruler who did not know anything about Joseph or how he had saved everyone from starvation. This ruler was afraid of the people of Israel, so he forced them to slaves.

Through Joseph, God saved the lives of Jacob and his sons. Now through Moses, God was about to bring their descendants—the Israelites—together as His chosen nation, free them from bondage, and lead them to the Promised Land.

---

11 THE GREAT LIBERATOR
Moses

Several centuries after his death, no one in Egypt seemed to remember who Joseph was anymore (Exodus 1:8). Even worse, the people of Israel had become slaves. However, God used their years in bondage to grow their numbers (Exodus 1:11-14). The time came when the Israelites grew tired of their oppression, and they cried out to God to save them. God heard their plea and sent a man to deliver them. This man was a unique individual—Hebrew by birth but raised as an Egyptian. His name was Moses.

EXODUS 2–4; 14:15-31; NUMBERS 12:6-8

Pharaoh became concerned with the growing number of Israelites (also called Hebrews), so he ordered the midwives to kill every Hebrew baby boy at birth. However, two brave Hebrew midwives refused to obey this evil command (Exodus 1:15-17). When one Hebrew woman, Jochebed, had a baby boy, she hid him from the Egyptians for as long as she could. After three months, hiding was no longer an option. Jochebed waterproofed a basket of papyrus leaves, placed her baby boy inside, and set him afloat on the Nile River.

Pharaoh's daughter often came to the river to bathe, and she soon found the basket. When she saw the crying baby boy inside, she had compassion on him. The princess knew this was a Hebrew baby, but she decided to adopt him as her own son. However, she needed someone to care for him until he could eat solid food. The baby's older sister had been watching from a distance, and she offered to help the princess find a nursing Hebrew mother. The princess agreed, and the sister knew just the right person: Jochebed! This remarkable Hebrew mother not only saved her son from imminent death, but she also had the blessing of rearing and teaching him for several years. Then she took her son to the palace, where the princess officially adopted him and named him *Moses* (Exodus 2:1-10).

While visiting his people many years later, Moses noticed an Egyptian beating a Hebrew slave. Enraged, Moses killed the Egyptian and hid the body. He thought he could keep his actions a secret. The next day, Moses saw two Hebrews fighting with each other, and he tried to break up the fight. He was very alarmed when one man retorted, "Are you going to kill me as you killed that Egyptian yesterday?" (Exodus 2:14). Even Pharaoh knew about the murder. Fearing for his life, Moses fled to the land of Midian and became a shepherd there (Exodus 2:11-15).

As he was herding sheep one day, Moses saw a bush on fire. This alone would have been a strange sight, but it became even stranger when he realized the bush wasn't burning up. How was this possible? As Moses came toward the bush for a closer inspection, God suddenly spoke to him from it. God told Moses to return to Egypt and to tell Pharaoh to set the Hebrew people free so they could worship God at the mountain. After many objections and excuses, Moses decided to obey God (Exodus 3:1-4:17).

Moses approached Pharaoh, but Egypt's ruler refused to free the Hebrews. He said, "I don't know the Lord, and I will not let Israel go" (Exodus 5:2). As a result, God sent nine terrible signs of His power to the land of Egypt. The Nile River turned into blood. Swarming animals, disease, and hail plagued the land. For three days, there was total darkness. God showed His favor to the Hebrews, though, and protected their community from these horrors. Still, Pharaoh refused to obey God. Then God delivered the tenth and final sign: the death of the firstborn son. Every Egyptian family felt this terrible loss, but God passed over the sons of the Hebrews, once again proving that Israel was His chosen people. With his land and his people devastated, Pharaoh relented and set the people of God free (Exodus 5-13).

Shortly after the Hebrews left, Pharaoh hardened his heart once again. He said, "What have we done, letting all those Israelite slaves get away?" (Exodus 14:5). Gathering his mighty army, Pharaoh chased after the people and soon caught up with them, trapping them against the Red Sea. Then God proved His power yet again by splitting the water and creating a dry path for the Hebrews to walk on to the other side. Pharaoh and his army tried to follow them, but God brought the water crashing down, and all the Egyptians drowned. God saved the Israelites, just as He promised (Exodus 14:5-15:20).

So God led Moses, Moses led the people, and God provided for their needs. God took them to Mount Sinai, where He gave Moses the Law for the people to follow. Once again, however, sin entered the picture. The people did not trust God to keep His promises, and they often tried to take matters into their own hands. They angered and disappointed Moses with their constant complaining and disobedience. While the people were at Kadesh, Moses became so frustrated that he disobeyed God's command. God wanted to give the people water to drink, so He told Moses to speak to a large rock, and water would come out of it. Instead, though, Moses hit the rock twice with his walking stick. God still provided water for the people, but because of his disobedience, Moses was not allowed to enter the Promised Land (Numbers 20:8-12).

God called Moses to deliver His people from slavery. However, they constantly tried to do things their own way, and even Moses failed to obey God on at least one occasion. The Israelites spent 40 years wandering in the wilderness until a new generation was ready to enter the Promised Land. Only two of the original Hebrews who came out of Egypt were allowed to enter as well.

Moses' life can teach us many lessons as we answer God's call:

Let God prepare you.
— Like Moses, you may sense God is calling you to do great things for Him. However, you must be ready to do them His way. God wants to do a work *in* you before He works through you. Let Him work.

God's timing may be different from yours.
— Moses was 40 years old when he ran away from Egypt, and then he spent 40 more years herding sheep. When he returned to Egypt, Moses was 80 years old. You are never too old to follow God's plan.

The more you receive, the more God expects your obedience.
— Moses was a great man of God, but he never entered the Promised Land because he disobeyed God's direct command. Moses knew God intimately, and he had a unique calling. God has also given you a special calling, but He requires your obedience.

Trust that God will provide.
— Moses learned that God would protect and care for His people, just as He had spared Moses from death as a baby. Moses saw the Israelites' suffering and liberated them from slavery by the power of God. In the wilderness, God miraculously provided food, water, and daily guidance.

God is present.
— God met Moses at the burning bush and on Mount Sinai. His glory was even seen on Moses' face (Exodus 34:35). God was with His people in a cloud by day and a pillar of fire by night. His

presence was with them in the Tabernacle. God wants to be with us.

God wants to protect, provide for, and be present with you. He will if you let Him. Moses didn't want to go anywhere unless God went with him, and truly, that is the only way to live.

1. Do you believe God is calling you to some type of service or ministry? If so, what is it? What are you doing now to prepare for it?
2. How do you remain patient while you wait on God to work in an area of your life?
3. What is one way you know God has provided for you in the past? How do you need Him to provide for you in the present?

4. How do you know God is present in your life?
5. How would you encourage others to believe God is present in their lives?

When God delivered the people of Israel from Egypt, it was a rescue mission. He freed them from captivity like a rescuer frees hostages. However, God did not simply want to free them; He wanted to make them His own. But for the Israelites to be God's people, they would have to follow His ways, obey His commands, and listen to His voice. And God spoke very clearly. He told them exactly how they were to live and obey Him. On Mount Sinai, God even wrote down the Law with His own finger and gave it to Moses.

12 THE LAWGIVER
The Ten Commandments

When God freed the Israelites from slavery and delivered them from Pharaoh's rule, He became their King. God didn't simply call His people out of Egypt; He called them to Himself (Exodus 19:4). He was their God, and they were His people. However, this would require Israel to walk in His ways, not in those of Egypt or any other nation.

EXODUS 20:1–17

At Mount Sinai, God gave Moses all the laws He wanted His people to follow. This covenant would separate the Israelites from every other nation and clearly mark them as the people of God. Foundational to these laws were the Ten Commandments, which God Himself wrote on two stone tablets (Exodus 31:18).

God gave laws by which His people could enjoy His provision and protection. He did not give them rules simply to make their lives difficult. God is good, and He wants His people to experience His goodness. Moses said, "Listen closely, Israel, and be careful to obey. Then all will go well with you" (Deuteronomy 6:3). God always wanted everything to go well with His people.

The Ten Commandments showed Israel how to respect God and treat others. The first four addressed the people's relationship with God. They were to serve and honor only Him. This mindset was very different from that of the Egyptians, who worshipped thousands of different gods. The Israelites had lived in Egypt for centuries, so it was imperative to begin their new life by establishing faithfulness to the one true God.

The last six commandments spoke about how the people were to treat others. They were to honor their parents. They were not to murder, commit adultery, steal, lie, or selfishly desire what others had. If Israel obeyed God's laws, they would know God's blessings.

Many times, the people of Israel failed to keep their covenant with God. Instead, they followed the practices of other nations, even though this disobedience often resulted in suffering. After God sent many warnings to His people through men called prophets, He removed the Israelites from the Promised Land, just as He had removed the nations that were there before them. Some of God's people were taken to Assyria. Later, others were taken to Babylon. Eventually, God brought the Israelites back to the land He had promised their ancestors, but their lives would have been much better if they had simply kept God's laws from the beginning.

God gave His people the Ten Commandments to teach them about His goodness. He had no desire to make their lives miserable. God loves us and really does know what is best for us. His desire is for you to be close to Him and to live in harmony with others.

Jesus said all of God's commandments could be summed up in two actions: love God and love others. When asked which commandment was the most important, Jesus answered, "You must love the LORD your God with all your heart, all your soul, and all your mind" (Matthew 22:37). He went on to say that a second commandment was just as important as the first: "Love your neighbor as yourself" (Matthew 22:39). The apostle John understood:

> If someone says, "I love God," but hates a fellow believer, that person is a liar; for if we don't love people we can see, how can we love God, whom we cannot see? (1 John 4:20).

When we fail to obey God's commandments, we prevent ourselves from experiencing all His blessings. God freed His people from bondage in Egypt, but they continuously disobeyed His laws and found themselves yet again under the control of other nations. God has also called us to obey Him, and like the Israelites, we often fail to live according to His standards. James says if we violate one commandment, we are guilty of breaking them all (James 2:10).

When Adam and Eve disobeyed God, sin entered the world and made it impossible for anyone to keep all God's laws all the time. Our only hope is in God's Son, Jesus Christ. On the cross, Jesus paid the price for all our disobedience. When you accept His sacrifice, God gives you a fresh start. He offers you a new nature—one that not only desires to but is also able to obey Him. This does not mean you will lead a perfect life. Rather, you will have the Holy Spirit to help you, and when you fail, you can turn away from your disobedience and receive God's forgiveness (1 John 1:9). God has all the resources you need to love Him and others, and He offers them to you today.

1. Before giving the Ten Commandments, God said, "I am the LORD your God, who rescued you from the land of Egypt, the place of your slavery" (Exodus 20:2). How are the Ten Commandments still applicable to God's people today?

2. Read Exodus 20:3-17. How is the tenth commandment different from the first nine?

3. Which commandment do people have the most difficulty obeying today? Why do you think this is?

4. How do you think the commands to love God and love your neighbor relate to the Ten Commandments? Why did Jesus say the whole Law relates to these two commands?

Moses said to the people of Israel:

"Be careful to obey all the commands I am giving you today. Then you will live and multiply, and you will enter and occupy the land the LORD swore to give your ancestors. Remember how the LORD your God led you through the wilderness for these forty years, humbling you and testing you to prove your character, and to find out whether or not you would obey his commands" (Deuteronomy 8:1-2).

Sadly, the Israelites were not always careful to obey God's commands. However, they did prove their character—and it was not godly! Consequently, God did not allow the first generation out of Egypt to enter the Promised Land.

13 THE WILDERNESS GENERATION
The People of Israel

God has always loved His people, Israel. He loved them when they were slaves, so He delivered them. He loved them when the Egyptians pursued them, so He rescued them. He loved them when they wandered in the wilderness, so He led them. However, the children of Israel did not always appreciate God's deliverance, rescue, or leading. They didn't always love Him in return.

EXODUS 16; 32; NUMBERS 10-14

In the wilderness, the Israelites were free from Egyptian oppression. However, the wilderness did not bear fruit in the same way Egypt had. It was a barren, dry, and uninviting place. Nevertheless, God was with His people the entire way, always meeting their needs. He led them with a cloud by day and a pillar of fire by night. He miraculously provided food and water for them and even kept their shoes and clothing from wearing out!

After leaving Egypt, the people of Israel wandered in the wilderness for 40 years. This wandering was not because they did not know how to read a map, but rather because they continuously rebelled and complained against God. Normally, it would only take a few weeks to cross the Sinai desert on foot. The shortest route is only about

250 miles (400 km). But the people were ungrateful for God's divine provision, so they grumbled. They complained to Moses when they were thirsty. They complained about the manna, a special type of bread God provided, and asked for meat instead. They even claimed to miss their lives in Egypt—where they had been slaves!

While Moses was on the mountain receiving God's Law, the people became impatient. They rejected God and formed a golden calf to worship. Moses pleaded with the Lord to forgive the people, and thus began the pattern of the Israelites rebelling and Moses interceding for them. However, when the Israelites refused to enter the Promised Land because they feared the current inhabitants, God declared:

"They have all seen my glorious presence and the miraculous signs I performed both in Egypt and in the wilderness, but again and again they have tested me by refusing to listen to my voice. They will never even see the land I swore to give their ancestors" (Numbers 14:22-23).

God forced the Israelites to wander in the wilderness for 40 years until an entire generation died.

They were not allowed to enter the Promised Land. One whole generation experienced a false start.

After being slaves for over 400 years, why did the children of Israel act so unfaithfully once they were set free? After they saw the great signs in Egypt, the parting of the Red Sea, and the miraculous presence and provision of God, how could they have been so foolish and unthankful? With a land of blessings ahead of them, how could they have thought about going back to Egypt? Because of their disobedience, God did not let His people make a direct journey to the Promised Land. He knew they would need to be tested to see if their hearts were turned toward Him or not (Deuteronomy 8:2). Sadly, almost every person proved to be unfaithful and therefore did not get to experience God's blessings.

What lessons can we learn from the Israelites who fled Egypt?

Guard your heart.

— When times are tough, it is easy to forget the goodness of God and how He has blessed you. However, you always have a choice—either you can be thankful for all God has done or complain about what you do not yet have. Like the Israelites in the wilderness, your attitude will affect your future.

Draw close to the Lord.

— Rather than grumble, you can actually grow in your relationship with the Lord when you face difficulties. When everything is fine, you may be tempted to spend less time with Him. God warned His people not to forget about Him when they came into the Promised Land. He knew they could easily get caught up in all the blessings and forget the One who blesses (Deuteronomy 6:10-12). The apostle Paul instructs us to learn from the example of the people of Israel in the wilderness (1 Corinthians 10:1-11). When things aren't going as we would like, we must remember that we were slaves to sin and darkness before Jesus saved us. When you find yourself feeling spiritually dry and thirsty, draw near to God rather than complain. You can trust Him to meet your needs during difficult times. God has promised, "I will never fail you. I will never abandon you" (Hebrews 13:5).

Trust God with your future.

— When you get discouraged, don't fall into the same trap the children of Israel did. In the wilderness, they wanted the food from Egypt while forgetting they had been slaves. Satan wants to convince you not to trust God. He wants you to take your future into your own hands. But remember the pain and emptiness in your life before Jesus saved you. In the wilderness, an entire generation experienced a false start. God set them free, but they failed to receive the blessings He had in store for them. *Trust God*. He has a "Promised Land" of blessings in store for you.

1. Have you ever turned away from God when bad things happened to you? If so, how did God bring you back to Himself?
2. Have you ever forgotten God when things went well for you? If so, how did God get your attention?
3. What are some ways you can guard your heart and keep yourself from disobeying God?
4. Do you know someone who has turned away from God, either because things were going badly or well? If so, take time to pray for that person right now.

Not every Israelite rebelled against God. Two men remained faithful: Joshua and Caleb. God blessed Caleb with the land he and his descendants would possess (Number 13-14). And God chose Joshua to be the next leader of the people. Joshua would take them into the Promised Land.

---

14 GOD'S STEADFAST WARRIOR
Joshua

Born into slavery in Egypt, Joshua was nearly 40 years old when he and the people of Israel followed Moses to freedom. Joshua witnessed God's mighty power firsthand as the Red Sea parted for the Israelites and then came crashing back into place, destroying Pharaoh and the Egyptian army. While the people struggled to obey God during the wilderness years, Joshua remained steadfast in his faith and proved himself worthy of his calling as the next leader of Israel.

JOSHUA 1; 3; 6; 23-24

When an enemy force confronted the Israelites for the first time, Moses chose Joshua to lead the battle. As they faced off against the Amalekites, Joshua obeyed God and defeated the enemy with the Lord's power. Then God gave a message to Moses and a promise to Joshua: "I will erase the memory of Amalek from under heaven" (Exodus 17:14).

Not long after, Moses climbed Mount Sinai to receive God's laws on stone tablets. Joshua accompanied him part of the way but then camped in place for 40 days. Meanwhile, at the foot of the mountain, the people of Israel became impatient and wavered in their faith. Thinking their leader had met with some terrible fate, they fashioned a golden calf to worship—in clear disobedience to God's commandment not to worship other gods or make any idols. Still, Joshua continued to wait, standing strong in his loyalty to God and Moses, God's chosen leader.

Years later, after wandering through the desert, the people finally arrived at the edge of Canaan, the Promised Land. God told Moses to send 12 spies, one from each tribe, to scout out the land. Joshua was the chosen representative from his tribe. Ten spies brought back a discouraging and even frightening report. They said the enemy was far too powerful to be defeated. Only Joshua and Caleb spoke with confidence: "If the Lord is pleased with us, he will bring us safely into that land and give it to us" (Numbers 14:8). The people of Israel did not believe God would be faithful to His promise, and this angered the Lord. He had repeatedly shown them His power—the miraculous signs in Egypt, the parting of the Red Sea, and the provision of food and water on their journey—but they continued to doubt Him. As a result of their unbelief and disobedience, God declared that none of that generation of Israelites would enter the Promised Land. Only Joshua and Caleb would be exceptions because they put their trust in the Lord.

For over 40 years, Joshua served as Moses' assistant and helped guide the people as they wandered in the wilderness. When Moses died, Joshua was appointed as the next leader of Israel. Then he received a second promise from God: "No one will be able to stand against you as long as you live. For I will be with you as I was with Moses. I will not fail you or abandon you. Be strong and courageous" (Joshua 1:5-6).

At 84 years old, Joshua led the new generation of Israelites across the Jordan River and into the land of their inheritance. They faced intense opposition from the people in the land—pagan nations who worshipped many false gods—but as Israel stayed faithful to the one true God, God proved Himself faithful to His promise. Over and over, He displayed His miraculous power, such as when the impenetrable walls of Jericho collapsed into dust (Joshua 6:20) and when the sun stood still during the battle with the Amorites (Joshua 10:12). By the time of Joshua's death at the age of 110, he had led the Israelites to victory over 31 kings and their territories (Joshua 12:24).

Though originally called "Hoshea," this famous warrior is remembered by the name Moses gave him: *Joshua*, which means 'God is salvation.' Though Moses led the people out of slavery in Egypt, it was Joshua who led them into the Promised Land. Centuries later, a young virgin gave this same name to her newborn Son, the fulfillment of another divine promise. *Jesus* (the English form of the translated name) is God's promised Savior, not just to the people of Israel but to all people everywhere (Romans 1:16).

1. When have you acted in boldness and faith when other people doubted? How did it make you feel at the time?
2. What calling has God put on your life that gives you confidence?
3. God often wants us to wait and submit to other leaders before He puts us in positions of authority. What should someone do to remain patient while waiting?
4. How would you encourage someone to remain strong and courageous in following God, even when others around them do not obey the Lord?

_____

God led His people to the land He had promised to give their ancestor Abraham. The land was not empty, though. The Israelites would have to take it from the current inhabitants by force. As they set out to conquer the city of Jericho, they found help from an unlikely source: a prostitute named Rahab.

15 JERICHO'S HEROINE
Rahab

God delivered His people and brought them through the wilderness. Before they entered the Promised Land, Joshua sent out spies to learn about the enemies they would face. When they came to Jericho, they met a woman of the city who would help them. Her name was Rahab.

JOSHUA 2; 6:22-23

Rahab was an unexpected choice to help God's people. She was a prostitute. However, when she heard how the God of the Israelites had delivered His people from Egypt, she knew His favor was with these spies. So Rahab agreed to hide the spies from the men in the city who wanted to harm them. At first, she hid the spies on the roof of her home. Then she helped them escape the city.

In return for Rahab's help, the spies promised to protect her and her family when the Israelites returned to capture the city. They told her to tie a scarlet rope in the window to identify her home. Not long after, an Israelite army, led by the priests, returned to Jericho. By the Lord's miraculous power, the walls fell when the people shouted, and the Israelites took the city. When they came to Rahab's home, they saw the scarlet rope and spared the lives of all who were inside.

Rahab had heard about how God had delivered the Israelites from Egypt. She recognized that God was with these people and would give her city into their hands. Rahab did not grow up among the Israelites and was not exposed to all the knowledge they had about the Lord. Still, she stepped out in faith on what she did know. The writer of Hebrews says, "It was by faith that Rahab the prostitute was not destroyed with the people in her city who refused to obey God. For she had given a friendly welcome to the spies" (Hebrews 11:31).

God's grace is deep and wide. The story of Rahab is a picture of that grace. She and her family may have been the least likely people in Jericho for God to spare. Rahab would not have been considered righteous or holy; she did not know the Law of Moses. The Lord spared her because of her faith. She believed God was with the Israelites. In the same way, when we place our faith in what Jesus did on the cross, we are saved! Like Rahab, we are not saved by our own knowledge or holiness but by the blood of Jesus. Maybe you would not expect God to spare a prostitute and destroy the rest of the city, but God doesn't always act as we would suppose. Many people criticized Jesus because He chose to spend time with people who were not holy. However, Jesus' response to those critics was, "I tell you the truth, corrupt tax collectors and sinners will get into the Kingdom of God before you do" (Matthew 21:31). It's also interesting to note that although He came to earth many

centuries later, Jesus was a descendant of Rahab (Matthew 1:5).

No matter what you've done, Jesus can save you. No matter where you've been, Jesus can save you. No matter what other people think of you or how unworthy you feel about yourself, Jesus can and will save you if you put your faith in Him. His blood will cleanse you from all your sins, and He will give you a fresh start.

One more interesting fact about Rahab: she was the mother of Boaz, and she became Ruth's second mother-in-law (the first being Naomi). No wonder Boaz showed such compassion to Ruth. He learned it from his mother.

1. Have you ever felt unworthy? How does the story of Rahab speak to you about your value to God?
2. What could you say to people who believe they can never be saved because of their past?
3. The writer of Hebrews says Rahab was saved by her faith. How are people saved by faith today?
4. Rahab was part of God's plan to bring us Jesus. Why do you think God used a person like Rahab as part of His plan?

God told the Israelites to destroy all the inhabitants of Jericho, except for Rahab and her family. He also told them not to take anything of value. Everyone obeyed God, except for one man. His name was Achan, and his greed cost him everything.

---

16 DESTRUCTIVE GREED
Achan

After God freed the Israelites from slavery in Egypt, He guided them through the wilderness and brought them into the Promised Land. However, the land was not empty. Other people lived there, but God had promised to remove them. The first city God's people encountered was the walled fortress of Jericho. Miraculously, God broke down those walls and allowed Israel to take the city. However, He commanded the Israelites not to take any of the property from the city. All the people followed God's command, except for one man—Achan.

JOSHUA 7:1–26

Greed destroys. It often causes people to make terrible decisions. God was very serious about His command, and Achan's disobedience came at a high cost—the price tag was his life and the lives of his entire family. He also brought pain to all the Israelites. Because Achan disobeyed God, the Israelites could not defeat the next city. Then God revealed to Joshua the reason for the army's

failure: one of the Israelites had disobeyed His command at Jericho. The next day, God showed Joshua the person who was guilty of not following His instructions: Achan. When asked why, Achan replied, "I saw a beautiful robe from Babylon, 200 silver coins, and a bar of gold weighing more than a pound. I wanted them so much that I took them" (Joshua 7:21).

When children are young, they do not yet know it is right to share their toys. No matter how many toys they have, they always want the toy in another child's hand. When they see it, they quickly express their dissatisfaction with the toy they have. Then they will fight over that one toy, no matter how many other toys are in the room. Greed has the same effect on us. It prevents us from enjoying what we have and makes us want more and more, even when it hurts others and us. Greed can cause us to do many harmful things.

Greed grows when we take our eyes off God's ways and all He has given us and focus on what we do not have. The writer of Proverbs tells us,

Guard your heart above all else,
for it determines the course of your life
(Proverbs 4:23).

In Genesis, God gave Adam and Eve every tree in the Garden of Eden for food, except for one (Genesis 2:16-17). Then the serpent tempted them to see *only* that tree. They began to desire it, and then they ate from it. Because of their disobedience, Adam and Eve had to leave Eden. Their desire for what God hadn't given them created horrible results for the entire world. God also promised many blessings to the people of Israel in the Promised Land, but they would have to obey Him. He told them to offer everything in Jericho to Him (Joshua 6:17). Obeying God's command would honor Him and help them remember He was the source of their blessings.

Achan could have enjoyed God's blessings, but instead, he took for himself what was to be offered to God. He entered the Promised Land but lost everything. Achan's greed led to a false start. He was like those whom Jesus spoke about who hear the Word of God but allow the lure of wealth to prevent them from living a blessed and fruitful life (Matthew 13:22).

God wants to bless us, but we must never desire the blessings more than the One who gives them. Jesus said, "Seek the Kingdom of God above all else, and live righteously, and he will give you everything you need" (Matthew 6:33). We don't have to live with constant worry. God has promised to provide for us. He knows what we need, and we can trust Him (Matthew 6:25).

Contentment and thankfulness will help you avoid the dangers of greed. Contentment will help you show gratitude for what God has given you rather than concerning yourself with what others have. Thankfulness will keep your eyes on God, the One who blesses you with all you need.

Greed brings misery because it is never satisfied. It brought great misery to Achan and his family. You can always dream of a bigger house, a better car, or more money. However, true joy comes from trusting God to provide for your needs, recognizing all He has already given you, and thanking Him for all His blessings.

1. Have you ever wanted something that was not yours? Maybe you even took something that did not belong to you. How did that experience make you feel?
2. How does generosity protect us from greed?
3. When you think about everything God has given you, how often do you thank Him for it? What can you do to remind yourself to tell God how grateful you are for what He has done?
4. Right now, take a few minutes to think about the good things you have. You may even want to make a list. Then tell God how thankful you are for His blessings to you.

Joshua and the Israelites continued to defeat their enemies and settle in the land of Canaan. Then they divided the land among the 12 tribes of Israel, and the people lived in peace. However, this time of peace did not last long.

17 A FEARLESS TRIO
Deborah, Barak, and Jael

Near the end of his life, Joshua called the people of Israel together and reminded them to follow all God's laws. He also warned them that disobedience would make life very difficult. However, the people did not remain faithful to God, and before long, their struggles with the nations around them resumed. Thus began an ongoing cycle:
— Israel serves the Lord.
— Israel falls into sin and idolatry.
— God allows Israel's enemies to oppress the people.
— The people cry out to the Lord for help.
— God raises up a military leader.
— The people are delivered.

The military leaders God raised up at that time were similar to local tribal chieftains or warlords. They would free the Israelites from oppression at the hands of the surrounding enemies. These leaders were called judges.

JUDGES 4-5

Because of their disobedience to God, the people of Israel suffered under the oppression of the Canaanites for 20 years. Finally, they cried out to God, and He sent Deborah to deliver them. She then sent for a man named Barak to gather an army for battle.

Deborah assured Barak that God would give the Israelite army victory over the enemy. Barak was willing to obey the Lord but under one condition—he would only go into battle if Deborah went with him. Deborah agreed to do so, but she told Barak he would receive none of the glory for the victory. Instead, it would go to a woman (Judges 4:9). At the time, Barak did not know that the woman Deborah spoke of was not herself. Rather, it was a woman named Jael.

With the Lord's help, Israel fought and defeated the armies of the Canaanites. Sisera, the commander of the Canaanite army, escaped and fled until he came upon Jael's tent. Jael went out to meet him and invited him inside. Sisera told Jael not to let anyone know he was there. Exhausted from his escape, he asked for a drink and then fell asleep. While Sisera slept, Jael took a tent peg and drove it through his head, killing him (Judges 4:21). Barak may have led the army of Israel into battle, but Jael was the one who killed the Canaanite commander. She received the credit for defeating Israel's enemy. Deborah and Barak wrote a song celebrating the victory and honoring Jael.

The story of Deborah, Barak, and Jael has valuable lessons for us:

Serve humbly.
— Deborah and Jael stand out as the heroines of this story, and Barak emerges as a man who humbled himself before the Lord and others. Barak knew he would not receive glory for the victory, even before the battle began. President Harry Truman once said, "It is amazing what you can accomplish if you do not care who gets the credit." As believers, we know God deserves the glory for our victories, and we willingly give honor to others for their good works.

God uses both men and women.
— Although the Bible contains numerous stories of great men like Abraham, Moses, and the apostle Paul, it also has many accounts of women doing great things for God. Deborah and Jael had more influence than Barak on Israel's victory. These characters are just two of the examples of God working through women to accomplish His will. God will continue working through women of faith, just as He works through men of faith.

Trust others to strengthen your faith.
— Barak had faith, but he was also a bit hesitant. He set conditions for his obedience: "I will

go, but only if you go with me" (Judges 4:8). However, Deborah didn't give up on Barak. She went with him and gave him strength and support. God will often pair us with someone who will encourage us when our faith is weak. Many of God's people have hesitated. Even Moses was slow to obey the Lord's command to go to Egypt and deliver the Israelites. As a result, God sent Moses' brother, Aaron, with him. God will send people to help you follow Him. Pray for godly friends who will strengthen your faith.

1. Have you ever been willing to do a task and allow someone else to have the credit? Ask God to give you the humility to lift up other believers.
2. Who are some of the great women of faith you know about? What great things did they do for God?
3. What women in your life have had great faith? Thank God for their desire to follow Him.
4. Has someone in your life had faith for you even when yours was weak? Thank God for bringing that person into your life. If possible, tell that person how much their faith encouraged you.
5. Do you have godly friends who encourage you? If not, ask God to send the right people into your life.

After Deborah's service as a judge, the Israelites once again turned to sin. As a result, God allowed their enemies to harass, defeat, and oppress them. The Midianites devastated their land, destroyed their crops, and killed their cattle for many years. God did not forget about His people, though. He raised up another military leader to guide the Israelites during this time of conflict. His name was Gideon.

18 A WARRIOR FOR GOD
Gideon

The people of Israel once again turned away from God and suffered for their actions. When they changed their hearts and minds and came back to God, He raised up Gideon to lead and deliver them.

JUDGES 6–8

One day, the angel of the Lord appeared to Gideon, saying, "Mighty hero, the LORD is with you!" (Judges 6:12). Gideon asked how God could be with the Israelites when their enemies were oppressing them so badly. The angel replied that God was calling Gideon to deliver the people of Israel from their enemies.

Gideon was unsure, though, so he asked God to give him a sign as proof. Gideon wanted the fleece

of a sheep to be wet with morning dew while the ground all around it was dry. The next morning, Gideon found exactly that. However, this sign still was not enough to convince him. Gideon then asked God to make the ground wet with dew but keep the fleece dry. Again, God did as Gideon had asked Him to do.

With this assurance from the Lord, Gideon gathered his army of 32,000 men. However, God told him there were too many soldiers. If all of those men went into battle, they would take the credit for God's victory over their enemies. So the Lord told Gideon to let anyone who felt afraid go home. Only 10,000 men remained.

God told Gideon 10,000 were still too many. So Gideon instructed the men to drink water from a spring. Only those who remained upright and alert, cupping water with their hands, were allowed to stay and fight. The army of 10,000 quickly dwindled to a mere 300. Gideon would now face an army of thousands with only 300 men!

That night, Gideon's small but fierce group blew rams' horns, held torches, and shouted, "A sword for the LORD and for Gideon!" (Judges 7:20). At this sight and sound, the enemies of Israel turned in terror and killed each other. Gideon's little army pursued those who fled from the battle and defeated them as well. God gave them the victory.

We can learn three important lessons from the story of Gideon:

We are often the cause of our own difficulties.
— Israel kept disobeying God, and bad things kept happening. Nevertheless, God is good. He will forgive us and reveal how to change our bad situations if we will reject sin and turn to Him. Through Gideon, the Lord miraculously delivered His people from harm, and He will do the same for us when we turn to Him for help.

God can handle any situation we face, no matter how difficult or impossible it may seem.
— God did not need a huge army to deliver the Israelites from their enemies. You do not need an entire battalion for God to rescue you either. God may not "need" us, but He wants to involve us. Like Gideon, the Lord requires you to do what He asks you to do. Obey Him, even if what He is asking you to do seems insignificant. If you are faithful to do your part, God will do what only He can do.

God can and will do amazing things through ordinary people who are willing to do what He calls them to do.
— There was nothing special about Gideon. He was hiding from his enemies when the angel of the Lord called him a hero! Gideon changed when the Spirit of the Lord came upon him (Judges 6:34). He became bold enough to confront a massive army with only 300 men. Before Gideon went into battle, the Lord encouraged him by allowing him to hear about a dream that one of his enemies had. The dream put fear into the hearts of his enemies, but it encouraged Gideon.

God will never ask you to do something without Him. He will lead you all along the way. If you want to see miracles in your life, do what God tells you to do and let Him do what only He can do. Then give God credit for the victory.

1. Have you ever suffered because you did not obey God? Did you realize at the time why you were experiencing such difficulties? What did you do in response?
2. Think of a time when God asked you to do something specific. Did you obey Him? What was the result?
3. Has God called you to do something special with your life? What has He called you to do?

_____

After Gideon, eight more judges served Israel in the book of Judges. The cycle of sin and deliverance continued. The final judge in the book was Samson. This man was flawed in many ways, yet God still used him.

---

19 THE FLAWED HERO
Samson

A people called the Philistines had a long history with the Israelites. The two peoples were often in conflict with each other. The Bible first mentions the Philistines in a list of the nations that descended from Noah (Genesis 10:14). They were in contact with both Abraham and Isaac (Genesis 21:32; 26:1, 8). The Philistines were vicious warriors, and when the people of Israel left Egypt, God directed them away from the Philistines' land, even though traveling through it would have made the journey to the Promised Land much shorter (Exodus 13:17). By the time of the judges, the Philistines had built five cities close to the Israelites. They were deadly enemies to the people of Israel and sometimes defeated them. However, God raised up a judge who could hold back and even overpower the Philistines. His name was Samson.

JUDGES 13–16
God had a special plan for Samson. Before his mother became pregnant, an angel told her that she was going to have a son who would deliver the Israelites from their worst enemies, the Philistines (Judges 13:5). From the moment of his birth, he would belong to God. The son would be a Nazirite—he must never cut his hair, drink alcohol, or eat certain foods. When the son was born, his mother named him *Samson*.

God gave Samson great strength. He could defeat entire armies and kill wild animals with his bare hands. Even though he had been set apart for God since birth, Samson had many flaws. One was a wrong desire for ungodly, foreign women. Samson pursued and married a foreign woman who was a Philistine. He also spent time with other immoral women. In spite of these flaws, the Spirit of the Lord gave Samson supernatural strength to fight against the Philistines. Samson's bad decisions continually got him into trouble, but time after time, God graciously delivered him and punished Israel's enemies.

One day, though, Samson's actions went too far. He became involved with a Philistine woman named Delilah. The Philistines wanted to use Delilah as a spy to discover the source of Samson's great strength. At first, Samson refused to tell her. However, Delilah persistently asked him, and after much persuasion, Samson foolishly revealed the secret of his strength: God had told him not to cut his hair as a sign of his special dedication (Judges 13:5).

With Delilah's help, the Philistines cut Samson's hair while he slept. When he woke up, his strength was gone. Then the Philistines gouged out his eyes and took him away. The very people whom God had called Samson to defeat carried him away as a defeated prisoner. This could have been the end of Samson's story; however, God did not forget about him.

During a festival the Philistines held to praise their false gods for giving them victory over Samson, they allowed him to lean between the two main pillars in their temple. They wanted to publicly ridicule their captive. Just then, Samson asked the Lord to give him strength one last time. God heard his prayer, and as Samson pushed on the pillars, they gave way. The temple came crashing down, killing all the Philistines inside as well as Samson. At his death, Samson killed more of Israel's enemies than at any other time in his life.

God chooses imperfect people to accomplish His will. Since no one is perfect, He works through people with flaws. Though God graciously does this, it is no excuse for people to live carelessly or take God's grace lightly. Samson is a fitting illustration of God working through an imperfect person. He is also an example of someone who didn't value his calling the way he should have. Samson's poor moral choices often got him in trouble with Israel's enemies; however, God continued to fulfill His purposes through Samson.

At one terrible point in his life, Samson's carelessness finally caught up with him. He lost his sight, his freedom, and most importantly, God's special anointing on his life. Samson's foolishness brought him great harm. But God still loved Samson.

We do not have to be perfect people for God to work through us. His grace is greater than any of our flaws. However, we may forfeit God's anointing if we are careless with His calling or casual about His grace. Without God, we cannot do anything

of eternal value. Thankfully, our God is good, and He gives us second, third, and fourth chances. In his weakened state, Samson called out to God and asked for His anointing one more time. God answered his prayer and gave Samson the power to defeat the Philistines for the final time.

When you fail to obey, God will give you an opportunity to change your heart and mind and return to Him. He wants to forgive you and give you a fresh start. Even so, do not be careless with God's calling or casual with your commitment. God will pick you up when you fall, but the fall itself can still be quite painful.

Yes, God calls imperfect people. In your weakness, He remains strong. In your failures, He remains faithful. God knows your heart and your shortcomings. If you fall and humbly return to Him, He will come to your rescue and lift you up again. God strengthened Samson one last time, and He will strengthen you as well. When you get off course, call out to Him. He will give you a fresh start.

1. Have you ever thought God could not use you because of mistakes in your past? How does the story of Samson relate to your life?
2. Have you had times of failure in your walk with God? How did God restore you? Even if you feel far from God, God wants to bring you back to Himself. Right now, ask God to show you what He wants you to do.
3. Do you know someone who has walked away from God? Pray for that person right now and ask God to send people who will help restore them. He may even send you!
4. Samson often got into trouble because he spent time with the wrong people. Are there people in your life who cause you to turn away from God? If so, ask the Lord to give you godly relationships. If you must continue those relationships, for whatever reason, ask God for wisdom and protection.

The period of the judges was a time of moral failure for the people of Israel. Because of their disobedience, God caused them to have conflicts with each other and wars with their enemies. Occasionally, however, the Israelites experienced relative peace with the people around them. The book of Ruth reflects one of those peaceful times. It tells the story of a woman from Moab and her connection to an Israelite family. The woman's name was Ruth.

20 THE LOYAL GENTILE WOMAN
Ruth

During the period of the judges, Israel had several times of prosperity and numerous times of hardship. There were also many times of war and some of peace. The story of Ruth happened during a time of peace, but it was also a time when the people suffered through a famine.

RUTH 1–4

The book of Ruth opens in the country of Moab (now part of modern-day Jordan). A Jewish woman named Naomi and her family fled there from Bethlehem because the famine in Judah was severe. While living in Moab, Naomi's sons married Moabite women. Then both sons, as well as Naomi's husband, died. With no blood relatives in Moab and news that food was once again available in Judah, Naomi decided to return to her home country. She advised her two widowed daughters-in-law, Orpah and Ruth, to stay in Moab. At first, they both told her they would follow her to Judah. Orpah changed her mind, but Ruth went back with Naomi.

When they arrived in Bethlehem, Ruth went into the fields to gather grain left behind by the harvesters. It just so happened that she picked a field owned by one of Naomi's relatives. His name was Boaz. Ruth caught the attention of Boaz, and he made sure she went home with plenty of grain. When Naomi learned about Boaz's kindness, she encouraged Ruth to continue working for him. Later, Naomi instructed her daughter-in-law to approach Boaz after he finished working at the threshing floor. As a relative of Naomi, and by extension Ruth, Boaz was a family redeemer; he had the right to rescue a relative who was in trouble, danger, or need. He could marry Ruth, and since he was a wealthy man, Naomi and Ruth would be redeemed from lives of poverty and given prosperity and blessing.

That night, Ruth obeyed Naomi's instructions and slept at Boaz's feet. When he saw her lying there, Boaz praised Ruth for being so loyal. He readily agreed to marry her if they could first resolve one issue—there was actually a closer relative who had the first right to marry Ruth. The next morning, Boaz spoke to that relative, but the man did not want to make Ruth his wife. Boaz then married Ruth, and together, they had a son.

At first glance, the book of Ruth may appear to be a simple, heartwarming love story, with a tragic beginning and a happy ending. However, the ending is actually the beginning of a much larger story:

Boaz was the father of Obed.
Obed was the father of Jesse.
Jesse was the father of David (Ruth 4:21–22).

Boaz and Ruth's son, Obed, was the grandfather of King David. David was a great king, and in his line of descendants is an even greater king: Jesus Christ, the Messiah (Matthew 1:1).

The story of Ruth teaches us some essential truths:

The Good News of Jesus is for everyone.
— This simple story about a Moabite woman shows God's great plan to save us. Ruth was not a Hebrew. God chose a woman from a foreign nation to be in the line of the Jewish Messiah, Jesus. God was already showing how He would call both Jews and non-Jews (Gentiles) to be part of His people. The book of Acts tells how the Good News about Jesus spread from the Jewish people to the entire world.

God loves ordinary people.
— Ruth was a common, ordinary person. She did not come from royalty or wealth. When she returned with Naomi to Bethlehem, she needed to pick up grain so they could eat. God rescued these women through a wealthy man named Boaz. This is a picture of God's love for us. The apostle Paul says that God even chooses the weak to shame the strong (1 Corinthians 1:27). God chose us to be His! Both the apostles Paul and John wrote about believers as the bride of Christ (Ephesians 5:31–32; Revelation 19:7; 21:9).

Ruth's loyalty and commitment to Naomi led to a fresh start for both of them. God will take those on the "outside" and bring them into His eternal plans and purposes. As you faithfully serve the Lord in everyday tasks and relationships, God will honor your life with eternal significance.

1. God called non-Jewish people to be part of His family. However, He never abandoned the Israelites. Begin making a habit today to pray for the people of Israel and the city of Jerusalem.
2. How have you seen God work in the lives of ordinary people? What would you say to someone who didn't feel important enough to be part of God's plan?
3. God will honor your loyalty and commitment. What can you do to show more loyalty to God and His people?
4. Have you ever lost hope and then God did something amazing to change your situation? How do you tell others about the amazing things God has done for you?

The era of the judges drew near to an end. Over time, kings would replace them. During the transition period, one man served as a bridge between the judges and Israel's first kings. His name was Samuel. He was a prophet, priest, and Israel's last judge.

21 THE LAST JUDGE
Samuel

Before Samuel's birth, his mother, Hannah, could not have any children. Just as in many other cultures, it was shameful for a married Jewish woman to be childless. The people assumed something was wrong with Hannah. This situation caused her much sorrow. While praying one day, Hannah promised God that if He gave her a son, she would dedicate the child back to Him. God heard her plea, and about a year later, Hannah's prayer was answered. She gave birth to a baby boy and named him Samuel.

1 SAMUEL 1; 3; 8-10; 12; 16

When Samuel could eat solid food, Hannah kept her promise to God; she left her son in the care of Eli, the priest. One night, God spoke to Samuel. He told the boy that He would one day remove Eli and his sons from serving as priests because Eli's sons did wicked things and their father failed to correct them. From that time on, people recognized God's special calling on Samuel to be a prophet. God's message came to pass, and Eli and his sons died. Then Samuel served as God's prophet-judge in Israel for many years.

When Samuel was an old man, the people of Israel asked him to appoint a king over them (1 Samuel 8:5). God wanted Israel to be different from all the other nations. He alone was to be their King. However, the people of Israel wanted to be like the other nations who had human kings to rule over them. Finally, Samuel told them God would grant their request, but he warned them of all the negative things a king would require. Rule by a human king would not have the benefits they thought. Even so, God's stern warning did not change their minds. Under God's leadership, Samuel anointed a man named Saul to be the first king of Israel. However, God later rejected Saul because of his disobedience. Then God told Samuel to anoint a young man named David as king.

Samuel remained God's faithful prophet throughout his life. He spoke the words God told him to speak and did whatever God commanded him to do. Before he was born, his mother had dedicated him to the Lord, and Samuel followed God until he died. The only fault the Bible mentions about this man is that he failed to raise his sons to serve the Lord as he had done (1 Samuel 8:3-5). Nevertheless, regarding his personal conduct, the Bible has nothing critical to say about Samuel. To the contrary, when Samuel challenged God's people to remember a time when he had ever cheated, stolen from, or oppressed any of them, not one person could recall a single instance. Samuel shows us it is possible to have a great start, faithful service to God, and a strong finish.

Even more, Samuel stayed faithful to the Lord in the midst of those who were not. He grew up among people who did not live godly lives. Samuel served as a prophet to people who often did not want to follow God's will. He even anointed a king who disobeyed the Lord. Still, Samuel was not negatively influenced by any of them. His life provides an example of a person who serves the Lord faithfully, even when those around him do not. In spite of your surroundings, you can both start and finish strong.

1. Hannah honored her commitment to God. What are some ways you can honor your commitments to God?
2. Eli and his sons did not follow God's ways, partly because they did not fulfill their responsibilities to each other. Even Samuel failed in the way he brought up his children. If you are a parent, how can you train your children to follow God? As a son or daughter, in what ways can you honor your parents no matter how old you are?
3. Even as we honor those who are rulers over us, how can we remind ourselves that God is our first priority and highest authority?
4. Do you know someone who has served God for a very long time? What can you learn from that person's experience that will help you follow God?

Samuel anointed two men to serve as kings of Israel: Saul and David. God chose both of them. Both of them sinned against God and others. However, one changed his heart and mind and returned to God while the other did not. King Saul is the one who did not.

22 THE FIRST KING
Saul

Many stories in the Bible do not end with "happily ever after." That observation is certainly the case for Saul, the first king of Israel. Although he started well, Saul finished poorly. He provides an example of how *not* to follow God.

1 SAMUEL 9–10; 13:8-13; 15:10-23

For centuries, the people of Israel were different from any other nation—they did not have a human king because God Himself was supposed to be their king. Although they were better off without one, the Israelites eventually wanted a human king to rule over them. Although God warned them about the consequences, He finally let them have what they demanded.

God told the prophet-judge Samuel to anoint Saul as king over Israel. When the time came for Saul to be named king, he hid among some baggage. The Bible does not give a reason why he did this. Perhaps Saul was shy, fearful, or humble. No matter the reason, Saul did not show confidence in his new anointing as king. At first, it seemed as if he might be a good king who would serve the Lord and His people well. Over time, however, Saul proved otherwise. He disobeyed God and did so on more than one occasion.

During a time of war with the Philistines, the king waited seven days for Samuel to arrive and offer a burnt offering so Saul and the Israelite troops could go into battle. However, Samuel was late in arriving, and the troops began to scatter. So Saul took matters into his own hands and made the burnt offering himself. Just as he finished, Samuel arrived. The prophet told Saul that because he had disobeyed God's command, God would remove him as king (1 Samuel 13:1-15).

Saul later disobeyed God a second time. Samuel told the king that God wanted him to destroy Israel's enemy, the Amalekites, completely. Not a single person or animal was to be left alive. Instead, Saul altered the plan. He captured the king alive and spared some of the best animals. When Samuel confronted him about his disobedience, Saul tried to justify it by saying he was going to sacrifice the animals to the God. Samuel made it clear there was no excuse; obedience to God was more important than offering sacrifices (1 Samuel 15:22). Because of Saul's disobedience, Samuel once again told him God had disqualified him as king.

When Saul learned of God's decision, he could have humbly accepted it, recognizing that his actions had cost him the kingship. Instead, he allowed bitterness and envy to fill his heart. Saul became so jealous that he spent many years trying to kill David, the man God chose to replace him. There were moments when Saul came to his senses.

When he did, he repented of his wicked desires and actions. However, these times were short-lived, and he continued on a downward spiral until his death.

Saul's story is tragic, but it can teach us these valuable lessons:

God is the One who elevates people.

— God chooses to put people in authority (Psalm 75:7). Saul became king because God chose him, not because Saul campaigned for it, fought for it, or took it by force. If you are in a position of authority, it is because God has placed you there. He can also remove you. When God places you in a position of authority, it is not up to you to protect it with your own strength. Obey God, and you will serve as long as He desires. Saul failed because he followed the will of the people, stopped serving the Lord, and believed it was up to him to hold onto his position. He started well but finished poorly.

Guard your heart against fear, bitterness, and jealousy.

— God may choose someone else to lead, or He may select someone to take your place. If either of these things happens, beware of fear, bitterness, and jealousy. You do not need to fear because God loves you and has a plan for your future. Take care in how you see and treat others. Rather than facing his own sin, Saul labeled David as his problem. Bitterness and jealousy caused Saul to follow a dangerous path, and they will lead you down one as well.

Saul started well, but his disobedience, self-will, and jealousy cost him everything. His mistakes serve as a warning for us today. If God has placed you in a position of authority, focus your attention on obeying Him rather than holding onto your position. Trust God to keep you where He's placed you as long as He desires. Guard yourself against jealousy. As you keep your heart right, God will make sure you finish well.

Have you ever found yourself trusting more in human authority than God's authority? Why do you think people have trouble trusting God to provide for their needs?

Think about a time when you decided to take matters into your own hands instead of waiting for God to act. What was the result?

When God places you in a position of authority, do you feel grateful, or do you feel worried that someone may try to take your place?

How do you react when you see God blessing other people? What should you do if you begin to feel bitter or jealous?

Saul was Israel's first king, but he is not remembered as their best king. He did not trust the Lord, and when confronted about his disobedience, he did not humble his heart. So God sent Samuel to anoint a new king: a young shepherd named David.

23 THE SHEPHERD SONGWRITER KING
David

Israel's first king, Saul, did not obey the Lord, so God removed him from power. God told the prophet Samuel to anoint a new king. Samuel went to the house of a man named Jesse because God had chosen one of this man's sons to rule over Israel. To everyone's surprise, God chose Jesse's youngest son, David.

1 SAMUEL 16–18; 24; 26; 2 SAMUEL 11–12; 1 KINGS 2:1–12

David was just a young shepherd when Samuel anointed him as the next king of Israel. Shepherds rarely become kings, but David was a special person. God described him as a man after His own heart (1 Samuel 13:14). Not long after, Israel once again went to war with the Philistines. A Philistine giant named Goliath challenged the entire army of Israel to a battle. No soldier was willing to fight him, though. Jesse told David to carry food to his brothers because they were encamped with Israel's army. When David saw Goliath, he believed God wanted him to fight and defeat the giant. David may have been the least likely Israelite to win against this enemy, but God gave him the victory. He killed Goliath with a single stone from a slingshot.

The people of Israel took notice of David's great victory, and they began to sing songs in his honor. King Saul became jealous and angry. Soon Saul's heart turned against David to the point that he attempted to kill him multiple times. For several years, Saul forced David to run and hide for fear of his life. Though the king wanted to kill David, David refused to harm the king, even when he had the chance to do so.

Many years passed after his anointing, but during this waiting period, God worked in David's life. Eventually, Saul died in battle, and David began to reign in Israel. God gave him the power to defeat many of Israel's enemies. God blessed Israel under David's rule.

One day, David made a terrible choice. He had a sexual relationship with Bathsheba, the wife of one of his best soldiers. She became pregnant from the encounter. Trying to cover his sin, David had Bathsheba's husband killed in battle. Many other brave soldiers also died that day because of David's order.

However, we cannot hide our sins from God. God sent the prophet Nathan to confront David. The king paid a high price for his sin: four of his sons died, including the child from the affair. David repented, but he could not escape the consequences of his actions.

David's life reveals these important truths, which encourage and challenge every believer:

God does not choose leaders based on outward appearances or accomplishments.

— God looks at the heart when He selects leaders. He looked at this young shepherd and saw someone who cared for his father's sheep in the way God wanted a king to watch over His people. David did not look the part, but he had the right heart in God's eyes. God can do great things through anyone with the right kind of heart.

We cannot cover our sins.

— David's sin and the efforts to hide his evil deed serve as a warning that no one is immune to temptation. Even God's anointed can fall. The more David tried to hide his sin, the more God revealed it. Repentance is always better than attempts to cover and hide. Only Jesus can cover our sins with His own righteousness (2 Corinthians 5:21).

God remembers His best, not our worst.

— David had sexual relations with another man's wife and then conspired to murder him. However, this king is best remembered as a "man after [God's] own heart." He fought and killed Goliath by faith. He wrote many of the psalms of the Bible out of his deep love for God. David led his people with a shepherd's heart. As a result, we do not remember this king as a womanizer; we think of him as a worshipper.

When confronted with his sin, David changed his heart and mind and returned to God. His willingness to repent gave him a fresh start. God does not call perfect people. He chooses those who have their hearts right with Him.

1. Have you ever tried to cover up your sin? What happened as a result?

2. When has God shown you mercy when you repented of sin?

3. Do you ever feel like your past prevents God from using you today? How does the life of David give you guidance for your future?

God is full of grace and mercy. After killing her husband, David married Bathsheba, the woman with whom he had sinned. Their first son died, but God chose their second son, Solomon, as Israel's next king. Before David died, he wanted to build a great temple as a place to worship God, but the Lord did not allow him to build it. However, God did not forget David, and He used his son Solomon to build the Temple.

---

24 THE WISE UNWISE KING
Solomon

After King David's death, one of his sons became the next king. Rather than seeking after wealth and power, the son prayed for wisdom to govern well. Because of his humble request, the Lord not only gave him wisdom but also great riches. Sadly, this king also made some very unwise decisions later in life, which hurt both himself and others. His name was Solomon.

1 KINGS 2:13–30; 3:3–28; 10:1–13; 11:1–13

King David sinned when he had sexual relations with Bathsheba, a woman who was not his wife. Then he had her husband killed to cover his sin. After that, David married Bathsheba, but the child they conceived died. Bathsheba and David later had another son named Solomon. In those days, kings had great power and could become extremely rich. At first, Solomon didn't seek power or wealth. God offered a gift to Solomon, and he chose wisdom. Because of that wisdom, Solomon grew to be the wisest and richest king on earth (1 Kings 10:23).

The Bible records an amazing event that shows Solomon's great wisdom. One day, two women in a dispute came to him with one baby. Both women claimed to be the child's mother. Only one could be telling the truth, and only these two women knew which one was. Then Solomon ordered one of his guards to cut the baby in half and give each woman a portion. One woman agreed to this compromise, but the real mother begged for the baby's life. Solomon knew this was the real mother, and he ordered the baby be given to her.

The Bible also tells how Solomon brought great wealth to himself and his kingdom. People traveled from all over the world to hear his wisdom and witness his wealth. Those who did were amazed to hear his unmatched wisdom and see all of his possessions (2 Chronicles 9:1–7).

Sadly, Solomon made some very unwise decisions later in his life. He made political alliances and married many women from foreign countries. Then he allowed his wives to bring their false gods (idols) with them. Eventually, Solomon's heart turned away from the Lord, and he worshipped the false gods as well (1 Kings 11:1–9).

King Solomon's life is an example of both a fresh start and a false start. Though David and Bathsheba's first son died, God blessed them with another. Solomon asked for wisdom, not wealth, and God gave it to him. The new king ruled well and brought both peace and prosperity to his people. However, when Solomon turned away from the Lord, his fresh start became a false start. At the end of his life, King Solomon was not the man nor the king he was at the start. The same king who recorded great pearls of wisdom in the book of Proverbs also wrote of despair and vanity in the book of Ecclesiastes.

King Solomon's example teaches us the importance of finishing well. His wisdom brought great blessing to himself and to others, but he did not heed God's warnings:

> "The king must not take many wives for himself, because they will turn his heart away from the Lord. And he must not accumulate large amounts of wealth in silver and gold for himself" (Deuteronomy 17:17).

In spite of his great wisdom, Solomon became unwise as he ignored God's commands.

We should take great care to ensure our strong start does not end tragically. Those around us can influence us either positively or negatively. The apostle Paul warns, "Don't team up with those who are unbelievers" (2 Corinthians 6:14). Consequently, we must surround ourselves with other believers who will encourage us to stay faithful to the Lord. We show true wisdom by our obedience to the Word of God. We must also guard against allowing the blessings of God to become more important to us than the One who blessed us. We cannot allow our gratitude and humility to turn into pride and carelessness toward God's commands. No person or possession should ever turn our hearts away from the Lord.

1. Have you ever let someone or something turn you away from God and His Word? What happened to bring you back to God?
2. What are some of the things that pull people away from God today?
3. What would you say to a friend who has turned away from God because of success?

While God blessed King Solomon despite his disobedience, the people of Israel suffered later for his sins. When Solomon's son Rehoboam became king,

10 of the 12 tribes refused to accept his rule. Those tribes submitted to the rule of King Jeroboam while the southern two tribes remained loyal to King Rehoboam. Both the northern and southern kingdoms had several successive rulers. Some of the kings were faithful to the Lord, but most were not. In the north, King Ahab and his wife, Jezebel, were very wicked rulers. During their reign, God raised up a prophet named Elijah to speak God's words of truth and judgment to them.

25 THE COURAGEOUS PROPHET
Elijah

King Ahab and Queen Jezebel were wicked rulers of the northern kingdom of Israel. During their reign, God sent the brave prophet Elijah to confront them about their sins and the idol worship they encouraged among the people. Elijah worked miracles that let all the people know the difference between the idols they worshipped and the Living God of Israel.

1 KINGS 17–19; 2 KINGS 2:1–12

Elijah declared to King Ahab that there would be no rain in Israel for the next few years. It would only rain again after the prophet gave the word (1 Kings 17:1). During this time of drought, God miraculously provided for Elijah. The prophet drank water from a brook, and God sent ravens to bring him food twice a day.

When the brook dried up, God sent Elijah to a widow who only had enough food for one more meal for herself and her son. She expected they would die after that. Elijah told the widow to take her last bit of flour and make some bread for him first. Then she could make some for herself and her son. The woman did as the prophet commanded, and God miraculously multiplied her supply. She had enough for her and her son to eat for many days. Sometime later, the widow's son became ill and died. She asked if Elijah had come to her to point out her sin and take her son's life. When Elijah heard her say this, he laid on top of the boy and prayed for God to restore his life. The Lord heard his prayer, and the boy came back to life (1 Kings 17:22).

Ahab and Jezebel allowed and encouraged the people of Israel to worship the false god Baal. One day, Elijah challenged the prophets of Baal to meet him at Mount Carmel. He proposed that both they and he place sacrifices on two separate altars. The prophets of Baal would then call out to their god, asking him to burn up their sacrifice. Then Elijah would call out to the God of Israel, asking Him to do the same.

The followers of Baal cried out, but they received no answer. Then Elijah soaked his sacrifice in water and prayed to the Lord. Just then, fire came down from heaven and burned up not only the sacrifice but also the wood, the stones, and all the water. Elijah gave the order, and all the prophets of Baal were killed that day. Israel now knew the difference between false gods and the one true God.

When the wicked Queen Jezebel heard what happened, she threatened to kill Elijah. When he learned of her plan, the prophet fled into the wilderness. There, Elijah found a cave and cried out to the Lord. God spoke to him and told him to anoint (or choose at God's command) a man named Elisha to take his place.

Elijah's life did not end in death. God sent a chariot and horses of fire to take him to heaven as Elisha watched (2 Kings 2:11). The Lord took the great prophet from the earth in a way that was as miraculous as the life he had led. Elijah is one of only two men who ever lived and did not die. The other was Enoch (Genesis 5:21–24).

Although Elijah is one of the most unique characters in the Bible, every believer can learn valuable lessons from his example:

God provides for His people.

— During a severe drought, God miraculously met Elijah's needs—first through food delivered by ravens and water from a brook, followed by the little food a widow had in her home. God will also provide for your daily needs. Jesus told us not to worry about things like clothing and food. If you put God first in your life, He will meet your needs (Matthew 6:31–33).

Stand for God even when others don't.

— In Elijah's day, many people had turned away from God, including the king and queen. Even so, the prophet remained faithful, and God defended him. Jesus said God will also defend you and give you the words to say when others challenge you for taking a stand for God (Luke 12:11–12).

Be bold for God—you are not alone.

— Elijah was a courageous prophet, but there was a time when he ran from Queen Jezebel and became discouraged. He felt like he was the only person in the land who still served God. The Lord told him there were 7,000 others who had also remained faithful to the Lord (1 Kings 19:18). From time to time, you may feel like Elijah, wondering if anyone else wants to serve God. Be encouraged! You are never alone. No matter who may be against you, God is always with you. He will lead you to other believers who will both encourage you and stand with you.

Keep the faith.

— Elijah remained faithful to the Lord until the end. He never let the people around him turn him away from the Lord, even when they abandoned God. Not only did Elijah finish well, but he also passed on his ministry to another prophet. Like Elijah, God will help you both finish well and pass on your spiritual legacy to others.

1. How has God provided for you in the past? How do you know He will provide for you in the future?

2. When have you seen someone take a stand for God even when it was unpopular? How did the Lord protect and use that person?

3. Who is supporting you right now as you follow God? Tell God you are thankful for that person in your life.

4. Who is an example for you as you follow the Lord? To whom do you want to leave a spiritual legacy?

Elijah lived an amazing life, full of miracles and intrigue, until God took him to heaven. Before he left, Elisha asked for a double portion of Elijah's spirit (2 Kings 2:9). God was good to Elisha and allowed him to experience the same miraculous power Elijah did and even more.

26 A MAN OF MIRACLES
Elisha

Elijah ran from Queen Jezebel because she wanted to have him killed. The prophet escaped to a cave where he cried out to the Lord. God answered Elijah and told him to choose a man by His command as his successor. When Elijah found Elisha plowing in a field, he threw his cloak on Elisha's shoulders as a sign that God had chosen him. Elisha sacrificed the animals with which he was plowing to the Lord, and then he followed Elijah.

1 KINGS 19:19–21; 2 KINGS 2; 4:1–6:23

The day came when Elisha discovered the Lord was going to take Elijah from the earth into heaven. Elijah told him to stay behind, but Elisha followed the older prophet. As they came to the Jordan River, Elisha asked Elijah for a double share of his spirit. When a fiery chariot took Elijah into heaven, Elisha took the cloak his mentor left behind and struck the waters of the Jordan River with it. The river divided, and Elisha walked across on dry land. Everyone recognized God was now with Elisha in the same way He had been with Elijah.

Miracles followed Elisha just as they had his predecessor:

— A widow who was desperately in debt came to Elisha for help. He told her to gather as many jars as she could and begin pouring into them the little oil she had remaining in a flask. The widow filled every container and sold the oil to pay her debt.

— Naaman, the army commander of one of Israel's enemies, came to Elisha because he had leprosy. Elisha told him to wash seven times in the Jordan River. At first, Naaman was angry about what the prophet told him to do, but Naaman's servant convinced him to obey Elisha's instructions. When he did, the leprosy was gone!

— One of the most amazing events in Elisha's life involved the Arameans, one of Israel's enemies. In an effort to capture Elisha, their army surrounded the city where the prophet was staying. Elisha prayed, and God blinded the eyes of every enemy soldier. Then the prophet led them before the king of Israel. God opened their eyes, and they were shocked to find themselves standing there. Rather than kill them, though, Elisha told the king to hold a great feast and then send them home. After that, the Arameans stopped attacking Israel.

— Just before Elisha's death, the king of Israel told the prophet he saw the "chariots and charioteers of Israel" (2 Kings 13:14). The king described something similar to what Elisha had seen when God took Elijah to heaven. Elisha did not leave the earth in a chariot of fire like his teacher did, but the power of God was with him so strongly that a dead man came to life when his body touched Elisha's bones (2 Kings 13:21).

We can learn two important truths from Elisha's example:

Godly influence leads to more godly influence.

— Elisha's life testifies to the value of godly influence. He learned firsthand from the great prophet Elijah and continually saw God's faithfulness. As a result, Elisha became a great prophet as well.

God will do great things through us if His glory is our first desire.

— Elisha did not seek God's special calling for his own fame or other selfish reasons. He did not use his position as a prophet for personal gain. When Naaman was healed of leprosy, he offered a reward for what Elisha had done, but the prophet refused to take it (2 Kings 5:16). However, Elisha's servant, Gehazi, deceived Naaman into giving him silver and clothing. As a result, Gehazi became sick from leprosy. When the apostle Paul describes leadership, he clearly states that leaders should not be those who love money (1 Timothy 3:3). Jesus said a person cannot serve both God and wealth (Matthew 6:24). Elisha used his anointing to bring glory to God, not material gain for himself. There is nothing wrong with ministry leaders receiving payment for what they do, but it shouldn't be their primary motivation.

1. What miracles have you seen in your life? How have they led others to glorify God?
2. Who are the godly influences in your life? To whom can you be a godly influence?

3. What are some ways others can see God working through you on a daily basis?
4. How can you make sure you have the right motivation as you serve God? What do you think are the results of the wrong motivation?

Elisha learned from a great man of God and kept his heart right before the Lord. His life serves as an example for others to follow. However, neither Elijah nor Elisha wrote down their prophecies, or if they did, no copies remain in existence. But God did call other prophets to deliver His messages to His people. Many of these messengers wrote down the things the Lord told them to say. These prophecies have been preserved as books of the Bible.

27 THE MESSIAH'S PROPHET
Isaiah

God often spoke to His people through individuals known as prophets. These messengers delivered words of warning and calls for repentance. They also spoke words of encouragement and foretold the coming of the Messiah. God instructed some of the prophets to write down the things He told them. One such prophet was Isaiah.

ISAIAH 6; 9:1-7; 11; 53

Isaiah is one of the longest books in the Bible. It is also the most quoted book in the New Testament. One theme repeatedly emerges throughout Isaiah: God alone can save. The Jewish people thought they could save themselves, but Isaiah told them they could not, nor could any other nation rescue them. The people from the northern kingdom of Israel had already been taken into captivity. The people in the southern kingdom of Judah fell into sin and idol worship. God would soon bring judgment on them as well because He wanted a holy people. God was going to use foreign nations to discipline His people and rid them of their sin. Even more, God was going to send His Servant, the Messiah, to make His people pure. The Messiah would bring in a time of peace and prosperity such as the world had never known. Then God would take a remnant of His people and use them to rule over the nations.

The Bible only gives a small amount of information about the prophet Isaiah's personal life. His name means 'the salvation of the Lord.' He was the son of Amoz but may also have been a member of the royal family. Isaiah ministered for at least 60 years and saw the reigns of four or five kings. During his lifetime, this prophet had one mission: to lead the nation back to God.

Isaiah began his ministry about the time the Assyrian army destroyed the northern kingdom and

threatened the southern kingdom. King Hezekiah survived the conflict, but he unwisely let visitors from Babylon see the palace treasures. Isaiah prophesied that this foolish act would lead to the future Babylonian Exile. The prophet did not know when the captivity would begin, so he began to prepare the people. Next, Isaiah prophesied about a time in the future when God would restore His people and the city of Jerusalem. Finally, the prophet saw a vision of the new heaven and new earth where the Messiah will reign over all creation. God will remove all evil from the world. The blessings of the Kingdom Jesus revealed during His ministry will come in fullness. Israel will be restored and her enemies defeated. War and suffering will be things of the past, and God will rule without opposition or interference.

Many people know about Isaiah's vision in the Temple (Isaiah 6:1-8). He saw the Holy God seated on His throne. Suddenly, Isaiah became painfully aware of his own sinfulness. Then an angel came to him and touched his lips with a purifying coal from the altar in heaven. This act served to prepare Isaiah for his ministry as a prophet. Isaiah willingly followed this call, and God showed him many wonderful and terrible things, which the prophet shared with the people.

When Isaiah prophesied about the coming Messiah, the Savior of Israel and the world, he described Him in a different way than the people expected. The Messiah would be born of a virgin (Isaiah 7:14). He would bring healing and set people free by the power of the Holy Spirit. However, the Messiah's own people would reject Him, and He would suffer greatly. The Suffering Servant would be beaten and bruised beyond recognition (Isaiah 52:13-14). Like a sacrificial lamb, the Messiah would give His life as an offering for the sin of every person. The New Testament writers clearly recognized Jesus as the Messiah about whom Isaiah wrote. When Isaiah received a vision of heaven, he also saw the coming of Jesus as God's loving response to Israel's waywardness. God would send His Son as a sacrifice for sin. Jesus would be not only the Messiah of the Jews but also the Savior of all people.

Isaiah proclaimed the heart of God. He warned the people of judgment, but he also spoke about God's great love revealed through the Messiah, Jesus Christ. In spite of the Israelites' rebellion and sin, God made a way for them to be forgiven. God doesn't warn His people about judgment because He hates them. No, He loves us and wants to remove those things in our lives that keep us from His blessings. When God convicts you of sin, He wants you to repent so you can enjoy all His blessings.

God offered Israel a fresh start, and He also offers it to you through His Son, Jesus. He wants us to see our sinfulness in light of His holiness. Jesus died in our place so we can be forgiven and experience a fresh start. Our whole world will change as a result.

1. Have you ever experienced a warning from God about sin in your life? If so, how did you respond? What were the results?
2. What do you think it means to repent so you can experience all of God's blessings?
3. How did Jesus fulfill Isaiah's prophecies about the coming Messiah?
4. Isaiah also prophesied about a new heaven and a new earth. How will this new earth differ from the one in which we currently live?

God often sent prophets to speak to the Jewish people. However, He loves everyone, and sometimes He sent messengers to people who were not Jews. Jonah was one of those prophets.

28 THE RUNAWAY PROPHET
Jonah

God often sent prophets to warn people who were living sinful lives to change their ways. Usually, He sent them to the Jewish people, but sometimes He sent them to other nations too. You might think God's prophets loved all people and wanted them to be saved. Sadly, this was not always true. Jonah knew God was loving and merciful, but he didn't want God to show that same compassion to the people of Nineveh.

JONAH 1–4

One day, God told Jonah to go to the sinful city of Nineveh to preach a message of judgment. Nineveh was the capital city of Assyria—located in modern-day Iraq. Assyria was a wicked nation that did many terrible things to the Jews.

At first, Jonah did not want to obey the Lord, so he boarded a ship heading in the opposite direction. Jonah's disobedience didn't come from his fear of the Ninevites. Instead, he knew God's character and didn't want God to forgive the people if they turned away from their sin.

Even so, God gave Jonah an opportunity to change his mind and obey. While at sea, the ship encountered a very intense storm. It was so violent that all the people on board thought they were going to die. When the sailors discovered Jonah was running from God, they became even more fearful. Seeing no other way to survive the storm, they threw Jonah into the raging sea. Suddenly, the storm stopped. As Jonah sank into the water, God sent a great fish to swallow him. For three days and three nights, the prophet lived inside the stomach of the fish (Jonah 1:17). Jonah cried out to God, changed his heart and mind, and agreed to do what God asked. Then God caused the fish to spit Jonah out onto the shore.

Jonah immediately went to Nineveh, where he spent three days telling people about God's coming judgment. Surprisingly, all the Ninevites, including the king, turned away from their wickedness. In response to their repentant hearts, God did not destroy the city.

Jonah should have been pleased that the people listened to his message, but he was not. In fact, he was furious. Jonah complained that he knew God would show mercy if the people repented, which was why he did not want to go to Nineveh in the first place (Jonah 4:1-2). The prophet wanted God to judge the Ninevites because they had treated the people of Israel so terribly.

Revenge fantasies are a common response to injustice. Has anyone ever treated you or someone you love so badly that you wanted that individual to suffer? Perhaps someone bullied you in school or made you the victim of a crime. Someone may have abused you, your family members, or your friends. If so, you may want that person to pay for what they have done. Maybe you have even imagined something terrible happening to them. Jonah certainly felt this way about the Ninevites. He did not want God to show them mercy. However, he forgot how often God had forgiven the Israelites. The Bible tells many stories of how the people of Israel frequently rebelled against God. Still, God loved them and forgave them whenever they repented.

Jonah is a story of God's love and mercy, both for us and for others. The prophet's life teaches us these two crucial lessons:

God wants us to help others find forgiveness, just as He has forgiven us.

— You may wish other people would "get what they deserve." Take a moment to think about that desire. Do you really want what *you* deserve? We all deserve God's judgment, but we receive His mercy and forgiveness when we turn from sin and turn toward Him. We should want the same for others.

Jesus tells us how to think about our enemies.

— Jesus said His followers should love their enemies (Matthew 5:43-44). He told a story about a man who was unwilling to forgive a small debt even after his own master had released him from an enormous debt (Matthew 18:23-35). God wants us to forgive others because He has forgiven us. God chose Abraham and through him, Israel. God desired to bless the people of Israel *and* all the nations of the world through them (Genesis 22:18). As the Israelites rebelled against God, they often suffered at the hands of other nations. Their experiences caused them to hate those nations. However, Israel's hatred did not change God's desire. He called Jonah to go to Nineveh so the people would have an opportunity to repent and find freedom from judgment. Jonah wanted them to be judged and not repent! He disobeyed the Lord, but God gave him a fresh start when Jonah changed his mind.

God "does not want anyone to be destroyed, but wants everyone to repent" (2 Peter 3:9). Like Jonah, God calls you to offer people His grace and mercy available to them through Jesus Christ. Has someone done things to hurt you? Ask God to give you the grace and mercy to forgive that person. If they do not have a relationship with Jesus Christ, ask God to send the right person to talk to them. If that person is no longer alive, ask God to remove the bitterness from your heart so you can find freedom and healing. This prayer may be difficult, but it is what God calls us to do.

1. Suppose someone says to you, "That person hurt me. I cannot forgive them." How would you respond?
2. Is it difficult to pray for your enemies? Why or why not?
3. Some people may think Jesus was unrealistic when He told His followers to forgive, show mercy, and pray for their enemies. Why are these actions necessary?
4. Have you ever refused to do something God called you to do? What were the results?

Jonah was one of the few prophets God called to warn people outside of Israel to turn away from their sins to avoid judgment. The Lord wants all people to turn from sin and toward Him, but He often spoke directly to the people of Israel because He had a special covenant relationship with them. When they violated this covenant, the people made God angry and sad. He continued to send prophets to warn them to change their ways. Hosea was one of those prophets.

29 THE PROPHET WITH GOD'S HEART
Hosea

In the days when kings ruled Israel, God spoke to His people through His chosen prophets. These messengers were rarely popular because they called the people to turn away from sin and idol worship. Through the prophet Hosea, God urged His people to stop their evil behavior and return to Him. The Lord often compared Israel's idolatry to the actions of an unfaithful wife, and it was this message God gave to Hosea to declare to His rebellious people.

HOSEA 1-2

God sometimes told His prophets to deliver His messages through unusual methods. What Hosea did was certainly unusual, and his actions caught the people's attention. God told Hosea to marry a wife who was unfaithful to him. She was even a prostitute. God told Hosea to do this as a sign of

Israel's unfaithfulness. Throughout Scripture, God often speaks of His relationship with His people as that of a husband and wife. Through Hosea, however, God said, "Israel . . . is no longer my wife, and I am no longer her husband" (Hosea 2:2).

Israel regularly turned away from God and worshipped idols. They had worshipped a golden calf while waiting for Moses at Mount Sinai, and centuries later, they returned to the same kind of false god (Hosea 8:5-6). Even though God had blessed them with everything they needed, they still turned away from Him. The people of Israel experienced great hardships because of their rebellion. As a result of their worship of other nations' gods, the Lord allowed their enemies to defeat them. Then He allowed their enemies to carry the Israelites away from the Promised Land into Babylonian captivity.

Hosea reveals that even while the Israelites were unfaithful to God, God remained faithful to them! God always wanted to draw His people back to Himself. The day would come when they would once again call God their husband (Hosea 2:16).

How could a nation that experienced God's blessings ever turn away from Him? Actually, each of us has done just that—"All of us, like sheep, have strayed away. We have left God's paths to follow our own" (Isaiah 53:6). We all have wandered away and turned our backs on Him. We often make decisions that do not please Him, and our sins separate us from God. However, our unfaithfulness to God does not change His faithfulness toward us. God sent His Son into the world to bring us back to Himself: "Yet the LORD laid on him the sins of us all" (Isaiah 53:6). God did not turn His back on us. Instead, Jesus suffered for us and made it possible for us to return to the Lord.

The apostle Paul writes that the Church's relationship with Christ is like a marriage; husbands should love their wives as Christ loved the Church—all of us who are believers (Ephesians 5:25). Paul also quotes from Genesis: "A man leaves his father and mother and is joined to his wife, and the two are united into one" (Ephesians 5:31; Genesis 2:24). In a surprising twist, Paul then reveals that this verse actually speaks about Christ's relationship with His people (Ephesians 5:32).

In the book of Revelation, God calls His people His bride (Revelation 21:9). Jesus is the Husband of His people. God desires an intimate relationship with us, and His love for us is even greater than the love of a husband for a wife. Consequently, our unfaithfulness to Him can be compared to the betrayal of an unfaithful wife. We may not take our wrong choices seriously enough, but God does. However, even though we turn away from Him, God will never turn away from us.

1. In what ways do God's people act unfaithfully toward Him today?
2. How do you think Hosea felt when God told him to marry an unfaithful wife? How do you think God feels about our unfaithfulness?
3. What are some ways a husband or wife shows faithfulness to their spouse? What are some ways we can show our faithfulness to God?

Through the prophet Hosea, God spoke in a very dramatic way. He wanted His people to know just how much their unfaithfulness hurt Him. However, Hosea was not the only prophet God used in this way. Known as "the weeping prophet," Jeremiah shed many tears as an expression of God's great love and sorrow when His people sinned.

30 THE SORROWFUL PROPHET
Jeremiah

Prophets in Israel seldom held popular opinions or safe positions in relationship to those who held political power or religious authority. The rulers particularly hated it when the prophets spoke of God's judgment coming at the hands of their enemies. Rather than repenting, the rulers vilified and abused God's messengers. One especially persecuted prophet was Jeremiah.

JEREMIAH 1–2; 17:1–18:17

Jeremiah boldly proclaimed the coming of God's judgment from Israel's hated enemy, the Babylonians. This enemy would destroy the city of Jerusalem. Then the Babylonians would take many people captive and carry them away. Jeremiah's message was not one people wanted to hear, but God told him to proclaim it boldly.

The people of Jerusalem refused to believe Jeremiah, especially when he said they should willingly go into captivity. Instead, they did all they could to resist the Babylonians. They even turned for help to Egypt, the nation that once enslaved them. Jeremiah received harsh treatment for his prophecies. First, the king's officers threw him into a well. Later, he was placed in prison. Nevertheless, Jeremiah continued to warn God's

people of the coming destruction.

In time, God did as He promised. The Babylonians destroyed Jerusalem. They captured the king of Judah and took him and many of the people to Babylon. Some of God's people fled to Egypt and took Jeremiah with them. Only a small number of poor people stayed in the city.

Jeremiah is often referred to as "the weeping prophet." The Bible says he wept over the destruction of Jerusalem, the rebellion of God's people, and their subsequent judgment. He proclaimed the word of the Lord boldly in the face of opposition, but he also had a tender heart. Some people might think a prophet with such strong words could not have a tender heart. There are even those who view God the same way. They see God only as a judge.

However, Jeremiah gives a different picture of God. The Lord told Jeremiah to deliver a message of judgment, but He also gave the prophet words of encouragement and restoration. God said to Jeremiah,

"Today I appoint you to stand up
against nations and kingdoms.
Some you must uproot and tear down,
destroy and overthrow.

Others you must build up and plant" (Jeremiah 1:10).

Although God said the Babylonians would destroy Jerusalem and the Jews would experience judgment, He also made this promise about His people: "I will bring them back here again. I will build them up and not tear them down. I will plant them and not uproot them" (Jeremiah 24:6). The same God who brought judgment would one day give His people a fresh start. God would deliver them and bring them back to the Promised Land.

Jesus also expressed great sorrow over God's people and the city of Jerusalem. He cried out:

"O Jerusalem, Jerusalem, the city that kills the prophets and stones God's messengers! How often I have wanted to gather your children together as a hen protects her chicks beneath her wings, but you wouldn't let me" (Matthew 23:37).

God has a loving and caring heart toward His people. He does not tell of coming judgment because He enjoys punishing them. Rather, He warns them because He loves them. God could have ignored those living in Jerusalem during the days of Jeremiah. Instead, He sent a prophet. In spite of their unwillingness to listen, God warned them, giving them a chance to repent and experience His blessings instead of judgment.

God so loved the world that He sent His Son, Jesus (John 3:16). Jesus was Israel's promised Messiah, but many rejected Him. They refused to believe His message and disregarded the miracles that confirmed the truth of His words. Like the

prophets they rejected in the past, the people of Israel also rejected Jesus. However, the apostle Paul says God's people can again find His grace and favor if they will turn from their sin and acknowledge Jesus as their Messiah (Romans 9-11).

Our sin separates us from God; it makes us worthy of His judgment. However, Jesus said He came to save the world, not to judge it (John 3:17). Through Him, God offers us a fresh start. If we believe His Word and turn from sin, we will experience eternal life rather than judgment.

1. How do you feel when you hear about a person rejecting God? How do you think God feels?
2. When you turned toward God, how did He restore your life?
3. Do you know someone who has suffered because of their bad choices? What could you tell them about God's love?
4. How would you balance the message of God's love and His judgment as you tell others about Him?

Both Jeremiah and Josiah were born during wicked King Manasseh's long reign. Manasseh encouraged idol worship and led the people of Israel away from the Lord. When he died, his son Amon became king. However, Amon only reigned for two years before his own officials assassinated him. The people of Judah remembered King David and still wanted a member of his family to take the throne. But at the time, Amoz's son Josiah, the royal heir, was only a boy. Even so, the people crowned him as king (2 Chronicles 33:21-25).

31 | THE BOY WHO BECAME KING
Josiah

For many years, kings ruled Israel. Most led the people away from God, while only a few feared the Lord and ruled according to His commands. Josiah was one of the kings who ruled righteously.

2 KINGS 22-23

Crowned about 600 years before the birth of Jesus, Josiah was only eight years old when he became king. Both his father and grandfather had been wicked rulers, but Josiah "did what was pleasing in the LORD's sight" (2 Kings 22:2). King Josiah used funds from the royal treasury to hire skilled laborers to repair the Lord's Temple. He also had every form of idol worship removed from the Temple and destroyed.

While Hilkiah the high priest was working in the Temple, he found a book containing the Law God gave His people. However, the people had neglected this Law for many years. Hilkiah

arranged to deliver the book to King Josiah. When the court secretary read the book to the king, Josiah realized he was hearing God's Word. He humbled himself and repented both personally and on behalf of the nation for having ignored it for so long. Josiah then read the book in public so the people of God could hear. They all agreed to obey God's Word and keep His commandments.

Josiah did more than just remove all the idols from the Temple. He also destroyed all the altars throughout the kingdom where the people had offered sacrifices to false gods. Then Josiah got rid of all the mediums, psychics, household idols, and every other form of false worship in the land (2 Kings 23:24). Even after he did all these good things, though, Huldah the prophetess declared Jerusalem would fall because of the people's wickedness. She said this fall would not happen during King Josiah's lifetime because the people had repented of their sins and returned to God.

King Josiah died unexpectedly in a battle with the Egyptians. Throughout his life, he had remained faithful to the Lord. No king before or after him had turned to the Lord like Josiah did (2 Kings 23:25). Josiah did not follow in the footsteps of previous generations. His father and grandfather were not good kings, but Josiah was nothing like them. It is true that ungodly parents and previous generations can negatively affect a person, but this does not mean we are doomed to repeat previous errors. Like Josiah, we can be different. We can live in a way that is pleasing to the Lord. God has given us the ability to choose what is right and make a fresh start for ourselves as well as for those who may follow us.

King Josiah's life teaches us two valuable lessons:

Obedience to God is more important than experience or age.
— Josiah's life demonstrates how a person can be influential for God at any age. He was still young when he ordered the repair of the Temple and its cleansing from idolatry. Wisdom should come with age, but this is not guaranteed. However, wisdom will come when a heart is right with God. Josiah's heart for God qualified him to change his kingdom for the better, even while he was young. At any age, we can have a positive influence on others if our hearts are submitted to the Lord.

The past does not define God's children.
— King Josiah did what was right in spite of his father and grandfather; he did not repeat their mistakes. Josiah refused to tolerate the idolatry

of God's people. He took action! When he heard the Word of the Lord, the king repented and provided a godly example for the people to follow.

Josiah successfully moved the entire nation in a new direction. His life exemplifies the importance of a leader's influence. No matter how you grew up or what your past was like, you can decide today to be different. Serve the Lord with all your heart and do what is right. Then you will have a position of influence on those around you as well as those who follow you in the future.

1. Despite your past or your family's past, how do you believe God wants you to serve Him?
2. As you think about the young people you know, how should you pray for them as they try to follow the Lord?
3. How can you influence others to turn away from doing wrong things and follow the Lord with all their hearts?

One person can lead a nation to follow God, but only if the people will obey. King Josiah led a great revival in the worship of the Lord, but the people soon forgot and returned to worshipping idols. It was only a matter of time until God lost His patience with them. When He did, the people suffered a great defeat—enemy forces destroyed their city and Temple, and many Jews were taken as captives to a foreign country. This period is known as the Babylonian Exile. For more than 70 years, God's people were kept away from the Promised Land. During this time, God raised up prophets to speak to the captive people. One such prophet was Ezekiel.

32 A PROPHET IN A TIME OF CRISIS
Ezekiel

Jerusalem fell to the Babylonians, and many of God's people were taken into captivity. While living in a foreign land, one Jewish man had a supernatural vision and received a divine call to declare God's word. This man was Ezekiel.

EZEKIEL 1; 37
Along with many other Jews, Ezekiel came to Babylon as a captive. One day, he saw a vision of heaven. Then God told Ezekiel that He was sending him as a prophet to speak God's word to His people. The Lord said Ezekiel should boldly declare the message given to him, regardless of whether the people received it or not (Ezekiel 2:7). God told Ezekiel it was not his responsibility to convince anyone to believe the words he spoke. However, God would hold him accountable for delivering the warning to the people. In the face

of rejection and suffering, Ezekiel had to speak the words given to him by God.

God required Ezekiel to communicate His message in some unusual and vivid ways. For example, Gold told the prophet to lay on his left side for 390 days and then on his right side for 40 days. This symbolic act would show the people their sinful rebellion and God's coming judgment.

Not every message God gave to Ezekiel was about judgment, though. One day, the Lord showed the prophet a valley of dry bones. As Ezekiel looked at the bones, God asked him if he thought the bones could become living people again. Ezekiel replied that only God knew the answer to that question (Ezekiel 37:3). God then told the prophet to speak His word to the bones. Ezekiel was to say that God would put muscle and skin on them and breathe life into them. At God's word, the people came back to life and stood on their feet as a great army. God told Ezekiel this vision was a picture of His people. Even though the Jews thought there was no hope of ever becoming a nation again, God was capable of raising them up once more. The prophet who spoke of judgment also declared words of hope and restoration.

Ezekiel's life offers challenges as well as hope:

Obey God. Share His message.

— God told Ezekiel to declare His word. The prophet was not responsible for how the people responded to the message, but he would be held accountable if he did not speak the words the Lord gave him. The Lord also asks us to share our faith and the gifts He has given us with others. We cannot force anyone to respond favorably to God's message. However, we are responsible for our own obedience.

God gives a message of hope.

— Ezekiel brought more than a message of judgment; he also shared words of encouragement and hope. Even when the Babylonians destroyed Jerusalem and took the Jews captive, God declared His people would be restored. God would bring them back home (Ezekiel 39:25-29).

God's promise is to all nations.

— Ezekiel spoke of a restoration beyond Israel. He envisioned a day when God would restore the world from the effects of sin. The Lord showed Ezekiel a river flowing from the Temple; this river brought life wherever it went. Trees on both sides of the river bore fruit each month, and their leaves brought healing (Ezekiel 47:12). The Bible also describes a river in the Garden of Eden. Beside the river was the tree of life and other trees for Adam and Eve to enjoy. When

the couple sinned, God evicted them from Eden. Later, Jesus offered living water to the woman at the well (John 4:10-11). She had come to get physical water, but He offered water to quench the thirsting of her soul. Jesus came to bring life to all who are dead in sin. In the book of Revelation, the apostle John writes about the river of life. Like the Garden of Eden and in Ezekiel's vision, this river has trees on each side that bear fruit with leaves for healing. Because of Jesus, anyone who believes in Him will gain what Adam and Eve lost.

In the book of Ezekiel, God offers a fresh start after His people have a terrible false start. Ultimately, Jesus is the One sent by God to rescue all humanity. He offers living water to every person in every nation.

1. God told Ezekiel to share His message regardless of the way people responded. How can you have confidence in sharing God's message no matter how others receive it?
2. Sometimes our actions have negative consequences, whether through natural causes or God's supernatural judgment. How would you share God's message of hope with someone who has suffered negative consequences for their actions?
3. How do you participate in fulfilling God's desire for all nations to follow Him?

Ezekiel was not the only prophet God called to deliver His message during the Babylonian Exile. God continued speaking to His people even while they experienced His correction and judgment. Many powerful words from God came through the prophet Daniel.

33 A FAITHFUL PROPHET
Daniel

Not everyone likes honest and loyal people. There are those who brag unjustifiably about how good they are while they secretly do evil things. Others quietly live admirable and honest lives. These humble people work hard and treat others right. Daniel was one such person. Though many admire this type of person, others do not.

DANIEL 1-2; 6

When God's people turned away from Him, He often allowed them to come under the control of other nations. The Babylonian Exile was the worst of those experiences—many Jews were forced to leave their homeland and taken to Babylon. Young men whom the king considered to have the most

potential benefit to him received special training. Daniel was one of them. After he was captured and taken to Babylon, this young man remained faithful to the Lord. Others began to see God's blessing on Daniel's life. One night, the king had a terrifying dream. No one could tell him its meaning except Daniel. When Daniel interpreted the dream, the king made the Jewish captive a ruler over Babylon (Daniel 2:48).

Later, the nation of Persia defeated Babylon. The Persian King Darius appointed Daniel as one of the three highest officials in the land. Because the king valued Daniel so highly, the other leaders became jealous. They looked for a way to make the king dislike Daniel, but they were unable to find any fault with the godly young man. Unable to use Daniel's character as an excuse for punishment, the leaders decided to use his faith in God to destroy him. They tricked the king into signing a law that made it illegal for people to worship anyone but the king himself for 30 days (Daniel 6:7-10). They knew Daniel would not stop praying to the Lord, and it would only be a matter of time before Daniel's actions would force the king to punish him.

Against the king's order, Daniel continued to pray three times each day. His enemies quickly reported this "crime" to the king. The news upset the king because he liked Daniel; however, he could not ignore his own law. The king reluctantly ordered Daniel to be thrown into a den of lions. That night, the king did not eat or sleep, and as soon as morning arrived, he rushed to the den to see if God had spared Daniel. To the king's great joy, Daniel was safe. God had sent an angel to keep the lions from hurting him. Then the king gave a new order: he had Daniel's accusers thrown into the den of lions. Because Daniel trusted God, he was spared. Those who hated him received the punishment they wanted for Daniel.

Daniel's life offers these two valuable lessons:

Your faithfulness will have influence on others.
— Even though Daniel was captured and taken to a foreign land, he remained faithful. God blessed him and gave him favor with his captors. Through Daniel's faithfulness, unbelieving rulers had to admit his God was the one true God. When we are faithful, we give others the

opportunity to follow God. Daniel also influenced his enemies, though they did not learn from his example. Their jealousy and hatred kept them from experiencing God's love and grace. When we are faithful to God, some people will respond positively and others negatively, but we will influence them all.

When we are faithful, God is even more faithful.
— After the king signed the law, Daniel continued to pray. He remained faithful even in the face of death, and God delivered him. The same lions Daniel's enemies hoped would kill him actually killed them! Daniel trusted God, and God protected him. We can always trust God to be faithful to His people.

1. In what ways have you positively influenced others through your faithfulness to God?
2. Has anyone ever bullied or even persecuted you because of your faith? How did you respond?
3. How would you encourage someone who is suffering because of their faith?
4. How has God shown you His faithfulness in difficult situations?

Daniel is an example of faithfulness. Away from his home and family, he faced intense persecution—to the point of death—but he remained loyal to the one true God. Daniel had three friends who also remained faithful under pressure, and God protected them as well.

34 THREE FAITHFUL FRIENDS
Shadrach, Meshach, and Abednego

The Babylonians defeated the nation of Israel and took many Jews captive. One of the best-known captives was Daniel, but he also had three friends with him. Their Hebrew names were Hananiah, Mishael, and Azariah, but they are better known by their Babylonian names: Shadrach, Meshach, and Abednego.

DANIEL 1; 3

The king of Babylon had special plans for Shadrach, Meshach, and Abednego. Like Daniel, they were specially trained to serve the king. Even though they were captives in a foreign land, things were going as well for them as could be expected. Everything changed, though, when the king made a large idol and required everyone in his kingdom to worship it. The three young men willingly served the king, but they would not bow down to an idol. They believed their God alone was worthy of worship.

When the king learned of their refusal, he threatened to have them thrown into a furnace

if they did not comply. However, his threat did not change their minds. Shadrach, Meshach, and Abednego told the king that their God was able to save them from the flames of the furnace. They went on to say, "But even if he doesn't, we want to make it clear to you, Your Majesty, that we will never serve your gods or worship the gold statue you have set up" (Daniel 3:18).

Their response made the king furious! He ordered the furnace to be heated seven times hotter than normal. Then Shadrach, Meshach, and Abednego were tied up and thrown into it. As the king looked on, he was shocked to see not three but *four* men in the furnace! He also saw they were untied and unharmed by the fire. Then the king called for Shadrach, Meshach, and Abednego to come out of the furnace. To the surprise of all the Babylonian officials, the three men were unharmed! In fact, not a single hair on their heads or any of their clothing had been burned. They didn't even smell like smoke! (Daniel 3:27). The king was so amazed by this miracle that he praised

God. He also decreed that no one could say anything against the God who had delivered Shadrach, Meshach, and Abednego. Then the king gave all three men higher positions in his kingdom.

Shadrach, Meshach, and Abednego demonstrated how we should live our lives in the midst of ungodly situations:

God will deliver those who are faithful to Him.
— The faith of these three men caught the attention of unbelievers in a remarkable way. Shadrach, Meshach, and Abednego displayed their faith in God through their confidence that He could deliver them and by their willingness to die rather than to worship a false god. Believers do not need to compromise their faith to be successful in this life. The three captives were elevated in Babylon before they were ordered to worship the idol, and they were promoted a second time after they remained faithful to God in the face of death. Though blessed in this way, Shadrach, Meshach, and Abednego had their priorities in order. They were not motivated by personal gain or fame, and they remained faithful to the Lord even when tested. God delivered them, and He will deliver you too.

Honor those in authority but honor God first.
— God wants us to honor those who are in authority over us until or unless they require us to deny our Lord. The apostle Paul affirms that God Himself places people in positions of power (Romans 13:1). The apostle Peter tells us to respect and honor those in authority (1 Peter 2:17). Shadrach, Meshach, and Abednego did just that until they were told to deny their God. Even then, they did not rebel against authority. They

were willing to submit, even unto death. They simply obeyed a higher authority—God. Even though the king of Babylon had them thrown into a furnace, they honored him after God delivered them.

Shadrach, Meshach, and Abednego demonstrated their faithfulness to God. They showed that obedience brings great blessings. However, our priority should always be obedience first; blessings are simply the result. Serve the Lord with all your heart in the abundance of blessings *and* in the face of death. God will protect and provide for you as you do.

1. When has God blessed you for your faithfulness?
2. When has God protected you as you stood firm in your faith?
3. We should obey those in authority. What is an example of someone who disobeys authority for the wrong reasons? What would be a right reason to disobey authority?

The Jewish people learned many important lessons over their 70 years in captivity. The Exile taught them how to remain faithful to God even when others mistreated or threatened them. Their experiences in Babylon formed them as a people who could live and thrive anywhere in the world, even until today. In time, the Babylonian Exile ended. Many Jews stayed in Babylon, but others returned home to the Promised Land. However, the land was in disrepair, the city in ruins, and the Temple destroyed. They would need to rebuild. God raised up two important men to complete the reconstruction of Jerusalem: Ezra and Nehemiah.

35 THE REBUILDERS
Ezra and Nehemiah

The Babylonians took God's people captive. Later, the Persians defeated the Babylonians, and after some time, the Persian king allowed God's people to return to Jerusalem. Their first tasks were to rebuild the city and its Temple. God worked through two men in particular to accomplish these goals: Ezra and Nehemiah.

EZRA 1; 7-10; NEHEMIAH 1-2; 4; 8-9

In the first year of his reign, King Cyrus of Persia declared that God had told him to have the Temple in Jerusalem rebuilt (Ezra 1:2). The king gave the Jews permission to return to their homeland, and he also returned the special worship items the Babylonians had stolen from the Temple in Jerusalem. When the rebuilding of the Temple began, the enemies of God's people tried to stop

the project. They wrote letters to King Cyrus asking him to stop the work. Then they told him it would be a threat to his kingdom if he allowed the work to continue.

At first, Cyrus agreed, and he issued a decree to halt the rebuilding. The next king, Darius, allowed the work to continue after finding the original decree from his predecessor. At that time, Ezra returned to Jerusalem with a letter from Darius that gave the Jews permission to complete the work. Through Ezra's leadership and encouragement, the people rebuilt the Temple.

Nehemiah was one of the Jews who served the king of Persia. One day, some men came from Judah and told Nehemiah about the conditions back in Jerusalem. The people were suffering, and the walls of the city were broken down. Nehemiah prayed and then asked the king for permission to return to Jerusalem. The king granted his request. When Nehemiah arrived, he inspected Jerusalem's walls and motivated the people to rebuild them. Enemies tried to stop the work, but Nehemiah rallied the people to continue. Some men stood guard with weapons while others built from dawn until dark until they finished rebuilding the wall (Nehemiah 4:21).

Ezra and Nehemiah played critical roles in the rebuilding of Jerusalem's city and Temple, and they made an even greater impact in rebuilding the people's use of and respect for God's Word. They knew the destruction of the city and Temple happened because the people failed to obey God. God had given the Jewish people a fresh start, but it would not last unless they honored His commands and worshipped Him alone. Thus, Ezra "determined to study and obey the Law of the LORD and to teach those decrees and regulations to the people of Israel" (Ezra 7:10). Ezra and Nehemiah gathered God's people to hear His Word as Ezra read it. When he finished, they confessed their sins and worshipped God (Nehemiah 9:3). Whenever Ezra and Nehemiah became aware of anyone not obeying God's word, they took action. They did not want to repeat the past.

Ignoring God and His Word are dangerous acts. God's Word told the people His will for their lives, but they had neglected it. The people were to worship God alone, but they had turned to idols. The Temple was the Jews' center of worship, but because of their sin and disobedience, God allowed the Babylonians to destroy it. The city walls were smashed too. God's people lost the place where the Lord's presence dwelt as well as the protection around them. Then they were taken captive by their enemies. They failed God. But God never fails, and He never abandons His people either (Deuteronomy 31:6). He eventually brought the Jews back to the land He had promised their ancestors Abraham, Isaac, and Jacob. God protected them from hostile enemies as they rebuilt the city, the Temple, and their relationship with Him. The people of Israel had once forfeited God's presence and protection through their disobedience. They now knew the consequences of sin were painful, and the only way to avoid bondage was to keep God first and follow His Word.

1. What are some ways you can keep God's Word at the center of your life?
2. Have you ever ignored God's Word and suffered the consequences? What was the result?
3. How would you tell someone to find freedom after they have made poor choices?

While many Jews returned to Jerusalem when their years in exile ended, some chose to stay in the foreign land where their families had lived for decades. Mordecai's family remained in Susa, the fortress of King Xerxes. Mordecai had a beautiful young cousin whom he adopted as his own daughter. Her name was Esther.

36 THE TIMELY QUEEN
Esther

God calls His people to be faithful no matter where they live or who rules over them. After the Babylonian Exile, many Jews returned to Jerusalem, but some remained in the land where their families had lived for the past 70 years. Mordecai's family continued living in Susa, where King Xerxes ruled over his vast empire of 127 provinces. Mordecai had a cousin whom he adopted as his daughter when her parents died. Though originally called Hadassah, this girl also went by another name: Esther.

As a young Jewish girl, Esther had little reason ever to imagine herself as a queen of Persia. However, her life's direction abruptly changed one day when agents of the king gathered all the attractive young women in the province—Esther included—and took them to the king's harem. King Xerxes was in search of a new queen. The former queen, Vashti, had infuriated the king by refusing to appear before him at a banquet. As punishment, King Xerxes banished Vashti from his presence and stripped her of her royal title. One of the young, beautiful women now gathered in the harem would replace Vashti.

Esther impressed the servant in charge of the harem, and she received special food, beauty treatments, and even her own maids. At the direction of Mordecai, Esther kept her Jewish identity a secret, even when King Xerxes chose her to be his queen. Esther remained in close contact with her cousin and continued obeying his instructions. When Mordecai, now a palace official, warned the queen of a plot against the king, Esther told King Xerxes and gave the credit to Mordecai. This information saved the king's life.

While Queen Esther kept her Jewish identity a secret, Mordecai did not hide his. One day, he found himself at odds with a powerful enemy: Haman. King Xerxes had given Haman authority to rule over all the officials of the Persian Empire. Everyone was required to bow down to Haman, but Mordecai refused. Haman was so enraged he wanted to destroy not only Mordecai but also Mordecai's people—the Jews.

Haman went to the king and told him a certain race of people were enemies of the crown and should be destroyed. King Xerxes agreed to let Haman destroy this race, and a decree was written and stamped with the king's own ring. The decree stated that on March 7 of the following year, "all Jews—young and old, including women and children—must be killed, slaughtered, and annihilated on a single day" (Esther 3:13).

Terrified of this impending doom, Jews all over the empire began mourning. When Esther, unaware of the king's decree, learned of Mordecai's deep sadness, she sent her servants to ask him about his troubles. Mordecai sent back a copy of the decree and asked Esther to plead with the king to spare the Jews. However, the queen had not been summoned to appear before the king in a month. Without an invitation, an appearance could be a death sentence. Mordecai reminded Esther that her position in the palace did not erase the fact she was Jewish; neither she nor her people were safe. He said, "Who knows if perhaps you were made queen for just such a time as this?" (Esther 4:14). Gathering her courage, Esther asked all the Jews in the city to fast with her for three days. Then, in spite of the risk, she would appear before the king.

Three days later, Esther dressed in her finest clothes and appeared before King Xerxes. He invited her to approach the throne and make her request. Esther then invited the king and Haman to a banquet. As they were feasting that evening, Esther invited the men to return again the next day, and she promised to tell the king the true nature of her request.

Haman was thrilled to receive a second invitation, but his hatred for Mordecai and the Jews still burned within him. He was temporarily appeased when King Xerxes asked how a man who had pleased the king should be honored. Thinking this pleasing man was himself, Haman gave his grand suggestions, only to be humiliated when he learned that the pleasing man was Mordecai! King Xerxes had never shown his appreciation for Mordecai's information that prevented an assassination attempt and wanted now to correct this oversight. Haman was forced to carry out the honors he had suggested for his most hated enemy.

Haman's troubles had only just begun, however. At the second banquet that evening, Esther asked King Xerxes to spare the lives of her people and revealed Haman to be the leader of this planned genocide. The king stormed out of the room in a fit of rage. Haman realized his life was in jeopardy, but as he attempted to beg for mercy, he fell onto Esther. King Xerxes thought Haman was attempting to hurt the queen, and Haman's fate was sealed. He was impaled on the very pole he had once hoped to use to kill Mordecai.

Esther and Mordecai were safe, but the Jewish people throughout the empire were still in danger. King Xerxes's first decree could not be revoked, but an additional decree was written that allowed the Jews to protect themselves from any enemy wishing to harm them. March 7 soon came, but unlike Haman's plan, the Jews were not harmed—"no one could make a stand against them, for everyone was afraid of them" (Esther 9:2). Instead, the Jews defeated their enemies and spent the next day in celebration. This celebration became an annual event known as the Festival of Purim. Every year, the Jews throughout the Persian Empire remembered and rejoiced that their lives had been spared, and Jewish people around the world celebrate this event even to this day.

Esther remained faithful even in the face of difficult and dangerous circumstances. When she became queen, she continued to honor and obey Mordecai. When she learned about Haman's plot, Esther advocated for the Jews, risking both her secret and her life. And even after securing her own safety, Esther used her position to rescue her people from annihilation. The book of Esther never directly mentions God, but His presence and power are evident throughout the life of the queen who saved His chosen people.

1. Has your life ever gone in an unexpected direction? How can you honor God even when you feel like you aren't in control of your circumstances?
2. What are some ways you can encourage others to trust God in difficult times?
3. Sometimes it takes great courage to stand for what is right. Why is it important to surround yourself with other believers who support you?

Whether the Jews lived in foreign lands or Jerusalem, God continued to show His faithfulness to His people. Time and again, He rescued them from their enemies. In the land of Israel, peace lasted for a short time after Ezra and Nehemiah oversaw the rebuilding of Jerusalem and the Temple.

Between the last Old Testament writing and the birth of Jesus, 400 years passed. Even though the Bible does not record the events during those centuries, many things happened. Judea had a brief time of self-rule but was also ruled by Persians, Greeks, Egyptians, Syrians, and finally Romans. A group of rabbis translated the Old Testament into a Greek version called the Septuagint. This version is the most often quoted text in the New Testament. Pharisees and Sadducees came to power, and scribes gained influence among the Jews. Many people began to hope and pray for the coming of the Messiah, although few would recognize His appearance (Matthew 16:13-16). Jesus was born during a time of uncertainty and unrest. It may have been a strange time, but as the apostle Paul says, "When the right time came, God sent his Son, born of a woman, subject to the law" (Galatians 4:4, emphasis added).

37 THE MOST BLESSED WOMAN
Mary

The last Old Testament book, penned by the prophet Malachi, had been written 400 years earlier. During the intervening years, the people of Israel had been under one foreign occupation after another. Some Jews cooperated with the invaders, some revolted against the enemy, and some simply waited and prayed for God's salvation. Most Jews knew the Old Testament prophets had promised that God would send a Messiah to rescue His people, although they did not agree on what kind of Messiah He would be. Almost no one expected the strange way God would send His Son to save the world.

The Gospel of Luke records the angel Gabriel's visit to a young woman named Mary. Angels visited other people in the Bible, but none like this. Gabriel gave Mary a unique message: even though she had never been intimate with a man, she would become pregnant and give birth to a son. The angel told her to call the baby *Jesus*.

LUKE 1:26–56; 2

Mary, a young Jewish woman, was engaged to a man named Joseph. The angel Gabriel told Mary that God favored her, and although she had never had a physical relationship with a man, she would become pregnant and give birth to a son. At first, Mary asked Gabriel how this could happen since she was a virgin. The angel replied that her pregnancy would be the work of the Holy Spirit. In response, Mary said, "I am the Lord's servant. May everything you have said about me come true" (Luke 1:38).

Joseph stayed with Mary, but he did not have a physical relationship with her until after the child was born. In time, Mary gave birth to a son and named him *Jesus* as Gabriel had instructed her to do. When Jesus was born, angels appeared to shepherds who were watching their flocks at night and declared the Savior had been born.

Mary and Joseph faithfully taught Jesus how to follow the Lord, and they watched Him grow "in wisdom and in stature and in favor with God and all the people" (Luke 2:52). Mary was present when Jesus performed His first public miracle by turning water into wine at a wedding feast (John 2:1–11). She was also at the cross where her Son suffered greatly and died. After Jesus rose from death, Mary stayed with His followers as they waited for the promised Holy Spirit to come (Acts 1:14).

God did amazing things through many of the Bible's men and women. Prophets and apostles heard from God and performed many miraculous signs. But there could be only one woman in all of history to give birth to God's Son, Jesus. Mary was undoubtedly the most favored among women.

Mary demonstrated that she was a woman of faith when she believed what Gabriel told her. As the Lord's servant, she willingly accepted God's call for her life. God chose Mary and honored her, though others likely did not. Few would have believed her story. After all, how many women have ever given birth without a man's involvement in the child's conception? If many Jews did not believe Jesus' claim to be the Messiah, imagine how many others doubted Mary's claim of divine intervention. Even so, she remained a virtuous woman.

The infant Messiah grew within Mary, which would have been evident to those who saw her. Even while John the Baptist was in his mother's womb, he recognized the great gift that was within Mary (Luke 1:39–45). Mary faithfully carried God's presence until the time came for her to give birth to the Savior of the world. None of us will ever carry and bring Jesus into the world the way Mary did. However, each of us can receive Him into our lives and carry Him to others.

In one sense, Mary was special and favored by the Lord, but in another, she was just like us. She was an ordinary person and typical of many women during that time, but God's call and the Holy Spirit's work made her extraordinary. In the same way, God can do amazing things in and through us by the power of the Holy Spirit if we will faithfully do whatever He asks.

1. Why was it important for Mary to have no physical relations with a man before Jesus was born? What does this fact say about Jesus?
2. Has God ever asked you to do something that seemed truly impossible? What does Mary's response teach us about trusting and obeying God?
3. How can you show God today that you are willing to do whatever He asks you to do?

Mary obeyed God and His messenger Gabriel even though it meant great personal risk. However, she was not the only person who dared to do something great for God at the time of Jesus' birth. Joseph, Mary's fiancé and eventual husband, also received special messages from God about how to care for this new baby. Joseph was not Jesus' biological father, but he parented Him in a loving and sacrificial way. As a good and honorable man, he had the faith to obey God.

38   A JUST MAN
Joseph, Mary's Husband

Most people have some familiarity with "the Christmas story." They probably know it centers on the birth of Jesus. They may also be aware that it involves angels, shepherds, and a special star in the sky. Beyond that, though, the details become fuzzy.

Jesus was born to a young virgin named Mary. While some Christians give meaning to her that others do not, all believers agree that she should be greatly esteemed because God held her in such high regard. Her relative Elizabeth said Mary would be blessed above all women, just as her child was blessed (Luke 1:42). As God chose a special woman to give birth to Jesus, He also selected a special man to be Jesus' earthly father. That man was Joseph.

MATTHEW 1:18–24; 2:13–14; LUKE 2

Joseph was a carpenter or builder by trade, and he likely taught this skill to his Son, Jesus (Mark 6:3). Joseph was probably not a wealthy or privileged person; he was a hardworking tradesman. As the Bible follows Jesus' adult life, it mentions Mary several times but does not mention Joseph. Some Bible scholars believe Joseph may have died sometime before the beginning of Jesus' earthly ministry. Perhaps this is the reason why Jesus, while hanging on the cross, asked the "disciple he loved" (probably John) to care for Mary as if she were his own mother (John 19:26–27).

The Bible has more to say about Mary than it does Joseph, yet it does reveal a few things about this man's character and faith. Matthew describes Joseph as a good man who obeyed the Lord (Matthew 1:19, 24). When Joseph first learned about his fiancée's pregnancy, he wanted to protect her from any shame or disgrace: "He decided to break the engagement quietly" (Matthew 1:19). Joseph had more concern for Mary's feelings and reputation than his own. He may even have been saving her life because women who became pregnant outside of marriage were often killed during that time.

The angel Gabriel told Mary she would become pregnant "through the power of the Holy Spirit" (Matthew 1:18). Few people have ever seen an angel, but Mary did. And so did Joseph. He actually had multiple angelic encounters. As Joseph thought about breaking off his engagement to Mary, an angel told him through a dream that Mary's pregnancy did not mean she had been unfaithful. God had done a great miracle in her, and Joseph was to name the baby *Jesus*. Joseph believed the angel's words, and he married Mary. They refrained from being physically intimate until after the baby arrived, and "Joseph named him Jesus" (Matthew 1:25).

King Herod later learned from the wise men that a new king had been born. Enraged and paranoid, the ruler ordered the murder of every boy from birth to two years old in the area. An angel warned Joseph in a dream, though, to escape with Mary and Jesus to Egypt. Joseph heeded the warning, and the family stayed in the foreign land until a third angelic dream told Joseph it was safe to return to Israel. Upon arriving in their home country, Joseph had a fourth dream that led him to settle his family in Nazareth.

The Bible offers many details about the lives of some people, such as Abraham, Moses, and David. For others, however, it includes little information. Joseph belongs to the latter group. Like Mary, Joseph was an ordinary person, but he demonstrated his character and faithfulness through his actions. He was a good man in the way he treated Mary, and he honored God through his quick obedience. Scripture never says Joseph performed great miracles or preached powerful sermons. Yet God chose him to be the earthly father—perhaps the most significant male role model—of Jesus. The Bible does not record a single negative thing about this Jewish tradesman. He feared God, protected his family, and led them well.

1. How can you show concern for someone's reputation and feelings even when you don't feel like it?
2. Joseph took a special role in protecting Jesus. How do you think God wants you to protect others who cannot protect themselves?
3. Joseph was quick to obey God. Why did the speed of his obedience make a difference?

Jesus grew up just like any other Jewish boy, with one significant difference—He was God's Son. Even from childhood, the Holy Spirit was working in Him in a special way. Jesus knew God was His Father, and He wanted to obey Him. As God was preparing Jesus for a world-changing ministry, He was also preparing another special boy: Jesus' cousin John the Baptist. God put a great calling on John's life. This man preached for people to repent—change their hearts and minds and turn to God. Then he baptized them as a sign of their repentance. John told the people that the Kingdom of God was very close; it was so near they could touch it. That Kingdom would come in the person of his own cousin Jesus.

39 THE FORERUNNER
John the Baptist

Throughout the history of the nation of Israel, God often sent prophets to speak to His people. These messengers told about what would happen in the future, and they also called God's people to change the way they were living in the present. Malachi was the last prophet God sent before the time of Jesus. This man spoke about another prophet who would come after him (Malachi 3:1). Centuries later, God sent John the Baptist as the fulfillment of Malachi's words.

MATTHEW 3; 14:1–12

John the Baptist preached a simple and clear message—he called for people to change their hearts and minds and return to the LORD in preparation for the coming Messiah. Hundreds of years earlier, the prophet Isaiah had said that John the Baptist would be "a voice shouting in the wilderness, 'Prepare the way for the LORD's coming! Clear the road for him!'" (Matthew 3:3). Many people believed John was a prophet of God. He baptized those who believed his message and repented of their sins. However, many of the religious leaders did not believe John was a prophet, so they refused to be baptized by him.

One day, John saw his cousin Jesus and called out, "Look! The Lamb of God who takes away the sin of the world!" (John 1:29). John preached a message of repentance, but Jesus was the One who came to take away sin. John knew Jesus was the promised Savior of the world, and he was surprised when Jesus came to be baptized by him. When John protested, Jesus answered, "It should be done, for we must carry out all that God requires" (Matthew 3:15). Jesus never sinned, but He was baptized so others would follow His example. When Jesus emerged from the water, the Holy Spirit came and settled upon him like a dove. Then God said, "This is my dearly loved Son, who brings me great joy" (Matthew 3:17).

Not long after, King Herod imprisoned John the Baptist for criticizing his ungodly marriage. While in prison, John sent some of his followers to ask Jesus if He really was the One God promised—the Messiah. Jesus confirmed His identity, and as John's followers left, He told the onlooking crowd that there was no one greater than John. However, Jesus also said that the "least person in the Kingdom of Heaven is greater" than John (Matthew 11:11). Jesus did not say this to criticize His cousin. Instead, He was giving the crowd a clue as to the importance of His own ministry for those who would believe in Him.

While John the Baptist was still in prison, a birthday party was held for King Herod. This ruler only served because the Romans allowed him to do so. Herod was married to his half-brother's former wife, Herodias. John condemned the marriage, and this disapproval infuriated Herodias. At the party, Herodias's daughter Salome danced before Herod. Her dancing pleased the king so much that he vowed to let her have whatever she requested. Herodias convinced her daughter to ask for the head of John the Baptist. At first, King Herod was reluctant to honor Salome's request, but he feared what his party guests might say if he went back on his word. Thus, he ordered John's execution. John the Baptist's life and ministry ended that day, but his legacy lives on.

For centuries, God spoke to His people through prophets. After many years of silence, God again spoke through John the Baptist. John announced the promises God would soon fulfill through Jesus; he prepared the way for the Messiah. God always sets things in order, according to His design and timing. He prepared the way for you to receive Jesus Christ as your Lord and Savior, using one of a variety of circumstances to gain your attention. You may have gone through a traumatic event, or God may have reached you through a gentle prodding in your heart. Perhaps you heard about Jesus from a friend. The Holy Spirit works through events and people to draw you to the Messiah. He prepares the way.

1. Think about someone who shared the gospel with you. What can you learn from their example as you tell others about Jesus?
2. Why did John the Baptist preach repentance? How is this message still relevant to today's culture?
3. What did John the Baptist mean when he called Jesus "the Lamb of God who takes away the sin of the world" (John 1:29)?

God orders our lives. He sent John the Baptist to prepare the way for the Messiah, Jesus. We will never know all the arrangements God made for us to come to Him in repentance and faith, but we can appreciate the beauty of His plan. Many of the encounters Jesus had with people occurred in ways we would not expect, but God designed them all. One night, Jesus met with an important Pharisee named Nicodemus. This inquisitive man came with many questions. Not only did Jesus provide answers, but He also corrected many of the questions. Little did Nicodemus know that this clandestine meeting would reveal some of the Bible's greatest teaching about God's plan for humanity.

40 THE NIGHT VISITOR
Nicodemus

A man once took a great risk and came to see Jesus late at night. He likely wanted to keep his visit a secret because he was a Pharisee, a Jewish religious leader. Most of the Pharisees did not believe Jesus was the Son of God. In fact, they were some of His most hostile opponents. However, this Pharisee saw something in Jesus that made him want to know more. His name was Nicodemus.

JOHN 3:1–21

Nicodemus approached Jesus and said, "We all know that God has sent you to teach us. Your miraculous signs are evidence that God is with you" (John 3:2). This statement may indicate what Nicodemus believed about Jesus, or it may reveal his inner conflict. He may have struggled to reconcile his fellow Pharisees' rejection of Jesus with the obvious miracles the latter performed.

In response, Jesus made a statement that confused Nicodemus: "Unless you are born again, you cannot see the Kingdom of God" (John 3:3). This announcement surprised Nicodemus because according to the Pharisees' religious beliefs, he was already "born again." He had already completed all the necessary steps, such as bar mitzvah, marriage, and leading a school for rabbis. How could he start all over now?

Then Jesus made it clear He was speaking not of a physical birth but a spiritual one. It is in the context of this conversation that we find perhaps the most famous verse in all of Scripture: "For this is how God loved the world: He gave his one and only Son, so that everyone who believes in him will not perish but have eternal life" (John 3:16). Nicodemus's nighttime visit with Jesus resulted in the great revelation that being born again had nothing to do with human efforts and everything to do with God's remarkable gift of His Son. Only by believing in Jesus can a person experience God's salvation—this is the Good News!

Nicodemus was an educated man, but he was also humble enough to recognize there was something special about Jesus. It took courage to seek out the truth, especially when the other leaders rejected everything this new Teacher had to say. This man may have been fearful at first, but when Jesus' body was taken down from the cross, Nicodemus was there to help wrap the Messiah's body and lay him in the tomb (John 19:39–42).

Like Nicodemus, we should seek Jesus' presence. No matter how much we've learned or how rich or poor our religious heritage may be, encounters with Jesus will always reveal truth to us. If we come to Him with seeking hearts, He will answer our questions and open our eyes. Every person needs a spiritual rebirth in Jesus Christ. Paul says that every person is spiritually dead because of sin (Ephesians 2:1). Therefore, we *all* need to be "born again." We must humble ourselves and ask the Holy Spirit to open our eyes to the truth about Jesus.

In Jesus' encounter with Nicodemus, He revealed the motive and purpose for His coming to earth—*God's love*. God loved the world so much that He was willing to send His own Son to die for us. The purpose was to bring us eternal life. Jesus died in our place so we could live forever. Although we were dead because of sin, Jesus came to give us eternal life. He did not come to judge us but to save us (John 3:17).

1. How would you tell someone what it means to be "born again"?
2. Some people move boldly toward Jesus while others take small, tentative steps. Do you know someone who is taking baby steps toward Jesus? If so, ask God to give them courage and open their eyes and heart.
3. Some people believe God only wants to judge them. What would you say to someone who thinks this way?

Like the evening encounter with Nicodemus, the Gospels record several one-on-one conversations Jesus had with people. Some of our Savior's most important teaching moments happened through these personal connections. One such meeting took place with a Samaritan woman at a water well on the edge of her town. It would change her life.

41 LIVING WATER
The Woman at the Well

Jesus often had conversations with unlikely people. Most religious leaders would avoid certain types of people because of their gender, social class, or identity. However, Jesus did not abide by these limitations. He came to reach lost people.

A Samaritan woman He met at a water well was one of those people.

JOHN 4:1–42

One day, Jesus and His disciples journeyed through an area called Samaria. Few Jews traveled that way because of a long history of conflict between Jews and Samaritans. Many years before, some Jews intermarried with people from other nations. The offspring produced from those relationships were the Samaritans.

Tired from the journey, Jesus stopped to rest by a well while His disciples went to buy food. As Jesus waited, a Samaritan woman came to draw water from the well. Jesus surprised her by asking for a drink. Jewish men did not usually talk to unfamiliar women and certainly not to a Samaritan woman. The woman expressed her astonishment: "You are a Jew, and I am a Samaritan woman. Why are you asking me for a drink?" Jesus responded, "If you only knew the gift God has for you and who you are speaking to, you would ask me, and I would give you living water" (John 4:9–10).

The woman did not understand that Jesus was speaking about something spiritual. She wondered how He could offer her a drink without having a bucket or utensil to draw water from the well. Jesus then said if she drank the water He was offering her, she would never be thirsty again (John 4:14). So the woman asked Him to give her this water.

Jesus replied in an unusual way—He told her to go get her husband. The woman revealed she didn't have a husband, but Jesus already knew that fact. He agreed with her and said she had five previous husbands and was not married to the man with whom she now lived. When Jesus made this revelation, the woman immediately recognized He was not an ordinary man. She turned the conversation toward religious matters and began to talk about the coming Messiah. Jesus said, "I AM the Messiah" (John 4:26). At that moment, the woman ran back to her town and told everyone about Jesus.

Sometimes Christians believe they should remain distant from those who are not believers. This separation is a wise practice if you know others will lead you to sin; however, it does not apply if you merely dislike someone. Jesus did not stay away from people who were not like Him. If He did, He would have avoided everyone. Jesus willingly spoke to this Samaritan woman, though most Jews had racial prejudice against her ethnicity. Among her own people, she would have been looked down on for her marital status and living arrangements. Even so, Jesus talked to this woman about living water. He used a natural truth about water and human thirst to share with her a spiritual truth. She went to the well to satisfy the physical need to drink, but her life showed that her true thirst was spiritual. Jesus did not condemn the woman for the way she was living, but He didn't excuse it either. Instead, He made her aware of her real need.

Jesus showed this Samaritan woman her moral condition and lack of spiritual understanding. In the same way, God brings us to a place where we cannot deny our shortcomings, our lack of understanding, or our inability to meet our deepest needs. He loves us enough not to let us stay in a state of spiritual hunger and thirst. Jesus loved the Samaritan woman so much that He revealed His true self to her. He also wants us to know Him and drink from the living water that will quench our spiritual thirst. When we drink from Jesus, we will never thirst again!

1. Before people meet Jesus, what are some ways they try to satisfy their spiritual thirst?
2. How is the living water that Jesus speaks of different from physical water?
3. Do you know someone who needs living water? How would you encourage them to let Jesus satisfy their deep spiritual needs?

Jesus taught great spiritual truths through His conversations with individuals. He also taught groups, both large and small. To teach these truths, Jesus often told simple stories called *parables*. The Gospels record 46 parables.

42 **DIFFERENT KINDS OF SOIL**
The Parable of the Farmer Scattering Seed

Jesus often taught spiritual truths through simple stories called *parables*. Not everyone understood these parables, but the Gospels do provide explanations for some of them. One of the most famous of these stories is the Parable of the Farmer Scattering Seed (sometimes called the Parable of the Sower). This story tells about a man who aimlessly threw seeds into a field. He was not a careful farmer, though the story does not focus on his lack of horticultural ability. The seed he was spreading represents God's Word, but the focus of the parable is on different types of soil and what each represents.

MATTHEW 13:1–23; MARK 4:1–20; LUKE 8:4–15

Seeds have amazing potential. They begin as small bundles of life and can eventually become entire orchards or fields of crops. However, if not planted in the right kind of soil with the right conditions, they are useless and will die.

Jesus told a story about a farmer who scattered seeds onto four kinds of soil:
— footpath
— rocky ground

— ground with thorns
— and fertile soil.

The farmer threw the same type of seed on all four surfaces, but each location produced different results:
— The seeds on the footpath never had a chance to grow because birds quickly ate them.
— The seeds that fell on the rocky ground started to grow, but they couldn't take root and quickly withered in the sun.
— The seeds that landed around thorns died because the thorns stole the space and nutrients needed by the seeds to grow.
— The seeds in the fertile soil took root and grew into healthy plants. They even bore fruit.

The seeds that landed on the fertile ground were the only ones that grew long enough and strong enough to reach their full potential.
What did Jesus want His followers to learn from this parable?
— The seeds represent God's Word.
— The different kinds of soil represent the different ways people receive or respond to God's Word.
— Three of the ways lead to a false start. Only one way leads to a fresh start.

The footpath represents people who hear God's Word, but either their hearts are hardened to the truth, or they cannot understand its importance. As a result, the devil removes the life-changing Word of God before it can have a positive effect on their lives. The rocky ground describes people who have initial excitement about God's Word, but their shallow faith falters when troubles come. The ground with thorns symbolizes those who believe and receive God's Word long enough for it to start growing. Over time, though, life's worries and the

desire for wealth become more important. When people allow these things to take precedence, the power of God's Word becomes absent in their lives.
The fertile ground represents people who not only hear God's Word but also believe it and live fruitful lives for Him. Like the seed in the parable, God's Word has the power to bring life. God's Word will change you, but you have to take part in the process. If your heart is hard toward God, His Word will have no real effect on your life. If you put your faith in God but then turn away when troubles come, you will be as shallow as the rocky soil. Your faith must go deeper. Like thorns, worry and temptation will stunt or even stop your spiritual growth. You can trust Jesus. He promises to take care of you (Matthew 6:25–33) and give you the strength to resist temptation (1 Corinthians 10:13).
God's Word will help you grow in your faith. It will change your life from one that is dry and empty to one that is full and vibrant. Read it, learn it, study it, and believe it. Then watch what God will do.

1. What kind of soil are you right now? What kind do you want to be?
2. What are some ways you can deepen your faith?
3. How would you talk to someone who struggles with worry or temptation?
4. Have you ever "fallen away" from God when life became difficult? What happened? How did you return to Him?

Jesus taught crowds and had conversations with many individuals, but sometimes He ministered to people who had no relationship with Him at all. He met those people for the first time and immediately knew how to meet their deepest needs. One such person was the woman caught in the act of adultery.

---

43 A FORGIVEN WOMAN
The Woman Caught in Adultery

The apostle John is the only writer who includes the following event in his Gospel. Several men wanted to shame and even kill a particular woman, but Jesus rescued her in more ways than one. He used the incident to teach an amazing lesson about judgment and forgiveness. Because John did not record her name, she is known only as the woman caught in adultery.

JOHN 8:1-11
Some Jewish religious leaders and teachers caught a woman in the act of adultery. They brought her to Jesus and told Him what she had done. Everyone present knew the Law of Moses said adultery was punishable by stoning

(Leviticus 20:10). These men thought they had Jesus trapped because if He showed mercy to this woman, it would appear as if He didn't honor God's commands. They could then use this to refute His claim to be the Messiah.
The accusers demanded an answer from Jesus, but He knelt down and wrote something in the dirt instead. After they kept pressing Him, Jesus replied, "All right, but let the one who has never sinned throw the first stone!" (John 8:7). When the accusers heard this, they walked away one at a time. Not a single man threw a stone—none of them were without sin.
When they had left, Jesus turned to the woman and asked her if any of her accusers were still willing to pass judgment on her. She replied that none

remained to condemn her. Then Jesus told her, "Neither do I. Go and sin no more" (John 8:11).

Some of the most amazing things Jesus said and did were in response to situations that appeared to have no simple solution. The Jewish religious leaders and teachers often sought to trick Jesus into hurting His credibility, and they thought they had the perfect opportunity with the woman caught in adultery. In their minds, no matter how Jesus responded, He would leave Himself open to criticism. Always one step ahead, though, Jesus did not fall into their trap. Instead, He put the focus back on their own shortcomings. If they were going to punish this woman for her sin, they would first have to declare themselves to be sinless. Unable to claim such perfection, each man had no choice but to walk away.

This event teaches several important truths:

Our judgment of others is never impartial.
— The teachers and leaders told Jesus that Moses' Law required the woman to be put to death. However, the Law actually required the punishment of both the man and the woman caught in adultery (Leviticus 20:10). If the man and woman had equally sinned, why did these accusers only condemn the woman?

All have sinned.
— The woman's accusers were quick to hold her accountable for her sin while ignoring their own. Challenged by Jesus to confront their own sinfulness, no one was left to judge her. We all have broken God's commands. Thankfully, Jesus did not come to condemn us according to the law, but to bring us salvation. The apostle Paul writes, "For the wages of sin is death, but the free gift of God is eternal life through Christ Jesus our Lord" (Romans 6:23).

God condemns sin and loves people.
— Jesus revealed God's heart in the two statements He made to the woman. First, He told her He did not condemn her. John 3:17 says Jesus came to save the world, not to judge it. Second, Jesus said, "Go and sin no more." Just as He did not condemn the woman, He did not ignore her sin either. The proper response to God's mercy and grace is to turn away from sin and choose to live in a way that pleases Him.

We should hope no one "gets what they deserve."
— All people are more deserving of judgment than they are qualified to judge. Jesus is the only One without sin in all of history, yet He did not condemn the woman others were so quick to judge. Jesus was qualified to throw stones, but He didn't.

Do not take God's grace for granted. Go and sin no more. You will never be perfect in this world, but you can choose each day to serve Jesus. By His grace, He did not—and does not—condemn you.

1. How would you explain to someone that God loves them no matter what they have done?
2. As a believer, why is it important to show mercy to others, even if it feels like they don't deserve it?
3. How do you think God wants you to deal with guilt and shame from your past?

The apostle John's account of Jesus and the woman caught in adultery is a dramatic demonstration of God's love and mercy. Jesus often did things that surprised even His closest followers. Nothing could be more amazing, though, than His ability to raise His friend Lazarus from death.

44 THE FRIEND WHO LIVED AGAIN
Lazarus

Lazarus, Jesus' friend and follower, became very sick. His sisters sent a messenger to tell Jesus about the seriousness of his illness. At first, it appeared as if Jesus did not show concern because He waited two days before traveling to see His friend. By the time Jesus arrived, Lazarus had died.

JOHN 11:1–44

In addition to the 12 disciples who traveled with Him, Jesus had other followers who supported and believed in Him. Lazarus and his two sisters, Mary and Martha, lived in the town of Bethany, and they were especially close to Jesus. When Lazarus became ill, his sisters sent word to Jesus: "Lord, your dear friend is very sick" (John 11:3). Jesus cared

very much for this family, but He also knew His Father had a miraculous plan that would require patience. After two days, Jesus told His disciples that Lazarus was dead and what they were about to witness would increase their faith (John 11:14–15).

Jesus and His disciples went to Bethany and learned that Lazarus had died four days earlier. Martha came out to meet Jesus with a heavy heart and mixed emotions. She said, "Lord, if only you had been here, my brother would not have died. But even now I know that God will give you whatever you ask" (John 11:21-22). Jesus replied that Lazarus would rise from the dead. Martha believed His words, but she thought Jesus was referring to a future time. Neither she nor her sister, Mary, had any idea what Jesus planned to do that very day.

Because He was both God and human, Jesus understood the overwhelming sorrow and heartache Mary and Martha felt. He even wept as He walked toward the tomb (John 11:35). Jesus told onlookers to roll away the stone covering the tomb's entrance. Then He prayed to His Father and shouted, "Lazarus, come out!" (John 11:43). Immediately, Lazarus emerged from the tomb, fully alive. Because of this miracle, many people believed in Jesus.

Jesus' followers had seen Him heal many people; consequently, they failed to understand why He did not come in time to heal Lazarus. If He healed strangers, why would He not also heal His friend? The choice to wait for two days had nothing to do with a lack of compassion or love for Lazarus; rather, Jesus knew His Father wanted to bring about an even greater miracle than simply curing a sickness. By raising Lazarus from death, Jesus demonstrated His power over death. It was one thing for Jesus to say, "I am the resurrection and the life" (John 11:25), but it was quite another to bring a man back to life.

Jesus told His disciples He would one day be crucified. They heard His words but did not understand what Jesus meant. As the promised Messiah, they thought He would defeat God's enemies and set up His Kingdom on earth. Jesus would indeed defeat His enemies, but they would be death, sin, hell, and the devil!

The apostle Paul wrote that Jesus defeated sin and Satan on the cross. Death is the final enemy to be defeated (1 Corinthians 15:26). No matter how strong, rich, or holy we may be, death is the inescapable end of every person's life. Death came to the human race because Adam and Eve sinned. Jesus came not only to pay the price for our sin but also to destroy death. He said to Martha, "I am the resurrection and the life. Anyone who believes in me will live, even after dying" (John 11:25). As proof, Jesus raised Lazarus from death. Then, after His own death on the cross, Jesus rose out of the grave!

God is not indifferent to the sorrow death brings. Jesus wept over the death of Lazarus and the sorrow it caused others. He was even angry (John 11:38). His anger was not toward the grieving people, though; it was toward the terrible effects of sin and death on the world. God sent His Son, Jesus, to remove sin and defeat death. Jesus said, "I am the way, the truth, and the life" (John 14:6). He is the only way to deal with the great enemy of death. Many people fear death, but believers can have confidence in Jesus. The apostle Paul even says that physical death brings believers into the presence of the Lord (2 Corinthians 5:8).

1. If someone told you Jesus does not still heal today, how would you respond?
2. What did Jesus mean when He called Himself "the resurrection and the life"?
3. How does Jesus' resurrection prove He has power over sin, death, hell, and the devil?

The story of Lazarus demonstrates Jesus' power over death, and when Jesus later rose again after the Crucifixion, He defeated death for all time. By faith, we have eternal life in Him, and death no longer has the final word. The Good News of Jesus cannot be told without His resurrection. For some people, though, Jesus was not Good News because they did not want to respond to Him in faith. The rich young religious leader was one of those people.

45 A VERY SAD MAN
The Rich Young Religious Leader

People came to Jesus for many different reasons. One day, a young religious leader who was very rich approached Jesus with a question. He asked Jesus what he needed to do to inherit eternal life. The answer Jesus gave caused the man to be very sad.

MATTHEW 19:16–22; MARK 10:17–22; LUKE 18:18–23

When a rich young religious leader asked Jesus what he needed to do to receive eternal life, Jesus responded by asking the man if he had kept several of the Ten Commandments. However, Jesus did not mention the tenth commandment, which lies at the heart of this encounter.

Bible scholars often divide the Ten Commandments into two major sections, which they sometimes call *tables*. The first table primarily addresses duties to God: no gods beside the God of Israel, no idols, no misuse of God's name, and the command to keep the Sabbath. Jesus did not address any of the commandments in the first table. Why? Because any good Jew would have readily kept those commandments. Jesus did refer to the second table, though. He asked if the man had honored his parents and avoided murder, adultery, stealing, and lying. However, Jesus did not ask the man if he coveted or had a greedy fixation on things that belonged to others.

Why did Jesus not mention the tenth commandment? Actually, He did—in a very subtle way. The ancient rabbis referred to the tenth commandment as "the fence around the Law," which means it holds a unique position among the commandments. If we were to follow someone very closely for many years, we could determine if that person had kept the first nine commandments. Simple observation will show if a person has stolen, killed, committed adultery, and so on. But how would we know if someone coveted? It is possible to covet something in one's heart and mind without ever showing an outward sign of breaking that commandment.

During Jesus' ministry, some rabbis taught that something could only be considered a "sin" if someone physically committed that action. But what about things that happen on the inside? Jesus knew that God also looks at the heart. He even strengthened the Law by telling His followers to avoid sinful thoughts. Jesus said, "For from the heart come evil thoughts, murder, adultery, all sexual immorality, theft, lying, and slander" (Matthew 15:19).

The man replied that he had kept the commandments Jesus mentioned. Then Jesus began to address the condition of the man's heart. He said, "There is still one thing you haven't done. Sell all your possessions and give the money to the poor, and you will have treasure in heaven. Then come, follow me" (Luke 18:22). What Jesus said made this man very sad. In Greek, his "face fell." It was not what the man wanted to hear, and he was not ready or willing to do what Jesus called him to do.

Was Jesus' directive specifically for this one man, or is it a command for every believer? The answer is clear, though not simple. God may call an individual believer to give away all earthly possessions to follow Him. However, He has not given that call to every Christian throughout history. Some believers have had great financial success and used it to further God's Kingdom. Several New Testament believers also fit into this category. While God may call certain individuals to give up all earthly possessions, this is not the usual calling for the majority of believers.

However, Jesus does give a command to every believer: *change your heart and mind and come follow Him.* Your desire for God must be greater than any other desire. Jesus knows the truth about your heart. You may follow God on the outside but have hidden sin on the inside. Jesus said, "No one can serve two masters. . . . You cannot serve God and be enslaved to money" (Matthew 6:24). In a letter to Timothy, the apostle Paul wrote, "For the love

of money is the root of all kinds of evil. And some people, craving money, have wandered from the true faith and pierced themselves with many sorrows" (1 Timothy 6:10). Beware—the love of money does not apply only to those who are wealthy. Many people who have little money love it just as much. Covetousness is an equal-opportunity sin.

The Holy Spirit stands ready to convict you and help you change. It is not true that only *you* know what you think and feel—God knows too. He is fully aware, but He is also available to forgive you and make you more like Him. God will not force you to serve Him. He lovingly calls you to draw closer. If you truly hunger for a deep relationship with Jesus, He will show you if there is something in the way. The rich young religious leader heard the voice of God, but then he walked away. Don't walk away.

After the conversation between Jesus and the rich man, Peter said he and the other disciples had left their homes to follow Jesus. In response, Jesus said anyone who had given up anything or anyone to follow Him would receive even more now and in the future Kingdom of God (Luke 18:29-30). Don't settle for things that are only temporary. God has so much more for you, both now and throughout eternity.

1. What do you believe is God's opinion about money and possessions?
2. God speaks to all believers about what they should do with their money. What has God specifically said to you?
3. How would you explain to someone that God cares as much about what is in our hearts and minds as what we do on the outside?
4. What is the Holy Spirit saying to you about your heart and mind?

The rich young religious leader allowed his money and possessions to control his heart and prevent him from truly serving God. However, there was another rich man who would not allow his wealth to stop him from following Jesus. This man's name was Zacchaeus, and he was a tax collector.

---

46 A VERY JOYFUL MAN
Zacchaeus

The Gospel of Luke closely links Jesus' encounters with the rich young religious leader and Zacchaeus in terms of sequence, time, distance, and major spiritual truth. Salvation is the primary theme in both stories. The rich young religious leader wanted to know what he needed to do to be saved. To Zacchaeus, Jesus said, "Salvation has come to this home today" (Luke 19:9). The rich young religious leader allowed his wealth to

prevent him from fully serving God. Zacchaeus, on the other hand, experienced a radical change of heart and was willing to give his wealth away to follow Jesus.

LUKE 19:1-10

Jesus drew a crowd wherever He went. As word spread about His teaching, compassion, and miracles, people gathered around Him. Some tried to discredit Him, but others saw Him as the great hope of Israel. When Jesus came to Jericho, a man named Zacchaeus desperately wanted to see Him. Zacchaeus could not see Jesus over the crowd, so he climbed a tree to get a better view. From his perch among the sycamore-fig tree's branches, he saw Jesus. More importantly, Jesus saw him. He told Zacchaeus, "Quick, come down! I must be a guest in your home today" (Luke 19:5). Zacchaeus hastily returned to the ground, and he "took Jesus to his house in great excitement and joy" (Luke 19:6).

The onlooking crowd did not share Zacchaeus's happy emotions. They didn't like this man because he was the area's lead tax collector. Jewish people of the day considered tax collectors to be some of the worst sinners. They often viewed these men as traitors for cooperating with the foreign occupiers. The Jews also knew that many of the tax collectors collected more than what was required and kept the extra for themselves. Even so, the crowd's opinion did not prevent Jesus from having dinner in Zacchaeus's home. While they ate, Zacchaeus told Jesus he was going to right the wrongs he had committed as a tax collector. He said, "I will give half my wealth to the poor, Lord, and if I have cheated people on their taxes, I will give them back four times as much!" (Luke 19:8). Zacchaeus had a genuine change in his heart and mind.

Jesus "came to seek and save those who are lost" (Luke 19:10). For Him, Zacchaeus was not a sinful tax collector, unworthy of love; instead, Jesus saw him as a "true son of Abraham" (Luke 19:9). Even though Zacchaeus had lost his way for a time, he was still one of God's chosen people. The crowd had rejected him, but Jesus came to find people just like Zacchaeus. The story began with Zacchaeus trying to get a brief glance of Jesus, but it ends with Jesus at Zacchaeus's dining

room table. God told the prophet Jeremiah, "If you look for me wholeheartedly, you will find me" (Jeremiah 29:13). The rich young ruler avoided the call of Jesus. But Zacchaeus looked for Jesus and found Him.

Every person is lost apart from Jesus. The Good News is that Jesus came to seek and save us. When we lost our way because of sin and selfishness, Jesus came looking for us. When we called out to Him, He forgave us of our sins and saved us. Jesus doesn't see you as others see you. He doesn't even see you as you see yourself. In your heart, you may label yourself in unflattering ways, just like the Jews labeled Zacchaeus as a sinful tax collector. Remember what Jesus called him, though—a true son of Abraham.

Just as Jesus saved Zacchaeus, He is willing to save all people who come to Him with simple faith and a sincere desire to change their hearts and minds. Jesus didn't reject Zacchaeus, and He won't reject you. Seek Him, and you will find Him.

1. What are the similarities between the rich young religious leader and Zacchaeus? What are the differences?
2. How does God see you differently than others do? How does He see you differently than you see yourself?
3. What are some ways you can show your commitment to God?

Jesus was changing *everything*. Outcasts like Zacchaeus were receiving forgiveness, and leaders were coming under God's judgment. The Jewish religious leaders were angry about these changes, so they began plotting to kill Jesus. They would need allies, though. Sadly, they found a willing coconspirator among Jesus' closest followers. The betrayer's name was Judas.

47 THE BETRAYER
Judas

Jesus called 12 men to be His closest followers. For over three years, the disciples traveled with Jesus, heard Him teach, and watched Him perform many miracles. Jesus chose these men to take His message to the world, which most of them did. However, one man named Judas didn't. Instead, he betrayed Jesus.

MATTHEW 26:14-16, 47-56; 27:1-10; LUKE 22:1-6

Near the end of Jesus' earthly ministry, Satan entered into Judas. This disciple then approached the religious leaders "to discuss the best way to betray Jesus to them" (Luke 22:3-4). These men were eager to destroy Jesus, but they preferred to

do it secretly, not in front of the crowds. Thrilled to accept the disciple's offer, they gave Judas 30 pieces of silver in exchange for helping them find the right time to arrest Jesus (Matthew 26:14-16).

As Jesus and His disciples gathered together to eat the Passover meal, Jesus revealed that one of them would betray Him. This deeply upset the disciples, and one by one, they began asking, "Am I the one, Lord?" (Matthew 26:22). Not wanting to appear suspicious, Judas asked as well. To him, Jesus replied, "You have said it" (Matthew 26:25).

Later that evening, Jesus and the disciples went to the Mount of Olives. Judas alerted the religious leaders that this was their opportunity to act. A group of men carrying weapons came to arrest

Jesus. Having arranged the signal beforehand, Judas went up to Jesus and kissed him. Jesus replied, "Judas, would you betray the Son of Man with a kiss?" (Luke 22:48).

The men arrested Jesus and brought Him to the religious leaders who wanted Him killed. Most of the disciples fled, but a few followed at a distance. When Judas realized his actions would result in Jesus' death, he returned to the religious leaders and confessed, "I have betrayed an innocent man" (Matthew 27:4). These men did not care about Judas's guilty conscience, and they were certainly not going to set Jesus free. Judas threw the 30 pieces of silver back at them and left. Overcome with remorse, he took his own life by hanging himself (Matthew 27:5).

Judas followed Jesus every day for over three years. He heard and saw everything the other 11 disciples did. How did his life end so differently from theirs? The Bible only provides a small amount of information about Judas, but what it tells is quite revealing. Shortly before Passover, the disciples attended a dinner held to honor Jesus who had recently raised Lazarus from death. Mary, a sister of Lazarus, poured costly perfume onto Jesus' feet as a sign of love. Judas harshly criticized Mary for expressing her love in such an extravagant way. He said it would have been better to sell the perfume and give the proceeds to people in need. Contrary to his words, Judas did not have a generous spirit; he wanted the money for himself. Judas was responsible for the disciples' money, and he frequently stole from the group's funds (John 12:6).

The encounter with Mary is even more significant considering Judas willingly betrayed Jesus for money. According to the Law of Moses, the value of

a slave was 30 pieces of silver (Exodus 21:32). Judas sold himself into slavery to Satan for that amount. Like the rich man, Judas had a problem with greed. He stole from Jesus and the other disciples and then betrayed the Lord for money.

We do not need to be afraid of ending up like Judas. No one was ever more evil. However, we would be wise to learn from his bad example. Slavery to his own greed destroyed Judas. Nothing should prevent you from following Jesus with all your heart. If something is standing in the way of complete surrender, let it go. If it is a struggle, ask the Holy Spirit to give you the power to overcome it. Jesus is more valuable than anything else you will ever find.

1. What kinds of things get in the way of people fully following Jesus?
2. What is the Holy Spirit saying to you about money and material possessions?
3. Some people act as if they are following Jesus, but their hearts are not committed to Him. How can you make sure you are following Him with all your heart?

Judas played a major role in Jesus' execution, but his was not the only part. Religious leaders plotted against Jesus and riled the people against Him. The disciples ran away, and one of them even denied knowing Jesus. The Roman governor Pilate sent Jesus to Herod Antipas, the ruler of Galilee, but Jesus refused to answer Herod's questions. In the end, Pilate sent Jesus to His death. No one was innocent, even if they proclaimed themselves to be so.

48 THE MAN WITH BLOODY CLEAN HANDS
Pilate

The Jewish religious leaders feared Jesus and hated His influence on the people. Time after time, they tried to discredit Him, but with no success. There seemed to be only one solution—Jesus had to die. With help from the disciple Judas, they had Jesus arrested, and they questioned Him in front of a religious tribunal. Then they brought Jesus to Pilate, the Roman governor. The governor found no cause to condemn Jesus, but the religious leaders vehemently demanded Jesus' death. In the end, Pilate's hands held Jesus' fate. Though he did not want to take on that responsibility, the governor soon found he could not wash his hands of Jesus, even when he tried.

MATTHEW 27:11–26; JOHN 18:28–19:16

Jesus' teaching and ministry captured the hearts of many but hardened the hearts of others. Most of

the Jewish religious leaders saw Jesus as a threat to their position and power. They paid Judas, one of the disciples, to help them find a time to arrest Jesus. After eating the Passover meal, Jesus and His disciples went to the Garden of Gethsemane to pray. Judas led a band of soldiers to the garden, and they arrested Jesus. They immediately brought Him to a tribunal of prominent religious leaders where He was falsely accused of speaking against God. Then they brought Jesus to Pilate, the Roman governor who ruled over their land. The religious leaders did not have the authority to execute Jesus, but Pilate did (John 18:31). They told Pilate that Jesus deserved to die on a cross.

Pilate questioned Jesus, but he discovered Jesus had not broken any Roman laws. The governor also realized the religious leaders did not want justice as they claimed; instead, hatred and jealousy motivated their actions. Every year during Passover, the

Jews asked Pilate to free one prisoner. Hoping to excuse himself from the situation, Pilate offered to release Jesus; however, the accusers wanted the criminal Barabbas released instead.

Pilate was in a difficult situation. He did not want to condemn Jesus because he could not find Him guilty of breaking any laws. However, the governor also feared that a riot would break out if he refused to give the religious leaders what they wanted. When Pilate attempted to set Jesus free, the angry men yelled, "If you release this man, you are no 'friend of Caesar.' Anyone who declares himself a king is a rebel against Caesar" (John 19:12).

Pilate felt trapped. If he released Jesus, someone might accuse him of opposing Caesar's rule, which would put his own life in jeopardy. But if he had Jesus crucified, he would be guilty of condemning an innocent man. The governor reasoned that his only choice was to give Jesus over to be crucified but publicly disown the decision. Rinsing his hands in water, Pilate told the crowd, "I am innocent of this man's blood. The responsibility is yours!" (Matthew 27:24).

God sent His Son to the world to pay the price for humanity's sins, but Pilate still had the authority to either release Jesus or have Him killed. Pilate's wife even warned him to "leave that innocent man alone" (Matthew 27:19). The Roman governor did not want to have an innocent man's blood on his hands and conscience. However, by succumbing to the pressure from the Jewish religious leaders, Pilate could not completely wash his hands of his involvement, even though he tried.

Many factors affect the choices we make, but God still holds us responsible. The actions and opinions of others may influence us, but in the end, we are responsible for our own actions. When faced with the drastic choice about Jesus, Pilate wrestled with his accountability to Rome, the words of Jesus, the demands of the religious leaders, and his own conscience. In the end, he yielded to the pressure from the crowds. He chose to protect himself, even though he knew it meant the death of an innocent man.

Making right choices is not always easy. We can often disappoint or even anger others. Sometimes the right decision isn't immediately obvious. However, God promises to help us when we face difficult choices. Stop focusing on "my decision" and spend your efforts on listening to the Holy Spirit. *There is a big difference between deciding and discerning.* Deciding implies your will takes precedence. Discerning means giving God's will first place. The Bible says,

Trust in the LORD with all your heart;
　do not depend on your own understanding.
Seek his will in all you do,
　and he will show you which path to take
　　(Proverbs 3:5–6).

If you want to do what is right, listen to the Holy Spirit.

God will forgive you for any bad choices you have made if you simply ask Him. You may have to live with some of the consequences of those choices, but you do not have to live with guilt and shame. Ask the Holy Spirit to speak to you clearly and trust Him to guide you to the right choices. He may tell you to go against the crowd, but you will experience joy and peace in your heart when you follow His voice.

1. Have you ever made your own choice and ignored the Holy Spirit? What happened?
2. Think of a time when you obeyed the Holy Spirit's voice, even though it meant going against the crowd. What was the result?
3. Do you need to hear the Holy Spirit's voice regarding a specific situation today? If so, ask Him to speak clearly to you right now.

Pilate sent Jesus to His death. Roman soldiers mocked Jesus, beat Him, and placed a crown of thorns on His head. They led Him outside the city of Jerusalem and nailed Him to a cross. It was the worst event in human history. However, it was also the best event in human history.

49　A NEW MAN IN PARADISE
The Thief on the Cross

Pilate reluctantly gave into the demands of the Jewish religious leaders and sentenced Jesus to death by crucifixion. Spurred on by the taunting crowd, Roman soldiers mocked Jesus and treated Him as a criminal. They also placed two actual criminals on crosses next to Him. As these men suffered and took their dying breaths, one chose to put his last hope in Jesus.

LUKE 23:33–43

Crucifixion is a gruesome way to die. A condemned person often hung on a cross for hours, slowly suffocating. The Romans used crucifixion as a cruel method to kill criminals and enemies of the state. They specifically designed this execution to torture and humiliate the condemned person as well as deter others from rebelling against Roman rule. The Jewish religious leaders demanded Jesus' crucifixion because they did not want Him simply to go away—they wanted Him to suffer as well.

Soldiers led Jesus and two convicted criminals to Golgotha (also known as The Skull) and nailed the three men to crosses. Onlookers taunted Jesus, "Let him save himself if he really is God's Messiah, the Chosen One" (Luke 23:35). They dared Jesus to prove Himself as the Messiah by coming down from the cross. One of the criminals hanging next to Jesus showed no remorse for his actions and joined in the crowd's mocking, saying, "So you're the Messiah, are you? Prove it by saving yourself—and us, too, while you're at it!" (Luke 23:39).

The other criminal, however, recognized there was something different about Jesus. Speaking to the first criminal, he said, "We deserve to die for our crimes, but this man hasn't done anything wrong" (Luke 23:41). Then he asked Jesus to remember him when Jesus entered His Kingdom. Recognizing this man's faith, Jesus responded, "I assure you, today you will be with me in paradise" (Luke 23:43).

The contrasting responses of the two criminals represent the ways people respond to sin and the Good News of Jesus Christ. One man showed no remorse for his crimes. Instead, he defiantly challenged Jesus. The other man acknowledged his guilt, accepted his punishment, and humbly asked Jesus for mercy. If we respond like the second man, we too can receive the promise of eternal life with the Lord.

In reality, we all deserve death, but Jesus offers us the incredible gift of eternal life. Our response to Him makes all the difference. At the very end of his life, one man received the promise of eternity with the Lord. The other did not. As long as we are alive, it is never too late. We are never too old to put our faith in Jesus Christ. The sooner we do, though, the more our lives will count for His Kingdom.

1. What would you say to someone who believes it is too late for them to put their faith in Jesus?
2. What would you say to someone who wants to be saved but says they will wait until a later date?
3. The criminal who put his faith in Jesus while on the cross was saved. However, what did he miss experiencing by waiting to be right with God until he was dying?

Jesus is in the business of forgiveness, and He wants to make us right with God. He is the God of second chances. As long as we live, He stands waiting for us to change our hearts and minds and turn to Him. Jesus gave forgiveness from the cross, and He even forgave those who once turned their backs on Him during His time of need. Simon Peter was one of those people. Not only did Jesus forgive him, but He also called Peter to lead other believers as Jesus was getting ready to return to heaven.

50 THE SECOND CHANCE
Simon Peter

Simon Peter, a fisherman by trade, had fished through the night without a single catch. The next morning, he was surprised to hear Jesus say, "Now go out where it is deeper, and let down your nets to catch some fish" (Luke 5:4). Peter was tired from the previous night's attempt, but he trusted Jesus. When the fisherman threw out his nets this time, he caught so many fish that both his boat and his partners' boat almost sank! Then Jesus told Peter, "Don't be afraid! From now on you'll be fishing for people!" (Luke 5:10).

JOHN 21:1-19

As one of Jesus' 12 disciples, Peter courageously (and impulsively) said and did things the other disciples would not. For example, he was Jesus' only follower to walk on water (Matthew 14:29). When Jesus asked the disciples who they believed Him to be, only Peter identified Him as the Son of God (Mathew 16:16). Bible scholars often note Peter's impulsivity. For example, only shortly after his declaration that Jesus was the Messiah, Peter scolded Jesus for speaking about His eventual death and

resurrection. Jesus rebuked the overzealous disciple, even saying Peter's words came from Satan (Matthew 16:21-23).

As the time came near for His death, Jesus gathered the disciples and told them they would all turn away from Him. Peter protested, "Even if everyone else deserts you, I will never desert you. . . . Even if I have to die with you, I will never deny you!" (Matthew 26:33-35). After soldiers arrested Jesus, Peter secretly followed them to the high priest's home. However, when questioned about his association with Jesus and faced with the danger of personal harm, Peter did the very thing he swore never to do. He denied knowing Jesus—not once but three times! Earlier that evening, Jesus had warned Peter this would happen: "Before the rooster crows, you will deny three times that you even know me" (Matthew 26:34). The usually audacious disciple was devastated when he realized what he had done. In bitter shame and disappointment, Peter returned to his previous profession as a simple fisherman (John 21:3).

Thankfully, Peter's story continues from there. Following the Resurrection, the newly risen Jesus appeared to His disciples several times, and it was by the Sea of Galilee—where Peter first met Jesus—that the broken disciple received a life-changing second chance. Peter had once again fished all night with no success. The next morning, he and the disciples with him could see someone standing on the shore, and this unknown person told them to throw their net on the other side of the boat. When they did, the net became so full of fish they could not pull it in. Immediately, they knew who the mysterious person was—Jesus! Peter jumped out of the boat and swam to Him while the other disciples brought the fish to the shore.

When the disciples reached Jesus, He was already cooking breakfast over an open fire. Following the meal, Jesus asked Peter if he loved Him, not once but three times. After each affirmative response, Jesus called Peter to care for His "sheep"—His people. Peter had denied his Lord three times, but Jesus forgave him and gave him a second chance. Peter became a great apostle and boldly proclaimed the gospel for the rest of his life.

Have you had moments of incredible success as well as times of embarrassing failure? Maybe you served the Lord faithfully for a while, but then in a critical moment, you yielded to temptation and did not obey what the Lord wanted you to do. You may have failed to stand for Jesus in the face of opposition, even though you had thought you were strong. If you have had any of these experiences, the devil wants you to believe God has given up

on you. Don't believe it! God never gives up on His sons and daughters.

Peter lost hope when he denied the Lord, but Jesus never lost hope in Peter. This fisherman eventually became a great evangelist and even wrote two of the New Testament's letters. Your past failures do not determine your future worth. Admit your weakness and put your hope in the Lord. Jesus can do in your life what He did for Peter. Turn your heart to the Lord and trust Him to give you a fresh start.

1. Have you ever experienced failure in your spiritual life? What does Peter's story say about God's ability to restore His people?
2. How would you encourage someone to believe God gives second chances?
3. What does it mean for you to be God's son or daughter?

Jesus told Peter to feed His people. A transformation was taking place in Peter's character, but he was not yet up to the task. He would need greater power than a changed heart or mind could bring. The resurrection of Jesus had certainly made a great difference, but one more event would equip Peter to assume leadership of this new movement. No one knew exactly what would happen next, but Jesus promised more power would come on the Day of Pentecost.

---

51 THE DAY THE CHURCH WAS BORN
Pentecost

Just before He returned to the Father, Jesus told Peter and the other disciples to wait for the power they would need to take the Good News about Him to the world. The disciples watched Jesus ascend to heaven, and then they gathered in Jerusalem, as instructed, to pray and wait for God's promised gift—the Holy Spirit.

ACTS 2

The sound of a mighty wind from heaven suddenly swept through the house where the followers of Jesus were meeting. Flames of fire settled over each person in the room, and they all began to speak in other languages. Jesus had promised to send a gift—the Holy Spirit— and an awareness rose with the crescendo of the voices: *this is it!* The Holy Spirit had come with presence and power (Acts 2:4). Once again, the disciples knew the words of Jesus were true—visibly, physically, and undeniably true. This is no subjective event; those present experienced it with all their senses. Everyone saw, heard, felt, and probably tasted and smelled. The Holy Spirit arrived on the

Day of Pentecost and changed the meaning of that day forever.

Pentecost was a Jewish feast that brought people from many nations to Jerusalem. For the Jewish people, it commemorated the annual harvest and the firstfruits that came from it. For those present at the Church's first Pentecost, it also commemorated a harvest of new souls and the firstfruits of Jesus' resurrection. People from many nations stood and marveled at hearing these Jews from Galilee speaking in their own mother tongues. Some wondered what this miraculous occurrence meant; others simply accused Jesus' followers of drunkenness (Acts 2:12-13).

Filled with the Holy Spirit's power, Peter spoke to the crowd. He began by assuring the onlookers that the disciples were sober; it was, after all, still morning. Then Peter made a most radical claim—*this is that*. What the people were seeing and hearing was the fulfillment of something the prophet Joel had predicted many years earlier: "In those days I will pour out my Spirit" (Acts 2:18). Next, Peter reminded the crowd of the miracles Jesus performed. He told them Jesus was crucified according to the will of God and had also risen from death. Then the disciple proclaimed, "So let everyone in Israel know for certain that God has made this Jesus, whom you crucified, to be both Lord and Messiah!" (Acts 2:36). When Peter finished, many in the crowd asked what they needed to do to be saved. He told them, "Each of you must repent of your sins and turn to God, and be baptized in the name of Jesus Christ for the forgiveness of your sins. Then you will receive the gift of the Holy Spirit" (Acts 2:38). Three thousand people were saved and baptized that very day.

After Jesus' arrest, Peter was powerless. After the Holy Spirit's arrival, the disciple was powerful. God wants to provide His people with the power we need to accomplish all He calls us to do. After His resurrection, Jesus instructed His disciples to go to the whole world and preach the Good News. However, they would need the supernatural power of the Holy Spirit to accomplish this task. That is why Jesus told them to wait.

On the Day of Pentecost, Jesus' followers received the power they needed. Peter said the Holy Spirit anointed Jesus with power. Now, every believer can receive that same anointing from the Holy Spirit, which empowers us to be witnesses for Jesus. The Holy Spirit was present throughout the Old Testament years. At various times, He would manifest Himself to God's people. Now, He can live inside every believer everywhere and all the time.

You *need* the Holy Spirit. You cannot do all God has called you to do without Him. Supernatural tasks require supernatural power to accomplish them. Jesus promised to give His disciples the power they needed to do what He called them to do. He can and will do the same for you. As you share and live out your faith, you may feel like Peter before Pentecost, but that does not have to be your experience. Ask Jesus to fill you with the Holy Spirit. Peter said this gift is for "all who have been called by the Lord our God" (Acts 2:39). *All* includes you.

1. How did the Holy Spirit change the lives of the first believers?
2. How does the Holy Spirit change a believer's life today?
3. If you have received the Holy Spirit, how has He changed your life?

Those who first believed in Jesus not only preached the Gospel but also ministered in the power of the Holy Spirit. The book of Acts records miracles taking place as believers proclaimed the resurrection of Jesus Christ. Their preaching and power led to many believing in Jesus as Lord. However, some people tried to destroy the new movement. The first person killed for his faith in Jesus was a man named Stephen.

52 A MAN FULL OF GOD'S GRACE
Stephen

After the outpouring of the Holy Spirit at Pentecost, new believers joined the Church every day. The numbers swelled so quickly the apostles had trouble managing the care of every person. It was a good problem to have, but it was still a problem. The apostles decided to choose more leaders to help carry the burden. They selected seven men to make sure every believer was treated fairly when it came to mealtimes. Though these men were not apostles, they preached the Good News of Jesus in powerful ways. One of those chosen men was Stephen.

ACTS 6–7

Stephen boldly proclaimed the Good News of Jesus, and miracles confirmed his preaching. People who opposed him could not match his persuasive message, so they falsely accused him of rejecting both the Temple and Moses. These lies led to Stephen's arrest, and he was forced to appear before the Jewish religious leaders. Speaking to this high council, Stephen responded by recounting the history of the Jewish people, starting with Abraham and continuing through the

captivity in Egypt and the Exodus. Then Stephen spoke about Solomon, the king God called to build His Temple.

Stephen ended his message by telling the religious leaders that just as their ancestors often refused to listen to the prophets who spoke for God, they were now rejecting what the Holy Spirit was speaking through him. At that moment, Stephen received a vision of heaven, where he saw Jesus standing at the right hand of the Father. Stephen infuriated his accusers by telling them what he was seeing, and they rushed to stone him to death. As they hit him with stones, Stephen focused on the vision of heaven. Just as Jesus did during the Crucifixion, he asked God to receive his spirit and not to hold his accusers accountable for their sin (Acts 7:59–60). Then Stephen died and went to be with the Lord.

The first Christians boldly proclaimed the Good News of Jesus and walked in the power of the Holy Spirit. However, they also experienced persecution, even to the point of death. Many people gladly received their message, but many others rejected it. The situation today is no different. Many receive the message of salvation while others reject it.

Believers around the world still suffer persecution, even unto death.

The Good News of Jesus remains the same. God has called us to follow Jesus and has anointed us to proclaim His truth. Some will joyfully receive the message; some will hatefully reject it. Like Stephen, we cannot allow the fear of rejection or persecution to prevent us from answering God's call. We should not seek conflict; rather we should make the gospel attractive to those who will listen. Even so, some people will have no desire to embrace the truth or to change their hearts and minds. Jesus was with Stephen, and He will be with you as well. As you obey God, He will watch over you. Jesus said He will acknowledge before the Father anyone who acknowledges Him before people.

God can work mightily through anyone. Stephen was not an apostle; he was a man the apostles appointed to ensure food was distributed fairly. Yet Stephen was also "a man full of God's grace and power, [who] performed amazing miracles and signs among the people" (Acts 6:8). No one was able to challenge his wisdom and the Holy Spirit within him (Acts 6:10). You may see yourself as just an ordinary person without any great spiritual position or title. Believe that God can and will do great things through you as you serve Him faithfully. The same Holy Spirit available to Stephen is available to you today.

1. What special calling has God placed on your life?
2. How can you remain faithful to proclaim the truth about Jesus even in the face of opposition?
3. How can we support and encourage persecuted believers around the world?

The book of Acts also includes events in the lives of other early church leaders. Philip in the book of Acts is often called the Evangelist or Deacon to distinguish him from the apostle Philip. He was one of the seven men chosen by the apostles to ensure the fair distribution of food. When the Jewish religious leaders killed Stephen and began persecuting the Church, many believers left Jerusalem. Philip went to Samaria and told people there about Jesus. Later, the Holy Spirit sent Philip to explain the gospel to a man who served as the treasurer of Ethiopia.

53 A TRUE SEEKER
Philip and the Ethiopian Eunuch

After His resurrection, Jesus told His disciples to go into the world and tell people the Good News about Him. He said they should start in Jerusalem and Judea. After Judea, Jesus told them to preach in Samaria and then the rest of the world (Acts 1:8). Jesus not only wanted the Jewish people to hear the Good News but the entire world too. Most of the people in Jerusalem and Judea were Jews. However, those who lived in Samaria were a mixed race of people who were descendants of Jews who married people from other nations.

Like Stephen, Philip was also chosen by the apostles to help with the daily needs of the Church. Philip had great spiritual power and authority, and when persecution began in Jerusalem, he went to preach the truth about Jesus to the Samaritans. The Lord then worked through Philip to tell the Good News to people from other parts of the world. One of those people was the treasurer for Kandake (Candace), the queen of Ethiopia.

ACTS 8:26–40

After Philip preached to the people of Samaria, an angel told him to head south toward the town of Gaza. As he did, he encountered the treasurer of Ethiopia who was traveling home after going to Jerusalem to worship God. The Holy Spirit told Philip to walk alongside the Ethiopian's carriage.

As he did, Philip learned that the Ethiopian was reading the words of the prophet Isaiah. By divine appointment, the man was reading Scripture that specifically addressed the death of Jesus.

Since the Ethiopian did not understand what he was reading, Philip took the opportunity to tell him about Jesus. When the Ethiopian heard and understood, he put his faith in Jesus and asked Philip to baptize him immediately. Philip did as the man requested, and immediately after, the Lord miraculously took Philip away. Then the Ethiopian treasurer continued on his journey home with great joy (Acts 8:39).

This event in Philip's life offers many words of encouragement:

The Holy Spirit can empower every believer.
— Philip was not one of the apostles. The apostles simply appointed him to care for the physical needs of some believers in the Church. However, Philip preached the Gospel in Samaria, and "many evil spirits were cast out. . . . And many who had been paralyzed or lame were healed" (Acts 8:7). You do not need to be famous or serve as the pastor of a large church for God to do great things through you.

God looks at the heart.
— The Ethiopian man was not only a treasurer; he was also a eunuch, which means he did not

have the typical body parts that distinguish a man from a woman. This procedure was often done to men who served in a royal palace in the ancient world. According to the Law of Moses, a man with such physical limitations was not allowed to enter the Temple (Deuteronomy 23:1). Even so, this man had a heart for God. The Ethiopian made the long journey from his homeland to Jerusalem to worship God, and God recognized his faith. The Holy Spirit led Philip to bring this man the message of salvation through Jesus Christ. God wanted to reach the Ethiopian with the Good News. He also put the right people in your life so you would hear about Jesus. As the Lord said through the prophet Jeremiah: "If you look for me wholeheartedly, you will find me" (Jeremiah 29:13).

God loves all people.
— Jesus told His disciples to take the Good News about Him throughout the earth because God loves every person in every nation. The Jewish people had rejected the Samaritans because they were a mixed race, but God sent Philip to reach them with the message of salvation. Then the Holy Spirit sent Philip on a special mission to explain God's Word to the Ethiopian. God loved the world so much that He sent Jesus to save *whoever* would believe in Him (John 3:16).

He loves every person, including you. If you seek Him, you will find Him. If you have come to know Jesus as your Savior, then allow the Holy Spirit to lead you as you tell others about the Good News, just as Philip did.

1. Has the Holy Spirit ever given instructions to you? What did He tell you to do?
2. God wants all believers to have a heart for global missions. What are some ways you can support missions around the world?
3. What can you do today to help other people understand God's Word?

As men and women began to tell the story of Jesus to people outside Jerusalem and Judea, the young Church faced new challenges. What would they do with people who did not understand Jewish laws or customs? They wondered what Jesus meant when He told them to tell *everyone* about Him. Should the Church expect new believers to conform to the same standards as the Jewish Christians? Would the same Holy Spirit be available to all people no matter where they lived? These were serious matters that could not be taken lightly. The Holy Spirit began to challenge their preconceptions, including the mindset of the apostles.

54 GOD LOVES ALL PEOPLE
Cornelius and Peter's Vision

Jesus is the promised Savior of the Jewish nation, but He also came to offer salvation to every person. "For this is how God loved the world: He gave his one and only Son, so that everyone who believes in him will not perish but have eternal life" (John 3:16). The first apostles did not yet understand all the implications of this verse. Over time, however, the Holy Spirit began to show them. The book of Acts contains an important story about salvation coming to someone who was not Jewish. This man's name was Cornelius, and his salvation changed many things, including the heart and mind of the apostle Peter.

ACTS 10

Cornelius was a devout and generous Roman officer who led a God-fearing household. This Gentile man prayed to God regularly (Acts 10:1-2). One day, an angel came to tell Cornelius to send for the apostle Peter who was staying in the city of Joppa. Cornelius obeyed what the Lord had told him to do. Through this meeting, Cornelius had a divine encounter, and soon Peter did as well. In a vision from the Holy Spirit, Peter saw a large sheet descend from heaven with many animals that the

Law of Moses forbid the Jewish people to eat. According to the Law, meat from these animals was "unclean."

Then a voice told Peter to eat the animals from the sheet. Peter had never eaten "unclean" food before, so he objected. The voice replied, "Do not call something unclean if God has made it clean" (Acts 10:15). Peter saw the same vision three times. As he mulled over what he had seen and heard, the men whom Cornelius sent arrived. At that moment, the Holy Spirit revealed to Peter that he should go with the men at the door. Peter obeyed the Lord and traveled with the men to the home of Cornelius the very next day.

When Peter arrived, he told everyone that even though the Jewish law prohibited him from entering a Gentile home, "God has shown me that I should no longer think of anyone as impure or unclean" (Acts 10:28). The apostle realized that the Lord's vision was less about food than it was about the people the Jews considered "unclean"—the Gentiles. Many Jews believed God had rejected these people. When Peter heard the reason Cornelius had sent for him, he responded, "I see very clearly that God shows no favoritism" (Acts 10:34). Peter told everyone in the household about

Jesus, and the Holy Spirit fell on those who were listening, just as He had come upon the Jewish believers on the Day of Pentecost. God worked through Cornelius and Peter to bring the Good News about Jesus beyond the Jewish nation and into the Gentile world.

God called Abraham to be the father of the Jewish nation. They were to be different from all the other nations. God gave the Jewish people His covenant and told them not to worship the false gods of other nations. However, God also told Abraham his descendants would bless all the nations. At the time when Peter encountered Cornelius, most Jewish people simply looked down on those who were not like them.

God did separate the Jewish people from other nations, but He did it to keep them holy, not to keep the other nations from knowing about His grace and goodness. Many of God's people forgot this greater mission. When some of the Jews began to believe in Jesus, they willingly shared their faith with other Jews, but not with Gentiles. God had to do something special and radical to change their attitudes, so He brought Cornelius and Peter together.

God loves people from every race, nation, language, and background. He wants to save anyone who will come to Him in faith. He shows no favoritism. Even today, many people in one group will not accept those in another. If we are to view everyone as God does, then we will recognize we are all the same in two important ways: God

created all of us in His image, and Jesus died for every one of us. Every person has sinned and is need of a Savior. God sent His Son, Jesus, to save the world, not just one group of people. He calls us to share the love of Jesus with everyone.

God will always accomplish His purposes. In the case of Cornelius and Peter, God was speaking to both of them in different places at the same time for the same purpose. He prepared them for what was about to happen. At times, the Holy Spirit will ask you to do something that may seem unusual, difficult, and even scary—but never impossible. If He calls you to do something, all of heaven is moving things into place to accomplish God's plan. As you obey, you will be amazed at what God has been doing behind the scenes.

1. What has God called you to do that seemed difficult at first but later revealed His hand at work?
2. How can you share the Good News about Jesus with people who are not like you?
3. What does "God shows no favoritism" mean to you?

The early church's mission to the Gentiles was just beginning. However, much more work remained. If Peter's actions broke down some of the barriers between Jews and Gentiles, Paul's activities shattered them.

55 A MESSENGER TO THE GENTILES
Paul

Paul was a devout Jewish Pharisee on a mission to stamp out the new movement of Jesus' followers. He believed he was accomplishing God's work until he encountered the resurrected Jesus. Soon, the Lord called Paul to preach the Good News in many places. The Holy Spirit also inspired this man to write a significant portion of the New Testament.

ACTS 7:58–8:3; 9:1–31; 11:25–30; 13–16

Not only was Paul present at the stoning of Stephen for his faith in Jesus Christ, but Paul may have thrown the first stone. Traditionally, one person threw the first stone, and then the others put their coats at his feet as a way to show their complicity in the stoning. In any case, Paul approved of Stephen's execution. Soon after, he traveled toward the city of Damascus. Paul intended to persecute the believers living there. While he was on his way, a light brighter than the noonday sun knocked him off his horse and blinded him. Then Paul encountered the risen Lord.

Paul was shocked to hear Jesus ask, "Why are you persecuting me?" (Acts 9:4). The Lord told Paul He was calling him to preach the gospel to the entire world (Acts 26:16-18). Then He told Paul to go to Damascus where he would receive further instructions. Paul remained blind for three days. The people traveling with him had to lead him into the city. The Lord called a man named Ananias to pray for Paul's healing and filling with the Holy Spirit. Ananias obeyed, and Paul regained his vision. Immediately, Paul began preaching the Good News about Jesus.

At first, Christian believers questioned Paul's sincerity. They wondered if he faked his conversion in an attempt to arrest more Christians. Over time, they realized Paul had experienced a miraculous transformation. The man who had once tried to silence the message of Jesus was now boldly proclaiming it!

The book of Acts describes Paul's three missionary journeys. He preached boldly, and the miracles he performed by the power of the Holy Spirit confirmed his message. Paul declared the gospel in much of the then-known world. For his efforts, he experienced persecution from both unbelieving Jews and Gentiles wherever he went. During one visit to Jerusalem, Paul nearly lost his life. He was later sent to Rome and imprisoned for a long time. During his imprisonment, the Holy Spirit inspired him to write letters to the churches; these communications now make up a significant portion of the New Testament. After many years of faithful service to the Lord, Paul died for his faith at the hands of the Roman government. Paul had one of the most amazing lives in all history. No other person had a greater impact on the world for the cause of Christ than Paul.

Although most of us will likely never have Paul's influence, we can still learn many things from his life and ministry:

Remember who you were before Jesus saved you.
— Paul never forgot the person he was before Jesus saved him. He had led a ruthless persecution of believers. As a result, Paul knew he was as unworthy of God's grace as any person, which made him all the more grateful to the Lord. He once said he was the worst of all sinners (1 Timothy 1:15). We must never forget who we were before God rescued us from our sin. We have no right to look down on others who have not yet accepted Jesus. Pride should have no place in our lives. The past humbles and reminds us that God's grace alone saved us.

Remember who you are now that you are saved.
— Paul knew how sinful he had been, but he did not let the past keep him from fulfilling God's call on his life. Instead, his past motivated him

to serve with greater zeal and passion (1 Corinthians 15:10). Your past does not disqualify you from God's service. Instead, it should motivate you to serve the Lord with all that you have.

Remember what Jesus has saved you to do.
— Paul brought Jesus' message of salvation to the Gentiles, the very people many believed unworthy of it. Remember, God so loved the *world*, not just those we consider acceptable. Like Paul, we must share the Gospel with everyone. Paul's conversion shows us that God's grace can reach any person. Who could have expected the man who mercilessly persecuted Christians to become a champion for Jesus? No one is beyond God's reach. The worst of sinners can become the greatest of Christ's followers. Someone simply must tell them about Jesus.

1. What was your life like before Jesus saved you? How is it different now?
2. What would you say to someone who believes their past disqualifies them from receiving God's grace?
3. Who in your life needs to hear the Good News about Jesus today? Ask God to give you the opportunity to share His love with that person.

During Paul's second missionary journey, he met a follower of Jesus named Timothy. This young man had a Jewish mother and a Greek father. All who knew Timothy spoke well of him, so Paul selected him as a traveling partner. Timothy became one of Paul's spiritual sons.

---

56 A SON IN THE FAITH
Timothy

During his second missionary journey, the apostle Paul met the young man Timothy while in the city of Lystra. Paul chose Timothy to accompany him for the remainder of his trip. Timothy was the child of a mixed marriage; his mother was Jewish while his father was Greek. Timothy had not been circumcised, so Paul encouraged him to submit to the procedure to avoid any unnecessary hindrances to Paul's ministry. For years, Timothy ministered under and alongside this great apostle.

ACTS 16:1–5; 1 TIMOTHY 4:11–13;
2 TIMOTHY 2; 3:14–17

In the book of Acts, Timothy faithfully served alongside Paul, both traveling with him and serving in whatever cities Paul asked him to go or stay. Paul wrote two letters to Timothy. Timothy was also the coauthor of the letters Paul

wrote to the Corinthians, Thessalonians, and Philippians.

While Paul was in prison towards the end of his life, he wrote the second letter to Timothy. Not only did Paul give instruction, but he also made a personal and urgent request for Timothy to visit him (2 Timothy 4:9). Before Paul's death, he greatly desired to see his apprentice. The writer of the book of Hebrews states that Timothy also spent time in prison for his faith (Hebrews 13:23).

Timothy's life provides many valuable lessons:

A godly upbringing has great value.
— Timothy's father may or may not have believed the Bible, but Timothy's mother and grandmother were women of faith (2 Timothy 1:5). Timothy himself learned about God's Word at an early age (2 Timothy 3:15). His upbringing certainly contributed to the godly man he came to

be. Do not underestimate the benefit of training children about the Lord from a young age. The influence of a godly parent, relative, or teacher can have a profound effect on a child's future. Children may not be able to understand everything in the Bible, but they can still receive great benefits from learning what it says, even at an early age. The Word of God can have a powerful influence on young children.

We need examples to follow.

— Timothy benefitted tremendously from Paul's example, training, and encouragement. When the young leader struggled, Paul encouraged him to let his character and calling qualify him (1 Timothy 4:12). Even the most gifted person requires good mentors, solid advisors, and positive role models. A wise person recognizes the need to learn from those who are more mature and experienced. Every "Timothy" should look for a "Paul" from whom to learn.

We need believing friends.

— Timothy held a special place in Paul's heart. They were fellow workers (Romans 16:21), but Paul also referred to Timothy as his son (1 Timothy 1:18). Over time, Timothy became more than a ministry partner to Paul; he became a dear friend. In Paul's letter to the Philippians, he said he had no one in his life like Timothy (Philippians 2:20). Learn from Timothy's example and find believing friends who will stand by you at all

times. God will bring people into your life who can nurture, train, and develop you. Consider these people a divine gift. As you grow in the Lord, He may place you in relationships with others who can teach you how to fulfill your calling. The best-known spiritual leaders always had others to help them fulfill their calling.

God wants you to reproduce.

— As you become a mature believer, be willing to take on a "Timothy" as Paul did. God wants spiritual leaders to raise up the next generation. Today, you may wonder if you will ever be qualified as an example for others to follow. Learn from the Lord as well as from those He places in your life.

1. Who are the spiritual mentors God has placed in your life?
2. How should you prepare to one day be able to take on a "Timothy"?
3. What are you doing today to surround yourself with believing friends?

While imprisoned in Rome, Paul received a visitor from Colossae named Onesimus. Onesimus was the escaped slave of Philemon, one of Paul's friends. Paul encouraged Onesimus to return home and sent a letter with him. This letter asked Philemon to welcome Onesimus back, not merely as a servant but also as a brother in Christ.

57 A BROTHER IN CHRIST
Philemon

During the time of the New Testament, slaves made up a large percentage of the population. Onesimus, the slave of Philemon, fled from his master to Rome where Paul was imprisoned. Onesimus became a useful helper to Paul (Philemon 11). Paul knew Onesimus needed to return to Philemon, but Paul wanted things to be different this time around.

PHILEMON 1–25

The runaway slave Onesimus had become a follower of Christ, possibly while he was spending time in Rome with Paul. Paul was his mentor, but the imprisoned missionary knew that Onesimus needed to make things right with his former master, Philemon. Philemon was a believer as well as one of Paul's friends. Paul wrote a letter to Philemon asking him to accept Onesimus back as his brother in Christ rather than as a mere slave. Paul did not demand obedience from his friend; rather, he made an appeal to Philemon to look at Onesimus in a different light (Philemon 10). As far

as society was concerned, Onesimus was merely a slave. However, in light of the work of Christ, he had become a brother in the Lord. Paul humbly asked Philemon to view Onesimus from a spiritual perspective. Doing so would completely change the nature of their relationship.

Philemon had every right to treat Onesimus as only a slave, but Paul asked him to lay that attitude aside and embrace Onesimus as a partner in Christ. To help his friend make this choice, Paul offered to cover any financial loss Philemon experienced while Onesimus served Paul. In his letter, Paul also appealed to their deep friendship and asked Philemon to receive Onesimus as if he were Paul himself.

At first glance, some people may wonder why the letter to Philemon is in the Bible. Is it only a personal letter from Paul to a friend about a slave? No, God put it there for very important reasons. Paul's letter teaches us that social differences and cultural prejudices have no place among the followers of Jesus. Philemon had a legal right to punish Onesimus for escaping. He could continue treating him as a slave. However, Paul asked Philemon to relate to Onesimus according to a "higher law" because of their shared faith. Paul urged Philemon to receive Onesimus back as a brother in the Lord, not as a slave.

Today, many distinctions still exist between people based on wealth, ethnicity, and other factors. Our society does not consider everyone as equal. These distinctions regard one person as better or lesser than another, but according to Paul, these differences disappear in Christ (Galatians 3:28).

Sadly, some believers do not always treat others as sisters and brothers. The book of James confronted and corrected believers who were favoring the wealthy over the poor. In the Church, those who were rich were not to receive any special favor or attention over those who were poor (James 2:1-4).

Paul reminded the believers that they had all been slaves to sin before coming to Christ. Now, every believer is a servant of Christ because of faith in Him (Romans 6:18). Jesus sets both slaves and non-slaves free from sin! Both slave and free can partake of the same Holy Spirit and join the same body of believers (1 Corinthians 12:13).

Paul's letter to Philemon shows that societal distinctions no longer apply to those in Christ. God so loved the *world*—not just those of a particular tribe, tongue, nation, or people. The Holy Spirit helps us love others without distinction. Every person is lost apart from Christ, but anyone can join His family of believers.

1. Why is it important for believers to love one another, regardless of differences? What message does this send to unbelievers?
2. How can you pray for your church to become a place where all races are included?
3. What is the Holy Spirit saying to you about your attitude toward others who are different from you?

Jesus chose 12 disciples who later became known as apostles. James and his brother were both fishermen before they became disciples. James's brother was likely only a teenager when Jesus called him, but he lived longer than any of the other apostles. The Bible describes him as the disciple whom Jesus loved. This brother's name was John.

---

58 THE BELOVED DISCIPLE
The Apostle John

While Jesus chose 12 men as His closest followers, only three spent almost all their time with Him. John was one of those three. Jesus gave John and John's brother James a nickname: "Sons of Thunder" (Mark 3:17). These men once asked if they should call down fire from heaven upon a village of people who did not welcome Jesus. The Lord corrected them for their rash request (Luke 9:51-55). John was on the mountain when Jesus met Moses and Elijah and His appearance was transformed (Mark 9:2-4). John stayed close to Jesus in the Garden of Gethsemane where Jesus prayed shortly before His arrest. During Jesus' final meal with His disciples, John sat right next to Jesus. This man referred to himself as "the disciple Jesus loved."

JOHN 1:1-16; 1 JOHN 4:7-21

The Holy Spirit inspired John to write one of the four Gospels. This apostle also wrote three letters and the book of Revelation. John's Gospel includes stories the other three do not. John 21 records the personal conversation Jesus had with Peter after His resurrection. Peter had previously denied Jesus three times, and now Jesus asked Peter three times if he loved Him. Jesus gave Peter a second chance to prove his love for Him.

John wrote a great deal about God's love for us and the love we should have for Him and other

believers. As the "disciple Jesus loved," he clearly understood the importance of loving God and loving others. John stated that if we truly love God, we will keep God's commandment to love others (1 John 4:11).

John had an amazing life as he faithfully served the Lord into old age. Jesus called him when he was young, and for decades, John followed as the Lord guided and instructed him. In his Gospel, John reveals Jesus as the Word that was from the beginning, the Light of the world, the Bread of Life, and the Good Shepherd. He experienced the love of Jesus. As a result, John encouraged other believers to love God and to love others. He truly understood the two most important commandments Jesus gave (Matthew 22:36-40).

Near the end of his life, John received a special revelation of heaven from the resurrected Jesus. He saw a new heaven and a new earth where God had removed sin and evil. One day God will rid us of all sorrow, pain, and tears. He will dwell with His people for all eternity.

John followed Jesus over many years. His teaching is the key to a long life of service to the Lord—love God and love others. It is possible for us to make the Christian life too complicated. We may begin with a sincere desire to do everything right, but if we are not careful, that pursuit may lead us to self-righteousness. John never forgot the example of love Jesus demonstrated in life and in death. John's heart and mind were changed by Jesus' love. Even in old age, that love remained the center of John's life and teaching.

1. Why do you think loving God and loving others is the most important Christian teaching? How is this teaching different from other beliefs?
2. Can you think of a person who has lived a long life for the Lord? If so, what is special about that person?
3. What are some ways you can express the love of God through your words and actions this week?

Many people find John's book of Revelation difficult to understand. The apostle received visions of things like a beast with seven heads and 10 horns coming out of the sea (Revelation 13:1). The descriptions of earthquakes, water turning to blood, and destruction fill some people with fear and dread. Others experience frustration as they try to grasp the book's meaning. However, God did not confuse John, nor will He lead us to confusion. The book of Revelation is in the Bible to encourage us and give us hope.

59 BEHOLD THE LAMB
Jesus in Revelation

God didn't give us the Bible to make us fearful nor to frustrate us. He gave us His Word to answer life's deepest questions and to introduce God as a loving Father. While some things in Revelation may seem hard to figure out, what is clear is that God wants to give us hope for the present and the future.

REVELATION 1; 21

Revelation does not focus primarily on judgment, war, or destruction. The central figure in the book is Jesus Christ, and the central message is hope. The apostle John encountered the risen Lord on the island of Patmos, where John lived in exile. Jesus shows John many things and commands him to write them down (Revelation 1:19).

Though much of what John wrote addresses what has and will happen on earth, he also gave us a picture of heaven. In Revelation, John is taken up into the heavenly realm, and there he sees the hand of God holding a scroll. No one is worthy to open the scroll except the Lamb. This Lamb is Jesus.

Lambs play an important role in Scripture. The people offered them as substitute sacrifices for sin. Before God judged the Egyptians for preventing the Israelites from leaving, every Jewish family killed a lamb and placed some of its blood on their doorway. When the Lord killed the firstborn of the Egyptians, He spared Israel's sons (Exodus 12:23–29).

When John the Baptist saw Jesus, he said, "Look! The Lamb of God who takes away the sin of the world!" (John 1:29). John knew why Jesus had come to earth. On the cross, Jesus bore the penalty for all our sins and died in our place. He was—and is—the Lamb whom all the other sacrificed lambs foretold.

In Revelation, John sees Jesus as the Lamb—the One who died for the sins of the world. Adam and Eve's sin corrupted God's perfect creation, but God had a plan to restore everything from the very beginning. This plan involved the Lamb. Jesus' death and resurrection broke the power of sin and death. God is now in the process of

restoring all things. That is the central message of John's Revelation.

John did have visions of earthquakes, death, and destruction. He described the judgment upon people who refused to repent. He wrote about water turning to blood, the sun and moon darkening, and stars falling from the sky. However, none of those events is the true focus of John's vision. The book of Revelation is not primarily about destruction; instead, it is about God's plan to put an end to everything that is evil, destructive, and not the way God designed it to be.

No one was found worthy to open the scroll except the Lamb. Likewise, none of us has the ability to save ourselves. Only the Lamb can save us from the effects of sin. Only the Lamb can restore us from our brokenness. When we make the Lamb our Lord, we have great hope for both the present and the future.

John's Revelation concludes with a picture of the new heaven and earth, in which God has restored His relationship with us. The world returns to the way He intended it. The time is coming when God will wipe away every tear from our eyes. Death, sorrow, and pain will be gone forever (Revelation 21:4)!

1. How does John's description of the new heaven and earth differ from our current earth?
2. Many people believe the book of Revelation is confusing. How would you encourage someone to discover its message of hope?
3. What does the image of Jesus as the Lamb mean to you?

No matter what your past looks like, God can restore you. He wants to give you a fresh start so you can spend the rest of your life and all of eternity with Him. John's Revelation clearly reveals Jesus as the Lord who will return for His people. If He is your Lord, you can look forward to a future in His presence without sorrow or pain.

WORSHIP WAY

WHAT IS WORSHIP?

ZACH NEESE

Worship is not a type of music. If it were, we could categorize it, consume it, and critique it. We could limit our engagement to our preferences and moods. Also, worship is not for people. If it were, people would be the objects of worship. And if people were the objects of worship, we would be gods unto ourselves.

Worship is for God. We worship Him with all three parts of ourselves: body, soul, and spirit. If one part is disengaged, we are not truly worshipping. As a tool, music helps us engage all three parts of ourselves with all three parts of God: Father, Son, and Holy Spirit. Music affects our heartbeats, communicates emotions, and moves our spirits. But music itself is not worship.

The word *worship* is a compressed form of the Old English term *worthship*, which means 'to give something worth.' We *worthship* God by communicating and demonstrating His value. When we value something, we put a price on it. That's why worship is so often associated with sacrifice. We only sacrifice for things (or people) that are important to us—things that are valuable.

The first mention of worship in the Bible is in Genesis 22:5 when Abraham brings his son Isaac up the mountain to offer him as a sacrifice to God. Abraham says to his servants, "Stay here with the donkey . . . The boy and I will travel a little farther. We will worship there, and then we will come right back." *Worship*. What Abraham really means is, "I will offer God the greatest sacrifice I have to offer, the most valuable thing in my world—my son—because God is worth even more to me." Now, God doesn't want us to sacrifice our children, so He provided a ram for Abraham to sacrifice instead. Today, God provides the sacrifice through Jesus, but the principle remains. Worship—valuing God—must cost the worshipper something. We sacrifice when we offer God our time, our money, our songs of praise when our circumstances don't look praiseworthy, and our attitude of gratitude when we feel like grumbling. Sacrifice is always uncomfortable and always has a price. Worship is sacrifice.

One Hebrew word that is sometimes translated as 'worshipper' is *abad*. This word means 'bondservant.' Deuteronomy 15:12-18 explains that when a slave was released from his time of servitude, he had a choice to make. He could go free, or if he loved his master, he could choose to remain with him and serve him as a bondservant. We do not serve God because of any religious requirement or the threat of hell. We choose to serve Him because He loves us. And we love Him so much that there is nothing we would rather do for the rest of our lives than serve Him with every faculty of our being. *That* is worship.

Bond service speaks directly to the difference between religion and worship. Slaves serve their masters out of compulsion. They obey because there is a constant threat of negative repercussions for disobedience. They *must* obey because it is their duty. A bondservant, however, serves his master out of love. The bondservant is free to go his own way, but he chooses to stay with his master for the rest of his life. He loves his master so much that there is nothing he would rather do than serve him. And there is nowhere he would rather be than in his master's house.

A religious person is like a slave. He serves God out of compulsion, fear, or a sense of duty. He is not truly free because he feels constrained to obey God, but his heart longs to be its own master. A worshipper, however, is a person who has complete freedom to choose but loves God so much that he chooses to serve and obey Him because there is nothing he would rather do.

Religion is motivated by fear and the sense that our identity and value are maintained through our work. Worship is always motivated by love. Two people can do the same thing, and God will receive one as an act of worship and reject the other as a religious work. The first biblical example of this can be seen in the sacrifices of the brothers Cain and Abel.

> When it was time for the harvest, Cain presented some of his crops as a gift to the LORD. Abel also brought a gift—the best portions of the firstborn lambs from his flock. The LORD accepted Abel and his gift, but he did not accept Cain and his gift (Genesis 4:3-5).

Worship begins with a motivation from the heart, but it never stops there. The motivation is love, and that love must find expression in order to be considered worship. *Unexpressed love is no love at all.* God is not convinced by mere lip service. He reads our body language. Incidentally, the world reads body language too. It is only the Church that seems to be deceived by hollow platitudes and empty songs of affection.

So how do we demonstrate adoration for God? How do we demonstrate worship? Worship is love expressed God's way. There are some ways we may think we are expressing love to God that He doesn't see as love at all. For instance, God does not feel loved just because we sing a song that says we love Him. God needs more from His people.

God's Word clearly teaches us how to express our love to God in a way He will recognize.
— "If you love me, obey my commandments" (John 14:15).
— "Those who accept my commandments and obey them are the ones who love me. And

because they love me, my Father will love them. And I will love them and reveal myself to each of them" (John 14:21).
— "All who love me will do what I say. My Father will love them, and we will come together and make our home with each of them" (John 14:23).
— "Anyone who doesn't love me will not obey me. And remember, my words are not my own. What I am telling you is from the Father who sent me" (John 14:24).

Salvation demonstrates God's love for us. Worship demonstrates our love for Him.[1]

1. Why does worship involve sacrifice?
2. What is the difference between worship and religion?
3. What are some ways you can express your love to God every day?

_____

1 Content adapted from *How to Worship a King* by Zach Neese © 2012. Used by permission.

WHOM DO WE WORSHIP?

AARON CRIDER, DMIN

Worship has always been a centerpiece in the history of humanity. From the beginning, human beings have been drawn to worship anything that looks good at the moment. In Exodus 32, the people of Israel worshipped a golden calf when they grew impatient for Moses to return from the mountain. Ancient Egyptian worship was polytheistic, meaning they practiced idol worship of many different gods. These gods could be virtually anything and often included animals or parts of animals. Ancient Geeks opted for worshipping people and idols that looked like people. Today, we can clearly see humanity offering their worship at the altar of the gods of fame, fortune, substance, and self. The question for us today is not *"Do you worship?"* but *"Whom do you worship?"*

For believers, there can only be one answer: We worship the one true God. This fundamental statement of faith creates a distinction between Christians and those who simply worship *a* god. The prophet Isaiah says,

God, the LORD, created the heavens and
  stretched them out.
He created the earth and everything in it.
He gives breath to everyone,
  life to everyone who walks the earth (Isaiah
  42:5).

Two chapters later, the Lord declares,

"How foolish are those who manufacture idols.
  These prized objects are really worthless.
The people who worship idols don't know this,
  so they are all put to shame.
Who but a fool would make his own god—
  an idol that cannot help him one bit?" (Isaiah
  44:9–10).

Isaiah plainly says there is one Creator of the heavens and one Giver of life on earth. That "One" is the *only* being deserving of glory and praise, and to give worship to any other is foolishness. That "One" is He whom we call God.

In Exodus 3:14–15, the one true God speaks to Moses and refers to Himself as "I AM . . . the God of Abraham, the God of Isaac, and the God of Jacob." As translated from the Hebrew, "I AM" expresses the nature of God—or *Yahweh* as verses 15–16 call Him—as the absolute, eternal, and unchanging Being who is and will always be. This one true God spoke the universe into existence in Genesis 1:1, and He breathed life into people in Genesis 2:7. All throughout Scripture, the God of Abraham, the God of Isaac, and the God of Jacob is revealed to us as eternal (Psalm 90:2), all-powerful (Matthew 19:26), unchanging

(James 1:17), and even personal (Deuteronomy 34:10). The great hymn of praise in Romans 11 concludes with verse 36:

For everything comes from him and exists
by his power and is intended for his glory. All
glory to him forever! Amen.

He is the original Cause of all things, He is the current Sustainer of all things, and He is the eternal Lord of all things. That is the God we worship!

Having a full understanding of who God is is truly exciting. He stands alone as the one true God of the universe. Throughout the Old and New Testaments, God is both one and triune. Scripture testifies that the one true God exists eternally in three persons. These three persons are the Father, Son, and Holy Spirit. These are not three separate gods, and they are not three gods in one. The Trinitarian doctrine articulates the testimony of Scripture by defining *God as one eternal God, whose singular nature expresses itself in three persons.* Genesis 1:26 says, "Then God said, 'Let us make human beings in our image, to be like us.'" This passage shows the Trinity being revealed through Scripture when God speaks to Himself in the plural.

So who are the three persons of the Trinity? God the Father is the eternal and loving Creator of the universe, the Source and Sustainer of all life and all things. The Father created people for the purpose of relationship, and He is now calling them back to Himself through the Son who died on the cross for our sins.

God the Son—*Jesus Christ*— is the eternal Son of God who has been one with the Father and Holy Spirit from the beginning. Through Him, all things were created. Jesus left His place in heaven and came to this earth by the Holy Spirit, through the virgin Mary. Being fully God, Jesus took on a second nature and became God and Man in one person. The Son fulfilled the sayings of the Old Testament prophets by living a perfect, sinless life and dying on the cross for our sins so that we might be saved. God the Father raised Jesus from death, and Jesus is now seated at the right hand of the Father, where He intercedes for us as our eternal High Priest.

God the Holy Spirit is also eternal God and the Lord of life. Active throughout the entire Bible, the Holy Spirit was given to the Church in the fullness of power on the Day of Pentecost. The Holy Spirit empowers, comforts, and guides believers and is manifested by the fruit and gifts of the Spirit in our lives.

This truth can be a lot to grasp, but the reality is that we worship the one true God of all Creation whose nature is expressed in the Father, Son, and Holy Spirit. There has never been, and there will never be any other like Him or above Him. He is the Kings of all kings and Lord of all lords. We worship the one true God who loves us with an everlasting love and wants nothing more than to have a relationship with us. Galatians 4:6 refers to Him as "Abba, Father," which means 'Daddy.' In Hebrew, Psalm 7:17 calls Him *El Elyon*, which means 'God Most High.' Psalm 91:1 says He is *El Shaddai*, which means 'God Almighty,' and Genesis 22:14 says He is *Yahweh-Yireh*, which means 'the LORD will provide.'

Deuteronomy 31:6 gives one of the most beautiful pictures of who the God we worship is:

"Do not be afraid and do not panic before them. For the LORD your God will personally go ahead of you. He will neither fail you nor abandon you."

1. How can God be both one and triune? What are the actions of the three persons of the Trinity?
2. How do the different names of God (such as *El Shaddai* and *Yahweh-Yireh*) demonstrate His desire to have a relationship with us?
3. What are some common "idols" that people worship today? Are any of these idols preventing you from truly worshipping God?

WHY DO WE WORSHIP?

THOMAS MILLER

Genesis 1:27 states, "God created human beings in his own image." To this crown of His creation, God gave the most remarkable gift: free will. From the moment we humans take our very first breath, we have the ability to choose how we will live and what we will do with our lives. The options may seem wide-ranging or even overwhelming at times. However, in the light of eternity, only one choice truly matters: Will we choose to live with God or without Him?

Worship is our prerogative. God created the first human, Adam, and assigned him to care for the Garden of Eden. The Lord also presented the man with his first opportunity to make a choice:

"You may freely eat the fruit of every tree in the garden—except the tree of the knowledge of good and evil. If you eat its fruit, you are sure to die" (Genesis 2:16-17).

Why did God allow there to be such a tree? Was He unfairly introducing temptation to lead humanity astray? Actually, God was extraordinarily fair. He created a choice so Adam could exercise his free will. The man could choose to obey, partake of all the acceptable trees in Eden, and be connected to God. Or he could choose to disobey, eat the forbidden fruit, and sever his connection to God. God clearly laid out the consequences of disobedience: death and disconnection.

God could have named the animals, but instead, He brought them to Adam "to see what he would call them, and the man chose a name for each one" (Genesis 2:19). In the same way, God could make us do what He wants us to do, but He gives us a choice. We do not worship because we have to. *We worship because we get to choose, and we choose the greater thing—connecting with God.*

In Romans 12:1, the apostle Paul instructs believers to give their bodies as a "living and holy sacrifice" to God because "this is truly the way to worship him." Jews in Paul's day were very familiar with the concept of sacrifice as required by the Law of Moses. The Law called for burnt offerings of doves, goats, bulls, and other animals as atonement for sin. However, once sacrificed, these animals were dead. What does Paul mean by "living . . . sacrifice"? How can a *sacrifice*—something burned and therefore dead—be *living* (alive)? How can followers of Jesus offer themselves as living dead things? Paul explains that every believer must make this choice. We must choose to give our lives entirely to God, dying to our own control and surrendering to His. We worship God by offering all that we are for all that He is.

Bible translators render several Hebrew words as *worship*, but the most common connotation is 'to bow low' or 'bow before.' Many consider bowing to be one-directional—down. When we bow, we bow down. However, bowing also means to move toward. When we kneel before God, our posture is toward Him. False humility, on the other hand, leans back. This is the posture of those who merely go through the motions of worship as they want it to be—acting as if they live for Christ but surrendering no control. True, submitted worship always leans down and forward.

Worship is our purpose. God created us to worship. In John 4:23-24, Jesus tells the woman at the well,

"True worshipers will worship the Father in spirit and in truth. The Father is looking for those who will worship him that way. For God is Spirit, so those who worship him must worship in spirit and in truth."

When we worship *in spirit*, our spirits connect with God's Spirit. We reach beyond the physical realm in which we live and connect with the spiritual realm where God dwells. When we worship *in truth*, we declare that we wholly and openly offer our lives to the Lord. There is no false humility or artificial harmony. Nothing is held back.

When God spoke creation into existence, He said it was "good" (Genesis 1:9, 12, 18, 21, 25). However, when He created man, He said it was "very good!" (Genesis 1:31). God is self-sustaining, self-governing, and utterly complete within Himself, yet He created humans because He wants a relationship with us. *Relationship* is why we were created; therefore, relationship is our purpose.

Some people look to culture or entertainment to find their purpose, but the real answer is in the Word of God. Jesus says,

"Those who accept my commandments and obey them are the ones who love me. And because they love me, my Father will love them. And I will love them and reveal myself to each of them" (John 14:21).

We were created to be with God, and we show our love to Him by doing what He commands. Worship is not about singing songs or showing emotions, though both can indeed be aspects of worship. At its core, worship is about fully offering ourselves to the Lord and obeying His commandments.

We are His pleasure. When we experience the incredible power of Christ's love and forgiveness, our hearts change. One sign of this heart-change is the transformation of our desires. We no longer want to live to please only ourselves. Instead, we want to be pleasing to the Lord. When the apostle John had a vision of worship in heaven, he saw 24 elders bowing before God's throne and saying,

> "You are worthy, O Lord our God,
>   to receive glory and honor and power.
> For you created all things,
>   and they exist because you created what you
>   pleased" (Revelation 4:11).

God created what He pleased and what pleased Him—us! We are His prized creation. Psalm 37:23 says the Lord "delights in every detail" of our lives, and Psalm 149:4 says, "The Lord delights in his people." When we understand how much God cares for us, we in turn desire to be pleasing to Him. *We can worship the Lord in spirit and in truth, choosing to fulfill our purpose and His greatest desire by giving our lives wholly to Him.*

1. Why did God create the tree of the knowledge of good and evil?
2. What does it mean to offer yourself as a "living and holy sacrifice" to God?
3. How can we worship "in spirit and in truth"?

HOW DO WE WORSHIP?

MARK HARRIS

As a believer, you may know that the Bible says you should worship God. You may even feel a deep desire to express your thankfulness to Jesus, your Savior, who rescued you from sin and gave you a brand-new life. But you have one question: *How do I worship?*

Should you stand reverently with a hymnal in your hands and sing softly? Or are you supposed to shout and wave your arms? What about bowing? Dancing? What about acts of service, like feeding the poor or helping those in need? What is the right way to worship?

Worship always begins with a heart submitted to God. The position of your heart determines whether your actions are merely physical gestures or also spiritual ones—if you are connecting to your emotions or connecting to God. If the position of your heart is not worship, then nothing you can do with your body will be either.

The apostle Paul simplifies the "how" of worship in his letter to the believers in Rome:

> Dear brothers and sisters, I plead with you to give your bodies to God because of all he has done for you. Let them be a living and holy sacrifice—the kind he will find acceptable. This is truly the way to worship him" (Romans 12:1, emphasis added).

But what does it mean to be a "living and holy sacrifice"? Paul goes on to explain that God has given every believer a unique gift.

> Just as our bodies have many parts and each part has a special function, so it is with Christ's body. We are many parts of one body, and we all belong to each other (Romans 12:4-5).

When we use the gifts God has given us for His glory, we worship Him. Many well-meaning Christians think worship only occurs during church services, but this is not true. On the contrary, worship *can* and *should* occur every day of our lives! Paul tells believers,

> If God has given you the ability to prophesy, speak out with as much faith as God has given you. If your gift is serving others, serve them well. If you are a teacher, teach well. If your gift is to encourage others, be encouraging. If it is giving, give generously. If God has given you leadership ability, take the responsibility seriously. And if you have a gift for showing kindness to others, do it gladly (Romans 12:6-8).

God does not require His people to become something they are not. He does not ask tone-deaf individuals to become expert singers or reserved introverts to become exuberant extroverts. Rather,

God allows us the amazing privilege of using the gifts He has already placed inside us. He has already equipped you with everything you need to worship Him. What an amazing Father!

Pastor Robert Morris says worship is "love expressed." If this is true, then the *how* of worship is any act of service to God. It does not have to be extravagant, but it does have to be an expression of a humble heart. Pride and worship cannot coexist. Though he was created to be heaven's worship leader, Satan fell because pride entered his heart. He wanted to "be like the Most High" (Isaiah 14:14). Pride is an easy trap to find ourselves tangled in; after all, it rarely presents itself as a dangerous sin. Instead, pride begins as the briefest notion of "I deserve . . ." When we begin to think we deserve more, we are entering the danger zone. We must remind ourselves of this truth: "Everyone has sinned; we all fall short of God's glorious standard" (Romans 3:23). The only thing we "deserve" through our own merit is death. How amazing it is, then, that "the free gift of God is eternal life through Christ Jesus our Lord" (Romans 6:23). God alone is worthy of all worship.

When you speak or act in God's name, you worship. This includes:
— raising your hands to the heavens,
— bowing your knees,
— singing songs of praise,
— comforting a hurting friend,
— working diligently at your job,
— teaching your children about God's love,
— buying groceries for a struggling single parent,
— give an encouraging word to a neighbor,
— and so much more.

Worship does not require a talented singing voice, the ability to play an instrument, or a résumé full of community service. None of these are wrong, of course, and they can all be forms of worship. However, unless they are used for the glory of God, they are simply human effort. And in the light of eternity, human effort is worthless. True worship, on the other hand, has eternal significance.

Perhaps you have a hard time believing you can worship anywhere and anytime. You may feel as if God is so holy that nothing you do or say will be meaningful enough. Take comfort in 1 Samuel 16:7: "The LORD looks at the heart." God does not require the "right" words or actions; He just wants the right heart.

While teaching His disciples about the final judgment, Jesus shared the following story:

> "The King will say to those on his right, 'Come, you who are blessed by my Father, inherit the Kingdom prepared for you from the creation of the world. For I was hungry, and you fed me.

I was thirsty, and you gave me a drink. I was a stranger, and you invited me into your home. I was naked, and you gave me clothing. I was sick, and you cared for me. I was in prison, and you visited me.'

Then the righteous ones will reply, 'Lord when did we ever see you hungry and feed you? Or thirsty and give you something to drink? Or a stranger and show you hospitality? Or naked and give you clothing? When did we ever see you sick or in prison and visit you?'

And the King will say, 'I tell you the truth, when you did it to one of the least of these my brothers and sisters, you were doing it to me!'" (Matthew 25:34-40).

1. How is the position of your heart related to worship?
2. Why can't pride and worship coexist?
3. What are some ways you can worship God in your everyday life?

FREEDOM PATH

BARKING UP THE WRONG TREE

ELIZABETH SETTLE

The LORD God made all sorts of trees grow up from the ground—trees that were beautiful and that produced delicious fruit. In the middle of the garden he placed the tree of life and the tree of the knowledge of good and evil.
—Genesis 2:9

When God placed Adam in the Garden of Eden, He gave the man free reign, with only one exception:

"You may freely eat the fruit of every tree in the garden—except the tree of the knowledge of good and evil. If you eat its fruit, you are sure to die" (Genesis 2:16-17).

God put trees in the garden for Adam's benefit. Adam and Eve, the helper God made for Adam, could receive all the nourishment they needed from the "delicious fruit" (Genesis 2:9). To enjoy a perfect existence in this paradise, the first humans simply had to stay away from one particular tree. God warned them that the tree of the knowledge of good and evil would be their tree of death. The choice was theirs, just as it is ours today. Will we choose life? Or will we choose death?

God designed people to depend on Him as their Supplier and Sustainer. When Adam and Eve chose to eat from the tree of the knowledge of good and evil (Genesis 3:6), they rejected God and elected their own knowledge to supply and sustain them. The sly serpent told Eve the forbidden fruit would make her like God, "knowing both good and evil" (Genesis 3:4). This deceitful serpent omitted the fact that with this knowledge came spiritual death. Adam and Eve's spirits died the moment they ate that fruit. From then on, their bodies began to deteriorate, and their souls exchanged peace for shame (Genesis 3:7). They disobeyed, and with this fateful choice, "creation was subjected to God's curse" and "has been groaning as in the pains of childbirth right up to the present time" (Romans 8:20, 22).

Even though the couple had eaten, the fruit of knowledge did not satisfy them. Imagine sitting down at a restaurant, hungry and eager to see the menu. You flip through its pages and consider how each dish might taste. The server pulls out a pad and pen to take your order, and you say, "I'll take the menu, please." The server seems puzzled and asks, "You mean you want to order every item on the menu?" Shaking your head, you clutch the menu to your chest and reply, "Oh, no, no, no. I mean I want to keep the menu. I'm going to study and memorize it, and then I will be full."

At first glance, this may seem like a ridiculous illustration, but it makes an important point. You will not get full simply by knowing *about* food. In

fact, you will die of malnourishment. In the same way, you cannot become fully alive merely by knowing *about* God. Again, the results are death—spiritual death. When the Pharisees boasted about how much they knew about God, Jesus confronted them: "You search the Scriptures because you think they give you eternal life. But the Scriptures point to me! Yet you refuse to come to me to receive this life" (John 5:39-40). Knowing about Jesus and knowing Jesus are two completely different kinds of "knowing." Knowledge may be good, and knowledge may be evil. Either way, knowledge itself is not life. Or to put it another way, knowledge without a relationship is a waste of a life.

"Barking up the wrong tree" is an English expression that refers to hunting dogs who mistakenly think their prey is in a particular tree. These dogs plant themselves in front of that tree and bark persistently, but their efforts are useless because their prey has actually gone into another tree. The tree at which they are standing does not have and cannot give the dogs what they want. The dogs can bark all day, but their prey is long gone.

We may be smarter than dogs are about prey and trees, but sin and Satan deceive us about other more important goals. Our sin nature drives us to "bark up" the tree of knowledge as we strive to do good and avoid evil. We mistakenly believe that wanting to know more will lead to doing better. Thus, we plant ourselves in front of the tree of knowledge, hoping to be satisfied and nourished. However, knowledge never delivers the life we are seeking. Despite what we might learn or achieve, it is a polluted tree rooted in death. We are barking up the wrong tree, and life has actually gone elsewhere.

The apostle Paul writes, "Just as everyone dies because we all belong to Adam, everyone who belongs to Christ will be given new life" (1 Corinthians 15:22). Where the first man, Adam, failed, the New Man, Jesus, succeeded. Jesus came into the world as fully God and fully human, and He accomplished the greatest do-over of all time (1 Corinthians 15:47). By grace through faith, God will make us alive in Christ and restore us to His original plan to eat from the tree of life—Him!

Jesus said again, "I tell you the truth, unless you eat the flesh of the Son of Man and drink his blood, you cannot have eternal life within you. But anyone who eats my flesh and drinks my blood has eternal life, and I will raise that person at the last day. For my flesh is true food, and my blood is true drink. Anyone who eats my flesh and drinks my blood remains in me, and I in him" (John 6:53-56).

Sin, shame, sickness, Satan, and death are life's greatest enemies. You can stand by the tree of knowledge for the rest of your life, but you will never overcome them. The only real option is to surrender to Jesus' finished work, which He accomplished on another "tree"—the cross of Calvary.

> Taste and see that the LORD is good.
> Oh, the joys of those who take refuge in him!
> (Psalm 34:8).

1. What happened to Adam and Eve's bodies when they ate the fruit from the tree of the knowledge of good and evil? What happened to their spirits?
2. Why is knowing *about* God not enough for your spirit to be alive?
3. Is there any sin, sickness, or shame in your life that you need to overcome? If so, tell God about it right now. He loves you, and He wants to make you fully alive through Jesus today!

UNBOUND

ELIZABETH SETTLE

Then Jesus shouted, "Lazarus, come out!" And the dead man came out, his hands and feet bound in graveclothes, his face wrapped in a headcloth. Jesus told them, "Unwrap him and let him go!"

—John 11:43-44

When Jesus called Lazarus to come out of the grave, the once-dead man emerged alive. *Fully alive!* Salvation works in a similar way. When you are born again, Jesus calls your name, and by grace through faith, you come forth from the grave of sin. No longer spiritually dead, you are "alive to God through Christ Jesus" (Romans 6:11). Like Lazarus, those of us who have accepted Christ are now fully alive!

However, one problem remains: we are still bound. Our spirits are alive, but the fallen world in which we live still affects our bodies and souls. This is not the way it should be! God designed us to be influenced by His life-giving Spirit, but sin entered the world through Adam and Eve's disobedience. From the moment we are born, we are subject to sin's effects, including pain, sickness, dysfunction, and fear.

Salvation does not take us out of this fallen world. Like the risen Lazarus, many new followers of Christ find themselves alive yet still bound. Our "graveclothes" include the ways we have learned to self-satisfy, self-protect, and self-soothe in this hostile and often traumatizing environment. However, when we become born again, we no longer need to use these methods. We are children of God, and our heavenly Father promises to satisfy, protect, and soothe us as members of His own family. We just have to learn how to receive His love and allow it to free us from our areas of bondage.

The good news is we have already taken the first step! Through salvation, we accept God's amazing grace, which rescues us from death and makes us truly alive for the first time.

> For God made Christ, who never sinned, to be the offering for our sin, so that we could be made right with God through Christ (2 Corinthians 5:21).

While we were still His enemies, Jesus paid the price to redeem our relationship with God (Romans 5:10). Jesus became rejected so we could belong. He became bound so we could be free.

As believers, we must mature into our new identity as children of God, which takes time. The apostle Paul explains,

> Don't copy the behavior and customs of this world, but let God transform you into a new person by changing the way you think. Then you will learn to know God's will for you, which is good and pleasing and perfect (Romans 12:2).

Our minds need to be transformed because we are accustomed to living in bondage. Satan does not want us to claim the freedom we rightfully have in Christ, so he tries to keep us trapped in old patterns of thinking and living. We may be tempted to think that our biggest problems are financial or relational; however, according to Ephesians 6:12, there is a more significant battle:

> We are not fighting against flesh-and-blood enemies, but against evil rulers and authorities of the unseen world, against mighty powers in this dark world, and against evil spirits in the heavenly places.

No wonder we need the comfort and encouragement of other believers! Consider Lazarus once again. When he came out of the grave, his freedom was greatly limited by the graveclothes binding him. Jesus did not leave Lazarus to unbind himself. No, the Healer told those standing nearby to help. When you are born again as a child of God, you instantly become part of a family. God will bring healthy influences, helpful leaders, and wise counsel into your life. He does not expect us to live godly lives on our own. Community is a powerful part of our healing.

Have you ever had someone quickly remove a bandage from your arm? It hurts! Sometimes removing graveclothes hurts too.

> Confess your sins to each other and pray for each other so that you may be healed (James 5:16).

When we emerge from the grave of sin, the graveclothes of our past are all we know. It can be painful to lay down the thoughts, words, and actions that defined our former lives. We need one another to help us break free from the bondage in our soul.

Lazarus was dead for four days before Jesus raised him (John 11:39). If there was hope for Lazarus, there is hope for us! Are you ready to exchange what you know—what is old and familiar—for what you need in God, who offers a new and better life? Are you ready to be unbound from the bondage of your past and walk into a free future? God wants to speak life to your spirit and freedom to your soul. Like Lazarus, you too can be unbound.

1. How can you be spiritually alive but still bound?
2. Why is being part of a godly community an essential step toward freedom?
3. Are you still wearing some "graveclothes" from your past? What old patterns of thinking and living do you need to lay down today?

PROMISED LAND OR PRISON?

BENJAMIN GILMORE

Pharaoh sent for Moses and Aaron during the night. "Get out!" he ordered. "Leave my people—and take the rest of the Israelites with you! Go and worship the LORD as you have requested."

—Exodus 12:31

Exodus contains the account of God's deliverance of His people from slavery in Egypt. The Lord went to great lengths to set His people free, and He revealed Himself through 10 amazing plagues. However, the Hebrew text refers to these events not as plagues but as "signs." Whether they are signs or plagues really depends on your perspective. God told Moses the reason for them: "I will show you that I am the LORD" (Exodus 7:17). If you were a Hebrew, you would have seen the "signs" of God's mighty hand; if you were the Pharaoh, you would have seen God's visitation as "plagues." God delivered two messages with a single act: follow God and be delivered, or stand against God and death will visit your house.

Pharaoh missed the signs and got the plagues. Each plague served as a message to him, but it wasn't until the tenth plague that he finally understood: *This God of the Hebrews is totally unlike the many gods of Egypt.* After the tenth and final plague—the death of the firstborn sons—Pharaoh finally yielded his stubborn heart and reluctantly agreed with the call of God to "let my people go" (Exodus 5:1).

There's much more to this story, though. It didn't begin with the 10 plagues, nor did it end when Pharaoh finally gave in to God's command. The people of Israel had spent centuries crying out for deliverance from Egyptian oppression. Like the Israelites, we all start with important areas in our lives that need to change. Our inability to bring about these changes by ourselves leaves us feeling trapped, bound, and enslaved. We can't escape our hurts from the past or our current troubles. We want out, but there's no way out on our own. So like the Israelites, we come to the Lord and cry out, "Set us free!"

God was listening to His people, the Hebrews, the entire time. Consider the great effort He made to secure their freedom. Here's an amazing revelation: *You are also one of God's people.* He will go to great lengths for your freedom too! God cares more about your freedom than you do. He created you to live for Him and with Him—worshipping Him "in spirit and in truth" (John 4:24). It won't even take centuries; God has already heard you. He purchased your freedom before you even knew you needed it (Romans 5:8).

For the Hebrews, Egypt was a prison, but God was going to take them to Canaan, the Promised Land. However, between the two places was another land—the wilderness of Sinai. Very soon after their escape, the Hebrews came to the border of the Promised Land. Following God's command, Moses sent 12 spies into Canaan to explore the area. Forty days later, they returned with a report. The majority (10 spies) gave their fearful account: *while the land is bountiful, the current inhabitants are too powerful, and they will destroy us.* Only two spies gave the minority report. Joshua and Caleb acknowledged the facts about the land, but they came to a different conclusion: *these Canaanites are big, but the Lord is bigger. With His help, we can defeat them.*

The Hebrews had witnessed God's strong hand of deliverance in Egypt and the destruction of Pharaoh's army in the Red Sea (Exodus 14:15-31). So why did they still have the minds and hearts of slaves? They were physically free yet spiritually bound by fear and doubt. It's one thing to know God is powerful, but it's quite another to believe He will use His power on your behalf. Given the "facts" about their circumstances, the Hebrews refused to trust God's faithfulness. Instead, they complained, saying they would be better off dead than to face the challenges of the Promised Land. Some even began plotting to return to Egypt (Numbers 14:4).

You might think God was toying with the Hebrews as He led them in circles through the wilderness for 40 years, but that is not the case. They were the ones who refused to enter the Promised Land because of their stubbornness and fear. They fell under judgment, but they actually brought it on themselves—they got what they wanted and didn't have to face the Canaanites. Eventually, everyone from that generation died, except for Caleb and Joshua. These men were the only two original participants of the Exodus to enter and occupy Canaan.

Sometimes on your journey to freedom, you may find yourself taking a detour through your own wilderness. Trust God. He is working things into you as well as working things out of you. He sees the areas where you need to grow and the areas that need to die. Though it may be difficult, even painful, the wilderness is an expression of God's kindness. He is working to get you to a place where the freedom before you is the freedom within you.

For four centuries, the Hebrews lived in bondage, and while their bodies left Egypt, their hearts and minds remained captive. God had taken them out of slavery, but He still had to take slavery out of them. The same is true for you today. When you find yourself looking toward the Promised Land but seeing only a prison, there is still work to be done inside of you. This work can only be accomplished by setting time apart with God.

Do you see a room full of strangers as a Promised Land or a prison? Do you think, *Look at all the people I can meet* or *Look at all the people who will reject me?* When you see a business opportunity, do you say to yourself, *I will never be good enough. I'll fail!* or *This could be what God is calling me to oversee!?*

God stands on the edge of the Promised Land, beckoning you. No giant is bigger than the Lord. He is calling you to a place of freedom where you can be who He called and created you to be. It's a place He had in mind for you when He rescued you from the bondage of sin and death. This Promised

Land is awaiting you. Embrace the process.

Welcome your wilderness journey, no matter how long it takes. Believe that God cares more about your freedom than you do and give Him the time and space to work the bondage out of you.

1. What messages did God send with the 10 plagues or signs?
2. How can you be physically free but spiritually bound?
3. Do you feel like you are on a detour through your own wilderness? Ask God to show you what things He wants to work into you and what things He wants to work out of you.

BOUND FOR FREEDOM

BENJAMIN GILMORE

This High Priest of ours understands our weaknesses, for he faced all of the same testings we do, yet he did not sin.
—Hebrews 4:15

Every believer faces obstacles along their journey to freedom. Financial difficulties, relationship struggles, and health problems can affect anyone and threaten to interfere with their relationship with God. When dealing with these issues in my own life, I often ask Jesus, "Lord, what would You do in this situation?"

You may be thinking, *But Jesus was perfect! He didn't have any issues.* And you're partially right. Jesus was perfect; Hebrews 4:15 says He never sinned. But look at the beginning of that verse: "He faced all of the same testings we do." In other words, Jesus dealt with issues too! He faced the same temptations and felt the same frustrations we do today. Knowing that Jesus understands my struggles encourages me in every area of life.

But what happens when your struggle is less a frustration and more a bondage? What if your issue has you wrapped up, tied down, and unable to see a way out? Does Jesus still understand? Most people would never relate Jesus to bondage. In fact, if I were to ask you to name a person who embodies the idea of freedom, you'd probably say "Jesus." Many of our prayers and worship songs are about the freedom we have in Jesus, and rightly so—"If the Son sets you free, you are truly free" (John 8:36). So how could such a free person understand bondage?

One day while I was praying about my own bondage, I asked Jesus, "Were You ever bound?" He immediately reminded me of the story of Judas's betrayal in the Garden of Gethsemane. I turned to John 18 and read:

So the soldiers, their commanding officer, and the Temple guards arrested Jesus and tied him up (v. 12).

I had probably read this verse dozens of times before, but I had never stopped to think about Jesus—the King of all Kings and Lord of all Lords—being literally tied up. And not only is He tied up, but He is *willingly* tied up. Several verses before, the soldiers and guards come to the garden in search of Jesus, but as soon as He identifies Himself, "they all drew back and fell to the ground!" (John 18:6). Jesus has the power to walk away and remove Himself from danger, but He chooses to stay. He allows Himself to be arrested, tied up, and led away.

If you're in bondage today, you may feel alone. You may also feel hopeless. Whether the bondage is of your own making or the fault of others, you just can't see a way out. For Jesus, there was no way out. His arrest led to questioning and mocking, which then led to torture and a horrific death on the cross. Everything Jesus had worked for in His ministry seemed to be lost. Perhaps you feel as if you have lost everything too.

No matter how painful, humiliating, or overwhelming your bondage is, Jesus understands. He experienced extreme pain and utter humiliation as He took on the most overwhelming task of all time—paying the penalty for humanity's sins. Why would Jesus endure all this for us? Because He wanted to give us something we could never earn—*freedom*. Jesus wanted you to be free, and He was willing to do whatever it takes. The apostle Paul writes about this divine sacrifice in his letter to the Philippians:

He gave up his divine privileges;
    he took the humble position of a slave
    and was born as a human being.
When he appeared in human form,
    he humbled himself in obedience to God
    and died a criminal's death on a cross
    (Philippians 2:7-8).

Jesus was the perfect sacrifice, and His death on the cross cleared our sin-stained record before God. Then three days later, He rose again, fully alive and fully free.

Jesus' temporary bondage paved the way for our eternal freedom. Any bondage you may be facing today, including the grip of death, is subject to His divine authority. You can bring any struggle, issue, or temptation to Him. He cares, He understands, and He wants to set you free.

1. What are some common obstacles believers face today?
2. How do you think Jesus felt as He saw the soldiers and guards coming to arrest Him?
3. How does it make you feel to know that you have a Savior who was willing to do whatever it takes to give you freedom?

BIBLE READING
BREAKTHROUGH

MY DAILY JOURNEY

JOEL STOCKSTILL

Without God's Word, I would have died long ago. For over 20 years, I have battled chronic illness, and I lost my first wife to cancer. No one volunteers for these kinds of experiences, and many have compared my life with Job's. However, I have found my refuge in the Bible.

1. **God's Word will give you victory over despair.** Many times, it seemed as if I would die. Other times, my soul grew weary, and I simply wanted the suffering to end. Despair comes when we face great hardships, and we cannot rely on natural things to help us through them. Our only rock of safety is the Word of God.

2. **God's Word will reveal and clarify your calling.** As you read the Bible, you will discover situations and characters that correspond to your specific calling in God's Kingdom. The Holy Spirit will use certain passages to speak directly to you.

3. **God's Word will help you understand mysteries.** God has revealed many things to me through the daily study of His Word. None is more precious than the revelation of Christ's suffering on the cross (1 Corinthians 2:2). I am so thankful for the death, burial, and resurrection of our precious Savior. God has marked my ministry through this revelation.

After spending more than 15 years making disciples, preaching sermons, and mentoring leaders, I can say without hesitation that the greatest asset to my leadership and spiritual walk has always been the daily reading of God's Word.

THE 15-MINUTE BREAKTHROUGH
PASTOR ROBERT MORRIS

If I told you that you could experience miracles by doing something for 15 minutes a day, would you do it? I am talking about having a daily quiet time. You might cringe when you hear that phrase because so many of us have had bad experiences in this area. We have tried to have a quiet time, but it wasn't very good. When we hear other people talking about their quiet times, it seems like Moses, Elijah, and Jesus show up—but some of us simply don't have quiet times like that. We might even fall asleep during our quiet times. And eventually, we just give up on the whole idea. We think, *I'm a Christian. I love God. I serve God and come to church, but I'm just never going to have a quiet time like other people.*

I used to feel that way too, so I want to help you by disproving *three common myths* about quiet times.

1. You can only have a quiet time from 4 am to 6 am. I used to travel and preach at crusades and revivals. Our services started at 7 pm, and most nights I didn't get to bed until midnight or later. For years, I was a late riser. But when I would get around my friends in ministry who were early risers, they always talked about how they met with God at 5 am. It sounded so spiritual, and it made me feel terrible because I didn't get up early to have a quiet time.

I want you to understand this: If you show up later than 7 am, God isn't going to say, "Sorry, we're closed. You should have come earlier when the spiritual people were here." You can have a quiet time whatever time of day you want. I suggest doing it at the start of your day, but it's important to realize you can have it anytime.

2. Your quiet time must last at least one hour. There is nothing in the Bible about a one-hour-minimum requirement for spending time with God. I know there are those who think that "spiritual" people need to spend at least an hour each day having a quiet time, but I'm a pastor, and I don't do that. The reason why is I am a bottom-line kind of person. I'm not a long-winded preacher. I like to get to the bottom line, and my prayers are that way too.

3. Your prayer journal must sound like the Bible. Have you ever had someone read to you from their prayer journal, and it was unbelievably awesome? I was with a group of ministers once when one of the guys said, "I want to read something to you that the Lord spoke to me this past Tuesday." As he read, I thought, "I have *never* heard anything like that in my life." There was such poetry to it! Wondering what God spoke to me on that Tuesday, I looked in my journal, and this is what I had written: "Try not to be a jerk today." That is

what the Lord had spoken to me! It wasn't eloquent or poetic. But it was real.

God doesn't want to burden you with "rules" about quiet times that other people have set. He just wants to spend time with you. Can you imagine what it would be like to have to go down a checklist when we are trying to spend time with God?

Now that we have cleared the air, I want to show you four things that have helped me tremendously in my quiet time. I absolutely believe 15 minutes with the Lord each day can change your life.

Quiet Your Mind
Let all that I am wait quietly before God,
for my hope is in him (Psalm 62:5).

In this passage, David tells his soul to be quiet before God, and we need to do the same. A quiet time is not a time to be busy; it's a time to slow down. In order to do that, you are going to have to quiet your mind and soul.

Focus Your Mind on God
Shout with joy to the LORD, all the earth!
Worship the LORD with gladness.
Come before him, singing with joy.
Acknowledge that the LORD is God!
He made us, and we are his.
We are his people, the sheep of his pasture.
Enter his gates with thanksgiving;
go into his courts with praise.
Give thanks to him and praise his name.
For the LORD is good.
His unfailing love continues forever,
and his faithfulness continues to each
generation (Psalm 100).

When I go to meet with the Lord and quiet my mind, God always puts a song in my heart. For the rest of the day, that song is my key into God's presence. If you will just listen, He will give you a song too. You can sing it out loud if you want to, but you don't have to. What is important is that you are focusing on Him. Singing to the Lord turns your focus toward God, and it can be your key into His presence.

Pray What's on Your Mind

Don't worry about anything; instead, pray about everything. Tell God what you need, and thank him for all he has done (Philippians 4:6).

Just talk to God like you talk to anyone else, and pray about whatever concerns you. You don't have to pray for world peace unless that is on your heart. Pray about what is burdening you. You are never going to pray passionately until you pray about something that burdens you. You can pray for your kids, your marriage, your job, or your finances. It doesn't matter. Simply pray about whatever God has put on your heart and mind.

Renew Your Mind

> Don't copy the behavior and customs of this world, but let God transform you into a new person by changing the way you think. Then you will learn to know God's will for you, which is good and pleasing and perfect (Romans 12:2).

Renewing your mind will transform every area of your life, and the process is simple: read God's Word every day. There have been so many times when something I read in the morning was exactly what I needed for that day. God's Word gives me life, peace, and strength. It's like lifting weights—sometimes it feels good, and sometimes it doesn't. But if you persevere and do it consistently, you are going to see results over time. The more regularly you read the Bible, the stronger you will become spiritually. Reading God's Word every day renews your mind, changes your thinking, and transforms you into His image!

On September 16, 1999, I had my quiet time like any other day, but something special happened as I met with God. After I prayed, I asked the Lord, "Where do You want me to read?" Very clearly, I heard God say, "Genesis 35 and Deuteronomy 11." So I opened up to Genesis 35 and read, "Move to Bethel and build an altar for Me there" (v. 1 paraphrase). As soon as I read that, the Holy Spirit immediately spoke to me and said, "Move to Southlake and start a church." As I kept reading, God began unfolding His plan for Gateway Church. Where Gateway is today all came out of that little quiet time several years ago!

What is five years down the road for you? What is 10 years down the road? God knows. Are you giving Him an opportunity to tell you? Please don't miss it because you are too busy. All it takes is 15 minutes.

THE PROMISE PRINCIPLE

PHILLIP HUNTER

The *Promise Principle* is based on 2 Peter 1:3–11. God has given us His promises to participate in His nature rather than to live in our nature, which tends to be ruled by our circumstances.

> In view of all this, make every effort to respond to God's promises (2 Peter 1:5).

HOW CAN I IDENTIFY GOD'S PROMISES?

His promises are either a truth or a commandment.

HOW DO I RESPOND TO GOD'S PROMISES?

1. Ask for by faith (Matthew 21:22; James 4:2)
2. Receive with thanks (1 Timothy 4:4; Ephesians 5:20)

Every truth and commandment is a promise from God. As you read, underline every promise from God and ask yourself if this is a promise you should ask God for in faith or receive with a thankful heart. Then pray it!

> Pray about everything (Philippians 4:6).

Example #1

> God decided in advance to adopt us into his own family by bringing us to himself through Jesus Christ. This is what he wanted to do, and it gave him great pleasure (Ephesians 1:5).

IS THIS A PROMISE YOU SHOULD ASK FOR BY FAITH OR RECEIVE WITH THANKS?

Receive with thanks!

ASK THE HOLY SPIRIT HOW YOU NEED TO RESPOND TO THIS PROMISE BASED ON THE CIRCUMSTANCES IN YOUR LIFE. THEN PRAY IT.

Lord, there are times when I feel unloved and struggle with loneliness, but I thank You that You picked me and made me a part of Your family. I am loved by You. I belong! Thank You that You desire me. In Jesus' name, Amen.

Example #2

> Asking God, the glorious Father of our Lord Jesus Christ, to give you spiritual wisdom and insight so that you might grow in your knowledge of God. I pray that your hearts will be flooded with light so that you can understand the confident hope he has given to those he called—his holy people who are his rich and glorious inheritance (Ephesians 1:17–18).

IS THIS A PROMISE YOU SHOULD ASK FOR BY FAITH OR RECEIVE WITH THANKS?

Ask for by faith!

ASK THE HOLY SPIRIT HOW YOU NEED TO RESPOND TO THIS PROMISE BASED ON THE CIRCUMSTANCES IN YOUR LIFE. THEN PRAY IT.

Lord, I want to know You and all that You have for me. I ask You to give me spiritual wisdom and insight. My desire is to grow in my knowledge of You. I need to know You because I feel despair, and I am anxious. I am filled with fear. Would You fill my heart with light and overcome the darkness? Help me understand the hope that I have in You. I want You to be my confidence. In Jesus' name, Amen.

Recap

1. Underline the promises as you read.
2. Identify the promise as a truth or a commandment.
3. Ask the Holy Spirit what circumstance in your life is touched by this promise.
4. Do you need to ask for by faith, receive with thanks, or both?
5. Pray it!
6. Journal what the Holy Spirit is saying to you.

TRAVELING THE SCRIPTURES

MARY JO PIERCE

People often ask me why I love prayer so much. My answer is that it works! This one word encompasses the whole of why we were created. Prayer is pure, powerful, and our greatest calling. We were created to pray—to connect with God and to connect others to God.

The Bible is often referred to as a Prayer Book. Through its pages, we come to understand how we develop and cooperate with the Trinity through prayer. In the Scriptures, Jesus demonstrates a lifestyle of prayer and teaches us how to pray. The Holy Spirit directs our prayers, and the Father releases His will in our lives and through our prayers. From Genesis to Revelation, we see God pursue people. In Psalms we see people pursue God, a relationship established through prayer.

What you are holding right now is the greatest single tool for growing a personal prayer life, one that delights God and brings you great joy. Early in my relationship with the Lord, I came across a book by John Sherrill entitled *My Friend, the Bible*. At first, this title did not make sense to me. How could the Bible be a friend? I was curious, so I bought a copy of the book and began to read it. I couldn't go to sleep until I finished it! This book opened my eyes to experiencing the Bible as an ongoing conversation with God.

Over the years, the Holy Spirit has taught me how to have a conversation with God through His Word. I'll often ask the Lord, "What do You want to talk about today?" Then I will sit still—in a hush—waiting for His answer. Suddenly a word, a situation, or a conversation with a friend will come to mind. The Holy Spirit can speak from many sources, and each time He directs me to the Word.

I have come to refer to this experience as "traveling the Scriptures," and I have discovered that it is the key to following God and finding His heart for my prayers. Often, a particular Bible selection will stand out and speak to my spirit, triggering me to look at another Scripture. It is an adventure in hearing God as I journey through His Word.

The Bible has become my close, intimate friend, and this friendship grows even stronger when I ask questions, listen, and seek to know the Father, Son, and Holy Spirit. The Scriptures become the "script" to my prayers as I dig deeper into God's will for my life. They mold my heart while also directing my path. The Bible is alive. God lives within its pages—so real and so close.

I listen for God's voice throughout the day. I may hear it as I read, or it may come as a thought, something spoken, or something seen. It can be a picture, a story, or a formed question. I can hear God's voice when I am talking to Him alone, writing in my journal, praying for others privately, or praying with others corporately.

After the Resurrection, Jesus met two of His followers on the road to Emmaus. The Bible says that while He spoke with them, their hearts burned (Luke 24:32). I can relate to this experience. The Bible can bring tears, laughter, joy, questions, and answers. It changes the way I see and understand things. I can barely describe the joy I experience when I am speaking with the Lord, and then I open the Bible and receive a perfect response. That is so God!

Prayer is a living, breathing relationship and partnership with God. I'm passionate about engaging God in every area of my life. His Word is a wonderful traveling companion and such good company.

All Scripture is inspired by God and is useful to teach us what is true and to make us realize what is wrong in our lives. It corrects us when we are wrong and teaches us to do what is right. God uses it to prepare and equip his people to do every good work (2 Timothy 3:16–17).

1. Why do you think prayer is such an important aspect of our relationship with God?
2. Would seeing the Bible as your "friend" change your prayer life? If yes, in what way?
3. What sources in your life do you think the Holy Spirit might use to direct you to God's Word?

ONE YEAR READING PLAN

JANUARY

01	09	17	25
Genesis 1-2	Genesis 17-18	Genesis 33-34	Genesis 49-50
Psalm 1	Psalm 5:7-12	Psalm 9:1-6	Psalm 14
Proverbs 1:1-7	Proverbs 2:9-22	Proverbs 3:21-26	Proverbs 4:20-24
Matthew 1	Matthew 7	Matthew 12:1-21	Matthew 16

02	10	18	26
Genesis 3-4	Genesis 19-20	Genesis 35-36	Exodus 1-2
Psalm 2:1-6	Psalm 6:1-5	Psalm 9:7-10	Psalm 15
Proverbs 1:8-9	Proverbs 3:1-4	Proverbs 3:27-30	Proverbs 4:25-27
Matthew 2	Matthew 8:1-17	Matthew 12:22-50	Matthew 17

03	11	19	27
Genesis 5-6	Genesis 21-22	Genesis 37-38	Exodus 3-4
Psalm 2:7-12	Psalm 6:6-10	Psalm 9:11-20	Psalm 16:1-6
Proverbs 1:10-19	Proverbs 3:5-6	Proverbs 3:31-35	Proverbs 5:1-6
Matthew 3	Matthew 8:18-34	Matthew 13:1-30	Matthew 18:1-20

04	12	20	28
Genesis 7-8	Genesis 23-24	Genesis 39-40	Exodus 5-6
Psalm 3:1-4	Psalm 7:1-5	Psalm 10:1-11	Psalm 16:7-11
Proverbs 1:20-23	Proverbs 3:7-8	Proverbs 4:1-6	Proverbs 5:7-14
Matthew 4	Matthew 9:1-17	Matthew 13:31-58	Matthew 18:21-35

05	13	21	29
Genesis 9-10	Genesis 25-26	Genesis 41-42	Exodus 7-8
Psalm 3:5-8	Psalm 7:6-9	Psalm 10:12-18	Psalm 17:1-5
Proverbs 1:24-27	Proverbs 3:9-10	Proverbs 4:7-9	Proverbs 5:15-20
Matthew 5:1-26	Matthew 9:18-38	Matthew 14:1-21	Matthew 19

06	14	22	30
Genesis 11-12	Genesis 27-28	Genesis 43-44	Exodus 9-10
Psalm 4:1-5	Psalm 7:10-17	Psalm 11	Psalm 17:6-15
Proverbs 1:28-33	Proverbs 3:11-12	Proverbs 4:10-13	Proverbs 5:21-23
Matthew 5:27-48	Matthew 10:1-15	Matthew 14:22-36	Matthew 20:1-16

07	15	23	31
Genesis 13-14	Genesis 29-30	Genesis 45-46	Exodus 11-12
Psalm 4:6-8	Psalm 8:1-2	Psalm 12	Psalm 18:1-6
Proverbs 2:1-5	Proverbs 3:13-18	Proverbs 4:14-17	Proverbs 6:1-5
Matthew 6:1-18	Matthew 10:16-42	Matthew 15:1-20	Matthew 20:17-34

08	16	24	
Genesis 15-16	Genesis 31-32	Genesis 47-48	
Psalm 5:1-6	Psalm 8:3-9	Psalm 13	
Proverbs 2:6-8	Proverbs 3:19-20	Proverbs 4:18-19	
Matthew 6:19-34	Matthew 11	Matthew 15:21-39	

FEBRUARY

01	09	17	25
Exodus 13-14	Exodus 29-30	Leviticus 5-6	Leviticus 19-20
Psalm 18:7-19	Psalm 20:6-9	Psalm 24:1-6	Psalm 27:4-6
Proverbs 6:6-11	Proverbs 7:6-23	Proverbs 9:7-9	Proverbs 10:10-12
Matthew 21:1-22	Matthew 25:1-30	Matthew 28	Mark 5:1-20

02	10	18	26
Exodus 15-16	Exodus 31-32	Leviticus 7-8	Leviticus 21-22
Psalm 18:20-29	Psalm 21:1-7	Psalm 24:7-10	Psalm 27:7-14
Proverbs 6:12-15	Proverbs 7:24-27	Proverbs 9:10-12	Proverbs 10:13-16
Matthew 21:23-46	Matthew 25:31-46	Mark 1:1-20	Mark 5:21-43

03	11	19	27
Exodus 17-18	Exodus 33-34	Leviticus 9-10	Leviticus 23-24
Psalm 18:30-42	Psalm 21:8-13	Psalm 25:1-7	Psalm 28:1-5
Proverbs 6:16-19	Proverbs 8:1-5	Proverbs 9:13-18	Proverbs 10:17-18
Matthew 22:1-22	Matthew 26:1-25	Mark 1:21-45	Mark 6:1-29

04	12	20	28
Exodus 19-20	Exodus 35-36	Leviticus 11-12	Leviticus 25
Psalm 18:43-45	Psalm 22:1-8	Psalm 25:8-15	Psalm 28:6-9
Proverbs 6:20-25	Proverbs 8:6-11	Proverbs 10:1-3	Proverbs 10:19-21
Matthew 22:23-46	Matthew 26:26-56	Mark 2	Mark 6:30-56

05	13	21	
Exodus 21-22	Exodus 37-38	Leviticus 13	
Psalm 18:46-50	Psalm 22:9-18	Psalm 25:16-22	
Proverbs 6:26-29	Proverbs 8:12-21	Proverbs 10:4	
Matthew 23:1-22	Matthew 26:57-75	Mark 3:1-19	

06	14	22	
Exodus 23-24	Exodus 39-40	Leviticus 14	
Psalm 19:1-6	Psalm 22:19-21	Psalm 26:1-5	
Proverbs 6:30-31	Proverbs 8:22-31	Proverbs 10:5-7	
Matthew 23:23-39	Matthew 27:1-31	Mark 3:20-35	

07	15	23	
Exodus 25-26	Leviticus 1-2	Leviticus 15-16	
Psalm 19:7-14	Psalm 22:22-31	Psalm 26:6-12	
Proverbs 6:32-35	Proverbs 8:32-36	Proverbs 10:8	
Matthew 24:1-35	Matthew 27:32-56	Mark 4:1-20	

08	16	24	
Exodus 27-28	Leviticus 3-4	Leviticus 17-18	
Psalm 20:1-5	Psalm 23	Psalm 27:1-3	
Proverbs 7:1-5	Proverbs 9:1-6	Proverbs 10:9	
Matthew 24:36-51	Matthew 27:57-66	Mark 4:21-41	

MARCH

01	09	17	25
Leviticus 26-27	Numbers 15-16	Numbers 31-32	Deuteronomy 11-12
Psalm 29:1-9	Psalm 32:1-5	Psalm 35:1-10	Psalm 37:16-22
Proverbs 10:22-25	Proverbs 11:16-18	Proverbs 12:1	Proverbs 12:12-14
Mark 7:1-23	Mark 11:1-19	Mark 14:53-72	Luke 2:1-24

02	10	18	26
Numbers 1-2	Numbers 17-18	Numbers 33-34	Deuteronomy 13-14
Psalm 29:10-11	Psalm 32:6-11	Psalm 35:11-16	Psalm 37:23-29
Proverbs 10:26-29	Proverbs 11:19-21	Proverbs 12:2	Proverbs 12:15-16
Mark 7:24-37	Mark 11:20-33	Mark 15:1-20	Luke 2:25-52

03	11	19	27
Numbers 3-4	Numbers 19-20	Numbers 35-36	Deuteronomy 15-16
Psalm 30:1-7	Psalm 33:1-5	Psalm 35:17-28	Psalm 37:30-36
Proverbs 10:30-32	Proverbs 11:22-23	Proverbs 12:3	Proverbs 12:17-19
Mark 8:1-21	Mark 12:1-27	Mark 15:21-47	Luke 3

04	12	20	28
Numbers 5-6	Numbers 21-22	Deuteronomy 1-2	Deuteronomy 17-18
Psalm 30:8-12	Psalm 33:6-15	Psalm 36:1-4	Psalm 37:37-40
Proverbs 11:1-3	Proverbs 11:24-26	Proverbs 12:4-6	Proverbs 12:20-22
Mark 8:22-38	Mark 12:28-44	Mark 16	Luke 4:1-30

05	13	21	29
Numbers 7-8	Numbers 23-24	Deuteronomy 3-4	Deuteronomy 19-20
Psalm 31:1-5	Psalm 33:16-22	Psalm 36:5-12	Psalm 38:1-8
Proverbs 11:4-6	Proverbs 11:27	Proverbs 12:7	Proverbs 12:23-25
Mark 9:1-29	Mark 13:1-27	Luke 1:1-25	Luke 4:31-44

06	14	22	30
Numbers 9-10	Numbers 25-26	Deuteronomy 5-6	Deuteronomy 21-22
Psalm 31:6-13	Psalm 34:1-7	Psalm 37:1-6	Psalm 38:9-22
Proverbs 11:7-11	Proverbs 11:28	Proverbs 12:8	Proverbs 12:26-28
Mark 9:30-50	Mark 13:28-37	Luke 1:26-38	Luke 5:1-16

07	15	23	31
Numbers 11-12	Numbers 27-28	Deuteronomy 7-8	Deuteronomy 23-24
Psalm 31:14-18	Psalm 34:8-14	Psalm 37:7-11	Psalm 39:1-6
Proverbs 11:12-14	Proverbs 11:29	Proverbs 12:9-10	Proverbs 13:1-3
Mark 10:1-31	Mark 14:1-26	Luke 1:39-56	Luke 5:17-39

08	16	24
Numbers 13-14	Numbers 29-30	Deuteronomy 9-10
Psalm 31:19-24	Psalm 34:15-22	Psalm 37:12-15
Proverbs 11:15	Proverbs 11:30-31	Proverbs 12:11
Mark 10:32-52	Mark 14:27-52	Luke 1:57-80

APRIL

01	09	17	25
Deuteronomy 25-26	Joshua 7-8	Joshua 23-24	Judges 15-16
Psalm 39:7-11	Psalm 43	Psalm 47	Psalm 51:1-5
Proverbs 13:4-6	Proverbs 13:22-23	Proverbs 14:14	Proverbs 14:31-32
Luke 6:1-26	Luke 9:37-62	Luke 13:22-35	Luke 18:1-25

02	10	18	26
Deuteronomy 27-28	Joshua 9-10	Judges 1-2	Judges 17-19
Psalm 39:12-13	Psalm 44:1-3	Psalm 48:1-7	Psalm 51:6-9
Proverbs 13:7-8	Proverbs 13:24-25	Proverbs 14:15-17	Proverbs 14:33-35
Luke 6:27-49	Luke 10:1-24	Luke 14:1-24	Luke 18:26-43

03	11	19	27
Deuteronomy 29-30	Joshua 11-12	Judges 3-4	Judges 20-21
Psalm 40:1-5	Psalm 44:4-19	Psalm 48:8-14	Psalm 51:10-19
Proverbs 13:9-10	Proverbs 14:1-2	Proverbs 14:18-19	Proverbs 15:1-3
Luke 7:1-35	Luke 10:25-42	Luke 14:25-35	Luke 19:1-27

04	12	20	28
Deuteronomy 31-32	Joshua 13-14	Judges 5-6	Ruth 1-2
Psalm 40:6-10	Psalm 44:20-26	Psalm 49:1-9	Psalm 52:1-7
Proverbs 13:11-12	Proverbs 14:3	Proverbs 14:20-21	Proverbs 15:4-5
Luke 7:36-50	Luke 11:1-28	Luke 15:1-10	Luke 19:28-48

05	13	21	29
Deuteronomy 33-34	Joshua 15-16	Judges 7-8	Ruth 3-4
Psalm 40:11-17	Psalm 45:1-9	Psalm 49:10-20	Psalm 52:8-9
Proverbs 13:13-14	Proverbs 14:4-5	Proverbs 14:22-24	Proverbs 15:6-7
Luke 8:1-25	Luke 11:29-54	Luke 15:11-32	Luke 20:1-26

06	14	22	30
Joshua 1-2	Joshua 17-18	Judges 9-10	1 Samuel 1-3
Psalm 41	Psalm 45:10-17	Psalm 50:1-6	Psalm 53
Proverbs 13:15-16	Proverbs 14:6	Proverbs 14:25-27	Proverbs 15:8-11
Luke 8:26-56	Luke 12:1-31	Luke 16	Luke 20:27-47

07	15	23
Joshua 3-4	Joshua 19-20	Judges 11-12
Psalm 42:1-4	Psalm 46:1-6	Psalm 50:7-15
Proverbs 13:17-18	Proverbs 14:7-11	Proverbs 14:28
Luke 9:1-17	Luke 12:32-59	Luke 17:1-19

08	16	24
Joshua 5-6	Joshua 21-22	Judges 13-14
Psalm 42:5-11	Psalm 46:7-11	Psalm 50:16-23
Proverbs 13:19-21	Proverbs 14:12-13	Proverbs 14:29-30
Luke 9:18-36	Luke 13:1-21	Luke 17:20-37

MAY

01	09	17	25
1 Samuel 4-5	1 Samuel 20-21	2 Samuel 5-6	2 Samuel 21-22
Psalm 54	Psalm 59:1-5	Psalm 63	Psalm 68:1-6
Proverbs 15:12-13	Proverbs 15:31-33	Proverbs 16:16-17	Proverbs 17:1-4
Luke 21:1-19	Luke 24:36-53	John 5:1-18	John 8:21-59

02	10	18	26
1 Samuel 6-7	1 Samuel 22-23	2 Samuel 7-8	2 Samuel 23-24
Psalm 55:1-8	Psalm 59:6-17	Psalm 64	Psalm 68:7-10
Proverbs 15:14	Proverbs 16:1-2	Proverbs 16:18-19	Proverbs 17:5-6
Luke 21:20-38	John 1:1-34	John 5:19-47	John 9:1-23

03	11	19	27
1 Samuel 8-9	1 Samuel 24-25	2 Samuel 9-10	1 Kings 1-2
Psalm 55:9-14	Psalm 60:1-5	Psalm 65:1-8	Psalm 68:11-14
Proverbs 15:15-17	Proverbs 16:3	Proverbs 16:20-21	Proverbs 17:7-9
Luke 22:1-23	John 1:35-51	John 6:1-21	John 9:24-41

04	12	20	28
1 Samuel 10-11	1 Samuel 26-27	2 Samuel 11-12	1 Kings 3-4
Psalm 55:15-23	Psalm 60:6-12	Psalm 65:9-13	Psalm 68:15-20
Proverbs 15:18-20	Proverbs 16:4-5	Proverbs 16:22-24	Proverbs 17:10-12
Luke 22:24-46	John 2	John 6:22-59	John 10:1-21

05	13	21	29
1 Samuel 12-13	1 Samuel 28	2 Samuel 13-14	1 Kings 5-6
Psalm 56:1-13	Psalm 61:1-3	Psalm 66:1-7	Psalm 68:21-27
Proverbs 15:21-23	Proverbs 16:6	Proverbs 16:25-26	Proverbs 17:13-15
Luke 22:47-71	John 3:1-21	John 6:60-71	John 10:22-42

06	14	22	30
1 Samuel 14-15	1 Samuel 29-31	2 Samuel 15-16	1 Kings 7-8
Psalm 57:1-3	Psalm 61:4-8	Psalm 66:8-15	Psalm 68:28-35
Proverbs 15:24-25	Proverbs 16:7-9	Proverbs 16:27-30	Proverbs 17:16-17
Luke 23:1-25	John 3:22-36	John 7:1-24	John 11:1-27

07	15	23	31
1 Samuel 16-17	2 Samuel 1-2	2 Samuel 17-18	1 Kings 9-10
Psalm 57:4-11	Psalm 62:1-4	Psalm 66:16-20	Psalm 69:1-4
Proverbs 15:26	Proverbs 16:10-12	Proverbs 16:31-32	Proverbs 17:18-19
Luke 23:26-56	John 4:1-42	John 7:25-53	John 11:28-57

08	16	24
1 Samuel 18-19	2 Samuel 3-4	2 Samuel 19-20
Psalm 58	Psalm 62:5-12	Psalm 67
Proverbs 15:27-30	Proverbs 16:13-15	Proverbs 16:33
Luke 24:1-35	John 4:43-54	John 8:1-20

JUNE

01	09	17	25
1 Kings 11–12	2 Kings 5–6	2 Kings 22–24	1 Chronicles 13–14
Psalm 69:5-12	Psalm 72:1-7	Psalm 74:18-23	Psalm 78:1-8
Proverbs 17:20-22	Proverbs 18:10-11	Proverbs 19:3	Proverbs 19:20-21
John 12:1-19	John 18:1-18	Acts 2:22-47	Acts 7:23-43

02	10	18	26
1 Kings 13–14	2 Kings 7–8	2 Kings 25	1 Chronicles 15–16
Psalm 69:13-21	Psalm 72:8-14	Psalm 75	Psalm 78:9-16
Proverbs 17:23-24	Proverbs 18:12-13	Proverbs 19:4-5	Proverbs 19:22-24
John 12:20-50	John 18:19-40	Acts 3	Acts 7:44-60

03	11	19	27
1 Kings 15–16	2 Kings 9–10	1 Chronicles 1–2	1 Chronicles 17–18
Psalm 69:22-28	Psalm 72:15-20	Psalm 76:1-10	Psalm 78:17-25
Proverbs 17:25-26	Proverbs 18:14-15	Proverbs 19:6-7	Proverbs 19:25-26
John 13:1-20	John 19:1-16	Acts 4:1-22	Acts 8:1-25

04	12	20	28
1 Kings 17–18	2 Kings 11–13	1 Chronicles 3–4	1 Chronicles 19–20
Psalm 69:29-36	Psalm 73:1-14	Psalm 76:11-12	Psalm 78:26-33
Proverbs 17:27-28	Proverbs 18:16-17	Proverbs 19:8-9	Proverbs 19:27-29
John 13:21-38	John 19:17-42	Acts 4:23-37	Acts 8:26-40

05	13	21	29
1 Kings 19–20	2 Kings 14	1 Chronicles 5–6	1 Chronicles 21–22
Psalm 70:1-5	Psalm 73:15-20	Psalm 77:1-3	Psalm 78:34-39
Proverbs 18:1-2	Proverbs 18:18-19	Proverbs 19:10-12	Proverbs 20:1-2
John 14	John 20	Acts 5:1-16	Acts 9:1-19

06	14	22	30
1 Kings 21–22	2 Kings 15–16	1 Chronicles 7–8	1 Chronicles 23–25
Psalm 71:1-6	Psalm 73:21-28	Psalm 77:4-10	Psalm 78:40-55
Proverbs 18:3-5	Proverbs 18:20-21	Proverbs 19:13-14	Proverbs 20:3
John 15	John 21	Acts 5:17-42	Acts 9:20-43

07	15	23	
2 Kings 1–2	2 Kings 17–18	1 Chronicles 9–10	
Psalm 71:7-16	Psalm 74:1-11	Psalm 77:11-15	
Proverbs 18:6-8	Proverbs 18:22-24	Proverbs 19:15-16	
John 16	Acts 1	Acts 6	

08	16	24	
2 Kings 3–4	2 Kings 19–21	1 Chronicles 11–12	
Psalm 71:17-24	Psalm 74:12-17	Psalm 77:16-20	
Proverbs 18:9	Proverbs 19:1-2	Proverbs 19:17-19	
John 17	Acts 2:1-21	Acts 7:1-22	

JULY

01	**09**	**17**	**25**
1 Chronicles 26-27	2 Chronicles 13-14	2 Chronicles 30-31	Nehemiah 1-2
Psalm 78:56-64	Psalm 81:1-5	Psalm 85:1-7	Psalm 88:11-18
Proverbs 20:4-5	Proverbs 20:22-23	Proverbs 21:9-11	Proverbs 21:25-26
Acts 10:1-23	Acts 15:22-41	Acts 20:1-16	Acts 25

02	**10**	**18**	**26**
1 Chronicles 28-29	2 Chronicles 15-16	2 Chronicles 32-33	Nehemiah 3-5
Psalm 78:65-72	Psalm 81:6-10	Psalm 85:8-13	Psalm 89:1-4
Proverbs 20:6-7	Proverbs 20:24-25	Proverbs 21:12	Proverbs 21:27
Acts 10:24-48	Acts 16:1-15	Acts 20:17-38	Acts 26

03	**11**	**19**	**27**
2 Chronicles 1-2	2 Chronicles 17-18	2 Chronicles 34-36	Nehemiah 6-7
Psalm 79:1-4	Psalm 81:11-16	Psalm 86:1-7	Psalm 89:5-10
Proverbs 20:8-9	Proverbs 20:26-28	Proverbs 21:13-14	Proverbs 21:28
Acts 11	Acts 16:16-40	Acts 21:1-16	Acts 27:1-26

04	**12**	**20**	**28**
2 Chronicles 3-4	2 Chronicles 19-20	Ezra 1-2	Nehemiah 8-9
Psalm 79:5-11	Psalm 82	Psalm 86:8-13	Psalm 89:11-18
Proverbs 20:10-12	Proverbs 20:29-30	Proverbs 21:15-16	Proverbs 21:29-31
Acts 12	Acts 17:1-15	Acts 21:17-40	Acts 27:27-44

05	**13**	**21**	**29**
2 Chronicles 5-6	2 Chronicles 21-22	Ezra 3-4	Nehemiah 10-11
Psalm 79:12-13	Psalm 83:1-8	Psalm 86:14-17	Psalm 89:19-29
Proverbs 20:13-14	Proverbs 21:1	Proverbs 21:17-18	Proverbs 22:1-2
Acts 13:1-25	Acts 17:16-34	Acts 22	Acts 28

06	**14**	**22**	**30**
2 Chronicles 7-8	2 Chronicles 23-24	Ezra 5-6	Nehemiah 12-13
Psalm 80:1-6	Psalm 83:9-18	Psalm 87	Psalm 89:30-37
Proverbs 20:15	Proverbs 21:2-3	Proverbs 21:19-20	Proverbs 22:3-4
Acts 13:26-52	Acts 18	Acts 23:1-22	Romans 1

07	**15**	**23**	**31**
2 Chronicles 9-10	2 Chronicles 25-27	Ezra 7-8	Esther 1-2
Psalm 80:7-13	Psalm 84:1-7	Psalm 88:1-2	Psalm 89:38-45
Proverbs 20:16-18	Proverbs 21:4-5	Proverbs 21:21-22	Proverbs 22:5-6
Acts 14	Acts 19:1-22	Acts 23:23-35	Romans 2

08	**16**	**24**	
2 Chronicles 11-12	2 Chronicles 28-29	Ezra 9-10	
Psalm 80:14-19	Psalm 84:8-12	Psalm 88:3-10	
Proverbs 20:19-21	Proverbs 21:6-8	Proverbs 21:23-24	
Acts 15:1-21	Acts 19:23-41	Acts 24	

AUGUST

01	09	17	25
Esther 3-4	Job 9-10	Job 26	Job 41-42
Psalm 89:46-52	Psalm 93	Psalm 96:11-13	Psalm 101:5-8
Proverbs 22:7-8	Proverbs 22:22-23	Proverbs 23:10-12	Proverbs 23:31-35
Romans 3	Romans 9:19-33	Romans 15:14-33	1 Corinthians 7:1-16

02	10	18	26
Esther 5-6	Job 11-12	Job 27-28	Ecclesiastes 1-2
Psalm 90:1-6	Psalm 94:1-11	Psalm 97:1-6	Psalm 102:1-11
Proverbs 22:9	Proverbs 22:24-25	Proverbs 23:13-14	Proverbs 24:1-2
Romans 4	Romans 10	Romans 16	1 Corinthians 7:17-40

03	11	19	27
Esther 7-8	Job 13-14	Job 29-30	Ecclesiastes 3
Psalm 90:7-17	Psalm 94:12-19	Psalm 97:7-12	Psalm 102:12-17
Proverbs 22:10-11	Proverbs 22:26-27	Proverbs 23:15-16	Proverbs 24:3-4
Romans 5	Romans 11:1-21	1 Corinthians 1	1 Corinthians 8

04	12	20	28
Esther 9-10	Job 15-16	Job 31-32	Ecclesiastes 4-6
Psalm 91:1-8	Psalm 94:20-23	Psalm 98:1-3	Psalm 102:18-28
Proverbs 22:12	Proverbs 22:28-29	Proverbs 23:17-18	Proverbs 24:5-6
Romans 6	Romans 11:22-36	1 Corinthians 2	1 Corinthians 9

05	13	21	29
Job 1-2	Job 17-18	Job 33-34	Ecclesiastes 7
Psalm 91:9-13	Psalm 95:1-5	Psalm 98:4-9	Psalm 103:1-5
Proverbs 22:13-14	Proverbs 23:1-3	Proverbs 23:19-21	Proverbs 24:7-9
Romans 7	Romans 12	1 Corinthians 3	1 Corinthians 10:1-22

06	14	22	30
Job 3-4	Job 19-20	Job 35-36	Ecclesiastes 8-10
Psalm 91:14-16	Psalm 95:6-11	Psalm 99	Psalm 103:6-14
Proverbs 22:15	Proverbs 23:4-5	Proverbs 23:22-25	Proverbs 24:10-12
Romans 8:1-17	Romans 13	1 Corinthians 4	1 Corinthians 10:23-33

07	15	23	31
Job 5-6	Job 21-22	Job 37-38	Ecclesiastes 11-12
Psalm 92:1-8	Psalm 96:1-6	Psalm 100	Psalm 103:15-22
Proverbs 22:16	Proverbs 23:6-8	Proverbs 23:26-28	Proverbs 24:13-14
Romans 8:18-39	Romans 14	1 Corinthians 5	1 Corinthians 11:1-16

08	16	24	
Job 7-8	Job 23-24	Job 39-40	
Psalm 92:9-15	Psalm 96:7-10	Psalm 101:1-4	
Proverbs 22:17-21	Proverbs 23:9	Proverbs 23:29-30	
Romans 9:1-18	Romans 15:1-13	1 Corinthians 6	

SEPTEMBER

01	09	17	25
Song of Songs 1-2	Isaiah 9-10	Isaiah 25-26	Isaiah 41-42
Psalm 104:1-9	Psalm 106:1-5	Psalm 107:23-32	Psalm 109:26-31
Proverbs 24:15-16	Proverbs 25:1-2	Proverbs 25:18-19	Proverbs 26:3-4
1 Corinthians 11:17-34	2 Corinthians 1	2 Corinthians 9	Galatians 3

02	10	18	26
Song of Songs 3-4	Isaiah 11-12	Isaiah 27-28	Isaiah 43-44
Psalm 104:10-23	Psalm 106:6-18	Psalm 107:33-43	Psalm 110
Proverbs 24:17-18	Proverbs 25:3-5	Proverbs 25:20	Proverbs 26:5-9
1 Corinthians 12	2 Corinthians 2	2 Corinthians 10	Galatians 4

03	11	19	27
Song of Songs 5-6	Isaiah 13-14	Isaiah 29	Isaiah 45-46
Psalm 104:24-30	Psalm 106:19-23	Psalm 108:1-5	Psalm 111
Proverbs 24:19-20	Proverbs 25:6-8	Proverbs 25:21-22	Proverbs 26:10
1 Corinthians 13	2 Corinthians 3	2 Corinthians 11:1-15	Galatians 5

04	12	20	28
Song of Songs 7-8	Isaiah 15-16	Isaiah 30-32	Isaiah 47-48
Psalm 104:31-35	Psalm 106:24-31	Psalm 108:6-13	Psalm 111:7-10
Proverbs 24:21-22	Proverbs 25:9-10	Proverbs 25:23-24	Proverbs 26:11-12
1 Corinthians 14:1-25	2 Corinthians 4:1-15	2 Corinthians 11:16-33	Galatians 6

05	13	21	29
Isaiah 1-2	Isaiah 17-18	Isaiah 33-34	Isaiah 49-50
Psalm 105:1-7	Psalm 106:32-39	Psalm 109:1-5	Psalm 112:1-4
Proverbs 24:23-25	Proverbs 25:11-12	Proverbs 25:25-26	Proverbs 26:13-15
1 Corinthians 14:26-40	2 Corinthians 4:16-5:21	2 Corinthians 12	Ephesians 1

06	14	22	30
Isaiah 3-4	Isaiah 19-20	Isaiah 35-36	Isaiah 51-52
Psalm 105:8-15	Psalm 106:40-48	Psalm 109:6-15	Psalm 112:5-10
Proverbs 24:26-27	Proverbs 25:13	Proverbs 25:27-28	Proverbs 26:16
1 Corinthians 15:1-34	2 Corinthians 6	2 Corinthians 13	Ephesians 2

07	15	23	
Isaiah 5-6	Isaiah 21-22	Isaiah 37-38	
Psalm 105:16-36	Psalm 107:1-9	Psalm 109:16-20	
Proverbs 24:28-29	Proverbs 25:14-15	Proverbs 26:1	
1 Corinthians 15:35-58	2 Corinthians 7	Galatians 1	

08	16	24	
Isaiah 7-8	Isaiah 23-24	Isaiah 39-40	
Psalm 105:37-45	Psalm 107:10-22	Psalm 109:21-25	
Proverbs 24:30-34	Proverbs 25:16-17	Proverbs 26:2	
1 Corinthians 16:1-24	2 Corinthians 8	Galatians 2	

OCTOBER

01	09	17	25
Isaiah 53-54	Jeremiah 3-4	Jeremiah 19-20	Jeremiah 35-36
Psalm 113:1-4	Psalm 116:15-19	Psalm 119:1-8	Psalm 119:65-72
Proverbs 26:17-19	Proverbs 27:2	Proverbs 27:13	Proverbs 27:22
Ephesians 3	Philippians 4	1 Thessalonians 4	1 Timothy 4

02	10	18	26
Isaiah 55-56	Jeremiah 5-6	Jeremiah 21-22	Jeremiah 37-38
Psalm 113:5-9	Psalm 117	Psalm 119:9-16	Psalm 119:73-80
Proverbs 26:20-21	Proverbs 27:3-4	Proverbs 27:14	Proverbs 27:23-27
Ephesians 4	Colossians 1	1 Thessalonians 5	1 Timothy 5

03	11	19	27
Isaiah 57-58	Jeremiah 7-8	Jeremiah 23-24	Jeremiah 39-40
Psalm 114	Psalm 118:1-4	Psalm 119:17-24	Psalm 119:81-88
Proverbs 26:22	Proverbs 27:5-6	Proverbs 27:15-16	Proverbs 28:1
Ephesians 5:1-20	Colossians 2	2 Thessalonians 1	1 Timothy 6

04	12	20	28
Isaiah 59-60	Jeremiah 9-10	Jeremiah 25-26	Jeremiah 41-42
Psalm 115:1-8	Psalm 118:5-9	Psalm 119:25-32	Psalm 119:89-96
Proverbs 26:23	Proverbs 27:7	Proverbs 27:17	Proverbs 28:2
Ephesians 5:21-33	Colossians 3	2 Thessalonians 2	2 Timothy 1

05	13	21	29
Isaiah 61-62	Jeremiah 11-12	Jeremiah 27-28	Jeremiah 43-44
Psalm 115:9-13	Psalm 118:10-14	Psalm 119:33-40	Psalm 119:97-104
Proverbs 26:24-26	Proverbs 27:8	Proverbs 27:18	Proverbs 28:3
Ephesians 6	Colossians 4	2 Thessalonians 3	2 Timothy 2

06	14	22	30
Isaiah 63-64	Jeremiah 13-14	Jeremiah 29-30	Jeremiah 45-46
Psalm 115:14-18	Psalm 118:15-21	Psalm 119:41-48	Psalm 119:105-112
Proverbs 26:27	Proverbs 27:9	Proverbs 27:19	Proverbs 28:4
Philippians 1	1 Thessalonians 1	1 Timothy 1	2 Timothy 3

07	15	23	31
Isaiah 65-66	Jeremiah 15-16	Jeremiah 31-32	Jeremiah 47-48
Psalm 116:1-4	Psalm 118:22-24	Psalm 119:49-56	Psalm 119:113-120
Proverbs 26:28	Proverbs 27:10	Proverbs 27:20	Proverbs 28:5
Philippians 2	1 Thessalonians 2	1 Timothy 2	2 Timothy 4

08	16	24	
Jeremiah 1-2	Jeremiah 17-18	Jeremiah 33-34	
Psalm 116:5-14	Psalm 118:25-29	Psalm 119:57-64	
Proverbs 27:1	Proverbs 27:11-12	Proverbs 27:21	
Philippians 3	1 Thessalonians 3	1 Timothy 3	

NOVEMBER

01	09	17	25
Jeremiah 49-50	Ezekiel 9-10	Ezekiel 25-26	Ezekiel 41-42
Psalm 119:121-128	Psalm 121	Psalm 128	Psalm 133
Proverbs 28:6	Proverbs 28:16	Proverbs 28:25	Proverbs 29:6
Titus 1	Hebrews 5	Hebrews 11:17-40	1 Peter 1

02	10	18	26
Jeremiah 51-52	Ezekiel 11-12	Ezekiel 27-28	Ezekiel 43-44
Psalm 119:129-136	Psalm 122:1-5	Psalm 129:1-4	Psalm 134
Proverbs 28:7-8	Proverbs 28:17-18	Proverbs 28:26	Proverbs 29:7
Titus 2	Hebrews 6	Hebrews 12	1 Peter 2

03	11	19	27
Lamentations 1-2	Ezekiel 13-14	Ezekiel 29-30	Ezekiel 45-46
Psalm 119:137-144	Psalm 122:6-9	Psalm 129:5-8	Psalm 135:1-7
Proverbs 28:9-10	Proverbs 28:19	Proverbs 28:27	Proverbs 29:8
Titus 3	Hebrews 7	Hebrews 13	1 Peter 3

04	12	20	28
Lamentations 3-5	Ezekiel 15-16	Ezekiel 31-32	Ezekiel 47-48
Psalm 119:145-152	Psalm 123	Psalm 130:1-4	Psalm 135:8-14
Proverbs 28:11	Proverbs 28:20	Proverbs 28:28	Proverbs 29:9
Philemon 1-25	Hebrews 8	James 1	1 Peter 4

05	13	21	29
Ezekiel 1-2	Ezekiel 17-18	Ezekiel 33-34	Daniel 1-2
Psalm 119:153-160	Psalm 124	Psalm 130:5-8	Psalm 135:15-21
Proverbs 28:12	Proverbs 28:21	Proverbs 29:1	Proverbs 29:10
Hebrews 1:1-14	Hebrews 9	James 2	1 Peter 5

06	14	22	30
Ezekiel 3-4	Ezekiel 19-20	Ezekiel 35-36	Daniel 3-4
Psalm 119:161-168	Psalm 125	Psalm 131	Psalm 136:1-9
Proverbs 28:13	Proverbs 28:22	Proverbs 29:2-3	Proverbs 29:11
Hebrews 2	Hebrews 10:1-18	James 3	2 Peter 1

07	15	23	
Ezekiel 5-6	Ezekiel 21-22	Ezekiel 37-38	
Psalm 119:169-176	Psalm 126	Psalm 132:1-9	
Proverbs 28:14	Proverbs 28:23	Proverbs 29:4	
Hebrews 3	Hebrews 10:19-39	James 4	

08	16	24	
Ezekiel 7-8	Ezekiel 23-24	Ezekiel 39-40	
Psalm 120	Psalm 127	Psalm 132:10-18	
Proverbs 28:15	Proverbs 28:24	Proverbs 29:5	
Hebrews 4	Hebrews 11:1-16	James 5	

DECEMBER

01	09	17	25
Daniel 5-6	Hosea 9-10	Obadiah 1-21	Haggai 1-2
Psalm 136:10-26	Psalm 139:13-16	Psalm 143:7-12	Psalm 147:7-11
Proverbs 29:12-13	Proverbs 29:21	Proverbs 30:5-6	Proverbs 30:20
2 Peter 2	3 John 1-15	Revelation 7	Revelation 15

02	10	18	26
Daniel 7-8	Hosea 11-12	Jonah 1-4	Zechariah 1-3
Psalm 137:1-6	Psalm 139:17-24	Psalm 144:1-8	Psalm 147:12-20
Proverbs 29:14	Proverbs 29:22	Proverbs 30:7-9	Proverbs 30:21-23
2 Peter 3	Jude 1-25	Revelation 8	Revelation 16

03	11	19	27
Daniel 9-10	Hosea 13-14	Micah 1-3	Zechariah 4-6
Psalm 137:7-9	Psalm 140:1-5	Psalm 144:9-15	Psalm 148:1-6
Proverbs 29:15	Proverbs 29:23	Proverbs 30:10	Proverbs 30:24-28
1 John 1	Revelation 1	Revelation 9	Revelation 17

04	12	20	28
Daniel 11-12	Joel 1-3	Micah 4-5	Zechariah 7-9
Psalm 138:1-3	Psalm 140:6-13	Psalm 145:1-7	Psalm 148:7-14
Proverbs 29:16	Proverbs 29:24	Proverbs 30:11-12	Proverbs 30:29-31
1 John 2	Revelation 2	Revelation 10	Revelation 18

05	13	21	29
Hosea 1-2	Amos 1-3	Micah 6-7	Zechariah 10-12
Psalm 138:4-5	Psalm 141:1-4	Psalm 145:8-16	Psalm 149:1-5
Proverbs 29:17	Proverbs 29:25	Proverbs 30:13-14	Proverbs 30:32-33
1 John 3	Revelation 3	Revelation 11	Revelation 19

06	14	22	30
Hosea 3-4	Amos 4-5	Nahum 1-3	Zechariah 12-14
Psalm 138:6-8	Psalm 141:5-10	Psalm 145:17-21	Psalm 149:6-9
Proverbs 29:18	Proverbs 29:26	Proverbs 30:15-16	Proverbs 31:1-9
1 John 4	Revelation 4	Revelation 12	Revelation 20

07	15	23	31
Hosea 5-6	Amos 6-7	Habakkuk 1-3	Malachi 1-4
Psalm 139:1-6	Psalm 142:1-7	Psalm 146:1-10	Psalm 150
Proverbs 29:19	Proverbs 29:27	Proverbs 30:17	Proverbs 31:10-31
1 John 5	Revelation 5	Revelation 13	Revelation 21-22

08	16	24	
Hosea 7-8	Amos 8-9	Zephaniah 1-3	
Psalm 139:7-12	Psalm 143:1-6	Psalm 147:1-6	
Proverbs 29:20	Proverbs 30:1-4	Proverbs 30:18-19	
2 John 1-13	Revelation 6	Revelation 14	

SELECT FAMOUS BIBLE PASSAGES

— Creation (Genesis 1:1-2:3).
— Noah's boat (ark) and the great Flood (Genesis 6:5-8:19).
— God's covenant with Noah (Genesis 8:20-22).
— God calls Abram (Abraham) (Genesis 12).
— God promises the land of Israel to Jacob and his descendants (Genesis 35:12).
— The people of Israel become enslaved in Egypt (Exodus 1).
— Moses and the burning bush (Exodus 3).
— The first Passover (Exodus 12:1-30).
— The Israelites cross the Red Sea (Exodus 14:5-31).
— The Ten Commandments (Exodus 20:1-17; Deuteronomy 5:6-21).
— Israel enters the Promised Land (Joshua 3).
— David and Goliath (1 Samuel 17).
— David becomes king (2 Samuel 2:1-7).
— Solomon asks for wisdom (1 Kings 3:1-15).
— Solomon builds the Temple (2 Chronicles 3-4).
— Prayer of national repentance (2 Chronicles 7:14).
— The nation of Israel is torn in two (2 Chronicles 10).
— Jerusalem conquered by Babylon and taken into captivity (2 Kings 25).
— The Temple rebuilt (Ezra 6).
— The Suffering Servant (Isaiah 53).
— The Lord is my shepherd (Psalm 23).
— God will command his angels concerning you (Psalm 91:9-13).
— The importance of God's Word (Psalm 119).
— Gabriel appears to Mary (Luke 1:26-38).
— The birth of Jesus (Luke 2:1-7).
— The angels and shepherds (Luke 2:8-20).
— The Word became flesh (John 1:1-18).
— God loved the world and sent His Son (John 3:16).
— Jesus is baptized (Matthew 3:13-17).
— Jesus is tempted (Matthew 4:1-11).

— The Lord's Prayer (Matthew 6:9-13).
— The Beatitudes (Matthew 5:1-12).
— The Golden Rule (Luke 6:31).
— The Greatest Commandment (Mark 12:29-31).
— The Good Samaritan (Luke 10:30-37).
— The Lost (Prodigal) Son (Luke 15:11-32).
— The Farmer (Sower) Scattering Seed (Matthew 13:3-23).
— The Triumphal Entry/Palm Sunday (Matthew 21:1-11).
— The Last Supper (Luke 22:7-23).
— Jesus is crucified (Matthew 27:32-56).
— Jesus is resurrected (Luke 24:1-12).
— The Great Commission (Matthew 28:18-20).
— The Holy Spirit is given to believers on the Day of Pentecost (Acts 2:1-4).
— The first new converts to faith in Christ (Acts 2:41).
— The first picture of New Testament Church life (Acts 2:42-47).
— The first recorded miracle after Jesus went back to heaven (Acts 3:1-11).
— The first persecution of the Church (Acts 4:1-31).
— The first Samaritans led to faith and filled with the Holy Spirit (Acts 8:4-25).
— The first Gentiles saved and filled with the Holy Spirit (Acts 10).
— The Church sends the first missionaries (Acts 13).
— The first Church council (Acts 15:1-21).
— The Good News of Jesus reaches Europe (Acts 16:6-10).
— Nothing can separate us from the love of God (Romans 8:38-39).
— The Love Chapter (1 Corinthians 13).
— The Resurrection Chapter (1 Corinthians 15).
— A new heaven and a new earth (Revelation 21).

TABLES OF WEIGHTS AND MEASURES

VOLUME

MEASUREMENT	CUSTOMARY	METRIC	REFERENCE
Omer (⅒ ephah)	2.1 qt	2.3 lt	Exodus 16:36
Ephah (10 omers)	.652 bu (21 qt)	23 lt	Ezekiel 45:11
Homer (10 ephahs)	6.52 bu (210 qt)	230 lt	Ezekiel 45:11
Bath	6.1 gal	23 lt	Ezekiel 45:11
Homer (10 baths)	61 gal	230 lt	Ezekiel 45:11

WEIGHT

MEASUREMENT	CUSTOMARY	METRIC	REFERENCE
Gerah	⅕₀ oz	0.567 gm	Ezekiel 45:12
Beka (10 gerahs)	⅕ oz	5.67 gm	Exodus 38:26
Shekel (2 bekahs)	⅖ oz	11.34 gm	Ezekiel 45:12
Mina (60 shekels)	1.25 lbs	0.567 kg	Ezekiel 45:12*

Elsewhere the mina is equated to 50 shekels.

NOTES

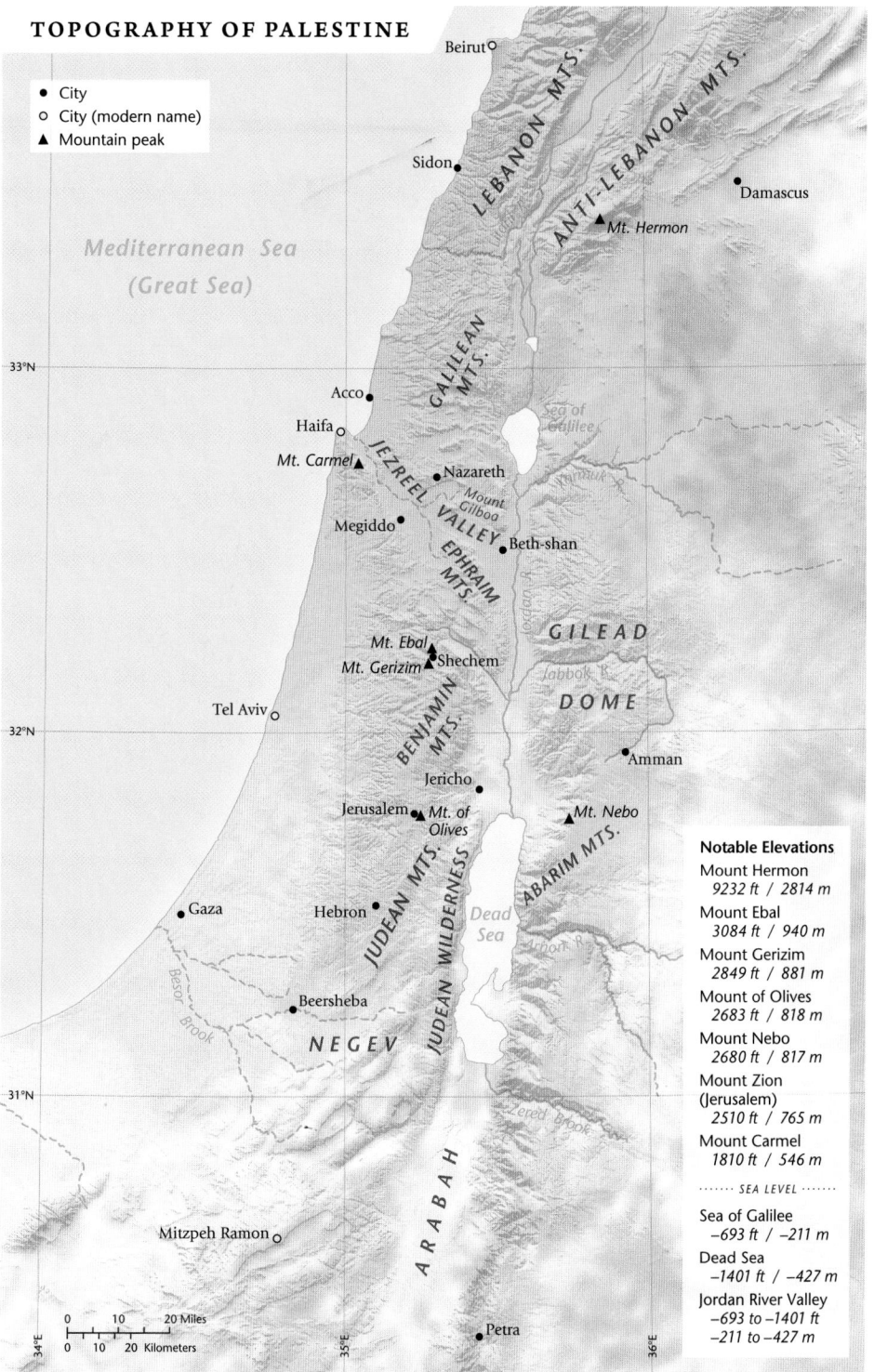

TOPOGRAPHY OF PALESTINE

- ● City
- ○ City (modern name)
- ▲ Mountain peak

Beirut○

LEBANON MTS.

ANTI-LEBANON MTS.

Sidon ●

Damascus ●

▲ Mt. Hermon

Mediterranean Sea

(Great Sea)

33°N

Acco ●

Haifa ○

GALILEAN MTS.

Sea of Galilee

Mt. Carmel ▲

JEZREEL VALLEY

Nazareth ●

Mount Gilboa

Yarmuk R.

Megiddo ●

● Beth-shan

EPHRAIM MTS.

GILEAD

Jabbok R.

Mt. Ebal ▲

Mt. Gerizim ▲ Shechem ●

DOME

Tel Aviv ○

BENJAMIN MTS.

32°N

● Amman

Jericho ●

Jerusalem ● ▲ Mt. of Olives

▲ Mt. Nebo

ABARIM MTS.

● Gaza

Hebron ●

JUDEAN MTS.

JUDEAN WILDERNESS

Dead Sea

Arnon R.

Notable Elevations

Mount Hermon
9232 ft / 2814 m

Mount Ebal
3084 ft / 940 m

Mount Gerizim
2849 ft / 881 m

Beersheba ●

Mount of Olives
2683 ft / 818 m

NEGEV

Besor Brook

Mount Nebo
2680 ft / 817 m

31°N

Zered Brook

Mount Zion
(Jerusalem)
2510 ft / 765 m

Mount Carmel
1810 ft / 546 m

······· SEA LEVEL ·······

Sea of Galilee
−693 ft / −211 m

ARABAH

Dead Sea
−1401 ft / −427 m

Mitzpeh Ramon ○

Jordan River Valley
−693 to −1401 ft
−211 to −427 m

0 10 20 Miles
0 10 20 Kilometers

34°E   35°E   36°E

● Petra

1238

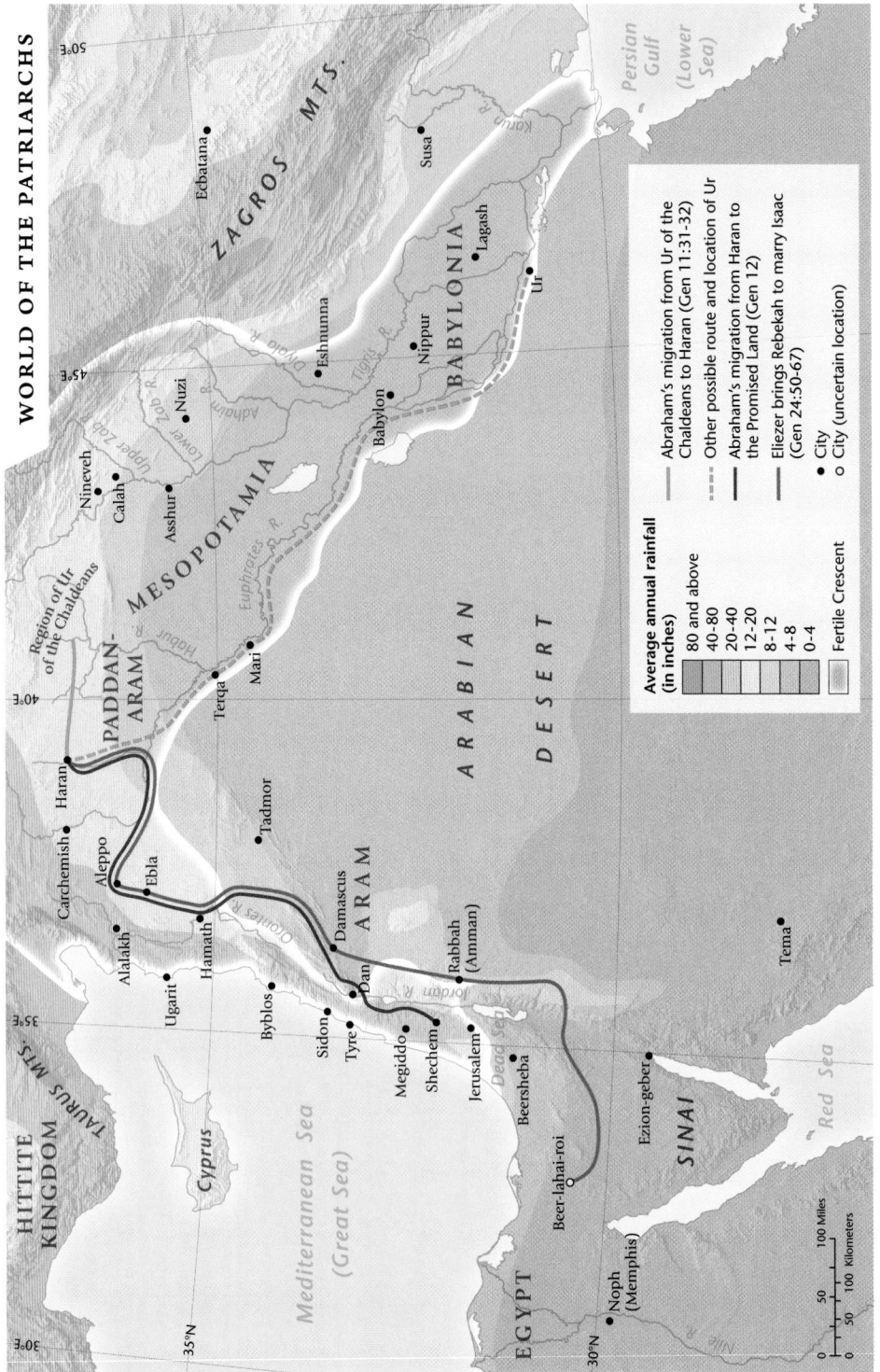

WORLD OF THE PATRIARCHS

Average annual rainfall
(in inches)
80 and above
40–80
20–40
12–20
8–12
4–8
0–4
Fertile Crescent

— Abraham's migration from Ur of the
Chaldeans to Haran (Gen 11:31-32)
--- Other possible route and location of Ur
— Abraham's migration from Haran to
the Promised Land (Gen 12)
— Eliezer brings Rebekah to marry Isaac
(Gen 24:50-67)
● City
○ City (uncertain location)

COPYRIGHT © 2018 TYNDALE HOUSE PUBLISHERS, INC.

EXODUS FROM EGYPT

Legend:

- ● City
- ○ City (modern name)
- ▲ Mountain peak (possible sites of Mt. Sinai)

- Route from Egypt to Mt. Sinai
- Route from Mt. Sinai to Kadesh-barnea
- Route from Kadesh-barnea to Acacia Grove
- – – – Annual bird migration path
- —— Ancient roadway

Mediterranean Sea (Great Sea), Lake Menzaleh, Lake Sirbonis, Lake Ballah, Lake Timsah, Zoan (Tanis), Rameses (Avaris), Ismalia, GOSHEN, Succoth, Pithom (uncertain location), On (Heliopolis), Noth (Memphis), Nile R., W. Tumilat, Great Bitter Lake, Little Bitter Lake, Suez, Darb el-Hajj, Gulf of Suez, Ras Gharib, WILDERNESS OF SHUR, Way to Shur, Way to the Land of the Philistines, Brook of Egypt, Besor Brook, Gaza, PHILISTIA, Beersheba, NEGEV, CANAAN, Jerusalem, Jordan R., Dead Sea, Acacia Grove, Amman (Rabbah), Heshbon, Dibon, Arnon R., MOAB, Zered Brook, King's Highway, Punon, Petra, EDOM, Kadesh-barnea, Jebel Karkom, WILDERNESS OF ZIN, WILDERNESS OF PARAN, Timna, Ezion-geber, Taba, Gulf of Aqaba, MIDIAN, Jebel el-Lawz, Darb el-Hajj, Sharm el-Sheikh, Ras Muhammad, Dahab, Jebel Musa, Jebel Katarina, RasSafsaf, Jebel Serbal, Ain Khadra, Nuweiba, SINAI, Serabit el-Khadim, WILDERNESS OF SIN, Abu Zeneimeh, Ras Gharib

Coordinates: 32°N, 30°N, 28°N, 36°E, 34°E, 32°E, 30°E

Scale: 50 Miles / 50 Kilometers, 0 25 50

1240

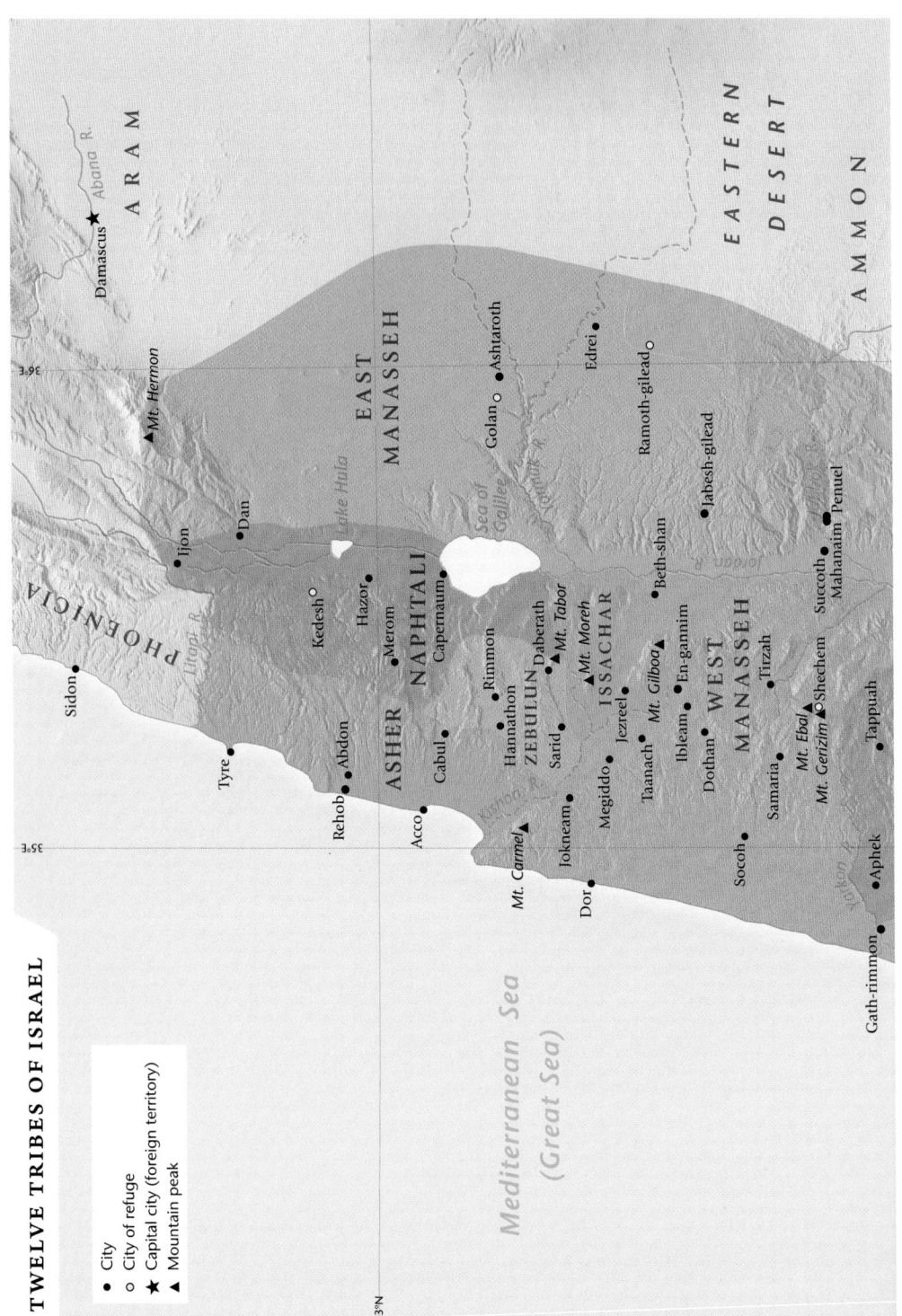

TWELVE TRIBES OF ISRAEL

- • City
- ○ City of refuge
- ★ Capital city (foreign territory)
- ▲ Mountain peak

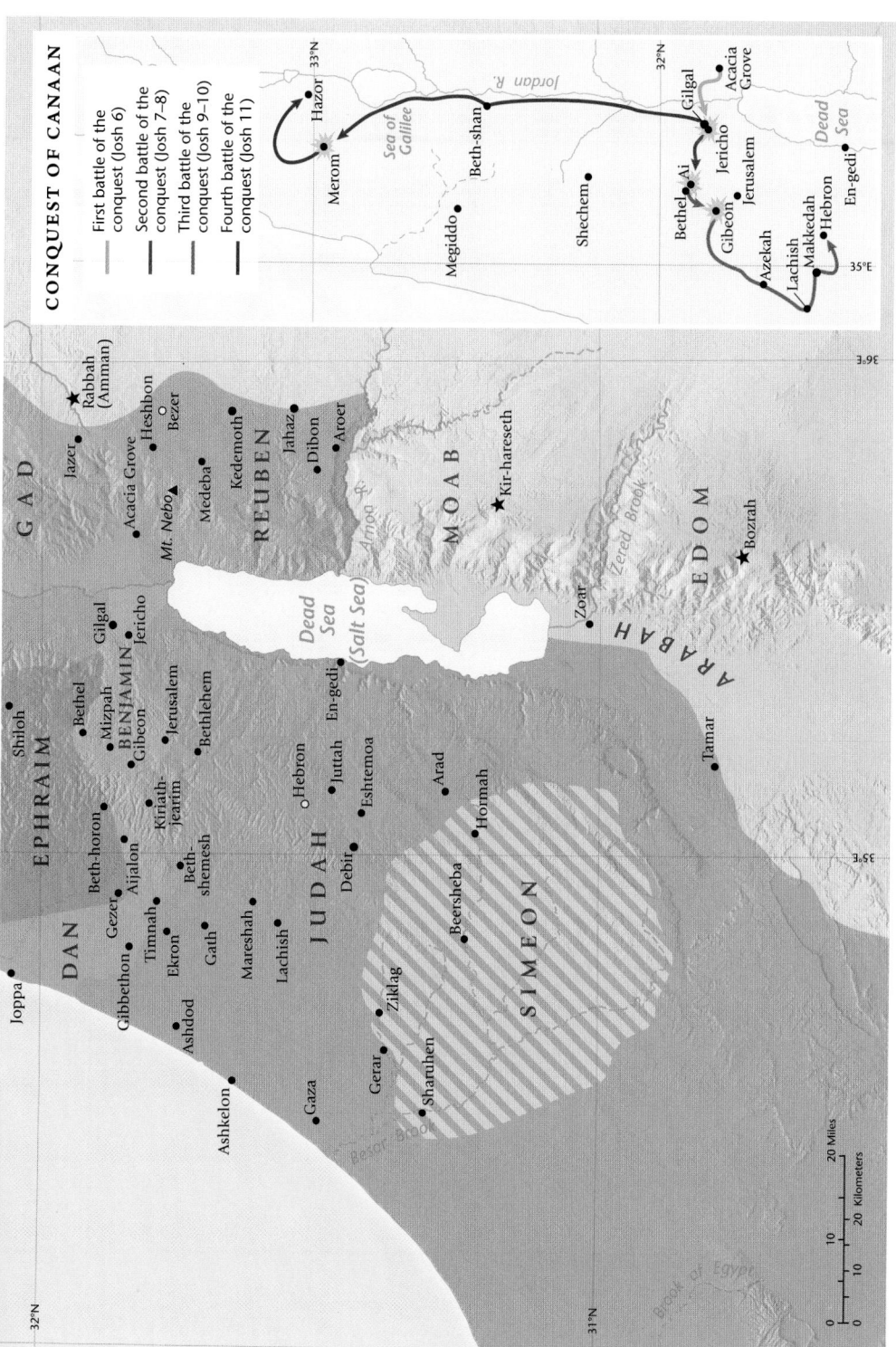

CONQUEST OF CANAAN

First battle of the
conquest (Josh 6)

Second battle of the
conquest (Josh 7–8)

Third battle of the
conquest (Josh 9–10)

Fourth battle of the
conquest (Josh 11)

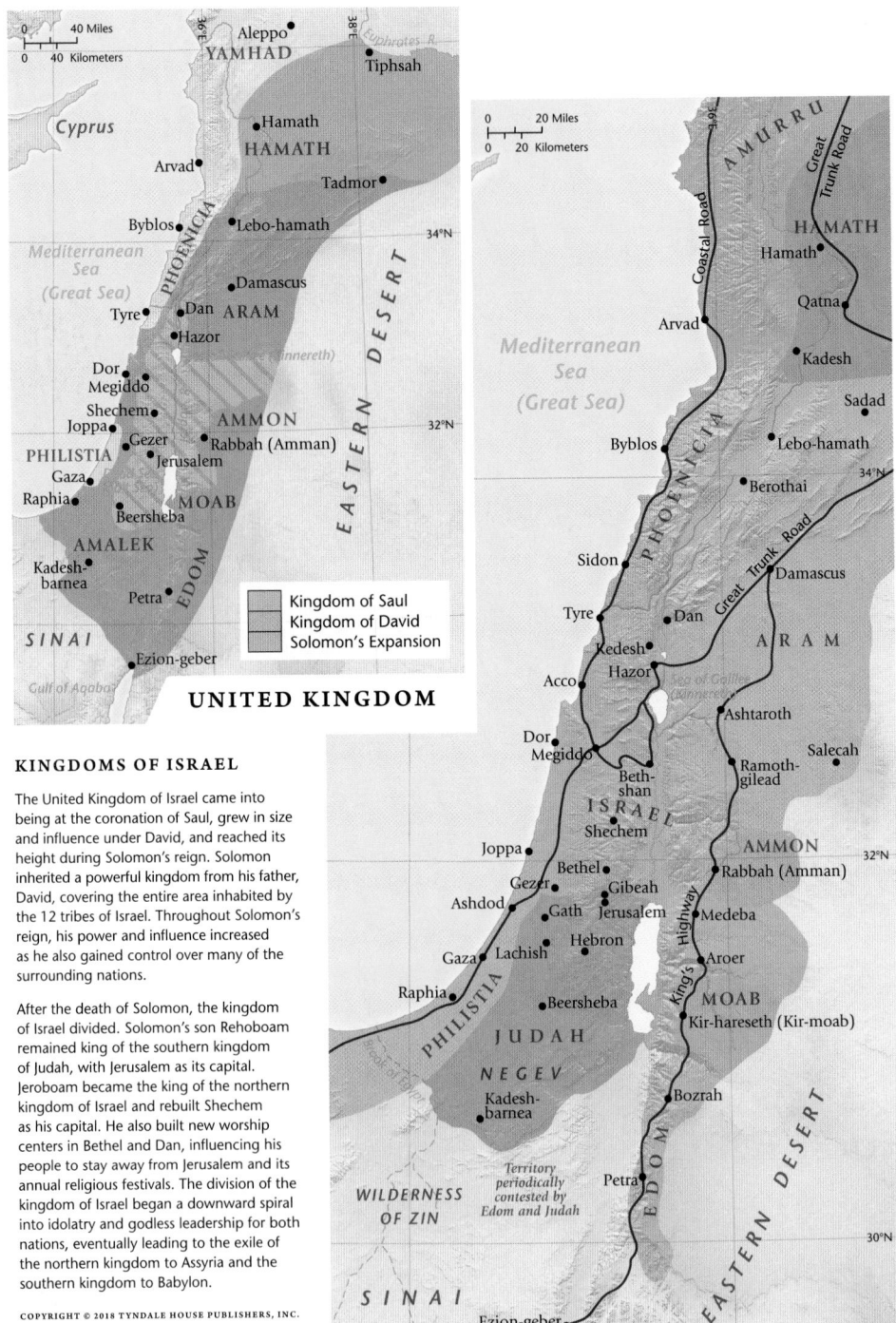

UNITED KINGDOM

KINGDOMS OF ISRAEL

The United Kingdom of Israel came into
being at the coronation of Saul, grew in size
and influence under David, and reached its
height during Solomon's reign. Solomon
inherited a powerful kingdom from his father,
David, covering the entire area inhabited by
the 12 tribes of Israel. Throughout Solomon's
reign, his power and influence increased
as he also gained control over many of the
surrounding nations.

After the death of Solomon, the kingdom
of Israel divided. Solomon's son Rehoboam
remained king of the southern kingdom
of Judah, with Jerusalem as its capital.
Jeroboam became the king of the northern
kingdom of Israel and rebuilt Shechem
as his capital. He also built new worship
centers in Bethel and Dan, influencing his
people to stay away from Jerusalem and its
annual religious festivals. The division of the
kingdom of Israel began a downward spiral
into idolatry and godless leadership for both
nations, eventually leading to the exile of
the northern kingdom to Assyria and the
southern kingdom to Babylon.

DIVIDED KINGDOM

DEPORTATIONS AND RETURNS UNDER ASSYRIA AND BABYLON

Caspian Sea

50°E

ELBURZ MTS.

MEDIA

Ecbatana

Hara

Susa

ELAM

Persian Gulf

ZAGROS MTS.

MANNAI

Avva

Hamath

CHALDEA

BABYLONIA

Ur

45°E

Arrapha

Arbela

Cutha

Nippur

Sepharvaim

URARTU

Nineveh

ASSYRIA

Sippar

Babylon

100 Miles

50

100 Kilometers

50

0

IZALLA

Gozan

Halah

40°E

Haran

BIT-ADINI

Rezeph

Tadmor

ARABIA

Carchemish

Aleppo

Qarqar

Hamath

Riblah

Damascus

Rabbah (Amman)

MUSHKU MTS.

TAURUS MTS.

35°E

AMURRU

Byblos

Sidon

Mediterranean Sea (Great Sea)

Samaria

Shechem

Jerusalem

35°N

30°N

Legend:

Assyria around 700 B.C.

Babylonia around 600 B.C.

● City

○ City (uncertain location)

Exiles from Canaan in Assyrian captivity to Gozan, Halah, the Habur River, and the cities of the Medes (2 Kgs 17:6; 18:11; 1 Chr 5:26)

Foreign exiles to Canaan in Assyrian captivity from Babylon, Cutha, Avva, Hamath, and Sepharvaim (2 Kgs 17:24-31; Ezra 4:10)

Exiles from Canaan in Babylonian captivity (2 Kgs 24:12-16; 25:11; Jer 52:28-30; Ezra 2:59-67; 3:15; 8:15-17)

Return of exiles under Sheshbazzar and Zerubbabel (Ezra 1–2)

Return of exiles under Ezra (Ezra 8:31); under Nehemiah (Neh 1–3)

ASSYRIAN AND BABYLONIAN EMPIRES

Assyria around 700 B.C.

Babylonia around 600 B.C.

Black Sea

Byzantium

40°N

URARTU

LYDIA

Lake

Tarsus KUE Carchemish
Haran
Nineveh
Calah
Aleppo
Asshur Arrapha
MEDIA
Riblah
Tadmor
Ecbatana
Mediterranean Sea Cyprus
(Great Sea)
Tyre Damascus
Sippar
Samaria
KEDAR
Babylon Nippur Susa
Jerusalem
Erech (Uruk)
Ur
ELAM
30°N
Memphis
Ezion-geber
Dumah
PERSIA

SAHARA
DESERT

ARABIAN
DESERT

Tema

Red Sea

Persian Gulf

0 100 200 Miles
0 100 200 Kilometers

GREEK EMPIRE

Danube R.

MACEDONIA
Black Sea
CAUCASUS MTS.

Pella
THRACE
Sinope

40°N

ARMENIA

Athens ASIA
HELLAS Ephesus
Sparta

Tarsus Carchemish
Haran
Aleppo
Gaugamela
Arbela
MEDIA
Ecbatana
Crete

Tadmor

Mediterranean Sea Cyprus
Cyrene (Great Sea)
Tyre Damascus
BABYLONIA
Opis
Babylon Susa
LIBYA
Alexandria
Jerusalem
Erech (Uruk)
Ur
30°N
EGYPT
Ezion-geber
Memphis

SAHARA
DESERT

ARABIAN
DESERT

Extent of Alexandrian empire
Ptolemaic realm
Seleucid realm
Antigonid realm
Minor Hellenistic provinces

Thebes

Red Sea

0 100 200 Miles
0 100 200 Kilometers

PALESTINE BETWEEN OLD AND NEW TESTAMENTS

Legend:

- Judea at the beginning of the Maccabean revolt
- Expansion of Jonathan
- Expansion of Simon
- Expansion of John Hyrcanus I
- Expansion of Aristobulus I
- Expansion of Alexander Janneus
- Herodian fortress
- • City
- ○ City (uncertain location)

0   10   20 Miles
0   10   20 Kilometers

ROMAN DIVISION OF PALESTINE

ABILENE
Abila

Sidon

PHOENICIA

ITUREA

Mt. Hermon

Damascus

Abana R.

SYRIA

Tyre

Litani R.

Caesarea Philippi

Cadasa (Kedesh)

TRACONITIS

Raphana

Thella

33°N

GALILEE

Ptolemais (Acco)

Mt. Meron

Korazin

Capernaum

Gennesaret

GAULANITIS

Bethsaida

Sea of Galilee (Kinnereth)

Mediterranean Sea

Magdala

Tiberias

Gergesa

Hippos

BATANEA

(Great Sea)

Mt. Carmel

Gebae

Mt. Tabor

Nain

Gadara

Abila

Edrei

AURANITIS

Dora

Caesarea

Scythopolis (Beth-shan)

Pella

Dion

DECAPOLIS

Great Trunk Road

Dothan

SAMARIA

Sebaste (Samaria)

Mt. Ebal

Sychar (Shechem)

Mt. Gerizim

Amathus

Gerasa

Antipatris (Aphek)

Joppa

Alexandrium

PEREA

32°N

Lydda (Lod)

Bethel

Ephraim

Tyrus

Philadelphia (Amman)

Jamnia

Jericho

Abila

Azotus (Ashdod)

Mt. of Olives

Jerusalem

Bethany

Cyprus

Esbus (Heshbon)

Ascalon

Bethlehem

Hyrcania

Medeba

Machaerus

Marisa

JUDEA

Herodium

Gaza

Hebron

Dead Sea

Adora

En-gedi

(Salt Sea)

Arnon R.

King's Highway

NABATEA

IDUMEA

Masada

Raphia

Beersheba

Malatha

Arad

31°N

Besor Brook

Division of Herod's kingdom to his three sons

Territory of Archelaus	● City
Territory of Herod Antipas	○ Decapolis city
Territory of Philip	▢ Herodian fortress
Territory of the Proconsul of Syria	▲ Mountain peak
Extent of Herod the Great's kingdom	

0   10   20 Miles

0   10   20 Kilometers

MINISTRY OF JESUS

Chronologically speaking, it is not possible to sequentially arrange the events in the life of Christ in any definitive way; none of the New Testament Gospels follows an overtly chronological pattern. Accordingly, the arrangement here follows a geographic order, basically proceeding from north to south on the map. Because the Gospel of Matthew most frequently contains information cited here, and because it is the most geographically particularistic Gospel, synoptic passages are keyed to the book of Matthew, except where they are unattested there or where more pertinent information about the event cited is available in another Gospel.

(A) *Region of Tyre:* Gentile woman's daughter healed (Mt 15:21-28)

(B) *Caesarea Philippi:* Peter's great declaration (Mt 16:13-20)

(C) *Mt. Meron/Mt. Tabor/Mt. Hermon:* (1) possible location of Transfiguration (Mt 17:1-13); (2) demon-possessed boy healed nearby (Mt 17:14-21)

(D) *Cana of Galilee:* (1) water changed to wine (Jn 2:1-11); (2) Capernaum official's son healed (Jn 4:46-54)

(E) *Gennesaret:* (1) possible location of feeding of multitudes (Mt 14:13-21; 15:32-39); (2) many healings (Mk 6:53-56)

(F) *Area of Korazin:* (1) judgment pronounced on the cities of Korazin, Bethsaida, and Capernaum (Mt 11:20-24); (2) possible area of Sermon on the Mount (Mt 5-7)

(G) *Capernaum:* (1) catch of fish (Lk 5:1-11); (2) evil spirit cast out (Mk 1:21-28); (3) Sermon on the Mount (Mt 5-7); (4) Peter's mother-in-law healed (Mt 8:14-15); (5) Roman officer's servant healed (Mt 8:5-13); (6) paralyzed man healed (Mt 2:1-12); (7) woman with a hemorrhage healed (Mk 5:25-34); (8) Jairus's daughter raised (Lk 8:40-56); (9) two blind men healed (Mt 9:27-31); (10) a mute, demon-possessed man healed (Mt 9:32-34); (11) the twelve apostles sent out (Mt 10:1-15); (12) man with deformed hand healed (Mt 12:9-13); (13) another demon-possessed man healed (Mt 12:22-37); (14) Temple tax provided (Mt 17:24-27); (15) Bread of Life discourse (Jn 6:22-59)

(H) *Bethsaida:* (1) possible location of feeding of multitudes (Mt 14:13-21; 15:32-39); (2) blind man healed (Mk 8:22-26)

(I) *Sea of Galilee near Bethsaida:* walking on water (Mt 14:22-33)

(J) *Sea of Galilee:* storm quieted (Mt 8:23-27)

(K) *Gergesa/Gadara:* possible location of casting out demons, which enter pigs; the pigs then rush down a steep bank and drown (Lk 8:26-39)

(L) *Nazareth:* (1) childhood home (Mt 2:19-23); (2) rejected by townspeople (Lk 4:16-30)

(M) *Nain:* widow's son raised (Lk 7:11-17)

(N) *Region of Galilee:* (1) leper cleansed (Mk 1:40-45); (2) post-resurrection appearances to the disciples (Mt 28:16-20)

(O) *Decapolis (Region of Ten Towns):* many healings (Mt 15:29-31; Mk 7:31-37)

(P) *Region between Galilee and Samaria:* (1) refused entry into village (Lk 9:51-56); (2) ten lepers healed (Lk 17:11-19)

(Q) *Sychar:* woman at the well of Samaria (Jn 4:1-42)

(R) *Ephraim:* enters into seclusion with the disciples (Jn 11:54)

(S) *Region of Perea:* (1) teaching on marriage (Mt 19:1-12); (2) possible location of healing of woman with infirmity (Lk 13:10-13); (3) possible location of healing of man with swollen limbs (Lk 14:1-6); (4) possible location of the rich young ruler (Lk 18:18-30)

(T) *Jericho:* (1) Bartimaeus healed (Mk 10:46-52); (2) Zacchaeus converted (Lk 19:1-10)

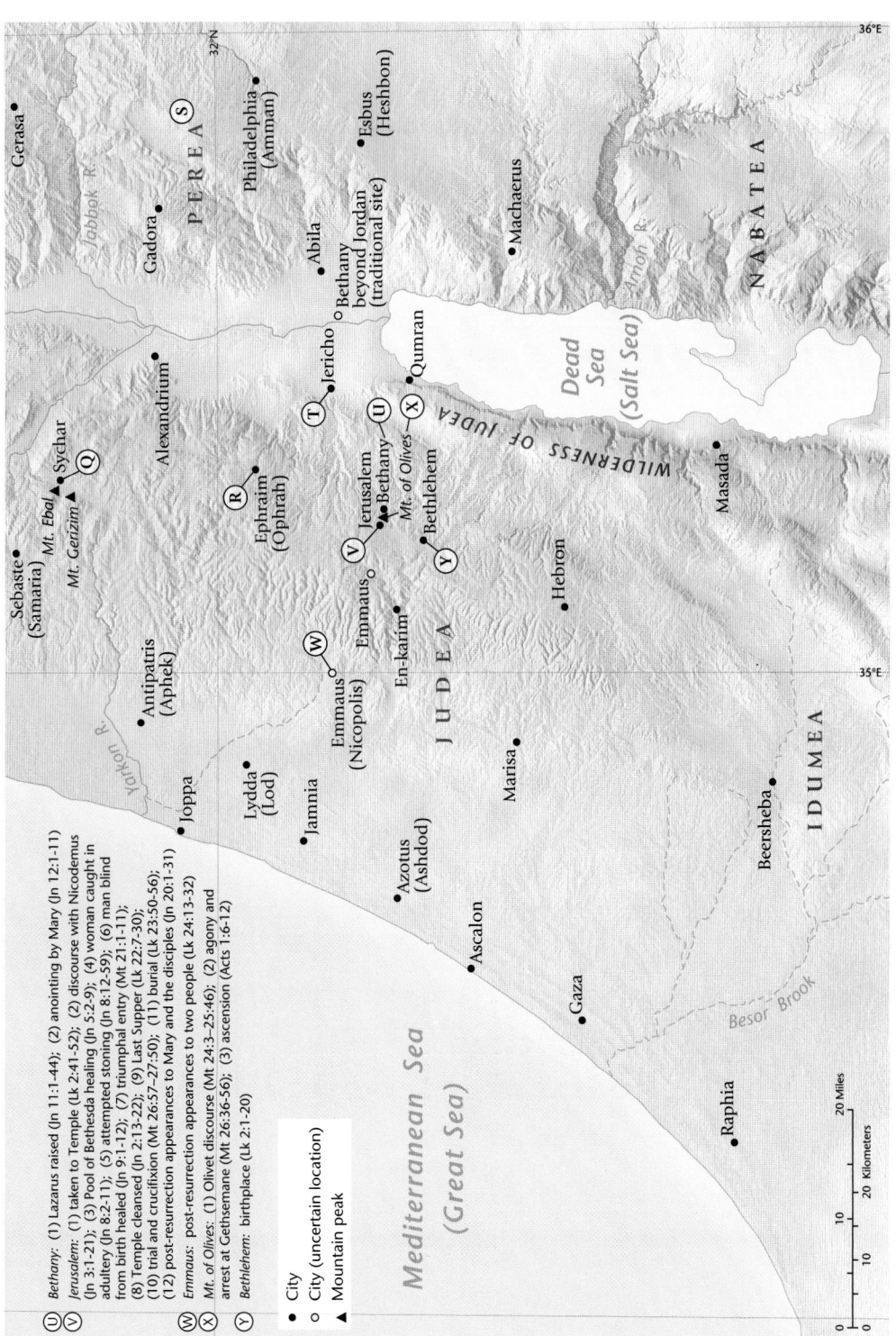

36°E

32°N

Gerasa

PEREA ⓢ

Jabbok R.

Philadelphia
(Amman)

Gadora

Abila

Esbus
(Heshbon)

Bethany
beyond Jordan
(traditional site)

Machaerus

NABATEA

Arnon R.

Alexandrium

Jericho

Qumran

ⓣ

ⓤ

ⓧ

Dead
Sea
(Salt Sea)

Sychar
ⓠ

Mt. Ebal
Mt. Gerizim

Sebaste
(Samaria)

ⓡ

Ephraim
(Ophrah)

Jerusalem
Bethany
Mt. of Olives
ⓥ

Bethlehem
ⓨ

WILDERNESS OF JUDEA

Masada

Hebron

Antipatris
(Aphek)

Emmaus
ⓦ

En-karim

JUDEA

35°E

Joppa

Emmaus
(Nicopolis)

Lydda
(Lod)

Jamnia

Marisa

Beersheba

IDUMEA

Azotus
(Ashdod)

Ascalon

Gaza

Besor Brook

Yarkon R.

Raphia

Mediterranean Sea
(Great Sea)

Bethany: (1) Lazarus raised (Jn 11:1-44); (2) anointing by Mary (Jn 12:1-11)
Jerusalem: (1) taken to Temple (Lk 2:41-52); (2) discourse with Nicodemus
(Jn 3:1-21); (3) Pool of Bethesda healing (Jn 5:2-9); (4) woman caught in
adultery (Jn 8:2-11); (5) attempted stoning (Jn 8:12-59); (6) man blind
from birth healed (Jn 9:1-12); (7) triumphal entry (Mt 21:1-11);
(8) Temple cleansed (Jn 2:13-22); (9) Last Supper (Lk 22:7-30);
(10) trial and crucifixion (Mt 26:57-27:50); (11) burial (Lk 23:50-56);
(12) post-resurrection appearances to Mary and the disciples (Jn 20:1-31)
Emmaus: post-resurrection appearances to two people (Lk 24:13-32)
Mt. of Olives: (1) Olivet discourse (Mt 24:3-25:46); (2) agony and
arrest at Gethsemane (Mt 26:36-56); (3) ascension (Acts 1:6-12)
Bethlehem: birthplace (Lk 2:1-20)

ⓤ
ⓥ

ⓦ
ⓧ

ⓨ

● City
○ City (uncertain location)
▲ Mountain peak

20 Miles

20 Kilometers

10

10

0

0

PAUL'S MISSIONARY JOURNEYS

Mediterranean Sea
(Great Sea)

// Cilician Gates
↑ First journey (outbound)
↑ First journey (inbound)
↑ Second journey (outbound)
↑ Second journey (inbound)
↑ Third journey (outbound)
↑ Third journey (inbound)
↑ Journey to Rome

PAUL'S JOURNEY TO ROME

ROMAN EMPIRE AND THE SPREAD OF CHRISTIANITY

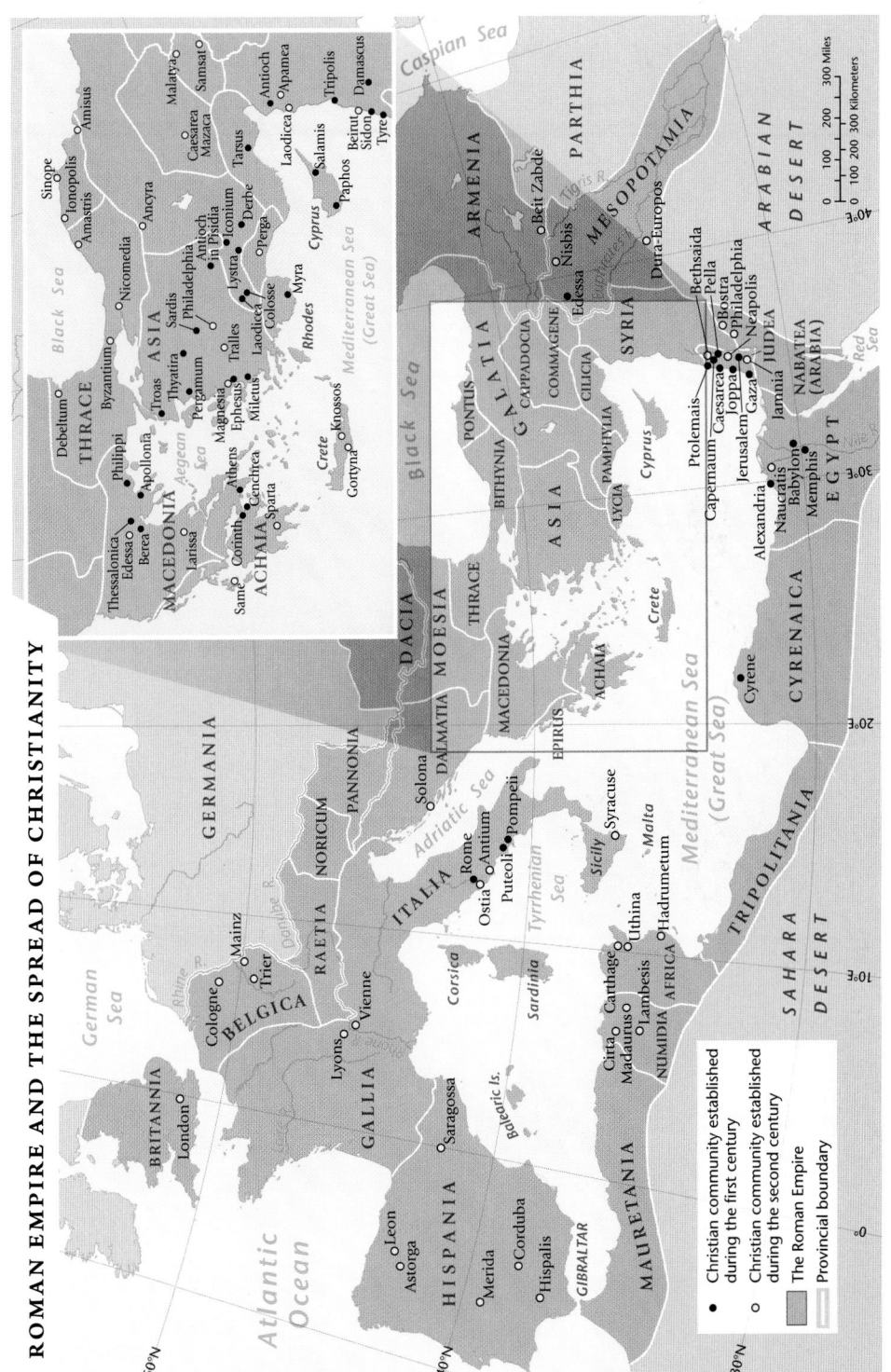

Christian community established during the first century
Christian community established during the second century
The Roman Empire
Provincial boundary

ISRAEL AND THE MIDDLE EAST TODAY

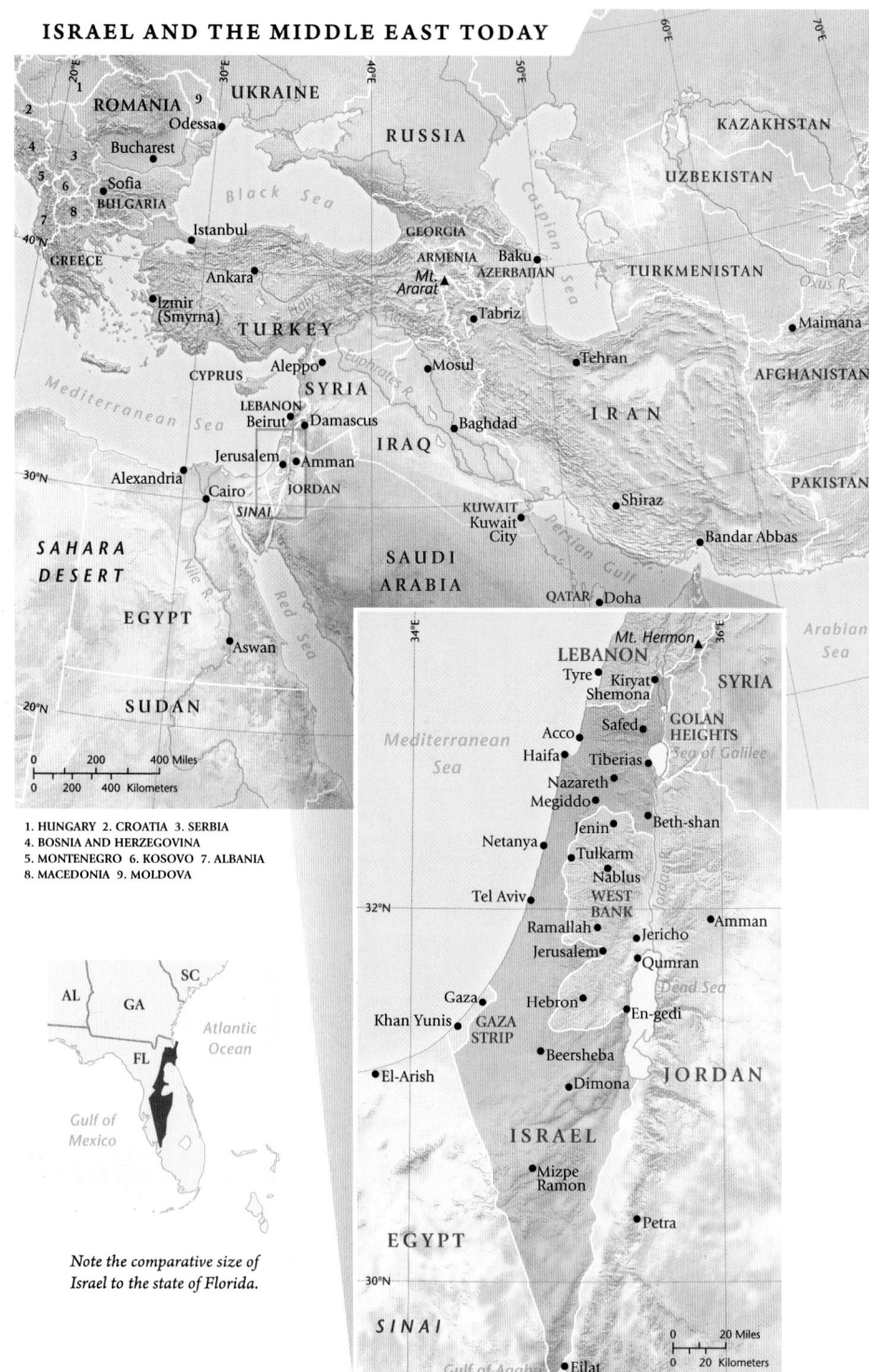

1. HUNGARY 2. CROATIA 3. SERBIA
4. BOSNIA AND HERZEGOVINA
5. MONTENEGRO 6. KOSOVO 7. ALBANIA
8. MACEDONIA 9. MOLDOVA

*Note the comparative size of
Israel to the state of Florida.*